North American
Women Artists
of the Twentieth Century

GARLAND REFERENCE LIBRARY OF THE HUMANITIES
(Vol. 1219)

North American
Women Artists
of the Twentieth Century
A Biographical Dictionary

Edited by
Jules Heller
and Nancy G. Heller

GARLAND PUBLISHING, INC.
New York & London
1995

Library of Congress Cataloging-in-Publication Data

North American women artists of the twentieth century : a biographical dictionary / edited by Jules
    Heller and Nancy G. Heller.
        p.   cm. — (Garland reference library of the humanities ; vol. 1219)
    Includes bibliographical references (p.   –   ) and index.
    ISBN 0-8240-6049-0
    1. Women artists—North America—Biography—Dictionaries.   I. Heller, Jules.   II. Heller,
Nancy.   III. Series.
N6503.N67 1995
709'.2'2—dc20
[B]   94-49710
                                                                              CIP

Cover illustration: Fanny Sanin. *Acrylic No. 2, 1989* (56 × 72 inches).
    Courtesy the artist.

Cover design by Larry Wolfson

Printed on acid-free, 250-year-life paper
Manufactured in the United States of America

To Eleanor Tufts

Contents

Acknowledgments

North American Women Artists of the Twentieth Century: A Biographical Dictionary owes its existence to the contributions of myriad persons and institutions. Most importantly, we are indebted to all of the contemporary artists who have lent their wholehearted support to this reference work. We thank the contributors for their pithy entries and for meeting deadlines (more or less); we appreciate the museum, gallery, library, and university personnel with whom we dealt for their staunch cooperation; we wish to recognize our friends, colleagues, and acquaintances in Canada, Mexico, and the United States for offering materials beyond what could be accommodated in this present work.

For particular kindnesses rendered, we wish to thank Lieschen A. Potuznik of the Art Institute of Chicago, Illinois; Susan Campbell of the National Gallery of Canada, Ottawa; Cristina Hijar G. of Centro Nacional de Investigación, Documentación y Información de Artes Plásticas, Instituto Nacional de Bellas Artes (CENIDIAP-INBA), Mexico City; Charles E. Brown of the Mercantile Library, St. Louis, Missouri; Lucinda Gedeon, director of the Neuberger Museum, State University of New York at Purchase; Leonard Lehrer of New York University; Ingo Hessel of the Inuit Art Section, Indian and Northern Affairs, Ottawa, Canada; Tamatha Kuenz of the Philadelphia Museum of Art, Pennsylvania; Anita Duquette, Whitney Museum of American Art, New York City; James Ballinger, Phoenix Art Museum, Arizona; and staff members James Hanley, Gretchen Herrig, and Clayton Kirking.

We are especially grateful to: Odette Leroux of the Canadian Museum of Civilization; Janet Mayhew of Dorset Fine Arts, Toronto, Canada; Elizabeth M. Weisberg of Artists Rights Society, New York City; Brian Hutchinson, University of Monterrey, Mexico; Diana Emery Hulick of Arizona State University, Tempe; Krystyna Wasserman, librarian, the National Museum of Women in the Arts, Washington, D.C., for help with knotty research problems, and Randi Greenberg, assistant registrar of the same institution, for supplying valuable illustrations; Sara J. MacDonald, reference librarian at the University of the Arts, Philadelphia; Pennsylvania, for her patience, good humor, and professional expertise; and Bonita Billman of Georgetown University, Washington, D.C., for many helpful discussions and suggestions.

It would be remiss if we did not thank Mary F. Williamson, fine arts bibliographer at Scott Library, York University, Toronto, Canada, and Margaret Archuleta of the Heard Museum, Phoenix, Arizona, for assistance in the early stages of this work; we wish to thank the reference staff of George Washington University's Gelman Library and Arizona State University's Hayden Library; and the many anonymous research assistants at various colleges, publications, museums, and community libraries in numbers of cities, including Phoenix, Scottsdale, Mexico City, Toronto, and Philadelphia, who answered our phone inquiries with both accuracy and kindness.

Thanks also to José Rogelio Alvarez, director general, Enciclopedias de México, for permission to translate certain articles; Pamela Posz of the Library of Congress, Washington, D.C.; Sylvia White, Contemporary Artists' Services, Santa Monica, California; Donald B. Goodall, independent Latin American art scholar; Lisa Sette of Lisa Sette Gallery, Scottsdale, Arizona; Brian C. Berg, computer consultant, Tempe, Arizona; Zoe Levy, independent Latin American lecturer; Norman Stevens, Sherman Oaks, California, for invaluable assistance; Krissy Kuramitsu of the Social and Public Art Resource Center (SPARC), Venice, California; David Silcox, Deputy Minister for

Culture, Ottawa, Canada; Mary Jane Williams, registrar, and Linda McAllister, associate curator, Latin American Art, University Art Museum, Arizona State University, Tempe; Joanne Greenbaum, Art Resource, New York City; Joan A. Geiser of the Indianapolis Museum of Art; Neil Winkel, Fishbach Gallery, New York City; and hundreds of others who offered services, suggestions, criticisms, and fruitful exchanges. If we have omitted your name, forgive us; *you* know that *we* know *you* were invaluable to this project.

Of course, we are indebted to our editor, Marie-Ellen Larcada, to Helga McCue and the many other Garland staffers who put so much time and effort into this volume. Without them it, literally, could not have been printed. And, finally, a special note of thanks to Gloria Heller, and also to Robert G. Regan, for their contributions to this book: Garland may have made its publication possible; but the two of them enabled us to *produce* it.

Jules Heller, Professor Emeritus of Art
Arizona State University, Tempe
Nancy G. Heller, Associate Professor of Art
University of the Arts, Philadelphia

Introduction

It is entirely appropriate to ask, "Why another work on women artists?" More specifically, "Why this North American Free Trade Agreement, this NAFTA-like approach which embraces women artists from Canada, Mexico, and the United States?"

Both questions have the same, relatively straightforward, set of answers. We decided to produce *North American Women Artists of the Twentieth Century: A Biographical Dictionary* because, to the best of our knowledge, there is no comprehensive reference work like this available, even though the bibliography in English on various aspects of the history of women artists has grown exponentially during the past ten years. As researchers, we both have been frustrated many times by being unable to locate basic information about many of the artists included in this volume—especially those working outside the United States. This leads directly to another reason for producing this particular kind of reference book—to try and create a better understanding between and among the artists and art audiences in these three countries.

Although the curricula of both the Canadian and Mexican public school systems routinely include units on the social, political, and cultural history of the United States, the reverse is not true. The Heller family has spent several years living in both our neighbor nations, to the north and south. Based on this experience we can state with certainty that, while the visual art of the United States is familiar to the members of the Mexican and Canadian art worlds, very few United States art students, or professionals, know anything about Canada's "Group of Seven" painters, or the "Great Four" of Mexico. Indeed, information about the art produced in these countries is notoriously difficult to obtain in the United States. We fervently hope that, sometime in the near future, the citizens of the United States will have learned so much about women artists—from Canada, Mexico, Lebanon, Ireland, Ethiopia, New Zealand, and the rest of the world—that there will no longer be any need for a book such as this.

Meanwhile, another question arises: how did we select these artists? Lists of names were drawn up by the editors and shared with colleagues, curators, research librarians, artists, art historians, consultants, and state or provincial arts councils; they are acknowledged elsewhere. In making these lists we tried to be as comprehensive as possible, given our self-imposed criteria: every artist included had to be a woman born before 1960, who lived and worked primarily in one or more of the three designated countries, and who had made a serious professional commitment to the visual arts—indicated by such factors as solo exhibitions and/or major gallery shows; the acceptance of her work in juried regional, national, or international exhibitions; and a "paper trail" of reviews, articles, monographs, histories, repeated mentions in journals, etc. Inevitably, certain quandaries arose—how much time could one spend, for example, in the nineteenth century, or in Asia, and still be eligible for inclusion in this book? After considerable cogitation, we decided that such matters would simply have to be decided on a case-by-case basis. And, though we tried our very best to be consistent, it goes without saying that some worthy individuals may have been inadvertently omitted from our master list; for this we apologize.

Another difficulty presented itself in the preparation of this volume, regarding the matter of artistic "categories"—drawing, painting, sculpture, and the like. More and more, in recent years, persons who had considered themselves "painters," for example, have suddenly started producing lithographs, or even sculpture. How, then, does one categorize these artists? More significantly, what does one call an artwork that is neither a painting nor a sculpture, in the traditional sense? Does it even matter, unless one is running an art competition which involves prize money specifically designated for one category or the other? Clearly, the old labels are no longer adequate at the end of the twentieth century. But, since we felt obligated to make some sort of designation that might prove useful to the reader, we have tried to choose the term that most clearly describes the sort of work for which each artist is best known. It's an imperfect solution, but the best we could devise.

The careful reader will note that many of the entries in this encyclopedia are signed by the individual contributors, while many others are not. All unsigned entries were written by the editors. It will also be apparent that the entries included here vary considerably in length. The length of a given artist's entry in no way suggests any greater, or lesser, accomplishment or reputation on her part. Moreover, the proportion of professional versus biographical information is quite different from one entry to another. In preparing this book we found that some artists wished us to present only their professional backgrounds; in other cases, we decided not to dwell on the lives of artists who have already been the subject of innumerable biographical studies.

Over one hundred illustrations of artworks, one apiece by a selection of the artists discussed here, are reproduced in three sections of this book. Since budgetary considerations precluded including more illustration, or reproducing them in color, once again we had to make some difficult decisions. Our primary concern was to present a cross-section of work by twentieth-century Canadian, Mexican, and United States women artists, working in as many different media and styles as possible. Of course, relatively little can be deduced about an artist's *oeuvre* from a single black-and-white reproduction, but we think that illustrations are a valuable part of any art reference book, and we thank Garland for agreeing to include these.

For any and all omissions and commissions that may appear in this volume, we take full responsibility and hope we will have an opportunity to correct them in the future. Meanwhile, let us simply add that for a long time, both of us have wanted to *use* a book like this. Finally, we can do so—and we hope that many other readers will find it useful, as well.

Nancy G. Heller
Associate Professor of Art
University of the Arts
Philadelphia, Pennsylvania

Jules Heller
Professor Emeritus of Art
Arizona State University
Tempe, Arizona

Contributors

Susan Aberth
Graduate student, graduate center
City University of New York (CUNY), New York City

Clinton Adams
Director Emeritus, Tamarind Institute
University of New Mexico, Albuquerque

Patricia Ainslie
Director, collections
Glenbow Museum, Calgary, Canada

Julie A. Aronson
Smithsonian Institution fellow
Washington, D.C.

Maria Balderama
Independent art historian
New York City

Miriam Basilio
Independent art historian
New York City

Susan F. Baxter
Independent art writer
Tempe, Arizona

Karen A. Bearor
Assistant professor of art history
Florida State University, Tallahassee

Lynne S. Bell
Department of Art and Art History
University of Saskatchewan, Saskatoon, Canada

Robert J. Belton
College professor
Okanagan University College, British Columbia, Canada

Janet Catherine Berlo
Professor of art history
University of Missouri, St. Louis

Allison P. Bertrand
Independent art historian
Paradise Valley, Arizona

Marilyn Lincoln Board
Associate professor of art history
State University of New York (SUNY), Genesco

Marie Bouchard
Baker Lake Fine Arts
Baker Lake, Northwest Territories, Canada

Christine Boyanoski
Curator
Art Gallery of Ontario, Toronto, Canada

Janine A. Butler
Independent art historian
Arva, Ontario, Canada

Kim Caldwell-Meeks
Registrar
Scottsdale Cultural Center, Scottsdale, Arizona

Elena Karina Canavier
Artist
Los Angeles, California

Deborah Caplow
Art historian
Seattle, Washington

Elizabeth Chew
Assistant curator
The Phillips Collection, Washington, D.C.

Julie Codell
Director, school of art
Arizona State University, Tempe

Caron Crane Compton
Independent art historian
Tempe, Arizona

Rhonda Cooper
Director, university art gallery
State University of New York (SUNY), Stony Brook

Barbara Cortright
Independent art historian
Tempe, Arizona

Dennis Costanzo
Associate professor of art
State University of New York (SUNY), Plattsburgh

Richard Cox
Professor of art history
Louisiana State University, Baton Rouge

Mary Craig
Fine arts director, retired
Kemptville, Ontario, Canada

Dawn-Starr Crowther
Independent writer/artist
Tempe, Arizona

Laura J. Crary-Ortega
Associate professor of art history
Western Washington University, Bellingham

Lori A. Cutler
Research and reference officer, Inuit art section
Indiana and Northern Affairs, Ottawa, Ontario, Canada

Martha Davidson
Grants manager, art museums
Harvard University, Cambridge, Massachusetts

Larry Day
Professor Emeritus
University of the Arts, Philadelphia, Pennsylvania

Kiana Dicker
Art writer
Laveen, Arizona

Karen Dugas
Artist
Tofield, Alberta, Canada

Bridget Elliott
Associate professor of art history
University of Alberta, Edmonton, Canada

Betsy Fahlman
Associate professor of art history
Arizona State University, Tempe

Ruth E. Fine
Curator, modern prints and drawings
National Gallery of Art, Washington, D.C.

Jean Gagnon
National Gallery of Canada
Ottawa, Ontario, Canada

Gretchen Garner
Academic dean
Moore College of Art, Philadelphia, Pennsylvania

Lucinda H. Gedeon
Director, Neuberger Museum of Art
State University of New York (SUNY), Purchase

Moira Geoffrion
Department of Art
University of Arizona, Tucson

Frank Gillette
Independent art critic
New York City

Cie Goulet
Artist and writer
New York City

Melissa J. Guenther
Graduate student, art history
Arizona State University, Tempe

Helen Hayes
Independent writer
Tempe, Arizona

Peggy J. Hazard
Independent art historian
Tucson, Arizona

Janice Helland
Associate professor, art history
Concordia University, Montréal, Québec, Canada

Jules Heller
Professor Emeritus of art
Arizona State University, Tempe

Nancy G. Heller
Associate professor of art
University of the Arts, Philadelphia, Pennsylvania

Victoria Henry
Visual arts curator
Ottawa, Ontario, Canada

Ingo Hessel
Coordinator, Inuit art section
Indian and Northern Affairs, Ottawa, Ontario, Canada

Delwyn Higgens
Independent art writer
Downsview, Ontario, Canada

Diana Emery Hulick
Professor of art history
Arizona State University, Tempe

Liz Ingram
Artist and professor
University of Alberta, Edmonton, Canada

Paul Ivey
Assistant professor of art history
University of Arizona, Tucson

Marion E. Jackson
Professor of art history
Carleton University, Ottawa, Ontario, Canada

Linda Jansma
Assistant curator
Robert Laughlin Gallery, Oshawa, Ontario, Canada

Ingrid Jenkner
Curator
Dunlop Art Gallery, Regina, Saskatchewan, Canada

Adeline Lee Karpiscak
Assistant director, museum of art
University of Arizona, Tucson

Ilona Katzew
Institute of Fine Arts
New York University, New York City

Martha Kearns
Independent art critic
New York City

Cynthia Lee Kerfoot
Independent scholar
Carmel Valley, California

Jeanne O. Snodgrass King
Museum curator, retired
Tulsa, Oklahoma

Nancy Knechtel
Assistant professor of fine arts
Niagara County Community College, Tonawanda, New York

Victor Koshkin-Youritzin
Associate professor of art history
University of Oklahoma, Norman

Marytka Kosinski
Professor Emeritus, Department of the History of Art and Design
University of Alberta, Edmonton, Canada

Barbara Kramer
Independent art scholar
Santa Fe, New Mexico

Travis Barton Kranz
Independent art writer
McLean, Virginia

Leonard Lehrer
Chair and professor, Department of Art and Art Professions
New York University, New York City

Vera Lemecha
Curator/writer/instructor
Regina, Sasketchewan, Canada

Odette Leroux
Curator, Canadian Museum of Civilization
Hull, Québec, Canada

Elaine Levin
Lecturer
University of California at Los Angeles (UCLA)

Heather Sealy Lineberry
Curator, art museum
Arizona State University, Tempe

Barbara Loeb
Associate professor of art
Oregon State University, Corvallis

Giancarlo Malvaioli von Nacher
Independent art critic
Nuevo León, Monterrey, Mexico

Virginia Hagelstein Marquardt
Associate professor of art history
Marist College, Poughkeepsie, New York

Patricia Mathews
Associate professor of art
Oberlin College, Ohio

Lynn McAllister
Independent art historian
Seattle, Washington

Cynthia Mills
Graduate student, art history and archeology
University of Maryland, College Park

Sylvia Moore
Freelance writer
Bronx, New York

Ann Lee Morgan
Independent scholar
Princeton, New Jersey

John Mraz
Graduate student
Mexico, D.F., Mexico

Maria Muehlen
Inuit art section
Indian and Northern Affairs, Ottawa, Ontario, Canada

Cynthia Navaretta
Publisher/writer
New York City

Melissa D. Olson
Editor/writer
Arizona State University, Tempe

Lyndal Osborne
Artist/professor
University of Alberta, Edmonton, Canada

Claire Campbell Park
Artist and lecturer
Tucson, Arizona

Phyllis Peet
Director, women's programs/women's studies
Monterey Peninsula College, Monterey, California

Frances K. Pohl
Associate professor of art and art history
Pomona College, Claremont, California

Elizabeth Poulson
Art historian
Glendale Community College, Glendale, Arizona

Cyril Reade
Professor of visual arts
University of Western Ontario, London, Canada

Deborah Anne Rindge
Assistant professor of art
New Mexico State University, Las Cruces

Spyro Rondos
Art writer
Montréal, Québec, Canada

Marie Routledge
National Gallery of Canada
Ottawa, Ontario, Canada

Judith Sealy
Independent art writer
Dallas, Texas

Janice Seline
Assistant curator of contemporary art
National Gallery of Canada, Ottawa, Ontario

Tryntje Van Ness Seymour
Independent art writer
Salisbury, Connecticut

Margaret Sheffield
Independent art critic
New York City

Judith P. Smith
Independent art writer
Scottsdale, Arizona

Karen E. Speirs
Independent art writer
Mesa, Arizona

Annalisa R. Staples
Northern Images
Yellowknife, Northwest Territories, Canada

Laine Sutherland
Curator of photography
Northern Arizona University, Flagstaff

Charlotte Townsend-Gault
Independent scholar
Bowen Island, British Columbia, Canada

Eleanor Tufts, deceased
Professor of art history
Southern Methodist University, Dallas, Texas

Rudy H. Turk
Director Emeritus, art museum
Arizona State University, Tempe

Frederick S. Voss
Curator
National Portrait Gallery, Washington, D.C.

Christine L. Wilson
Independent art historian
Edmond, Oklahoma

Paula Wisotzki
Professor, Department of the history of architecture and art
University of Illinois, Chicago

Independent scholars Tess Sidey and Lana Pitkin were also contributors of several entries.

Credits

Cecile Abish. *Chinese Crossing*. 1985. Gelatin silver photograph. 11 × 14 inches. Courtesy the artist.

Pat Adams. *Interstitial*. 1987. Oil, isobutyl methocrylate (mica and shell) on linen. 80 × 131½ inches. Courtesy the artist.

Lola Alvarez Bravo. *Triptico de los martirios* 3, n.d. Silver gelatin photograph. Archivo CENIDIAP-INBA.

Edna Andrade. *Blue Cylinder*. 1989. Acrylic on canvas. 18 × 76 inches. Greitzer and Locks Collection.

Judith Francisca Baca. *Balance*, a panel of the *World Wall: A Vision of the Future Without Fear*. 1989. Acrylic on canvas. 120 × 360 inches. Courtesy Social and Public Arts Resource Center (SPARC).

Peggy Bacon. *The Untilled Field*. 1937. Pastel on paper. 19⅛ × 25¼ inches. Collection of Whitney Museum of American Art. Gift of Mr. and Mrs. Albert Hackett.

Sofia Bassi. *Te Estoy Viendo*. 1970. Oil on masonite. 0.59 × 0.49 m. Courtesy the artist.

Cecilia Beaux. *Dorothea and Francesca*. 1898. Oil on canvas. 80⅛ × 46 inches. The Art Institute of Chicago. A.A. Munger Collection.

Leigh Behnke. *Civic Fame*. 1990. Oil on canvas. 48 × 36 inches. Courtesy the artist.

Susanne Bergeron. *Barques dans le port de Saint-Jean (Boats in the Harbor of Saint-Jean)*. 1958. Oil on canvas. 60.0 × 120.2 cm. National Gallery of Canada.

Rosemarie T. Bernardi. *She Lives in Three Houses*. 1985. Intaglio with photo. 24 × 36 inches. Courtesy the artist.

Louis Etherington Betteridge. *Jewish Wedding Cup*. 1993. Silver, moonstone, and lapis lazuli. 12 inches high. Courtesy the artist.

Isabel Bishop. *Subway Scene*. 1957–1958. Egg tempera and oil on composition board. 40 × 28 inches. Collection of Whitney Museum of American Art.

Nell Blaine. *Gardens Near Harbor*. 1992. Oil on canvas. 28 × 34 inches. Courtesy Fischbach Gallery, New York.

Kittie Bruneau. *La terre tourne (The World Turns)*. 1965. Oil on canvas. 160.8 × 127.8 cm. National Gallery of Canada.

Diane Burko. *Saule Pleurer—Giverny*. 1989. Oil on Arches paper. 37 × 68 inches. Courtesy the artist.

Mary Callery. *Perhaps*. 1950. Bronze. 27½ × 22 × 14 inches. Courtesy Arizona State University Art Museum, Tempe. Gift of Oliver B. James.

Wendy Calman. *Franklinstein.* 1982. Photo/mechanical construction. 276 × 168 × 96 inches. Courtesy the artist.

Florence Carlyle. *Grey and Gold.* 1910. Oil on canvas. 101.8 × 81.0 cm. National Gallery of Canada.

Emily Carr. *Cumshewa*, c. 1912. Watercolor over graphite. 52.0 × 75.5 cm. National Gallery of Canada.

Mary Cassatt. *Maternal Caress.* 1891. Etching and aquatint. 36.8 × 26.8 cm. The Art Institute of Chicago. Mr. and Mrs. Martin A. Ryerson Collection.

Elizabeth Catlett. *Woman Fixing Her Hair.* 1993. Wood. 28 × 19 × 15½ inches. Courtesy June Kelly Gallery.

Olga Costa. *Desnudo.* 1945. Oil on canvas. 22 × 15½ inches. Phoenix Art Museum. Gift of Mr. and Mrs. Orme Lewis.

Elaine de Kooning. *Jardin de Luxembourg.* 1977. Lithograph. 30 × 22 inches. The National Museum of Women in the Arts. Gift of Mr. and Mrs. James E. Foster.

Dora De Larios. *Goddess* (detail). 1990. Stoneware, porcelain, and gold leaf. 90 × 36 inches. Courtesy the artist.

Jennifer Dickson. *Crystalline Morning, Stourhead.* 1992. Hand-tinted etching. 24 × 32 inches. Courtesy the artist.

Geny Dignac. *Fire Sculpture E.D.M.* 1969–1971. Cor-ten steel, gas, 6 jets of fire. 222 × 12 × 12 inches. Courtesy the artist.

Sydney Drum. *Untitled (SD//P42).* 1991. Oil on canvas. 60 × 69 inches. Courtesy the artist.

Susan Macdowell Eakins. *Portrait of Thomas Eakins*, c. 1889. Oil on canvas. 50 × 40 inches. Philadelphia Museum of Art. Given by Charles Bregler.

Helen Escobedo. *Give Us This Day Our Daily Bread.* 1993. Two tons of rubble, 40 loaves, white cloth. 18 m. Courtesy the artist.

Aurora Estrada. *Peregrinacion.* 1976. Engraving on copper. 13 × 20 cm. Archivo CENIDIAP-INBA.

Gathie Falk. *Picnic with Birthday Cake and Blue Sky.* 1976. Glazed ceramic with acrylic and varnish in painted plywood case. 63.6 × 63.4 × 59.7 cm. National Gallery of Canada.

Elen A. Feinberg. *Sea Clouds.* 1990. Oil on linen. 56 × 70 inches. Courtesy the artist.

Jackie Ferrara. *M 165.* 1976. Masonite. 3 × 9¼ × 12¼ inches. The National Museum of Women in the Arts. Gift of Wallace and Wilhelmina Holladay.

Dorothy Fratt. *Spanish Drum.* 1992. Acrylic on canvas. 54 × 50 inches. Courtesy the artist and Riva Yares Gallery.

Jane Freilicher. *From the Studio.* 1989–1991. Oil on linen. 76 × 77¾ inches. Courtesy Fischbach Gallery, New York.

Sue Fuller. *String Construction #746.* 1987. Acrylite and teflon. 36 × 10½ × 8 inches. Courtesy the artist.

Flor Garduño. *Caracola.* 1957. Silver gelatin photo. 26.5 × 35.0 cm. Archivo CENIDIAP-INBA.

Judith Golden. *Earth* from the series, *The Elements.* 1993. Polaroid color photo with paint and collage. 30 × 26 inches. Courtesy the artist.

Andrea Gómez. *Madre contra la guerra*, n.d. Linoleum engraving. 32 × 39 cm. Collection INBA.

Betty Goodwin. *Vest with Plaster and Feathers.* 1974. Collage, acrylic, and plaster on construction paper. 61.0 × 45.7 cm. National Gallery of Canada.

Angela Gurría. *Tzompantli floreado.* 1993. Stone relief (detail). 1.8 × 4.0 m. Courtesy the artist.

Eva Hesse. *Study for Sculpture.* 1967. Sculpmetal, cord, acrylic medium, glue, and varnish on masonite. 10 × 10 × 1 inches. The National Museum of Women in the Arts. Gift of Wallace and Wilhelmina Holladay.

Prudence Heward. *Rollande.* Oil on canvas. 139.9 × 101.7 cm. National Gallery of Canada.

Kati Horna. *Calle Mariana, Barcelona.* 1938. Silver gelatin print. Archivo CENIDIAP-INBA.

Harriet Hosmer. *Beatrice Cenci.* 1856. Marble. 24 × 61½ × 24 inches. Collection of the St. Louis Mercantile Library Association.

Graciela Iturbide. *Untitled*, n.d. Silver gelatin print. Archivo CENIDIAP-INBA.

Maria Izquierdo. *El circo o Payasos de circo.* 1939. Gouache. 40 × 49 cm. Archivo CENIDIAP-INBA. Private collection.

Tamarra Kaida. *Hawks.* 1988. Silver gelatin print. 16 × 20 inches. Courtesy the artist.

Frida Kahlo. *Suicide of Dorothy Hale.* 1939. Oil on masonite panel with painted frame. 50.80 × 40.64 cm. Phoenix Art Museum. Gift of an anonymous donor.

Maryon Kantaroff. *The Wave.* 1992. Bronze with blue-green patina. 60 × 180 × 24 inches. Canadian Embassy, Tokyo, Japan.

Kenojouak. *The Woman Who Lives in the Sun.* 1960. Stonecut on laid paper. 54 × 65 cm. Courtesy West Baffin Eskimo Cooperative, Cape Dorset, NWT, Canada.

Lee Krasner. *The Guardian.* 1960. Oil on canvas. 53 × 58 inches. Collection of Whitney Museum of American Art. Purchase with funds from the Uris Brothers Foundation, Inc.

Joy Laville. *Playa en Baja California.* 1978. Oil on canvas. 140 × 180 cm. Archivo CENIDIAP-INBA. Collection the artist.

Rita Letendre. *After the Storm.* 1983. Acrylic on canvas. 30 × 40 inches. Courtesy the artist.

Edmonia Lewis. *Hagar.* 1875. Carved marble. 52⅝ × 15¼ × 17 inches. National Museum of American Art, Washington, D.C./Art Resource, New York.

Beth Lo. *Untitled Platter.* 1989. Porcelain. 18 × 18 × 2½ inches. Courtesy the artist.

Helen Lucas. *Paradise.* 1993. Acrylic on canvas. 54 × 84 inches. Courtesy the artist.

Bertha Lum. *Point Lobos.* 1920. Woodcut. 16¼ × 10¾ inches. Collection, Library of Congress, Prints and Photographs Division.

Loren MacIver. *Venice.* 1949. Oil on canvas. 59 × 93 inches. Collection of Whitney Museum of American Art.

Jo Manning. *Shirtseries.* 1993. Pen and ink. 13½ × 10½ inches. Courtesy the artist.

Sandra Meigs. *Purgatorio, A Drinkingbout (Four Room Bar with Smoke: Drinkingroom, Billiard Room, Dancing Room, Lounge No. 1).* 1981. Watercolor and pencil on wove paper. 27.9 × 33.0 cm. National Gallery of Canada.

Tina Modotti. *Nina con cubeta.* 1926. Silver gelatin print. Archivo CENIDIAP-INBA.

Ellen Murray. *Collection: Pinwheel Painting #3.* 1987. Watercolor. 39 × 59 inches. Courtesy the artist.

Louise Nevelson. *Young Shadows.* 1959–1960. Painted wood. 115 × 126 × 7¾ inches. Collection of Whitney Museum of American Art. Purchase with funds from the Friends of the Whitney Museum of American Art and Charles Simon.

Marion Nicoll. *Thursday's Model.* 1959. Oil on canvas. 92.0 × 51.1 cm. National Gallery of Canada.

Katie Ohe. *Night Watch.* 1988–1989. Cast aluminum, steel. 48½ × 124 × 124 inches. Courtesy the artist.

Georgia O'Keeffe. *Red Hills and Bones.* 1941. Oil on canvas. 30 × 40 inches. Philadelphia Museum of Art: The Alfred Stieglitz Collection.

Marta Palau. *La bufadora.* 1978. Mural tapestry. 187 × 182 × 28 cm. Collection Museo de Arte Moderno, INBA.

Irene Rice Pereira. *Landscape of the Absolute.* 1955. Oil on canvas. 40 × 50 inches. Collection of Whitney Museum of American Art. Gift of Richard Adler.

Leona Pierce. *Stilts #1.* Color woodcut. 26 × 20 inches. Courtesy the artist.

Ashoona Pitseolak. *Happy Family.* 1963. Engraving. 24.50 × 29.75 cm. Courtesy West Baffin Eskimo Cooperative, Cape Dorset, NWT, Canada.

Mary Pratt. *Red Currant Jelly.* 1972. Oil on masonite. 45.9 × 45.6 cm. National Gallery of Canada.

Georgina Quintana. *Untitled.* 1956. India ink on paper. 46 × 33 cm. Archivo CENIDIAP-INBA.

Fanny Rabel. *Callejon de la amagura.* 1949. Tempera and oil on masonite. 95 × 122 cm. Archivo CENIDIAP-INBA. Private collection.

Genevieve Reckling. *Cave of the Poet.* 1988. Oil on paper. 23 × 30 inches. Courtesy the artist.

Holly Roberts. *Bound Man Kneeling* (6 panels). 1992. Oil on gelatin silver print. Courtesy the artist.

Mariette Rousseau-Vermette. *Portes Secretes (Secret Doors).* 1983–1984. Wool and twine. 4 units, each 250 × 250 cm. Courtesy the artist.

Kay Sage. *No Passing.* 1954. Oil on canvas. 51¼ × 38 inches. Collection of Whitney Museum of American Art.

Norie Sato. *Wings of Transmission: Vertical Sync.* 1990. Wood, wax, pigment, etched glass. 76 × 37 × 15 inches. Courtesy the artist.

Helen Sawyer. *Arrangement with Pitcher and Green Glass,* n.d. Oil on canvas. 30 × 25 inches. Copyright ©1994 by the Indianapolis Museum of Art. Gift of Mrs. and Mrs. Wendell F. Coler in memory of their daughter Jean Coler.

Barbara Schwartz. *Head Land.* 1992. Painted cast aluminum. 35 × 34 × 13 inches. Courtesy the artist.

Marian Scott. *Artifact.* Acrylic on duck canvas. 152.4 × 152.4 cm. National Gallery of Canada. Royal Canadian Academy of Arts diploma work, deposited by the artist, Montréal, 1976.

Sarai Sherman. *Tower of Babel.* 1983. Majolica porcelain. 36 × 6 inches. Courtesy the artist.

Susana Sierra. *Forma silente.* 1983. Oil on canvas. 130 × 160 cm. Archivo CENIDIAP-INBA.

Clarissa T. Sligh. *Who We Was.* 1993. Installation: Caran d'Ache crayon on Cyanotype and engraved plastic. 90 × 240 inches. Courtesy the artist.

Lila Snow. *DNA Birds.* 1992. Oil on canvas. 40 × 40 inches. Courtesy the artist.

Lisa Steele. *The Ballad of Dan Peoples.* 1976. B/w videotape, 8:00 minutes on 3/4" cassette. National Gallery of Canada.

Dorothea Tanning. *Paris and Vicinity.* 1962. Oil on canvas. 100 × 78 3/4 inches. Collection of Whitney Museum of American Art. Gift of Alexander Iolas Gallery.

Anne Truitt. *Summer Dryad.* 1971. Acrylic on wood. 76 × 13 × 8 inches. Courtesy The National Museum of Women in the Arts. Gift of the Holladay Foundation.

Agnese Udinotti. *Stele #2* (detail). Welded steel. 42 × 12 × 10 inches. Private collection, Paris, France.

Lucinda Urrusti. *Desnudo gris.*, n.d. Pigment. 33 × 25 cm. Archivo CENIDIAP-INBA. Collection of the artist.

Cordelia Urueta. *Al filo de la obsidiana.* 1964. Oil on canvas. 109 × 150 cm. Archivo CENIDIAP-INBA. Private collection.

Charmion von Wiegand. *Triptych, Number 700.* 1961. Oil on canvas. 3 panels, overall: 42 1/4 × 54 inches. Collection of Whitney Museum of American Art. Gift of Alvin M. Greenstein.

Esther Warkov. *Memorial to a Dead Lover.* 1966. Oil on canvas. 113.8 × 162.3 cm. National Gallery of Canada.

June Claire Wayne. *Empyrealite Two.* 1988. Lithograph, molded paper, silver leaf. 31 × 22 inches. Courtesy the artist.

Ruth Weisberg. *Alone, Together.* 1989. Charcoal, graphite, oil, and wax on unstretched canvas. 46 1/2 × 63 3/4 inches. Courtesy the artist.

Mia Westerlund. *Untitled No. 2.* 1980. Charcoal on wove paper. 151.5 × 107.5 cm. National Gallery of Canada, Ottawa.

Catherine E. Wild. *Eyes of Fire I.* 1991. Lithograph. 41 × 29 inches. Courtesy the artist.

Jane Wilson. *Salt Marsh.* 1993. Oil on linen. 70 × 60 inches. Courtesy Fischbach Gallery, New York.

Mariana Yampolsky. *Carisia-Caress.* 1992. Silver gelatin print. 6 1/4 × 8 1/4 inches. Courtesy the artist.

North American
Women Artists
of the Twentieth Century

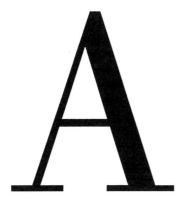

Aarons, Anita (1912–)

Born in Sydney, Australia, sculptor Anita Aarons studied at technical colleges and the National Art School in Sydney, Australia, before studying at Columbia University, New York City (1964), where she showed work in the First World Crafts Conference Exhibition. Aarons also exhibited work in the National Crafts Exhibition, Toronto, Canada (1968); the National Sculpture Exhibition, Melbourne, and the First Outdoor Exhibition, Sydney—both in Australia; among others.

A teacher of sculpture and crafts in institutions in Australia and Canada, Aarons also designs stained glass windows, furniture, and jewelry which, in effect, are sculptures to wear. Her work is represented in private and public permanent collections, including the Charlottetown National Craft Collection, Prince Edward Island, and National Collection of the Canadian Craftsmen Guild, Toronto—both in Canada; and others.

Bibliography

Munk, Linda, and May Ebbit Cutler. "The Jeweller as a Sculptor—Jack Pocock, Anita Aarons, Walter Schluep." *Canadian Art* 22:4 (September–October 1965): 44–48.

Who's Who in American Art. 15th ed. R.R. Bowker Co., 1982.

Abadi, Fritzie

Daughter of a rabbi, Fritzie Abadi was born in Aleppo, Syria, lived in Jerusalem (then Palestine), and emigrated to New York when she was nine years old. Abadi's interest in art was kindled when she won a drawing competition at Bay Ridge High School, Brooklyn.

Married at eighteen, Abadi moved to Oklahoma City, gave birth to two daughters, and "forgot about art." She returned to Brooklyn in 1945 and the following year enrolled in the Art Students League, New York City, where her mentor and sole teacher was Nahum Tschacbasov.

Abadi has had ten solo exhibitions in New York institutions and has had her paintings and sculpture invited to many group shows, including the Brooklyn Museum, New York; the various annuals at the Whitney Museum of American Art, New York City; the Carnegie Institute, Pittsburgh, Pennsylvania; and the Library of Congress. Her works are in the permanent collections of the Butler Institute of American Art, Youngstown, Ohio; the Evansville Museum of Arts and Science, Indiana; the Slater Memorial Museum, Norwich, Connecticut; and the Georgia Museum of Art in Athens.

Abadi won the Acrylic Painting Award from the National Association of Women Artists (1974); the American Society of Contemporary Artists honored her with their Box Assemblage Award (1978) and an award for oil painting (1979), among others. *America's First Hurrah* (1976), a two-by-three-foot collage, reveals Abadi's wit and sophistication in a potpourri of colonial history, including George Washington.

She is a member of a clutch of institutions, including the National Association of Women Artists (member of the board, 1970); American Society of Contemporary Artists (president, 1970–1972); New York Society of Women Artists (member of the board, 1980); Women in the Arts; and the Hudson River Contemporary Artists.

Bibliography
"Fritzie Abadi." *Arts* 51:32 (October 1976): 32.
"Fritzie Abadi." *Arts* 53:42 (June 1979): 42.
Who's Who in American Art. 19th ed. R.R. Bowker Co., 1990–1991.

Abascal, Amelia (1923–)

Born in Madrid, Spain, Amelia Abascal was primarily self-taught. When she came to Mexico in 1940, she took advanced studies in chemistry, as it applies to the plastic arts. Painter, ceramist, and designer—Abascal specializes in relief works, though she has also painted murals.

In 1968, along with three other artists, Abascal represented Mexico at a Latin American painting exhibition held in Argentina. That same year she won acclaim in a highly contentious and original solo exhibition at the Misrachi Gallery in Mexico City, Mexico. By and large, she treats laminated sheets of bronze and copper with acids in her abstract works, which seem to evoke the textures and patinas of eroded, natural phenomena.

Bibliography
Alvarez, José Rogelio, et al. *Enciclopedia de México.* Secretaría de
    Educación Pública, 1987.
The Texas Quarterly: Image of Mexico I. The University of Texas,
    Autumn 1969.

Abascal, Graciela (1939–)

Born in Mexico, Graciela Abascal studied at the Ibero-American University, Mexico City, for three years, then spent five years learning the discipline of painting under the aegis of José Marquez F.

A figurative artist who occasionally approached the surreal or fantastic in her work, Abascal has had her work in myriad solo exhibitions, including twenty-five watercolors titled "Rincones de Puebla," in Puebla (1968); twenty-five oils (painted with a spatula) at the Unión de Artes Plásticas, Puebla (1969); the Galerías de la Ciudad de Mexico de la Alameda Central, and a special invitation to show at the Ayuntamiento de Teziutlán, Puebla (1970); "Mexican Landscape" in the Galería de Arte of the Hotel Camino Real (1971)—all in Mexico; "Spatula Oil Colors" and "Paisaje de Graciela Abascal," shown in the Friendship Gardens, Brownsville, Texas (1972); "Mexican Landscape" exhibited at the Hotel Fremont, Los Angeles, and the St. Francis Hotel, San Francisco, California (1972); the Henkle Galleries in Houston, Texas (1973); the Galería Romano in Mexico (1974); "Puebla en Oleos y Acrílicos" at the Sala Agustín Arrieta, Casa de la Cultura, Puebla (1977); and the exhibitions in the "Eliseo" and the "Jardín del Arte" in Oaxaca (1978)—both in Mexico. Abascal has also shown her work throughout Mexico and abroad in group exhibitions for many years.

Bibliography
Alvarez, José Rogelio, et al. *Enciclopedia de México.* Secretaría de
    Educación Pública, 1987.
*Biografico Enciclopedia Diccionário de la Pintura Mexicana: Siglo Arte
    Contemporaneo.* Quiniéntos Años Editores, 1979.

Abbe, Elfriede (1919–)

Born in Washington, D.C., the sculptor and graphic artist Elfriede Abbe earned her Bachelor of Fine Arts degree from Cornell University, Ithaca, New York, in 1940. Her prints are in many permanent collections throughout the United States and abroad, including the Grolier Club, New York City; Beinecke Library, Yale University, New Haven, Connecticut; the Watson Library in the Metropolitan Museum of Art, New York City; National Library of Australia, Canberra; National Library of Ottawa, Canada; Museum of Fine Arts, Venice, Italy; Kew Gardens Library, London, England; and many others.

Abbe carved "The Explorer" and fabricated a bronze head of Napoleon for the library at McGill University, Canada; she created a thirty-foot frieze for the Mann Library of Cornell University, Ithaca, New York; and sculpted works in bronze, a portrait bust of Liberty Hyde Bailey, a marble sculpture in Morrison Hall, and six memorial plaques. She created a bronze bust for the Herzog August Bibliothek, Wolfenbuttel, Germany; a nine-foot sculpture, "The Hunter," for the New York World's Fair (1939); and much more.

Abbe has had no less than fourteen solo exhibitions of her work in various museums and institutions in the United States and has had her sculpture and graphic output invited by the National Academy of Design, New York City (1970); Carnegie-Mellon University, Pittsburgh, Pennsylvania (1968, 1972, 1977); National Society of Mural Painters, New Hampshire (1981); and the Columbia University Fine Printing Conference (1982), to name a few invitations. She has won myriad awards, grants, and prizes for her work.

A member of the National Arts Club, National Society of Mural Painters; Phi Kappa Phi; and a fellow of the National Sculpture Society, Abbe is also the proprietor of the Press of Elfriede Abbe—a one-person establishment—which she founded in 1950. During her five-decade career, in which she has been sculptor, author, printer, and printmaker, Abbe has worked on the highest qualitative levels. Her most recent hand-set book (which she printed, illustrated with thirty-eight wood engravings, and bound), *The City of Carcasonne* by Eugène Viollet-le-Duc (1991), has an edition of one hundred and ten copies. Abbe's wood engravings capture the feeling of the famed medieval fortress with a minimum of burin strokes.

Bibliography
Archives. Ithaca, New York: Cornell University.
Archives of American Art. Washington, D.C.: Smithsonian Institution.
    Elfriede Abbe Papers.
Who's Who in American Art. 15th ed. R.R. Bowker Co., 1982.

Abbott, Berenice (1898–1991)

An early advocate of realism in photography, Berenice Abbott has emerged as one of the most prolific artists and technicians in twentieth-century photography. Born in Springfield, Ohio, she studied at the Ohio State University, Columbus (1917–1918) and at Columbia University, New York City, where she received some training in journalism. For the three years following her brief exposure to académie she studied painting and sculpture in New York City, then went to Paris, France, in 1921, where she studied at the Studio of Emil Bourdelle and frequented the Grand Chaumière and the studio of Constantin Brancusi until 1923. She then travelled to Berlin, Germany, where she enrolled as a student in the Kunstschule before returning to Paris where she worked for two years as an assistant to the surrealist photographer and painter Man Ray until 1925. This period is a pivotal one in her life, since Man Ray's studio is where she learned to print and develop. It also was in this studio that she became acquainted with the Parisian avant-garde—many of whom would pose for her when she opened her own studio in 1926. From 1926 to 1929 Abbott's portraits formed a visual history of literary and artistic Paris. André Gide, Jean Cocteau, James Joyce, Marie Laurencin, Marcel DuChamp, André Maurois, and Princess Eugènie Marat posed for her to create insightful portraits lighted primarily by natural light. She acknowledged the influence of the nineteenth-century photographer Nadar (Gaspard Félix) in her attempt to express the character of her sitters. Like Nadar, Abbott was fascinated with the potential of photography as a historical record.

Prior to her encounter with the work of Nadar, however, Abbott had a first solo exhibit in 1926 at the Au Sacre du Printemps Gallery where her "Portraits Photographiques" were introduced by Jean Cocteau. The following year she purchased prints and negatives from the estate of Eugène Atget—a chronicler of Paris, with whom she had recently become acquainted but who died that same year. Atget's objective yet human documentary photographs of Paris made primarily between 1900 and 1920 may have inspired Abbott to document the city of New York.

Abbott was also convinced of Atget's greatness and reprinted many of his works from the original negatives; she later donated many of the prints to the Museum of Modern Art (MoMA) in New York City. In this way she functioned as an important historian as well as a photographer.

When she arrived in New York in 1929, Abbott conceived the idea of photographing the changing aspects of the city. Her project "Changing New York," which she began that same year, did not receive financing until 1935 when the Federal Art Project of the Works Progress Administration hired Abbott to photograph the city for $35 a week. To complete this task she first made brief records with a Curt Bentzin—a German medium format single-lens reflex camera. At this time Walker Evans was also using a small format camera for his studies of the New York City subways. Both photographers shared similar modernist sensibilities in their search to capture the ephemeral quality of city life using the objectivity of the camera. Neither went through a pictorialist phase in their development, as did so many of their contemporaries in photography. Rather, like Matthew Brady and William Henry Jameson, whom Abbott also admired, Evans and Abbott were documentary photographers from the beginning.

By using an eight-by-ten view camera for her final images of "Changing New York," Abbott was able to control its swings and tilts to create meaningful juxtapositions of objects as well as exposures whose meticulously focused receding parallels brought the salient details of city architecture and its ambient life into play. She was a deliberate, methodical, and superb technician and was granted six photographic patents. She also authored over ten books, including such technical classics as *The View Camera Made Simple* (1948).

Although documentary in style, her photographs are not without internal commentary. "Changing New York" includes many photographs that reveal the ethnic diversity of the city. Other images show carefully composed storefronts, with little reflection to hide the plethora of objects available to the consumer. Images of skyscrapers and the Wall Street financial district comment on the power represented by these buildings and institutions. Abstractions and distortions produced by the camera were occasionally used to expressive ends in this last group of work.

In 1939 *Fortune* magazine hired Abbott to take portraits of American businessmen, and *Life* magazine hired her to take a series of photographs of scientific subjects. These latter constitute investigations of new subject matter and continue from 1940 to 1961, culminating in her work for the physical sciences study committee of Educational Services, Inc. of New York. During these years she produced illustrations of physical phenomena, such as electricity and principles in physics. During this period she also completed a book on photographs of Maine, where she settled in 1968. Since then, Abbott has been included in numerous retrospectives, books, and catalogs, including MoMA, New York City (1970), "The Women of Photography," San Francisco Museum of Art, California (1975), "Paris Berlin 1900 to 1933" at the Centre G. Pompidou, Paris, France (1978); and the International Center for Photography, New York City (1981). The years since her retirement were spent reprinting her photographs as eight-by-ten-inch contact silver prints or, more rarely, enlarging them to eleven-by-fourteen-inch or to sixteen-by-twenty-inch.

Diana Emery Hulick

Bibliography
Abbott, Berenice. Text by Elizabeth MacCausland. *Changing New York*. Dutton, 1939.
———. *A Guide to Better Photography*. Crown, 1941.
———. *The View Camera Made Simple*. Ziff Davis, 1948.
———. Text by E.G. Valens. *Magnet*. World, 1964.
———. *The World of Atget*. Horizon Press, 1964.
———. Text by E.G. Valens. *Motion*. World, 1965.
——— with Chenoworth Hall. *A Portrait of Maine*. Macmillan, 1968.
———. Text by E.G. Valens. *The Attractive Universe*. World, 1969.
Mann, Margery, and Ann Noggle, eds. "Women of Photography." San Francisco Museum of Art, 1975.
Tucker, Ann, ed. *The Women's Eye*. Alfred A. Knopf, 1973.
Vestal, David. *Berenice Abbott Photographs*. Horizon Press, 1970.

Abeles, Kim (1952–)

Originally from Missouri, Kim Abeles spent a year in Japan during high school and befriended a Buddhist priest who introduced her to the traditional Japanese arts. From 1970 to 1974 Abeles pursued a Bachelor of Fine Arts degree in painting at Ohio University, Athens, and discovered the socially-conscious assemblages of Edward Kienholz in an art history text. Abeles moved to Southern California in 1978 to attend graduate school and completed a Master of Fine Arts degree at the University of California, Irvine, in 1980. Her Master's research thesis focused on Shingon Buddhism and included a highly-acclaimed series of Kimonos that explored philosophical issues. Abeles's assemblages and multi-part installations are constructed primarily from found objects and focus upon social or historical concepts.

After graduation Abeles established a studio in downtown Los Angeles, California, where she continues to live and work. In 1982 she began creating shrine-like assemblages and contraption pieces with photo-documentation. For "Experiment to Identify Change" (1983) Abeles photographed her hands every day for seven and one-half months with a specially built contraption. The "St. Bernadette" series is a major and characteristic work that explores the life of the saint and the commercialization of religion. "The Image of St. Bernadette" installation of 1987 included a pachenko game and orthopedic chair adorned with the saint's image and a travelling sales bag full of St. Bernadette souvenirs. Other major series of the 1980s include the "Dead Sea Scrolls" sculptures and biographical portraits of Alma Mahler, Calamity Jane, and Julius and Ethel Rosenberg.

In the 1990s Abeles has become increasingly concerned with contemporary issues. "L.A. Smog" documented the build-up of smog residue on objects on the roof of the artist's studio. "Living with AIDS" was a collaborative installation to increase the awareness of the epidemic.

Abeles's work was included in the landmark exhibition "Object/Concept—Forty Years of California Assemblage" at the University of California at Los Angeles (UCLA) in 1989.

Heather Sealy Lineberry

Bibliography

Brown, Betty Ann. "Kim Abeles." *Forty Years of California Assemblage.* University of California, 1989.

Sims, Patterson, and Michael McMillan. *Kim Abeles.* A.R.T. Press, 1989.

Smith, Richard. "Tradition and Transition in Southern California Art." *New Art Examiner* (March 1989).

Zimmerer, Kathy. "The Image of St. Bernadette." *Visions* 1:3 (Summer 1987).

Aber, Ita (1932–)

Sculptor, painter, fiber artist, art historian, and curator, Ita Aber was born in Montréal, Canada. Between 1968 and 1981 Aber studied at Queens College, New York University, Columbia University, and the Jewish Theological Seminary—all in New York. She received her Bachelor's degree in cultural studies from Empire State College, New York, and did graduate work at the Valentine Museum in Richmond, Virginia.

Aber studied painting with Ann Savage in Canada, sculpture with Hana Geber and Jessica Holden, and fiber arts at the Valentine Museum and Embroiderers Guild of America. She has had eight solo exhibitions in New York museums and galleries, including Empire State College (1989); Seltzer Gallery (1987, 1988); Columbia University (1981); and the Judaica Museum, Riverdale (1988).

Her works have been invited to many national and international group exhibitions, among which are Hebrew Union College, New York (1991); the Flagler Museum, Palm Beach, Florida (1991); Lever House, New York (1990); Phoenix Gallery, New York (1988); Joods Historisches Museum, Amsterdam (1986); Cooper-Hewitt Museum, New York City (1983); and the Yeshiva University Museum (1976, 1982).

Aber's many-faceted works are in major permanent collections such as the National Museum of American History, Smithsonian Institution, Washington, D.C.; the Cooper-Hewitt Museum, New York City; Valentine Museum, Richmond, Virginia; the Fashion Institute of Technology, New York City; the Israel Museum, Jerusalem; the Jewish Museum, New York City; the Skirball Museum, Los Angeles, California; and many others. *Gamma #10*, an embroidery with paint on silk, is based upon a pre-Christian symbol that was applied to a woman's garment. Aber re-creates the symbol in bold,

contemporary colors, striking composition, and multilayered meanings.

Author of many articles and books from 1969 onward, Aber has taught and lectured extensively throughout the United States on fiber arts, women's craft, Jewish art, textile restoration, and needlework. She is a member of New York Artists Equity, the Hudson River Contemporary Artists, Women's Caucus for the Arts, the National Association of Corporate Art Managers, and the American Institute for Conservation. Among other affiliations Aber is curator at the Hebrew Home for the Aged, Riverdale, New York, and adjunct curator of the Park Avenue Synagogue, New York City.

Bibliography

Aber, Ita. *The Art of Judaic Needlework.* Charles Scribner's Sons, 1979.

Langer, Cassandra. "Ita Aber: Refabricated Mysteries." *Women Artists News* (Spring 1988): 17.

Who's Who in American Art. 19th ed. R.R. Bowker Co., 1991.

Abercrombie, Gertrude (1908–1977)

Gertrude Abercrombie's appreciation of the alien and the theatrical may be traceable to early childhood years in Berlin, Germany, where her mother pursued a career in opera. It was in Chicago, Illinois, however, that Abercrombie matured and pursued an art of surrealist illusion.

Abercrombie earned a degree in romance languages at the University of Illinois, Urbana, but had little formal art training. "There on the Table" (1935) marks the emergence of her personal sensibility. In this odd still life of uneasily coexisting objects, a stiff realism emphasizes underlying and unresolved tensions.

In the 1940s Abercrombie left the Works Progress Administration (WPA), which had provided her income for several years, married twice, and bore a daughter. Her home became a gathering place for unconventional writers, artists, and jazz musicians. As Abercrombie's paintings now became more controlled and smaller, they gained psychological richness. The autobiographical impetus behind much of her art is evident in the obscure but tantalizing "Marble Top Mystery" (probably after 1950). Here, a ghostly self-portrait and a dead tree rise through twin holes in a table set in a vast, inhospitable landscape.

By the late 1950s Abercrombie began to accumulate misfortunes: divorce, financial reverses, and illnesses. She responded by further constricting the size of her work, tightening her technique, and enlarging her symbolism. The meticulously executed "Ostrich Egg" (1963) is a meditation on perfection, failure, and emptiness.

Ann Lee Morgan

Bibliography

Gillespie, Dizzy, Wendell Wilcox, and James Purdy. *Gertrude Abercrombie: A Retrospective Exhibition.* Hyde Park Art Center, 1977.

Weininger, Susan. *Gertrude Abercrombie and Friends.* Illinois State Museum, 1983.

Abish, Cecile

A native New Yorker, Cecile Abish was a successful urban planner until 1965, when she devoted herself full-time to art. Abish is a graduate of Brooklyn College, New York, with a Bachelor of Fine Arts degree in sculpture. For the past twenty-five years, she created works that may be termed post-minimalist, if, indeed, it can be labelled at all. However, hers is an additive art concerned with appropriating institutional surfaces, temporarily, for aesthetic purposes. According to Abish: "the surfaces upon which I work do not belong to me." Hers is an art that reprocesses information—that makes the viewer reexamine that which has always been taken for granted. Abish's art is a subtle, highly-sophisticated, witty, old-master-inspired series of site sculptures—and work in other media—to elicit cogitation.

A sampling of Abish's recent solo exhibitions encompasses work using "marbles"—the familiar variegated cat's eye marbles—baking soda, particle board, carpets and other indoor floors, lawns and excavations in the earth, steel rods, photographs, and ordinary, garden-variety houses in the following institutions: "Say When," the Center for Creative Photography, Tucson, Arizona (1984); "From the Marble Works 1974–1979," the State University of New York (SUNY) at Stony Brook (1982); "Fogg," Anderson Gallery, Virginia Commonwealth University, Richmond (1981); "Past Projects," Harvard University, Cambridge, Massachusetts (1979); Wright State University Art Gallery, Dayton, Ohio (1978); "Near/Next/Now," Alessandra Gallery, New York City (1977); "Shifting Concern," Douglass College, Rutgers University, New Brunswick, New Jersey (1975); "Surface Clearance," Institute of Contemporary Art, Boston, Massachusetts (1974); and "Field Coil," 112 Greene Street Gallery, New York City (1971).

Abish has had her work in myriad group exhibitions from Rhode Island to Vienna, Austria; New York City; Stuttgart, Germany; Tokyo, Japan; Peoria, Illinois; and Stockholm, Sweden. She has published eight photo works, including "99: The New Meaning, Burning Deck" (1990); "Chinese Crossing Conjunctions 9" (1986); and "Firsthand," Wright State University, Dayton, Ohio (1978).

In addition to offering workshops, serving on panels, and giving lectures, Abish has been visiting artist at Harvard University, Cambridge, Massachusetts; the Cooper Union, New York City; University of Massachusetts, Amherst; North Carolina School for the Arts, Winston-Salem; and Queens College, New York City. She has won a Creative Artist Public Service (CAPS) fellowship (1974); National Endowment for the Arts (NEA) fellowships (1975, 1977, 1980); and a DAAD award in Berlin, West Germany (1987), among others.

Bibliography
Alloway, Lawrence. "Cecile Abish: Recent Sculpture." *Arts Magazine* 51:6 (February 1977): 140–41.
Glueck, Grace. *The New York Times* (July 11, 1980): C19.
Keeffe, Jeffrey. "Cecile Abish: From the Ground Up." *Artforum* 17:2 (October 1978): 35–39.
Kingsley, April. "Six Women at Work in the Landscape." *Arts Magazine* 52:8 (April 1978): 108–12.
Kuspit, Donald B. "Cecile Abish's Museum of the Absurd." *Art in America* (January 1982): 111–15.

Abraham, Carol Jeanne (1949–)

Born in Philadelphia, Pennsylvania, the ceramist/assemblage artist Carol Jeanne Abraham studied at a number of institutions of higher learning, including the Tyler School of Art, Temple University, Philadelphia (1964–1967); Boston Museum School of Fine Arts, Massachusetts (1967–1971); Tufts University, Medford, Massachusetts, where she earned a Bachelor's degree (1967–1971); Rochester Institute of Technology, School for American Craftsmen, New York, where she received a Master of Fine Arts degree (1973). She also attended the Penland School for Crafts, North Carolina (1975) and received a diploma from the Brooks Institute for Photography (1988).

Abraham, who has taught various media in schools and colleges, has exhibited work in museums and galleries in the United States and abroad: from New York to Spokane, Washington; from University Park, Pennsylvania to Auckland, New Zealand; and many other venues.

Examples of her work are in private and public permanent collections, including Brigham Young University, Provo, Utah; Museum of Ceramics, Bassano Del Grappa, Italy; Renwick Gallery, Smithsonian Institution, Washington, D.C.; Rochester Institute of Technology, New York; and others.

Bibliography
"Review." *Ceramics Monthly* 23 (May 1975): 24–26.
"Review." *Ceramics Monthly* 24 (October 1976): 34.
"Review." *Ceramics Monthly* 36 (April 1983): 71.

Abramowicz, Janet

A native New Yorker, Janet Abramowicz attended Columbia University, New York, and studied with Morris Kantor and Robert Beverly Hale at the Art Students League. She earned a Bachelor of Fine Arts degree in painting and printmaking (1953) and a Master of Fine Arts degree in painting and art history (1955) from the Accademia di Belle Arti, Bologna, Italy, where she was a teaching assistant to Giorgio Morandi (1952–1955).

Abramowicz held solo exhibitions of her work at the Nantenshi Gallery, Tokyo, Japan (1981); the Susan Caldwell Gallery, New York (1980); and La Strozzina di Palazzo Strozzi, Florence, Italy (1955). Her graphic work has been invited to group exhibitions throughout the United States, Italy, Japan, and England, including the 11th British International Biennale, Royal College of Art, London, and Bradford, England (1990–1991); "Public and Private: American Prints Today," travelling, Brooklyn Museum, New York City (1986–1987); "Prints Recently Acquired," Metropolitan Museum of Art, New York City (1985); 24th National Exhibition," Tokyo, Japan (1979); "National Exhibition of Prints," Library of Congress, Washington, D.C. (1973); the Weyhe Gallery, New York City (1956, 1959, 1971); and many others.

Abramowicz has garnered many honors for her work between 1962 and 1992, including fellowships from the Guggenheim Foundation (1992), and the American Council of Learned Societies (1990–1991). She was elected an honorary fellow of the Accademia Clementina, Bologna, Italy (1990); won a Fulbright fellowship to Italy (1989); held a residency at the Rockefeller Foundation's Study and Conference Center, Bellagio, Italy (1989); and held the post of visiting artist at the American Academy in Rome (Summers 1984, 1985, 1989); to name a few. In addition to her studio expertise, she is a writer, lecturer, panelist and expert on Giorgio Morandi.

Her work is in the permanent collections of the Metropolitan Museum of Art, New York City; the Fogg Art Museum, Cambridge, Massachusetts; Boston Public Library, Massachusetts; New York Public Library; Museo di Arte Moderna, La Spezia, Italy; Galleria d'Arte Moderna, Bologna, Italy; the New Museum, Hokkaido, Japan; Ohara Museum, Kurashiki, Japan; the Tokyo Gallery, Japan; and many others.

Since 1955 Abramowicz has taught the history of materials and techniques in painting, drawing, and printmaking at various museums and universities, including the University of Illinois at Chicago (1955–1957); School of the Worcester Art Museum (1957–1958); Boston Museum of Fine Arts (1958–1970); the Radcliffe Institute Seminar Program (1965–1971); and Harvard University, Cambridge (1971–1979)—all in Massachusetts.

Bibliography
Haas, Irving. "Print Collector." *Art News* 56 (January 1958): 63–65.
Walker, Barry. *The American Artist as Printmaker: 23rd National Print Exhibition.* Brooklyn Museum, 1984.
Who's Who in American Art. 19th ed. R.R. Bowker Co., 1991–1992.

Abrams, Jane (1940–)
During the 1970s and early 1980s Jane Abrams established a growing reputation for her work as a printmaker. Her color intaglio prints, notable both for their technical complexity and sophisticated wit, were regularly included in national and international exhibitions, receiving many awards and prizes. At the height of her career as a printmaker Abrams suffered adverse effects from the chemicals that are used in the intaglio process. Unable to continue her work in printmaking, Abrams turned to painting, and while artist-in-residence at the Roswell Museum and Art Center, New Mexico (1985–1986) created a series of large, expressionist landscapes which proclaimed a total shift in direction. Working in oil and encaustic Abrams used a palette of deep reds and blues to evoke a foreboding world of swirling waters and silent, autumnal forests. Since 1986 her paintings have been seen in a series of impressive solo exhibitions at the Roswell Museum and Art Center, New Mexico (1986); Robischon Gallery, Denver, Colorado (1987, 1989); Norman R. Eppink Gallery, Emporia State University, Emporia, Kansas (1988); Marilyn Butler Fine Art, Santa Fe, New Mexico (1988); and Nora Eccles Harrison Museum of Art, Logan, Utah (1989).

Abrams was born in Eau Claire, Wisconsin, attended the University of Wisconsin-Stout, Menomonie, and earned Bachelor of Science (1962) and Master of Science (1967) degrees. After graduate study in printmaking at the University of Indiana, Bloomington, where she earned a Master of Fine Arts degree (1971), she received a faculty appointment at the University of New Mexico, Albuquerque, where she is now professor of art. Her prints and paintings are included in many public collections, principally in the Midwest and Southwest.

Clinton Adams

Bibliography
Jane Abrams: Recent Paintings. New Mexico: Roswell Museum and Art Center, 1986.
Deats, Suzanne. "Jane Abrams: Designing a Life for Art." *Artlines* (July–August 1987).

Abrams, Joyce Diana (1945–)
Native New Yorker Joyce Diana Abrams received her Bachelor of Fine Arts degree from the Cooper Union in New York City (1966) and a Master of Fine Arts degree from Columbia University, New York, six years later. She studied with Leon Goldin, John Heliker, Charles Cajori, and Philip Guston.

Abrams's most recent solo exhibition was held at the Edward Williams Gallery, Fairleigh Dickinson University, Hackensack, New Jersey (1988). Her work has been selected for group exhibitions in many institutions throughout the United States, including "Black and White on Paper," National Arts Club (1982); "The Painting Tradition," Houghton Gallery, the Cooper Union (1982); "5 and Japan," The Nippon Gallery (1982); "Newscapes Land and City-States of Mind," One Penn Plaza (1984)—all in New York City; "Painted Constructions—Constructed Paintings," Rockland Center for the Arts, Nyack, New York (1985); "Mid-America Biennial," Owensboro Museum of Fine Arts, Kentucky (1988); the Knoxville Museum of Fine Art, Tennessee (1989); and others.

Abrams taught painting at the City University of New York (CUNY) (1978–1981) and since 1989 has been on the teaching staff of the Parsons School of Design, New York City. She was a MacDowell Colony fellow (1985, 1987) and a resident fellow at Yaddo, Saratoga Springs, New York (1988).

In addition to their metaphoric interpretations, Abrams's wall constructions celebrate and reveal the process of construction: *Winter Night* contains an abstract oil as part of the piece, which allows the viewer to see the wooden support beneath the work. Her work is in many corporate collections throughout the United States and Canada—from New York to Colorado; from Alaska to Canada.

Bibliography
Bush, Steve. "See Here, Now-Back to the Present." *Artspeak* (February 16, 1986).
Morris, Diana. "Summer Group Show." *Arts Magazine* 58:5 (October 1983).
Who's Who in American Art. 19th ed. R.R. Bowker Co., 1991–1992.

Abrams, Ruth (1912–1986)
Ruth Abrams was born in Brooklyn, New York, and studied art at several institutions, including the Art Students League, Columbia University, and the New School for Social Research—all in New York City; she also enrolled in workshops tutored by William Zorach and Alexander Archipenko. Abrams is known for her spacescape paintings, including one entitled, "There Are Unknown Elements in the Universe as Old as Mankind" (1962).

Solo exhibitions of Abrams's work were displayed in museums and galleries in the United States and abroad, including the Museum of Fine Arts, Caracas, Venezuela (1963); the Massachusetts Institute of Technology (MIT), Cambridge (1964, 1969); Delson-Richter Galleries, Jerusalem, Israel (1976); Contemporary Art Gallery, New York University (1977); Amarillo Art Center, Texas (1977–1978); Virginia Commonwealth University, Richmond (1977–1978); and others. Abrams's work was also invited to many group exhibitions, including the Riverside Museum, New York; Art: USA (1958); Critics Choice (1960); Dallas Museum of Fine Arts, Dallas, Texas (1963); and many others.

Abrams taught at the New School for Social Research, New York City (1976); the Loeb Center, New York University (1977); and the Ringling School of Art, Sarasota, Florida (1979). Previously, she was art director of the New School for Social Research (1965–1966), member of the editorial staff of Public Pictures on Exhibit, and author/codirector of an art film, "Paradox of the Big."

Abrams's work is housed in the permanent collections of public and private institutions in the United States and South America, including the Carnegie Institute of Technology, Pittsburgh, Pennsylvania; Corcoran Gallery of Art, Washington, D.C.; New York University; the Rose Art Museum, Brandeis University, Waltham, Massachusetts; Smith College, Northampton, Massachusetts; and many others.

Bibliography
"Ruth Abrams." *Arts* 51:46 (March 1977).
Who's Who in American Art. 15th ed. R.R. Bowker Co., 1982.

Abrams, Vivien (1946–)

Born in Cleveland, Ohio, the painter Vivien Abrams received her Bachelor of Fine Arts degree from the Carnegie Mellon University, Pittsburgh, Pennsylvania, and a Master of Fine Arts degree from the Instituto Allende, San Miguel de Allende, Guanajuato, Mexico.

Between 1976 and 1986 Abrams held six solo exhibitions of her work in various institutions, including the Akron Art Institute, Ohio (1976); the New Gallery of Contemporary Art, Cleveland, Ohio (1977, 1980); Luise Ross Gallery, New York City (1984); Manhattanville College, Purchase, New York (1986); and others.

Abrams's work has been invited to more than thirty group exhibitions throughout the United States and Canada. Winner of many honors, awards, and commissions, she has had a Cleveland Foundation Grant, Ohio (1976); and fellowships at the MacDowell Colony, Peterborough, New Hampshire (1979, 1981, 1985). Abrams was also a fellow at Yaddo, Saratoga Springs, New York (1979, 1982); she won First Prize at the 62nd May Show, Cleveland Museum of Art, Ohio (1981); and was artist-in-residence at Bennington College, Vermont (1980).

Abrams is a lecturer and art teacher at many colleges, including the State University of New York (SUNY) at Purchase, Manhattanville College in the same city, and others. Her work is in the permanent collections of museums and corporations, including the Cleveland Museum of Art; Aldrich Museum of Contemporary Art, Ridgefield, Connecticut; Currier Gallery of Art, Manchester, New Hampshire; Case Western Reserve University, Cleveland, Ohio; and many others.

Bibliography
Cullinan, Helen. "Art: A Matter of Math and Logic." *Cleveland Plain Dealer* (September 25, 1977): 46–55.
Gottlieb, Mark. "Getting Around." *Northern Ohio Live* (July 1981): 14, 16.
Westfall, Stephen. "Reviews." *Arts* (November 1984).

Adams, Alice (1930–)

A native New Yorker, Alice Adams began as a painter at Columbia University, New York City, where she earned a Bachelor of Fine Arts degree (1953). After receiving a French government fellowship to study the art of tapestry making at L'École Nationale d'Art Décoratif, Aubusson, France (1953–1954), Adams became a successful fiber artist, whose large-scale three-dimensional woven works led her, naturally, to sculpture.

Adams's work began with yarn, moved to sisal and tarred rope

and then to metals, chain link fencing, and chicken wire, to walls and "houses" made of wood, including Douglas fir, bass, cypress, oak, pine, spruce, and three-quarter-inch plywood. She progressed from tapestry artist to one who dealt with site-specific sculpture and then to large public spaces. She has held a MacDowell Colony fellowship (1967); grants from the National Endowment for the Arts (NEA) (1978–1979, 1984–1985); Creative Artists Public Service (CAPS) grants (1972–1973, 1976–1977); a Guggenheim fellowship (1981–1982); an American Academy and Institute of Arts and Letters award in sculpture (1984); and a short-term humanities fellowship at Princeton University, New Jersey (1980).

"Big Aluminum" (1965), a twenty-foot-long, open-ended wire tube with biomorphic connotations was exhibited at the Fischbach Gallery, New York City, in 1956; it seems to presage Adams's large "architectural" works of the mid-1970s and, at the same time, it holds its own in the Fischbach "Eccentric Abstraction" show. One of her permanent on-site installations, "Leveling"—a red oak abstraction of a "building" on the campus of Wilson College, Chambersburg, Pennsylvania—is typical of her work from that period.

Adams has had many solo shows and has exhibited in many major institutions throughout the United States and abroad, including the Whitney Museum of American Art, New York City (1970–1971, 1973, 1978); the Museum of Modern Art (MoMA), New York City (1971, 1984); the Kunsthaus, Hamburg, Germany (1972); 55 Mercer Street, New York City (1970, 1972, 1973, 1974); Hal Bromm Gallery, New York City (1975, 1981); the Neuberger Museum, State University of New York (SUNY) at Purchase (1979–1980); University of Houston, Texas (1981); Bronx Museum of the Arts, New York (1986); Contemporary Arts Center, Cincinnati, Ohio (1987); Long Island University, and Blum-Helman Gallery, New York City (1989); and many others. Her work may be viewed in many noteworthy permanent collections, including L'École Nationale d'Art Décoratif, Aubusson, France; Weatherspoon Gallery, University of North Carolina, Greensboro; Wilson College, Chambersburg, Pennsylvania; University of Nebraska, Lincoln; Haags Gemeentemuseum, the Hague, the Netherlands; Rutgers University, New Brunswick, New Jersey; and others.

Bibliography
Fenn, Gloria. "Alice Adams." *Craft Horizons* 20:3 (May–June 1960): 16–20.
Kramer, Hilton. "Alice Adams." *The New York Times* (June 26, 1979).
Lippard, Lucy. "The Abstract Realism of Alice Adams." *Art in America* 67:5 (September 1979): 72–76.

Adams, Martha (1893–1978)

Born in Westphalia, Germany, to a Spanish mother and a Swedish father, Martha Adams travelled constantly as a child and youth with her diplomat-father in Africa, Central Europe, China, India, and Japan. In 1916 she married Edward B. Adams and, six years later, studied art in the United States under the aegis of Karl Knappe. Her first sculpture exhibition took place in the United States in 1931.

In 1937 Adams established herself in Mexico and became a friend of Diego Rivera, who helped her find her way toward a lyrical interpretation of Mexican popular art. In 1962 she exhibited three figures in the Palacio de Bellas Artes, Mexico City. She formed part of the group, or stable, that exhibited at the Galería de Arte Mexicana, but in her last years she showed in the Galería Misrachi, Mexico City. She concentrated her efforts in the three-dimensional elaboration of archaic portraits and heads, humanized plants and animals, simple in line, based on pre-Columbian fragments. Adams died in Mexico City in 1978.

Bibliography

Alvarez, José Rogelio, et al. *Enciclopedia de México*. Secretaría de
    Educación Pública, 1987.
The Texas Quarterly: Images of Mexico. The University of Texas,
    Autumn 1969.

Adams, Pat (1928–)

Born in Stockton, California, Pat Adams received her Bachelor's degree, Phi Beta Kappa, from the University of California at Berkeley in 1948. As a child during the Great Depression she benefitted from the Works Progress Administration (WPA) artists-in-schools program and the Haggin Museum's focus on children's art. The Haggin Collection (Bierstadt, Moran, Bougereau, and advanced French painting) and its director, Earl Rowland, pointed the way to the world of art, suggesting such reading as Robert Henri's *The Art Spirit* and studies of Degas and Renoir. The turbulent 1940s, punctuated by the war and the atomic bomb and also, for her, by such events as J. Robert Oppenheimer's lectures at Berkeley and the opening session of the United Nations at the San Francisco Opera House, made their mark upon an imagination already exercised by lessons in music and dance, and by nature in the San Joaquin Delta. At Berkeley she studied with Worth Ryder, Erle Loran, and Margaret Peterson O'Hagan, who themselves were actively considering the teachings of Hans Hofmann, Albert Barnes's theories of visual elements, Northwest Indian sacred art, and the structurings of Cézanne.

Coming to New York City in the fall of 1950, Adams worked with Max Beckmann, Reuben Tam, and John Ferren at the Brooklyn Museum Art School. Her first New York City exhibition was held at the Korman Gallery (shortly to become the Zabriskie Gallery) in the 1953–1954 season. In 1956–1957, she went as a Fulbright fellow to France to examine the neolithic cumulus at Gavr'Inis in Brittany and other megaliths there and in Ireland. This absorption with prehistoric and sacred art subsequently directed her travels to Malta, Egypt, Lebanon, Syria, Iran, Turkey, and most recently to Thailand, Pagan in Burma (now Myanmar), and Borobudur in Indonesia.

Adams teaches painting at Bennington College, Vermont (1964 to present) and Yale University School of Art, New Haven, Connecticut (1971–1972, 1983, 1990 to present). She has taught graduate seminars at Queens College, New York City (1972) and the Rhode Island School of Design, Providence (1981), and has visited as artist/critic in the graduate schools of the University of Iowa, Iowa City (1976); Western Kentucky University, Bowling Green (1978); the University of New Mexico, Albuquerque (1978); Columbia University, New York City (1979); Kent State University, Ohio (1980); the Rhode Island School of Design, Providence (1980, 1989); Mills College, Oakland, California (1987); and the University of Massachusetts, Amherst (1989).

Summer residencies at Yaddo, Saratoga Springs, New York, and the MacDowell Colony were an early major creative support. A member of the Yaddo Corporation since 1972, Adams has served on its board of trustees, executive council and as vice-chair. She also served on the boards of the Vermont Council on the Arts (1977–1981), the Williamstown Regional Conservation Laboratory in Massachusetts (1985–1986), and the College Art Association of America (1986–1990). In 1990 she was elected a fellow of the Vermont Academy of Arts and Sciences.

Awards and honors for her work include awards from the National Council on the Arts (1968); the National Endowment for the Arts (NEA) (1976, 1987); the American Academy and Institute of Arts and Letters Childe Hassam purchase award (1980, 1984, 1989) and their award in art (1986). Her contributions as visiting artist and professor of art were cited in the Distinguished Teaching of Art award of the College Art Association for 1984.

Not atypical of her work is "Interstitial" (1987), a large oil/isobutyl methacrylate painting on linen which plays upon the morphological runs of texture-become-shape. Visual events create an alertness to configurations between items such as disc and scrawl. Adams has evolved a personal technique to move toward the reaches of her awareness, in the process realizing new visual situations.

Adams has been exhibited biennially at Zabriskie Gallery, New York City, since 1954. Her paintings have been selected for many group and solo exhibitions, including the "Annuals" at the Whitney Museum of American Art (1956, 1961), and the Museum of Modern Art (MoMA) travelling exhibition—both in New York City; "41 Aquarellistes," France (1957); the "New Acquisitions" exhibits at the Hirshhorn Museum and Sculpture Garden, Washington, D.C. (1974, 1976); the survey of twenty-five years of work at the Contemporary Arts Center, Cincinnati, Ohio (1979); the exhibition at the Rutgers University Art Museum, New Brunswick, New Jersey (1978); "Islamic Allusions" at the Alternate Museum, New York (1980); "Acquisitions" at the Montclair Art Museum, New Jersey (1981); "Invitational" at the University of Hawaii, Hilo (1983); "Artist/Printmaker" at the Maryland Institute of Art, Baltimore (1987–1988); "Pat Adams: Circles, Spheres and Other Correspondences" at the New York Academy of Sciences, New York City (1988); "Pat Adams: Paintings, 1968–1988" at the Berkshire Museum, Pittsfield, Massachusetts; "New England Now: Contemporary Artists from Six States," Currier Gallery, Manchester, New Hampshire (1989); "Yale Art Faculty: 1950–1990," Marilyn Pearl Gallery, New York City (1990); and "Transformations" at the Brattleboro Museum, Vermont (1991).

Her work is in the permanent collections of major private and public institutions, among which are the Fleming Museum, University of Vermont, Burlington; the University of California at Berkeley; the Whitney Museum of American Art, New York City; the Hirshhorn Museum and Sculpture Garden, Washington, D.C.; the Yale Art Gallery, New Haven, Connecticut; the University of North Carolina, Greensboro; the Berkshire Museum, Pittsfield, Massachusetts; and the New Britain Museum of American Art, Connecticut.

Bibliography

Kimmelman, Michael. *The New York Times* (February 26, 1988): C29.
Langhorne, Elizabeth. "Paintings of Pat Adams." *Realizations*.
    University of Virginia, 1986.
Meyer, Ruth K. *Pat Adams Paintings: A Survey (1952–1979)*.
    Contemporary Arts Center, 1980.
Pat Adams: Circles, Spheres and Other Correspondences. The New York
    Academy of Sciences, 1988.
Perl, Jed. "Art Scene." *Salmagundi*. 25th Anniversary Issue, 1991.

Adan, Suzanne Rae (1946–)

Born in Woodland, California, Suzanne Rae Adan earned her Bachelor's degree from California State University at Sacramento in 1969, and two years later was awarded a Master's degree. She has won many awards for her work in California, including the Ayling Waterseler Award and a Purchase Award from the Crocker Art Museum, Sacramento (1968, 1973); a New Works Grant from the Sacramento Metropolitan Arts Commission (1990); and others.

Adan has had seven solo exhibitions between 1982 and 1991, at galleries such as the Betsy Rosenfield Gallery, Chicago, Illinois (1982, 1983, 1985); Himovitz/Salomon Gallery, Sacramento (1984, 1986); the John Berggruen Gallery, San Francisco (1987); and a show titled, "The Seven Deadly Sins . . . More or Less," at the Michael Himovitz Gallery, Sacramento (1991). Her work has been invited to forty-seven group shows between 1970 and mid-1991, including the San Francisco Art Institute (1970); the Whitney Museum of American Art (1973); Del Mar College, Corpus Christi, Texas (1974); Fuller Goldeen Gallery, San Francisco (1980); New Mexico State University, Las Cruces (1985); and the Michael Himovitz Gallery (1989, 1990).

Adan's work is in a number of permanent public and private collections throughout the United States. *Trick or Treat*, an amusing oil on canvas, reveals the wit and humor of the artist in the 1980s.

Bibliography

Albright, Thomas. "A Drawing Invitational at the S.F. Art Institute." *San Francisco Chronicle* (August 1970).
"Exhibitions." *ArtWeek* 17:19 (May 17, 1986): 5.
"Art in the Park." *On the Wing* IX:9 (November 1990): 2–3.

Adele, Sister (1915–)

Born in Massachusetts, Sister Adele earned a Bachelor's degree from the University of Southern California, Los Angeles (1938) and, two years later, received from the same institution her Master of Science degree; earlier on (1934–1935), she studied at the Carnegie-Mellon University, Pittsburgh, Pennsylvania. In 1949, Sister Adele was awarded a Ph.D. degree from the University of California at Berkeley.

Sister Adele has taught at several institutions of higher learning, including California State University, Fresno (1940–1950); Dominican College, San Rafael, California (1940–1974) at which time she became an artist-in-residence.

Her work has been exhibited widely in the United States and abroad and is in private and public permanent collections, including the Bibliothèque Nationale, Paris, France; Dunedin Public Art Gallery, New Zealand; the Library of Congress, Washington, D.C.; Metropolitan Museum of Modern Art, Manila, the Philippines; Oakland Art Museum, California; and others.

Bibliography

Browne, Turner, and Elaine Partnow. *Macmillan Biographical Encyclopedia of Photographic Artists & Innovators*. Macmillan, 1983.
Photo & Audio (August 1979).

Adler, Myril (1920–)

Painter, printmaker, puppeteer, mother, wife, and teacher, Myril Adler was born in Vitebsk, in the former USSR. She received her art education at various institutions in New York City, including the Brooklyn Museum Art School, the Art Students League, the Young Men's Hebrew Association (YMHA) Theatre Arts Workshop of Moi Solitaroff, and the Pratt Graphics Center.

Between 1944 and 1990 Adler has had many solo exhibitions of her work in museums and galleries, such as the Museum Gallery, University of Colorado at Boulder (1944); Galerie Bernheim Jeune, Paris, France (1950); Casa Municipale, Merano, Italy (1952); a "10 Year Retrospective," Scarborough School, New York (1960); Hudson River Museum, Yonkers, New York (1972, 1974); Katonah Gallery, Katonah, New York (1972, 1976, 1980); Art Expo, New York City (1986); "Faces of New York," Ossining Public Library, New York (1990); and others.

Her work has been selected for exhibition in innumerable juried and travelling group exhibitions throughout the United States, Europe, Japan, Korea, Central and South America, China, Taiwan, and the USSR. A sampling of her shows includes the National Academy of Design, New York City; Sarah Lawrence College, Bronxville, New York; the Jewish Museum, New York City; Lincoln Center, New York City; Boston Printmakers Society, Massachusetts; University of California at Berkeley; National Watercolor Society, New York; International Miniature Print Exhibitions, Pratt Center, New York City; Round Tower, Copenhagen, Denmark; Contemporary North American Prints, Museum of Modern Art, Caracas, Venezuela; and others.

Her works are in the permanent collections of the Hudson River Museum, Yonkers, New York; Museum of Modern Art, Caracas, Venezuela; New York Public Library; University of California at Berkeley; University of Rhode Island, Providence; and others.

Winner of more than twenty-five awards and honors, including first prizes, for more than four decades at the Westchester Art Society, Hudson River Contemporary Artists, and others, Adler received the Abel M. Sylvan award for printmaking (1983), the Hortense Ferne memorial award for printmaking (1989), and an award at the 100th Anniversary Exhibition of the National Association of Women Artists.

Director of the Myril Adler Arts Workshop since 1955, Adler has given workshops, has been guest artist, has organized art programs for emotionally disturbed children, and been artist-in-residence at the Pratt Graphics Center, New York City. She has been a member of Artists Equity Association, the National Assocation of Women Artists, Abraxas Artists Group, and the Hudson River Contemporary Art Association.

Adler has come full-circle in her prolific printmaking career: she began by exploring the faces of inner city children on wood, copper, and other printmaking media; today she digs into the inner essence of the homeless, using the latest computer technology in conjunction with intaglio and multi-media to express what is behind the face.

Bibliography

Cheever, Mary. *The Changing Landscape*. Phoenix Press, 1990.
Laliberté, Norman, and Alex Mogelon. *The Reinhold Book of Ideas*. Van Nostrand Reinhold, 1977.
Romano, Clare, and John Ross. *The Complete Printmaker*. The Free Press, 1990.
Who's Who in American Art. 19th ed. R.R. Bowker Co., 1991–1992.

Aguilar Suro, Teresa (1931–)

Born in Guadalajara, Jalisco, Mexico, Teresa Aguilar Suro studied art from 1950 to 1953 in the Academy of San Carlos; was professor of art in the Association for Cultural Studies (1975–1979); and was director of the Galería del Claustro Sor Juana (1980).

A member of the Mexican Society of Watercolorists, Aguilar won a silver medal (1980) in a show commemorating the 450th anniversary of the founding of Taxco, Guerrero. She has exhibited her work in forty-nine group shows, including the Mexican Society of Watercolorists (biannually, 1974–1978), Galerías Misrachi and Danilo Ongay, Mexico City (1974), Galería KIN, Mexico (1977, 1978), Galería José Guadalupe Posada, Mexico (1978), and Salón Nacional de Bellas Artes, Mexico City (1979, 1980, 1981); *El Informalismo en México* in the Palacio de Minería (1980); and the American Watercolor Society in New York City.

Aguilar had seven solo exhibitions in Mexico, including Centro Universitario Cultural (1979), Instituto de Artes de Mexico, Mexico City (1976), the Galería KIN (1980–1981), and the Palacio de Minería.

Bibliography

Alvarez, José Rogelio, et al. *Enciclopedia de México*. Secretaría de Educación Pública, 1987.

Ahrendt, Mary (1940–)

Born in Chicago, Illinois, Mary Ahrendt studied sculpture at the University of Illinois in her native city, where she received her Bachelor's degree in 1978. Two years later, after graduate work at the School of the Art Institute of Chicago, Ahrendt was awarded a Master of Fine Arts degree in painting and performance.

Ahrendt has had many solo exhibitions of her photographs, including the Ehlers-Caudill Gallery (1991); Deson-Saunders Gallery (1981, 1984, 1986); N.A.M.E. Gallery (1981); and Artemisia Gallery (1978)—all in Chicago; and CEPA Gallery, Buffalo, New York (1984).

In the last decade her work has been invited to more than a dozen major group shows, including "Summer Exhibition," Jayne H. Baum Gallery, New York (1991); "Toward the Future: Contemporary Art in Context," Museum of Contemporary Art, Chicago (1990); "First Person Singular: Self-Portrait Photography," High Museum of Art, Atlanta, Georgia (1988); "Nude, Naked, Stripped," Albert and Vera List Visual Arts Center, Massachusetts Institute of Technology (MIT), Cambridge (1986); "Constructed Works," Institute of Contemporary Art of the Virginia Museum, Richmond (1984); "New Photography," Just Above Midtown Gallery, New York City (1983); "Recent Color," the San Francisco Museum of Art, California (1982); and others.

Ahrendt has received grants from the Illinois Arts Council (1981, 1983, 1984, 1987), and has her work represented in the permanent collection of the Museum of Contemporary Art, Chicago. Her most recent exhibition at the Ehlers-Caudill Gallery, Chicago (1991) was comprised of torn recombinations, collages, of earlier photographs of her family bearing her hallmark: displacement and the liquidity of identity.

Bibliography

Aletti, Vince. "Summer Group." *Village Voice* (August 13, 1991): 100.
Artner, Alan G. "Mary Ahrendt's Photoworks Show Conceptual Development . . . ." *Chicago Tribune* (March 14, 1991): 15c.
Hagen, Charles. "Group Show." *The New York Times* (August 23, 1991).
Reeve, Catherine, and Marilyn Sward. *The New Photography*. Prentice-Hall, 1984.
Who's Who in American Art. 19th ed. R.R. Bowker Co., 1991–1992.

Akeley, Mary L. Jobe (1878–1966)

Explorer, photographer, and writer, Mary L. Jobe Akeley was born January 19, 1878, on the family farm in Tappan, Ohio. Virtually unknown until the 1980s when her photographic work was "rediscovered," she was nonetheless an important early twentieth-century photographer, working from 1905 to the mid-1950s. Her subject matter ranged from the Rocky Mountains of British Columbia to the plains of East Africa.

She received a Bachelor of Philosophy degree from Scio College (now Mt. Union College) in Alliance, Ohio; did two years of graduate work at Bryn Mawr College, Pennsylvania, from 1901 to 1903; and received her Master of Arts degree from Columbia University, New York City, in 1909. She was awarded an honorary Doctorate degree in 1930 from Mt. Union College in recognition of her accomplishments.

Prior to her marriage in 1924 to the African explorer Carl Ethan Akeley (inventor of the Akeley movie camera later photographed by Paul Strand), she travelled and photographed extensively in British Columbia. From 1905 to 1918 she made ten expeditions to the Canadian Rockies. In 1913 she made an ethnographic expedition to study a group of Native Americans known as the "Carrier" Indians who lived along the Skeena and Peace Rivers. On this journey she photographed the villages and their occupants. These images are sensitive records of these people and their customs, including images of women, children, ceremonial objects, and totem poles. In 1914 she was commissioned by the Canadian government to map the headwaters of the Fraser River and also made the first two attempts to climb Mt. Sir Alexander.

The images she made during this period were transformed into hand-painted lantern slides, which she used to illustrate her numerous lectures on British Columbia—over forty lectures in 1912.

Two years after her marriage, Akeley accompanied her husband on the 1926 Akeley-Eastman-Pomeroy expedition, organized under the aegis of the American Museum of Natural History. This expedition was undertaken to make collections for various dioramas for African Hall—a hall designed by Carl Akeley with dioramas of African animals in their natural habitats. Her husband died while on this expedition, and Akeley assumed leadership of the expedition, making the photographs, film footage, and collections necessary to complete the work. She returned twice to Africa after the 1926 expedition, in 1935 and in 1947, again photographing and filming extensively. She continued her lecturing, becoming deeply involved in African conservation, and published numerous articles and seven books, most of which were illustrated with her photographs.

Akeley's photographic work is housed in two collections, one at the American Museum of Natural History in New York City, the other at the Mystic River Historical Society in Mystic, Connecticut.

Akeley's photographs span an important period for women artists, and through her work she often seemed to be resolving for herself the dilemma of many women who were struggling to shake off the tenets of Victorianism and find meaningful ways through which to express themselves. Over two thousand of her lantern slides survive as beautifully-colored objects, and her black-and-white images, many of which have only recently been printed, are testaments to her clear vision of the world around her.

Dawn-Starr Crowther

Bibliography
Preston, Douglas J. *Dinosaurs in the Attic.* New York: St. Martin's Press, 1986.
Sicherman, Barbara, and Carol Hurd Green, eds. *Notable American Women: The Modern Period.* The Belknap Press of Harvard University Press, 1980.

Akers, Adela (1933–)

Adela Akers, a lover of mathematics, chemistry, and above all weaving, was born in Santiago de Compostela, Spain, and grew up in Havana, Cuba, where she received a Bachelor's degree in science from the University of Havana (1955). Two years later Akers enrolled in the School of the Art Institute of Chicago, Illinois, and discovered the loom and weaving in 1959. She went on for further study in weaving at the Cranbrook Academy of Art, Bloomfield Hills, Michigan (1960–1961 and 1962–1963).

She carried out commissions for designers and architects on her return to Chicago in 1963, began to exhibit her work on a regional and national level, and went to Peru in 1965 on behalf of the Alliance for Progress as a weaving consultant.

Solo exhibitions of Akers's weaving have been held in many galleries, institutions, and universities, including Bloomsburg State College (now Bloomsburg University), Pennsylvania (1977); Fiberworks Gallery, Berkeley, California (1980); Triangle Gallery, San Francisco, California (1981); Mandell Gallery, Los Angeles, California (1981); Modern Master Tapestries, New York City (1984); Pennsylvania Academy of Fine Arts, Philadelphia (1986); Patrick King Contemporary Art, Indianapolis, Indiana (1987); Helen Drutt Gallery, New York (1990); and others.

Her weavings have been selected for numerous group exhibitions throughout the United States, including the Inaugural Exhibition of the American Crafts Museum, New York City (1986); "Fiber: The Next Generation," Illinois State University, Normal (1987); Maple Hill Gallery, Portland, Maine (1988); among others.

Akers was an instructor in the crafts program sponsored by the city of Chicago, Illinois (1965–1967); she taught at the Penland School for Crafts, North Carolina, during the summers of 1968, 1969, and 1970; Akers also served on the faculties of the New School for Social Research (1970–1971); the Cooper Square Art Center, New York City (1971); San Francisco State University, California (1981); and since 1972 has been a professor of weaving at the Tyler School of Art, Temple University, Philadelphia, Pennsylvania.

She was a lecturer at "Fiberworks," Center for Textile Arts, Berkeley, California (1984); the North Carolina Weaver's Guild, Charlotte (1986); Philadelphia Textile Society, Pennsylvania (1986); and the Philadelphia Weaver's Guild, Pennsylvania (1988); Akers was a designer for Oaxaca Loom and directed cottage weavers in Diaz Ordas, Oaxaca, Mexico (1981), as she had done earlier on in Yucatan.

Akers has been the recipient of many awards and honors, including artist-in-residence at the Penland School for Crafts, North Carolina (1969, 1971); a National Endowment for the Arts craftsman's fellowship (1974, 1980); a New Jersey Council on the Arts grant (1971); research grants, Temple University, Philadelphia, Pennsylvania (1975, 1979, 1984, 1988); and a Pennsylvania Council on the Arts grant (1983).

A selected list of her weavings in permanent collections in the United States and Canada would include the Olympia-York Building, Toronto, Canada; Sumitomo Bank, New York; Manchester Community College, Connecticut; Chase Manhattan Bank, New York; W.B. Saunders Publishers, Philadelphia, Pennsylvania; and others.

Bibliography
Creager, Clara. *Weaving.* Van Nostrand Reinhold, 1980.
Held, Shirley. *Weaving: A Handbook for the Fiber Artist.* Holt, Rinehart & Winston, 1980.
Janeiro, Jan. "The Line as Movement: Adela Akers." *Fiber Arts Magazine* (March–April 1981).
Scheinman, Pamela. "Adela Akers: The Loomed Plane." *Crafts Horizons* 37:1 (February 1977): 24–25, 61–62.
Znamierowski, Nell. *Fiber: The Artist's View.* Hillwood Art Gallery, Long Island University, 1983.

Akin, Gwen (1950–)

A native New Yorker, the photographer Gwen Akin studied at Tufts University, Medford, Massachusetts, and received her Bachelor of Fine Arts degree from the Boston Museum School, Massachusetts.

Akin has had ten solo exhibitions of her work in the United States and abroad, including the Galerie Farideh Cadot, Paris, France (1990); the XYZ Gallery, Ghent, Belgium (1989); the O'Kane Gallery, Houston, Texas (1988); White Columns, New York City (1987–1988); the Shadai Gallery, Tokyo, Japan (1987); and the Center for Creative Photography, Tucson, Arizona (1986). Between 1985 and 1990 her work has been invited to more than forty group exhibitions in galleries, museums, and festivals of photography throughout the world.

Akin's work is in the permanent collections of the San Francisco Museum of Modern Art, California; the Museum of Fine Arts, Houston, Texas; Espace Photographique de Paris, France; the Tokyo Institute of Technology, Japan; and many others. A recipient of a National Endowment for the Arts (NEA) grant in photography (1990–1991), Akin has lectured at many colleges, universities, and museums. She photographs sensuous, sometimes grotesque, still-life material to entice or repel the viewer; her earlier subjects included octopi, rats, and other specimens in formaldehyde.

Bibliography
Adams, Brooks. "Grotesque Photography." *The Print Collector's Newsletter* 21:6 (January–February 1991): 206–211.
———. "Prints and Photographs Published." *The Print Collector's Newsletter* 28:1 (March–April 1987): 19–20.
Levi, Jan Heller, ed. *The Interrupted Life.* The New Museum, 1991.
Rapier, April. *SPOT: A Publication of the Houston Center for Photography.* 1985, p. 20.
Righter, Lisa. "Tableau Mort." *CEPA Quarterly* 3:1 (Fall 1987).

Alarcon Madrigal, Flor Beatriz (1954–)

Born in Ameca, Jalisco, Mexico, Flor Beatriz Alarcon Madrigal studied painting in the Escuela de Artes Plásticas of the Universidad de Guadalajara, Mexico, and in Palomar College, San Marcos, California.

From 1970 onward Alarcon Madrigal exhibited her work in Mexico in the capital of Jalisco and in Mexico City. The critic Juan Crespo de la Serna has written that "the creatures portrayed by this artist are diagrams or schemas of visible reality; for that reason, it is not strange that they bear a resemblance to the faces and figures painted by Picasso and Matisse."

Bibliography

Alvarez, José Rogelio, et al. *Enciclopedia de México*. Secretaría de Educación Pública, 1987.

Alaupovič, Alexandra Vrbanič (1921–)

One of the most versatile and noted sculptors in the Southwest, Alexandra Vrbanič Alaupović was born of a cultured, artistic family in Podravska Slatina, Yugoslavia. From 1944 to 1949 she attended the Academy of Visual Arts in Prague, Czechoslovakia. In 1947 she married Pierre Alaupović, who became an internationally distinguished biochemist. Along with her husband and daughter, Alaupović emigrated to the United States and, between 1957 and 1958, took courses in advertising design and photography at the University of Illinois, Champaign-Urbana. Following a 1960 move to Oklahoma—where the Alaupovićs continue to reside—she graduated from the University of Oklahoma with a Master of Fine Arts degree in sculpture (1966) and won the university's prestigious Jacobson award (1964) for her exquisitely refined and enigmatic plaster head, "Moon Girl." Interested from the outset of her career in nature, movement, organic growth, and the importance of form triumphing over chaos, she has said: "I am intuitively attracted to the order in nature. My goal is to express this conviction in balanced and harmonious relationships." These concerns have repeatedly manifested themselves in her work, which has alternated between realism and a total or often cubist-related abstractionism. Her early art between 1936 and 1965 concentrated on the human figure and portraiture, often of a highly expressive, human flavor (the powerful figural bronze "Struggle I" [1952] remains one of her finest pieces).

In the early 1960s Alaupović added welding to her arsenal of sculptural techniques; this helped allow her, at times, to move from her earlier realism and concentration upon sculpture as mass to a new emphasis on linear construction and open form (as, for example, in the whimsical, Duchampesque 1966 "Firebird," which consists of pipe and motorbike chain). While influenced in Europe by Charles Despiau and Aristide Maillol, it was not until reaching America that Alaupović became actively aware of other masters with whom her art would often share strong affinities: these were Alexander Archipenko, Constantin Brancusi, Jean Arp, Barbara Hepworth, and Elie Nadelman. A sculptor of great energy and creative range, Alaupović is also a sensitive draftsperson. A participant in numerous group shows in the United States and abroad, she has had solo exhibitions at the University of Oklahoma Museum of Art, Norman (1975); La Mandragore Internationale Galerie d'Art, Paris, France (1984); and the Oklahoma Art Center in Oklahoma City, where she was honored by a retrospective (1987–1988). The recipient of many awards, Alaupović has work in the permanent collections of museums in Yugoslavia, as well as the University of Oklahoma Museum of Art, the Oklahoma Art Center, and the state of Oklahoma Art Collection.

Victor Koshkin-Youritzin

Bibliography

Watson-Jones, Virginia. *Contemporary Women Sculptors*. Oryx Press, 1986, pp. 7–8.

———, and Sue Scott. *Struggle, Growth, and Whimsy: An Alexandra Alaupović Retrospective*. Exhibition Catalog. Oklahoma Art Center, Oklahoma City, 1987.

Who's Who in American Art. 18th ed. R.R. Bowker Co., 1989–1990.

Who's Who of American Women, 1975–1985/1986, 1989–1990. Chicago: Marquis Who's Who.

Albee, Grace (1890–1985)

Born in Sceituate, Rhode Island, the painter/printmaker Grace Albee is best known for her brilliant black-and-white wood engravings. She studied at the Rhode Island School of Design, Providence, and later with Paul Bornet in Paris, France.

Winner of many prizes and honors, Albee, especially in the 1950s, received awards from the Audubon Artists Society, New York City; Boston Printmakers Society, Massachusetts; the Connecticut Academy; National Academy of Design, New York City; the Providence Art Club, Rhode Island; Society of American Graphic Artists, New York City; and many others.

Her work is represented in prestigious private and public permanent collections in the United States and abroad, including the Carnegie Institute, Pittsburgh, Pennsylvania; the Cleveland Museum of Art, Ohio; the Library of Congress; the Metropolitan Museum of Art, New York City; the National Museum, Israel, and the National Museum, Stockholm, Sweden; New York Public Library; Rhode Island School of Design; and others.

Bibliography

Fielding, Mantle. *Dictionary of American Painters, Sculptors, and Engravers*. Modern Books and Crafts, 1974.

Albers, Anni (1899–1994)

A weaver and printmaker, Anni Albers was born Annelise Fleischmann in Berlin, Germany. As an adolescent she had art lessons at home and in 1922 she became a student at the Bauhaus. She entered the weaving workshop, not because of any initial enthusiasm for the medium, but because it seemed the lesser evil of the workshops available to her. In keeping with Bauhaus theories, she learned to produce textiles with abstract, geometric patterns where the threads and process of weaving determined the design. This modernist approach—in which truth to materials was viewed as a way to connect with eternal order—became the foundation of her art-making philosophy. She embraced new materials and received her Bauhaus diploma in 1930 on the basis of sound-absorbing material of cellophane, chenille, and cotton designed for an auditorium in Bernau.

Married in 1925 to Josef Albers, a fellow student who became master of the glass workshop, she worked as a free-lance textile designer and part-time instructor in the Bauhaus weaving workshop after having earned her diploma. With the closing of the Bauhaus in 1933, the couple was without any steady income and recognized that, although she had been raised as a Protestant, Albers's Jewish heritage was a threat to their safety in Nazi-controlled Germany.

The couple emigrated to the United States in November 1933. Philip Johnson, whom they had met in Berlin, arranged an invitation for both to teach at newly-founded Black Mountain College in North Carolina. Albers was asked to set up a weaving workshop at this innovative college, serving as a tutor during the first year and as assistant professor from 1934 to 1949. Her teaching was a continuation of the Bauhaus principle that material and technique should determine the look of the object.

Through her work, as well as her teaching, Albers advocated a dual role for textile artists: producing both pictorial weavings and fabric samples for industry. While she viewed machine weaving as a practical way to eliminate the boredom of hand weaving, she disliked the gulf between process and product that resulted from industry's reliance on designers who worked on paper and never on the loom. Her use of the term "pictorial weavings" to designate works of art, indicated that she did not think of them as traditional tapestries. Indeed, she had many works framed and placed behind glass. The paucity of extant drawings from the 1930s and 1940s emphasizes that she "drew" on the loom.

In 1949 the Alberses resigned from the Black Mountain, North Carolina, faculty. They moved north, first to New York—where Albers had an uprecedented solo exhibition of weavings at the Museum of Modern Art—and in 1950 to New Haven, Connecticut, where Josef Albers became chairman of the department of design at Yale University. With no new teaching post of her own, Albers concentrated on writing and weaving, publishing two major treatises: *Anni Albers: On Designing* (1959) and *Anni Albers: On Weaving* (1965). This was the most productive period of her career in terms of pictorial weavings, and she received a number of important commissions, including a 1966–1967 memorial to victims of the Nazi concentration camps for the Jewish Museum in New York.

Albers began producing prints in 1963, when she accompanied her husband to the Tamarind Lithography Workshop in California. While there she too was invited to try her hand. One year later, she returned as artist-in-residence in her own right. In these early prints, line determined form, as thread did in her weavings. Later prints were based on repetitive patterns of small geometric forms. Fascinated with the possibilities of the technical processes involved, Albers worked with several additional printing methods—including embossing, photo-offset, and silk-screen—enjoying the opportunity to collaborate with printers. Gradually, printing replaced weaving as her chosen medium, and she produced her last pictorial weaving in 1967. When the Alberses moved to Orange, Connecticut, in 1970, she gave away her looms, although she continued to produce occasional textile designs.

Albers responded to the multiples possible in the print medium, which, unlike her unique pictorial weavings, allowed her to reach a wider audience. Ironically, despite Albers's success in destroying the boundaries between art and craft with her weavings, her prints, beyond reproach as part of the "high art" tradition, seem to have secured her reputation.

Paula Wisotzki

Bibliography
Baro, Gene. *Anni Albers: Drawings and Prints*. Essay by Nicholas Fox Weber. New York: Brooklyn Museum, 1977.
The Woven and Graphic Art of Anni Albers. Essays by Richard S. Field, Mary Jane Jacob, and Nicholas Fox Weber. Renwick Gallery, 1985.

Albizu, Olga (1924–)

Born in Ponce, Puerto Rico, the painter Olga Albizu earned her Bachelor's degree from the University of Puerto Rico (1948), where she studied with Esteban Vicente. During the next three years, on a graduate scholarship awarded by her undergraduate university, she studied with Hans Hofmann at the Art Students League in New York City. Albizu took further study in France and Italy at the Académie de la Grande Chaumière, Paris, and the Accademia di Belle Arte, Florence (1951). Five years later, she took up residence in the United States.

Albizu has held solo exhibitions in the United States and abroad, including the Ateneo Puertorriqueño, San Juan, Puerto Rico (1957, 1958, 1961); Roland de Aenlle Gallery, New York City (1959, 1960); Pan American Union, Washington, D.C. (1960); Galería Santiago, San Juan (1969); and others.

Her work has been included in group exhibitions, such as the City Center, New York City (1956); Riverside Museum, New York (1957, 1959, 1960); Instituto de Cultura Puertorriqueño, San Juan (1957, 1962); and many others.

Examples of the abstract paintings of Olga Albizu are in private and public permanent collections, including the University of Miami, Florida; Ateneo Puertorriqueñno and the Instituto de Cultura Puertorriqueño, San Juan; Museum of Modern Art of Latin America, Washington, D.C.; and many others.

Bibliography
Benítez, M. *The Latin American Spirit: Art and Artists in the United States*. Harry N. Abrams, 1988.
Bloch, Peter. *Painting and Sculpture of the Puerto Ricans*. Plus Ultra Educational Publishers, 1978.

Albright, Gertrude Partington (1874–1959)

Born in Heysham, England, the painter/printmaker Gertrude Partington Albright studied with J.H.E. Partington and G.X. Prinet.

One of her oils, "Portrait of an Actress," is in the permanent collection of the city of San Francisco, California; Albright was a member of several professional arts organizations, including the Beaux-Arts Club, San Francisco; the San Francisco Art Association; and the San Francisco Society of Women Artists. She was a recipient of a bronze medal at the Panama-Pacific International Exposition of San Francisco (1915).

Bibliography
Dawdy, Doris Ostrander. *Artists of the American West*. Vol 1. Swallow Press, 1974.
Fielding, Mantle. *Dictionary of American Painters, Sculptors, and Engravers*. Modern Books and Crafts, 1974.
A Woman's Vision: California Painting into the 20th Century. San Francisco: Maxwell Galleries, 1983.

Albro, Maxine (1903–1966)

The Iowa-born painter and printmaker Maxine Albro, active in the 1930s and the 1940s, exhibited in museums and galleries, including the Delphic Studios, New York City (1931); the California Palace of the Legion of Honor, San Francisco, California (1936); and many others.

A member of the San Francisco Art Association and the American Artists Congress, Albro's work is in private and public permanent collections, including a mosaic in San Francisco State College; a fresco in Coit Tower, San Francisco; and others.

Bibliography

"Maxine Albro in New York." *Art Digest* 6:6 (December 15, 1931): 11.
"Maxine Albro Exhibition." *Arts & Architecture* 62 (October 1945): 22.
A Selection of American Prints: A Selection of Biographies of Forty Women Artists Working between 1904–1979. Santa Rosa, California: The Annex Galleries, 1987.

Albuquerque, Lita (1946–)

Like the early masters of abstract painting—Wassily Kandinsky, Kasimir Malevich, and Arthur Dove—Albuquerque believes that art can serve a spiritual purpose. She delves into her own subconscious for clues to the relationship between humankind, nature, and the cosmos.

Albuquerque's ambitious project reflects her origins in a cosmopolitan childhood replete with visual stimulation. Although she was born in Santa Monica, California, she spent her early years principally in Paris and Tunisia and did not learn to speak English until she was eleven, when she returned to live in California. She earned her Bachelor of Arts degree in art history at the University of California at Los Angeles (UCLA) (1968), and became involved in the arts, including photography, filmmaking, and acting as well as painting. She also renewed her contacts with Europe, establishing a penchant for travel as a means of enlarging her knowledge of art, other cultures, and nature.

Albuquerque's early abstract expressionist paintings were followed by large, paint-laden works in red oil on wood. A series of autobiographical and contemplative little paintings, "The Moments" (1976), set her on her way as a mature and individual artist. In these paintings Albuquerque combined simple geometric forms signifying order with unpremeditated marking and layering. Soon Albuquerque embarked on the striking and evocative outdoor works and indoor installations for which she is best known. In these latter works there is evidence of her aesthetic relationships with earth art, with process art, and, most particularly, with that loosely-defined school of southern California artists who emphasize light and space for ends that are simultaneously sensuous and mystical.

Between 1978 and 1984 Albuquerque experimented vigorously with ephemeral interventions in the landscape. For one of the most compelling of these, "Malibu Line" (1978), she filled a shallow trench with ultramarine powder. This straight, unnaturalistic blue line on the Malibu cliffs directed the eye out to the ocean and the distant horizon, thereby using the simplest of man-made means to emphasize the sublimity of nature. "Rock and Pigment Installation" (1978) in the Mojave Desert, comprising pigment-dusted rocks set in a desolate landscape, suggested a Tanguy landscape made real.

In 1980 Albuquerque employed similar means to create what may be her best known work, the "Red Pyramid" in Washington, D.C. In this instance she used red pigment to trace the triangular tip of the Washington Monument's shadow on the ground at the three points where it fell due west, north, and south on one day in June. The effect was to transform the monument, at least momentarily, from a memorial to a national hero into a marker of celestial patterns and of man's relationship to space and time.

In the later 1980s Albuquerque continued to produce indoor installations, such as "Spheres of Influence/Sphere of Influence" (1989) for California State University at Fullerton, but she also returned to smaller individual pieces, such as the "Dark Iris" series (1987–1989) of images in oil, iridescent powders, and gold leaf on paper. Her major project underway since 1988 has been the design and implementation of "Sit/Memory/Reflection," an ambitious indoor-outdoor permanent installation for 550 South Hope Street, Los Angeles, California.

Ann Lee Morgan

Bibliography

Butterfield, Jan. *Lita Albuquerque: Reflections.* Exhibition Catalog. Santa Monica Museum of Art, 1990.
Campbell, Clayton. "Lita Albuquerque." *Art Gallery International* 11 (December 1990): 22–26.
McClintic, Miranda. *Directions 1981.* Catalog of an exhibition at the Hirshhorn Museum and Sculpture Garden. Smithsonian Institution Press, 1981.

Aldaco Salido, Esther (1924–)

Born in Monterrey, Nuevo León, Mexico, Esther Aldaco studied painting at the University of Sonora, Mexico, as a scholarship student, before taking further work at Escuela de Pintura y Escultura (La Esmeralda). She also studied with professors Raúl Anguiano, Castro Pacheco, Chavez Morado, "Nacho" Aguirre, and Erasto Córtez. Aldaco left Mexico City to live in Navojoa, Sonora, and finally settled in Ensenada, Baja California, Mexico.

Aldaco has had a number of solo exhibitions, including eight years (1950–1958) of showing her work annually at the Academy of Painting of the University of Sonora; the Yoga Institute of Ensenada, Baja California (1971); the Complejo Turístico Baja California—all in Mexico (1978); and others.

With respect to group exhibitions, Aldaco's work has been shown at the Exposition of Women Painters, Ensenada, Baja California (1961–1963); the VI Exhibition of Baja California Painting in the city of Tijuana, Mexico (1961); the Exhibition of Self-Portraits in Tijuana, Mexico (1962); the Exhibition in the "Lion's Cave," Ensenada, Baja California (1972)—all in Mexico; the Exhibition of Baja California Painters in San Diego, California (1976); the Ensenada Exhibition sponsored by Radio Ensenada, Baja California, Mexico (1977); and others, especially the painting competition held in the National Auditorium in Mexico City, Mexico, where Aldaco won two first prizes and a third prize.

Aldaco has mastered the disciplines requisite to creating artistic work; her students, no doubt, have been aware of and thankful for that mastery. She has lectured at conferences, given seminars on the pictorial arts, taught many students, and produced a significant body of work as a painter.

Bibliography
Alvarez, José Rogelio, et al. *Diccionario Biográfico Enciclopedico de la Pintura Mexicana.* Quinientos Años Editores, 1979.

Alf, Martha (1930–)

Born in Berkeley, California, Martha Alf grew up in southern California, where she attended San Diego State University and received her Bachelor's degree in clinical psychology at the age of twenty-two. (She had begun post-secondary work as an art major.) She married Edward Franklin Alf, a fellow student in psychology, while in her third year of university study; they moved to Seattle, where he worked toward a doctorate degree.

Persuaded by Everett Gee Jackson to return to art, Alf earned a Master of Arts degree from San Diego State University, California, in 1963 and started to "haunt" the museums and galleries in major urban areas across the United States. She did research on women artists of the past; authored works on Joyce Treiman and Clair Falkenstein; and, in 1968, decided to take up post-graduate study at the University of California at Los Angeles (UCLA) and work toward a professional fine arts degree. Two years later, after study with William Brice, Richard Diebenkorn, and James Weeks, she received her Master of Fine Arts degree and was ready to take on the art world.

Using the photograph as a point of departure, Alf began to make monochromatic pencil drawings of herself and of fruits and vegetables; then works in color, which she identified as "color field representational painting." "Pear No. 1 (for Andy Wilfe)," a twelve-by-eighteen-inch work in colored pencil, reveals the quiet, sensuous "atmosphere" that surrounds and permeates her work—work that demands to be seen, not just looked at.

Alf's work has been exhibited in many museums and galleries, including the Whitney Museum of American Art, New York City (1975); Scripps College, Pomona, California (1979); the Henry Gallery, University of Washington, Seattle (1980); the Art Center College of Design, Los Angeles, California (1981); and the Laguna Beach Museum of Art, California (1981). A self-confessed "romantic realist" and prize-winning artist, Alf received a grant from the National Endowment for the Arts (NEA) (1979), and was given a solo exhibition at Pomona College, Claremont, California, in 1981.

Bibliography
Hines, Diane C. "Martha Alf Explores Simple Forms." *American Artist Magazine* 40 (December 1976): 56–60, 77–79.
Perlmutter, Elizabeth. "300 Years of Drawing." *Art News* 74:9 (November 1975): 85.
Rubin, David S. "Martha Alf." *Arts Magazine* 53:1 (September 1978): 12.
Schipper, Merle. "Martha Alf." *Art News* 86:2 (February 1987): 24, 27.
Wight, Frederick S. "Martha Alf at Pomona College and Newspace." *Art in America* 69:8 (October 1981): 150–51.

Alford, Gloria (1928–)

Printmaker/sculptor Gloria Alford was born in Chicago, Illinois, and attended the University of California at Berkeley, where she received her Bachelor of Arts degree. Alford also studied at various institutions, including the Art Institute of Chicago, Illinois; Penland School of Crafts, North Carolina; Columbia University, and Pratt Graphics Center—both in New York City; and the University of California at Santa Cruz.

Among the solo exhibitions of her work seen in the United States and abroad are the Monterey Museum of Art, California (1980) and the Netherlands Institute for Advanced Study, Wassenaar, Holland (1982). Her work has been exhibited in more than two scores of juried and invitational shows between the early 1970s and 1990 in the United States, such as the Brooklyn Museum of Art, New York City (1974, 1976); Western Association of Art Museums Travelling Show (1974); "Contemporary Musical Notation," Sesnon Art Gallery, University of California at Berkeley (1980, 1990); "Alternative Applications: Computer Technology in the Arts," University of California at Santa Cruz (1989); and many others.

Alford's work is housed in permanent collections of museums and corporations, including Time-Life Corporation, New York City; Monterey Museum of Art, California; Elvehjem Art Center, University of Wisconsin, Madison; Silicon Graphics, Mountain View, California; and many others.

Alford, who was a visiting artist in the France-United States Cultural Exchange Program, has explored and keeps searching for "high-tech" approaches to her sculpture and printmaking vocabulary, wedding the past and the present, as in her investigations of the old and new art of handmade paper, color xerox prints, and the monotype.

Bibliography
Who's Who in American Art. 19th ed. R.R. Bowker Co., 1991–1992.
Maurello, Donna. "Gloria Alford of Santa Cruz." *Monterey Life Magazine* (November 1984).

Alhilali, Neda (1938–)

A mixed-media artist of great versatility, Neda Alhilali was born in Czechoslovakia and lived in Baghdad as a young adult. She studied art at St. Martin's School of Art, London, England in 1957, and at the Kunstakademie München, West Germany in 1957. She continued her studies at the University of California at Los Angeles (UCLA), where she received a Bachelor of Fine Arts degree (1965) and a Master of Fine Arts degree (1968). Her concentration was in the textile area headed by Bernard Kester. Since this time she has maintained a studio in the Los Angeles, California, area.

In the late 1960s and early 1970s Alhilali was creating large-scale knotted sculptures, such as "Nightmare," exhibited in "Deliberate Entanglements," which opened at the Wight Gallery in Los Angeles, California, and traveled throughout the United States (1971). By the mid-1970s she was plaiting, pressing, dyeing, and painting paper. This work is included in the collection of the Central Museum of Textiles, Lodz, Poland, among others. In 1975 she created an environment of "Tongues" on Venice Beach, California. The patterned surfaces of her plaited work became of prime importance in the "Cassiopeia" series. This consisted of installations of draped paper, hanging from walls and ceiling, with both sides painted in contrasting patterns. This work was exhibited in solo exhibitions at the Allrich Gallery, San Francisco (1981) Hunsaker/Schlesinger Gallery, Los Angeles (1982), and the Scripps College, Eucalyptus Court, Claremont (1982)—all in California. Recent work includes pattern-painted constructions of hundreds of pieces of aluminum, shown in the solo exhibits "Plumed Serpent Works in Paper and Metal," Modern Masters Tapestries, New York City

(1985), and "Burning Bush," the Allrich Gallery, San Francisco, California (1986).

"Neda Alhilali Selected Works 1968–1985," was a retrospective at the Municipal Art Gallery, Barnsdall Park, Los Angeles, California. Alhilali's work was included in "Fibres Art 85," Musée des Arts Décoratifs, Paris, France (1985); "The Art Fabric Mainstream," the San Francisco Museum of Modern Art, California (1981), the "Triennale of Tapestry," Lodz, Poland; and the "5th Biennale Internationale de la Tapisseries," Lausanne, Switzerland (1971); among others.

Alhilali was the recipient of a National Endowment for the Arts (NEA) fellowship in 1974 and 1979 and was a professor of art at Scripps College, Claremont, California, from 1971 to 1988.

Claire Campbell Park

Bibliography

Constantine, Mildred, and Jack Lenor Larsen. *The Art Fabric Mainstream.* Van Nostrand Reinhold, 1981.

Los Angeles Municipal Art Gallery. *Neda Alhilali.* Los Angeles, California. 1985.

Norklun, Kathi. "Sculptural Transformations." *Artweek* (June 5, 1982).

Allen, Constance O. (1923–)

Painter and designer of jewelry, Constance O. Allen was born in Camphill, Alabama. She received her formal and artistic education at George Washington University, Washington, D.C.; the Instituto Allende, San Miguel de Allende, Mexico; and from private study with Richard Goetz, Oklahoma City, Oklahoma, and at the Gemological Institute of America, Santa Monica, California.

Widely travelled, Allen founded the Chickasha Art Guild in Oklahoma. Her work has been seen in many solo and group exhibitions throughout the United States, including juried shows in Florida, New Mexico, Arizona, Montana, and others.

Recipient of many awards for her work, Allen has executed a number of commissions, including "20 Indian Chiefs," A.C. Leftwich Indian Hall of Fame, Duncan, Oklahoma (1972); "4 Historical Paintings of Southwest Oklahoma," Restaurateur Collection, Moore, Oklahoma (1977); and others.

Allen offered private classes in drawing and painting (1969–1974) and taught at the University of Science and Arts, Chickasha, Oklahoma (1974–1975). Her work is in the permanent collections of the Jane Brooks School for the Deaf; the Chickasha Public Library, Oklahoma; and others.

Bibliography

Paris, Dale. "Artist Paints Favorite Subjects." *Green Valley News* (December 2, 1983).

Who's Who in American Art. 19th ed. R.R. Bowker Co., 1991–1992.

Allen, Marion Boyd (1862–1941)

At forty, the Boston-born Marion Boyd Allen entered the Boston Museum School, Massachusetts, and studied with Edmund C. Tarbell and Frank W. Benson. Upon graduation in 1910 she had a solo exhibition of portraits and genre scenes at the Copley Society Gallery, where she continued to exhibit regularly until about 1930. Her painting "Enameling" was accepted for the Panama-Pacific International Exposition

of 1915, and thereafter her work began receiving a succession of awards, including the popular prize of the Newport Art Association in 1919 for her arresting portrait of "Anna Vaughn Hyatt" (1915, Maier Museum of Art, Randolph-Macon Women's College), in which she depicts Hyatt in her Annisquam, Massachusetts, studio, creating the maquette for her "Joan of Arc" statue.

A change occurred in Allen's work in the 1920s when she travelled west and discovered its natural phenomena. She became a landscape painter, recording the scenic wonders of the Grand Canyon, Mt. Rainier, and Mt. Olympus. In the following summers she visited the Canadian Rockies, painting Lake Louise, Lake O'Hara, Pinnacle Mountain, Valley of the Ten Peaks, Emerald Lake, and additional majestic views. In her seventies she continued to exhibit at galleries in Boston and New York and to win prizes for her paintings, including the club prize at the New Haven Paint and Clay Club, Connecticut, in 1932. In an age when men dominated landscape painting, Allen was one of the women pioneers in this type of painting.

Eleanor Tufts

Bibliography

Fairbrother, Trevor J. *The Bostonians: Painters of an Elegant Age, 1870–1930.* Boston Museum of Fine Arts, 1986.

Tufts, Eleanor. *American Women Artists, 1830–1930.* National Museum of Women in the Arts, 1987.

Allen, Roberta (1945–)

Native New Yorker Roberta Allen attended the Fashion Institute of Technology, New York, where she received an Associate's degree in 1964. She won fellowships or grants from the MacDowell Colony, Peterborough, New Hampshire (1971, 1972); the Ossabaw Island Project (1972); and a Creative Artists Public Service (CAPS) grant from New York State (1978–1979). She was a resident fellow at Yaddo, Saratoga Springs, New York (1983, 1987) and at the Virginia Center for the Creative Arts (1985); and was artist-in-residence at the Art Gallery of Western Australia, Perth (1989).

Known for her artist's books, as a conceptual artist, sculptor, writer of fiction and non-fiction, Allen had twenty-two solo exhibitions in the United States and abroad between 1967 and 1989, including Galerie 845, Amsterdam, the Netherlands (1967); four shows at the John Weber Gallery, New York (1974, 1975, 1977, 1979); the Galleria Primo Piano, Rome, Italy (1981); the Perth Institute of Contemporary Arts, Australia (1989); and others.

Allen's work has been invited to more than seventy group and travelling exhibitions throughout the world (1971–1991), such as Women's Interart Center, New York (1971); "Artists' Books," National Art Gallery, Wellington, New Zealand (1978); "Primera Bienal Internacional del Deporte en las Artes Plásticas," Museo Nacional de Artes Plásticas, Montevideo, Uruguay (1980); "Arteder 82, International Graphic Arts Exhibition," Bilbao International Exhibition Center, Spain (1982); "Verbally Charged Images," the Queens Museum, New York City (1984); "Estampes et 'livres d'artistes' du XXe siècle: Enrichissements du Cabinet des Estampes 1978–1986," Bibliothèque Nationale, Paris, France (1986); "Rotating Group Show," Rosa Esman Gallery, New York City (1991); and many others.

Allen's works are in many permanent museum, private, and corporate collections, including the Metropolitan Museum of Art, Museum of Modern Art (MoMA), and Cooper-Hewitt Museum—all in New York City; the Bibliothèque Nationale, Paris, France; Stadtische Galerie im Lenbachhaus, Munich, Germany; the Art Gallery of Western Australia, Perth; Reader's Digest; and others.

The most widely-known artist's book published by Allen (1981) in an edition of 300, the title of which provides a possible clue to her work, is: *Everything in the World There Is to Know Is Known by Somebody, but Not by the Same Knower.*

Bibliography

Harrison, Helen A. "When the Word Meets the Picture." *The New York Times* (September 15, 1985): 11, L.I.
Lopes Cardozo, Judith. "Roberta Allen." *Artforum* (February 1978): 73, 74.
Siegle, Robert. *Suburban Ambush, Downtown Writing and the Writing of Insurgency.* Johns Hopkins University Press, 1989.
Who's Who in American Art. 19th ed. R.R. Bowker Co., 1991–1992.

Allen (Atkins), Louise (d. 1953)

Born in Lowell, Massachusetts, the sculptor Louise Allen [Atkins] studied at the Rhode Island School of Design, Providence, and also at the Boston Museum School of Fine Arts. Examples of her work are in Smith College, Northampton, Massachusetts; the Cleveland Museum of Art, Ohio; and other institutions.

Bibliography

American Art Annual. Vol 30. American Federation of Arts, 1934.
Kohlman, Rena Tucker. "America's Women Sculptors." *International Studio* 76 (1922): 225–235.
National Sculpture Society. A Catalog. *Exhibition of American Sculpture.* California Palace of the Legion of Honor, 1929.

Alloucherie, Jocelyne (1947–)

Born in Québec City, Canada, Jocelyne Alloucherie first studied fine arts at Laval University, Québec, completing her Bachelor of Fine Arts degree in 1973. She held her first solo exhibition at the Musée du Québec and has since been a prolific exhibiting artist, showing in solo and group shows in several Canadian cities, as well as New York, and Lyons, France. She received her Master of Fine Arts degree from Concordia University, Montréal, Canada, in 1980 and presently lives in Montréal. She is represented by the Galerie Chantal Boulanger, also in Montréal.

Alloucherie made a decided break with the formalism and insularity of modernism at the outset of her career. The work, by its very nature, resists definition on both symbolic and formal levels. Her installations, described by some critics as "sculpture-environments," combine elements and images in various media, blurring the boundaries of painting, sculpture, photography, and architecture. Critic James D. Campbell summarized her pieces as "radically open structures that obviate the distinction between object, image, and site . . . . In the end she creates an architectural entity that is architectonic, a labyrinth that lures the viewer within it—even the gaps between the masses are experienced as negative volumes in a topology without boundaries—and yet remains inviolate." In "Specchio, Speculaire (Not Yet and Already)" (1989, National Gallery of Canada, Ottawa) a typical work of the late 1980s, the cultural elements might suggest buildings, monuments, or furniture—a vanity, or perhaps a lamp—while the photographic images set around the objects are distant, exterior—tree shapes, sky, a rounded courtyard defined by columns. The evocations change as one moves and lingers within this theater of shapes, images, and surfaces; and there is a sense, at once, of the integrity of each element, as well of totality, of a fleeting sense of the impermanent present, of memory and anticipation.

Janice Seline

Bibliography

Alloucherie, Jocelyne, and Cyril Reade. *Specchio, spéculaire.* Éditions Parachute, 1989.
Boulanger, Chantal. "Au-delà de l'in situ. Jocelyne Alloucherie, Mario Bouchard, Louise Viger." *Parachute* 42 (March–May 1986): 16–20.
Campbell, James D. *Jocelyne Alloucherie.* 49th Parallel, 1988.

Allyn, Jerri (1952–)

Conceptual and performance artist Jerri Allyn was born in Paterson, New Jersey, and earned a Master's degree in art and society from Goddard College and a two-year certificate from the Feminist Studio Workshop—both in Los Angeles, California (1976–1978).

Working with audio, video, artist's books, and other "new genres" in public places, Allyn elects to work in any medium that fits the idea behind a particular work of art. Her performances, interactive art structures, exhibitions, radio and television works have reached audiences throughout the United States and abroad, including "New Work," C.W. Post College, Brookville, New York (1991); "Origins: Gift of the Story," Tyler Gallery, Philadelphia, Pennsylvania, and Spaces Gallery, Cleveland, Ohio (1992); "Video Festival," American Film Institute, Los Angeles, California (1987); and "New American Radio Series," New York, 200 public radio stations via satellite (1991). Certain of her works have travelled to Canada, Brazil, Australia, and New Zealand.

Allyn teaches on the faculty of the New School for Social Research, New York City (1988 to present) and has taught one fourth of each year at Western Washington University, Bellingham (1987–1990). She was artist-in-residence in a number of colleges and universities, including the University of Washington, Pullman (1990); Humboldt College, California (1988); University of Illinois, Champaign-Urbana (1987); Women's Graphic Center, Los Angeles, California (1983); and others.

A member of the Bessies Dance and Performance Art Awards committee and the Artists' Board of the New Museum of Contemporary Art, Allyn was the recipient of arts media grants from the New York State Council on the Arts (1989, 1991); grants from the National Endowment for the Arts (NEA), Washington, D.C. (1981, 1985, 1990); an Art Matters grant, New York, for "Angels Have Been Sent to Me," her interactive work on aging and disability (1989); and a scholarship from the Corporation for Public Broadcasting to attend the National Radio Training Workshop (1987).

Allyn's work, sometimes humorous, explores social concerns, is filled with political insights, and grows out of her rich life experience.

Bibliography

Burnham, Linda. "Jerri Allyn: Apron . . ." *Artforum* (November 1981): 89.

Raven, Arlene. "The L Word." *Village Voice* (August 4, 1987): 85.
Smith, Roberta. "A Show on Issues . . ." *The New York Times* (June 27, 1990): C24.

Almeida Ramírez, Laura (1954–)

Born in Mexico, Laura Almeida Ramírez studied painting at the Casa del Lago, Mexico City, Mexico (1972), and then went to Paris, France, to work under the aegis of Pierrakos. The following year she worked in the studio of the painter Juan Berruecos and, in 1975, entered the El Molino printmaking workshop in Santo Domingo, Dominican Republic, to study with Octavio Bajonero. Almeida Ramírez also took a printmaking course from José Lazcarro T. (1970) and took a printmaking seminar with the noted engraver Mauricio Lasansky. These techniques and processes were supplemented by research and study of color, drawing, and aesthetic theory under the guidance of the painter Felipe Dávalos. Finally in 1977 Almeida Ramírez travelled to Imperial Valley College, California, to study artisanry and other aspects of artistic expression with Michael Chailé and Willis C. Bernard.

Almeida Ramírez has held many solo shows, including the Galería del Unicornio, Coyoacán, Mexico (1976); an exhibition of drawings and prints at Imperial Valley College, California (1977); a drawing exhibition at the Galería San Angel, Mexico (1978); and others. She has had her work accepted in numerous group exhibitions, such as the Galería del Molino de Santo Domingo, Dominican Republic (1975); Galería de la Ciudadela, "Diez Artistas Plásticos de Vanguardia" (1976); Galería Altamira, "Seis Artistas Latinoamericanos," the Galería Rosales, San Miguel de Allende, Guanajuato, and the Galería Gabriela Orozco—all in Mexico in 1977. The following year she showed prints at the Galería San Angel in Mexico.

Almeida Ramírez is a disciplined printmaker and painter. This allows and encourages her to express her deepest feelings to truly create, in her own words, "complete and humanistic paintings."

Bibliography
Alvarez, José Rogelio, et al. *Diccionario Biográfico Enciclopedico de la Pintura Mexicana.* Quinientos Años Editores, 1979.

Almy, Max (1948–)

Born in Omaha, Nebraska, the video artist Max (Marilynn Irene) Almy earned a Bachelor of Fine Arts degree at the University of Nebraska, Omaha (1970); did advanced work at the University of Minnesota, Minneapolis; and received a Master of Fine Arts degree from the California College of Arts and Crafts, Oakland (1978).

Almy's work has been exhibited in many venues in the United States and abroad, including "Electronic Art," Museum of Contemporary Art, Chicago, Illinois, "Biennale Paris," Musée d'Art Moderne, Paris, France, "California Video," Long Beach Museum of Art, California—all in 1980; "Exchange Show," Berlin, Germany (1981); "Performance Art," Museum of Modern Art (MoMA), New York City (1982); "National Video Festival," American Film Institute, Los Angeles, California (1983); "Video Art: A History, Part II," MoMA, New York City (1983); and many others.

Among the awards and honors she has received are a fellowship from the National Endowment for the Arts (NEA) (1982); a U.S. Film and Video Festival award the same year; a Western States Regional Media Arts fellow (1983); and others.

Almy's work is represented in private and public permanent collections in the United States and abroad, including the Long Beach Museum of Art, California; MoMA, New York City; San Francisco Museum of Art, California; Stedilijk Museum, Amsterdam, the Netherlands; and others.

Bibliography
"MoMA—TV: The Push to Artsify Video." *Village Voice* (1983).
Seid, Steve. "Deadline for the Future." *Networks* (1982).

Alquilar, Maria (1935–)

Known for her richly-imaginative paintings, ceramic murals, and sculpture, Maria Alquilar was born in Brooklyn, New York, of a Russian-Jewish mother and a Spanish father. She attended Hunter College, where she earned a Bachelor of Arts degree in 1955.

Alquilar has had a number of solo exhibitions of her work, including the Gorman Museum, University of California at Davis (1983). She has also had her work invited to numerous group exhibitions, such as "Animal Imagery," and "The Inedible Renwick Birthday Cake," at the Renwick Gallery, Smithsonian Institution, Washington, D.C. (1979 and 1982, respectively); "Raku and Smoke," Newport Art Museum, Newport Harbor, Rhode Island (1984); various shows at the Downey Museum, California (1982, 1983, 1984, 1987); "Works in Cast Iron and Brass," the result of a residency at the John Michael Kohler Art Center, Sheboygan, Wisconsin (1990); "Modern Mythology," Joan Robey Gallery, Denver, Colorado (1991); and others.

Alquilar received many major commissions, including eighteen pavement works, "Arkeology," for a Sacramento, California, Light Rail Station (1987); a ceramic and metal altar, "Bien Venida y Vaya Con Dios," for the U.S. Port of Entry, San Luis, Arizona (1985); a seventeen-foot ceramic mural, "Los Viajeros Viennen a San José," for the San José International Airport, California (1990); a ceramic tile project for an underpass in Denver, Colorado (1991); and many others.

Her works are in the permanent collections of the Chase Manhattan Bank, New York, and Phoenix, Arizona; National Museum of American Art, Smithsonian Institution, Washington, D.C.; San Francisco Arts Commission, California; the Kohler Company, Wisconsin; the Downey Museum, California; and others.

Bibliography
Dalkey, Victoria. "The Art of Inspiration." *The Sacramento Bee* (January 20, 1991).
Schlesinger, Ellen. "Sunday Woman-Artist in Residence." *The Sacramento Bee* (August 1983).
Who's Who in American Art. 19th ed. R.R. Bowker Co., 1991–1992.

Altwerger, Libby (1921–)

Born in Toronto, Canada, Libby Altwerger attended the Ontario College of Art in her native city as a scholarship student, graduating with the silver medal for drawing and painting. She earned a certificate for recreation at the University of Toronto and resided at the University Settlement House for three years as art director.

Widely travelled, Altwerger toured through Europe, the United States, Mexico, and Canada, including England, France, Italy, Spain, Cape Cod, Massachusetts, and San Francisco, California, visiting art galleries, museums, churches, and other cultural icons.

Altwerger taught art and design at Ryerson Polytechnical Institute for eleven years; offered art seminars throughout Ontario communities; demonstrated working procedures before numerous art clubs and art societies; and taught also at the YMCA—all in Toronto, Ontario, Canada.

A full-time painter, Altwerger exhibited her watercolors and prints in many solo and group shows in Canada and abroad, and won many awards and honors, including a gold medal and a purchase award at the Institute Feminine Culturelle, Vichy, France (1963); the Sterling Trust award for lithography (1965); the Royal Bank of Canada purchase award, Ontario Society of Art Show (1979); and many others.

Altwerger's works are in many permanent public and private collections, such as the Hamilton Art Gallery, the London Art Gallery, the Windsor Art Gallery—all in the province of Ontario, and others. Altwerger is a member of the Ontario Society of Art, the Canadian Society of Watercolor Painters, and a former member of the Canadian Society of Painter-Etchers and Engravers.

Bibliography
Correspondence with the artist.
Who's Who in American Art. 19th ed. R.R. Bowker Co., 1991–1992.

Alvarez, Candida (1955–)

Born in Brooklyn, New York, Candida Alvarez was educated at Fordham University, where she received her Bachelor of Arts degree in 1977; she also studied at the Skowhegan School of Painting and Sculpture, Maine, four years later.

Alvarez has held solo exhibitions in the United States and abroad, including "Red Spirit, White Sail," at P.S.1, Long Island City, New York (1980); "The Hybrid Series," Real Art Ways, Hartford, Connecticut (1983); "Paintings and Drawings," June Kelly Gallery (1989); "John Street Series," Galerie Schneiderei, Cologne, Germany (1990); "Paintings and Works on Paper," The Queens Museum, Flushing, New York (1991); and others.

Her work has been invited to many group exhibitions in the United States and abroad (including travelling shows), such as "Recollections: Candida Alvarez and Vincent Smith," the Brooklyn Museum, New York (1979); "Books Alive," the Metropolitan Museum of Art, New York City (1983); "American Women in Art: Works on Paper," United Nations International Women's Conference, Nairobi, Kenya (1985); "Latina Art Showcase '87," Mexican Fine Arts Center Museum, Chicago, Illinois (1987); "The Blues Aesthetic: Black Culture and Modernism," travelling, Washington Project for the Arts, Washington, D.C. (1989); "Third International Bienal of Painting," travelling, Cuenca, Ecuador (1991); and many others.

Winner of many honors, awards, and fellowships, Alvarez has been the recipient of an artist fellowship from Art Matters, New York City (1991); a National Endowment for the Arts (NEA) Mid-Atlantic Regional fellowship (1988); an international exchange program with Cologne, Germany (1987); fellowships and residencies at the MacDowell Colony, Peterborough, New Hampshire; the New York Foundation for the Arts; and the Brandywine Workshop, Pennsylvania—all in 1986; artist's grants from Artists Space, New York City (1983, 1985); an artist residency fellowship from the Studio Museum in Harlem, New York (1984, 1985); and others.

Alvarez's works are in private, corporate, and public permanent collections, including the German Consulate, Philadelphia, Pennsylvania; the Studio Museum in Harlem, New York; the University of Delaware at Newark; American Telephone and Telegraph, New York City; and many others.

Bibliography
Pacheco, Patrick. "The New Faith in Painting." *Art & Antiques* (May 1991): 61–62.
Richard, Paul. "WPA's 'Blues' Symphony." *The Washington Post* (September 14, 1989).
Who's Who in American Art. 19th ed. R.R. Bowker Co., 1991–1992.

Alvarez Bravo, Lola (1906–)

Lola Alvarez Bravo was born Dolores Martínez Vianda in the small city of Lagos de Moreno in Jalisco—a state on the Pacific coast of Mexico. At an early age she moved with her family to Mexico City, where she was educated in the manner traditional for daughters of her social class. She grew up in the turbulent years of the Mexican Revolution and came of age among the artists and intellectuals who led the cultural renaissance that followed the political upheaval.

Alvarez had the good fortune to know personally many of these painters and writers—including Diego Rivera, José Clemente Orozco, David Alfaro Siqueiros, Carlos Pellicer, and others—and she began to feel that she, too, wanted to contribute to the creative life of her country. In 1925 she married a young artist, Manuel Alvarez Bravo, who was then just beginning a career in photography; he would later emerge as Mexico's most renowned practitioner of the medium. The couple separated in 1934. It was around that time that Alvarez herself began working professionally as a photographer.

During the 1940s and 1950s Alvarez photographed nearly all of Mexico's artists and intellectuals in an effort to document for posterity the great cultural leaders of that period. Although a master of portraiture, she did not confine herself to that genre. She travelled widely throughout the country, observing and learning from the monuments of Mexico's past and the people of urban and rural Mexico. She made photographs to express her feelings about what she saw, creating often haunting images that captured the mystery of moments of everyday life.

For more than thirty years, Alvarez worked for the Instituto Nacional de Bellas Artes. She also taught photography at the Academia de San Carlos—Mexico's most distinguished school of fine arts—and at the Universidad Nacional Autónoma de Mexico. Her photographs have been widely published and exhibited. A major solo exhibition was held at the Museo del Palacio de Bellas Artes in Mexico City in 1965, and she has participated in many group exhibitions in Mexico and abroad. In recognition of her artistic work she was awarded the José Clemente Orozco medal by the state of Jalisco.

Martha Davidson

Bibliography
Alvarez Bravo, Lola. *100 Fotos de Lola Alvarez Bravo.* Introduction by
Luis Cardoza y Arragón. Mexico City: Instituto Nacional de Bellas
Artes, 1965.
————. *Escritores y artistas de México: Fotografías de Lola Alvarez Bravo.*
Introduction by Salvador Elizondo. Mexico City: Fondo de Cultura
Económica, 1982.
Eder, Rita, et al. *Künstlerinnen aus Mexiko.* Berlin: Die Gesellschaft/Das
Künsterhaus, 1981.
Fernández Perera, Manuel. *Lola Alvarez Bravo: Recuento fotográfico.*
Mexico City: Editorial Penélope, 1982.

Alvarez Golzarri de Salazar, Rosa (1925–)

Born in Puebla, Mexico in 1925, Rosa Alvarez Golzarri de Salazar,
from childhood, knew she was going to be a painter. Thus, in 1948 she
studied privately with Julieta Sarmiento and two years later she enrolled in the Academy of Fine Arts in Puebla and took the usual art
courses: perspective, landscape painting, anatomy, life drawing, and
others. Still searching for artistic guidance, she enrolled in other academies, but was not satisfied with the instruction she received until she
met and took further work from Faustino Salazar in 1953.

Alvarez attempted relief printmaking on linoleum and, with several friends, helped found the "First Nucleus of Printmakers" in
Puebla and showed with this group in Puebla and in Peking, China,
in 1952. The previous year she was part of the Grupo Plástica Poblana.
In 1952 she was a member of the Unión de Artes Plásticas in the
Artist's Quarter, Puebla, and in 1969 she participated in the painting competition, "Revolución Mexicana." Her work was seen in shows
at the Sala Arrieta of the House of Culture, Puebla (1974–1975) and
in the Museum of the City of Mexico in an exhibition titled "10
Pintoras y Escultoras Poblanas." In 1978 she was a participant in a
national show organized by the University of Puebla and in the Quinta
Feria de Zacapoaxtla.

Alvarez has also had a number of solo exhibitions in various cities throughout Mexico. Her work carries on the tradition of the great
Mexican School of Painting coupled simultaneously with a seeming
romantic streak.

Bibliography
*Biográfico Enciclopedia Diccionario de la Pintura Mexicana: Siglo Arte
Contemporaneo.* Quinientos Años Editores, 1979.

Ames, Scribner (1908–)

A native of Chicago, Illinois, Scribner Ames received her Bachelor of
Philosophy degree from the University of Chicago; she attended the
School of the Art Institute of Chicago and was a scholar at the Chicago
School of Sculpture. In addition to study with Hans Schwegerle in
Munich, Germany, Ames took further study with José de Creeft and
Hans Hofmann in New York City.

Teacher, portraitist, commissioned sculptor, and writer (her pen
name is Polly Scribner Ames), Ames has held many solo exhibitions of
her work in the United States and abroad, including the Cultural Center, Netherlands West Indies (1947); Galerie Chardin, Paris, France
(1949); Cercle Université, Aix-en-Provence, France (1950); Esher-Sur-
rey Gallery, The Hague, Holland (1950); and other shows in Cincin-

nati, Ohio; St. Louis, Missouri; New York City; Milwaukee, Wisconsin;
and others.

Her work has been invited to group exhibitions for many years
and is to be seen in the permanent and private collections of the Quad-
rangle Club, University of Chicago; the Fort Nassau Asiento Club,
Curaçao, Netherlands West Indies; Plejehospitaet, Copenhagen, Denmark; Aix-en-Provence and Versailles, France; and others.

Turning more to writing, Ames recently completed a manuscript,
"Chance of My Making," based upon her experiences as an exhibiting
artist in post-occupation France and The Hague, Holland.

Bibliography
Correspondence with the artist.
Who's Who in American Art. 19th ed. R.R. Bowker Co., 1991–1992.

Amézcua, Consuelo González (1903–)

Born in Mexico, Consuelo (Chelo) González Amézcua, a self-taught
artist, was raised in Del Rio, Texas. She won a scholarship to the San
Carlos Academy in Mexico City, Mexico, in the 1930s, but her father's
death created problems that would not allow her to take up the award.

From early childhood it was apparent that Amézcua possessed
both the talent and the desire to draw everything about her. Despite a
lack of encouragement from her family, and other difficulties, Amézcua
showed her "filigree art"—her term for her precisely-drawn religious
and secular ballpoint images, many with colored inks, on cardboard or
paper—in institutions in San Antonio, and Dallas, Texas; Monterrey,
Mexico; New York City; and Springfield, Massachusetts.

Bibliography
Quirarte, Jacinto. *Mexican-American Artists.* University of Texas Press, 1973.

Amos, Emma (1938–)

Painter, printmaker, designer/weaver Emma Amos was born in Atlanta,
Georgia, and attended Antioch College, Yellow Springs, Ohio, where
she received a Bachelor of Arts degree in 1958. The following year
she enrolled in the London Central School, England, where she earned
a Bachelor of Fine Arts degree. Amos took her graduate work at New
York University and was awarded a Master of Arts degree in 1966.

Between 1960 and 1992 Amos held 19 solo exhibitions of her
work throughout the United States, Italy, and Sweden, including the
Alexander Gallery, Atlanta, Georgia (1960); Gallery 62, National Urban League, New York (1980); Galleri Oscar, Stockholm, Sweden
(1986); Zimmerman Saturn Gallery, Nashville, Tennessee (1989, 1990);
Clemson University Gallery, Genoa, Italy (1989); the Bronx Museum,
New York (1991); the Pump House Gallery, Bushnell Park Foundation, Hartford, Connecticut (1992); and others.

Amos's works have been invited to more than sixty group exhibitions throughout the United States and abroad, such as "Dream Singers, Story Tellers: An African-American Presence," Fukui Fine Arts
Museum, Fukui, Japan (1993); "Presswork: The Art of Women
Printmakers," National Museum of Women in the Arts, Washington,
D.C. (1991–1993); "African-American Works on Paper," travelling,
New Visions Gallery, Atlanta, Georgia (1991); "Committed to Print,"
travelling, the Museum of Modern Art (MoMA), New York City (1988–
1991); "Art in Print: A Tribute to Robert Blackburn," the Schomburg

Center for Research in Black Culture, New York (1984); "Impressions/ Expressions," Smithsonian Institution, Washington, D.C. (1979); "30 Contemporary Black Artists," Minneapolis Institute of Art, Minnesota (1968); and many others.

Social and political concerns, myth and fable, the fact that she does not swim, Afro-American culture, aesthetic considerations, drug addiction, life in New York City—all of these and more are fused together in her visual works, her prints, her paintings edged with *kente* cloth, and her textiles. What once may have been a painting of a diving figure (Icarus?) in her "Water Series" is now plummeting into nowhere: *Into the Dangerous World I Leapt* (1989), a large acrylic painting with African fabric on canvas, portrays Amos's fears for the time of AIDS, homelessness, etc.

She has been associate professor at the Mason Gross School of Art, Rutgers University, New Brunswick, New Jersey, since 1980; governor of the Skowhegan School of Painting and Sculpture, Maine, since 1987; holder of fellowships from the New York Foundation for the Arts in painting (1989), and the National Endowment for the Arts (NEA) in drawing (1983).

Amos's work is in permanent collections throughout the United States, Sweden, and England, including the Dade County Museum of Art, Miami, Florida; Minnesota Museum of Art, Minneapolis, Minnesota; Newark Museum, New Jersey; MoMA, New York City; Skandinaviska Enskilda Bankn, Stockholm, Sweden; the U.S. Embassy, London, England; and others.

Bibliography

Hess, Elizabeth. "Breaking and Entering." *The Village Voice* (June 5, 1990).

Lippard, Lucy. "Floating, Falling, Landing: An Interview with Emma Amos." *Art Papers*. Atlanta. (November–December 1991).

Raven, Arlene. "Laws of Falling Bodies: Emma Amos, 'The Falling Series.'" *The Village Voice* (May 7, 1991): 86.

Amoss, Berthe (1925–)

Born in New Orleans, Louisiana, Berthe Amoss is an author and illustrator of fourteen children's books and four young adult novels, a watercolorist, and a professor of children's literature and folklore at Tulane University in her native city. She is also a columnist for the *Times Picayune*, and the mother of six sons. Amoss received her Bachelor of Arts degree in English literature and art from Sophie Newcomb College, Tulane University, New Orleans, Louisiana, and her Master of Arts degree from Tulane University.

Widely travelled, Amoss attended art schools at the University of Hawaii, and the Academy of Fine Arts—both in Honolulu, Hawaii; the Kunsthalle, Bremen, Germany; and the Académie des Beaux-Arts, Antwerp, Belgium. Her etchings and watercolors have been in solo and group exhibitions and are housed in the permanent collections of the University of Minnesota, Minneapolis; the State Library of Louisiana; the University of Southern Mississippi at Hattiesburg; the Howard Tilton Memorial Library of Tulane University, New Orleans, Louisiana; and others.

Bibliography

Who's Who in American Art. 19th ed. R.R. Bowker Co., 1991–1992.

Anderson, Laurie (1947–)

Laurie Anderson is an American performance artist, whose multi-media concert-style productions express ironic, piercing insights into the omnipresent nature of electronic media in contemporary life. Anderson's extension of these live performances into musical recordings, videos, and film fueled her successful cross-over from the elite strata of performance art to the commercial arena of popular music.

United States I–IV (1979–1981), the first of Anderson's electronically sophisticated live performances, began an international tour at the Brooklyn Academy of Music (BAM), New York, on February 3, 1983. Her use of back-up singers and musicians and her recording contract with the Warner Brothers label beginning in 1981 have focused considerable attention on the musical component of her work, but her performances are powerfully visual as well. Anderson is simultaneously composer and instrumentalist, lyricist and vocalist; her figure is isolated on the vast stage, dwarfed by projected moving and still images of her own design. Gleaned from commercial graphics, the projected imagery and text appear in deft synchronization with lyrics and sound, constructing alternately poignant and amusing juxtapositions between the subjects of nature and technology. In *O Superman* (1981) from *United States* II, the lyrics linguistically transform a maternal embrace into the international arms race, while projected cartoon graphics of chubby airplanes and a faintly heard chorus of birds reinforce the chilling narrative through opposition.

With musical training in violin in her background, Anderson compositionally mixes classical and electronic instruments. She develops dramatically-built tension within romantic melody lines against the pulsing sameness of a repetitive minimalist beat. Her body movements make both contemporary and historical references as well. Angular and stiff, the robotic style is vaguely reminiscent of early twentieth-century Russian dance master Sergei Diaghilev and, by association, his collaborations with visual artists such as Pablo Picasso (*Parade*, 1917). Anderson's performances resonate with futurist and dada ancestry, but her incorporation of gender issues and semiotics places the work in an undeniably contemporary context. On stage her boxy monochromatic suits, short spiked hair, and electronically-filtered voice form the anonymous personas of corporate anti-individuals. These androgynous characters are framed by lyrics and images which alter gender roles and expectations. Speaking in a hypnotically quiet voice, Anderson invokes mass-speak. Her lyrics—rife with commercial slogans—acknowledge the power of language in contemporary life, as well as its intrinsic inability to convey precise expression.

Born in the Chicago, Illinois, area, Anderson took her Master of Fine Arts degree in sculpture from Columbia University, New York City, in 1969. In the 1970s she wrote art criticism for journals such as *Art News*, *Artforum*, and *Art in America* and taught art history for several years in New York. Her first performance event, *Automotive* (1972), was a site-specific orchestration for automobile horns in Rochester, Vermont. Before engaging the commercial theater and film circuit in the 1980s Anderson's conceptual art and performances were presented in museum and gallery spaces. Her conceptual pieces consisted of series of photographs, contextualized with captions, storyboard narrations, and musical compositions. Early performances were offered in New York City at the Kitchen and the Whitney Museum of American Art. In 1978 Anderson exhibited sound sculptures at the Museum of Modern Art (MoMA). A fifteen-year retrospective of her work was organized by the Institute of Contemporary Art in Philadelphia, Pennsylvania, in 1983, a travelling show to Los Angeles, California; New York City; and Houston, Texas. She was awarded a Guggenheim Foundation fellowship in 1983.

Anderson's only venture into commercial film to date is *Home of the Brave* (1985). Filmed as a live performance on a stage in New Jersey, it was an effort to take her work into yet another medium. Although the film flattened the multi-dimensional aspects of the live experience, Anderson has expressed interest in exploring this medium further.

Tickets for Anderson's two-and-one-half- to three-hour performances are sold through commercial entertainment vendors. Her intent is to graft the vitality of theatrical performance—a major fixture of contemporary popular culture—into a visual arts context. Although those who question any possible coexistence of intellectual insight and mass appeal regard her work with some suspicion, her inventive contributions to performance art have been highly praised. A smooth, professional, and innovative performing artist, Anderson has engaged audiences far beyond the esoteric realm of the avant-garde.

Deborah Anne Rindge

Bibliography
Anderson, Laurie. *United States.* Harper & Row, 1984.
Kardon, Janet. *Laurie Anderson: Works from 1969 to 1983.* Institute of Contemporary Art, University of Pennsylvania, 1983.
Smagula, Howard. *Currents: Contemporary Directions in the Visual Arts,* 2nd ed. Prentice-Hall, 1989, pp. 241–52.

Andrade, Edna Davis Wright (1917–)

Edna Davis Wright Andrade was born in Portsmouth, Virginia, and grew up in a rural environment. Encouraged by her parents in her intense interest in drawing, Andrade attended the Pennsylvania Academy of Fine Arts and the University of Pennsylvania, both in Philadelphia, and graduated with a Bachelor of Fine Arts degree in 1937. She studied there with Henry McCarter, George Harding, and Daniel Garber. At the age of nineteen, and again at twenty, Andrade was awarded the first and second Cresson European travel fellowships from the Pennsylvania Academy, and by 1938 she had travelled extensively throughout Western Europe, Greece, Egypt, and Scandinavia.

Long known for its geometric abstractionism, Andrade's work evolved gradually from the traditional academic orientation—through her experience as a designer during the war years in Washington, D.C., in the Office of Strategic Services, and her architectural drafting projects after the war—to more formalist concerns and images in the late 1950s and early 1960s. Greatly affected by the writings of Lancelot Law Whyte and by the work of Josef Albers and Paul Klee, Andrade sought to reconcile scientific observation and phenomena with the sensuality of color and light. Through the 1960s she applied these interests to her paintings and architectural commissions, and, in 1971, through a residency at the Tamarind Institute, Albuquerque, New Mexico, was able to add lithography to her mastered mediums.

Andrade began her equally distinguished teaching career as an art supervisor in the Norfolk, Virginia, elementary schools in 1938 and taught at Tulane University, New Orleans, Louisiana, from 1939 to 1951. She

married the architect Preston Andrade in 1941; they divorced in 1960.

Andrade was appointed to the faculty of the Philadelphia College of Art, Pennsylvania, in 1958 and became professor emeritus in 1982. She also held another faculty appointment briefly at Temple University, Philadelphia, Pennsylvania, and has been visiting artist at Skidmore College, Saratoga Springs, New York; the Tyler School of Art at Temple University; the University of New Mexico, Albuquerque; the University of Zulia, Maracaibo, Venezuela; the Pennsylvania Academy of Fine Arts, Philadelphia; Rutgers University, New Brunswick, New Jersey; Hollins College, Virginia; and Arizona State University, Tempe, where she has continuing adjunct professor status.

Among Andrade's numerous awards are the honor award for achievement in the visual arts from the National Women's Caucus for Art (1983); the governor of Pennsylvania's Hazlett memorial award for excellence in the arts (1980); the Klein prize, American Color Print Society (1973); Childe Hassam memorial purchase awards, American Academy and Institute of Arts and Letters (1967, 1968); and others. Her commissioned works include the Philadelphia "Art Now" Bus Stop Poster (1988); Poster for *Circus 1984*, Philadelphia Please Touch Children's Museum (1983); an edition of silk-screen prints, Institute of Contemporary Art, Philadelphia (1973); mobile sculpture, marble intarsia mural, and mosaic mural for three branches of the Free Library of Philadelphia (1960, 1967, and 1969, respectively). Numerous museum and corporate collections have acquired her paintings and prints, including the Albright-Knox Art Gallery, Buffalo, New York; Baltimore Museum of Art, Maryland; Atlantic Richfield; AT&T; Marion Koogler McNay Art Museum, San Antonio, Texas; Philadelphia Museum of Art, and Pennsylvania Academy of the Fine Arts—both in Philadelphia, Pennsylvania; Arizona State University Art Museum, Tempe; University of New Mexico Art Museum, Albuquerque; Federal Reserve Bank; University of Houston, Texas; Addison Gallery of American Art, Andover, Massachusetts; and others.

Andrade's first one-woman exhibition was held in 1954 at the Philadelphia Art Alliance, Pennsylvania. She has had twelve solo shows since, including five at the Marian Locks Gallery, Philadelphia, in 1971, 1974, 1977, 1983, and 1989. Her work continues to embrace the worlds of art and science in her particular unique manner. Her travels over the years to India, Japan, and Europe, as well as her long-standing love of Islamic decoration, have synthesized into a fully integrated vision of experience. Andrade maintains the graciousness of the traditional southern lady coupled with the thoroughly urbane professional artist—a combination that is at the core of her reputation as both world-class artist and salon hostess to art-world circles in the city of Philadelphia.

Leonard Lehrer

Bibliography
Bregman, Lillian. "Portraits of Artists." *Philadelphia Magazine* (October 1983): 206–09, 215.
Burko, Diane. *SCA Honor Awards.* Philadelphia: National Women's Caucus for Art Conference, 1983, pp. 4–5, 18–19.
D'Harnoncourt, Anne. *Philadelphia: Three Centuries of American Art.* Philadelphia Museum of Art, 1976, pp. 636–37.
Rubinstein, Charlotte S. *American Women Artists.* Avon, 1982, pp. 136.

Andrea (1940–)

A native of Liverpool, England, the artist known simply as Andrea studied various art media in Austria, Belgium, Germany, Greece, Holland, and other European countries, before immigrating to Mexico and taking further work with Ernesto Kubli (1954–1956), Guillermo Silva Santamaría (1957), Gilberto Aceves Navarro (1956–1958), and the sculptor Heinz Leinflellner at the University for the Applied Arts—all in Mexico.

Andrea has had a number of solo shows in Mexico, including the Galería Diana (1962); Galería GDA (1975); Galería Fénix (1976); Galería de Arte Danilo Ongay (1977). She also held solo exhibitions in the Erste Oesterreichische Spar Casse, Vienna, Austria, and at J & L Lobmeyr in the same city, in 1977. The following year, she showed at the Alpha-Omega Galerie in Vienna, Austria.

Among the myriad group exhibitions in which Andrea's work has been seen are the Convento del Desierto de los Leones, Mexico (1957); Bad Godesberg Stadthalle, Germany (1960); and a number of galleries in Mexico City, including Galería Diana (1962–1963), Galería Misrachi (1962–1964; 1975–1976), Galería Nios (1964–1965), Galería GDA (1975), Galería Rive-Gauche (1976), and Tane, S.A. Arte-Objecto (1976). She also showed abroad in Paris, Moscow, and Leningrad in 1976. Andrea has worked as sculptor, ceramist, and painter and has shown her work in all these media; her work is abstract in nature: subtle, strong, and sensitive.

Bibliography
Biográfico Enciclopedia Diccionario de la Pintura Mexicana: Siglo Arte Contemporaneo. Quinientos Años Editores, 1979.

Andreson, Laura (1902–)

An American potter known for her functional wheel-thrown porcelain embellished with unique glazes of her own formulation, Laura Andreson is also known for her pioneering role as an educator in the ceramics field. Born and raised in San Bernardino, California, Andreson graduated from the University of California at Los Angeles (UCLA) in 1932 with a Bachelor of Education degree. Here she was the valedictorian of her class and graduated with the highest honors. From 1932 to 1933, she did graduate work at Claremont College, California, after which she attended Columbia University, New York City, receiving a Master of Arts degree in 1937.

Andreson is credited as a pioneer in bringing high-fired ceramics methods and technologies to Southern California through her teaching at UCLA (1933–1970). When she began to teach ceramics, the prevailing technology consisted of low-fired earthenware cast in molds or hand-built. There were no throwing wheels or high-fire kilns, and no stoneware clays or glazes for students to use. Through experimentation and with the assistance of her students Andreson gradually created high-temperature kilns, kick wheels, stoneware clays and glazes, often aided by the notes and pottery she brought home from her extensive travels throughout the world. Under her direction the ceramics department grew into a large, well-equipped facility which produced many academic generations of potters on the West Coast.

Not only a teacher but a potter of distinction, Andreson made pots to be used and to be "felt with the eyes and seen with the hands."

Her love of glazes led her to make simple forms of high purity and refinement of surface in order to best show off the coloration and subtleties of her glazes. Her interest and research in glazes led to the redevelopment of a number of elusive glazes of early foreign cultures, which she documented and shared through papers and lectures.

An indefatigable traveler, Andreson made a point of visiting ceramic artists, museums, and institutions in other countries, broadening her knowledge of the medium and its history. To illustrate her studies, she became an avid collector of ceramics both historic and contemporary. Her unique and educational collection has been divided into two—one given to UCLA and the other to the Los Angeles County Museum of Art.

Andreson was elected in 1976 to the Academy of Fellows by the American Craft Council and the same year was made an honorary member in the National Council on Education in the Ceramic Arts.

Her ceramics have been included in numerous exhibitions, among them the touring exhibitions "A Century of American Ceramics" organized by the Everson Museum, Syracuse, New York; and "American Porcelain: New Expressions in an Ancient Art," organized by the Renwick Gallery, Smithsonian Institution, Washington, D.C. Twelve pieces of her work are in the collection of the Museum of Fine Arts, Boston, Massachusetts.

Elena Karina Canavier

Bibliography
Levin, Elaine. *History of American Ceramics*. Harry N. Abrams, 1988, pp. 175, 180, 184–186, 187, 188, 213, 220.
Rico, Diana. "Laura Andreson, An Interview." *American Ceramics* (March 1984): 12–19.
Washington, D.C., Smithsonian Institution, Archives of American Art. Laura Andreson Papers, June 1991.

Andrews, Marietta M. (1869–1931)

Born in Richmond, Virginia, the painter Marietta Minnigerode Andrews first studied at the Corcoran School of Art, Washington, D.C., with her husband-to-be, Eliphalet Fraser Andrews. She later studied under William Merritt Chase of New York; Luigi Chialiva of Paris, France; and Ernest Lieberman of Munich, Germany.

Andrews is the author and illustrator of several books, including *My Studio Window* (1928), *Scraps of Paper* (1929), and *George Washington's Country* (1930), all published by E.P. Dutton & Co. In addition to painting and creating silhouettes, she created many commissioned stained-glass windows at venues, including St. Paul's Church, Steubenville, Ohio; the American Society for Psychical Research, New York; University of Virginia, Charlottesville; George Washington University, Washington, D.C.; and many others.

Bibliography
Andrews, Marietta M. *My Studio Window*. Dutton, 1928.
Cosentino, Andrew J., and Henry H. Glassie. *The Capital Image: Painters in Washington, 1800–1915*. Smithsonian Institution Press, 1983.
Obituary. *American Art Annual*. Vol. 28. American Federation of Arts, 1932.

Andrews, Sybil (1898–)

Sybil Andrews is known for her powerful color linocuts which reflect the dynamism of the modern world. She is considered the most important of a vital group of artists working in London, England, under the influence of Claude Flight in the 1920s and 1930s.

Born in Bury, Saint Edmunds, England, Andrews initially studied art using John Hassal's correspondence course. She also became friendly with Cyril E. Power—an architect and artist who guided and encouraged her early work.

In 1922 Andrews moved to London, England, to attend Heatherley's School of Fine Art. There she did intensive study in life drawing, oil painting, and composition, and developed a very accomplished facility as a draftsperson. She also studied part-time with Henri Glicenstein—a Polish sculptor—who made her understand the importance of simplification and formal qualities. Through him she made her first prints—drypoints on copper of popular architectural subjects—completing more than thirty-four by 1929.

In 1925 Andrews joined the newly-formed Grosvenor School of Modern Art, London, England, as a secretary. While there she met Claude Flight and began to make color linocuts under his influence. Flight was committed to the use of the linocut—a modern material not burdened with a tradition—for making prints which combined the ideas of futurist motion and cubist flattened planes using simplified forms with strong color and decorative patterning.

Already an accomplished artist, Andrews was inspired by Flight and realized the potential of the color linocut. In her prints forms are simplified and linked through repeated shapes to create an inner rhythm and dynamic sense of movement. Diaphanous layers of transparent color are built up to a rich surface in these bold and powerful images. With Flight and other students, Andrews exhibited regularly in the linocut exhibitions held at the Redfern Gallery in London until the war. In 1938 Andrews moved to the New Forest, southwest of London. During the war she worked in the yards of the British Power Boat Company at Hythe near Southampton.

Andrews was also an accomplished artist in other media. Vigorous watercolors of gnarled, twisted, and heavy forms of the ancient trees of the New Forest have a very dense and vibrant color. In an oil painting self-portrait of 1940 the form is modelled with vigorous brushstrokes in high-keyed, saturated color. She produced landscapes with the sweep and rhythm and short slabs of paint reminiscent of Van Gogh. Oils later painted in Canada were often extremely abstracted with repeated forms linking broad areas of color. A group of these were given the title "Opus," denoting an association with the rhythm and modulation of music.

In 1947 Andrews emigrated to Canada and settled in Campbell River on Vancouver Island. She continued to make art and exhibited her work quite actively in Canada in the 1950s but infrequently after that. She continued to make the color linocuts for which she is now famous, completing seventy-six between 1929 and 1988.

A major retrospective exhibition of her prints and the catalog *Sybil Andrews: Colour Linocuts* by Peter White, Glenbow Museum, Calgary (1982) brought her to the attention of a broad public. The Glenbow Museum houses the largest and most complete collection of her work and archives.

Patricia Ainslie

Bibliography

Ainslie, Patricia. Taped Interviews with Sybil Andrews. Calgary: Glenbow Museum. August 18–20, 1990.

Looy, Jean. Taped Interviews with Sybil Andrews. Calgary: Glenbow Museum. April–August 1990.

Urbanelli, Lora S. *The Grosvenor School: British Linocuts Between the Wars.* Providence: Rhode Island School of Design, 1988.

White, Peter. *Sybil Andrews: Colour Linocuts.* Calgary: Glenbow Museum, 1982.

Anglin, Betty L. (1937–)

Born in Greenwood, South Carolina, Betty Lockhart Anglin studied at Agnes Scott College, Decatur, Georgia (1956–1958); the University of Georgia, Athens, where she studied with Lamarr Dodd (1958–1960); and the College of William and Mary, Williamsburg, Virginia (1970–1972), where she earned her Bachelor's degree in Art. Anglin also studied with Leone Cooper in St. Louis, Missouri, and with Barclay Sheaks in Newport News, Virginia, among others.

Anglin has held a number of solo exhibitions of her work, in galleries, associations, and universities, including Hampton University, Virginia (1986); Virginia Wesleyan College, Norfolk, and the Peninsula Arts Association, Newport News, Virginia (1987); Blue Skies Gallery, Hampton, Virginia (1990); and Cottey College, Nevada, Missouri (1991).

She has had her work invited to many group exhibitions, such as the Irene Leach Juried Shows at the Chrysler Hermitage Museum, Norfolk, Virginia (1964, 1966, 1971); Biennial Exhibition, Virginia Museum, Richmond (1969, 1971); Hampton University, Virginia (1985); Cecil Rawls Museum, Courtland, Virginia (1988); Cottey College, Nevada, Missouri (1990, 1991); and many others.

Anglin has been a widely respected teacher of art and award winner for more than two score years. Her works are in the public, private, and corporate permanent collections of many institutions, including the Cecil Rawls Museum, Courtland, Virginia; Hampton University, Virginia; Peninsula Arts Association, Newport News, Virginia; City of Hampton, Virginia; Owens-Corning, Anderson, South Carolina; and many others.

Bibliography

Who's Who in American Art. 19th ed. R.R. Bowker Co., 1991–1992.

Anker, Suzanne (1946–)

One of the original pioneers in cast-paper work, Suzanne Anker is also a painter and, primarily, a sculptor. Her *oeuvre* is interconnected by a highly-focused regard for the images, processes, and structures of the natural world. This attention devoted to organic form manifests itself as an indexical sign in which natural phenomena—boughs, leaves, stones, shells—are cast directly into bronze, iron, or aluminum. In her encaustic graphite paintings natural fragments are directly impressed or printed upon the surface, while in the cast-paper work they emerge from the surface within a continuous texture. In each instance abstraction is combined with imagistic devices that generate poetic metaphors based on the integration of cultural artifacts and organic forms.

In 1989 Anker began incorporating refracting optical lenses into her sculpture, opening up an entirely novel direction in both site-specific outdoor pieces and still-life tableaux in steel, bronze, and copper. This development in her work invites the viewer to peer through a vessel shape in which a kaleidoscope prism refracts, multiplies, and patterns other components of the sculpture. Thus the lenses transform the viewer's experience of sculpture into a cinematic visual field.

Anker's interests in the natural world through this issue of privileged viewing extended her investigation into the microscopic domain of chromosomes and genes. By incorporating the helical X–Y structure of the chromosome into her motif index, she completed the cycle from the directly observable in nature to its invisible realm. Appropriating scientific images, she created a body of work—under the collective title "Gene Pool"—that includes suspended pigment on large vellum sheets and expansive sculptural arrays made of metallic fibers of stainless steel, copper, aluminum, and bronze. This development combines the apparent polarities that have always characterized her work; that is, an intense regard for the sensuality of her chosen materials and a rigorous conceptual framework within which to manifest them.

Born in Brooklyn, New York, Anker received her initial training in art as part of a liberal arts program at Brooklyn College, New York, studying closely with her mentor Ad Reinhardt and graduating in 1967 with honors in art and the all arts award. The influence of Reinhardt's metaphysical philosophy is readily apparent in the monochromatic and phenomenological aspects of her work. She received her Master of Fine Arts degree from the University of Colorado, Boulder (1976), where she also taught for one year. She was appointed to the faculty at Washington University, St. Louis, Missouri (1976), where she remained for two years. In 1978 Anker returned to New York City and is currently the director of the painting and drawing program at New York University.

Frank Gillette

Bibliography
Ash, John. *Art in America* (October 1990): 208.
Heller, Jules. *Papermaking*. Watson-Guptill Publications, 1978.
Ratcliff, Carter. "Swamp Things." *Vogue* (April 1989): 282–87.
Risatti, Howard. *Artforum* (Summer 1990): 170.
Rubinstein, Meyer Raphael. "Suzanne Anker." *Arts* (December 1988): 85.
Schwabsky, Barry. "Natural Anti-Naturalism." *Flash Art* (1988): 102–04.

Antin, Eleanor (1935–)

A native New Yorker, the videographer and performing artist Eleanor Antin earned a Bachelor's degree from the College of the City of New York (CUNY) and also studied at the Tamara Daykarhanove School for the Stage.

Antin has given many solo exhibitions and performances in galleries and museums, including the Museum of Modern Art (MoMA), New York City (1973); Everson Museum, Syracuse, New York (1974); "Art: A Woman's Sensibility," California Institute of the Arts, Valencia (1975); Clocktower, New York City (1976); "Eleanor Antin: The Angel of Mercy," La Jolla Museum of Contemporary Art, California (1977); "Eleanor Antinova, Recollections of My Life with Diaghilev," Ronald Feldman Fine Arts Gallery, New York City (1980); and others.

Her work has been included in other shows, such as "Invisible/Visible," Long Beach Museum of Art, California (1972); "In Her Own Image," Fleisher Art Memorial, Philadelphia, Pennsylvania (1974); Wadsworth Atheneum, Hartford, Connecticut (1977); Whitney Museum of American Art, New York City (1978); "Intimate/Intimate," Indiana State University, Terre Haute (1986); and many others.

Winner of awards and honors and a university professor of note, Antin received, among others, a grant from the National Endowment for the Arts (NEA) (1979).

Bibliography
Henry, Gerrit. "Eleanor Antinova at Ronald Feldman." *Art in America* 69:1 (January 1981): 128–129.
Munro, Eleanor. *Originals: American Women Artists*. Simon and Schuster, 1979.
Raven, Arlene, and Deborah Marrow. "Eleanor Antin: What's Your Story." *Chrysalis* 8 (Summer 1978): 43–51.
Russell, John. "Eleanor Antin's Historical Daydream." *The New York Times* (January 30, 1977).

Apel, Barbara (1935–)

Born in Falls City, Nebraska, Barbara Apel attended the Kansas City Art Institute, Missouri, where she received a Bachelor of Fine Arts degree in 1965. Two years later, after graduate study with the printmaker Lee Chesney at the University of Illinois, Urbana, Apel received a Master of Fine Arts degree.

Apel had solo exhibitions of her prints at Gallery East, Boston (1974); the Newton Public Library (1981); Impressions Gallery, Boston (1982)—all in Massachusetts; and at the Davenport Gallery, Ltd., Greenville, South Carolina (1988); and others.

Her work was invited to group exhibitions throughout the United States, including the Potsdam National Print Exhibition, State University of New York (SUNY) at Potsdam (1978); "Contemporary Monotypes," Impressions Gallery, Boston, Massachusetts, and Smith-Andersen Gallery, Palo Alto, California (1979); "New American Monotypes," Smithsonian Institution, Washington, D.C. (1978–1980); "Winter Exhibition," Davenport Gallery, Ltd., Greenville, South Carolina (1989); and many others.

Winner of many prizes for her prints and recipient of a MacDowell Colony fellowship, Peterborough, New Hampshire (1979), Apel has taught from 1967 to 1981 at various institutions, including the Art Institute of Boston, the DeCordova & Dana Museum, Lincoln, and the Cambridge Center for Adult Education—all in Massachusetts.

Apel's works are in the permanent collections of museums, universities, and other institutions, including the Museum of Fine Arts, Boston, Massachusetts; Hood Museum of Art, Dartmouth College, Hanover, New Hampshire; Worcester Fine Arts Museum, Massachusetts; University of Illinois, Urbana; University of Wisconsin, Fond du Lac; Salomon Brothers, New York City; and many others.

Bibliography
Goldstein, Nathan. *The Art of Responsive Drawing*. 3rd ed. Prentice-Hall, 1983.
Puniello, Francoise S. *Female Artists in the United States: A Research and Resource Guide*. State University of New Jersey, 1986.
Who's Who in American Art. 19th ed. R.R. Bowker Co., 1991–1992.

Appel, Thelma (1940–)

Born in Tel Aviv, Israel, the painter Thelma Appel earned diplomas from St. Martin's School of Art (1961) and Hornsey College of Art (1962)—both in London, England.

Appel has exhibited widely in solo and group shows in museums and galleries in the United States; her solo exhibitions include the Fischbach Gallery, New York City (1979, 1982); Westchester County Center for the Arts, White Plains, New York (1992); and others.

Appel is a teacher of art and an award-winning painter who was a resident fellow at Yaddo, Saratoga Springs, New York (1974), among others. Her work is represented in private, public, and corporate permanent collections, including the Chase Manhattan Bank, New York City; IBM Corporation, Lawrence, New Jersey; the Milwaukee Arts Center, Wisconsin; Vermont State Legislature, Montpelier; and many others.

Bibliography
André, M. "Review." *Art in America* (November 1975).
Who's Who in American Art. 20th ed. R.R. Bowker Co., 1993–1994.

Apple, Jacki

Native New Yorker, performance and media artist, audio composer, curator, writer, director and producer, Jacki Apple attended Syracuse University, New York (1959–1960), Parsons School of Design, New York City (1960–1963), studied dance with Andy De Groat, Rudy Perez, and Satoru Shimazaki, and also studied ballet.

From her 1970s base in New York City to the 1980s and 1990s in Los Angeles, Apple had scores of solo exhibitions, performances, audio productions and compositions, installations, conceptual pieces, and screenings produced throughout the United States, Canada, Europe, Australia, and New Zealand, including performance pieces such as "Transfer," "The Mexican Tapes," and "Voices in the Dark"; film and video works, including "Performance Live from the Franklin Furnace," "Free Fire Zone," and "Fluctuations of the Field"; audio/radio pieces, including "Black Hole/Blue Sky Dreams," "Redefining Democracy in America," and "The Culture of Disappearance"; installations such as "Digging" and "Bedtime Stories, Lullabies, and Other Lies"; conceptual pieces and artist's books, including *Activity Exchanges, Positions, Partitions,* and *Trunk Pieces;* exhibitions, performances, and screenings at the Museum of Modern Art (MoMA), the Whitney Museum of American Art, P.S.1, Martha Jackson West, and Franklin Furnace—all in New York City; and myriad works performed, literally, throughout the world.

Apple has taught at the Visual Studies Workshop, Rochester, New York (1979); Concordia University, Montréal, Canada (1980); California State University at Long Beach (1983); Otis-Parsons School of Design, Los Angeles, California (1984–1985, 1991); and has been on the faculty of the Art Center College of Design, Pasadena, California, since 1983.

Winner of many honors and awards for her work, Apple received a ZBS Foundation grant (1978); several grants from the National Endowment for the Arts (NEA) (1979, 1980, 1981, 1984, 1992); other grants from the New York State Council on the Arts (1981); the Cactus Foundation (1987); the Los Angeles Cultural Affairs Department (1990); a VESTA award (1990); commissions from the Museum of Contemporary Art, Los Angeles, California; the Santa Monica Arts Commission, California; New American Radio; and others.

Author of *Doing it Right in L.A.: Self-Producing for Performing Artists* (1990), Apple was curator of exhibitions and performances at Franklin Furnace, New York City (1977–1980). She is an active participant in the arts community of Los Angeles and a busy lecturer at national conferences and universities. A member of the National Writers Union and the International Association of Art Critics, she is a cofounder of the Cactus Foundation.

Bibliography
Goldberg, Roselee. *Performance, Live Art 1909–Present.* 1979.
Lippard, Lucy R. *From the Center: Feminist Essays on Women's Art.* E.P. Dutton, 1976.
Wooster, Ann. "Reviews." *Artforum* (February 14, 1976): 62.

Applebroog, Ida (1929–)

Born in the Bronx, New York, the painter/printmaker Ida Applebroog studied at the New York Institute of Applied Arts and Sciences (1948–1950), and at the Art Institute of Chicago, Illinois (1965–1968).

Applebroog has held solo exhibitions in museums and galleries in the United States and abroad, including the Whitney Museum of American Art, New York City (1978); Ronald Feldman Gallery, New York City (1981, 1983, 1985, 1986, 1987, 1989, 1991); Contemporary Arts Museum, Houston, Texas (1990); Kunsthallen Brandts Klaedefabrik, Odense, Denmark; and Realistmus Studio, Berlin, Germany (1992); and others.

Her work has been included in many prestigious group shows, such as "Painting and Sculpture Today," Indianapolis Museum of Art, Indiana (1980); "Directions '83," Hirshhorn Museum and Sculpture Garden, Washington, D.C., and the 23rd National Print Exhibition, Brooklyn Museum, New York City (1983); Museum of Modern Art (MoMA), New York City (1984); "El Bienal de la Havana," Cuba (1986); Documenta 8, Kassel, Germany (1987); Los Angeles Museum of Art, California (1992); and many others.

Winner of honors and awards, and a former teacher of painting and sculpture, Applebroog has received grants from the National Endowment for the Arts (NEA) (1980, 1985); the New York Foundation on the Arts (1986, 1990); and a Guggenheim fellowship (1990).

Examples of her work are in private and public permanent collections, including the Guggenheim Museum, Metropolitan Museum of Art, and MoMA—all in New York City; the Wadsworth Atheneum, Hartford, Connecticut; and many others.

Bibliography
Bass, Ruth. "Ordinary People." *Art News* 87:5 (May 1988): 151–154.
Cohen, Ronny H. "Ida Applebroog: Her Books." *The Print Collector's Newsletter* 15:2 (May–June 1984): 49–51.
Erotik in der Kunst. Bonn, Germany: Bonner Kunstverein, 1982.
McGreevy, Linda F. "Ida Applebroog's Latest Paradox: Dead-Ends=New Beginnings." *Arts Magazine* 60:8 (April 1986): 29–31.

Aragón, Pilar (1946–)

Born in Tampico, Tamaulipas, Mexico, Pilar Aragón studied art at the Academía de San Carlos, Mexico City (1967–1970); in Argentina with Libero Bandi, and in France with Cardot. Her earliest works were bronze and wood sculptures in an abstract style.

Bibliography
Alvarez, José Rogelio, et al. *Enciclopedia de México*. Secretaría de Educación Pública, 1987.

Arbus, Diane (Nemerov) (1923–1971)

Diane (Nemerov) Arbus's work has acquired an almost monumental status because of her compelling subject matter, the directness of its treatment, and her tragic death by suicide. Yet art historical literature about her photographs has largely been confined to speculative statements about Arbus's relationship to her sitters, who were often marginal characters in society—dwarfs, nudists, transvestites, the retarded—and more conventional people seen at leisure. Her work contemporizes traditionally mythic and prototypical aspects of humanity by photographing androgyny, witches, giants, and dwarfs within the context of the modern photographic document. Her more ordinary subjects, such as men and women on the street, combine with others in her *oeuvre* to form a world in which the interpenetration of ordinary and extraordinary reality exists within an alienated society. In this way, Arbus objectivizes social disintegration within the context of the individual. Arbus considered herself to be a self-taught visual anthropologist, and her personal work was primarily concerned with the problems of personal identity within the context of modern culture. Human appearance is shown as a series of visual possibilities, for one photograph may present a sitter or sitters who are both parent and child, male and female, or witch-like yet powerless, at once. Nor does her work separate public and private identities.

Arbus was born on March 14, 1923, in New York City of well-to-do parents. Her brother is the poet Howard Nemerov. She attended the Ethical Culture and Fieldston Schools in her native city, where she was an adept student; she also studied painting. In 1941 she married Allan Arbus, and they began a successful working partnership in fashion photography, which lasted until 1957. During these years her husband was primarily responsible for the actual exposure of the images, while she concerned herself with their layout. Not surprisingly, her later work includes frontally-positioned sitters whose mannered gestures and self-conscious awareness partake of fashion photography's characteristics. Her often blank backgrounds which isolate the sitter and emphasize human outline and details of clothing may also derive from her early fashion work.

In 1943 Arbus took a short course in basic photographic technique from Berenice Abbott—a noted documentary photographer. In 1954 she studied photography with art director and photographer Alexei Brodovitch. From 1955 to 1957 she enrolled in courses taught by Lisette Model at the New School for Social Research, New York City. Model was to be her most influential teacher and remained her mentor throughout her life. While working with Model Arbus was encouraged to photograph that which was meaningful to her, and she came to the conclusion that she wanted to photograph "evil." Seen within the context of her work her desire was not to literally photograph evil, but to photograph the forbidden and chaotic in human life.

Once she had defined this goal, Arbus pursued it with the tenacity that characterized her professional life. Her photograph "Jewish Giant at Home with His Parents in the Bronx" (1970) was the culmination of ten years of photographing Eddie Carmel—the main subject. She first encountered him at Hubert's Freak Show and Flea Circus—a now-defunct establishment on 42nd Street in New York City, where she and Model often photographed. It is evident from the number of exposures of Carmel and others that she would gradually refine her vision of an individual or a type over a period of time.

Until 1957 Arbus primarily used a 35-mm camera for her personal photographic work. During her first contact with Model, the first medium format 2-by-2-inch negatives appeared in her contact sheets, and she started to photograph for *Esquire Magazine*. In 1959 she separated from her husband, with whom she had two daughters—Doon and Amy. In 1961 she began work for *Harper's Bazaar*, and in 1962 her first major article, "The Full Circle," was published in *Infinity* magazine (five of the six images that appeared in *Infinity* were reprinted from a November 1961 *Harper's Bazaar* article titled "Five Singular People"). These images are accompanied by a text Arbus had written about each character. Beginning about 1959, she kept small notebooks that included notes made on subjects she had photographed. Both the quality of her published prose and of her photographs display characteristics of magic realism, for the seemingly impossible is placed within the context of the psychologically real and intensity of experience is combined with fact.

Arbus also displayed an eye for the symbolic qualities of her sitters. The photograph "Man in an Indian Headdress" (New York City, 1968) is one example of how contradictory roles may be symbolically embodied in one human being. Although the man is at a parade, he appears isolated. As a white man in an Indian headdress, he is the oppressor dressed in the ceremonial garb of the oppressed, and is both a historical symbol and one that is part of American national mythology. While he carries an American flag and displays a flag pin on his lapel, his Indian quiver of arrows has been ironically reduced to the arrow-shaped clip of a Parker pen. At the same time, the man's dazed look and half-opened mouth offer no interpretation of his mood or of the symbols he bears.

Arbus was awarded a Guggenheim Foundation fellowship in 1963 and again in 1966. In the application for her 1963 project titled *American Rites, Manners and Customs* she wrote about her desire to photograph the ephemeral rituals of American society; parades, beauty pageants, carnivals, and other aspects of life which often go unrecorded. Thus she can be seen as a photographer who wished to reassert a balance in the twentieth-century documentary, since she recorded images of marginal subjects who thus became part of our acknowledged history. In 1967 she was included along with Gary Winogrand and Lee Friedlander in the seminal "New Documents" exhibit at the Museum of Modern Art (MoMA), New York City. This exhibit established her reputation as a photographic innovator whose work has the capacity to shock and at the same time enlighten her audience.

In the late 1960s Arbus began to teach part-time at the Parson's School of Design, and Cooper Union, New York City; and Rhode Island School of Design, Providence. From 1970 to 1971 she lived and taught at Westbeth—a New York artists' cooperative. During this period she produced a portfolio of ten photographs, for which her friend art director Marvin Israel designed a plexiglass case. This limited edition portfolio, which sold only five copies during her lifetime, provides a paradigm for the presentation of her mature images made between 1962 and 1970. The plexiglass case was designed to double as a frame for her unmatted silver prints, which were usually printed on sixteen-by-twenty-inch paper with an approximate image size of twelve-by-twelve inches.

In 1972 a Museum of Modern Art retrospective of her work travelled for three years throughout the United States. That same year a monograph of eight images of her work was published. The monograph, which contains excerpts from tape recordings made during her workshops, was edited by Doon Arbus and Marvin Israel. In 1972 Arbus also became the first American photographer to be given a solo exhibition at the Venice Biennale.

Until Arbus's photography, marginal has often meant underprivileged. Her work, however, proposes no social solutions. Rather, it provides a reassessment of the marginal subject through a complex iconography and formal vision. These characteristics enable her work to partake of both artistic and documentary traditions and establishes it as photography whose essential subject is the interpretation of personal identity and culture.

Diana Emery Hulick

Bibliography
Arbus, Diane. "Five Singular People." *Harper's Bazaar* 3000 (November 1961).
————. "The Full Circle." *Infinity* 11 (February 1962): 2.
————. *Diane Arbus*. Aperture, 1972.
————. "A Monograph of Seventeen Prints." *Picture Magazine* 16 (September 1980).
Bosworth, Patricia. *Diane Arbus: A Biography*. Alfred A. Knopf, 1984.
Stevens, Robert B. "The Diane Arbus Bibliography." *Exposure* 15 (September 1977): 3.

Archambault, Anna Margaretta (1856–1956)

The centenarian and portrait painter who specialized in miniatures, Anna Margaretta Archambault was born (and died) in Philadelphia, Pennsylvania. She studied at Miss Anne Longstreth's School for Girls and the Pennsylvania Academy of Fine Arts, both in her native city, before going on to the Académie Julian, Paris, France. She also worked in Paris under Debillemont and Chardon.

Archambault, who exhibited at the Royal Miniature Society, London, England, won prizes for work at the Pennsylvania Society of Miniature Painters (1922, 1925) and the Pennsylvania Academy of Fine Arts (1941). She wrote *Art, Architecture, and Historic Interest in Pennsylvania* and was a lecturer and director at the Philadelphia School of Miniature Painting.

Examples of her work are in private and public permanent collections, including the Butler Art Institute, Youngstown, Ohio; Independence Hall, Philadelphia; the University of Pennsylvania Engineering School; the Philadelphia College of Physicians and Surgeons; United States Naval Academy, Annapolis, Maryland; and others.

Bibliography
American Art Annual. Vol. 28. American Federation of Arts, 1932.
Fielding, Mantle. *Dictionary of American Painters, Sculptors, and Engravers*. Modern Books and Crafts, 1974.
Obituary. *The New York Times* (July 1, 1956): 56.

Arenal Huerta, Electa (1935–1969)

Daughter of artists Luis Arenal and Elena Huerta, Electa Arenal Huerta was privileged to grow up in an arts environment. Arenal was born in Mexico City, Mexico and spent part of her childhood (from the age of six to eleven) in the Soviet Union.

Arenal took her formal art training at the Academy of San Carlos and at Escuela de Pintura y Escultura (La Esmeralda)—both in Mexico City, Mexico.

At the age of nineteen, she exhibited a self-portrait and a portrait of Benita Galeana—a noted feminist and activist—in the First Biennial of the Palacio de Bellas Artes in Mexico City, and, in 1959, she moved to Itolquin, Cuba, where she founded an artist's workshop.

Arenal painted several murals, including "Canto a la Revolución" on the facade of a hospital in Puerto Padre (Eastern Cuba); "Pascuas Sangrientas" at the Worker's Centre; and "Homenaje a los Mártires Revolucionarios" on the City Hall. In 1965 she worked along with David Alfaro Siqueiros and Francisco Zuñiga in a mural painting in Mexico. Arenal died in 1969 as a result of a fall from a scaffold in the Polyforum Siqueiros in Mexico City.

Bibliography
Alvarez, José Rogelio, et al. *Enciclopedia de México*. Secretaría de Educación Pública, 1987.

Ariss, Margot Joan (Phillips) (1929–)

Born in Belleville, Ontario, Canada, Margot (Joan Phillips) Ariss moved to London, Ontario, and studied art at H.B. Beal Secondary School, which was soon to become famous in Canadian circles for fostering a very active regional school under the guidance of nationalistic pop artists such as Greg Curnoe. There she met her husband, Herb Ariss, whose own work was very accomplished, though considerably more traditional. His local celebrity was more a matter of his openness to new ideas and his avuncular nurturing of unconventional talents. Inspired partly by this model, Ariss began to explore all white ceramics, some in softer organic forms, others with positively threatening profusions of spikes. After a time—and perhaps inspired by Curnoe's often verbose images—she began adding written texts to her objects, raising the letters in high relief from the surfaces. Showing quite regularly in regional centers since 1952, Ariss was finally given a retrospective of substance at the London Regional Art and Historical Museums in 1989. The show's title, "Zen Song," clarified her preoccupation with organic form, infrequent visual incident, invariable white surfaces, and poetic statements quietly evocative of a meditative state of mind.

Robert J. Belton

Bibliography
Artscanada (August 1969): 14.

Armington, Caroline (1875–1939)

Born in Brampton, a small community west of Toronto, Canada, the painter and etcher Caroline Armington studied design and painting at the Ontario College of Art, Toronto. She pursued further art study in Paris, France, at l'Académie Julian and La Grande Chaumière.

Between 1908 and 1910 Armington exhibited paintings in the Salons des Artistes Français, Paris, France. A number of her etchings were prominently displayed in 1913 in the Salon of the Société Nationale des Beaux-Arts, Paris, and, seven years later, on the strength of her work, Armington was elected to membership. Armington was also a member of the Société de la Gravure Originale en Noir and the Société des Graveurs Français, Paris, France, as well as the Chicago Society of Etchers, Illinois.

Armington held three solo exhibitions in the United States in 1924, one of which was at the Corcoran Gallery of Art, Washington, D.C. The others were in New York City and Cleveland, Ohio. The previous year, she exhibited oils at Simonson's, Paris, from which the government of France purchased a painting. In 1926 she exhibited her work in Chicago, Illinois; Cleveland, Ohio; Detroit, Michigan; and Toledo, Ohio.

She etched many European cities and scenes; her "Pont de la Tournelle" recorded for posterity the bridge since destroyed by the Paris authorities in the name of progress.

Armington's work is in the permanent collections of museums and libraries in Europe, Canada, and the United States, including the Bibliothèque de Belgique, Brussels; the British and South Kensington Museums, London, England; the New York Public Library; Library of Congress, Washington, D.C.; the National Gallery, Ottawa, Canada; the Art Museums of Cleveland, Ohio; Syracuse, New York; Dayton, Ohio; and others.

Bibliography
Art News 14 (November 1925): 4.
Art News 12 (February 1927): 9.

Armstrong, Jane B. (1921–)

Known primarily for her stone carvings, the sculptor Jane B. Armstrong was born in Buffalo, New York. After attending Middlebury College, Vermont, Armstrong studied at Pratt Institute, Brooklyn, New York, before becoming a student of José de Creeft and John Hovannes at the Art Students League in 1964.

She has been given nearly 100 gallery, museum, and university exhibitions of her work in the United States and abroad, ten of which were in New York City galleries. Armstrong showed at the Frank Rehn Gallery (1971, 1973, 1975, 1977), the Sculpture Center (1981), the Schiller-Wapner galleries (1987), the Grand Central Art galleries (1989)—all in New York City, and she held four solo shows at the Foster Harmon Galleries of American Art, Sarasota, Florida (the last in 1992). Armstrong also had solo shows at the Marjorie Parr Gallery, London, England (1976), and the Glass Gallery, Toronto, Canada (1985).

Her work has been included in numerous invitational group exhibitions, among which are "Reflections: Images of America," a travelling exhibition which toured Europe, including the former Soviet Union (1976–1977); "Critic's Choice," the Sculpture Center, New York City (1972); and many more.

An award-winning artist, Armstrong has garnered almost forty medals in national juried shows, including four gold medals, two medals of honor, and a plaque of honor. The Knickerbocker Artists, a national art society, awarded her its gold medal of honor for "distinguished achievement in sculpture" (1986). In 1990 she won the award of excellence at the "Artists of America 10th Exhibition," a show of representational painters and sculptors held at the Denver Heritage Museum, Colorado.

Recently Armstrong wrote, ". . . after twenty-five years of carving marble, I am still drawn to a particular piece by its veining, shear lines, fissures and fossils, which tell the unique history of that stone. I try to respect and preserve these special characteristics . . . ."

Armstrong is a fellow of the National Sculpture Society and a member of the Sculptors Guild. Her works are in more than 800 private and public permanent collections throughout the United States, Canada, and Europe.

Bibliography
Loercher, Diana. "Jane Armstrong—Late Blooming Sculptor." *Christian Science Monitor* (December 19, 1977).
Wyckes-Joyce, Max. "Review." *International Herald Tribune* (May 15–16, 1976).
Who's Who in American Art. 19th ed. R.R. Bowker Co., 1991–1992.

Arngna'naaq, Ruby (1947–)

Among the first of the young Inuit women to become involved in the new printmaking program at Baker Lake, Northwest Territories, in the early 1970s, Ruby Arngna'naaq had no previous training in the arts but quickly demonstrated her natural talents and management skills. She became one of the Sanavik staff printmakers, printing six editions of fine art prints for the Baker Lake annual print collections between 1969 and 1973. During this time she printed images based on drawings by prominent Baker Lake artists: Myra Kukiiyaut, Victoria Mamnguqsualuk, Jessie Oonark, and Armand Tagoona. The best known of Arngna'naaq's prints is her delicate stencil print, "Keeveeok's Journey" (1969), based on a line drawing by Mamnguqsualuk. Through experimentation in the preparation of this print, Arngna'naaq developed a method for suffusing color to imitate the appearance of the shaded edge of an accidental coffee stain which had inspired her.

Arngna'naaq also served as manager of the fledgling Baker Lake Sanavik Cooperative during its formative years in the 1970s and, versatile in her talents, has since gone on to work in the broadcast media and in Inuit leadership organizations.

Marion E. Jackson

Bibliography
Goetz, Helga. *The Inuit Print/L'estampe Inuit.* Ottawa: National Museums of Canada, 1977.

Arngnaqquaq, Elizabeth (1916–)

A textile artist, working in embroidery and felt appliqué on duffle, Elizabeth Arngnaqquaq is one of the pioneer members of the group of Inuit women who work in this medium at Baker Lake, Northwest Territories. She was born in a nomadic camp in the Garry Lake area and was already in her forties when she and her family had to be evacuated from their camp to avoid certain death by starvation.

A decade later Arngnaqquaq learned to apply her skill of sewing skin clothing to the art of producing images with the needle. Her strength is in the embroidery on her duffle wallhangings using stitching freely as a painter would use the paint on his brush, lengthening or shortening the individual stitches and the density between them as she pleases. This gives her richly embroidered scenes of Arctic life on the tundra a fluidity and energy remarkable for the medium.

Arngnaqquaq's work has appeared in numerous exhibitions, including two solo exhibitions at the Inuit Gallery of Eskimo Art in Toronto (1981, 1986) and one at the Upstairs Gallery in Winnipeg (1988). Her work has also been shown in group shows in San Francisco and Los Angeles, California; New York City; and Washington D.C., between 1979 and 1981. In 1976 she was commissioned by Public Works Canada to create a wallhanging for the post office in Lakefield, Ontario.

Maria Muehlen

Bibliography
Butler, Sheila. "Wallhangings from Baker Lake." *The Beaver* (Autumn 1972): 26–31.
Schrager, Reissa. "Embroidered and Appliquéd Wall Hangings by Elizabeth Arngnaqquaq of Baker Lake." *Inuit Art Quarterly* 1 (Summer 1986): 9–10.

Arnold, Anne (1925–)

The sculptor Anne Arnold was born in Melrose, Massachusetts, and was educated at the University of New Hampshire, Durham, and the Ohio State University, Columbus, where she received her Bachelor's and Master's degrees in 1946 and 1974, respectively. She did graduate study at the University of Guadalajara, Mexico (1949), and spent the next four years at the Art Students League in New York City.

Arnold has been a member of the board of governors, Skowhegan School of Painting and Sculpture, Maine, since 1980, and an associate of the National Academy of Design, New York City, since 1981. She was recently honored by the American Academy and Institute of Arts and Letters through receipt of the Louise Nevelson award in art (1989). She has been on the art faculty of Brooklyn College, City University of New York (CUNY), since 1971, and has also taught or been visiting critic at many other universities and art institutions, including New York State University at Geneseo; Wagner College, Staten Island, New York; Philadelphia College of Art, Pennsylvania; Columbia University, New York; and the University of Pennsylvania, Philadelphia.

Arnold has had eighteen solo exhibitions of her sculpture in New York City and Hannover, Germany, half of which were held at the Fischbach Gallery, New York City, between 1960 and 1988. Arnold's sculpture has been invited to more than ninety-five major group shows throughout the United States and abroad and may be seen in the permanent collections of the Metropolitan Museum of Art, New York City; the Albright-Knox Art Gallery, Buffalo, New York; the Walter Chrysler Museum, Norfolk, Virginia; the University of North Carolina, Greensboro; and Housatonic Community College, Stratford, Connecticut.

Arnold has created sculptures of animals unlike those of any other contemporary three-dimensional artist; there is a particular presence, a certain wit evident, a mastery of technique and materials fused in a delightful manner, not without a spiritual component. "Monte I," 1988, a carved and joined pine sculpture of her Russian wolfhound, singularly reveals Arnold at her best.

Bibliography
Anne Arnold: A Retrospective. A Catalog. University of New Hampshire, 1983.
Campbell, Lawrence. "The Animal Kingdom of Anne Arnold." *Art News* 63:8 (December 1964): 32–33, 64–65.
———. "Anne Arnold at Fischbach." *Art in America* (November 1988): 173–74.

Arnold, Eve (1913–)

After studying medicine Eve Arnold turned to photography at the New School for Social Research, New York City, where she studied with Alexy Brodovitch (1947–1948). Arnold was the first woman to have joined Magnum Photos, a noted cooperative agency with offices in New York City and Paris, France (1951).

Widely travelled and published, Arnold has held solo exhibitions and has had her work included in prestigious group shows in museums in the United States and abroad, including "Lichtbildnisse Das Porträt in der Fotografie," Rheinisches Landesmuseum, Bonn, Germany (1982); "Photography in America 1910–93," Tampa Museum, Florida (1983); "Sammlung Gruber," Museum Ludwig, Cologne, Germany (1984); and many others. Examples of her work are in private and public permanent collections in the United States and Europe.

Bibliography
Arnold, Eve. *The Unretouched Woman.* Alfred A. Knopf, 1976.
Naylor, Colin, ed. *Contemporary Photographers.* 2nd ed. St. James Press, 1988.
Peters, Pauline. "Eve Arnold." *You and Your Camera* (May 10, 1979).

Aronson, Irene H. (1918–)

Born in Dresden, Germany, the painter/printmaker Irene Aronson studied at many institutions, including the Eastbourne School of Art, England; the Ruskin School of Drawing, Oxford University, England, the Slade School of Fine Arts, University of London, England; Columbia University, New York City, where she earned a Bachelor's degree (1960) and two years later, a Master of Arts degree. Aronson also studied at the Art Students League and Parsons School of Design, New York City; and with Stanley William Hayter, Polunin, and Professor Schwabe.

Aronson has held solo exhibitions in galleries and museums in the United States and abroad, including the Museo de Arte Moderno, Mexico (1959); the Towner Art Gallery, Eastbourne, England (1961); the National Association of Women Artists, New York City (1974–1975); and others.

Her work has been invited to, or included in, major group exhibitions from Bern, Switzerland to Boston, Massachusetts; from Brooklyn, New York to Ljubljana, Yugoslavia.

Winner of awards and honors, examples of Aronson's works are in private and public permanent collections throughout the world, including the National Collection of Fine Arts, Washington, D.C.; the Bibliothèque Nationale, Paris, France; the Victoria and Albert Museum, London, England; the Metropolitan Museum of Art and the Museum of Modern Art (MoMA), both in New York City; and others.

Bibliography
Aronson, Irene H. "How to Make a Linocut." *Artist Magazine*. London
     (July 1975).
Who's Who in American Art. 15th ed. R.R. Bowker Co., 1982.

Aronson, Sanda (1940–)

A native New Yorker, Sanda Aronson was born in Manhattan and grew up in (as she puts it) a "quiet place in Brooklyn." She received her Bachelor's degree from the State University of New York (SUNY) at Oswego and, except for two years spent in New Orleans, Louisiana, and one in Denver, Colorado, has lived in Manhattan all of her adult life.

A curious combination of a February 29th (leap year) birthday, an unusually-spelled first name, and a myopic condition have provided her with sufficient stimuli to have developed early on a delightful sense of humor wedded to a love for detail—evident in her collages and assemblages.

In 1975 Aronson had a triple entry into group exhibitions of her work: she participated in the Brooklyn Museum's year-long travelling show, "Works On Paper/Women Artists"; she won an award in "Women Showing/Women Sharing" at the U.S. Military Academy at West Point, New York; and she showed in the "Exhibition for Women Artists" at the Manhattan Community College for the Performing Arts. Since then she has participated in more than twenty national and international juried group exhibitions, has received more than ten awards and honors, including two Pollack-Krasner Foundation grants (1986–1987, 1987–1988), and has had two solo shows, one of which was at Barnard College, New York (1985).

Aronson's assemblages allow and encourage her to utilize her hand-made papers in conjunction with the urban flotsam of New York City to create everyday objects with surreal, playful, new meanings, quite different from those of Joseph Cornell. She also creates editions of xerographics; a recent one titled, "Xeroaeroplane" contains xeroxed images of zebras, giraffes, an African elephant, insects, a nineteenth-century Scottish machine, a valve, a woodcut and the word "LOVE," a flying bat, an addax, and a clutch of other phenomena. The print contains precise instructions for folding so it may be flown.

Bibliography
Hogg, Gary. "Bits, Pieces, and Beauty: The Art of Sanda Aronson."
     Alternatives (January–May 1985): 6–7.
1987 Artists' Society International Exhibition. San Francisco: ASI
     Galleries, 1987.
Tufts, Eleanor. *American Women Artists, A Selected Bibliographical Guide*.
     Vol. II. Garland, 1989.

Asawa, Ruth (1926–)

A sculptor whose work explores conventional and unorthodox materials in both figurative and abstract forms, Ruth Asawa was born in Norwalk, California. Asawa received a scholarship to Black Mountain College, North Carolina, where she studied under Buckminster Fuller, Josef Albers, and Adolf Dehn from 1946 to 1949.

Asawa began exhibiting her work in 1948. She quickly gained recognition with her suspended, crocheted, wire sculptures revealing lacy geometric forms floating within a transparent framework. Her first solo exhibit was at the Peridot Gallery, New York City, in 1956. She had a retrospective at the San Francisco Museum of Art, California, in 1973. Her sculptures are in the permanent collections of the Whitney Museum of American Art, New York City; the Oakland Museum of Art, California; Williams College, Williamstown, Massachusetts; the Guggenheim Museum, New York City; and the Josef Albers Bequest.

Asawa cofounded the Alverado School Art Workshop and helped establish the School of the Arts—both in San Francisco, California. She was an artist-in-residence for the San Francisco Foundation twice during the 1970s and once during the early 1980s for the National Endowment for the Arts (NEA). From 1974 to 1978 she was sponsored by the NEA Education "Artists in Schools." During 1977 and 1978 Asawa was on the National Council, NEA Task Force, Education and Training of Artists.

Asawa has received many public commissions—several of them for fountains within the city of San Francisco, California. In 1966 she was commissioned to create a figurative cast bronze fountain for Ghiradelli Square; between 1970 and 1974 she involved the community at large in depicting life in San Francisco in baker's clay, which she then cast in bronze for the steps of the Grand Hyatt on Union Square; in 1983 she sculpted a concrete bas-relief fountain for the Motor Court Entry Park Fifty-Five; and in 1986 an abstract stainless-steel fountain for Bayside Plaza, on the Embarcadero. In 1966 Asawa was the first recipient of the Dymaxion award for artist/scientist, and in 1974 she received the Robert Kirkwood award from the San Francisco Foundation, as well as the fine arts gold medal from the American Institute of Architects (AIA). In 1990 she won the Cyril Magnin award for outstanding achievement in the arts, and the Women's Caucus for Art national honor award in 1993.

Susan F. Baxter

Bibliography
Harris, Mary Emma. "Ruth Asawa." Women's Caucus for Art. *Honor Award
     Catalog* (1993): 6–9.
Nordland, Gerald. "Reviews." *Artforum* (June 1962): 8.
Rubinstein, Charlotte Streifer. *American Women Sculptors*. Boston:
     G.K. Hall, 1990, pp. 351–55.

Ascher, Mary

Born in Leeds, England, the painter/printmaker/author Mary Ascher studied at the New York School of Applied Design for Women; Hunter College, and the Art Students League, all in New York City, with Will Barnet, Morris Kantor, and Vaclav Vytlacl.

Her work has been widely exhibited in the United States and abroad in museums and galleries in Japan and Argentina, including a "30-Year Retrospective," National Arts Club (1973), and Metropolitan Museum of Art, both in New York City (1979); and myriad others.

Winner of awards and honors, Ascher received a Huntington Hartford Foundation fellowship (1960); a medal of honor and other distinctions from the National Painters and Sculptors Society, National Association of Women Artists, and the National League of American Penwomen; International Women's Year award (1975–1976); first prize in oil, Womanart Gallery, New York City (1977); and others.

Chaplain of the National Society of Arts and Letters, New York, she holds the rank of Fellow in the Royal Society of Artists, London, England; is a Life Member of the Art Students League, New York City; and a member of the Society of Contemporary Artists and the National Association of Women Artists, among others.

Her work is represented in private and public permanent collections in the United States and abroad, including Ein Harod Museum, Israel; Butler Institute of American Art, Youngstown, Ohio; National Collection of Fine Arts, Smithsonian Institution, Washington, D.C.; Norfolk Museum of Fine Arts, Virginia; the United States National Museum of Sport, New York City; and others.

Bibliography

Krantz,Les. *American Artists: An Illustrated Survey of Leading Contemporary Americans.* The Krantz Company, Publishers, Inc. 1985.

Opitz, Glenn B. *Mantle Fielding's Dictionary of American Painters, Sculptors, and Engravers.* Apollo. 1986.

Radio Interview. WNYC. 1979.

Asher, Elise

A native of Chicago, Illinois, the poet/painter Elise Asher has lived in New York City since 1948. She studied at the School of the Art Institute of Chicago; Bradford Junior College, Massachusetts; and Simmons College, Boston, Massachusetts, where she earned a Bachelor's degree.

Between 1953 and 1991 Asher has held twenty-three solo exhibitions, including shows at the Tanager Gallery (1953) and Grand Central Moderns (1958)—both in New York City; Bradford Junior College, a retrospective, Massachusetts (1964); Bertha Schaefer Gallery, New York City (1973); National Academy of Sciences, Washington, D.C. (1983); Ingber Gallery, New York City (1981, 1983, 1985, 1987); University of Connecticut, Storrs (1988); and others.

Her work has been invited to more than forty group exhibitions, including "Greetings," Museum of Modern Art (MoMA), New York City (1964); the "Biennial," Corcoran Gallery, Washington, D.C. (1966); "The Words as Image," Jewish Museum, New York City (1970); "The Book as Art," Fendrick Gallery, Washington, D.C. (1976, 1977); and "Women Painters and Poets," New York University (1978); "Candidates for Art Awards," American Academy and Institute of Arts and Letters (1980, 1989); "The Expanding Figurative Imagination," Anita Shapolsky Gallery (1990), June Kelly Gallery (1991)—all in New York City; and many others.

Her work is represented in private and public permanent collections, including the University of California at Berkeley; Brandeis University, Waltham, Massachusetts; Ciba-Geigy Corporation, Ardsley, New York; Corcoran Gallery of Art, Washington, D.C.; New York University, New York City; Provincetown Art Association and Museum, Massachusetts; National Academy of Sciences, Washington, D.C.; and others.

Bibliography

Little, Carl. "Elise Asher at Ingber." *Art in America* (June 1987).

O'Doherty, Brian. "Elise Asher Ut Pictura Poesis." *Art in America* (November–December 1973).

Rubenstein, Charlotte S. *American Women Artists.* Avon Press, 1982.

Asher, Lila Oliver

Known for the sensitive and flowing line in her relief prints, Lila Oliver Asher was born in Philadelphia, Pennsylvania. A graduate of the Philadelphia College of Art, which she attended on a four-year scholarship, Asher also studied with Joseph Grossman, Frank B.A. Linton, and Gonippi Raggi; she took further work at the Graphic Sketch Club in her native city.

Asher has held more than thirty-five solo exhibitions of her work in the United States and abroad between 1951 and 1991, including the Barnett-Aden Gallery, Washington, D.C. (1951); American Club, Tokyo, Japan (1973); United States Information Agency (USIA) Headquarters, Ankara and Adana, Turkey (1976); National Museum of History, Taipei, Taiwan (1982); Kastrupgardsamlingen Kunst Museum, Denmark (1982); several retrospective exhibitions at Howard University, Washington, D.C. (1978, 1991); and many others.

Her work has been invited to many group exhibitions throughout the United States, such as the Pennsylvania Academy of Fine Arts, Philadelphia; Library of Congress, Washington, D.C.; Baltimore Museum of Art, Maryland; the Krannet Museum, University of Illinois, Champaign; and others.

Muralist, portraitist, and professor, Asher has taught art at Howard University, Washington, D.C., since 1947, except for a brief stint at Wilson Teachers College (1953–1954). She is a member of many professional art associations, including the Society of Washington Artists, Artists Equity, the Maryland Printmakers Association, the Print Consortium of Kansas City, Missouri, the Print Club of Philadelphia, and others.

Asher's works are in the permanent collections of museums and corporate institutions throughout the world, including the National Museum of American Art, the Corcoran Gallery of Art, the National Museum of Women in the Arts, the Art Gallery of Howard University, and Georgetown University—all in Washington, D.C.; Embassies of the United States in Tel Aviv, Israel, and Mexico City, Mexico; the National Museum of History, Taipei, Taiwan; the Kastrupgardsamlingen Kunst Museum, Denmark; and others, including private collections.

Bibliography

American Prints from Wood. A Catalog. Smithsonian Institution Publishers, n.d.

Falk, Peter H., ed. *Who Was Who in American Art?* Sound View Press, 1985.

Who's Who in American Art. 19th ed. R.R. Bowker Co., 1991–1992.

Ashoona, Mayureak (1946–)

A Candian Inuit, known primarily for her prints and drawings (although she has also done some sculpture), Mayureak lives outside of Cape Dorset, Northwest Territories, and is an artist member of the West Baffin Eskimo Co-operative. Born at Saturituk—a camp located on the southwest coast of Baffin Island—Mayureak grew up living a traditional Inuit life on the land with her father, Aggeak and mother Sheouak (1923–1961)—one of the first Inuit to take up drawing in the late 1950s. In 1964 she married Kaka Ashoona, a sculptor and the son of graphic artist Pitseolak Ashoona. They continued to live at Saturituk until about 1970 or 1971, when they moved into the community of Cape Dorset. Mayureak states that it was with the encouragement of her mother-in-law Pitseolak that she began to draw about this time. In 1987 her first print appeared in the Cape Dorset annual graphics collection, and through 1990 she has had some thirty works published through the studios of the West Baffin Eskimo Co-operative. About 1982 Mayureak, along with her husband and children, returned to their present outpost camp, believing that life away from the community was better for both the family and their artistic endeavors.

Along with her sisters-in-law, Napatchie Ashoona and Sorosiluto Ashoona, Mayureak belongs to a group of younger artists who follow Pitseolak's interest in depicting Inuit traditions and camp activities. Yet, unlike their mentor, these women usually interpret their subject matter in a style that is much more realistic and concerned with Western notions of spatial development and perspective than has been associated with Inuit art in the past. From her earliest lithographs, such as "Tornaq" (1978) and "First Goose Hunt" (1979), Mayureak has evolved a dense, compact style of drawing to explore both mythological subjects and landscapes. In more recent works, such as "Walrus Watch Newborn" (1984) and "Nocturnal Raven" (1989), her love of detail and sense of texture combines with the close-up, over-sized forms of the walruses and the sensuous patterns of the raven's feathers to add a new element of drama to her compositions.

Mayureak is represented in the collections of the Winnipeg Art Gallery, Manitoba; the Canadian Museum of Civilization, Hull, Québec; Canadian Guild of Crafts, Montréal; and Prince of Wales Northern Heritage Centre, Yellowknife, Northwest Territories—all in Canada. Her work has been included in important exhibitions of Inuit art in Canada, Germany, and Japan.

Marie Routledge

Bibliography

Barz, Sandra. *Inuit Artists Print Workbook*. Arts & Culture of the North, 1981.
——. *Canadian Inuit Print Artist/Printer Biographies*. Arts & Culture of the North, 1990.
——. *Inuit Artists Print Workbook, Vol. II*. Arts & Culture of the North, 1990.
Cape Dorset, West Baffin Eskimo Co-operative. Catalogs of the Cape Dorset Annual Graphics Collections, 1978–1980, 1982–1987, 1989–1990.
Jackson, Marion E. "The Ashoonas of Cape Dorset: In Touch with Tradition." *North/Nord* 29:3 (Fall 1982): 14–18.

Ashoona, Sorosiluto (1941–)

Born at Nanuqtu, a traditional Inuit camp on the southwest coast of Baffin Island, Northwest Territories, Canada, Sorosiluto Ashoona grew up in the care of her adoptive parents, Kanayuk and Solomonie, and grandparents, Ningeeookaluk and Pootoogook (d. 1959; a strong, highly-respected traditional camp leader). About 1959 to 1960 the family moved into the settlement of Cape Dorset, and in 1961 Sorosiluto married Kiawak Ashoona, a sculptor and the son of graphic artist Pitseolak Ashoona. She began to draw about 1962 with the prompting and encouragement of her mother-in-law, Pitseolak, who even at this early date was one of the leading artist-members of the West Baffin Eskimo Co-operative and featured prominently in the annual graphic collections published at their printmaking studio since 1959.

Sorosiluto's first print "Woman Juggling" was published in 1965, although she was most active between 1970 and 1980, producing some thirty-five prints. Her work, like that of her sisters-in-law, Mayureak

Ashoona and Napatchie Pootoogook, may be seen as bringing a new degree of realism and interest in Western drawing concepts to contemporary Inuit art. In 1974 Sorosiluto was commissioned by the art section of Indian and Northern Affairs—a department of the Canadian government—to produce a series of drawings illustrating the process of making a parka, from the hunt to the finished product, for the exhibition "Inuit Women in Transition." A second commission followed the next year for a series of animated pen-and-ink drawings on traditional Inuit games for "Inuit Pinguangit." Sorosiluto was part of a group of artists who participated in an acrylic painting/drawing project in 1976 inspired by the presence of Toronto painter K.M. Graham, in the community. In 1979 she also was part of an etching and engraving workshop that again was part of a continued trend toward more sophisticated and varied graphic options for Inuit expression.

Sorosiluto and her family moved away from Cape Dorset in 1979 to an outpost camp some distance from the settlement. Since that time she has done very little drawing, although in 1991 she has renewed her interest and activity. Sorosiluto is represented in the collections of the Art Gallery of Ontario, Toronto; the Winnipeg Art Gallery, Manitoba; Canadian Museum of Civilization, Hull, Québec; National Gallery of Canada, Ottawa, Ontario; Macdonald Stewart Art Centre, Guelph, Ontario—all in Canada; and the Amon Carter Museum, Fort Worth, Texas. In 1979 her profile became the subject of two lithographs by Joyce Wieland, produced during the Toronto artist's visit to the print studio of the West Baffin Eskimo Co-operative.

Marie Routledge

Bibliography

Barz, Sandra. *Inuit Artists Print Workbook*. Arts & Culture of the North, 1981.
——. *Canadian Inuit Print Artist/Printer Biographies*. Arts & Culture of the North, 1990.
——. *Inuit Artists Print Workbook, Vol. II*. Arts & Culture of the North, 1990.
Cape Dorset, West Baffin Eskimo Co-operative. Catalogs of the Cape Dorset Annual Graphics Collections, 1978–1980, 1982–1987, 1989–1990.
Jackson, Marion E. "The Ashoonas of Cape Dorset: In Touch with Tradition." *North/Nord* 29:3 (Fall 1982): 14–18.

Asmar, Alice

Born in Flint, Michigan, and reared in Portland, Oregon, Alice Asmar drew and painted from her surroundings, knowing that she would one day become an artist. In 1949 Asmar received her Bachelor of Arts degree *magna cum laude* from Lewis and Clark College, Portland, Oregon, and, two years later, received a Master of Fine Arts degree from the University of Washington, Seattle, where she studied sculpture with Alexander Archipenko and Edward Melcarth.

Asmar worked at a variety of jobs, including engineering drafting for the Boeing Aircraft Company (1952–1954); engraving for Nambe Mills, Santa Fe, New Mexico (1968); and free-lance illustrating for the *Los Angeles Times* (1977–1981). A prolific artist who works in many media, Asmar has shown her work in hundreds of national and international solo and group exhibitions, including the Galerie de Fondation des États-Unis, Paris, France; Museo de Arte Contemporaneo, Ibiza, Spain; the Public Art Museum, Gabrova, Bulgaria; the Minneapolis Institute of Art, Minnesota; Seattle Art Museum, Washington; and others.

Asmar has won many awards and honors for her work, including the H.H. Wooley grant to study with M. Souverbie at l'École Nationale Supérieure des Beaux-Arts, Paris, France (1958–1959); fellowships from the MacDowell Colony, Peterborough, New Hampshire, and the Huntington Hartford Foundation, Pacific Palisades, California; honorable mention at the Galleria Europa Arte, Biennale delle Regione, Ancona, Italy (1968–69); and more.

Though she is widely travelled in Europe and the Near East, Asmar, in a trip to the Southwest in 1966, became obsessed with the culture of the Native Americans in New Mexico and Arizona. This near-obsession has formed the basis of her work in oils, watercolors, tapestries, murals, the several print and other mediums in which she works, and is nourished through annual visits to, and interaction with members of the Santa Clara pueblos.

Asmar, who has taught at Lewis and Clark College, Portland, Oregon (1955–1958) and elsewhere, has work in numerous permanent museum and private collections, including the Smithsonian Institution, Washington, D.C.; Roswell Museum and Art Center, New Mexico; Portland Art Museum, Oregon; Southwest Museum, Los Angeles, California; Huntington Hartford Museum, New York; the Public Art Museum, Gabrova, Bulgaria; and many others.

Bibliography
Samuels, Peggy, and Harold Samuels. *Contemporary Western Artists*. 1982.
Who's Who in American Art. 19th ed. R.R. Bowker Co., 1991–1992.

Astman, Barbara (1950–)

Barbara Astman was born in Rochester, New York, on July 12, 1950. After an unexceptional childhood she entered the Rochester Institute of Technology School for American Craftsmen, New York, from which she received an Associate's degree in silversmithing in 1970. Until this point most of her work was in sculpture; in 1971, however, she began to turn to photography and textiles, often with passages of hand-tinting. Along with this change came a move to Toronto, Canada, where she entered the Ontario College of Art. There she received the W.O. Forsyth award in 1973—the year of her graduation.

A restless innovator, Astman began to experiment with color xerography in January 1976, then an unfamiliar technology in Toronto. Many of these works are reminiscent of old, faded postcards, both in their superficial appearance and in their curious fusion of the public and the private.

Up to this point Astman was relatively obscure, but in 1977 she joined the faculty of the Ontario College of Art and in 1978 that of York University's Faculty of Fine Arts—both in Canada. In 1980 she attracted widespread public attention with the first exhibition of her so-called "Red Series" at the prestigious Sable-Castelli Gallery in Toronto. These works were photographic self-portraits in which virtually all of the clothing and domestic artifacts were painted bright red, manipulated by the artist in a variety of ways, and photographed with a Polaroid SX-70 instant camera. Since the artist's head was usually cropped, a compensatory autobiographical dimension was added by typing a letter to a friend on the print while it was still developing. The resulting curious deformations of the image (which were not at all like Lucas Samaras's distantly related photo-transformations) were then re-

photographed and commercially enlarged to mural size. The results were so arresting that she became a sort of celebrity, and works were chosen for more commercial contexts, such as record album covers.

Astman has since returned to sculpture. In 1982 she began the "Places" series which consisted largely of brilliantly decorative reliefs fabricated from a wide variety of commercial linoleum pieces. "Settings for Situations," in 1984, returned to wood sculpture.

Despite Astman's sometimes bewildering switches of medium and style, her reputation is sufficiently great that she figures in the most recent *Canadian Encyclopedia*, which generally accords very little space to contemporary art, especially that of women.

Robert J. Belton

Bibliography
Visual Facts: Photography and Video by Eight Artists in Canada. Glasgow: Third Eye Centre (June 8–July 6, 1985).
Wright, Judy. "A Discussion of the Work of Barbara Astman and Fern Helfand." *Artmagazine* 6:19 (Fall 1974): 13–15.

Atitu, Siasi (1896–1983)

Siasi Atitu, a Canadian Inuit graphic artist, was born near the Arctic Québec settlement of Ivujivik around 1896. She eventually settled in Povungnituk with her husband, the camp leader Adam Amamartua, who died in 1967. The couple raised ten children, four of whom were adopted.

Printmaking was first introduced to Povungnituk in 1961. Siasi was one of the first to become interested in the new medium in spite of the fact that, by local standards, she was already an old woman. As a member of the female minority in the Povungnituk print shop, her individuality was never in question. Proof of her independence is manifest in her choice of imagery for her stonecut prints. Siasi seemed obsessed by the darker side of life, including murder and even cannibalism. Some of her prints were more typical of the mainstream "lifestyle in the old days" school.

Siasi was featured in six Povungnituk annual print collections between 1962 and 1972. Her works have been exhibited in several group shows in Canada and abroad and are represented in the collections of the Canadian Museum of Civilization and the Avataq Cultural Institute.

Mary Craig

Bibliography
Barz, Sandra. *Canadian Inuit Print Artist/Printer Biographies*. Art & Culture of the North, 1990.

Attie, Dotty (1938–)

Known for her pencil drawings since the 1970s, Dotty Attie was born in Pennsauken, New Jersey. She earned a Bachelor of Fine Arts degree from the Philadelphia College of Art (now part of the University of the Arts) in Pennsylvania (1959); was a Beckmann fellow at the Brooklyn Museum Art School, New York City (1960); and studied at the Art Students League, New York (1967).

Attie has held solo exhibitions in museums and galleries, including A.I.R. Gallery, New York City (1973, 1977); O.K. Harris Gallery, New York City (1977); the University of Rhode Island, Kingston (1978); and others. She has shown in group exhibitions, such as "In Her Own

Image," Fleisher Art Memorial, Philadelphia (1974); "Words as Images," Chicago Renaissance Society, University of Chicago, Illinois (1981); "New Dimensions in Drawing," Aldrich Museum of Contemporary Art, Ridgefield, Connecticut (1981); and many others.

A winner of awards and honors, Attie received a Creative Artists Public Service (CAPS) grant from the New York State Council on the Arts (1976–1977), and grants from the National Endowment for the Arts (1976–1977, 1983–1984); and others. Examples of her work are in private and public permanent collections including the University of Massachusetts, Amherst; Fairleigh Dickinson University, Rutherford, New Jersey; National Museum of Women in the Arts, Washington, D.C.; Smith College, Northampton, Massachusetts; and many others.

Bibliography
Berger, Maurice. "The Empty Frame: Dotty Attie's 'J. and Armand Tour the World.'" *Arts Magazine* 56:1 (September 1981): 150–153.
Orenstein, Gloria. "13 Ways of Looking at a Portrait: Dotty Attie." *Womanart* 1:2 (Fall 1976): 4–7, 33.
Putterman, Susan. "Dotty Attie." *Arts Magazine* 55:4 (December 1980): 9.
Wortz, Melinda. "Dotty Attie." *Art News* 81:4 (April 1982): 103.

Aubin, Barbara (1928–)

Painter, professor of art, and assemblage artist—Barbara Aubin was born in Chicago, Illinois, and received her Bachelor of Arts degree from Carleton College, Northfield, Minnesota (1949). Five years later she received a Bachelor of Art Education degree from the School of the Art Institute of Chicago, Illinois, and a Master of Art Education degree from the same institution in 1955.

Aubin has exhibited her work in more than two dozen solo shows between 1954 and 1990, including the Fairweather Hardin Gallery, Chicago, Illinois (1978, 1980, 1985, 1990); the Centre d'Art, Port-au-Prince, Haiti (1960); and many others. Her work has been invited to more than three-score group and travelling exhibitions throughout the United States, such as "Flora '92," Chicago Botanic Garden, Glencoe, Illinois (1992); "15th Annual Alice and Arthur Baer Competition," Beverly Art Center, Chicago, Illinois (1991); "Fulbright Art Exhibit," East/West Center, Honolulu, Hawaii (1990); "The Aesthetic Excursion," Wustum Museum of Fine Arts, Racine, Wisconsin (1989); "Herself," Womens Caucus for Art, International Exhibition, Broward Community College, Ft. Lauderdale, Florida (1985); "Postcard-Size Art," Bologna, Italy; and P.S.1, New York City (1978); and others.

Winner of many honors and awards, Aubin won a George D. Brown foreign travel fellowship to France and Italy (1955–1956); a Fulbright fellowship to Haiti (1958–1960); a Huntington Hartford grant (1963); two completion grants from the Illinois Arts Council (1978, 1979); a number of purchase prizes and awards from the Michigan Watercolor Society; the Walker Art Center, Minneapolis, Minnesota; the Pennsylvania Academy of Fine Arts, Philadelphia; and still others. She was professor of art at Chicago State University, Illinois, from 1971 until her retirement in 1991; she taught at the School of the Art Institute of Chicago, Illinois (1956–1958, 1960–1967), and other art schools and institutions. She was visiting artist at the University of Wisconsin, Green Bay, and Marinette (1981) and at St. Louis Community College, Forest Park, Missouri (1980–1981).

Aubin's work is in the permanent collections of the Illinois State Museum, Springfield; Ball State Museum, Muncie, Indiana; the Art Institute of Chicago, Illinois; Centre d'Art, Port-au-Prince, Haiti; Shimer College, Waukegan, Illinois; and many private and corporate collections.

Bibliography
Mihopoulos, Effie. "Personal Visions." *Women Artists News* (Fall 1990): 17.
Morrison, Carolee. "Chicago Barbara Aubin: Fairweather Hardin Gallery." Review. *Artforum* (October 1978): 72–73.
Who's Who in American Art. 19th ed. R.R. Bowker Co., 1991–1992.

Audette, Anna Held (1938–)

A native New Yorker, the painter/printmaker Anna Held Audette earned a Bachelor's degree from Smith College, Northampton, Massachusetts (1960) before going on to Yale University, New Haven, Connecticut, where she received a Bachelor of Fine Arts degree (1962) and a Master of Fine Arts degree (1964).

Audette has held solo exhibitions in museums and galleries in the United States and abroad, including Gallery Fikrun Wa Fann, Alexandria, Egypt (1977); Clark Art Institute, Williamstown, Massachusetts (1978); Wesleyan University, Middletown, Connecticut (1982); Munson Gallery, New Haven, Connecticut (1985, 1987, 1990); Fitzwilliam Museum, Cambridge, England (1986); and others.

Audette has been a professor of art at Southern Connecticut State University, New Haven, since 1964. Her work has been included in group exhibitions for many years. Examples of her work are in private, public, and corporate permanent collections, including the Fitzwilliam Museum, Cambridge, England; Metropolitan Museum of Art, New York City; the National Gallery of Art, Smithsonian Institution, Washington, D.C.; Rijksprentenkabinett, Rijksmuseum, Amsterdam, the Netherlands; and others.

Bibliography
Anna Held Audette: Drawings and Prints at the Slater Memorial Museum. Norwich, Connecticut: The Slater Memorial Museum, 1974.
"Anna Held Audette, Under Glass (1979)." *The Print Collector's Newsletter* 10:3 (July–August 1979): 92.
Boorsch, Suzanne. "Anna Held Audette." *Art News* 79:7 (September 1980): 43–44.

Auerbach, Ellen (1906–)

Born in Karlsruhe, Germany, the widely-travelled photographer Ellen Auerbach studied sculpture at the Karlsruhe Kunstakademie, Germany (1924–1927), photography at the renowned Bauhaus, Berlin, Germany, with Walter Peterhans and Grete Stern; she created 16mm experimental films (1929–1932). Auerbach emigrated to Israel, then to London, England, and then to the United States (1937), where she has since lived and worked.

Auerbach has held solo exhibitions in museums and galleries in the United States and abroad, including "Mexican Church Interiors," Sander Gallery, Washington, D.C. (1978); the Bauhaus Archives, Berlin (1981); "Ellen Auerbach, Pictures after 1934," Photographers' Gallery, London, England (1982); and others.

Auerbach's work has been included in group exhibitions, such as "Avant-Garde Photography in Germany, 1919–1939," a travelling show across the United States (1980); "When Words Fail," a travelling show,

International Center for Photography, New York City (1980); "22 Fotografinnen," Kunsthaus, Hamburg, Germany (1983) and Schlossgallerie, Bruhl, Germany (1984); "Photography of the '30s," Sander Gallery, New York (1984); and others. Examples of her work are in private and public permanent collections.

Bibliography
Auer, Michel. *Photographers Encyclopedia International: 1839 to the Present*. Geneva: Editions Camera Obscura, 1985.

Austen, E. Alice (1866–1952)

Born in Clifton, Staten Island, New York, the photographer (Elizabeth) Alice Austen received her education in private schools in Manhattan and Staten Island.

At the age of twelve, Austen began the practice of photography and developed her "hobby" over the next fifty-two years during more than a score of trips to England, France, and Germany—until arthritis and the collapse of the stock market combined to cut short her taking further outdoor "shots" of the sights and scenes that intrigued her.

She chronicled noteworthy national phenomena, playing the earliest role of photo-journalist, and recorded the rich and the poor in her environment.

Several thousand of her negatives are in the permanent collections of the Alice Austen House, Staten Island, New York, and the Staten Island Historical Museum, New York.

Bibliography
Gover, C. Jane. *The Positive Image*. Albany: State University of New York, 1988.
Kramer, Hilton. "E. Alice Austen Photographed Earlier Gracious Days of S.I.[Staten Island]." *The New York Times* (April 9, 1976).
Novotmy, Ann. *Alice's World, The Life and Photography of an American Original: Alice Austen, 1866–1952*. Old Greenwich, CT: Chatham Press, 1976.

Austin, Amanda Petronella (1859–1917)

Amanda Petronella Austin, a California artist, was prolific in painting, sculpture, and drawing; an inventory of her estate after her death revealed 300 works. Born in Carollton, Missouri, she studied with the genre painter George Caleb Bingham at the University of Missouri from 1877 to 1879 before moving to Sacramento, California, to care for an ailing great-uncle. She continued her studies at the San Francisco School of Design, California, with Virgil Williams from 1882 to 1885, and in January of 1886 she opened her own studio in the Oddfellow building in Sacramento for a painting class which attracted large enrollments. Throughout these years Austin was exhibiting, beginning in 1881 with one oil painting and four charcoal drawings at the California State Fair, followed by "Morning Glories" (1881, Crocker Art Museum) at the state fair the next year. From 1895 to 1906 she exhibited regularly with the San Francisco Art Association, California.

In 1908 she sailed for Europe, maintaining a studio in Paris, France, until 1912 and studying with Eugène Delécluse, Jean Escoula, and Émile Renard. Here she began working in sculpture, encouraged

by Escoula, Auguste Rodin's chief cutter. Austin's marble bust of "Miss Quinn," an American student in Paris, France (1909, Crocker Art Museum), was accepted at the Salon of the Société Nationale des Beaux-Arts, which won Austin membership in the Union Internationale des Beaux-Arts et des Lettres.

On her return to Sacramento, California, three works were accepted for the Panama-Pacific International Exposition of 1915: "Miss Quinn," a sculpture of "St. John," and her painting of "Market Street." The two sculptures travelled on to the Buffalo Fine Arts Academy, New York, and to the 29th Exhibition of Sculpture at the Art Institute of Chicago, Illinois. In the summer of 1916 Austin went to Paris to execute a commissioned monument for the city of Sacramento, only to be advised by her Paris physician to return home, for she was dying of cancer. She died in New York City, en route to California.

Austin's paintings, although realistic, are softened with impressionism, and her subject matter encompasses both landscape and the human figure. Some of her sculptures are neoclassical, while others are more individualistic and vigorous, showing an influence from Rodin.

Eleanor Tufts

Bibliography
Peterson, Margaret. "Rescued from Oblivion." *The Sacramento Bee*, "Scene" section (September 10, 1978): 1:3.
Tufts, Eleanor. *American Women Artists, 1830–1930*. National Museum of Women in the Arts, 1987.

Autry, Carolyn (1940–)

Internationally-known intaglio printmaker Carolyn Autry was born in Dubuque, Iowa, and was a Phi Beta Kappa graduate of the University of Iowa, where she studied with Mauricio Lasansky and received a Bachelor of Arts degree (1963). Two years later she earned a Master of Fine Arts degree in painting from the same institution.

Between 1973 and 1991 Autry exhibited her etchings in more than three score group exhibitions in the United States and abroad, including such prestigious shows as the "World Print Competition," San Francisco Museum of Modern Art, California (1973); Ljubljana International Biennial, Moderna Galerija, Yugoslavia (1975, 1981, 1987); "Premio Internazionale Biella per L'Incisione, Galleria Leonardo da Vinci, Italy (1976); "Grafik Aus Amerika," Volkshochschule Leverkusen, Germany (1977); "One Hundred Prints by Twenty Artists," Grunwald Center, University of California at Los Angeles (UCLA) (1981); "Inter-Grafik '84 and '87," International Invitational Exhibition, the Television Tower Exhibition Centre, Berlin, Germany (1984, 1987); "International Print Exhibitions," Taipei Fine Arts Museum, Taiwan (1985, 1987, 1989, 1991); and many others.

Autry's work was included in many international exchange exhibitions and travelling shows in Korea, the United Kingdom, and elsewhere and two major solo exhibitions of her intaglio prints were held in the American Embassy's Cultural Center, Belgrade, Yugoslavia (1983) and at Drake University, Des Moines, Iowa (1985).

Autry has been the recipient of more than thirty-two awards and honors for her prints, including the Pennell Award, Library of Congress (1971, 1975); the Dayton Art Institute Exhibition Award, Ohio (1972); J.B. Speed Art Museum Exhibition Award, Louisville, Kentucky (1973); George Roth Prize, Philadelphia Print Club (1975); Bradley

University National Exhibition Award, Peoria, Illinois (1975, 1981, 1991); Jo Miller Memorial Prize, Society of American Graphic Artists, New York City (1985); Hunterdon Art Center Award, 35th National Print Exhibition, Hunterdon Art Center, Clinton, New Jersey (1991); and others.

Recipient of a Yale-Norfolk Summer School of Art and Music fellowship (1962), Autry earned a Ford Foundation grant (1961–1964), two Ohio Arts Council grants for printmaking (1979, 1989), and a residency at the School of the Arts, Lacoste, France (1984, 1987). She taught at Baldwin-Wallace College, Berea, Ohio (1965–1966), and has been an adjunct associate professor of Art of the University of Toledo at the Toledo Museum of Art, Ohio, since 1966.

Autry's works are in the permanent collections of Albion College, Michigan; the University of Dallas, Texas; Istituto per la Cultura e l'Arte, Catania, Italy; Library of Congress, Washington, D.C.; Los Angeles Printmaking Society, California; Philadelphia Museum of Art, Pennsylvania; Worcester Art Museum, Massachusetts; and many others. Autry describes her medium as follows: "The question is always the relationship of things—what is problematic are the spaces between. Dark, then light, then dark, the condition—in the midst of that intervening light, I scratch."

Bibliography
Stasik, Andrew. "Toward a Broader View and Greater Appreciation of America's Graphic Artist: The Printmaker, 1956–1981." *Print Review* 13: 25.
Who's Who in American Art. 19th ed. R.R. Bowker Co., 1991–1992.

Avaalaaqiaq, Irene (1941–)

Irene Avaalaaqiaq was born in the Kazan River area of the Keewatin region of the Northwest Territories. In 1958 she and her family resettled in Baker Lake. She began making art in the early 1970s as a way to earn money to help feed her family. Since that time she has mastered several media—including drawing, printmaking, sculpture, and fabric art.

Avaalaaqiaq's lively, narrative wallhangings burst onto the southern art scene in 1973 in a solo exhibition mounted by the Inuit Gallery of Eskimo Art in Toronto, Ontario, Canada. In 1975 she contributed her first drawings to the Baker Lake annual print collection. She printed these herself using a stencil technique and also printed the work of other artists while employed as a printmaker at the Baker Lake print shop.

Over a span of two decades Avaalaaqiaq's works have been included in major private, corporate, and public collections and featured in more than twenty national and international group exhibitions. Some thirty prints by the artist have been published in the Baker Lake annual print collections. Wall hangings, however, have remained Avaalaaqiaq's strongest medium of artistic expression. In 1979 one of her hangings was presented to the state of Minnesota by the Canadian ambassador to the United States and now hangs in the State Legislature in Minneapolis. Another hangs in the foyer of l'Esplanade Laurier, Ottawa. Most recently Avaalaaqiaq's wall hangings were featured along with those of fellow Baker Lake artists Jessie Oonark and Marion Tuu'luq in the 1989 Canadian Museum of Civilization touring exhibition "In the Shadow of the Sun": *Zeitgenossische Kunst der Indianer und Eskimos in Kanada*. Iqaluit Fine Arts Studio in Iqaluit, Northwest Territories, mounted a solo exhibition of Avaalaaqiaq's wall hangings in the spring of 1990.

Avaalaaqiaq's style is bold and colorful, much like the artist herself. Her subject matter tends always to be shamanic in origin and is based on the Inuit myths, legends, and beliefs of traditional times as told to her by her grandmother. The shamanic belief system practiced in traditional times called for an easy interplay between man and animals. Avaalaaqiaq's hybrid, flowing figures aptly portray this harmonious relationship—the forms are fluid and flat—half human, half animal; their heads are often in profile or duplicate halves, with staring eyes and gaping mouths. Her unique figures are readily recognizable. Avaalaaqiaq often sews a border around her imagery, perhaps to contain its unworldly content.

Marie Bouchard

Bibliography
Blodgett, Jean. *Grasp Tight the Old Ways: Selections from the Klamer Family Collection of Inuit Art.* Art Gallery of Ontario, 1983.
Bouchard, Marie. "Making Art in Baker Lake." *Inuit Art Quarterly* 4:3 (Summer 1989).
Butler, Sheila. "Wallhangings from Baker Lake." *The Beaver* (Autumn 1972).
"Eskimo Learned Craft at Grandmother's Knees." *Globe and Mail* (October 6, 1973).
Jackson, Marion, and Judith Nasby. *Contemporary Inuit Drawings.* Guelph: Macdonald Steward Art Centre, 1987.
Muehlen, Maria. "Baker Lake Wall-hangings: Starting from Scraps." *Inuit Art Quarterly* 4:2 (Spring 1989).

Ayaq Anowtalik, Mary (1938–)

Mary Ayaq Anowtalik is a Canadian Inuit sculptor living in Arviat (Eskimo Point), Northwest Territories, on the west coast of Hudson Bay. Born 200 miles west near Ennadai Lake, Ayaq Anowtalik and her family were air-lifted to the community at the height of a famine in 1957. Ayaq Anowtalik's mother is the prominent sculptor Elizabeth Nutaraluk Aulatjut; her husband, Luke Anowtalik, is also a stone carver.

Although Ayaq Anowtalik started carving while still living on the land in the 1950s, her artistic career began in the mid-1960s. Her strong sense of family and tradition is very much evident in her work; like many Arviat artists, Ayaq Anowtalik concentrates on maternal and family themes. Although her sculptures are conceived as figural compositions, individual subjects are often difficult to distinguish as they emerge, sometimes only as faces, from the compact mass of the stone. Ayaq Anowtalik and her husband often work together, and even sometimes finish each other's pieces; consequently their sculptures, when not signed, present problems of attribution.

Ayaq Anowtalik's sculptures have been included in fifteen group shows in Canada, the United States, and Europe. Her work is represented in the collections of the Canadian Museum of Civilization, the Art Gallery of Ontario, and the Winnipeg Art Gallery.

Ingo Hessel

Bibliography
Hessel, Ingo. "Artists from Ennadai Lake." *Inuktitut* 62 (Winter 1985): 25–30.
Winnipeg Art Gallery. *Eskimo Point/Arviat.* Winnipeg Art Gallery, 1982.

Aycock, Alice (1946–)

Born in Harrisburg, Pennsylvania, Alice Aycock attended Douglass College, Rutgers University, New Brunswick, New Jersey, where she earned her Bachelor's degree in 1968. Three years later, at Hunter College, New York, under the aegis of Robert Morris, she obtained a Master's degree. Widely-read, Aycock has practiced her craft as a sculptor and assemblage artist since 1972.

Between 1972 and 1987 Aycock has held thirty-eight solo exhibitions in the United States and abroad, including the Nova Scotia College of Art and Design, Halifax (1972); the Museum of Modern Art (MoMA), New York City (1977); "Machinations," Protech-McIntosh Gallery, Washington, D.C. (1979); "Drawings," Locus Solus, Genoa, Italy (1982); "New Work," John Weber Gallery, New York (1984; 1986); Galerie Walter Storms, Munich, Germany (1987); and many others.

Her work has been invited to many group exhibitions throughout the world, such as "Documenta 6," Kassel, Germany (1977); "Biennale," Venice, Italy (1978); "Whitney Biennial," Whitney Museum of American Art (1979, 1981); "International Sculpture Conference," Washington, D.C. (1980); "Mythos und Ritual in der Kunst der 70er Jahre," Kunsthaus, Zurich, Switzerland (1981); "Avant-Garde in the Eighties," Los Angeles County Museum of Art, California (1987); and others.

Aycock has been visiting artist, artist-in-residence, and visiting member of the sculpture faculty at a number of colleges and professional art schools, including a teaching position at Hunter College, New York City (1982–1985). The recipient of a National Endowment for the Arts (NEA) fellowship (1975) and a Creative Artists Public Service (CAPS) grant from the New York State Council on the Arts (1976), Aycock is well-known for her use of industrial materials in creating precision-crafted mega-sculptures. These machine-like, variable-dimensioned, three-dimensional works tease the viewer with respect to understanding their functions. "The Savage Sparkler" (1981), a large-scale work ten-by-fourteen-by-eight feet, for example, is composed of fans, fluorescent lights, heating coils, motors, sheet metal, and steel, yet it possesses a certain difficult-to-describe spirituality, as do most of her pieces. "How to Catch and Manufacture Ghosts" (1970), questions, in a wry manner, the all-knowing attitude of scientists. Aycock's interest in assemblage art may have been kindled by watching her father, who was in the construction business.

Her works are in the permanent collections of museums, corporations, and the private sector, including MoMA, the Guggenheim Museum, and the Whitney Museum of American Art—all in New York City; the Hirshhorn Museum and Garden, Washington, D.C.; and others.

Bibliography

Environment and Sculpture. Lake Biwa, Japan: International Contemporary Sculpture Symposium, 1984.

Fry, Edward. "The Poetic Machine of Alice Aycock." *Portfolio* 3:6 (November–December 1981): 60–65.

Hauser, Reine. "Alice Aycock." *Art News* 83:9 (November 1984): 145.

Watson-Jones, Virginia. *Contemporary American Women Sculptors*. Oryx Press, 1986.

Aylon, Helene (1931–)

Listening to the soft-spoken, gentle Helene Aylon, it is difficult to imagine her organizing defiant performance demonstrations across the United States to all Strategic Air Command (SAC) stations, the United Nations, Israel and Russia, promoting peace through an art-and-words exchange.

Married at an early age to an Orthodox Jewish rabbi, Aylon, a native New Yorker, adhered to all the constraints of such a marriage until her children started school. Then, with her husband's approval, she enrolled in Brooklyn College, where she studied with Ad Reinhardt, completing her Bachelor of Arts degree *cum laude* (1960), followed by a Master of Fine Arts degree and a Master of Arts degree in women's studies.

She obtained commissions for murals in hospitals, chapels, and community centers, in places as disparate as Hadassah Hospital in Jerusalem, a high-school drop-out center in Brooklyn's Bedford-Stuyvesant area, and the chapel at New York City's Kennedy Airport.

Aylon held her first show in an important New York City gallery, Max Hutchinson (1969). A late starter, by the end of the decade she had succeeded in showing at prestigious galleries in New York City (Betty Parsons and Susan Caldwell) and in galleries and museums throughout the United States. Aylon's early work was mysterious, shimmering, and abstract, with an intensely physical, yet also metaphysical, quality.

The next decade witnessed Aylon's making her art one with her fierce dedication to peace and the elimination of nuclear testing sites. In 1981 Aylon staged "Border Dust/Border Earth sac," throwing cloth over the barbed-wire gate between Israel and Lebanon. The folds that formed were filled with Israeli earth on one side and Lebanese earth on the other.

Perhaps the most serious and awesome of all of Aylon's artworks was the "Rescued Earth/Endangered Earth sac," also known as the Women's SAC (Survive and Continue) Caravan, which traveled across the country in an "Earth Ambulance," rescuing earth from thirteen Strategic Air Command (SAC) nuclear sites. Women delivered sacs to U.S. Army bases, where they sang and read lists of all the sites doing nuclear testing. The project culminated at the United Nations in New York City.

In the spring of 1989 Aylon presented "The Trial of the Sands of Time," a multimedia installation performance documenting her suit against a fine arts storage company for malfeasance and destruction of her art work (sacs from the 1981 performances filled with sand and earth from the San Andreas Fault line, the Pacific shoreline, and Death Valley). Three years later she brought this ten-year project to a close with a ceremonial performance and reading at the Brooklyn Bridge Anchorage, New York City. There, with accompanying text and music, she emptied the remaining sand sacs, pouring them from her position some forty feet high onto the floor below at the audience's feet. Appropriately concluding this decade-long conceptual work was the artist's distribution of seeds to the audience to replant the earth.

Cynthia Navaretta

Bibliography

Atkins, Robert. "Pro and Con Artists." *The Village Voice* (January 24, 1989).

Aylon, Helene. "Coming of Age: On Common Ground." *Heresies Magazine* 23 (1988).

Orenstein, Gloria. "Creation and Healing: An Empowering Relationship for Women Artists." *Women's Studies International Forum* 8:5 (1985).

"The Helene Aylon Case." *Artweek* (February 25, 1989).

Azara, Nancy (1940–)

A native New Yorker, the painter/sculptor Nancy Azara studied stage design at the Polakov Studio, New York (1960–1962); studied sculpture and painting at the Art Students League, New York City, with John Hovannes and Edwin Dickinson, respectively (1964–1967); and received a Bachelor's degree in sculpture from Empire State College, New York City (1974), whereupon she went to Italy for further study, research, and exhibition of her work.

Long associated with the women's movement, Azara has exhibited her abstract, carved, and painted wood sculptures widely, including SoHo 20 Gallery (1981, 1984, 1987); A.I.R. Gallery (1989, 1992)—both in New York City; Artemisia Gallery, Chicago, Illinois (1985); and has published many visual diaries and artist's books. She has taught at several universities and museum schools of art, and was the founder and administrator of the New York Feminist Art Institute (1977) in addition to giving workshops and teaching there.

Bibliography
La Rose, Elise. "Nancy Azara." *Arts Magazine* 59:1 (September 1984): 18.
Melf, Terry Hope. "Women's Autobiographical Artist's Books." *New Art Examiner* 15:5 (January 1988): 64–65.
Rosser, Phyllis. "Nancy Azara at SoHo 20." *Women Artists News* 12:3 (Summer 1987): 29–30.

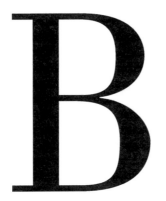

Baber, Alice (1928–1982)

Alice Baber's earliest years were divided between summers in her native Illinois and winters in Florida, necessitated by ill health. The abstract oils and watercolors of her maturity reflect both clear Midwestern light and the lush colors of the semitropics.

Baber began to study drawing at age eight and by age twelve was so advanced she was enrolled in a college-level class. She spent two years at Lindenwood College in Missouri, then transferred to Indiana University, Bloomington, where she studied with figurative expressionist Alton Pickens. Completing the Master of Arts degree in 1951 she travelled through Europe, studying briefly at the École des Beaux-Arts in Fontainebleau, France. She settled in New York City, supporting herself by writing and eventually becoming art editor of *McCall's*. At this time Baber joined the March Gallery, New York City, one of the Tenth Street artists' co-ops.

The year 1958 was a crucial one for Baber. She had her first solo show at March Gallery and her first residency at the Yaddo Colony, Saratoga Springs, New York. She began a period of living in Paris, France for six months of each year. And while working on an oil painting "Battle of the Oranges," she first perceived that the circle possessed an infinite range of possibilities for exploration of color and light, an insight that directed her toward a more distinctive personal image in her art.

In 1959 Baber was selected to show in the first "Jeune Biennale" by the director of the American Cultural Center in Paris, France. Over the next few years her paintings were in exhibitions in Paris, France, London, and Edinburgh—both in England, and Hamburg, Germany. Baber married another expatriate American, painter Paul Jenkins, in 1964. (They divorced in 1970.) The marriage was important to the artistic growth of both, since they had a mutuality of interests and shared basic theories about light and color, although their work differed in method and result. In 1964 the couple travelled to Japan for a joint exhibition at the Osaka Pinacotheca Museum. Avid collectors, they brought back many treasures of Asian art.

Baber developed a unique stain and lift technique of painting, while her distinctive palette evolved through many stages. For a time she worked solely with reds, but as she progressively eliminated opacity, she explored yellows, greens, and lavender, largely monochromatically. By the early 1960s she began to use a great variety of colors on a single canvas, and by the mid-1970s introduced black, achieving some of her most subtle and delicate effects.

Baber's work appeared in many women-only exhibitions. An active feminist, in 1975 she organized a show at the Women's Interart Center in New York City in celebration of the United Nations' International Women's Year. Called "Color, Light, and Image," it was comprised of works by women from Europe, Asia, Africa, and the United States.

Another exhibition curated by Baber was the 1972 "Color Forum" at the University of Texas, Austin, for which she wrote a lyrical essay on color. Baber was also active as a teacher and lecturer on painting, design, and art history. In 1979 she was artist-in-residence at the Tamarind Institute print-workshop, University of New Mexico, and she became a skilled color lithographer.

Baber travelled widely and exhibited her work all over the globe. In the 1970s she twice visited India and had a solo show in New Delhi in 1974. In the same year she exhibited in Teheran, Iran. The U.S.

Information Agency (USIA) sent her on a four-month tour of thirteen Latin American countries in 1976. She exhibited her paintings, demonstrated her working methods, and gave color slide lectures. This trip resulted in a series of paintings based on the jaguar.

Critics often tried to associate Baber's work with various stylistic trends, but the paintings elude categorization. Her circles, ovals, and free-form shapes are always imbued with undulating, sensuous movement, and her pure, translucent colors create a sense of radiance that is her artistic signature.

Baber's work is in dozens of private, corporate, and university collections, as well as most of the major U.S. museums and many other museum collections worldwide. An Alice Baber Memorial Art Library has been established at the Guild Hall Museum of East Hampton, New York. The Greater Lafayette Museum of Art, Lafayette, Indiana, has several of Baber's paintings as the nucleus of the Baber Midwest Modern Art Collection, which includes paintings by Baber's colleagues and contemporaries.

Toward the end of her life, despite pain and debilitation from cancer, Baber continued to paint and produced a group of luminous small watercolors in prismatic colors. She died on October 2, 1982.

Sylvia Moore

Bibliography

Baber, Alice. "Color." Color Forum. A Catalog. Austin, Texas: 1972.

de Lallier, Alexandra. "The Watercolors of Alice Baber." *Woman's Art Journal* (Spring–Summer 1982).

Derfner, Phyllis. "Color, Light and Image." *Art International* (March–April 1976).

Dodge, Norton T., ed. *Alice Baber: Color, Light and Image*. A Catalog. St. Mary's City, Maryland, 1977.

Jones, James. "The Tragedy of Color." *Studio International* (September 1965).

McCoy, Ann. "Alice Baber: Light as Subject." *Art International* (September–October 1980).

Moore, Sylvia. "Alice Baber." *Woman's Art Journal* (Spring–Summer 1982).

Baca, Judith Francisca (1946–)

A prominent muralist and artistic director of the Social and Public Art Resource Center (SPARC) in Venice, California, Judith Francisca Baca has maintained a lifelong commitment to the creation and preservation of community-based art.

Baca was born and raised in the Los Angeles area and currently resides in Venice, California. As a studio art major at California State University at Northridge in the 1960s she joined in the many demonstrations calling for an end to racial discrimination and for the establishment of ethnic studies programs. Baca was convinced that survival for peoples of color in the United States meant the preservation of their cultures and the presence of these cultures within the educational system. Upon completing her undergraduate degree in 1969 she began teaching at a Catholic high school in Los Angeles. It was here that she organized her first mural project in an attempt to bring together students from different neighborhoods. The following summer, while working for the Los Angeles Recreation and Parks Department, California, she organized another mural team of twenty youths from four different neighborhoods. She taught not only about making art, but also about the history of ethnic communities of Los Angeles, California, and about

making connections between the present and the past.

In 1974 Baca submitted a proposal for a citywide mural program to the Los Angeles City Council, California. The program was funded and, over its ten-year existence, 250 murals were produced and over 1,000 crew members employed (in 1988 the mural program was revived under Baca's direction by Los Angeles, California Mayor Tom Bradley). Baca was also contacted in 1974 by the U.S. Army Corps of Engineers, who wanted her to design a mural for a segment of the Tujunga Wash drainage channel in the San Fernando Valley, California. This was the beginning of "The Great Wall of Los Angeles" (1976–1983), a 2,435-foot mural painted during the summers of 1976, 1978, 1980, 1981, and 1983 by eighty youths, ten artists, and five historians who collaborated under Baca's direction. Baca wanted "The Great Wall" to be an alternative history of California, one that acknowledged, for example, the presence of ethnic peoples, racial and class conflict, sexism, and homophobia. She wanted to give a public voice to those who had been silenced. A conglomeration of young people worked on the mural, including black, white, Mexican, Jewish, and Asian-American peoples, bringing with them a lifetime of experiences of interracial struggle. Through their work on the mural they began to understand the roots of this racial conflict and to break down some of the barriers that existed between them. To facilitate the organization and execution of this mural, Baca, filmmaker Donna Deitch, and artist Christina Schlesinger founded SPARC in 1976. Located in the old Venice City jail, it has served over the years as a multicultural arts center devoted to the production, exhibition, distribution, and preservation of public art works.

In 1977 Baca travelled to Cuernavaca, Mexico, to study further the art of mural painting at the Taller Siqueiros and in 1979 completed her Master of Fine Arts degree at California State University at Northridge. During the 1980s she continued her work with the peoples of color living in southern California but also began to organize public art projects that stretched across broader geographic and racial boundaries. In the two nine-by-twenty-inch billboards "Be Skeptical of the Spectacle" (1985) and "Respect Your Perspective" (1985) she calls upon the viewer to be aware of the propagandistic nature of media images and to have greater faith in a perspective based on personal experience. "The Street Speaks" (1986), a pair of murals located on Skid Row in Los Angeles, California, maps out the Skid Row area and provides the homeless people who live there with information on food, shelter, and medical care available nearby. In a series of four murals erected in the town of Guadalupe, California (1990), Baca treats not only the specific history of this farm workers' community, but also the exploitative system of migrant labor in place in the United States. And in one of her most recent works, a portable mural project entitled "The World Wall: A Vision of the Future without Fear" (1987–), she explores the material and spiritual transformation of an international society seeking peace. Having read Jonathon Schell's *Fate of the Earth*, which argues that we must imagine the eventuality of nuclear war before we can change our destiny, Baca realized that what is more important—and more difficult—than imagining nuclear destruction is imagining peace, particularly as an active rather than passive concept. The seven, ten-by-thirty-foot panels arranged in a circle that make up "The World Wall" attempt such imagining.

Baca has been active during the 1970s and 1980s not only as an artist but also as a teacher and public spokesperson for artists of color. She has taught in the art department of the University of California at Irvine since 1981 and has served on the boards of directors of the American Council of the Arts and the Los Angeles Museum of Contemporary Art, California. Jude McGee of *Los Angeles Magazine* described her in October 1988 as "the voice of the street-level community frequently ignored by the established art world." The description is an accurate one. Baca has helped shape a public art program in the Los Angeles, California area that has shown the benefits of multi-ethnic cooperative projects and that has given both the artists and the communities in which the murals are located a greater sense of pride in the cultural achievements and traditions of the many different peoples of southern California. She hopes that "The World Wall" will bring a similar message concerning the benefits of global cooperation to an international audience.

Frances K. Pohl

Bibliography

Baca, Judith Francisca. "Our People Are the Internal Exiles." Interview with Diane Neumaier in *Cultures in Contention*. Ed. Douglas Kahn and Diane Neumaier. Real Comet Press, 1985.

Pohl, Frances. "The World Wall: A Vision of the Future without Fear: An Interview with Judith F. Baca." *Frontiers* 2 (January 1990).

Rickey, Carrie. "The Writing on the Wall." *Art in America* 69 (May 1981): 54–57.

Bacon, Peggy (1895–1987)

One of America's most delightful and penetrating caricaturists during the 1930s and 1940s, Margaret Frances (Peggy) Bacon was born in 1895 to Elizabeth and Charles Chase in Ridgefield, Connecticut. Both parents were artists: her mother was a painter of miniatures, and her father was a painter of landscapes, figures, and murals. Peggy began to draw as a toddler, designing dinner place cards with historical and literary figures and including drawings and poetry with letters to family members.

Bacon's art education began after graduating from the Kent Place School, a private boarding school in Summit, New Jersey, in 1913. Instead of attending college she enrolled in the School of Applied Arts for Women in New York City in November 1913. Beginning in the summer of 1914 she studied landscape painting with Jonas Lie in Port Jefferson, Long Island, New York, and gouache and tempera with Lie in New York City during the following fall and spring. In 1915 Lie mounted Bacon's first one-person show in his studio. In the fall of 1915 Bacon enrolled at the Art Students League in New York City, where she studied until May 1920. At the Art Students League, she attended classes by George Bellows, George Bridgeman, Andrew Dasburg, Kenneth Hayes Miller, John Sloan, and Max Weber. Of these, Miller and Sloan were the most influential instructors for Bacon. In her spare time she visited galleries and museums where she particularly enjoyed the work of Honoré Daumier, Gustave Courbet, and Georges Seurat. Bacon taught herself drypoint technique in 1917, learned lithography in 1928, and began to make etchings in 1929. During her years at the League, she always preferred caricature to portraiture.

In 1919 Bacon began to establish a format of combining her drawings and prints with prose or poetry that was to be continued the rest of her life. In that same year her prints were shown at exhibitions of the Society of Independent Artists and the Painter-Gravers of America and were reproduced in *World Magazine. The True Philosopher and Other Cat Tales*, a book which she wrote and illustrated, was also published that year. Other books—satirical and children's books—followed. *Off With Their Heads!* (1934), which included thirty-nine black-and-white satirical portraits accompanied by written descriptions and small vignettes, established her reputation as a prominent American caricaturist. Other books which she wrote and illustrated include: *Funerealities* (1925), *The Ballad of Tangle Street* (1929), *The Terrible Nuisance, and Other Tales and Animosities* (1931), *Mischief in Mayfield* (1933), *Cat-Calls* (1935), *The Mystery at East Hatchett* (1939), *The Good American Witch* (1957), *The Oddity* (1962), *The Ghost of Opalina* (1967), and *The Magic Touch* (1968). She also illustrated many more books written by others.

Caricature and satire were the hallmarks of Bacon's mature style. Her satirical drawings were published in numerous magazines, including *Mademoiselle, New Masses, The New Yorker, Promenade, The New Republic, Town and Country,* and *Vanity Fair*. Most notable were the series of caricatures of important figures in Washington, D.C., which *The New Republic* commissioned Bacon to do in 1935. In 1937 Bacon began to make humorous genre pictures in pastels which she grouped into the series "Manhattan Genre" (1937), and "Manhattan Cats" (1937–1939). Other series of reportorial genre subjects followed in the 1940s: "Life on the Maine Coast" (1939–1940), "Summer Folks, Provincetown," Massachusetts (1945).

Recognition of her work came early. After her 1915 exhibition at Lie's studio, she had a major exhibition of her drypoints at the Joseph Brummer Gallery, New York City, and William Murrell wrote the first monograph on her work in 1922. The Montross Gallery, New York City, mounted two one-person exhibitions of Bacon's work in 1925. In 1928 Alfred Stieglitz held a one-person show of her work at the Intimate Gallery, and the Downtown Gallery—both in New York City, and held three one-person shows from 1931 to 1934. In 1942 the Association of American Artists held a major retrospective of her work, and the Kraushaar Galleries, New York City, held four one-person shows from 1953 to 1972. In 1975, the National Collection of Fine Art held a comprehensive retrospective of Bacon's work.

Bacon lived a comfortable life. She and her husband, Alexander Brook, a painter whom she married in 1920, resided in New York City and summered in Woodstock, Westchester—both in New York, or Maine until they divorced in 1940. Bacon taught at the Art Students League, New York City, beginning in 1935 and again from 1949 to 1951; thereafter she taught at the Stella Elkins Tyler School of Fine Arts, Temple University, Philadelphia, Pennsylvania (1940), the Corcoran School of Art, Washington, D.C. (1942–1944), and Moore College of Art, Temple University, Philadelphia, Pennsylvania (1963–1964) as well as private secondary schools in New York and New Jersey. In 1961 Bacon moved to Maine. After 1955 Bacon became exclusively a painter, working on problems of color and composition and in combinations of watercolor, gouache, and ink, and, after 1958, in oil. She abandoned the penetrating satirical approach in her late paintings; and despite her near blindness during the 1970s, she persisted to paint with the aid of a magnifying glass.

Virginia Hagelstein Marquardt

Bibliography
Peggy Bacon: Personalities and Places. Washington, D.C.: Smithsonian Institution, 1975.

Baer, Jo (1929–)

Born in Seattle, Washington, the hard-edged abstractionist painter, Jo Baer (born Josephine Gail Kleinberg) received her Bachelor's degree in 1949 from the University of Washington, Seattle, where she majored in biology and art. Three years later she did graduate work in physiological psychology at the New School for Social Research, New York City.

Baer held more than a dozen solo exhibitions of her work in the United States and abroad between 1966 and 1975, including the Fischbach Gallery (1966), and Noah Goldowsky Gallery—both in New York City (1967, 1968, 1970); Galerie Rolf Ricke, Cologne, Germany (1969, 1970, 1973); Galleria Toselli, Milan, Italy (1974); the Whitney Museum of American Art, New York City (1975); and others.

Baer's work was selected for many group exhibitions throughout the world, such as "Systematic Painting," Guggenheim Museum, New York City (1966); "Documenta 4," Kassel, West Germany (1968); "Eine Tendenz Zeitgenossischer Malerei," Kölnischer Kunstverein, Cologne, Germany (1969); "Drawings," Art Institute of Chicago, Illinois (1971); "Hand Colored Prints," a travelling show organized by Brooke Alexander, Inc., New York City (1975); and others.

Among the many permanent collections that house Baer's work are: the Albright-Knox Art Gallery, Buffalo, New York; Australian National Gallery, Canberra; Guggenheim Museum, New York City; Kölnischer Kunstverein, Cologne, Germany; Museum of Modern Art (MoMA), New York City; Suermondt Museum, Aachen, West Germany; University of North Carolina at Greensboro; and the University of Texas at Austin.

Baer taught at the School of Visual Arts, New York City (1969–1970), received a National Endowment for the Arts (NEA) grant (1969) and, early on, before her marginal affiliation with the Ferus Gallery, Los Angeles, in 1957, worked on a kibbutz in Israel.

An abstract-expressionist in the 1950s, Baer found her metier a decade later in hard-edge abstraction or "minimal" painting. The black or colored bands in her diptychs or triptychs gave way, in the 1970s, to hedonistic, figurative, splintered, yet composed, human and animal forms.

Bibliography
Haskell, Barbara. *Jo Baer.* Whitney Museum of American Art, 1975.
Naylor, Colin. *Contemporary Artists.* 3rd ed. St. James Press, 1989.
Poirier, Maurice, and Jane Necol. "The '60s in Abstract: 13 Statements and an Essay." *Art in America* 71:9 (October 1983): 129, 136–137.
Who's Who in American Art. 19th ed. R.R. Bowker Co., 1991–1992.

Baez, Myrna (1931–)

Born in Santurce, Puerto Rico, the painter/printmaker Myrna Baez initially studied the sciences at the University of Puerto Rico (1951), then took up art studies at the Academia de San Fernando, Madrid, Spain (1957). She studied printmaking at the Taller de Artes Gráficas, Instituto de Cultura Puertorriqueño, San Juan, Puerto Rico (c. 1960) and did further study in the techniques of printmaking at Pratt Institute, Brooklyn, New York (1969–1970).

In addition to solo exhibitions at the Instituto de Cultura Puertorriqueño (1962); Galería Colibri, San Juan, Puerto Rico (1966); and others, Baez has had her work shown in many group exhibitions, including the Riverside Museum, New York City (1961); University of Puerto Rico, San Juan (1962, 1968); Galería Sudamericana, New York City (1966–1970); and many others.

Baez has been the recipient of honors and awards, including an award at the Pratt Graphic Center Exhibition, New York City (1970). Her work is housed in private and public permanent collections, including the Instituto de Cultura Puertorriqueño, San Juan, Museo de Arte de Ponce, and University of Puerto Rico, San Juan—all in Puerto Rico; Metropolitan Museum of Art, and Museum of Modern Art (MoMA)—both in New York City; and others.

Bibliography
Bloch, Peter. *Painting and Sculpture of the Puerto Ricans.* New York: Plus Ultra Educational Publishers, 1978.
The Latin American Spirit: Art and Artists in the United States, 1920–1970. New York: Abrams, 1988.

Bagley, Frances Stevens (1946–)

Born in Fayetteville, Tennessee, the Texas sculptor Frances Stevens Bagley earned a Bachelor of Fine Arts degree (1969) and a Master of Arts degree (1971) from Arizona State University, Tempe. Bagley was in England between 1971 and 1973 where, early on, she was an apprentice to Michael Leach at a pottery in Devon. In 1973 she engaged in travel and research throughout Great Britain and, seven years later, received a Master of Fine Arts degree from North Texas State University at Denton.

Bagley has held solo exhibitions in a number of Texas galleries and universities and has had her work included in many group exhibitions throughout Texas and elsewhere, including "American Women Artists 1980," University of São Paulo, Brazil (1980); "Showdown," Alternative Museum, New York City (1983); "Fifth Texas Sculpture Symposium," Dallas, Texas: Connemara Conservancy (1985); and others.

Bagley has won awards and honors from Del Mar College, Corpus Christi, Texas (1975) and the University of Texas at Arlington (1976). Examples of Bagley's work are in private, public, and corporate permanent collections, including the Arkansas Arts Center, Little Rock; Southwestern Bell Telephone Company, Dallas, Texas; the University of Texas at Arlington; and others.

Bibliography
Kutner, Janet. "The Southwest Texas Ranges: Dallas, Acquisitions Are Only Part of the Action." *Art News* 81:10 (December 1982): 86–88.
McFadden, Sarah. "Going Places, Part II: The Outside Story, Creedmoor Psychiatric Center." *Art in America* 68:6 (Summer 1980): 51–55, 57–59.
Moore, Sylvia, ed. *No Bluebonnets, No Yellow Roses: Essays on Texas Women in the Arts.* Midmarch Arts Press, 1988.
Watson-Jones, Virginia. *Contemporary American Women Sculptors.* Oryx Press, 1986.

Baizerman, Eugenie (1899–1949)

Proclaimed by some to be the first abstract impressionist in America, Eugenie Baizerman was born in Warsaw, Poland. But her family remained there only a short time after her birth, and her earliest recollections of childhood date from periods of residence in the Russian province of Bessarabia and the seaport city of Odessa in the Russian

Ukraine. All that is known of her original surname is that it became Silverman when her family emigrated to the United States.

Baizerman's mother was a semi-professional actress while her father, whose wanderlust led to prolonged absences from home, made his living as a teacher of languages. Both of them encouraged their daughter's early interest in art. After enlisting a young artist to instruct her privately, they enrolled her in the Odessa Art School.

Soon after the family settled in New York City following its arrival in America in 1910, Baizerman began taking art classes at the National Academy of Design, New York City and, later, at the Educational Alliance, a settlement house on the lower East Side of New York City. While at the National Academy of Design she earned money by overseeing the school's models. One of those models was the Russian-born sculptor Saul Baizerman who had also studied at the Odessa Art School and whom she eventually married. Although the date of their union is not certain, surviving correspondence between them indicates that it must have occurred in 1924 or 1925.

Through much of her adult life Baizerman suffered from an asthmatic condition that was partly psychosomatic. She was also an intensely shy individual and was unwilling to risk even the minor stresses that might have come with trying to promote her professional reputation aggressively. As a result she contented herself with advancing her art in privacy and only rarely did she consent to public exhibitions of her work.

In her stylistic approach Baizerman's starting point was French impressionism. But as she developed the broad brushwork and bold coloring that characterized her mature work she moved well beyond this initial inspiration to create a form of expression uniquely her own. Ultimately the figures, objects, and natural landscapes discernible in her pictures became only pretexts for creating dramatic harmonies of color, movement, and atmosphere. Ever anxious to avoid repeating the effects created in her previous compositions, Baizerman often defined her work as "color conversations" and likened her brush strokes to the "notes of music." Speaking of her later canvases, one critic described them as "abstractions with figural content."

By the time Baizerman died from her respiratory ailments in 1949 her work had been accorded only two significant showings—a solo exhibition in 1938 and another just before her death, in which her paintings appeared in tandem with her husband's sculpture. In effect, very few knew of her pictures, and that remained the case for many years. In 1961, however, the Artists' Gallery of New York City exhibited a selection of her paintings from the estate of her recently deceased husband. The results were startling. At show's end, virtually every piece had found a buyer, and the Whitney Museum of American Art, and the Museum of Modern Art (MoMA)—both in New York City, had acquired two of her most important works.

Frederick S. Voss

Bibliography

Art News 60:11 (March 1961); 61:12 (January 1963).

Baizerman, Saul. *Eugenie Baizerman and Her Art.* Privately printed, 1950 (copy in vertical files, library of the National Museum of American Art and National Portrait Gallery).

Debakis, Melissa. *Vision of Harmony: The Sculpture of Saul Baizerman.* Black Swan Books, 1989.

Saul Baizerman Papers. Archives of American Art, Smithsonian Institution.

Baker, Dina Gustin (1924–)

Born in Philadelphia, Pennsylvania, Dina Gustin Baker attended the College of Fine Arts (1940, 1942) and the Tyler School of Fine Arts at Temple University (1943)—both in her native city. She won scholarships for further study at the Art Students League (1945), and Atelier 17 (1953)—both in New York City, where her award allowed her to study with Peter Grippe; and a scholarship to the Barnes Foundation, Merion, Pennsylvania in 1946, after study with Dr. Albert C. Barnes and Violet DeMazia.

Between 1960 and 1991 Baker held eighteen solo exhibitions of her work in the United States and Germany, including Roko Gallery, New York City (1960, 1963); Regensburg Museum, Germany, and the Amerika Haus in Hamburg and Munich, Germany (1974); Ingber Gallery, New York City (1974–1987); Utah State University, Logan (1983); Adlena Adlung Gallery, New York City (1990, 1991); and others.

Her paintings have been invited to group exhibitions in New York City, including the Brooklyn Museum and Whitney Museum of American Art; as well as the Philadelphia Academy of Fine Art Biennial, Pennsylvania; Hudson River Museum, New York; Art USA, and many others throughout the United States.

Baker has won much recognition for her painting, including the Gold Medal award, Parrish Art Museum, Southampton, New York (1965); "Artist of the Region," from the Guild Hall, East Hampton, New York (1963); and others. She was a MacDowell Colony fellow, Peterborough, New Hampshire (1959).

Baker's paintings are in the permanent collections of the Barnes Foundation, Merion, Pennsylvania; Gannett Foundation, the Philadelphia Museum of Art, Pennsylvania; Columbia University, New York City; the Bergen Museum of Arts and Sciences, Paramus, New Jersey; the Butler Academy, Ohio; and others.

Bibliography

Glueck, Grace. "Review of Solo Show at Ingber Gallery." *The New York Times* (March 24, 1984).

Schumacher, Marie Louise. "Das Amerika Haus zeigt Bilder von Dina Gustin Baker." *Die Welt* (March 1974).

Who's Who in American Art, 19th ed. R.R. Bowker Co., 1991–1992.

Baker, Jill (1942–)

The widely-travelled painter Jill Baker was born in Ilion, New York, and attended Baylor University, Waco, Texas, where she received her Bachelor of Arts degree in 1964. Baker enrolled in graduate study at Florida State University, Tallahassee, with Karl Zerbe (1966–1969) and, six years later, took further graduate work at the Accademia de Belle Arti, Florence, Italy. In 1981 she obtained a Master of Fine Arts degree from Pratt Institute, Brooklyn, New York.

Between 1969 and 1990 Baker had eighteen solo exhibitions of her work in the United States and abroad, including Goethe House, New York City (1974); Palazzo Strozzi, Florence, Italy (1975); the American Embassy, Seoul, South Korea (1977); Ward-Nasse Gallery, New York City (1977, 1979, 1982, 1984, 1986); Sunset Studio, Huntington Beach, California (1990); and others.

Baker's work has been invited to more than thirty group exhibitions throughout the world in cities as widespread as Florence, Italy; Paris, France; and Seoul, South Korea. She has taught at Pierce College, Northridge, California (1984–1986); led colloquia for honors students at Bowling Green Junior High School, Kentucky (1978); lectured at Korean universities (1977); taught in the adult art education program in Bowling Green, Kentucky (1969–1974); served as president of Los Angeles' Artists Equity, California (1984–1986) and serves as regional vice-president of its national board; illustrated nine books and has supported herself as an artist since 1969.

Baker's work is represented in permanent collections, such as Goethe House, New York City; Purdue University, West Lafayette, Indiana; Bellarmine College, Louisville, Kentucky; Western Kentucky University, Bowling Green; the Herman Rath Collection, Houston, Texas; and many others. "Rock House on Water" (1979), a not atypical oil collage, provides clues to the artist's wit and sensibilities through its juxtaposition of elements.

Bibliography
Wheeless, Karen, "Jill Baker, An artist who . . ." *Baylor Line Quarterly* (December 1975).
Who's Who in American Art. 19th ed. R.R. Bowker Co., 1991–1992.

Baker, Sarah M. (1899–1983)

Born in Memphis, Tennessee, the painter Sarah M. Baker studied at the Maryland Institute of Art, Baltimore; and also with Hugh Breckenridge, Arthur Charles, and André L'Hôte.

Baker has been a teacher at various schools, including the Bryn Mawr School for Girls, Baltimore (1929–1937); St. Timothy's School, Catonsville, Maryland (1931–1945); and American University, Washington, D.C. (1945–1983). She has exhibited widely and won prizes in venues such as the Washington Society of Independent Artists, Washington, D.C. (1935); the Baltimore Museum of Art, Maryland (1945); and others.

Baker is the winner of a fellowship gold medal at the Pennsylvania Academy of Fine Arts, Pennsylvania (1926). Her work is represented in private and public permanent collections, including the Brooklyn Museum, New York; American University, Washington, D.C.; St. John's Church, McLean, Virginia; the Phillips Collection, Washington, D.C.; and others.

Bibliography
American Art Annual. Vol. 28. American Federation of Arts, 1932.
Archives of American Art. *Collection of Exhibition Catalogs.* G.K. Hall & Co., 1979.
The Phillips Collection, A Summary Catalog. Washington, D.C., 1985.

Baldaugh, Anni von Westrum (1881–1953)

Born in the Netherlands the painter Anni von Westrum Baldaugh studied privately with masters in Austria, Germany, and the Netherlands.

A member of many art institutions, Baldaugh was associated with the Beaux-Arts, Paris, France; the California Watercolor Club and California Society of Miniature Painters—both in Los Angeles; Connecticut Academy of Fine Arts, Westport; Laguna Beach Art Association, and San Diego Fine Arts Society—both in California; and others.

Resident in San Diego, California, she exhibited work in museums and galleries and won prizes and honors throughout California, including a gold medal from the Los Angeles County Museum of Arts and Science (1922); prizes from the California Society of Miniature Painters (1929); the Fine Arts Gallery of San Diego (1930, 1934, 1935, 1936); and others.

Examples of her work are in private and public permanent collections, including the Fine Arts Gallery, San Diego, California; and others.

Bibliography
Kamerling, Bruce. "Painting Ladies: Some Early San Diego Women Artists." *Journal of San Diego History* 32:3 (Summer 1986): 152–154.
A Selection of Paintings by Early San Diego California Artists. San Diego Museum of Art, 1987.

Ball, Lillian (1955–)

Lillian Ball was born in Augusta, Maine, and was educated at many institutions, including the Instituto Bellas Artes, San Miguel de Allende, Mexico (1971); Nordenfiords Verdens Universitet, Copenhagen, Denmark (1972–1973); Harvard University, Cambridge, Massachusetts (1975–1976); Parsons School of Design (1978); Columbia University (1984–1985); and the New School for Social Research—all in New York City (1985).

Ball has had solo exhibitions of her outdoor public sculpture at the Snug Harbor Cultural Center, Staten Island, New York (1989); Socrates Sculpture Park, Long Island City, New York (1989–1999); the Hudson River Museum, Westchester County, New York (1990); and others.

She has had her work invited to numerous group exhibitions in the United States and abroad, including "Sculptural Forms," Aldrich Museum of Contemporary Art, Ridgefield, Connecticut (1980); Sculpture Center, New York City (1986, 1987); "Personal Poetics," Sala Uno Galleria, Rome, Italy (1987); "Artists Working," Bard College, Annandale-on-Hudson, New York (1988); "Mixed Messages," Ruggerio Henis Gallery, New York (1989); "A Lick of the Eye," Shoshana Wayne Gallery, Santa Monica, California (1991); and many others.

Ball has been the recipient of honors and awards, such as the National Heritage Trust grant, Art Park, Lewiston, New York (1979); a National Endowment for the Arts (NEA) fellowship grant in sculpture (1986–1987); an award from Triangle Artists, International Sculpture Symposium, Pine Plains, New York (1989); a New York State Foundation for the Arts fellowship grant in printmaking (1991); and others.

Ball has been a visiting artist and lecturer at many institutions, including New York University, New York City; the New York Feminist Art Institute; the Rhode Island School of Design, Providence; and Boston University, Massachusetts. She has also been an assistant to Jackie Winsor, an invited artist to Garner Tullis' Print Workshop in Santa Barbara, California, and one of the invited artists to the 2nd Contemporary Artist Cruise and Show to France, Spain, and Italy.

Ball's work is housed in a number of corporate permanent collections, such as Nynex Corporation, White Plains, New York; Best Products, Inc., Ashland, Virginia; Bingham, Dana & Gould, Boston, Massachusetts; and others.

Bibliography
Ball, Lillian. "What is Missing from Contemporary Art Discourse?" *M.E.A.N.I.N.G. Magazine* (Spring 1989).
Brenson, Michael. "Bold Sculpture for Wide Open Spaces." *The New York Times* (July 21, 1989).
Zimmer, William. "An Intersection of Art and Nature." *The New York Times* (June 17, 1990).

Baltzell, Jan C. (1948–)

Painter and teacher Jan Baltzell was born in Philadelphia, Pennsylvania and educated at the Philadelphia College of Art (now the University of the Arts), in her native city, where she received a Bachelor of Fine Arts degree in 1971, and at Miami University in Ohio, where she earned a Master of Fine Arts degree in 1976. She now teaches at the Pennsylvania Academy of Fine Art and the University of the Arts, both in Philadelphia, Pennsylvania.

Baltzell's work, which is highly personal, reflects a knowledge of the history of art, a deep love of nature, and a clarifying structural awareness. Her large gesturally-abstract paintings and drawings have been seen in eleven one-person shows and a large number of group shows throughout the country, and her work is represented in numerous major collections.

Baltzell received a fellowship to the Virginia Center for the Creative Arts at Mt. Angelo, Virginia (1983); she was visiting artist at Towson State University in Maryland (1983–1984); and was visiting artist at the Vermont Studio Center at Johnson, Vermont (1991).

Baltzell is the youngest of a highly creative family: her mother was the painter Jane Piper, and her sister Eve is an architect in Boston; her father is the sociologist E. Digby Baltzell.

Larry Day

Bibliography
Donohoe, Victoria. "The Arts." *Philadelphia Inquirer* (January 13, 1989); (May 25, 1985).
Milstein, Alan. *The Philadelphia Bulletin* (November 22, 1981).
Purchase, Steven. "Baltzell's Abstracts at Holtzman." *Baltimore Sun* (March 29, 1984).
Walker, Alice. *In Search of Our Mother's Garden* (Cover), Keizersgracht 321, Amsterdam.
Wolanin, Barbara. *The New Art Examiner* (December 1981); (rpt., January 1982).

Banks, Ellen

Born in Boston, Massachusetts, African-American painter Ellen Banks earned a Bachelor's degree from the Massachusetts College of Art and also studied at the School of the Museum of Fine Arts—both in Boston.

Banks's first solo exhibition took place at the Dunbarton Galleries, Boston, Massachusetts (1962); five years later, she received the Prix de Paris, France. "Black and White Plus #194" (1970), a large non-representational acrylic on board, is typical of Banks's work of this period: it posits a sensitive yet strong composition of two-dimensional forms in a cool arrangement. Her work is represented in private and public permanent collections in the United States and Canada.

Bibliography
Afro-American Artists: New York and Boston. A Catalog. The Museum of the National Center of Afro-American Artists and the Museum of Fine Arts, Boston, 1970.

Baranceanu, Belle (1902–1988)

Born in Chicago, Illinois, the painter/printmaker Belle Baranceanu learned her craft at the Minneapolis School of Art, Minnesota, and through further study with Anthony Angarola. A resident of San Diego, California, Baranceanu has been associated with a number of institutions, including the Chicago Society of Artists, Illinois; La Jolla Art Center, California; San Diego Artist's Guild; and others.

In addition to the murals she created in the U.S. Post Office, and the Auditorium of the La Jolla High School—both in La Jolla, California, Baranceanu exhibited in museums and galleries, including the "Annual American Exhibition," Art Institute of Chicago, Illinois (1926, 1928, 1931, 1938); Kansas City Art Institute, Missouri (1927); California Pacific Exposition, San Francisco (1935); Carnegie Institute, Pittsburgh, Pennsylvania (1943); Library of Congress, Washington, D.C. (1943, 1945, 1946); National Academy of Design, New York City (1943–1946); Denver Art Museum, Colorado (1945); and many others.

Examples of her work are in private and public permanent collections, including the Fine Arts Society and Fine Arts Gallery—both in San Diego, California; Library of Congress, Washington, D.C.; and others.

Bibliography
Belle Baranceanu—A Retrospective. La Jolla: University of California at San Diego, 1985.
Kamerling, Bruce. "Painting Ladies: Some Early San Diego Women Artists." *The Journal of San Diego History* 32:3 (Summer 1986): 154–157.
Park, Marlene, and Gerald E. Markowitz. *Democratic Vistas: Post Offices and Public Art in the New Deal.* Philadelphia: Temple University Press, 1984.

Barker, Lucy Hayward (1872–1948)

Born in Portage Lake, Maine, the painter Lucy Hayward Barker learned her craft at the School of the Boston Museum of Fine Arts, Massachusetts, under the tutelage of Frank Benson, Alger V. Currier, Philip Hale, and Edmond Tarbell.

Examples of her work are in private and public permanent collections, including St. Luke's Cathedral, Portland, Maine, and the Wayland Public Library, Maine.

Bibliography
Who's Who in American Art. 2nd ed. Washington, D.C.: American Federation of Arts, 1937.
Women Pioneers in Maine Art 1900–1945. Portland, Maine: Joan Whitney Payson Gallery of Art, Westbrook College, 1985.

Barney, Alice Pike (1857–1931)

Born in Cincinnati, Ohio, the painter Alice Pike Barney, despite her husband's protestations, studied painting with Ellizabeth Nourse, went to Europe to study with Carolus-Duran, Henner and, most importantly, with James McNeil Whistler. Barney exhibited widely in the United States and before returning home, showed at the Salon of 1889, Paris, France; and in other venues. Whether in pastel or in oil her landscape paintings, portraits, studies of women and children, and the occasional male portrait reveal a keen eye and a sure hand. Barney and her husband were active patrons and champions of art and artists.

Representative examples of her work are in private and public permanent collections in the United States and abroad, including the Folger Shakespeare Library; the National Collection of Fine Arts; and the Studio House—all in Washington, D.C.; the Paris Opera House, France; University of Virginia, Charlottesville; and others.

Bibliography
Cosentino, Andrew J., and Henry H. Glassie. *The Capital Image: Paintings in Washington 1800–1915*. National Museum of American Art, 1983.
Hall, Delight. *Catalogue of the Alice Pike Barney Memorial Lending Collection*. National Collection of Fine Arts, 1965.
McClelland, Donald R. *Where Shadows Live: Alice Pike Barney and Her Friends*. National Collection of Fine Arts, 1978.

Barr-Sharrar, Beryl (1935–)

Born in Norfolk, Virginia, the painter and art critic Beryl Barr-Sharrar earned her Bachelor's degree at Mount Holyoke College, South Hadley, Massachusetts, and a Master's degree from the University of California at Berkeley. She also holds a Master's degree and a Ph.D. from the Institute of Fine Arts, New York University.

Barr-Sharrar has held many solo exhibitions throughout her painting career, including shows at the Galerie Steinstrasse, Kaiserlautern, Germany (1963); Galerie Lefranc, Paris, France (1964); Galerie Lucien Durand, Paris, France (1967); and others.

Her work has been invited to numerous group exhibitions in the United States and Europe, such as the "San Francisco Annual National Exhibition," San Francisco Museum, California (1958); "Prix Lefranc," Galerie Lefranc, Paris, France (1964); "Prix International du Chateau de la Saraz," Lausanne, Switzerland (1965); "U.S.A. Groupe 67," travelling through museums in France, United States Information Agency (USIA) (1967); Sachs Gallery (1973), Livingstone-Learmonth Gallery (1975), and Art Galaxy (1981)—all in New York City; and many others.

Winner of a summer scholarship to the Yale-Norfolk Summer School, Connecticut (1955) and a travelling fellowship to Europe from Mount Holyoke College (1958), Barr-Sharrar was co-founder of Art Study Abroad, Paris (1961) and co-director from 1961–1968, when she lived in Paris. She has been the recipient of grants and awards for her work as a critic and a painter, including two grants from the American Philosophical Society (1980, 1982); a grant from the American Council of Learned Societies (1982); a fellowship from the Center for Advanced Study in the Visual Arts, National Gallery, Washington, D.C. (1985); and an award, the *Prix de France pour le jeune peinture*, Paris, France (1964). She has lectured on painting and art history at many colleges and universities in the United States, including Mount Holyoke College, South Hadley, Massachusetts (1968–1969); Pratt Institute (1978), and Fordham University—both in New York City (1981); and Vassar College, Poughkeepsie, New York (1982).

In her solo exhibition at Lucien Durand in Paris (1967), the critic Michel Seuphor suggested that her abstract acrylics followed the line of succession from Arshile Gorky. "Les Bois Sourverains" (1967) pays homage to Sylvia Plath in a strong, forthright composition.

Barr-Sharrar's work is in many private, corporate, and public permanent collections in the United States and Europe, including Mount Holyoke College, South Hadley, Massachusetts; the Los Angeles Savings and Loan, California; and many others.

Bibliography
Seuphor, Michel. "Beryl Barr-Sharrar." A Catalog. Paris: Galerie Lucien Durand, 1967.
Who's Who in American Art. 19th ed. R.R. Bowker Co., 1991–1992.

Barry, Ann Meredith (1932–)

Born in Toronto, Canada, the environmental painter and printmaker Ann Meredith Barry studied at the Ontario College of Art, Toronto, graduating in 1954. Between 1969 and 1990 Barry has held more than three dozen solo exhibitions throughout Canada: from the Lillian Morrison Art Gallery, Toronto (1969–1971) to the Emma Butler Gallery, St. John's, Newfoundland (1990); from exhibitions in Vancouver, B.C., to Edmonton, Alberta, and Halifax, Nova Scotia.

Her work has been included in many prestigious group exhibitions throughout Canada and abroad since 1973, including the "III American Biennale of Graphic Arts," Museum of Modern Art, São Paulo, Brazil (1976); "International Exhibition of Miniature Prints," Pratt Institute, New York City (1977); "Printmakers and Apprentices," a travelling exhibition, Harbourfront Art Gallery, Toronto (1979–1980); "From Sea to Sea," Buschlen-Mowatt Gallery, Vancouver, B.C. (1989); and others.

Barry has completed numerous commissions, is a much-sought-after teacher, and has been active in professional arts organizations.

Examples of her work are in private, corporate, and public permanent collections, including Memorial University, St. John's, Newfoundland; the Canada Council Art Bank, Ottawa; Emily Carr College of Art and Design, Vancouver, B.C.; Bank of Montréal, Canada; and myriad others.

Bibliography
Barry, A.M. *The Printmobile*. Fifteen-Minute Video. ECCAD, B.C. producer, 1982.
Hicks, P. "Review." St. John's: *Evening Telegram* (June 1988).
Kritzwiser, Kay. "Review." *Arts Atlantic* (Spring 1983).
Warner, G. "Review." *Canadian Art Magazine* (Winter 1985).

Barry, Edith Cleaves (1884–1969)

Born in Boston, Massachusetts, the painter/sculptor Edith Cleaves Barry studied at the Art Students League and the Institute of Fine Arts—both in New York City; she also studied her craft in Paris, France.

Winner of many prizes and awards, Barry exhibited in museums and galleries, including Yale University's Museum of Fine Arts, New Haven, Connecticut (1916); National Association of Women Artists, New York City (1916, 1922, 1926, 1932, 1942, 1945); and with a host of other institutions, such as the Art Institute of Chicago, Illinois; National Academy of Design, New York City; the Pennsylvania Academy of Fine Arts, Philadelphia; and others.

Barry was the director of the Brick Store Museum, Kennebunk, Maine (1936–1946). Examples of her work are in private and public permanent collections.

Bibliography
American Art Annual. Vol. 28. Washington, D.C.: American Federation of Arts, 1932.
Who's Who in American Art. Vol. 1. Washington, D.C.: American Federation of Arts, 1935.

Bartlett, Jennifer (1941–)

Born in Long Beach, California, the well-known painter/printmaker/writer Jennifer Bartlett earned a Bachelor's degree from Mills College, Oakland, California (1963); the following year, she received a Bachelor of Fine Arts degree from Yale University, New Haven, Connecticut; and, in 1965, after graduate study with Jim Dine, Al Held, James Rosenquist, and Jack Tworkov, received a Yale University Master of Fine Arts degree.

Bartlett has held many solo exhibitions in the United States and abroad, including Dartmouth College, Hanover, New Hampshire (1975); Baltimore Art Museum, Maryland (1978); and the San Francisco Museum of Modern Art, California (1978); Tate Gallery, London, England (1982); the Rose Art Museum, Brandeis University, Waltham, Massachusetts (1984); the Walker Art Center, Minneapolis, Minnesota (1985); and others.

Bartlett's work has been invited to prestigious group exhibitions in the Art Institute of Chicago, Illinois; the Corcoran Gallery of Art, Washington, D.C.; Museum of Modern Art (MoMA), New York City; Los Angeles County Museum of Art, California; the Whitney Museum of American Art, New York City; and many others. "2 Priory Walk" (1977), a major work composed of sixty-four one-foot-square units of baked enamel, silkscreen, and enamel on steel plates, represents but one of several approaches employed by Bartlett through the years. Her stylistic changes herald new ways of looking.

Bartlett has been the recipient of awards and honors including a Creative Artists Public Service (CAPS) grant from the New York State Council on the Arts (1974); the Harris Prize from the Art Institute of Chicago, Illinois (1875); the Lucas Visiting Lecture Award from Carleton College, Northfield, Minnesota (1979); the Brandeis University Creative Arts award, Waltham, Massachusetts (1983); election to the American Academy and Institute of Arts and Letters (1983); and others.

Examples of her work are in private and public permanent collections, including the Metropolitan Museum of Art, and Whitney Museum of American Art—both in New York City; Philadelphia Museum of Art, Pennsylvania; Walker Art Center, Minneapolis, Minnesota; and others.

Bibliography

Amaya, Mario. "Conversation with Jennifer Bartlett." *Architectural Digest* 38:12 (December 1981): 50–60.

At the Lake; Up the Creek; In the Garden; Jennifer Bartlett. Essay by Richard Francis. London: Tate Gallery, 1982.

Russell, John. "Archetypes in Jennifer Bartlett's Pastels." *The New York Times* (February 27, 1987): 25, 29.

Tomkins, Calvin. "Profiles: Getting Everything In." *The New Yorker* (April 15, 1985): 50–68.

Bartol, Elizabeth Howard (1842–1927)

Born in Boston, Massachusetts, the painter Elizabeth Howard Bartol learned her craft at the Boston School of Design, Massachusetts, where she was one of the better students of William Morris Hunt; while there, she also studied with William Rimmer and S.S. Tuckerman.

Bartol exhibited in museums and galleries, including the William & Everett Gallery (1888), and the Boston Art Club (during the 1870s and 1880s)—both in Boston, Massachusetts; the Society of American Artists (1880); and in other venues.

Examples of her work are in private and public permanent collections, including the Lancaster Historical Society, Massachusetts; among others.

Bibliography

"Boston Exhibition." *The Art Journal* 5 (1879): 190.

Carter, S.N. "The New York Spring Exhibitions, The Society of American Artists." *The Art Journal* 6 (1880): 156.

Hoppin, Martha. "Women Artists in Boston, 1870–1900: The Pupils of William Morris Hunt." *The American Art Journal* 13:1 (Winter 1981): 17–46.

Barton, Loren (1893–1975)

Born in Oxford, Massachusetts, the painter/printmaker Loren Barton studied at the University of Southern California, Los Angeles, and taught at the Chouinard Art Institute in the same city.

Winner of many honors and awards, Barton exhibited and won prizes in many shows in museums and galleries, including the Arizona Art Exhibition, Phoenix (1922, 1923, 1926, 1927); National Association of Women Painters and Sculptors (1926), National Association of Women Artists (1928), American Watercolor Society (1941), and National Academy of Design (1945)—all in New York City; and others.

Examples of her work are in private and public permanent collections in the United States and abroad, including the Bibliothèque Nationale, Paris, France; the Art Institute of Chicago, Illinois; Brooklyn Museum, and Museum of Modern Art (MoMA)—both in New York City; Los Angeles County Museum of Art, and San Diego Fine Arts Society—both in California; National Gallery of Fine Art, Smithsonian Institution, Washington, D.C.; and many others.

Bibliography

American Art Annual. Vol. 28. Washington, D.C.: American Federation of Arts, 1932.

"Loren Barton and Rome." *Art Digest* 6:11 (March 1, 1932): 6.

Moure, Nancy Dustin Wall. *Los Angeles Painters of the 1920s.* Claremont, California: Pomona College Gallery, 1972.

Southern California Artists, 1890–1940. Laguna Beach, California: Laguna Beach Museum of Art, 1979.

Bassi, Sofia (1930–)

A self-taught painter from Ciudad Mendoza, Veracruz, Mexico, Sofia Bassi began to paint in 1964. Known for her dream images, Bassi has been referred to as a surrealist. She has exhibited widely throughout Mexico and internationally, and her works are in the permanent collections of the Smithsonian Institution, Washington, D.C.; Museo de Arte Moderno, Mexico City, Museo Liceo Selma Lagerloff de Estocolmo, Suecia, and Museo de Guadalajara—all in Mexico; the Museum of Modern Art of Tel-Aviv, Israel; and others.

Bassi has exhibited in both group and individual exhibitions including "Frida Kahlo acompañada de siete pintoras," Museo de Arte Moderno, Mexico City (1967), "La mujer en la plástica," Museo Nacional de Antropología, Mexico City (1971), the IV Festival Internacional de Cultura de la Universidad Autónoma del Estado de Morelos (1971)—all in Mexico. In 1973 she exhibited in a group show at the Museo de Arte Contemporaneo de Patzcuaro, and her work appeared at auction at Sotheby Parke Bernet, New York City.

Bassi's individual exhibitions include, among many others, the Lys Gallery, New York City (1965); the Salón de la Plástica Mexicana, under the auspices of the Instituto Nacional de Bellas Artes, Mexico City (1969); and the Museo de Arte Contemporáneo, Morelia, Michoacán (1974)—all in Mexico; the Maison de l'Amérique Latine, Paris, France (1976); Galería Mer-Kup (1981), and the Galería de Arte del Partido Revolucionario Institucional—both in Mexico City, Mexico (1987); and others.

Many of her paintings were exhibited in Mexico through government-sponsored commemorative exhibitions. In 1971, for example, the Secretaría del Patrimonio Nacional presented her work in the Federal Palace of Guadalajara, Mexico, to commemorate the sacrifice of the heroic children of Chapultepec for the anniversary of the Independence.

Bassi received a number of honors, including awards from the Universidad Autónoma de Guerrero (1969); La Escuela Preparatoria No. 3 de Acapulco (1970); and El Cine Experimental de Orizaba (1973)—all in Mexico. In Terni, Italy, in 1971 she received the Copa Trofeo, the award of "San Valentino di Arti Figurative." She was made an Honorary Member of the Instituto Mexicano de Ciencias y Humanidades, Mexico City, Mexico (1992).

Travis Barton Kranz

Bibliography

Elizondo, Salvador. *Los continentes del sueño*. Mexico City: Artes de Mexico, 1974.

Washington, D.C., Columbus Memorial Library-Organization of American States, Archives of the Museum of Modern Art of Latin America. Sofia Bassi file.

Bates, Mary (1951–)

Mary Bates is known for her large- and small-scale bronze sculptures which appear to resemble unfunctional tools or implements. Born in Billings, Montana, Bates received a Bachelor of Fine Arts degree from Colorado State University, Fort Collins (1973), and a Master of Fine Arts degree from Indiana University, Bloomington (1981). She is currently professor of sculpture at Sonoma State University, Rohnert Park, California, after having served as department head (1986–1989).

Bates's work has ranged in scale from four inches to ten feet in height and width. During the past two years she has worked on a series of 200 bronze implements. Each form alludes to scientific and artistic potential, yet reveals no actual application. The ninety completed forms incorporate a physical and psychological energy in states of containment and release. Bates believes that many of the images project a quality of animation as the shapes appear to grow, probe, or reach out toward the viewer.

Her numerous exhibitions include "The Implement Series," Barclay Simpson Gallery, Lafayette, California (1991); and *An Archeology of the Mind,* Loveland Museum and Gallery, Colorado (1991). Bates has been a recipient of honors and awards, including a grant from the Washington State Arts Council, Art in Public Places purchase award (1984); a sculpture fellowship from the New Jersey State Council on the Arts (1982); and a Ford Foundation fellowship in the visual arts at Indiana University, Bloomington (1978–1981).

Moira Geoffrion

Bibliography

Baker, Kenneth. "Sculpture: In Search of an Audience." *San Francisco Chronicle* (October 6, 1991): 33.

Watson-Jones, Virginia. *Contemporary American Women Sculptors*. Oryx Press, 1986.

Bates, Pat Martin (1927–)

Born in Saint John, New Brunswick, Canada, Pat Martin Bates studied painting under Stanley Royale, a professor at Mount Allison University, at age thirteen. Some years later (1957) she received a Fine Arts Diploma from the Royale Académie des Beaux-Arts, Belgium. Bates also studied at the Académie de la Grand Chaumière, and at the Sorbonne—both in Paris; the Pratt Graphic Center in New York City under an Ingram–Merrill scholarship; Dalhousie University, the University of Victoria, and the Banff School of Fine Arts—all in Canada; the Royal Palace Library in Iran; the Topkapi Royal Library in Istanbul, Turkey; and the Asian Art Society in Japan. Since 1965 she has been teaching art at the University of Victoria, although she maintains her interest in movement, travel, and other cultures.

One of Bates's most important and innovative series of works involved poking holes through pieces of handmade paper which were then back lit. "Inscape of the Sea-Sailor Moon-Star" (1985), for example, is representative of work that shows her move away from traditional printmaking into the realm of mixed media. Introducing other media is in keeping with her own explorations of mysticism and symbol, culture, and religions. Her work is informed by a knowledge of ancient prehistoric sites, particularly those in Britain; an interest in Islamic mysticism, especially the Sufic traditions; by alchemy, by numerology, and by an intensive study of esoteric subjects in general. Often these interests can be located in the titles and the content or the appearance of her work: "Garden of Shiraz" (c. 1985) refers to the ancient city in the Middle East but also recalls the exquisitely produced eleventh-century Iranian manuscript: the "Shahnama" (Book of Kings); or, "Sung Night in China and the Porcelain Lady's Star" (c. 1985) reminds us of tenth- and eleventh-century China when the goddess Kuanyin was revered and elegant Sung dynasty porcelain flourished. From western European culture, in addition to prehistoric sites, she finds the cathedrals of the Medieval era fascinating, not as signifiers of Christianity but for their mysticism and magic, and she admires the work of the fourteenth-century alchemist, Nicolas Flamel. Her range is wide; her interests are intense; and her searching is incessant.

Bates's art can be found in almost seventy major collections around the world, including the Museum of Modern Art (MoMA), New York City; the National Gallery of Art, Oslo, Norway; the Museums of Modern Art, Tokyo and Osaka, Japan; the National Gallery of Art, Ottawa, Canada; and the Art Gallery of Greater Victoria, Canada. Her work has appeared in exhibitions across Canada, as well as in Europe, China, and Japan, and she has often been invited to judge and jury prints in Europe and North America. In addition, she has won many awards herself, including a gold medal in Norway's prestigious international Biennial (1986); an Edinburgh Arts Bursary, Scotland (1980) to crew on the Darwin barque *Beagle*, thereby providing sketches for the Edinburgh Festival; and a "Critic's Choice" award in the 12th Biennale Internationale de gravure, Poland. In 1990 she was awarded a research grant to investigate the art of papermaking in India, and while there she lectured at Banasthall University, Rajasthan, and the Institute of Fine Arts and Crafts, New Delhi. One of her most recent accomplishments was the receipt of the University of Victoria's Teaching Excellence award (1991), attesting to Bates's concern for her students' progression as well as her own.

In 1985 Bates and a young Canadian artist, Marlene Creates,

shared an exhibition at The Art Gallery, Mount Saint Vincent University in Halifax, Canada, titled "Traces: From the Travels of Marlene Creates and Pat Martin Bates." The exhibition wove together the interest these two artists share in travelling, megalithic astronomy, and standing stone sites. It also attested to concepts of cooperation, exploration, and a willingness to share her own knowledge with others that makes Bates such a unique figure in the world of printmaking.

Janice Helland

Bibliography

Brodzky, Anne, Barry Lord, and P.K. Page. *Black and White Almost: Pat Martin Bates*. Victoria: Art Gallery of Greater Victoria, 1972.

Lord, Barry. *Eleven Canadian Printmakers*. Hanover: Dartmouth College, Hopkins Centre Art Galleries, 1967.

Page, P.K. "Darkinbod the Brightdayler. Transmutation Symbolism in the Work of Pat Martin Bates." *Artscanada* 154/155 (April–May 1971): 35–40.

Traces: From the Travels of Marlene Creates and Pat Martin Bates. Halifax: The Art Gallery, Mount Saint Vincent University, 1985.

Bauermeister, Mary (1934–)

Combining intellectualism and whimsy, the lens boxes made by German-born artist Mary Bauermeister in New York during the 1960s remain to Americans her best known work. These constructions comprise all manner of small natural and manmade objects—shells, stones, buttons, etc.—combined often with miniaturistic line-drawings and cryptic written messages, and visible through the glass front to which lenses are affixed. Bauermeister was born in Frankfurt in 1934 and began to paint in the early 1950s. Later in that decade she lived in Cologne, where she associated with a dynamic group of artists and intellectuals, who were interested in rebuilding post-war cultural life. Here she met Karlheinz Stockhausen, already well-known as a musical avant-gardist who espoused electronic music. Through Stockhausen, whom she later married, Bauermeister came into contact with stars of the international post-war art constellation, including Americans John Cage and Merce Cunningham, the Korean-born peripatetic Nam June Paik, and Yves Klein and Jean Tinguely from Paris. They helped to shape her nontraditional aesthetic valuing chance, fluid notions of form, and direct responses to any and all of life's experiences.

In 1961 Bauermeister began to make assemblages of odd materials, such as sand and drinking straws, composed by applying the serial techniques of musical composition. The next year she emphasized the passage of time as an aesthetic element by spatially separating components of a single work, so that the viewer could not apprehend it at a glance.

In 1962 Bauermeister moved to New York City for a decade. In that city she showed pebbles and sand on a gallery floor and linen sculptures, sewn collages lit from behind, as well as assemblages. Soon she began to produce the pristine white box constructions that are particularly associated with her name, such as "No Faces" (1964). In these constructions small objects and drawings can be observed through the front glass or, in some cases, through lenses which offer a focused, magnified, or distorted view, thus playing on ideas of reality and illusion. By the mid-1960s the written elements included in these charming settings often referred to problematic aspects of social reality, such as the civil rights movement or the Vietnam war. Like the boxes larger installation-assemblages she produced at the end of the decade combined aspects of 1960s conceptualism, pop art, and political consciousness into works that tease the mind and eye without moralizing.

After returning to Germany Bauermeister continued to produce the signature boxes but she added living plants to the range of materials in her art. In several German cities she created gardens which combine plantings with fanciful components, such as glass prisms that project rainbows and hanging elements covered with lenses. She also produced studio works, such as "Contemplation Pyramid" (1979–1990), which attaches to the wall. A hinged top allows access to an interior replete with mirrors, lenses, and her familiar black calligraphy.

Ann Lee Morgan

Bibliography

Rubinstein, Charlotte S. *American Women Artists*. Avon, 1982, 356–58.

———. *American Women Sculptors*. G.K. Hall, 1990, 412–13.

Baxter, Bonnie (1946–)

Born in Texarkana, Texas, the printmaker Bonnie Baxter was a student at several institutions, including Monticello College, Illinois; the University of Kansas, Lawrence; and Cranbrook Academy of Art, Bloomfield Hills, Michigan. Baxter is a master-printer, printmaker, papermaker, university professor of printmaking, and creator of artist's books.

Baxter has held solo exhibitions in galleries in Italy, the United States, and Canada, including the Galleria Fenwick Forano, Italy (1970, 1975); Quivira Gallery, Kansas (1976); Centre Culturel de Val-D'Or, Québec (1979); "Fetiches," Galerie L'Imagier, Aylmer, Québec (1987); "Shazam," Galerie Barbara Silverberg, Montréal, Québec (1992); Centre d'exposition du Vieux Palais, Saint Jerome, Québec (1993); and many others.

Her work has been included in or invited to group exhibitions, including Paris, France; Valparaiso, Chile; Montréal, Québec; Morelia, Mexico; Tokyo, Japan; Madrid, Spain; Boston, Massachusetts; New York City; and Atlanta, Georgia. "Fatima II" (1992), a color woodcut, reveals a keen wit and a mastery of technical control in its handling of the figure.

Baxter has won many honors and awards. Examples of her work are in private and public permanent collections, including the Art Bank, Canada Council; Bibliothèque Nationale du Québec; Brenau College, Gainesville, Georgia; the National Library of Canada, Ottawa; the National Museum of Prints, Mexico; and others.

Bibliography

Olivier, Sylvie. "Bonnie Baxter Spirit-Figures." *Vie des Arts* (June 1990).

Rivard, Yoland. "Des Fetiches a l'Imagier." Hull-Aylmer: *Le Droit*. (March 18, 1987).

Tomalty, Nansea. "Time Machine." *Montréal Mirror* 5:18 (1989).

Baxter, Martha Wheeler (1869–1955)

Born in Castleton, Vermont, the painter of miniatures Martha Wheeler Baxter studied in many venues in Europe, including the Académie Julian and the Académie Colarossi—both in Paris, France; privately with Chardon and Schmidt in Paris; with Behenna in London, England; Sartorelli in Venice, Italy; and at the Institute of Design in Boston, Massachusetts.

Winner of honors and awards, Baxter exhibited work in galleries and museums in Europe and South America; she also showed work and won prizes at presentations of the California Society of Miniature

Painters (1919, 1922, 1923, 1929, 1932, 1936, 1937); and the Los Angeles County Museum of Art, Science, and Industry (1936); she also exhibited work at the Art Institute of Chicago, Illinois (1940); the American Society of Miniature Painters, New York City; Palace of the Legion of Honor, San Francisco, California; Pennsylvania Academy of Fine Arts, Philadelphia; and others.

Examples of her work are in private and public permanent collections, including the Frick Collection, Washington, D.C.; Los Angeles County Museum of Art, California; National Collection of Fine Arts, Smithsonian Institution, Washington, D.C.; Philadelphia Museum of Art, Pennsylvania; and others.

Bibliography
American Art Annual. Vol. 28. Washington, D.C.: American Federation of Arts, 1932.
Moure, Nancy Dustin Wall. *Los Angeles Painters of the Nineteen Twenties.* Claremont, California: Pomona College, 1972.
Woman's Who's Who in America. New York: American Commonwealth Company, 1914.

Beals, Jessie Tarbox (1870–1942)

Born in Hamilton, Ontario, Canada, the photographer Jessie Tarbox Beals' first job was to teach in a one-room schoolhouse near Williamsburg, Massachusetts. Her first camera was received gratis when she subscribed to a magazine.

During summer vacations, Beals worked as an itinerant photographer and, in 1893, taught in Greenfield, Massachusetts. Within seven years she and her husband, Alfred T. Beals, became full-time itinerant photographers.

Among her many honors, Beals was named official photographer for the World Exposition in St. Louis, Missouri (1904); earlier, she worked for the *Buffalo Inquirer and Courier* and, finally, established herself in New York.

Beals' photographic documents of people and places in New York were widely published in newspapers and magazines, including *American Art News*, *New York-Herald*, *Vogue*, and *Harper's Bazaar*. Her interests encompassed major architectural sights, cityscapes, landscapes, and the unfortunate children of the Big Apple who lived in wrenching poverty.

Bibliography
Alland, Alexander Sr. *Jessie Tarbox Beals: First Woman News Photographer*, 1978.
Browne, Turner, and Elaine Partnow. *Macmillan Biographical Encyclopedia of Photographic Artists and Innovators.* Macmillan, 1983.
Mann, Margery. *Women of Photography.* A Catalog. San Francisco Museum of Art, 1975.

Bean, Caroline van Hook (1879–1980)

Born in Washington, D.C., the painter Caroline van Hook Bean, after earning a Bachelor's degree from Smith College, Northampton, Massachusetts, studied her craft with the painters B.J. Blommers, William Merritt Chase, and John Singer Sargent.

A member of the Society of Washington Artists, Society of Washington Etchers, and the Washington Art Club—all in Washington, D.C., Bean exhibited work in museums and galleries, including the Bresler Gallery, Milwaukee, Wisconsin; Closson Gallery, Cincinnati, Ohio; High Museum of Art, Atlanta, Georgia; and others. Examples of her work are in private and public permanent collections.

Bibliography
Cosentino, Andrew J., and Henry H. Glassie. *The Capital Image, Painters in Washington, 1800–1915.* Washington, D.C.: National Museum of American Art, Smithsonian Institution Press, 1983.
New York City in Wartime (1918–1919). New York: Chapellier Galleries, 1970.

Bear, Shirley (1936–)

Maliseet artist Shirley Bear, from Perth-Andover, New Brunswick, Canada, derives inspiration for her realist and surrealist oils from petroglyphs, a deep spiritualism, political activism, and her feminist perspectives.

Bear has had a number of solo exhibitions of her work, including the Clement Cormier Gallery, Moncton (1982–1983); Restigouche Gallery, Campbellton (1982–1983); the University of St. Louis, Edmonston (1982–1983); and the Connexion Gallery, Frederickton (1988)—all in New Brunswick, Canada. She also showed at the House Gallery, Ottawa, Ontario (1988); at Mount St. Vincent University Gallery, Halifax, Nova Scotia (1990); and others.

She has had her work invited to many group exhibitions, such as the North American Indian House Gallery, New York City (1983); Atlantic Print Festival, Nova Scotia Gallery, Halifax (1984); Artistas Indigenas, Austin, Texas (1985); Galleria Principal, Altos de Chavon, Dominican Republic (1988); the Saw Gallery, Ottawa (1989); Mount St. Vincent University Gallery, Halifax (1990); and many others.

Board member of the Omniiak Native Artists and the Tobique Women's Group, Bear was artist-in-residence in the Dominican Republic (1988) and at St. Michaels Print Shop in Newfoundland (1983). Among other professional activities she held a Ford Foundation fellowship (1969–1970), curated exhibitions, served on the Women's Political Lobby to change the Indian Act (1980–1985), and was program director of the Fine Arts Program of T.R.I.B.E., Inc., Bar Harbor, Maine (1971–1972).

Bear describes her oil "Old Lady in Rocking Chair—Sogoi" (1986) as follows:

"Because we are the sum of what we have experienced, there comes into our lives persons who contribute to either the good or the bad of these experiences . . . (to) give us the sense of ourselves . . . Sogoi . . . a sense of solitary strength aided by the eagle spirit, is a contradiction. My view of this person personally does not sympathize with the feeling the painting conveys."

Bear's works are in the permanent collections of the New Brunswick Art Bank, the National Indian Art Centre, the National Museum of Civilization, the University of Moncton, and other public and private collections throughout Canada.

Bibliography
Bear, Shirley. *Changers: A Spiritual Renaissance.* A Catalog. National Indian Arts and Crafts Corporation, 1990.
Heard Museum Archives, Phoenix, Arizona.
Lippard, Lucy R. "Native Intelligence." *Voice* (December 27, 1983): 102.

Beauchemin, Micheline (1931–)

Born in Longueil, Québec, Canada, the artist Micheline Beauchemin studied art at the École des Beaux-Arts, Montréal. She continued her studies in Paris, France, at the Académie de la Grande Chaumière with Ossip Zadkine, and at the École des Beaux-Arts, Paris, where she learned printmaking and the art of stained glass.

Widely travelled in Europe, North Africa, and the Far East, Beauchemin made tapestries for the first time in 1953. The following year she exhibited tapestries and a stained-glass piece for a show at the Palais des Beaux-Arts, Chartres, France. In 1957 she had an exhibition at the Maison Canadienne of the Cíte Universitaire in Paris, France, and, two years later, returned to Canada.

Beauchemin exhibited two tapestries at the Canadian Pavilion, Brussels, Belgium (1958), and continued to show and accept commissions. In 1963 she created a large eighteen-by-nine-foot tapestry for the Grande Salle of the Place des Arts, Montréal. In 1966 she won the competition to create a curtain for the Opera House at the National Arts Centre, Ottawa—a project that won great acclaim. Examples of Beauchemin's work are in private and public permanent collections in many venues.

Bibliography

Gagnon, Claude-Lise. "Au mur: Micheline Beauchemin." *Vie des arts* 65 (Winter 1971–1972): 34–37, 92–93.

Jaque, Louis. "Un cas de jeunesse ardente." *Vie des arts* (Spring 1959): 13–17.

Sabbath, Lawrence. "Art in the Place des Arts." *Canadian Art* 21:1 (January–February 1964): 32–35.

Beaumont, Mona

A painter whose works reveal a certain wit and elegance, Mona Beaumont was born in Paris, France. She received her Bachelor's and Master's degrees from the University of California at Berkeley; took further graduate work at Harvard University and the Fogg Art Museum—both in Cambridge, Massachusetts; and studied painting with Hans Hofmann in New York City.

Beaumont has had many solo exhibitions of her work in the United States and abroad, including Galería Proteo, Mexico City, Mexico; Palace of the Legion of Honor, San Francisco, California; L'Armitière Gallery, Rouen, France; Galerie Alexandre Monnet, Brussels, Belgium; Honolulu Academy of Arts, Hawaii; and others. Her work has been invited to numerous group exhibitions throughout the world, including the Galerie Zodiaque, Geneva, Switzerland; the Grey Foundation, U.S. Artists "Tour of Asia," Washington, D.C.; the San Francisco Art Institute Travelling Exhibitions, California; and hosts of others.

Beaumont's work has received a number of important awards and honors, including the Grey Foundation Purchase Award (1963); the San Francisco Arts Festival Purchase Award and One-Person Exhibit Award (1966, 1975); the Ackerman Award, San Francisco Women Artists Annual (1968); and more.

Her works are in the permanent collections of the Hoover Foundation, Palo Alto, California; the Grey Foundation, Washington, D.C.; the Bulart Foundation, San Francisco, California; the Oakland Art Museum, California; and others.

Bibliography

Albright, Thomas. *Art in the San Francisco Bay Area: An Illustrated History*. University of California at Berkeley Press, 1985.

DeShong, Andrew. "Works on Paper—San Francisco Art Institute." *Artweek* (November 1974).

Who's Who in American Art. 19th ed. R.R. Bowker Co., 1991–1992.

Beaux, Cecilia (1855–1942)

Born in Philadelphia, Pennsylvania, in 1855, Cecelia Beaux lost her mother when she was young, and her distraught father returned to France, leaving his two daughters in the care of their maternal grandmother and two aunts in Philadelphia. As Beaux related in her autobiography, *Background with Figures*, she had the example of her Aunt Eliza Leavitt who always carried her sketchbook and pencil with her. As a consequence, Beaux observed in the home how both art and music were not playthings to be taken up lightly: "I already possessed the materials for oil painting, and had used them quite a little but without advice." Instruction in drawing and copying art were given to her in the studio of another relative, Katharine Drinker, who painted historical and Biblical subjects. Finally, Beaux's uncle, William Biddle, contributed financially to an arrangement for oil classes, whereby she and a classmate from Miss Lyman's School were to work from a model three mornings a week, and the painter William Sartain was to come from New York every fortnight to give a critique.

Once trained, Beaux attempted an ambitious composition of two full-length, life-size figures in a living room; she posed her older sister Aimée Ernesta, with her three-year-old son Henry S. Drinker Jr. seated in her lap. This painting, entitled "Les Derniers Jours d'Enfance," became a pivotal work in her career. Not only was it accepted into the Annual Exhibition of the Pennsylvania Academy of Fine Arts, but it won the Mary Smith prize for "the best painting by a resident woman artist." Another Philadelphia painter, Margaret Lesley Bush-Brown, was so impressed with this painting that she took it to France and entered it in the Paris Salon of 1887.

In January 1888 Beaux and a cousin left for a nineteen-month trip to Europe. In Paris Beaux studied at the Académie Julian with the painters Tony Robert-Fleury and William Bouguereau. She spent the summer with three Americans (her cousin May, the painter Lucy Conant, and Lucy's mother, Mrs. Catherine Scarborough Conant) at Concarneau on the coast of Brittany near Pont-Aven, where she studied with the plein-air painters Alexander Harrison and Charles Lazar. In the fall she visited Switzerland, Italy, and southern France. She had already copied Old Master paintings in the Louvre and was particularly delighted in the opportunity that this travel provided to see the Veroneses, Titians, and Tintorettos in Venice. After her return to Paris she enrolled in an evening class at Académie Colarossi in 1889 and also had her work critiqued at the atelier of Benjamin Constant. The Paris Salon of 1889 accepted her portrait of "Louise Kinsella." Before returning home she travelled to England that spring to visit an old friend who had married the eldest son of Charles Darwin and visited the National Gallery where she was enchanted by the Velázquez and Rembrandt paintings.

Back in her Philadelphia studio she firmly established herself as a portraitist. She won the Mary Smith prize at the Pennsylvania Academy again in 1891 and 1892 and was elected an associate of the National

Academy of Design in New York City in 1892 (rising to full member in 1903). In 1895 she became the first woman to be engaged as a full-time member of the faculty of the Pennsylvania Academy. She taught drawing and painting until 1916 and was in charge of portrait classes.

Some of her most impressive paintings come from this period: "Sita and Sarita" (1893–1894), of a woman dressed in white who is accompanied by a black cat posed on her shoulder, was purchased by the Luxembourg Museum in Paris; "Ernesta with Nurse" (1894, Metropolitan Museum), depicts a winsome child at her own short level and only the skirt of the attendant nurse is seen; "New England Woman" (1895, Pennsylvania Academy of Fine Arts), enlivens the white dress of the sitter by lavender passages; "Henry Sturgis Drinker" (1898, National Museum of American Art), shows the subject sitting near a window holding a contented yellow cat on his sparkling white suit. "Mother and Daughter" (1898, Pennsylvania Academy of Fine Arts), a painting of two women standing in long evening cloaks, won more prizes than any other (first prize at Carnegie Institute, a gold medal at the Exposition Universelle, Paris) (1900), and others.

She returned to Europe in 1896 when six of her portraits were exhibited at the Paris Salon. Her international reputation grew with this large a showing, and she was elected an associate of the Société Nationale des Beaux-Arts. In 1898 she became the first female recipient of the Pennsylvania Academy's gold medal of honor.

Beaux opened a studio in Washington Square, New York City at the turn of the century and experienced a surge of commissions from Mrs. Theodore Roosevelt (1902–1903), Mr. Richard Watson Gilder, editor of Century Monthly Magazine, and others.

After two sizable exhibitions of her works at the St. Botolph Club in Boston, Massachusetts (1897, 1904) and an exhibition at Durand-Ruel Gallery in New York City (1903) as well as receipt of a number of awards, such as a gold medal at the Pan-American Exposition in Buffalo, New York (1901), and a gold medal at the Universal Exposition, St. Louis, Missouri (1904), Beaux made a third trip to Paris in 1904, followed two years later by a trip to several countries, this time including Spain in order to see the Velázquez and Titian paintings in the Prado Museum. An honorary Doctoral degree was conferred on her by the University of Pennsylvania, Philadelphia, in 1908 and an honorary Master of Arts degree by Yale University, New Haven, Connecticut, in 1912. She had an exhibition at the Corcoran Gallery of Art, Washington, D.C. (1912), and at the Knoedler Gallery, New York City (1915, 1917).

In 1919 Beaux was among eight American painters chosen to do three portraits each of important international personages at the close of World War I for a national portrait gallery. Her three subjects were Cardinal Mercier, whom she painted in Malines, Belgium; the British Admiral Lord Beatty, whom she painted in London; and the French Premier Georges Clemenceau, who had just signed the Peace Treaty of Versailles. All three portraits are now in the National Museum of American Art, Washington, D.C. Beaux continued to be honored with awards, including a gold medal at the Art Institute of Chicago, Illinois (1921), and a gold medal in 1926 from the American Academy of Arts and Letters, New York City, which elected her a member in 1933 and which gave her the largest exhibition of her work during her lifetime in 1935 and 1936. In Paris in 1924 she suffered a broken hip which never healed properly, forcing her to walk with crutches toward the end of

her life and severely curtailing her artistic output. She died in Gloucester, Massachusetts, at "Green Alley," the spacious house and studio she had built in 1905 for her summer residence.

Beaux's style of painting had much in common with John Singer Sargent's: well-grasped facial features on tall, slim, elegant figures, often portrayed in their homes—sometimes depicted in shimmering daylight and other times bathed in a darker, warmer evening glow.

Eleanor Tufts

Bibliography
Bailey, Elizabeth Graham. "The Cecelia Beaux Papers." *Archives of American Art Journal* 13: 4 (1973): 14–19.
Beaux, Cecilia. *Background with Figures.* Houghton Mifflin, 1930.
Drinker, Jr., Henry S. *The Paintings and Drawings of Cecilia Beaux.* Pennsylvania Academy of Fine Arts, 1955.
Goodyear, Frank H., Jr. *Cecilia Beaux: Portrait of an Artist.* Pennsylvania Academy of Fine Arts, 1974.
Grafly, Dorothy. "Beaux, Cecilia." *Notable American Women*, Vol. 1. Belknap Press of Harvard University Press, 1971.
Stein, Judith. "Profile of Cecilia Beaux." *The Feminist Art Journal* 4 (Winter 1975–1976): 25–31.
Tufts, Eleanor. *American Women Artists, 1830–1940.* National Museum of Women in the Arts, 1974.
Whipple, Barbara. "The Eloquence of Cecilia Beaux." *American Artist* 38 (September 1974): 44–51, 80–85.

Beck, Margit

The painter Margit Beck was born in Tokay, Hungary, and studied art at the Institute of Fine Arts, Oradea Mare, Rumania; and the Art Students League, New York City.

Beck has held more than twenty-two solo exhibitions in museums and galleries and has had her work shown in group exhibitions, including the Art Institute of Chicago, Illinois; the Corcoran Gallery, Washington, D.C.; the Biennials at the Brooklyn Museum, New York; the Childe Hassam Purchase Award exhibitions at the American Academy and Institute of Arts and Letters, New York City; the Pennsylvania Academy of Fine Arts Annuals, Philadelphia, Pennsylvania; the Annuals at the Whitney Museum of American Art, New York City; and many others.

Winner of honors and awards, Beck was a resident fellow at the MacDowell Colony (1956, 1957, 1959, 1960, 1975); she won Childe Hassam Purchase Awards at the American Academy and Institute of Arts and Letters (1968, 1970, 1971); and medals of honor (1968, 1972) and the Stephen Hirsh Memorial Award—both from the Audubon Artists Society, New York City.

Examples of her work are in private and public permanent collections, including the Lyman Allyn Museum, New London, Connecticut; Norfolk Museum of Arts and Sciences, Virginia; J.B. Speed Museum. Louisville, Kentucky; the Whitney Museum of American Art, New York City; and others.

Bibliography
Gruen, John. "Margit Beck." *SoHo News* (March 3, 1975).
Paris, Jeanne. "Margit Beck." *Long Island Press* (March 30, 1975).
Who's Who in American Art. 20th ed. R.R. Bowker Co., 1993–1994.

Beck, Rosemarie (1925–)

Rosemarie Beck studied at several institutions of higher education, including Columbia University and New York University—both in New York City; and Oberlin College, Ohio.

Beck has held more than a dozen solo exhibitions in galleries and museums, including the Ingber Gallery, Peridot Gallery, and Poindexter Gallery—all in New York City. Her work has also been shown at the Art Institute of Chicago, Illinois; the National Academy and Institute of Arts and Letters, New York City; the Pennsylvania Academy of Fine Arts, Philadelphia; the Whitney Museum of American Art, New York City; and others.

A teacher of painting for many years at several colleges in New York and Connecticut, Beck has won honors and awards, such as grants from Ingram-Merrill (1967, 1979), and others. Examples of her work are in private and public permanent collections, including the Hirshhorn Museum and Sculpture Garden, Washington, D.C.; State University of New York (SUNY) at New Paltz; Vassar College, Poughkeepsie, New York; the Whitney Museum of American Art, New York City; and others.

Bibliography
Edgar, Natalie. "Rosemarie Beck." *Art News* 71:3 (May 1972): 10.
Kramer, Hilton. "Rosemary Beck (Ingber Gallery)." *The New York Times* (February 29, 1980).
O'Beil, Hedy. "Rosemarie Beck." *Arts Magazine* 54:10 (June 1980): 35–36.

Beckington, Alice (1868–1942)

Born in St. Charles, Missouri, the painter Alice Beckington learned her craft at the Art Students League, New York City, under the aegis of Beckwith; she also studied in Paris with Constant, Lazar, and Lefébvre.

Beckington exhibited work and won honors and awards in prestigious group shows, such as the Pan-American Exposition, Buffalo, New York (1901); St. Louis Exposition, Missouri (1904); the Brooklyn Society of Miniature Painters, New York City (1935); and others.

Beckington has been a member of the American Federation of Arts, the American Society of Miniature Painters, and the Pennsylvania Society of Miniature Painters. Examples of her work are in private and public permanent collections, including the Museum of Modern Art (MoMA), New York City; the Philadelphia Museum of Art, Pennsylvania; and others.

Bibliography
Fuller, Lucia Fairchild. "Modern American Miniature Painters." *Scribner's Magazine* 67 (March 1920): 381–384.
Merrick, Lula. "The Miniature in America." *International Studio* 76:310 (March 1923): 509–514.
Obituary. *Who's Who in American Art.* 4th ed. Washington, D.C.: American Federation of Arts, 1947.

Beerman, Miriam

The painter/printmaker Miriam Beerman was born in Providence, Rhode Island, and earned a Bachelor of Fine Arts degree at the Rhode Island School of Design in her native city; she did further study with Yasuo Kuniyoshi at the Art Students League, New York City; at the New School for Social Research, New York City, with Adja Yunkers; and studied printmaking in Atelier 17, Paris, France, with Stanley William Hayter.

Beerman's work has been exhibited in many solo and group shows in galleries and museums in the United States and abroad: from New York City to Cassis, France; from Newark, New Jersey, to Jerusalem, Israel. A "40-Year Retrospective" exhibition was held at the State Museum of New Jersey, Trenton, in 1991.

Winner of many awards and honors, Beerman, who served as a guest artist and teacher in several venues, has been the recipient of a CAPS grant from the New York State Council on the Arts (1971); a Childe Hassam purchase award from the American Academy and Institute of Arts and Letters, New York City (1977); a Camargo Foundation Award, France (1980); a distinguished artist grant from the New Jersey State Council on the Arts (1987); and others.

Examples of her oils and intaglio prints are in private and public permanent collections, including the Brooklyn Museum, the New School for Social Research, and the Whitney Museum of American Art—all in New York City; University of Oregon, Eugene; and others.

Bibliography
Schiff, Gert. *Images of Horror and Fantasy.* Harry N. Abrams, 1979.
Who's Who in American Art. 20th ed. R.R. Bowker Co., 1993–1994.

Behnke, Leigh (1946–)

Leigh Behnke is a representational painter known for her work with repetitive and sequential imagery. She was born in Hartford, Connecticut and received her early education in the Connecticut public school system. After one year at Southern Connecticut State College (now Southern Connecticut State University), she transferred to Pratt Institute in Brooklyn, New York, where she received a Bachelor of Fine Arts degree in 1969. She has since then lived in New York City, earning a Master of Arts degree at New York University in 1976. She has been on the faculty of the School of Visual Arts since 1978.

Originally known for her large-scale, conceptually-based watercolors, Behnke began showing with the Fischbach Gallery, New York City, in 1978. She was included, along with others in this group, including Jane Freilicher and Neil Welliver, in a revival of interest in "Painterly Realism," which gained national attention through several travelling shows. The first of these, "Real, Really Real, Super Real," was organized by the San Antonio Museum of Art, Texas, and travelled to museums throughout the United States in 1980 and 1981. A second show, "American Realism: Twentieth-Century Drawings and Watercolors," originated at the San Francisco Museum, California (1985) and travelled extensively until 1987. Her work has been seen in major museums across the country, including the downtown branch of the Whitney Museum, in a show called "Lower Manhattan from Sea to Sky" and at the Springfield Art Museum in Missouri in a watercolor survey entitled "Watercolor USA 1986: The Monumental Image."

The general format for Behnke's work has remained constant throughout her career, consisting of a series of multiple images presented together as a single painting. Initially these were identical in composition, but with alterations made to some aspect of the color system. Her interest in these paintings came out of an involvement with perceptual theory and are concerned with how the alteration of one component changes the perception of that image in both formal and associative ways. Since 1980 Behnke has been using this device of multiple imagery to explore a series of more complicated relationships, often in oil paint. She has stated that it is not the image itself that interests her, but rather the visual dialogue between the images. In her more recent work these are no longer always identical, and often not even related in their original source. The intent is to explore the commonality on a formal or associative level of what are often quite disparate sources. Her roots seem to come out of both conceptual art and from cinema.

Cie Goulet

Bibliography
Bastian, Linda. "Leigh Behnke." Women's Caucus for Art, *National Art Education Bulletin* (1985).
Chwast, Seymour, and Steven Heller. *The Art of New York*. Harry N. Abrams, 1983.
Finch, Christopher. *Twentieth-Century Watercolors*. Abbeville Press, 1989.
Friedman, Jon. Review, "Leigh Behnke." *Arts Magazine* (January 1980).
LeClaire, Charles. *The Art of Watercolor*. Prentice-Hall/Spectrum Books, 1985.
Marberger, Aladar. "New Faces/New Images." *Ocular Magazine* 5:4 (1980).
Martin, Alvin. *American Realism: Twentieth-Century Drawings and Watercolors*. Harry N. Abrams, 1986.

Beker, Gisela

The painter Gisela Beker was born in Zoppott, Germany; studied at the Kunstinstitut, Rostock, Germany (1948–1950); and did further study with Rudolf Kroll in Düsseldorf, Germany.

Beker has held many exhibitions of her work, including solo shows in museums and galleries: from New York City to Paris, France; from Phoenix, Arizona, to Terme, Turkey; and others.

Beker is the recipient of honors and awards at international venues. Examples of her work are in private and public permanent collections, including the Aldrich Museum of Contemporary Art, Ridgefield, Connecticut; Arts and Science Center, Baton Rouge, Louisiana; Palm Springs Museum, California; Syracuse University, New York; and others.

Bibliography
Battcock, Gregory. *Why Art?* Dutton, 1977.
"Gisela Beker's Art at Arts and Science Center." *Arts Magazine* (February 1975).
Who's Who in American Art. 20th ed. R.R. Bowker Co., 1993–1994.

Belfort-Chalat, Jacqueline (1930–)

The painter and sculptor Jacqueline Belfort-Chalat, a figurative artist, was born in Mt. Vernon, New York, and enjoyed a rich and varied education in the arts, including the study of sculpture with Frederick V. Guinzburg (1943) and Ruth Nickerson (1944). At Columbia University, New York City, she took further work with Oronzio Maldarelli and Ettore Salvatore (1947), then went to the Art Students League to work under Stuart Klonis in life drawing (1948). For the next two years, Belfort-Chalat studied dress design at the Fashion Institute of Technology, New York City, and attended the University of Chicago, Illinois, where she received a Bachelor of Arts degree (1948). From 1960 to 1962 she did graduate work at the Royal Academy of Fine Arts,

Copenhagen, Denmark.

Belfort-Chalat has had many solo and group exhibitions of her work, including the video, "Idea to Image," shown on CBS and the Religious Cable Network (1989); Hartwick College, Oneonta, New York (1985); Everson Museum, Syracuse, New York (1984, 1979); St. Joseph's College, Philadelphia, Pennsylvania (1976, 1986); Boston College, Chestnut Hill, Massachusetts (1974); Washington Gallery of Art, Washington, D.C. (1966); the National Collection of Fine Arts, Washington, D.C.; Charlottenborg Slot, Copenhagen, Denmark (1962); and others.

Belfort-Chalat received many commissions throughout the United States and abroad, such as "Tree Trunks" (1985–1987), a hammered copper piece twelve-by-fourteen-feet, Skaneatleles, New York; "Holy Family" (1983), a lifesize terra cotta relief for Central Square, New York City; "Ecce Homo" (1973), a lifesize acrylic painting on wood, Jesuit Curia, Rome, Italy; "Many Hands" (1964–1965), a three-ton wood carving, Government of Nigeria, Enugu, Nigeria; and many others.

Since 1969 Belfort-Chalat has been associated with LeMoyne College, Syracuse, New York from founding and continuing chair of fine arts (1969) to full professor (1985); she is active in church, cultural, community, and sporting activities.

Bibliography
Perry, Barbara. *American Ceramics*. Rizolli Publishers, 1989.
Who's Who in American Art. 19th ed. R.R. Bowker Co., 1991–1992.

Beling, Helen (1914–)

A native New Yorker, the sculptor Helen Beling studied at the National Academy of Design, New York, with Lee Lawrie and Paul Manship (1930–1937); she also studied with William Zorach at the Art Students League, New York City (1944–1945).

In addition to having held nine solo exhibitions in major museums and galleries, Beling has had her work shown in group exhibitions at the Pennsylvania Academy of Fine Arts, Philadelphia (1950–1966, 1984); the Metropolitan Museum of Art (1951); Sculptors Guild (1954–1983); Whitney Museum of American Art (1955); and the American Academy and Institute of Arts and Letters (1981)—all in New York City; and others.

Winner of honors and awards, Beling has received medals of honor (1965, 1980, 1986) and medals of merit (1980–1986) from the Audubon Artists Society, New York City; and others. Examples of her work are represented in private and public permanent collections.

Bibliography
Who's Who in American Art. 20th ed. R.R. Bowker Co., 1993–1994.

Bell, Lilian A. (1943–)

Internationally-known for her sculpture, assemblages, and, currently, for her installations, artists books, and fax art, Lilian A. Bell was born in Epping, Essex, England, and emigrated to the United States when she was twenty years old.

Bell was educated at the William Morris Technical School in London, England (1956–1960) and, during summers in 1959 and 1960, attended the University of Strasbourg, France, and the University of

Besançon, France, where she earned certificates in the German language, and French civilization and language respectively.

Bell has had solo exhibitions of her work in the United States and abroad, including the Keller Gallery, Salem, Oregon (1978); Willamette University, Salem, Oregon (1979); the São Paulo Museum of Art, Brazil (1982); the National Museum, San José, Costa Rica (1991); and many others.

Between 1972 and 1991 her work has been invited to more than eighty group exhibitions throughout the world, such as "The Paper Show," Portland Art Museum, Oregon (1972); "Biennial of the Pacific," Metropolitan Museum of Manila, the Philippines (1980); "Paper 3 Conference Exhibition," Visual Arts Center, Beer Sheva, Israel (1981); "Mini Paper Exhibition," Gallery Momoyo, Tokyo, Japan (1981); "Sculptural Books," Brighton Polytechnic Faculty of Art, England (1984); "Kunst aus papier," University of Basel, Switzerland (1991); and others.

Winner of honors and awards for her work as a paper artist, Bell was the recipient of a visual arts fellowship from the Western States Arts Foundation (1977) and an individual artist fellowship from the Oregon Arts Commission (1989). Widely travelled, she has done research on papermaking techniques in Japan, Polynesia/Hawaii, Samoa and Tonga, Israel, Brazil, and Mexico. She has offered workshops, lectured, and written extensively about her research throughout the world.

Her recent *Under the Table* series of paperworks, composed of rocks (made of cast paper), architectural fragments, and tables, provides an insight to Bell's wit and political satire. Her works are in private, public, and corporate permanent collections, including the Visual Art Center, Beer Sheva, Israel; Portland Art Museum, Oregon; University of Guam Isla Center, Mangilao, Micronesia; Western Oregon State College, Monmouth; the University of Oregon Museum of Art, Eugene; and many others.

Bibliography
Flores, Juan Carlos. "The Death of the Icon: The Post Modern Paper Sculpture of Lilian A. Bell." *Reflex* 4:2 (March–April 1990): 14–15.
Watson-Jones, Virginia. *Contemporary American Women Sculptors.* Oryx Press, 1986.
Who's Who in American Art. 19th ed. R.R. Bowker Co., 1991–1992.

Belmore, Rebecca (1960–)

"When I do anything (work), I ask myself . . . will it benefit the people?" This question, which Rebecca Belmore, born in Thunder Bay, northern Ontario, learned to ask, was learned from Freda McDonald, one of her Ojibwe elders. It has been the touchstone of her work, which combines the roles of performer, community animateur, instructor, as well as the maker of "powerful" objects. In the face of the ignorance and racism prevalent in the non-native population, Belmore's work has been marked by a search for ways to represent native women and, in doing so, to give them back their own voices—voices that have been forgotten, silenced, or ignored—and to find ways of ensuring that those voices will be heard by several different audiences.

Her major works include: "I'm a High-Tech Teepee Trauma Mama" (1986), in which Belmore, accompanied by her sisters, gives voice to the fraught and ironic contradictions under which they must live, with the refrain, "I'm a plastic replica of Mother Earth"; "Twelve Angry Crinolines" (1987), a performance through the streets of Thunder Bay; "Nah-Doe-Tah-Moe-Win" (1989), a series of "audio boxes," small, multi-dimensional representations of her heroines and one villain, including a sound component, shown in a circular configuration on the floor; and "Ayum-ee-aawach Oomama-mowan" (1991), dramatizes the fact that her people have a direct and loud voice. In a meadow in the Rocky Mountains, Belmore set up an enormous megaphone—two meters in diameter—through which the group of First Nations people she had assembled, including the chief of the local Stoney band, were able to address the earth directly. Belmore's own words began: "My heart is beating like a small drum, and I hope that you, Mother Earth, can feel it . . . I have watched my grandmother live very close to you, my mother the same. I have watched my grandmother show respect for all that you have given her . . ."

Charlotte Townsend-Gault

Bibliography
Bear, Shirley. *Changers: A Spiritual Renaissance.* A Catalog. National Indian Arts and Crafts Corporation, 1990.
Podedworny, Carol. "Okanata." *C Magazine*: 32 (Winter 1991).
Townsend-Gault, Charlotte. "Having Voices and Using Them." *Arts Magazine* (February 1991).

Beloff, Angelina (1879–1969)

Born in St. Petersburg, Russia, in 1879, Angelina Beloff came from a middle-class intellectual family; her father was a magistrate who did not appreciate his daughter's artistic sensibilities, despite the fact that she sketched constantly, from childhood on. In university, Beloff studied mathematics, science, and biology—acceding to her father's wishes—but she also took night classes in painting to satisfy her own.

In 1904 Beloff won a scholarship to the St. Petersburg Academy of Fine Arts, where after four years she was licensed as a teacher of drawing.

The deaths of her parents and her oldest brother, soon after she graduated, provided her with a certain freedom, a modest income, and little need to concern herself with her other two brothers, as they were already married. Consequently, in 1909, she continued her art education in Paris and spent several baffling and frustrating months studying with Henri Matisse. Beloff then worked in the Montmartre atelier of a Catalan painter, Anglada Camarassa. Still thirsting for more art experiences, she learned metal engraving from an English engraver and wood engraving from a Swedish woman printmaker.

With a close friend, the painter Maria Blanchard, she took a trip to Brugge, Belgium, and there met Diego Rivera—who was to become her husband. They spent the summer of 1914 on a walking, sketching tour, exploring Spain. Ever painting, their friends included many of the best-known artists of the time, including Pablo Picasso, Henri Matisse, André Derain, Amedeo Modigliani, Aristide Maillol, Charles Despiau, and the poets and writers Jean Cocteau, Guillaume Apollinaire, and Max Jacob, among others. A child, Diego, was born in 1916; he died fourteen months later. When Rivera left her in Paris to return to Mexico, Beloff worked mornings as a restorer for seven years; she painted and made prints in the afternoons. Those early engravings are in the permanent collections of the Bibliothèque de Beaux-Arts et Archeologie, Paris, and the Musée de l'Havre.

Beloff illustrated many books between the years 1925 and 1931, among which were works by André Maurois, Charles Vidrac, Jack London, a complete edition of Jean Baptist Molière, and others.

In 1932 Beloff settled in Mexico to remain there until her death in 1969. She was employed as a teacher by the Secretaría de Educación Pública and had her first show in Mexico in the art gallery of the Secretariat. For fifteen years she taught drawing classes in the Secondary Technical School, No. 6; later on, she taught a class in French at the School of the Book Arts, Mexico City, Mexico.

Her interest in the puppet theater led to a commission by the Teatro Guiñol in 1938 to write a book on the subject; Beloff completed it after six months of study and travel in Paris, Brussels, and Geneva. The Secretaría de Educación Pública published her landmark study, *Muñecos animados: Historia, técnica, y función educativa del teatro de muñecos en México y en el mundo* (Animated Puppets: History, Technique, and Educative Function of Puppet Theatres in Mexico and in the World), in 1945.

Beloff exhibited her paintings in Mexico and abroad; she did landscapes, portraits, still lifes, and flowers in oil, gouache, and watercolor. Her prints were shown with the Society of Mexican Engravers in Mexico, the United States, and Europe. Her work, from its beginning in Mexico, was shown by Inés Amor in her Galería de Arte Mexicano. Beloff was also a founding member of the Salón de la Plástica Mexicana and myriad other groups.

The retrospective of her work in the Museo del Palacio de Bellas Artes, Mexico City, in 1986, brought together the life of an artist, an artist whose work was versatile, eloquent, harmonious, and full of life.

Bibliography
Alvarez, José Rogelio, et al. *Enciclopedia de México.* Secretaría de
    Educación Pública, 1987.
Angelina Beloff: Su Obra, 1879–1969. A Catalog. Museo del Palacio de
    Bellas Artes, 1986.
Beloff, Angelina. *Muñecos animados: Historia, tecnica, y función educativa
    del teatro de muñecos en México y en el mundo.* Secretaría de
    Educación Pública, 1945.
———. *My Art, My Life.* Citadel Press, 1960.
———. *Memorias.* Universidad Nacional Autónoma de Mexico, 1986.

Bender, Beverly (1918–)

Born in Washington, D.C., Beverly Bender is a sculptor whose preferred medium is stone, and whose preferred subjects are animals. She received her Bachelor's degree from Knox College, Galesburg, Illinois, and studied sculpture in New York City at the Art Students League, the Sculpture Center, and the Museum of Natural History.

During World War II Bender worked in the testing laboratories of Chance-Vought and modeled children in miniature in her spare time; later, in the Art Department of Johns-Manville, where she worked for thirty-two years, Bender used her off-hours to produce her first stone sculptures of animals.

She has held solo exhibitions of her work throughout the United States, including the Dawson Grist Mill Gallery, Chester, Vermont; the Southern Vermont Art Center, Manchester; and the Hiram Halle Memorial Library, Pound Ridge, New York. Her work has been selected in juried group exhibitions throughout the country for many years.

Bender serves on the board of the Society of Animal Artists and has been on the boards of the Catharine Lorillard Wolfe Art Club and the Pen and Brush Art Club—both in New York City. She is also a participant in the American Artists Professional League, the Knickerbocker Artists, and others in the same city.

Bender has won awards from many arts groups for her work, including the Catharine Lorillard Wolfe Art Club (1969–1990); the Knickerbocker Artists (1974, 1975, 1983); the Hudson Valley Art Association, and the Pen and Brush Art Club, Knox College, Galesburg, Illinois (1979); and the Society of Animal Artists award of excellence presented for the highest standards of artistic achievement in the field of animal art (1987, 1989).

Bender's commissioned works are in many private collections and include a memorial work at Mystic Seaport, Connecticut, and another in the Schmidgall Collection of 19th and 20th Century Animal Sculpture. She is represented in the Children's Wing of the Museum in Norwich, Connecticut.

Bibliography
Dictionary of American Sculptors: 18th Century to the Present. Glenn B.
    Opitz, ed. Apollo, 1984.
*Mantle Fielding's Dictionary of American Painters, Sculptors, and
    Engravers.* Glenn B. Opitz, ed. Apollo, 1986.
Who's Who in American Art. 19th ed. R.R. Bowker Co., 1991–1992.

Bengelsdorf (Browne), Rosalind (1916–1979)

A painter and art writer, Rosalind Bengelsdorf was a New York City native who studied with realist artists at the Art Students League before spending a year (1934–1935) at Germany's Annot School of Art, where she was trained in the principles of abstract form. She returned to America and in 1935 enrolled in Hans Hofmann's New York school; there she was profoundly affected by his teachings, including his "pushpull" theory relating to the interaction of forms and colors. In 1936 Bengelsdorf co-founded the American Abstract Artists—a small group committed to unifying abstract artists in America and continuing European experimentation with abstraction. She participated in the American Abstract Artists' (A.A.A.) first group show in 1937 at New York's Squibb Building. A pioneering spokeswoman for American abstractionism during a historical period generally hostile to it, Bengelsdorf in 1938 wrote an essay, "The New Realism," maintaining that abstract art could communicate a deeper, "keener account of reality" than traditional, representational art. In her view, the abstract artist, rather than avoiding social responsibility, was helping to improve society. Between 1936 and 1939 Bengelsdorf was employed in the Federal Art Project's Mural Division and in 1937 to 1938 produced a large mural for the Central Nurses' Home on New York City's Welfare Island; this mural's hard-edged and biomorphic forms invite comparison with not only Pablo Picasso's work but also Arshile Gorky's contemporaneous abstract mural for the Newark, New Jersey, airport. After Bengelsdorf in 1940 married the avant-garde painter George Byron Browne and had a son, she reduced her painting activity and turned instead to a new career as a writer, critic, and teacher. She published widely, was until 1972 an editorial associate for *Art News,* and, up to her death, conducted courses treating the creative process at New York's School for Social Research.

Victor Koshkin-Youritzin

Bibliography

Bengelsdorf, Rosalind. "The New Realism." *American Abstract Artists.* New York: American Abstract Artists, 1938. n.p. Essay VII.

Dunford, Penny. *A Biographical Dictionary of Women Artists in Europe and America since 1850.* Philadelphia: University of Pennsylvania Press, 1989, 26.

Marling, Karal Ann, and Helen A. Harrison. *7 American Women: The Depression Decade.* New York: A.I.R. Gallery, 1976, 18–20.

Rubinstein, Charlotte Streifer. *American Women Artists: From Early Indian Times to the Present.* Avon, 1982, 245–46.

Benglis, Lynda (1941–)

Born in Lake Charles, Louisiana, and educated at H. Sophie Newcomb College, Tulane University, New Orleans, where she received her Bachelor's degree in 1964, Lynda Benglis won a Yale-Norfolk Summer School scholarship, Connecticut (1963) and a Max Beckmann scholarship (1965), which allowed her to attend the Brooklyn Museum Art School, New York.

Since 1969 Benglis has held more than seventy-five solo exhibitions of her work in galleries, universities, and museums throughout the United States and abroad, a dozen of which were shown at the Paula Cooper Gallery in New York City. Benglis's work in painting, papermaking, printmaking, glass, ceramics, video, and sculpture has been invited to many two-person and myriad group exhibitions (almost 300) throughout the world, including New York City; Boston, Massachusetts; Denver, Colorado; Los Angeles, California; Houston, Texas; Chicago, Illinois; Trenton, New Jersey; Palm Beach, Florida; Toronto, Canada; Monte Carlo, Monaco; Stockholm, Sweden; Madrid, Spain; Tokyo, Japan; Genoa, Italy; Paris, France; and Auckland, New Zealand.

Winner of many honors for her work, Benglis won a Guggenheim Foundation fellowship (1975); an Artpark grant (1976); an Australian Art Council Award (1976); a National Endowment for the Arts grant (1979); a Minos Beach Art Symposium grant and another from the Delphi Art Symposium (1988); a grant from the Olympiad of Art Sculpture Park, Korea (1988); and a grant from the National Council of Art Administration (1989).

She has been a member of the professoriate or a visiting artist at various art schools, institutes, colleges, and universities, including the University of Rochester, New York (1970–1972); Princeton University, New Jersey (1975); University of Arizona, Tucson (1982); School of Visual Arts (1985–1987); and others.

Benglis weds technology and a state of excitement, using seemingly contradictory materials, to re-create new spatial experiences for the viewer. A recent, not atypical sculpture, "Eclat" (1990), transmutes ordinary accordion-pleated steel mesh, through a magical process, into a series of golden, spiral-shelled conches.

Her work is housed in public, private, and corporate permanent collections, including the High Museum, Atlanta, Georgia; the Albright-Knox Art Gallery, Buffalo, New York; the National Gallery of Australia, Canberra; Israel Museum, Jerusalem; the New Orleans Museum of Art, Louisiana; the Museum of Modern Art (MoMA), Guggenheim Museum, New York University, and the Whitney Museum of American Art—all in New York City; the Hokkaido Museum of Modern Art, Sapporo, Japan; the Corcoran Gallery of Art and the National Museum of American Art—both in Washington, D.C.; and others.

Bibliography

Contemporary Sculpture: Selections from the Collection of the Museum of Modern Art. New York: The Museum of Modern Art, 1979.

Lippard, Lucy R. "Intruders: Lynda Benglis and Adrian Piper." *Breakthroughs: Avant-Garde Artists in Europe and America, 1950–1990.* 1991, 124–31.

Plagens, Peter. "Objects of Affection." Newsweek (June 3, 1991): 68.

Watson-Jones, Virginia. *Contemporary American Women Sculptors.* Oryx Press, 1986.

Bennett, Philomene (1935–)

Born in Lincoln, Nebraska, the painter/ceramist/printmaker Philomene Bennett attended the University of Nebraska in her native city, where she received her Bachelor of Fine Arts degree in 1956.

Bennett has had almost 100 solo, two-person, and group exhibitions of her work throughout the United States between 1956 and 1991, including her first honorable mention and purchase award at the 6th Mid-America Exhibition, Atkins Museum, Kansas City, Missouri (1956); an award at "Women Artists," University of Missouri, Kansas City (1977); "Art from HELICON NINE," Women's Bank, New York City (1979); "Women in Art," (National exhibition), Suzanne Brown Gallery, Scottsdale, Arizona (1981); "Solo Exhibition," Topeka Library, Kansas (1983); "Invitational: 2-Person Exhibition," Wesleyan University, Lincoln, Nebraska (1985); "Inaugural Exhibition: Group Show," National Museum of Women in the Arts, Washington, D.C. (1987); "Coast to Coast: 4 Women," Andrea Ross Gallery, Santa Monica, California (1990); and many others.

Bennett has executed many commissions, including "Tornado-Emerald City," (1987), a sculpture for the Hickok-Dible Co.; "Celebration" (1983), a monotype suite for the Kansas City Arts Council; a ten-by-twelve-foot abstract mural (1974) for the Western Crown Center Hotel, Kansas City, Missouri; "Thirteen Stained-Glass Windows" (1975) for St. Charles' Church, Kansas City North, Missouri; "Fourteen Stations of the Cross" (1977) for Conway Chapel, Rockhurst College, Kansas City, Missouri; and others for major corporations.

Member of a number of professional art organizations, lecturer and keynote speaker, cofounder and past-president of the Kansas City Artists Coalition, Bennett has been a nominee for the National Artist's Award (1984, 1985, and 1987). Her work is in the permanent collections of museums and corporations throughout the United States, including the National Museum of Women in the Arts, Washington, D.C.; Nelson-Atkins Museum of Art, Kansas City, Missouri; Muchnic Art Museum, Atchison, Kansas; Albrecht Museum, St. Joseph, Missouri; Prudential Life Insurance, New York City; American Express, Salt Lake City, Utah; and many others.

Bibliography

Collins, J.L. *Women Artists in America II.* University of Tennessee Press, 1975.

Hoffman, Don. "Portraits." *The Kansas City Star* (October 13, 1985).

Who's Who in American Art. 19th ed. R.R. Bowker Co., 1991–1992.

Benson, Patricia S. (1941–)

The printmaker Patricia S. Benson was born in Philadelphia, Pennsylvania, and earned a Bachelor of Fine Arts degree from Michigan State

University, East Lansing (1963), where she studied with John De Martelly. She received a Master of Fine Arts degree from Florida State University, Tallahassee, four years later, under the direction of Arthur Deshaies.

Benson has shown her intaglio and embossed Lucite prints in major exhibitions in the United States and abroad, including the Whitney Museum of American Art, New York City (1971); an extensive tour of South American venues (1972–1975); Belgrade, Yugoslavia and a tour of Eastern Europe (1971); the University of Hawaii, Hilo (1976–1977); the Library of Congress National Print Exhibition, Washington, D.C. (1969); an exhibition of Maine Coast Artists, Rockport (1979); and many others.

Winner of purchase awards and honors in Alaska, North Dakota, and California, among others, Benson taught printmaking in universities and art institutes in Florida and California. Examples of her work are in private and public permanent collections in the United States and abroad, including the Anchorage Fine Arts Museum, Alaska; Brooklyn Museum, New York; California Palace of the Legion of Honor, San Francisco; Cincinnati Museum of Art, Ohio; U.S. embassies throughout the world; and others.

Bibliography
Lippe, Stewart. *Prints of Patricia Benson.* A Film. 1973.
"Review." *Artforum* (April 1971).
Who's Who in American Art. 15th ed. R.R. Bowker Co., 1982.

Benton, Suzanne (1936–)

Suzanne Benton was born in Brooklyn, New York, and received her Bachelor of Fine Arts degree from Queens College, New York, in 1956. She is a maker of welded metal masks used in performances that grow out of history, myth, and religion; a printmaker with a fondness for monotypes created on handmade papers showing evidence of *chine collé*; and a sculptor of multimedia works containing secret compartments not to be opened before the year 2000.

Benton expanded her art vocabulary through further study at the Art Students League, New York City; the Brooklyn Museum School, New York; the Silvermine College of Art, New Canaan, and the Wooster Community Art Center, Danbury—both in Connecticut; and through worldwide contacts with various cultures.

During the last three decades Benton has held myriad solo and group exhibitions and performances in the United States and abroad, including Yale University, New Haven, Connecticut (1963); Ruth White Gallery, New York City (1969); Lincoln Center, New York City (1971); the Metropolitan Museum of Art, New York City (1976); "Masks and Other Works," exhibited and performed in fourteen Asian, African, and European countries on a worldwide journey (1976–1977); a clutch of universities, colleges, and art schools in the United States, Germany, England, the Netherlands, Turkey, and Greece (1977–1991).

Winner of many honors for her work Benton was the recipient of artists grants from the Connecticut Commission on the Arts (1973, 1974); and U.S. Information Service grants to Yugoslavia (1978) and Tunis (1983). She was voted Outstanding Connecticut Woman Sculptor, United Nations, New York (1988); and many others.

She is an ardent feminist; founder and organizer of Connecticut Feminists in the Arts; active in N.O.W. (National Organization of Women); a prodigious research worker seeking ever new sources for her work; set designer and producer; national coordinator for the International Womens Arts Festival (1973–1975); artist-in-residence, teacher, presenter of workshops at many universities; art consultant; art and mythology tour leader to Greece (1985); panelist; guest artist; and world traveller.

Benton's work is in many private, corporate, and public permanent collections throughout the world, including the National Museum of Modern Art, New Delhi, India; Tokyo School of Fine Arts, Japan; Birla Academy, Calcutta, India; Ewha University, Seoul, Korea; Deree Pierce Colleges, Athens, Greece; and others.

Bibliography
Benton, Suzanne. *The Art of Welded Sculpture.* Van Nostrand Reinhold, 1975.
Who's Who in American Art. 19th ed. R.R. Bowker Co., 1991–1992.

Berge, Dorothy (1923–)

Born in Ottawa, Illinois, the sculptor Dorothy Berge won a summer session scholarship to the Cranbrook Academy of Art, Bloomfield Hills, Michigan (1944); earned a Bachelor's degree from St. Olaf College, Northfield, Minnesota (1945); attended the School of the Art Institute of Chicago, Illinois (1946); received a Bachelor of Fine Arts degree from the Minneapolis School of Art, Minnesota (1950); studied with Ivan Mestrovic at Syracuse University, New York, the following year; and was a recipient of a Master of Visual Arts degree from Georgia State College, Atlanta (1976).

Berge has held solo exhibitions at the Walker Art Center (1960); and the Kilbride-Bradley Gallery (1964)—both in Minneapolis, Minnesota; the High Museum of Art (1968); and Image South Gallery (1972)—both in Atlanta, Georgia; St. Olaf College, Northfield, Minnesota (1990); and others. Her work has been invited to many group exhibitions throughout the United States, including "Recent Sculpture, USA," at the Museum of Modern Art in New York City.

A former teacher at art schools and colleges, Berge has received awards and honors and has executed many sculpture commissions for private, public, and corporate sponsors. Examples of her work are sited in many venues, including the High Museum of Art, Atlanta, Georgia; Iowa State Teachers College (now Iowa State University), Ames; Minneapolis Institute of Art, University of Minnesota and Walker Art Center—all in Minneapolis, Minnesota; St. Olaf College, Northfield, Minnesota; the Nelson Rockefeller Collection, New York City; and others.

Bibliography
"Abstract Sculptures, Paintings in Dual Show at Heath Gallery." *The Atlanta Journal* (September 12, 1979).
"Recent Sculpture U.S.A." *Museum of Modern Art Bulletin* 26:3 (Spring 1959).
Watson-Jones, Virginia. *Contemporary American Women Sculptors.* Oryx Press, 1986.

Bergeron, Suzanne (1930–)

Known as an abstract painter of managed fury, Suzanne Bergeron was born in Causapscal, Gaspé Peninsula, Québec. She studied painting with Jean-Paul Lemieux and others at the École des Beaux-Arts, where she graduated with honors in 1953. Two years later she received second prize at the Concours Artistiques de la Province de Québec and went to Paris, France, the following year, where she won the Prix de la Ville de Paris and a bursary from the Canadian government. Bergeron took further study at the École du Louvre, Paris (1957–1958); and exhibited a painting, "Arrière Port," at the 2nd Biennial Exhibition of Canadian Art, 1957, which was acquired by the National Gallery of Canada, Ottawa.

Bergeron has held many solo exhibitions of her work in galleries and museums, including the Agnes Lefort Gallery, Montréal, Québec (where she held her first solo show); the Roberts Gallery, Toronto, Canada; and others. Her paintings have been invited to numerous group exhibitions in Europe and North America, such as the École de Paris, which travelled through France (1957); the 3rd and 5th Biennial Exhibition of Canadian Painting, National Gallery, Ottawa (1959, 1963); the New Delhi International, India (1956); the International Guggenheim Exhibition (1957); the Biennial Museo de Arte Moderna, São Paulo, Brazil (1959); and many others.

Bergeron's work is housed in the permanent collections of museums and galleries, including the Art Gallery of Ontario, Toronto; Montréal Museum of Fine Arts; the National Gallery, Ottawa; the Québec Provincial Museum—all in Canada; and others.

Bibliography

Folch, Jacques. "Une Romantique." *Vie des arts* 14 (Spring 1959: 23–25.
Fulford, Robert. "Suzanne Bergeron." *Canadian Art* 18:1 (January–February 1961): 10–11.
National Gallery of Canada Catalogue of Painting and Sculpture. Vol. 3, Canadian School. R.H. Hubbard, 1960.

Berlin, Beatrice (1922–)

Born in Philadelphia, Pennsylvania, the printmaker/painter Beatrice Berlin received her art education at the Moore College of Art in her native city. She also studied printmaking with Sam Maitin and Hitoshi Nakazato. Recently, she wrote: "I don't think it's so terrible to start a career when you're mature . . . . For me, art isn't simply a matter of creating images—it's a way of life."

Between 1965 and 1989 Berlin has held more than forty solo exhibitions of her drypoints, watercolors, and collagraphs in galleries, museums, and universities in the United States and abroad; and more than four score group exhibitions, including the "Annuals" at the Philadelphia Watercolor Club, Pennsylvania (1968–1989); the American Color Print Society, Philadelphia, Pennsylvania (1969–1984); the Philadelphia Print Club, Pennsylvania (1969, 1973, 1975); Metropolitan Museum of Art, Tokyo, Japan; and many others.

Berlin has been a teacher and lecturer in the Philadelphia area and New Jersey for a number of years; a winner of honors and awards for her prints and watercolors between 1966 and 1984; and a board member of Artists Equity Association (1982–1990) and the California Society of Printmakers, Los Angeles (1983–1984). Her work is represented in private, public, and corporate permanent collections, including the Philadelphia Museum of Art, Pennsylvania; Brooklyn Museum, New York; the Fred Grunwald Collection, University of California at Los Angeles (UCLA); New York Public Library, New York City; Temple University, Philadelphia, Pennsylvania; University of Pennsylvania, Philadelphia; Atlantic Richfield Company (ARCO) collection; Bank

of San Francisco, California; Achenbach Collection, San Francisco Museum of Art, California; and many others.

Bibliography

Frym, Gloria. *Second Stories.* Chronicle Books, 1979.
Haber, Karen. "Beatrice Berlin." *American Artist Magazine* (May 1989): 64–67.
Wenninger, Mary Ann. *Collagraph Printmaking.* Watson-Guptill, 1975.
Who's Who in American Art. 19th ed. R.R. Bowker Co., 1991–1992.

Berman, Ariane R. (1937–)

Born in Danzig, Poland, the painter/printmaker Ariane R. Berman earned a Bachelor of Fine Arts degree at Hunter College, New York (1959), and a graduate scholarship to Yale University, New Haven, Connecticut. From 1959 to 1962, until she received a Master of Fine Arts degree, Berman was on full scholarship to Yale University. She took further study in Paris, France, on fellowships awarded by the American Association of University Women and the Fondation des États-Unis (1962–1963).

Berman has held more than fifty solo exhibitions of her acrylic paintings and screen prints in museums and galleries in the United States and abroad, including Gallery 84, New York City (1992); Concordia College, Bronxville, New York (1989); Phoenix Gallery, New York City (1985, 1987); Northwood Institute, Michigan (1984); Philadelphia Art Alliance, Pennsylvania (1980); Galleria d'Arte Helioart, Rome, Italy (1974); Fontana Gallery, Pennsylvania (1963, 1971, 1974); Galleria San Sebastianello, Rome, Italy; Graphic Art Gallery, Tel Aviv, Israel (1973); and many others.

Berman has been the recipient of many honors and awards from universities and art associations for her precisionist, richly-hued representational imagery. Her work has been invited to more than 150 group exhibitions throughout the world. She has executed many painting and print editions on commission and was visiting artist at the artist's colony, Mishkenot Sha'ananim, Jerusalem, Israel (1993–1994).

Berman's work is represented in private, public, and corporate permanent collections, including the Metropolitan Museum of Art, New York City; Philadelphia Museum of Art, Pennsylvania; Purdue University, Bloomington, Indiana; Hearst Corporation; American Color Print Society, Philadelphia, Pennsylvania; Israel Ministry of Tourism; and many others. "Seaside" (1992), a not atypical work, presents a barefoot, stylized female sitting on a railing overlooking the water; the ordered composition is rendered in a cool, subtle palette.

Bibliography

"Ariane R. Berman alla Galleria San Sebastianello." *Il Giornale del Mezzogiorno.* Rome. (December 27, 1973): 6.
"Berman: Pain Behind the Plastic." *The Milwaukee Journal* (April 21, 1974).
Farber, Howard. "Ariane R. Berman's Extended Family of Colorful Forms." *Artspeak* (October 1992).
Who's Who in American Art. 19th ed. R.R. Bowker Co., 1991–1992.

Berman, Vivian (1928–)

A native New Yorker, the printmaker Vivian Berman earned a Bachelor of Fine Arts degree at the Cooper Union, New York City, and also studied at Brandeis University, Waltham, Massachusetts, and the Art Students League, New York City.

Berman has held more than a dozen solo exhibitions of her prints between 1969 and 1991; she has had her work in many two- and four-artist shows in galleries, including the University of Wyoming, Laramie (1982); Gallery on the Green, Lexington, Massachusetts (1981, 1988); Rhode Island College of Design, Providence (1973); and many others. Her work has been invited to myriad prestigious group exhibitions—from Hong Kong to Brooklyn, New York; from Boston, Massachusetts, to Bradford, England; from Darien, Connecticut, to Haifa, Israel.

Berman has been the recipient of honors, purchase prizes, and awards for her prints from the Library of Congress, Washington, D.C.; Western New Mexico University, Silver City; Springfield Museum of Art; Boston Printmakers; and Cambridge Art Association Print Show—all in Massachusetts; and she was the recipient of a MacDowell Colony fellowship (1981).

Her work is represented in private, public, and corporate permanent collections in the Library of Congress, Washington, D.C.; Dartmouth College, Hanover, New Hampshire; Boston Public Library, Massachusetts; Pennsylvania Academy of Fine Arts, Philadelphia; De Cordova Museum, Lincoln, Massachusetts; IBM; Drexel-Burnham; and many others.

Bibliography

Romano, Clare, and John Ross. *The Complete Collagraph*. Macmillan, 1980.
Wenninger, Maryanne. *Collagraph Printmaking*. Watson-Guptill, 1978.
Who's Who in American Art. 19th ed. R.R. Bowker Co., 1991–1992.

Bernardi, Rosemarie T. (1951–)

Printmaker, artist, educator, Rosemarie T. Bernardi's passions for literature, psychology, drawing, and photography have led to her creative work in the exploration of photo etching processes. Born in Detroit, Michigan, Bernardi studied art at the Detroit Society of Arts and Crafts (1965–1970), under the tutelage of Brenda Goodman; she received her Bachelor of Fine Arts degree with honors from St. Mary's College, Orchard Lake, Michigan in 1974 and won her Master of Fine Arts degree in printmaking from the University of Cincinnati, Ohio, in 1977. Bernardi also worked with Douglas Kinsey in printmaking at the University of Notre Dame, Indiana, and in 1970–1971 was in Rome, Italy, obtaining a liberal and aesthetic education in the Eternal City.

Bernardi has participated in more than 100 national and international juried print exhibitions, including the Philadelphia Print Club International, Pennsylvania (1981); Cabo Frio International Exhibition, Brazil (1983); and the 3rd International Biennial Print Exhibition, Taipei, Taiwan (1988). She has garnered over twenty awards from such long-established national print exhibitions as the Bradley National, Peoria, Illinois (1989); the North Dakota National, Minot (1986); and Potsdam Prints, New York (1982).

Since 1977 Bernardi has taught at the University of Alabama, Huntsville (1977–1980); the University of Delaware, Newark (1980–1988); and the University of Arizona, Tucson (1988 to present). She holds professional memberships in the Society of American Graphic Artists, the Boston Printmakers, the Philadelphia Print Club, and the College Art Association.

"Studies in Hysteria" (1991), an ongoing installation of intaglio, charcoal, text, and xerox works, is Bernardi's most recent deconstructive study of nineteenth-century science, psychology, and media. Her work is in the permanent collections of the Philadelphia Museum of Art, Pennsylvania; the Montgomery Museum of Art, Alabama; the Roswell Museum and Art Center, New Mexico; and others. Bernardi has been the recipient of many grants, including a National Endowment for the Arts (NEA) individual artists fellowship in printmaking (1980); a year-long artist-in-residence grant at the Roswell Museum and Art Center, New Mexico (1980–1981); and a clutch of MacDowell Colony fellowships, Peterborough, New Hampshire (1983, 1984, 1986, 1988, and 1990).

Bibliography

Printed by Women. A Catalog. A National Exhibition of Prints and Photography. Essays by Ofelia Garcia and Judith Brodsky. Port of History Museum, 1983.
Romano, Clare, and John Ross. *The Complete Printmaker*, 3rd ed. The Free Press, 1989.

Bernhard, Ruth (1905–)

Born in Berlin, Germany, Ruth Bernhard studied the history of art and typography at the Akademie der Künste in Berlin (1926–1927). She emigrated to New York City (1927) and, after several years, started a career as a freelance photographer. On a visit to California (1935), Bernhard, by chance, met Edward Weston and was indelibly influenced by his powerful photographic statements.

Bernhard moved to Los Angeles, California, in 1936 and held her first solo exhibition of photographs at the Jake Zeitlin Gallery, which was soon followed by "Eye Behind the Camera," at the Pacific Institute of Music and Art—both in Los Angeles. She has held solo exhibitions of her photographs in more than fifty public and private institutions in the United States and abroad, including a major retrospective at the Institute for Cultural Relations, Mexico City, Mexico (1956); Neikrug Gallery (1971); and the Witkin Gallery (1977)—both in New York City; Canon Gallery, Amsterdam, The Netherlands (1978); Galerie Athanor 538, Marseille, France (1983); and P.G.I. Gallery, Tokyo, Japan (1983). "The Eternal Body," a travelling show which toured the United States and Europe, opened at the San Francisco Museum of Modern Art (1986) and closed at the Preus Fotomuseum, Horten, Norway (1989).

Her work has been invited to group exhibitions at prestigious institutions throughout the world, such as "Photography in the Fine Arts," Metropolitan Museum of Art, New York City (1967); "Recollections: 10 Women of Photography," a travelling show which toured the United States; Museum of Art, University of Oregon, Eugene (1982); "Photography in California," a travelling show which toured the United States and Europe; San Francisco Museum of Modern Art, California (1984); and others.

In the mid-1950s Bernhard offered private classes and workshops on "Photographing the Nude" and "The Art of Feeling," and critiquing sessions for amateur and professional photographers; she began to teach for the University of California (Berkeley) Extension in San Francisco in 1967 and offered seminars on "Seeing and Awareness." She also taught at Utah State University, Logan, and Columbia University, New York City.

Winner of many honors and awards for her work, Bernhard was

the recipient of the National Urban League Award (1961); the Dorothea Lange Award, Oakland Museum, California (1976); the City and County of San Francisco Award, California (1978); the Award of Honor for Outstanding Achievement in Photography, San Francisco Art Commission (1984); and others. She regards herself as "a catalyst . . . whose function it is to arouse in the photographer an intensified awareness of his potential creativity."

Her photographs are in many private, public, and corporate permanent collections, including the Museum of Modern Art, the Metropolitan Museum of Art, and the International Center of Photography—all in New York City; Massachusetts Institute of Technology (MIT), Cambridge; Norton Simon Museum, Pasadena, California; the Bibliothèque Nationale, Paris, France; and many others.

Bibliography
Alinder, James. *Collecting Light.* The Friends of Photography, 1979.
Bernhard, Ruth. *The Eternal Body: Photographs by Ruth Bernhard.* Ed. Margaretta Mitchell. Photography West Graphics, 1986.
Mann, Margery, and Anne Noggle. *Women in Photography: An Historical Survey.* San Francisco Museum of Modern Art, 1975.
Mitchell, Margaretta. *Recollections: Ten Women of Photography.* Viking Press, 1979.

Bernstein, Judith (1942–)

Born in Newark, New Jersey, Judith Bernstein earned a Bachelor of Science degree (1963) and a Master of Science degree a year later from the Pennsylvania State University, State College, Pennsylvania; she received Bachelor of Fine Arts and Master of Fine Arts degrees from the School of Art and Architecture, Yale University, New Haven, Connecticut (1967).

Recipient of grants from the National Endowment for the Arts (1974, 1985) and a fellowship from the New York Foundation for the Arts (1988) Bernstein has held a number of solo exhibitions of her work, including a mini-retrospective, "Drawings," at the University of Colorado, Boulder (1976); Brooks Jackson Iolas Gallery, New York City (1978); A.I.R. Gallery, New York City (April 1973; October 1973; 1984); University of Arkansas, Fayetteville (1987); and others.

Bernstein's work has been invited to myriad group exhibitions throughout the United States and abroad, including the "First International Exhibition of Erotic Art," Lund Kunsthall Museum of Art, Sweden (1968); "Erotica," Allan Stone Gallery, New York City (1973); "5 Americaines À Paris," Galerie Gerald Piltzer, Paris, France (1975); "Contemporary Women—Consciousness and Content," Brooklyn Museum, New York (1977); "Venerazia-Revenice, Titian's Forbidden Fruit," Palazzo Grassi, Venice, Italy (1978); "The Great Big Drawing Show," P.S.1, Long Island City, New York (1979); "International Impact Art Festival," Kyoto International Art Center, Japan (1982); "100 Drawings by Women," a travelling exhibition sponsored by the United States Information Agency (USIA) shown throughout the United States and Europe (1989–1991); and others.

Bernstein is a professor of art at the State University of New York (SUNY), Purchase, as well as a popular lecturer. Her work is represented in private and public permanent collections, including the Museum of Modern Art (MoMA), New York City; the Kronhausen Collection, Sweden; Colgate University, Hamilton, New York; University of Colorado, Boulder; Yale University, New Haven, Connecticut; Brooklyn Museum, New York; William N. Copley; Lawrence Alloway; and many others.

Bibliography
Gadon, Elinor. "Phantasmagoria: The Sexual Metaphors of Judith Bernstein." *The Once and Future Goddess.* Harper & Row, 1989.
Lubell, Ellen. "Judith Bernstein." *Art in America* (November 1984): 159–60.
Russell, John. "Judith Bernstein." *The New York Times* (April 27, 1984): C2.

Bernstein (Meyerowitz), Theresa F. (1890–)

Born in Philadelphia, Pennsylvania, Theresa F. Bernstein was an only child whose talent for art was encouraged by her family. Bernstein studied at the Philadelphia School of Design for Women (now the Moore College of Art) from 1907 to 1911; she took further work at the Pennsylvania Academy of Fine Arts with Daniel Garber and Elliott Daingerfield; and in 1912, when Bernstein's family moved to New York City, she continued her art education at the Art Students League, with a short course under the aegis of William Merritt Chase.

Painter and printmaker of the New York scene from 1919, when her solo show at the Milch Galleries in New York City was reviewed favorably as "a woman painter who paints like a man," Bernstein exhibited her prints in institutions and museums holding group shows and/or competitions, including the American Color Print Society at the Print Club of Philadelphia, Pennsylvania; the Brooklyn Society of Etchers, New York; the Library of Congress, Washington, D.C. (1922); the Victoria and Albert Museum, London, England; the Pitti Palace, Florence, Italy, with the Society of American Etchers (1931–1932); the 1933 inaugural color print show at the Brooklyn Museum, New York; and a solo exhibition of her intaglio work at the National Museum of Art, Smithsonian Institution, Washington, D.C. (1948).

Beginning in 1916 Bernstein spent summers painting scenes of Gloucester, Massachusetts, in myriad watercolors, in a fresh, direct, personal style, which convey an impression of movement through the tilted perspective she employed, as in "Gloucester Harbor" (1927). Working in oils as well, she received many commissions to paint portraits, including those of Harvard professors David Lyons (1954), Robert Pfeiffer (1956), and Henrietta Szold, the founder of Hadassah (1959). In 1950 Bernstein was represented in the Exhibition of American Painters at the Metropolitan Museum, New York City; the Biennial of American Art at the Corcoran Gallery of Art, Washington, D.C.; the Carnegie Institute, Pittsburgh, Pennsylvania; the New York Annual at the National Academy of Design, a solo show at Summit Gallery (1978); another solo exhibition, "Echoes of New York: The Paintings of Theresa Bernstein" at the Museum of the City of New York (1990–1991); and still another solo show at Srago Gallery (1991)—all in New York City—to name a few.

Winner of a number of awards and prizes, Bernstein holds the John Sartain Prize (1911); the Shilliard gold medal from the Plastic Club (1925); the Jeanne d'Arc Medal from the French Institute of Arts and Letters (1929); the John A. Johnson award from the North Shore Art Association (1971); the Matson Memorial award from the Rockport Art Association (1979), and an honor award for outstanding achievement in the visual arts from the Women's Caucus for Art (1991); among others.

Bernstein has written articles on intaglio for the *Christian Science Monitor*, most of which are illustrated with an etching by her husband, William Meyerowitz; she also penned a history of color printing for the *Brooklyn Museum Bulletin*, as well as histories and biographies of people and associations.

With more than forty solo exhibitions in her career and a distinguished record of publishing, printmaking, and painting, Bernstein's remarkable work is in the permanent collections of the Brooklyn Museum, New York; the Art Institute of Chicago, Illinois; the Library of Congress, Washington, D.C.; the Metropolitan Museum of Art, and the New York Public Library—both in New York City; and the Phillips Collection, Washington, D.C.; and others.

Bibliography

Catalogue of an Exhibition of Paintings by Theresa F. Bernstein and a Group of Colored Etchings by William Meyerowitz, Theresa F. Bernstein, Ellen Day Hale, Gabriella de V. Clements. Syracuse Museum of Fine Arts, 1921.

Echoes of New York: The Paintings of Theresa Bernstein. A Catalog. Michele Cohen, guest curator. Museum of the City of New York, 1990.

"A Salute to Theresa Bernstein in Her 100th Year." *Journal of the Print World* (Winter 1991).

Who's Who in American Art. 15th ed. R.R. Bowker Co., 1982.

Berry, Carolyn (1930–)

Born in Sweet Springs, Missouri, the painter/writer Carolyn Berry earned a Bachelor's degree from the University of Missouri, Columbia (1953) and attended Humboldt State College (now Humboldt State University), Arcata, California (1971).

Berry has held numerous solo exhibitions in galleries and museums, including the Monterey Peninsula Museum of Art, California (1967, 1974); the State University of New York (SUNY) at New Paltz (1967); Pacific Grove Art Center, California (1973, 1985, 1989); University of California at Los Angeles (UCLA) (1985); "Women Artists Series," Douglass College, Rutgers University, New Brunswick, New Jersey (1988); Texas Woman's University, Denton (1988); and others.

Her paintings and books have been invited to group exhibitions in the United States and abroad: from Irvine, California, to Marcius, Hungary; from Tempe, Arizona, to Laon, France; from New York City to Bologna, Italy—in museums, art centers, galleries, colleges, universities, and foundations. Berry has also participated in myriad national and international mail-art exhibitions, including the 16th São Paulo Biennale, Brazil, and the 1st International Fax Art Biennial, Tangente, Liechtenstein (1990).

Berry's books, collages, and other works are in private and public permanent collections, including the Art Institute of Chicago, Illinois; Museum of Modern Art (MoMA), New York City; University of California at Santa Cruz; University of California at Los Angeles (UCLA); King Steven Museum, Marcius, Hungary; National Institute of Design, Ahmedabad, India; and many others.

Bibliography

Berry, Carolyn. "Quill Art." *Heresies.* 1978.

———. *Artists and Their Cats.* Midmarch Publications, 1990.

Lauter, Estella. "Women as Mythmakers Revisited." *Quadrant* XXIII: 1. University of Wisconsin, 1990.

Who's Who in American Art. 19th ed. R.R. Bowker Co., 1991–1992.

Bertoni, Christina (1945–)

Born in Ann Arbor, Michigan, the ceramist Christina Bertoni earned a Bachelor's degree at the University of Michigan, Ann Arbor (1967) and received a Master of Fine Arts degree from Cranbrook Academy, Bloomfield Hills, Michigan (1976).

From forms that had black interiors and white exteriors to relief wall sculptures to writing "legends" on works which speculate on profundities and superficial matters, her work has unfolded creatively.

Bibliography

Clark, Garth. *American Ceramics: 1896 to the Present.* Abbeville Press, 1987.

Wechsler, Susan. "Celestial Bodies: Christina Bertoni." *American Ceramics* 2:2 (1983).

Betteridge, Lois Etherington (1928–)

Born in Drummondville, Québec, Canada, Lois Etherington Betteridge studied at the Ontario College of Art in Toronto (1947–1948); received a Bachelor of Fine Arts degree from the University of Kansas, Lawrence (1951); and, five years later, a Master of Fine Arts degree from the Cranbrook Academy of Art, Bloomfield Hills, Michigan. Betteridge describes her passion for her craft as follows:

"The allure of the next idea, the challenge of realizing it, and the ephemeral exaltation, or "moment of truth" that may or may not result from its realization are sequential factors that have driven me throughout my life as a silversmith."

A studio artist since 1952, Betteridge has held twenty-one solo exhibitions of her silver, gold, and bronze pieces; her work has been selected in more than 120 juried group exhibitions held throughout Canada, Belgium, France, Japan, the United Kingdom, and the United States. A selection of these include "Canadian Abstract Art—Centennial Exhibition," Commonwealth Institute Gallery, London, England (1967); "Contemporary Ontario Crafts," Agnes Etherington Gallery, Kingston, Ontario, Canada (1977); "Grand Prix des Metiers d'Art," Paris, Brussels, London (1985–1987); and hosts of others.

Betteridge has taught intermittently in colleges, guilds, universities, and institutions throughout the United States, Canada, and Europe since 1952, as a lecturer and as a visiting artist. She has been a board member, advisor, or officer of many guilds, councils, and institutions, including the Canadian Guild of Crafts, Ontario; the Royal Canadian Academy of Art, Ottawa; Society of North American Goldsmiths; Algonquin College, Ottawa; L'Atelier Joallerie Enregistre, Montréal; and the Haliburton School of Fine Art, Fleming College, among others.

Her commissioned work in jewelry, ecclesiastical silver, and secular hollowware have included trophies and presentation pieces for statesmen in Canada and elsewhere; baptismal fonts, communion sets, and processional crosses for churches; and bronze sculptures for lay institutions.

Winner of many awards and honors for her functional hollowware, sculpture, and jewelry in bronze, silver, and gold, Betteridge was the 1987 recipient of the Saidye Bronfman award for excellence in crafts, and the M. Joan Chalmers 15th Anniversary award for contributions to the crafts in 1991. She received a citation for distinguished professional achievement from the University of Kansas (1975); was elected a distinguished member to the Society of North American Goldsmiths (1974); received two commendations in the De Beers International Ring Competition, London (1966); and, four years later, was elected to the Royal Canadian Academy of Art.

Betteridge's work is in the permanent collections of many public galleries throughout North America and Europe, such as the Royal Scottish Museum, Edinburgh; National Museum of Natural Sciences, Ottawa, Canada; Cranbrook Art Gallery, Bloomfield Hills, Michigan; the National Museum of Civilization, Ottawa, Canada; and others.

Bibliography
Betteridge, Lois Etherington. *The Function of the Artist in Canada*. Ontario Crafts Council Review, 1958.
————. *The Techniques of Chasing and Repoussé*. Crafts Canada, 1975.
Who's Who in American Art. 19th ed. R.R. Bowker Co., 1991–1992.

Bettinson, Brenda (1929–)

Known for her figurative, neo-expressionist paintings and prints, Brenda Bettinson was born in King's Lynn, England, and studied art in London, Paris, and Rome. She had her first solo exhibition at the Twenty Brook Street Gallery, London, England (1948), and since then has had many solo and group exhibitions in the United States and abroad. Bettinson has painted numerous murals and large panels on commission, including the Vatican Pavilion, New York World's Fair; Calvary Hospital, the Bronx, New York; and others.

Art editor for Riverside Radio, WRVR-FM, New York (1961–1965), Bettinson was professor of art at Pace University, New York, for twenty-seven years until her retirement (1990) as Professor Emerita. She also lectured at the Katonah Gallery, New York, taught in its docent program, and was consultant to the Society for the Renewal of Christian Art (1969–1992).

Winner of a gold medal from the National Arts Club, New York (1966), Bettinson is at work on a series of two and three-dimensional, free-form paintings, plus woodcuts and monotypes, on aspects of the ecology of Barter's Island, Maine, her current residence.

Bibliography
Gordon, Rosemary. *Dying and Creating*. Society of Analytical Psychology, 1978.
The Beginning. A Film. Columbia University Press, 1962.
Who's Who in American Art. 19th ed. R.R. Bowker Co., 1991–1992.

Bevlin, Marjorie E. (1917–)

Born in The Dalles, Oregon, the painter Marjorie Elliott Bevlin earned a Bachelor of Fine Arts degree from the University of Colorado, Boulder; attended the College of Architecture at the University of Washington, Seattle; received a Master of Science degree from New York University; and studied painting with Jimmy Ernst.

Bevlin had numerous solo exhibitions of her work in Colorado and Washington; her work was invited to group shows in the United States and Europe, including the annual exhibitions between 1963 and 1971 at the National Academy of Design, New York; "Scottish-American Women's Exhibition," Edinburgh Royal Gallery, Scotland (1963); British Women's Exhibition, Liverpool, England (1964); 8th Annual Prix de Deauville, France (1972); Prix de Rome, Italy (1972); La Galerie Mouffe, Paris, France (1972); and others.

She was founding chair of fine arts at Otero Junior College, La Junta, Colorado, where she was commissioned to paint two six-by-twenty-four-foot murals (1955); and director and founder of the Arkansas Valley School Arts Festival, La Junta, Colorado (1956–1975). Member and officer of several artist's organizations, Bevlin is the author of *Design Through Discovery*, a work that has appeared in five editions, as well as in two brief versions.

Bevlin's paintings are in many private and public permanent collections, including Orcas Island Historical Museum, Australia, and throughout the United States, England, and Canada.

Bibliography
Bevlin, Marjorie E. *Design Through Discovery*. Holt, Rinehart & Winston, 1989.
Who's Who in American Art. 19th ed. R.R. Bowker Co., 1991–1992.

Bienvenue, Marcella (1946–)

Known across Canada and in the United States for her performance artworks, Marcella Bienvenue has also produced paintings, prints, video tapes, films, and installations. Born in Stettler, Alberta, Bienvenue was trained as a painter at the Alberta College of Art (1965–1969) in Calgary, which she has since made her home. After graduating she began making prints in silk-screen and offset lithography. In 1975 she became involved in performance art, film, and video.

Her performances and film and video work have been seen across Canada and in the United States since 1979. Bienvenue's work during the 1980s examined the effects of mass media and advanced technology on society. In 1986 the Alberta Motion Picture Industries Association selected her film, *The Heart is a Lonely Monitor*, for an award for innovation. She has produced installations for the Nickle Museum (1989) and the Glenbow Museum (1990)—both in Calgary. Her work has been included in numerous group exhibitions.

Bienvenue has held many administrative positions, including assistant director, Parachute Centre for Cultural Affairs (1976–1977); assistant director, Arton's (1977–1978); assistant editor, *Centerfold* (1977–1978) (now *Fuse* magazine); coordinator and executive director, the Calgary Society of Independent Filmmakers (1981–1987); as well as others. She has served on arts advisory boards and in 1987 was appointed to the Canada Council Media Arts Advisory Committee.

Vera Lemecha

Bibliography
Conley, Christine. "Seeing Clearly: An Interview with Artist Marcella Bienvenue." *The Newsmagazine for Alberta Women* (Fall 1985): 34–36.
Earl, Linda. "Performance Art/Putting a Frame Around Life." *Cityscape* 2, 4 (Fall 1985): 17–19, 72–75.
Garneau, David. "Introverted Presence." *Artichoke* (Fall 1989): 22–24.
Pike, Bev. "Mixing Art and Politics." *The Newsmagazine of Alberta Women* (Summer 1986): 32–34.

Biggs, Electra Waggoner (1916–)

Born in Fort Worth, Texas, Electra Waggoner Biggs studied sculpture with Katherine Breeze in her New York atelier; took courses in the School of Business at Columbia University, New York; learned bronze casting techniques at the Valzauni Foundry, Paris, France; and mastered marble-cutting in a Paris atelier. She was awarded an honorary Doctorate of Fine Arts degree from the Texas Women's University, Denton.

Her many portrait sculptures and busts have celebrated a cross-section of American society and include persons as diverse in background and accomplishment as Victor McLaglen, Amon G. Carter, Harry S Truman, Dwight D. Eisenhower, John Nance Garner, and Bob Hope—to name a few. Biggs's most important work, "Into the Sunset" (1942), is a monumental ten-by-twelve-foot bronze which depicts Will Rogers on his favorite horse, "Soapsuds."

Her work has received numerous honors and recognition, including third prize at the Salon d'Automne, Paris; it has been exhibited throughout the United States, including Griffith Park, Los Angeles, California; the National Museum of Women in the Arts, Washington, D.C.; the Red River Valley Museum, Vernon, Texas (where many of her original plasters and other works are on permanent display); the University of Notre Dame, Indiana; Duke University, Durham, North Carolina; and Texas Tech University, Lubbock.

Bibliography

Broder, Patricia Janis. *Bronzes of the American West.* Harry N. Abrams, 1974.

National Museum of Women in the Arts. Harry N. Abrams, 1987.

Watson-Jones, Virginia. *Contemporary American Women Sculptors.* Oryx Press, 1986.

Billian, Cathey (1946–)

Born in Chicago, Illinois, Cathey Billian has achieved the title of sculptor, videographer, printmaker, arts activist and environmental and public artist. She earned her Bachelor of Fine Arts degree from the University of Arizona, Tucson (1969), after brief stints at the Art Institute of Chicago (1964) and the Art Students League, New York City (1967). Billian was an honors fellow at Pratt Institute, Brooklyn, New York, where she received a Master of Fine Arts degree (1977).

Billian has exhibited her work in numbers of solo exhibitions, including "Cross-Cut/Piedra Lumbre," Pratt Institute, Brooklyn, New York (1990); "Frozen Moments," Gallery of New York Experimental Glassworks (1988); "Future Antiquities," Whitney Museum of American Art (1984); "Two Views of Nature," Elise Meyer Gallery—all in New York City (1982); and others.

Her work has been invited to many group exhibitions throughout the United States, such as "New York Experimental Glass," Society for Art in Craft, Pittsburgh, Pennsylvania (1989); "Four Sculptors . . .," Nina Owen Ltd., Chicago, Illinois (1986); "Recent Acquisitions" (Louis Comfort Tiffany Foundation Purchase), Brooklyn Museum, New York (1985); "Cathey Billian, Michael Graves, Charles Simonds at Liberty State Park," Jersey City Museum, New Jersey (1984); "Nature Transformed," Virginia Commonwealth University, Richmond (1982); and many others.

Billian has taught at art schools and universities and was visiting artist (1978–1988) at Columbia University, New York City; Brown University, Providence, Rhode Island; Maryland Institute of Art, Baltimore; University of Illinois, Champaign-Urbana; Parsons School of Environmental Design, New York City; and others. She was artist-in-residence at Carson-Santa Fe National Forests/Ghost Ranch Museum, New Mexico (1988–1991); the New York Experimental Glass Workshop (1985–1986); the Printmaking Workshop, New York (1977–1982) and Delaware Water Gap National Park (1975, 1979, 1981).

Winner of many awards and honors for her work, Billian won sculpture commissions for Deer Valley Airport, Phoenix, Arizona (1990–1991) and a commission for Prospect Park, Brooklyn, New York, from the New York State Council on the Arts (1985). She was the recipient of fellowships from the Hirsch Farm Project, Wisconsin (1990); the New York State Foundation for the Arts (1985–1986); and the National Endowment for the Arts (1983).

Her work is in a number of private, public, and corporate permanent collections, including the Philadelphia Museum of Art, Pennsylvania; the New York/New Jersey Port Authority; Brooklyn Museum, New York; Newark Museum, New Jersey; Saks Fifth Avenue, New York; the New York Public Library; and others.

Bibliography

Wagner, Cheryl. "Rio Chama (N.M.) Visitor Center to Challenge Visitors." *Public Art Review* 2:1 (Spring–Summer 1990).

Who's Who in American Art. 19th ed. R.R. Bowker Co., 1991–1992.

Bills, Linda (1943–)

Born in Long Island, New York, the artist Linda Bills earned a Bachelor of Fine Arts degree from Beaver College, Glenside, Pennsylvania (1965).

Bills has exhibited her bark constructions, bark kimonos, and other objects in many galleries and museums, including "Meeting Ground: Basketry Traditions and Sculptural Forms," The Forum, St. Louis, Missouri, and Arizona State University, Tempe (1990); "Expanding Traditions," Maryland Art Place, Baltimore (1990); "Maryland Invitational 1989," The Baltimore Museum of Art (1989); "The Tactile Vessel: New Basket Forms," a travelling show through 1991, Erie Art Museum, Pennsylvania (1989); "American Baskets: The Eighties," Chicago Public Library Cultural Center, Illinois, and Grand Rapids and Jackson, Michigan (1988); and others.

"Armor Corbu" (1989), a folded and tacked bark kimono, in a reference to the plunging roof of LeCorbusier's Chapel of Notre Dame du Haut, Ronchamp, France; a vessel or basket of sorts; and Japanese clothing, offer the viewer a set of engaging contradictions.

Winner of awards and honors, Bills received a grant-in-aid from the Maryland State Arts Council (1989); and a National Endowment for the Arts (NEA) fellowship (1988). Her work is in private and public permanent collections.

Bibliography

Giuliano, Mike. "Invitation Only." *The Columbia Flyer* (March 9, 1989).

Meeting Ground: Basketry Traditions and Sculptural Forms. A Catalog. The Forum, St. Louis, Missouri, and Arizona State University, Tempe, 1990.

Shermeta, Margo, and Kathy Malec. *American Baskets: The Eighties.* Chicago: Department of Cultural Affairs, 1988.

Birnbaum, Dara (1946–)

Native New Yorker Dara Birnbaum earned her Bachelor's degree in architecture from the Carnegie Institute of Technology, Pittsburgh, Pennsylvania (1969) and, five years later, a Bachelor of Fine Arts degree from the San Francisco Art Institute, California.

Birnbaum has held a Creative Artists Public Service (CAPS) fellowship (1981) and won a video production grant from the New York State Council on the Arts (1983). She has had solo exhibitions of her work in the United States and abroad, including the Musée d'Art Contemporain, Montréal, Canada (1983); Hudson River Museum (1982); Institute of Contemporary Art, London, England (1982); Museum van Hedendaagse Kunsten, Ghent, Belgium (1982); Museum of Modern Art (MoMA), New York City (1981); and others.

Her work has been invited to many group exhibitions, such as "Deconstruction/Reconstruction," New Museum, New York City (1980); "60 '80 Attitudes/Concepts, Images," The Stedelijk Museum, Amsterdam (1982); "74th American Exhibition," the Art Institute of Chicago, Illinois (1982); "Documenta 7," Kassel, Germany (1982); and installations, including Grand Central Station, New York City; various rock clubs; the American Film Institute; USA Cable Network; and many others.

Employing high-tech effects including image-processing, sound, lighting, and color, Birnbaum's videos seek to sharpen the dialogue on mass culture and high art.

Bibliography

Buchloh, B.H.D. "Allegorical Procedures: Appropriation and Montage in Contemporary Art." *Artforum* 21 (September 1982): 54–56.

Furlong, L. "Mixed Blessing: 1981 San Francisco International Traveling Video Festival." *Afterimage* 9 (May 1982): 18.

Owens, C. "Phantasmagoria of the Media . . ." *Art in America* 70 (May 1982): 98–100.

Birstins, Inese (1942–)

Born in Madona, Latvia, Inese Birstins is known for her work in fiber art, jewelry, and sculpture. She studied at Sydney University, Australia, where she earned a Bachelor's degree in 1963.

For more than two decades Birstins has held solo and group exhibitions in universities, museums, and galleries in Canada and abroad, including "Habitat," Vancouver, British Columbia (1976); Capilano College, Vanouver, and The Fraser Valley College, British Columbia; Place des Arts, Vancouver (1978); "Fibre Interchange," Banff Centre for the Arts, Alberta (1979); and many others. A recent solo exhibition at the Museu de Arte Contemporanea da Universidade de São Paulo, Brazil (1989), brought to fruition Birstins's ironic installations of chimerical, soft, felted wool figures in a world of their own. Recently, the artist wrote, "I wonder about the almost-impossibility of ever really knowing the 'other'—and, so, of ever being known by them."

Birstens is a teacher of weaving and design in Vancouver, Banff, and elsewhere. Her work is represented in private and public permanent collections in Australia, Canada, Germany, and the United States.

Bibliography

Berzins, Daina. *Birstins: Felt Contradictions*. A Catalog. Museu de Arte Contemporanea da Universidade de São Paulo, 1989.

Constantine, Mildred, and Jack Lenor Larsen. *The Art Fabric: Mainstream.*

Van Nostrand Reinhold, 1981.

Inese Birstins & Anne Flaten Pixley. A Catalog. Walter Phillips Gallery, the Banff Centre School of Fine Arts, Canada, 1983.

Bischoff, Ilse (1903–)

A native New Yorker, the painter/printmaker/illustrator Ilse Bischoff studied at the Art Students League, New York City; travelled and studied in Europe; and took further work with Joseph Pennell and George Buchner.

Bischoff is a winner of honors and awards in exhibitions at the Philadelphia Print Club, Pennsylvania (1927); the American Institute of Graphic Artists (1930); and others. She has been a member of the American Institute of Graphic Artists and the Art Students League.

Bischoff also illustrated children's books. Examples of her work exist in private and public permanent collections, including the Brooklyn Museum of Art, New York; Boston Museum of Fine Arts, Massachusetts; Museum of Modern Art (MoMA); the New York Public Library—both in New York City; and others.

Bibliography

American Art Annual. Vol. 28. Washington, D.C.: American Federation of Arts, 1932.

The Intimate Realism of Ilse Bischoff, Paintings and Drawings 1964–1976. Hanover, New Hampshire: Carpenter Galleries, Dartmouth College, 1976.

Bishop, Isabel (1902–1988)

Born in Cincinnati, Ohio, the painter/printmaker Isabel Bishop is best known for her works based upon light and the people of Union Square, New York City. Bishop studied at the New York School of Applied Design for Women (1918) and, two years later, studied with Guy Pène du Bois and Kenneth Hayes Miller at the Art Students League—both in New York City. Much later, in 1941, she studied etching and other intaglio work with Stanley William Hayter in his Atelier 17, New York City.

Bishop held many solo exhibitions in museums and galleries, including the Midtown Galleries, New York City (1932, 1936, 1939, 1942, 1955, 1960); the Herbert Institute, Atlanta, Georgia (1940); the Smithsonian Institution, National Museum of American Art, Washington, D.C. (1945); and others.

Her works were included in prestigious group exhibitions throughout the United States: from Atlanta, Georgia, to Bloomfield Hills, Michigan; from Clearwater, Florida, to Colorado Springs, Colorado; from New York City to Lincoln, Nebraska; to name a few.

Winner of many awards and honors, Bishop was elected an academician of the National Academy of Design (1941); member (1943) and vice-president (1946) of the National Institute of Arts and Letters (the first woman officer since 1898); and received a host of awards from institutions, including the American Artists Group, New York City; the Art Association of Newport, Rhode Island; Society of American Etchers, New York City (1940, 1947); Butler Institute of American Art, Youngstown, Ohio; Corcoran Gallery of Art; and the Library of Congress (1946)—both in Washington, D.C.; the Pennsylvania Academy of Fine Arts, Philadelphia; and others.

Bishop taught at the Art Students League, New York City; the Skowhegan School of Painting and Sculpture, Maine; and Yale University, New Haven, Connecticut. Her drawings, prints, and paintings capture the essence of an informal gesture; they are real beyond reality and sing praises of and to the person on the street, the model in her studio—all with that special quality of light that permeates the world of Isabel Bishop.

Examples of her work are in private and public permanent collections, including Atlanta University, Georgia; Baltimore Museum of Art, Maryland; the Brooklyn Museum, New York; Columbus Gallery of Fine Arts, Ohio; Cranbrook Academy of Art, Bloomfield Hills, Michigan; Dallas Museum of Art, Texas; Des Moines Art Center, Iowa; the Los Angeles County Art Museum, California; Metropolitan Museum of Art, New York City; Nebraska Art Association, Lincoln; the Phillips Collection, Washington, D.C.; University of Arizona, Tucson; Whitney Museum of American Art, New York City; and many others.

Bibliography
Alloway, Lawrence. "Isabel Bishop, the Grand Manner and the Working Girl." *Art in America* 63:5 (September–October 1975): 61–65.
Bishop, Isabel. "Isabel Bishop Discusses 'Genre' Drawings." *American Artist* 17 (Summer 1953): 46–47.
Johnson, Una, and Jo Miller. *Isabel Bishop*. The Brooklyn Museum, 1964.
Reich, Sheldon. *Isabel Bishop: The First Retrospective Exhibition Held in American Museums of Paintings, Drawings, Etchings and Aquatints.* Tucson: University of Arizona, 1974.

Bittleman, Dolores Dembus (1931–)

A native New Yorker, fiber artist and conservator Dolores Dembus Bittleman earned a Bachelor of Science degree *cum laude* from Columbia University, New York City (1952) and did her graduate work at the University of Calcutta, India (1955–1956).

Bittleman's silk and natural fiber tapestries have been shown in myriad exhibitions in the United States and abroad, including "New Weavings to Look At," Silvermine College of Art, New Canaan, Connecticut (1967); "Wall Hangings," Museum of Modern Art (MoMA), New York City (1969, 1970, 1972); "The Fifth International Tapestry Biennale," Palais de Rumine, Lausanne, Switzerland, and the "Biennial" at the Zacheta Gallery, Warsaw, Poland—both in 1971; "Artists and Craftsmen of Central New York," Munson-Williams-Proctor Institute, Utica, New York (1973); "Collaborations in Art, Science, and Technology," Everson Museum of Art, Syracuse, New York (1975); and others.

Winner of honors and awards for her fiber structures, Bittleman was a recipient of a Fulbright fellowship to Paris, France (1954–1955); a purchase prize at a Columbia University exhibition (1952); a Master Craftsman and Apprentice grant from the National Endowment for the Arts (NEA) (1975–1976); and others.

She has taught her craft at institutions, including the Creative Arts Workshop, New Haven, Connecticut (1962); Troy Arts Workshop (1966), and Union College, Schenectady (1969–1974)—both in New York; and others, and founded Cambridge Textiles, New York, in 1979.

Bittleman was one of only ten Americans invited to exhibit her weaving in the "greatest craft show on earth" (the 1971 Lausanne international biennial). Examples of her work are housed in private, public, and corporate permanent exhibitions, such as MoMA, and Columbia University, New York City; Yale University, New Haven, and Silvermine College of Art, New Caanan—both in Connecticut; and others.

Bibliography
Bittleman, Dolores Dembus. "Gemini." *Craft Horizons*. Vol. 31 (October 1971): 30.
Larson, Jack Lenor. "Two Views of the Fifth Tapestry Bienniale: The Greatest Craft Show on Earth." *Craft Horizons*. Vol. 31 (October 1971): 23, 62.
Who's Who in American Art. 15th ed. R.R. Bowker Co., 1982.

Black, Lisa (1934–)

Born in Lansing, Michigan, the painter/graphic artist/photographer Lisa Black earned a diploma at the University of Paris, Sorbonne (1955); she received a Bachelor's degree from the University of Michigan, Ann Arbor the following year. Black also attended classes at the Detroit Institute of Art, Michigan; Museum of Modern Art (MoMA), New York City; Rowayton Arts Center, Connecticut; and the Art Students League, New York City; and took further courses from Leo Manso and Robert Francis.

Between 1971 and 1992 Black exhibited her work widely and has won sixty-eight awards in painting, drawing, sculpture, mixed media, and photography, including first prize in photography at the Rowayton Arts Center (1991); the Fred Kraus Memorial award at the "22nd Annual Competition of Art," Stamford Museum and Nature Center, Connecticut, for a work in mixed media (1992); "Off the Wall and Out of the Frame," Stamford Art Association, Connecticut (1989); "Stamford's Heritage, Then & Now—and Into the Future," Stamford Art Association (1991); and myriad others.

Black's work is in many public and private permanent collections. She is an active member of many art societies in Connecticut, including the New Haven Paint and Clay Club, Old Greenwich Art Society, Stamford Art Asociation, Rowayton Arts Center, Westport Arts Center, New Canaan Society for the Arts, Darien Arts Council, and the Greenwich Art Society, for which she was a member of the nominating committee (1991–1992) and historian (1992–1993).

Bibliography
"Photographs by Lisa Black." *Greenwich Times* (July 24, 1991): A8.
Who's Who in American Art. 19th ed. R.R. Bowker Co., 1991–1992.

Black, Mary McCune (1915–)

Born in Broadwell, Ohio, the watercolorist Mary McCune Black earned a Bachelor's degree (1937) and a Master of Fine Arts degree (1958) from Ohio University, Athens; she studied with Hilton Leech at the Amagansett School of Art, Sarasota, Florida (1946–1947); and enrolled in various workshops offered by Charles Burchfield, Aaron Bohrod, John Carroll, Eliot O'Hara, William Thon, and others.

A former director/curator of the Charleston Art Gallery, Sunrise, West Virginia (1963–1977), Black has held solo shows in West Virginia galleries, including the Charleston Art Gallery; West Virginia State College Institute; South Charleston Women's Club; Kanawha County Public Library; University of Charleston; and the Commercial Bank and Studio 7—both in Parkersburg. Her work has been invited to state, regional, and national group shows, including "International Women's Year and West Virginia Juried Exhibition," Department of Culture and History, Capitol Complex, Charleston (1979, 1981, 1983, 1992).

A charter member of the West Virginia Watercolor Society and the Charleston branch of the National League of American Pen Women and associate member of the American Watercolor Society and the

Southern Watercolor Society, Black has been active in many professional arts associations, including the Women's Caucus for Art, Sarasota Manatee Florida Chapter. Between 1937 and 1963 she has taught children and adults, organized art-in-schools and related programming during her directorship of the Charleston Art Gallery, and attended seminars on museum education—regionally and abroad.

Her work is represented in private, public, and corporate permanent collections in West Virginia, including West Virginia State College, Institute; First Christian Church, Charleston; the Kanawha County Public Library; Lutheran Church, Parkersburg; Pediatric ward, Charleston General Division, CAMC; WZAZ-TV Offices, Huntington; and others.

Bibliography

Taylor, Della Brown. "Art Exhibit Proves Work Rewarding." *The Charleston Gazette* (November 5, 1969).

Who's Who in American Art. 19th ed. R.R. Bowker Co., 1991–1992.

Blackburn, Linda (1941–)

Born in Baltimore, Maryland, the painter/printmaker Linda Blackburn earned a Bachelor of Fine Arts degree at the University of Texas, Austin (1962), and a Master of Arts degree from the University of California at Berkeley (1965).

Blackburn has held many solo exhibitions of her work in museums, galleries, and universities in Texas, including the Southwest Crafts Center, San Antonio; James Gallery, Houston; and the Peregrine Gallery, Dallas—all in 1991. She also showed at the Tyler Museum of Art (1989); Mattingly Baker Gallery, Dallas (1981, 1983, 1985); Texas Christian University, Denton (1981); and others.

Her work was invited to numerous group exhibitions, such as "Creative Partners," Rice University (1991), and "Monoprints," James Gallery (1990)—both in Houston, Texas; "Glass Prints," Municipal Art Collections, Coburg, Germany (1988); "Mid-America Biennial," Nelson-Atkins Museum of Art, Kansas City, Missouri (1989); "Luminous Expressions," Mint Museum, Charlotte, North Carolina (1987); "Women of the American West," Bruce Museum, Greenwich, Connecticut (1985); "Four Texas Painters," University of Illinois at Chicago (1984); and many others.

Her work is represented in private, public, and corporate permanent collections in Texas, including the Crescent Collection, Dallas; Longview Art Museum, Tyler; Modern Art Museum of Fort Worth; Southwestern Bell; and others.

Bibliography

Freudenheim, Susan. "A Survey of Texas Art: Linda Blackburn." *Arts and Architecture* (Winter 1981): 23.

Thistlewaite, Mark. "Linda Blackburn." *Artspace* (Summer 1984): 24–25.

Who's Who in American Art. 19th ed. R.R. Bowker Co., 1991–1992.

Blackey, Mary

Painter and printmaker Mary Blackey was born in Glen Cove, New York. She earned a certificate after study at the Albright Art School (1952); received her Bachelor's degree from the State University of New York (SUNY) at Buffalo the following year; and did graduate work at Columbia University, New York City (1953–1955). Blackey also studied at the Art Students League (1954–1955, 1961–1963) and Donn Steward's Etching Workshop (1977–1979)—both in New York City, and did further work at the Fleisher Art Memorial Printmaking Workshop in Philadelphia, Pennsylvania (1989 to the present).

Blackey began exhibiting her work in a solo travelling watercolor show in New Hampshire (1972), which travelled to several sites, including the Manchester Institute of Arts, Sharon Arts Center, and the Nashua Arts and Science Center; her first solo museum exhibition took place at the Nassau County Fine Arts Museum, Roslyn, New York (1975).

Her work has been invited to scores of group exhibitions throughout the United States, including "Works on Paper," Widener University Museum, Chester, Pennsylvania (1991); "Annual Watercolor Exhibition," National Arts Club, New York (1967, 1969, 1976, 1977, 1983, 1985); National Academy of Design Annual, New York (1965, 1966, 1968, 1976, 1978, 1980); "Watercolor West," Utah State University, Logan (1976, 1977); "Watercolor—USA," Springfield Art Museum, Missouri (1973, 1975, 1992); Wichita Centennial National Art Exhibition, Kansas (1970); and others.

Winner of scores of awards and honors for her work between 1971 and 1991, Blackey taught printmaking at the Roslyn Creative Arts Workshop (1968–1980) and watercolor at the Jackson Heights Art Club (1976). She also was an instructor at the Five Towns Music and Art Foundation (1977–1979).

Her works are in many public and private permanent collections, such as Hofstra University, New York; College of Eastern Utah, Price; Columbia Broadcasting System, New York; IBM, New York and Colorado; and many others.

Bibliography

Nechis, Barbara. *Watercolor—The Creative Experience.* Van Nostrand Reinhold, 1979.

Shirey, David. "Good News in Old Westbury." *The New York Times* (November 7, 1976): 21.

Who's Who in American Art. 19th ed. R.R. Bowker Co., 1991–1992.

Blackstone, Harriet (1864–1939)

The painter Harriet Blackstone was born in New Hartford, Connecticut, and studied at Pratt Institute, Brooklyn, New York (1903–1905). Earlier on, she taught drawing and the theater arts to children. Blackstone engaged in further study, over two years, in Paris, France, where she enrolled in the Académie Julian; analyzed Leonardo's paintings in the Louvre; and exhibited in the Salon of 1907.

On her return to the United States, Blackstone settled in Glencoe, Illinois and was inundated with portrait commissions. In 1912 she travelled again to Europe to take a summer course in Brussels, Belgium, with the American painter William Merritt Chase, whose influence on her brushwork and use of color was visible in future work.

During World War I the U.S. government sent Blackstone to New Mexico, where she painted the Native Americans and their environment. Her work is in many private and public permanent collections, including the National Portrait Gallery, Washington, D.C.

Bibliography

A Mystical Vision: The Art of Harriet Blackstone 1864–1939. Vermont: Bennington Museum, 1984.

Cuthbert, Lee. *Contemporary American Portrait Painters.* W.W. Norton, 1929.

D'Unger, Giselle. "Harriet Blackstone: Portrait Painter." *Fine Arts Journal*

(February 1912): 97–101.

National Portrait Gallery: Permanent Collection Illustrated Checklist. Smithsonian Institution Press, 1987.

Blaedel, Joan Stuart Ross (1942–)

Born in Boston, Massachusetts, the painter/printmaker Joan Stuart Ross Blaedel (formerly Bloedel) was educated at several institutions, including Connecticut College, New London, where she earned a Bachelor's degree (1964); and the University of Iowa, Iowa City, where she received a Master of Arts degree (1967) and a Master of Fine Arts degree (1968). Blaedel also studied at Yale University, New Haven, Connecticut (1965); and the Boston Museum School of Fine Arts; and the Massachusetts College of Art—both in Boston, Massachusetts.

Between 1971 and 1993 Blaedel held more than thirty solo exhibitions of her work throughout the Northwestern United States, including a show at Surrey Art Gallery, Surrey, British Columbia, Canada (1982); and one at Galleri 7, Oslo, Norway (1979).

Her paintings and prints have been invited to myriad group shows in the United States and abroad, such as "Breaking and Entering," Josef Gallery, New York City (1983); "New Directions—New Work" (1982), and "The Food Show" (1985), Equinox Gallery, Vancouver, British Columbia, Canada; "Northwest Print Council in China," Beijing (1986); "Seattle Style," travelling show in France, Musée de Carcassone (1986–1988); "Through the Eyes of Women," Italia, Seattle, Washington (1987); "Regional Prints," Washington State University, Pullman (1990); "Printmakers and Book Artists," Pratt Fine Art Center, Seattle, Washington (1991); and many others.

Blaedel has been the recipient of honors and awards for her work. From 1968 to 1992, she taught drawing, painting, and printmaking in numbers of colleges, art centers, universities, and workshops. Her work is in private, public, and corporate permanent collections in the United States and Canada, including the Seattle Art Museum, Washington; University of Illinois, Chicago; Pan-Pacific Hotel, Vancouver, British Columbia, Canada; IBM, San Francisco, California; NBC, Chicago, Illinois; U.S. West, Denver, Colorado; and many others.

Bibliography

Guenther, Bruce. *50 Northwest Artists.* Chronicle Books, 1983.
Nichols, Ellen, ed. *Northwest Originals: Washington Women and Their Art.* Matrimedia, 1990.
Who's Who in American Art. 19th ed. R.R. Bowker Co., 1991–1992.

Blaine, Nell (1922–)

Born in Richmond, Viriginia, the painter Nell Blaine has had fifty solo exhibitions throughout the United States since 1945. Despite her parents' opposition Blaine chose to be an artist and enrolled in what is now Virginia Commonwealth University (1939–1942). She was grounded in abstraction through study with Hans Hofmann in New York City (1942–1944) and acquired intaglio printmaking techniques and processes with Stanley William Hayter at Atelier 17, New York City the following year. Blaine also studied at the New School for Social Research, New York City (1952–1953). She taught painting intermittently between 1945 and 1957.

Widely travelled, Blaine's paintings have been invited to group exhibitions throughout the United States and abroad, including the Museum of Modern Art (1956, 1963); and the Whitney Museum of American Art (1959, 1974)—both in New York City; the Tate Gallery, London, England (1979); Museum of Modern Art, Tokyo, Japan (1955); Antonio Sousa Gallery, Mexico (1957); the "Festival of Two Worlds," Spoleto, Italy (1958); and a host of others.

From 1944 to 1957, Blaine was a member of the American Abstract Artists in New York. Around 1950 she gradually turned back to representational painting. She was also a member of the Jane Street Group (1945–1949) and was secretary/coordinator in 1948–1949 of the Jane Street Gallery—both in New York City.

Blaine's awards and grants for her work through the years include fellowships from the Virginia Museum of Fine Arts, Richmond (1943, 1946); residencies at the MacDowell Colony, Peterborough, New Hampshire (1957), and Yaddo, Saratoga Springs, New York (1957, 1958, 1964); a Guggenheim fellowship (1974), and a grant from the National Endowment for the Arts (1975); honorary doctorate degrees from Moore College of Art, Philadelphia, Pennsylvania (1980), and Virginia Commonwealth University, Richmond, Virginia (1985); and the Louise Nevelson Award in Art from the American Academy and Institute of Arts and Letters, New York City (1990); to name a few.

Blaine's works are housed in many major permanent public, private, corporate, and foundation collections, such as the Whitney Museum of American Art, the Metropolitan Museum of Art, the Brooklyn Museum, and the National Academy of Design—all in New York City; the Hirshhorn Museum and Sculpture Garden, the National Museum of Women in the Arts, and the Corcoran Gallery—all in Washington, D.C.; the Virginia Museum of Fine Arts, Richmond; the Carnegie Institute of Technology, Pittsburgh, Pennsylvania; the Civici Musei e Gallerie de Storia e Arte, Udine, Italy; Matsushita, Osaka, Japan; Dorado Hotel, Puerto Rico; and the Ministry of Food Industries, Moscow, Russia.

"Fog and Sunset, Autumn" (1989) and "Fog Coming In" (1990), both modest-sized watercolors and pastel works, reveal the same view from Blaine's East Gloucester, Massachusetts, home, under different conditions, not unlike the methods and procedures used by the impressionists—except that the "handwriting" is pure Blaine with her qualitative and complementary colors placed judiciously on her wet and dry grounds.

Bibliography

Campbell, Lawrence. "Blaine Paints a Picture." *Art News* (May 1959).
Gill, Susan. "Nell Blaine." *Women's Caucus for Art Honor Awards for Outstanding Achievement in the Visual Arts.* 1986.
Marks, Claude. *World Artists 1950–1980.* H.W. Wilson Company, 1984.
Mellow, James R. "The Flowering Summer of Nell Blaine." *The New York Times* (October 11, 1970).

Blair Crosbie, Helen (1910–)

Born in Hibbing, Minnesota, Helen Blair Crosbie graduated from the Massachusetts School of Art, Boston, after study with Cyrus Dallin; she attended classes at the Boston Museum School for two years; and also studied with Alexander Archipenko for a year in New York City.

Blair Crosbie has had many solo exhibitions of her sculptures, including the Arden Studios, New York City (1938); Portraits Inc., New York City (1941, 1942); Robert Vose Gallery, Boston, Massachusetts (1944); Martin Gallery, Phoenix, Arizona (1973, 1974); C.G. Rein Galleries, Scottsdale, Arizona; Palm Beach, Florida (1979); and others.

She taught at Boston University, Massachusetts, between 1937 and 1940 and was a volunteer art teacher at a number of hospitals and schools, such as the Hudson River State Hospital, New York; Colorado State School for the Retarded; St. Joseph's Hospital, Phoenix, Arizona; and at several Veteran's Administration hospitals for the mentally disturbed, including Minneapolis, Minnesota; Detroit, Michigan; Denver, Colorado; and Phoenix, Arizona. Blair Crosbie's sculpture captures the essence of a character or a situation in three-dimensional bronze. She recently wrote, ". . . portraiture has been my first love . . . in between portrait commissions I'm attempting to say something about my own era."

Her sculptures are in many private and public permanent collections throughout the United States, including portrait plaques of Dr. James Waring and James Porter in the Colorado Medical School and the Porter Hospital, Denver, Colorado respectively; and Dr. John Barrows in the Barrows Institute, Phoenix, Arizona. Blair Crosbie also fashioned the bronze portraits of Mr. and Mrs. Robert Herberger in the lobby of the Herberger Theater, Phoenix, Arizona.

Bibliography

Barrett, Marjorie. "Helen Blair's Little People." *Denver Post* (1970).
Martin, Peter. "Moulder of Youth." *American Magazine* (1946).
Who's Who in American Art. 19th ed. R.R. Bowker Co., 1991–1992.

Blakeslee, Sarah (1912–)

Born in Evanston, Illinois, the painter Sarah Blakeslee studied at the Art Institute of Chicago, Illinois; the Corcoran School of Art, Washington, D.C.; and the Pennsylvania Academy of Fine Arts, Philadelphia. She was the recipient of a Cresson Travelling Scholarship to Europe and did further study with Catherine Critcher.

Blakeslee exhibited her work at the "Annuals" held by the Art Institute of Chicago (1939, 1940); the "Biennial" at the Corcoran Gallery, Washington, D.C. (1940); the Pennsylvania Academy of Fine Arts, Philadelphia; the "Collector's Exhibition," North Carolina Museum of Art (1968); the Golden Gate International Exposition, 1939 World's Fair, San Francisco, California; and others. She has also showed at the National Academy of Design, New York City; and elsewhere.

Winner of awards and honors for her paintings, Blakeslee received the Mary Smith prize from the Pennsylvania Academy of Fine Arts, Philadelphia (1940); the Ranger Fund purchase prize from the National Academy of Design, New York City; first prize at Woodmere Gallery, Chestnut Hill, Pennsylvania (1952); and first prize and a gold medal at the National Exhibition, Ligonier, Pennsylvania (1961). As a Works Progress Administration (WPA) artist, she painted a mural for the post office in Strasburg, Virginia (1938).

Blakeslee's work is represented in private, public, and corporate permanent collections throughout the United States, including the Pennsylvania Academy of Fine Arts; Greenville Museum of Art, North Carolina; North Carolina Museum of Art; Muskegon Museum, Illinois; St. John's Museum, Wilmington, North Carolina; and many others.

Bibliography

Litt, Steven. "Sarah Blakeslee Paints with Calm Strokes from Past."
New Observer (September 8, 1985): E3.
Who's Who in American Art. 19th ed. R.R. Bowker Co., 1991–1992.

Blanch, Lucile (1895–1981)

Lucile (Linquist) Blanch, a painter and lithographer, was one of several prominent artists to emerge from the Minneapolis Art Institute during the World War I years. She was born December 31, 1895, in Hawley, Minnesota. Winning a scholarship, Blanch came to New York City and studied at the Art Students League with Boardman Robinson, Vincent DuMond, Frederick Gruger, and Kenneth Hayes Miller. After marrying the artist Arnold Blanch in 1922 she lived in Woodstock, New York, where she exhibited in local group shows as well as with the New York Society of Women Artists and the Whitney Studio club.

In 1931 Blanch won a first prize in graphics at the San Francisco Art Association's annual exhibit. The following year the Whitney Museum of American Art purchased her painting "August Landscape" from its first biennial, adding to its already substantial collection of her work. In 1934 Wanamaker Galleries acquired her painting "Tumblers" from the Regional Art Exhibition. The award of a Guggenheim fellowship in 1933 enabled Blanch to study abroad.

Blanch taught at the Ringling School of Art in Sarasota, Florida, from 1935 to 1936, and the following year she painted a mural at the Fort Pierce, Florida, post office. By the time of her solo exhibit at the Milch Galleries in 1937, socially conscious subjects began to appear among her usual circus themes, flowers, and landscape scenes. The Metropolitan Museum of Art purchased "Florida Wildflowers" from this show. In 1938 and 1939 Blanch exhibited with the American Artists' Congress and An American Group.

Peggy J. Hazard

Bibliography

Archives of American Art: Checklist of the Collection. Smithsonian Institution, 1977.
"Lucile Blanch Talks of Art." *New York Sun* (October 20, 1934): 26.
Marling, Karl Ann. *Woodstock, An American Art Colony, 1902–1977*.
Vassar College Art Gallery, 1977.
Reese, Albert. *American Prize Prints of the Twentieth Century*. American Artists Group, 1949.

Bland, Erlena Chisom

Born in Washington, D.C., African-American painter/sculptor/educator Erlena Chisom Bland earned a Bachelor of Fine Arts degree from Howard University, Washington, D.C., and did graduate work at the University of Maryland, College Park, where she received a Master's degree in library science.

Bland has held solo exhibitions in galleries, including the Overseas Development Council, Washington, D.C. (1989); the Capitol Gallery, Maryland Parks and Planning Commission, Landover (1988); and others. Her work has been included in many group shows, such as "Visions 1990," Westbeth Gallery, New York City (1990); the Bethune Museum-Archives, Inc., Washington, D.C. (1989); "Coastal Exchange Show," a travelling exhibition, Arts Council of Richmond, Virginia (1988); "14 Washington Women Artists," Evans-Tibbs Collection, Washington, D.C. (1986); and others.

Bland's work is in private and corporate permanent collections, including Bronson, Bronson, and McKinnon Law, Los Angeles, California; McKay Enterprises, New Orleans, Louisiana; and others. "Random Abstract" (1990) is not unlike Bland's other work of this period:

bold acrylic color on abstract plywood forms (some are heavily textured), extemporaneously interlocked, combine painting and sculpture to provide a joyous sensation in the viewer.

Bibliography

Cohen, Jean Lawlor. "News and Notes." *Museum & Arts Washington* (May–June 1989).

Hall, Robert L. *Gathered Visions: Selected Works by African American Women Artists.* Anacostia Museum, Smithsonian Institution Press, 1992.

Wilcox, Claire. "Washington, D.C.: Mid-Atlantic Artist's Page." *New Art Examiner* (November 1988).

Blayton-Taylor, Betty (1937–)

Born in Williamsburg, Virginia, Betty Blayton-Taylor earned a Bachelor of Fine Arts degree with honors from Syracuse University, New York (1959); she studied sculpture with Arnold Prince at the Art Students League, New York City (1960–1962), and at the Brooklyn Museum School, New York, with Minoria Nizuma (1964–1967). She also attended the City College of New York, where she took a summer course in educational psychology and art education (1961). In 1968 she seconded Victor D'Amico in founding the Museum of Modern Art's Children's Art Carnival, as an independent and community-based outreach program in the visual arts, designed for the education and delight of children.

Blayton-Taylor has been a productive and exhibiting artist for more than thirty years throughout the United States in universities and galleries. In addition, she has been executive director of the Children's Art Carnival since its move to Harlem in 1969; consultant to the Board of Education of the City of New York (1968 to present), member of the board of the Arts and Business Council, New York City (1975 to present), member of the board of Robert Blackburn's the Printmaking Workshop, New York City (1978 to present); and a founding member of the Studio Museum in Harlem, New York (1965).

A trip to Egypt in 1988 allowed Blayton-Taylor to realize her abiding interest in the exploration of her African heritage and its folklore. This resulted in a solo exhibition of a series of her monotypes, "Aswan Legacy" and "From the Garden of Isis" at the Isabel Neal Gallery, Chicago, Illinois (1990).

Blayton-Taylor's work has been documented on television and radio in the United States and Europe; the artist and her work are presented in the film "Five," a documentary of five black artists. Widely known as a lecturer, she has been an adjunct professor at City College of New York, and has been artist-in-residence at a number of colleges and universities, including Brown University, Fisk University, Tugaloo College, and Virginia State University at Norfolk.

Her work is in numerous private and public permanent collections, including the Metropolitan Museum of Art, New York City; the Studio Museum in Harlem; and many others.

Bibliography

Grigsby, Eugene. "Betty Blayton." *Arts & Activities* (February 1991): 38–39.

Who's Who in American Art. 19th ed. R.R. Bowker Co., 1991–1992.

Blitt, Rita (1931–)

Born in Kansas City, Missouri, the sculptor/painter Rita Blitt earned a Bachelor's degree at the University of Missouri, Kansas City (1952), having also attended the University of Illinois, Urbana. After graduation, she studied painting at the Kansas City Art Institute with Wilbur Niewald before pursuing the challenge of sculpture.

Blitt has held more than thirty solo exhibitions in museums and galleries in the United States and abroad, including Scotts, Kansas City, Missouri (1959); Spectrum Gallery, New York City (1969); Battle Creek Civic Art Center, Michigan (1975); Harkness Gallery, New York City (1977); St. Louis University, Missouri (1980); Joy Horwich Gallery, Chicago, Illinois (1987); Goldman Gallery, Haifa, Israel (1989); Bet Shmuel, Jerusalem, Israel (1989); Singapore National Museum (1991); Aspen Institute, Colorado (1992); and others.

Her sculptures have been invited to exhibitions throughout the United States and are sited in public places from Joliet, Illinois, to Singapore; from Kansas City, Missouri, to Rockaway, New Jersey; from Long Island, New York, to Davies, Florida.

Blitt has painted murals, designed banners, wall hangings, and wall sculptures on commission. Her "dancing hands" have transmuted two-handed drawings into powerful sculpted works of steel, aluminum, and acrylic sheets—some that soar high in the air, such as "One" (1984), a steel sculpture sixty-by-six-by-two-feet.

Her work is represented in public, private, and corporate permanent collections, including the Albrecht-Kemper Art Museum, St. Joseph, Missouri; St. Louis University, Missouri; National Museum of Singapore; Spertus Museum, Chicago, Illinois; Skirball Museum, Los Angeles, California; the Haifa Symphony, Israel; John F. Kennedy Library, Cambridge, Massachusetts; AT&T, Kansas City, Missouri; and others.

Bibliography

"Dancing Hands: Visual Arts of Rita Blitt." Film and Video. Pentacle Productions, 1984.

Hanani, Hannah. "Georgia O'Keefe and Other Women Artists." *Kansas Quarterly* 19:4 (1987).

Rita Blitt: Sculpture. A Catalog. Essay by David Knaus. 1989.

Sabapathy, T.K. "Dances of Life." *The Straits Times* (April 16, 1991): 7.

Watson-Jones, Virginia. *Contemporary American Women Sculptors.* Oryx Press, 1986.

Bloch, Lucienne (1909–)

Daughter of the composer Ernest Bloch, the painter/printmaker Lucienne Bloch was born in Geneva, Switzerland. She won a scholarship to the Cleveland School of Art, Ohio (1924–1925); continued her study of painting and sculpture in Paris, France, with André L'Hôte and Antoine Bourdelle respectively; and also attended the École National et Supérieure des Beaux-Arts, where she studied anatomy and drawing (1925–1928).

In addition to travel and study in Europe over the next three years, Bloch created glass sculptures for the Royal Leerdam Factory in the Netherlands. She returned to the United States in the fall of 1931, at which time Frank Lloyd Wright had occasion to see her small glass sculptures and employed her briefly as a teacher of sculpture at Taliesin East in Spring Green, Wisconsin. But it was an apprenticeship with Diego Rivera that led to her expertise and love of true fresco and more than two score mural commissions throughout the United States; her marriage to another of Rivera's apprentices, Stephen P. Dimitroff; and a deep and abiding friendship with Frida Kahlo.

"The Evolution of Music" (1937–1938), a five-by-eighty-six-foot true fresco of four panels painted for the then music room of George Washington High School, New York City, is Bloch at her best. The mural unites her sensitive reaction to and meaningful understanding of the music of many cultures gleaned from her upbringing; her technical knowledge of buon fresco learned from Rivera; and her personal approach to the visual arts based on the principles of dynamic symmetry espoused by Jay Hambidge.

Though some of her murals have been destroyed, examples still exist scattered throughout the United States in many different sites. Her children's books and other graphic works are in private and public permanent collections.

Bibliography
Bloch, Lucienne. "Murals for Use." In *Art for the Millions*. Ed. F.V. O'Connor. New York Graphic Society, 1973.
Marling, Karal Ann, and Helen A. Harrison. *7 American Women: The Depression Decade*. Vassar College, 1976.
Rubinstein, Charlotte S. *American Women Artists*. G.K. Hall & Co., 1982.
Vishny, Michele. "Lucienne Bloch: The New York City Murals." *Woman's Art Journal* (Spring–Summer 1992): 23–28.

Blondeau, Barbara (1938–1974)

A native of Detroit, Michigan, the photographer/teacher Barbara Blondeau earned a Bachelor of Fine Arts degree from the School of the Art Institute of Chicago, Illinois (1961); and a Master of Science degree from the Institute of Design of the Illinois Institute of Technology, Chicago (1968), where she studied with Joseph Jachna and Aaron Siskind.

Blondeau's teaching career included posts at St. Mary's College, Notre Dame, Indiana (1966–1968); Moore College of Art, Philadelphia, Pennsylvania (1968–1970); and the Philadelphia College of Art (now in the University of the Arts) (1970–1974).

Her photographs, which explored the use of a wide body of materials, processes, scales, and format, served as sample solutions to some of the current aesthetic problems of the photographer. Representative examples of her work are in permanent collections, including the Visual Studies Workshop, Rochester, New York; the National Gallery of Canada, Ottawa; and others.

Bibliography
Art in America (September 1976).
Camera (November 1971).
Browne, Turner, and Elaine Partnow. *Macmillan Biographical Encyclopedia of Photographic Artists & Innovators*. Macmillan.

Blum, Andrea (1950–)

A native New Yorker known for her exhibitions and installations and art in public places, Andrea Blum was educated at the Boston Museum School of Fine Arts, Massachusetts; Tufts University, Medford, Massachusetts, where she earned a Bachelor of Fine Arts degree (1973); and the Art Institute of Chicago, where she received a Master of Fine Arts degree three years later.

She has had many solo exhibitions in the United States, including the N.A.M.E. Gallery, Chicago, Illinois (1976); "Room 218," Institute for Art and Urban Resources, Long Island City, New York (1979); "Primary Pits," DeCordova Museum, Lincoln, Massachusetts (1981); Tibor de Nagy Gallery, New York City (1982); University of Colorado, Boulder (1985); "New York Diary," Institute for Contemporary Art, P.S.1, Long Island City, New York, an installation (1991); and many others. Blum has been engaged in public projects throughout the world, such as "Surveillance Marquée," Galerie des Archives, Paris, France (1992); "Surveillance Stations," STROOM, Centre for Visual Arts, The Hague, Holland (1992); "Livonia," Art in Public Places Commission, Livonia, Michigan (1991); "Street Link," Dayton City Beautiful, Ohio (1989); "Benches and Walkways," East Carolina University, Greenville, North Carolina (1985); and others.

Blum's work has been invited to many group exhibitions in the United States and abroad, such as "A Marked Difference," Maatschappij Arti et Amicitiae, Amsterdam, Holland (1992); "Projects and Proposals," 1 Percent Program, Department of Cultural Affairs, New York (1988); "Beyond the Monument," a travelling show, Massachusetts Institute of Technology (MIT), Cambridge (1983); "Architectural Sculpture," Galleria d'Arte Del Cavallino, Venice, Italy (1977); and others.

A faculty member at Hunter College, New York City (1986 to present), Blum has taught for or been a visiting artist at a number of distinguished colleges and universities in the United States from 1976 to the present. She has been the recipient of many honors and awards for her work, such as artist fellowships from the National Endowment for the Arts (NEA) (1976, 1978); a Graham Foundation fellowship (1983); a design award from the American Institute of Architects (AIA), New York State (1991); an arts award in architecture from the New York Foundation for the Arts (1992); and others.

Blum's work is represented in private, public, and corporate permanent collections, including the Art Institute of Chicago, Illinois; National Collection of Fine Arts, Washington, D.C.; University of Iowa, Iowa City; IBM; AT&T; and public projects in the cities of Paris, France; The Hague, Holland; Carlsbad, California; San Francisco, California; New York City; and many others.

Bibliography
Barrière, Philippe. "D'Est En Ouest." *L'Architecture D'Aujourd'hui* (October 1990).
Grout, Catherine. "Andrea Blum, Jacques Vielle: Une Nouvelle Vision de L'Espace Public." *Art Press* (February 1992): 40–42.
Ollman, Leah. "Art Review." *Los Angeles Times*, San Diego County (March 14, 1992).
Princenthal, Nancy. "Elasticizing Urban Spaces: Andrea Blum's Public Art Projects." *Art in America* (April 1992): 130–138.

Blumenthal, Lyn (1949–1988)

Born in Chicago, Illinois video artist Lyn Blumenthal was founding director of the Video Data Bank (1976). She earned a Master of Fine Arts degree from the School of the Art Institute of Chicago, Illinois, the same year.

Blumenthal held many solo exhibitions, screenings, installations, and some collaborative work in museums and alternate spaces from New

York to California, including "Ice Piece" (Parts I, II, and III), Museum of Contemporary Art, Chicago, Illinois (1976); "Clean Slate" (Parts I and II), the Detroit Institute of Arts, Michigan (1978); "The Pleasure of His Company," The Kitchen, New York City (1983); "Special Studies" (Parts I and II), the Institute of Contemporary Art, Boston, Massachusetts, and Hallwalls, Buffalo, New York, and a tour (1984); and others.

Winner of awards and honors, Blumenthal received a National Endowment for the Arts (NEA) fellowship (1977); grants from the New York State Council on the Arts (1983, 1985); a fellowship from the New York Foundation for the Arts (1985); and others. Examples of her work are represented in public permanent collections, including the Museum of Modern Art (MoMA), New York City; Institute of Contemporary Art, Boston, Massachusetts; and others.

Bibliography
Kirshner, Judith R. "The Science of Fiction/The Fiction of Science." *Artforum* 23 (December 1984): 92–93.
Wooster, Ann-Sargent. "Lyn Blumenthal." *The Village Voice* (June 7, 1983).
Zeichner, Arlene. "Re(Tele)visionists." *The Village Voice* (December 20, 1983).

Bobak, Molly Lamb (1922–)

A woman of many talents, Molly Lamb Bobak's first love is painting. As a student of Jack Shadbolt from 1938 to 1941 at the Vancouver School of Art, Canada, she simply "fell in and caught fire." Through painting, Bobak conveys a worldview which embraces an unshakeable faith in humanity and an intense interest in all living things. The artist most often depicts what she considers to be the "good things" in life—public celebrations, leisure activities, and flowers, which represent, for her, "pure energy." She works as a gatherer and transmitter of impressions employing sparing and, over the years, increasingly free line and brushy, glorious color. Bobak's paintings possess light and transparency, whether executed in oil or watercolor, her preferred mediums.

The artist joined the Canadian Womens' Army Corps in 1942 and became the first commissioned woman war artist in 1945. Her paintings and drawings from that time are included in many collections, including those of the National Gallery, Ottawa, Canada, and the Art Gallery of Ontario, Toronto, Canada. She is currently writing a book based on her illustrated war diary.

Bobak has received a French government scholarship for study in France, 1950–1951, and a Canada Council scholarship for study in Europe, 1960–1961. More recently she has been given the honorary degrees of Doctor of Letters, University of New Brunswick in 1983, and Doctor of Fine Arts, Mount Allison University in 1984 in recognition of her work as an artist and art educator.

Bobak has taught painting at the Vancouver School of Art (1947–1950); University of British Columbia (1958–1959); University of New Brunswick Art Centre (1960)—and continues to teach at workshops held in various centers throughout Canada. She has participated in a CBC-TV series on teaching drawing and art appreciation (c. 1956), and was instructor of a televised art course on CHSJ-TV in St. John, New Brunswick (1964–1965).

Bobak has served on the National Film Board of Canada; Stamp Design Council; National Capital Commission; and is presently on the National Gallery, Ottawa Advisory Board. Though best known for her paintings, she has also illustrated Frances Itani's book, *Linger by the Sea* (1979), and in 1989 designed three stained-glass windows for the chapel in the old arts building, University of New Brunswick. Regardless of the medium, Bobak's works invariably exhibit freshness and honesty as reflections of the artist's ability to discover all that is new in the familiar.

Delwyn Higgens

Bibliography
Bauer, Nancy. "Molly Lamb Bobak: A Painter of Silent Space." *Arts Atlantic* 9 (Winter 1989): 35–38.
Bobak, Molly Lamb. *Wildflowers of Canada*. Pagurian Press, 1978.
———. *The Queen Comes to New Brunswick: Paintings and Drawings by Molly Lamb Bobak*. Fredricton: Beaverbrook Art Gallery, 1977–1979.
———. "I Love the Army." *Canadian Art* II (April–May 1945): 147–49.
Nowlan, Alden. "Molly Bobak: A Gift for Finding Joy." *Atlantic Insight* 3 (November 1981): 72–74.

Bobrowicz, Yvonne Pacanovsky (1928–)

Born in Maplewood, New Jersey, Yvonne Pacanovsky Bobrowicz is known for her richly textured fiber art. She attended the Cranbrook Academy of Art, Bloomfield Hills, Michigan (1946–1949); studied with Anni Albers and Paolo Soleri; and, since 1950, has maintained a professional studio.

In addition to a recent solo exhibition at the "Gross McLeaf" Gallery, Philadelphia, Pennsylvania, her work has been invited to many group shows in the United States and abroad, including a miniature exhibition in Como, Italy (1992); "Art Now," Philadelphia Museum of Art, Pennsylvania (1990), and "3 Centuries of American Art," at the same museum (1976); "20th Century Textiles," Art Institute of Chicago, Illinois (1990); "Textile Biennale," Netherlands Museum, Tilburt (1989); "14th Biennale," Lausanne, Switzerland (1989); and others at the Detroit Museum of Art, Michigan; the American Craft Museum, New York City; Helen Drutt Gallery, Philadelphia, Pennsylvania; and many others.

Bobrowicz has been on the faculty of Drexel University, Philadelphia, Pennsylvania, teaching textiles and weaving since 1966. She has offered weaving and fiber art workshops at craft schools, colleges, and universities throughout the United States and Canada.

Bobrowicz has completed many important commissions for permanent collections, including a major work at the Kimball Museum, Fort Worth, Texas, for the architect Louis I. Kahn; and others for the University of Pennsylvania, Philadelphia; RCA Corporation; Sheraton Hotel; E.I. Du Pont de Nemours & Co.; and for many private collections.

Bibliography
Philadelphia Museum of Art. *Three Centuries of American Art*. Philadelphia: Philadelphia Museum of Art, 1976: 530, 628–29.
Who's Who in American Art. 19th ed. R.R. Bowker Co., 1991–1992.

Bohlen, Nina (1931–)

A painter and printmaker known for her sensitive studies of birds and animals, Nina Bohlen was born in Boston, Massachusetts. She earned her Bachelor's degree at Radcliffe College, Cambridge, Massachusetts (1953), and studied drawing and painting with Hyman Bloom (1952–1957). In the 1950s Bohlen studied sculpture with Frank Tock and Harold Tovish; she also studied painting, for a brief period in 1957, with Morton Sacks; and, three years later, she studied lithography with John Brennan at the Boston Museum School.

Bohlen had her first solo exhibition of drawings at the Carl Siembab Gallery, Boston, Massachusetts (1959), and her first solo show of drawings and monotypes twenty years later at the FAR Gallery in New York City .

She has had her work invited to group exhibitions throughout the United States, including "Salute to Boston," Boston Public Library, Massachusetts (1990–1991); DeCordova Museum, Lincoln, Massachusetts (1987); Hassam Fund Exhibition, American Academy of Arts and Letters, New York City (1978, 1982); Westmoreland Museum, Greensburg, Pennsylvania (1973); and others.

Widely travelled in Kenya, Thailand, and Venezuela, Bohlen illustrated her sister's book, *Baboon Orphan*, in 1981. Winner of awards and honors for her work, Bohlen received an art award from the American Academy of Arts and Letters, New York City (1977) and was artist-in-residence at the Camargo Foundation, Cassis, France (1989).

Bohlen taught a monotype workshop in Lubec, Maine (1984); and also taught in Massachusetts at the Newton Arts Center (1984–1988); Pine Manor College, Chestnut Hill (1985–1992); and to private students (1970–1992). Her work is in private and public permanent collections, including the Fogg Art Museum, Harvard University, Cambridge, Massachusetts; Fuller Memorial Museum, Brockton; Boston Public Library—all in Massachusetts; and others.

Bibliography
Stephan, Karin. *Nina Bohlen: Her Life and Art*. Boston Public Library, 1987.
Who's Who in American Art. 19th ed. R.R. Bowker Co., 1991–1992.

Bohnen, Blythe (1940–)

Born in Evanston, Illinois, the painter/photographer/muralist Blythe Bohnen earned a Bachelor's degree in art from Smith College, Northampton, Massachusetts (1962); received a Bachelor of Fine Arts degree five years later from Boston University's School of Fine and Applied Art; and obtained a Master of Fine Arts degree in painting from Hunter College, New York City (1972).

Bohnen has held a number of solo exhibitions of her work in the United States and abroad, including A.I.R. Gallery, New York City (1972, 1974, 1976, 1977); Rhode Island University, Providence (1973); Douglass College, Rutgers University, New Brunswick, New Jersey (1976); International Cultural Center, Antwerp, Belgium (1978); Artline Gallery, The Hague, Holland (1979); Contemporary Arts Center, New Orleans, Louisiana (1980); Galerie Mukai, Tokyo, Japan (1984); and others.

Her work has been invited to myriad group exhibitions throughout the world, including New York City; Stamford, Connecticut; Indianapolis, Indiana; State College, Pennsylvania; Hamburg, Germany; Vienna, Austria; Paris, France; and Rome, Italy. Of special import are her drawings, which were included in Documenta 6, Kassel, Germany (1977); "Extraordinary Women," Museum of Modern Art (MoMA), New York City (1977); and others.

Bohnen, who was commissioned to create a fifteen-by-thirty-foot ceramic tile relief mural for the Library for the Blind/Record Storage Center, Trenton, New Jersey (1980–1982), was the subject of a television production, "Art Show—Blythe Bohnen," for WABC-TV (1977). She received a National Endowment for the Arts (NEA) fellowship (1978), and was artist-in-residence at Rutgers University as a result of an earlier NEA grant (1976).

Her work is in private, public, and corporate permanent collections, including the Metropolitan Museum of Art, Brooklyn Museum, MoMA, Whitney Museum of American Art—all in New York City; Dallas Museum of Fine Art, Texas; Albright-Knox Art Gallery, Buffalo, New York; Boston Museum of Fine Art, Massachusetts; Art Institute of Chicago, Illinois; High Museum, Atlanta, Georgia; National Gallery of Art, Osaka, Japan; and many others.

Bibliography
Alloway, Lawrence. "Blythe Bohnen." *Artforum* (November 1976).
Heine, Ellen. "Blythe Bohnen." *Arts Magazine* (November 1980).
Kuspit, Donald. "Blythe Bohnen at Light." *Art in America* (December 1984).
Moss, Jacqueline. "Anatomy of a Brush Stroke." *Christian Science Monitor* (January 14, 1974).

Bontecou, Lee (1931–)

Born in Providence, Rhode Island, the sculptor Lee Bontecou studied painting at the Art Students League, New York City, then switched to study sculpture there with William Zorach (1952–1955). She did further study at the Skowhegan School of Painting and Sculpture, Maine, and, on a two-year Fulbright fellowship to Italy, did still further research and travel.

Bontecou is best known for her outsized (betweeen four- and twenty-feet high) canvas and welded-steel-frame reliefs centered about voids which shock and rock the viewer. Bontecou held her first solo exhibition in New York City in 1959. She has since had her work viewed both in solo and group exhibitions in the United States and abroad, including the "Annual Exhibition of American Paintings and Sculpture," Art Institute of Chicago, Illinois (1962, 1963); "Twenty-Eighth Biennial Exhibition," Corcoran Gallery, Washington, D.C. (1963); "Annual Exhibition of Sculpture and Prints," Whitney Museum of American Art, New York City (1963, 1964); "Contemporary Painters and Sculptors as Printmakers," MoMA, New York City (1966); "Prints and Drawings by Lee Bontecou," Wesleyan University, Middletown, Connecticut (1975); "American Artists '76: A Celebration," Marion Koogler McNay Art Institute, San Antonio, Texas (1976); and many others.

Her work is represented in private and public permanent collections, including the Albright-Knox Art Gallery, Buffalo, New York; the Guggenheim Museum, and the Whitney Museum of American Art—both in New York City; the Hirshhorn Museum and Sculpture Garden and the National Museum of Women in the Arts, Washington, D.C.; the Stedelijk Museum, Amsterdam, the Netherlands; Walker Art Center, Minneapolis, Minnesota; and many others.

Bibliography
Ashton, Dore. *Modern American Sculpture*. Harry N. Abrams, 1968.
Mellow, James R. "Art: Bontecou's Well-Fed Fish and Malevolent

Flowers." *The New York Times* (June 6, 1971): D19.

Watson-Jones, Virginia. *Contemporary American Women Sculptors.* Oryx Press, 1986.

"What I Do Just Is." *Vogue* (May 1969).

Borden, Linda (Lizzie) (1957–)

Educated at Wellesley College, Massachusetts, where she studied painting and art history, Lizzie Borden went to New York City, where she wrote criticism for *Artforum* before making films. Her preparation includes editing *From Mao to Mozart*, sculptor Richard Serra's *Stahlwerk*, and Michael Oblowitz's *Minus Zero*, examples of art films made from documentary footage. She has made three films: *Regrouping* (1976), *Born in Flames* (1983), and *Working Girls* (1986). Her central theme is the sexual politics of work, and her presentation is the pseudo-documentary shot in cinema verité style. She avoids advocating easy political solutions and typifies the independent filmmaker who writes, directs, coproduces, edits, and distributes her films. Borden has been grouped with the new New York Cinema of Sara Driver, Jim Jarmusch, and Spike Lee.

Born in Flames is considered an important feminist film, although it has been criticized for its occasional agitprop content. Borden casts nonactors in this film to emphasize a spontaneous collaborative intention and to match the purposely budget production values which express the narrative's lower Manhattan world. The film took five years to finish because of the problems financing it. The film's theme is the impossibility of true female liberation and the continuing power of men in the workplace. Her vision for *Born in Flames* was to create a utopian world in which women from different social, economic, ethnic, and sexual camps worked together for their collective liberation. The film portrayed African-American liberationists, and its actors included Florence Kennedy, the black civil rights activist, and Jeanne Satterfield, a basketball player. The narrative is constructed by a complex series of montages and improvised political discussions and accompanied by fast-paced music.

Working Girls, which was shown in the Directors' Fortnight Showcase at Cannes and at film festivals in Montréal, Telluride, and Toronto, depicts a day in the life of several call girls working in an apartment which is their "office" and which is run by a madam. The sex scenes are shot from the woman's point of view, and Borden avoids using any traditionally erotic content or shooting techniques to portray the sex without eroticism or titillation. Between customers the women talk about their lives and do their schoolwork (one attends college). The main character, Molly, is a lesbian and Yale graduate with degrees in English and art history. While some feminists criticized the film for not taking a position against prostitution, Borden argued that the prostitution portrayed in the film allows women some control over their labor and that the conflicts are not strictly along gender lines: several men appear kind and vulnerable, and the madam is cheated by the girls as repayment for her greed. Prostitutes are symbolic of women's work for Borden and may be less enslaved to their employers than office workers, for example, while women in prostitution re-enact sexual codes and rituals which are enacted generally in all intimate relationships, or the routinizing of sex, in Borden's view. One of Borden's intentions was to remove the stigma of second-class citizenship of prostitutes. For her, prostitution is about work, not sex. Borden's camera technique is simply to observe, rather than to film from special angle shots or use editing for emotional effect.

Julie F. Codell

Bibliography

Beauvais, Paul Jude. "Lizzie Borden's Working Girls: Interpretation and the Limits of Ideology." *Postscript: Essays in Film and the Humanities* 10 (Winter 1991): 50–63.

De Lauretis, Teresa. *Technologies of Gender: Essays on Theory, Film, and Fiction.* Indiana University Press, 1987.

Dika, Vera. "Critical/Mass." *Art in America* (1987): 39–41.

Fusco, Coco. "Working Girls: An Interview with Lizzie Borden." *Afterimage* 14 (1986): 6–7.

Haskell, Molly. *From Reverence to Rape.* 2nd ed. University of Chicago Press, 1987.

Jackson, Lynne. "Labor Relations: An Interview with Lizzie Borden." *Cineaste* 15 (1987): 4–9.

Judge, Maureen, and Lori Spring. "An Interview with Lizzie Borden." *CineAction* 8 (1987): 69–76.

Kuhn, A., and S. Radstone, eds. *Women in Film.* Fawcett, 1990, 47–48.

Macdonald, Scott. "Interview with Lizzie Borden." *Feminist Studies* 15 (Summer 1989): 327–45.

Perlmutter, Ruth. "Lizzie Borden: An Interview." *Post Script: Essays in Film and the Humanities* 6 (Winter 1987): 2–11.

Boretz, Naomi (1935–)

A native of New York City, Naomi Boretz earned her Bachelor's degree from Brooklyn College, New York (1957); received a Master's degree in art history from Rutgers University, New Brunswick, New Jersey (1976); and obtained a Master's degree in studio art from the City University of New York (CUNY) (1971). She also studied at the Art Students League, New York City (1968), and the Boston Museum Art School, Massachusetts (1956).

Associate professor of fine arts and department chair at Wilson College, Chambersburg, Pennsylvania, Boretz has held a number of solo exhibitions of her work between 1970 and 1992, including Fordham University (1973); Nicholas Roerich Museum (1972); and the Hudson River Museum (1978)—all in New York City; Brockton Municipal Gallery, Massachusetts (1973); University of Richmond, Virginia (1976); and many others.

Her work has been invited to group exhibitions in the United States and abroad, such as the Condeso-Lawler Gallery, New York (1987); Brooklyn Museum, New York (1972); Carnegie-Mellon University, Pittsburgh, Pennsylvania (1990); San José Art Museum, California (1982); Crawford Municipal Museum and Art Gallery, Cork, Ireland (1988); University of East Anglia, England (1989); and many others.

Recipient of many honors and grants for her work, Boretz was an artist fellow at the Ossabaw Foundation, Georgia (1975); Virginia Center for Creative Arts (1980, 1986); New Jersey State Council on the Arts (1985–1986); Tyrone Guthrie Arts Centre, Ireland (1987); Writers-Artist Guild, Saskatchewan, Canada (1988); and others.

Her work is represented in private and public permanent collections throughout the world, including the Metropolitan Museum of Art and the Guggenheim Museum—both in New York City; Yale University Art Gallery, New Haven, Connecticut; the British Museum, London, England; Bibliothèque Nationale, Paris, France; Galería Nazionale d'Arte Moderna, Rome, Italy; National Central Library, Taipei, Taiwan; and hosts of others.

Bibliography
Raynor, Vivian. "Art." *The New York Times* (March 29, 1981).
"Today's World." A Radio Interview. *Archives of American Art*. 1980.
Who's Who in American Art. 19th ed. R.R. Bowker Co., 1991–1992.
Who's Who in the East. 24th ed. Marquis, 1992–1993.

Borgatta, Isabel Case (1922–)

Born in Madison, Wisconsin, sculptor Isabel Case Borgatta attended Smith College, Northampton, Massachusetts (1938–1940) and completed her Bachelor of Fine Arts degree at Yale University, New Haven, Connecticut (1944). She studied in New York City at the New School for Social Research, the Art Students League, and with José de Creeft. Known primarily for her sculptures of women in stone or wood, Borgatta has also worked with two-dimensional abstract landscapes and figurative bas-reliefs.

Borgatta's females represent women in all guises, as seen in such works as: "Expectation" (1954), depicting a pregnant woman; "Trojan Woman" and "Danae I" and "II" (1974); "Triad" of nymphs for the Grand Hyatt Hotel in New York City (1980); and "Enid," the earth-mother for the Haupt Glass Pavilion at the New York Botanical Garden (1982), New York City.

First exhibiting at the Village Art Center, New York City, in 1947, Borgatta has continued to exhibit in individual and group exhibitions, including: Frank Rehn Gallery; "Women Choose Women," New York Cultural Center; and "20th Century Sculpture"—all in New York City; Hudson River Museum, Yonkers, New York; Galerie Coach, Paris, France; and International Sculpture Conference, 1992.

Borgatta received the D'Orsay Prize from the National Association of Women Artists (1952); Jacques Lipshitz Award (1961); Yaddo fellowship (1971, 1973); the Virginia Center for Creative Arts fellowship (1985, 1992); and a grant from the Greek government to carve in Delphi (1990).

Borgatta's works are represented in the permanent collection of the Hartford Atheneum, Connecticut; Norfolk Museum of Fine Arts, Virginia; and Hudson River Museum, Yonkers, New York, as well as varied private, corporate, and university collections. She is active in the Women's Caucus for the Arts, Artist's Equity, Municipal Art Society of New York, Sculptors League, and College Art Association. She is coeditor of *The Guild Reporter* of the Sculptors Guild, to which she is a regular contributor.

Judith Sealy

Bibliography
Jones, Virginia Watson. *American Women Sculptors*. Oryx Press, 1986.
Podavano, Anthony. *The Process of Sculpture*. Doubleday, 1981.
Van Doren, Mark. *The Sculptures of Isabel Borgatta*. Galerie St. Etienne, 1954.

Boris, Bessie (1917–)

Born in Johnstown, Pennsylvania, the painter Bessie Boris attended Pratt Institute, Brooklyn, New York (1934–1936) and studied painting with George Grosz and Vaclav Vytlacil at the Art Students League, New York City (1940–1942).

Boris has held solo exhibitions in galleries and art centers in the United States, including Washburn University, Topeka, Kansas (1949); Cober Gallery, New York City (1960–1961, 1963, 1965, 1968); Image Gallery, Stockbridge, Massachusetts (1970, 1976, 1980, 1983, 1986); Berkshire Museum, Pittsfield, Massachusetts (1987); Katharina Rich Perlow Gallery, New York City (1990, 1992); and others.

Her work has been invited to group exhibitions, including those at the Virginia Museum of Fine Arts, Richmond (1945); Norfolk Museum of Fine Arts, Virginia (1947); "21st Biennial," Corcoran Gallery of Art, Washington, D.C. (1949); "Six Americans," Institute of Contemporary Art, Boston, Massachusetts (1951); Silvermine Guild of Artists, New Canaan, Connecticut (1963); "Annual Exhibitions," Pennsylvania Academy of Fine Arts, Philadelphia (1961, 1963, 1969); Nominee for the Childe Hassam Purchase Fund, American Academy and Institute of Arts and Letters (1970, 1972, 1976); "The Human Face," Image Gallery, Stockbridge, Massachusetts (1977); and others.

Boris's works are represented in private, public, and corporate permanent collections, including the Norfolk Museum of Fine Arts, Virginia; Denver Museum, Colorado; Montclair Museum of Art, New Jersey; University of Massachusetts, Amherst; Smith College, Northampton, Massachusetts; Berkshire Museum, Pittsfield, Massachusetts; Chase Manhattan Bank, New York City; and others.

Bibliography
Balken, Debra Bricker. "Bessie Boris." A Catalog. Berkshire Museum, 1987.
Russell, Gloria. "Berkshire Museum Showing Works by Bessie Boris." *Springfield Republican* (May 24, 1987): G-6.
Waisins, Edward. "Bessie Boris." *Art New England* 7:8 (September 1986): 17.
Who's Who in American Art. 19th ed. R.R. Bowker Co., 1991–1992.

Borochoff, Sloan

The painter/printmaker (Ida) Sloan Borochoff was educated at various institutions, including the High Museum of Art, Atlanta, Georgia (1939); the University of Georgia, Athens (1939–1940); Georgia State University, Atlanta (1940); the Atlanta Art Institute, Georgia (1968); and the Chicago School of Interior Decorating, Illinois, where she earned a diploma (1966).

Borochoff exhibited her work in many solo and group shows throughout the United States and examples of her output are in private and public permanent collections, such as the White House, Washington, D.C.; Hebrew Academy, Atlanta, Georgia; Designs Unlimited, Inc.; Temple Emanu-El, Tucson, Arizona; and many others.

A multi-faceted individual, active in the social and cultural life of her community, Borochoff has won many honors for her work. She has been consultant for a national art exhibit; artistic director for the Atlanta Playhouse Theatre (1972); and author and one of the artists of "Images of Women," a television production for WGTV (1972). She was selected as "Atlanta's Leading Lady" (1976); coedited a newsletter for the Atlanta Music Club (1989); and was a former President of B'nai Brith Women, among other achievements.

Bibliography
Collins, J.L. *Women Artists in America II*. Collins. 1975.
Who's Who in American Art. 19th ed. R.R. Bowker Co., 1991–1992.

Bothwell, Dorr (1902–)

Widely-travelled painter-printmaker Dorr Bothwell was born in San Francisco, California, in 1902. At the age of nineteen she attended the California School of Fine Arts in her native city, where she studied under the aegis of Rudolph Schaeffer. Three years later Bothwell became a student at Schaeffer's own School of Design, soaking up his philosophy of *notan* (a Japanese-based systems approach to design based on the unity of opposites). In 1949 she was awarded an Abraham Rosenberg Fellowship for independent art study in France.

A veritable globe-girder, Bothwell was in American Samoa (1928–1929), where she painted and studied tapa cloth design; she devoted herself to art history and painting when in England, France, and Germany (1930–1931) and spent a sabbatical year in England, three decades later, preparing for a show of paintings. Bothwell was in Tunisia and western Nigeria (1966–1967) absorbing the practice of the crafts in those countries; in 1970 she was in England, France, and Holland investigating twelfth-century enamels; and four years later Bothwell went to Bali, Java, and Sumatra to examine batik, woodcarving, and folk design. In the 1980s she toured China, Mexico, France, and Italy on separate journeys.

Her first solo exhibition of paintings, a group of semi-abstract works on canvas, occurred in 1927 at the Modern Gallery in San Francisco, California; two years later another solo show of Samoan work opened at the San Diego Fine Arts Museum, California, and in 1930 still another one-person exhibit of Samoan paintings was shown at the Beaux-Arts Gallery in San Francisco, California; Bothwell has had ten solo shows at the Bay Window Gallery in Mendocino, California, including a retrospective of forty-three years of printmaking (1986). She has had solo shows in the M.H. De Young Memorial Museum, San Francisco, California (1952, 1963), and the Meltzer Gallery, New York City (1958); and has exhibited her work in many group shows throughout the United States and abroad, including the III Bienale, São Paulo, Brazil, and the Carnegie International, Pittsburgh, Pennsylvania (1952, 1958).

Her most recent solo shows of screenprints, drawings, and paintings reflecting a synthesis of cultures, color, and abstract form were shown at the Tobey C. Moss Gallery, Los Angeles, California (1989, 1991). With respect to her prints, Bothwell won a Purchase prize at the Brooklyn Museum's 2nd National Print Exhibition (1948), received the award for visual arts from the Mayor of San Francisco, California (1979), and had a retrospective of her screen prints at the Mendocino Art Center, California (1985). Examples of her work are in the permanent collections of the Metropolitan Museum of Art, the Museum of Modern Art (MoMA), and the Whitney Museum of American Art—all in New York City; the Fogg Museum at Harvard University, Cambridge, Massachusetts; the Victoria and Albert Museum and the British Museum of London, England; the Bibliothèque Nationale of Paris, France; and the National Museum of Women in the Arts, Washington, D.C.

Bothwell has taught design, color, and composition on the faculties of many art institutions, including her alma mater, the California School of Fine Arts (1944–1948; 1955–1958); Parsons School of Design in New York City (1952); and the San Francisco Art Institute (1959–1961); the Mendocino Art Center (1983), and the Ansel Adams Photography Workshop, Yosemite National Park—all in California (1964–1978).

Bibliography

Bothwell, Dorr, and Marlys Frey. *Notan: The Dark-Light Principle of Design.* Van Nostrand Reinhold, 1968.

Chipp, Herschel B. "San Francisco: One-Man Shows." *Art News* 57:48 (April 1958).

Who's Who in American Art. R.R. Bowker Co., 1980.

Botke, Jessie Arms (1883–1971)

A passion for birds—especially those with extravagant plumage—dominates the art of Jessie Arms Botke. Born in Chicago, Illinois, she received her initial training at that city's Art Institute under John Johanson and Charles Woodbury; she also studied with Albert Herter. Inspired by a view of white peacocks at the Bronx Zoo, New York City, Botke devoted the major part of her career to creating meticulously-detailed, brilliantly-colored images of such birds, in lush settings, generally depicted in oil on canvas (with tempera underpainting), and frequently embellished with gold leaf. She also worked in watercolor.

Beginning in 1916 Botke exhibited regularly, especially in New York, her native Illinois, and her adopted state: California. Her work has been shown at the Art Institute of Chicago, Illinois (1916, 1917, 1918, 1919, 1920–1925, and 1926); as well as the National Academy of Design, New York City; the Pennsylvania Academy of Fine Arts, Pennsylvania; the Los Angeles County Museum of Art, and the Palace of the Legion of Honor, San Francisco—both in California; and many other institutions. During the course of her career Botke won nearly a dozen prizes. In addition to easel paintings she produced a number of murals, sometimes working in collaboration with her husband, the Dutch-born painter and printmaker, Cornelius Botke (1887–1954). For many years Botke lived with her husband and son on a ranch near Santa Paula, California, though she continued to travel extensively, visiting zoos all across the United States and Europe to study and sketch birds.

Bibliography

Hughes, Edan. *Artists in California, 1786–1940.* Hughes Publishing Co., 1989, 62–63.

"Jessie Arms Botke: A Painting Career that has Revolved Around Peacocks." *American Artist* 13:6 (issue 126) (June 1949): 27–30.

Bouchard, Mary (1912–1945)

Mary Bouchard was born at Baie Saint-Paul, Charlevoix County, Québec. She and her sisters, Marie Cécile and Emily, taught themselves to paint. Their "primitive" paintings were very much in demand at the end of the 1930s and their studio was often visited by professional painters, such as Marius Barbeau, Jean-Paul Lemieux, and Jori Smith.

Winner of prizes and honors in Montréal and Québec, Bouchard became a member of the Society of Contemporary Art and exhibited annually with the group. In addition her work was shown in New York City (1938); Andover, Massachusetts (1942); Rio de Janeiro, Brazil (1945); and other venues. Two memorial exhibitions of her paintings were mounted by the Dominion Gallery, Montréal (1947, 1952).

Bibliography

Eber, Dorothy. "What Québec's 'Primitives' Don't Know About Art is Making Them Rich." *Maclean's* 78:7 (April 3, 1965): 17–19.

Boucher, Tania Kunsky (1927–)

Born in Wilno, Russia, the painter/sculptor Tania Kunsky Boucher was educated at a number of institutions, including the College of the City of New York, where she received a Bachelor of Science degree; the University of Pennsylvania, Philadelphia, where she earned a Master of Science degree; and the University of Delaware, Newark, which awarded her a Bachelor of Arts degree. Boucher also studied with Tom Bostelle.

Boucher held a number of solo exhibitions of her work, including the Westtown Friends School, Pennsylvania (1971); University of Delaware (1973); Station Gallery, Wilmington, Delaware (1989–1992); and others. Her work was invited to group shows, such as the Carspecken Scott Art Gallery, Wilmington, Delaware (1974); Woodmere Art Museum, Chestnut Hill, Pennsylvania (1980); Baltimore Museum Loan Library, Maryland (1989); Aeolian Palace, Pocopson, Pennsylvania (1991); "Women's Exhibition," University of Delaware, Newark (1992); and others.

Describing her craft, Boucher recently wrote: "For the past fifteen years, my work has centered around the 'mask' which, in my paintings, is rendered in paint, pastel and collage and, in my sculptures, in bronze (thinly cast) finished with acid or painted."

Bibliography
Collins, Clint. "Tania Kunsky Boucher." *Delaware Today Magazine* (September 1981).
Hope, Warren. "Tania Kunsky Boucher." *Wilmington News Journal* (April 23, 1978).
Who's Who in American Art. 19th ed. R.R. Bowker Co., 1991–1992.

Boughton, Alice (1869–1943)

Born in Brooklyn, New York, the photographer Alice Boughton attended Miss Rounds' School in her native borough and studied painting in Paris, France. Boughton was an associate of Gertrude Kasebier.

A member of the Cosmopolitan Club of New York City, Boughton had a photographic studio in that city from 1890 until she retired in the 1930s. Her specialties were portraits of major writers and theater personalities, nudes, and photographs of children.

Representative examples of her work are in private and public permanent collections, including the Duse Memorial Library, Asola, Italy; International Museum of Photography, George Eastman House, Rochester, New York; and the Metropolitan Museum of Art and Museum of Modern Art (MoMA)—both in New York City.

Bibliography
Browne, Turner, and Elaine Partnow. *Macmillan Biographical Encyclopedia of Photographic Artists & Innovators.* Macmillan, 1983.
Green, Jonathan, ed. *Camera Work: A Critical Anthology.* 1973.

Bourgeois, Louise (1911–)

A sculptor whose work owes much of its inspiration to surrealism, Louise Bourgeois was born in Paris, France. Her parents, Josephine and Louis Bourgeois, were proprietors of a tapestry restoration business and, at about the age of ten, she became a part of that enterprise when, at her mother's urging, she began making drawings for use in reconstructing lost portions of tapestries.

Upon graduating from the Lycée Fénélon in Paris, France, in 1932, Bourgeois enrolled at the Sorbonne, where she studied mathematics. But art was her primary interest, and she soon left the university to enter the École des Beaux-Arts. Finding the curriculum there too restrictive, she later moved onto other schools, including the Académie Julian and the Académie de la Grand-Chaumière and worked in the atelier of Fernand Léger whom she later credited with first whetting her interest in sculpture. Initially, however, she concentrated mostly on painting and drawing, manifesting a preference for cubist abstraction. Also at that time she became aware of the surrealist movement that currently held sway over much of the French art world and that several years later would play a central part in molding her mature work.

In 1938 Bourgeois met Robert Goldwater, a young American art historian who was just completing his doctoral thesis. Following their marriage that year she accompanied him to the United States. Shortly after settling in New York City, she enrolled in the Art Students League. Though generally a loner throughout her career, she also began forming associations within the New York art community and eventually became friends with such figures as Willem de Kooning and Jackson Pollock. In her work she concentrated on painting, drawing, and printmaking, and by the latter half of the 1940s her pieces in these media fell into a style best defined as surrealist expressionism. Many of them carried strong feminist overtones: a good case in point being "Femme-Maison," an ink and oil composition showing the limbs of a woman extruding from a house.

Following two solo exhibitions (1945 and 1947) Bourgeois became increasingly dissatisfied with the constraints of working in two dimensions. By 1940 she had turned to sculpture, and toward the end of that year seventeen of her works in wood went on view at a New York gallery. She continued to work primarily in wood for many years, producing pieces that consisted largely of columnar figural abstractions. In the early 1960s, however, she began experimenting with a host of other materials that included bronze, stone, and plaster. At the same time her compositions became more varied and complex—a shift that Bourgeois herself characterized as a "change from rigidity to pliability" and that critics claim marks the advent of her best work.

Despite the substantial alterations in her work, certain elements of it remained constant. Eschewing the strictly formal preoccupations that came to prevail among so many American modernists following World War II, Bourgeois never forsook her interest in investing her art with subjective meaning. Working in a semi-abstract surrealistic idiom, she made her sculptures vehicles for expressing the feelings of love, fear, hostility, and eroticism that had their origin in memories of her French childhood. As the artist herself often put it, the creation of one of her pieces in large degree represented a kind of personal exorcism. An often-cited example of that is "Destruction of the Father" (1974), which evokes a scene of a man devoured by his children and is reflective of the artist's own troubled memories of her father.

Broad critical recognition of Bourgeois's work was slow in coming, due partly at least to the artist's abiding preference for the solitary life. But the quickening ferment of the feminist movement in the 1970s brought with it an escalating interest in Bourgeois's sculptural visualizations of her feelings, particularly as they related to sexuality and male-female relationships. At the same time the personal content of her art, in general, seemed to fill a need that had long gone unmet in the contemporary art world, in the face of the art establishment's longstanding and overriding concern with form. Among the signs of greater appreciation spanned by these developments was an honorary degree from Yale University, New Haven, Connecticut, and an award for outstanding achievement from the Women's Caucus of Art, New York City. But the most significant testimony to Bourgeois's late-life admission into the ranks of American art notables was her retrospective exhibition at the Museum of Modern Art (MoMA), New York City, in 1982, a form of recognition rarely accorded to a living artist.

Frederick S. Voss

Bibliography

Gardner, Paul. "The Discreet Charm of Louise Bourgeois." *Art News* 79 (February 1980): 80–86.

Hughes, Robert. "A Sense of Female Experience." *Time* 120:116 (November 22, 1982).

Kuspit, Donald. "Louise Bourgeois—Where Angels Fear to Tread." *Artforum* 25 (March 1987): 115–120.

———. *Bourgeois: An Interview with Louise Bourgeois by Donald Kuspit.* Random House/Vintage Books, 1988.

Pels, Marsha. "Louise Bourgeois: A Sear for Gravity." *Art International* 23 (October 1979): 46–54.

Rubin, William S. "Some Reflections Prompted by the Recent Work of Louise Bourgeois." *Art International* 13 (March 20, 1969): 17–20.

Wye, Deborah. *Louise Bourgeois.* The Museum of Modern Art, 1982.

Bourke-White, Margaret (1904–1971)

Born in New York City, Margaret Bourke-White was an American photojournalist known for her photos that captured world events during the dramatic decades of the 1920s through the 1950s. Daughter of a successful engineering designer and a self-taught mother, Bourke-White's early interests included biology and technology. In 1921 she attended Rutgers University, New Brunswick, New Jersey, and then went on to Columbia University, New York City, where she took a course at the Clarence H. White School of Photography. She continued as an amateur photographer during her college years and finally graduated from Cornell University, Ithaca, New York, in 1927. She then moved to Cleveland, Ohio, where her family lived, and started her professional career. From 1928 until 1936 Bourke-White produced a series of photographs based on a wide variety of industries: pigs, watches, automobiles, paper mills, etc. She began this period of industrial photography with the steel industry. Otis Steel Mill in Cleveland hired her for a promotional booklet for the Otis stockholders. She brought a new dramatic view and visual excitement to these photos that previously had not existed. The steel industry was at its peak in the 1920s, and Bourke-White wanted to convey the power, energy, drama, and beauty that steel was to the Industrial Age.

Other steel companies, such as Republic Steel and Chrysler, Inc., then commissioned her to photograph their plants. She prided herself on the ability to produce a picture under any condition. Her passion and enthusiasm are perceived in her industrial subject as well as the idea of the interpretation of the age in which she lived. This is the conception of photography as an art which Bourke-White helped to originate. Her aim was to interpret history through her photographs.

Her Otis Steel photographs interested Henry Luce, the publisher of *Time Magazine*, who sent for her in 1929. He was captured by the dignity and excitement of industry that Bourke-White had photographed.

In 1930 Luce launched *Fortune Magazine*, whose central focus was industry. Bourke-White photographed meat packing, stockyards, shoemaking, commercial orchid growing, watch factories—anything to do with industry.

Her reputation grew as she was able to photograph the most harsh industries, such as logging and mining, under extreme conditions.

Bourke-White saw an aesthetic quality and inherent beauty to the industries that she captured on film as well as their greatness to an age.

During her "Industrial" years, Bourke-White had the opportunity to travel to the then very closed society of the Soviet Union. The Soviets were struggling to develop from an agrarian society to an industrial one, and Bourke-White captured this. She wanted to convey the dramatic change that the Soviets encountered as well as the birth of industry. Bourke-White photographed Moscow's bread factories and textile mills, Dnieperstroi's dam construction and Rostov's collective farms, among others.

The Soviet people were a large part of these industrial photographs in that they were the driving force behind the emerging industry. Bourke-White's own recollections and anecdotes can be found in her book, *Eyes on Russia.* Bourke-White made three trips to Russia to photograph its industry and people during this decade—the last being in 1933. She made 3,000 negatives and the first complete documentary of the new industrial Soviet Russia.

Bourke-White returned to the United States and began advertising work. This consisted of food pages for the *Saturday Evening Post*, *Vanity Fair*, and other popular magazines. She also was hired by the Pan-American Airline Corp. in 1934 to photograph their new Miami terminal. Eastern Airlines used her in 1935 to photograph their routes from the air, and this in turn led to a lifelong love for flying.

She became less and less satisfied and more bored by advertising photography and made a resolution that her photographic assignments must be creative and purposeful.

So began her romantic and professional alliance in 1936 with Erskine Caldwell, the author of *Tobacco Road.* From their collaboration came "You Have Seen Their Faces," which documented American social conditions—specifically those of the American farmer, the sharecropper, and laborer. They produced a photo-documentary of social injustice focused on the South. The poverty, despair, sickness, and apathy that Bourke-White's photos reflected were new and different from what she had previously done. The drama and dignity of her photos remained but were veiled with the pathos and pain of real people. This was one of the great photography projects of her life—the other being *Life Magazine.*

Henry Luce again called on Bourke-White's gift for photography for his new magazine *Life*; this magazine was based on photos and their being able to tell a story. During her collaboration with *Life*, she was able to maintain her freedom to do personal projects such as her book, *Say, Is this the U.S.A.*, of 1940.

In 1936 Bourke-White's photo of a Northwest dam sponsored by the New Deal project became the first *Life* magazine cover, along with a ten-page essay of the life of the workers. A new magazine with a photo-documentary style was born.

A number of early *Life* assignments by Bourke-White focused on Americana trivia—small-town life. This changed in 1938 when *Life* sent Bourke-White to Czechoslovakia to cover the developing upheaval of Europe. Erskine Caldwell went with her, and together they produced a book, *North of the Danube*, which exposed the dangerous politics of the time. In 1939 Bourke-White and Caldwell married.

Bourke-White and Caldwell found themselves in Russia in 1941 at the request of *Life*. In July when the German bombs fell on Moscow Bourke-White was the only foreign photographer present. The book, *Shooting the Russian War* (1942), was published from this experience since *Life* couldn't give the extensive coverage needed for all the photos taken at this time.

During the early war years Bourke-White went to London and photographed that city during the Blitz, as well as Winston Churchill. While in Russia she captured Stalin on film and became fearfully aware of the change that he had inflicted on the Soviet Union.

When America entered the war in 1942 Bourke-White was eager to become a war correspondent. She was again assigned to England and a bomber base, although she was not allowed to go on flying missions; the men correspondents were. During the North African campaign she was assigned to a ship convoy and was torpedoed by the Germans in the Mediterranean. After this event she was given permission to go on a bombing mission. Bourke-White became the first woman to accompany an Air Force crew on a bombing mission.

During the war her marriage ended, and she went on to photographing the war on the ground in Italy with the Army service forces in 1944. Bourke-White followed the conquering American army into Germany in 1945. She recorded the devastation and total destruction of the German cities and the battered society. Most shocking are her photos of Buchenwald and Erla—the Nazi death camps. The atrocities and painful suffering are captured and locked in time. In 1946, *Dear Fatherland, Rest Quietly*, Bourke-White's diary on the fall of Germany, was published.

Next came the "India Years," 1946–1948, in which the photographer was sent by *Life* to cover the birth of the nations of India and Pakistan. Through her photographs she tried to present an understanding of India and its people.

Her photos of Gandhi, Indian refugees, and camps, as well as the street violence, presented the struggle for freedom of the Indian people. Another photo-documentary book was published, *Halfway to Freedom: A Report on the New India*.

During the Korean War, Bourke-White got a new slant on war—focusing on a Communist guerrilla who surrendered and was repatriated. She wanted to relate war to people—the soldiers as well as the civilians.

In 1953 Bourke-White contracted Parkinson's disease, which slowly crippled her, and, after 1957, she was forced to give up photography. In 1955 she started her biography, *Portrait of Myself*, which was published in 1963. She retired from *Life* magazine in 1969 and died in 1971.

Karen E. Speirs

Bibliography

Bourke-White, Margaret. *Portrait of Myself*. Simon and Schuster, 1963.

Callahan, Sean. *The Photographs of Margaret Bourke-White*. Bonanza Books, 1972.

Goldberg, Vicki. *Margaret Bourke-White: A Biography*. Addison-Wesley Publishing Company, Inc., 1987.

Silverman, Jonathan. *For the World to See: The Life of Margaret Bourke-White*. The Viking Press, 1983.

Silverman, Jonathan, and Jonathan White. *Margaret Bourke-White: The Taste of War*. Gyernsey Press Co. Ltd., 1985.

Bowes, Betty (1911–)

Known for her semi-abstract acrylic paintings, Betty Bowes was born in Philadelphia, Pennsylvania, and studied at the Moore College of Art and the University of Pennsylvania—both in her native city. She was a recipient of the George W. Elkins European fellowship.

Bowes has had numerous solo and group exhibitions of her work throughout the United States and was elected into membership at a number of prestigious organizations, including the American Watercolor Society, National Academy of Design, National Society of Painters in Casein and Acrylic, Audubon Artists, and Knickerbocker Artists—all in New York City.

She has won myriad awards and honors for her work, including seventeen medals of honor at American Watercolor Society's exhibitions; certificates of merit or prizes at the National Academy of Design (1963, 1980, 1984, 1987), New York City; Audubon Artists; Philadelphia Sketch Club, Pennsylvania; Springfield Museum, Illinois; Georgia Museum, Atlanta; Canton Art Institute, Ohio; and many others.

Bowes's work is represented in private, public, and corporate permanent collections, including the Philadelphia Museum of Art; Pennsylvania Academy of Fine Arts; National Academy of Design, New York City; University of Southern California, Los Angeles; and others.

Bibliography

Blake, Wendon. *Complete Guide to Acrylic Painting*. Watson-Guptill, 1971.

Kent, Norman. *100 Watercolor Techniques*. Watson-Guptill, 1968.

Who's Who in American Art. 19th ed. R.R. Bowker Co., 1991–1992.

Bracken, Clio Hinton (1870–1925)

Born in Rhinebeck, New York, the sculptor Clio Hinton Bracken studied with Augustus Saint-Gaudens, among others. In addition to lyrical works, Bracken created portraits of well-known generals, including General Fremont and General John J. Pershing. Examples of her work are in private and public permanent collections, including "Chloe," which is sited in Brookgreen Gardens, South Carolina.

Bibliography

Bracken, Clio. "Freehand Modeling." *The Touchstone* 5 (July 1919): 346–47.

Fanton, Mary A. "Clio Hinton Bracken, Woman Sculptor and Symbolist of the New Art." *The Craftsman* 8 (July 1905): 472–81.

Fielding, Mantle. *Dictionary of American Painters, Sculptors, and Engravers*. Modern Books and Crafts, 1974.

"Six Women Sculptors at Work in Their Studios." *Arts and Decoration* 16 (November 1921): 26.

Bradley, Susan H. (1851–1929)

The landscape painter Susan H. Bradley was born in Boston, Massachusetts, and studied at the School of the Boston Museum; she also studied with William Merritt Chase and Edward Boit, among others.

Bradley was a member of the Boston Watercolor Club, the New York Watercolor Club, the Philadelphia Watercolor Club, and the Society of Independent Artists.

Her work is represented in private and public permanent collections, including the John Herron Art Institute, Indianapolis, Indiana.

Bibliography

An Exhibition of Women Students of William Merritt Chase. New York: Marbella Gallery, 1973.

Fielding, Mantle. *Dictionary of American Painters, Sculptors, and Engravers.* Modern Books and Crafts, 1974.

Obituary. *American Art Annual.* Vol. 26. Washington, D.C.: American Federation of Arts, 1929.

Richards, Laura E. "Susan H. Bradley." *American Magazine of Art* 15 (July 1924): 370–74.

Brady, Carolyn (1937–)

Born in Chickasha, Oklahoma, the realist painter/printmaker/photographer Carolyn Brady studied at Oklahoma State University, Oklahoma City (1955–1958). She transferred to the University of Oklahoma, Norman, where she earned both a Bachelor of Fine Arts degree (1959) and, two years later, a Master of Fine Arts degree.

Brady has exhibited work in museums and galleries from New York to California, including "Contemporary Naturalism," Nassau County Museum, Roslyn, New York (1980); "Realism, Photo Realism," Philbrook Art Center, Tulsa, Oklahoma (1980); "Real, Really Real, SUPER REAL," San Antonio Museum of Art, Texas (1981); "Contemporary American Realism Since 1960," the Pennsylvania Academy of Fine Art, Philadelphia (1981); "Focus on Realism," San Francisco Museum of Modern Art, California (1985); and others.

Examples of Brady's work are in private and public permanent collections, including the Delaware Art Museum, Wilmington; Metropolitan Museum of Art, New York City; Mint Museum, Charlotte, North Carolina; St. Louis Art Museum, Missouri; Worcester Art Museum, Massachusetts; and others.

Bibliography

Ffrench-Frazier, Nina. "Carolyn Brady." *Art International* 24:1–2 (September–October 1980): 183–89.

Martin, Alvin. *American Realism, 20th Century Drawings and Watercolors from the Glenn Janss Collection.* San Francisco Museum of Modern Art, 1985.

McManus, Irene. "'The Ultimate Risk': New Watercolors by Carolyn Brady." *Arts Magazine* 61:10 (Summer 1987): 86–87.

"Prints & Photographs Published . . . Carolyn Brady." *Print Collector's Newsletter* 14:4 (September–October 1983): 143.

Bramson, Phyllis (1941–)

Though she did some serious thinking about the theater at one time, Phyllis Bramson always knew that she would be an artist. Born in Madison, Wisconsin, Bramson earned her Bachelor of Fine Arts degree from the University of Illinois, Champaign, in 1963; a Master of Arts degree from the University of Wisconsin, Madison, the following year; and a Master of Fine Arts degree from the Art Institute of Chicago, Illinois, in 1973. Earlier on, she spent a summer at the Yale Summer Art School in Norfolk, Connecticut (1962), was awarded a Vilas fellowship from the University of Wisconsin, Madison (1964), and held Illinois Arts Council fellowships (1981, 1988).

Bramson has shown her work in exhibitions in the United States and abroad, including the Art Institute of Chicago, Illinois (1974, 1978); Smithsonian Institution, Washington, D.C. (1976); Museum of Contemporary Art, Chicago, Illinois (1979); the New Museum, New York City (1979); Farideh Cadot, Paris, France (1980); Dart Gallery, Chicago, Illinois (1980, 1983, 1985, 1988, 1992); Marilyn Butler Gallery, Scottsdale, Arizona (1983); and others. She has had solo exhibitions at the Monique Knowlton Gallery (1977, 1979, 1981, 1982, 1984, 1986) and G.W. Einstein (1990)—both in New York City.

In addition to her position as associate professor of art at the University of Illinois, Chicago, since 1985, Bramson has taught at Columbia College, Chicago, Illinois (1972–1982), and has been a visiting artist at a number of universities throughout the United States (including Alaska) and Australia.

A board member of the College Art Association (1989–1992), Bramson won a Louis Comfort Tiffany grant (1980), National Endowment for the Arts (NEA) fellowship grants (1976, 1983), and was a Fulbright fellow to Australia (1988).

Bramson's work is in the permanent collection of many museums, including the Museum de Toulon, France; the Illinois State Museum; the Museum of Contemporary Art, Chicago, Illinois; the Art Institute of Chicago, Illinois; the Hirshhorn Museum and Sculpture Garden, Washington, D.C.; and many others.

On one level Bramson's oils and mixed media works tend to reflect her early concern with the theater. On another, she probes her innermost feelings and her physical and psychological reactions to the so-called outside world. The two levels, as they say in the hacker's world, do not compute; thus, her struggle to make things right, knowing that as she paints another canvas, the world will have changed again.

Bibliography

Brown, Betty Ann, and Arlene Raven. *Exposures: Women & Their Art.* NewSage Press, 1989.

Butera, Virginia F. "Phyllis Bramson." *Arts Magazine* 56:9 (May 1982): 32.

Henry, Gerrit. "Phyllis Bramson." *Art News* 80:9 (November 1981): 196, 199.

Intimate/Intimate. A Catalog. Turman Gallery, Indiana University, 1986.

Who's Who in American Art. 19th ed. R.R. Bowker Co., 1991–1992.

Brandford, Joanne Segal (1933–)

Joanne Segal Brandford earned a Bachelor's degree from the University of California at Berkeley (1955) and received a Master of Arts degree from the same institution (1969).

Brandford has taught aspects of the fiber arts at Montclair State College, Upper Montclair, New Jersey (1979); Fiberworks Center for Textile Arts, Berkeley, California (1977); Rhode Island School of Design, Providence (1977); Wheelock College, Boston, Massachusetts (1975–1976); Radcliffe College, Cambridge, Massachusetts (1972–1976); Massachusetts College of Art, Boston (1971–1974); Cambridge

Center for Adult Education and Project, Inc., Massachusetts (1970–1972); and the University of California at Berkeley (1967–1969).

A fellow of the Radcliffe Institute, Cambridge, Massachuestts (1971–1973), Brandford has exhibited widely, including the Herbert F. Johnson Museum, Ithaca, New York; "Dyer's Art," Museum of Contemporary Crafts, New York City; and many others. Between 1972 and 1978 Brandford was a resident fellow in textile arts at the Peabody Museum of Archeology and Ethnology, Harvard University, Cambridge, Massachusetts.

Her work is represented in private and public permanent collections.

Bibliography
Constantine, Mildred, and Jack Lenor Larsen. *The Art Fabric: Mainstream.* Van Nostrand Reinhold, 1980.

Brandt, Helene (1936–)
A sculptor whose welded pipe structures invite active participation and whose recent welded steel serial "progressions" redefine movement in space, Helene Brandt earned a Bachelor's degree in fine arts at the City College (CUNY) (1970); and a Master of Fine Arts degree at Columbia University (1975)—both in New York City. The following year, she received a Certificate of Advanced Studies from St. Martin's School of Art, London, England.

Brandt has held many solo exhibitions, primarily in New York City museums and galleries, including the Bernice Steinbaum Gallery, New York City, and the Hudson River Museum, Yonkers, New York (1991); Trabia-MacAfee Gallery, New York City (1989); Pennsylvania Academy of Fine Arts, Philadelphia (1987); A.I.R. Gallery, New York City (1985); Bronx Museum of the Arts, New York (1984); Sculpture Center, New York City (1982); and others.

Her work has been invited to group exhibitions throughout the world: from Mexico City, Mexico, to Yonkers, New York; from Florence and Prato, Italy, to Fort Wayne, Indiana; from New York City to Caracas, Venezuela; from Harlow, England, to Greenwich, Connecticut.

Brandt has been a visiting artist, artist-in-residence, and faculty member at several colleges, universities, and art schools between 1973 and 1989, and has won honors for her work, such as the BRIO Excellence in the Arts award (1991); a Guggenheim fellowship (1985–1986); the Betty Brazil Memorial Fund career development award (1982); a National Endowment for the Arts (NEA) artist-in-residence grant to Northern State College, Aberdeen, South Dakota; and others.

Her work is represented in private, public, and corporate permanent collctions, including the Israel Museum, Jerusalem; Columbia University, New York City; Hudson River Museum, Yonkers, New York; AT&T, Bedminster, New Jersey; Ward's Island Sculpture Garden, New York; and others.

Bibliography
Brenson, Michael. "Helene Brandt." *The New York Times* (May 12, 1989): C28.
Gonzales, Aliana. "En el arte tambien se discrimina a la mujer." *El Nacional.* Caracas, Venezuela (March 9, 1990)
Van Wagner, Judy C. *Lines of Vision: Drawings by Contemporary Women.* Hudson Hills Press, 1989.
Watson-Jones, Virginia. *Contemporary American Women Sculptors.* Oryx Press, 1986.

Brawer, Gladys R.
Born in Buenos Aires, Argentina, Gladys R. Brawer received her undergraduate degree in architecture at the University of Buenos Aires and took a postgraduate course in the same field at Stanford University, California, in 1971. Three years later, she did research in textile and glass design in the Scandinavian countries.

Brawer delights in using glass as her medium: playing its fragility against its strength; transparency against translucency or the opaque quality that derives from sanding her medium; engraving line, form, and content into her glass pieces—searching for a certain balance.

Brawer has had solo exhibitions at the College of Architecture (1977) and in the Galería Pro Arte (1979)—both in Mexico City, Mexico.

Her work has been seen in many group shows, including "Salon '78" in the Museum of Modern Art, Mexico City, and at the 13th World Congress of the International Union of Architects, the Exhibition of Architecture and Fine Arts, at the Palace of Fine Arts, Mexico, to name a few.

Bibliography
Alvarez, José Rogelio, et al. *Diccionario Biográfico Enciclopedico de la Pintura Mexicana.* Quinientos Años Editores, 1979.

Breiger, Elaine (1938–)
Born in Springfield, Massachusetts, the printmaker/painter Elaine Breiger studied at the Art Students League and the Cooper Union—both in New York City; she also worked with the intaglio artist, Krishna Reddy.

Breiger has exhibited her prints and paintings widely: from the Brooklyn Museum, New York, to the Library of Congress, Washington, D.C.; from the Martha Jackson Gallery, New York City, to the Source Gallery, San Francisco, California; and others.

A winner of awards and honors Breiger received a Creative Artists Public Service (CAPS) grant from the New York State Council on the Arts (1974); a grant from the National Endowment for the Arts (NEA) (1975); and others. Examples of her work are in private, public, and corporate permanent collections, including the Brooklyn Museum, New York; Chase Manhattan Bank, New York City; DeCordova Museum, Lincoln, Massachusetts; Honolulu Academy of Art, Hawaii; Library of Congress, Washington, D.C.; and others.

Bibliography
Johnson, Una. *American Prints and Printmakers.* Doubleday, 1980.
Who's Who in American Art. 21st ed. R.R. Bowker Co., 1993–1994.

Brendel, Bettina
Daughter of the German Expressionist poet, Dr. Robert Brendel, the painter/printmaker/computer artist Bettina Brendel was born in Luneburg, Germany. Despite persecution and the interruption of her education during the Hitler regime, Brendel matriculated at several institutions, including the Oberlyceum Lerchenfeld, Hamburg, Germany (1940); the Hamburg Academy of Art (1945–1947); the University of Southern California, Los Angeles (1955–1958, 1962); and the New School for Social Research, New York City (1968–1969), where she studied the history and theory of physics.

Brendel has held many solo exhibitions of her work throughout the United States and abroad, most recently at the Los Angeles Artcore Gallery, California (1984), and Gallery 16.34, Santa Monica, California

(1991), where she held a mini-retrospective of two decades of paintings and computer graphics. Earlier on, she showed in solo shows at the Santa Barbara Museum of Art, California (1966); Long Beach Museum of Art, California; Pasadena Art Museum, California; Spectrum Gallery, New York City; the University of Southern California, Los Angeles; and others.

Brendel's work has been invited to myriad group exhibitions in the United States and Germany, such as the "Annuals" at the Los Angeles County Museum of Art (1955, 1957, 1959, 1961); San Diego Fine Arts Gallery, California; Tucson Art Museum, Arizona; Pennsylvania Academy of Fine Arts, Philadelphia; Beaumont Art Museum, Texas; Staatliche Kunsthalle, Baden-Baden, Germany (1986); Galerie Objecta, Rhineland, and Munich, Germany (1991); Museum für Konkrete Kunst, Ingolstadt, Germany (1992); and many others.

Lecturer and author, her work is in private, public, and corporate permanent collections, including the Los Angeles County Museum of Art; La Jolla Art Museum; University of Southern California, Los Angeles; and University of California at Los Angeles (UCLA)—all in California; State University of New York (SUNY) at Stony Brook; Kunstmuseum, Hannover, Germany; Max Planck Institute, Munich, Germany; and others.

Bibliography
Maler in Hamburg. Hans Christian Verlag, 1974.
Museum für Konkrete Kunst. A Catalog. Ingolstadt, Germany, 1992.
Who's Who in American Art. 19th ed. R.R. Bowker Co., 1991–1992.

Breschi, Karen Lee (1941–)

Born in Oakland, California, the sculptor/mixed media artist Karen Lee Breschi earned a Bachelor of Fine Arts degree from the California College of Arts and Crafts in her native city (1963); received a Master's degree from San Francisco State University, California (1965); studied at the San Francisco Art Institute (1968–1971); and received a Doctorate from the California Institute of Integral Studies, San Francisco (1987).

In addition to solo exhibitions at many venues, including Braunstein/Quay Gallery, San Francisco, California, and New York City (1973, 1975, 1978, 1981, 1984), Breschi has shown in group exhibitions, such as "Clay," Whitney Museum of American Art, New York City (1974); "Illusionistic-Realism Defined in Contemporary Ceramic Sculpture," Laguna Beach Museum, California (1977); "The Great American Foot," Museum of Contemporary Crafts, New York City (1978); "Clayworks," University of Santa Barbara, California (1979); "A Century of Ceramics in the United States: 1878–1978," Renwick Gallery, Smithsonian Institution, Washington, D.C. (1979–1980); and many others.

A winner of awards and honors, Breschi has taught sculpture in several California institutions; her work is represented in private and public permanent collections, including Arizona State University, Tempe; Crocker Art Gallery, Sacramento, California; Oakland Museum of Art, California; San Francisco Museum of Art; University of California at Berkeley; and others.

Bibliography
"Review." *Arts Magazine* 53 (January 1979): 16.
"Review." *Craft Horizons* 38 (June 1978): 58.
"California Clay." *Art News* 77 (March 1978): 173.
"California Clay." *Arts Magazine* 51 (April 1977): 36.

Brewster, Anna Mary (Richards) (1870–1952)

The daughter of renowned marine and landscape painter William Trost Richards, Anna Mary (Richards) Brewster was born in Germantown, Pennsylvania. Her Quaker mother educated her at home; the only outside schooling consisted of art classes. Two of her three brothers, who were educated at home until college age, went on to pursue science. One became a Nobel Prize-winning chemistry professor at Harvard; the other taught botany at Barnard College, Columbia University, New York City. While attending Cowles Art School in Boston, Massachusetts, Brewster enjoyed early artistic success when she won "First Scholarship in Ladies Life Classes" in 1888. The next year she studied in New York City with William Merritt Chase and John LaFarge, winning the Dodge Award at the National Academy for the best exhibited work by a woman artist. With her father she travelled abroad often during the early 1890s; in Paris she was the pupil of Benjamin Constant and Jean Paul Laurens. In 1895 she moved to England and lived alone for one year in the Devon village of Clovelly. Two prominent people, Thomas Carlyle and James Abbott McNeill Whistler, lived near the studio she rented at Cheyne Gardens, Chelsea. Thirteen of the paintings she made during this first year were exhibited in Baltimore, Maryland, in May 1896. One of these works, "Storm at Clovelly" (1895), which depicts a group of men dismantling a wrecked ship on a windswept shore, evokes the work of Winslow Homer both in style and subject. She kept her Cheyne Gardens studio for nine years; between 1896 and 1905 she exhibited twice at the Royal Academy in London, where one of her admirers was the English painter George Frederic Watts. When Brewster in 1898 published her own illustrated version of her mother's sonnets, *Letter and Spirit, Dramatic Sonnets of Inward Life*, Watts wrote to Brewster's publisher, George Allen, praising her illuminations: "They are more than illustrations, they are interpretations."

In 1905 she married William Tenney Brewster, a Barnard College professor. Their only child, a son, died in 1910. Settling in Scarsdale, New York, the couple spent the rest of their lives travelling whenever they could, both in the United States and abroad, Brewster sketching and painting everywhere she went. A passionate lover of nature, her favorite subject was the landscape. Her landscapes are peaceful, lovely scenes, often impressionistically tinged, and her inclusion of figures is rare; when they do appear, they seem incidental. Brewster also composed cityscapes, notably "The Steam Counter" (1933), showing customers at a restaurant counter. One senses in her treatment of the scene the same type of human isolation found in the work of Edward Hopper, for none of the figures appears to have any real contact with the others. In addition to her other artistic talents, Brewster was an accomplished portraitist. Her eight paintings of Columbia professors adorn the walls of the university, and in the Scarsdale Library is her official portrait of the library's founder, John W. Dickinson. Brewster continued to paint and draw until she reached eighty, at which point her health began to fail. She died at eighty-two, a few months after suffering a stroke.

Cynthia Lee Kerfoot

Bibliography
Brewster, Anna Richards. *He Knew the Sea: William Trost Richards, N.A.* New Britain Museum of Art, 1973.
Brewster, William Tenney. *A Book of Sketches by Anna Richards*

Brewster. William Tenney Brewster, 1954.

Karlstrom, Paul J. "Papers of Anna Brewster." *Archives of American Art* 26, 1 (1986): 36–38.

Rubinstein, Charlotte Streifer. *American Women Artists: From Early Times to the Present.* Avon, 1982.

Briansky, Rita (1925–)

Born in Grajewa, Poland, Rita Briansky emigrated to Canada when she was four years old. In her mid-teens, Briansky studied art at the Montréal Young Women's Hebrew Association (YWHA) with Alexandre Bercovitch and spent the next two years as a student of Jacques de Tonnancour at the Montréal Museum of Fine Arts, Canada (1942–1944). From 1944 to 1946 she worked at the École des Beaux-Arts with M. Charpentier, then took further study at the Art Students League, New York City, with Louis Bosa, Jon Corbino, Harry Sternberg, and Vyclav Vytlacil (1946–1948).

Briansky's first solo exhibition occurred at the Montréal Museum of Fine Arts (1957); another solo show opened there five years later. Subsequent solo exhibitions were held at the Upstairs Gallery, Toronto (1960); Elca London Studio, Montréal (1963, 1965); Gallery Pascal, Toronto (1964, 1966); Artlenders, Montréal (1964); Alice Peck Gallery, Burlington, Ontario (1964); and many others.

She has shown in national and international group shows, including the prestigious Second International Biennial Exhibition of Prints, Tokyo and Osaka, Japan (1960–1961); the Salon Internationale Feminine de Vichy, Algiers (1960–1961); the United Nations UNICEF exhibition, New York City (1965); and others.

Her paintings and prints, visionary and eloquent, based upon the life around her, are in permanent and corporate collections, such as the Art Gallery of Hamilton, Ontario; Vancouver Art Gallery, British Columbia; Mendel Art Gallery, Saskatoon, Saskatchewan; London Art Museum, Ontario; New Brunswick Museum, St. Johns; McMaster University, Hamilton, Ontario; Dofasco, Hamilton, Ontario—all in Canada; and others.

Briansky holds memberships in the Canadian Painters, Etchers, and Engravers Society and the Canadian Society of Graphic Art. She won many awards and honors for her work, including third prizes at the National Exhibition of Prints, Burnaby, British Columbia (1960, 1963); the Diplôme d'Honneur at the Salon Internationale Feminine de Vichy, Algiers (1961); and grants and awards from the Canada Council, Ottawa (1962, 1967); among others.

Bibliography
Globe & Mail (March 5, 1960).
Montréal Gazette (September 29, 1962).
Who's Who in American Art. 19th ed. R.R. Bowker Co., 1991–1992.

Bridges, Fidelia (1834–1923)

Born in Salem, Massachusetts, Fidelia Bridges is best known for her landscapes with birds and for her delicate paintings of flowers. She also illustrated several books, such as Celia Thaxter's *Poems* (1976) and *Familiar Birds and What the Poets Sing of Them* (1886). Louis Prang and Company reproduced many of her paintings on cards. Her association with Prang, the chromolithographer, began in 1875 when he bought a series of her paintings of the months for a calendar; in 1881 she entered his Christmas card competition and was selected as one of his permanent designers.

Bridges met Anne Whitney, who encouraged the younger artist to join her for lectures to be given in Philadelphia by William Trost Richards and for drawing classes at the Pennsylvania Academy of Fine Arts, Philadelphia. By 1862 Bridges had her own studio in Philadelphia and was exhibiting at the Pennsylvania Academy of Fine Arts. After a trip to Europe in 1867–1868 she obtained a studio in New York City and began exhibiting at the National Academy of Design, which elected her an associate in 1873. She was invited to exhibit three paintings at the Philadelphia Centennial Exhibition of 1876.

In 1871 Bridges began spending summers in Stratford, Connecticut, where she could paint the birds and wildflowers along the banks of the Housatonic River and in the salt marshes. She moved to Canaan, Connecticut, in 1892. She continued to paint and exhibit her works at the Pennsylvania Academy until 1896, the National Academy of Design until 1908, and the American Society of Painters in Watercolors until 1912, all told exhibiting several hundred works. Her paintings have been included in such recent exhibitions as "Reflections of Nature," Whitney Museum of American Art, New York City (1984), and "The New Path, Ruskin and the American Pre-Raphaelites," Brooklyn Museum, New York (1985).

Eleanor Tufts

Bibliography
Hill, Mary Brawley. *Fidelia Bridges, American Pre-Raphaelite.* New Britain Museum of American Art, 1981.
Sharf, Frederic A. "Fidelia Bridges." *Notable American Women.* Vol. 1. Belknap Press of Harvard University Press, 1971.
Tufts, Eleanor. *American Women Artists, 1830–1930.* National Museum of Women in the Arts, 1987.

Brigman, Anne W. (Nott) (1869–1950)

Born December 3, 1869, in Honolulu, Hawaii, Anne W. (Nott) Brigman was an American photographer and later poet whose Hawaiian upbringing gave her an appreciation of the natural world and human interaction with it. Brigman attended Abigail Smith's Nuuanu School, Hawaii, where she received a classical education. From 1882 to 1883 she attended Punahou School, Hawaii, after which her family moved to Los Gatos, California, when Brigman was approximately sixteen years old. In 1894 she married Martin Brigman, a sea captain with whom she occasionally travelled in the Pacific. Both she and her sister Elizabeth Nott appear to have been self-taught free-lance photographers. The earliest known notice of Brigman's work in photography appears in 1903, when she exhibited a piece titled "Soldier of Fortune" in the 3rd San Francisco Photographic Salon, California. A separate showing by the Photo-Secession was also included in this exhibit, permitting Brigman to see works by Stieglitz, Steichen, Kasebier, and other members of this group. By 1907 she was elected a fellow of the Photo-Secession, although she did not meet Stieglitz until 1909, when she travelled to New York City and showed him her work, and met with other members of the organization. By this time she had begun to establish her reputation through a series of important exhibitions between 1903 and 1904. These included the Corcoran Gallery, Washington, D.C., the Carnegie Institute in Pittsburgh, as well as an exhibit with the Photo-

Secession in Hamburg, Germany.

In 1909 Brigman won a gold medal at the Alaska Yukon Exhibition, and also had seven prints in a show at the National Art Club in New York City. The first issue of *Camera Work* that year contained the first critical piece on her work, written by J. Nilson Laurvik. He noted the brooding elemental themes of her work, as well as its idyllic and mysterious lyricism.

Her photographs were evocative and to some degree symbolist in tone, for they depicted a dream-like photographic reality whose primary subjects consisted of lithe androgynous nudes photographed as extensions of the natural world of the California High Sierras. A declared pagan, Brigman had an early artistic Epiphany in these mountains which prompted her to visualize humans as part of the natural landscape, and as models for the spirits that she believed inhabited the land. Her models were friends and family who agreed in many cases to pose as nude embodiments of dryads, nymphs, or other sylvan entities. Although she also printed on bromide paper and made palladium and platinum prints, her favored medium, the gum-bichromatic print, was a process she could manipulate. Using gum, she created images in which obscurity was pierced by sudden light or by light flesh appearing against dark rocks or foliage. The painterly quality of the gum surface also gave her figures an aloof undetailed classicism. A 1912 edition of *Camera Work* contains some of her best known photographs: the "Cleft in the Rock," "Dawn," "The Wondrous Globe," and "The Pool." A 1913 issue of the periodical contains her photograph, "Dryads."

In 1910 she separated from her husband and began living with her mother in Oakland, California. The following year sixteen of her prints were exhibited in the International Exposition of the Albright Art Gallery, Buffalo, New York. Between 1914 and 1920 her record of publications and exhibitions was sporadic, but in 1922 she exhibited five prints in the 1st Annual International Exhibition of Pictorial Photography at the San Francisco Palace of Fine Arts, California. In 1923 she exhibited at the 2nd International Exhibition and continued to do so for some years. By 1933 failing eyesight caused Brigman to turn to poetry as a means of expression. In 1949 Caxton Printers published *Songs of a Pagan*, a compendium of her photographs from 1903 to 1933, coupled with poems written between 1935 and 1942. This year, before her death at age eighty-one, she also began a second book called *Child of Hawaii*.

Diana Emery Hulick

Bibliography
Brigman, Anne. *Songs of a Pagan*. Caxton Printers, 1949.
Green, Jonathan, ed. "*Camera Work*: A Critical Anthology." *Aperture*, 1973.
Heyman, Therese Thau. *Anne Brigman: Pictorial Photographer/Pagan/Member of the Photo-Secession*. The Oakland Museum, 1974.
Mann, Margery, and Ann Noggle, eds. *Women of Photography: An Historical Survey*. San Francisco Museum of Art, 1975.

Brito, Maria (1947–)

Born in Havana, Cuba, the sculptor Maria Brito earned an Associate's degree at Miami-Dade Community College, Florida, where she studied sculpture (1967); received a Bachelor's degree in Education from the University of Miami, Coral Gables, Florida (1969); a Master of Education degree from Florida International University, Miami (1976); a Bachelor of Fine Arts degree in ceramic sculpture from Florida International University (1977), after study with William Burke; and a Master of Fine Arts degree from the University of Miami, Florida, after study with Christine Federighi and David Vertacnik.

Brito has held solo exhibitions in museums and galleries in the United States including The Gallery at 24, Miami, Florida (1980, 1982); "Architecture of the Mind," Kennesaw College, Marietta, Georgia (1987); Museum of Contemporary Hispanic Art, New York City (1989); "Cabinet of Wonders: Sculpture by Maria Brito," Spirit Square Center for the Arts, Charlotte, North Carolina (1990); the Ann Jaffe Gallery, Bay Harbour, Florida, and "Maria Brito: A Retrospective," Barry University, Miami Shores, Florida (1991); and others.

Her work has been invited to many group exhibitions in the United States and abroad, such as "Islands in the Stream: Seven Cuban-American Artists," State University of New York (SUNY) at Cortland (1993); "South Florida Cultural Consortium 1992 Fellowship Recipients," Museum of Art, Fort Lauderdale, Florida, and Galería de la Raza, San Francisco, California (1992); "Southern Exposures," the High Museum, Atlanta, Georgia (1991); "CUBA/USA," a travelling show, Museum of Contemporary Art, Chicago, Illinois (1991); "Twenty-Five in Miami: An Invitational Exhibition," Miami-Dade Community College, Florida (1990); "Exhibition of World Invitational Open-Air Sculpture, Olympic Park, Seoul, Korea (1988); "Fifth Iberoamerican Art Biennial," Mexico City, Mexico (1986); and others.

Winner of a number of awards, Brito was the recipient of a Pollack-Krasner Foundation grant and two South Florida Consortium fellowships (1990, 1992); National Endowment for the Arts (NEA) fellowships (1984, 1988); Cintas fellowships from the Institute for International Education (1981, 1985); a resident fellowship at the Djerassi Foundation, Woodside, California (1983); and others.

Her work is represented in private, public, and corporate permanent collections, including Olympic Sculpture Park, Seoul, Korea; Archer M. Huntington Museum, Austin, Texas; Metro-Dade Center, Miami, Florida; Cintas Foundation, New York City; Southeast Banking Corporation, Miami, Florida; the Lowe Museum, Coral Gables, Florida; and others.

Bibliography
Alvarez-Bravo, Armando. "Maria Brito." *El Miami Herald* (January 31, 1989): 1C, 4C.
Lippard, Lucy. *Mixed Blessings*. Pantheon Books, 1990.
Turner, Elisa. "Maria Brito." *Art News* (March 1989): 187.
Who's Who in American Art. 20th ed. R.R. Bowker Co., 1993–1994.

Brockman, Ann (1896–1943)

The painter Ann Brockman was born in Alameda, California and studied her craft at the Art Students League, New York City, as a student of John Sloan and Gifford Beal.

Brockman exhibited her oils and watercolors widely and examples of her work may be found in private and public permanent collections. Three years after her death, a memorial exhibition of her work was held at the Kraushaar Galleries, New York City.

Bibliography
Bénézit, E. *Dictionnaire critique et documentaire des peintres, sculpteurs, dessinateurs, et graveurs de tous les temps et de tous les pays*. New ed. Paris: Librairie Grund, 1976.

Falk, Peter H. *Who Was Who in American Art*. Madison, Connecticut: Sound View Press, 1985.

Memorial Exhibition of Paintings and Watercolors by Ann Brockman. New York: Kraushaar Galleries, 1946.

Brodsky, Beverly (1941–)

Born in Brooklyn, New York, Beverly Brodsky earned a Bachelor's degree from Brooklyn College, New York (1965), where she studied with Ad Reinhardt and Burgoyne Diller; she also attended classes at the Brooklyn Museum and the New School for Social Research, and studied textile design at the School of Visual Arts—all in New York City.

Brodsky has held many solo and group exhibitions of her work, including the B.E.L. Gallery, Westport, Connecticut (1979); State University of New York (SUNY) at Plattsburgh (1980); Wilson Arts Center, Rochester, New York (1982); Yeshiva University Museum, New York City (1983); Parsons School of Design, New York City (1986, 1989); Galerie Lohrl, Monchengladbach, Germany (1990); "Inaugural Exhibition," the Kimberly Gallery, New York City (1990); "Eccentric Abstraction," M-13 Gallery, SoHo, New York City (1992); and others.

A Caldecott Honor award-winning illustrator of children's books, Brodsky has executed poster commissions between 1971 and 1982 for a variety of patrons, such as the Fête de L'Oliviers, Grasse, France (1971); and the New York City Opera, Lincoln Center, New York City. Other honors for her work include painting fellowships from the Connecticut Commission on the Arts (1979); the Triangle Artists Workshop (1988); and the Monchengladbach Exchange Program, Germany (1990).

"Flight" (1990), a large abstract, bird-like oil/sand work on canvas, is not atypical of her style during this period. A teacher at Parsons School of Design, New York City, her work is represented in private and public collections, such as the Elizabeth Stone Gallery and the Mazza Collection, Toledo, Ohio.

Bibliography

New York Magazine (January, 29 1990).

Who's Who in American Art. 19th ed. R.R. Bowker Co., 1991–1992.

Winz, Horst, ed. "Dossier: New York! New York!" *Juni* 2–3, 1991.

Brodsky, Judith (1933–)

Educator and printmaker Judith Brodsky studied art history at Radcliffe College, Cambridge, Massachusetts, and completed her formal education with a Master of Fine Arts degree at the Tyler School of Art at Temple University, Philadelphia, Pennsylvania. She has taught at the Tyler School of Art, Glenside, Pennsylvania; Beaver College; and Rutgers University, New Brunswick, New Jersey. At Rutgers she was chair of the Art Department (1978–1981), associate dean (1981–1982), and associate provost (1982 to the present). In addition to being active in the academic world Brodsky was associate director of the Princeton Graphic Workshop, Inc. (1966–1968) and is the owner of Castle Howard Press.

Exhibitions of Brodsky's works include Brown University, Providence, Rhode Island (1973); New York State Museum, Albany, New York (1975); Douglas College, New Brunswick, New Jersey (1978); the Philadelphia Association of Artists, Pennsylvania (1979); plus many group shows in the United States and abroad. She received purchase prizes from the New Jersey State Museum, Trenton (1970, 1971), and Boston Printmakers, Massachusetts (1971). Brodsky was awarded the Stella C. Drabkin Memorial award of the American Color Print Society, Philadelphia, Pennsylvania (1977).

Brodsky is a member of the College Art Association, Philadelphia Print Club, California Society of Printmakers, Boston Society of Printmakers, and Society of American Graphic Artists. She is also active in women's art organizations as a founding member of the Coalition for Women's Art Organizations and the spokesperson and president of the Women's Caucus for Art (1976–1977). This interest in women in the arts can also been seen in Brodsky's works, such as "Woman, A Portfolio" (1978), which she designed and published; plus her own writings, "Rediscovering Women Printmakers: 1500–1850" (1979); and "The Status of Women in Art, Feminist Collage" (1979).

Examples of Brodsky's prints can be found in the Library of Congress, Washington, D.C.; Fogg Art Museum, Harvard University, Cambridge, Massachusetts; New Jersey State Museum, Princeton University, and the Newark Museum—both in New Jersey.

Judith Sealy

Bibliography

Brodsky, Judith. "Some Notes on Women Printmakers." *Art Journal* 35, 4 (Summer 1976): 396–98.

Miller and Swenson. *Lives and Works: Talks with Women Artists*. Scarecrow Press, 1981, 267–68.

Bromberg, Faith (1919–1990)

Painter Faith Bromberg was born in Los Angeles, California, and attended Sacramento Junior College, the University of California at Los Angeles (UCLA), Otis Art Institute, and the School of Fine Art in Los Angeles. She also studied with Wayne Thiebaud and June Wayne. She won a National Endowment for the Arts (NEA) fellowship (1980) and two American Academy and Institute of Arts and Letters awards (1975, 1976).

Working in oil and spray paint, Bromberg had her first solo exhibition at Sacramento Junior College, California, in 1966. She continued to exhibit throughout the country with shows at the Roko Gallery, New York City (1975, 1977); Art Space, Los Angeles, California (1979); and Arizona State University, Tempe (1983). Her work also appeared in diverse group shows, including San Diego Museum, California; Butler Institute of Art, Ohio; Springfield Art Museum, Missouri; Las Vegas Annual, Nevada; and Michael Fagan Gallery, Colorado.

Active in feminist art groups, Bromberg was a contributor to *Feminist Art Journal*, as well as taking an active role in organizations such as Womanspace and Women's Caucus for the Arts. Her paintings typically explore the conflict between the sexes with abstracted, expressionistic figures. Paintings on this theme include "Three Little Words" (1975), "Lovers and Other Strangers" (1977), and "Barbie and Ken in the Hamptons" (1975). She was also an active participant in the Los Angeles Institute for Contemporary Art, Artists for Economic Action, and the Artists Equity Association.

Judith Sealy

Bibliography

Arts Magazine 51:37 (June 1977).

Arts Magazine 52:35 (September 1977).

Brooks, Ellen (1946–)

Born in Los Angeles, California, the photographer Ellen Brooks spent two years at the University of Wisconsin, Madison (1963–1965) before she transferred to the University of California at Los Angeles (UCLA), where she earned a Bachelor's degree (1968), a Master of Arts degree (1970), and a Master of Fine Arts degree (1971); while at UCLA, she studied under the aegis of Robert Fichter, Lynn Foulkes, and Robert Heinecken, among others.

Brooks has held many solo exhibitions in museums and galleries in the United States and abroad, including shows in Santa Monica, California; Paris, France; New York City; Boston, Massachusetts; Cleveland, Ohio; Washington, D.C.—all between 1991 and 1994. There were others earlier on.

A teacher in prestigious schools, colleges and universities, her work has been included in many group and travelling shows and has won honors and awards, such as fellowships from the National Endowment for the Arts (NEA) (1976, 1979, 1991); the Phelan Award, Oakland, California (1972); and others.

Examples of her work are in private and public permanent collections, including the Albright-Knox Art Gallery, Buffalo, New York; Musée d'Art Contemporain, Montréal, Québec, Canada; Museum of Modern Art (MoMA), New York City; National Gallery of Canada, Ottawa; National Museum of American Art, Smithsonian Institution, Washington, D.C.; UCLA, Los Angeles, California; and others.

Bibliography

Tonkonow, Leslie. "Ellen Brooks." *Journal of Contemporary Art* (Fall–Winter 1991).

Who's Who in American Art. 20th ed. R.R. Bowker Co., 1993–1994.

Witkin, Lee D., and Barbara London. *The Photograph Collector's Guide.* 1979.

Brooks, Romaine Goddard (1874–1970)

An expatriate artist, who was born in Rome and died in Nice, France, Romaine Goddard Brooks was American in her parentage and in some of her schooling. Her father, major Harry Goddard, whose wealth came from Pennsylvania coal, separated from his wife but left the family well off. Romaine Brooks grew up in Europe with her eccentric mother and mentally-ill older brother. She attended St. Mary's Hall (an Episcopalian school) in New Jersey, a convent school in Italy, and Mlle Tavan's Finishing School in Geneva, Switzerland, before she began seriously the study of painting in Rome, Italy, at the Scuola Nazionale by day and the Circolo Artistico in the evening during the years from 1896 to 1899. After a summer on Capri, Italy, she studied at the Académie Colarossi in Paris, France. In 1902 she married John Ellingham Brooks, an Englishman whom she took to London, England, and then discarded. The years in England gave her exposure to James Whistler's paintings, which made an indelible impression on her style. Her career peaked when she settled in Paris, France, in 1905; the Durand-Ruel Galleries gave her a solo exhibition in 1910 which went on to the Goupil Gallery in London, England, the next year. Five years later she had a solo exhibition in London, England, that travelled to Wildenstein Galleries in New York City. In 1935–1936 she returned to New York City, where she rented a studio in Carnegie Hall and painted portraits of Americans.

Provided with a substantial inheritance, Brooks did not depend upon commissions, and she returned to Europe where she had a circle of friends in the orbit of Natalie Barney, the American renowned for her literary salon in Paris, France. Barney and Brooks lived together in a villa in Fiesole overlooking Florence, Italy during World War II, after which Brooks retired to her apartment in Nice, France.

A resurgence of interest in Brooks occurred in 1971 when Adelyn Breeskin arranged an exhibition entitled "Romaine Brooks, 'Thief of Souls.'" It opened at the National Collection of Fine Arts and travelled to the Whitney Museum of American Art in New York City. In 1980 the National Collection of Fine Arts gave Brooks a second exhibition, showing eighteen of the sixty-three works by her in its collection, and this was followed by an exhibition of her drawings at this same institution (now renamed National Museum of American Art) in 1986.

Her paintings generally consist of a human figure accompanied by some germane attribute. The Eiffel Tower appears behind Jean Cocteau (1914), Gabrielle d'Annunzio in a dashing black cape stands before an infinite expanse of sea (1912); Natalie Barney called "L'Amazone" is posed next to a small horse (1920), Renata Borgatti is seated at a piano (1920), and Una, Lady Troubridge, the lesbian friend of the author Radclyffe Hall, wears a tuxedo and a monocle (1924). These portraits are painted in a monochromatic gray, Whistlerian style, and most are signed with her first name and her symbol: the wing of a butterfly held down by a chain.

Eleanor Tufts

Bibliography

Breeskin, Adelyn D. *Romaine Brooks, "Thief of Souls."* Smithsonian Institution Press, 1971.

Secrest, Meryle. *Between Me and Life: A Biography of Romaine Brooks.* Doubleday, 1974.

Brown, Alice Dalton (1939–)

Born in Danville, Pennsylvania, Alice Dalton Brown studied art at the Académie Julian, Paris, France; at the Université de Grenoble, France; and at Cornell University, Ithaca, New York, before winning her Bachelor's degree from Oberlin College, Ohio, in 1962.

Brown has had a dozen solo exhibitions of her paintings between 1975 and 1991; four were held at the Fischbach Gallery, New York City. Her work has been seen in many group shows, including the Marion Koogler McNay Art Museum, San Antonio, Texas (1981, 1989, 1990); A.M. Sachs Gallery, New York City (1981, 1982, 1983, 1984, 1985); Columbus Museum, Ohio (1985); Swain Galleries, Plainfield, New Jersey (1986); the William Sawyer Gallery, San Francisco, California (1988); and the Maier Museum of Art, Lynchburg, Virginia (1991).

She was the recipient of the Judges Award Exhibition of the New York State Council on the Arts (1979); and won a purchase award in the exhibition, "The West Collection '85: Art and the Law," which travelled to museums and other institutions throughout the United States. Her work is in the permanent collections of major public and corporate institutions.

"The Coral Wall" (1990), shows Brown's approach to realist painting: this large oil of a cool, shadowed Victorian porch, dappled with sunlight, is tightly organized, with shrubbery breaking across the vertical columns to contrast both formally and evocatively with the variegated coral wall.

Bibliography
Cooper, James F. "Beautiful Flame Burns under Brown's Victorian Facade." *New York City Tribune* (March 1987).
Gill, Susan. "Alice Dalton Brown." *Arts Magazine* (November 1985).
Howard, Henrietta. "Inside and Outside." *House and Garden Magazine.* British ed. (January 1991).
The New Fillmore. Vol. 3:2 (June 1988).

Brown, Carol K. (1945–)

After studying at Tulane University, New Orleans, Louisiana, and the New School for Social Research in New York City, sculptor Carol K. Brown took a Bachelor of Fine Arts degree from the University of Miami, Florida, in 1978. She completed her formal education with a Master of Fine Arts degree from the University of Colorado, Boulder, in 1981. She received a State of Florida Fine Arts fellowship in 1983 and National Endowment for the Arts (NEA) fellowships in 1984 and 1986. She also won a Southeastern Center for Contemporary Arts fellowship in 1986.

Brown's first solo exhibition took place at Miami-Dade Community College, Miami, Florida, in 1977. Since then she has had solo exhibitions at the University of Florida, Miami; Contemporary Arts Center, New Orleans, Louisiana; University of Colorado, Boulder; Gloria Luria Gallery, Miami, Florida; Bass Museum of Art, Miami Beach, Florida; and the Bacardi Sculpture Plaza and Gallery, Miami, Florida.

Throughout the 1980s Brown worked on a series of abstracted, anthropomorphic sculptures made of steel and, later, aluminum. These works range up to eight feet high and are always in groups of three or more figures. Both menacing and whimsical, this surrealistic series included: "Seven More of Them" (1987), bought by Metro-Dade County Art in Public Places collection; "Some Were Not Sure" (1987), for the University of Florida; and "They Have No Name" (1988), built under the auspices of the Miami Sculpture Exhibition. A serious illness in 1990 forced Brown to find a new format for her personal iconographic figures. These forms reappeared adapted to four-inch tondos of mixed media in an exhibition entitled "Dark Tondos" (1991).

Brown's sculptures are also part of the permanent collection of the University of Colorado, Boulder; Denver Art Museum, Colorado; Jacksonville Art Museum, Florida; ARCO; Prudential Life Insurance Company; and Southeastern Banking Corporation; among others.

Judith Sealy

Bibliography
Blanc, Giulio V. "Bombs and Oranges, Discovering Miami's Explosive Art Scene." *Arts Magazine* 64:79 (November 1990).
Espinosa, Juan. *Carol K. Brown.* Bacardi Art Gallery, 1988.

Brown, Catharine H. (1944–)

Born in Washington, D.C., the ceramist Catharine H. Brown earned a Bachelor's degree from Mills College, Oakland, California, where she studied with Antonio Prieto; she received a Master of Fine Arts degree, after study with Lyle Perkins and others, from the University of Massachusetts, Amherst; Brown did further study in summers with Arline Fisch at Haystack Mountain School of Crafts, Deer Isle, Maine.

Brown has exhibited widely throughout the United States; she has won honors and awards for her ceramic works, which are housed in private, public, and corporate permanent collections.

Bibliography
Who's Who in American Art. 15th ed. R.R. Bowker Co., 1982.

Brown, Charlotte Harding (1873–1951)

Charlotte Harding Brown, born in Newark, New Jersey, was one of the artists who helped to popularize the "Golden Age of Illustration in America." Brown studied at the Philadelphia School of Design for Women, Pennsylvania.

Winner of honors and prizes, Brown received a fellowship from the Pennsylvania Academy of Fine Arts, Philadelphia; and silver medals at the Woman's Exposition, London, England (1900); the St. Louis Exposition, Missouri (1915); and others. She also worked as an illustrator for *The Century Magazine.* She was a member of the Philadelphia Watercolor Club, Pennsylvania, and the Plastic Club.

Bibliography
The American Personality: The Artist-Illustrator of Life in the United States, 1860–1930. University of California at Los Angeles, 1976.
Fallows, Alice K. "Working One's Way Through Women's Colleges," with pictures by Charlotte Harding. *The Century Magazine* 62:3 (July 1901): 323–41.
Mayer, Anne E. *Women Artists in the Howard Pyle Tradition.* Chadds Ford, Pennsylvania: Brandywine River Museum, 1975.

Brown, Joan (1938–1990)

A native of San Francisco, California, who died in a tragic accident in Proddaturn, India, Joan Brown was given a solo painting exhibition by the Sparta Gallery, San Francisco, California, when she was nineteen years old. She studied at the California School of Fine Arts, San Francisco, and received her Bachelor of Fine Arts degree in 1955. Between 1957 and 1962 Brown took further tuition in art from Bay Area artists, including Elmer Bischoff, Richard Diebenkorn, Sonia Gechtoff, Robert Howard, Frank Lobdell, Manuel Neri, and, especially, David Park.

She had more than forty solo exhibitions of her work in museums, galleries, and institutions throughout the United States and abroad, from her teenage first show until her death; Brown's work was selected for many group exhibitions, such as "Art in the San Francisco Bay Area: 1945–1980," Oakland Art Museum, California (1985); "The Figurative Mode," New York University (1984); "Content: A Contemporary Focus: 1974–1984," Hirshhorn Museum and Sculpture Garden, Washington, D.C. (1984); "San Francisco Painting," the University of Nebraska, Omaha (1984); and myriad others.

Brown was a Guggenheim Foundation fellow in 1977; she received two National Endowment for the Arts grants (NEA) (1976, 1980), and won the San Francisco Art Institute Adaline Kent award in 1973. Her teaching career included stints at the San Francisco Art Institute; Sacramento State College; the Academy of Art, San Francisco; and the University of California at Berkeley—all in California.

Brown's work is in the permanent collection of many museums and institutions, including the Albright-Knox Art Gallery, Buffalo, New York; University of California at Berkeley; University of Colorado, Denver; Long Beach Museum of Art, California; Miami-Dade Community College, Florida; Museum of Modern Art (MoMA), New York City; Oakland Art Museum, and the San Francisco Museum of Art—both in California.

In a memorial exhibition at the Frumkin/Adams Gallery, New York City (1990) which brought together twenty-one of her self-portraits (to 1983), especially three from her cartoonlike series, the "Alcatraz Swim," it was evident that Brown drew on personal events in her life to create large detailed, brightly-colored, richly-painted canvases of shiny enamel. She travelled widely through Europe, Egypt, South America, China, and India, studying the various cultures, not uninfluenced by mysticism and Eastern thought.

Bibliography
Cummings, Paul. *Dictionary of Contemporary American Artists.* 5th ed. St. Martin's Press, 1988.
Lucie-Smith, Edward. *Art in the 70's.* Cornell University Press, 1980.
Richardson, Brenda. *Joan Brown.* University of California Press, 1974.
Schwartz, Sanford. "Between Bonnard and Dick Tracy." *The New York Times* (October 6, 1991).

Brown, Judith (1931–1992)

Native New Yorker Judith Brown was known for her direct metal welded sculpture. Brown studied art with Theodore Roszak at Sarah Lawrence College, Bronxville, New York. Soon after receiving her Bachelor's degree (1954) under Roszak's guidance, Brown established her own sculpture studio in New York City; later, she worked during the summer months in Reading, Vermont, where she set up another studio.

Brown's three-dimensional works were welded and pounded from scrap metal material, crushed auto parts, found objects—the detritus of junkyards—which were transformed, magically it seemed, into striking figurative pieces. Her work was commissioned by churches, lay institutions, and synagogues, including store windows for Tiffany & Co., New York City (1957–1979); a menorah for the Fritz-Nathan Jewish Museum, New York City (1978); "Caryatids," a monumental piece for the Donald M. Kendall Sculpture Garden, Purchase, New York; a wall sculpture for the Federal Courthouse building, Trenton, New Jersey (1992); and others.

Brown held solo exhibitions of her work at New York University (1977, 1980); and other institutions. Two weeks after her death, a solo show of her smaller sculptures opened at Meisner SoHo, New York (1992). Her work was invited to many group exhibitions throughout the United States, such as the Dallas Museum of Fine Arts, Texas (1958); Pennsylvania Academy of Fine Arts, Philadelphia (1959); "Recent Acquisitions," Aldrich Museum of Contemporary Art, Ridgefield, Connecticut (1966); New Britain Museum of American Art, Connecticut (1968); William Penn Museum, Harrisburg, Pennsylvania (1973); Artists Equity, New York City (1977); and others.

Brown's work is represented in private, public, and corporate permanent collections, including the Museum of Modern Art (MoMA), New York City; Brooklyn Museum, New York; Dallas Museum of Fine Arts, Texas; Riverside Museum, New York City; Bundy Art Gallery, Waitsfield, Vermont; Dartmouth College, Hanover, New Hampshire; and others.

Bibliography
Anonymous. "Judith Brown . . ." *The New York Times* (May 15, 1992): C19.
Who's Who in American Art. 19th ed. R.R. Bowker Co., 1991–1992.

Brown, Lawrie (1949–)

Born in San José, California, the photographer Lawrie Brown earned a Bachelor's degree from San José State University (1972) and, three years later, received a Master of Arts degree from San Francisco State University—both in California.

Brown has exhibited widely in museums and galleries in the United States and abroad: from the Everson Museum of Art, Syracuse, New York (1977) to Il Diaframma-Canon, Milan, Italy (1982); from the Alternative Museum, New York City (1984) to the Houston Center for Photography, Texas (1987); and many others.

Director of the Department of Photography at Cabrillo College, Aptos, California, since 1979, and winner of honors and awards, Brown received a National Endowment for the Arts (NEA) fellowship in photography (1979) and grants from the Polaroid Corporation (1985, 1986, 1987).

Examples of her photographic prowess are in private and public permanent collections, including the Bibliothèque Nationale, Paris, France; Center for Creative Photography, Tucson, Arizona; and Oakland Art Museum; San Francisco Museum of Modern Art; and Stanford University—all in California; and others.

Bibliography
Fischer, Hal. "Don Worth, Barbara Thompson, Lawrie Brown, Casey Williams." *Art Week* (September 25, 1976).
Rice, Leland. *Contemporary California Photography.* A Catalog. Camerawork Gallery, 1978.

Brown, Sonia Gordon (1890–late 1960s)

Born in Moscow, Russia, the painter/sculptor Sonia Gordon Brown studied with Nicolas Andrieff and others before going to Paris, France, where she worked under Antoine Bourdelle.

Brown exhibited in prestigious group exhibitions, including "Contemporary American Sculptors," sponsored by the National Sculpture Society and the California Palace of the Legion of Honor, San Francisco (1929); the 1st Biennial Exhibition of Contemporary American Sculpture, Watercolors, and Prints. Whitney Museum of American Art, New York City (1933); and others.

Brown was a member and past president (1927) of the New York Society of Women Artists. Her work is represented in private and public permanent collections in the United States and abroad.

Bibliography
American Art Annual. Vol. 28. American Federation of Arts, 1932.
Fielding, Mantle. *Dictionary of American Painters, Sculptors, and Engravers.* Modern Books and Crafts, 1974.
Wolf, Amy J. *New York Society of Women Artists, 1925.* New York: ACA Galleries, 1987.

Browne, Margaret Fitzhugh (1884–1972)

Born in West Roxbury, Massachusetts, Margaret Fitzhugh Browne attended the Massachusetts Normal Art School, and the School of the Boston Museum of Fine Arts—both in Massachusetts, where her instructors included Joseph DeCamp and Frank W. Benson.

Known primarily as a portraitist, Browne included among her subjects Admiral D.W. Taylor, Secretary of State Robert Lansing, and Dean Everett W. Lord, and Dean Arthur H. Wilde of Boston University, Massachusetts. An especially prestigious commission in 1927 sent her to Spain to paint King Alphonso XII for the New York Yacht Club, and among her sitters at the height of her career in the 1930s was Henry Ford. One of the portraits from the next decade was that of her friend the painter Jane Peterson (private collection, Boston, Massachusetts), who is colorfully accompanied by flowers. In 1933 Browne wrote a book entitled *Portrait Painting*, advising painters on how to capture their sitter's natural likeness.

Browne also painted genre subjects and floral still lifes. She was active in a number of art associations, such as the Copley Society in Boston, Massachusetts; the North Shore Arts Association (of which she was president beginning in 1935), Long Island, New York; Connecticut Academy of Fine Arts, Westport, Connecticut; Allied Artists of America, New York City; and the Boston Art Club, Massachusetts. Her work was often shown in the Annual Exhibition of the National Association of Women Painters and Sculptors in New York City. She received such awards as the popular prize, North Shore Arts Association, Long Island, New York (1925), and founder's special award, Society for Sanity in Art, Chicago, Illinois (1941).

Eleanor Tufts

Bibliography

Browne, Margaret Fitzhugh. *Portrait Painting*. Isaac Pitnam and Sons, 1933.
Lee, Cuthbert. *Contemporary American Portrait Painters*. W.W. Norton, 1942.
Tufts, Eleanor. *American Women Artists, 1830–1930*. National Museum of Women in the Arts, 1987.

Browne, Vivian E. (1929–1993)

Born in Laurel, Florida, the African-American abstract and mixed-media painter Vivian E. Browne earned her Bachelor's and Master's degrees from Hunter College, New York City; she attended the Art Students League, Pratt Graphics Center, the New School for Social Research—all in New York City—and did further study at the University of Ibadan, Nigeria in 1979.

Browne held solo exhibitions in galleries and museums, including "African Memories," Rhode Island College, Providence (1973); SoHo 20 Gallery, New York City (1982, 1984, 1987, 1989, 1992); "Paintings and Drawings," Franklin Marshall College, Lancaster, Pennsylvania (1983); Western Michigan University, Kalamazoo (1984); "Recent Works," The Bronx Museum, New York City, and "Paintings and Drawings," the University of California at Santa Cruz (1985); Virginia Technical University, Blacksburg (1990); and others.

Her work has been included in prestigious two-person and group exhibitions from the Museum of Modern Art (MoMA), New York City (1988) to the Orlando Gallery, Sherman Oaks, California (1985); from Mexico City, Mexico (1986) to the Black Art Festival, Atlanta, Georgia (1988); and many others.

Prior to 1970, when Browne joined the faculty in the Department of Art and Design at Rutgers University, Newark, New Jersey, she taught in high schools in South Carolina and New York. She was a full professor and administrator of the art education program at Rutgers University.

Widely travelled, a founder of SoHo 20, a women's cooperative gallery in New York City, and a much sought-after artist-in-residence at universities, Browne was a recipient of many honors and awards,

including the College Art Association's "Distinguished Art Teacher of the Year" (1989); a MacDowell Colony fellowship (1980); research grants from Rutgers University (1975, 1973); a Huntington Hartford Foundation painting fellowship (1964); and others.

Browne was a member of several professional arts organizations. Her work is represented in private, corporate, and public permanent collections, such as the Chase Manhattan Bank, MoMA, New York Public Library, and Schomburg Center for Research—all in New York City; Fisk University, Nashville, Tennessee; Tougaloo College, Mississippi; and many others.

Bibliography

Cederholm, Theresa D. *Afro-American Art: A Bio-Bibliographical Directory*. The Boston Public Library, 1973.
Henkes, Robert. *The Art of Black American Women*. McFarland & Co., 1993.
Igoe, Lynn Moody. *250 Years of Afro-American Art*. R.R. Bowker Co., 1981.
Who's Who in American Art. 20th ed. R.R. Bowker Co., 1993–1994.

Browning, Colleen (1929–)

Born in Ireland, painter Colleen Browning received a fellowship to and studied at the Slade School of Art in London, England. She first worked as a movie set designer, but after moving to New York City in 1949, she began a career as a painter. Browning's oil paintings show a constant interest in texture and design. She creates realistic scenes by combining bold color and abstract patterns.

In the 1950s and 1960s, Browning painted a series of works which concentrate on the urban scenes of New York City—often Harlem. In works such as "Lennox and Mondrian" (1951) and "Door Street" (1953), Browning explores humanity trapped in a decaying environment. Children play on the graffiti-covered, cracked sidewalks of the inner city with little hope, already alienated and distrustful. In a series of paintings of telephone booths, adults are enclosed—caught—in a confining urban environment. In "Telephones" (1954), seven people stand next to each other without interacting—alone in their closeness.

Urban scenes continued to hold Browning's attention throughout the 1970s, when she did a series of subway paintings. In "Clyde's Car" (1976), the passengers on the subway car appear to be confined as much by the sweeping, bold graffiti on the outside of the car as by the subway car itself. Again, the participants do not interact, but stay isolated in their own spaces.

While most of Browning's paintings include people, the figures only interact with their environment—they are usually trapped or overwhelmed by it. This can be seen in paintings from the early 1980s, which show women—often the artist—in luxuriant gardens. The patterning and texture Browning favors is very obvious in this group of works. In "Gardner" (1980) and "Noon" (1981), the bold color is even repeated in the design of the woman's dress.

In a series of firework paintings, including "Fireworks I" (1983), the environment has taken over completely, and no humanity is involved.

Paintings by Browning are part of the permanent collections of the New York State Museum, Albany; Detroit Art Institute, Michigan; Columbia Museum, South Carolina; Milwaukee Art Center, Wisconsin; and St. Louis Art Museum, Missouri. Browning's first exhibition was at the Hewitt Gallery, New York City, and since then she has been included in exhibitions throughout the United States. She has shown at the Whitney Museum of American Art, New York City; Art Institute of Chicago, Illinois; National Academy of Design, New York City; Cleveland Museum, Ohio; and Indianapolis Museum, Indiana. She presently exhibits with the ACA Gallery in New York City.

Judith Sealy

Bibliography

Berman, Greta. "Colleen Browning and the Texture of Life." *Art International* 27 (August 1984): 18–25.
Colleen Browning—Recent Paintings. New York: Kennedy Galleries, 1949.
"Colleen Browning—The Evolution of a Painting." *American Artist* 53 (July 1989): 54–59.

Brownscombe, Jennie Augusta (1850–1936)

The most famous painting done by Jennie Brownscombe, a history and genre painter, is "The First Thanksgiving" (1914), seen by droves of tourists every year when they visit the Museum of Pilgrim Treasures in Plymouth, Massachusetts. Brownscombe attended high school in her hometown of Honesdale, Pennsylvania, and taught for two years in the late 1860s before moving to New York City. She graduated from the School of Design for Women of the Cooper Union in 1871, and for the next four years studied at the National Academy of Design—both in New York City. She was one of the founders of the Art Students League, New York City, where she taught classes to support herself, and in the late 1870s alternated her studies with Lemuel Wilmarth between this institution and the National Academy of Design. She was very active at the National Academy of Design, exhibiting annually from 1874 to 1887 and on an occasional basis until 1910; she won honorable mention and then first prize and was named an associate.

In 1882–1883 Brownscombe travelled to Europe to study in Paris, France, with the American genre painter Henry Mosler, and on her return she exhibited "Brittany Peasant Girl" at the National Academy of Design. From 1888 to 1895 she spent part of each year in Europe, maintaining a studio near Rome, Italy, in the winter. She exhibited her work at the Royal Academy in London in 1900 and at the Watercolor Society in Rome. She also exhibited in Philadelphia, Pennsylvania, and Chicago, Illinois.

Her illustrations in *Scribner's Magazine* and *Harper's Weekly* and on Louis Prang's cards and calendars were popular as well as income-producing for the artist. In 1927 she produced color illustrations for Pauline Bouvé's *Tales of the Mayflower Children.*

Among her works in public museums are "The New Scholar," Thomas Gilcrease Institute of American History and Art (1878), "Love's Young Dream," National Museum of Women in the Arts (1887), and "The Peace Ball at Fredericksburg, Virginia," Newark Museum, New Jersey (1897). Her penchant was for narrative painting rendered with realism.

Eleanor Tufts

Bibliography

Ahrens, Kent. "Jennie Brownscombe: American History Painter." *Woman's Art Journal* 1: (Fall 1980–Winter 1981): 25–29.
Hazzard, Florence W. "Brownscombe, Jennie Augusta." *Notable American Women.* Vol. 1. Belknap Press of Harvard University Press, 1971.

Tufts, Eleanor. *American Women Artists, 1830–1930.* National Museum of Women in the Arts, 1987.

Brumback, Louise Upton (1872–1929)

Born in Rochester, New York, the painter Louise Upton Brumback was a student of William Merritt Chase. Brumback's work was exhibited in many venues, including group shows with the New York Society of Women Artists and the National Association of Women Painters and Sculptors, among others. Examples of her paintings are in private and public permanent collections.

Bibliography

American Art at the Newark Museum. Newark Museum, 1981.
An Exhibition of Women Students of William Merritt Chase. New York: Marbella Gallery, 1973.
Seachrest, Effie. "Louise Upton Brumbach." *American Magazine of Art* 10:9 (July 1919): 336–37.

Brumer, Miriam (1939–)

A native New Yorker, the painter Miriam Brumer earned a Bachelor's degree from the University of Miami, Florida; and received a Master of Fine Arts degree from Boston University, Massachusetts.

Brumer has exhibited in solo and group shows in museums and galleries, including the Lotus Gallery, New York City (1976, 1977); the Salon des Femmes Peintres, Museum of Modern Art, Paris, France (1975); New York University (1979), and Fordham University (1980)—both in New York City; Virginia Miller Gallery, Miami, Florida (1981); and others.

Winner of honors and awards, including a grant from the Ludwig Vogelstein Foundation (1976–1977), Brumer was a studio teacher and once and future writer for the *Feminist Art Journal.* Examples of her work are in private, public, and corporate permanent collections, including Boston University, Massachusetts; the Chase Manhattan Bank and Citibank—both in New York City; and others.

Bibliography

Orenstein, Gloria. "Evocative Images." *Arts Magazine* (May 1980).
Zimmer, William. "Miriam Brumer." *Arts Magazine* (September 1977).

Bruneau, Kittie (1929–)

Born in Montréal, Québec, Canada, Kittie Bruneau studied at the École des Beaux-Arts in her native city under the aegis of Chicoine, Simard, and Raymond (1945–1949). She also worked with Ghitta Caiserman in Montréal, Québec, and attended the Académie Julian in Paris, France—her home between 1950 and 1958.

Bruneau also danced professionally in Paris, France (1952–1956) and with Madame Chiriaeff's company in Montréal, Québec (1954). She returned to Canada in 1958 and experimented with various materials with which to create her non-figurative works.

Her paintings were shown in solo exhibitions in France and Canada, including the Montmartre Gallery, Paris, France (1956); the Galerie Libre (1960, 1963, 1964); Montréal Museum of Fine Arts (1962); Thomas Moore Institute (1976); Bibliothèque Nationale (1972, 1978); the Musée d'Art Contemporain—all in Montréal, Québec; "4 Graveurs," Libraire du Québec, Paris, France (1980); "2nd Biennale

Gravure," Krakow, Poland (1968); and the Centre Culturel de Canada, Paris, France (1975).

Bruneau's work has been invited to many group exhibitions, such as the Spring Exhibitions at the Montréal Museum of Fine Arts, Québec; the National Gallery; the 4th and 5th Biennial Exhibition of Canadian Painting (1961, 1963); and others.

Honored for her work, Bruneau was awarded a Canada Council fellowship (1964); and a grant from the Conseil des Arts de la Province de Québec, Montréal (1965). She is a member of La Guilde Graphique.

Her work is in the permanent collections of the Montréal Museum of Fine Arts, Québec; the National Gallery, Ottawa; the Musée d'Art Contemporain, Montréal; Sir George Williams University (now Concordia University), Montréal; the Musée du Québec; and others.

Bibliography
Creative Canada: A Biographical Dictionary of Twentieth-Century Creative and Performing Artists. University of Toronto Press, 1971.
Viau, Guy. *Kittie Bruneau—Peintre et Sculpteur.* Cité Libre, Montréal, 1962.
Who's Who in American Art. 19th ed. R.R. Bowker Co., 1991–1992.

Bry, Edith (1898–1991)

Best known for her work in fused glass, Edith Bry was born in St. Louis, Missouri. In addition to her works in glass, Bry also worked in assemblage, collage, oils, enamels, printmaking, and mosaics. She studied at the Ethical Culture School, New York City (1917) and then went on to the Art Students League, New York City, where she worked with Guy Pène du Bois, Charles Locke, Winold Reiss, and Alexander Archipenko; in the 1950s, she also studied with Abraham Rattner.

A retrospective of her work was held at the Loeb Student Center, New York University, New York City, in 1983. Bry had a successful solo show at the John Heller Gallery, New York City, in 1940. Bry's work was invited to many group exhibitions throughout the United States, including the annuals held by the Federation of Modern Painters and Sculptors, New York City, and the American Society of Contemporary Artists, New York City; as well as those held at the Pennsylvania Academy of Fine Arts, Philadelphia; Whitney Museum of American Art, New York City; Los Angeles County Museum of Art, California; Seattle Art Museum, Washington; Union Theological Seminary, New York City; Butler Institute of American Art, Youngstown, Ohio; and others.

Bry's prints and oils are in the permanent collections of museums and other institutions, such as the Lincoln Center Library; the Museum of the City of New York; Museum of Fine Arts, Boston, Massachusetts; the New York Historical Society; Wichita State University Art Museum, Kansas; and more.

In her seventy-five-year career (at age fifteen, she worked in a batik studio), Bry received a number of major commissions, including fused glass works for the Central Synagogue and the Park Avenue Synagogue—both in New York City; the Second Reformed Church, Tarrytown, New York; and others.

Bry, who gave public lectures and demonstrations before the National Academy of Design, New York City, the Donnell Public Library, and Wave Hill, garnered a clutch of awards, including those from the National Association of Women Artists, the American Society of Contemporary Artists, and the Painters and Sculptors Society of New Jersey.

Member of several artist's associations, Bry belonged to the Federation of Modern Painters and Sculptors, the American Society of Contemporary Artists, and the Artist-Craftsmen of New York. She kept up a spirited correspondence with major figures in the arts, such as George Gershwin, Marc Blitzstein, George Biddle, Marsden Hartley, Abraham Rattner, Franklin Watkins, and Harold Weston.

Bibliography
Edith Bry. An Exhibition. John Heller Gallery, 1940.
Edith Bry. A Retrospective. New York University: Loeb Student Center, 1983.
National Association of Women Painters and Sculptors. *Forty-Fifth Annual Exhibition.* 1936.
Obituary. *The New York Times* (January 30, 1991).
Who's Who in American Art. 15th ed. R.R. Bowker Co., 1982.

Buba, Joy Flinsch (1904–)

Born in Lloyd's Neck, New York, Joy Flinsch Buba was destined to be an artist. At the age of nine she sat in on her first life drawing class and also created her first sculpture. A fellow of the National Sculpture Society, New York City, Buba studied at the Eberle Studio in Greenwich Village, New York; did further study in Frankfurt and Munich, Germany; Paris, France; and Rome, Italy. She also worked with Theodor Kaerner and Angelo Yank.

In describing her portrait busts, Buba claimed to have sought "the difference between things or people." She added, "There was a time that everyone said, 'Simplify. Simplify.' I said, 'Why?' I lose myself in the delight of detail . . . . The thing I am driving at from the very first is the quintessence of the person."

In addition to her sculpted portraits of fishermen and the elderly, Buba has been commissioned to sculpt international leaders in politics, medicine, the arts and the humanities, the sciences, and religion, including such luminaries as John D. Rockefeller Jr.; Chancellor Konrad Adenauer; Norman Thomas; Pope Paul VI and Pope John Paul II; Justice Stanley Mathews; and myriad others.

Her work is represented in private and public permanent collections, including the Metropolitan Museum of Art, New York City; Statuary Hall, Capitol Building, Washington, D.C.; National Portrait Gallery, Washington, D.C.; Rockefeller Plaza, New York City; Vatican Museum, Vatican City, Italy; Schaumburg Palais, Bonn, Germany; Iona Abbey, Scotland; Museum of Natural History, New York City; Historical Museum, Frankfurt, Germany; Princeton University, New Jersey; Museum of the American Indian, Browning, Montana; Kress Foundation, New York City; St. Patrick's Cathedral, New York City; and others.

Bibliography
National Portrait Gallery, Permanent Collection Illustrated Checklist. Smithsonian Institution Press, 1982.
Gardner, Albert TenEyck. *American Sculpture: A Catalogue of the Collection in the Metropolitan Museum of Art.* New York Graphic Society, 1965.
Langley, Lynne. "Sculptor Likes Difference between Things and People." *The News and Courier/The Evening Post* (November 20, 1983).
Who's Who in American Art. 19th ed. R.R. Bowker Co., 1991–1992.

Buchanan, Beverly (1940–)

Born in Fuquay, North Carolina, the African-American painter/sculptor/photographer Beverly Buchanan earned a Bachelor's degree at Bennett College, Greensboro, North Carolina (1962); received Master's degrees in public health and parasitology from Columbia University, New York City (1968, 1969) and, after working as a medical technologist and health educator, studied at the Art Students League, New York City, with Norman Lewis.

Buchanan has held solo exhibitions in museums and galleries in the United States, including "Beverly Buchanan: In Celebration of Improvisational Architecture," Schering-Plough Headquarters Gallery, Madison, New Jersey (1992); "Beverly Buchanan: Drawings, Sculptures, Legends, Photography," and "A Celebration of the Architecture of the Shack in Two and Three Dimensions," Bernice Steinbaum Gallery, New York City (1991, 1990); "Beverly Buchanan," Museum of Arts and Sciences, Macon, Georgia (1990); Heath Gallery Inc., Atlanta, Georgia (1981, 1986, 1987); University of Alabama, Birmingham (1982); Cinque Gallery, New York City (1972); and many others. Between 1963 and 1992 her work has been invited to more than seventy group exhibitions: from New York City to Tampa, Florida; from Atlanta, Georgia, to Minneapolis, Minnesota; from Ketchum, Idaho, to New Orleans, Louisiana.

Buchanan has won many honors and awards, including a Guggenheim fellowship and a National Endowment for the Arts (NEA) fellowship in sculpture (1980). Buchanan's environmental installations are sited in museums, parks, botanical gardens, and rail stations in Georgia, North Carolina, and Florida.

In drawings, photographs, legends, table-top and full-scale sculptures (re-presentations) of wood and metal shacks, Buchanan has found a metaphor to celebrate and honor the families and the handmade architecture of the poor. Her work is represented in private, public, and corporate permanent collections, including the Metropolitan Museum of Art, New York City; Columbia Museum of Art, South Carolina; High Museum of Art, Atlanta, Georgia; Newark Museum, New Jersey; AT&T Corporation, New Jersey; ARCO Corporation, Pennsylvania; and others.

Bibliography
Bertoia, Buchanan, Edwards, Mitchel: Sculpture Update. A Catalog. Winston-Salem State University, 1991.
Brenson, Michael. "Beverly Buchanan: Evocations of Poor Black Southern Life." *The New York Times* (May 24, 1991).
Kangas, Matthew. "Common Ground Separate Choices." *Art in America* 80:3 (March 1992).
Lippard, Lucy R. *Mixed Blessings: New Art in Multicultural America.* Pantheon Books, 1990.

Buchanan, Ella (d. 1951)

Born in Preston, Ontario, Canada, the sculptor Ella Buchanan studied her craft at the Art Institute of Chicago, Illinois (1908–1911), under the aegis of Charles J. Mulligan. After graduation, she taught sculpture at her alma mater (1911–1915).

Long associated with the art scene in Southern California, Buchanan exhibited her work and won awards at the California Liberty Fair, Los Angeles (1918); Pomona Fair (1928); California Art Club (1918); Ebell Spring Exhibition (1934); the Los Angeles Museum of Science, Industry, and Art (1932)—all in California; and others.

Member of the Chicago Society of Artists, the California Art Club, Los Angeles, she was vice-president of the Sculptors' Guild of Southern California, Los Angeles.

Examples of her work are in public and private collections, including the Baker Memorial, Chicago; Southwest Museum, Los Angeles; and others.

Bibliography
American Art Annual. Vol. 28. Washington, D.C.: American Federation of Arts, 1932.
Moure, Nancy. *Dictionary of Artists in Southern California before 1950.* Los Angeles: Dustin Publications, 1975.
Obituary. *The New York Times* (July 17, 1951): 27.

Buchanan, Nancy (1946–)

Born in Boston, Massachusetts, the video and performance artist Nancy Buchanan earned both her Bachelor's (1969) and Master of Fine Arts degrees (1971) from the University of California at Irvine.

Buchanan has held many solo performances and screenings of her work in universities, museums, and alternate spaces, including "Pie Piece," the Woman's Building, Los Angeles, California (1974); "Tar Baby," Mills College, Oakland, California (1976); "Glossing the Text," Franklin Furnace, New York City (1980); "It's Been Asked Before," Washington State University, Pullman (1982); and "Freedom Suites," sponsored by the California Institute of the Arts, Valencia, the Los Angeles Institute of Contemporary Art, and the Japan-American Theater, Los Angeles—all in California (1985); and others.

Winner of awards and honors, Buchanan received National Endowment for the Arts (NEA) fellowships (1978, 1980, 1983); a research grant from the University of Wisconsin at Madison (1983); and residencies at the Experimental Television Center, Oswego, New York (1984, 1993); and others. Her work is represented in public permanent collections, including the Museum of Modern Art (MoMA), New York City; Oberlin College, Ohio; and others.

Bibliography
Aber, Buchanan, Holste. A Catalog. Newport Beach, California: Newport Harbor Art Museum, 1976.
Burnham, Linda, and Steven Durland. "It's All I Can Think About: An Interview with Nancy Buchanan." *High Performance* 18:25 (1984).
Harrison, Helen A. "Trying to Express the Outrage of War." *The New York Times* (April 24, 1983).

Buchner, Barbara (1950–)

Born in Chicago, Illinois, the video artist Barbara Buchner earned a Bachelor of Fine Arts degree from the Institute of Film and Technology, New York University, New York City (1972).

Buchner has held solo exhibitions in museums, galleries, and alternate spaces, including The Kitchen (1973); and Anthology Film Archives—both in New York City (1975, 1981); the Experimental Television Center, Binghamton, New York, and the Museum of Modern Art (MoMA), New York City (1977); the School of the Art Institute of Chicago, Illinois (1978); Video Free America, San Francisco, California

(1979); the Whitney Museum of American Art, New York City (1980); and many others.

Winner of awards and honors, Buchner received a second prize at the Yale Film Festival, New Haven, Connecticut (1972); grants from the National Endowment for the Arts (NEA) (1977, 1978, 1980); grants from the New York State Council on the Arts and a Creative Artists Public Service (CAPS) grant (1979); a grant from Channel 13, WNET, New York City (1981); and others.

Examples of her work are in public permanent collections, including MoMA and New York University—both in New York City; and others.

Bibliography

Rosen, Randy, and Catherine C. Brawer, compilers. *Making Their Mark: Women Artists Move into the Mainstream 1970–1985*. A Catalog. Abbeville Press, 1989.

Sturken, Marits. "An Interview with Barbara Buchner." *Afterimage* (May 1985).

Buller, Cecil (1886–1973)

Cecil Buller was a talented printmaker who produced prints in an unusually powerful modernist style. She was among the first American artists to produce black-and-white block prints at the time of the international revival. Born in Montréal, Canada, she studied there at the Art Association and then at the Art Students League in New York City. In late 1912 she went to Paris, where the art of Cézanne, Gauguin, Léger, Fallotton, and the Cubists profoundly affected the development of her work. She studied with the French symbolist Maurice Denis who inspired her early, uncomplicated compositions produced in a rhythmical, linear style with figures set in decorative, exotic landscapes.

In 1915 Buller made her first print—a linocut—"Summer Afternoon." In 1916 she studied with master wood engraver Noel Rooke at the Central School of Art and Design in London. Here she met American artist-printmaker John J.A. Murphy and after their marriage, settled in New York City in 1918. She began wood engraving and exhibited widely in print exhibitions.

Buller maintained a lifelong interest in the figure. Her early prints were primarily classical and represented an idyllic, harmonious world. In 1929 this work culminated in eleven dramatic and sensuous wood engravings for *Song of Solomon*. The blocks were reused for the subsequent book, *Cantique des Cantiques*, published in Paris by Éditions du Raisin in 1931.

In the late 1930s Buller produced mainly lithographs of "American Scene" subjects and then in the 1940s resumed wood engraving. Her prints became more personal, detailed, and expressive. They included mythical and allegorical figures which had a psychological power. She had two one-person exhibitions, in Oxford, England (1951) and at the Montréal Museum of Fine Arts, Canada (1959). She was elected an associate of the National Academy of Design, New York City (1949). In 1989 Glenbow Museum, Calgary, Alberta, Canada produced a retrospective exhibition and catalogue raisonné of her prints.

Buller stopped printmaking in 1956. In 1959 she returned to Montréal, Québec, where she died in 1973.

Patricia Ainslie

Bibliography

Ainslie, Patricia. *Images of the Land: Canadian Block Prints 1919–1945*. Calgary: Glenbow Museum, 1984.

———. *Cecil Buller: Modernist Printmaker*. Calgary: Glenbow Museum, 1989.

Martin, Denis. *L'Estampe Au Québec, 1900–1950*. Québec City: Musée du Québec, 1988.

Bulnes, Rosalinda (1938–)

Painter and sculptor Rosalinda Bulnes changed from figurative work to abstraction; from sculpture and drawing to creating pictorial compositions in relief—using handmade paper pulp beaten from cotton and palm fibers. Bulnes was born in Monterrey, Nuevo León, Mexico, where she resides at present. In 1960 she began her art production, creating sculptures and paintings.

Bulnes's works have been in exhibitions and competitions locally, nationally, and internationally—receiving praise from art critics. Her first solo exhibition took place in 1981 at the Casa de la Cultura in Monterrey. Bulnes studied art at the University of Nuevo León and at the Institute of Arts and Letters, Monterrey; and at the Instituto Allende, San Miguel de Allende, Guanajuato—all in Mexico; as well as at the Massana School in Barcelona, Spain; at the University La Mirial, Toulouse, France; at l'École des Beaux-Arts, Dijon, France; and at l'École La Migros in Lausanne, Switzerland.

From 1984 to 1987 Bulnes worked as an arts administrator for the Secretariat of Public Education in Monterrey. In 1983 she received first prize in the annual exhibition organized by Arte Vitro, S.A., for her sculpture, "Discipline." Bulnes won first prize for her paper pulp painting, "Mexican Fantasy," in 1984. In 1990 her work, "Composition," obtained second prize in the International Exhibition of the Art League of Brownsville, Texas.

Bulnes's work has been selected for over 100 group and over twenty solo exhibitions in Mexico and abroad, including "Favorites" in Blosstoff, Illinois (1983); Bienal Latinoamericana, Buenos Aires, Argentina (1986); Grand Prix de Paris, France; Internationale Chapelle de la Sorbonne, Paris, France; Grand Prix d'Aquitaine, Musée La Commanderie, Bordeaux, France (1990); International Art Connection, City Hall, Miami, Florida (1990); and others.

Bulnes is a member of the International Association of Art, International Association of Mexican Artists (IAA-AIAM) of Mexico. She studied the techniques and processes of handmade paper in 1980 and, for the last ten years, has manually produced the paper pulp she uses in her pictorial works.

Bulnes's work is fundamentally abstract; however, she sometimes returns to a symbolic, figurative mode. The importance of her work resides in the coloration of the paper, in her unique compositions that truly define her style, that express a feeling of serenity, of liberation, of the alienation of our times—where emotion overflows, repressing any attempt at intellectualization. Her compositions are frequently geometric or geometrizing, inspired by abstract pre-Hispanic motifs and also by the chromatic richness of popular Indian art.

Giancarlo Malvaioli v. Nacher

Bibliography
Alvarez, José Rogelio, et al. *Diccionario Biográfico Enciclopedico de la Pintura Mexicana.* Quinientos Años Editores, 1979.
Vitaver, Pablo Raul. *Who's Who in Mexico.* Worldwide Reference Publications, Inc., 1990.

Bunt, Leslie P. (1943–)

Leslie Patricia Bunt first studied art at the National Institute of Fine Arts, Mexico City, Mexico (1963) and, two years later, worked in the studio of Robin Bond. Bunt did further study at the Academy of San Marcos (1969) and the Esmeralda (1975–1980)—both in Mexico City, Mexico.

Between 1975 and 1985 Bunt's sculpture was exhibited in more than twenty-five group shows, including Galería Castellanos, Hotel Camino Real (1975); Sección Trienal de Escultura, Salón Nacional de Artes Plásticas del Auditorio Nacional INBA (1979); "Latinoamerica Hoy," Salón de la Plástica Mexicana (1983); "A la Sazon de los 80s," Casa del Lago, University of Mexico (1984); Salón de Dibujo de la Plástica Mexicana (1985)—all in Mexico City; and many others. Bunt has held solo exhibitions at the World Bank, Washington, D.C. (1985), among other venues.

Winner of awards and honors, Bunt won a prize at the Salón de la Plástica Mexicana (1983); and two years later, received honorable mention at the Concurso de Escultura Torre Lomas—both in Mexico City. Her work is represented in private and public permanent collections.

Bibliography
"Image of Mexico I." *The Texas Quarterly.* A Special Issue (Autumm 1969).

Buonagurio, Toby (1947–)

A sculptor best known for her complex ceramic pieces, Toby Buonagurio received a Bachelor of Arts degree in Fine Arts in 1969 and a Master of Arts degree in art education in 1971, both from the City College of New York, New York City.

Buonagurio began exhibiting in 1973 and had her first solo exhibition at Westbroadway Gallery in New York City in 1974. She has since presented her work in seventeen solo exhibitions, including the Everson Museum of Art in Syracuse, New York (1982); the Bronx Museum of the Arts, New York, and the Contemporary Arts Center in New Orleans (1983); and the University Art Gallery at the State University of New York (SUNY) at Stony Brook (1986); as well as in approximately ninety group exhibitions in galleries and museums throughout the United States, Europe, and Japan. Buonagurio is a tenured professor at SUNY, Stony Brook, New York, where she has been teaching since 1976.

Buonagurio's awards include a Creative Artists Public Service fellowship (CAPS) grant for drawing in 1980–1981, a Contemporary Arts Center grant for participation in the New Orleans Artists' Mardi Gras "Krewe of Clones" Parade in 1983, and a research support grant from SUNY, Stony Brook, New York, in 1984.

Buonagurio's diverse and wide-ranging influences include Spanish reliquaries, art deco jukeboxes, the Chicago imagists, the pyramids of ancient Mexico, surrealism, and pop art. Originally inspired by the ironically humorous work of ceramicist Robert Arneson, Buonagurio has created a body of work that is strongly flavored by her own distinctive sense of humor. She sees her work as a form of imagi-native play in which images are juxtaposed in ways that initially seem absurd but somehow make perfect sense when taken on their own terms. High-heeled shoes, robots, mermaids, shrines, mythic female heads, and ironic hunting trophies are just a few of the images Buonagurio employs. Technically flawless, each sculpture includes recognizable images taken from popular culture, which are then assembled in unusual configurations. Buonagurio skillfully juxtaposes diverse images, relocates image parts, and plays with abrupt changes in scale, color, and surface texture.

Buonagurio's robot series, which began in 1978 and has been included in every solo show since, was part of the American Craft Museum's exhibition entitled "The Robot Exhibition: History, Fantasy, Reality." In 1988 Buonagurio collaborated with the Tallix Foundry in Beacon, New York, to produce her first cast metal—bronze, stainless steel, and anodized aluminum—polychromed sculpture, "Snake Charmer Robot." Working with metal has extended her range for larger-scale outdoor sculptural possibilities. Other recent subjects explored by Buonagurio include altered self-portraits placed within a dreamlike setting, such as "Radiant Creatures of the Blue Coral Sea" (1990) and ironic hunting trophies such as "Forest Genie Trophy" (1988).

Buonagurio's sculptures are included in public and corporate collections throughout the United States, including the Everson Museum of Art in Syracuse, New York, the Mint Museum of Art in Charlotte, North Carolina, and the Alternative Museum in New York City.

Rhonda Cooper

Bibliography
Cooper, Rhonda. "Toby Buonagurio." Exhibition Catalog. University Art Gallery, State University of New York at Stony Brook, 1986.
Everson Museum of Art. *American Ceramics.* Rizzoli, 1989, 217–18.
Klein, Ellen Lee. "Toby Buonagurio: More Optical Bounce to the Ounce." *Arts Magazine* (March 1986): 55–57.
Wechsler, Susan. *Ceramics Today, T. Buonagurio, U.S.A.* Geneva, Switzerland: Editions Olizane, 1984.

Burgess, Catherine (1953–)

A sculptor formed in the male-dominated Edmonton, Canada tradition of formalist artmaking, Catherine Burgess constructs her abstract and non-representational work in wood and metal. After graduating with a Bachelor of Fine Arts degree from the University of Alberta, Canada, in 1975 Burgess attended the Emma Lake Artists' Workshop led by Anthony Caro in 1977. At the end of the 1970s she was producing small- to medium-sized constructed masses using roughly-hewn chunks of wood. Her preoccupations with structure and material were markedly different from those of her mentor Caro, though she later assimilated aspects of his more expansive, pictorial, and referential vocabulary. Burgess's precocity was acknowledged in solo exhibitions at the Edmonton Art Gallery (1979), and the Mendel Art Gallery, Saskatoon (1980)—both in Canada.

In 1982 she worked with Anthony Caro at the Triangle Workshop, New York. This led to a softening of her rigorously structural approach, evident in works of welded scrap steel, such as "Scimitar I" (1982) and "Mustard Seed" (1982). These works maintain the architectonic forms and sectioned open box-shape elements of the earlier, wooden pieces, but with a more playful deployment of soaring planes and vanes.

Steadily distancing herself from the parochial formalism of the Edmonton milieu, Burgess produced the "Altarpiece" series of small, space-enclosing floor sculptures containing small geometric forms (1986–1987). The works embody references to fireplaces, temples, and shrines. No longer simply objects, they function as sites for psychological projection and spaces in which to act.

Burgess's shift toward subjective expression was apparently influenced by viewing an exhibition of David Smith's early production in 1981, and by her subsequent involvement with Jungian psychology. The "Altarpieces" herald the narrative symbolism of the (primarily) welded steel "Table" series. The upper surfaces of the "Tables" manage to connote place—a landscape topography, for example—while the overall sculpture remains a monolithic, furniture-like object.

"Things as They Are: Guelph, September 27, 1990" is an eleven-foot-long table structure supporting sparsely distributed geometric objects. The elements in the tableau function as non-specific signifiers of psychological and metaphorical meanings. The bronze sculpture was commissioned for the Donald Forster Sculpture Park adjacent to the Macdonald Stewart Art Centre in Guelph, Ontario.

Ingrid Jenkner

Bibliography

Burnett, David, and Marilyn Schiff. *Contemporary Canadian Art.* Hurtig, 1983.

Fenton, Terry. *Catherine Burgess Recent Sculpture.* Exhibition Catalog. Banff: Peter Whyte Gallery, 1982.

Tousley, Nancy. *Catherine Burgess.* Exhibition Catalog. Edmonton Art Gallery, 1990.

Burke, Rebecca (1946–)

Born in Kalamazoo, Michigan, the painter/printmaker, creator of so-called flamboyant pictures, Rebecca Burke, studied at Ohio State University, Columbus.

Burke has had her work included in solo and group exhibitions, including "Die Funfies," University of Waterloo, Ontario, Canada (1973); "Follies," Gallery III, Montréal, Québec, Canada (1973); and many others. Examples of her work are in private and public permanent collections.

Bibliography

Hume, Christopher. "Women Artists: Bright Young Newcomers on Canada's Art Scene." *Chatelaine* 54:10 (October 1981): 84–87.

Burke, Selma (1900–)

Selma Burke's stylistically and technically varied figurative sculpture encompasses both portraiture and imaginative work. Although she admires the abstract modernists, in her own creations she treats the human form with dignity, using distortions only to convey expressive content. Burke has also pursued a distinguished career as an art educator, working primarily within the African-American community.

One of ten children born to a Methodist minister (who worked also as a train porter to make ends meet) in Mooreshead, North Carolina, Burke started modeling with clay from a nearby riverbed when she was a child. Instead of going to art school, however, she studied nursing at St. Agnes Hospital in Raleigh, North Carolina. After earn-

ing her R.N. in 1924, she practiced in New York City, where she associated with the artists and writers of the Harlem Renaissance. Burke married one of them, the Jamaican-born novelist and poet Claude McKay. Among many portraits that reveal her ties to African-American culture are depictions of Duke Ellington, Mary McLeod Bethune, and A. Philip Randolph.

Burke travelled twice to Europe in the 1930s. In 1933–1934, she studied in Vienna, and in 1936 she returned on a sculpture scholarship, this time to Paris, France, where she studied with Aristide Maillol, whose sympathy for both classical and modern form reinforced her own interests. Her sensitive portrait head of "Frau Keller" (1937), a German-Jewish mother, captures the psychic tensions of the mounting Nazi threat, which convinced Burke to leave at the end of 1937. Subsequently Burke worked on the Federal Art Project, for which she completed "Lafayette" (1938), earned her Master of Fine Arts degree from Columbia University in New York City in 1941, and worked with Oronzio Maldarelli. In 1942 she was one of the first African-American women to join the navy. In competition the next year she won a commission for a bronze relief portrait of President Franklin Delano Roosevelt (officially unveiled in 1945). This was subsequently adapted for the portrait of Roosevelt on the American dime.

During the Depression Burke had taught at the Harlem Community Art Center, and after the war, in 1946, she went on to found the Selma Burke Art School in Greenwich Village—both in New York City. This enterprise lasted for ten years, during which she continued to work and exhibit. In such works as "Despair" (1951), a kneeling figure in travertine, and "Falling Angel" (1958), a cantilevered vision executed in wood, Burke demonstrated her commitment to her self-described role as "a people's sculptor," an artist whose work can speak to a wide audience.

In the late 1960s Burke moved to Pittsburgh, Pennsylvania. There she reached thousands of children through her teaching at the art center renamed in her honor and her visits to schools. Her bronze relief "Together" (1975), depicting a family group, and a monumental portrait of "Martin Luther King" (1980s) for Charlotte, North Carolina, represent her continuing dedication to both symbolic and realistic purposes for sculpture. Today she lives in New Hope, Pennsylvania.

Ann Lee Morgan

Bibliography

Gangewere, Robert J. "An Interview with Selma Burke." *Carnegie Magazine* 49 (January 1975): 6–12.

Rubinstein, Charlotte Streifer. *American Women Sculptors.* G.K. Hall, 1990, 296–97.

Burko, Diane (1945–)

Born in Brooklyn, New York, Diane Burko received her Bachelor of Science degree in painting and art history from Skidmore College, Saratoga Springs, New York, in 1966; and her Master of Fine Arts degree in painting in 1969 from the University of Pennsylvania, Philadelphia. Burko has been committed to landscape painting for virtually her entire professional career and clearly has made a strong niche for herself in the history of the American landscape tradition. Her painterly approach and dramatic sense of composition invariably combine to revitalize a landscape image whether the actual subject is the Delaware Water Gap or the coast line of Normandy.

Since 1967 Burko has had seventeen one-person exhibitions, including three at the Marian Locks Gallery in Philadelphia, Pennsylvania, and has also shown in seventy group exhibitions in that same span of time, including shows at the Princeton University Art Museum, New Jersey; Institute of Contemporary Art, Philadelphia, Pennsylvania; Carnegie-Mellon University, Pittsburgh, Pennsylvania; Stefanotti Gallery and Armstrong Gallery—both in New York City; Art Institute of Chicago, Illinois; Philadelphia Museum of Art, and Pennsylvania Academy of Fine Arts—both in Philadelphia, Pennsylvania; and others. Examples of her work are included in the permanent collections of the Philadelphia Museum of Art, Pennsylvania Academy of Fine Arts, and Reading Public Museum—all in Pennsylvania; Prudential Insurance Company of America; AT&T; the CIGNA corporate collection; and others.

Burko received a National Endowment for the Arts (NEA) Artists fellowship (1985–1986), and Pennsylvania Council on the Arts individual artists grants (1981, 1989). She received a guest artist fellowship from the Tamarind Institute of the University of New Mexico (1980, 1982), and was invited to collaborate on prints in Arizona State University's Print Research Facility (1981). She was the recipient of a six-month residence fellowship at Giverny, France, sponsored by the Reader's Digest Foundation in 1989, and the next several exhibitions she has scheduled will focus on her response to Monet's great gardens and total experience in France. Burko serves on the mayor of Philadelphia's Cultural Advisory Council and served as a board member for the National Women's Caucus for Art (1984–1987). Burko has been a visiting professor at Princeton University, New Jersey, and other institutions such as Hollins College and has taught since 1969 at the Community College of Philadelphia, Pennsylvania, where, since 1985, she has held the rank of professor.

Leonard Lehrer

Bibliography

Alloway, Lawrence, and Lenore Malin. *Diane Burko*. Philadelphia: Marian Locks Gallery, 1988.

Berlind, Bob. "Diane Burko at Stefanotti and PAFA." *Arts in America* (February 1981).

Boyle, Richard J. *Waterways of Pennsylvania: Drawings and Prints by Diane Burko*. Allentown Museum of Art, 1983.

Goodyear, Frank H., Jr. *Contemporary American Realism Since 1960*. New York Graphic Society, Boston (in association with the Pennsylvania Academy of Fine Arts), 1981.

Rubenstein, Charlotte Streifer. *American Women Artists*. G.K. Hall and Co. and Avon Books, 1982.

Sozanski, Edward J. "Diane Burko at Marian Locks." *The Philadelphia Inquirer* (April 7, 1988).

Burrage, Mildred Giddings (1890–1983)

Born in Portland, Maine, the painter Mildred Giddings Burrage learned her craft at the Académie de la Grande Chaumière, Paris, France; she also studied with Richard Miller.

Burrage held solo exhibitions in museums and galleries in the 1930s, including the Montclair Art Museum, New Jersey (1932), among others.

Her work was included in many prestigious group shows, such as the Pennsylvania Academy of Fine Arts, Philadelphia (1911, 1913, 1928, 1931, 1935); the Art Institute of Chicago, Illinois (1913); the Architectural League, New York City (1921); Boston Museum of Fine Arts, Massachusetts (1927); Ogunquit Art Association, Maine (1935, 1936); Kennebunk, Maine (1936–1944); and others.

Examples of Burrage's paintings are in private and public permanent collections, including the National Collection of Art, Smithsonian Institution, Washington, D.C.; a mural in the Science Library of Bryn Mawr College, Pennsylvania; and others.

Bibliography

American Art Annual. Vol. 28. Washington, D.C.: American Federation of Arts, 1932.

Archives of American Art. A Checklist of the Collection. 2nd ed. Washington, D.C.: Smithsonian Institution, 1977.

Burroughs, Edith Woodman (1871–1916)

Born in Riverdale-on-Hudson, New York, the celebrated sculptor Edith Woodman Burroughs entered the Art Students League, New York City, to study with Augustus Saint-Gaudens (1886)—and, in several years, this very young woman was able to support herself by teaching and executing sculpture commissions for churches. She did further study with Injalbert and Merson in France and, seven years before her death, on another trip to France, was motivated by Aristide Maillol to simplify her work.

In addition to a solo exhibition in New York City (1915), two examples of her work were shown, the same year, at the Panama-Pacific International Exposition, San Francisco, California. The National Sculpture Society, New York City, honored her with a memorial exhibition.

Representative examples of Burroughs's work are in private and public permanent collections, including the Metropolitan Museum of Art, New York City; the Corcoran Gallery, Washington, D.C.; Brookgreen Gardens, South Carolina; and others.

Bibliography

Calder, A. Stirling, and Stella G.S. Perry. *The Sculpture and Mural Decorations of the Exposition: A Pictorial Survey of the Art of the Panama-Pacific International Exposition*. San Francisco: Paul Elder & Co., 1915.

Gardner, Albert TenEyck. *American Sculpture: A Catalogue of the Collection of the Metropolitan Museum of Art*. New York Graphic Society, 1965.

Perry, Stella G.S. *Little Bronze Playfellows*. Paul Elder & Co., 1915.

Burroughs, Margaret T.G. (1917–)

Born in St. Rose Parish, Louisiana, the multi-talented African-American artist Margaret T.G. Burroughs received her education in many institutions, including the Chicago Normal School, Illinois; the Art Institute of Chicago, Illinois, where she earned a Bachelor's degree in art education (1944) and a Master's degree in art education (1948); Teachers College, Columbia University, New York City (1958–1961); and Northwestern University, Chicago, Illinois. Additionally, she studied in Mexico City, Mexico.

Burroughs has held solo exhibitions throughout the United States and abroad in museums and galleries for half a century, including Mexico City, Mexico (1952–1953); the Soviet Union and Poland (1965);

South Side Art Center (1972, 1974, 1978) and the YWCA (Young Women's Christian Association) (1973)—both in Chicago, Illinois. Her work has been invited to many group exhibitions: from New York City to San Francisco, California; from Kenosha, Wisconsin, to Moscow, Russia; from Chicago, Illinois, to Leipzig, Germany.

Winner of awards and honors, Burrroughs was a recipient of an honorary Doctorate from Lewis University, Romeoville, Illinois; first watercolor award, Atlanta University, Georgia (1955); best in show, National Conference of Artists, Lincoln University, Jefferson City, Missouri (1963); third place in sculpture, Atlanta University, Georgia (1969); and others.

Founder of the Du Sable Museum of African-American History (1961), the National Conference of Artists, the South Side Community Art Center, and founder and director of the Ebony Museum of Negro History and Art—all in Chicago, Burroughs taught in the same city at Du Sable High School (1946–1969), School of the Art Institute (1968–1969), and Kennedy-King City College (1969). She illustrated and wrote books for children, juveniles, and adults and served as art director and research assistant for the Negro Hall of Fame.

Her work is represented in private and public permanent collections, including Alabama A&M University, Normal; Atlanta University, Georgia; Howard University, Washington, D.C.; Jackson State University, Mississippi; and others.

Bibliography
Bontemps, Arna Alexander, ed. *Forever Free: Art by African-American Women*. Illinois State University, 1980.
Dover, Cedric. *American-Negro Art*. Graphic Society, 1960.
Driskell, David C. *Two Centuries of Black American Art*. Knopf and Los Angeles County Museum of Art, 1976.
Fine, Elsa Honig. *The Afro-American Artist: A Search for Identity*. Holt, Rinehart & Winston, 1971.
Women's Caucus for Art Honor Awards. Houston: National Women's Caucus for Art, 1988.

Burwell, Lilian Thomas (1927–)

Born in Washington, D.C., the African-American painter/sculptor/educator Lilian Thomas Burwell studied at Pratt Institute, Brooklyn, New York; and earned a Master of Fine Arts degree at the Catholic University of America in Washington, D.C.

Burwell has held solo exhibitions in the "O" Street Studio, Washington, D.C. (1990); and CRT's Craftery Gallery, Hartford, Connecticut (1988); among others. Her work has been included in many group shows in the United States and abroad, such as "African-American Contemporary Art," Museo Civico d'Arte Contemporanea di Gibellina, Sicily, Italy (1990); "Coast to Coast: Women of Color National Artist's Book Project," a travelling exhibition, Baltimore Museum of Art, Maryland (1990); "Afro-American Art, Now," George Washington University, Washington, D.C. (1987); Martin Luther King Jr. Memorial Library, Washington, D.C. (1985); and others.

Burwell's installations are based upon a personal analysis and response to the natural world, using painting and sculpture in ever-new configurations, to create her delightfully ambiguous illusions. Her work is in private and corporate permanent collections, including ARCO, Philadelphia, Pennsylvania; Parasio, Huelva, Spain; and others.

Bibliography
Abromowitz, Benjamin. "Lilian Thomas Burwell." *Eyewash* (March 1990).
Hall, Robert. *Gathered Visions: Selected Works by African American Women Artists*. Anacostia Museum, Smithsonian Institution Press, 1992.
Kernan, Michael. "Burwell's Breakouts." *Washington Post* (March 1983).

Bush-Brown, Margaret White Lesley (1856–1944)

Margaret White Lesley Bush-Brown was a painter and etcher who first worked for her father, J. Peter Lesley, professor of geology and mining engineering at the University of Pennsylvania, Philadelphia, making geological models. Bush-Brown was known for her portraits in oil. Her mother, Susan Lyman Lesley, a writer and social reformer, supported her studies at the Philadelphia School of Design for Women and the Pennsylvania Academy of Fine Arts—both in Philadelphia, Pennsylvania. She studied first at the academy with Christian Schussele and then with Thomas Eakins from 1876 to 1880. Travelling to Paris, France, in 1880 she studied in the studio of Emile-Auguste Carolus-Duran and with Tony Robert-Fleury, Jules Lefèbvre, and Gustave Boulanger at the Académie Julian. Gabrielle De Vaux Clements taught her to etch in Philadelphia, Pennsylvania, in October 1883. She had a lifelong friendship with Clements and Ellen Day Hale, both of whom were painters and etchers. She married sculptor Henry Kirke Bush-Brown in 1886 after obtaining his commitment to respect her intention to continue to work as an artist. They spent 1888–1890 in France and Italy, where she gave birth to her daughter and first son. She continued to work in New York City until 1910, when she and her family moved to Washington, D.C. She set up a studio there and frequently travelled to execute portrait commissions.

Bush-Brown began to exhibit in 1880. She showed oil paintings regularly at the Pennsylvania Academy of Fine Arts, Philadelphia; the National Academy of Design, New York City; the Paris Salon, France; the Boston Art Club and the St. Botolph Club—both in Boston, Massachusetts; and the Woman's Art Club of New York City. Bush-Brown exhibited in several world expositions and painted a mural, "Spring," for the ladies' reception room of the Pennsylvania State Building at the Columbian Exposition in Chicago, Illinois. She won her first medal at the Charleston Exhibition, South Carolina (1902). The Corcoran Gallery, Washington, D.C., sponsored her first solo exhibition of oil paintings in 1911. In 1923 Doll and Richards Gallery in Boston, Massachusetts, hung a solo exhibit of her portrait drawings. She exhibited etchings with the New York Etching Club, the Union League Club, the Salmagundi Club, and the National Arts Club—all in New York City; and the Art Institute of Chicago, Illinois.

She supported the Women's suffrage movement and was active in the National Alliance of Unitarian Women, as well as many art organizations, including the Woman's Art Club, the National Association of Women Painters and Sculptors, the Washington Society of Mural Painters, and the National Arts Club. She lectured on "The Relations of Women to the Artistic Professions."

Her self-portrait, which exemplified the academic realism which she learned from Eakins and her French teachers, is in the Pennsylvania Academy of Fine Arts, Philadelphia. Other works are in the National Museum of American Art, the National Museum of Women in the Arts, and the Library of Congress—all in Washington, D.C.; the Boston Museum of Fine Arts, Massachusetts; the New York Public Library, New York City; and the Sophia Smith Collection, Smith College,

Northampton, Massachusetts.

    Phyllis Peet

Bibliography

Bush-Brown Family Papers. Northampton, Massachusetts.: Sophia Smith Collection, Smith College.

Corcoran Gallery of Art. *Exhibition of Portraits and Pictures by Mrs. Henry K. Bush-Brown*. Washington, D.C.: Corcoran Gallery of Art, 1911.

Doll and Richards Gallery. *Portrait Drawings by M. Lesley Bush-Brown*. Boston: Doll and Richards, 1923.

"Mrs. H. Bush-Brown, Portrait Painter, 87 [Obituary]." *The New York Times* (November 18, 1944): 13.

National Museum of Women in the Arts, Washington, D.C. *American Women Artists: 1830–1930*. NMWA, 1987: cat. no. 15.

Peet, Phyllis. *American Women of the Etching Revival*. Atlanta: High Museum of Art, 1988: 51–52.

Butler, Frances (1940–)

Frances Butler is a remarkably versatile artist, who is not only an accomplished printmaker, but who has also made assemblages and installations, designed textiles, run a fabric printing company, taught book design and graphic arts techniques on the college level, published numerous articles and books, and cofounded a small publishing company. The St. Louis, Missouri, native did not decide to devote herself to visual art until her mid-twenties. Before that time Butler was a student of literature and history, receiving a Bachelor of Arts degree in history from the University of California at Berkeley (1961) and a Master of Arts degree from Stanford University (1963). In 1966 Butler earned a Master of Arts degree in design from the University of California at Berkeley; she also did extensive doctoral work in the architecture department at that institution.

Since the early 1970s Butler has participated in group shows all over her adopted state of California, and in many other parts of the United States, as well as Holland and France. Her work was also included in "American Bookworks in Print," a USIA-sponsored show that travelled through Europe and to several African nations, in 1984. The artist has had many solo exhibitions—of her books, posters, prints, fabrics, and sculptures—including a retrospective at the University Art Museum, University of California at Davis (1982), and a one-person show at Pyramid Atlantic, Riverdale, Maryland (1991). In 1986 she was commissioned to do a piece called "Shadow Garden" for the University Hospital in Seattle, Washington.

In addition Butler has had a distinguished career as a college professor—teaching typography, commercial design, and experimental color printing at Berkeley (1968–1970), and the University of California at Davis (1970 to the present)—where she is currently a professor of environmental design. Between 1973 and 1979 Butler was the proprietor, designer, and manufacturer of Goodstuffs Handpainted Fabrics, and in 1975 she cofounded (with Alastair Johnston) the Poltroon Press—a Berkeley-based company which published innovative books by Butler, and many other people (often designed by her), through 1981.

Butler has received numerous National Endowment for the Arts (NEA) grants (1973, 1977, 1979, 1980), and many other awards; she served as artist-in-residence at the Visual Studies Workshop, Rochester, New York (1984); the San Francisco Center for Interdisciplinary and Experimental Studies, California (1985); and the School of the Art Institute of Chicago, Illinois (1986). She has published more than eighteen articles and more than half a dozen books. Butler's art is found in many collections, including those of the Victoria & Albert Museum, London, and the Museum of Modern Art (MoMA), New York City.

Bibliography

Miller, Lancaster. *Colored Reading: The Graphic Art of Frances Butler*. Berkeley: 1980.

Treib, Marc. "The Turning of the Page: The Work of Frances Butler." *Idea* (Tokyo) 163 (November 1980): 68–75.

———. "Design in Two and a Half Dimensions." *Print* 29: 6 (November–December 1975): 60–65.

Butler, Sheila (1938–)

Sheila Butler was born in Teesport, Pennsylvania. The first art instruction she received was at the Carnegie Institute in Pittsburgh, Pennsylvania, which held Saturday morning art classes for children. Butler received a Bachelor of Fine Arts degree with honors from the Carnegie Institute of Technology in Pittsburgh (now the Carnegie-Mellon University) in 1960, majoring in painting and printmaking. Her teachers included Douglas Wilson and Robert Gardiner.

Moving to Canada in 1962 and settling there permanently in 1969, Butler became a citizen of that country in 1975. From 1969 to 1972 Butler was employed as a special projects officer for the government of the Northwest Territories at Baker Lake, Canada, where she developed a printmaking project for Inuit artists. Butler continued to be involved with the Inuits until 1976 in various capacities, including director of the Baker Lake Sewing Shop and fine arts consultant. She has lectured at the University of Winnipeg, University of Manitoba School of Art, and the University of Western Ontario School of Visual Art in London, Ontario—all in Canada.

Butler's work concentrates on the investigation of the figure to express the human condition. She often works in series which include subjects such as humans as swimmers, humans in tents, figures sleeping, and works dealing with violent images from television news, news magazines, and newspapers. Works such as "Walking on Water" (1980) explore the ambiguous nature of the figure in water—an environment alien to them—while "The Black Sedan #1" (1990) is a haunting image that uses time and memory as a device to create tension. Stylistically, Butler's paintings show line that has been consciously developed, while the color is more intuitive. Butler's work has been shown in numerous solo and group exhibitions, and her work is included in the collections of the National Gallery of Canada, the Winnipeg Art Gallery, and the Art Gallery of Hamilton—all in Canada, among others. Butler is a fellow of the Royal Canadian Academy.

    Linda Jansma

Bibliography

Butler, Sheila. *Sheila Butler: New Paintings & Drawings*. Toronto: Evelyn Aimis Gallery, 1990.

Dillow, Nancy E. *Sheila Butler: Recent Paintings*. Winnipeg, Manitoba: the Winnipeg Art Gallery, 1981.

Moppett, George. *Sheila Butler: Paintings 1986*. Saskatoon, Saskatchewan: Mendel Art Gallery, 1986.

Butterfield, Deborah (1949–)

Throughout her career Deborah Butterfield has created life-sized sculptures of horses in sticks and mud, found objects, and industrial detritus. Butterfield uses the horse as a vehicle to explore material and form, and as a metaphor for the human experience.

Since her childhood in San Diego, California, Butterfield has been fascinated by horses. When she enrolled at the University of California at Davis, she was torn between pursuing art and veterinary medicine. She decided upon the former and completed her Bachelor of Arts degree with honors in 1972 and a Master of Fine Arts degree in 1973. While at the University of California at Davis, Butterfield bought her first horse and lived and worked on a thoroughbred farm. In the studio, however, she avoided the image of the horse and concentrated at first on ceramic pots.

Butterfield sculpted her first horse in 1973, working with plaster over a steel armature to create a highly realistic representation. William T. Wiley, Butterfield's professor at the University of California at Davis, encouraged her new and unusual direction, and from the beginning Butterfield's sculptures were about a great deal more than horses. She is frequently quoted as saying, "I first used the horse images as a metaphorical substitute for myself—it was a way of doing a self-portrait one step removed from the specificity of Deborah Butterfield." Butterfield's early works embodied highly personal feminist and political statements inspired by her anti-Vietnam War activities in graduate school. She consciously chose to depict mares, countering the masculine, military equestrian statues found throughout art history. Her horse sculptures were positive images of procreation and nurturing rather than destruction.

In 1976 Butterfield abandoned realism and made a dramatic change in materials, leading to her mature style. From 1975 to 1976 Butterfield taught sculpture at the University of Wisconsin at Madison, and in 1976 she moved to Montana to teach at Montana State University in Bozeman. Butterfield began experimenting with natural materials found in the mountain terrain. Still using a handmade steel-and-chicken-wire armature, her life-sized horses became sketches in mud and sticks that hover between representation and abstraction. Butterfield manages to convey distinct presences with downstretched heads and paunchy girths, yet her images are stripped of all but the most basic anatomical characteristics, and evoke rather than represent the horse. The seemingly random clustering of mud and sticks is actually a careful examination of line and mass in space. In an early installation at the Zolla/Lieberman Gallery in Chicago, Illinois (1977), Butterfield's standing and reclining horses were dense brown masses with sticks crisscrossing their torsos. Sensual and vulnerable, the reclining mares predominated and purposefully echoed images of women throughout art history.

After 1979 the interior dynamics of Butterfield's horses increased when she began working with found industrial objects. These works range from three to seven feet in height and are composed of barbed wire, pipes, fencing, old tires, tin cans, and colorful and corroded scraps of metal. An untitled work of 1986 includes the remains of an old tricycle found in Colorado and "Green Horse #3" (1980) is formed from rusted wire fencing and green stakes. These powerful sculptures are alternately skeletal and dense in construction. The reclining "Mardi" (1986) is a graceful, curving outline of rusted steel, with only the flank and rump formed by blue corrugated metal fragments. By contrast the standing "Vermillion" (1988) is one solid mass of battered, orange steel balancing on spindly steel legs. The horses are quiet and still, but there is a great deal of internal movement—the contrasts of solids and voids, colors and textures. Patches of rust become painterly passages, and light plays over the beaten, corroded metal as it would over a twitching flank.

As in much assemblage art, Butterfield's later horses echo junkyards and ghost towns, and art writers have interpreted the sculptures as new images of the American West. Terse letters and words often emerge from the complex structure of the horses, hinting at the previous industrial use of the materials. In "Ferdinand" (1990), large orange letters form the horse's musculature.

In the mid-1980s Butterfield began casting many of her horses in bronze, particularly those made of ephemeral materials. The delicate lace-like structure of the six-foot-high "Solo" was formed by casting twigs and sticks in bronze and assembling them in a crisscrossing pattern. "Laka" (1990), also cast in bronze and similar in height, is composed of bold, circular rhythms of beaten found metal. In the late 1980s Butterfield completed a small cast bronze edition of thirty-two-inch-high horses for the Kentucky Derby Festival Arts Commission. The work's spindly legs and massed body resembled beaten steel sheets and was painted the color of rust.

The horse has a long tradition as a political and philosophical symbol in the history of Western art, and Butterfield's work has often been linked to this tradition. Butterfield refutes this comparison. She finds her inspiration in the art of Africa and Asia and, most importantly, in her own experiences as a horsewoman. Butterfield rides and trains horses for dressage, a discipline in which the horse and the rider work together to perform a set of specific tasks. She describes this process as a "kinetic language" and as her attempt to "try to communicate with another species." Butterfield projects onto her horses her desire, and that of humans throughout history, to connect with nature.

Butterfield continues to live on a ranch in Montana, dividing her time between her horses and sculpting. Since 1986 she has spent her winters in Hawaii, where she continues to work in natural materials. Butterfield's work has been exhibited internationally and is represented in most major collections in the United States, including the Whitney Museum of American Art, New York City; the San Francisco Museum of Modern Art, California; the Walker Art Center, Minneapolis, Minnesota; and the Metropolitan Museum of Art, New York City.

Heather Sealy Lineberry

Bibliography

Martin, Richard. "A Horse Perceived by Sighted Persons: New Sculptures by Deborah Butterfield." *Arts Magazine* 61 (January 1987): 73–75.

Rosen, Randy, and Catherine C. Brawer. *Making Their Mark: Women Artists Move into the Mainstream, 1970–1985.* Abbeville Press, 1989.

Tucker, Marcia. "Equestrian Mysteries, An Interview with Deborah Butterfield." *Art in America* 77 (June 1989): 155–57, 203.

Buyers, Jane (1948–)

Born in Toronto, Ontario, Canada, Jane Buyers spent six months at the Instituto Allende in Mexico in 1969, where her choice to become an artist was confirmed. She earned an Honors Bachelor of Arts degree in printmaking at York University, Toronto in 1973. She spent the next year working at the Montréal printer's collective, La Guilde Graphique. For the following eight years she produced figurative prints, working mainly with lithography and silk-screening. Her first images were of clothes and prints. Buyers's first important solo exhibition was at Mount Allison University's Owen's Art Gallery in Sackville, New Brunswick, Canada (1975). This exhibition toured Canada's Atlantic provinces extensively. She began showing with the Miriam Perlman Gallery, first in Flint, Michigan (1980) and then in Chicago, Illinois. Her work was acquired by such corporate collectors as Detroit Edison and First Federal Savings. As her imagery moved to ladders and stairs as in "Construction Site" (1981), Buyers began to work with mixed media, incorporating sculpture and architectural references. In her 1983 exhibition "Mixing Memory and Desire" at the Art Gallery of Hamilton, Ontario, Canada, her constructions of interiors included lights and audio tapes, as in "La Vie en Rose" (1982). In 1988 Buyers went to Pietrasanta, Italy, where she learned bronze casting which she incorporated in mixed-media assemblages. This work, such as "La Rosa Che Viaggia" (1990), was included in her exhibition of the same title at the Garnet Press in Toronto. She obtained a Master of Arts degree in women's Studies from the University of Toronto's Ontario Institute for Studies in Education in 1990. Buyers currently teaches at the University of Waterloo, Ontario, Canada.

Cyril Reade

Bibliography

Andreae, Janice. "Jane Buyers." *C Magazine* 26 (Summer 1990): 60–61.
Cheetham, Mark. *Remembering Postmodernism: Trends in Recent Canadian Art*. Oxford University Press, 1991.
Fabo, Andy. "Jane Buyers." *Vanguard* 13, 2 (March 1984): 45.

Buzio, Lydia (1948–)

Born in Montevideo, Uruguay, the ceramist Lydia Buzio studied drawing and painting with several teachers, including Fernández, Montez, and Horacio Torres (1964–1966); and she was a ceramics student of José Collel (1976).

In 1972 Buzio set up a ceramics studio in New York City. The primary influence on her work derived from the constructionist paintings of Joaquin Torres-García (1874–1949) and his followers, which graced the environment in which she grew up. (Also, her sister married the son of Torres-García.) Yet, Buzio's work is her own; the painted cityscapes on her ware exude a certain spatial phenomenon, difficult to describe.

Bibliography

Beardsley, John, Jane Livingston, and Octavio Paz. *Hispanic Art in the U.S.: 30 Contemporary Painters and Sculptors*. Houston Museum of Fine Arts, 1987.
Clark, Garth. *American Ceramics 1896 to the Present*. Abbeville Press, 1987.
Lebow, Edward. "Lydia Buzio in Perspective." *American Ceramics* 2:2 (1983).

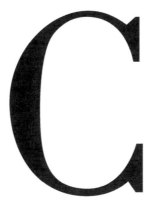

Cabrera, Geles (Angeles) (1929–)

Born in Mexico, Geles Cabrera studied art at the Academy of San Carlos when she was fifteen years old. Three years later she moved to Havana, Cuba, and attended the Academy of San Alejandro. Returning to Mexico in 1949, Cabrera continued her art studies at the Escuela de Pintura y Escultura (La Esmeralda) in Mexico City.

In 1949 Cabrera became professor of drawing at the Escuela Nacional Preparatoria, Mexico. A sculptor, she renounced naturalism and the figurative style and reduced all forms in her three-dimensional work to their most basic elements.

In 1966 she opened the Museo Escultorio at 181 Xicoténcatl in Coyoacan, Mexico. Five years later she produced several lyrical and poetic works in Plexiglas. In 1975 Cabrera was part of the group called "Gucadigose," which was comprised of Cabrera, Angela Gurría, Juan Luis Díaz, Mathias Goeritz, and Sebastián—with whom she exhibited five sculptures on the periphery of the Villahermosa, Tabasco, Mexico.

Cabrera has produced sculpture in myriad materials, including wood, metal, stone, clay, bronze, scrap iron, laminated copper, wire, plastics, and *papier maché*. From 1948 to 1981, she had many solo and group exhibitions and won a number of prizes in Mexico and abroad.

Bibliography

Alvarez, José Rogelio, et al. *Enciclopedia de México*. Secretaría de
    Educación Pública, 1987.

Caesar, Doris Porter (1892–1971)

Doris Porter Caesar was born in Brooklyn, New York. Alfred Haynes Porter, her father, a successful lawyer and entrepreneur, took his twelve-year-old motherless child on trips to England, France, and Italy.

Caesar was initially enrolled in Miss Chapin's and then the Spence School from which, at the age of sixteen, she would rush to her anatomy class with George Bridgeman at the Art Students League—all in New York City; she studied at the Art Students League until she married in 1913.

Between 1914 and 1922 she gave birth to two sons and a daughter, took care of the household and her children and, in this World War I period, had little opportunity to further her career as a sculptor.

Caesar studied sculpture with Alexander Archipenko (1925–1930) without becoming a clone of her instructor; she noted that Archipenko was a teacher from whom she learned a great deal, one who did not impose his style on his students. She approached sculpture, not as a carver, but as one who modelled expressionistic figures of women from clay—revealing powerful three-dimensional statements. She cast her first bronze in 1927.

Caesar's first solo exhibition took place at the Montross Gallery, New York City, in 1931; it was followed by another three years later in the same gallery. The E. Weyhe Bookshop and Gallery gave her a solo show in 1935, the first of many in that New York City landmark. At Weyhe, she was able to study his collection of German sculpture, including the work of Emile Nolde, Käthe Kollwitz, and, especially, Rudolph Belling, who exerted a profound influence upon her work. Regrettably, most of her work from the 1920s and 1930s has been destroyed.

Caesar experimented with extending the nude female body beyond its "normal" height; the results, not always successful from her point of view, always portrayed living, breathing beings, and Curt Valentin showed this stage of her efforts in an exhibition in New York

City in 1943.

Her finest work was done in the late 1940s and 1950s, when she moved fifty miles north of New York City to Salem Center, New York, and later to Litchfield, Connecticut: "Torso 1955," a fifty-three-inch bronze, and "Ascent 1957," a sixty-inch brass, each representing a nude female figure, reveal Caesar at her best.

Bibliography
Devree, Howard. "Doris Caesar Displays Sculpture." *The New York Times* (October 17, 1957).
Doris Caesar, Philip Evergood. Exhibition Catalog. Wadsworth Athenaeum, 1960.
Goodrich, Lloyd, and John I.H. Baur. *Four American Expressionists.* Whitney Museum of American Art, 1959.
Weyhe, Erhard. *Caesar.* Weyhe Gallery, 1952.

Caiserman-Roth, Ghitta (1923–)

Born in Montréal, Québec, Canada, Ghitta Caiserman-Roth studied painting with Alexander Bercovitch and, at the age of twelve, showed her work at the Montréal Museum of Fine Arts, Québec. Caiserman received a Bachelor of Arts degree at the Parsons School of Design, New York City, and was awarded a post-graduate scholarship for further study in Europe (1941). In New York City she worked under the aegis of Moses Sawyer at the New York Art School, and with Harry Sternberg at the Art Students League. Caiserman also did work at the Nova Scotia College of Art, and the École des Beaux-Arts—both in Canada, under Albert Dumouchel.

In the late 1940s Caiserman and Alfred Pinsky opened an art school and held a two-person show at the Montréal Museum of Fine Arts, Québec. Together, they painted a sixteen-foot mural for a clothing factory in Montréal, Québec.

Caiserman won the O'Keefe art award (1951) for travel and study in France and Italy. The following year, she received a scholarship for study at the well-known Instituto Allende in Mexico. The recipient of a Canada Council senior fellowship (1962), Caiserman has held memberships in the Federation of Canadian Artists, the Canadian Group of Painters, and the Canadian Society of Graphic Art. She received the Canadian Government Centennial Medal in 1967. In 1956 the Royal Canadian Academy of Art elected her to the rank of associate. She has been on the faculties of universities in Canada, including Queen's University (1963); Sir George Williams (now Concordia University) in 1960; and the Sadye Bronfman Centre, Montréal—all in Canada (1970).

Her paintings and prints have been shown in solo and group shows throughout Canada and are represented in many permanent collections, including the Vancouver Art Gallery and the University of British Columbia; the Saskatoon Art Centre, Saskatchewan; the London Public Library and Art Museum, Ontario; the National Art Gallery, Ottawa; Hart House, University of Toronto, Ontario; Montréal Museum of Fine Arts, Québec—all in Canada; and hosts of others.

Bibliography
Duval, Paul. *Canadian Prints and Drawings.* Burns & MacEachern, 1952.
McCullough, Norah. "Ghitta Caiserman." *Canadian Art* 17:2, pp. 84–89.
Who's Who in American Art. 19th ed. R.R. Bowker Co., 1991–1992.

Calderon de la Barca, Celia (1921–1969)

Born in Mexico, the painter/printmaker Celia Calderon de la Barca was the daughter of a landholder whose family traced its roots back to the Spanish poet, Calderon. She lived in Mexico City, Mexico, and studied art at the San Carlos Academy (1942) with further study in lithography and engraving at the School of the Book Arts in her native city.

Calderon de la Barca won many awards and prizes, including a scholarship in 1944; first prize in a competition sponsored by the Anglo-American Institute for Cultural Relations (1945); and an award from the British Council in 1950, which led to the "grand tour" through France, Italy, and England.

In 1947, Calderon de la Barca was one of the founders of the Sociedad Mexicana de Grabadores. She travelled throughout North America in 1951 and became a member of the Taller de Gráfica Popular soon afterward. Her work has been widely exhibited in group and solo shows in institutions in Mexico and North America.

Bibliography
Haab, Armin. *Mexican Graphic Art.* George Wittenborn, Inc., 1957.

Callery, Mary (1903–1977)

American sculptor Mary Callery worked primarily in metal. Her portrait busts and thin, linear abstract and figurative subjects were regularly featured in New York City galleries from 1944 through the 1960s. Callery's professional prominence is indicated by a photographic feature on her sculptures which appeared in *Life* magazine and several commissions she received for large-scale pieces in the 1950s.

Born in New York City, Callery studied at the Art Students League, New York City, in the 1920s under Edward McCartan. At age twenty-seven she went to Paris, France, where she lived for the next ten years. She studied there under Jacque Loutchansky, Henri Laurens, and Pablo Picasso, and began collecting Picasso's work at the same time. In 1940, due to the outbreak of World War II, she returned to the United States. She lived briefly in Montana and Wyoming before settling in New York and thereafter maintained residences in Long Island, New York; Paris, France; and Spain.

In 1943 Callery collaborated with Fernand Léger on a series of polychrome reliefs of acrobats in plaster and bronze. These served as a point of departure for the colorful metal sculptures for which she became best known. Her work is characterized by spindly, stick-like forms which tumble through open spaces as figures in the round or in screens or reliefs. Although she occasionally exhibited work in terra cotta and plaster, her preferred medium was metal. In the 1940s Callery worked almost entirely in bronze, but in the 1950s she favored steel, and she made abstract forms of brass and steel in the 1960s. A 1953 commission for the Pittsburgh headquarters of the Aluminum Company of America consisted, appropriately, of three sculptures in aluminum, "Constellation I," "Constellation II," and "Three Birds in Flight."

The elongated, rubbery limbs of the acrobatic figures she portrayed so often were employed in other subjects as well. In Callery's delightful polychromed steel screen, "Fables of La Fontaine" (1954), a commission executed for P.S.34 in New York City, playful animals and figures from the well-known stories are set off in geometric compartments which function as foot and handholds for climbing schoolchildren. Following this she received another large-scale commission,

"Acrobats" (1955), a sculpture for the Wingate Public School in Brooklyn, New York. Most of Callery's sculpture was done on a small scale, however, intended for interior display.

The figurative emphasis of Callery's work in the 1940s and 1950s was gradually displaced by non-objective forms and abstractions of subjects from the natural world. She exhibited frequently with the Buchholz Gallery, Curt Valentin Gallery, and M. Knoedler—all in New York City, and her work is in many collections, including the Museum of Modern Art (MoMA), also in New York City. Throughout her career, critics Christian Zervos and Henry McBride championed her work. Following her death in Paris, France, a retrospective exhibit was held at the Washburn Gallery in New York City in 1978.

Deborah A. Rindge

Bibliography
Callery, Mary. "The Last Time I Saw Picasso." *Art News* 41 (March 1942): 23, 36.
Rubinstein, Charlotte Streifer. *American Women Artists: From Early Indian Times to the Present.* Avon, 1982, 310–11.
"Stretched Statues." *Life* 33 (November 17, 1952): 143.

Callis, Jo Ann (1940–)
As a photographer, Jo Ann Callis was known for her works based on the society she saw around her. Born on November 25, 1940, to a middle-class, Jewish family in Cincinnati, Ohio, Callis attended Ohio State University, Columbus, where she studied painting and sculpture. She remained there until her marriage to David Callis in 1960. After the birth of two children she began taking night classes at California State University at Long Beach, which she continued until 1965. When Callis and her husband separated in 1970 she was determined to achieve a degree from the University of California at Los Angeles (UCLA), which she did in 1975. In obtaining her Master of Fine Arts degree in photography, she remained there for three more years and studied under Robert Heinecken. Callis is currently an instructor of photography at the California Institute of the Arts in Los Angeles, California, and has been so since 1976. She also taught at California State at Fullerton from 1977–1978 and regularly at UCLA from 1977–1983.

Callis has consistently exhibited her works throughout her career, beginning in 1974, with a solo exhibition at Grandview Gallery, Los Angeles, California. Her work is also in the permanent collections of the George Eastman House, Rochester, New York; the Museum of Modern Art (MoMA), New York City; Bibliothèque Nationale, Paris, France; and the National Museum of Modern Art, Kyoto, Japan; to name a few. Her work has been recognized with two National Endowment for the Arts (NEA) grants in 1980 and 1985. Callis has also received the Ferguson grant, Friends of Photography, in 1978, as well as the Mellon Leave grant of the California Institute of the Arts, Valencia, in 1982.

In her use of the medium of photography, Callis expresses her inner feelings and thoughts by beginning with her imagination, where she conjures up scenes which are based in the everyday world. These dream-like images, like "Morphe" (1975) and "Black Tablecloth" (1979), are theatrically staged with anonymous models and objects. She photographs in color, which emphasizes the emotional impact of the work, and she creates tension by producing beautiful pictures that deviate from reality. "Still Life with Lobster" (1980), an example of her more recent work, is a photograph of isolated objects on a large black and white print, and the concentration is on the associations between the objects, while being less emotional or theatrical.

Melissa J. Guenther

Bibliography
Browne, Turner, and Elaine Partnow. *Macmillan Biographical Encyclopedia of Photographic Artists and Innovators.* Macmillan, and Collier Macmillan, 1983.
McMann, Jean. "Callis." *San Francisco Camera Work Quarterly* 10:3 (Autumn 1983).
Walsh, George, Coline Naylor, and Michael Held, eds. *Contemporary Photographers.* St. Martin's Press, 1982.

Calman, Wendy (1947–)
Born in New York City, Wendy Calman received a Bachelor of Arts degree in art history from the University of Pittsburgh, Pennsylvania, in 1969, and her Master of Fine Arts degree in printmaking from the Tyler School of Art of Temple University, Philadelphia, Pennsylvania, in 1972. At Tyler School of Art, she studied with photographer William Larson, from whom she learned about the photographic methods essential to her work in printmaking.

Calman's work is in mixed media with virtually all media, including sound, fully integrated with the overall effect. Her proficiency in print and photographic media are most evident in the great variety of surface effects she achieves. She has become extremely adept at three-dimensional constructions with moving mechanical parts. Calman is sensitive to issues concerning language, humor, and the processes by which her pieces are constructed. Her work is based on specific themes involving equivocal dichotomies such as human/mechanical, male/female, and secular/religious, and have titles such as "Franklinstein," "Ben Her," "Annilla the Nun," etc. In the case of "Franklinstein," the mixed-media piece evolved into a life-size installation piece which she refers to as a "photo-mechanical construction."

Calman's work has appeared in several books, including *Contemporary American Women Sculptors, Innovative Printmaking*, and *Photographer's Choice*, and she is represented in the permanent collections of the International Center for Photography, George Eastman House, New York City; Honolulu Academy of the Arts, Hawaii; Arkansas Art Center, Little Rock; and House of Humor and Satire, Gabravo, Bulgaria. Winner of numerous awards in competitive exhibitions, Calman has been included in international exhibitions such as "Works on Paper," in Hamburg, Germany; "Sights Unseen," A.I.R. Gallery; "Photofusion," Pratt Manhattan Center Gallery; "Photographer's Choice," Witkin Gallery; "Photo/Synthesis"—all in New York City; Herbert F. Johnson Museum, Cornell University, Ithaca, New York; "Photography Unlimited," Fogg Art Museum, Harvard University; and others.

Calman has served as a juror for the printmaking and drawing panel for artists' fellowships, National Endowment for the Arts (NEA) in 1979, and serves as advisory panelist, visual arts, Indiana Arts Commission since 1988. She has taught at the University of Tennessee (1972–1976), and Indiana University, Bloomington (1976–present).

Leonard Lehrer

Bibliography
Newman, Thelma. *Innovative Printmaking.* Crown Publications Inc., 1977.
Photographer's Choice. Addison House Foundation, 1975.
Watson-Jones, Virginia. *Contemporary American Women Sculptors.* Oryx Press, 1986.

Campos, Susana (1942–)

Born in Mexico, Susana Campos studied art at the Academy of San Carlos from 1962 to 1967. The following year she won a scholarship from the French government for study in Paris, France. One of the founding members of the group New Engravers, she has been a member of the Salón de la Plástica Mexicana, Mexico City, Mexico, since 1966 and has shown her prints and paintings in many group shows in Mexico and abroad. Her solo exhibitions include: the French Institute, Mexico City, and Galería de Bellas Artes, Monterrey, Nuevo León—both in Mexico, and the Hebrew Cultural Center, Philadelphia, Pennsylvania (1967–1968); between 1970 and 1980 she has had three solo shows at the Salón de la Plástica Mexicana in Mexico City, Mexico.

A prizewinner for her prints, Campos received a "best engraving" award for an engraving in a show sponsored by the National Institute of Youth at the Galería de la Plástica Mexicana, Mexico City, Mexico in 1968. The previous year, she won the national prize in painting in Guadalajara, Jalisco, Mexico. Her work is noted for its portrayal of the illusion of motion—abstractly. Campos created a series of paintings titled "Obsessive Rhythms," which parallel a true musician's improvisation on an aural theme.

Campos's work has been accepted in many juried group exhibitions, including the Interamerican Biennial Printmaking show held in Cordova, Argentina (1964); the ORTF French scholarship winners, Paris (1986); the National Polytechnic Institute, Mexico City, Mexico (1971); the International Year of the Woman, INBA, and the Siqueiros Cultural Polyforum, Mexico City, Mexico (1975); the "23 Young Painters" exhibition in the Palace of Fine Arts, Mexico City, Mexico (1976), and many others.

Bibliography
Alvarez, José Rogelio, et al. *Enciclopedia de México.* Secretaría de Educación Pública, 1987.
SAHAGUN: Segundo Concurso Nacional de Pintura. A Catalog. INBA, 1981.

Canavier, Elena Karina (1931–)

Born in Tientsin, China, Elena Karina Canavier moved three years later with her parents to Los Angeles, California. She studied painting at the Jepson Art Institute in that city between 1950 and 1953. Attracted to clay for its durability, she studied at Los Angeles City College and the University of Southern California—both in California, earning a Bachelor of Arts degree in 1961. Although continuing her interest in painting and printmaking, by the mid-1960s ceramic sculpture became her medium of choice.

As an art history major Canavier earned a Master's degree from California State University, Long Beach, in 1971, shortly thereafter becoming a contributing editor to *Artweek* and *Southeast Art.* After her move to Washington, D.C., in 1974 where she relocated her studio, she was appointed crafts coordinator for the National Endowment for the Arts (NEA). Canavier contacted artists and assisted in organizing a unique group of place settings of American crafts, for First Lady Rosalyn Carter's 1977 luncheon for senator's wives, Washington, D.C. This interest by the White House in American crafts continued with changing exhibits in the vice-president's home, where Canavier functioned as an advisor on the arts to Mrs. Joan Mondale, wife of the vice-president.

Promoting art and especially sculpture in public places led Canavier to the position of executive director of the Public Art Trust, a nonprofit group organized in 1982. In 1986 Canavier opened her own curatorial group working with a number of clients in Washington, D.C., as the coordinator for annual exhibitions.

Public and private assignments did not interfere with the artist's attention to multi-chambered porcelain sculptures. Since the 1970s when her studio was near ocean tide pools, structures recalling conch and mussel shells, sea kelp, or a chambered nautilus have taken these vessel forms far from traditional paths. Rococo, energetic, gestural, and elegant, the lustered, sensual interiors contrast with encrusted exterior matt glazes. The scallop shell in art can be traced back to Greek statuettes of Aphrodite and forward to eighteenth-century English ceramics as sweetmeat stands. Canavier's "tide pools," as she has named them, are a contemporary offering to this tradition.

During a ten-year period beginning in 1973 the artist had twelve solo exhibitions and was a participant in a number of group shows, including several organized by the Smithsonian Institution, Washington, D.C. She maintains a studio in Washington, D.C., commuting frequently since 1989 to Los Angeles, California.

Elaine Levin

Bibliography
Axel, Jan, and Karen McReady. *Porcelain: Traditions and New Visions.* Watson-Guptill, 1981.
Herman, Lloyd. *American Porcelain: New Expressions in an Ancient Art.* Timber Press, 1981.
Levin, Elaine. "Elena Karina, A Sense of the Sea." *American Craft* 41:1 (February–March 1981): 28–31.
———. *The History of American Ceramics.* Harry N. Abrams, 1988.
Scott, Bill. "Elena Karina Canavier's Tide Pool Ceramics." *Southwest Art* (September 1974).

Caparn, Rhys (1909–)

A sculptor of animal and landscape abstractions, Rhys Caparn was born July 18, 1909, in Onteora Park, a resort in New York's Catskill Mountains. She said she "became aware of the basic dignity of natural and life forms" when watching her father, a landscape architect, work in the garden as a small girl. She attended Bryn Mawr College, Pennsylvania, from 1927 to 1929, then went to Paris, France, from 1929 to 1930 to study with animal sculptor Edouard Navellier. When she returned to New York, she attended Alexander Archipenko's school of art from 1931 to 1933—studying the human figure—but determined still to become an animal sculptor. "Archipenko freed me," she told an interviewer. She said his lessons about reaching for infinity in art—the point where form and idea become one—remained with her throughout her career. Her first show in 1933 at Delphic Studios in New York City was mostly comprised of torsos and other figurative work, with Archipenko writing in the introduction for the catalog that Caparn has created "lyrical poetry with pure form." Dozens of solo and group shows followed throughout a half-century-long career.

From the late 1930s to the late 1940s, Caparn made frequent trips to New York City's Bronx and Central Park zoos to sketch, and she concentrated on animal abstractions. "I explored the basic form and characteristic of the animal, the shape of the bovine or the bird in flight," she wrote. From subjects such as "Bird of Prey," "Wild Sow," and "Stalking Cat," she moved toward abstractions of landscape themes, however, by 1948. After a trip to Poland, she made sculptures of ruins, preserving only one, "Warsaw 1948." Other landscape themes included New York City scenes, "Cycladic Harbor," after a 1950s trip to Greece and "Mountain Meadow," following a trip to the Grand Tetons. She also created reliefs suggesting architectural forms and weathered fragments. Usually, she modeled her forms in plasticene or plaster, then cast them in bronze where possible, but she also worked in tattistone, densite, and hydrostone. Many of her pieces were two feet in height or less, with larger works measuring about six feet. In addition, she exhibited ink, conté crayon, and litho pencil drawings, which she described as "notes" to jog her memory for her sculpture. Her works were interpreted as primarily about form, sometimes including angry, irregular shapes. She said they all were based on the "endless well" of nature.

In 1935 she married Herbert Johannes Steel, a New York businessman. She was active in arts organizations over the years, serving as president of the Federation of Modern Painters and Sculptors, founded in 1940. In that role, she wrote the Museum of Modern Art (MoMA), New York City, in 1944 criticizing its "increasingly reactionary policies" toward the work of American artists. From 1946 to 1972 she taught at the Dalton School of Art in New York City. Later she lived in Newtown, Connecticut, writing art comments in the 1960s for the Danbury, Connecticut, *News-Times*.

Caparn's public works included bas-reliefs in 1958 for the Wolman Library at Barnard College in New York City. Her works also were in the Brooklyn Botanic Garden and Whitney Museum of American Art—both in New York City; St. Louis Art Museum, Missouri; and Yale University Art Gallery, New Haven, Connecticut; among others. Her "Animal Form I" won second prize at New York City's Metropolitan Museum of Art's American Sculpture 1951 show. She won first prize for sculpture at the New York State Fair in 1958 and the medal of honor for sculpture at the National Association of Women Artists annual exhibition in 1960. Retrospectives of her work were held at Riverside Museum (1961), and the Gallery Felicie (1984)—both in New York City. She took part in group shows at many major museums, including MoMA, the Whitney Museum of American Art, and Metropolitan Museum of Art—all in New York City, and the Musée du Petit Palais, Paris, France.

Cynthia Mills

Bibliography

Hale, Robert Beverly. *Rhys Caparn*. Retrospective Press, 1972.

Hoffman, Marilyn. "Sculptures Landscapes." *Christian Science Monitor* (April 14, 1961).

Longman, Robin. "Rhys Caparn: The Eloquence of Form." *American Artist* 45 (August 1981): 60–65, 86–88, 92–93.

Smithsonian Institution. Archives of American Art. Rhys Caparn papers (microfilm rolls 680, 1007).

Watson-Jones, Virginia. *Contemporary American Women Sculptors*. Oryx Press, 1986, pp. 86–87.

Cardiff, Janet (1957–)

A multi-media artist whose production has included printmaking, painting, photography, video, bookworks, and installation, Janet Cardiff was born and raised on a farm in Brussels, Ontario, Canada. Having found it remarkable that people in the city did not all look like the glamorous media images through which she had developed assumptions, she realized the power that these images had on the construction of notions about the world. These images have formed the basis for the investigations in her work.

During the summer of 1976 Cardiff took courses in drawing and painting at the Ontario College of Art, Canada. In 1978 she apprenticed with Carl Heywood in photography and silk-screen. She was awarded a Bachelor of Fine Arts degree from Queen's University, Kingston, Ontario, in 1980 and a Master of Fine Arts degree from the University of Alberta, Edmonton, in 1983.

Cardiff's work has been included in numerous Canadian exhibitions, and since 1984 she has had solo exhibitions in Ontario, Alberta, and Saskatchewan—all in Canada, as well as in Minnesota. She has been invited to exhibit in international exhibitions, including the "British Biennale" in England (1984), where she was named best artist under thirty-five. She exhibited in the "International Exhibition of Graphic Art," Yugoslavia (1985, 1987); the "Miami International Biennale," Florida (1985), as well as West Germany (1987); and in Chile (1988). She has received numerous awards including Canada Council awards; best print, Graphex 9, Brantford, Ontario; and an award of merit and Nick Novak scholarship, Open Studio Juried Exhibition, Toronto, Ontario.

Vera Lemecha

Bibliography

Jenkner, Ingrid. *Tabl'eau*. Macdonald Stewart Art Centre, 1988.

Lemecha, Vera. *Dualisms: Janet Cardiff and William MacDonell*. Glenbow Museum, 1989.

Maranl, Celine. *Scripta Manent*. La Gallerie des Arts Lavalin, 1988.

Traer, Patrick. *Chronicle and Symbol*. Memorial University Art Gallery, 1988.

Wylie, Liz. *Another Fiction*. Glendon Gallery, 1987.

Cardinal-Schubert, Joane (1942–)

Joane Cardinal-Schubert was born in Red Deer, Alberta, Canada; graduated with a diploma from the Alberta College of Art in 1968; and completed a Bachelor of Fine Arts degree in 1977 at the University of Calgary, Alberta. From 1978 until she left in 1985 to be a full-time artist, Cardinal-Schubert worked as a curator at the University of Calgary Art Gallery and the Nickle Arts Museum. In 1986 she became a member of the Royal Canadian Academy and was one of the first artists of Native American ancestry to be included in an exhibition, "Cross Cultural Views," the National Gallery of Canada, Ottawa (1986).

Cardinal-Schubert's earliest work was "herstory": paintings in which she included family portraits and Native legends. Already concerned with the environment and the misuse of native materials in museums, her work as a documentary of injustices to native peoples became increasingly politicized during the exhibition "The Spirit Sings," Glenbow Museum, Calgary (1988), where her protest work on behalf of the Lubicon Band was burned.

Cardinal-Schubert paints in series; six solo exhibitions, some versions of "Preservation of the Species," have been created from 1986 to 1990, including "Keeper of the Vision," Ufundi Gallery, Ottawa (1987); "Preservation of a Species: Deconstructivists," Ottawa School of Art (1990); and "Preservation of a Species: Cultural Currency, The Lesson," Articule Gallery, Montréal (1990). Within the presentations are blackboards with chalked information, labelled artifacts, wrapped angry "babies," warshirts of crumpled paper, and references to the environment and extinct animal species.

Cardinal-Schubert is a great communicator. She writes well, debates well, and has a clear focus to each of her works. An example of that focus; ten plaster-wrapped babies are lined up in a row and titled "One Little, Two Little," Canadian Museum of Civilization (1987). *In the Red*, a controversial article first published in *Fuse* magazine (Fall 1989), charged non-native artists with misappropriating native images. She is continuously invited to speak at art forums on artists' rights and native rights.

During the past five years, there have been several important group exhibitions of contemporary native artists, all of which included Cardinal-Schubert: "Stardusters," Thunder Bay, Canada (1986); "In the Shadow of the Sun," Germany (1989); "Beyond History," Vancouver, Canada (1989); "Why Do You Call Us Indians . . . ?," Ottawa, Canada (1989–1990); and "Seeing Red," Kingston, Canada (1990).

Victoria Henry

Bibliography
Baele, Nancy. "Keeping the Vision, Searching for Salvation." *The Citizen*, Ottawa (October 15, 1987).
———. "Native Artist Puts Writing on the Wall." *The Citizen*, Ottawa (April 26, 1990).
Cardinal-Schubert, Joane. "In the Red." *Fuse*, Toronto (Fall 1989).
Duffek, Karen, and Tom Hill. *Beyond History*. Vancouver Art Gallery, 1989.
Hammond, Lois. "Joane Cardinal-Schubert, Translator." *Visual Arts Newsletter*, Calgary, 1985.
Henry, Victoria. "Curator's Statement." *Why Do You Call Us Indians . . . ?*, Greensboro, North Carolina: Guilford Native American Association, 1990.
Soe, Valerie. "Universalizing Cultural Oppression." *Artweek* (October 28, 1989).
Townshend, Nancy. "Joane Cardinal-Schubert at Gulf Canada Gallery." *Artpost*, Toronto (Summer 1988).

Carey, Ellen (1952–)

A native New Yorker, the photographer Ellen Carey earned a Bachelor of Fine Arts degree in printmaking from the Kansas City Art Institute, Missouri (1975), and, three years later, received a Master of Fine Arts degree in photography from the State University of New York (SUNY) at Buffalo, New York. Earlier on, she attended classes at the Art Students League, New York City.

Recipient of a Creative Artists Public Service (CAPS) grant from the New York State Council on the Arts (1979), Carey is a member of the Visual Studies Workshop, Rochester, New York.

Employing mixed media on her large format photographs, Carey creates unique, distinctive, original prints. Representative examples of her work are in private and public permanent collections, including the Albright-Knox Art Gallery, Buffalo, and Colgate University, Hamilton—both in New York; the University of Colorado at Boulder; and others.

Bibliography
Browne, Turner, and Elaine Partnow. *Macmillan Biographical Encyclopedia of Photographic Artists and Innovators*. Macmillan, 1983.
Coleman, A.D. *The Grotesque in Photography*. Summit Books, 1977.
Popular Photography Annual 1979 (Fall 1979).

Carhartt, Elaine (1951–)

Born in Grand Junction, Colorado, the ceramist Elaine Carhartt earned a Bachelor of Fine Arts degree from Colorado State University, Fort Collins (1975), and, the following year, set up a ceramics studio in Pasadena, California.

Winner of honors and awards, Carhartt was a recipient of the new talent award offered by the Los Angeles County Museum, California (1980). Working in a figurative manner, Carhartt creates creatures that, if encountered in real life, would probably go bump in the night. She displays a wry sense of humor.

Bibliography
Clark, Garth. *American Ceramics 1896 to the Present*. Abbeville Press, 1987.
Muchnic, Susan. "The Art Galleries: Elaine Carhartt." *The Los Angeles Times* (November 29, 1985).

Carlson, Cynthia (1942–)

Born in Chicago, Illinois, Cynthia Carlson always wanted to be an artist. She studied with Ray Yoshida at the School of the Art Institute in her native city, where she received her Bachelor of Fine Arts degree in 1965 and, two years later, acquired a Master of Fine Arts degree from Pratt Institute, Brooklyn, New York, to begin a twenty-year teaching relationship at the Philadelphia College of Art, Pennsylvania (now part of the University of the Arts).

Artist, consultant, art juror, panelist, professor of art, lecturer, workshop leader in many art schools, colleges, and universities, Carlson arrived at her site-specific and installation format, for which she is well known, after a decade or so of heavily-impastoed painting that soon found itself on the walls without benefit of canvas. Carlson's paintings of the late 1960s reveal a wry approach to nature and the machine. For example, one of her 1967 works depicts a giant sewing machine stitching a quilt-like landscape.

Carlson's forty solo exhibitions from 1967 to 1990 include retrospective shows at the Queens Museum, Flushing, New York (1990); the Freedman Gallery, Albright College, Reading (1989), and the Philadelphia Art Alliance—both in Pennsylvania (1988); Albright-Knox Art Gallery, Buffalo, New York (1985); and the Milwaukee Art Museum, Wisconsin (1982); among others. Her work has been invited to more than 100 group and travelling exhibitions in Europe and the United States.

Winner of grants and fellowships, Carlson received the Professional Staff Congress-City University of New York (CUNY) research award (1988, 1990); National Endowment for the Arts (NEA) fellowships (1975, 1978, 1987, 1980); Philadelphia College of the Arts, Pennsylvania faculty venture fund grant (1983, 1986); Creative Artists Public Service (CAPS) grant, New York State Council on the Arts (1978); Natural Heritage Trust artist-in-residence grant, Artpark, Lewiston, New

York (1977); and a MacDowell Colony fellowship, Peterborough, New Hampshire (1976).

Carlson's work is represented in the permanent public collections of major museums, including the Brooklyn Museum, the Metropolitan Museum of Art, and Guggenheim Museum—all in New York City; and the Philadelphia Art Museum, Pennsylvania; as well as many corporate and private collections. She has been a professor of art at Queens College, and City University of New York (CUNY)—both in New York City, since 1987.

"Vietnam: Sorry About That" (1987), a commemorative piece with haunting overtones, contains wall-mounted framed collages and drawings based on memorabilia left by visitors to the Vietnam Memorial in Washington, D.C. The title of the work derives from an emblem on a soldier's beret that was photographed by Carlson.

Bibliography

Brown, Betty Ann, and Arlene Raven. *Exposures: Women and Their Art.* NewSage Press, 1989.

Jensen, Robert, and Patricia Conway. *Ornamentalism.* Clarkson N. Potter, 1982.

Robbins, C. *The Pluralist Era-American Art 1968–1981.* Harper & Row, 1984.

Rubin, David S. *Cynthia Carlson: Installations 1979–1989 (A Decade, More or Less).* Albright College, 1989.

Carlyle, Florence (1864–1923)

Born in Galt, Ontario, Canada, the painter Florence Carlyle studied with her mentor and friend, Paul Peel, in Canada, and then was a student at the Académie Julian, Paris, France, where she worked under Adolphe Bouguereau, Jules Lefèbvre, and T. Robert-Fleury after 1890.

Widely travelled in Europe and the United States, painter of landscapes, figures, and interiors shown in many venues, interested in music and literature in addition to art, Carlyle exhibited paintings in the Paris Salons, France (1893–1895). Returning to Canada, she was elected an associate in the Royal Canadian Academy (1897)—the first woman to be so honored. In 1900 she was elected to membership in the Ontario Society of Artists.

Winner of honors and awards for her paintings, Carlyle served in the Women's Land Army during World War I, doing hospital work and supporting the Red Cross from the sales of her work. Examples of her paintings are in private and public permanent collections in Canada, including the Art Gallery of Ontario; National Gallery of Art, Ottawa; Ontario Parliament; and others.

Bibliography

Charlesworth, Hector. "Pictures by Florence Carlyle: Memorial Exhibition of Works by a Famous Canadian Painter." *Saturday Night* 40:29 (June 6, 1925): 3.

MacBeth, Madge. "Canadian Women in the Arts." *Maclean's* 27:12 (October 1914): 23–25, 105–08.

Carman, Nancy (1950–)

Born in Tucson, Arizona, the ceramist Nancy Carman earned a Bachelor's degree from the University of California, Davis (1972) and, four years later, a Master of Fine Arts degree from the University of Washington, Seattle.

Among the honors and awards she garnered, Carman received a National Endowment for the Arts (NEA) grant (1980). Her modest figurative sculptures are, primarily, autobiographical.

Representative examples of her work are in private and public permanent collections.

Bibliography

Bell, Michael S. *Nancy Carman.* A Catalog. Philadelphia: Helen Druitt Gallery, 1985.

Clark, Garth. *American Ceramics 1896 to the Present.* Abbeville Press, 1987.

Carnwath, Squeak (1947–)

Known for her emotive canvases containing formal and textual fragments, Squeak Carnwath was born in Abington, Pennsylvania, and received her Master of Fine Arts degree from the California College of Arts and Crafts, Oakland, in 1977. Originally a sculptor and ceramist, Carnwath gained notoriety for her paintings in the 1980s.

Carnwath's paintings have appeared in several one-person exhibitions, including an exhibition at the San Francisco Museum of Art, the Palo Alto Cultural Center, and the Fuller-Goldeen Gallery in San Francisco—all in California, and the Brentwood Gallery in St. Louis, Missouri. Her work has been collected by a number of museums, including the Oakland Museum and the San Francisco Museum of Art—both in California.

Carnwath was awarded a grant from the National Endowment for the Arts (NEA) in 1980. She has taught as a guest instructor at the University of California at Berkeley and is represented by Fuller-Goldeen in San Francisco, California, and Getler-Pall in New York City.

Carnwath's canvases are thickly covered with oil paints and wax and have rich-textured surfaces. Her paintings often include text lists, handwriting, numbers, small everyday objects, such as beds and coffee cups, and even graffiti. Carnwath's often symbolic iconography of the everyday is wedded with creamy painting surfaces which have been compared by writer Gerrit Henry to those of Albert Pinkham Ryder. Carnwath's texts, images, and pictographs are enticing to many critics because they invite viewers to interpret the personal observations of a female artist in more public ways. They are schematic views of the fragments of daily life and are often eccentric and enigmatic in their lushness.

Bibliography

Henry, Gerrit. "Review of Squeak Carnwath at Shea and Beker." *Art in America* 78:10 (October 1990): 212–13.

Tamblyn, Christine. "Review of Squeak Carnwath at John Berggruen Gallery in San Francisco." *ArtNews* 88:10 (December 1989): 174–75.

Carr, Emily (1871–1945)

Partly because her father was a bit of a rebel who encouraged her and partly because Victoria, British Columbia, Canada, was not a thriving center of visual art when she was growing up, Emily Carr went to San Francisco, California, in 1889 to study, returning to Canada in 1895. After a period of the doldrums, she resolved to further her studies in England, which she did from 1899 both in "official" schools in Westminster, England and Hertfordshire, England, and in a more bohemian manner in an artists' colony at St. Ives, England. Her studies were interrupted by an illness—acute anemia and/or clinical depression—which necessitated a very lengthy stay in a hospital before she was able to return to British Columbia, Canada. Back in Victoria Carr was able to derive occasional income from drawings made for the local newspaper. She found the activity uninspiring, however, and turned to sketching aspects of the area Native Americans' cultural heritage. By 1905 she had given up the newspaper work altogether and moved to Vancouver, Canada.

In 1910 she made her way to France for more advanced study, but once again her endeavors were thwarted by illness. After a period of convalescence in Sweden she briefly studied watercolor techniques in Brittany, most likely with Frances Hodgkins, a New Zealander whom she may have met during an earlier stint at the Académie Colarossi in Paris, France. Carr's works of this period were somewhat Fauvist in their departures from naturalism, and she managed to get some work hung in the advanced "Salon d'automne" in 1911. Back in Canada in 1912 she fused the expressive modernity of her new style and her fascination with Northwest Coast native culture, as in "Totem by Ghost Rock" (1912). The public response to a small show of these in Vancouver, Canada, in 1913 was entirely negative. Disappointed, Carr returned to Victoria and a period of virtual oblivion that would last for fourteen years.

In the middle 1920s the National Gallery of Canada in Ottawa began planning an exhibition of West Coast art to be held in 1927. Then-director Eric Brown had been in touch with the National Museum of Canada's ethnologist and folklorist Marius Barbeau, who had earlier heard stories from his Native American acquaintances of a rather strange white woman making frequent visits. Barbeau had sought her out in 1915 and again in 1921, when she was doing very little painting, busy as she was with a boarding house of sorts to keep food on the table. With Barbeau's recommendation, Brown was pleased to show more than two dozen of Carr's early pictures in his exhibition, greatly encouraging the deeply disillusioned artist. Also instrumental in her rehabilitation were some of the members of the Group of Seven, whose rhetoric of Canadian national identity and cultural uniqueness struck a responsive chord when she travelled through Ontario, Canada on the occasion of the National Gallery show.

Newly determined to translate her impressions of her region's "primitive" culture into modernist forms, Carr returned to Victoria, Canada and immediately began to paint. She recommenced her travels through the British Columbian forests, deeper and farther than she had gone before and not without hardship. Her style grew denser, darker, and more monumental ("Blunden Harbour," 1929), no doubt inspired by the massive simplicity of the Group of Seven's Lawren Harris, whose work she described as "rising into serene, uplifted planes, above the swirl into holy places" (Carr, *Hundreds* 6–7). By 1930 she was exhibiting in the East with the Group to slowly growing acclaim, but she still received little notice in western Canada. Her attempts to operate a small gallery in Victoria in 1932 were doomed to failure, and she generally had more success in her contacts with artists in the Seattle area, such as Mark Tobey. Meanwhile, she read Whitman and Emerson, among others and, like them, became increasingly absorbed by the ineffable character of nature. From 1930–1931, she was more concerned with a modernist sublimity than with Indian culture, and her paintings were

of the encompassing forest alone. Many of these have a superabundance of cùrvilinear, convoluted forms that are spiritually akin to some of the more ecstatic landscapes of Vincent van Gogh, though much less heavily textured (e.g., "Forest," "British Columbia," c. 1932).

Carr's fame reached a lifetime height in the mid-1930s, when she had a string of solo shows in publically-funded institutions. Her first commercial exhibition, however, was not held until 1944, at the Dominion Gallery in Montréal, Canada. Exactly 95 percent of the work was sold. Ironically, she was having heart problems by this time and had not painted regularly for two years. Instead, she turned to publishing autobiographical books which straddled the line between simple historical narrative and creative fiction. She won the prestigious Governor General's literary award for the first of these, *Klee Wyck*.

Still plagued by poor health Carr finally succumbed in 1945. A major memorial exhibition was immediately organized by the National Gallery in cooperation with the Art Gallery of Toronto—Ontario's two largest public art institutions. The Vancouver Art Gallery organized a retrospective in 1972, and Carr's contributions to Canadian culture further took on near-mythic proportions—helped, no doubt, by the nationalistic fervor that gripped the country for some time after its Centennial year (1967).

Robert J. Belton

Bibliography
Blanchard, Paula. *The Life of Emily Carr*. 1989.
Carr, Emily. *Klee Wyck*. Oxford University Press, 1941.
———. *Book of Small*. Oxford University Press, 1942.
———. *House of All Sorts*. Oxford University Press, 1944.
———. *Growing Pains: The Autobiography of Emily Carr*. Oxford University Press, 1946.
———. *Hundreds and Thousands, the Journals of Emily Carr*. Clarke, Irwin, 1966.
Turpin, Marguerite. *The Life and Work of Emily Carr: A Selected Bibliography*. 1965.

Carrillo, Lilia (1930–1974)

Lilia Carrillo, who was born and died in Mexico City, Mexico, began to paint with Manuel Rodriguez Lozano. She studied painting from 1947–1951 at the Escuela de Pintura y Escultura ("La Esmerelda"), Mexico City, Mexico, with Agustin Lazo, Antonio Ruiz, and Carlos Orozco Romero. From 1953–1955 she lived in Paris, France, and was enrolled at the Académie de la Grande Chaumière and, at that time, participated in her first group show at the Petite Palais. After returning to Mexico in 1956 she began teaching at the Instituto Nacional de Bellas Artes and painted her first abstract works. Carrillo's work was in the vanguard in Mexico, and she began to have one-person shows and participate in numerous group exhibitions.

At this time her paintings were associated with the styles of Enrique Echeverria, Alberto Gironella, and Manuel Felguérez (whom she married in 1960). Carrillo was the only woman associated with "La Ruptura" ("The Break")—an art movement in Mexico (c. 1952–1965) that began in defiance of the muralist movement and which stressed a more universal and international vision. In the early 1960s Carrillo designed sets for Alejandro Jodorowky's theatrical productions. In 1966 she lived in the United States with Felguérez and was also part of the famous exhibition "Confrontación 66" at the Palacio de Bellas Artes.

The following year one of Carrillo's works was exhibited at the Mexican Pavillion at the Montréal World's Fair. Also in 1967 she participated in the "Tendencias del Arte Abstracto en Mexico" show at the Museo de la Ciudad Universitaria where in 1968 she took part in a collective mural project in support of the student movement. Her last exhibition during her lifetime took place at the Galería Juan Martin. Carrillo's work is in such collections as the Bezabel Museum in Jerusalem, Israel, and the Museo de Arte Moderno in Mexico City, Mexico.

Susan Aberth

Bibliography

Espejo, Beatriz. *Historia de la Pintura Mexicana*. Mexico City, 1989, pp. 239–40.

Pintura Mexicana (Mexican Painting) 1950–1980. New York: IBM Gallery, 1990, pp. 42–43.

Ponce, Juan Garcia. *Homenaje a Lilia Carrillo*. Mexico City: Palacio de Bellas Artes, 1974.

Sullivan, Edward. *Women in Mexico*. Mexico City: Centro Cultural, Arte Contemporaneo, 1990, pp. 46–49.

Carrington, Leonora (1917–)

For more than half a century, Leonora Carrington's surrealist paintings have reported on the no-man's land between reality and illusion. Born into a wealthy family in Lancashire, England, Carrington received only brief formal training in art, at Amédée Ozenfant's school in London, England. A period of rapid creative growth was stimulated by her association with Max Ernst, whom she met in 1937. They fell in love and moved to a village near Lyon, France, where Carrington produced her earliest masterworks, including the fanciful portraits of Ernst (c. 1938) and herself (c. 1938).

When Ernst was interned as an enemy alien at the outbreak of World War II, Carrington made her way, via Spain, Lisbon, Portugal, and New York City, to Mexico City. There, she married the Hungarian photographer Emerico "Chiqui" Weisz, raised two sons, and associated with the international community of artists and writers, among whom were a number of surrealists. Intense collaboration with Remedios Varos during the mid-1940s initiated the full flowering of Carrington's art. "The House Opposite" (c. 1947) summarizes significant aspects of this work: meticulous technique, dream-like imagery, feminist consciousness, and historical continuity with past masters of the imagination, such as Hieronymus Bosch and Pieter Brueghel.

Beginning in the 1960s Carrington divided her time between New York and Mexico. Since 1987 she has lived in the Chicago suburb of Oak Park, Illinois. Much of her recent work has focused on the meaning of ageing for women in Western society. Intermittently throughout her career, Carrington has also published fiction.

Ann Lee Morgan

Bibliography

Chadwick, Whitney. "Leonora Carrington: Evolution of a Feminist Consciousness." *Woman's Art Journal* 62 (Spring–Summer 1986): 37–42.

———. "Painting on the Threshold." Introductory essay in *Leonora Carrington: Recent Works*. New York: Brewster Gallery, 1988.

Carroll, Patty (1946–)

Born in Chicago, Illinois, the photographer Patty Carroll earned a Bachelor of Fine Arts degree from the University of Illinois, Urbana (1968), and, four years later, received a Master of Science degree from the Institute of Design, Illinois Institute of Technology, Chicago. Carroll studied under Arthur Siegel, Art Sinsabaugh, and Garry Winogrand.

Carroll is on the faculty of the Institute of Design, Chicago; earlier, she taught at the University of Michigan, Ann Arbor (1974–1976) and at Pennsylvania State University, University Park (1973–1974).

A member of the College Art Association and the Society for Photographic Education, Carroll has won various prizes and honors, including a faculty research grant from Pennsylvania State University, University Park (1974); an award from the Illinois Arts Council and the Arts and Riverwoods award from the Art Institute of Chicago, Illinois (1977).

Representative examples of her photographs are in private and public permanent collections, including the Illinois State Museum, Springfield; the Library of Congress, Washington, D.C.; Museum of Contemporary Art, Chicago; Smithsonian Institution, Washington, D.C.; and others.

Bibliography

Sunset After Dark. A Portfolio. New York: Frumkin Gallery, 1979.

Hayes, Dannielle B. *Women Photograph Men*. William Morrow, 1977.

Carter, Carol Ann (1947–)

Born and raised in Indianapolis, Indiana, Carol Ann Carter earned a Bachelor of Fine Arts degree from the Herron School of Art in her native city and received a Master of Fine Arts degree in printmaking from the University of Notre Dame, Indiana (1974). She was awarded a National Endowment for the Arts (NEA) fellowship (1988) and a Ford Foundation grant (1986). Her work is represented in private and public permanent collections, including the Indianapolis Museum of Art, Indiana; First Service Bank; Chevron Oil Company; and the Atlanta Life Insurance Company.

Carter works in mixed media painting, creating small-scale sculptural forms and wall pieces that range from three to 101 inches. She also creates large-scale installations of dyed, stitched, pinned, collaged, and painted works of ripped raw silk, canvas, wire, wood, buttons, and other materials. The surfaces of her work are lush and sensuous, abstract, color-filled textural tracings that are based upon her cultural heritage, which were further sensitized while on a Lily Grant sabbatical leave to Nigeria (1984), and which also reflect certain aspects of her many years as a printmaker and intaglio teacher. African-American quilts and African fabrics are reinvented, are transmuted, through her use of paint layering; one senses, in her works, the disparities that obtain between persons and cultures—bringing lost and forgotten cultural and personal information to the forefront. Carter's works display a sense of order and focus within a free and spontaneous use of material and color.

Carter's work has been exhibited in the "Women of Color Box Project," Cinque Gallery, New York City (1990). She has exhibited and lectured throughout the United States, including the University of Cincinnati, Ohio; Cranbrook Academy of Art, Bloomfield Hills, Michigan; and Pennsylvania State University, University Park.

Moira Geoffrion

Bibliography

Lippard, Lucy. *Mixed Messages: New Art in Multicultural America.*
  Pantheon Books, 1991.

Stephenson, Mary Brecht. *Carol Ann Carter.* A Catalog. Detroit Institute
  of Arts, 1990–1991.

Carter, Yvonne Pickering (1939–)

Born in Washington, D.C., the African-American painter/performance
artist/educator Yvonne Pickering Carter earned both her Bachelor's
degree and a Master of Fine Arts degree from Howard University in
her native city. Her multimedia performances include "Confessions:
The Making of a Sinner or a Saint," National Museum of Women in the
Arts, Washington, D.C. (1990); "Installation . . . Lament," Walters Art
Gallery, Baltimore, Maryland (1988); "Relic, Ritual, and Region,"
University of Maryland, Baltimore (1988); and others.

Carter's work has been included in group exhibitions in the United
States and abroad, including "African-American Contemporary Art," Museo
Civico d'Arte Contemporaneo di Gibellina, Sicily, Italy (1990); "Coast to
Coast: Women of Color National Artist's Book Project," Baltimore Museum
of Art, Maryland (1990); "Introspectives: Contemporary Art by Americans
and Brazilians of African Descent," Museum of the Arts, New York City
(1990); "Celebrate African American Art: Yesterday and Today," Art at
100 Pearl, Hartford, Connecticut (1989); "Pillar to Post: Wall Works by Contemporary Artists," Kenkeleba Gallery, New York City (1989); and others.

Carter's performance pieces wed illusion and reality, life and
death, yin and yang, in complex and mysterious visual and aural metaphor. A recent multimedia work, "Doors, Entrances, Exits and
Trances—Known and Unknown," captures her perceptual and conceptual approaches to life employing the door as symbol. Her work is represented in galleries and museums, including the University of the District of Columbia, Washington, D.C.; Gibbes Gallery, Charleston, South
Carolina; North Carolina Museum of Art, Raleigh; and others.

Bibliography

Brenson, Michael. "Sculptors Using the Wall as Venue and Inspiration."
  The New York Times (February 24, 1989).

Gamble, Allison. "Mayor's 1988 Black History Art Exhibit." *New Art
  Examiner* (June 1988).

Hall, Robert L. *Gathered Visions: Selected Works by African American Women
  Artists.* Anacostia Museum. Smithsonian Institution Press, 1992.

Caso, Beatriz (1933–)

Born in Mexico, Beatriz Caso was fascinated with pre-Columbian art from
early childhood—a factor which would play an important role in her future career as a sculptor. She used to accompany her father, Alfonso
Caso (the famous archaeologist who discovered Tomb 7 in Monte Albán)
on his archeological digs. Caso became infatuated with the art of the
Toltecs as a result of this exposure and got the urge to reproduce that
which she had seen in plaster of Paris, clay, and other media—from
memory spiced with imagination. Caso married Carlos Solórzano, the
playwright who wrote, "Doña Beatriz la sin ventura," in which Caso de-
buted as an actress. She studied at the Faculty of Philosophy and Letters in the University of Mexico (1956) and spent two years in Paris studying ceramics at the Académie de Beaux-Arts, France.

Self-taught in sculpture, Caso works in stone, bronze, onyx, clay, and
other materials—frequently with incrustations or embedments of precious
stones in the pieces, not unlike the works she had seen as a child—works
with inlays of turquoise, coral, or conch shells. She has had solo exhibitions in the Galerías Excelsior (1965); the Salón de la Plástica Mexicana
(1969, 1975, 1981); and Tasende, Acapulco (1970)—all in Mexico; Hiram,
Cleveland, Ohio (1972); Bel'Art, Estocolmo (1978); D'Endt, Amsterdam
(1979); Contemporary Art, Houston, Texas (1979); Palacio de Bellas Artes
(1984), and the Galería Misrachi (1985)—both in Mexico City, Mexico.
She participated in many group shows in Mexico and abroad.

In 1975 Caso's eldest child, Diego, died at the age of twenty-three;
she has two daughters, Juana Inés and Beatriz. Caso created monuments
to Benito Juárez in San Pablo Guelatao, Oaxaca (1973), to Rosario
Castellanos in the Rotonda de los Hombres Ilustres del Panteon Civil de
Dolores (1975), to her father in Monte Albán, Oaxaca (1976), to her mother,
Maria Lombardo, in the state of Oaxaca (1976)—all in Mexico; to Sor Juana
Ines de la Cruz for the Organization of American States, Washington, D.C.,
and in the cloister that bears her name in Mexico; to *Dualidad* in the
Instituto Nacional Indigenista; to José Hernández in Tlacochahuya, Oaxaca;
"A la migracion azteca" in Aztlan, Nayarit; "A la maternidad" in the
Instituto Nacional de Perinatologia; and "Continuidad" for the Associacion
Psicoanalítica Mexicana—all in Mexico.

In 1984, Caso was given an exhibition at the Palacio de Bellas
Artes, Mexico City, Mexico; she completed a monumental stone sculpture weighing fifteen tons, titled "Tonantzin," in 1986 and a bronze
titled "Semillas y Columpios."

Bibliography

Alvarez, José Rogelio, et al. *Enciclopedia de México.* Secretaría de
  Educación Pública, 1987.

En escultura una revelación: Beatriz Caso. A Catalog. Museo del Palacio
  de Bellas Artes, 1984.

Cassatt, Mary (1844–1926)

Mary Cassatt, the only American in the French impressionist movement,
was born in the Pittsburgh suburb of Allegheny City, where her father served
as mayor before moving his family into Pittsburgh, Pennsylvania. The peripatetic businessman next took his family to Philadelphia, Pennsylvania, and
scarcely two years later, in 1851, to Europe, where they remained for four
years. When the family returned to Philadelphia, Cassatt began her artistic
training, enrolling at the Pennsylvania Academy of Fine Arts in 1861, Philadelphia. After four years of study she knew she must go back to Europe and
in 1866 moved to Paris, France. Because the École des Beaux-Arts did not
admit women at that time, she arranged to study privately with Jean Léon
Gérôme, one of the principal masters of the École des Beaux-Arts. In 1867
she took private lessons with Pierre Edouard Frère and Paul Constant Soyer
at Ecouen and in 1868 with Thomas Couture. Her first recognition came in
1868 when the Paris Salon, France, accepted her painting "La Mandoline"
and was reinforced in 1870, when the Paris Salon accepted a painting she
had just done on an Italian trip, "Contadina di Fabello." The Franco-Prussian War forced her to return to Pennsylvania, but by December of 1871 she
was back in Europe. Early in 1872 she and the artist Emily Sartain painted
in Parma, Italy, where Cassatt fulfilled a commission to make a copy of a
religious painting for the cathedral of Pittsburgh. In the fall she satisfied her
long-time wish to see Italian Renaissance and Spanish Baroque paintings in
the Prado Museum, Italy. She then moved on to Seville, Spain, where she

had a studio at the Casa de Pilatos. One of the Seville paintings, "Torero and Young Girl," (Sterling and Francine Clark Art Institute), was accepted for the Paris Salon of 1873. After looking at old masters in Holland and Belgium and returning to Parma (for Correggio) and Rome—both in Italy, she settled for good in Paris in 1874. Both "Torero and Young Girl" and "On the Balcony during the Carnival," (Philadelphia Museum of Art), Pennsylvania, were shown at the annual exhibition of the National Academy of Design in New York City in 1874.

Edgar Degas had admired Cassatt's portrait, "Ida," in the Paris Salon of 1874 and invited her to exhibit with his group of independent artists known as the impressionists. Since, as she said in her own words, she liked the prospect of working "in complete independence, without bothering about the eventual judgment of a jury," she accepted. In 1877 her parents and sister Lydia arrived to take up residence with her in Paris, France, and became frequent subjects of her brush.

In the 1879 impressionist exhibition (the fourth), Cassatt was represented by eleven paintings which were praised in the press for their effects of light and shade. One of these paintings was "Lydia in a Loge, Wearing a Pearl Necklace" (1879, Philadelphia Museum of Art, Pennsylvania), in which Lydia is radiantly seen in a soft light reflected from a chandelier that is visible in the mirror painted behind her.

For the next exhibition of 1881 she showed her recent plein-air paintings and again experienced success, this time selling almost all her entries; the critic Elie de Mont asserted that Cassatt and Berthe Morisot were the only interesting artists exhibiting. One of the most striking paintings was Cassatt's "The Garden" (1880, Metropolitan Museum of Art) in which Lydia is depicted crocheting in the garden at Marly. Another was "The Tea" (1880, Boston Museum of Fine Arts) in which the tea service glistens with the reflective colors of the room.

Of her seven paintings in the final eighth impressionist show of 1886, one was "Young Girl at the Window" (1883, Corcoran Gallery of Art, Washington, D.C.) in which Susan, a cousin of Cassatt's housekeeper, sits on the balcony of Cassatt's Paris apartment, holding the artist's Belgian griffin "Battie." Cassatt catches the effect of sunlight on the sitter's white dress and hat, while the brim of Susan's bonnet partially shades her face. Another outdoor scene in this exhibition was her "Children on the Beach" (1884, National Gallery of Art, Washington, D.C.) in which two little girls (one hatless) play with their sand buckets on the shore.

Unfortunately between these two exhibitions Lydia died from Bright's disease in 1882. One of the most imposing of Cassatt's paintings had been of Lydia driving a two-wheel carriage through the Bois de Boulogne: "Woman and Child Driving" (1879, Philadelphia Museum of Art). Placed beside Lydia is Degas's niece and seated at the rear of the buggy is the groom. The dresses are painted in rich impastos of pink, white, red, and violet and stand out in contrast to the subdued greens of the park behind.

Cassatt's first venture into printmaking occurred in 1879, when she worked with Degas on etchings for a proposed print journal, entitled *Le Jour et la nuit*, to suggest the effects of light and dark to be found in the etchings. In 1889 she joined impressionist friends in a group called Société des Peintre-Graveurs which exhibited at Durand-Ruel Gallery, Paris, France. One reason she liked prints is because working people could buy them, and thus her art could reach a wider audience. The Durand-Ruel Gallery initiated a one-woman exhibition of Cassatt's paintings in 1891, followed by a second major retrospec-

tive two years later. In the interim Cassatt received a commission to paint a tympanum mural for the Woman's Building at the World's Columbian Exposition in Chicago, Illinois. A suffragist herself, Cassatt spent a year working on the fifty-by-twelve-foot triptych, "Modern Woman." In 1895 Durand-Ruel Gallery organized a large Cassatt exhibition in New York. She was doing so well financially from her sales that in 1894 she had been able to buy a country château (fifty miles northwest of Paris, France) which she renovated and used as a summer retreat the rest of her life.

In the 1890s the figures in her paintings became a little more solid and linear, perhaps partly influenced by her graphic art; for example, two strongly-outlined figures are at the forefront of "Women Picking Fruit" (1891, Carnegie Institute Museum of Art), and three solid figures constitute "The Boating Party" (1893, National Gallery of Art, Washington, D.C.). In this decade mother-and-child paintings feature prominently in her output: from substantially-defined ones such as "Mother and Daughter, Both Wearing Large Hats" (1900–1901, Amon Carter Museum, Fort Worth, Texas) to softly-suggested figures in "Mother Wearing a Sunflower on Her Dress" (c. 1905, National Gallery of Art, Washington, D.C.), a painting in which there are mirror reflections, a popular device of Cassatt's. When her eyesight weakened she turned more often to painting with pastels, continuing frequently with the mother-and-child subject matter. She and Degas both appreciated Japanese prints, and one aspect she incorporated in some of her works was the high eye-level as in "The Bath" (1892, Art Institute of Chicago, Illinois) in which there is a high floor line, and the viewer looks down upon the woman bathing the child.

The French government recognized Cassatt's achievements in 1904 by making her a chevalier of the Legion of Honor. She also travelled extensively in the twentieth century: to Italy and Spain in 1901, to the United States for the last time in 1908–1909, and to Egypt in 1910–1911. In 1915 she displayed a touch of feminism in enthusiastically sending her paintings and Degas's to a benefit exhibition for women's suffrage at the Knoedler Gallery in New York City.

Operations for cataracts in her eyes were not successful, and finally in 1915 she gave up painting. She died on June 14, 1926 at her château in Mesnil-Beaufresne.

Throughout her career Cassatt encouraged American collectors, particularly the Havemeyers, to buy the paintings of her colleagues, and thus she is responsible for building up a strong representation of impressionist art in United States museums. Her own paintings, of which more than 600 have been cataloged, can be found today in the major museums of the world.

Eleanor Tufts

Bibliography

Breeskin, Adelyn Dohme. *A Catalogue Raisonné of the Oils, Watercolors, and Drawings*. Smithsonian Institution Press, 1970.

———. *A Catalogue Raisonné of the Graphic Work*. Smithsonian Institution Press, 1980.

Gerdts, William. *American Impressionism*. University of Washington, 1980.

Mathews, Nancy Mowll. *Cassatt and her Circle, Selected Letters*. Abbeville Press, 1984.

Moffett, Charles S. *The New Painting: Impressionism 1874–1886*. The Fine Arts Museums of San Francisco, 1986.

Pollock, Griselda. *Mary Cassatt*. Harper & Row, 1980.

Castañeda, Pilar (1941–)

Born in Mexico, Pilar Castañeda attended the Academy of San Carlos, Mexico, for four years, from the age of twenty. Painter and printmaker, Castañeda received the Nuevos Valores prize in the Salón de la Plástica Mexicana, Mexico, in 1962.

Castañeda taught painting from 1964 to 1966 at the Ibero-American University and, three years later, founded the Centro Activo de Arte Infantil in Mexico City—both in Mexico.

Since 1963, Castañeda has had twenty solo exhibitions and has participated in ten group shows in Mexico and abroad (without counting the last six years which were spent in Europe). She has illustrated books and made drawings for newspapers and reviews, such as *Presencia del Salón de la Plástica Mexicana*, 1981. Castañeda is a neorealist.

Bibliography
Alvarez, José Rogelio, et al. *Enciclopedia de México*. Secretaría de Educación Pública, 1987.

Castanis, Muriel (1926–)

Born in New York City, self-taught sculptor and fiber artist Muriel Castanis first exhibited two-dimensional board and acrylic compositions in a one-person show at the Ruth White Gallery in New York City in 1968. Solo exhibitions of her works include: O.K. Harris (New York City; Scottsdale, Arizona; and Miami, Florida), City University of New York (CUNY) Graduate Center; Carpenter Center for the Visual Arts at Harvard University, Cambridge, Massachusetts; Women's Interart Center in New York City; and Hokin Gallery in Palm Beach, Florida.

After her early paintings, Castanis began working with fabric and resins in the late 1960s. At first she draped resin-soaked cloth over domestic objects which would be familiar to her audience—chairs, bathtubs, or tables—then removed the object so only the stiffened fabric remained. She later added needlework from both personal sources and second-hand shops. "Cleopatra's Needle" (1976) is a monument to the anonymous craftswomen who created with fabric and thread.

Since the late 1970s, Castanis has made a series of draped works reminiscent of the classical forms of Greece and Rome. These sculptures are different in that they are only drapery without an inner figure. Her most important work to date is a group of three, twelve-foot-high draperies for the cornice of 580 California Street, San Francisco (1983–1984). The architect of the building, Philip Johnson, asked Castanis to adapt her figureless draperies for the facade of his building. Her contemporary exploration of traditional figures compliments the post-modern style of the building.

Castanis won a Tiffany Foundation sculpture grant in 1977, the award of distinction from the Virginia Museum of Fine Arts Biennial, Richmond, in 1979, and the O.K. Harris medal of honor in 1989. Her commissions include works for Malcolm Forbes; Palais Mendoub; Prudential Life Insurance Company Gateways in Newark, New Jersey; Montgomery County Court House, Rockville, Maryland; Mount Holyoke College, South Hadley, Massachusetts; Arizona State University, Tempe, Arizona; and the Portland State Office Building, Oregon.

Judith Sealy

Bibliography
Marter, Joan. "Muriel Castanis." *Arts Magazine* 52:23 (April 1978).
Robertson, David. *Context and Collaboration for Contemporary Art: The Sculptural Program for 580 California Street*. The Trout Gallery, Dickenson College, 1986.

Castoro, Rosemarie (1939–)

The Brooklyn-born sculptor Rosemarie Castoro received a scholarship to the Museum of Modern Art (MoMA) in New York City in 1955. She completed her formal education at Pratt Institute, Brooklyn, New York, where she received a Bachelor of Fine Arts degree *cum laude*. Castoro creates two- and three-dimensional objects using a variety of media, including wood, graphite, wire, concrete, and steel.

Exhibiting in group shows since "Invitational, 1966" at the Park Place Gallery, New York City, Castoro's first solo exhibition was in 1971 at Tibor de Nagy, New York City, where she continues to show. Castoro received a Guggenheim fellowship (1971) and two National Endowment for the Arts (NEA) grants (1974, 1984). She has taught at several colleges, including Hunter College, New York City; California State University, Fresno; Syracuse University, New York; and the University of Colorado, Boulder.

Castoro's earliest exhibited works are gestural, abstract paintings, many exploring the letter "Y." In the late 1960s she worked with political-conceptual pieces such as installations where she "cracked" sidewalks or buildings by delineating a proposed crack with silver tape—one such work was commissioned by the Seattle World's Fair Center, Washington (1969).

In 1971 Castoro exhibited minimalist sculptural pieces which were wood and masonite panels covered with the gestural strokes of her earlier paintings—"Free-standing Works." These strokes later became separate sculptural entities, and Castoro began a series of examinations of thin, stick-like forms which lasted throughout the 1970s. Free-standing, on the wall, or suspended from the ceiling, these became "exoskeletal" or vaguely figurative, organic, tree-like figures and ladders, as in "Compound" (1976). These forms are always black or neutral, but the material varies—wood, epoxy, and steel.

In the 1980s Castoro moved toward more weighty, figurative forms with cubist overtones—"Flashers" (1979), "Kings and Queens" (1986), and a series of works based on dance and opera (1989). In these works large steel sheets are crimped and molded to suggest human forms, and then discolored with a blow torch to add color.

Castoro's public commissions include "Trap a Zoid" (1978) in New York City and installations of "Flashers" in New York City (1984), Paris, France (1983), and the Artpark, Lewiston, New York (1979). She is represented in the permanent collection of the Museum of Modern Art (MoMA), New York City; the Newark Museum, New Jersey; and various university, private, and corporate collections.

Judith Sealy

Bibliography
Lippard, Lucy. "Rosemarie Castoro: Working Out." *Art Forum* 13 (Summer 1975): 60–62.
Ratcliff, Carter. "Rosemarie Castoro: Gesture as Object." *Art in America* 67 (January 1979): 98–101.

Catchings, Yvonne Parks (1935–)

Throughout her adult life Yvonne Parks Catchings has combined two professions— public school art teacher, and prolific painter.

Born in Atlanta, Georgia, she was educated in that city's public schools but spent childhood summers on her paternal grandmother's nearby farm, where she has said she was profoundly affected by the natural world around her. Education has always been important for Catchings; she received a Bachelor of Arts degree in studio art from Spelman College in Atlanta, Georgia, where she studied with Leo Katz in 1955; three years later she earned a Master of Arts degree in art education from Teachers College, Columbia University, New York City; during the intervening years she did additional coursework at Atlanta University, Georgia, and Wayne State University, Detroit, Michigan. In 1970 she was awarded a second Master of Arts degree, in museum practices, from the University of Michigan, Ann Arbor, and in 1981 Catchings received a Doctorate in education from the same university.

Since 1955 Catchings has been an art teacher in the Detroit, Michigan, public school system. Meanwhile, she has been making her own art, working in various media—including watercolor, acrylics, oils, and collage—and in several different subjects and styles—ranging from lyrical landscapes and still lifes to highly-simplified figurative images, to powerful examples of pure abstraction.

Catchings has been exhibiting her work regularly since 1953, all over the eastern United States and beyond. Her first solo show was presented in Detroit, Michigan, in 1973 by the National Dental Association at its annual conference; subsequent solo exhibitions occurred at the Plymouth United Church of Christ in Detroit, Michigan (1976); at the American Automobile Association Gallery in Dearborn, Michigan (1984); and at the NCA Gallery (1990). She also took part in the important travelling exhibition, "Forever Free: Art by African-American Women, 1862–1980" (1980–). Her work is represented in private collections in Michigan, Georgia, and Washington, D.C.; it is also in the permanent collections of Spelman College and the Apex Museum— both in Atlanta, Georgia.

Catchings is a member of the National Art Education Association, the American Art Therapy Association, and the Detroit Institute of Arts Founders Society, along with many other professional and civic organizations. She is also the recipient of numerous awards and honors, including the Jerome Award for Sculpture, Spelman College, Atlanta, Georgia (1955); the Mayor's Award of Merit (1978); and the James D. Parks Special Award, the National Conference of Artists (1979). In 1984 Catchings received a Fulbright Hayes fellowship to visit Zimbabwe; this trip resulted in an exhibition later that same year of her watercolors on African subjects.

An avid writer, Catchings has published a number of articles and other works concerning the United States civil rights struggles of the 1960s, entitled *You Ain't Free Yet: Notes From a Black Woman*, published in 1976 by DuSable Museum of African-American History, Chicago, Illinois. She is married to Dr. James Catchings; they have two children.

Bibliography

Bontemps, Arna A., ed. *Forever Free: Art by African-American Women, 1862–1980*. Illinois State University, 1980, p. 66.

Henkes, Robert. *The Art of Black American Women: Works of 24 Artists of the 20th Century*. McFarland & Co., 1993.

Leis, Samella S., and Ruth G. Waddy. *Black Artists on Art*. Vol. 2. Los Angeles: Contemporary Crafts, Inc., 1970, pp. 25–26.

Catlett, Elizabeth (1919–)

Elizabeth Catlett, primarily a sculptor, is one of a small number of women who has achieved a lifelong career. Born April 15, 1919, in Washington, D.C., to Mary and John Catlett, she grew up in a middle-class home marked by the industry and nurturance of her mother, who became a widow near the time of Elizabeth's birth. From Dunbar High School, Washington, D.C., where her drawings and paintings had received attention, Catlett applied to the Carnegie Institute of Technology, Pittsburgh, Pennsylvania, where her paintings were included in the final round of applicants. However, Catlett was denied entrance because the school did not admit African-American students.

In 1933 she entered Howard University, Washington, D.C., the only black college in the United States then offering an undergraduate degree in art. A painting major, Catlett studied with Lois Jones, James Porter, and James Wells; her greatest influence in drawing, painting, and aesthetics was James Porter. While there was a brief introduction to the art of Mexican muralists, Diego Rivera and Miguel Covarrubias deeply impressed her. She also absorbed and fully appreciated the aesthetic principles of Alain Locke, whose classic critical essay, "The New Negro," written a decade earlier, helped to shape the artistic and social dynamism of the Harlem Renaissance. Locke's pioneering aesthetic theory analyzed that the American artist of African descent had, in the aesthetic traditions of Africa, inspiration in style and use from which a new modern art, especially in painting and sculpture, could arise. Catlett's own artistic vision was deepened further at this time by her viewing of an exhibit at Howard University of African art reproductions on tour from the Barnes Collection, Philadelphia, Pennsylvania.

Graduating *cum laude* from Howard University, Washington, D.C., in 1937, Catlett for the next decade blended work as a student and teacher of art and artist, and life as a wife and activist in North Carolina; Louisiana; Iowa; Texas; Chicago, Illinois; New York City; and Mexico City, Mexico. Her artistic mentors—two artist teachers, Grant Wood and Ossip Zadkine, and two organizations, the George Washington Carver School, New York City; and the Taller de Gráfica Popular, Mexico City, Mexico—gave the base of technique and purpose from which the work of her career would come.

From painter Grant Wood she gained discipline in technique and the process of creating. In a form new to her, sculpture, she achieved success in a short period of time. Her thesis sculpture, "Mother and Child" (1940) was awarded first prize in sculpture at the 1941 Golden Jubilee National Exposition, Chicago, Illinois. After leaving Wood's instruction at the University of Iowa, where she was the first to receive the Master of Fine Arts degree in sculpture in 1941, she taught art in Texas and New Orleans and studied ceramics at the Art Institute of Chicago, Illinois. Shortly after this, she went to New York City.

In New York City Catlett became associated for the first time with peers, an informal group of artists and intellectuals including Gwendolyn Bennett, Bob Blackburn, Ernest Critchlow, Aaron Douglas, Ralph Ellison, Langston Hughes, Jacob and Gwen Lawrence, Norman Lewis, Ann Petry, and Hale Woodruff. She exhibited with the painters of this group at Edith Halpert's Downtown Gallery, New York City, and with all, in various groupings, worked on social, political, and cultural causes in Harlem.

Staying with Dorothy and Kenneth Spencer at 409 Edgecombe, a hubbub of New York City artists and activists, Catlett joined the faculty of Harlem's George Washington Carver School and, almost at the same time, became the only private student of French abstract sculptor Ossip Zadkine. With Zadkine she developed freedom of expression in the process of creating, and intensified her skill as an abstract sculptor. At George Washington Carver School, a night school of art and crafts for African-American working people, Catlett witnessed firsthand the great need working people have for beauty and art.

A few years later, in 1946, enabled to travel and work in Mexico City, Mexico, by a Rosenwald Foundation grant, Catlett joined the collective of master printmakers of el Taller de Gráfica Popular. Working in collaboration, Catlett acquired the cooperative and individual disciplines required in an artist's collective, skill in the art of the linocut, and the belief that the purpose of art is social and political as well as aesthetic. At el Taller de Gráfica Popular she met painter and printmaker Francisco Mora, whom she married.

By 1947 Catlett's artistic purposes—to create art, to respond to the need for art by minority working people, and to create art which could be felt by and used in their lives by the public—were set. So too was the rhythm of her life as a wife, mother, artist, and teacher.

Although not consciously creating heroic imagery of the African-American woman, mother, and child, Catlett, in oil paintings and sculpture, had already depicted her as beautiful in body and strong in character. With the suite of fifteen linocuts "I am the Black Woman" (1946–1947) Catlett expanded this aesthetic view. "I am the Black Woman" is the first graphic series in Western art to portray the image of the African-American woman as heroic. Originally titled "The Negro Woman," it shows new iconography of the African-American woman as a heroine and as a complex person; Catlett portrays her strength and suffering as a field and domestic worker, victim of housing segregation, and as a protestor against racial lynching. Although each work is small (ten-by-fifteen centimeters), the suite, in each work and as an artistic unity, shows monumentality; this is especially true of the powerfully ironic "I have Special Reservations." The timeless classicism of these works is revealed by their effective use as complimentary accompaniments, published in a book forty-six years later, to the verses of "Lift Every Voice and Sing," considered the United States Negro National Anthem.

While raising her three sons Catlett worked exclusively on prints, working at night after the children were in bed. Still members of the Taller de Gráfica Popular, Catlett and Mora, working as a supportive and professional team which has become their signature, founded their own gallery, Salón de la Plástica Mexicana, Mexico City, Mexico, in 1951. Members of the Salón de la Plástica Mexicana included Diego Rivera, whom, with his wife Frida Kahlo, they befriended. Living at the house of the mother-in-law of David Alfaro Siqueiros in Mexico during this time, Catlett would visit the studios of Rivera, Orozco, and Siqueiros, and returning to sculpture, studied with José L. Ruiz and Francisco Zuñiga. Working in wood with Ruiz, Catlett learned the artistic tradition of Mexican woodcarving, while Zuñiga, at the Escuela de Pintura y Escultura (La Esmeralda), taught her the Mexican Indian tradition of ceramic sculpture.

In 1959, Catlett created "Mother and Child," in style close to the realistic classicism of sculptures in the 1940s, showing a young Mexi-

can mother with child in her lap. In that same year she became the first woman appointed professor of sculpture at the National School of Fine Arts, Mexico City, Mexico, where a few years later she became the first woman to head the department.

During the 1960s and the 1970s Catlett's graphic art and sculpture received international awards and commissions from the Biannual Exhibition of Sculpture in Mexico; the city of New Orleans, Louisiana; the Atlanta University Annual Exhibition, Georgia; and the International Graphics Exhibition, Leipzig, Germany. Her style in both media matured, integrating new formal elements. Primarily realistic in style, an abstraction of shape and the three-dimensionality of sculpture in spatial organization now influenced compositions in lithograph, serigraph as well as linocut; an example is "The Torture of Mothers" (1970) in which the profile of an African-American mother's head is set, neckless and open, in a white background, while set within the interior of her profile is her son, outlined in red and dead.

Some works of sculpture from this period transcend the stylistic trends of the twentieth century, at times unifying both Western and non-Western artistic traditions. These works combine the figurative and abstract principles of composition and reflect the Western love and respect for pure form, yet also use form symbolically, borrowing from the West-African tradition of shaping sculpture to communicate the spirit or purpose of the piece. This unity of Western and West-African sculptural traditions is shown in ten works, in wood and stone, and include both versions of "Singing Head" (1969, 1979), "Pregnancy" (1970), and "Recognition" (1970).

Catlett's oeuvre dates from 1941, and includes nearly thirty paintings, hundreds of drawings, more than 100 prints (linocut, lithograph, and serigraph), one graphic series, more than 100 sculptures (marble, onyx, limestone, terra cotta, bronze, cedar, walnut, apricot wood, and tropical wood), one relief-mural, and ten public sculptures (United States and Mexico). The dominant subject matter is the minority working woman in the United States, Mexico, and Latin America. Catlett's oeuvre contains the largest number of images of the minority working woman numbering nearly 120 in Western art. The seven themes of Catlett's oeuvre are: the life-experience of the minority working woman, the mother-child relationship, heroism, human solidarity, the spirit of life, seen especially in the faces and movements of children, the physical beauty of African-American people, and white-against-black violence. Her contributions to art history include the pioneering iconography of the African-American woman as heroic and complex, her stylistic unity of Western and West-African sculptural traditions, and achievement of a career as an African-American woman sculptor.

Since 1947 the work of Catlett has been seen in fifty individual exhibitions in Mexico City, Mexico, and throughout the United States, and in fifteen group shows in Mexico, the United States, and Germany. Commissions include the city of New Orleans, Louisiana, for "Louis Armstrong," a ten-foot bronze sculpture, presented in the 1976 Bicentennial Celebration, and the city of Atlanta, Georgia, for "The People of Atlanta," a thirty-six-by-ten-foot bronze relief set in Atlanta City Hall, Georgia in 1991. Her work is included in the collections of the Metropolitan Museum and Museum of Modern Art (MoMA)—both in New York City; the National Institute of Fine Arts and Museo de Arte Moderno—both in Mexico; and the National Museum of American Art, Washington, D.C. She is the recipient of many awards, including an honor award for outstanding achievement in the visual arts from the National Women's Caucus for Art (1981) and "Artist of the Year" (1991) from the New York City Art Teacher's Association, United Federation of Teachers.

Catlett attributes her professional career to the devotion and support of her husband, Francisco Mora, and living in Mexico. Continuing to be in demand as a sculptor and printmaker, Catlett, now a grandmother, works six hours daily in her studio, part of the custom-built home she and her husband designed in Cuernavaca, Morelos, Mexico.

Martha Kearns

Bibliography

Billips, Camille, and Glory Van Scott. "Elizabeth Catlett." *Artist and Influence* 1991. Vol. X.

Gouma-Peterson, Thalia. "Elizabeth Catlett: The Power of Human Feeling and of Art." *Women's Art Journal* (Spring–Summer 1983).

Kearns, Martha. "The Art of Elizabeth Catlett: Book Review." *M.S.* 13:10 (April 1985).

Lewis, Samella. *The Art of Elizabeth Catlett.* Hancraft Studios, 1984.

Mora, Juan. *E.C.: The Work of Elizabeth Catlett.* Elizabeth Catlett Productions, Inc., Third World Newsreel, 1978.

Tibol, Raquel. "Elizabeth Catlett: Museo de Arte Moderno." *National Institute of Fine Arts*, Mexico City, 1970.

Cavat, Irma (1928–)

A native New Yorker, the painter Irma Cavat studied at the New School for Social Research, New York City; the Art School of Alexander Archipenko; the Académie de la Grande Chaumière, Paris, France; with Amadée Ozenfant in Paris, and also with Hans Hofmann.

Cavat has been commissioned to paint murals in Port-au-Prince, Haiti (1948); the Faculty Club at the University of California at Santa Barbara (1968), where she has been a professor of drawing and painting since 1964; in a hotel in Athens, Greece (1970); and others. She has held solo exhibitions in museums and galleries, including the Santa Barbara Museum of Art, California, and the Phoenix Museum of Art, Arizona (1966–1967); Kennedy Galleries, New York City (1982, 1984); Feingarten Gallery, Los Angeles, California (1986); Preston Burke, Detroit, Michigan (1987); and others. Her work has been included in prestigious group shows, such as the Festival of Two Worlds, Spoleto, Italy (1958–1959); "Ten Americans," Palazzo Venezia, Rome, Italy (1960); and many others.

Cavat has been the recipient of numerous awards and honors. Her work is represented in private and public permanent collections, including the Art Institute of Detroit, and Flint Museum—both in Michigan; Isaac Delgado Museum, New Orleans, Louisiana; the Museum of Modern Art (MoMA), New York City; and others.

Bibliography

"Prizes (1984)," *Arts Magazine* 59 (September 1984).

"Prizes (1984)," *Art News* 83 (September 1984): 8.

Who's Who in American Art. 20th ed. R.R. Bowker Co., 1993–1994.

Celmins, Vija (1939–)

From Riga, Latvia, the Celmins family went to Germany in 1944 and finally to the United States in 1949, where they settled in Indianapo-

lis, Indiana. Following her graduation (1962) from the John Herron Art Institute in that city, Vija Celmins continued her study of art at the University of California at Los Angeles (UCLA), where she received her Master of Fine Arts degree in 1965. Her first one-person exhibition took place at the David Stuart Galleries in Los Angeles, California, the following year. Her numerous awards include a Cassandra Foundation award (1968) and fellowships from the National Endowment for the Arts (NEA) (1971, 1976).

Celmins's paintings and sculptures of the 1960s suggest pop art origins. Glorified household objects (as in "Comb," 1969–1970) were often interspersed with themes of disasters ("Burning Man," 1966). In the late 1960s Celmins utilized photographic prototypes in conjunction with imagery of highway driving ("Freeway," 1966). While many of these early canvases were in tones of gray, by the 1970s she worked almost exclusively in pencil in an effort to eliminate any supplementary elements. She ultimately abandoned color, gesture, and painting itself. Best known during the 1970s for her airless, serene, silent views of the Pacific Ocean, Celmins went on to describe through her work the surface of the moon, the desert floor, and the night sky ("Desert—Galaxy" [1974] and "Coma Bernices" series [1973–1975]). These large-scale natural phenomena are depicted suddenly devoid of human life. Still working from photographs, Celmins is occasionally associated with "photorealism" in general. She pronounces a certain distillation of the movement essentially derivative of abstraction.

The graphite medium itself has influenced Celmins's style as it translates easily to the lithographic stone. Experimenting with textures and techniques, more recently, her etchings and mezzotints have added further dimension to an already varied career.

Adeline Lee Karpiscak

Bibliography

Armstrong, R. "Of Earthly Objects and Stellar Sights: Vija Celmins." *Art in America* 69 (May 1981): 100–07.

Knight, Christopher. "Vija Celmins, Newport Harbor Art Museum." *Artforum* 18 (March 1980): 80.

Krantz, Les. *American Artists: An Illustrated Survey of Leading Contemporary Americans.* Facts on File Publications, 1985.

Solomon, Elke M. *Recent Drawings: William Allan, James Bishop, Vija Celmins, Brice Marden, Jim Nutt, Alan Saret, Pat Steir, Richard Tuttle.* American Federation of Arts, 1975–1976.

Turnbull, Betty. *Vija Celmins: A Survey Exhibition.* Newport Harbor Art Museum, 1979.

Chabot, Aurore (1949–)

Internationally-known for her ceramic sculpture, Aurore Chabot was born in Nashua, New Hampshire. She employs a rich interweave of colored, glazed surfaces and inlays in her sculptured shapes to create a rich and sensuous complexity within large, minimal forms. There is a sense of history and archeology within Chabot's sculptures which deal, in an abstract manner, with layerings, recesses, sharp edges, and aggressive, yet playful, forms. She deals with issues of protection versus vulnerability in her work.

Chabot received a Bachelor of Fine Arts degree from Pratt Institute, Brooklyn, New York (1971) and a Master of Fine Arts degree from the University of Colorado, Boulder (1981). She moved from the University of Vermont to the University of Arizona (1988), where she heads the ceramics program.

Her important honors and awards include the Governor's Arts Award (1990); first prize in the "All Fired Up" exhibition at the University of Arizona Museum of Art (1989), and selection as an affiliate member of the A.I.R. Gallery, New York City. Chabot has exhibited her work at the Anderson Ranch Art Center, Colorado; Kohler Arts Center, Wisconsin; Scottsdale Center for the Arts, Arizona; A.I.R. Gallery, New York City; and other shows in various venues, including San Diego, California; Montpelier, Vermont; Las Cruces, New Mexico; Cincinnati, Ohio; Chicago, Illinois; and Taipei, Taiwan, Republic of China.

Moira Geoffrion

Bibliography
Chabot, Aurore. *NCECA Journal* 10:8 (1989).
Who's Who in American Art. 19th ed. R.R. Bowker Co., 1991–1992.

Chaffee, Ada Gilmore (1883–1955)

Born in Kalamazoo, Michigan, Ada Gilmore Chaffee was one of the original Provincetown, Massachusetts, painter/printmakers. She was one of four children in an upper-middle-class household who were orphaned by the time she was twelve years old and sent to Belfast, Ireland, to be brought up by an aunt.

Gilmore studied art at the Belfast School of Design, Ireland, and did further study at the Art Institute of Chicago, Illinois; in 1912 she worked under the tutelage of Robert Henri, as did her future husband, Oliver Newberry Chaffee. The following year, Gilmore went to Paris, France, and became a student of Ethel Mars—the result of attending one of Mars' exhibits of color woodcuts.

The onset of World War I sent Gilmore back to the United States, where she settled in Provincetown, Massachusetts, to paint and develop her "white-line" color woodcuts using a technique not unlike that employed by Bror J.O. Norfeldt.

In 1915 her prints were shown at the Panama-Pacific International Exposition in San Francisco, California; the initial exhibition of the Provincetown Art Association, Massachusetts, the New York Watercolor Club, which exhibited her work annually; and the Berlin Photographic Company—both in New York City. For the next several years, Gilmore's work elicited distribution in many New York and Boston shows.

On a 1923 visit to Vence, in southern France, to renew her friendship with Ethel Mars, Gilmore remet and married Oliver Chaffee, Jr., and, through him and his painter-colleagues (Albert Gleizes, Marsden Hartley, Jules Pascin, and others) was truly influenced to work toward their "modern" direction. Her printmaking subsided; her paintings multiplied.

Returning to Provincetown in 1928, Gilmore broke with the Provincetown Art Association and painted until her death in 1955.

Bibliography
Acton, David. *A Spectrum of Innovation: Color in American Printmaking 1890–1960.* Worcester Art Museum, 1990.
Seckler, Dorothy Gees. *Provincetown Painters 1890s–1970s.* Everson Museum of Art, 1977.
Flint, Janet. *Provincetown Printers: A Woodcut Tradition.* Exhibition Catalog. National Museum of American Art, Smithsonian Institution, 1983.

Chapa, Martha (1946–)

Born in Monterrey, Nuevo León, Mexico, Martha Chapa de Ortiz Quesada (Martha Chapa) studied painting with the maestros Juan E. Mignornace (1965–1968) and Luis Sahagún (1964–1970); she was also a pupil of Carlos Navarro and José Vásquez Quiñones. Chapa participated in many group exhibitions in galleries and in cultural institutions in Mexico and abroad.

In her first visual essays, she painted pitchers, earthenware, fruit, vegetables, and flowers; in her second stage, the fruit disappeared from the still life to reappear on open windowsills, which fronted on landscapes; in her third approach, she returned to the human figure and the symbol of the apple as a metaphor for the complexity of life.

Also an excellent chef, Chapa has brought high cultural status to the art of cuisine: in 1983, the publishing house, Everest, of León, Spain, brought out her book, *La cocina mexicana y su arte*, which contains myriad recipes of Mexican dishes she created or renewed.

Among her most important painting exhibitions are the Monterrey Casino (1974); Galería "Chaplin," Caracas, Venezuela (1978); Panama Institute, Panama (1978); Galerie "C. Rarte," Paris, France (1978); Canning House, London, England (1982); Galería "Sloane Racotta," Mexico City, Mexico (1983); Mexico House in Paris, France (1985); Misrachi Gallery, Mexico City, Mexico (1987); Santo Domingo Gallery, Dominican Republic (1988); House of Art, La Jolla, California (1988); and the Museum of Art and History, San Juan, Puerto Rico (1989).

Bibliography
Alvarez, José Rogelio, et al. *Enciclopedia de México.* Secretaría de Educación Pública, 1987.
Presencia de Monterrey en México: Muestra plástica de pintura y escultura. The Historical Museum of the City of Mexico, 1990.

Chapin, Cornelia van Auken (1893–1972)

Born in Waterford, Connecticut, the sculptor Cornelia van Auken Chapin tested herself in many areas: she engaged in European travel; frequented museums, especially the Metropolitan Museum of Art, New York City; and learned, early on, how to pilot a plane. She decided to become a sculptor in the early 1920s and studied with Gail Corbett.

Chapin exhibited animal sculptures at the National Academy of Design, New York City, and decided to study stone carving with Hernández in Paris, France, where she lived, worked, and exhibited from 1934 to 1939—until World War II drove her back to New York City.

One of her direct stone carvings won her election to the Salon d'Automne, France, and also the Anna Hyatt Huntington Prize at the National Association of Women Artists, New York City (1936). Among many other awards Chapin, a member of the National Academy of Design, and the National Sculpture Society—both in New York City, won the second grand prize at the Paris Exposition of 1937, France, held a number of solo exhibitions when she was again in the United States, and was one of the founding members of Artists for Victory.

Examples of her sculpture are represented in private and public permanent collections, including the Pennsylvania Academy of Fine Arts, Philadelphia; Cathedral of St. John the Divine, New York City; Brookgreen Gardens, South Carolina; the Zoological Gardens in Washington, D.C.; and others.

Bibliography
Dunford, Penny. *Biographical Dictionary of Women Artists in Europe and America since 1850.* University of Pennsylvania Press, 1989.
Fairmount Park Association. *Sculpture of a City: Philadelphia's Treasures in Bronze and Stone.* Walker Publications Co., 1974.
Schnier, Jacques. *Sculpture in Modern America.* University of California Press, 1948.
Who's Who in American Art. 8th ed. American Federation of Arts, 1962.

Charkow, Natalie (1933–)

Natalie Charkow is considered one of the finest figurative sculptors in the United States. She went to the Tyler School of Art of Temple University in Philadelphia, Pennsylvania, earning a Bachelor of Fine Arts degree in 1955 and a Bachelor of Science degree in education in 1956.

Charkow's work has changed from a strongly abstract mode in the 1950s and 1960s to a strongly representational mode since the 1970s. In a memorable and highly acclaimed exhibition in 1988 at the Schoelkopf Gallery, New York City, she showed work, mainly in relief, and mainly growing from and commenting on two-dimensional structures of the past. This practice is ongoing as suggested by a complex set of carved reliefs based on a series of prints by Antonio Tempesta (1555–1630) illustrating scenes from Ovid, completed in the early 1990s.

Charkow is a slow worker and a very demanding one, always seeking the elusive gratifications of her vision, a vision that links the present and the past together in the forms and structures of her art.

In 1962 and 1963 Charkow received a Fulbright fellowship and an Italian government grant. She has received other awards, including a Tiffany Foundation grant in 1981.

Charkow has taught during most of her artistic career. She was a professor at the Philadelphia College of Art, Pennsylvania, from 1959 to 1972; acting chairperson of the culture department at Indiana University, at Bloomington, 1966–1967; and associate professor at Queens College, Flushing, New York, 1973–1976. She taught at Bard College, Annandale-on-Hudson, New York, 1978–1979; Boston University, Massachusetts, 1977–1979, and has been teaching at Yale University, New Haven, Connecticut, since 1979.

Charkow is married to the poet John Hollander and lives in Woodbridge, Connecticut.

Larry Day

Bibliography
Hollander, John, and Gabriel Laderman. *Natalie Charkow, Sculpture.* New York: Robert Schoelkopf Gallery, 1981.

Chase, Doris (1923–)

Born in Seattle, Washington, the painter/sculptor/video artist Doris Chase studied at the University of Washington, Pullman (1941–1943) and also with the Northwest painter, Mark Tobey.

Chase began her art career as a successful painter and sculptor and, over the years, changed genres to television artist. She has held many solo exhibitions and broadcasts in museums and galleries in the United States and abroad, including the Formes Gallery, Tokyo, Japan (1963, 1970); University of Washington, Seattle (1971, 1978); Metropolitan Museum of Art, New York City (1974); Wadsworth Atheneum, Hartford, Connecticut (1973); Anthology Film Archives, New York City (1975); University of Michigan, Ann Arbor (1977, 1980); Hirshhorn Museum and Sculpture Garden, Washington, D.C. (1977); Museum of Modern Art (MoMA), New York City (1978, 1981); "Table for One," broadcast from WNYC-TV, New York City (1985); and many others.

Chase has completed monumental kinetic sculpture commissions and other works at sites as varied as Expo '70, Osaka, Japan (1970); Atlanta Sculpture Park, Georgia; the Seattle Opera Association, Washington (1972); Museum of Art, Montgomery, Alabama (1974); the Open Eye Theater, New York City (1975); Lakeside Park, Anderson, Indiana (1976); and others.

Winner of awards and honors, Chase received a fellowship from the National Endowment for the Arts (NEA) (1976); the American Film Festival award (1972, 1979); a grant from the New York State Council on the Arts (1981); first prize at the National Women's Film Festival (1985); and others.

Examples of Chase's work are in private and public permanent collections, including the Art Institute of Chicago, Illinois; Museum of Fine Arts, Boston, Massachusetts; the Museum of Modern Art, Kobe, Japan; MoMA, New York City; the Smithsonian Institution, National Collection of Fine Arts, Washington, D.C.; and others.

Bibliography
Lorber, Richard. "Doris Chase." *Arts Magazine* 51 (September 1976): 10.
Making Their Mark: Women Artists Move into the Mainstream, 1970–1985. Abbeville Press, 1989.
Sturken, Marita. "Video as a Performance Medium." *Sightlines* (Spring 1983).
Weisman, Velia. "Doris Chase: Video and the Dramatic Monologue." *Film Quarterly* 17:2–4 (1984).

Chase, Louisa L. (1951–)

Painter/printmaker Louisa Chase was born in Panama City, Panama; she attended Syracuse University, New York, where she obtained a Bachelor of Fine Arts degree in 1973. Two years later Chase received a Master of Fine Arts degree from Yale University, New Haven, Connecticut.

Chase has had many solo exhibitions of her work in the United States and abroad, including Brooke Alexander, New York City (1989); The Texas Gallery, Houston (1987); Robert Miller Gallery, New York City (1981, 1982, 1984, 1986); Margo Leavin Gallery, Los Angeles, California (1985); Mira Goddard Gallery, Toronto, Canada (1984, 1989); Gallerie Inge Baker, Cologne, Germany (1983); and others.

Her work has been invited to significant group shows, such as "Landscape Painting in the East and West," Shizuoka Prefectural Museum of Art, Kobe, Japan (1984); and "The New Generation, the 1980s, American Painters and Sculptors," Metropolitan Museum of Art, New York City (1988); "The Figure Speaks," Bard College, Annandale-on-Hudson, New York (1989); "Works on Paper," Pamela Auchincloss Gallery (1988); and "Drawing Acquisitions, 1981–1985," the Whitney Museum of American Art (1985)—both in New York City; and many others.

Chase won grants from the National Endowment for the Arts (NEA) (1978–1979 and 1982–1983), and from the New York Council on the Arts Creative Artists Public Service (CAPS) (1979–1980).

She taught painting at the Rhode Island School of Design, Providence (1975–1979) and at the School for Visual Arts, New York City (1980–1982).

"Untitled 88–327" (1988), a not atypical color lithograph, was pulled at Tamarind Institute, Albuquerque, New Mexico. Linear squiggles of brush-filled gray to black tusche are superimposed upon squares and rectangles of primary colors, creating an energy-laden, reticulated surface.

Her work is in permanent public, corporate, and private collections, including the Albright-Knox Art Gallery, Buffalo, New York; the Corcoran Gallery, Washington, D.C.; Denver Art Museum, Colorado; Library of Congress, Washington, D.C.; the Morton Neumann Family Collection, Chicago, Illinois; the Museum of Modern Art (MoMA), the Metropolitan Museum of Art, the New York Public Library, and the Whitney Museum of American Art—all in New York City; and the University of Massachusetts, Worcester.

Bibliography

Brenson, Michael. "Works from Nature, Louisa Chase." *The New York Times* (February 17, 1989).

Cotter, Holland. "Louisa Chase at Robert Miller." *Art in America* 74:6 (June 1986): 123.

Field, Richard S., and Ruth E. Fine. *A Graphic Muse.* Hudson Hills Press, 1987.

Moore, Margaret. "Louisa Chase." *Art News* (Summer 1989).

Chase-Riboud, Barbara Dewayne (1939–)

Born in Philadelphia, Pennsylvania, the African-American sculptor Barbara Dewayne Chase-Riboud earned a Bachelor of Fine Arts degree from Temple University, Philadelphia (1957), and, three years later, received a Master of Fine Arts degree from Yale University, New Haven, Connecticut.

Chase-Riboud has held many solo exhibitions in galleries and museums in the United States and abroad, including the University of California at Berkeley (1973); the Museum of Modern Art, Paris, France (1974); Kunstmuseum, Düsseldorf, Germany (1974); Kunstmuseum, Baden-Baden, Germany (1979); and others.

She has been commissioned to create aluminum wall reliefs, fountains, forged steel sculptures and bronzes for various public and private collections and, early on, she exhibited work in the First Spoleto Festival, Italy (1958); the First World Festival of Negro Art, Dakar, Senegal (1966); and myriad others.

Winner of awards and honors, Chase-Riboud was a recipient of a John Hay Whitney fellowship (1957–1958); a grant from the National Endowment for the Arts (NEA) (1973); a travelling grant from the U.S. State Department (1975); the outstanding alumni award from Temple University, Philadelphia, Pennsylvania (1975); and many others. Her "Monument to Malcolm X #2" (1969), a bronze and wool three-dimensional homage to the black leader, is not atypical of her work of this period.

Chase-Riboud's work is represented in private and public permanent collections, including the Metropolitan Museum of Art, the Museum of Modern Art (MoMA), and St. John's University—all in New York City; the Newark Museum of Art, New Jersey; the University of California at Berkeley; and others.

Bibliography

Afro-American Artists: New York and Boston. The Museum of the National Center of Afro-American Artists and the Museum of Fine Arts, 1970.

Waller, Irene. *Textile Sculptures.* Taplinger Publishing Co., 1977.

Who's Who in American Art. 15th ed. R.R. Bowker Co., 1982.

Chavez, Margaret Herrera (1912–)

The widely travelled painter/printmaker Margaret Herrera Chavez was born in Las Vegas, New Mexico, and attended the schools in her area. The fact that Chavez was the daughter of ranchers may help to explain her subjective approach to the northern New Mexico landscape. Examples of her oils, watercolors, or prints are in private and public permanent collections.

Bibliography

Quirarte, Jacinto. *Mexican-American Artists.* Austin: University of Texas Press, 1973.

Chavous, Barbara (1936–)

Born in Columbus, Ohio, the painter/sculptor Barbara Chavous earned a Bachelor's degree from Central State University, Wilberforce, Ohio (1960). An elementary school teacher in New York City for a decade, Chavous, in a lifelong pursuit of the fine arts in the 1970s, began to experiment with the visual arts.

Beginning with "Jazz Totem #2" (1980), shown at the Columbus Honolulu Exchange, City Hall, Hawaii, Chavous has had her work invited to many group exhibitions, including the Atlanta Life National Art Competition and Exhibition, Georgia (1981–1983); Mississippi Museum of Art, Jackson (1981); the New Gallery of Contemporary Art, Cleveland, Ohio (1983); University of Cincinnati, Ohio (1983); Dayton Art Institute, Ohio (1985); University of Youngstown, Ohio (1985); "African-American Artists' Showcase," Central State University, Wilberforce, Ohio (1986); "Focus: 88, The Black Artist," Cincinnati, Ohio (1988); "Acts of Reclamation," Ohio State University, Columbus (1988); and others.

Her first solo exhibition of paintings and sculpture, "The Gathering of Elders," was shown at the Museum of Art, Oxford, Ohio, and a retrospective exhibition of her work took place at the Columbus Cultural Arts Center, Ohio (1991). "The City," her most recent commissioned work, among many, a large steel sculpture, is permanently sited in Bicentennial Park, Columbus, Ohio.

Winner of honors and grants, Chavous was the recipient of artist fellowships from the Ohio Council on the Arts (1980–1981, 1984–1985, 1986–1987); she was one of four Ohio artists awarded an art residency by the government of China with respect to the Shaanx-Ohio Artists Exchange Project (1990); and was resident artist at Wittenburg University, Springfield, Ohio, and Kenyon College, Gambier, Ohio, during the academic year 1991–1992.

Art juror, consultant, lecturer, workshop and seminar leader on African-American and other concerns, Chavous serves many arts and community organizations locally, nationally, and internationally. Her work is represented in private, public, and corporate permanent collections, including the Columbus Museum of Art, Ohio; Ohio Council on the Arts; Port Columbus International Airport; Atlantic Richfield Company, Dublin, Ohio; and others.

Bibliography
Chavous: Visual Artist. WOSU-TV Special. Ohio State University, 1989.

Chernow, Ann (1936–)

A native New Yorker, the painter/printmaker Ann Chernow, after study at Syracuse University, New York (1953–1955) earned both a Bachelor's degree (1957) and a Master of Arts degree from New York University, New York City (1969). Her mentors during this period were Howard Conant, Jules Olitski, Irving Sandler, Lawrence Alloway, and Hale Woodruff. From 1966 to 1971, she worked with Victor D'Amico at the Museum of Modern Art (MoMA), New York City, in his innovative art education program. Chernow's work derives from the faces and forms of women in films of the 1930s and 1940s which are transmuted to expressive drawings, paintings, and prints that move the spectator beyond the evocative.

Chernow has held solo exhibitions of her work in galleries and museums every year between 1980 and 1993, including the Suzanne Maag Gallery, Zurich, Switzerland (1980); Beall/Lambremont, New Orleans, Louisiana (1981); Snug Harbor Cultural Center, Staten Island, New York (1984); Munson Gallery, New Haven, Connecticut (1986, 1988); UFO Gallery, Provincetown, Massachusetts (1988, 1991, 1992, 1993); Virginia Lust Gallery, New York City (1992); Uptown Gallery, New York City (1993); and others.

Chernow's drawings, paintings, and prints have been invited to numerous group exhibitions, such as "Particular People," Alex Rosenberg Gallery, New York City (1982); "Two Hundred Eight Years of American Drawing," Morris Museum, New Jersey (1984); "American Art/American Women," Stamford Museum and Nature Center, Connecticut (1986); "As They See Themselves," John Szoke Gallery, New York City (1989); "42nd North American Printmakers Exhibition," Fitchburg Art Museum, Massachusetts (1990); National Museum of Women in the Arts, Washington, D.C. (1991); Printmaking Council of New Jersey, a travelling show (1992); "Resonance," Lyman Allyn Museum, New London, Connecticut; and others.

Winner of many awards and honors for her etchings and lithographs, Chernow recently received an award from the Printmaking Council of New Jersey (1992) and was awarded a painting fellowship from the Connecticut Commission on the Arts (1980–1981). Presently the chairman of the department of art, Norwalk Community College, Connecticut, Chernow has been a guest lecturer and visiting artist at many institutions. Her works are in private and public permanent collections, including Wesleyan University, Middletown, Connecticut; Elvehjem Museum of Arts, Madison, Wisconsin; Hofstra University, New York City; Neuberger Museum Study Collection, Purchase, New York; Aldrich Museum of Contemporary Art, Ridgefield, Connecticut; the New York Public Library Print Collection; and many others.

Bibliography
Alloway, Lawrence. "Ann Chernow: New Paintings and Drawings." A Catalog. Alex Rosenberg Gallery, 1984.
Dickson, Janet S. "New Works." A Catalog. New Haven, Connecticut: Munson Gallery. 1988.
Lust, Herbert. "Chernow's Modular Expressionism." A Catalog. Virginia Lust Gallery, 1992.
Who's Who in American Art. 19th ed. R.R. Bowker Co., 1991–1992.

Chicago, Judy Gerowitz (1939–)

The artist most often associated with the feminist movement in art, Judy Chicago has been one of its most important instigators on the West Coast. The issues that define her work became the crucial concerns for the early feminist movement in art as a whole: female experience and sensibility, central core imagery, rewriting women's history, and high art versus craft. Chicago has consistently raised issues never dealt with openly before, with the goal of reversing the way women are seen in our culture.

Chicago was born Judy Gerowitz in Chicago, Illinois. She received her Master of Fine Arts degree from the University of California at Los Angeles (UCLA) in 1964. After making well-received minimalist sculpture in the late 1960s she began to create an abstract art with more personal content. In 1970 she exhibited her "Pasadena Lifesavers" series (1969), large paintings (five-foot-by-five-foot) that used central core forms with dissolving color to represent the experience of female orgasm. This solo exhibition show in Fullerton, California, marked her break with the conventional art world in other ways as well. A statement on the wall proclaimed that "Judy Gerowitz hereby divests herself of all names imposed upon her through male social dominance and freely chooses her own name, Judy Chicago." When the critics and public failed to see the female sexual content of the work, she broke with the male art world altogether. She single-handedly developed the Fresno Feminist Art Program at California State University in 1970 for women students (later moved to California Institute of the Arts, Valencia), where one would not have to choose between "being a woman and being an artist."

Chicago and Miriam Schapiro, who joined the program at Chicago's request the following year, taught workshops in performance and autobiographical journal writing, respectively, both of which had tremendous impact on emerging feminist art. Their work with students culminated in the first feminist exhibition, "Womanhouse" (1972), in which the group took over and renovated an entire house to express their particular experience of women's lives as shaped by their new feminist consciousness. "Womanhouse" contained a series of installations that ranged from expressions of outrage to irony and humor, including Chicago's infamous "Menstruation Bathroom," featuring a garbage container overflowing with used tampons. The performance workshop group held numerous and now canonic performances, such as Faith Wilding's "Waiting," and "Ablutions" by Chicago, Suzanne Lacy, Sandra Orgel, and Aviva Rahmani. A record of the building and its artworks is preserved in an exhibition catalog containing statements by Chicago and Schapiro, as well as a film, *Womanhouse,* showing its interior and recording several of the performances.

After this project Chicago left the California Institute of the Arts, because the harsh criticism and intimidation of the women students by male faculty had further convinced her that she could not work within the system. She did a series of works in 1972–1973 based on flower/vaginal imagery that articulated both female history and female sexuality. These works were made with a female audience in mind and were closely identified with her own body. Her "Female Rejection Drawing" (1974), for example, is a vaginal icon, whose painfully peeled-back forms reveal a vulnerable center. By 1974 she no longer veiled the content of her works in abstractions, but directly based them on the vagina/butterfly image. As a form symbolizing freedom, this motif became the foundation of her first major project, and arguably her most important work, "The Dinner Party" (1974–1978).

"The Dinner Party," a carefully-researched sculptural installation, highlights women left out of history from the prehistoric goddess to Georgia O'Keeffe. As Chicago describes it in her book on the project, the place settings around the three-sided table move chronologically from the development of goddess worship to the eventual patriarchal domination and institutionalization of women's oppression. Each setting includes a carved and glazed plate in the shape of a butterfly-vagina, a porcelain goblet and flatware, and a runner embroidered and ornamented with traditional stitchery related to the historical period of the woman represented. Chicago and hundreds of volunteer collaborators not only extensively researched women's history, but also learned the various arts of needlework, ceramics, and china painting in order to complete this enormous undertaking. They found so many names of women that the original thirteen place settings (representing both the Last Supper for women and a witches' coven) were increased to thirty-nine, and Chicago wrote the names of 999 women whom they would have liked to include onto the white porcelain tiles on the floor space in the middle of the table. As one moves around the table, the names appear and disappear, a metaphor for the role of women in history.

"The Dinner Party" was an empowering experience for a number of women when it toured the United States in 1979, but the art world and some feminist critics received it less favorably. Writer Alice Walker was offended by the fact that African-American ex-slave and abolitionist Sojourner Truth was the only woman not represented by a vaginal image; others have also complained that the choices of women do not represent cultural diversity. A number of feminists charge that women should not be represented merely by their genitals and condemn what they consider to be its essentialism. Despite criticisms, "The Dinner Party," a major monument of early feminism, has not yet found an institutional home.

Because of the difficulty exhibiting and storing "The Dinner Party," Chicago executed with her collaborators a series of variously scaled needlework pieces that could be shown in smaller segments for her next large work, "The Birth Project" (1980–1985). The images deal with the female act of giving birth as a metaphor for the creation of life in general. Although Chicago claimed she wanted to dispel the myth surrounding the act of birth, the works are themselves mythical, as well as celebratory and/or painful. The needlework, done by women across the country based on Chicago's design, is of very high quality, and the images are quite striking. Once again, however, criticism has been leveled at the work for its presentation of "woman as nature," and its essentialism.

Chicago is now engaged in a series of paintings depicting the Holocaust. Although she is still a controversial and outspoken artist, her two major projects remain among the major accomplishments of feminist art.

Patricia Mathews

Bibliography

Chicago, Judy. *Through the Flower. My Struggle as a Woman Artist.* Anchor, 1975.

———. "The Dinner Party." *A Symbol of Our Heritage.* Anchor, 1979.

———. *The Birth Project.* Doubleday & Co., 1985.

Chicago, Judy, with Susan *Hill. Embroidering Our Heritage.* "The Dinner Party" *Needlework.* Anchor, 1980.

Lippard, Lucy. "Judy Chicago, Talking to Lucy R. Lippard." *Artforum* 13:1 (September 1974): 60–65.

———. "Judy Chicago's 'Dinner Party,'" *Art in America* 68:4 (April 1980): 114–26.

Withers, Josephine. "Judy Chicago's Birth Project: A Feminist Middle?" *New Art Examiner* 13 (January 1986): 28–30.

Chitty, Elizabeth (1953–)

Formerly based in Toronto, Canada, Elizabeth Chitty is an interdisciplinary artist whose work in performance, video, and installation has received national exposure. She is also active as an administrator, curator, editor, producer, and writer.

After graduating from the York University Dance Department, Toronto, in 1975, Chitty began to exploit the durational implications of dance and video together in her performances. As she gained distance from the minimalist dance theater, her work acquired more of a basis in linguistic theory. Early multimedia performance works such as "Demo Model" (*A Space*, Toronto, 1978) tended to foreground the codedness of various signifying systems including semaphores, sign language, news media. and photography, and their potentially dissociative effects on the receiving individual.

Chitty's critique of communications technologies, sexual norms, and language is often sublimated as metaphor in her work, which relies on an interdependence between the chosen content and the means of its representation. An early example of this tendency, "History, Colour T.V. & You" (3 symposium d'art performance, Lyon, France, 1981) used slide projection, live and pre-recorded performance, "self-referential" video, live and recorded sound to evoke the culturally-determined parameters of present-day subjectivity.

The performance "Moral/Passion" (Winnipeg Art Gallery, Manitoba, 1986) marked the beginning of an enhanced theatricality in Chitty's work. This large-scale production in twelve scenes incorporated multiple performers and slide projectors, live and recorded sound, music, text, shadowplay, light, fire, and wind. Disconnected narrative elements elaborated themes of overcoming loss and grief.

The artist's growing preoccupation with redemption and healing, and her aesthetic commitment to orchestrated grand spectacle, are extended in "Lake" (Bill Bolton Arena, Toronto, Ontario, 1990). The work focuses on environmental issues, while reintroducing Chitty as a performer and dance as an expressive element, in addition to the techniques deployed in "Moral/Passion." Around the same time, as an outgrowth of concerns exemplified in "Lake," Chitty began to produce interactive video installations, such as "The View of the Landscape from Here" (Niagara Artist's Centre, St. Catharines, Ontario, 1990).

Ingrid Jenkner

Bibliography

Bronson, A.A., and Peggy Gale. *Performance by Artists.* Toronto: Art Metropole, 1979.

Chitty, Elizabeth, ed. *Artists Talk About Technology.* Toronto: ANNPAC, 1985.

Gale, Peggy. "Elizabeth Chitty: Demo Model." *Centerfold* (December 1978): 8–12.

Lynch, Peter, and Renya Onasick. *Prime Time Video.* Exhibition Catalog. Saskatoon: Mendel Art Gallery, 1984.

Chryssa (Vardea) (1933–)

Chryssa (Vardea) was brought up and educated in Athens, Greece. The Greek Ministry of Social Welfare sent this neophyte social worker to the Dodecanese Islands and later to the earthquake-ravaged island of Zante in the Ionian Sea. Chryssa, realizing that monies were available to restore monasteries but not to provide food and shelter for children, renounced social work and returned to Athens to study painting with Anghelos Prokopion.

She left for Paris, France, to further her art education, had a brief association with the Académie de la Grande Chaumière, met André Breton, Max Ernst, and Edgard Varèse, savored the post-war surrealist atmosphere, took off for San Francisco, California, in 1954, the California School of Fine Arts in San Francisco a year later, and then settled in New York City.

It is utterly clear that Chryssa's mature work grew out of the Greek experience, before and after World War II, wedded to the raucous letters, signs, symbols, and lights of Times Square, New York City, and transmuted through her sensibilities to her two- and three-dimensional innovative work with neon, Plexiglas, steel, aluminum, enamel, and other materials.

Chryssa's first commission in 1969 was to paint six panels, thirteen feet in height, for Count Peter Metternich's family castle in Adelebsen. Eight years earlier, she had a retrospective exhibition at the Guggenheim Museum in New York City.

Her sculptural light assemblages are truly wonders to behold: "Gates to Times Square" (1964–1966), a monumental cubic assemblage of neon, Plexiglas, timers, and mixed-media fragments in the form of a giant letter "A" reveals Chryssa as the shaman of light sculpture. Her twenty-two-foot-long "Untitled Light Sculpture" (1980), hanging in the eight-story atrium lobby of a Chicago, Illinois, building at 33 West Monroe, is electronically programmed to provide patterns of changing light intensity through 900 feet of white neon tubing.

Chryssa has had a great many solo exhibitions in the United States and abroad—including the Museum of Modern Art (MoMA) (1963), the Guggenheim Museum (1961), the Whitney Museum of American Art (1972), the Pace Gallery (1966, 1967)—all in New York City; Harvard University, Cambridge, Massachusetts (1968); Galerie Rive Droite (1969), and the Musée de l'Art Moderne de la Ville de Paris, France; the Kunsthaus, Zurich, Switzerland (1979); and other institutions. Her work is held in major public and private collections, including the Albright-Knox Art Gallery, Buffalo, New York, and others.

Bibliography

Campbell, Vivian. "Chryssa—Some Observations." *Art International* 17:4 (April 1932): 18–30.

Chryssa (Vardea). *Selected Prints and Drawings: 1959–1962*. Whitney Museum of American Art, 1972.

Hunter, Sam. *Chryssa*. Harry N. Abrams, 1974.

Mellow, James. *The New York Times* (April 21, 1973).

Restany, Pierre. *Chryssa*. Harry N. Abrams, 1977.

Chunn, Nancy (1941–)

Beginning in the early 1980s Los Angeles native Nancy Chunn has created paintings that use maps of various parts of the world as the basis for political commentary. Chunn received her Bachelor of Fine Arts degree in 1969 from the California Institute of the Arts, Valencia. Twelve years later she was an established artist.

Since 1981 Chunn has had eight one-person shows, including three (in 1987, 1989, and 1992) at the Ronald Feldman Gallery in New York City; others were held at New York City's Concord Gallery (1984); the Carnegie Mellon College of Fine Arts, Pittsburgh, Pennsylvania (1986); and Chicago's Festival Gallery (1987), and the Museum of Contemporary Art in Chicago—both in Illinois (1987). She has participated in several group exhibitions every year since 1981, at venues in more than a dozen states in the United States plus Toronto, Canada.

While they are rich from a purely aesthetic standpoint—featuring dramatic, asymmetrical compositions and a combination of tightly-controlled drawing with complex, multi-layered textures—many of Chunn's works are also overtly political. For example, she depicts the continent of South America hanging upside-down, its narrow stem held by the hook of a construction crane, and presumably destined for destruction. She has also contributed her art to exhibitions dedicated to such issues as environmental destruction and human reproductive rights. In 1985 Chunn was awarded a National Endowment for the Arts (NEA) fellowship in painting, and her work was selected for the Corcoran Biennial of Contemporary American Painting, Washington, D.C. in 1991.

Bibliography

Kuspit, Donald. "42nd Biennial: Corcoran Gallery of Art." *Artforum* 36:332 (February 1992): 122.

Lawson, Thomas. "The Apocalyptic Vision: Four New Imagists." *Artforum* 20:1 (September 1983): 71.

Richard, Paul. "Abstract and Personal." *The Washington Post* (September 6, 1991): F-1.

Cifolelli, Alberta (1931–)

Born in Erie, Pennsylvania, the painter Alberta Cifolelli received a diploma in painting (1953) from the Cleveland Institute of Art, Ohio, where she studied on a four-year National Scholastic scholarship; earned a Bachelor's degree from Kent State University, Ohio, while on a state scholarship (1955); and received a Master's degree in video and communication from Fairfield University, Connecticut (1975).

Cifolelli has held solo exhibitions of her paintings in museums and galleries, including the University of Connecticut, Storrs (1978, 1992); Cortland Jessup Gallery, Provincetown, Massachusetts (1992); Harmon Meek Gallery, Naples, Florida (1987); Kaber Gallery (1983), and Noho Gallery (1982)—both in New York City; Silvermine Guild Arts Center, New Canaan, Connecticut (1978); and others.

Her work has been invited to group exhibitions in the United States and abroad, such as the "Permanent Collection Show," Stamford Museum, Connecticut (1992); Reece Galleries, New York City (1991, 1992); "Connecticut Biennial," Bruce Museum, Greenwich, Connecticut (1991); "Four Hundred Years of Women Artists," a travelling show to major museums in Japan, and National Museum of Women in the Arts, Washington, D.C. (1990–1991); "The Natural Image Invitational," Stamford Museum, Connecticut (1989); "The Artists' Mark," Armstrong Gallery, New York City (1984); "Art of the Northeast," Silvermine Galleries, New Canaan, Connecticut (1979, 1980, 1981); and others.

Winner of honors and awards for her painting, Cifolelli has been the recipient of arts education grants from the National Endowment for the Arts (NEA) (1975, 1977); the Connecticut Commission on the Arts (1972); the Doris Kriendler Award, National Academy of Design, New York City (1974); a residency at the Djerassi Foundation, Woodside, California (1986); and others.

Her richly-hued metaphorical, large-scale paintings of landscapes and flowers reflect, in part, inward visual journeys, the feminine mystique, fertility, and reproduction. She recently wrote, "[My landscape] deals with an autobiographical theme or an attitude. The images are not derived referentially; [instead] everything in the picture is invented by me."

Her work is represented in private, public, and corporate permanent collections, including the National Museum of Women in the Arts, and the Smithsonian Museum—both in Washington, D.C.; Stamford Museum, Connecticut; Cleveland Art Association, Ohio; Djerassi Foundation; Xerox Corporation; Dean Witter; and many others.

Bibliography
Alberta Cifolelli. A Catalog. Essay by Virginia Mann. Stamford Museum, 1987.
Alberta Cifolelli. Connecticut Biennial Catalog. Essay by Nancy Hall Duncan. Bruce Museum, 1991.
Moss, Jacqueline. "Alberta Cifolelli." *Arts Magazine* (April 1982).
Zimmer, William. "Connecticut Biennial Displays Diversity." *The New York Times* (April 14, 1991).

Citron, Minna Wright (1896–1991)

A painter and graphic artist, Minna Citron was born in Newark, New Jersey, and did not begin studying art until 1924. Married and the mother of two sons, Citron was weary of her conventional life. She studied painting under Benjamin Kopman at the Brooklyn Institute of Arts and Sciences, New York City, then did three years of studies at the New York School of Applied Design for Women, New York City, from which she graduated with honors. In 1928 she enrolled at New York City's Art Students League; here, her primary mentor and strong early influence was Kenneth Hayes Miller, the leader of what was often called "the 14th Street School," home to such artists as Reginald Marsh, muralist Edward Laning, Moses and Rafael Soyer, and Isabel Bishop. Following the lure of freedom, Citron divorced her husband in 1934 and turned completely to her art career, never remarrying. Like many of her fellow 14th Street artists, during the 1930s she painted numerous scenes of Union Square, New York City, where she had her studio. The Daumier-influenced Citron tended to observe Union Square humanity and society in general with a humorous eye, satire being her favorite mode of expression. "Feminanities" (1935), one of her first solo exhibitions, was typical of her witty style as she depicted women in unflattering situations; "Beauty Culture," for example, mocks the vanity of beauty parlor patrons, who seem virtually imprisoned by their hair-dryers. Citron could find humor almost anywhere: while finalizing her divorce in Reno, Nevada, she visited some casinos and came away with several "spicy scenes" of the players and dealers she encountered. Some time after that, she served on a jury and recorded in paint her wry testimony of that experience.

With the growth of government-sponsored art in the late 1930s, Citron's artistic interests evolved from satire to social awareness. Employed by the Work Projects Administration (WPA) Federal Art Project in New York City, she taught painting from 1935–1937, and between 1938 and 1942 she travelled to Tennessee, enthusiastically creating Tennessee Valley Authority (TVA) murals at the Newport and Manchester post offices. She also painted a series of Tennessee Valley scenes, which she exhibited at Manhattan's Midtown Galleries.

Citron was drawn to printmaking in the late 1930s after seeing some unusual work by Stanley William Hayter, whose Atelier 17 had been forced to relocate from Paris, France, to New York City with the beginning of World War II. This famous graphics workshop attracted many refugee artists from Europe, notably Jacques Lipchitz, André Masson, Salvador Dali, and Marc Chagall. Citron spent much time at the Atelier 17, learning new techniques from the Europeans and embarking upon her own innovations. She combined the deliberate with the accidental, happily exploiting the opportunity a broken etching plate provided to recreate a design. Her goal was to find "an actual third dimension in painting as well as printmaking," and toward this end, she piled on paint and varnish, creating raised surfaces on her canvases or plates. Later, she began cutting into the surfaces. Her art became progressively more abstract, thanks in part to her continuing association with Atelier 17, which she visited often after it was moved back to France at war's end. In the 1950s she exhibited a series of experimental prints at the Peter Deitsch Gallery in a show titled "The Uncharted Course," the journey of a plate through several incarnations made possible by breakage, other accidental effects, and Citron's own creative energy.

Citron, whose art hangs in the Metropolitan Museum of Art, and the Museum of Modern Art (MoMA)—both in New York City; and the National Gallery of Art, Washington D.C. (among other leading museums), was honored at Rutgers University's Douglass College Library, New Jersey, on her ninetieth birthday; the celebration, part of the library's Women Artists Series, included a retrospective of Citron's work. "Models of Persistence" was the show's theme, which the ebullient Citron epitomized as she continued to create and display works of art into her nineties. Her last exhibit was held in 1990 at the Susan Teller Gallery in SoHo, New York City; the following year Citron died in New York City at the age of ninety-five.

Cynthia Lee Kerfoot

Bibliography
Bird, Payul. "Gambling and Minna Citron." *The Art Digest* 12 (November 1, 1937): 18–19.
Citron, Minna. "Communication Between Spectator and Artist." *College Art Journal* 14:2 (1955): 147–53.
———. "Minna Citron." *The Journal of Decorative and Propaganda Arts* 1:1 (Spring 1986): 51–53.
Davidson, Martha. "Minna Citron, Critical Commentator of American Life." *The Art News* 34:5 (October 30, 1937): 16.
Dunford, Penny. *A Biographical Dictionary of Women Artists in Europe and America Since 1850*. University of Pennsylvania Press, 1989.
Lane, James W. "Citron's Light Tones for Humor and Civics." *The Art News* 38:7 (November 18, 1939): 22.
Marxer, Donna. "Minna Citron at Ninety." *Women Artists News* 12:13 (March 1987).
Masters, Greg. "From the 1930s–40s, 50 Years Ago. WPA/AAA." *Arts Magazine* 62:106 (February 1987).
Rubenstein, Charlotte Striefer. *American Women Artists from Early Times to the Present*. Avon, 1982.
Smith, Roberts. Obituary of Minna Citron. *The New York Times* (December 24, 1991).

Clark, Lygia (1920–1988)

Born in Belo Horizonte, Brazil, the neo-concrete sculptor Lygia Clark initially studied in Rio de Janeiro, Brazil, with landscape architect and artist Robert Burle Marx before going on to Paris, France, for further study with Fernand Léger and Arpad Szenes (1950–1952).

Clark held solo exhibitions in galleries and museums, including the Louise Alexander Gallery, New York City (1963); the Venice Biennale, Italy, a ten-year retrospective (1968); and others. Her work was invited to prestigious group shows, including the Museum of Modern Art (MoMA), New York City (1960); Pan American Union, Washington, D.C. (1962); "Art of Latin America since Independence," Yale University, New Haven, Connecticut, and the University of Texas at Austin (1966); and others.

Examples of Clark's work, which moved from geometric construction to the organic, are in private and public permanent collections, including the MoMA, New York City, and others.

Bibliography
Arte Brasileira Contemporanea. *Lygia Clark*. Rio de Janeiro: Edicao
    FUNARTE, 1980.
The Latin American Spirit: Art and Artists in the United States, 1920–1970.
    Harry N. Abrams, 1988.

Clark, Paraskeva (1898–1986)

Born in St. Petersburg, Russia, and trained there in both pre-revolutionary and post-revolutionary systems, Paraskeva Clark moved to Paris, France, in 1923 before the reactionary Russian movement closed the borders. She lived in obscurity until 1931, when she married a Canadian, Philip Clark, who took her to Toronto, Canada. In 1936 Pegi Nicol MacLeod introduced her to Norman Bethune, the Canadian doctor who would become a national hero two years later in Communist China. Presumably inspired by his socially conscious convictions, Clark participated in the Committee to Aid Spanish Democracy. A few of her works are charged with similar outcries against social injustice. A notable example is "Petroushka" (1937), which is a falsely naive allegory of American police brutality and political graft in the guise of a public puppet show. Curiously, she seems not to have made any comment on similar events in Canada. Other works, such as "Pink Cloud" (1937), are not overt political statements but formal meditations on the landscape, partly influenced by some of the members of the Canadian Group of Painters, with whom she exhibited in the 1930s. The National Gallery of Canada organized a touring exhibition of her work in 1982–1983.

Robert J. Belton

Bibliography
Cameron, V. "The Useful and the Human." *Vanguard* 12 (April 1983): 6–9.
Redgrave, F. "The Divine Grumpiness of Paraskeva Clark." *Artmagazine*
    63:4 (June–August 1983): 58–59.

Clarke, Anne (1944–)

Born in Norfolk, England, the painter Anne Clarke emigrated to Canada in 1968. Clarke studied painting and printmaking at the Slade School of Art, London, England.

Clarke has held solo exhibitions in many venues, including Gallery One, Toronto, Ontario (1980), and has had her work included in group shows, such as "Alberta '73," Edmonton Art Gallery, a travelling show (1974); "Canada x Ten," Edmonton Art Gallery, a travelling show (1974); Espace 5 (1974), and "Prairies," Saidye Bronfman Centre—both in Montréal, Québec. Examples of her work are in private and public permanent collections.

Bibliography
Carpenter, Ken. "Anne Clarke." *Artmagazine* 12:53–54 (May–June
    1981): 32–35.
Changes: 11 Artists Working on the Prairies. A travelling show.
    Saskatchewan: University of Regina, 1975–1976.

Clement, Kathleen (1928–)

Born on the Willow Dell Stock Farm outside of Ord, Nebraska, Kathleen Clement attended the University of Nebraska, Lincoln, where she received a Bachelor of Arts degree in 1950. She took additional courses at Milton College, Wisconsin (1946–1948); studied privately with Frank Gonzales in Mexico (1967–1969); attended the University of the Americas, where she worked under the aegis of Toby Joysmith (1977–1980); enrolled in Museum Studies in Paris, France (1980); and, four years later, studied hand papermaking in Mexico.

Between 1969 and 1991 Clement held twenty-two solo exhibitions of her work in Mexico and the United States, including the Museo de Bellas Artes, Toluca, Mexico (1992), and Casa de la Cultura, Puebla (1980, 1991)—both in Mexico; Margolis Galleries, Vail, Colorado (1985); Walker Gallery, Kearney, Nebraska (1980); and others.

Her work was invited to more than forty group exhibitions in the United States and abroad, including the Museo Nacional de Antropologiá, Mexico City, Mexico (1989, 1990, 1991); Biennial of Humour and Satire, Gabrovo, Bulgaria (1989–1991); Sheldon Memorial Art Gallery, Lincoln, Nebraska (1980); Triennial Latinoamericana del Grabado, Salas Nacionales de Exposicion, Buenos Aires, Argentina (1979); "Arte Contemporaneo de México," Abbia Gallery, Sydney, Australia (1971); and many others.

Examples of Clement's works are housed in the permanent collections of the Isidro Fabela Cultural Center and Institute of North American Cultural Relations, Mexico City, Mexico; the House of Humour and Satire, Gabrovo, Bulgaria; and elsewhere. "Still Life in April" (1989), from the series, "Illuminations," a polymer emulsion painting on canvas, is not atypical of Clement's work: it is multi-layered, mysterious, and moving.

Bibliography
Folch, Mireya. "Influencia de Camboya en la Obra de Kathleen Clement."
    El Sol de México (October 8, 1977).
Taracena, Berta. "Microestructuras." *Tiempo* (May 24, 1982): 54.
Who's Who in American Art. 19th ed. R.R. Bowker Co., 1991–1992.

Clements, Gabrielle De Vaux (1858–1948)

A painter and etcher, Gabrielle De Vaux Clements was known especially for her mural paintings commissioned for public and private buildings. Clements is the daughter of Dr. Richard Clements of Philadelphia and Gabrielle De Vaux of South Carolina, descendant of General Francis "Swamp Fox" Marion, hero of the American Revolution. She earned a Bachelor of Arts degree from Cornell University, Ithaca, New York, in 1880. She studied art at the Philadelphia School of Design for Women, Pennsylvania, in 1875, and from 1880 to 1883 with Thomas Eakins at the Pennsylvania Academy of Fine Arts, Pennsylvania, where she won the Toppan Prize for the best painting by a student. Clements learned to etch from Stephen Parrish in Philadelphia, Pennsylvania, in 1883 and subsequently taught Ellen Day Hale, Margaret Lesley White Bush-Brown, and other women to etch. In 1884–1885 she studied at the Académie Julian in Paris, France, with Tony Robert-Fleury and William A. Bouguereau.

Clements has an extensive exhibition record. The list includes the Pennsylvania Academy of Fine Arts, Philadelphia; the National Academy of Design, New York City; the Philadelphia Society of Artists, Pennsylvania; the New York Etching Club, New York City; the Boston Art Club, Massachusetts; the Association of Canadian Etchers; the Boston Art Students' Association, Massachusetts; the Boston Watercolor Club, Massachusetts; the Chicago Society of Etchers, Illinois; National Arts Club; National Museum of American History; the Library of Congress, Washington, D.C.; the J.B. Speed Museum, Louisville, Kentucky; the Rockport Art Association, Massachusetts; the Folly Cove Etchers; and the North Shore Arts Association. She was included in the Boston Museum of Fine Arts' "Women Etchers of America," Massachusetts, the first museum exhibition of women artists. She also participated in major expositions, including the 1893 World's Columbian Exposition; 1904 Louisiana Purchase Exposition; and Philadelphia's 1926 Sesqui-Centennial International, Pennsylvania.

Her murals included "Harvest" for the Ladies' Reception Room of the Pennsylvania State Building at the Columbian Exposition, those for the New Century Club Building in Philadelphia, and religious subjects for five churches in the Washington, D.C.-Maryland area and for one in Detroit, Michigan. Clements's etchings were published in deluxe portfolios by Prang & Co., Christian Klackner, and J.R.W. Hitchcock. Between 1896 and 1931 she was commissioned by the Bendann Galleries to etch a series of views of Baltimore, Maryland. She taught at Baltimore's Bryn Mawr School, Maryland, for many years.

For twenty years beginning in 1918 Clements and her friend Ellen Day Hale experimented with printing soft-ground etchings and aquatints in color à la poupée based on modern French techniques. As in earlier etchings the influence of Whistler and of Japanese prints was evident. Clements's subjects included landscapes, seascapes, architectural views and a variety of scenes of life observed in her travels in Europe, Algiers, and Palestine. In their Rockport, Massachusetts, studio and in Charleston, South Carolina, where they spent the winters, Clements and Hale taught a new generation of etchers, including Elizabeth O'Neill Verner (1883–1979), Alice Ravenel Huger Smith (1875–1945), and Lesley Jackson.

Clements's etchings are in the National Museum of American Art and the National Museum of American History; Smithsonian Institution, and the Library of Congress—both in Washington, D.C.; the Boston Museum of Fine Arts, Massachusetts; the New York Public Library, New York City; and the National Museum of Women in the Arts.

Phyllis Peet

Bibliography
Artist Files, Graphic Arts Division, National Museum of American History, Smithsonian Institution, Washington, D.C. *Exhibition and Sale of Etchings and Soft-ground Aquatints in Color of French, Italian and American Subjects by Ellen Day Hale and Gabrielle DeV. Clements, . . . January 14, . . . January 26, 1924.* Goodspeed's Bookshop, 1924.
Exhibition of Etchings in Color by Ellen Day Hale, Gabrielle DeVeaux Clements, Lesley Jackson, Margaret Yeaton Hoyt, Theresa F. Bernstein, and William Meyerowitz, November 30 to December 30, 1935. J.B. Speed Memorial Museum, 1935.
"Gabrielle De Vaux Clements, . . . ; Chancel Decorations for the Mission Chapel of St. Paul, Baltimore." *Art Digest* 8:11 (October 15, 1933).
Gabrielle De Vaux Clements Papers, Archives of American Art, Smithsonian Institution, Washington, D.C.
"Gabrielle D. Clements [Obituary]," *The New York Times* (March 28, 1948): 2.
Peet, Phyllis. *American Women of the Etching Revival.* High Museum of Art, 1988.
Prints and Photographs Division, Museum and Library of Maryland History, Baltimore, Maryland.

Climent, Elena (1955–)
Daughter of the Spanish exiled artist Enrique Climent, the painter Elena Climent was born and raised in Mexico City, Mexico. Although she has studied painting in Mexico City, Mexico; Valencia, California; and Barcelona, Spain, she is basically self-taught. In 1973 she won second prize in a drawing competition held by the state government of Aguascalientes in Mexico.

Climent's first exhibition was held at the Helen Lavista Gallery, Mexico City, Mexico (1972). Her work has been the subject of solo exhibitions at the Palacio de Bellas Artes, Mexico City, Mexico (1988); the Mary-Anne Martin/Fine Art gallery, New York City (1992); and the Galería de Arte Mexicano, Mexico City, Mexico (1993). She has also participated in several important group exhibitions including "Women in Mexico," National Academy of Design, New York City (1990); and "Pasado y presente del Centro Histórico," Palacio de Iturbide, Mexico City, Mexico (1993).

While her work prior to 1986 is in a surrealist vein, in her recent paintings Climent depicts the mundane realities of urban life in Mexico City, Mexico. Works such as "Altar in a Car" (1988), "Kitchen Cupboard" (1991), and "Altar of the Dead with Relatives" (1991), are carefully arranged compositions filled with commonplace objects and foods.

A draftsperson, Climent has also executed numerous illustrations for literary magazines, volumes of poetry, and children's books. She currently lives in Mexico City, Mexico, and New York City.

Ilona Katzew

Bibliography
Elena Climent: Flor de asfalto. A Catalog. Mexico City: Palacio de Bellas Artes, 1988.
Elena Climent: In Search of the Present. A Catalog. New York: Mary-Anne Martin/Fine Art, 1992.
Elena Climent: En busca del presente. A Catalog. Mexico City: Galería de Arte Mexicano, 1993.
Herrera, Hayden. "Elena Climent at Mary-Anne Martin/Fine Art." *Art in America* (October 1993): 151.
Sullivan, Edward J. *Women in Mexico.* A Catalog. Centro Cultural Televisa, A.C., 1990.

Coe, Sue (1952–)
Born in Tamworth, Staffordshire, England, the painter Sue Coe studied at the Royal College of Art, London, England (1970–1973).

Coe has had work shown in galleries and museums in the United

States and abroad, including PPOW, New York City, where she held solo exhibitions (1983, 1984, 1985); Virginia Commonwealth University, Richmond (1987); and others. She has exhibited in group shows, such as the Kresge Art Museum, Michigan; and "Committed to Print," Museum of Modern Art (MoMA), New York City (1988); held exhibitions in England and Ireland (1989); "Porkopolis," a show which travelled to Bloomington, Indiana; Portland, Maine; and St. Louis, Missouri (1989–1991); and others. Examples of her work are in private and public permanent collections, including MoMA and the New York Public Library—both in New York City; the National Museum of American Art, Smithsonian Institution, Washington, D.C.; and others.

Bibliography
Coe, Sue. *How to Commit Suicide in South Africa.* Raw Books and Graphics, 1986.
Coe, Sue. *X.* Raw Books and Graphics, 1986.
McGreevy, Linda F. "Policing the State: The Art of Sue Coe." *Art Magazine* 61:6 (February 1987): 18–21.
Scala, Mark. "The Dictates of Conscience: An Interview with Sue Coe." *New Art Examiner* 14 (April 1987): 21–23.

Cohen, Elaine Lustig (1927–)

Born in Jersey City, New Jersey, the painter/designer Elaine Lustig Cohen is also known for her work as a sculptor, printmaker and quilt maker. Cohen studied at Sophie Newcomb College, Tulane University, New Orleans, Louisiana; and at the University of Southern California, Los Angeles, where she earned a Bachelor of Fine Arts degree.

Cohen was a commercial designer (1948–1955); worked as a freelance graphic designer (1955–1967); and held her first of several solo painting exhibitions at the John Bernard Meyers Gallery, New York City (1970). Other shows include the Mary Boone gallery and Galerie Denise Rene—both in New York City; Modernism, San Francisco, and Kanus Gallery, Los Angeles—both in California; Nina Freudenheim Gallery, Buffalo, New York (1981); and others.

Her work has been included in many prestigious group shows, such as "American Painting: The Eighties," Grey Gallery, New York University, New York City (1980); "Eight Painters," Jersey City Museum, New Jersey; and "Geometric Abstraction," Bard College, Annandale-on-Hudson, New York. Examples of her work are in private and public permanent collections.

Bibliography
"Across the Sky." *Art in America* (December 1984): 6. (A reproduction).
"Mrs. Oliver Byrne's Quilt." *New Art Examiner* (February 1986): 63. (A reproduction).
Robinson, Charlotte, ed. *The Artist & The Quilt.* Alfred A. Knopf, 1983.

Cohen, Lynne (1944–)

Born in Racine, Wisconsin, the photographer Lynne Cohen earned a Bachelor's degree from the University of Wisconsin, Madison (1967); attended the Slade School of Art, University of London, England (1964–1965); the Ox-Bow Summer School of Painting, Michigan (1967); and the University of Michigan, Ann Arbor (1968); and received a Master of Arts degree from Eastern Michigan University, Ypsilanti (1969).

Cohen has held many solo exhibitions in the United States and abroad, including A Space, Toronto, Canada (1973); University of New Mexico, Albuquerque (1975); International Center of Photography, New York City (1978); Yarlow/Saltzman Gallery, Toronto, Canada (1979); Light Work, Syracuse, New York (1979); Nova Scotia College of Art and Design, Halifax (1984); Printworks, Chicago, Illinois (1987, 1990); Galerie Samia Saouma, Paris, France (1988); Museum für Gestaltung, Zurich, Switzerland (1989); Sweger Konst, Stockholm, Sweden (1989); York University, Toronto, Canada (1992); PPOW, New York City (1992); FRAC, Limousin, France (1992); Hotel des Arts, Paris, France (1993); and many others.

Her photographs have been invited to group exhibitions throughout the world: from Banff, Alberta, Canada, to Prague, Czechoslovakia; from Albuquerque, New Mexico, to Brussels, Belgium; from Marseille, France, to Seattle, Washington; from Hollywood, California, to London, England.

Cohen has taught at Eastern Michigan University, Ypsilanti; Algonquin College, Ottawa, Canada; School of the Art Institute, Chicago, Illinois; and has been teaching photography since 1974 at the University of Ottawa, Canada. Winner of awards and honors for her work, Cohen was a recipient of the Logan Award, Chicago Art Institute, Illinois (1967); the 11th Ann Arbor Film Festival, Michigan (1973); and grants from the Canada Council (1975, 1978–1979, 1983, 1985–1986, 1988–1989, 1991).

Her work is represented in private, public, and corporate permanent collections, including the Metropolitan Museum of Art, New York City; Art Bank, Canada; Australian National Gallery, Canberra; Bibliothèque Nationale, Paris, France; Center for Creative Photography, Tucson, Arizona; National Gallery of Canada, Ottawa; Musée de Nîmes, France; Museum voor Fotografie, Antwerp, Belgium; Prudential Insurance Co., New York City; and many others.

Bibliography
Loke, Margarett. "Review." *Art News* (May 1992).
Lost and Found/L'Endroit du Decor. A Catalog. F.R.A.C., Limousin and Hotel des Arts, Paris, 1992.
No Laughing Matter. A Catalog. New York: Independent Curators, 1991.
Occupied Territory: Lynne Cohen. A Monograph. Texts by David Byrne, David Mellor, and William Ewing. Aperture, 1988.
Stages Without Wings. A Catalog. Text by Johanne Lamoureux. Toronto: York University, 1992.

Cohen, Sorel (1936–)

Born in Montréal, Canada, Sorel Cohen was a little too young to appreciate the early generation of Québecois modernists and their radical subversion of authority, but their implicitly political stance influenced her indirectly in her studies at Corcordia University, Montréal, where she received a Bachelor of Fine Arts degree with the completion of a thesis entitled "Feminist Art of the Seventies." By that time she had already had her first solo exhibition (Galerie Mira Godard, Montréal, 1977). Since then she has distinguished herself with exhibitions all over Canada, twice in New York City (49th Parallel, 1981, and P.S.1, 1983), and once in Paris, France (1984).

Cohen is an articulate feminist artist, and she has explored very deeply veiled aspects of gender issues in recent modernist art. Her

"Grid #1" (1975) was a soft, stuffed sculpture intended to undermine some of the dogmatic principles of grid-making in the minimalist period. In 1976 she turned to photographic documentation of female domestic rituals—such as making the bed every morning—which had been overlooked by the patriarchal art establishment in its blind rush toward male ritual and primitive shamanism. She is now most well known for her photo-performance series under the general title "An Extended and Continuous Metaphor," begun in 1983. This consists of various strategic revisions of the artist and his [sic] model mythos, with Cohen playing the roles of both protagonists. Many of the works are straightforward feminist interventions of the iconography of the studio, and some are directly patterned after well-known historical works, such as Francisco José de Goya's two "Maja" paintings and the works of painter Francis Bacon and photographer Edweard Muybridge.

Cohen has received numerous Canada Council grants. She was represented in the very influential "Songs of Experience" exhibition of contemporary art mounted by the National Gallery of Canada in 1986. She continues to live and work in Montréal, Quebec.

Robert J. Belton

Bibliography
An Extended and Continuous Metaphor. Lethbridge: Southern Alberta Art
  Gallery (January 7–29, 1984).
Bradley, Jessica, and Diana Nemiroff. *Songs of Experience.* Ottawa:
  National Gallery of Canada, 1986.
Sorel Cohen . . . et les ateliers de femmes (ou se jouent les regards) Musée
  d'art contemporain de Montréal (September 24–November 2, 1986).

Coles, Ann Cadwallader (1882–1969)
Born in Columbia, South Carolina, the painter Ann Cadwallader Coles studied with several painters and printmakers, including F.L. Mora, Harry Sternberg, Vincent Tack, and C.A. Whipple.

Coles exhibited her work in museums and galleries, including the Art Institute of Chicago, Illinois; the Art League, Columbia, South Carolina; the Southern States Art League; the Women's Club, Charlotte, North Carolina; and others.

Examples of her work are in private and public permanent collections, such as the Columbia Museum, South Carolina; Confederate Museum, Richmond, Virginia; Parish House, Charlotte, North Carolina; Yale University, New Haven, Connecticut; and others.

Bibliography
Chambers, Bruce. *Art and Artists of the South: The Robert P. Coggins
  Collection.* University of South Carolina Press, 1984.
Parris, Nina G. *South Carolina Collection 1779–1985.* Columbia
  Museum, 1985.

Collings, Betty (1934–)
Born in Wanganui, New Zealand, the sculptor/writer/museum professional Betty Collings has been a resident of the United States since 1962. After receiving a professional diploma from Teachers College, Wellington, and extra credit from Victoria University, Wellington, New Zealand, Collings earned a Bachelor of Fine Arts degree *cum laude* (1970) from Ohio State University, Columbus, and a Master of Fine

Arts degree in 1974. In 1980 Collings attended the Museums Management Institute, Berkeley, California.

Collings has held fifteen solo exhibitions in university museums and other sites, including the Gallery Vistavka of the Ukraine Union of Artists, Kiev, Ukraine (1992); Bertha Urdang (1979, 1980, 1983, 1989–1990); the City University of New York (CUNY) (1983)—both in New York City; Antioch College, Yellow Springs, Ohio (1982); Ohio Wesleyan University, Delaware (1977); Purdue University, West Lafayette, Indiana (1975); and others. Her work has been invited to more than thirty group exhibitions in the United States and abroad: from Lancaster, Ohio, to Sydney, Australia; from Lisbon, Portugal, to Israel, and Islip, New York.

Winner of seven awards for sculpture, Collings was a recipient of artist fellowships in sculpture and criticism from the Ohio Arts Council (1981–1982, 1983–1984) and the Columbus Art League distinguished service award for contributions to the visual arts (1980). Her huge, inflated vinyl sculptures, painted with acrylics, provide intellectual/mathematical/aesthetic delight in visual studies of the helix.

Collings is active in many associations and organizations; former Director of Ohio State University Gallery of Fine Art, freelance writer for *Dialogue* and *Arts Magazine*; curator of thought-provoking exhibitions; panelist; founding president of The Artists' Organization (TAO); as well as coordinator of an exchange of art and artists between Ohio and Shaanxi Province, People's Republic of China (1989–1990) and another exchange between four artists of Ukraine and four artists from the United States (1992–1993). Her sculpture is represented in private and public permanent collections.

Bibliography
Burnside, Madeline. "Betty Collings." *Arts Magazine* (September 1979): 19.
Constable, Lesley. "Exhibition Pushes New Boundaries." *Columbus
  Dispatch* (April 1, 1990): 10F.
Smith, Roberta. "Could It Be the '70s Again. Artist Looks Back." *The
  New York Times* (December 22, 1989).
Who's Who in American Art. 19th ed. R.R. Bowker Co., 1991–1992.

Collyer, Nora (1898–1979)
Member of the Beaver Hall Group, the painter Nora Collyer was born in Montréal, Canada. She studied her craft at the Art Association of Montréal with William Brymner, Maurice Cullen, and Alberta Cleland; Collyer shared a studio on Beaver Hall Hill with her good friend, Anne Savage, one of her classmates at the art school.

Solo exhibitions of Collyer's work were held at the Dominion Gallery, Montréal (1946); Klinkhoff Gallery, Montréal (1964); a travelling retrospective show organized by the National Gallery of Canada, Ottawa (1969); and others. Her works were invited to group exhibitions in Canada and abroad, including the Annual Spring Exhibitions of the Art Association of Montréal (1919–1937); the Canadian Group of Painters; the New York World's Fair (1939); British Empire Exposition, Wembley, England (1924–1925); and others.

A teacher of art at a private school for girls, Trafalgar School, Montréal (1925–1930), Collyer also taught at the Art Association of Montréal, Québec. Her work is represented in private and public permanent collections.

Bibliography

Gwyn, Sandra. *Women in the Arts in Canada*. Ottawa: Royal Commission on the Status of Women, 1971.

McCullough, Nora. *The Beaver Hall Group*. Ottawa: National Gallery of Canada, 1966.

Millar, Joyce. "The Beaver Hall Group: Painting in Montréal 1920–1940." *Woman's Art Journal* 13:1 (Spring–Summer 1992): 3–9.

Colton, Mary-Russell Ferrell (1889–1971)

Mary-Russell Ferrell Colton is known today for her paintings in oil and in watercolor of the Southwest—both its landscapes and its Native Americans. She has preserved in her paintings many images of the Hopis and the Navajos, some in the form of portraiture and others as genre, showing the Native Americans working at their crafts.

Colton was born in Louisville, Kentucky, and began her artistic career in Philadelphia, Pennyslvania, where she studied at Moore Institute and at the Philadelphia School of Design for Women from 1904 to 1909 under Elliott Daingerfield and Henry Snell. Upon graduation she and a friend opened their own studio and supported themselves with the restoration of paintings and commercial art projects. Perhaps more significantly for the history of women artists, Colton was a founding member of "The Ten," a group of ten women artists, all professionally trained in Philadelphia. From 1910 to 1941 The Ten sustained an active exhibition schedule in Philadelphia, which expanded to touring up and down the Eastern seaboard, out to the Middle West, and even occasionally to Europe.

In 1912 she married Harold S. Colton and they spent their honeymoon on the Colorado Plateau of Arizona, hiking in the San Francisco peaks. Fourteen years later they settled in Flagstaff, Arizona, and a few years later returned to Hart Prairie, so Colton could record in a memorable painting "Aspens on the San Francisco Peaks" (1930, Museum of Northern Arizona, Flagstaff). The Coltons were cofounders of the Museum of Northern Arizona. Colton worked at first as curator and initiated exhibitions of Indian art, while continuing to pursue her own work as a painter of Southwestern subjects. Her husband served as director of the museum for more than four decades. Distance made it difficult for Colton to send large oil paintings to the exhibitions of "The Ten," so in 1934, for example, she was represented by simply a portfolio of watercolors and prints.

Eleanor Tufts

Bibliography

Chase, Katherin L. *Brushstrokes on the Plateau*. Museum of Northern Arizona, Flagstaff, 1984.

Tufts, Eleanor. *American Woman Artists, 1830–1930*. National Museum of Women in the Arts, 1987.

Condit, Cecilia (1947–)

Born in Philadelphia, Pennsylvania, the video artist Cecilia Condit attended the Pennsylvania Academy of Fine Arts (1967–1969); earned a Bachelor of Fine Arts degree from the Philadelphia College of Art (now the University of the Arts) in 1971; and received a Master of Fine Arts degree from the Tyler School of Art, Temple University (1978)—all in her native city.

Condit's specialization in still photography moved naturally to video when her narratives needed more space and time in which to redefine and reinterpret themes and variations thereof of the role of woman in society. She has held solo exhibitions and screenings in museums and galleries, including Michigan State University, East Lansing, and the Woodmere Museum of Art, Philadelphia (1981); the Carnegie Institute of Technology, Pittsburgh, Pennsylvania (1985); and others.

Winner of honors and awards, Condit received grants from the Ohio Arts Council (1981, 1983, 1984); fellowships from the National Endowment for the Arts (NEA) (1983, 1985); a first place video award at the Atlanta Film and Video Festival, Georgia (1984); and others. Examples of Condit's work are in public and private permanent collections, including the Museum of Modern Art (MoMA), New York City; Oberlin College, Ohio; the New York Public Library, New York City; and others.

Bibliography

Husler, Kathleen. "Love Stories." *American Film* 11 (November 1985): 63–65.

Sturken, Marita. "Difference: On Representation and Sexuality." *Afterimage* 12 (April 1985): 10.

White, Mimi. "Resimulation, Video Art, and Narrative." *Wide Angle* (Fall 1985).

Cone, Claribel (1947–)

Daughter of classical musicians, the painter/writer/musician Claribel Cone was born in New York City. She studied at the Anthology Archives, New York City, with Ken Jacobs; learned her craft from Leland Bell and Mercedes Matter at the New York Studio School; worked with Kendall Shaw at the Brooklyn Museum School, New York City; studied the cello with Lesli Parnas; and was helped and inspired by Richard Diebenkorn.

Cone has held solo exhibitions in museums and galleries in the United States, including the MK Vance Gallery, Chicago, Illinois (1993); Bentley Tomlinson Gallery, Scottsdale, Arizona (1992); the Capital of the State of Arizona, Phoenix (1991); Wade Gallery, Los Angeles, California (1987, 1988, 1990); Morehead Gallery, North Carolina (1986); Leland Stanford Museum, Palo Alto, California (1985); Udinotti Gallery, Scottsdale, Arizona (1981); Clarke Benton Gallery, Santa Fe, New Mexico (1976); Brooklyn Museum, New York City (1974); and others. Her work has been invited to many group exhibitions throughout the United States: from New York City to La Jolla, California; from Brooklyn, New York, to Santa Fe, New Mexico, in museums, galleries, and art centers—sometimes on behalf of programs concerned with drug abuse, AIDS, and other matters.

Cone's works, including her clutch of books, are represented in private and public permanent collections, including the Museum of Modern Art (MoMA), New York City; Walker Art Center, Minneapolis, Minnesota; National Museum of Women in the Arts, Washington, D.C.; San Francisco Museum of Art, Los Angeles County Museum of Art, and J. Paul Getty Museum, Malibu—all in California; Arizona State University, Tempe; and the libraries of distinguished universities throughout the United States.

"The Figure Resting on Radio Waves" (1986), "Mandolin Seeding Red" (1990), and her ten pastels for Robert Tzudiker's recent book,

Unnatural History (1992) all reveal joyous, inventive, witty compositions in which rich and vibrant color forms play point/counter-point with delicate/powerful linear elements.

Bibliography

Beaudin, Victoria. "Artistic Heritage: She Got a Message From Paris." *Scottsdale Daily Progress* (July 29, 1983): 22.

Lenke, Hal. "Versatile Artist Speaks Her Mind." *Scottsdale Daily Progress* (February 19, 1982): 16.

Loniak, Walter. "New—and Not-So-New—Directions." *The Santa Fe Reporter* (November 23, 1978): 11.

Connell, Clyde (1901–)

A sculptor whose work often evoked the mystery and night sounds of Louisiana's bayous, Clyde Connell did not begin making her haunting constructions until she was in her sixties. Her art gained public attention when she was in her seventies, and she worked actively through her eighties.

Born Minnie Clyde Dixon on September 19, 1901, on a cotton plantation near Belcher, Louisiana, she attended Brenau College in Gainesville, Georgia, where she took painting courses, and Vanderbilt University in Nashville, Tennessee, between 1918 and 1920. In the 1920s she married T.D. Connell and began raising the couple's three children. She continued to study painting in the mid-1920s in Shreveport, Louisiana. She also was a volunteer at a Presbyterian church school for African-American children. It was there that she began inventing a "swamp orchestra" of sounds—night herons, cicadas, frogs, and winds—for the children.

In 1949 Connell moved with her husband to the minimum-security Caddo Parish Penal Farm, where he became superintendent. She studied during this time at the Louisiana State Museum in Shreveport, doing figural work, including woodblock prints of prisoners. After many years of church activism and civil rights work she began in 1954 travelling twice a year to New York City as a church delegate. There she discovered abstract expressionism, a turning point in her artistic development. She soon started experimenting with collages of painted-and-torn paper glued on canvas and helped form the Contemporary Art Group in Shreveport, Louisiana.

When Connell's husband lost his prison post in 1959 the couple moved to a cabin on Lake Bistineau, Louisiana, an area of dense trees with Spanish moss and vines. Her collages became layered and heavier, with wooden rather than canvas bases, and with found objects attached. By 1963 she said, "the urge to surround the house with sculpture became so strong that I began to experiment in three dimensions." She began making totems or earth figures over six feet tall and giving them *papier-maché* "skin," which she related "to dirt dobber, wasp and moth nests." Then she developed constructions of cedar, cypress, and twisting rattan vines, with the joints tied together and bound with the molded paper pulp "skin." By the late 1970s she created her habitat series—pieces with the aspect of timeless artifacts that include hollowed-out spaces serving as ritual altars, hiding places, or havens for contemplation. Connell also made "Swamp Songs," large wall hangings on bark and pulpy papers with "automatic" notations that she said were responses to "the movement and sounds of the bayou." In the 1980s she focused on more geometric sculptures and smaller-scale works on paper.

Works by Frederick Kiesler, Adolph Gottlieb, and Eva Hesse influenced her development, and she said Judy Chicago's comments on her sculpture in the late 1970s had an impact on it. Connell's first solo exhibition was held in 1973, when she was seventy-two, at Louisiana State University at Alexandria, where her oldest son taught. Her first exhibition in New York City was at the Clocktower in 1981. In 1990 she was given a show at the Galerie Vallois in Paris, France. Her work is in the Alexandria Museum, and the Louisiana State University Library—both in Alexandria, Louisiana; the Laguna Gloria Museum of Art, Austin, Texas; Jay R. Broussard Memorial Gallery in the Old State Capitol, Baton Rouge, Louisiana; and in corporate and private collections. In 1984 she was honored by the National Women's Caucus for Art.

Cynthia Mills

Bibliography

Detroit, Michigan. Smithsonian Institution. Archives of American Art. Clyde Connell Papers (microfilm rolls 2837, 2838).

Moser, Charlotte. "Review of Exhibition. Houston: Clyde Connell at Lawndale Annex, University of Houston." *Art in America* 68 (February 1980): 136–37.

———. *Clyde Connell.* University of Texas Press, Austin, 1988.

Randolph, Lynn M. "Clyde Connell." *Woman's Art Journal* 6 (Fall 1985–Winter 1986): 30–34.

Sims, Lowery Stokes. "Clyde Connell: Speaking the South." *Artforum* 29 (September 1990): 148–51.

Watson-Jones, Virginia. *Contemporary American Women Sculptors.* Oryx Press, 1986, pp. 108–09.

Connor, Linda (1944–)

A photographer who has concentrated since the early 1970s on landscape, particularly sacred landscape, Linda Connor has chosen to use the techniques of an earlier era, which seem to reinforce the timeless quality of her photographs. In 1972 she began using her great-aunt Ethelyn McKinney's Century view camera with its soft semi-achromatic lens, and since that time an eight-by-ten-inch view camera and contact printing on slow printing-out-paper have been her chosen photographic method. Connor's time-consuming process seems to fit her subjects, as her interest is not in the fleeting moment but in connection across time. Influential in the resurgence of a feminist landscape sensibility in the 1970s and 1980s, Connor has been articulate in her emphasis on the intimate relationship to an earth felt to be an organic whole, not territory to be conquered.

With McKinney's camera Connor produced a group of photographs later published in the collection *Solos* (Apeiron, 1979). In this work—which ranged from commonplace backyard scenes to the exotic sacred sites of foreign cultures, all given a mystical aura through the soft-focus lens—she established a symbolic emphasis in her work. Subsequently, using a sharp-focus lens, she has sought out and photographed people along with their mystical and sacred sites all over the world. Particularly interested in Asian spirituality, she has done much work in India and Nepal. Egypt, Peru, Hawaii, the megalithic sites of old Europe, and the petroglyphs of the American Southwest have also drawn her attention. Something of a spiritual tourist, Connor informs herself but does not claim to be a scholar of the cultures she visits. Nevertheless she feels the sacred place can speak to her across cultures and across time, and her photographs embody a kind of universal iconic power.

Critic Rebecca Solnit gives credit for this power to "a compositional strategy that centers the subject as though to enshrine it, but does so without the rigidity, the perfect symmetry, and flattening frontality of the wholly formal. The subject is given something of the icon's concentrated power without being severed from its surroundings." Her early set-up still lifes of the late 1960s often incorporated a photograph as an iconic presence within a natural environmental scene. Others involved natural objects such as shells laid over old pictures. Family history—both her adoptive family and her recently found biological family—has been a continuous theme as well.

Trained in photography at the Rhode Island School of Design, Providence, where she earned a Bachelor of Fine Arts degree (1967) and at the Institute of Design in Chicago, Illinois, where she received her Master of Science degree (1969), Connor names Harry Callahan and Aaron Siskind, her teachers, as well as Walker Evans, Eugene Atget, and Frederick Sommer as influences.

Since moving to northern California in 1969 Connor has taught, primarily at the San Francisco Art Institute, California, and given numerous workshops throughout the country. Widely exhibited and published, she has received numerous professional honors, including a National Endowment for the Arts (NEA) fellowship (1976), a Guggenheim Foundation fellowship (1979), and an AT&T Photography Project grant (1978). In 1986 she was honored with a peer award from the Friends of Photography, Carmel, California, as "Photographer of the Year." Connor's work is in many public collections, including the California Museum of Photography, University of California, Riverside; the Museum of Fine Arts, Boston, Massachusetts; the Art Institute of Chicago, Illinois; the Museum of Modern Art (MoMA), New York City; the Center for Creative Photography, University of Arizona, Tucson; the Hallmark Photographic Collection, Kansas City; the International Museum of Photography, George Eastman House, Rochester; the San Francisco Museum of Modern Art, California; and the Corcoran Gallery of Art, Washington, D.C.

Gretchen Garner

Bibliography

Aperture #93 (Esalen Arts Symposium 1982 issue), 1983, pp. 48–52.

Asbury, Dana. "Linda Connor: Solos and Landscapes." *Afterimage* 7:5 (December 1979): 1, 5–6.

Cahn, Robert, and Robert Glenn. *American Photographers and the National Parks*. National Park Foundation and Viking Press, 1981.

Connor, Linda. "Gesture of Faith." In *Marks in Place*. University of New Mexico Press, 1988.

———. *Spiral Journey: Photographs 1967–1990*. Introduction by Denise Miller-Clark, essay by Rebecca Solnit. Museum of Contemporary Photography at Columbia College, 1990.

Danese, Renato. *American Images: New York by Twenty Contemporary Photographers*. McGraw-Hill, 1979, pp. 50–59.

Enyeart, James. *Decade by Decade: Twentieth-Century American Photography*. Center for Creative Photography, University of Arizona, and Bullfinch Press, Little, Brown and Co., 1989.

Garner, Gretchen. *Reclaiming Paradise: American Women Photograph the Land*. Tweed Museum of Art, University of Minnesota, 1987, pp. 56–57.

Jussim, Estelle, and Eliz Lindquist-Cock. *Landscape as Photograph*. Yale University Press, 1985.

Lifson, Ben. "Linda Connor at Light." *Art in America* 66:5 (September–October 1978): 125–26.

Cook, Lia (1942–)

Known for her many innovative explorations of the woven surface, Lia Cook was born on November 25, 1942, in Ventura, California. She was raised in the San Francisco Bay area and attended the University of California, Berkeley. Although she took art classes during this period she received her Bachelor of Arts degree in political science. Continuing her interest in art, she spent 1967 studying weaving in Sweden and looking at art in Europe. In 1969 she began to exhibit professionally in the Designer Craftsman Annual at the Richmond Art Center, California. She returned to the University of California at Berkeley, and received a Master of Arts degree in art in 1973. Cook cites professor Ed Rossbach's belief in her as a creative being, and his ability to inspire yet create an atmosphere of freedom and independence, as a lifelong influence.

Cook first received international attention in 1973, when she participated in the 6th International Biennial of Tapestry in Lausanne, Switzerland, where she exhibited a ten-by-twelve-foot, optic, black-and-white work titled "Space Continuum." In 1978 she had a solo exhibit at the Allrich Gallery in San Francisco, California, which marked the transition of her work from the large optic pieces and photo-silkscreen series into complexly-woven and pressed rayon works which are the forerunners of her current direction. These works mark the beginning of her signature process. Cook uses intricate pattern weaves to create a textured surface of industrial rayon. This is then altered by shrinking, pressing, stiffening, dyeing, and painting. Variations of this unique process have evolved into many related series of work. Cook chooses to work with the woven cloth because it evokes powerful memories of protection, warmth, security, and sensuality. In the various series of work she explores the curtain and our relation to fabric in many forms and contexts.

Cook received National Endowment for the Arts (NEA) fellowships (1974, 1977, 1986), and a NEA special projects grant (1981), which allowed her to study Jacquard weaving in Europe and led to her explorations on computerized looms. At her 1987 solo exhibition at the Allrich Gallery, San Francisco, California, Cook introduced the Crazy Quilt series, inspired by her great-grandmother's crazy quilt. Her current series exhibited at the National Academy of Science, Washington, D.C. (1990) is concerned with the painted image of draped cloth.

Cook has participated in the International Biennial of Tapestry (1975, 1977, 1989), as well as her initial participation in 1973. She has had solo exhibitions at the Renwick Gallery, Washington, D.C., and the Galerie Nationale de la Tapisserie et d'Art Textile, Beauvais, France, among others. Her work won the excellence award at the International Textile Competition '89 in Kyoto, Japan, and is included in the "Eloquent Object," a travelling exhibition that originated at the Philbrook Art Center in Tulsa, Oklahoma (1987).

Cook's work is in numerous public collections, including the Metropolitan Museum of Art, the Museum of Modern Art (MoMA), and the American Craft Museum—all in New York City; and the Galerie Nationale de la Tapisserie et d'Art Textile, Beauvais, France.

Cook played an active role at Fiberworks Center for the Textile Arts both as an instructor (1975) and as a member of the advisory committee (1977–1979). She has held the position of professor of art at the California College of Arts and Crafts, Oakland, from 1976 to the present.

Claire Campbell Park

Bibliography
Alexander, Judy. "Lia Cook: Exploring the Territory Where Painting and Textile Meet." *Fiberarts* (September–October 1982).
Constantine, Mildred, and Jack Lenor Larsen. *The Art Fabric Mainstream.* Van Nostrand Reinhold, 1981.
Janiero, Jan. "Lia Cook: On the Loom of Contradiction." *American Craft* (June–July 1980).
University Art Museum, University of Wisconsin, Milwaukee. *Fiber R/Evolution.* 1986.
Scarborough, Jessica. "Lia Cook: A New Approach to Weaving Images. *Fiberarts* (March–April 1990).

Cooke, Judy (1940–)

Born in Bay City, Michigan, the painter/collagist/printmaker Judy Cooke received a diploma with honors in printmaking from the Boston Museum School of Fine Arts, Massachusetts (1963); earned a Bachelor of Fine Arts degree from Tufts University, Medford, Massachusetts (1965); and a Master of Arts degree in teaching from Reed College, Portland, Oregon.

Cooke has held solo exhibitions in galleries and universities in the Northwest, including Portland State University, Oregon (1973); Foster/White Gallery, Seattle, Washington (1978); Blackfish Gallery, Portland, Oregon (1979, 1982–1983); Traver Sutton Gallery, Seattle, Washington (1985, 1989); "Recent Monotypes," Elizabeth Leach Gallery, Portland, Oregon (1991); Mount Hood Community College, Gresham, Oregon (1992); and others.

Her work has been invited to group exhibitions, such as "14 Women Survivors," University of Washington, Seattle (1972); "Aesthetics of Graffiti," San Francisco Museum of Modern Art, California (1978); Cheney Cowles Memorial Museum, Spokane, Washington (1980); Lane Community College, Eugene, Oregon (1982); "Expo '86," Oregon Pavilion, Vancouver, British Columbia (1986); "De Warande," a travelling show through France and Japan, Ministry of Culture, Turnhout, Belgium (1988); Esther Saks Gallery, Chicago, Illinois (1990); "Unabandoned Abstraction," Marylhurst College, Oregon (1991); and many others.

Winner of awards and honors, Cooke received a National Endowment for the Arts (NEA) fellowship (1989); was artist-in-residence at the University of Nevada, Las Vegas (1985); received a fellowship in painting from the Boston Museum School of Fine Arts, Massachusetts (1974); and won cash and purchase awards from the Seattle Art Museum, Washington (1974); Portland Art Museum, Oregon (1973); University of Oregon, Eugene (1971); and many others.

Her work is represented in private, public, and corporate permanent collections, including the Portland Art Museum, Oregon; Hewlett-Packard, Portland, Oregon; Boston Museum School of Fine Arts, Massachusetts; Bank of America, San Francisco; collections of the cities of Seattle, Washington and Portland—all in Oregon; and many others.

Bibliography
Hopkins, Terri. A Catalog. *Unabandoned Abstraction.* Marylhurst College, 1991.
Lippard, Lucy R. "Northwest Passage." *Art in America* (July–August 1976).
Who's Who in American Art. 19th ed. R.R. Bowker Co., 1991–1992.

Coombs, E. Grace (1890–)

Born in Hamilton, Ontario, Canada, the painter E. Grace Coombs earned a diploma from the Ontario College of Art, Toronto, Canada (1918), and did further work at the New York School of Fine and Applied Arts, New York City (1929).

Coombs held solo exhibitions at many galleries in Toronto, including Eaton's, Laing Galleries, Maloney Galleries, and Mellors Galleries. She also showed at the Robertson Galleries, Hamilton. Her work was included in many prestigious group shows, such as the Willingdon Exhibition, Ottawa, Canada. Using thematic material from Native American legends, Coombs painted several murals, two of which are in the North American Indian section of the National Museum of Canada.

Coombs has been a teacher of art at the Ontario College of Art for many years, as well as a painter who was associated with Canada's well-known Group of Seven. Examples of her work are in private and public permanent collections, including the Hamilton Art Gallery; Queen's University, Kingston, Ontario; Sarnia Public Library; and others.

Bibliography
Pierce, Lorne. *E. Grace Coombs.* Ryerson Press, 1949.

Cordero, Helen (1915–)

Born in Cochiti Pueblo, New Mexico, in 1915, Helen Cordero is a self-taught ceramist, who is best known for her "Little People" (small clay representations of seated human figures, eyes closed, mouths open, telling stories, singing, each painted in black and terra cotta on whiteware, no two of them alike).

In the late 1950s, after attempts at pottery and leathercraft frustrated her, Cordero began to model birds and animals in clay. These first essays in modeling led inevitably to the human figure and, in 1964, she found her "style," and sent some work off to the New Mexico State Fair, which presented her with first, second, and third prizes for her clay figures. She was a consistent winner at the fair for the next seven years.

In 1968 and 1969 Cordero won first prize at the Heard Museum Guild's Annual Indian Arts and Crafts Exhibition in Phoenix, Arizona; the following year, at the same museum, she won best of show for her "Nativity Scene." Four years later her "Storyteller" was selected to be shown at the World Craft Council Exhibit, "In Praise of Hands," in Toronto, Canada. Cordero's first solo show took place in 1973 at a Scottsdale, Arizona, art gallery: it was sold out before the doors officially opened.

Cordero has taught ceramics at a local school, at Kent State University, Ohio (1972), and at Pecos Monument, New Mexico (1974).

Married to painter/former two-term governor of Cochiti Pueblo, and noted drum-maker Fred Cordero, Helen Cordero can communicate fluently in the three languages of the region in which she lives: English, Keresan, and Spanish. Her themes derive from the history and culture of her Rio Grande pueblo, filtered through time and the circumstance of daily life, touched with humor and a rich creative sensitivity.

Bibliography
Monthan, Guy, and Doris Monthan. Art and Indian Individualists. *The Art of Seventeen Contemporary Southwestern Artists and Craftsmen.* Northland Press, 1975.

Corkidi, Matusha
Born in Egypt, the sculptor Matusha Corkidi, a nationalized Mexican citizen, studied her craft at the Academia de San Carlos, Mexico. She is a professor of sculpture, as well as a photographer, painter, published writer and poet.

Corkidi has held solo exhibitions and her work has been included in many group shows. Examples of her creative output are in private and public permanent collections, including the Palacio de Bellas Artes, and the Hotel Presidente, Chapultepec—both in Mexico.

Bibliography
Mujeres Mexicanas: Quien es Quien. Mexico: Editorial Antena S.A., 1980–1981.

Corpron, Carlotta M. (1901–1988)
Trained first as a designer and later as a photographer, Carlotta M. Corpron describes herself as a designer with light. Born in Blue Earth, Minnesota, on December 9, 1901, she attended British boarding schools in India where her missionary-surgeon father served. In 1920 she returned to the United States to complete her education, receiving a Bachelor of Science degree in 1925 from what is now Eastern Michigan University, Ypsilanti, and a Master of Arts degree from Teachers College, Columbia University, New York City, in 1926. After several academic appointments in the South and in the Midwest she was appointed in 1935 to be an instructor in design, art history, and creative photography at Texas Women's University, Denton, Texas. She remained there until her retirement in 1968.

In 1933 she began to use black-and-white photography as an instructional aid at the University of Cincinnati, Ohio, where she taught textile design. After she arrived at Texas Women's University, Denton, she was asked to teach photography and so spent the summer of 1936 at the Art Center in Los Angeles, California.

Her earliest photographs, titled "Nature Studies," demonstrate the abstraction inherent in the natural world. From there she moved to the creation of "Light Drawings" from 1940 to 1943. In these images light was both the creator and subject. The photographs themselves often looked like drawings made with a "light" pen. These ranged from "Church in Havana," where the camera is still and the subject discernible, to images such as "Commentary on Civilization," where the camera has been moved during exposure to record the subject as a delicate tracing of light.

Until 1942 Corpron worked in near isolation. That year Moholy Nagy taught for a term at Texas Women's University, Denton, and Corpron conducted a light workshop under his supervision. Together they taught students how to explore the shapes and solidity of materials by making photograms, as had been practiced in photography

courses at the Bauhaus. In 1944 Gyorgy Kepes, then Moholy Nagy's associate at the Institute of Design in Chicago, Illinois, arrived at North Texas State University to work on his book, *Language of Vision*. Kepes became Corpron's mentor and told her about the light box, a tool which served as a surround for constructed still lifes and which admitted light in controlled amounts. This discovery led to experiments with groups of work she titled "Light Patterns" and "Light Follows Form." These works often made reference to other art forms and occasionally resembled cut paper collages or photographs of sculptural forms in space. At this time venetian blinds figured prominently in Corpron's work as well, functioning both to modulate light and to give it repetitive form.

In 1945, Corpron met with Alfred Stieglitz at his New York Gallery, An American Place. He was impressed by her original vision of the world and interested in offering her an exhibition. Unfortunately, Stieglitz died in 1946, and Corpron didn't receive her first solo exhibition until 1948 at the Dallas Museum of Fine Arts, Texas.

Her fifth group of work, which she pursued after her return to Texas in 1946, was a series of "Space Compositions," photographs made using nautilus shells, eggs, paperweights, and a curved ferrotype plate to reflect light. The images are original explorations of the changes familiar forms may undergo as a result of changing light and space. These images were followed by her last group of experiments, "Fluid Light Designs," which sought to capture the abstract patterns of light as reflective surfaces. Along with her photograph of eggs made during her "Space Composition" series, Corpron considers this last work to be her best.

In 1953 she had a second major solo exhibition at the Art Institute of Chicago, Illinois. Failing health forced her to curtail her photography in the 1950s. However, she continued to reprint her work, and in 1980 the Amon Carter Museum, Fort Worth, and Texas Women's University, Denton, exhibited her work in conjunction with a major monograph titled *Carlotta Corpron: Designer with Light*.

Diana Emery Hulick

Bibliography
Amon Carter Museum, *Carlotta Corpron: Designer with Light*. Text by Martha A. Sandweiss. University of Texas Press, 1980.
Mann, Margery, and Ann Noggle, eds. *Women of Photography: An Historical Survey*. San Francisco Museum of Art, 1975.
Mitchell, Margaretta K. *Recollections: Ten Women of Photography*. New York: International Center for Photography, 1979.

Cosindas, Marie (1925–)
Born in Boston, Massachusetts, the photographer Marie Cosindas developed her craft through study at various institutions, including the Modern School of Fashion Design and the Boston Museum School—both in her native city, and participated in workshops with noted photographers, including Ansel Adams (1961) and Minor White (1961, 1964).

A free-lance photographer since 1960, Cosindas has held solo exhibitions in museums and galleries in the United States and abroad, including Harvard University, Cambridge, Massachusetts (1963); "Polaroid Color Photographs," Museum of Modern Art (MoMA), New York City (1966), and the Art Institute of Chicago, Illinois (1967); Bi-National Cultural Institute, Mexico City, and Monterrey—both in

Mexico (1969); Kunstlerhaus, Vienna, Austria (1977); and many others. Her work has been included in prestigious group exhibitions throughout Canada and the United States—from California to New York to Cologne, Germany.

Winner of honors and awards, Cosindas received, among others, an honorary Doctor of Fine Arts degree from the Moore College of Art, Philadelphia, Pennsylvania; a Guggenheim fellowship; an artist-in-television award from WGBH, Boston; and an award from the National Academy of Television Arts and Sciences.

Examples of her work are in private and public permanent collections, including the Addison Gallery of American Art, Andover, Massachusetts; Art Institute of Chicago, Illinois; International Museum of Photography, George Eastman House, Rochester, New York; Metropolitan Museum of Art and MoMA—both in New York City; National Gallery of Canada, Ottawa; and others.

Bibliography
Browne, Turner, and Elaine Partnow. *Macmillan Biographical Encyclopedia of Photographic Artists and Innovators.* Macmillan, 1983.
Marie Cosindas, Color Photographs. Essay by Tom Wolfe. New York Graphic Society, 1978.
Szarkowski, John. *Mirrors and Windows, American Photographs Since 1960.* New York: Museum of Modern Art, 1966.

Costa, Olga (1913–)

Although Olga Costa was born in Leipzig, Germany, she has said that her "passion for Mexico" inspired her to paint. Her parents, Jacob and Ana Kostakovsky, were both from Odessa, Russia. Her father was a violinist and symphonic music composer. World War I led the family to move to Berlin the year after Costa's birth. In 1925 the family, including Costa's sister Lia, emigrated to Mexico. Costa attended the Colegio Alemán (German School), where she studied piano and voice until 1929.

Meeting artists such as Diego Rivera, Frida Kahlo, and Rufino Tamayo motivated her to abandon her musical studies and enroll at the San Carlos Academy of Art, Mexico City, in 1933. Given the need for her to help her family's economic situation, her studies with the painter and muralist Carlos Mérida lasted only four months.

In 1935 Costa married painter/muralist José Chávez Morado, whom she had met during her brief period as a student at San Carlos. The couple lived in Jalapa, Veracruz, from 1936 to 1937, and while Chávez worked on a mural, Costa again began to paint. Her first works, which were influenced by Rufino Tamayo and the Mexican muralists, especially Diego Rivera, included portraits, still lifes, and landscapes. Chávez Morado's establishment of an art school took the couple to San Miguel de Allende in 1940. In addition to painting Costa took part in other projects. She was one of the founders of the Galería Espiral in Mexico City, which was open from 1941 to 1943. She designed sets and wardrobe for the Waldeen Ballet in 1942. The following year, she took part in the founding of the Sociedad de Arte Moderno, Mexico City, which was one of the first galleries to organize exhibitions of foreign artists, including Pablo Picasso, who had his first Mexican exhibition there in 1944. Costa's own first solo exhibition was at Ines Amor's Galería de Arte Mexicano, Mexico City, in 1945.

Color, light, and atmosphere are important protagonists in Costa's work. Her themes reflect her love for Mexico, its landscape and culture. Her still lifes and portraits, such as "Recuerdo de Silao" (1954) and "Niño muerto" (1944), depict native Mexican fruits, flowers, and popular art objects such as masks, and "Dia de los Muertos" (Day of the Dead) skulls. Her work has been shown in both group and solo exhibitions from the 1940s onward. She continued to participate in organizations for the promotion of art in Mexico, such as the Sociedad para el Impulso de las Artes Plásticas, Mexico City, of which she became a member in 1948. The following year, she was one of the founders of the Salón de Artes Plásticas, Mexico City.

One of her most well-known paintings, "La Vendedora de Frutas" (The Fruit Vendor, 1951) was commissioned for the National Institute of Fine Arts. This painting depicts the abundance of nature and suggests the physical and emotional strength of women. During the late 1950s Costa focused on unpopulated landscapes reflecting her distaste for the growing urbanization of Mexico. Her work of the late 1950s and early 1960s became more abstract and geometric. However, she continued to paint pictures such as "Ofrenda" (1691), whose theme is taken from Mexican folk art and described in tones of particularly intense color. Mexico's countryside and architecture also figure prominently in her art.

In addition to painting, Costa worked on a mosaic (1952) for the Agua Hedionda Spa in Cuautitlán, Morelos. Costa has travelled extensively. The influence of a trip to Japan (1964) can be seen in a series of mixed-media works, done on Japanese paper.

The couple moved to Guanajuato (Chávez's birthplace) in 1966. Both artists are promoters of museums in Guanajuato, donating their collection of pre-Hispanic, colonial, and popular art to the Museo de la Alhóndiga de Granaditas in 1975. They founded the Museo del Pueblo de Guanajuato in 1979 and donated their collection of eighteenth-, nineteenth-, and twentieth-century painting to it. Costa travelled in 1985 to Albuquerque, New Mexico, where she was invited to participate in the Mexico Nine lithography workshop at the Tamarind Institute of New Mexico. She continues to paint, and her work has been shown in museums and galleries in many countries.

Miriam Basilio

Bibliography
Billeter, Erika. *Images of Mexico.* Dallas Museum of Art, 1987.
Olga Costa Exposición Homenage. Guanajuato and Mexico City, 1989.
Debroise, Oliver. *De la naturaleza del tropico (los dibujos de Olga Costa).* Mexico, 1985.
Pitol, Sergio. *Olga Costa.* Gobierno del Estado de Guanajuato, Mexico, 1984.
Sullivan, Edward J. *Women in Mexico/La Mujer en México.* Centro Cultural/Arte Contemporáneo, Mexico City, 1990.

Couch, Clara (1921–)

Born in Decatur, Georgia, the ceramist/sculptor Clara Couch earned a Bachelor's degree from Agnes Scott College, Decatur, Georgia (1943), and also studied at Sacred Heart, Belmont, North Carolina. Couch has held many solo exhibitions in galleries and art centers, including the Reedy Riverworks, Greenville, South Carolina, and Chastain Gallery, Atlanta, Georgia (1982); Jerald Melberg Gallery, Charlotte, North Carolina (1985, 1986); Southeastern Center for Contemporary Art, Winston-Salem, North Carolina (1988); and others. Her work has been invited to group exhibitions from Athens, Georgia, to Rome, and Cortona, Italy, to Davidson, North Carolina; and many others.

Couch's work is represented in private and public permanent collections. "Cyclical Time—Artemis II" (1985), a delicate yet strong terracotta, an O'Keeffe-like vessel, reveals a mysterious eroticism that challenges the viewer to reconsider long-held beliefs about life, love, and the unknown.

Bibliography
Nine from North Carolina: An Exhibition of Women Artists. A Catalog for a Travelling Show. North Carolina State Committee and the National Museum of Women in the Arts, Washington, D.C., 1989. University of North Carolina at Chapel Hill Archives.

Coulombe, Carmen (1946–)

Primarily known for small-scale prints and drawings, Carmen Coulombe was born in Courcelles, Québec, and studied art at the École des Beaux-Arts de Québec until 1971. Attending Laval University, she became a certified teacher a year later.

She has preferred to exhibit mostly in Montréal, Québec, and the small surrounding communities. Canadians elsewhere know her best for her participation in a group show of feminist art in Montréal in the early 1980s, where she exhibited drawings of nude women blindfolded and tightly bound.

Robert J. Belton

Bibliography
Art et Féminisme. Montréal: Musée d'art Contemporain. (March 11–May 2, 1982).

Coulter Clark, Mary Jenks (1880–1966)

Mary Jenks Coulter Clark was a nationally known art activist whose accomplishments cover many fields; she was a painter, etcher, lithographer, potter, weaver, textile designer, jeweler, bookbinder, lecturer, administrator, curator, and writer. Born in Newport, Kentucky, her mother is identified as Mrs. Courtland Baker.

Coulter Clark studied at the Cincinnati Art Academy, Ohio, with Frank Duveneck, Vincent Nowottny, and Lewis Henry Meakin; at the University of Chicago, Illinois, and in Florence, Italy. She worked at Cincinnati's renowned Rookwood Pottery and served as the first curator of etchings and engravings at the Cincinnati Art Museum, Ohio. Coulter Clark moved to San Francisco, California, and was on the staff of the Department of Fine Arts of the 1915 Panama-Pacific International Exposition and chaired the arts and crafts Jury. While she maintained a studio in Honolulu in 1916 to 1918, Coulter Clark studied painting with Lionel Walden and produced over-mantel decorations for ships owned by the Matson Navigation Company. In 1972 she produced her "California Hawaii Series" of etchings for that company. In 1918 she went to Provincetown, Massachusetts, studied painting with Charles Hawthorne, and produced her "Cape Cod" series of etchings. Returning to California Coulter Clark moved from San Francisco to San Diego to serve as assistant director of the Fine Art Gallery of San Diego in the mid-1920s. Later she lived in Santa Barbara. In 1959 she married Orton Loring Clark and moved to Amherst, Massachusetts.

Coulter Clark began to exhibit frequently in 1905, winning a silver medal at the Lewis and Clark Exposition in Portland, Oregon. She exhibited at the Art Institute of Chicago, Illinois; the Cincinnati Art Museum, Ohio; the Philadelphia Print Club, Pennsylvania; the Uffizzi Gallery, Florence, Italy; the Bibliothèque Nationale, Paris, France; and the Victoria and Albert Museum, London, England. Coulter Clark had solo exhibitions at the California Palace of the Legion of Honor and the M.H. de Young Memorial Museum, San Francisco; the Los Angeles Museum of Art; the Print Rooms, Inc., San Francisco; and the Albert Roullier Art Galleries, Chicago. She won the Atlan Prize for porcelain in 1909 at the Art Institute of Chicago, Illinois; two bronze medals—one for ceramics and one for jewelry—and an honorable mention for weaving at the 1915 Panama-Pacific International Exposition in San Francisco, California, and honorable mention for landscape at the Los Angeles Museum Exposition of 1936.

She was a member of the American Federation of Arts, the Chicago Society of Etchers, the California Printmakers, the Provincetown Art Association, San Francisco Art Association, the National Association of Women Painters and Sculptors, San Francisco Society of Women Artists, the Japan Society of America, and the California Society of Etchers.

Coulter Clark's work was collected by the Cincinnati Art Museum, Ohio; the Art Institute of Chicago, Illinois; the Museum of Fine Arts, Boston, Massachusetts; the Metropolitan Museum of Art, New York City; the British Museum; the Chalcographie du Louvre, Paris; the University of California at San Diego; the Cooke Gallery, Honolulu; the Library of Congress; the National Gallery of Art; the New York Public Library; the Huntington Library; and the Herron Institute, Indianapolis.

Phyllis Peet

Bibliography
Albert Roullier Art Galleries. *Catalogue of an Exhibition of Original Etchings and Dry Points by Mary J. Coulter*. Foreword by Wilma Frances Minor. Chicago: Albert Roullier Art Galleries, 1927.
"Art Career of Mary J. Coulter." *San Francisco Chronical* (January 29, 1939): 4:1.
M.H. de Young Memorial Museum and California Palace of the Legion of Honor. *Paintings, Drawings, Prints, Textiles by Mary J. Coulter*. Fine Arts Museums of San Francisco, 1931.
"Mary J. Coulter." *American Magazine of Art* (April 1920): 196–98. Mary J. Coulter Papers. Archives, Cincinnati Art Museum.

Courtice, Rody Kenny (Hammond) (1895–1973)

Painter and graphic artist Rody Kenny (Hammond) Courtice was born in Renfrew, Ontario, Canada. Courtice studied at the Ontario College of Art in Toronto, under the instruction of Group of Seven members Arthur Lismer and A.Y. Jackson, among others. She graduated from that school in 1925. Later studies included a season at the Art Institute of Chicago, Illinois (1927), where, in addition to figure work, she studied puppets and stagecraft at the Institute's theater, and a session at Hans Hofmann's summer school in Provincetown, Massachusetts (1950). Teaching was an important facet of Courtice's own career; during the late 1920s and 1930s she worked as an assistant to Arthur Lismer for children's classes at the Art Gallery of Toronto, in addition to teaching various summer school courses and instructing children in the use of discarded materials for art.

Courtice's own work reflects an interest in exploring various media and techniques: her earliest paintings are oils, but during the 1940s egg tempera became her favorite medium. She also worked in watercolor, casein, and collage, while her graphic work includes etching, aquatint, scratchboard, and drypoint prints. "The White Calf" (c. 1941) was reproduced as a silk-screen print for distribution in schools and other public venues during the 1940s and 1950s, as part of a program organized by A.Y. Jackson and the National Gallery of Canada to promote Canadian art.

Courtice was an active exhibitor and member in many Canadian artists' societies throughout her career, including the Canadian Group of Painters, the Ontario Society of Artists, the Canadian Society of Painters in Watercolour, and the Canadian Society of Graphic Art. Her work was shown internationally at such exhibitions as "A Century of Canadian Art," Tate Gallery, London, England (1938), and the New York World's Fair (1939); "Pintura Canadense Contemporanea," Rio de Janeiro, Brazil (1944); and "Canadian Women Artists," Riverside Museum, New York City (1947). She is best known, perhaps, for her many animal studies and treatments of rural life, and for the humor and whimsy of such works as "Just Cows" (c. 1939) and "The Silly Ass" (c. 1937).

Janine A. Butler

Bibliography
Cameron, Janice, Frances Ferdinands, Sharon Snitman, et al. *Eclectic Eve*. Toronto: Ontario College of Art, n.d.
"Who's Who in Ontario Art, Part 18." *The Ontario Library Review* (August 1952).

Cowan, Aileen H. (1926–)

Born in Windsor, Ontario, Canada, the sculptor/painter Aileen H. Cowan earned a Bachelor's degree from the University of Toronto, Canada, and did further graduate work there as well as at Queen's University, Kingston, Ontario.

Cowan has held solo and group exhibitions in Canada and abroad, including a show in Greece (1972); the Art Gallery of Hamilton, Ontario (1973); Queen's University, Kingston (1974); Merton Gallery (1979), and the McDowell Gallery (1980)—both in Toronto; Sculptors Society of Canada, Robson Square Media Centre, Vancouver, British Columbia (1980); and many others.

Cowan has won several awards and honors, such as the Augusta Kopmanis Memorial award (1980). Her non-representational paintings and sculpture are represented in private and public permanent collections, including the McLaughlin Art Centre, Oshawa, Ontario; the University of Western Ontario, London; and others.

Bibliography
"What Is It Like to Be a Woman in Art?" *Art Magazine* 5:15 (Fall 1973): 11–12.
Who's Who in American Art. 15th ed. R.R. Bowker Co., 1982.

Cowley, Reta Madeline (1910–)

Born in Moose Jaw, Saskatchewan, Canada, the painter/printmaker Reta Madeline Cowley studied at the Murray Point Summer School of Art workshops, Emma Lake, Saskatchewan (1937–1940, 1963, 1981– 1985); at the Banff School of Fine Arts, Alberta, where she studied with A.Y. Jackson (1931–1944), among others; at the University of Saskatchewan, Saskatoon, where she earned a Bachelor's degree and worked with Eli Bornstein and Nikola Bjelajak (1966)—both of whom greatly influenced her work.

Cowley has held many solo exhibitions across Canada, including the Mendel Art Gallery, Saskatoon (1969); the Edmonton Art Gallery, Alberta (1976); Gallery One, Toronto, Ontario (1983); "Reta Cowley: A Survey," a travelling exhibition (1986); and others. Her work has been included in prestigious group shows throughout North America, including the National Gallery of Canada, Ottawa (1964, 1966, 1971); and many galleries from British Columbia to Montréal and New York City.

Cowley has received awards and honors for her paintings and prints. Her works are represented in private, public, and corporate permanent collections, including the Art Gallery of Hamilton, Ontario; Canada Council Art Bank, Ottawa; Glenbow Museum, Alberta; Mendel Art Gallery, Saskatoon; Winnipeg Art Gallery, Manitoba; Shell Oil Corporation, Calgary, Alberta; and many others.

Bibliography
Burnett, David, and Marilyn Schiff. *Contemporary Canadian Art*. Hurtig Publishers, 1983.
Greenberg, Clement. "Clement Greenberg's View of Art on the Prairies." *Canadian Art* 22:2 (March–April 1968): 103.
Millard, Peter. "Reta Cowley." *Arts West* 3:3 (May–June 1978): 4–7.

Craig, Kate (1947–)

A Canadian video artist, Kate Craig is associated with the Western Front, one of Canada's oldest artist-run centers, of which she was a founding member in 1973. In the early 1970s she was involved with mail art activities and performance work. "Spots Before Your Eyes" was a piece made in collaboration with Eric Metcalfe, in which she and Metcalfe played Lady and Dr. Brute searching for "leopard reality" and involving mailings from fellow "correspondence artists" worldwide. A number of exhibitions, performance, and media pieces, such as those published in *FILE*, an artists' magazine, resulted from the project. Craig was also involved in Image Bank, an image exchange network. This early period of Craig's work is best understood within the context of artists' efforts to not only question the status of the work of art in the tradition of Marcel Duchamp, but also to redefine and possibly merge art and life. The Western Front—with Craig at its heart—continues to operate with an idea of "l'art vivant," influenced in this by the late French artist Robert Filiou.

Craig initiated and continues to direct the video program at the Western Front; since 1976 she has produced hundreds of videotapes with artists while they were in residence at the Front. Her own video art is characterized by its simplicity of production, using a camera with good sound and little post-production intervention. Her works are intimate, personal, and laconic, both in their making and their statement. One of her best-known video pieces is *Delicate Issue* (1979, 12 min.), where in extreme close-up the artist explores her own body, while her voiceover asks questions like "What is the dividing line between the private and the public?" Here she examines such issues from a feminist perspective, as well as questioning the nature of representation by

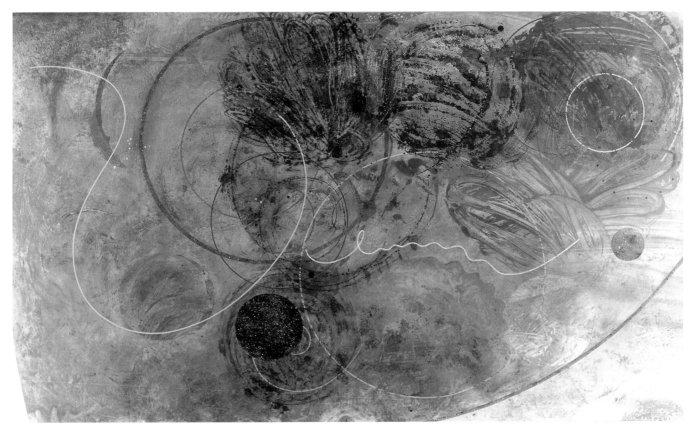

Pat Adams. Interstitial. *1987. Oil, isobutyl methocrylate (mica and shell) on linen.*
80 × 131¹/₂ inches. Courtesy the artist.

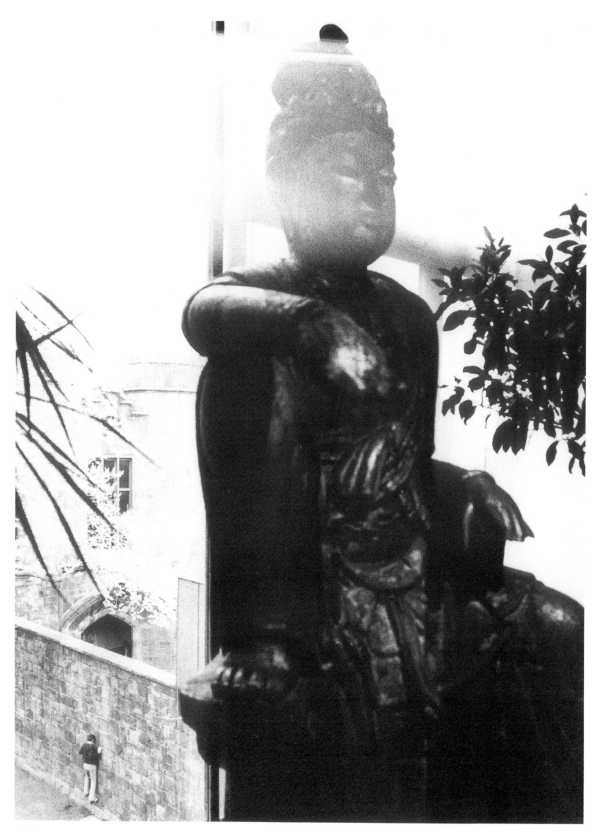

Cecile Abish. Chinese Crossing. 1985. Gelatin silver photograph. 11 × 14 inches.
Courtesy the artist.

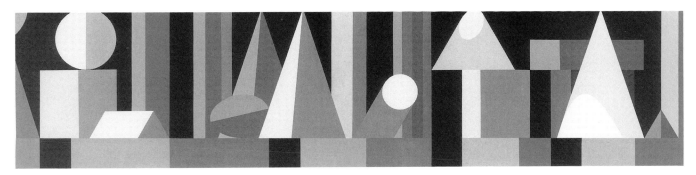

Edna Andrade. Blue Cylinder. *1989. Acrylic on canvas. 18 × 76 inches.*
Greitzer and Locks Collection.

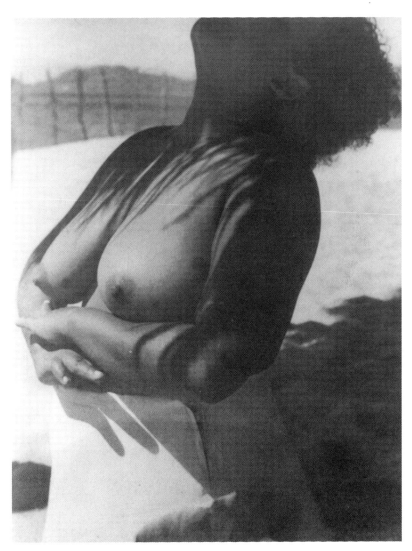

Lola Alvarez Bravo. Triptico de los martirios 3, *n.d. Silver gelatin photograph.*
Archivo CENIDIAP-INBA.

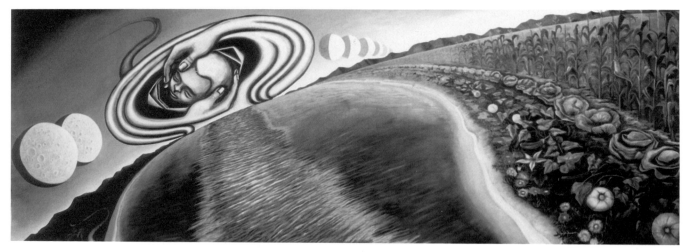

Judith Francisca Baca. Balance, *a panel of the* World Wall: A Vision of the Future Without Fear. *1989. Acrylic on canvas. 120 × 360 inches. Courtesy Social and Public Arts Resource Center (SPARC).*

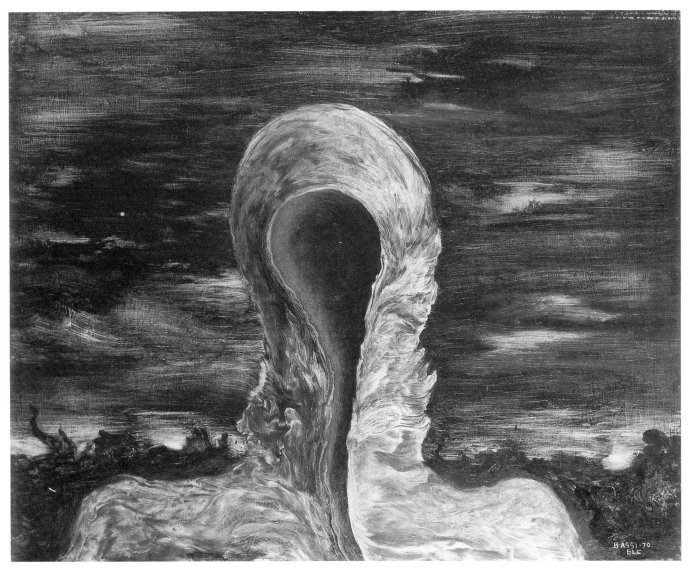

Sofia Bassi. Te Estoy Viendo. *1970. Oil on masonite. 0.59 × 0.49 m. Courtesy the artist.*

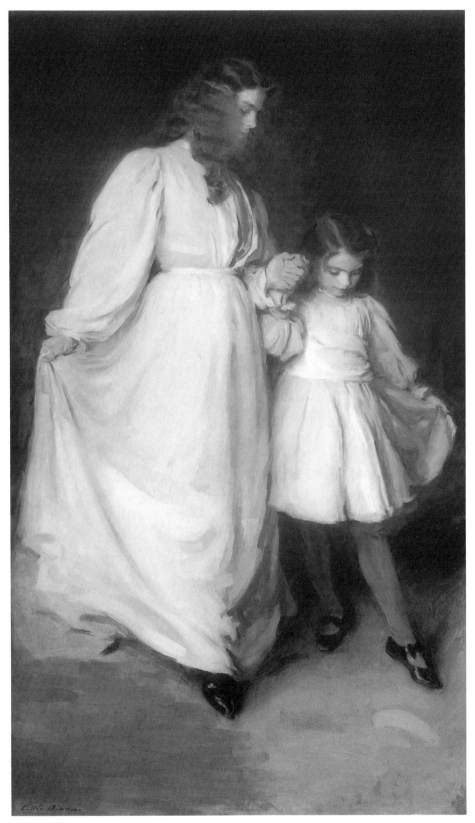

Cecilia Beaux. Dorothea and Francesca. *1898. Oil on canvas. 80¹/₈ ×46 inches.*
The Art Institute of Chicago. A.A. Munger Collection.

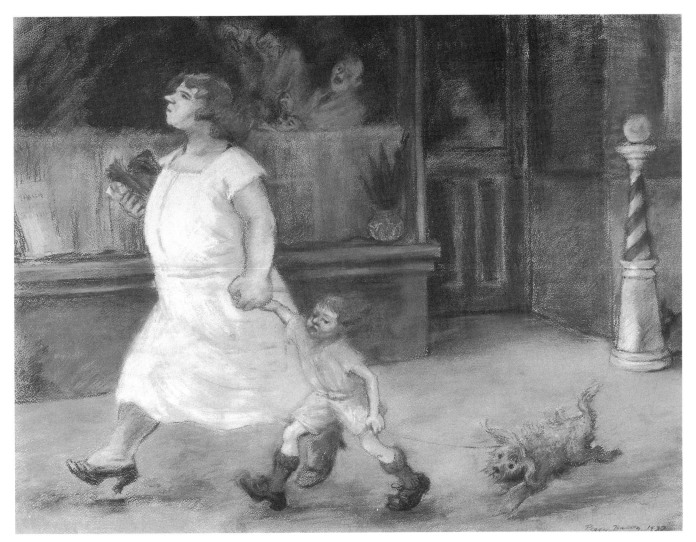

Peggy Bacon. The Untilled Field. 1937. Pastel on paper. 19¹/₈ × 25¹/₄ inches.
Collection of Whitney Museum of American Art. Gift of Mr. and Mrs. Albert Hackett.

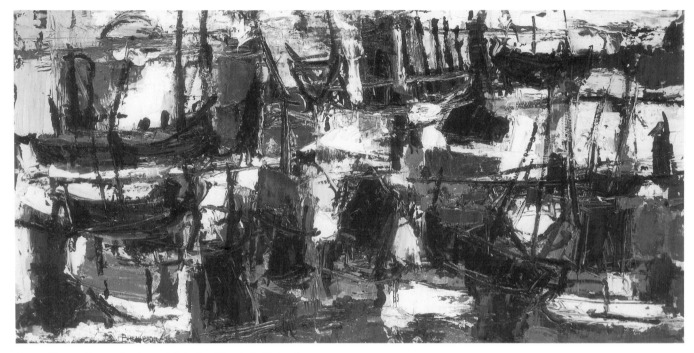

Susanne Bergeron. Barques dans le port de Saint-Jean (Boats in the Harbor of Saint-Jean). *1958. Oil on canvas. 60.0 × 120.2 cm. National Gallery of Canada.*

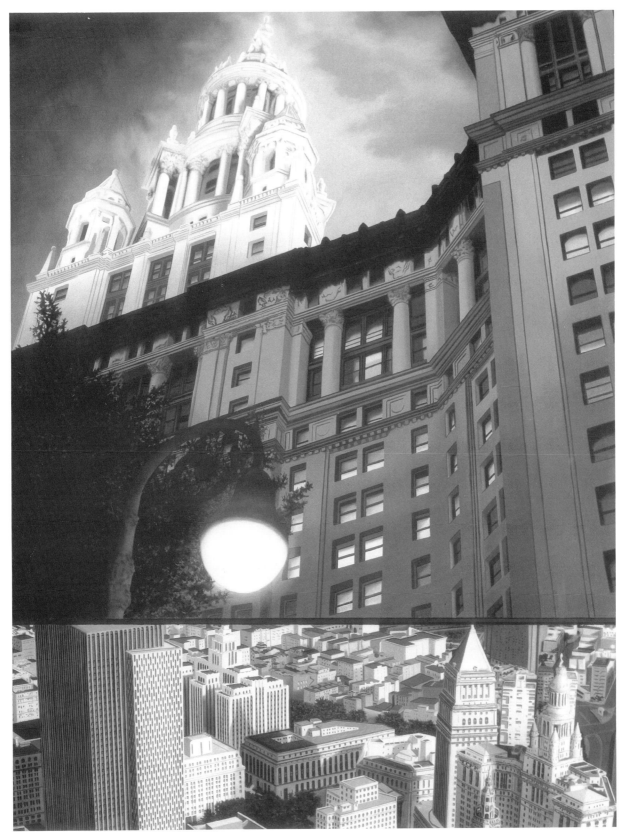

Leigh Behnke. Civic Fame. *1990. Oil on canvas. 48 × 36 inches. Courtesy the artist.*

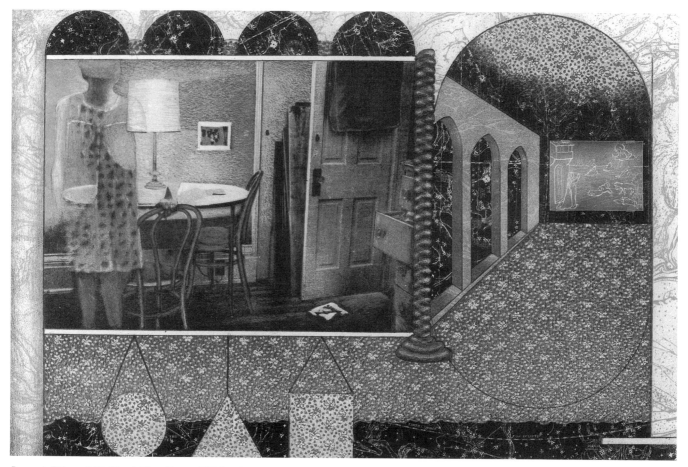

Rosemarie T. Bernardi. She Lives in Three Houses. *1985. Intaglio with photo.*
24 × 36 inches. Courtesy the artist.

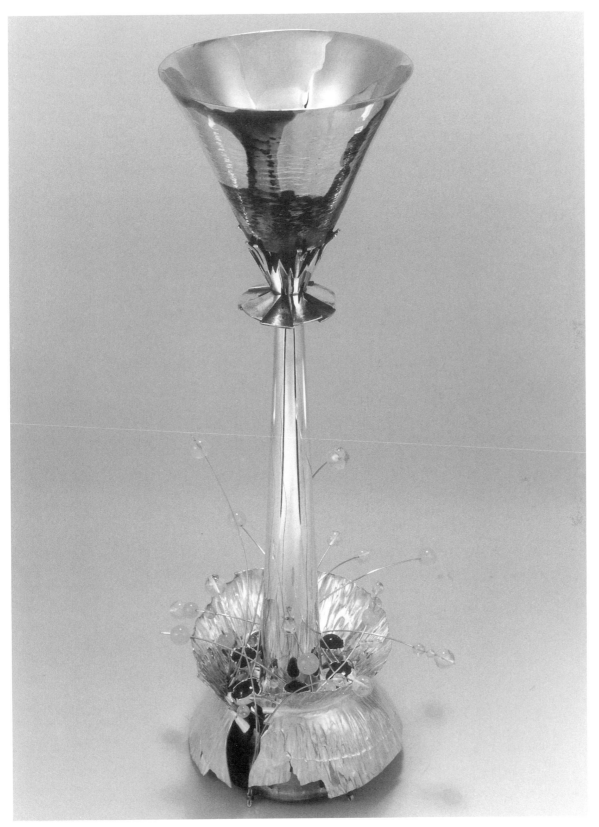

Louis Etherington Betteridge. **Jewish Wedding Cup.** *1993. Silver, moonstone, and lapis lazuli. 12 inches high. Courtesy the artist.*

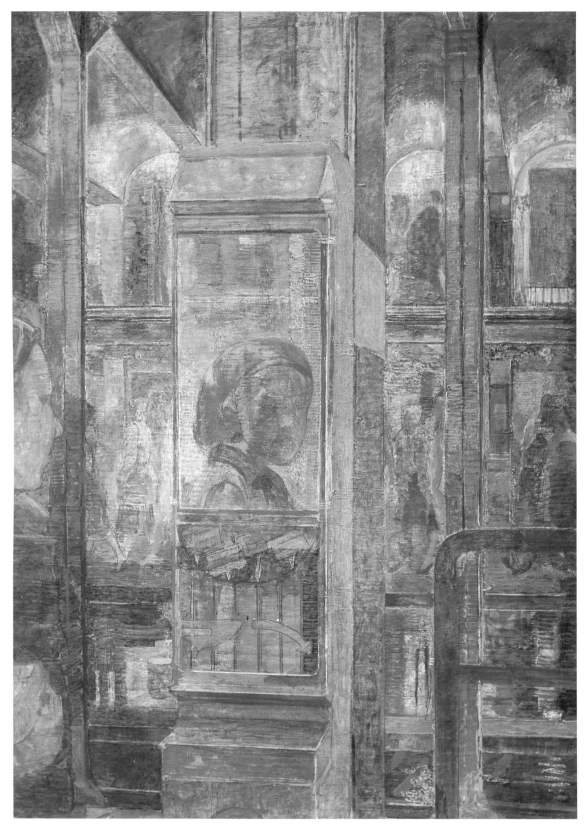

Isabel Bishop. Subway Scene. 1957–1958. Egg tempera and oil on composition board.
40 × 28 inches. Collection of Whitney Museum of American Art.

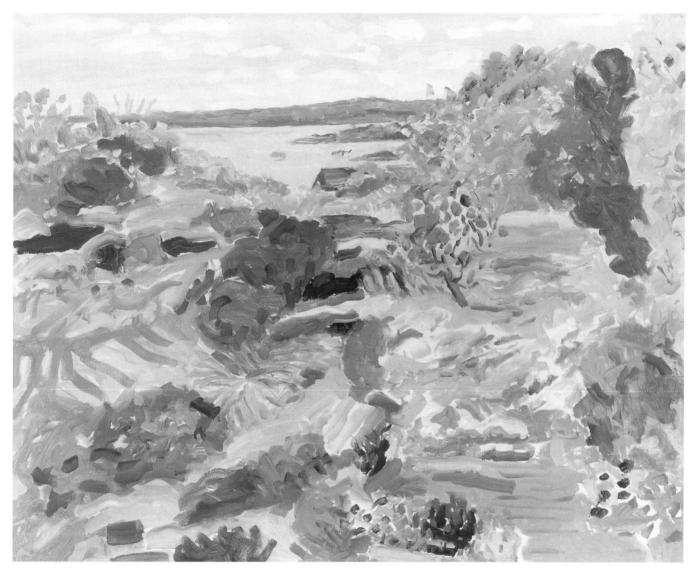

Nell Blaine. Gardens Near Harbor. *1992. Oil on canvas. 28 × 34 inches.*
Courtesy Fischbach Gallery, New York.

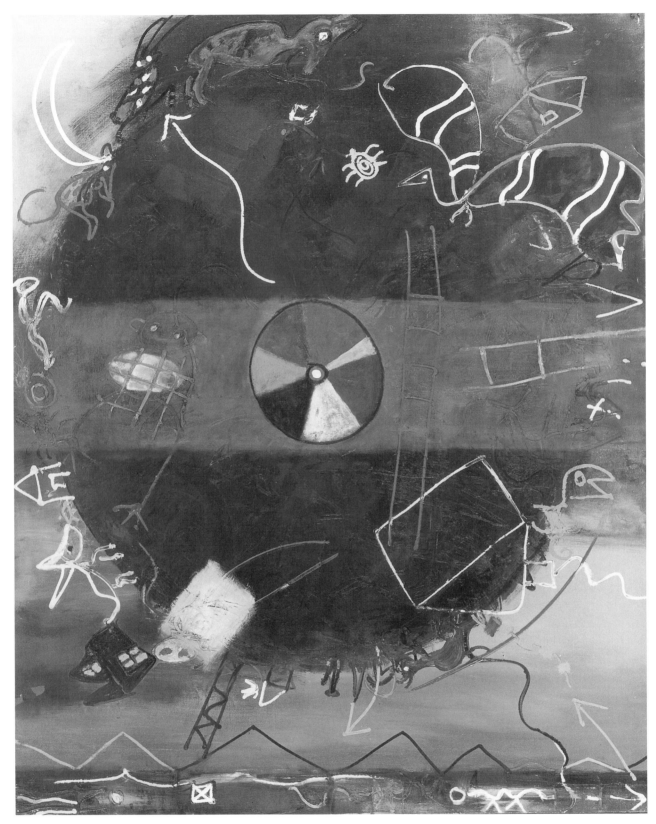

Kittie Bruneau. La terre tourne (The World Turns). *1965. Oil on canvas.*
160.8 × 127.8 cm. National Gallery of Canada.

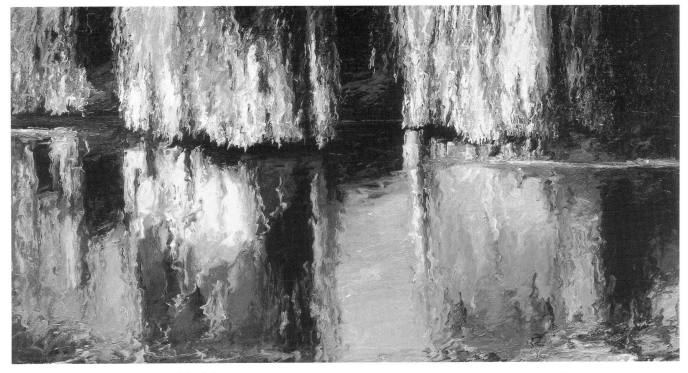

Diane Burko. Saule Pleurer—Giverny. *1989. Oil on Arches paper.*
37 × 68 inches. Courtesy the artist.

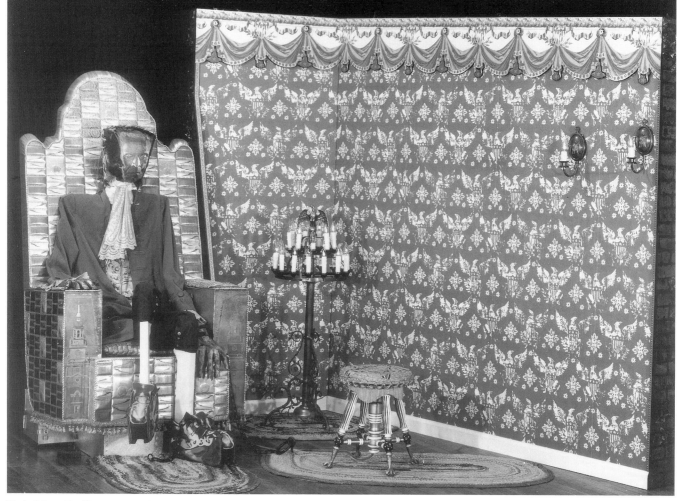

Wendy Calman. Franklinstein. 1982. Photo/mechanical construction.
276 × 168 × 96 inches. Courtesy the artist.

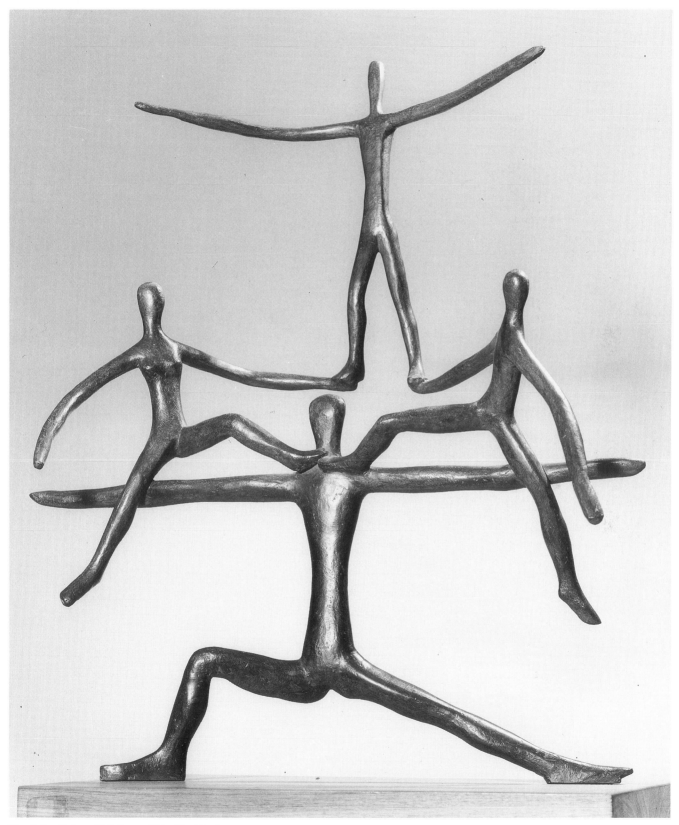

Mary Callery. Perhaps. 1950. Bronze. 27½ × 22 × 14 inches.
Courtesy Arizona State University Art Museum, Tempe. Gift of Oliver B. James.

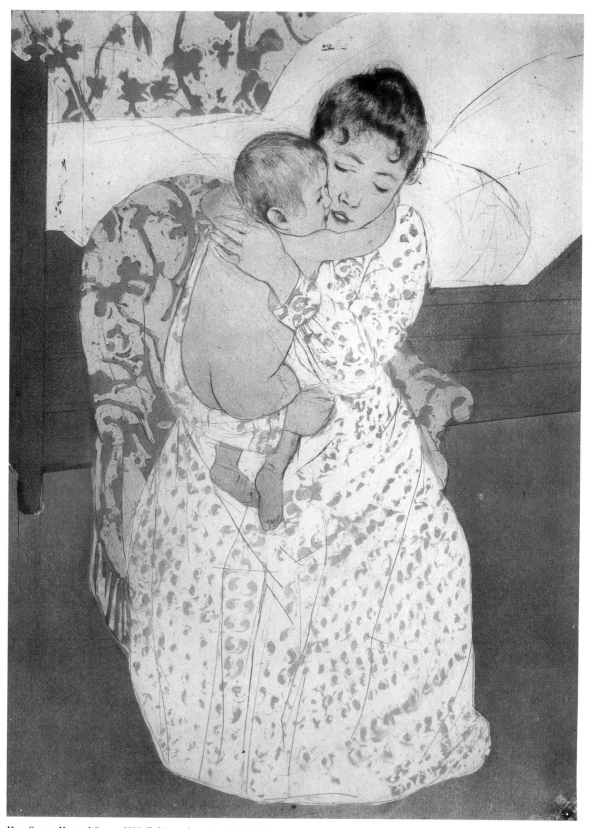

Mary Cassatt. Maternal Caress. *1891. Etching and aquatint. 36.8 × 26.8 cm.*
The Art Institute of Chicago. Mr. and Mrs. Martin A. Ryerson Collection.

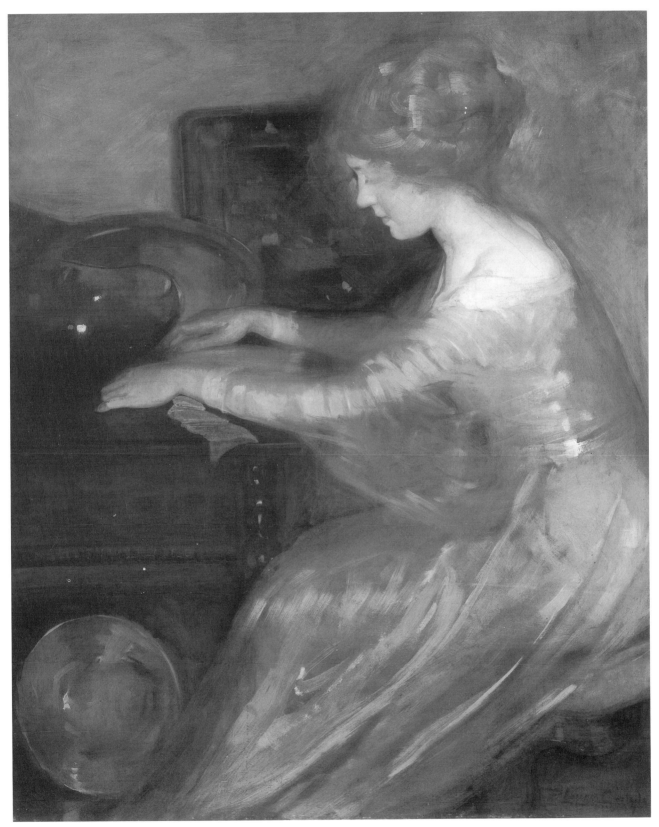

Florence Carlyle. Grey and Gold. *1910. Oil on canvas. 101.8 × 81.0 cm.*
National Gallery of Canada.

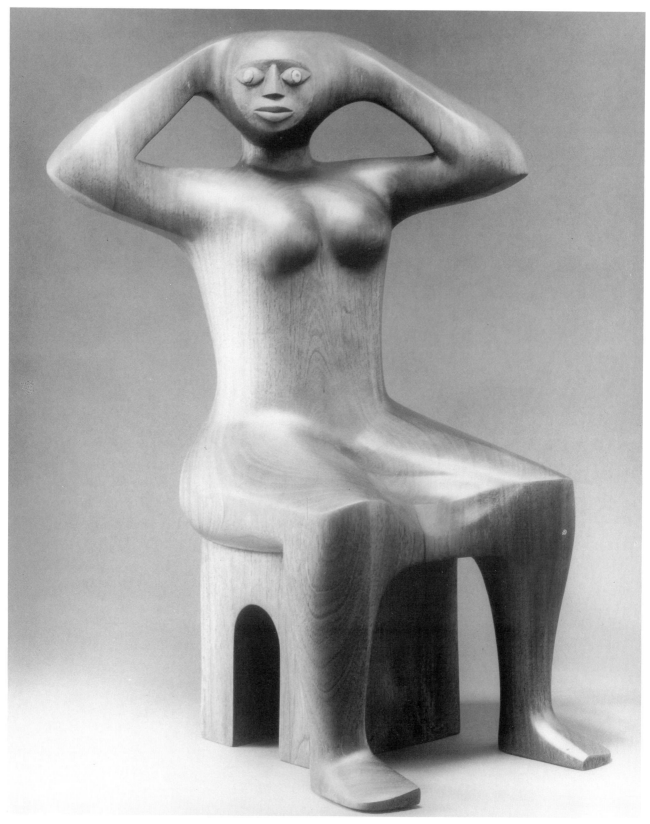

Elizabeth Catlett. Woman Fixing Her Hair. *1993. Wood. 28 × 19 × 15¹⁄₂ inches.*
Courtesy June Kelly Gallery.

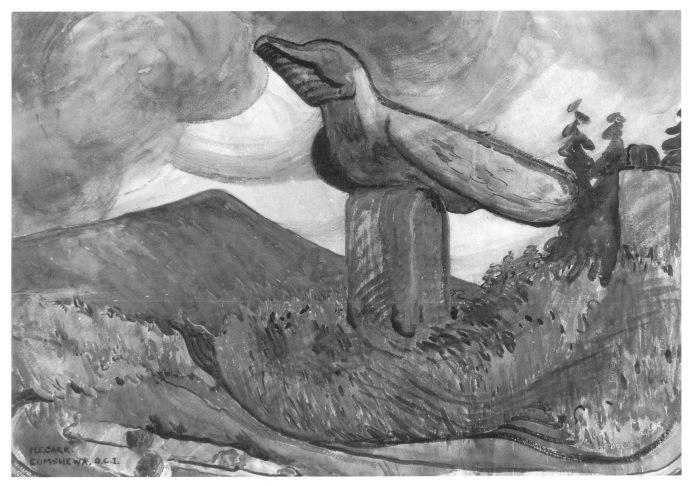

Emily Carr. Cumshewa, c. 1912. Watercolor over graphite. 52.0 × 75.5 cm.
National Gallery of Canada.

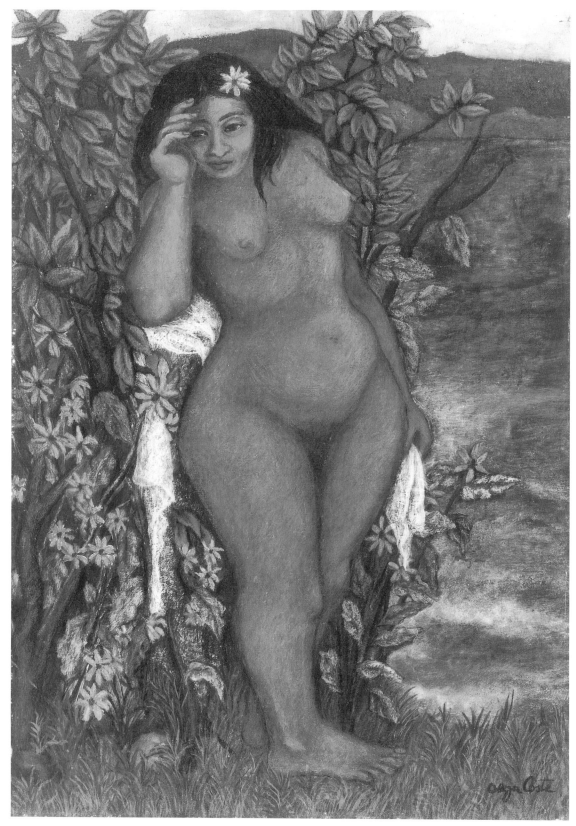

Olga Costa. Desnudo. 1945. Oil on canvas. 22 × 15¹/₂ inches.
Phoenix Art Museum. Gift of Mr. and Mrs. Orme Lewis.

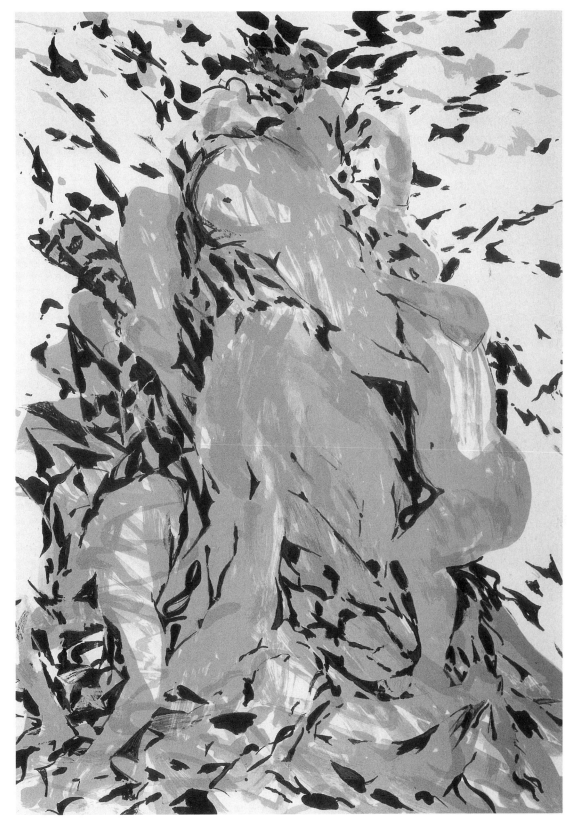

Elaine de Kooning. Jardin de Luxembourg. *1977. Lithograph. 30 × 22 inches.*
The National Museum of Women in the Arts. Gift of Mr. and Mrs. James E. Foster.

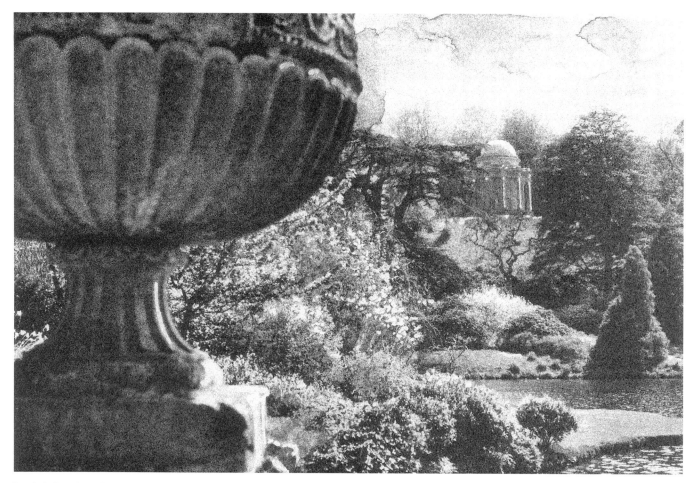

Jennifer Dickson. Crystalline Morning, Stourhead. *1992. Hand-tinted etching.*
24 × 32 inches. Courtesy the artist.

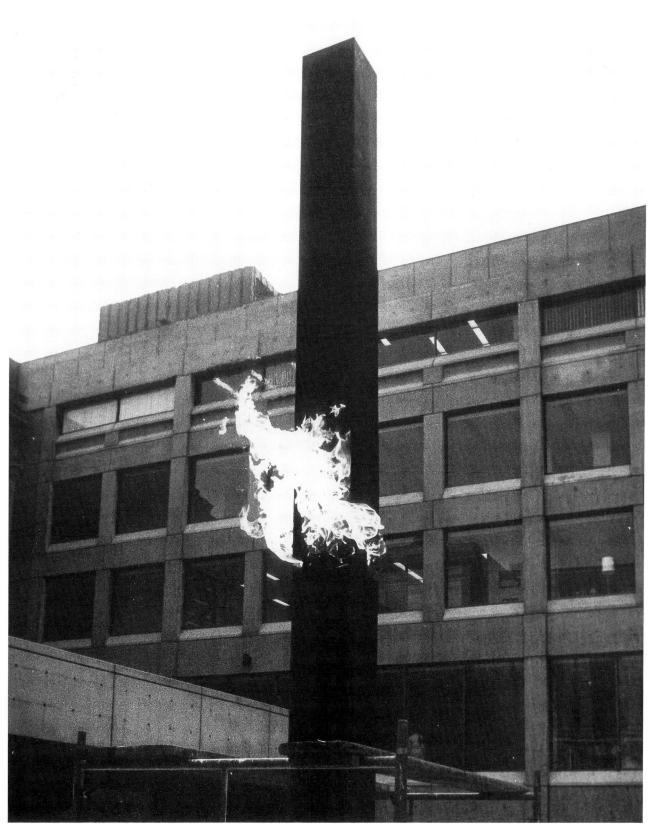

Geny Dignac. Fire Sculpture E.D.M. *1969-1971. Cor-ten steel, gas, 6 jets of fire.*
222 × 12 × 12 inches. Courtesy the artist.

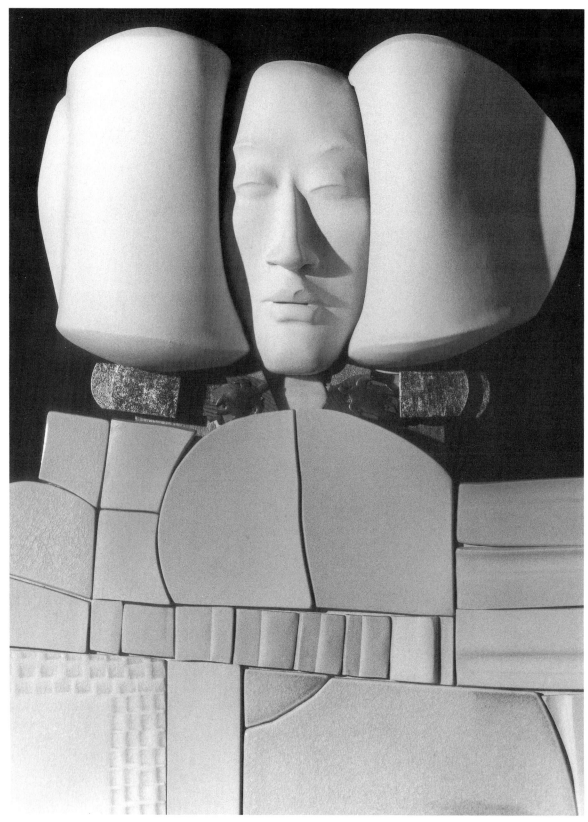

Dora De Larios. Goddess *(detail). 1990. Stoneware, porcelain, and gold leaf.*
90 × 36 inches. Courtesy the artist.

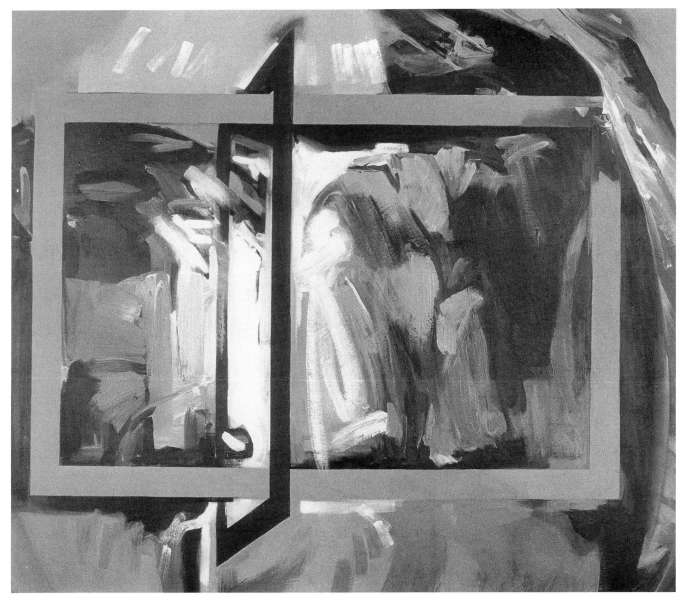

Sydney Drum. Untitled (SD//P42). *1991. Oil on canvas. 60 × 69 inches. Courtesy the artist.*

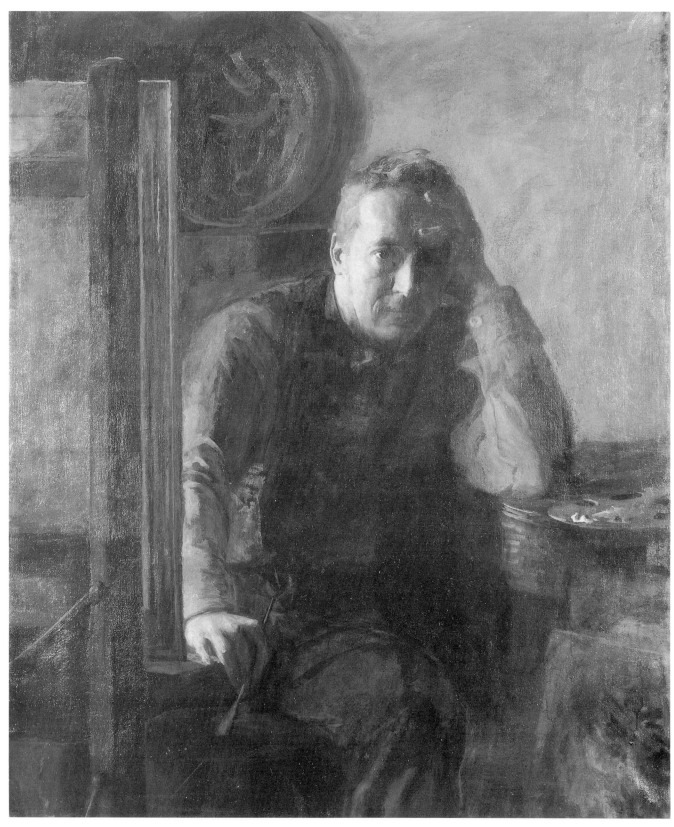

Susan Macdowell Eakins. Portrait of Thomas Eakins, *c. 1889. Oil on canvas.*
50 × 40 inches. Philadelphia Museum of Art. Given by Charles Bregler.

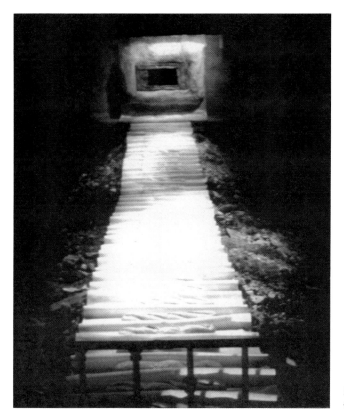

Helen Escobedo. Give Us This Day Our Daily Bread. *1993. Two tons of rubble, 40 loaves, white cloth. 18 m. Courtesy the artist.*

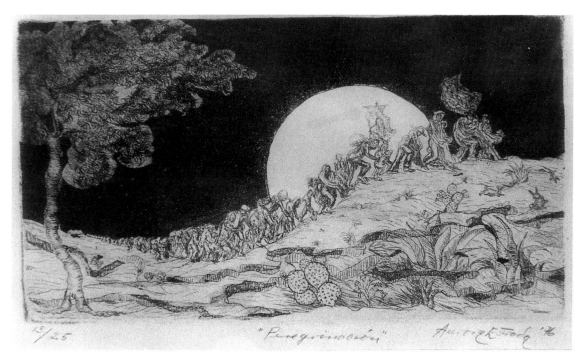

Aurora Estrada. Peregrinacion. *1976. Engraving on copper. 13 × 20 cm. Archivo CENIDIAP- INBA.*

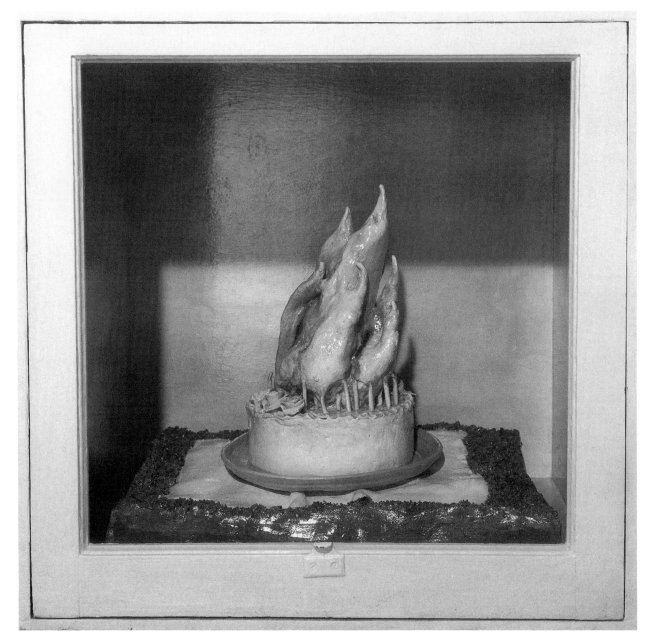

Gathie Falk. Picnic with Birthday Cake and Blue Sky. *1976. Glazed ceramic with acrylic and varnish in painted plywood case. 63.6 × 63.4 × 59.7 cm. National Gallery of Canada.*

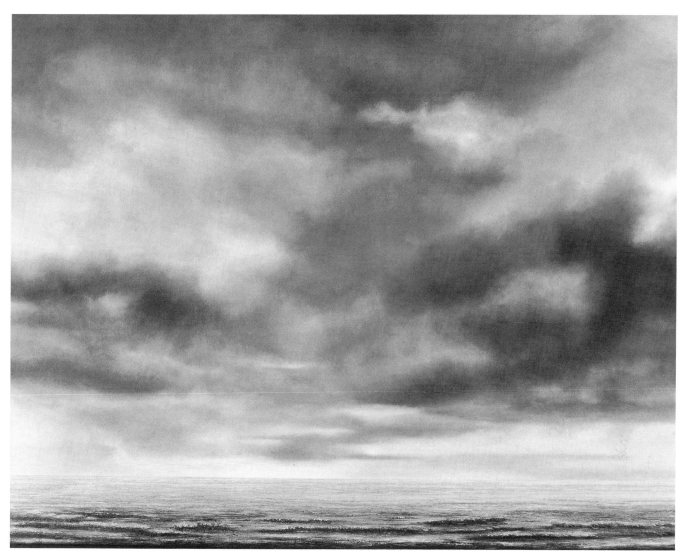

Elen A. Feinberg. Sea Clouds. *1990. Oil on linen. 56 × 70 inches. Courtesy the artist.*

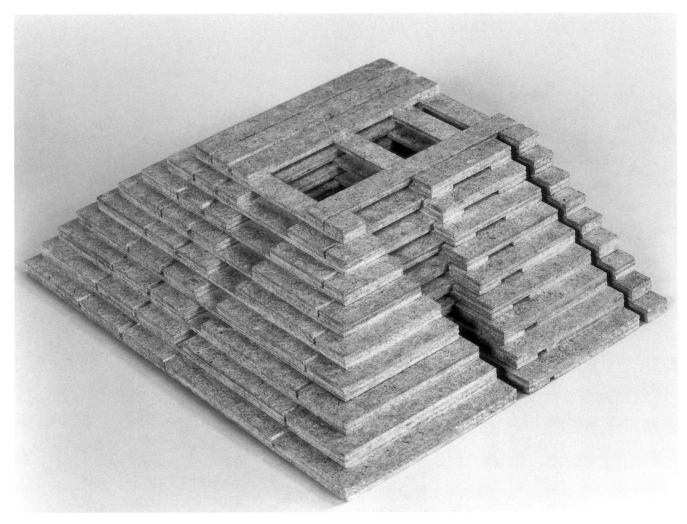

*Jackie Ferrara. M 165. 1976. Masonite. 3 × 9¼ × 12¼ inches. The National Museum
of Women in the Arts. Gift of Wallace and Wilhelmina Holladay.*

the close camera work that is characteristic of most of her videotapes. In the early 1980s Craig travelled to Japan, India, and other Asian countries. Her videotapes *Ma* (1986, 17 min.), shot while travelling in India, and *Mary-Lou* (1989, 28 min.), shot in Japan, reflect her interest in Eastern cultures. In all her works, as curator Karen Henry wrote in 1987, sounds and images play an equal part in the creation of a "sensual evocative whole."

Jean Gagnon

Bibliography

Craig, Kate. "Artist Statement." *Parachute* 20 (Fall 1980): 9–10.

Dragu, Margaret. "Delicate Issue: A Videotape by Kate Craig." *Fuse* 4 (January 1980): 12.

Sharp, Willoughby, and Lisa Bear. "Business as Usual at the Western Front." *Avalanche Magazine* (Summer–Fall 1973): 34–39.

Art and Correspondence from the Western Front. Vancouver: Western Front, 1987.

Western Front Video. Montréal: Musée d'art Contemporain, 1987.

Crane, Barbara Bachmann (1928–)

The photographer Barbara (Bachmann) Crane is strongly associated with Chicago, Illinois, where she was born; educated in photography, receiving her Master of Science degree from the Institute of Design (1966); and where she has taught since 1967 at the School of the Art Institute. Crane has explored both the street-life and the gridded visual aspect of that most architectural American city. Despite the great variety of projects Crane has undertaken, ranging widely both technically and in scale, she has written that she "consistently worked with the dual concepts of abstraction and social documentation."

Crane's unusually strong sense of design was fostered by the formal training and radical experimentation that were the hallmarks of photography at the Institute of Design, where Aaron Siskind was an important teacher. Crane herself has been an active teacher, influencing students at the Art Institute as well as at many workshops and visiting professorships at other institutions. Her undergraduate training in the history of art and architecture at Mills College, Oakland, California, and at New York University, as well as her exposure to advanced music and art in New York City, where she lived in the early 1950s, also stimulated her aesthetic development. Chance, which she encountered in the ideas of composer John Cage, has been an element she has used throughout: "Chance extends the boundaries of my imagination. I try to set up a framework to allow this to happen: I choose where I stand; I determine the tonalities; I select the forms; I look for the right light. Then I give chance a little room to perform for me."

Repetition within a grid has been the framework for some of her best series: "Whole Roll" (grids) (1968–1978), "Repeats" (1974–1979), "Petites Chose" (1974–1975), and the huge murals she produced for the Baxter/Travenol Labs in Deerfield, Illinois (1975). Incorporation of "found objects" in the "Combines" (1974–1975), "On the Fence" (1980), and "Objet Trouve" (1982–1983) reflects her interest in collecting fantastic bits of urban detritus. Although her serious work began with abstract, intimate studies of the human form in graduate school (her models were sometimes her three young children), Crane's subsequent interest in humans has been concentrated on public street-life: "People of the North Portal" (1970–1971), "Chicago Beaches and Parks" (1972–1978), "Commuter Discourse" (1978), and "Chicago Fest/Taste of Chicago/Mardi Gras" (1980–1984). Most recently her attention has been focused on landscape motifs, photographed either using an overpowering flash that renders near objects white (i.e., "Wipe-Outs," 1986–1988), or with new Polaroid color materials she has explored ("Visions of Enarc," 1983–1990), both techniques rendering strikingly aggressive, disquieting landscapes.

Crane has received major fellowships and awards from the National Endowment for the Arts (1974, 1988), the Polaroid Corporation (for materials support, 1979 to the present), and the Guggenheim Foundation (1979). She has exhibited widely and often in the United States and abroad, with a major touring retrospective and catalog, *Barbara Crane: 1948–80*, organized in 1982 by the Center for Creative Photography, University of Arizona, Tucson. Her work is in numerous public collections, including the Polaroid International Collection, Offenbach, Germany; the International Museum of Photography, George Eastman House, Rochester; the Art Institute of Chicago and the Museum of Contemporary Photography at Columbia College, Chicago; the Museum of Fine Arts, Houston; the International Center for Photography, New York City; and the Center for Creative Photography, University of Arizona, Tucson.

Gretchen Garner

Bibliography

Bach, Ira J. *Chicago's Famous Buildings*. Chicago: University of Chicago Press, 1980.

Crane, Barbara. *Barbara Crane: 1948–80*. Essay by Estelle Jussim. Tucson: Center for Creative Photography, University of Arizona, 1981.

———. *Barbara Crane: The Evolution of a Vision*. Baltimore: The Alvin O. Kuhn Library and Gallery, University of Maryland, and Polaroid Corporation, 1983.

Enyeart, James. *Decade by Decade: Twentieth-Century American Photography*. Tucson: Center for Creative Photography, University of Arizona, and Bullfinch Press, Little, Brown and Co., 1989: 86, plate 75.

Garner, Gretchen. *Reclaiming Paradise: American Women Photograph the Land*. Duluth: Tweed Museum of Art, University of Minnesota, 1987: 32–33.

Jussim, E., and E. Lindquist-Cock. *Landscape as Photograph*. Yale University Press, 1985, 125, 129.

Reeve, C., and M. Sward. *The New Photography: A Guide to New Images, Processes, and Display Techniques for Photographers*. Prentice-Hall, 1984.

Rice, Shelley (cur.). *Deconstruction/Reconstruction*. New York: The New Museum, 1980.

Traub, Charles (cur.). *The New Vision: Forty Years of Photography at the Institute of Design*. Millerton: Aperture, 1982.

Creates, Marlene (1952–)

Order and meaning in the landscape, legends and mysteries in landscape, and the relationship between human being and landscape are the elements that inform the art of Marlene Creates. Her solo exhibition, "The Distance between Two Points is Measured in Memories, Labrador 1988" (1989–1990), which travelled across Canada from St. John's to Vancouver, speaks to the viewer of the relationship between the "natural" sites found in remote areas with the "cultural," or the people who live closest to these places. Creates assembled photographs of her subjects along with a "memory map" of their own environment—

a story told to the artist by each subject and an object from the landscape that each subject considers home. The resulting associations cause the viewer to examine and explore the distinctions between nature and culture as well as the separation of ourselves from nature. Earlier exhibitions, for example, "Paper, Stones and Water" (1984), "The Physicality of Landscape: Cristo, Paterson Ewen, Marlene Creates" (1985), and "Landworks: Baffin Island 1985" (1986), had already explored relationships with the land as Creates developed her love for remote regions (she travelled around Britain on a motorcycle) and her interest in earlier prehistoric peoples and their monuments (for example, the Callanish standing stones on the remote Scottish Isle of Lewis). Whether she works with the wild, northern regions of her native Canada or with the still wild, but more accessible parts of the British Isles, Creates brings to her work an understanding of and sensitivity to the environment. She infuses her art work with this sensitivity and, in turn, the art work compels the viewer to respond actively to the explorations, whether that be following the "memory map" of her Labrador peoples or tracing her photographed paper paths through a wilderness.

Since graduating from Queen's University, Kingston, Ontario, in 1974, Creates has taught and participated in numbers of group and solo exhibitions throughout Canada. In addition, she has curated exhibitions, one of the most important being a retrospective exhibition of art works made by Canadian artist Don Wright, "Don Wright 1931–1988, A Retrospective," which originated at the Art Gallery of Memorial University, St. John's. She currently lives and works in St. John's Newfoundland.

Janice Helland

Bibliography

Fry, Jacqueline. *Marlene Creates: The Distance Between Two Points is Measured in Memories, Labrador 1988.* Presentation House Gallery, North Vancouver, B.C., 1990.

Lippard, Lucy. *Overlay: Contemporary Art and the Art of Prehistory.* Random House, 1983.

McFadden, David. "The Physicality of Landscape." *Canadian Art* (March 1986).

Crile, Susan (1942–)

Painter/printmaker Susan Crile was born in Cleveland, Ohio, and studied at Bennington College, Vermont, where she received her Bachelor of Fine Arts degree at the age of twenty-three. Crile also attended New York University (1962–1964) and Hunter College (1971–1972)—both in New York City.

Crile has held a number of solo exhibitions throughout the United States, including the Droll/Kolbert Gallery, New York (1978, 1980); Nina Freudenheim Gallery, Buffalo, New York (1980); Ivory Kimpton Gallery, San Francisco, California (1981); and others. Her work was selected for many major group exhibitions in museums and galleries, including the Annual at the Whitney Museum of American Art, New York City; the Art Institute of Chicago Annual, Illinois (1972); "The Way of Color," 33rd Corcoran Biennial, Corcoran Gallery of Art, Washington, D.C. (1973); "Works on Paper," Virginia Museum of Fine Arts, Richmond (1975); "MacDowell Colony Artists," James Yu Gallery, New York (1976); "American Drawing in Black and White: 1970–1980," Brooklyn Museum, New York (1980); "Geometric Abstraction: A New Generation," Institute of Contemporary Art, Boston, Massachusetts

(1981); "22nd National Print Exhibition, Brooklyn Museum, New York (1981); and many others.

Crile has taught at or been visiting artist at several colleges and universities, including Princeton University, New Jersey (1974–1976); Sarah Lawrence College, Bronxville, New York (1976–1978); the School of Visual Arts, New York (1976–); and the University of Pennsylvania, Philadelphia (1980).

Early in her career Crile painted still life; later the objects disappeared from her work and richly-patterned works took their place. Currently, her paintings and prints are abstract, based in part on aerial landscape and/or on her intuitive manipulation of surface, color, and form.

Crile's work is housed in the permanent collections of the Albright-Knox Art Gallery, Buffalo, New York; the Brooklyn Museum, New York; Carnegie Institute, Pittsburgh, Pennsylvania; the Hirshhorn Museum and Sculpture Garden, and the Phillips Collection, Washington, D.C.; the Whitney Museum of American Art, New York City; and others.

Bibliography

Field, Richard, and Ruth Fine. *A Graphic Muse.* Hudson Hills Press, 1987.

Poling, Clark V. *Geometric Abstraction: A New Generation.* Institute of Contemporary Art, 1981.

Raynor, Vivien. "Susan Crile." *The New York Times* (February 28, 1987).

Rose, Barbara. *American Painting: The Eighties.* Urizen Books, 1980.

Who's Who in American Art. 19th ed. R.R. Bowker Co., 1991–1992.

Critcher, Catharine Carter (1868–1964)

Born in Virginia, Catharine Critcher studied at Cooper Union in New York City and at the Corcoran School of Art in Washington, D.C. Her first professional activity was painting portraits of prominent Virginia families. In 1904 she went to Paris and enrolled at the Académie Julian. On her return to Washington, D.C., in 1909 she became an instructor at the Corcoran School of Art, where she remained for ten years, leaving only to start her own institution, the Critcher School of Painting, which remained open in Washington, D.C., until 1940.

During the 1920s Critcher spent many summers in Taos, New Mexico, enchanted by her new subject matter, the Native Americans. In the autumns, when she returned East, her paintings of the Taos and Hopi Indians were accepted for the Corcoran biennial exhibitions and the international exhibitions for the Carnegie Institute in Pittsburgh, Pennsylvania. One of her greatest satisfactions occurred in 1924 when she was unanimously elected to the Taos Society of Artists—the first woman ever admitted.

Critcher's wanderlust spirit took her to Mexico in 1936; to Canada where she painted the French Canadians of the Laurentian Mountains and the Nova Scotia fishermen; and to Gloucester, Massachusetts, for scenes of fishermen in 1941. She joined the Provincetown Art Association, Massachusetts, and showed her work in its exhibitions. As her fame spread, her commissions proliferated; she painted portraits of Woodrow Wilson (at Princeton), Senator Harry F. Byrd, and twenty generals, including George Marshall and Mark Clark. The Corcoran Gallery of Art gave her a solo exhibition in 1940 and the Washington County Museum of Fine Arts in Hagerstown, Maryland, a retrospective exhibition in 1949.

Eleanor Tufts

Bibliography

Broder, Patricia Janis. *Taos, A Painter's Dream*. New York Graphic Society, 1980.

Nelson, Mary Carroll. "Catharine Critcher." *Southwest Profile* (January–February 1986): 47–48.

Tufts, Eleanor. *American Women Artists, 1830–1930*. National Museum of Women in the Arts, 1987.

Crosby, Suzanne Camp (1948–)

Born in Roanoke, Virginia, the photographer Suzanne Camp Crosby earned a Bachelor of Fine Arts degree in painting from the University of Florida, Gainesville (1970), and, six years later, received a Master of Fine Arts degree in photography from the University of South Florida, Tampa. She took further study in workshops with Ralph Gibson and George A. Tice (1979).

Winner of awards and honors, Crosby received a National Endowment for the Arts/Southeastern Center for Contemporary Art fellowship (1978); a Florida Fine Arts Council fellowship (1979); and others. She has taught at Hillsborough Community College, Tampa, Florida, since 1977. Prior to that post, she worked in various institutions, including Florida Technological University, Orlando; Tampa Bay Art Center; and the University of South Florida.

Crosby's photographic images grow out of her life experience and are represented in private and public permanent collections.

Bibliography

Browne, Turner, and Elaine Partnow. *Macmillan Biographical Encyclopedia of Photographic Artists and Innovators*. Macmillan, 1983.

Cohen, Joyce T. *In/Sights: Self-Portraits by Women*. 1978.

Petersen's Photographic Magazine (January 1976).

Cueto, Lola (1897–1978)

Dolores Vásquez Rivas de Cueto (Lola Cueto) was born in Mexico. She studied at the Academy of San Carlos with Alberto Lago and Carlos Alvarado Lang. In collaboration with the former, she published *Titeres populares Mexicanos* (1947), which contained forty hand-pulled aquatints.

A distinguished printmaker, Cueto is equally known for her tapestries which were woven in Paris about 1940. Major pieces from her work of this period include: "Tropical o La casa del tigre de Rousseau" and "La Cruz de Palenque." She also reproduced a number of church windows from Chartres and Bourges: "La natividad"; "La última cena"; "La anunciación"; "La visitación"; "La dormición de la Virgen"; "El lavatorio de los pies"; and "A San Eustaquio en cacería."

The critic Arqueles Vela wrote: "Lola Cueto weaves her silken tapestries on a loom not unlike a painter using oils or pastels."

As a printmaker, she made aquatints, engravings, woodcuts, soft-ground etchings, lithographs, and monotypes. Cueto exhibited her prints and tapestries in many exhibitions in Mexico and abroad.

Bibliography

Alvarez, José Rogelio, et al. *Enciclopedia de México*. Secretaría de Educación Pública, 1987.

Cuillery, Magdalena (1945–)

Born in Mexico, Magdalena Cuillery studied printmaking with Silvia Santamaría, and oil painting and sculpture with José Enrique Rebolledo. She worked as a designer for the Platería Tane.

In 1985 Cuillery had her first solo exhibition titled "Esculturas Utilitarias." She employs basalt and silver on some of her demountable pieces.

Bibliography

Alvarez, José Rogelio, et al. *Enciclopedia de México*. Secretaría de Educación Pública, 1987.

Cunningham, Imogen (1883–1976)

A photographer whose career spanned three quarters of the twentieth century, Imogen Cunningham began as a soft-focus pictorialist in 1901 in her native city of Seattle, Washington. In the 1920s she switched to a sharp-focus realism, and Cunningham ended her career primarily as an environmental portraitist working with roll-film Rolleiflex cameras, which she started to use in 1945. Throughout her long career she was primarily a photographer of people, and within that field a specialist in nudes and in portraits, interested in unique individuality rather than documenting societal issues. Even her well-known plant photographs have been considered individual portraits for their emphasis on unique, particular form.

Although Cunningham was university-trained, her education was in chemistry and not art. She was visually talented and participated in the photographic movements of her time, but essentially without systematic training in visual matters. Although she was widely read in art, this lack of training may account for the somewhat varied quality of her work, and, along with her inbred disgust at pretense of any kind, it may also account in part for the wise-crack pronouncements of her later years, which often seemed to deflate the seriousness of her work. Yet she was a lifelong worker, completely serious about the photography that was always the center of her life. In 1970 she told a class at the University of California, "Everyone has to find his own way in photography. If you want help in photography, don't go to famous photographers."

In high school Cunningham had seen reproductions of Gertrude Käsebier's portraits in 1901 and decided to become a photographer by way of a correspondence course. Her early efforts had the romantic, soft, symbolist qualities of Käsebier's pictorialist images. While studying for a degree in chemistry at the University of Washington, which at the time had no art curriculum, Cunningham got a job as a commercial platinum printer in the Curtis Studio, printing the hundreds of Native American portraits Edward S. Curtis was producing for his mammoth study of the North American Indians. In 1909, on a Pi Beta Phi scholarship she left for Dresden, Germany, to study photographic chemistry at the Technische Hochschule, and on her return opened a commercial portrait studio in Seattle. Throughout her life she identified herself as a commercial photographer, although she participated in art movements such as "Group f/64."

After her marriage to the etcher Roi Partridge in 1915 and their move to northern California, the next twenty years of Cunningham's life included her three children, Gryffydd, Padraic, and Rondal, and the busy social life of a faculty wife (Partridge taught at Mills College in Oakland). Even so, she continued photographing, both portraits for hire and the plant forms made in her own garden when her children were small. Through the recommendation of Edward Weston, ten of these plant studies were included in the "Film and Foto" exhibition of 1929, sponsored by the Deutscher Werkbund, an association of German designers and architects.

Along with Weston and several other West Coast photographers (Ansel Adams, John Paul Edwards, Sonia Noskowiak, Willard Van Dyke, and Henry F. Swift), Cunningham was a founding member of "Group f/64," an informal and short-lived association formed in 1932 based on a commitment to sharp-focus realism in photography. The name "f/64" comes from the lens setting that renders maximum sharp detail. Although their association lasted only three years, the group did sponsor one exhibit at the M.H. de Young Memorial Museum, San Francisco, California, in 1932, and they formalized a shift in photographic style that was to remain firmly established for the rest of Cunningham's life. During the same period Cunningham was making commercial portraits of movie stars for *Vanity Fair* and continuing to work for hire. A trip to New York City in 1934 to meet with the editor of *Vanity Fair* triggered the breakup of her marriage, although Cunningham and Partridge remained cordial friends.

Armed with her Rolleiflex camera, Cunningham began exploring the San Francisco street in the 1940s, and her portraits became increasingly environmental and candid. To these portraits Cunningham brought a lifetime of deepening understanding of light, of natural symbols, and of the cycles of life. The late portraits are considered by many to be her lifework's culmination. Her two portraits of the painter Morris Graves (1950 and 1973) offer approximate brackets for this period of greatest power.

In 1970, at age 87, Cunningham received a Guggenheim fellowship to enable her to print earlier neglected negatives. In 1974 she founded the Imogen Cunningham Trust, which handled print sales and after her death has continued to sell prints made from her original negatives. Her last major project, begun the year before her death and published the year after, was a book called *After Ninety*, portraits of the aged.

Gretchen Garner

Bibliography
Borden, Elizabeth. "Imogen Cunningham." *U.S. Camera World Annual* (1970): 60–65, 206.
Cooper, Thomas Joshua, and Gerry Badger. "Imogen Cunningham: A Celebration." *British Journal of Photography Annual*. London, 1978.
Cunningham, Imogen. *After Ninety*. Essay by Margaretta Mitchell. University of Washington Press, 1977.
———. *Imogen!* Essay by Margery Mann. University of Washington Press, 1974.
Dater, Judy. *Imogen Cunningham: A Portrait*. New York Graphic Society, 1979.
Garner, Gretchen. *Reclaiming Paradise: American Women Photograph the Land*. Tweed Museum of Art, University of Minnesota, 1987.
[Jay, Bill.] "Imogen Cunningham." *Album* 5 (June 1970): cover, 22–38.
Mann, Margery. "Imogen Cunningham." *Infinity* 15 (November 1966): 25–28.
Maschmedt, Flora Huntley. "Imogen Cunningham—an Appreciation." *Wilson's Photographic Magazine* 51 (March 1914): 96–99, 113–20.
Newhall, Beaumont. Intro. to *Imogen Cunningham: Photographs 1921–1967*. Stanford, Calif.: Stanford Art Gallery, 1967.
White, Minor. "An Experiment in 'Reading' Photographs." *Aperture* 5 (1957): 66–71.

Currelly, Judith (1946–)

Although Judith Currelly was born in Toronto—one of Canada's most important cities as well as a major art center—she has spent almost twenty years of her life living and working in the Yukon. Her first trip to this northern region took place in 1972 soon after she had completed her studies in painting and drawing at the Ontario College of Art, Toronto (1970). Although her first experience was brief, she returned to Frances Lake in the Yukon in 1974 and lived alone there for ten months. This began a relationship with the Northern landscape that would direct both her painting and her photography as well as her life.

Her early paintings show a concern with light and shape such as we might find reflected upon snow or water, or in grey overcast skies. Although they would be formally defined as abstract, Currelly's experience with solitude in nature is a major part of the work and, therefore, seemingly without content; the pictures speak to the viewer of experiences. Similarly, her photographs evoke this response with the added interest of ephemeral but recognizable forms: light, sky, and water.

Between 1975 and 1978 Currelly learned to fly, purchased a Piper PA12 and flew it back to the Yukon. Then, in 1978, she moved to Atlin, in northern British Columbia, and began to fly commercially. Her artistic production was further developed by her experience with aerial landscape and has led to her latest researches into nature, the North, and mapping.

Since 1970 when she was awarded "best of the show" in the Young Canadian Artists' Exhibition, Currelly has continued to play an important role within Canadian art. Her work was in "Young Contemporaries '76," London Regional Art Gallery, London, Ontario (1976); "Ontario Now, Part 2—A Survey of Contemporary Art," Art Gallery of Hamilton, Ontario (1977); and "Art in Victoria: 1960–1986," Art Gallery of Greater Victoria, B.C. (1986). In addition to these group exhibitions she has had a number of solo exhibitions in Vancouver, Victoria, and Toronto. She currently lives and works in Victoria and Atlin.

Janice Helland

Bibliography
Johnson, Nick. "Judith Currelly: Photography and Painting." *Artscanada* 32:1 (March 1975): 54–55.

Currier, Anne C. (1950–)

Born in Louisville, Kentucky, the ceramist Anne C. Currier earned a Bachelor of Fine Arts degree from the Art Institute of Chicago, Illinois (1972), and, two years later, received a Master of Fine Arts degree from the University of Washington, Seattle. A teacher at the New York State College of Ceramics, Alfred, New York, Currier initially created work that reflected a minimal aesthetic; her more recent, non-figurative pieces reflect a more spatial approach within a linear configuration. Winner of several awards and honors, Currier was the recipient of National Endowment for the Arts fellowship in 1986.

Bibliography
Clark, Garth. *American Ceramics 1896 to the Present*. Abbeville Press, 1987.

Curry, Gwen (1950–)

Born in the lush rainforest area of British Columbia, Gwen Curry has maintained an interest in her environment and its vulnerability in her iconic prints and installations. Curry obtained her Bachelor of Fine Arts degree at the University of Victoria, British Columbia, and completed her Master of Fine Arts degree at Arizona State University, Tempe.

Curry's solo exhibitions "Icons: Images of Power and Transformation" (1987) and "Mapping the Coast" (1989) represent the power, the solitude, and the intensity of a personal relationship with nature and with human intrusions into nature. Her work shares some of the same concerns as work done earlier in the century by another West Coast artist, Emily Carr, but while Carr was able to reconstruct a still relatively unspoiled natural environment, Curry infuses her work with a human presence that suggests domination, if not destruction. Given this potential for violence, Curry also indicates the bond that can be forged between intruder and environment as well as between artist and viewer.

The artist/viewer bond and the discursive aspect of that bond is readily seen in Curry's recent work, a series of large black-and-white charcoal and oil stick drawings. These drawings continue the searches into intimacy with elements that are seen and comprehended but remain somehow out of our control. Birds are the dominant subject of the drawings, and because of their large size and portrait-like quality, they enter the space of the viewer demanding an interaction that implies understanding. The recent drawings were exhibited at the Cologne Art Fair, Cologne, Germany (1990), and the Los Angeles Art Fair, Los Angeles, California (1990).

Curry is an associate professor in the visual arts department at the University of Victoria and exhibits nationally and internationally. As early as 1977, while she was still a graduate student, her prints were included in the "12th International Biennale of Graphic Art" in Ljubljana, Yugoslavia and, in 1979, in the "6th British International Print Biennale," Bradford, England. Her work is held by a number of public collections, including the Canada Council Art Bank; Imperial Esso of Canada; Rothman's Pall Mall of Canada; Skopje Museum, Yugoslavia; and the Art Gallery of Victoria.

Janice Helland

Bibliography

Bellerby, Greg. "Gwen Curry." *Society of Northern Alberta Print Artists' Newsletter* (February 1991).

Malbert, Roger. "Marks and Surfaces." *Vanguard* (March 1983): 30.

Cuthbert, Virginia (1908–)

The magic realist Virginia Cuthbert was born in West Newton, Pennsylvania, and knew from childhood that she would become an artist. She earned a Bachelor of Fine Arts degree from Syracuse University, New York (1930), and received the coveted August Hazard travelling fellowship for European study. Cuthbert studied with Charles Hawthorne at the Provincetown Art Colony, Massachusetts (summer 1930); took classes at the Académie de la Grande Chaumière, Paris, France; did private study with Felice Carena in Florence, Italy; studied with Colin Gill, was given critiques by Augustus John, and took classes at the Chelsea Polytechnical Institute—all in London, England. Back in the United States she studied with George Luks in New York City (1932); did graduate work in art history at the University of Pittsburgh, Pennsylvania (1933–1934); and did further graduate study in painting with Alexander Kostellow at the Carnegie Institute of Technology, Pittsburgh (1934–1935).

Cuthbert has held many solo exhibitions, including Syracuse University, New York (1930); the Carnegie Institute Museum of Art, Pittsburgh, Pennsylvania (1938); Butler Art Institute, Youngstown, Ohio, and the Syracuse Museum of Fine Arts, New York (1939); Contemporary Arts, New York City (1945, 1949, 1953); American Academy and Institute of Arts and Letters, New York City (1954); Rehn Gallery, New York City (1958, 1966); "A Retrospective," Nina Freudenheim Gallery, Buffalo, New York (1990); and others.

Cuthbert's work has been invited to more than sixty-five distinguished group exhibitions throughout the United States from 1933 to 1992. A teacher of painting at the Albright Art School, the University of Buffalo (1942–1966); art critic for brief periods with the *Buffalo Courier-Express* (1954–1955) and the *Buffalo Evening News* (1955–1956); winner of honors and awards, she was the recipient of an American Academy and Institute of Arts and Letters grant (1954) for contributions to American painting. Her work is represented in many private and public permanent collections.

Bibliography

Burrows, Carlyle. "Virginia Cuthbert Show." *New York Herald-Tribune* (May 19, 1953).

Virginia Cuthbert: A Retrospective. A Catalog. Essay by Albert L. Michaels. Nina Freudenheim Gallery, 1990.

Who's Who in American Art. 19th ed. R.R. Bowker Co., 1991–1992.

Cutler-Shaw, Joyce

Born in Detroit, Michigan, the intermedia artist Joyce Cutler-Shaw earned a Bachelor's degree from New York University, New York City (1953); enrolled in graduate work at Columbia University, New York City, the following academic year, and was awarded a Master of Fine Arts degree from the University of California at San Diego (1972). She also studied painting and textile design in New York City.

Between 1974 and 1993 Cutler-Shaw has held twenty-six solo exhibitions—ranging from drawings, texts, new imaging systems, books, scrolls, word sculptures, wingwall collages, installation projects, public events, performances and readings—in museums and galleries throughout the United States and abroad, including "The Anatomy Lesson: Re-Vision," School of Medicine, University of California, San Diego (1992–1993); "Into Flight," Teylers Museum, Haarlem, the Netherlands (1990); "Seacrest Donor Namewall," Seacrest Village Retirement Community, Encinitas, California (1989); "In the Garden of Exotic Blooms," and "The Banquet," Volt Corporate Park, Orange, California (1987–1990); "Wingtrace/The Sign of its Track," National Academy of Sciences, Washington, D.C., and Cornell University, Ithaca, New York (1986); "Messenger: A Performance" (with Arthur Wagner), Sushi Performance Gallery, San Diego, California (1986); "The Lady and the Bird," Apropos Gallery, Lucerne, Switzerland (1979); "Wings for the Voyageur de Beyrouth," Galerie Gaetan, Geneva, Switzerland (1979); "The Namewall," Los Angeles International Airport, California (1974); and others.

Her work has been invited to myriad group exhibitions throughout the world: from Washington, D.C., to Moscow, Russia; Potsdam, New York; Normandie, France; Morgantown, West Virginia; Brussels, Belgium; San Diego, California; Bilbao, Spain; Paris, France; Budapest, Hungary; Mexico City, Mexico; São Paulo, Brazil; Liverpool, England; Walnut, California, and other venues.

Cutler-Shaw has won many awards and honors for her work over the last two decades; her book, *Three Cages*, was a winner in the competition sponsored by the Center for the Book Arts, New York City (1992); her "*Alphabet of Bones: The Art of Broadside* received a purchase prize at an exhibition held at the State University of New York (SUNY) at Potsdam (1991); her project, *Museum of Seasonal Change*, was awarded a grant from the National Endowment for the Arts (1985–1987) as well as a project development grant (1981–1982). Television grants from the California Arts Council allowed her to hone her particular skills (1982–1983, 1983–1984); and her *We the People* project was endorsed by the United States Congressional Joint Committee on the Bicentennial (1976); among other honors.

Cutler-Shaw is the author of thirty-seven publications, including many handbound, limited editions; a faculty member and visiting artist at colleges and universities in California; a television interviewer and project director for various arts-oriented educational television series; and founding director of Landmark Art Projects, Inc. (1979). A self-employed artist since 1981, her work is in private and public permanent collections, including the Guggenheim Museum, New York City; Cornell University, Ithaca, New York; Klingspor Museum, Offenbach, Germany; Museum of Modern Art (MoMA), New York City; Museum of Natural History, San Diego, California; Tate Gallery, London, England; New York Public Library Special Collections; Teylers Museum, Haarlem, the Netherlands; the Universities of California at San Diego and Santa Barbara; and others.

Bibliography

Courtney, Cathy. "Birds and Oblivion Boys." *Art Monthly* 108 (July–August 1987): 37–38.

Roth, Moira. A Catalog. "The Lady and the Bird." *Wingtrace/The Sign of its Track*. Cornell University, 1986.

Vanden Hoek Ostende, Menalde M. "Kunst-En Vliewerk." *Teylers Magazijn* No. 28. Teylers Museum. The Netherlands, 1990.

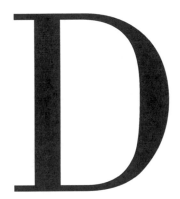

Dahl-Wolfe, Louise (1895–1989)

Louise Dahl-Wolfe helped define and advance the art of color photography. Following the arrival of Kodachrome color film her photographs were party to displacing fashion illustrations in American magazines and clothing advertisements during the 1930s. Between 1936 and 1958 Dahl-Wolfe produced eighty-five cover photographs for *Harper's Bazaar*. The magazine also published more than 600 of her color pictures and countless black-and-white photos.

Her fashion photographs and celebrity portraits were noted for their strong design and composition and their mastery of color and light. In her photography Dahl-Wolfe drew on five years of training at the California School of Fine Arts (now the San Francisco Institute of Art), studies in interior design and architecture in New York City, and work with interior decorators on both coasts.

Dahl-Wolfe, a self-taught photographer, began experimenting with a Brownie fixed-focus camera after seeing nude pictures taken by Anne Brigman in 1921. She did her own "Anne Brigmans," posing nude with fellow art students among the cypress trees near Point Lobos, California, in 1922.

Dahl-Wolfe's first published photograph, "Mrs. Ramsey—Tennessee Mountain Woman," was printed in the November 1933 issue of *Vanity Fair*. The documentary-style picture was included in the first photography exhibition, "Photography 1839–1937," held at the Museum of Modern Art (MoMA), New York City (1937).

During the Great Depression Dahl-Wolfe photographed food for *Woman's Home Companion* in her New York City studio. She also did free-lance fashion photography for Saks Fifth Avenue and a variety of stores and clothing manufacturers until she joined the *Harper's Bazaar* staff in 1936.

At *Harper's Bazaar* Dahl-Wolfe started by photographing still lifes of shoes and accessories. She graduated to fashion shoots, and soon she was among the first to take color photography out of the studio. Her locations included the *haute couture* runways of the French collections and destinations in Brazil, Cuba, Mexico, Spain, the United States, and other countries during the years following World War II.

Also at *Harper's Bazaar* Dahl-Wolfe began to photograph celebrities. Portraiture freed her from the commercial concerns associated with representing fashions true to designers' intentions. One of her best-known portraits is of "Colette," taken in 1951 at the novelist's bedside.

Dahl-Wolfe acknowledged her need for independence and maintained her own studio throughout her career. It was a violation of her independence that robbed her enthusiasm for photography—when a new *Harper's Bazaar* art director came into her studio and looked through her ground glass. No one had done this to her before. She resigned her position at *Bazaar*, and after doing some work for *Vogue* and *Sports Illustrated*, she retired from photography in 1960.

Dahl-Wolfe's photographs have been featured in the exhibition of "Women of Photography: An Historical Survey" at the San Francisco Museum of Modern Art, California, and the Sidney Janis Gallery, New York City (1975–76). Her work also appeared in the group show "Recollections: Ten Women of Photography" at the International Center of Photography, New York City (1979). Among the collections holding Dahl-Wolfe's photographs are the Fashion Institute of Technology, and the Museum of Modern Art (MoMA)—both in New York City.

Melissa D. Olson

Bibliography

Dahl-Wolfe, Louise. *Louise Dahl-Wolfe: A Photographer's Scrapbook*. St. Martin's/Marek, 1984.

"Louise Dahl-Wolfe, A Photographer, 94." *The New York Times* (December 13, 1989): IV, 21.

Goldberg, Vicki. "Profile: Louise Dahl-Wolfe." *American Photographer* 6:6 (June 1981): 38–47.

Daly (Pepper), Kathleen (1898–)

Kathleen Daly (Pepper) has described herself as a painter of portraits, landscapes, and genre subjects, and an engraver and etcher. She was born in Napanee, Ontario, Canada. Daly studied at the Ontario College of Art from 1920 to 1924 with J.W. Beatty, George Agnew Reid, Arthur Lismer, and J.E.H. MacDonald; attended the Académie de la Grande Chaumière in Paris, France and Parsons School of Design, New York City; and studied wood engraving with René Pottier. Between 1924 and 1930 she made annual trips to Europe but after 1930 focused her attention on Canadian subjects.

The work Daly executed along the north shore of Lake Superior and in Charlevoix County in the province of Québec shows a stylistic indebtedness to the Group of Seven, Canada's national school of landscape painters who were in their heyday during her student years. This is evident in the bold patterning and strong design quality which she imposed on her subjects. However, Daly went beyond the Group, particularly in terms of her subject matter, which included portrait studies of Canadian native peoples, fishermen, and miners, whom she observed on her extensive travels. These travels took her to northern Ontario, Nova Scotia, and the Gaspé Peninsula (1931), the Laurentians (from 1932), Alberta (1944–1946), the Rockies, Newfoundland, and Labrador (1950–1953), Mexico (1952), Spain and Morocco, and northern Québec.

Daly became an associate member of the Royal Canadian Academy in 1937 and a full academician in 1961 and was a member of the Ontario Society of Artists (1936) and the Canadian Group of Painters (1934). She is also the author of *Morrice*, published in 1966, and collaborated on the illustrations for *The Kingdom of the Saguenay*, by Marius Barbeau, published in 1936.

Christine Boyanoski

Bibliography

Hills, Charles, and Pierre Landry. *Catalogue of the National Gallery of Canada: Canadian Art*. Vol. 1 A–E. National Gallery of Canada, 1989.

MacDonald, Colin S. *A Dictionary of Canadian Artists*. Vol. 1. Canadian Paperbacks Publishing Ltd., 1975.

Reid, Dennis. *A Concise History of Canadian Painting*. 2nd ed. Oxford University Press, 1988.

Who's Who in Ontario Art. Part 3. Reprint from the *Ontario Library Review* (May 1948).

Damon, Betsy (1940–)

A performance and environmental artist known for her participatory performances and installations, Betsy Damon was born in New York City and raised in Washington, D.C. In 1966 she received a Master of Fine Arts degree from Columbia University in her native city.

Damon began exhibiting in 1967 and had her first solo painting exhibit in 1968 at Amerika Haus, Munich, Germany. The year 1977 marked the beginning of her gallery performances involving the audience as performers. She was first known for her feminist performances of the "7,000-Year-Old Woman" and "The Blind Beggarwoman."

Damon has received many grants and awards, including a New York Foundation for the Arts fellowship (1988), and a National Endowment for the Arts (NEA) fellowship, to create "Homage to Rivers" (1990). She also won grants from the Jerome Foundation for Workshops for Artists and Scientists, Arts Midwest, 3M Corporation, and the Hubert Humphrey Institute for Affairs, for "Keepers of the Waters," a 250-foot hand-made paper cast of a dry creek bed near Castle Rock, Utah. Damon involved each community in which the piece was shown in a dialogue focusing on local water conservation and related water issues. In 1989 the Women's Caucus for Art awarded Damon the Mid-life Career Award.

Damon has travelled and worked as an artist and teacher in Japan, Africa, Europe, and the United States. In 1993 she was the distinguished guest artist at Trinity University in San Antonio, Texas.

Susan F. Baxter

Bibliography

Gadin, Elinor. "Betsy Damon's 'A Memory of Clear Water.'" *Arts Magazine* 61:10 (Summer 1987): 76–77.

Larson, Kay. "For the First Time Women Are Leading, Not Following." *Art News* 79:8 (October 1980): 64–72.

Lippard, Lucy. *Overlay, Contemporary Art and the Art of Prehistory*. Pantheon Books, 1983, p. 266.

Tufts, Eleanor. "First International Festival for Women in the Arts." *Arts Magazine* 55:2 (October 1980): 136–37.

Danziger, Joan (1934–)

A native New Yorker, the sculptor Joan Danziger earned a Bachelor of Fine Arts degree at Cornell University, Ithaca, New York (1954), and studied at the Art Students League, New York City (1955). She took further work at the Academy of Fine Arts, Rome, Italy (1956–1958). Board member of the International Sculpture Center and Sculptor Source and president of the Washington Sculptors Group, Danziger served as a visual arts panelist for the Commission on the Arts and Humanities, Washington, D.C., and the New Jersey State Council on the Arts. She was also artist-in-residence at the Cité International des Arts, Paris, France.

Danziger has held solo exhibitions in museums and galleries throughout the United States, including the Southwest Art Center, San Antonio, Texas (1987); the Textile Museum, Washington, D.C. (1985); Louisiana World Exposition, New Orleans (1984); Rutgers University, New Brunswick, New Jersey (1983); Joy Horwich Gallery, Chicago, Illinois (1982); Terry Dintenfass Gallery, New York City (1980); Jacksonville Museum of Arts and Sciences, Florida (1979); the Fendrick Gallery (1978); the Corcoran Gallery of Art, Washington, D.C. (1975); and others. The animal-human figures and human-animal fantasies that comprise her mysteriously-elegant sculptures have been invited to many group exhibitions from coast to coast.

Danziger has executed several site-specific public commissions, such as the Washington, D.C., Convention Center; and Frostburg State College and the George Meany Labor Studies Center—both in Maryland. Her work is represented in private, public, and corporate permanent collections, including the National Museum of American Art,

Washington, D.C.; the New Orleans Museum of Art, Louisiana; Artery Corporation, Chevy Chase, Maryland; New Jersey State Museum, Trenton; National Museum of Women in the Arts, Smithsonian Institution, Washington, D.C.; and others. "Orion's Ride" (1992), mixed media, a recent public commission for the State of Maryland's George Taylor Multi-Service Center, Glen Burnie, is composed of three larger-than-life, three-dimensional, meticulously-crafted, enigmatic, suspended sculptures in a forty-foot atrium and two wall sculptures.

Bibliography

Donohue, Victoria. "Danziger's Sculptures Are Mythology in 3-D." *The Philadelphia Inquirer* (May 11, 1984): 38.

Watson-Jones, Virginia. *Contemporary American Women Sculptors*. Oryx Press, 1986.

Welzenbach, Michael. "The Magical Menagerie." *The Washington Post* (December 19, 1984): D9.

Who's Who in American Art. 19th ed. R.R. Bowker Co., 1991–1992.

Daoust, Sylvia (1902–1974)

Born in Montréal, Québec, Canada, the liturgical sculptor Sylvia Daoust studied at the École des Beaux-Arts in her native city (1922–1930). She won a Québec government scholarship for study and research in Europe (1929) where, in France, she worked with Henri Charlier and also became familiar with the work of leading French and English sculptors.

Daoust's commissioned work is sited in many venues, including a bronze head and a monument at the Montréal Botanical Gardens, Québec; a crucifix and a sculpture of St. Benoit at the Monastery at St. Benoit du Lac; many medallions of notable persons, and trophies for various Canadian activities (e.g., the Canadian Drama Festival); and others. A memorial retrospective exhibition of her work was shown at the Musée du Québec (1974).

Daoust earned honors and awards early on: she shared a first prize with Elizabeth Wyn Wood at the Willingdon Arts Competition (1929); won the Royal Architectural Institute of Canada Allied Arts Medal (1961); and others. She was a professsor at the École des Beaux-Arts, Québec, and then at the École des Beaux-Arts, Montréal, for many years. Examples of her works are in private, corporate, and public permanent collections, including the Art Gallery of Ontario, Toronto; IBM, Montréal; the National Gallery of Canada, Ottawa; the Québec Provincial Museum; and others.

Bibliography

Cloutier, Albert. "Sylvia Daoust." *Canadian Art* 8:4 (Summer 1951): 154–57.

Hambleton, Josephine. "Canadian Women Sculptors." *Dalhousie Review* 29:3 (October 1949): 327–37.

Lasnier, Rina. "Sylvia Daoust." *Carnets Viatoriens* 11:3 (July 1946): 202–07.

Dater, Judy (1941–)

Born in Hollywood, California, the photographer Judy Dater studied at the University of California at Los Angeles (UCLA) (1959–1962) before transferring to San Francisco State University, California, where she earned both Bachelor's and Master's degrees in photography (1963, 1966).

Dater has held many solo exhibitions in the United States and abroad in the 1970s; recent shows include the Spectrum Gallery, Fresno, California (1981); Yuen Lui Gallery, Seattle, Washington (1982); "New

Works . . ." Silvereye, Pittsburgh, Pennsylvania (1989); "Judy Dater: A Retrospective," Stockton State College, Pomona, New Jersey (1991); "Cycles," Matsuya Department Store, Tokyo, Japan (1992); and many others.

Her work has been included in many prestigious group exhibitions, such as "Photography in America," Whitney Museum of American Art, New York City (1974); "Women of Photography," San Francisco Museum of Art, California (1975); "Mirrors and Windows," a travelling show, Museum of Modern Art (MoMA), New York City (1978–1980); "Similar Images/Dissimilar Motives," Sonoma State University, Rohnert Park, California (1990); "Odalisque," Jane Baum Gallery, New York City (1990); "Suburban Home Life: Tracking the American Dream," Whitney Museum of American Art, New York City (1990); and many others.

Dater is a founding member of the photographer's group called the Visual Dialogue Foundation; instructor of photography intermittently (1966–1990); National Endowment for the Arts (NEA) fellow (1976, 1988); Guggenheim Foundation fellow (1978); and recipient of an individual artist's grant from the Marin Arts Council, California. She is well known for her posed works of female nudes which, among a host of other effects, seem to haunt one's memory.

Examples of her work are in private and public permanent collections, including the Bibliothèque Nationale, Paris, France; Boston Museum of Fine Arts, Massachusetts; Fogg Art Museum, Harvard University, Cambridge, Massachusetts; Museum of Modern Art (MoMA), New York City; University of Maryland, Baltimore; and many others.

Bibliography

Dater, Judy, and Jack Welpott. *Women and Other Visions/Photos*. Dobbs Ferry: Morgan and Morgan, 1975.

Enyeart, James. *Judy Dater: Twenty Years*. University of Arizona Press, 1986.

Munsterberg, Hugo. *A History of Women Artists*. Clarkson N. Potter, 1975.

Phillips, Donna-Lee. "Personas of Women." *Artweek* 15:13 (March 31, 1984): 15–16.

Davidson, Carol Kreeger (1931–)

The sculptor Carol Kreeger Davidson was born in Chicago, Illinois; earned a Bachelor's degree at Northwestern University, Evanston, Illinois (1953); received a Bachelor of Fine Arts degree *cum laude* in sculpture from the University of Hartford Art School, Connecticut (1967); and a Master of Fine Arts degree from the Rhode Island School of Design, Providence (1973).

Davidson has held more than twenty-five solo exhibitions in museums and galleries, including the New Britain Museum of American Art, Connecticut (1974, 1990); Institute of Contemporary Art, Boston, Massachusetts (1976); Gloria Cortella Gallery, New York City (1978); Hudson River Museum, Yonkers, New York (1980); Terry Dintenfass Gallery, New York City (1982); "Ten Year Retrospective," Joseloff Gallery, University of Hartford, Connecticut (1984); Humphrey Gallery, New York City (1986, 1988, 1991, 1992); Perimeter Gallery, Chicago, Illinois (1991, 1993); and others. Her work has been invited to many distinguished group exhibitions in the United States and abroad: from New York City to Madrid, Spain; from San Francisco, California, to Kanokke, Belgium; Detroit, Michigan; Waltham, Massachusetts; Stamford, Connecticut; and many other cities.

Davidson taught sculpture for the Peace Corps at Kent College, Tuaran (1967), and at Guya College, Kota Kinabalu—both in Sabah, Malaysia (1968). She has received a number of commissions for bronze and cast aluminum sculptures and has been the recipient of honors and awards, including grants from the Connecticut Commission on the Arts (1975–1976); Hyatt International and the Cottonwood Foundation (1981); the National Endowment for the Arts (NEA), New York State Council for the Arts, and the Asia Foundation (1983); and others.

Davidson's work is represented in private, public, and corporate permanent collections, including the Wadsworth Atheneum, Hartford, Connecticut; New Jersey State Museum, Trenton; National Museum of Women in the Arts, Washington, D.C.; Bucknell University, Lewisburg, Pennsylvania; Northwestern University, Evanston, Illinois; and many others.

Bibliography
Hanson, Henry. "Review." *Chicago Magazine* (January 1991).
Ten Year Retrospective. A Catalog. University of Hartford, 1984.
Watson-Jones, Virginia. *Contemporary American Women Sculptors*. Oryx Press, 1986.
Zimmer, William. "Review." *The New York Times* (November 11, 1984).

Davison, Betty (1909–)

Known for her humorous cast paper reliefs of Canadian genre scenes and everyday objects, Betty Davison came to international acclaim later in life. She credits the encouragement of her second husband, Arthur Davison, and the tutelage of Alma Duncan at the Ottawa Municipal Art Centre in the early 1960s with her return to the career she had abandoned in the 1940s.

In the 1930s and 1940s Davison danced and acted with the Ottawa Little Theatre, where she was frequently photographed by Yousuf Karsh. Her first solo exhibition was in the foyer of that theater in 1945. The success of her original process of creating hand-painted cast paper prints was assured when she won the Ontario Arts Council Award in 1974 and the inclusion in the touring exhibition, "Editions 1." Davison has won numerous other awards, including the Martha Jackson Gallery purchase award for "Lazy Sunday" (1977), the Harold Pitman prize for "Highrise II" (1978)—both at the Pratt Graphics Center, New York City; and a purchase award from the Art Gallery of Brant for "Portraits at a Vernissage" (1983).

In 1987 the work exhibited in her retrospective, "A Slice of Life," Ufundi Gallery, Ottawa, became part of many permanent institutional and corporate collections.

Victoria Henry

Bibliography
Belshaw, Linda. *Graphex 5*. The Art Gallery of Brant, Brantford (1977): 24.
Henry, Victoria. *Betty Davison, A Slice of Life*. Ufundi Gallery, Ottawa, 1988.
Knowles, Valerie. "Betty Davison, Award-Winnning Printmaker." *The Canadian Art Investor's Guide*. Vol. 1 (1981): 34–35, 41.
Pottruff, Richard. *Graphex 9*. The Art Gallery of Brant, Brantford (1984): 26.

Daw, Leila (1940–)

The printmaker/installationist/performance artist Leila Daw earned a Bachelor's degree from Wellesley College, Massachusetts (1962); took further work at the Boston Museum School of Fine Arts, Massachusetts, and the Maryland Institute of Arts, Baltimore; and, after marriage, children, and a teaching assistantship, received a Master of Fine Arts degree from Washington University, St. Louis, Missouri (1974).

Daw uses techniques of mapping the earth and sky—drawings, focussed on themes of change, renewal, the human voyage, and the Mississippi River, among others—documented in artist's books, collages, prints, paintings, and diagrams, in layered veils which evoke physical and visual metaphors. She uses the earth and the sky as her canvas.

A professor of art at Southern Illinois University, Carbondale, since 1976, Daw has held solo exhibitions in galleries in New York City and elsewhere and has exhibited in myriad group shows in the Midwest. Examples of her work are represented in private and public permanent collections.

Bibliography
Frueh, Hoanna. "St. Louis. Leila Daw at Atrium." *Art in America* 75:7 (July 1987): 133.
Melf, Terry Hope. "Women's Autobiographical Artists' Books." *New Art Examiner* 15:5 (January 1988): 64–65.
Schwartz, Helen. "Leila Daw, Opening New Layers of Women in Art." *Curtain Call, the Magazine of St. Louis Arts* (September 1977): 9.
Sky Art '83. Massachusetts Institute of Technology, 1983.

Day, Worden (1916–1986)

Known for her technical innovations in two- and three-dimensional media, Worden Day was born in Columbus, Ohio, daughter of a Methodist minister. At the age of eighteen Day received her Bachelor's degree from Randolph-Macon Woman's College in Richmond, Virginia, and then studied in New York City with Maurice Sterne and George Grosz. In New York City she also worked under Jean Charlot and Emilio Amero at the Florence Crane School; at the Art Students League with Harry Sternberg, Will Barnet, and Vaclav Vytlacil; and with Hans Hofmann at his school.

At the onset of World War II Day won a Julius Rosenwald Foundation fellowship; about a decade later she was awarded two back-to-back Guggenheim Foundation fellowships for painting and printmaking (1952–1953). Soon after winning a fellowship from the Virginia Museum of Fine Arts, Richmond (1940), Day had her first solo show at the Perls Gallery in New York City. Her paintings, not unlike her prints, are layered, collaged, and on occasion, incised; "Prehistoric Horizon," a study in red, has a chunk of glass embedded in the painted surface.

In 1943 Day worked at Stanley William Hayter's Atelier 17, New York City, and six years later taught at the University of Wyoming in Laramie; she was also on the faculty of the New School for Social Research (1961–1966) and the Art Students League (1966–1970)—both in New York City. New York University, New York City, awarded Day a Master's degree in 1966 upon the completion of her studies.

In the late 1960s Day abandoned painting and edition printmaking and concentrated her efforts on sculpture and the monotype; after more than thirty years of experimentation in sculpture Day held a solo exhibition of three-dimensional work at the Sculpture Center, New York City (1972). The New Jersey State Museum, Trenton, prepared a forty-year retrospective of her work in 1986; Day died of cancer prior to the formal opening.

Bibliography

Acton, David. *A Spectrum of Innovation in American Printmaking: 1890–1960.* Worcester Art Museum, Massachusetts, 1990.

Breuning, Margaret. "Worden Day Debut." *The Art Digest* 22:7 (January 1, 1948): 10.

Johnson, Una, and Worden Day. *Worden Day 40-Year Retrospective.* Exhibition Catalog. New Jersey State Museum, 1966.

Sawin, Martica. "Worden Day." *Arts Magazine* 33:8 (May 1959): 65.

de Gogorza, Patricia (1936–)

The sculptor/printmaker Patricia de Gogorza was born in Detroit, Michigan. She earned a Bachelor's degree from Smith College, Northampton, Massachusetts (1958); and received a Master of Arts degree from Goddard College, Plainfield, Vermont (1975). De Gogorza studied with Seong Moy in Provincetown, Massachusetts (summer 1956) and with the printmaker Stanley William Hayter at Atelier 17, Paris, France (1956–1959).

De Gogorza has held fourteen solo exhibitions in universities and galleries, including Smith College (1989); a retrospective show, Vermont College, Montpelier (1988); A.V.A. Gallery, Hanover, New Hampshire, and Moonbrook Gallery, Rutland, Vermont (1985); Johnson State College, Vermont, and the Garage Gallery, Montpelier, Vermont (1984); Bundy Museum, Waitsfield, Vermont (1982); and others. Her stone sculptures have been invited to group exhibitions throughout the northeastern United States; and her prints have been exhibited in group shows in the United States and abroad: from Provincetown, Massachusetts, to Paris, France; from New York City to Ljubljana, Yugoslavia; and have travelled through Australia.

De Gogorza has garnered honors and awards, including first prizes in sculpture, Norwich Art Annual, Connecticut (1980, 1983, 1986); first prize in the All Vermont Juried Show, Bundy Museum, Waitsfield (1982); a grant from the Vermont Council on the Arts (1975); and others. She has been a visiting artist and critic, a faculty member at many art schools and universities, a panelist, seminar leader, and a lecturer. Active in many professional art organizations and a professional violinist with the Vermont Philharmonic Orchestra, de Gogorza has executed commissions of granite and marble sculptures and engaged in on-site group projects (1987–1992). Her work is represented in private and public permanent collections, including the Collection de la Ville de Paris (Louvre), France; Victoria and Albert Museum, London, England; Boston Museum of Fine Arts, Massachusetts; Library of Congress, Washington, D.C.; University of Illinois, Urbana; Provincetown Museum, Massachusetts; and others.

Bibliography

Watson-Jones, Virginia. *Contemporary American Women Sculptors.* Oryx Press, 1986.

Who's Who in American Art. 19th ed. R.R. Bowker Co., 1991–1992.

de Kooning, Elaine (1918–1989)

Associated with the abstract expressionists, Elaine de Kooning was a well-known painter who also wrote extensively about art. Born the oldest child of Irish-German parents, de Kooning grew up in Brooklyn. She credited her mother with exposing her as a child to a variety of cultural events: the theater, opera, and museums, including the Metro-politan Museum of Art and the Brooklyn Museum—both in New York City. The reproductions in the family home—Rosa Bonheur and Elizabeth Vigée-Lebrun, along with Raphael and Rembrandt—led her to assume that half of all artists were women. Praise for her childhood drawings from family and friends encouraged her to spend hours on her own making art. She attended Erasmus Hall High School, Brooklyn, New York, where it was possible for her to major in art.

In the late 1930s she studied sculpture and painting in New York City, first at the Leonardo da Vinci School, and then at the American Artists School. Perhaps more important than her actual classes was the fact that her fellow students introduced her to the New York art scene. She was exposed to a wide range of styles but chose to express her support for various causes, such as the Spanish Civil War, by working in a social realist style. However, when she became the private pupil of Willem de Kooning, he persuaded her to turn to still lifes and emphasized the importance of developing spatial relationships in her paintings. They were married in 1943.

In the 1940s, as an active member of the emerging abstract expressionist group, de Kooning considered her spouse and Arshile Gorky to be the greatest influences on her painting. She had her first solo exhibition in 1952 at the Stable Gallery, New York City. In the late 1940s she began to write art criticism, setting down her lively assessment of developments in the New York art world. Encouraged by Thomas Hess, editor of *Art News*, her articles appeared regularly in that periodical throughout the 1950s. After an amicable separation from her husband in 1956, she began a series of visiting professorships at major universities throughout the country. She found teaching a way to fill the gap that resulted when success destroyed the camaraderie of the New York School in the late 1950s.

Although de Kooning sometimes worked on the enormous canvases typically associated with abstract expressionism, she insisted that size was not important to her and often had several pieces of vastly different scale in process at the same time. She worked quickly, varying her materials frequently—charcoal, ink, pastels, oils, and acrylics—always marking the canvas in a gestural process that was ultimately more about drawing than arranging patches of color.

De Kooning produced non-representational works, but became best known for her figurative paintings, including portraits. Many of these portraits were of her family and friends, but she accepted commissions, including one to paint "President John F. Kennedy," which occupied her from December 1962 until the time of his assassination. Her method of working resulted in an emphasis on the physical appearance of her portrait subjects, and she captured the individual through physiognomy and gesture.

De Kooning's other figurative works were painted serially, in large thematic cycles, which, as Eleanor Munro pointed out, often involved the "Towering Male," or his surrogate—bull. The first of these cycles consisted of seated portraits of faceless men. Newspaper photographs of sports events stimulated a series of paintings of baseball and basketball players. Her bullfight series, begun in 1957, was inspired by weekend trips to the corrida in Juárez while she was a visiting artist in Albuquerque, New Mexico. In 1976, during a stay in Paris, she began a series based on a nineteenth-century, baroque-revival statue of Bacchus in the Luxembourg Gardens. Her final series began in 1983, when de Kooning visited several prehistoric sites in Northern Spain and Southern France. Reacting to the immediacy of the cave paintings, she saw in the works of paleolithic artists a sensibility similar to her own lyrical expressionism.

Paula Wisotzki

Bibliography

Campbell, Lawrence. "Elaine de Kooning Paints a Picture." *Art News* 59 (December 1960): 40–44.

de Kooning, Elaine. "Pure paints a picture." *Art News* 56 (Summer 1957): 57, 86–87.

———. "Subject: What, How or Who?" *Art News* 54 (April 1950) 26–29, 61–62.

Munro, Eleanor. *Originals: American Women Artists.* Simon and Schuster, 1979, pp. 248–60.

De Larios, Dora (1933–)

A sculptor known for her architectural ceramic murals and public art commissions, Dora De Larios was born and raised in Los Angeles, California, where she currently maintains her studio.

She studied ceramics with Vivika and Otto Heino and Susan Peterson at the University of Southern California (USC), Los Angeles, where she earned a Bachelor of Fine Arts degree in 1957. Upon graduation De Larios set up her ceramic studio, returning to USC to teach ceramics in 1959 and, later, teaching at the University of California at Los Angeles (UCLA). In 1968 De Larios became a design consultant to the International Pipe and Ceramic Corporation and in 1966 she completed her first large-scale ceramic mural commission for the company's headquarters in New Jersey. In 1977 she was one of twelve American potters to make place settings of dinnerware for the White House in Washington, D.C., used for Mrs. Carter's luncheon honoring the senators' wives. The dinnerware then toured six cities throughout the United States in an exhibition titled "American Crafts at the White House."

De Larios has executed architectural commissions for such far-flung sites as Central Park Development in Nagoya, Japan; Tetiaroa in Tahiti, French Polynesia; and the Makaha Inn Resort in Oahu, Hawaii. In the United States her sculptural murals can be seen at the Contemporary Hotel at Disney World in Orlando, Florida, as well as at the Alan Sieroty Building, Famco Investments, Lawry's California Center in Los Angeles, and at many other sites throughout Southern California. Her most recent commission is a public art project for the City of Pasadena, completed in 1992.

Elena Karina Canavier

Bibliography

Rubenstein, Charlotte Streifer. *American Women Sculptors.* G.K. Hall & Co., 1991.

Levin, Elaine. *History of American Ceramics.* Harry N. Abrams, 1988, p. 304.

De Pédery-Hunt, Dora (1913–)

Dora De Pédery-Hunt was born in Budapest, Hungary. She studied sculpture and design at the Royal School of Applied Arts, Budapest, receiving her Master's degree in 1943. While in Hungary she executed several sculpture commissions for the government and various churches and in 1943 won the city of Budapest sculpture award. From 1945 she lived and worked in Germany, finally coming to Canada late in 1948 to settle in Toronto.

The early part of De Pédery-Hunt's career in Canada was spent designing church interiors and religious sculpture. Her commissions included liturgical sculpture for St. Joseph's College chapel, Toronto (1957); the convent of the Ursuline Sisters, Chatham (1962); and the chapel of the Grey Nuns General Hospital in Sault Ste. Marie (1964). In 1956 she designed the interior fittings for the chapel of Notre Dame Academy, Waterdown, Ontario. Two of her bronze sculptures were included in the Canadian section of the 1964 "Biennial of Religious Art" at Saltzburg, Austria.

De Pédery-Hunt is probably best known, however, for her miniature sculptures and as Canada's foremost medallist. Her medal designs run into the hundreds and include many private commissions. Among her public commissions are the reverse of the Canadian Centennial Medal (1967), and Canada's official medal for Expo '70 in Osaka, Japan. She also designed Canada's $100 gold coins commemorating the Montréal Olympics (1976), and the International Year of Peace (1986). A portrait medal of Dr. Norman Bethune by the artist was presented by Canadian prime minister Pierre Elliot Trudeau to Chairman Mao Tsetung of China on the occasion of his 1973 visit to that country. Recently De Pédery-Hunt has designed the new effigy of Queen Elizabeth II for use on all Canadian coins.

De Pédery-Hunt has been a member of the Sculptors' Society of Canada since 1953, serving as its president from 1966 to 1968. An associate of the Royal Canadian Academy of Arts since 1956, she was made a full member of that society in 1967. In addition to numerous solo exhibitions of her work since 1959, De Pédery-Hunt has also participated in many international medal exhibitions from the early 1960s and is Canada's representative at the Fédération Internationale de la Médaille. In 1971 she organized "Ten Contemporary Canadian Medallists" (the first all-Canadian medal exhibition) for the Public Archives of Canada; the National Gallery of Canada, Ottawa; the Smithsonian Institution, Washington, D.C.; the British Museum, London, England; the Royal Cabinets of Medals in Brussels, Belgium; The Hague, Holland; and Stockholm, Sweden; and in numerous other public and private collections around the world.

Janine A. Butler

Bibliography

De Pédery-Hunt, Dora, and Elizabeth Frey. *Medals.* Canadian Stage and Art Publications Ltd., 1974.

———. *Sculpture.* Trans. by Raynald Desmeules. Prince Arthur Galleries and Canadian Stage and Arts Publications Ltd., 1978.

Mullaly, Terence. "Dora De Pédery-Hunt: A Medallist with a Message." *The Medal* 15 (Autumn 1989): 68–71.

de Saint-Phalle, Niki (1930–)

Niki de Saint-Phalle was born in Neuilly-sur-Seine (near Paris), France, and educated at the Convent of Sacre Coeur, New York City (1936–1945). A self-taught postmodernist sculptor, de Saint-Phalle was married in 1948, gave birth to two children, returned to Paris in 1951, separated from her husband nine years later, and created her first paintings in 1952. She formed her first assemblages and object-reliefs four years later and, in the 1960s, produced her rifle-shot paintings. She lived with Jean Tinguely and collaborated with him in many happenings throughout Europe, fashioned her first "Nana" sculptures, and, in the following decade, produced her first films.

De Saint-Phalle has shown her works in more than three score solo exhibitions throughout the world, including the Moderna Muséet, Stockholm, Sweden (1961, 1963); Galerie Rive Droite, Paris, France (1962); Gallery Iolas, Geneva, Switzerland (1964, 1969); Stedelijk Museum, Amsterdam, the Netherlands (1967); Galerie der Spiegel, Cologne, Germany (1970); Gimpel and Weitzenhoffer, New York (1971, 1973, 1979, 1982, 1985); Museum of Fine Arts, Columbus, Ohio, toured the United States (1980); Centre Georges Pompidou, Paris, retrospective, toured Germany, Austria, Great Britain, Sweden, and Israel (1980); Space Niki/Sagacho Exhibit Space, Tokyo, Japan (1987); and many others. Her works have been invited to significant group shows, such as "The Art of Assemblage," Museum of Modern Art (MoMA), New York City (1961); "Biennale de Paris," Musée d'Art Moderne, Paris, France (1963); "Collection Hammer," Kunstmuseum, Basel, Switzerland (1978); "The Figurative Tradition," Whitney Museum of American Art, New York City (1980); "Sacred Spaces," Everson Museum of Art, Syracuse, New York (1987); and hosts of others.

De Saint-Phalle's works are in permanent public collections throughout the world, including the Metropolitan Art Museum, Tokyo, Japan; Museum of Modern Art, Kamakura, Japan; Rockefeller Collection, New York City; Museum of Fine Arts, Houston, Texas; Rijksmuseum Kroller-Muller, Otterlo, the Netherlands; and many others. "HON" (1963) (which means "she" in Swedish), an eighty-two-foot-long, twenty-foot-high hollow sculpture of a female lying on her back, is not atypical of de Saint-Phalle's work. The viewing public entered the figure through a door between her legs to find a theater, bar, aquarium, and a planetarium. A work designed to épater le bourgeois.

Bibliography
Matsumoto, Michiko. *Portrait of Niki de Saint-Phalle*. Parco Co., Ltd., 1986.
Picard, Denis. "Sut la Colline Embellie." *Conaissance des Arts*. No. 431 (January 1988): 78–81.
Schulz-Hoffman, Carla, et al. *Niki de Saint-Phalle*. Prestel-Verlag, 1987.

Dehner, Dorothy (1901–1994)

Dorothy Dehner has produced art steadily since 1920; however, she sought few exhibition opportunities until 1952—the year of her divorce from sculptor David Smith.

Born in Cleveland, Ohio, Dehner lived in Pasadena, California, with her mother's sisters after she was orphaned in 1916. Exposed by her family to liberal views and avant-garde culture, Dehner developed an interest in acting that brought her to New York City in 1922 to study and perform. In 1925 she travelled to Europe, where, in addition to visiting monuments of the past, she sought out works by contemporary artists, including the Fauves and Cubists. She returned to New York City and enrolled at the Art Students League, determined to become a sculptor, but quickly switched to painting classes when she discovered, despite the school's avant-garde reputation, the sculptors on the faculty were decidedly "old-fashioned."

Dehner met Smith in 1926, and they were married in 1927. She was instrumental in aiding his development as an artist, steering him to the Art Students League and introducing him to recent advanced art. During the twenty-five years of their marriage Dehner continued to produce paintings and drawings, but did little to advance her professional career. Works from this period were often Cubist-inspired abstractions, but in the early 1940s she chronicled her daily life with Smith on their farm at Bolton Landing in a series of realistic works. Other works from the 1940s directly reflected the contemporary New York avant-garde interest in surrealism.

Dehner's professional life blossomed when she left Smith in 1940. Her first one-person exhibition in New York City was a 1952 showing of watercolors at the Rose Fried Gallery. Despite her early interest in sculpture, Dehner did not work in three dimensions until 1955, but her first experiments with sculpture were so satisfying that she stopped painting. For the next twenty years, Dehner worked primarily in bronze, using the lost-wax process to achieve an assembled rather than a modeled appearance. Although small in size, her bronzes conveyed a sense of monumentality. The imagery frequently involved the archetypal symbols common among post-war artists in the United States.

Beginning in 1955 Dehner was represented by the Willard Gallery. That same year she married Ferdinand Mann. After his death in 1974 Dehner began to work with wood, the angular shapes of her assemblages modified by patterns of the natural grains of their unpainted surfaces. From 1981 she has also worked on Corten steel. In the later years of her career the size of her sculptures has increased considerably.

Dehner is a published poet and has written incisive articles about figures from the New York art world, including Smith, John Graham, and Jan Matulka.

Paula Wisotzki

Bibliography
Dorothy Dehner and David Smith: Their Decades of Search and Fulfillment. Essays by Joan Marter and Judith McCandless. Jane Voorhees Zimmerli Art Museum, 1983.
Keane-White, Dorothy. *Dorothy Dehner: Sculpture and Works on Paper.* Twining Gallery, 1989.
Marter, Joan M. "Dorothy Dehner." *Woman's Art Journal* 1 (Fall 1980–Winter 1980): 47–50.
Obituary. *The New York Times* (September 23, 1984): A14.

Del Riego, Yolanda (1943–)

Born in Santo Domingo, Dominican Republic, the printmaker Yolanda Del Riego studied drawing, painting, ceramics, photography, and other arts in many institutions in the United States between 1967 and 1975. Beginning in 1976 she began to specialize in printmaking, working at various times and places with Lee Chesney, Clinton Cline, Bob Evermon, Jules Heller, Misch Kohn, Bill Kimura, Kathryn Lipke, John Sommers, Carol Summers, and Toshi Yoshida.

Del Riego has held solo exhibitions in museums and galleries in the United States and abroad, including the Kittery Art Association, Maine (1970); Carriage House Gallery, Portsmouth, New Hampshire (1972); The Gallery (1976), Old Store Gallery (1977), Artique (1978), Collectors Gallery (1979, 1980), and Anchorage Historical and Fine Arts Museum (1979)—all in Anchorage, Alaska; Galería de la Mota (1980); Centro Cultural de los Estados Unidos (1983), Instituto de

Cooperacion Iberoamericana (1983), and "Yolanda Del Riego, Obra Gráfica, 1976–1986," Biblioteca Nacional (1986)—all in Madrid, Spain; and others. Her work has been included in many group exhibitions from the Ibiza, Balearic Islands to Ogunquit, Maine; from Spokane, Washington, to Boston, Massachusetts; and Anchorage, Alaska. Her imaginative, abstract, viscous intaglios have won honors and awards and are represented in private and public permanent collections.

Bibliography
Yolanda Del Riego, Obra Gráfica, 1976–1986. A Catalog. Madrid, Spain: La Biblioteca Nacional, 1986.

DeLange, Stephanie (1944–)

Born and raised in Los Angeles, California, Stephanie DeLange spent her childhood and adolescence enjoying the extensive geographic variety within California. The national parks, the beaches, the deserts, and lush farmlands became familiar territory and entered her ceramic sculptures when she became a research assistant in a graduate ceramics program at the University of California at Los Angeles (UCLA). After receiving a Bachelor of Arts degree in 1966 from the Santa Barbara campus of the university, DeLange returned to Los Angeles to work with professor Laura Andreson, whose extensive glaze research fired her imagination.

Certain rugged glaze surfaces recalled the beauty of rocks meeting the ocean surf while others suggested the desert contrasting with a cloudless sky. How to express landscape in which mass meets mass was a dilemma she solved through geometric shapes; a wedge resembles a mountain, a cylinder a butte, and a dome mimics the earth's curve. In the 1980s DeLange's work progressed toward evoking a sense of place, a time of day, or a season of the year for a less literal and more ethereal interpretation of nature.

Graduating in 1971 with a Master of Fine Arts degree, DeLange participated in numerous group exhibitions in California, Arizona, Iowa, Washington State, and Washington, D.C. She has had four solo exhibits since 1977, the most recent titled "Attending to the Earth" (1990). She established a studio in Venice, California in 1972 and as visiting faculty, taught at California State University (1974), Pitzer College in Claremont (1975–1976), Santa Monica College (1977, 1978), and at the two university campuses she had attended (1981, 1983–1984). Since 1987 she has been an adjunct faculty member at Pepperdine University in Malibu, California.

Elaine Levin

Bibliography
Lane, Peter. *Ceramic Form.* Rizzoli International Publications, Inc., 1988.
Levin, Elaine. *Attending to the Earth.* Los Angeles: Laband Art Gallery, Loyola Marymount University, 1990.
"West Coast Clay Spectrum." *Ceramics Monthly* (January 1980): 40–41.

Delano, Irene (1919–1982)

Painter, printmaker, designer, writer, and editor, Irene Delano was born in Detroit, Michigan, and studied at the Pennsylvania Academy of Fine Arts, Philadelphia (1933–1937). A visit to Puerto Rico in 1946 prompted Delano to found the Motion-Picture and Graphic Arts Workshop of the Commission of Public Recreation. (Her husband was a photographer for the Farm Security Administration in the United States.) Delano, along with Felix Bonilla-Norat, taught the techniques and processes of serigraphy in the workshop to Puerto Rican artists (1949–1952).

Early on, Delano was an assistant to Anton Refregier on the mural commissioned for the World's Fair, New York City (1939). From 1970 until her death Delano was editor of *Que Pasa,* a Puerto Rican magazine. Examples of her award-winning works are in private, public, and corporate permanent collections, including the American Institute of Graphic Arts, New York City; Division of Community Education, San Juan, Puerto Rico; Smith, Kline and French, Puerto Rico; UNESCO, New York City; and others.

Bibliography
The Latin American Spirit: Art and Artists in the United States 1920–1970. Harry N. Abrams, 1988.

Delgado, Maria Elena (1921–)

Born in Monclova, Coahuila, Mexico, Maria Elena Delgado studied painting and sculpture at the Technological Institute of Monterrey, Nuevo León, Mexico, from 1946 to 1955 where, as a distinguished alumna, she taught classes in those selfsame studio fields between 1954 and 1957. She painted a fresco in "Old Main" on the campus of the University of Nuevo León (1955). Delgado was a student of Mignorances, though she took up ceramics with Guillermo Cataño (1958), lacquerware and calligraphy with J. Tovar (1960), the three-dimensional uses of resins, fiberglass, and lithography (1973).

Delgado had a great number of solo exhibitions, including Arte, A.C., in Monterrey, Nuevo León (1956), the National College of Architects (1957), the Regional Institute of Bellas Artes, Acapulco (1958), and Salón de la Plástica Mexicana, INBA, Mexico City—all in Mexico; and the Velna Gallery, Chicago, Illinois (1968); Museum of the City of Juárez, Chihuahua, the Museo Pape, Monclova Coahuila, and Arte A.C., Monterrey, Nuevo León (1969), and Escudero Galería de Arte—all in Mexico (1970); the Organization of American States, Washington, D.C.; and the Institute of Mexican Culture, San Antonio, the Museum of Science and Industry, Fort Worth (1972), and the McAllen International Museum, McAllen (1980)—all in Texas. Delgado produced a number of sculptures that may be found in her native city. She participated in myriad group shows throughout Mexico and abroad.

She is founder of the Ateneo del Arte de la Academía Mexicana de Bellas Artes and of the Sociedad Mexicana de Artes Plásticas.

Bibliography
Alvarez, José Rogelio, et al. *Enciclopedia de México.* Secretaría de Educación Pública, 1987.
Diccionario Biográfico Enciclopedico de la Pintura Mexicana. Quinientos Años Editores, 1979.

Delisle, Roseline (1952–)

Born in Québec, Canada, the ceramist Roseline Delisle is known for her small black-and-white porcelains. Delisle studied at the College du Vieux Montréal, Québec, Canada (1975), and, three years later, emigrated to the United States, where she set up a ceramic studio in Venice, California.

Winner of awards and honors, Delisle was commissioned by the

J. Paul Getty Center for the History of Art and Humanities, Santa Monica, California (1985), to create vases for their entry area. Her work, as a result, has grown in scale to a certain monumentality.

Bibliography
Clark, Garth. *American Ceramics 1896 to the Present.* Abbeville Press, 1987.
Clark, Garth, et al. *Pacific Connections.* Los Angeles Institute of
    Contemporary Art, 1985.

Dembus, Dolores (1931–)
A native New Yorker known for her weavings in silk, Dolores Dembus earned a Bachelor of Science degree *cum laude* from Columbia University, New York City (1952); won a Fulbright fellowship in painting to Paris, France, the following year; and did post-graduate work at the University of Calcutta, India (1953–1955). She also studied weaving (c. 1958) with Anni Albers and audited a class in color offered by Josef Albers at Yale University, New Haven, Connecticut. While in India Dembus researched the fiber arts and visited major monuments in the course of more than 15,000 miles of travel.

On her return to New York, Dembus worked as a commercial artist and did freelance work for a variety of clients, including *Seventeen*, CBS, Grey Advertising, and others. She had two solo exhibitions of her paintings at the end of her Fulbright year: one in Paris, France; the other in London, England. Her weavings were invited to many group exhibitions in the United States and abroad, including shows at the Museum of Modern Art (MoMA), New York City (1969, 1970, 1972); the International Biennale of Weaving. Lausanne, Switzerland (1971), and Warsaw, Poland (1971); and exhibitions at the Munson-Williams-Proctor Institute, Utica, New York; the Everson Museum of Art, Syracuse, New York (1975); and others.

Dembus taught at several institutions, including the Creative Arts Workshop, New Haven, Connecticut (1962); Troy Arts Workshop (1966); and at Union College, Schenectady, New York (1969–1974). Winner of honors and awards for her work, Dembus was the recipient of grants from the National Endowment for the Arts (NEA) (1975, 1976). Her work is in private, public, and corporate permanent collections, such as MoMA, New York City; Yale University, New Haven, Connecticut; Silvermine College of Art, New Canaan, Connecticut; Columbia University, New York City; and others.

Bibliography
Larson, Jack Lenor. "Two Views of the Tapestry Biennale." *Craft Horizons*
    (October 1971).
Who's Who in American Art. 19th ed. R.R. Bowker Co., 1991–1992.

DeMeritt, Carolyn (1946–)
Born in Charlotte, North Carolina, the photographer Carolyn DeMeritt has held solo exhibitions in universities and colleges, including Queens College, Charlotteville (1984); Virginia Intermont College, Bristol, Virginia (1988); and others.

DeMeritt's work has been invited to, or included in group exhibitions, such as the "Annual Light Factory National Juried Exhibition," Charlotte, North Carolina (1983, 1984, 1985); "Light Images '84," Chrysler Museum, Norfolk, Virginia (1984); "Photographing Children," Santa Fe Center for Photography, New Mexico (1987); "Flashpoint/Ten

Photographers," Art on the Tracks, Pensacola, Florida (1989); and others.

Winner of honors and awards, DeMeritt won first place at the exhibition, "Black and White," Southern Visions (1984); best of competition at the Raleigh Photographic Arts Association, North Carolina (1985); the Linda Weaver Achievement award, National Aperture (1986); and others. "Untitled" (1986) is one of a series of unsettling photographic studies of teenage girls in various, seemingly unposed, situations. Her work is represented in private and public permanent collections.

Bibliography
Nine from North Carolina: An Exhibition of Women Artists. North Carolina
    State Committee and the National Museum of Women in the Arts, 1989.

Denes, Agnes (1938–)
Born in Budapest, Hungary, the environmental sculptor and printmaker Agnes Denes studied at the City University of New York (CUNY); the New School for Social Research; and Columbia University—all in New York City.

Denes has held solo exhibitions in museums and galleries in the United States, including the Corcoran Gallery of Art, Washington, D.C. (1974); Centre Culturel Americain, Paris, France (1978); Amerika Haus, Berlin, Germany (1978); Institute for Contemporary Art, London, England (1979); "Agnes Denes: Drawings, Objects, Graphics, Photos," the Galleriet, Lund, Sweden (1980); and others. Her work has been included in group shows, such as "Women Choose Women," New York Cultural Center (1973); "New Acquisitions," Museum of Modern Art (MoMA), New York City (1973); "In Her Own Image," Fleisher Art Memorial, Philadelphia, Pennsylvania (1974); "Thirty Years of American Printmaking," including the 20th National Print Exhibition, Brooklyn Museum, New York City (1976); Newport Harbor Art Museum, Newport, California (1976); and others.

Examples of Denes's work are in private and public permanent collections, including the Allen Memorial Art Museum, Oberlin, Ohio; National Collection of Fine Arts, Smithsonian Institution, Washington, D.C.; Moderna Muséet, Stockholm, Sweden; MoMA, and the Whitney Museum of American Art—both in New York City; and many others.

Bibliography
Agnes Denes: Sculptures of the Mind, Philosophical Drawings. Berlin,
    Germany: Amerika Haus, 1978.
Cohen, Ronny H. "Agnes Denes: Triumph of the Visual Will." *Print
    Collector's Newsletter* 13:5 (November–December 1982): 159–61.
Johnson, Una E. *American Prints and Printmakers.* Doubleday & Co., 1980.
Kuspit, Donald B. "Agnes Denes: The Ironies of Comprehension." *Arts
    Magazine* 56:4 (December 1981): 152–53.

Dennis, Donna (1942–)
Born in Springfield, Ohio, the sculptor Donna Dennis earned a Bachelor's degree at Carleton College, Northfield, Minnesota (1964); studied in Paris, France, with College Art Studies Abroad (1964–1965); and studied with Stephen Greene at the Art Students League, New York City (1965–1966).

Dennis has held more than thirty solo exhibitions in museums and galleries, including the Sculpture Center, New York City (1993);

"Tunnel Tower/Donna Dennis," Neuberger Museum, State University of New York (SUNY), Purchase (1991); "Subway with Silver Girders," Florida International University, Miami (1990); "26 Bars," Institute of Contemporary Art, Boston, Massachusetts (1989); "Deep Station," Indianapolis Museum, Indiana (1991); Muhlenberg College, Allentown, Pennsylvania, and Delaware Art Museum, Wilmington (1988), and Brooklyn Museum, New York (1987); "Subway with Silver Girders and Skowhegan Stairway," Holly Solomon Gallery, New York City (1983); and many more. Her sculpture, paintings, drawings, and prints have been invited to group exhibitions throughout the United States and Europe: from New York City to Venice, Italy; from Joplin, Missouri, to Halifax, Nova Scotia; from London, England, to Corpus Christi, Texas; from Aachen, Germany, and Surrey, British Columbia, to Minneapolis, Minnesota, and Fullerton, California.

Winner of honors and awards, Dennis has received painting and sculpture fellowships from the New York State Foundation for the Arts (1985, 1992); won a Bessie award in visual design for the sets of "Quintland, The Musical" (1992); received the Bard award of merit in architecture and urban design from the City Club of New York, and other recognition for the P.S.234, New York City fence and ceramic medallion designs (1987, 1989); sculpture fellowships from the National Endowment for the Arts (NEA) (1977, 1980, 1986); an art award from the American Academy and Institute of Arts and Letters (1984); New York State Creative Artist Public Service (CAPS) grants (1975, 1981); and a Guggenheim fellowship (1979).

Visual arts associate professor at the State University of New York (SUNY) at Purchase since 1990, Dennis has taught at various art schools and universities and has been a visiting artist and lecturer throughout the United States. Panelist, curator, board member of professional arts organizations and artist's needs advocate with respect to the Loft Law in New York City, Dennis has offered seminars for high school art teachers (1988) and gifted high school art students (1989, 1992, 1993) through the Alliance of Independent Colleges of Art and the Marie Walsh Sharpe Foundation, respectively. Her work is represented in private and public permanent collections in the United States and Europe, including the Geneva Art Museum, Switzerland; Neue Galerie-Sammlung Ludwig, Aachen, Germany; and many others.

Bibliography

Brenson, Michael. "Donna Dennis—Dreaming of Faraway Places: The Ships Come to Washington Market." *The New York Times* (July 23, 1989).
Heartney, Eleanor, and Victoria Hansen. A Catalog. *Presswork: The Art of Women Printmakers*. Lang Communications, 1991.
Megerian, Maureen. A Catalog. *Enclosures and Encounters: Architectural Aspects of Recent Sculpture*. Storm King Art Center, 1991.
Rubenstein, Charlotte Streifer. *American Women Sculptors*. G.K. Hall, 1990.

DeSwaan, Sylvia (1941–)

Born in Chernowitz, Rumania, Sylvia DeSwaan emigrated to the United States when she was ten years old. She went to Hunter College, New York City, and then took classes at the Art Students League in the same city.

At the age of twenty-one DeSwaan settled in Mexico where she has pursued three separate, yet related, careers: painting, stage designing, and photography.

She had a solo exhibition at the Carmel Gallery in New York City in 1963 and since then has had a number of shows in Mexico and elsewhere. The Safad Museum in Israel has one of her works in its permanent collection, and her work was shown repeatedly at the Galeriá Edvard Munch and the Galeriá de Antonio Souza—both in Mexico City. A portfolio of her work titled "Drawings of Life and Death" was published in 1966. A number of her drawings have graced the pages of literary reviews and magazines.

Bibliography

The Texas Quarterly: Image of Mexico I. The University of Texas. Autumn 1969.

Dey, Kris (1949–)

A mixed-media artist known for her complex color constructions of thread and painted fabric wrapped on a variety of materials, Kris Dey was born on October 17, 1949, in Buffalo, New York. She was raised in Oakland, California, and studied art at the University of California at Los Angeles (UCLA), where she received a Bachelor of Arts degree in 1972, a Master of Arts degree in 1974, and a Master of Fine Arts degree in 1976. Bernard Kester, a professor of textiles, and Vasa, a sculptor and painter, were strong influences on Dey's artistic development.

Dey first exhibited professionally in the exhibit "Design '76" at the Pacific Design Center, Los Angeles, California. Her interest in layered systems of color has produced compositions of increasingly complex color relationships. Initially these were created by wrapping yarn on vertical bundles of sisal twine. However, in the late 1970s Dey introduced compositions made of hand-painted cloth, torn into strips and wrapped on wooden slats and plastic tubing. These were exhibited in "The New Classicism," Museum of Modern Art (MoMA) New York City (1977); and the "Third Textile Triennale," Lodz, Poland (1978). Variations of this process of painting, striping, and wrapping have continued to evolve into color compositions with illusions of depth, transparency, and emanating light sources. Exhibits of this work include "Craft Today: Poetry of the Physical," American Craft Museum, New York City (1986); and "Fiber Directions: West Coast," Schneider Museum of Art, Ashland, Oregon.

Dey's work is included in numerous corporate collections, including the Shaklee Corporation, San Francisco, and California Federal Savings and Loan, Beverly Hills—both in California; the Vesti Corporation, Boston, Massachusetts; and Metropolitan Life Insurance Company, Houston, Texas. Her work is also in the collection of the Art Institute of Chicago, Illinois. Dey was the recipient of a National Endowment for the Arts (NEA) fellowship in 1979.

Claire Campbell Park

Bibliography

American Craft Museum. *Craft Today: Poetry of the Physical*. Weidenfeld & Nicolson, 1986.
Constantine, Mildred, and Jack Lenor Larsen. *The Art Fabric Mainstream*. Van Nostrand-Reinhold, 1981.
Paley, Aaron. "Los Angeles: Four Artists." *Textile/Art* (Fall 1983).

Dickinson, Eleanor (1931–)

Born in Knoxville, Tennessee, the painter/printmaker/video artist Eleanor Dickinson is known for her huge, spiritual pastel figure drawings and paintings of the lower Appalachian Pentecostal Peoples. Dickinson earned a Bachelor's degree from the University of Tennessee, Knoxville (1952); she also studied at the San Francisco Art Institute, California (1961–1963); Académie de la Grande Chaumière, Paris, France (1971); University of California at Berkeley (1967, 1971, 1981); the California College of Arts and Crafts, Oakland, where she received a Master of Fine Arts degree in film and video (1982); and at Golden Gate University, San Francisco (1984).

Dickinson has held more than seventy solo exhibitions in museums and galleries since 1958, including Independent Curators, Inc., New York, a travelling show (1993–1997); the Museum of Contemporary Religious Art, St. Louis, Missouri (1993); Diverse Works, Houston, Texas (1990); Gallery 10, Washington, D.C. (1989); Tennessee State Museum, Nashville (1981); the Oakland Museum, California (1979); Galerie de Arte y Libros, Monterrey, Mexico (1978); Triton Museum, Santa Clara, California (1977); the Fine Arts Museum of San Francisco (1975); "Sky Drawings" from an airplane over San Francisco and the Central Valley, California (1963–1964); and many others. Her work has been invited to myriad group exhibitions in the United States and abroad—from Knoxville, Tennessee, to Paris, France; from Sacramento, California, to Nairobi, Kenya; from Toronto, Canada, to London, England; and from Brussels, Belgium, back to the Cumberland Gap, Kentucky.

Recipient of more than thirty honors, awards, and grants for her work, Dickinson, a widely-travelled professor of art at the California College of Arts and Crafts, Oakland, since 1971, has created set designs; produced videos and television programs; chaired panels and held high office in regional and national professional organizations; has served as art juror for competitions; and has lectured widely and written extensively. Along with three other artists, she holds the record (according to the *Guinness Book of Records*) for the "longest continuous drawing time: three days and three nights."

Dickinson's large-scale pastels on black velvet, "Crucifixions," are powerful metaphors for life and death, reflecting, among other concerns, man's inhumanity to man. Her works are represented in private, public, and corporate permanent collections, including the National Museum of American Art, Smithsonian Institution, the Corcoran Gallery of Art, the Library of Congress, the Archives of American Art, and the National Museum of Women in the Arts—all in Washington, D.C.; Stanford Art Museum, San Francisco Museum of Modern Art, Oakland Museum, and Santa Barbara Museum—all in California; Tennessee State Museum, and Knoxville Museum—both in Tennessee; Museum of Contemporary Religious Art, St. Louis, Missouri; Butler Institute of American Art, Ohio; and many others.

Bibliography

"Artist and Social Documentarian." *The Quarterly Journal of the Library of Congress.* (Summer 1981).

Cohn, Terri. "Paul Mavrides and Eleanor Dickinson." *Artweek* (March 1991).

Epstein, Helga. "Eleanor Dickinson, Social Historian and Artist." *American Artist* 44:461 (December 1980): 80–83, 95–96.

Hanson, Jo. "Eleanor Dickinson: The Crucifixion Series." *Women Artists News* (Spring–Summer 1989).

Selz, Peter. "Eleanor Dickinson at Hatley Martin." *Art in America* (September 1989).

Wasserman, K. *A Salute to Women.* National Museum of Women in the Arts, 1991.

Dickson, Jennifer (1936–)

Born in Piet Retief, South Africa, the printmaker Jennifer Dickson knew early on that she would become an artist. Contrary to her father's desires she studied at Goldsmith's School for Art, University of London, England (1954–1959) and at Atelier 17, Paris, France, with Stanley William Hayter (1961–1965). Founder and chair of printmaking at Brighton College of Art, England, during the 1960s, Dickson emigrated to Canada in 1969 and has taught and lectured widely in Canada, the United States, and Jamaica since 1974. Her lectures on the nude and on feminist issues in the history of art are singularly informed.

Winner of many awards and honors, Dickson is a prolific artist; by 1978 she had held more than thirty solo exhibitions in six countries and showed in scores of group exhibitions. A sampling of her exhibition record includes the Biennale de Paris, Museum of Modern Art, France (1963); "Modern Prints," Victoria & Albert Museum, London, England (1965); "The Secret Garden," University of British Columbia, Vancouver (1978); Art Gallery at Harbourfront, Toronto, Canada (1980); "Canadian Camera Works: A Bracketed View," Bemidji State University, Montana (1981); and many others. With respect to "The Secret Garden" she recently wrote, "This sequence of photo-etchings is a form of private theatre in which the gestalt of events is complete—whereas in reality it often is not. To be the director of the *mise-en-scéne*, and also the participant: to be *in* and, simultaneously, to *look-at* (a voyeur of one-self)."

Dickson was elected to membership in the Royal Academy of Arts, London, England (1976) and, two years later, to the Royal Canadian Academy of Arts. Her work is represented in private and public permanent collections throughout the world, including the Bibliothèque Nationale, Paris, France; the Hermitage, St. Petersburg, Russia; National Gallery of Canada, Ottawa; Smithsonian Institution, Washington, D.C.; Victoria & Albert Museum of Art, London, England; and many others.

Bibliography

Heviz, Judy. "Jennifer Dickson: An Art That Transcends Time." *Vie des arts* 18:71 (Summer 1973): 17–19, 88–89.

Lucie-Smith, Edward. *Art in the Seventies.* Phaidon, 1980.

Rosenberg, Avis Lang. "Before Narcissus, Before Paradise: Jennifer Dickson's Secret Garden." *Print Voice.* University of Alberta, pp. 36–40.

Rothenstein, Michael. *Frontiers of Printmaking.* Studio Vista, 1970.

Dienes, Sari (1898–1992)

Born in Debreczen, Hungary, Sari Dienes (Sari Chylinska von Daivitz) studied dance, music, and philosophy before deciding upon the visual arts as a career. She studied at the Académie Moderne, Paris, France, with Ferdinand Léger, André L'Hôte, and Amedée Ozenfant (1930–1935). Two years later Dienes became director at the Ozenfant School, London, England, and in 1938 she studied with Henry Moore. In 1939 she worked at Ozenfant's school in New York City.

The outbreak of World War II caused Dienes's visit to the United States to become a lifetime stay. She began holding a series of solo and group exhibitions of her work in various galleries and institutions, including the New School for Social Research (1942); Wittenborn Gallery (1942); Betty Parsons Gallery (1950, 1954, 1959); "The Art of Assemblage," Museum of Modern Art (MoMA) (1961); and A.I.R. Gallery (1973,

1975, 1977, 1979, 1981, 1990)—all in New York City; "Sari Dienes: A Retrospective," Thorpe Intermedia Gallery, Sparkill, New York (1986); Galerie J & J Donguy, Paris, France (1990); and "Sari Dienes: Memorial Celebration," Sari Dienes Gallery, New York City (1992–1993).

Dienes had an experimental attitude toward art and, early on, used found materials in her work. She travelled widely, learned the art of woodcut and ceramics in Japan; worked at printmaking in Atelier 17, New York City, with Stanley William Hayter; was a founding member of the A.I.R. Gallery, the first women's cooperative art gallery in the United States; taught at Parsons School of Design, New York City, and the Brooklyn Museum School of Art, New York, as well as in her own studio; was a fellow in residence at the MacDowell Colony, Peterborough, New Hampshire (1952, 1953, 1955); began her series of "rubbings" when in residence at the Cummington School of Art, Massachusetts (1954); was the recipient of a Ford Foundation grant (1965); experimented with color xerox and was commissioned to create silk-screened murals for the New York State House, Albany, New York (1972); won grants from the National Endowment for the Arts (NEA), the Gottlieb Foundation, and a gold medal from the Accademia Italia Delle Arti di Lavoro, Parma, Italy (1979); and had a three-month residency at Atlos de Chavon, Santo Domingo, Dominican Republic, where she worked with local materials. Her works are represented in numerous private and public permanent collections throughout the United States and abroad.

Bibliography
Frank, Peter. "Sari Dienes (A.I.R.)." *Art News* 75:1 (January 1976): 125–26.
Miodoni, Cate. "The Natural Order of Things: Sari Dienes." *Women Artists News* 8:1 (Fall 1982): 18–19.
Smith, Roberta. "Sari Dienes, 93, Artist Devoted to the Value of the Found Object." *The New York Times* (May 28, 1992).
Von Baron, Judith. "Sari Dienes." *Craft Horizons* 34 (April 1974): 48.

Diesing, Freda (1925–)

Born in Prince Rupert in northern British Columbia, Canada, Freda Diesing attended the Vancouver School of Art. A Haida, Diesing is one of those rare women (Ellen Neel, the Kwagiulth carver, was another) who has proved the exception to the historical rule of Northwest Coast cultures—that wood carving is the preserve of men. Diesing has shown that the historical art tradition is neither closed nor moribund, in terms of the inventiveness of its vocabulary, as well as the social roles of its practitioners.

She learned her carving skills from Bill Holm, Tony Hunt, and Robert Davidson in Hazelton, B.C. just before the Kitanmax School of Northwest Coast Indian Art (known as 'Ksan) opened there in 1970. She went on to make her own contribution there and has taught many young Tsimshian, Tlingit, and Haida artists, primarily in Prince Rupert but also in Terrace, British Columbia, and in Ketchikan and Sitka, Alaska. Doing her part to increase the number of artists who understand the principles of the style, Diesing considers the 'Ksan style to be a mixture of the styles of those who taught there; her own carving style derives from Masset, the principal Haida community on the Queen Charlotte Islands (now known as Haida Gwaii). She cites as important influences both Ellen Neel and Bill Reid (Reid's father was Haida from Masset, while Diesing's mother was Haida from Skidegate).

Diesing has designed and carved many bowls and masks, panels, rattles, talking sticks, and totem poles, including the large pole made for the city of Prince Rupert. She also paints and makes silk-screen prints—a widely-favored medium for the translation of Northwest Coast designs. Diesing has also contributed to the reflorescence of the button blanket form which had evolved with the advent of stroud cloth and pearl buttons from China in the post-contact period, from the older, woven cedar bark forms. The making and wearing of these ceremonial blankets, in red and black, or navy blue, with the owners' family crest motif outlined with rows of pearl buttons, is an integral part of the potlatches and naming ceremonies which mark the renewed vigor of Haida culture. Diesing inherits the Eagle crest from her mother; her given name is Skil-que-wat, which derives from her family story about the Skil (a small supernatural woman who carries a baby).

In the wider community of Northwest Coast artists, Diesing is well-respected as a teacher and designer who helps and encourages others. Her best-known pupils include Dempsey Bob, Don Yeomans, and Norman Tait.

Charlotte Townsend-Gault

Bibliography
Jensen, Doreen, and Polly Sargent, eds. *Robes of Power Totem Poles on Cloth.* University of British Columbia Press, 1984.
Macnair, Peter L., Alan L. Hoover, and Kevin Neary, eds. *The Legacy: Tradition and Innovation in Northwest Coast Indian Art.* University of Washington Press, 1984.
Sargent, Polly, and Doreen Jensen. *Robes of Power: Totem Poles on Cloth.* University of British Columbia Press, 1986.
Stewart, Hilary. *Totem Poles.* Douglas and McIntyre, 1990.

Dignac, Geny (1932–)

Born in Buenos Aires, Argentina, Geny Dignac is a sculptor and environmental artist who works with fire, light, and temperature. After living in the Washington, D.C. area (1954–1972), Dignac settled in Arizona, where she continues to push the limits of her magical thinking in projects such as "Sand Fire," "Fire Over Water," and "Forms of Fire in Mid-Air"—works going beyond technology—works for the future.

Dignac has held myriad solo exhibitions of her "Fire Gestures" (drawings with fire; sculpture, veritable monuments where fire is the primary element; and mixed-media fire configurations) in the United States and abroad. From 1958 to the present, her works have been invited to major group exhibitions throughout the world: from Medellin, Colombia; to Antwerp, Belgium; from New York City and many venues in the United States to Paris, France; from Pamplona, Spain, to Caracas, Venezuela, and San Juan, Puerto Rico.

Dignac has lectured on the use of fire as an art medium since 1969 at museums and schools in the United States and South America. She collaborated with a metallurgist and the Naval Ordinance Laboratory to fabricate sculpture employing fire and nitinol alloys (1971) and has been the subject of several films and videos by R. Osuna and J.Y. Bermudez (1967–1980).

With respect to her use and love of fire, Dignac recently wrote, "Lightning is the gesture of the storm. Flames are the gesture of the fire. Fire is a magical element. Magical thinking is art."

Examples of her work are represented in private, corporate, and public permanent collections, including the Fundación Joan Miró, Barcelona, Spain; Palazzo Dei Diamanti, Ferrara, Italy; Museo La Tertuliam Cali, Colombia; Museo del Banco Central de Ecuador, Guayaquil; the Latinoamerican Art Foundation, San Juan, Puerto Rico; and others in the United States, Germany, Chile, Venezuela, Italy, Spain, and Argentina.

Bibliography
Davis, Douglas. *Art and the Future.* Praeger, 1973.
Glusberg, Jorge. *Art in Argentina.* Giancarlo Politi Editore, 1986.
————. *Del Pop a la Nueva Imagaen.* Ediciones de Arte Gaglianome, 1985.
Rubenstein, Charlotte Streifer. *American Women Artists.* G.K. Hall, 1982.

Dillaye, Annie Blanche (1851–1931)

A painter, etcher, illustrator, poster designer, jeweler, silversmith, teacher, and writer, Annie Blanche Dillaye specialized in seascape, landscape, and architectural views in the United States, England, Europe, and Canada. The daughter of Charlotte B. Malcolm and Stephen D. Dillaye, a lawyer and businessman, she attended private schools in Philadelphia, Pennsylvania, before studying art with Thomas Eakins at the Pennsylvania Academy of Fine Arts, Philadelphia, from 1877 to 1882. She learned to etch from Stephen Parrish in Philadelphia in 1883 before travelling abroad from 1885 to 1887 to study with Eduardo-Leon Garrido in Paris, France.

Dillaye began exhibiting her work in 1882, showing often at the Pennsylvania Academy of Fine Arts, Pennsylvania; and the Boston Art Club, Massachusetts; in the Paris Salon, France, five times; with the Philadelphia Society of Artists, and the Philadelphia Society of Etchers—both in Pennsylvania; the Royal Society of Painter-Etchers, London, England; the New York Etching Club; the American Art Society; the Woman's Art Club of New York; the Philadelphia Art Alliance, Pennsylvania; the Brooklyn Society of Etchers, New York; the Boston Museum of Fine Arts, Massachusetts; and the Syracuse Museum of Art, New York. The expositions which included her work were the 1888 Ohio Valley Centennial; the 1893 World's Columbian; the 1895 Cotton States and International, where she won a silver medal; the 1901 Pan-American; the 1903 Exposition Universelle in Lorient, France; the 1904 Louisiana Purchase; the 1913 National Conservation Exposition, Knoxville, Tennessee, where she won a gold medal; the 1915 Panama-Pacific; and the Philadelphia, Pennsylvania 1926 Sesqui-Centennial. The Syracuse Museum of Fine Arts, New York; the Plastic Club; and the Williams & Everett Gallery, Boston, Massachusetts, held special exhibitions of her work.

An art-activist all her life, she was president of the Philadelphia Watercolor Club and the Fellowship of the Pennsylvania Academy, and a founder and president of the Plastic Club—all in Philadelphia, Pennsylvania. She was also a member of the Philadelphia Society of Etchers (founded 1928), Pennsylvania; the Black and White Club; Association of Women Painters and Sculptors, New York City; the American Women's Art Association, Paris, France; the New York City Watercolor Club and Chicago Watercolor Club, Illinois; and the Daedalus Arts and Crafts Guild of Philadelphia, Pennsylvania. Dillaye directed the art education program for the Pennsylvania Academy of Fine Art, Philadelphia.

Phyllis Peet

Bibliography
Dillaye, Blanche. "Etching." The Congress of Women, Held in the Woman's Building, World's Columbian Exposition, Chicago, U.S.A., 1893. Chicago and Philadelphia: S.I. Bell & Co., 1894.
Peet, Phyllis. *American Women of the Etching Revival.* Atlanta: High Museum of Art, 1988, p. 54.
Philadelphia Art Alliance. *Memorial Exhibition of Watercolors and Etchings by Blanche Dillaye.* Philadelphia: Philadelphia Art Alliance, 1932.
The Plastic Club. *A Catalogue of Etchings, Pencil Sketches and Auto-Lithographs by Blanche Dillaye, April 4–16, 1902.* Philadelphia: The Morris Press, 1902.
Obituary. *The New York Times* (December 21, 1931): 21.

Diska (Patricia) (1924–)

Born in New York City, Diska (Patricia Diska) earned a Bachelor's degree at Vassar College, Poughkeepsie, New York, and studied at the Académie Julian, Paris, France, with Joseph Rivière.

Diska has held many solo exhibitions of her work between 1961 and 1992 in Europe and the United States, including the Galerie Colette Allendy (1961), and Galerie Suzanne de Coninck (1964)—both in Paris, France; Galleria XXII Marzo, Venice, Italy (1961); Southern Methodist University, Dallas, Texas (1965); Galerie Jacques Casanova, Paris, France (1966); Ruth White Gallery, New York City (1969); Municipal Gallery, Mainz, Germany (1986); Galerie Hansma, Paris, France (1992); and others. Her work has been invited to numerous group exhibitions throughout the world, such as the "Exposition Internationale de Sculpture," Musée Rodin, Paris (1961, 1966); "Internazionale Bildhauerzeichnungen," Museum des XX Jahrhunderts, Vienna, Austria (1964); "École de Paris," Musée des Beaux-Arts, Istanbul, Turkey (1966); "Exposition de Sculpture Americaine," Musée des Augustins, Toulouse, France (1966); and the various "Annuals" of the Salon des Réalites Nouvelles and Salon de Mai, Paris; the Sculptors Guild, New York City; Union des Femmes Peintres, Sculpteurs, Graveurs and the Salon d'Art Sacre, Paris; and others.

Diska has been a participant in international symposia in Yugoslavia (1961), Israel (1962), Austria (1966), Czechoslovakia (1968), and France (1970). She has executed twenty large-scale, site specific commissions in limestone, cast-iron, wood, ceramic tile, and flame-treated stone and concrete for municipal projects and school playgrounds throughout France, including a monument to the French Resistance movement in Saint Ouen, composed of cast-iron on a pedestal of rough-cut stone.

Her work is represented in private and public permanent collections (and in various sites), including the Musée d'Art et d'Industrie, St. Étienne, France; Cornell University, Ithaca, New York; the Public Gardens, Vitry-sur-Seine, France; Palm Springs Desert Museum, California; the Sculpture Garden, Chateauvert (Var) France; the French Cultural Ministry; and others.

Bibliography
Dunford, Penny. *Biographical Dictionary of Women Artists in Europe and America Since 1850.* University of Pennsylvania Press, 1989.
Hichisson, Marjorie. *Architectural Association Journal* 80:892 (1965).
Watson-Jones, Virginia. *Contemporary Women Sculptors.* Oryx Press, 1988.

Dix, Eulabee (1878–1961)

Born in Greenfield, Illinois, but raised in Grand Rapids, Michigan, Eulabee Dix was a prominent painter of portrait miniatures whose circle included many of the most interesting visual artists and writers active in turn-of-the-century New York City. As a young girl she demonstrated a strong interest in, and talent for making art, and became intrigued with the technique of miniature painting. After two years at the St. Louis School of Art—where she won several medals for her drawing skills—Dix moved to New York in 1899. There she studied at the Art Students League under William Whittemore; she also worked privately with miniaturist Isaac A. Josephi and briefly took classes from William Merritt Chase.

Between 1902 and 1909 Dix lived and worked in a studio on the fifteenth floor of the towers at Carnegie Hall. Her neighbors included Frederick Church (who drew her portrait), Charles Dana Gibson, and many other noted artists. In 1900 Dix participated in the first annual exhibition mounted by the American Society of Miniature Painters, an organization founded the preceding year (by Whittemore and Josephi, among others) to revive interest in, and regard for miniature painting, which had been eclipsed during the late 1800s by the popularity of photography. The commission to paint a well-known British socialite in 1904 quickly led to a series of solo exhibitions for Dix, in New York, London, and elsewhere. She also garnered critical acclaim and, quite quickly, a steady income from her art. As Dix's fame spread, she painted the portraits of such notable actresses as "Ellen Terry" and "Ethel Barrymore," and was herself the subject of photographic portraits by Gertrude Käsebier; she was good friends with John Butler Yeats (who drew her likeness), Robert Henri (who painted her, twice), and John Sloan (who included Dix in his informal group portrait, "Yeats at Petipa's" [1910], a popular New York café).

In 1910 Dix married New York lawyer Alfred Becker, by whom she had two children. In subsequent years her husband's career necessitated moves to Buffalo and then Albany, New York, which put additional strains on their relationship and limited her artistic output. By 1925 the marriage had ended, but Dix never stopped producing art, spending the remaining three-and-a-half decades of her life working in New York, London, and Lisbon, travelling and exhibiting her art all over the United States and Europe. Toward the end of her life, as miniatures once again fell out of favor, Dix adapted, creating large-scale oil portraits and popular series of floral still lifes. She was also in demand as a lecturer. As her (unpublished) memoirs indicated, throughout her long life Dix explored many areas of creativity—including acting, hat and doll design, and the writing and illustrating of poetry and children's books. But it was her portrait miniatures that made her name—celebrated, as they were, for their close attention to detail, combined with pleasingly sensual colors and textures, to produce objects of great beauty which reveal the personalities, not merely the likenesses, of Dix's sitters.

Dix had her first important solo show at the Fine Arts Society of London, England in 1960; thereafter, she had one-person exhibitions at the Bauer Folsom Gallery, New York City (1907); the St. Louis Museum of Fine Arts, Missouri (1908); the Thurber Gallery, Chicago, Illinois (1910); Milch Galleries, New York City (1928, 1958); Knoedler Gallery, London, England (1934); the Marie Sterner Gallery, New York City (1936); and the National Museum of Portugal, Lisbon (1957). She also participated in numerous group exhibitions, winning silver medals at the Paris Salon, France (1927), and the American Society of Miniature Painters (1929), and a bronze medal from the Pennsylvania Society of Miniature Painters (1929). Other group venues include the Corcoran Gallery of Art, Washington, D.C. (1933); the Walker Art Gallery, Liverpool (1906), and the Royal Academy, London—both in England; and others. Her work is in the permanent collections of many institutions, including the National Museum of Women in the Arts, Washington, D.C., which, in her honor in 1991, inaugurated the Eulabee Dix Gallery of Portrait Miniatures.

Bibliography

Rabbage, Lewis Hoyer. "Eulabee Dix." Catalog Essay. Grand Rapids Art Museum, 1987, unpaged.

Unsigned. "Precious Objects: Eulabee Dix and the Revival of Portrait Miniatures." *Women in the Arts*. National Museum of Women in the Arts—Newsletter 11:1 (Spring 1991): 1–2.

Dodd, Lois (1927–)

Born in Montclair, New Jersey, Lois Dodd is known particularly for her nighttime landscapes, although she displays her keen wit and painterly approach in sunlit works as well. Dodd studied at the Cooper Union in New York City, under the aegis of Peter Busa and Byron Thomas.

Between 1954 and 1990 Dodd held twenty-six solo exhibitions of her paintings in museums and galleries in the United States, including the Tanager Gallery (1954, 1957, 1958, 1961, 1962), the Green Mountain Gallery (1969, 1970, 1971, 1974, 1976), and the Fischbach Gallery (1978, 1980, 1982, 1986, 1988, 1990)—all in New York City; and others from Maine to Maryland.

Her work has been invited to more than 100 group exhibitions, such as the "Stable Annual," Stable Gallery (1956, 1958), and "Art U.S.A.," New York Coliseum (1959)—both in New York City; "Artisti Americani Residenti a Roma," Palazzo Venezia, Rome, Italy (1960); "Eighteen Painters," curated by Fairfield Porter, Parrish Art Museum, Southampton (1965), and "Childe Hassam Purchase Exhibition," American Academy and Institute of Arts and Letters (1973); "New Images," Queens Museum (1974)—both in New York City; "American Realism," College of William and Mary, Williamsburg, Virginia (1978); "Nightworks," the Bronx Museum of the Arts (1987), "A Little Night Music—Manhattan in the Dark," curated by Gerrit Henry, One Dag Hammarskjold Plaza, New York (1990), and "An Artist in the Garden," National Academy of Design (1991)—all in New York City; and many others.

Winner of many honors for her work, Dodd has been a professor of art at Brooklyn College, New York, since 1970; and has won an Italian Study grant (1959–1960); a Longview Foundation purchase award (1962); an Ingram Merrill Foundation grant (1971); an American Academy and Institute of Arts and Letters award (1986), a distinguished alumni award from the Cooper Union (1987), a Leonilda S. Gervase award from the National Academy of Design (1987), and a Henry Ward Ranger Purchase Prize from the same institution (1990)—all in New York City.

Dodd's works are in private, corporate, and public permanent collections in the United States, including the Whitney Museum of American Art, Cooper Union, the National Academy of Design, and Ciba-Geigy—all in New York City; Wadsworth Atheneum, Hartford, Connecticut; Colby College, Waterville, Maine; Kalamazoo Art Center, Michigan; and others.

Bibliography
Bass, Ruth. "Lois Dodd (Fischbach)." *Art News* 80:1 (January 1981): 168.
Campbell, Lawrence. "Lois Dodd at Fischbach." *Art in America* 71:4 (April 1983): 184–85.
Smith, Roberta. *The New York Times* (February 9, 1990).
Turner, Norman. "Lois Dodd." *Arts Magazine* 52:7 (March 1978): 8.

Dodson, Sarah Paxton Ball (1847–1906)

One of the finest, though today too-little-known women painters of her time, Sarah Paxton Ball Dodson is most noted for her monumental religious and mythological paintings in the academic grand manner. A native of Philadelphia, Pennsylvania, she entered the Pennsylvania Academy of Fine Arts, Philadelphia, in 1872 and was there a pupil of Christian Schussele (who also taught Thomas Eakins); by 1873 she moved to Paris, France, where she studied for three years with Evariste Vital Luminais and around 1890 turned for further instruction to Jules-Joseph Lefèbvre and Louis-Maurice Boutet De Monvel. Dodson was one of the many late-nineteenth-century American women who trained under distinguished academic masters in Paris, France, and competed with French painters through exhibiting in the Salon. Her first exhibited painting, "La Danse" (1876), appeared at the 1878 Paris Exposition Universelle, France. As Barbara Gallati has pointed out, Dodson's "L'Amour Ménétrier" (1877) is suggestive in its mythological subject and complex design of Titian's "Bacchus and Ariadne" (1522–1523) but also carries a light French Rococo flavor. Dodson subsequently turned away from the Rococo manner to a monumental classicism influenced by a newly acquired attraction to the painters of the Italian Renaissance. One of her major canvases, the Old Testament-inspired "Deborah" (c. 1879) was shown at the 1879 Exposition Universelle, and the 1880 Paris Salon—both in Paris, France; and the 1883 Annual Exhibition of the National Academy of Design, New York City; "Deborah" and "The Invocation of Moses" (exhibited at the 1882 Paris Salon, France) reflect Dodson's strong inspiration from Michelangelo. Her powerful, brilliantly composed, and psychologically bizarre 1883 Salon entry, "The Bacidae," was called, by an anonymous critic in the August 1883 *The Art Amateur*, "the most important work by an American woman this year, both in size and merit . . . [the] one that shows the strongest and freest hand among all the women artists in our country." "The Bacidae"—probably Dodson's best-known work—manifests her continuing interest in depicting arcane themes and partially nude figures unusually posed. Her next significant canvas was her only pure history painting, "The Signing of the Declaration of Independence in the State House, Philadelphia, Fourth of July, 1776" (c. 1883), reminiscent of John Trumbull's 1818 compositional treatment of the same subject. After returning to the United States about 1885, Dodson turned away from her earlier monumental, dramatic canvases to a concentration on landscape, perhaps feeling this was a subject more suited to contemporary American collecting tastes. Along with pure, often plein-air landscapes, she also produced figure pieces which incorporated landscape elements; her new poetic style—as seen in "The Morning Stars" (c. 1886)—suggests connection with French symbolism and the English pre-Raphaelites. An expatriate most of her life, Dodson by 1891 left France and moved permanently to Brighton, England. She had long suffered from fragile health and was further weakened by an 1893 illness and accident; however, she still managed to paint until her death.

Although the list of her extant work is short—which may help explain her relative obscurity—paintings by her can be found in the permanent collections of the Brooklyn Museum, New York; Boston Museum of Fine Arts, Massachusetts; Indianapolis Museum of Art, Indiana; and Philadelphia Museum of Art, Pennsylvania.

Victor Koshkin-Youritzin

Bibliography
Artist Index, Inventory of American Paintings, National Museum of American Art, Smithsonian Institution, pp. 5, 361–65.
Catalogue of Paintings by Sarah B. Dodson. Essay by John Ellingwood Donnell Trask. Exhibition Catalog. The Pennsylvania Academy of Fine Arts (April 16–May 14, 1911).
Gallati, Barbara. "The Paintings of Sarah Paxton Ball Dodson (1847–1906)." *The American Art Journal* (Winter 1983): 67–82.
"Pictures by American Women in the Paris Salon." *The Art Amateur* 9:3 (August 1883): 46.
Quick, Michael. *American Expatriate Painters of the Late Nineteenth Century*. Dayton Art Institute, 1986, p. 96.
Rubinstein, Charlotte Streifer. *American Women Artists: From Early Indian Times to the Present*. Avon, 1982, 109, 116–17.
Sturgis, Russell. "The Work of Miss Sarah Dodson." *Scribner's Magazine* 43 (April 1908): 509–12.
Trask, John E.D. "Sarah Ball Dodson: An Appreciation." *The International Studio* 45 (December 1911): xxxvii–xli.

Dondé, Olga (1937–)

Born in Campeche, Mexico, Olga Dondé is a self-taught artist. She saw her first pictorial works when she was thirty-one years old in a show titled "Confrontación 68," organized by the Instituto de Bellas Artes, Mexico.

Dondé works in oils, lithography, engraving, tapestries, sculpture, stained glass, and architectural design. She has had many solo shows in the interior of Mexico and in various cities throughout the United States, including: the Galería Mexicana de Arte, Mexico City, and the Museo de Queretaro (1968)—both in Mexico; East Tennessee State University, Johnson City (1969); the Pan American Union, Washington, D.C.; the Janus Gallery, Greensboro, North Carolina (1970); Galería Arvil, Mexico City, Mexico; the Museum of Houston, and the Fort Worth Museum—both in Texas (1973); the Museum of Contemporary Art, Bogotá, Columbia; the Serra Galería de Arte, Caracas, Venezuela; the Municipal Museum and Gallery of the City of Puebla (1974), and Galería Arvil, Mexico City—both in Mexico; the Galería 1-2-3, San Salvador, El Salvador (1977); the Galería Gabriela Orozco, Mexico City, the Michoacán House of Culture, Morelia (1979); and the National Polytechnic Institute (1980)—all in Mexico; and many others.

Dondé employs the metaphor of the outsized strawberry (and other fruit) in her painting: sensual, erotic, sexual symbols of life and love and a certain magic. Her works are in the permanent collection of the Museo de Arte Moderno and the Banco Nacional—both in Mexico; the Museum of Modern Latin American Art, Washington, D.C.; the Museo Nacional de Arte, Costa Rica; and the Institutos Panamericano de Arte and Panameno de Arte, Panama.

Dondé has had work exhibited in innumerable group shows in Mexico and abroad. Her work has been published in many books and in reviews. She has won prizes and awards in exhibitions throughout the Americas.

Bibliography
Alvarez, José Rogelio, et al. *Enciclopedia de México*. Secretaría de
    Educación Pública, 1987.
Diccionario Biográfico Enciclopedico de la Pintura Mexicana. Quinientos
    Años Editores, 1979.

Donneson, Seena

A native New Yorker, the sculptor/printmaker Seena Donneson studied at Pratt Institute, Brooklyn; the Art Students League, under the
aegis of Morris Kantor; and with printmaker Michael Ponce de León,
at the Pratt Graphics Center—all in New York City.

Donneson has held exhibitions of prints and sculpture in galleries and museums throughout the United States, including the "15th
and 19th Biennials," Brooklyn Museum, New York (1965, 1975); "Re-
flections/Refractions," Fort Lauderdale Museum of Fine Art, Florida
(1978); and "Relief Sculpture," Danville Museum of Art and History,
Virginia (1988); among many others. She has been commissioned to
pull editions of prints, create tapestry designs, and produce outdoor
sculpture for many patrons.

Teacher and intermittent lecturer at universities and schools since
1961, Donneson is a member of Artists Equity Association, New York
City; the Women's Caucus; and the National Association of Women
Artists. She was a recipient of a fellowship from the MacDowell Foundation (1963, 1964); an award from Clayworks, New York City (1981);
and a Creative Artists Public Service (CAPS) grant from the New York
State Council on the Arts (1983–1984).

Examples of Donneson's work are in private, public, and corpo-
rate permanent collections, including the Fort Lauderdale Museum of
Art, Florida; Los Angeles County Art Museum, California; Museum of
Modern Art (MoMA), and Phillip Morris International—both in New
York City; and others.

Bibliography
Pennington, Mary Anne. *Seena Donneson: Relief Sculptures*. Greenville
    Museum of Art, North Carolina, 1987.
Who's Who in American Art. 19th ed. R.R. Bowker Co., 1991–1992.

Doray, Audrey Capel (1931–)

Born in Montréal, Québec, Canada, Audrey Capel Doray is a painter,
electronic artist, muralist, and filmmaker. Doray studied at McGill
University, Montréal, where she earned a Bachelor of Fine Arts degree
and worked under the tutelage of Arthur Lismer and John Lyman (1952);
four years later, she finished a course of intaglio printmaking with
Stanley William Hayter in his Atelier 17, Paris, France.

Doray has held solo exhibitions in galleries and museums and has
had her work included or invited to many group shows in Canada and
abroad, such as the Vancouver Art Gallery, British Columbia (1961);
National Art Gallery, Ottawa, Ontario (1966); "Vancouver Print Show,"
Heidelberg, Germany (1969); Museum of Contemporary Crafts, New
York City (1972); and "Arteder '82," Bilbao, Spain; among many others. Her
works combine robust social criticism with her own interpretation of
luminist theory; she deals with pop art and the feminist archetype, themes
of perpetual motion and endless transition, and light and sound.

Doray was an instructor at the Vancouver Art School (1959–1962),
as well as the recipient of a Bursary Award from the Canada Council

(1968–1970). Examples of her work are in private, public, and corporate permanent collections, including an electronic mural commissioned
by Mazda Motors (1973), and paintings commissioned by the Mandarin Hotel (1984)—both in Vancouver.

Bibliography
Rhodes, Michael. "Audrey Capel Doray." *Artscanada* 25:5 (December
    1968): 50–53.
Rosenberg, Ann. "Audrey Capel Doray at Bau-Xi." *Vanguard* 7:2 (March
    1978): 20.

Drier, Katherine Sophie (1877–1952)

Katherine Sophie Drier's contribution to modern art surpasses her
achievement as a painter. Motivated by belief in the spiritual powers
of art and concern for social improvement, she crusaded on behalf of
the most advanced international art of her day. Among the artists she
championed were Piet Mondrian, Paul Klee, Vassily Kandinsky,
Fernand Léger, Kurt Schwitters, Kasimir Malevich, and Alexander
Archipenko.

Brooklyn-born Drier studied art in New York City, where Walter
Shirlaw was her most important mentor; and in Europe, where she
supplemented formal studies with extensive travel. After exhibiting in
the 1913 Armory Show, she determined to educate the public about
modern art. Her most significant undertaking was the Société
Anonyme, which she founded in 1920 along with Marcel Duchamp and Man Ray
but ran more or less single-handedly. In addition to lectures and publications, her organization presented exhibitions of the major European
and American modernists and amassed a museum-quality collection
of more than 600 objects.

Drier's evocative early landscapes displayed a Whisterlian lyricism. Later she developed a personal abstract style indebted to
Kandinsky and exemplified by "Abstract Portrait of Marcel Duchamp"
(1918). In Paris between 1930 and 1933 she belonged to the new ab-
straction-creation group. Drier exhibited frequently until the final decade of her life when, in poor health, she nevertheless continued to
write and lecture.

Ann Lee Morgan

Bibliography
Bohan, Ruth. *The Société Anonyme's Brooklyn Exhibition: Katherine Drier
    and Modernism in America*. UMI Research Press, 1982.
Herbert, Robert, Eleanor Apter, and Elise Kenney, eds. *The Société
    Anonyme and the Drier Bequest at Yale University*: A Catalogue
    Raisonné. Yale University Press, 1984.

Drexler, Rosalyn (1926–)

Rosalyn Drexler has only intermittently given her full attention to making art—a fact not surprising given her other accomplishments, which
have ranged from university teaching to professional wrestling. In addition she has published seven novels, written five other books under
the pseudonym Julia Sorel, seen two dozen of her plays produced and
several published, and won an Emmy for a Lily Tomlin television special she wrote.

Drexler has achieved all this without benefit of training in either
art or writing. She grew up in New York City and was married at nine-

teen to the painter Sherman Drexler, who turned her attention to art during visits to New York museums. While they were living in Berkeley, California, she began to make sculpture from scavenged materials. Back in New York City in 1959 she showed eighty-four pieces ranging from abstract to figurative; these sculptures (virtually all now lost) in varied sizes and materials made uninhibited use of found elements.

Despite some favorable critical responses to her sculpture, Drexler moved on to the painted photo-collages that account for her reputation as an important artist of the 1960s. Instead of searching for detritus she now scoured magazines and newspapers. As in "Baby, It's Allright" (1963) she snipped figures from these sources, pasted them down, and painted around and/or over them. Soon she began photographically enlarging the illustrations, so she could work in a much larger format.

Most of the 1960s paintings consist of fairly simple images against backgrounds of flat, hot color, as in "Where Is the Loot!" (1963) and "Chubby Checker" (1964). Drexler had an eye for figures whose physical demeanor reflects psychic forces, such as people engaged in violence or sex—or, not infrequently, both. The implicit but unexplicit narrative meaning of these canvases seemed frequently sinister, sometimes amusing, always unsettling. Because her art was rooted in popular culture, it was often associated with contemporary pop art, but in fact her work was more closely related to the surrealist search for the bizarre in modern life than to the pop embrace of indifference.

At the end of the 1960s Drexler abandoned the visual arts for nearly twenty years. In 1986 a travelling show of her work from the 1960s revealed surprising correspondence with the work of younger artists—Robert Longo is probably the best example—who were interested in both media appropriation and loaded statements. Stimulated by her own relevance to a new generation, Drexler once again began to paint, turning now to more complex images. Subjects she has addressed in series include the life of Jean-Michel Basquiat and the circus seen with a feminist eye. In these brightly colored works, which are generally based on photographs but do not incorporate collage, Drexler continues to comment on the passing scene.

Ann Lee Morgan

Bibliography

De Kooning, Elaine, with Rosalyn Drexler. "Dialogue." In *Art and Sexual Politics: Why Have There Been No Great Women Artists?* Edited by Thomas B. Hess and Elizabeth C. Baker. Collier Books, 1973. [Reprint from *Art News* 69 (January 1971).]

Driggs, Elsie (1898–1992)

Elsie Driggs's fame rests on a handful of precisionist paintings acclaimed in the late 1920s, when they were first shown. In the fifty years between 1930 and 1980, she did not have a one-person show. Nevertheless, she was continuously and inventively productive for nearly seventy years.

Born in Hartford, Connecticut, Driggs moved with her family to suburban New Rochelle, New York, in 1908. In 1918 she enrolled at the Art Students League, New York City, where she encountered as teachers George Luks, John Sloan, and Maurice Sterne. From late 1922 until early 1924, Driggs studied and travelled in Italy.

Almost immediately upon her return to New York City, she exhibited in a group show at the Daniel Gallery. Her single entry, "Cabbage" (1924), was well received, giving her an entree into the New York art world. In the late 1920s and 1930s, her work appeared in the first biennial at the Whitney Museum of American Art, and in the first exhibition at the Museum of Modern Art (MoMA)—both in New York City, as well as in group and solo shows at several commercial galleries.

The work with which her name has always been particularly associated was initiated in 1926, when she returned to Pittsburgh in search of a childhood memory of the steel mills. Her best-known painting, "Pittsburgh" (1926–1927), came out of this experience. It was followed by "Blast Furnaces" (1927) and other industrial subjects, including "Queensborough Bridge" (1927). In these works celebrating the new industrial landscape, Driggs independently formulated a hard-edged precisionist style that put her in the aesthetic company of such artists as Charles Demuth, Niles Spencer, Louis Lozowick, Charles Sheeler, and others who concurrently sought a modern expression of American life. Even then, however, Driggs's output was varied, reflecting her dual interests in the "quick" and the "classical." This self-described polarity aptly evokes her lifelong attraction to animated, lively, even playful form on the one hand and to stability, order, monumentality, and repose on the other.

During the Depression of the 1930s Driggs worked for the Works Projects Administration (WPA), producing both murals and watercolors. In 1935 she married painter Lee Gatch. To save on expenses they bought a small farmhouse in Lambertville, New Jersey, their home until Gatch's death in 1968. With no studio and shortly a daughter to care for, Driggs's work was mostly confined to what she could accomplish on the kitchen table between meals.

Although in the 1960s she had a studio, after her husband's death Driggs moved back to New York City, where she continued to incorporate contemporary interests into her art. In the 1970s she concentrated on assemblages encased in Lucite boxes. In works such as "Cobbles" (1979) she imaginatively juxtaposed disparate objects and images in evocative ensembles. These clearly belong to the heritage of surrealism and confirm that all along Driggs's work was ultimately unified by an interest in drawing attention to objects as emotional stimulants. In the 1980s many of her paintings directly reflected the visual impact of the contemporary city; "N.Y." (1984) and "C's Convertibles" (1985), for example, bear witness to the advertising-infested urban landscape.

Ann Lee Morgan

Bibliography

Fillin Yeh, Susan. "Elsie Driggs." *Arts* 54:3 (May 1980).
Loughery, John. "Blending the Classical and the Modern: The Art of Elsie Driggs." *Woman's Art Journal* 7 (Fall–Winter 1986–1987): 22–26.
Lyle, Cindy. "An Interview with Elsie Driggs: Return from 30 Years 'at the Edge of a Ravine.'" *Women Artists News* 6 (May 1980): 1, 4, 6.

Drum, Sydney (1952–)

Sydney Drum was born in Calgary, Alberta, Canada, receiving a Bachelor of Fine Arts degree from the University of Calgary, in 1974. In 1976 she received her Master of Fine Arts degree from York University in Toronto, specializing in printmaking and drawing. Since 1975 Drum has taught fine arts at a number of universities, including York University, the Nova Scotia College of Art and Design in Halifax, the University of Illinois at Chicago, and Rutgers University in New Jersey, where she presently works. Drum has lived in New York City since 1984.

Drum's paintings, drawings, and prints have been included in numerous solo and group exhibitions. Among other exhibitions, she has shown at the Art Gallery of Ontario, Toronto (1978); Getler/Pall Gallery, New York City (1981); and has had a solo travelling exhibition in Yugoslavia (1983) that was sponsored by the U.S. Embassy in that country. Recent paintings have been shown at Yeshiva University, New York City (1988); and Bau-Xi Gallery, Toronto (1990). She has completed a commissioned painting for Harmann-Reimer Corporation, New York City; and a print edition commissioned by Zimmerli Museum at Rutgers University, New Jersey.

Drum's work can best be described as gestural and expressionistic. Her work became wholly abstract while she studied at York University, where print specialist Jules Heller was a major influence. Drum's personal style includes making the physical gesture visible. This characteristic is obvious in such works as "Drawing" (1977), which was included in the Art Gallery of Ontario exhibition. In this drawing the viewer can follow each repeated extension of the artist's body. Recent work continues to develop Drum's interest in movement and abstract tradition in both printmaking and painting. Her work is found in both public and private collections, including the Museum of Modern Art (MoMA), New York City; the Philadelphia Museum of Art, Pennsylvania; the National Museum of American Art, Smithsonian Institution, Washington, D.C.; the Canada Council Art Bank, Ottawa; and the Robert McLaughlin Gallery, Oshawa.

Linda Jansma

Bibliography

Mays, John Bentley. "Drum Developing in Intriguing Ways." *The Globe and Mail* (January 27, 1981): 18.

Tousley, Nancy. "Sydney Drum." *Artscanada* 226–227 (May–June 1979): 62.

Zemans, Joyce. "Beyond the Boreer at Harbourfront Art Gallery." *Art Magazine* 47 (February–March 1980): 36–38.

Dryer, Moira (1950–1992)

Born in Toronto, Canada, Moira Dryer is known for her abstract paintings on plywood sheets. Dryer received her education, in part, at Sir George Williams University (now Concordia University), Montréal, Canada, and at the School of Visual Arts, New York City, where she studied with Elizabeth Murray and graduated with honors (1981). Dryer's mother was an architect; her father was a professor of philosophy at the University of Toronto. By June 1983 Dryer had been married and already widowed.

Dryer's first solo exhibition was held at the John Good Gallery, New York City (1986). Her last solo exhibition was held in February 1992 at the Mary Boone Gallery in SoHo, New York City. In between these dates there were other solo shows at the Institute of Contemporary Art and the Mario Diacono Gallery—both in Boston, Massachusetts; the Fred Hoffman Gallery, Santa Monica, California; and others. Her work was invited to many group exhibitions in galleries and museums throughout the United States.

Bibliography

Smith, Roberta. "Moira Dryer, 34, An Abstract Artist; Painted on Wood." *The New York Times* (May 21, 1992): C23.

Dryfoos, Nancy Proskauer (1918–1991)

A sculptor known for her stone and terra cotta works, Nancy Proskauer Dryfoos was born in New Rochelle, New York. She received a diploma from Sarah Lawrence College, Bronxville, New York, where she studied sculpture with Oronzio Maldarelli and painting with Curt Roesch; at Columbia University, New York City, she continued further study with Maldarelli and, later, worked privately with José de Creeft. She also attended classes at the Art Students League, New York City.

Dryfoos had more than a dozen solo exhibitions in Connecticut, New York, and Washington; her work was selected for many group shows in the United States, including the "Annuals" between 1948 and 1972 held by the Allied Artists of America at the National Academy of Design, New York City; Syracuse Museum, New York; Brooklyn Museum, New York; the Whitney Museum of American Art, New York City; Philadelphia Art Alliance, Pennsylvania; Dallas Museum of Fine Arts, Texas; Pennsylvania Academy of Fine Arts, Philadelphia; the Corcoran Gallery of Art, Washington, D.C.; and others.

Dryfoos won many honors and awards for her work, such as the gold medal of honor from the Allied Artists of America; the Edel award for fine arts; the Constance K. Livingston award from the American Society of Contemporary Artists; the Knickerbocker award; the Naomi Lehman memorial award; and others. She was a member, board member, or officer of many organizations, including the National Sculpture Society; the New York Society of Women Artists; the Allied Artists of America; the American Society of Contemporary Artists; the Creative Arts Commission of Brandeis University; and other professional associations. Her work is in the permanent collections of the Boca Raton Museum, Florida; Brandeis University, Waltham, Massachusetts; Columbia University, New York City; Sarah Lawrence College, Bronxville, New York; Kean College of New Jersey, Union; and many other institutions.

Bibliography

Collins, Glenn. "Nancy Proskauer Dryfoos Dies: Prize-Winning Sculptor Was 73." *The New York Times* (October 15, 1991): C18.

Who's Who in American Art. 19th ed. R.R. Bowker Co., 1991–1992.

Duble, Lu (1896–1970)

Born in Oxford, England, the sculptor Lu Duble studied her craft with Alexander Archipenko, José de Creeft, and Hans Hofmann, among others.

In addition to solo exhibitions, Duble's work was seen in many prestigious group shows, such as the "National Sculpture Society Exhibition," Whitney Museum of American Art, New York City (1940); Philadelphia Museum of Art, Pennsylvania (1940); Museum of Modern Art (MoMA) New York City (1942); the "Annuals," Pennsylvania Academy of Fine Arts, Philadelphia (1942–1946); the "Annuals," the National Association of Women Artists, and the National Academy of Design—both in New York City; the "1954 Annual Exhibition of Contemporary American Sculpture, Watercolors and Drawings," Whitney Museum of American Art, New York City (1954); and many others.

Winner of honors and awards, Duble received Guggenheim Foundation fellowships (1937, 1938) and was a fellow of the Institute for International Education. Examples of her work are in private and public permanent collections.

Bibliography
American Art at the Newark Museum. The Newark Museum, 1981.
"Guggenheim Fellows." *Art Digest* 11:13 (April 1, 1937): 10.
Sculpture 1962 (Lever House). Sculptors Guild, 1962.

Duckworth, Ruth (1919–)

Working in stoneware and porcelain, Ruth Duckworth has explored many directions during her prolific career, from reductive vessels, to chunky sculptures and massive murals. Duckworth was born in Hamburg, Germany, and emigrated to Liverpool, England, in 1936. Because of her Jewish heritage, Duckworth was denied entrance to art school in Nazi Germany. She graduated from the Liverpool School of Art, England, in 1940 with a degree in sculpture and, fifteen years later, while living in London, England, started experimenting with clay. At the suggestion of ceramist Lucie Rie, Duckworth studied glazes at the Hammersmith School of Art in 1955 and the Central School of Arts and Crafts from 1956 to 1960. English ceramics of the 1950s were dominated by the teachings of Bernard Leach, who advocated simple, rustic vessels inspired by the Far East. By contrast, Duckworth's ceramic forms were inspired by modernist sculpture and often denied the nature of the vessel. In "Dish" (1962), the vessel's function is negated by the abstract designs incised on its surface. Duckworth is one of three European emigres credited with liberating English ceramics in the 1960s.

In 1964 Duckworth was offered a teaching position at the University of Chicago, Illinois. There Duckworth became one of the first ceramists to experiment with large expanses of clay on the wall. The 240-square-foot mural "Clouds Over Lake Michigan" (1976), created for the Chicago Board of Trade Building, Illinois, resembles a monumental topographical map. Its abstract organic patterning and undulating surface alludes to the "windy city"'s environment.

In the late 1970s and 1980s Duckworth concentrated on wall panels and small, hand-built porcelain forms that continue to explore and revise the nature of the vessel. In "Bowl (Six Dividers)" (1977), the interior volume is divided by six delicate monochromatic walls. "Bowl with Lid and Many Rocks" (1981) is glazed in delicate hues and covered with a lid that allows a glimpse of four mysterious mounds in the body of the vessel. Although Duckworth denies the comparison, her sensual forms have been compared frequently to female sexual organs.

Duckworth is represented in international collections, including the Smithsonian Institution and the Victoria & Albert Museum in London. She retired from teaching in 1977 but maintains a studio in Chicago and continues to exhibit internationally.

Heather Sealy Lineberry

Bibliography
Clark, Garth. *American Ceramics, 1876 to the Present.* Abbeville Press, 1988.
Duckworth, Ruth, and Alice Westphal. *Ruth Duckworth.* Exhibit A, Gallery of American Ceramics, Evanston, May 1977.
Levin, Elaine. *The History of American Ceramics, 1607 to the Present.* Harry N. Abrams, 1988.
Luecking, Stephen. "Ruth Duckworth." *New Art Examiner* (January 1991): 40.

Duesberry, Joellyn (1944–)

Born in Richmond, Virginia, Joellyn Duesburry is known for her strongly interpreted plein-air paintings and monotypes. Duesberry received her art education at several institutions, including Smith College, Northampton, Massachusetts, where she earned a Bachelor of Arts degree with distinction and a Phi Beta Kappa key (1966); and the Institute of Fine Arts, New York University, New York City, where she earned a Master of Arts degree (1967). She spent the summers (1974–1977) in study at Pietrasanta, Italy; attended classes intermittently at the National Academy of Design and the Art Students League (1966–1984), and did further study at the New York Academy—all in New York City (1984–1985).

Duesberry has held many solo exhibitions across the United States, including the Tatischeff Gallery, New York City (1982, 1985); Gerald Peters Gallery, Santa Fe, New Mexico (1986, 1988, 1990, 1992); "Joellyn Duesberry," Graham Modern, New York City (1991); "Joellyn Duesberry, Landscapes 1972–1992," Denver Art Museum, Colorado (1993); and others. Her work has been invited to many group exhibitions in the United States and abroad, such as the Tatischeff Gallery, New York City (1979, 1980, 1989); "Contemporary Realism," New York State Council on the Arts, Museum Gallery, White Plains, New York (1982); "Artists of America," Colorado History Museum, Denver (1987); "Invitational," a travelling show, the Hubbard Museum, Ruidoso, New Mexico, the Soviet Union, Germany, and Japan (1990); "Art in the Woods," Overland Park, Kansas (1991–1992); and many others.

Duesberry's work is represented in a number of private, public, and corporate permanent collections, including AT&T and Citibank, New York City; General Electric, Fairfield, Connecticut; Goddard Center for the Visual Arts, Ardmore, Oklahoma; Mobil Oil Corporation, Houston, Texas; Pittsburgh Plate Glass Industries, Pennsylvania; and the Denver Art Museum, Colorado.

Bibliography
Bolt, Thomas. "Joellyn Duesberry." *American Artist* (October 1986): 48–53, 111, 113–15.
Brenson, Michael. "In the Arts: Critics' Choices." *The New York Times* (November 13, 1983): 2A:3.
Hill, May Brawley. "Joellyn Duesberry." *Arts* (October 1985): 127.
Little, Carl. "Joellyn Duesberry at Graham Modern." *Art in America* (March 1992): 122–23.

Dugas, Karen (1957–)

A printmaker, mixed-media artist, and teacher, Karen Dugas was born and raised in Cornwall, Ontario, Canada. She enrolled in the Bachelor of Fine Arts program at Queen's University, Kingston, Ontario (1975–1979), studying under Carl Heywood and Jennifer Dickson. Interests in painting and sculpture yielded to etching and photographic printmaking processes.

Dugas moved to Edmonton, Canada, in 1979 to undertake Master of Visual Arts studies at the University of Alberta working in photo-etching with Walter Jule (her future husband) and Lyndal Osborne. Her graduate prints, the "Boiler Room series," were derived from nights spent exploring the miles of service tunnels which circulate heat and power to the buildings on the University of Alberta campus. In works such as "Dissolved Shelter" (1980) and "Zero Grounding" (1982), the machines and the idea of automation represent Dugas's suspicion of developing technologies in industry and weapons of war.

Working as the technician for a special spring session course at the University of Alberta in 1981 with Jule and Shoichi Ida (Japan) intensified Dugas's belief in the importance of printmaking as a viable contemporary art form. The experience supplied new insights and critical tools that she transferred to her work.

While Dugas was still a student, the following works were accepted in international print competitions: "Espace" (1979), exhibited at the 8th International Print Biennial in Cracow, Poland; and "Proceeding Towards Condition" (1981), selected for the 14th International Biennial of Graphic Art in Ljubljana, Yugoslavia. "Shifted Impulse" (1980) won a purchase award and the David Moore award for a young professional in Graphex 8, Brantford, Ontario, Canada. "Mysteries: Falling Plane" (1981) and "Hot Segment" (1980) won purchase awards respectively in Boston Printmakers 34th National Exhibition, Massachusetts, and the 5th Miami International Print Biennial, Florida.

In 1982, after teaching a summer session course at the University of British Columbia, Dugas began making palm-sized clay sculptures which she refers to as internal gestures. Key works such as "Blue Hot in Deep Freeze" (1983) and "Position of Exchange" (1983) have a raw primitive look and function as crude masks. Dugas became the first Canadian artist to win a prize at the prestigious 16th International Biennial of Graphic Art (1985), Ljubljana, Yugoslavia.

After spending two months as artist-in-residence at Tokyo National University of Fine Arts and Music, Japan, in 1985, Dugas challenged her work by introducing the human figure in the "Sensation and Sentiment" series (1985–1989). An almost androgynous female stands facing the viewer reminiscent of ancient Egyptian sculpture in the large-format photo-etching triptych "Guards" (1986). Parts of the figure are obscured by bits of matter now literally redefining parts of the body and immediate environment. This play with known and abstract forms evokes complex objective and subjective responses. From this series, "History of the Observed" (1985) was chosen for the superior class prize in the 5th Seoul International Print Biennial, Korea. The portfolio of nine etchings "W.H.O.L.E.S." (1989) and the mixed-media installation "Boundaries," Latitude 53 Gallery, Edmonton, Alberta (1989) conclude various experiments during this period.

Dugas's work has been collected by the Canada Council Art Bank, Ottawa; the Alberta Art Foundation; Air Canada; the Art Gallery of Brant, Brantford, Ontario; the Edmonton Art Gallery, Alberta; Hamilton Art Gallery, Ontario; the Metropolitan Museum and Art Center, Coral Gables, Florida; the Modern Gallery, Ljubljana, Yugoslavia; Hart House, Toronto; and Kelly Lavoie, Montréal.

She has been teaching as a sessional lecturer at the University of Alberta since 1982. Dugas and her husband Walter Jule live near Elk Island National Park outside Edmonton, Alberta.

Liz Ingram

Bibliography

Cochran, Bente Roed. *Contemporary Edmonton Prints*. A Catalog. Edmonton Art Gallery, 1988, pp. 6, 10, 12.

———. *Printmaking in Alberta 1945–1985*. The University of Alberta Press, 1989, p. 47.

Cracow. A Catalog. The 8th International Print Biennial, Cracow, Poland, 1980.

Edmonton Prints: Brazil. A Catalog. Society of Northern Alberta Print-Artists, Edmonton, 1988.

Gee, Gary. "Environmental Exploration." *The Edmonton Sun* (March 23, 1989): 67.

Graphex 8. A Catalog. The Art Gallery of Brant, Brantford, Ontario, 1981, p. 23.

Ingram, Liz. "International Print Biennial, Yugoslavia." *Carfac News* (Winter 1986): 8, 9.

Kosinski, Marytka. "Karen Dugas: Prix 1985." A Catalog. *17th International Biennial of Graphics Art*, Ljubljana, Yugoslavia, 1987.

Nygard, Soren. "A Review, Karen Dugas in Ljubljana." *Precarious Balance*, Print Voice 2. University of Alberta Press, 1990, 72–77.

Sybesma, Jetske. "Karen Dugas: Habits of Vision/Collages of Thought." *Inside-Out: Four Artists from Edmonton, Canada*. A Catalog. Society of Northern Alberta Print-Artists, Edmonton, and the 13th International Print Biennial, Cracow, Poland, 1991.

Seoul. A Catalog. The 5th International Print Biennial, Seoul, Korea, 1986, p. 17.

Wylie, Liz. "Canadian Impressions." *Vanguard* (September 1984): 40, 41.

Dukes, Caroline

Born in Ujpest, Hungary, the painter/printmaker Caroline Dukes studied in the studio of sculptor Sigiesmund de Strobl, Hungary; she took further study at the Academy of Fine Arts, Budapest, Hungary, and received a diploma from the School of Art at the University of Manitoba, Winnipeg, Canada (1972), after working with Ivan Eyre.

Between 1974 and 1991 Dukes has had ten solo exhibitions of her work in Canada and the United States, including "At the Focus of Forces," Winnipeg Art Gallery (1991), Melnychenko Gallery (1991); "Ten Year Survey," Gallery 111, School of Art, University of Manitoba—all in Winnipeg (1983); Pollock Gallery, Toronto, Ontario (1980); Gilman Gallery, Chicago, Illinois (1976); and others.

Since 1968 Dukes's work has been selected for showing in more than eighty juried group exhibitions in Spain, the United States, Canada, and Israel, including shows, such as "Introductions: The Artists Who Live Among Us," North Dakota Museum of Art, Grand Forks (1991); "All Over the Map: Women and Place," Plains Museum, Fargo/Moorehead, North Dakota (1991); "Third Open Print Exhibition," Manitoba Printmaking Association, Winnipeg (1990); "Mini Print International-Cadaque," Taller Galería Fort, Barcelona, Spain (1989); Yad Vashem Art Museum, Jerusalem, Israel (1987, 1985); "Occurrences: Four Manitoba Painters," Winnipeg Art Gallery, Manitoba (1981); "Patronat Premi Internacional Dibuix Jean Miro," Barcelona, Spain (1973–1974); and many others.

Dukes has been the recipient of many grants and awards. Her work has been recognized for outstanding interpretation of the landscape in the Midwestern International Juried Art Show at the Winnipeg Art Gallery (1976); and for highest quality and originality at the Manitoba Society of Artists Exhibition (1973). She received grants in 1990 from the Winnipeg Arts Advisory Council and the Canada Council and eight grants from the Manitoba Arts Council between 1974 and 1987.

Member of Canadian Artists Representation, the Manitoba Artists for Women's Art Association, and the Manitoba Printmakers Association, Dukes pulled editions of prints for the Winnipeg Art Gallery in 1981 and in 1988.

Her work is in permanent public, corporate, and private collections in Canada, the United States, and Israel, including the Canada

Council Art Bank; Winnipeg Art Gallery; Bronfman Collection, Montréal Museum of Fine Arts; Yad Vashem Art Museum; Toronto Dominion Bank; St. John's College, Winnipeg; and many others.

Bibliography
Cramer, David, dir., and John Prentice, prod. *C. Dukes, Artists Series*. Video. Winnipeg Video, 1987.
Hughes, Kenneth James. *Caroline Dukes*. St. John's College, University of Manitoba, 1983.
Lovatt, Tom. *The Trellis of Memory: At the Focus of Forces*. Exhibition Catalog. Winnipeg Art Gallery, 1991.
Who's Who in American Art. 19th ed. R.R. Bowker Co., 1991–1992.

Dunkelman, Loretta (1937–)

Born in Paterson, New Jersey, the painter Loretta Dunkelman earned a Bachelor's degree in art from Douglass College, Rutgers University, New Brunswick, New Jersey (1958); and received a Master's degree from Hunter College, New York City (1966).

Dunkelman has held solo exhibitions in galleries and museums in the United States, including 1708 East Main Gallery, Richmond, Virginia (1987); A.I.R. Gallery, New York City (1973, 1974, 1978, 1981, 1983, 1987); University of Rhode Island, Kingston (1975); University of Cincinnati, Ohio (1974); and others. Her work has been invited to group exhibitions, such as Michael Walls Gallery, New York City (1989); Virginia Commonwealth University, Richmond (1987); "Let's Play House," Bernice Steinbaum Gallery, New York City (1986); "13th Anniversary Exhibition," A.I.R. Gallery, New York City (1985); Kulturhuset, Stockholm, Sweden (1981–1982); "A Taft Menagerie," Taft Museum, Cincinnati, Ohio (1980); "Waves: An Artist Selects," Cranbrook Academy of Art, Bloomfield Hills, and Grand Rapids Art Museum—both in Michigan (1974); "Whitney Biennial of Contemporary Art," Whitney Museum of American Art, New York City (1973); and others.

Winner of awards and honors, Dunkelman was a recipient of an Adolph and Esther Gottlieb Foundation grant, and a fellowship from the New York Foundation for the Arts (1991); a fellowship from Hand Hollow Foundation (1984); National Endowment for the Arts (NEA) grants (1975, 1982); fellowships from the MacDowell Colony, Peterborough, New Hampshire, and Yaddo, Saratoga Springs, New York (1981); American Association of University Women (1976–1977); and a Creative Artists Public Service (CAPS) grant from the New York State Council on the Arts (1975–1976). Her work is represented in private, public, and corporate permanent collections, including Colgate University, Hamilton, New York; University of Cincinnati, Ohio; University of Kansas, Lawrence; City University Graduate Center, New York; Chase Manhattan Bank; Bristol-Myers Squibb; and others.

Bibliography
Bell, Tiffany. "Review." *Arts Magazine* (February 1979): 26–27.
Frank, Peter. "Gifts of the Imagi." *Village Voice* (January 8, 1979): 57.
Merritt, Robert. "Romantic Views: Light and Dark." *Richmond Times Dispatch* (October 3, 1987).
Proctor, Roy. "Romantic View." *The Richmond News Leader* (October 3, 1987).

Duran Reynals, Francisca (1939–)

Born in New Haven, Connecticut, in 1939, Francisca Duran Reynals is the child of parents who fled from Spain during the Civil War. Reynals received her Bachelor of Arts degree in Latin from Bryn Mawr College in Pennsylvania and did graduate work in the same field at Columbia University in New York City. She attended the Cooper Union School of Art for two years and worked for a New York City experimental theater group as a stage and poster designer.

Reynals's first exhibition was held in Boston in 1967; she has had a number of solo shows, including the Galería de Antonio Souza in Mexico City and others. Noted for her collages, she designed the cover for America Hurrah by Jean-Claude Van Itallie.

Bibliography
The Texas Quarterly: Image of Mexico I. The University of Texas. Autumn, 1969.

Durieux, Caroline (Wogan) (1898–1989)

An American satirist, best known for her lithographs of the 1930s, Caroline (Wogan) Durieux also pioneered the electron print after World War II.

Durieux grew up in the Vieux Carré in New Orleans, Louisiana; French was her first language until she was seven. After graduating from Sophie Newcomb College, Tulane University, New Orleans, she spent two years (1917–1919) studying painting with Henry McCarter at the Pennsylvania Academy of Art, Philadelphia. In Philadelphia she first saw the work of nineteenth-century satirists, including the lithographs of Honoré Daumier, which would have a lasting effect upon her art. In 1921 she married a New Orleans, Louisiana export-import businessman, Pierre Durieux; they lived in Havana, Cuba, for six years before moving to Mexico City, Mexico, in 1928. In Mexico Durieux was coaxed into trying lithography by Diego Rivera and Howard Cook. Two master printers, Dario Mejia and George Miller (whom she met through Carl Zigrosser), showed her how to draw on the stones. Mejia printed her first set of twelve lithographs at the Senefelder Lithographic House in Mexico City in 1932—this "Mexico Series" was exhibited at Zigrosser's Weyhe Gallery, New York City, in 1934. In these prints and in a second series, the "North Americans" (1936), Durieux avoided imitating the revolutionary Mexican artists who had either honored the heroic Native Americans or attacked the corrupt Spanish aristocrats. Instead she focused on the up-and-coming Latin American bourgeoisie, as well as the "Yankee" diplomats and businessmen living high in Mexico City in the 1920s and 1930s. The Mexican Series prints were indebted to Daumier: The drawing had a wide range of grays, and the caricature was understated. The North American prints, done on zinc plates, were wire-thin, caustic renderings lit by a frozen white glare that exposed the arrogant north-of-the-border interlopers who provided a dubious model for the emerging Latin American middle class.

Durieux returned to New Orleans in 1936 where she directed the Louisiana branch of the Federal Arts Project and taught art at Tulane University. Over the next decade she produced more than thirty lithographs. Many took aim at a subject she knew intimately—the Creole subculture with its religious rituals, dinner parties, society balls, and Mardi Gras. Her new satires were more wounding than savage. She mocked the pretenses of academics and the peculiarities of the Creole clans whose values were at odds within Durieux's own—thrift, forthrightness, reason, and secular humanitarianism. Other lithographs lampooned French Quarter prostitutes and American expatriate writers and artists in Paris, France, where Durieux lived briefly in 1950. Occasionally, Durieux's lithographs went outside the boundaries of satire. "The Visitor" (1944) and "Persuasion" (1948) evoked the gloom of the 1940s when totalitarian governments, the carnage of World War II, and the specter of nuclear holocaust cast doubt about the good prospects of the human race.

In the 1950s a chronic back ailment forced Durieux to give up the heavy labors of lithography. She became a professor of printmaking at Louisiana State University and experimented with print techniques, new and old. She worked out a new color variation of the cliché verre print, and with the aid of university science professors she invented the electron print, in which isotope drawings were exposed to photographic paper and printed by chemical means. Unfazed by the abstract and formalist thrust of American printmaking after the War, Durieux continued to produce realistic satires of contemporary people and events. Electron prints, "Fashion" (1953), "Creole Mermaids" (1973), and "Gigolo" (1977), pillared the fads of the post-war era through wry caricatures of shoes, belts, glasses, and hairdos. There were also burlesques of literature and mythology mixed with mordant observations on modern culture.

Durieux's prints have been collected by the Brooklyn Museum, New York; the Boston Museum of Fine Arts, Massachusetts; the Metropolitan Museum of Fine Art, New York City; and the Philadelphia Museum of Art, Pennsylvania, among others. She was honored, along with Anni Albers, Louise Bougeois, Ida Kohlmeyer, and Lee Krasner, in 1980 by the National Women's Caucus. A series of strokes ended Durieux's career in August 1980. She lived in a Baton Rouge nursing home until her death in 1989.

Richard Cox

Bibliography
Cox, Richard. *Caroline Durieux: Lithographs of the Thirties and Forties.* Louisiana State University Press, 1977.
Exposición Caroline Durieux, Oleos, Lithographs y Dibujos. Galería Central, 1934.
Zigrosser, Carl. *The Artist in America.* Louisiana State University Press, 1948.

Durr, Pat (1939–)

Three things have remained consistent in Pat Durr's life—her tenaciousness as a practicing artist, her personal symbolic imagery, and her continuous involvement in the Ottawa arts community.

A native of Kansas City, Missouri, Durr graduated from the University of Kansas in 1961. She then studied for a Master of Arts degree at the University of Southampton in 1962, and in 1963 emigrated to Canada.

In 1975 Durr helped organize the first Visual Arts Ottawa Exhibition, and for the next seven years taught in the visual arts department at Algonquin College. In 1987 and 1988 Durr curated the Person's Award Exhibition. She is currently chair of the visual arts advisory committee for the city of Ottawa and has been instrumental in establishing policy for the new Arts Court. In 1989 Durr was awarded the Victor Tolgesy arts award.

Her earliest work was a fine drawing line that explored the possibilities of space and nature. Later Durr added color in a layering process that continues to the present. Her work explores the context of space as defined by objects swirling around or layering the surface of it. Frogs, chairs, airplanes, and letters of the alphabet are her visual vocabulary that she identifies with her dreams.

Durr is included in many public and private collections, including the Canada Council Art Bank, Petro Canada, the Toronto Dominion Bank, and the Corporation of the city of Ottawa.

Victoria Henry

Bibliography
Blouin, Rene. "Art in Situ." *Canadian Art* (Spring 1986).
Gibson, Susan. "Pat Durr, Dreams of Black Rainbows." *Arts Atlantique* 7:4 (Spring 1987).
Knowles, Valerie. "Pat Durr, près de la nature." *Vie Des Arts* 27 (Autumn 1982).

Duval, Jeanne (1956–)

The large-scale, colorful, super-realist figure paintings, genre scenes, landscapes, and still lifes created by Jeanne Duval have an intense, sometimes surreal, component that makes them particularly haunting. Born in Peterborough, New Hampshire, Duval studied painting under Bruno Civitico at the University of New Hampshire, Durham, where she earned her Bachelor of Fine Arts degree in 1978. Three years later she received her Master of Fine Arts degree from Brooklyn College, New York, after working with Joseph Groell, Paul Gianfagnia, and Richard Piccolo. Duval also cites the influence on her art of the Queens College, Huntington, New York, Landscape Painting Program, directed by Gabriel Laderman, which she attended in 1981, and an extended period spent working in Italy two years later.

Duval has been exhibiting her paintings regularly since her early twenties, including group shows held in fifteen states, plus Mexico and Switzerland. Her first solo exhibition was at the Jaffrey Civic Center, New Hampshire (1980); since then, she has had one-person exhibits at the Walt Kuhn Gallery, Cape Neddick, Maine (1981); the First Street Gallery (1983), and the Sherry French Gallery—both in New York City (1984, 1987, 1991); and the Contemporary Realist Gallery, San Francisco, California (1993). Duval's work is in numerous private and public collections; the latter include the Metropolitan Museum of Art, New York City; the Bayly Art Museum, Charlottesville, Virginia; and the Carey Ellis Company, Houston, Texas.

Bibliography
Doherty, Stephen. "Jeanne Duval." *American Artist* 48 (March 1984): 43–50.
O'Beil, Hedy. "Jeanne Duval." *Arts* 59:7 (March 1985): 40.

Dwight, Mabel (1876–1955)

Known for her humorous lithographs illustrating aspects of contemporary American life, Mabel Dwight did not embark upon her artistic career until relatively late in life. Born in Cincinnati, Ohio, on January 29, 1876, she grew up in New Orleans, Louisiana, and studied with Arthur Mathews at the Hopkins School of Art in San Francisco, California. It was not until the 1920s, after travelling in Europe and Asia, that Dwight began her career as a lithographer with a set of picturesque views of Paris made with the French printer Duchatel. Returning to the United States in 1928, she established her reputation over the following years with a series of genre scenes of New York City. Comparable in spirit to Honoré Daumier's work, these lithographs, such as "Ferry Boat" (1930) and "Queer Fish" (1936), exposed the absurdities of life in the city, but their satire was tempered by the artist's sympathy for her subjects.

Dwight's work was exhibited extensively through the 1930s in the United States as well as internationally. Her prints were frequently shown in the Fifty Prints of the Years, Philadelphia Print Club, Pennsylvania; and New York City American Printmakers exhibitions. The Wehye Gallery, New York City, sponsored a one-woman show of Dwight's watercolors and lithographs in 1932 and another show, "A Decade of Lithography," in 1938. Her work has been collected by the Tamarind Institute, Albuquerque, New Mexico, and several museums, including the Museum of Modern Art (MoMA), New York City; the Boston Museum of Fine Arts, Massachusetts; and the Victoria & Albert Museum, London, England.

From 1935 to 1939 Dwight was employed by the Works Projects Administration (WPA), Federal Art Project to make lithographs and watercolors. "Satire in Art," an essay she wrote for the WPA, expresses her opinion that aesthetic quality is vital to the success of satirical art, and that the artist need not deliberately distort form in order to reveal the imperfections inherent in human nature.

Peggy J. Hazard

Bibliography

Adams, Clinton. *American Lithographers 1900–1960*. University of New Mexico Press, 1983.

The Federal Art Project: American Prints from the 1930s in the Collection of the University of Michigan Museum of Art. University of Michigan Museum of Art, 1985.

O'Connor, Francis V., ed. *Art for the Millions: Essays from the 1930s by Artists and Administrators of the WPA Federal Art Project*. New York Graphic Society, 1973.

Pirog, John, and Susan Barnes Robinson. *Mabel Dwight: Catalogue Raisonné of the Lithographs*. (In preparation.)

Rubinstein, Charlotte Streifer. *American Women Artists from Early Indian Times to the Present*. Avon, 1982.

Zigrosser, Carl. *The Artist in America: Twenty-four Close-ups of Contemporary Printmakers*. Knopf, 1942.

Dyer, Carolyn Price (1931–)

Born in Seattle, Washington, the widely-travelled, multi-talented fiber artist Carolyn Price Dyer is also known for her paintings, sculpture, photographs, writing, editing, and criticism. Dyer received her education at Mills College, Oakland, California, where she earned a Bachelor of Arts degree (1953), and a Master of Arts degree two years later. Dyer also studied at the University of Washington, Seattle.

Dyer has held many solo exhibitions of her work in fiber and mixed media throughout the United States, most recently at the Kennedy-Douglass Center, Florence, Alabama (1992). Dyer's work has been invited to myriad group exhibitions in the United States and abroad, including "Form & Object," a travelling show through 1993, University of Wyoming, Laramie (1992); "Invitational," Maude Kerns Art Center, Eugene, Oregon (1991); "Art to Wear," Larson Gallery, Yakima, Washington (1990); "Wearable Art: Color in Motion," Pasadena City College, California (1989); "Art Couture X," Elements Gallery, Greenwich, Connecticut (1987); and many others.

Winner of honors and awards for her work, Dyer was a trustee scholar and a graduate fellow in art history at Mills College, 1950–1953, and 1953–1955, respectively. She won the gold crown award for visual arts from the Pasadena Arts Council (1982) "in recognition of continuous contributions to the arts." She has taught at various institutions, including Los Angeles Community College (1970–1976); the Creative Arts Group, Sierra Madre (1965–1970); Pasadena Art Museum (1972–1973)—all in California; and Yakima Valley Community College, Washington (1959–1960).

Dyer's works are represented in private, public, and corporate permanent collections, such as Pepperdine College, Malibu, California; Tokio Marine and Fire Insurance, Los Angeles; Huntington Hospital, Pasadena, California; General Electric Corporation, Fairfield, Connecticut; EPCOT, Orlando, Florida; International Gas Company, Boise, Idaho; Nestle USA, Inc., Glendale, California; and many others.

Bibliography

Browne-Del Mar, Claire. "Challenging Tradition." *L'art dans la mode*. A Catalog. Chaffee College, 1991.

Pace, Terry. "From Coats to Documents: Dyer Considers Herself Correspondent of Art." *Times Daily* (March 29, 1992): B1.

Who's Who in American Art. 19th ed. R.R. Bowker Co., 1991–1992.

Who's Who in the West. 23rd ed. R.R. Bowker Co., 1992–1993.

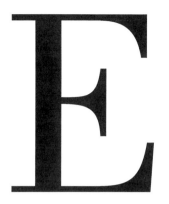

Eakins, Susan Macdowell (1851–1938)

The painter Susan Macdowell Eakins, the fifth of eight children, was fortunate to grow up in an artistic home. Her father was an engraver who worked with many of the leading artists in Philadelphia, Pennsylvania, and he provided his daughter with a studio in the attic. She painted portraits of the numerous members of the family during the years she took courses at the Pennsylvania Academy of Fine Arts, Philadelphia (1876–1882), where she studied with both Christian Schussele and Thomas Eakins (her future husband). She realized success in her first year when the portrait that she showed in the Academy of Fine Art's annual exhibition of 1876 was sold. In 1877, as class secretary, she requested and obtained a life class for women, and in the painting "Female Life Class" (1879) by her classmate Alice Barber, Eakins can be seen seated at her easel. The Academy of Fine Art's 1878 Annual exhibited two of her paintings: "The Picture Book" and "Portrait of a Gentleman." In 1879 she became the first recipient of the Mary Smith prize for the best picture submitted by a woman artist residing in Philadelphia, Pennsylvania, and three years later she received the Charles Toppan prize for "The Old Clock on the Stairs" (based on Henry Wadsworth Longfellow's poem of the same name), a painting which was purchased by Fairman Rogers who had earlier commissioned a work of Thomas Eakins. Her younger sister Elizabeth who was also studying painting was included in this 1882 competition.

After their marriage in 1884 both Eakins maintained studios on the fourth floor of their home in Philadelphia, Pennsylvania. She was primarily a portraitist who skillfully gave her sitters realistic three-dimensionality in interior settings. Though her palette was often rather dark, she cast a strong light on her sitters' carefully-studied physiognomies. Perhaps this desire to scrutinize faces was the impetus that led her into photography early in the 1870s, even before she met Eakins—who also became adept with the potentialities of the camera. She was among the first members of the Philadelphia Photographic Society, Pennsylvania, and in its first show of 1898 exhibited a photograph entitled "Child with Doll." Occasionally she, like her husband, used photographs in conjunction with her paintings, such as "Grandfather Macdowell" (1879, private collection) and "Portrait of a Soldier" (1917, French Benevolent Society, Philadelphia). One of her most riveting portraits is that of "Thomas Eakins," Philadelphia Museum of Art, Pennsylvania, quite possibly painted after his death in 1916, in which he is shown wedged between his easel and the table on which his palette lies; he holds his paint brush in his right hand, and his face, gazing forward, is modeled in chiaroscuro.

In the 1920s she added a few still lifes to her usual subject matter of portraiture and in the 1930s expanded her study of single figures to a rather complete living room scene of two seated women ("The Lewis Sisters," private collection), extending the depth farther than in her earlier painting of "Two Sisters" (1879, private collection). In 1936 she helped to organize an exhibition, sponsored by the Philadelphia Art Club, which included paintings by her husband, her sister Elizabeth, and twenty of her own. Since her death in Philadelphia, there has been a retrospective of fifty-two of her works at the Pennsylvania Academy in 1973.

Eleanor Tufts

Bibliography
Casteras, Susan P. *Susan Macdowell Eakins, 1851–1938.* Pennsylvania Academy of Fine Arts, 1973.

Eberle, Abastenia St. Léger (1878–1942)

The sculptor Abastenia St. Léger Eberle was born to Canadian parents living in Webster City, Iowa. She grew up in Canton, Ohio, where she began her first art training with a local sculptor, Frank Vogan, who was a patient of her physician-father. In 1899 she began the three-year program at the Art Students League in New York City, studying with C.Y. Harvey, George Grey Barnard, and Kenyon Cox, and was able to pay her way through school with prizes and scholarships. She received her first public recognition in 1904 when a large sculpture, "Men and Bull," made jointly with Anna Vaughn Hyatt, was highly praised by Augustus Saint-Gaudens in the exhibition of the Society of American Artists and recommended for the St. Louis Exposition, Missouri, where it won a bronze medal.

Eberle's realistic renditions of New York street scenes began with "Roller Skating" (Whitney Museum of American Art, New York City) in 1906, followed by "Girls Dancing" (also called "Ragtime") (Corcoran Gallery of Art, Washington, D.C.) in 1907. Her first trip abroad was in 1907 when she went to Naples, Italy, in order to cast her works in bronze more cheaply than she could in New York City. She caused a bit of sensation because the Neapolitans had never seen a woman at work in a foundry before. On her return to New York City she took a studio in Greenwich Village and resumed working on such urban subjects as "Woman Picking up Coal" (1907) and "Ragpicker" (1911). Two of her sculptures were exhibited in the New York Armory Show of 1913: "Girls Wading" (1913, Corcoran Gallery of Art) and "White Slave" (1913, private collection). During this period she exhibited regularly at the Macbeth Gallery, and the National Academy of Design—both in New York City; and the Pennsylvania Academy of Fine Arts, Philadelphia. Her work was included in three international exhibitions: Venice (1909), Rome (1911), and Paris (1913). She was also active in the suffrage movement, leading the section of sculptors in a Fifth Avenue parade in 1911 and contributing to an exhibition for the benefit of woman's suffrage at the Macbeth Gallery in 1915.

The work of Eberle was the sculptural counterpart of the Ashcan School of painting early in the twentieth century in New York City. She was so taken with the naturalism of life on the Lower East Side of New York amid the recently arrived immigrants that she rented two rooms under the Manhattan Bridge, using one as a studio and the other as a playroom with toys for tenement children who posed for her. "Playing Jacks," "Yetta and the Cat Wake Up," and "On Avenue A" (also called "Dance of the Ghetto Children") were among the sculptures of this period, 1914–1916 (all three of these works are in Kandall Young Library, Webster City, Iowa).

In 1920 the National Academy of Design, New York City, elected her an associate member, but a heart condition was beginning to sap her energy, and she failed to achieve full membership. She won a bronze medal for "The Windy Doorstep" (1910, Worcester Art Museum) at the Panama-Pacific International Exposition in 1915 and the Garden Club of America prize for her fountain "Boy Teasing Fish" in 1929; two years later the Allied Artists of America awarded her the Lindsey Morris memorial prize for a small bronze sculpture.

Eberle bought an old barn in Westport, Connecticut, which she converted into a studio in 1931 for summer use and eventually expanded and winterized for year-round living. Her last sculpture, "Madam Pharazan," was shown at the National Sculpture Society exhibition at the Whitney Museum of American Art in 1940.

Eleanor Tufts

Bibliography
Noun, Louise R. *Abastenia St. Léger Eberle, Sculptor.* Des Moines Art Center, 1980.
Tufts, Eleanor. *American Women Artists, 1830–1930.* National Museum of Women in the Arts, 1987.

Eckhardt, Edris C. (c. 1907–)

Born in Cleveland, Ohio, the pioneering glass artist and ceramist Edris Eckhardt studied on a scholarship to the Cleveland School of Art (1928–1932). After graduation Eckhardt set up a ceramic studio, where she specialized in glaze chemistry.

Eckhardt was appointed director of the department of ceramic sculpture in Cleveland, Ohio under the Work Projects Administration (WPA), Federal Arts Project (1935–1941). She exhibited widely and in 1947 showed a major piece, "Painted Mask," in the May exhibit at the Cleveland Museum, Ohio.

Six years later Eckhardt turned her attention to glassworking and rediscovered an ancient Egyptian technique: fusing gold leaf between glass sheets. This led to ever-new discoveries and creations which include multiple laminations, among others. Winner of awards and honors, Eckhardt was a recipient of a Tiffany fellowhip in stained glass; Guggenheim fellowships (1956, 1959); and others.

Bibliography
Barrie, Dennis. "Edris Eckhardt Interviewed." *Line* 12:3 (1978).
Clark, Garth. *American Ceramics 1896 to the Present.* Abbeville Press, 1987.
Marling, Karal Ann. *Federal Art in Cleveland (1933–1943).* Cleveland Public Library, 1976.

Edell, Nancy (1942–)

Edell's interest in traditional forms of representation was expanded and changed when she studied animated film for a year at the University of Bristol, England (1968–1969). However, returning to Manitoba (she had moved from Omaha, Nebraska, to Canada in 1966) she continued, throughout the 1970s, to develop her interest in lithography and drawing. The year 1980 marked the first significant change in her visual direction when she moved to Nova Scotia and became interested in the local tradition of rug-hooking. It is at this point that her original training, her interest in animation, and her new interest in folk art came together to produce a unique style. Using found wool rag (used clothing) and a traditional method of shrinking, she began to construct images that spoke of enclosed interior (indoor) spaces as related to the gender issue. She explores a socially-constructed gender that is developed through the use of myth (often Assyrian) and stereotype.

In addition to her work with fabric pieces Edell continued to explore monotypes. For example, "Home Entertainment: Flying Saucer" (1985) combines etching, ink, charcoal, and conté with colorful, embossed children's (found) stickers. Other pieces from her "Home Entertainment" series, such as "Boudoir Lemur" are less humorous and more poignant in their suggestions of gender exploitation. Her more recent work moves further into multi-media by including large paintings.

Edell has received recognition for her work in animation, including awards from the First Festival of Women's Films, New York City (1972); Canada Council Show, Paris, France (1972), and Edinburgh, Scotland (1969). Edell has exhibited widely in Canada and has had prints, drawings, and hooked rugs purchased by permanent collections, including Canada Council Art Bank, Ottawa; Vancouver Art Gallery; Nova Scotia Art Bank, Halifax; among others. Since 1982 she has taught part time at the Nova Scotia College of Art and Design in Halifax.

Janice Helland

Bibliography
Gill, Dennis. "Nancy Edell." *Vanguard* (September 1984).
Metcalfe. "Nancy Edell, Men and Women, Women and Men." *Arts Atlantic* (Winter 1987).
Pope, Robert. "Charlotte Wilson Hammond and Nancy Edell." *Arts Atlantic* (Fall 1988).

Edelson, Mary Beth (Johnson) (c. 1934–)

Mary Beth Edelson is an artist whose work has utilized many means—performance, photography, installation, sculpture, drawing, and painting—and whose original contributions to the feminist art movement place her at the forefront of artists of the late-twentieth century. Born in Indiana, Edelson received her Bachelor of Arts degree from DePauw University, Greencastle, Indiana (1955) and her Master of Arts degree from New York University, New York City (1959).

Edelson broke through to new areas of expression through the bold use of her nude figure in the private rituals she photographed in the early 1970s. In assertive and powerful poses, her body often painted, the photographs were sometimes painted or collaged as well. In later private rituals (late-1970s to 1980s) her figure was clothed, and with long exposure and moving lights it became an eerie, mystical presence.

Strongly feminist and spiritual in intent, Edelson's work is informed by her study of Jungian archetypes as well as the feminist rediscovery of a female-centered spirituality. She has written about her rituals that "In using my own body as a sacred being, I broke the stereotype that the male gender is the only gender that can identify in a first-hand way with the body and, by extension, the mind and spirit of a primary sacred being." In 1977 she performed a ritual, "Grapčeva Neolithic Cave: Pilgrimage/See for Yourself," in an ancient goddess-worship site in a cave on Hvar Island, Yugoslavia. In the same year she initiated public ritual performances with "Memorials to the 9,000,000 Women Burned as Witches in the Christian Era" at New York City's A.I.R. Gallery. In many subsequent public ritual performances, such as "Your 5,000 Years are Up!" at the University of California at San Diego (UCSD), California (1977), as well as collaborative works such as her "Story-Gathering House Boxes" at the Franklin Furnace, New York (1978), she has involved the audience as participants.

Continuing to perform and to exhibit her photographs, Edelson returned to painting as well in 1980. In the 1980s her work has expanded toward broader political and historical issues that also generally incorporate her feminist concerns. In a series of large wall-paintings, drawings, and smaller paintings, Edelson developed a vocabulary of personal symbols, such as a burning candle/serpent, the baby's head, the whirling vortex, and the hummingbird, that recur as motifs in much of the work. A 1990 New York City gallery exhibition of these works was titled "Universal Pictures." Her recent emphasis on the ecological concerns of the Green movement can be seen in "Black Spring: Room for New Beginnings," a 1989 installation at the Washington Project for the Arts. In symbolic language (death's heads, the hummingbird, and the central image of the baby's head) Edelson created a piece to grieve the recent oil spill in Alaska from the Exxon Valdez.

Edelson is the mother of a son and daughter. After living in Indianapolis and Washington, D.C., she has lived in New York City since 1975. Widely exhibited and published, a frequent panelist and lecturer, Edelson has also been artist-in-residence at several universities although she has no regular academic affiliation. Her work is included in the permanent collections of the Walker Art Center, Minneapolis, Minnesota; the National Museum of American Art, Smithsonian Institution, Washington, D.C.; the Guggenheim Museum, New York City; the Museum of Contemporary Art, Chicago, Illinois; the Corcoran Gallery of Art, Washington, D.C.; the Indianapolis Museum of Art, Indiana; and the Detroit Institute of Art, Michigan.

Gretchen Garner

Bibliography
Battcock, Gregory, and Robert Nickas, eds. *The Art of Performance: A Critical Anthology*. E.P. Dutton, 1983.
Burnham, Jack. "Mary Beth Edelson's Great Goddess." *Arts Magazine* (November 1975): 75–78.
Edelson, Mary Beth. "Pilgrimage/See for Yourself: A Journey to a Neolithic Cave." *Heresies*, Great Goddess issue, 5 (1978): 96–99.
———. "An Open Letter to Thomas McEvilley." *New Art Examiner* (April 1989): 34–38.
———. *Shape Shifter: Seven Mediums*. M.B. Edelson, 1990.
Garner, Gretchen. *Reclaiming Paradise: American Women Photograph the Land*. Tweed Museum of Art, University of Minnesota, 1987, pp. 58–59.
Levy, Mark. "The Shaman is a Gifted Artist: Kelin, Beuys, Edelson, Finley." *High Performance* (Fall 1988): 54–61.
Lippard, Lucy. *Overlay: Contemporary Art and the Art of Prehistory*. Pantheon, 1983.
Raven, Arlene. *Crossing Over: Feminism and Art of Social Concern*. UMI Press, 1988.
Rosen, Randy. *Making Their Mark: Women Artists Move into the Mainstream*. New York: Abbeville Press, 1989.
Weinberg, Adam. *Vanishing Presence*. Minneapolis: Walker Art Center and Rizzoli, 1989, pp. 108–15.

Ehrlich, Millie (1923–)

Collage artist Millie Ehrlich was born and raised in Chicago, Illinois, where she studied at the Art Institute of Chicago, later completing her degree at the University of Illinois. She moved to Phoenix, Arizona, in 1949 and continued to paint. Her style evolved from the traditional/representational to the non-objective and color-field approach.

In the early 1970s Ehrlich began to concentrate on paper collages as her primary idiom and had her first solo show in 1974. Other solo and group exhibitions followed, including participation in a national travelling show of selected American collage artists sponsored by the Mississippi Museum of Art. Her most recent mini-retrospective museum exhibition, "On the Edge: Contemporary Collages—Work by Millie Ehrlich and Contemporaries," was held at the Nelson Art Center, Arizona State University, Tempe (1991–1992), in conjunction with a display of notable works from the university collection.

Since the early 1990s Ehrlich has also been working in mixed media and assemblages, utilizing odd-shaped pieces of wood within a bas-relief and/or boxed structure. Her style is spare—in her own words, "I strive for the maximum effect with the minimum of means." She has appeared on the Arizona affiliate of Public Broadcasting System (PBS) in a discussion of her methodology, and is represented in private and corporate permanent collections, such as Bullock's, IBM, Levi-Strauss, Talley Industries, and others.

Bibliography
Cortright, Barbara. "Millie Ehrlich." *Artspace* (Winter 1980): 23–26.
Kotrozo, Carol Donnell. "Millie Ehrlich." *Arts Magazine* (December 1980).

Eisenstadt, Eve (1953–)
Born in Detroit, Michigan, Eve Eisenstadt, an art educator associated with New York University and the Hunter College Campus Schools, received her Bachelor of Fine Arts degree from the University of Michigan, Ann Arbor (1974); secured her Master of Fine Arts degree from the Cranbrook Academy of Art, Bloomfield Hills, Michigan (1976); and a Doctorate degree in education from Teachers College, Columbia University, New York City (1984).

Eisenstadt held solo exhibitions of her paintings at the Just Above Midtown/Downtown Gallery, New York City, and the Hadler-Rodriguez Gallery, New York City (1981). Her work was selected for many group painting and handmade paper exhibitions, including the Oscarson-Hood Gallery, New York City (1981); the Smithsonian Institution, a travelling exhibition (1978–1981); the Düren Museum of Art, Germany (1982); American Craft Museum, New York City (1982); Beyer Museum, Chicago, Illinois (1983); Cleveland Art Institute, Ohio (1986); Pindar Gallery, New York City (1988); Hartwick College, Foreman Gallery, Oneonta, New York (1990); Untitled Gallery, San Francisco, California (1991); and others.

Eisenstadt has lectured widely, served as artist-in-residence at Lincoln Center, New York City (Summers 1980, 1981); received a creative development grant from City University of New York (CUNY) (1990); and faculty development grants from William Patterson College, Wayne, New Jersey (1978, 1979, 1980). Early on, Eisenstadt discovered handmade paper, along with painting. At ease with the old/new paper medium, she "paints" with colored pulp, creating works not unlike her paintings.

Bibliography
Blum, Michael. "Pulp Dreams." *New Haven Advocate* (April 18, 1983).
Cohen, Ronny. "Paper Routes." *Art News* (October 1983): 79–85.
Toale, Bernard. *The Art of Papermaking*. Davis Publications, 1982.

Elliott, Lillian (1930–1994)
In 1992 Lillian Elliott was elected a fellow of the American Craft Council—the highest honor which can be achieved by an American craftsman. This contemporary textile pioneer long has been recognized for her exceptionally high level of craftsmanship, innovation, and her influence on other craftsmen through her art, teaching, and writing.

A native of Detroit, Michigan, Elliott took a Bachelor of Arts degree at Wayne State University, Detroit (1952), her primary fields being drawing, painting, and art education; this was followed in 1955 with a Master of Fine Arts degree from Cranbrook Academy of Art, Bloomfield Hills, Michigan, with a major in ceramics and a minor in painting. Although Elliott has painted, potted, and designed throughout her career, she has always regarded herself as a "textile artist." After graduation she worked for a few years designing textiles in the styling division of the Ford Motor Company and taught courses at the University of Michigan, Ann Arbor.

In 1960 she moved to California and concentrated her energies into creative activity. Within a short time her unique woven tapestries and off-loom textiles were being recognized in competitive and invitational exhibitions, for Elliott worked with non-traditional as well as traditional materials. She astounded the California craft worlds by the quantity, diversity, and quality of her production, the dynamic expression, even "primitive nature" of her imagery. During the 1970s Elliott expanded her work by experimenting with machine appliqués, serigraphed textiles, knotless netting, colored xeroxed textiles, printed fabrics, miniature tapestries, and works combining many techniques.

Since the mid-1970s Elliott, challenged by the concept of basketry, has produced hundreds of works, again using non-traditional materials and treating baskets as sculpture. Natural materials abound in her works: bark, reed, twigs, branches. Her baskets are volumetric, often ungainly and insouciant. She has said that her baskets are "if not beautiful, at least compelling." For many years Elliott has collaborated with Pat Hickman on baskets of all types, but their most notable successes have been with works with gut (sausage casing) as the prime element. They have had numerous joint exhibitions in the United States, Japan, and Europe. In 1985 Elliott was one of twenty California craftspeople designated as "Living Treasures of California" by the Creative Arts League and the Crocker Art Museum of Sacramento, California.

Elliott has had notable solo exhibitions at the Henry Gallery, University of Washington, Seattle; the Arizona State University Art Museum in Tempe; San José Museum of Art, California; and the Evanston Art Center, Illinois. Major group shows in which she participated include "Tapestry—Tradition and Technique" at the Los Angeles Art Museum, California (1971), "Vannerie" at the Musée des Arts Décoratifs in Lausanne, Switzerland (1981), and "Poetry of the Physical" at the American Craft Museum, New York City (1987).

Among the many institutions that feature Elliott's work in their collections are the American Craft Museum, New York City; Detroit Institute of the Arts, Michigan; Arizona State University Art Museum, Tempe; Cranbrook Academy of Art, Bloomfield Hills, Michigan; Renwick Gallery of the Smithsonian Institution, Washington, D.C.; Rhode Island School of Design, Providence; the Oakland Art Museum, California; and the Wadsworth Atheneum, Hartford, Connecticut.

Rudy H. Turk

Bibliography
California Crafts XIV: Living Treasures of California 1985. Creative Arts League of California, 1985.

Janeiro, Jan. "A Conversation with Lillian Elliott." *Fiberarts* (March–April 1982): 67–73.

Rossbach, Edward. "Lillian Elliott: Baskets and Textiles." *American Craft* (October–November 1992): Cover, 30–35.

Smith, Paul J., and Edward Lucie-Smith. *Poetry of the Physical.* Weidenfeld & Nicolson, 1986.

Emery, Lin (1928–)

A native New Yorker, the kinetic sculptor Lin Emery was an apprentice to Ossip Zadkine in Paris, France (1950–1951); she also studied at the Sculpture Center, New York City.

Between 1957 (the year she created her first kinetic work) and 1992 Emery was given many solo exhibitions in the United States and Canada, including the Brevard Art Center, Melbourne, Florida (1992); Arthur Roger Gallery, New Orleans, Louisiana (1990, 1992); Glass Art Gallery, Toronto, Canada (1985); Max Hutchinson Gallery, New York City (1982, 1984); Lauren Rogers Museum, Laurel, Mississippi (1977); Orleans Gallery, New Orleans, Louisiana (1962, 1964, 1967, 1968); and others.

Her work has been invited to myriad group exhibitions in the United States and abroad, such as "World Expo '88," Brisbane, Australia (1988); International Sculpture Conference, Washington, D.C. (1980); "Awards Candidates," American Academy and Institute of Arts and Letters (1977); "Art in Louisiana," German-American Folkfest, Berlin, Germany (1968); "Catastrophe," Raymond Cordier Gallery, Paris, France (1962); "Orleans Gallery Group," a United States Information Agency (USIA)-sponsored travelling show to Tokyo, Manila, and Hong Kong (1961); and many others.

Emery has worked solo or has collaborated with architects, composers, mathematicians, and other sculptors on team projects involving design proposals throughout the United States; she has executed many commissions, including large-scale kinetic sculptures, up to thirty-six-by-twenty-two-feet in orbit, for parks, marinas, corporate, and governmental places and spaces.

Visiting artist and critic, lecturer, panelist, and seminarian at colleges, museums, and international conferences, Emery has won many awards and honors for her work, including the Lazio Aranyi award of honor for public art (1990); YWCA "Role Model" award (1989); a National Endowment for the Arts (NEA) "Interart" grant (1983); the Mayor's Award for Achievement in the Arts, New Orleans (1980); and others. She recently wrote, "My forms are derived from symmetries found in nature and I borrow natural forces (wind, water, gravity) to set them in motion."

Emery's work is represented in private, public, and corporate permanent collections, including the National Collection of American Art, Washington, D.C.; Flint Institute of Arts, Michigan; New Orleans Museum of Art, Louisiana; Museum of Foreign Art, Sofia, Bulgaria; the Campus of Hofstra University, New York; Jewish Community Center, New Orleans; Emanuel Baptist Church, Alexandria, Virginia; Chevron Headquarters, Oxnard, California; and many others.

Bibliography
Feldman, Edmund Burke. *Art as Image and Idea.* Prentice-Hall, 1967.

Watson-Jones, Virginia. *Contemporary Women Sculptors.* Oryx Press, 1988.

Who's Who in American Art. 19th ed. R.R. Bowker Co., 1991–1992.

Emmet, Lydia Field (1866–1952)

Lydia Field Emmet, a painter of portraits and of figures in landscapes, came from a family of artists. Her grandmother and mother had been painters and both of her sisters, Rosina and Jane, as well as her cousin Ellen, became professional painters. Born in New Rochelle, New York, Emmet in 1884 accompanied her older sister Rosina to Europe, where she enrolled for classes at the Académie Julian, Paris, France. After her return to New York City she studied with William Merritt Chase, H. Siddons Mowbray, and Kenyon Cox at the Art Students League from 1889 to 1895. When Chase began his summer school at Shinnecock Hills on Long Island, New York, in 1891, she was sufficiently advanced that he put her in charge of the preparatory class.

In her early work Emmet painted a wide range of subjects, including a mural, "Art, Science, and Literature," for the Woman's Building at the World's Columbian Exposition of 1893 in Chicago, Illinois, but soon her reputation as a portraitist of children superseded all else, and she was able to command handsome prices for her many commissions. Among her portraits are "Olivia Stokes" (1911, National Gallery of Art), Washington, D.C., "Cynthia Pratt" (c. 1917, private collection), "The Four Daughters of Winthrop Aldrich" (1927, Museum of the City of New York), and "Mrs. Herbert Hoover" (The White House, Washington, D.C.).

Emmet received countless prizes for her paintings and was elected a member of the National Academy of Design.

Eleanor Tufts

Bibliography
Hoppin, Martha J. *The Emmets: A Family of Women Painters.* Berkshire Museum, 1982.

Tufts, Eleanor. *American Women Artists, 1830–1930.* National Museum of Women in the Arts, 1987.

Ente, Lily (1905–1984)

Born in Ukraine, the sculptor Lily Ente studied in Russia and France before coming to the United States in 1925. She learned stone carving through the good works and services of those who carved monuments in the Washington Cemetery, Brooklyn, New York.

Ente held many solo exhibitions in galleries and universities, including the Loeb Center, New York University, New York City (1955, 1959); East Hampton Gallery, New York (1965); Fordham University, Rosedale, New York (1966); Fordham University at Lincoln Center, New York City (1967); and others. Her work was invited to group exhibitions in the United States and abroad, such as "New Jersey Artists Annual Exhibition," Riverside Museum, New York City (1954); Contemporary American Painting and Sculpture, University of Illinois, Champaign-Urbana (1957); "New Sculpture Group: Guests and Members Fifth Annual Exhibition," Stable Gallery, New York City (1960); "Aspects de la Sculpture Americaine," Galerie Claude Bernard, Paris, France (1960); "Louise Nevelson, Sari Dienes, and Lily Ente" (1973) and "Eight Artists," Buecker and Harpsicord Gallery, New York City (1982); and others.

Ente won an honorable mention at the "Biennial" of the Brooklyn Museum, New York (1954); a bronze medal of honor at the Newark Museum, New Jersey (1956); the Amelia Peabody Award for Sculpture, "National Association of Women Artists Annual," National Academy of Design, New York City (1966); and others. Her sculpture is represented in private and public permanent collections, including Brandeis University, Waltham, Massachusetts; Chrysler Museum, Norfolk, Virginia; Phoenix Art Museum, Arizona; Safad Municipal Museum, Israel; Wichita State University, Kansas; and others.

Bibliography

Ashton, Dore. "About Art and Artists." *The New York Times* (November 15, 1956): 32.

Schwartz, Sanford. "New York Letter." *Art International* 17:2 (February 1973): 60–61.

Tillim, Sidney. "New York Exhibitions: In the Galleries, Contemporaries." *Arts Magazine* 37:5 (February 1963): 55.

Watson-Jones, Virginia. *Contemporary American Women Sculptors.* Oryx Press, 1986.

Erla, Karen (1942–)

Born in Pittsburgh, Pennsylvania, the printmaker/painter/sculptor Karen Erla attended the Carnegie Institute of Technology in her native city (1958–1959); studied at Boston University, Massachusetts (1960–1962); and earned a Bachelor of Fine Arts degree from George Washington University, Washington, D.C. (1965). She also studied independently with John Ross at Manhattanville College, Purchase, New York, and at Pratt Institute, New York City.

Between 1976 and 1988 Erla has held solo exhibitions in galleries and colleges, including Manhattanville College, New York (1982, 1987); University of the South, Sewanee, Tennessee (1983); Paul Rosen Gallery, Washington, D.C. (1984); Bertha Urdang Gallery, New York City (1986); E.L. Stark Gallery, New York City (1987, 1988); and others. Her work has been invited to many group exhibitions throughout the United States and abroad, such as the Fay Gold Gallery, Atlanta, Georgia (1982); Chaffey Museum of History and Art, Ontario, California (1983); Pochoir Gallery, Sydney, Australia (1984); "37th National Exhibition," Boston Printmakers, Massachusetts (1985); National Museum of American Art, Smithsonian Institution, Washington, D.C. (1986); Los Angeles Printmaking Society, California (1986); the Print Club, Philadelphia, Pennsylvania (1987); Atlanta College of Art, Georgia (1988); Australian National Gallery, Canberra (1989); Stark Gallery, New York City (1990); and others.

A virtuoso painter and printmaker, Erla has recently turned to monotypes as her medium—allowing her to wed multiple original concepts and ideas derived from music, the dance—from life, itself—to unique originals, using not only an etching press and many inkings, but myriad mark-making approaches. "Jazz at Marty's" (1980), a not atypical layered abstraction of this period, reveals Erla's mastery of the medium.

Erla's work is represented in private and public permanent collections, including the Australian National Gallery, Canberra; Baltimore Museum of Art, Maryland; Brooklyn Museum, New York; Los Angeles County Museum of Art, California; Metropolitan Museum of Art, New York City; National Museum of American Art, Smithsonian Institution, Washington, D.C.; Philadelphia Museum of Art, Pennsylvania; and others.

Bibliography

Cohen, Ronny. *Karen Erla: Works on Paper.* A Monograph. 1988.

Thompson, Mary Lee. *Karen Erla: Monoprints 1979–1983.* A Monograph. 1984.

Urdang, Bertha, and Eric L. Stark. *Karen Erla: Paintings 1987.* A Monograph. 1987.

Who's Who in American Art. 19th ed. R.R. Bowker Co., 1991–1992.

Esa, Marjorie (1934–)

Inuit artist Marjorie Esa was born near Iglulik and adopted as a newborn child by Louis Tapatai and Hannah Siksik who were living in the area around Baker Lake, Northwest Territories. Tapatai was associated with the Hudson Bay Company traders and worked and travelled with them regularly. Esa grew up, therefore, in close contact with the traditions of her own Inuit culture and had, as well, sustained contact with the Euro-Canadian influences which were introduced into the Canadian Arctic in the twentieth century. During the 1950s and 1960s, when Esa was already a young adult, the settlement of Baker Lake grew rapidly with starving and sick Inuit from the wide surrounding area being relocated in Baker Lake by the Canadian federal government. At this time the federal government introduced experimental arts and crafts projects as a means to encourage a new local economy, and Esa was one of the first to respond to this new opportunity. She began making soapstone carvings and fashioning miniature artifacts modeled after tools and equipment traditionally used by the Central Arctic Inuit. She also tried her hand at a few wool duffel wall-hangings. However, Esa's favored artistic medium was to be drawing, and she has drawn regularly since the mid-1960s, always striving to improve her skill at observing and rendering the world that she sees around her.

Esa developed her own distinctive graphic style, and her drawings are among the most naturalistic of those created at Baker Lake during the early years. While she sometimes draws imaginary figures from her mind, she more frequently concentrates on observed reality. Esa favors birds and fish, singly or in flocks, and people as the subject matter for her art. Working almost exclusively in colored pencil, she uses soft colors, frequently blending one color into another with great subtlety to imitate the appearance of light falling across the feathers of birds or scales of fish.

Esa's drawings have served as the basis for sixteen prints produced at Baker Lake's Sanavik Cooperative between 1971 and 1990. Her images are included in the annual collections for 1971, 1972, 1973, 1980, 1981, 1983–1984, 1985, and 1990; she was also involved briefly in the printmaking shop, aiding in the production of the 1983–1984 print collection. Esa's drawings and prints have been included in internationally touring exhibitions of Canadian Inuit graphic art—"The Inuit Print/L'estampe Inuit" and "Contemporary Inuit Drawings"—and she has been represented in a number of group shows at public and commercial galleries in Canada. Significant public collections holding works by Esa include the Canadian Museum of Civilization, Ottawa; Winnipeg Art Gallery, Manitoba; Macdonald Stewart Art Centre, Guelph, Ontario; and the Prince of Wales Northern Heritage Center, Yellowknife, Northwest Territories—all in Canada.

Marion E. Jackson

Bibliography

Baker Lake Annual Print Collection Catalogs: 1971, 1972, 1973, 1980, 1981, 1983–1984, 1985, 1990.

Beaverbrook Art Gallery. *The Murray and Marguerite Vaughan Inuit Print Collection.* Beaverbrook Art Gallery, 1981.

Driscoll, Bernadette, and Sheila Butler. *Baker Lake Prints and Print Drawings 1970–76.* Winnipeg Art Gallery, 1983.

Goetz, Helga. *The Inuit Print/L'estampe Inuit.* National Museums of Canada, 1977.

Fry, Jacqueline, and Sheila Butler. *Baker Lake Drawings.* Winnipeg Art Gallery, 1972.

Jackson, Marion, and Judith Nasby. *Contemporary Inuit Drawings.* Macdonald Stewart Art Centre, 1987.

Escobedo, Helen (1934–)

Helen Escobedo, internationally-known environmental sculptor, was born in Mexico City, where she studied with Germán Cueto. She was awarded a scholarship to the Royal College of Art, London, England, from which she received her ARCA diploma (1952).

Escobedo was director of the museums and galleries of the National University of Mexico (1974–1978); director of the Museo de Arte Moderno, Mexico City, Mexico (1982–1984); received a Guggenheim fellowship for her sculptural work (1991); and was one of six artists who created the monumental circular environmental work, "El Espacio Escultorico," which focuses on the volcanic and archeological origins of the site at the National University of Mexico. Her concern with ecological and urban problems is embodied in the numerous ephemeral environments she has built in Mexico, the United States, Europe, and Japan. In these sited works she uses materials such as standing trees, painted branches, garbage, leaves, straw, and stones to focus the viewer on ecological issues and the environmental pollution that obtains from human existence patterns.

In "Gateway to the Wind" (1968), one of her public commissions sited on the Olympic Friendship Route in Mexico, Escobedo incorporates transparent materials, open wire mesh, and metal structures. Similarly, the "Great Cone Series" (1968), in Jerusalem, Israel; and "Liquid Column" (1988), Hamburg, Germany, reveal her singular use of materials.

Escobedo has participated in more than 100 group exhibitions and twenty-six solo shows in museums and galleries throughout the world, including the Ordrupgaard Museum, Copenhagen, Denmark (1990); a site sculpture, "Black Garbage," Chapultepec Park, Mexico City, Mexico (1991); and another at the Helsingin Kaupungin Taidemuseo, Helsinki, Finland (1991); "Dawn Figures," Balliol, St. John's University College, England (1992); and a two-person show at the Museo Tamayo, Mexico City, Mexico (1992).

Moira Geoffrion

Bibliography

Eder, Rita. *Helen Escobedo.* UNAM. 1982.

Escobedo, Helen. *Only a Tree.* HJR zur Ausstellung im Helsingin Kaupungin Taidemuseo. Helsinki, 1991.

Escobedo, Helen, and Paulo Gori. *Mexican Monuments, Strange Encounters.* Abbeville Press, 1987.

Estrada, Aurora (1940–)

Born in San Miguel de Allende, Guanajuato, Mexico, Aurora Estrada studied painting in the Centro Cultural Ignacio Ramirez, and printmaking in the Instituto San Miguel de Allende, and at the University of Iowa, Iowa City.

She has had a number of solo exhibitions, including her first showings in Mexico City (1967–1968). She exhibited her prints at the Galería Kreisler, Madrid, Spain (1976); the Casa de la Cultura, Queretaro (1977); the Galería Romano (1978), and the Bienal de la Gráfica del Palacio de Bellas Artes—both in Mexico City, Mexico. Estrada has also shown acrylics and etchings in various galleries in Mexico.

Estrada did a portrait of the liberator of Peru, Mariscal Ramon Castilla, for the art gallery of the Museum of Natural History in Chapultepec, Mexico. She was named "Favorite Daughter of San Miguel de Allende" for having painted Castilla's likeness, and the Peruvian government awarded her a medal of honor and a certificate for her work. In the beginning of her career Estrada worked in an academic manner; her subsequent production has veered toward the fantastic, the symbolic, and is expressed through mythic means.

Between 1963 and 1975 Estrada's paintings were seen in many group exhibitions throughout the Republic of Mexico. In 1976 she showed work in the Museum of Contemporary Art, San Miguel de Allende; the Printmaking Biennial at the Palace of Fine Arts, Mexico City; and the Regional Museum in Acoponeta, Nayarit. Three years later, her prints were in the Printmaking Biennial, Galería del Auditorio Nacional, Mexico; and in the Art Center of Atlantic City, New Jersey.

Bibliography

Alvarez, José Rogelio, et al. *Enciclopedia de México.* Secretaría de Educación Pública, 1987.

Diccionario Biográfico Enciclopedico de la Pintura Mexicana. Quinientos Años Editores, 1979.

Etidlooie, Kingmeata (1915–1989)

Born at Itinik camp near Lake Harbour, Northwest Territories, Canada, Kingmeata Etidlooie grew up and spent most of the first half of her life in similar sites along the southwest coast of Baffin Island. She began to carve and to draw in the late 1950s after the death of her first husband, Elijah. As with most Inuit artists of her generation, Kingmeata's creative endeavors mark a second phase in her life—one that parallels the significant changes experienced by the indigenous people of the Canadian Arctic over the past five decades. With her second husband, Etidlooie Etidlooie (1910–1981), and their family, Kingmeata moved into the settlement of Cape Dorset in the mid-1960s, exchanging a seasonally-based camp life for a permanent residence. Both she and her husband became artist-members of the West Baffin Eskimo Cooperative, recognized internationally for its printmaking studio and the strength of the graphic artists it represents.

A relatively prolific artist, Kingmeata had more than fifty of her prints published between 1970 and her death in 1989. Her work is characterized by a strong sense of order and structure. Using predominantly simplified animal and bird motifs, she concentrated on the formal rather narrative qualities of her subjects. However, her most important contribution to Inuit art has probably been her experimentation with media that are more painterly than linear. In the late 1960s to the early 1970s Kingmeata became one of the first Cape Dorset artists to work with watercolors, which had been given to her by Terry Ryan—co-op manager and arts advisor—who recognized the painterly qualities of her drawings. In the mid-1970s the presence of Toronto painter K.M. Graham provided a further catalyst who came North to sketch and work with acrylic paints in her own color-field style. Graham was impressed by Kingmeata's watercolors and offered her acrylics upon her departure. When a painting studio was established by the cooperative in 1976 Kingmeata, along with Pudlo Pudlat (b. 1916), was one of the most committed and enthusiastic users. The rich, saturated colors that were now attainable seemed to mesh perfectly with her formal sense of composition. In works such as "Sea Creatures with Birds" (1976), color, shade, texture, and shape are enmeshed in a delightful, lyrical image.

Kingmeata is represented in the collections of the National Gallery of Canada, Ottawa; the Art Gallery of Ontario, Toronto; the Winnipeg Art Gallery; the Canada Council Art Bank, Ottawa; and the Canadian Museum of Civilization, Hull/Ottawa.

Marie Routledge

Bibliography
Barz, Sandra. *Inuit Artists Print Workbook*. Arts & Culture of the North, 1981.
———. *Canadian Inuit Print Artist/Printer Biographies*. Arts & Culture of the North, 1990.
———. *Inuit Artists Print Workbook*, Vol. II. Arts & Culture of the North, 1990.
Blodgett, Jean. *Grasp Tight the Old Ways: Selections from the Klamer Family Collection of Inuit Art*. Exhibition Catalog. Art Gallery of Ontario, 1983.
Cape Dorset, West Baffin Eskimo Cooperative. Catalogs of the Cape Dorset Annual Graphics Collections: 1970–1983, 1986, 1988.
Jackson, Marion E., and Judith Nasby. *Contemporary Inuit Drawings*. Exhibition Catalog. Macdonald Stewart Art Centre, 1987.
Kingston, Ontario, Agnes Etherington Art Centre. *Inuit Art in the 1970s*. Exhibition Catalog by Marie Routledge, 1979.

Evans, Jessie Benton (1866–1954)

Born in Uniontown, Ohio, Jessie Benton Evans was a painter of western landscapes in general and the Salt River Valley, Arizona, in particular. Evans initiated her study of art at Oberlin College, Ohio, and, thanks to financial support first from her father and then her husband, travelled to Europe regularly. Evans earned a diploma from the Art Institute of Chicago, Illinois (1904), and studied in Europe and America with distinguished artists, including William Merritt Chase, Charles Hawthorne, Lawton Parker, Zanetti Zilla of Italy, and others.

For reasons of health Evans went to Arizona in 1911. Once there she fell in love with the desert; built a palatial home in Paradise Valley; painted myriad oils and watercolors which were shown in European and American venues; and remained in her Southwestern home until her death.

Evans has won prizes and honors for landscape and portraiture at the Arizona State Fair, including first prize at the Phoenix Municipal Exposition, Arizona. Her work is represented in private and public permanent collections, including the Phoenix Country Club, Arizona; the Municipal Collection of Phoenix, Arizona; the Municipal Collection of Akron, Ohio; the Vanderpoel Art Association, and the College Club, Chicago, Illinois; and many others.

Bibliography
Berryman, Florence Seville. "An Artist of the Salt River Valley." *The American Magazine of Art* 20:8 (August 1929).
Dvoino, Dee. "Noted Painters Arizona's Own." *Arizona: The State Magazine and the Pathfinder*. (October 1922).
Kovinick, Phil. *The Woman Artist in the American West, 1860–1960*. Muckenthaler Cultural Center.

Evans, Jessie Benton (1938–)

Born in Phoenix, Arizona, the painter/writer Jessie Benton Evans earned a Bachelor's degree from Arizona State University, Tempe (1960); and received a Master's degree from the University of Iowa, Iowa City, where she worked under the aegis of Mauricio Lasansky (1972).

Evans has held many solo and two-person exhibitions in the United States and has had her work invited to numbers of group exhibitions. Some of her recent shows include Adelphi University, Garden City, New York (1981, 1982); Lincoln Center (1984, 1985, 1986), and Art Students League—both in New York City (1983, 1986); C.G. Rein, Scottsdale, Arizona (1987, 1988); Hartley-Hill Gallery, Carmel-by-the-Sea, California (1988, 1989); Es Possible Gallery, El Pedregal, Carefree, Arizona (1992); and others.

Painter of large-scale expressionistic skies over improbable landscapes that challenge the imagination, Evans wrote art criticism for the *New York Arts Journal* (1975–1979), and *Art World* (1986–1991); she moderated a weekly Manhattan cable television show, "Personalities" (1979–1985), and held forth on WTBQ Radio, Warwick, New York (1978–1985). Recipient of a grant from the Institute for Art and Urban Resources, New York (1981), Evans has taught in Goshen, New York (1968–1969) and Warwick, New York (1971). Her work is represented in private and public permanent collections throughout the United States.

Bibliography
Campbell, Lawrence. "Jessie Benton Evans at Western Images." *Art in America* (November 1989).
Harrison, Helen A. "The Cool and the Emotional." *The New York Times* (July 11, 1982).
Parks, Stephen. "Ecstatic Expressionism." *Southwest Profile* (March–April 1987): 25–28.
Wolff, Theodore F. "Out in the Sun and the Wind." *The Christian Science Monitor* (October 9, 1986): 30.

Evans, Minnie Jones (1892–1987)

The African-American folk painter Minnie Jones Evans was born in Long Creek, Pender County, North Carolina; she became a painter in the mid-1930s.

Evans's work was exhibited widely in the United States and abroad in galleries and museums, including the Little Gallery, Wilmington, North Carolina (1966); Church of the Epiphany, and St. Clement's Episcopal Church—both in New York City; The Art Image, New York (1969); Wesleyan University, Middletown, Connecticut (1969); Portal Gallery, London, England (1970); Indianapolis Museum of Art, Indiana (1970); St. John's Art Gallery, North Carolina (1970); American Federation of Arts, a travelling show (1970–1972); Museum of Modern Art (MoMA) (1972); the Studio Museum, Harlem (1973); and the Whitney Museum of American Art—all in New York City (1975); and many others.

Her symmetrical compositions, filled with strange and wondrous things, were based in large part on the Book of Revelations. Evans believed that her work "is just as strange to me as they are to someone else." That comment aptly describes the complicated symmetrical composition, "Design Made at Airlie Garden" (1967), which is crammed with exotic flowers, feathers, and several faces. Her works are represented in private and public permanent collections.

Bibliography
Kahan, Mitchell D. *Heavenly Vision: The Art of Minnie Evans*. North Carolina Museum of Art, 1986.

Meyer, Jon. "Minnie Evans (North Carolina Museum of Art)." *Art News* 85:4 (April 1986): 144.

"Minnie Evans, 95, Folk Painter Noted for Visionary Work." *The New York Times* (December 19, 1987): Y12.

Star, Nina Howell. *Minnie Evans*. A Catalog. Whitney Museum of American Art, 1975.

Eyetoaq, Ada (1934–)

Baker Lake Inuit artist Ada Eyetoaq is best known for her roughly-carved miniature soapstone sculptures of human figures, though she has also explored other artistic media. She has created a number of drawings for the Sanavik Cooperative's print program and a few wool duffel and felt wall-hangings. Two of Eyetoaq's drawings were produced as prints in the 1971 Baker Lake print collection and two more in the 1972 collection. Her subject matter is generally inspired by her long years of experience living in the traditional Inuit hunting culture. She and her family were among the last to move into the settlement of Baker Lake from their traditional camp near Beverly Lake in the Keewatin District of the Central Arctic, and she initially turned to soapstone sculpture as a means of securing some income at a time when her family could no longer depend on hunting and trapping for their livelihood. Eyetoaq's husband, James Kingilik, is also an artist and produces primarily soapstone sculpture.

Eyetoaq's work has been included in a number of group exhibitions, including the internationally touring exhibition, "The Inuit Print/ L'Estampe Inuit," and a number of exhibitions at the Winnipeg Art Gallery, Manitoba. Her work is also represented in numerous private and public collections, including the Prince of Wales Northern Heritage Centre, Yellowknife, Northwest Territories; Amon Carter Museum, Fort Worth, Texas; Canadian Museum of Civilization, Ottawa; Macdonald Stewart Art Centre, Guelph, Ontario; Montréal Museum of Fine Art, Québec; and the Red Deer and District Museum and Archives Collection, Alberta.

Marion E. Jackson

Bibliography

Baker Lake Annual Print Collection Catalogs: 1971, 1972.

Blodgett, Jean. *The Coming and Going of the Shaman*. Winnipeg Art Gallery, 1978.

Driscoll, Bernadette. *The Inuit Amautik: I Like My Hood to Be Full*. Winnipeg Art Gallery, 1980.

———, Bernadette, and Sheila Butler. *Baker Lake Prints and Print Drawings 1970–76*. Winnipeg Art Gallery, 1983.

Furneaux, Patrick, and Leo Rosshandler. *Arts of the Eskimo: Prints*. Signum Press in Association with Oxford Press, 1974.

Goetz, Helga. *The Inuit Print/L'estampe Inuit*. National Museums of Canada, 1977.

Queens Museum. *Eskimo Art*. Queens Museum, 1974.

University of Alberta. *Inuit Games and Contests: The Clifford E. Lee Collection of Prints*. University of Alberta, 1978.

Eyre de Lanux, Elizabeth (1894–)

The daughter of a New York lawyer, Elizabeth Eyre de Lanux was the niece of Wilson Eyre—one of Philadelphia's leading late-nineteenth-century domestic architects. Studying at the Art Students League, New York City, under Edwin Dickinson, Robert Henri, George Bridgman, and Charles Hawthorne, Eyre de Lanux first exhibited in 1917 at the Society of Independent Artists, also in New York City. The following year she married the French writer and diplomat, Pierre de Lanux, and she settled with him in Paris, France. Dropping Elizabeth from her professional name, she enrolled in the Académie Colarossi and in the Académie Ranson, and her teachers included Maurice Denis, Demetrius Galanis, and Constantin Brancusi.

Throughout the 1920s Eyre de Lanux maintained a wide variety of contacts with writers and artists. She soon became a regular participant in the salon of Natalie Clifford Barney, whose Paris, France residence she overlooked. The individuals she encountered there and elsewhere inspired a series of Cubist portraits, including one of Barney (1921, National Museum of American Art, Washington, D.C.) and another of Romaine Brooks (1923), who had earlier painted Eyre de Lanux's portrait, "Chasseresse" (1920, National Museum of American Art). Other sitters included Eva le Gallienne, Marion Tiffany, Liane de Pougy, Carlotta Monterey, Martha Gelhorn, and Malvina Hoffman. When she exhibited some of these in 1921 in New York City, she collectively titled them "Outlines of Women." Also during this period she became actively involved in decorative arts design, working with Evelyn Wyld, and designing furniture and interiors.

Betsy Fahlman

Bibliography

Anscombe, Isabelle. "Expatriates in Paris: Eileen Gray, Evelyn Wyld and Eyre de Lanux." *Apollo* 115 (February 1982): 117–18.

———. *A Woman's Touch: Women in Design from 1860 to the Present Day*. Penguin, 1984.

Fahlman, Betsy. "Eyre de Lanux." *Woman's Art Journal* 3 (Fall 1982– Winter 1983): 44–48.

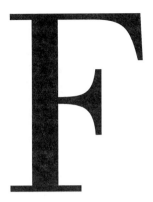

Falk, Gathie (1928–)

Born in Alexander, Manitoba, Canada, Gathie Falk studied part-time at the University of British Columbia in the late 1950s and early 1960s. She remained in the Vancouver area and has become generally associated with its artist's-run Western Front, founded in 1973. Falk's work cannot be easily categorized, for she is equally at home in ceramics, painting, and performance art. Most of her work alternates between a sensuous neo-expressionism and a kind of folk-art sensibility, at least in terms of superficial appearances. Her painted images are often of simple domestic items such as arm-chairs or family photographs. A well-known sculpture, "Herd Two" (1974–1975), consists of more than a dozen plywood cut-outs of carousel horses, relatively muted in color and suspended just off the floor. The effect is one of nostalgia and the not-quite-graspable nature of memory.

Robert J. Belton

Bibliography
G. Bellerby. *Gathie Falk: Paintings 1978–1984.* Art Gallery of Greater Victoria, 1985.

Falkenstein, Claire (1908–)

Reared in North Bend, Oregon, the sculptor Claire Falkenstein earned a Bachelor's degree from the University of California at Berkeley (1930); in the 1940s she turned away from ribboned-clay abstractions to wood, and produced jointed wood sculptures that could be uncoupled and re-formed by the viewer. Still later she learned to weld, made jewelry and wire sculpture, and briefly attended Stanley William Hayter's Atlelier 17, New York City.

A teacher at the California School of Fine Arts, San Francisco, Falkenstein went to Paris, France (1950); lived there for more than a decade; was supported (as were other Americans) by Michel Tapie; and exhibited her work throughout Europe. Falkenstein returned to the United States in 1962; held solo exhibitions in galleries and museums; and was invited to show in major group exhibitions, including the Annuals at the Whitney Museum of American Art, New York City (1960, 1964); "Artiste Objets," Musée des Arts Décoratifs, Paris, France (1962); "Pittsburgh International Exhibition of Painting and Sculpture," Carnegie Institute, Pennsylvania (1964); "Painting and Sculpture in California: The Modern Era," San Francisco Museum of Art, California, and the National Collection of Fine Arts, Washington, D.C. (1976); "Claire Falkenstein: In San Francisco, Paris, Los Angeles, and Now," Palm Springs Desert Museum, California (1980); "The Continuing Vision of Claire Falkenstein: 1947–1984," University of California at Berkeley (1984); and many others.

Falkenstein has executed monumental and other works, many on commission, and her work is represented in private and public permanent collections, including the Tate Gallery, London, England; Carnegie Institute, Pittsburgh, Pennsylvania; the Guggenheim Museum, Venice, Italy; the National Museum of American Art, Washington, D.C.; and myriad others.

Bibliography

Americans in Paris: The Fifties. California State University, Northridge, 1979.

An Exhibition of the Sculpture, Paintings, and Ceramics of Claire Falkenstein. Commentaries by Henry Seldis and Katherine Kuh. Los Angeles: California Federal Savings, 1970.

Roth, Moira, ed. *Connecting Conversations: Interviews with 28 Bay area Women Artists.* Mills College, Eucalyptus Press, 1988.

Watson-Jones, Virginia. *Contemporary American Women Sculptors.* Oryx Press, 1986.

Faller, Marion (Sudol) (1941–)

A prolific photographer generally working in a documentary tradition, Marion (Sudol) Faller's particular emphasis has been on collections of types and their repetition, usually picturing commonplace phenomena. Influenced perhaps by her father, Walter Sudol, who made monthly photographs of Faller and her sisters throughout childhood, she works almost exclusively in series. Rarely does the single image stand alone in her work, and rarely does a series exist without gentle wit as well as perfect photographic technique. Subjects have been the familiar and domestic for the most part, including, for example, the contents of her son's pockets, recorded over two years ("Time Capsule," begun in 1979, printed in 1985). In "Local Conventions" (1979–1983), Faller documented in an extensive series the kinds of things householders in Central New York State do to their property in response to seasons and holidays. A more recent series begun in 1987 and ongoing, "Ritual Renewal: Polish-American Easter Traditions" produced in collaboration with folklife historian Kate Koperski, explores devotional displays, traditional food, and customs of Buffalo's Polish-American community.

Faller is an associate professor at the State University of New York (SUNY) in Buffalo, where she has been on the faculty since 1982. She received her Master of Fine Arts degree in 1979 through the same institution's program at the visual studies workshop in Rochester, after earning a Bachelor of Arts degree from Hunter College in 1971. Filmmaker and theorist Hollis Frampton was Faller's companion and collaborator from 1971 until his death in 1984, and together they produced such works as "Rites of Passage" (1983–1984), "False Impressions" (1979), and "Vegetable Locomotion" (1975), the last a spoof of the locomotion series made by pioneer motion photographer Eadweard Muybridge in the 1880s. Instead of animals, however, Faller and Frampton showed advancing apples, zucchini, and the like.

Although Faller tends to use the camera and color film in a straightforward manner in most of her work, she has utilized alternative processes when they best fit her concept, such as "Patchwork Pieces" (1977–1979), collages made of color xeroxes, and "Flora" (1977), photograms of flowers and old glass-plate negatives on Cibachrome paper.

Widely exhibited, particularly in New York State and the Northeast, Faller has also curated exhibitions. Faller's work is included in the permanent collections of the Albright–Knox Art Gallery, Buffalo; the Buscaglia-Castellani Art Gallery, Niagara University, Niagara Falls; the International Museum of Photography, George Eastman House, Rochester; and the Visual Studies Workshop Research Center, Rochester—all in New York; the Carnegie Institute Museum of Art, Pittsburgh, Pennsylvania; and the Museum of Fine Arts, Houston, Texas.

Gretchen Garner

Bibliography

Asbury, Dana. "Shows We've Seen: Observations of Domestic Realities." *Popular Photography* 89:6 (June 1982): 19.

Berger, P., L. Searle, and D. Wadden. *Radical/Rational Space/Time: Idea Networks in Photography.* Henry Art Gallery, University of Washington, 1983, pp. 7, 43–45.

Faller, Marion, and K. Koperski. *Ritual Renewal: Polish American Easter Traditions* and *The Iconography of Rebirth: Aspects of the Polish American Easter Celebration.* Buscaglia-Castellani Art Gallery, 1989.

Garner, Gretchen. *Reclaiming Paradise: American Women Photograph the Land.* Tweed Museum of Art, University of Minnesota, 1987, 40–41.

———, ed. "Connections: An Invitational Portfolio of Images and Statements by Twenty-Eight Women." *Exposure* (Journal of the Society for Photographic Education) 19:3 (Fall 1981): 26.

Grundberg, Andy, and Kathyleen McCarthy Gauss. *Photography and Art: Interactions Since 1946.* Los Angeles County Museum of Art, and Abbeville Press, 1987: 151.

Krane, Susan. *Hollis Frampton: Recollections/Recreations.* Buffalo: Albright-Knox Art Gallery, and MIT Press, 1984.

Lord, Catherine. "Women and Photography: Some Thoughts on Assembling an Exhibition." *Afterimage* 7:6 (January 1980): 6–13.

"Marion Faller: A Portfolio of Photographs." *Creative Camera,* Coo Press Ltd., London (July 1974): 220, 228–229.

Peterson, Christian. *Photographs Beget Photographs.* The Minneapolis Institute of Arts, 1987, pp. 21–23.

"Portfolio: Marion Faller." *Ms. Magazine* (April 1975): 17.

Farnham, Sally (1876–1943)

Born in Ogdensburg, New York, the sculptor Sally Farnham, except for the advice and counsel of Frederick Remington, was self-taught. The advantages of European travel with her father and visits to art collections culminated, five years after her marriage, in the desire to work at sculpture (1901). Mother of three children, her singular work in clay, bronze, and marble grew in scale and quality through the years.

Farnham's work was exhibited widely in group shows, including the National Sculpture Society and the National Academy of Design—both in New York City. She has been the recipient of many major commissions, such as equestrian sculptures, portrait busts, and war memorials; she was responsible for the relief panels in the Pan-American Union, Washington, D.C. (1910); "Simon Bolivar," an equestrian work in Central Park, New York City (1921); and portrait busts of presidents Frankin Delano Roosevelt, Warren G. Harding, and Herbert C. Hoover; among many others. Her work is represented in private and public permanent collections, including the Brookgreen Gardens, South Carolina; Corcoran Gallery of Art, and the National Portrait Gallery—both in Washington, D.C.; the War Memorial, Fultonville, New York; and others.

Bibliography

Dunford, Penny. *Biographical Dictionary of Women Artists in Europe and America Since 1850.* University of Pennsylvania Press, 1989.

Kohlman, Rena Tucker. "America's Women Sculptors." *International Studio* 76:307 (December 1922): 225–35.

Proske, Beatrice Gilman. *Brookgreen Gardens Sculpture.* Vol. II. South Carolina, 1955.

Fasnacht, Heide (1951–)

Born in Cleveland, Ohio, the sculptor Heide Fasnacht earned a Bachelor of Fine Arts degree from the Rhode Island School of Design, Providence (1973); and received a Master of Arts degree in studio art from New York University, New York City (1982).

Working primarily in wood, and occasionally from recycled works, Fasnacht constructs painted, laminated wooden "portraits" which reveal the yin and the yang, the outer and the inner, the skull and the brain in abstract and figural configurations.

Winner of honors and awards, she received a fellowship from the National Endowment for the Arts (NEA) (1979); fellowships at Yaddo, Saratoga Springs, New York (1980, 1985); and the MacDowell Colony, Peterborough, New Hampshire (1981, 1983); awards and fellowships from foundations, including Athena (1983); Hand Hollow (1983); Edward Albee (1984); and others.

Fasnacht has shown widely and her work is represented in private and public permanent collections, including the Columbus Museum of Art, and Cincinnati Art Museum—both in Ohio; University of North Carolina, Greensboro; and others.

Bibliography
Brenson, Michael. "A Sculpture Revival All Around Town." *The New York Times* (November 2, 1985).
Klein, Ellen L. "Heide Fasnacht." *Arts Magazine* 58 (December 1983): 35.
Smith, Roberta. "Irregulars." *The Village Voice* (December 18, 1984).

Feinberg, Elen A. (1955–)

Born in New York City, Elen A. Feinberg received her Bachelor of Fine Arts degree in 1976 from Cornell University, Ithaca, New York, and her Master of Fine Arts degree in 1978 from Indiana University, Bloomington. She has had twenty one-person exhibitions since 1982 at such galleries as Bill Bace Gallery, New York City; Roger Ramsay Gallery, Chicago, Illinois; and Mekler Gallery, Los Angeles, California. Her expansive luminous landscape paintings have received considerable recognition as witnessed by her receiving an award in painting from the Ingram Merrill Foundation, New York City (1988), an artists' fellowship in painting, from the National Endowment for the Arts (NEA) (1987), a MacDowell Colony Fellowship, Peterborough, New Hampshire (1987), and an artist-in-residence award from the Roswell Museum and Art Center, New Mexico (1985–1986).

Characterized by deep landscape/seascape space, and often permeated by engaging and soft-edged cloud formations, Feinberg's images evoke very personal psychological states of mind. Using the formal elements of the landscape tradition she incorporates a classical sense of painting with potent metaphorical significance. Critical response to Feinberg's paintings has been positive and perceptive. Her work has been acquired for the permanent collections of the Los Angeles County Museum of Art, the University of California at Santa Cruz Art Museum, and the Fresno Art Museum—all in California; the Israel Museum, Jerusalem, Israel; Milwaukee Museum, Wisconsin; Roswell Museum and Art Center, New Mexico; IBM, Enron Corporation; Shell Oil Company, and others. Feinberg has also participated in group exhibitions throughout the United States in such shows and galleries as the Chicago Navy Pier Show, Illinois; Los Angeles Contemporary Art Fair, California; the Ruth Siegel Gallery, and G.W. Einstein Gallery—both in New York City, and numerous others.

Feinberg lives in Albuquerque, New Mexico, and holds a faculty position in the Department of Art and Art History at the University of New Mexico.

Leonard Lehrer

Bibliography
Adams, Clinton. *Printmaking in New México.* University of New Mexico Press, 1991.
Donahue, Marlena. "The Galleries, La Cienega." *Los Angeles Times* (September 29, 1989): part 6.
Frank, Peter, and Emily Kass. *Elen Feinberg.* Los Angeles: Mekler Gallery, 1988.
Van Gelder, P. "Representing Realist Artists." *American Artist* (May 1987).

Feldman, Bella (1940–)

A native New Yorker, the sculptor Bella Feldman earned a Bachelor's degree from Queens College, New York City, and received a Master's degree from San José State University, California.

Feldman has held twenty-nine solo exhibitions in museums and galleries in the United States and abroad, between 1975 and 1993, including Shidoni, Santa Fe, New Mexico (1993); Jan Baum Gallery, Los Angeles, and Barclay Simpson Gallery, Lafayette—both in California (1992); Zaks Gallery, Chicago, Illinois (1989, 1991); SPACE Gallery, Los Angeles, California (1987–1988, 1991); "New Sculpture: Bella Feldman," Miller/Brown Gallery, San Francisco, California (1984, 1987); "Bella Feldman," California State University, Hayward (1979); "The Origin of Birds," Grapestake Gallery, San Francisco, California (1976); "Bella: Sculptures," Galerie Bernard Letu, Geneva, Switzerland (1975); and others.

Feldman's work has been invited to many group exhibitions, such as the Oakland Museum, California (1991); "Crossovers," University of Colorado, Colorado Springs (1990); "Tangents: Seven Artists," a travelling show, Maryland Art Institute, Baltimore (1987–1988); "Menagerie: Contemporary Animal Images," San Francisco Airport Commission, California (1985); "Six Artists of the Biennale," Focus Gallery, and "Fibre/Sculpture Biennale," Musée des Beaux-Arts, Lausanne, Switzerland (1983, 1985); "Art and/or Craft USA," a travelling show through Japan (1982); "Paper as Medium," a travelling show, Smithsonian Institution, Washington, D.C. (1978–1980); and many others.

Feldman is a professor of sculpture at the California College of Arts and Crafts, Oakland. Since 1965 she has executed many architectural commissions; was a lecturer in the School of Fine Arts and a cultural specialist at Makerere University, Kampala, Uganda (1968–1970, 1990); received a National Endowment for the Arts (NEA) fellowship (1986–1987); and a travel award from Harvard University, Cambridge, Massachusetts, for research and study in East Africa (1975); and has been a visiting artist, workshop leader, and lecturer at many colleges and universities in the United States.

Feldman's work is represented in private, public, and corporate permanent collections, including the Oakland Museum, University of California at Berkeley; Federal Home Loan Bank, San Francisco; IBM, San José; and Temple Rodef Sholom, San Rafael—all in California; Nora Eccles Harrison Museum of Art, Utah State University, Logan; and others.

Bibliography
Cohn, Terri. "Bella Feldman." *Artweek* (January 9, 1992).
Fibre/Sculpture. A Catalog. Lausanne: Musée des Beaux-Arts, 1985.
Watson-Jones, Virginia. *Contemporary American Women Sculptors*. Oryx Press, 1986.
Who's Who in American Art. 19th ed. R.R. Bowker Co., 1991–1992.

Fenton, Beatrice (1887–1983)

Born in Philadelphia, Pennsylvania, the sculptor Beatrice Fenton learned her craft at the Pennsylvania Academy of Fine Art in her native city and at the School of the Philadelphia Museum of Art.

Fenton exhibited her work widely, and won honors and awards in shows, including the Pan-Pacific Exposition of San Francisco, California (1915); the Pennsylvania Academy of Fine Arts (1922, 1942–1945); "Exhibition of American Sculpture," National Sculpture Society, New York City (1923); the Sesquicentennial Exposition (1926), and "Exhibition of Paintings and Sculpture by Beatrice Fenton, Marjorie D. Martinet, and Anne W. Strawbridge," the Art Club of Philadelphia (1929)—both in Philadelphia, Pennsylvania. She also exhibited with the National Association of Women Painters and Sculptors, New York City (1936); the World's Fair, New York City (1939); the Art Institute of Chicago, Illinois; the National Academy of Design, New York City; Philadelphia Museum of Art, Pennsylvania; (1976); and many others.

Examples of her work are in private and public permanent collections, including the Academy of Music, Children's Hospital, Fairmount Park, the Philadelphia Art Club, the University of Pennsylvania—all in Philadelphia, Pennsylvania; and others in Baltimore, Delaware, and South Carolina.

Bibliography
American Art Annual. Vol. 28. American Federation of Arts, 1932.
Fairmount Park Association, Philadelphia. *Sculpture of a City: Philadelphia's Treasures in Bronze and Stone*. Walker Publishing Co., 1974.
Proske, Beatrice Gilman. *Brookgreen Gardens Sculpture*. Brookgreen Gardens, 1943.

Ferguson, Kathleen E. (1945–)

Born in Chicago, Illinois, the sculptor Kathleen E. Ferguson attended Stephens College, Columbia, Missouri (1963–1964); earned a Bachelor of Fine Arts degree with honors at the Layton School of Art, Milwaukee, Wisconsin (1969) and, two years later, was awarded a Master of Fine Arts degree from the Rhode Island School of Design, Providence.

From 1972 to 1992 Ferguson held nineteen solo exhibitions of her work, including a mini-retrospective show (1968–1985) titled, "Precious Objects," at Transylvania University, Lexington, Kentucky (1985). She also had solo shows at the Smithsonian Institution, Washington, D.C. (1972); Nobe Gallery, New York City (1977, 1979); Jan Cicero Gallery, Chicago, Illinois (1984); Graham Modern, New York City (1985); High Museum of Art, Atlanta, Georgia (1986); "Kozmic Kingdom," an environmental installation commissioned by the J.B. Speed Museum, Louisville, Kentucky (1987); and others.

Ferguson's work has been invited to many group exhibitions in the United States and Japan, such as "Small Sculpture," Philip Bareiss Contemporary Exhibitions, Taos, New Mexico (1990); "Kentucky Women Sculptors," Northern Kentucky University, Highland (1987);

"American Abstract Artists Group Exhibition," Betty Parsons Gallery, New York City (1979); "Group Show," Ginza Nissan Gallery, Tokyo, Japan (1976); "Biennial of Contemporary Art," Whitney Museum of American Art, New York City (1975); and others.

Ferguson has won many awards and honors for her work, and has been visiting artist, lecturer, and faculty member at colleges and universities in the United States. Ferguson has been an administrator, coordinator, and consultant to corporations and other institutions, including E.I. Dupont de Nemours, Wilmington, Delaware; General Electric, Daytona Beach, Florida; and many others.

Bibliography
Glueck, Grace. "Review." *The New York Times* (July 26, 1985).
Meyer, John. "Southern Abstraction." *Art News* (November 1987): 220.
Watson-Jones, Virginia. *Contemporary American Women Sculptors*. Oryx Press, 1986.
Who's Who in American Art. 19th ed. R.R. Bowker Co., 1991–1992.

Ferrara, Jackie (1929–)

Born in Detroit, Michigan, the "Post-Minimalist" sculptor Jackie Ferrara fuses geometry and the pyramidal structure into another realm of personal, meticulously-crafted form-building.

Ferrara held more than thirty-four solo exhibitions of her work between 1973 and 1991, ten of which were at the Max Protetch Gallery, New York. Her public works range from the 1973 work, "Stacked Pyramid," at Storm King Art Center, Mountainville, New York (an eight-and-one-half-foot treated fir structure) to the "Terrace" (16,200 square feet of materials, including slate, concrete, gravel, maple benches, and Australian willows) at the University of California at San Diego (1991). Between those dates she created architectural and site works in various locales in the United States and abroad. Her works have been invited to more than 117 group exhibitions in the United States and abroad, including the "Sculpture Annual," Whitney Museum of American Art, New York City (1970); "GEDOK American Women Artists Show," Kunsthaus, Hamburg, Germany (1972); "Ferrara, Lichtenstein, Nevelson, Ryman," Sarah Lawrence College, Bronxville, New York (1977); "Artists and Architects: Challenges in Collaboration," Cleveland Center for Contemporary Art, Ohio (1985); Michael Klein, Inc., New York (1991); and others.

Winner of many honors for her work, Ferrara received grants from the New York State Council on the Arts (1975, 1971); a Guggenheim Foundation fellowship (1976); grants from the National Endowment for the Arts (NEA) (1973, 1977, 1987); a design excellence award from the Art Commission of the City of New York (1988); and further recognition from the American Institute of Architects (AIA) (1990). She has served on many jury panels for a variety of projects in the visual arts and engineering competitions, as well as policy advisory panels for public art programs.

Ferrara's works are in the permanent collections of major museums and corporations in the United States and abroad, including the Beijer Collection, Stockholm, Sweden; the Louisiana Museum, Humlebaek, Denmark; the Whitney Museum of American Art, Metropolitan Museum of Art, Museum of Modern Art (MoMA), the Brooklyn Museum, the Guggenheim Museum, and the Seagrams Collection—all in New York City; Mobil Oil Corporation, Fairfax, Virginia; and others.

Bibliography
Anonymous. "Jackie Ferrara." *The New Yorker* (April 29, 1991).
Bourdon, David. "Jackie Ferrara: On the Cutting Edge of a New Sensibility." *Arts Magazine* 50:5 (January 1976): 90–91.
Feinberg, Jean. "The Museum as Garden." *Landscape Architecture* (April 1989): 69–73.
Heartney, Eleanor. "Jackie Ferrara." *Arts Magazine* 57:7 (March 1983): 9.

Ferron, Marcelle (1924–)

Born in Louiseville, Québec, Canada, the internationally-known automatist painter Marcelle Ferron learned her craft at the École des Beaux-Arts de Québec and studied under the aegis of Jean-Paul Lemieux and Simone Hudon. Ferron lived, worked, and exhibited paintings from her base in Paris, France (1953–1965), to prestigious shows throughout the world. She has also created major works in stained glass, as in the Metro station, Champs-de-Mars, Montréal.

Ferron has held solo exhibitions in prestigious museums and galleries in Canada and abroad: from Paris, France, to Montréal, Québec, Canada, to Brussels, Belgium. Her work has also been shown in Rome, Turin, Milan, and Spoleto, Italy; London, England; Zurich, Switzerland; and in many shows in Canada. A major retrospective exhibition was held in 1973 at the Musée du Québec and the University of Sherbrooke; there have been many others.

Ferron has been the recipient of many prizes and honors, including the silver medal at the São Paulo Biennial, Brazil (1961), and several from the Canada Council. Her work has been invited to prestigious group exhibitions throughout Canada and Europe, and is represented in myriad private and public permanent collections, including the National Gallery of Canada, Ottawa; Musée des Beaux-Arts, Montréal; and others.

Bibliography
Pocock, Jasmine, and Philip Pocock. "Canadian Artists in Paris." *Canadian Art* 14:4 (Summer 1957): 154–59, 166.
Sarazin, Jean. "Marcelle Ferron or the Joyous Search for Light." *Vie des arts* 61 (Winter 1970–1971): 30–33, 81–82.
Trois Generations d'Art Québecois, 1940, 1950, 1960. Montréal: Musée d'Art Contemporain, 1976.

Fesenmaier, Helene (1937–)

Born in New Ulm, Minnesota, the painter/sculptor Helene Fesenmaier earned a Bachelor's degree from Smith College, Northampton, Massachusetts (1959), and received a Bachelor of Fine Arts degree from Yale University, New Haven, Connecticut (1961).

One of several founders of the New York Studio School of Drawing, Painting, and Sculpture (1964), Fesenmaier travelled and painted in Europe and South America (she spent a year in Caracas, Venezuela, in 1969–1970) and, when no models were available, made constructions. In 1971 she settled on England as a base from which to work.

She exhibits her singular work in solo and group shows in Europe, South America, and the United States, and has executed commissions for the Victoria & Albert Museum, London, England (1979), among others. Examples of her output are to be found in private and public permanent collections, including the Museum of Modern Art (MoMA), New York City; the Fitzwilliam Museum, Cambridge, England; and many others.

Bibliography
Dunford, Penny. *Biographical Dictionary of Women Artists in Europe and America since 1850.* University of Pennsylvania Press, 1989.
Four American Sculptors Working in Britain. University of East Anglia, Norwich, England, 1981.

Fife, Phyllis (1948–)

Born near Dustin, Oklahoma, of Creek Indian ancestry, Phyllis Fife was a student of the late California painter Howard Warshaw. Early in her career Fife had her first educational experiences in a rural school and then enrolled in the Institute for American Indian Arts in Santa Fe, New Mexico, from 1963 to 1966. Fife took further study in painting with Warshaw at the University of California at Santa Barbara, transferred to the University of Oklahoma, Norman, in 1970, and was awarded her Bachelor of Fine Arts degree in 1973.

She has been on the art faculty of Northeastern Oklahoma State University, Tahlequah, and also taught at Southeastern Oklahoma State University, Durant.

Fife's work has been exhibited in many major museums and institutions, including the Heard Museum, Phoenix, Arizona; Oregon State University, Corvallis; the University of Oklahoma Art Museum, Norman; and many others.

One of her works, "The Poet in Painter's Clothing" (1977), expresses in strong, yet subtle, color and brush strokes, visual metaphors for thought; there is a certain assurance about her style, layered with meaning.

Bibliography
Highwater, Jamake. *The Sweet Grass Lives On: Fifty Contemporary North American Indian Artists.* Lippincott & Crowell, 1980.

Filkosky, Josefa (1933–)

The sculptor/designer/metalsmith Josefa Filkosky was born in Westmoreland City, Pennsylvania. On a four-year scholarship she earned a Bachelor's degree at Seton Hill College, Greensburg, Pennsylvania (1955); did graduate work at the School for American Craftsmen, Rochester, New York (Summer 1959); received a Bachelor of Fine Arts degree from Carnegie-Mellon University, Pittsburgh, Pennsylvania (1963), which she followed with a year of graduate study; was awarded an assistantship at the Cranbrook Academy of Art, Bloomfield Hills, Michigan (1966) which, two years later, bestowed its Master of Fine Arts degree upon her.

A professor of art at Seton Hill College, Filkosky has held solo exhibitions at universities, museums, and galleries, including the Art Image in All Media, New York City (1970); Pittsburgh Plan for Art, Pennsylvania (1971, 1973); Indiana University of Pennsylvania (1972); Bertha Schaefer Gallery, New York City (1973); RM Gallery, Toronto, Canada (1974, 1975); Southern Alleghenies Museum of Art, Loretto, Pennsylvania (1992–1993); and others. Her work has been invited to many group exhibitions throughout the United States and has won awards and honors, including the Mellon award, Associated Artists of Pittsburgh, and a purchase award, St. Lawrence University, Canton,

New York (1976).

In addition to their aesthetic and metaphorical meanings, the titles of many of Filkosky's sculptures (e.g., "Pipe Dreams" and the "Pipe Theme" series) describe the ten-inch diameter aluminum and steel pipe she has employed to create her monumental works. Her works are fabricated in one and one-eighth inch steel plate and are represented in private and public permanent collections in the United States.

Bibliography
Benton, Suzanne. *Art of Welded Sculpture*. Reinhold, 1975.
Miller, Donald. "Art International." *Pittsburgh Post-Gazette* (December 1971): 50–51.
Watson-Jones, Virginia. *Contemporary American Women Sculptors*. Oryx Press, 1986.

Fine, Joan (1942–)

A native New Yorker, the sculptor Joan Fine earned a Bachelor's degree at Queens College, New York City, and received a Master of Fine Arts degree from Columbia University, New York City. Fine also studied at St. Martin's School of Art, London, England, with Anthony Caro and others, and at the bronze foundry of the Camberwell School of Arts, also in London, England. She took additional work in ceramics at the Pittsburgh Museum, Pennsylvania, and studied sculpture with Toshio Odate at the Brooklyn Museum School, New York.

Fine has held solo exhibitions at the Old Church Cultural Center, Demarest, New Jersey (1991); John Harms Center for the Arts, Englewood, New Jersey (1989); 14 Sculptors Gallery (1979, 1983, 1985, 1987); National Art Center, New York City (1979), and 5th Street Gallery—both in New York City (1978); and others. She took part in a two-person show, "Origins," at the Jan Weiss Gallery, New York City (1992). Her work has been invited to many group exhibitions throughout the United States—from New York City to Atlanta, Georgia; Pittsfield, Massachusetts; Philadelphia, Pennsylvania; and Greenwich, Connecticut.

A teacher of sculpture at various institutions in New York and New Jersey, Fine is a member of the Sculptors Guild and the Women's Caucus for Art. She received a fellowship in sculpture from the New Jersey State Council on the Arts (1985) and, in 1979, created a notable children's book.

Bibliography
Ehrlich, Robbie. "Arts Reviews: Joan Fine." *Arts Magazine* 53:9 (May 1979): 40.
Watson-Jones, Virginia. *Contemporary American Women Sculptors*. Oryx Press, 1986.
Who's Who in American Art. 19th ed. R.R. Bowker Co., 1991–1992.

Fine, Miriam Brown (1913–)

Dedicated to both painting and writing poetry, Miriam Brown Fine is a devoted admirer of William Blake, whose great illuminated books inspired a series of unique volumes—some filled with paintings alone, some combining her own poetry with painted imagery—completed in the 1980s when the artist was in her seventies. Born in New Jersey, Fine moved to Philadelphia, Pennsylvania, as a one-year-old and has spent the rest of her life in that city. From 1931 to 1935 she attended the Philadelphia Museum School of Industrial Art (now the University of the Arts) and the University of Pennsylvania, majoring in design, although her subsequent career has been devoted to painting and drawing.

Fine works in a variety of media and her art encompasses religious and genre subjects and landscapes, but her foremost and most powerful focus has been her flower compositions, for one of which she received the Philadelphia Art Teacher's Association Mary Marshall award in 1955. Flower subjects were also featured in jewelry she painted through the 1970s, and they dominate her books of the 1980s.

During the 1950s Fine taught art in the Philadelphia, Pennsylvania public school system, then in several community centers as well as privately. From 1976, she has been an active participant in the Temple University Association for Retired Professionals (TARP), Philadelphia, Pennsylvania, teaching watercolor classes and serving as president, then president emeritus of the group. A member of the Artists Equity Association, the American Watercolor Society, the Philadelphia Watercolor Club, the Women's Caucus for Art, and several literary groups, Fine has had more than a dozen one-person shows throughout the Philadelphia, Pennsylvania, area and also has participated in numerous national and international group exhibitions, including the albums at the United Nations Conference on Women, Nairobi, Kenya (1986, now at the National Museum of Women in the Arts, Washington, D.C.) and "The Book as Art IV" (1992–1993, at the National Museum of Women in the Arts, Washington, D.C.).

Ruth E. Fine

Bibliography
Donahue, Victoria. "Exhibition Reviews." *Philadelphia Inquirer* (November 22, 1974).
Grafley, Dorothy. *Art in Focus* (June 1976).
Onufer, Lourie. "Miriam Brown Fine, Creative at 71." *Northeast Times* (February 1, 1984).
Wasserman, Krystyna. *The Book as Art IV*. Washington, 1992.

Fine, Ruth E. (1941–)

A painter and printmaker known for her abstract landscapes, Ruth Fine works at her art in spite of an extremely busy schedule as curator of modern prints and drawings at the National Gallery of Art in Washington, D.C.

Fine was educated at the Philadelphia College of Art, Pennsylvania (now the University of the Arts) where she studied with, among others, George Bunker and Mercedes Matter, graduating with a Bachelor of Fine Arts degree in 1962. She then went to the University of Pennsylvania and received a Master of Fine Arts degree in printmaking in 1964.

Fine taught for a number of years, first at the Philadelphia College of Art from 1965 to 1969, then at Beaver College, Glenside, from 1968 to 1972—both in Pennsylvania. In 1972 she was invited by Lessing Rosenwald to become curator of his famous collection of prints, drawings, and rare books, and when the collection moved to Washington, D.C., she went with it and has been there ever since.

Fine has also written a number of books and catalogs: *Lessing J. Rosenwald: Tribute to a Collector* (1981); *Drawing Near: Whistler Etchings from the Zelman Collection* (1984); *Gemini G.E.L.: Art and Collaboration* (1984); *A Graphic Muse: Prints by Contemporary American Women*

Artists (with Richard S. Field) (1987); *Michael Heizer* (1988); *The 1980s: Prints from the Collection of Joshua P. Smith* (1989); *John Marin* (1990); *The Drawings of Jasper Johns* (with Nan Rosenthal) (1990).

Fine's work is characterized by strong, spontaneous, gestural forms that delight in the sensuous qualities of the particular medium with which she is working. In addition to oil paintings she does large, colorful drawings in pastel and oil-stick. Her prints include lithographs and screenprints, but since the mid-1980s she has concentrated on etching in collaboration with Simmelink/Sukmmoto Editions in Southern California.

Fine has also done the illustrations for the fine press edition of the poems of Francis Goffing published by Abattoir Editions in 1980, and Clifford Burke's *A Landscape with Cows In It* in 1987 and *Bone Songs* in 1992, both published by Janus Press. Her most recent one-person exhibitions were at Rider College in Lawrenceville, New Jersey, and Gallery 72 in Omaha, Nebraska, both in 1991.

Larry Day

Bibliography
Ruth Fine Works on Paper: A Retrospective View. Introduction by the Artist. Beaver College, Glenside, Pennsylvania, 1979.
Day, Larry. *Ruth Fine: California Landscapes.* Interview with the Artist by Harry Naar. Rider College Gallery, Lawrenceville, New Jersey. April 11–May 5, 1991.
Geoffrion, Moira M. *Women Artists, Here and Now.* University of Notre Dame, June 1976.

Finke, Leonda F. (1922–)

Leonda F. Finke is known for her large outdoor figurative sculpture commissions as well as her work as a medallist. Finke was born in Brooklyn, New York, and studied at the Art Students League, the Education Alliance, and the Brooklyn Museum Art School—all in New York City.

Finke has held solo exhibitions of her work in many galleries, including the Cast Iron Gallery (1991), and the Sculpture Center Gallery—both in New York City (1986); the Harbor Gallery, Cold Spring Harbor, New York (1972, 1975, 1980); and others. Her work has been invited to numerous group exhibitions in the United States and abroad, such as the F.I.D.E.M., the British Museum, London, England (1992) and Helsinki, Finland (1990), where she showed medals; the Newark Museum, New Jersey (1991); and the Cast Iron Gallery, and the Sculptors Guild—both in New York City (1990, 1991). Finke also showed with the National Association of Women Artists in Israel (1981); with a U.S. Information Agency (USIA) exhibition which travelled to the Soviet Union and Eastern Europe (1976); and many others.

Finke is the winner of more than thirty prizes, honors, and awards; she is active in many professional art organizations; has been commissioned to create medals, reliefs, and larger-than-life outdoor sculptures; and has been a lecturer and teacher at colleges and universities since 1969. Her work is represented in private and public permanent collections in the United States and abroad, including Brookgreen Gardens, Murrells Inlet, South Carolina; the British Museum, London, England; National Portrait Gallery, and the National Museum of American History—both in the Smithsonian Institution, Washington, D.C.; Chrysler Museum, Norfolk, Virginia; Museum of Foreign Art, Sofia, Bulgaria; the collection of Senator and Mrs. Eugene McGovern; and others.

Bibliography
Contemporary Sculpture at Chesterwood. A Catalog. Artist's Statement. Stockbridge, Massachusetts. 1989.
Watson-Jones, Virginia. *Contemporary American Women Sculptors.* Oryx Press, 1986.
Who's Who in American Art. 19th ed. R.R. Bowker Co., 1991–1992.

Finley, Karen (1956–)

Born and raised in Chicago, Illinois, Karen Finley, after making art for more than a decade in 1990, suddenly achieved national notoriety by being denied a grant for which she had previously been recommended by the National Endowment for the Arts (NEA). Although Finley, and the other three performance artists who were "de-funded" at the same time (John Fleck, Holly Hughes, and Tim Miller) had all received earlier NEA grants, the political climate of the time led the NEA to withdraw its support from these artists, based on the premise that their work—which often dealt with homosexuality, nudity, four-letter words, and other unconventional subjects—was too controversial to warrant federal funding. As a result of its actions the NEA was accused of censorship and became the focus of numerous protests, legal actions, and other pressures.

An unintentional catalyst for all this furor, Finley, who was initially a painter, received her Master of Fine Arts degree from the San Francisco Art Institute, California, in 1982. After two years back in her native city Finley moved to the New York City area; she currently makes her home in Rockland County, north of Manhattan. In addition to painting Finley has worked in several creative fields—writing and directing plays, authoring a book (*Shock Treatment*, published in 1990), and experimenting with billboards, videos, and other media. However, she is known primarily for her performance art—a broad term encompassing the work of such diverse individuals as Laurie Anderson, Spaulding Gray, and Pat Oleszko. In Finley's case, her "signature" performance pieces, such as "Deathcakes and Autism" (1979), "The Constant State of Desire" (1986), and "The Summer of Hate" (1987), typically featured the artist, alone onstage at one of the nightclubs—the Palladium, the Cat Club, Danceteria—"alternative art spaces" (P.S.122, the Kitchen—frequented by the members of New York's avant-garde scene. Finley would recite texts she had written, often savagely attacking the U.S. government for its failure to move faster to help AIDS patients or victims of sexual abuse, or American society as a whole, for its homophobia, racial intolerance, and dysfunctional families. These dramatic monologues were punctuated with surprising changes in costume and odd props. Often Finley used her body as the centerpiece of the action, slathering herself with yellow paint, covering her torso with glitter and confetti and—in her most-quoted gesture—smearing her nude skin with chocolate. Finley's deliberately shocking, obscene language, and confrontational presentations of her body were intended, not to titillate, but rather to call attention to what she regards as the most important political issues of the day.

In the period immediately following the NEA brouhaha, Finley—who had received the bulk of mass-media coverage—was clearly distressed, and unable to create new art. She lamented that she wanted to be known for her work, not for being "the blacklisted artist." Finley also noted her fear that the institutions that had supported her in the past might be unwilling to risk the loss of their own funding, by book-ing her—a fear that proved to be well-founded in several cases. However, in the past few years Finley has returned to the stage, touring the United States with new performance pieces. She has also published her book and created a series of installations for more conventional art galleries and museum spaces. For example, "Memento Mori," a three-room installation at Los Angeles' Museum of Contemporary Art, California (1992), combined painted portraits with wall-texts and volunteer "performers" who interacted with each other, museumgoers, and a series of set-pieces and props, most notably beds. One of her most moving, and simplest installations—"Written in the Sand," the Amy Lipton Gallery, New York City (1992)—consisted of lighted votive candles and a layer of sand covering the gallery floor; a short wall-text requested visitors to trace the names of friends who have died of AIDS, and then cover the names over again with sand.

Bibliography

Hart, Linda. "Karen Finley's Dirty Work: Censorship, Homophobia, and the NEA." *Genders* 14 (Fall 1992). University of Texas Press.

Nadotti, Maria. "Karen Finley's Poisoned Meatloaf." *Artforum* 27:7 (March 1989): 113–16.

Span, Paula, and Carla Hall. "Rejected! Portraits of the Performers the NEA Refused to Fund." *The Washington Post* (July 8, 1990), G1ff.

Finnegan, Sharyn Marie (1946–)

A native New Yorker, the painter Sharyn Marie Finnegan studied at several venues, including the Art Students League, New York City; Accademia di Belli Arti, Rome, Italy; Marymount College, Tarrytown, New York, where she earned a Bachelor of Fine Arts degree; and New York University, New York City, where she studied with Esteban Vicente and received a Master of Arts degree.

Finnegan's paintings have been exhibited in galleries and museums, solo and group shows, including "Artists' Choice: Figurative Art in New York," Bowery Gallery, New York City (1976); Roswell Museum and Fine Arts Center, New Mexico (1977); Prince Street Gallery (1974, 1975, 1977, 1980, 1986, 1989), "Painted Light," Queens Museum (1983), and "Interiors," One Penn Plaza—all in New York City (1986); and others.

Finnegan has taught art and the history of art; has been artist-in-residence at the Roswell Museum, New Mexico (1976), the Palisades Summer, New Jersey (1979), and held a residency at the MacDowell Colony, Peterborough, New Hampshire (1979). Her work is represented in private and public permanent collections.

Bibliography

Dreiss, J. "Review." *Arts Magazine* (April 1981).

Lubel, Ellen. *Views by Women Artists*. New York Women's Caucus for Art, 1982.

Mellow, J. "Review." *The New York Times* (January 1974).

Firestone, Susan Paul (1946–)

Born in Madison, Wisconsin, the sculptor/printmaker Susan Paul Firestone earned a Bachelor's degree from Mary Baldwin College, Staunton, Virginia. Firestone grew up in Charleston, South Carolina. She studied at the Pennsylvania Academy of Fine Arts, Philadelphia; the Corcoran School of Art, Washington, D.C.; Skowhegan School of Painting and Sculpture, Maine; and received a Master of Fine Arts degree from American University, Washington, D.C.

Firestone's most recent solo exhibitions include a Studio Invitational, New York City (1988); the "Rites of Passage," at Gallery K (1991), other solo exhibitions at Gallery K (1983, 1988), Covington and Burling (1985), Jack Rasmussen Gallery (1982), and the Corcoran School of Art (1981)—all in Washington, D.C.; and others. Her work has been invited to many group exhibitions in the United States and abroad: from Washington, D.C., to Cortina, Italy; from Tempe, Arizona, to New York City; from Havana, Cuba to Nigeria, Iceland, Nepal, and Canada.

Winner of honors and awards, Firestone was the recipient of residencies at Pyramid Atlantic (1992); and the University of Georgia Abroad, Cortina, Italy (1989). Her prints, paintings, and sculpture are represented in private, public, and corporate permanent collections, including the Corcoran Gallery of Art, National Museum of Women in the Arts; the Washington Post, Riggs National Bank of Washington, Peat Marwick Company, and the National Museum of American Art—all in Washington, D.C.; and others.

Bibliography

"Hope/Even." *New Art Examiner*. Vol. 16 (November 1988): 6.

"Dare 2?" *Artforum*. Vol 26 (January 1988): 18.

"Stay in Line." *New Art Examiner*. Vol. 13 (January 1986): 9A.

Fisch, Arline M. (1931–)

Born in Brooklyn, New York, Arline M. Fisch earned her Bachelor's degree at Skidmore College, Saratoga Springs, New York (1952) and a Master's degree in art at the University of Illinois, Urbana, two years later. She attended the Kunsthaandvaerkerskole (School of Arts and Crafts) Copenhagen, Denmark (1956–1957), and also pursued further study in jewelry fabrication at the Bernhard Hertz Guldvaerefabrik (1957). Fisch studied weaving at the Haystack Mountain School of Crafts, Liberty, Maine (1959); metalsmithing at the School for American Craftsmen, Rochester, New York (1964); and returned to Copenhagen to learn chasing and engraving at the Apprentice School for Gold and Silversmiths (1966–1967).

In almost four decades of exhibitions of her work throughout the world, Fisch has had twenty-nine solo exhibitions, a number of duo shows, and no less than 290 group exhibitions between 1955 and 1991. Her work has been shown in a U.S. Information Agency (USIA) travelling exhibition to Latin America (1964); a solo show at the Museum of Contemporary Crafts, New York City (1968); and "Form and Quality," the International Handicrafts and Trade Fair, Munich, Germany (1966, 1968–1975). She has exhibited in Zurich, Switzerland; Toronto, Canada; Celje, Yugoslavia; Adelaide, Australia; London, England; Sheboygan, Wisconsin; Pforzheim, Germany; Tokyo, Japan; Vienna, Austria; Anchorage, Alaska; Honolulu, Hawaii; Seoul, Korea; and many other venues.

Fisch has received honors and awards, including Fulbright Foundation fellowships to Denmark (1956–1957; 1966–1967); Austria (1981–1982); and Uruguay (1989); Danforth grants for study and creative work in weaving (1959, 1960); National Endowment for the Arts (NEA) grants (1974–1975, 1976–1979, 1981); and awards from San Diego State University, California, including a research grant, and meritorious performance awards (1970, 1984, 1986, 1990). She was declared a "Living Treasure of California" by the California State Assembly (1985); and others.

Goldsmith, weaver, metalsmith, jeweler, all-around craftsperson—Fisch has taught on the faculties of many colleges and universities, including the University of Illinois, Urbana (1952–1954); Wheaton College, Norton, Massachusetts (1954–1956); Skidmore College, Saratoga Springs, New York (1957–1961); and San Diego State University, California (1961 to the present). She has served as visiting artist to many art schools, such as the Haystack Mountain School of Crafts, Liberty, Maine; Penland School of Crafts, North Carolina; School of Arts and Crafts, Copenhagen, Denmark; and has been visiting professor at Boston University, Massachusetts; Bezalel Academy of Art, Jerusalem, Israel; and the Academy of Applied Art, Vienna, Austria.

Fisch has given workshops and seminars in textiles and in "textile techniques in metal," lectures on contemporary American jewelry and metalsmithing, and large-scale jewelry literally all over the world. She has held prominent positions in the Society of North American Goldsmiths, the World Crafts Council, the American Crafts Council, the U.S. National Commission for UNESCO, and others. Her work is housed in many corporate, private and public permanent collections, including the Renwick Gallery, Smithsonian Institution, Washington, D.C.; Detroit Institute of the Arts, Michigan; Victoria & Albert Museum, London, England; Vatican Museum, Rome, Italy; Worshipful Company of Goldsmiths, London, England; and many others.

Bibliography
Bell, Jeanine Keefer. "The Art of Wearable Magic." *Metalsmith* (Summer 1988).
Ramshaw, Wendy. "Ornamenting the Body." *American Crafts* (April–May 1986).
Tudor, Robyn. "The Aesthetics of Ornamentation." *Craft Arts* 4 (October–December 1986).
Who's Who in American Art. 19th ed. R.R. Bowker Co., 1991–1992.

Fish, Janet (1938–)

Janet Fish, a painter in oil, pastel, and watercolor, was born in Boston, Massachusetts. She studied sculpture and printmaking with Leonard Baskin at Smith College, Northampton, Massachusetts, graduating in 1960. She studied painting at the Yale University School of Art, New Haven, Connecticut, obtaining a Bachelor of Fine Arts degree and in 1963 a Master of Fine Arts degree. During the summer of 1961 she attended the Skowhegan Art School and in her early work did Maine landscapes. She also painted people sitting in a room, but because models were hard to get and her recruits did not want to sit for such a long period, she turned to painting vegetables. Her breakthrough occurred when she started painting fruits in cellophane packages—such as "Green Apples" (1970, Colby College Museum of Art)—and then moved to table compositions of reflective, transparent glassware. Many of the paintings were simply of glasses half-filled with water—such as "Glass Garden" (1974)—and others were of brand-name bottles, for example, Heinz vinegar as in "Eight Vinegar Bottles" (1972–1973, Dallas Museum of Art), "Smirnoff's Vodka and Don Q Rum" (1973), and Tanqueray gin as in "Tanqueray Bottles" (1973, private collection). She became famous as a still-life painter with these close-up views of transparent containers. An artist whose skill keeps growing, she next enriched her still lifes with differently-shaped containers—some holding fruit and others flowers—such as "Red Vase, Yellow Tulips" (1980, McMurray and Gihon Foundations, Dallas) and "Black Vase with Daffo-

dils" (1980, private collection, Philadelphia). The scale of the subjects in these is a little smaller in relation to the canvas, and the differently-shaped vases are grouped in a specified locale; the color is more high-keyed and lush. Some are even set against wooded landscapes, such as "Blue Flag and Honeysuckle" (1980) and "Peaches, Black-Eyed Susans and Teacups" (1980). Although she resides in New York—with an extensive collection of glasses—she also paints in Vermont. In the 1980s goldfish or seashells were added to her still life for their intrinsic colors, for example, "Raspberries and Goldfish" (1981, Metropolitan Museum of Art) and a variety of butterflies in "Butterfly Collection" (1984, Robert Miller Gallery). In 1985 Fish said in an interview, "For the last five years I've been doing still-lifes—breakfast kitchen scenes, or just objects on a table. Since I work from life, the still-life is the actual sketch. In one piece, "Eggs and Cereal," I arranged breakfast things on a table—flowers, orange juice, a morning newspaper and shirred eggs in ceramic containers. . . . I started with some wallpaper. The paper was 'springy,' so I wanted the scene to evoke a sunny morning."

She has also occasionally reintroduced the human figure into her paintings, such as "Barry" (1982), in which a man sits before a typewriter; "Ruth Sewing" (1983) with patterned material in front of the seated figure; "Toby and Claire Reading" (1984), of children lying on the grass; "Howard and Athena" (1985), in which a man is juxtaposed with the head of Athena; and "Kite" (1986), which includes a running dog.

Although her paintings are realistic, they are poetic with their layers of transparency, and she focuses attention on shapes, patterns, and refracted light. Her first solo exhibition was at Fairleigh Dickinson University, Rutherford, New Jersey, in 1967. This was followed by early exhibitions at the Kornblee Gallery (1971–1976) and at the Robert Miller Gallery—both in New York City. Among the group shows in which her paintings have been included are "Seven Realists," Yale University Art Gallery, New Haven, Connecticut (1974); "Super Realism," Baltimore Museum, Maryland (1975); "America 1976—A Bicentennial Exhibition," which travelled across the country from the Brooklyn Museum, New York, to the San Francisco Museum of Modern Art, California; and "8 Contemporary American Realists," Pennsylvania Academy of Fine Arts, Pennsylvania (1977). She has several times been a recipient of a MacDowell Colony fellowship, Peterborough, New Hampshire, and won the Harris award at the Art Institute of Chicago Biennale of 1974, Illinois.

Eleanor Tufts

Bibliography
Gardner, Paul. "When Is a Painting Finished?" *Art News* 84, 9 (November 1985): 91–92.
Henry, Gerrit. *Janet Fish.* Burton & Skira, 1987.
Janet Fish. Robert Miller Gallery, New York, 1985.
Nemser, Cindy. "Conversation with Janet Fish." *Feminist Art Journal* 5:3 (Fall 1976): 4–10.

Fisher, Elaine (1939–)

Born in Newark, New Jersey, the photographer Elaine Fisher earned a Bachelor of Fine Arts degree from Carnegie-Mellon University, Pittsburgh, Pennsylvania (1961), and took further study in photography with Minor White (1966, 1968, 1973).

Fisher has taught at schools and universities, including the School of Fashion Design, Boston, Massachusetts and, currently, Southeastern Massachusetts University, North Dartmouth, and has presented workshops in several states during the 1970s.

Winner of awards and honors, Fisher received a fellowship in photography from the National Endowment for the Arts (NEA) (1972); won first prize the same year at "Photovision '72 of New England Photographers"; and others. Her expressive, autobiographical photographs are in private and public permanent collections, including the Chrysler Museum, Norfolk, Virginia; and others.

Bibliography
Alinder, J., ed. *Self-Portrayal*. 1979.
Cohen, Joyce T., ed. *Insights—Self-Portraits by Women*. 1978.
White, Minor, ed., *Light*. 1968.

Flack, Audrey (1931–)

The photo-realist painter Audrey Flack was born in New York. After graduating from Cooper Union, New York City, in 1951, she obtained a Bachelor of Fine Arts degree the next year from Yale University, New Haven, Connecticut, where she studied with Josef Albers. From 1960 to 1968 she taught at Pratt Institute in Brooklyn and at New York University, and from 1970 to 1974 at the School of Visual Arts—all in New York City. She was the Albert Dorne professor at the University of Bridgeport, Connecticut, in 1975 and received an honorary Doctorate degree from Cooper Union, New York City, in 1977.

Her first solo exhibition was at the Roko Gallery in 1959, and her periodic one-woman exhibitions at the Louis K. Meisel Gallery—both in New York City—began in 1974. Among the earliest group shows in which she participated were "Twenty-Two Realists" (1970) and the "Annual Exhibition of Contemporary American Paintings" (1972)—both at the Whitney Museum of American Art, New York City. She was also included in "New Photo-Realism" at the Wadsworth Atheneum, Hartford, Connecticut (1974); "Super Realism" at the Baltimore Museum of Art, Maryland (1975); "American Painting of the Seventies" at the Albright-Knox Art Gallery, Buffalo, New York (1979); "Contemporary American Realism" at the Pennsylvania Academy of Fine Arts, Philadelphia (1981); and "Real, Really Real, Super Real" at the San Antonio Museum, Texas (1981).

Flack began to use photographs in the 1960s. One of her most effective uses of photographic journalism resulted in her painting entitled the "Kennedy Motorcade, November 22, 1963" (1964, private collection). She further saw the potentialities of photographs when Oriole Farb commissioned her to do a family portrait and provided a 35-mm. slide of the Farb family. The projection of the slide on a large canvas eliminated the need for individual sittings and preliminary drawings; the completed painting, "The Farb Family" (1969–1970), is at the Rose Art Museum at Brandeis University, Waltham, Massachusetts. Flack went on to paint an especially impressive image of the "Macarena Madonna" sculpted by Louisa Roldán in the eighteenth century. With her camera in hand she found the church in Seville, Spain, that houses this famous object of worship which is paraded through the city during Holy Week. Not only did Flack then paint her "Macarena Esperanza" (1971, private collection, Virginia) but did her own "Self-Portrait" (1974, private collection, Basel, Switzerland) emulating the same kind of pearly, unblemished skin that the Spanish sculpture possessed.

Whereas other photo-realists often chose the mundane—such as store fronts and street scenes—as their subjects, Flack wanted more enduring monuments; she painted Michelangelo's "David" and "Siena Cathedral" in 1971. Also in the 1970s she concentrated heavily on painting still lifes, first a series composed of playing cards. Closely-viewed money and cards are the subjects of "Royal Flush" (1973, private collection, Paris) of which she has said, "my family gambled." In "Solitaire" (1974, private collection, Harrison, New York) we see the right hand of her mother, a woman who suffered from insomnia, holding the king of hearts while her cigarette rests in an ashtray and the clock indicates 2:50 a.m. The "Gray Border Series" of still lifes, exhibited in 1976, contain sumptuous displays of tempting desserts, fruits, and jewels. In 1976 Flack saw Maria van Oosterwyck's "Vanitas" of 1668 and found in this type of painting a way to express her anguish over the "Holocaust: World War II (Vanitas)" (1976–1977), composed of sweet pastries and pearls superimposed on Margaret Bourke-White's photograph "Buchenwald 1945."

Flack in her work has sought the "universal." She has studied both Eastern and Western philosophies and in some of her paintings of the 1980s arrived at the image of the woman goddess. Her exploration may have begun with her large "Marilyn Monroe" painting of 1977 (ninety-six-by-ninety-six-inch, University of Arizona Museum of Art, Tucson) and culminated in the monumental paintings of "Hannah" (1982) and "Isis" (1983). Now she is searching for the universal significance three-dimensionally in sculpture which she has titled: "Islandia, Goddess of the Healing Waters"; "Rock Hill Goddess," a commission for North Carolina; "The Art Muse"; and "Diana" (all of 1988), gilded, slim figures adorned by headdresses and representing timeless ideas.

Eleanor Tufts

Bibliography
Audrey Flack on Painting. Introduction by Lawrence Alloway. Harry N. Abrams, 1981.
Gouma-Peterson, Thalia. "Icons of Healing Energy: The Recent Work of Audrey Flack." *Arts Magazine* 58:3 (November 1983): Cover, 136–41.
Nemser, Cindy. "Audrey Flack: Photorealist Rebel." *Feminist Art Journal* 4:3 (Fall 1975): 5–11.

Florsheim, Lillian H. (1896–)

Born in New Orleans, Louisiana, the sculptor Lillian H. Florsheim studied painting with Henry Hensche, Provincetown, Massachusetts (1946–1947); Rudolph Weisenborn, Chicago, Illinois (1948–1950); and George Buehr, Chicago (1948–1954). Florsheim studied sculpture at the Institute of Design, Illinois Institute of Technology, Chicago (1951).

She exhibited widely in the United States and abroad, including the Denise René Gallery, Paris, France (1965); Tel Aviv, Israel, the same year; and a major solo show at the Main Street Galleries, Chicago, Illinois (1966); and many others.

Florsheim's work is represented in many private and public permanent collections, including the Isaac Delgado Museum, New Orleans, Louisiana. Her abstract sculptures of plexiglas, such as "Squares on Diagonal with Rods" (1966), reveal a sense of geometric peace, free of chaos, and a deep respect for the qualities of synthetic material.

Bibliography
Krantz, Claire Wolf. "Reviews Chicago: Lillian Florsheim, Fairweather Hardin Gallery." *New Art Examiner* 10:6 (March 1983): 16.
Lillian H. Florsheim. Chicago: Museum of Contemporary Art, 1970.
Watson-Jones, Virginia. *Contemporary American Women Sculptors.* Oryx Press, 1986.

Follett, Jean Frances (1917–)

Born in St. Paul, Minnesota, the painter/sculptor Jean Frances Follett earned an Associate of Arts degree from the University of Minnesota, Minneapolis; attended painting classes at the Minneapolis School of Art; studied at the Hans Hofmann Art School, New York City; and, after World War II, did further study at the School of Fernand Léger, Paris, France (1946–1951). During her last year in Paris Follett also studied with Ossip Zadkine.

Follett has held solo exhibitions at the Hansa Galleries (1950s), Leo Castelli Gallery (1960), SoHo Gallery (1977), Landmark Gallery (1977)—all in New York City; and has had her work included in many prestigious group shows, such as the "Pittsburgh International Exhibition of Painting and Sculpture," Carnegie Institute, Pennsylvania (1958).

A pioneer in utilizing junk and other discards in her sculpture, Follett creates assemblages of painted wood, metal, and other materials to form powerful, yet sensitive three-dimensional structures. Examples of her work are in private and public permanent collections, including the Museum of Modern Art (MoMA) and the Whitney Museum of American Art—both in New York City.

Bibliography
Hess, Thomas B., and Elizabeth C. Baker, eds. *Art and Sexual Politics.* Macmillan, 1973.
Kaprow, Allan. *Assemblage, Environments and Happenings.* Harry N. Abrams, 1966.
Sandler, Irving. *The New York School: The Painters and Sculptors of the Fifties.* Harper & Row, 1978.
Watson-Jones, Virginia. *Contemporary American Women Sculptors.* Oryx Press, 1986.

Forbes, Elizabeth A. (1859–1912)

Born in Ottawa, Ontario, Canada, the painter/printmaker Elizabeth A. Forbes was reared in England and attended the South Kensington School of Art, London, England. In 1877 Forbes enrolled in the Art Students League, New York City, where she studied for several years under William Merritt Chase and others. She also studied with Chase in Europe during the summer of 1884, when he taught in Zandvoort, near Haarlem, Holland.

A number of Forbes's drypoints were exhibited in England at the Royal Academy and the Royal Society of Painter/Etchers (1885)—both in London; however, she is best known for her fishing scenes and landscapes near Newlyn, Cornwall, and her paintings of children.

Poet, editor, illustrator, printmaker, painter, wife, and mother—Forbes was elected an associate member of the Royal Watercolor Society and has exhibited her plein-air work widely. Examples of her output are in private and public permanent collections in England.

Bibliography
Birch, Mrs. Lionel. *Stanhope A. Forbes and Elizabeth Stanhope Forbes.* 1906.
Dunham, Penny. *Biographical Dictionary of Women Artists in Europe and America since 1850.* University of Pennsylvania Press, 1989.

Ford, Lauren (1891–1973)

Although she identified herself primarily as a painter, Lauren Ford was also a writer and illustrator of children's books. Daughter of hotel owner Simeon Ford and Author Julia Ellsworth Ford, she was born in New York City on January 23, 1891, and was raised in New York, Connecticut, and Brittany. Ford was encouraged by her mother toward an artistic career, learning to draw as a young child. She received training at the Art Students League in New York City and studied with George Bridgman and Frank DuMond, as well as at the Académie Colarossi in Paris, France.

Ford's first exhibit of paintings in 1928 at the Ferargil Galleries in New York City commenced a long relationship with the gallery and a series of annual shows. She was also a regular exhibitor at the Carnegie International Exhibitions in Pittsburgh, Pennsylvania, through the 1930s; in 1937 her painting, "Country Doctor," took second place in the popular poll for best picture. Ford's "Choir Practice" was acquired by the Corcoran Gallery of Art, Washington, D.C., from its 1935 Biennial of "Contemporary American Oil Paintings." Her works have also been collected by the Metropolitan Museum of Art, New York City, and the Art Institute of Chicago, Illinois.

Ford's paintings and etchings usually contain children and depict Christian themes set in contemporary environments—often that of her Connecticut farm. *Life's* Christmas issues of 1938 and 1944 featured her pictures on the boyhood of Christ and other religious scenes. Ford's children's books include *The Little Book About God* (1934) and *The Ageless Story* (1939).

Peggy J. Hazard

Bibliography
Boswell, Peyton. *Modern American Painting.* Dodd, 1939.
Gambone, Robert L. *Art and Popular Religion in Evangelical America, 1915–1940.* University of Tennessee Press, 1989.
Mahoney, Bertha E., Louise Payson Latimer, and Beulah Folmsbee. *Illustrators of Children's Books, 1944–1945.* Horn Book, 1965.

Forner, Raquel (1902–)

Born in Buenos Aires, Argentina, the painter Raquel Forner studied painting at the National Academy of Fine Arts in her native city, and also studied in Paris, France, with Emile Othon Friesz (1929–1930).

Forner has held solo exhibitions in museums and galleries, including the Pan American Union, Washington, D.C. (1957); Roland de Aenlle Gallery, New York City (1958); and others. Her work has been included in many group shows, such as the "Pittsburgh Internationals" at the Carnegie Institute, Pennsylvania (1935, 1958, 1964, 1967); National Gallery of Art, Washington, D.C. (1958); "South American Art Today," Dallas Museum of Fine Arts, Texas (1959); Duke University, Durham, North Carolina (1963); "Art of Latin America since Independence," University of Texas at Austin; and Yale University, New Haven, Connecticut (1966); and others.

Forner was one of the founders of the Curso Libre de Arte

Plástico—the first private art school in Argentina devoted to modern art. Her spirited abstractions are in private and public permanent collections, including the Bronx Museum of the Arts, and the Museum of Modern Art (MoMA)—both in New York City; Dallas Museum of Fine Arts, Texas; Museum of Modern Art of Latin America, Washington, D.C.; the Walker Art Center, Minneapolis, Minnesota; and others.

Bibliography

Iturburu, Cordoba. *La Pintura Argentina del Siglo XX*. Buenos Aires: Editorial Atlantida, 1958.

Kirstein, Lincoln. *The Latin American Collection of the Museum of Modern Art*. Museum of Modern Art, 1943.

The Latin American Spirit: Art and Artists in the United States 1920–1970. Harry N. Abrams, 1988.

Forrester, Patricia Tobacco (1940–)

Born in Northampton, Massachusetts, Patricia Tobacco Forrester won a scholarship to Smith College, Northampton, Massachusetts, where she received her Bachelor's degree, *Phi Beta Kappa* in 1962. Forrester earned her Bachelor of Fine Arts and Master of Fine Arts degrees from Yale University, New Haven, Connecticut, in 1963 and 1965, respectively. She worked under the aegis of Leonard Baskin at Smith College, and studied with realist painters Alex Katz, Philip Pearlstein, and Neil Welliver at Yale University.

Printmaker and watercolorist, Forrester won a Guggenheim Foundation fellowship in printmaking (1967) and has held residencies at the Yaddo Foundation, Saratoga Springs, New York (1979, 1981); the MacDowell Colony, Peterborough, New Hampshire; and the Hand Hollow fellowship (1980, 1981).

She has taught or has been a guest artist at several colleges and universities, including Chabot Junior College, Hayward (1971) and the California College of Arts and Crafts, Oakland (1972–1981)—both in California; Kent State University, Ohio (1981); University of Iowa, Iowa City (1981); the Art Institute of Chicago, Illinois (1982); and the New Orleans Academy of Fine Art, Louisiana (1984).

Forrester, a world-traveller, explores new gardens and parks, grist for her large-scale watercolors, which she paints directly from nature—some, such as the diptych, "Purple Eclipse," 1988, as wide as ten feet. Irises abound everywhere in this dense yet freely-painted watercolor of flowers and tree limbs.

Forrester has had thirty-six solo exhibitions of her work in galleries from New York to Hawaii from 1968 to 1991. Her work was invited to more than fifty major group exhibitions throughout the United States, and is in permanent public, corporate, and private collections such as the Achenbach Foundation, San Francisco, California; the Art Institute of Chicago, Illinois; the British Museum, London, England; the Brooklyn Museum, New York; the Library of Congress, and the National Collection of Fine Arts—both in Washington, D.C.; and Citibank, New York City.

Bibliography

Geracimos, Ann. "Patricia Tobacco Forrester." *American Artist* (November 1983): 62–65.

Richard, Paul. "Holding a Mirror to Nature." *The Washington Post* (December 1981).

Wolff, Theodore F. "Landscapes Live Again." *World Monitor* (December 1988): 82–85.

Forsyth, Constance (1903–1987)

The daughter of William Forsyth, a prominent Native American artist, Forsyth was born in Indianapolis, Indiana, where, after receiving her undergraduate degree at Butler University, she studied painting and etching at the John Herron School of Art. Her work in lithography began in 1932 at the Broadmoor Art Academy in Colorado Springs, Colorado, where she studied with Boardman Robinson and Ward Lockwood. Subsequently, after Lockwood became head of the art department at the University of Texas, Austin, he invited Forsyth to join the University of Texas faculty in 1940. In 1941–1942, when the painter-printmaker B.J.O. Nordfeldt came to Austin, Texas as visiting professor, he became a close friend of Forsyth and an influence upon her work.

Forsyth's knowledge of lithography was greatly advanced through study in 1945 with the master printer George C. Miller at his studio in Vermont, with the result that in her later lithographs she used the medium with new force and assurance. Among her best works are expressionist landscapes (lithographs and aquatints) inspired by her excursions into the hill country west of Austin.

Throughout her more than forty years as a member of the faculty of the University of Texas, Austin, Forsyth was an influential teacher and a leader among the printmakers of Texas. Her work received recognition in national exhibitions and entered many museum collections; in 1985 she was the recipient of the Printmakers Emeritus Award from the Southern Graphics Council. Two years later she died in Austin at the age of eighty-three.

Clinton Adams

Bibliography

Adams, Clinton. *American Lithographers, 1900–1960: The Artists and Their Printers*. University of New Mexico Press, 1983.

Farmer, David. "Constance Forsyth: Printmaker." *Tamarind Papers* 12 (1989): 46–54.

Forsyth, Mina (1920–1987)

A painter known for her landscapes, figure compositions, portraits, and large-scale flower paintings, Mina Forsyth was born in Estevan, Saskatchewan, Canada. Since the late 1970s many of Forsyth's portraits and figurative paintings were concerned with representing the people she had known during her childhood in the small prairie community of Carnduff, Saskatchewan, in the 1920s and 1930s.

After working for a bank and then for the British government in Washington, D.C., and New York City, Forsyth began to paint full-time in the late 1940s. She received her Bachelor of Fine Arts degree from the University of Manitoba, Winnipeg, in 1955 and her Master of Fine Arts degree from Michigan State University, East Lansing in 1957, where she studied with Abraham Rattner. She attended Emma Lake Artists' Workshops under Jack Shadbolt in 1955, Jules Olitski in 1964, Lawrence Alloway in 1965, Harold Cohen in 1966, and Frank Stella in 1967. She did one year of post-graduate study in education at the University of British Columbia, 1958–1959. Since the 1960s her work has been included in group exhibitions across Canada and in a number of solo exhibits in Saskatchewan; Forsyth's paintings are represented in the collections of the Saskatchewan Arts Board and the Mendel Art Gallery, among others.

In addition to producing and exhibiting her work Forsyth played a significant role in the development of art education in Saskatchewan. From 1964 to 1966 she taught in the College of Education, University of Regina; and from 1966 to 1985 she was on the faculty of the Department of Art and Art History, University of Saskatchewan.

Lynne S. Bell

Bibliography
Arnold, Grant. *Mina Forsyth: Flowers and Heads.* Mendel Art Gallery, 1985.
Heath, Terrence. "Three Prairie Pieces." *Artscanada* 30 (February–March 1973): 74–78.

Fosdick, Marion Lawrence (1888–1973)

Born in Fitchburg, Massachusetts, the ceramist Marion Lawrence Fosdick learned her craft from institutions and individuals, including the Boston Museum of Fine Arts, Massachusetts; she took further study in Berlin, Germany; and did additional work with G. Demetrios, Hans Hofmann, E. Thurn, and C.H. Walker.

Fosdick exhibited in museums and galleries, such as "Contemporary American Ceramics," the Syracuse Museum of Fine Arts, New York (1932–1933, 1937); the Boston Society of American Ceramists (1939), Massachusetts; and many others. Winner of awards and honors for her ware, Fosdick was also a teacher of ceramics at the New York State College of Ceramics (now the Alfred University College of Ceramics). Examples of her work are in private and public permanent collections.

Bibliography
Garth, Clark. *A Century of Ceramics in the United States 1878–1978.* E.P. Dutton, 1979.
Fosdick, Marion L. "Modeled Treatment of Pottery." *American Ceramic Society Journal* 9 (1926).

Foss, Harriet Campbell (1860–1938)

A painter of genre, still life, and portraits, Harriet Campbell Foss was born in Middletown, Connecticut, where her father, a Methodist minister, taught at Wesleyan University. After graduation from Wilbraham Academy, Massachusetts, Foss attended Smith College, Northampton, Massachusetts (1883–1884) but then decided to pursue her artistic interests by enrolling at the Woman's School of Design at Cooper Union, New York City. She also studied painting in New York City with J. Alden Weir and in Paris, France, in the late 1880s with Alfred Stevens. She stayed in Paris, France, for five years, studying with William Bouguereau at the Académie Julian and with Gustave Courtois at the Académie Colarossi.

In 1887 Foss began exhibiting at the Paris Salon and continued to exhibit in both Paris, France, and New York City in the 1890s. She signed her paintings "H. Campbell Foss" in order to escape any possible prejudice against women artists. An especially handsome example from this period is "The Flower Maker" (1892, private collection, New York), which was accepted in the Paris Salon of 1892, France, the World's Columbian Exposition in Chicago, Illinois (1893), and in an exhibition at the Royal Academy, London, England, in 1899. A woman, making flowers in imitation of real ones, is shown in a dark interior,

working by the light of a window and warmed by a fireplace. Through the window shoppers are depicted—some are seen through the clear glass and others through a transparent curtain.

From 1892 to 1895 Foss taught painting at the Women's College of Baltimore, Maryland (now Goucher College). Starting in 1905 Foss maintained a studio in New York City and a home in Stamford, Connecticut. In 1909 she moved to Darien, Connecticut, where she was active with the Seven Art League and continued painting a wide range of subject matter.

Eleanor Tufts

Bibliography
Tufts, Eleanor. *American Women Artists, 1830–1930.* National Museum of Women in the Arts, 1987.

Foster, Velma A. (1938–)

Born in Maidstone, Saskatchewan, Canada, the painter/printmaker Velma A. Foster studied with Illingworth Kerr, Stan Perrot, Ron Spickett, and Ken Sturdy at the Alberta College of Art, Calgary (1957–1962); with the British artist, Harold Cohen, at the Emma Lake Summer School Workshop, Saskatchewan (1966); and with the Japanese printmaker Toshi Yoshida (1968), and the American printmaker Andrew Stasik (1969), at workshops offered by the University of Calgary. Foster also studied intaglio printmaking at Pratt Institute, New York City (1969–1970).

Foster has held a number of solo exhibitions of paintings and prints in museums and galleries in Alberta in the mid-1970s, and her work has been included in many prestigious group shows in Canada and abroad, including the "4th International Miniature Print Show," Pratt Institute, New York City (1971); "4th International Print Show," Krakow, Poland (1972); "Calgary Printmakers," Edmonton Art Gallery, Alberta (1974); Hokkaido Museum of Modern Art, Sapporo, Japan (1983); "Multiples: Contemporary Prints from the Glenbow Collection," Glenbow Museum, Calgary (1987); and others.

Foster has won honors and grants from the Canada Council (1970, 1974). Examples of her work are in private and public permanent collections, including the Alberta College of Art and the Glenbow Museum, Calgary; Canada Council Art Bank, Ottawa; University of North Carolina, Chapel Hill; Edmonton Art Gallery, Alberta; and others.

Bibliography
Cochran, Bente Roed. *Printmaking in Alberta 1945–1985.* University of Alberta Press, 1989.
Greenberg, Clement. "View of Art on the Prairies." *Canadian Art* 20:2 (March–April 1963).

Frackelton, Susan S.G. (1848–1932)

Author of *Trial by Fire* (1885), the most popular handbook for decorators of chinaware, Susan Stuart Goodrich Frackelton founded the Frackelton China and Decorating Works in Milwaukee, Wisconsin, in 1883. Her weekly factory production was enormous. Frackelton also founded the National League of Mineral Painters (1892) and patented Frackelton's Dry Colors (1894); key members of the league were the ceramists Mary Chase Perry and Adelaide Robineau.

Frackelton showed her salt-glazed ware at the World's Columbian

Exposition, Chicago, Illinois (1893) and, seven years later, perfected delftwares which were exhibited at the Exposition Universelle in Paris, France. A fine representative cross-section of her work is in the permanent collection of the State Historical Society, Madison, Wisconsin.

Bibliography
Clark, Garth. *American Ceramics: 1896 to the Present.* Abbeville Press, 1987.
Stover, Frances. "Susan Goodrich Frackelton and the China Painters." *Milwaukee County Historical Society* (March 1954).
Weeden, George A. *Susan S. Frackelton and the American Arts and Crafts Movement.* Box Press, 1975.

Frank, Mary (1933–)

Born in London, England, the sculptor Mary Frank studied modern dance for four years with Martha Graham; attended the Children's Professional School in New York City; and, for a short time, was a student of Max Beckmann and Hans Hofmann in New York City.

Frank has been the recipient of many awards and honors, including election to the American Academy and Institute of Arts and Letters, New York City (1984); Guggenheim fellowships (1973, 1983); the Brandeis University Creative Arts award, Waltham, Massachusetts (1977); a Creative Artists Public Service (CAPS) grant (1973); a fellowship from the National Endowment for the Arts (NEA) (1972); Longview Foundation grants (1962–1964); and a grant from the Ingram Merrill Foundation (1961).

Frank has held numerous solo exhibitions in museums and galleries in the United States and abroad between 1958 and 1992, including Galerie Zabriskie, Paris, France (1992); Allene Lapidus Gallery, Santa Fe, New Mexico (1992); Zabriskie Gallery, New York City (fourteen solo shows between 1968 and 1990); the Pennsylvania Academy of Fine Arts, Philadelphia (1989); De Cordova Museum, Lincoln, Massachusetts (1988); Brooklyn Museum, New York (1987); Neuberger Museum, Purchase, New York (1978); Stephen Radich Gallery, New York City (1961, 1963, 1966); and others. Frank's sculpture, drawings, and prints have been invited to myriad group exhibitions from Hamburg, Germany, to Santa Clara, California; Orono, Maine; Houston, Texas; New York City; Portland, Oregon; and many others.

Holder of the Milton Avery chair, Frank was distinguished professor of art at Bard College, Annandale-on-Hudson, New York (1992); taught on the graduate faculty at the Pennsylvania Academy of Fine Arts, Philadelphia (1992–1993); offered workshops and lectures at Smith College, Northampton, Harvard University, Cambridge, and gave the Beckwith lecture at the Boston Museum School of Fine Arts (1992)—all in Massachusetts. She also taught at the New York Academy of Art, New York City; and the Santa Fe Institute of Art, New Mexico (1993).

Her chimerical figures in motion—slabs of clay defining form in space—may reflect her early dance training. Frank's works are in private and public permanent collections, including the Akron Art Institute, Ohio; Art Institute of Chicago, Illinois; Connecticut College, New London, and Yale University, New Haven—both in Connecticut; Hirshhorn Museum and Sculpture Garden, and the Library of Congress—both in Washington, D.C.; Metropolitan Museum of Art, and Whitney Museum of American Art—both in New York City; and others.

Bibliography
Edelman, Robert. "Mary Frank." *Art News* (February 1991).
Herrera, Hayden. *Mary Frank.* Harry N. Abrams, 1990.
Jones, Bill. "Mary Frank." *Arts Magazine* (February 1991).
Matthiessen, Peter, and Mary Frank. *Shadows of Africa.* Harry N. Abrams, 1992.
Ratcliff, Carter. "Mary Frank's Monotypes." *The Print Collector's Newsletter* (November–December 1978).

Frankenthaler, Helen (1928–)

The painter Helen Frankenthaler was born in New York City, and, showing early promise, studied with Rufino Tamayo while still in high school. She received a Bachelor of Arts degree from Bennington College, Vermont, and then returned to New York City, where she studied art history at Columbia University for a short time. Later she studied briefly with Hans Hofmann in Provincetown, Massachusetts. Frankenthaler is considered a second generation abstract expressionist and is also often labelled as a color field painter.

In 1950 Frankenthaler met the art critic Clement Greenberg, who introduced her to the artists of the New York School, including Jackson Pollock, Arshile Gorky, and Willem de Kooning. Trained by a cubist, Paul Feeley, at Bennington College, Vermont, Frankenthaler was painting Picasso-inspired heavy-lined figures and still lifes at this time. Greenberg was unimpressed with "Woman on a Horse" (1950) and encouraged Frankenthaler to open up to the freer forms of abstract expressionism. Works such as "Abstract Landscape" (1951) and "Winston's Tropical Gardens" (1951–1952) earned her a place in the 1951 "Ninth Street Show" set up by the artists of the New York School. That same spring she was given her first solo show at the Tibor de Nagy Gallery, New York City, which included: "August Weather," "Great Meadows," and "Cloudscape."

A major breakthrough in Frankenthaler's paintings came after a visit to the Long Island, New York, home and studio of Jackson Pollock. While she was there she watched Pollock spread his canvas on the floor and literally dance around the composition dripping and spreading paint in a controlled accident. On her return to her own studio she used Pollock's technique as a starting point to develop her own style. Spreading an unprimed, raw canvas on the floor, Frankenthaler diluted oil paint to watercolor thickness and flooded the canvas with pale, luminescent color which created puddles and seeped into the weave of the canvas. No longer was the canvas a support for the composition—it was now an integral part of the whole. Her most famous painting, "Mountains and Sea" (1952), was the result of this experiment and the beginning of a unique technique which Frankenthaler has continued to explore throughout her career.

Frankenthaler was strongly influenced by the older abstract expressionists; she took from them the right to create purely abstract art, the use of large canvases and Pollock's basic technique. However, she developed her own personal style and strongly differs from their basic outlook—Frankenthaler's paintings are about light and color. As opposed to the dark and heavy color of Pollock, de Kooning, and Gorky, Frankenthaler's canvases glow with pools of brilliant color. This same difference gives a more tranquil and less didactic quality to Frankenthaler's canvases, setting them aside from the heavier works of the older abstract expressionists.

Frankenthaler's new canvases were quickly accepted, and she won first prize at the 1959 Paris Biennale with "Jacob's Ladder" (1957). Early retrospectives of her work were held in 1960 at the Jewish Museum of New York and in 1969 at the Whitney Museum of American Art—both in New York City. She has had solo shows at venues throughout the world, including the Metropolitan Museum of Art, the Guggenheim Museum, and André Emmerich Gallery—all in New York City; Knoedler Gallery, London, England; and Galerie Ulysses, Vienna, Austria.

Frankenthaler's paintings have developed over the years so that there are periods within her distinctive style. Early works used thin diluted oil paint which left halos of turpentine around the edges of the painted areas. Early work also relied more on her early influences—Arshile Gorky, Joan Miró, and Vassily Kandinsky—with calligraphic details surrounding the washed areas.

Although Frankenthaler never sets out to paint a specific scene or subject, the works that she creates as controlled accidents often recall some natural formation and are named accordingly. Such works as "Flood" (1967), "Eden" (1957), and "Mount Sinai" (1956), reflected something of the forms for which they are named. The complete abstraction with which Frankenthaler works does not deny the existence of spatial depth and this depth is used in naming works for exhibition. "Caravan" (1967) is a large canvas—seven-feet-by-nine-feet, six inches—in tones of yellow, gold, and brown with a bright blue streak across the bottom. The desert hues of the background and the straightness of the accent suggested a caravan moving through the desert to the artist and now, with the name displayed, clearly shows that to the viewer as well.

In 1958 Frankenthaler was married to Robert Motherwell—one of the first generation abstract expressionists. When their marriage was dissolved in 1971, such titles as "Passage" and "New Paths" showed a new period in the artist's life. In the 1970s Frankenthaler began new paths in other ways as well, by trying a variety of other media. She has done some sculpture in clay and prints with woodcuts and lithography. These new media stretch the artist and make her rethink what she has already done.

Frankenthaler was very influential upon the Washington School of Color Field artists, particularly Kenneth Noland and Morris Louis, who use the stain technique she developed. She can also be classed as a color field artist, except that she continues to use a freedom which is often expressed in the gestural brushstrokes of the abstract expressionists. Frankenthaler also maintains a sense of depth and natural form which color field artists eliminate. In a work such as "Tangerine" (1964), where intense color overwhelms the viewer, Frankenthaler comes closest to being a pure color field artist. She can be seen as a pivotal figure, taking what she needs from one group and influencing the other while remaining unique.

Works by Frankenthaler are in the permanent collections of museums throughout the world, including the Guggenheim Museum, Whitney Museum of American Art, Metropolitan Museum of Art, and Museum of Modern Art (MoMA)—all in New York City; Art Institute of Chicago, Illinois; Cleveland Museum of Art, Ohio; National Gallery of Art, Washington, D.C.; Boston Museum of Fine Arts, Massachusetts; and Carnegie Institute, Pittsburgh, Pennsylvania.

Judith Sealy

Bibliography

Baro, Gene, and Roy Slade. *Helen Frankenthaler: Paintings 1969–74.* Catalog. Corcoran Gallery of Art, 1975.

Carmean, E.A. *Helen Frankenthaler.* Catalog. Harry N. Abrams, 1989.

Goossen, Eugene C. *Helen Frankenthaler.* Catalog. Whitney Museum of American Art, 1969.

Rose, Barbara. *Helen Frankenthaler.* Harry N. Abrams, 1971.

Sandler, Irving. *The New York School: The Painters and Sculptors of the Fifties.* Harper & Row, 1978.

Fraser, Laura Gardin (1889–1966)

Born in Chicago, Illinois, the sculptor Laura Gardin Fraser studied at the Art Students League, New York City (1907–1911) and, two years later, married her instructor, James Earle Fraser.

Known for her fountains and monumental sculptures of animals, Fraser was still better known for her medal designs, including the Morse medal for the American Geographic Society; the Centenary medal for the American Numismatic Society; the George Washington Bicentennial medal; and others.

During World War I, Fraser served as a captain in the Ambulance Service Motor Corps and was a recipient of the Barnett prize at the National Academy of Design, New York City (1916). Winner of many awards and honors for her work, Fraser was elected to membership in the National Academy of Design, the National Institute of Arts and Letters, and the National Sculpture Society—all in New York City.

Examples of her work are in private and public permanent collections, including Brookgreen Gardens, South Carolina; the Corcoran Gallery of Art, Washington, D.C.; the U.S. Military Academy, West Point, New York; and many others.

Bibliography

Adams, Adeline. *The Spirit of American Sculpture.* National Sculpture Society, 1929.

Kohlman, Rena Tucker. "America's Women Sculptors." *International Studio* 76:307 (December 1922): 225–35.

Reuter, Ed. "The Proposed Washington Commemorative: Is the Time Finally Right for Laura Gardin Fraser's Design." *The Numismatist* (May 1981): 1192–94.

Taft, Lorado. *The History of American Sculpture.* Macmillan, 1924.

Fratt, Dorothy (1923–)

Born in Washington, D.C., Dorothy Fratt is the daughter of a photographer-journalist who worked for the *Washington Post*. Fratt won multiple scholarships to Mount Vernon College, the Corcoran School of Art, and the Phillips Memorial Gallery Art School—all in Washington, D.C. She studied painting with Nikolai Cikovsky and Karl Knaths.

Fratt held her first solo exhibition in 1946 at the Washington, D.C., City Library and since then has shown her work in many other solo shows, including the Tucson Art Center (1964), the Phoenix Art Museum (1964), Yares Gallery, Scottsdale (1965, 1966, 1982, 1984, 1987, 1989), and a major retrospective exhibition, "Dorothy Fratt: 1970–1980," Scottsdale Center for the Arts (1980)—all in Arizona; Thomas Babeor Gallery, La Jolla, California (1985); and others. Her work has been invited to many group exhibitions, such as the Corcoran Gallery of Art, Washington, D.C. (1948, 1964); the Roswell Museum of Art, New Mexico (1961); California Palace of the Legion of Honor, San Francisco (1965); "Gottlieb's Contemporaries," Phoenix Art Museum, Arizona (1979); "4 Women," Carson-Sapiro Gallery, Denver, Colorado (1981); Wade Gallery, Los Angeles, California (1989); and others.

Fratt taught at Mount Vernon College, Washington, D.C. (1946–1951) and offered private instruction in painting and color theory after settling in Phoenix, Arizona (1958–1972). Winner of several honors and awards for her work, she won her first prize at the age of fifteen in a student show at the Corcoran School of Art. Despite some of the titles of her huge acrylic paintings which, in themselves, suggest representational works to certain viewers, Fratt uses color as an expressive tool, uniquely, personally, from deep within her being, to create and explore ever-new color phenomena. She is indeed a colorist in the purist sense of the word. Her work is in many private, public, and corporate permanent collections, including the Phoenix Art Museum, Arizona; Tucson Museum of Art, Arizona; Museum of Northern Arizona, Flagstaff; Arizona State University, Tempe; Burlington Northern, Seattle, Washington; IBM; General Electric; and many others.

Bibliography

Cone, Claribel. "Dorothy Fratt at the Scottsdale Center for the Arts." *Artspace* (June 1980): 48–49.

Dorothy Fratt: Paintings 1970–1980. A Catalog. Scottsdale Center for the Arts, 1980.

Holusha, Rosemary. "Dorothy Fratt." *Art Voices South* (September–October 1979): 47.

Freckelton, Sondra (1936–)

Well-known painter and printmaker Sondra Freckelton was born in Dearborn, Michigan, and was educated at the School of the Art Institute of Chicago and the University of Chicago—both in Illinois.

Between 1961 and 1992, Freckelton has held twenty solo exhibitions of her works in galleries throughout the United States. Her work has been represented exclusively by the Tibor de Nagy Gallery (1959–1969), the Brooke Alexander Gallery (1975–1984), Robert Schoelkopf Gallery (1985–1991), and, presently, by the Maxwell Davidson Gallery—all in New York City. Her most recent solo shows were held at Eastern Michigan University, Ypsilanti (1991), and Dennos Museum, Traverse City (1991)—both in Michigan; and the Maxwell Davidson Gallery, New York City (1992).

Freckelton's work has been invited to scores of group and travelling exhibitions in the United States and abroad, such as the "Whitney Annual," Whitney Museum of American Art, New York City (1964); "Colored Sculpture," a travelling show, American Federation of the Arts, New York City (1965); "Sixth British International Print Biennale," Bradford Art Gallery and Museum, England (1979); "American Realism," a travelling show, San Francisco Museum of Modern Art, California (1985–1987); "Prints by Contemporary American Women Artists," a travelling show, Mt. Holyoke College, South Hadley, Massachusetts (1987–1988); "Realist Watercolors," Pennsylvania State University, University Park (1990); and many others.

Initially a sculptor of abstract forms, Freckelton moved to painting realistic, large, rich watercolors of still lifes and working in lithography, screen printing, and *pochoir* (a stencil process). "Openwork" (1986), a not atypical screenprint composed of apples, a glass vase, and a hand-stitched fabric, reveals Freckelton's mastery of her medium.

Freckelton's work is in private, corporate, and public permanent collections, including the Virginia Museum of Fine Arts, Richmond; Springfield Art Museum, Missouri; Amerada Hess Corporation, New York; Owens Corning, Toledo, Ohio; and many others.

Bibliography

Bolt, Thomas. "Reckless, Brave, or Both: New Paintings by Sondra Freckelton." *Arts Magazine* 60:5 (January 1986): 52–53.

Field, Richard S., and Ruth E. Fine. *A Graphic Muse: Prints by Contemporary American Women.* Hudson Hills Press, 1987.

Ward, John L. *American Realist Painting, 1945–1980.* UMI Research Press, 1989.

Freilicher, Jane (1924–)

A native of Brooklyn, New York, Jane Freilicher received her Bachelor's degree from Brooklyn College (1947) and, the following year, won a Master of Arts degree in art education from Teachers College, Columbia University—both in New York City. Earlier, she had studied at the Hans Hofmann School of Fine Arts, both in New York City and Provincetown, Massachusetts.

Freilicher's work, by and large, has been realistic in *her* sense of the term. There must be a beginning, an emotional "reason" for wanting to paint something: a landscape seen from her home in Long Island, New York, giving vent to her feelings, as in "Changing Scene" (1981), a still life or cityscape viewed from her Greenwich Village apartment; but, she proceeds to paint, responding to the whole canvas, using what is out there as a reference, but often inventing or changing the motif, following the dictates of the painting.

She has won many awards and honors, including an American Association of University Women (AAUW) fellowship (1974); a grant from the National Endowment for the Arts (NEA) (1976); a membership in the National Academy of Design (1982), the Saltus gold medal, National Academy of Design (1987), and membership in the American Academy and Institute of Arts and Letters—all in New York City (1989).

Freilicher has been commissioned to create theater sets, book jackets, and illustrations for the works of numbers of her friends, including John Ashbery, Frank O'Hara, Kenneth Koch, James Schuyler, and others.

Her first solo exhibition was at the Tibor de Nagy Gallery, New York City, in 1952, followed by eleven more at the same gallery by 1970. Freilicher has had many solo shows at the Fischbach Gallery, New York City (1977, 1979, 1980, 1983, 1985, 1988, and 1990). She has also held solo exhibitions at Cord Gallery, Southampton, New York (1968); John Bernard Myers Gallery, New York (1971); a major retrospective show at the Currier Gallery of Art, Manchester, New York, that was also seen at the Parrish Art Museum, Southampton, New York; the Contemporary Arts Museum, Houston, Texas; and the Marion Koogler McNay Art Museum, San Antonio, Texas (1986–1987); and others. There have been more than 175 group exhibitions regionally, nationally, and internationally in which one or more of Freilicher works have been exhibited from 1955 to mid-1991.

Freilicher's work hangs in major permanent private, public, and corporate collections throughout the nation, including the American

Federation of the Arts, the Brooklyn Museum, the Metropolitan Museum of Art, and the Museum of Modern Art (MoMA)—all in New York City; the Cleveland Museum of Art, Ohio; Corcoran Gallery of Art, and Hirshhorn Museum and Sculpture Garden—both in Washington, D.C.; Hampton University, Virginia; the San Francisco Museum of Art, California; and many others.

Bibliography
Arthur, John. *Realism/Photo Realism*. Philbrook Art Center, 1980.
Doty, Robert. *Jane Freilicher: Paintings*. Taplinger Publishing Co., Inc., 1986.
Henry, Gerrit. "Jane Freilicher and the Real Thing." *Art News* (January 1985): 78–83.
Kramer, Hilton. "Art: Jane Freilicher Is Back." *The New York Times* (February 7, 1975).
Porter, Fairchild. "Jane Freilicher Paints a Picture." *Art News* 55:5 (September 1956): 46–49, 65–66.
Westfall, Stephen. "Vanishing Acts." *Art in America* (June 1991): 130–35.

Freiman, Lillian (1908–)
The painter Lillian Freiman was born in Guelph, Ontario, Canada, and studied her craft at the École des Beaux-Arts, Montréal, and the Art Students League in New York City. In 1925 she went to Paris, France, for additional study and research with respect to her work. Freiman stayed in Paris until the onset of World War II, when she returned to Toronto and then to New York City.

Mining the theater and recital halls for content Freiman has created sensitive, yet vigorous drawings and watercolors. She has exhibited her highly personal works in galleries and museums in Canada and abroad, including the Bienal de São Paulo, Brazil (1951); "Rehearsal III: Callas with Fausto Cleva," Canadian Watercolors, Drawings, and Prints (1966); and many others. Examples of her works are in private and public permanent collections.

Bibliography
Abell, Walter. "Some Canadian Moderns." *Magazine of Art* 30:7 (July 1937): 422–27.
Buchanan, Donald W. "Painter of Sensitive Vision." *Canadian Art* 7:3 (Spring 1950): 99–104.
Nasby, Judith. *Lillian Freiman: Paintings and Drawings*. A Catalog and Travelling Exhibition. Kingston, Ontario: Queen's University, 1978.

Frenkel, Vera (1938–)
Born in Bratislava, Czechoslovakia, the artist/poet/writer Vera Frenkel emigrated to Canada via London and Leeds—both in England, to escape the havoc of World War II. She earned a Bachelor's degree in fine arts and anthropology from McGill University, Montréal, Canada, where she took studio courses with John Lyman and Guy Viau. Along with her undergraduate work at McGill University, she studied with Arthur Lismer at the Montréal Museum School of Fine Arts. Frenkel finished the course work and research for a McGill postgraduate degree, but decided to travel and paint in Europe. In the early 1960s in London, she worked in a print shop to finance her creative efforts and, on her return to Canada, did further study with Albert Dumouchel at the École des Beaux-Arts, Montréal.

Frenkel has held myriad exhibitions and performances, text installations, slide cycles, tapes (aural and visual), videos, prints, and paintings in galleries and museums in Canada and abroad, including "Sensory Perceptions," a travelling show, Art Gallery of Ontario, Toronto, Canada (1970); "Print and Mirror Assemblages," a solo travelling show organized by the National Gallery of Canada, Ottawa (1971–1972); "Mostra Grafica," Venice Biennale, Italy (1972); "Mystic Circle," Vancouver Art Gallery, British Columbia and "Segunda Bienal Americana de Artes," Cali, Colombia (1973); "String Games: Improvisations of Inter-City Video," Espace 5, Montréal (1974); "The Big Book," The Gallery, Stratford, Ontario (1976); "No Solution—A Suspense Thriller," York University, Toronto (1976); and many others.

A minor clue to one aspect of Frenkel's approach may be found in this sentence: "My absorption with randomness and control . . . makes it possible for me to enter the process and to rediscover its elusiveness and balance." Her works deal with illusion and reality—with truth and lies—in brilliant metaphor. Professor of art at York University, Toronto, Ontario, Frenkel has received many honors, awards, and commissions. Her work is represented in private, public, and corporate permanent collections, including the Art Gallery of Ontario, Toronto; the Canada Council Art Bank; Erindale College of the University of Toronto; Rothman's of Pall Mall, Canada; York University; and many others.

Bibliography
Dault, Gary Michael. *Lies and Truths: An Exhibition of Mixed Format Installlations by Vera Frenkel*. A Catalog. Vancouver Art Gallery, 1978.
Lowndes, Joan. "Vera Frenkel: Printmaking Plus." *Artscanada* 28:6 (December–January 1971–1972): 130–32.
Perrin, Peter. "Mapping Time: Three New Works by Vera Frenkel." *Artscanada* 31:1 (Spring 1974): 36–41.

Frey, Viola (1933–)
Born in Lodi, California, Viola Frey was an integral member of the new figuration movement in ceramics in the San Francisco Bay area in the 1970s. Frey has since built an international reputation with her monumental earthenware polychrome figures. She consistently produces two other types of work—sculptures that meld figurines and vessels, and encrusted plates.

Frey enrolled at the California College of Arts and Crafts, Oakland, in 1953; studied painting with Richard Diebenkorn; and took an elective ceramics class with Vernon Coykendall and Charles Fiske. After receiving her Bachelor of Arts degree, Frey moved to New Orleans, Louisiana, in 1956 to pursue a graduate degree at Tulane University. She studied color theory with Mark Rothko and ceramics with abstract expressionist Katherine Choy. After completing her Master of Fine Arts degree in 1958, Frey moved to Port Chester, New York, to participate with Choy in the Clay Art Center—an early forum to explore ceramics as a fine art medium. Choy's death caused the demise of the Clay Art Center, and in 1960 Frey returned to the San Francisco Bay area. Since 1965 she has taught color and ceramics at the California College of Arts and Crafts, Oakland.

In the 1950s Frey's work consisted primarily of pots in the Japanese and Chinese tradition, but in the 1960s, the figure began appearing in her work, emerging half-formed from a columnar base as in "Hiding Figure" (1968) or painted in bold colors on plates. By the mid-1970s Frey's work had expanded in scale and complexity. Influenced by the funk art sculptures of Robert Arneson and the writings of anthropologist Claude Levi-Strauss, Frey was drawn to everyday objects and mass-produced ceramics. She amassed a large collection of dimestore figurines, whose case and molded forms began appearing in her work. "Journey Teapot" of 1975 to 1976 merges frolicking nudes with a gilded rooster teapot. "Junkman" (1977) and "Junked Vessel" (1978) show a continued interest in the melding of vessel with figurine and are painted with an exaggerated use of color and line to imitate chiaroscuro effects. Frey's work received national attention in the 1979 exhibition, "A Century of Ceramics in the United States," and was the subject of a retrospective in 1981 at the Crocker Art Museum in Sacramento, California.

In the 1970s Frey also began creating life-sized portraits of family and self. Standing figures dominated Frey's production in the 1980s and were featured at her solo exhibition in 1984 at the Whitney Museum of American Art, New York City. "Man in Blue I" of 1983 is characteristic of the iconic nature of these sculptures. Dressed in the corporate uniform of suit and tie, the hunched figure is frozen in mid-gesture. Reaching eleven feet in height, these figures are created in segments and painted with bold washes of color that have been called fauve and expressionistic.

In 1985–1986 Frey began a series of reclining nude figures, still on a monumental scale, that are cartoon versions of the classical nude. She also has returned to platters encrusted with permutations of mass-produced figurines.

Frey's sculptures are included in numerous major collections, including the Metropolitan Museum of Art and the Whitney Museum of American Art—both in New York City; and the Los Angeles County Museum of Art, California; and others.

Heather Sealy Lineberry

Bibliography
Clark, Garth. *Viola Frey Retrospective*. Crocker Art Museum, Sacramento, March 21–April 26, 1981.
———. *American Ceramics, 1876 to the Present*. Abbeville Press, 1987.
Kelley, Jeff. "Viola Frey." *American Ceramics* 3 (1984).
Miedzinski, Charles. "Images of Paradox." *Artweek* 16 (September 21).
Noland, Garry. "Viola Frey." *New Art Examiner* (March 1983).
Simms, Patterson. *Viola Frey*. Whitney Museum of American Art, 1984.

Frick, Joan (1942–)

Born in Toronto, Ontario, Canada, the painter Joan Frick studied her craft at the École des Beaux-Arts, Montréal, Québec.

In addition to a solo exhibition she held at the Fleet Galleries, Winnipeg, Manitoba, Canada (1973), Frick held another in 1975, the result of four years of work. She has had her linear-oriented paintings included in group shows, such as the Beth Tzedec Synagogue, Toronto (1973); and others. Examples of her work are in private and public permanent collections.

Bibliography
Swain, Robert. "Joan Frick: Drawing and Painting." *Artscanada* 32:1 (March 1975): 52–53.

Frishmuth, Harriet Whitney (1880–1979)

Born in Philadelphia, Pennsylvania, the sculptor Harriet Whitney Frishmuth learned her craft from many artists in the United States and abroad, including Injalbert and Auguste Rodin in Paris, France; Cuno von Enschtritz in Berlin, Germany; and Gutzon Borglum and H.A. Macneil at the Art Students League in New York City.

Frishmuth exhibited widely in museums and galleries in the United States and abroad, such as the Paris Salon, France (1903); "Exhibition of American Sculpture," National Sculpture Society (1923), and "Fortieth Annual Exhibition and Forty-Fifth Annual Exhibition," National Association of Women Painters and Sculptors—both in New York City (1931, 1936). She also exhibited work at the Architectural League of New York, and the National Academy of Design—both in New York City; the Pennsylvania Academy of Fine Arts, Philadelphia; San Francisco Fine Arts Museums, California; and others.

Winner of hosts of honors and awards, Frishmuth received honorable mention at the Panama-Pacific International Exposition, San Francisco, California (1915); the Joan of Arc silver medal and other awards from the National Association of Women Painters and Sculptors (1921, 1924), and a gold medal from the Catharine Lorillard Wolfe Art Club, National Academy of Design (1922)—both in New York City; and many others.

Examples of Frishmuth's work are in private and public permanent collections, including the Botanical Gardens, St. Paul, Minnesota; Brookgreen Gardens, South Carolina; the Capitol, Richmond, Virginia; Dallas Museum of Fine Arts, Texas; Hunter Museum of Art, Chattanooga, Tennessee; Los Angeles Museum of Art, California; Metropolitan Museum of Art, New York City; Museum of Fine Arts, Dayton, Ohio; and many others.

Bibliography
Aronson, Charles N. *Sculptured Hyacinths*. A Biography. Charles N. Aronson Publisher, 1973.
"Harriet W. Frishmuth, Sculptor of Women, 99." *The New York Times* (January 4, 1980).
"Philadelphia's Outdoor Sculpture Show." *International Studio* 75:302 (July 1922): 299.

Frissel, Toni (1907–)

A native New Yorker, the photographer Toni Frissel learned her craft from her brother, a documentary filmmaker. Her photographs have appeared in a variety of publications, including *Life*, *Look*, *Sports Illustrated*, and *Vogue*. Prior to her photographic work, Frissel prepared herself for a career as an actress; was employed by a painter; and worked in the advertising field. Her photographs are represented in private and public permanent collections, such as the Library of Congress, Washington, D.C.; the Metropolitan Museum of Art, New York City; and others.

Bibliography
Beaton, Cecil, and Gail Buckland. *The Magic Image*. 1975.
Browne, Turner, and Elaine Partnow. *Macmillan Biographical Encyclopedia of Photographic Artists & Innovators*. Macmillan, 1983.

Fry, Laura Anne (1857–1943)

Born in Indiana, the ceramist Laura Anne Fry was the daughter of William Henry Fry, a well-known woodcarver. She studied sculpture, drawing, china painting, and wood carving at the Cincinnati School of Design, Ohio (1872–1876), and took further instruction in Trenton, New Jersey, before embarking on additional study and travel in France and England. On her return to the United States Fry became a member of the decorating team at the Rookwood Pottery, incising designs on the ware and rubbing cobalt oxide in the intagliates.

Six years after she invented the technique of spraying slips from an atomizer to greenware (1889), Fry received a patent. It is interesting to note that she tried, unsuccessfully, through the years, to keep Rookwood from using her patented technique. However, she lost the suit in the courtroom of Judge William Howard Taft (1898).

She taught briefly at Purdue University, Lafayette, Indiana (1891), went to work for the Lonhuda Pottery, Steubenville, Ohio, and returned to teach at Purdue University until 1922. A leader in the women's art movement in Cincinnati, Ohio, Fry's work is well represented in the St. Louis Art Museum, Missouri, and in other public and private permanent collections.

Bibliography
Clark, Garth. *American Ceramics 1896 to the Present*. Abbeville Press, 1987.
Macht, Carol, and Kenneth Trapp. *The Ladies, God Bless 'Em*. Cincinnati Art Museum, 1976.

Fuller, Lucia Fairchild (1872–1924)

Born in Boston, Massachusetts, Lucia Fairchild Fuller studied painting at the Cowles Art School with Dennis Bunker after attending Mrs. Shaw's private school. She then moved to New York City, where, beginning in 1889, she attended the classes of William Merritt Chase and H. Siddons Mowbray at the Art Students League. She was invited to paint a mural, "The Women of Plymouth," for the Woman's Building at the World's Columbian Exposition of 1893 in Chicago, Illinois.

On October 25, 1893, she married Henry Brown Fuller, a painter whom she had met at the Cowles Art School, and, as she combined her career and family, she turned to portraiture on ivory. In 1897 the Fullers and their two children began to spend summers in the art colony that sprang up around Augustus Saint-Gaudens at Cornish, New Hampshire. They all participated in the dramatic productions; for example, in 1906 Fuller painted the scenery for *The Rose and the Ring*, while Ethel Barrymore coached the performers. In addition to portraits, which Fuller painted of the summer residents, she did one large mural, a colonial scene for which the local citizens posed, that is preserved today in Blowmedown Grange, Plainfield, New Hampshire.

In 1899 Fuller was one of the founding members of the American Society of Miniature Painters, of which she later served as president, and she was among the first women to be elected to the Society of American Artists. She was elected an associate of the National Academy of Design, New York City, in 1906.

In her New York studio Fuller's sitters included "Mrs. J.P. Morgan and the Morgan children," "Mrs. H.P. Whitney and her children," "James J. Higginson," and "Dr. Edwin A. Tucker." Among her prizes were a bronze medal at the International Exposition, Paris, France (1900); a silver medal for "Girl Drying Her Foot" at the Pan-American Exposition in Buffalo, New York, of 1901; and gold medals for "The Chinese Jacket" and "In the Days of King Arthur" at the St. Louis Exposition of 1904, Missouri. Her work can be found today in such major museums as the Metropolitan Museum of Art, and the Museum of the City of New York—both in New York City; the National Museum of American Art, Smithsonian Institution, Washington, D.C.; and the Boston Athenaeum, Massachusetts.

Eleanor Tufts

Bibliography
A Circle of Friends: Art Colonies of Cornish and Dublin. University of New Hampshire Galleries and Thorne-Sagendorph Art Gallery, 1985.
Tufts, Eleanor. *American Women Artists, 1830–1930*. National Museum of Women in the Arts, 1987.

Fuller, Meta Warrick (1877–1968)

The talented African-American sculptor Meta Warrick Fuller was born in Philadelphia, Pennsylvania, and studied at the Pennsylvania Museum School of Industrial Arts in her native city (1894–1898); the following year she won a postgraduate fellowship and went to Paris, France, to study at L'École des Beaux-Arts and the Académie Colarossi. She stayed in Paris three years and benefitted further from studio critiques and the wise counsel and encouragement of Auguste Rodin. "The Head of Medusa," an early work, reflects her fanciful interests at that time. She exhibited work at Bing's l'Art Nouveau Galleries, Paris, that elicited great excitement. "Thief on a Cross" offers a good example of this period.

Fuller returned home to confront racism, sexism, and a lack of opportunity barring her growth and development—until 1907, when she won a gold medal at the Jamestown Exposition—a state fair with more than 550 works, including drawings, paintings, sculpture, and china painting. Much of her early work was destroyed in a fire (1910), to the benefit of the sculpture that followed: form and content became a unified whole. She was married to Dr. Solomon Fuller; gave birth to three sons, and, until they were of a certain age, slowed down her creative efforts. Fuller employed African-American models to pose, and, for the next five decades, despite physical infirmities, produced figurative sculptures, including portraits, such as "Richard B. Harrison as De Lawd," and many others.

Bibliography
Dannett, Sylvia G.L. "Meta Warrick Fuller." *Profiles of Negro Womanhood*. Vol. 2. Educational Heritage, 1966.
Harlem Renaissance: Art of Black America. Introduction by Mary S. Campbell. Studio Museum in Harlem and Harry N. Abrams, 1987.
Kennedy, Harriet Forte. *An Independent Woman: The Life and Art of Meta Warrick Fuller (1877–1968)*. Danforth Museum, 1985.

Fuller, Sue (1914–)

Born and raised in Pittsburgh, Pennsylvania, Sue Fuller was the daughter of a construction engineer, and the second-niece and cousin of two New England female mathematics teachers, which may help to explain, in part, her early string constructions. Fuller entered the Carnegie Institute of Technology in her native city at the age of eighteen and earned her Bachelor's degree four years later. At the end of her sophomore year she spent a summer at the Thurn School of Art and studied with Hans Hofmann, who was visiting artist at the school. In 1944 she also encountered Josef Albers in a two-month-long Bauhaus class.

A postgraduate year at Teachers College, Columbia University, New York City, under Arthur Young (1939) grounded Fuller in printmaking and related studies, and initiated her as a printmaker; she served as an assistant to Stanley William Hayter in his New York Atelier 17 (1943–1945) and won the privilege of doing what studio assistants do—ordering and managing materials and supplies, teaching beginning printmaking, preparing acid baths, and whatever else was required—including printing editions for Marc Chagall, André Masson, and Hayter.

"Hen" (1945), Fuller's best-known soft-ground etching, reflects use of lace in the ground, and what was to become her obsession: threads in two- and three-dimensional constructs. All along Fuller had been making string constructions. Later, in the 1960s, she embedded the strings in plastic, titling them with numbers.

Two grants for printmaking—a Tiffany fellowship (1948), and a Guggenheim fellowship (1949)— plus a grant from the National Institute of Arts and Letters, New York City (1950) were awarded Fuller when her interest in the graphic arts was declining.

Ever concerned about permanence and complete control of her material, Fuller apprenticed in glassmaking in England and Italy (1950); calligraphy in Japan (1953); and lacemaking in 1962. In 1969 Fuller obtained a patent for her embedment system—the outcome of her constructivist growth and development. From the early 1950s she never looked back at printmaking, and her numbered string compositions kept appearing in the collections of major museums and institutions in the United States and abroad. Fuller's first solo show was held at the Bertha Schaefer Gallery in New York City (1949); she showed there for the next several decades as well as at the Guggenheim Museum, the Metropolitan Museum of Art, and the Whitney Museum of American Art, and the Museum of Modern Art (MoMA)—all in New York City; the Tate Gallery, London, England; the National Collection of Fine Arts, Smithsonian Institution, Washington, D.C.; the First Bienale, São Paulo, Brazil; and others.

Fuller has taught at MoMA (1945–1947), New York City; the University of Minnesota (1950); the University of Georgia (1951–1952); Teachers College, Columbia University (1952, 1958), and Pratt Institute (1965–1966)—both in New York City.

Bibliography

Browne, Rosalind. "Sue Fuller." *Art International* 16 (January 1972): 37–40.
Dunford, Penny. *A Biographical Dictionary of Women Artists in Europe and America since 1850.* University of Pennsylvania Press, 1989.
Fuller, Sue, and Maurice Amar. *String Composition.* Video Cassette, 1974.
Watson-Jones, Virginia. *Contemporary American Women Sculptors.* Oryx Press, 1986.

Funk, Charlotte (1934–)

Known as an award-winning fiber artist, Charlotte Funk was born in Milwaukee, Wisconsin, and received her education at several institutions, including Wisconsin State College, Milwaukee (1952–1954); the University of Hawaii, Honolulu (1954–1955); the University of Wisconsin at Whitewater, where she earned a Bachelor of Science degree (1970–1972); the University of Wisconsin at Milwaukee (1972–1973); Illinois State University, Normal, where she received a Master of Science degree (1975), and, a year later, a Master of Fine Arts degree.

Funk has had solo exhibitions of her work in museums, galleries, and universities throughout the United States, including Bradley University, Peoria, Illinois (1990); the Krannert Center, University of Illinois, Champaign-Urbana (1976); the Marine Bank, Milwaukee, Wisconsin (1977); and others. Her work has been invited to myriad group exhibitions in the United States and Switzerland, such as "Woven Structures in the Computer Age," a travelling show, Purdue University, West Lafayette, Indiana (1991); "Fiber Structure National V," Downey Museum, California (1987); "Fiber/Paper," Hand and Spirit Gallery, Scottsdale, Arizona (1985); "Contemporary Tapestry," Pratt Institute, Brooklyn, New York (1980–1981); "Contemporary Trends in American Weaving," University of Miami, Florida (1977); "7th International Biennial of Tapestry," Lausanne, Switzerland (1975); and many others.

Funk has been an instructor in the fiber arts at Texas Tech University, Lubbock, since 1978. Her works are housed in private, public, and corporate permanent collections, including the University of Chicago, Illinois; the City of Lausanne, Switzerland; Illinois State University, Normal; Rockwell International, Dallas, Texas; First National Bank, Lubbock, Texas; and many others.

Bibliography

Regensteiner, Else. *Geometric Design in Weaving.* Schiffer Publishing, 1986.
Tennant, Donna. *Nine in Fiber. Artspace Magazine* (January–February 1990): 62–63.
Who's Who in American Art. 19th ed. R.R. Bowker Co., 1991–1992.

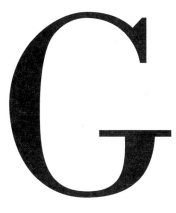

Gablik, Suzi (1934–)

Native New Yorker Suzi Gablik spent a summer session at Black Mountain College, North Carolina (1951) and studied with Robert Motherwell at Hunter College, New York City, where she received her Bachelor of Arts degree in 1955.

Artist, author, critic, teacher, and lecturer—Gablik has had seven solo exhibitions of her work at galleries, including the Alan Gallery (1963, 1966) and the Landau-Alan Gallery—both in New York City (1967); the Henri Gallery, Washington, D.C. (1971); the Hester Van Toyen Gallery, London, England (1978); and the Terry Dintenfass Gallery, New York City (1972, 1978). Her work was also invited to group exhibitions in institutions such as the Guggenheim Museum, New York City (1966); the Institute of Contemporary Arts, London, England (1969); and the New York Cultural Art Center (1973).

Her published books include *Pop Art Redefined*, co-authored with John Russell (1969); *Magritte* (1979); *Progress in Art* (1977); *Has Modernism Failed?* (1984); and *The Reenchantment of Art* (1991).

Gablik was critic for *Art News* (1962–1966); London correspondent for *Art in America* since 1975; and author of many articles and reviews for major art journals. She has been visiting professor of art and artist-in-residence at colleges throughout the United States and elsewhere; the most recent post was as visiting professor of art history and criticism at the University of Colorado, Boulder, during the summer of 1990.

Gablik has lectured in myriad colleges, universities, museums, and art associations throughout the world, including the United States, Hungary, Pakistan, India, Bangladesh, Nepal, Jordan, Egypt, Sri Lanka, Finland, Sweden, Australia, New Zealand, the Philippines, Canada, and Mexico since 1974.

Bibliography

Mecklenburg, Virginia M. *Modern American Realism: The Sara Roby Foundation Collection*. National Museum of American Art, 1987.

Ratcliff, Carter. "Suzi Gabllik at Dintenfass." *Art in America* 67:2 (March– April 1979): 149–50.

Gadbois, Louise (1896–)

Born in Montréal, Québec, Canada, the painter Louise Gadbois studied with Edwin Holgate in her native city (1932–1934); and also with John Lyman.

A prolific painter, Gadbois exhibited fifty-four works at the Montcalm Palace, Québec (1941), including some portraits. Three years later she showed in a joint exhibition with her daughter, Denyse, at the Royal Victoria College, Montréal; that same year she also showed jointly with Philip Surrey.

Winner of prizes and honors, Gadbois won the K.R. MacPherson prize for drawing at the Art Association of Montréal (1938); and others. Examples of her works are in private and public permanent collections, including the National Gallery of Canada, Ottawa.

Bibliography
Brunet-Weinmann, Monique. "Connaître et reconnaitre Louise Gadbois."
    Vie des arts 25:100 (Autumn 1980): 23–25.
Hubbard, R.H. *National Gallery of Canada Catalogue of Paintings and
    Sculpture.* Vol. 3.

Gag, Wanda Hazel (1893–1946)

Born in New Ulm, Minnesota, the printmaker Wanda Hazel Gag studied at the Art Students League, New York City, with many of the art world's best-known artists of that time, including John Sloan.

A prolific illustrator of children's books and translator of *Tales from Grimm* (1936), *Three Gay Tales from Grimm* (1943), and *More Tales from Grimm* (1947) Gag, early on, wrote and illustrated one of her most popular works, *Millions of Cats* (1928). Her solo exhibition of drawings, lithographs, and woodcuts at the Weyhe Gallery in New York City (1926) was most successful and led to many other shows, including "Art in Our Time," at the Museum of Modern Art (MoMA), New York City (1939). The year 1940 saw her memoirs based upon her journals, *Growing Pains: Diaries and Drawings for the Years 1908–1917*, published by Coward-McCann.

"Lamplight" (1929), a not atypical lithograph, reveals the wit and humor in her work; "Cats at a Window" (1930), a tiny wood engraving of three cats looking out the window, further proves Gag's magic with graver or lithographic crayon. Her work is represented in many private and public permanent collections, including the Philadelphia Museum of Fine Arts, Pennsylvania.

Bibliography
Fourteen American Women Printmakers of the '30s and '40s. New York:
    Weyhe Gallery, 1973.
Johnson, Una E. *American Prints and Printmakers.* Doubleday & Co., 1980.
Parker, Alice Lee. "American Prints to be Shown in Italy." *Magazine of
    Art* 23:4 (October 1931): 289–94.
Rubenstein, Charlotte S. *American Women Artists.* G.K. Hall & Co., 1982.

Gage, Frances Marie (1924–)

Known as a prolific and accomplished sculptor, Frances Marie Gage was born in Windsor, Ontario, Canada, and studied at a number of institutions, including Oshawa Collegiate and Technical Institute, Ontario (1943); Ontario College of Art, Toronto, where she studied sculpture (1951); the Art Students League, New York City, and the École des Beaux-Arts, Paris, France, where she held two-year scholarships—the latter from the Royal Society of Canada.

From 1962 to 1992 Gage has executed many commissions, including a twice-life-sized sculpture and four walnut relief panels for Fanshaw College, London, Ontario (1962); a portrait relief of Dr. Bertram Collip for the University of Western Ontario (1963); "Song in the Wind," a memorial at the Music Building, Mount Allison University, Sackville, New Brunswick (1968); a bust of Gordon Nikiforuk at the University of Toronto, Ontario (1975); "Woman," a marble sculpture for the Women's College Hospital, Toronto, Ontario (1969); a portrait bust of Elmer Iseler for Roy Thompson Hall, Toronto, Ontario (1990), a portrait head of the late Colonel R.S. McLaughlin, founder of General Motors of Canada, for the Royal College of Physicians and Surgeons, Canada (1992); and many others.

Member of the Council of the Royal Canadian Academy of Art and winner of the Rothman purchase award (1965), Gage designed the Jean P. Carrière award (medal) for the Standards Council of Canada and a commemorative medal of Samuel Bronfman (1971). Her work has been invited to many group exhibitions in Canada and abroad, including the International Congress of Medallic Arts, Florence, Italy (1984); Colorado City, Colorado (1987); Helsinki, Finland (1990); London, England (1992); and others.

Bibliography
The Canadian Who's Who. Who's Who Canadian Publications, 1992.
Who's Who in American Art. 19th ed. R.R. Bowker Co., 1991–1992.

Gammell, Linda (1948–)

Photographer Linda Gammell was born in 1948 in Austin, Minnesota, and has remained in the state for her education and professional life. After receiving her Bachelor of Arts degree in journalism from the University of Minnesota (1972), Gammell studied photography at a workshop with Ruth Bernhard. Subsequently she returned to the university for a Master of Fine Arts degree in photography (1979). Since 1981 she has been on the faculty of the Minneapolis College of Art and Design, Minnesota. With this lifelong home-base in one state, Gammell is also a keen traveller, and her intense involvement with the concept of "place" is demonstrated in works such as "Landscape of Hope and Despair" (1989), "White Pine Pages" (1989), and numerous multi-paneled landscapes of domestic gardens, each made from a grid of intimate views (1985–1988).

Gammell's early training as a journalist may account for the complex narrative content of much of her work. Frequently her photographs incorporate several levels of content—visual and textual—and meaning always merges from the complex layering in the work. Formats in Gammell's work range from the book to the wall-mural. Issues and themes range from the intimate pleasures of nature to the politics of ecology and cultural conflict. In her "East/West: False Portrait of a Culture" (1980–1983), images and symbols of American and Asian cultures were combined as color xerox transfers on translucent Japanese paper. This work also reflects her strong interest in Chinese and Japanese painting. The subsequent "American Stories" series (1983–1985) combined black-and-white photographs of commonplace scenes with texts taken from newspaper stories. With artist Sandra Menefee Taylor and historian Jo Blatti, Gammell produced *Landscape of Hope and Despair*, a limited-edition book that is a textual and visual account of the demise of an American family farm in Minnesota. The book, subtitled *SE Section 6, Township N, Range 21W of the 5th Principle Meridian 160 Acres*, combines photography and oral history. Its production was supported by a Jerome Foundation/Minnesota Center for Book Arts fellowship. "White Pine Pages" (1989), four large diptychs, was a collaboration with her father, a former forester.

Gammell has received several fellowships and awards, including a regional fellowship from the National Endowment for the Arts (NEA) (1989), two McKnight Foundation/Film in the Cities Photography fellowships (1984, 1988), a Bush Foundation fellowship (1984), and two Minnesota State Arts Board fellowships (1980, 1986). She was a founding member of the Women's Art Registry of Minnesota (WARM) and WARM Gallery (1974–1949). Widely exhibited, Gammell's work is included in several public collections in Minnesota, including the Minnesota Historical Society; the Minneapolis Institute of Arts, and the Walker Art Center—both in Minneapolis; Cray Research; Film in the Cities; and the Minnesota Center for Book Arts. Other public collections include the International Museum of Photography, George Eastman House, and the Visual Studies Workshop—both in Rochester, New York; and the Grand Rapids Art Museum, Michigan.

Gretchen Garner

Bibliography

Brush, Gloria DeFilipps. "On Photography: The Limits of Responsibility." *Artpaper* (March 1985).

Fling, Shelly. "The Life of Bath." *Minnesota Monthly* (December 1989): 93–97.

Gammell, Linda, and Sandra Menefee Taylor and Jo Blatti. *Landscape of Hope and Despair: SE Section 6, Township N, Range 21W of the 5th Principle Meridian 160 Acres*. Minnesota Center for Book Arts, 1989.

Garner, Gretchen. *Reclaiming Paradise: American Women Photograph the Land*. Tweed Museum of Art, University of Minnesota, 1987, pp. 42–43.

Hartwell, Carroll T., and Owen Edwards. "Twin Cities Reflex." *American Photographer* (September 1984).

Jerome Book Arts Fellowship Exhibition. Catalog essay by Joan Lyons. Minnesota Center for Book Arts, 1989.

Lauter, Estella. *Women as Mythmakers: Poetry and Visual Art by Twentieth Century Woman*. University of Indiana Press, 1985.

Gardiner, Eliza Draper (1871–1955)

Born in Cranston, Rhode Island, Eliza Draper Gardiner was a nationally-known printmaker who was associated with the Provincetown Printmakers, a Massachusetts group of graphic artists. Gardiner studied with Sophia L. Pittman at the Friends School and continued her studies at the Rhode Island School of Design—both in Providence, Rhode Island—where she received her Bachelor's degree in 1897.

Gardiner took the Grand Tour of Europe and, on her return, did further study with Charles H. Woodbury in Boston, Massachusetts. Between 1910 and 1920 Gardiner exhibited her color woodcuts widely in the United States and Europe. In 1919 she showed seven color woodcuts at the Berlin Photographic Company in New York City. Three years later she exhibited four relief prints at the Provincetown Art Association, Massachusetts; showed a dozen more at the Detroit Institute of Arts, Michigan; and held her first solo show at Goodspeed's in Boston, Massachusetts. In 1932 the New York lithographer George Miller printed no less than ten of her crayon-drawn, stone lithographs.

Beginning in 1908 Gardiner taught drawing, watercolor, and color woodcut technique at the Rhode Island School of Design, Providence, for thirty-one years. Her woodcut technique was based upon that employed by the Japanese: her blocks were inked with a mixture of rice paste and watercolor and were, on occasion, further worked upon with pastel or crayon. Gardiner's subjects were drawn from the life around her—children, landscapes, still lifes.

Bibliography

American Art Annual. Volume 28. American Federation of Arts, 1932.

Falk, Peter H., and E.D. Gardiner. *Master of Color Woodcut*. Sound View Press, 1987.

Who's Who in American Art. Obit. Vol. 6. American Federation of Arts, 1956.

Gardner, Elizabeth Jane (Bouguereau) (1837–1922)

After attending school in her native town of Exeter, New Hampshire, Elizabeth Jane Gardner studied language and art at Lasell Female Seminary (now a junior college) in Auburndale, Massachusetts, and graduated in 1856. During the next few years she taught French at the Worcester School of Design and Fine Arts, Massachusetts, and in 1864 moved to Paris, France, with Imogene Robinson, her former art teacher at Lasell Female Seminary; they worked that first summer as copyists—filling orders from America for copies of paintings at the Louvre, France and Luxembourg museums. When Gardner tried to enroll in the fall at the École des Beaux-Arts, Paris, France, she found that classes were open to men only. The solution was a woman's cooperative studio in which the women hired their own models. Her first big success occurred in 1868 when two of her pictures (a still life and a figure painting) were accepted for the annual Paris Salon, France, and one of these paintings sold for $400. Her teacher at this time was Hughes Merle.

Gardner is thought to have been the first American woman in the nineteenth century to try to study in Paris, France. She dressed as a boy to accompany Robinson's nephew to all-male drawing classes and later to attend drawing classes at the Gobelin Tapestry School, Paris, France. Rodolphe Julian was impressed with Gardner's determination and admitted her into his academy, where she studied with Jules Joseph Lefèvre. By 1879 Gardner had attained the right to have paintings accepted at the annual Paris Salon, France, without subjecting her work to the jury, and she received an honorable mention for an entry. William Bouguereau was her teacher at this time, and they announced their engagement also in this year. The actual marriage did not take place until after his mother died in 1896.

Gardner painted a wide range of subject matter: portraits, genre, and history (both religious and mythological), but always in the academic tradition. Although she and Mary Cassatt were contemporaries in Paris, France, Gardner adhered to the conservative style. At her zenith she was selling her paintings for $1,600. Her work was recognized with prizes, including a gold medal at one of the Paris Salons, France, and a bronze at the Exposition Universelle of 1889. She was the first American woman to win a gold medal at the Paris Salon, France (1887).

Eleanor Tufts

Bibliography

Fidell-Beaufort, Madeleine. "Elizabeth Jane Gardner Bouguereau: A Parisian Artist from New Hampshire." *Archives of American Art Journal* 24:2 (1984): 2–9.

Tufts, Eleanor. *American Women Artists, 1830–1930*. National Museum of Women in the Arts, 1987.

Garduño, Flor (1957–)

Born in Mexico City, Mexico, the photographer Flor Garduño studied painting at San Carlos Academy, Mexico City, Mexico, under the aegis of Cati Horna (1976) and took further study with Horna at the National Plastic Arts School of the National University of Mexico (1976–1978). Turning to photography she assisted Manuel Alvarez Bravo (1978–1981) and also studied the graphic arts at the Universidad Autonoma Metropolitana, Mexico City, Mexico (1978–1980).

Garduño has published many portfolios and photoessays of work related to Mexico, Guatemala, Ecuador, Bolivia, Peru, and elsewhere. She also collaborated with Alvarez to photograph the indigenous peoples and places in Chinanteca, Mixteca, Nahuatl, Zapoteca—all in Mexico, and more. Her work has appeared in many group exhibitions in Mexico and abroad, including Escuela de Pintura y Escultura (La Esmeralda; 1979), Biblioteca Benjamin Franklin (1979), and "Exposicion Colección Manuel Alvarez Bravo" (1980)—all in Mexico City, Mexico; Museum of Modern Art, San Francisco, California (1981, 1983); "Bienal de Grafica," Havana, Cuba (1984); and others.

Garduño has held solo exhibitions in museums and galleries, such as the Escuela Nacional de Artes Plásticas, San Carlos (1980), and Galería José Clemente Orozco, Mexico City (1982)—both in Mexico; Art Institute of Chicago, Illinois (1992); and others.

Examples of her work are in private and public permanent collections, including the Museum of Modern Art, Mexico City, Mexico.

Bibliography
Auer, Michel. *Photographers Encyclopedia International: 1839 to the Present.* Editions Camera Obscura, 1985.
Garduño, Flor. "Cemetery in Cumen, Guatemala." *British Journal of Photography.* Vol. 139 (June, 4 1992): 3.
Hugunin, James. "The Art Institute of Chicago: Exhibit." *New Art Examiner.* Vol. 20 (November 1992): 32–33.

Garner, Gretchen (1939–)
Currently chair of the art department at the University of Connecticut, Storrs, Gretchen Garner has functioned as an editor and photographer, as well as a curator and photo-historian. In 1965 she received her Bachelor of Arts degree with honors in art history from the University of Chicago, Illinois, followed by a Master of Fine Arts from the School of the Art Institute, Chicago, Illinois, in 1975. To this end she received a Danforth Foundation grant for graduate study from 1973 to 1975. After receiving her degree she worked as the photography editor for the *New Art Examiner* from 1975 to 1977 and as editor of *Exposure* magazine (the organ of the Society for Photographic Education) from 1981 to 1982.

Between 1975 and 1989 she has had more than twenty-five solo or two-person exhibitions, including the Friends of Photography, Carmel, California (1979), and exhibits at the Chicago Center for Contemporary Photography, Illinois (1982, 1988). She has also been involved in numerous invitational exhibits throughout the country and her work is in public collections both in this country and Scandinavia.

Garner's most important work has been both as a curator and an artist. In 1987 she was guest curator at the Tweed Museum of Art at the University of Minnesota, Duluth. There she wrote and assembled the exhibition: "Reclaiming Paradise: American Women Photograph the Land." This exhibit, which travelled to thirteen sites between 1987 and 1989, contributed substantially to the scant literature available on contemporary landscape photography and in particular the landscape as seen by women. In this catalog Garner has collected the landscape photographs of nineteenth- and twentieth-century American women and accompanied their works with a text about each of them. Her introductory essay hypothesizes that women have a more intimate relationship to the landscape than men and that theirs is a landscape of gardens, still lifes, and secluded valleys, rather than the expansive

views that characterize traditional landscapes. This catalog also investigates the vision women have of the earth as a mother and explores the rebirth of feminist paganism with the context of twentieth-century photography.

This exhibit was preceded in 1982 by Garner's own book of urban landscapes titled *An Art History of Ephemera: Gretchen Garner's Catalog,* a collection of her work from 1976–1978. The beginning of the catalog quotes Linnaeus and establishes the photographs that follow as depictions of objects that fall into representative categories. However, the categories she establishes for these color and black-and-white photographs are not based on objective and logical order, as phyla would be; rather they are both arbitrary and ambiguous groupings of photographs. Her category "Signs," for example, shows blank signs that are not signs but shapes, stressing their visual rather than their verbal qualities. A section titled "Topiary" contains small ornamental plant groupings. All of the plants, however, are trimmed into unnatural shapes, thereby illuminating the unnaturalness of nature. The cityscape is also included in such sections as "Tingling Lines," whose title is borrowed from the rhetoric of advertising. In these images of car lots, only one contains cars, and the viewer is confronted with the irony of advertising without the goods. Garner's catalog forms a satiric commentary on the categorizing prevalent in Western civilization and more particularly in art history. Like many contemporary artists Garner chooses to comment on the conceptual framework of contemporary criticism by creating works where the signs and signifiers are one.

In her landscape photographs of the 1980s Garner has expressed less irony, concentrating on more lyrical single images. Movement, intense color, and an intimate point of view mark these works, which have become increasingly complex spatially. Most recently her landscapes are two- or three-panel panoramas taken from a very close vantage point. Another body of work developed from 1983, and ongoing, are her portraits. Many of Garner's portraits incorporate still-life elements, which have developed from her portfolio *Vanitas* (1980), essentially an extended self-portrait in still-life form.

Diana Emery Hulick

Bibliography
Garner, Gretchen. *An Art History of Ephemera: Gretchen Garner's Catalog.* Tulip Press, 1982.
Gruber, Dan. "Gretchen Garner, Klaus, Frahm." *Artweek* (October 19, 1979).
Hellekson, Diane. Essay. *Gretchen Garner, Landscapes 1981–1988.* Grand Rapids Art Museum, 1989.
Tweed Museum of Art. *Reclaiming Paradise: American Women Photograph the Landscape.* University of Minnesota, Duluth, 1987.

Garrett, Paula (1954–)
Born in Stuttgart, Germany, the jeweler/sculptor/metalsmith Paula Garrett earned a Bachelor of Fine Arts degree from North Texas State University, Denton (1976); attended the Penland School of Crafts, Penland, North Carolina (1978–1980); and received a Master of Fine Arts degree from Southern Illinois University, Carbondale (1982).

Garrett has exhibited work in galleries and museums in the United States and abroad, including "The Accessory as Art," Art Gallery, Tokyo, and "American Metalwork," Kyoto Municipal Museum of Traditional Industry—both in Japan (1983); "Small Sculpture Exhibition," Central Michigan University, Mt. Pleasant (1984); "Metals Invitational," Southeastern Center for Contemporary Art, Winston-Salem, North Carolina (1985); "Mainstreams in Metals," Galveston Art Center, Texas (1986); and others.

"Ghost Nets" (1988), a small sculpture composed of a variety of metals—including gold, silver, and copper—makes a strong statement about ecological responsibilities. Garrett received a Southern Arts Federation/National Endowment for the Arts (NEA) regional fellowship for emerging visual artists (1985); the following year her work was included in a travelling show under the same auspices. Representative examples of her work are in private and public permanent collections.

Bibliography
Nine from North Carolina: An Exhibition of Women Artists. North Carolina State Committee and the National Museum of Women in the Arts: 1989.

Gascón, Elvira (1911–)

Born in Almenar, Soria, Spain, Elvira Gascón studied at the Academía de Bellas Artes, Madrid, Spain, and specialized in painting, particularly of nudes.

She arrived in Mexico in 1939 and worked with the Fondo de Cultural Económica and, from 1946 to 1956, was an illustrator for the newspapers *El Nacional* and *Novedades*.

In 1942 Gascón exhibited her work in a group show, along with Mexican artists and Spanish artists resident in Mexico and, from then on, participated in some forty solo and group exhibitions.

Gascón produced the following murals alfresco: "Epifanía" (1952) in the church of La Milagrosa; "Estampida de caballos" and "Guarida de tigres" on exterior walls of the Instituto de Seguridad y Servicios Sociales de los Trabajadores del Estado (1961); "Gatos" and "Grupos de caballos" at her residence (1964); "San Antonio de las Huertas" (1964) and "San José y la Virgen" (1968) in the convent of Los Padres Josefinos—all in Mexico City, Mexico. Her easel paintings include the following series: "Adan y Eva, expulsión del paradiso," "Cristo hombre," "Centauro y Centauresa," and many others. Gascón is also recognized for her splendid drawings—notable for their purity of line—that grace books, reviews, and cultural supplements; a fine example of her work as illustrator may be seen in Laura Villaseñor's translation of José Gorostiza's *Death Without End.* The fundamental theme throughout her work is the human nude figure. In 1982 she received the highly valued Sor Juana Ines de la Cruz award, and in 1984 exhibited a special group of works titled, "A Spanish Exile in Mexico."

Bibliography
Alvarez, José Rogelio, et al. *Enciclopedia de México.* Secretaría de Educación Pública, 1987.
The Texas Quarterly: Image of Mexico I. The University of Texas. Autumn 1969.

Gates, Margaret (Casey) (1903–1989)

A native of Washington, D.C., Margaret (Casey) Gates made a career as a painter in watercolor, oil, and tempera, and as a teacher. Gates received her training at the Corcoran School of Art in Washington, D.C., Colorado Springs Fine Arts Center, Colorado, under Henry Varnum Poor, and the Phillips Memorial Gallery Art School, Washington, D.C., under C. Law Watkins. In 1933 the artist married painter Robert Franklin Gates and was appointed to the teaching faculty of the Phillips Gallery Art Schools. She taught there through 1946.

Gates accompanied her husband in 1936 to Saint Thomas, Virgin Islands, where he had been sent on a government-sponsored watercolor project. There, in works such as "The White Gate" (private collection), she painted brilliant watercolors of the sun-drenched island and native population with her characteristic eye for decorative motifs and patterns formed by gates, wrought-iron furniture, and other ornamental elements.

The year 1941 was a significant one, as her watercolor, "Live Oaks," was purchased by the U.S. government for the hospital at Fort Stanton, New Mexico, as part of a New Deal program initiated by Edward Bruce. She also received an honorable mention in a mural competition of the Section of Fine Arts of the Public Building Administration, resulting in a commission for the post office in Mebane, North Carolina, entitled "Landscape—Tobacco Curing" (destroyed; copy by Henry D. Rodd installed 1964).

Gates exhibited regularly in group shows, including the Richmond Bi-Annual, the Critics Choice Exhibition of the Cincinnati Art Museum, Ohio (1945), and the shows of the Society of Washington Painters and Sculptors, who awarded her a prize in 1945. In 1946 the Whyte Gallery of Washington mounted her first solo exhibition. This was followed by an exhibition at the Corcoran Gallery of Art in 1948.

Seven works by Gates, principally land and townscapes of northern Virginia, are in the Phillips Collection. Her work is also represented in the Watkins Memorial Collection at American University, Washington, D.C., where she was given a retrospective in 1981. She died in Mitchellsville, Virginia.

Julie A. Aronson

Bibliography
E.E.P. "Who's Who in Washington Art Circles." *Washington Times-Herald* (December 18, 1939).
The Phillips Collection: A Summary Catalogue. Washington, D.C.: The Phillips Collection, 1981, p. 85.
Falk, Peter Hastings, ed. *Who Was Who in American Art.* Madison, Connecticut: Soundview Press, 1985, p. 225.

Gatewood, Maud (1934–)

Born in Yanceyville, North Carolina, the painter Maud Gatewood earned a Bachelor's degree from the Women's College of the University of North Carolina at Greensboro (1954); received a Master of Fine Arts degree from Ohio State University, Columbus, the following year; and did further work at the University of Vienna, and the Academy of Applied Arts—both in Vienna; and a summer course at Harvard University, Cambridge, Massachusetts.

Between 1965 and 1981 Gatewood held more than two dozen solo exhibitions in galleries and museums, including the Mint Museum of Art, Charlotte, North Carolina (1965, 1966, 1972); Heath Gallery, Atlanta, Georgia (1969, 1971, 1974, 1976, 1978, 1980, 1983, 1986, 1988); Willard Gallery, New York City (1972); Henri Gallery, Washington, D.C. (1976); Hodges Taylor Gallery, Charlotte, North Carolina (1982, 1984, 1986, 1988); and others. Her work has been invited to many distinguished group exhibitions, such as the American Academy and Institute of Arts and Letters, at which she received a painting award (1972), and the Fischbach Gallery (1978)—both in New York City; "Five North Carolina Artists," Green Hill Center for North Carolina Art, Greensboro (1979); "Painting in the South," a travelling show, the Virginia Museum, Richmond (1983); and others.

Winner of awards and honors Gatewood received a Fulbright fellowship to Vienna, Austria (1962–1963); an artists fellowship from the North Carolina Arts Council (1980); a grant from the National Endowment for the Arts (NEA) (1981); and others. "A Sudden Gust" (1985), a large acrylic painting, provides one aspect of Gatewood's imagery, her masterly control of the medium, and the wry humor of the artist: on an asphalt parking lot, autumnal leaves swirl around a strongly-painted, three-quarter view of a female figure wearing a greenish coat and one blue glove, walking down a stairway toward the viewer. Fused together these separate elements furnish much food for thought.

Gatewood's work is represented in private and public permanent collections, including the Mint Museum of Art, Charlotte; the National Collection of Fine Arts, Washington, D.C.; the North Carolina Museum of Art, Raleigh; and others.

Bibliography
Nine from North Carolina: An Exhibition of Women Artists. North Carolina State Committee and the National Museum of Women in the Arts: 1989.
Who's Who in American Art. 19th ed. R.R. Bowker Co., 1991–1992.

Gauthier, Suzanne (1948–)

Born in Lorette, Manitoba, Canada, Suzanne Gauthier stayed in her native province to study art, obtaining her Honors Bachelor of Fine Arts degree from the University of Manitoba, Winnipeg, in 1969. Although she studied printmaking at the University of Iowa, Iowa City, for a year (1970–1971), she returned to Canada to found and direct a printmaking studio in Winnipeg, Manitoba. She was active in the Print Studio which opened an adjacent gallery (1974) until 1975. By 1977 she was actively engaged in arts and education—first as a visiting artist at Mount Allison University, Sackville, New Brunswick (1977); then as a teacher at the School of Art, University of Manitoba, Winnipeg (1977–1979) and as a participant in the Manitoba and Ontario "Artists in the Schools Programme" (1979–1982). More recently, in addition to answering invitations as a guest artist at various Canadian institutions, she has lectured at the Nova Scotia College of Art and Design.

Although she currently lives and works in Montréal, Gauthier exhibits widely across Canada. In keeping with her diverse interests in art production she has exhibited work in the International Exhibition of Ceramic Art in Faenza, Italy, as well as in the 2nd Biennale of the Print and Drawing Council of Canada. The motifs evident in her sculptural work are often repeated in her more formal graphic explorations on paper; and her work on paper is often a richly textured expansion and exploration of her sculptural work. The result is a highly integrative body of work that constantly examines and develops a formal language of line, space, and volume. This intense interest in the formal language of art is enhanced by Gauthier's particularly adept use of a black-and-white graphic on paper and a carefully planned integration of mixed media.

In addition to being the recipient of a prestigious Canada Coun-

cil grant (1984, 1987), Gauthier's work is held by major Canadian collections such as Canada Council Art Bank and the Massey Foundation—both in Ottawa; the Macdonald Stewart Art Centre, Guelph, Ontario; the Winnipeg Art Gallery, and the Manitoba Art Council—both in Manitoba.

Janice Helland

Bibliography
Enright, Robert. "Preying and Predatoring: The Recent Painting of Suzanne Gauthier." *Border Crossings* 5:1 (Winnipeg) (1986): 18–20.
Xuriguera, Gerard. *Le Dessin, le pastel, l'aquarelle dans l'art contemporain.* Paris: Editions Meyer, 1987.

Gearhart, Frances Hammel (1869–1958)

One of the founding members of the Printmakers of Los Angeles (now California Printmakers Society), Frances Hammel Gearhart was born in Sagetown (Gladstone), Illinois. Before she reached the "age of consent," the family moved to Southern California. Gearhart studied art with Charles H. Woodbury and Henry R. Poore; then taught English history for many years in the Los Angeles public schools, before becoming a full-time artist.

Gearhart and her sister, May, exhibited watercolors in a two-person show at the Walker Theatre Building in Los Angeles (1911). Three years later Gearhart, along with her sister and Benjamin and Howell Brown, founded the Los Angeles Printmakers. A self-taught pioneer "western" printmaker, Gearhart specialized in landscapes, including the Sonora Desert, Yosemite National Park, the Rockies, and others, printed with rice paste and watercolor, in the Japanese manner. Her woodcuts reveal a certain awareness of the works of Pedro Lemos, Frank Morley Fletcher, and Hiroshi Yoshida—all of whom exhibited widely.

Twenty-seven of Gearhart's color woodcuts were shown at the Los Angeles Museum of History, Science, and Art in Exposition Park, California (1923) in a duo show with her sister. Seven years later the American Federation of Arts organized a travelling exhibition of her prints. In 1933 a solo exhibition of her work was mounted at the Grand Central Galleries, New York City, and that same year, Gearhart won a purchase prize when the California Printmakers exhibited their member's prints at the Los Angeles County Museum, California.

Gearhart's works are in permanent public and private collections, including the Art Gallery of Ontario, Toronto, Canada; the Rhode Island School of Design, Providence; the Los Angeles County Museum of Art, California; the Isaac Delgado Museum, New Orleans, Louisiana; and many others.

Bibliography
Hughes, Edan Milton. *Artists in California: 1786–1940.* Hughes, 1986.
Moure, Nancy D. *Dictionary of Artists in Southern California 1950.* Dustin Publications, 1975.
Who's Who in American Art. 3rd ed. American Federation of Arts, 1940.

Gearhart, May (1872–1951)

Born in Sagetown (Gladstone), Illinois, May Gearhart was one of three daughters of a middle-class businessman. Gearhart studied art at the Los Angeles State Normal School, California, and the School of the Art Institute of Chicago, Illinois. She took further work at the California School of Fine Arts, San Francisco, under the aegis of Rudolph Schaeffer; completed a summer course at Teachers College, Columbia University, New York City, with Arthur Wesley Dow; and studied under Hans Hofmann at the University of California at Berkeley in 1930.

At the age of twenty-eight Gearhart began to teach art in the public schools of Berkeley, California, before moving to Los Angeles, California, where she was appointed art supervisor for the city school system from 1903 to 1939. Gearhart travelled frequently to Mexico, gathering visual material for her technically-complex, figurative etchings. She was also a delegate, on four separate occasions, to the International Art Congress in London, England (1908), Dresden, Germany (1912), Prague, Czechoslovakia (1928), and Paris, France (1937).

Gearhart, along with her etching instructor, Benjamin Chambers Brown, Howell Brown, and her sister, Frances, founded the Los Angeles Printmakers (now California Printmakers Society) in 1914. Gearhart exhibited her color etchings in museums and with various print groups throughout the United States, including the Los Angeles County Museum of History, Science, and Art, California; the Pacific Artists Association; the Chicago Society of Etchers, Illinois; and the Society of American Etchers, New York City. Her work is in the permanent collection of the Los Angeles County Museum of Art, California; the California State Library, Sacramento; and others.

Bibliography

Feinblatt, Ebria, and Bruce Davis. *Los Angeles Prints 1883–1980*. Exhibition Catalog. Los Angeles County Museum of Art, 1980.
Gearhart, May. *Sketches of a Late Etcher*. J.D. Schneider, 1939.
Who's Who in American Art. 5th ed. American Federation of Arts, 1953.

Gechtoff, Sonia (1926–)

Sonia Gechtoff has wrestled to the ground two classic polarities. One, which is as old as painting itself, is the balance between abstraction and representation—between the formal properties of art and imitation of visually available reality. The other opposition, more acutely modern, is the tension between freedom and constraint—between feeling and discipline.

Born in Philadelphia, Pennsylvania, Gechtoff grew up there, learning about painting first from her Russian-born father, Leonid Gechtoff, a painter of expressionistic landscapes, and later at the Philadelphia Museum School of Art, Pennsylvania, where she received her Bachelor of Fine Arts degree in 1950. The following year she moved to San Francisco, California. There she took a course in lithography with James Budd Dixon at the California School of Fine Arts and came to admire the brand of West Coast abstraction led by Clyfford Still, Frank Lobdell, and Ernest Briggs. At the same time she began to associate with a freewheeling group of young artists, including action painter James Kelly, whom she married. Gechtoff's expressionistic figure paintings soon evolved into tempestuous abstract expressionist works which brought her national acclaim as one of the most promising artists of her generation.

In 1958 Gechtoff and Kelly moved to New York City, where they have resided since. She had already had a one-person show at the DeYoung Museum in San Francisco, California, and had appeared in prestigious group shows, including the Whitney Annual (as it was then) at the Whitney Museum of American Art, New York City, and the Carnegie International in Pittsburgh, Pennsylvania. Her first solo show in New York City took place the following year. Apparently poised for success, she instead fell into relative obscurity in the sixties when pop art and minimalism abruptly supplanted abstract expressionism.

By the mid-1970s, when she began to exhibit regularly again, she had revised her approach, in terms of both medium and style. Her new works, which originated during a year of teaching at the University of New Mexico, Albuquerque, were pencil drawings on rag paper prepared with acrylic paint in saturated hues; the compositions were geometric. Nevertheless, her precise and delicate pencil chiaroscuro communicated the same intensity of feeling that had motivated earlier works, although now with more lyric and meditative overtones. Throughout the 1980s, as she expanded this technique in size and scope, the works became larger and less programmatic. She increasingly stressed visual allusions to architecture—as in the "Small City Facades" series (1983)—and landscape—as in "Double Waterfall" (1986–1987).

In the late 1980s Gechtoff returned to painting, building upon the freest of her previous pencil drawings. Working in acrylic on large canvases, she creates triumphant abstractions, which acknowledge Matisse's continuing inspiration and sometimes allude to representational origins, as in "Odessa" (1992). In these recent paintings, geometric and eccentric shapes mingle freely; hard-edge and painterly approaches combine without contradiction; and audacious colors coexist. The conflicts between abstraction and representation or between freedom and discipline don't even come to mind.

Ann Lee Morgan

Bibliography

Mellow, James. "Concerning the Landscapes of Sonia Gechtoff." In *Sonia Gechtoff: New Works*. New York: Gruenebaum Gallery, 1980.
———. "Sonia Gechtoff: A Different Kind of Knowledge." *Arts Magazine* 56 (February 1982): 158–60.
Loughery, John. "The Theater of the Visible." In *Sonia Gechtoff* Exhibition Brochure. New York: Kraushaar Galleries, 1992.

Gego (Gertrude Goldschmidt) (1912–)

Born in Hamburg, Germany, the painter, sculptor, printmaker, and architect, Gego (Gertrude Goldschmidt) studied architecture at the University of Stuttgart, Germany, in the early 1930s.

A university professor in Caracas, Venezuela, for many years, Gego has held solo exhibitions in museums and galleries, including the Center for Inter-American Relations, New York City (1969); and many others abroad. Gego received a lithography award from the Tamarind Institute, Los Angeles (1966). Her work has been included in prestigious group shows, such as the Betty Parsons Gallery (1960); Museum of Modern Art (MoMA) (1960, 1965, 1967), and the Whitney Museum of American Art—all in New York City (1969); Graphics Gallery, San Francisco, California (1970); and others.

Examples of Gego's pristine sculptures and other works are represented in private, public, and corporate permanent collections, including the Amon Carter Museum, Fort Worth, University of Texas at Austin, and Braniff Airlines, Dallas—all in Texas; La Jolla Museum of Art, and University of California at Los Angeles (UCLA)—both in California; Art Institute of Chicago, Illinois; Library of Congress, Washington, D.C.; and many others.

Bibliography
Boulton, Alfredo. *Historia de la Pintura en Venezuela*. Caracas: Coleccion
    Libros de Arte, 1972.
Ossott, Hanni. *Gego*. Caracas Museum of Contemporary Art, 1977.

Gehr, Mary

Born in Chicago, Illinois, the painter/printmaker Mary Gehr studied at
several institutions, including Smith College, Northampton, Massachusetts; the Art Institute of Chicago, Illinois, where she worked under
Paul Wieghardt; and the Institute of Design, Illinois Institute of Technology, Chicago, with Misch Kohn.

Widely-travelled, Gehr has held myriad solo exhibitions in the
United States and abroad and has shown in major professional
printmaking shows for many years.

Her work is represented in private and public permanent collections, including the Art Institute of Chicago, Illinois; Free Library of
Philadelphia, and Philadelphia Museum of Art—both in Pennsylvania; Library of Congress, Washington, D.C.; the Nelson Rockefeller
Collection, New York City; and others.

Bibliography
Carbol, T.J., ed. *The Printmaker in Illinois*. Illinois Art Education
    Association, 1971–1972.
Who's Who in American Art. 15th ed. R.R. Bowker Co., 1982.

Geiger, Anna Bella (1933–)

Born in Rio de Janeiro, Brazil, the painter/printmaker Anna Bella Geiger studied intaglio printmaking with Fayga Ostrower, and the history
of art with Hannah Levy at the Metropolitan Museum of Art, New York
City (1953–1955).

Geiger has held solo exhibitions at the European Gallery (1963), and
Columbia University—both in New York City (1968); and others. Examples
of her work are in private and public permanent collections, including the
Franklin Furnace Archives, the Museum of Modern Art (MoMA), the New
York Public Library—all in New York City; and others.

Bibliography
*The Latin American Spirit: Art and Artists in the United States, 1920–
    1970*. Harry N. Abrams, 1988.

Genn, Nancy

Born in San Francisco, California, the multi-talented Nancy Genn studied at the San Francisco Art Institute, California, and the University of
California at Berkeley.

Genn has held many solo exhibitions in galleries and museums,
including the M.H. De Young Memorial Museum, San Francisco (1955,
1963), San Francisco Museum of Art (1961), and Los Angeles Institute of Contemporary Art—all in California; and others.

Her work, which includes non-objective handmade paper compositions, commissioned bronze fountains and fountain sculptures, ceramic tile murals, and menorahs, has been invited to myriad group
shows from New York to California, and she has garnered her share of
honors and awards, including a Creative Artists Public Service (CAPS)
grant to Japan (1978–1979).

"Sedona 10" (1981), typical of her sensitive, creative work of this
period is a non-objective, layered, handmade, colored paperwork containing partially-seen, embedded fibers.

Genn's work is represented in private and public permanent collections, such as the Albright-Knox Art Gallery, Buffalo, New York;
Aldrich Museum of Contemporary Art, Ridgefield, Connecticut; Cincinnati Art Museum, Ohio; Oakland Art Museum, and San Francisco
Museum of Modern Art—both in California; and others.

Bibliography
Farmer, Jane M. *New American Paperworks*. A Catalog. The World Print
    Council, 1982.
Heller, Jules. *Papermaking*. Watson-Guptill, 1978.

Genth, Lillian Mathilde (1876–1953)

A highly successful artist, Lillian Mathilde Genth was well known for
her scenes of nude women in a landscape which she painted at her
summer home, a seventy-acre estate in the Berkshires. She participated in more than 233 exhibitions between 1904 and 1935. Her paintings were collected by the Metropolitan Museum of Art, and the Brooklyn Institute of Arts and Sciences—both in New York City; the National
Gallery of Art, Washington, D.C.; the Carnegie Institute, Pittsburgh,
Pennsylvania; the Cincinnati Art Museum, Ohio; and many other large
museums during her lifetime, yet her career fell into oblivion as the
histories of art were written.

Genth was born in Philadelphia, Pennsylvania, to Matilda Caroline
Rebscher and Samuel Adam. She attended the Philadelphia School of
Design for Women, Pennsylvania, on a scholarship and worked through
the school as a dress designer. Her teachers included Elliott
Daingerfield, the principal painting and drawing teacher. After graduation in 1900 she went to Europe for three years, one year of which
was supported by the William L. Elkins European fellowship for at-
tainment in art from the Philadelphia School of Design. She attended
James McNeill Whistler's Académie Carmen from October 1890 until
it closed in March 1901.

Upon her return to the United States in 1904 she settled in New
York City and participated in exhibitions at the National Academy of
Design, New York City; the Philadelphia Art Club, Pennsylvania; the
Worcester Art Museum, Massachusetts; and had her first solo show at
the Pennsylvania Academy of Fine Arts, Philadelphia. She was also
awarded the Mary Shaw prize for the best landscape in the Annual
Exhibition that year. Within three years she had exhibited at the Art
Institute of Chicago, Illinois; the Boston Art Club, Massachusetts; the
Carnegie Institute, Pittsburgh, Pennsylvania; the Cincinnati Art Museum, Ohio; and the Corcoran Gallery of Art, Washington, D.C. In 1908
she won the Shaw prize and was elected an associate of the National
Academy of Design, New York City. The next year she won the National Academy of Design's first Hallgarten prize for the best painting
by an American.

Genth travelled to Spain and Northern Africa several times during the 1920s. After 1928 she abandoned the nudes for which she had
become famous and produced mostly scenes from her travels, especially of Spanish festivals and bullfights. Three years later she again
abruptly changed subject matter after a tour of Japan, China, Pago-
Pago, Bali, Fiji, New Guinea, and Thailand (Siam), where she was commissioned to paint a portrait of the King.

The most important influence on her style has been attributed to Whistler. However, the thick paint and strong tonalist qualities of the intimate landscape scene as well as the poetic approach to nature in her paintings of women in the landscape are even more like the work of her first teacher, Elliott Daingerfield. Daingerfield was one of several artists who helped to formulate tonalism's aesthetic based upon the ideas and methods of the Barbizon painters. Like him Genth used a highly coloristic approach within the tonalist mode.

In New York City Genth was a member of the American Federation of Arts and the National Arts Club. She also was a member of the Royal Society of Arts, London, England; and the Union Internationale des Beaux-Arts et des Lettres, Paris.

Phyllis Peet

Bibliography

Artist Files, National Museum of American Art, Smithsonian Institution, Washington, D.C.

Carroll, Dana H. "A Painter of Independence: Miss Lillian M. Genth; Women Painters of Today—Second Article." *Arts and Decoration* (December 1912): 54–56.

Genth, Lillian. "A Painting Trip in North Africa." *The American Magazine of Art* 18 (May 1927): 227–37.

Lillian Genth Papers and William H. Bender Jr. Papers. Archives of American Art, Smithsonian Institution, Washington, D.C.

Lillian Mathilde Genth: A Retrospective. Exhibition Catalog. Hickory, North Carolina: Hickory Museum of Art, 1990.

Rainey, Ada. "A Painter of the Figure in Sunlight: Lillian Genth." *The International Studio* 50 (October 1913): LV–LXI.

Genush, Luba (1924–)

Born in Odessa, Ukraine, the painter/printmaker Luba Genush learned her several arts disciplines at the School of Fine Arts, Kiev (1938–1941); the Vienna Academy of Fine Arts, Austria (1944–1948); and the École du Meuble, Montréal, Canada, under the aegis of J. Cartier (1956).

Genush has exhibited paintings and prints in museums and galleries, including the "Third Biennial Exhibition of Canadian Art," National Gallery, Ottawa (1959); the "Fourth Biennial Exhibition of Canadian Art," National Gallery, Ottawa (1961); and others. She has shown "collagraphs" (collaged and cannibalized prints reprinted to form a new print), along with her other works. Examples of these works are in private and public permanent collections, including the National Gallery of Canada, Ottawa, Ontario.

Bibliography

Third Biennial Exhibition of Canadian Art. A Catalog. National Gallery of Canada, 1959.

Geoffrion, Moira Marti (1944–)

Both a sculptor and educator/administrator, Moira Geoffrion was born in Olney, Maryland; received her Bachelor of Fine Arts degree from Boston University, Massachusetts, in 1965; studied at Indiana University, Bloomington, and went on to Southern Illinois University at Edwardsville to finish a Master of Fine Arts degree in 1974.

Geoffrion has exhibited widely in the 1970s and 1980s. Her sculptures have appeared in more than seventy-five group shows, and one-person exhibitions have been held in many museums and galleries, including Gallery Route One, Point Reyes, California; Zaks Gallery, Chicago, Illinois; Pleiades Gallery, New York City; the University of Texas at Irving; Miami University, Florida; Ball State University, Muncie, Indiana; and Slippery Rock College, Pennsylvania. Her work is represented in a number of private and public collections, including collections of the South Bend Art Center, and the Indianapolis Museum of Art—both in Indiana; the Midwest Museum of American Art; the University of Dallas, Texas; the Snite Museum; and several corporate collections. She has received many public commissions for her sculpture and is represented by Zaks Gallery in Chicago, Illinois.

Geoffrion has won many grants and awards, among them a Mellon Foundation research grant, a National Endowment for the Arts (NEA) grant for visiting artists (1984–1985, 1988), an ICIP/Fulbright grant, and an Exxon distinguished scholars grant. A consultant and juror for a number of national sculpture venues, Geoffrion is also an educator; she taught at the University of Notre Dame in Indiana, and was most recently the department head and professor of art at the University of Arizona, Tucson. She has also lectured widely on sculpture and gender issues, coordinated workshops, and has been a visiting artist at a number of colleges and universities. Geoffrion has also contributed several catalog essays to national sculpture shows. Most recently she has served as the president (1991–1992) of the Mid-America College Art Association. She is also on the board of the National Council of Art Administrators.

Geoffrion's sculptural work often consists of linear structures made of cast polychromed bronze, sometimes with hand-made paper, wood, or vinyl fragments attached. Most of them are natural tree-like sculptures, which evoke a decaying or deformed sense of once-living materials. Light is also important to Geoffrion, and often the sculptures are specifically lit in order to create shadow-play on the spaces surrounding the sculptures. Geoffrion has also combined dance/performance elements in some of her recent work. Many of her sculptures and oil paintings are brilliantly colorful, reminding us of African or Indian color combinations, and she and her husband have lived in Africa and collect African art. Her sculptures are created and cast but appear strangely natural. As writer April Kingsley has observed, "the enigma of her enchanted forest is that nothing is ever quite as it seems."

Paul Ivey

Bibliography

Kingsley, April. "The Enigmatic Artistry of Moira Marti Geoffrion." Catalog essay in *Geoffrion: Stonewall IV.* Tucson Museum of Art, 1988.

Mahoney, Robert. *Arts Magazine* (December 1985).

Geoffrion. Exhibition Catalog. Art Gallery, University of Notre Dame, 1978.

Gershoy, Eugenie (1902–)

Born in Krivoi Rog, Russia, the sculptor Eugenie Gershoy studied at the Art Students League, New York City, under the direction of Alexander Calder, Kenneth Hayes Miller, and Boardman Robinson (1921–1922).

Gershoy has held solo exhibitions in galleries and museums throughout the United States, including the Baltimore Museum of Art, Maryland; Brooklyn Museum, New York; Dallas Museum of Art, Texas; Isaac Delgado Museum, New Orleans, Louisiana; Wichita Museum of Fine Arts, Kansas; and others. Her work has been included in many prestigious group shows, including the "Annuals" and "Biennials" offered by the Whitney Museum of American Art, New York City; "Sculpture Invitationals," Philadelphia Museum of Art, Pennsylvania (1940, 1952); "15 Young American Sculptors," a travelling show, Museum of Modern Art (MoMA), New York City (1942); the "Annuals" of the San Francisco Museum of Art, California (1948–1965); "Women Artists of America," Newark Museum, New Jersey (1964); and many others.

Gershoy is an inspirational teacher and winner of awards and honors. Her polychromed papier-mache sculptures enjoyed wide acceptance and were commissioned through the mid-1970s by a great variety of clients. Her work is represented in private and public permanent collections, including the Metropolitan Museum of Art, and Whitney Museum of American Art—both in New York City; the National Museum of Art, Smithsonian Institution, Washington, D.C.; San Francisco Museum of Art, California; Syracuse University, New York; and others.

Bibliography
Gerdts, William H. *Women Artists of America, 1707–1964.* The Newark Museum, 1965.
Goodrich, Lloyd, and John I.H. Baur. *American Art of Our Century.* Praeger, 1961.
Woodstock's Art Heritage: The Permanent Collection of the Woodstsock Artists Association. Overlook Press, 1987.

Gersovitz, Sarah (1920–)
Born in Montréal, Québec, Canada, the painter/printmaker Sarah Gersovitz studied at MacDonald College; took graduate work at Concordia University; the School of the Montréal Museum of Fine Arts; and the École des Arts Appliqués—all in Montréal.

Gersovitz has held solo exhibitions in galleries and museums in Canada and abroad, including the Montréal Museum of Fine Arts (1962, 1965); 1640 Gallery, Montréal (1964); Instituto Cultural Peruano, Lima, Peru (1973); St. Mary's University (1976); London Art Gallery (1981); and others. Her work has been included in many group shows, such as "Printmaker's Showcase," Carleton University, Ottawa (1973); the "Tenth Anniversary Exhibition," Galerie Pascal, Toronto (1973); Art Gallery of Ontario, a travelling show, Toronto (1974); "C.P.E.," a travelling exhibition, Commonwealth Centre, London, England, and Edinburgh, Scotland (1974); McGill University, Montréal (1974); Ontario Society of Artists, Toronto (1974); the International Biennial of Colored Graphics, Grenchen, Switzerland; "Primera Bienal del Grabado Americana," Maracaibo, Venezuela (1977); "15th International Bienal de São Paulo, Brazil (1979); "Biennale des Arts Graphiques," Brno, Czechoslovakia (1980); and many others.

Gersovitz has earned honors and purchase awards for her work. Examples of her prints and paintings are represented in private and public permanent collections, including the Art Gallery of Greater Victoria, British Columbia; the Library of Congress, Washington, D.C.; Museum of Contemporary Art, Montréal; National Gallery of Canada, Ottawa; National Gallery of Southern Australia; New York Public Library, New York City; the University of Waterloo, Ontario; and many others.

Bibliography
Balfour, Lisa. "Artist's Abstract Designs Printed on Old Proof Press." *Montréal Star* (December 17, 1964).
Robert, Guy. *L'Art au Québec depuis 1940.*

Gervais, Lise (1932–)
Born in Saint-Césaire, Québec, Canada, the painter/sculptor Lise Gervais studied painting under the aegis of Jacques de Tonnancour and Stanley Cosgrove, and sculpture under the direction of Louis Archambault at the École des Beaux-Arts, Montréal, Québec (1950–1954).

Winner of many prizes and honors, teacher for more than a decade at her alma mater and the University of Québec, Montréal, Gervais has held solo exhibitions in museums and galleries, including the Galerie Denyse Delrue, Montréal (1961–1963); Moos Gallery, Toronto (1962–1965); Galerie du Siècle, Montréal (1964, 1965, 1967); Galerie de Montréal, Québec (1970–1972); and many others.

Her work has been included in prestigious group shows in North America and Europe: from Montréal, Québec to Paris, France; from Philadelphia, Pennsylvania to Spoleto, Italy; from one end of Canada to the other.

Examples of her paintings and sculpture are housed in private and public permanent collections in Canada and abroad.

Bibliography
Henault, Gilles. "Lise Gervais." *Vie des arts* 42 (Spring 1966): 48–51.
O'Leary, Marie-France. "Lise Gervais à la Galerie de Montréal." *Vie des arts* 59 (Summer 1970): 60–61.

Getchell, Edith Loring Peirce (1855–1940)
Highly regarded for the exquisite tonal qualities in her etchings, drypoints, and watercolors, Edith Loring Peirce Getchell was a painter and etcher of landscapes of Holland and the United States. She was the daughter of Unitarians Joseph S. and Ann Moore Peirce, who in 1874 sent her to study at the Philadelphia School of Design for Women, Pennsylvania, with Peter Moran. Getchell returned to her home town of Bristol, Pennsylvania, in 1877 to work as a designer at Livingston Mills. In the early 1880s she studied in New York City with William Sartain and R. Swain Gifford. Getchell set up a studio in Philadelphia, Pennsylvania, in 1883 while she studied painting with Thomas Eakins at the Pennsylvania Academy in Philadelphia, and etching with Stephan Parrish in his studio. After her marriage to Albert C. Getchell, a graduate of Philadelphia's Jefferson Medical School, in 1886 she moved to Worcester, Massachusetts, where she established her studio and was a founder of the Worcester Museum of Art.

Getchell exhibited at the Philadelphia School of Design for Women, the Pennsylvania Academy, and the Philadelphia Society of Artists—all in Philadelphia, Pennsylvania; the National Academy of Design, the American Watercolor Society, and the New York Etching Club—all in New York City; the Paris Salon and Galerie Durand-Ruel—both in Paris, France; the Boston Museum of Fine Arts, the Boston Art Club, and the Twentieth Century Club—all in Boston, Massachusetts; the Royal Society of Painter-Etchers, London, England; the Chicago Society of Etchers, and Albert Roullier's Art Galleries—both in Chicago, Illinois; and the California Society of Etchers. The 1888 Ohio Valley Centennial, the 1893 World's Columbian, the 1904 Louisiana Purchase, and the 1915 Panama-Pacific International Expositions also included her paintings and etchings. Special exhibitions of her work were organized by the Williams and Everett Gallery, Boston, and the Worcester Art Museum—both in Massachusetts.

Selected several times for publication, her etchings were included in *Twenty Original American Etchings, Gems of the American Etchers,* and *American Women of the Etching Revival,* as well as in special exhibition catalogs.

Getchell was a member of the Philadelphia Society of Artists, and the Philadelphia Sketch Club—both in Pennsylvania; the New York Etching Club, New York City; and the Chicago and California Societies of Etchers.

Phyllis Peet

Bibliography
"Another Exhibition of Etchings by Peirce and Dillaye at Williams and Everett's Gallery on Boylston Street." *The Art Interchange* 32 (January 16, 1886): 16.
"Edith Loring Getchell [Obituary]." *The New York Times* (September 19, 1940): 23.
Peet, Phyllis. *American Women of the Etching Revival.* Atlanta: High Museum of Art, 1988, pp. 56–57.
Worcester Art Museum. *Exhibition of Etchings by Edith Loring Getchell, December 5 to December 14, Nineteen Hundred and Eight.* Worcester Art Museum, 1908.

Getz, Ilse (Bechold) (1917–1992)

Born in Nuremberg, Germany, Ilse (Bechold) Getz left Germany for the United States (1933) and studied with Morris Kantor and George Grosz at the Art Students League, New York City. She was best known for her paintings, collages, and assemblages.

Getz has held solo exhibitions at the Phoenix Museum of Art, Arizona (1964); Kostiner-Silvers Gallery, Montréal, Canada (1975); a retrospective show at the Neuberger Museum, Purchase, New York (1978); the Kunsthalle, Nuremberg, Germany (1978); Goethe Institute, New York City (1981); Alex Rosenberg Gallery, New York City (1981); and many others.

A Yaddo fellow at Saratoga Springs, New York, Getz designed the set for the 1960 production of Ionesco's *The Killer* at the Seven Arts Theater, New York City. (The backdrop to this set is in the permanent collection of Dartmouth College, Hanover, New Hampshire.) Her work is represented in private and public permanent collections, including the Aldrich Museum of Contemporary Art, Ridgefield, Connecticut; Carnegie Institute, Pittsburgh, Pennsylvania; Hirshhorn Museum and Sculpture Garden, Washington, D.C.; Kunsthalle, Nuremberg, Germany; Tel Aviv Museum, Israel; and others.

Bibliography
"Collages and Constructions by Ilse Getz." *Arts Magazine* (April 1980).
Who's Who in American Art. 19th ed. R.R. Bowker Co., 1991–1992.

Gibson, Cathy (1942–)

In 1987 Cathy Gibson's graduation from the University of Ottawa, *cum laude,* with a Bachelor of Fine Arts degree, was more important than the mere acquisition of the degree itself. As a craftsperson Gibson had earlier felt discriminated against by the visual arts community. Her earlier arts background—the arts program at University of British Columbia (1961–1963), and the Vancouver School of Art (1963–1964)—both in Vancouver, British Columbia, had encouraged her creative expression but had done little to develop her understanding of theory

and practice of an art scene dominated by male culture.

In her earlier work she expressed her frustrations by creating the myths of the female body, such as "Woman in Bed Eating Chocolate" (1981), as tiny creations of baked and lacquered bread dough. Her "Cow Pie" (1979) included in "Kids and Kows" at the Burnaby Art Gallery, British Columbia, and "Venus Reborn in a Kippers Can" (1979) rely on the irony of scale and the restrictive containment of the objects.

Gibson's first solo exhibition, "Marjorie" (1989) at the Ufundi Gallery, Ottawa, is "about the role of memory in human interactions"; it alludes to the ethical dilemma of euthanasia for the elderly when the quality of life no longer exists. Gibson created an installation of two chairs, a paper quilt, and a row of transparent silver photographs. One of the chairs, Marjorie's own, was painted and covered with photographic transfers of her life; the other was a geriatric chair under a harsh light with a list of intrusions on a clipboard. Gibson's feminist sensibilities have not changed; the practical applications have.

Victoria Henry

Bibliography
Baele, Nancy. "Art As Tribute." *Ottawa Citizen* (October 12, 1989).
Herbert, Walter. *Visual Arts Survey Exhibition #1.* Landsdowne Park, Ottawa, 1975.

Gikow, Ruth (1915–1982)

Russian-born, the painter/printmaker Ruth Gikow studied at the Cooper Union, New York City. A member of the United American Artists, Gikow held solo exhibitions at the Weyhe Gallery (1946), and the National Serigraph Gallery—both in New York City (1947), among others. She also exhibited work at Rockefeller Center in New York City and, earlier on, at the Golden Gate Exposition, San Francisco, California (1939).

Gikow illustrated *Crime and Punishment* (1946) and was a teacher at the American Artists School, Inc., New York City. Her work is represented in private and public permanent collections, including murals at Rockefeller Center, New York City, and for the Works Projects Administration (WPA); the Metropolitan Museum of Art, and the Museum of Modern Art (MoMA)—both in New York City; the Philadelphia Museum of Art, Pennsylvania; and others.

Bibliography
Gerdts, William. H. *Women Artists of America 1707–1964.* The Newark Museum, 1965.
"Ruth Gikow Dead: Painter of People." *The New York Times* (April 3, 1982).
Tannenbaum, Judith. "Ruth Gikow (Kennedy)." *Arts Magazine* 51:3 (November 1976): 17–18.

Gilbert, Helen (1922–)

Born in Mare Island, California, Helen Gilbert is known as an environmental artist who creates paintings, prints, and light structures. Gilbert earned a Bachelor's degree from Mills College, Oakland, California (1943); attended the Central School of Art, London, England (1960); received a Master of Fine Arts degree from the University of Hawaii, Honolulu (1968); and took post-graduate work at the University of California at Berkeley. She also studied printmaking at Pratt Graphics Center, New York City (1979), on a Ford Foundation grant.

Currently professor of art at the University of Hawaii, Gilbert has held solo exhibitions in museums and galleries in the United States and abroad, including the Karin Fesel Galerie, Düsseldorf, Germany (1990); Contemporary Art Museum, Honolulu, Hawaii (1983, 1989); Sande Webster Gallery, Philadelphia, Pennsylvania (1985, 1988, 1992); Northeastern University, Boston, Massachusetts (1986); Galerie Meissner Edition, Hamburg, Germany (1984); Galerie Maghi Bettini, Amsterdam, the Netherlands (1984); "Light and Paper Works: Helen Gilbert," Honolulu Academy of Art, Hawaii (1971, 1977); "Works on Paper Made in Paris," North American Cultural Center, Barcelona, Spain (1976); and others. Her work has been invited to myriad group exhibitions throughout the world: from Philadelphia, Pennsylvania to Cadaques, Spain; Paris, France; Wichita, Kansas; New York City; Kyoto and Tokyo—both in Japan; Varese, Italy; and Summit, New Jersey.

Gilbert has created environmental installations in Osaka, Japan; Philadelphia, Pennsylvania; and Honolulu, Hawaii, the most recent being "Island Light" (1992), the HonFed Building, Honolulu, Hawaii, a marble mural forty-five inches high by thirteen feet in length. She is a member of the American Abstract Artists Association and the National Arts Club—both in New York City; the Honolulu Printmakers Association and the Hawaii Artists League—both in Hawaii. Her work is represented in private, public, and corporate permanent collections, including the Museum of Modern Art (MoMA), Brooklyn Museum, and Guggenheim Museum—all in New York City; the Walker Art Center, Minneapolis, Minnesota; the British Museum, London, England; Bibliothèque Nationale, Paris, France; Honolulu Academy of Art, and the Contemporary Art Museum—both in Hawaii; the Museum Für Kunst Und Gewerbe and the Deutsche Bank, Hamburg—both in Germany; and others.

Bibliography
Presswork: The Art of Women Printmakers. Lang Communications, 1992.
Watson-Jones, Virginia. *Contemporary American Women Sculptors.* Oryx Press, 1986.
Who's Who in American Art. 19th ed. R.R. Bowker Co., 1991–1992.

Gilder, Helena De Kay (1848–1916)

The painter Helena De Kay Gilder initially studied with Winslow Homer and John La Farge before studying at the Cooper Union and the National Academy of Design—both in New York City. In 1871 Gilder and her friend, Maria R.O. Dewing, were the first women to take a life-drawing class at the National Academy of Design.

Gilder painted still lifes, portraits, and the figure and, with her husband, held a veritable salon of influential writers and artists, including Cecilia Beaux and others. She was a founding member of the Art Students League (1875), and the Society of American Artists (1877)—both in New York City, both of which were organized as alternatives to the academic training offered by the Academy and as opportunities for the study of art by women.

Bibliography
Beaux, Cecilia. *Background with Figures.* Houghton Mifflin, 1930.
Gilder, Rosamond. *Letters of Richard Watson Gilder.* Houghton Mifflin, 1916.

Low, Will H. *A Chronicle of Friendships 1873–1900.* Charles Scribner's Sons, 1908.
Nineteenth Century American Women Artists. Whitney, Downtown Branch, 1976.

Gillespie, Dorothy (1920–)

Born in Roanoke, Virginia, Dorothy Gillespie is known as a painter, sculptor, printmaker, curator, lecturer, and administrator. Gillespie received her education at various institutions, including the Maryland Institute College of Art, Baltimore; the Art Students League, and Atelier 17—both in New York City—with master printmaker Stanley William Hayter.

In addition to solo exhibitions held at the Museum of Contemporary Arts, Lima, Peru (1963), and at the Fenster Gallery, Frankfurt, Germany (1964), Gillespie held sixty-eight additional solo shows throughout the United States in galleries, museums, and universities between 1960 and 1991. Further, she created solo happenings and environments at the Champagne Gallery, New York City (1964, 1965) and other sites, and executed sculptural sets for the Cleveland Ballet, Ohio (1986).

Gillespie's work has been invited to myriad group exhibitions, including the Virginia Museum of Fine Art, Richmond (1963); Brooklyn Museum, New York (1976); Maryland Institute College of Art, Baltimore (1980); "Art in Fashion/Fashion in Art," a two-year travelling show to museums in Canada and the United States, Bernice Steinbaum Gallery, New York City (1987); "American Women Artists: The Twentieth Century," Knoxville Museum of Art, Tennessee, and Queensborough Commonwealth College, Bayside, New York (1990); "Children in Crisis," Lorence Monk Gallery, New York (1991); and others in Kenya and Iran.

Gillespie is the founder of the Women Artists Historical Archives of the Women's Interart Center, New School for Social Research, New York City (1973); as well as a Woodrow Wilson visiting fellow (1986–1991). She has won many honors and awards for her work, including a grant from the Alice Baber Art Fund, Inc., New York City (1990); two honorary Doctorate degrees (1976, 1990); and the Governor's Arkansas travelers award (1983). She was commissioned to create silk-screened posters and major public sculpture for a wide variety of corporate and other patrons, Gillespie has been a visiting artist and lecturer in colleges and universities throughout the United States.

Gillespie's work is in many private, public, and corporate permanent collections throughout the United States and abroad, such as Yale University, New Haven, Connecticut; Guggenheim Museum, Brooklyn Museum, and New York University—all in New York City; Newark Museum of Art, New Jersey; The Museum of Art, Fort Lauderdale, Florida; the State Collections of the cities of Kessel, Darmstadt, and Frankfurt—all in Germany; Institute of Contemporary Arts, Lima, Peru; Helena Rubenstein Pavilion, Tel Aviv, Israel; Corroon and Black, Washington, D.C.; and many others.

Bibliography
Dorothy Gillespie. A Catalog. Sarasota, Florida: Corbino Galleries, 1991.
First of May. A thirty-minute documentary film. Roanoke, Virginia: WBRA Public Television, 1984.
Martin, Richard. "Review." *Arts Magazine* (October 1986).
Shirey, David L. "Review." *The New York Times* (January 13, 1983).

Gilmour, Gina (1948–)

Born in Charlotte, North Carolina, the painter Gina Gilmour earned a Bachelor's degree from Sarah Lawrence College, Bronxville, New York (1972).

Gilmour has held many solo exhibitions in museums and galleries, including the Vanderwoude/Tananbaum Gallery, New York City (1984, 1986); Gibbes Museum, Charleston, South Carolina (1985); New Southern Paintings Gallery, Savannah, Georgia (1987, 1989); Brody's Gallery, Washington, D.C. (1988); Robert Cheek Fine Arts, Charlotte, North Carolina (1989); and others.

Gilmour's work has been invited to or included in group exhibitions, such as the "Southern Realism Travelling Exhibition," Mississippi Museum of Art, Jackson (1980); "Demons, Dreams and Madness," Alternative Museum (1983), "Nocturnes," Ruth Siegel Gallery (1983), and Kenkeleba Gallery—all in New York City (1985, 1986); "North Carolina Artists," Fayetteville Museum of Art, North Carolina (1986); "100 Women's Drawings," Long Island University, New York (1989); and others.

Winner of awards and honors, Gilmour received a MacDowell Colony fellowship, Peterborough, New Hampshire (1979); a Karolyl Memorial Foundation fellowship in Vence, France (1980–1981); a fellowship from the Virginia Center for the Creative Arts, Sweetbriar (1987); a grant from the Southeastern Center for Contemporary Art/National Endowment for the Arts (NEA) (1989); and others.

"Night Swimming" (1981–1983), a large oil on canvas, is part of the metaphoric "Waterfall Series," which grew out of her personal experiences in the south of France, yet the dream series which encompasses water, stones, and androgynous figures suggests far greater and more profound themes and variations on the human discourse with nature. Gilmour's work is represented in private and public permanent collections.

Bibliography
Nine from North Carolina: An Exhibition of Women Artists. North Carolina State Committee and the National Museum of Women in the Arts: 1989.

Gilpin, Laura (1891–1979)

Photographer Laura Gilpin was born in Colorado Springs, Colorado. Her cousin was photographer Henry Gilpin. She received her first camera, a Brownie, at the age of twelve and made her first Autochrome plate photograph at age nineteen. Gilpin attended the Clarence H. White School in 1916–1917 at the recommendation of family friend Gertrude Käsebier, studying with Clarence White and Max Webber. In 1918 she took a post-graduate class with Anton Bruehl on photogravure process. She had her first one-person exhibition in 1924. Between 1926 and 1930 she taught photography at the Chappell School of Art in Denver, Colorado. She was staff photographer in 1933 for the Central City Opera House Association in Colorado. Gilpin taught photography at Colorado Springs Fine Arts Center in 1940–1941.

Gilpin published *The Pikes Peak Region* (1926), *The Mesa Verde National Park* (1927), *The Pueblos: A Camera Chronicle* (1941), *Temples of Yucatan, a Camera Chronicle of Chichen Itzá* (1948), and *The Rio Grande: River of Destiny; An Interpretation of the River, the Land, and the People* (1947).

During World War II Gilpin worked in Kansas as a public relations photographer for Boeing Airplane Company. After the war she moved to New Mexico and started her lifelong project of documenting the life and environment of the Native Americans in the region. She not only made the photographs but also did the research and writing for *The Enduring Navaho*, published in 1968.

Gilpin is regarded as a master of the platinum printing process, hand-coating her own paper. In 1975 she received a Guggenheim fellowship to make platinum prints of the best of her life's work.

Laine Sutherland

Bibliography
Auer, Michel. *Photographers Encyclopedia International: 1839 to the Present*. Editions Camera Obscura, 1985.
Hill, Tom, and Tom Cooper. "Interview." *Camera* 55:11 (November 1976): 27, 35–37.
Mitchell, Margaretta K. *Recollections: Ten Women of Photography*. Viking Press, 1979.
Vestal, David. "Laura Gilpin: Photographer of the Southwest." *Popular Photography* 80 (February 1977): 100–05, 130–34.
Walsh, George, Colin Naylor, and Michael Held. *Contemporary Photographers*. St. Martin's Press, 1982.

Giorgi, Vita

Born in Italy, Vita Giorgi has been an active painter/printmaker in Mexico City, Mexico, since 1960. Her color etchings and tempera paintings, revealing a sort of sophisticated naiveté, have elicited praise from the art critics of her adopted city.

She has had a number of solo exhibitions of her intaglio work at the Galería Pecanins, Mexico City, and in other institutions throughout the Americas.

Giorgi is a member of the printmaking group, La Ciudadela, under the direction of master printmaker Guillermo Silva Santamaría.

Bibliography
The Texas Quarterly: Image of Mexico II. The University of Texas, Autumn 1969.

Girouard, Tina (1946–)

Born in De Quincy, Louisiana, the video and performance artist Tina Girouard earned a Bachelor of Fine Arts degree from the University of Southwestern Louisiana, Lafayette (1968).

She has given performances and solo exhibitions in museums and galleries in the United States and abroad, including "Juxtaposed, Contained, Revealed," The Kitchen, New York City (1974); "Swiss Self," Centre d'Art Contemporain, Geneva, Switzerland (1976); "Even Odd," Forum Stadtpark Museum, Graz, Austria (1979); "Remoat/Remote," De Vleeshal, Middelburg, the Netherlands (1982); "Vamonos," Museo Tamayo, Mexico City, Mexico (1983); "Tasting the Blaze," Austin Opera House, Texas (1985); and others.

Winner of honors and awards, Girouard received a Creative Artists Public Service (CAPS) grant (1973); grants from the National Endowment for the Arts (NEA) (1976, 1983); a grant from the Louisiana Department of the Arts (1984); and others. Her works are noted for their multi-faceted, stimulating levels of wonderment, and examples are to be found in permanent collections, including the Metropolitan

Museum of Art, New York City; Museo Tamayo, Mexico City, Mexico; the New Orleans Museum of Art, Louisiana; and others.

Bibliography

Lippard, Lucy R. "Gardens: Some Metaphors for a Public Art." *Art in America* 69 (November 1981): 136–50.

Russell, John. "Art: American Finds of a Great Collector." *The New York Times* (June 26, 1981).

Silverthorne, Jeanne. "Review: Alternatives in Retrospect." *Artforum* 21 (October 1982): 78–79.

Glatt, Linnea (1949–)

Born in Bismarck, North Dakota, the post-modern sculptor and installationist Linnea Glatt earned a Bachelor's degree from Moorhead State University, Minnesota (1971) and a Master of Arts degree from the University of Dallas, Irving, Texas (1927).

In addition to several major projects in which she has been engaged, Glatt has had recent work invited to several installations and travelling shows, such as "Circum-stance," Blue Star Art Space, San Antonio (1990); "A Century of Sculpture in Texas 1889–1989," a travelling show to the University of Texas at Austin, San Angelo Museum of Art, El Paso Museum of Art, and Amarillo Art Center (1989–1990)—all in Texas; "Third Coast Review: A Look at Art in Texas," a travelling show to Aspen Art Museum, Colorado, University of Colorado at Boulder, Powerplant Visual Arts Center, Fort Collins, Colorado, and Blue Star Art Space, San Antonio, Texas (1987–1988).

Winner of awards and honors for her sculpture and installations, Glatt is a former instructor on the art faculties of Richland College (1974–1984) and Southern Methodist University (1985–1988)—both in Dallas, Texas. Her work is represented in private and public permanent collections, including the Dallas Museum of Art, collection of the city of Dallas, and collection of the city of Houston—all in Texas; collection of the city of Phoenix, Arizona; and others. Her permanent site installations in Texas include "Harrow," Lubben Plaza, Dallas (1992); "Passage Inacheve," Buffalo Bayou, Houston (1990); "A Place to Perform," Bath House Cultural Center (1984); and "A Place to Gather," Richland College (1983)—both in Dallas.

Bibliography

Hickey, Dave. "Linnea Glatt and Patricia Tillman: Post-Modern Options." *Artspace* (Summer 1985): 28–31.

Freudenheim, Susan. "Glatt's Sculpted Sanctuaries." *Texas Homes* (June 1984): 22–25.

Mitchell, Charles Dee. "Linnea Glatt and Frances Merritt Thompson." *Artforum* (Summer 1991): 120.

Godwin, Judith Whitney (1930–)

Producing powerful, gestural, richly-colored and extremely large canvases for the past three-and-a-half decades, Judith Whitney Godwin has been a quintessentially abstract expressionist painter. Born in rural Suffolk, Virginia, Godwin started painting at the age of twelve. In 1948 she entered Mary Baldwin College, in Staunton, Virginia, later transferring to Virginia Commonwealth University, Richmond, from which she received her Bachelor of Fine Arts degree in 1953. That same year Godwin moved to New York City, where her work became more and more abstract, and more painterly. There she studied at the Art Students League with Will Barnett, Harry Sternberg, and Vaclav Vytlacil, and also with Hans Hoffmann, whose summer art school in Provincetown, Massachusetts, she attended. Godwin remained in New York City, then the headquarters for the abstract expressionist movement, and became close to many other members of this avant-garde group.

Godwin had her first one-person show in New York City in 1959. From then on she has had regular solo exhibitions—at the Ingber Gallery, New York City (1977, 1979, 1981–1982, 1984, 1990); Womensbank, Richmond, Virginia (1981); the Loonam Gallery, Bridgehampton, New York (1982); Phoenix II Gallery, Washington, D.C. (1983); Mukai Gallery, Tokyo, Japan; and the Lockwood-Matthews Mansion, Norwalk, Connecticut (1985). She has also had retrospective exhibitions at several institutions, including Northern Michigan University, Marquette; Virginia Polytechnic Institute, Blacksburg; and Northern Virginia Community College, Alexandria; and has participated in group exhibitions all across the United States.

The winner of several awards, Godwin received an honorary Doctorate degree (1989) from Virginia Commonwealth University. Examples of her work can be found in numerous private, corporate, and public collections, including the Chase Manhattan Collection, New York City; Cornell University, Ithaca, New York; the Metropolitan Museum of Art, New York City; the Milwaukee Art Center, Wisconsin; the National Museum of Art, Osaka, Japan; the National Museum of Wales, Cardiff; the Newark Museum, New Jersey; and Yale University, New Haven, Connecticut.

Bibliography

Cohen, Ronny. "Judith Godwin." *Art News* 84:2 (February 1985): 156.

Henry, Gerritt. "Judith Godwin (at Ingber)." *Art News* 79:3 (March 1980): 196.

Nadelman, Cynthia. "Judith Godwin." *Art News* 80:7 (September 1981): 242.

Godwin, Phyllis (1930–)

Born in Fir Ridge, Saskatchewan, the painter Phyllis Godwin earned a teaching certificate from the University of Saskatchewan, Saskatoon (1950); studied with Ken Lochead at an Emma Lake Summer Workshop (1951); studied with Illingworth Kerr at Southern Alberta Institute of Technology, where she received a diploma (1954); and did research and travel in Greece (1962–1963) and Ireland (1971–1972).

Godwin has held many solo exhibitions in museums and galleries throughout Canada: from Calgary, Alberta, to Toronto, Ontario; from Victoria, British Columbia, to Fredericton, New Brunswick. Her work has been included in major group exhibitions in Canada and abroad, including the London Art Gallery, Ontario (1965); Kenny's Gallery, Galway, Ireland (1972); "Phantasmagoria," Dunlop Art Gallery, Regina, Saskatchewan (1977); "Watercolor Painting in Saskatchewan 1905–1980," Mendel Art Gallery, Saskatoon (1980); and others.

Examples of Godwin's work are in private and public permanent collections, including the Alberta Art Foundation, Edmonton; Beaverbrook Art Gallery, Fredericton, New Brunswick; Norman Mackenzie Art Gallery, Regina, Saskatchewan; Shell Canada Ltd.; and others.

Bibliography

Burke, Lora. "The Godwins: Artists in Residence." *Artswest* 1:6 (1976): 21.

Christie, Robert. *Watercolor Painting in Saskatchewan 1905–1980.* A Catalog. Saskatoon: Mendel Art Gallery, 1980.

Gold, Betty (1935–)

Born in Austin, Texas, Betty Gold studied art history at the University of Texas, Austin (1955–1956). A decade later, she studied sculpture in the studios of Octavio Medellin and Ruth Tears (1966–1970)—both in Dallas, Texas.

Widely-travelled throughout the world, Gold has held more than fifty solo exhibitions in galleries and museums in the United States and abroad between 1971 and 1991, including the Beni Gallery, Kyoto, Japan, and the Expositum Galería de Arte, Mexico City (1991); Nishida Gallery, Nara, Japan (1989); Walker Hill Art Center, Seoul, Korea (1987); Purdue University, West Lafayette, Indiana (1986); Gallery 10, Aspen, Colorado (1984); University of Texas, Austin (1981); Phoenix Art Museum, Arizona (1979); Esther Robles Gallery, Los Angeles, California (1975); and many others.

Her major sculptural works—monumental permanent installations—are sited in venues from San Juan Cosala, Mexico, to the Bronx, New York; from Brea, California, to Biloxi, Mississippi; from Sayo, Japan, to Birmingham, Alabama, and Seoul, Korea. "M.H. Triptych I" (1990), a twelve-by-eighteen-foot, painted, welded steel sculpture at Florida Atlantic University, Boca Raton, is typical of Gold's recent work in that it plays monumental yellow forms against one another, redefining space.

Gold has been a professional sculptor for twenty-four years; her work is represented in private, public, and corporate permanent collections, including the Hawaii State Foundation of the Arts, Honolulu; Hofstra University, Hempstead, New York; Loyola-Marymount University, Los Angeles, California; Michigan State University, East Lansing; New York University, New York City; RCA Building, Chicago, Illinois; University of California at Irvine, Riverside, and Santa Barbara; Washington University, St. Louis, Missouri; and many others.

Bibliography
Ball, Maudette. "Angles and Curves in Steel." *Artweek* 11:30 (September 20, 1980): 5.
Brown, Betty Ann. "Harmonies of Duality." *Artweek* 15:7 (February 18, 1984): 5.
Watson-Jones, Virginia. *Contemporary American Women Sculptors*. Oryx Press, 1986.

Gold, Sharon (1949–)

Painter and performance/video artist, Sharon Cecile Gold was born in the Bronx, New York, and received her education at several New York schools, including Hunter College, City University of New York (1967–1968); Columbia University (1968–1970); and Pratt Institute (1974–1976), where she earned a Bachelor of Fine Arts degree.

Gold has held seventeen solo exhibitions between 1971 and 1991 throughout the United States and Switzerland, among which are the Stephen Rosenberg Gallery, New York City (1987, 1989, 1991)—the most recent of which included a video installation titled, "A Video Tape 1990–1991"; John Davis Gallery, Akron, Ohio (1986); Virginia Commonwealth University, Richmond (1982); San Francisco Art Institute, California (1981); Galerie Michael Storrer, Zurich, Switzerland (1981); O.K. Harris Gallery, New York City (1976, 1977); and others.

Gold's work has been invited to numerous group exhibitions across the United States and abroad, including "New Acquisitions," Everson Museum of Art, Syracuse, New York (1991); "The Image of Abstract Painting in the 80's," Brandeis University, Waltham, Massachusetts (1990); "Painting Beyond the Death of Painting," Kuznetsky Most Exhibition Hall, Moscow, USSR (1989); "Abstraction/Abstraction," a travelling show, Carnegie-Mellon University, Pittsburgh, Pennsylvania (1986); "Earsight: Sound and Image in the Contemporary Arts," Nexus Gallery, Philadelphia, Pennsylvania (1985); "Multiples," Jack Tilton Gallery, New York City (1983); "Donne in Arte—Viaggio a New York," a travelling show, Galleria Arco d'Alibert, Rome, Italy (1981); and many others.

Lecturer, visiting artist, guest critic, visiting professor at scores of colleges and universities in the United States, Gold has been a permanent member of the faculty at Syracuse University since 1986; she has been the recipient of honors and awards, including fellowships at the MacDowell Colony, Peterborough, New Hampshire (1972), Pratt Institute, New York City (1974–1976), a grant from the National Endowment for the Arts (NEA) (1981); and an award in painting from the Penny McCall foundation (1988). Her work is represented in many private, public, and corporate permanent collections, such as the Everson Museum of Art, Syracuse; Chemical Bank; and Chase Manhattan Bank—all in New York; Rose Art Museum, Brandeis University, Waltham, Massachusetts; Prudential Insurance Company of America, New Jersey; and others.

Bibliography
Gold, Sharon. "Essay." *M/E/A/N/I/N/G* #5 (May 1989).
Masheck, Joseph. "Sharon Gold." *Arts Magazine* (October 1987).
Stoops, Susan. A Catalog. "Ardent Abstraction in a Decade of Doubt." *The Image of Abstraction in the 80's*. Brandeis University, 1990.
Westfall, Stephen. "Review." *Art in America* (January 1988).

Golden, Judith (1934–)

As a photographer Judith Golden is known for her unique, and often humorous self-portraits. Born on November 29, 1934, in Chicago, Illinois, Golden studied painting and printmaking at Indiana University in Bloomington and Washington University in St. Louis, Missouri, where she remained until her marriage to David Golden in 1955—a union that lasted thirteen years. After the births of two children her interests turned rapidly toward photography. In 1973 Golden received her Bachelor of Fine Arts degree in printmaking and photography from the School of the Art Institute of Chicago, Illinois, while studying under Paul Welghardt. Continuing her education, Golden attended the University of California at Davis, where she completed her Master of Fine Arts Degree in 1975. While at Davis Golden received the Chancellor's Graduate Fellowship. Since 1981 she is currently an associate professor at the University of California at Davis, and the California College of Arts and Crafts in Oakland, as well as the University of California at Los Angeles (UCLA).

Golden has participated in a variety of group and individual exhibitions in the United States, British Columbia, and West Germany since 1977. Retrospectives of her work were held at the Tucson Museum of Art, Arizona (1987) and at the Museum of Photographic Arts in San Diego, California (1986). Golden has produced a large body of work, which can be found in numerous collections, including the Museum of Modern Art (MoMA) in New York City; the San Francisco Museum of Modern Art, California; the Center for Creative Photography at the University of Arizona, Tucson; and the George Eastman House in Rochester, New York. Golden has been recognized for her photographic work by such awards as a National Endowment for the Arts (NEA) grant in 1979 and an Arizona Foundation grant in 1984.

Melissa J. Guenther

Bibliography

Browne, Turner, and Elaine Partnow. *Macmillan Biographical Encyclopedia of Photographic Artists and Innovators.* Macmillan and Collier Macmillan, 1983.

Goldstein, Yvette. "Myths and Masquerades." *Women Image Now: Arizona Women in Art.* Vol. 3. 1986–1987, pp. 13–15.

Walsh, George, Colinen Naylor, and Michael Held, eds. *Contemporary Photographers.* St. Martin's Press, 1982.

Goldin, Nan (1953–)

Nan Goldin's work references one of the most traditional of photographic conventions, that of the family picture album. It is the public nature of her examination of the traditionally private issues of gender, power, and dependency within this framework that has made her images controversial. Her style evokes the documentary quality of casual snapshots. She works in the tradition of Garry Winogrand, Lisette Model, Larry Clark, and Diane Arbus.

Goldin started to take photographs in 1972 when she was eighteen years old. She had her first exhibition in 1973. "The Ballad of Sexual Dependency," one of the first works to receive critical attention, consisted of a large number of 35-mm. color slides which were continually re-edited and projected accompanied by a musical soundtrack. This piece was exhibited internationally in a number of galleries and museums, including the Whitney Biennial at the Whitney Museum of American Art, New York City (1985), the Walker Arts Center, Minneapolis, Minnesota (1986), the Stedelijk Museum, Amsterdam (1987), and the Centro Reina Sofia, Madrid, Spain (1987). Excerpts from this body of work, which represented over a decade of her professional life, were published in a book in 1986. In 1990 she turned her attention to subjects of mixed gender, photographing transsexuals in New York, Europe, and Asia. Examples of these images were exhibited in Berlin, Germany (1992) and in the Whitney Biennial at the Whitney Museum of American Art, New York City (1993), where Goldin covered a large wall with twenty-two color prints. Selections from this work are included in the book *The Other Side* (1993).

Allison P. Bertrand

Bibliography

Armstrong, David, and Walter Keller, eds. *The Other Side.* Introduction by Nan Goldin. 1993, pp. 5–8.

The Ballad of Sexual Dependency. Introduction by Nan Goldin. 1986, pp. 6–9.

Kozloff, Max. "The Family of Nan." *Art in America* 75:11 (November 1987): 38–43.

Goldthwaite, Anne (1869–1944)

Anne Goldthwaite was a portrait and landscape painter in oil and watercolor, specializing in Fauvist-influenced landscapes and narrative scenes of Alabama. She was also well known for her etchings, dry-points, and lithographs. Goldthwaite was born in Montgomery, Alabama, to Lucy Armistead, a homemaker, and Confederate army captain Richard Goldthwaite, who moved the family to Dallas, Texas, after the Civil War. An aunt who raised her after the death of her parents observed her talent for drawing and sent her to New York City in 1893 to study art.

Goldthwaite studied first with Henry McBride, then with Walter Shirlaw from 1898 to 1904. She learned to etch from Charles Frederick William Mielatz after 1904 at the National Academy of Design, New York City, where she also studied with Francis Coates Jones. In 1906 she went to Paris, France, where she frequently was a guest of Gertrude Stein and made friends with many avant garde artists. With friends she helped form a group called the Académie Moderne. Members worked together and received criticism from David Rosen, Charles Guérin, Albert Marquet, and Émile-Othon Friesz. In 1913 World War I forced her to return to New York City, where she immediately opened a studio.

While still in Paris, France, living at the American Girls' Club, Goldthwaite joined the National Society of Women Painters and Sculptors and sent work to exhibit with them as well as at the National Academy of Design—both in New York City. She also sent work for exhibition in the 1913 Armory Show.

Goldthwaite taught at the Art Students League in New York City for twenty-three years, beginning in 1922. In the mid-1930s she received a Works Projects Administration (WPA) commission to paint murals in the Atmore and Tuskegee post office buildings—both in Alabama. Prizes she won included the McMillan prize for her 1915 entry in the National Association of Women Painters and Sculptors exhibition, New York City, and a bronze medal for etching in the 1915 Panama Pacific Exposition, San Francisco, California.

She exhibited with the National Academy of Design, the New York Society of Women Artists, the American Society of Painters, Sculptors and Gravers, the American Printmakers, the Society of American Etchers, and the Society of Painters of New York—all in New York City; the Philadelphia Society of Etchers, Pennsylvania; the Printmakers Society of California, Los Angeles; the Portland Art Association, Oregon; and in the 1939 New York World's Fair. Museums that showed her work include the Corcoran Gallery of Art, Washington, D.C.; the Syracuse Museum of Fine Arts, New York; the Metropolitan Museum of Art, New York City; and the Montgomery Museum of Fine Arts, Alabama. Important galleries that showed her work include the Downtown Gallery, the Milch Galleries, the Georgette Passedoit Gallery, the Brummer Galleries, and M. Knoedler and Company—all in New York City; and Goodspeed's of Boston, Massachusetts.

Goldthwaite's work was collected during her lifetime by the Bibliothèque Nationale and the Museum of rue Spontini—both in Paris, France; Art Institute of Chicago, Illinois; New York Public Library, Museum of Modern Art (MoMA), the Whitney Museum of American Art, the Metropolitan Museum of Art, and the Brooklyn Museum of Art—all in New York City; Phillips Memorial Gallery, and the Library of Congress—both in Washington, D.C.; Rhode Island School of Design, Providence; Carnegie Institute, Pittsburgh, Pennsylvania; the Baltimore Museum of Art, Maryland; the Cleveland Museum of Art, Ohio; and the Delgado Museum, New Orleans, Louisiana.

Phyllis Peet

Bibliography
"A Modern Painter with a Strong Sense of Style." *The New York Times Magazine* (October 24, 1915): 21–22.
Anne Goldthwaite, 1869–1944. Montgomery Museum of Fine Arts, 1977.
Breeskin, Adelyn Dohme. *Anne Goldthwaite: A Catalogue Raisonné of the Graphic Work*. Montgomery Museum of Fine Arts, 1982.
Defries, A.D. "Anne Goldthwaite as a Portrait Painter." *The International Studio* 59 (July 1916): 3–8.
Memorial Exhibition: Anne Goldthwaite. M. Knoedler and Company, 1944.

Gómez, Andrea (1926–)

Born in Mexico City, Mexico, the printmaker Andrea Gómez was encouraged by her grandmother, Dona Juana B. Gutierrez—a noted revolutionary—to engage in art activities throughout her childhood.

After her schooling in Mexico City, Mexico, Gómez turned to commercial art. She worked in several studios and, in 1950, became a member of the Taller de Gráfica Popular, where Leopoldo Méndez, Pablo O'Higgins, and Alberto Beltrán introduced her to the several techniques of printmaking.

Gómez, who exhibited with the Taller de Gráfica Popular, worked in the Instituto Nacional Indigenista, Mexico City, Mexico, and occasionally in the Centro Coordinador Tzeltal-Tzotzil (the Institute for Indian Language and Culture), San Cristobal de las Casa, Chiapas.

Gómez, who is married to Alberto Beltran, has illustrated many books with her incisive prints.

Bibliography
Biografico Enciclopedia Diccionario de la Pintura Mexicana: Siglo Arte Contemporaneo. Quinientos Anos Editores, 1979.

González Amezcua, Consuelo (1903–1975)

Born in Villa Acuña, Mexico, the self-taught artist/poet Consuelo Gonzáles Amezcua ("Chelo") was raised in Del Rio, Texas. She drew works of fantasy, religion, and other images with a ball-point pen, creating complex, "filagree" compositions.

González was given a solo exhibition at the Marian Koogler McNay Art Institute, San Antonio, Texas (1968); this show led to many others in the early 1970s in Dallas, Texas; Monterrey, Mexico; New York City; Springfield, Massachusetts; and others.

Bibliography
Meier, Matt S. *Mexican American Biographies: A Historical Dictionary, 1836–1987*. Greenwood Press, 1988.
Quirarte, Jacinto. *Quetzal* 1:2 (Winter 1970–1971).
The Latin American Spirit: Art and Artists in the United States, 1920–1970. Harry N. Abrams, 1988.

González, Esther (1936–)

Painter/printmaker Esther González was born in Tampico, Tamaulipas, and resides at present in Monterrey and Mexico City; in both Mexican cities she has a studio-home that she shares with her husband, Guillermo Ceniceros, also a painter, whom she married in 1973.

After creating her early lithographic works on stone and plates, González began to experiment by making prints on acrylic plates with a special acrylic paste. Unable to find a paper that met her needs, she researched and studied the techniques and processes of hand-made paper and, in 1978, produced her own, which she used as a means to create pictorial works in relief over a foundation of the same material. She obtained results not unlike those of intaglio prints, providing a certain new life to her work.

González's figurative approach is inspired by fossils, which she interprets and outlines through a display of textures and contrasts of dark and light (chiaroscuro). In her oils and, very frequently, in her lithographs, she takes her subjects from the Byzantine "Madonna" and from German and Flemish portraits such as those of Jan van Eyck, Hans Memling, Jan Vermeer, Petrus Christus, Lucas Cranach, and from the Italians: Giovanni Bellini, Raphael, and Leonardo da Vinci.

These portraits are reinterpreted by changing certain details, adding an abstract background, modifying secondary details, giving them a modern touch of texture, color, and simplifying the design.

González has participated in more than ninety exhibitions in Mexico, the United States, and Europe, including the 9th International Printmaking Biennial, Ljubljiana, Yugoslavia (1971); the 4th and 5th International Printmaking Biennials in Krakow, Poland (1972; 1974); the International Printmaking Show in Spoleto, Italy (1973); the First International Engraving Biennial in Puerto Rico (1974); the Contemporary Mexican Plastics Exhibition in Rotterdam, Holland (1976); the Museum of Mexican Art, San Francisco, California (1976); and the 4th Triennial in New Delhi, India (1978). Further, she participated in exhibitions in Miami, Florida; Washington, D.C.; and Harvard University, Cambridge, Massachusetts.

González is a member of the International Association of Plastic Arts (AIAP/UNESCO) in Paris, France. Among other distinctions González received first prize at the Salón de la Plástica Mexicana, Mexico City, Mexico (1971), for her print, "Moon Wall"; first prize in painting for "Echo of the Earthquake" (1985); and first prize in drawing for "The Three Sisters" (1987), also in the Salón de la Plástica Mexicana.

Giancarlo Malvaioli von Nacher

Bibliography
Alvarez, José Rogelio, et al. *Enciclopedia de México*. Secretaría de Educación Pública, 1987.
Fuentes, Arturo, and Alfredo de Neuvillate. *Ecos del Pasado, Esther González*. Galería Universitaria Aristos—Universidad Nacional Autónoma de México, 1990.

González, Patricia (1958–)

Born in Cartagena, Colombia, Patricia González was eighteen when she attended the Central School of Art and Design in London, England, where she completed the foundation course. Transferring to the Wimbledon School of Arts, England, she received her Bachelor of Fine Arts degree in painting and printmaking in 1980. González also studied printmaking at the Glassell School of Art in Houston, Texas, during the 1982–1983 academic year. Not until she discovered the films of Satjayit Ray and Frida Kahlo's painting, however, did she find her direction: "They pointed toward a place where the personal becomes the universal."

González has had annual solo exhibitions at the Graham Gallery (1984–1987) and in "Perspectives" at the Contemporary Arts Museum

(1989)—both in Houston, Texas. She has also been invited to show her work at the Corcoran Gallery of Art, Washington, D.C. (1987, 1988); the Los Angeles County Museum of Art, California (1989); the Brooklyn Museum, New York (1989); and at Rice University, Houston, Texas (1990); among many others. A prize winner for her paintings, González won the Anne Giles Kimbrough Fund, Dallas Museum of Art Award, Texas (1985); and was awarded a National Endowment for the Arts (NEA) grant (1987).

Bibliography

Beardsley, John, and Jane Livingston. *Hispanic Art in the U.S.* Abbeville Press, 1987.

Brown, Betty Ann, and Arlene Raven. *Exposures: Women and Their Art.* NewSage Press, 1989.

The 1985 Show, "Self Images. Women's Caucus for Art, 1985.

Who's Who in American Art. 19th ed. R.R. Bowker Co., 1991–1992.

Goodacre, Glenna (1939–)

Sculptor/painter Glenna Goodacre was born and raised in Lubbock, Texas, and attended Colorado College, Colorado Springs, from which she graduated in 1961. She studied portraiture with Frank Gervasi in 1965–1966 and at the Art Students League, New York City, in 1967. Goodacre exhibited figurative oil paintings regionally, but her primary interest shifted to sculpture when she visited a foundry in 1970.

In 1974 Goodacre was awarded the Allied Artists of America prize for sculpture in that organization's annual exhibition in New York City. Since that date she has been awarded medals for figurative bronze sculptures: a gold medal by the National Academy of Design (1978), and the Therese and Edward H. Richard memorial prize by the National Sculpture Society (1981)—both in New York City; an award of merit by the National Academy of Western Art, Oklahoma City, Oklahoma (1982); the Joyce and Eliot Liskin award by the Pen and Brush Club (1983), and the Excalibur bronze works award by the Catherine Lorillard Wolfe Art Club, National Academy of Design (1985)—both in New York City; plus numerous other awards.

In addition to creative pieces Goodacre also fulfills commissions for large-scale and life-size bronze portraits—corporate, public, and private. She has sculpted portraits of former Texas governor Preston Smith for Texas Technical College, Lubbock (1986), and monuments to Dwight D. Eisenhower, Barbara Jordan, Kathryn Anne Porter, and Scott Joplin for Sea World of Texas, San Antonio (1987)—both in Texas; and philanthropist Robert P. Holding, Jr., for Ravencroft School, Raleigh, North Carolina (1988).

Goodacre and painter Eric Sloane held three two-person shows: two at Fenn Galleries, Santa Fe, New Mexico (1980, 1984), and one at Gilcrease Museum, Tulsa, Oklahoma (1982). Fenn Galleries presented a show by Goodacre and landscape painter Wilson Hurley in 1989.

Sculptures by Goodacre are in the permanent collections of the Colorado Springs Fine Arts Center; Denver Art Museum; and Denver Museum of National History—all in Colorado; Thomas Gilcrease Museum, Tulsa; National Cowboy Hall of Fame, Oklahoma City; and Western Heritage Center, Oklahoma City—all in Oklahoma; the U.S. Agency for International Development (US AID), Washington, D.C.; and banks, corporations, educational institutions, and branches of government throughout the United States.

Goodacre moved to Santa Fe, New Mexico, in 1983 and is a member of the National Academy of Western Art, Oklahoma City; the Catherine Lorillard Wolfe Art Club, National Academy of Design; the National Sculpture Society, of which she is a fellow; and Allied Artists of America—all in New York City.

Barbara Kramer

Bibliography

Deats, Suzanne. "Grace and Fluidity." *Focus Santa Fe* (November–December 1989): 41–47.

Kramer, Barbara. "Glenna Goodacre: Lyric Expressions." *Southwest Art* 13:12 (May 1984): 86–92.

Luce, Ralph. "Artist Glenna Goodacre." *The Santa Fean* 18:1 (January 1990): 8–10.

Samuels, Harold, and Peggy Samuels. *Contemporary Western Artists.* Southwest Art Publishing, 1983.

Goodman, Eileen (1937–)

Born in Atlantic City, New Jersey, Eileen Goodman is a painter known primarily for her still lifes in oil and watercolor, although since the mid-1980s she has been working exclusively in watercolor. Goodman's paintings are characterized by a strong moody palette, boldly authoritative drawing, and a highly personal point of view. She is a highly respected member of the Philadelphia, Pennsylvania art world—an individualistic artist who has established a sense of her artistic world and has imbued it with dignity and force.

Goodman's professional life has taken place in and around Philadelphia, Pennsylvania. She went to the Philadelphia College of Art, Pennsylvania (now the University of the Arts) and received a Bachelor of Fine Arts degree in 1958. She has also taught at that institution since 1967 and in the late 1980s taught at the Philadelphia Community College and the Abington Art Center—both in Pennsylvania.

Goodman has had one-person shows at various locations, including Swarthmore College, Pennsylvania; Hollins College, Virginia; and Hinkley and Brohel, Washington, D.C. She has participated in numerous group shows in Pennsylvania and New York City. She is now represented by the Locks Gallery in Philadelphia, Pennsylvania.

Goodman has received several awards, including a purchase award from Beaver College, Glenside (1978); the Greater Harrisburg Arts Festival painting prize (1988); and a venture fund award from the Philadelphia College of Art (1985)—all in Pennsylvania.

Larry Day

Bibliography

Le Clair, Charles. *The Art of Watercolor/Techniques and New Directions.* Prentice-Hall, 1985.

Scott, William P. *Contemporary Women Artists.* Engagement and Address Book. Bo-Tree Productions, 1987.

———. *American Artist.* January 1982.

Zaferatos, Olga. *Painting the Still Life.* Watson-Guptill, 1985.

Goodman, Janis (1951–)

Janis Goodman's art combines the old and the new in strange and wonderful ways. For the past decade she has been producing large (five-by-five-foot) paintings, on gessoed wooden panels, which combine sensitively-rendered black-and-white drawings in graphite pencil with colorful and often iconographically-rich egg-tempera designs. Critics typically compare Goodman's recent works with medieval illuminated manuscripts and, indeed, there are similarities—for example, in the playfulness with which a *trompe-l'oeil* strand of ivy crawls across a painted border, or the care with which the artist paints the most minute details. At the same time, however, Goodman's pictures are thoroughly modern. Her off-center archways, through which worried figures can be seen interacting with a series of props (most often mysterious, battered leather valises), could only have been created at the end of the present century.

A New York City native, Goodman was educated at Queens College of the City University of New York (CUNY), from which she received her Bachelor of Arts degree in 1972. She did further study at the Corcoran School of Art in Washington, D.C. (1973–1974), followed by a brief stint at the Etruscan Foundation in Siena, Italy. One year later in Washington, D.C., Goodman completed her Master of Fine Arts degree at the George Washington University, and was a co-founder of the Washington Women's Art Center.

Since 1980 Goodman's art has appeared in many group exhibitions, held in a dozen states, plus London, England, and Moscow, Russia. Her first one-person exhibition was at the Hodson Art Gallery of Hood College, Frederick, Maryland (1975); subsequent solo shows occurred at the Woodbury Forest School's Walker Art Center, Orange (1976), and George Mason University's Renwick Art Gallery, Fairfax (1979)—both in Virginia; the Georgetown Art Gallery (1981), Catholic University (1982), and the Hom Gallery (1983)—all in Washington, D.C.; the Forum Gallery, New York City (1984); the Reynolds/Minor Gallery, Richmond, Virginia (1988); the Jane Haslem Gallery, Washington, D.C. (1988, 1989, 1993); the Steven Scott Gallery, Baltimore, Maryland (1990); Marymount University's Barry Gallery, Arlington, Virginia (1990); and the Deer Isle Artists Association, Maine (1993).

Goodman has had extensive teaching experience—at Northern Virginia Community College, Annandale (1976–1980); American University, Washington, D.C. (1981); Montgomery College, Rockville, Maryland (1981–1993); Trinity College, Washington, D.C. (1981–1983); Hofstra University, Hempstead, New York (1984); and Parsons School of Design, New York City (1985–1986). Since 1982 she has also been on the faculty of the Corcoran School of Art, Washington, D.C.

Goodman has received numerous awards, including two grants from the Commission on the Arts, Washington, D.C. (1981, 1990); an artist's book grant from the Writers Center, Glen Echo, Maryland (1982); and the Montpelier cultural award in the Maryland drawing competition (1983). Her work is in many private and public collections, among them the Hirshhorn Museum and Sculpture Garden, Washington, D.C.; the University of Virginia, Charlottesville; the Knoxville Museum of Art, Tennessee; the Tera Collection, Chicago, Illinois; and Shearson Lehman, Bethesda, Maryland.

Bibliography

Allen, Jane Adams. "A Giant Step Forward for Washington Artist." *The Washington Times* (June 16, 1983): B1, B3.

North, Percy. "Janis Goodman: The Content of History." *Washington Review*: 19:1 (June–July 1993): 17.

Goodwin, Betty (1923–)

Betty Goodwin was born and raised in Montréal, Canada. Well known for her large figure drawings, she has also worked in etching, collage, assemblage, sculpture, and installation. She worked quietly for many years and began exhibiting figure drawings, street scenes, and still lifes in 1955. She studied etching in 1968 and 1969 at Sir George Williams University (now Concordia University, Montréal) and worked with color field painter Yves Gaucher. She produced a series of etchings of gloves, vests, shirts, and hats. Her "Vest" series—the subject of her 1972 solo show at Galerie B, Montréal—was produced by taking impressions of vests on copper plates. These prints brought her national and international recognition. From 1974 to 1976 she investigated pictorial surfaces in the "Tarpaulin" series, introduced again at Galerie B.

The work from 1977 to 1983, more abstract and geometric, investigated the theme of passage. In the 1977 Clark Street project entitled "Four Columns to Support a Room," she installed large sheets of treated paper to redefine an interior space of an unoccupied warehouse. She transformed the surfaces and volumes of a Montréal flat in the "Mentana Street Project" (1979). In the same year Goodwin created "An Altered Point of View" at P.S.1 in New York City, where an empty room was viewed from the top of a ladder set up in a corridor. She presented "Passage in a Red Field," a long narrow corridor bounded by two thick walls covered with pigment, at the National Gallery of Canada, Ottawa, in the 1980 exhibition "Plurality." She was invited to participate in the 1982–1983 exhibition "OKanada" at the Akademie der Künste in Berlin, Germany. Here the megaphone and the bridge, as symbols of communication, were integrated as sculptural elements in the installation "In Berlin, A Triptych: The Beginning of the Fourth Part." As well she introduced large superimposed drawings of figures on transparent paper in this exhibition.

In 1982 Goodwin began her "Swimmer" series—large drawings in which she combined oil, oil pastels, charcoal, and graphite, working first on vellum and later on Transpagra and Geofilm. Using media images and photographs of people as a point of departure, she gradually erased the identifiable physiognomic characteristics, resulting in a figure floating in an aquatic environment. Goodwin's "Moving Toward Fire" (1985)—a large figure drawing in oil pastels and acrylics executed directly on a seven-meter wall for the Centre International d'Art Contemporain de Montréal's "Aurora Borealis"—combined both her earlier spatial concerns and her more recent investigation of the solitary figure. In 1986 she was the recipient of the Paul-Émile Borduas award for visual arts from the Province of Québec's Ministry of Cultural Affairs.

In 1987 the Montréal Museum of Fine Arts organized a large survey of Goodwin's work which travelled to Toronto's Art Gallery of Ontario and the Vancouver Art Gallery, British Columbia. This tour included an installation at the New Museum of Contemporary Art and work from 1984 to 1987 at the 49th Parallel, Centre for Contemporary Canadian Art—both in New York City.

In 1989 Goodwin was chosen as Canada's representative at the XX São Paolo International Biennial, Brazil. Densely rendered figures interacted with each other in the large mural "Carbon," where she worked with charcoal powder rubbed into wax and with oil and oil pastel on large sheets of galvanized aluminum. She also presented a series of small wall sculptures entitled "Steel Notes," which included objects squeezed between magnets on a steel plate on which a short quote was inscribed. The Künst Museum in Bern, Switzerland, organized a one-person show of Goodwin's work in 1989.

In 1991 Goodwin was selected to create a permanent installation entitled "Triptych" for the Montréal Museum of Fine Arts' new wing. The work includes a quote from Carolyn Forche, "How long does it take for one voice to reach another?," which she had used as the title of a 1985 drawing. The commission included a large copper ear and its reflection on an opposing wall installed high above the inscription. Goodwin's work is found in many Canadian public and private collections, and she has been the recipient of many grants and prizes. Goodwin lives and works in Montréal, where she is represented by Galerie René Blouin and in Toronto by the Sable-Castelli Gallery.

Cyril Reade

Bibliography

Bogardi, Georges. *Betty Goodwin, Passages.* Concordia Art Gallery, Concordia University, 1986.

Ferguson, Bruce. "Rue Mentana, Betty Goodwin and Marcel Lemyre." *Parachute* 20 (Autumn 1980): 28–33.

Gosselin, Claude, Norman Thériault, and René Blouin. *Aurora Borealis*, Centre international d'art contemporain de Montréal, 1985.

Morin, France. *Steel Notes, Betty Goodwin.* National Gallery of Canada, 1989.

Parent, Alain. *Betty Goodwin.* Musée d'art contemporain, 1976.

Pontbriand, Chantal. "Betty Goodwin." *Pluralities/1980/Pluralités*, National Gallery of Canada, 1980.

Racine, Yolande. *Betty Goodwin, Works from 1971 to 1987.* The Montréal Museum of Fine Arts, 1987.

Théberge, Pierre. "Betty Goodwin in Berlin." *OKanada.* Akademie der Künste, 1982.

Gordon, Bonnie (1941–)

A native of New York State, the photographer Bonnie Gordon earned a Bachelor of Fine Arts degree in illustration from Syracuse University, New York (1962), and, eight years later, received a Master of Fine Arts in printmaking from the Rochester Institute of Technology, New York.

Winner of awards and honors, Gordon received Creative Artists Public Service (CAPS) grants from the New York State Council on the Arts (1975, 1978); a National Endowment for the Arts (NEA) grant (1977); and others. She has been a designer/illustrator in Rochester and Syracuse (1967–1969)—both in New York, and has taught on the faculty of the State University of New York (SUNY) at Buffalo since 1970.

Representative examples of Gordon's work are in private and public permanent collections, including Colgate University, Hamilton; Syracuse University; and Rochester Institute of Technology—all in New York; and others.

Bibliography

Browne, Turner, and Elaine Partnow. *Macmillan Biographical Encyclopedia of Photographic Artists and Innovators.* Macmillan, 1983.

Gordon, Hortense (Mattice) (1887–1961)

Hortense (Mattice) Gordon was born in Hamilton, Ontario, Canada. She showed an interest in art at an early age, and as a child attended classes at the Hamilton Art School. In 1903 she left home to set up her own studio and teach art part-time in Chatham, Ontario. Returning to Hamilton in 1916 Gordon continued to teach art and design at her former school (renamed the Hamilton Technical Institute in 1923) until 1951. A dedicated educator, Gordon was also the instructor for a unique art teachers' course at the Institute, and in 1928 she (along with husband John Gordon) organized an exhibition of fine and applied art by Institute students for the Canadian section of the 6th International Congress for Art Education in Prague, Czechoslovakia. Gordon was also a member of the Hamilton branch of the Women's Art Association of Canada and a charter member of that city's Contemporary Artists group.

Her earliest work included painted china, and she continued to work in this medium into the 1930s. Her oils, watercolors, and sketches of this period vary stylistically from impressionism and post-impressionism to works influenced by the Group of Seven. Summers from 1920 until the early 1930s were spent in Europe, and Gordon's many landscapes from these years reflect locations in France and the British Isles, as well as in areas of Ontario, Québec, and the New England states. During the 1940s her painting became increasingly abstract, influenced by sessions at Hans Hofmann's summer school, Provincetown, Massachusetts. By the time Gordon joined the Toronto-based abstract group Painters Eleven in 1953, her work was almost completely abstract, reflecting Hofmann's theories of composition. It is for these later paintings, such as "Orange and Yellows, Bound in Space" (1952) and "Composition Red and Gold" (1956), that she is perhaps best known.

A regular exhibitor with the Ontario Society of Artists, the Art Association of Montréal, and the Royal Canadian Academy of Arts from the 1920s, Gordon was made an associate of the latter institution in 1930. She also exhibited with the Canadian Society of Painters in Water Colour and was a member of the Canadian Society of Graphic Art. In addition to her participation in numerous group shows, solo exhibitions of her paintings and sketches were held in Hamilton, Ontario (1928); New York City; Detroit, and Ann Arbor—both in Michigan (1952); Montréal, Québec (1961), and Toronto (1961). A major memorial exhibition of her work was organized by the Art Gallery of Hamilton, Ontario, in 1963. Gordon's work was also included in "Canadian Women Artists," Riverside Museum, New York (1947), and the travelling "Canadian Abstract Exhibition" (1952–1953). As a member of Painters Eleven, her paintings were shown across Canada and in New York (1956) and Dallas, Texas (1958). Gordon's work is represented in the National Gallery of Canada, Ottawa, and the Art Gallery of Ontario, as well as in numerous other public collections across Canada.

Janine A. Butler

Bibliography

MacCuaig, Stuart. *Climbing the Cold White Peaks: A Survey of Artists in and from Hamilton 1910–1950.* Hamilton: Hamilton Artists' Inc., 1986.

Oshawa, Ontario, Robert McLaughlin Gallery. Hortense Gordon Archives and artist's file.

Gorelick, Shirley (1924–)

Shirley Gorelick is one of few contemporary artists who has devoted a career largely to portraiture. Vigorous handling of paint, life-size (or sometimes even larger) scale, strong lighting, and obsessively-detailed naturalism contribute to expressive intensity in her treatment of this subject. She does not flatter her sitters, most of whom display a solemn demeanor that emphasizes the seriousness of her art and their lives. Pursuing psychological insights, she has often depicted figures in pairs or small groups in order to explore relationships between them. She has sometimes also used objects or environments drawn from the sitter's life to enhance her analysis of character. In the 1980s Gorelick began to place her figures in landscapes, then turned to landscape alone. In these too her close scrutiny of form and serious tone convey the grandeur and complexity of her subject.

A native of Brooklyn, New York, Gorelick earned a Bachelor of Arts degree at Brooklyn College, New York, and a Master of Arts degree at Columbia University, New York City. She studied with Hans Hofmann in the late 1940s. In 1956 she moved to Great Neck, Long Island, where she still lives.

Gorelick's early paintings were in the prevailing abstract expressionist style. During the 1960s, after working her way into figurative art through reinterpretations of master works by such canonical painters as Giorgione and Picasso, she treated the nude with free, gestural brushwork. By the early 1970s she was working in the realistic manner that has since characterized her work. An early powerful statement, "Willie, Billie Joe, and Leroy" (1972), represents three black men standing warily before one of her own large canvases. "Three Sisters II" (1976) explored the character of three self-absorbed adolescents, each portrayed twice. Later as Gorelick probed sensitively into the lives of her middle-aged friends, her portraits lost some of the confrontational edge seen earlier. In several double portraits of "Gunny and Lee Benson" (1978–1979) and separate depictions of the psychiatrist-couple "Dr. Tess Forrest" and "Dr. Joseph Barnett" (1980–1982), she sympathetically explored the human condition through exact rendering of individuals.

Ann Lee Morgan

Bibliography
Harrison, Helen A. "People as Paint in Shirley Gorelick's Works." *The New York Times* (February 11, 1979).
Rubenstein, Charlotte Streifer. *American Women Artists: From Early Indian Times to the Present.* G.K. Hall, 1982, p. 403.
Shirey, David L. "Portraits That Tell a Lot." *The New York Times* (January 13, 1980).

Gornik, April (1953–)

Born in Cleveland, Ohio, the painter/printmaker April Gornik studied at the Cleveland Institute of Art, Ohio (1971–1975), then took further study leading to a Bachelor of Fine Arts degree at the Nova Scotia College of Art and Design, Halifax, Canada (1975–1976).

Gornik has held solo exhibitions in museums and galleries, including the Edward Thorp Gallery, New York City (1981, 1983, 1985, 1986, 1988); "The Reality of Perception," Rutgers University, Newark, New Jersey (1981); "Landscape," University of Akron, Ohio (1981); and others.

Her work has been included in many prestigious group exhibitions and is represented in private, public, and corporate permanent collections, including the Chase Manhattan Permanent Collection, London, England; the Frito-Lay Collection, Plano, Texas; the Nova Scotia Art Bank; and others.

Bibliography
Grimes, Nancy. "April Gornik (at Edward Thorp)." *Art in America* 87:1 (January 1988): 153–54.
Pincus-Witten, Robert. "Entries—Analytical Pubism." *Arts Magazine* 59:6 (February 1985): 89.
Sources of Light, Contemporary American Luminism. A Catalog. Seattle: Henry Art Gallery, University of Washington, 1953.

Gouin, Judy (1947–)

The printmaker Judy Gouin was born in Toronto, Ontario, Canada, and studied at the Chelsea School of Art, London, England.

Gouin, who specialized in photographic serigraphy, created very large original prints at Open Studio in her native city. She has held a number of solo exhibitions, including the Agnes Etherington Art Centre, Kingston, Ontario (1974); and others. Her work has been included in prestigious group shows, such as "Graphic II," Art Gallery of Brant, Brantford, Ontario (1974); "Fourth British International Print Biennale," Bradford, England (1975); "Sixth British International Print Biennale," Bradford, England (1979); and many others. Examples of her work are in private and public permanent collections.

Bibliography
Sixth British International Print Biennale. A Catalog. Cartright Hall. Lister Park, Bradford, England.

Goulet, Cie (1940–)

A landscape painter, Cie Goulet has drawn upon varied terrain—the valleys, mountains, skies, and shoreline—primarily of the West and Southwest.

Born in Glendale, California, Goulet moved to the Northwest at the age of six. In college she studied with Wally Hedrick at the San Francisco Art Institute, California; at Parsons School of Design in New York City; and with Jack Wilkinson at the University of Oregon, Eugene, where she graduated in 1965.

Goulet's first solo exhibition was held at A Clean Well-Lighted Place, Austin, Texas (1969). This first show consisted of photo-realistic, black-and-white airbrushed paintings of shiny automobile details. The paintings evolved over the ensuing two decades into an energetic, painterly realistic style.

Early influences include Charles Burchfield, Albert P. Ryder, and George Bellows and are reflected in her interpretation of the landscape in which aspects of the countryside become energy-laden participants in a changing drama. Her paintings and works on paper are worked over a black ground. Intense colors and exaggerated, anthropomorphic forms describe the trees, water, hillsides, and skies.

Since 1983 Goulet has split her year between studios on the Oregon coast and in the SoHo section of New York City. In addition to the dramatic Western landscape, her work has been affected by the landscape in other parts of the world.

Goulet has also curated a number of notable exhibitions—both as a university curator at the State University of New York (SUNY) at Potsdam and, most recently, as an independent curator in New York City.

Goulet's paintings are in the permanent collections of the Portland Art Museum, and Oregon Arts Commission—both in Oregon; the Federal Reserve Bank; the U.S. State Department, Washington, D.C.;

and others.

Lynn McAllister

Bibliography

Allen, Lois. "Retrospective Promises." *Reflex* (March–April 1991).

Frank, Peter, ed. "Dialogue with Four Artists." *Visions Magazine* (January 1993).

Heartney, Eleanor. "Abstract Painting, Redefined." *Art News* (Summer 1985).

Johnson, Barry. "Critics Choice, West Coast Monotypes." *The Oregonian* (January 1989).

Goulet, Lorrie (1925–)

Born in Riverdale, New York, the sculptor Lorrie Goulet studied at the Inwood Potteries Studios, New York City (1932–1936), and at Black Mountain College, North Carolina (1943–1944).

Goulet has held a score of solo exhibitions of her work in many galleries, including the Clay Club Sculpture Center (1948, 1955), the Kennedy Galleries (1971, 1973, 1975, 1978, 1980, 1983, 1986)—all in New York City; Temple Emeth, Teaneck, New Jersey (1969); Caldwell College, New Jersey (198); and others. Her work has been invited to myriad group exhibitions in the United States and abroad, such as the Whitney Museum of American Art, New York City (1948–1950, 1953, 1955); "12 Women Sculptors," Philadelphia Art Alliance, Pennsylvania (1950); World Trade Fair, Zagreb, Yugoslavia, and Barcelona, Spain (1957); Memorial Museum, Johnson City, Tennessee (1965); National Academy of Design (1966, 1975, 1977), and "Women in the Making of Art History," Art Students League—both in New York City (1982); "Collector's Choice," paintings, the McNay Museum, San Antonio, Texas (1990); "The Coming of Age of American Sculpture," a show travelling to colleges in Pennsylvania, Iowa, Wisconsin, and Maryland; and many others.

Goulet has executed two ceramic relief public sculpture commissions: a work for a public library branch (1958); a Bronx municipal hospital (1961); and a stainless-steel relief for a Bronx police and fire station (1971)—all in New York City. Winner of awards and honors for her work, she has appeared intermittently on network television and in schools and museums from 1957 to the present; Goulet has taught at the Art Students League, New York City, since 1981. Her work is represented in private and public permanent collections, including the Hirshhorn Museum and Sculpture Garden, and the National Museum of Women in the Arts—both in Washington, D.C.; National Academy of Design, and the Archdiocese of New York—both in New York City; Boston University, Massachusetts; New Jersey State Museum, Trenton; Wichita Museum of Art, Kansas; and others.

Bibliography

Eliscue, Frank. *Slate and Soft Stone Sculpture.* Chilton Book Co, 1973.

Watson-Jones, Virginia. *Contemporary American Women Sculptors.* Oryx Press, 1985.

Who's Who in American Art. 19th ed. R.R. Bowker Co., 1991–1992.

Gow, Isabel Dowler (1933–)

The environmental artist, photographer, and "constructionist," Isabel Dowler Gow lives and works in Montréal, Québec, Canada. She learned her craft at the School of the Montréal Museum of Fine Arts; studied intaglio printmaking at Atelier 17, Paris, France, with Stanley William Hayter; and studied at Sir George Williams University (now Concordia University), Montréal.

Gow has held solo exhibitions in galleries and museums, such as "Egg Box Ends," La Galerie de la S.A.P.Q., Montréal (1973); her work has been included in many prestigious group shows in Canada and abroad, including "Dessins," Vehicle Art, Inc. (1973), and "Repeats," Powerhouse (1974)—both in Montréal; "Slide Exhibition," International Fair, Basel, Switzerland (1974); and many others. Examples of her work are in private and public permanent collections.

Bibliography

Vehicle Art: In Transit. A Travelling Exhibition. Simon Fraser University, Burnaby, British Columbia, 1975.

Vehicle's Vehicle. Centre for Experimental Art and Communication. Toronto, 1976.

Graham, Gloria (1940–)

Born in Beaumont, Texas, the sculptor Gloria Graham apprenticed to Jacques Manessier in Paris, France (1965), three years after having received a Master of Fine Arts degree from Baylor University, Waco, Texas. She also attended the University of California at Berkeley (1962); the University of Wisconsin, Madison (1964); and the University of New Mexico, Albuquerque (1966).

Graham has held solo exhibitions in museums and galleries, including the Motel Gallery, Albuquerque, New Mexico (1975–1977); George Belcher Gallery, San Francisco, California (1979); Scottsdale Center for the Arts, Arizona (1980); Linda Durham Gallery, Santa Fe, New Mexico (1980, 1983); Craig Cornelius Gallery, New York City (1984); Graham Gallery, Albuquerque (1987, 1989); Angles Gallery, Santa Monica, California (1991, 1992).

Her work has been invited to group exhibitions throughout the United States for almost two decades and has made her the recipient of grants from the National Endowment for the Arts (NEA) (1977), and the Asian Cultural Council for study and research in Japan (1987).

Examples of Graham's work are in private and public permanent collections, including the Albuquerque Museum, and Roswell Museum and Art Center, Albuquerque—both in New Mexico; CinemaLine, Los Angeles, California; Denver Art Museum, Colorado; the Panza Collection, Milan, Italy; University of North Dakota, Grand Forks; and others.

Bibliography

Artists of the 20th Century: The Museum of New Mexico Collection. Museum of New Mexico Press, 1992.

Panza de Biumo: The Eighties and Nineties from the Collection. A Catalog. Umberto Allemande & Co., 1992.

Watson-Jones, Virginia. *Contemporary American Women Sculptors.* Oryx Press, 1986.

Wiggins, Susan. "Gloria Graham." *Art Issues* 21 (1992): 38.

Graham, K.M. (1913–)

Born in Hamilton, Ontario, Canada, and educated at Trinity College, University of Toronto, K.M. (Kate) Graham took up painting as a full-time profession only in 1962. Prior to that Graham's exposure to art was through international travel with her husband, Wallace Graham, a medical doctor. It was after his death in 1962 that she turned her attentions fully to art.

As a docent at the Art Gallery of Toronto, Graham honed her skills of observation and was particularly struck by a large retrospective exhibition of Piet Mondrian at the Art Gallery in 1966. It was undoubtedly the Dutchman's distillation of nature into patterns based on careful observation that attracted her to his work.

Graham's own work has always been inspired by colors and patterns in nature. She has been influenced by the American color field painters whose work was exhibited at the David Mirvish Gallery in Toronto beginning in the 1960s. This group included Helen Frankenthaler, Kenneth Noland, Jules Olitski, and Morris Louis. In 1970 work by Milton Avery and the Canadian Jack Bush began to be exhibited; both artists have been relevant to Graham's development as an artist.

Bush was a personal friend of Graham and first encouraged her to exhibit her work. It was he who selected and installed her first exhibition at a commercial gallery—the Carmen Lamanna Gallery, Toronto, in 1967. While her paintings bear some affinity to Bush's late works in which strokes of color dance across large stained fields, and she was included in a show entitled "The Heritage of Jack Bush" in 1981–1982, the artists with whom Graham has been most closely associated are a generation younger than herself: David Bolduc, Paul Fournier, Alex Cameron, and Paul Sloggett. Her work was exhibited in the company of these artists in "Fourteen Canadians: A Critic's Choice," an exhibition selected by critic Andrew Hudson for the Hirshhorn Museum and Sculpture Garden in 1977.

Initially Graham's work was highly abstract, inspired by the flowers in her garden, or views of lily pads at close range, reminiscent of Monet's lily pads. In the 1970s there is a fine balance between color and line in her painting. During the 1980s she stepped back from the motif to take in the larger rhythms and patterns of nature, relinquishing the close-up focus, and choosing to delineate the topography of the Arctic and Newfoundland. Trips to the North began in 1971, the year she first went to Cape Dorset, and have continued ever since. She is attracted by the shape, texture, and color of the hills of the Hudson Strait, and the unique quality of light and color found in the North. Graham has executed oils, watercolors, and prints based on this subject matter.

Christine Boyanoski

Bibliography

Burnett, David, and Marilyn Schiff. *Contemporary Canadian Art.* Hurtig Publishers, 1983.

Carpenter, Ken. *The Heritage of Jack Bush.* Robert McLaughlin Gallery, 1981.

Hudson, Andrew. *Fourteen Canadians: A Critic's Choice.* Hirshhorn Museum and Sculpture Garden, 1977.

Reid, Dennis. *A Concise History of Canadian Painting.* 2nd ed. Oxford University Press, 1988.

Grambs, Blanche (1916–)

Known for her strong lithographs and intaglio prints of workers, Blanche Grambs was born in China and emigrated to the United States when she received a scholarship from the Art Students League, New York City (1930s). Subsequently she worked on the Federal Arts Project in New York City, wielding her expressive crayon on the stone, portraying the lives and times of miners and others.

"Miner's Head" (1930s), an intaglio work employing etching and aquatint, is not atypical of her output. It is a powerful close-up composition of a hard-hatted miner on whose visage one can read a life's experiences. Grambs's work is represented in private and public permanent collections.

Bibliography

Beall, Karen F., and David W. Kiehl. *Graphic Excursions: American Prints in Black and White, 1900–1950: Selections from the Collection of Reba and Dave Williams.* David R. Godine and the American Federation of Arts, 1991.

Granbery, Henrietta Augusta (1829–1927)

A painter of still lifes and landscapes, Henrietta Augusta Granbery, who was born in Norfolk, Virginia, grew up in New York City, where she studied painting. She taught at Professor West's Seminar in Brooklyn, New York, while maintaining a studio in New York City. She exhibited several paintings annually at the National Academy of Design in New York City from 1861 through 1890, including such works as "Apple Blossoms," "Near Elizabeth, New Jersey," "View in Central Park," "Magnolia Grandiflora," "Basket of Fruit," and "Late Flowers." Among the works exhibited at the Pennsylvania Academy of the Fine Arts, Philadelphia, between 1863 and 1869 were "Garden Flowers," "Cherries," "Azaleas," "Roses," "Gladiolus," "Sweet Peas," "Roses in the Finger Bowl," and "Fruit." She was also included in the Philadelphia Centennial Exhibition of 1876, Pennsylvania.

An example of her decorative still lifes is "Peonies in an Oriental Vase" (1891, Collection of Marge and Leslie Greenbaum), a tall, vertical composition of luxuriant blossoms painted in subtle tonalities and an ornate vase with an intricate design that includes a man wearing a wide-brimmed hat. Her style can be characterized as realistic with occasional decorative flourishes.

Eleanor Tufts

Bibliography

Gerdts, William H., and Russell Burke. *American Still-Life Painting.* Praeger, 1971.

Tufts, Eleanor. *American Woman Artists, 1830–1930.* National Museum of Women in the Arts, 1987.

Grauer, Sherri (1939–)

Born in Toronto, Ontario, Canada, Sherri Grauer has spent nearly all her life and active career in Vancouver, British Columbia. In later years she claimed her mother was her first art teacher but that her most memorable instruction concerned the proper way to clean brushes. Perhaps of greater significance was a period of study in Paris, France, in 1958–1959 at the École du Louvre and the Atelier Ziegler. This was followed by a three-year stay at the San Francisco Art Institute, California. Grauer's first solo show was in 1964 at the Mary Frazer Gallery of West Vancouver, British Columbia, but she came to national attention only in 1967, when she was represented in the art exhibition of the Canadian Pavilion at Expo '67, Montréal, Québec. This exposure led to several commissions for public works of art in federal ministries and other such institutions.

Grauer's work is rather unlike that of other Vancouver artists, ranging from Emily Carr to Gathie Falk. This is due in part to the unconventional materials she now uses and in part to the origins of the works in childhood play, in memory and in fantasy. In the mid-1960s her paintings were relatively conventional scenes of ordinary people in peculiar circumstances. After a time she began to add extra bits of canvas and other material to the surface of her works, as in "Former Wife on Terrace" (1964). Then, during a stay in Montréal, she happened upon some wire mesh in a hardware store and became enchanted by its power to suggest both the presence and the absence of a form. "Five Dog-Faced Boys" (1969), arguably her most well-known work, was the result: a suggestive arrangement of wire figures topped with solid, baleful heads. More recently, "Snakes and Ladders" (1985) has confronted complicated installation-art conventions with allusions to childhood games.

Robert J. Belton

Bibliography

Markiewicz, Cherie. *Still Life, Snakes and Ladders, and Bogeymen: Marcie Pitch and Sherri Grauer.* Vancouver: Emily Carr College of Art and Design, Charles H. Scott Gallery, 1985.

Sherri Grauer . . . so far . . . Vancouver: Surrey Art Gallery (September 18–October 19, 1980).

Grauerholz, Angela (1952–)

Angela Grauerholz was born in Hamburg, Germany, where she trained in graphic design at the Kunstschule Alsterdamm. She subsequently received a grant from the Canada Council to do graduate work and earned a Master of Fine Arts degree in photography from Concordia University, Montréal, in 1980. Grauerholz was a founding member of Montréal's Artexte, a nonprofit contemporary art catalog distribution and information center. She started a graphic design studio in 1984 and won numerous awards for her work. Grauerholz has been teaching graphic design at the Université du Québec à Montréal since 1988. In her first one-person show at Centre Vu in Québec City in 1984 and then again at Art 45 in Montréal in 1985, Grauerholz presented a series of photographs of young women, among them "Martha Townsend" (1985). The blurred, grainy, out-of-focus quality of these prints, achieved by long exposure and over-printing, became characteristic of Grauerholz's work. She turned her lens to landscape, interiors, and paintings, working with original material as well as re-photographing archival sources. Large black-and-white photographs, such as "Basel" (1986)—a tourist-like photo of a stream in the Swiss city—examined how images of the natural sentimentalize their subjects. These works were shown at Art 45 in 1987 and then extensively across Canada. Grauerholz began to work with cibachrome and produced "Sofa" (1988) with brownish tints that emphasize the distancing effects of photography. In 1990 Grauerholz exhibited in the Sydney Biennial, Australia, and was offered a one-person show at the Westfälisher Kunstverein, Münster, Germany, in 1991. Grauerholz was invited to participate in Kassel's Documenta IX, where she occupied some of the galleries of the Neue Galerie, Germany. Her large cibachrome photographs mounted in heavy wooden frames, such as "Hospital" (1987) and "Interior" (1988), were installed along with paintings selected from the permanent collection, creating a dialogue between painting and photography.

Grauerholz's work is included in the collections of the Stedelijk Museum, Amsterdam, Holland, as well as in major Canadian collections such as those of the Art Gallery of Ontario, Toronto, and the Montréal Museum of Fine Arts.

Cyril Reade

Bibliography

Bérard, Serge. *Paysage.* Dazibao, 1987.

Documenta IX. Edition Cantz and Harry N. Abrams, 1992.

Pontbriand, Chantal. *The Historical Ruse: Art in Montréal.* The Power Plant, 1988.

———. "Le regard vertigineux de l'ange." *Parachute* 63 (July, August, September 1991): 4–11.

Seaton, Beth. "Mundane Remembrances." *Parachute* 56 (October, November, December 1989): 23–25.

Simon, Cheryl. "The Déjà Vu of Angela Grauerholz." *Vanguard* 15:2 (April–May 1986): 27–29.

Graves, Ka (1938–)

Born in Detroit, Michigan, the assemblage, mixed media artist Ka Graves earned an Associate in Arts degree from the American College in Paris, France (1974). The rest of her academic career was accomplished at Arizona State University, Tempe, where she received a Bachelor of Fine Arts degree (1974); a Master of Fine Arts degree (1979); and did graduate work in anthropology (1987–1988).

Graves has held solo exhibitions in museums and galleries, including "Haunting Space, Public Places," Elaine Horwitch Gallery, Scottsdale, Arizona (1990); Winged Horse Gallery, Las Vegas, Nevada (1989); "The Tea Party," Fine Arts Center of Tempe (1985); "The Artist and the Magician," John Douglas Cline Gallery, Phoenix (1984); and "Mother, Daughter & Wholly Beastie," Scottsdale Center for the Arts (1982)—all in Arizona; and others. Her transmuted assemblages celebrate the magic of ritual, especially ceremonies based upon religious and ethnic happenings; she has been invited to participate in many shows throughout the United States: from Mesa, Arizona to Chicago, Illinois; Palm Springs, California; Elkins Park, Pennsylvania; New Brunswick, New Jersey; and others.

Artist-in-residence, teacher of life drawing in Arizona schools and colleges, mask maker, maker of witty and imaginative works—Graves created the costumes and scenic design for *Wilbur,* an original opera by Randall Shinn (1986), among other commissions. Her work is represented in private and public permanent collections.

Bibliography

Donnell-Kotrozo, Carol. "The Mythic Core." *Artweek* 13:21 (June 5, 1982): 6.

Perlman, Barbara H. "PHOENIX: A 'Sun Palace' in the Land of 'GOVT PROPERTY' and Four-Wheel Drive Cowboys." *Art News* 80:10 (December 1981): 119–21.

Watson-Jones, Virginia. *Contemporary American Women Sculptors.* Oryx Press, 1986.

Graves, Nancy (1940–)

As a sculptor, painter, film producer, printmaker, and stage designer, Nancy Graves is prolifically successful in combining scientific disciplines with nature and art. At an early age Graves was introduced to exhibits which dealt simultaneously with art, history, and science by her father who was assistant to the director of the Berkshire Museum, Massachusetts. It is an influence that is evident in her earliest work and can still be seen in her present-day sculpture.

Born in Pittsfield, Massachusetts, Graves recognized by the age of twelve her desire to be an artist. She attended Vassar College in Poughkeepsie, New York, receiving her Bachelor of Arts degree in 1961. She later studied at Yale University's School of Art and Architecture, New Haven, Connecticut, from which she earned her Bachelor of Fine Arts and Master of Fine Arts degrees in 1964. After graduating, Graves received a Fulbright–Hayes grant in painting in 1965 and went to Paris, France, to work and do independent research; study in Florence followed a year later. She was awarded a Vassar College fellowship (1971); a National Endowment for the Arts (NEA) grant (1972); and a spirit achievement award from the Albert Einstein College of Medicine, New York City (1988). Graves' pieces can be found in major art collections throughout the world. She has also enjoyed numerous solo exhibitions, including those at the Whitney Museum of American Art, and the Museum of Modern Art (MoMA)—both in New York City.

Graves's work initially focused on images from natural history, such as the reconstruction of bones, skeletons, and animals. In "Camels" (1969), she employed polyurethane, latex, plaster, wood, and steel along with painted skins to re-create the "natural appearance" of lifesized, two-humped camels.

Still keenly interested in science and its disciplines in the early 1970s, Graves turned to painting, temporarily abandoning sculpture. In 1974 the artist made "Reflection on the Moon," a lunar topography film which recorded the changing nature of the moon. It was followed by purely abstract paintings derived from photographs by NASA of the ocean floor, maps of Mars, and the lunar surface.

Graves then became intrigued by the casting process and began to cast organic forms in bronze. The free-standing configurations were made from objects welded into structures and then coated with brilliant colors using patinas, enamels, and polyurethane paints. The forms "float, touch and intertwine with one another," achieving the appearance of weightlessness by ignoring the basic concepts of gravity and symmetry.

In the 1980s Graves continued to assemble directly cast forms in structures of "unexpected balances and weight dispersements," combining organic forms with found objects. In the piece "Le Sourire" (1985) botanical images are placed adjacent to machine parts and architectural elements; once again illustrating the artist's interest in melding science with nature and art.

Graves's sculptures become increasingly less organic in the latter part of the decade. "Spanse" (1987) and "Struck By Their Guns" (1989) continue to explore the complexities of weight and balance with their asymmetry and juxtaposition of forms; however, these later works suggest a seriousness not found in the earlier and sometimes more whimsical pieces.

Christine L. Wilson

Bibliography

Berman, Avis. "Nancy Graves' New Age of Bronze." *Art News* 85 (February 1986): 56–64.

Collins, Amy Fine, and Bradley, Jr. "The Sum of the Parts." *Art in America* 76 (June 1988): 112–19.

Shapiro, Michael Edward. "Nature Into Sculpture: Nancy Graves and the Tradition of Direct Casting." *Arts Magazine* 59 (November 1984): 92–96.

Storr, Robert. "Natural Fictions." *Art in America* 72 (March 1983): 118–21.

Green (Youritzin), Glenda Allen (1945–)

One of the finest realist painters and portraitists in the United States, Glenda Allen (Youritzin) Green is a native of Weatherford, Texas. A child prodigy, Green won first prize in a national intercollegiate painting competition when she was a student at Texas Christian University, Fort Worth, from which she obtained a Bachelor of Fine Arts degree in painting *magna cum laude* (1967). From 1968 to 1969 she served as research assistant to the director of the Kimbell Art Museum, Fort Worth, Texas. In 1970, as a Kress fellow, she received her Master of Arts degree in art history from Tulane University, New Orleans, Louisiana (having written a thesis on French Gothic sculpture); there she also taught art history and was curator of collections at the Newcomb Art School. She married the art historian and critic Victor Koshkin-Youritzin in 1970; two years later they moved to Norman, Oklahoma, where, at the University of Oklahoma, she continued to teach art history and was also guest artist on the faculty from 1972 to 1976. After she had completed only two portraits, U.S. Senator Allen J. Ellender commissioned her to paint his official portrait, which was reproduced in the Fall 1972 *Art Journal* (College Art Association of America). Other distinguished portrait commissions quickly followed. Her 1972 oil portrait of the world's then-foremost living medical artist, "Dr. Paul Peck," hangs in the Smithsonian Institution, Washington, D.C. A. Hyatt Mayor, Curator Emeritus of Prints for the Metropolitan Museum of Art, New York City, commissioned an internationally-acclaimed, astonishingly life-like portrait (1974), which hangs in the Museum of the City of New York. Of his portrait, Mayor wrote: "I thought I was looking into a reducing mirror when I [viewed] your 'speaking' likeness of me. Can anyone do more?" Her ("terrifyingly objective"—Sir John Pope-Hennessy) 1975 portrait of the former Williams College Art Department chairman, "S. Lane Faison, Jr.," is in the Williams College Museum of Art, Williamstown, Massachusetts. By the mid-1970s, after having established herself as one of the premier living realist portraitists, Green (who then was using her married name, Youritzin) also embarked on a series of figure paintings treating the contemporary woman. Solo shows of her portraits and figure paintings were held at the Museum of the Southwest, Midland, Texas (1975); Museum of Art, University of Oklahoma, Norman (1975); Oklahoma Museum of Art, Oklahoma City (1976); and Philbrook Art Center, Tulsa (1978)—all in Oklahoma, among other public institutions in the Southwest. In 1986–1987 the Oklahoma Art Center in Oklahoma City honored her with a retrospective of her paintings and portraits. In the early 1980s Bruce McGaw Graphics, Inc., New York City, published internationally-distributed editions of her paintings, most notably the radiant "Flight of Spring" (1977). Possessing a photographic memory and a medical knowledge of anatomy, Green (who remarried to Brian Bibb in 1980) lives in Fort Worth, Texas, and continues to paint primarily in an old master oil technique employing numerous glazes, with an occasional use of airbrush. Her paintings often communicate an exceptional energy and contain a magical luminosity, which can in part be explained by a highly complex, nuclear physics-based color system that she has invented and is currently preparing for publication.

Cynthia Lee Kerfoot

Bibliography

Browning, Boo. "More Than Meets the Eye [Glenda Youritzin]." *Oklahoma Monthly* (January 1987): 44–49.

Glenda Green: Retrospective at the Oklahoma Art Center/New York at Artspace II. Exhibition Catalog. Oklahoma Art Center, Oklahoma City (November 1, 1986–January 11, 1987).

Glenda Youritzin: Paintings. Exhibition Catalog. The Oklahoma Museum of Art, Oklahoma City (March 7–18, 1976).

Kimball, V. "A New Search for Humanism in Art: An Interview with Glenda Green Youritzin." *Southwest Art Magazine* (January 1974): 60–62.

Longley, Cynthia. "Glenda Green [Artist Profile]." *Art Voices/South* 21 (September–October 1978).

Multiple Realities: Paintings by Glenda Youritzin. Exhibition Catalog. Philbrook Art Center, Tulsa, Oklahoma (February 19–March 19, 1978).

Ramses, Jim. "Glenda Youritzin: A Feminine Humanist." *Southwest Art Magazine* (September 1976): 76–80.

Greenbaum, Dorothea Schwarcz (1893–1986)

A native New Yorker, the representational sculptor/printmaker Dorothea Schwarcz Greenbaum studied at the New York School of Fine and Applied Art and the Art Students League—both in New York City, with Charles W. Hawthorne, Jonas Lie, and Kenneth Hayes Miller, among others.

Greenbaum held twenty-eight solo exhibitions and exhibited in group shows, including the New York World's Fair (1939); Pennsylvania Academy of Fine Arts, Philadelphia (1941); Society of Washington Artists, Washington, D.C. (1941); the Art Institute of Chicago, Illinois; Whitney Museum of American Art, New York City; San Francisco Museum of Art, California; and many others.

A member of the American Academy and Institute of Arts and Letters; the American Artists Congress; Sculptors Guild; American Society of Painters, Sculptors, and Gravers; and the Whitney Studio Club—all in New York City, Greenbaum executed sculpture commissions for the Princeton Public Library, New Jersey, and the Museum of Art, Ogunquit, Maine, her work is represented in private and public permanent collections, including the American Academy and Institute of Arts and Letters, and Whitney Museum of American Art—both in New York City; Brookgreen Gardens, South Carolina; Lawrence Museum, Williamstown, Massachusetts; Oberlin College, Ohio; and others in the United States and abroad.

Bibliography

Gerdts, William H. *Women Artists of America 1707–1964*. The Newark Museum, 1965.

Rubinstein, Charlotte S. *American Women Artists*. G.K. Hall, 1982.

The New York Times (April 9, 1986): Y45.

Greenberg, Gloria (1932–)

Painter and printmaker Gloria Greenberg was born in New York City; received her Bachelor of Fine Arts degree at Cooper Union Art School, New York City (1952), won a Yale-Norfolk summer fellowship, Connecticut (1953), to study painting with Nicholas Marsicano; and worked with Gabor Peterdi at the Brooklyn Museum Art School, New York (1953), where she secured a scholarship to study printmaking.

Between 1970 and 1990 Greenberg exhibited her work in seventeen solo shows at the Mercer Gallery, New York City. Earlier on she had exhibited her work in European and United States institutions, including the Brooklyn Museum Print Show, New York (1953–1954); the Musée d'Orbigny, La Rochelle, France (1959); the Joslyn Art Museum, Omaha, Nebraska (1953); the Waverly Gallery, New York City; "Post-Card Size Art," Organization of Independent Artists, Bologna, Italy (1978); "The Sixties and Seventies: Looking Back, Looking Forward," A Retrospective at Marist College, Poughkeepsie, New York (1979); and many others.

Greenberg's work has received awards and honors, including two MacDowell Colony fellowships, Peterborough, New Hampshire (1965, 1973); and the medal of honor, Société des Beaux-Arts, Dordogne, France (1959); and others. A book designer and teacher, Greenberg has received several important commissions, such as her "4 Squares," an installation at the International Arrivals Building, Kennedy Airport, New York City (1971); her seven panel installation for IBM, Tarrytown, New York (1981); and others.

Bibliography

"Gloria Greeenberg." *Art News* (April 1972).

Who's Who in American Art. 19th ed. R.R. Bowker Co., 1991–1992.

Greene, Ethel (1912–)

Born in Malden, Massachusetts, Ethel Greene always wanted to be an artist; even in first grade she was in competition to be the best in the class. "High school was rather a drag for me, but four years at the Massachusetts School of Art (now Massachusetts College of Art) were pure joy." Greene also studied painting at the Boston University School of Art and at the School of the Boston Museum—both in Massachusetts.

To support herself during the Great Depression in and around metropolitan Boston, Greene worked at various art-related jobs: she painted sales samples for a greeting card company and did free-lance work, mainly in fashion illustration. She went west to San Diego, California, early in World War II and drew airplane parts for Consolidated Vultee (now General Dynamics). At war's end Greene worked at the University of California, Division of War Research, Point Loma, then moved on to work as a technical illustrator for the U.S. Navy Electronic Laboratory until she retired in 1955. Prior to this time Greene painted as time permitted; now she could devote her energies to becoming a full-time artist.

She moved inexorably toward surrealism "along about the 1960s" and, as the style seemed to fit her personality, has stayed with it ever since. The world of Ethel Greene is filled with irony, wry humor, mystery, and psychological punch—the contemporary visual equivalent of "an umbrella and a sewing machine upon a dissecting table." "Waterbed," for example, portrays a bedroom in which a woman is asleep on a waterbed that has become a pool of water about to engulf the sleeper.

Greene's work has been invited to many group exhibitions in the United States and abroad, including the University of California at San Diego (1990); the Yokohama Citizen's Gallery, Japan (1979); Bertha Schaefer Gallery, New York City (1966); the La Jolla Museum, California (1966); and myriad others. An award winner for many years, Greene has had seventeen solo exhibitions between 1956 and 1990 in major commercial galleries, museums, and university art galleries throughout the United States.

Greene's work is in the permanent public and private collections of the San Diego Museum of Art, California; Western University; La Salle College, Philadelphia, Pennsylvania; the collections of Elizabeth Taylor and Larry Bell—to name but a clutch of her collectors. A member of Artists Equity Association, Greene is also in the San Diego Artists Guild, California, and is an advocate for women artists.

Bibliography
Ethel Greene. A Catalog. Introduction by Henry F. Robert, Jr. Arizona State University, 1972.
Pincus, Robert L. "For the Most Part, the 'Echoes of Surrealism' are Hollow and Faint." *The San Diego Union* (October 19, 1990): E3.
Vreeland, Susan. "Ethel Greene: Idea Woman." *Hill Courier* 2:8 (October 1984): 14–15.

Greene, Gertrude (Glass) (1904–1956)

Born in Brooklyn, New York, Gertrude (Glass) Greene was one of America's pioneering abstract painter/sculptors. Greene began her study of sculpture at New York City's Leonardo da Vinci Art School from 1924 to 1926. She married the painter Balcomb Greene in 1926, and until 1931 they travelled several times to and from Europe, finally settling in New York City, where they lived until 1942. After that they maintained two residences—one a house that the couple built completely themselves over several years at Montauk Point, Long Island, New York; the other in Pittsburgh, Pennsylvania. Greene also kept her Greenwich Village, New York City, studio until she died. An early constructivist, she helped found the American Abstract Artists, as well as the Federation of Modern Painters and Sculptors, the Painters and Sculptors Guild, and the Artists Union. Combining elements of constructivism, Cubism, suprematism, and neo-plasticism, her art reflects the influence of such European masters as Jean Arp, Pablo Picasso, and Constantin Brancusi. Greene's work took many forms, beginning with free-standing sculpture, and progressing to wooden relief constructions, abstract painting, and collage. She even made a foray into the medium of sheet-metal sculpture in 1935 when she and sculptor Ibram Lassaw purchased steel-forging equipment.

During the 1930s and 1940s Greene exhibited her work via her several organizations, but her major exhibitions did not take place until the last years of her life. She exhibited her abstract expressionist oil paintings at the Whitney Museum of American Art (1950), and "Abstract Painting and Sculpture in America," the Museum of Modern Art (MoMA) (1951)—both in New York City. Her first one-woman show took place the same year at the Grace Borgenicht Gallery; her second was at the Bertha Schaefer Gallery in 1955—both in New York City. The following year Greene died of cancer; an exhibition of her work, including drawings, collages, and wooden constructions, was shown posthumously at the Bertha Schaefer Gallery in 1957.

Cynthia Lee Kerfoot

Bibliography
Armstrong, Tom, et al. *Two Hundred Years of American Sculpture*. David R. Godine, in association with the Whitney Museum of American Art, 1976.
Moss, Jacqueline. "Gertrude Greene: Constructions of the 1930s and 1940s." *American Art Journal* 15 (Winter 1983): 67–82.
Rubinstein, Charlotte Streifer. *American Women Artists: From Early Times to the Present*. Avon, 1982.

Greene-Mercier, Marie Zoe (1911–)

Born in Madison, Wisconsin, the sculptor Marie Zoe Greene-Mercier earned a Bachelor's degree in Fine Arts at Radcliffe College, Harvard University, Cambridge, Massachusetts (1933); on a scholarship grant to the New Bauhaus, Chicago, Illinois, she took further work with Alexander Archipenko, Laszlo Moholy-Nagy, and Gyorgy Kepes (1937–1938). Greene-Mercier lived and exhibited in Canada (1941–1946).

Greene-Mercier's early solo exhibitions were held in galleries in the United States and abroad, including the Photographic Stores, Ltd., Ottawa, Canada (1946); Well of the Sea Gallery, Chicago, Illinois (1949); Argent Gallery, New York City (1950); Layton Gallery and School of Art, Milwaukee, Wisconsin (1951); Marguerite Hobenberg Gallery (1951, 1952), Art Institute of Chicago, Prints and Drawings Department (1955), Chicago Public Library (1956), and American Institute of Architects (AIA) (1957)—all in Chicago, Illinois; Galerie Raymond Duncan, Paris, France (1963); Galleria d'Arte Arno, Florence (1965), Galleria Numero, Milan, Rome, and Venice (1966), and Galleria San Stefano, Venice (1968)—all in Italy; and most recently at the Galerie Loeht, Frankfurt, Germany (1991).

Between 1945 and 1992 Greene-Mercier's work has been invited to more than 180 group exhibitions in the United States, Canada, and Europe—from Montréal, Québec, to Paris, France; London, England; Trieste and Rome, Italy; Chicago, Illinois; New York City; Washington, D.C.; and other venues. Her work of the 1960s, especially her bronzes—such as "Orpheus and Eurydice XV" (1965), a four-foot piece—reveals the remarkable energy in her abstract forms as they weave and dart through space.

Greene-Mercier's work is represented in private, public, and corporate permanent collections, including Roosevelt University, Chicago; University of Chicago; Smart Museum; and International Film Bureau, Chicago—all in Illinois; Southwest Missouri State College, Springfield; Musée des Sables, Barcares, France; Museum of Modern Art, Venice, Italy; Radcliffe College, Cambridge, Massachusetts; Bauhaus Archiv Museum, Berlin, Germany; First Baptist Church, Bloomington, Indiana; and many others.

Bibliography
Elgar, Frank. *Greene-Mercier*. Le Musée de Poche, 1978.
Greene-Mercier, Marie Zoe. "The Role of Materials in My Sculpture." *Leonardo* XV:1 (1982).
Redstone, Louis G. *Public Art, New Directions*. McGraw-Hill, 1981.
Rubinstein, Charlotte Streifer. *American Women Sculptors*. G.K. Hall, 1990.
Who's Who in American Art. 19th ed. R.R. Bowker Co., 1991–1992.

Greenwood, Marion (1909–1970)

The painter/muralist/printmaker Marion Greenwood was born in Brooklyn, New York; studied with George Bridgman and John Sloan at the Art Students League, New York City, at the age of fifteen, and then attended the Académie Colarossi in Paris, France. Returning to America in 1930 she derived income from portraits and also published sketches in *The New York Times*. After visiting the Southwest to paint aspects of the Pueblo and Navajo cultures, she crossed over into Mexico in 1932 and became the first woman muralist commissioned by the Mexican government. Her art typically showed a concern for accurately depicting physical types and people's social interaction. After a year studying the Tarascan Indians in Mexico, she produced a huge fresco of Indian life at the University of San Hidalgo in Morelia. Impressed by her work, the famed Mexican muralist Diego Rivera—director of his country's mural program—engaged Greenwood and her accomplished sister Grace Greenwood to paint part of a mural in Mexico City's central market and civic center. Under the influence of Rivera and José Clemente Orozco, Greenwood's art assumed a revolutionary flavor (her work would also later suggest influences from Thomas Hart Benton). Back in America in 1936 she was employed by the Treasury Relief Art Project to produce, in Camden, New Jersey, a now covered-over mural treating the theme of collective bargaining achieved by Camden shipyard laborers under the New Deal. In 1938, commissioned by the Treasury Department section of fine arts, she secured a socially-optimistic Tennessee Valley Authority (TVA)-supportive post office mural entitled "The Partnership of Man and Nature" in Crossville, Tennessee. Further demonstrating her optimism and abiding concern for the betterment of social conditions was Greenwood's now also covered-over fresco, "Blueprint for Living" (1940), in Brooklyn, New York's Red Hook housing project. During World War II she and Anne Poor were the only U.S. government-appointed artist-correspondents. After 1940 easel painting and printmaking absorbed Greenwood's principal attention, and she had her first solo exhibition in 1944 at New York's Associated American Artists Gallery. Many other exhibits followed, in the United States and abroad, and she travelled widely to such destinations as Hong Kong, India, and North Africa. She twice returned to mural work: in 1954–1955, while teaching at the University of Tennessee, Knoxville, and in 1965 at Syracuse University, New York. Recipient of several prestigious awards, she was in 1959 elected a member of the National Academy of Design, New York City.

Victor Koshkin-Youritzin

Bibliography
Dunford, Penny. *A Biographical Dictionary of Women Artists in Europe and America Since 1850*. University of Pennsylvania Press, 1989, pp. 118–19.
Marling, Karal Ann, and Helen A. Harrison. *7 American Women: The Depression Decade*. New York: A.I.R. Gallery, 1976, pp. 28–30.
Rubinstein, Charlotte Streifer. *American Women Artists: From Early Indian Times to the Present*. Avon, 1982, pp. 216–20, 501.
Salpeter, Harry. "Marion Greenwood: An American Painter of Originality and Power." *American Artist* 12 (January 1948): 14–19.

Grenkie, Hazel J. (1916–)
Born in Zealandia, Saskatchewan, Canada, the painter/printmaker Hazel Jensen Grenkie graduated from the Saskatoon Normal School, Saskatchewan (1935); and studied intermittently with a host of artists at the University of Saskatchewan, including Eli Bornstein, Reta Cowley, Stanley Day, Mina Forsyth, Charles Ringness, and others (1964–1982).

Grenkie has held solo exhibitions in museums and galleries, such as "Hazel Grenkie: Reliefs and Acrylic Paintings," Mendel Art Gallery, Saskatoon (1972) and others, including retrospective shows at Cranston Galleries, Saskatoon (1983) and the Rosetown Gallery and Museum (1984)—both in Saskatchewan. Her work has been included in major juried and travelling group exhibitions in Saskatchewan for

more than a decade and a half. Examples of her work are in private, corporate, and public permanent collections of the University of Alberta, and Guarantee Trust Company—both in Edmonton; the *Star Phoenix*, Saskatoon; and others.

Bibliography
Canadian Artists in Exhibition. Roundstone Press, 1974.
Newman, Marketa. *Biographical Dictionary of Saskatchewan Artists: Women Artists*. Fifth House Publishers, 1990.

Grigoriadis, Mary (1942–)
Born in Jersey City, New Jersey, Mary Grigoriadis is a painter of "secular icons," and a founder of the A.I.R. Gallery in New York City. Mary Grigoriadis earned a Bachelor's degree from Barnard College (1963) and a Master of Fine Arts degree from Columbia University (1965)—both in New York City.

Grigoriadis has held sixteen solo exhibitions of her work between 1972 and 1989, nine of which were at the A.I.R. Gallery, New York City. She has also shown at Barnard College, New York City (1988); Helen Shlien Gallery, Boston, Massachusetts (1978, 1981, 1983); Douglass College, Rutgers University, New Brunswick, New Jersey (1979); Gallery K, Washington, D.C. (1978); and O.K. Harris, New York City (1976). Her work has been invited to myriad group exhibitions in the United States and abroad, including "Artists for Choice," SoHo 20 Gallery, New York City (1991); "The Definitive American Quilt," travelling in the United States and Japan until 1993, Bernice Steinbaum Gallery, New York City (1990); "New Acquisitions of the Vorres Museum, Athens, Greece (1988); "A.I.R.," Lunds Kunsthall, Stockholm, Sweden (1982); "Islamic Allusions," Alternative Museum, New York City (1980); Gallery Ginza Kaigakan, Tokyo, Japan (1978); "Award Exhibition," American Academy and Institute of Arts and Letters, New York City (1974); and many others.

Winner of awards and honors for her work, Grigoriadis received a fellowship award from the New York Foundation for the Arts (1989) and was chosen by Arts in Transit to create murals for the Metropolitan Transit Authority, New York City (1986). "Persian Steepe" (1978), a typical heavily-patterned work of the period, is rooted in icons and images of the Byzantine church—remembrances of Grigoriadis's childhood. Her work is represented in private, public, and corporate permanent collections, including New York University, New York City; Oberlin College, Ohio; Voores Museum, Athens, Greece; Virginia Museum of Fine Arts, Richmond; Chase Manhattan Bank; IBM; the National Museum of American Art, Washington, D.C.; and others.

Bibliography
Herrera, Hayden. "Reviews." *Art in America* (March–April 1977).
Lerman, Ora. "Autobiographical Journey: Can Art Transform Personal and Cultural Loss?" *Arts Magazine* (May 1985).
Marter, Joan. "Mary Grigoriadis." *Arts Magazine* (November 1984): 12.
Robins, Corinne. *The Pluralist Era: 1968–1981*. Harper & Row, 1984.

Grilo, Sarah (1921–)
Born in Buenos Aires, Argentina, the painter Sarah Grilo lived in New York City (1962–1970), where she had come to activate a fellowship from the Guggenheim Foundation.

Grilo has held solo exhibitions in the United States and abroad, in galleries and museums, including Galería Bonino, Buenos Aires, Argentina (1961); the Organization of American States (OAS) Headquarters (1957) and Obelisk Gallery (1963)—both in Washington, D.C.; Bianchini Gallery (1963), and Byron Gallery (1963, 1967)—both in New York City; and many others. Her paintings have been included in prestigious group exhibitions, such as the National Gallery of Art, Smithsonian Institution, Washington, D.C. (1956); "The United States Collects Latin American Art," Art Institute of Chicago, Illinois and "South American Art Today," Dallas Museum of Fine Arts, Texas (1959); "Painters Residing in the U.S. from Latin America," Institute of Contemporary Arts, Washington, D.C. (1964); "The "Emergent Decade," Guggenheim Museum, New York City, and Cornell University, Ithaca, New York (1965); "Art of Latin America since Independence," Yale University, New Haven, Connecticut, and the University of Texas at Austin (1966); and many others.

Examples of Grilo's work are in private and public permanent collections, including the Museo de Arte Contemporaneo, Buenos Aires, Argentina; Modern Museum of Latin American Art, Washington, D.C.; and many others.

Bibliography

Iturburu, Cordoba. *La Pintura Argentina del Siglo XX*. Buenos Aires: Editorial Atlantida, 1958.

Traba, Marta, et al. *Museum of Modern Art of Latin America—Selections from the Permanent Collection*. Washington, D.C.: Organization of American States, 1985.

The Latin American Spirit: Art and Artists in the United States, 1920–1970. Harry N. Abrams, 1988.

Grimes, Frances (1869–1963)

Born in Braceville, Ohio, the sculptor Frances Grimes studied at Pratt Institute, Brooklyn, New York, with Augustus Saint-Gaudens and others.

Grimes was elected an associate member of the National Academy of Design, New York City (1931); and a member of the National Sculpture Society (1912), the National Association of Women Painters and Sculptors, and the American Federation of Arts—all in New York City; and the Cornish Colony, New Hampshire. She has won many awards and honors, including a silver medal for numismatic design at the Pan-Pacific Exposition, San Francisco, California (1915); the McMillan sculpture prize at the National Association of Women Painters and Sculptors, New York City (1916); a memorial award for work in the permanent collection of the Washington Cathedral, Washington, D.C.; and others.

Examples of Grimes's work may be found in many locations in the United States, including an overmantel for Washington Irving High School, busts of "Charlotte Cushman" and "Emma Willard" for the Hall of Fame, New York University, and relief panels "Girls Singing," the Metropolitan Museum of Art—all in New York City; "Girl by Pool," and "Boy with Duck," Toledo Museum of Art, Ohio.

Bibliography

American Art Annual. Vol. XXX. American Federation of Arts, 1933.

Gardner, Albert TenEyck. *American Sculpture: A Catalog of the Collection of the Metropolitan Museum of Art*. New York Graphic Society, 1965.

Who Was Who in American Art. Vol. IV (1961–1968). Chicago, 1968.

Grizá, Irma (1946–)

Born in Mexico in 1946, Irma Grizá studied at the Academy of San Carlos in Mexico City from 1952 to 1956. Member of the Salón de la Plástica Mexicana since 1975, she has participated in fifteen solo and many group shows in Mexico and abroad. Grizá recently was a prize-winner in the Nuevos Valores competition in Mexico City.

Bibliography

Alvarez, José Rogelio, et al. *Enciclopedia de México*. Secretaría de Educación Pública, 1987.

Grobet, Lourdes (1940–)

A Mexican photographer, now living and working in Mexico City, Mexico, Lourdes Grobet studied with the artist Mathias Goeritz, switching from painting to photography in 1970. She participated in a number of individual and group exhibitions of photography in Mexico between 1970 and 1975. In 1976 she studied graphic art at Cardiff College of Art, Wales, and in 1977 she studied photography at Derby College of Art and Technology, England. In addition to exhibitions of her work at the University of Wales, Cardiff, and St. Michael's Gallery in Derby, England, Grobet mounted a "travelling exhibition" in elevators of an office building in Derby. The concept of a moving show is typical of Grobet's sense of humor and leaning toward experimentation. Her work often crosses into other media and makes use of conceptual art strategies.

On her return to Mexico in 1977 Grobet participated in the First Colloquium of Mexican Photography held by the Mexican Council of Photography. She has also participated in the three Colloquia of Latin American Photography held since 1978. In 1979 Grobet began a five-year photographic investigation of popular wrestling (which is known as *la lucha libre* in Mexico City), during which she documented the lives of male and female wrestlers—in the ring, at work, and at social gatherings with their families, fans and managers, and one another. Grobet was also a member of a women's collective theater group which put on a performance called *De Mujir a Mujer* (roughly translated as Women Mooing) in which she was both actor and photographer. Grobet performed a photographic strip tease, discarding a costume made of photographs of herself. The group travelled around Mexico, bringing this somewhat shocking work to both cities and small towns.

Grobet has also documented the work of a peasant theater group, the *Teatro Campesino* of Tabasco, and went with them to Joseph Papp's Latin American Theater Festival in New York in 1987. Her book of photographs of the Garcia Lorca play, *Boda de Sangre* (Blood Wedding), put on by the *Teatro Campesino*, won the Premio Juan Pablos Editores in 1988. Among other projects Grobet has photographed the streets of Chicago, Illinois, and political rallies in Mexico City, Mexico, produced a photographic work about Mother's Day inspired by religious imagery, and has made multi-media artist's books.

Deborah Caplow

Bibliography

Hecho en Latinoamerica: Primera Muestra de la Fotografia Latinoamericana Contemporanea. Mexico: Instituto Nacional de Bellas Artes. Consejo Mexicano de Fotografia, 1978.

Hecho en Latinoamerica 2/Segundo Coloquio Latinoamericano de Fotografia. Mexico: Instituto Nacional de Bellas Artes. Consejo

Mexicano de Fotografia, 1981.

Grobet, Lourdes. *Bodas de Sangre*. Mexico: Gobierno del Estado de Tabasco, 1987.

Mandoki, Katya. "The Double Struggle: Photographing 'La Lucha Libre.'" *Exposure* (Summer 1984).

Gross-Bettelheim, Jolán (1900–1972)

Through her powerful etchings and lithographs of bridge and viaduct forms, completed before, during, and after World War II, Jolán Gross-Bettelheim gained prominence among American printmakers. Her constructivist compositions depict an Orwellian world in which man is displaced by the forms of the industrial age; when human figures are present among the bridges, cables, and industrial forms, they are reduced to automations.

Born in Nyitra, Hungary (now Nitra Czechoslovakia), in 1900, Gross-Bettelheim began her study of art in Budapest. At the age of nineteen she went to Vienna, Austria, then moved to Berlin, Germany, in 1920, where she continued her studies. The work she did during her two years in Berlin reveals the influences of Wassily Kandinsky, Karl Hofer, George Grosz, and Otto Dix. Between 1922 and 1924 she studied in Paris, France, then emigrated to the United States and in 1925 married Frigyes Bettelheim, a medical doctor, and moved with him to Cleveland, Ohio. At this point she began to sign (and re-sign) her work Gross-Bettelheim. Her drawings, etchings, lithographs, and pastels of the late 1920s and 1930s are divided between satirical figures, echoing her Berlin years; constructivist cityscapes; and depictions of the city, particularly of crowded tenement buildings in working-class neighborhoods. Some of her prints were made while working on the Works Projects Administration (WPA) Federal Art Project in Cleveland, Ohio, and New York. She was a communist and a member of the John Reed Society, and many of her works from the 1930s and 1940s have a content that reflects her political beliefs.

Before 1937 Gross-Bettelheim exhibited principally in Cleveland, Ohio; between 1937 and the mid-1950s her work was regularly seen in national print and watercolor exhibitions, where they received numerous prizes and purchase awards. In 1945 she had a one-woman show of pastels at the Durand-Ruel Gallery, New York City. After her husband's death, perhaps motivated by her political beliefs, Gross-Bettelheim returned to Hungary in 1956. Her timing was unfortunate. As a communist she did not find her place in the art scene of the country she had left as a young woman. Affected by personal problems, her work lost its creative tension; the late drawings and paintings are loosely composed and lacking in direction. Since her death in 1972 retrospective exhibitions of her work have been presented in several Hungarian galleries and museums.

Clinton Adams

Bibliography

Arnold, Laureen, ed. *The Federal Art Project: American Prints from the 1930s in the Collection of the University of Michigan Museum of Art.* University of Michigan Museum of Art, 1985.

Jolán Gross-Bettelheim: Graphic Works Selected from Vörösváry's Collection. Kecskeméti Galéria, Kecskemét (Hungary), 1987.

Jolán Gross-Bettelheim: Retrospektív Kiállítása (Retrospective Exhibition). Introduction by Lóránd Hegyi. Budapest Kiállítóterem, 1988.

Grossen, Francoise (1943–)

Born in Neuchatel, Switzerland, the fiber artist/sculptor Francoise Grossen earned a Bachelor's degree from the School of Architecture, Polytechnical University, Lausanne, Switzerland (1963). After travel in Africa, which proved influential in her work, Grossen graduated in textile design from the School of Arts and Crafts, Basel, Switzerland (1967). She received a Master of Arts degree from the University of California at Los Angeles (UCLA), where she studied with Bernard Kester (1969). The following year Grossen worked for Jack Lenor Larsen, Inc., New York City.

Grossen has held solo exhibitions in the United States and abroad, including the Hadler Galleries, New York City, and the Museum Bellerive, Zurich, Switzerland (1976); "Fiberworks—The Americas and Japan," National Museum of Modern Art, Tokyo and Kyoto—both in Japan (1977); "Soft-Art, Weich, Plastisch," Kunsthaus, Zurich, Switzerland (1979); and others. Her work has been invited to many group exhibitions, such as "Wall Hangings," Museum of Modern Art (MoMA), New York City (1968); "Biennale Internationale de la Tapisserie," Lausanne, Switzerland (1969, 1971, 1973, 1975); "Deliberate Entanglements," University of California at Los Angeles (UCLA) (1972); "Fiber Structures," Denver Art Museum, Colorado (1972); "Sculpture in Fiber," Museum of Contemporary Crafts, New York City (1972); "In Praise of Hands," World Crafts Council, Toronto, Canada (1974); "First International Exhibition of Miniature Textiles," British Crafts Centre, London, England (1974); "Three Dimensional Fiber," New Plymouth, New Zealand (1974–1975); and many others.

Grossen taught weaving and macramé at the New School for Social Research, and the Brooklyn Museum Art School (1971–1973)—both in New York City; Kansas City Art Institute, Missouri (Summer 1974); and the University of California at Los Angeles (UCLA) (Summer 1975). She has her work represented in private, corporate, and public permanent collections, including the Bank of Texas, San Antonio, and North Texas State University, Dallas—both in Texas; Dreyfus Fund, and Rudin Management—both in New York City; Museum Bellerive, Zurich, Switzerland; One Embarcadero Center, San Francisco, California; O'Hare Regency Hyatt House, Chicago, Illinois; and others.

Bibliography

Constantine, Mildred, and Jack Lenor Larsen. *Art Fabric: Mainstream.* Van Nostrand Reinhold, 1981.

Fiberworks. A Catalog. Essay by Evelyn Svec Ward. Cleveland Museum of Art, 1977.

Grossman, Nancy (1940–)

Born in New York City, Nancy Grossman, from the age of six, was reared on a dairy farm in Oneonta, New York, and attended Pratt Institute, New York City, despite difficult economic circumstances. Grossman's three-dimensional, leather-covered, powerful figures and heads achieved instant renown in 1969—after more than a decade of figurative drawing and painting which explored and expressed basic human conditions; and after having exhibited work at the Corcoran Gallery of Art, Washington, D.C. (1963), and the Whitney Museum of American Art, New York City (1968).

Grossman has shown her two- and three-dimensional works at the Whitney Biennial, Whitney Museum of American Art, New York City

(1973); "Recent Figure Sculpture," Fogg Art Museum, Harvard University, Cambridge, Massachusetts (1972); "Perceiving Modern Sculpture," Grey Art Gallery, New York University (1980), Hamilton Gallery (1980), "Drawing Acquisitions," Whitney Museum of American Art (1981), and "Figuratively Sculpting," P.S.1 (1981)—all in New York City; "The Americans: The Collage," Contemporary Arts Museum, Houston, Texas (1982); "The Sculptor as Draftsman," Whitney Museum of American Art, New York City (1983); and many others.

Grossman taught sculpture at the Boston Fine Arts School, Massachusetts in 1985 and drawing at Cooper Union, New York City, in 1989. She has won many honors, including a Guggenheim Foundation fellowship (1965); and an American Academy and Institute of Arts and Letters award, New York City (1974). Grossman was granted a National Endowment for the Arts (NEA) sculpture award (1985); a New York Foundation for the Arts fellowship in sculpture (1991); and was commencement honoree at the Massachusetts College of Art in Boston (1974).

Grossman held three retrospective exhibitions of her work in 1991: "Nancy Grossman: Collages, Constructions, Drawings and Sculptures, 1965–1990," Exit Gallery, and "Nancy Grossman: Collages & Heads, 1970–1991" at Sculpture Center—both in New York City; and "Nancy Grossman: 25 Years," Hillwood Art Gallery, Long Island University, New York. In her recent bronzes Grossman has achieved the same or similar qualities evident in her leather-covered work: anonymous twentieth-century icons that haunt the viewer.

Bibliography
Blau, Douglas. "Nancy Grossman." *Arts Magazine* 55:6 (February 1981): 3.
Brown, Betty Ann, and Arlene Raven. *Exposures: Women and Their Art.* NewSage Press, 1989.
Kuspit, Donald. "Nancy Grossman (Terry Dintenfass)." *Artforum* 23:4 (December 1984): 85–86.
Raven, Arlene. *Nancy Grossman.* Hillwood Art Museum, 1991.
Watson-Jones, Virginia. *Contemporary American Women Sculptors.* Oryx Press, 1986.

Grotell, Maija (1899–1973)

Born in Helsinki, Finland, Maija Grotell emigrated to the United States in 1927. She had graduated from the Central School of Industrial Art, Finland, but felt she would have more opportunities to pursue a career in ceramics in America. Her first job as an instructor at the Inwood Pottery Studios of New York City set her on the path of teaching ceramics. Settlement houses in New York City had become schools for craft classes which led Grotell to a nine-year teaching career (1929–1938) at the Henry Street Settlement House Craft School.

Grotell began exhibiting her work shortly after her arrival in the United States and in 1929 received the Diploma Di Colaborador at the International Exposition, Barcelona, Spain. The Paris International Exposition, France, of 1937 awarded her ceramics a silver medal; a year later the Arts and Crafts Society of Boston, Massachusetts, brought her work to national attention by honoring her with the title of master craftsman. This award probably attracted Finnish architect Eliel Saarinen, president of the Cranbrook Academy of Art, Bloomfield Hills, Michigan, who subsequently asked her to chair the ceramics department.

The Michigan art school became her home for twenty-eight years

(1938–1966) and made the development of her art possible. Her interest in glaze research blossomed on her favored forms—cylinders and globes. At the same time she built a reputation for ceramic education at the Cranbrook Academy of Art that attracted students from around the country. Active in Michigan artist organizations, Grotell consistently took prizes for her vessels at the annual exhibitions as well as from the Michigan Academy of Science, Arts, and Letters. She had a solo show at the Art Institute of Chicago, Illinois, in 1950, and in 1961 she received a medal from Alfred University, New York, for excellence in ceramics. A retrospective of her work opened at the Cranbrook Academy of Art in 1967 and travelled to Syracuse and the Museum of Contemporary Crafts (now the American Craft Museum) in New York City.

Between 1936 and 1949 Grotell's ceramics were also recognized by her peers through regular awards from the National Ceramic Exhibitions of the Syracuse Museum of Fine Arts, New York (now the Everson Museum). Many of her undergraduate and graduate students became the ceramic teachers for the next generation of ceramists and led the studio pottery movement of the 1960s.

Elaine Levin

Bibliography
Hakanson, Joy. "A Visit with Maija Grotell." *The Detroit News* (August 28, 1960): 28.
Levin, Elaine. "Maija Grotell." *American Ceramics* 1:1 (Winter 1982): 42–45.
Schlanger, Jeff. "Maija Grotell." *Craft Horizons* 29:6 (November–December 1969): 14–23.

Groves, Naomi Jackson (1910–)

Born in Montréal, Québec, Canada, the painter/writer Naomi Jackson Groves studied at various institutions, including Rannows Art School, Copenhagen, Denmark; Sir George Williams University (now Concordia University), and McGill University—both in Montréal, where she earned Bachelor's and Master's degrees; Heidelberg University, the University of Berlin, and the University of Munich—both in Germany; and Radcliffe College, Harvard University, Cambridge, Massachusetts, where she received Master of Arts and Doctorate degrees. Groves was awarded honorary Doctorates from McMaster University, Hamilton, Ontario, and Carleton University, Ottawa, Canada (1972, 1990).

Groves has held solo exhibitions at Radcliffe College, Harvard University, Cambridge, and Wheaton College, Norton—both in Massachusetts; McMaster University, Hamilton, Ontario; Godthaab, Greenland; and the Montréal Museum of Fine Arts; her work has also been invited to many group exhibitions. Assistant to the director of the National Gallery of Canada, Ottawa (1942–1943), she was later its consultant, and also taught at McGill, Carleton, and McMaster Universities—all in Canada.

A member of Canadian Artists Representation and an honorary member of the Ernst Barlach Society of Hamburg, Germany, Groves was a recipient of the Governor General's gold medal, McGill University, Montréal (1933) and a travelling fellowship from the Canadian Federation of University Women (1936–1937). Her work is represented in private and public permanent collections, including the National Gallery of Canada, Ottawa; McMaster University Collection, Hamilton, Ontario; McLaughlin Art Gallery, Oshawa, Ontario; and others.

Bibliography

Groves, Naomi Jackson. *A.Y. Jackson, dessins, un été au Québec.* Roussan Editeur, Inc., 1991.

———. *Greenland Diary 1941.* Penumbra Press, 1983.

Who's Who in American Art. 19th ed. R.R. Bowker Co., 1991–1992.

Gruber, Aaronel de Roy (1928–)

Born in Pittsburgh, Pennsylvania, the painter/photographer/sculptor Aaronel de Roy Gruber earned a Bachelor's degree from Carnegie-Mellon University in her native city.

Gruber has been given many solo exhibitions in the United States and abroad, including the Photo Forum, Pittsburgh, Pennsylvania (1991); Anita Shapolsky Gallery, New York City (1984); "Artist of the Year," Pittsburgh Center for the Arts (1981), and Carnegie Museum of Art—both in Pittsburgh, Pennsylvania (1977); Electric Gallery, Toronto, Canada (1974, 1977); William Penn Memorial Museum, a retrospective, Harrisburg, Pennsylvania (1976); Everson Museum, Syracuse, New York (1973); Galería Juana Mordo, Madrid, Spain (1969); Galleria 88, Rome, Italy (1965); Bertha Schaefer Gallery, New York City (1969, 1971); and others.

Between 1963 and 1992 her work has been invited to myriad group exhibitions throughout the United States, Canada, Switzerland, Germany, Hungary, Japan, Italy, the Near East, and South Asia. Gruber has won more than eighty awards and honors for her photography, sculpture, and painting. Her twenty-four-foot "Steelcityscape" won a purchase and sites award at the Western Pennsylvania Society of Sculptors at Fort Duquesne Park, Pittsburgh, Pennsylvania (1976); an award from General Mills, Inc., Minneapolis, Minnesota; and others. Most recently, she received the "100 Friends of Art Purchase Prize" at the Carnegie Museum, Pittsburgh, Pennsylvania (1992).

Gruber's work is represented in private, public, and corporate permanent collections, including the Aldrich Museum of Contemporary Art, Ridgefield, Connecticut; Butler Institute of American Art, Youngstown, Ohio; Carnegie Museum and Westinghouse Electric—both in Pittsburgh, Pennsylvania; Rose Art Museum, Brandeis University, Waltham, Massachusetts; Chase Manhattan Bank, New York City; Mobil Oil Corporation; Blue Cross and Blue Shield of Western Pennsylvania; and many others.

Bibliography

Evert, Marilyn, and Vernon Gay. *Discovering Pittsburgh's Sculpture.* University of Pittsburgh Press, 1983.

Seventy-Fifth Anniversary Associated Artists of Pittsburgh. Carnegie Institute Museum of Art, 1985.

Watson-Jones, Virginia. *Contemporary American Women Sculptors.* Oryx Press, 1986.

Who's Who in American Art. 19th ed. R.R. Bowker Co., 1991–1992.

Grygutis, Barbara (1946–)

Known as a sculptor and ceramist, Barbara Grygutis creates site-specific public art works that also incorporate aspects of architecture and environmental design.

Grygutis was born in Connecticut; spent most of her childhood in Israel; and moved to New Jersey with her family while in high school.

In 1964 Grygutis opted for the desert terrain of Tucson, Arizona, and attended the University of Arizona. She began her studies as an architecture student, but quickly changed her focus to art, completing a Bachelor of Fine Art degree in 1968 and a Master of Fine Art degree in 1971. During her student years Grygutis travelled to Japan to study pottery villages and to Europe, where she was entranced by monumental sculptures in public areas. Back in Tucson she established a studio for functional ceramics and lobbied for public art projects, completing murals and fountains as early as 1972. Since 1975 Grygutis has completed more than twenty major public art works throughout the nation.

Grygutis's work is characterized by its use of handmade ceramic tile and indigenous materials, combined in environments that reflect the site and participate in the daily life of the community. In the "Arlene Dunlop Smith Garden" (1985) in Tucson, Grygutis turned a destitute inner-city plot into a contemplative park of antique brick walkways, totems of blue stoneware and volcanic rock, and carefully chosen foliage. "Temple" (1988) was commissioned by the Tempe Arts Commission, Arizona, to reclaim a drainage area for a local neighborhood. Grygutis literally sculpted the earth to create a land bridge, crowned by a plaza of cobalt-blue architectural fragments. In 1990 Grygutis completed the controversial "San Mateo Gateway" in Albuquerque, New Mexico, in which she covered an actual 1954 Chevrolet in sky-blue tile and mounted it on a turquoise, twenty-six-foot-high triumphant arch. Grygutis is currently working on a number of projects, including a memorial to Martin Luther King, Jr., in Columbia, Missouri.

Heather Sealy Lineberry

Bibliography

Lowe, Charlotte. "Galleries Can't Hold Her Work." *Tucson Citizen* (June 3, 1991): 1B.

Sealy Lineberry, Heather. "A Temple for Tempe." *Artspace* (March–April 1991): 63.

Watson-Jones, Virginia. *Contemporary American Women Sculptors.* Oryx Press, 1986.

Guay, Nancy Allen (1945–)

The fiber artist Nancy Allen Guay studied at Haystack Mountain School of Crafts, Deer Isle, Maine (1963–1967) and earned a Master of Fine Arts degree from the University of Wisconsin at Madison (1976).

A studio assistant to Jack Lenor Larsen, Guay exhibited work in "10 Boston Fiber Artists," Northeastern University, Boston, Massachusetts (1978); the Skidmore College "Invitational," Saratoga Springs, New York (1978); "Contemporary Weaving," Clark Gallery, Lincoln, Massachusetts (1978); Boston Atheneum, Massachusetts (1977); Museum of Modern Art (MoMA), New York City (1976); and many others.

Winner of awards and honors, Guay received an artist's fellowship from the Massachusetts Council on the Arts and Humanities (1979); grants from the American-Scandinavian Foundation, the government of Finland, and the League of Finnish-American Societies, Helsinki (1975); the Denny award, University of Wisconsin Crafts Show, Madison (1974); the Marguerite Mergentime award for textile design, Skidmore College, Saratoga Springs, New York (1967); and others. Her work is represented in private and public permanent collections, including the United Nations, New York City; Calvary Lutheran Chapel, Madison, Wisconsin; and others.

Bibliography
Constantine, Mildred, and Jack Lenor Larsen. *The Art Fabric: Mainstream.* Van Nostrand Reinhold, 1980.

Guerrilla Girls (1985–)

The Guerrilla Girls came into being as a direct result of the "International Survey of Contemporary Painting and Sculpture," at the Museum of Modern Art (MoMA), New York City (1985), which represented 169 artists—less than 10 percent of whom were women.

The Guerrilla Girls are a congregation of women who, in public appearances, wear intimidating gorilla masks to protect their anonymity; trumpet themselves as the "conscience of the art world"; and, through pithy, boldly-designed posters laden with statistics, feel free to roundly criticize collectors, critics, galleries, museums, and white male artists—the entire elite art world—for its sexist and racist practices. Guerrilla Girls pursue a single-issue campaign unconcerned with style or quality.

Lecturers at colleges, museums, and on television throughout the United States, the Guerrilla Girls received an award from the borough president of Manhattan, New York. Complete sets of their posters are in private and public permanent collections, including the New York Public Library, New York City, and the Spencer Museum of Art, University of Kansas, Lawrence.

There is little doubt that, in part, the Guerrilla Girls have been responsible for raising the consciousness of the power players in the art world, effecting change in the number of women artists visible on the art scene, and providing hope for future generations of women artists.

Bibliography
Smith, Roberta. "Waging Guerrilla Warfare Against the Art World." *The New York Times* (June 17, 1990): Sect. 2:1, 31.

Gugler, Frida (1874–1966)

Born in Milwaukee, Wisconsin, the painter Frida Gugler studied at the School of the Art Institute of Chicago, Illinois, and took further work in France, Germany, and Italy. Her landscape paintings are represented in private and public permanent collections, including the Vanderpoel Memorial Association, Chicago, Illinois, and the Milwaukee Art Institute, Wisconsin.

Bibliography
American Art Annual. Vol. 30. American Federation of Arts, 1933.
Who's Who in American Art. 5th ed. American Federation of Arts, 1953.

Guité, Suzanne (1927–1981)

Born in New Richmond, Gaspe, Québec, Canada, the sculptor/painter Suzanne Guité studied sculpture at the Institute of Design, Chicago, Illinois, under the aegis of Laszlo Moholy-Nagy and Alexander Archipenko (1949). She then studied with Constantin Brancusi (1950); did further study at the Academy of Fine Arts, Florence, Italy (1951); did research at the Instituto Polytechnico, Mexico (1953), and painted murals (1956–1960). She explored the possibility of contemporary glass murals and mosaics in Venice, Italy; and did additional study of archeology and art history in Crete and Rhodes.

Guité, who lived in Perce, Québec, has held solo exhibitions in museums and galleries, including Douglass College, Rutgers University, New Brunswick (1974), and the Public Library, Princeton—both in New Jersey (1975); the Musée Régionale de Rimouski, Québec (1976); the Wells Gallery, Ottawa, Canada (1976); the Musée du Québec (1977); and many others. Her work was included in numerous prestigious group shows, such as the Museum of Contemporary Art, Montréal; the Musée Rodin, Paris, France; and the Musée du Québec—all in 1970; and others.

Examples of her sculptural work and tapestries grace many venues in Canada and the United States and are in private, public, and corporate permanent collections, including the National Gallery of Canada, Ottawa; Québec Museum of Art; Seagram's Art Collection, Montréal; and others.

Bibliography
Boulanger, Roland. "Suzanne Guité." *Arts et penseé* 14 (November–December 1953): 55–57, 59.
Boulanger, Roland, et al. *La Sculpture de Suzanne Guité.* Montréal: Aquila, 1973.
Gagnon, Claude-Lyse. "Une terre cuite murale de Suzanne Guité." *Vie des arts* (Autumn 1965): 28–31.
Masse, Ginette. *Suzanne Guite: Sculptures et tapisseries.* Musée du Québec, 1977.

Gurría, Angela (1929–)

Born in Mexico City, Angela Gurría is the daughter of José Maria Gurría Urgell, lawyer, salient poet, and rector of the University of Tabasco, Zacatecas. She attended classes in the School of Philosophy and Letters of the University of Mexico between 1946 and 1948 and then enrolled at Mexico City College to study sculpture (1949–1951).

Over the next six years, Gurría studied with maestro Germán Cueto and, later, with Abraham González. Still later, she completed her studies in sculpture at Montiel Blancas' studio.

Gurría became a professor of art in 1961 at the Iberoamerican University in Mexico City. Her work in sculpture, which has been exhibited in myriad exhibitions in Mexico and elsewhere, can be described in three words: monumental and important.

Bibliography
Camp, Roderic A. *Who's Who in Mexico Today.* Westview Press, 1988.

Gutiérrez, Judith

Born in Guayaquil, Ecuador, Judith Gutiérrez studied painting at the School of Fine Arts in Guayaquil and then went on for further study at the Casa de Cultura in Quito—both in Ecuador.

She emigrated to Mexico in 1964 and initially showed her work at the Galería Pecanins. Gutiérrez has had exhibitions throughout Mexico and Ecuador, as well as in the United States and Venezuela. Her abstract oils are vigorous and brilliant in color.

Bibliography
The Texas Quarterly: Image of Mexico I. The University of Texas. Autumn 1969.

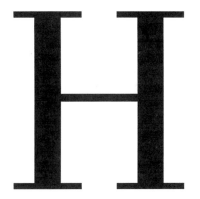

Haeseker, Alexandra (1945–)

Alexandra Haeseker produces prints, watercolor and acrylic paintings, and three-dimensional painted constructions in a representational style. She records details of everyday life and personal experience. Compiled from family archives and photographs she has taken, elements are re-combined in collage-like images.

Born in Breda, Holland, in 1945, Haeseker settled in Calgary, Alberta, Canada, in 1955. She has a fine arts diploma from the Alberta College of Art (1968) and a Bachelor of Arts degree (1966) and Master of Arts degree (1972) from the University of Calgary, Alberta. Since 1973 she has been an instructor at the Alberta College of Art.

Haeseker has exhibited widely in Canada, the United States, Britain, Europe, Australia, and Asia, including "Contemporary Canadian Art," New York City, 1982; the International Juried Print Biennales, Poland, Yugoslavia, Italy, and Spain; "Interaction," touring Australia; she was a prize winner at the International Exhibit in Seoul, Korea (1983).

Influenced by Edweard Muybridge's photographic studies of a young amputee, Haeseker initially made paintings and constructions which dealt with the theme of a legless boy. The collaging and juxtaposition of elements creates an ambiguous and surrealistic quality.

Subsequent work depicts legless figures hovering in the landscape while accompanying dogs are firmly anchored to the ground, an abstracted painterly field of subdued and mottled color. The simple treatment suggests the limitless space of the Canadian prairie. The isolation of the figures provides a formal and psychological tension.

Haeseker shows dogs, which became a dominant theme for her after 1976. From the mid-1980s Haeseker has focused behind the scenes at dog shows. A shallow space is set up by the grid of the pens which are draped with canvas, nylon and silver-reflective tarps and decorated with banners, ribbons, and pennants in vivid primary colors. These are in fact manufactured images or "set-ups" staged by the artist. They are complex compositions with careful formal structures. Clarity of color and light is all important. The luminous light plays over the intricate surfaces and textures.

Haeseker's work is not straightforward representation. Rather, through careful rendering of individual forms, it presents the illusion of reality.

Patricia Ainslie

Bibliography

Baker, Suzanne Devonshire. *Alberta Artists*. University of Alberta Press, 1980.

Murray, Joan. *The Best of Contemporary Canadian Art*. Hurtig Publishers, 1987.

Szabados, Bela. "Alexandra Haeseker and Derek Michael Besant at Galerie Royale." *Artmagazine* 6:21 (Spring 1975): 32–33.

Hafif, Marcia (1929–)

A native of California, born in Pomona, the painter Marcia Hafif earned a Bachelor's degree at Pomona College, Claremont, California (1950); did graduate work in art history at Claremont Graduate School, California (1960); and was awarded a Master of Fine Arts degree from the University of California at Irvine (1971).

Hafif is the holder of two National Endowment for the Arts (NEA) fellowships (1980–1981, 1990) and a Creative Artists Public Service (CAPS) grant from the New York State Council on the Arts (1976–1977) for her visual work. She has published widely, made films, and given performances, such as "Language Exchange," with Pavel Sobczak in Lodz, Poland (1990).

Between 1964 and 1992 Hafif has held myriad solo exhibitions of her drawings and paintings in the United States and abroad, including Galleria La Sallita, Rome, Italy (1964, 1968); "Mass Tone Paintings," Sonnabend Gallery, New York City (1974); "Transparent Paintings," Galerie Nordenhake, Malmö, Sweden (1983), and Raum für Malerei, Cologne, Germany (1984); "Enamel on Wood," Julian Pretto/Berland Hall, New York City (1989); "From the Table of Pigments," Galerij S65, Aalst, Belgium, and "Local Color," Galleria Plurima, Milan, Italy (1992); and many others.

Hafif's work has been invited to major group exhibitions in the United States and throughout the world: from Rome, Italy, to San Francisco, California; Dijon, France; New York City; Chapel Hill, North Carolina; and Belmont-sur-Lausanne, Switzerland. She has been a visiting artist, faculty member, and lecturer at several colleges and universities in the United States and her work is represented in private, public, and corporate permanent collections, including the Massachusetts Institute of Technology (MIT), Cambridge; the American embassy in Japan; Chase Manhattan Bank; First National Bank of Chicago; and others.

Bibliography
Dagbert, Anne. "Marcia Hafif." *Art Press* (June 1991): 102.
Gibson, Ann. "Color and Difference in Abstract Painting: The Ultimate Case of Monochrome." *Genders* 13 (Spring 1992): 123.
Massera, Jean-Charles. "Marcia Hafif, From the Inventory: Bleu Parisien." *Opus International* 125 (Summer 1991): 47.
Wei, Lily. "Talking Abstract." *Art in America* (July 1987): 80–81, 96–97.

Hafner, Dorothy (1952–)

The ceramist Dorothy Hafner was born in Woodbridge, Connecticut, and earned a Bachelor's degree from Skidmore College, Saratoga Springs, New York (1974).

After receiving her degree Hafner worked as production manager for the International Craft Film Festival and directed the international department of the Museum of Contemporary Crafts, New York City (1976). For the next two years she was artist-in-residence at Artpark, Lewiston, New York, before setting up "Art in Dining" (1979), in New York City, where she designed porcelain tableware for elegant department stores and other such retailers, including Neiman Marcus and Tiffany's in New York City and, since 1982, Rosenthal in Germany.

Winner of awards and honors for her work, Hafner was the recipient of the Westerwald Industrial Design award; a certificate of honor from the Women in Design, Ross, California; and others.

Bibliography
Clark, Garth. *American Ceramics: 1896 to the Present*. Abbeville Press, 1987.
Herman, Lloyd E. *American Porcelain: New Expressions in an Ancient Art*. Timber Press, 1980.
Horn, Richard. *Fifties Style: Then and Now*. Beach Trees Press, 1985.

Hagin, Nancy (1940–)

Born in Elizabeth, New Jersey, Nancy Hagin earned her Bachelor of Fine Arts degree from Carnegie-Mellon University, Pittsburgh, Pennsylvania, in 1962. Two years later, after graduate study at Yale University, New Haven, Connecticut, she received a Master of Fine Arts degree.

A New York City resident for six months of each year, Hagin spends the spring and summer in her country home in Glenco Mills, New York. Her medium is watercolors in her upstate New York house and acrylics in the city.

An award-winning painter, Hagin won a scholarship to the Yale–Norfolk Summer School of Music and Art, Connecticut (1961); a Fulbright fellowship to Rome, Italy (1966–1967); three fellowships to the MacDowell Colony, Peterborough, New Hampshire (1974, 1979, 1982); two grants from the National Endowment for the Arts (NEA) (1982, 1991); and an award from the National Academy of Design, New York City (1989); among others.

Hagin has been teaching at the Fashion Institute of Technology (1974 to the present), and the Cooper Union (1982 to the present)—both in New York City, after stints at the Maryland Institute College of Art, Baltimore (1964–1973); Pratt Institute, New York City (1973–1974, 1985); and the Rhode Island School of Design, Providence (1974). Between 1974 and 1986 she was a visiting artist at various colleges and universities, including Kean College of New Jersey, Union; Bowling Green University, Ohio; Auburn University, Alabama; Kent State University, Ohio; and Lafayette College, Easton, Pennsylvania.

"Enamel Top" (1989), an acrylic, and "Squirrel Cage" (1989), a large watercolor, are prime examples of Hagin's painting techniques in the two mediums. Both are still lifes: the former is a pristine arrangement of objects on the kitchen table, meticulously painted, a study of light; the latter presents a highly-organized, riotous jumble of objects, including quilts, a squirrel cage, a coffee pot, flour container, a wooden box, eggs and a pitchfork, and a box in a wicker basket—all in an interior setting, rich in color and texture, showing a mastery of light.

Hagin has had eighteen solo exhibitions at major galleries in the United States to 1991, six of which were at the Fischbach Gallery in New York City. Her works have been seen in more than sixty group shows of importance, and are in many permanent public and private collections, including the Boston Museum of Fine Arts, and Rose Art Museum, Brandeis University, Waltham—both in Massachusetts; the Butler Institute of American Art, Youngstown, Ohio; Yeshiva University, New York City; the Utah Museum of Fine Arts, the Delaware Museum, and the art in embassies program of the U.S. Department of State, and others.

Bibliography
Henry, Gerrit. "Nancy Hagin at Fischbach." *Art in America* 75:10 (October 1987): 185–86.
Nancy Hagin. A Catalog. Introduction by John Arthur. Fischbach Gallery, 1989.
Roberts, Nancy. "Nancy Hagin: A Double Life." *U.S. Art* (January–February 1990): 37–41.

Hahn, Betty (1940–)

Born in Chicago, Illinois, Betty Hahn studied photography with Henry Holmes Smith at Indiana University, Bloomington, where she earned a Master of Fine Arts degree in 1966. She was assistant professor of photography at Rochester Institute of Technology, New York, between 1969 and 1975 and has taught non-traditional forms of photography at the University of New Mexico, Albuquerque, since 1976.

Hahn's work—evidence of Henry Holmes Smith's influence—encompasses a wide range of process, technique, and imagery. In her early work she used multiple imagery with the gum bichromate process. In 1969 the George Eastman House displayed this work in the exhibition "Vision and Expression," one of the first surveys of non-traditional photography. During the early 1970s Hahn began combining gum bichromate on fabric with embroidery. Hahn states, "They really had more [of a] feminist intent, I saw myself connected to a whole generation of women who expressed themselves through stitched pieces." These pieces also had feminist themes, such as the family, flower gardens, and vegetables. During the 1970s she also began a long series of process variations on the same image of Lone Ranger and Tonto, which questions our ideas of the American hero and popular culture, and flowers. Hahn also used the Mick-a-matic toy camera for her series, "Passing Shots," of gardens. Employing the Polaroid twenty-by-twenty-four-inch camera she produced the series, "Botanical Layout" (1979–1980) with the recurrent themes of flowers. She also played the role of detective in the series "Scenes of the Crime and Surveillance," fictional crime scenes that question criminal photography as evidence. In 1984 Hahn's travels in Japan inspired the filmatic series "Shinjuku," eleven images that combine color with black-and-white negatives printed on color paper. Influence of film can again be seen in "Arrival or Departure (After Hitchcock)," (1987), a series of gelatin silver prints.

Hahn has had more than thirty solo exhibitions nationally and internationally and has work displayed in major collections worldwide. She received National Endowment for the Arts (NEA) photographers fellowships in 1978 and again in 1983.

Laine Sutherland

Bibliography
Auer, Michel. *Enciclopédie Internationale des Photographes de 1839 á nos jours.* Editions Camera Obscura, 1985.
Bloom, John. "Interview with Betty Hahn." *Photo Metro* 51 (August 1987): 7–17.
Garner, Gretchen. *Reclaiming Paradise: American Women Photograph the Land.* University of Minnesota, 1987.
Walsh, George, Colin Naylor, and Michael Held. *Contemporary Photographers.* St. Martin's Press, 1982.

Hailman, Johanna K. Woodwell (1871–)

Born in Pittsburgh, Pennsylvania, the painter Johanna K. Woodwell Hailman has won many honors and awards, including a silver medal at the exhibition of the Art Association of Pittsburgh (1911); a silver medal at the Pan-Pacific Exposition in San Francisco, California (1915); and others. She also exhibited work in a group exhibition at the Saint Louis City Art Museum, Missouri (1918). Examples of her work appear in private and public permanent collections, such as the Carnegie Institute of Technology (now Carnegie Mellon University), Pittsburgh, Pennsylvania; and others.

Bibliography
American Art Annual. Vol. 30. American Federation of Arts, 1933.
Archives of American Art. *Collection of Exhibition Catalogs.* G.K. Hall, 1979.
Who's Who in American Art. 3rd ed. American Federation of Arts, 1940.

Hale, Ellen Day (1855–1940)

A member of the Beecher-Hale family of Boston, Massachusetts, Ellen Day Hale was a painter, etcher, and writer. Her father, author/orator/clergyman Edward Everett Hale, who was a daguerreotypist, taught her photography. Her mother, Emily Baldwin Perkins Hale (granddaughter of Lyman Beecher) encouraged Hale and her seven brothers, including artist Philip Lesley Hale, to draw while they were growing up. Hale's role models included her grandaunts, authors Harriet Beecher Stowe and Catherine Beecher, and her aunt, artist and author Susan Hale (1833–1910), who probably gave Ellen Day Hale her first painting lessons.

In Boston Hale studied art with William Rimmer in 1873 and with William Morris Hunt and Helen Knowlton from 1874 to 1879. She opened her own studio in 1877 and began teaching in grammar schools and taking private pupils. She took classes at the Pennsylvania Academy of Fine Arts, Philadelphia, when she visited her cousin, Margaret Lesley Bush-Brown.

Hale was fluent in six languages when she and Knowlton went to Europe in 1881. In Paris she took Emmanuel Frémiet's drawing class at the Jardin des Plantes, then studied briefly at the Académie Colarossi with Louis-Joseph-Raphael Collin and Gustave-Claude-Étienne Courtois before she joined the class for women taught by Émile-Auguste Carolus-Duran and Jean-Jacques Henner. The next year she returned to Europe and studied at the Académie Julian. She again attended Julian's in 1885, studying with Rodolphe Julian, William Adolphe Bouguereau, and Tony Robert-Fleury. That summer Gabrielle Clements taught her to etch while they were touring the French countryside.

Hale began to exhibit in the mid-1870s with the Boston Art Club, Massachusetts, and at the 1876 U.S. Centennial Exposition. She exhibited with the Royal Academy, London, England; the Paris Salon, France; the Pennsylvania Academy of Fine Arts, Philadelphia; the Boston Museum of Fine Arts, St. Botolph Club, Boston, the Guild of Boston Artists, and the Worcester Art Museum—all in Massachusetts; the National Academy of Design, the New York Etching Club, and the National Arts Club—all in New York City; the Art Institute of Chicago and the Chicago Society of Etchers—both in Illinois; the Corcoran Gallery of Art and the U.S. National Museum—both in Washington, D.C.; the J.B. Speed Art Museum, Louisville, Kentucky; the American Society of Painters in Watercolors; and the Salmagundi Club—all in New York City. She was included in the first art museum exhibition featuring women's work, "The Women Etchers of America," at the Boston Museum, Massachusetts, in 1887.

Hale lived in Washington, D.C., from 1904 to 1909 when she played hostess for her father while he served as chaplain of the U.S. Senate. She and Clements spent summers in the artist colony of Rockport, Massachusetts, and winters in Charleston, South Carolina. With Clements, she travelled in Europe, Algiers, and the Middle East.

Hale translated French etcher René Ligeron's *Original Engraving in Colors* into English. Using his method she and Clements experimented with color soft-ground etchings and aquatints in the 1920s and 1930s.

Hale painted and etched in a broad, bold style which she had learned from Hunt, who had introduced Barbizon painting to America. She gradually incorporated the lessons of Whistler and the impressionists into her work. In the twentieth century, photography influenced her to use tighter drawing and more careful modeling.

Her striking self-portrait in the Boston Museum of Fine Arts, Massachusetts, reveals the intensity with which she viewed herself as an independent woman and artist. Paintings and etchings are in the National Museum of American History, Washington, D.C.; the Philadelphia Museum of Art and the Pennsylvania Academy of Fine Arts—both in Philadelphia, Pennsylvania; and in many private collections.

Phyllis Peet

Bibliography

Bush-Brown Family Papers and Hale Family Papers. Sophia Smith Collection, Smith College, Northampton, Massachusetts.

Chesebro, Alanna. *Ellen Day Hale, 1855–1940.* October 17–November 14, 1981. Richard York Gallery, 1981.

Ellen Day Hale Papers and Philip Lesley Hale Papers, Archives of American Art, Smithsonian Institution, Washington, D.C.

Exhibition and Sale of Etchings and Soft-Ground Aquatints in Color of French, Italian and American Subjects by Ellen Day Hale and Gabrielle DeV. Clements, . . . January 14, . . . January 26, 1924. Goodspeed's Bookshop, 1924.

Exhibition of Etchings in Color by Ellen Day Hale, Gabrielle DeVeaux Clements, Lesley Jackson, Margaret Yeaton Hoyt, Theresa F. Bernstein, and William Meyerowitz, November 30 and December 30, 1935. J.B. Speed Memorial Museum, 1935.

Hale, Ellen Day. *History of Art; A Study of the Lives of Leonardo, Michelangelo, Raphael, Titian, and Albert Dürer.* Charles H. Kerr & Company and George H. Ellis, 1888.

Hale, Nancy. *The Life in the Studio.* Little, Brown and Co., 1969.

Peet, Phyllis. *American Women of the Etching Revival.* High Museum of Art, 1988.

Tufts, Eleanor. *American Women Artists 1830–1930.* National Museum of Women in the Arts, 1987.

Hale, Lilian Westcott (1881–1963)

A painter of portraits and of figures in interiors—in oil and in charcoal—Lilian Westcott Hale also occasionally painted landscapes in the vicinity of her Dedham, Massachusetts, home. She was born in Hartford, Connecticut, and began her studies at the Hartford Art School. About 1897 she attended William Merritt Chase's summer class at Shinnecock, New York. She won a scholarship to study at the Boston Museum School, Massachusetts, and entered Edmund C. Tarbell's painting class in 1899. She married the painter/teacher Philip Leslie Hale in 1901.

Hale had her first solo exhibition in 1908 in Boston, Massachusetts—four years after her graduation from the Boston Museum School. Her first prize came in 1910—a bronze medal at the Buenos Aires International Exposition, Argentina, and was followed in 1915 by a gold medal at the Panama-Pacific International Exposition in San Francisco, California.

Hale exhibited regularly in Boston, Massachusetts, at the Guild of Boston Artists, the Copley Society, and Rowlands Galleries as well as numerous showings in New York City. She was elected an associate of the National Academy of Design, New York City, in 1927 and achieved full membership in 1931.

Her soft, atmospheric paintings are intimate and have often been described as impressionistic. Her work can be found in the Museum of Fine Arts, Boston, Massachusetts; the National Academy of Design and Metropolitan Museum of Art—both in New York City; the Pennsylvania Academy of Fine Arts, Philadelphia; the Corcoran Gallery of Art,

Washington, D.C.; and many private collections.

Eleanor Tufts

Bibliography

Fairbrother, Trevor J. *The Bostonians: Painters of an Elegant Age, 1870–1930.* Boston Museum of Fine Arts, 1986.

Hale, Nancy. *The Life in the Studio.* Little, Brown and Co., 1969.

Tufts, Eleanor. *American Women Artists, 1830–1930.* National Museum of Women in the Arts, 1987.

Hall, D.J. (1951–)

Born in Los Angeles, California, the painter D.J. Hall earned a Bachelor of Fine Arts degree *magna cum laude* from the University of Southern California, Los Angeles (1973).

Hall has held many solo exhibitions in galleries, including the Albert Contreras Gallery, Los Angeles, California (1975, 1977); O.K. Harris, New York City (1981, 1982, 1985, 1988, 1991); Tortue Gallery, Santa Monica (1983, 1985), "Selected Works 1974–1985," Barnsdall Park, Municipal Art Gallery, Los Angeles (1986), and "A Ten-Year Survey," Santa Monica Heritage Museum (1992)—all in California; and others.

Between 1974 and 1992 Hall's work has been invited to myriad group exhibitions in the United States and abroad, such as "The Figure in Contemporary Realism," Long Beach City College, California (1976); "Billboards" (a fifteen-by-sixty-foot hand-painted billboard), Eyes and Ears Foundation, Los Angeles (1977); "Contemporary American Realism Since 1960," a travelling show from the Pennsylvania Academy of Fine Arts, Philadelphia, Pennsylvania, to the eastern United States, Portugal, Spain, and Germany (1981–1983); "Los Angeles Today: Contemporary Visions," Amerika Haus, Berlin, Germany (1987); "American Pop Culture Today III," La Fôret Museum, Harajuku, Japan (1989); "New Work—New York," Galerie Barbara Silverberg, Montréal, Canada (1990); "Individual Realities," a travelling show from the Sezon Museum of Art, Tokyo, to Osaka, Japan (1991); "The 56th Annual Mid-Year Exhibition," Butler Institute of American Art, Youngstown, Ohio (1992); and others.

Hall has taught in several California universities and was the 1992 recipient of the 6th Annual Heritage Award "for contributions to the cultural heritage of the Santa Monica Bay Community." Earlier on she was awarded a National Endowment for the Arts (NEA) fellowship in painting (1977). Her work is represented in private, public, and corporate permanent collections, including the Metropolitan Museum of Art, New York City; Kemper Insurance, Chicago, Illinois; BankAmerica, Los Angeles; GTE of California; and others.

Bibliography

Martin, Victoria. "Los Angeles Realism: A Conversation with D.J. Hall." *Artweek* 22:25 (August 1, 1991): 17.

Moore, Sylvia. *Yesterday and Tomorrow: California Women Artists.* Midmarch Arts, 1989.

Raynor, Vivien. "The Figure Revisited: Figural Energy Is Explored." *The New York Times* (April 30, 1989): 32.

Wilson, William. "Art Review: D.J. Hall Unmasks Los Angeles' Excruciating Aging Process." *Los Angeles Times* (June 2, 1992): F5.

Hall, Norma Bassett (1889–1957)

Born in Halsey, Oregon, the printmaker Norma Bassett Hall studied at the Art Institute of Chicago, Illinois; the School of the Portland Art Association, Oregon; and in London, England. Winner of honors and awards at a number of printmaking exhibitions, Hall showed at the Kansas State Federation of Arts (1937); the Southern Printmakers (1938); and many others.

Hall exhibited with and was a member of the American Color Print Society; California Printmakers; Chicago Galleries Association; National Serigraph Society; Prairie Printmakers; and Southern Printmakers. Examples of her prints are in private and public permanent collections, including the Brooklyn Public Library, New York; California State Library, Sacramento; Honolulu Academy of Art, Hawaii; Smithsonian Institution, Washington, D.C.; University of Tulsa, Oklahoma; and many others.

Bibliography
American Art Annual. Vol. 28. American Federation of Arts, 1932.
Kovinick, Phil. *The Woman Artist in the American West 1860–1960.* Fullerton, California: Muckenthaler Cultural Center, 1976.
A Selection of American Prints. A Selection of Biographies of Forty Women Artists Working between 1904–1979. Santa Rosa, California: The Annex Galleries, 1987.

Hall, Pam (1951–)

Since her move to St. John's, Newfoundland, Canada, in the 1980s, Pam Hall has explored and developed her relationship with this northern and rugged landscape in conjunction with her already established commitment to feminism. These concerns have surfaced in her art but, more important for the art community in Newfoundland, they have also taken the form of active involvement in artists' groups and in lobbying provincial and federal governments on behalf of artists. In 1984 Hall was a founding member of St. John's artist-run, Eastern Edge Gallery, which retains its importance as an alternative gallery in Canada's maritime area; in 1985 she was chair of the Citizens' Coalition Against Cultural Cutbacks in St. John's as well as secretary of the Association of National Non-Profit Artists' Centres (ANNPAC); in 1986 and 1987 she was national spokesperson for ANNPAC; and in 1988 she was a member of the Canadian Advisory Committee on the Status of the Artist.

Hall's commitment to a Canadian, and specifically a Newfoundland arts community is enhanced by her own commitment to her art. Born in Kingston, Ontario, she completed her Honors Bachelor of Fine Arts degree at Sir George Williams University (now Concordia University) in Montréal in 1973 and then proceeded to complete a Master's degree in education at the University of Alberta in Edmonton. Within four years of her graduation she had moved to Newfoundland and opened her first solo exhibition, "On the Edge of the Eastern Ocean" (1982), in that province's most important art gallery, Memorial University Art Gallery, St. John's. The show toured provincially and resulted in a publication by the same name being released by GLC Publishers in Toronto.

In 1984 and 1986 Hall held two more solo exhibitions still in keeping with her maritime theme, "Saltwater Rock," Memorial University of Newfoundland (1982), and "Newfoundland Scotch on the Rocks," Contemporary Graphics (1986)—both in St. John's, Newfound-

land. In 1987 she exhibited a series of drawings with Don Wright at Contemporary Graphics, St. John's, as well as with a number of other artists in "Innovation: Subject and Technique" at the Scarborough Campus Art Gallery, University of Toronto, Ontario. This same year she began to explore and develop her metaphysical interests in the landscape, resulting in "Worshipping the Stone," Memorial University of Newfoundland (1987), and "In the Temple," Eastern Edge Gallery (1988)—both in St. John's, Newfoundland. An important result of her metaphysical and esoteric searches was a recent show, "The Coil that Binds, the Line that Bends," Memorial University of Newfoundland, Sir Wilfred Grenfell College, Corner Brook (1990). This exhibition combined Hall's concern for the Newfoundland fishing industry with her interest in myth and story. Her mixed-media drawings with their inclusion of topographical maps of the coastline, color photographs, xeroxes, and text hung on the gallery walls formed the "frame" for the central sculpture—"the Coil." The coil was a found cod-net, altered by Hall, with red polyester fishing twine that assumed a spiral shape (105 feet by approximately nine inches in diameter) in the center of the gallery floor. The chant-like text accompanying the drawings invoked the mystery as well as the repetitiveness of interaction between humans and environment in life-giving or life-supporting situations: "first sign—first sight/coiled line—in-sight"; "—his net, her nest, at rest"; "serpentine/on the snakeless land"; "lie lightly on the land."

In 1989, in addition to producing her "Coil" exhibition, Hall presented a paper, "The Contents of Artistic Creation: Some Speculations on the Role of the Artist in Society," at a colloquium, "Creating in Context: Issues Affecting Art and Artists," Victoria, British Columbia, thereby continuing her active role as artists' advocate as well as producer. And, as multi-dimensional artist she was art director for the Canadian films, *Finding Mary March* (1987) and *The Lost Salt Gift of Blood* (1989).

Janice Helland

Bibliography
O'Neill, Colleen. *Pam Hall: The Coil that Binds/The Line that Bends.* St. Johns, Memorial University, 1990.

Hall, Susan (1943–)

Born in Point Reyes Station, California, the painter/printmaker Susan Hall earned a Bachelor of Fine Arts degree from the California College of Arts and Crafts, Oakland (1965), and two years later received a Master of Arts degree from the University of California at Berkeley.

Between 1967 and 1991 Hall has held thirty-two solo exhibitions of her work throughout the United States, including the Ovsey Gallery, Los Angeles, California (1981, 1982, 1984, 1987, 1989, 1991); the Trabia Macafee Gallery, New York City (1988, 1989); Wyckoff Gallery, Aspen, Colorado (1990–1992); Ted Greenwald Gallery (1986), Hamilton Gallery (1978, 1979, 1981, 1983), and the Whitney Museum of American Art (1972)—all in New York City; and many others.

Hall's work has been invited to myriad group exhibitions in the United States and abroad, such as "Drawing Invitational," Sunrise Museum, Charleston, West Virginia (1992); "Presswork: The Art of Women Printmakers," a travelling show, the National Museum of Women in the Arts, Washington, D.C. (1991); "Lines of Vision," a travelling show, Blum Helman Downtown, New York City—then to major museums in Mexico, Venezuela, Chile, Colombia, Argentina, Brazil, Portugal, and Spain (1989); "Hommage aux Femmes," Berlin, Germany (1985); "Painting," Sarah Lawrence College, Bronxville, New York (1975, 1976, 1977); "Extraordinary Realities," Whitney Museum of American Art, New York City (1973); "98.5," a documentary Holly Solomon film, including Susan Hall, 26th Edinburgh Film Festival, Scotland (1971); and many others.

Between 1967 and 1992 Hall was a faculty member at art schools and universities throughout the United States. She is the recipient of fellowships and grants from the National Endowment for the Arts (NEA) (1979, 1987), the Krasner Pollack Foundation (1986), the New York State Council on the Arts (1977), and the Palace of the Legion of Honor, San Francisco (1967). Her work is represented in private, public, and corporate permanent collections, including the Whitney Museum of American Art, New York City; Hudson River Museum, Yonkers, New York; San Francisco Museum of Art, California; St. Louis Art Museum, Missouri; Chase Manhattan Bank, New York City; Warner Brothers, Los Angeles; the Brooklyn Museum, New York; and others.

Bibliography

Clark, John R. "Image, Technique and Spirituality in Susan Hall's New Work." *Arts Magazine* (Summer 1988).

Glueck, Grace. "Susan Hall." *The New York Times* (April 19, 1981).

Hornick, Lita. "Susan Hall/Out of the Shadows." *Nine Martinis*. Kulchur Foundation, 1987.

Hallauk, Joy Kiluvigyuak (1940–)

Joy Kiluvigyuak Hallauk is a Canadian Inuit (Eskimo) artist born at Padlei near Henik Lake, west of Hudson Bay in the Northwest Territories. Her family gave up their traditional semi-nomadic camp life and moved into the community of Arviat (Eskimo Point) in 1954; there she met and married Luke Hallauk. Kiluvigyuak began stone carving in 1964 and started producing wall-hangings and dolls around 1970.

Kiluvigyuak depicts maternal or multiple head motifs in stone, using small axes and files. The bulky volumes of her figures, with their juxtaposed rounded and angular masses, present dynamic as well as powerful images. Kiluvigyuak also produces exquisite dolls and is probably the most gifted maker of appliqué wall-hangings in Arviat. Her wall-hangings generally consist of rows of figures with carved antler faces, dressed in traditional bleached caribou skin clothing decorated with elaborate bead trim, sewn onto duffle cloth. Her largest such wall-hanging measures fourteen-by-four-and-one-half feet.

Kiluvigyuak's sculptures, wall-hangings, and dolls have been exhibited in about twenty-five group shows in Canada, the United States, and Europe. She is represented in the collections of the Winnipeg Art Gallery, the Art Gallery of Ontario, and the New Brunswick Museum.

Ingo Hessel

Bibliography

Hessel, Ingo. "Arts and Crafts in the Keewatin." *Inuktitut* 6 (Fall 1986): 43–48.

Hammond, Harmony (1944–)

Born in Chicago, Illinois, the African-American painter/sculptor Harmony Hammond studied at the Junior School of the Art Institute of Chicago, Illinois (1960–1961); Milliken University, Decatur, Illinois

(1961–1963); and earned a Bachelor's degree from the University of Minnesota, Minneapolis (1967). During the summers of 1967 and 1969, Hammond also studied at the Alliance Française, Paris, France.

Hammond has held solo exhibitions in the United States and abroad, including the Trabia Macafee Gallery, and Bernice Steinbaum Gallery (1986)—both in New York City; the Linda Durham Gallery, Santa Fe (1988); and the University of New Mexico, Albuquerque (1987)—both in New Mexico; "Luxuriance," American Center, Paris, France (1983); Lerner-Heller Gallery, New York City (1979, 1981, 1982); Amherst College, Massachusetts (1981); "Retrospective Exhibition," Glen Hanson Gallery, Minneapolis, Minnesota, and the Denver Art Museum, Colorado (1981); "International Feminist Art," Haag Gementemuseum, The Hague, the Netherlands (1980); and many others. Her work has been invited to many major group exhibitions in the United States since the mid-1960s.

Hammond has written numerous articles on feminist art and has taught at the School of the Art Institute, Chicago, Illinois (1973), and Richmond College, the City University of New York (CUNY) (1975). She has won honors and awards for her work, including a Creative Artists Public Service (CAPS) grant (1982); a residency and a fellowship at the MacDowell Colony, Peterborough, New Hampshire (1979, 1981); fellowships from the National Endowment for the Arts (NEA) (1979–1980, 1983–1984); and a Pollack-Krasner fellowship (1989–1990).

Hammond's work is represented in private, public, and corporate permanent collections in the United States and abroad, such as the Art Institute of Chicago, Illinois; Brooklyn Museum and Metropolitan Museum of Art—both in New York City; Denver Art Museum, Colorado; Walker Art Center, Minneapolis, and General Mills Corporation—both in Minnesota; Museum of Fine Arts, Santa Fe, New Mexico; Wadsworth Atheneum, Hartford, Connecticut; and many others.

Bibliography

Harmony Hammond: Ten Years, 1970–1980. Essay by Lucy Lippard. Women's Art Registry of Minnesota, 1981.

Hess, Elizabeth. "Sanctuary." *Village Voice* (May 24, 1988).

Raven, Arlene. *Crossing Over: Feminism and the Art of Social Change.* University of Michigan Press, 1988.

Van Wagner, Judith C. "Harmony Hammond's Painted Spirits." *Arts Magazine* 60:5 (January 1986): 22–25.

Watson-Jones, Virginia. *Contemporary American Women Sculptors.* Oryx Press, 1986.

Hanson, Jo

Born in Carbondale, Illinois, Jo Hanson is a sculptor who transmutes paper and metal urban trash found outside her San Francisco, California, home into forms that speak to the myriad problems endangering society. Hanson earned a Master of Arts degree in art at San Francisco State University, California (1973), making an abrupt mid-career switch after having worked in the fields of teaching, journalism, and social work. Earlier on, she received a Master of Arts degree in education from the University of Illinois, Urbana.

Hanson has held solo exhibitions in museums and galleries including the Lucien Labaudt Art Gallery, San Francisco, California (1969); Corcoran Gallery of Art, Washington, D.C. (1974); University of California at San Diego (1975); Pennsylvania Academy of Fine Arts,

Philadelphia (1976); Utah Museum of Fine Arts, Salt Lake City (1977); San Francisco Museum of Modern Art (1980), was artist-in-residence at The Farm (1981); and exhibited at the International Sculpture Conference—all in San Francisco, California (1982); held solo exhibitions at Base Internationale, Lyon, France (1983); Hatley Martin Gallery, San Francisco, California (1986); and others. Her work has been invited to many group exhibitions in the United States and abroad: from Cupertino, California, to Auckland, New Zealand; Walnut Creek, California; São Paulo, Brazil; Brattleboro, Vermont; New York City; Ames, Iowa; and Worcester, Massachusetts.

Lecturer, curator, teacher, art juror, and panelist at many universities, museums, and professional art groups—Hanson has been commissioner of the San Francisco Arts Commission, California (1982–1989) and is active on the advisory boards of the San Francisco Exploratorium, the Northern California Women's Caucus for Art, and Open Studios of San Francisco—all in California; among others. Winner of awards and honors, she has been the recipient of a National Endowment for the Arts (NEA) fellowship (1977); an NEA/NAP regional projects grant (1979); a San Francisco, California, Board of Supervisor's citation for her exhibit, "Public Disclosure: Secrets from the Street" (1980); and a lifetime achievement award from the Northern California Regional Women's Caucus for Art (1992).

Hanson's work is represented in private, public, and corporate permanent collections, including the San Francisco Museum of Modern Art; the San Francisco Arts Commission; Cornell University, Ithaca, New York; Fresno Art Museum, California; Knoxville Museum of Art, Tennessee; Bank of America, San Francisco; and many others.

Bibliography

Baker, Kenneth. "New Art That Sticks Together and Stands Apart." *San Francisco Chronicle* (November 3, 1988).

Cline, Alan. "You See Garbage—She Sees Art." *San Francisco Examiner* (August 13, 1982).

Hanson, Jo. *Artist's Taxes, The Hands-On Guide: An Alternative to Hobby Taxes.* Vortex Press, 1987.

Lacy, Suzanne. "Broomsticks and Banners: The Winds of Change." *Artweek* (May 3, 1980).

Watson-Jones, Virginia. *Contemporary American Women Sculptors.* Oryx Press, 1986.

Hardin, Helen (1943–1984)

Born in Albuquerque, New Mexico, the painter/printmaker Helen Hardin was the daughter of Pablita Velarde—the distinctive Santa Clara painter—and Herbert O. Hardin. Her mother, who attended The Studio at Santa Fe Indian School, New Mexico gave Hardin the Santa Clara name, Tsa-sah-wee-eh, which means "Little Standing Spruce." As an artist Hardin placed a symbolic spruce tree after the name on all her art works. In about 1970 she added stylized initials—four vertical lines with one horizontal line running through them—under the spruce.

Hardin graduated from St. Pius X High School and attended the University of New Mexico, Albuquerque, where she studied anthropology, art history, and design and drawing classes for one year. At age seventeen she received a Rockefeller Foundation scholarship to attend the University of Arizona's Indian Art Project—an innovative program concerned with the future of Indian art.

Initially Hardin utilized soft, pale colors in fairly uncomplicated designs. The Arizona Project exposed her to other designs and techniques, but exposure to the tools she saw being used in a high school drafting class became even more influential. The early pale colors in tempera and casein were generally set aside for rich, vibrant colors in acrylic applied to very complicated designs which were constructed, in part, with the use of drafting tools.

Using watercolor board, she would commonly apply iridescent acrylic in twenty or more layers; often she used a sponge for a stippling effect, as well as an airbrush. The final designs were frequently varnished with polymer. The application became exact and precise, as were the themes which developed into various series such as figures in robes, prehistoric designs derived from pottery, and kachinas (religious carved dolls of the Hopi Indians).

Faithful to her Native American roots, her kachinas were never specific or identifiable. Hardin's precisely engineered lines, original color schemes, and designs are uniquely her own.

Hardin's first solo show was in 1962 at Coronado Monument—a prehistoric site where her ancestors had probably lived. Her next solo show was two years later at Enchanted Mesa—a shop in Albuquerque, where her art was exhibited for several years. Before 1968 she exhibited in group and competitive shows in Detroit, Michigan, at Wayne State University's First Annual American Art Exhibition; the Museum of New Mexico, and the Annual Indian Art market, in Santa Fe; and at the Inter-Tribal Indian Ceremonials, Gallup, New Mexico, where very early in her career she exhibited with her mother.

The United States Information Agency (USIA) invited Hardin to exhibit in Bogotá, Colombia, in 1968, and in Guatemala City, Guatemala, the following year. Other solo shows, between 1969 and 1970, were at the Heard Museum, Phoenix, Arizona; and at Kansas State University, Manhattan, Kansas, where there were two shows. During one of these, a retrospective, she was also a guest lecturer.

Even as a young child Hardin won awards in art competitions. As an adult she received awards in the Scottsdale National Indian Art Exhibition, Scottsdale, Arizona. In 1972 the Scottsdale show awarded her best-in-show, the grand award, and a special award for "Winter Awakening of the O-Khoo-Wah" (Cloud People), a fifteen-by-thirty-inch acrylic of kachinas. This painting has the distinction of receiving more major awards in the show than any other, and was shown in color in Lou Ann Faris Culley's article in *American Indian Art Magazine*. It is in the James T. Bialac Collection.

In 1973 Hardin was given best-in-show and the grand award at Tanner's First Annual Invitational Painting and Pottery Exhibit in Scottsdale, Arizona. In 1974 the Santa Fe Indian Art Market honored her with the first Patrick Swazo Hinds Memorial award for excellence in painting. The Heard Museum presented her with the 1975 Avery Memorial grand award at its Annual Indian Art Exhibit. In 1977 the Inter-Tribal Indian Ceremonials in Gallup, New Mexico, honored Hardin with the grand award.

Hardin was a survivor of the tumultuous 1960s. She succumbed to the atmosphere of the time, expressing her own rebellion through her art in forms that characterized the age. Her work was sporadic, and her output was uneven. While incorporating traditional Indian themes with contemporary designs, she occasionally used psychedelic colors and overtones.

By 1973 Hardin's life began to swing upward. She married Cradoc Bagshaw, a free-lance photographer, who encouraged her to create her art and provided a stable home atmosphere for her and her daughter, Margarete. In 1979 Sue DiMaio—the owner of Galería Capistrano, San Juan Capistrano, California—convinced Hardin to begin to develop etchings. By the following year she had not only learned the etching process, but had produced several. Later she advanced to four-color etchings and started her "Woman" series. She seemed driven to produce art works that took endless hours of uninterrupted work to complete.

Although 1981 was Hardin's best year professionally it was not a good year physically. Diagnosed with cancer, she had a mastectomy. Alternating with periods of feeling better, the cancer spreading, and treatments for cancer, in 1984 she prepared for her last show at Western Images in Chester, New Jersey. Her health rapidly declined, her last painting (unfinished) was "Last Dance of the Mimbres" (1984).

Between 1980 and 1990 Galería Capistrano featured Hardin's work and produced posters from her 1980 original acrylics, "Messengers of Winter," "Water Bearers," and "Original Robes."

Hardin is represented in the collections of the Heard Museum, Phoenix, Arizona; Museum of New Mexico, Santa Fe; the U.S. Department of the Interior's Indian Arts and Crafts Board, Washington, D.C.; University of California, Long Beach, and Loyola Marymount College of Law, Los Angeles—both in California.

Jeanne O. Snodgrass King

Bibliography

Bisgyer-Lauer, Magda, ed. "National Indian Women's Art Show." Via Gambaro Studio-Gallery, Washington, D.C., 1980: 12–13.

Culley, Lou Ann Faris. "Helen Hardin: A Retrospective." *American Indian Art Magazine* 4 (Summer 1979): 68–75.

Scott, Jay. *Changing Woman: The Life and Art of Helen Hardin.* Northland Publishing, 1989, pp. 1–165.

Silberman, Arthur. *100 Years of Native American Painting.* Oklahoma Museum of Art, Oklahoma City, 1978, p. 84.

Snodgrass, Jeanne O. *American Indian Painters. A Biographical Dictionary.* Museum of the American Indian, Heye Foundation, 1968, pp. 69–70.

Hardy, Anna Elizabeth (1839–1934)

Born in Bangor, Maine, the still-life painter Anna Elizabeth Hardy was the daughter and niece of practicing artists, and learned her craft from her father. She also studied in Paris, France, with Jeannin and with Thayer.

Hardy's precisionist, *trompe-l'oeil* still-life paintings sold well and examples of them are in private and public permanent collections, including Colby College, Waterville, and the Public Library, Bangor—both in Maine; and others.

Bibliography

Gerdts, William H., and Russell Burke. *American Still-Life Painting.* Praeger, 1971.

Groce, George C., and David H. Wallace. *The New York Historical Society's Dictionary of Artists in America, 1564–1860.* Yale University Press, 1957.

Simpson, Corelli C.W. *Leaflets of Artists.* John H. Bacon, 1893.

Harkavy, Minna R. (1895–1987)

Born in Estonia, the sculptor Minna R. Harkavy earned a Bachelor's degree from Hunter College and studied at the Art Students League—both in New York City; and with Antoine Bourdelle in Paris, France.

Harkavy exhibited work throughout the United States, including the Metropolitan Museum of Art and the Whitney Museum of American Art—both in New York City; Art Institute of Chicago, Illinois; Carnegie Institute, Pittsburgh, and Pennsylvania Academy of Fine Arts, Philadelphia—both in Pennsylvania; Munson-Williams-Proctor Institute, Utica, and Albright-Knox Art Gallery, Buffalo—both in New York; the San Francisco Museum of Art, California; and others. She belonged to many arts organizations, such as the American Artists Congress; American Society of Painters, Sculptors, and Gravers; Artists Equity Association; Boston Art Club; Collaborative Group of Painters, Sculptors, and Architects; Salon de Tuileries, Paris, France; National Association of Women Artists; New York Society of Women Artists; and the Society of American Sculptors.

Harkavy's work is represented in private and public permanent collections in the United States and abroad, including the Museum of Modern Art (MoMA), New York City; Ain Harod Museum, Tel Aviv, Israel; Biro-Bidjan Museum and Museum of Western Art, Moscow—both in the Soviet successor states; Municipal Museum, St. Denis, France; the U.S. Post Office, Winchester, Massachusetts; and others.

Bibliography

Baur, John I.H. *Revolution and Tradition in Modern American Art.* Harvard University Press, 1951.

Goodrich, Lloyd, and John I.H. Baur. *American Art of Our Century.* Praeger, 1961.

"Minna Harkavy, 101, Sculptor and Teacher." *The New York Times* (August 5, 1987): Y14.

Harkness, Madden (1948–)

Born in Montclair, New Jersey, Madden Harkness attended Boston Museum School, Massachusetts; the Nova Scotia College of Art and Design, Halifax, Canada; earned a Bachelor's degree in art education from Tufts University, Medford, Massachusetts; and received a Master of Fine Arts degree with high distinction from the California College of Arts and Crafts, Oakland (1985).

Harkness has held solo exhibitions of her work in the United States and abroad, including "Mixed Media Drawings," Pepperdine University, Malibu (1990), and Southern California Art Institute, Laguna Beach (1989)—both in California; "Forum '88," Hamburg, Germany (1988); Roy Boyd Gallery, Santa Monica, Ivory Kimpton, San Francisco (1987), and the Slant Gallery, Sacramento (1985)—all in California; and others. Her work has been invited to group exhibitions, such as "Addictions," Santa Barbara Contemporary Arts Forum, California (1991), and Tatistcheff Gallery, Santa Monica (1991)—both in California; "National Drawing Invitational," Arkansas Art Center, Little Rock (1990); "Contemporary Southern California," Taipei Fine Arts Museum, Taiwan, Republic of China (1987); "Extraordinary Perceptions," Los Angeles City Museum, California (1986); "Drawing National," Everson Museum of Art, Syracuse, New York (1985); and many others.

Harkness was a visiting artist at the American Academy in Rome, Italy (1990), and at the Ragdale Foundation, Lake Forest, Illinois

(1987). She won a purchase award in the "Drawing National" at the Everson Museum of Art, Syracuse, New York, where the jury was composed of Clement Greenberg, Nancy Hoffman, and John Perreault. In "Past Tense" (1986), a mixed-media, large-scale drawing on drafting film—a not atypical work of the period—we are witness to a group of powerful, enigmatic nude figures on a mysterious black ground. Examples of Harkness's work can be found in private and public permanent collections, including the Everson Museum of Art, Syracuse, New York; Arkansas Art Center, Little Rock; Fresno Art Museum, California; and others.

Bibliography
Brown, Betty Ann, and Arlene Raven. "Art Throb." *Lears* (November 1989): 62–67.
Muchnic, Suzanne. "Review." *The Los Angeles Times* (September 1991).
Pagel, David. "When Reason Dreams—Madden Harkness." *Visions* 2:3 (June 1988): 12–14.
Turner, Nancy Kay. "Dark Visions." *Artweek* (December 26, 1987).

Harries, Mags (1945–)

Born in Barry, Wales, Great Britain, Mags Harries earned a diploma from the Leicester College of Art and Design, England (1967), and, three years later, received a Master of Fine Arts in sculpture from Southern Illinois University at Carbondale.

A member of the sculpture faculty at the School of the Museum of Fine Arts, Boston, Massachusetts, since 1978, Harries has held solo exhibitions in the United States at such venues as Pine Manor College, Chestnut Hills (1987), De Cordova Museum, Lincoln (1982); Bunting Institute, Radcliffe College, Harvard University, Cambridge (1978), School of the Museum of Fine Arts, Boston (1978); Harcus Krakow Gallery, Boston (1973, 1976)—all in Massachusetts; Terry Dintenfass Gallery, New York City (1974); and others. Her work has been invited to many group shows in the United States and abroad—from Framingham, Massachusetts, to Cologne, Germany; from Dayton, Ohio, to Cardiff, Wales.

Harries, whose work has garnered many awards and honors, has fulfilled major sculpture commissions since the mid-1970s on sites from Boston, Massachusetts, to Scottsdale, Arizona, employing bronze, wood, concrete, steel, aluminum and landscape materials. In 1990 she formed a collaboration with the architect, Lajos Heder, to create works on an urban scale. Her work is represented in private, public, and corporate permanent collections, including the Boston Public Library; Museum of Fine Arts, Boston; Polaroid Corporation, Cambridge; Rose Art Museum, Brandeis University, Waltham; De Cordova Museum, Lincoln; and Dana Museum and Park, Lincoln—all in Massachusetts; Southern Illinois University, Carbondale; Welsh National Museum, Cardiff, Wales; and others.

Bibliography
Allara, Pamela. "Mags Harries." *Art News* (March 1983).
Hansen, Dana. "Art That Transforms Space." *Space Design*, Tokyo (November 1992): 58–59.
Kuspit, Donald. *Runic Ruins: Mag Harries' Archeology of the Present.* A Catalog. De Cordova Museum, 1982.
Tarlow, Lois. "Sculptor, Mags Harries." *Art New England* (December–January 1993): 20–22.

Harrison, Carole (1933–)

A commissioned sculptor since 1966, Carole Harrison is also a member of the Sculptors Guild and Artist's Equity—both in New York City; a Fulbright fellow to England (1957); recipient of a Tiffany Foundation fellowship (1960); and an Ossawbaw Island Project fellow (1975). Harrison was born in Chicago, Illinois, and earned a Bachelor of Fine Arts and Master of Fine Arts degrees from the Cranbrook Academy of Art, Bloomfield Hills, Michigan.

Harrison has held solo exhibitions in many galleries, including the Sculpture Center, New York City (1985); Converse College, Spartanburg, South Carolina (1983); Kalamazoo Institute of the Arts, Michigan (1976); Ludlow-Hyland Gallery, New York City (1979); Gilman Galleries, Chicago, Illinois (1963, 1965); House of Prints, Toronto, Canada (1962); and others.

Harrison has been associate professor and head of the department of sculpture at Western Michigan University, Kalamazoo (1960–1974) and the State University of New York (SUNY) at Fredonia (1975–1978). Her work has been invited to group exhibitions, such as "The Expressive Figure," SoHo Building, New York City (1990); Imprimature, Minneapolis, Minnesota (1985); Olivet College, Michigan (1980); "75 Women Artists," SUNY at Buffalo (1975); "Painting and Sculpture Today," Herron Museum of Art, Indianapolis, Indiana (1967); and many others.

Harrison's work is represented in private, public, and corporate permanent collections, including the National Museum of Women in the Arts, Washington, D.C.; Cranbrook Academy of Art, Bloomfield Hills, and Kalamazoo Institute of Art—both in Michigan; Springfield Art Museum, the city of Oak Park, and Uptown Savings and Loan, Chicago—all in Illinois; The New Wilderness Foundation, New York City; and others.

Bibliography
Berry, Vern. "Review." *Kalamazoo Gazette* (November 4, 1975).
Hendry, Fay. "Outdoor Sculpture in Kalamazoo." *Artspeak* 1:6 (February 1980).
Watson-Jones, Virginia. *Contemporary American Women Sculptors.* Oryx Press, 1986.

Harrison, Helen Mayer (1929–)

Native New Yorker Helen Mayer Harrison was born in 1929 to a family of professional men and women. Early in her career she evinced an interest both in science and art. She earned her Bachelor's degree from Queens College and her Master's degree from New York University (1953)—both in New York City. Her marriage to Newton Abner Harrison, after a four-year stint at teaching in the New York City school system, formed the basis of a continuing collaboration in the arts that began to flower in 1970. Their portable fifty-ton fish farm was presented at the Hayward Galleries in London, England, that year and the controversy that sizzled when they electrocuted the catfish, fried, and served them to 500 invited guests cemented their ongoing collaborative efforts.

The Harrisons regard themselves and their work as post-conceptual. They deal in ecosystems on a gigantic scale: through hand-colored maps, photographs, text, performance, poetry, posters, billboards, media advertisements, and sidewalk graffiti; they employ the rhetoric of the sciences and social sciences in long-term survival projects. Their works comprise micro-farming systems, through proposals for fish farms in the deserts, by creating a meadow on a rocky site, by re-creating the estuarial lagoons of Sri Lanka to breed a Sinhalese crab as a source of food for the world, by altering the paths of waterways and creating new political areas, and researching and presenting environmental impact reports.

Their "Lagoon Cycle" was an outgrowth of the "Survival Series," wherein they progressed from breeding fish, crabs, and other creatures in indoor tanks or ponds to engage enormous outdoor ecosystems rivalling nature. "Meditations on the Conditions of the Sacramento River" offers a didactic view on water distribution in California. Their presentation, "Meditation on the Gabrielino, Whose Name for Themselves Is No Longer Remembered Although We Know That They Farmed with Fire and Fought Wars by Singing," speaks eloquently for itself.

The Harrisons' work has been exhibited and collected by museums and various institutions in the United States and abroad. Their work, including travelling exhibitions, has been shown at the Los Angeles County Museum of Art, California, and the Hayward Galleries, London, England (1971); the Kunsthalle, Cologne, Germany, and Donald Feldman Fine Arts, New York City (1974); the Muséet Moderna, Stockholm, Sweden, and the Venice Biennale, Italy (1976); the Museo de Arte Contemporánea, Universidad de São Paulo, Brazil (1980); the Berlines Gallery, Barcelona, Spain (1981); and many others.

Bibliography
Cavaliere, Barbara. "Helen Mayer Harrison and Newton Harrison." *Arts Magazine* 54:10 (June 1980): 40.
Franks, Peter. "Newton and Helen Mayer Harrison." *Art News* 75:2 (February 1976): 118.
Harrison, Helen M., and Newton Harrison. *The Lagoon Cycle.* Exhibition Catalog. Cornell University, 1985.
Levin, Kim. "Helen and Newton Harrison: New Grounds for Art." *Arts Magazine* 52:6 (February 1978): 126–29.
Selz, Peter. "Helen and Newton Harrison: Art as Survival Instruction." *Arts Magazine* 52:6 (February 1987): 130–31.
Yard, Sally. "Shadow of the Bomb." *Arts Magazine* 58:8 (April 1984): 78–79.

Hartigan, Grace (1922–)
American painter Grace Hartigan was identified with New York School second generation abstract expressionism in the 1950s. In 1960 she left New York City for Baltimore, Maryland, where she resides today. In a studio in an industrial waterfront neighborhood, she paints fanciful figurative subjects with an intensely colored, luminous palette.

Born in Newark, New Jersey, Hartigan worked as a mechanical draftsperson during World War II. A high school graduate, she studied painting with Isaac Lane Muse in night classes until she moved to New York in 1945. There she became one of few women accepted into the abstract expressionist fold. Her contacts with Jackson Pollock, Franz Kline, and Willem de Kooning were crucial to her artistic development in the late 1940s and early 1950s.

After seeing Pollock's drip paintings in 1948, Hartigan experimented with non-objective painting. By 1952, however, she shifted to figurative abstraction, inspired by the work of Willem de Kooning. More confident of her direction at this point she developed an independent approach. She looked back to the work of such past artists as Albrecht Dürer, Diego

Velázquez, Francisco Goya, and Henri Matisse, conflating their figures with contemporary urban scenes. In paintings such as "Grand Street Brides" (1954, Whitney Museum of American Art), subjects of seventeenth-century portraits occupy a shop window from her lower East Side neighborhood. Some of her work from this early period is signed "George" Hartigan in homage to women writers George Sand and George Eliot.

Recognized for their abstract expressionist qualities, Hartigan's paintings were featured in the seminal Ninth Street Show in 1951, and included in the Museum of Modern Art (MoMA) exhibit "Twelve Americans" in 1959—both in New York City. At the Cedar Bar and the Club—important New York City gathering places for artists and writers—she met New York School poet and museum curator Frank O'Hara. Their friendship inspired them to sometimes refer to one another in their work.

New York museums acquired paintings such as "Persian Jacket" (1952, MoMA). Hartigan developed a characteristic style of figurative subjects, broken in intense color segments and articulated by solid outlines. Once she moved from New York to Baltimore, however, her work drew considerably less attention. While she continued to paint she also became interested in teaching. In 1967 she became the director of the Hoffberger Graduate School of Painting at the Maryland Institute of Art in Baltimore.

Her recent paintings are characterized by the "Great Queens and Empresses" series, which she began in 1983. These feature royal women, identifiable from well-known historical portraits, who appear as mildly abstracted forms on thin, stained surfaces made tactile with dripping paint. Interest in Hartigan's work has grown in the past decade, beginning with a thirty-year retrospective at the Fort Wayne Museum of Art in Texas in 1981. A forty-year retrospective was shown at the Camillos Kouros Gallery in New York City in 1989.

Deborah Anne Rindge

Bibliography
Grace Hartigan: Four Decades of Painting. New York: Camillos Kouros Gallery, 1989.
Mattison, Robert. "Grace Hartigan: Painting Her Own History." *Arts Magazine* 59 (January 1985): 66–72.
———. *Grace Hartigan: A Painter's World.* Hudson Hill's Press, 1990.
Sandler, Irving. *The New York School: The Painters and Sculptors of the Fifties.* Harper & Row, 1978, pp. 111–15.
Schoenfeld, Ann. "Grace Hartigan in the Early 1950s: Some Sources, Influences, and the Avant-Garde." *Arts Magazine* 60 (September 1985): 84–88.
Washington, D.C. Transcript of Interview with Grace Hartigan by Julie Haiflen, May 10, 1979. Archives of American Art, Smithsonian Institution.

Hartwig, Cleo (1911–1988)
Born in Webberville, Michigan, the sculptor Cleo Hartwig attended classes at the School of the Art Institute of Chicago, Illinois (1930–1931); earned a Bachelor's degree from Western Michigan University, Kalamazoo (1932); attended the summer art program at the International School of Art, New York City, which allowed her to travel in Hungary, Poland, and Rumania (1935); and studied with José de Creeft at the New School for Social Research, New York City (1937).

Hartwig held solo exhibitions in museums and galleries, including the Sculpture Center, New York City (1943, 1947, 1981); Western Canada Art Circuit, a travelling show, Calgary, Alberta, Canada (1949–

1950); Art Guild, New York City, a travelling show in the United States (1965–1966); Montclair Art Museum, New Jersey (1971); and others. She exhibited her work in galleries and museums throughout the United States and abroad: from New York City to Minneapolis, Minnesota; Manchester, Vermont; Denver, Colorado; Newark, New Jersey; Lincoln, Nebraska; as well as Eastern and Western Europe.

Winner of honors and awards for her direct carving in stone, Hartwig received an honorary Doctorate degree from Western Michigan University, Kalamazoo (1973); the Ellin P. Speyer Prize at the "Annual Exhibition" of the National Academy of Design, New York City (1979); the Edith H. and Richard Proskauer prize from the National Sculpture Society, New York City (1984); and others. Her work is represented in private and public permanent collections.

Bibliography
Bell, Enid. "The Compatibles: Sculptors Hartwig and Glinsky." *American Artist* 32:6 (June 1968): 44–49, 91.
Glinsky, Vincent, and Cleo Hartwig. "Direct Carving in Stone." *National Sculpture Review* (Summer 1965): 23–25.
Meilach, Dona Z. *Contemporary Stone Sculpture: Aesthetics, Methods, Appreciation.* Crown, 1970.
Watson-Jones, Virginia. *Contemporary American Women Sculptors.* Oryx Press, 1986.

Hassan, Jamelie (1948–)

A politically-engaged artist working in whatever medium best suits her purpose, Jamelie Hassan addresses both social and artistic questions, working to communicate a political position through art in a manner that reflects her own necessarily subjective experience. Always provocative, Hassan avoids the informational tendencies of widely accepted genres, such as political documentary—approaches that disregard the loaded intrusions of medium and claim the artist's objectivity. Hassan was born in London, Ontario, Canada, in 1948 of Lebanese immigrant parents with an Islamic background. Her youthful interest in art began as a need to express feelings of cultural alienation; travelling has been another way of confronting rootlessness. Her effort to understand cultural experience and the politics underlying it are evident in both the empathy and the broad international perspective visible in Hassan's art. War has been an important theme for Hassan. In "A Primer for War" (1984) she juxtaposes a World War I text rationalizing American engagement in the war with images of swans that play on dual symbolism of serenity and aggressiveness. Image and text are brought together on ceramic prayer book forms displayed on a pew-like bench. Here Hassan touches both our fear and involvement in war, embracing our prayers and our sometimes fallible reason.

Hassan has studied at the Academy of Fine Arts, Rome, Italy (1967); the École des Beaux-Arts, Beirut, Lebanon (1968); the University of Windsor, Ontario (1969); and the University of Mustansyria, Baghdad (1979–1987). Another important formative influence was the supportive, innovative, and to some extent politicized atmosphere of the London, Ontario, arts community, in which Hassan continues to be involved. Public collections holding her work include the National Gallery of Canada, Ottawa; the Art Gallery of Ontario, Toronto; and the Art Bank of the Canada Council, Ottawa.

Janice Seline

Bibliography
Dewdney, Christopher. *Jamelie Hassan: Material Knowledge: A Moral Art of Crisis.* London, Ontario: London Regional Art Gallery, 1984.
Gagnon, Monika. "Al Fannanah 'I Rassamah: The Work of Jamelie Hassan." *Third Text.* London, England (Summer 1989): 23–32.

Hassinger, Maren (1947–)

Born in Los Angeles, California, the African-American sculptor Maren Hassinger earned a Bachelor's degree from Bennington College, Vermont (1969), where she studied with Michael Todd and Isaac Witkin; four years later, Hassinger received a Master of Fine Arts degree in fiber structure from the University of California at Los Angeles (UCLA), where she studied with Bernard Kester.

Hassinger has held solo exhibitions in museums and galleries, including Just Above Midtown/Downtown Gallery, New York City (1980); the Los Angeles County Museum, California (1981); Los Angeles City College, and California State College, Northridge (1985). Her work has been included in many group exhibitions: from New York City to Long Beach, California; from Grand Central Station, New York City, to Illinois State University, Normal; and others.

Winner of awards and honors, Hassinger received fellowships from the National Endowment for the Arts (NEA) (1981, 1984); a grant from the Betty Brazol Memorial Fund, Tarrytown, New York (1983); and others. Her site-specific sculptures (some created with wire rope, others with natural materials) reveal the ongoing conflict between man and nature in this technologically-oriented society. Examples of her work are in private, public, and corporate permanent collections.

Bibliography
Bontemps, Arna Alexander, ed. *Forever Free: Art by African-American Women 1862–1980.* Illinois State University, 1980.
East/West: Contemporary American Art. Museum of African-American Art, 1984.
"Maren Hassinger." *The International Review of African-American Art* 6:1 (Spring 1984): 34–41.

Hatch, Emily Nichols (1871–1959)

The multi-talented artist Emily Nichols Hatch was born in Newport, Rhode Island. Painter, printmaker, lecturer, teacher, and writer—Hatch studied painting with William Merritt Chase, Charles Hawthorne, and John Ward Stimson.

Winner of honors and awards, Hatch was a recipient of the McMillan portrait prize at the New York Women's Art Club (1912), and first prize at the annual exhibition of the Pen and Brush Club—both in New York City (1931); and others. She was a member of several art organizations, including the Hudson Valley Art Association; the National Association of Women Painters and Sculptors; the Pen and Brush Club; and the Society of Painters—all in New York City. Her work is represented in private and public permanent collections, including the Smithsonian Institution, Washington, D.C.

Bibliography
American Art Annual. Vol 30. American Federation of Arts, 1933.
Pisano, Ronald G. *The Students of William Merritt Chase.* Heckscher Museum, 1973.
Who's Who in American Art. 8th ed. American Federation of Arts, 1962.

Hawley, Margaret Foote (1880–1963)

A painter of both miniatures and portraits, Margaret Foote Hawley was elected president of the American Society of Miniature Painters in 1923 and regularly exhibited in the society's annual shows. She also exhibited in London, England, from 1926 to 1929, giving as her studio address 58 West 57th Street, New York City, and was elected to the Royal Miniature Society in 1927.

Both Hawley and her older sister, the painter Mary Foote, were born in Guilford, Connecticut, but orphaned when Hawley was only five. She was adopted by her aunt Harriet Foote Hawley and her husband, a U.S. senator, who took her to live with them in Washington, D.C., where she attended public schools before enrolling at the Corcoran Art School, Washington, D.C. She also studied privately with the painter Howard Helmick, of Georgetown. After graduating from the Corcoran School of Art and receiving a gold medal for the best drawing from life, Hawley taught at a girls' boarding school and earned enough money to travel to Paris, France, for two summers of study at the Académie Colarossi.

Her oeuvre is estimated at 400 miniatures, most commissioned portraits in private collections. Among the major museums holding her works are the Metropolitan Museum of Art and the Brooklyn Museum—both in New York City; the National Museum of American Art and Corcoran Gallery of Art—both in Washington, D.C.; and the Wadsworth Athenaeum, Hartford, Connecticut.

Hawley's paintings received awards from the Pennsylvania Society of Miniature Painters (1918), and the Pennsylvania Academy of Fine Arts (1920)—both in Philadelphia; the Baltimore Watercolor Club, Maryland (1925); the Sesquicentennial Exposition, Philadelphia, Pennsylvania (1926); the Brooklyn Society of Miniature Painters, New York (1931), and the National Association of Women Painters and Sculptors (1931)—both in New York City.

Eleanor Tufts

Bibliography
Portraits of Americans by Americans. National Association of Portrait Painters, The New York Historical Society, 1945.
Tufts, Eleanor. *American Women Artists, 1830–1930*. National Museum of Women in the Arts, 1987.

Haworth, Zema Barbara Cogill (1900–1988)

A painter in many media, ceramist, illustrator, and teacher, Zema Barbara Cogill Haworth was born in Queenstown, South Africa. She studied at the Royal College of Art in London, England, under Sir William Rothenstein, Dora Billington, and Eric Gill, specializing in ceramics. It was in this field that she was first known after arriving in Toronto, Canada, in 1923. Haworth taught ceramics at Central Technical School, Toronto, from 1929 until 1963, and instructed in the fine arts department at the University of Toronto, Canada, from 1943 to 1956.

"Bobs" Haworth was married to artist Peter Haworth (1889–1986) with whom she collaborated on illustrations for Marius Barbeau's *The Kingdom of the Saguenay* (1936), and later illustrated J.E. Rossignol's *The Habitant Merchant* (1939). Both Haworths were involved in recording home front activity on Canada's west coast during World War II, which gave her the opportunity to work on marine scenes for which she showed a particular talent. She also painted on the east coast. One of her works, "Port au Persil" (c. 1944), was used in a series of silk-screen reproductions featuring the work of leading Canadian painters produced under the auspices of the National Gallery of Canada during World War II.

Haworth was a member of the Canadian Society of Painters in Watercolour—the society with which she was most closely affiliated—and acted as its president from 1954 to 1956. She was also a member of the Canadian Guild of Potters, the Canadian Group of Painters, the Ontario Society of Artists, and the Royal Canadian Academy.

Christine Boyanoski

Bibliography
Farr, Dorothy, and Natalie Luckyj. *From Women's Eyes: Women Painters in Canada*. Agnes Etherington Art Centre, 1975.
Hare, Irene B. "Close-Ups of Toronto's Women Artists." *Sunday World* 11 (August 10, 1924).
MacDonald, Colin S. *A Dictionary of Canadian Artists*. Vol. 2. Canadian Paperbacks Publishing Ltd., 1968.
Who's Who in Ontario Art. Vol. 3. Reprint from the *Ontario Library Review*, Toronto (May 1948).

Hawthorne, Marion Campbell (1870–1945)

The painter Marion Campbell Hawthorne was born in Joliet, Illinois, and studied at the School of the Art Institute of Chicago, Illinois, and with William Merritt Chase in New York City. She was a member of the Pen and Brush Club and the National Association of Women Painters and Sculptors—both in New York City.

Bibliography
American Art Annual. Vol. 30. American Federation of Arts, 1933.
Pisano, Ronald G. *The Students of William Merritt Chase*. Heckscher Museum, 1973.
Who's Who in American Art. 4th ed. American Federation of Arts, 1947.

Hazelton, Mary Brewster (1868–1953)

Born in Milton, Massachusetts, the painter Mary Brewster Hazelton studied painting under the aegis of Edmund C. Tarbell.

Winner of many awards and honors, Hazelton won the first Hallgarten prize at the National Academy of Design, New York City (1896); the Paige travelling scholarship from the School of the Boston Museum of Fine Arts, Massachusets (1899); honorable mention at the Pan-American Exposition, Buffalo, New York (1901); the Pan-Pacific Exposition, San Francisco, California (1915); the popular prize at the Newport Art Association, Rhode Island (1916); and others.

Hazelton was a member of the Copley Society, the Guild of Boston Artists, and the Concord Art Assocation—all in Massachusetts, and the Connecticut Academy of Fine Arts. An example of her work is the decoration for the chancel of the Wellesley Hills Congregational Church, Massachusetts.

Bibliography
American Art Annual. Vol 30. American Federation of Arts, 1933.
Clement, Clara E. *Women in the Fine Arts*. Houghton Mifflin, 1904.
Fielding, Mantle. *Dictionary of American Painters, Sculptors, and Engravers*. Modern Books and Crafts, 1974.

Hazen, Bessie Ella (1862–1946)

Born in Waterford, New Brunswick, Canada, the painter and printmaker Bessie Ella Hazen studied at Columbia University, New York City, and at the University of California at Los Angeles (UCLA).

Winner of awards and honors, Hazen was the recipient of second prizes for watercolor at the Arizona State Fair, Phoenix (1916, 1917, 1919); first prize for realism in painting at the Art Teachers Association of Los Angeles (1924); a gold medal for watercolor at West Coast Arts (1926); first prizes, Ebell Club, Los Angeles (1931, 1932)—all in California; and others.

She was a member of the California Art Club, the California Watercolor Society, California Art Teachers Association, Women Painters of the West, Arthur Wesley Dow Foundation, and Pacific Art Association. Her work is represented in private and public permanent collections, including the City Library, Springfield, Massachusetts; Dixie College, St. George, Utah; Exposition Park Museum, Los Angeles (now the Los Angeles County Museum of Art), and public libraries of Sacramento and Los Angeles—all in California; the Vanderpoel Collection, Chicago, Illinois; and others.

Bibliography

American Art Annual. Vol. 30. American Federation of Arts, 1933.

A Selection of American Prints. A Selection of Biographies of Forty Women Artists Working Between 1904–1979. Santa Rosa, California: The Annex Galleries, 1987.

Who's Who in American Art. 4th ed. American Federation of Arts, 1947.

Head, Lydia Bush-Brown (1887–)

Lydia Bush-Brown Head was a well-known painter and designer. She was the daughter of portrait painter Margaret White Lesley Bush-Brown and sculptor Henry Kirke Bush-Brown. After attending the Pratt Institute in Brooklyn, New York, from 1906 to 1908, Head studied with Ralph H. Johonnot (d. 1940). She maintained a studio in Greenwich Village, New York City, until 1911, when she moved to Washington, D.C. In 1919 she settled permanently in New York City and developed her silk murals. She married Francis Head (d. 1947) in 1926.

Head directed the art programs for the Luther Gulick Camps for Girls and for the Camp Fire Girls. During World War I she served as an occupational therapist for wounded soldiers in France and the United States. Her subjects for wax-resist painting on silk were those of oil and watercolor painters—city views, landscapes, and seascapes. Many were scenes from her travels in Brittany, Greece, Egypt, Syria, Persia, Panama, Bermuda, and Mexico. She also painted scenes of Manhattan and Washington, D.C. Contemporary reviewers referred to her wall-hangings, often inspired by Medieval and Asian carpet design, as "murals," considered them "modern" in conception, and "naturalistic" and "decorative" in treatment.

Head exhibited at the Corcoran Gallery of Art, Washington, D.C.; the Montclair Art Museum, New Jersey; the Santa Fe Art Museum, New Mexico; the Architectural League and the Ehrich Gallery—both in New York City, and at the 1937 Paris Exposition, France. She was a member of the Arts and Crafts Society of New York City; National Arts Club, New York City; the Civic Club; the Arts Club of Washington, D.C.; the Philadelphia Art Alliance, Pennsylvania; and the Arts and Crafts Society of Boston, Massachusetts.

Phyllis Peet

Bibliography

"Artists Are Made, Not Born, Is Proved by Record of Artistically Perfect Family." *Evening Public Ledger* [Philadelphia] (January 16, 1923): 29.

Becker, Babette M. "Silk Murals of Lydia Bush-Brown." *The American Magazine of Art* (October 1928): 556–60.

Bush-Brown Family Papers, Sophia Smith Collections, Smith College, Northampton, Massachusetts.

Cameron, Mabel Ward, Compiler. *The Biographical Cyclopedia of American Women.* 3 vols. The Halvord Publishing Company, Inc., 1924. Vol. 3, pp. 26–27.

Exhibition of Silk Murals by Lydia Bush-Brown, March 2–19, 1927. New York: Ehrich Galleries, 1927.

Healy, Anne (1939–)

A native New Yorker, the sculptor Anne Healy earned a Bachelor's degree from Queens College, New York City (1962).

Healy has held many solo exhibitions in museums and galleries throughout the United States, including the A.I.R. Gallery (1972, 1974, 1978, 1981, 1983), City University of New York (CUNY) Graduate Center (1974), Zabriskie Gallery (1975, 1978)—all in New York City; Art Museum of South Texas, Corpus Christi (1977); Alfred University, New York (1979); Rutgers University, New Brunswick, New Jersey (1984); Museum of Modern Art Rental Gallery, San Francisco (1988); Art Institute of Southern California, Laguna Beach (1989); Saint Peter's Church, New York City (1990); and others. Her work has been invited to national and international group exhibitions, such as the outdoor installations of FIAC '76, Paris, France, and ART '76, Basel, Switzerland (1976); A.I.R. Artists, Ginza, Kaigakan, Tokyo—all in Japan (1978), Lund (1981), and Stockholm (1981)—both in Sweden; Museum of Contemporary Crafts, New York City (1972); "Painting and Sculpture Today 1974," Indianapolis Museum of Art, Indiana (1974); "Site Sculpture," Zabriskie Gallery (1975, 1977), "Views by Women Artists: Sculptor's Drawings," Max Hutchinson Gallery (1982), and "In Three Dimensions: Recent Sculpture by Women," Pratt Institute, Brooklyn (1985)—all in New York City; "Diversity and Presence," a travelling show, University of California system (1987–1989); "Art at Gateway Center," Newark, New Jersey (1990); and others.

Healy has been creating installations and sited sculpture since 1971; her recent commissions include a temporary sited work, "Spiritus Sanctus," sixty-by-forty-by-twelve-feet and "Golden Boughs/Glowing Embers," twenty-three-by-sixty-by-sixty-feet for Stanford University, Palo Alto, California (1990). She is commissioner for sculpture, chair of the visual arts committee, member of the civic design committee and president of the San Francisco Arts Commission, California (1989 to the present), plus a lecturer, art juror, curator, visiting artist, panelist, board member of the Northern California chapter of Artist's Equity, and symposium moderator. She has been teaching at the University of California at Berkeley since 1981. She has been the recipient of honors and awards, including a sculpture award from the American Association of University Women (1976–1977); a Yaddo fellowship, Saratoga Springs, New York (1979); a sculpture award from the American Academy and Institute of Arts and Letters, New York City (1979–1980); a MacDowell Colony fellowship, Peterborough, New Hampshire (1980); and others. Her work is represented in private, public, and corporate permanent collections, including the Museum of Contemporary Crafts, New York City; Michigan State University, East Lansing; Allen Art Museum, Oberlin, Ohio; CUNY, New York City; Prudential Insurance Company, New Jersey; city of Oakland, California; Washington State Arts Commission, Olympia; and many others.

Bibliography
Donnaly, Trish. "Fashionable Art." *San Francisco Chronicle* (February 6, 1989): B6.
Lippard, Lucy R. "Get the Message? A Decade of Art for Social Change." E.P. Dutton, 1984.
Raven, Arlene, ed. *Art in the Public Interest.* University of Michigan Research Press, 1989.
Who's Who in American Art. 19th ed. R.R. Bowker Co., 1991–1992.

Hecht, Mary (1931–)

A native New Yorker, the sculptor Mary Hecht emigrated to Canada in 1970. She earned a Bachelor's degree from the University of Cincinnati, Ohio (1952), and did postgraduate work at the University of Iowa, Iowa City (1957). Hecht initiated her art education at the Art Academy of Cincinnati, Ohio (1948–1952); the Art Students League, New York City (summer 1949, 1952); Columbia University, New York City (summer 1950, winter 1952–1953); and the Camberwell School of Art, London, England (1958–1960).

Since 1957 Hecht has held many solo exhibitions in Canada, the United States, and abroad, and has had her sculpture invited to myriad group shows, such as the 2nd International Watercolor Exhibition, Kaoshiung City, Taiwan (1992); "In-Script-Art," University of Toronto, Canada (1990); 1st to 6th Annual International Exhibition of Miniatures, Toronto, Ontario, and New York City (1986–1992); and 6th to 9th International Dantesca, Ravenna, Italy (1985–1992); among others.

Hecht has won honors and awards, including grants from the Ontario Arts Council (1975, 1979, 1987); honorable mention at the International Exhibition of Liturgical Art and Architecture, Boston, Massachusetts (1976); and the Excalibur bronze award, Catherine Lorillard Wolfe Exhibition, New York City (1983). She was elected to membership in the American Society of Contemporary Artists (1978) and the Sculptors' Society of Canada (1982). She is both a teacher and illustrator of magazines, including *Middle East Focus* and *Wagner Notes*. Her work, such as "Bear" (1988) (a wax for a bronze) and "Bach" of the same year—both additive works—emit an expressionistic warmth and the sense of camouflaged power.

Hecht's work is represented in public permanent collections, including the Kitchener-Waterloo Art Gallery, Ontario; Ramapo College, New Jersey; Fairfield University, Connecticut; Indianapolis Museum of Art, Indiana; Mount Sinai Hospital, New York City; The Reconstructionist Rabbinical College, Philadelphia; University of Iowa, Iowa City; and many distinguished private collections in England, Italy, Germany, Israel, Holland, Canada, and the United States.

Bibliography
Fountain, Tom. *Mary Hecht: Myth, Theatre, and Music: An Exhibition of Sculpture.* A Catalog. London, England: Driian Gallery, 1984.
Kettlewell, James. *Introduction to Mary Hecht.* A Catalog. New Jersey: Ramapo College, 1981.
Webb, Marshall. *Figurative Sculpture.* A Catalog. Toronto: Koffler Gallery, 1987.

Heino, Vivika T. (1909–)

The ceramist Vivika T. Heino was born in Caledonia, New York, and earned her Bachelor's degree at the New York State College of Ceramics, Alfred, New York; she received a Master of Arts degree from the California School of Fine Arts, San Francisco.

In the late 1940s Heino taught ceramics at the League of New Hampshire Arts and Crafts, Concord, where she met and later married Otto Heino. When Glen Lukens, the "Dean" of ceramists in California went on sabbatical leave, Heino was employed by the University of Southern California, Los Angeles, to take his place. She also taught ceramics at the Chouinard Art Institute, Los Angeles, and the Rhode Island School of Design, Providence. In the mid-1960s the Heinos reopened their home and studio in Hopkinton, New Hampshire; they returned to California to open a pottery, where they worked on architectural commissions and also produced decorative and functional ware. Winner of awards and honors, Heino was the recipient of a silver medal from the International Ceramics Exhibition, Ostend, Belgium (1959); and others.

Bibliography
Bray, Hazel. *California Ceramics and Glass: 1974.* The Oakland Museum, 1974.
Clark, Garth. *American Ceramics: 1896 to the Present.* Abbeville Press, 1987.
Levin, Elaine. "Otto and Vivika Heino." *Ceramics Monthly* (October 1977).

Helfand, Fern Miriam (1952–)

Born in Toronto, Ontario, Canada, Fern Miriam Helfand remembers making collages as early as four years of age. Although her immediate family showed no particular art interests—apart from a grandfather who was a professional photographer whom she had never met—she attended classes at the Children's Art Centre directed by William Withrow at the Art Gallery of Toronto (renamed the Art Gallery of Ontario in 1966) for several years from the age of eight. A young friend from the influential Eaton family encouraged her to attend gallery openings and the like. This must have been very intellectually stimulating, for she accelerated in elementary school around the same time. When she was in junior high school she won an art award which enabled her to study in Saturday morning art classes at the Ontario College of Art, Toronto, where she drew from live models for the first time. In high school she studied painting formally with John Mergler. However, her reputation is now firmly based on her photography—a technique she did not try until the third year of an Honors Bachelor of Arts program at York University in Toronto. Graduating in 1974, she later took a Master of Fine Arts degree at the University of Florida in Gainesville (1980). She taught part-time at York University (1981–1982), and joined the full-time faculty at the University of Western Ontario (1982–1989). Since 1989, she has taught at the Pusat Seni (Art Center) of the University Sains in Penang, Malaysia.

Helfand's first works of note were the kind of fabric-based assemblages made popular in Toronto when Joyce Wieland first started to question the traditional canon of accepted art media. She discovered when making maquettes for such works that the cutting and pasting activity—no doubt remembered from her youth—appealed to her more than the finished products, so she began to cast about for ways to incorporate this into new works. Like her contemporary Barbara Astman, Helfand found the answer in the manipulation of photography. With sociological and environmental issues in mind, Helfand has turned her eye on the phenomenon of tourism. Her very large works are collages of dozens of figures, many operating cameras and camcorders, at famous sites such as the Great Wall of China, Niagara Falls, or even Disneyland. Where photographic images can't be spliced together, she simply draws in the missing details. With this, both form and content ask the viewer to consider what is real and what is false. The works usually end up as deeply ironic meditations on the ways in which touristic vision and experience have become nothing more than an unthinking collection of images.

Robert J. Belton

Bibliography
Dewdney, Christopher. *London/Havana Exchange*. Havana: Casa de las Americas, December 1988.
Gilchrist, Rodney. *Photo Life* (Summer 1989).
Miles, Geoffrey. "Fern Helfand: The Photography Gallery, Harbourfront." *Vanguard* 16:1 (January–February 1987): 43–44.

Helfond, Riva (1910–)

Born in Brooklyn, New York, the painter/printmaker Riva Helfond studied at the Art Students League, New York City, with Alexander Brook, Morris Kantor, Yasuo Kuniyoshi, Harry Sternberg, and William Von Schlegell; she also studied at the School for Industrial Arts, also in New York City.

Helfond taught printmaking at New York University, New York City, and instructed students in art appreciation and painting at Union College, Cranford, New Jersey. She has participated in solo and group exhibitions throughout the United States and abroad in galleries and museums, including the Serigraph Galleries, New York City (1946); Galerie Collette Allendy, Paris, France (1957); "Art USA" (1958, 1959); and Juster Gallery (1959)—both in New York City; Corcoran Gallery of Art, Washington, D.C. (1960); Newark Museum of Fine Arts, New Jersey (1964, 1967); Bethesda Art Gallery, Maryland (1983); Ellen Sragow Gallery, New York City (1988 to the present); and others.

Winner of honors and awards, Helfand received a painting prize from the Audubon Artists, New York City (1983); Pennell purchase prizes for lithography from the Library of Congress, Washington, D.C.; honors from the Museum of Modern Art (MoMA), New York City; and others. She is a member and, in some cases, an officer of several professional artists organizations, and her work is represented in private and public permanent collections, including the Library of Congress, Washington, D.C.; MoMA, New York City; Newark Museum of Fine Arts, New Jersey; Springfield Museum of Fine Art, Massachusetts; and others.

Bibliography
Greengard, Stephen. "Ten Crucial Years: A Panel Discussion by Six WPA Artists." *Journal of Decorative and Propaganda Arts* 1:1 (Spring 1986): 46–48.
Riva Helfond. New York: Serigraph Galleries, 1946.
Riva Helfond. New York: Juster Gallery, 1959.

Helioff, Anne G.

Born in Liverpool, England, the painter/collagist Anne G. Helioff studied with Yasuo Kuniyoshi and others at the Art Students League and the Hans Hofmann School of Art—both in New York City.

Helioff has held solo exhibitions in galleries and museums, including the Capricorn Gallery (1964, 1966, 1969), and Phoenix Gallery (1971, 1973, 1976, 1982, 1983, 1985)—both in New York City; Woodstock Artists Association, New York City (1988); and others. Her work has been included in many prestigious group shows in the United States and abroad: from New York City to Florence, Italy; from Philadelphia, Pennsylvania, to Cluse, France.

Winner of awards and honors in exhibitions at the Museum of Art and Science, Albany, New York; Riverside Museum, New York City; and the Berkshire Museum, Pittsfield, Massachusetts, Helioff has lectured at the Yasuo Kuniyoshi Summer School, Woodstock, New York (1942–1944). Her work is represented in private and public permanent collections, including the Archives of American Art and the Smithsonian Institution, Washington, D.C.; the New York Historical Society; the Woodstock Historical Society, New York; and others.

Bibliography
Frachtman, N. *Arts Magazine* (January 1977).
Hall, Dorothy. *Park East* (November 1976).
Offin, C. *Pictures on Exhibit* (November 1976).

Heller, Dorothy

A native New Yorker, the painter Dorothy Heller studied with Hans Hofmann in New York City before striking out on her own.

Heller has exhibited in solo and group shows in museums and galleries, including the Wadsworth Atheneum, Hartford, Connecticut (1964); Betty Parsons Gallery, New York City (1972–1981); Albright-Knox Art Gallery, Buffalo, New York (1974); University of Pennsylvania, Philadelphia (1976); Transcendental Art Center, New York (1977); Metropolitan Museum of Art, New York City (1979); Dorothy Heller Studio Exhibition (1984, 1988); Brooklyn College, New York (1990); and many others.

Heller's acrylic paintings are represented in private and public permanent collections, such as the Allen Memorial Art Museum, Oberlin, Ohio; Johnson Museum, Cornell University, Ithaca, New York; Metropolitan Museum of Art, New York City; Wadsworth Atheneum, Hartford, Connecticut; and others.

Bibliography
Loercher, Diana. "Review." *Christian Science Monitor* (October 22, 1976).
Wolfe, James R. "Review." *Meditation Today* (September 1976).
Wolff, Theodore. *Christian Science Monitor* (May 22, 1979).

Heller, Helen West (1885–1955)

Painter, printmaker, writer, and illustrator—Helen West Heller was born in Rushville, Illinois, and lived and worked in New York City. She studied at the Art Students League, New York City, and at the St. Louis School of Fine Arts, Missouri.

Heller's woodcuts were exhibited widely in museums and other institutions throughout the United States, including the Brooklyn Museum (1929–1932), the Whitney Museum of American Art (1935), the American Artist's Congress (1936), the Works Projects Administration (WPA) Federal Art Project [with Louis Schanker] (1939), the National Academy of Design (1942–1946), the Artist's Gallery [with Louis

Monza] (1942), and the American Federation of Arts travelling exhibition (1943–1945)—all in New York City; the Library of Congress (1943, 1944, 1945), and a retrospective at the Smithsonian Institution (1949)—both in Washington, D.C.; and many others.

A prize-winning printmaker and elected member of the National Academy of Design, New York City (1948), Heller was the artist/author of the books *Migratory Urge* and *Woodcuts U.S.A.* Her work is in the permanent print collections of museums and other institutions throughout the United States, such as the Library of Congress, Washington, D.C.; the Brooklyn Museum, New York, and the New York Public Library, New York City; Chicago Municipal College, Illinois; Lindsborg Artists Guild, Kansas; the Grosvenor Library, Buffalo, New York; the Berkshire Museum, Pittsfield, Massachusetts; and myriad others.

Bibliography
American Art Annual. Vol. 30. American Federation of Arts, 1933.
Heller, Helen West. *Woodcuts U.S.A.* Introduction by John Taylor Arms. Oxford University Press, 1947.
Reese, Albert. *American Prints of the Twentieth Century.* American Artists Group, 1949.
Who's Who in American Art. 5th ed. American Federation of Arts, 1956.

Heller, Susanna (1956–)

Born in New York City, the painter Susanna Heller studied at the Nova Scotia College of Art and Design, Halifax, Canada, where she earned a Bachelor of Fine Arts degree (1977); the previous year, she studied art history with Robert Rosenblum at New York University, New York City.

Heller has held solo and group exhibitions in galleries and museums in Canada and abroad, including the Anna Leonowens Gallery, Halifax, Nova Scotia (1985); Galerie Paul Andriesse, Amsterdam, the Netherlands (1986); the 49th Parallel, New York City (1986); Grunwald & Watterson, Toronto, Canada (1987, 1989); Tomoko Ligouri Gallery, New York (1988, 1989); Mount St. Vincent University, Halifax (1989); Chicago International Art Exposition, Illinois (1990); and others.

Winner of awards and honors, Heller has received various grants from the Canada Council (1978, 1980, 1983, 1985, 1986); and fellowships from the Millay Colony Residence (1982), the Leighton Art Colony, Banff, Alberta (1986), and the Guggenheim Foundation (1988). Her work is represented in private, public, and corporate permanent collections, including Air Canada Corporation; the Canada Council Art Bank, Ottawa; Concordia University, Montréal; Osler, Hoskin & Harcourt, Toronto; and the Toronto Dominion Bank—all in Canada.

Bibliography
Berlind, Robert. "Review." *Art in America* (February 1989).
Clark, John. "No Apologies." *Vanguard* (February–March 1989).

Helman, Phoebe (1929–)

A native New Yorker, the painter/sculptor Phoebe Helman studied with Paul Burlin at Washington University, St. Louis, Missouri, where she earned a Bachelor of Fine Arts degree; she also studied at the Art Students League, New York City, under the aegis of Raphael Soyer.

Helman is an adjunct professor of art at Pratt Institute, New York City. Her work has been exhibited in solo and group exhibitions in the United States and abroad: from New York City to Moscow, Russia; from Miami, Florida, to Dayton, Ohio. She has won awards and honors, including a Creative Artists Public Service (CAPS) grant (1975); a Guggenheim fellowship (1979); a grant from the National Endowment for the Arts (NEA) (1983–1984); a New York Foundation for the Arts grant (1986); and others.

In addition to commissioned steel wall pieces sited in New York City and Raleigh, North Carolina, Helman's work is represented in private, public, and corporate permanent collections, including Ciba-Geigy, Ardsley, New York; the Guggenheim Museum, New York City; Hampton Institute, Virginia; and many others.

Bibliography
Kuspit, Donald. "Phoebe Helman at Sculpture Now." *Art in America* 67:3 (May–June 1979): 142–43.
Robins, Corinne. "American Urban Art Triumphant: The Abstract Paintings of Arthur Cohen, Al Held, Phoebe Helman, and Frank Stella." *Arts Magazine* 56:9 (May 1982): 86–89.
Watson-Jones, Virginia. *Contemporary American Women Sculptors.* Oryx Press, 1986.

Henri, Florence (1895–)

Florence Henri is a photographer/painter known for her avant-garde style of photography and her association with the Bauhaus.

Born of a French father and a German mother in New York in 1895, Henri began as a musician and then shifted to the visual arts in 1914. She attended the Academy of Art in Munich, Germany, for three years and studied painting with Hans Hofmann in New York City. By 1918 she was associated with Hans Richter, Hans Arp, and John Heartfield, who were all Dadaists.

Henri moved to Berlin in 1921 and there met Moholy-Nagy, who had a great influence on her. In 1924 she studied painting with Fernand Léger and Amédée Ozenfant. She later attended the Bauhaus in Dessau in 1927; it was then that she became interested in photography.

She settled in Paris, France, in 1929 and opened a studio on Rue Froideveaux as a professional photographer. She specialized in portraits and became successful with her next studio in Rue de Varennes by 1931.

She continued to experiment in avant-garde photography and appeared regularly in *Arts et Metiers* graphics. Her work has also been published in *Vogue, Art et Décoration, Image Bravo,* and *Varietá.*

Her photographs during the Bauhaus and early Paris years are a mix of constructivism and surrealism. Henri is usually identified with the Neue Sachlichkeit, but a greater interest in pure design is found in her work than is usual in the Neue Sachlichkeit. Her first photographs included mirrors which caused a spatial complexity and a surrealistic mood. After she arrived in Paris, she began making collages of her photographs.

After 1945 Henri again turned to painting, and her works can be seen in the collections of the Museum of Modern Art (MoMA), New York City; San Francisco Museum of Modern Art, California; Bibliothèque Nationale, Paris, France; and Universitá di Parma, and Museo della Fotographica—both in Italy.

By 1975 Henri was living in Picardy, France, and as of 1980 was in poor health and unable to pursue any artistic activities.

Karen E. Speirs

Bibliography
Art and Artists 14 (July 1979): 41.
Arts Magazine 51 (December 1976): 38.
Avant-Garde Photography in Germany, 1919–1939. Exhibition Catalog.
Camera 54 (November 1975): 11:40.
San Francisco Museum of Modern Art, 1980.

Heon, Michelle (1948–)

Fiber artist Michelle Heon earned a Master of Fine Arts degree from the University of Montréal, Québec, Canada (1978), after study at Jagiellon University, Poland (1972–1973), and the Superior School of Fine Arts, Poznan, Poland (1973–1974). She was also a tapestry student of Magdalena Abakanowicz and Ursula Plewka-Schmidt. In 1975 Heon studied theater and costume design on a study tour of France; she was on a Fibre Interchange at the Banff Centre for the Arts, Alberta, at various times in 1977, 1978, and 1979.

Heon has held solo exhibitions at Pod Jaszezury, Poland (1974, 1979) and has had her work invited to group exhibitions, including "Fibre 1," Powerhouse Gallery, Montréal (1977); First Biennale Québecoise, Montréal (1977); "First Biennale of New Tapestry in Québec," Museum of Contemporary Art, Montréal (1979); and others.

Winner of honors and awards, Heon received scholarships from the Ministry of Art and Culture, Warsaw, Poland (1972–1973, 1973–1974); and the government of Québec (1976, 1977). Her tapestries are in private and public permanent collections, including the Museum of Contemporary Art, Montréal.

Bibliography
Constantine, Mildred, and Jack Lenor Larsen. *The Art Fabric: Mainstream.* Van Nostrand Reinhold, 1980.

Hera (1940–)

Public and environmental sculptor Hera was born in New Orleans, Louisiana, and received her education at a number of institutions, including the University of Dallas, where she earned a Bachelor of Arts degree (1970) and Southern Methodist University—both in Dallas, Texas, where she received a Master of Arts degree, four years later. She also studied at Mount Holyoke College, South Hadley, Massachusetts, and the School of the Art Institute, Chicago, Illinois.

Hera has held many solo exhibitions of her work, including "Spirit House," Cadman Plaza, Brooklyn, New York (1986); "Family Room," Contemporary Art Center, New Orleans, Louisiana; Nexus Gallery, Philadelphia, Pennsylvania; the Women's Interart Center (1982), and "Butcher Shop," Brooks Jackson, Gallery Iolas (1979)—both in New York City; and others. Her public commissions include a community-based design pilot for the Philadelphia Art Commission, Pennsylvania (1991); "Tower as Inland Lighthouse," Hillsborough Area Regional Transit, Tampa, Florida (1990); "Niagara-Knossos-Carranza Connector," Artpark, Lewiston, New York (1982); "Stormflower," University of New Orleans, Louisiana (1980); and others.

Hera has won many awards and honors for her sculptural creations—especially her public and environmental works—for more than a dozen years. Examples of her output are in many public and corporate permanent collections throughout the United States.

Bibliography
Fleming, Ronald, and Renata Von Tscharner. *Placemakers.* Hastings House, 1981.
Hatton, E.M. *The Tent Book.* Houghton-Mifflin, 1979.
Lippard, Lucy R. "Gardens: Some Metaphors for a Public Art." *Art in America* 69:9 (November 1981): 136–50.

Hergesheimer, Ella Sophonisba (1873–1943)

Born in Allentown, Pennsylvania, the painter/printmaker Ella Sophonisba Hergesheimer studied with Cecilia Beaux and William Merritt Chase at the Pennsylvania Academy of Fine Arts, Philadelphia. She did further study in France, Italy, and Spain.

Hergesheimer has received many honors and awards, including a gold medal for her portraits at the Appalachian Exposition in Knoxville, Tennessee (1910); honorable mention at the Southern States Art League Exhibition (1922, 1925); first prize at the Tennessee State Exhibition (1924); first prizes for portrait, still-life, and flower studies (1926); and honorable mention for a woodcut, Ogunquit, Maine (1932); and others. A fellow of the Pennsylvania Academy of Fine Arts, Philadelphia, she held memberships in the Nicholson Art Lodge, Knoxville, Tennessee; National Arts Club, New York City; American Federation of Arts, Washington, D.C.; Philadelphia Print Club, Pennsylvania; Northwest Printmakers; Nashville Studio Club, Tennessee; and the Southern States Art League.

Bibliography
American Art Annual. Vol. 30. American Federation of Arts, 1933.
Pisano, Ronald G. *The Students of William Merritt Chase.* Heckscher Museum, 1973.
Who's Who in American Art. 4th ed. American Federation of Arts, 1947.

Hering, Elsie Ward (1874–1923)

Born in Fayette, Missouri, the sculptor Elsie Ward Hering was a student of Augustus Saint-Gaudens, and also completed his "Baker Memorial," in Mount Kisco, New York, begun a short time before his death.

Winner of honors and awards, Hering exhibited work in museums, galleries, and expositions, including the Charleston Exposition, South Carolina (1902); the St. Louis Exposition, Missouri (1904); "Exhibition of American Sculpture," National Sculpture Society, New York City (1923); and others. Examples of her work are in private and public permanent collections, including the Chapel of Our Saviour, Denver, Colorado; the fountain of the Women's Christian Temperance Union, St. Louis, Missouri; and others.

Bibliography
American Art Annual. Vol. 18. American Federation of Arts, 1921.
Kohlman, Rena Tucker. "America's Women Sculptors." *International Studio* 76 (1922): 225, 228–29.
Saint-Gaudens, Homer. *Reminiscences of Augustus Saint-Gaudens.* Century Co., 1913.

Hernández, Camila (c. 1937–)

Born in San Pablito at the foot of El Brujo, Puebla, Mexico, the Otomí artist Camila Hernández paints solely on *amate* paper which she fashions herself. To make the paper, she cuts approximate one-inch strips from the inner bark of the tree (*amate* or *anacahuite*), separates the sap-filled fibers, soaks and boils them with lime or ashes for about ten hours in water in which corn had been soaking, places the strips together, side by side on a rectangular board, and pounds them with a beater.

In 1964 Hernández exhibited her works at the Organization of American States building in Washington, D.C.

Bibliography

Alvarez, José Rogelio, et al. *Enciclopedia de México.* Secretaría de Educación Pública, 1987.

Heller, Jules. *Papermaking.* Watson-Guptill Publications, 1978.

Herrera, Carmen (1915–)

Born in Havana, Cuba, the non-figurative painter Carmen Herrera has a varied arts background. She studied art and the history of art at the Academía de San Alejandro, Havana (1948–1952), and Marymount College, Paris, France (1952–1953); architecture at the Universidad de Havana (1953); moved permanently to the United States in 1954, where she enrolled in courses at the Art Students League, New York City.

Herrera has held solo exhibitions in museums and galleries, including the Galería Sudamericana (1956); Trabia Gallery (1963); Cisneros Gallery (1965); and "Carmen Herrera," a retrospective, Alternative Gallery (1986)—all in New York City; and others. Her work has been included in group shows, such as City Center, New York City (1956); State University of New York (SUNY) at Syracuse (1967, 1969); Center for Inter-American Relations, New York City (1968); and others. Examples of her paintings can be found in private and public permanent collections in New York City, including the Cintas Foundation, Cornell University Medical Center, Rusk Institute of Rehabilitation, and others.

Bibliography

Nearman, Judith. *Carmen Herrera.* A Catalog. New York: Alternative Museum, 1986.

The Latin American Spirit: Art and Artists in the United States, 1920–1970. Harry N. Abrams, 1988.

Herreshoff, Louise (1876–1967)

A painter of landscapes, still lifes, and portraits, Louise Herreshoff was born in Brooklyn, New York, the only child of a prominent Rhode Island family. Her mother died when she was only four, so she was raised by her aunts in Providence, Rhode Island. She attended the Lincoln School and took art classes at the studio of Mary C. Wheeler, beginning at the age of six and continuing until she graduated from the Lincoln School in 1890. A progressive educator, Wheeler introduced her students to painting from live models and also took classes abroad in the summertime. For the next five summers Herreshoff was a member of these classes, and in 1895 at Fontenay-aux-Roses she met Raphael Collin, a leader in plein-air painting. She returned the next two summers to study with him and then moved to France in 1898 for more sustained study with him as well as travel to other European countries. In 1899 she enrolled at the Académie Julian to study with Jean-Paul Laurens whose use of vivid colors had a strong impact on her later art.

In 1900, her "Le Repos" (1899, Washington and Lee University) was accepted in the Paris Salon exhibition and "An Interior" was exhibited at the National Academy of Design in New York City.

Herreshoff returned to the United States in 1903 and exhibited at the Rhode Island School of Design in Providence. She married Charles Eaton in 1910, but the two separated after three months. Between 1921 and 1925 she exhibited at the Pennsylvania Academy of Fine Arts, the Philadelphia Watercolor Club—both in Philadelphia, Pennsylvania; the North Shore Art Association; and the Providence Art Club, Rhode Island. By this time her style had evolved from nineteenth-century Romanticism to Fauvism. On the death of her beloved Aunt Lizzie in 1927 she stopped painting and spent the last forty years of her life collecting fine porcelain. In 1941 she married Euchlin D. Reeves, a graduate of the School of Law at Washington and Lee University, Lexington, Virginia, and after twenty-six years together she bequeathed her art collection to his university.

Eleanor Tufts

Bibliography

Louise Herreshoff: An American Artist Discovered. Washington and Lee University, 1976.

Tufts, Eleanor. *American Women Artists, 1830–1930.* National Museum of Women in the Arts, 1987.

Herter, Christine (1890–)

Born in Irvington-on-Hudson, New York, Christine Herter studied her craft with fellow painter Sergeant Kendall.

Herter has won many awards and honors, including the popular vote prize at the Newport Art Association, Rhode Island (1915); the second Hallgarten prize at the National Academy of Design (1916); and a prize at the National Association of Women Painters and Sculptors—both in New York City (1922).

Herter is a member of the New York Watercolor Club, the National Association of Women Painters and Sculptors, and the American Federation of Arts—all in New York City; and the Newport Art Association, Rhode Island. A religious work by Herter was commissioned by St. Luke's Episcopal Church, Hot Springs, Virginia.

Bibliography

American Art Annual. Vol. 30. American Federation of Arts, 1933.

Fielding, Mantle. *Dictionary of American Painters, Sculptors, and Engravers.* Modern Books and Crafts, 1974.

Who's Who in American Art. 3rd ed. American Federation of Arts, 1940.

Hesse, Eva (1936–1970)

Sculptor/painter Eva Hesse wanted more than anything to be a major artist, and a brain tumor nearly robbed her of this opportunity when it claimed her life at the age of thirty-four. But the large volume of drawings and sculptures that she left behind assures her a secure place in the annals of American art.

Born in Hamburg, Germany, on January 11, 1936, Hesse was sent to Holland with her older sister to escape the Nazi persecution when she was only two years old. When Hesse was three, her family emigrated to the United States, settling in New York City. Her father kept journals for both Hesse and her sister when they were young children, filling them with photographs, written material, memorabilia, and newspaper clippings. These books inspired Hesse to keep her own journals, which survive as a chronicle of her development as an artist.

In September 1954 Hesse's art career was launched when *Seventeen Magazine* printed her illustrations as part of a contest titled "It's All Yours." She had studied at Pratt Institute in New York City but didn't like the advertising design course she had signed up for. "The only painting I knew, and that was very little, was Abstract Expressionism, and at Pratt they didn't stress painting at all," she said.

Hesse went on to study at Cooper Union, the Art Students League—both in New York City, and the Yale School of Art and Architecture, New Haven, Connecticut, where she earned a Bachelor of Fine Arts degree in 1959. At the Yale School of Art and Architecture, Hesse did abstract figurative paintings but did not have much confidence in her work.

A turning point occurred in Hesse's life in April 1961. She had her first show, at the John Heller Gallery, New York City, and met Tom Doyle, a sculptor who was to become her husband. They were married November 21, 1961, and rented a big loft studio on Fifth Avenue in New York City. Her former college roommate, who sublet part of the loft, said Hesse's work at the time featured thick brushstrokes and "had the look of de Kooning with signs and symbols."

Another turning point came in 1964–1965—the year Hesse and her husband spent working in Germany. It was Hesse's first trip back since she left as a child. Hesse had not yet found the artistic vision that would guide her through her last years of creating art, and she felt very inadequate. For a time after they arrived in Germany her drawings became simple and almost crude. When she felt she could not work, her husband suggested she work with some of the materials, including old weavings, that were lying around in the warehouse where they had their studios in Germany.

The string from the weavings—along with plaster—set her on a new course, from which her mature work was to come. Breaking away from the expressionist and surrealist direction of her art, she began to concentrate on extending two-dimensional spatial concepts into three-dimensional work. When she returned to New York from Germany she renewed her friendship with Sol LeWitt and began to change the images of her work under the influence of LeWitt and other minimalists.

Hesse's work could not be strictly labeled sculpture. It was a hybrid of sculpture and painting. All of her work was characterized by the potential for random arrangement of the elements, such as "Repetition III," which consisted of nineteen fiberglass "pots," or "Addendum"—a series of wall-mounted, nipple-like papier-maché figures with rubber tubing cascading to the floor. Hesse was fascinated by materials that she could manipulate herself. She turned to papier-maché, then cloth-covered wire, of which she constructed "Metronomic Irregularity."

In November 1967 her work was included in the first show of the Museum of Normal Art, New York City, which was considered one of the birthplaces of conceptual art. Earlier that year she had discovered latex rubber, which took the place of papier-maché. The next year she began working with fiberglass—a material that embodied her fascination with chemistry, materials, and fabrication.

Art from this period was shown at the Fischbach Gallery in New York City in November 1968. About this show Hesse said, "I would like the work to be non-work. This means that it would find its way beyond my preconceptions." Included in this show were "Sans II,"

"Accretion," "Repetition Nineteen III" and "Accession II," all in fiberglass. This work was described by one critic as "surreal serialism" and "anti-form," while another said her work was "toys," though admitting there was a "bland, quiet pleasure to these loony pieces."

Her next show, in May 1969, was at the Whitney Museum of American Art, New York City, titled "Anti-Illusion: Procedures/Materials." In this show, which included "Vinculum I" and "Expanded Expansion," a critic noted that Hesse used only those materials that she could use without casting or molding. Hesse died May 29, 1970, leaving behind work that, toward the end, moved again toward abstract expressionism. Her last sculpture, "Right After," was described by *Life Magazine* as unfinished, but Hesse said in the article that it was "ordered." She explained, "Chaos can be structured as non-chaos. That we know from Jackson Pollock."

Judith P. Smith

Bibliography

Eva Hesse: A Memorial Exhibition. New York: The Solomon R. Guggenheim Museum, 1970s.

Gula, Kasha Linville. "Eva Hesse: No Explanation." *Ms. Magazine* (April 1973): 39–42.

Lippard, Lucy R. *Eva Hesse*. New York University Press, 1976.

Nemser, Cindy. "Eva Hesse: Her Life." *Feminist Art Journal* (Winter 1973): 13–14.

Pincus-Witten, Robert, ed. "Eva Hesse: Last Words." *Artforum* (November 1972): 74–76.

Rose, Barbara. "A Special Woman, Her Surprise Art." *Vogue* (March 1973): 50.

Shapiro, David. "The Random Forms in Soft Materials and String by the Late Young Innovator Eva Hesse." *Craft Horizons* (February 1973): 40–45, 77.

Hessing, Valjean McCarty (1934–)

A Choctaw Native American painter, Valjean McCarty Hessing prefers to use water-based paints to create her culturally-oriented themes. She is best known for earth tones—browns, dusty mauves, siennas, and muted reds—on a stark white field in a flat, two-dimensional style which she taught herself in 1962. An effect of three-dimensional shading is created by closely aligned stripes of one color with increasing or diminishing values. As a secondary interest she creates small, painted clay maternal figures holding children. She titles these "Singers."

At the age of eleven Hessing was awarded a scholarship to art classes at Philbrook Art Center (now, Philbrook Museum of Art) in Tulsa, Oklahoma. At age eighteen she accepted one of three scholarships and attended Mary Hardin-Baylor College in Texas for two years. A native of Tulsa, Oklahoma, Hessing returned there to study with Alexander Hogue at the University of Tulsa.

Although her work had been acquired by collectors since 1945, Hessing did not seriously pursue an art career until 1963, when her children started school. As she rapidly improved her skills in her chosen style of painting, she often exhibited with her sister, Jane McCarty Mauldin, also an accomplished painter. In 1972 the Heard Museum, Phoenix, Arizona, honored the pair with an exhibit of their paintings. The following year the staff at Philbrook Museum of Art gave their former protegé a solo exhibit. She was presented in another solo showing at Via Cambaro Gallery in Washington, D.C., in 1980.

In 1985 Hessing and seven other Oklahoma Native American

women artists organized and participated in the travelling exhibition, "Daughters of the Earth." She has exhibited in more than 100 shows in galleries and institutions, including the Denver Art Museum, Colorado; the Thomas Gilcrease Institute of American History and Art, Tulsa, Oklahoma; John F. Kennedy Center for the Performing Arts, and the Smithsonian Institution—both in Washington, D.C. Hessing has served as juror for Native American artists competitions at the Five Civilized Tribes Museum, Philbrook Museum of Art, and the Red Earth Festival—all in Oklahoma.

Hessing has received ninety awards for her paintings, including nine grand awards. In 1976 she was proclaimed master artist by the Five Civilized Tribes Museum of Muskogee, Oklahoma. Her paintings are in the permanent public collections of the Amerindian Circle, and the U.S. Department of the Interior's Indian Arts and Crafts Board—both in Washington, D.C.; Heard Museum, Phoenix, Arizona; Philbrook Museum of Art, Tulsa, Oklahoma; Southern Plains and Indian Museum, Anadarko, Oklahoma; and Wheelwright Museum, Taos, New Mexico. In the Southeast Missouri University Museum, Cape Giradeau, her painting "Some Died Along the Way" depicts her tribal ancestors passing over the University's land during their forced march (more commonly called the "Trail of Tears") from their ancestral lands in the southeastern United States to present-day Oklahoma.

Hessing's painting "Chief Joseph" (1970) was on the cover of the catalog for the "Ninth Scottsdale National Indian Arts Exhibition," held in Arizona in 1970. Her "Long Hair Corn Woman" (1981), illustrating an elderly woman feeding her children, was on the cover of *American Indian Journal* in 1981. Also in 1981 "Tornado," her distinctively-colored single figure of a wind-swept female, was given a full page in *Oklahoma Today*.

Jeanne O. Snodgrass King

Bibliography
"Daughters of the Earth." *Oklahoma Today* 35 (July–August 1985): 18, 20.
Clark, Jean Noe. "Indian Art Quietly Ignites Fame." *Chicago Tribune* (March 23, 1979): 16, 18.
Fitzpatrick, Mary, et al. *Contemporary North American Indian Art.* Smithsonian Institution, 1986, pp. 6, 9.
Night of the First Americans. John F. Kennedy Center for the Performing Arts, 1982, p. 22.
Rubenstein, Charlotte Streifer. *American Women Artists: From Early Indian Times to the Present.* Avon, 1982, p. 19.
Snodgrass, Jeanne O. *American Indian Painters. A Biographical Directory.* Museum of the American Indian, Heye Foundation, 1968, p. 74.
Wall, Judith. "Oklahoma's Indian Art." *Oklahoma Today* 32 (Winter 1981): 5–6.
Yvain, M.L. "Radically Different, Yet Extremely Similar: Bidner and Hessing." *Washington Post, Aura* (November–December 1980): 7.

Heustis, Louise Lyons (c. 1865/78–1951)

Born in Mobile, Alabama, the painter Louise Lyons Heustis studied at the Art Students League, New York City, under the aegis of William Merritt Chase and Kenyon Cox. She took further work in Paris, France, at the Académie Julian with Lazar and Frederick Macmonnies.

Heustis has won honors and awards, including the Brown and Bigelow National Competition (1925); prizes at the Newport Art Association, Rhode Island (1921, 1927, 1928, 1930); a prize at the Nashville Art Association, Tennessee (1926); a prize for portraits at an exhibition in Birmingham, Alabama (1928); and the Nobel prize for figure composition at the National Association of Women Painters and Sculptors, New York City (1932), where she held membership. She was also a member of the Newport Art Association, Rhode Island.

Bibliography
American Art Annual. Vol. 30. American Federation of Arts, 1933.
Clement, Clara Erskine. *Women in the Fine Arts.* Houghton-Mifflin, 1904.
50th Anniversary Exhibition 1889–1939. New York: National Association of Women Painters and Sculptors, 1939.
Pisano, Ronald G. *The Students of William Merritt Chase.* Heckscher Museum, 1973.

Heward, Efa Prudence (1896–1947)

Efa Prudence Heward was born in Montréal, Québec, Canada, and attended classes at the Art Association of Montréal. The principal instructor was then William Brymner, who imparted to her a taste for academic naturalism. She also spent some time sketching with Maurice Cullen, whose inclinations were more toward impressionism. She served with the Red Cross in England in World War I, following which she studied for a time at Académie Colarossi in Paris, France. The latter institution fostered a taste for the watercolors of Frances Hodgkins, who had earlier taught there and who had also inspired Emily Carr. Heward returned to Montréal in 1920 and joined the so-called Beaver Hall Hill group—a small exhibition society comprised mainly of former female students of Brymner. This group was short-lived, but it fostered a number of interesting talents which might otherwise have been lost. Heward, for instance, won first prize at the Willingdon Arts Competition of 1929 with "Girl on a Hill," a portrait of a local dancer, Louise McLea.

In 1933 Heward became a charter member of the Toronto-based Canadian Group of Painters, organized by former Group of Seven members in part to avoid accusations of central Canadian bias. She also played a role in the Montréal-based Contemporary Art Society, founded by Matisse-devotee John Lyman in 1939 to combat what he saw as the Group of Seven's insular, provincial mentality. Heward's talent enabled her to bridge the gulf between these organizations, for she could paint landscape in the monumental, vigorous manner of the Torontonians without compromising the sensuous modernism of the human figure common to the Montréal group. An earlier painting, the famous "Girl Under A Tree" of 1931, reveals her unique admixture of both tendencies. At the same time, the color scheme and mildly Cézannesque handling of certain simplified details shows her continuing interest in Hodgkins, two of whose works she owned.

She travelled widely in the late 1930s and 1940s, sketching in Bermuda, Manitoulin Island, Québec, and Los Angeles. She died rather suddenly in California in 1947. The following year the National Gallery of Canada organized a memorial show which travelled across the country.

Robert J. Belton

Bibliography
Expressions of Will: The Art of Prudence Heward. Agnes Etherington Art Centre, Queen's University, 1986.

Hickman, Pat (1941–)

Born in Fort Morgan, Colorado, the artist Pat Hickman earned a Bachelor's degree from the University of Colorado, Boulder (1962), and received a Master of Arts degree from the University of California at Berkeley (1977).

Hickman has exhibited in solo and group shows in the United States and abroad, including "Pat Hickman," Purdue University, West Lafayette, Indiana (1980); "K18-Stoffwechsel Projektgruppe Textilforum," Kassel, Germany (1982); "The Modern Basket at the Edge," Visual Arts Center of Alaska, Anchorage (1984); "12e International Biennale Lausanne," Musée des Beaux-Arts, Switzerland (1985); "Meeting Ground: Basketry Traditions and Sculptural Forms," The Forum, St. Louis, Missouri, and Arizona State University, Tempe (1990); and others.

Hickman was the recipient of an artist's grant from the National Endowment for the Arts (NEA) (1986). "Free to Change" (1989), a basket made of interlaced gut, seemingly defies reality: structure and surface are one; a pliant material, gut, woven in large interstices stands as skeleton and skin. Her work is represented in private and public permanent collections.

Bibliography
Hickman, Pat. "Gutwork." *Fiberarts Magazine* (November–December 1980).
Meeting Ground: Basketry Traditions and Sculptural Forms. A Catalog. The Forum, St. Louis, Missouri, and Arizona State University, Tempe, 1990.
Stofflet, Mary. "Collaboration: Elliott/Hickman." *American Craft Magazine* (December 1981–January 1982).
Wickman, Erstin. "Textilart from the USA." *Form Magazine.* Stockholm, Sweden (November 1985).

Hill, Abby Rhoda Williams (1861–1943)

Painter of more than 100 canvases of western landscapes and of Native Americans, Abby Rhoda Williams Hill was born in Grinnell, Iowa. In 1880 she enrolled at the Art Institute of Chicago, Illinois, to study with Henry Fenton Spread. Upon graduation she taught painting from 1884 to 1886 at a girls' private school in Berthier-en-haut in the province of Québec, Canada. From 1888 to 1889 Hill studied with William Merritt Chase at the Art Students League in New York City. She married Frank Hill in December 1888, and the following year moved with him to Tacoma, Washington, to enable him to open his medical practice. Hill devoted the next twelve years of her life to raising a family in Washington. One year during that time (1896–1897), however, was spent travelling in Germany when her husband was doing post-doctoral work; Hill studied with the illustrator Hermann Haase during the six months they lived in Hamburg.

In 1903 Hill was commissioned by the Great Northern and the Northern Pacific Railway companies to paint the Cascade Range in order to advertise rail travel at the Louisiana Purchase Exposition of 1904 in St. Louis. She created a "painting tent-studio," and the twenty canvases she painted on site were so successful that she was awarded a second contract for Yellowstone National Park, Montana, and Idaho for exhibition at the Lewis and Clark Exposition of 1905 in Portland, Oregon. At the Alaska-Yukon-Pacific Exposition of 1909 in Seattle her work received two gold medals.

After approximately 100 panoramic paintings Hill began painting portraits of Native Americans on reservations in 1906. The family moved to Laguna Beach, California, in 1909. Paintings of more national parks were done in the period of 1924–1932. A large corpus of her work today can be seen at the University of Puget Sound, Tacoma, Washington.

Eleanor Tufts

Bibliography
Fields, Ronald. "Northwest Frontier Painter." Landmarks 2:4 (1984): 2–7.
———. *Abby Williams Hill and the Lure of the West.* Washington State Historical Society, 1989.
Tufts, Eleanor. *American Women Artists, 1830–1930.* National Museum of Women in the Arts, 1987.

Hill, Joan (1930–)

Joan Hill is a Native American painter whose ancestors were Cherokee Chiefs and Creek Kings. She often signs her paintings with her Native American name, Chea-sequah (Redbird). She has lived most of her life on land that has been in her family since 1859, near Muskogee, Oklahoma.

Her instinctive drive and ability to excel was apparent as early as the seventh grade when she knew she would be an artist. It was then she was chosen by the American Legion as "outstanding girl" in the Harris Township School, near Muskogee.

At Muskogee Junior College Hill earned membership in Phi Theta Kappa, an honorary scholastic fraternity. In 1953 she received her Bachelor of Arts degree in education from Northeastern State College (now Northeastern Oklahoma State University), Tahlequah, Oklahoma, and began teaching art at Theodore Roosevelt Junior High School in Tulsa, Oklahoma. Four years later Hill resigned this position to pursue her own art studies.

From 1958 to 1964 Hill studied with Cheyenne artist Dick West at Bacone College in Muskogee, Oklahoma; with George E. Calvert at Northeastern State College; and nineteen series of classes from eight painting instructors, including Jack Vallee, Roger Lee White, Johnny Arthur, Bob Bartholic, and Paul Maxwell. She studied with Frederick Taubes of New York at Philbrook Museum of Art, Tulsa, Oklahoma, in 1964.

Hill has been offered the position of painting instructor at several schools, including the Institute of American Indian Arts, Santa Fe, New Mexico; Northeastern State College, Tahlequah; and Haskell College, Lawrence, Kansas. She has always declined as she feels called to paint, not teach.

Hill enjoys working in all painting and drawing media, but she most often uses oil, acrylic, or transparent watercolor, and is proficient in various print and sculpture media. Her collages often combine tissue paper and sandpaper with loose sand, scattered with control. The combined media are held together by using polymer.

Since 1964 Hill has travelled the world extensively with T.H. Hewitt's workshop painting tours. Through these tours she has studied with Dong Kingman, Millard Sheets, Rex Brandt, and George Post, gaining from their critique and advice. Her paintings of Native American themes are frequently in the flat, two-dimensional technique with the distinctive styles and color schemes for which she has become recognized.

Hill finds most themes for her Native American art from extensive research in her personal library. Through the study of noted men and women of history she gains insight into the subject's appearance. The resultant historical insight has led to her excellent reputation for the accuracy of her portraiture. She utilized her research practice on a commissioned portrait of "Diana Rogers," the Cherokee wife of Sam Houston. It shows a striking resemblance to Hill, a distant cousin of Rogers. The Rogers portrait appears as the frontispiece in the publication, *Sam Houston with the Cherokees, 1829–1833*.

Hill's biography has been included in thirty-five publications, including *American Indian Painters: A Biographical Dictionary*; *The World Who's Who of Women*; *The Dictionary of International Biography*; *The Two Thousand Women of Achievement*; *International Platform Association*; *Who's Who in American Art*; *Who's Who of American Women*; *Encyclopedia of the American Indian*; and *Indians of Today*. Her art has been used on the cover, slip jacket, or frontispiece of twelve important publications.

Hill has shown in more than 300 exhibitions since 1956. In competitions throughout the United States, she has received more than 254 awards, including twelve grand awards. In 1973 the Philbrook Museum of Art singled her out for the Waite Phillips Trophy (their highest award), given to the artists who had made significant contributions to Native American art. She was invited to participate in the Outstanding Indian Painters and Sculptors Honorary Exhibition, held at Princeton University, New Jersey, during the 1st Convention of American Indian Scholars in 1970.

The Seattle Arts Commission mural competition for Daybreak Star Performing Center selected her oil "Origin of the First Fruits of the Land," depicting a Cherokee legend.

Hill's first solo show was at Northeastern State College in 1952. Since then there have been sixteen solo shows at such institutions as Heard Museum in Phoenix, Arizona; Philbrook Museum of Art, Tulsa; Southern Plains Indian Museum, Anadarko; and Langston University, Langston—all in Oklahoma.

Hill's tempera paintings, "Dressing for the Ribbon Dance" and "Seminole Women Preparing Koonti Bread," were included in the Museum of New Mexico's touring exhibition. A solo show of her paintings by means of color photographs was arranged by the Central Art Academy of Peking to tour the Peoples Republic of China in May–June 1978. At this same time Hill and twenty-three other American artists participated in the first Painters Cultural Exchange, under the auspices of the U.S. Department of State.

Her acrylic painting, "Voices of the Drum Circle the Sun" was in the 1980 Bacone College Centennial Touring Art Exhibit. Her painting, "Medicine Flowers," was shown in a tour conducted by the Institute of American Indian Arts in 1976, and a color depiction appeared in the catalog.

By invitation Hill's acrylic painting, "The Appointed Day of the Sacred Fire" (predominantly in tones of yellow, orange, and brown), was shown at the John F. Kennedy Center for the Performing Arts in Washington, D.C., in 1982, and then it was displayed in a ten-month showing at the Smithsonian Institution, also in Washington, D.C.

Hill is represented by sixty-six paintings, eighteen drawings, and two prints, in fourteen public collections which include the Museum of Fine Arts, Santa Fe, New Mexico; the U.S. Department of the Interior's Indian Arts and Crafts Board (from this collection,

Hill's art can be seen at the Southern Plains Indian Museum, Anadarko, Oklahoma); and the U.S. Center of Military History, Smithsonian Institution—both in Washington, D.C.; and the Museum of the American Indian, Heye Foundation; and the American Indian Arts Center—both in New York City. In Oklahoma, Hill's works are in the collections of Bacone College; the Five Civilized Tribes Museum, Muskogee; Philbrook Museum of Art, and the Performing Arts Center, Tulsa; Central State University, Edmond; Cherokee Historical Center, and the Cherokee Cultural Center—both in Tahlequah.

The U.S. Department of the Interior commissioned Hill to produce four large paintings for federal buildings in Albuquerque, New Mexico. She is in the Telex corporation's collection in London, England, and has almost 1,000 paintings and prints in private collections throughout the world. Hill's 1973 acrylic, "Evening of the Busk" (now in the Tulsa Performing Arts Center), was published (in color) in *HRW Art Works, Teacher's Level 4* as a comparison study to Henri Rousseau's "Carnival Evening."

Hill has distinguished herself with a long record of involvement in activities on state, national, and international levels. She was the guest of Americans for Indian Opportunity while representing women artists on a panel discussion at the 1972 Smithsonian Institution's Festival of American Folklife. That same year she was honored as one of the Ten Outstanding Indians in the United States by the Fashion Industry of New York. She was appointed co-chairperson for the Oklahoma State Art Exhibition which was held during Indian Achievement Week, 1973.

Chosen in 1980 as one of the eminent men and women who have made outstanding contributions to mankind, Hill signed a commemorative stamp for the collection called "People of the Century." The collection will be housed at the Smithsonian Institution. Also in 1980 the under-secretary of the U.S. Department of the Interior appointed Hill to the Review Panel of American Indian Art and Culture, and to the advisory committee to the U.S. government's task force to save the Santa Fe Indian School. In that same year she was invited to testify before a U.S. Senate Select Committee on Indian Affairs because of her experience and knowledge relating to Indian art and culture. Her record of artistic excellence prompted the governor of Oklahoma to appoint Hill to the Commission on the Status of Women, in 1981. At the same time she was selected to exhibit in the "Living Women—Living Art" exhibit, which was held in conjunction with Women's Day at the State Capitol.

In 1982 Hill was chosen from a national membership of more than 6,000 women, as one of fourteen honorees to receive the Distinguished Pen Women award for professional excellence in her field. The Accademia Italia, in Calvatone, Italy, honored her in 1985 with the *Oscar d'Italia*, which is given to a select list of masters throughout the world.

Due to poor health, and the health and eventual deaths of both her parents, Hill was relatively inactive between 1980 and 1987. However, 1988 found her painting and exhibiting again. She accepted an appointment to the Oklahoma Governor's Commission on the Status of Women, and she remains active on the board of directors of Oklahomans for Indian Opportunity.

Jeanne O. Snodgrass King

Bibliography
Bucklew, Joan. "Traditions of the Indian Tribes Depicted." *The Arizona Republic* (February 14, 1965): 20C.
Burton, Wilma W. "Joan Hill Immortalizes Her People in Art." *The Pen Woman* 52 (November 1976): Cover, 14–15.
Harmon, Bill. "Not Bound by Tradition." *Oklahoma's Orbit Magazine* (July 21, 1963): 8–9.
Highwater, Jamake. *Song From the Earth*. American Indian Paintings. New York Graphics Society, 1976, pp. 123–24, 128.
Hill, Joan. "Indian Art: A Form of Visual Prayer." *The Creative Woman* 8 (Fall 1987): Cover, 19–21.
Humphrey, Donald G., and Jeanne O. Snodgrass King. *Centennial Touring Art Exhibit*. Bacone College, 1980, p. 12.
Litchfield, Yvonne. "Cherokee Customs Shown by Oklahoma Indian Artist." *Tulsa Daily World, World of Women* (June 27, 1968): 1.
National American Indian Women's Art Show. Gambaro Studio-Gallery, 1980, Cover, pp. 14–15.

Hills, Laura Coombs (1859–1952)

Born in Newburyport, Massachusetts, the painter Laura Coombs Hills studied with Helen M. Knowlton; attended the Cowles Art School in Boston, Massachusetts, and the Art Students League in New York City.

Winner of awards and honors, Hills was the recipient of a bronze medal at the Paris Exposition, France (1900); a silver medal at the Pan-American Exposition, Buffalo, New York (1901), and another at the Charleston Exposition (1902); a gold medal at the St. Louis Exposition (1904), and medals of honor at the Pan-Pacific Exposition, San Francisco (1915), and the Pennsylvania Academy of Fine Arts, Philadelphia (1916); and others. Four years later she won the Lea prize at the Pennsylvania Academy.

Hill was a member of many arts organizations, including the National Academy of Design, New York City, where she was elected an associate; the Boston Watercolor Club, Massachusetts; Copley Society, Philadelphia (1892); American Society of Miniature Painters, New York City; Pennsylvania Society of Miniature Painters, Philadelphia; American Federation of Arts, Washington, D.C.; and others. Her work is in permanent collections, including the Metropolitan Museum of Art, New York City.

Bibliography
American Art Annual. Vol. 30. American Federation of Arts, 1933.
Clement, Clara Erskine. *Women in the Fine Arts*. Houghton-Mifflin, 1904: 159–60.
Duncan, Frances. "The Miniatures of Miss Laura Hills." *International Studio* 41:162 (August 1910): xlvi–xlviii.
Who's Who in American Art. 5th ed. American Federation of Arts, 1953.

Hillsmith, Fannie (c. 1913–)

Born in Boston, Massachusetts, the painter/collagist Fannie Hillsmith studied at several venues, including the Boston Museum School of Fine Arts, Massachusetts; University of London and the Slade School, both in London, England (1930–1934); the Art Students League, with Alexander Brook, Yasuo Kuniyoshi, John Sloan, and William Zorach (1934–1935); and Atelier 17—both in New York City, with the printmaker Stanley William Hayter (1946–1950).

Hillsmith exhibited in many solo and group shows, including the Charles Egan Gallery (1949, 1954); Swetzoff Gallery (1949, 1950, 1954, 1957, 1963); Boston Arts Festival (1950–1954, 1956–1963)—all in Boston, Massachusetts; Colby College, Waterville, Maine (1950); Santa Barbara Museum of Art, California (1950); Brockton Museum, Massachusetts, a retrospective (1971); Bristol Museum, Rhode Island (1972); and many others.

Hillman has won many prizes and honors, including first prizes at the Portland Museum of Art, Maine (1958), and the Boston Arts Festival, Massachusetts (1957, 1963); a purchase award at the 29th Illinois Invitational Exhibition (1976); and many others. An abstract cubist, Hillsmith has taught at the University of Illinois, Champaign, for many years. Her works are in many private and public permanent collections, including the Decatur Art Museum and Illinois Art Museum, Springfield—both in Illinois; DeWaters Art Institute, Flint, and Western Michigan University, Kalamazoo—both in Michigan; Indianapolis Museum of Art, Indiana; and others.

Bibliography
"Abstractions at Egan Gallery." *Art Digest* 23:28 (April 15, 1949).
"Exhibition of Recent Oils at Egan." *Art News* 48:47 (April 1949).
"Exhibition at Peridot Gallery." *Art News* 56:14 (April 1957).
"Exhibition at Peridot Gallery." *Art News* 64:11 (May 1965).

Hinsley, Tanis (1951–)

Tanis Hinsley, who is half Tlingit Indian, was born in Skagway, Alaska. She has taught metalsmithing, papermaking, drawing, and sculpture since the early 1980s. Hinsley studied at Utah State University, Logan (1979–1980); earned a Bachelor of Fine Arts degree in printmaking from the University of Alaska, Fairbanks (1987); and received a Master of Fine Arts degree from the University of Arizona, Tucson (1992).

Hinsley's numerous exhibitions include shows at the University of Arizona Museum of Art, Tempe (1992); Sacred Circle Gallery of American Indian Art, Seattle, Washington (1991); and the Civic Center Gallery, Fairbanks (1987, 1988, 1990). Her work was also included in "Vision of New Eyes," Visual Arts Center of Alaska, Anchorage (1992), and was in "Arts from the Arctic," a travelling show to Alaska, Canada, Greenland, Scandinavia, and Siberia (1993).

Hinsley's sculptural works during the late 1980s incorporated mixed media: handmade paper, paint, wood, and metal. These works formed abstract references to forms from her cultural traditions, powerful elements of societal rituals and beliefs. She believes that her art work functions to educate the contemporary viewer, creating an awareness of Native Americans, their sources of ideas, and their place in the twentieth century.

Hinsley's current large-scale, mixed-media drawings incorporate figurative imagery and traditional symbols which are overlaid with dynamic, aggressive, and sensuous markings. In Hinsley's words, "This creates a 'way in' for the viewer to understand what it is I deal with . . . to break the stereotypic ideas surrounding Native Americans today."

Color, line, and shape move from recognizable imagery to distortions of form and space, implying an emotional spiralling and layering. This, in turn, refers, in a surreal way, to cultural overlays, pain, suffering, anger, sharing, memories, and travels through the subconscious.

Moira Geoffrion

Bibliography
Portfolio, Eleven Indian Artists. 1987.
Native Artists Newsletter. Institute of Alaska. (May 1987).

Hirsch, Gilah Yelin (1944–)

Born in Montréal, Québec, Canada, the painter Gilah Yelin Hirsch earned a Bachelor's degree from the University of California at Berkeley (1967) and, three years later, received a Master of Fine Arts degree from the University of California at Los Angeles (UCLA). At various times Hirsch also studied at Boston University, Massachusetts; Hebrew University, McGill University, and Sir George Williams University (now Concordia University), Montréal.

A university professor, Hirsch has held solo exhibitions in museums and galleries, such as the Los Angeles County Museum of Art, California (1969); Tibor de Nagy Gallery, New York City (1972); the Woman's Building (1978), and JLK Gallery—both in Los Angeles, California (1984); and others. Her work has been in group exhibitions, including "Southern California Attitudes," Pasadena Museum, California (1972); the "Annual," the Whitney Museum of American Art, New York City (1973); University of California at Irvine (1982); and others.

Winner of honors and awards, Hirsch was artist-in-residence at the Tamarind Lithography Workshop, Albuquerque, New Mexico (1973); a fellow at the Dorland Mountain Colony (1981, 1983); a fellow at the Banff Centre for the Arts, Alberta, Canada (1985); and the recipient of a fellowship from the National Endowment for the Arts (1985). Her work is represented in private, public, and corporate permanent collections.

Bibliography
Arelianes, Roberto. "Two Views of Nature." *Artweek.* Vol. 17 (November 29, 1986): 8.
Brown, Betty Ann. "Finding Patterns of Harmony." *Artweek.* Vol. 20 (January 7, 1989): 4.
Lazzari, Margaret R. "The Power of Writing." *Artweek.* Vol. 20 (February 25, 1989): 5.
Weisberg, Ruth. "Illuminations of Nature." *Artweek.* Vol. 15 (November 17, 1984): 3.
Who's Who in American Art. 19th ed. R.R. Bowker Co., 1991–1992.

Hirst, Claude Raguet (1855–1942)

Named for her grandmother of French descent, Claudine Raguet Hirst submitted her paintings to art juries under the name Claude R. Hirst to conceal her sex and thus avoid discrimination against female artists. A painter of still life, Hirst grew up in Clayton, Ohio—a suburb of Cincinnati—and studied at the Cincinnati School of Design, Ohio, from 1874 to 1878. She then moved to New York City, where she took lessons from Agnes D. Abbott, George Smillie, and Charles Curran. The first dated record of her appearance in a New York exhibition was in the year 1882 when two of her flower paintings were accepted for the National Academy of Design's, New York City, annual show. Her entries in the next four consecutive years continued to be still lifes of flowers. But in 1890 a change occurred: the three titles were "A Bachelor's Solace," "Crumbs of Comfort," and "Ye Ancient Tales." These titles describe Hirst's new subject matter of pipes and books inspired by fellow artist William C. Fitler, who smoked a meerschaum

pipe. Hirst and Fitler married in 1901.

Another event that may have affected her painting was the return to New York City from Europe of William M. Harnett, who in 1886 took a studio on East 14th Street next to Hirst's. A similar *trompe l'oeil* quality to realistic, sharply-delineated still-life objects exists in the paintings of both artists. The major difference is that Hirst almost invariably, and always astonishingly, achieved her effect through the medium of watercolor.

Hirst was a longstanding member of the National Association of Women Artists, which was formed in 1889. She often exhibited in the Association's annual juried shows. In 1922 and 1927 her work won honorable mention, and in 1931 her oil, "The Title Page," received the painting prize.

Her still lifes are generally composed of open books, pipes, one vase, and a tobacco pouch, seen against an opaque background and resting on a wooden table top; they are often signed on the edge of the table at the right. Many are in private collections today, and others are in the hands of art dealers.

Eleanor Tufts

Bibliography
Tufts, Eleanor. *American Women Artists, 1830–1930.* National Museum of Women in the Arts, 1987.

Hobson, Katherine Thayer (1889–1982)

Born in Denver, Colorado, the sculptor Katherine Thayer Hobson studied at the Art Students League, New York City, and with Walter Sintenis in Dresden, Germany. Her work was exhibited in many galleries and shown with the Allied Artists of America, American Artists Professional League, the Catharine Lorillard Wolfe Art Club, Hudson Valley Art Association, the National Academy of Design—all in New York City; and many others.

Hobson executed commissions of busts and other sculptural work sited in the Bahnhofs Platz, Göttingen; the universities of Göttingen and Königsberg—all in Germany; and a war memorial for the St. James Episcopal Church in New York City. She was a member of many professional art societies, and a lecturer on sculpture. She won many honors and awards for her three-dimensional work and was made a fellow of the National Sculpture Society, New York City.

Bibliography
The New York Times (September 23, 1982): Y23.
Who's Who in American Art. 15th ed. R.R. Bowker Co., 1982.

Hoff, Margo (1912–)

Rethinking the relationship between art and life has preoccupied many twentieth-century artists. Some radicals have attempted to eradicate any distinction at all between the two, but others, including Margo Hoff, have sought to incorporate their life experiences into aesthetically independent works of art. In her work Hoff addresses human and creative issues infrequently encountered in recent art, which often represses her central concerns: the transcendent purpose of art; the validity of beauty, or even the purely decorative; and interest in what is intimate, sensuous, personal, indeed valuable.

Everywhere she goes Hoff gathers visual impressions that crystallize a moment. These images, sometimes hastily sketched on the spot, provide the raw material for memories of shapes, colors, and textures. As she transforms these into art she communicates a life-affirming psychological reality rather than a literal view of the world. Her work confirms that Hoff relishes the act of seeing, which she further intensifies through lively and sophisticated dialogue with modern formal experiments in color, space, composition, and surface texture. Henri Matisse, Pierre Bonnard, and post-cubist George Braque are especially relevant to her aesthetic.

Hoff was born and grew up in Tulsa, Oklahoma. In 1938 she arrived in Chicago, Illinois, to study at the School of the Art Institute. She married Chicagoan George Buehr and made the city her home for another two decades. In the late 1940s and 1950s, she was among the most successful artists of her emerging generation. She was, for example, cited in Art in America's "New Talent" series, while her work won numerous prizes and was acquired by major institutions.

During these early years Hoff's work evolved from a rather tightly painted magic realism, evident in "Doorways" (1944), to a broader and more abstract mode, exemplified by "Intersection" (1953) and "Grownup Party" (1953). This work of the 1950s, which made Hoff's early reputation, is characterized by simplified, flattened shapes and richly painted surfaces, recalling the work of Milton Avery and other less well-known post-war artists who attempted to strike a balance between abstraction and representation.

In the early 1960s Hoff moved to New York, where she still lives, and began to work with collage, which remains her most frequent medium. Simultaneously her work has evolved away from representation. In her most completely realized recent works, of which the acrylic-and-collage "Rose Mystery" (1987) and "Studio Inside" (1987) are large and dramatic examples, the abstracted stimulus all but disappears in a vibrant expanse of color.

Besides the paintings and collages for which she is best known, Hoff has produced works in other media, including lithographs and wood-block prints, tapestry designs, mosaics, murals, book illustrations, and costumes for theater and dance. She has travelled widely, often living for periods of time abroad, and has taught at numerous schools and workshops in this country and elsewhere.

Ann Lee Morgan

Bibliography
Morgan, Ann Lee. "Margo Hoff." *New Art Examiner* 15 (September 1987): 42.
Weller, Allen S. "Margo Hoff." *Art in America* 43 (February 1955): 36–38.

Hoffman, Malvina Cornell (1885–1966)

An indomitable and prolific artist, highly praised by her contemporaries for her realistic portraits, Malvina Cornell Hoffman was one of America's most prominent sculptors by the time she was thirty. Hoffman was born in New York City to Fedelia Marshall Lamson Hoffman, who taught her at home until she was ten years old, and Richard Hoffman, a composer and pianist for the New York Philharmonic Orchestra. Hoffman attended the Chapin School for Girls and the exclusive Brearly School.

While attending high school at the Brearly School, Hoffman took evening classes at the Woman's School of Applied Design and the Art Students League—all in her native city. For several years she studied painting with John White Alexander and Harper Pennington. Then turning to sculpture she studied with Herbert Adams, George Grey Barnard, and Gutson Borglum, whose modernistic style appears occasionally in her symbolic pieces. She became expert in both cast and carved sculpture.

After the death of her father Hoffman and her mother went abroad. In London, England, she became fascinated by the juxtaposition of motion and control when she saw a performance of Anna Pavlova and Mikhail Mordkin in their dance to Glazunov's *Autumn Bacchanale*, which she translated into sculpture. Later she met Pavlova, who was to have an ongoing influence on her work and serve as a subject for some of her most significant sculptures. Hoffman and her mother settled in Paris, France, from 1910 to 1914. Supporting herself as Janet Scudder's studio assistant, she convinced Auguste Rodin to take her as a pupil and studied at the Académie Colarossi, Paris, France, at night. She also studied with Emanuele Rosales. In 1912 she made a trip home to study anatomy with George S. Huntington at the College of Physicians and Surgeons, Columbia University. She returned permanently to New York at the outbreak of World War I.

During the war she worked in New York City as the American representative of Appui aux Artistes, a French war charity for the benefit of needy artists which she had helped to organize. She also was one of the organizers of the American-Yugoslav relief fund designed to support destitute children after the war. Years later, during World War II, she raised money for the Red Cross and for national defense.

Hoffman began to exhibit in 1910 at the National Academy of Design, New York City. The next year she won an honorable mention at the Paris Salon, France. Her many solo exhibitions began with the Leicester Gallery in 1914 and included prominent New York City galleries—the Ferargil Gallery, the Painters and Sculptors Gallery, the Cloisters, and Grand Central Galleries—as well as the Carnegie Institute, Pittsburgh, and the Philadelphia Art Alliance—both in Pennsylvania; the Virginia Museum of Fine Arts, Richmond; the Corcoran Gallery of Art, Washington, D.C., and the M.H. de Young Memorial Museum, San Francisco, California.

Hoffman's best-known commission was from Chicago's Field Museum in 1930 to sculpt 105 life-size heads and figures depicting the most typical physical characteristics of various peoples of the world for the Field Museum's "Hall of Man." Before this project was conceived Hoffman had travelled in the mid-1920s to Africa to sculpt. For the Field Museum work she went to Hawaii, Japan, China, Bali, Java, the Malay Peninsula, India, and Ceylon. She produced most of the figures in bronze. Among other important commissions are her "Bacchanale Russe" (1917); "The Sacrifice" war memorial for Harvard University, Cambridge, Massachusetts (1918); the memorial to the "Friendship of the English Speaking People," London, England (1924); the "International Dance" fountain for the New York World's Fair (1939); the memorial to members of the 71st Regiment in New York (1956); and three statues of Polish pianist "Ignace Paderewski." Her work was collected by the Luxembourg Museum in Paris, France; the Stockholm Art Museum, Sweden; the Metropolitan Museum of Art, the American Museum of Natural History, the Brooklyn Museum, the National Academy of Design, and the Frick Collection—all in New York City; the Corcoran Gallery of Art, Washington, D.C.; the Buffalo Museum of Science, New York; and the Art Institute of Chicago, Illinois.

Long after establishing herself as a successful sculptor, Hoffman married British violinist Samuel Bonarios Grimson in 1924. She wrote two books about her life—her autobiography, *Heads and Tales*, in 1936, and a personal family history, *Yesterday Is Tomorrow*, in 1965. She became an expert in sculpture methodology and wrote a technical book, *Sculpture Inside and Out*, in 1939. She published the story of her travels to create the Field Museum sculptures, *A Sculptor's Odyssey*, in 1937, and also wrote several magazine articles about her experiences.

Widely recognized for her public service as well as for her art, Hoffman was awarded the Palmes Académiques (1920); Royal Order of St. Sava III of Yugoslavia (1921); the Woman of Achievement award by the New York League of Business and Professional Women; the Award for Eminent Achievement of the American Woman's Association (1937); the French Legion of Honor (1951); "Woman of the Year" by the American Association of University Women (1957); and fellow of the National Sculpture Society (1958). She was awarded the George D. Widener memorial medal of the Pennsylvania Academy of Fine Arts, Philadelphia (1920); Helen Foster Barnett prize by the National Academy of Design, New York City (1921); and its Elizabeth Watrous gold medal (1924); honorable mention for sculpture at the Panama-Pacific International Exposition (1915); the Shaw memorial prize (1917), the Joan of Arc gold medal by the National Association of Women Painters and Sculptors (1925); and the gold medal of honor from the Allied Artists of America (1962); the medal of honor of the National Sculpture Society (1964), and the first prize for sculpture of the National Council of the Arts (1966). The University of Rochester, New York, Northwestern University, Evanston, Illinois, and Bates College, Lewiston, Maine, each conferred upon her Doctor of Fine Arts degrees; Smith College, Northampton, Massachusetts, gave her a Doctor of Humanities degree; and Mt. Holyoke College, South Hadley, Massachusetts, honored her with a Doctor of Literature degree.

A national academician, Hoffman was also a member of the National Association of Women Painters and Sculptors, the National Institute of Arts and Letters, the National Sculpture Society, the Painters and Sculptors Gallery Association, the National Arts Club, the American Women's Association, the Pen and Brush Club, the Society of Women Geographers, the Architectural League, the Spanish Institute, the Art Alliance of America, the Architectural League of New York, the National Institute of Social Sciences, and the Three Arts Club of New York.

Phyllis Peet

Bibliography
Hill, May Brawley. *The Woman Sculptor: Malvina Hoffman and Her Contemporaries*. Berry-Hill Galleries, 1984.
Hoffman, Malvina. *Heads and Tales*. Charles Scribner's Sons, 1936.
———. *Sculpture Inside and Out*. W.W. Norton & Co. and Bonanza Books, 1939.
———. *Yesterday Is Tomorrow: A Personal History*. Crown Publishers, 1965.
Nochlin, Linda. "Malvina Hoffman: A Life in Sculpture." *Arts Magazine* 59:3 (November 1984): 106–110.

Hofmann, Kitzia Domenge De (1924–1987)

Born in Mexico, Kitzia Domenge De Hofmann was initially the student and then the wife of the sculptor, Herbert Hofmann-Ysenbourg.

Hofmann specialized in the art of stained glass; her finest effort culminated in the panels she designed for the chapel of the Misioneros del Espíritu Santu in the convent of El Atillo in Coyoacán, Mexico.

This masterwork was commissioned by the architect, Enrique de la Mora y Palomar; the panels are situated behind the altar in such positions as to evoke a "jubilation of colors" and form in movement.

Hofmann created many other works in sacred and secular places in Monterrey, Guadalajara, and Cuernavaca. She died in 1987 in the city of her birth.

Bibliography
Alvarez, José Rogelio, et al. *Enciclopedia de México*. Secretaría de Educación Pública, 1987.

Holsenbeck, Bryant (1949–)

Born in Kingsport, Tennessee, the sculptor Bryant Holsenbeck earned a Bachelor's degree from the University of North Carolina at Chapel Hill (1971), and received a Master's degree in education (1972) from the same institution. As a sculptor, Holsenbeck works with natural and man-made materials in seemingly unusual combinations.

Holsenbeck has held solo exhibitions in galleries, including the New Morning Gallery, Asheville, North Carolina (1982, 1985, 1986); "Recent Weavings," The Works, Philadelphia, Pennsylvania (1988); and others. Her work has been invited to, or included in group exhibitions in the United States and abroad, such as "Fiber and Wood Invitational," Columbia Museum of Art, South Carolina (1980, 1982); "American Crafts in Iceland," Reykjavik (1983); "U.S.A. Volti del Sud," Palazzo Venezia, Rome, Italy (1984); "After Her Own Image: Woman's Work," Salem College, Winston-Salem, North Carolina (1986); "Let's Play House," curated by Miriam Schapiro, Bernice Steinbaum Gallery, New York City (1986); "Women in Sculpture," Wabash College, Crawfordsville, Indiana (1987); and others.

Winner of awards and honors, Holsenbeck received a fellowship from the Atlantic Center for the Arts to study with Miriam Schapiro (1983); an emerging artist grant from the Durham Arts Council, North Carolina (1985); and others.

"Passage" (1986), a mixed-media, sculptural work of natural and man-made cast-offs, is typical of this period.

Bibliography
Nine from North Carolina: An Exhibition of Women Artists. North Carolina State Committee and the National Museum of Women in the Arts: 1989.

Holt, Nancy (1938–)

Through landscape sculpture, video-tape, and film, Nancy Holt controls her viewer's sight, guiding and shaping it in an effort to enlarge the experience of perception. She challenges pre-existing notions of order through intricate spatial relationships involving the earth, sky, sun, moon, and stars. Normal vision is altered by deflecting, reflecting, and otherwise revising one's visual perception of the universe.

Born in Worcester, Massachusetts, Holt graduated from Tufts University in Medford, Massachusetts, in 1960. She coauthored the video-tape, *East Coast—West Coast*, in 1969 with her husband and fellow artist, Robert Smithson, and later the film, *Swamp*, in 1971. Other video-tapes by Holt include *Locating Z* (1972), *Zeroing In* (1973), *Going Around in Circles* (1973), and *Underscan* (1974), as well as the film, *Pine Barrens* (1975).

Holt's earliest landscape pieces involve focusing sight through devices she calls "locators"—small, steel pipes framing specific views. In 1973 the artist followed a natural progression to her only non-commissioned piece, "Sun Tunnels," which again employs the use of locators, only this time on a monumental scale. Four concrete cylinders measuring eight feet in length with diameters of nine feet, two-and-a-half inches were placed in an open "X" configuration in the Great Basin Desert in northwestern Utah. The tunnels are aligned in accordance with the rising and setting of the sun on the summer and winter solstices. Holes drilled into the tunnels cast the constellations of stars into the darkened interior, reproducing the vastness of the cosmos for the earthbound viewer and, thus, inverting perception by turning the earth into sky.

Holt successfully integrates her sculpture with the environment, taking advantage of the natural phenomena which surround it to emphasize the fluctuation of visual reality. Spatial relationships perceived through the tunnels and the changing landscape heighten the viewer's awareness of an infinite number of perceptions heretofore unseen.

"Rock Rings" (1977–1978) at Western Washington University in Bellingham, Washington; "Annual Ring" (1980–1981) at the Federal Building in Saginaw, Michigan; and "Star-Crossed" (1979–1981) in Oxford, Ohio, at the Miami University Art Museum continue to question visual perceptions, making the viewer conscious of space and reality.

In 1979 Holt began what was to be an important and successful commission for an urban renewal project. As sculptor and landscape architect she created "Dark Star Park" (completed in 1984) in Rosslyn, Arlington County, Virginia. The park, as a result, is a complete work of art consisting of five spheres, two tunnels, two circular pools, and four steel pipes standing upright. Holt likens the spheres to fallen stars. The visitor becomes involved in an ever-changing interplay of relationships with the elements as he or she walks through the park. Again, Holt combines what she believes to be a basic human desire, "the need to look at the sky—at the moon and stars . . ." with intriguing aspects of perception.

Christine L. Wilson

Bibliography
Castle, Ted. "Nancy Holt, Siteseer." *Art in America* 70 (March 1982): 84–91.
Holt, Nancy. "Stone Enclosure: Rock Rings, 1977–78." *Arts* 53 (June 1979): 152–55.
———. "Sun Tunnels." *Artforum* 15 (April 1977): 32–37.
Marter, Joan. "Nancy Holt's Dark Star Park." *Arts Magazine* 59 (October 1984): 137–39.

Holzer, Jenny (1950–)

Born in Gallipolis, Ohio, the conceptual artist Jenny Holzer earned a Bachelor of Fine Arts degree from Ohio University, Athens (1972), and, five years later, received a Master of Fine Arts degree from the Rhode Island School of Design, Providence. She was also a fellow in the Whitney Museum of American Art Independent Study Program, New York City (1977).

Holzer has held solo exhibitions in prestigious museums and galleries throughout the United States and abroad and has executed commissions in diverse venues; her innovative printed art works filled with social and political overtones have been included in group exhibitions from New York City to London, England; from San Francisco, California, to Wiesbaden, Germany; from Boston, Massachusetts to Venice, Italy, Barcelona, Spain; and many others.

Holzer has won honors and awards, including the Blair Award from the Art Institute of Chicago (1982), and others. Examples of her work are in private, public, and corporate permanent collections, including the Museum of Contemporary Art, Chicago, Illinois; Museum of Modern Art (MoMA) Lending Service, New York City; Van Abbe Museum, Eindhoven, the Netherlands; and others.

Bibliography
Ferguson, Bruce. "Wordsmith: An Interview with Jenny Holzer." *Art in America* 74:12 (December 1986): 108–15, 153.
Handy, Ellen. "Jenny Holzer." *Arts Magazine* 63:1 (September 1988): 91.
Siegel, Jeanne. "Jenny Holzer's Language Games." *Arts Magazine* 60:4 (December 1985): 64–68.
Westerbeck, Colin. "Jenny Holzer." *Artforum* 25:9 (May 1987): 154–55.
Who's Who in American Art. 20th ed. R.R. Bowker Co., 1993–1994.

Hood, Dorothy (1919–)

Unlike most mature artists who dwell lovingly on their early lives and childhood memories, Dorothy Hood, in conversation, offers only facts: born in Bryan, Texas, an only child, she was brought up mostly by household help. Her mother was sickly and spent long stretches of time at sanitariums where Hood joined her during school vacations. Her father travelled extensively on business. Her childhood was a time when children were expected to be seen but not heard. It was lonely growing up; she felt isolated and forced upon her own inner resources, spending vacation time at mountain spas—places populated only by adults.

Hood's talent was obvious from an early age. She always knew she would be an artist. Her mother, despite her long absences, encouraged Hood's early efforts. When she was in high school, an art teacher submitted one of her paintings to a competition that won her a National Scholastic Scholarship to Rhode Island School of Design, Providence. Transferring to New York City's Art Students League, Hood completed her studies in 1941 and took off for Mexico on a vacation trip. It was twenty years after the Revolution, and although the Mexican Renaissance was fading, there were new influences from surrealism—the most important international "ism" of the time. The young artist responded to the beauty, danger, excitement, and intellectual climate of the country, and was befriended by leading Mexican and European artists and writers exiled there. The artists virtually adopted her, giving her the warmth and circle of friends missing from her isolated childhood. It was for Hood the beginning of her life and her career as an artist.

She was to spend most of the next nineteen years in Mexico, marrying Bolivian composer and conductor Velasco Maidana and travelling extensively from Mexico to Central, South, and North America.

Hood's first exhibition was at the Gama Gallery in Mexico City, Mexico, in 1941. Her oils and gouaches were realist—children and animals, self and family portraits. The Chilean poet Pablo Neruda wrote a prose poem in lieu of the usual catalog essay. The work reflected the impact of Mexico, as well as the influence of her close friend, José Clemente Orozco. The eruption of the Volcano Paricutín the night before the scheduled opening was incidental; despite the damage and disruption the show opened as scheduled.

In 1945 Hood spent most of the year in New York to study some more and catch up with her Mexican friends whose cultural background so exceeded hers. A wonderful string of coincidences occurred at this time, starting with the gift from a Texas neighbor of James Thrall Soby's book, *After Picasso*, which enthralled her. A friend in New York, John McAndrews, curator of architecture at the Museum of Modern Art (MoMA), showed one of her drawings (by now much influenced by her study of the book) to Soby, who was also at MoMA. Much taken with it, Soby hung it in his office and shortly after included it in a major exhibition which travelled the United States. And so, the young artist found her work hanging with Pablo Picasso and Henri Matisse.

In 1950, she had a one-person show at the Marian Willard Gallery, New York City—a highly unusual feat for a woman at that time. Asked how this came to pass, Hood explained that on another short visit to the United States that year, she rented a room near Columbia University, New York City, hung her paintings, and invited curators, gallery directors, and such up to see them. Hood says it took about a month to get everyone in to see the work. Marian Willard came on the very last day and liked what she saw. It was through Willard that Hood later met Mark Tobey, an artist whom she had long admired, and the Swiss collector and patron who subsequently invited her to work at the Ahrensberg Atelier of which he was director. Needless to say, this was wonderful exposure for the artist. There Hood worked alongside important European artists, and met many visiting European art dealers.

Gradually through the 1950s Hood's style changed from a tentative exploration of surrealist imagery to weaving plant and animal forms into increasingly abstract patterns. Although acknowledging the influence of Max Ernst (to whom she dedicated a major painting in 1984), she also recognized the significance of the Mexican Native American culture underlying her work. Hood's unique style was soon aptly labeled "Abstract Surrealism."

In 1961 Hood returned to Texas and shortly began teaching at the School of Art of the Museum of Fine Arts in Houston. Recalling her own unsatisfying student years, she sought new ways to meet the needs of her students. It was a good time to return to her roots. She had already gained great recognition and respect in Mexico. In Texas her teaching, her readings and studies in Taoism, the Yoga of Sri Aurobinda and comparative religions, in addition to the hovering presence of the great space research center and its projected moon trip, all gave new energy to her work. She became a member of a prestigious local gallery by 1962 and has shown there ever since. She won commissions and was included in numerous exhibitions; by 1971 she had five one-person shows at major Texas museums.

Although Hood may by that time have been the best-known Texas artist, she was little known in the rest of the United States until 1974, when a retrospective exhibition of thirty years of drawings, originating at the Everson Museum, Syracuse, New York, travelled the country. In 1973 her work was selected for the Childe Hassam purchase prize of the American Academy and Institute of Arts and Letters, New York City. From that time important invitations, commissions, and exhibitions in New York, Europe, and Canada have secured her national and international reputation.

Aesthetically there has been little change in Hood's work. She has always been a traveller—bodily, to faraway places, and spiritually, probing the secrets of the universe. Her paintings are full of mysteries, emerging largely from her unconscious in grand gestural sweeps, filled with the textures of the earth and the galaxies of the heavens. She works with mythic intensity, as is reflected in the titles and alluded to in the imagery. She is concerned with color, texture, form, line, and scale; her technique encompasses the automatic methods of pouring combined with other unique skills of her own invention. Her references are to natural phenomena of earth, oceans, sky; the pouring patterns are reminiscent of landscapes as seen in aerial photographs with more specific forms in applied areas; the elements are transformed by means of poetry. Brush strokes are rarely evident; the subjects become expression based solely on the movement of paint and form. Intense, emotionally urgent painting reveals the artist's need to reach new meanings—to literally probe outer space. Her colors have moved from an intentionally limited palette to an astonishing juxtaposition of colors—that shouldn't work together, but do, emitting a miraculous resonance. A documentary film produced in 1985 is aptly titled *Dorothy Hood: The Color of Life*. She was also included in a 1982 documentary of thirteen women artists—*From the Heart*.

Dorothy Hood's career does much to dispel several myths: she has lived most of her life in Houston, outside the center, yet has had one-person shows in New York and in major capitals at a time when it was nigh impossible for a woman even to show in a prestigious gallery; her works were selected by major museums for national travelling exhibitions, and working in abstract surreal imagery she became Texas's most famous artist at a time when Texas was mostly famous for cowboy art and prairie scenes.

Hood writes in a mystically poetic way and is frequently quoted. The prose and poetry plumbing similar depths evoke the same terrain as her paintings. Although none of her writing has been formally published, it has gained an audience.

Dorothy Hood lives and works in a gorgeous clutter—an overflow of books and magazines on every surface, indigenous artists' wall-hangings obscured by stacks of canvases, and in the winter months a jungle of plants moved in from their summer sojourn in the backyard. There she continues to be highly productive, to take risks and to probe the mysteries of the universe, extending the boundaries of art with panache.

Cynthia Navaretta

Bibliography
Camfield, William. "New Work from a New City." Catalog. Salzburg, Austria: Kuntsverein, 1983.
Cathcart, Linda. "The Americans: Collage." Catalog. Houston, Texas: The Contemporary Arts Museum, 1982.
Glueck, Grace. "Art: A Houston School Emerges." *New York Times* (May 24, 1985).
Hayes, Jr., Bartlett. *Drawings of the Masters: American Drawings*. Shorewood Publishers, 1965.
Kalil, Susi, and Barbara Rose. "Fresh Paint." Catalog. Houston, Texas: Museum of Fine Arts, 1985.
Mahoney, J.W. "Dorothy Hood." Catalog. Washington, D.C.: Wallace Wentworth Gallery, 1986.
Marvel, Bill. "Fresh Paint." *Dallas Times Herald* (April 1985).
Moore, Sylvia. "Dorothy Hood." *Women's Art Journal* 2 (Fall–Winter 1981).
Navaretta, Cynthia. "American Women in Art: Works on Paper." Catalog. Nairobi, Kenya: U.N. Focus International Exhibition, July 1985.
Neruda, Pablo. *There is a Painting That Not Only Caresses*. Prose poem. Mexico City, 1943.
Tufts, Eleanor. *American Women Artists*. Garland, 1984.
Wego, Nina. "Variert og Moderne Kunst fra Houston." *Aftenpotten, Aftengutgaven*. Oslo, Norway (January 17, 1983).

Hood, Ethel Painter (1908–1982)

Born in Baltimore, Maryland, the sculptor Ethel Painter Hood studied at the Art Students League, New York City, and at the Académie Julian in Paris, France.

In addition to four solo exhibitions held in New York City, Hood exhibited work at the Baltimore Museum of Art, Maryland; Corcoran Gallery of Art, Washington, D.C.; National Academy of Design and the Whitney Museum of American Art—both in New York City; the Pennsylvania Academy of Fine Arts, Philadelphia; and others.

Hood is a fellow of the National Sculpture Society, New York City, and a member of the National Association of Women Artists. Her work is represented in the Brookgreen Gardens, South Carolina, and elsewhere.

Bibliography

Proske, Beatrice G. *Brookgreen Gardens Sculpture.* Vol. II. South Carolina, 1955, pp. 112–13.

Reed, Judith Kaye. "Heads by Hood." *Art Digest* 21:9 (February 1, 1947): 18.

Hopkins, Edna Boies (1872–1937)

Born to an affluent household in Hudson, Michigan, Edna Boies Hopkins is known for her color woodcuts printed in the Japanese manner. Two years after she married, in 1892, her husband died of tuberculosis and, three years later, she enrolled in the Art Academy of Cincinnati, Ohio, where she began lifetime friendships with Ethel Mars, Maud Squire, and James R. Hopkins, whom she married in 1904. She attended Pratt Institute, Brooklyn, New York, in 1899, and studied Japanese woodcut technique with Arthur Wesley Dow; the following year, she taught at the Veltin School for Girls, New York City.

Following her second marriage, Hopkins and her husband, also an artist, travelled extensively. While in Japan, she focussed particularly on the printing techniques employed by local printmakers. Settling in Paris, France, Hopkins produced many successful editions of prints. She and her husband did not return to Cincinnati until the onset of World War I. Medal-winner at the Panama-Pacific International Exposition in San Francisco, California (1915), Hopkins was a member of the Societé du Salon Automne; Societé Internationale des Graveurs au Couleurs; Societé des Artistes Decorateurs; and the Societé Nationale des Beaux-Arts, Paris, France, in addition to the Provincetown Association, Massachusetts, with which she exhibited for many years.

Hopkins had solo and group exhibitions of her prints at many galleries and museums in the United States and Europe. Her work is in the permanent collection of the Library of Congress, Washington, D.C.; Walker Art Gallery, Liverpool, England; the National Museum, Stockholm, Sweden; the Kunstgewerbe Museum, Berlin, Germany; the Bibliothèque d'Art et Archeologie, Paris, France; Cincinnati Art Museum, Ohio; Detroit Institute of Fine Arts, Michigan; and many others.

Bibliography

A Selection of American Prints. A Selection of Biographies of Forty Women Artists Working between 1904–1979. The Annex Galleries, 1987.

Flint, Janet A. *Provincetown Printers: A Woodcut Tradition.* National Museum of American Art, 1983.

Who's Who in American Art. 2nd ed. American Federation of Arts, 1937.

Hopkins, Elisabeth Margaret (1894–after 1976)

The naive or "primitive" Canadian painter Elisabeth Margaret Hopkins created visual compositions continuously from childhood. Yet, it was not until 1973 that her work elicited interest, and in 1975 she was offered a solo exhibition at the Bau-Xi Gallery, Toronto, Ontario, Canada.

Hopkins cared neither for the words "naive" or "primitive" nor for the kind of aesthetic, religious, philosophical, or metaphorical speculation that followed the public showing of her work. She just painted children and animals in Eden-like surroundings in a naive manner.

Bibliography

Australian and New Zealand, American, and Canadian Oil Paintings and Water Colour Drawings. London, England: Burlington Gallery, 1888.

Hopkins, Elisabeth Margaret. "Grandmama." *Beaver* 397:3 (Winter 1976): 25–29.

Thomas, Audrey. "The Unwalled Garden, Elisabeth Hopkins Finds Wonder Everywhere." *Interface* 4:8 (1981): 8–13.

Hopkins, Frances Ann (1838–1918)

The painter Frances Ann Hopkins emigrated from England to Canada with her husband in 1858. She accompanied him on his travels through Canada on behalf of the Hudson's Bay Company and, in 1870, was the only woman on the Red River expedition. Her paintings of the *voyageurs*, their canoes, the flora and fauna seen on those trips, were faithfully recorded in her sketchbooks, many of them to become formal oils or watercolors. She showed paintings at eleven of the Royal Academy of Art Exhibitions, London, England (1869–1918).

Bibliography

Chalmers, John W. "Frances Ann Hopkins: The Lady Who Paints Canoes." *Canadian Geographical Journal* 83:1 (July 1971): 18–27.

Johnson, Alice. "M. Edward and Frances Hopkins of Montréal." *Beaver* 302:2 (Autumn 1971): 4–19.

Nute, Grace Lee. "Voyageurs' Artist." *Beaver* 218 (June 1947): 32–37.

Horna, Kati (1912–)

The photographer Kati Horna is one of a number of artists who found a home in Mexico during the late 1930s. Although born in Hungary Horna has spent most of her life in Mexico and considers herself Mexican. Her work includes photojournalism, photomontage, and photographs in which her personal version of surrealism emerges.

Horna's interest in photography began while attending the University of Berlin, Germany (1931–1933). She studied with Pesci in Paris, France, where she spent extensive periods of time between 1933 and 1939. Her early work includes a series of photographs taken at flea markets titled "Marché aux Puces" (1933) in which her later interest in chance and elements of surprise are already apparent. In 1937 she received a commission from the Republican government to document the Civil War in Spain. Her work was published in the anarchist magazines *Umbral* and *Libre Estudio*. She met her husband, the sculptor José Horna, while working with him on *Umbral*. Like many artists who had sided with the Republic, they emigrated to Mexico in 1939. In Mexico the Hornas were part of a close-knit group of exiles which included Remedios Varo, Leonora Carrington, her husband Emerico

(Chiqui) Weisz, Gunther Gerszo, and Benjamin Péret.

Since the publication of her photo essay "Así se va otro año, 1939" (*Todo* magazine; published as *Lo que va al cesto* in Paris, 1939), Horna's first work published in Mexico, much of her work has been for magazines. Her work has been published in periodicals such as *Diseño*, *Siempre*, *Nosotros*, *Muros de México*, and *Mexico This Month*. Many important figures in the world of Mexican culture artists, writers, playwrights, art dealers, and stage personalities have posed for Horna. Many of her portraits were published in the magazine *Mujeres*. For this publication she took the cover photographs as well as those for the center pages, which focused on women artists and artisans, from 1958 to 1963.

Aside from her commissioned work, Horna creates what she calls her *"creación personal."* Horna's particular sensibility emerges in both her commercial and personal work, however. In a series commissioned in 1945 of the inmates at the insane asylum of La Castañeda, titled *Los olvidados* (the forgotten ones), Horna portrays the inmates as seers possessed of special insight and creativity. From 1962 to 1964 she collaborated on the journal *S.nob*, which published fiction, criticism, drawings, and photography. Her photographic series for *S.nob*, known as *Fetiches*, include "Oda a la necrofilia" and "Impromptu con arpa." In these series, as in much of her other work, Horna sought to depict the unexpected lurking in everyday spaces. Masks, dolls, nocturnal environments, and sinister juxtapositions often play key roles in her photographs.

Since 1958 Horna has taught photography in Mexico City, Mexico, and is currently professor at the Escuela Nacional de Artes Plásticas in Mexico City, Mexico.

Miriam Basilio

Bibliography
Billeter, Erika, and José Pierre. *Images of Mexico*. Dallas Museum of Art, 1987.
Centro Nacional de Investigación, Documentación e Información de Artes Plásticas, Kati Horna Archive. Mexico City.
Prampolini, Ida Rodríguez. *El Surrealismo y el Arte Fantástico en México*. Universidad Autónoma de Mexico, 1969.
Sánchez Mejorada de Gil, Alicia. "Las series fotograficas de Kati Horna." *Signos, El art y la investigacion*. Instituto Nacional de Bellas Artes, Mexico City, 1989.
El Surrealismo Entre Viejo y Nuevo Mundo. Centro Atlántico de Arte Moderno, Las Palmas de Gran Canaria, 1989.
Sullivan, Edward J. *Women In Mexico/La Mujer en México*, Centro Cultural/Arte Contemporáneo, Mexico City, 1990.

Hornbacher, Sara

The multi-media sculptor, film and video artist, and writer—Sara Hornbacher was reared in Minnesota and educated at Moorhead State University in her native state; she did graduate work in film and video at the State University of New York (SUNY) at Buffalo, where she studied with Hollis Frampton, Paul Sharits, and Woody Vasulka (1975–1978). Hornbacher also did research at the Experimental Television Center, Oswego, New York, beginning in 1976.

Hornbacher has been the recipient of a Creative Artists Public Service (CAPS) award from the New York State Council on the Arts (1980); an award from the Media Bureau of The Kitchen, New York City (1983); and others. Her installations, films, and videos have been broadcast and/or screened in the United States and abroad, including

"A Film and Video Retrospective," Hallwalls, Buffalo (1980); Kijkhus World-Wide Video Festival, The Hague, the Netherlands (1982, 1984); Oakland Museum, California (1983); "Videoville 1985," a broadcast from WNYC-TV, New York (1985); and many others.

Hornbacher's work reveals a sensitive artist who utilizes the new technology as a tool—one of many—to transmute and re-create images, both political and aesthetic, from various sources. Examples of her work are in permanent collections, including the Bronx Museum of the Arts, Whitney Museum of American Art, and the New York Public Library—all in New York City; and others.

Bibliography
Hagen, Charles. "Review." *Artforum* 21 (April 1983): 74.
Slaton, Amy. "Review." *East Village Eye* (April 1985).
Video Music: New Correlations. New York City: Whitney Museum of American Art, 1982.

Horrell, Deborah (1953–)

A sculptor known for spectacular technical achievements with clay, wood, and mixed-media, Deborah Horrell was born and raised in Tempe, Arizona. She studied with noted ceramists Jeanne Otis and Randall Schmidt at Arizona State University in her native city where she received a Bachelor of Fine Arts degree in 1975. At the University of Washington in Seattle she worked under the direction of highly acclaimed and innovative ceramist-sculptor Patti Warashina. It was there that Horrell developed unique imagery and technical authority which won her early material recognition, as well as a Master of Fine Arts degree in 1979.

From 1979 to 1985 Horrell's elegantly crafted, ceramic satiric figures and her complex cast porcelain works were exhibited at major museums and galleries throughout the United States. Among her most significant early solo exhibitions were those at the Whatcom Museum in Bellingham, Washington (1981); Alfred University, New York (1982); and the Kohler Art Center, Sheboygan, Wisconsin (1983). Her work was also included in significant group exhibitions at the Renwick Gallery in Washington, D.C. (1980, 1981); and at the Museum of Fine Arts, Boston, Massachusetts (1985).

It was during this period that Horrell had major residencies through the Arts/Industry Program (1983, 1984) and the Limited Edition Program (1984) at the Kohler Company in Kohler, Wisconsin. There Horrell worked with state-of-the-art ceramic equipment and industrial craftsmen to produce "Flesh & Bones," a monumental and complex interlacing of porcelain bones with a complementary acrylic graphic on a sculptured porcelain slab. This 1983 masterpiece dealing with death, transition, and transfiguration prefigures much of her artistic production in the 1980s.

In 1985, during a residency at the Otsuka Ohmi Chemical Company in Shigaraki, Japan, Horrell carved, painted, and pieced together monumental ceramic slabs, many of which were nine to ten feet in length, although often not even two inches wide. Her technically and artistically acclaimed Ohmi residency masterpiece, "Passages: Heaven, Hell and the In-Between," is a dynamic series of monumental archways designed to make visual and to hold up for scrutiny physical, intellectual, and psychological passages—a Dantean journey for 1985. In her 1987 piece "Pappa Can You Hear Me?" Horrell arrived at a mixed-media synthesis (wood, etched glass, paper, acrylic, and slate) that was acclaimed by critics and visitors to its exhibition at Syracuse University, New York.

By 1985 Horrell's interest in clay was superseded by involvement with mixed-media and, especially, wood. Mastery of woodcarving techniques is apparent in her 1991 masterwork, "Discovery/Recovery," a piece commissioned by the Arthur G. James Cancer Hospital in Columbus, Ohio. This ten-foot-long inspirational work is composed of hard-carved geometric pieces joined in a fluid abstract composition.

Horrell taught ceramics and sculpture at Ohio State University from 1983 to 1993. She was exhibitor and U.S. representative to the 1st International Ceramic Symposium in Canberra, Australia.

Major works are in the collection of the Kohler Company, the John Michael Kohler Art Center, Wisconsin; the Tucson Museum of Art, Arizona; and the Washington State Arts Commission, Olympia.

Rudy H. Turk

Bibliography

Horrell, Deborah. "From Real to Ethereal." *Ceramics Monthly* (December 1987).
———. "Figure." *Studio Potter* (September 1987).
———. "Working at Otsuka." *Ceramics Monthly* (February 1987).

Hosmer, Harriet (1830–1908)

The first of the American nineteenth-century women sculptors to move to Rome, Italy, Harriet Hosmer, who was born in Watertown, Massachusetts, displayed pioneering instincts early in life. After completing Mrs. Sedgwick's School at Lenox, Massachusetts, in 1849, she returned home and created a studio for herself on the family property abutting the Charles River. She became a student of the sculptor Peter Stephenson in Boston. When no medical school in the East would admit a woman, she made arrangements to study anatomy in St. Louis at what is now the Washington University School of Medicine and took her lessons privately for nine months in the doctor's library. Upon receiving her certificate of accomplishment from Dr. Joseph McDowell, she embarked upon some regional sightseeing down the Mississippi River to New Orleans, Louisiana. Later in the spring of 1851 she took another boat north to Minnesota. When a race to climb a tall bluff along the river was proposed, Hosmer entered the race and won; the 400-foot-bluff (near the present town of Lansing, Iowa) was named "Mount Hosmer" in her honor.

In 1852 Hosmer arrived in Rome, Italy, and persuaded the English sculptor John Gibson to take her as his first and only pupil by showing him daguerreotypes of her idealized sculpture of "Hesper" (today in the Watertown Free Public Library, Massachusetts). Her next two marble busts, "Daphne" and "Medusa," were exhibited in Boston, Massachusetts, in 1853. Her life-size figure of "Oenone" (Washington University Gallery of Art), based on Tennyson's poem, followed in 1855. When the Prince of Wales visited her studio in Rome, Italy, he was so impressed with her marble statue of "Puck" that he bought it instantly. This created a demand for replicas and ensured the self-sufficiency of the artist. Commissions came from St. Louis, Missouri, for a sculpture of "Beatrice Cenci" (1857) and in 1860 for her first public monument, a ten-foot bronze statue of "Senator Thomas Hart Benton," which still stands in Lafayette Park, also in St. Louis, Missouri. During these years she modeled portrait busts, the statue of "Zenobia" (shown at the In-

ternational Exhibition of 1862 in London, England), and sculptures of fauns (Hosmer was the inspiration for one of the artists in Nathaniel Hawthorne's *The Marble Faun*), all in a neo-classical style. She was the first American to be given a commission for a work in a Roman church: the tomb of Judith Falconnet in S. Andrea della Fratte (1957, one of the few tomb sculptures in Italy by a woman).

Many fountains and chimney pieces were requested of Hosmer during the 1860s and 1870s, especially by English tourists who then invited the witty American to their country estates. Early in 1900 she returned to Watertown, Massachusetts, where she died; she was buried in Mt. Auburn Cemetery in Cambridge, Massachusetts.

Eleanor Tufts

Bibliography

Carr, Cornelia, ed. *Harriet Hosmer, Letters and Memories*. New York: Moffat, Yard & Co., 1912.
Faxon, Alicia. "Images of Women in the Sculpture of Harriet Hosmer." *Woman's Art Journal* 2:1 (Spring–Summer 1981): 25–29.
Groseclose, Barbara S. "Harriet Hosmer's Tomb to Judith Falconnet: Death and the Maiden." *American Art Journal* 12:2 (Spring 1980): 78–89.
Tufts, Eleanor. *American Women Artists, 1830–1930*. National Museum of Women in the Arts, 1987.
Zastoupil, Carol. "Creativity, Inspiration, and Scandal: Harriet Hosmer and *Zenobia*." *The Italian Presence in American Art, 1760–1860*. Fordham University Press, 1989, pp. 195–207.

Housser, Yvonne McKague (1898–)

Born in Toronto, Ontario, Canada, the landscape painter Yvonne McKague Housser studied at the Ontario College of Art (OCA) and earned a diploma in 1917. After further study at OCA, the administration appointed Housser as a teacher—a post she kept until her retirement in 1949.

Housser took additional work at the Académie de la Grande Chaumière, the Académie Colarossi, and the Académie Ranson—all in Paris, France, on her first trip to Europe (1921). Subsequent summer visits to Europe for research and study involved travel in Austria, England, France, and Italy. She has won awards and honors for her work, and has exhibited regularly with the Ontario Society of Artists, the Royal Canadian Academy, the Canadian Group of Painters, and others.

Not unlike the Group of Seven, Housser memorialized the rough Canadian landscape of Northern Ontario and, later on, ever seeking new ways of expression, she worked under Emil Bisttram in Mexico and Hans Hofmann in Provincetown, Massachusetts. Examples of her paintings are in private, public, and corporate permanent collections, including the Art Gallery of Ontario, Toronto; National Gallery of Canada, Ottawa; University of Toronto, Ontario; Canadian Pacific Railway Collection; Bank of Montréal; and others.

Bibliography

Frye, Helen Kemp. "Yvonne McKague Housser." *Canadian Forum* 18 (September 1938): 176–77.
Harper, J. Russell. *Canadian Paintings in Hart House*. University of Toronto Press, 1955.
Housser, Frederick B. "The Amateur Movement in Canadian Painting." *Yearbook of the Arts on Canada, 1928–1929*. Macmillan Company of Canada, 1929.

Howard, Linda (1934–)

An artist known for her aluminum monumental sculpture, Linda Howard was born in Evanston, Illinois. She attended the Art Institute of Chicago (1953–1954), and Northwestern University, Evanston (1954–1955)—both in Illinois; the University of Denver, Colorado, where she received her Bachelor of Arts degree (1957); Hunter College, New York City, where she earned a Master of Arts degree (1971); the School of Architecture, City College, New York City (1982); and Manatee Community College, Bradenton, Florida, where she studied mathematics and computer science (1988–1989).

Howard had her first solo exhibition at the Silvermine Guild, Norwalk, Connecticut, in 1971; there have been nine solo shows since then, three of which were at the Max Hutchinson Gallery, New York City (1979, 1980, 1981). Her work has been invited to more than 100 group exhibitions in the United States and abroad, and is housed in the permanent collections of the Springfield Art Museum; Lake Placid, New York—the site of the 1980 Winter Olympics; the city of Chicago, Illinois; Allstate Insurance, Bush Corporate Center, Columbus, Ohio; and others.

Between 1970 and 1989 Howard has taught intermittently and been a visiting artist at colleges and universities in the United States. She has received major commissions, including "Stepped Arch" (1981; a seventeen-foot-high aluminum sculpture whose straight lines form curved planes creating interesting shadow patterns) for the city of Chicago, Illinois; "Zig-Zag" (1987; an eight-by-ten-by-nine-foot sculpture) for the city of Tampa, Florida; "Centerpiece" (1991; a fourteen-foot-high aluminum work) for Bradley University, Peoria, Illinois, where Howard was the first artist working in the master print program; and numerous others.

Bibliography
Watson-Jones, Virginia. *Contemporary American Women Sculptors.* Oryx Press, 1986.
Who's Who in American Art. 19th ed. R.R. Bowker Co., 1991–1992.

Howell, Felicie Waldo (1897–1968)

Born in Honolulu, Hawaii, the painter Felicie Waldo Howell studied with E.C. Messer at the Corcoran School of Art, Washington, D.C.; the Philadelphia School of Design for Women, Pennsylvania; and privately with Henry B. Snell.

An instructor of painting at the New York School of Fine and Applied Art, Howell won many awards and honors, including a prize at the National Association of Women Painters and Sculptors, also in New York City (1916); first honorable mention at the Concord Art Association, Massachusetts (1919); a silver medal at the Society of Washington Artists, Washington, D.C. (1921); a second Hallgarten prize at the National Academy of Design, New York City (1921); and a silver medal at the Washington Watercolor Club, Washington, D.C. (1921); the Peabody prize at the Art Institute of Chicago (1921), and the William H. Tuthill purchase prize at the International Watercolor Exhibition (1926)—both in Chicago, Illinois.

Howell was elected an associate member of the National Academy of Design, New York City (1922) and also belonged to several other art organizations, including the Concord Art Association, Massachusetts. She held a lifetime membership in the National Arts Club, New York City; and was a member of the American Watercolor Society; New York Watercolor Club, the Painters and Sculptors Gallery Association, and the Society of Painters of New York—all in New York City; and others. Her work is represented in private and public permanent collections, including the Metropolitan Museum of Art and the National Arts Club—both in New York City, Corcoran Gallery of Art and the National Gallery, Smithsonian Institution—both in Washington, D.C.; Telfair Academy, Savannah, Georgia; and many others.

Bibliography
American Art Annual. Vol. 30. American Federation of Arts, 1933.
McMahan, Virgil E. *Washington D.C. Artists Born Before 1900: A Biographical Dictionary.* Washington, D.C., 1976.
Who's Who in American Art. 8th ed. American Federation of Arts, 1962.

Howland, Edith (1863–1949)

Born in Auburn, New York, the sculptor Edith Howland studied her craft with several instructors, including Gustave Michel in Paris, France, D.C. French; and Augustus Saint-Gaudens. She received an honorable mention in the Paris Salon, France, of 1913 and was a member of the Art Students League, the National Sculpture Society, and the National Association of Women Painters and Sculptors—all in New York City. One of her works, "Between Yesterday and Today," is represented in the permanent collection of the Brooklyn Museum, New York.

Bibliography
American Art Annual. Vol. 30. American Federation of Arts, 1933.
Weimann, Jeanne M. *The Fair Women.* Academy Chicago, 1981, p. 295.
Who's Who in American Art. 5th ed. American Federation of Arts, 1953.

Howland, Isabella (1895–1974)

Born in Brookline, Massachusetts, the painter/sculptor Isabella Howland is associated with the women pioneer artists of Maine. In addition to examples of her work that grace the permanent collection of the Smithsonian Institution, Washington, D.C., Howland's "Horses in Pasture," "Landscape with Factories," and "Rodeo" are housed in the collection of the Whitney Museum of American Art, New York City.

Bibliography
Archives of American Art. *A Checklist of the Collection.* Smithsonian Institution, 1975.
Who's Who in American Art. 3rd ed. American Federation of Arts, 1940.
Women Pioneers in Maine Art 1900–1945. Portland: Westbrook College, 1985.

Hu, Mary Lee (1943–)

Born in Lakewood, Ohio, the widely-travelled educator, metalsmith, and jeweler Mary Lee Hu attended Miami University, Oxford, Ohio; earned a Bachelor of Fine Arts degree from the Cranbrook Academy of Art, Bloomfield Hills, Michigan (1965); and, two years later, received a Master of Fine Arts degree from Southern Illinois University, Carbondale.

In addition to two-person exhibits, Hu has held many solo exhibitions in museums and galleries throughout the United States, including the Crafts Alliance Gallery, St. Louis, Missouri (1967); University of Iowa, Iowa City (1974); Eastern Kentucky University, Richmond (1979); University of North Dakota, Grand Forks (1981); Middle Tennessee State University, Murfreesboro (1982); University of Southwest Louisiana, Lafayette (1983); the Hand and Spirit Gallery, Scottsdale, Arizona (1984);

Concepts Gallery, Carmel, California (1988); Concepts Gallery, Palo Alto, California, and the Merrin Gallery, New York City (1989). Her work has been invited to distinguished national and international exhibitions in the United States and abroad: from Taxco, Mexico, to Toronto, Canada; Memphis, Tennessee; Jackson, Mississippi; El Paso, Texas; Manila, the Philippines; Tokyo, Japan; Vienna, Austria; La Paz, Bolivia; Taipei, Taiwan; Perth, Australia; and virtually all of Europe.

Hu has earned many honors and awards for her work, including National Endowment for the Arts (NEA) fellowships (1976, 1984, 1992). She has been an art juror, curator, and panelist at world conferences, and has given myriad lectures, workshops, and demonstrations of her singular approach to jewelry-making throughout the United States, Canada, New Zealand, Australia, Korea, and New Guinea. Past president of the Society of North American Goldsmiths, craftsman trustee of the American Crafts Council, and former deputy vice-president for North America of the World Crafts Council, Hu has taught at a number of universities in the midwestern United States and has been associated with the University of Washington, Seattle, where she is currently professor, since 1980. Her work is represented in private and public permanent collections, including Goldsmith Hall and the Victoria & Albert Museum—both in London, England; Renwick Gallery, Washington, D.C.; American Crafts Museum, New York City; Yale University, New Haven, Connecticut; the Art Institute of Chicago, Illinois; and many others.

Bibliography
Biskeborn, Susan. *Artists at Work: 25 Northwest Glassmakers, Ceramists, and Jewelers.* Alaska Northwest Books, 1990.
Lynn, Vanessa. "Review." *American Craft* (February–March 1990).
Stein, Margery. "The World of Wearable Art." *New York Magazine* (November 1989).
Who's Who in American Art. 19th ed. R.R. Bowker Co., 1991–1992.

Hudon-Beaulac, Simone (1905–)
Born in Québec City, Canada, the printmaker Simone Hudon-Beaulac earned a diploma from the École des Beaux-Arts, Québec, after study with Lucien Martial and H. Ivan Neilson (1931). Hudon-Beaulac has won many prizes and awards and has had her prints of the Canadian landscape included in myriad prestigious exhibitions in Brazil, Canada, England, and the United States, including the Biennial at São Paulo, Brazil (1947); and others.

A teacher for many years at the École des Beaux-Arts, Québec, Hudon-Beaulac held an exhibition of liturgical works there with Sylvia Daoust. Examples of her work are in private and public permanent collections.

Bibliography
Canadian Graphic Arts in Brazil. A Catalog. Brasilian Press, 1947.
Deziel, Julien. "Simone Hudon-Beaulac." *Arts et penseé* 7 (January–February 1952): 19–22.
Levesque, Albert et Pierre Dagenais. "La Canadienne française et les arts." *Almanach de la langue Française* (1936): 59–69.

Hudson, Grace Carpenter (1865–1937)
Born in Potter Valley, California, the widely-travelled painter Grace Carpenter Hudson studied at the Mark Hopkins Institute, San Fran-

cisco, California; and with Virgil Williams.

Winner of awards and honors, Hudson exhibited paintings and won prizes at the Mark Hopkins Institute, San Francisco, California; the Columbian Exposition, Chicago, Illinois (1893); the San Francisco Industrial Exposition, California; and others. Examples of her work are in private and public permanent collections.

Bibliography
A Woman's Vision: California Painting into the 20th Century. San Francisco: Maxwell Galleries, 1983.
Clement, Clara Erskine. *Women in the Fine Arts.* Houghton-Mifflin Co., 1904.
Kovinick, Phil, and Gloria Ricci Lothrop. "Women Artists: The American Frontier." *Art News* 75:10 (December 1976): 75.

Huerta, Elena (1908–)
Born in Saltillo, Coahuila, Mexico, in 1908, Elena Huerta studied painting in the State Academy of Fine Arts with Rubén Herrera (1923–1927) and then at the Academy of San Carlos, Mexico City, Mexico (1929–1923), while she taught in the public schools. She was one of the founders of the League of Revolutionary Writers and Artists (LEAR) and directed its theater arts department. She began working as a guest artist with the Taller de Gráfica Popular in 1939.

Huerta was director of the gallery, José Guadalupe Posada, which was later renamed, José Maria Velasco. She also served as director of the José Clemente Orózco gallery.

In 1957, after a trip to China, Huerta published a portfolio of engravings and lithographs of Chinese female peasants. Her first solo exhibition occurred in 1977, and she has exhibited her work in group shows in Mexico, the Soviet Union, Czechoslovakia, Hungary, China, Hong Kong, Canada, and Japan. Huerta also painted a mural in the Escuela Superior de Agricultura Antonio Narro de Coahuila.

Bibliography
Alvarez, José Rogelio, et al. *Enciclopedia de México.* Secretaría de Educación Pública, 1987.
The Texas Quarterly: Image of Mexico I. The University of Texas. Autumn 1969.

Hughes, Daisy Marguerite (1883–1968)
Born in Los Angeles, California, the painter Daisy Marguerite Hughes studied under the aegis of George Elmer Browne, Ralph Johonnot, L.E.G. Macleod, Rudolph Schaefer, and C.P. Townsley. She was a member of many arts organizations, including the Allied Artists of America and National Association of Women Painters and Sculptors—both in New York City; American Federation of Arts, Washington, D.C.; California Art Club; California Watercolor Society, Los Angeles; and the Provincetown Art Association, Massachusetts.

Bibliography
American Art Annual. Vol. 30. American Federation of Arts, 1933.
Archives of American Art. *Collection of Exhibition Catalogs.* G.K. Hall, 1979.
Moure, Nancy D. *Dictionary of Artists in Southern California.* Dustin Publications, 1975.

Hughto, Margie (1944–)

Born in Endicott, New York, the ceramist Margie Hughto earned a Bachelor's degree at the State University of New York at Buffalo (SUNY) (1966) and received a Master of Fine Arts degree from the Cranbrook Academy of Art, Bloomfield Hills, Michigan (1971). Upon graduation, she moved to Syracuse, New York, to take on the responsibility for the teaching of ceramics at Syracuse University, where she is presently associate professor of ceramics.

From 1979 to 1991 Hughto has held solo exhibitions of her work in the United States and abroad, including the James Yaw Gallery, Birmingham, Michigan (1979, 1982, 1987, 1989); Nina Freudenheim Gallery, Buffalo, New York (1979, 1982); Thomas Segal Gallery, Boston, Massachusetts (1980); André Emmerich Gallery, New York City, and Galerie L, Hamburg, Germany (1981); Gallery One, Toronto, Canada (1983); Meredith Contemporary Art, Baltimore, Maryland (1983, 1984, 1986); Eva Cohon Gallery, Highland Park, Illinois (1984, 1986, 1987, 1989); Albers Fine Art Gallery, Memphis, Tennessee (1990); Everson Museum of Art, Syracuse, New York (1991); and others. Her work has been invited to myriad major group exhibitions, many of them travelling shows: from Syracuse, New York to Nagoya, Japan; from Scottsdale, Arizona to Toronto, Canada; from Grand Rapids, Michigan, to Vallouris, France.

Hughto has received a number of commissions for large-scale ceramic and paper wall reliefs, including "Summer Days, Summer Nights" (1987; ceramic, three-by-forty-five-feet) for the World Trade Center, New York City; "Spring in the Village" (1991; four ceramic murals, eight-by-forty-feet) for the Port Authority of New York City; and others. "Lake Reflections" (1989; forty-one-by-ninety-six inches), a richly-glazed ceramic wall piece with gold leaf, is not atypical of her recent work: It is "painterly," bold yet subtle, rich in texture, evocative.

Hughto's work is represented in private and public permanent collections, such as the Albright-Knox Art Gallery, Buffalo, New York; Cincinnati Museum of Art, Ohio; Cranbrook Academy of Art, Bloomfield Hills, Michigan; Everson Museum of Art, Syracuse, New York; Montgomery Museum of Fine Arts, Alabama; Museum of Fine Arts, Boston, Massachusetts; the Rockefeller Foundation, New York City; and many others.

Bibliography

Clark, Garth. *American Ceramics: 1976 to the Present.* Rev. ed. Abbeville Press, 1988, pp. 9, 141, 143, 144, 273–74.
Howe, Katherine, and Joanne Mattera. "Fans and Fan Imagery." *Fiberarts* (July–August 1982): 26–31.
Perry, Barbara, ed. *American Ceramics.* Rizzoli, 1989, pp. 203, 262–64.
Who's Who in American Art. 19th ed. R.R. Bowker Co., 1991–1992.

Hull, Marie Atkinson (1890–1980)

Born in Summit, Mississippi, the painter Marie Atkinson Hull studied at the Pennsylvania Academy of Fine Arts, Pennsylvania; the Art Students League, New York City; and with George Elmer Browne, John F. Carlson, and Robert Reid.

Winner of many awards and honors, Hull was the recipient of a gold medal at the Mississippi Art Association (1920); first prize at the Southern States Art League (1926); second prize at the Davis Wildflower Competition, San Antonio, Texas (1929); watercolor prizes, Southern States Art League (1931); and the New Orleans Art Association and the Benjamin prize at the New Orleans Arts and Crafts Club (1932)—both in Louisiana. Her work is represented in private and public permanent collections, including the Mississippi Art Association; high schools in Laurel and Jackson, Mississippi; Southwestern Texas Normal School; the Witte Memorial Museum, San Antonio, Texas; and others.

Bibliography

American Art Annual. Vol. 30. American Federation of Arts, 1933.
Norwood, Malcolm M., Virginia M. Elias, and William S. Haynie. *The Art of Marie Hull.* University Press of Mississippi, 1975.
Who's Who in American Art. R.R. Bowker Co., 1978.

Humphrey, Margo (1942–)

One of the most original and forceful artists making prints today, Margo Humphrey made her first lithographs in the early 1960s, while a student of Helen Dozier at Merritt College in Oakland, California. Subsequently, in study at the California College of Arts and Crafts, Oakland, and at Stanford University (with Nathan Oliveira), lithography became her principal medium of expression. Her images, which she characterizes as "narrative symbolism," derive directly from her personal experience as an African-American artist in America. In her view, art is "a testament to one's culture, one's intelligence, one's instincts for survival, and one's personal concepts of beauty and aesthetics." Despite their technical complexity and sophistication, her color lithographs (many of which were created at Tamarind Institute in Albuquerque, New Mexico) often recall the directness and naiveté of Haitian and Brazilian painters, whose work she greatly admires.

Humphrey's work has been seen in numerous group and one-person exhibitions during the 1970s and 1980s, and she has received many awards, including fellowship grants from the Ford Foundation, National Endowment for the Arts (NEA), and the Tiffany Foundation. She has taught at the University of California, Santa Cruz; School of the Art Institute of Chicago, Illinois; University of Texas, San Antonio; and the University of Maryland, College Park. In 1988 she travelled to Africa under the auspices of the U.S. Information Agency (USIA), which also organized an exhibition of her lithographs in Lagos, Nigeria.

Clinton Adams

Bibliography

Adams, Clinton. "Art As a Testament: A Conversation with Margo Humphrey." *Tamarind Papers* 9 (Spring 1986): 16–26.
Tamarind Impressions, Recent Lithographs: A Cultural Presentation of the United States of America, 1986.
Tamarind 25 Years, 1960–1985. Catalog of exhibition circulated by the Art Museum Association of America. Essay by Carter Ratcliff. Albuquerque: University Art Museum, University of New Mexico, 1985.

Hunter, Clementine (c. 1885–1988)

African-American folk artist Clementine Hunter was born on Little Eva Plantation, Natchitoches, Louisiana, where she picked cotton and cooked. It was not until the 1930s that Hunter began to express herself in paint in a manner not unlike the two-dimensional works of Horace Pippin.

Hunter's paintings were exhibited throughout the United States in museums and galleries, including the Saturday Gallery, St. Louis, Missouri (1954); Isaac Delgado Museum, New Orleans (1955), and Grambling State University—both in Louisiana (1970); La Jolla Museum of Contemporary Art, California (1971); Fisk University, Nashville, Tennessee (1974); Barnwell Center, Shreveport, Louisiana (1975); and others.

The undated oil, "Funeral on Cane River," captures the essence of the experience of death—in local color: fifteen mourners carrying bouquets of flowers, a casket, a freshly-dug grave and two gravediggers, a church, and a four-wheeled vehicle are all depicted in the two-dimensional composition. Her work is represented in private and public permanent collections, including the Louisiana State Library.

Bibliography
Bishop, Robert. *Folk Painters of America*. E.P. Dutton, 1979.
Bontemps, Arna A., ed. *Forever Free: Art by African-American Women 1862–1980*. Normal: Illinois State University, 1980.
Driskell, David C. *Two Centuries of Black American Art*. Alfred A. Knopf and Los Angeles County Museum, 1976.
Morris, Steven. "The Primitive Art of Clementine Hunter." *Ebony* (March 1969): 144.

Hunter, Debora (1950–)

Born in Chicago, Illinois, the photographer Debora Hunter earned a Bachelor of Arts degree from Northwestern University in her native city (1972) and after study with Harry Callahan, Aaron Siskind, Lisette Model, and Minor White at the Rhode Island School of Design, Providence, received a Master of Fine Arts degree in her chosen field (1976).

Hunter has held many solo exhibitions of her work throughout the United States, including Colin County Community College, Plano, Texas (1992); Emporia State University, Kansas (1989); Museum of Contemporary Photography, Chicago, Illinois (1985); International Museum of Photography/George Eastman House, Rochester, New York (1980); the University of New Mexico, Albuquerque (1977); and others. Her work has been invited to myriad group exhibitions in the United States and abroad, such as "Sitting Pretty, Photographs by Debora Hunter and Sue Packer," Art Institute of Chicago, Illinois (1992); "Contrast/Comparison IV," University of Dallas, Texas (1990); "Trains, Boats and Planes," Witkin Gallery, New York City (1988); "Texas Women Photographers Today," Stichting Amsterdam Foto Gallery, the Netherlands (1984); "Second Sight," a travelling show, Carpenter Center for the Arts, Harvard University, Cambridge, Massachusetts (1981); "Invisible Light," a travelling show, Smithsonian Institution, Washington, D.C. (1980); "Photo Video Invitational," Anyart Gallery, Bristol, Rhode Island (1975); and many others.

Hunter has won awards and honors, including a National Endowment for the Arts (NEA) regional photo fellowship (1987); she has been a lecturer, visiting faculty member at the School of the Art Institute of Chicago (1984–1985) and the University of New Mexico (summer 1980); and has been teaching at Southern Methodist University, Dallas, Texas, since 1976. Her work is represented in private and public permanent collections in the United States, including the Houston Museum of Fine Art and Amon Carter Museum, Fort Worth—both in Texas; Yale University, New Haven, and Wesleyan University, Middletown—both in Connecticut; Rhode Island School of Design, Providence; Massachusetts Institute of Technology (MIT), Cambridge; and many others.

Bibliography
Medlin, Kayoko. "Review." *Photo Journal Asahicamera* (August 1990): 118.
Rickey, Carrie. "Curatorial Conceptions, The Hirshhorn: Danger, Curves Ahead." *Artforum* (April 1981): 48.
Tate, Lawson. A radio interview. "Art Matters." WRR-FM, Dallas, 1989.
Who's Who in American Art. 19th ed. R.R. Bowker Co., 1991–1992.

Hunter, Florence Kent (1917–1989)

A native New Yorker, the painter/printmaker Florence Kent Hunter studied at the Cooper Union and the New School for Social Research—both in New York City. During her second marriage Hunter took further study at the University of Bern, Switzerland (early 1950s); she also studied in the 1970s with painter Anthony Toney.

In the mid-1930s, Hunter, who was also known by the painting name Kent, and her first husband, Theodore Herzl Emanuel, set up the Artist's Union. During that time Hunter became associated with the Works Projects Administration (WPA) Federal Arts Project, teaching in settlement houses and creating intaglio and planographic prints.

Hunter's style changed several times, even as her life underwent dislocation and alteration: from social content and representation to Picassoid works, paintings of her Jewish heritage and, finally, a visual concern for the environment. Representative examples of Hunter's work are in private and public permanent collections.

Bibliography
Beale, Karen F., and David W. Kiehl. *Graphic Excursions: American Prints in Black and White, 1900–1950: Selections from the Collection of Reba and Dave Williams*. David R. Godine and the American Federation of Arts, 1991.

Hunter, Isabel (1878–1941)

Born in San Francisco, California, the painter Isabel Hunter studied at the San Francisco Art Institute, California; the Art Students League, New York City; and with Emil Carlsen and Arthur Mathews. She was a member of the San Francisco Art Association and the San Francisco Society of Women Artists—both in California.

Bibliography
American Art Annual. Vol. 30. American Federation of Arts, 1933.
Dawdy, Doris O. *Artists of the American West*. Swallow Press, 1974.
Spangenberg, Helen. *Yesterday's Artists on the Monterey Peninsula*. Monterey Peninsula Museum of Art, 1976.

Huntington, Anna Vaughn Hyatt (1876–1973)

A giant among artists, Anna Vaughn Hyatt Huntington lived to be ninety-seven and capped her seventy-year career as sculptor with the last of her seven heroic equestrian monuments, "General Israel Putnam," completed when she was ninety.

Born in Cambridge, Massachusetts, Huntington, along with her older sister Harriet, was encouraged to pursue sculpture classes with Henry Hudson Kitson in the 1890s. Huntington's father was a professor of paleontology at Massachusetts Institute of Technology (MIT), Cambridge, Massachusetts, and her mother painted landscapes and sketched diagrams for her husband's books.

For her first exhibition in 1900 at the Boston Arts Club, Massachusetts, Huntington already had forty animal sculptures to display. She moved to New York City to further her studies at the Art Students League with Hermon MacNeil and to obtain criticism from Gutzon Borglum. She also spent much time at the Bronx Zoo, New York, studying the wild animals, often carrying two or three models with her on the subway so that she could work on several different poses at once. The "Men and Bull" sculpture on which she and Abastenia St. Léger Eberle collaborated received a bronze medal at the Louisiana Purchase Exposition of 1904.

In 1923 she married Archer Milton Huntington in the studio that she shared with sculptor Brenda Putnam on 12th Street in New York City. Among the massive sculptures she subsequently modeled were "El Cid Campeador," erected in Seville, Spain, in 1927, and many Spanish subjects for the terrace of the Hispanic Society of America. The Spanish government was moved to decorate her with the Grand Cross of Alfonso the Twelfth in 1929. When the Huntingtons were returning home by ship from Spain, they noticed an advertisement for the Brookgreen plantation in South Carolina. Huntington bought the ten thousand acres, and in 1932 the outdoor museum at Brookgreen Gardens was opened. Not only did this enable Huntington to show her work, but she and her husband commissioned works of other sculptors during these lean years of the Depression. The American Academy of Arts and Letters, New York City, awarded Huntington the gold medal for distinction in 1930 and six years later organized a retrospective exhibition of 171 of her sculptures.

A true lover of animals since her childhood, Huntington did not enjoy the city life of New York, so in 1940 the couple settled at Stanerigg, an estate in Redding Ridge, Connecticut. In her specially-built studio she developed huge works such as "Fighting Stallions: Lincoln," which she gave to New Salem, Illinois; and the energetic equestrian statue of "José Martí," the Cuban patriot, for Central Park in New York City. Her first equestrian commission was awarded in 1915 when she won the competition in New York to create a "Joan of Arc" statue for Riverside Drive, New York City. The young maiden from Orleans, garbed in armor and standing up on her stirrups, holds aloft a sword as she looks heavenward for guidance. Additional castings are in Blois, France; Gloucester, Massachusetts; Québec City, Montréal; and the park of the California Palace of the Legion of Honor in San Francisco.

In addition to bronze, some of her works were cast in aluminum, and she was thus one of the first American sculptors to use this lightweight metal in her work. Her realistic, vivacious sculptures are located today in more than 200 museums and parks around the world.

Eleanor Tufts

Bibliography
Proske, Beatrice Gilman. "Anna Hyatt Huntington." *Brookgreen Bulletin* (Fall 1973): 1–15.
———. "Anna Hyatt Huntington." *Brookgreen Bulletin* 13 (1983): 1–15.
Tufts, Eleanor. *American Women Artists, 1830–1930*. National Museum of Women in the Arts, 1987.

Huntington, Margaret W. (1867–1958)

A brilliant watercolorist who lived, worked, and exhibited in New York City galleries (Midtown Gallery and Passedoit Gallery, for example), Margaret W. Huntington's luminous still-life paintings and wry visual comments on the sculpture that graced New York City's World Fair (1939), were noted for posterity by the erstwhile critic, Alfred M. Frankfurter.

Member of the National Association of Women Painters and Sculptors, New York City, Huntington won awards in that group's exhibitions, including an honorable mention (1927); a prize (1931); and the Penman prize in flower painting (1937).

Bibliography
Clendenen, Janet. "Margaret Huntington at Barbizon." *Art Digest* 20:17 (June 1, 1946): 19.
Lowe, Jeanette. "Margaret Huntington." *Art News* 35:14 (January 2, 1937): 18.
Frankfurter, Alfred M. "Watercolorist Amusingly Records the Fair's Sculpture." *Art News* 37 (September 16, 1939): 15.
Who's Who in American Art. 1st ed. American Federation of Arts, 1937.

Huntley, Victoria Hutson (1900–1971)

A painter and lithographer, Victoria (Ebbels) Hutson Huntley is best known for her work in the print medium. Born in Hasbrouck Heights, New Jersey, on October 9, 1900, she obtained her early art training at the New York School of Fine and Applied Art, New York City. Huntley studied at the Art Students League, also in New York City, with John Sloan, George Luks, and Max Weber, leaving to teach at the College of Industrial Arts in Denton, Texas, from 1921 to 1923. She later took classes from Kenneth Hayes Miller and studied mural painting with William C. Palmer.

Huntley's first New York City exhibit was a solo show of paintings and drawings at the Weyhe Gallery in 1930. Subsequently Huntley turned her attention to lithography, winning a Logan prize for "Interiors" at the Art Institute of Chicago's 1930 International Exhibition, Illinois, and a first prize in 1933 for "Kopper's Coke" at the Philadelphia Print Club's National Exhibition, Pennsylvania. Huntley received a grant from the American Academy and Institute of Arts and Letters, New York City, in 1947 and a Guggenheim fellowship in 1948.

Precisionistic industrial forms in Huntley's early works were later replaced by sensitive portrayals of flowers, birds, and landscapes, culminating in the 1940s series of lithographs inspired by the Florida Everglades. Huntley also painted murals for post offices in Springfield, New York, and Greenwich, Connecticut, and was the author and illustrator of *Portraits of Plants and Places* (1948). Her prints have been collected by major museums, including the Metropolitan Museum of Art, New York City; the Art Institute of Chicago, Illinois; and the Boston Museum of Fine Arts, Massachusetts.

Peggy J. Hazard

Bibliography
Adams, Clinton. *American Lithographers 1900–1960*. University of New Mexico, 1983.
Kraeft, June, and Norman Kraeft. *Great American Prints 1900–1950*. Dover, 1984.
One Hundred Prints by One Hundred Artists of the Art Students League of New York, 1875–1975. Art Students League of New York, 1975.
Whiting, F.A. "Victoria Hutson Huntley." *Magazine of Art* 31 (November 1938): 838–42, 872–73.
Who's Who of American Women. 7th ed. Marquis Who's Who International, 1971.

Hurd, Henriette Wyeth (1907–)

Born in Wilmington, Delaware, the painter Henriette Wyeth Hurd studied at the Normal Art School in Boston, Massachusetts; the Pennsylvania Academy of Fine Arts, Philadelphia; and with her father N.C. Wyeth.

Winner of awards and honors, Wyeth Hurd has been the recipient of four first prizes at the Wilmington Society of Fine Arts, Delaware; the Pennsylvania Academy of Fine Arts, Philadelphia; the governor's award, Santa Fe, New Mexico (1981); and others. Her work has been in exhibitions throughout the United States, including the Art Institute of Chicago, Illinois; Carnegie-Mellon University, Pittsburgh, Pennsylvania; Metropolitan Museum of Art, New York City; the Roswell Museum of Art, New Mexico; and many others.

Wyeth Hurd's work is represented in private and public permanent collections, such as the Lubbock Museum of Art and Texas Tech University—both in Texas; New Britain Museum of Art, Connecticut; Roswell Museum of Art, New Mexico; and others.

Bibliography

Barnitz, Jacqueline. "Henriette Wyeth." *Arts Magazine* 39:4 (January 1965): 64.

Bell, David L. "Santa Fe." *Art News* 81:10 (December 1982): 92.

Bywaters, Jerry. *The American Woman as Artist*. Pollack Galleries. Southern Methodist University, 1966.

Husar, Natalka (1951–)

Born in New Jersey and currently residing in Toronto, Canada, Natalka Husar is best known for large representational oil paintings. The daughter of Ukrainian immigrants, Husar often draws on the particular expectations which that community places on its female members in her recurring explorations of personal relationships, gender role expectations, ethnic identification, and consumer alienation. Her paintings juxtapose larger-than-life-sized people and objects in disturbing combinations, layers, and distorted perspectives which utilize realist, surrealist, and expressionist approaches to the painted surface.

Receiving her Bachelor of Fine Arts degree from Rutgers University, New Brunswick, New Jersey, in 1973, Husar began her exhibiting career after moving to Toronto, Ontario. Her first solo exhibition was held at the Ukrainian Canadian Art Foundation in Toronto (1977). Since then she has had several important solo shows focusing on different themes in her work: "Faces-Facades" at Nancy Poole's Studio in Toronto (1980); "Behind the Irony Curtain" at Garnet Press in Toronto (1986); and a travelling exhibition entitled "Milk and Blood" (1988–1989), which was exhibited in Vancouver, Winnipeg, Toronto, Sudbury, and Edmonton. Works such as "Our Lady of Mississauga" (1987) have been shown in a number of group exhibitions. Husar has received various awards from the Canada Council, Ontario Arts Council, and the Secretary of State. Her work is represented in private and public collections, including the Canadian Museum of Civilization in Ottawa and the Toronto Sun Collection.

Bridget Elliott

Bibliography

Elliott, Bridget, and Janice Williamson. *Dangerous Goods: Feminist Visual Art Practices*. Edmonton Art Gallery and Latitude 53, 1990, pp. 13–15, 26.

Enright, Robert. "Desperately Seeking Ukrainian: The Recent Paintings of Natalka Husar." *Border Crossings* (Summer 1986): 29–30.

Thompson, Grace Eiko. "Natalka Husar's Tarantella." *Milk and Blood: Natalka Husar's Paintings*. Garnet Press, 1988.

Walsh, Meeka. "Gentle Savagery: The Felicities of Biting the Hand that Feeds You." *Border Crossings* (Spring 1989): 11–16.

Hutchinson, Nora (1951–)

Nora Hutchinson is known primarily as a video artist and is closely identified with the pioneering years of artists' video and artist-run production facilities in Canada (1970s), especially Ed Video Media Arts Centre, Guelph, Ontario (founded 1976). She is also a performance artist. In 1991 she began to produce sound sculpture and installations.

While majoring in music at the University of Guelph, Hutchinson began to work with artists Noel Harding and Eric Cameron, who were introducing video to the University's visual arts curriculum. Starting with their somewhat narcissistic, self-referential approach to the medium, Hutchinson quickly grounded herself in "personal politics displayed in the form of poetry." Her early work lets music and dialogue establish a rhythmic "score" for the flow and pulse of visual images. Incorporating layered sound, musical and performative elements, Hutchinson's *Salem* (five minutes, color, sound, 1980) and *Granny and Me* (15 minutes, color, sound, 1982) play with narrative structure while exploiting only the most basic camera and editing techniques. Her *Go Away Heart* (16 minutes, color, sound, 1979) won first prize at the Athens Video Festival, Greece, in 1979.

Later in the 1980s Hutchinson's performance and video production brought her lyrical, narrative approach into confrontation with pressing social issues. The feminist subtext of *Opera Around the House* (35 minutes, color, sound, 1987), is voiced through a highly intensive use of processed images, vocal music, mime, and a larger-than-usual cast of performers. *Dick and Jane (Spot and Puff)* draws personal politics further into the realm of the social by turning a conventional elementary school reader (*Dick and Jane*) into a metaphor for alienation and media saturation. The work exists in video (22 minutes, color, sound, 1989) and was also performed at Burlington Cultural Centre in 1989.

Hutchinson's work has been screened at the following international venues: *O Kanada*, Akademie für Künste, Berlin, Germany (1982); *A Space/Canada House Video Exchange*, London, England (1984); and *Montevideo*, Amsterdam, Netherlands (1985).

Ingrid Jenkner

Bibliography

Hallas, Nancy. *Nora Hutchinson: Dick and Jane (Spot and Puff)*. Exhibition Catalog. Guelph: Ed Video Media Arts Centre, 1990.

Moving Images: An Introduction to Video Art. Exhibition Catalog. Sarnia Public Library and Art Gallery, 1988.

Hyde, Helen (1868–1919)

A pioneer in color etching and color woodblock printmaking in the United States, Helen Hyde was born to upper-middle-class parents Marietta Butler Hyde, a school teacher, and William Birelie Hyde, an engineer and railroad builder, in Lima, New York. She was brought up in Oakland, California, and from ages twelve to fourteen studied drawing with

Ferdinand Richardt. She set up a studio in her home and entered the California School of Design to study with Emil Carlsen in 1887. She spent a year, between 1888 and 1889, studying at the Art Students League, New York City, with Kenyon Cox, then returned to the California School of Design. In 1890 she studied with Franz Skarbina at the Hochschule für Bildende Künste in Berlin, Germany, before she went to Paris, France, for three years (1891–1894), studying with Raphael Collin, Albert Sterner, and Félix Régamey, from whom she acquired expertise in Japanese art. She also saw Japanese prints on exhibition and viewed Mary Cassatt's 1893 exhibition of color aquatints, which influenced her interest in Japanese style and in the mother-and-child theme.

When Hyde returned to San Francisco she bought a press and began to experiment with etching, producing her first etching à la poupée in 1896. She began to exhibit and sell her prints in New York City at the Macbeth Gallery in 1899, the year she and her friend Josephine Hyde went to Japan, where Helen settled until 1914. In Japan Austrian artist Emil Orlik taught her how to cut and print woodcuts. Her first illustrated book, *The Moon Babies*, was published in 1900. Late in 1901 she made one of several long visits to the United States. While in San Francisco, California, she and her sister Mabel Hyde published a book of poems, *Jingles from Japan*, illustrated with forty-three relief prints by Hyde.

In Tokyo, Japan, Hyde met Arthur Wesley Dow, whose writings had introduced Japanese printmaking and design principles in the United States. Her friend, Chicago etcher Bertha Jaques, visited her in Tokyo, Japan, in 1908. Hyde made several trips to China and one to India. In 1911, the year after her long bout with cancer began, she travelled in Mexico with her friend, artist Edith Emerson. Hyde returned to the United States permanently in 1914, moving to Chicago, Illinois, the next year.

Hyde began to exhibit her work at the 1894 California Midwinter Fair. She was included in the 1896 Mechanics Institute Exhibition, San Francisco, California; the 1897 St. Louis Exposition, Missouri; and the 1901 Pan-American Exhibition, Buffalo, New York. She won a gold medal at the 1909 Alaska-Yukon-Pacific Exposition in Seattle, Washington; first place for ink drawing at the 1901 Tokyo Exhibition of Native Art, Japan; and a bronze medal at the Panama-Pacific International Exposition in San Francisco, California, in 1915. Hyde exhibited in the Paris Salon, the Société de Gravure Originale en Couleur, and the Société de la Gravure sur Bois Originale—all in Paris, France; with the California Society of Etchers, Los Angeles, and the Sketch Club, Oakland; the Chicago Society of Etchers, Illinois; the Pennsylvania Academy of Fine Arts Watercolor Annual, Philadelphia; the Milwaukee Art Society, Wisconsin; and the Detroit Institute of the Arts, Michigan. Hyde exhibited for at least ten years with each of the following galleries: W.K. Vickery in San Francisco, California; the Macbeth Gallery in New York City; the Christian Klackner Gallery in New York City and London, England; the Swan Gallery, Kansas City, Missouri; the R.L. Boutwell Gallery, Denver, Colorado; Doll and Richards, Boston, Massachusetts; and at the Albert Roullier Gallery, Chicago, Illinois. Hyde held solo exhibitions at most of those galleries as well as at the Newark Museum, New Jersey (1913), Art Institute of Chicago, Illinois (1916), and at the Hill Tolerton Print Rooms, San Francisco, California (1915, 1919).

Phyllis Peet

Bibliography
Blattner, E.L. "Helen Hyde, An American Artist in Japan." *The International Studio* 45 (November 1911): 50–57.
Helen Hyde Papers. California Historical Society, San Francisco.
Jaques, Bertha E. *Helen Hyde, An Appreciation*. Libby Press, 1922.
Mason, Lynn, and Tim Mason. *Helen Hyde*. Washington and London: Smithsonian Institution Press, 1991.
Peet, Phyllis I. *The Emergence of American Women Printmakers in the Nineteenth Century*. Ph.D. dissertation, University of California, Los Angeles. Ann Arbor: University Microfilms International, 1987.

Iannone, Dorothy (1933–)

Born in Boston, Massachusetts, Dorothy Iannone received her Bachelor's degree Phi Beta Kappa from Boston University in 1957. The following year she did graduate work in English at Brandeis University, Waltham, Massachusetts. At the age of eighteen she spent one year serving as transportation agent at the Boston army base, Massachusetts.

Between 1964 and 1990 Iannone held twenty-nine solo gallery exhibitions in the United States and Europe, including the Stryke Gallery, New York City (1964–1967); Sum Galerie, Reykjavik, Iceland (1974); Galerie Bama, Paris, France (1976); Galerie Ars Viva, Berlin, Germany (1982); Boekie Woekie, Amsterdam, the Netherlands (1986); Petersen Galerie, Berlin, Germany (1989); Galerie Bernharad Steinmetz and Kunstfonds, Kunstraum, Bonn, Germany (1990); and others. Her work has been invited to many group exhibitions and has toured Europe in such shows as: "Dieter Roth and Dorothy Iannone," Galerie Zwirner, Cologne, Germany (1967); "Erotic Art Show: Collection of Drs. Phyllis and Eberhard Kronhausen," Lund, Sweden, a travelling show to Denmark and Germany (1969); "Biennale," Moulin des Jouissances, Venice, Italy (1975); "Daily Bul Exposition" (1976), and "Daily Bul Show," organized by Pol Bury and André Balthazar, a travelling show to France, Belgium, and Germany—both from Fondation Maeght, St. Paul-de-Vence, France (1976); "L'Estampe Aujourd'hui," Bibliothèque Nationale, Paris, France (1978); Karl Gerstner's Private Pinakothek, Kunst Museum, Solothurn, Switzerland (1983); "Art in Bookform," the Alvar Aalto Museum, Jyväskylä, Finland (1986–1987); "Nutidskunst . . ." Silkeborg Kunstmuseum, Copenhagen, Denmark (1989); "La Caravane Passe et . . . ," Musée d'Art Moderne et d'Art Contemporain, Nice, France (1991); "Interferenzen," Berlin Video, curated by Mike Steiner, Riga, and St. Petersburg, Russia; and many others.

Employing sound and visual means, using words and erotic images of sensuous desire, in highly ornate works, Iannone explores the heterosexual world of carnality. Widely-travelled in Europe and the Far East (1961–1967), Iannone conducted open workshops at the College of Arts, Berlin (1977, 1979); was a guest artist at the Jan Van Eyck Académie, Maastricht, the Netherlands (1982, 1983); the Rijks Académie, Amsterdam, the Netherlands (1982, 1984); and the Enschede Kunst Académie (1983). Honored for her works, she has been a recipient of the Senate for Science and Art grant, Berlin, Germany (1980, 1982, 1984); received fellowships from Brandeis University, Waltham, Massachusetts (1958) and Stanford University, California (1959); an Art Foundation of Bonn grant (1988); and others. Iannone has written many books—all published in Germany.

Iannone's works are in permanent public and private collections in the United States and Europe, including the National Museum of Women in the Arts, Washington, D.C.; Musée Municipale de Toulouse, France; Victoria & Albert Museum Book Collection, London, England; Collection Kornfeld, Zurich, Switzerland; International Museum of Erotic Art, San Francisco, California; Museum of Modern Art (MoMA) Book Collection, New York City; the Kunstverein, Berlin, Germany; the Bibliothèque Nationale, Paris, France; the Kunstmuseum, Basel, Switzerland; and others.

Bibliography
Becker, Wolfgang. *Dorothy Iannone*. Catalog of an Exhibition. Aachen, 1980.
Kaps, Andreas. *Tageszeitung* (March 15, 1989).
Kreis, Elfie. Article. *Kunstblatt* 61 (1989).
Richter, Wolfgang. *Aachener Volkszeitung* (April 25, 1980).
Sommer, Ed. *Kunstforum International* (Spring 1973).

Ingram, Judith (1926–)

Born in Philadelphia, Pennsylvania, the sculptor/papermaker Judith Ingram studied at the Philadelphia College of Art (now the University of the Arts), Pennsylvania; and with printmaker Carol Summers. Her work has been exhibited in many galleries and museums throughout the United States, including the annual exhibitions of the Society of Graphic Artists and the Florence Duhl Gallery (1979)—both in New York City; Hooks-Epstein Galleries, Houston, Texas (1979, 1981, 1988); Rosenfeld Gallery, Philadelphia, Pennsylvania (1980, 1982, 1984, 1986, 1989); Sutton Gallery, New York City (1981); the annual exhibitions of the Philadelphia Print Club, Pennsylvania; Portland Museum of Art, Maine (1988); and others.

Winner of awards and honors, Ingram has given handmade paper workshops at many institutions, including the University of Delaware, Newark; Philadelphia Museum of Art, Pennsylvania; Arrowmont School of Crafts, Gatlinburg, Tennessee; Haystack Mountain School of Crafts, Deer Isle, Maine; and others. Her work is represented in private, public, and corporate permanent collections in the United States and abroad, including Bank of America; Collection of the Emperor of Japan; International Paper Company; Kimberly-Clark; Philadelphia Museum of Art; and many others.

Bibliography
Constantine, Mildred, and Jack Lenor Larsen. *The Art Fabric: Mainstream.* Van Nostrand Reinhold, 1981.
Who's Who in American Art. 19th ed. R.R. Bowker Co., 1991–1992.

Ingram, Liz (Elizabeth) L. (1949–)

Liz Ingram was born in Buenos Aires, Argentina, and was raised in New Delhi, Bombay, and Toronto. She went under the name of Liz Gagnon from 1974 to 1980 but returned to her maiden name after her first marriage. She received her Honors Bachelor of Fine Arts degree in 1972 from York University in Toronto, where she studied with Anthony Benjamin and Deli Sacilotto. In 1975 she completed her Master of Visual Arts degree in printmaking at the University of Alberta under the supervision of Lyndal Osborne and Walter Jule.

Graduate school was a profound experience for Ingram, providing the opportunity to focus on printmaking and to develop confidence and commitment. In lithographs from this period, like "Presss . . ." (1975), and "Releasing Squeeze" (1975), magnified photographic views of her own body were combined with gestures on nebulous sheets of white paper. Metaphors for transitions between the physical and the spiritual, these prints are indicative of the conceptual direction for all her works to follow.

After graduate school, Ingram began teaching at the University of Alberta, and set up a shared studio with Walter Jule and Bonnie Sheckter. For the next six years this joint studio proved to be very stimu-lating and productive. Lithographs from this period employed photo fragments of organic debris, revealed and dissolved by interior light. In 1978, a print from this period, "Beginning Under Ice" (1978), won the award of merit and a purchase award at the Graphex 6 exhibition at the Art Gallery of Brant in Ontario. In 1981 the lithograph "Outside Interior's Rubied Ground" (1981), won a purchase award in the International Exhibition of Graphic Art at the Museum of Modern Art in Ljubljana, Yugoslavia.

In 1983 Ingram stopped working in lithography and after producing a small etching for the publication *Print Voice*, began to develop her imagery in the etching medium. Her works became more confrontational and less romantic, relying more heavily on tonal variation and less on subtle color transitions. Light remained a constant presence in these prints, dissolving and revealing forms, and implying relationships between energy and matter.

In 1985 "Primal Vision, State III" (1984) received an award at the Cabo Frio International Print Exhibition in Brazil, and in 1987 the etchings "Bird of Paradise" (1985) and "Revealed Matrix" (1986), won second prize in the International Exhibition of Graphic Art at the Museum of Modern Art in Ljubljana, Yugoslavia. In 1989, Ingram won a purchase award for her etching, "Coincidental Realities" (1987), again at the biennial in Ljubljana.

Ingram has had over one dozen solo, duo, and three-person exhibitions in Toronto, Montréal, Washington, D.C., Hong Kong, Edmonton, and Calgary, including a solo retrospective exhibition in 1989 at the International Center of Graphic Art in Ljubljana, Yugoslavia. Her works have been accepted into more than thirty juried exhibitions in Canada, the United States, Japan, Yugoslavia, Poland, Taiwan, Brazil, and Spain. Permanent collections include: the Canada Council Art Bank; the Alberta Art Foundation; the Art Gallery of Brant; the Owens Art Gallery, Newfoundland; the Edmonton Art Gallery; the Glenbow Museum, Calgary; the Cultural Redaction Delo, Lujubljana, Yugoslavia; and many corporate, university, and private collections.

Lyndal Osborne

Bibliography
Baxter, Charlotte. "Alberta Printmakers." *Art Magazine* 31:32 (March–April, 1977).
Bradley, Ross. "Liz Ingram: Etchings Blur Distinction Between Reality and Illusion." *Muttart Art Gallery Newsletter* 2:12. Calgary, 1989.
Cochran, Bente Roed. "Edmonton Printmakers." *Arts West Magazine* 7:9 (1982).
———. *Contemporary Edmonton Prints.* Exhibition Catalog. Edmonton Art Gallery, 1988.
———. *Printmaking in Alberta 1945–1985.* University of Alberta Press, 1989, pp. 83–86.
Devonshire-Baker, Suzanne. "Liz Gagnon." *Alberta Artists.* University of Alberta Press, 1978.
Jule, Walter, ed. *Print Voice.* Edmonton: Department of Art and Design, 1985, p. 89.
Kosinski, Marytka. "Elizabeth Ingram." *International Exhibition of Graphic Art Catalogue.* Ljubljana, Yugoslavia: International Center of Graphic Art, 1989, pp. 324–29.
Menzies, Susan. "Liz Ingram." *Society of Northern Alberta Print Artists Newsletter.* Edmonton: August 1989.

Ipcar, Dahlov (1917–)

Daughter of artists William and Marguerite Zorach, the painter/author/ illustrator Dahlov Ipcar was born in Windsor, Vermont. Self-taught, she has won many honors and awards for her work and has been the recipient of several honorary Doctorate degrees from colleges and universities, including the University of Maine, Orono (1978); Colby College, Waterville (1980); and Bates College, Lewiston (1991)—all in Maine. Ipcar has held solo and two-person exhibitions in museums and galleries throughout the United States, including the Museum of Modern Art (MoMA), New York City (1939); Philadelphia Art Alliance, Pennsylvania (1944); A.C.A. Gallery, New York City (1946); Children's Museum, Oakland, California (1956); University of Maine (1965, 1967, 1969, 1970, 1971, 1975); "30-Year Retrospective," Westbrook College, Portland, Maine (1966); Dalzell-Hatfield Galleries, Los Angeles, California (1970); Delaware Art Museum, Maryland (1976); Frost Gully Gallery, Portland, Maine (1977, 1985); Bates College, Lewiston, Maine (1990); and others. Her works have been invited to many group exhibitions—from Washington, D.C., to Bangkok, Thailand; from Pittsburgh, Pennsylvania, to Houston, Texas; from Hobe Sound, Florida, to Ottawa, Canada.

Ipcar has written adult fiction and has written and illustrated more than thirty-six children's books between 1947 and 1986 in her singular brand of imaginative realism. A muralist whose works grace post offices and schools in Tennessee, Oklahoma, and Maine, she recently received the Living Legacy award from the Central Maine Area Agency on Aging (1986); and others. Her work is represented in private, public, and corporate permanent collections, including the Brooklyn Museum, Metropolitan Museum of Art, and Whitney Museum of American Art—all in New York City; Bates College, Lewiston; Colby Museum of Art, Waterville; University of Maine at Orono, Farmington, and Southern Maine; and the Farnsworth Museum of Art, Rockland—all in Maine; University of Maryland, College Park; L.L. Bean, Inc.; and many others.

Bibliography

Nakamura, Joyce, ed. *Something about the Author Autobiography Series.* Vol. 8. Gale Research, 1989.
Reef, Pat Davidson. *Dahlov Ipcar, Artist. Maine Art Series for Young Readers.* Kennebec River Press, 1987.
Who's Who in American Art. 19th ed. R.R. Bowker Co., 1991–1992.

Irvine, Sadie (1887–1970)

Though little is known of her personal life, Sadie Irvine earned a Bachelor's degree from Sophie Newcomb Memorial College for Women, Tulane University, New Orleans, Louisiana, and became one of the noted decorators who worked for the Newcomb Pottery, in that same city. The creation of the live oak designs used by the pottery were her contribution—a fact that eventually disturbed her—in that the tasteful, refined forms of the vases and that specific design did not marry well. Irvine taught at Sophie Newcomb College until the early 1950s; she also made relief prints and watercolors.

Bibliography

Blasberg, Robert W. "The Sadie Irvine Letters." *Antiques* 100 (August 1971).
Clark, Garth. *American Ceramics: 1896 to the Present.* Abbeville Press, 1987.

Isaac, Lucero (1936–)

Known primarily for her boxes and assemblages, Lucero Isaac was born in Mexico City, Mexico. She was raised in a family attracted to the arts; her grandfather was an antiques dealer and a curator. Her first incursion into the world of art was as a dancer. After her marriage to the film director Alberto Isaac, however, she began work as an art director and set designer for films, including *Los días del amor* (1971), *Foxtrot* (1975), *Las apariencias engañan* (1977), *La viuda de Montiel* (1979), and *Missing* (1981). She has also worked as a set designer in the theater, most notably for the play *Gigi*, directed by Manolo Fábregas in Mexico City, Mexico, and *Women*, directed by Rafael Buñuel in Los Angeles.

Isaac's work has been the subject of solo exhibitions at the Galería Honfleur, Mexico City (1988); the Gerald Peters Gallery, Santa Fe, New Mexico (1991); and the Galería Arte Contemporáneo, Mexico City, Mexico (1992). She has also participated in several important group exhibitions, including "Women in Mexico," National Academy of Design, New York City (1990); "Encountering the Others," Universitat Kassel, Germany (1992); "Pasado y Presente del Centro Histórico," Palacio Iturbide, Mexico City, Mexico (1993); and "Latin America and Surrealism," Museum of Bochum, Germany (1993).

The importance of space in Isaac's work as a dancer, and later as a set designer, is manifest in her carefully constructed boxes and assemblages. In a number of these works, including *No Turning Points* (1991) and *The Date* (1992), the artist ventures into the realm of dreams. Other works, such as *I Wish I Could be a Singer* (1989), allude to the past and its grandeur, always with an element of ambiguity. Isaac currently lives and works in Cuernavaca, a town near the nation's capital.

Ilona Katzew

Bibliography

Krulik, Barbara, and Robert Littman. *Night People's Theater.* Gerald Peters Gallery, 1992.
Melkonian, Neery. "Lucero Isaac." *Arts Magazine* 71 (December 1991).
Podany, Jim. "Lucero Isaac Relies on Dreams to Create Stuff of Assemblages." *The New Mexican Pasatiempo* (July 7, 1991).
Sullivan, Edward J. *Women in Mexico.* A Catalog. Centro Cultural Televisa, A.C., 1990.

Ishulutaq, Elizabeth (c. 1925–)

Equally talented in drawing as in carving stone, Ishulutaq started her career as an artist relatively late in life. She was born in 1925 at Kanirterjuak on the east side of Cumberland Sound, on Baffin Island in Canada's Northwest Territories. The artist experienced the traditional Inuit lifestyle until 1970 when, at the age of 45, she moved into Pangnirtung on Baffin Island.

Ishulutaq's deceptively simple but brilliant drawings capture with a few pencil lines narrative episodes out of her childhood. These pencil drawings have been used at the Pangnirtung Weave Shop as designs for tapestries and at the print shop for stencil prints of extraordinary lyricism. Her designs charm us with their humor and immediacy. Through the use of multiple perspective using frontal, profile, and bird's eye view in the same image, she draws the viewer into the picture plane where usually everyday domestic happenings are depicted.

Her carvings, using equally simplified forms, have the same appeal and charm as her drawings.

Annual collections both by the Pangnirtung Weave Shop and Print Shop have contained several works by the artist since 1973. The artist's work has been shown in numerous national and international exhibits. Among these, the international travelling exhibit, "The Inuit Print," which travelled from 1977 until 1982, and "Chisel and Brush," which toured Canada between 1985 and 1987, should be highlighted.

Maria Muehlen

Bibliography
Hickman, Deborah. "Pangnirtung Weaving Workshop." *About Arts and Crafts* III, 2 (Autumn 1982): 24–27.
Hoffmann, Gerhard, ed. *Im Schatten der Sonne: Zeitgenoessische Kunst der Indianer und Eskimos in Kanada* (In the Shadow of the Sun: Contemporary Art of the Canadian Indians and Eskimos). Stuttgart: Edition Cantz. Ottawa: Canadian Museum of Civilization, 1988, pp. 588–91.

Isserkut Kringayark, Madeleine (1928–1984)

Canadian Inuit artist Madeleine Isserkut Kringayark was born on Southampton Island, Northwest Territories, in 1928. After she married in 1942, her family lived on the land, moving as far south as Chesterfield Inlet and finally settling in Repulse Bay.

Isserkut was among the first in her community to begin carving in the early 1950s. Her sculptures of hunting and domestic scenes, made up of finely detailed elements, often depict the regular and necessary interaction between the Inuit and the animals of the north. Usually carved from ivory or antler and arranged on a stone base, these tableaus serve as sculptural narratives, and are typical of Repulse Bay. In addition to her carving, Isserkut was also a talented jewelry artist. In a 1978 competition she won an award of merit for a necklace made of caribou antler and sinew.

Isserkut's work has been represented in many group exhibitions in Canada and the United States since the 1960s. Her sculpture "Drum Dancer" was reproduced on a Canadian postage stamp in 1979. Examples of Isserkut's sculpture and jewelry are included in the collections of the National Gallery of Canada, the Canadian Museum of Civilization, and the Winnipeg Art Gallery, among others.

Lori Cutler

Bibliography
Blodgett, Jean. *Grasp Tight the Old Ways: Selections from the Klamer Family Collection on Inuit Art.* Toronto, 1983.
Winnipeg Art Gallery. *Repulse Bay.* Winnipeg, 1979.

Itami, Michi (1938–)

Born in Los Angeles, California, the artist Michi Itami earned a Bachelor's degree in English literature from the University of California at Los Angeles (UCLA) (1959); did graduate work in Japanese and English language and literature at Columbia University, New York City (1959–1962); apprenticed to Kimpei Nakamura, a ceramist in Kanazawa, Japan (1967–1968); and received a Master of Arts degree from the University of California at Berkeley (1971).

Itami has held solo exhibitions in galleries in the United States and abroad between 1975 and 1992, including Phoenix Gallery, San Francisco, California (1975, 1976); Beni Gallery, Kyoto (1979, 1980, 1982) and Miyazaki Gallery, Osaka—both in Japan (1980, 1982); Soker-

Kaseman Gallery, San Francisco, California (1978, 1980, 1983, 1984); Richard Kauffman Gallery, Houston, Texas (1985); A.I.R. Gallery and 55 Mercer Gallery—both in New York City (1991); Shinsegae Dongbang Plaza Art Gallery, Seoul, Korea (1992); and others. Her paintings and prints have been invited to many group exhibitions from Sag Harbor, New York, to Buenos Aires, Argentina; San Francisco, California; Salisbury, North Carolina; Houston, Texas; Tokyo, Japan; and others.

"The Irony of Being American" (1992), a computer-generated, photo-collage print on vellum, reflects Itami's keen utilization of the new technology in a work packed with metaphor. Winner of awards and honors, Itami was the recipient of grants and fellowships, including a National Defense Foreign Language fellowship (1961); a printmaking fellowship, Festival of the Arts, Asilah, Morocco (Summer 1984); a National Endowment for the Arts (NEA) grant (1981–1982); an ACM Siggraph Educator's grant (1991); and a research grant from the City University of New York (CUNY) (1992). An assistant professor of art at CUNY since 1988, Itami has taught printmaking at the San Francisco Art Institute (1974–1985), and art at California State University, Hayward—both in California. Her work is represented in private and public permanent collections, including the Achenbach Foundation, Legion of Honor Museum, San Francisco; Oakland Museum; San Francisco Museum of Modern Art, and the University Art Museum, Berkeley—all in California; Brooklyn Museum, New York; Cincinnati Art Museum, Ohio; State of Hawaii Collection; the National Museum of Modern Art, Kyoto, Japan; and others.

Bibliography
Chroman, Eleanor. *The Potter's Primer.* Hawthorn Books, 1974.
Davis, Suzanne. "Review." *Atlanta Art Papers* (May–June 1989).
Dickson, Joanne A. "Michi Itami Zimmerman: Paintings and Prints." *Artweek* 6:4 (February 25, 1975).
Roche, Harry. "Samplings." *San Francisco Bay Guardian* (June 27, 1990).

Itatani, Michiko (1948–)

Born in Osaka, Japan, the painter Michiko Itatani graduated from Kobe Jogakuin University, Japan, having studied literature, philosophy, and calligraphy; she attended the University of Chicago, Illinois; studied painting at the Skowhegan School of Painting and Sculpture, Maine (1974); and earned Bachelor of Fine Arts and Master of Fine Arts degrees from the School of the Art Institute of Chicago, Illinois (1976), where she is presently a professor.

Itatani has held solo exhibitions in galleries and museums throughout the United States and abroad, including "Michiko Itatani: Paintings since 1984," Chicago Cultural Center, Illinois (1992); University of Western Ontario, Canada (1991); Deson/Saunders Gallery, Chicago, Illinois (1980, 1982, 1984, 1987–1988, 1990–1991); Kyoni Gallery, Tokyo (1988, 1990), and Amano Gallery, Osaka—both in Japan (1988, 1990); University of Colorado, Boulder (1989); "Solo Series," Rockford Art Museum, Illinois (1987); "Paintings," Alternative Museum, New York City (1985); "Painting/Installation," Ukranian Institute of Modern Art, Chicago, Illinois (1981); and others. Her work has been invited to many group exhibitions, such as the "20th Anniversary of Visiting Artists Program," University of Colorado, Boulder (1992); "Osaka Triennale '90." Japan (1990); "Bramson, Itatani, Klement," Amerika Haus, Stuttgart, Germany (1989); "Connections Project/

Conexus," Museum of Contemporary Hispanic Art, New York City (1987); "Fine Line: Drawing with Silver in America," Norton Gallery, West Palm Beach, Florida (1985); "Drawing from Chicago," University of Nebraska, Omaha (1982); "American Women Artists," Museu de Arte Contemporanea, São Paulo, Brazil (1980); and many others.

Winner of awards and honors for her painting, Itatani is the recipient of a number of grants and fellowships, including Illinois Arts Council Project completion grants and fellowships (1979, 1981, 1984, 1985); a National Endowment for the Arts (NEA) fellowship (1980); Chicago Artists Abroad (1988, 1989, 1990); a Guggenheim fellowship (1990); a grant from the Marie Walsh Sharp Foundation (1991); and others.

Itatani's current paintings are monumental, expressionistic, polygonal works of nude figures in ambiguous space. They are metaphors for finding one's way in life. Recently, she wrote, "For me, to be an artist is an intellectual choice and a carefully chosen commitment. There is no intoxication." Her work is represented in private, public, and corporate permanent collections, including the Art Institute of Chicago, Illinois; University of Colorado, Boulder; Musée du Québec, and University of Western Ontario—both in Canada; American Embassy in Brasilia, Brazil; Rockford Art Museum, Illinois; KDI Corporation, New York City; Yamanouchi Pharmaceutical Co., Ltd., Japan; and others.

Bibliography
Cook, Katherine. "In Search of a New Cosmology." *Artweek* 2:32 (April 1992): 12.
Holg, Garrett. "Michiko Itatani: Printworks." *Art News* 91:91 (April 1992): 129.
Lippard, Lucy R. *Mixed Blessings*. Pantheon Books, 1990.
Michiko Itatani. A Catalog. Essay by Janet Koplo, Interview by Lanny Silverman. Chicago Cultural Center, 1992.

Ito, Miyoko (1918–1983)

When Ito died of a heart attack at the age of sixty-five, she was one of the most revered artists in the Chicago art community. Because her luminous and allusive little canvases synthesize cubism and surrealism, they appealed to abstract artists and Imagists alike. Moreover, artists admired Ito's personal example of steadfast commitment to the highest ideals of art, even at the cost of speed, sales, or professional advancement.

Ito's refined yet deeply emotional sensibility owed much to her East-West heritage. Born into a prospering Japanese family in Berkeley, California, she was taken at the age of five to provincial Japan for five years. Her early childhood had therefore passed when she began to be Westernized upon her return to Berkeley, where she earned a B.A. degree at the University of California in 1942. She continued her education at Smith College, Northampton, Massachusetts, and the School of the Art Institute of Chicago, Illinois. Thereafter, she and her husband, Harry Ichiyasu, a toy manufacturer, remained in Chicago.

Ito began as a watercolorist influenced by synthetic cubism, Dufy, Bonnard, and Hofmann. Surrealism gradually entered her work in Chicago. Two children born in the early 1950s occupied most of her time for several years, during which she mastered oil painting. As "Miraculous Mandarin" (1959) demonstrates, by the end of the decade she had initiated her mature approach dominated by simplified, biomorphic

shapes, later often combined with architectonic forms. A late masterwork, "Door to the Sea" (1981) summarizes her achievements. At once adventurous and serene, her representation and imagination converge, alluding to experience, memory, and the dream of a perfect work of art.

Ann Lee Morgan

Bibliography
Adrian, Dennis. *Miyoko Ito: A Review*. Chicago: Renaissance Society at the University of Chicago, 1980. [Catalog of retrospective exhibition.]
Gedo, Mary Mathews. "Abstraction as Metaphor: The Evocative Imagery of William Conger, Miyoko Ito, Richard Loving, and Frank Piatek." *Arts Magazine* 57 (October 1982): 112–17.

Itter, Diane (1946–1989)

Born in Summit, New Jersey, the fiber artist Diane Itter earned a Bachelor's degree at the University of Pittsburgh, Pennsylvania (1969); and received a Master of Fine Arts degree in textiles from Indiana University, Bloomington (1974).

Itter's small, jewel-like fiber pieces have been exhibited regionally, nationally, and internationally; they reflect a sensitive awareness of the textiles of other cultures, particularly with respect to color and form. The National Endowment for the Arts, starting in 1977, awarded Itter the first of three craftsman's fellowship grants. Her work is represented in private and public permanent collections.

Bibliography
Fiber Concepts. A Catalog. Tempe: Arizona State University, 1989.
Koplos, Janet. "The Knot as Brush Stroke: Diane Itter's Fiber Paintings." *American Craft* (February–March 1980): 21–23.
Park, Betty. "Diane Itter: Recent Work." *Fiberarts* (September–October 1981): 68.

Ittuluka'naaq, Martha (1912–1981)

Martha Ittuluka'naaq was born along the Kazan River in the barren grounds of the Canadian Central Arctic in the first decade of the twentieth century and lived the first fifty years of her life pursuing a caribou-hunting lifestyle similar to that of her Inuit ancestors. In her early years, Ittuluka'naaq had very little contact with the Euro-Canadian traders and missionaries who were already establishing small permanent settlements in the Canadian Arctic. However, illness and starvation among her people in the 1950s and 1960s led Ittuluka'naaq and others from the barren grounds to relocate in the settlement of Baker Lake where medical care, food, and housing was provided by the federal government. At the time she moved into Baker Lake in 1961, Ittuluka'naaq was a widow with no independent means of support. Her well-developed survival instincts may have led her to respond to the opportunity to make and sell drawings to the fledgling arts and crafts projects initiated in Baker Lake by the federal government in the 1960s.

Ittuluka'naaq's pencil and crayon drawings—often viewed as crude in their simplicity and in their wavering quality of line—are stylistically similar to those of other Inuit artists, such as Anguhadluq and Parr, whose life experiences were also largely within the traditions of the Inuit culture. Ittuluka'naaq's sketchy stick-drawings also relate stylistically to early engraved Eskimo ivories of the Central and

Western Canadian Arctic and Alaska. Ittuluka'naaq's subject matter is limited almost exclusively to stick drawings of humans and of the Arctic animals hunted and trapped in the Kazan River area (primarily caribou, Arctic hare, wolves, and fish). Many of her drawings are characterized by repetition of isolated figures, often placed in parallel lines on the page.

Ittuluka'naaq's drawing served as the basis for eight prints produced by the Baker Lake Sanavik Cooperative between 1970 and 1977; her works were included in Baker Lake print collections in the years 1970, 1971, 1972, 1973, and 1977. Examples of Ittuluka'naaq's artwork have been included in the internationally touring exhibitions, "The Inuit Print/L'Estampe Inuit" and "Contemporary Inuit Drawings" and in several Baker Lake group exhibitions organized by the Winnipeg Art Gallery. Her work is represented in important collections of contemporary Inuit art, including the Canadian Museum of Civilization, Ottawa; Winnipeg Art Gallery, MacDonald Stewart Art Centre, Guelph, Ontario; and the Prince of Wales Northern Heritage Centre, Yellowknife, Northwest Territories.

Marion E. Jackson

Bibliography
Baker Lake annual print collection catalogues: 1970, 1971, 1972, 1973, 1977.
Driscoll, Bernadette. *The Inuit Amautik: I Like My Hood To Be Full.* Winnipeg: Winnipeg Art Gallery, 1980.
Driscoll, Bernadette, and Sheila Butler. *Baker Lake Prints & Print Drawings 1970—76.* Winnipeg: Winnipeg Art Gallery, 1983.
Goetz, Helga. *The Inuit Print/L'Estampe Inuit.* Ottawa: National Museums of Canada, 1977.
Jackson, Marion, and Judith Nasby. *Contemporary Inuit Drawings.* Guelph, Ontario: MacDonald Stewart Art Centre, 1987.

Iturbide, Graciela (1942–)

Graciela Iturbide, one of the most notable of Mexico's new generation of photographers, was born in Mexico City in 1942. She studied film-making at the Centro Universitario de Estudios Cinematográficos of the Universidad Nacional Autónoma de Mexico (1969–1972). In 1970 she became an assistant to and disciple of photographer Manual Alvarez Bravo, and by 1974 she had abandoned cinematography to work exclusively in still photography.

She was a member of the Salón de la Plástica Mexicana (1976–1978) before becoming a founding member of the Foro de Arte Contemporaneo in Mexico City (1978) and joining the Consejo Mexicano de Fotografía (1980).

Iturbide began showing her photographs in group exhibitions in Mexico City in the early 1970s (Instituto Mexicano Norteamericano de Relaciones Culturales, 1972; Galería José Clemente Orozco, 1975). Within a few years her work began to be known in the United States (the Midtown Gallery, New York City, 1975; Center for Creative Photography, Tucson, Arizona, 1978). In 1980, she had two solo exhibitions in Mexico (Galería de Fotografía, Universidad Nacional Autónoma de Mexico; Casa de la Cultura, Juchitan, Oaxaca) and began to show her work in Europe (Centre Cultural Mexicain, Paris, 1980; Kunsthaus, Zurich, 1981; Centre Georges Pompidou, Paris, 1982; and other exhibitions in England and Finland).

She tends to work in essay form, in black and white, photographically exploring a subject over a period of time. Her study of the Seri Indians of the coast of Sonora, in northwestern Mexico, was published in 1980 (*Los que viven en la arena*). A second book, *Sueños de papel*, was published in 1985. A photo essay entitled *Juchitan de las mujeres* (published in 1989, with a text by Elena Poniatowska) celebrates the culture of a city in Tehuantepec, Oaxaca, a region legendary for its strong and beautiful women. Juchitan was the birthplace of the artist Francisco Toledo, who was supportive of Iturbide's work there. The essay on Juchitan was exhibited in Paris in 1988, where it received the Grand Prix du Mois de la Photographie.

Iturbide is the recipient of other honors as well: the W. Eugene Smith award (1987) and a Guggenheim fellowship (1988). Her work has continued to be widely exhibited and published in catalogs and journals of photography. She participated in the First, Second, and Third "Muestra de Fotografía Latinoamericana Contemporánea" (Mexico City, 1978, 1981; Havana, 1985) and in the "Primera Bienal de Fotografía (Mexico City, 1980). In 1989 Iturbide was one of the few women photographers and one of the few Latin Americans whose work was included in the National Gallery of Art, Washington, D.C., retrospective exhibition, "On the Art of Fixing a Shadow: 150 Years of Photography." Her photographs are in the collections of the Center for Creative Photography, Tucson; the Casa de las Américas, Havana; the Bibliothèque Nationale, Paris; and in other public and private collections in Mexico and abroad.

Martha Davidson

Bibliography
Iturbide, Graciela. *Los que viven en la arena.* Mexico City: Instituto Nacional Indigenista, 1980.
———. *Sueños de papel.* Introduction by Veronica Volkow. Mexico City: Fondo de Cultura Económica, Collección Río de Luz, 1985.
———. *Juchitan de las mujeres.* Text by Elena Poniatowska. Mexico City: Ediciones Toledo, 1989.
Iturbide, Graciela, Paulina Lavista, and Colette Urbajtel. *Fotografías.* Texts by Julieta Campos and others. Mexico City: Instituto Nacional de Bellas Artes, 1975.
7 Portafolios mexicanos. Mexico City: Universidad Autónoma de México, 1980.

Iwata, Kiyomi (1941–)

Born in Kobe, Japan, the sculptor Kiyomi Iwata studied at several institutions, including the Penland School of Crafts, North Carolina (1967, 1968); Haystack Mountain School of Crafts, Deer Isle, Maine (1970, 1973, 1976); and the New School for Social Research, New York City (1971, 1974, 1975).

Iwata has exhibited work in solo and group shows in the United States and abroad, including "Meeting Ground: Basketry Traditions and Sculptural Forms," The Forum, St. Louis, Missouri, and Arizona State University, Tempe (1990); "The Tactile Vessel: New Basket Forms," a travelling show through 1991, Erie Art Museum, Pennsylvania (1989); "Fiber R/Evolution," a travelling show through 1987, Milwaukee Art Museum and the University of Wisconsin-Milwaukee (1986); "13e International Biennale Lausanne," Musée des Beaux-Arts, Switzerland (1985); "Kiyomi Iwata, in Collaboration with American Silk Mills Presents Sculptures," Paul Mellon Arts Center, Wallingford, Connecticut

(1985); and others.

"Sea Creature One" (1987), a silk organza and gold leaf work, is typical of her delicate sculptures. Winner of awards and honors, Iwata received an artists' fellowship from the New York Foundation on the Arts (1987); a visual artists fellowship from the National Endowment for the Arts (NEA); and others. Her work is represented in private and public permanent collections.

Bibliography

Larson, Jack Lenor. *The Tactile Vessel: New Basket Forms.* Erie Art Museum. 1989.

Meeting Ground: Basketry Traditions and Sculptural Forms. St. Louis, Missouri: The Forum, and Tempe: Arizona State University, 1990.

Malaracher, Patricia. "Review." *The New York Times* (February 17, 1985).

Izquierdo, María (1902–1955)

The first Mexican woman to exhibit her paintings in the United States, Maria Izquierdo participated in the Mexican Renaissance in painting that developed after the Mexican Revolution of 1910–1920. Although her early life in many ways was that of the average rural Mexican woman, her choices to study art, pursue painting, and later to write outspokenly feminist articles about the situations of women in Mexico and women artists in general distinguish her not just from other Mexican women, but from her more notoriously revolutionary colleagues, such as Diego Rivera. While they championed the rights of oppressed workers and peasants of Mexico, they neglected to include women in their revolutionary propositions.

Izquierdo was born in 1902 in San Juan de los Lagos in rural Jalisco. Her upbringing and education were in a conservative Catholic tradition. Her father died when she was five years old, and her mother worked as a travel agent. Not surprisingly, Izquierdo married her first husband in 1917 at the age of fourteen.

In 1923, she, her husband, and three children moved to Mexico City. Soon after, her husband left the family. In 1927, Izquierdo made the unusual decision to enter the School of Fine Arts (formerly the Academy of San Carlos) in Mexico City, where she studied painting with Germán Gedovius and Manual Toussaint. Gedovius granted her permission to work at home in order to take care of her children, although this did not estrange her from her fellow students. In keeping with the politically charged atmosphere of the period, in a student group exhibition in 1928 she showed *The Jury of Toral*, a reference to the man who had assassinated President Obregon the previous July, as well as a painting more typical of her subject matter, a *Still Life with Camera*. The school's director, Diego Rivera, singled out Izquierdo's work as being the only authentically Mexican of the exhibit. Her painting style and technique that so attracted Rivera, based on Mexican popular paintings, ceramics, and textiles, was also highly contested in the School of Fine Arts, which still retained many of the values it inherited from its earlier incarnation as the traditional Academy. Soon after, Izquierdo was asked to leave the school by her professors.

In 1919, Izquierdo met Rufino Tamayo, the Oaxaca painter with whom she lived and worked for the next three years. His influence on her work is particularly noteworthy in her use of color. Her earlier reliance on dark, opaque colors that robbed her paintings of perspective gave way to brighter colors and juxtapositions of light and dark that,

while she continued to flatten space in her work, served to highlight certain elements and animate her work.

That same year Rivera organized Izquierdo's first solo exhibition in the Gallery of Modern Art of the National Theater in Mexico City. The exhibit travelled to the Art Center in New York City in 1930, making her the first Mexican woman to exhibit her work in the United States. In that same year, her work was included in the Metropolitan Museum's exhibit, "Mexican Arts." From then on, her work appeared in most exhibits of modern Mexican art, and in 1933 she had a solo exhibit in Paris. In the years following, her work was seen in San Francisco, California, Buffalo, New York, and Chicago, Illinois. In Mexico she exhibited in the states of Veracruz, Jalisco, Puebla, and Oaxaca, as well as in Mexico City. She travelled extensively, and after meeting the Chilean painter Raul Uribe in 1938, she went to Chile. She lived there with him for two years and married him in 1944.

While she enjoyed some financial success as a painter, she also taught painting at the Ministry of Public Education's School of Painting and Sculpture beginning in 1931 in order to support her family. Despite her gaining international recognition, Izquierdo, like other women artists in Mexico such as Frida Kahlo, declared that she did not consider herself a painter but that she painted out of the necessity of her soul. The image of Izquierdo as an intuitive painter was also promoted by the French writer Antonin Artaud, who came to Mexico in 1936 in search of a more primitive, pure expression of the spiritual. This he found in Izquierdo's painting while rejecting all other modern Mexican art as too European. Those characteristics of Izquierdo's work that appealed to Artaud, in addition to her popular art style and use of color, were her repeated themes of circuses, household altars often in landscapes, small cupboards full of fruits, vegetables, and figurines of people and animals. In many paintings, such as "The Virgin of Sorrows" (1947), she mixed religious and domestic content. In this painting, the Virgin looks upon the altar dedicated to her from behind some curtains, treating the magical relationship between popular religious practice and spirituality. Among her other admirers were the Chilean and Mexican poets Pablo Neruda and Carlos Pellicer. Inspired by her work, they found in it an appeal that contrasted to the didactic, politically-motivated art of the Mexican muralists. Although she did paint one series called "Tragedies of War," she was considered to be an apolitical artist. This, along with professional jealousy, is probably what prompted both Rivera and David Alfaro Siqueiros to move against a commission Izquierdo received to paint a mural in the government palace of Mexico City. The two muralists wanted to dictate the theme of the mural, ensuring that it had a political base; yet they cited her lack of experience as the principal reason for denying her the commission. Severe heart problems at the time led her to concede that commission and another less important one offered in consolation. The experience fed her sense of injustice, however; its effects can be read in her later journal articles.

Izquierdo's activism first appeared publicly when she organized a travelling exhibition, "Revolutionary Posters of the Female Section of Plastic Arts, Department of Fine Arts." In 1950 she published in the journal *Zocalo* "A Letter to the Women of Mexico," in which she criticized the view of working women as "morally inferior" to the wives and mothers who stay at home. She also pointed out the neglect and limitations of women in Mexican society. She carefully insisted that as she was not a man-hater or believer in women's superiority, she could not be called a "classic feminist." In an earlier article about the Chilean painter Mireya Lafuente, she attacked art critics for judging women's art ". . . as if color, line, volumes, landscape or geography had sex [gender]." Her strong defense of women's rights and more subtle observations of the dynamics of machismo, in addition to her own life choices, show her to have been one of the few voices of the time to speak on behalf of women's issues. In her paintings, she often depicted women and children, or women alone, often peasant women, showing her concern with the sphere of influence designated to women: nature, the home, and children.

In her last paintings, including "Landscape" (1953), "The Dream" (ca. 1953), and "Woman with Flower" (1955), she abandoned her use of jewel-like color and shallow space and adopted a palette of dry earthtones, browns, and greens, and often attempted to define a deep, almost infinite space through repetition of receding forms. The trees in *Landscape* all have their limbs cut as if amputated, and lead back in two seemingly endless rows along a brown, barren road. "The Dream" shows her holding her own decapitated head in her hand as she leans out a window to watch nude headless female figures go running down a road. These pessimistic images, contrasting greatly with her earlier work, coincide with her divorce from Uribe and her own increasing heart trouble from which she died in December 1955 in Mexico City. The next year a large retrospective, that had been in the planning stages before her death, opened in Mexico City.

Laura J. Crary-Ortega

Bibliography
Helm, Mackinley. *Modern Mexican Painters*. New York, 1941.
Images of Mexico. Exhibition Catalog. Dallas Museum of Art, Dallas, Texas, 1988.
Maria Izquierdo. Exhibition Catalog. Centro Cultural/Arte Contemporaneo, Mexico City, 1989.
Monsivais, Carlos, et al. *Maria Izquierdo*. Mexico City, 1986.

Jackson, Edna Davis (1950–)

Papermaking artist Edna Davis Jackson (Ka-Swoot), a member of the Tlingit tribe, was born in Petersburg, a small Alaskan village, and studied art at Oregon State University, Corvallis, where she received her Bachelor of Fine Arts degree in fiber arts (1980). Three years later Jackson did graduate work at the University of Washington, Seattle, and earned a Master of Fine Arts degree in the same discipline. She also studied spruce root and cedar bark weaving with Delores Churchill; and Chilkat weaving with Cheryl Samuel and Jennie Thlunaut.

Jackson's work has been shown in solo exhibitions at the Southern Plains Indian Museum and Crafts Center, Anadarko, Oklahoma (1988), and at AICA, San Francisco, California (1990). Her work has been invited to many group shows, including "Women of Sweetgrass, Cedar and Sage," American Indian Community House Gallery, New York (1985); "New Directions Northwest," Portland Art Museum, Oregon (1987); "Annual Native Show," Stonington Gallery, Anchorage, Alaska (1990); and many others. She uses certain cellulosic materials found in her immediate environment to make pulp for her art, including tree bark, grasses, and other plant materials. "Ka-oosh and Coho Salmon," a paperwork collage of handmade paper, string, copper wire, and gouache, is not atypical of her work. It reveals four netted, leaping Coho salmon, Tlingit motifs, and three visages in certain tension.

Jackson taught at the University of Alaska at Juneau, offering classes in papermaking from 1983 to 1985 and both papermaking and weaving from 1985 to 1988. Recipient of many honors, she completed a collaborative project with Robert Davis for the Institute of Alaskan Native Arts titled, "Dissent Is Not a Bad Word" (1986–1987); won a grant from the Alaska State Council on the Arts (1985); received a Chevron fellowship from the Institute of Alaskan Native Arts (1985); and a Sealaska Heritage Foundation graduate fellowship (1981–1983). Her works are in public, private, and corporate permanent collections, including the Department of Interior, Indian Arts and Crafts Board, Washington, D.C.; the Seattle Arts Commission and Alaska Airlines—both in Seattle, Washington; Anchorage Performing Arts Center, Alaska; the Heard Museum, Phoenix, Arizona; and others.

Bibliography

Fitzhugh, William W., and Aron Crowell. *Crossroads of Continents, Cultures of Siberia and Alaska*. Smithsonian Institution Press, 1988.

Heard Museum Archives. Phoenix, Arizona.

Kenagy, Suzanne G. "Eight Artists: Contemporary Indian Art at the Southwest Museum." *American Indian Art Magazine* (Winter 1987): 59.

Jackson, Hazel Brill (1895–1991)

An award-winning sculptor, Hazel Brill Jackson was primarily noted for her bronzes of animals in general and of horses and dogs in particular. She also made wood engravings. Born in Philadelphia, Pennsylvania, Jackson studied at the Boston Museum School of Fine Arts, Massachusetts, and the Scuola Rosatti in Florence, Italy. She also worked in Rome, Italy, with Angelo Zanelli and took further instruction from Bela Pratt and Charles Grafly.

A fellow of the National Sculpture Society, New York City, Jackson exhibited her work in the National Academy of Design, New York City; the National Museum of Modern Art, Rome, the Art Museum of Florence, and the Art Museum of Trieste—all in Italy; the

Royal Academy of Scotland, the Springfield Museum of Fine Arts; and others. Jackson won the Altman prize in an exhibition at the National Academy of Design (1945), and, four years later, was awarded the Ellen P. Speyer Memorial prize for "Indian Antelope." Her several solo exhibitions included one held at the Boston Artists Guild, Massachusetts, and the other at the Corcoran Gallery of Art, Washington, D.C.

Jackson was an inveterate mountain climber who belonged to both American and Italian alpine clubs. Her work is in the permanent public collections of many colleges and museums in the United States and abroad, including Dartmouth College, Hanover, New Hampshire; Vassar College, Poughkeepsie, New York; Wellesley College, Massachusetts; and the Calgary Museum, Alberta, Canada.

Bibliography
"Hazel Brill Jackson, A Sculptor Known for Animal Statues." Obituary. *The New York Times* (May 1991).
Who's Who in American Art. 19th ed. R.R. Bowker, 1990–1991.

Jackson, May Howard (1877–1931)

Born in Philadelphia, Pennsylvania, the academic sculptor May Howard Jackson was a graduate of the Pennsylvania Academy of Fine Arts in her native city. Jackson's work is represented in private and public permanent collections, including St. Thomas' Church, Philadelphia, Pennsylvania; Dunbar High School and Howard University—both in Washington, D.C.

Bibliography
Fielding, Mantle. *Dictionary of American Painters, Sculptors, and Gravers.* Apollo Books, 1986.

Jackson, Sarah (1924–)

Born in Detroit, Michigan, the multitalented sculptor Sarah Jackson earned a Bachelor's degree from the University of London, England (1946), and received a Master's degree from Wayne State University, Detroit, Michigan.

Jackson has held many solo exhibitions in Canada and abroad, including the Apollinaire Gallery, London, England (1951); New Vision Gallery, London (1956); the Art Club, Montréal, Québec, Canada (1957); Roberts Gallery, Toronto, Canada (1961, 1962); Galerie Libre, Montréal, Canada (1962, 1963, 1967); Carmen Lamanna Gallery, Toronto (1967); and others. Her commissioned work, wall sculptures and other three-dimensional works that are integral parts of the architecture of a project, are in many venues in England and Canada. Other aspects of her sculpture exhibit a full range of emotions. Examples of her drawings, xerographs, and sculpture are in private and public permanent collections.

Bibliography
Charent, Brian. "An Interview with Sarah Jackson." *Artmagazine* 6:20 (Winter 1975): 14–17.
McKeeman, Karl. "Printmaking in Nova Scotia." *Artmagazine* 8:31–32 (March–April 1977): 18–22.
Pacey, Elizabeth. "The Artist and the Machine." *Atlantic Advocate* 67:9 (May 1977): 62–65.

Jackson, Suzanne Fitzallen (1944–)

Born in St. Louis, Missouri, Suzanne Fitzallen Jackson has been known as a writer, a costume designer, and for her work in the ballet. It is for her creative abilities as a painter, however, that she is best known and for which she has received national recognition. Her paintings—washed acrylics applied in layers—are filled with a juxtaposition of abstract and figurative imagery as she combines reminiscences from her African-American background with an interest in the metaphysical.

Jackson's involvement in the arts led her to pursue a Bachelor of Arts degree from San Francisco State College, California, and a Master of Fine Arts degree from Yale University, New Haven, Connecticut. Since then her work has been exhibited in many exhibitions across the country. In 1974 she was one of twenty artists included in "Directions of Afro-American Art," exhibited at the Herbert F. Johnson Museum of Art at Cornell University, Ithaca, New York. She also participated in the travelling exhibition, "19-Sixties," organized by the California Museum of African-American History and Culture (1981–1989).

Jackson's creative talents have also been used in other professional pursuits. She was selected as vice chairperson for the California Arts Council (1975–1978) and served on the Century City Cultural Commission, California (1977–1978). In 1985 her endeavors extended to work overseas as project director of the Cultural Exchange Program, Lagos, Nigeria, which was a part of the Wajumbe Cultural Institute in San Francisco, California. Additionally, she has lectured and accepted fellowships at a number of institutes and schools, including San Francisco State University and the California Institute for Women—both in California.

Jackson's paintings have been acquired for several public and private permanent collections, including the Palm Springs Desert Museum, California; the Indianapolis Museum of Art, Indiana; and the California Museum of Afro-American Art. She was a nominee for the first national award in the visual arts in 1981.

Kim Caldwell-Meeks

Bibliography
Hazlitt, Gordon J. "Creating Her Own World." *ArtNews* 73 (November 1974): 38–39.
Igoe, Lyn Moody. *250 Years of Afro-American Art: An Annotated Bibliography.* R.R. Bowker Co., 1981.
Who's Who in American Art: 1993–1994. 20th ed. R.R. Bowker Co., 1993.

Jackson, Vera (1912–)

A photographer active in the 1930s, Vera Jackson was born on July 21, 1912, in Wichita, Kansas. She spent her teenage years living on a farm in Corona, California, with her father, who was a book collector and amateur photographer. After she finished high school she married Vernon Jackson and had two sons. Her interest in the camera stemmed from her love and admiration for her father.

In 1936 Jackson began to take government-sponsored photography classes taught by George Manuel, where she learned about the use of camera equipment, as well as processing techniques. Receiving recognition for her photographs of family and friends while attending classes at Frank Wiggins (a career high school), Jackson was hired as a staff photographer for the *California Eagle*, where she photographed all aspects of society, ranging from sports events to the theater. After accumulating a large body of works in the 1940s Jackson left the newspaper to continue her education, receiving her Bachelor of Arts and Master of Arts degrees in education and began to teach in the Los Angeles City School System.

Jackson took her photographic skills around the world, including four trips to Africa. Through these works she brought understanding and value to the human condition, opening new horizons while creating beautiful photographs. Jackson's exhibitions include the Vernon Library; the Los Angeles County Public Library and the Afro-American Museum of History and Culture—both in Los Angeles, California; and the Museum of Art in San Francisco, California. Her works can be found in permanent collections throughout the state of California.

Melissa J. Guenther

Bibliography

Moutoussamy-Ashe, Jeanne. *Viewfinders: Black Women Photographers.* Dodd, Mead & Co., 1986.

Willis-Thomas, Deborah. *An Illustrated Bio-Bibliography of Black Photographers 1940–1988.* Garland, 1989.

Jacobi, Lotte (1896–1990)

Born in West Prussia, Germany, and noted for her searching portraits of world figures in the arts and sciences—as well as abstract compositions—the photographer Lotte Jacobi came from a line of photographers reaching back to her great-grandfather. She received instruction at the Bavarian State Academy of Photography and the University of Munich, Germany, in the mid-1920s. From 1927 until 1935, when she left Nazi Germany for the United States, Jacobi managed her father's photo studio in Berlin. Later on, in the early 1960s, she studied at the University of New Hampshire, Durham, which honored her with an honorary Doctorate degree in 1974.

Winner of many awards and honors, Jacobi was the recipient of a silver medal from the Royal Photography Salon, Tokyo, Japan (1931); first prize in *Life* magazine's "British War Relief Photography Competition" (1941); first prize at the New Hampshire Art Association exhibition (1970); an honor award from the National Women's Caucus for Art, Philadelphia, Pennsylvania (1983); and others. Representative examples of her work are in private and public permanent collections, including the National Portrait Gallery, Smithsonian Institution, Washington, D.C.; and many others.

Bibliography

Brodsky, Judith E., and Ofelia Garcia. *Printed by Women: A National Exhibition of Photographs and Prints.* Philadelphia: Port of History Museum, 1983.

Greve, Ludwig. *Berlin-New York: Portrats von Lotte Jacobi.* Marbach am Necker. 1982.

Moore, Gaylen. "Lotte Jacobi: Born with a Photographer's Eye." *The New York Times Magazine* (September 16, 1979): 43–44, 69–71, 74–81.

Jacobs, Ferne (1942–)

Born in Illinois, the sculptor/fiber artist Ferne Jacobs attended several undergraduate schools, including Art Center College of Design, Los Angeles, California (1960–1963); Pratt Institute, New York City (1964–1965); and California State University at Long Beach (1966–1967). She taught at California State University at Los Angeles (1972), and earned a Master of Fine Arts degree from Claremont College, California, in 1976.

Jacobs's work has been invited to many group exhibitions in the United States and abroad, including "Fiber Structures," Denver Art Museum, Colorado (1972); "Sculpture in Fiber," Museum of Contemporary Crafts, New York City (1972); "In Praise of Hands," World Crafts Council, Toronto, Canada (1974); "First International Exhibition of Miniature Textiles," British Crafts Centre, London, England (1974); "Opening Group Exhibition," the Hadler Galleries, New York City (1975); "American Crafts '76," Museum of Contemporary Art, Chicago, Illinois (1976); and others. Her work is represented in private and public permanent collections in the United States and elsewhere, including the Royal Scottish Museum, Edinburgh.

Bibliography

Fiberworks. A Catalog. Essay by Evelyn Svec Ward. Cleveland Museum of Art, 1977.

Jacobs, Helen Nichols (1924–)

Born in Kent, Connecticut, Helen Nichols Jacobs studied at Marot Junior College (1940–1942) and learned composition in oil painting from her father, Spencer B. Nichols, a member of the National Academy of Design, New York City. Jacobs also studied for many years at the Ridgewood Art Institute, New Jersey, with Arthur Maynard, who shared his knowledge of the effects of light on form. The advice and counsel of these two sources of painting techniques is synthesized in Jacobs's convincing landscapes, seascapes, and still-life works.

Jacobs has exhibited her paintings in regional and national exhibitions, including Lever House, the National Academy of Design, the National Arts Club, and the Salmagundi Club—all in New York City; the Kent Art Association, Connecticut; Bergen County Museum, New Jersey; and others. She has won many honors and awards for her paintings, including the memorial award from the Hudson Valley Art Association, New York (1991), and the non-member award of the Salmagundi Club, New York City (1992). She also received an award from the Grand National juried show of the American Artists Professional League (1991) and, two years earlier, their award for "best atmospheric effect."

Jacobs has been an instructor at the Ridgewood Art Institute for more than two decades; a member of the Kent Art Association, Connecticut; the Hudson Valley Artists Association, New York; the Ridgewood Art Institute; the Catherine Lorillard Wolfe Art Club, New York City; and a fellow of the American Artists Professional League. Her work is represented in private and public permanent collections throughout the United States, including the American Broadcasting Company, New York Life Insurance Company, Burns & Roe, Ernst & Whinney, and many others.

Bibliography

Anonymous. "KAA's Final Exhibition for the 1987 Season." *Kent Good Town Daily* (September 17, 1987).

Safran, Rose. "PS Galleries Offer New Exhibits." *The York Weekly*, Maine. (June 26, 1991): 7A.

Who's Who in American Art. 19th ed. R.R. Bowker Co., 1991–1992.

Jacobs, Katja (1939–)

Katja Jacobs was born in Germany and studied printmaking at the Akademie der Bildenden Künste in Freiburg, Germany, and the École des Beaux-Arts in Brussels, Belgium. She arrived in Canada in 1963, where she is known in Toronto principally as a painter. Her work generally has a boldly abstract appearance, sometimes consisting of slips of indeterminate space generated by nervously calligraphic lines reminiscent of Jackson Pollock. In some respects, however, the work is not abstract at all, for on some surfaces she collages various kinds of materials, each with an implicit association or memory. In other instances, the calligraphic streams seem to swirl and eddy around vaguely suggestive images, each of which, presumably, has its own metaphoric possibilities.

Robert J. Belton

Bibliography

Wilken, Karen. *Katja Jacobs: Recent Works.* Agnes Etherington Art Centre, Queen's University, 1986.

Jacquette, Yvonne (1934–)

Best known for her night views of urban cities, Yvonne Jacquette was born in Pittsburgh, Pennsylvania, and attended the Rhode Island School of Design, Providence (1952–1956), where she studied with John Frazier and Robert Hamilton. Jacquette also worked with Herman Cherry and Robert Roche.

Between 1965 and 1991 Jacquette has held nineteen solo exhibitions of her work in the United States and abroad, including Swarthmore College, Pennsylvania (1965); Brooke Alexander, New York City (1976, 1979, 1981–1983, 1986, 1988, 1991); Yurakucho Seibu, Takanawa, Tokyo, Japan (1985); "Looking Down: Prints by Yvonne Jacquette," Syracuse University, New York (1988); and others. Her work has been invited to more than three score group exhibitions, some of which travelled throughout the United States, such as "Exhibition of Work by Newly Elected Members and Recipients of Awards," American Academy and Institute of Arts and Letters, New York City (1990); "Nocturnal Visions in Contemporary Painting," Whitney Museum of American Art at Equitable Center, New York City (1989): "Making Their Mark: Women Artists Today—A Documentary Survey 1970–1985," a travelling show to Cincinnati, Ohio; New Orleans, Louisiana; Denver, Colorado; and Philadelphia, Pennsylvania (1989): "Interiors & Exteriors: Contemporary Realist Prints," Yale University, New Haven, Connecticut (1986); "An International Survey of Recent Painting and Sculpture," Museum of Modern Art (MoMA), New York City (1984): "The American Artist as Printmaker: 23rd National Print Exhibition," the Brooklyn Museum, New York (1983); and many others.

Set designer and illustrator of several books of poetry, Jacquette lives and works in New York City and on a farm in Maine. She has been a visiting artist at the University of Pennsylvania, Philadelphia, and the Nova Scotia College of Art, and has also taught at Parsons School of Design, New York City. "Northwest View from the Empire State Building" (1982), a not atypical lithograph of Jacquette's print output, reveals her remarkable love for the aerial panorama.

Jacquette's work is in many permanent museum and university collections, including the Staatliche Museum, Berlin, Germany; the Metropolitan Museum of Art, the Museum of Modern Art (MoMA), Museum of the City of New York, the Brooklyn Museum, the American Academy and Institute of Arts and Letters, and the Whitney Museum of American Art—all in New York City; and others.

Bibliography

Field, Richard S., and Ruth E. Fine. *A Graphic Muse.* Hudson Hills Press, 1987.

McGeevy, Linda. "Yvonne Jacquette." *Arts Magazine* 63: 1 (September 1988): 92.

Storr, Robert. "Yvonne Jacquette at Brooke Alexander." *Art in America* 74:7 (July 1986): 118, 120.

Jagger, Gillian (1930–)

Born in London, England, Gillian Jagger earned her Bachelor of Fine Arts degree from the Carnegie Institute of Technology, Pittsburgh, Pennsylvania; studied with Vaclov Vytlacil at the Colorado Springs Fine Arts Center, Colorado; and completed further studies at the University of Buffalo, New York, and Columbia University, New York City, obtaining a Master of Arts degree from New York University, also in New York City.

Jagger has held a number of solo exhibitions of her work in the Ruth White Gallery (1961, 1963, 1964); Finch College Museum (1964); Lerner-Heller Gallery (1971, 1973, 1975, 1977); and Anita Shapolsky Gallery (1991)—all in New York City; and others. Her work has been invited to numerous group exhibitions and two-person shows throughout the United States.

Jagger is a Guggenheim Foundation fellow (1983), was a textile designer for Wamsutta Mills (1955–1957), a lecturer on art for Radio Free Europe, a teacher and a professor of art at many institutions, including New York University, Post College, New Rochelle Academy, and Pratt Institute, Brooklyn—all in New York. Jagger has also taught at several other professional art schools. Her most recent sculptures are formed of hammered lead sheets, somewhat reminiscent of the torsos and heads created by the late Saul Baizerman.

Jagger's work is in private, corporate, and public permanent collections, including the Finch College Museum, New York City; the Carnegie Institute of Technology, Pittsburgh, Pennsylvania; Brompton's, Montréal, Québec, Canada; and many others.

Bibliography

Brenson, Michael. "Art in Review: Hammered Lead from Gillian Jagger." *The New York Times* (July 12, 1991).

Who's Who in American Art. 19th ed. R.R. Bowker Co., 1991–1992.

James, Ann (1925–)

Born in Hove, Sussex, England, the sculptor/ceramist/painter Ann James emigrated to Canada in 1945 after having studied at the Brighton School of Art in her native country. James took further study at the University of Saskatchewan, Regina, Canada, under the tutelage of Ric Gomez, Kenneth Lochhead, Arthur McKay, and Jack Sures.

James's wry humor was revealed in a solo exhibition at the Regina Public Library, Saskatchewan (1968), which evoked the full range of middle-class emotions to an avant-garde show. Her work has been included in many group exhibitions, including the Saskatchewan Arts Board Show, Regina (1965); the Diamond Jubilee Show (1966), at which one of her paintings was singled out by the noted critic Clement Greenberg; and others.

James has travelled widely in Europe and the Far East for research and study. Her work is represented in private and public permanent collections.

Bibliography
Fitzrandoph, Katie. "Nothing Tame About James' Art at the Central Library." *Regina Leader Post* (October 1, 1968).
Shuebrook, Ron. "Regina Funk." *Art and Artists* 8:5 (August 1973): 38–41.

James, Rebecca Salsbury (1891–1968)

Born in London, England, the self-taught painter Rebecca Salsbury James exhibited in museums and galleries, including Alfred Stieglitz's American Place, New York City (1932); the "Annual Exhibitions" offered by the Painters of the Southwest; and others. Examples of her work are in private and public permanent collections, such as the Denver Art Museum, Colorado; Museum of Art, Albuquerque, New Mexico; and others.

Bibliography
Dawdy, Doris Ostrander. *Artists of the American West*. Vol. 1. Swallow Press, 1974.
Samuels, Peggy, and Harold Samuels. *The Illustrated Biographical Encyclopedia of Artists of the American West*. Doubleday and Co., 1976.

Janvier, Catharine Ann (Drinker) (1841–1922)

A Philadelphia native, Catherine Ann (Drinker) Janvier spent her early youth in China, where her sea-captain father, Sandwith Drinker, had become a merchant. Upon his death in 1857 the family set sail for America—a journey made notable by young Janvier's navigation of the ship when the captain was drunk. Not long after the family was settled in Baltimore, Maryland, her mother died. Janvier again took the helm, managing her mother's school for girls and supporting her sister, brother, and grandmother. During this time Janvier began the study of art at the Maryland Institute in Baltimore. Moving to Philadelphia, Pennsylvania, she taught at Miss Sanford's Girls' School and subsequently studied at the Pennsylvania Academy of Fine Arts, Pennsylvania, where two of her teachers were Thomas Eakins and the Dutch painter Adolph van der Whelan. Janvier promoted the cause of female art students by calling for a "serious" women's class in life drawing and eventually became the first woman to teach at the Pennsylvania Academy, giving a series of lectures on perspective. (Cecilia Beaux, a relative and protégée of Janvier, later was hired at the Academy as its first permanent female faculty member.)

In 1878 she married Thomas Allibone Janvier; in 1880 she won the Mary Smith prize—a major award at the Pennsylvania Academy of Fine Arts—for her painting "The Guitar Player." Travelling abroad with her husband, she became noted for her translations of French romantic novels, and she published her own works, including *Practical Keramics for Students* (1880) and *London Mews* (1904). Her intense love of literature is reflected in her paintings and illustrations, many of which are historical, mythological, and Biblical scenes.

Cynthia Lee Kerfoot

Bibliography
Beaux, Cecilia. *Background with Figures*. Houghton Mifflin Co., 1930.
Dunford, Penny. *A Biographical Dictionary of Women Artists in Europe and America since 1850*. University of Pennsylvania Press, 1989.
Rubinstein, Charlotte Streifer. *American Women Artists: From Early Times to the Present*. Avon, 1982.

Jaques, Bertha Evelyn Clausen (1863–1941)

A prolific etcher, Bertha Evelyn Clausen Jaques organized the Chicago Society of Etchers in 1910. Composed of members from around the United States and abroad, the Society under her leadership initiated the twentieth-century etching revival. Jaques was born in Covington, Ohio. She wrote poetry and worked as a reporter to support herself and her mother before she married surgeon W.K. Jaques in 1889 and moved to Chicago, Illinois. Except for two months of drawing instruction from Caroline Wade at the Art Institute of Chicago, Illinois, around 1900, Jaques was self-taught. Using Maxime Lalanne's *A Treatise on Etching* as her instruction book, she began to experiment with etching in 1893. She reportedly pulled the first etching ever to be printed in Chicago in 1897 on a press she had imported from Milwaukee. Jaques first exhibited her work in 1903 at the Art Institute of Chicago, Illinois.

Among her contributions to the art of etching are her own instruction book, *Concerning Etchings*, which she published in 1912. As secretary-treasurer for twenty-seven years, she was instrumental in organizing two annual travelling exhibitions a year for the Chicago Society of Etchers. They were often co-sponsored by the Art Institute of Chicago. Her etchings were exhibited with the Society throughout the country, including the New York Public Library, New York City; the University of Chicago Art Gallery, Illinois; the Detroit Public Library and Society of Arts and Crafts—both in Detroit, Michigan; the Boston Public Library and Massachusetts State College, Amherst—both in Massachusetts; the University of Oregon Art Museum, Eugene; the City Art Museum, St. Louis, Missouri; Crocker Art Gallery, Sacramento, California; University of Kentucky Museum, Lexington; Antioch College, Yellow Springs, Ohio; and the Smithsonian Institution, Washington, D.C. Works by many artists were sold through these exhibitions.

Jaques made direct, straight-forward etchings of urban and rural views, landscapes, and seascapes while gradually assimilating into her work the use of drypoint, aquatint, color, and various formal devices which had been developed in the late nineteenth century. Subjects include scenes from her travels in the United States, Europe, Egypt, and Japan, where she visited her friend and fellow printmaker, Helen Hyde. She also produced almost 100 simple floral and plant compositions based on Japanese flower design. She drew the images with etching and drypoint, then used aquatint to add color. The Smithsonian Institution, Washington, D.C., exhibited her color aquatints in 1930.

Jaques's prints were collected by the Art Institute of Chicago, Illinois; the Philadelphia Museum of Art, Pennsylvania; the New York Public Library, New York City; the Library of Congress, Washington, D.C.; the Fine Arts Museum of San Francisco, California; the National Museum of American Art, and the National Museum of American History—both in Washington, D.C.

Phyllis Peet

Bibliography
"A Leader Retires." *Art Digest* 12 (October 15, 1939): 25.
Bertha E. Jaques Papers. Archives of American Art, Smithsonian Institution, Washington, D.C.

Bertha E. Jaques (1863–1941): An American Printmaker, A Retrospective, April–May 1982. Houston, Texas: Gerhard Wurzer Gallery, 1982.

Exhibition of Etchings–Aquatints–Drypoints and Drypoints in Color by Bertha E. Jaques. Chicago: The Chicago Society of Etchers and Albert Roullier Art Galleries, 1939.

Jaques, Bertha E. *Concerning Etchings.* 1912.

Jaramillo, Virginia (1939–)

Born in El Paso, Texas, the painter Virginia Jaramillo studied at Otis Art Institute, Los Angeles, California (1958–1961). She has received many honors and grants, including grants from the Ford Foundation (1962); National Endowment for the Arts (NEA) (1972–1973); and a Creative Artists Public Service (CAPS) grant from New York State (1975).

Jaramillo has exhibited work in solo and group exhibitions, including the "Annual," Whitney Museum of American Art, New York City (1972); "Contemporary Reflections 1971–1972," Aldrich Museum of Contemporary Art, Ridgefield, Connecticut (1972); Douglas Drake Gallery, Kansas City, Kansas (1975, 1976); "Contemporary Art," a travelling show throughout Eastern Europe (1976); and others. Representative examples of her work are in private and public permanent collections, including the Aldrich Museum of Contemporary Art, Ridgefield, Connecticut; Long Beach Museum of Art and Pasadena Art Museum—both in California; National Museum of Women in the Arts, Washington, D.C.; Schenectady Museum, New York; and others.

Bibliography
¡Mira! The Canadian Club Hispanic Art Tour III. Farmington Hills, Michigan: Canadian Club, 1988.
1972 Annual Exhibition. Whitney Museum of American Art, 1972.
National Museum of Women in the Arts. Harry N. Abrams, 1987.

Jaudon, Valerie (1945–)

Born in Greenville, Mississippi, the painter Valerie Jaudon learned her craft in several venues, including Mississippi State College for Women, Columbus (1963–1965); Memphis Academy of Art, Tennessee (1965); University of the Americas, Mexico City, Mexico (1966–1967); and St. Martin's School of Art, London, England (1968–1969).

Jaudon has shown her unique pattern paintings in museums and galleries in the United States and abroad, in solo and in group shows, including the Museum of Modern Art (MoMA), New York City (1975); the Albright-Knox Art Gallery, Buffalo, New York (1976); the Pennsylvania Academy of Fine Arts, Philadelphia (1977); Galerie Bishofberger, Zurich, Switzerland (1979); Galerie Hans Strelow, Dusseldorf (1980), and Quadrat Museum, Bottrop—both in Germany (1983); and many others. In collaboration with the architect Romaldo Giurgola she has executed many commissions, including tile work, ceiling murals, fountains, and courtyards. "Yazoo City" (1975), a six-by-six-foot oil on canvas, is not atypical of her work of this period: it consists of a meticulous, complex, linear pattern painting that transports the viewer to Jaudon's world.

Examples of Jaudon's work are in private and public permanent collections, including the Aldrich Museum of Contemporary Art, Ridgefield, Connecticut; Hirshhorn Museum and Sculpture Garden, Washington, D.C.; Louisiana Museum, Denmark; and others.

Bibliography
Goldin, Amy. "The Body Language of Pictures." *Artforum* 16 (March 1978): 54–59.
Perreault, John. "Allusive Depths: Valerie Jaudon." *Art in America* 71 (October 1983): 162–65.
Westfall, Stephen. "Review." *Arts Magazine* 60 (December 1985): 125.

Jencks, Penelope (1936–)

Born in Baltimore, Maryland, the figurative sculptor Penelope Jencks studied at the Hans Hofmann School, Provincetown, Massachusetts (1956); attended the Skowhegan School of Painting and Sculpture, Maine, where she studied with Harold Tovish (1957); earned a Bachelor of Fine Arts degree in drawing and painting from Boston University (1958), and studied sculpture with Ernest Morenon at the School of the Museum of Fine Arts—both in Boston, Massachusetts (1959); and did advanced work at the Staatliche Akademie der Bildenden Künste, Stuttgart, Germany (1960).

Jencks has held solo exhibitions in galleries and museums, including the Landmark Gallery, New York City (1977, 1981); the Art Institute of Boston (1978), and the Helen Shlien Gallery—both in Boston, Massachusetts (1981, 1985). She has been artist-in-residence at the MacDowell Colony, Peterborough, New Hampshire (1975), received a grant from the Massachusetts Artists Foundation (1977), and a commendation for design excellence from the National Endowment for the Arts (NEA) (1981).

Jencks's work has been included in many group shows throughout the Northeastern area of the United States since 1966 and is represented in private, public, and corporate permanent collections and sites, such as the bronze and granite fourteen-foot monument to "Samuel Eliot Morrison" (1982), on Commonwealth Avenue near Exeter Street, Boston; and works at Brandeis University, Waltham; Bunker Hill Pavilion, Charlestown; Chelsea Square, Chelsea, Garrett Associates, Cambridge—all in Massachusetts; the Federal Courthouse, Danbury, Connecticut; Promenade Park, Toledo, Ohio; and others.

Bibliography
Faxon, Alicia, and Sylvia Moore. *Pilgrims and Pioneers.* Midmarch Arts Press, 1987, pp. 85–86, 96.
Living American Artists and the Figure. The Pennsylvania State University, 1974.
Parry, Marian. "An Interview with Penelope Jencks." *American Artist* 37:373 (August 1973): 36–39, 64.
Watson-Jones, Virginia. *Contemporary American Women Sculptors.* Oryx Press, 1986.

Jenkins, Connie (1945–)

Born in Lubbock, Texas, the realist painter Connie Jenkins earned a Bachelor of Fine Arts degree from the University of Colorado, Boulder (1967), and, five years later, received a Master of Fine Arts degree from the same institution.

Jenkins has held solo exhibitions of her work in galleries, including the 1309 Gallery, Boulder, Colorado (1972); and Artspace, Los Angeles (1978); California State University, Long Beach (1978); Los Angeles Municipal Gallery, Barnsdall Park (1981); and Koplin Gallery, Los Angeles (1982, 1984–1985, 1988, 1993)—all in California.

Her paintings have been invited to many group exhibitions in the United States, such as "A Mighty Fortress is Our Art," Denver Center, Colorado (1971); "Opening Show," Womanspace (1973); "Current Concerns," Los Angeles Institute of Contemporary Art (1975); and "Directions in Southern California Realism," Cedars-Sinai Medical Center (1977)—both in Los Angeles, California; "California Realist Painters," Nevada Fine Arts Center, Reno (1978); "Painting and Photography: Relationships," Harbor College, San Pedro, California (1981); "West Coast Realism," a travelling show from Spiva Art Center, Joplin, Missouri, to Texas, Nevada, and Florida (1985); "Artists Recall: Art against U.S. Intervention in Central America," Los Angeles City College (1987); and "Group Show," Koplin Gallery (1989)—both in Los Angeles, California; and others.

From 1974 to 1989 Jenkins has taught drawing and painting at a number of art schools and universities in California; she has been a three-term elected member and a past-president of the Santa Monica-Malibu Board of Education and plays an active role in the aesthetic, political, and spiritual affairs of Southern California. "Cycles: In Memory of Ken Edwards" (1991), a not atypical six-by-fifteen-foot oil on canvas, reveals her meticulous approach to reality and illusion. In 1987 the California Legislature named her "Woman of the Year," 44th District. Her works are represented in private and public collections in the United States and abroad.

Bibliography
Anderson, Isabel. "Connie Jenkins at Koplin." *Images and Issues* (March–April 1983).
Brown, Betty Ann, and Arlene Raven. *Women and Their Art*. New Sage Press, 1989.
Morrow, Maria. *Inside the LA Artist*. Peregrine Smith, 1988.
Nieto, Margaret. "The Political and the Esthetic." *Artweek* (November 9, 1985).

Jewett, Maude Sherwood (1873–)

Born in Englewood Cliffs, New Jersey, the sculptor Maude Sherwood Jewett studied her craft at the Art Students League, New York City. Her sculptural works are represented in a number of permanent collections and sites, including the Fountain in the Cleveland Museum, Ohio; and the Soldiers and Sailors War Memorial, East Hampton, New York. Jewett fashioned numbers of sundials of more than passing interest.

Bibliography
American Art Annual. Vol. 30. American Federation of Arts, 1933.
Fielding, Mantle. *Dictionary of American Painters, Sculptors, and Engravers*. Modern Books and Crafts, 1974.
Kohlman, Rena Tucker. "America's Women Sculptors." *International Studio* 76 (1922): 225–35.

Jiménez Gutiérrez, Eloísa (c. 1917–)

Born in León, Guanajuato, Mexico, Eloísa Jiménez was a disciple of Antonio Segoviano from the age of thirteen; from him she learned how to mix color, to shade, and to develop visual compositions.

Jiménez's work comprises three stages: until 1940 she painted only portraits; from 1940 to 1950 she perfected the technique of painting miniatures in oil; and after 1950, she went full-circle, by returning to the portrait, but in a more imaginative style and in larger format. Jiménez uses her own special formulae and her own techniques in the preparation of canvas and paper. She works exclusively in oils, and her favorite themes are portraits of village people, ancestors, and contemporaries.

In 1962 Jiménez was heralded as the prime restorer of the miniature in Mexico and was compared with Eugène Isabey. She has shown her work in many institutions in Mexico and abroad, but has not left León because of her fallible health situation; in 1988 she continues to be active in her native city.

Bibliography
Alvarez, José Rogelio, et al. *Enciclopedia de México*. Secretaría de Educación Pública, 1987.

Jiménez, Sarah (1928–)

Born in Piedras Negras, Coahuila, Mexico, Sarah Jiménez studied at la Escuela de Pintura y Escultura (La Esmeralda) in Mexico City. Since 1957 she has participated in group printmaking shows at the Salón de Grabado of the Instituto Nacional de Bellas Artes and in many solo and group exhibitions in Mexico and abroad. Jiménez is a member of the Taller de Gráfica Popular and is a teacher of drawing.

Jiménez works in woodcut, linoleum, and lithography; her themes are social in character. The protagonists of daily life populate her prints, which speak eloquently for the indigent.

Bibliography
Alvarez, José Rogelio, et al. *Enciclopedia de México*. Secretaría de Educación Pública, 1987.

Johanson, Patricia (1940–)

A native New Yorker, Patricia Johanson is known for her sensitive integration of architecture, landscape architecture, painting, and sculpture in large-scale projects, employing local flora as food and dwelling for insects, animals, birds, and reptiles. Johanson received her formal education in several institutions, including a Bachelor of Arts degree from Bennington College, Vermont (1962), where she studied with Tony Smith and worked for Joseph Cornell during the non-resident term; a Master of Arts degree in art history from Hunter College, New York City (1964); and a Bachelor of Architecture degree from the City College (CUNY) School of Architecture, New York (1977).

Winner of many awards and honors for her work, Johanson was a Guggenheim fellow (1970, 1980); a National Endowment for the Arts (NEA) fellow (1975); recipient of the International Women's Year award (1976) and a gold medal from the Accademia Italia Delle Arti, Parma, Italy (1979); and delegate to "Survival and the Arts," a global forum, Sundance Institute, Utah (1991).

Widely travelled and even more widely published, Johanson has been commissioned to plan and design sites throughout the United States. Her work has been shown in myriad solo and group exhibitions throughout the world. "Fair Park Lagoon," Dallas, Texas (1981), a not impressive aquatic site over five blocks long, was transmuted by Johanson into a unique environmental "sculpture" that was designated a national historic landmark five years later. Commenting on it recently, she wrote, "As one walks out onto these vast sculptures, the 'art' dissolves and the person is left with his or her own focus and thoughts. So instead of the imposed vision of the artist, the lagoon allows for the development of a multitude of subjective situations." "Endangered Garden" at Candlestick Cove in the San Francisco area, transformed a sewer into a sculptural landscape haven (over a third-of-a-mile long) for birds, insects, and aquatic life at risk. Johanson recently completed a public art master plan for Rockland County, New York and a "Park for a Rainforest" for "Projeto Omame" in Brasilia, Brazil (1992).

Johanson's works are represented in many permanent collections and on sites in the United States and abroad, including the Metropolitan Museum of Art, and Museum of Modern Art (MoMA)—both in New York City; National Museum of Women in the Arts, Washington, D.C.; Dallas Museum of Art, Texas; Bennington College, Vermont; Brandeis University, Waltham, Massachusetts; Storm King Art Center, Mountainville, New York; and many others.

Bibliography
Campbell, Laurence. "Patricia Johanson." *Art in America* (December 1983): 148.
Garris, Laurie. "The Changing Landscape: Patricia Johanson." *Arts and Architecture* 3:4 (1985): 56–59.
Johanson, Patricia. *Art and Survival: Creative Solutions to Environmental Problems*. Vancouver, B.C.: Gallery Women Artists Monographs, 1992.
———. "Patricia Johanson." *Gallerie*. Vancouver, B.C.: An Annual. 1989.
Matilsky, Barbara. *Fragile Ecologies: Artists Interpretations and Solutions*. Universe Books/Rizzoli International, 1992.

John, Grace Spaulding (1890–1972)

Born in Battle Creek, Michigan, the painter/writer/lecturer Grace Spaulding John studied with Daniel Garber, Charles Hawthorne, and Fred Weber. Examples of her portraits and murals are represented in private and public permanent collections, including the Museum of Fine Arts, Houston; Sam Houston Normal Library, Huntsville; and Houston Central Library—all in Texas; the Historical Society, Oklahoma City, Oklahoma; and others.

Bibliography
American Art Annual. Vol. 30. American Federation of Arts, 1933.
Moore, Sylvia. *No Bluebonnets, No Yellow Roses: Essays on Texas Women in the Arts*. Midmarch Arts Press, 1988.
O'Brien, Esse F. *Art and Artists of Texas*. Tardy Publishing Co., 1935.

Johnson, Adelaide (1859–1955)

Reared in Plymouth, Illinois, the talented young sculptor Adelaide Johnson attended the St. Louis School of Design, Missouri. Despite perennial financial difficulties Johnson did further study in Chicago, Illinois, and the generous settlement for an accident allowed her still further study in Dresden, Germany, and Rome, Italy (1883–1884).

An early feminist, Johnson exhibited four busts of prestigious American suffragettes in the Women's Building at the Chicago International Exposition of 1893, Illinois. She set up studios in a number of cities in the United States and Europe, including New York City; Chicago, Illinois; Washington, D.C.; London, England; and Rome, Italy.

In 1921 Johnson reached a long-term goal: she sited a monumental work, addressed to the women's movement in the U.S. Capitol building at Washington, D.C. Both her work and her financial health were in decline after 1930. Her works are represented in private and public permanent collections, including the U.S. Capitol and the Smithsonian Institution—both in Washington, D.C.; the Metropolitan Museum of Art, New York City; and others.

Bibliography
Mayo, Edith. "Johnson, Adelaide." *Notable American Women: The Modern Period*. Harvard University Press, 1980.
Smith, Jean B. Cook. "Life in Marble—Speech in Silence: Adelaide Johnson and Her Work." *The New American Woman* (June 1917).
Weimann, Jeanne Madeline. *The Fair Women*. Academy Chicago, 1981.

Johnson, Buffie (1912–)

A native New Yorker, the painter Buffie Johnson studied at the Académie Julian, Paris, France; the Art Students League, New York City; with Francis Picabia at Atelier 17, Paris, France; and earned a Master of Arts degree from the University of California at Los Angeles (UCLA).

Johnson taught at Parsons School of Design, New York City (1946–1950), and has held solo exhibitions of her work in many galleries and museums, including the New School for Social Research, Betty Parsons Gallery, and the Max Hutchinson Gallery—all in New York City; the Stamford Museum, Connecticut; and others. Johnson's work has been included in major group shows in galleries and museums, including showings at the Biennials of the Whitney Museum of American Art, New York City.

Johnson has been the recipient of awards and honors, including a Yaddo fellowship, Saratoga Springs, New York; a Bollingen Foundation award; an Edward Albee Foundation fellowship; and others. Her work is represented in private and public permanent collections, including the Boston Museum of Fine Arts, Massachusetts; National Collection of Fine Arts, Washington, D.C.; Walker Art Center, Minneapolis, Minnesota; Whitney Museum of American Art, New York City; Yale University, New Haven, Connecticut; and many others.

Bibliography
De Lallier, Alexandra. "Buffie Johnson: Icons and Altarpieces to the Goddess." *Woman's Art Journal* 3:1 (Spring–Summer 1982): 29–34.
Kingsley, April. "The Primal Plants of Buffie Johnson." *Art International* (January–March 1981): 195–203.
Who's Who in American Art. 17th ed. R.R. Bowker Co., 1986.

Johnson, Grace Mott (1882–1967)

A native New Yorker, the sculptor Grace Mott Johnson studied her craft under the aegis of Gutzon Borglum. Winner of awards and honors, Johnson won the Macmillan sculpture prize at New York City's National Association of Women Painters and Sculptors (1917); their Joan of Arc medal (1927); and others. She was a member of the National Sculpture Society; the National Association of Women Painters and Sculptors; and Grand Central Galleries—all in New York City. Examples of her work appear in the Whitney Museum of American Art, New York City, as well as other public and private permanent collections.

Bibliography
American Art Annual. Vol. 30. American Federation of Arts, 1933.
Moore, Isabel. "A Sculptor of Animals." *The American Magazine of Art*
    14:2 (February 1923): 59–61.
Who's Who in American Art. 8th ed. American Federation of Arts, 1962.

Johnson, Lois M. (1942–)

A "cowgirl in the city" is how Lois M. Johnson has viewed herself since 1967, when she moved to Philadelphia, Pennsylvania, to join the printmaking department of the Philadelphia College of Art (now the University of the Arts). Born in Grand Forks, North Dakota, and raised there as well as in Fargo, North Dakota and Oslo, Minnesota, Johnson remains intrigued by the contrasts between the city's soaring, ornate architectural structures and the wide open spaces and big sky she experienced during her early years. Autobiographical experience rooted in these contrasting environments as well as the artist's frequent travels (mainly in the United States and Canada) have provided her essential subject matter; and in layering that rich visual texture she has embraced a conceptual forming that grows from collage, peppered by a film-strip format that probably developed from her early interest in pop art.

Johnson's primary work is in printmaking, and she has worked in virtually every major method—lithography and offset (the latter introduced to her by Claire Van Vliet), screenprinting, etching, the relief methods of woodcut and collagraph, and a number of photographic techniques such as cliché verre. She has explored these print media within a wide range of formats—single sheet works and portfolios, books (under her own Peripatetic Press imprint and with Janus Press), and environmental installations including site-specific pieces, some of which have been worked with her long-time collaborator, Phillips Simkin.

Johnson received her Bachelor of Fine Arts degree from the University of North Dakota (1964) and her Master of Fine Arts degree from the University of Wisconsin, Madison (1966). Her primary teaching has been at the University of the Arts, Philadelphia, Pennsylvania, although she has been a visiting artist and lecturer throughout the country. In Philadelphia she has twice been chair of the printmaking department, where she pioneered the use of waterbase screenprinting ink (for safety and health reasons) and was founding chair of the University's Master of Fine Arts program in the book arts.

Johnson's work has been in approximately twenty solo exhibitions and dozens of juried and invitational group shows throughout the United States; and it is in many important public and private collections.

Ruth E. Fine

Bibliography
Contemporary Philadelphia Artists: A Juried Exhibition. Philadelphia, 1990.
Courtney, Julis. *Artists Choose Artists.* Philadelphia, 1991.
Glassman, Elizabeth, and M.F. Symmes. *Cliché-Verre: Hand-Drawn, Light-Printed, A Survey of the Medium from 1939 to the Present.* Detroit, 1980.
Johnson, *Porett Simkin: Art in Science V.* Philadelphia, 1986. With two essays about Johnson and her work by Ruth E. Fine and a statement by the artist.
Johnson, Lois M., and Hester Stinnett. *Water-Based Inks: A Screenprinting Manual for Studio and Classroom.* Philadelphia, 1987. Rev. 1990.
Ross, John, Clare Romano, and Tim Ross. *The Complete Printmaker,* rev. ed. New York, 1990.

Johnson, Rae (1953–)

Born in Winnipeg, Manitoba, Canada, Rae Johnson studied art at the New School of Art, New York City (1975–1976), and at the Ontario College of Art (1977–1980) in Toronto. In 1981 Johnson became a founding member of the artist collective ChromaZone gallery that supported the rebirth of figurative painting. Johnson's work was included in the ChromaZone organized exhibitions: "Mondo Chroma" (1981), "Destroy Those Pictures!" (1981), "Monumenta" (1982), an exhibition held in conjunction with A Space, Gallery 76 and YYZ, all of Toronto, and "O KromaZone: die anderen von Kanada," held in Berlin, Germany. Since 1979 she has had numerous solo exhibitions and since 1983 she has been represented by the Carmen Lamanna Gallery in Toronto.

In her figurative paintings Johnson explores the role of women in society in the guise of virgin, whore, and displaced woman. The "Madonna Series" and the "Rachel Series" exemplify this exploration into feminine and sexual icons in which Johnson feels she shows the "dehumanization of woman . . . the detachment of the soul from the body." In 1987 Johnson moved to Northern Ontario and began to use the landscape as the subject of her work. Her out-of-doors sketches on small panels are in the tradition of the Group of Seven—painters whose work she had studied at the National Gallery of Canada in Ottawa as a youth. These sketches were later used as studies for larger landscape paintings that have a similar sense of tension and drama than her figurative work.

Linda Jansma

Bibliography
Genereux, Linda. *The Displaced Woman: Figure Paintings by Rae Johnson.* MacLaren Art Centre, 1990.
Lypchuk, Donna. "Back to the Landscape." *Canadian Art* 5:3 (Fall–September 1988): 106–09.

Johnson-Calloway, Marie E. (1920–)

Born in Baltimore, Maryland, the African-American artist Marie E. Johnson-Calloway attended what is now Coppin State College in her native city, then earned a Bachelor's degree in art education from Morgan State College, Baltimore (1952). Johnson-Calloway did further study at San José State University, California, where she received a Master of Arts degree in painting (1968).

Johnson-Calloway has exhibited her two- and three-dimensional painted plywood constructions in museums and galleries, including San José State University (1952, 1968); Horse's Mouth, Saratoga (1964); Oakland Art Museum (1967, 1968); Foothill College, Los Altos Hills (1967); San Francisco Women Artists Annual (1970)—all in California; and others.

Johnson-Calloway's figurative, painted constructions and environments transcend the specific and reveal her concerns about race and man's inhumanity to man. In addition to her professional work as a teacher and exhibiting artist, she is identified with the Bay Area Women Artists of Northern California, and is an active participant in community concerns. "Hope Street" (1971), a three-foot-square mixed-media work, reveals an aged African-American male looking out a window next to a live canary in a bird cage.

Johnson-Calloway, who taught at San José City College for many years, is represented in private, public, and corporate permanent collections, including the Johnson Publishing Company, Chicago, Illinois; the Oakland Art Museum, San Francisco Art Commission, San José City College, and San José State University—all in California; and others.

Bibliography
Bontemps, Arna Alexander, ed. *Forever Free: Art by African-American Women 1862–1980*. Illinois State University, 1980.
Fine, Elsa Honig. *The Afro-American Artist: A Search for Identity*. Holt, Rinehart & Winston, 1973.
Hedgepeth, Chester M. *Twentieth-Century African-American Writers and Artists*. Chicago: American Library Association, 1991.
Lewis, Samella, and Ruth G. Waddy. *Black Artists on Art*. Vol. 1. Contemporary Crafts, 1969.

Johnston, Frances Benjamin (1864–1952)

Known as a journalist, portraitist, architectural photographer, and recorder of social history, Frances Benjamin Johnston was born in Grafton, West Virginia, in 1864. She grew up in Rochester, New York, and then Washington, D.C. Johnston graduated from the Notre Dame Convent in Maryland and then studied painting and drawing at the Académie Julien in Paris during the years of 1883–1885. She returned to Washington and attended the Art Students League, New York City, and later, the Corcoran Gallery School, Washington, D.C.

Johnston began her career as a correspondent to a New York magazine and illustrated her articles with her own artwork. Eventually she used photographs to accompany her articles. George Eastman was a family friend, and it was from him that Johnston obtained a Kodak camera and began her apprenticeship with T.W. Smilie at the photographic laboratory of the Smithsonian Institution, Washington, D.C.

A two-part series on the U.S. Mint published in *Demorest's Family Magazine* in 1889 and 1890 was the first article illustrated with Johnston's own photographs. Other subjects photographed by Johnston include the Pennsylvania coal fields, Mammoth caves, West Point, Annapolis, and the interiors and exteriors of millionaires' homes such as the Astor and Vanderbuilt mansions.

In 1890 Johnston opened her own studio. It enjoyed immediate artistic and financial success.

The presidents' wives, first ladies "Mrs. Cleveland" and "Mrs. McKinley," came to the studio to pose with their cabinet ladies. Johnston also had the opportunity to photograph "Theodore Roosevelt's children" with text by Jacob A. Riis for a photographic story.

Also in 1892 Johnston photographed "The Evolution of A Great Exhibition" in Chicago, Illinois. She was then an assistant photographer to the U.S. government, and it was in Chicago that she took a group portrait of the delegates signing the Spanish-American peace protocol, which then became the basis for Theodore Chartran's painting of the event.

Beginning in 1896 Johnston's photos were being accepted for exhibitions both in America and abroad.

In 1899 Johnston was commissioned to photograph the "Hampton Institute," part of a pictorial essay on the Washington, D.C., school system for the Paris Exhibition of 1900. Hampton Institute of Virginia trained African-American and Native American youths in an integrated coeducational system of hands-on training consisting of domestic and agricultural arts and crafts.

Johnston photographed the members of African-American families in the Hampton community before and after a Hampton Institute education. These photos were later used by Booker T. Washington for articles on African-American education.

Johnston was the only American woman invited to attend the 3rd International Photographic Congress, held as an adjunct to the Exposition, and she was one of three American women to win a gold medal at the exposition.

In the summer of 1899 Johnston was commissioned by a news syndicate to photograph "Admiral George Dewey" on the U.S.S. *Olympia* on his return voyage after the triumphant battle of Manila. She became friends with Gertrude Käsebier when they served together as jurors for the Philadelphia Salon of Pictorial Photographers. Like Käsebier, not only did Johnston encourage women to become photographers, she championed those already in the profession. In 1897 she wrote an article for the *Ladies Home Journal*, entitled "What a Woman Can Do with a Camera." In 1991 "The Foremost Women Photographers in America," a series of six articles for *Ladies Home Journal*, was published by Johnston.

Johnston and Mattie Edward Hewitt went into partnership and began a foray into architectural photography. They received commissions from the New Theater in New York City, as well as architectural firms. During the twentieth century Johnston continued to photograph colonial and federal architecture. In 1945 she was made an honorary member of the American Institute of Architects (AIA), and in 1948 she gave her negatives, prints, and correspondence to the Library of Congress, Washington, D.C. Johnston died in 1952 at the age of eighty-eight. Her name was virtually forgotten until 1966 when *The Hampton Album* was published by the Museum of Modern Art (MoMA), New York City.

Johnston's work carefully documents with detail and care the events and people of her time. She once wrote that she relied on a schooled eye, Eikonogen (a now obsolete developing agent), and the inspiration of old masters such as Rembrandt, Van Dyck, Sir Joshua Reynolds, Romney, and Gainsborough.

Karen E. Speirs

Bibliography
Camera 51 (1972): 4, 13, 31.
Maddox, Jerald C. "Photography in The First Decade." *Art in America* 61 (1973): 72–78.
The Hampton Album–1966. New York: Museum of Modern Art.
Tucker, Anne. *The Woman's Eye*. Alfred Knopf, 1973.
Time Magazine. Obituary. "Milestones." (June 2, 1952).

Johnston, Ynez (1920–)

Guggenheim fellow, painter, and printmaker—Ynez Johnston, a highly literate and much-travelled individual, was born in Berkeley, California. She was educated at the University of California at Berkeley, where she received her Bachelor of Fine Arts degree (1941) and her Master of Fine Arts degree (1947).

Johnston has been winning awards and receiving honors for her work for more than four and one-half decades: she won a prize for an oil at the San Francisco Museum of Art, California (1946); travelled and painted in Italy while on a Guggenheim grant (1952); held a Louis Comfort Tiffany grant for painting and printmaking (1955–1956); was awarded two Huntington Hartford grants (1951, 1957); a Senator James

D. Phelan grant (1958), and a MacDowell Colony grant, Peterborough, New Hampshire (1959). She held a Tamarind workshop fellowship for lithographic research (1966); and received two grants from the National Endowment for the Arts (NEA) (1976, 1986).

Johnston developed a particularly strong, playful, personal, mythic, serendipitous approach to art early on. This singularly sensitive "style" has burgeoned in her oils, watercolors, prints, ceramic murals, and bronzes and has led to many commissions. In confronting her work of the mid-1970s and musing about influences upon her innermost past and present concepts and ideas (*The Cosmic Mountain* and *Mirage with Charloteers*), Johnston writes, "I feel an affinity for the Moghul and Rajput painters and the Tibetan *thanka* artists, the medieval artists, Blake, also Thomas Traherne, Eckhart, Juan de la Cruz . . . ." The breadth of her vision and the depth of her feelings are still being realized in her current works.

Johnston has taught in many universities and schools of art through the years, including the University of California at Berkeley (1950–1951); the Colorado Springs Fine Arts Center, Colorado (1954–1955); Chouinard Art Institute (1956); California State College (1966, 1967, 1969, and 1973); the School of Fine Arts, University of Judaism (1967); and the Otis Art Institute of Parsons Schools of Design (1978–1980)—all in Los Angeles, California. She has exhibited in 141 group shows and has had sixty-two solo exhibitions in major institutions between 1943 and early 1991. Her prints and paintings are in the permanent collections of noteworthy public and private institutions, including the Museum of Modern Art (MoMA), the Whitney Museum of American Art, and the Metropolitan Museum of Art—all in New York City; the San Francisco Museum of Art, California; the Hirshhorn Museum and Sculpture Garden, Washington, D.C.; the National Museum of Israel, Jerusalem, and Ethicon (Johnson & Johnson) of Chicago, Illinois.

Bibliography
Acton, David. *A Spectrum of Innovation, Color in American Printmaking, 1890–1960.* Massachusetts: Worcester Art Museum, 1990.
Berry, John, and Ynez Johnston. *Selected Works 1950–1977.* New York: Wiener Gallery, 1977.
Leopold, Michael. "Los Angeles Letter." *Art International* 17 (Summer 1973): 86.
Tufts, Eleanor. *American Women Artists, Past and Present.* Garland, Vol. I, 1984. Vol II, 1989.

Jolicoeur, Nicole (c. 1950s–)

Apart from acknowledging receipt of a Master of Fine Arts degree from Rutgers University, New Brunswick, New Jersey, Jolicoeur has kept her biography to herself. Given the nature of her work, this seems fitting. Since 1980 she has developed doubled references to the nineteenth-century theory of hysteria proposed by French neuropathologist Jean-Martin Charcot and to the cartographic expeditions of Charcot's son, Jean-François. The work of Charcot *père* involved photographs of female patients undergoing fits of hysteria, some of which were later discovered to be simulated according to the demands of the male doctors and attendants. Jolicoeur overlays images appropriated from these documents with implications drawn from the works of Charcot *fils*, whose explorations of *terra incognita* provide the springboard into an extended metaphor: the social basis of the construction of gender-knowl-

edge predetermines that "Woman" will always be unexplored, uncharted territory. The artist's autobiographical silence thus seems appropriate.

In 1984 Jolicoeur participated in an international project involving twenty-seven women artists from Canada and the United States. Organized by a nonprofit organization entitled "La chambre blanche," two exhibitions were mounted to expose stereotypical responses to women's art practices, including the mechanisms of gender-based exclusion expressed in language itself.

Jolicoeur currently lives and works in Laval, Québec, where she teaches at l'École des arts visuels, Université Laval. She has exhibited throughout Canada, the United States, and Western Europe.

Robert J. Belton (with Lana Pitkin)

Bibliography
Gravel, Claire. "L'extase photographique: Quelques photographes montréalaises." *Vie des arts* 136 (Autumn 1989).
Isaak, JoAnna. "Mapping the Imaginary." *PsychCritique* 1:3 (1985).
Jolicoeur, Nicole. *Charcot: deux concepts de nature.* Montréal: Artexte, 1988.
———, et al. *Féministe toi-même/féministe quand même.* Québec: La chambre blanche, 1986.

Jonas, Joan (1936–)

The performance artist Joan Jonas was born in New York and educated at various institutions, including Mount Holyoke College, South Hadley, and the Boston Museum School—both in Massachusetts; and Columbia University, New York City, where she received her Master of Fine Arts degree in sculpture. Under the aegis of Trisha Brown, she studied dance and, in 1968, with Peter Campus, produced "Wind," her first film.

Between 1968 and 1984 Jonas held solo exhibitions and performances in more than fifty sites in the United States and abroad, including "Documenta," Kassel, West Germany (1972); The Kitchen, New York City (1974); Institute of Contemporary Arts, Los Angeles, California (1975); Kunsthalle, Basel, Switzerland (1977); Van Abbemuseum, Eindhoven, the Netherlands (1978); the DAAD Galerie, West Germany (1984); and many others. Her work has been invited to group exhibitions throughout the world, such as the "Festival d'Automne," Paris, France (1973); the "Bienal," São Paulo, Brazil (1974); "The Video Show," Serpentine Gallery, London, England (1975); "Documenta 7," Kassel, West Germany (1982); and many others.

Jonas has been a visiting artist or guest lecturer at a number of universities and art schools, including the Video School of Visual Arts, New York City (1972); Princeton University, New Jersey (1974); Yale University, New Haven, Connecticut (1974); the Minneapolis College of Art, Minnesota (1974); San Diego State University, California (1975); Otis Art Institute of Parsons School of Design, Los Angeles, California (1975); Kent State University, Ohio (1977); University of California at Berkeley; and California State College, Long Beach (1980); among others.

Ever concerned with movement in space, Jonas used the mirror in 1970, and incorporated video in 1972 to further her efforts in shaping and redefining the visual and aural message; narrative components, colored lights, household objects, audio tapes, paintings and props, including skeletons—all provide metaphoric allusions to the eternal questions of the human condition.

Honored through awards for her pieces, Jonas is the recipient of two grants from the National Endowment for the Arts (NEA) (1973, 1975); three Creative Artists Public Service (CAPS) grants from New York State (1972, 1973, 1975); a DAAD artist's fellowship from West Berlin, Germany (1982); and others. Her work is in the permanent collection of the Museum of Modern Art (MoMA), New York City.

Bibliography
Anderson, Laurie. "Joan Jonas." *Art Press* (November–December 1973).
Carroll, Noel. "Joan Jonas: Making the Image Visible." *Artforum* 12 (April 1974): 52–53.
Wortz, Melinda. "Wolf Calls and Frog Songs—Upside Down and Backwards." *Art News* 79:7 (September 1980): 213.

Jones, Amy (1899–)

Born in Buffalo, New York, the painter/printmaker Amy Jones studied at Pratt Institute, Brooklyn, New York. She also took further study with Peppino Mangravite, Xavier Gonzales, Carlus Dyer, and others.

Jones has exhibited work in solo and group shows in the United States and abroad, including Wave Hill, Riverdale, New York (1977); Galleria Il Sigillo, Padua, Italy (1974); Gallery of Glory Be, Kingston, Jamaica (1975); and many others.

She has won awards, honors, and commissions for murals, including purchase prizes at the Washington County Museum, Hagerstown (1958); and the Baltimore Watercolor Club—both in Maryland. She also won first prize for graphics at an exhibition of the Northern Westchester Artists, New York (1961).

Jones is a member of several professional artists organizations and her work is represented in private, corporate, and public permanent collections, including the Chrysler Museum, Norfolk, Virginia; New Britain Museum of American Art, Connecticut; New York Hospital, New York City; the Hudson River Museum, Yonkers, New York; Pepsicola Corp.; and others.

Bibliography
Archives of American Art. *Collection of Exhibition Catalogs.* G.K. Hall, 1979.
Peck, Marlene, and Gerald E. Markowitz. *Democratic Vistas: Post Offices and Public Art in the New Deal.* Temple University Press, 1984.
Who's Who in American Art. 15th ed. R.R. Bowker Co., 1982.

Jones, Lois Mailou (1905–)

The first significant African-American painter/teacher, the "Grande Dame of African-American Art," Lois Mailou Jones was born in Boston, Massachusetts. During a forty-seven-year teaching career at Howard University, Washington, D.C., she taught a number of now-prominent artists, including Elizabeth Catlett, L. Howardena Pindell, Alma Thomas, and others.

Jones had a rich and varied education in the arts, which laid the groundwork for everything in her future career—except the discrimination that dogged her early on. She won a four-year scholarship to the Boston Museum School of Fine Arts; studied at the Boston Normal Art School; and went to Harvard University, Cambridge—all in Massachusetts; attended the Designer's Art School; took classes at Columbia University, New York City; earned her Bachelor's degree at Howard University, Washington, D.C.; won a scholarship to the Académie Julian, where she studied under the aegis of Adler, Berges, Maury, and Montezin; and also attended the Académie de la Grande Chaumière—both in Paris, France.

Jones has held more than sixty solo exhibitions of her work, and has had her work invited to many group exhibitions in the United States and abroad, including the National Academy of Design, New York City; the Rhodes National Gallery (in what was then Southern Rhodesia); the Salon Artistes Français, Paris, France; the San Francisco Museum of Art, California; the Trenton Museum, New Jersey; and many others.

Honored and esteemed for her figurative oils and landscapes, Jones won an award for painting at the Corcoran Gallery of Art, Washington, D.C. (1941); and the same year received the National Order of Merit from the government of Haiti for achievement in art. In addition to other forms of recognition through the years (honorary Doctorate degrees from universities, prizes for painting, etc.), Howard University presented her with its alumni award in 1978.

Jones designed the commemorative stained-glass window for the Andrew Rankin Chapel at Howard University (1978) and a mural, "The Light," for Cook Hall at the same institution. Her work is in many permanent collections in the United States and elsewhere, including the Hirshhorn Museum and Sculpture Garden, the Corcoran Gallery of Art, and the Phillips Collection—all in Washington, D.C.; the Palais Nationale, Haiti; the Brooklyn Museum, New York; and many others.

Bibliography
Barbour, Floyd B., ed. *The Black Seventies.* Extending Horizons Books, 1972: 133–34.
Dannett, Sylvia G.L. *Profiles of Negro Womanhood.* 2 vols. Educational Heritage, Inc., 1964.
Jones, Lois M. *Lois Mailou Jones. Peintures 1937–1951.* Presses Georges Frére, 1952.
Laduke, Betty. "Lois Mailou Jones: The Grande Dame of African-American Art." *Woman's Art Journal* 8:2 (Fall 1987–Winter 1988): 28–32.
Lewis, Samella. *Art: African-American.* Harcourt, Brace, Jovanovitch, 1978.
Romero, Patricia, ed. *In Black America: 1968.* Washington, D.C.: International Library of Negro Life and History, 1969: 224, 226, 230, 233.
Who's Who in American Art. 19th ed. R.R. Bowker Co., 1991–1992.

Jones, Nell Choate (1879–1981)

Born in Hawkinsville, Georgia, the painter Nell Choate Jones attended Adelphi Academy, Brooklyn, New York, in the 1920s as a result of her artist-husband's urging. She also studied privately with a number of painters and began to exhibit in 1927. Two successful years later a scholarship allowed her a year of freedom to paint her impressionist landscapes in Fontainebleau, France, and for additional research and study in England.

Jones returned to Georgia in 1936. Her powerful, expressionist paintings of African-American men and women pointed to future concerns in her work.

Jones won many honors and awards for her work. She was president of the National Association of Women Artists, New York City, and the American Society of Contemporary Artists in the same city. Her art expressed a concern about the problems of women as well as those in art. Her work is represented in private and public permanent collections in the United States and abroad.

Bibliography

Chambers, Bruce W. *Art and Artists of the South*. University of South Carolina Press, 1984.

Paintings by Nell Choate Jones. New York: Marbella Gallery, 1979.

Who's Who in American Art. 10th ed. American Federation of Arts, 1970.

Jones, Phyllis Jacobine (1898–1976)

Born in London, England, Phyllis Jacobine Jones emigrated to Canada in 1932. Earlier, Jones had studied under Harold Brownsword at the Regent Street Polytechnic, and in Italy, Denmark, and France. It was during these years that she formed her classical approach to sculpture. Her strength was in animal modeling. She was a member of the Sculptors' Society of Canada (1933), and became an associate of the Royal Canadian Academy in 1943, and a full academician in 1951.

In 1933 Jones was invited to execute a number of animal sculptures for the Ontario Agricultural College at Guelph, Ontario. Her "Black Cavalry" (c. 1930, private collection), a stylized horse and rider executed in Belgian black marble, was exhibited at the Paris Salon, France, in 1935.

Jones became known primarily as an architectural sculptor. Her main achievements include the Gore Vale Fire Insurance Building in Galt, Ontario (1934); seven relief figures representing the trades of Canada on the Bank of Canada Building, Ottawa (1938); relief panels on the Bank of Montréal, Toronto in 1946 (a collaborative venture); and a large marble relief for the Bank of Nova Scotia (1951). She held one-person shows at the Mellors Gallery, Toronto (1936), and at Rodman Hall, St. Catharines, Ontario (1969).

Jones also taught at Northern Vocational School, Toronto, and at the Ontario College of Art where she was director of sculpture from 1951 to 1953. Her work is represented in the collections of the National Gallery of Canada, Ottawa; the Art Gallery of Hamilton; the Art Gallery of Ontario, Toronto; and the University of Guelph Collection, Guelph, Ontario—all in Canada.

Christine Boyanoski

Bibliography

Luckyj, Natalie. *Visions and Victories: Ten Canadian Women Artists 1914–45*. London Regional Art Gallery, 1983.

McInnes, Graham. *A Short History of Canadian Art*. The MacMillan Company of Canada Ltd. at St. Martin's House, 1939.

MacDonald, Colin S. *A Dictionary of Canadian Artists*. Vol. 3. Canadian Paperbacks Publishing Ltd., 1975.

Jones, Ruthe Blalock (1930–)

Primarily a painter and printmaker, Ruthe Blalock Jones was born and raised in Oklahoma. She is one-half Delaware, one-quarter Shawnee, one-quarter Peoria, and a member of the Peoria tribe of Native Americans. The noted Cheyenne artist Dick West was a major influence on her developing technique when she was studying to earn her Bachelor of Arts degree at Bacone College, Muskogee, Oklahoma (1970). Two years later she had earned her Bachelor of Fine Arts degree in painting at the University of Tulsa, Oklahoma. It was there (1973–1974) that she was awarded a graduate research grant in anthropology for "The Delaware Big House Ceremony," which served as the inspiration for several later works of art.

Jones usually paints in the flat, two-dimensional style associated with many Native Americans. She produces this style in water-based paint on rag paper and board. Although she portrays the wide scope of tribal customs, she has specialized in women, dance apparel, and the Peyote ritual. Alternatively Jones executes non-Indian styles, from representational to semi-abstract, in oils and acrylics on canvas or masonite. Doing graduate work at the University of Tulsa, studying painting and graphic arts under Carol Coker, Jones mastered serigraphy, etching, linoleum and woodblock printmaking on fine papers, in low-numbered editions.

In 1979 Jones became the first woman director of the well-established art department at Bacone College in Muskogee, Oklahoma. She took a two-year leave of absence (1985–1986) to devote herself to full-time painting. She returned to teaching at Bacone College, and was appointed to the rank of associate professor in 1988.

The first painting competition Jones entered (1954) brought her an award. Between 1956 and 1989, with the encouragement of her husband and four children, she participated throughout the United States in eighty-nine group exhibits which included the Fogg Museum at Harvard University, Cambridge, Massachusetts; the John F. Kennedy Center for the Performing Arts and the Smithsonian Institution—both in Washington, D.C. She received thirty-eight awards, served as art juror for twenty-one competitions, and presented numerous slide lectures on Native American painting. Her first major solo exhibit (1967) was at the Heard Museum, Phoenix, Arizona, and, by the end of 1985, she was presented in fifteen more solo exhibitions across the United States.

Jones took part in two touring exhibits, "Contemporary Indian Prints and Posters" and "Daughters of the Earth" (1985). The latter was composed of paintings by eight Oklahoma Native American women. In 1982 her painting "Shawl Woman" was chosen for a poster to promote the "Contemporary Native American Art" show at the Smithsonian Institution. In 1984 she was one of four artists whose paintings were used as a poster to accompany the show "Ornament and Symbol: The Illuminated Garment of American Indian Women," presented at the University of Oklahoma's Museum of Art. Jones's work has been published in newspapers, magazines, and calendars, and her "Plains Dancer" (in color) was the 1980–1982 cover of the Bacone College catalog.

Jones is represented in fifteen permanent public collections which include the Heard Museum, Phoenix, Arizona; Museum of the American Indian, Heye Foundation, New York City; U.S. Department of the Interior, Washington, D.C.; Bacone College, Muskogee; the Five Civilized Tribes Museum, Muskogee; Northeastern Oklahoma State University, Tahlequah; University of Tulsa, Philbrook Museum of Art, Tulsa; and Southern Plains Indian Museum, Anadarko—all in Oklahoma.

Jeanne O. Snodgrass King

Bibliography

Bucklew, Joan. "Art Works by Ruthe Jones Something Bit Different." *The Arizona Republic* (August 6, 1967).

Callahan, Cathy. "Artist Portrays Indian Lifestyles." *The Tulsa Tribune* (December 23, 1976): 1B, 4B.

"Daughters of the Earth." *Oklahoma Today* 20 (July–August 1985).

Fitzpatrick, Mary, et al. *Contemporary North American Indian Art.*
Smithsonian Institution, 1982, pp. 13, 15.
Humphrey, Donald G., and Jeanne O. Snodgrass King. *Centennial Touring
Art Exhibit.* Bacone College, 1980, 8.
Night of the First Americans. John F. Kennedy Center for the Performing
Arts, 1982, p. 28.
Paintings by Ruthe Blalock Jones. An Exhibition. U.S. Department of the
Interior, Southern Plains Indian Museum, 1981, pp. 1–4.
Snodgrass, Jeanne O. *American Indian Painters. A Biographical Directory.*
Museum of the American Indian, Heye Foundation, 1968, p. 88.

Joysmith, Jean (1920–)

Born in Scotland in 1920 Jean Joysmith, whose father was an artist,
was raised in London, England. Her talent was nurtured at home: she
was awarded the Princess Louise Gold Medal for sketching in an all-
British Empire contest in 1936. She studied at Gray's School of Art on
scholarship and won her degree handily.

In the late 1960s Joysmith was an assistant professor of fine arts
at the University of the Americas, Mexico City, Mexico; she has worked
in many media, including costume and mosaic design, portraiture, and
mural painting, but her forte is drawing. Her strong, realistic works
reveal—at the same time—a delicate sensitivity to the culture and
ambiance of Mexico.

Joysmith's work is in many important permanent collections and,
since 1942, has been exhibited in solo shows at the Royal Scottish
Academy and the Royal Scottish Institute, both in the United Kingdom, and elsewhere, including a number of group exhibitions in London, England and Mexico.

Bibliography
The Texas Quarterly: Image of Mexico I. The University of Texas, Autumn 1969.

Juárez Green, Saskia (1943–)

Born in Monterrey, Nuevo León, Mexico, Saskia Juárez Green majored
in art during her four-year curriculum at the University of Nuevo León
and then was awarded a scholarship for advanced study at the Academy of San Carlos in Mexico City, Mexico. She has had her work exhibited in many group shows throughout Mexico.

A number of her original prints were purchased for special use
by OPIC, a cultural arm of the Ministry of Foreign Affairs of the Mexican government. In 1964 Juárez Green was sent by OPIC to Santiago
de Chile to delineate a mural designed by Juan O'Gorman. At the end
of the 1960s Juárez Green was teaching printmaking at the department of art at the University of Nuevo León, Monterrey, Mexico.

Bibliography
The Texas Quarterly: Image of Mexico I. The University of Texas. Autumn 1969.

Judah, Doris Minette (1887–1965)

Born in Montréal, Québec, Canada, the sculptor Doris Minette Judah
studied in her native city at the École des Beaux-Arts, Montréal, and
the Monument Nationale under the aegis of Albert Laliberté and
Edmond Dyonnet. While a student, she won a gold medal for accomplishment in life drawing from the Conseil des Arts et Métiers, Montréal
(1918–1919); and other honors.

Judah held numerous solo exhibitions in museums and galleries,
including the Coffee House Gallery, Montréal (1936). She also participated in many group shows with the Art Association of Montréal and
the Royal Canadian Academy of Arts. Examples of her portrait busts
and other works are in private and public permanent collections.

Bibliography
Exhibition of Sculpture by Doris M. Judah. A Catalog. Montréal, Québec:
The Coffee House Gallery, 1936.
MacLachlan, Mary E. *The Portrait Sculpture of Doris M. Judah.* A Catalog.
Halifax, Nova Scotia: Mount Saint Vincent University, 1980.

Judge, Mary Frances (1935–)

Born in Minneapolis, Minnesota, the painter Mary Frances Judge earned
a Bachelor's degree at the College of New Rochelle, New York (1961);
took additional work at Webster College, St. Louis, Missouri; and received a Master of Fine Arts degree from the University of Notre Dame,
Indiana (1971).

Judge's work has been exhibited in galleries and museums in the
United States and abroad, including the "Annual Exhibition," Springfield Museum, Missouri (1970); "Annual Mid-States Exhibition,"
Evansville Museum, Indiana (1971); "Midwest Biennial," Joslyn Museum, Omaha, Nebraska (1972); "American Women Artists," Museum
of Contemporary Art, São Paulo, Brazil (1980); and many others.

Judge has been a board member of the Women's Art Center, St. Louis,
Missouri (1972–1974); Artists Equity, Dallas, Texas (1974–1978); Dallas
Museum of Fine Arts, Texas (1976–1977). Her work is represented in private and public permanent collections, including the Carnegie Institute
of Arts and Letters, Pittsburgh, Pennsylvania; Springfield College, Illinois; Nobles County Art Center, Worthington, Minnesota; and others.

Bibliography
American Women Artists. São Paulo Museum of Contemporary Art. A
Catalog. 1980.
Trucco, Terry. "How Can You Be a Nun if You're an Artist." *Art News* 78:5
(May 1979): 7.
Who's Who in American Art. 17th ed. R.R. Bowker Co., 1986.

Judson, Sylvia Shaw (1897–1978)

Born in Chicago, Illinois, the sculptor Sylvia Shaw Judson studied with
the masters Polasek and Bourdelle. She has received many honors and
awards, including an honorable mention in an exhibition at the Chicago Art Club (1926) and the Logan prize three years later. One of her
works, "the Belle Austin Jacobs Memorial," is sited in Kosciusko Park,
Milwaukee, Wisconsin.

Bibliography
American Art Annual. Vol 30. American Federation of Arts, 1933.
Schnier, Jacques. *Sculpture in Modern America.* University of California
Press, 1948.
Who's Who in American Art. Vol. 1. American Federation of Arts, 1935.

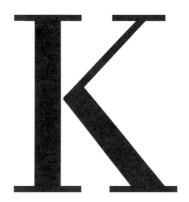

Kahane, Anne (1924–)

Born in Vienna, Austria, Anne Kahane has lived in Canada since 1926. Her earliest art studies included commercial art and engraving, but it was at Cooper Union Art School in New York City (1945–1947) that she was introduced to woodcarving—the sculpture technique that would dominate her career.

Recognition came early when in 1953 Kahane was awarded a prize in the first international sculpture competition, held in London, England, on the theme "The Unknown Political Prisoner." In 1956 her "Ball Game" (1955) won the grand prize for sculpture at the Concours Artistique de la Province du Québec, Canada. In addition Kahane's work was among that chosen to represent Canada at the Venice Biennale and the Brussels World's Fair in 1958, and she was also included in the 1958–1959 Carnegie International in Pittsburgh, Pennsylvania.

Kahane has been included in such group exhibitions in Canada as "A Trio of Canadian Sculptors" (circulated 1964–1966); "300 Years of Canadian Art" (circulated 1967); 3-D into the 70s (circulated 1970); and "Spectrum Canada" (held in conjunction with the Montréal Olympics, 1976). She was a member and exhibitor with the Sculptors' Society of Canada, a regular exhibitor in the annual shows at the Montréal Museum of Fine Arts from the late 1940s until the mid-1960s, and an associate member and exhibitor with the Royal Canadian Academy of Arts from 1961 to 1971. Numerous solo exhibitions of her work have been held across Canada since 1957, including a major retrospective at McMaster University Art Gallery in Hamilton in 1981. Her sculpture commissions include a memorial to "Captain F.J. Stevenson" for the Winnipeg International Airport (1963–1964); "Chant de la Terre" for Place des Arts in Montréal (1963); "Man on His Head" for Expo '67 in Montréal; and "La Mer" for the Canadian Embassy in Islamabad, Pakistan (1972–1973). Kahane's work is also represented in major public and private collections across Canada.

While her media have included drawing and printmaking, sculpture remains Kahane's primary form of expression. Her early work is of laminated and carved wood, sometimes polychromed or combined with metal. Concentrating on the human figure either alone or in groups, her themes range from the everyday, as in "Rain" (1958), to the symbolic, as in "Icarus" (1974). Beginning in the early 1970s her figures have become flatter, emphasizing the silhouette, and since 1976 she has worked primarily in sheet metal, cutting out and "folding" her figures into more abstract forms.

Janine A. Butler

Bibliography

Antoniou, Sylvia A. *Anne Kahane: Sculpture, Prints and Drawings, 1953–1976*. Hamilton: McMaster University Art Gallery, 1981.

Spencer, Charles. "Anne Kahane, Canadian Sculptor." *The Studio* 160:807 (July 1960): 21–23.

Kahlo, Frida (1907–1954)

Frida Kahlo is best known for her self-portraits in which she often painted herself undergoing graphic physical suffering. She also engaged in the debates in Mexico around establishing a national and cultural identity in the years following the Mexican Revolution. In her self-portraits, which comprise approximately 40 percent of her total paintings, she investigated her various roles as a woman, a Mexican, and as the wife of the internationally famous mural painter, Diego Rivera.

Kahlo was the daughter of Mathilde Calderón, a *mestiza* (of Spanish and indigenous Mexican ancestry) and Guillermo (Wilhelm) Kahlo, a German-Jewish immigrant. She lived most of her life in her childhood home in Coyoacán, an area just outside of Mexico City. The favored child of her father, a well-respected photographer in turn-of-the-century Mexico, Kahlo was one of the first women to attend the national Preparatory School in Mexico City, where she studied medicine and medical illustration. Among her companions at the school she could count members of the Mexican literary vanguard, such as Salvador Novo, and young radical leftists like Germán de Campo.

In September 1925 a trolley-bus slammed into the bus on which Kahlo was riding, and the injuries she sustained in the accident plagued her the rest of her life. The broken bones included her right foot and leg, her pelvis, collar bone, and a few vertebrae. A steel handrail pierced her abdomen and, according to Kahlo, exited through her vagina. While bedridden for one and one half years, Kahlo began to paint. In her earliest efforts, such as her first self-portrait from 1926 and a portrait of her sister Adriana from 1927, Kahlo attempted to mimic traditional portraiture, drawing on influences such as Italian Renaissance painter Sandro Botticelli and the nineteenth-century Mexican artist José Maria Estrada. She also experimented with various European avant-garde styles as can be seen in her "Portrait of Miguel N. Lira" (1927) and "Pancho Villa and Adelita" (1927), in which she combined cubist flattening of space with unusual juxtapositions of objects such as seen in the work of Russian painter Marc Chagall. In these paintings Kahlo also began to show an interest in Mexican popular arts, with the inclusion of such elements as the skull, or *calavera*, in the portrait of Lira, and the painting of Pancho Villa's soldiers and the women who accompanied them during the Mexican Revolution that she included in "Pancho Villa and Adelita." The name "Adelita" derives from a revolutionary ballad, "If Adelita . . . ," associated with Villa—another element drawn from Mexican popular culture.

Kahlo's reference to Mexican popular arts demonstrates her awareness of debates going on in Mexico in the 1920s related to the formation of a Mexican national culture distinct from the European influences that had dominated the country since the Spanish Conquest and particularly during the period immediately preceding the revolution of 1910. In 1929, when Kahlo met and married Diego Rivera, one of the "Big Three" of the Mexican muralism movement, she became more deeply involved in those debates, choosing to explore the problem of a Mexican national identity often in strikingly personal ways. In addition, her marriage to Rivera brought her into contact with many of the most important artists and intellectuals of the time, including surrealist leader André Breton and the Russian revolutionary Leon Trotsky, as well as some of the wealthiest and most powerful industrialists and financiers in the United States such as Henry Ford and John D. Rockefeller Jr. Kahlo recorded her responses to each of these associations, including that with her husband, through complicated images of herself in which she explored her own self and identity within varying social contexts.

In 1930 Kahlo moved to the United States with Rivera while he worked on a mural for the San Francisco Stock Exchange. This was to be the first of several important commissions, the next being in Detroit and then New York City. A highly vocal supporter of communism and a member of the anti-Stalinist left, Rivera drew attention and controversy from all political fronts. As Rivera's wife, Kahlo attracted attention more for her Mexican style of dress and her flamboyant manner of speaking than for her art work, although she too, if less vocally, supported a socialist political agenda. During the four years spent in the United States Kahlo increasingly emphasized her Mexican nationalism in her dress and manner of painting. She developed a sophisticated pictorial vocabulary drawn from numerous Mexican sources as well as European avant-garde movements, especially surrealism.

Two of the paintings from that period, "Henry Ford Hospital" and "My Birth," contributed greatly to Kahlo's image as a painter of unflinchingly graphic images of female suffering. The first shows Kahlo on a hospital bed in a stark landscape in front of the Detroit skyline. The bedsheet is soaked in blood, an obvious reference to the miscarriage. In the second Kahlo painted a woman on a bed giving birth. The sheet covering her face indicates that she is dead. The child's head is Kahlo's own adult head. Once again blood stains the sheet. The fact that she painted these images in the style and technique of Mexican ex-votos—small religious paintings of miracles—shows how Kahlo often subverted traditional forms and motifs to create startling contrasts of meaning.

In the late 1930s, after her return to Mexico, Kahlo concentrated on images exploring her own ancestry in terms of her relationship to Mexico and its indigenous culture. The complexity of Mexico's racial and cultural heritage created philosophical and political problems for many artists and intellectuals of the time, who tried to establish just what exactly it meant to be "Mexican." In numerous self-portraits Kahlo worked not only on her genealogy, but also her socialization into *mestizo* culture, in which the European and indigenous merged to create entirely new social and cultural formations. Her painting "My Nurse and I" (1937) exemplifies Kahlo's investigations into the expression of the two cultures as distinct yet synthesized into a third.

Kahlo's first solo exhibition was not held until 1938, when she exhibited at predominantly surrealist Julien Levy Gallery in New York City. She had come to the attention of André Breton, who went to Mexico that same year to see Leon Trotsky, the exiled Russian revolutionary leader who lived with Kahlo and Rivera from 1937 to 1939. Breton hailed Kahlo as a surrealist, even though she herself denied any connection to the group. In 1938 she did paint one clearly surrealist work, "What the Water Gave Me," but by and large the fantastic elements of her work derived from her interest in Mexican art forms rather than surrealism.

In 1939 Kahlo and Rivera divorced. She painted "The Two Fridas" in that year to show the images of herself that Rivera had loved and the one he no longer loved. This work also continues to show Kahlo's interest in the problem of Mexican identity, as the Frida on the left wears early twentieth-century European-style dress and the other a dress from Juchitán in Mexico. The exposed hearts of the two figures are joined by a common artery though, again referring to the combined European and indigenous ancestry of most Mexicans, including Kahlo.

The following year Kahlo and Rivera remarried each other. From 1940 on Kahlo's work centered primarily on bust-length self-portraits and still lifes. In this series of self-portraits Kahlo moved away from the explicit exploration of Mexican identity and toward more ambiguous representations. Almost always she included a background of dense foliage, and the additional elements of animals (monkeys, parrots, and cats), as well as her elaborate hairstyles, jewelry, and dress, create an exotic image. By this time, Kahlo had undergone numerous surgical procedures on her back and leg, and she was confined to bed or a wheelchair for extended periods. The intense concentration on her own image may have come from an increased awareness of her body as it progressively failed her.

In 1953, Kahlo's left foot became gangrenous and had to be amputated. Shortly after the operation she was honored with a large retrospective exhibition in Mexico City. Rivera and several other friends carried Kahlo to the opening on a stretcher, from which she viewed the exhibit and greeted those in attendance. In July of 1954 Kahlo died in her home in Coyoacán.

During her lifetime Kahlo sold very few of her paintings. She was best known for her flamboyant appearance, political sentiments, and romantic attachments, not just with Rivera but others, including Leon Trotsky. Since the 1970s reassessments of her work have uncovered the extensive process of self-examination Kahlo undertook through her paintings.

Laura J. Crary-Ortega

Bibliography

Herrera, Hayden. *Frida: A Biography of Frida Kahlo.* New York, 1983.
Prignitz-Poda, Helga. *Frida Kahlo: das Gesamtwerk.* Frankfurt am Main, 1988.
Rico, Araceli. *Frida Kahlo: fantasía de un cuerpo herido.* Mexico City, 1988.
Zamora, Martha. *Frida Kahlo: el pincel de la angustia.* Mexico City, 1987.

Kaida, Tamarra (1946–)

Born in Lienz, Austria, Tamarra Kaida emigrated with her parents to the United States in 1950, settling in New Jersey. She received her Bachelor of Arts degree in 1974 from Goddard College, Vermont, and her Master of Fine Arts degree from the State University of New York (SUNY) at Buffalo, and Visual Studies Workshop, Rochester—both in New York (1979). From 1976 to 1979 Kaida was assistant director of the education department at the International Museum of Photography at the George Eastman House, Rochester, New York. She was appointed to the faculty of Arizona State University as a visiting lecturer in 1979 and became a permanent member of the faculty in 1980; she is presently an associate professor. She has lectured extensively throughout the United States at various museums, universities, and photography conferences.

Kaida has received numerous awards and honors, including the Ferguson award from the Friends of Photography (1983); a 1986 National Endowment for the Arts (NEA) visual artist fellowship grant; and an Arizona Commission on the Arts visual arts photography fellowship (1990). While at the George Eastman House, she had additional responsibility for four exhibitions in the three years of her tenure there, and at Arizona State University has been a guest curator or co-curator for three exhibitions at the School of Art's Northlight Gallery. She collaborated with the poet Rita Dove on *The Other Side of the House* in 1988 (published by Pyracantha Press and the Visual Arts Research Studios of the School of Art, Arizona State University), and also produced *Tremors From the Faultline*, an artist's book published by the Visual Studies Workshop Press, Rochester, 1989.

Kaida's reputation was initially based on the inordinate success of her portraits of children in which hidden meanings seemed to abound just below the surface of the pose. She captured in very direct and poetic terms the growing awareness of the curious adolescent being transformed into the young, sexually cognizant adult. Her work has since embraced narrative considerations, the social landscape, and formal concerns of the classical still life. Implicit to her various subjects is a strong sense of the desert environment, both symbolically and literally. Her interest in photographing children remains very much in the forefront of ideas for future projects as is her need for continuing to challenge the basic photographic format.

Examples of Kaida's work are included in the International Museum of Photography at the George Eastman House, Rochester, New York; the Center for Creative Photography, Tucson, Arizona; the Polaroid Corporation; the Museum of Modern Art (MoMA) Library, New York City; the Santa Fe Museum of Fine Arts, New Mexico; and other museum and corporate collections. Her exhibition record is extensive and includes participation in group shows throughout the United States, such as "Mothers and Daughters," an invitational travelling exhibition organized by Aperture, and she has had exposure to European audiences through several invited group exhibitions in Salzburg, Munich, Vienna, Rome, and others. She had solo shows at the OPSIS Foundation Gallery in New York in 1990 and at the Rhode Island School of Design, Providence, in 1989. Reviews and reproductions of her photographs have appeared in the *Los Angeles Times*; *American Photographer*; *Das AKTFOTO: Artspace*; *Photographing Children, Life Library of Photography*; *Exposure*; *New American Nudes*; *Between Twelve and Twenty*; and others.

Kaida has authored several short stories and essays both as works of literature and as narratives in support of her photographic essays. Most recently Kaida has collaborated with poet Rita Dove, and writer/video artist Fred Viebahn, on an installation entitled "With Hammer and Chisel," which addresses the demise of the Berlin Wall, Germany. This project is the result of her trip to that site in December of 1989.

Leonard Lehrer

Bibliography

Dove, Rita, and Tamarra Kaida. *The Other Side of the House.* Rochester: Visual Arts Research Studios and Pyracantha Press, Arizona State University School of Art, 1988.
Jenkins, William. "Tamarra Kaida." *Artspace.* Southwestern Contemporary Arts Quarterly (Winter 1983–1984).
Krantz, Les, ed. *American Artists: An Illustrated Survey of Leading Contemporaries.* Chicago, 1989.
Photographing Children. Time Life Books, 1983.

Kaish, Luise (1925–)

Born in Atlanta, Georgia, the sculptor Luise Kaish earned a Bachelor of Fine Arts degree in visual arts from Syracuse University, New York (1946); worked at the Escuela de Pintura y Escultura (La Esmeralda), Mexico City, Mexico (1946–1947); received a Master of Fine Arts degree in sculpture from Syracuse University, New York, where she worked with Ivan Mestrovic (1951); and studied bronze casting and stone carving at the Instituto d'Arte, Florence, Italy (1951–1952).

Kaish has received honors and awards, including a Tiffany Foundation grant (1951), a Guggenheim Foundation fellowship (1959), and a Rome Prize fellowship from the American Academy in Rome, Italy (1970). She has held solo exhibitions in museums and galleries in the United States and abroad since the mid-1950s, including Staempfli

Gallery and Jewish Museum—both in New York City; Minnesota Museum of Art, St. Paul; American Academy in Rome, Italy; Hopkins Center, Dartmouth College, Hanover, New Hampshire; the University of Haifa, Israel; and others. Her work has been included in many major group shows at the Albright-Knox Art Gallery, Buffalo, New York; Metropolitan Museum of Art and Whitney Museum of American Art—both in New York City; Pennsylvania Academy of Fine Arts, Philadelphia; and many others.

Kaish's commissioned work encompasses arks and ark doors, menorahs, memorials to the Holocaust, and Christ figures, for a variety of sponsors, including Export Khleb, Moscow, Russia; Hebrew Union College, Jerusalem, Israel; Jewish Museum, Metropolitan Museum of Art, and Whitney Museum of American Art—all in New York City; Container Corporation of America; Temple Beth Shalom, Wilmington, Delaware; Holy Trinity Mission Seminary, Silver Spring, Maryland; among many others.

Bibliography

Annual Exhibition of Contemporary American Sculpture. Whitney Museum of American Art, 1962, 1964, 1966.

Henry, Gerrit. "Luise Kaish: A Lyrical Essay." *Arts Magazine* 62:7 (March 1988): 86–88.

Kampf, Avram. *Jewish Experience in the Art of the Twentieth Century.* Bergin and Garvey, 1984.

Watson-Jones, Virginia. *Contemporary American Women Sculptors.* Oryx Press, 1986.

Kalvak, Helen (1901–1984)

Born on Victoria Island in the northwest portion of Canada's Northwest Territories, graphic artist Helen Kalvak lived the traditional migratory life of most early twentieth-century Inuits (Eskimos) for most of her life. Soon after she moved into the settlement of Holman Island in 1960 Kalvak was given the opportunity to draw by Father Henri Tardy, an Oblate missionary who introduced graphic arts to the community. Kalvak made more than 1,800 drawings between 1962 and 1978, of which 154 were made into stencil prints and lithographs issued in the annual Holman Island print editions from 1965 to 1985.

Kalvak's childhood training as a shaman informed the artwork she made in her old age, long after her conversion to Christianity. More than most Inuit graphics, her work depicts women in the roles of healer, sorcerer, and transformational figure. "Bird Tracks," "Enchantress," and "Dream"—all from 1973—represent this theme. Through her prints Kalvak became a well-known Inuit artist. She was elected to membership in the Canadian Royal Academy of Arts in 1975 and was made a member of the Order of Canada in 1979.

Kalvak's first print retrospective was held at the Canadian guild of Crafts, Montréal, in 1968, followed by an exhibition of her drawings held there in 1970. Her work appeared in many group exhibits of Inuit art, including "The Coming and Going of the Shaman," Winnipeg Art Gallery (1978) and "The Inuit *Amautik*," Winnipeg Art Gallery (1980). Kalvak's prints are in the permanent collections of the Toronto Dominion Bank, the Canadian Museum of Civilization, the Amon Carter Museum, and the Winnipeg Art Gallery—all in Canada.

Janet Catherine Berlo

Bibliography

Annual Holman Island Print Catalogues: 1965–1985. Holman Eskimo Co-op, Holman Island, N.W.T., Canada. Distributed by Canadian Arctic Producers, Ottawa.

Driscoll, Bernadette. *Kalvak/Emerak Memorial Catalogue.* Holman Eskimo Co-op, Holman N.W.T., Canada, 1987.

Kamen, Rebecca (1950–)

In addition to creating powerful, sensual, and evocative mixed-media sculptures, for the past half-dozen years Rebecca Kamen has been working on an ambitious cross-cultural project involving artists, educators, and young children in both the United States and the People's Republic of China.

Kamen was born in Philadelphia, Pennsylvania, and trained in three different states—receiving a Bachelor of Science degree in art education from the Pennsylvania State University, University Park (1972), a Master of Arts degree in art education from the University of Illinois, Urbana (1973), and a Master of Fine Arts degree in sculpture from the Rhode Island School of Design, Providence (1978). Since 1978, she has been an associate professor of art at Northern Virginia Community College, Alexandria.

In 1980 Kamen began participating in group exhibitions; her resumé lists numerous shows of collages and sculptures in ten states in the United States, and Sheffield, England. She had her first one-person show in 1980 at the University of Richmond, Virginia. Subsequent solo shows were held at: Gallery 10, Washington, D.C. (1982); Washington & Lee University, Lexington, Virginia (1984); the law firm of Arnold & Porter, Washington, D.C. (1985); the J. Walter Thompson advertising agency, New York City (1986); Brody's Gallery, Washington, D.C. (1986); the Leslie Cecil Gallery, New York City (1987): Middle Tennessee State University, Murfreesboro (1988); the Winston Gallery, Washington, D.C. (1988); FOTA Gallery, Alexandria, Virginia (1987); the Jones Troyer Fitzpatrick Gallery, Washington, D.C. (1990 and 1992); and the Cortland Jessup Gallery, Provincetown, Massachusetts (1993).

Kamen has won several honors, including third prize at "Artery '89," Strathmore Halls Arts Center, Rockville, Maryland; cash awards at "Sculpture '84," Public Art Trust, Washington, D.C.; and "Artscape 1983," Baltimore, Maryland; and honorable mention at the Alexandria Sculpture Festival, Virginia (1983). Her work is represented in the collections of many organizations, including the First National Bank of Jackson, Tennessee; Binion & Butler, Washington, D.C.; the Gannett Corporation, Rosslyn, and Advisors Financial, Inc., Arlington—both in Virginia; IBM, Baltimore, Maryland, and Raleigh-Durham, North Carolina; the Tower Construction Company, Bethesda, Maryland; and the Levy Organization, Chicago, Illinois. Kamen has also served as a panelist at many symposia and given guest lectures from Tennessee to Alaska, Hong Kong, and China.

After half a decade exhibiting her boldly-colored sculptures all across the eastern United States, Kamen's professional focus underwent a profound change with her first trip to the People's Republic of China in 1985. There she delivered a series of lectures, got to know local artists, and became intrigued with many aspects of traditional Asian art. On another trip to China in 1987 Kamen met the noted sculptor Zhao Shu Tong, with whom she began a six-year collaboration, culminating in "The China Project," a three-part cultural exchange program that will eventually involve a video documentary; an educational program—using advanced telecommunications technology to teach children about the relationships between science and art, and United States and Chinese culture; and a visual-art exhibition, emphasizing the influence of Chinese art on Kamen's work, and of Western art on Zhao.

In recent years Kamen's sculpture has reflected her growing interest in traditional Asian culture—especially Chinese and Japanese gardens. Many of her works are indoor "environments," which contrast reality and illusion, by combining actual rocks—used as the centerpieces of her constructions—with wood, carved and painted in rich, muted colors to represent other stones, plants, or water.

Bibliography
Forgey, Benjamin. "Galleries: The Shape of Local Sculpture." *The Washington Post* (August 21, 1986): C1.
Lewis, JoAnn. "Galleries: Rebecca Kamen at Winston." *The Washington Post* (November 5, 1988): E2.
Mahoney, J.W. "Washington, D.C.—Rebecca Kamen at Winston." *Art in America* 77:9 (September 1989): 217–18.
Welzenbach, Michael. "Galleries—Rebecca Kamen at Jones Troyer Fitzpatrick." *The Washington Post* (September 15, 1990): D2.

Kantaroff, Maryon (1933–)

The Canadian sculptor Maryon Kantaroff was born to Bulgarian parents in Toronto, Ontario, and graduated with honors from the University of Toronto in art and archaeology (1957). After working as an assistant curator at the Art Gallery of Ontario Kantaroff moved to Great Britain, studying American ethnology at the British Museum. She became interested in sculpture and studied for six years. She received a Canada Council grant and did postgraduate work at the Berkshire College of Art in Reading; studied sculpture with Eric Stanford, and took further instruction at the Sir John Cass College of Art, and the Chelsea College of Art in London. Her first solo exhibitions in 1962 were at the Temple Gallery in London and the Galleria Verritre in Milan. In 1968 she exhibited a strong frieze of aluminum and cast fiberglass in resin and cement in the main lobby of the City Hall in Toronto. She has had shows at the Stenzel Gallery in Munich, Germany; the Galerie Martal in Montréal, the de Vooght Galleries, Vancouver, the Fleet Gallery, Winnipeg, and the Prince Arthur Galleries, Toronto—all in Canada. Her works are expressive with complementary motifs of tension and relaxation and symbolic snake and egg shapes.

A versatile sculptor, Kantaroff is also a member of the Society of Portrait Sculptors in London, which she considers to be academic representation. She also has designed many awards, including the Xerox of Canada award, the Golden Cloud award for the Association of TV Producers and Directors in Toronto, the Canadian Film Editors Guild, and the Women's Art Festival award in Toronto.

She was resident sculptor at the Seneca College in Toronto in 1971 and has done many commissioned sculptures, including "Prometheus," a bronze work for the Fred Gans Memorial in Toronto; the "Bird of Paradise," a concrete and fiberglass sculpture in the Sheridan Mall in Mississauga; "Totems," in the Sheridan Mall in Pickering; and the "Song of Deborah," a bronze work at the Baycrest Centre for Geriatric Care in Toronto. The three main pieces of the twelve-foot, two-ton bronze sculpture had to be cast in England as no foundry in North America could handle the size.

Kantaroff has an international reputation for her work with steel, resin, and concrete doing sculpture, architectural commissions, and even work for television in Canada.

Nancy Knechtel

Bibliography
Images of Origin: Sculpture by Maryon Kantaroff. Prince Arthur Galleries, 1979.
MacDonald, Colin. *A Dictionary of Canadian Artists.* Canadian Paperbacks, 1982, p. 605.
Toronto Globe and Mail (June 13, 1979): 5.

Karnes, Karen (1925–)

A native New Yorker, Karen Karnes is known for her salt glaze and wood-fired ware. Karnes received a Bachelor's degree from Brooklyn College, New York (1946), and studied at Alfred University College of Ceramics, New York, for a year in 1951. She has received many honors and awards for her ceramic work, including fellowships from the National Endowment for the Arts (NEA) (1976, 1988); National Council on Education in Ceramic Arts (1980); Tiffany Foundation (1958); a medal of excellence from the Society of Arts and Crafts, Boston, Massachusetts (1990); a silver medal at the Trienale de Milano, Italy (1964); and others.

Karnes has held twenty-nine solo exhibitions of her ceramic ware between 1953 and 1992 in galleries in the United States and abroad—from New York City to Honolulu, Hawaii; from Scottsdale, Arizona, to London, England; from Shreveport, Louisiana, to Boston, Massachusetts. A "traditional" ceramist whose ware steadily grows aesthetically, Karnes has taught at many institutions, including Camberwell School of Art, London, England (1986); Frog Hollow Craft Center, Middlebury, Vermont (1980–1982, 1985, 1989); Royal College of Art, London, England (1977); and others. Her work has been invited to more than three-score group exhibitions, many of which were travelling shows, including the "Vermont Bicentennial Ceramics Invitational," Johnson State College (1991); "Ashen Beauty," University of Oregon, Eugene (1990); "Fired with Enthusiasm," Campbell Museum, Camden, New Jersey (1987); "Art in Craft Today: Poetry of the Physical," American Craft Museum, New York City (1986); "High Styles: American Design since 1900," Whitney Museum of American Art, New York City (1985); "Pots & Potters," Aldeburgh, England (1982, 1984); "Craft Art & Religion," the Vatican Museum, Rome, Italy (1978); "International Ceramics," Victoria & Albert Museum, London, England (1968, 1972); and many others.

Karnes's work is represented in private, public, and corporate permanent collections throughout the world, such as the American Crafts Museum and the Metropolitan Museum of Art—both in New York City; Cranbrook Museum of Art, Bloomfield Hills, Michigan; Delaware Museum of Art, Wilmington, Delaware; Johnson Wax Collection of Contemporary Crafts, Racine, Wisconsin; Los Angeles Museum of Art, California; Arizona State University, Tempe; Victoria & Albert Museum, London, England; and others.

Bibliography
Hynes, Reggie. "Karen Karnes Workshop." *Ceramic Review* (May–June 1982).
Peterson, Susan. *The Art and the Craft of Clay.* Prentice Hall, 1991.
Rubin, Michael. "Karen Karnes." *Ceramics Monthly* (April 1986).
Wright, Nancy M. "Clay and Clouds." *Stratton Bromley.* 1986.

Käsebier, Gertrude (1852–1934)

Born in Des Moines, Iowa, and raised in Leadville, Colorado, the photographer Gertrude Kasebier attended Moravian College for Women in Bethlehem, Pennsylvania. After marriage and three children Käsebier enrolled at Pratt Institute, Brooklyn, New York, to study portrait painting. However, she soon gave up painting and took up photography. In 1892 she was awarded a $50 prize in "The Monthly Illustrator" photography competition. After four years of studying photography in Germany and in Brooklyn, New York, she opened a portrait studio in New York City in 1897. That same year she exhibited 150 photographic portraits at the Boston Camera Club, Massachusetts, and at the Pratt Institute, Brooklyn, New York. The following year she exhibited ten photographs in the first Philadelphia Photographic Salon, Pennsylvania, and received a very enthusiastic review in *Camera Notes*. In 1899 her pictorialist photograph, "The Manger," was sold for an unprecedented $100. Her work was also reproduced in the Camera Club of New York Portfolio: *American Pictorial Photography*. She became one of the leading portrait photographers. In 1900 Käsebier became a member of the Camera Club of New York and was the first woman elected to The Linked Ring, a society organized to promote photography as an independent art. In 1902, along with Alfred Stieglitz and Clarence H. White, Kasebier was one of the founding members of the Photo-Secession, a group whose aims were to advance pictorial photography, to hold exhibitions of photography, and to organize Americans interested in art. Six of her photogravures were published in Stieglitz's first issue of *Camera Work* in 1905. The following year Käsebier and Clarence H. White were joint exhibitioners at Stieglitz's Little Galleries of the Photo-Secession ("291"). In 1910 the "International Exhibition of Pictorial Photography" exhibited twenty-two of Käsebier's photographs at the Albright-Knox Art Gallery, Buffalo, New York. The Gallery also purchased "The Manger."

Käsebier heavily manipulated her prints, so, when Stieglitz and his "291" group broke from pictorialism and began championing unmanipulated, "straight" photography, Käsebier resigned from the Photo-Secession. In 1916 she and Clarence H. White were among the founding members of a rival organization, the Pictorial Photographers of America.

Käsebier had her last exhibition at the Brooklyn Institute of Arts and Sciences, New York, in 1926. In 1929, at the age of 77, she liquidated her portrait studio.

Laine Sutherland

Bibliography
Green, Jonathan. *Camera Work: A Critical Anthology.* Aperture, 1973.
Kennedy, Anne, and David Travis. *Photography Rediscovered: American Photographs, 1900–1930.* Whitney Museum of American Art, 1979.
Naef, Weston J. *The Collection of Alfred Stieglitz: Fifty Pioneers of Modern Photography.* Viking Press, 1978.
Tighe, Mary Ann. "Gertrude Käsebier Lost and Found." *Art in America* 65 (March–April 1977): 94–98.
Tucker, Anne. *The Woman's Eye.* Alfred A. Knopf, 1973.

Kass, Deborah (1952–)

Born in San Antonio, Texas, Deborah Kass earned a Bachelor of Fine Arts degree at Carnegie-Mellon University, Pittsburgh, Pennsylvania (1974), after previous study in the Whitney Museum of American Art Independent Studies Program (1972) and the Art Students League (1968–1970)—both in New York City.

Kass has been given solo exhibitions at galleries and museums, including Simon Watson (1990, 1992); Scott Hanson Gallery (1988); Baskerville and Watson Gallery (1984, 1986)—all in New York City; Zolla/Lieberman Gallery, Chicago, Illinois (1982); and others. Her work has been invited to myriad group exhibitions in the United States and abroad, such as "In Your Face: Politics of the Body and Personal Knowledge," A.C. Project Room, New York City (1992); "Rope," Fernando Alcolea Gallery, Barcelona, Spain (1991); "Painting Culture," Fiction/Non-Fiction Gallery (1991), and "The Last Laugh: Irony, Humor, Self-Mockery, and Derision," Massimo Audiello Gallery—both in New York City (1990); "Young New York," Bellarte, Helsinki, and Turku—both in Finland (1989); "Awareness and Desire," Galerie Rahmel, Cologne, Germany (1989); "Romantic Science," One Penn Plaza (1987), "Red," Stefanotti Gallery (1982); and "Artists by Artists," Whitney Downtown—all in New York City (1979); and many others.

Kass's recent parody of Andy Warhol's image, based on an advertisement for plastic surgery, "Before and Happily Ever After," adds a scene from Disney's *Cinderella* to transform it into a biting, worrying painting. Her paintings are represented in private and public permanent collections, including the Jewish Museum and the Guggenheim Museum—both in New York City; Cincinnati Museum of Art, Ohio; McCrory Corporation; Commodities Corporation; and others.

Bibliography
Cameron, Dan. "The Outlaw Academy." *Art and Auction* (May 1992): 96–98.
Cunningham, Michael. "After AIDS Gay Art Aims at a New Reality." *The New York Times* (April 26, 1992): 17.
Hess, Elizabeth. "Spiritual America." *The Village Voice* (May 19, 1992): 101.
Smith, Roberta. "Women Artists Engage the Enemy." *The New York Times* (August 16, 1992): H1, H23.

Katzen, Lila Pell (1932–)

Born in Brooklyn, New York, the environmental sculptor Lila Pell Katzen studied at the Art Students League and the Cooper Union School of Art—both in New York City; and with Hans Hofmann at his schools in New York City and Provincetown, Massachusetts.

Between 1954 and 1992 Katzen has held more than seventy solo exhibitions in museums and galleries, including "Paintings," Tirca Karlic Gallery, Provincetown, Massachusetts (1958); "Shaped Painting," Maryland Institute of Art, Baltimore (1965); "Light Floors" (plastic and light sculpture), National Museum of American Art, Washington, D.C. (1968); "Sculpture & Site," Baltimore Museum of Art, Maryland (1975); "City Spirit" (large-scale sculpture), Fordham University, Lincoln Center, New York (1978); "Fan, Ribbon & Plate Works," University of North Carolina, Chapel Hill (1979); "Sculpture Returns to the Garden" (1982) and "Ruins & Reconstructions" (1984)—both at the Alex Rosenberg Gallery, New York City; "Double Rainbow" (large-scale sculpture), "World Expo '88, Brisbane, Australia (1988); "Maya Queen Empowered," Dante Park, New York City (1989); "Dawn Double Rainbow" (large-scale sculpture), Chicago International Art Exposition, Navy Pier (1990); "Columbus and the Statue of Liberty," College of William and Mary, Williamsburg, Virginia (1992); and many others. Her work has been invited to myriad group exhibitions throughout the

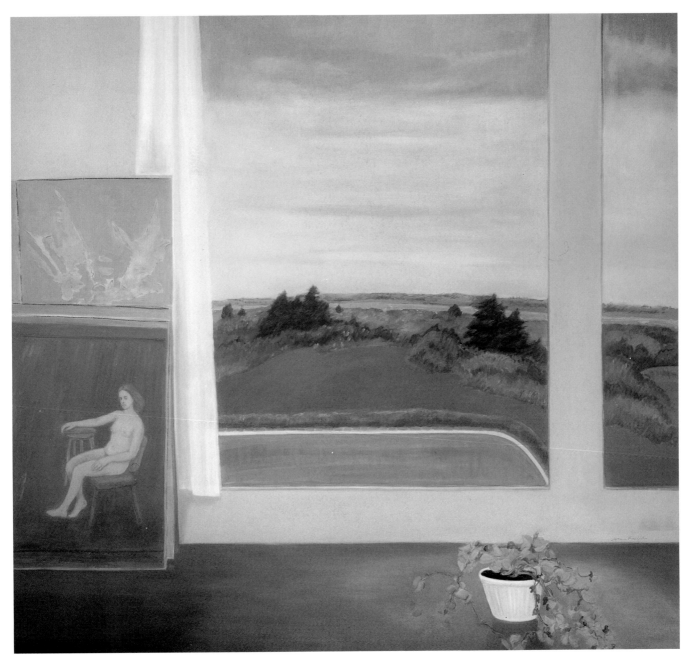

Jane Freilicher. From the Studio. *1989-1991. Oil on linen. 76 × 77³/4 inches.*
Courtesy Fischbach Gallery, New York.

Dorothy Fratt. Spanish Drum. 1992. Acrylic on canvas. 54 × 50 inches.
Courtesy the artist and Riva Yares Gallery.

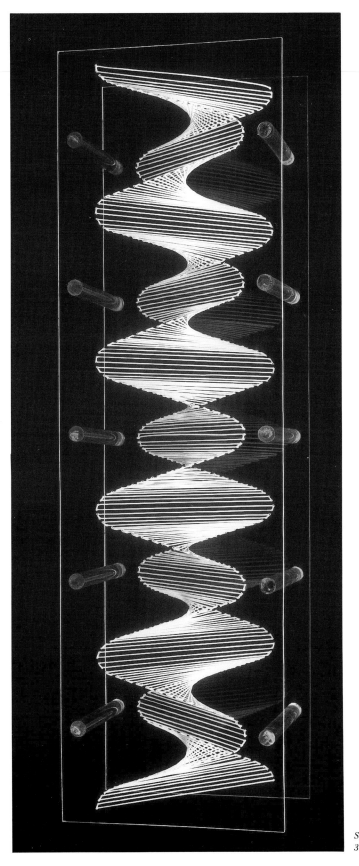

Sue Fuller. String Construction #746. 1987. Acrylite and teflon. 36 × 10¹/₂ × 8 inches. Courtesy the artist.

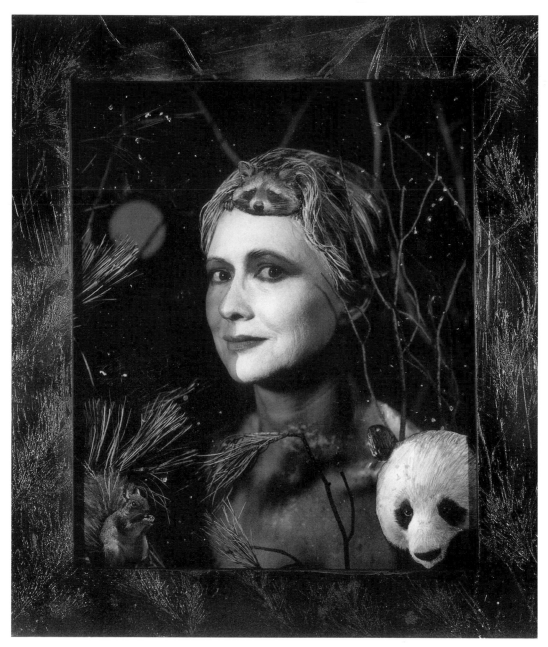

Judith Golden. Earth *from the series,* The Elements. *1993.*
Polaroid color photo with paint and collage. 30 × 26 inches. Courtesy the artist.

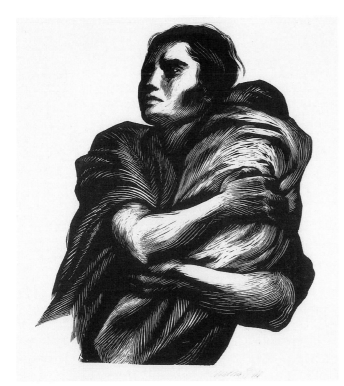

Andrea Gómez. Madre contra la guerra, *n.d. Linoleum engraving.*
32 × 39 cm. Collection INBA.

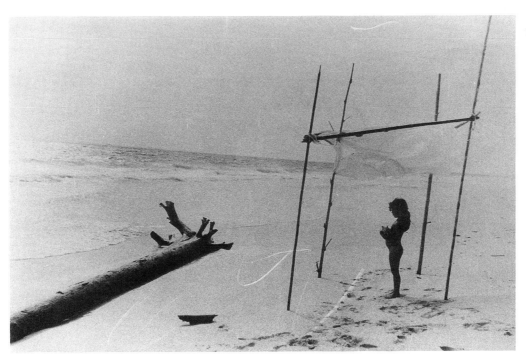

Flor Garduño. Caracola. 1957. Silver gelatin photo. 26.5 × 35 cm.
Archivo CENIDIAP-INBA.

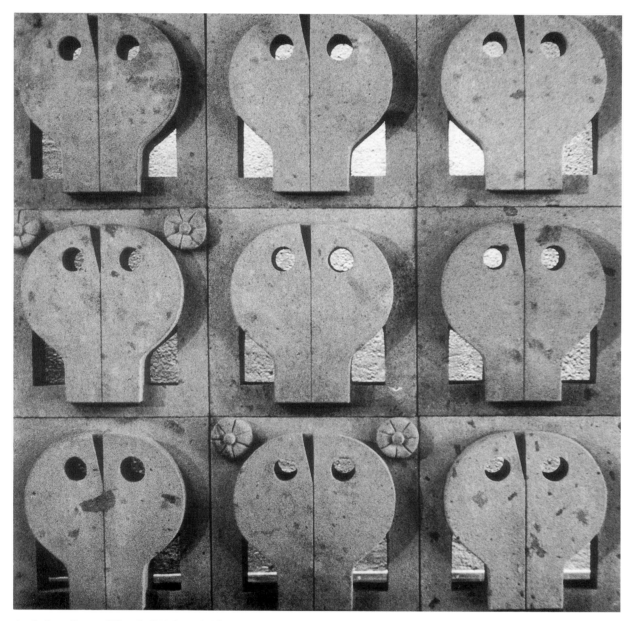

Angela Gurría. Tzompantli floreado. *1993. Stone relief (detail).*
1.8 × 4.0 m. Courtesy the artist.

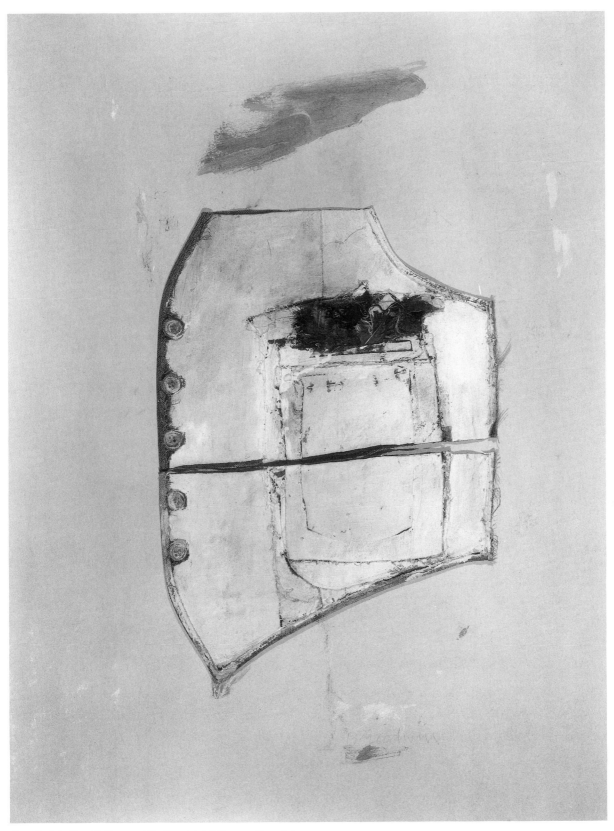

Betty Goodwin. Vest with Plaster and Feathers. *1974. Collage, acrylic, and plaster on construction paper. 61.0 × 45.7 cm. National Gallery of Canada.*

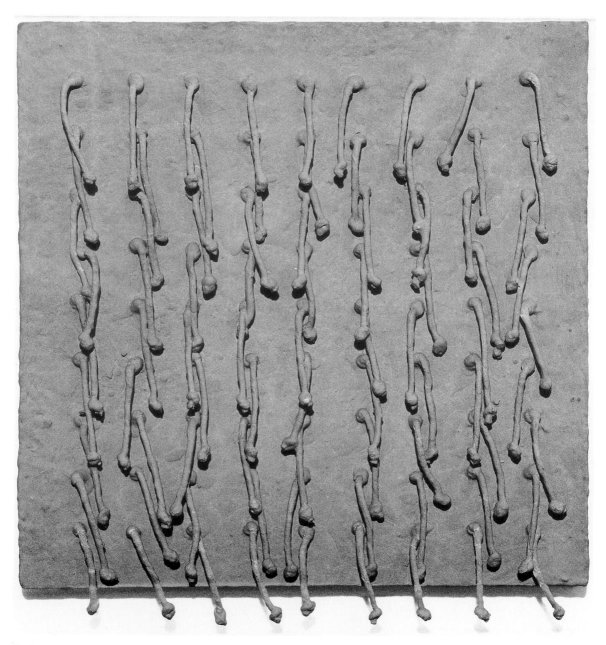

Eva Hesse. Study for Sculpture. 1967. Sculpmetal, cord, acrylic medium, glue, and varnish on masonite. 10 × 10 × 1 inches. The National Museum of Women in the Arts. Gift of Wallace and Wilhelmina Holladay.

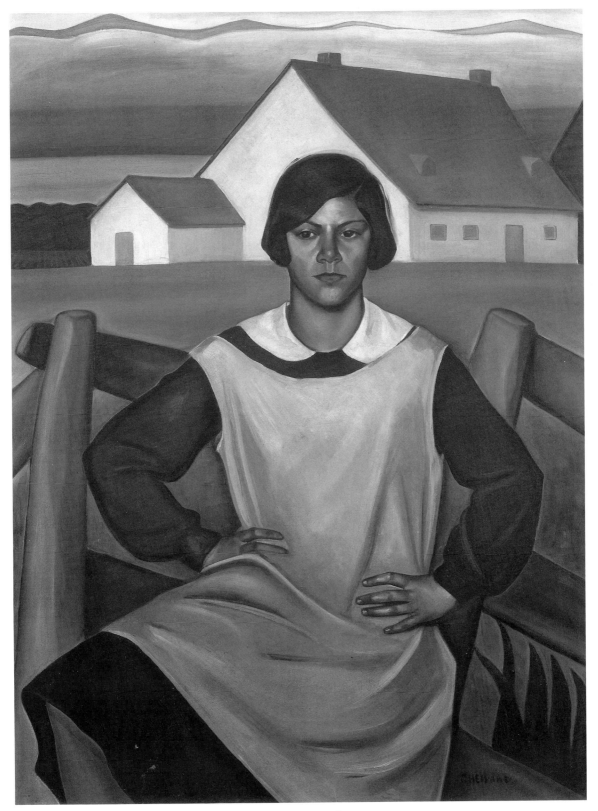

Prudence Heward. Rollande. Oil on canvas. 139.9 × 101.7 cm. National Gallery of Canada.

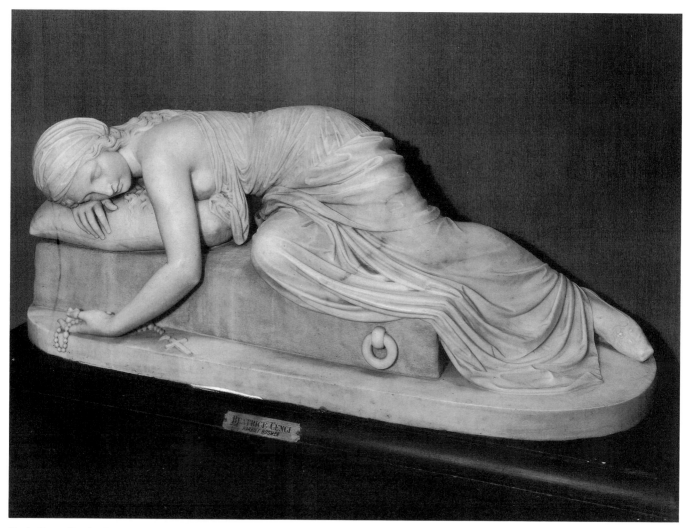

Harriet Hosmer. Beatrice Cenci. *1856. Marble. 24 × 61.5 × 24 inches.*
Collection of the St. Louis Mercantile Library Association.

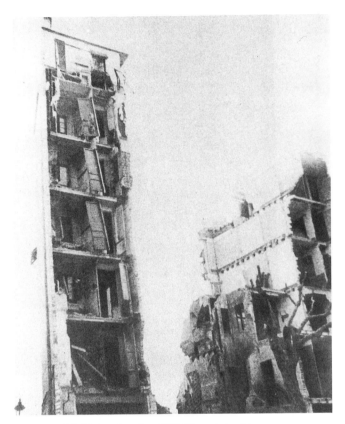

Kati Horna. Calle Mariana, Barcelona. *1938. Silver gelatin print.*
Archivo CENIDIAP-INBA.

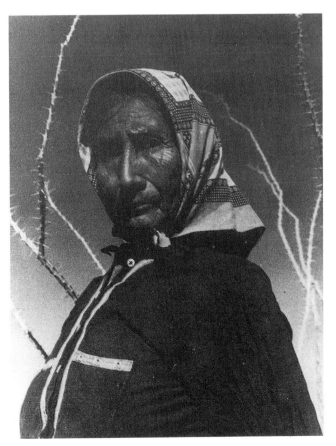

Graciela Iturbide. Untitled, *n.d. Silver gelatin print. Archivo CENIDIAP-INBA.*

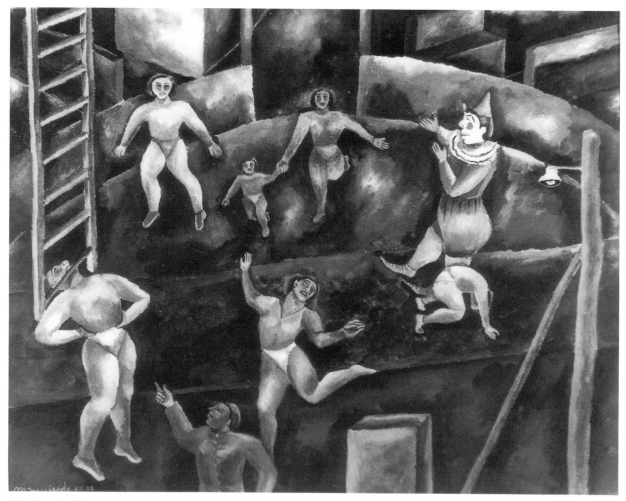

Maria Izquierdo. El circo o Payasos de circo. 1939. Gouache. 40 × 49 cm.
Archivo CENIDIAP-INBA. Private collection.

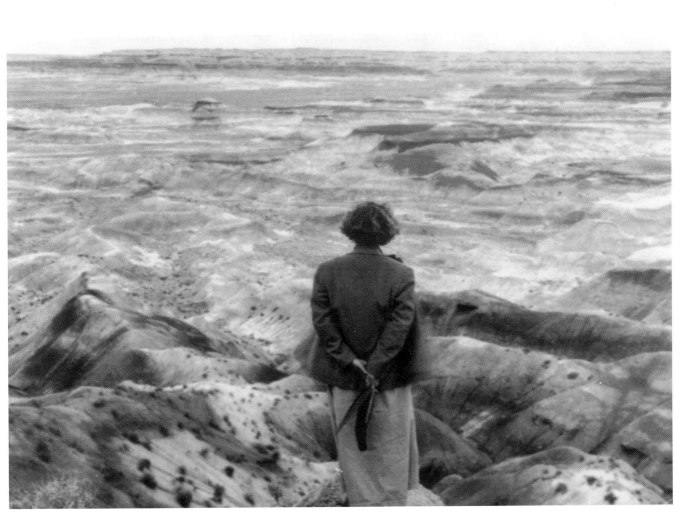

Tamarra Kaida. Hawks. 1988. Silver gelatin print. 16 × 20 inches. Courtesy the artist.

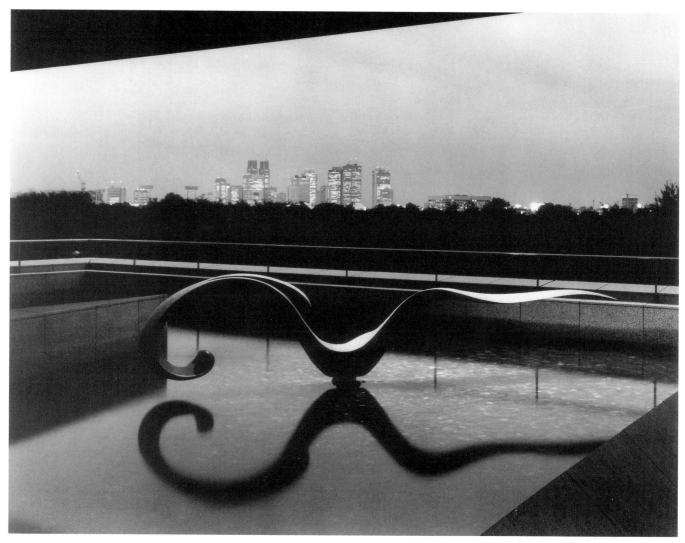

Maryon Kantaroff. The Wave. 1992. Bronze with blue-green patina.
60 × 180 × 24 inches. Canadian Embassy, Tokyo, Japan.

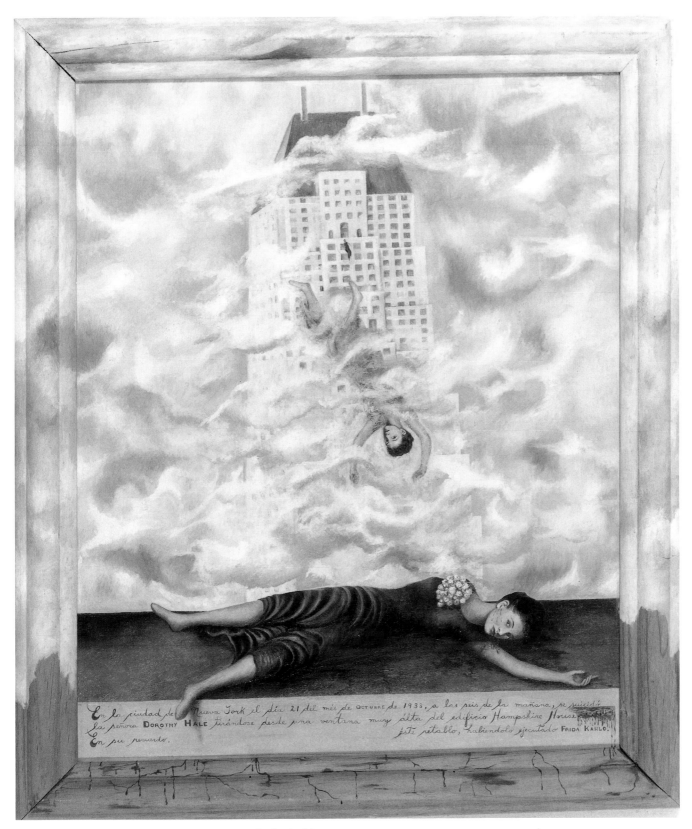

Frida Kahlo. Suicide of Dorothy Hale. *1939. Oil on masonite panel with painted frame.*
50.8 ×40.64 cm. Phoenix Art Museum. Gift of an anonymous donor.

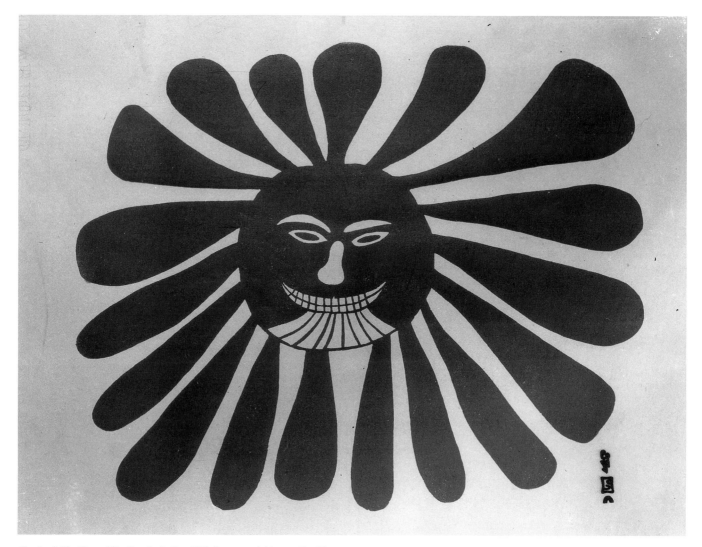

Kenojouak. The Woman Who Lives in the Sun. *1960. Stonecut on laid paper. 54 × 65 cm.*
Courtesy West Baffin Eskimo Cooperative, Cape Dorset, NWT, Canada.

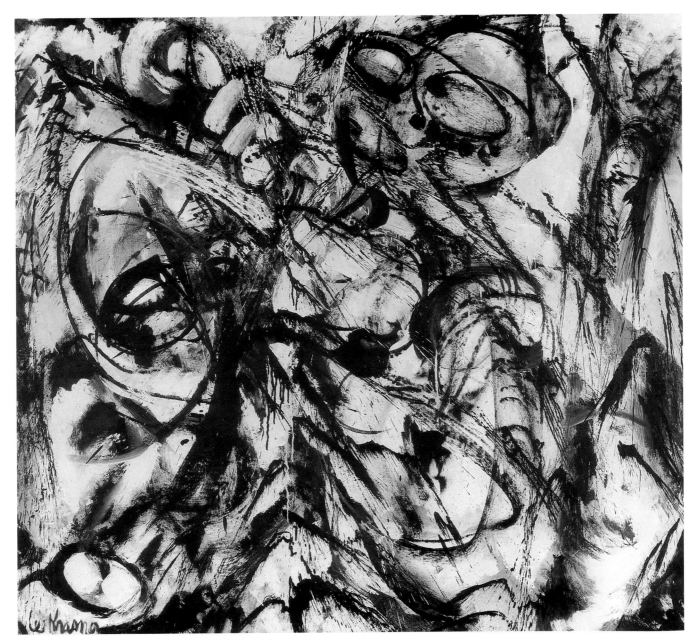

Lee Krasner. The Guardian. *1960. Oil on canvas. 53 × 58 inches. Collection of Whitney Museum of American Art. Purchase with funds from the Uris Brothers Foundation, Inc.*

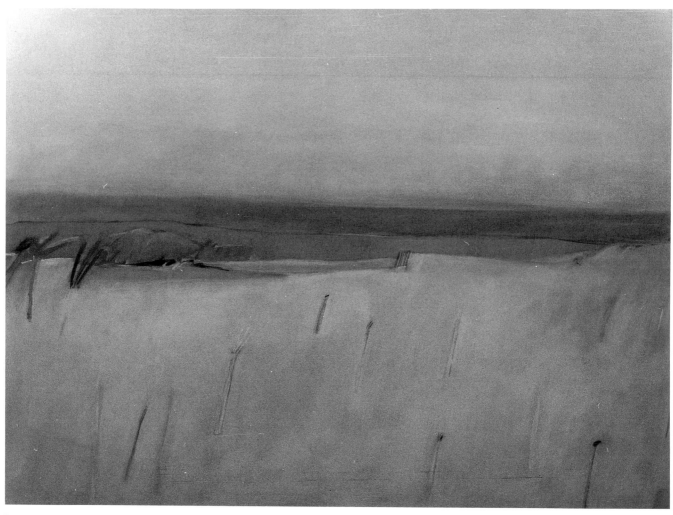

Joy Laville. Playa en Baja California. *1978. Oil on canvas. 140 × 180 cm.*
Archivo CENIDIAP-INBA. Collection the artist.

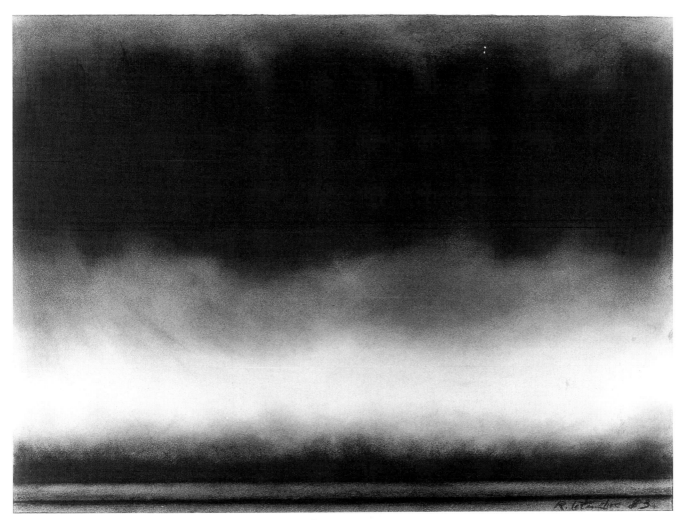

Rita Letendre. After the Storm. *1983. Acrylic on canvas. 30 × 40 inches. Courtesy the artist.*

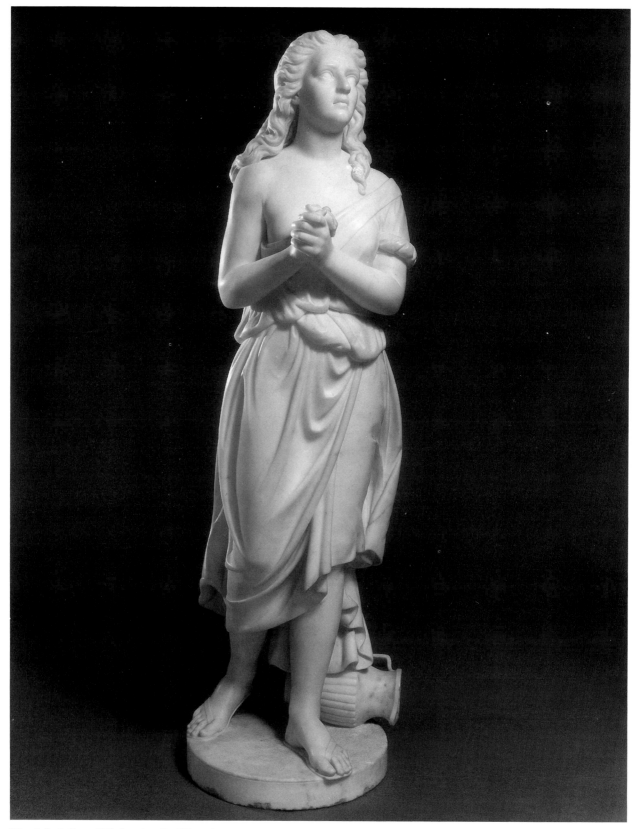

Edmonia Lewis. Hagar. *1875. Carved marble. 52⁵/₈ × 15¹/₄ × 17 inches. National Museum
of American Art, Washington, D.C./Art Resource, New York.*

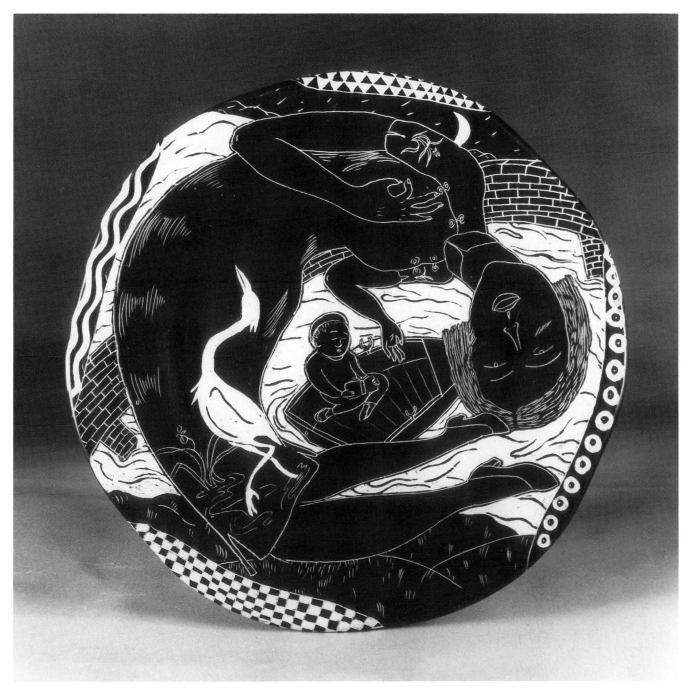

Beth Lo. Untitled Platter. *1989. Porcelain. 18 × 18 × 2¹/₂ inches. Courtesy the artist.*

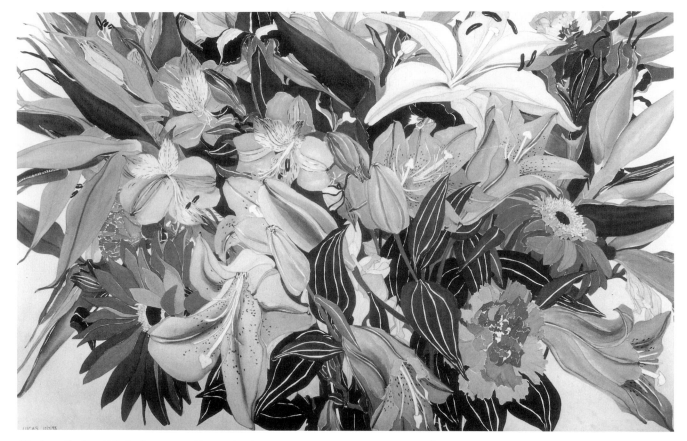

Helen Lucas. Paradise. 1993. Acrylic on canvas. 54 × 84 inches. Courtesy the artist.

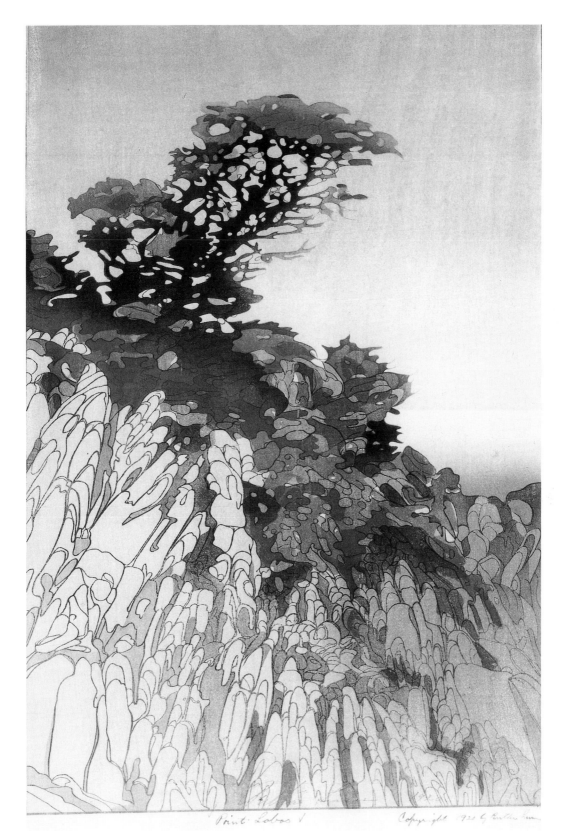

Point Lobos

Copyright 1920 by Bertha Lum

Bertha Lum. Point Lobos. *1920. Woodcut. 16¼ × 10¾ inches. Collection*
Library of Congress, Prints and Photographs Division.

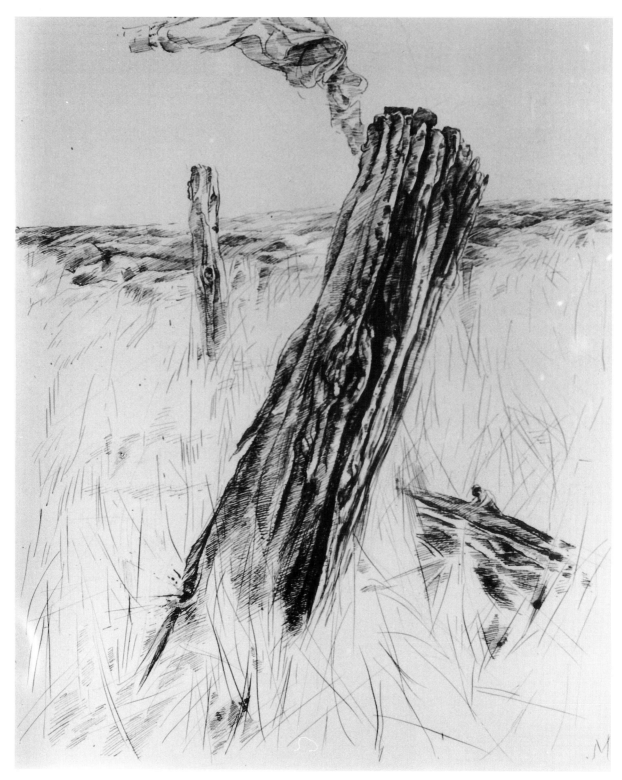

Jo Manning. Shirtseries. 1993. Pen and ink. 13¹⁄₂ × 10¹⁄₂ inches. Courtesy the artist.

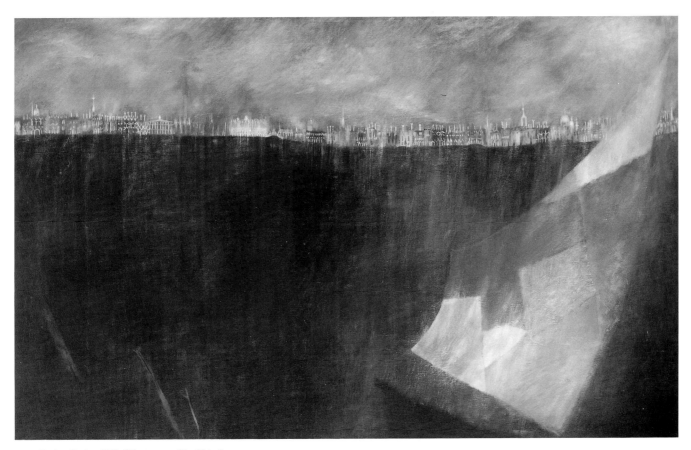

Loren MacIver. Venice. 1949. Oil on canvas. 59 × 93 inches.
Collection of Whitney Museum of American Art.

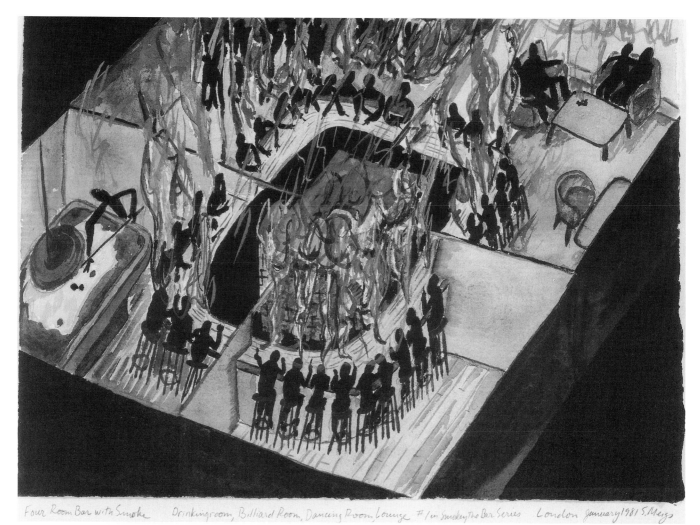

Four Room Bar with Smoke   Drinkingroom, Billiard Room, Dancing Room, Lounge #1 in smoky the Bar Series   London January 1981 S. Meigs

Sandra Meigs. Purgatorio, A Drinkingbout (Four Room Bar with Smoke: Drinkingroom,
Billiard Room, Dancing Room, Lounge No. 1). *1981. Watercolor and pencil on wove paper.*
27.9 × 33.0 cm. National Gallery of Canada.

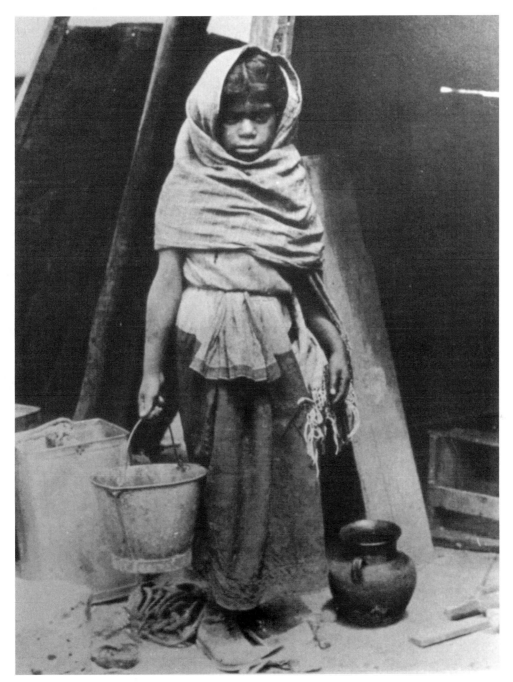

Tina Modotti. Nina con cubeta. *1926. Silver gelatin print. Archivo CENIDIAP-INBA.*

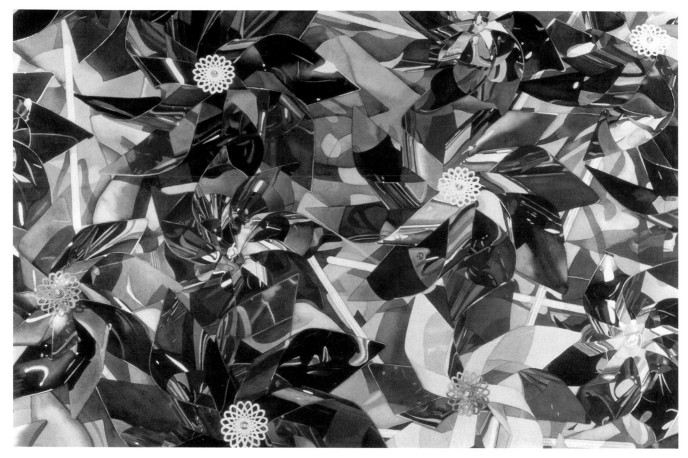

Ellen Murray. Collection: Pinwheel Painting #3. *1987. Watercolor. 39 × 59 inches. Courtesy the artist.*

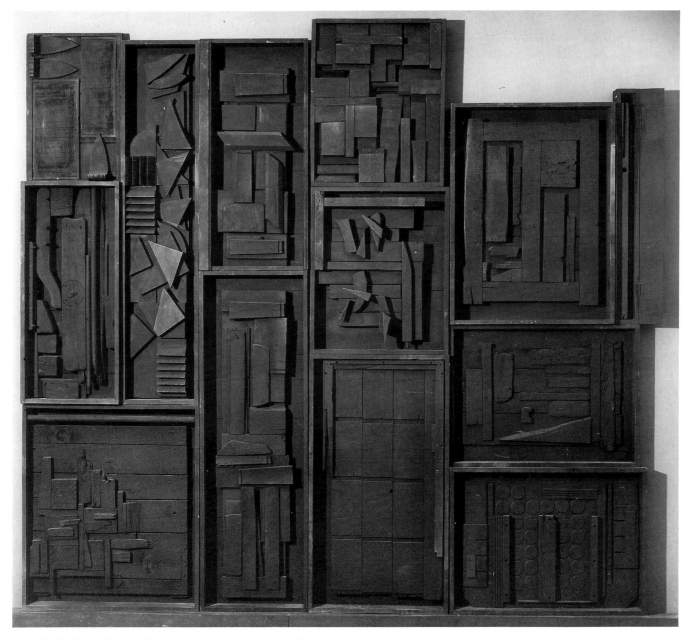

Louise Nevelson. Young Shadows. 1959–1960. Painted wood. 115 x 126 x 7³/₄ inches.
Collection of Whitney Museum of American Art. Purchase with funds from the Friends of
the Whitney Museum of American Art and Charles Simon.

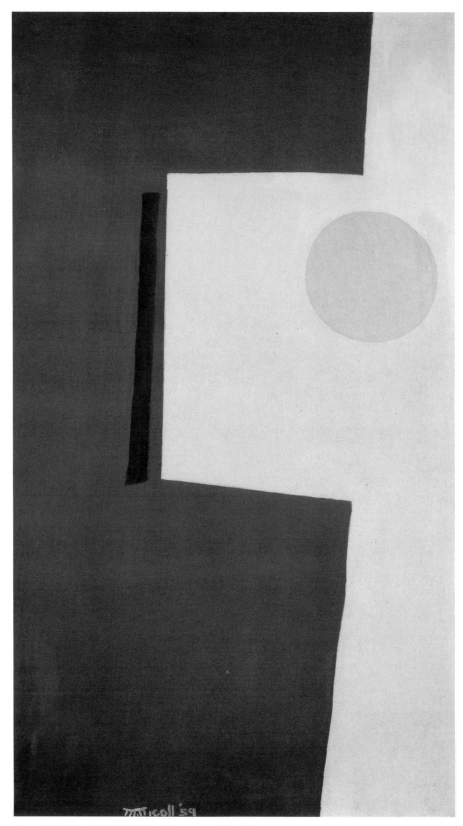

Marion Nicoll. **Thursday's Model.** *1959. Oil on canvas. 92.0 × 51.1 cm.*
National Gallery of Canada.

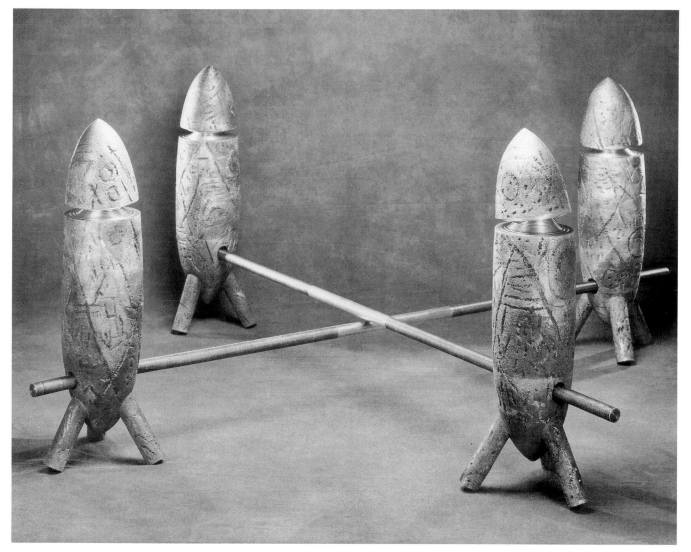

Katie Ohe. Night Watch. *1988-1989. Cast aluminum, steel. 48¹/₂ × 124 × 124 inches.*
Courtesy the artist.

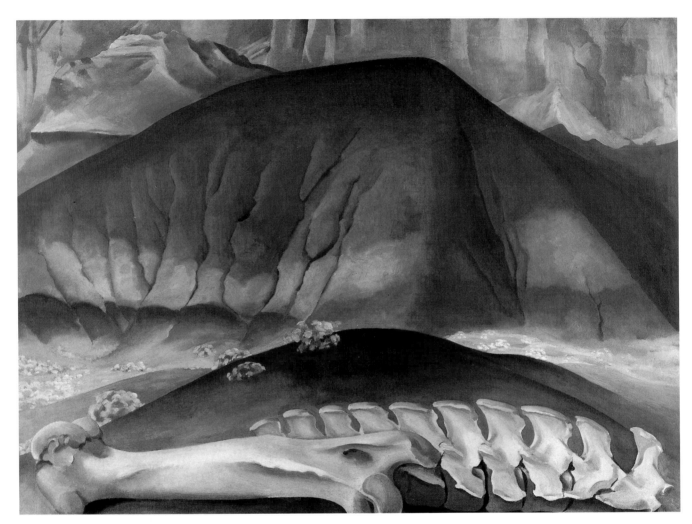

Georgia O'Keeffe. Red Hills and Bones. *1941. Oil on canvas. 30 × 40 inches.*
Philadelphia Museum of Art: The Alfred Stieglitz Collection.

United States and abroad, and has been commissioned by various individuals and institutions from New York City to Hamburg, Germany; São Paulo, Brazil; Washington, D.C.; Paris, France; Riyadh and Jeddah—both in Saudi Arabia; and others.

Katzen has won honors and tributes for her painting and sculpture, including awards and fellowships from the Tiffany Foundation (1964); Lannan Foundation (1966); Architectural League of New York (1967); National Endowment for the Arts (NEA) fellowship (1973); Goodyear fellowship (1974); and others.

The titles of Katzen's steel, bronze, and aluminum abstract sculptures often provide further clues to more deeply experience that which is aesthetically revealed; her large-scale work floats and twists sensuous ribbons of steel to provide illusions and allusions of feminine power. Her work is represented in private, public, and corporate permanent collections, including the Aldrich Museum of Contemporary Art, Ridgefield, Connecticut; Baltimore Museum of Art, Maryland; Chrysler Museum, Norfolk, Virginia; Everson Museum, Syracuse, New York; Milwaukee Art Center, Wisconsin; National Gallery of Art, Washington, D.C.; University of Iowa, Iowa City; Wadsworth Atheneum, Hartford, Connecticut; CIBA-GEIGY; Atlantic Records, New York; and many others.

Bibliography
Ahlander, Leslie Judd. "Lila Katzen: Free-Flowing Sculpture." *Arts Magazine* 55:7 (March 1981): 158–60.
Kuspit, Donald. "Lila Katzen's Ruins and Reconstructions." *Lila Katzen.* 1985–1986.
Lila Katzen: Wall Sculpture, 1978–1988. A Catalog. University of North Carolina, 1988.
Zimmer, William. "Mayan Themes in Stamford Sculpture Show." *The New York Times* (August 24, 1986): CN28.

Kaufman, Jane (1938–)

A native New Yorker, the painter/sculptor Jane Kaufman earned a Bachelor's degree from New York University (1960) and received a Master of Arts degree from Hunter College (1965)—both in New York City.

Kaufman has held a number of solo exhibitions, including the Bernice Steinbaum Gallery (1985, 1988); P.M. & Stein Gallery (1982); Droll/Kolbert Gallery (1978, 1980); Alessandra Gallery (1975); the Whitney Museum of American Art (1971); A.M. Sachs Gallery (1968, 1970)—all in New York City; and others. Her work has been invited to many group exhibitions throughout the United States and abroad, such as "Absolute Henri," Henri Gallery, Washington, D.C. (1991); "Americans in Glass," Leigh Yawkey Woodson Art Museum, Wausau, Wisconsin (1984); "Eight from New York Selected by Lawrence Alloway," Stony Brook Gallery, New York (1980); "The 1970's: New American Painting," travelling throughout Europe; the New Museum (1978), and the Whitney Museum of American Art (1971, 1972)—both in New York City; "Lyrical Abstraction," Aldrich Museum of Contemporary Art, Ridgefield, Connecticut (1970); and others.

Kaufman has taught art continuously since 1960 in the United States and Canada, in public high schools, colleges, art schools and universities; she has been an instructor of fine arts at the Cooper Union School of Art, New York City, since 1981 and has given workshops and lectures at major colleges and universities from 1972 to 1982. She has won awards and honors for her work, including grants and fellowships

from the National Endowment for the Arts (NEA) (1979, 1989); the Adolph and Esther Gottlieb Foundation (1988); the Ariana Foundation (1982); and the Guggenheim Foundation (1974). She also received a commission from the General Services Administration (GSA) to create a suspended crystal structure in the atrium of the Thomas P. O'Neill Building in Boston, Massachusetts (1986).

Kaufman's work is represented in private, public, and corporate permanent collections in the United States and abroad, including the Whitney Museum of American Art and Brooklyn Museum—both in New York City; Aldrich Museum of Contemporary Art, Ridgefield, Connecticut; Worcester Art Museum, Massachusetts; Museum of Modern Art, Adelaide, Australia; Levi-Strauss Company, San Francisco; the Rhone-Poulenc Rorger Co., Philadelphia, Pennsylvania; and many others.

Bibliography
Doe, John. "Jane Kaufman at Steinbaum." *The New York Times* (August 12, 1991): 24–25.
Langer, Cassandra L. "Jane Kaufman: Quilted Pieces and Screens." *Women Artist News* (Winter 1991): 9:26.
Who's Who in American Art. 19th ed. R.R. Bowker Co., 1991–1992.

Kaula, Lee Lufkin (1865–1957)

Born in Erie, Pennsylvania, the painter Lee Lufkin Kaula studied her craft with C.M. Dewey in New York City and with Aman-Jean in Paris, France. A member of the National Association of Women Painters and Sculptors, Kaula won an honorable mention at the Connecticut Academy of Fine Arts (1925).

Bibliography
American Art Annual. Vol. 30. American Federation of Arts, 1933.
Fielding, Mantle. *Dictionary of American Painters, Sculptors, and Engravers.* Modern Books and Crafts, 1974.
Weber, Nicholas F. "Rediscovered American Impressionists." *American Art Review* 3:1 (1976): 100.

Kelly, Mary (1941–)

The work of conceptual artist Mary Kelly is exemplary of what might be termed postmodern feminist art. It is based in a critique of representation, which is defined not as a mimesis of some ultimate reality but as the way a culture reflects its vision of itself. Kelly utilizes psychoanalytic and poststructuralist approaches to reveal the constructed nature of naturalized ideologies concerning women in our culture, such as motherhood or aging. She often relates these cultural constructions to her own personal experience.

Her best known work is "The Post-Partum Document" (1973–1979). Kelly documented the mother-child relationship from her son's birth to age six in this six-section, 135-part, multimedia installation work. The pieces include traces of the child such as his nappies, plaster hand prints, and scribblings, as well as typed text that documents events such as the child's speech acts or her musings on motherhood and the mother/child relationship, a veritable "archeology of everyday life" as Kelly refers to it. There are no images of mother or child in the piece. Kelly wanted to avoid the objectifying connotations that images of the female body automatically inspires. This piece thus represents an intimate relationship, yet offers no comfortable viewing position because of its non-illusionistic, non-narrative format.

Kelly tracks the inscription of her son into the social order as a process defined particularly through patriarchal language. She draws on the French psychoanalytic theorist Jacques Lacan for much of her interpretation of her son's sexual and social formation through language. Her analysis relates this complex theory to actual documented events in the life of the child, particularly that of language acquisition. At the same time she reveals the psychic and social processes through which motherhood itself is constructed in Western cultures, thus dismantling the ideology which deems motherhood instinctual and inherent. "The Post-Partum Document" has had a tremendous impact on both feminist and other forms of postmodern art, both in the United States and abroad.

Kelly's second large installation, entitled "Interim" (1984–1989), in four sections ("Corpus," "Pecunia," "Historia," "Potestas"), questions the construction of the feminine through issues ranging from attitudes toward aging to shopping, fashion, and beauty. Once again the female body is not present, but represented this time by a series of photographic images of fetish-like objects, such as a leather jacket folded and finally knotted, shoes, shopping lists, etc. Text accompanies these images. The work reveals Kelly's continuing concern with language.

Her most recent work, "Gloria Patri," concerns the masculine ideal and its social consequences. The installation consists of thirty-one etched and screenprinted images on polished aluminum.

Kelly's writings have been almost as influential as her art work. She is very well versed in postmodern theory, and her perspectives on modernism, the reception of artwork, essentialism, the role of the subject, female spectatorship, and language have been very widely published and sought after.

Kelly was born in Minnesota. She lived and worked in London for a number of years, but now resides in New York City and teaches at the Whitney Museum of American Art, Independent Study Program, New York City. Her Master of Arts degree comes from the Pius XII Institute in Florence, Italy, and she received a postgraduate diploma from St. Martin's School of Art in London, England. She has lectured and exhibited her work widely both in the United States and abroad, and her work is represented in major museums throughout the world.

Patricia Mathews

Bibliography
Adams, Parveen. "The Art of Analysis: Mary Kelly's *Interim* and the Discourse of the Analyst." *October* 58 (Fall 1991): 81–96.
Apter, Emily. "Fetishism, Visual Seduction and Mary Kelly's *Interim*." *October* 57 (Fall 1991): 97–108.
Mary Kelly: Interim. Essays by Hal Foster, Griselda Pollock, and Marcia Tucker. New Museum of Contemporary Art, 1990.
Mulvey, Laura. "Impending Time: Mary Kelly's *Corpus*." *Visual and Other Pleasures.* Bloomington and Indianapolis, 1989, pp. 148–55.

Kemenyffy, Susan B. (1941–)

Born in Springfield, Massachusetts, the ceramist Susan B. Kemenyffy studied at Syracuse University, New York, where she earned a Bachelor of Fine Arts degree after study with Robert Marks (1963); Kemenyffy received a Master of Arts degree at the University of Iowa, Iowa City (1966) and, the following year, a Master of Fine Arts degree with honors after study with Mauricio Lasansky.

Kemenyffy's work in ceramics has been viewed in solo and group exhibitions in major museums and galleries throughout the United States and Europe: from San Antonio, Texas, to Wellington, New Zealand; from Sheboygan, Wisconsin, to Nottinghamshire, England; from Kansas City, Missouri, to Montgomery, Alabama, and Philadelphia, Pennsylvania. She has taught and lectured widely in the United States and abroad and has been the recipient of many awards and honors, including a grant from the National Endowment for the Arts (NEA) (1973); Associated Artists of Pittsburgh award, Carnegie-Mellon University Museum, Pennsylvania (1981, 1983, 1987); the Annual Ceramic and Small Sculpture Show award, Butler Museum of Art, Youngstown, Ohio (1982); and others.

Kemenyffy's work is represented in private, public, and corporate permanent collections, including the Canton Art Institute and Cincinnati Art Museum—both in Ohio; Erie Art Museum, Pennsylvania; Everson Museum, Syracuse University, New York; Rohm & Haas Pharmaceuticals, Philadelphia, Pennsylvania; and others.

Bibliography
Brody, Regis. *Energy-Efficient Ceramics.* Watson-Guptill Publications, 1982.
Gamble, Harriet. "Review." *Arts & Activities* (February 1986).
Gibson, John. *Contemporary Pottery Decoration.* Chilton, 1987.

Kendall, Marie Boening (1885–1953)

Born in Mount Morris, New York, the painter Marie Boening Kendall studied under the aegis of William Merritt Chase in New York City, and then, at the Los Angeles College of Fine Arts, California, worked under Jean Mannheim.

Kendall's paintings are in the collections of many institutions, including Teachers College, Mount Pleasant, Michigan; Seaside Hospital and the Polytechnic High School, Long Beach, California; the Hollywood Riviera Club House, California; and many others. She was a member of the California Art Club; Laguna Beach Art Association; the National Association of Women Painters and Sculptors; Society of Independent Artists; and West Coast Artists.

Bibliography
American Art Annual. Vol. 30. American Federation of Arts, 1933.
Fielding, Mantle. *Dictionary of American Painters, Sculptors, and Engravers.* Modern Books and Crafts, 1974.
Moure, Nancy D. *Dictionary of Artists in Southern California Before 1950.* Dustin Publications, 1975.

Kennedy, Harriet Forte

Born in Cambridge, Massachusetts, the African-American sculptor Harriet Forte Kennedy studied at the School of the Museum of Fine Arts, Boston (1960–1965); and did graduate work at Boston University (1965)—both in Massachusetts.

Winner of honors and awards, Kennedy received the Boit award from the School of the Museum of Fine Arts, Boston, Massachusetts; and others. "Head of Michael," a strong, dignified, bronze male head is not atypical of the work shown by Kennedy at the exhibition of "Afro-Americian Artists: New York and Boston," at the Museum of the National Center of Afro-American Artists and the School of the Museum of Fine Arts—both in Boston, Massachusetts (1970).

Bibliography
Afro-American Artists: New York and Boston. A Catalog. The Museum of the National Center of Afro-American Artists and the School of the Museum of Fine Arts, Boston, 1970.

Kenojuak (1927–)

Internationally-known Inuit printmaker and sculptor Kenojuak was born on the south coast of Baffin Island. She credits James Houston, a Canadian artist sent by his government to assist the Inuit, for encouragement and influence on her sculpture, drawing, and printmaking.

A prolific artist, Kenojuak has held but two major solo exhibitions in galleries, including "Kenojuak Drawings," Inuit Gallery of Eskimo Art, Toronto, Canada (1971), and "Kenojuak," Walter G. Phillips Gallery, Banff, Alberta, Canada (1979). Her work has been exhibited in two-person shows with that of her first husband, Johnniebo (d. 1972), including the National Library of Canada, Ottawa (1967); "Sculptures by Kenojuak and Johnniebo," Nova Scotia Technical College, Halifax (1974); and "The Inuit Print," National Museum of Man, Ottawa, a show which toured Canada, Denmark, France, Holland, and the United States.

Kenojuak's prints, sculpture, and drawings have been included in many group shows and group travelling exhibitions: from Canada to Russia and throughout Europe and the United States. "Enchanted Owl" (1960), her best-known print, is typical of her brilliant imagination.

Kenojuak has received many commissions; she is a member of the Royal Canadian Academy; and has won honors and awards, including the Order of Canada. Her work is represented in many private, public, and corporate permanent collections.

Bibliography
Blodgett, Jean. *Kenojuak.* Firefly Books, 1985.
Eber, Dorothy. "The History of Graphics in Dorset." *Canadian Forum* (March 1975): 29–31.
Houston, James. "Eskimo Graphic Art." *Canada Today/d'Aujourdhui* (April 1971): 1–7.

Kent, Adaline (1900–1957)

Born in Kentfield, California, the sculptor Adaline Kent studied at Vassar College, Poughkeepsie, New York; the California School of Fine Arts, San Francisco, California; with Emile Bourdelle and others at the Académie de la Grande Chaumière, Paris, France; and with Ralph Stackpole.

Winner of honors and awards, Kent exhibited work in museums and galleries, including the "Annuals" of the San Francisco Art Association (1935–1946), and San Francisco Museum of Art (1937)—both in California; New York World's Fair (1939); Palace of the Legion of Honor, San Francisco, California (1946, 1948); "Adaline Kent and Jeanne Miles," Betty Parsons Gallery, New York City (1956); and others. Examples of her work are in private and public permanent collections, including Mills College, Oakland; San Francisco Museum of Art; and Stanford University, Palo Alto—all in California; and others.

Bibliography
Painting and Sculpture in California: The Modern Era. San Francisco: California Palace of the Legion of Honor, 1976.
Ritchie, Andrew C. *Abstract Painting and Sculpture in America.* New York:
The Museum of Modern Art, 1951.
Ventura, Anita. "Adaline Kent and Jeanne Miles." *Arts Magazine* 30:8 (May 1956): 55.

Kent, Corita (1918–1986)

Born in Fort Dodge, Iowa, and raised in Hollywood, California, the printmaker and designer Corita Kent (the nun, Sister Mary Corita) joined the Sisters of the Immaculate Heart, Los Angeles, California, early on, and taught art at Immaculate Heart College in the same city.

Kent's colorful and dynamic screen prints (which included anti-war posters, book jackets, greeting cards, the *Love* stamp design for the U.S. Post Office, and other projects) created, singlehandedly, the "Immaculate Heart printmaking style," which was imitated widely in national print exhibitions. Her work, which fused dazzling color, pop art, graffiti, and bold form, was shown in many museums and galleries throughout the United States, including several national print exhibitions in the 1950s at the University of Southern California, Los Angeles; "American Printmakers 1962," Emily Lowe Art Center, Syracuse University, New York (1962); "Corita," a retrospective, De Cordova Museum, Lincoln, Massachusetts (1980); Suzanne Brown Gallery, Scottsdale, Arizona (1981); and many others.

In 1968 Kent left the sisterhood to live in Boston, Massachusetts, where she worked until her death. Driving along the Southeast Expressway, near the Boston harbor, one can see her spectrum-like decoration of the Boston Gas Company's gas tank. Examples of her work are in private and public permanent collections.

Bibliography
"Corita Kent, Artist and Nun, Designed 'Love' Stamp of 60's." *The New York Times* (September 19, 1986).
Kent, Mary Corita, et al. *Sister Corita.* Pilgrim Press, 1968.
Rothon, Pamela. "A Conversation with Corita Kent." *American Way* (November 1970): 7–14.
Rubinstein, Charlotte S. *American Women Artists.* G.K. Hall, 1982.

Kerr, Estelle (1879–1971)

Born in Toronto, Ontario, Canada, the painter/illustrator Estelle Kerr initially studied with M.E. Dignam and Laura Muntz in her native city; she did further study at the Art Students League, New York City, and at the Académie de la Grande Chaumière, Paris, France.

Widely travelled during summers in Europe, she sketched and made notes for future works while touring Belgium, France, Italy, the Netherlands, and Switzerland.

Kerr illustrated books of poetry, children's books, and non-fiction works in Canada and the United States, and exhibited paintings in museums and galleries, including a joint show with Edgar Noffke at the Gavin Henderson Galleries, Toronto (1948); and others. Examples of her work are in private and public permanent collections.

Bibliography
Burgoyne, St. George. "Some Canadian Illustrators." *Canadian Bookman* (January–April 1919): 21–25, 27–30.
Kerr, Estelle. "The Artist." *Saturday Night* 26:35 (June 7, 1913): 29.
MacBeth, Madge. "Canadian Women in the Arts." *Maclean's* 27:12 (October 1914): 23–25, 105–08.

Kerrigan, Maurie (1951–)

New wave imagist Maurie Kerrigan was born in Jersey City, New Jersey, and earned a Bachelor of Fine Arts degree in sculpture from Moore College of Art, Philadelphia, where she studied with William Walton (1973). She received a Master of Fine Arts degree in sculpture from the School of the Art Institute, Chicago, Illinois, under the aegis of Whitney Halstead (1977); and, the same year, completed an independent study program at the Whitney Museum of American Art, New York City.

Kerrigan has held solo exhibitions in museums and galleries in Philadelphia and New York City since the mid-1970s, and has had her work included in group shows, such as "Flora and Fauna," Jeffrey Fuller Fine Art, Philadelphia, Pennsylvania (1981); "Beast Show," P.S.1, Institute for Art and Urban Resources, Long Island City, New York (1982); "Return of the Narrative," Palm Springs Desert Museum, California (1984); and others.

Winner of awards and honors, Kerrigan received an artist's fellowship from the Pennsylvania Council on the Arts (1982); a sculpture award at "Sculpture/Penn's Landing," Port of History Museum, Philadelphia (1983); and others. Examples of her work are in private, public, and corporate permanent collections, including the Philadelphia Museum of Art, and Please Touch Museum, Philadelphia, Pennsylvania; the Lannan Foundation, West Palm Beach, Florida; the Phillips Collection, and the National Museum of Women in the Arts—both in Washington, D.C.; and others.

Bibliography

Projects Made in Philadelphia. Institute of Contemporary Art of the University of Pennsylvania, 1982.

Slatkin, Wendy. "Maurie Kerrigan." *Arts Magazine* 57:9 (May 1983): 12.

Watson-Jones, Virginia. *Contemporary American Women Sculptors.* Oryx Press, 1986.

Wooster, Ann-Sargent. "Maurie Kerrigan at Touchstone." *Art in America* 69:10 (December 1981): 147, 149.

Kever, Honor (1948–)

Born in Boise, Idaho, the printmaker/photographer/installationist Honor Kever attended a number of institutions, including San Antonio College, Texas (1966–1967); Cleveland Institute of Art, Ohio (1967–1968); University of Texas at Austin (1968–1969); Arizona State University, Tempe (1974–1975); and the University of Saskatchewan, Saskatoon, where she earned a Bachelor of Fine Arts degree (1977).

Kever has held solo exhibitions in museums and galleries, including "Drawings and Aquatint Etchings," Shoestring Gallery, Saskatoon (1980); "Who Knows Best (A Fine Line)," travelling show, Centre Eye Photography Gallery, Calgary, Alberta (1984); "The Brooding Rooms: Mother-and-Childhood Reassembled," travelling show, Photographers Gallery, Saskatoon (1986); "Stations along the Way," Mendel Art Gallery, Saskatoon (1989)—all in Canada; and others. Her work has been included in group shows, such as "Rockford Prints," Rockford College, Illinois (1979); "Miami International Print Biennial," Metropolitan Museum, Florida (1980); Mendel Art Gallery, Saskatoon (1980, 1981, 1982, 1987); "Making Space," Presentation House, Vancouver, British Columbia, and Mercer Union, Toronto, Ontario (1988); and others.

Kever's work is represented in private and public permanent collections in Canada, including the Mendel Art Gallery, Saskatoon; the Saskatchewan Arts Board, Regina; and others.

Bibliography

Cochran, Bente Roed. "Saskatchewan Printmakers." *Arts West* 7:10 (November 1982): 20–23.

Crozier, Lorna, and Bruce Grenville. *Honor Kever: Stations along the Way.* A Catalog. Saskatoon: Mendel Art Gallery, 1989.

Laing, Carol. "Making Space." *Parachute* 54 (March–June 1989): 65–66.

Kigusiuq, Hannah (1931–)

Born near Garry Lake in the Central Canadian Arctic, Hannah Kigusiuq grew to adulthood living much the same as her Inuit ancestors had before her—residing in snow houses in the winter and skin tents in the summer. Married as a very young woman, Kigusiuq remembers travelling on the land and following the Arctic game animals in order to survive. She was in her mid-twenties in 1956 when her husband, Kuuk, and others from her camp were afflicted with tuberculosis—a condition that forced them to move to the settlement of Baker Lake, Northwest Territories, where he could receive medical treatment. During her husband's subsequent two-year hospitalization in the South of Canada and as a means to supplement her meager income while she awaited his return to Baker Lake, Kigusiuq responded to encouragement from the local crafts officer, Boris Kotelewitz, to try her hand at drawing. Feeling clumsy at first because her only previous experience with drawing was to make "pictures" on the ice window of her igloo as a child, Kigusiuq rapidly became engaged by this new activity and quickly proved herself to be a talented and inventive draftsperson with a distinctive personal style.

Kigusiuq draws inspiration for her art from her experience living on the land as a young woman, and she typically depicts communal activities from traditional Inuit lifestyle. Winter camp scenes, groups travelling on the land by foot or dogteam, and Inuit celebrating traditional drum dances are among her favored subjects, though Kigusiuq occasionally illustrates episodes from traditional Inuit mythology and from the Christian Bible as well. She is best known for her carefully-controlled graphite pencil line drawings in which she situates large numbers of people and animals in complex relationships with one another frequently adding Inuktitut syllabic notations to clarify her intent or to present conversation among individuals. She rarely incorporates color, preferring instead the clarity of carefully-drawn line.

Kigusiuq's drawings have served as the basis for twenty-three prints produced at the Baker Sanavik Cooperative between 1970 and 1990; she was represented in fifteen of the annual Baker Lake print collections between 1970 and 1990. In addition Kigusiuq's prints and drawings have been included in a number of important exhibitions, including "The Inuit Print/L'Estampe Inuit," "Looking South," "Baker Lake Prints and Print Drawings," and "Contemporary Inuit Drawings," and her work is represented in important North American museum collections, including the Canadian Museum of Civilization, Ottawa: Winnipeg Art Gallery; Macdonald Stewart Art Centre, Guelph, Ontario; Prince of Wales Northern Heritage Centre, Yellowknife, Northwest Territories; Amon Carter Museum, Fort Worth, Texas; and the University of New Brunswick Art Centre, Frederickton, New Brunswick.

Marion E. Jackson

Bibliography

Baker Lake annual print collection catalogues: 1970–1972, 1974, 1976, 1978–1979, 1981–1988, 1990.

Blodgett, Jean. *The Coming and Going of the Shaman.* Winnipeg Art Gallery, 1978.

———. *Looking South.* Winnipeg Art Gallery, 1978.

Driscoll, Bernadette, and Sheila Butler. *Baker Lake Prints and Print Drawings 1970–76.* Winnipeg Art Gallery, 1983.

Goetz, Helga. *The Inuit Print/L'Estampe Inuit.* National Museums of Canada, 1977.

Fry, J, and S. Butler. *Baker Lake Drawings.* Winnipeg Art Gallery, 1972.

Jackson, Marion, and Judith Nasby. *Contemporary Inuit Drawings.* Macdonald Stewart Art Centre, 1987.

Kigusiuq, Janet (1926–)

Janet Kigusiuq is best known for her graphics but has also gained significant recognition in the medium of fabric art. She was born in the Back River area of the Keewatin region of the Northwest Territories and is the eldest daughter of Jessie Oonark. Oonark was one of Baker Lake's—and Canada's—most distinguished artists. Kigusiuq was encouraged by her mother to draw as a means of making money to supplement her family's meager income.

Kigusiuq began drawing in 1967 and in 1970 contributed two drawings to the inaugural Baker Lake Print Collection. Since that time more than thirty of her drawings have been published in the annual print collection. Her drawings have also been frequently selected to appear in national and international group exhibitions and remain her strongest medium.

With uncanny clarity and a steady hand, Kigusiuq draws intimate portrayals of neighbors, friends, and relatives engaged in the daily activities of camp life rendered in minute detail, often from multiple viewpoints. She also enjoys portraying the myths and legends told to her as a young child by her grandmother. Over the years her style has evolved from a strong linear style with color as a decorative accent to a more painterly style where vibrant colors are applied in thick overlays of colored pencil. Kigusiuq's graphic art incorporates, in a limited manner, Western conventions of spatial perspective—shapes sometimes overlap, and there are subtle implications of volume and space.

Kigusiuq's wall-hangings were first exhibited in 1976. Her wall-hangings, like her drawings, feature clearly delineated shapes and bold compositions. Whereas Kigusiuq uses colored pencil to create line and texture on paper, she uses intricate embroidery stitching in a variety of colors to achieve a similar effect on fabric.

In 1984 Kigusiuq was chosen to travel to Ottawa, Ontario, to present Oonark's print "Giver of Life" to Pope John Paul II as a gift from the Inuit of Canada. She has travelled south on other occasions to attend exhibitions featuring her work but has never had a solo exhibition. Kigusiuq's prints, drawings, and wall-hangings are represented in many private and corporate collections and can be found in the permanent collections of the Winnipeg Art Gallery; the Canadian Museum of Civilization, Hull; the Macdonald Stewart Art Centre, Guelph, Ontario; the Agnes Etherington Art Centre, Kingston; the Prince of Wales Northern Heritage Centre, Yellowknife; and the Klamer Family Collection, Art Gallery of Ontario, Toronto—all in Canada.

Marie Bouchard

Bibliography

Arngna'naaq, Ruby. "Janet Kigusiuq." *Inuktitut* (Winter 1984).

Blodgett, Jean. *Grasp Tight the Old Ways: Selection from the Klamer Family Collection of Inuit Art.* Art Gallery of Ontario, 1983.

Bouchard, Marie. "Making Art in Baker Lake." *Inuit Art Quarterly* 4:3 (Summer 1989): 6–9.

Driscoll, Bernadette. *Inuit Myths, Legends and Songs.* The Winnipeg Art Gallery, 1982.

Furneaux, Patrick, and Leo Rosshandler. *Arts of the Eskimo: Prints.* Signum Press, in association with Oxford University Press, 1974.

Jackson, Marion E. *Contemporary Inuit Drawings.* Guelph: Macdonald Stewart Art Centre, 1987.

Parkin, Jean. "The People Within—Art from Baker Lake." *Artmagazine* (Summer 1976).

Swinton, George. "Eskimo Art Reconsidered." *Arts Canada* 28, 6 (1971–1972).

Kilbourn, Rosemary (1931–)

Born in Toronto, Ontario, Canada, the painter/printmaker Rosemary Kilbourn learned her craft at the Ontario College of Art, Toronto, and took further study at the Chelsea School of Art and the Slade School of Art, London, England.

Best known for her wood engraving and other prints, Kilbourn is also a painter; she executed a large mural in the dining hall of the University of Western Ontario (1957); illustrated one of her husband's books with a series of wood engravings (1960); and completed a number of other projects.

Kilbourn has received many honors and awards, including the C.W. Jefferys award from the Canadian Society of Graphic Arts (1962). She has exhibited with this distinguished printmaker's society, as well as at "Canadian Water Colours, Drawings and Prints 1966," National Gallery of Canada, Ottawa (1966); and many others. Examples of her work are in private and public permanent collections.

Bibliography

Kilbourn, Elizabeth. "18 Printmakers." *Canadian Art* 18:2 (March–April 1961): 100–13.

Kilbourn, William. *The Elements Combined.* Clarke, Irwin & Co., Ltd., 1960.

Kimball, Katharine (1866–1949)

A sculptor, architecture and landscape illustrator, etcher, and writer—Katharine Kimball was born in Fitzwilliam, New Hampshire, and was sent abroad to attend the Jersey Ladies College at St. Helier on the island of Jersey in the Channel Islands. She returned to the United States to study at the National Academy of Design, New York City, in the mid-1890s, then with her cousin W.J. Whittimore. In London, where she established residence, she continued her art studies with Sir Frank Short at the Royal College of Art.

Kimball travelled through England and Europe, sketching in Spain, Italy, Holland, Belgium, Switzerland, and France. She became well known for her architectural studies in pen and ink. Among the many periodicals that published her illustrations were *The Century Magazine, Scribner's, Outlook, The Studio,* and *Gazette des Beaux-Arts.* She illustrated Thomas Okey's *Paris and Its Story* (1904), Gilliat Smith's *Brussels* (1906), Sterling Taylor's *Canterbury,* and *Rochester* of the "Artist's Sketch Book Series" (1912).

Kimball began to exhibit in London in 1902. She exhibited at the Royal Academy, London; the Walker Art Gallery, Liverpool; the Salon des Artistes Français, and the Salon d'Automne, Paris, France; the Royal Society of Painter-Etchers and Engravers, London, England; the Royal Swedish Academy, Stockholm; the Albert Roullier Gallery and the Art Institute of Chicago, Illinois; the Worcester Art Museum, Massachusetts; the New York Public Library, New York City; and in the Philadelphia Sesqui-Centennial International Exposition, Pennsylvania (1926). She won a bronze medal at the 1915 Panama-Pacific International Exposition in San Francisco, California.

Kimball was a member of the Royal Society of Painter-Etchers, London; the Associé du Salon des Beaux-Arts, Paris, France; the Chicago Society of Etchers, Illinois; and served on the jury of the Salon d'Automne, Paris, France.

Her work has been collected by the Library of Congress, Washington, D.C.; the Museum of Fine Arts, Boston, Massachusetts; the New York Public Library, New York City; the Oakland Museum, California; the British Museum and Victoria & Albert Museum—both in London, England; and the Bibliothèque d'Art et d'Archéologie, Paris, France.

Phyllis Peet

Bibliography
Catalogue of an Exhibition of Original Etchings by Katharine Kimball. Chicago: Albert Roullier's Art Gallery, 1913.
Chatterton, E. Keble. *"Miss Katharine Kimball's Work in Black and White."* Brush and Pencil (1902): 20–24.

Kimball, Yeffe (1914–1978)

An Oklahoma-born American painter of Osage Indian heritage, Yeffe Kimball worked in various media but chose for her major works either oil, acrylic, or acrylic resin. Throughout most of her career she used Native American themes as subject matter while also delving into strong periods based on atomic and space exploration themes.

Between 1935 and 1939 Kimball studied at the Art Students League in New York City, with independent study in France and Italy. She studied intermittently with Fernand Léger between 1940 and 1941 in New York City. It was while studying in Europe that she first discovered, and was influenced by primitive African art. This led her in 1939 to undertake serious study of Native American painting and history. Her interest in hide-paintings by early Plains Indians is reflected in her 1947 stylized painting "To the Happy Hunting Ground." This painting of three leaping horses, each carrying a rider with flowing headdress, was shown in *The Art Digest* (1947) in an article written by Kimball.

In 1948 Kimball married Harvey L. Slatin, an atomic scientist. David Jones reported that Slatin's work and interests were a major influence during her "fused earth" period. Kimball said that her husband had been given a sample of the fused earth from the first atomic explosion site and that, without conscious planning, her new paintings were influenced by that sample. By the early 1960s she was creating paintings two feet taller than her under-five-foot self, and she had entered into her "space concept" period of burning planets, spewing atmospheric gases, and flashing comets.

Between 1942 and 1965 Kimball exhibited in more than 100 shows at galleries and museums in the United States. Kimball's first participation in a major exhibition was in 1942 at the National Acad-

emy of Art, followed in 1945 at the Armory's Critic's Choice, and the Whitney Museum of American Art—all in New York City, where she maintained a studio on West 55th Street. Rounding out 1945 she exhibited at the Carnegie Institute of Arts and Letters in Pittsburgh, Pennsylvania, and in various museums in Georgia and the Carolinas.

The following year (1946) she had her first solo showing at Rehn Gallery in New York City. By 1987 she had given more than 55 solo exhibitions in such major galleries and institutions as the Crocker Art Gallery, Sacramento, California (1947); Dayton Art Institute, Ohio (1958); Denver Art Museum, Colorado (1947); Davenport Municipal Art Gallery (1947), and Des Moines Art Center (1950)—both in Iowa; the Fine Arts Gallery of San Diego, California (1950); Galerie Giroux, Brussels, Belgium (1948); Isaac Delgado Museum of Art, New Orleans, Louisiana (1947); Joslyn Art Museum, Omaha, Nebraska (1947); John F. Kennedy International Airport, New York City (1964); Museum of New Mexico, Santa Fe (1948, 1957); Norfolk Museum, Virginia (1963); Nova Gallery, Boston, Massachusetts (1961, 1962); Portland Art Museum, Oregon (1949); Pasadena Art Museum, California (1947); Rochester Art Center, Minnesota (1951); Santa Barbara Museum of Art, California (1950); Toledo Museum of Art, Ohio (1949); Tirca Karlis Gallery, Provincetown, Massachusetts (annually, 1959–1965); the University of New Mexico, Albuquerque (1948, 1957); and the University of Virginia Museum of Fine Arts, Charlottesville (1963).

Philbrook Art Center (now Philbrook Museum of Art), Tulsa, Oklahoma, honored Kimball with four major exhibitions: solo shows in 1947 and 1948 ; a group show titled "American Indian Paintings" in 1961–1964; and a thirty-year (1935–1965) retrospective exhibition which toured in the United States in 1966–1967.

Kimball is represented in the permanent collections of the Baltimore Museum of Art, Maryland; Boston Museum of Fine Arts, Massachusetts; Cincinnati Art Museum, and Dayton Art Institute—both in Ohio; Chrysler Art Museum, Provincetown, Massachusetts; Museum of the American Indian, Heye Foundation, and Trans-World Airways, Inc.—both in New York City; Mattatuck Museum, Waterbury, Connecticut; Norfolk Museum of Arts and Sciences, Virginia; Philbrook Museum of Art, Tulsa, Oklahoma; Portland Art Museum, Oregon; Wadsworth Atheneum, Hartford, Connecticut; and Washington and Lee University, Lexington, Virginia. Following her death in 1978 her husband donated sixty-five of her paintings to the U.S. Department of the Interior's Indian Arts and Crafts Board, Washington, D.C. These paintings are housed at the Southern Plains Indian Museum in Anadarko, Oklahoma.

Kimball became a consultant on arts of the American Indian to the Chrysler Art Museum and the Portland Art Museum. She selected the Indian art section of *America 1953*, a publication of the U.S. Department of State. She was advisor to Americana Foundation and Young America Films for thirteen films. She did research and the illustrations for the *Book of Knowledge* and the *World Book of Knowledge* in 1957 and 1958. She served as vice-president, and member of the board of control of the Art Students League in New York City. She illustrated four books and illustrated and coauthored *The Art of American Indian Cooking* in 1965. She has written several articles on Indian art for *The Art Digest*, 1946 to 1949. Kimball was included in *Who's Who in American Art*.

Jeanne O. Snodgrass King

Bibliography

Highwater, Jamake. *The Sweet Grass Lives On: Fifty Contemporary North American Indian Artists.* Lippincott & Crowell, 1980, pp. 127–29.

Humphrey, Donald G. *Yeffe Kimball. A 30-Year Retrospective of An American Woman Painter.* Philbrook Art Center, 1966, pp. 1–8.

Jones, David. "Yeffe Kimball: From Caves to the Cosmos." *The Tulsa Tribune* (January 6, 1966): 44.

Snodgrass, Jeanne O. *American Indian Painters. A Biographical Directory.* Museum of the American Indian, Heye Foundation, 1968, p. 94.

Kipling, Ann (1934–)

Born in Victoria, British Columbia, the painter/sculptor Ann Kipling was a painting student of Jan Zack and Herbert Siebner before she studied at the Vancouver School of Art (1955–1960) where, in addition to the normal art curriculum, she learned the mysteries of printmaking from Rudy Kovak.

Kipling has held many solo exhibitions in galleries, including the Bau-Xi Gallery, Vancouver (1968), and "Ann Kipling," Vancouver Art Gallery—both in British Columbia (1976); she was given a large, ten-year retrospective at the Bau-Xi Gallery in Toronto, Ontario (1977); and others. Her calligraphic drawings and lyrical intaglio prints have been included in numerous group exhibitions.

Kipling has received awards and honors for her work, including the Emily Carr scholarship, a grant from the Koerner Foundation, and the Vancouver School of Art Travel scholarship—all in 1960. Examples of her work are in private and public permanent collections, including the National Gallery of Canada, Ottawa.

Bibliography

Murray, Joan. "Joan Murray Talks to Ann Kipling." *Artmagazine* 10:41 (November–December 1978): 24–26.

———. *Twelve Canadian Artists.* A Catalog. Robert McLaughlin Gallery, 1980.

Varley, Christopher et al. *Ann Kipling.* A Catalog. Vancouver Art Gallery, 1976.

Kitson, Theo Alice Ruggles (1871–1932)

Born in Brookline, Massachusetts, the sculptor Theo Alice Ruggles Kitson studied her craft in Paris, France, and took further work with her future husband, Henry Kitson.

Kitson received awards and honors for her work, including honorable mentions at the Exposition Universelle (1899), and the Salon of 1890—both in Paris, France. She exhibited four works at the World's Columbian Exposition, Chicago, Illinois (1893).

The primary breadwinner in the family (her husband's weak physical condition cut down his production), Kitson was the recipient of numerous sculpture commissions, including monuments to the veterans of the Civil War, the Spanish-American War, portrait busts, and others. Examples of her praiseworthy public memorials are represented in Arlington Cemetery, Washington, D.C.; Admiral Hopkins Square, and Roger Williams Park, Providence, Rhode Island; and other public and private venues.

Bibliography

Adelman, Joseph. *Famous Women.* John L. Rogers, 1926.

Freemann, Robert, and Vivienne Lasky. *Hidden Treasures: Public Sculpture in Providence.* Rhode Island Bicentennial Foundation, 1980.

"Mrs. Kitson, Sculptor, Dies." *Art Digest* (November 15, 1932): 18.

Klavun, Betty (1916–)

Born in Boston, Massachusetts, the artist Betty Klavun earned a Bachelor's degree in theater design from Bennington College, Vermont (1938); studied sculpture in 1960 at the studio of Fred Farr, and the School of the Brooklyn Museum—both in New York City—with Reuben Kadish.

Klavun's witty and playful three-dimensional works have appeared in many solo and group exhibitions throughout the United States and are sited in venues including the Civic Center Plaza, Scottsdale, Arizona; the General Theological Seminary, and the Manhattan Laboratory Museum—both in New York City; Manhattan Children's Psychiatric Center, Ward's Island, New York; and others.

Klavun has won many honors and awards, including a National Endowment for the Arts (NEA) fellowship (1974); artist-in-residence at Artpark, Lewiston, New York (1977); and an exhibition grant from the Plumsock Foundation, Indianapolis, Indiana.

Bibliography

"Betty Klavun." *Scottsdale Daily Progress* (June 20, 1975).

Hoffman, Marilyn. "Artist Designs Sturdy 'Sculpture' Playhouses for Children." *The Christian Science Monitor* (March 30, 1981): 18.

National Association of Women Artists Annual Exhibition. National Academy of Design, 1973, 1975.

Watson-Jones, Virginia. *Contemporary American Women Sculptors.* Oryx Press, 1986.

Klement, Vera (1929–)

Vera Klement was born between the world wars, to Russian emigré parents, when Danzig/Gdansk was still a free city. In earlier times, this 1,000-year-old Baltic port and cultural center had been a coveted possession of both Poland and Germany. Hitler wanted it so badly—along with access through Poland to isolated German territory—that he invaded Poland and precipitated World War II. Klement escaped, but her art did not. The "Strandkorb" series (1981), for example, is based on childhood images of sun-blazed beach furniture on the shore. But usually Danzig's impress is more general. Like the city, Klement's art is independent, intellectually and morally engaged, burdened—even troubled—by history and memories. Her forced departure and subsequent lack of community inclined her sensibility toward alienated brooding.

After graduating from Cooper Union, New York City, in 1950, Klement stayed on in New York, where she was first known as a printmaker. In the tradition of Munich and the German expressionists, the emotionally-charged woodcut, "The Wake" (1953), demonstrates a rough-hewn sensitivity to material, along with mastery of dramatic pattern. As her attention turned increasingly toward painting, she absorbed important aspects of abstract expressionism; in particular, the taste for large, painterly, emotion-laden, and even heroic art is a continuous presence in her work. Nevertheless, few of her paintings are abstract. "Woman at the Window" (1962) is a luscious exception, but even here the structure reflects a figurative image. A mid-1960s sequence integrates representation with the free brushwork of abstract expressionism, recalling the contemporary work of Richard Diebenkorn and San Francisco Bay area figurative painters.

In 1965 Klement moved to Chicago, Illinois. By 1969 she started teaching at the University of Chicago, Illinois, where she is still on the faculty, and began painting highly stylized, hard-edge landscape forms, as exemplified by "Avenue" (1969). This search for essences soon ran dry, however, and by the early 1970s, she had turned to purely abstract compositions, often given the titles of musical forms, such as "Phrase" and "Partita." These works related to a lifelong love of music, which had been intensified by her marriage to composer Ralph Shapey.

Klement's mature personal style began to appear in the late 1970s. This work is marked by heavily impastoed, rich and dramatic brushwork; simple, almost archetypal images; and a recurrent format of two images (on occasion, one may be abstract) juxtaposed upon a white ground. The impossibility of reconciliation between the images is emphasized by Klement's habit of either abutting two physically separate canvases or adhering a smaller canvas to the surface of the larger.

By emphasizing duality Klement comments on contemporary fragmentation. At the same time the exuberant beauty of her paint surfaces celebrates life. Usually the two images are figure and landscape, as in "Blue Figure" (1983) or their surrogates, such as the bowl and tree trunk of "Ancient Witness" (1985). In the triptych, "Expulsion from Eden" (1989), perspectivized doors on the wings frame a lyrical, pastel landscape, which is interrupted and marred at the center by two dark and sinful rectangles.

Ann Lee Morgan

Bibliography
Ashton, Dore. "Two Part Connection: Vera Klement's Painting." *Arts Magazine* 58 (March 1984): 78–79.
Ashton, Dore, and James Yood. *Vera Klement: A Retrospective.* Renaissance Society at the University of Chicago, 1987.
Suhre, Terry, and James Yood. *Locations of Desire: Phyllis Bramson, Michiko Itatani, and Vera Klement.* State of Illinois Art Gallery, 1990.

Klinker, Orpha (1891–1964)

Born in Fairfield, Iowa, the painter/printmaker Orpha Klinker studied at the University of California at Los Angeles (UCLA); the Académie Julian, Paris, France; and with Mildred Bryant Brooks, Will Foster, and Edgar Payne.

Klinker's work was exhibited in many galleries and museums in the United States and abroad, including the Grand Central Art Galleries (1940), Museum of Modern Art (1943), and the National Academy of Design (1943, 1944, 1946)—all in New York City; Mexico; the Library of Congress, Washington, D.C. (1944); Denver Art Museum, Colorado (1945); many "Annuals" of the Los Angeles County Art Museum, the California Society of Etchers (1939–1956), and Oakland Art Gallery, California (1940–1956)—all in California; and others.

Author of several books, Klinker has lectured widely and was a member of several arts organizations, including the American Society of Heraldry; California Society of Etchers; Los Angeles Art Association; the Academias Nacionales de Bellas Artes, Brazil and Argentina; National Society of Science and Arts, Mexico; Society of Graphic Artists; and others.

Klinker won many awards and honors from institutions in India, Panama, and the United States; and was also a recipient of the Croix de Commandeur from Belgium. Examples of her work are in private and public permanent collections, including the Campo de Cahuenga, and Los Angeles City Hall—both in Los Angeles, California; and many others.

Bibliography
Moure, Nancy D. *Dictionary of Artists in Southern California before 1950.* Dustin Publications, 1975.
Southern California Artists, 1890–1940. Laguna Beach Museum of Art, 1979.
A Woman's Vision: California Painting into the 20th Century. Maxwell Galleries, 1983.

Klitgaard, Georgina (1893–1976)

Born in Spuyten Duyvil, New York, the painter/etcher/muralist Georgina Klitgaard, whose Works Projects Administration (WPA) murals graced U.S. post offices in Poughkeepsie and Goshen—both in New York, and in Pelham, Georgia—studied at Barnard College and the National Academy of Design—both in New York City.

Klitgaard was a member of the American Society of Painters, Sculptors, and Gravers and also belonged to the Audubon Artists. She showed her work annually at the Pennsylvania Academy of Fine Arts, Philadelphia, where she won a gold medal in 1930. Her work was also seen every year at the Virginia Museum of Fine Arts, Richmond; the Corcoran Gallery of Art, Washington, D.C. (1928–1946); Carnegie Institute, Pittsburgh, Pennsylvania (1929–1946); and many others.

Klitgaard's work garnered many awards and honors, including prizes at the Carnegie Institute, Pittsburgh, Pennsylvania; San Francisco Art Association, California (1932); the Pan-American Exposition (1931); and others. She received a Guggenheim fellowship in 1933.

Examples of her work are in private and public permanent collections, including the Museum of Modern Art (MoMA), the Whitney Museum of American Art, and Brooklyn Museum—all in New York City; Art Institute of Chicago, Illinois; Dayton Art Institute, and Toledo Museum of Art—both in Ohio; Wood Gallery of Art, Montpelier, Vermont; and others.

Bibliography
American Art Annual. Vol 28. American Federation of Arts, 1932.
American Art in the Newark Museum. The Newark Museum, 1981.
First Biennial Exhibition of Contemporary American Sculpture, Watercolors, and Prints. Whitney Museum of American Art, 1933–1934.
Gerdts, William H. *Women Artists of America 1707–1964.* Newark Museum, 1965.
Goodrich, Lloyd, and John I.H. Baur. *American Art of Our Century.* Praeger, 1961.
Mechlin, Leila. "The Art of Today at Pittsburgh." *The American Magazine of Art* 20:12 (December 1929): 685.
Zaidenberg, Arthur, comp. *The Art of the Artist: Theories and Techniques of Art by the Artists Themselves.* Crown Publishers, 1951.

Klonarides, Carole Ann (1951–)

Born in Washington, D.C., the video artist, curator, and independent video producer Carole Ann Klonarides earned a Bachelor of Fine Arts degree from Virginia Commonwealth University, Richmond (1973); attended the Whitney Museum of American Art Independent Study Program, New York City (1972–1973); and received a Master of Arts degree from the New School for Social Research, New York City (1983).

Klonarides has had many of her works broadcast or screened from venues as scattered as Grant Park, Chicago, Illinois; New York City; Schiedam, the Netherlands; and elsewhere. At "The Science of Fiction/

The Fiction of Science" screening in Chicago (1985), a collaborative work, "Arcade," with Lyn Blumenthal and Ed Paschke received its premiere.

Winner of honors and awards, Klonarides received a media grant from The Kitchen, New York City (1983); the following year, she won a fellowship from the National Foundation for the Arts (NEA), and a production grant from the Illinois Arts Council. Examples of her work are in private and public permanent collections in the United States and abroad, including the Centre Pompidou, Paris, France; Milwaukee Art Museum, Wisconsin; Museum of Modern Art (MoMA), New York City; the Rhode Island School of Design, Providence; and others.

Bibliography

Gardner, Paul. "Thinking of Leonardo Wielding a Pixel and a Mouse." *The New York Times* (April 22, 1984): 1.

Kirshner, Judith R. "The Science of Fiction/The Fiction of Science." *Artforum* 23 (December 1984): 92–93.

Pelfrey, Robert H., and Mary Hall-Pelfrey. *Art and Mass Media.* Harper & Row, 1985.

Kloss, Gene (1903–)

Born in Oakland, California, the painter/printmaker Gene Kloss (Alice Geneva Glasier) received a Bachelor's degree with honors from the University of California at Berkeley (1924), and did graduate work at the California School of Fine Arts, Oakland, and the Oakland School of Arts and Crafts (1924–1925)—all in California.

An academician of the National Academy of Design, New York City, Kloss has won many awards and honors for her work in painting and etching, including the Eyre gold medal, Pennsylvania Academy of Fine Arts, Philadelphia (1936); the Henry B. Shope prize, Society of American Etchers, New York City (1951); first prize, the Chicago Society of Etchers, Illinois (1952); a purchase award, Library of Congress, Washington, D.C. (1953); honorable mention, Museum of New Mexico, Albuquerque (1964); and others. She is particularly proud of her appointment as colonel aide-de-camp on the staff of the Governor of New Mexico.

Kloss's work, rooted in a sympathetic interpretation of life in the Southwest, has been seen in solo exhibitions and has been invited to myriad group shows in the United States and abroad. Her paintings and prints are represented in private, public, and corporate permanent collections, including the Metropolitan Museum of Art and New York Public Library—both in New York City; Carnegie Institute, Pittsburgh, Pennsylvania; the National Museum of American Art, Smithsonian Institution, Washington, D.C.; Dallas Museum of Art, Texas; San Francisco Museum of Art, California; Museum of Tokyo, Japan; Honolulu Museum of Fine Arts, Hawaii; and many others.

In addition to the National Academy of Design, Kloss is a member of the Society of American Graphic Artists, New York; the Philadelphia Watercolor Club, Pennsylvania; and the Albany Print Club, New York.

Bibliography

Nelson, Mary Carrol. "Intaglios by Gene Kloss." *American Artist* (February 1978).

Who's Who in American Art. 19th ed. R.R. Bowker Co., 1991–1992.

Klotz, Suzanne (1944–)

Born in Shawno, Wisconsin, a prolific painter Suzanne Klotz attended Washington University, St. Louis, Missouri, and received a Bachelor of Fine Arts degree from the Kansas City Art Institute in 1966. The following year she received a secondary art teaching certificate from the University of Missouri, Kansas City, and was awarded a Master of Fine Arts degree from Texas Technical University, Lubbock, in 1972.

Klotz's work has been in many solo exhibitions in museums, universities, and art centers throughout the United States, including the Phoenix Art Museum, Arizona; Museum of South Texas, Corpus Christi, and University of Texas, San Antonio—all in Texas; Spencer Art Museum, Lawrence, Kansas; and the Schneider Museum of Art, Ashland, Oregon. A travelling solo show of her work, between 1985 and 1987, was viewed in many other institutions. Since 1970 her work has been selected for more than 200 exhibitions; her public art works may be seen at the Mesa Centennial Conference Center, Arizona; "Art for Roosevelt Park," Phoenix, Arizona; and the University of Arizona Medical Center, Tucson.

The recipient of numerous honors and awards in painting, drawing, ceramics, sculpture, and mixed media—Klotz received National Endowment for the Arts (NEA) craftsman's fellowships (1975, 1978), and shared a National Endowment for the Arts fellowship for performance and dance in 1983. Her work is in permanent collections throughout the United States and abroad, including the National Museum of American Art, Smithsonian Institution, Washington, D.C.; the San Francisco Museum of Modern Art, California; Baha'i World Center, Haifa, Israel; Baha'i National Centers, Wilmette, Illinois and Sydney, Australia; Spencer Art Museum, Lawrence, Kansas; Minnesota Museum of Art, St. Paul; and the Scottsdale Center for the Arts, Tucson Museum of Art, and the Phoenix Art Museum—all in Arizona.

Klotz taught art for five years in public secondary schools; spent an additional seven years on the full-time teaching staff in universities in Arizona, Texas, and California; and, since 1978, has been a visiting artist at other distinguished university art schools and departments. In 1990–1991, Klotz was artist-in-residence at Hilai International in Mitzpe Ramon and Ma'alot, Israel, where she conducted integrated workshops for Hebrew and Arab students and teachers, and another for Bedouin children.

During 1991 Klotz was an art consultant in South Australia for the Ngarrindjeri aboriginals; she organized and coordinated an exhibition of their aboriginal art and her own creative works for Northern Arizona University, Flagstaff, and arranged to have guest Ngarrindjeri speakers at the opening of the show. She had a show of paintings at Hebrew Union College, Jerusalem, Israel; and was a guest artist at Lakeside Studio, Michigan.

In 1992 Klotz was guest artist at Mishkenot Sha'ananim, Jerusalem, Israel, and consultant at the Jerry Mason Aboriginal Centre, Glossop, South Australia; had a solo exhibition at Chelouche Gallery, Tel Aviv; a two-person show at Ben Gurion University of the Negev; and conducted a workshop at the Municipal Gallery of Jerusalem—all in Israel; she had a solo exhibition at the Elaine Horwitch Gallery, Scottsdale, Arizona; and was visiting associate professor at the University of Utah, Salt Lake City.

Klotz views art as a vehicle to accomplish and express individuality and universal understanding. She wrote, "To achieve unity, harmony, and peace, we must consider all citizens of this world as our brothers and sisters, and all people as the fingers of one hand."

Bibliography
Arizona Clay Sculpture. Gross Gallery, University of Arizona, 1984.
Levine, Melinda. "Suzanne Klotz-Reilly at Jeremy Stone." *Images and Issues* 4:2 (September–October 1983): 60–61.
Return of the Narrative. Palm Springs Desert Museum, 1984.
Watson-Jones, Virginia. *Contemporary American Women Sculptors*. Oryx Press, 1986.

Klumpke, Anna Elizabeth (1856–1942)

A painter of portraits, genre, and landscapes in oil, pastels, and watercolors—Anna Elizabeth Klumpke was born in San Francisco, California, and studied at the Académie Julian in Paris, France, under Tony Robert-Fleury and Julian Joseph Lefèbvre. Her first awards were accorded her by the Académie: a medal and, in 1888, first prize. Also, at the Paris Salon of 1885, France, she received an honorable mention. Funds to cover her study expenses were augmented by the sale of her copy of Rosa Bonheur's painting, "Plowing in Nivernais," bought by an American visitor who admired Klumpke as she learned how to paint by copying this work in the Luxembourg Museum.

Klumpke painted many portraits in her Paris studio, including "Mrs. Randolph Coolidge and her Son," which was exhibited in the Salon and subsequently purchased by the Coolidge family of Boston, Massachusetts. This led to Klumpke's being invited to Boston for additional portrait commissions and also resulted in an exhibition of her work at the St. Botolph Club. In 1889 she became the first woman to receive Philadelphia's Pennsylvania Academy of Fine Arts Temple gold medal for her large genre painting "In the Wash House" (1888) in the annual exhibition.

Klumpke returned to Paris, France, continued to exhibit in the Salon, and visited her former idol, Rosa Bonheur. While painting portraits on a trip to the United States, Klumpke became determined to paint Bonheur's portrait. After an exchange of letters in which Bonheur assented, Klumpke arrived at Bonheur's estate on the edge of Fontainebleau Forest just the year before the French artist died. Klumpke not only did memorable portraits of Bonheur (including the portrait in the Metropolitan Museum of Art, 1898) but also wrote the artist's biography. Klumpke stayed at the château, which she inherited, for the next thirty years. In 1924 she was made a chevalier of the Legion of Honor and in 1936 an officer. In 1932 Klumpke returned to the United States for further exhibitions in Boston and San Francisco and settled in San Francisco, where she died.

Eleanor Tufts

Bibliography
Klumpke, Anna Elizabeth. *Memoirs of an Artist*. Ed. Lilian Whiting. Boston, 1940.
Tufts, Eleanor. *American Women Artists, 1830–1930*. National Museum of Women in the Arts, 1987.

Knee, Gina (1898–1982)

Born in Marietta, Ohio, the painter/printmaker Gina Knee studied at Smith College, Northampton, Massachusetts, and won honors and awards for her semi-abstract oils and watercolors.

A widow of the painter Alexander Brook, Knee held solo exhibi-

tions in galleries and museums, including the Willard Gallery, New York City (1943); a solo show in Santa Fe, New Mexico (early 1980s); and others. Her work was seen in many group shows throughout the United States and is represented in private and public permanent collections, such as the Buffalo Fine Arts Academy, and Guild Hall, East Hampton—both in New York; Denver Art Museum, Colorado; Phillips Memorial Gallery, Washington, D.C.; and others.

Bibliography
Eldredge, Charles, Julie Schimmel, and William H. Truettner. *Art in New Mexico, 1900–1945: Paths to Taos and Santa Fe*. National Museum of American Art, 1986.
Gerdts, William H. *Women Artists of America 1707–1964*. Newark Museum, 1965.
The Phillips Collection. A Summary Catalogue. The Phillips Collection, 1985.

Knight, Gwendolyn (1913–)

Born in Barbados, West Indies, the painter Gwendolyn Knight arrived in the United States at the age of seven. After living in St. Louis, Missouri for six years, her family moved to Harlem in New York City. Knight studied at Howard University, Washington, D.C.; the New School for Social Research, New York City; and the Skowhegan School of Painting and Sculpture, Maine. She also studied sculpture and the techniques of Graham modern dance. Knight has shown her paintings and drawings in exhibitions throughout the United States. Jacob Lawrence writes, "Her feeling for color is very lyrical and her work has a certain kind of rhythm . . . ."

Knight has been the recipient of two awards from Arizona State University, Tempe, in 1985: the centennial award of merit and the black caucus centennial medallion. Her work is represented in private and public permanent collections, including the Museum of Modern Art (MoMA), New York City; the Seattle Arts Commission, Washington; the King's County Arts Commission, New York; and others.

Bibliography
Artists of the Black Community/USA. A Catalog. The Arizona Bank Galleria, 1988.

Knopf, Nellie Augusta (1875–1962)

Born in Chicago, Illinois, the American Impressionist painter/lecturer/teacher Nellie Augusta Knopf studied at the School of the Art Institute of Chicago, Illinois, with Freer and John H. Vanderpoel; she also studied with John F. Carlson, Birger Sandzen, and Charles H. Woodbury.

Professor of art and director of the School of Fine Arts, Illinois Women's College (now Illinois College), Jacksonville, Knopf exhibited work with many professional arts organizations, including the "Fortieth Annual Exhibition" of the National Association of Women Painters and Sculptors, New York City (1931).

She was active in the American Watercolor Society; the Art Institute of Chicago Alumni; Chicago Galleries Association; the College Art Association; Illinois Academy of Fine Arts; and the Society of Independent Artists.

Knopf's work is represented in private and public permanent collections, including the John H. Vanderpoel Memorial Collection, the Art Association, Lafayette, Indiana; and others.

Bibliography
Weber, Nicholas Fox. *American Painters of the Impressionist Period Rediscovered*. Maine: Colby College, 1975.
Women Painters in Maine Art 1900–1945. Maine: Westbrook College, 1981.
Who's Who in American Art. 1st ed. American Federation of Arts, 1935.

Knowles, Alison (1933–)

A native New Yorker, visual artist and performer Alison Knowles attended Middlebury College, Vermont, as a scholarship student (1952–1954); she received another scholarship to Pratt Institute, Brooklyn, New York, where she graduated with honors and received her Bachelor of Fine Arts degree in 1957. Knowles took a graduate course in painting at Syracuse University, New York, under the aegis of Josef Albers. Returning to Pratt Institute she studied with Adolph Gottlieb and Richard Lindner (1957–1959) and, three years later, studied printing at the Manhattan School of Printing in New York.

Knowles's work has been in more than three dozen solo exhibitions and performances in the United States and Europe between 1958 and 1987, including the Nonagon Gallery, New York City (1958); "Identical Lunch," Galerie Inge Baecker, Bochum, Germany (1973); "Take a New Name," Whitney Museum of American Art, and "Japanese Bean Garden," St. Marks Church, New York City (1977); "I Am Festival," Remont Gallery, Warsaw, Poland (1978); "House of Dust," California Institute of the Arts, Valencia, and Galerie A, Amsterdam, the Netherlands (1980); "20 Years of Performance Art: Dick Higgins and Alison Knowles," University of Massachusetts, Amherst (1980); Nordyllands Kunstmuseum, Aalborg, Denmark (1987); and others.

Knowles was one of the cofounders of Fluxus (1962), and she was the only woman in the group of male artists to participate in the Fluxus Festivals early on (1962–1963). Her commitment to the group was longstanding, as evidenced by her participation in the following group exhibitions: "Happenings and Fluxus," Kunstverein, Cologne (1970); and "Fluxus Group," Galerie Rene Block, Berlin (1974)—both in Germany; "Fluxus Exhibition," Ecart Gallery, Switzerland (1978); "Fluxus Group Show on Food Art," Maison de la Culture, Châlon-Sur-Saône, France (1980); and "Fluxus 1962–1982," Kunstverein, Wiesbaden, Germany (1982). Her work was also selected for group shows, such as "Fascina della Carta," Museo Civico, Reggio Emilia, Italy (1984); "Breath River Route," 537 Artworks, New York (1986); and many others.

The mother of two daughters, Knowles has cultivated many roles: she established the Something Else Gallery in New York City with Dick Higgins (1966); was associate professor directing the graphics laboratory at the California Institute of the Arts, Valencia, California (1970–1972); performed at Douglass College, Rutgers University, New Brunswick, New Jersey (1977); was cofounder, with Dick Higgins, of Printed Editions, New York City (1978–1985); and established a studio/shop in Barrytown, New York (1984). She was a recipient of a Guggenheim Foundation fellowship in 1968; won a National Endowment for the Arts (NEA) grant in 1981; the Karl Sczuka award, Westdeutscher Rundfunk, Germany (1982); and a DAAD grant from Berlin (1984). She has completed residencies in Salzburg, Austria, and Banff, Alberta, Canada, in the 1990s. In 1991 she completed her fourth radio play for West German Radio, which had its premiere at the Whitney Museum of American Art Equitable, New York City.

Knowles's work is in the permanent collections of the Aarhus Museum, Denmark; Galerie De Appel, Amsterdam; Bibliothèque Nationale, Paris, France; Inga Baecker, Bochum, Germany; Rene Block Gallery, New York City and Berlin, Germany; Kunstbibliotek, Hellerup, Denmark; Pepe Morra Gallery, Naples, Italy; Nordyllands Kunstmuseum, Aalborg, Denmark; Hans Sohm Archives, Markgroeningen, Germany; and others.

Writer, editor, printmaker, performer, and painter—Knowles has based her imagery on the seeming mundane: beans, books, fishes, and shoes. As she states, "The objects used in my artworks are commonplace, often ephemeral and always changed from use. I often use food in artworks, for example, beans. I interact with the working process automatically, letting the materials speak for themselves . . . ."

Bibliography
Hale, B. "Follow Alice But . . ." *The Telegram*. Toronto (September 1967).
Knowles, Alison. *A Bean Concordance*. Vol 1. Printed Editions, 1983.
Marks, Claude. *World Artists: 1950–1980*. H.W. Wilson, Publishers, 1984.
Who's Who in American Art. 19th ed. R.R. Bowker Co., 1991–1992.

Knowles, Dorothy (1927–)

One of Canada's more distinguished contemporary interpreters of the prairie landscape, Dorothy Knowles originally had no intention of becoming a painter. Born in Unity, Saskatchewan, Canada, on April 7, 1927, she studied at the University of Saskatchewan to be a lab technician. Graduating in 1948 Knowles had no summer plans in mind, and her friend, Alice McNab, suggested that they go to the summer school for the arts at Emma Lake. There she met the painter Reta Cowley, who inspired her to take evening art classes at the University of Saskatchewan for the next four years. The principle instructor at the university was Eli Bornstein, whose interests then were in early American modernism of the sort practiced by John Marin. Profoundly affected by this fertile cultural environment, Knowles resolved to study at the Goldsmith School of Art in London, England, and she registered in 1952. Not long after, however, the Saskatchewan painter William Perehudoff arrived and spirited her off to the continent, where they married in the British embassy in Paris. Her academic studies were thus interrupted, but she was thereby exposed to a great deal of art in London, Paris, and Italy.

The couple returned to Canada later in 1952, and Knowles seems to have been inactive for about four years. In 1956, however, she began attending the Emma Lake Artists Workshops, which would become western Canada's most important forum for advanced contemporary art in the 1960s. Arguably the most influential of these was led by the critic Clement Greenberg in 1962. In spite of Greenberg's reputation as a champion of post-painterly abstraction, he advised Knowles to be true to her nature, which was thoroughly imbued with a sensitivity to nuances of the landscape. (It has been argued that this was the result of her childhood, when she was so much younger than her brothers that she was alone with the land all the time.) She was then painting fairly heavily on masonite, but in 1963 another distinguished painter, Kenneth Noland, advised her to use much thinner paint. This she did, and her technique began to resemble watercolor washes. (Some have further linked this to a local tradition of watercolor landscapes begun by Augustus Kenderine, who started the original Emma Lake summer school in 1935. However, Kenderine died in 1947, the year before Knowles first went to the school. One could just as effectively adduce the very thinly painted late landscapes of Emily Carr.)

In 1964 Knowles began to paint from the back of a van, which greatly facilitated a wider range of prairie motifs. The practice was well-established in western Canada—both Kenderdine and Carr had done the equivalent—but Knowles seems to have been influenced as much by John Steinbeck's *Travels with Charlie*. Since her first major show at the powerful David Mirvish Gallery in Toronto in 1965, Knowles has grown steadily in accomplishment and fame.

Robert J. Belton

Bibliography
Fenton, Terry. *Dorothy Knowles: Paintings 1964–1982*. Exhibition Catalog. Regina: Norman Mackenzie Art Gallery (April 15–May 22, 1983).

Knowles, Elizabeth (1958–)

Born in St. Louis, Missouri, the sculptor Elizabeth Knowles earned a Bachelor's degree from Pomona College, Claremont, California (1981) and, two years later, received a Master of Fine Arts degree from the School of the Art Institute of Chicago, Illinois.

Knowles has exhibited work in solo and group shows in the United States and abroad, including "Three New York Sculptors," Wake Forest College, Winston-Salem, North Carolina (1990); "Air Lines," Long Island University, C.W. Post College, Greenvale, New York (1989); "Fiber R/Evolution," a travelling show, Milwaukee Art Museum and the University of Wisconsin, Milwaukee (1986–1987); "12e International Biennale Lausanne," Musée Cantonal des Beaux-Arts, Switzerland (1985); and others.

Winner of honors and awards, Knowles received a grant from the Ludwig Vogelstein Foundation (1989) and another from the Joyce Caryle Memorial Fund, The Banff Centre, Alberta (1984). "Continuum" (1990), a large, biomorphic wire, paint, and plaster sculpture is not atypical of her work of this period: the painted, layered wire form appears to destabilize space. Examples of her work are represented in private and public permanent collections.

Bibliography
Billeter, Erika. *Sculpture Textile: 12th International Biennal of Tapestry*. Lausanne, Switzerland: Musée Cantonal des Beaux-Arts. 1985.
Braff, Phyllis. "Lines Redefining Space." *The New York Times* (April 9, 1989).
Sandler, Irving. *Queens Museum Annual 88*. New York: Queens Museum, 1988.

Knowlton, Grace F. (1932–)

Born in Buffalo, New York, the sculptor/photographer Grace Knowlton earned a Bachelor's degree from Smith College, Northampton, Massachusetts (1954), and a Master of Arts degree in art and education from Teachers College, Columbia University, New York City (1981).

Knowlton has held solo exhibitions of her work in sculpture, drawing, and photography throughout the United States and has had her work invited to group exhibitions from Northampton, Massachusetts, to Tucson, Arizona; New York City; San Francisco, California; Bridgehampton, New York; Dallas, Texas; Cincinnati, Ohio; and Atlanta, Georgia. A sampling of exhibition sites, including public installations, ranges from the Spectrum Gallery, New York City; San Francisco Museum of Modern Art, California; Metropolitan Museum of Art, New York City; Center for Creative Photography, Tucson, Arizona; M-13, New York City; Dallas Museum of Modern Art, Texas; and many others.

Knowlton has won several awards and honors, including a grant from the East Hampton Center for Contemporary Art, Long Island, New York (1989), resulting in a public installation at that site. Other installation sites include the C.W. Post Campus, Long Island University, New York (1987–1988); City Hall Park and Socrates Park, New York City (1987); and the Stamford Art Museum, Connecticut (1986).

Knowlton's work is represented in private, public, and corporate permanent collections in the United States and abroad, including the Corcoran Gallery of Art, Washington, D.C.; Cathedral of St. John the Divine, New York City; Houston Museum of Fine Arts, Texas; Victoria & Albert Museum, London, England; Mobil Corporation, Washington, D.C.; and others.

Bibliography
Burstyn, Ellen. A Film. "Balls of Grace." 1988.
"Grace Knowlton, Layers and Traces." A Catalog. Smith College Museum of Art, 1992.
Johnson, Ken. "Grace Knowlton at Bill Bace. *Art in America* (January 1990).
Smith, Roberta. "Review." *The New York Times* (April 14, 1992).

Knowlton, Helen Mary (1832–1918)

A painter, writer, and art teacher, Helen Mary Knowlton was born in Littleton, Massachusetts, and was raised in Worcester, where her father was mayor and editor of the *Worcester Palladium*—a newspaper which she and her sister ran for a few years following his death in 1871. She studied painting in Boston, Massachusetts, in the early 1860s and established her own studio there in 1867. The next year she was one of about forty women artists who approached the city's premier portraitist and figure painter, William Morris Hunt, to teach an art class for them. The French-trained, Barbizon-influenced Hunt consented and conducted this course from 1868 to 1871, when he asked Knowlton—one of his foremost pupils—to take over the class, which she then directed in 1875. That conservative Boston would have a professional art course for women was a novel development. Based on notes she compiled from Hunt's frequent critique-visits to this class, Knowlton in 1875 produced the instruction manual, *Talks on Art*. In 1879 she wrote another book, *Hints for Pupils in Drawing and Painting*, which reflected Hunt's ideas about teaching and was illustrated with his charcoal drawings. Around this period she started what would be a long career writing art criticism for the *Boston Post*, continued her painting, and also began conducting other art courses. Out of both genuine interest and economic necessity Knowlton would teach for the next two decades; William Rimmer and Frank Duveneck were visiting lecturers in her classes. Through her as well as Hunt's efforts, Boston collectors began acquiring works by Gustave Courbet, Jean-François Millet, and Edouard Manet. While much of her best art was lost in an 1870s studio fire in Boston, her many charcoal drawings and broadly-massed, loosely-brushed oil paintings—ranging from figure pieces to landscapes—show Hunt's influence and suggest comparison with the work of such Barbizon painters as Charles François Daubigny, Millet, and Camille Corot. Influenced also by Duveneck, with whom she probably studied in Munich, Knowlton directed her attention from landscapes to portraits, the first of these being a dramatic likeness of "Hunt" painted the year following his death in 1879. Between 1873 and 1897 she contributed work almost annually to the Boston Art Club. Her paintings were also exhibited at the Boston Museum of Fine Arts, the Pennsylvania Academy of Fine Arts, and New York's National Academy of Design. Described as America's first female Boswell, she in 1899 published a biography, *The Art-Life of William Morris Hunt*, which provides insights into Hunt's personality. Details of Knowlton's later life are vague, and she died relatively forgotten. Her highly accomplished oil portrait of Hunt is in the Worcester Art Museum, and her "Haystacks" (c. 1878) is in the Boston Museum of Fine Arts.

Victor Koshkin-Youritzin

Bibliography
Dunford, Penny. *A Biographical Dictionary of Women Artists in Europe and America since 1850.* University of Pennsylvania Press, 1989.
Hoppin, Martha J. "Women Artists in Boston, 1870–1900: The Pupils of William Morris Hunt." *The American Art Journal* (Winter 1981): 17–46.
Rubinstein, Charlotte Streifer. *American Women Artists: From Early Indian Times to the Present.* Avon, 1982, pp. 109, 114, 118–19, 167.
Sharf, Frederic A. "Knowlton, Helen Mary." *Notable American Women 1607–1950: A Biographical Dictionary.* Ed. Edward T. James. Harvard University Press. Vol. 2, pp. 342–43.

Knowlton, Win (1953–)

Born in Boston, Massachusetts, the sculptor Win Knowlton studied at the Instituto Allende, San Miguel de Allende, Mexico (1974); did further work at Winchester College of Art, England (1977); and earned a Bachelor of Fine Arts degree from Parsons School of Design, New York City (1978).

Knowlton has held solo exhibitions in museums and galleries in the United States and abroad, including " Projects," Museum of Modern Art (MoMA) (1986), and "Win Knowlton: New Sculpture," BlumHelman Gallery (1987, 1990)—both in New York City; "Win Knowlton," Galerie Montenay, Paris, France (1988); and others. Her work has been invited to many group exhibitions, such as "On Ward's Island," Organization for Independent Artists (1980), and "Selections," Artists Space (1982)—both in New York City; "Group Sculpture Exhibition," Dart Gallery, Chicago, Illinois (1986); "Drawings," Marc Richards Gallery, Los Angeles, California (1987); "Abstract Expressions, Recent Sculpture," The Lannan Museum, Lake Worth, Florida (1988); "For the Collector: Important Contemporary Sculpture," Meredith Long & Company, Houston, Texas (1989); "It Must Give Pleasure: Erotic Perceptions," Vrej Baghoomian Gallery, New York City (1990); and others.

Knowlton is the recipient of a Guggenheim Foundation fellowship at Chesterwood, Stockbridge, Massachusetts (1988). Her sculptural works elicit haunting metaphors of our age, using reinforced concrete, glass, rubber, and copper tubing in strange and wondrous ways. Her work is represented in private and public permanent collections.

Bibliography
Brenson, Michael. "Art: Knowlton's Work on Show at the Modern." *The New York Times* (March 28, 1986): C30.
Cyphers, Peggy. "New York in Review." *Arts Magazine* (January 1989): 107.

Gillette, Frank. *Win Knowlton: New Sculpture.* A Catalog. New York: BlumHelman, 1990.

Knox, Susan Ricker (1875–1959)

Born in Portsmouth, New Hampshire, the painter/printmaker Susan Ricker Knox studied her craft in New York, Philadelphia, Pennsylvania, and Europe.

Knox garnered many awards and honors for her work, including an honorable mention at the Connecticut Academy of Fine Arts, Westport (1927); honorable mention at the Springfield Art League, Massachusetts (1927); and honorable mention at the Ogunquit Art Association, Maine (1931); second prize in printmaking, Museum of Northern Arizona, Flagstaff (1932); and many others. She was a member of the Pen and Brush Club, Society of Painters, National Association of Women Painters and Sculptors; and American Artists Professional League—all in New York City; Connecticut Academy of Fine Arts, Westport; North Shore Art Association, Long Island, New York; Ogunquit Art Association, Maine; and Phoenix Art Association, Arizona. Examples of her work are in the collection of the Board of Trade, Kansas City, Missouri; a public school in Jamestown, New York; and other sites.

Bibliography
American Art Annual. Vol. 30. American Federation of Arts, 1933.
Fielding, Mantle. *Dictionary of American Painters, Sculptors, and Engravers.* Modern Books and Crafts, 1974.
Samuels, Peggy, and Harold Samuels. *Illustrated Biographical Encyclopedia of Artists of the American West.* Doubleday, 1976.

Koblitz, Karen Estelle (1951–)

Italian plates of painted fruits and vegetables inspired Karen Estelle Koblitz's ceramics during her junior college years in Italy. Born in Los Angeles, California, Koblitz graduated with a Bachelor of Fine Arts degree from the California College of Arts and Crafts, Oakland, in 1973. Three years later she earned her Master of Fine Arts degree from the University of Wisconsin, Madison. After five years of teaching at Baker University in Baldwin City, Kansas, and two years as chair of the ceramics department at the University of South Carolina in Columbia, Koblitz returned to Los Angeles to become a full-time artist.

Still-life images in vivid colors continued to dominate her work, progressing from painted fruit, fish, and vegetables to three-dimensional, slip-cast objects on platters and in buckets. The early trompe-l'oeil effect soon gave way to intricate patterns, transforming familiar objects into complex compositions. Wall reliefs of common objects show the influence of della Robbia arched wall reliefs framed by foliage. Seventeenth-century Dutch still-life paintings and the patterns on Mayan ruins in Mexico also are reflected in her work.

Invited to design dinnerware at a pottery in Deruta, Italy, Koblitz spent the summer of 1990 and 1991 at Dr. Ubaldo Grazia's factory. Since 1981 Koblitz has participated in group exhibitions; in 1987 she was commissioned to do a mural, and her work was featured in five shows from Washington, D.C., to Santa Fe, New Mexico. In 1991–1992, Koblitz taught a course in design at the University of California (UCLA) at Los Angeles.

Elaine Levin

Bibliography

Horowitz, Jacki. "Ceramic Artist Bakes Vivid Color, Humor into Her Pieces." Life/Arts, *The Outlook* 112:28 (February 2, 1987): C1+.

Koblitz, Karen. "A Love Affair with Italy." *Ceramics Art and Perception* 6 (1991): 37–40.

Levin, Elaine. "Mixes of Color and Pattern." *Artweek* (April 21, 1984): 4.

Kohlmeyer, Ida (1911–)

Ida Kohlmeyer, a prolific and successful painter and sculptor with a truly unique style, began making art only in her late thirties. Born in New Orleans, Louisiana, Kohlmeyer's first love was English literature, in which she majored at Newcomb College, where she earned her Bachelor of Arts degree in 1933. After graduation Kohlmeyer married a local businessman, raised two children, and played a great deal of golf. But her husband's service in World War II made Kohlmeyer keenly aware that something was missing in her life; she took some neighborhood art classes, then enrolled at Tulane University's Newcomb Art School. There art professor Pat Trivigno encouraged her to complete the Master of Fine Arts degree in painting, which she did in 1956.

Kohlmeyer's work at this time was exclusively figurative, mostly portraits of children. But her art underwent a profound change during the summer of 1956, when she was exposed to abstraction—specifically, abstract expressionism—at Hans Hofmann's Provincetown, Massachusetts, school. For several years after that her art was quite gestural, and she also notes the influence of Mark Rothko, who was artist-in-residence at Newcomb Art School, Tulane University, New Orleans, Louisiana, when she began teaching there in 1957. She continued teaching there until 1965, and also taught at the University of New Orleans (1975–1975)—also in New Orleans, Louisiana.

Kohlmeyer developed her characteristic, mature style during the 1970s. These paintings are large and energetic, filled with eccentric pictographic elements, arranged in grids. Over the years Kohlmeyer gradually simplified her work, and began experimenting with sculpture—using everything from wood to styrofoam, sewn and stuffed fabric, and welded steel.

Kohlmeyer has also participated in group exhibitions throughout the United States since 1962, including such prestigious venues as the Corcoran Gallery of Art Biennial, Washington, D.C. (1963, 1967); the "Inter-American Annual Exhibition of Painting" in Colombia, South America (1963). The artist has had well over forty solo shows, at the New Orleans Museum of Art, Louisiana (1957, 1967, 1974); the Ruth White Gallery, New York City (1959, 1961, 1965); the Heath Gallery, Atlanta, Georgia (1968, 1971, 1973, 1977, 1981); the David Findlay Galleries, New York City (1976, 1978, 1980, 1982); the William Sawyer Gallery, San Francisco, California (1977, 1980, 1983); the Elaine Horwitch Gallery, Scottsdale, Arizona (1979); Giimpel Fils, London, England (1984); and elsewhere. She has had retrospectives at the Turman Gallery, Indiana State University, Terre Haute (1972); and the Mint Museum, Charlotte, North Carolina (1983), which travelled to six other museums through 1985.

Kohlmeyer's work is in numerous important collections, such as the Addison Gallery of American Art; Phillips Academy, Andover, Massachusetts; the Smithsonian Institution's National Museum of American Art, the Corcoran Gallery of Art, and the National Museum of Women in the Arts—all in Washington, D.C., the High Museum of Art, Atlanta, Georgia; the Jewish Museum, New York City; the San Francisco Museum of Modern Art, California; the Houston Museum of Fine Arts, Texas; and the Milwaukee Art Center, Wisconsin. Kohlmeyer has received many honors, including the annual achievement award of the National Women's Caucus for Art (1980), and the (New Orleans) Mayor's Art Award; moreover, March 1985 was officially declared "Ida Kohlmeyer Month" in her home city.

Bibliography

Donnell-Kotrozo, Carol. "Ida Kohlmeyer: Pictographic Grids that Feel." *Arts* 188:9 (April 1980): 188–89.

Green, Roger. "Ida Kohlmeyer Month." *Art News* 84: 6 (Summer 1985): 104–05.

Kolbowski, Silvia (1953–)

In the late 1970s a number of feminist artists embraced postmodern theory as the basis of their work. Conceptual artist Silvia Kolbowski was particularly interested in Lacan's psychoanalytic theory of woman as existing only as a spectacle for male desire. She created a series of photographic collages that exposed the way in which women are imaged in the media as silent spectacles. The piece, "Model Pleasures" (1984), appropriates media images of glamorous female models representing idealized images for the male gaze, but reveals them to be veiled, barred from speech, only objects of consumer exchange. As such the viewer is implicated in a voyeuristic position of domination and control. These images are juxtaposed with texts that employ a slippage of meaning from one word to the next (craved/carved) based on French psychoanalytic theorist Julia Kristeva's notion that such slippage can disrupt the patriarchal language that she believes constructs culture generally. According to Kristeva this slippage is founded in the period prior to language acquisition—the "pre-oedipal"—and thus has the power to subvert the positioning of women as absent spectacles within a patriarchal language structure. Kolbowski thus unmasks the cultural construction of women as spectacle in the media.

In the later 1980s and early 1990s Kolbowski did a series of "Enlargements" of art catalogs that reproduce parts of the text with the addition of her own typeset commentary on the text. The methodology of documentation itself is questioned in these pieces and raises issues of exhibitions, art institutions, and the ideological nature of representation.

Kolbowski is also an important critic and theorist. Her writing appears in a number of the landmark texts on postmodern art, as well as in important publications such as *Artforum, Flash Art, Afterimage,* and *m/f.*

Kolbowski was born in 1953 in Buenos Aires, Argentina, and received her Bachelor of Arts degree from Hunter College, the City University of New York (CUNY). Her art has been shown in a variety of contexts and places, including Paris, France; Amsterdam, the Netherlands; Lyons, France; Documenta in Kassel, Germany (1987); and Israel, as well as in a variety of galleries and museums in New York City. One-person exhibitions of her most recent work, "Once More, with Feeling" (1992), were held in New York City and in Paris. She now lives in New York City and has taught theory and studio art in the Whitney Museum of American Art Independent Study program for several years.

Patricia Mathews

Bibliography
The Desire of the Museum. Exhibition Catalog. The Whitney Museum of
American Art, 1989.
Kolbowski, Silvia. "Discordant Views." *Blasted Allegories: An Anthology
of Writings by Contemporary* Artists. Ed. Brian Wallis. New Museum
of Contemporary Art, 1987, pp. 386–94.
Linker, Kate. "Ex-posing the Female Model." *Parachute* (Fall 1985).
Owens, Craig. "Posing." *Difference. On Representation and Sexuality*. New
Museum of Contemporary Art, 1985.
Silvia Kolbowski, XI Projects. Border Press, 1992.

Koop, Wanda (1951–)

Wanda Koop's work has been called "one of the most audacious uncompromising painting projects in contemporary Canadian art" (John Bentley Mays, *The Globe and Mail*, August 27, 1987). Working in series on large format plywood panels, using bold simplified images, the heroic scale of her work has the impact of billboards. Her direct expressive method and vibrant palette gives an impressive physicality to the work.

Born in Vancouver, British Columbia, Canada, Koop now lives in Winnipeg where she graduated from the University of Manitoba in 1973. Regular one-person exhibitions include "Nine Signs," Glenbow Museum, Calgary, Alberta (1983); "Airplanes and the Wall," Winnipeg Art Gallery, Manitoba (1985); and "The Northern Suite," Canada House, London, England (1987). Her work has been shown in important national exhibitions including "Songs of Experience," National Gallery of Canada (1986).

Early gestural and impressionistic landscapes in the 1970s expressed Koop's understanding of the limitless prairie landscape. Summer travels since 1980 have provided Koop with hundreds of visual notes. In 1982 she travelled 10,000 miles across Canada making sketches and small panel paintings. Sixty large charcoal drawings were developed in her Winnipeg studio and nine were selected to translate into eight-by-twelve-foot paintings for "Nine Signs." Huge central images, for example "Raven," "Hayroll," and "Incinerator," were transformed into psychologically charged symbols. "Raven," a black silhouette on a field of brilliant yellow, signifies life and death.

Koop sites her work carefully, and each exhibition becomes a single installation. "Building" (1983), eleven eight-by-twelve-foot paintings, was installed following the curve of the elegant rotunda, known as the Pool of the Black Star, in the Manitoba Legislative Building. "Reactor Suite" (1985), exhibited at the National Gallery, shows the dangers of technology in paintings which suggest a post-holocaust world. In some paintings from the late 1980s Chinese opera masks are fractured, split down the center, and then reassembled in powerful and disturbing images. Others, such as "Flying to the Moon" (1987), feature masks and Chinese symbols, the chrysanthemum, and carp, in brilliantly-colored images of harmony and serenity which celebrate human spiritual values.

Patricia Ainslie

Bibliography
Bradley, Jessica, and Diana Nemiroff. *Songs of Experience*. National
Gallery of Canada, 1986.
Burnett, David, and Marilyn Schiff. *Contemporary Canadian Art*. Hurtig, 1983.
Enright, Ribert. "Thinking Big." *Canadian Art* 1:1 (Fall 1984): 36–41.

Koppelman, Dorothy (1920–)

A native New Yorker, the painter Dorothy Koppelman studied at several New York City institutions, including Brooklyn College, American Artists School, and the Art Students League; and also with Eli Siegel. Koppelman has won many awards and honors, including prizes for her paintings in exhibitions at the City Center Gallery (1957); the Brooklyn Society of Artists (1960); and a grant from the Tiffany Foundation (1965–1966)—all in New York City; and others. "The Grip" (1959), a figurative oil on canvas, is typical of the work of this period and may be characterized as an example of "aesthetic realism," encompassing the push and pull of visible tensions.

Art teacher and consultant, Koppelman has shown work in exhibitions, including the Museum of Modern Art (MoMA), a travelling show (1962–1963); Pratt Graphics Center, a travelling show (1962–1963); and Terrain Gallery (1969, 1970)—all in New York City; and many others. Examples of her work are in private and public permanent collections, among them Yale University, New Haven, Connecticut; Hampton University, Virginia; and others.

Bibliography
Recent Painting USA: The Figure. A Catalog. Museum of Modern Art, 1962.
Who's Who in American Art. 15th ed. R.R. Bowker Co., 1982.

Kopriva, Sharon (1948–)

Born in Houston, Texas, the painter/sculptor Sharon Kopriva earned a Bachelor's degree in art education from the University of Houston, Texas (1970), and a Master of Fine Arts degree in painting from the same institution in 1981.

Kopriva has held a number of solo exhibitions of her work in the United States, including "Conflicting Rituals," Corpus Christi State University (1992), "Rite of Passage," the Art Center Museum, Waco (1991), Graham Gallery, Houston (1986, 1990), "Penances," and the Art Museum of Southwest Texas, Beaumont (1991)—all in Texas; "Sharon Kopriva," J. Rosenthal Gallery, Chicago, Illinois (1990); Brazosport Fine Arts Center, Lake Jackson, Texas (1981); and others. In addition to many shows in her native state, her work has been invited to numerous group exhibitions in the United States and abroad, such as the LewAllen Gallery, Santa Fe, New Mexico (1992); "Dreams and Shields," Salt Lake City Art Center, Utah (1992); Hall-Barnett Gallery, New Orleans, Louisiana (1990); Allan Stone Gallery, New York City (1985, 1987, 1980); "Memento Mori," Centro Cultural Arte Contemporaneo, Mexico City, Mexico (1986); "Arteder," Graphic Arts International, Bilbao, Spain (1982); and others.

Kopriva has received honors and awards for her work, including an individual artist's grant from the Cultural Arts Council, Houston (1991) and an outdoor installation grant for "Landscapes" (1990). She won first prize at an area exhibition held at the University of Houston (1988); an honorable mention at a Texas Invitational, Fort Worth Art Festival (1986); and a best of show at the Brazosport Fine Arts Center, Lake Jackson (1979)—all in Texas; and others. Her work is represented in private, public, and corporate permanent collections in the United States, including the Menil Museum and the Museum of Fine Arts, Houston, Texas; Museum of New Mexico, Santa Fe; Edward and Nancy Kienholz, Hope, Idaho; the Barrett Collection, Dallas, Texas; and others.

Bibliography
Bloom, Suzanne, and Ed Hill. "Review." *Artforum* (May 1989).
Ganbrell, James. "Texas: State of the Art." *Art in America* (March 1987).
Tennant, Donna. "Sharon Kopriva at Graham Gallery, Houston." *Artspace* (Fall 1986).
Who's Who in American Art. 19th ed. R.R. Bowker Co., 1991–1992.

Korzybska, Mira Edgerly (c. 1872–1954)

Painter, writer, and lecturer—Mira Edgerly Korzybska (the Countess Alfred Skarbek de Korzybska) was born in Aurora, Illinois. Her portraits "Mrs. Lawrence Drummond with Jim" and a portrait of her husband are in the permanent collections of the Metropolitan Museum of Art (MoMA), New York City, and the Art Institute of Chicago, Illinois, respectively.

Bibliography
American Art Annual. Vol. 30. American Federation of Arts, 1933.
Earle, Helen L. *Biographical Sketches of American Artists.* Michigan State Library, 1912.
Who's Who in American Art. 3rd ed. American Federation of Arts, 1940.

Kowalsky, Elaine (1948–)

Elaine Kowalsky is one of the few artists currently based in Britain who has chosen to concentrate on printmaking as her main medium of expression. Using "the battleground between men and women, between basic emotional needs and psychological confrontation" (Pauline Barrie, *Works From The Rouge Press*, 1988), she has created an uncompromising visual language about male/female relationships.

Born in Winnipeg, Canada, in 1948, Kowalsky now lives and works in the East End of London, England. She attended the University of Manitoba, Canada (1967–1971), which was followed by a post-diploma in printmaking at St. Martin's School of Art, London, and a year at Brighton Polytechnic—both in England—as part of a specialist printmaking group. She was a major mover in the establishment of North Star Studios print workshop in Brighton, England in 1977 and is a leading member of the women's print group, The Rouge Press. In 1987 her work as a printmaker was acknowledged with the awarding of the first Henry Moore fellowship in printmaking at Leeds Polytechnic, England.

From producing small black-and-white engravings, the "Larger Than Life" exhibition at Canada House, London, England, in 1986 marked Kowalsky's emergence into a full-blown large format. She works principally with woodcut and linocut in sizes of up to four-by-five feet, or more recently on a foundation of silk-screened color. Dark blues, pinks, reds, and yellows notably fight for attention within the confines of restless black-and-white contours and cross-marking. Relief from this emotional onslaught is seen in titles drawn from the cliché of pulp magazines and books: "He Couldn't Help Himself"; "She's Seen It All Before"; "It's Heart-Rendering Stuff"; "Yes, Love Hurts." Within the acknowledgement of these crude, frequently funny myths, Kowalsky has found a space to retrieve a sense of joy and strength.

Tessa Sidey

Bibliography
Barrie, Pauline. *Work from the Rouge Press.* Touring Exhibition Catalog. Clwyd: Oriel Gallery, 1988.
Bear, Griselda. *Larger Than Life.* Exhibition Catalog. London: Canada House, 1986.
Sidey, Tessa. *Hearts and Vessels: Elaine Kowalsky, The Henry Moore Printmaking Fellow, 1987–88.* Exhibition Catalog. Leeds City Art Gallery.

Kozloff, Joyce (Blumberg) (1942–)

Born in Somerville, New Jersey, Joyce (Blumberg) Kozloff earned her Bachelor of Fine Arts degree at the Carnegie Institute of Technology, Pittsburgh, Pennsylvania (1964) and her Master of Fine Arts degree from Columbia University, New York City (1967). She also studied at the Art Students League, New York City; Rutgers University, New Brunswick, New Jersey; and the University of Florence, Italy.

Kozloff has held several professional positions, from teaching elementary and junior high school art to painting instructor and visiting artist at several colleges and institutions, including the School for Visual Arts in New York City; the Chicago Art Institute, Illinois; the San Francisco Art Institute and California State University at Fresno—both in California. She was awarded a grant from the Tamarind Institute in Albuquerque, New Mexico (1972), a New York Creative Artists Public Service (CAPS) grant (1972–1973) in printmaking and in painting (1975–1976); and a National Endowment for the Arts (NEA) grant for painting in 1977.

Kozloff's first one-person show took place in 1970 at the Tibor de Nagy Gallery, New York City, and it was in the early years of that decade that she began her use of patterning. These paintings and prints are, in her own words, "deliberately decorative."

Initially inspired by the decoration on Mexican cathedrals during a trip to that country one summer, Kozloff studied its origin in both Spanish and Islamic (North African) traditions. She has since incorporated into her work patterns derived from folk arts and styles from the past, such as art nouveau and art deco. Thus her work links international as well as historical crafts traditions from countries as diverse as Egypt, Morocco, Persia, and China.

For Kozloff the use of colorful, flat, abstract patterning is based on these historic examples (Homage to Robert Adam, 1980). Others who compose work of this nature, such as Miriam Shapiro, Kim MacConnel, and Valerie Jaudon, produce a different form based on other criteria. Pattern painting (as opposed to patterns in painting) has its roots in the "decorative" arts (textiles, wallpapers, etc.) and has frequently been associated with feminist ideology. In Kozloff's work the repetitive geometric forms are produced with strongly varied elements of line, shape, and color. Kozloff seeks an art that is, in her own words, "nonethnocentric"—it becomes purely decorative and pleasurable without any alliance to any particular nationality or period.

In the 1980s Kozloff produced a number of site-specific public art pieces using tiles and mosaics—two of the original formats for these patterning motifs. These include "New England Decorative Arts" (1979–1985) for the Harvard Square Subway Station, Cambridge, Massachusetts; "Galla Placidia in Philadelphia" and "Topkapi Pullman" (1985) in the lobby of that city's One Penn Plaza, Pennsylvania; and "'D' is for Detroit" (1987) for the Financial Station of the Detroit's Downtown People Mover, Michigan.

A recent project has involved a series of thirty-two watercolors, each twenty-two inches square. "Patterns of Desire" (subtitled "Pornament is Crime") involves the manipulation of a series of erotic art historical images whose sources include, among others, Pompeiian frescoes, Greek vase painting, Japanese prints, and Indian and Persian patterns. One composition may be based on a series of up to ten Eastern and Western motifs forming "patterns" of color and texture.

Adeline Lee Karpiscak

Bibliography
Kozloff, Joyce. *Patterns of Desire*. Introduction by Linda Nochlin. Hudson Hills Press, 1990.
Perrault, John. "Issues in Pattern Painting." *Artforum* 16 (November 1977): 32–36.
Phelan, Peggy. "Crimes of Passion." *Artforum* 28 (May 1990): 173–77.
Webster, Sally. "Pattern and Decoration in the Public Eye." *Art in America* 75 (February 1987): 118–24.
White, Robin. "Joyce Kozloff." *View*. Crown Point Press, 1981.

Kraft, Polly

A resident of Washingon, D.C. and Wainscott, Long Island, New York, the painter Polly Kraft is a graduate of the Corcoran School of Art, Washington D.C.; and the University of Maryland, College Park.

Kraft has had sixteen solo exhibitions of her work between 1972 and 1991. Her watercolors and oils have been included in many group shows, such as the "De Menil Invitational," at the Guild Hall Museum, East Hampton, New York (1975); "Long Island Artists of the Region," Parke Bernet, New York City (1976); the Heckscher Museum, Huntington, Long Island, New York; and the Diane Brown and Osuna Galleries in Washington, D.C. Kraft's paintings are included in numerous corporate and private collections throughout the United States.

While her earlier work was centered primarily on the domestic still life with particular emphasis on the disorder of everyday living (e.g., rumpled bedsheets, books opened, objects askew), Kraft has moved on to such works as "Zinnias I" (1990), a directly painted, figure-ground watercolor which evokes the very essence of these flowers.

Bibliography
Florescu, Michael. "Polly Kraft." *Arts Magazine* (April 1981).
Newhall, Edith. "Arts and Kraft." *New York* (March 7, 1988).
Russell, John. "Peter Loftus and Polly Kraft." *The New York Times* (April 4, 1986).

Kramer, Linda (1937–)

A native New Yorker, the ceramist/sculptor Linda Kramer earned a Bachelor's degree from Scripps College, Claremont, California (1959), and received a Master of Fine Arts degree from the School of the Art Institute of Chicago, Illinois (1981).

Kramer has been a guest speaker, visiting artist, or faculty member at a number of colleges and universities between 1979 and 1986, such as Southern Illinois University, Carbondale (1986); University of Wisconsin, Green Bay (1984); Columbia College, Chicago, Illinois (1981); Purdue University, Lafayette, Indiana (1979); and others. She has held solo exhibitions and has had her work invited to numerous group shows throughout the United States, including "Solo American Transformed," Loyola University, Chicago (1993); Artemisia Gallery, Chicago (1973–1980); "Landscapes," Jean Albano Gallery, Chicago (1992); and "Still Light," Octagon Gallery, Evanston (1990)—all in Illinois; "Chicago Contemporary Sculpture," CAGE Gallery, Cincin-

nati, Ohio (1987); "Scripps College Invitational International Ceramics," Claremont, California (1984); "Linda Kramer," University of Arizona, Tucson (1984); "Magic Mystery Tour," Los Angeles Municipal Gallery, Barnsdall Park, California (1982); and others.

Winner of awards and honors for her work, Kramer received several prizes at exhibitions held at the Art Institute of Chicago, Illinois, including the Levy fund prize (1984), the Arts & Riverwoods award (1980), and the Eisendrath prize (1977); she was a fellow at the Dorland Mountain Colony for Creative Arts, Temecula, California (1986); and was invited to the Karolyi Foundation in Vence, France (1989). Her work is represented in many private and public permanent collections in Illinois, Indiana, New York, and California, such as the Museum of Contemporary Art, Chicago; Purdue University; Lafayette, Indiana; and others.

Bibliography
Carroll, Patty. *Portraits of Chicago Artists*. University of Illinois Press, 1991.
Elliot, David. "Chicago Enjoys its Own Eclecticism." *Art News* (May 1982).
Koplos, Janet. "Linda Kramer." *American Ceramics* (Winter 1984).

Kramer, Margia

A native of Brooklyn, New York, the installationist, video artist, and painter Margia Kramer earned a Bachelor's degree from Brooklyn College and a Master of Arts degree from New York University—both in New York City.

Kramer has won many awards and honors for her videos, which delve into politically-sensitive and aesthetically-innovative, camouflaged subjects. She has received grants from the National Endowment for the Arts (NEA) (1976, 1982), the Illinois Arts Council Project (1981), the New York State Council on the Arts (1981), and the Jerome Foundation (1985); she also received fellowships from the MacDowell Colony, Peterborough, New Hampshire (1982, 1984, 1985); and others.

Kramer has held solo exhibitions in museums and galleries, including "New Paintings," Sarah Lawrence College, Bronxville, New York (1977); and others. She has presented installations in venues in the United States and abroad, including A Space Gallery, Toronto, Canada; the Institute for Contemporary Art, London, England; the Whitney Museum of American Art and the Museum of Modern Art (MoMA)—both in New York City; and others. Examples of her works are in private and public permanent collections, including MoMA and the Guggenheim Museum—both in New York City; the University of California at San Diego; and others.

Bibliography
Linker, Kate. "Margia Kramer, Progress (Memory)." *Artforum* 22 (Summer 1984): 89.
Lippard, Lucy R. "They've Got FBEyes for You." *The Village Voice* (November 1981).
Wooster, Ann-Sargent. "Manhattan Short Cuts." *Afterimage* 9 (February 1982): 19.

Krasner, Lee (Lenore) (1908–1984)

Best known as the wife of Jackson Pollock, Lee (Lenore) Krasner was a significant contributor to the first generation of abstract expressionist art.

Born in Brooklyn, New York, of Russian emigré parents, Krasner attended the public schools in Manhattan. Her formal education included the Woman's Art School of Cooper Union (1926–1929), the Art Students League (1928), the National Academy of Design (1929–1932), City College of New York, and Greenwich House (1933)—all in New York City. During the early 1930s Krasner painted fantastical, surrealistic cityscapes for a brief period, reflecting the influence of Giorgio de Chirico, Arshile Gorky, and Joan Miró. By far the most influential figure in Krasner's training was Hans Hofmann with whom she studied from 1937 to 1940. Hofmann introduced her to the structuralism of Cubism, the colorism of Henri Matisse, and his "push-pull" theory of the spatial effects of color. In her work done for Hofmann—mainly figure drawings and compositions based on still lifes—Krasner worked on problems of integrating form and color. Krasner was employed intermittently by the Works Progress Administration (WPA) from 1934 to 1941. Initially under the supervision of Burgoyne Diller and subsequently a supervisor herself, Krasner was introduced to large-scale compositions through her work for the mural division. In 1940 she became affiliated with the American Abstract Artists group (AAA), a group of artists working along lines similar to those of the Dutch DeStijl movement—and through this group met Piet Mondrian, whose work she greatly admired. Krasner exhibited with the AAA in its annual exhibitions from 1940 to 1943. During these years her work combined curvilinear synthetic cubistic forms with black lines recalling Mondrian.

Although Krasner met Pollock in the mid-1930s she did not see his work until 1942, when they were both preparing for "American and French Painting," an exhibition organized by John Graham for the McMillan Gallery. Krasner immediately became an ardent supporter of Pollock's work and after their marriage in 1945 largely worked in directions that paralleled those of Pollock. Her small-scale (generally less than two feet) "Little Images" paintings of 1946 to 1949 included works reflecting the couple's investigations of techniques of improvisation and free-association. These included: paintings done with palette knife or open tube of paint; drip paintings, which approximated Pollock's all-over canvases; and hieroglyphic or grid compositions that were begun in the upper-right and worked across in a manner suggesting Hebraic writing or cuneiform, but most directly inspired by automatic games and free-associational lettering. These transitional works were exhibited at Betty Parson's Gallery, New York City, in 1951.

Beginning in 1951 Krasner began to work in collage. From 1951 to 1953 she made a series of painted paper collages by cutting up unsuccessful paintings or drawings in black ink or wash. In 1953 she began her first major series of collage paintings in which she used paintings left over from the Parsons show as backgrounds onto which she painted large configurations cut out of discarded works. This group of large-scale (over six feet tall) collages was exhibited at Eleanor Ward's Stable Gallery, New York City, in 1955. After these collages Krasner turned to new imagery and formats: figurative expressionist paintings in a style reminiscent of Gorky's use of anatomical motifs (1956–1957), a series of mural-sized action paintings (1959–1962), and small works on paper begun in 1969. In 1976 she began her second major series of collage paintings in which compositions dating from the Hofmann years (1937–1940) were cut and placed on sized, but unpainted canvas along with passages of muted colors resulting from paint bleeding through colored sheets that had been reversed to use as collage elements. This group of collage compositions was exhibited in 1977 at the Pace Gallery, New York City.

Until the 1970s historians and critics viewed Krasner's work as dependent upon that of Pollock. The first major retrospective of Krasner's work curated by Bryan Robertson was held at Whitechapel, London, England, in 1965 and was circulated throughout England by the Arts Council of Great Britain the following year. Recognition in the United States occurred with the mounting of an exhibition of Krasner's large-scale paintings at the Whitney Museum of American Art, New York City, in 1973–1974 and a retrospective at the Corcoran Gallery of Art, Washington, D.C., in 1975. More recently Barbara Rose has reassessed the work of Krasner in "Krasner/Pollock: A Working Relationship," an exhibition held at the Guild Hall, East Hampton, and the Grey Art Gallery, New York City, in 1981, and a retrospective at the Houston Museum of Fine Art, Texas, in 1983. Such studies and exhibitions demonstrate that Krasner was a significant figure in the first generation of abstract expressionism.

Virginia Hagelstein Marquardt

Bibliography
Landau, Ellen G. "Lee Krasner's Early Career." *Arts Magazine* 56:2 (October 1981): 110–22; (November 1981): 80–89.
Rose, Barbara. *Lee Krasner: A Retrospective.* Houston: Museum of Fine Arts, and New York: Museum of Modern Art, 1983.
Tucker, Marcia. *Lee Krasner: Large Paintings.* New York: Whitney Museum of American Art, 1973.

Kreyes, Marielouise (1925–)

Born in Lobberich, Germany, the realist painter Marielouise Kreyes earned a Bachelor's degree in the arts at the School of Fine Arts, University of Manitoba, Canada (1959–1963), under the aegis of George Swinton and others.

Kreyes has held solo exhibitions in museums and galleries in Canada, including the Albert White Gallery, Toronto, and the Yellow Door Gallery in Winnipeg (1965); and others. Her work has been included in group shows, such as the "Second Annual McLaren Acquisition Show," Winnipeg (1966); the Manitoba Society of Artists Exhibition, a travelling show (1967); and others.

Kreyes has won honors and awards, including a gold medal and the Grand Prix du Salon International de Vichy, France (1960); her work is in private and public permanent collections.

Bibliography
Payne, Anne. "Kreyes." *Emerging Arts West* 1:3 (March–April 1976): 15–18.

Kruger, Barbara (1945–)

Born in Newark, New Jersey, the multi-faceted artist Barbara Kruger studied at Syracuse University, New York (1965), and the following year attended classes at Parsons School of Design, New York City, where she studied photography with Diane Arbus and graphic art with Marvin Israel. Kruger has moved from soft sculpture to painting to photography to photographic images with words, where content is as important, or more so, than form—where her feminist inclinations have become more precise.

Kruger has been a popular teacher at art schools and universities, and has won awards and honors for her work, including a Creative Artists Public Service (CAPS) grant from the New York State Council on the Arts (1976); a National Endowment for the Arts (NEA) fellowship (1982); a fellowship from the New York Foundation on the Arts (1985); and others.

Kruger has held solo exhibitions in museums and galleries in the United States and abroad, including the Institute of Contemporary Art, London, England (1983); and others. She has had her work included in many prestigious group exhibitions, such as the "Biennials" at the Whitney Museum of American Art, New York City (1973, 1983, 1987); and many others. Examples of her work are represented in private and public permanent collections, including the Museum of Modern Art (MoMA) and the Whitney Museum of American Art—both in New York City; the Milwaukee Art Museum, Wisconsin; and others.

Bibliography

Barbara Kruger: 'We Won't Play Nature to Your Culture.'" London: Institute of Contemporary Arts, 1983.

Brenson, Michael. "Art: Whitney Biennial's New Look." *The New York Times* (April 19, 1987): 17.

Kunst mit Eigen-Sinn. Aktuelle Kunst von Frauen. Vienna and Munich: Locher Verlag, 1985.

Siegel, Jeanne. "Barbara Kruger: Pictures and Words." *Arts Magazine* 51:10 (Summer 1987): 17–21.

Kruger, Louise (1924–)

Born in Los Angeles, California, the sculptor/printmaker Louise Kruger studied at Scripps College, Claremont, California; the Art Students League, New York City; and was an apprentice to several masters, including Captain Sundquist (a shipbuilder from whom she learned wood joinery); and F. Guastini, Pistoia, Italy, and Chief Opoku Dwumfuor, Kumasi, Ghana, who imparted the secrets of foundry work.

Kruger has held many solo exhibitions, including the Artist's Gallery (1949, 1950, 1955), Martha Jackson Gallery (1957, 1959), and Schoelkopf Gallery (1968, 1970)—all in New York City; Squibb Gallery, Princeton (1975), and Drew University, Madison—both in New Jersey (1976); Bowdoin College, Brunswick, Maine (1977); Condeso-Lawler Gallery, New York City (1979, 1980, 1982); Port Washington Library, Long Island, New York (1985); Martin Sumers Graphics, New York City (1986); and many others. Her work has been invited to many group exhibitions in major galleries and museums in the United States and abroad: from New York City to Zurich, Switzerland; Philadelphia, Pennsylvania; Oslo, Norway; Oakland, California; and São Paulo, Brazil. Examples of her prints and sculpture are represented in many private and public collections, including the Museum of Modern Art (MoMA), the New York Library Print Collection, and the Brooklyn Museum—all in New York City; Museu de Arte Contemporaneo, São Paulo, Brazil; and others.

Bibliography

Glueck, Grace. "Art: Sculptured Figures of the 70's at Pratt." *The New York Times* (November 7, 1980): C19.

Henry, Gerrit. "Louise Kruger: Expressions in Wood." *American Craft* 40:6 (December 1980–January 1981): 26–29.

Mainardi, Patricia. "Louise Kruger." *Arts Magazine* 55:7 (March 1981): 13.

Watson-Jones, Virginia. *Contemporary American Women Sculptors.* Oryx Press, 1986.

Krugman, Irene (1925–1982)

A native New Yorker, the sculptor Irene Krugman studied at several institutions, including the Kansas City Art Institute, Missouri; New York University; and the New School for Social Research—both in New York City, with Yasuo Kuniyoshi.

Krugman held solo exhibitions in museums and galleries, such as the Summit Art Center, New Jersey (1971); the New Jersey State Museum, Trenton (1975–1976); Bertha Urdang Gallery (1980), and 55 Mercer—both in New York City (1981); and others. Her work appeared in many group exhibitions, including "Some More Beginnings" (1968), and "Works on Paper: Women Artists" (1975–1976), Brooklyn Museum, New York; "Contemporary Americans," Riverside Museum, New York (1970); and many others.

Krugman's work is represented in private and public permanent collections in the United States, including Michigan State University, East Lansing; Newark Museum, New Jersey; New Jersey State Museum, Trenton; University of Notre Dame, Indiana; and others.

Bibliography

Alloway, Lawrence. "Irene Krugman: An Obituary." *Woman's Art Journal* 5:2 (Fall 1984–Winter 1985): 53–54.

Glueck, Grace. "Irene Krugman." *The New York Times* (February 4, 1977).

Malen, Lenore. "Irene Krugman." *Arts Magazine* 52:8 (April 1978): 24.

Who's Who in American Art. 15th ed. R.R. Bowker Co., 1982.

Kubota, Shigeko (1937–)

Known for her video art and video curating expertise, Shigeko Kubota was born in Niigata, Japan, and earned a Bachelor's degree in sculpture at the University of Tokyo, Japan.

Kubota's videos have been exhibited in museums and galleries in the United States and abroad, including "Video Sculpture: Duchamp's Grave," The Kitchen, New York (1975), also viewed at the Everson Museum, Syracuse, New York (1976), and the Kunstakademie, Berlin, Germany (1976); "Nude Descending a Staircase," Seattle, Washington (1976), and "Dokumenta 6," Kassel, Germany (1977); "Video Sculptures," René Block Gallery, New York City (1977); and many others.

Video curator at Anthology Film Archives (1974), and video faculty member at the School of Visual Arts, New York City (1978 to the present), Kubota has won honors and awards, including a documentary video grant from the National Endowment for the Arts (1976); a Creative Artists Public Service (CAPS) grant from the New York State Council of the Arts (1976) to create three video sculptures; and more.

Bibliography

Bourdon, David. "A Critics Diary: The New York Art Year." *Art in America* (July–August 1977).

———. "The Young Generation: A Cross-Section." *Art in America* (September–October 1977).

Kukiiyaut, Myra (1929–)

Myra Kukiiyaut was born in Baker Lake, Northwest Territories, Canada, where her father worked for the Royal Canadian Mounted Police, but was raised on the land where she lived a traditional nomadic existence subsisting on caribou and fish, living in an igloo in winter and a caribou skin tent in summer. Kukiiyaut, along with her young daughter and newborn son, moved permanently to Baker Lake in 1957 after her husband, artist Luke Argna'naaq, became ill with tuberculosis and was evacuated from their camp. He was hospitalized in the South, where he remained for the next three years, leaving Kukiiyaut and her children dependent on government relief.

To supplement her income Kukiiyaut sewed traditional clothing for sale to local white people. She experimented with art making for the first time in 1960, when the federal government established an arts and crafts program in Baker Lake. She made small carvings and crafts. Her sculpture was included in the exhibition, "Eskimo Fantastic Art," mounted in 1972 at Gallery 111 in Winnipeg, Manitoba. She also made a tentative attempt at drawing in 1967 but did not pursue this medium in earnest until artists Jack and Sheila Butler, advisors for the arts and crafts program, arrived in 1969. Over the years Kukiiyaut has developed primarily as a graphic artist and printmaker but has also experimented with wall-hangings and weaving in recent years.

From the outset Kukiiyaut favored depicting abstract concepts—"The Wind" (1971), "Dreaming" (1972), "As It Is Given, So We Accept" (1973) are the subjects of her early prints. Her subject matter is derived from memories of traditional songs, legends, and beliefs, as well as from her own astute observation of the world around her. According to Kukiiyaut, the enchanting, flowing, rhythmic forms characteristic of her work originate from the fluid shapes found in nature—cloud formations floating across an expanse of clear, blue sky; wind-swept figures and their shadows, spilled juice on the linoleum floor.

Kukiiyaut draws in a subliminal fashion: "I just start drawing and then it becomes different from what I thought I was going to draw." The Butlers encouraged this freedom of expression, and under their nurturing eye Kukiiyaut developed a distinctive, highly personal style. Her drawings first appeared in the 1971 Baker Lake Annual Print Collection and have been included in each annual collection since. She began printing her own drawings in 1978 using the techniques of stenciling, stonecut/stenciling, and woodcutting. She prints other artists works as well.

Drawings and prints by Kukiiyaut have been featured in thirty-one national and international group exhibitions in such noted shows as "The Inuit Print," mounted by the Department of Indian Affairs and the National Museum of Man (now the Canadian Museum of Civilization, Ottawa) (1977–1982); "The Coming and Going of the Shaman: Eskimo Shamanism and Art," Winnipeg Art Gallery, Manitoba (1978); "Polar Vision: Canadian Eskimo Graphics," Jerusalem Artists' House Museum, Israel (1978); "Grasp Tight the Old Ways: Selections from the Klamer Family Collection of Inuit Art," Art Gallery of Ontario, Toronto (1983–1985); "Contemporary Inuit Drawings," Macdonald Stewart Art Centre, Guelph, Ontario (1987–1989); "In the Shadow of the Sun: Zeitgenossische Kunst der Indianer und Eskimos in Kanada," Canadian Museum of Civilization, Ottawa, Ontario (1988–1989)—all in Canada; and "Art Inuit, la Sculpture des Esquimaux du Canada," mounted by L'iglou Art Esquimau, Douai, France (1989).

In 1973 Kukiiyaut's drawings were featured alongside those of her peers—Luke Anguhadluk, Ruth Annaqtussi, and Janet Kigusiuq—at Robertson Galleries in Ottawa. The artist has never had a solo exhibition of her work.

Kukiiyaut is an accomplished throat singer and performed at the Inuit Pavilion at Expo '86 in Vancouver, British Columbia. She was also invited to attend the opening of the exhibition "In the Shadow of the Sun," at the Canadian Museum of Civilization in 1989.

Drawings and prints by Kukiiyaut can be found in the collections of the National Gallery of Canada, Ottawa; the Canadian Museum of Civilization, Ottawa; the Canada Council Art Bank, Ottawa, the Musée des Beaux-Arts de Montréal, Québec; the Macdonald Stewart Art Centre, Guelph, Ontario; the Klamer Family Collection, Art Gallery of Ontario, Toronto; the Winnipeg Art Gallery, Winnipeg; the Clifford E. Lee Collection, University of Alberta, Edmonton; the Saskatoon Gallery and Conservatory Corporation, Yellowknife, Saskatchewan; and the Prince of Wales Northern Heritage Centre, Yellowknife.

The artist continues to reside in Baker Lake. She has nine children and numerous grandchildren.

Marie Bouchard

Bibliography

Blodgett, Jean. *The Coming and Going of the Shaman: Eskimo Shamanism and Art.* Winnipeg Art Gallery, 1979.

———. *Grasp Tight the Old Ways: Selections from the Klamer Family Collection of Inuit Art.* Art Gallery of Ontario, 1983.

———. "Christianity and Inuit Art." *The Beaver* (Autumn 1984): 16–25.

Collinson, Helen. *Inuit Games and Contests: The Clifford E. Lee Collection of Prints.* The University of Alberta Collections, 1978.

Driscoll, Bernadette. *Inuit Myths, Legends and Songs.* The Winnipeg Art Gallery, 1982.

Jackson, Marion E. *Contemporary Inuit Drawings.* Macdonald Stewart Art Centre, 1987.

Merlinger, Elizabeth Schotten. "In the Shadow of the Sun: Exhibition Review." *Inuit Art Quarterly* 4:4 (Fall 1989): 20–23.

National Museum of Man. *The Inuit Print/L'Estampe Inuit.* National Museums of Canada, 1977.

Shamans and Spirits: Myths and Medical Symbolism in Eskimo Art. Canadian Arctic Producers and the National Museum of Man, 1979.

Kurz, Diana (1936–)

Born in Vienna, Austria, the painter Diana Kurz earned a Bachelor's degree *cum laude* at Brandeis University, Waltham, Massachusetts and received a Master of Fine Arts degree from Columbia University, New York City, where she studied with Robert Beverly Hale, John Heliker, and Ralph Mayer.

Kurz has held many solo exhibitions in galleries and museums throughout the United States and abroad, including the Thomas Center Gallery, Gainesville, Florida (1991); Mercer County Community College, Trenton, New Jersey (1990); Bienville Gallery, New Orleans, Louisiana (1989); Brooklyn Botanic Gardens, New York (1989); Palais de Justice, Aix-en-Provence, France (1986); and Alex Rosenberg Gallery (1984), Snug Harbor Cultural Center (1982), Green Mountain Gallery (1972, 1974, 1977, 1979), Queens College (1977), and Brooklyn College (1974)—all in New York City; and others. Between 1963 and 1992 her work has been invited to more than eighty two-person and group exhibitions, some of them travelling shows—from Moscow, Russia, to Cherry Hill, New Jersey; from New York City to Paris, France; from Boulder, Colorado, to Louisville, Kentucky.

Kurz loves contrasts in her many-layered works: elegant flowers sitting in American Art Pottery of the 1930s, 1940s, or 1950s; decoration and pattern versus three-dimensionality; transparency and luminosity versus opaqueness. Her most recent work is narrative in content. She has taught widely from 1968 to 1990 in various art schools and colleges, including the Philadelphia College of Art, Pennsylvania; Queens College and Pratt Institute—both in New York City; State University of New York (SUNY) at Stony Brook; University of Colorado, Boulder; Virginia Commonwealth University, Richmond; Cleveland Institute of Art, Ohio; Art Institute of Chicago, Illinois; Vermont Studio Center; and others.

Kurz has won many honors and awards for her pastels and oils, including a Hambidge Center fellowship (1992); an American Center residency at the Cité International des Arts, Paris, France (1985–1986); a Creative Artists Public Service (CAPS) grant from the New York State Council on the Arts (1977); fellowships at the MacDowell Colony, Peterborough, New Hampshire (1977), Yaddo, Saratoga Springs, New York (1968–1969); and Brevoort-Eickemeyer (1959–1960); and a Fulbright grant to France (1965–1966). Her work is represented in private and public permanent collections.

Bibliography
Campbell, Lawrence. "Diana Kurz at Alex Rosenberg." *Art in America* (May 1984).
Hurwitz, Laurie S. "Mixing Styles and Patterns with Assurance." *American Artist* (August 1991): 38–43, 81–82.
Langer, Sandra L. "Diana Kurz." *Arts Magazine* (February 1984).
McClelland, Elizabeth. "Profile: Diana Kurz." *Nova News* (February 1981).

Kusama, Yayoi (1929–)

Painter, sculptor, filmmaker, novelist, and performance artist—Yayoi Kusama was born in Matsumoto City, Nagano, Japan. She studied at the Arts and Crafts School, Kyoto, Japan (1948–1951) and took classes at the Art Students League, the Brooklyn Arts School, and Washington Irving School (1957–1958)—all in New York City. She relocated to the United States in 1960; became a naturalized citizen six years later, and returned to Tokyo in 1974.

Kusama has held more than three score solo exhibitions, happenings, or performances in Japan, Europe, and the United States between 1952 and 1987, including her first one of 240 paintings at the Matsumoto Civic Hall, Japan (1952); Stephen Radich Gallery, New York City (1960, 1961); Stedelijk Museum, Schiedam, the Netherlands (1964); Galleria del Naviglio, Milan, Italy (1966, 1982); Fuji Television Gallery, Tokyo, Japan (1982, 1984, 1986); "Mirror Ball Sale Happening," Giardina della Biennale, Venice, Italy (1966); "Phallics Festival," St. Patrick's Cathedral (1968), "Nixon Orgy," New School for Social Research (1968), and "Naked Orgy Performance," Museum of Modern Art (MoMA) Garden (1969)—all in New York City; "Infinity Nets," Video Gallery Scan, Tokyo, Japan (1984); and many others. Her work has been selected for inclusion in group exhibitions throughout the world, such as the "International Biennial of Watercolor," Brooklyn Museum, New York (1955, 1959); "Monochrome Malerei," Stadtische Museum, Leverkusen, Germany (1960); "The Object Transformed," MoMA, New York City (1966); "Soft-Art," Kunsthaus, Zurich, Switzerland (1979); "Le Japon des Avantgardes," Centre Georges Pompidou, Paris, France (1986); and others.

Kusama is an artist of uncommon visions; as a child she is reported to have seen haloed objects and listened to the speech of the flora and fauna around her. Her works in many media burgeoned after 1957: she created works with polka-dot surfaces; made soft sculptures; used mirrors and electric circuitry to fashion kinetic sculptures; staged happenings; made a film, *Kusama's Polka Dot Obliteration*; founded entrepreneurial outlets for her dress designs and films, such as Kusama Enterprises, Kusama Polka Dot Church, Kusama Fashion Company, Ltd., Kusama International Film Company, Ltd., and others; founded and edited *Kusama Orgy* in New York (1968), a weekly newspaper; was a member of the editorial board of *Kindai Foudo*, a Tokyo magazine; and wrote novels.

Winner of many honors and awards, Kusama won a Rockefeller Foundation scholarship, New York City (1965); a film prize at the Belgian International Short Film Festival, Knokke-le-Zoute (1968); a gold award from the Accademia di Belle Arti, Rome, Italy (1982); the Kadokawa Shoten novelist prize, Tokyo, Japan (1983); and others. Her works are in the permanent collections of the Chrysler Museum, Provincetown, Massachusetts; Oberlin College, Ohio; the Stedelijk Museum, Schiedam, the Netherlands; and others.

Bibliography
Kusama, Yayoi. *Manhattan Suicide Addict*. Tokyo, 1978.
Marks, Claude. *World Artists: 1950–1980*. H.H. Wilson Company, 1984.
Who's Who in American Art. 19th ed. R.R. Bowker Co., 1991–1992.
Yayoi Kusama. Exhibition Catalog. Essay by Toshiaki Minemura. Tokyo, 1986.

Kuunnuaq, Marie (1933–1990)

Canadian Inuit artist Marie Kuunnuaq was born December 21, 1933, in the Mallery Lake area, just southwest of Baker Lake, Northwest Territories, Canada. She lived with her husband and seven children in Baker Lake until her death in March 1990.

A versatile artist, Kuunnuaq was known for her appliquéd wall-hangings as well as her sculpture. Her sense of imagination and creative ability are demonstrated by her obvious comfort with a variety of materials. Her natural skills with skins, fabric, and stone allowed her to develop her talent as a multi-media artist. In both sculpture and wall-hangings, Kuunnuaq concentrated on important relationships for her subject matter. The bonds of mother and child, families, animals, and the land were commonplace in her life, and therefore common themes in her work. Her sculptures are roughly carved masses of stone, often abstract in form, yet they express feelings of intimacy and sensitivity. The depth of these feelings in her interpretations lend warmth to the hard, dark stone of Baker Lake.

In the last twenty years of her life Kuunnuaq's work was exhibited in many shows across Canada, the United States, and Greenland, including three solo exhibitions in the early 1980s. Examples of her work are now in major collections at the Winnipeg Art Gallery, Manitoba; the Canada Council Art Bank, Ottawa; and the Inuit Cultural Institute.

Lori A. Cutler

Bibliography
Marie Kuunnuaq: Recent Sculpture. Canadian Arctic Producers Cooperative Limited, 1980.
Marie Kuunnuaq Sculpture. Canadian Arctic Producers Cooperative Limited, 1980.

Kyra (Belán) (1947–)

Born in China and reared in Argentina, the multi-talented, multi-media artist Kyra (Belán) became an American citizen; earned a Bachelor of Fine Arts degree at Arizona State University, Tempe (1973); and received a Master of Fine Arts degree from Florida State University, Tallahassee, two years later.

Kyra has held thirty-two solo exhibitions of environmental sculpture, installations, video and ritual performances, and documentary works on paper in the United States and abroad, including "The Magic Circle Goddess Series 1978–1985," Nova University, Fort Lauderdale, Florida (1985); "Nature Goddess Sekhmet: Magic Circle XII," Key Biscayne, Florida (1987); "Cosmic Goddess Demeter: Magic Circle XV," Washington and Lee University, Lexington, Virginia (1988); "Great Goddess Rhea: Magic Circle XVI," Crete, Greece (1988); and others. Her works have been invited to more than eighty group exhibitions, such as SoHo 20 Gallery (1977), Womanart Gallery (1977, 1978), Jeanne Taylor Gallery (1978), and Alain Bilhaud Gallery (1981)—all in New York City; Hanson Galleries, New Orleans, Louisiana (1980); University of Wisconsin, Milwaukee (1984); Kassel Museum, Germany (1986); the Divine Feminine, Monterey, California (1990); and myriad others throughout the state of Florida.

Kyra has been the recipient of awards and honors for her work; she is a member of several professional art associations; and a professor of art at Broward Community College, Pembroke Pines, Florida. Her work is represented in private, public, and corporate permanent collections, including Metro-Dade Art in Public Places; Broward County Art in Public Places; Bass Museum of Art, Miami Beach—all in Florida; and others.

Bibliography

Alioto, Susanne. "Kyra: Giving a Shape to Magic Realism." *The Miami Herald* (February 11, 1982).

Comini, Alessandra. "Titles Can Be Troublesome: Misinterpretations in Male Art Criticism." *Art Criticism* 1:2 (1979): 50–54.

Lauter, Estella. "Women as Mythmakers Revisited." *Quadrant* XXIII (1990).

Wynn, Patrice, ed. *The Womanspirit Sourcebook*. Harper & Row, 1988.

Labowitz, Leslie (1946–)

Following study at Otis Art Institute, Los Angeles, California, the performance artist Leslie Labowitz, intrigued by the work of Joseph Beuys, went to Germany for a four-year stay. On her return to the United States, allied with the women's movement in Los Angeles, she worked on collaborative performances with various groups, but predominately with Suzanne Lacy.

One of the works Labowitz created in Germany was *Menstruation Wait* (1971); six years later, at the City Hall in Los Angeles, Labowitz conducted a public ceremonial lamenting the women killed by the "Hillside Strangler," which also searched out strategies to resist such atrocities. Her main performance concerns are those of a feminist ardently expressing her views.

Bibliography

Dunford, Penny. *Biographical Dictionary of Women Artists in Europe and America since 1850.* University of Pennsylvania Press, 1989.

Lippard, Lucy. Issue: *Social Strategies by Women Artists.* London: ICA, 1980.

Roth, M. *The Amazing Decade: Women and Performance Art, 1970–1980.* 1983.

Lackey, Jane (1948–)

A mixed-media artist, known for her constructions of textiles, wood, and paint as well as her related drawings, Jane Lackey was born on August 3, 1948, in Chattanooga, Tennessee. She attended the California College of Arts and Crafts in Oakland, where she studied with Trude Guermonprez and received a Bachelor of Fine Arts degree with distinctions in 1974. Lackey received a Master of Fine Arts degree in 1979 from Cranbrook Academy of Art, Bloomfield Hills, Michigan, where she studied with Gerhardt Knodel.

Lackey's first professional exhibition was a one-person show at the Pacific Basin School of Textile Arts, Berkeley, California, in 1976, where she exhibited woven work with ikat imagery. Her imagery gradually became more narrative in her weavings with surfaces of telephone wire that were first introduced in a solo exhibition at the Charlotte Crosby Kemper Gallery, Kansas City Art Institute, Missouri (1982). By 1986 Lackey's weavings had evolved into "totem figures" combined with painted, wooden constructions and exhibited in the travelling exhibition "Craft Today: Poetry of the Physical," American Craft Museum, New York City.

Her constructions are often shown in conjunction with related drawings and the imagery of the two processes enrich and influence each other. In 1988 she introduced her diptych series, filled with evocative shapes and contrasting hard and soft materials. These were shown at the Hokin/Kaufman Gallery, Chicago, Illinois (1988) and the "14th International Biennial of Tapestry," Lausanne, Switzerland (1989).

Lackey is the recipient of National Endowment for the Arts (NEA) fellowships (1984, 1988); she was selected for the NEA-sponsored U.S./France Exchange and completed an artists' residency at La Napoule Art Foundation, La Napoule, France, in 1989. Lackey has been an associate professor and chairman of the fiber department at the Kansas City Art Institute, Missouri, since 1980.

Claire Campbell Park

Bibliography

Corwin, Nancy. "Jane Lackey: A Vision into Past and Future." *Fiberarts* 14:4 (1986).

Fiber R/Evolution. Milwaukee: University Art Museum, University of Wisconsin, 1989.

14th Biennale Internationale de la Tapisserie. Lausanne, Switzerland: Musée Cantonal des Beaux-Arts, 1989.

Lacy, Suzanne (1945–)

A performance artist known for collaborative productions focusing on social issues, Suzanne Lacy was born in Wasco, California. While studying psychology at Fresno State College in California, Lacy met Judy Chicago and decided instead to earn her Master of Fine Arts degree in the woman's design program at the California Institute of Arts, Valencia, where she studied under Allan Kaprow.

Lacy's first performance, *Ablutions*, took place in 1972, when Lacy, together with Judy Chicago, Sandra Orgel, and Aviva Rahmani, put on a production in Venice, California, focusing on rape. In 1977 *Three Weeks in May*, another production concerning rape, was her first performance to receive national media coverage. She erected twenty-five-foot maps of Los Angeles in a shopping mall and identified specific addresses where rapes had taken place and also where victims could get help. Coupled with daily performances, group discussions, and a gallery installation, the frequency of rape began to be acknowledged. *Mourning in Rage*, with Leslie Labowitz, in response to the "Hillside Strangler," was nationally televised. In the *International Dinner Party*, Lacy organized two thousand women from around the world to participate in dinner parties celebrating the opening of Judy Chicago's *Dinner Party* in 1979. Addressing the issues of women over sixty-five in America, Lacy created the *Crystal Quilt* in Minneapolis, Minnesota, while she was an artist-in-residence at the Minneapolis College of Art and Design. Women aged sixty-five to ninety sat at 150 tables arranged in a black, yellow, and red grid designed by Miriam Shapiro. This performance, like most of Lacy's work, is sculptural, more in the tradition of the tableau vivant rather than relying on movement or dialogue. As are many other works it is documented by a book, video, slides, and articles.

Lacy began teaching in 1974 and became the dean of the School of Fine Arts at the California College of Arts and Crafts, Oakland, in 1987. She has won many awards and grants, including National Endowment for the Arts (NEA) individual artists fellowships (1978, 1981, 1985). In 1992 she received the Lila Wallace Reader's Digest fellowship, a Guggenheim Foundation fellowship, and the National Endowment for the Visual Arts grant.

Susan F. Baxter

Bibliography

Lacy, Suzanne. "The Forest and the Trees." *Heresies* 15 (1982): 62–63.

Lippard, Lucy. "Some of Her Own Medicine." *TDR* (Spring 1988): 71–76.

Roth, Moira. "Social Reformer and Witch." *TDR* (Spring 1988): 42–60.

Rothenberg, Diane. "Social Art/Social Action." *TDR* (Spring 1988): 61–70.

Rubinstein, Charlotte Streifer. *American Women Sculptors*. G.K. Hall, 1990.

Ladd, Anna Coleman (1878–1939)

Born in Bryn Mawr, Pennsylvania, the sculptor Anna Coleman Ladd studied her craft in Paris, France, and Rome, Italy. A member of several professional art organizations, Ladd exhibited widely and won an honorable mention in the Panama-Pacific International Exposition, San Francisco (1915); she was also made a chevalier of the Legion of Honor by the government of France.

Examples of Ladd's work are in private and public permanent collections and venues in the United States and abroad, including the Borghese Collection, Rome, Italy; Boston Art Museum, Gardner Museum, and the Boston Public Gardens Fountain—all in Boston, Massachusetts; the Rhode Island School of Design, Providence; and memorial sculptures in many cities, such as Grand Rapids, Michigan; South Bend, Indiana; and others.

Bibliography

American Art Annual. Vol. 28. American Federation of Arts, 1932.

Ladd, Anna Coleman. *The Life of Anna Coleman Ladd*. Seaver Howland Press, 1920.

Proske, Beatrice G. *Brookgreen Gardens*. Brookgreen Gardens, South Carolina, 1943.

Laemmle, Cheryl (1947–)

Born in Minneapolis, Minnesota, the painter Cheryl Laemmle earned a Bachelor's degree from Humboldt State University, Arcata, California (1974); four years later, after trying various jobs, she received a Master of Fine Arts degree from Washington State University, Pullman.

Laemmle has won honors and awards, including a Creative Artists Public Service (CAPS) grant (1980); the Vera G. List award (1984); a National Endowment for the Arts (NEA) fellowship (1985); and others. Her surreal-like paintings of animals and the environment have been exhibited in many group and solo exhibitions in the United States and are represented in private and public permanent collections, including the Metropolitan Museum of Art, New York City; the Corcoran Gallery of Art, Washington, D.C.; and others.

Bibliography

Russell, John. *The New York Times* (March 11, 1983).

Vettese, Angela. "Europe and America: Two Aspects of the New Surreal." *Flash Art* 122 (April–May 1985): 20–25.

White, John. "Cheryl Laemmle." *Metropolis M* (July–August 1984): 42–45.

Lagunes, Maria (1936–)

Born in Vera Cruz on the Bay of Campeche in the state of Vera Cruz, Mexico, Maria Lagunes immersed herself in learning to play the classical guitar, hoping for a career in music. She studied interior design at the University for Women (1952–1953). Until 1956 Lagunes drew caricatures for various newspapers while studying at the School of Fine Arts in Vera Cruz. At this juncture, believing that art (which she decided upon as her vocation) required the mastery of many approaches, she took further work in the Centro Superior de Artes Aplicados in Mexico City, Mexico. She studied printmaking with Yukio Fukasawa and Ismael Ishikawa; sculpture with Francisco Zuñiga and Tomás Chavez Morado; engraving with Arturo García Bustos and Guillermo Silva Santamaria; and painting with Antonio Rodríguez Luna. She also studied ceramics with Juan Soriano. In 1966 Lagunes was awarded a scholarship from the French government to study sculpture; she toured the studios of St. Maur, Ossip Zadkine, Étienne-Martin François Stahly, and André Bloc.

Lagunes first exhibited her work in 1961 and has participated in many shows in Mexico and abroad. In 1974, and again between 1976 and 1978, Lagunes was invited to exhibit her sculpture in the Salon de Mai, Musée d'Art Moderne, Paris, France. She has been teaching drawing and three-dimensional form in the faculty of architecture of the University of Mexico, Mexico City.

Lagunes's primary theme in her work embraces man and his environment. Her principal sculptures are executed in wood, onyx, and bronze. "Rosario Castellanos," a monumental sculpture completed in 1976, is sited in Chapultepec Park, Mexico City, Mexico, as is her bronze portrait, "Leon Felipe."

Bibliography
Alvarez, José Rogelio, et al. *Enciclopedia de México*. Secretaría de Educación Pública, 1987.
The Texas Quarterly: Image of Mexico II. The University of Texas, August 1969.

Laky, Gyöngy (1944–)

Known for her constructions in a variety of media, Gyöngy Laky was born in Budapest, Hungary. Her family left Hungary when she was five and came to the United States. They eventually settled in Carmel, California, where her father ran an art gallery and her mother was a painter. Laky studied art at the University of California, Berkeley, where she received a Bachelor of Arts degree in 1970 and a Master of Arts degree in 1971. Her professor Ed Rossbach's respect for the process of inquiry and his belief that someone has to champion the things that everyone else rejects have remained lifelong influences. She also studied with Peter Voulkos and Joanne Brandford.

Much of Laky's original training was in textiles. She has explored the textile sensibility in a variety of materials as her creative work has evolved. She began to exhibit professionally in 1971, and her work was included in "California Design XI" at the Pasadena Art Museum, California. Also in 1971 she spent a year in India researching textiles under the auspices of the University of California professional studies program. In 1976 Laky was weaving three-dimensional works. One of these was commissioned by the federal government art-in-architecture program for the Social Security Administration building in Richmond, California. Not easily categorized she is known for working in a variety of humble materials such as rope, tape, wire, and, since 1978, her signature material: branches and twigs. These are transformed into dimensional constructions both on-the-wall and free-standing; they are often symbols of the familiar—baskets, houses, or, since 1983, sometimes simply sketches. Laky has also created site-specific works; notably the "Red Piece," "Yellow Piece," and "Blue Piece"—large grids of surveyor tape which were part of the inauguration of the Headland's Art Center in 1984 in Marin's Golden Gate National Recreation Area. Laky participated in the 14th Biennale Internationale de la Tapisserie, Lausanne, Switzerland (1989) with an eight-foot-tall sculpture of the word "ART" made of almond and walnut prunings and titled "That Word."

Laky has championed art in the craft media through a variety of positions of leadership. She founded Fiberworks Center for the Textile Arts in Berkeley, California, in 1973 and remained the director of this important catalyst for creative explorations in textiles until 1977. Laky was the guest curator of "Matter, Memory, and Meaning," which originated at the Honolulu Academy of the Arts, Hawaii, in 1980 and travelled for two years. She has been a trustee of the American Craft Council from 1988 to the present.

In conjunction with her interest in site-specific work she served as chairperson of the board of directors for the Capp Street project in San Francisco, California, from 1986 to 1989. Her work has been exhibited at the University of Louisville, Kentucky (1987), the Oakland Museum, California (1986), Musée des Arts Décoratifs, Paris, France, among others. Examples of her constructions can be found in the collections of the Monterey Peninsula Museum of Art, the Oakland Museum, and the San Francisco Museum of Modern Art—all in California. Laky has been a professor at the University of California, Davis, from 1978 to the present.

Claire Campbell Park

Bibliography
Curtis, Cathy. "Fiberworks: When Everything Was Possible." *Goodfellow Review of Crafts* 10:4 (1982).
14th Biennale Internationale de la Tapisserie. Lausanne, Switzerland: Musée de Cantonal des Beaux-Arts, 1989.
Matter, Memory, Meaning. Honolulu Academy of Art, 1980.
Miedzinski, Charles. "Art on the Headlands." *Artweek* 15:35 (1984).

Laliberté, Madeleine (1922–)

Born in Victoriaville, Québec, Canada, the painter Madeleine Laliberté studied at the École des Beaux-Arts, Québec; she took further work at the Académie de la Grande Chaumière, Paris, France, and also with Marcel Gromaire (1937–1938). Laliberté did additional study in New York City with Amedée Ozenfant (1942–1944).

Laliberté held a two-person exhibition with Jean Soucy in Québec City (1940), and a solo show in Québec the following year. She exhibited widely for almost two more decades; held a major solo exhibition of eighty paintings at the Compagnie Paquet Limitée, Québec City (1950); and quit painting in 1958. She returned to her craft ten years later. Examples of her work are in private and public permanent collections.

Bibliography
Ostiguy, Jean-Rene. "Le langage technique et poétique de Madeleine Laliberté." *Vie des arts* 20:81 (Winter 1975–1976): 20–22.

Lam, Jennet Brinsmade (1911–1983)

Born in Ansonia, Connecticut, the painter Jennet Brinsmade Lam earned Bachelor of Fine Arts and Master of Fine Arts degrees from Yale University, New Haven, Connecticut, where she studied with Josef Albers.

Lam achieved the title of Professor Emerita at the University of Bridgeport, Connecticut, retiring from that institution in 1972. She exhibited paintings in museums and galleries in the United States and abroad, including the Whitney Museum of American Art, New York City (1965); the Carnegie Institute International Exhibition, Pittsburgh, Pennsylvania (1964); the University of Illinois, Champaign (1963); the University of Bridgeport, Connecticut (1972); Le Point Cardinal Galerie, Paris, France (1965, 1969); Grand Central Moderns, New York City (1963, 1964, 1966); and others. Her work is represented in major museums, including the Brooklyn Museum, Museum of Modern Art

(MoMA), and Whitney Museum of American Art—all in New York City; Philadelphia Museum of Fine Arts, Pennsylvania; Yale University, New Haven, Connecticut; and others.

Bibliography
Sokol, David M. *Solitude: Inner Visions of American Art.* Terra Museum of American Art, 1982.
Waldberg, Patrick. "Jennet Lam." *Quadrum* (December 1965).
Who's Who in American Art. 15th ed. R.R. Bowker Co., 1982.

LaMarr, Jean (1945–)

Born in Susanville, California, Jean LaMarr of the Paiute/Pit River tribe studied at San José City College, California (1970–1973); the University of California at Berkeley (1973–1976); and the Kala Institute, Berkeley, California (1976–1986). She specialized in printmaking and mastered all of its processes—though she is also a muralist.

Between 1973 and 1990 LaMarr taught at many institutions, including the College of Marin, Kentfield; San Francisco State University; the California College of Arts and Crafts, Oakland; and Lassen Community College, Susanville—all in California; and the Institute of American Indian Art, Santa Fe, New Mexico, with which she is still affiliated.

LaMarr has held exhibitions of her work at Bakersfield Community College Gallery, California (1990); and the University of California at Davis (1989). She has also shown her prints in more than seventy-five major group exhibitions in the United States and abroad, including "Intergrafik 90," 90th International Triennial of Committed Graphic Arts, Berlin, Germany (1990); "LaMarr and Fonseca," Galería Esquina de la Libertad, San Francisco, California (1989); "Committed to Print," the Museum of Modern Art (MoMA), New York City, a travelling exhibit (1988–1990); and "Progressions of Impressions," Heard Museum, Phoenix, Arizona (1988), to name some recent shows.

In "Some Kind of Buckaroo" (1990), a photorealistic screenprint not atypical of her work, LaMarr depicts the present state of the Native Americans through metaphor and irony. A popular lecturer, consultant, and curator of exhibitions, LaMarr won mural commissions, grants, printmaking fellowships, and appointments as artist-in-residence from organizations as diverse as the California Arts Council; the Brandywine Workshop, Philadelphia, Pennsylvania; and the Berkeley Arts Commission, California; among others.

Bibliography
Lippard, Lucy. "Review." *The Village Voice* (1987).
Our Land/Ourselves: American Indian Contemporary Artists. A Catalog. State University of New York at Albany, 1990.
"Review." *American Indian Art Magazine.* Heard Museum Biennial, 1986.

Lambert, Beverly (1943–)

Born in Biggar, Saskatchewan, Canada, the artist Beverly Lambert enrolled in art classes at the University of Saskatchewan, Regina, where she studied with Ronald Bloore, Kenneth Lochhead, and Art McKay (1961–1963); she earned a Bachelor of Fine Arts degree from the University of Saskatchewan at Saskatoon (1967); and did further study in workshops offered by the National Film Board, Regina, and at Emma Lake, Saskatchewan, with Allan King.

In addition to solo exhibitions at museums and galleries in Canada,

Lambert's work has been included in many group shows, such as "Heart of London," National Gallery of Canada, Ottawa (1968); Norman MacKenzie Art Gallery, Regina (1969, 1970, 1971, 1973, 1978); "12th Annual Show," Winnipeg Art Gallery, Manitoba (1970); Mendel Art Gallery, Saskatoon (1972); and many others.

Lambert has won awards and honors, and her work is represented in private and public permanent collections, including the Mendel Art Gallery, Saskatoon; Saskatchewan Arts Board, Regina; and others.

Bibliography
Canadian Artists in Exhibition, 1973–1974. Roundstone Press, 1974.
McConnell, Clyde. "Two Regina Artists: Fafard and Lambert." *Artscanada* 148–149 (October 1970): 79.
Saskatchewan Arts Board Collection. Regina: Norman Mackenzie Art Gallery, 1978.

Landau, Myra (1934–)

Born in Bucharest, Rumania, Myra Landau lived for a time in Brazil before she settled in Mexico at the close of 1959. She became a naturalized citizen of Mexico in 1976. Landau was a student in Brazil, England, France, Italy, Rumania, and the United States and learned the art of intaglio from Oswaldo Goeldi.

Landau's first exhibition was held in 1963 at the Galería Juan Martín in Mexico City, Mexico. She created a most unusual mixed technique in the late 1960s which fused painting, sculpture, letterpress, and printmaking, on metal and plastic plates, into three-dimensional, textured works. A self-taught painter, Landau has exhibited her work in more than fifty group and twenty solo shows in Mexico and abroad, including a solo show in 1967 at the Galería Pecanins in Mexico City, Mexico. Her work has been exhibited at the Pan American Union in Washington, D.C., and in Argentina, Brazil, Cuba, Chile, Colombia, Ecuador, Uruguay, and other South American countries.

Landau was a professor of art at the University of Veracruz, Mexico (1974), and a year later was appointed to do research at the Institute of Esthetic Investigation and Artistic Creation, Mexico City, Mexico; she has been coordinator of the free visual and plastic arts workshops offered by the university since 1981. In 1976, commissioned by the university, she painted four murals, one of which has since been destroyed.

A twenty-year retrospective of her work titled, "Myra Landau: 1965–1985" was held in the Museum of Modern Art, Bosque de Chapultepec, Mexico City, in 1987.

Bibliography
Alvarez, José Rogelio, et al. *Enciclopedia de México.* Secretaría de Educación Pública, 1987.
The Texas Quarterly: Image of Mexico II. The University of Texas, August 1969.

Lane, Lois

Born in Philadelphia, Pennsylvania, the "New Image" painter Lois Lane spent a summer at the Yale-Norfolk Summer School of Art and Music, Connecticut (1968), then went on to receive her Bachelor of Fine Arts degree from the Philadelphia College of Art (now part of the University of the Arts), Pennsylvania, the following year. She returned to Yale University, New Haven, Connecticut, for graduate work and secured her Master of Fine Arts degree in 1971.

Lane has had many solo exhibitions of her work, including shows at Willard Gallery, New York City (1977, 1979, 1980, 1983); Greenberg Gallery, St. Louis, Missouri (1980); Akron Art Museum, Ohio (1981); and others. Her work has been selected for group exhibitions in the United States and Canada, such as the "Ronald Greenberg Collection," Brooks Memorial Art Gallery, Memphis, Tennessee (1978); the well-known "New Image Painting," at the Whitney Museum of American Art, New York City, and its Biennial (1979); "10 Artists/Artists Space," Neuberger Museum, State University of New York (SUNY) at Purchase (1979); "American Painting: The '80s," Grey Art Gallery, New York University, New York City, which travelled to Texas and Europe (1979–1980); "Painting and Sculpture Today," Indianapolis Museum of Art, Indiana (1980); "Printed Art: A View of Two Decades," Museum of Modern Art (MoMA), New York City (1980); "American Prints 1960–1980," Sadye Bronfman Centre, Montréal, Québec, Canada (1980); and many others.

Lane received a New York State Council on the Arts Creative Artists Public Service (CAPS) grant in 1977, and a National Endowment for the Arts (NEA) fellowship in painting the following year. Her work is housed in the permanent collections of the Museum of Modern Art (MoMA), and the Whitney Museum of American Art—both in New York City; the Akron Art Museum, Ohio; the Art Museum of South Texas, Corpus Christi; the Museum of Fine Art, Houston, Texas; and others.

Bibliography

Marks, Claude. *World Artists: 1950–1980.* H.W. Wilson Publishers, 1984.
Siegel, Jeanne. "Lois Lane and Robert Longo: Interpretation of Image." *Arts Magazine* 55:3 (November 1980): 154–57.
Staniszewski, Mary Anne. "Lois Lane (Willard Gallery)." *Art News* 80:3 (March 1981): 230.
Who's Who in American Art. 19th ed. R.R. Bowker Co., 1991–1992.

Lanfear, Marilyn (1930–)

A native of Texas, the sculptor/performance artist Marilyn Lanfear earned a Master of Fine Arts degree in 1978 and has had her work included in prestigious group shows in galleries and museums in the United States and abroad, including the Dallas Museum of Fine Art, Laguna Gloria Art Museum, McNay Art Institute, the San Antonio Art Institute, and the Witte Museum—all in Texas. She has exhibited work at the Museo de Arte Contemporanea da Universidad de São Paulo, Brazil (1980); the Museo de Monterrey, Mexico; and in many alternative spaces.

Lanfear's work—including her lead blouses—exists on many levels: autobiographical, psychological, sociological, filled with commentary and wry humor, but always presented in formal aesthetic terms. Examples of her work are in private and public permanent collections.

Bibliography

"Artistas Americanas." *Folma de São Paulo.* (October 26, 1980).
Moore, Sylvia, ed. *No Bluebonnets, No Yellow Roses: Essays on Texas Women in the Arts.* Midmarch Arts Press, 1988.
Neal, Patsy. "Lead Blouses: A Stunning Exhibit." *San Antonio Light* (September 3, 1982).
Sieberling, Dorothy. "A New Kind of Quilt." *The New York Times Magazine* (October 3, 1982): 42–50.

Lange, Dorothea (1895–1965)

Although she produced thousands of photographs during her lifetime, Dorothea Lange could have established her reputation on one widely reproduced photograph: her "Migrant Mother, Nipomo, California" (1936). Indeed, the artist occasionally complained that this image, which has become synonymous with the American Depression, unfairly overshadowed a lifetime of work.

Dorothea Lange was born on May 26, 1895, in Hoboken, New Jersey. At the age of seven she was stricken with polio, and her right leg, impaired from the knee down, caused her to limp. When Lange was twelve her father left the family and her mother worked, first as a librarian and later as a court investigator of probation cases. Her primary school years were spent in New York City P.S.62, where most of her classmates were the children of Jewish immigrants. These aspects of her childhood had an important bearing on her later work. Her early illness, abandonment, and exposure to poor immigrants gave her a first-hand knowledge of adversity that resulted in documentary portraits of great dignity and compassion. When she began to photograph the poor during the Depression in 1932, her limp provided her subjects with visual evidence that she, too, had suffered. While accompanying her mother on her investigative work, she learned both observation and interview techniques.

During 1912–1917 Lange worked at a number of studios as a photographic assistant. At this time she studied with Arnold Genthe, a prominent photographer of the well-to-do. He had also photographed San Francisco's Chinatown before the 1906 earthquake, and had photographed the quake's aftermath. Like Genthe, Lange would first become a photographer of the well-to-do and later become a photographer of social change.

From 1915 until 1917 Lange became a student at the Training School for Teachers in New York City, and in 1917 she briefly attended a class given by Clarence White at Columbia University, also in that city. Lange was struck by the pure quality of his work and may have absorbed this quality herself.

In 1908 she set out with her friend, Florence Ahlstrom, to work her way around the world. In San Francisco a pickpocket left them almost penniless, and Lange got a job photofinishing at Marsh Dry Goods and Photo Supply. From 1919 to 1934 she became a free-lance photographer, establishing her own portrait studio and becoming, by the early 1920s, one of the best-known portraitists in San Francisco. These early studio images were often soft in focus and reflected the pictorialist aesthetic which was also the hallmark of White and Genthe's work.

In 1920, Lange married Maynard Dixon, who was a well-known painter of the Western landscape and its people. Lange's first sustained efforts at photographing outside her studio took place in 1922, when she and Dixon travelled through Arizona's high country. Here she was exposed to the difficult lives of Native Americans and took one of her first strong documentary images: a frontal portrait of a Hopi Indian. In 1930 and 1931 Lange and Dixon spent time in northern New Mexico, where they saw the first of the Depression's homeless move through Taos. At this time, she made a decision to concentrate on taking pictures of all the people who interested her.

When she returned to San Francisco in 1932 she took her first major image of the Depression: "White Angel Bread Line." She began to photograph in the city streets and had small invitation-only showings of her work. In 1934 the photographer Willard Van Dyke, a member of the avant-garde Group F.64, showed her work in his Oakland studio, and five of her images appeared in *Camera Craft*. This same year she began to work with the sociologist Paul Schuster Taylor in the California Rural Rehabilitation Administration and was under the direction of Roy E. Stryker.

In 1935 Lange divorced Dixon, with whom she had two sons, and married Paul Taylor, with whom she would work until her death. Taylor taught her how to take field notes which she turned into pithy and telling annotations or titles for her photographs.

From 1934 to 1939 she and Taylor traveled often throughout California and then throughout all parts of the United States, with the exception of New England. Between 1935 and 1939, while working for the Farm Security Administration, she took her best-known photographs and developed a consistent approach to her sitters. She would strike up a conversation with her intended subjects, ask if she might take pictures, and allow the children, if present, to handle her medium-format Rolleiflex and four-by-five Graflex. Seldom photographing indoors or using artificial light, Lange usually exposed her subjects for her eight-by-ten silver prints from a low angle, stressing outlines and bold composition. Detail is subordinated to large effects in her work, and all the people she photographed—most of whom were poor, jobless, or dispossessed—are treated with dignity. Her subjects appear to have settled into their postures, and their faces usually express worry or stoic resignation. Their hands were often expressive as well, and along with arm gestures form reiterated triangles in Lange's compositions.

After an often-stormy relationship with Roy Stryker, which revolved around the issue of artistic control, Lange left the Farm Security Administration in 1939. This same year she published *An American Exodus: A Record of Human Erosion*, collaborating with Taylor. In 1941 she was awarded a Guggenheim Foundation grant to photograph Utopian communities; the Hutterites of South Dakota, the Amana Society in Iowa, and the Mormons in Utah. She abandoned this study to work, as did Ansel Adams, for the Office of War Information, photographing the internment of Japanese-Americans following Executive Order 9066. Although these images demonstrate her compassion and ability to elicit the telling detail, Lange's Depression photographs remain the strongest in her oeuvre. In 1945 she was commissioned by the State Department to photograph the San Francisco conference establishing the United Nations. Soon afterward she was hospitalized and was found to have severe ulcers—an illness that curtailed her travel. Thus, she began to photograph her family and her immediate environment. In the mid-1950s she completed a series of assignments for *Life* and *Look*, which included a series on the public defender system in California and on the rural people of Ireland for *Life*. In 1956 she collaborated on a photo essay with Pirkle Jones, titled "Death of a Valley," it depicted an excavated and devastated dam site. The essay was first published in the periodical *The New California*, and later as a book. It also formed the subject of a museum exhibit originating at the San Francisco Museum of Art, California. This was to be her last major exhibit until her 1966 retrospective at the Museum of Modern Art (MoMA), New York City.

From the late 1950s to the end of Lange's life, her husband held appointments as an international consultant on rural settlements and agrarian sociology. Despite her ill health, Lange accompanied him on his travels to Asia, Latin America, and the Middle East. These last photographs of people are more records of design than demonstrations of emotional empathy, yet they are clear indicators of her ability to seek the articulate detail while stressing the exoticism as well as the beauty of the individual within the context of a foreign culture.

Diana Emery Hulick

Bibliography

Conrat, Maisie, and Richard Conrat. *Executive Order 9066: The Internment of 110,000 Japanese Americans*. California Historical Society, 1972.

Hexman, Therese Thau. *Celebrating A Collection, The Work of Dorothea Lange*. Oakland Museum of Art, 1978.

Lange, Dorothea, with Paul Taylor. *An American Exodus: A Record of Human Erosion*. Reynal and Hitchcock, 1935. Rev. ed. Yale University Press, 1969. Rpt. Arno, 1975.

———, with Pirkle Jones. *Death of a Valley*. Aperture 8:3 (1960).

———. *Dorothea Lange*. Essay by George P. Elliott. Museum of Modern Art, 1966.

———. *Dorothea Lange Looks at the American Country Woman*. Text by Beaumont Newhall. Amon Carter Museum and Ward Ritchie, 1967.

———, with Margetta K. Mitchell. *To a Cabin*. Grossman, 1973.

———. *Photographs of a Lifetime*. Text by Robert Coles. Aperture (1982).

Levin, Howard M., and Katherine Northrup, eds. *From the Library of Congress: Dorothea Lange Farm Security Administration Photographs 1935–39*. Vols. I and II. Text-Fiche Press, 1980.

Meltzer, Milton. *Dorothea Lange: A Photographer's Life*. Farrar, Strauss, and Giroux, 1973.

Ohrn, Karin Becker. *Dorothea Lange and the Documentary Tradition*. Louisiana State University Press, 1980.

Lansner, Fay (1921–)

Born in Philadelphia, Pennsylvania, the painter/tapestry artist Fay Lansner attended the Tyler School of Fine Arts, Temple University in her native city (1945–1947); the Art Students League, New York City, where she studied with Vaclav Vytlacil (1947–1948); Columbia University, New York City, where she studied aesthetics with Suzanne Langer; she did further study with Hans Hofmann in Provincetown, Massachusetts, and New York City (1948–1949); and still further study with Fernand Léger and André l'Hôte in Paris, France (1950–1951).

Lansner has held many solo exhibitions in galleries in the United States and abroad, including her first solo show at the Galerie Huit (1951), which was followed by Le Gerrec (1952)—both in Paris, France; Hansa Gallery, New York City (1954, 1956, 1958); Elaine Benson Gallery, Bridgehampton, New York (1972, 1976, 1977, 1980–1982, 1984, 1992); Douglass College, Rutgers University, New Brunswick, New Jersey (1975); Lehigh University, Bethlehem, Pennsylvania (1976); Ingber Gallery, New York City (1980, 1983); Phoenix II, Washington, D.C. (1982); Benron Gallery, Southampton, New York (1986, 1988, 1991); and many others. Her work has been invited to distinguished landmark exhibitions in such venues as New York City; Madrid, Spain; Knoxville, Tennessee; Paris, France; the Hamptons, New York; Hamilton, Ontario and Montréal—both in Canada; Tucson, Arizona; La Jolla, California; Greensboro, North Carolina; and Houston, Texas.

Lansner's works have unfolded from her untitled abstract pastel and charcoal drawings of the late 1940s, through an intuitive personal series of "abstract expressionist" figurative paintings in the 1950s (coupled with feminist concerns), with explorations along the way of visual homage to certain of her forebears (including the Aubusson tapestries she created beginning in 1969), to the large, strong charcoal drawing, "Portrait of George Sand" (1992). Her work is represented in private, public, and corporate permanent collections, including New York University, and the Metropolitan Museum of Art—both in New York City; Corcoran Gallery of Art, Washington, D.C.; Neuberger Museum, State University of New York (SUNY) at Purchase; Cité Des Arts, Paris, France; Philadelphia Museum of Art, Pennsylvania; and many others.

Bibliography
Anonymous Was a Woman. California Institute of the Arts, 1974.
De Lallier, Alexandra. "Fay Lansner: Woman as Metaphor." *Woman's Art Journal* 7:2 (Fall 1986–Winter 1987): 41–46.
Fay Lansner. A Monograph. Intro. by Barbara Guest. AVA Books, 1977.
Harrison, Helen. "Realism to Abstraction." *The New York Times* (December 21, 1986): 29.
Sandler, Irving. *Conversation with Fay Lansner.* AVA Books, 1976.

Lanyon, Ellen (1926–)

Ellen Lanyon's most typical paintings address the phenomenon of ceaseless and inevitable metamorphosis, particularly with respect to the evolution of personal consciousness. Her repertoire of techniques, which alternately jolt and seduce the viewer, includes improbable juxtapositions, distortions of scale, exquisite ornamentation, wry wit, alarmingly grotesque apparitions, and endearing sentimentality. Although Lanyon's oeuvre fits within the larger tradition of surrealism, her work has nevertheless long been concerned with such post-modern issues as representation, gender identification, and ecological survival.

A native of Chicago, Illinois, Lanyon earned a Bachelor of Fine Arts degree from the School of the Art Institute of Chicago, Illinois, in 1948 and a Master of Fine Arts degree from the University of Iowa, Iowa City, two years later. Following additional study in London, England, she returned to Chicago, Illinois, married abstract painter Roland Ginzel, and embarked on the familiar triple career of wife, mother, and artist. Later she moved to New York, where she has worked and taught for many years.

In graduate school Lanyon pursued painstakingly detailed imagery in the old-fashioned technique of egg tempera. In the 1950s she worked with oil (later she switched to acrylic) but continued to paint representationally, despite the prevalence of abstract expressionism. This interest loosely allied her with other Chicagoans who were more interested in European surrealism, in the ethnographic collections richly represented in Chicago's natural history museum, and in popular culture than in New York-style abstraction.

Lanyon's first distinctive body of mature work was a "nostalgia series," consisting of paintings based on old photographs. Initiated about 1960 this approach evolved into another body of paintings inspired by magazine and newspaper illustrations. Her interest in the imagery of mass culture paralleled similar concerns in pop art of the same period, but in the mid-1960s Lanyon began to pursue the more personal meaning of illusion. At that time the seemingly antagonistic subjects of magic and natural science particularly stimulated her imagination. When feminism became a cultural force in the early 1970s Lanyon actively participated, and her art from those years often reflects the period's heightened consciousness of women's values. In "Chinese Wonder Bowl II" (1970) Lanyon dramatically links science, magic, and feminism in one compelling image: animals, insects, and reptiles, rendered with near scientific accuracy, are unleashed in a tabletop world furnished with domestic accoutrements of middle-class life.

A 1976 sojourn in the Florida Everglades intensified Lanyon's interest in wildlife, which has since played a central role in her narratives. In "The Pond," a poignant meditation on nature and culture, a long-legged bird wades through a lavish floriated inkwell; ironically, the elegant art nouveau forms of the idealized "pond" derive from the natural habitat of the bird, who stalks his prey oblivious to the mutilation/transformation of his habitat.

Ann Lee Morgan

Bibliography
Frueh, Joanna. "The Psychological Realism of Ellen Lanyon." *Feminist Art Journal* 6 (Spring 1977): 17–21.
Kuspit, Donald. *Introduction to Strange Games: A Twenty-Five Year Retrospective.* Champaign, Illinois: Krannert Art Museum, 1987.
Lippard, Lucy. "Ellen Lanyon's Natural Acts." *Art in America* 61 (May 1983): 132–38.
Sawin, Martica. "Altar Piece, Alter Peace: The Recent Work of Ellen Lanyon." *Arts* 57 (April 1983): 117–19.

Lark, Sylvia (1947–1991)

Born in Buffalo, New York, the Native American painter/printmaker Sylvia Lark attended the Academy of Art, University of Siena, Italy (1967). Two years later, after a stint at Mills College, Oakland, California, she earned a Bachelor's degree from the State University of New York (SUNY) at Buffalo. Lark received a Master of Arts degree (1970) and a Master of Fine Arts degree (1972) from the University of Wisconsin, Madison.

Between 1970 and her death in 1991 Lark held twenty-eight solo and two-person exhibitions in the United States and abroad, including the North Dakota Museum of Art, Grand Fork (1991); Jeremy Stone Gallery, San Francisco, California (1983, 1985, 1987, 1990); Galerie Hartje, Frankfurt, Germany (1985); Galerie Akmak, Berlin, Germany (1983); Allan Stone Gallery, New York City (1982); Sacred Circle Gallery, Seattle, Washington (1982); Bhirasri Institute of Modern Art, Bangkok, Thailand (1980); N.A.M.E. Gallery, Chicago, Illinois (1978); School of the Art Institute of Chicago, Illinois (1976); and others. Lark's work was invited to myriad group exhibitions throughout the world: from Anchorage, Alaska to Tokyo, Japan; Nairobi, Kenya; Stillwater, Oklahoma; Fredrikstad, Norway; Sackville, New Brunswick, Canada; New York City; Maracaibo, Venezuela; Berkeley, California; and others.

Lark taught for eight years at the California State University, Sacramento (1972–1980) and was a professor at the University of California at Berkeley (1977–1990). Winner of honors and awards, she was named distinguished teacher of studio art by the College Art Association (1991); received research and travel grants from the University of California at Berkeley (1977, 1978, 1980, 1981, 1982, 1986); won a Fulbright grant to Korea and Japan (1977); and others. Her works are represented in private and public permanent collections.

Bibliography
Boettger, Suzanne. "Decoration and Transcendence." *Artweek* 12 (January 21, 1981).
Frueh, Joanna. "Chicago: Kathe Keller and Sylvia Lark." *Art in America* (January 2, 1979).
Loach, Roberta. "Sylvia Lark." *Visual Dialogue* (January 2, 1979).

Larkin, Anna (1855–1939)

Born in Sweden, the folk artist and sculptor Anna Larkin emigrated to Arkansas City, Kansas around 1890. As a child she carved small wooden sculptures of people and animals and, after the purchase of two of her three-dimensional horses by the royal family of Sweden, her work and reputation prospered.

Larkin's work reveals the pioneer at work and at play—mingling with the animals—or separately, as in "Standing Woman," a white pine and steel brad work just under one foot in height.

Bibliography
American Folk Art. A Catalog. Tulsa, Oklahoma. Philbrook Art Center, 1975.
Arts and Crafts of Kansas. A Catalog. Lawrence, Kansas: Community Center, 1948.
Hyland, Douglas, and Marilyn Stokstad, eds. *Catalogue of the Sculpture Collection*. Helen Foresman Spencer Museum of Art, the University of Kansas, 1981.

Lasch, Pat (1944–)

A native New Yorker, the conceptual artist/painter/sculptor Pat Lasch earned a Bachelor's degree from Queens College, City University of New York (CUNY), New York City.

Lasch has exhibited work in solo and group shows in the United States and abroad, including A.I.R. Gallery, New York City (1973, 1977, 1979–1980); Galerie Ahlner, Stockholm, Sweden; "Out of House," Whitney Museum of American Art Downtown (1978); "Hommage: 1929–1979," a sculpture commissioned by the Museum of Modern Art (MoMA) (1979); and Lerner-Heller Gallery (1982)—all in New York City; "Art 1981," Chicago Navy Pier, Illinois (1981); Kathryn Markel (1982); and "Heresies," Grey Art Galleries—both in New York City; and others. Examples of her work are in private and public permanent collections, including Queens College and MoMA—both in New York City; and others.

Bibliography
Handy, Ellen. "10th Anniversary Show." *Arts Magazine* 61:4 (December 1986): 121.
Lasch, Pat, and Fred Lasch. *Art Book/Pastry Book. If You Make a Mistake Put a Rose On It*. New York, privately printed, 1985.
Twenty-Five Conceptual Artists. (Curated by Lucy Lippard). Valencia: California Institute of the Arts, 1974.

Latham, Barbara (1896–1989)

Content for more than fifty years to live and work in the shadow of her husband, printmaker Howard Cook, Barbara Latham has not received the recognition that should have come to her. Active throughout her married years as a painter and printmaker, Latham was also preeminent as an illustrator of fine books for children.

After studying at the Pratt Institute, Brooklyn, New York, and the Art Students League, New York City, and with Andrew Dasburg, Latham travelled west in 1925 as a visitor to Taos, New Mexico. It was there that she met Cook, who was in New Mexico to complete illustrations for Willa Cather's book, *Death Comes to the Archbishop*. During the 1930s and 1940s Latham completed a series of lithographs which, though influenced by Dasburg, are highly personal in style and spirit. This work, printed by George C. Miller & Son, led directly to her book, *Pedro, Nina and Perrito* (1939), illustrated by a series of original color lithographs, hand-drawn on zinc plates. Other children's books followed, including *Maggie*, selected by the American Institute of Graphic Arts among the best books published between 1945 and 1950.

Latham had one-woman exhibitions at the Weyhe Gallery, New York City; Dallas Museum of Fine Arts and Witte Memorial Museum, San Antonio—both in Texas; Roswell Museum and Art Center, New Mexico; and elsewhere. Her work is included in the collections of the Metropolitan Museum of Art, New York City; Philadelphia Museum of Art, Pennsylvania; and the Library of Congress, Washington, D.C.

Clinton Adams

Bibliography
Adams, Clinton. *Printmaking in New Mexico*. University of New Mexico Press. Forthcoming.
Barbara Latham papers (microfilm reels 2839–2841. Smithsonian Institution, Archives of American Art.

Lathrop, Gertrude K. (1896–1986)

Born in Albany, New York, the sculptor Gertrude K. Lathrop studied at the Art Students League and the School for American Sculpture—both in New York City; and with Solon Borglum and Charles Grafly.

First recognized with an honorable mention in a sculpture exhibition at the Art Institute of Chicago, Illinois (1924), and again in 1931, Lathrop has won many honors and awards, including the Helen F. Barnett prize at the National Academy of Design (1928), and honorable mention at the National Association of Women Painters and Sculptors (1930)—both in New York City; the Anna Hyatt Huntington prize (1933); medal of honor, Allied Artists of America (1964); silver medal, Pen & Brush Club, New York City (1967); the Saltus gold medal for merit, National Academy of Design, New York City (1970); and others. She was commissioned to design medals for the Garden Club of America (1942, 1950); the Hispanic Society of America (1950); the Mariners' Museum (1954); the Hall of Fame, New York State University (1962, 1966); National Steeplechase & Hunt Association (1964); and others.

Lathrop has held solo exhibitions of her work at the Albany Institute of History and Art, New York (1957, 1966), and the Woodmere Art Gallery, Philadelphia, Pennsylvania (1963); and group shows such as the "Fortieth Annual Exhibition," National Association of Women Painters and Sculptors, New York City (1931) and others. Her work includes "Sammy Houston" in the Children's Room of the Public Library, Houston, Texas; a relief portrait of "Leonard W. Richardson" at the New York State College for Teachers; "Nancy Lee" at the Smithsonian Institution, Washington, D.C.; and others.

Lathrop was elected an associate member of the National Academy of Design (1933), and was a member of the National Association of Women Painters and Sculptors—both in New York City; National

Sculpture Society; Society of Medalists; American Numismatic Society; and others.

Bibliography
American Art Annual. Vol. 30. American Federation of Arts, 1933.
Proske, Beatrice G. *Brookgreen Gardens Sculpture.* South Carolina, 1943.

Lavenson, Alma (1897–1989)

Born in San Francisco, California, the photographer Alma Lavenson Wahrhaftig earned a Bachelor's degree from the University of California at Berkeley (1919); except for the influence of Edward Weston and, particularly, Imogen Cunningham, Lavenson was self-taught.

Her work was exhibited in many solo and group shows, including the "F64 Show," M.H. De Young Memorial Museum, San Francisco, California (1932); the Brooklyn Institute of Art, New York (1933); "Alma Lavenson," "California Mother Lode," and "Photographs of a Vanishing Life," San Francisco Museum of Art (1942, 1948, 1960); "Three Photographers and the Place," Focus Gallery, San Francisco (1970); "Retrospective Exhibitions," at the California Museum of Photography, Riverside (1979), Oakland Art Museum, California (1979), and the University Art Museum, University of New Mexico, Albuquerque (1979); "Alma Lavenson," Focus Gallery, San Francisco (1981); and others.

The well-travelled winner of honors and awards, Lavenson was a recipient of a National Endowment for the Arts (NEA) fellowship (1979); and a Dorothy Lange award, Oakland Art Museum, the same year.

Her photographs of the California environment and, especially, the Mother Lode country, are noteworthy visual chronicles; Lavenson's work is represented in private and public permanent collections, including the Metropolitan Museum of Art and Museum of Modern Art (MoMA)—both in New York City; Mills College and Oakland Art Museum—both in Oakland, California; National Gallery of Art, Washington, D.C.; and others.

Bibliography
Browne, Turner, and Elaine Partnow. *Macmillan Biographical Encyclopedia of Photographic Artists & Innovators.* Macmillan, 1983.
Who's Who in American Art. 15th ed. R.R. Bowker, 1982.

Laville, Joy (1923–)

Born in Ryde on the Isle of Wight, England, Joy Laville showed an early talent for drawing. After living in Canada since 1947 she moved to Mexico in 1956, where she studied painting at the Instituto Allende in San Miguel, Guanajuato until 1958. In 1965 she met the well-known author Jorge Ibargüengoitia, and they were married in 1972. Laville began to exhibit in 1964, and her first solo exhibition was in 1966 in Mexico City, Mexico. Also in 1966 she was selected to participate in the historical show "Confrontación 66" in the Museo del Palacio de Bellas Artes, Mexico City, Mexico, and this same institution awarded her an acquisition prize in 1968 in its "Exposición Solar" exhibition. In 1967 the Galéria de Arte Mexicano—the oldest and one of the most prestigious art galleries in Mexico City—gave her a solo show and has represented her ever since.

Laville has had more than twenty-five individual exhibitions in various countries, and her works are in major public collections in Mexico. She held one-woman exhibitions at the Museo de Arte Moderno, Mexico City, Mexico (1977); the Centro Cultural de Mexico en Paris (1984); and the Palacio de Bellas Artes, Mexico City, Mexico (1985). Laville was included in the exhibition, "Diez Artistas de la Galería de Arte Mexicano" at Mary-Anne Martine/Fine Art Gallery (1983), and "Eight Women in Mexico" at the National Arts Club (1990)—both in New York City. Also in 1990 Laville was shown in SoHo, New York City, as part of Parallel Project's "New Moments in Mexican Art," a series of exhibitions which showcased leading contemporary Mexican painters.

Laville paints abstracted, sun-drenched landscapes in subtle and rich pastel colors in which the human figure is often a small presence in the foreground, surveying a lyrical and vast ocean panorama. These gentle yet emotional seaside scenes are set in Baja, California, and other coastal areas in Mexico.

Susan Aberth

Bibliography
Garcia Ponce, Juan. *Joy Laville: Un mundo luminoso y transparente.* Museo de Arte Moderno, Mexico, 1977.
Grimberg, Salomon. "Landfalls and Departures: Images of Mourning in Joy Laville's Art." *Woman's Art Journal* 10 (Fall 1989–Winter 1990): 3–6.
Ibargüengoita, Jorge. *Joy Laville.* Galería de Arte Mexicano, 1967.
Krauze, Enrique. *Joy Laville, pintura en su isla.* Museo de Monterrey, Nuevo Leon, 1988.
Mekler, Gilda. "Joy Laville." *Nuevos Momentos del Arte Mexicano (New Moments in Mexican Art).* Exhibition Catalog for Parallel Project, New York, 1990, pp. 158–61.

Lawson, Adelaide J. (1889–1986)

A native New Yorker, the painter Adelaide J. Lawson studied her craft at the Art Students League, New York City. She was a member of several professional arts organizations, including the Society of Independent Artists, the Salons of America, and the New York Society of Women Artists.

Bibliography
American Art Annual. Vol. 30. American Federation of Arts, 1933.
Braff, Phyllis. "An Adventurous Landscapist at 93." *The New York Times,* Long Island Section (September 12, 1982): 17.
Fielding, Mantle. *Dictionary of American Painters, Sculptors, and Engravers.* Modern Books and Crafts, 1974.
Wolf, Amy J. *New York Society of Women Artists 1925.* New York: ACA Galleries, 1987.

Lawson, Katharine Stewart (1885–)

Born in Indianapolis, Indiana, the sculptor Katharine Stewart Lawson studied with Lorado Taft and Hermon A. MacNeil. She was a member of the National Association of Woman Painters and Sculptors, New York City, and the Independent Society of Sculptors. In 1921 Lawson won the Shaw prize in an exhibition at the National Academy of Design, New York City.

Bibliography
American Art Annual. Vol. 30. American Federation of Arts, 1933.
Burnet, Mary Q. *Art and Artists of Indiana.* Century Co., 1921.
National Sculpture Society. *Exhibition of American Sculpture.* California Palace of the Legion of Honor, 1929.

Lazo, Rina

Born in Guatemala, Central America, the painter Rina Lazo studied in the school of fine arts in her country and continued her art education in Mexico. She graduated from the Escuela de Pintura y Escultura (La Esmeralda) in 1954.

From 1947 Lazo was an assistant to Diego Rivera, with whom she collaborated on the murals for the Del Prado Hotel, the Cárcamo of Dolores, the stadium of the city university in Cárcamo, and the Hospital de la Raza. She also participated in the execution of the mural, "La Gloriosa Victoria," which dealt with the aggression of president Arbenz's government, and she painted "Venceremos," which represents the struggle of the people of the third world (Museum of Toluca). Lazo was imprisoned during the student movement of 1968; she was introduced to the black art of printmaking by Arturo García Bustos, whom she married.

Lazo has taught in several institutions and has received many prizes and awards, including first prize for engraving in the Festival Mundial de la Juventud, Bucharest (1963). Among her better-known works are "Tierra Fértil," Guatemala (1954); and in collaboration with Bustos, the murals: "La Lucha de los Campesinos por la Creación de la Cooperativa Cañera;" "Hidalgo Enseña a los Campesinos las Ideas de Libertad;" and "El Fusilamiento de José Maria Morelos"—all in 1959; facsimiles of the Bonampak murals for the Museo Nacional de Antropología; and the illustrations for the book, *Pinturas Rupestres de Baja California Sur*, written by Francisco Gonzáles Rul and Miguel Angel Asturias. Her style and expression have been as diverse as her thematic material: political matter; still life; portraits; landscapes; and the human figure.

Bibliography

Alvarez, José Rogelio, et al. *Enciclopedia de México*. Secretaría de Educación Pública, 1987.

Lazzell, Blanche (1878–1956)

One of the earliest American interpreters of abstract art, Blanche Lazzell was born in 1878 near Maidsville, West Virginia, the ninth in a family of ten children. Her formal education was grounded in the liberal arts, humanities, and the fine arts at the West Virginia Conference Seminary; the South Carolina Co-educational Institute; and West Virginia University, Morgantown.

In 1908 Lazzell enrolled at the Art Students League, New York City, to study with William Merritt Chase. Four years later she took her first trip to Paris, France, to work under Charles Guérin and David Rosen at the Académie Moderne. The onset of World War I forced her to return to America and to take further study of the white-line color woodcut (the "Provincetown print") with Oliver Newberry Chaffee, and painting with Charles W. Hawthorne. Most of her summers thereafter were spent in Provincetown, Massachusetts. By 1918 Lazzell was *the* avant-garde Provincetown printmaker and teacher, a member of the Société Anonyme, and a well-known exhibitor with the Provincetown Art Association, Massachusetts.

Lazell returned to Paris, France, in 1923 for still further study with Fernand Léger, Albert Gleizes, and André L'Hôte and, for a decade or so, exhibited her abstract work at the Salon d'Automne. Her bold paintings reveal an experimental mind well aware of Cubism and, especially, of Léger's compositional approaches which she wedded to her personal sense of color.

In 1933 Lazzell moved to Morgantown, West Virginia, where she worked for the Federal Art Project painting murals and pulling prints. At Forum '49–a summer-long festival of the arts in Provincetown, Massachusetts (1949)—the artist Elaine de Kooning singled out four paintings of the fifty invited works on exhibit, one of which was "Painting #12" by Lazzell. De Kooning termed the Lazzell work "most contemporary."

Bibliography

Campbell, Lawrence. "Blanche Lazzell at Martin Diamond Fine Arts." *Art in America* 74:7 (July 1986): 122–23.

Dunford, Penny. *Biographical Dictionary of Women Artists in Europe and America since 1850*. University of Pennsylvania Press, 1989.

Flint, Janet. *Provincetown Printers: A Woodcut Tradition*. National Museum of American Art, 1983.

Fort, Ilene Susan. "Blanche Lazzell." *Arts Magazine* 57:2 (October 1982): 20–21.

Marks, Matthew. "Provincetown Prints." *The Print Collector's Newsletter* 15 (September–October 1984): 132–33.

Leaf, June (1929–)

Born in Chicago, Illinois, the all-media artist June Leaf studied at the School of the Art Institute of Chicago, Illinois, and also in Paris, France.

Leaf's work has been seen in group and solo exhibitions in museums and galleries, including "Torment," the Whitney Museum of American Art, New York City (1970); "Drawings by Contemporary American Artists," Cranbrook Academy Museum, Bloomfield Hills, Michigan (1974); "Contemporary Drawings," Boston University, Massachusetts (1975); "A Retrospective Exhibition," Museum of Contemporary Art, Chicago, Illinois (1978); "Alternative Realities in Contemporary American Photography," University of Minnesota, Minneapolis (1981); and others. Her work is represented in major museums, such as the Art Institute of Chicago, Illinois; Madison Art Center, Wisconsin; Museum of Contemporary Art, Chicago; Museum of Modern Art (MoMA), New York City; National Collection of Fine Arts, Smithsonian Institution, Washington, D.C.; and others.

Bibliography

Lippard, Lucy R. "June Leaf: Life Out of Life." *Art in America* 66:2 (March–April 1978): 112–17.

Rubinfien, Leo. "June Leaf, Terry Dintenfass Gallery." *Artforum* 15:4 (December 1976): 63.

Who's Who in American Art. 17th ed. R.R. Bowker Co., 1986.

Leak, Viola Burley (1944–)

Born in Nashville, Tennessee, the African American fiber artist/printmaker/educator Viola Burley Leak earned a Bachelor's degree from Fisk University, Nashville; a Bachelor of Fine Arts degree from Pratt Institute, Brooklyn, New York; a Master's degree from Hunter College, New York City; and a Master of Fine Arts degree from Howard University, Washington, D.C.

Leak has held solo exhibitions at Northern Virginia Community College, Annandale (1990); and Montgomery College, Rockville, Maryland (1989); among other venues. She has had her work included or invited to many group shows, including Strathmore Hall Arts Center,

Rockville, Maryland (1989); "The Seventh Atlanta Life African-American National Art Competition and Exhibition," Atlanta Life Insurance Company, Georgia (1987); "Black Women Visual Artists in Washington, D.C.," Bethune Museum Archives, Inc., Washington, D.C. (1986); Dusable Museum of African American History, Inc., Chicago, Illinois (1984); and others.

Leak's work is represented in museums and corporate permanent collections, including Atlanta Life, Georgia; Howard University, Washington, D.C.; Manufacturers Hanover Trust, New York City; and others. "Field Trilogy" (1985), not unlike other work of this period, depicts a soft sculpture of female cotton pickers, more or less triangular in form, in a magical arrangement of earth-colored fabric, batting, and thread.

Bibliography
Hall, Robert L. *Gathered Visions: Selected Works by African American Women Artists.* Anacostia Museum, Smithsonian Institution Press, 1992.
Igoe, Lynn. *250 Years of Afro-American Art: An Annotated Bibliography.* 1981.
Tower, Samuel A. "Stamps: International Women's Year." *The New York Times* (April 20, 1975).

Lecky, Susan (1940–)

Born in Los Angeles, the painter Susan Lecky earned a Bachelor of Fine Arts degree from the University of Southern California, Los Angeles (1961).

Lecky has held many solo exhibitions in museums and galleries, including the University of Illinois, Champaign (1977); and Millikin University, Decatur (1983)—both in Illinois; Eastfield College, Mesquite (1985); Conduit Gallery, Dallas; East Texas State University, Commerce (1986); Richland College, Dallas (1991); and the Art Center, Waco (1992)—all in Texas; and others. Her work has been invited to, or included in group exhibitions from Lawton, Oklahoma, to St. Charles, Illlinois; Omaha, Nebraska; Los Angeles, California; and throughout the state of Texas.

Lecky's work is represented in private and corporate permanent collections, including the Los Angeles County Museum, California; and others. "And Then There is Tomorrow" (1986), a large acrylic on canvas, is not atypical of her work of this period: subtly-hued, irregular, textured configurations are enclosed or pierced by vertical and oblique broad lines. In her own words, "I am intrigued with the random and fixed patterning found in nature and how the intrusion of human-made forms interacts with these patterns."

Bibliography
Kagle, Joe. *The Studios.* A Video. Waco, Texas: The Art Center, 1992.
Who's Who in American Art. 20th ed. R.R. Bowker Co., 1993.

Lee, Amy Freeman (1914–)

Born in San Antonio, Texas, Amy Freeman Lee was educated at St. Mary's Hall in her native city and graduated in 1931; she attended the University of Texas, Austin, between 1931 and 1934; and Incarnate Word College, San Antonio, from 1934 to 1942, receiving an honorary Doctorate degree from that institution in 1965. Lee's work profited from critiques offered by Ralph M. Pearson, Charles Rosen, and Edward John Stevens.

Lee has held 149 solo exhibitions of her work between 1947 and 1989; the most recent include the Meredith Long Galleries, Houston, Texas (1980); Incarnate Word College, San Antonio (1981, 1985); St. Mary's Hall (1981); and a mini-retrospective at Sol del Rio Gallery (1989)—all in San Antonio, Texas, and at Arte A.C., Monterrey, Mexico. She has won awards and honors for her work, including the *hors de concours*, which was presented to her at the 40th Anniversary Exhibition of the Texas Watercolor Society, McNay Art Museum, San Antonio (1989). She has exhibited her watercolors and other works in 639 group exhibitions in the United States and abroad, between 1945 and 1992.

Art critic for the San Antonio Express (1939–1941) and KONO Radio, San Antonio (1942–1950)—both in Texas, Lee was elected to membership in the International Association of Art Critics, Paris, France (1952), and to its American section in New York (1977). She has been a public member of the Texas chapter of the American Institute of Architects (AIA) from 1986–1988; a juror of the several arts; and a lecturer who has presented nearly 2,500 lectures between 1948 and 1992 at local, regional, national, and international civic, educational, and humane organizations. A member of scores of distinguished professional societies, Lee has also published three books and over 250 works, including essays, poems, critiques, and forewords (1937–1992). She was presented with the "First Living Treasure of San Antonio Award" for "Outstanding Achievements as Artist, Scholar, and Humanist" by the Center for Peace through Culture, San Antonio, Texas (1988).

Lee's work is represented in private and public permanent collections, including Baylor University, Waco; Texas A&M College, Prairie View; D.D. Feldman Collection, University of Texas, Austin; and McNay Art Museum, San Antonio—all in Texas; Smith College, Northampton, Massachusetts; Norfolk Museum of Arts and Science, Virginia; and others.

Bibliography
Archives of American Art. Smithsonian Institution, Washington, D.C.
Collins, J.L. *Women Artists in America.* University of Texas, 1973.
Who's Who in American Art. 19th ed. R.R. Bowker Co., 1991–1992.

Lee, Caroline (1932–)

Born in Chicago, Illinois, the sculptor Caroline Lee earned a Bachelor's degree from the University of Chicago, Illinois (1953); received a Bachelor of Fine Arts degree in drawing and painting from the School of the Art Institute of Chicago, Illinois, where she also studied sculpture with Edouard Chassaing (1957). The following year Lee went to Paris, France, where she apprenticed in sculpture to the Fonderie André Susse and also apprenticed in welding at the Oxhydrique Française.

Lee has been the recipient of an independent research grant from the Cassandra Foundation, Paris, France (1961); a professional achievement award from the University of Chicago, Illinois (1980); and a first prize at the "Concours pour un Monument: Hommage à la Résistance," Montreuil, France (1981). She has held solo exhibitions in museums and galleries, including the Galerie Lahumière, Paris (1965); Galerie d'Eendt, Amsterdam, the Netherlands (1967, 1972); Galerie Latina, Stockholm, Sweden (1968); and others. Her work has been included since the late 1950s in group exhibitions in galleries and museums throughout France, and is sited in private and public permanent collections in towns and cities throughout France, as well as the New Britain Museum of American Art and Emhart Corporation—both in Connecticut.

Bibliography
La Part des Femmes dans l'Art Contemporain. Vitry-sur-Seine: Galerie Municipale, 1984.
Visions/Painting and Sculpture: Distinguished Alumni 1945 to Present. School of the Art Institute of Chicago, 1976.
Watson-Jones, Virginia. *Contemporary American Women Sculptors.* Oryx Press, 1986.

Lee, Catherine (1950–)

Born in Pampa, Texas, the painter/printmaker Catherine Lee studied at the College of Alameda, California, and earned a Bachelor's degree from San José State College, California (1975).

Lee held a solo exhibition at the Duffy-Gibbs Gallery, New York City (1977), and has since had her work invited to many solo and group exhibitions, including "Lee, Lewczuk, Witek: Paintings and Prints," Pamela Auchincloss Gallery, Santa Barbara, California (1987); "Prints from Garner Tullis," Laurie Rubin Gallery, New York City (1987); and others.

Lee has earned awards and honors for her work, including a Creative Artists Public Service (CAPS) grant (1978), and an award from the Edward Albee Foundation, New York City (1982). She has taught at Princeton University, New Jersey (1980); Rochester Institute of Technology, New York (1982); and the University of Texas at San Antonio (1983).

Lee's work is represented in private and public permanent collections. "Unica 39" (1987), an abstract monotype in color, reflects a certain minimal structural ambiguity that teases the eye and derives, in large measure, from the constructivist and minimalist camps.

Bibliography
Bell, Tiffany. "Catherine Lee." *Arts Magazine* (June 1986): 124.
Davis, John. *Catherine Lee: Paintings.* A Catalog. John Davis Gallery, 1987.
Plous, Phyllis. *Collaborations in Monotype.* A Catalog. Santa Barbara: University Art Museum, 1988.
Russell, John. "Catherine Lee." *The New York Times* (April 17, 1987).

Lee, Doris Emrick (1905–1983)

Doris Emrick Lee is a well-known realistic painter whose name is associated with the Woodstock Art Colony—she was president of the Woodstock Art Association in 1952. She acquired early recognition as an artist in 1935 when she received first prize and the Logan gold medal in the American Art Annual at the Art Institute of Chicago, Illinois, and won the Country Post and General Store and Post Office mural commissions from the U.S. Treasury Department (1938).

Born in Aledo, Illinois, Lee attended Rockford College in that state. Upon graduation in 1927 she married Russell Lee—an engineer who became an art photographer during their years together—and they departed for Europe. In 1928–1929 she studied at the Kansas City Art Institute, Missouri, with Ernest Lawson before returning to Paris to study with the Cubist painter André L'Hôte. Abstractions did not hold her attention long, and she enrolled at the California School of Fine Arts, San Francisco, where her teacher, Arnold Blanch, advised her to paint from nature. In 1931 she moved to Woodstock, New York, and painted in the company of Peggy Bacon, Alexander Brook, Leon Kroll, Yasuo Kuniyoshi, and Blanch, whom she married in 1939, having divorced Lee. Her marriage to Blanch would also end in divorce.

The painting that catapulted Lee into prominence was "Thanksgiving" (1935, Art Institute of Chicago), not only because the painting won first prize at the Art Institute of Chicago, Illinois, but because Mrs. Josephine Logan, wife of the benefactor who sponsored the award, called this kitchen scene, in which nine people scurry about preparing the Thanksgiving dinner, "atrocious," and a "Sanity in Art" campaign ensued. The Art Institute of Chicago rose to the challenge and acquired the painting for its permanent collection.

Typical of Lee's anecdotal realism is "April Storm, Washington Square" (1932, Rhode Island School of Design Museum of Art), in which numerous encounters of humans and animals are narrated under a darkening sky, and "Catastrophe" (1936, Metropolitan Museum of Art), in which passengers drop by parachute from a burning dirigible over New York City and descend around the Statute of Liberty. *Life* magazine commissioned her in 1947 to travel and paint and then published four picture essays of her works: Negroes of the American South, North Africa, the Caribbean and Mexico, and Hollywood. Her painting, "Harvest," was included in the Biennial Exhibition at the Whitney Museum of American Art, New York City (1934). Her work was shown at the New York World's Fair and the San Francisco Golden Gate Exposition of 1939. She won a prize at the Carnegie Institute, Pittsburgh, Pennsylvania (1943), at the Library of Congress, Washington, D.C. (1943), and at the Pennsylvania Academy of Fine Arts, Philadelphia (1944). With Arnold Blanch she wrote the book, *It's Fun to Paint* (1947).

In her paintings Lee drew heavily upon her own rural beginnings in Illinois, reinforced by her later years of living at Woodstock in the Catskill Mountains. Her scenes of Americana are often populated by animated, gesturing individuals. Occasionally one detects a caricaturish quality in her otherwise naturalistic paintings. She died in Clearwater, Florida.

Eleanor Tufts

Bibliography
Lee, Doris. *Doris Lee.* New York: American Artists Group, 1946.
Lewis, Alice. *Doris Lee, 1905–1983.* Woodstock Artists Association, 1984.
Marling, Karal Ann. *Wall-to-Wall America.* University of Minnesota Press, 1982.
Tufts, Eleanor. *American Women Artists, 1830–1930.* National Museum of Women in the Arts, 1987.

Leeper, Doris (1929–)

Born in Charlotte, North Carolina, the sculptor/painter/printmaker Doris Leeper earned a Bachelor's degree, Phi Beta Kappa, from Duke University, Durham, North Carolina (1951). She spent the next decade or so doing studio work in Atlanta and Charlotte; and spent a dozen years on environmental concerns in Florida. Recently (1986–1991) Leeper channeled her efforts to aid the Atlantic Center for the Arts—a unique interdisciplinary international arts project which she conceived and many others helped bring to fruition.

Leeper has held more than thirty solo exhibitions in galleries and museums in the United States between 1966 and 1993; her work has been included in major group shows from Sarasota, Florida, to Fortaleza, Brazil; from New York City to Portales, New Mexico; from Dover, Delaware, to Laramie, Wyoming.

Winner of honors and awards, Leeper received fellowships from the National Endowment for the Arts (NEA) (1972), the Fine Arts Council of Florida (1977), and the Rockefeller Foundation (1977); she was the 1993 recipient of the Florida Arts Recognition award and, earlier on, was appointed to the advisory commission to oversee the planning and development of the Canaveral National Seashore (1975).

Representative works are located in private, public, and corporate permanent collections, including the Chase Manhattan Bank, New York City; Columbus Museum of Art, Ohio; Duke University, Durham; and Salem College, Winston-Salem—both in North Carolina; ; Mississippi Museum of Art, Jackson; National Museum of American Art, Washington, D.C.; University of South Florida, Tampa; Wadsworth Athenaeum, Hartford, Connecticut; and others. "Steel Quilt," a monumental, modular, non-objective commissioned wall sculpture from the 1980s over an entrance to the Orlando International Airport, Florida, is one of a score of commissions executed by Leeper.

Bibliography
Doris Leeper's Art for Public Places. A Catalog. Orlando: Loch Haven Art Center, 1979.
Martin, Francis, Jr. "Doris Leeper." *Art Voices South* (March–April 1979): 35.
Rubenstein, Charlotte Streifer. *American Women Sculptors.* G.K. Hall, 1990.

Leff, Juliette (1939–1987)

A native New Yorker, the painter Juliette Leff earned a Bachelor's degree with honors from the City College of New York (1962); and received a Master of Arts degree from Hunter College (1976)—both in New York City, where she studied with Mark Rothko, Tony Smith, and Eugene Goosen. She was also a Max Beckmann painting fellow at the Brooklyn Museum, and a Margaret Lowengrund scholar at the Pratt Graphic Center—both in Brooklyn, New York.

Leff held solo and group exhibitions in the United States and abroad, including a two-person show at New York University (1971); and "Year of the Woman: Reprise," Bronx Museum of the Arts (1976)—both in New York City; "What is Feminist Art? Writings of 200 Women Artists," Women's Building, Los Angeles, California (1977); "International Festival of Women Artists," Copenhagen, Denmark (1980); and others.

Recipient of a Tiffany Foundation grant, among others, Leff was a member of College Art Association of America and the Women's Caucus for Art. Examples of her work are represented in private and public permanent collections, including the Cathedral Museum of Religious Art; Chase Manhattan Bank; and the U.S. Information Agency (USIA), Washington, D.C.

Bibliography
Klein, Ellen Lee. "Juliette Leff." *Arts Magazine* 62:1 (September 1987): 94.
Who's Who in American Art. 17th ed. R.R. Bowker Co., 1986.

Leff, Rita

A native New Yorker, the painter/printmaker Rita Leff studied at the Art Students League, the Brooklyn Museum, and Parsons School of Design—all in New York City; she also studied under Letterio Calapai, Worden Day, Abraham Rattner, Louis Shanker, and Adja Yunkers.

Leff's work has been included in major printmaking group exhibitions, including the "Annuals" at the Library of Congress, Washing-

ton, D.C., and the Pennsylvania Academy of Fine Arts, Philadelphia. She has also held solo exhibitions at Esterhazy Gallery (1971) and Gallery Cassell (1973), Palm Beach, Florida; Lighthouse Gallery, Tequesta, Florida (1975); and others.

Winner of honors and awards, Leff won medals of honor at exhibitions of the National Association of Women Artists (1964, 1966, 1968, 1969); the grand prize at the Salon Internationale de Femmes, Cannes, France (1969); first prize at the Norton Gallery, Palm Beach, Florida (1971, 1972); and others. Examples of her work are in private and public permanent collections, including the Brooklyn Museum and Metropolitan Museum of Art—both in New York City; Dallas Museum of Fine Arts, Texas; Library of Congress, Washington, D.C.; Pennsylvania Academy of Fine Arts, Philadelphia; and others.

Bibliography
Who's Who in American Art. 15th ed. R.R. Bowker Co., 1982.

Leibovitz, Annie (1949–)

A portraitist and photo-journalist who has made her reputation in the world of advertising and editorial photography, Annie Leibovitz has photographed some of the most famous figures of the past two decades. The daughter of a career military officer, Leibovitz and her family moved a number of times during her childhood. She enrolled in the San Francisco Art Institute, California, in 1967 as a student of painting. She first used a camera the next summer while visiting her family in the Philippines, where her father was stationed.

In 1970 she began her career by photographing John Lennon for the cover of *Rolling Stone.* Largely self-taught, she cites books by Henri Cartier-Bresson and Robert Frank as having important bearing on her photo-journalism and Richard Avedon and Irving Penn as impacting the style of her portraits. While her initial work was in black-and-white, she began working in color in 1974. The style of the portraits of celebrities for which she is so well-known was developed to fit the requirements of the offset printing process.

In 1981 she did her first work for *Vanity Fair*—the publication with which she is presently associated. She published her first book and had her first solo exhibition in the same year. In 1984 she was named "Photographer of the Year" by the American Society of Magazine Photographers. In 1990 she first began to make images not intended for the print media. In 1991 a retrospective exhibition of her work was organized by the International Center for Photography, New York City, in conjunction with the National Portrait Gallery in Washington.

Allison P. Bertrand

Bibliography
Annie Leibovitz: Photographs. Introduction by Tom Wolfe. New York, 1983.
Hagen, Charles. "Annie Leibovitz Reveals Herself." *Artnews* 91:3 (March 1991): 91–95.
Sischy, Ingrid. "A Conversation with Ingrid Sischy." *Photographs: Annie Leibovitz 1970–1990.* New York, 1991, pp. 7–12.

Leighton, Clare Veronica Hope (c. 1901–)

Born in London, England, Clare Veronica Hope Leighton is the daughter of authors Robert Leighton (1859–1934) and Marie Flora Barbara Connor (active 1898–1920). She had two gifted brothers, one of whom was engaged to the novelist Vera Brittain and died at the age of eighteen in World War I. The Leighton home was a salon for London's literati, social reformers, and intellectuals. Poetry, music, and art were family hallmarks. Leighton often did illustrations for her father's books, but it was not until 1918 that her formal schooling began, first at the Brighton School of Art and later at the Slade School of Fine Arts of the University of London—both in England—where she studied with British painter and draughtsman, Henry Tonks (1862–1937).

In 1922 Leighton began to study with Noel Rooke (1881– c. 1940) at the London Central School, England, where she made her first wood-engraving. This print was seen by the artist Eric Gill (1882–1940), who encouraged her efforts and helped launch her career as a printmaker. Success came while still in her twenties, when she was commissioned to illustrate such works as *The Return of the Native* (1929) by Thomas Hardy, several editions of *The Bridge of San Luis Rey* (1929) by Thornton Wilder, and *Wuthering Heights* (1930) by Emily Brontë. In 1933, by the suggestion of her publisher, she was to write her own text and design the entire volume of large wood-engravings based upon the twelve months on an English farm entitled *The Farmer's Year: A Calendar of English Husbandry*. Over the years Leighton has authored and illustrated fourteen of her own books and illustrated some fifty others.

With her subtle skills of technical improvisation Leighton has achieved an extraordinary range of expression and sensitivity in her intense love of nature's infinite moods and aspects. She taught wood-engraving continually until the 1940s when she served as a visiting lecturer at Duke University in Durham, North Carolina. She became fascinated by America during two earlier visits in the 1920s, and in 1939 settled permanently in this country, becoming a citizen in 1945. In 1952, partly at the encouragement of her friend the American etcher, John Taylor Arms, Leighton settled in Woodbury, Connecticut.

Among her numerous awards are an honorary degree in fine arts from Colby College in Waterville, Maine; membership in the National Academy and Institute of Arts and Letters and the National Academy of Design—both in New York City; and the Royal Society of Painters, Etchers, and Engravers, London, England. She received first prize and a Logan medal from the Art Institute of Chicago, Illinois. A major retrospective of her work was held at the Boston Public Library, Massachusetts, in 1977. She has designed stained glass windows, including thirty-three for St. Paul's Cathedral, Worcester, Massachusetts, and Wedgewood Plate designs were also executed by Leighton.

Wood-engravings by Leighton may be found in collections of the Metropolitan Museum of Art and New York Public Library—both in New York City; the Library of Congress, Washington D.C.; the Art Institute of Chicago, Illinois; the Baltimore Museum, Maryland; Cleveland Museum, Ohio; Los Angeles Museum, California; and Boston Museum, the Boston Public Library, and the Fogg Art Museum, Harvard University, Cambridge—all in Massachusetts; the National Gallery of Canada, Ottawa; National Gallery of Stockholm, Sweden; the British Museum and the Victoria & Albert Museum, London, England.

Caron Crane Compton

Bibliography
Clare Leighton: Wood-Engravings. Exhibition Catalog. Associated American Artists, 1983.
Ferguson, Charles B. *Clare Leighton: A Retrospective Exhibition*. Connecticut: New Britain Museum of American Art, 1967.
Fletcher, William Dolan. *Clare Leighton: An Exhibition: American Sheaves, English Seed Corn*. Boston Public Library, 1977.
Hardie, Martin. "The Wood-Engravings of Clare Leighton." *Print Collector Quarterly* 22 (April 1935): 139–65.
———. "How I Made My Book: Where Land Meets Sea." *American Artist* 19 (February 1955): 40–45.
Leighton, Clare. *Wood-Engravings and Woodcuts*. New York: Studio Publications, 1944.

Leighton, Kathryn W. (1876–1952)

Born in Plainfield, New Hampshire, the painter Kathryn W. Leighton studied at the Boston Normal Art School, Massachusetts. A member of the California Art Club and West Coast Arts, Leighton was particularly known for her studies of Native Americans. Her work is in private and public permanent collections.

Bibliography
American Art Annual. Vol. 28. American Federation of Arts, 1932.
Moure, Nancy. *Los Angeles Painters of the Nineteen Twenties*. Pomona College Gallery, 1972.
Southern California Artists 1890–1940. Laguna Beach Museum of Art, 1979.

Leisenring, Mathilde Mueden (c. 1870–1949)

The portrait painter Mathilde Mueden Leisenring was born in Washington, D.C., and studied her craft at the Art Students League, New York City, and in Paris, France, with Constant, Henner, and Laurens.

Leisenring, an instructor at the School of the Corcoran Gallery of Art, was a member of the Society of Washington Artists, the Washington Watercolor Club, and the Washington Art Club—all in the District of Columbia. She won many prizes, including the Third Corcoran prize at the Society of Washington Artists (1903); the Second Corcoran prize at the Washington Watercolor Club (1903); and second honorable mention at the Appalachian Exposition, Knoxville, Tennessee (1910). Representative examples of Leisenring's work are in private and public permanent collections.

Bibliography
American Art Annual. Vol. 30. American Federation of Arts, 1933.
Fielding, Mantle. *Dictionary of American Painters, Sculptors, and Engravers*. Modern Books and Crafts, 1974.
Mathilde Mueden Leisenring: A Memorial Exhibition. Corcoran Gallery of Art, 1950.

Lekberg, Barbara (1925–)

Born in Portland, Oregon, the sculptor Barbara Lekberg earned a Bachelor of Fine Arts degree from the University of Iowa, Iowa City (1946), where she studied her craft with Humberto Albrizio and, the following year, received a Master of Arts degree from the same institution. She took further work at the Sculpture Center, New York City (1948), where she acquired skills in foundry work and welding from Sahl Swarz.

Lekberg has held more than two dozen solo exhibitions in the United States and Canada, including the Sculpture Center, New York City (1959, 1965, 1971, 1975, 1977, 1983); a major retrospective at Mount Holyoke College, South Hadley, Massachusetts (1978); the Glass Art Gallery, Toronto, Canada (1984, 1987); Percival Galleries, Des Moines, Iowa (1985, 1987, 1990); courtyard installations at the Katonah Gallery, New York (1985, 1988); and others. In addition to two- and three-person exhibitions, her work has been invited to myriad group exhibitions in the United States and abroad—from Palo Alto, California, to Helsinki, Finland; New York City; London, England; Santa Fe, New Mexico; and Toronto, Canada.

Lekberg has won many awards and honors, including Guggenheim fellowships (1957, 1959), and prizes and medals from the National Sculpture Society (1974, 1988, 1991, 1992). She has been a visiting artist at several colleges, a member of professional art organizations, and a faculty member and academician of the National Academy of Design, New York City, since 1990. Lekberg has completed steel and bronze commissions on sites in New York City; Chicago, Illinois; Bermuda; Birmingham, Alabama; and Clifton, New Jersey—some of them ten feet in height, such as "Sea Wind" (1989), a life-sized expressionistic, figural bronze which conjures up both motion and serenity.

Lekberg's work is represented in national and international private, public, and corporate permanent collections, including the Whitney Museum of American Art, the New School for Social Research, and the National Academy of Design—all in New York City; the Des Moines Art Center, Iowa; Knoxville Art Center, Tennessee; General Electric, Fairfield, Connecticut; and many others.

Bibliography
Annual Exhibition. National Academy of Design, 1982, 1984.
Annual Exhibition: Contemporary American Art. Whitney Museum of American Art, 1952–1956.
Chapin, Louis. "The Home Forum: Dancing in Bronze." *The Christian Science Monitor* (July 19, 1978): 20.
Lekberg, Barbara. "Expressionism: Subjective Response to Reality." *Sculpture Review* (Summer 1990).
Raynor, Vivien. "Art: Noise in the Attic, Barbara Lekberg (Sculpture Center)." *The New York Times* (December 9, 1977): C19.
Rubenstein, Charlotte S. *American Women Sculptors*, 1990.
Watson-Jones, Virginia. *Contemporary American Women Sculptors.* Oryx Press, 1986.

Lempicka, Tamara de (1898–1980)

Many facts about the life of the art deco painter Tamara de Lempicka are unknown. It is speculated that she was born in Warsaw, Poland; that her family name was Gorska; that she studied art in St. Petersburg, Russia; that she fled Russia with her husband and child when the Revolution broke out; that she studied painting with André L'Hôte in Paris, France; that she exhibited widely and won prizes in the United States and in Europe, and that she had myriad admirers; that she was a mysterious femme fatale, the toast of Paris, whose affair with the Italian poet Gabriele d'Annunzio created grist for the gossip mills; that she married a Hungarian baron and emigrated to the United States; that she used her art deco home as a setting for lavish parties and as a background for the sleek portraits she painted.

Bibliography
Bojko, Szymon. "Tamara de Lempicka." *Art and Artists* 15 (June 1980): 6–9.
Gilot, Francoise. "Tamara." *Art and Antiques* (January 1986): 64–69, 88.
McKay, Gary. "And the Baroness Was an Artist, The Brushstrokes of Tamara de Lempicka." *Ultra* (March 1988): 52–57.
Seiberling, Dorothy. "Siren of a Stylish Era." *The New York Times Magazine* (January 1, 1978): 14–15.

Leonard, Joanne (1940–)

Born in Los Angeles, California, the photographer Joanne Leonard earned a Bachelor's degree at the University of California at Berkeley (1962).

Leonard has held solo exhibitions in museums and galleries in the United States and abroad, including "Not Losing Her Memory," University of Michigan, Ann Arbor (1992); "Photographs and Photo Collage," and "Ten Years," Jeremy Stone Gallery, San Francisco, California (1985, 1988); "Inside and Beyond," a ten-year retrospective, Laguna Gloria Art Museum, Austin, Texas (1980); Stephens College, Columbia, Missouri (1977); Bristol Polytechnic Art Gallery, England (1975); "100 Photographs and Collages," San Francisco Art Institute, California (1974); Seligman Gallery, Seattle, Washington (1969); "Our Town," M.H. de Young Memorial Museum, San Francisco (1968); and others. Her work has been invited to many group exhibitions: from Amherst, Massachusetts, to San Francisco, California; from Philadelphia, Pennsylvania, to Texas City, Texas; from New York City to Stanford, California; from Ithaca, New York, to Exeter, England—and throughout the world with the Art in Embassies Program.

"Not Losing Her Memory: Stories in Photographs, Words, and Collage" (1992), re-presents and transmutes (as the title suggests) the lives of four generations of women in Leonard's family juxtaposed against the horrors of the Holocaust and the mental derangement of Alzheimer's Disease. Her work is represented in private and public permanent collections.

Bibliography
Joanne Leonard: Photographs and Photo Collage. A Catalog. Jeremy Stone Gallery, 1988.
Library of Photography: The Great Themes. Time-Life, 1970.
Lippard, Lucy R. *Inside and Beyond.* A Catalog. Laguna Gloria Art Museum, 1980.
Noggle, Ann, and Margery Mann. *Women of Photography.* San Francisco Museum of Modern Art, 1975.
Velick, Bruce. *Baby Baby Sweet Baby.* Pomegranate Art Books, 1992.

Lerman, Ora (1938–)

Growing up in rural Kentucky as part of a lively Jewish immigrant family influenced the character of Ora Lerman's colorful, imaginative paintings. Sensitive to the loss of her parents' cultural heritage, Lerman tried to salvage family biography in fantasy. Her oils and watercolors, replete with time/space dislocations and ambiguities, focus on carefully rendered objects—typically, an inventive arrangement of toys, photographs, dolls, and other still-life items—framed by block-lettered phrases that simultaneously serve as spatial foil, commentary, and personal reference. Theatrical in form, near to surreal, the work blends memory with fancy in a timeless construct.

Lerman earned a Bachelor of Arts degree in fine arts from Antioch College, Yellow Springs, Ohio, and a Master of Fine Arts degree in painting from Pratt Institute, in conjunction with art history studies at Columbia University (1969)—both in New York City. She also studied painting at the Brooklyn Museum Art School, New York.

Lerman's awards include fellowships at MacDowell Colony, Peterborough, New Hampshire (1977); Ossabaw Island Foundation (1980), an Andrew Mellon fellowship (1984), and a Pennsylvania State Council on the Arts grant (1988). She is a four-time recipient of State University of New York (SUNY) research grants in painting (1972, 1974, 1976, 1977). In addition, she won a Fulbright research award to Japan, where she studied at Tama Art University and pursued private studies in calligraphy and *sumi-ye* (1963–1965).

In 1988 Lerman was chosen for the coveted six-month residency, sponsored by *Reader's Digest*, at Monet's renowned garden in Giverny, France. This technicolor paradise inspired her to examine the plants, birds, and serpents of Eden within the parameters of her own magical imagery.

A year later Lerman went to India, where she had travelled in the 1960s, on an International Exchange of Scholars program, Indo-American fellowship. Settling in Manipal, she continued her exploration of myths and legends, a long-time interest.

Lerman, a full professor of art at SUNY, Suffolk, has taught for nearly twenty-five years in the New York City area. She lectures frequently at colleges and conference locations across the United States and writes articles for art magazines and exhibition catalogs.

Ora Lerman has participated in many group exhibitions at U.S. museums, such as the Speed Museum, Louisville, Kentucky; the Hudson River Museum, Yonkers; and the Brooklyn, Queens, and Bronx museums—all in New York City. She has had several solo gallery shows, including Prince Street Gallery, New York City (1972, 1974, 1977); Rutgers University, New Jersey (1977); and Bernice Steinbaum Gallery, New York City (1982). Lerman has also had a solo show at the Poulain Museum, Vernon, France (1988).

Sylvia Moore

Bibliography
"Combining Mysticism with Simplicity." *The Hindu* (July 7, 1989).
Lerman, Ora. "Autobiographical Journey: Can Art Transform Personal and Cultural Loss." *Arts* (May 1985).
Marter, Joan. "Narrative Painting, Language, and Ora Lerman's Trilogies." *Arts* (May 1982).
"In Monet's Garden." *The New York Times* (January 15, 1989).
"Some American Painters at Giverny." *Le Monde* (August 1, 1988).
"To the Side of Claude Monet's House." *Le Figaro* (July 26, 1988).

Lerner, Marilyn (1942–)

Born in Milwaukee, Wisconsin, the neo-abstractionist painter/printmaker Marilyn Lerner earned a Bachelor's degree from the University of Wisconsin at Milwaukee (1964), and, two years later, received a Master of Fine Arts degree from Pratt Institute, Brooklyn, New York.

Lerner has held solo exhibitions of her work in galleries since 1969, when she showed at the Zabriskie Gallery; she has most recently shown at the John Good Gallery (1987, 1989) and the Kornblee Gallery (1976)—all in New York City. In addition to having her work in-vited to myriad group exhibitions at major galleries in the United States since 1965, Lerner has shown at "Painting between the Sacred and the Profane" and "Painting between Paradigms," Galerie Rhamel, Cologne, Germany (1989); "Sightings," a travelling show, Institute of North American Studies, Barcelona, Spain (1988–1989); "Art from the City University of New York: Approaches to Abstraction," Shanghai, China (1986); the Basel Art Fair, Switzerland (1974); and others.

Lerner has won awards and honors for her work, including a Fulbright fellowship to India (1990–1991); grants and fellowships from the New York State Council on the Arts (1976, 1981, 1989); a National Endowment for the Arts (NEA) grant in painting (1987); a summer fellowship from the MacDowell Colony, Peterborough, New Hampshire (1989); and others. Her work is represented in private and public permanent collections, including Chase Manhattan Bank, New York City; IBM, Endicott, New York; Progressive Corporation, Cleveland, Ohio; Commerce Bankshares, Kansas City; and many others.

Bibliography
Frank, Peter. "Reconstructivist Painting: New Modern Abstraction in the U.S." *Artspace* (March–April 1990): 45–50.
Meyers, Terry R. "Controlled Substance." *Arts Magazine* (September 1989).
Morgan, Robert C. "Review." *Arts Magazine* (May 1989).

Letendre, Rita (1929–)

Rita Letendre was born in Drummondville, Québec, Canada, partly of Iroquois descent. Her interest in art began at a young age, and although she attended the École des Beaux-Arts in Montréal for a brief time around 1949, she is largely self-taught. Her artistic development was facilitated by contact with Paul-Émile Borduas, the leader of the revolutionary group of automatistes who introduced surrealist-inspired irrationalism into Québec culture. She exhibited with them from 1952 on. In 1964 she married the sculptor Kosso Eloul, who may have encouraged her to participate in an International Symposium of Sculpture at Long Beach State College in California the following year. Curiously, however, her contribution was not three-dimensional: instead, "Sunforces" (1965) was a huge mural almost twenty feet on each side. As she was working on it she discovered that bright sunlight tended to flatten the space in her work. To compensate, she adopted an extremely intense palette within a reduced vocabulary of form, so that the pictorial drama was chiefly an effect of color. With that, she left behind the spontaneous, gestural mannerisms of the automatistes, moving instead into a repetitive series of brilliantly colored radiating stripes, such as diagonal fan formations crossing the canvas entirely. She continued to explore this scheme until very recently, as in "A Recurrent Dream of Mine" (1986), where she used an airbrush to create more atmospheric, organic, and impassioned versions of similar motifs. She now lives and works in Toronto.

Robert J. Belton (with Lana Pitkin)

Bibliography
Murray, Joan, ed. *The Best of Contemporary Canadian Art*. Hurtig, 1987.
The Non-Figurative Artists' Association of Montréal. National Gallery of Canada, 1960.
The Third Biennial Exhibition of Canadian Art. Ottawa: National Gallery of Canada, 1959.

Levine, Marilyn Anne (1935–)

Born in Medicine Hat, Alberta, Canada, the superrealistic ceramist and sculptor Marilyn Ann Levine earned a Master's degree in chemistry from the University of Alberta, Canada (1959). An unemployed chemist, she had earlier studied art at the University of Alberta (1955–1956) and, making a "career change," she worked under the aegis of Kenneth Lochead, Arthur McKay, and Beth Hone at the University of Saskatchewan, Regina (1961–1962) and, later, with W.E. Godwin and, especially, Jack Sures (1964–1966). She also attended the University of California at Berkeley, where she received Bachelor of Fine Arts and Master of Fine Arts degrees (1970, 1971).

Levine's work takes soft materials—such as a woman's leather purse—and magically transforms them into superrealistic ceramic sculptures. She has held exhibitions in solo and group exhibitions in myriad venues, including O.K. Harris, New York (1974, 1976, 1979, 1981); "Canada Trajectories," Musée d'Art Moderne, Paris, France (1973); "Retrospectives," Norman MacKenzie Gallery, Regina, Saskatchewan (1974); "Illusion and Reality," Australian National Gallery, Canberra; and many others. Levine has been an inspiring teacher and winner of international honors and awards. Examples of Levine's work are in private, public, and corporate permanent collections, including the Australian National Gallery, Canberra; Montréal Museum of Fine Arts; the National Museum of Modern Art, Kyoto and Tokyo, Japan; and many others.

Bibliography

Clay as Sculpture. A Catalog. Alberta College of Art, 1977.

Peterson, Susan. "The Ceramics of Marilyn Levine." *Craft Horizons* 37:1 (February 1977): 40–48, 63–64.

Shuebrook, Ron. "Regina Funk." *Art and Artists* 8:5 (August 1973): 38–41.

Levine, Marion Lerner (1931–)

Marion Lerner Levine's paintings transform the traditional form of the still life into whimsical portraits of everyday life. Using both watercolor and oil paints, Levine characteristically places items such as imported canned foods, postcards, and botanical plants against a stark white background in an effort to illuminate in a new way the objects of daily consumption and reflection.

Levine was born in England of Polish and Rumanian parents; her family later emigrated to the United States when her father was offered a Rockefeller Foundation grant in economics. While attending the University of Chicago, Illinois, Levine was inspired to pursue a career in art; she eventually went on to study with Paul Wieghardt, Max Kahn, and Vera Berdich at the Art Institute of Chicago, Illinois, where in 1954 she received a Bachelor of Fine Arts degree in printmaking and painting.

Most of Levine's exhibitions during the 1970s occurred at the Prince Street Gallery in New York City. It was during this period that her still-life paintings took shape and became her trademark. Levine went on to have solo exhibitions at the Albright-Knox Art Gallery, Buffalo, New York (1981); the Springfield Art Museum, Missouri (1983), the Butler Institute of American Art, Youngstown, Ohio (1987), and the Carey Arboretum (1990), returning to the Prince Street Gallery in 1992.

Levine has been awarded a number of grants, including an Adolf and Esther Gottlieb grant in painting (1982), a Creative Artists Public Service Program (CAPS) fellowship (1983), and a National Endowment for the Arts (NEA) fellowship (1986). She resides in New York, where she has lived since the early 1970s.

Kim Caldwell-Meeks

Bibliography

ArtNews 72 (May 1973): 96.

Cutler, June. "Marion Lerner Levine." *American Artist* 48 (January 1984): 62–65 ff.

Who's Who in American Art. 20th ed. R.R. Bowker Co., 1993.

Levine, Sherrie (1947–)

Born in Hazleton, Pennsylvania, Sherrie Levine earned a Bachelor's degree (1969) and, four years later, a Master of Fine Arts degree in photo-printmaking from the University of Wisconsin at Madison. By re-photographing photographic and other works of art and re-presenting them out of context, Levine has re-created the efforts of male master photographers and painters and made these works her own, not unlike the "borrowings" of Andy Warhol and others.

Recipient of a National Endowment for the Arts (NEA) fellowship (1985), Levine has held many solo exhibitions in the United States and abroad, including Hallwalls, Buffalo, New York (1978); The Kitchen, New York City (1979); Ace, Montréal, Québec, Canada (1984); Northwestern University, Evanston, Illinois (1985); Mary Boone Gallery, New York City (1987); and others. Examples of her work are in private and public permanent collections, including the Museum of Contemporary Art, Los Angeles, California; the High Museum of Art, Atlanta, Georgia; and others.

Bibliography

Grimes, Nancy. "Sherrie Levine [at] Mary Boone." *Art News* 86:9 (November 1987): 191–92.

Hoy, Anne H. *Fabrications: Staged, Altered, and Appropriated Photographs.* Abbeville Press, 1987.

McGill, Douglas C. "An Original Slant on Originality." *The New York Times* (November 12, 1987).

Wei, Lilly. "Talking Abstract." *Art in America* 75:12 (December 1987): 112–14.

Levitt, Helen (1913–)

A native New Yorker, the free-lance photographer Helen Levitt—known for her lyrical and remarkable street photographs of children in Spanish Harlem, other New York City subjects, and the land and people of Mexico—began photographing city life in 1936. Levitt studied under the aegis of Walker Evans (1938–1939); and did further study at the Art Students League, New York City (1956–1957).

Levitt received many honors and awards, including fellowships from the Guggenheim Foundation (1959, 1960). Her work was exhibited widely in major newspapers (*The New York Post* and *The New York Times*), magazines (*Fortune, Harper's Bazaar,* and *Time*), and museums and galleries, including "Children," the Museum of Modern Art (MoMA) (1943); the Carlton Gallery (1977); and Sidney Janis Gallery (1980)—all in New York City; Corcoran Gallery of Art, Washington, D.C. (1980); and many others.

Levitt also has made films, including *The Quiet One* (1949, with James Agee), and *In the Street* (1952, with James Agee and Janice Loeb). Representative works are in private and public permanent collections, such as the Metropolitan Museum of Art, MoMA, and the New York Public Library—all in New York City; Springfield Art Museum, Missouri; and many others.

Bibliography
Auer, Michèle, and Michel Auer. *Encyclopedie International des Photographes de 1839 a Nos Jours.* Hermance, Switzerland: Editions Camera Obscura, 1985.
Coles, Robert. "Children of Poverty Making Do with Ease and Zest." *The New York Times* (April 26, 1992): 37–38.
Hellman, Roberta, and Marvin Hoshino. "The Photographs of Helen Levitt." *Massachusetts Review* (Winter 1978).
Levitt, Helen. *A Way of Seeing.* Viking Press, 1965.

Levy, Beatrice (1892–1974)

Born in Chicago, Illinois, the painter/printmaker Beatrice Levy studied at the School of the Art Institute of Chicago, Illinois, with Charles Hawthorne; and others.

Winner of awards and honors, Levy exhibited work in group shows in museums and galleries, including the Pan-Pacific Exposition, San Francisco, California (1915); the Art Institute of Chicago, Illinois (1917, 1919, 1923, 1928–1930, 1931–1940, 1942–1946); the Pennsylvania Academy of Fine Arts, Philadelphia (1923, 1924, 1929, 1931); National Academy of Design, (1945–1946); and Society of American Etchers (1938, 1940, 1944–1945)—both in New York City; Library of Congress, Washington, D.C. (1945–1946); and others.

Levy was a member of professional art societies, including the Chicago Art Club; Chicago Society of Artists; Chicago Society of Etchers; and the Renaissance Society of the University of Chicago—all in Illinois. Her work is represented in private and public permanent collections, such as the Art Institute of Chicago; Bibliothèque Nationale, Paris, France; Los Angeles County Museum of Art, California; Library of Congress and the Smithsonian Institution, Washington, D.C.; and others.

Bibliography
American Art Annual. Vol. 28. American Federation of Arts, 1932.
American Prints in the Library of Congress: A Catalog of the Collection. Johns Hopkins Press, 1970.
A Selection of American Prints. A Selection of Biographies of Forty Women Working Between 1904–1979. The Annex Galleries, 1987.

Lewczuk, Margrit (1952–)

A native New Yorker, the painter Margrit Lewczuk studied at Queens College (1969–1972) before attending the Brooklyn Museum School (1972–1975)—both in New York City.

Lewczuk's work has been invited to many group exhibitions and her first solo exhibition occurred at the Brooklyn Museum (1975); further solo exhibitions took place at the Pamela Auchincloss Gallery, New York City, and the Healand Thorden Wetterling Galleries, Stockholm, Sweden. She is the recipient of a Creative Artists Public Service (CAPS) grant, among others. Lewczuk's "Well" (1987), is a typical monotype reflecting nature in an earth-colored ambiguous form in an equally ambiguous space. Her works are represented in private and public permanent collections.

Bibliography
Brenson, Michael. "Drawing with Respect to Painting." *The New York Times* (March 2, 1984).
Plous, Phyllis. *Collaborations in Monotype.* A Catalog. Santa Barbara: University Art Museum, 1988.
Russell, John. "Four Painters." *The New York Times* (June 1, 1984).

Lewis, Edmonia (1844–c. 1911)

Half Native American and half African-American, Edmonia Lewis was raised by her mother's tribe—the Chippewa Indians. The exact dates of her birth and death have been difficult to determine because of varying anecdotal accounts, but in a sworn document the artist stated that she was born near Albany, New York, in 1844. Orphaned early, she was given new direction by her older brother, a California gold miner. He financed her schooling near Albany, New York, and helped her in 1859 to attend Oberlin College, Ohio, where she completed high school courses and enrolled in the college's liberal arts program. Among her courses were drawing and painting, and Oberlin College today owns one of her drawings done after an engraving of "The Muse, Urania" (1862).

Boston, Massachusetts, attracted Lewis, and with a letter of introduction to the anti-slavery advocate William L. Garrison she travelled there in 1863 in hopes of pursuing a musical career. Once there she was fascinated by the sculptured busts in the State House and the monuments that decorated the city in honor of early patriots. Garrison, aware of her new interest, introduced her to the neoclassical sculptor Edward Brackett who became her teacher. Her first sculpture was a portrait medallion in memory of John Brown, the abolitionist martyr. In 1864 and 1865 she had a studio on Tremont Street in the same building where Anne Whitney worked, and she asked Whitney to give her sculpture lessons. At the Soldiers' Relief Fair of 1864 Lewis exhibited a portrait bust of colonel Robert Gould Shaw, the Bostonian who had been killed leading the first Black regiment in the Civil War, and it became such a popular work that 100 replicas of it were sold, providing Lewis with enough money to buy a boat ticket to Europe. A marble version of the Shaw (signed and dated Rome 1867), made after she moved to Italy, is today on loan from the Afro-American History Museum to the Boston Athenaeum.

Lewis visited England and France before settling in Rome, Italy, where she became a member of the American colony, taking a succession of studios in the area around the Spanish Steps. One of her most imposing works is "Forever Free" (signed "Fecit a Rome, 1867," Howard University Art Gallery), composed of two former slaves who have broken their chains of bondage. After this emancipation work Lewis turned to her other ethnic interest and made a number of sculptures based upon *The Song of Hiawatha* by Henry Wadsworth Longfellow, for example, the marble group sculpture entitled "Old Arrow Maker and His Daughter" (1872, National Museum of American Art), as well as a bust portrait of Longfellow (Schlesinger Library, Radcliffe College). She did portraits of many eminent Americans, among them Senator Charles Sumner, William Lloyd Garrison, Wendell Phillips, president of the Anti-Slavery Society; Charlotte Cushman, the actress; Maria Weston Chapman, head of the Boston Female Anti-Slavery Society; and President Ulysses S. Grant.

Lewis made some full-length statues of historical and mythological personages, such as "Death of Cleopatra," which created a sensation at the Philadelphia Centennial Exhibition of 1876, Pennsylvania; "Hagar" from the Old Testament (1875, National Museum of American Art); and "Hygeia," goddess of health, which stands on the tomb of a woman physician in Mount Auburn Cemetery, Cambridge, Massachusetts.

Lewis visited the United States in 1873 when five of her sculptures were being exhibited at the San Francisco Art Association, California. Two pieces, "Poor Cupid" and "Hiawatha's Marriage," were sold there, and Lewis took the remaining three sculptures to nearby San José, California, for an exhibition. Her "Bust of Lincoln" was bought for the San José Library, and the other two ("Awake" and "Asleep"), which were privately purchased, are now at the San José Library. Lewis returned to Rome and was last noted there in 1911. References to forty-six different compositions have been found. Her sculptures are of marble and are neoclassical in style.

Eleanor Tufts

Bibliography

Hartigan, Lynda Roscoe. *Sharing Traditions, Five Black Artists in Nineteenth-Century America.* National Museum of American Art, 1985.

Porter, James A. "Lewis, Edmonia." *Notable American Women.* Vol. 2. Belknap Press of Harvard University Press, 1971.

Richardson, Marilyn. "Edmonia Lewis." *Harvard Magazine* 88:4 (March–April 1986): 40.

Tufts, Eleanor. *American Women Artists, 1830–1930.* National Museum of Women in the Arts, 1987.

Lewis, Golda

Native New Yorker Golda Lewis studied sculpture with Robert Laurent; painting with Hans Hofmann, Jack Tworkov, and Vaclav Vytlacil; and found her true love—papermaking—after study with Douglass Morse Howell.

A productive and innovative papermaker, Lewis has held seventeen solo exhibitions of her work throughout the world between 1963 and 1989, including a mini-retrospective at the Leopold-Hoesch Museum, Düren, Germany (1986); Galerie Faust, Geneva, Switzerland (1986); "Relieves," Galería Enrique Echandi, San José, Costa Rica (1984); "Sidewalks of New York," Rhode Island School of Design, Providence (1981); Gallery K, Washington, D.C. (1979); Alonzo Gallery, New York (1971, 1974); Court Gallery, Copenhagen, Denmark (1970); Balin-Traube Gallery, New York City (1963); and others. Her work has been invited to myriad group exhibitions in the United States and abroad: from Nysted, Denmark to Kasama, Japan; the Hague, Holland; Arad, Israel; New York City; San Francisco, California; Southampton, England; and the University of Guam, Micronesia. Lewis also recently prepared a travelling exhibition of her work to tour throughout Latin and South America in 1993.

Lewis is a teacher at the Ballard School (1961–1971) and at Marymount College (1971)—both in New York; a lecturer and workshop presenter at schools, museums, and universities in the United States, Europe, Latin and South America (1961–1992); and a winner of awards and honors. She built the papermaking department for the Wildcliff Museum, New Rochelle, New York (1978). One of the first artists to experiment with paper pulp (in 1961), to use as a medium for two- and three-dimensional expression, Lewis writes, ". . . technical mastery in making the pulp is no substitute for the rigor of intellectual content and aesthetic vision . . . I stick close to the 100 percent cotton for my working material and combine the uses of painterly and sculptural language to convey a particular vision and use of this medium."

Lewis's work is in a number of private, public, and corporate permanent collections throughout the world, including the Foundations of Paper History, Haarlem, Holland; Ciba-Geigy, Ardsley, New York; Hercules Powder Company, Wilmington, Delaware; and many others.

Bibliography

Alexander, Ron. "Making Paper from Scratch." *The New York Times* (February 1978).

Chacon, Luis. "Pieces of Timeless History." *La Nacion* (April 15, 1984). San José, Costa Rica.

Turner, Silvie, and Birgit Skiold. *Handmade Paper Today.* Lund Humphries, 1983.

Lewis, Lucy M. (c. 1895–1992)

Born a Keresan-speaking Native American in the Mesa pueblo of Acoma, New Mexico, Lucy M. Lewis made pottery souvenirs such as vase forms, candlesticks, and ashtrays for tourists as a child. Traditional hand-coiled, utilitarian pottery had been replaced by manufactured goods at the turn of the century, so women and children made trinkets that they could sell.

By the 1930s, however, Lewis had revived the polychrome jar forms of her ancestors, vessels with extremely thin walls, red slip base and white slip body with intricate designs in black, sometimes with the addition of yellow, orange, and red. By the 1940s she had perfected fine-line repetitions that covered the entire body of the jar. Prior to 1950, she merely printed "Acoma N.M." on the bottom of her pieces without identifying herself.

In 1950 Lewis entered work in the Gallup Intertribal Indian Ceremonial, New Mexico, and won an award of merit; from that point on she began signing the bottom of each pot, "Lucy M. Lewis, Acoma, N.M." When she attended the Southwestern American Indian Art Market in Santa Fe, New Mexico, in 1958, photographer Laura Gilpin took Lewis to the Laboratory of Anthropology to show her the fine collection of prehistoric and historic pueblo pottery. The extensive collection inspired her to make corrugated ware and to develop her own interpretations, particularly of Hohokam and Anasazi (fifth to thirteenth centuries) and Mimbres (tenth to thirteenth centuries) designs. Shapes included miniatures, seed jars, bowls, animal effigies, and water jars, rarely larger than ten inches in height.

The Museum of North Orange County, Fullerton, California, gave Lewis her first major show in 1976 in which work by her daughters was also included. She has been invited to show in most major Native American art markets throughout the West and Southwest.

Lewis works in the ancient coil-and-scrape method with local grey clay tempered with ground pot sherds, slipped with several coats of white and polished with a wet stone after each application. Paints made from ground minerals to which boiled vegetal matter is added as a binder are applied with a chewed yucca leaf brush. Vessels are fired outdoors with dried cow dung. Lewis's daughters help her prepare the clay and fire the vessels, but Lewis still shapes and paints her own work.

Lewis and her husband Toribio Lewis raised a family of nine children at their home in McCartys near the Mesa of Acoma where they maintain their ancestral home. Vessels by Lewis are included in permanent collections of the School of American Research, Santa Fe, New Mexico; Smithsonian Institution, Washington, D.C.; and the Southwest Museum, Los Angeles, California.

Barbara Kramer

Bibliography

Dillingham, Rick. "The Pottery of Acoma Pueblo." *American Indian Art* 2:4 (Autumn 1977): 44–51.

Dockstader, Frederick J. *A Tribute to Lucy M. Lewis, Acoma Potter.* Museum of North Orange County, Fullerton, California, 1975.

Peterson, Susan. *Lucy M. Lewis: American Indian Potter.* Kodansha International, 1984.

Lewis, Marcia

Born in Washington, D.C., the goldsmith/metalsmith Marcia Lewis earned a Bachelor's degree at San Diego State University, California (1969), and received a Master of Fine Arts degree from California State University at Long Beach two years later, when she became an apprentice goldsmith to Ingrid Hansen in Zurich, Switzerland. In 1972 Lewis was an assistant to the silversmith Tony Laws in London, England.

Lewis has been a professor at Long Beach City College, California, since 1978, and has taught her craft at a number of colleges and universities, including the University of Wisconsin, Whitewater (1973–1975); San José State College, California (1976); Cabrillo College, Aptos, California (1977); Haystack School of Crafts, Maine (1977, 1981); and Penland School of Crafts, North Carolina (1974, 1989). She has held a number of solo exhibitions of her work in the United States, including the Elements Gallery, Greenwich, Connecticut (1975); the Craft and Folk Arts Museum, Los Angeles, California (1977); Prairie House Gallery, Salem, North Carolina (1977); "Flights of Fancy," Long Beach City College, California (1980); and others.

Lewis's work has been invited to numerous group exhibitions in the United States and abroad, such as "Contemporary Metals," Yaw Gallery, Birmingham, Michigan (1973); "Goldsmiths '74," Renwick Gallery, Smithsonian Institution, Washington, D.C. (1974); "The S.N.A.G. (Society of North American Goldsmiths) European Exhibition," a travelling show, Pforzheim, Germany, including Finland and England (1979); "The State of Metal in the United States," Visual Arts Center, Anchorage, Alaska (1980); "Beasties," Aaron Faber Gallery, New York City (1989); "Metal Expressions," National Ornamental Metal Museum, Memphis, Tennessee (1991); and others.

Winner of several awards and honors for her work, Lewis received two separate grants from the National Endowment for the Arts (NEA); the George C. Marshall memorial fellowship to Denmark; and a Sterling Silversmiths Design Competition. Her work is in many private and public permanent collections, including the Museum of Contemporary Crafts, New York City; Oakland Museum of Art, California; the Renwick Gallery, Smithsonian Institution, Washington, D.C.; and others.

Bibliography

Evans, Chuck. *Jewelry: Contemporary Design and Techniques.* Davis Publishing Co, 1983.

Untracht, Oppi. *Jewelry Concepts and Technology.* Doubleday & Co., 1982.

Who's Who in American Art. 19th ed. R.R. Bowker Co., 1991–1992.

Lewis, Samella Sanders (1924–)

Born in New Orleans, Louisiana, the African-American multi-talented artist Samella Sanders Lewis earned a Bachelor's degree from Hampton Institute, Virginia (1945) and received her Master of Arts degree (1948) and Doctorate degree (1951) from Ohio State University, Columbus. Lewis also studied at Tunghai University, Taiwan; the Institute of Fine Arts at New York University, New York City; and the University of Southern California, Los Angeles.

Working across many fields, including history, education, painting, sculpture, printmaking, writing, and more—Lewis has exhibited examples of her work in many museums and galleries across the United States: from the Whitney Museum of American Art, New York City, to the La Jolla Museum of Art, San Diego, California.

A commissioned painter and muralist, Lewis has won awards and honors, including a Fulbright fellowship and two grants from the Ford Foundation. She has served on the art faculties of universities and colleges since 1953. Representative examples of her work are in private and public permanent collections, including the Atlanta University Museum of Contemporary Art and High Museum—both in Atlanta, Georgia; Baltimore Museum of Fine Art, Maryland; Denison University, Granville, Ohio; Hampton Institute, Virginia; Oakland Art Museum, California; the Pennsylvania State University, University Park; and others.

Bibliography

Cederholm, Theresa. *Afro-American Artists: A Bio-Bibliographical Directory.* Boston Public Library, 1973.

Hedgepeth, Chester M. *Twentieth-Century African-American Writers and Artists.* American Library Association, 1991.

Glueck, Grace. "Black Show under Fire at the Whitney." *The New York Times* (January 31, 1971).

Liebes, Dorothy (1899–1972)

Born in Santa Rosa, California, the fiber artist Dorothy Liebes studied at the California School of Fine Arts, San Francisco; the University of California at Berkeley; and Columbia University, New York City.

Liebes has exhibited work in solo shows in museums and galleries, including the San Francisco Museum of Art, California; the Brooklyn Museum, New York; and many others. She has won prizes and awards, and her work has been included in many prestigious group shows, such as the American Institute of Architects (AIA); Museum of Modern Art (MoMA) and the New York World's Fair—both in New York City in 1939; and the Golden Gate Exposition the same year, San Francisco, California; the Walker Art Center, Minneapolis, Minnesota; the International Exposition, Paris, France; and many others.

Examples of Liebes's work are included in private and public permanent collections, including the Honolulu Academy of Art, Hawaii; the Fort Worth Museum of Art, Texas; and many others.

Bibliography

Anonymous. "American Craft Council Gold Medalists." *American Craft.* Vol. 53 (August–September 1993): 118.

Lijn, Liliane (1939–)

A native New Yorker, the sculptor/writer Liliane Lijn has been interested in art and the reflection, refraction, and re-emission of light since she was a teenager. Self-taught, Lijn studied archaeology and art history at L'École dǔ Louvre, Paris, France. At the age of sixteen she settled in Lugano, Switzerland, and began painting symbolic/surrealistic works. This was followed by an unbroken series of three-dimensional experimental projects, in various European cities and in New York, employing myriad plastic materials and fire, in a search for getting light to "move." When the poet Nazli Nour challenged Lijn to make poems move, Lijn created her first "poem machines." These were revolving cylinders (and then cones) on which poems, in single words, were inscribed. In 1963 her initial kinetic poems were given a solo exhibition at the Galerie de la Librairie Anglaise, Paris, France.

Lijn embarked on further experiments to get light to move in plastic: injecting drops of polymer; spinning plastic discs; working with mercury; placing crystal balls on plastic containing drops of water; using prisms fastened to stones to create light sculptures; and more.

Lijn has had further solo exhibitions of her work in English venues including Indica Gallery (1967), Hanover Gallery (1970), Serpentine Gallery (1976)—all in London; Germain Gallery, Paris, France (1972); an Arts Council touring exhibition in Durham, Sheffield, and Liverpool (1977)—all in England; and many others. Her work was invited to a number of group exhibitions, including "Light and Movement," "Musée d'Art Moderne, Paris (1967); "Prospekt '68," Düsseldorf, Germany (1968); "Art Vivant," Fondation Maeght, St. Paul-de-Vence, France (1968); "Kinetic Art," Kunstnernes Hus, Oslo, Norway, Helsinki, Finland, and Göteborg, Sweden (1969); "Agam Bury Lijn Soto Takis," Delson-Richter Galleries, Tel Aviv, Israel (1973); "The Video Show," Serpentine Gallery, London, England (1975); Boîtes," Musée d'Art Moderne de la Ville de Paris, Musée de Rennes (1976); "Art in the Sixties," Tate Gallery, London, England (1978); "Objects," Marion Goodman Gallery, New York City (1978); "Hayward Annual," Hayward Gallery, London, England (1978); "British Sculpture in the Twentieth Century, Part II," Whitechapel Art Gallery, London (1981); "Electra," Musée d'Art Moderne, Paris (1983); "20th Century Drawings and Watercolors," Victoria & Albert Museum, London, England (1985); "Livres d'Artistes," Centre George Pompidou, Paris, France (1985); "Technologia e Informatica," Venice Biennale, Venice Italy (1986); "Imagine the Goddess," Fisher Fine Arts, London, England (1987); "Licht und Transparenz," Museum Bellerive, Zurich, Switzerland (1988); and others.

Lijn's work may be seen in major public permanent collections, including the Tate Gallery, London, England; Musée de la Ville de Paris, France; the Arts Council of Great Britain, the University of Warwick, Coventry, England; the Victoria & Albert Museum, London, England; Glasgow Museum, Kelvingrove, Scotland; the Wasserman Collection, Boston, Massachusetts; and a host of others.

Resident in England, Lijn has won a number of awards, including the Alecto Print award at the Bradford Print Biennale (1976); a publishing award from the Arts Council of Great Britain (1981); and a Bursary from the same Council in 1982 for holography. She has written many thought-provoking articles, fulfilled numbers of commissions, and classifies herself as a user of "all industrially used materials."

Bibliography
Barrett, Cyril. "Art as Research: The Experiments of Liliane Lijn." *Studio International* 173 (June 1967): 314–16.
Burr, James. "Around the Galleries." *Apollo* 89 (April 1969): 314.
Hayward Annual '78. A Catalog. Arts Council of Great Britain, 1978.

Lindgren, Charlotte (1931–)

Born in Toronto, Ontario, Canada, the sculptor/fiber artist Charlotte Lindgren earned her undergraduate education at several institutions, including the University of Toronto and others in the United States. Lindgren was awarded a scholarship to study with Jack Lenor Larsen at the Haystack School of Arts and Crafts, Deer Isle, Maine (1964); and the Canada Council granted her an arts scholarship for research and study in England, Finland, and Sweden (1965).

Lindgren has held many solo exhibitions in Canada and abroad, including the Rourke Gallery, Moorhead, Minnesota (1964); and the Nova Scotia Technical College, Halifax (1965). She has participated in other exhibitions in Confederation Centre, Charlottetown, Prince Edward Island, Canada; New York City; and the University of Manitoba, Winnipeg. Examples of her work are in private and public permanent collections, including the National Gallery, Ottawa, Canada. Among her many commissions is a large, three-dimensional metallic tapestry created for "Osaka '70," Japan; and others. Her work has been included in many prestigious group shows in Canada and abroad, such as the Dorothy Cameron Gallery, Toronto (1965); the Montréal Museum of Fine Arts, Canada (1966); the 3rd and 4th International Biennials of Ancient and Modern Tapestry, Lausanne, Switzerland (1967, 1969); and others.

Bibliography
Cowan, Harvey. "Fibre Art: A Canadian View." *Art Magazine* 9:37 (March–April 1978): 52–56.
Murray, Joan. "Joan Murray in Conversation with Charlotte Lindgren." *Arts Atlantic* 2:3 (Winter–Spring 1980): 28–31, 44.
Rombout, Luke. "The East—Environment of Cultural Vacuity." *Vie des arts* 54 (Spring 1969): 55–57, 92–93.

Lindroth, Irene

Born in California, Irene Lindroth won a scholarship to the Chouinard Art Institute in Los Angeles, California. Lindroth was awarded still another scholarship to Scripps College, Claremont, California, where she honed her talent.

Winner of many prizes and awards, Lindroth has had her work exhibited throughout California and at many museums and institutes, including the Carnegie Institute, Pittsburgh, and the Philadelphia Museum of Art—both in Pennsylvania; the Chicago Art Institute, Illinois; the Metropolitan Museum of Art and the Museum of Modern Art (MoMA)—both in New York City; and the National Gallery of Art, Washington, D.C.

Lindroth wrote *Color Vision and Painting* and, during World War II, made a significant contribution to enhancing the military uses of camouflage.

Bibliography
The Texas Quarterly: Image of Mexico II. The University of Texas. August 1969.

Liu, Hung (1948–)

Caught up in the cultural revolution and forced to work four years in the fields, the installationist/painter/assemblage artist Liu Hung was born in the village of Changchun in Northeast China. She earned the equivalent of a Bachelor of Fine Arts degree in art education at Beijing Teachers College, China (1975); a Master's degree in mural painting at the prestigious Central Academy of Fine Arts, Beijing; and received a

Master of Fine Arts degree from the University of California at San Diego (1986), where she studied with Allan Kaprow.

Liu has held many solo exhibitions in museums and galleries throughout the United States since her arival in California in 1984, including "Sittings," Bernice Steinbaum Gallery, New York City (1992); "Bad Women," Rena Bransten Gallery, San Francisco, California (1991); "Trauma," Diverseworks, Houston, Texas (1990); "Goddesses of Love and Liberty," Nahan Contemporary, New York City (1989); "Resident Alien," Capp Street Project, San Francisco, California (1988); "Once There Were Ten Suns," South Dallas Cultural Center, Texas (1987); "Art and the Tao," a permanent mural, Media Center and Communications Building, University of California at San Diego (1986); "Grotto Variations," University of Nevada, Reno (1985); and others.

Liu has been a speaker, writer, panelist and seminar participant, and a faculty member at Mills College, Oakland, California. Her work has been invited to group exhibitions throughout the United States and Mexico, and has garnered many awards and honors, such as the Society for the Encouragement of Contemporary Art (SECA) arts award, San Francisco Museum of Modern Art, California (1992); National Endowment for the Arts (NEA) fellowships (1989, 1991); Artist's Award: Contemporary Art by Women of Color (1990); Capp Street Project, a stipend, San Francisco, California (1988); stipends, tuition scholarships and research grants from the University of California at San Diego (1984–1987); and others. Her most recent commission was a twenty-five-by-forty-foot mural on the history of San Francisco in the lobby of the Moscone Center's Esplanade Ballroom, Yerba Buena Gardens, California.

"Goddess of Love and Liberty" (1989), a six-by-eight-foot diptych, re-presents a frontally-seated Chinese woman exposing her bound feet juxtaposed against a Ming dynasty vase portraying an amorous couple coupling. Both panels scream "possession." Liu fuses metaphors of the Chinese past and the contemporary present (e.g., Tiananmen Square), cultural differences between East and West, the role of the female in Confucianism, media-age history painting (her term), male domination and political, sexual, and social repression—as she wrote, ". . . to comment on the true condition of liberty in China as seen through the voyeuristic lens of the Western media." Her work is represented in public permanent collections, including the Dallas Museum of Fine Arts, Texas, and in many private collections.

Bibliography
Graves, Donna, and Lydia Mathews. "Evacuations Through Community History." *Artweek* 23:22 (August 20, 1992).
Li, Xiarong. "Painting the Pain: An Interview with Hung Liu." *Human Rights Tribune* (Spring 1992).
Machida, Margo. "(re) Orienting." *Harbour* 1:3 (August–October 1991).
Watten, Barrett. "The Powers of Imbalance." *Artweek* (November 28, 1991).

Livingston, Sidnee

A native New Yorker, the painter Sidnee Livingston learned her craft at the National Academy of Design, New York City, and has exhibited widely throughout the United States, including the Art Institute of Chicago, Illinois; the Library of Congress, Washington, D.C.; the Pennsylvania Academy of Fine Arts, Philadelphia; St. Louis Museum, Missouri; and many others.

Livingston has received awards and honors, including two prizes from the National Association of Women Artists: the Mildred Tommy Atkins prize (1971) and the award in oil painting (1977); a MacDowell Colony fellowship, Peterborough, New Hampshire; and first prize in watercolor in an exhibition of the New Jersey Painters and Sculptors Society. She was a member of Artists Equity Association, New York City, and the National Association of Women Artists. Her work is represented in private and public permanent collections, including the Columbus Museum, Georgia; Princeton University, New Jersey; University of Miami, Coral Gables, Florida; University of Mississippi, University, Mississippi; and others.

Bibliography
Havlice, Patricia P. *Index to Artistic Biographies.* Scarecrow Press, 1973.
Who's Who in American Art. 19th ed. R.R. Bowker Co., 1991–1992.

Livingstone, Joan (1948–)

Born in Portland, Oregon, the sculptor Joan Livingstone studied and worked at several institutions including Beloit College, Wisconsin (1966–1967); Portland State University, Oregon, where she earned a Bachelor of Arts degree (1972); the Portland Shakespeare Company, where she was a graphic and stage designer (1969–1972); Hillside Center for the Arts, Portland (1970–1972); and Cranbrook Academy of Art, Bloomfield Hills, Michigan, where she received a Master of Fine Arts degree (1974).

Livingstone has held many solo exhibitions in the United States, such as "Installation: Harlequin," Fiberworks Gallery, Berkeley, California, and "Figures and Curtains: 1980–1984," 341 West Superior Street, Chicago, Illinois (1984); "Joan Livingstone: Sculpture from 1980–1985," Contemporary Craft Association, Portland, Oregon (1985); "Joan Livingstone: Recent Sculpture and Collage," Tyler School of Art, Temple University, Philadelphia, Pennsylvania (1986); "Joan Livingstone: Recent Sculpture 1988," and "Joan Livingstone: New Sculpture 1990," Artemisia Gallery, Chicago, Illinois; and others.

Livingstone's work has been invited to group exhibitions in the United States and abroad, including "Three Spatial Attitudes," Central Michigan State University, Mount Pleasant (1976); the Hadler Galleries, New York City (1975, 1976); the 12th Biennale, Musée Cantonal des Beaux-Arts, Lausanne, Switzerland (1985); "Imagining Form: Six Sculptors," State of Illinois Art Gallery (1988); "Five Chicago Sculptors," University of Wisconsin-Eau Claire and "Seven Chicago Sculptors," Randolph Street Gallery, Chicago, Illinois (1989); "Crossroads: Contemporary Fiber," University of Colorado, Colorado Springs (1990); "USA/Columbia: Fibers," a show initiated by Florida State University, Tallahassee, which travelled to Bogotá, Calle, and Medellín—all in Colombia—through 1991; and many others.

Livingstone has taught at the Kansas City Art Institute, Missouri (1976–1980); the Cranbrook Academy of Art, Bloomfield Hills, Michigan (1980–1982); and has been associate professor of fiber art at the School of the Art Institute of Chicago, Illinois, since 1983. She was an artist-in-residence at the Banff Centre for the Arts, Alberta, Canada, received artist's fellowships from the Illinois Arts Council and the Tiffany Foundation (1989); and another from the Howard Foundation, Brown University, Providence, Rhode Island (1990). Her work is represented in private, public, and corporate permanent collections, including the Cranbrook Academy of Art, Bloomfield Hills, Michigan.

Bibliography
Abell, Jeff. "Imagining Form." *New Art Examiner* 15:7 (April 1988).
Fiberworks. A Catalog. Essay by Evelyn Svec Ward. Cleveland Museum of Art, 1977.
Richerson, Suzanne. "Paper/Fiber XI." *New Art Examiner* 15:11 (Summer 1988).

Lo, Beth (1949–)

Beth Lo was born in West Lafayette, Indiana, to parents who had recently immigrated to the United States from mainland China. After graduating from the University of Michigan Phi Beta Kappa in 1971, she turned to studying ceramic art with Rudy Autio at the University of Montana, Missoula, receiving her Master of Fine Arts degree in 1974. Subsequently, she opened a studio in rural southwestern Montana, taught art classes, and began playing bass in a nationally recognized jazz and rhythm and blues sextet, the Big Sky Mudflaps. In 1982 she married David Horgan, a fiction writer and the band's guitar player. In 1985 she was hired to be Autio's replacement as assistant professor of ceramics at the University of Montana. The birth of her son Tai in 1987 brought about major changes in Lo's ceramic work. She made a shift from standard vessels to sculptural stacking forms and from abstract markmaking to more direct figuration.

Lo's extensive exhibition record includes participation in "El Arte Contemporaneo del Estado de Montana," State Museum of Oaxaca, Mexico (1989); "Sculptural Ceramics Invitational," New Mexico State University (1987); and "Northwest Ceramics Today," Boise State University, Idaho (1987). She has also shown her work in the American Craft Museum and World Trade Center—both in New York City; Portland Museum of Art, Oregon; and many others. Her work is in the collection of the Hallmark Card Corporation Ceramics Collection; Missoula Museum of the Arts Permanent Collection, Montana; and others. In 1989 Lo received a Montana Arts Council individual artist fellowship and in 1986 received an American Craft Museum design award, New York City. Lo has been on the faculty of the University of Montana since 1985. Lo continues to pursue her multiple interests as mother, artist, teacher, and musician.

Leonard Lehrer

Bibliography
"American Ceramics." *New York Times Sunday Magazine* (April 13, 1987).
Biskeborn, Susan. *Artists at Work*. Alaska Northwest Books, 1990.
Ceramics Monthly (March 1980): 85–87.
Craft Range 15:5 (September–October 1984).

Lockerby, Mabel (1887–1976)

Born in Montréal, Québec, Canada, the landscape painter Mabel Lockerby studied for many years at the Art Association of Montréal with several teachers, including William Brymner and Maurice Cullen. While learning her craft at the Art Association, she received a drawing award in the "antique class" (1902) and was a prizewinner for composition (1911).

Lockerby was a member of the Canadian Group of Painters and the Contemporary Arts Society of Montréal. She showed her work in the annual spring exhibitions of the Art Association of Montréal beginning in 1914. Her work was also invited to major group exhibitions in Canada and abroad, including the British Empire Exposition, Wembley, England (1924–1925); Royal Canadian Academy (1925); National Gallery of Canada, Ottawa; Contemporary Arts Society, Montréal; the Beaver Hall Group, Montréal; New York World's Fair, New York City (1939); "400th Anniversary Exhibition, São Paulo, Brazil (1954); and others.

Lockerby's work is represented in private and public permanent collections. "Marie et Minou" (c. 1928), a not atypical oil, presents a portrait of a girl and her cat seen against a background containing houses, fence posts, and a road in a refreshing composition.

Bibliography
Catalog of Painting and Sculpture. National Gallery of Canada, 1940.
Gwyn, Sandra. *Women in the Arts in Canada*. Ottawa: Royal Commission on the Status of Women, 1971.
Meadowcroft, Barbara. *Mabel Irene Lockerby*. A Catalog. Montréal: Walter Klinkhoff Gallery, 1989.

Loloma, Otellie (1922–)

Born on Second Mesa of the Hopi Reservation in 1922, Otellie Loloma went to Second Mesa Day School before attending Phoenix Indian High School in Arizona. Her artistic talents were noted by her teachers early on and in 1945 Loloma won a scholarship to the eminent ceramics institution at Alfred University in New York. On receipt of her Bachelor's degree she took further study at Northern Arizona University in Flagstaff, which was followed by attendance at the College of Santa Fe in New Mexico.

Loloma has combined the professions of teaching and full-time artist: she first taught at the Shungopovi Day School in Second Mesa. Between 1958 and 1962 she ran a pottery shop with her then husband, Charles Loloma, at the Kiva Craft Center, Scottsdale, Arizona; worked at ceramics, jewelry, and painting in her own Scottsdale studio; and taught summer session courses for Arizona State University in Sedona. Loloma taught for the Southwest Indian Art Project, sponsored by the Rockefeller Foundation, at the University of Arizona in Tucson and also became a founding member of the American Indian Arts Center in Santa Fe, New Mexico (1962).

The Arizona State Fair in Phoenix—the first group competition she entered in 1960—awarded her first prize in ceramic sculpture; two years later, at the Scottsdale National Indian Arts Exhibition, she won another first award and in 1965 still another first prize and two second prizes in ceramic sculpture and pottery. The Philbrook Art Center, Tulsa, Oklahoma, awarded her first prize at the Annual American Indian Artists Exhibition in 1963.

Loloma also had work in the international travelling exhibition sponsored by the Institute of American Indian Arts titled, "Art of Indian America—Traditional and Contemporary." She was one of three artists from Santa Fe whose work was shown at the Center for Arts of Indian America in Washington, D.C., in 1968. Her work was also included in a show at Princeton University, New Jersey, in 1970 during the First Convocation of American Indian Scholars, and has been exhibited and placed in major permanent collections of Native American art throughout the United States.

Loloma has fused traditional Hopi symbols with a personal style in her pottery, large ceramic sculpture, paintings, and jewelry to win a prestigious place in her field.

Bibliography
Monthan, Guy, and Doris Monthan. *Art and Indian Individualists, The Art of Seventeen Contemporary Southwestern Artists and Craftsmen.* Northland Press, 1975.

Lomahaftewa, Linda (1947–)

Born in Phoenix, Arizona, of the Hopi/Choctaw tribe, Linda Lomahaftewa (Linda Joyce Slock) earned her Bachelor of Fine Arts (1970), and Master of Fine Arts degrees (1971), from the San Francisco Art Institute, California. She also studied at the Institute for American Indian Studies in Santa Fe, New Mexico.

Lomahaftewa's work has been invited to many group exhibitions throughout the United States and Canada, including "Contemporary Printmaking in New Mexico: A Native American Perspective," Governor's Gallery, Santa Fe, New Mexico (1990); "Native Proof: Contemporary American Indian Printmakers," and "As in Her Vision," American Indian Contemporary Arts, San Francisco, California (1989); "Progressions of Impressions," Heard Museum, Phoenix, Arizona (1988); "Harmony and Rhythm in Balance," Indo-Hispano/Nuevo Mexicano, San Antonio, Texas (1987); and "Women of Sweetgrass, Cedar and Sage," a travelling exhibition, Gallery of the American Indian Community House, New York City (1985). In 1985 Lomahaftewa also had a solo exhibition of her work at American Indian Contemporary Arts in San Francisco, California.

Winner of many prizes for her paintings and prints, Lomahaftewa won the Helen Hardin award for creative excellence in painting and a third place for printmaking at the South Western Association on Indian Affairs (SWAIA) 67th Annual Indian Market, Santa Fe, New Mexico (1988), and a visiting artist fellowship, the same year, at the Brandywine Workshop, Philadelphia, Pennsylvania. She won third place for mixed media at the 66th Annual (1987), and another for painting at the 61st (1982). "Star Gatherers" (1990), not atypical of her work, is a large monotype of petroglyphic figures engaged in a sacred, spiritual task in space.

A member of the faculty at the Institute of American Indian Arts, Santa Fe, New Mexico, since 1976, Lomahaftewa has also taught at the University of California at Berkeley; California State College, Sonoma and Rohnert Park campuses; the Fort Sill Indian School, Lawton, Oklahoma; and the San Francisco Art Institute, California. Her work is in permanent collections such as the Southern Plains Indian Museum, Anadarko, Oklahoma; the Millicent Roger Museum, Taos, New Mexico; the University of Lethbridge, Alberta, Canada; the Native American Center for the Living Arts, Inc., Niagara Falls, New York; and the Center for the Arts of Indian America, Washington, D.C.

Bibliography
Highwater, Jamake. *The Sweet Grass Lives On: 50 Contemporary Native American Indian Artists.* Lippincott & Crowell, 1980.
Our Land/Ourselves: American Indian Contemporary Artists. A Catalog. State University of New York at Albany, 1990.
Who's Who in American Art. 19th ed. R.R. Bowker Co., 1990–1991.

London, Edith (1904–)

Born in Berlin, Germany, Edith London studied art in various institutions and with several individuals, including the Verein Berliner Kunstlerinnen, Germany, with Wolf Roehricht (1929–1930); the British Academy in Rome, Italy (1931); again, with Roehricht in Berlin (1932); with Marcel Gromaire (1936–1937) and at the Académie André L'Hôte, Paris, France (1937–1939); and took further study with André L'Hôte in Paris (1951).

London has had many solo exhibitions of her work at such venues as La Citadella, Ascona, Switzerland (1966); Biberach Kunstgalerie, Germany (1966); Stetson University, DeLand, Florida (1968); Duke University, Durham, North Carolina (1968, 1980); City Hall Art Gallery, Berlin, Germany (1971); St. John's Museum of Art, Wilmington (1983), North Carolina Museum of Art, Raleigh (1988), and Marita Gilliam Gallery, Raleigh (1990)—all in North Carolina; "Edith London: A Retrospective," Durham Art Guild, North Carolina (1992); and others. Her work has been invited to group exhibitions, such as "The Art Train," sponsored by the National Endowment for the Arts (NEA) (1974); "200 Years of Visual Art in North Carolina," North Carolina Museum of Art, Raleigh (1976); "Art on Paper," Weatherspoon Gallery, Greensboro, North Carolina (1981); "Paintings in the South: 1564–1980," Virginia Museum of Art, Richmond (1983); American Academy and Institute of Arts and Letters, New York City (1990); and others.

London has won honors and awards for her paintings and collages, including the Young Women's Christian Association (YWCA) "Woman of Achievement Award," Durham, North Carolina (1985); the North Carolina award in fine arts, Raleigh (1988); a purchase award at the 1990 exhibition of the American Academy and Institute of Arts and Letters, New York City; and others. Her works are in private permanent collections in the United States, Canada, France, Germany, Great Britain, and Switzerland. Her works are also in public and corporate permanent collections, including Duke University, Durham, and North Carolina Museum of Art, Raleigh—both in North Carolina; the Phillip Morris Collection; St. John's Museum of Art; and many others.

Bibliography
Carnuffe, Mark. "60 Years, 60 Pieces." *Raleigh NC: News and Observer* (March 8, 1992): H1.
Godfrey, Robert. "Edith London's Quiet Collages Explore Nuances." *Ashville Citizen Times* (November 27, 1988).
Halperen, Max. "Painter's Study in Contrasts." *News and Observer* (April 5, 1992): H3.

Longman, Evelyn Beatrice (1874–1954)

Evelyn Beatrice Longman is best known today for her statue of "Genius of Electricity" which for sixty-four years stood atop the twenty-six-story AT&T building at 195 Broadway in New York City, and which was again in the news in 1981 when it travelled uptown to be installed in the lobby of the new AT&T building designed by Philip Johnson and John Burgee at 550 Madison Avenue. Renamed "The Spirit of Communications," and more popularly called "Golden Boy," this twenty-two-foot-tall gilded bronze nude, holding symbolic bolts of electricity over his head with coils of cable wound around his torso, was initially installed four hundred thirty-four feet above street level in 1916 and became a familiar figure over the years by its continued appearance on the cover of telephone books.

Born in a cabin in Winchester, Ohio, into a family of six children, Longman took a job at fourteen in a wholesale house in Chicago,

Illinois, while attending classes at the Art Institute of Chicago. She saved enough money to enroll at Olivet College in Michigan, but after a year and a half there, she realized that she wanted training in sculpture with Lorado Taft. She returned full-time to the Art Institute of Chicago, serving as Taft's studio assistant during the summers of 1898 and 1899. She accelerated her studies in order to finish within two years and graduated with highest honors. In 1900 she went to New York City, where she assisted Hermon A. MacNeil and Isidore Konti on the decorations for the Pan-American Exposition of 1901. She met Daniel Chester French at this time and subsequently worked for him for three years. She was the only woman ever admitted as an assistant in French's studio. During this period she modeled the daughter of the Frenches, "Peggy," a smiling young girl with grape leaves in her hair, which she cast in bronze. Meanwhile she also opened her own studio and was chosen to provide a "Victory" statue for the Varied Industries Building at the St. Louis Exposition of 1904. It was so well received that instead of placing it on this building it was put on the dome of Festival Hall, the centerpiece of the entire exposition, and the sculptor was awarded a silver medal. A small-size replica was later used as a trophy that was awarded in athletic competitions by the Atlantic Fleet of the U.S. Navy.

In 1906 she entered the competition for the bronze doors of the chapel of the U.S. Naval Academy in Annapolis, Maryland, and won the $20,000 commission over thirty-three other sculptors. The success of these reliefs resulted in a second commission for doors, this time on the library at Wellesley College, Massachusetts (1911). Among the many bust portraits she made was one of educator Alice Freeman Palmer, Wellesley's second president, for the Hall of Fame. When Longman and the architect Henry Bacon collaborated on the "Fountain of Ceres" for the Panama-Pacific International Exposition of 1915, they received an award for their work; they collaborated again on the Illinois Centennial Monument for Logan Square, Chicago, Illinois, in 1918. In both instances Longman created allegorical figures in a classical style. She also did much of the decorative work on Daniel Chester French's Lincoln Memorial in Washington, D.C.

Longman lived in New York City until her marriage in 1920 to Nathaniel H. Batchelder, headmaster of the Loomis School in Windsor, Connecticut. She then moved her studio to Windsor and thereafter took on commissions for many monuments in Connecticut: war memorials in Naugatuck and Windsor; the Spanish War Memorial of Victory on a ship's prow for Bushnell Park, Hartford (1927); and a decorative frieze for the post office and federal building in Hartford, Connecticut (1933). Her most famous portrait was done in this period: a six-foot bust of "Thomas A. Edison," the only one for which he sat. She spent two weeks at Edison Laboratories in Fort Myers, Florida, shortly before the inventor's death in 1931. Her bust of Edison was among the portraits to be seen at her 1932 exhibition at the Grand Central Galleries, New York City. She was the first woman sculptor elected to full membership in the National Academy of Design, New York City. Among the many awards she received were the W.M.R. French gold medal at the Art Institute of Chicago, Illinois, in 1920, the Widener gold medal at the Pennsylvania Academy of the Fine Arts, Philadelphia, in 1921, and the Watrous gold medal at the National Academy of Design, New York City, in 1923.

Eleanor Tufts

Bibliography

Adams, Adeline. "Evelyn Beatrice Longman." *American Magazine of Art* 14:5 (May 1928): 237–49.

Rawson, Jonathan A., Jr. "Evelyn Beatrice Longman: Feminine Sculptor." *International Studio* 45 (February 1912): 99–103.

Tufts, Eleanor. *American Women Artists, 1830–1930.* National Museum of Women in the Arts, 1987.

Look, Dona (1948–)

Born in Port Washington, Wisconsin, the artist Dona Look earned a Bachelor's degree from the University of Wisconsin at Oshkosh (1970).

Look has exhibited work in solo and group shows in the United States and abroad, including "Tapestry to Vessel," Palo Alto Cultural Center, California (1990); "Meeting Ground: Basketry Traditions and Sculptural Forms," The Forum, St. Louis, Missouri, and Arizona State University, Tempe (1990); "The Tactile Vessel: New Basket Forms," a travelling show, Erie Art Museum, Pennsylvania (1989–1991); "Craft Today, Poetry of the Physical," a travelling show, American Craft Museum, New York City (1986–1988); "Craft Today: USA," a travelling show in Europe, Musée des Arts Décoratifs, Paris, France (1991); and others. Look was a recipient of an Arts Midwest fellowship (1987), and a visual artists fellowship—both from the National Endowment for the Arts (NEA) (1988).

Look's work is represented in private and public permanent collections, including the Neutrogena Corporation; Bellas Artes Gallery, Santa Fe, New Mexico; Garth Clark Gallery, New York; and others. "#895" (1989), is a white birch bark and silk thread basket, so perfect in execution, so reminiscent of another time—another culture—that one stands in awe of its physical poetry.

Bibliography

"A Life in Crafts." *Creative Ideas for Living* (April 1988): 14.

Larson, Jack Lenor. *The Tactile Vessel: New Basket Forms.* Erie Art Museum, 1989.

Meeting Ground: Basketry Traditions and Sculptural Forms. The Forum, 1990.

López, Julia (1935–)

Born in Ometepec, Guerrero, Mexico, Julia López is a self-taught painter, who was introduced to art through modelling for other artists. Since 1959 López has exhibited her work in exhibitions in Mexico and abroad. She was awarded first prize in the Salón de la Plástica Mexicana.

Her portraits, which she terms, "similitudes," uniquely catch the likenesses of her subjects. López employs a color palette of purples, magentas, blues, greens, and white that seem to evoke the fiestas and the ambiance of her village.

"Las Amantes del Rio" and "Rapto de la Serena" are two of her better-known works of fancy, embracing mermaids, wild flowers, coral reefs, and angels. Among her most recent projects is a series of lithographs pulled for the casa Olivetti.

Bibliography

Alvarez, José Rogelio, et al. *Enciclopedia de México.* Secretaría de Educación Pública, 1987.

Loring, Frances (1887–1968)

Frances Loring was born in Idaho; spent the first twelve years of her life in Spokane, Washington; another year in Washington, D.C.; and then moved with her family to Europe, where she enrolled in the École des Beaux-Arts of Geneva, Switzerland. She lived in Munich, Germany, for about a year (1903–1904) and studied at the Académie Colarossi in Paris, France, for another year (1904–1905). In 1905 she went to the School of the Art Institute of Chicago, Illinois, and a year later did a stint at the School of the Museum of Fine Arts in Boston, Massachusetts. With a background so varied, it is curious that she was to become a well-known "Canadian" sculptor.

By 1909 Loring had realized that New York City offered the best opportunities. She was soon joined there by Florence Wyle, a promising sculptor whom she had met in Chicago in 1905. By 1912, with things not working out quite as she had hoped, she moved to Toronto, Canada—where she had travelled briefly in 1908. Wyle joined her there a year later, and from that moment on they were indivisible.

Loring joined the Women's Art Association in 1917, after some success in local exhibitions. Her works of this period are striking: small bronzes of women workers in factories and munitions plants. Both she and Wyle later became involved in a number of important Canadian art associations, among them the Ontario Society of Artists and the Sculptor's Society of Canada, of which they were charter members. An associate of the Royal Canadian Academy from 1920, Loring became a full member only in 1947. A tireless defender of sculpture, until then of relatively little celebrity in Canada, she was awarded a gold medal by the University of Alberta in 1954 and an honorary degree from the University of Toronto in 1955. Her example encouraged a number of other women sculptors, among them Frances Gage and Elizabeth Wyn Wood.

Loring received a number of important commissions for memorials and portraits in her lifetime. One of the more celebrated was her 1955 series of works for a statue of "Sir Robert Borden," Canada's eighth prime minister. Since Borden was one of the prime movers behind the country's heroic involvement in World War I, the commission would have been considered a plum. She also portrayed a number of other Canadian cultural icons, including various members of the nationalistic Group of Seven, the discoverer of insulin, "Sir Frederick Banting" (c. 1934), and the inevitable hockey player. Her works are generally described as more "masculine" than those of Wyle, which might be interpreted to mean that they have a greater interest in broader, forceful planes, and less interest in reductive, polished surfaces.

Though she was certainly well known, the critical community paid relatively little attention to her work until 1983, when her estate made a substantial donation of works by both she and Wyle to the Art Gallery in Ontario. In 1987 that institution mounted a comprehensive exhibition with an exemplary catalog.

Robert J. Belton

Bibliography
Boyanoski, Christine. *Loring and Wyle: Sculptors' Legacy*, 1987.
Sisler, Rebecca. *The Girls: A Biography of Frances Loring and Florence Wyle*, 1972.

Lounder, Barbara (1955–)

Barbara Lounder was born in Iserlohn, West Germany, in 1955 on a Canadian Armed Forces base and grew up in Germany and in Canada. She completed her Bachelor of Fine Arts degree at Queen's University, Kingston, Ontario, Canada (1980) and her Master of Fine Arts degree at the Nova Scotia College of Art and Design, Halifax (1984). She has travelled extensively in Canada, the United States, Mexico, Great Britain, and Europe and, for the past ten years, has been actively involved with the feminist movement and with the peace movement. Both her role as a teacher (at the Nova Scotia College of Art and Design) and an activist play a large part in her art making, which is essentially "idea-driven."

A recent exhibition at the Art Gallery, Mount Saint Vincent University, Halifax (1990), was an intermedia installation done with Montréal artist Lani Maestro, in which the artists explored their roots and motherhood but extended beyond this to include social and political concerns that evolve out of these issues. Nature, human interaction with nature, and the politics of our bodies and desires inform much of Lounder's work which inevitably begins with personal experience but always radiates out from this and engages with the larger issues of the community.

Lounder's most recent solo exhibitions in Canada include "Heaters," 00 Gallery, Halifax (1991); "Churchill," Eye Level Gallery, Halifax (1989); "Trouble Dolls (for Beatrice Marroquin)," Articule, Montréal (1987); and "Caring/Curing: Women and Medicine," Gallery 940, Toronto (1985). Group exhibitions include "Re-enactment: Between Self and Other," the Power Plant, Toronto (1990); "Memory Track," Walter Phillips Gallery, Banff, Alberta, Canada (1988); "Two Cities/Two Countries," Galeria Labirynt, Lublin, Poland (1988); "N.A.T.O.: Nova Scotia Artists on the Threat of Militarism," Anna Leonowens Gallery, Halifax (1986); "Halifax-Auckland Exchange," Artworks Gallery, Auckland, New Zealand (1986).

In addition to her gallery installation Lounder has participated in a number of performances, including *Is War Entertainment?* at the Metro Centre, Halifax (1984), and has been active in speaking about issues of concern to artists in seminars and panels; for example, she was a participant on the panel, "Feminist Art and Cultural Production Strategies," held in Toronto (1987), and on the panel, "Artists and Art Criticism," in Winnipeg (1988).

Lounder received Canada Council grants (1984, 1985, 1991), a Canada Council travel grant (1987), and a Canada Council project grant (1989). Her work has been purchased by the Canada Council Art Bank and by the Nova Scotia Art Bank.

Janice Helland

Bibliography
Gault, Charlotte Townsend. "Barbara Lounder." *Vanguard* 15:5 (October–November 1986).
Lounder, Barbara, and Lani Maestro with Carol Laing. *Refuse*. Halifax: Mount Saint Vincent University, 1990.

Love, Arlene (1937–)

Born in Philadelphia, Pennsylvania, the sculptor Arlene Love earned a Bachelor of Fine Arts degree and a Bachelor's degree in education from the Tyler School of Art, Temple University, Philadelphia.

Love has held many solo exhibitions in universities and galleries, including the Bennett Siegel Gallery, New York City (1990, 1991); "Mexican Journeys: Myth, Magic, and Mummies," Moore College of Art (1990);

"Arlene Love: In Retrospect 1960–1987," Temple University (1987); and Lawrence Oliver Gallery (1986) and "Freaks & Victims," Pennsylvania Academy of Fine Arts, Philadelphia (1979)—all in Philadelphia, Pennsylvania; Museum of the Surreal & Fantastique, New York (1982); and others. Between 1959 and 1992 her work has been invited to group exhibitions throughout the United States: from New York City to San Diego, California; Philadelphia, Pennsylvania; Los Angeles, California; Winston-Salem, North Carolina; Denver, Colorado; and more.

Winner of honors, including grants from the Pennsylvania Council on the Arts (1989) and the Tiffany Foundation (1960), Love has been an active guest lecturer, visiting artist, and juror at universities and art schools. She has created monumental bronzes and other works, on commission, for the Dorchester, Philadelphia (1987); Franklin & Marshall College, Lancaster (1985); the University of Scranton (1982); and Wells Fargo, Philadelphia (1981)—all in Pennsylvania; and others.

Bibliography
Arlene Love: In Retrospect 1960–1987. A Catalog. Temple University, 1987.
Brenson, Michael. "Going Beyond Slickness." *The New York Times* (March 3, 1989).
Stein, Judith. "Arlene Love at Lawrence Oliver." *Art in America* 75:2 (February 1987): 153–54.
Watson-Jones, Virginia. *Contemporary American Women Sculptors.* Oryx Press, 1986.

Lowengrund, Margaret (1902–1957)

As founder of the Contemporaries Graphic Arts Center Margaret Lowengrund had a crucial role in the print renaissance of the 1960s. Later called The Pratt—Contemporaries Graphic Art Center (and still later, the Pratt Graphics Center), this workshop gave important impetus to the use of lithography by American artists.

Born in Philadelphia, Pennsylvania, Lowengrund studied art at the Pennsylvania Academy of Fine Arts in that city before entering upon a career in journalism. In 1923 she moved to New York City and enrolled in Joseph Pennell's printmaking class at the Art Students League. With Pennell's encouragement she then went to England for study of lithography with A.S. Hartrick and to France for study of painting with André L'Hôte. One of her paintings was included in the Salon d'Automne, and one of her lithographs was purchased by the British Museum. In 1928, after returning to New York, she had her first solo show of paintings and prints at the Kleeman-Thorson Galleries.

Although Lowengrund enjoyed substantial success as an exhibiting painter and printmaker during the 1930s and 1940s, it was as a writer, gallery director, and administrator that she made her most important contribution to the history of the print. In her position as associate editor of *Art Digest*, she became a strong advocate of lithography, "a medium which knows few limitations." As director of the Contemporaries, she invited leading American artists to make lithographs in the workshops she established in Manhattan and in Woodstock, New York. In 1956, after developing an association with Pratt Institute, she received a grant from the Rockefeller Foundation to expand and support the Manhattan workshop; Fritz Eichenberg then became its co-director. Shortly thereafter, her work was interrupted by cancer, and she died in 1957 at the age of fifty-five.

Clinton Adams

Bibliography
Adams, Clinton. *American Lithographers, 1900–1960: The Artists and Their Printers.* University of New Mexico Press, 1983, pp. 182–89.
———. "Margaret Lowengrund and The Contemporaries." *Tamarind Papers* 7 (Spring 1984): 17–23.

Lownes, Anna (professionally active 1884–1905)

Anna Lownes was a painter of powerful, realistic still lifes. She studied at the Philadelphia School of Design for Women, Pennsylvania, and at Eugène Delécluse's academy in Paris, France. Little more is known about this Pennsylvania painter except that she studied with Milne Ramsey, a Philadelphia still-life painter. From 1885 to 1887 she lived in Media, Delaware County, Pennsylvania, and then moved to Chestnut Street, Philadelphia.

Lownes exhibited at the Pennsylvania Academy of Fine Arts, Philadelphia, beginning in 1884 and concluding in 1890; among the works were "Still Life," "Yellow Roses," "A Study: 'Perchance a thing oe'r which the raven flaps its funeral wing,'" "An Interior," "Carnations," "A Cup of Tea," "Study of Wild Azalea," and "Study of Apples."

Lownes also exhibited two paintings at the World's Columbian Exposition of 1893 in Chicago: "The Raven" in the Palace of the Fine Arts and a still life in the Board Room of the Woman's Building.

Eleanor Tufts

Bibliography
Tufts, Eleanor. *American Women Artists, 1830–1930.* National Museum of Women in the Arts, 1987.

Loyd, Jan Brooks (1950–)

Born in Quanah, Texas, the metalsmith/sculptor Jan Brooks Loyd earned an Associate in Arts degree from Columbia College, Missouri (1970), and, four years later, received a Master of Fine Arts degree from Southern Illinois University, Carbondale.

Loyd has held solo exhibitions of her work in galleries and universities, including the Southeastern Center for Contemporary Art, Winston-Salem (1981); and Davidson College—both in North Carolina (1983); and others. Her work has been invited to, or included in many group exhibitions in the United States and abroad, such as "Feria Mundial de la Plata," National University of Mexico, Mexico (1974); "The Metalsmith," Phoenix Art Museum, Arizona (1977); "Young Americans: Metal," American Craft Museum, New York City (1980); "Towards a New Iron Age," Victoria & Albert Museum, London, England (1982); "American Metalwork," Kyoto Municipal Museum, Japan (1983); "Ironing," Fire & Iron Gallery, Leatherhead, England (1986); and others.

Loyd has received honors and awards in her field: "Tornadic Vessel" (1983), reflects a technical wizardry fused, inextricably, to private expression. Her work is represented in private and public permanent collections.

Bibliography
Nine from North Carolina: An Exhibition of Women Artists. North Carolina State Committee and the National Museum of Women in the Arts, 1989.

Lozano, Agueda (1944–)

Born in Cuahtemoc, Chihuahua, Mexico, Agueda Lozano began her studies at the University of Nuevo Léon in 1961 under the aegis of Pablo Flórez and at the Monterrey Academy of Plastic Arts in the same city. Later on, she studied in Paris, France, where her creativity seemed to unfold.

A serious student, she had her first solo exhibition while still learning her craft at the academy. Then there followed exhibitions in Chihuahua, San Luis Potosi, Juárez, and Mexico City. In 1969 her work was seen at the Galería Edvard Munch. Since that time, she has won many honors and awards for her highly-personalized geometric works and has exhibited her efforts in many shows in Mexico and abroad.

Critics label her work "fantastic geometry," in an attempt to explain her search for a personal language with which to communicate her concerns and her anxieties as an artist coming to grip with reality— through organic, textured, geometric forms.

Bibliography
Pintura Mexicana: 1950–1980. A Catalog.
The Texas Quarterly: Image of Mexico II. The University of Texas, August 1969.

Lucas, Helen (1931–)

Canadian painter Helen Lucas was born in Weyburn, Saskatchewan, Canada, and studied at the Ontario College of Art in Toronto; and earned a Master's degree in drawing and painting at Sheridan College in Oakville, Ontario (1979). Her first solo exhibit was at the Saskatoon Art Gallery in Saskatchewan in 1953, and her first show in Toronto was at the Upstairs Gallery in 1962. Much of her earlier work during the 1960s was of a solitary female figure showing a need for self-expression, using simple black-and-white tones. Later figures were classical in stance and expression with softer warmer tones. In 1965 she was one of four Canadian figurative painters whose work was in an exhibit that travelled throughout the United States.

While Lucas was raising her two children she gravitated toward images of mothers and children, primarily done in charcoal. Her images became intensely personal after her marriage broke up with distorted drawings of embryonic men and women.

In the 1970s a trip to Mexico City, Mexico, started her painting colorful biomorphic floral images where flowers literally give birth to animal and human forms that indicate the closeness of nature in the life experience. In the 1980s she abandoned the figures and concentrated on floral imagery in vibrant colors. She has had solo exhibits in Toronto and its surrounding areas, including the Bonli Gallery, Variety Club, Peel County Museum, Shaw-Rimmington Gallery, and Oakville Centennial Gallery.

Lucas has illustrated two books: *A Christmas Birthday Story*, written by Margaret Laurence and published in 1980, and *Angelica*, which she also wrote, published in both French and English in 1973. She has works in several Ontario collections, including Sheridan College, Oakville; the Mississauga Library; and the Provincial Court in Toronto. She also has works in numerous private collections in the United States, Europe, and Mexico.

Nancy Knechtel

Bibliography
MacDonald, Colin S. *A Dictionary of Canadian Artists*. Canadian Paperbacks, 1982, p. 923.
Helen Lucas/1980. Oakville Galleries, 1980.

Luce, Molly (1896–1986)

The American art critic Henry McBride called Molly Luce "the American Breughel." Her oeuvre consists for the most part of realistic views of American towns inhabited by brightly garbed citizenry. Her first solo exhibition was held at the Whitney Studio Club, New York City, in 1924; at this exhibition the Whitney Museum of American Art, New York City, purchased two of her paintings. In 1934 the Metropolitan Museum of Art, also in New York City, acquired its first painting by her; the museum later reproduced her "Winter in the Suburbs" (1940) as a Christmas card. More recently the Rhode Island School of Design, Providence, held a retrospective exhibition of fifty-five of her paintings (1979), and "Eight Decades," a travelling exhibition of her work, circulated among thirteen American museums (1980–1983).

Born in Pittsburgh, Pennsylvania, Luce cited Rosa Bonheur's "The Horse Fair" as the first picture to affect her. She studied at Wheaton College in Norton, Massachusetts, with Amy Otis, a miniaturist; and at the Art Students League, New York City, with F. Louis Mora, George Bellows, and Kenneth Hayes Miller. She travelled through Europe in 1922–1923 and lived in Minneapolis, Minnesota, in 1925. Upon her marriage in 1926 to Alan Burroughs, a conservator at Harvard University's Fogg Art Museum, she moved to Cambridge, Massachusetts, before settling three years later in Belmont, Massachusetts. Her last paintings were done in Little Compton, Rhode Island, her final home.

Luce's early style in the 1920s has a parallel in Charles Burchfield's urban realism. Then in the late 1920s her style evolved into a precisionist mode, seen in the sharply-defined cylindrical grain storage tanks in "Backyards of Minneapolis" (1925–1926). Some of her later paintings of people in landscapes and homes (e.g., "Women Working," 1946) are comparable to Norman Rockwell's illustrations. She maintained an active exhibition schedule, and her paintings were included in the Whitney Museum's regular exhibitions up to 1950 as well as in many other national shows.

Eleanor Tufts

Bibliography
Howlett, D. Roger. *Molly Luce, Eight Decades of the American Scene*. Boston: Childs Gallery, 1980.
Tufts, Eleanor. *American Women Artists, 1830–1930*. National Museum of Women in the Arts, 1987.

Lucero-Giaccardo, Felice (1946–)

A painter and poet, Felice Lucero-Giaccardo is noted as a mainstream artist and innovator in contemporary Native American art.

Raised in the traditional Pueblo of San Felipe, New Mexico, at age fourteen she began formal training with Pueblo painter Manuel Chavez. Like most Native American artists of that time, Lucero-Giaccardo first painted romanticized, realistic Indian subjects in the studio style, but she almost immediately shifted to modernism. In 1962 she studied at the controversial new Institute of American Indian Art in Santa Fe, New Mexico, and later attended the Fletcher Arts Memorial in Philadelphia, Pennsylvania, and the University of New Mexico in Albuquerque, where she earned a Bachelor of Fine Arts degree in 1979.

Lucero-Giaccardo's work applies acrylics, pastels, and mixed media to paper or canvas, with compositions organized around grid patterns reminiscent of Louise Nevelson or wavy lines recalling minimalist Agnes Martin. Most works tell a story via overlays of found objects, personal symbols, and fragments of the artist's poetry. Themes emphasize political issues such as racism, religious oppression, and feminism, but also include family subjects such as the parent-child relationship and the impact of television. Although she presently lives in the east, San Felipe remains her main inspiration.

Lucero-Giaccardo was accepted in her first juried show in 1979, was published the same year in *ArtSpace Magazine*, and had her initial solo exhibition in 1980. Her work is contained in permanent collections of the Chase-Manhattan Bank, New York City; the U.S. Department of the Interior, Washington, D.C.; Miami University Art Museum, Oxford, Ohio; Albuquerque Museum of Fine Art, New Mexico; Museum of the American Indian, New York City; the Heard Museum, Phoenix, Arizona; the Millicent Rogers Museum in Taos, New Mexico; and numerous private collectors.

Barbara Loeb

Bibliography
Kenagy, Suzanne G. "Eight Artists II." *American Indian Art Magazine* 13:1 (Winter 1987): 60–62.
Loeb, Barbara. *Felice Lucero-Giaccardo: A Pueblo Painter*. University Art Museum, Arizona State University, 1991.
Traugott, Joseph. "Native American Artists and the Post-Modern Cultural Divide." *Art Journal* 51:3 (Fall 1992): 36–43.

Lucier, Mary (1944–)

Born in Bucyrus, Ohio, the video artist Mary Lucier earned a Bachelor's degree from Brandeis University, Waltham, Massachusetts, with honors in English and American literature and she also received the president's award in sculpture.

Between 1971 and 1991 Lucier has held twenty-nine solo exhibitions of her work throughout the United States, including Greenberg Wilson, New York City (1989, 1991), the Museum of Contemporary Art, Los Angeles, California (1988); the Whitney Museum of American Art, New York City (1981, 1985, 1986); Carnegie Museum of Art, Pittsburgh, Pennsylvania (1983); The Kitchen, New York City (1975, 1978); and others. Her work has been invited to numerous group exhibitions in the United States and abroad, including "Videoskulptur retrospectiv und aktuell 1963–1989," Kolnischer Kunstverein, Cologne, Germany, a travelling show to Neuer Berliner Kunstverein, Berlin (1989); "American Landscape Video," Carnegie Museum of Art, Pittsburgh, Pennsylvania, a travelling show to the San Francisco Museum of Modern Art, California (1988); "The Luminous Image," Stedelijk Museum, Amsterdam (1984); "Biennial Exhibition," Whitney Museum of American Art, New York City (1983); and many others.

Lucier has been a visiting artist and/or member of the faculty of colleges and universities across the United States; artist-in-residence at the Atlantic Center for the Arts, Florida (1990), Capp Street Project, San Francisco, California (1986), and the Television Laboratory, WNET, in New York City. She has won awards, fellowships, honors, and public commissions from the Guggenheim Foundation, American Film Institute, Jerome Foundation, National Endowment for the Arts (NEA), and the New York State Council on the Arts, among others. Lucier has had her work aired on PBS and cable television, and on Spanish television

and elswhere in the decade of the 1980s. Her work is represented in private, public, and corporate permanent collections in the United States, Canada, and Europe, inluding the Whitney Museum of American Art, New York City; San Francisco Museum of Art, California; Stedelijk Museum, Amsterdam; National Gallery of Canada, Ottawa; Reader's Digest Foundation, Endicott, New York; the Banff Center, Alberta, Canada; and others.

Bibliography
Gookin, Kirby. "Mary Lucier." *Artforum* (April 1991).
Heartney, Eleanor. "Ten for the 90's." *Art News* (April 1990).
Raven, Arlene. "Refuse Refuge." *The Village Voice* (January 15, 1991).
Russell, John. "Mary Lucier: Wilderness." *The New York Times* (March 25, 1989).

Luke, Alexandra (1901–1967)

Alexandra Luke (then called Margaret) first went to school in Westmount, an affluent English-speaking quarter of the city of Montréal, Québec, Canada. Soon after, her family moved to Oshawa, a mid-sized city east of Toronto, where she graduated from high school in 1919. In neither of these educational situations did she give any particular indication of her later career. She was married for a brief four-month period to Marcus Everett Smith in 1924, but the marriage ended with his sudden death. Four years later she was exposed to the work of a visiting Dutch landscapist, Jan van Empel (1880–1931). That, plus her marriage to the very supportive Clarence Ewart McLaughlin, sealed her fate. By 1930 she was a charter member and art convenor of the Oshawa Lyceum Club and Women's Art Association. Within a few years she had become a staunch local defender of avant-garde tendencies in art, particularly those that tended toward abstraction based on analogies to music, although her own work remained conventional for the time. Nevertheless, her first group show in 1933 at the Lyceum Club provided the occasion for a public debate with the conservative president of the Royal Academy of Art, Sir Wyly Grier.

Luke's output dwindled during the war years, when she worked in a blood donor clinic, but she did manage to complete a few canvases roughly in the manner of the nationalistic Group of Seven, at least two of whom (Arthur Lismer and A.J. Casson) she knew personally. However, it seems she studied in the mid-1940s with Leonard Brooks, who advised her to abandon the Group's manner and be truer to her own sensibilities.

The first opportunity to do so came in 1945, when she enrolled in the Banff School of Fine Arts in Alberta. Group of Seven member A.Y. Jackson was there then, but she was more moved by the younger, more experimental Jock MacDonald, who advocated an admixture of Kandinsky, and Ouspenskian spirituality. The first results of these new influences were exhibited in a two-person show with Isabel McLaughlin in 1946 in Oshawa. Because her married name was McLaughlin as well, she decided thereafter to sign herself Luke. The second opportunity to find herself came when she participated in a show of "Canadian Women Artists" in New York City in 1947, for she then learned of the school of Hans Hofmann, with whom she would study from 1947 to 1953. She was deeply influenced by his teachings: her notes are filled with direct quotations of his "push and pull" theory of abstraction, and some of her titles are allusions to his work.

Luke's first solo show was in 1952 at the local picture loan society, and in the same year she organized a show of contemporary Canadian abstraction at the Young Men's Christian Association (YMCA). The venue is an indication of that era's lack of commercial support for this type of art. For that matter, so was her next public outing, the "Abstracts at Home" show organized for a major Toronto department store by the young, rebellious painter William Ronald. It was to be her greatest claim to fame, for it led directly to the creation of the first "official" abstract school of painting in Canada, the Painters Eleven. She was the only female member, but her colleagues remember her as a prime mover, and the first official meetings took place in her studio. However, her work of the time still had some vestiges of traditional subjects such as still life, despite a vigorous impasto ("Golden Glow," 1953).

A visit to Europe in 1955 provided Luke with a wealth of ideas, and her work became bolder. In 1956 the Painters Eleven showed in New York, eventually coming to the attention of Clement Greenberg, who paid a critical visit to the artists' studios a year later. Greenberg advised Luke to make her compositions less busy and to let the color speak for itself. She was able to do this more readily in watercolor than in oil, so her smaller works immediately became freer, more colorful, and more translucent. It is not surprising that in 1958 she formally became a member of the Canadian Society of Painters in Watercolor. By 1961 she was painting small works in a manner somewhere between those of Helen Frankenthaler and Jules Olitski. Works like "Yellow Space" (1961) won her the diploma of honor at the Vichy Salon in 1961. But for their size, they would be true color-field paintings.

Luke was nothing if not committed to the cause of art in her community. She constantly organized art-related activities, frequently donating works as prizes for fundraisers and the like. She taught painting classes in her own home from 1933 to 1939, and she ran a community ceramics program of sorts from about 1939 to 1951. In 1949 she even taught an early modern art history class for the Community Recreation Association. She was a dedicated member of several arts organizations, including the Ontario Society of Artists, the International Institute of Arts and Letters, and the Canadian Group of Painters. Her affliction with cancer around 1963 curtailed virtually all such activities.

Robert J. Belton

Bibliography

Watson, Jennifer C. *Alexandra Luke: A Tribute*. Catalog. Oshawa: Robert McLaughlin Gallery (July 6–August 7, 1977).

Lum, Bertha Boynton Bull (1869–1954)

An illustrator and early practitioner of color woodcut and hand-colored raised line prints in the United States, Bertha Boynton Bull Lum was the daughter of Tipton, Iowa, attorney Joseph Bull and homemaker Harriet Bull—both artists. She studied at the Art Institute of Chicago, Illinois, in 1895–1896 and again in 1901 following classes with illustrator Frank Holme and stained-glass artist Anna Weston. At Holme's school she apparently was exposed to woodblock cutting from Holme and the reading of Arthur Wesley Dow's *Composition, A Series of Exercises Selected from a New System of Art Education*. In 1903 she married corporate lawyer Burt F. Lum. The couple spent their seven-week honeymoon in Japan, where she met with a woodcut printmaker. When she returned to Japan for fourteen weeks in 1907 she spent most of her

time working in the studio of block cutter Bonkotsu Igami. She made four additional trips to Japan. She and her family moved from Minneapolis, Minnesota, to San Francisco, California, in late 1917. Lum spent 1922 through 1924 in China, returning to San Francisco, California, to live until 1927, when she, by then divorced, and her two daughters moved to China, living there until 1939. After World War II she again lived in China until 1953, when she went to Genoa, Italy, to join her daughter and grandchildren. Between her many moves, Lum travelled frequently among the continents.

Her first major exhibition was in 1912 at the 10th Annual Art Exhibition in Uyeno Park, Tokyo. She exhibited at the Panama-Pacific International Exposition, San Francisco (1915); Exposition Park Art Museum, Los Angeles; California Society of Etchers; and the Printmakers Society of California—all in California; the Post Exposition Exhibition (1916); the Art Institute of Chicago and Chicago Society of Etchers—both in Illinois; the New York Public Library, New York City; the U.S. National Museum, Washington, D.C.; and the Institute of Fine Arts, Peking. She also exhibited with the American Federation of the Arts; among others.

Lum is known for her color woodcuts and illustrations inspired by her travels and by Asian myths and legends. She published her first illustrated book, *Gods, Goblins, and Ghosts*, based upon her Japanese experiences, during her first trip to China in 1922. In her second book, *Gangplanks to the East* (1936), she told Asian folk tales as well as stories of her travels in Asian countries. Her drawings illustrate fiction for the *New York Herald Tribune* Sunday Magazine, the *Golden Phoenix, Jades and Dragons*, and *Imperial Incense* by Princess Der Ling, and *Good Housekeeping* and *World Traveller* magazines. She also illustrated a book by her daughter Eleanor (Peter) Lum, *Peiping and North China*, and articles by Peter and her other daughter.

Phyllis Peet

Bibliography

Gravalos, Mary Evans O'Keefe, and Carol Pulin. *Bertha Lum*. Washington and London: Smithsonian Institution Press, 1990.

Wright, Helen. "Bertha Lum's Wood-Block Prints." *American Magazine of Art* 8 (August 1917): 408–11.

Lundeberg, Helen (1908–)

Throughout the more than fifty-five years that separate Helen Lundeberg's remarkably assured "Self-Portrait" of 1933 from her elegant paintings of the 1980s, her work has reflected a belief that a truly creative artist must seek "the personal solution." From beginning to end she has accomplished this, creating an art of subtle color, ambiguous space, classical restraint, and quiet authority.

Born in Chicago, Illinois, Lundeberg spent her childhood in Pasadena, California, and attended school there. In the summer of 1930 she studied drawing with the modernist painter Lorser Feitelson. In ensuing years she actively participated with Feitelson in development of the new classicism, later known as post-surrealism. Lundeberg wrote the group's theoretical manifesto and took part in its exhibitions together with Feitelson, Lucian Labaudt, Knud Merrild, Grace Clements, Philip Guston, Reuben Kadish, and others. Among her more important post-surrealist paintings are "Double Portrait of the Artist in Time" (1935; Collection, National Museum of American Art, Smithsonian Institution, Washington, D.C.) and "Cosmicide" (1935), which was included in the historic 1936 exhibition, "Fantastic Art, Dada, Surrealism," at the Museum of Modern Art (MoMA), New York City. While working on the Federal Art Project (FAP/WPA) between 1936 and 1942, Lundeberg created several lithographs of outstanding quality and a number of petrachrome and painted murals in public sites in Los Angeles and vicinity. Her work was again shown at MoMA in "Americans 1942/18 Artists from 9 States."

Partially in response to the "impersonality" of her mural paintings, Lundeberg often worked at very small scale—as in "The Abandoned Easel" series—during the 1940s. Beginning in 1950 her work became increasingly abstract—more concerned with the ambiguities of complex space than with the forms that occupy that space. Although Lundeberg and Feitelson were married and continued to share studios, her use of surreal, illusionist space and evocative, close-valued color served to place her work on a path which—while still related to his—was increasingly distinct. Her steady development as an artist brought many honors, including invitations to participate in major exhibitions at the Whitney Museum of American Art, New York City; Carnegie Institute, Pittsburgh, Pennsylvania; University of Illinois, Urbana; and the Bienal de São Paulo, Brazil; among others.

A series of retrospective exhibitions of Lundeberg's paintings has been presented in California museums, first, at the Pasadena Art Institute (1953); subsequently, at Scripps College, Claremont (jointly with Feitelson, 1958); La Jolla Museum of Contemporary Art (1971); San Francisco Museum of Modern Art (jointly with Feitelson, 1980); and the Los Angeles County Museum of Art (1988).

Clinton Adams

Bibliography
Americans 1942/18 Artists from 9 States. New York: Museum of Modern Art, 1942.
A Birthday Salute to Helen Lundeberg. Los Angeles County Museum of Art, 1988.
Geometric Abstraction in America. New York: Whitney Museum of American Art, 1962.
Helen Lundeberg: A Retrospective Exhibition. La Jolla, California: La Jolla Museum of Contemporary Art, 1971.
Helen Lundeberg: A Retrospective Exhibition. Barnsdall Park, Los Angeles: Los Angeles Municipal Art Gallery, 1979.
Lorser Feitelson and Helen Lundeberg: A Retrospective Exhibition. San Francisco Museum of Modern Art, 1980.

Lutkenhaus, Almuth (1927–)

Born in Hamm, Westfalia, Germany, the sculptor Almuth Lutkenhaus studied with Kurt Schwitters and was a student at the Fine Arts institutes in Dortmund and Münster, Germany (1948–1952). A teacher, Lutkenhaus had completed more than twenty large figures and sculptural murals for governmental buildings in Germany (1952–1966) before she emigrated to Canada that same year.

Lutkenhaus's first solo exhibition in Canada was held at the Pollock Gallery, Toronto (1968); it was followed by solo shows at Goethe House, Toronto (1969); Gallery House Sol, Georgetown (1970, 1971); University of Toronto (1971); Sheridan College, Oakville (1971)—all in Ontario; and others. She has won awards and honors in Germany

and Canada, and examples of her work are in private and public permanent collections, including the Oakville Civic Centre and St. James' Church, Oakville, Ontario.

Bibliography
Kirkwood, Hilda. "Space and Sculpture: An Interview with Almuth Lutkenhaus." *Canadian Forum* 60:705 (December–January 1980–1981): 5–9.

Lutz, Winifred Ann (1942–)

Born in Brooklyn, New York, the sculptor/environmental artist/papermaker Winifred Ann Lutz earned a Bachelor of Fine Arts degree from the Cleveland Institute of Art, Ohio (1965); studied in Atelier 17, New York City, with Stanley William Hayter during the same year; and, three years later, received a Master of Fine Arts degree from Cranbrook Academy of Art, Bloomfield Hills, Michigan.

One of the most experienced artists working with handmade paper today—Lutz received a Hollander beater as a gift when she was a mere child—she is particularly inventive with respect to casting techniques as her "Dayfinder" series demonstrates. "Reserve" (1981), reveals an elegant cast paperwork exhibited in a ninety-degree wall corner.

Lutz has had her work invited to major group exhibitions and has held solo shows in museums and galleries in the United States and abroad, including "Paper Reliefs," American Craft Museum, New York City (1975); "Handmade Paper Objects," Santa Barbara Museum of Art, California (1976); "Handmade Paper, Prints, and Unique Works," Museum of Modern Art (MoMA) (1976); and Marilyn Pearl Gallery (1977–1979, 1984–1985, 1986, 1988, 1990)—both in New York City: "Paper about Paper," Albright-Knox Art Gallery, Buffalo, New York (1980); "New American Paperworks," an international travelling show (1982–1986); "Paper as Image," Arts Council of Great Britain (1983); Dolan-Maxwell Gallery, Philadelphia, Pennsylvania (1990); and many others.

Lutz's work is represented in private, corporate, and public permanent collections, including the Albright-Knox Art Gallery, Buffalo, New York; the Art Institute of Chicago; and National Bank of Chicago—both in Illinois; Cleveland Museum of Art, Ohio; Crocker Art Gallery, Sacramento; and Desert Museum, Palm Springs—both in California; International Paper Corporation, New York City; Jan van Eyck Akademie, Maastricht, the Netherlands; Mount Holyoke College, South Hadley, Massachusetts; Newark Museum, New Jersey; and others.

Bibliography
Feinberg, Jean. "Findings of Winifred Lutz." *Craft Horizons* (April 1979).
Heller, Jules. *Papermaking.* Watson-Guptill, 1978.
Lutz, Winifred. "Casting to Acknowledge the Nature of Paper." *International Conference of Hand Papermakers.* Boston: Carriage House Press, 1981.

Lux, Gwen (1908–)

Born in Chicago, Illinois, the multi-talented sculptor Gwen Lux studied at the Maryland Institute of Arts, Baltimore; the Fine Arts School of the Boston Museum, Massachusetts; in Paris, France; and in Yugoslavia with Ivan Mestrovic.

Lux has had her work exhibited in many galleries, including the Whitney Museum of American Art, New York City (1934, 1935); Detroit Museum of Art, Michigan (1948); Pomeroy Galleries, San Francisco, California (1968); Contemporary Arts Center (1970), and the Downtown

Gallery (1976)—both in Honolulu, Hawaii (1976); and many others.

Sculptor, teacher, designer, lecturer, and writer—Lux created the fountains for the Detroit Institute of Art, and taught at the Detroit Society of Arts and Crafts (1944–1946)—both in Michigan; wrote for many art journals, including *Art Digest*, and *Parnassus*; won numerous awards and honors, including a Guggenheim Foundation fellowship (1933); prizes at exhibitions held at the Detroit Institute of Art, Michigan (1943–1945, 1956); a national prize in lithography and awards from the National Association of Women Artists (1947), Audubon Artists (1954), and the Architectural League (1958)—all in New York City; and others. Her work is represented in private, public, and corporate permanent collections, including the Association of American Artists, New York City; Detroit Museum of Art, Michigan; McGraw-Hill Building, Chicago, Illinois; Northland Shopping Center, Detroit, Michigan; University of Arkansas, Fayetteville; Victoria Theatre, New York City; and many others.

Bibliography
Clute, Eugene. "New Materials, New Triumphs." *Craft Horizons* 13:2 (March–April 1953): 22–26.

Lyall, Laura Adeline Muntz (1860–1930)

Laura Adeline Muntz Lyall was born in Radford, Warwickshire, England, but her family moved to Canada when she was a child. She began painting in her teens, and her first formal art instruction was with William Charles Forster in Hamilton, Ontario, in 1881. She continued her instruction from 1882 to 1883 at the Ontario School of Art in Toronto, then in 1887 travelled to England to study for three months at the St. John's Wood School of Art in London. Back in Canada she worked under George Reid (1890–1891). From 1891 to 1898 she lived in Paris, France, where she studied for a short period at the Académie Colarossi.

While in Paris Lyall's paintings were included in the salons of the Société des Artistes Français on five occasions: her "Fairy Tale" (c. 1893) received an honorable mention in 1895. She also exhibited in the "World's Columbian Exposition," Chicago, Illinois, in 1893, and won a silver medal at the "Pan-American Exhibition" in Buffalo, New York, in 1901, and a bronze medal at the "Louisiana Purchase Exhibition," St. Louis, Missouri, in 1904. A regular exhibitor with the Art Association of Montréal and the Royal Canadian Academy of Arts, Lyall was made an associate of the latter institution in 1895. She was also a member of and regular exhibitor with the Ontario Society of Artists, and the only woman to exhibit with the Canadian Art Club (in 1909).

Upon her return to Canada from Europe in 1899 Lyall continued the portraits and figure works for which she had become so well known. Working both in oil and watercolor, her loose, fluid brushwork shows the influence of impressionism and the years spent in Paris. Her favorite subjects were mothers and children, and many of her works, such as "Protection" (n.d.) and "Admiration" (n.d.) are less portraits than idealized renderings of a broader theme. Lyall's work is represented in the National Gallery of Canada and the Art Gallery of Ontario as in numerous other public and private collections across Canada.

Janine A. Butler

Bibliography
Duval, Paul. *Canadian Impressionism*. McClelland and Stewart, Inc., 1990.
MacCuaig, Stuart. *Climbing the Cold White Peaks: A Survey of Artists in and from Hamilton 1910–1950*. Hamilton Artists' Inc., 1986.

Lysohir, Marilyn (1950–)

Born in Sharon, Pennsylvania, Marilyn Lysohir is known for her outsized ceramic sculpture. Lysohir earned a Bachelor's degree from Ohio Northern University, Ada (1972) and received a Master of Fine Arts degree from Washington State University, Pullman, seven years later.

"BAMS" (1980), is composed of eleven three-quarter-sized ceramic sculptures of women marines on a tiled platform. "Bad Manners" (1985), which dominated her solo exhibition at Asher/Faure Gallery, Los Angeles, California, contains a six-foot, food-laden dining table around which are seated the clothes of four bodiless "figures." "The Dark Side of Dazzle" (1986), also shown at Asher/Faure Gallery along with anti-war drawings, depicts a twenty-four-foot-long ceramic and wood battleship. Her works speak eloquently for themselves; her mother was a U.S. Marine.

Bibliography
Clark, Garth. *American Ceramics: 1896 to the Present*. Abbevillle Press, 1987.
Muchnic, Suzanne. "Reviews: Lysohir." *The Los Angeles Times* (July 15, 1986).
Okazaki, Arthur. "Marilyn Lysohir." *American Ceramics* 4:1 (1985).

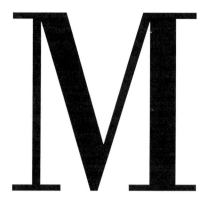

MacAdams, Cynthia (1939–)

Currently a resident of both New York City and Los Angeles, California, Cynthia MacAdams was born on an Indian reservation near Webster, South Dakota, in 1939. In 1961 she earned a Bachelor of Arts degree while studying theater at Northwestern University in Evanston, Illinois. From there she moved to New York City, where she worked on and off Broadway and at the Actor's Studio. She also acted in films such as *Me and My Brother* (1966), *Wild in the Streets* (1968), *The Last Movie* (1970), and *Mad Bomber* (1972). In 1972 she went on a spiritual pilgrimage to the Far East, where she meditated and studied in Buddhist monasteries. After her return to the United States MacAdams began to examine the natural world in Colorado—where she started her first serious photography. Her subject matter changed when she began to examine her own life and realized that the roles she had played as an actress were, in her opinion, women created by men. Thus she started to photograph other women who were also in the process of self-definition and who were emerging as individuals with strong feminine identities. These women appear in both urban and natural settings and are seen in a casual documentary style embodied by the carefully considered snapshot. The pictures are somewhat uneven in their visual impact, but convey the strength of each subject. These images were published in her first monograph, *Emergence* (1977), a title designed to call attention to the emerging characters of her sitters as embodiments of various archetypes of the great goddess.

Her second monograph, *Rising Goddess*, published in 1983, is a series of nudes of women and girls photographed in the desert, at the ocean, and in pool and prairie settings. Here women appear as separated from civilization, in a primordial state in which sacred aspects of the feminine are examined through a contemporary re-creation of Artemis and Aphrodite archetypes. In this second monograph she has moved into a more experimental use of black-and-white film—her preferred medium. Many of the images in *Rising Goddess* are exposed using infrared film. The infrared film causes the vegetation and human skin to appear as if emanating light. Its fine even grain gives flesh an almost opalescent quality. MacAdams's technique is enhanced by the custom printing of her negatives by Keith Williamson, with whom she works to create a flowing sense of surface. In this manner, MacAdam's printing contributes to her feminist iconology, for her nudes emerge not only as glorified bodies, but as spiritual entities. Originally titled *Island of Women*, this book represents MacAdams's attempt to create affirmative female images because she believes that such photographs have the power to change people's perceptions of women and hence to change civilization itself.

Diana Emery Hulick

Bibliography

Lacey, Peter. *Nude Photography, The Technique of Nine Modern Masters.* Amphoto, 1985.

MacAdams, Cynthia. Emergence. E.P. Dutton, 1979.

———. *Rising Goddess.* Essays by Kate Millett and Margaretta Mitchell. Morgan and Morgan, 1983.

MacDougall, Anne (1944–)

Born in Winchester, Massachusetts, the painter/printmaker Anne MacDougall received her Bachelor of Arts degree from Randolph-Macon Woman's College, Lynchburg, Virginia (1966), and, the following year, did graduate study at Syracuse University, New York.

MacDougall, known as Anne Ballou prior to 1979, has held solo exhibitions of her work at Long Island University, South Hampton, New York (1975); and Boston University (1977), Andover Gallery of American Art (1980), Pucker Safrai Gallery, Boston (1981), and Howard Yezerski Gallery, Boston (1987)—all in Massachusetts; and others. Her work has been invited to many group exhibitions throughout the United States, including "Virginia Artists," Virginia Museum of Fine Arts, Richmond (1976); "Boston Printmakers National," De Cordova Museum, Lincoln, Massachusetts (1974, 1976, 1977, 1979); "Contemporary Landscapes," Fairleigh Dickinson University, Teaneck, New Jersey (1984); "Watercolor U.S.A. The Monumental Image," Springfield Art Museum, Missouri (1986); "A Sense of Place—Whistler to the Present," John Szoke Gallery, New York City (1989); and others.

MacDougall has received many honors, including a grant from the Artists Foundation, Boston, Massachusetts (1981); a fellowship at the MacDowell Colony, Peterborough, New Hampshire (1980); and a grant from the Virginia Center, Sweet Briar, Virginia (1978). Her work is in private, corporate, and permanent museum collections in the United States, including the Museum of Fine Arts, Boston, and Fogg Art Museum, Harvard University, Cambridge, and the Boston Public Library —all in Massachusetts; Indianapolis Museum of Art, Indiana; Cleveland Museum of Art, Ohio; Springfield Art Museum, Missouri; the Virginia Museum, Richmond; and others.

Bibliography
Secrest, Meryle. Article. *Washington Post* (April 1975).
Who's Who in American Art. 19th ed. R.R. Bowker Co., 1991–1992.

MacIver, Loren (1909–)

Born in New York City, painter Loren MacIver had no formal art training, except for one year of children's classes at the Art Students League, New York City, in 1919. She has lived and worked in New York all of her life, spending summers on Cape Cod, Massachusetts. Often compared to the surrealists because of her use of indeterminate natural forms, MacIver adheres to no group or school.

MacIver's early work—prior to 1935—developed many of the themes she continues to use. Painting in oil, she uses a specific natural form—leaf, puddle, bird's egg—and transforms it into a glowing, floating, abstracted object. She worked for the Works Projects Administration Federal Art Project between 1936 and 1939, and one of her easel paintings, "Shack," was purchased by the Museum of Modern Art (MoMA), New York City, in 1938. MacIver was included in the "Fantastic Art, Dada and Surrealism" exhibition mounted by MoMA (1936). Her first solo show was at the East River Gallery, New York City, in 1938.

In the 1940s MacIver did a series of city paintings which included "Hopscotch" (1940); "Pushcart" (1944); "Window Shade" (1948); "The Violet Hour" (1943); "Oil Slick" (1940); and "Taxi" (1951). Each work highlights a mundane city object—as in the asphalt where a child's game is marked—against a glowing stained background. Generally lyrical and romantic, sometimes the sharp details of the personal imagery in her work brings into focus the decay of city life.

During travels in Europe MacIver carried notebooks for her "scrawls" which she later put to use in completed composition. These European works are indicated quite clearly by their titles: "Cathedral" (1949); "Venice" (1949); and "Dublin and Environs" (1950). The general composition remains similar to her earlier works, as in "Cathedral," where the glowingly painted stained glass of Chartres is used to symbolize all European cathedrals. MacIver is often compared with the imagist poets in her artistic vision. Married to the poet Lloyd Frankenberg, she seems to visually interpret the same ideal he expressed in words. It is also interesting that her only human subjects have been a series of portraits of poets and clowns.

MacIver received a Ford Foundation grant in 1960 and a Guggenheim Foundation fellowship in 1976. She won first prize at the Art Institute of Chicago, Illinois, in 1961 and a purchase prize at the Krannert Art Museum, University of Illinois, Urbana, in 1963. MacIver is one of the few women who have been elected to the American Academy and Institute of Arts and Letters, New York City. She has exhibited widely in the United States as well as in Europe, including the Venice Biennale, Italy (1967); Toulouse Museum of Fine Arts, France; Musée des Beaux-Arts, Lyons, France; Musée d'Art Moderne, Ville de Paris, France; Musée Ponchettes, Nice, France; Whitney Museum of American Art and Museum of Modern Art (MoMA)—both in New York City.

Paintings by MacIver are part of the permanent collection of the Whitney Museum of American Art, Metropolitan Museum of Art, and MoMA—all in New York City; Corcoran Gallery of Art, Washington, D.C.; Los Angeles County Museum of Art, California; and the Addison Gallery of American Art, Andover, Massachusetts.

Judith Sealy

Bibliography
Baigell, Matthew. *Dictionary of American Art.* Harper & Row, 1979, p. 219.
Baur, John I.H. *Loren MacIver—Rice Pereira.* New York: Whitney Museum of American Art, 1953.
Rubinstein, Charlotte Streifer. *American Women Artists.* G.K. Hall, 1982, pp. 250–52.

MacKendrick, Lilian (1906–)

A native New Yorker, the artist Lilian MacKendrick earned a Bachelor's degree at New York University, New York City; studied drawing and painting with Dorothy Block, and sculpture with Louis Keila.

MacKendrick's work has been exhibited in many solo shows, including the Mortimer Levitt Gallery (1949), and Feigl Gallery (1953, 1958)—both in New York City; and has been in group exhibitions in the United States and abroad, including the Witte Museum of Art, San Antonio, Texas (1952); "Third Biennial of American Painting," Bordighera, Italy (1955); "Eleven Americans," a travelling show through French museums (1956–1957); and others.

Winner of awards and honors, MacKendrick received an honorable mention at the Brooklyn Society of Artists (1953); a gold medal at the Biennial in Bordighera, Italy (1955); an award for public service, Northside Center for Child Development (1961); and others. Examples of her work are in private and public permanent collections in the United States and abroad, including the Georgia Museum of Art, Athens; Hirshhorn Museum and Sculpture Garden, Washington, D.C.; Israel Museum, Jerusalem; Metropolitan Museum of Art, New York City; Museum of Fine Art, Houston, Texas; and others.

Bibliography
Del Carlo, Omar, and Inglis Remy. "Lilian MacKendrick." *The Connoisseur* 186:747 (May 1974).
Who's Who in American Art. R.R. Bowker Co., 1978.

MacKenzie, Alix (1922–1962)

The ceramist Alix MacKenzie earned a Bachelor's degree from the School of the Art Institute of Chicago, Illinois (1946). She organized the momentous U.S. lecture-demonstration tour of the potters Shoji Hamada, Bernard Leach, and Soetsu Yanagi (1952) and, in the mid-1950s, with her husband, apprenticed for two years to Leach at his studio in St. Ives, England. MacKenzie and her husband opened a studio in Stillwater, Minnesota, where they threw low-cost, functional, reduction-fired ware.

Bibliography
Clark, Garth. *American Ceramics: 1876 to the Present.* Abbeville Press, 1987.

MacKenzie, Elizabeth (1955–)

Since the early 1980s Elizabeth MacKenzie's installations have been concerned with the representation of women within contemporary narratives, such as film, television, magazines, family histories, and medical and scientific discourse. Since 1986 her installations have consisted of large graphite drawings done from slide projections directly on the gallery walls. The images derive from photographs produced by MacKenzie while the texts have been appropriated from a variety of sources including newspapers, novels, mythology, self-help manuals, and scientific texts.

MacKenzie was born in Trois Rivières, Québec. From 1974 to 1979 she attended the Ontario College of Art and spent the next year in New York on an off-campus program. Since 1980 solo exhibitions of her work have been held in Canada in Toronto, Halifax, Vancouver, Sudbury, Kingston, and Regina. Her work has been included in group exhibitions across Canada and in the United States.

Along with Judith Schwarz, MacKenzie produced the video tape, *I Am An Artist. My Name is . . .* (1986)—one of numerous collaborative projects in which MacKenzie has been involved. In 1989 she collaborated with Anna Gronau and Carol Laing on an installation for the Morgentaler Clinic in Toronto. "Eating Virtue" is the title of an artist's project she produced for *Border/Lines* magazine (9/10, Fall–Winter 1987–1988). MacKenzie's work is included in the collection of the Canada Council Art Bank and private Canadian collections.

In addition to producing and exhibiting her own work, MacKenzie has been active in the art community as a curator, teacher, and guest lecturer. She was a founding member and served on the board of directors of YYZ, an artist-run gallery in Toronto, for eight years.

Vera Lemecha

Bibliography
Elliot, Bridget, and Janice Williamson. *Dangerous Goods.* Edmonton Art Gallery, 1990.
Gagnon, Monika. "Elizabeth MacKenzie." *Parachute* 46 (Spring 1987): 125.
Isaak, Jo Anna. *Mothers of Invention.* Hobart and William Smith Colleges, 1989.
Nemiroff, Diana. *Dessin-Installation-Drawing-Installation.* Sadye Bronfman Centre, 1984.

Mackenzie, Landon (1954–)

Landon Mackenzie was born in Boston, Massachusetts, of Canadian parents. She earned a Bachelor of Fine Arts degree at the Nova Scotia College of Art and Design, Halifax, in 1976, following it with a Master of Fine Arts degree from Montreal's Concordia University in 1979. Although she has taught and exhibited throughout Canada, since 1986 she has been associated with the Emily Carr College of Art and Design in Vancouver, British Columbia.

Like those of Emily Carr, Mackenzie's paintings could be loosely described as gently expressionist pastoral landscapes painted in a simple, direct manner. Unspoiled by the encroachment of signs of culture Mackenzie's arcadian vistas provide a home for hazily described animals to graze undisturbed. Despite the aura of innocence, the darkness of the images has generated some different responses. These vary from allusions to a lost world of implicitly religious simplicity, in which animals are at one with their natural environment, to the failure of a sombre nature to provide any solace or escape from the anxiety of urban life.

Robert J. Belton (with Lana Pitkin)

Bibliography
Dault, Gary Michael. *Some Version of Pastoral: Painting Against Cynicism.* Toronto: The Art Gallery at Harbourfront, 1986.
Fleming, Martha. "Geneviève Cadieux, Landon Mackenzie, Lyne Lapointe at Galerie France Morin, Montréal." *Artforum* (April 1982): 86–87.
Nemiroff, Diana. "Rhetoric and Figure in Montréal Painting Now." *Parachute* 27 (Summer 1982): 22–27.
Rabinovitch, R. Bella. *Landon Mackenzie: Paintings.* Lethbridge: The Southern Alberta Art Gallery, 1985.

MacLane, Jean (1878–1964)

Born Myrtle MacLane in Chicago, Illinois, the painter went through various name transformations, finally settling on Jean for her first name but for a period spelling her last name "McLane." After studying with John Vanderpoel at the Art Institute of Chicago, Illinois, from which she graduated in 1897, MacLane studied with Frank Duveneck in Cincinnati, Ohio, and William Merritt Chase in New York City. In 1905 she married the painter John Christen Johansen, who had earlier been a student at the Art Institute of Chicago, Illinois. They set up adjoining studios in New York and travelled to Europe whenever they could afford it. Among her paintings are many art deco-like beach scenes of Devonshire from the 1920s and sunlit portraits of her children—Margaret and John.

In 1912 the National Academy of Design, New York City, made MacLane an associate and, in 1926, a full academician. The long list of her awards begins with a bronze medal at the St. Louis Exposition, Missouri, in 1904, and includes first prize at the International Art League, Paris, France (1907, 1908); prizes at the National Association of Women Painters and Sculptors (1907, 1919); prizes at the National Academy of Design (1912, 1913, 1923, 1935)—both in New York City; prizes at the Pennsylvania Academy of Fine Arts, Philadelphia (1914, 1936); silver medal at the Panama-Pacific International Exposition, San Francisco (1915); and a prize at the Art Institute of Chicago, Illinois (1924).

MacLane was chiefly a portraitist. An early painting is a full-length figure entitled "The Visitor" (1907, Balogh Gallery). When a movement was initiated in 1919 to establish a national portrait gallery in the United States, MacLane was one of the eight American painters chosen to do three portraits of important international personages. MacLane's subjects were the Queen of Belgium and the prime ministers of Australia and Greece. Overseas travel funds were provided to carry out the commissions, but MacLane completed only the trip to Brussels, probably because travel to Australia and Greece may have posed a problem in view of distance and her family responsibilities. Her portrait of Elizabeth, "Queen of the Belgians" (1921, National Museum of American Art), is softly painted with iridescent colors glowing in the long dress set off by the encircling dark fur mantle.

MacLane's paintings are in the Toledo Museum of Art, Ohio; the Art Institute of Chicago, Illinois; Berkshire Museum, Massachusetts; Everson Museum, Syracuse, New York; and Milwaukee Art Museum, Wisconsin; and others.

Eleanor Tufts

Bibliography
Platt, Frederick. *Jean MacLane*. Charlottesville, Virginia: Balogh Gallery, 1984.
Ruthrauff, Florence Barlow. "The Unfeminized Art of M. Jean MacLane." *Art and Decoration* 3:9 (July 1913): 299–301.
Tufts, Eleanor. *American Women Artists, 1830–1930*. National Museum of Women in the Arts, 1987.

MacLeod, Pegi Nicol (1904–1949)

An energetic, intuitive painter, Pegi Nicol MacLeod was a consummate modernist whose stylistic affinities lie in the areas opened up by the formal experimentation of Cézanne and Kandinsky's validation of subconscious expression. MacLeod gravitated mainly toward urban subject matter interpreted as color and movement.

Born in Listowel, Ontario, MacLeod grew up in Ottawa, where she first studied art with the painter Franklin Brownell. She spent a year of further study at the newly-founded École des Beaux-Arts in Montréal, Québec, in 1923–1924, taking prizes in several categories. The works of the late 1920s were mainly portraits and landscapes of the hilly Gatineau area near Ottawa where she lived intermittently until 1934, maintaining close contact with Montréal. She won the Willingdon prize in 1931 for "The Log Run" (c. 1931), a strongly stylized landscape. By 1933 the loose expressionist style characteristic of her mature work emerged in paintings depicting school children gardening. Here she conveyed the excitement and movement of many active figures with sweeping lines and overlapping forms. Her tendency to make numerous rapid studies lent itself to the medium of watercolor, in which she excelled; her work in oils would develop toward the lightness and vivacity of the watercolors.

Moving to Toronto in 1934 MacLeod continued to paint, supporting herself by working on theater sets, as a window dresser and as art editor and contributor to the left-leaning magazine *Canadian Forum*. An important work from this period was the theatrical and dream-like "Descent of Lilies" (1935)—a self-portrait with organic forms flowing around her semi-nude figure—a concerted flirtation with surrealism. She married and settled in New York in 1937; a daughter, Jane, was born the same year.

Life in New York brought both stimulation and disillusionment to MacLeod. Her interests, she found, were peripheral to both surrealism and the social realism then current. Her commitment to realist observation was confirmed—the city with its crowds and rush proved a rich source of subject matter, as did her child. "The Manhattan Cycle," painted in the 1940s, was an important series of works depicting the changing seasons reflected by New York's street life—the flower carts on Good Friday; a wedding in September; and the burning of Christmas trees, among other events. The compositions, described as showing "Gothic complexity" by reviewer R.C. Hicklin, are crowded with figures often drawn from the bird's-eye viewpoint of MacLeod's apartment window.

MacLeod returned frequently to Canada. Always an activist, she was a co-founder of the University of New Brunswick Art Centre, Fredericton, and taught summer art courses there from 1940 to 1948. In the last years of World War II she served as a war artist, painting the women's division of the Canadian armed forces.

MacLeod had a distinguished career as an exhibiting artist, with several solo exhibitions to her credit. She showed regularly in the various annual exhibitions in Canada; she was elected to and exhibited with the Canadian Society of Painters in Watercolour (from 1936) and the Canadian Group of Painters (from 1937). She participated in group shows featuring Canadian painting abroad. Several touring retrospectives have honored MacLeod since her death. Significant holdings of her work can be found at the National Gallery of Canada, Ottawa, and the Art Gallery of Ontario, Toronto.

Janice Seline

Bibliography
Buchanan, Donald. *Pegi Nicol MacLeod: Memorial Exhibition*. National Gallery of Canada, 1949. Essay reprinted from Canadian Art 6 [Summer 1949]: 158–162.)
Hill, Charles C. *Canadian Painting in the Thirties*. National Gallery of Canada, 1975.
MacLeod, Pegi Nicol. *Daffodils in Winter: The Life and Letters of Pegi Nicol MacLeod*. Ed. and Intro. by Joan Murray. Penumbra Press, 1984.
Smith, Stuart Allen. *Pegi Nicol MacLeod*. University of New Brunswick Art Centre, 1981.

MacMonnies (Low), Mary Louise Fairchild (1858–1946)

A painter of figure pieces, portraits, and landscapes, Mary Louise Fairchild MacMonnies (Low) was born in New Haven, Connecticut; spent the Civil War years in New Orleans, Louisiana; and then moved with her family to St. Louis, Missouri. A talented pianist, she discovered her ability as a painter by accident while tinting photographs with her mother. MacMonnies subsequently enrolled in what was to become the St. Louis School of Fine Arts, Missouri, whose director arranged a scholarship for her to study in Paris, France, from 1885 through 1888. There she entered the Académie Julian and also studied with the painter Charles Carolus-Duran, who had been John Singer Sargent's teacher. In 1888 she married Frederick MacMonnies, who would become one of America's most famous sculptors. The two soon achieved financial success and eventually took up fashionable quarters in Paris.

In 1886 MacMonnies had her first painting accepted at the Paris Salon, France; in 1889 the Paris Salon exhibited her "June Morning," which was acquired by the St. Louis Museum of Fine Arts, Missouri. That year her glamorous "Self-Portrait" received a bronze medal—and considerable attention—at the Paris Exposition Universelle, France. While her husband began making frequent business trips to New York, MacMonnies continued to paint in Paris. Her celebrated copies of some Botticelli frescoes in the Louvre led to her being awarded one of the two major commissions: "Primitive Woman," for the woman's building at the 1893 World Columbian Exposition in Chicago, Illlinois, and a mural, "Modern Woman," being given to Mary Cassatt. MacMonnies's mural received critical acclaim and was generally considered a more effective work than Cassatt's. At the same Chicago Exposition two of MacMonnies's other paintings—"Tea al Fresco" and the above-mentioned "June Morning"—brought her awards and further recognition. Her international fame was now established, as was her husband's, who had designed the central fountain for the Paris Exposition. From 1894 the couple rented a summer home near Paris in Giverny, France, where Claude Monet and other artist-friends resided; in 1898 the MacMonnies took a permanent home in Giverny, while still maintaining a house in Paris. They had two daughters, one born in 1895, the other in 1897. Her husband, however, continued his prolonged visits to the United States, and in 1909 the couple's part-time marriage ended in divorce. MacMonnies remarried that year, to the academic muralist Will Hickok Low—a long-time admirer of hers. In 1910 they settled in Bronxville, New York. On the insistence of her new husband, who was afraid of scandal resulting from marriage to a divorced woman, MacMonnies began obliterating her former name from her art and substituting that of Low. Because of financial concerns, she turned increasingly to portraiture and to a tighter, darker, more academic style than that of her two previous styles: a light-infused impressionist manner followed by a misty or tonalist stage. By the end of her life, MacMonnies had won many major awards and had received the distinction of becoming an associate of New York City's National Academy of Design (1906).

Victor Koshkin-Youritzin

Bibliography

Dunford, Penny. *A Biographical Dictionary of Women Artists in Europe and America since 1850.* University of Pennsylvania Press, 1989.

Fielding, Mantle. *Dictionary of American Painters, Sculptors and Engravers,* 2nd ed. Ed. Glenn B. Opitz. Apollo Books, 1986, p. 557.

Rubinstein, Charlotte Streifer. *American Women Artists: From Early Indian Times to the Present.* Avon, 1982, pp. 139–40, 154.

Smart, Mary. "Sunshine and Shade: Mary Fairchild MacMonnies Low," *Woman's Art Journal* (Fall 1983–Winter 1984): 20–25.

Weimann, Jeanne Madeline. *The Fair Women.* Intro. by Anita Miller. Academy Chicago, 1981.

Macomber, Mary Lizzie (1861–1916)

A painter of allegorical and religious works in a Pre-Raphaelite or symbolist manner, Mary Lizzie Macomber was born in Fall River, Massachusetts, of a Quaker family that traced its ancestors to the Plymouth Pilgrims. When nineteen she embarked for three years on a series of flower and fruit paintings under the instruction of the noted Fall River master Robert S. Dunning, after which she spent a year at the Boston Museum of Fine Arts, Massachusetts, studying figure painting. Three years later she was a pupil of Frank Duveneck for a brief time and established a studio in Boston, Massachusetts.

About 1890 Macomber had developed a rarefied, idealizing style similar to that of the nineteenth-century English Pre-Raphaelites, who, dismayed by the materialism of the new industrial age, looked back to what they felt was the purer, more sincere period of the early Renaissance painters preceding Raphael. The influences of such Pre-Raphaelite artists as Sir Edward Burne-Jones or Dante Gabriel Rossetti appear strong in many of Macomber's tender, nobly-conceived, and spiritual paintings—some of them decorative panels—which often feature Annunciations, Magdalenes, and Madonnas. Following the destruction of many of her paintings in a 1903 studio fire, Macomber visited France, England, and Holland for several weeks. Her encounter with Rembrandt's art led to the looser brushwork and dramatic lighting of her later paintings.

Macomber was a technically accomplished painter with an excellent ability to compose her works and, through the subtlety and considerable refinement of her artistry, lift her idealized subjects beyond mere sentimentality to a level of genuine poetry. Among her fine paintings are "Memory Comforting Sorrow," "The Nightingale," "Singing Stars," and "Life." Her oil, "Saint Catherine" (1896), was awarded the Dodge prize in 1897 at New York City's National Academy of Design.

Victor Koshkin-Youritzin

Bibliography

Parker, Charles A. "Mary L. Macomber." *The International Studio* 47:188 (October 1919): lx–lxiv.

Rubinstein, Charlotte Streifer. *American Women Artists: From Early Indian Times to the Present.* Avon, 1982, p. 116.

MacRae, Emma Fordyce (1887–1974)

Born of American parents in Vienna, Austria, Emma Fordyce MacRae grew up in New York City. After attending Miss Chapin's School and the Brearley School she studied at the Art Students League, New York City, with F. Luis Mora and Ernest Blumenshein, and at the New York School of Art with Kenneth Hayes Miller. Her extensive exhibition activity began in 1914 with a two-woman show at the Anderson Galleries in New York City in which she was represented by twenty-nine paintings—mainly landscapes. She married Thomas MacRae in 1910 and subsequently gave birth to a daughter; but when her husband wished to move to Arizona, the city-bred artist balked and obtained a divorce. In 1922 she married Homer Swift of Rockefeller University and was able to continue to paint in her studio on West 69th Street. Many summers were spent in Gloucester, Massachusetts, where flowers became the subject of her paintings.

In addition to landscapes and floral still lifes MacRae created her own very distinctive compositions of a human figure in a decorative interior in which the many elements were woven together into a flat tapestry effect, e.g., "Stelka" (1926, cover of *Town and Country,* April 15, 1929) and "Naida Gray," shown at the "Exhibition of Paintings by Emma Fordyce MacRae," Roerich Museum, New York City (1930). Her paintings were shown in many solo exhibitions and were included in exhibitions at the Pennsylvania Academy of Fine Arts, Philadelphia; Corcoran Gallery of Art, Washington, D.C.; and Metropolitan Museum of Art, New York City. She received awards in New York City at the Pen & Brush Club, the National Association of Women Artists, the National Arts Club, and Allied Artists of America. In 1951 MacRae, who had been elected an associate of the National Academy of Design at forty-four, was raised to the status of academician.

Eleanor Tufts

Bibliography
Emma Fordyce MacRae. New York: Richard York Gallery, 1983.
Tufts, Eleanor. *American Women Artists, 1830–1930.* National Museum of Women in the Arts, 1987.

Magafan, Ethel (1916–1993)

Born in Chicago, Illinois, to a Polish mother and a Greek father, Ethel Magafan and her twin sister Jenne became known for their mural paintings done during the Depression. The Magafan twins were raised in Colorado, where they began painting at an early age. Encouraged by their grade school teachers as well as by a scholarship they shared, they enrolled for further study at the Colorado Springs Fine Arts Center, Colorado. Ethel studied chiefly with Frank Mechau and Peppino Mangravite and became Mechau's assistant on several mural commissions. Later Mangravite invited her to assist him on murals he was completing in Atlantic City, New Jersey.

The Magafan twins entered the national competition for murals sponsored by the U.S. Treasury Department in the 1930s, and Ethel, in her early twenties, won her first commission: "Wheat Threshing" for the post office in Auburn, Nebraska. A total of seven governmental commissions were awarded to her—five through national competitions. One of her commissions is in the Senate Chamber; one in the Recorder of Deeds building; one in the Social Security Building—all in Washington, D.C.; and three are in post office buildings in Wynne, Arkansas ("Cotton Pickers"); Mudill, Oklahoma ("Prairie Fire"); and South Denver, Colorado ("Horse Corral"). "Lawrence Massacre" (1936, Denver Art Museum) was never executed on the wall of Fort Scott, Kansas, post office because the Kansans were trying to forget this embarrassing moment in their history when Bushrangers in 1863 burned the town of Lawrence, which had become a center for the underground railway. However, after the forty-inch panel of "Lawrence Massacre" was exhibited in the Inaugural Exhibition at the National Museum of Women in the Arts, Washington, D.C. (1987), a seven-foot mural *was* commissioned of the artist, and she completed it in 1988.

The Magafan twins also exhibited together, making their New York City debut at the Contemporary Arts Gallery in 1940. Ethel continued at the Ganso Gallery in the 1950s, Seligman Galleries in the 1960s, and since the 1960s at the Midtown Galleries—all in New York City.

In 1946 Magafan married the painter Bruce Currie, and in 1951 they both won Fulbright grants which they used to paint landscapes in Greece. By this time Ethel and Bruce, as well as Jenne and her husband, the painter Edward Chavez, had moved to Woodstock, New York. Tragedy struck in 1952 when Jenne suddenly died of a cerebral hemorrhage. The loss of her sister deeply affected Magafan, and she strove to make certain that her sister's work was included in exhibitions.

A realistic painter in the 1930s, Magafan continued to paint mountainous landscapes but in an abstract style, occasionally with horses or goats suggested in the foreground. "Lonesome Valley" (egg tempera, 1950, Metropolitan Museum of Art) has a horse in a fenced-in pasture with a mountain range behind. Magafan's prizes include a Tiffany Foundation fellowship (1959); honorable mention in "American Painting Today" at the Metropolitan Museum of Art (1950); and the Altman prize at the National Academy of Design (1951, 1964)—all in New York City (1950); purchase prize in "Contemporary Arts of the USA," Pomona, California (1956); purchase award, Museum of Art, Columbia, South Carolina (1956); and many more. As recently as 1976 she won another mural commission: "General Grant in the Battle of the Wilderness" for the National Military Park in Fredericksburg,

Virginia. She has also had one-woman exhibitions at several museums across the country. She was the mother of the painter Jenne Currie.

Eleanor Tufts

Bibliography
Marling, Karal Ann. *Wall-to-Wall America.* University of Minnesota, 1982.
Tufts, Eleanor. *American Women Artists, 1830–1930.* National Museum of Women in the Arts, 1987.

Magafan, Jenne (1916–1952)

Born in Chicago, Illinois, the painter Jenne Magafan studied at the Colorado Springs Fine Arts Center, Colorado; and also with Peppino Mangravite, Frank Mechau, and Boardman Robinson. She shared her painting debut with her twin Ethel—also a painter—in 1940. Examples of her work are in many venues, including the Grafton Street Junior High School, Worcester, Massachusetts; Woodstock Artist's Association, New York; and others. Muralist, landscape and figure painter, Magafan showed work primarily at the Ganso Gallery, New York City; at her memorial exhibition at the Ganso Gallery, homage was paid her by fellow artists, including Yasuo Kuniyoshi, Peppino Mangravite, Fletcher Martin, and Eugene Speicher.

Bibliography
Jenne Magafan. Albany Institute of History and Art, 1954.
"Miss Magafan to Paint Grafton Street Junior High Murals." *Worcester Daily Telegram* (May 29, 1947).
"Twin Girls Score as Muralists." *Los Angeles Times* (April 23, 1944): Part III.
Woodstock's Art Heritage: The Permanent Collection of the Woodstock Artist's Association. Essay by Tom Wolf. Overlook Press, 1987.

Magenta, Muriel (1932–)

An installation sculptor and video artist known for her surreal images and plots drawn from an examination of popular culture, Muriel Magenta was born and raised in New York City. She received her Master of Fine Arts and Doctorate degrees at Arizona State University, Tempe.

Magenta began exhibiting environmental sculpture and audio work in 1975. Her films and videos have been shown throughout the United States and Europe. Her videos are distributed by ART COM in the United States, and Centre Simone De Beauvoir in France. In 1978 her photographic essays and art were published by the Wittenborn Publishing Company in New York. Between 1985 and 1986 she published photographs in *Women Artist News* and *The Humanist* covering the United Nations Conference of Women in Nairobi, Kenya. Her work is in the permanent collection at Arizona State University, Tempe.

In 1986 Magenta was awarded a video/computer art grant for *Salon Doo: Synthesis of Video and Computer Art Formats* from the Southwestern Interdisciplinary Arts Fund sponsored by the National Endowment for the Arts and the Rockefeller Foundation. She received the mid-career achievement award from the Women's Caucus for Art at the National Conference in Washington, D.C., in 1991.

Magenta began teaching at Arizona State University, Tempe, in 1979 and was an artist-in-residence at the University of Wisconsin also in 1979, and at St. Mary's College, Notre Dame University, Indiana, in 1984. She was the national president of the Women's Caucus for Art from 1982 to 1984.

Susan F. Baxter

Bibliography
Knight, Robert, and J. Grey Sweeney. *Coiffure Carnival: The Art of Muriel Magenta*. Exhibition Catalog. Scottsdale Center for the Arts.
Lippard, Lucy R. *Overlay: Contemporary Art History and The Art of Prehistory*. Avon Books, 1982, p. 52.
Rubenstein, Charlotte Streifer. *American Women Artists*. Pantheon Books, 1983, p. 279.
Tufts, Eleanor. *American Women Artists, Past and Present*. Vol. II. Garland, 1989, pp. 269–70.

Mailman, Cynthia (1942–)

Born in the Bronx, New York, a painter/educator known for her cool, pared-down representations of the urban landscape, Cynthia Mailman earned a Bachelor's degree in fine art and education from Pratt Institute, Brooklyn, New York (1964) and received a Master of Fine Arts degree in painting from Rutgers University, New Brunswick, New Jersey (1978).

Mailman has held eighteen solo exhibitions of her work between 1976 and 1988, including "Staten Island Visions/Nature and Technology," the Greenbelt (1988); the Newhouse Gallery, Snug Harbor Cultural Center (1980, 1983, 1986–1987); SoHo 20 Gallery (1974, 1976, 1978)—all in New York City; Everson Museum of Art, Syracuse, New York (1981); Douglass College, Rutgers University, New Jersey (1976); and others. Her work has been invited to myriad group exhibitions throughout the United States, including "Women for Choice," Women's Caucus for Art, SoHo 20 Gallery, New York City (1992); "Women Printmakers," Queensborough Community College, Queens, New York (1991); "West Art and the Law," Sunrise Art Museum, Charleston, West Virginia, Minneapolis Museum of Art, St. Paul, and Blandon Memorial Art Museum, Fort Dodge, Iowa—all in 1987; the Columbus Museum, Columbus, Ohio (1985); Joy Tash Gallery, Scottsdale, Arizona (1981); "Hassam Invitational," American Academy and Institute of Arts and Letters, New York City (1978); and many others.

Mailman has won awards and honors, including grants from the New York State (1976, 1987) and Staten Island, New York (1987) councils on the arts; large mural commissions at the Port Authority of New York and New Jersey, World Trade Center (1979) and City Walls, Inc., Staten Island, New York (1977). She has been a teacher, lecturer, and artist-in-residence at many schools and colleges across the United States since 1963, including adjunct assistant professor at Queensborough Community College since 1985. Her work is represented in private and public permanent collections, such as the Everson Museum, Syracuse; Staten Island Museum; the Port Authority of New York and New Jersey—all in New York; New Jersey State Museum, Trenton; and Prudential Insurance Company of America, Newark—both in New Jersey; and others.

Bibliography
Raynor, Vivian. "Review." *The New York Times–New Jersey* (September 21, 1991): 12.
Perreault, John. *The Staten Island Invitational*. A Catalog. The Newhouse Center, 1989.
Swenson, Sally. *Lives and Works, Talks with Women Artists*. Scarecrow Press, 1981.

Maka (Maria del Carmen Hernandez Fernandez) (1925–)

Maka, a Mexican national, was born in 1925 in Paris, France, of a Russian father and a Mexican mother. Born Maria del Carmen Hernandez Fernandez, she studied at the University of Mexico, where she earned a certificate in advertising and where she also took courses in photography and engraving in wood and metal. She began to paint in 1951 in the studio of Manuel Rodriguez Lozano. Her professional signature is Maka.

Maka's first solo exhibition occurred in 1955. She wrote for *Excelsior* (1968–1969) and, since 1969, has been writing for *Kena*. In 1973 Maka exhibited thirty-five works titled "Espacios del Espacio" in the Salón de la Plástica Mexicana and also displayed her book which carried the same title; she exhibited "Las Mutantes" in 1984, a show of thirty works of prehistoric animals evoking the theme of creation—also in the Salón de la Plástica Mexicana. Maka's technique for these paintings included using sand to encrust and texture her paint.

Maka's earlier solo shows were held at the Galería Pecanins, Mexico City, Mexico; the Proteo Gallery in New York; and the Galería Norte-Sur in Caracas, Venezuela; among others. By 1988 she had shown her work in 100 institutions and galleries in Mexico and elsewhere. She most recently exhibited her paintings in the Casa de la Cultura de Tlcaxcala, the Galería de Agora, and the Biblioteca de la Tesoreria. The portrayal of the human figure dominates her work, which can be found in the permanent collections of the Museum of Modern Art, Mexico City, Mexico, and the Museum of Tel Aviv, Israel, to name but two from a very large number of institutions. Actress Helen Hayes and actor Anthony Quinn have collected her work as have the late John Houston and Stan Getz.

Bibliography
Alvarez, José Rogelio, et al. *Enciclopedia de México*. Secretaría de Educación Pública, 1987.
The Texas Quarterly: Image of Mexico II. The University of Texas, Autumn 1969.

Malach, Josephine Lorraine (1933–)

Born in Regina, Saskatchewan, Canada, the painter Josephine Lorraine Malach studied with Kenneth Lochhead and Art McKay at the University of Regina, where she earned an art diploma (1951–1953). From 1952 to 1956, Malach won successive tuition and travel scholarships, which allowed her further study at the Pennsylvania Academy of Fine Arts, Philadelphia (1953–1957), the Albert Barnes Foundation, Merion (1953–1955)—both in Pennsylvania, and travel throughout Europe. She also won further grants from the Saskatchewan Arts Board, Canada (1975–1977, 1978, 1989).

Malach has held solo exhibitions in museums and galleries, and has had her work included in many group shows, including the Regina Public Gallery (1962, 1965, 1968); the Norman MacKenzie Art Gallery, Regina (1963, 1971, 1973, 1975–1976, 1978)—both in Saskatchewan; and others. Examples of her work are in private and public permanent collections, including the government of Saskatchewan; Saskatchewan Arts Board; the Vatican Collection of Papal Nuncio, Ottawa, Ontario; and others.

Bibliography
Newman, Marketa, ed. *Biographical Dictionary of Saskatchewan Artists: Women Artists*. Fifth House Publishers, 1990.
Phillips, Carol A. *Changes: 11 Artists Working on the Prairies*. Catalog of a travelling show. University of Regina, 1975.

Malamud, Tosia (1923–)

Born in Ukraine, the former USSR, Tosia Malamud was brought to Mexico the same year. A nationalized citizen of Mexico, Malamud studied the plastic arts with Francisco Goitia, Luis Ortiz Monasterio, Ignacio Asúnsolo, and Benjamin Coria.

Since 1925 Malamud has dedicated herself to sculpture—in wood, bronze, marble, resins, plastics, and other mediums. Her work has been exhibited in Mexico, Israel, the United States, Canada, Switzerland, and Spain—and has received many prizes and much recognition.

Bibliography

Alvarez, José Rogelio, et al. *Enciclopedia de México.* Secretaría de Educación Pública, 1987.

Maltais, Marcelle (1933–)

Born in Chicoutimi in the province of Québec, Canada, the painter Marcelle Maltais studied at the École des Beaux-Arts, Québec (1950–1955), under the aegis of Jean-Paul Lemieux and Jean Dallaire.

After her first solo exhibition at the Palais Montcalm, Québec (1955), Maltais showed in museums and galleries in Canada and abroad, including the Greenwich Art Gallery, Toronto (1956); Galerie l'Actuelle, Montréal (1957); Galerie Agnes Lefort, Montréal (1960–1962); Galerie "Nees Morphes," Athens, Greece (1961); Dorothy Cameron Gallery, Toronto (1963); "Atlantic Provinces Art Circuit," a travelling show throughout the Maritimes (1967); Galerie Pierre Dollmec, Paris, France (1969); Canadian Cultural Center, Paris, France (1972); and many more. Her work has been included in prestigious group shows throughout Canada, Czechoslovakia, Germany, Italy, Poland, the United States. Examples of her work are in private and public permanent collections in Canada and abroad.

Bibliography

O'Leary, Marie-France. "Entretiens avec les peintres québecois à Paris." *Culture vivant* 2 (1966): 28–39.

———. "Maltais/Marcelle Maltais." *Vie des arts* 64 (Autumn 1971): 38–41, 89.

Saucierm, Pierre. "Jeunes peintres au travail." *Vie des arts* 22 (Spring 1961): 37–45.

Mamnguksualuk, Victoria (1930–)

Victoria Mamnguksualuk is one of the best-known Canadian Inuit artists of her generation. Born near Garry Lake, Northwest Territories, she lived a migratory existence on the land until she was in her early thirties. Because of widespread disease and famine in the hunting camps of the Barren Lands region, Mamnguksualuk and her family, like many Inuits, moved to Baker Lake in 1963. Mamnguksualuk is the daughter of Jessie Oonark (c. 1906–1985), one of the best-known of all Inuit artists. Both mother and daughter became active in the artistic co-operative at Baker Lake.

Mamnguksualuk has done sculpture, drawings, and fabric wallhangings, but is best known for her silk-screen and stencil prints. Eight of her prints were included in the first edition of prints issued at Baker Lake in 1970; and her work has been included in annual print editions almost every year since then.

As a second generation Inuit artist to live in the settlements, Mamnguksualuk's art has been somewhat influenced by her exposure to images from the outside world. More than some of her predecessors she uses the conventions of European art in her depictions of three-dimensional space and sequential action. Her work is characterized by its complex scenes involving multiple figures and vigorous activity. Mamnguksualuk is particularly interested in the depiction of Inuit myth.

Mamnguksualuk's work has appeared in numerous group shows of Inuit art, including "Sculpture/Inuit: Masterworks of the Canadian Arctic," Canadian Eskimo Arts Council, Ottawa (1971–1973); "Baker Lake Drawings," Winnipeg Art Gallery (1972); "The Inuit Print," National Museum of Man, Ottawa (1977); and "Baker Lake Wallhangings," Vancouver Art Gallery (1979). Her work is represented in numerous museum collections, including the Winnipeg Art Gallery, the Canadian Museum of Civilization, the Macdonald Stewart Art Centre in Guelph, Ontario, the McMichaels Canadian Collection in Kleinberg, Ontario, and the Glenbow Museum in Calgary.

Janet Catherine Berlo

Bibliography

Driscoll, Bernadette. *Inuit Myths, Legends, and Songs.* Winnipeg Art Gallery, 1982, pp. 49–59.

Moore, Charles, ed. *Keeveeok, Awakel Mamnguksualuk and the Rebirth of Legend at Baker Lake.* Boreal Institute for Northern Studies, University of Alberta.

Mangold, Sylvia Plimack (1938–)

Born in the Bronx, New York City, Sylvia Plimack Mangold was aware of and sensitive to the clamor and the cultural cutting edge of the Big Apple. Mangold attended the High School of Music and Art, and the Cooper Union School of Art, New York City, before receiving her Bachelor of Fine Arts degree from Yale University, New Haven, Connecticut, in 1961.

Between 1974 and 1986 Mangold averaged about one solo exhibition of her work each year in the United States and abroad, including shows at the Fischbach Gallery, New York City (1974, 1975); Galerie Annemarie Verna, Zurich, Switzerland (1978); Brooke Alexander, Inc. (1982, 1984, 1986); and others. Her work was selected for inclusion in many group exhibitions in Europe and America, such as "Twenty Contemporary Women Artists," Aldrich Museum of Contemporary Art, Ridgefield, Connecticut (1971); "New York Realism," Espace Cardin, Paris, France (1973); "Documenta 6," Kassel, Germany (1977); "New Vistas: Contemporary American Landscapes," Hudson River Museum, Yonkers, New York (1984); and many others.

Working for a decade as an instructor of painting and drawing at the School of Visual Arts, New York City (1971–1981), Mangold was the recipient of a grant from the National Endowment for the Arts (NEA) (1974–1975); and a special purchase award in the Davidson National Print and Drawing Competition (1976). Her drawings, prints, watercolors, and oils are faithful, yet illusory re-presentations. There is an ever-deepening quality of lyrical realism in Mangold's work. It burgeons from the representational interiors of the 1960s to the masking-taped illusions of landscapes seen from her studio window in Washingtonville, New York. Since 1983 Mangold has been painting her landscapes out-of-doors in the fields that surround her house. Her work is in permanent private, corporate, and major museum collections, including the Whitney Museum of American Art, New York City; Yale University, New Haven, Connecticut; Baltimore Museum of Art,

Maryland; American Federation of Art, Washington, D.C.; McCrory Corporation, New York; and others.

Bibliography
Cathcart, Linda L. *Sylvia Plimack Mangold: Nocturnal Paintings*. Exhibition Catalog. Houston Contemporary Arts Museum, 1981.
Field, Richard, and Ruth Fine. *A Graphic Muse*. Hudson Hills Press, 1987.
Garver, Thomas H. *Sylvia Plimack Mangold: Paintings: 1965–1982*. Madison Art Center, 1982.
Mangold, Sylvia Plimack. *Inches and Fields*. Lapp Princess Press, 1978.
Who's Who in American Art. 19th ed. R.R. Bowker Co., 1991–1992.

Mann, Sally (1951–)

Born in Lexington, Virginia, the photographer Sally Mann earned a Bachelor's degree *summa cum laude* from Hollins College, Roanoke, Virginia (1974); and, the following year, received a Master of Arts degree in writing. Earlier on, she had attended Bennington College, Vermont, and Friends World College (1966–1972); studied photography at Praestigaard Film School (1971); Aegean School of Fine Arts (1972); Apeiron (1973); and the Ansel Adams Yosemite Workshop (1973).

Mann has held many solo exhibitions in galleries throughout the United States, including the Southeastern Center of Contemporary Art, Winston-Salem, North Carolina (1988); Museum of Photographic Art, San Diego, California (1989); Edwynn Houk Gallery, Chicago, Illinois (1990); Maryland Art Place, Baltimore (1991); Houk Friedman, New York City (1992); and others. Her photographs have been invited to myriad group exhibitions in the United States and abroad (some of them travelling up to three years), including the Metropolitan Museum of Art, Whitney Museum of American Art, and the Museum of Modern Art (MoMA) (1991)—all in New York City; New Orleans Museum of Art, Louisiana (1990); Aperture Foundation, Inc., New York City (1987–1989, 1991); Virginia Museum of Fine Arts, Richmond (1988); La Grande Halle, la Villette, Paris, France (1990); Friends of Photography, Carmel, California (1982); and many others.

A winner of honors and awards for her work, and a widely-noted workshop leader and lecturer, Mann has been the recipient of grants and fellowships from the National Endowment for the Arts (NEA) (1973, 1976, 1982, 1988); including a visual arts fellowship (1989); and others. Her work is represented in private, public, and corporate permanent collections, including the Metropolitan Museum of Art and Museum of Modern Art (MoMA)—both in New York City; Fogg Art Museum, Harvard University, and Polaroid Corporation—both in Cambridge, Massachusetts; Center for Creative Photography, Tucson, Arizona; Corcoran Gallery of Art, and Hirshhorn Museum and Sculpture Garden—both in Washington, D.C.; Hallmark Cards, Kansas City, Missouri; and many more.

Bibliography
Immediate Family. A Monograph. Aperture Foundation, Inc., 1991.
Second Sight: The Photographs of Sally Mann. David Godine, Publishers, 1982.
Hagen, Charles. "Childhood Without Sweetness." *The New York Times* (June 5, 1992).
Woodward, Richard B. "The Disturbing Photography of Sally Mann." *The New York Times* (September 27, 1992): 29–34, 36, 52.

Manning, Jo (1923–)

Born in Sidney, British Columbia, Canada, Jo Manning is well-known for her incisive etchings and drawings. Manning was an honors graduate in drawing and painting at the Ontario College of Art, Toronto (1945); returned there as a special student in printmaking (1960); and studied process camera techniques and color separation at George Brown College, Toronto, Ontario (1971).

Manning has held solo exhibitions of her graphic work throughout Canada in galleries and universities, including Pollack Gallery (1965, 1968), Gallery Pascal (1974, 1977, 1980), and Gadatsy Gallery (1984)—all in Toronto; Mira Godard Gallery, Montréal, Québec (1976); Earlscourt Gallery, Hamilton, Ontario (1979); Bishop's University, Lennoxville, Québec; and others. Her prints have been invited to myriad group shows throughout Canada and the world, such as "Contemporary Canadian Drawings and Prints," a travelling show in Australia, National Gallery, Ottawa, Canada (1967); "4th American Print Biennale," Santiago, Chile (1970); International Print Biennale, Bradford, England (1970, 1972); Print Biennale, Ljubljana, Yugoslavia (1971, 1973, 1975, 1977, 1979); "Graphics Exhibition," Venice Biennale, Italy (1972); "4th Print Biennale," Gamlebyen, Norway (1978, 1980); "5th Biennale de Artes Plásticas," Lisbon, Portugal (1985); and many others.

Manning freely shared her expertise through numerous lectures and demonstrations of the intaglio process at many Canadian institutions; she has taught (in a mobile printmaking workshop) for the Ontario Department of Education's community programs (1965–1970). Over the next two decades, she either taught, offered workshops, or lectured at Centennial College (1967–1971); Sheridan College (1971–1974); summer sessions at Hockley Valley School of Art (1970–1974) and Elliot Lake (1970–1972); University of Toronto (1975); workshops at the Ojibway Cultural Center, West Bay, Manitoulin (1980); a lecture-demonstration at Beal Secondary School, London, Ontario (1990); and others.

Winner of many awards and honors for her work, Manning has won purchase prizes at the National Gallery of Art, Ottawa (1964); the London Spring Show, Ontario (1965); Graphex II and III, Brantford, Ontario (1974, 1975). She won a gold medal at the 2nd Print Biennale, Florence, Italy (1970); first prize at the 4th American Print Biennale, Santiago, Chile (1970); the medal of honor in Frechen, Germany, at the International Graphic Biennale (1980); and others.

Manning's work is represented in many private, public, and corporate permanent collections in Canada, including the National Gallery, Ottawa; Montréal Museum of Fine Arts; Art Gallery of Windsor; Canada Council Art Bank; London Library and Art Museum; Department of External Affairs, Ottawa; University of Waterloo; University of Guelph; University of Calgary; National Library of Canada; Toronto-Dominion Bank; Ciba-Geigy; and many others.

Bibliography
Heller, Jules. "Jo Manning." *Artscanada* (December–January 1981): 43.
Inglis, Grace. "Artist's Prints Strong Statement." *The Hamilton Spectator* (December 9, 1978): 26.
Tousley, Nancy. "Three Canadian Artists Offer Varied Visions of Nature." *The Calgary Herald* (November 19, 1981): D8.

Mansell, Alice (1945–)

Alice Mansell was born in the small community of Hanna, Alberta, where, apart from the principal university cities in the province, there were few opportunities for art education. Not surprisingly, then, Mansell gravitated toward the nearest large center offering sophisticated training. Her first calling was art education, and she took a Bachelor of Education degree from the University of Calgary in 1967, followed by teaching stints in secondary schools in Calgary, Burnaby, British Columbia, and Sudbury, Ontario. She then turned her attention to a Master of Arts degree from the University of British Columbia in 1970. Since then, outside of her painting, Mansell has directed most of her energies toward teaching and administration at the university level. All of this bears mentioning in one place because there is no clear break between her painting and her other professional activities.

Mansell is very committed to new critical perspectives and interdisciplinary activities in the humanities, especially feminism. As such, she sees her contribution to art not only in terms of her painting practice—which is a kind of painterly naturalism which she varies considerably, depending upon the intellectual content of any given work—but also in terms of activities normally considered scholarly. The result is a prodigious parallel series of exhibitions on the one hand (the first solo one taking place in Calgary in 1977), and on the other, a notable number of papers presented at learned conferences and the like.

Mansell was named assistant professor in the department of art at the University of Calgary in 1977, joining the faculty of graduate studies in 1981. She was named associate professor at the same institution in 1984 and in 1986 became assistant dean (administration and research) of the faculty of fine arts. At each stage of her career Mansell has become increasingly conscious of the need to increase the intellectual, rather than purely technical commitment of artists working jointly in a post-modernist society. Her most intense efforts in this regard have been since 1987, when she was named chair of the department of visual arts at the University of Western Ontario in London, Ontario—a city that has had an intensely active regional art scene for decades. Mansell's distinctive contribution has been to awaken a great interest in art and ideas of a pronouncedly theoretical and socially sensitive sort. One such is to question the inevitability of a male-dominated canon of masterpieces. Her painting, "Canadian Masterpiece: Maligne Lake" (1989), is partly a parody of a famous work by a member of the Group of Seven, Canadian art "hero" Lawren Harris.

Not only has Mansell continued to exhibit as a practicing artist—most recently at the Pentimento Gallery in Toronto (1989) and the London Regional Art Gallery (1989, 1990)—she has played important roles in ongoing research on gender bias in art education and in Western's recently developed interdisciplinary Graduate Centre for Theory and Criticism. To bring these varied activities together, Mansell is currently developing a unique proposal for an entirely new type of graduate art education concentrating on feminist and post-modernist aesthetics.

Robert J. Belton

Bibliography

Mansell, Alice. "Gender Bias in Art Education." In *Gender Bias and Research: The Pervasive Prejudice*. Ed. W. Tomm and G. Hamilton. University of Waterloo Press, 1988, pp. 99–117.

Manville, Elsie (1922–)

Born in Philadelphia, Pennsylvania, the painter Elsie Manville received her art education at the Tyler School of Fine Arts, Temple University, in her native city, where she earned Bachelor of Fine Arts and Bachelor of Science degrees (1943).

Manville has held many solo exhibitions of her work, including the Kraushaar Galleries, New York City (1958, 1966, 1969, 1975, 1978, 1982, 1985, 1988, 1991); "Art: Progress, Process and Materials," East Hampton Free Library, New York (1990); "Distinguished Alumni," Tyler School of Fine Arts, Temple University, Philadelphia, Pennsylvania (1988); "Thirty Year Retrospective," Newhouse Gallery, Snug Harbor Cultural Center, Staten Island, New York (1983); and others. Her work has been invited to distinguished group exhibitions throughout the United States—from East Hampton, New York, to Boise, Idaho; from St. Paul, Minnesota, to Columbia, South Carolina; from New York City to San Antonio, Texas.

Winner of many awards and honors for her work, Manville received a grant from the New York Federation for the Arts (1990); fellowship grants from the National Endowment for the Arts (NEA) (1981, 1985); purchase prizes at the Hassam purchase fund exhibitions (with the Institute of Arts and Letters); National Academy of Design, New York City (1978, 1989, 1981); many awards and purchase prizes from the Tyler School of Art annual exhibitions (1947, 1948, 1950, 1956, 1966, 1967) and a certificate of honor from her alma mater (1988); plus others. Her work is represented in private and public permanent collections in the United States, Canada, and Europe, including the Butler Institute of American Art, Youngstown, Ohio; Guild Hall, East Hampton, New York; Museum of Art, University of Iowa, Iowa City; Temple University, Philadelphia, Pennsylvania; 3M Corporation, Minnesota; and many others.

Bibliography

Brown, P.S. "Elsie Manville." *Arts Magazine* 52:8 (April 1978): 8.
Frank, Peter. "Elsie Manville." *Art News* 77:8 (October 1978): 175.
Martin, Richard. "Elsie Manville." *Arts Magazine* 56:6 (February 1982): 6.
Who's Who in American Art. 19th ed. R.R. Bowker Co., 1991–1992.

Marcus, Marcia (1928–)

A native New Yorker, Marcia Marcus is known for her representational paintings and prints. Marcus earned a Bachelor's degree from New York University (1947), attended the Cooper Union (1950–1952) and studied with Edwin Dickinson at the Art Students League (1954)—all in New York City.

Marcus has held solo exhibitions of her work throughout the United States, including the Benton Gallery, Southampton, New York (1986); Canton Art Institute, Ohio (1984); Terry Dintenfass Gallery, New York City (1979); Everson Museum, Syracuse, New York (1975); ACA Gallery, New York City (1974); Rhode Island School of Design, Providence (1966); and many others. Her work has been invited to major group exhibitions since 1951, when Roko Gallery, New York City, requested her entry. A cross-section of her group shows includes the "Annuals," Stable Gallery (1953, 1954); "Young American Artists," Whitney Museum of American Art (1960); and American Academy and Institute of Arts and Letters (1970, 1971)—all in New York City; "Contemporary Painting," McNay Art Institute, San Antonio, Texas (1976); "The Selective Eye," State University of

New York (SUNY) at Albany (1985); "Partitions and Personages," Benton Gallery, Southampton, New York (1992); and others.

Winner of several awards and honors for her work, Marcus was the recipient of a Fulbright grant to France (1962–1963); Ingram-Merrill awards (1963, 1977, 1982); a Ford Foundation grant; and a National Endowment for the Arts (NEA) grant (1991–1992). Visiting artist and a visiting member of the faculty at a number of major colleges and universities, she has curated and juried important exhibitions.

Marcus's work is represented in private, public and corporate permanent collections, such as the Whitney Museum of American Art, New York City; Phoenix Art Museum, Arizona; Everson Museum, Syracuse, New York; Rhode Island School of Design, Providence; Purdue University, Lafayette, Indiana; Philadelphia Museum of Art, Pennsylvania; and many others.

Bibliography
Ashton, Dore. "What About the Figure?" *Studio* (August 1962): 60.
Bourne, Juliet. "In Painting, Intensity Tells the Story." *Chatauqua Daily* (July 30, 1990): 3.
Frackman, Noel. "The Attic Mind of Marcia Marcus." *Arts* (September 1975).
Who's Who in American Art. 19th ed. R.R. Bowker Co., 1991–1992.

Margoulies, Berta (1907–)

Born in Lovitz, Poland, the sculptor Berta Margoulies earned a Bachelor's degree in anthropology from Hunter College (1927); studied at the Art Students League (1928)—both in New York City; and did further work in Paris, France, at the Académies Julian and Collarossi (1929).

Margoulies has been elected to membership in the American Academy and Institute of Arts and Letters, New York City (1944), and received a fellowship from the Gardner Foundation, Boston, Massachusetts (1929), and the Guggenheim Foundation (1946). She has held solo exhibitions at the ACA Gallery (1949); and Forum Gallery (1964)—both in New York City; Heritage Arts, Orange, New Jersey (1972); and others. Her work has been included in myriad group exhibitions throughout the United States since 1934 in venues such as the Pennsylvania Academy of Fine Arts, Philadelphia; the Whitney Museum of American Art and Metropolitan Museum of Art—both in New York City; Art Institute of Chicago, Illinois; Montclair Art Museum, New Jersey; and others.

Representative examples of her expressionist sculpture are located in private and public permanent collections, including the Des Moines Art Center, Iowa; Whitney Museum of American Art, New York City; Willamette University, Salem, Oregon; Wyandotte County Museum, Bonner Springs, Kansas; and others.

Bibliography
"Interview with Berta Margoulies." Washington, D.C.: Archives of American Art, June 9, 1978.
Roth, Cecil. *Jewish Art.* McGraw-Hill, 1961.
Watson-Jones, Virginia. *Contemporary American Women Sculptors.* Oryx Press, 1986.
Who's Who in American Art. 19th ed. R.R. Bowker Co., 1991–1992.

Marisol (Escobar) (1930–)

Born to Venezuelan parents in Paris, France, the sculptor Marisol (Escobar) first studied art at the École des Beaux-Arts in Paris. After her move to California as a teenager she studied at the Jepson School with Howard Warshaw and Rico Lebrun. Moving to New York City in the early 1950s Marisol completed her formal education at the Art Students League with Yasuo Kuniyoshi and then with Hans Hofmann. All of her formal training was in two-dimensional art, and she is basically a self-trained sculptor. When she first seriously began to show work in the mid-1950s, Marisol dropped her last name as a simple way to gain publicity and make her stand out from the crowd.

Marisol's first sculptures, done during the 1950s, were a series of erotic terra cottas which relied on American folk art and primitive art sources for inspiration. By the late 1950s she was making constructions out of lumber with found objects attached. These sculptures are assembled as figurative *tableaux* with carved or molded pieces creating the details of face and hands—often cast from her own features. During this period, Marisol exhibited with a group at the Tanager Gallery or with other cooperatives, then, in 1957, she had a solo show at the Leo Castelli Gallery, New York City.

Marisol became part of the New York pop art scene with assemblages such as "The Party" (1966), "The Wedding" (1963), and "The Family" (1963, 1969). In "The Family" (1969), she used neon, wood, plastic, and glass to create a contemporary, slick version of the Holy Family. In other works she used 1960s American personalities such as Lyndon B. Johnson and John Wayne in the iconic manner common to pop art. Marisol lived in the glamour and publicity that surrounded this group of artists throughout the 1960s—even starring in the film *The Kiss,* made by Andy Warhol. In "The Party" (1966) Marisol parodies this world by showing the superficial side of glamour as one of the figures which speaks inane small-talk through a television set used as a head. Other exquisitely-dressed and coiffed women—all with Marisol's face—stand waiting to be served by a three-headed butler.

Breaking with the artificial life of New York society, Marisol travelled in the Far East during the late 1960s. She became interested in scuba diving and did a series of works which show her own face joined to sea creatures—sharks and dolphins—or men with fish heads. These works seek to show man and beast living in harmony in a more peaceful world than the superficial party scene she had portrayed earlier. In the 1980s, however, she returned to the acerbic quality of her earlier *tableaux* with portraits of "Georgia O'Keeffe," "Pablo Picasso," and "Marcel Duchamp." Again, parodying her life questions the icons of modern American art.

Both Moore College of Art in Philadelphia, Pennsylvania, and the Rhode Island School of Design, Providence, have given Marisol honorary Doctorate of Arts degrees; she is also a member of the American Institute and Academy of Arts and Letters in New York City. She has contributed to several books about sculpture and the pop art period. These include: *The Art of Assemblage* (Doubleday); *Pop Art* (Praeger); *The New American Arts* (Collier); and *Stamps Indelibly* (Multiples, Inc.).

Marisol has exhibited on an ongoing basis with the Sidney Janis Gallery, New York City, since 1966. She has also exhibited at the Contemporary Arts Museum of Houston, Texas; the Bronx Museum, Brooklyn Museum, New York Sculpture Center, and the Whitney Museum of American Art—all in New York City; the Hirshhorn Museum and Sculpture Garden and National Portrait Gallery—both in Washington, D.C., and Philadelphia Art Museum, Pennsylvania. Her sculptures are in the permanent collections of the Museum of Modern Art (MoMA) and

Whitney Museum of American Art—both in New York City; Albright-Knox Art Gallery, Buffalo, New York; Museo Bellas Artes, Caracas, Venezuela; National Portrait Gallery, Washington, D.C.; and the Hakone Open-Air Museum, Japan.

Judith Sealy

Bibliography

Campbell, Lawrence. "Marisol's Magic Mixtures." *Art News* 63 (March 1964): 38–41.

Fine, Elsa Honig. *Women & Art: A History of Women Painters and Sculptors from the Renaissance to the 20th Century.* Alanheld & Schram, 1978, p. 254.

Rubinstein, Charlotte Streifer. *American Women Artists.* G.K. Hall, 1982, pp. 347–50.

Marisol: [New Sculptures by Marisol at Sidney Janis]. New York: Sidney Janis Gallery, 1973.

Mark, Mary Ellen (1940–)

Born in Philadelphia, Pennsylvania, the internationally-known photographer Mary Ellen Mark earned a Bachelor of Fine Arts degree in painting and art history (1962), and, two years later, was awarded a Master of Arts degree in photojournalism—both from the University of Pennsylvania, Philadelphia.

Mark has held more than thirty solo exhibitions of her work between 1976 and 1993 in the United States and abroad, including "Bars," Photographers Gallery, London, England (1976); "Ward 81," Gallery Forum, Stradpack, Graz, Austria (1976–1977); Photography Gallery, Yarra, Australia (1978–1979); "Falkland Road," Castelli Gallery, New York City (1981); "Mother Teresa and Calcutta," Arizona State University, Tempe (1986); "Mary Ellen Mark: Twenty-Five Years," International Center for Photography, New York City (1991); "Indian Circus," Robert Koch Gallery, San Francisco, California (1992)—a travelling show to galleries in Los Angeles, Boston, Chicago, Houston, and New Orleans; and others. Her work has been invited to myriad group exhibitions throughout the world—from Cologne, Germany, to Teheran, Iran; Paris, France; Denver, Colorado; New York City; Great Barrington, Washington; and many others.

Winner of numerous awards and honors for her work, Mark has given workshops and lectured widely in the United States and abroad; she has published more than three score articles on the less fortunate among us; and her photographs have appeared in several dozen books, major magazines, and journals, including *American Photographer, Connoisseur, Il Fotografo, Leica Magazine, Life, Paris-Match, Rolling Stone, World Press Photography, Zero,* and many others.

Bibliography

"The Indian Circus Comes to Town." *The Los Angeles Times* (December 22, 1991).

Goldberg, Vicki. "The Unflinching Eye." *The New York Times Magazine* (July 12 1987), 12–18, 20, 57–58, 61.

Hagen, Charles. "25 Years of Being There (with Camera)." *The New York Times* (September 6, 1991), 210K.

Mary Ellen Mark: Twenty-Five Years. Bullfinch Press, in conjunction with George Eastman House/Kodak, 1991.

Markham, Kyra (1891–1967)

Born in Chicago, Illinois, the painter/printmaker/actress Kyra Markham (born Elaine Hyman) quit high school (c. 1907) and attended the School of the Art Institute in her native city. She then quit art school (1909) to begin a career as an actress with Chicago's Little Theater. After a significant relationship of some years with the novelist Theodore Dreiser, Markham, in 1916, performed with the Provincetown Players, Massachusetts, augmenting her earnings as an illustrator and mural painter. Markham returned to the study of art in New York City at the Art Students League in 1930 and, four years later, studied printmaking in general and lithography in particular. As with so many other artists of the period Markham became part of the New York City Federal Arts Project (WPA/FAP) in the mid-1930s.

"Fourth of July" (1936), a not atypical lithograph of a host of people watching the fireworks on Independence Day, reveals Markham's mastery of the lithographic crayon on stone, the broad range of "color" from white to black, and her keen sense of composition. Her work is represented in private and public permanent collections.

Bibliography

Beall, Karen F., and David W. Kiehl. *Graphic Excursions: American Prints in Black and White, 1900–1950: Selections from the Collection of Reba and Dave Williams.* David R. Godine and the American Federation of Arts, 1991.

Marks, Roberta B. (1936–)

Born in Savannah, Georgia, Roberta B. Marks is known for her constructions, paintings, and ceramics. Marks earned a Bachelor of Fine Arts degree from the University of Miami, Florida (1980), and, the following year, received a Master of Fine Arts degree from the University of South Florida, Tampa.

Marks has held solo exhibitions in many galleries in the United States and abroad, including "Recent Constructions," Helander Gallery, Palm Beach, Florida (1992); "Recent Constructions and Painting," Le Mieux Gallery, New Orleans, Louisiana (1991); "Backerie Paintings," Galerie Alte Krone, Biel (1990), and Galerie Scapa, Berne—both in Switzerland (1988); Lucky Street Gallery, Key West, Florida (1987, 1992); Garth Clark Gallery (1985); and Elements Gallery—both in New York City (1978, 1981); Galerie du Manoir, La Chaux-de-Fonds, Switzerland (1978); Franklin Art Center, Ocala, Florida (1973); and many others. Her work has been invited to myriad group exhibitions and travelling shows: from San Francisco, California, to London, England; Aspen, Colorado; Tuscaloosa, Alabama; New York City; Ames, Iowa; Bal Harbour, Florida; and Santa Cruz, California.

Marks has lectured widely in the United States and abroad, has curated exhibitions, and has won many honors and awards from distinguished art jurors. Her work is represented in private, public, and corporate permanent collections, including the Québec Government Office of Atlanta, Georgia; University of South Florida, Tampa, and IBM, Jacksonville—both in Florida; Victoria & Albert Museum, London, England; University of Utah, Salt Lake City; University of Notre Dame, Indiana; Rochester Institute of Technology, New York; Renwick Gallery, Smithsonian Institution, Washington, D.C.; and many others.

Bibliography
Clark, Garth, and Oliver Watson. *American Potters Today*. Victoria & Albert Museum, 1986.
———. *American Ceramics: 1876 to the Present*. Abbeville Press, 1987.
Who's Who in American Art. 19th ed. R.R. Bowker Co., 1991–1992.

Mars, Ethel (1876–c. 1956)

Born in Springfield, Illinois, the painter/printmaker Ethel Mars studied at the Cincinnati Art Academy, Ohio (1892–1897), where she met and thereafter lived with artist Maud Squire. Together they took trips to Europe beginning in 1900 and, six years later, made their home in Paris, France.

A member of the Société des Beaux-Arts and an elected member of the Salon d'Automne—both in Paris—Mars showed regularly at the latter venue (1907–1913) and even juried several exhibitions there. She was a source of color woodcut techniques, one who generously shared her technical skill with visiting American women artists. At the beginning of World War I, Mars was an ambulance driver, but she and Squire soon returned to the safety of the United States and lived in Provincetown, Massachusetts, where she created and exhibited her work. Her relief prints soon acquired the "Provincetown look"—a white outline encompassed each form in the composition on the block.

Mars returned to France with Squire in the late 1920s where the two artists illustrated children's books. Examples of her work are represented in private and public permanent collections, including the National Museum of American Art, Smithsonian Institution, Washington, D.C.

Bibliography
Dunford, Penny. *Biographical Dictionary of Women Artists in Europe and America since 1850*. University of Pennsylvania Press, 1989.
Flint, Janet. *Provincetown Printers: A Woodcut Tradition*. National Museum of American Art, 1983.
Marks, Matthew. "Provincetown Prints." *The Print Collector's Newsletter 15* (September–October 1984): 132–33.

Marshall, Vicky (1952–)

Vicky Marshall was born in Sheffield, England, and spent her early childhood there. She moved to Canada in 1966 and attended the Emily Carr College of Art in Vancouver in the late 1970s. In 1985 she was one of eight painters of a more-or-less neo-expressionist orientation in an exhibition entitled "Young Romantics" at the Vancouver Art Gallery.

Marshall's paintings have included traditional still-life subjects with heavily-textured surfaces and apparently spontaneous brushwork. *Scavengers and Sunflowers* (1988), commissioned by the Cineplex Odeon Corporation for its Station Square Five Cinemas, in Burnaby, British Columbia, is an ironic social comment: it features vibrant sunflowers springing from a garbage dump otherwise filled only with old stoves, rubber tires, and the like.

Robert J. Belton

Bibliography
Burnett, David. *Cineplex Odeon: The First Ten Years*. 1989.

Marshall-Nadel, Nathalie (1932–)

Born in Pittsburgh, Pennsylvania, the painter/poet/educator Nathalie Marshall-Nadel (Nathalie Van Buren from 1952–1975) completed her formal education at the University of Miami, Florida, where she earned a Bachelor of Fine Arts degree *magna cum laude* (1977), and Master of Arts and Doctorate degrees (1982). Previously she studied at the Silvermine College of Art, New Canaan, Connecticut, with George Chaplin, Robert Gray, Richard Lytle, Nicholas Marsicano, and Charles Seide, where she received an Associate of Fine Arts degree with honors.

Marshall-Nadel has held more than sixty solo, juried, and invitational group exhibitions in the United States and abroad, including a recent solo show, "Earth Mandala"—a sixty-by-twenty-four-foot sacred circle celebrating cycles and seasons—installed at the Pyramid Lake Paiute Reservation, Nixon, Nevada (1987–1988). Her primary focus is oil painting; she executed "Star Cycle" (1985), a six-panel work on the life cycle of stars, which was commissioned by the Einstein Library, Nova University, Fort Lauderdale, Florida. She also has created codices, experimental books, poetry chapbooks, and "book poems."

Art juror, teacher of art, editor, illustrator, poet, lecturer, designer, and winner of many awards and honors—Marshall-Nadel has been an active participant in the life of many civic, social, political, and aesthetic organizations. Since 1987, for example, she has served as art consultant to Nah-Yah-Ee, a Native American Children's Art Exhibition seen throughout the world. In attempting to define her works to others, she recently wrote, ". . . the viewer is invited to participate with the artist/writer by exploring visionary realms which intertwine these challenges (inner consciousness and outer universes) and present them together in beauty and harmony."

Bibliography
"Nathalie Van Buren." *Arts Magazine* (November 1969).
Crawford, Mark. "Creativity Unbounded in Multi-Media Reno Artist." *Reno-Gazette Journal* (November 2, 1986): 5E, 10E.
Hurlburt, Roger. "'Star Cycle' Paintings Trace Nebula from Birth to Rebirth." *News/Sun-Sentinel* (May 26, 1985).
Who's Who in American Art. 19th ed. R.R. Bowker Co., 1991–1992.

Martin, Agnes (1912–)

Agnes Martin is an abstract painter whose work is characterized by delicate, repeated patterns of lines and grids. Her style has been associated with the minimal art movement of the 1960s and such related tendencies as systemic painting. Although her work may have influenced such movements, Martin's intentions are too personal and her career too independent to be understood in relation to any group style. During a ten-year period of direct involvement in the New York art scene (1957–1967), Martin developed and refined her mature style and built a considerable reputation. She then left New York City, settled in New Mexico, and stopped painting for six years (1967–1973). Her resumption of artistic activity was heralded by retrospective exhibitions in Philadelphia, Pennsylvania (1973); Munich, Germany (1973); and London, England (1977). Since then Martin has continued to live and work in New Mexico. Throughout her career she has exhibited regularly in New York and other cities, and her reputation has remained impressively consistent.

Martin was born in Saskatchewan, Canada. Her father, a farmer, died when she was young, and her mother moved the family to Vancouver, where Martin attended primary and secondary schools. In 1932 she moved to the United States, studied at Western Washington

State College for three years, and became a U.S. citizen in 1940. Between 1941 and 1954 she attended Columbia University in New York City periodically, where she eventually earned a Master of Arts degree. During these years she also studied at colleges in Oregon and New Mexico, and she taught at public schools in various locations. In 1954 she returned to New Mexico to teach at the State University in Albuquerque, and, two years later, she moved to Taos, where she joined the Ruins Gallery group. In 1957, with the assistance of the gallery owner, Betty Parsons, Martin moved back to New York City. She lived in Coenties Slip, a warehouse district in lower Manhattan, where her neighbors included Ellsworth Kelly, Jack Youngerman, and Robert Indiana. Her association with these artists, who were all involved in reacting against the predominant abstract expressionist styles of the time, may have encouraged Martin to move toward the more rigid, impersonal style which soon came to characterize her work. She had her first individual exhibition at the Betty Parsons Gallery in 1958, and, by the time she switched to the Robert Elkon Gallery in 1961, the essential features of her style had emerged. Her frequent one-woman shows over the next several years made a distinctive impression on the volatile art world of the time.

Martin's earlier work had developed from a biomorphic figuration in the early 1950s into an increasingly systematic and symmetrical abstraction after her return to New York in 1957. By about 1960 she had settled on a consistently square format (usually six-feet-square for paintings and nine-inches-square for drawings), upon which she developed grid patterns of horizontal and vertical lines. Within this austere personal vocabulary Martin's works of the 1960s evolved from richly-textured oils with stitch-like patterns to smoother acrylics with sharper grids. The persistent quality throughout these works is the tension between the rigorously systematic grids and the subtle irregularities of pattern and facture. Especially characteristic is Martin's use of pencil on thinly painted canvas, in which the sharpness of the lines is broken by the weave of the surface. When viewed from up close these pencil grids can bristle with irregularity; when seen from a distance they often dissolve into delicate veils.

Martin's departure from New York in 1967 was abrupt and decisive. The death of Ad Reinhart and the demolition of the building in which her loft was located may have been contributing factors, but her overriding motivation for leaving was probably a general exhaustion with the pressures of the New York art world. She settled on a remote piece of land near Cuba, New Mexico, and did not paint for six years. During this period her creative energies were directed toward building activities on her property and writing. Several of her poetic notebook reflections, begun during these years, have been published in subsequent exhibition catalogs and art journals. These writings are deeply personal but often highly revealing of Martin's attitudes and intentions as an artist. She stresses the importance of humility and inspiration and the need for detachment from both the natural world and the concerns of everyday life. She describes the artistic sensibility as seeking to awaken an awareness of a perfection underlying life, which can only be glimpsed in moments of inspiration and hinted at in the finest works of art. This highly spiritual outlook reflects on both Chinese philosophy and Western classicism, but is ultimately her own personal perspective on her art and life.

Martin returned to pictorial activity with a suite of prints in 1973,

and she resumed painting the following year. Since then she has worked consistently and exhibited frequently. She has maintained and further refined the reductive format established in the 1960s, with ever softer colors and spare, horizontal lines or stripes often replacing the grids. As with the earlier works, her titles occasionally allude to nature, but her relation to nature is more than ever one of detachment, contemplation, and memory. Her works strive to represent a perfection of mind and spirit glimpsed through the delicately inscribed veil of an individual sensibility.

Dennis Costanzo

Bibliography

Agnes Martin. Philadelphia: Institute of Contemporary Art, University of Pennsylvania, 1973.

Agnes Martin. Munich: Kunstraum, 1973.

Agnes Martin: Paintings and Drawings 1957–1975. London: Hayward Gallery/Arts Council of Great Britain, 1977.

Alloway, Lawrence. "Agnes Martin." *Artforum* 11 (April 1973): 32–37.

Bordon, Lizzie. "Early Work." *Artforum* 11 (April 1973): 39–44.

Gruen, John. "Agnes Martin: 'Everything, everything is about feeling . . . feeling and recognition.'" *Art News* 75 (September 1976): 91–94.

Haskell, Barbara. *Agnes Martin.* New York: Whitney Museum, 1992.

Martin, Agnes. "Reflections." *Artforum* 11 (April 1973): 38.

McEvilley, Thomas. "Grey Geese Descending: The Art of Agnes Martin." *Artforum* 25 (Summer 1987): 94–99.

Martin, Jane (1943–)

During Jane Martin's childhood in Montréal, Canada, few women artists were available to act as role models for this talented and interested young woman. Instead Martin's education took the normal route prescribed for young women—a solid arts degree from Bishops College, Lennoxville, and a Masters degree from Carleton University, Ottawa. Then she took "art" and was expelled.

Martin's work is so richly original, decorative, and personal, that for those who do not want to share another's experiences, it is too aggressive to like. In her earlier work, Martin created people in typical situations made bizarre by the distorted bodies, strange color combinations and references to wrapped hair, wrapped fabrics, and clotheslines holding up floating segments of the scene. The irony in Martin's "Orchid Couple" (1983)—a bride and groom tied and constricted with wrapped ribbons while the bride picks her nose—is a negation of the sexual promise of a young bride. The allusion to feminist concerns of containment and powerlessness are evident in the faces that she creates, yet are also the means by which the viewer finally comes to know the person inside each character that she portrays.

In 1985 an exhibition at the SAW Gallery began the portrayal of a lonelier world of aging body parts and the pain of medical interventions which continued after her move to Toronto in the 1987 exhibition, "Berkeley Castle Works, 1984–1987." In 1989, in the introduction to "Jane Martin Gathie's Cupboard Emblems Transfigurations 1986–1989" at Gallery 101, Susan Crean writes, "the body continues to serve as the site of decorative display."

Martin's work has also been included in the 1990 exhibition, "Canadian Women Artists in the Permanent Collection," National Gallery of Canada, Ottawa. Her frustration with the patriarchal dominance of the arts establishment is evident in everything she does—her work, her distrust of the Gallery system, and her continuous involvement in CAR (Canadian Artists' Representation). In 1988 Martin was on the founding board of the Reprography Collective. In 1989–1991 she was the CARFAC national representative and a member of the first CARFAC copyright collective board of directors.

Victoria Henry

Bibliography
Baele, Nancy. "Artist Uses Prettiness in Sinister Fashion." *The Citizen*, Ottawa (May 11, 1985).
Crean, Susan. "The Female Gaze, Women's Bodies, Women's Selves; Reclaiming an Artistic Identity." *Canadian Art* (Summer 1989).
———. "Body Language." *Jane Martin*. Ottawa: Gallery 101, 1989.

Martin, Louise (1914–)

Born in Brenham, Texas, the African-American photographer Louise Martin received recognition for her coverage of the funeral of Dr. Martin Luther King, Jr., in Atlanta, Georgia, for two Houston, Texas newspapers (*The Forward Times* and *The Informer*). From an early age Martin knew that she wanted to pursue a career in photography. Also, knowing that there were no schools open to her in the South, Martin left Texas for Chicago, Illinois, where she studied photography at the School of the Art Institute of Chicago and the American School of Photography. After receiving her degree in photography from Denver University, Colorado, in 1946, Martin returned to Houston, where she opened a portrait and commercial studio. In photographing the people and events around her Martin was successful.

Martin's first exhibition was in 1952 as part of the Southwestern Photographer's Convention—of which she was the only African-American member. She continued exhibiting throughout the Houston area, including a solo exhibition in 1984 at the Houston Public Library. Martin was involved with the Professional Photographers of America, the Texas Professional Photographers Association, the Southwestern Professional Photographers of Texas, and the Business and Professional Woman's Association.

By the early 1970s Martin had received twenty-seven awards in photography, and, in 1973, she founded the Louise Martin School of Photography, Houston, offering classes in all areas of black-and-white photography. The school closed in 1976 because of financial difficulties, but Martin resumed her free-lance career, photographing the people of Houston.

Melissa J. Guenther

Bibliography
Moutoussamy-Ashe, Jeanne. *Viewfinders: Black Women Photographers*. Dodd, Mead & Co., 1986.
Willis-Thomas, Deborah. *An Illustrated Bio-Bibliography of Black Photographers 1940–1988*. Garland, 1939.

Martín, Maria Luísa (1927–1982)

Born in Salamanca, Spain, Maria Luísa Martín (Mary Martin) emigrated to Mexico when she was twelve years old. She received her formal training in art at la Escuela de Pintura y Escultura (La Esmeralda) in Mexico City, Mexico.

Martín's first solo exhibition took place at the Galería de Cristalin, Mexico City, Mexico (1950), and one of her engravings, "Paz y amistad," was used as an announcement for the "V Festival Mundial de la Juventad," Warsaw, Poland (1955). She was one of Diego Rivera's assistants when he painted the murals for the city university and "El Teatro de los Insurgentes" (1949–1956).

Martín was a member of the world-famous Taller Grafica Popular in Mexico City (1954–1966), the printmaking workshop led by Leopoldo Méndez. She painted murals and other works in the Hotel Emporio and in the laboratories of CIBA. She illustrated a monumental edition of the works of Polish poet Adam Michiewicz, and taught drawing at the Colegio Madrid and the University of Mexico.

Martín's work was exhibited in a number of solo and group exhibitions. She showed regularly at the Salón de la Plástica Mexicana from 1960 onward; at the Polyforum Cultural Siqueiros, the Allianza Francesa and the Ateneo Cultural de Madrid (1976); at the Museo de Salamanca (1978), and at the Museum of Graphic Arts in Sofia, Bulgaria (to which she donated fifteen prints) in 1979. In 1981 Martín held three solo exhibitions: "Mary Martin in the SPM"; an engraving show at the Galería de Arte; and "Nudes" (1974–1981), a collection of oils, drawings, prints, and watercolors. Martín died in Mexico City in 1982; the following year, the Salón de la Plástica Mexicana organized a posthumous retrospective of her work, titled "Desnudo Feminino."

Bibliography
Alvarez, José Rogelio, et al. *Enciclopedia de México*. Secretaría de Educación Pública, 1987.

Martinez, Maria Poveka (c. 1886–1980)

The legendary potter Maria Poveka Martinez, along with her late husband, Julian, created the ware and the seemingly-magic process that transformed red clay pottery into black-on-black ceramic ware. Born in San Ildefonso Pueblo, New Mexico, Martinez grounded her children, grandchildren, and great-grandchildren in the art and life of clay.

Martinez demonstrated her remarkable approach to pot-making at every World's Fair until the advent of World War II. She was awarded two honorary Doctorate degrees for her work, and was honored by four presidents of the United States; Martinez was given the honor of laying the cornerstone at Rockefeller Center in New York City and her work, which received scores of awards and prizes, is in prestigious private, corporate, and public permanent collections throughout the world.

Bibliography
Clark, Garth. *A Century of Ceramics in the United States: 1878–1978*. E.P. Dutton, 1979.
"Maria Poveka Martinez, Potter, 94." *The New York Times* (July 22, 1980).
Peterson, Susan. *The Living Tradition of Maria Martinez*. Kodansha International and Harper & Row, 1977.
Trucco, Terry. "Pond Lily Has Them Lining Up." *Art News* 80:2 (February 1981): 26.

Martins, Maria (1900–1973)

Born in Minas Gerais, Brazil, the surrealist sculptor Maria Martins (Maria de Lourdes Alves Martins Peréira de Souza) studied painting in Paris, along with music, in the early 1930s; she travelled widely, including a trip to Japan; and studied sculpture in Brussels, Belgium, with Oscar Jesper (1939). In the early 1940s she lived and worked in New York City, where she knew Alexander Calder, Marcel Duchamp, Piet Mondrian, and Yves Tanguy.

In addition to exhibitions held abroad, Martins's solo shows in the United States include the Corcoran Gallery of Art, Washington, D.C. (1941); the Valentine Gallery, New York City (1942, 1943, 1944, 1946); and others. Her work was included in group exhibitions, such as the "Pittsburgh International," Carnegie Institute, Pennsylvania (1940); "Latin American Exhibition of Fine Arts," Riverside Museum, New York City (1940); Dayton Museum, Ohio (1944); "Origins of Modern Sculpture," City Art of St. Louis, Missouri (1946); "International Surrealist Exhibition," Paris, France (1947); and others.

Winner of awards and honors, Martins won prizes at the International Biennials, São Paulo, Brazil (1953, 1955). She established the São Paulo Biennial in 1951, and was cofounder of the Fundação do Museu de Arte Moderna do Rio de Janeiro, Brazil. Examples of her sculpture are in private and public permanent collections, including the Metropolitan Museum of Art, New York City; the Philadelphia Museum of Art, Pennsylvania; and others.

Bibliography

The Latin American Spirit: Art and Artists in the United States, 1920–1970. Harry N. Abrams, 1988.

Martins, Sylvia (1954–)

Born in Bage, Brazil, the painter Sylvia Martins studied at the Museu de Arte Moderna, Rio de Janeiro, Brazil (1973–1976); the School of Visual Arts (1978); and the Art Students League (1979–1982)—both in New York City.

Martins has held solo exhibitions in galleries in the United States and abroad, including the Contemporary Museum of Modern Art, Fukuoka, Japan (1992); Galería Claudio Bernardes, Rio de Janeiro, Brazil (1991); "Tantra Paintings," Charles Cowles Gallery (1991); Trabia Gallery (1990); and 56 Bleeker Gallery (1989)—all in New York City; GB Arte and Galería Ipanema, Rio de Janeiro, Brazil (1982, 1988); Fahey/Klein Gallery, Los Angeles, California (1989); and others. Her work has been invited to many group exhibitions in the United States and elsewhere—from Muttontown, New York, to Rio de Janeiro, Brazil; from Washington, D.C., to Amsterdam, the Netherlands; from Frankfurt, Germany, to New York City—and is represented in private, public, and corporate permanent collections, such as Citibank, New York City; the Asher Edelman Foundation, Switzerland; Chase Manhattan Bank, New York City; and many others.

Bibliography

Eco Art. A Catalog. Rio de Janeiro: Museu de Arte Moderna, 1992.
The Art of Femininity. A Catalog. Fukuoka, Japan: Museum of Modern Art Contemporary Gallery, 1992.
Nathan, Jean. "Gypsy." *The New York Observer* (September 24, 1990).
O'Rourke, Meg. "Sylvia Martins." *Arts Magazine* (Summer 1990): 80.
Pecorelli, Rosa. "Sylvia Martins." *Desfile Magazine* (July 1992).

Mason, Alice Trumbull (1904–1971)

Acting on the belief that abstraction liberated the artist to work with universal, purely visual elements, Alice Trumbull Mason not only set an example with her work but vigorously promoted the art she believed in.

Mason was born in Litchfield, Connecticut. Her cultured upbringing included long sojourns in Europe, where she received her earliest training. Later, in New York City, Charles Hawthorne and Arshile Gorky were important mentors. Marriage in 1930 and the subsequent birth of two children only briefly intervened in Mason's career, and, in 1936, she participated in founding the American Abstract Artists—an organization she actively supported into the 1960s.

In the 1930s Mason developed a sensitive, intellectually-controlled style of biomorphic abstraction, related to precedents in the work of Wassily Kandinsky and Joan Miró, as is evidenced in "Free White Spacing" (1939). Under the influence of Piet Mondrian in the early 1940s Mason developed a more geometric manner, as exemplified by "L'Hasard" (1948). In the mid-1940s she also took up printmaking, working with Stanley William Hayter at Atelier 17 in New York City. Throughout the 1950s and early 1960s she continued to work abstractly in both media, investigating the properties of color and texture as complements to form, and producing unsentimental, non-doctrinaire works of great refinement. Her tendency to simplify shapes in later years is visible in "Memorial" (1958–1959), painted in response to her son's death, and in the etching, "March Time" (1965).

Ann Lee Morgan

Bibliography

Brown, Marilyn R. "Three Generations of Artists." *Woman's Art Journal* (Spring–Summer 1983): 1–8.
Johnson, Una E. *Alice Trumbull Mason: Etchings and Woodcuts.* Taplinger, 1985.
Pincus-Whitten, Robert. *Alice Trumbull Mason Retrospective.* Whitney Museum of American Art, 1973.

Mason, Molly Ann (1953–)

A sculptor best known for her large-scale metal and environmental public works, Molly Mason received her Bachelor of Fine Arts degree (1973) and her Master of Fine Arts degree (1976) from the University of Iowa School of Art and Art History, Iowa City.

Mason began exhibiting her work in 1974 and had her first solo exhibition at the Minneapolis Institute of the Arts Museum, Minnesota, in 1977–1978. She has since presented her work in fourteen solo exhibits and in approximately eighty-five juried and group exhibitions in galleries and museums throughout the United States. Mason's sculptures are included in public and corporate collections in the United States, Europe, and Australia.

In the mid-1980s Mason was the only American sculptor invited to participate in two prestigious international sculpture symposia, where she created large public sculptures in wood and stone for the National Sculpture Parks of Yugoslavia and Hungary. In 1991 she was awarded a senior research Fulbright fellowship in sculpture in Japan to study the sculptural aspects of Japanese gardens and the work of contemporary Japanese sculptors. Mason has also taught at the State University of New York (SUNY) at Stony Brook; Tulane University, New Orleans, Louisiana; the University of New Mexico, Albuquerque; Southern Illinois University, Carbondale; the University of Minnesota, Morris; and as a visiting artist at the University of California, Davis. She was awarded a Lilly Foundation teaching fellowship at the SUNY at Stony Brook (1987–1988).

Mason has received many other prestigious awards, fellowships, and grants for her sculpture, including a Ford Foundation fellowship (1975–1976); a Minnesota State Arts Board fellowship (1977); a city of Albuquerque, New Mexico, one percent for arts grant for a fifty-foot-long-by-eight-foot-deep-by-eight-foot-high concrete and ceramic tile public sculpture for the city of Albuquerque, New Mexico (1983); a Millay Colony for the arts fellowship that resulted in a series of Mason's sculptures being created at the estate of Edna St. Vincent Millay in Austerlitz, New York (1982); an American Association of University Women individual research grant for creative work in 1984–1985; and a state of Louisiana individual artist fellowship in 1985–1986. Mason was one of seven artists-in-residence at the Louisiana World Exhibition in New Orleans in 1984. Her stainless-steel and copper sculpture, "Ikembana" (1988), was acquired by the city of Brisbane, Australia, from the "1988 World Expo International Large Scale Sculpture Exhibit" held in Brisbane; Mason was one of nine American sculptors to show work in that exhibition.

Mason's sensitivity to the materials she employs and her technical range in working with a wide range of materials such as stainless-steel, glass, wood, bronze, cast concrete, and ceramic tiles enables her to create elegant forms that are monumental in their impact and yet delicate and airy at the same time. Her juxtapositions of textures, colors, densities, and intentions create a powerful duality that is evident in her large-scale outdoor works—a series of private environments which mediate with the individual viewer and larger, more public spaces. Mason's large-scale structures are intimate but, at the time same, echo the surrounding environment, reaffirming the aesthetic placement and form of her pieces. Her sensitivity to space and form enhance the power of both her individual works and sculptural environments.

Rhonda Cooper

Bibliography
Bookhardt, D. Eric. "Molly Mason." *Art Papers, Journal of Art in the Southeast United States* 12:3 (May–June 1988): 58–59.
Green, Roger. "A Lifelong Fascination with Nature." *New Orleans Times-Picayune* (September 25, 1983): 3:2.
Harrison, Helen. "Sculpture as Outdoor Experiment." *New York Times* (September 20, 1987): E27.
Miller, Stephen Paul. "Molly Mason." *Cover Arts New York* 3:3 (March 1989): 14.
"Scale, Spirit and Energy: Forma Viva." *International Sculpture Magazine* (March–April 1987): 16–47.
Watson-Jones, Virginia. *Contemporary American Women Sculptors: An Illustrated Bio-Bibliographical Directory*. Oryx Press, 1985, pp. 390–91.
Who's Who in American Art. 19th ed. R.R. Bowker Co., 1991–1992.
The World Expo '88 Collection. Exhibition Catalog. Brisbane, Australia: World Expo 1988, International Exhibit of Outdoor Sculpture, pp. 59, 95.

Massaro, Karen Thuesen (1944–)

Born in Copenhagen, Denmark, the ceramist/sculptor Karen Thuesen Massaro earned a Bachelor's degree in art education at the State University of New York (SUNY) at Buffalo (1966); did graduate work at the University of Massachusetts, Amherst (1967–1968); and received a Master of Fine Arts degree from the University of Wisconsin, Madison (1972).

Massaro has held solo exhibitions in galleries throughout the United States, including "New Work," Winfield Gallery, Carmel, California (1992); the Canyon Art Gallery, Santa Cruz, California (1984); Rochester Art Center, Minnesota (1980); Michigan State University, East Lansing (1979); Sun Valley Center for the Arts and Humanities, Idaho (1978); Beloit College, Wisconsin (1975); University of Wisconsin, Stevens Point (1973); and others. Between 1967 and 1992 her work was invited to more than seventy group exhibitions throughout the United States—from Scottsdale, Arizona, to Louisville, Kentucky; La Jolla, California; New York City; Kalamazoo, Michigan; and Baton Rouge, Louisiana.

Massaro has won many awards and honors for her ceramic sculpture, including a National Endowment for the Arts (NEA) fellowship (1976–1977). She has been a visiting artist at distinguished colleges and universities, a workshop leader and lecturer, and a practicing studio artist since 1972. Her work is represented in private, public, and corporate permanent collections, including Beloit College, University of Wisconsin, Madison, and Kohler Company Collection—all in Wisconsin; Arizona State University, Tempe; University of Kansas, Lawrence; Michigan State University, East Lansing; National Gallery of Art, Washington, D.C.; Decorative Arts Museum, Little Rock, Arkansas; and others.

Bibliography
Lloyd, Herman. *Art That Works*. University of Washington Press, 1990.
Nigrosh, Leon. *Sculpting Clay*. Davis, 1992.
Who's Who in American Art. 19th ed. R.R. Bowker Co., 1991–1992.

Mather, Margrethe (c. 1885–1952)

Despite several posthumous exhibitions and essays that have attempted to redress her scant reputation, even today Margrethe Mather remains a relatively unexamined but important figure in American West Coast photography of the 1920s and 1930s.

Mather's early origins are somewhat obscure. She was born around 1885 in Salt Lake City, Utah. An orphan, she was adopted by a mathematics professor named Mather and his common-law wife. At an early age, possibly as young as twelve or thirteen, she became a prostitute and ran away to San Francisco, California. She then moved to Los Angeles, California, where she was kept for a time by an admirer. Later she again became a streetwalker, giving up this lifestyle when an elderly client died of a heart attack.

Around 1911–1912 she was apparently introduced to the avant-garde art world as it then existed in Los Angeles. She made contacts with Jean Heap and Margaret Anderson, who were launching *The Little Review*, as well as meeting with poets and anarchists, such as Emma Goldman, who Mather is said to have frequently quoted and who may have served to justify Mather's own unconventional lifestyle.

In 1912 or 1913 Mather met the photographer Edward Weston at the Los Angeles Camera Club. She became his business partner in a studio in what was to become Glendale, California. They worked together for nearly ten years, and she took over the studio when he went to Mexico in 1992. Together they became founding members of the Los Angeles Pictorialists in 1914.

Mather, who is perhaps best known for her portrait work, admired the portraits of Gertrude Käsebier—a member of the Photo-Secession. Mather believed that a portrait should present an attractive and characteristic appearance; in short, it should be a good likeness. Her composition, both in portraiture and in her other commercial work—including many interiors—was asymmetrical and often had large areas of negative space, which functioned actively in structuring the piece. These characteristics are possibly due to the influence of Japanese art, which she collected. In particular Mather's portraits are evocative and introspective, with the subject apparently unaware of the camera. They demonstrate great economy of means and the subject is shown with few, if any, accessories. Some of these portraits focus on heads, hands, or other body parts. They share a common concern for gesture which is revealed through a concentration on line and form as evocative of expression. All of her work evinces a kind of classical restraint that may be partially the product of the large format (eight-by-ten-inch) camera she used for her black-and-white work, which consisted of both silver and platinum prints.

Mather contact-printed her negatives and did not use a light meter, preferring instead to expose intuitively using the softly filtered daylight characteristic of her work. Weston's prints share these qualities as well, and contemporaries such as Imogene Cunningham suggest that Mather's images, many of which were made during the early 1920s, were a great influence on her partner at a time when he was developing a new aesthetic. Weston himself has described her as "the first important person in my life."

Beginning in the late 1920s Mather gradually did less portrait work and made a series of platinum prints of William Justema's erotic drawings, which were produced for sale to collectors. Justema was a designer who became her closest companion and occasional photographic collaborator from 1922 until the mid-1930s. In 1930, while Justema was working at the M.H. De Young Memorial Museum, San Francisco, California, he persuaded its director to exhibit Mather's work in a 1931 exhibited titled "Patterns in Photography." Justema collaborated with Mather in producing photographs of overall pattern forms using such objects as cigarettes, clam shells, and egg protectors to produce images such as "Japanese Combs," created by Justema and Mather in 1930. This exhibition was the last major one of her career, and, although she did not entirely give up photography, she made few images after this period, a notable exception being a portrait of the critic, "Sadakichi Hartmann," in 1935. At this time she also became an antique dealer in Glendale, California, where she died from multiple sclerosis in 1952.

Mather's death went virtually unnoticed by the art community, and it was not until 1979, when Mather's work was included in the "Photography Rediscovered" exhibit at the Whitney Museum of American Art, New York City, that notice was taken of her work. The same year the Center for Creative Photography in Tucson, Arizona, collaborated in an exhibit with the Witkin Gallery of New York City to display a collection of 132 of Mather's images which the Center had acquired. Thus her work still remains to be explored, as does her critical influence on twentieth-century photography.

Diana Emery Hulick

Bibliography
Center for Creative Photography. *Margrethe Mather: Questions of Influence.* University of Arizona, 1979.
Travis, Davis, and Anne Kennedy. *Photography Rediscovered.* New York: Whitney Museum of American Art, 1979.

Matheson, Elizabeth (1942–)

Born in Hillsborough, North Carolina, the photographer Elizabeth Matheson earned a Bachelor's degree from Sweet Briar College, Virginia (1964). She also studied at the Penland School, North Carolina (1972).

Matheson has held solo exhibitions in many venues, including Duke University, Durham, North Carolina (1974); Virginia Polytech Institute, Blacksburg (1979); "Welsh Dreams and Summer Pleasures," Duke University, and St. John's Museum, Wilmington, North Carolina (1986); Hollins College, Roanoke, Virginia (1987); Virginia Intermont College, Bristo (1988); and others. Her work has been invited to, or included in group exhibitions in the United States and abroad, such as the "North Carolina Artists Exhibition," Museum of Art, Raleigh (1973–1976, 1980, 1984, 1987); "North Carolina Photographers Show," Meredith College, Raleigh (1982–1984, 1986, 1988); "U.S.A. Volti del Sud," Palazzo Venezia, Rome, Italy (1984); "The Psychological Landscape," Green Hill Center for North Carolina Art, Greensboro (1988); and others.

"San Malo, Brittany" (1985), a black-and-white photograph, exudes an almost surrealist atmosphere, despite its title; it is truly an environment waiting for its players: serene, mysterious, aesthetically pleasing—of a particular place. Matheson's work has won honors and awards and is represented in private and public permanent collections.

Bibliography
Nine from North Carolina: An Exhibition of Women Artists. North Carolina State Committee and the National Museum of Women in the Arts, 1989.

Maxwell, Kathryn (1959–)

Born in Centralia, Illinois, Kathryn Maxwell received her Bachelor of Arts degree from Northwestern University, Evanston, Illinois, in 1979, and her Master of Fine Arts degree from the University of Wisconsin, Madison, in 1982. Primarily a printmaker, she inventively combines printmaking, painting, and papermaking to create the final works.

Maxwell has held six solo exhibitions of her work at such venues as Whittier College, California; Florida A&M University, Tallahassee; Wesleyan College, Macon, Georgia; Alabama A&M, Normal; the Company Gallery, Montgomery, Alabama; and Alabama State University, Montgomery. She has participated in international group exhibitions, including "Artists' Books—USA," sponsored by the American Cultural Center, New Delhi, India; and the International Art Competition at the 112 Green St. Gallery in New York City. She has also shown in almost fifty national, regional, and local group exhibitions, including "Paper Valley: A National Exhibition Celebrating Color and Patterns in Handmade Paper," Moyer Gallery, Green Bay, Wisconsin; "Paper/Fiber XII," the Arts Center, Iowa City, Iowa; and "Currents '86," Middle Tennessee State University, Murfreesboro. Her work has been reproduced in a number of these exhibition catalogs.

Maxwell's awards include a Basil H. Alkazzi travel award to London (1988); medal winner in the International Art Competition at the 112 Green St. Gallery, New York City; merit award, "Spotlight '86," University of Florida; and others. Her work is included in such collections as the University of Montevallo, Huntsville Museum of Art, Birmingham Museum of Art, Fine Arts Museum of the South, Montgomery Museum of Art—all in Alabama; Salt River Project's Information System Building in Phoenix, Arizona; and others. Since 1988 Maxwell has been a faculty member of the School of Art of Arizona State University in Tempe.

Leonard Lehrer

Bibliography
Martin, Robert. "The Paper Works of Kathryn Maxwell." *Fiberarts* 14:2 (March–April 1987): 8.
Mathews, Kate, ed. *Fiberarts Design Book 3*. Lark Books, 1987, p. 96.

May, Mabel (1884–1971)

Born in Montréal, Québec, Canada, the impressionist painter Mabel May was a student of William Brymner at the Art Association of Montréal (1910–1912). With her colleague, Emily Coonan, May engaged in research and travel in Europe, the year following her graduation, and was influenced by the works of Monet and Renoir. Slowly May's paintings evolved into landscapes that seem, at first glance, not unlike those of Lawren Harris. However, an example such as "Melting Snow" (c. 1925), after careful study, reveals May's personal touch.

May has won awards and honors during a long and successful career; she was the three-time recipient of the Jessie Dow prize at the annual spring exhibitions of the Art Association of Montréal (1913, 1915, 1917); she was elected an associate of the Royal Canadian Academy in 1915; and she was the supervisor of art classes at the National Gallery of Canada, Ottawa, between 1937 and 1947.

May held solo exhibitions at James Wilson and Co., Ottawa, Canada (1939); a retrospective at the Dominion Gallery, Montréal, Québec (1950); Roberts Gallery, Toronto, Canada (1951); Vancouver Art Gallery, British Columbia, Canada (1952); and others. Her work was invited to many group exhibitions in Canada and abroad, including the British Empire Exposition, Wembley, England (1924–1925); "Contemporary Canadian Artists," Corcoran Gallery of Art, Washington, D.C. (1930); "A Century of Canadian Art," Tate Gallery, London, England (1938); the Riverside Museum, New York City (1947); and many others. Her paintings are represented in private and public permanent collections, including the National Gallery of Canada, Ottawa.

Bibliography
From Women's Eyes: Women Painters in Canada. Kingston, Ontario: Queen's University, 1975.
McCullough, Nora. *The Beaver Hall Group*. National Gallery of Canada, 1966.
Ontario Free Press (London) (November 17, 1966).
The Montréal Star (February 11, 1950).

Mayer, Rosemary (1943–)

Through the combination of visual images and written text Rosemary Mayer explores patterns of change and continuity. Born in Ridgewood, New York, the artist became acutely aware of the "transience of everything, person and circumstance" at an early age, due to the death of her father in 1957 and her mother in 1959. It was to become a recurring theme in her art.

As a young child Mayer drew and painted under the tutelage of her father—a factory worker. In 1964 she received her Bachelor of Arts degree in the classics from the University of Iowa, Iowa City. Wanting to study art, Mayer turned down a Woodrow Wilson fellowship to Harvard University, Cambridge, Massachusetts, so that she could attend the Brooklyn Museum School, New York, from 1965 to 1967, and, later, the School of Visual Arts in Manhattan from 1967 until 1969. Mayer was a writer and reviewer for *Arts Magazine* from 1971 to 1973 and also wrote for *Art in America*, in 1974 and 1975. She has taught at the Art Institute of Chicago, Illinois, as a visiting artist in 1974, as well as at Hartwick College at Oneonta, New York, in 1976 and Baruch College, New York, in 1987.

Mayer's work first received attention through the women's movement of the early 1970s. Seeking to promote the position of women in societies past and present, she became a strong supporter and an original member of A.I.R. (Artists in Residence)—one of the first women's cooperative galleries. Her first solo exhibition in 1973 was at the A.I.R. Gallery, New York City, later going on to one-person shows at the Whitney Museum Art Resources Center in New York City in 1975; the State University of New York (SUNY) at Stony Brook in 1978; and the Art Gallery at Cornell University, Ithaca, New York, in 1980; among many others.

Early work by Mayer centers around diaphanous fabric which is draped from or wrapped around a structural system of supports that are held in varying degrees of tension. Each piece is named for a woman or group of women from the historical past. Next, drapery is replaced with wire mesh which the artist ties, rolls, paints, and again incorporates into a support system.

Mayer's later pieces have employed such varied materials as paper, snow, balloons, and, most recently, rag vellum, which when shaped and allowed to harden resembles vases, jars, and baskets reminiscent of antiquity and the sculptor's classical education. By choosing perishable mediums Mayer is able to focus on aspects of transformation so important in her art.

The cyclical nature of life and its issues is perhaps what prompted Mayer, in 1982, to write *Pontormo's Diary*, a translation of the diary written by the sixteenth-century Mannerist Jacopo Pontormo. Mayer's translation accompanies the original Italian along with comments on the text, as well as drawings by the twentieth-century artist in a style compatible with the movement that followed the High Renaissance in Italy.

Drawing from the historical past and using traditional along with nontraditional resources, Mayer is able to translate patterns of change and continuity into the twentieth-century concerns of historical enlightenment, equal rights, and the transitory nature of life.

Christine L. Wilson

Bibliography
Connor, Maureen. "The Pleasure of Necessity: The Work of Rosemary Mayer." *Woman's Art Journal* 6 (Fall–Winter 1985–86): 35–40.
Mayer, Rosemary. "Passages." Tracks 2 (Fall 1976): 23–36.
———. "Surroundings." *Art-Rite* 15 (April 1977): 1–24.
———. *Pontormo's Diary*. Out of London Press, 1979.

Mayes, Elaine (1938–)

Born in Berkeley, California, the photographer/filmmaker Elaine Mayes earned a Bachelor's degree from Stanford University, California (1959). She did further study at the San Francisco Art Institute, California, with John Collier, Paul Hassel, and Minor White.

Winner of honors and awards, Mayes won photographic grants from America the Beautiful Foundation, the Federal Bureau of Public Roads

(1966), and the University of Minnesota Graduate School, Minneapolis (1969); research funds from Hampshire College, Amherst, Massachusetts, for film projects (1971, 1975); a film grant from the Royal Film Archive, Belgium (1974); National Endowment for the Arts (NEA) fellowships (1971, 1978); and others.

Mayes has taught photography and filmmaking at the University of Minnesota, Minneapolis, and, presently, teaches the same courses at Hampshire College, Amherst, Massachusetts. Her work is represented in private and public permanent collections, including the Boston Museum of Fine Arts, Harvard University, Cambridge, and Smith College, Northampton—all in Massachusetts; Corcoran Gallery of Art, Washington, D.C.; Metropolitan Museum of Art and Museum of Modern Art (MoMA)—both in New York City; and many others.

Bibliography
Browne, Turner, and Elaine Partnow. *Macmillan Biographical Encyclopedia of Photographic Artists and Innovators.* Macmillan, 1983.
Trachtenberg, Alan, Peter Neill, and Peter Bunnel. *The City.* 1971.
Wagstaff, Sam. *A Book of Photographs.* 1978.

Mayor, Harriet Hyatt (1868–1960)

Born in Salem, Massachusetts, the painter/sculptor Harriet Hyatt Mayor studied in Boston, Massachusetts, under the aegis of Henry H. Kitson and Dennis Bunker.

Mayor's work was included in many exhibitions, including the "Exhibition of American Sculpture," National Sculpture Society, New York City (1923); "Contemporary American Sculpture," National Sculpture Society and the California Palace of the Legion of Honor, New York City (1929); and others.

Mayor was the winner of a silver medal at an exhibition in Atlanta, Georgia (1895), and a member of the American Federation of Arts, Washington, D.C., and the Boston Art Club, Massachusetts. Her sculpture and/or memorial tablets are in many private and public permanent collections throughout the United States, including Princeton University, New Jersey; Woods Hole and Gloucester—both in Massachusetts; Annapolis, Maryland; Mariner's Park, and Newport News—both in Virginia; Brookgreen Gardens, South Carolina; and others.

Bibliography
American Art Annual. Vol. 28. American Federation of Arts, 1932.
Clement, Clara Erskine. *Women in the Fine Arts.* Houghton Mifflin and Co., 1904.
Who's Who in American Art. 3rd ed. American Federation of Arts, 1940.

McAfee, Ila (1897–)

Born in Gunnison, Colorado, the painter Ila McAfee studied at Western State College of Colorado, Gunnison; the Art Students League and the National Academy of Design—both in New York City.

One of many artists employed by the Works Projects Administration (WPA) to paint murals, McAfee exhibited work in the Denver Art Museum in her native state (1936); and in other venues. Her murals were painted in U.S. post offices in Clifton, Texas; Cordel, Oklahoma; Edmond, Oklahoma; and Gunnison, Colorado. Further examples of her work are in private and public permanent collections, including Baylor University, Waco, Texas; the Denver Art Museum, Colorado; and others.

Bibliography
Nelson, Mary C. "Ila McAfee of the White Horse Studio." *American Artist* 45 (January 1981): 64–69.
———. *The Legendary Artists of Taos.* Watson-Guptill Publications, 1980.
Park, Marlene, and Gerald E. Markowitz. *Democratic Vistas: Post Offices and Public Art in the New Deal.* Temple University Press, 1984.

McCormick, Pam (1946–)

Born in Grand Rapids, Michigan, the sculptor Pam McCormick earned a Bachelor's degree and a Master of Arts degree from San José State University, California (1972), after study with Sam Richardson; four years later, she took post-graduate work in art history at Stanford University, California.

McCormick's singular work has been exhibited in solo and group shows throughout the United States and abroad, including "Experimental Arts Projects," Morris Museum, Morristown, New Jersey (1980); "Captured by Gypsy Moths," Central Park, New York City (1981); "New Sculpture: Icon & Environment," a travelling show, Guild Hall, East Hampton, New York (1984); "Video Contemporary New York," Athens, Greece (1985); "Four Sculptors," Public Art Trust, Washington, D.C. (1986); "Unconventional Constitutional Convention," Cooper Union, New York City (1986); and others. Representative examples of her environmental sculpture include "Drawing Water from a Rock," Central Park, New York City (1984); "World Win," a water sculpture, Harbor Festival, New York City (1985); "Sculpture in the Mall," Corcoran Gallery of Art and Washington Sculptor's Group—both in Washington, D.C. (1986); and others.

Bibliography
Lunde, Karl. "Art and the Environment." *Arts Magazine* (March 1985).
Richards, Paul. "Review." *The Washington Post* (September 18, 1986).

McCoy, Ann (1946–)

Known for her large-scale drawings aimed at the perceptual rather than the conceptual in nature, Ann McCoy is especially concerned with photographing and exploring that which lives underwater. McCoy was born in Boulder, Colorado, and attended the local university, where she studied the classics, philosophy, and theology, and earned her Bachelor of Fine Arts degree in 1969. Three years later, after graduate work in drawing and sculpture at the University of California at Los Angeles (UCLA), she received a Master of Arts degree.

Between 1970 and 1981 McCoy held nineteen solo exhibitions of her work in the United States and abroad, including the Esther Bear Gallery, Santa Barbara, California (1970); Institute of Contemporary Art, Boston, Massachusetts (1975); Margo Leavin Gallery, Los Angeles, California (1976, 1979); Wallraf-Richartz Museum, Cologne, Germany (1977); Chandler Coventry Gallery, Paddington, Australia (1978); Brooke Alexander, Inc., New York City (1978, 1979, 1981); and others.

McCoy's work was selected for many group exhibitions such as "15 Young Artists," Pasadena Art Museum, California (1972); "New American Landscapes," Vassar College, Poughkeepsie, New York (1973); "America 1976," Corcoran Gallery of Art, Washington, D.C., a travelling exhibition (1976); "Painting and Sculpture Today," Indianapolis

Museum of Art, Indiana, a travelling exhibition (1980); "Myths and Symbols," Bruno Facchetti Gallery, New York City (1986); and many others.

McCoy teaches at the School of Visual Arts (1977 to the present), Barnard College (1980 to the present), and Columbia University (1985 to the present)—all in New York City. Winner of many honors and awards, McCoy won the new talent award from the Los Angeles County Museum of Art, California (1972); the Norman Wait Harris award from the Art Institute of Chicago, Illinois (1974); the American Association of University Women award (1976); the highly-prized D.A.A.D. Kunstlerprogramm Berlin fellowship, Germany (1977); National Endowment for the Arts awards (NEA) (1978, 1989); and the Prix de Rome Award in the Visual Arts (1989). McCoy's works are in the permanent collections of galleries and museums in the United States and abroad, including the Museum of Modern Art (MoMA) and the Whitney Museum of American Art—both in New York City; Allen Memorial Art Museum, Oberlin, Ohio; the National Gallery of Australia, Canberra; the Art Institute of Chicago, Illinois; the Denver Art Museum, Colorado; Los Angeles County Museum of Art, California; and many others.

Bibliography
Bordeaux, Jean-Luc. "The Silent World of Ann McCoy." *Art International* 21:1 (January–February 1977): 30–31, 63.
Brenson, Michael. "They Seek Spiritual Meaning in an Age of Skepticism." *The New York Times* (May 11, 1986). Arts and Leisure Section: 37, 41.
Lorint, John. "Looking for Ann McCoy." *Arts Magazine* 53:4 (December 1978): 146.
Marks, Claude. *Contemporary Artists*. H.H. Wilson, 1985.

McCullough, Geraldine (1922–)

Born in Kingston, Arkansas, the African-American artist/teacher Geraldine McCullough earned a Bachelor's degree from the School of the Art Institute of Chicago, Illinois (1948); and received a Master of Art Education degree in sculpture from the same institution, after study with Egon Wiener (1955)—thus realizing a dream held since childhood: to become an artist.

McCullough has held solo exhibitions in museums and galleries, including Ontario East Gallery (1967) and Johnson Publishing Company (1973)—both in Chicago, Illinois; Studio Museum in Harlem, New York City (1976); Fermi Laboratory, Batavia, Illinois (1981); and others. Her work has been included in many group shows, such as that held by the Brooklyn Museum, New York (1969); "Afro-American Art: Sculpture," Herbert F. Johnson Museum of Art, Ithaca, New York (1975); "Twentieth Century Black American Artists," San José Museum of Art, California (1976); "Second Annual Atlanta Life National Art Competition and Exhibition, Georgia (1981); and others. Examples of her public sculpture are sited in many public and private permanent venues throughout the United States.

Bibliography
Bims, Hamilton. "A Sculptor Looks at Martin Luther King." *Ebony* 28:6 (April 1973).
Riedy, James L. *Chicago Sculpture*. University of Illinois Press, 1981.
Watson-Jones, Virginia. *Contemporary American Women Sculptors*. Oryx Press, 1986.

McCurdy, Maggie (1932–)

Born in Fairview, West Virginia, the sculptor Maggie McCurdy earned a Bachelor's degree from West Virginia University, Morgantown (1954); she also attended the Yale School of Art and Architecture, New Haven, Connecticut.

McCurdy has held solo exhibitions and has had her work in many group shows, including the Museum of Contemporary Crafts, New York City (1973); the Art Institute of Chicago, Illinois (1974); and others. "Guardian of Small Beasts" (1972), is typical of her work of this period: a wood assemblage with etching on fabric, weds religio-mysticism and a wry sense of humor in a mixed-media work of surprising unity. Examples of her work are represented in private and public permanent collections.

Bibliography
Hyland, Douglas, and Marilyn Stokstad. *Catalogue of the Sculpture Collection*. Helen Foresman Spencer Museum of Art, the University of Kansas, Lawrence, 1981.

McEnery, Kathleen (1885–1971)

The painter Kathleen McEnery was born in Brooklyn, New York, and spent one academic year (1897–1898) at a convent in Tildonc, Belgium, where a sister of her Irish-born father was a teaching nun. When she returned to New York, she first studied at the Pratt Institute and then became a student of Robert Henri's at the New York School of Art—both in New York City. She was a member of Henri's class in Madrid, Spain in the summers of 1906 and 1908. A surviving painting from this period is her copy of Velàzquez's "Portrait of the Infanta Dona Margarita." In addition to having his students learn by copying in the Prado Museum, Henri encouraged outdoor painting. McEnery next moved to Paris, and many paintings from these productive years are preserved by her heirs, such as "Girl with Umbrella" (c. 1912), "Luxembourg Gardens," and "Seated Woman in Striped Dress with Red Flower in Hat" (c. 1912). On return to America she took a studio in New York. Two of her paintings of female nudes were accepted in the New York Armory Show of 1913 ("Going to the Bath," National Museum of American Art, and "The Dream," 1912, private collection).

In 1915 McEnery showed her paintings at the Macdowell Club in New York City, where she had previously exhibited, and at the University of Rochester Art Gallery, New York. Another New York City exhibition was held at the Ferargil Gallery in the early 1930s. Family and community interests thereafter commanded her attention. Her style of painting at first had the realism and dark palette of Henri but then changed to the bright colors and strong forms of post-impressionism.

Eleanor Tufts

Bibliography
Kathleen McEnery Cunningham Memorial Exhibition. New York: Memorial Art Gallery of the University of Rochester, 1972.
Tufts, Eleanor. *American Women Artists, 1830–1930.* National Museum of Women in the Arts, 1987.

McIlvain, Isabel (1943–)

Born in West Chester, Pennsylvania, the artist Isabel McIlvain earned a Bachelor's degree from Smith College, Northampton, Massachusetts (1966); studied painting with Michael Aviano in New York City (1969–

1970); and received a Master of Fine Arts degree in sculpture from Pratt Institute, Brooklyn, New York (1972).

McIlvain has held solo exhibitions in museums and galleries, including Washington and Lee University, Lexington, Virginia (1975, 1979); Haverford College, Pennsylvania (1978); Roanoke College, Salem, Virginia (1980); Robert Schoelkopf Gallery, New York City (1982, 1985); University of Virginia, Charlottesville (1982); and others. Her figurative sculpture has been included in group shows, some of them travelling throughout the United States, since the mid-1970s.

Winner of awards and honors, McIlvain received a Glenn grant from Washington and Lee University, Lexington, Virginia (1980); and a fellowship from the Massachusetts Council for the Arts and Humanities (1983). Her work is represented in private, public, and corporate permanent collections, such as Sweet Briar College, Virginia; Washington and Lee University; *Forbes Magazine* Collection, New York City; Weatherspoon Art Gallery, Greensboro, North Carolina; and others.

Bibliography
"Model of Kennedy Statue Unveiled in Boston." *The New York Times* (April 8, 1988): 8Y.
Stolbach, Michael Hunt. "Artists' Choice." *Arts Magazine* 55:3 (November 1980): 23–24.
Watson-Jones, Virginia. *Contemporary American Women Sculptors.* Oryx Press, 1986.
Zimmer, William. "Isabel McIlvain." *Arts Magazine* 51:10 (June 1977): 37.

McLaughlin, Isabel (1903–)

Isabel McLaughlin was born in Oshawa, Ontario. She received her first formal art training while attending school in Paris, France, from 1921 to 1924. While in Paris, painter Louise Saint taught McLaughlin drawing and watercolor. Upon her return to Canada, she studied under Arthur Lismer and Yvonne McKague at the Ontario College of Art in Toronto until 1927, when she and several other students set up an Art Students' League, roughly modelled on the New York City school. From 1929 to 1930 she studied at the Scandinavian Academy in Paris. Later instruction included studies in Dynamic Symmetry with Emil Bisttram in New Mexico, and sessions at Hans Hofmann's summer school in Provincetown, Massachusetts.

A charter member of the Canadian Group of Painters in 1933, McLaughlin also served as its president in 1939, and was a regular contributor to Group exhibitions, including those circulated abroad. Outside the Group her work was shown internationally at such exhibitions as the "Southern Dominions Exhibition" (Africa, Australia, and New Zealand, 1936–1939); "Artists of the British Empire Overseas" (Royal Institute Galleries, London, 1937); "Contemporary Canadian Painting" (Brazil, 1944–1945); and "Canadian Women Artists (Riverside Museum, New York, 1947). McLaughlin also exhibited with the Ontario Society of Artists. Her first solo exhibition was held at the Art Gallery of Toronto in 1933, with subsequent one-woman shows held at the Picture Loan Society, Toronto (1937), and Hart House, University of Toronto (1948). A major retrospective of her work was circulated in Ontario by the Robert McLaughlin Gallery, Oshawa, in 1983.

McLaughlin's earliest paintings included landscapes and cityscapes influenced in both subject matter and treatment by her contact with members of the Group of Seven. During the early 1940s her style began to evolve into one which emphasized strong color and more decorative, less sculptural patterning and design. Many of her works from the later years abandon the vista landscapes of earlier paintings for more intimate, close-up views of nature. Examples of this later style include "September Flowers" (1952) and "Autumn Fantasy" (1960). McLaughlin's work is represented in the National Gallery of Canada, the Art Gallery of Ontario, and in numerous public and private collections across Canada.

Janine A. Butler

Bibliography
Findley, Timothy. "Comparing Notes." *Canadian Art* 2:2 (Summer 1985): 54–57.
Murray, Joan. *Isabel McLaughlin: Recollections.* Oshawa: Robert McLaughlin Gallery, 1983.

McLaughlin, Mary Louise (1847–1939)

Born in Cincinnati, Ohio, the noted ceramist Mary Louise McLaughlin studied life drawing with Frank Duveneck, and china painting at the Cincinnati School of Design, Ohio (1874–1877), after some years of private art study.

McLaughlin first exhibited in the Centennial Exposition, Philadelphia, Pennsylvania (1876), and, three years later, showed her Limoges faience pieces, produced at the Patrick L. Coultry Pottery, in Cincinnati, Ohio and at the Exposition Universelle in Paris, France, where she won an honorable mention. Founder and president of the Cincinnati Pottery Club, McLaughlin produced her well-known "Ali Baba Vase" there and showed it in the 1st Annual held by the club (1880). She exhibited china painting and decorative metalwork at the Exposition Universelle, Paris, France (1889), where she won a silver medal. McLaughlin won another silver medal at the same exhibition in 1900, and a bronze medal at the 1901 Buffalo Exposition, New York—both for her porcelains.

McLaughlin turned away from ceramics in 1914 and wrote and published a work on great military battles. For several decades McLaughlin set ceramic high-water marks in aesthetics and professional standards.

Bibliography
Clark, Garth. *American Ceramics 1896 to the Present.* Abbeville Press, 1987.
Levin, Elaine. "Mary Louise McLaughlin and the Cincinnati Art Pottery Movement." *American Craft* 42 (December 1982).
"Mary Louise McLaughlin: Originator of Plastic Slip Underglaze Painting . . ." *The Bulletin of the American Ceramic Society* 17 (May 1938).

McLeary, Bonnie (1890–)

Born in San Antonio, Texas, the sculptor Bonnie McLeary studied her craft in several venues, including the Académie Julian, Paris, France; the Art Students League, New York City; and also with James E. Fraser.

McLeary is a member of the National Association of Women Painters and Sculptors, Allied Artists of America, and the American Artists' Professional League—all in New York City. Her work is represented in private and public permanent collections and sites, including the Children's Museum within the Brooklyn Museum, New York; the Metropolitan Museum of Art, New York City; the Muños Rivera monument in Rio Piedras, Puerto Rico; the World War Memorial in San Juan, Puerto Rico; and others.

Bibliography
American Art Annual. Vol. 26. American Federation of Arts, 1929.
Gardner, Albert TenEyck. *American Sculpture: A Catalogue of the Collection of the Metropolitan Museum of Art*. New York Graphic Society, 1965.
O'Brien, Esse Forrester. *Art and Artists of Texas*. Tardy Publishing Co, 1935.

McMillen, Mildred (1884–c. 1940)

A product of the School of the Art Institute of Chicago, Illinois (1906–1913), the printmaker Mildred McMillen is known for her woodcuts of Provincetown, Massachusetts, and vicinity. McMillen also studied in Paris, France, at the Académie Colarossi and, earlier on, with Ethel Mars, an American printmaker then resident in Paris.

The eruption of World War I caused many American artists in Europe to return home and McMillen was no exception. She established herself in Provincetown and exhibited her relief prints in many shows with the Provincetown Art Association. "Provincetown Housetops" (1918), a not atypical black-and-white woodcut, reveals McMillen's mastery of the medium: precise lines and jabs with the burin; light against dark, dark against light; a minimum of strokes to obtain effect—a brilliant composition. Representative examples of her work are in private and public permanent collections.

Bibliography
Beall, Karen F., and David W. Kiehl. *Graphic Excursions: American Prints in Black and White, 1900–1950, Selections from the Collection of Reba and Dave Williams*. David R. Godine and the American Federation of Arts, 1991.

McNicoll, Helen (1879–1915)

Born in Toronto, Ontario, Canada, the plein air painter Helen McNicoll studied with the popular teacher William Brymner, in Montréal. Her impressionist oils, which were shown by her estate at the Morris Gallery, Toronto (1974), suggest paintings not unlike those by Berthe Morisot.

McNicoll was a member of several arts organizations, including the Ontario Society of Artists, the Royal Canadian Academy, the Royal British Artists, and others. Her work is represented in private and public permanent collections. "The Tent" (1913)—a study of a seated female figure reading inside a canvas shelter—is in reality an investigation of light in a strong, yet delicate, composition.

Bibliography
Fleisher, Pat. "Love or Art." *Art Magazine* 5:15 (Fall 1973): 19, 20.
Murray, Joan. *Helen McNicoll, 1879–1915: Oil Paintings from the Estate*. Toronto: Morris Gallery, 1974.

McVey, Leza (1907–1984)

Born in Cleveland, Ohio, the innovative ceramist/weaver Leza McVey studied at the Cleveland Institute of Art, Ohio (1927–1932); the Colorado Springs Fine Arts Center, Colorado (1943–1944); and Cranbrook Academy of Art, Bloomfield Hills, Michigan.

McVey worked as a ceramist in Houston, Austin, and San Anto-

nio, Texas, before moving to Cranbrook Academy of Art, where she taught a summer course for Maija Grotell and stayed to teach there (1948–1953). In 1953 she returned to her native city, where she set up her studio, Pepper Pike.

In addition to fulfilling a ceramic mural commission for the Flint Art Center, Michigan (1961), with her husband, the sculptor William McVey, she completed other commissions and exhibited her work in major shows throughout the United States and abroad, including the International Congress for Contemporary Ceramics, Ostend, Belgium (1960). Her last major solo exhibition took place at the Cleveland Institute of Art, Ohio (1965).

McVey's large, novel asymmetrical forms expressed her displeasure with wheel-thrown pieces and revealed a certain strength. Examples of her work are in private, corporate, and public permanent collections, such as the Butler Institute of American Art, Youngstown, Ohio; General Motors Corporation; Smithsonian Institution, Washington, D.C.; and others.

Bibliography
Clark, Garth. *American Ceramics, 1896 to the Present*. Abbeville, 1987.
Clark, Robert Judson, et al. *Design in America: The Cranbrook Vision, 1925–1950*. Harry N. Abrams, 1983.

Mears, Helen Farnsworth (1872–1916)

Born in Oshkosh, Wisconsin, the sculptor Helen Farnsworth Mears learned her craft in New York City and Paris, France, and took further study with Augustus Saint-Gaudens.

Mears exhibited her sculptures of famous persons and other works in major museums, including "Portrait of Edward MacDowell" in the collection of the Metropolitan Museum of Art, New York City; "Statue of Miss Frances E. Willard" in the Capitol building, Washington, D.C.; and many others. Winner of honors and awards, Mears received a $500 prize from the Milwaukee Women's Club at the Columbian Exposition, Chicago, Illinois (1893); a silver medal at the St. Louis Exposition, Missouri (1904); an honorable mention at the Panama-Pacific International Exposition, San Francisco, California (1915); and others. She was elected to membership in the National Sculpture Society, New York City (1907).

Bibliography
Fairman, Charles E. *Art and Artists of the Capitol of the United States of America*. U.S. Government Printing Office, 1927.
Green, Susan Porter. *Helen Farnsworth Mears*. Oshkosh, Wisconsin: Paine Art Center, 1972.
Obituary. *American Art Annual*. Vol. 13. American Federation of Arts, 1916.
Statue of Miss Frances E. Willard. Proceedings in the Senate and House of Representatives on the Occasion of the Reception and Acceptance of the Statue from the State of Illinois. U.S. Government Printing Office, 1905.

Medel, Rebecca

A native of California, the fiber artist Rebecca Medel earned a Bachelor of Fine Arts degree from Arizona State University, Tempe (1970); and received a Master of Fine Arts degree from the University of California at Los Angeles (UCLA) (1982).

Medel's colored, knotted, diaphanous, netted fiber veils are shrouded in mystery; she employs an age-old technique in new ways, using light to heighten or emphasize feelings of composure. Her work—recognized internationally in many group exhibitions such as the "Tapestry Biennials" in Lausanne, Switzerland—is represented in private and public permanent collections.

Bibliography
Fiber Concepts. A Catalog. Tempe: Arizona State University, 1989.
Reuter, Laurel. "The Net Result: Californian Transcends Her Materials to Create Remarkable Works of Art." *Grand Forks Herald* (March 29, 1985): D1.
Taylor, Diane, and Elmer Taylor. "Twelfth International Biennial of Tapestry." *Fiberarts* (November–December 1985): 50–54.

Medicine Flower, Grace (1938–)

Born in Santa Clara, New Mexico, Grace Medicine Flower (Grace Tafoya) comes from a five-generation family of potters. She learned the art of pottery from her father, Camilio Tafoya, with whom she collaborated early on. The black and red ware produced between 1968 and 1972 bears both of their names.

Medicine Flower combines meticulous, delicate detail in matte or highly-polished ware, in an ever-burgeoning adventure in form and technique. A favorite symbol incised on her pots, from her small seed bowls to her large, elegant bottle shapes, is the plumed serpent (*Avanyu*)—a mythic reference of power, protector of life, guardian of the waters.

Medicine Flower entered her first show in 1968 and, since then, has won a great many awards. The New Mexico State Fair in 1971 granted her first prize and purchase award, and, that same year, she won a first prize, best of show, and a certificate of merit award at the Inter-Tribal Indian Ceremonial in Gallup, New Mexico. The following year, at the same ceremonial, Medicine Flower sent in three works and was awarded a first prize for each as well as a special award. Medicine Flower also was a prize-winner in shows in Beverly Hills and San José—both in California; Portland, Oregon; and Las Vegas, Nevada,

Medicine Flower's first solo exhibition occurred at the Gila River Indian Arts and Crafts Center, Sacaton, Arizona, in 1973. The next year her work was shown in the East Foyer of the White House in Washington, D.C., jointly with twenty-seven Hopi and New Mexican pueblo potters. Along with forty of her relatives who also showed their work, Medicine Flower exhibited ware at the Maxwell Museum of Anthropology, University of New Mexico, Albuquerque, in a show titled "7 Families in Pueblo Pottery." She is married to John C. Hoover.

Bibliography
Art and Indian Individualists, the Art of Seventeen Contemporary Southwestern Artists and Craftsmen. Northland Press, 1975.

Medina Castro, Elsa (1952–)

In Mexico art is often a product of the struggle for daily bread. Given this reality—as well as the fact that it is only in recent years that a few photographers have been able to make a living by selling their work in galleries—it should come as no surprise that photojournalism has been a vital seedbed of Mexican photography. Several of Tina Modotti's and Manuel Alvarez Bravo's more interesting photos fall within this category; and in more recent years, artists of the camera, such as Héctor García and Nacho López, have earned their livings essentially as pho-

tojournalists. Elsa Medina Castro is a direct descendent of this tradition, having been initiated in López's Photographic Expression Workshop at the Universidad Nacional Autónoma de Mexico. Earlier Medina had studied photographic techniques and graphic design at San Diego State University, California, but she feels that it was López who most influenced her art by teaching her "to see."

In 1986 Medina entered the staff of the newspaper *La Jornada*. From its inception *La Jornada* has provided an extraordinary space for photojournalism, where exceptional visual images are often printed whether or not they are related to news stories. Medina made good use of the opportunities this newspaper offered and has been able to publish many significant photos. For example her very first image to appear in the periodical received an award in a photo contest on the 1985 earthquake. The editors of *La Jornada* were so impressed with her striking photo of smoking ruins topped by workers clearing rubble, over all of which flies an upside-down Mexican flag, that they published it before she actually started working for the newspaper. Another memorable prize-winning photo is "Illegal," in which an undocumented Mexican worker lies in wait of darkness to enter into the United States which stretches out infinitely behind him. Much of this image's impact comes from the way the wide-angle lens details the lines of the hand held in front of his face. Medina favors the wide-angle lens, which has enabled her to capture forceful scenes such as the already-old boy photographed up through her car's windshield, which he is cleaning, while Christmas decorations hang over the street behind him.

In 1990 Medina travelled to New York City to study in Jeff Jacobson's workshop, "Personal Photojournalism: The Psyche and the World," at the International Center of Photography. She feels that this experience enabled her to discover worlds of photojournalism she had not previously considered. During 1991 she took a leave of absence from *La Jornada* to spend a month in Haiti documenting the *Lavalas* (Avalanche) movement of Jean Bertrand Aristide. She is presently preparing those photos for publication in a special supplement of *La Jornada*, as well as to appear in book form. If they are anywhere near as powerful as the images she has produced up to this point, they will no doubt further enhance her reputation as the outstanding woman photojournalist-artist of Mexico.

John Mraz

Bibliography
Mraz, John. "From Positivism to Populism: Towards a History of Mexican Photojournalism." *Afterimage* 18:6 (January 1991).

Medrez, Miriam (1958–)

Sculptor and designer Miriam Medrez was born in Mexico City, Mexico, and resides, at present, in Monterrey, Nuevo León. Medrez studied graphic design and sculpture at Concordia University, Montréal, Canada, from 1977 to 1979. From 1979 to 1982 she attended the School of Visual Arts of the San Carlos Academy, Mexico City, where she received her degree based, in part, upon her thesis, "Development of a program in sculptural perception for pre-school children."

Essentially figurative and expressionistic, Medrez creates a world of her own, filled with feminine figures intermingled with dogs—interpreting the simple relationships of daily life. Her favorite sculptors are Constantin Brancusi, Alberto Giacometti, and Henry Moore. However, she also draws inspiration for her compositions from Pablo Picasso: her synthetic and schematic figures combine the essential geometric lines and the bi-dimensional with three-dimensional shapes. In her ceramic sculpture—primarily her bas-reliefs—she plays more with sets of figures (persons and animals), arriving at complicated, but always interesting, effective, and original compositions.

Since 1981 Medrez has participated in more than thirty exhibitions—primarily in Mexico City and Monterrey. In 1986 she exhibited a series of drawings at the Institute of Mexican Culture, San Antonio, Texas. She received an honorable mention in the Ceramics Biennial at the Museum of Modern Art in Mexico City (1985), and an honorable mention in the Ceramic State Competition in Monterrey.

Giancarlo Malvaioli von Nacher

Bibliography
Glanz, Margo. *Doscientos Ballenas y Cuatro Caballos*. Ilustraciones de Miriam Medrez. Textos de Humanidades n.27. UNAM, 1981.
Museo de Arte Moderno. *Catálogo del Dibujo de Mujeres Contemporáneas Mexicanas*, 1990.

Meeko, Lucy (1929–)

Lucy Meeko is a Canadian Inuit artist born on the land near Kuujjuaraapik, Arctic Québec, Canada. Her husband Noah Meeko is also a talented artist, and together they attended print workshops and were involved with several of the annual Arctic Québec print collections. They still live and work in the Kuujjuaraapik area.

Meeko was approaching middle age before a new creative outlet opened up for her, and with it, recognition as an artist. After studying various print techniques in Povungnituk she went on to be a prolific and important contributor to the Arctic Québec print collections of the 1970s. Relying on traditional themes for subject matter, Meeko's prints are often stylized collages illustrating an almost spiritual relationship between Inuit and animals of the North. Among Meeko's other talents are sewing and carving. Here again she concentrates on the things she knows. Familiar images of mother and child, or walrus on an ice flow are naturally and simply depicted in her sculptures.

In 1989 Meeko was the guest of the McCord Museum of Canadian History in Montréal, where she demonstrated caribou skin tailoring and sealskin bootmaking. She is often called upon to conduct workshops in other communities. This versatile artist's work has been exhibited around the world, and is included in the collections of the Canadian Museum of Civilization and the Avataq Cultural Centre.

Mary Craig

Bibliography
Barz, Sandra. *Canadian Inuit Print Artist/Printer Biographies*. Art & Culture of the North, 1990.

Meeser, Lillian Burk (1864–1943)

Born in Ridley Park, Pennsylvania, the painter Lillian Burk Meeser studied at the Pennsylvania Academy of Fine Arts, Philadelphia; the Art Students League, New York City; and the Worcester Art Museum, Massachusetts.

Founder of the Detroit Society of Women Painters and Sculptors, Meeser was a fellow of the Pennsylvania Academy of Fine Arts, Penn-sylvania, and a member of several arts organizations, including the Philadelphia Art Alliance, the Plastics Club, the Northshore Art Association, the Provincetown Art Association, and the American Federation of Arts. She received an honorable mention (1921) and a silver medal (1922) from exhibitions at the Plastic Club, and the Mary Smith prize at the Pennsylvania Academy of Fine Arts (1923).

Examples of Meeser's work are in private and public permanent collections, including the Pennsylvania State University, University Park; the Reading Museum, Pennsylvania; the Pennsylvania Academy of Fine Arts; and others.

Bibliography
American Art Annual. Vol. 28. American Federation of Arts, 1932.
Bye, Arthur. *Pots and Pans*. Princeton University Press, 1921.
Moore, Julia G. *History of the Detroit Society of Women Painters and Sculptors, 1903–1953*. Michigan: Victory Printing Co., 1953.

Meiere, Hildreth (1892–1961)

A native New Yorker, the muralist/mosaicist Hildreth Meiere attended the Convent of the Sacred Heart, New York City; studied art in Florence, Italy; and took further work at the Art Students League, New York City.

Meiere was commissioned to create works in many venues, including murals for the Medical and Public Health Building at the New York World's Fair (1939); murals for the Irving Trust Company; mosaics and stained-glass windows for St. Bartholomew's Protestant Episcopal Church; metal wall pieces for Rockefeller Center, and the liner *America*; and design of the Lady Altar at St. Patrick's Cathedral—all in New York City; crypt mosaics at the National Cathedral, Washington, D.C.; murals for the Travellers Life Insurance Company, Hartford, Connecticut; a variety of works for the Nebraska State Capitol, Lincoln; and many others.

Meiere has received awards and honors, including a gold medal from the Architectural League (1928); an honorary Doctorate from Manhattanville College of the Sacred Heart (1953); a fine arts medal from the American Institute of Architects (AIA) (1956); and others.

Bibliography
Alexander, H.B. "Hildreth Meiere's Work for Nebraska." *Architecture* 63 (June 1931): 34–38.
Lee, Anne. "Hildreth Meiere: Mural Painter." *Architectural Record* 62 (August 1927): 103–12.
Watson, Ernest. "Hildreth Meiere: Mural Painter." *American Artist* 5 (September 1941): 4–9.

Meigs, Sandra (1953–)

Born in Baltimore, Maryland, and currently living in Toronto, Canada, Sandra Meigs uses a wide range of media in her work—from installations of found and manufactured objects to painting and drawing through to film and text. She is especially interested in the ways in which high and popular culture intersect, often drawing on cartoons, advertising, and kitsch. Similarly her installations, many of which have been in community-oriented spaces such as laundromats, as well as in galleries, explore how institutions, viewing expectations, and spatial arrangements affect the meaning of images. Since Meigs is especially interested in critically examining the systems and structures that govern the production and reception of cultural narratives and visual art practice, her installations often contain multiple images, which fracture, disrupt, and ultimately deny simple interpretations. The familiar popular imagery that she draws from is playfully manipulated to offer her viewers both the pleasures of recognition and insights into the way the popular becomes mythologized.

Meigs received her Bachelor of Fine Arts degree from the Nova Scotia College of Art and Design and a Master of Arts degree in philosophy from Dalhousie University—both in Halifax, Novia Scotia. Her solo exhibitions have included "The Maelstrom" at A-Space in Toronto (1980); "The Western Gothic" at the Montréal Museum of Fine Arts; "The Scab Picker" at the Ydessa Gallery in Toronto (1984); "The Room of 1,000 Paintings" at the YYZ in Toronto (1986); "Creative Management" (1988) and "The Power of Love" (1989) both at the Galerie Chantal Boulanger in Montréal; and "Sandra Meigs" at the Powerplant in Toronto (1990). She also participated in a collective exhibition in Toronto, titled "It All Comes Out in the Wash" (1989). Her work is in the permanent collections of the National Gallery of Canada, Ottawa, and the Canada Council Art Bank.

Bridget Elliott

Bibliography
Elliott, Bridget, and Janice Williamson. *Dangerous Goods: Feminist Visual Art Practices.* Edmonton Art Gallery and Latitude 53 (1990): 15–16, 27.
Hanna, Deirdre. "Sandra Meigs' Cartoon Kitsch and Classic Corn." *Now* 31:32 (September 11–17), 1986.
Racine, Yolande. *Avant-scene de l'imaginaire/Theatre of the Imagination.* Montréal Museum of Fine Arts, 1985.
Town, Elke. "Sandra Meigs: It's a Strange World." *Vanguard* (April–May 1987): 19–22.

Mellon, Eleanor Mary (1894–1980)

Born in Narberth, Pennsylvania, the sculptor Eleanor Mary Mellon studied her craft with a number of teachers, including Robert Aitken, Harriet Frishmuth, Charles Grafly, Edward McCartan, V.D. Salvatore, and A.A. Weinman.

Mellon's work was included in many exhibitions, such as the "Exhibition of American Sculpture," National Sculpture Society (1923); "Contemporary American Sculpture," National Sculpture Society, and California Palace of the Legion of Honor (1929)—all in New York City; and others. Winner of awards and honors, Mellon received the Barnet prize from the National Academy of Design, New York City; a bronze medal from the Society of Washington Artists (1931); honorable mention from the National Association of Women Painters and Sculptors (1932); and others.

Mellon was a member of the National Sculpture Society and the Americian Federation of Arts. Her work is represented in private and public permanent collections, such as the Brookgreen Gardens, South Carolina.

Bibliography
American Art Annual. Vol. 28. American Federation of Arts, 1932.
National Sculpture Society. *Exhibition of American Sculpture.* A Catalog. New York, 1923.
Who's Who in American Art. 8th ed. American Federation of Arts, 1962.

Menassé, Eliana (1930–)

Though she was born in New York of Russian parents, Eliana Menassé regards herself as truly Mexican, in that she was a mere two-year-old when her family emigrated to Mexico City, Mexico. Her identification with Mexico is so complete that the kind and quality of color one associates with that country is visible in her painting.

Menassé is an industrious, serious, and business-like painter who prepared for her craft and her profession by running the gamut of courses in life drawing, still life, design, and all the usual techniques and procedures in an art curriculum. There is a certain elegance to her work which has been seen in myriad exhibitions throughout Mexico and abroad.

Bibliography
The Texas Quarterly: Image of Mexico II. The University of Texas, Winter 1969.

Méndez, Mariángeles

Born in Mexico, Mariángeles Méndez is a prolific printmaker whose work has been exhibited in group shows since 1978. Together with Susana Carlson, Méndez showed a portfolio of six colored woodcuts at the Galería Maren in 1981. Each artist made three prints.

Méndez works in many print media, including etching, aquatint, drypoint, and mixed-media. She seems fascinated with trees, as they are a recurring theme running throughout her work.

Bibliography
Alvarez, José Rogelio, et al. *Enciclopedia de México.* Secretaría de Educación Pública, 1987.

Mendieta, Ana (1948–1985)

Born in Havana, Cuba, the multifaceted, energy-laden, ill-fated earth and body artist Ana Mendieta studied art at the University of Iowa, Iowa City, where she earned Bachelor's (1969), Master's, and Master of Fine Arts degrees (1972).

Mendieta held many solo performances and exhibitions in museums and galleries in cities across the United States; Mexico City; São Paulo, Brazil; Antwerp, Belgium; Belgrade, formerly Yugoslavia; Havana, Cuba; and elsewhere from 1972 until her death. Her work was centered in women's concerns and in the use of her own mud-covered, flower-covered, or grass-covered body to express, through performance, concepts, materials, and percepts related to the true nature of events, including rape, *Santería* images from her childhood, and other incidents meant to disturb the complacent.

Mendieta won many honors and awards, including a grant from the Iowa Arts Council (1977); fellowships from the National Endowment for the Arts (NEA) (1978, 1980, 1982, 1983); a Creative Artists Public Service (CAPS) grant (1979); a Guggenheim Foundation fellowship (1980); a grant from the New York State Council on the Arts (1982); a Prix de Rome fellowship from the American Academy in Rome, Italy (1983, 1984); and others. Examples of her works are in private and public permanent collections, including the Metropolitan Museum of Art, New York City; and others.

Bibliography
Ana Mendieta: A Retrospective. Curated by Peter Barreras del Rio and John Perreault. New Museum of Contemporary Art, 1987.
Katz, Robert. *Naked by the Window, The Fatal Marriage of Carl André and Ana Mendieta.* The Atlantic Monthly Press, 1990.

Lippard, Lucy. "Ana Mendieta: 1948–1985." *Hue Points* 14:1 (Spring 1986): 54–55.

Orenstein, Gloria F. "The Reemergence of the Archetype of the Great Goddess in Art by Contemporary Women." *Heresies* (Spring 1978): 74–84.

Merrill, Katherine (1876–)

Born in Milwaukee, Wisconsin, the painter/etcher Katherine Merrill studied at the School of the Art Institute of Chicago, Illinois; and with Frank Brangwyn in London, England.

Merrill's etchings are in major print cabinets and permanent collections in the United States and abroad, including the Art Institute of Chicago and University of Chicago—both in Illinois; Beloit College, Wisconsin; the Bibliothèque Nationale, Paris, France; Corcoran Gallery of Art, Washington, D.C.; Milwaukee Art Institute, Wisconsin; Metropolitan Museum of Art and New York Public Library—both in New York City; Newark Public Library, New Jersey; Widener Memorial Library, Harvard University, Cambridge, Massachusetts; and others.

Merrill was a member of the Chicago Society of Etchers, the Society of American Etchers, the California Society of Etchers, and the National Association of Women Painters and Sculptors.

Bibliography
American Art Annual. Vol. 28. American Federation of Arts, 1932.

Fielding, Mantle. *Dictionary of American Painters, Sculptors, and Engravers.* Modern Books and Crafts, 1974.

Thieme, Ulrich, and Felix Becker. *Allgemeines Lexikon der Bildenden Kunstler.* . . . Leipzig: E.A. Seeman, 1930.

Merritt, Anna Massey Lea (1844–1930)

Anna Massey Lea Merritt was prominent in England and the United States as a portrait and landscape painter and etcher of narrative subjects and portraits. Her Unitarian parents, Joseph Lea Jr., a Philadelphia manufacturer, and Susanna Massey Lea, a homemaker, took the family to Europe to live in 1865.

Merritt taught herself to paint from instruction books. She studied briefly with Stefano Ussi in Florence, Italy, and Heinrich Hofmann in Dresden, Germany. In 1870 she established a studio in London, England, spending part of the year there and part in Philadelphia working on commissions. Beginning in 1872 she studied art with London critic Henry Merritt, marrying him in 1877, three months before he died.

With technical help from Charles West Cope and Elizabeth Ruth Edwards, Merritt taught herself to etch in 1877 in order to illustrate *Henry Merritt. Art Criticism and Romance, with Recollections and Twenty-three Etchings by Anna Lea Merritt.* Merritt produced frontispiece portraits for many books, and her etchings were published in *The Etcher,* and in Sylvester Koehler's the *American Art Review, American Etchings,* and *American Artists and Their Works.* Individual etchings were published by Christian Klackner, Wunderlich, and Co., and Eyre & Spottswood. With her paintings she illustrated books and articles that she wrote.

Merritt's long exhibition career included participation at the Pennsylvania Academy of Fine Arts, Philadelphia, and the Philadelphia Society of Artists—both in Pennsylvania; London's Royal Academy and the Royal Society of British Artists—both in England; the Paris Salon, France; the Brooklyn Art Association, the National Academy of Design, and the National Arts Club—all in New York City; the Boston Museum of Art and the Boston Art Club—both in Massachusetts; and the Plastic Club. Her etchings were shown at the New York Etching Club and the Salmagundi Club—both in New York City; the Philadelphia Society of Etchers, Pennsylvania; the Royal Society of Painter-Etchers, England; and the Berlin Society of Etchers, Germany. Her work was included in many expositions. For the 1893 Columbian Exposition she painted panels of "Needlework," "Benevolence," and "Education" for the Woman's Building.

Phyllis Peet

Bibliography
Anna M. Lea Merritt Papers. New York: Manuscript Division, New York Public Library.

Chester, Austin. "The Art of Anna Lea Merritt." *Windsor Magazine* 38 (November 1913): 605–20.

Gorokhoff, Galina, ed. *Love Locked Out: The Memoirs of Anna Lea Merritt with a Checklist of Her Works.* Boston: Museum of Fine Arts, 1983.

Koehler, Sylvester Rosa. "The Works of the American Etchers. VIII. Anna Lea Merritt." *American Art Review* 1:1 (1880): 229–30.

Merritt, Anna Lea. "A Letter to Artists: Especially Women Artists." *Lippincott's Monthly Magazine* 65 (March 1900): 463–69.

"Mrs. Anna Lea Merritt, Noted Artist, Dies." [Obituary] *The New York Times* (April 8, 1930): 26.

Peet, Phyllis. *American Women of the Etching Revival.* Atlanta: High Museum of Art, 1988, pp. 23, 60.

Mihalcheon, Jean Lapointe (1929–)

Born in Domremy, Saskatchewan, Canada, the ceramist/painter Jean Lapointe Mihalcheon earned a diploma from the Alberta College of Art, Calgary (1952), where she had studied with Illingworth Kerr, Luke Lindoe, Marion Nicoll, William Perehudoff, and Stanford Perrott. She returned to the college for technical, post-graduate work in ceramics (1975).

A teacher and curator of ceramics, Mihalcheon has held solo exhibitions in museums and galleries in Canada, including the Calgary Galleries, Alberta (1974); Fleet Galleries, Winnipeg, Manitoba (1975); Lefèvre Gallery, Edmonton, Alberta (1976); Mount Royal College, Calgary (1978); Gulf Canada Ltd., Calgary (1986); and others. Her work has won awards and honors and has been included in prestigious group shows throughout the province. Examples of her work are in private, corporate, and public permanent collections in Canada and abroad, including Alberta House, London, England; Civic Collection, City of Calgary, Alberta; Government House, Edmonton, Alberta; the National Trust, Calgary; Northwest Utilities Ltd., Calgary; University of Calgary, Alberta; and others.

Bibliography
Alberta Clay Comes of Age. Potter's Association, 1986.

Baker, Suzanne Devonshire. *Artists of Alberta.* University of Alberta Press, 1980.

Payne, Anne. "Jean Mihalcheon." *Arts West* 3:2 (1978): 8.

Mikpiga, Annie (Nuvalinga) (1900–1984)

The Canadian Inuit graphic artist Annie (Nuvalinga) Mikpiga was born in 1900 near the Arctic Québec community of Povungnituk, where she lived until her death in 1984. Widowed in 1955, Nuvalinga was among the first of the Inuit artists to experiment with printmaking in the early 1960s. Nuvalinga was among the most prolific Povungnituk graphic artists in the years 1962 to 1973, carving about sixty stonecut images and printing many of them herself as well.

Small in scale and rather tentative at first, Nuvalinga's images quickly grew in size, complexity, and vitality, but always retained their naiveté. Nuvalinga illustrated scenes of traditional life, legends, and personal history. In Povungnituk stoneblock prints the excess stone is rarely cut away from the edges. Nuvalinga cut even less, removing hardly any material around and between figures in her compositions. Her images are usually black on white on black. In Povungnituk art paper images are almost a by-product of the stonecarver's craft. Nuvalinga's prints, especially, are more like rubbings taken from rock engravings than graphic art.

Nuvalinga's prints were represented in seven Povungnituk annual collections, as well as about fifteen group exhibitions. Her work is in the collections of the Canadian Museum of Civilization, the Glenbow Museum, and the Musée de la Civilisation, Québec.

Ingo Hessel

Bibliography
Barz, Sandra. *Canadian Inuit Print Artists/Printer Biographies.* Art & Culture of the North, 1990.

Mikus, Eleanore (1927–)

Born in Detroit, Michigan, the painter Eleanore Mikus earned Bachelor of Fine Arts and Master of Fine Arts degrees from the University of Denver, Colorado; she also studied in Central Europe and at the Art Students League in New York City.

Mikus has had her work invited to many group shows throughout the United States, including Cornell University, Ithaca, New York (1979–1990); "The 25-Year Tamarind Retrospective," Los Angeles City Museum of Art, California (1984); Mary Baskett Gallery, Cincinnati, Ohio (1982–1983); O.K. Harris, New York City (1980–1983); Weatherspoon Art Gallery, Greensboro, North Carolina (1977); Museum of Modern Art (MoMA), New York City (1974); and others. Her solo shows include the Mary Baskett Gallery (1983–1985, 1988); O.K. Harris (1970–1974); Pace Gallery, New York City (1963, 1964, 1965); and others.

Mikus received fellowships from the Guggenheim (1966–1967) and Ford Foundations (Tamarind Lithography fellowship, 1968); and the MacDowell Colony, Peterborough, New Hampshire (1969). She has taught painting at Monmouth College, West Long Branch, New Jersey (1966–1970); Cooper Union, New York City (1970–1972); the Central School of Art and Design, London, England (1973–1977); and Cornell University, Ithaca, New York (1979 to present), where she is currently an associate professor of art. Her work is represented in private and public permanent collections, including the Indianapolis Museum of Art, Indiana; Los Angeles County Museum of Art, California; Museum of Modern Art (MoMA) and Whitney Museum of American Art—both in New York City; National Gallery of Art, Washington, D.C.; Victoria & Albert Museum, London, England; and others.

Bibliography
Hobbs, Robert, and Judith Bernstock. *Eleanore Mikus: Shadows of the Real.* Seattle, Washington. University of Washington Press, 1991.
Wesley, Laura. "Gayil Nalls, Claudia DeMonte, Joy Parsons, Eleanore Mikus." *Q, A Journal of Art* (July 1988): 28–31.
Women Artists: Selected Works from the Collection. A Catalog. Ithaca, New York: Herbert F. Johnson Museum of Art, Cornell University, 1983.

Who's Who in American Art. 19th ed. R.R. Bowker Co., 1991–1992.

Miles, Jeanne Patterson (1908–)

Born in Baltimore, Maryland, the painter/sculptor Jeanne Patterson Miles earned a Bachelor of Fine Arts degree from George Washington University, Washington, D.C.; studied at the Grande Chaumière, Paris, France; and with Marcel Gromaire.

Miles has held solo exhibitions in museums and galleries in the United States, including eight at the Betty Parsons Gallery (1943–1982) and the Marilyn Pearl Gallery (1988–1989)—both in New York City; and others. She has had her work shown in group exhibitions—some of them travelling—such as "Mysticism in Art," Rome-New York Foundation, Italy (1957); "Geometric Art," the Whitney Museum of American Art, New York City (1963); "Three American Purists," Museum of Fine Arts, Springfield, Massachusetts (1975); and many others.

A teacher of painting and life drawing at several colleges, Miles has also been a docent at the Guggenheim Museum, New York City, and elsewhere; as well as a writer and researcher of the mandala in the history of art. Her work has won honors and awards and is represented in private and public permanent collections, including Cornell University, Ithaca, New York; Guggenheim Museum, New York City; Munson-Williams-Proctor Institute, Utica, New York; Newark Museum, New Jersey; Santa Barbara Museum, California; and others.

Bibliography
Brooks, Perry. "Jeanne Miles." *Arts Magazine* 56:8 (April 1982): 4.
Davis, Mary. "Jeanne Miles: An Interview." *Arts Magazine* 51:8 (April 1977): 139.
Hill, May Brawley. *Three American Purists: Mason, Miles, Von Weigand.* A Catalog. Springfield, Massachusetts: Museum of Fine Arts, 1975.
Rubinstein, Charlotte S. *American Women Artists.* G.K. Hall, 1982.

Miller, Brenda

Born in the Bronx, New York, the sculptor and conceptual artist Brenda Miller earned a Bachelor of Fine Arts degree from the University of New Mexico, Albuquerque (1965), and, two years later, received a Master of Fine Arts degree from Tulane University, New Orleans, Louisiana.

Miller's work has been in many group and solo exhibitions throughout the United States and abroad: from a solo show at the Whitney Museum of American Art in New York City to the Portland Center for Visual Art, Oregon; from Hartford, Connecticut, to the Netherlands. Recently, she received a private commission for a project on Block Island, Rhode Island, titled "A is for Anonymous."

Miller has earned honors and awards for her work, including a Creative Artists Public Service (CAPS) grant from the New York State Council on the Arts (1975); a Guggenheim Foundation fellowship (1978); grants from the National Endowment for the Arts (NEA) (1976, 1979, 1987–1988); and others. Examples of her work are in private and public permanent collections, including the Haag Gemente Museum, the Netherlands; Hartford Atheneum, Connecticut; Museum Boymans-Van Beuningen, Rotterdam, the Netherlands; the University of Texas, Austin; and others.

Bibliography
Lippard, Lucy. "Brenda Miller: Woven Stamped." *Art in America* 64:3 (1976).
Tower, Susan. "The Object Perceived, The Object Apprehended." *Artforum* 12:5 (1974).

Miller, Kay (1946–)

Born in Houston, Texas, Kay Miller earned a Bachelor of Science degree from the University of Houston, Texas (1970); she enrolled at the University of Texas, Austin, where she received a Bachelor of Fine Arts degree (1975), and a Master of Fine Arts degree four years later. Miller has lectured throughout the United States with respect to her paintings—direct and bold visual statements incorporating sources from her own cultural perspective. The lush surfaces of her works are built up in layerings of pigment and texture, creating a complex, deep surface, and content history. These large-scale paintings, for which Miller is nationally known, are multidimensional and powerful painterly works. She sees art as ". . . raw, living material (through which) we can embrace the mystical and mundane forces of inexhaustible possibilities." She believes in the coexistence of the sacred and the humorous, through which new meanings evolve.

Among Miller's numerous major exhibitions are "America/Re-America," Hunter College, New York City (1992); "Laughing Matters," Artemisia Gallery, Chicago, Illinois (1991); "The Price of Power," Cleveland Contemporary Art Center, Ohio (1990); "The Biennial of American Contemporary Painting," Corcoran Gallery of Art, Washington, D.C. (1985); and others. Her works are in major collections, such as the Denver Museum of Art, Colorado; the New Museum of Contemporary Art, New York City; the Djerassi Foundation, Woodside, California; and others. Winner of awards and honors, Miller has received a PSI residency award (1990–1991); a National Endowment for the Arts (NEA) grant (1985); a Ford Foundation research grant (1978); and others.

Moira Geoffrion

Bibliography
Lippard, Lucy R. *Mixed Blessings*. Pantheon Books, 1990.

Miller, Lee (1908–1977)

Film actress, photographer's model, and noted fashion photographer—the American-born Lee Miller played these and other roles during her lifetime. Wife of Sir Roland Penrose, Miller studied in Paris, France, and in New York City at the Art Students League (1926–1929).

In the early 1920s Miller was employed as a model by Edward Steichen in New York City, and worked as an assistant and model for Man Ray in Paris, France (1929–1932). Also in 1929 she starred in Jean Cocteau's film, *Blood of a Poet*. She owned and operated photographic studios both in Paris, France, and New York City. At the start of World War II she enlisted and served in the London War Correspondents Corps (1939–1945), sending her words and images from the theater of war to the magazine, *Vogue*. Representative examples of her work are in private and public permanent collections.

Bibliography
Chadwick, Whitney. *Women Artists and the Surrealist Movement*. Boston: New York Graphic Society, 1985.
Krauss, Rosalind, Jane Livingston, and Dawn Ades. *L'Amour Fou, Photography and Surrealism*. Abbeville Press, 1985.
Penrose, Antony. *The Lives of Lee Miller*. Holt, Rinehart & Winston, 1985.

Miller, Lee Anne (1938–)

Born in Salt Lake City, Utah, the painter/printmaker Lee Anne Miller earned a Bachelor's degree from Utah State University, Logan (1960); received a Master of Fine Arts degree from Cranbrook Academy of Art, Bloomfield Hills, Michigan (1961); and also studied at the Pratt Graphic Art Center, New York City (1961–1962).

Miller has participated in many solo exhibitions of her paintings and prints in galleries throughout the United States: from Chicago, Illinois, and Cleveland, Ohio, to Kansas City, Missouri, and Manhattan, Kansas. Her work has been included in major group exhibitions since the 1960s, including the "Eighth Utah Annual of Painting and Sculpture," Salt Lake Art Center (1966); "Watercolor USA," Springfield Art Museum, Missouri (1968–1974); "Works on Paper, 17th Dixie Annual," Montgomery Museum of Fine Arts, Alabama (1976); and others.

Winner of honors and awards, Miller received a Fulbright Foundation fellowship in painting, which took her to the Slade School, London, England (1962–1963); a Tamarind Institute grant (1975); a purchase award at the 9th Annual Prints, Drawings, and Crafts Exhibition, Arkansas Art Center, Little Rock (1976); second place award, 36th Annual Cedar City National Exhibition, Utah (1977); and others. She is a professor and administrator at universities and art institutes, and her work is represented in private and public permanent collections, including the Arkansas Art Center; the University of Missouri, Kansas; and others.

Bibliography
"Studio: Lee Anne Miller Paintings." *Helicon Nine* 9 (Spring 1982): 54–58.
Who's Who in American Art. R.R. Bowker Co., 1978.

Miller, Melissa (1951–)

Born in Houston, Texas, the painter Melissa Miller attended the University of Texas, Austin (1969–1971), and the Museum of Fine Arts School, Houston (1971)—both in Texas; the Yale-Norfolk Summer School of Music and Art, Connecticut (1974); and earned a Bachelor of Fine Arts degree from the University of New Mexico, Albuquerque (1974).

Miller has held solo exhibitions of her work in museums and galleries, including the Texas Gallery, Houston (1983, 1985); Holly Solomon Gallery, New York City (1985); Albright-Knox Art Gallery, Buffalo, New York; the Contemporary Arts Museum, Houston, the Fort Worth Art Museum (1986); and "Melissa Miller: The Artist's Eye," Kimbell Art Museum, Fort Worth (1991)—all in Texas; and others. Her work has been invited to group exhibitions throughout the United States and abroad, such as the "1983 Biennial Exhibition," Whitney Museum of American Art and "The End of the World: Contemporary Visions of the Apocalypse," the New Museum (1983)—both in New York City; "Paradise Lost/Paradise Regained," the Venice Biennale, Italy, and "Biennial III," San Francisco Museum of Modern Art, California (1984); "Fresh Paint," the Museum of Fine Arts, Houston (1985); "Directions," Hirshhorn Museum and Sculpture Garden, Washington, D.C. (1986); "Making Their Mark: Women Artists Today, A Documentary Survey 1970–1985," a travelling show, Cincinnati Art Museum, Ohio (1989); "Mind and Beast: Contemporary Artist and the Animal Kingdom," a travelling show, Leigh Yawkey Woodson Art Museum, Wausau, Wisconsin (1992); and many others.

Winner of honors and awards, Miller received a full scholarship to the Yale-Norfolk Summer School of Art and Music (1974); grants from the National Endowment for the Arts (NEA) (1979, 1982, 1985); an award from the Anne Giles Kimbrough Fund, Dallas Museum of Art, Texas (1982); and the 1987 Texas arts award. Her work is represented in private, public, and corporate permanent collections, including the Museum of Modern Art (MoMA), New York City; Albright-Knox Art Gallery, Buffalo, New York; Museum of Fine Arts, Houston, Texas; the Contemporary Museum, Honolulu, Hawaii; and Modern Art Museum of Fort Worth; ARCO, Dallas, AMOCO, Houston—all in Texas; and others.

Bibliography
Brenson, Michael. "In Melissa Miller's Wild Kingdom Lurks a World of Wonder." *The New York Times* (July 1986): H27, 29.
Ennis, Michael. "Double Visions." *Texas Monthly* (November 1991): 76.
Gregor, Katherine. "Melissa Miller's Animal Kingdom." *Art News* 85: 10 (December 1986): 106–15.
Tyson, Janet. "Animal Magnetism." *Fort Worth Star Telegram* (September 23, 1991): E1.

Miller, Nancy Tokar (1941–)

Though Nancy Tokar Miller was born in Detroit, Michigan, and earned her Bachelor of Arts degree at the University of California at Los Angeles (UCLA), and her Master of Fine Arts degree at the University of Arizona, Tucson, the primary influence on her painting has been Japanese. Based more on the experience of nature than its portrayal, these highly abstracted works evoke rather than describe. The goal, like Mark Rothko's, is contemplation growing out of this experience.

Miller has made several trips to Japan, which intensified and confirmed her bent toward simplified designs and flat fields of color working against space: the filled contrasted with the void. Her early works were characterized by veil-like areas of stain; later she introduced a second tension, that between brushstrokes and flat, evenly colored planes. The brushstroke as gesture records its own motion, and this motion—the movement of carp in water, or tidal water, for example, or an arm in a kimono sleeve—is suggested by the way these colored areas interact. This is motion, however, not against the flat surface of the picture, but against a shifting, receding space. The idea of receding depths is central to Miller's idea of color and motion and a major reason for the affinity she feels with Japanese art.

Though her large acrylic paintings are very large—even including some in the format of the room-sized Momoyama screen—she also works in watercolor on paper. Here the importance of the brushstroke and the accomplished use of white paper also owe much to the Japanese example, and to the oriental idea that the universal may be as well expressed in the deep observation of something small, such as a flower, as in something as large as mountain peaks.

In addition Miller's use of a range of color beyond and outside the conventional European scale, a palette that exploits the myriad possibilities in black and grey, relates her work to the Eastern tradition.

Miller's paintings have been exhibited regularly in galleries and museums in the Southwest and California since the 1970s. She has been consistently represented in the Western States Exhibitions since their inception and was visiting artist at Amarillo Art Center, Texas, and Arizona Western College, Yuma. In 1975 she received a fellowship from the Western States Arts Foundation. She has received a number of juror's and purchase awards from southwestern museum exhibitions, including the Southwestern Invitational held in Yuma, Arizona, and the Four Corners States Biennial at the Phoenix Art Museum, the Arizona Biennial at the Tucson Museum of Art.

Barbara Cortright

Bibliography
Kotik, Charlotta. *Third Western States Exhibition*. Catalog. New York: The Brooklyn Museum, 1986, pp. XXII, 57.
The World Who's Who of Women, 4th ed. 1977.
Who's Who in American Art. Jacque Cattell Press, 1976.

Millioud, Elizabeth (1939–)

Painter/sculptor Elizabeth Millioud was born in Mexico City, Mexico, in 1939. Primarily self-taught, Millioud received some formal instruction in ceramics and in mosaics. Her first solo exhibition occurred in 1963 at the Mexican-North American Institute of Cultural Relations, Mexico City. Millioud's work has appeared in many group exhibitions in Mexico and abroad, including the Seventh Salon for Women Painters in Barcelona, Spain (1968), and others.

Bibliography
The Texas Quarterly: Image of Mexico II. The University of Texas, Winter 1969.

Milne, Eleanor (1926–)

Born in Saint John, New Brunswick, Canada, the sculptor Eleanor Milne studied at the School of the Montréal Museum of Fine Arts, Québec, Canada, under the aegis of Arthur Lismer, Jacques de Tonnancour and others, earning her diploma in 1945. She then studied human anatomy at the Medical School, McGill University, Montréal, and took further study at the Central School of Arts and Crafts, London, England, from John Farleigh. Milne also learned wood sculpture from Sylvia Daoust at the École des Beaux-Arts, Montréal; and did an apprenticeship under Ivan Mestrovic.

Milne has worked in many media, travelled widely, and filled so many sculpture commissions successfully that she was appointed as Canada's official sculptor (1962)—the fifth person to be named "Dominion Stone Carver" on Parliament Hill, Ottawa, since 1867. She has been responsible for the one-hundred-twenty-foot-long bas reliefs in Parliament depicting the history of Canada; twelve stained-glass windows in the Chamber, and the ceiling of the House of Commons; among other works commissioned for private and public collections and institutions. Milne has also pulled wood engravings, and completed book illustrations, in addition to her three-dimensional work—which has been exhibited throughout North America and Europe.

Bibliography
Coulon, Jacques. "Canada's Official Sculptor." *En route* 2:4 (April 1974): 10–11.
Fetherling, Doug. "Light and Shadow on the Hill." *Imperial Oil Review* 63:2 (1979): 2–7.
Fidler, Vera. "Canada's Story in Stone." *Canadian Geographical Journal* 81:1 (July 1970): 2–9.

Mina (Guillermina Dulché) (1942–)

Born in Silao, Guanajuato, Mexico, Mina (Guillermina Dulché) studied in the Academy of San Carlos in Mexico City from 1958 to 1962, and in the École Nationale Superieure des Beaux-Arts and the Musée de l'Homme, Paris, France (1964–1966).

A painter, Mina has exhibited her work in eighty-six shows, twenty-two of which were solo presentations—in Mexico and abroad. She painted a mural in the Museum of the Insurgencia, in the Hidalgo Pavilion, in Aguascalientes (1964) and in 1980 Mina was a juror for the First National Watercolor Salon in Guatemala. Subsequently her work has been on exhibit in the Villa Olímpica and in the Sala Ollin Yolíztli.

Bibliography

Alvarez, José Rogelio, et al. *Enciclopedia de México*. Secretaría de Educación Pública, 1987.

Minkowitz, Norma (1937–)

A native New Yorker, the fiber artist Norma Minkowitz studied at the Cooper Union, New York City, where she received a Bachelor of Fine Arts degree (1958).

Minkowitz has exhibited work in solo and group shows in the United States and abroad, including "Meeting Ground: Basketry Traditions and Sculptural Forms," the Forum, St. Louis, Missouri, and Arizona State University, Tempe (1990); "The Vessel: Studies in Form and Media," Craft and Folk Art Museum, Los Angeles, California (1989); "The Tactile Vessel: New Basket Forms," a travelling show, Erie Art Museum, Pennsylvania (1989–1991); "A Sensitivity of Textile—A Proposal for a New Century," International Textile Competition '87, Kyoto, Japan (1987); "Fiber R/Evolution," a travelling show, Milwaukee Art Museum and the University of Wisconsin at Milwaukee (1986–1987).

Minkowitz has won awards and honors, including a National Endowment for the Arts (NEA) fellowship (1986) and a first place in fiber at "ArtQuest '86." Her work is represented in private and public permanent collections. "The Jealous Eye" (1989), a crocheted cotton, inverted basketlike form that has little to do with baskets, reveals Minkowitz's careful approach to surface and structure—where they are one and the same phenomenon.

Bibliography

Meeting Ground: Basketry Traditions and Sculptural Forms. The Forum, St. Louis, Missouri, and Arizona State University, Tempe, 1990.
Shermeta, Margo. "Norma Minkowitz: Shadow Boxes." *American Craft* (December 1989–January 1990): 38–41.

Minujin, Marta (1943–)

Born in Buenos Aires, Argentina, the intermedia artist Marta Minujin studied at the Escuela Nacional de Bellas Artes in her native city (1953–1959); at the Escuela Superior de Bellas Artes, Buenos Aires (1960–1962); and did postgraduate study in Paris, France, as a result of a French Embassy scholarship (1962).

Minujin has held solo exhibitions in museums, galleries, and other sites, including the Bianchini Gallery (1966); Howard Wise Gallery (1968); the Center for Inter-American Relations (1968)—all in New York City; and others. A New York City resident between 1965 and 1969 and again between 1970 and 1974, Minujin showed her work in group shows, such as the "Art of Latin America since Independence," Yale University, New Haven, Connecticut, and the University of Texas

at Austin (1966). Her "Happenings," for which she became well-known in New York City, embraced "Three Country Happenings" with Allan Kaprow and Wolf Vostell (1966); "Minuphone," Howard Wise Gallery, New York City (1967); "Golden Gate Park Happening," San Francisco, California (1969); and others.

Winner of honors and awards, Minujin received the first national prize from the di Tella Institute, Buenos Aires (1964); a Guggenheim Foundation fellowship two years later; a grant from the Center for Inter-American Relations (1968); and others. Examples of her work are in collections, including the Chase National Bank and the United Nations, New York City.

Bibliography

Collier, Barnard L. "Aperture Happenings." *The New York Times* (October 29, 1966).
Davis, Douglas. *Art and the Future*. Praeger, 1973.
The Latin American Spirit: Art and Artists in the United States, 1920–1970. Harry N. Abrams, 1988.

Miss, Mary (1944–)

Incorporating sculpture, engineering, landscape design, and archaeology into her architectural structures, Mary Miss explores space and its fundamental impact on people. Her interest in buildings, ranging from the classical to the primitive, generates a rich resource base from which to draw when presenting her recurrent themes of passages and boundaries. Doors, walls, partitions, towers, tunnels, and enclosures all elicit responses from the viewer as he or she interacts with the structure and the space which surrounds and permeates it.

Although born in New York, Miss grew up in the West. In 1966 she received her Bachelor of Arts degree from the University of California, Santa Barbara, and later her Master of Fine Arts degree from the Maryland Art Institute in Baltimore (1968). Highly successful, Miss has received commissions for permanent installations in Arizona, California, Colorado, Connecticut, Illinois, Missouri, Massachusetts, Ohio, and Washington, D.C., as well as purchases by the Hague, the Netherlands; the La Jolla Museum of Contemporary Art, and the Los Angeles County Museum of Art—both in California; the Dallas Museum of Fine Arts, Texas; and the Museum of Modern Art (MoMA), and the Guggenheim Museum—both in New York City.

Miss's earliest work focuses on changing perceptions as common building materials are subjected to close observation, as in "Bent Pipe" (1967) and "Awning" (1966). This study of ordinary objects evolved into the questioning of the space they occupy.

In the early 1970s Miss installed a number of temporary environmental sculptures. She was one of a group of artists working in public sculpture whose structures were determined by the site and not simply placing predetermined designs in an outdoor space. An untitled wood structure consisting of five forms made from planks of wood was placed on a lower-Manhattan landfill in 1973. Each form contained a cut-out circle which gradually descended from the top of the first structure into the ground of the last, creating for the viewer what critic Lucy Lippard noted as a telescopic experience.

In 1977 Miss constructed "Perimeters/Pavilions/Decoys" at the Nassau County Museum of Fine Arts in Roslyn, Long Island, New York—a complex of five structures spread over four acres and three levels of land. By placing her pieces outdoors and stretching them across large areas Miss avoids overpowering monolithic structures and is able to create more personal forms by encouraging the viewer to interact with the work on an intimate level as they walk in and around it.

Later work by Miss involves the exploration of two-dimensional problems. "Folding Screen," "Door Mask," and "Wallpiece"—all done in 1984—employ a variety of patterns and textures to question the function of form and its relationship to the decorative.

In 1988 Miss, in collaboration with architect Stanton Eckstut and landscape architect Susan Child, completed a successful urban landscape project on a two-and-a-half-acre site along the Hudson River at the end of the riverfront esplanade in Battery Park City. Paths in the form of a circular jetty lead out onto the water, while a pair of metal staircases curve upward toward a steel lookout tower. This latest project by Miss continues to explore multiple levels, effectively layering space and perspectives. Perception is altered as structures and space form endless relationships.

Christine L. Wilson

Bibliography

Anderson, Laurie. "Mary Miss." *Artforum* 12 (November 1973): 64–65.

Berman, Avis. "Space Exploration." *Art News* 88 (November 1989): 130–35.

Lippard, Lucy R. "Mary Miss: An Extremely Clear Situation." *Art in America* 62 (March 1974): 76–77.

Onorato, Ronald J. "Illusive Spaces: The Art of Mary Miss." *Artforum* 17 (December 1978): 28–33.

Mitchell, Janet (1915–)

Born in Medicine Hat, Alberta, Canada, the painter of inner and outer landscapes, Janet Mitchell won a scholarship for study at the Banff School of Fine Arts, Alberta, Canada, after part-time attendance at the Institute of Technology and Art (1942). Primarily a self-taught painter, Mitchell enrolled in a summer seminar offered by Gordon Smith at the Banff School (1959), and attended a seminar at the University of Saskatchewan two years later.

Mitchell has held many solo exhibitions in museums and galleries, including the Robertson Galleries, Ottawa (1956, 1959); Calgary Allied Arts Centre, Alberta (1963); Canadian Art Galleries, Calgary (1964); Jacox Galleries, Edmonton (1965); Bonli Gallery, Toronto (1967); and others. She is a member of the Alberta Society of Artists and the Canadian Society of Painters in Water Colour, and her work has been included in their group exhibitions, as well as many others.

Examples of Mitchell's work are in private and public permanent collections in Canada, including the National Gallery of Canada, Ottawa; Calgary Allied Arts Centre; University of Calgary; Willistead Art Gallery, Windsor, Ontario; and many others.

Bibliography

Cochran, Bente R. "The Alberta Visual Arts Scene." *Visual Arts Newsletter* 3:1 (Winter 1981): 3–15.

Oko, Andrew J. *Janet Mitchell*. A Catalog. Calgary, Alberta: Glenbow-Alberta Institute, 1977.

Mitchell, Joan (1926–1992)

Joan Mitchell was one of the most important and independent painters associated with the second generation of abstract expressionists. Although she established her personal style and reputation in the context of the New York School of the 1950s, she subsequently moved to France and spent most of the remainder of her career there. Thus removed from the shifting trends of the New York art scene, her work evolved in a distinctively slow and consistent manner. This resulted in a decline in her reputation during the 1960s—a period of sharp reactions against the expressive styles of abstract painting of her generation. Recognition of her work subsequently reemerged, however, and included one-woman shows at major museums, notably the Whitney Museum of American Art, New York City (1974), and the Musée d'Art Moderne in Paris, France (1982), and a retrospective exhibition that travelled to five United States cities in 1988–1989.

A native of Chicago, Illinois, Mitchell was born into a wealthy family, and her interest in art was encouraged from an early age. Her mother was a poet who invited such guests as Thornton Wilder and T.S. Eliot to the Mitchell home, and her father was a cultivated doctor who took his daughter on sketching trips in the countryside. The rich collections of French painting at the Chicago Art Institute became a focal point of Mitchell's childhood, from early visits with her parents to regular Saturday classes. After spending two somewhat unsettled years as an English major at Smith College, Northampton, Massachusetts, Mitchell returned to Chicago in 1944 and entered the School of the Art Institute, where she earned a Bachelor of Fine Arts degree in 1947. She then moved to New York for several months, where she had her first extensive exposure to the works of the abstract expressionists, and attended one of Hans Hofmann's painting classes, before departing for Paris, France, on a travel fellowship. Her stay in France (1948–1949) was a difficult but decisive point in her career. By the time she received her Master of Fine Arts degree from the School of the Art Institute of Chicago, Illinois, in 1950, she had abandoned figural representation in her work and returned to New York.

Following a brief marriage to Barney Rossett, a high school friend and founder of the Grove Press, Mitchell settled into a studio on St. Mark's Place in lower Manhattan. She was becoming increasingly involved with the group of young abstract painters who frequented the Cedar Tavern and exchanged ideas at meetings of The Club. A visit to Franz Kline's studio in 1950 made a strong impression, and she developed a keen interest in the paintings of Arshile Gorky and Willem de Kooning. Her own work achieved recognition in 1951, when she was invited by the charter members of The Club and the dealer, Leo Castelli, to show in their important "Ninth Street Show." She had her first one-woman show in New York City that same year at the New Gallery, and she continued to show regularly in New York for the rest of the decade. This was a period of considerable success for the young artist. Her works began to sell, and she received serious critical recognition. Her painting evolved from the strong early influence of Gorky and de Kooning to a more distinctly personal style by 1957, when she was included in the Jewish Museum's important exhibition, "Artists of the New York School: The Second Generation." By the later 1950s Mitchell's large canvases with their characteristic webs of slashing strokes on whitish grounds had developed a maturity of rich color and sweeping breadth.

In 1955 Mitchell returned to France for the summer and met the Canadian painter Jean-Paul Riopelle, who would become her companion for the next twenty-five years. After dividing her time between Paris, France, and New York City for several years, she moved to Paris in 1959. In 1968 she purchased a house at Vétheuil—a small village west of Paris—adjacent to the house where Claude Monet had lived and painted from 1978 to 1981. Once settled into the relative seclusion of Vétheuil, Mitchell was able to surround herself more fully with the natural landscape which had been a central source of inspiration throughout her career.

Although her work had been consistently non-representational since the early 1950s, nature had remained a persistent focal point of Mitchell's art. The desire to evoke—through color and form—memories of specific feelings experienced before nature, was an overriding concern of her painting. Her titles often allude to aspects of landscape such as lakes, rivers, beaches, and fields, but her slashing strokes of vivid color are concerned with memory and emotion rather than description. The basic elements of her style remained relatively consistent, and true to her abstract expressionist roots: large canvases, often expanded into vast, multi-paneled compositions; and thickly oil-painted surfaces in which intense, sweeping gestures are stabilized by a delicately calculated organization. Within this general framework Mitchell's work evolved from hectic linearity through dense color areas to explosive luminosity. Over a period of four decades her art came to represent one of the most fully developed and richly personal extensions of abstract expressionism.

Dennis Costanzo

Bibliography

Bernstock, Judith E. *Joan Mitchell*. Hudson Hills, 1988.

Gaugh, Harry. "Dark Victories." *Art News* 87 (Summer 1988): 154–59.

Joan Mitchell: Choix de peintures 1970–1982. Paris: Musée d'Art Moderne de la Ville, 1982.

Munro, Eleanor. *Originals: American Women Artists*. Simon and Schuster, 1979, pp. 233–47.

Nemser, Cindy. "An Afternoon with Joan Mitchell." *The Feminist Art Journal* 3 (Spring 1974): 5–6, 24.

Sandler, Irving. "Mitchell Paints a Picture." *Art News* (October 1957): 44–47, 69–70.

Tucker, Marcia. *Joan Mitchell*. New York: Whitney Museum of American Art, 1974.

Model, Lisette (1906–1983)

Lisette Model's photography is a passionate social comment with subjects pressing to the edge of the frame, seemingly jutting out of the picture. A stark, tightly-cropped and massive image is her signature. Working in small- and medium-format, her disorderly, unbalanced, and sometimes blurred, documentary style, becomes a grotesque and eccentric reality.

Born in Austria, Model was raised in a wealthy Viennese family. Educated by a private tutor, she studied with avant-garde composer Arnold Schoenberg from an early age, in the hope of pursuing a professional musical career.

Studying art in Paris, France, in the 1930s, Model stumbled into the beginnings of her life as a photographer while searching for an income in the face of hardships of the impending war. She first developed darkroom skills as her trade, and practiced taking photographs of people she encountered on the streets of Paris. With husband and artist Evsa Model, she came to New York for a brief visit in 1937. She stayed for the rest of her life.

Model sought employment as a darkroom technician with *P.M.*, a New York newspaper. On seeing her work, the editor Ralph Steiner published the vital, spirited, gritty, and bizarre "Promenade des Anglais" images shot on the pre-war French Riviera. This led to a staff position at *Harper's Bazaar* and exposure in art galleries and museums.

Model taught photography at the San Francisco Institute of Fine Arts, California, and was encouraged, in 1950, by friend and fellow photographer Berenice Abbott to become an instructor at the New School for Social Research in New York City. She maintained this educational post until her death.

The impact of Model's raw and strident portraiture was at its height in the 1950s. Renowned as an artist, Model had an equally strong influence as a teacher. One of her more famous students, who also became a close friend, was Diane Arbus.

There is a similarity in intent between both photographers. But whereas Arbus selected the strange and made it stranger, Model often took ordinary folk from everyday encounters and captured a startling oddness in their commonplace presence.

Kiana Dicker

Bibliography

Abbott, Berenice. *Lisette Model*. 1979.

Greene, Jonathan. *The Snapshot*. 1974.

"Lisette Model." *Center for Creative Photography Bulletin* (May 1977).

Newhall, Beaumont. *The History of Photography from 1839 to the Present Day*. 1964.

White, Nancy. *Hundred Years of the American Female*. 1967.

Modotti, Tina (1896–1942)

Photographer and political activist Tina Modotti was born in Udine, Italy, on August 16, 1896; immigrated to and became a citizen of the United States; and produced her most significant artistic work in Mexico, where she died—after a decade of exile and political activity in Europe—at the age of forty-six.

Modotti was the daughter of working-class parents with socialist leanings. As a teenager she worked in an Italian silk mill before emigrating in 1913 to join other members of her family who already had settled in California. There she again found work in the textile industry—first in a factory in San Francisco and later in a dressmaking establishment. She had some talent for acting and began participating in amateur theater.

In 1917 Modotti married a young poet and painter of French-Canadian origin, Robaix de l'Abrie ("Robo") Richey. They moved to Los Angeles, California, where the strikingly beautiful Modotti began a career in Hollywood as a minor actress in silent films. Along with her husband she became part of a group of artists and intellectuals (among them, the photographer Edward Weston) who had an avid interest in Mexico, which was then experiencing a surge of cultural activity following the Revolution of 1910.

Modotti made her first trip to Mexico in 1922 to join her husband, who had preceded her there; he died of smallpox before she arrived, however, and she stayed only long enough to deal with matters surrounding his death. Modotti returned to Mexico in 1923 with Edward Weston. They made their way to Mexico City, where they began to move in a circle of painters, writers, and other artists, including the muralists Diego Rivera, Jean Charlot, José Clemente Orozco, and David Alfaro Siqueiros.

Modotti had by this time begun working in photography. Like Weston, she used a large-format, heavy Graflex camera. When Weston returned to the United States in 1926, Modotti remained in Mexico. She made a living through commissioned work—photographing the murals of Rivera and Orozco, for example, or later, with Weston, illustrating Anita Brenner's book about Mexico, *Idols Behind Altars* (Boston, 1929). Her own preferred subjects, however, were women and children, workers, and carefully composed arrangements of symbols of revolutions: a bandolier, a sickle, ears of corn, a guitar. In 1927 she became a member of the Mexican communist party.

Her photographs, which displayed a strong graphic sensibility, began to be published in Mexico and abroad—in *El Machete* (the paper of the communist party); the United States journal, *Creative Art*, and the review, *Mexican Folkways*; the Belgian journal, *Variétés*; the British *Journal of Photography*, and the *Agfa Papers* (Prague, Czechoslovakia). Her photos also illustrated volumes of poetry of the *estridentista* movement. (*Estridentismo*, similar to the constructivist and futurist movements in Europe, celebrated technology, industrialization, and the urban environment, as well as revolution.)

A major exhibition of Modotti's work was held at the Biblioteca Nacional in Mexico in 1929. That same year she introduced a young Mexican photographer named Manuel Alvarez Bravo, with whom she had become acquainted a couple of years earlier and whose photographs she found promising, to Edward Weston, Diego Rivera, and other influential figures in the art world. In this way she played a key role in the career of Alvarez Bravo, who was to emerge as Mexico's first internationally recognized master of photography.

Regarding her own photography Modotti remarked that she did not like the terms "art" or "artistic" to be applied to it (interview, *Mexican Folkways* 5:4, 1929). She wanted to produce "not art, but honest photographs" that accepted the limitations and exploited the possibilities unique to that medium, and she was critical of photography that tried to imitate painting or other art forms.

It was also in 1929 that Modotti's companion, Julio Antonio Mella, founder of the Cuban communist party, was assassinated; Modotti was at his side when he was shot. The event marked the beginning of a new period in Modotti's life—one in which her commitment to antifascist activity became stronger. It also marked the beginning of her political persecution in Mexico: she was suspected of participating in Mella's assassination and then, in 1930, accused of conspiring against the new Mexican president, Pascual Ortiz Rubio. She was arrested and, when she refused to give up her political activities, she was expelled from Mexico and denied reentry into the United States. Given only two or three days to leave the country, Modotti took few possessions with her. She gave her camera to Manuel Alvarez Bravo, who was the only person who saw her to her train when she departed Mexico City. Her political views also made it dangerous for her to return to Mussolini's Italy; she went instead to Germany. In Berlin Modotti experienced a creative conflict between the type of deliberate, large-format photography she had practiced and the new trend toward journalistic photography, using the smaller 35-mm. Leica camera. Finally she gave up photography altogether for eight years, dedicating herself exclusively to political and humanitarian work in Europe in the period leading up to World War II. She worked for International Red Aid in Moscow, Poland, France, and particularly in Spain during the Civil War. Under the name of "comrade Maria," she served as director of International Red Aid in Spain, procuring medical aid and other relief for the Republican forces.

After the defeat of the Republicans in 1939, Modotti finally returned to Mexico, this time in the company of the Italian communist Vittorio Vidali, with whom she had worked and lived in Europe since 1932. In Mexico City Modotti and Vidali subsisted on the meager incomes they earned through her work as a translator and his as a journalist. Her interest in photography was rekindled when a friend, Constantina de la Mora, asked her to collaborate on a book about regional art in Mexico. They began planning and researching the project. Perhaps due to the hardships Modotti had undergone in Europe, her health began failiing. She died of a heart attack in Mexico City on January 6, 1942, and was buried there in the Pantheon of Dolores. Pablo Neruda, who had known her in Spain, commemorated her life in the Poem "Tina Modotti ha muerto."

Martha Davidson

Bibliography

Barckhausen, Christiane. *Auf den Spuren von Tina Modotti*. Pahl-Rugenstein, 1988.

Caronia, Maria, and Vittorio Vidali. *Tina Modotti: Photographs*. Idea Editions & Belmark Book Company, 1981.

Modotti, Tina. "Sobre la fotografía/On Photography." *Mexican Folkways* 5 (October–December 1929).

Neruda, Pablo, and Vittorio Vidali. *Tina Modotti*. Rome: Galleria l'Obelisco, 1978.

Vidali, Vittorio. *Ritratto di Donna: Tina Modotti*. Milan: Vangelista, 1982.

Whitechapel Art Gallery. *Frida Kahlo and Tina Modotti*. London: Whitechapel Art Gallery, 1982.

Mondragón, Carmen (d. 1978)

Although we do not know the date of her birth, the artist Carmen Mondragón spent the majority of her life in Mexico, and died in Tacubaya in 1978. The daughter of General Manuel Mondragón, she married the painter Manuel Rodríguez Lozano in 1913 and travelled with him to Europe where she met Diego Rivera, Roberto Montenegro, and other artists.

Mondragón returned to Mexico in 1920 and established a torrid relationship with Dr. Atl (Gerardo Murillo), which he noted in his diary in red ink and capital letters, under the date of July 27, 1921. Atl named his lover *Nahui Ollin* which, in Náhuatl, means "The Mistress of the Universe"—one who has the power to move the sun and radically alter the solar system. At the termination of her affair with Atl, Mondragón undertook another stormy romance with the painter Matías Santoyo.

Rivera painted her portrait in "La creación," an encaustic mural he executed in the Escuela Nacional Preparatoria. Jean Charlot also used her as a model. Mondragón published several books of poetry, including: *Calinemel*; *Energía cósmica*; *Dix ans sur mon pupitre* (1924); and *Optica cerebral* (1922), about which an unidentified critic wrote the following, "The apocalyptic visions herein reveal a powerful personality, audacious and without literary prejudice. It is the product of an exquisite sensibility. *Optica cerebral* is the work of a very young and marvelously beautiful woman."

There is proof that Mondragón played the piano and composed music. As a painter she worked on unprepared board in a *naive* style, on an intensely-colored background. She painted folkloric scenes of daily life, fruit sellers, christening parties, popular festivals with fireworks, landscapes, and cats—plus many self-portraits associated with the men who loved her.

Toward middle life Mondragón removed herself from her circle of admirers and isolated herself in her home in Tacubaya. Posthumously she inspired a dramatic work, *Nahui Ollin*, written by Emilio Carballido.

Bibliography

Alvarez, José Rogelio, et al. *Enciclopedia de México*. Secretaría de Educación Pública, 1987.

Lourdes, Andrade, and Tomás Surian. "Nahui Ollin, Musa de Pintores y Poetas." *México en el arte* 10 (1985).

Mones, Carmen (1926–)

Born in Mérida, Yucatan, Carmen Mones studied the plastic arts in general and printmaking in particular at the Universidad Iberoamericana. Her work has been seen in many group shows since 1967. The critic Jorge Juan Crespo de la Serna noted that "her etchings of nudes and landscapes were excellent."

Bibliography

Alvarez, José Rogelio, et al. *Enciclopedia de México*. Secretaría de Educación Pública, 1987.

Montano, Linda (1942–)

Born in Kingston, New York, the performance artist Linda Montano earned a Bachelor's degree from the College of New Rochelle, New York (1965); received a Master's degree from the Villa Schifanoia, Florence, Italy (1966); and, three years later, earned a Master of Fine Arts degree from the University of Wisconsin, Madison.

In the 1970s Montano gave her wry performances in the streets of San Francisco, California; the unforeseen death of her ex-husband in 1978 prompted her to create several performances and a video tape to explore feelings in the innermost recesses of her life and art. In addition to many performances given on the West Coast, from Seattle, Washington, to San Diego, California, Montano screened "Mitchell's Death" at the Museum of Modern Art (MoMA), New York City (1981); "Presentation of One Year Performance," at the Fleming Museum, Burlington, Vermont (1984); and many others. Winner of awards and honors, Montano was a recipient of a National Endowment for the Arts (NEA) fellowship ((1977); a collaboration grant from the Women's Studio Workshop (1983); and others. Examples of her work can be found in private and public permanent collections.

Bibliography

Burnham, Linda. "Review." *Artforum* 22 (October 1983): 75.

Johnson, Jill. "Hardship Art." *Art in America* 72 (September 1984): 176.

Shank, Theodore. "Mitchell's Death." *Drama Review* 23 (March 1979).

Montgomery, Evangeline J. (1933–)

A native New Yorker, the African-American sculptor Evangeline J. ("E.J.") Montgomery studied at California State University, Los Angeles (1958–1962) and earned a Bachelor of Fine Arts degree from the California College of Arts and Crafts, Oakland (1969).

Montgomery's work has been in solo and group exhibitions in museums and galleries, including Southern Illinois University, Carbondale (1972); Bowie State College, Maryland (1973); Berkeley Art Center, California (1974); "African-American Crafts," Brookmen Gallery, Memphis, Tennessee (1979); and others. Using natural and/or cast-off human materials or objects, Montgomery creates expressive jewelry and sculpture to fulfill inner, spiritual needs.

Winner of awards and honors, Montgomery has been an officer in several arts organizations and was special consultant to the Oakland Art Museum, California. Her work is represented in private and public permanent collections, such as the National Center of Afro-American Artists, Boston, Massachusetts; Oakland Art Museum, California; Rainbow Sign Gallery, Berkeley, California; Southern Illinois University, Carbondale; and others.

Bibliography

Cederholm, Theresa. *Afro-American Artists; A Bio-Bibliographical Directory*. Boston Public Library, 1973.

Hedgepeth, Chester M. *Twentieth-Century African-American Writers and Artists*. Chicago: American Library Association, 1991.

Lewis, Samella. *Art: African American*. Harcourt Brace Jovanovich, 1978.

Montoya, Geronima Cruz (Potsunu) (1915–)

Geronima Cruz Montoya has established a reputation as both artist and teacher of art. She was born September 22, 1915, to Pablo Cruz and Crucita Trujillo, both of San Juan Pueblo, New Mexico. One of the Rio Grande Pueblos in northern New Mexico, San Juan Pueblo is the home of Tewa-speaking people, and, four days after her birth, Cruz was given her Tewa name, *Potsunu*, meaning "shell." It was this name that Cruz later chose to use as her professional name when signing her work.

Cruz was exposed to art early through the traditional arts of her village—textiles, pottery, ceremonial items—and particularly through her mother's award-winning pottery, which was shown in the Nationwide Pottery Exposition in Syracuse, New York (1941). As a girl Cruz joined her sisters taking pottery to the nearby highway to sell to tourists.

After early schooling at the government day school in San Juan Pueblo, Cruz was transferred to the Santa Fe Indian School, and there she studied art under Dorothy Dunn. In 1932 Dunn had created the art program at the school, and soon the program achieved renown as the Studio. Believed to be the first official art department in Indian School history, the goal of the Studio was to help students to "maintain and develop their own art" by encouraging them to draw on their own rich artistic heritage while applying themselves to the Anglo-European-introduced art form of easel painting. The result, said Dunn, would be "a very valuable contribution to art in general." Works from the Studio were regularly exhibited in Santa Fe and beyond, and many of the students went on to full-time careers in art.

After earning the Henry Dendahl award for outstanding student, Cruz graduated from Santa Fe Indian School (1935) and was then appointed as Dunn's assistant to teach art to the younger classes at the

Studio. When Dunn left the Studio in 1937 Cruz was made the head of the program—a position she continued to hold until the Studio's dissolution in 1962. In 1939 she married Juan A. Montoya. Of their three sons, Robert (1947–) and Paul (1950–) have followed artistic careers as painters.

Working with assistant teachers who were fellow Native American artists (including, at different times, José Rey Toledo of Jemez Pueblo and Vicenti Mirabal of Taos Pueblo), Cruz carried on the principles and goals that Dunn had set in founding the Studio. "The main thing was to encourage the Indian students to carry on their traditions," she says, "—to know what is the beauty in the Indian world and to bring it out in painting." Among her many students who went on to become well-known artists in their own right were Jimmy Toddy (*Beatien Yazz*) (Navajo); Ignatius Palmer (Apache); Joe Herrera, Theodore Suina, and Ben Quintana (all of Cochiti Pueblo); and Popovi Da and Gilbert Atencio (both of San Ildefonso Pueblo). In 1940, while still a student of hers, Ben Quintana won first prize over 50,000 other contestants for a painting entered in the National Youth Contest sponsored by *American Magazine*. Many of Cruz's students-turned-professional artists credit her teaching as having been a critical point of encouragement and guidance.

While teaching at Santa Fe Indian School Cruz attended classes in art and education at the University of New Mexico, Albuquerque, where she studied under Kenneth Chapman (of the Laboratory of Anthropology in Santa Fe). She graduated with a Bachelor of Science degree from St. Joseph's in 1958.

In 1959 Cruz had her first solo show, at the Museum of New Mexico, Albuquerque. Other solo shows were held at the Philbrook Art Center, Tulsa, Oklahoma; the Yonemoto Art Gallery, Albuquerque, New Mexico; and in Nuremberg, Germany. She was a regular participant in group shows and in annual juried exhibitions of Indian art, winning prizes at several. Her work is in the permanent collections of the M.H. De Young Memorial Museum, San Francisco; the Museum of the American Indian, Heye Foundation, New York City; the Museum of New Mexico, Albuquerque; and the Millicent Rogers Museum, Taos, New Mexico; among others.

Cruz has painted in tempera, gouache, casein and dry brush, as well as making occasional block prints. Inspired by the Pueblo world, "music, scenery, [ceremonial] dances," she says, Cruz's work ranges from representational figures to abstractions. One particular source for these has been the pictographs and petroglyphs—ancient rock art created by her Pueblo ancestors—found near San Juan Pueblo.

After leaving her post at Santa Fe Indian School in 1962, Cruz was hired to conduct the just-started adult education program in San Juan Pueblo. The villagers requested that she teach arts and crafts, and so she did. Then, aware that the people of San Juan needed a sales outlet for their work, Cruz began to formulate plans for an artists' cooperative, which resulted in the founding, in 1968, of the O'ke Oweenge Crafts Cooperative in San Juan. The cooperative was a success and has continued to grow over the years, with Cruz a regular participant and volunteer.

Tryntje Van Ness Seymour

Bibliography

Dunn, Dorothy. *American Indian Painting of the Southwest and Plains Areas*. University of New Mexico Press, 1968.
Seymour, Tryntje Van Ness. *When the Rainbow Touches Down*. Phoenix: The Heard Museum, 1989.
Snodgrass, Jeanne O. *American Indian Painters: A Biographical Directory*. Contributions from the Museum of the American Indian, Heye Foundation. Vol. XXI, Part 1. New York: Museum of the American Indian, Heye Foundation, 1968.
Tanner, Clara Lee. *Southwest Indian Painting: A Changing Art*. University of Arizona Press, 1973.

Moonelis, Judy (1953–)

Judy Moonelis's three-foot-tall ceramic heads of the early 1980s are in the tradition of Greek theatrical masks. Each head bears two profiles with no frontal view. The faces are aggressive—one side grimacing in anger, the other side at times calmer—both textured and lightened by lyrical color from deep, rich glazes. As artist-in-residence at the Heckscher Museum, Huntington, New York, Moonelis produced more than twenty works, shown in a solo exhibition—her fifth one-person show—at the museum in 1983.

A Jackson Heights, New York, native, Moonelis opened a studio in Manhattan after earning a Bachelor of Fine Arts degree *cum laude* at Tyler School of Art, Temple University, Philadelphia, Pennsylvania (1975) and a Master of Fine Arts degree from New York State College of Ceramics, Alfred University (1978). That same year she received the Menno Alexander Reeb Memorial award for sculpture from the Albright-Knox Art Gallery of Buffalo, New York. The National Endowment for the Arts (NEA) granted her an individual artist's fellowship in 1980. Since then Moonelis has been a guest artist or visiting artist at museums, workshops, and colleges on the East Coast and is currently an instructor of ceramics at New York University, New York City.

Around 1985 Moonelis shifted from profiles to two heads suggesting an interaction between people. This concern with relationships evolved into a series featuring two figures at times in a shared bed. Exploring the emotions of dependency and caring for another person, Moonelis uses parts of figures, fragments in a flattened style that is a continuation of her earlier profiles. But unlike their nightmarish tone there is a suggestion of healing in the way the partners recline, embrace, or cradle one another.

Elaine Levin

Bibliography

Goldberg, Beth. "Fragments that Express a Whole." *Artweek* (November 19, 1988): 7.
Porges, M.F. "Exhibitions: Judy Moonelis." *American Ceramics* 7:2 (Summer 1989): 47.
Preston, Malcolm. "Art Review/Gold Sculpture at the Heckscher." *Newsday*, part 11 (April 19, 1983): 22.
Wechsler, Susan. *Low Fire Ceramics*. Watson-Guptill, 1981.

Moraga, Eva Laura (1946–)

Born in Monterrey, Nuevo León, Mexico, Eva Laura Moraga studied printmaking at la Escuela de Pintura y Escultura (La Esmeralda); painting at the Casa del Lago; and letterpress printing at the Molino de Santo Domingo. In particular she worked under the tutelage of José Lascarro, Mariano Paredes, and Nunik Sauret.

In 1970 Moraga first showed her work at the School of the Ballet Folklorico de Mexico and, from that time, has exhibited in twenty-five group and twenty solo shows. Her exhibition in the Casa de la Cultura de Hermosilla,

Sonora (1986), consisted of twenty-four watercolors all titled "Alegorías." Her most recent show of thirty-two oils and watercolors took place (1990) in the Galería of the Casa de la Cultura in the city of Aguascalientes. She is especially noted for the sensitive color in her oils and acrylic paintings.

The artist and art critic Alfredo Zalce noted that, "Her exhibition impressed me by its high level of technique expressed with brilliance and force."

Bibliography
Alvarez, José Rogelio, et al. *Enciclopedia de México*. Secretaría de Educación Pública, 1987.
Escenarios: Exposición de Eva Laura Alvarez. Exhibition Catalog. Galería de la Ciudad de la Casa de Cultura de Aguascalientes, Mexico.

Morath, Inge (1923–)
Born in Graz, Austria, the photographer Inge Morath earned a Bachelor's degree from the University of Berlin, Germany, and was awarded an honorary Doctorate of Fine Arts degree from the University of Hartford, Connecticut, in 1984.

Translator, editor, and free-lance writer for magazines—Morath has held many solo exhibitions of her extraordinary photographs in the United States and abroad, including the Wuehrle Gallery, Vienna, Austria (1956); Leitz Gallery, New York City (1958); Art Institute of Chicago, Illinois (1964); Oliver Woolcott Memorial Library, Litchfield, Connecticut (1969); University of Miami, Florida (1972); Museum of Modern Art, Vienna, Austria (1980); Kunsthaus, Zurich, Switzerland (1980); Sala del Canal, Madrid, Spain (1988); American Cultural Center, Brussels, Belgium (1989); Museum Rupertinum, Salzburg, Austria (1991); "Russian Journey," Nathan Berman Gallery, New York City (1992); "Inge Morath," a retrospective exhibition, Neue Galerie Museum, Linz, Austria (1992); and others. Her work has been invited to myriad major group exhibitions of photography throughout the world, such as "Photokina," in Cologne, Germany, and the World's Fair, Montréal, Québec, Canada.

Long associated with Magnum Photos, Paris, France, and New York City (since 1952), Morath has been the photographer of record for sixteen books authored by a diverse group, including Mary McCarthy, Yul Brynner, Boris Pasternak, Arthur Miller, and others. She has contributed photographs to magazines and anthologies of photography in Europe, the United States, South America, and Japan; and has been the recipient of many prizes and honors, such as the "Great Austrian State Prize for Photography," Vienna (1992).

Morath's work is represented in private, public, and corporate permanent collections, including the Metropolitan Museum of Art, New York City; Boston Museum of Art, Massachusetts; Art Institute of Chicago, Illinois; Bibliothèque Nationale, Paris, France; Kunsthaus, Zurich, Switzerland; the Prague Art Museum, Czechoslovakia; and many others.

Bibliography
Browne, Turner, and Elaine Partnow. *Macmillan Biographical Encyclopedia of Photographic Artists and Innovators*. Macmillan, 1983.
Carlisle, Olga. *Inge Morath*. Bucher Verlag, 1975.
Copyright: Inge Morath. A Film. Berlin Film Festival, 1992.
Morath, Inge, and Arthur Miller. *Chinese Encounters*. Farrar, Straus, Giroux, 1979.
Who's Who in American Art. 19th ed. R.R. Bowker Co., 1991–1992.

Morez, Mary (1940–)
Born on the Navajo reservation in Tuba City, Arizona, Mary Morez was reared by her grandparents in the traditions and beliefs of the Navajo until she was five years old. She received her Bachelor's degree from the University of Arizona, Tucson, and won a scholarship to the Ray Vogue Art School, Chicago, Illinois, to study fashion illustration. Morez suggests that she has been going to school all of her life: she has studied anthropology, psychology, philosophy, and photography—to name just a few of the areas that have attracted her interest.

Not unlike many artists whose careers began in commercial art, Morez opted to devote her talents to full-time painting in 1969. "The Fall" (1977), is typical of her early work: a mixed-media painting, it weds Navajo symbols, dreams, and Anglo culture in a two-dimensional, vividly colored effort.

"The Weaver's Yei" (1977), an oil painting, re-presents Morez's female goddess in symbolic form, a goddess for all seasons and moods. Morez writes, " I paint my impressions of Navajo spiritual beings. It's a way of getting closer to the unseen . . . I relive my dreams in my paintings. I can visit many places in my dreams."

Bibliography
This Song Remembers: Self-Portraits of Native Americans in the Arts. Ed. Jane B. Katz. Houghton Mifflin, 1980.

Morgan, Barbara (1900–)
Born and raised in California, the photographer Barbara Morgan is best known for her photomontages and photographs of modern dance, she began her career as a painter. Morgan became an art major in 1919 at the University of California. Always interested in continuous movement, she studied with the dance teacher Bertha Wardell in order to learn more about movement and the sense of living energy.

Morgan became fascinated with the meditative methods of Japanese painters and the empathy of subject and artist.

In 1925 she became a member of the art faculty at the University of California at Los Angeles (UCLA) teaching basic design, landscape painting, and woodcut. During this time she married free-lance writer and photographer Willard Morgan, who would later help to influence her interest in photography.

Morgan and her husband travelled extensively throughout the Southwest, where she became acquainted with Native American dance rituals. She was captivated by the spirituality of the rhythm and the idea of intrinsic visual movement and vitality that was exhibited. In 1930 Morgan and her husband moved to New York City. She established a studio for painting and lithography and exhibited graphics at Weyhe Gallery, New York City, in 1931. In 1932 her first son was born, and, in 1934, she had her first solo show at Mellon Gallery in Philadelphia, Pennsylvania. She continued to paint, and in 1935, when her second son was born, Morgan realized she had less time to paint—an activity that requires total absorption.

Morgan's husband had always encouraged her to create and express herself through photography. This idea was further enhanced by her previous experience and admiration of Edward Weston, whom she had met at UCLA in 1925 when helping to mount his show. Morgan delved into the medium and became a serious photographer, capturing New York and its visual excitement, rhythm, and movement through photomontage. Her purpose in photography was not to produce the obvious, but to use her creative imagination.

In 1935 Morgan attended a performance of the Martha Graham dance company. Morgan again became aware of the dance that connected to the spiritual beauty and motion of the Southwest Native American dance rituals which also had inspired Graham in her modern choreography. Morgan admired Graham's artistic sense of dance and interpretation of visual gesture. She worked together with Graham on a photography book based on Graham's modern dance. Published in 1941 and entitled *Martha Graham: Sixteen Dances in Photographs*, it embodies the camera's image of intrinsic motion, Morgan's previsualization of each gesture and movement that the individual dancer makes.

In 1951 Morgan's second book was published, *Summer's Children: A Photographer's Cycle of Life at Camp*, a pictorial essay of her love of children and creative spirit. The year 1961 brought Morgan a solo exhibition at Sherman Gallery and in 1967 her husband Willard died. Morgan worked as an unofficial consultant for her husband's publishing activities, and it was Morgan and Morgan that produced her book, *Barbara Morgan: Monograph* (1972). She was elected a fellow of the Philadelphia Museum of Art, Pennsylvania (1970), and received a grant from the National Endowment for the Arts (NEA) (1975). That same year she participated in "Women of Photography: An Historical Survey" exhibition at the San Francisco Museum of Art, California.

Morgan received an honorary Doctorate of Fine Arts degree from Marquette University, Milwaukee, Wisconsin, in 1978. Her contributions to publications are included in *Aperature, Dance Magazine, Image*, and *Magazine of Art*.

Karen E. Speirs

Bibliography
Beaton, Cecil, and Gail Buckland. *The Magic Image*. Little, Brown and Company, 1975.
Mitchell, Margaretta K. *Recollections: Ten Women of Photography*. Viking Press, 1979.
Szarkowski, John. *Looking at Photographs*. New York Graphic Society, 1973.
Tucker, Anne. *The Woman's Eye*. Alfred A. Knopf, 1973.

Morgan, Judith P.

Kitwanga artist Judith P. Morgan had the good fortune to attend the Alberni Indian Residential School in Canada, where she came under the influence of George Sinclair, who encouraged and promoted her painting. Morgan won a two-year scholarship to Cottey College, Nevada, Missouri, married Willis O. Fitzpatrick in 1953, mothered five children, and returned to the University of Kansas, Lawrence, to complete her Bachelor's degree in art education (1976).

Morgan began exhibiting her work in the mid-1940s; she held solo shows of her work at the National Museum, Ottawa, Canada, which travelled across the country (1949–1950); Museum of Northern British Columbia, Prince Rupert (1986); the Kitimat Centennial Museum, British Columbia (1987); Northwestern National Exhibition Centre (1987, 1990), and the 'Ksan Gallery, Hazelton, British Columbia (1987); Artropolis 90, Vancouver, British Columbia 1990; and many others in Canada and the United States.

Morgan has won many awards, including a first prize at the Pacific National Exhibition, Vancouver, British Columbia (1947); and another first prize at the Arts and Crafts Society Exhibition, Victoria,

British Columbia (1948). The provincial government purchased five of her early paintings for the Archives in Victoria, British Columbia in 1949. These works, based upon Morgan's experiences, have been loaned and exhibited widely.

Bibliography
Anonymous. "Indian Girl's Paintings Have Been Purchased by the British Columbia Government." *The Native Voice* 3:8 (August 1949).
Cooper, Ruth. "Centre Shows Legend Artist." *Three Rivers Report* (1987).
Hendrickson, Gwen. "Speaking of Art." *Enid Daily Eagle* (September 15, 1966).

Morgan, Mary De Neale (1868–1948)

Born in San Francisco, California, the painter/printmaker Mary De Neale Morgan studied at the San Francisco Art Institute, California, and with William Merritt Chase in New York City.

Morgan exhibited widely and her work is represented in private and public permanent collections, including the Memorial Museum (now the Los Angeles County Museum of Art); San Francisco Art Association; Stanford University; University of California at Berkeley; University of Southern California, Los Angeles—all in California; University of Texas, Austin; and many others. She was a member of the California Watercolor Society; National Association of Women Painters and Sculptors; and the Laguna Beach Art Association, California.

Bibliography
American Art Annual. Vol. 28. American Federation of Arts, 1932.
Kovinick, Phil. *The Woman Artist in the American West 1860–1960*. Muckenthaler Cultural Center, California, 1976.
A Selection of American Prints . . . . Santa Rosa, California: The Annex Galleries, 1987.

Morgan, Maud (1903–)

A native New Yorker, Maud Morgan attended Barnard College, in the city of her birth, where she received her Bachelor's degree in 1926. Three years later she studied with Kimon Nicolaides at the Art Students League, New York City, and also worked under the aegis of Hans Hofmann, off and on, between 1932 and 1940.

Morgan has held many solo exhibitions in the United States and abroad, and no less than two major retrospective exhibitions, including the Julian Levy Gallery (1938, 1940), and Betty Parsons Gallery (1948, 1952, 1957)—both in New York City; Margaret Brown Gallery, Boston, Massachusetts (1950–1955, 1957); Fitchburg Art Museum, Massachusetts (1967–1968, a retrospective); Modern Art Galerie, Vienna, Austria (1976); Wanda Batavia Gallery, Doesburg, Holland (1977); and the Addison Gallery of American Art, Andover, Massachusetts (1977, a retrospective).

Morgan has exhibited her work in two- and five-person shows with Alexander Calder; with her husband the painter Patrick Morgan at the Yale University Art Gallery, New Haven, Connecticut (1951); and with Jackson Pollack, Mark Rothko, Richard Pousette-Dart, Walter Murch, and Calvert Coggeshall at the Agnes Lefort Gallery in Montréal, Canada (1960). She has had her work selected for many group shows, including the Art Institute of Chicago, Illinois (1942); the Edinburgh Art Festival, Scotland (1974); the Goethe Institute, Boston, Massachusetts

(1973); the USIA (U.S. Information Agency) travelling show, which toured Belgium, Finland, Norway, Sweden, and Turkey (1975–1976)—and many others.

Morgan taught at Abbot Academy, Andover, Massachusetts, for five years beginning in 1943, and also at Lesley College, the Institute for the Arts and Human Development, Cambridge, Massachusetts, in 1975. She lectured and offered seminars at various institutions, including the Harvard Divinity School and Radcliffe College—both in Cambridge, Massachusetts. Her work is in many permanent public, private, and business collections, including the Addison Gallery of American Art, Andover, and the Fogg Museum of Art, Harvard University, Cambridge—both in Massachusetts; and the Museum of Modern Art (MoMA), the Metropolitan Museum of Art, and the Whitney Museum of American Art—all in New York City.

Noted for the elegant, long-fibered paper collages she has been doing most of her life as "studies" for other mediums, Morgan has also created lithographs, oils, screen prints, pastel drawings, and etchings.

Bibliography
Keyes, Norman, Jr. "Maud Morgan: A Life on Canvas." *The Boston Globe* (February 6, 1986): Calendar section.
Maud Morgan: A Retrospective Exhibition: 1927–1977. Addison Gallery of American Art, Phillips Academy, 1977.
Women's Caucus for Art Honor Awards. National Women's Caucus for Art, 1987.

Morgan, Norma (1928–)

Born in New Haven, Connecticut, and raised in New Rochelle, New York, the painter-printmaker Norma Morgan studied under Julian Levi at the Art Students League; took courses from Hans Hofmann at his School of Fine Art, and learned the art of engraving from Stanley William Hayter at Atelier 17—all in New York City. Morgan and her mother had moved to New York City from upstate, in the late 1940s.

Morgan won a scholarship to study in England and Scotland—an award that led, and keeps leading her to the moors of those countries and to her beloved rocks and water, to the ancient, wild landscape she conjures up in her prints and paintings of the Catskill Mountains, New York, the Isle of Skye, or the "Bronté country" of Arms Tor, Dartmoor.

Requiring a year or more to complete her large paintings, Morgan employs her burin on copper plates to create fanciful engravings which, because they are editioned, enjoy a wider audience and are housed in the permanent collections of museums and institutions throughout the United States and Europe, including the Library of Congress and the National Gallery of Art—both in Washington, D.C.; the Art Institute of Chicago, Illinois; Museum of Modern Art (MoMA), and the Metropolitan Museum of Art—both in New York City; the Philadelphia Museum of Art, Pennsylvania; Yale University, New Haven, Connecticut; and hosts of others.

Morgan's work has been exhibited in the Whitney Museum of American Art, New York City; the Walker Art Center, Minneapolis, Minnesota; the Victoria & Albert Museum, London, England; the Pennsylvania Academy of Fine Arts, Philadelphia; Los Angeles County Museum of Art, California; Boston Museum of Fine Arts, Massachusetts; and the Cincinnati Museum of Art, Ohio; to name a sampling of invitations.

"Ethel, Mother of the Artist" (1986), an etching, reveals a strong

woman, seated in a magical Rembrandt-lit cavern, facing outward, at ease with herself and the world. Morgan has made prints using all or most of the intaglio processes, including etching, engraving, aquatint, drypoint, and others, occasionally employing watercolor on the original print. She won the gold medal of honor for graphics from the Audubon Artists, New York, for a 1990 engraving and completed a major four-by-seven-foot acrylic painting, "Elk Lake (Adirondack Mountains)," in 1991.

Morgan divides her time between Woodstock and an apartment she shares with her mother in New York City; a loner, she is never lonely.

Bibliography
Eichenberg, Fritz. *The Art of the Print.* Harry N. Abrams, 1976.
Exler, E. "Romanticism and Printmaking." *Journal of the Print World* 13:3 (Summer 1990): 17.
Who's Who in American Art. 19th ed. R.R. Bowker Co., 1991–1992.

Morreau, Jacqueline (1929–)

Born in Los Angeles, California, the painter/printmaker Jacqueline Morreau attended art classes in her native city before she was a teenager. She also studied with Rico Lebrun—a noted California artist and teacher—at Chouinard in Los Angeles, California, and at Yale University, New Haven, Connecticut, among other institutions.

In Los Angeles Morreau turned to medical illustration to support herself; the City of Angels was a difficult place to be an artist. Married and with children, she had time, at that juncture in her life, only for drawing and some intaglio work. In the 1970s in London, England, Morreau's concern with woman as subject flowered through ideas of metaphor-made-visible and via themes from the fates, other aspects of Greek mythology, and from Adam and Eve. Her figurative paintings found support in the woman's movement and she was one of the organizers of the pioneer feminist art exhibition at the ICA, London, England (1980). In 1984, the same group organized a travelling show of women artists on the theme of "Pandora's Box." Examples of her work are represented in private and public permanent collections.

Bibliography
Dunford, Penny. *Biographical Dictionary of Women Artists in Europe and America since 1850.* University of Pennsylvania Press, 1989.
Women's Images of Men. ICA, London, 1980.

Morris, Kathleen (1893–1986)

An invalid most of her life, the impressionist painter Kathleen Morris was born in Montréal, Québec, Canada. She was associated with the Beaver Hall Group and studied with William Brymner and Maurice Cullen at the Art Association of Montréal. She learned to sketch and compose quickly on summer sketching trips with Cullen.

Morris's first solo exhibition occurred at the Art Association of Montréal (1939), and her work was shown there regularly until the mid-1950s. Among others, she held a solo exhibition at the Montréal Arts Club (1956) and a joint exhibition with Lincoln Morris in 1962. Her work was invited to many group exhibitions in Canada and abroad, including the Art Association of Montréal; Montréal Museum of Fine Arts; the Royal Canadian Academy (which elected her an associate in 1929); various Canadian artist's shows in Brussels, Belgium; Buenos Aires,

Argentina; London, England; Paris, France; the Riverside Museum, New York City (1947); the British Empire Exposition, Wembley, England (1924–1925); and others.

Morris's work is represented in major private and public permanent collections. "McGill Cab Stand" (c. 1927), typical of her genre work, depicts a snow scene with three raggedy-looking horses hitched to unoccupied sleds; a clutch of sinuous, bare-branched trees on rounded hillocks; a steepled church; and occasional touches of red-orange to heighten the composition. The government selected this work as one of a series of Christmas stamps in 1931.

Bibliography
From Women's Eyes: Women Painters in Canada. Agnes Etheridge Art Centre, Queen's University, 1975.
Millar, Joyce. "The Beaver Hall Group: Painting in Montreal 1920–1940." *Woman's Art Journal* 13:1 (Spring–Summer 1992): 3–9.
Smith, Frances. *Kathleen Moir Morris.* Intro. by Robert Swain. Queen's University, 1983.

Morrow (De Forest), Julie (c. 1882–1979)

A native New Yorker, the painter Julie Morrow (De Forest) studied with Jonas Lie, Hawthorne, and Carlson. The wife of Cornelius Wortendyke De Forest, Morrow was a member of several professional and related arts organizations, including the Allied Artists of America, American Federation of Arts, American Artists Professional League, Cincinnati Art Club, the MacDowell Society of Cincinnati, Ohio, Marblehead Art Association, National Arts Club of New York, National Association of Women Painters and Sculptors, and the Provincetown Art Association. Her work is represented in private and public permanent collections, including the Wadleigh Library, New York City, and the Farnsworth Museum, Wellesley College, Massachusetts.

Bibliography
American Art Annual. Vol. 28. American Federation of Arts, 1932.
Clark, Edna. *Ohio Art and Artists.* Richmond, Virginia: Garrett and Massie, 1932.
Gerdts, William. *American Impressionism.* Abbeville Press, 1984.

Morton, Ree (1936–1977)

Born in Ossining, New York, the painter/sculptor Ree Morton earned a Bachelor of Fine Arts degree from the University of Rhode Island, Providence (1968); and two years later, received a Master of Fine Arts degree from the Tyler School of Art, Temple University, Philadelphia, Pennsylvania.

Morton held many solo exhibitions and installations in museums and galleries, including "Biennials" of the Whitney Museum of American Art, New York City (1973, 1977); "Something in the Wind," an installation, South Street Seaport, New York (1975); University of Rhode Island, Kingston (1976); and others. After her death in an automobile accident, retrospective shows were held at New York University (1977); Droll/Colbert Gallery (1977, 1978); and the New Museum of Contemporary Art (1980)—all in New York City; and others.

Morton received awards and honors, including a Creative Artists Public Service (CAPS) grant (1974) and a National Endowment for the Arts (NEA) fellowship (1975). She worked the field between

painting and sculpture in works that dared to use decoration and, occasionally, *kitsch* to produce seemingly innocent and wry images. Examples of her work are in private and public permanent collections, including the Aldrich Museum of Contemporary Art, Ridgefield, Connecticut; Guggenheim Museum, New York City; Oberlin College, Ohio; the Pennsylvania Academy of Art, Philadelphia; and others.

Bibliography
Kramer, Hilton. "Art: Suspiciously Easy to Like." *The New York Times* (September 23, 1977).
Lippard, Lucy R. *From the Center.* E.P. Dutton, 1976.
Russell, John. "The Legacy of Ree Morton." *The New York Times* (February 22, 1980).
Tatransky, Valentin. "Ree Morton." *Arts Magazine* 52:3 (November 1977): 28–29.

Moses, Cherie (1949–)

Born in Cleveland, Ohio, Cherie Moses is a mixed-media artist who works in photography, printmaking, painting, video, and performance. She received a Bachelor of Arts degree in English literature from Case Western Reserve University in her native city, a Bachelor of Fine Arts degree from the Nova Scotia College of Art and Design, Halifax; and a Master of Visual Arts degree from the University of Alberta, Edmonton. Currently Moses teaches in the fine art program at Grant MacEwan Community College in Edmonton, Alberta, Canada.

In terms of photo-works Moses's series from the 1980s, "Imposed Image: Other Woman" and "Imposed Image: Mother," explore the limitations of gender stereotyping and social posing. These issues also underlie a mixed-media installation and performance piece entitled "Brides and Opening Ceremonies" in 1981 at the SUB Art Gallery in Edmonton, Alberta, Canada, and later in Calgary and Oakville, Ontario. Similarly the social pressures faced by immigrant women and female office workers are at issue in Moses's videos: *Placing the Talent* (1985), *The Measure of Success* (1987), and *Say It* (1988), which have been exhibited at various North American galleries and international film and video festivals. In a solo painting exhibition entitled "Vignettes/Short Stories" at Galerie Powerhouse in Montréal (1987), Moses addresses the spatial structuring and imag(in)ing of social relationship in urban spaces. Her performance, *Pressure/Pressure* at the Chinook Theatre in Edmonton and the Winnipeg Art Gallery (1988) looks at how stereotypical male personalities are formed, while her *Not Suitable for Mature Audiences* performed at the Edmonton Art Gallery (1990) addresses the engendering of cultural authority in institutions of "high" art. More recently, Moses has been producing paintings and works on paper which draw inspiration from hieroglyphic symbols in their playful exploration of emotional states. These were exhibited at the Ingrid Cusson Gallery in New York City (1989).

Moses has received awards from the Canada Council, the Banff Centre for the Arts, and Alberta Culture. Her work has been acquired by the Art Gallery of Windsor, the University of Alberta, the Alberta Art Foundation, Esso Resources, and the National Gallery of Canada.

Bridget Elliott

Bibliography
Blais, Denise. "'In Process': An Interview with Cherie Moses." *Atlantis* 10:1 (Fall 1984): 77–93.

Elliott, Bridget, and Janice Williamson. *Dangerous Goods: Feminist Visual Art Practices*. Edmonton Art Gallery and Latitude 53 (1990): 11–13, 27.
"In From the Cold: Feminism and Art in Edmonton." *Parallelogramme* (February–March 1986).
Wylie, Liz. "The Art Scene in Edmonton." *NeWest Review* (March 1985): 8–9.

Moses, Grandma (Anna Mary Robertson Moses) (1860–1961)

The art of Anna Mary Robertson Moses and the personality of Grandma Moses are inseparable. Together the aged artist and her childlike art charmed much of the world.

Moses took up painting in lieu of embroidery in her late seventies, because brushes and paint were easier on her arthritic fingers than needles and thread. In 1938 Moses's work was discovered by amateur art collector Louis J. Caldor, who saw her paintings in a drugstore window in Hoosick Falls, New York.

Moses had her first exhibition, outside of fairs and drugstore windows, in the members' rooms at the Museum of Modern Art (MoMA) in New York City, where three of her paintings were included in "Contemporary Unknown American Painters" (October 1939). Her first solo exhibition was hung a year later at Galerie St. Etienne in New York City. The show, "What a Farm Wife Painted," featured thirty-three paintings and one embroidered piece.

Moses's work was encouraged by Caldor and Galerie St. Etienne owner, Otto Kallir. They supplied her with professional tools that notably improved her art, for example, when she began using brushes instead of matchsticks and pins to paint fine details. Because she had no professional painting experience, Moses was classified as a primitive painter. Her autobiographical artworks were noted for their naive approach to painting the scenes and situations of growing up on a farm, working in other families' houses, and running farms with her husband. Through her paintings Moses depicted life in rural America with the changing seasons, holiday celebrations, and never-ending tasks, such as making maple syrup, candles, and quilts.

Often the stories underlying Moses's art were stressed more than the artworks themselves. Critics said her reputation outran her aesthetic skills and that, by the standards of art, Moses was not a very good painter. At times her work was dismissed as illustration. Nevertheless, exhibitions of Moses's art have been featured at museums and galleries throughout the United States. Travelling shows, sponsored by such organizations as the U.S. Information Agency (USIA) and the Smithsonian Institution, Washington, D.C., received large audiences while travelling throughout Europe, as well as in North America.

All of Moses's more than 1,500 paintings were copyrighted through the corporation, Grandma Moses Properties. Some of her works were reproduced as posters, patterned fabrics, plates, Christmas cards, and greeting cards. The reproductions made Moses's work accessible to a wider audience and increased her popularity.

The news of Moses's death on December 13, 1961, at age 101 was broadcast worldwide and published on the front pages of newspapers across the United States. President John F. Kennedy issued a statement marking her passing and paying tribute to the artist.

Kennedy was not the only U.S. president to appreciate Moses's art. Harry S. Truman had presented Moses with an award for achievement in art through the Women's National Press Club in 1949. Later, members of Dwight D. Eisenhower's cabinet commissioned a Moses painting as a gift for the president. In 1969, a detail of her painting, "July Fourth," which is owned by the White House, was issued as a six-cent commemorative stamp by the U.S. Postal Service as a tribute to the artist.

Melissa D. Olson

Bibliography
"An American Grandmother." *The New York Times* (December 15, 1961): 36.
Canaday, John. "Art of Grandma Moses." *The New York Times* (December 14, 1961): 46.
"Grandma Moses Is Dead at 101; Primitive Artist 'Just Wore Out,'" *The New York Times* (December 14, 1961): 1.
Grandma Moses: Anna Mary Robertson Moses (1860–1961). Washington, D.C.: National Gallery of Art, 1979.
Kallier, Otto. *Grandma Moses*. Harry N. Abrams, 1973.
Kallir, Jane. *Grandma Moses: The Artist Behind the Myth*. Clarkson N. Potter, 1982.
"Kennedy Pays Tribute." *The New York Times* (December 14, 1961): 46.
Moses, Anna Mary Robertson. *Grandma Moses: My Life's History*. Harper and Brothers, 1952.

Moss, Irene

Born in Hungary, the lyrical painter Irene Moss, a U.S. citizen, studied art at the Brooklyn Museum School of Art; the School of Visual Arts; and, privately, with the painter Moses Soyer—all in New York City.

Moss has held many solo exhibitions of her paintings at galleries and universities, including Contemporary Arts Gallery (1961–1963); East Hampton Gallery (1966, 1968, 1970); Columbia University (1970, 1971); Peter Rose Gallery (1974, 1975); Hansen Galleries (1976, 1980); and Reece Galleries (1988, 1990–1992)—all in New York City. She has also held solo shows at Nora Galleries, Great Neck, New York (1986); Bacardi Gallery, Miami, Florida (1974); New York University (1970); and Brooklyn College (1970)—both in New York City; and others. Her work has been invited to many group exhibitions in the United States, such as the Fort Worth Art Center, Texas (1968); Rochester Memorial Art Gallery, New York (1968); Stamford Museum, Connecticut (1972); Philadelphia Civic Center Museum, Pennsylvania (1974); and many others.

Coeditor of *The Feminist Art Journal* (1972–1977), Moss wrote articles and essays for *SunStorm*, *Artspeak*, and other magazines and journals. "City Figures on City Streets," a series of paintings, juxtaposes—in abstract form—people and the environment in hot, dazzling color; the paintings have been reproduced on the covers of two social psychology texts.

Moss's work is represented in private and public permanent collections, including the Akron Art Institute, Ohio; Brooklyn College, New York; New Britain Museum, Connecticut; Lehigh University, Bethlehem, Pennsylvania; Brandeis University, Waltham, Massachusetts; AT&T; IBM; and many others.

Bibliography
Collins, Jimmie Lee. *Women Artists in America II*. University of Tennessee, 1975.
Poroner, Palmer. "Irene Moss: Fusing Existence with a New Alchemy." *SunStorm* (October–November 1986): Sec III, 2–6.
Who's Who in American Art. 19th ed. R.R. Bowker Co., 1991–1992.

Moty, Eleanor (1945–)

Born in Glen Ellyn, Illinois, the goldsmith Eleanor Moty, one of the technological pioneers in metalsmithing, earned a Bachelor of Fine Arts degree at the University of Illinois at Urbana (1968), and, three years later, received a Master of Fine Arts degree from the Tyler School of Art, Temple University, Philadelphia, Pennsylvania.

Moty has shown her work in numerous international exhibitions, including "Crafts Today USA," a travelling show to France, Finland, Germany, Switzerland, and throughout the Soviet successor states (1989–1990); "Korean Metalworks Exhibition," Walker Hill Art Center Museum, Seoul, Korea (1988); "Jewelry 1900–1985," Electrum Gallery, London, England (1985); "International Jewelry Art Exhibition," Nihon Keizai Shimbun, Tokyo, Japan (1976); and others. She has held a number of solo exhibitions of her jewelry throughout the United States, including the Tweed Museum of Art, University of Minnesota, Duluth (1986); Perimeter Gallery, Chicago, Illinois (1984); Joseph Gross Gallery, University of Arizona, Tucson (1983); Birmingham Art Museum, Alabama (1981); Craft Alliance Gallery, St., Louis, Missouri (1978); and others. Her work has been invited to numerous group exhibitions in galleries throughout the United States—from Chicago, Illinois, to Atlanta, Georgia; San Diego, California; Philadelphia, Pennsylvania; New York City; Sheboygan, Wisconsin; Malibu, California; and Palm Beach, Florida.

Moty has received honors and awards for her work, including a Vilas fellowship (1986), and an H.I. Romnes fellowship (1980) from the University of Wisconsin, Madison; and Arts and Crafts fellowships from the National Endowment for the Arts (NEA) (1975, 1988). She has been professor of art at the University of Wisconsin since 1981. Her work is represented in private and public permanent collections including the Minnesota Museum of Art, St. Paul; Tyler School of Art, Temple University, Philadelphia, Pennsylvania; Georgia State University, Atlanta; Birmingham Art Museum, Alabama; the Lannon Foundation, Palm Beach, Florida; and many others.

Bibliography

Packard, Roger. "Eleanor Moty." *WARF Research Sampler*. Madison: University of Wisconsin, 1984.

Benesh, Carolyn. "Eleanor Moty." *Ornament* 7:2 (1983).

Foley, Suzanne. "Eleanor Moty." *American Craft* (June–July 1987).

Moulton, Sue Buckingham (1873–)

Born in Hartford, Connecticut, the painter Sue Buckingham Moulton studied under Andrews, Frisbie, and Moser.

Moulton was a member of the Philadelphia Art Alliance, Pennsylvania; and the American Artists Professional League, New York City. She won honors and awards, including the Micherson memorial prize, and she created many miniature paintings, fore-edge paintings, and murals. One of her murals is sited in the Philomusian Club, Philadelphia, Pennsylvania.

Bibliography

American Art Annual. Vol. 28. American Federation of Arts, 1932.

Weber, Carl J. *Fore-Edge Painting*. Harvey House, 1966.

Who's Who in American Art. Vol. 6. American Federation of Arts, 1956.

Mulcahy, Kathleen (1950–)

Born in Newark, New Jersey, the glass sculptor Kathleen Mulcahy earned a Bachelor's degree in art education from Kean College of New Jersey, Union (1972) and, two years later, was awarded a Master of Fine Arts degree in glass sculpture from Alfred University, New York.

Between 1980 and 1992 Mulcahy held seventeen solo exhibitions of her work in centers and galleries throughout the United States, including "Artist of the Year," Pittsburgh Center for the Arts, Pennsylvania (1992); "The Whirling Works," Kimzey Miller Gallery, Seattle, Washington (1991); Ruth Volid Gallery, Chicago, Illinois (1990); Glass Gallery, Bethesda, Maryland (1986); "Collaborations in Glass," Rudolph Lee Gallery, Clemson University, South Carolina (1981); "Juror's Exhibition," Butler Institute of American Art, Youngstown, Ohio (1980); and others. Her work has been invited to myriad group exhibitions in the United States and abroad, such as the "1992 Stockbridge Glass Invitational," Holsten Gallery, Stockbridge, Massachusetts (1992); "Crafts/USA," a travelling exhibition that was shown in centers, museums, and galleries in Ireland, Greece, Norway, Germany, Poland, the Soviet successor states, France, Spain, Turkey, Finland, and Belgium (1989–1992); Sandra Ainsley Gallery, Toronto, Canada (1990); "Women in Glass," the Hand and the Spirit Gallery, Scottsdale, Arizona (1988); "Glass National," Downey Art Museum, California (1986); "New Glass Review 3," Corning Museum of Glass International Survey, New York City (1983); and many others.

Winner of awards, honors, and commissions, Mulcahy designed and fabricated the cultural awards for the Pittsburgh Center for the Arts, Pennsylvania (1991, 1992), and others for corporations, universities, and synagogues. She was named Pittsburgh's "Artist of the Year" (1992), and has won fellowships from the Fulbright Commission (1984), the Pennsylvania Council on the Arts (1981, 1983), the National Endowment for the Arts (NEA) (1979), and others. Recently, she wrote, "I am inspired by things that have an intrinsic spiraling motion . . . moved by the sensual experience of music, dance and ideas that have their inception in 'centering.' The spinning which occurs in the core of my being is released in my work, translated into form." Mulcahy's glass sculptures encompass these words. Her work is represented in private, public, and corporate permanent collections in the United States, Canada, France, and Switzerland, including the Corning Museum of Glass, New York City; Carnegie-Mellon University, the University of Pittsburgh, Westinghouse Corporation, Blue Cross, and Steelcase Corporation—all in Pittsburgh, Pennsylvania; Wabash College, Crawfordsville, Indiana; and others.

Bibliography

Lowry, Patricia. "Artist of the Year Gives New Twist to Glass." *The Pittsburgh Press* (April 18, 1992).

Miller, Donald. "Mulcahy's 'Vapors' a Breath of Artistry." *Pittsburgh Post Gazette* (April 12, 1992).

Who's Who in American Art. 19th ed. R.R. Bowker Co., 1991–1992.

Mulcaster, Wynona C. (1915–)

Born in Prince Albert, Saskatchewan, Canada, the painter of landscapes and animals Wynona C. Mulcaster learned her craft from many artists in many venues. She earned her Bachelor's degree from the University of Saskatchewan; studied at the renowned Emma Lake Summer Workshops, and the Banff School of Fine Arts, with Will Barnet, Y.A. Jackson, Ernest Lindner, Kenneth Noland, Joe Plaskett, Jack Shadbolt, and others; took further study in art education with Dr. Arthur Lismer at the School of Art and Design, Montréal, Québec; a year of research and travel in Europe; and further study at Instituto San Miguel de Allende, Mexico.

Between 1954 and 1988 Mulcaster has held solo exhibitions throughout Canada: from Saskatoon, Saskatchewan, to Montréal, Québec, and has had her work included in numerous prestigious group exhibitions. Examples of her work are in private, public, and corporate permanent collections, including the Art Gallery of Hamilton, Ontario; Canada Council Art Bank, Ottawa; Edmonton Art Gallery, Alberta; Imperial Oil, Toronto, Ontario; Mendel Art Gallery, Saskatoon, Saskatchewan; University of Saskatchewan, Saskatoon; and many others.

Bibliography

Burnett, David, and Marilyn Schiff. *Contemporary Canadian Art.* Hurtig Publishers, 1985.

Millard, Peter. "Painting in Saskatoon." *Arts Manitoba* 2:2 (Winter 1983): 26–32.

Varley, Christopher. *Winnipeg West: Painting and Sculpture in Western Canada, 1945–1970.* Edmonton Art Gallery, 1983.

Murphy, Alice Harold (1896–1966)

Born in Springfield, Massachusetts, the painter/printmaker Alice Harold Murphy studied at the Art Students League and the National Academy of Design—both in New York City. At the latter institution she worked under the eminent painter Charles Wesley Hawthorne. Murphy took further work in Paris, France, at the Académie Colorossi and the Académie de la Grande Chaumière.

A popular teacher, Murphy instructed many pupils at the National Academy of Design and the Art Students League, yet always found time for her own work. Her last solo exhibition took place at the Chapellier Gallery, New York City (1954). Her figurative work revealed a spiritual approach, which can still be sensed in one of her titles: "Cave of Imagination."

Murphy's work is represented in private and public permanent collections, including the Library of Congress, Washington, D.C.; Metropolitan Museum of Art, and the New York Public Library—both in New York City; Philadelphia Art Alliance, Pennsylvania; Springfield Art Museum, and Williams College, Williamstown—both in Massachusetts; University of Maine, Orono; and others.

Bibliography

American Prints in the Library of Congress: A Catalog of the Collection. Johns Hopkins Press, 1970.

Clark, Eliot Candee. *History of the National Academy of Design.* Columbia University Press, 1954.

Obituary. *The New York Times* (April 12, 1966): 35.

Murphy, Catherine (1946–)

The realist painter Catherine Murphy was born in Cambridge, Massachusetts. She studied at Pratt Institute, Brooklyn, New York, where she received her Bachelor of Fine Arts degree in 1967, and also took additional work with Elmer Bischoff one summer at the Skowhegan

School of Painting and Sculpture, Maine.

Murphy has had a number of solo exhibitions of her work in galleries throughout the Eastern United States, including the First Street Gallery, New York City, and the Piper Gallery, Massachusetts (1972); "Recent Paintings," Fourcade Droll, Inc., New York City (1975); "Catherine Murphy: A Retrospective Exhibition," Phillips Collection, Washington, D.C., which also travelled to the Institute of Contemporary Art, Boston, Massachusetts (1976); and "Recent Paintings," Xavier Fourcade Inc., New York City (1975, 1985). Her work has been selected for many group exhibitions in major museums throughout the United States, such as the "Annual Painting and Sculpture Exhibition," Whitney Museum of American Art, New York City (1972) and its "Biennial" (1973); "Painting and Sculpture Today," Indianapolis Museum of Art, Indiana (1974); "A Selection of American Art: The Skowhegan School 1974–1976," Institute of Contemporary Art, Boston, Massachusetts (1976); "Awards Exhibition," American Academy and Institute of Arts and Letters (1979); and "Lower Manhattan from Street to Sky," Whitney Museum, Downtown Branch (1982)—both in New York City; "The Window in 20th Century Art," Neuberger Museum, State University of New York (SUNY) at Purchase (1986); and others.

Murphy's work is housed in permanent museum and corporate collections, including the Chase Manhattan Bank, and Whitney Museum of American Art—both in New York City; Hirshhorn Museum and Sculpture Garden, and Phillips Collection—both in Washington, D.C.; New Jersey Art Museum, Trenton, and the Newark Museum—both in New Jersey; Security Pacific National Bank, Los Angeles, California; Weatherspoon Art Gallery, University of North Carolina at Greensboro; and others.

Murphy has won awards and honors for her work, including a grant from the National Endowment for the Arts (NEA) in 1979, and won a Guggenheim Foundation fellowship three years later. "Scrub" (1987), if superficially examined, reveals an analogous approach to the work of Andrew Wyeth. Murphy's slow-paced output, on the other hand, bares a keen wit, coupled with a more intimate, almost cryptic approach.

Bibliography

Brodsky, Judith K., and Ofelia Garcia. *Printed by Women.* The Port of History Museum, 1983.

Marks, Claude. *World Artists: 1950–1980.* H.W. Wilson, Publishers, 1984.

Silverthorne, Jeanne. "Catherine Murphy." *Artforum* 24:6 (February 1986): 103.

Stavisky, Gail. "Catherine Murphy." *Arts Magazine* 60:6 (February 1986): 136–37.

Who's Who in American Art. 19th ed. R.R. Bowker Co., 1991–1992.

Murray, Elizabeth (1940–)

Born in Chicago, Illinois, Elizabeth Murray grew up in Bloomington, Illinois, one of three children whose Irish-Catholic family enjoyed difficult times. Early on Murray knew that she was going to be an artist. She was a scholarship student at the Art Institute of Chicago in her native city at the age of eighteen, and earned her Bachelor of Fine Arts degree in 1962. Two years later, she was awarded a Master of Fine Arts degree from Mills College, Oakland, California.

Internationally-known, Murray has had more than thirty solo exhibitions of her paintings and prints (aside from several travelling shows of her work) between 1974 and 1990, including the Jared Sable Gallery, Toronto, Canada (1974); Galerie Mukai, Tokyo, Japan (1980, 1990); Mayor Rowan Gallery, London, England (1989); and nine solo shows at Paula Cooper Gallery, New York City (her dealer), since 1976. To mid-1991, Murray's work has been invited to 266 group exhibitions throughout the world, many of which travelled to additional museums and institutions.

At various times in the 1970s Murray taught at distinguished universities and art schools, including Bard College, New York City (1974–1975, 1976–1977); the Art Institute of Chicago, Illinois (1975–1976); Princeton University, New Jersey (1977); Yale University, New Haven, Connecticut (1978–1979); and at the New York Studio of Drawing, Painting, and Sculpture (1987). Her recent honors embody the Walter M. Campana award, Art Institute of Chicago (1982); the American Academy and Institute of Arts and Letters, New York (1984); and the Skowhegan School medal for painting, Maine (1986).

Murray's work may be seen in the permanent public collections of major institutions in the United States, Japan, England, and France, such as the Museum of Modern Art (MoMA), the Metropolitan Museum of Art, the Whitney Museum of American Art, and the Guggenheim Museum—all in New York City; the Saatchi Collection, London, England; Fukuoka Sogo Bank, Japan; the European Fine Art Foundation, Paris, France; and many others.

Schooled in the traditional approach to painting at the Art Institute of Chicago, Murray, in her graduate work at Mills, admits to being influenced by Max Beckmann, Bosch, Chagall, Leon Golub, and Jasper Johns. At the institute, on her way to classes, she would have to traverse the galleries and, like it or not, truly sense the paintings of Paul Cézanne, Pablo Picasso, and Willem de Kooning, no mean role models. The turning point in Murray's work occurred in "Join" (1980), her inaugural "shattered" painting which her friend Jennifer Bartlett suggested was reminiscent, on one level, of a broken heart. From that time Murray's work has consistently grown in scale and strong colors toward the shaped, abstract canvases one associates with her recent work.

Bibliography
Field, Richard S., and Ruth E. Fine. *A Graphic Muse*. Hudson Hills Press, 1987.
Graze, Sue, and Kathy Halbreich. *Elizabeth Murray: Paintings and Drawings*. Harry N. Abrams, 1987.
Russell, John. "Elizabeth Murray's Shaped Canvases." *The New York Times* (June 9, 1981).
Solomon, Deborah. "Celebrating Paint." *The New York Times* (March 31, 1991): Magazine section 20–25, 40, 46, cover.

Murray, Ellen (1947–)

A native of Raleigh, North Carolina, Ellen Murray received her Bachelor of Fine Arts and Master of Fine Arts degrees in 1969 and 1971, respectively, from the University of North Carolina at Greensboro. She studied with Peter Agostini, among others. Exclusively known for her watercolors, Murray began exhibiting professionally in North Carolina while barely into graduate school. Among her many exhibition credits are regular showings in the annual "Watercolor USA" and "National Watercolor Society Annual Exhibition" plus numerous regional competitions, including those held by watercolor societies in California, Kansas, Oklahoma, Arkansas, and Colorado.

Murray's watercolors are characterized by richness of texture, complexity of composition, and the play between the verbal (title) and visual (subject). She usually focuses on commonplace objects for her subject matter, often things that are indigenous to the Western environment in which she has lived since 1971. In that year she was appointed as instructor in the department of art of Oklahoma State University, Oklahoma City; in 1986 she was appointed professor in the School of Art at Arizona State University, Tempe.

Murray's "Collection Series" began travelling to various cities in 1988 under the sponsorship of the Mid-America Arts Alliance and Arizona State University. In 1982 she was elected to membership in the National Watercolor Society, and in 1986 was invited to charter membership in the Watercolor USA Honor Society.

Murray has received a best of show award, a juror's award, and a judge's award from National Watercolor Oklahoma; a museum cash award from Watercolor USA at the Springfield Art Museum, Missouri; and a Besser Museum purchase award from the 1985 National Watercolor Exhibition at the Midland Center for the Arts, Michigan. Her work is included in the collections of Jesse Besser Museum, McDonald's Corporation, IBM, and others.

Married in 1975 to Lonnie Dean Meissinger, Murray has a son, Logan Don Meissinger, born in 1979. Often it is her son's toys which she incorporates into her complex compositions.

Leonard Lehrer

Bibliography
Landwehr, William C., Leonard Lehrer, and Ellen Murray. *Ellen Murray: The Collection Series*. "Exhibits USA," a Mid-America Arts Alliance Program, 1988.

Murray, Judith (1941–)

A native New Yorker, the painter Judith Murray earned a Bachelor of Fine Arts degree from Pratt Institute, Brooklyn, New York (1962); attended the San Fernando Academy of Fine Arts, Madrid, Spain (1963); and returned to Pratt for graduate work and receipt of a Master of Fine Arts degree the following year.

Murray has held solo and two-person exhibitions in galleries and museums, including the Jan Turner Gallery, Los Angeles, California (1987); "Three Aspects of Abstraction," Pam Adler Gallery, New York (1986); "Judith Murray: Painting—Ursula von Rydingsvard: Sculpture," C.W. Post College, Long Island University, New York (1985); "Concentration V," Dallas Museum of Fine Arts, Texas (1982); Janus Gallery, Los Angeles, California (1982); Betsy Rosenfield Gallery, Chicago, Illinois (1981); Pam Adler Gallery, New York City (1980, 1979); and others. Her work has been invited to many group exhibitions in the United States and abroad: from New York City to Leningrad, Russia; from Minneapolis, Minnesota, to Berlin, Germany; from Greensboro, North Carolina, and Dallas, Texas, to Helsinki, Finland, and Warsaw, Poland, as well as museums throughout Central and South America.

Murray has taught at several universities and has been artist-in-residence in Poland for the United States Information Agency (USIA); she designed the Mozart Festival and Bicentennial posters for Lincoln Center, New York City (1981, 1986, 1991–1992); and she received a National Endowment for the Arts (NEA) fellowship (1983–1984). Representative examples of her work can be found in private, public, and corporate permanent collections, including the Brooklyn Museum, New York; Honolulu Academy of Art, Hawaii; Library of Congress, Washington, D.C.; New York Public Library, New York City; National Museum of Art, Warsaw, Poland; Carnegie-Mellon University, Pittsburgh, Pennsylvania; Chase Manhattan Bank, New York City; Bendix Corporation; and many others.

Bibliography

Braff, Phyllis. "Two Artists on the Cutting Edge." *The New York Times* (November 10, 1985): LI28.

Kutner, Janet. "Ms. Murray's Style Defies Categorization." *Dallas Morning News* (April 1982): 1C, 3C.

Stavitsky, Gail. "Three Aspects of Abstraction." *Arts Magazine* (April 1986): 112.

Who's Who in American Art. 19th ed. R.R. Bowker Co., 1991–1992.

Murrill, Gwynn (1942–)

Born in Ann Arbor, Michigan, Gwynn Murrill is known for her sleek bird and animal sculptures in wood, bronze, aluminum, and stone. Murrill earned a Master of Fine Arts degree at the University of California at Los Angeles (UCLA).

Murrill has held nineteen solo exhibitions of her work in the United States between 1972 and 1992, including the Gail Severn Gallery, Ketchum, Idaho (1988, 1992); Asher/Faure, Los Angeles, California (1981, 1983, 1985, 1987, 1990, 1991); Rutgers Barclay Gallery, Santa Fe, New Mexico (1990); John Berggruen Gallery, San Francisco, California (1987); the University of California at Santa Barbara (1980); Nicholas Wilder Gallery (1977); and the Mizuno Gallery (1972)—both in Los Angeles, California; and others. Her work has been invited to many group exhibitions in the United States and abroad, such as "Mind and Beast: Contemporary Artists and the Animal Kingdom," Leigh Yawkey/Woodson Art Museum, Wasau, Wisconsin (1992); "Individual Realities," Sezon Museum of Art, Tokyo Tsukashin Hall, Osaka, Japan (1991); "Los Angeles," Scott Hanson Gallery, New York City (1987); "Fellows Exhibition," American Academy in Rome, Italy (1980); "Gwynn Murrill and Judy Pfaff," Artists Space, New York City (1974); and others.

Winner of honors and awards for her work, Murrill was the recipient of a Guggenheim fellowship (1986); a grant from the National Endowment for the Arts (NEA) (1984–1985); a Prix di Roma fellowship from the American Academy in Rome, Italy (1979–1980); and a new talent purchase award, Los Angeles County Museum of Art, California (1978). Her work is represented in many private, public, and corporate permanent collections in the United States, including the Los Angeles County Museum of Art, California; TransAmerica Corporation, San Francisco, California; Salt River Project, Phoenix, Arizona; the cities of Santa Monica and Culver City, California; Hyatt Regency Hotels, Tampa, Florida; and others.

Bibliography

Clothier, Peter. "Gwynn Murrill: Wood, Bronze, Stone, Aluminum." A Catalog. Asher/Faure, 1991.

Geer, Susan. "Review." *The Los Angeles Times* (January 12, 1990).

McCloud, Mac. "The Richness of Wood." *Art Week* (March 10, 1984): 3.

Mussoff, Jody (1952–)

While the term "colored pencil" conjures up images of delicate Rococo portraits in pastel hues, Jody Mussoff uses this medium to create a dramatic, erotic, and thoroughly modern world. Her large-format (often three-by-four-foot) drawings feature one or two female figures, built up from vividly colored and densely textured marks, and depicted in surreal situations.

Born in Pittsburgh, Pennsylvania, Mussoff was educated at Carnegie-Mellon University in her native city (1970–1971) and the Corcoran School of Art in Washington, D.C. (1974–1976). Since 1976 Mussoff has been participating in group shows throughout the United States and abroad, including the "2nd International Triennial of Emerging Artists," at the Kunsthalle Nürnberg, Germany (1982); "Lithograph Review" at the Machida City Museum in Tokyo, Japan (1991), and "NY, New York Generation" at Origrafica in Malmö, 1982, and "12 Samtida utländska mästure" at Tammviks Kursgård (1993)—both in Sweden. Her first one-person exhibition took place at Gallery K in Washington, D.C., in 1980; she has had additional solo shows there in 1981, 1984, 1985, 1989, 1990, and 1993. In addition her work has been featured in one-person exhibits at the Monique Knowlton Gallery in New York City (1981, 1983, 1984, 1986), the Pittsburgh Center for the Arts, Pennsylvania (1985); and galleries in Illinois, Ohio, Colorado, Virginia, and at Origrafica, in Malmö, Sweden (1986, 1988, 1991).

Mussoff is based in the Washington, D.C., area, and her work is represented in the permanent collections of several prestigious institutions there, including *The Washington Post Company,* the Hirshhorn Museum and Sculpture Garden, and the National Museum of American Art. Her work is also part of numerous corporate collections, such as those of Chemical Bank, Kidder, Peabody, the Philip-Morris Corporation, and Prudential Insurance Corporation, as well as the Kunsthalle Nürnberg, Nuremberg, Germany; Clarion University, Pennsylvania; the George Washington University, Washington, D.C.; University of South Florida, Tampa; University of Tennessee, Knoxville; University of Oklahoma, Norman; and Tokyo National University of Fine Arts, Japan.

Bibliography

Hess, Elizabeth. "Jody Mussoff." *Art News* 83:4 (April 1984): 132, 134.

Klein, Ellen Lee. "Jody Mussoff." *Arts Magazine* 57:9 (June 1984): 55.

Richard, Paul. "Mussoff's Temptresses." *The Washington Post* (November 30, 1986): D1, D16.

Shannon, Joe. "Jody Mussoff at Monique Knowlton." *Art in America* 71:8 (September 1983): 176–77.

Myers, Ethel (1881–1960)

Born in Brooklyn, New York, the sculptor/printmaker Ethel Myers studied at Hunter College and Columbia University—both in New York City—and also with William Merritt Chase, Robert Henri, and Kenneth Hayes Miller.

Myers's small sculptures and drawings were exhibited in museums and galleries, including the Art Institute of Chicago, Illinois; the Brooklyn Museum, New York; Corcoran Gallery of Art, Washington, D.C.; National Academy of Design, New York City; Pennsylvania Academy of Fine Arts, Philadelphia; Whitney Museum of American Art, New York City; and others. She was a member of the New York Society of Women Artists and the New York Ceramic

Society, and her work is represented in private and public permanent collections.

Bibliography
Campbell, Lawrence. "Ethel Myers." *Art News* 65:1 (March 1966): 18.
Fourteen American Women Printmakers of the '30s and '40s. Mount Holyoke College and Weyhe Gallery, 1973.
Katz, Leslie. *The Sculpture and Drawings of Ethel Myers.* Robert Schoelkopf Gallery, 1966.
Wolf, Amy J. *New York Society of Women Artists, 1925.* ACA Galleries, 1987.

Myers, Rita (1947–)

Born in Hammonton, New Jersey, the video artist/installationist Rita Myers earned a Bachelor's degree from Douglass College, Rutgers University, New Brunswick, New Jersey (1969); and did graduate work at Hunter College, New York City, where she received a Master's degree (1974).

Myers has held many solo exhibitions in museums and galleries in the United States and abroad, including "Barricade to Blue," The Kitchen, New York City (1977); "The Points of a Star," Whitney Museum of American Art, New York City (1980); "Dancing in the Land Where Children Are the Light," Art Gallery of Ontario, Toronto, Canada, and The Kitchen, New York City (1981); "Gate," Virginia Commonwealth University, Richmond, and "The Allure of the Concentric," Whitney Museum of American Art, New York City (1985); and others. Winner of awards and honors, Myers has received Creative Artists Public Service (CAPS) grants (1976, 1981); fellowships from the National Endowment for the Arts (NEA) (1976, 1980, 1984); grants from the New York State Council on the Arts (1983, 1985), and the Jerome Foundation (1984); and others.

Earlier Myers embraced the philosophy of minimalism and had a performance background; her videos are centered in the exploration of nature versus technology in mystic worlds of her own invention. Examples of her work are represented in private and public permanent collections, including the Museum of Modern Art (MoMA), New York City; and others.

Bibliography
Rice, Shelley. "Review." *Artforum* 19 (May 1981): 78.
Sturken, Marita. "The Circle Game." *Afterimage* 13 (December 1985).
Wooster, Ann-Sargent. "Review." *Art News* 75 (October 1976): 125.

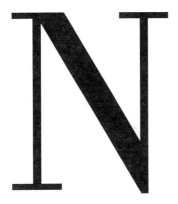

Nampeyo (c. 1860–1942)

Born a Hopi-Tewa on First Mesa of the Hopi Reservation, Arizona, Nampeyo learned to make utilitarian pottery in the traditional coil-and-scrape method of her ancestors. During Nampeyo's youth the Hopi mesas were relatively isolated and few outsiders visited the pueblos. In the 1880s, however, the National Museum in Washington, D.C. sent representatives to the Southwest to make extensive collections of material goods and artifacts from Native peoples who were thought to be nearing extinction. At some time during that decade Hopi potters revived the ancient polychrome style of ceramics made in Sikyatki, a prehistoric pueblo at the base of First Mesa, between about 1375 and 1625. Thereafter the Sikyatki revival style of pottery became an art form to be collected.

Acknowledged by outside visitors as the best potter on First Mesa, Nampeyo adapted the old designs and shapes of Sikyatki ceramics and other prehistoric periods to her own contemporary style that reached perfection in form and pattern the first decade of the twentieth century. Small seed jars and bowls to low-shouldered vessels, some twenty to twenty-two inches in diameter, and large storage jars eighteen to twenty inches high were decorated with stylized birds and feathers, graceful curvilinear motifs, or asymmetrical designs before firing. She dug her own clay and worked it by hand with water until malleable; made her paint from organic elements; and painted the designs with a yucca brush. Vessels fired outside with sheep dung and occasionally with soft coal turned a warm honey color with red-and-black design. Occasionally she added an accent of white or applied a white slip to the unpainted vessel that gave it a cream color after firing.

Around the turn of the century Nampeyo was photographed by all major photographers visiting the mesas, and she became a symbol of the Hopi people in tour books and guides. From about 1900 the Fred Harvey Company that managed hotels and dining rooms for the Santa Fe Railway sold her pottery through its many gift shops throughout the Southwest. She sold directly to visitors who found their way to her stone house on the mesa, as well as through traders Tom Pavatea, Thomas V. Keam, and Don Lorenzo Hubbell. As more museums and individuals made collections of her pottery Nampeyo was assisted by her family. While Nampeyo coiled and shaped the vessels and occasionally painted the designs, her husband Lesso, their daughters, and eventually granddaughters also painted designs before the vessels were fired. Because Nampeyo could neither read nor write, she did not sign her pottery. Attribution is therefore difficult unless there is an impeccable provenance with the piece.

In 1905 the Fred Harvey Company took Nampeyo and her family to the newly-completed Hopi House adjoining El Tovar Hotel Grand Canyon to demonstrate pottery-making to visitors. The family remained three months and was taken again to Hopi House in 1907 for the same purpose. In 1910 the Santa Fe Railway took Nampeyo, Lesso, and daughter Nellie to Chicago, Illinois, to be part of its Southwest exhibit at the U.S. Land and Irrigation Show at the Coliseum.

Nampeyo's sight diminished as she aged, though she continued to shape pots for family members to paint until she died. Because of the lack of records or personal journals very little accurate information has been published about her. She has been acknowledged as the most important potter in Hopi history, and as such, she was elected to the Arizona Women's Hall of Fame in 1986.

A retrospective of Nampeyo's work was held at the Muckenthaler Cultural Center, Fullerton, California, in 1974. Major collections are held by the Denver Museum of Art, Colorado; the Milwaukee Public Museum, Wisconsin; the Gilcrease Museum, Tulsa, Oklahoma; and Mesa Verde Visitor Center, Mesa Verde National Park, Colorado.

Nampeyo and Lesso parented six children. Their three daughters—Annie Healing, Nellie Douma, and Fannie Polacca—became fine potters in their mother's tradition, and four generations of descendants have continued her art.

Barbara Kramer

Bibliography

Kramer, Barbara. "Nampeyo, Hopi House, and the Chicago Land Show." *American Indian Art Magazine* 14:1 (Winter 1988): 46–53.
[Note: All other published references contain gross errors and would contradict information contained in this entry. I have written a book manuscript, *Nampeyo: History and the Old Lady*, after many years of research that will be going to a publisher for consideration after the first of the year.]

Nanogak, Agnes (1925–)

Agnes Nanogak, a Canadian Inuit graphic artist, was born November 12, 1925, on Baillie Island, in the Northwest Territories, Canada. Her mother was of Mackenzie Delta/Copper Eskimo background; her father, William Natkutsiak (Billy Banksland), came from Alaska as a guide to explorer Vilhjalmur Stefannson. Nanogak moved to Holman, Northwest Territories, at the age of twelve, married William Goose, and raised seven children. She is one of Holman's most prominent and prolific artists, having contributed a total of about one hundred forty images to twenty annual print collections since 1967, when her artistic career began.

Nanogak is an enthusiastic storyteller and illustrator. In 1972 Nanogak created the illustrations for the book *Tales from the Igloo*. 1986 saw the publication of *More Tales from the Igloo*, this time not only illustrated but also narrated by Nanogak herself. Nanogak's fascination with Aesop-like animal tales, stories of shamans, and myths has been a constant throughout her career. Stylistically, her works are characterized by their bold colors, fluid lines, and nervous energy. This is in large part the result of her use of narrow felt tip pens.

Nanogak's prints and drawings have been included in about fifty group and two solo exhibitions in Canada, the United States, and Europe. Works by her can be found in the collections of at least fifteen institutions in Canada and the United States, including the Canadian Museum of Civilization and the National Gallery of Canada—both in Ottawa; the Montréal Museum of Fine Arts, Québec; and the Winnipeg Art Gallery, Manitoba. In 1985 Nanogak received an honorary Doctorate degree from Mount Saint Vincent University in Halifax, Novia Scotia.

Ingo Hessel

Bibliography

Metayer, Maurice, ed. *Tales from the Igloo.* Hurtig Publishers, 1972.
Nanogak, Agnes. *More Tales from the Igloo.* Hurtig Publishers, 1986.

Napartuk, Mina (1913–)

Canadian Inuit artist Mina Napartuk was born in Kuujjuaraapik (Great Whale River), Arctic Québec. She lived and worked there until the mid-1980s, when she moved north to Umiujaq with her daughter and grandchildren.

After years of training in the traditional way of life, Napartuk is an expert seamstress, working easily with skins, furs, and fabric. A natural leader, she managed the women's craft workshop in Kuujjuaraapik with very high standards. Her wall-hangings, the most impressive of which tended to be of quite heroic proportions, provided a panoramic vision of the lifestyle that she and her contemporaries vividly remembered. These appliqued images cut from sealskin, superimposed on a black stroud background and integrated with syllabic captions, were the signature wall-hangings of Napartuk and the workshop. In addition she concentrated her considerable energies on making expertly tailored Kamiks (sealskin boots) and other finely crafted traditional clothing and dolls.

Napartuk's talents have brought her south to participate in crafts workshops in Toronto and Montréal. Her award-winning dolls and crafts have been exhibited throughout Canada and internationally. One of her mural-sized wall-hangings was the focal point of a reception in 1974 at the Optional Arts Centre in Ottawa, Ontario, where it was on display for one year.

Mary Craig

Bibliography

Inuit Art Index Arranged by Last Name. Indian and Northern Affairs Canada, 1990.

Naranjo-Morse, Nora (1953–)

The potter/poet Nora Naranjo-Morse—a widely-travelled Santa Clara Indian from a distinguished three-generation family of ceramists—received her Bachelor's degree from the College of Santa Fe, New Mexico in 1980. Her mother and three of her sisters are also potters.

Naranjo-Morse has exhibited her ware in solo and two-person shows in many galleries and museums, including "Rising Stars" at Gallery 10, Scottsdale, Arizona (1980), Many Goats Gallery, Tucson, Arizona (1983, 1987), and the Squash Blossom Gallery (1984–1986); "Earth, Hands Life: Southwestern Ceramic Figures" at the Hearing Museum, Phoenix, Arizona (1988), and The Four Winds Gallery, Pittsburgh, Pennsylvania (1988); and "Contemporary Native American Art" at the Quintana Galleries, Portland, Oregon (1988); and others.

A lecturer at prestigious institutions, panelist, and poet whose readings are well-attended—Naranjo-Morse has been the recipient of many honors for her work, including awards for her figurative pieces at the South Western Association on Indian Affairs (SWAIA) Indian Market (1979–1980, 1982–1983, 1985–1987); The Deer Dancer, annual pottery show, Denver, Colorado (1981–1982, 1984); and many others. She received a fellowship from SWAIA (1982), and was one of four artists filmed in the documentary, "A Separate Vision," Museum of Northern Arizona, Flagstaff (1988–1989). Her figurative ware—especially her creation, "Pearlene," a female subject that epitomizes her concept of the Native American woman on the contemporary scene—graces many collections, both private and public.

Bibliography
Bryan, Susan M. "Naranjo-Morse: Pearlene Plays Poker at the Pueblo." *Phoenix Home and Garden* (April 1988): 43–44.
Lichtenstein, Grace. "The Evolution of a Craft Tradition: Three Generations of the Naranjo Women." *Ms. Magazine.* 1983.
Pyne, Lynn. "Making Ceramic Figures Remains a Living Art Form." *Phoenix Gazette* (April 13, 1988): C4.

Nash, Anne Taylor (1884–1968)

Born in Pittsboro, North Carolina, the painter Anne Taylor Nash was an active member of the Southern States Art League and the Carolina Art Association. Examples of her portraits are in private and public permanent collections, including the Robert P. Coggins Collection; the Roper Hospital; the Hibernian Society, and St. Andrews Society—all of which are sited in Charleston, South Carolina.

Bibliography
American Art Annual. Vol. 28. American Federation of Arts, 1932.
Chambers, Bruce W. *Art and Artists of the South: The Robert P. Coggins Collection.* University of South Carolina Press, 1984.
Who's Who in American Art. Vol. 8. American Federation of Arts, 1962.

Nason, Gertrude (1890–1969)

Born in Everett, Massachusetts, the painter Gertrude Nason learned her craft at the Massachusetts School of Art, Boston, under the aegis of Joseph De Camp; and at the Boston Museum School of Fine Arts with Edmund Tarbell.

Nason exhibited widely in museums and galleries, including the Pennsylvania Academy of Fine Arts, Philadelphia (1925, 1932, 1934); National Academy of Design (1933, 1935); National Association of Women Artists (1939, 1945); and Riverside Museum (1942, 1944, 1946)—all in New York City; American-British Art Center (1943); Dayton Art Institute, Ohio (1946); and many others.

Winner of honors and awards, Nason was a member of the Brooklyn Society of Modern Art, New York; the Creative Arts Association; Lyme Arts Association, Connecticut; National Association of Women Artists; and the New York Society of Women Artists. Examples of her work are in private and public permanent collections.

Bibliography
American Art Annual. Vol. 28. American Federation of Arts, 1932.
Vose Winter 1987–88. Boston: Vose Galleries, 1987.
Obituary. *Who's Who in American Art.* Vol 13. American Federation of Arts, 1978.

Natzler, Gertrud Amon (1908–1971)

Born in Vienna, Austria, the well-known ceramist Gertrud Amon Natzler studied at the Handelsakademie and, briefly, with Franz Iskra (1934). Essentially self-taught, Natzler, along with her husband Otto, set up a ceramic studio in 1935 and turned out classic forms: she threw the pots and he glazed them. Two years later, at the Galerie Wurthle, their work met with success, which was reinforced by a silver medal awarded them the same year at the Exposition Universelle, Paris, France.

In 1938 the couple emigrated to the United States and, the following year, to Los Angeles, California, where they taught ceramics for three years. A first prize in the Ceramic National Exhibition in Syracuse, New York (1939), assisted greatly in the appreciation of their craftsmanship. Their work was invited to major museum exhibitions and was given several retrospective shows. Examples of their work are represented in private and public permanent collections, including the Art Institute of Chicago, Illinois; Los Angeles County Museum of Art, California; Metropolitan Museum of Art and the Museum of Modern Art (MoMA)—both in New York City; and many others.

Bibliography
Andreson, Laura. "The Natzlers." *California Arts & Architecture* 58 (July 1941).
Clark, Garth. *American Ceramics: 1896 to the Present.* Abbeville Press, 1987.
Henderson, R. "Gertrud and Otto Natzler." *Design* 49 (January 1948).

Nay, Mary Spencer (1913–1993)

Born in Crestwood, Kentucky, the painter/printmaker Mary Spencer Nay studied at several institutions, including the Art Center Association School, Louisville, Kentucky (1934–1940); the Cincinnati Art Academy, Ohio (1942); the University of Louisville, Kentucky, where she earned both a Bachelor's degree (1941), and a Master of Arts degree (1960). Nay also studied at the Art Students League, New York City (1942); and in Provincetown, Massachusetts, with Boris Margo (1950–1951).

Nay exhibited work in solo and group shows, including the New York World's Fair (1939); "Artists for Victory," Metropolitan Museum of Art, New York City (1941); the "International Color Lithography Annuals" at the Cincinnati Art Museum, Ohio (1950, 1952, 1954); a "Retrospective," the J.B. Speed Art Museum, Louisville, Kentucky (1976); and others.

Among other positions, she taught painting and printmaking for twenty years at the University of Louisville, retiring as Marcia S. Hite professor of painting in 1979.

Winner of many purchase awards, Nay was a member of the Provincetown Art Association and Museum, Massachusetts; the Heritage Museum; the Historical Association; and the Visual Artists Cooperative.

Her forceful abstractions are represented in private and public permanent collections, including the Evansville Museum of Arts and Science, Indiana; J.B. Speed Art Museum, Louisville, Kentucky; Kentucky Wesleyan College, Owensboro; Ohio University, Athens; and others.

Bibliography
Contemporary Art of the United States. Corcoran Gallery of Art. 1940: no. 18.
Mary Spencer Nay. A Catalog. J.B. Speed Art Museum, 1976.
Who's Who in American Art. 17th ed. R.R. Bowker Co., 1986.

Neel, Alice (1900–1984)

Alice Neel is one of the most powerfully original American portrait painters in the twentieth century. During a period when critics proclaimed the primacy of abstraction as a universal art form purified of the contaminations of history, she depicted the human image brutalized by social forces. Her style is deliberately inelegant, revealing the ravages of time and struggle on the human body and soul with uncompromising candor. More than for most artists her art and her biography are organically entwined.

Neel had an abiding disdain for "normality" that grew out of the debilitating boredom she experienced growing up in a small suburban town outside Philadelphia, Pennsylvania. Although she had no role models she knew from the beginning that she wanted to be an artist. She took the secretarial course in high school and worked in civil service jobs, but began to take art courses secretly at night. After three years she left her job to attend the Philadelphia School of Design for Women (now called Moore College of Art). Already rebellious, she rejected popular impressionist influences to paint expressionistic portraits and still lifes in a coarse, unconventional style.

While still a student, Neel met and married Carlos Enriquez, an aristocratic bohemian artist from Havana. From 1926 to 1927 they lived with his wealthy family in Cuba, where Neel had a baby girl and an exhibition of her work. Shortly after they returned to New York City the baby died of diphtheria. Neel was distraught, but, by the end of 1928, she had given birth to another daughter, Isabetta. During this period she painted "Well Baby Clinic" (1928), which juxtaposes the precision of the hospital's angular white walls with the ragged contours of the undisciplined human clientele. Here, as in all of her work, the rectangular contour of her canvas becomes a cage that seems to exert an invisible pressure upon her fragile subjects.

Poverty put a strain on Neel's marriage, and her husband abandoned her in 1930, taking their daughter to Cuba. She suffered a severe nervous breakdown and was hospitalized for a year, during which she continuously attempted suicide. A pencil drawing, "Suicidal Ward, Philadelphia General Hospital" (1931), depicts a mental ward with a group of female patients attended by an authoritative male doctor. The rigid geometrical structure of the room, its lack of windows, and its institutional barrenness impart a sensation of unrelenting and tedious confinement. Neel's life was traumatic, yet she always transformed it into art.

During the 1930s and 1940s Neel lived with a series of men, all of whom, along with her children, figure prominently in her work. In 1932 she moved to Greenwich Village in New York City with Kenneth Doolittle, a former Wobbly turned sailor. Later that year, John Rothschild, a Harvard-educated travel agent, saw her work at an exhibition, and she began an on-and-off relationship with him that lasted until his death in 1975. In response Doolittle destroyed most of her early work in 1934. In 1935 Neel met José Santiago, a Puerto Rican nightclub entertainer, and moved with him to Spanish Harlem. Shortly after the birth of their son, Richard, in 1939, Santiago ran off with a glamorous salesclerk. Sometime around 1940 Sam Putnam, a temperamental Marxist intellectual, translator, and newspaper writer, entered Neel's life, and, by 1941, they had a son, Hartley, but soon drifted apart. After Putnam, Neel lived alone with her children, remaining in Spanish Harlem until 1962.

In 1933 Neel had entered the Public Works of Art Project (PWAP), and by 1935 she was an easel painter in the Works Projects Administration Federal Art Project (WPA/FAP), producing expressionistic cityscapes, such as "Synthesis of New York (The Great Depression)" (1933). The picture appears deceptively conventional at first glance, recalling the solid naturalism of the Ash Can School, but, upon closer inspection, the faces of the dour, heavily-bundled inhabitants are revealed as skulls. An eerily empty subway tunnel occupies a separate register at the bottom of the canvas, and in a pocket of fragmented space in the sky, two winged mannequins, one of them headless, display an insignia showing the conjunction of the sun and the moon, which, like the painting itself, represents eternity and the ephemeral moment united in a single mysterious image.

Both in Greenwich Village and in Spanish Harlem Neel painted her neighbors: local eccentrics, poets, Left Wing activists, children, delinquents, and old people—all of them struggling to survive with dignity. "T.B. Harlem" (1940) depicts a young Puerto Rican neighbor who points mutely to his surgically collapsed lung with the martyr-like serenity of a Christian saint. His direct, melancholy gaze engages the viewer in a painfully intimate encounter with his suffering. When Neel moved to West 107th Street in 1962 she continued to chronicle her family of growing boys, their friends, and eventually their wives and children. With increasing frequency her subjects were members of the avant-garde art world: patrons, such as Linda Nochlin; as well as artists, such as Benny Andrews, the Soyer brothers, Robert Smithson, Duane Hanson, Faith Ringgold, Red and Mimi Grooms, and Andy Warhol.

Many of Neel's pictures treat human sexuality with an unprecedented freshness that ignores conventional sexual stereotypes. "Geoffrey Hendricks and Brian" (1978) explores the complex dynamics of a homosexual relationship with a psychological honesty that transcends sensationalism. "Pregnant Woman" (1971), a nude portrait of her daughter-in-law, Nancy, in the pose of a reclining Venus, removes female sexuality from the fantasy realm of aesthetic voyeurism by recording the physical burdens and emotional consequences of conception. "John Perreault" (1973), a nude portrait of a well-known *Village Voice* art critic, breaks new ground by depicting a male model in a passive position of receptivity which had previously been reserved only for women. Unlike most female nudes by male artists, Perreault's gentle gaze lacks the slightest hint of coquetry. He is portrayed with such empathy that the viewer is prevented from commodifying the image.

During most of her career Neel painted in poverty and isolation. She did not exhibit regularly until the 1960s, and only with the burgeoning feminist movement in the early 1970s did her work begin to receive public confirmation. Her first major one-woman exhibition was organized under the pressure of a petition from the art community when she was already seventy-four years old. But, in the last years before her death, her art was the subject of accolades, exhibitions, a book, and numerous articles. Her integrity and commitment to her own vision in the face of the discrimination and neglect has been an inspiration for a new generation of women artists.

Marilyn Lincoln Board

Bibliography

Board, Marilyn Lincoln. "The Legend of Alice Neel: Re-envisioning the Cinderella Story." *Women's Artistry: Re-envisioning the Female Self.* Ed. Kathryn Benzel. Edwin Mellen Press, 1990.

Fine, Elsa Honig. *Women and Art.* Allandheldt and Schrem, 1978.

Hills, Patricia. *Alice Neel.* Harry N. Abrams, 1983.

Munro, Eleanor. *American Women Artists.* Simon and Schuster, 1979.

Nemser, Cindy. *Alice Neel: The Woman and Her Work.* University of Georgia Press, 1975.

Nochlin, Linda. "Some Women Realists: Painters of the Figure." *Arts Magazine* 48 (May 1974): 29–33; rpt. *Women, Art and Power and Other Essays.* Harper & Row, 1988.

———. *Art Talk: Conversations with 12 Women Artists.* Charles Scribner's Sons, 1975.

Rubenstein, Charlotte. *American Women Artists: From Early Indian Times to the Present.* G.K. Hall, 1982.

Neimanas, Joyce (1944–)

Born in Chicago, Illinois, on January 22, 1944, Joyce Neimanas is known as a photographer who uses unorthodox methods in producing mixed-media imagery, which contains two recurrent themes—the anxiety of personal relationships and the male/female stereotypes. She received her Bachelor of Fine Arts degree (1966) and her Master of Fine Arts degree (1969) from the School of the Art Institute of Chicago, Illinois, where she studied under Kenneth Josephson. The program at the Art Institute emphasized an interdisciplinary approach that encouraged experimentation and manipulation of the photographic medium.

Since 1970 Neimanas has been an associate professor at the School of the Art Institute of Chicago, Illinois. Over the past twenty-five years she has participated in a number of group and individual exhibitions, from California to Rhode Island. Her work is included in the permanent collections of the Art Institute of Chicago, Illinois; the Fogg Museum of Art, Harvard University, Cambridge, Massachusetts; the George Eastman House, Rochester, New York; and the Center for Creative Photography, Tucson, Arizona, to name a few. Her work has been recognized with the National Endowment for the Arts individual artists grant in 1978.

Neimanas's unorthodox approach incorporates the use of anonymous negatives, cutting and tearing prints and negatives, manipulating photographs and rephotographing them, as well as hand-coloring and drawing on the surface. These procedures cause tension between the photograph as an art object and as a reproduction of reality. Neimanas's recent work varies in size and scale, creating a collage of SX-70 prints. By layering these Polaroids, she creates a surface texture of patterns and colors that mimic actual domestic space.

Melissa J. Guenther

Bibliography

Browne, Turner, and Elaine Partnow. *Macmillan Biographical Encyclopedia of Photographic Artists and Innovators.* Macmillan, and Collier Macmillan, 1983.

Moore, Sarah. *Joyce Neimanas.* Tucson: Center for Creative Photography, University of Arizona, 1984.

Nettles, Bea (1946–)

Born in Gainesville, Florida, the mixed-media photographer Bea Nettles earned a Bachelor of Fine Arts degree from the University of Florida in her native city (1968) and, two years later, received a Master of Fine Arts degree from the University of Illinois, Chicago Circle.

Nettles's first post in higher education was at Nazareth College, Rochester, New York (1970–1971); she then taught at the Tyler School of Art, Temple University, Philadelphia, Pennsylvania (1972–1974). Between 1971 and 1972 Nettles taught at the Rochester Institute of Technology, New York, and has been there on the faculty since 1976.

Winner of honors and awards, she received a Creative Artists Public Service (CAPS) grant from the New York State Council on the Arts (1976); a National Endowment for the Arts (NEA) fellowship in photography (1979); and others.

Nettles's work is represented in private and public permanent collections in the United States and abroad, including the Baltimore Museum of Art, Maryland; Center for Creative Photography, Tucson, Arizona; Colgate University, Hamilton, New York; the Metropolitan Museum of Art, New York City; Museum of Fine Arts, Houston, Texas; Pomona College, Claremont, California; the National Gallery of Art, Ottawa, Canada; and others.

Bibliography

Browne, Turner, and Elaine Partnow. *Macmillan Biographical Encyclopedia of Photographic Artists and Innovators.* Macmillan, 1983.

Cohen, Joyce T. *In/Sights: Self-Portraits by Women.* 1978.

Wade, Kent. *Alternative Photographic Processes.* 1978.

Witkin, Lee D., and Barbara London. *The Photograph Collector's Guide.* 1979.

Nevelson, Louise (1899–1988)

One of America's most well-known and distinctive sculptors, Louise Nevelson was born in Kiev, Russia, to Isaac Berliawsky and Ninna Ziesel Smolerank. She emigrated to the United States with her family in 1905, settling in Rockland, Maine. By the age of six Nevelson was assembling and carving scraps of wood from her father's contracting business.

Nevelson's formal art training began when she moved to New York City after her marriage to Charles Nevelson, a shipowner, in 1920. In New York City, she began to study all the arts, drama, and voice, as well as painting and drawing. In 1929–1930 she studied with Kenneth Hayes Miller and Kimon Nicolaides at the Art Students League, New York City. In 1931 she separated from her husband, left her son Myron (Mike), born in 1922, with her parents in Maine; and went to Munich, Germany, to study with Hans Hofmann. After the closing of Hofmann's academy approximately six months after her arrival, Nevelson travelled to Berlin, Vienna, Italy, and Paris. Upon her return to New York City in 1932, Nevelson resumed her art classes at the Art Students League, where she studied with Hofmann, now in New York, and George Grosz. She also worked as an assistant to Diego Rivera for a series of twenty-one murals, "Portrait of America," in the New Workers' School on Fourteenth Street—an experience that introduced her to mural scale and format.

In 1933 Nevelson exhibited several paintings at the Secession Gallery, New York City; and, in 1935, one of her terra-cotta figures was included in an exhibition of young sculptors at the Brooklyn Museum, New York, her first museum show. The following year five wood sculptures were exhibited in the ACA Gallery competition in New York City and received honorable mention. In 1937 Nevelson was employed by the Works Progress Administration (WPA), painting, sculpting, and teaching at the Educational Alliance School of Art.

Nevelson's distinctive sculptural style began to emerge during the 1940s. Her formal and thematic evolution can be marked by the one-person shows held principally at the Nierendorf Gallery, New York City, with which she was affiliated from 1941 to 1948. In her 1942 one-person show at the Nierendorf Gallery Nevelson introduced found objects in her work; and in 1943 she organized her first exhibit based on a theme, "The Circus: The Clown is the Center of His World," at the Norlyst Gallery, New York City. Her first exhibition of abstract wood sculpture, "Sculpture Montages," was held at Nierendorf Gallery in 1944. Beginning in 1943 Nevelson lived with her work. From 1943 to 1959 she lived in a four-story house with a garden on East Thirtieth Street. She divided the garden into tools on one side and a "farm" of odd objects which she had painted black on the other.

While principally a sculptor, Nevelson also was a printmaker. In 1947 she studied printmaking with Stanley William Hayter at the Atelier 17 in New York City and had her first exhibition of etchings, "Moonscapes," at the Lotte Jacob Gallery, New York City, in 1950. Printmaking remained an active interest for Nevelson, who received a Ford Foundation grant to work at the Tamarind Lithography Workshop in 1963. Her prints—etchings, lithographs, and serigraphs—usually produced in series, were published by Pace Editions during the 1960s.

Beginning in 1948 Nevelson underwent a personal crisis that resulted in an artistic retrenchment for a period. In 1948 the death of Karl Nierendorf had a debilitating effect on Nevelson: she was unable to work, became ill, and had surgery for a benign tumor. After a trip to Europe with her sister, Anita Berliawsky, Nevelson returned to making terracotta sculpture at the Sculpture Center on Eighth Street in New York City in 1949. She cut unmolded forms from clay and applied textures and lines by imprinting fabrics and drawing with sharp tools into the wet clay, creating faces, torsos, and geometric shapes which she stacked into totemic pieces called "Game Figures." In 1950 and 1951 Nevelson made trips to Mexico City and the Yucatan Peninsula, Mexico, and Quirigua, Guatemala, where she studied pre-Columbian sculpture.

Beginning in 1955 Nevelson resumed active productivity as a sculptor, reaching artistic maturity, exhibiting regularly, and receiving critical acclaim. From 1955 to 1958 she was affiliated with the Grand Central Modern Gallery in New York City, directed by her friend Coretta Roberts, which held annual one-person shows of her work. Her first show at Grand Central Modern Gallery, "Ancient Places, Ancient Games," included her "Game Figures." The presentation of some of the pieces on bases of crates, altered by eliminating some of the joining boards and adding triangular corner supports, which were painted black, or placed on the floor directly anticipated her mature style. In 1956 the Whitney Museum of American Art, New York City, acquired "Black Majesty" from her exhibition, "The Royal Voyage (of the King and Queen of the Sea)," at the Grand Central Modern Gallery; it was the first Nevelson piece acquired by a major museum. In 1957 she began to enclose wood reliefs in boxes and to assemble her first wall pieces, which resulted in her first environmental exhibition, "Moon Garden + One," at the Grand Central Modern Gallery in 1958. This installation consisted of black wall sculptures of boxes and columnar units, "Sky Cathedrals," which were illuminated by blue lights. The Museum of Modern Art (MoMA), New York City, acquired a "Sky Cathedral" from this show, and Hilton Kramer, reviewing the show for *Arts*, wrote enthusiastically of her work. Nevelson's work was included in the Pittsburgh International Exhibition, Carnegie Institute, Pennsylvania (1958), and collectors, such as Philip Johnson, Nelson Rockefeller, and Burton Tremaine, acquired her work. From 1958 to 1962 Nevelson was affiliated with the Martha Jackson Gallery, also in New York City, one of the most prestigious and best-financed galleries in America and one that reflected the international art scene.

After 1958 Nevelson began to depart from monochromatic black color for her wall pieces. She introduced white wall sculptures with the exhibit of "Dawn's Wedding Feast" as part of the "Sixteen Americans," show at MoMA. In 1961 she exhibited the first gold sculptures in the entitled show, "The Rodyal Tides," at the Martha Jackson Gallery. For the XXXI Biennale Internazionale at Venice, Italy, in 1962, Nevelson created three distinct environments, one each of black, white, and gold.

During the 1960s Nevelson began to explore new techniques and materials. Unlike her usual practice of making her own boxes, she be-

gan to have boxes made for her, perhaps reflecting the current minimalist direction in American sculpture. She also began to make plexiglass wall sculptures ("Transparent Sculptures" [1967–1968]) and in 1965 began to work with Cor-ten metal. The first large Cor-ten sculpture, "Atmosphere and Environment X" (1969), was commissioned by Princeton University, New Jersey, the first of many large commissions.

Since the 1960s Nevelson has been recognized for her distinctive contribution to American sculpture. The Whitney Museum of American Art mounted the first major retrospective of her work in 1967; and, in 1972, Arnold Glimcher wrote the first monograph on Nevelson, in which he places Nevelson's work in the context of contemporary sculpture and painting. According to Glimcher Nevelson's formal style and aesthetic derive from diverse sources: the geometric vocabulary and collage technique of Cubism and the mural-scale of American abstract painting of the 1940s and 1950s.

Virginia Hagelstein Marquardt

Bibliography
Glimcher, Arnold B. *Louise Nevelson*. Dutton, 1976.
Lipman, Jean. *Nevelson's World*. Hudson Hills Press in association with the Whitney Museum of American Art, 1983.
Nevelson, Louise. *Dawns + Dusks*. Charles Scribner's Sons, 1976.
Wilson, Laurie. *Louise Nevelson: Iconography and Sources*. Garland, 1981.

Nevin, Blanche (1841–1925)

Born in Philadelphia, Pennsylvania, the sculptor Blanche Nevin studied with Joseph Bailly and attended the Pennsylvania Academy of Fine Arts in her native city. Ironically, little is known today about this once popular figure.

Two examples of Nevin's sculpture, "Cinderella" and "Eve," were exhibited at the Centennial International Exposition, Philadelphia, Pennsylvania (1876); and her "Maud Muller" (from the poem by John Greenleaf Whittier) was shown at the International Exposition, Chicago, Illinois (1893). Nevin's work is also represented in the U.S. Capitol building.

Bibliography
Art in the United States Capitol. U.S. Government Printing Office, 1976.
Paine, Judith. "The Women's Pavillion of 1876." *The Feminist Art Journal* 4:4 (Winter 1975–76): 5–12.
Weimann, Jeanne Madeline. *The Fair Women*. Academy Chicago, 1981.

Newdigate, Ann (1934–)

Since the early 1970s Ann Newdigate has been known for her work in Gobelin-style tapestry. Woven in a wide variety of materials, her pictorial tapestries use layered images and text to explore issues around identity and location. Her series "Look at It This Way" (1988) examined the traditional art/craft hierarchy and the cultural politics surrounding the tapestry medium. Her most recent series of drawings and tapestries, "Sentences" (1990), uses found newspaper text and landscape imagery to represent the situation of apartheid in South Africa.

Newdigate was born in Grahamstown, South Africa. In 1964 she received a Bachelor of Arts degree in English literature and African studies before immigrating to Saskatoon, Saskatchewan, Canada, in 1966. She received Bachelor of Fine Arts (1975) and Master of Fine Arts (1986) degrees from the University of Saskatchewan, and completed a year of post-graduate studies at the tapestry department of the Edinburgh College of Art, Scotland (1981–1982).

Since the early 1980s Newdigate's tapestries have been included in group exhibitions across Canada, the United States, and Australia. Her work is represented in the collection of the Canada Council Art Bank and the Canadian Museum of Civilization, among others.

Besides producing and exhibiting her own work Newdigate is active as a teacher, writer, and guest-lecturer in the art community. She taught classes in studio and art education at the University of Saskatchewan (1982–1987), and was a visiting fellow at Monash University, Australia (1990), where she taught drawing and inaugurated the tapestry course for the fine art program.

Lynne S. Bell

Bibliography

Bell, Lynne. *Ann Newdigate Mills: Look At It This Way.* Mendel Art Gallery, 1988.

Clausen, Valerie, ed. *Tapestry: Contemporary Imagery/Ancient Tradition— United States, Canada, United Kingdom.* Cheney Cowles Memorial Museum, 1986.

Gourlay, Sheena. "Ann Newdigate Mills—The Gordon Snelgrove Gallery." *Vanguard* 15 (Summer 1981) 58–59.

Jones, Miranda. "Weaving Through Art History." *Border Crossings* (Summer 1989): 46–49.

Marcus, Sharon, ed. *Tapestry: The Narrative Voice.* The Centre for Tapestry Arts, 1989–1991.

Newmark, Marilyn (1928–)

A native New Yorker, the equestrian sculptor Marilyn Newmark received her formal education at Alfred University, and Adelphi College (now Adelphi University), Garden City—both in New York. Her informal learning started at age seven, when she first rode a horse. She also worked under the aegis of Paul Brown in Garden City, New York.

Newmark has won more than seventy awards for her bronze sculptures of horses and other animals between 1971 and 1992, including prizes from the National Sculpture Society, National Academy of Design, American Artists Professional League, Allied Artists of America, and others. She has held solo exhibitions of her work at Fasig-Tipton, Saratoga (1976), and Belmont Park, Elmont (1977, 1979)—both in New York. Her bronzes have been invited to numerous group exhibitions throughout the United States and abroad, including the National Sculpture Society, where she served on the council (1973–1979, 1981–1983, 1991 to the present), National Academy of Design, and Allied Artists of America—all in New York City; North American Sculpture Exhibition, Foothills Art Center, Colorado; Society of Animal Artists, where she served on the jury of admissions (1972–1975, 1989 to the present), and as a member of the board of directors (1990 to the present); Pen & Brush, New York City; U.S. Information Agency (USIA) tour of eastern and western Europe (1976–1977); and many others.

Newmark is a fellow of a great many professional art societies; academician-elect of the National Academy of Design; and founding member of the American Academy of Equine Art, as well as its director of sculpture (1981 to the present). She has been graced with commissions to sculpt the leading thoroughbred horses in bronze, and/or to create medallions and other awards for a number of equestrian or-

ganizations. Her work is represented in many private and public permanent collections, including the National Museum of Racing, Saratoga, New York; the National Art Museum of Sport, Indianapolis, Indiana; American Saddle Horse Museum; the International Museum of the Horse, Kentucky Horse Park, Lexington, Kentucky; and others.

Bibliography

Malmstrom, Margit. "The Bronze Horses of Marilyn Newmark." *American Artist* (April 1971): 28–33, 80–81.

Mackay-Smith, Alexander. "The American Academy of Equine Art." *The Chronicle of the Horse* (September 12, 1980): 2.

"Marilyn Newmark, Horsewoman and Artist Extraordinaire." *Horse of Course* (May 1977): 32, 34, 36–37.

Who's Who in American Art. 19th ed. R.R. Bowker Co., 1991–1992.

Newton, Lilias Torrance (1896–1980)

A leading portrait painter in Canada for several decades, Lilias Torrance Newton was an artist whose style embraced the keen interest in a formalist aesthetic that marked the work of figure painters in Montréal prior to World War II. Newton, whose father had been an amateur artist and poet, was born in Lachine, Québec. She developed an interest in painting in her youth and began to study seriously with William Brymner at the art school of the Art Association of Montréal around 1914.

During World War I Newton served overseas and while in England found time to study briefly with Alfred Wolmark, an eastern European painter. Returning to Montréal she continued to paint, and by 1920 became a member of the Beaver Hall Group, a group of painters who shared studio space and exchanged ideas. The group included Edwin Holgate, Randolph Hewton, and Mabel May, among others. She married Fred Newton in 1921 and he encouraged her to continue painting.

In 1923 Newton studied for four months in Paris, France, with Alexandre Jacovleff, a Russian artist known for his strong draftsmanship, and Adolf Milman, an associate of Holgate's. Newton and Holgate were colleagues in the 1930s as teachers at the art school of the Art Association of Montréal and as founding members of the Canadian Group of Painters.

Newton's career as a portraitist was established in the 1920s. Her works using friends or models as subjects have been noted by Charles Hill as her best, showing "a greater personal identification between sitter and artist" than her commissioned works. Her portraits of Group of Seven artists "A.Y. Jackson" and "Lawren Harris" (both National Gallery of Canada), for example, are considered among her best works. The portrait of artist "Louis Muhlstock," Newton's diploma piece for the Royal Canadian Academy into which she was received as a full member in 1937, is a full statement of her style—the half-length casually-posed figure is cropped to form an interesting composition in which the angular face is echoed in the repeated triangles within the figure as well as in the surrounding negative spaces. The planar structure of the picture is strongly and simply stated.

Newton was included in a number of prestigious group exhibitions of Canadian art, among them, "Exposition d'art Canadien," Jeu de Paume, Paris, France (1927); "Contemporary Canadian Artists," Corcoran Gallery of Art, Washington, D.C. (1930); Coronation Exhibition, London, England (1937); and "A Century of Canadian Art," Tate Gallery, London, England (1938). She had one-person exhibitions in

1930, 1939, 1945, and 1958; a retrospective was organized in 1981. She was commissioned to paint portraits of "Queen Elizabeth II" and "Prince Philip" of Britain in 1957. Her work may be found in the following public collections in Canada: Edmonton Art Gallery, Glenbow Museum, Art Gallery of Ontario, National Gallery of Canada, Montréal Museum of Fine Arts, Musée du Québec, and others.

Janice Seline

Bibliography

Farr, Dorothy. *Lilias Torrance Newton 1896–1980*. Exhibition Catalog. Kingston, Ontario: Agnes Etherington Art Centre, 1981.

Hill, Charles C. *Canadian Painting in the Thirties*. Exhibition Catalog. National Gallery of Canada, 1975.

MacDonald, C.S. *A Dictionary of Canadian Artists*. Vol. 5. Canadian Paperbacks, 1977.

Ney, Elisabet (1833–1907)

The daughter of a Münster, Germany, stonemason, Elisabet Ney persuaded the art academies, first in Munich (1852–1854) and then in Berlin (1854–1857), to admit her as a sculpture student. In Berlin she studied with the neoclassical sculptor Christian Daniel Rauch. Once a trained sculptor, Ney cultivated luminaries as subjects of bust portraits or medallions, including: "Jacob Grimm," "Alexander von Humboldt," "Cosima and Hans von Bülow," "Joseph Joachim," "Arthur Schopenhauer," and "King George V of Hanover." In 1865 she went to Italy to model Giuseppe Garibaldi, and, on her return to Germany the King of Prussia commissioned her to portray "Otto von Bismarck." From 1867 through 1870 she served King Ludwig II as his personal sculptor in Munich, creating an over-life-size, full-length marble statue of the young Bavarian King for his castle on the island of Herrenchiemsee. But, with the outbreak of the Franco-Prussian War, Ney was suspected of being a Bismarck plant in the Bavarian court, and, on January 14, 1871, she and her "best friend," Edmon Montgomery (whom she had married on the island of Madeira in 1864), departed by ship for America.

After living in a German-founded commune in Georgia and giving birth to two sons, Ney moved the family to Texas, finally settling in Austin. In the summer of 1892 Ney was commissioned to model statues of "Sam Houston" and "Stephen F. Austin" for the World's Columbian Exposition. Her full-length plaster statues of these two Texans are in the Elisabet Ney Museum in Austin, Texas (formerly her studio) and marble statues are in both the U.S. Capitol building in Washington, D.C., and in the entranceway to the Texas Capitol building in Austin. Her last dramatic sculpture, "Lady Macbeth" (National Museum of American Art), was completed in 1905.

Eleanor Tufts

Bibliography

Cutrer, Emily Fourmy. *The Art of the Woman: The Life and Work of Elisabet Ney*. University of Nebraska Press, 1988.

Tufts, Eleanor. *American Women Artists, 1830–1930*. National Museum of Women in the Arts, 1987.

Nicholls, Rhoda Holmes (1854–1930)

Born in Coventry, England, the painter/writer Rhoda Holmes Nicholls studied at the Bloomsbury School of Art, London, England; she took further work with William Merritt Chase, and with Cammerano and Vertuni in Rome, Italy. Nicholls emigrated to the United States in 1884.

Winner of honors and awards, Nicholls exhibited widely and won medals in many venues, including the World Columbian Exposition, Chicago, Illinois (1893); the Exposition in Atlanta, Georgia (1895); the Exposition in Nashville, Tennessee (1897); and expositions in Boston, Massachusetts; Charlotte, North Carolina; the Pan-American Exposition in Buffalo, New York (1901); the expositions in Charleston, South Carolina (1902); the St. Louis Missouri Exposition (1904); she also exhibited at the National Academy of Design, New York City, and others.

Member of a number of professional arts organizations, Nicholls' work is represented in private and public permanent collections, including the Boston Art Club and the Boston Museum of Fine Arts—both in Massachusetts; and others.

Bibliography

Benson, Frances M. "Five Women Artists in New York." *Essays in American Art and Artists*. American Art Co., 1895.

Elliot, Maud H. *Art and Handicraft in the Women's Building of the World's Columbian Exposition, Chicago, 1893*. Rand McNally and Co., 1894.

Fielding, Mantle. *Dictionary of American Painters, Sculptors, and Engravers*. Modern Books and Crafts, 1974.

Pisano, Ronald. *Students of William Merritt Chase*. Huntington, New York: Heckscher Museum, 1973.

Nicoll, Marion (1909–)

Born in Calgary, Alberta, Canada, the painter/printmaker Marion Nicoll studied with J.W.G. MacDonald at the Ontario School of Art, Toronto (1927–1929); then worked with A.C. Leighton at the Provincial Institute of Technology and Art, Calgary (1929–1932), as well as in three of his summer classes at the Banff School of Fine Arts, Alberta. She also studied at the Central School of Arts and Crafts, London, England, with Duncan Grant (1937–1938), and attended the well-known Emma Lake Workshops, where she worked with Will Barnet (1957). MacDonald taught her "automatic drawing," and she studied at the Art Students League, New York City (1958–1959).

Nicoll has held solo exhibitions in museums and galleries in Canada, including the Alberta College of Art, Calgary (1959); Studio 61, Edmonton, Alberta (1961); Focus, Edmonton (1962, 1963, 1964); Upstairs Gallery, Toronto (1963); Yellow Door Gallery, Winnipeg, Manitoba (1964, 1966); the Western Canadian Art Circuit, Victoria, British Columbia to Winnipeg (1966); Sears, the Vincent Price Collection, Chicago, Illinois (1968); and others.

The first Alberta woman to be elected to the Royal Canadian Academy, Nicoll has received honors and awards from the Canada Council and other institutions for her abstract paintings and prints. Her work has been included in prestigious group shows, such as the 5th, 6th, and 7th Biennial Exhibitions of Canadian Painting (1963, 1965, 1967); and others. Examples of her work are in private and public permanent collections in Canada, including the Edmonton Museum of Art, Alberta; Memorial University, Newfoundland; University of Alberta, Calgary; Winnipeg Art Gallery, Manitoba; and many others.

Bibliography
Barnet, Will, intro. *Marion Nicoll: A Retrospective, 1959–1971.* A Catalog. Edmonton Art Gallery, 1975.
Joyner, J. Brooks. *Marion Nicoll R.C.A.* Calgary, Alberta: Masters Gallery, 1979.
Payne, Anne. "Jim and Marion Nicoll." *Arts West* 2:3 (1977): 7–15.

Nilsson, Gladys (1940–)

Born in Chicago, Illinois, the painter Gladys Nilsson earned a diploma from the School of the Art Institute of Chicago (1960).

Nilsson has shown widely in museums and galleries in the United States and abroad, including the Whitney Museum of American Art, New York City (1973); Phyllis Kind Gallery, New York City (1976); "Who Chicago?" Ceolfrith Gallery, Tyne and Wear, England (1981); "Parallel Vision: Modern Artists and Outsider Art," a travelling show, Los Angeles County Art Museum, California (1992–1993); and many others.

Examples of Nilsson's work are in private and public permanent collections, including the Art Institute of Chicago; the Museum of Contemporary Art, Chicago, Illinois; Museum of Modern Art (MoMA), New York City; Museum of Modern Art, Vienna, Austria; the Whitney Museum of American Art, New York City; and others.

Bibliography
Bowman, Russell. "Gladys Nilsson." *Arts Magazine* 53:8 (April 1979): 11.
Cohrs, Timothy. "Gladys Nilsson." *Arts Magazine* 61:7 (March 1987): 111.
Victor, Polly. "Women Artists—Restoring the Balance." *Artweek* 18:14 (11 April 1987): 1.

Niviaxie, Annie (Sala) (1930–1989)

A Canadian Inuit sculptor, Annie (Sala) Niviaxie was born in the Arctic Québec community of Inukjuak (Port Harrison) in 1928. She moved to Kuujjuaraapik (Great Whale River) after her marriage to Josephie Niviaxie. Kuujjuaraapik is one of two Arctic Québec communities with an unusually large number of talented women carvers.

Early in her career, Niviaxie was able to indulge in more experimentally creative forms of her perennial theme: mother and child. As her husband and adopted son were unable to contribute to household finances, the demands fell increasingly on Niviaxie. "Equal pay for equal work" was not part of the purchasing policy of her cooperative, whose manager was not a woman. She worked harder and produced more than her male counterparts. This probably contributed to her more stylized, "stone doll." Even so, she managed to infuse originality into each one. An expert seamstress, Niviaxie joined a sealskin wall-hanging project in 1972, cooperating with two other artists in the creation of several large appliqué hangings. The production of hangings, dolls, and baskets was more lucrative, but Niviaxie preferred stone carving. Niviaxie's works have been shown in about twenty-five group exhibitions in Canada and the United States. She is represented in the collections of the Canadian Museum of Civilization, the National Gallery of Canada, and the Winnipeg Art Gallery.

Mary Craig

Bibliography
Inuit Artist Index Arranged by Community. Indian and Northern Affairs Canada, 1990.

Noble, Karen L. (1955–)

A Chimariko/Hupa/Karuk tribe member, Karen L. Noble was born in Arcata, California, and studied art there at Humboldt State College.

Between 1976 and 1987 Noble exhibited her paintings in twenty shows in New York, California, and Arizona, including the New York Center for the Living Arts, New York City (1981); and Native Americans Now, Santa Rosa (1982); a solo exhibition at the University of California at Davis (1982); "Keeping the Home Fires Burning," Humboldt Cultural Center, Eureka (1987); "Beyond Boundaries of Land and Water," AICA, San Francisco (1988); and "Paths Beyond Tradition," San Diego Museum of Art (1989)—all in California; and others.

Noble works in many media, including oils, watercolor, lithography, and seashell jewelry created for ceremonial purposes. "The Flood" (c. 1985) is a typical oil on canvas, which represents seven nude humans riding in a huge Northern California basket, on a rain-swept stormy sea, while three eagles soar overhead. In Noble's words, "To be an artist is to be a Channel through a higher intelligence which may manifest itself on our earthly plane."

Bibliography
Heard Museum Archives. Phoenix, Arizona.

Noel, Maxine (1946–)

Born on the Birdtail reservation in southwest Manitoba, Canada, Maxine Noel is a member of the Santee Oglala Sioux tribe. A self-taught artist and the eldest of eleven children, she was encouraged to draw by her mother and grandmother and, though she spent more than a decade as a legal secretary in Edmonton and Toronto, became a full-time artist in 1979 and had her first solo exhibition a year later.

Between 1980 and 1989 Noel has had her work exhibited in more than seventy museums and galleries in Canada, including the Thompson Gallery, Toronto (1980); "Directions—An Exhibition of Masterworks," Northwestern National Exhibition Centre, K'san, British Columbia (1983); Canada House, Banff, Alberta (1985, 1989); Whetung Art Gallery, Curve Lake, Ontario (1981, 1984, 1986, 1987, 1989); and hosts of others. She is widely known as a lecturer and an active participant with the Native Earth Performing Arts, the Canadian Native Arts Foundation, and the Association for Native Development in the Performing and Visual Arts. Her work has been commissioned to grace walls, ballets, books, and other printed materials.

Noel's works are in the permanent collections of the National Museum of Man, Ottawa; Western University, London; Whetung Art Gallery, Curve Lake; the Canadian Native Arts Foundation, Toronto—all in Ontario, Canada; and many others.

Bibliography
Collins, Allan. "The Spirit of Turtle Island." Video. Canadian Broadcasting Company, 1989.
Santarossa, Lauretta. "Beyond Appearances: A Conversation with Maxine Noel." *Catholic New Times* (December 1987).
Wood, Chris. "The Spirit Soars: A Native Ballet Keeps Indian Legends Alive." *Macleans* (November 1988).

Noggle, Anne (1922–)

Discovering photography at middle age, Anne Noggle had already lived a first life as a pilot, beginning as a woman air force service pilot (WASP) in World War II. After the war she was a flight instructor, stunt pilot, and crop duster. On active duty with the U.S. Air Force during the Korean War as an intercept controller, Noggle was retired for disability (resulting from crop-dusting) in 1959. It was at this point that her life as an artist began.

In 1959 Noggle moved to New Mexico and enrolled as an undergraduate art history student at the University of New Mexico, Albuquerque, studying with Van Deren Coke, the photo historian. After receiving her Bachelor of Arts degree in 1966, Noggle enrolled in the University of New Mexico graduate program in photography, and she received her Master of Arts degree in 1969. Since 1970 she has been adjunct professor of art at the University of New Mexico, and simultaneously (from 1970–1976) she served as curator of photography at the Fine Arts Museum of New Mexico in Santa Fe. With Margery Mann she was guest curator for the San Francisco Museum of Modern Art's exhibition, "Women of Photography: An Historical Survey" (1975).

From the beginning Anne Noggle has been a portrait photographer, and her work is remarkable both for her subjects (elderly persons, generally) and for the unsentimental candor with which she portrays them. Diane Arbus and August Sander were strong influences, yet Noggle's vision differs both from the aggressive style of Arbus and the scientific style of Sander in its mixture of honesty, humor, and respect for the complexity of the inner life. Self-imagery has been a substantial part of her work, and nowhere has Noggle been more candid and revealing than when the camera was directed at herself. Nude self-images and the more well-known close-up studies after a facelift in 1975 pioneered new territory in the portrayal of the aging subject. Critic Jan Grover has written, "In Noggle's work, age is the impersonal catalyst of character, and she documents its encroachments sedulously, watches as it gradually displaces personality with death."

Besides her substantial work in self-imagery, Noggle has done extensive studies of her aging (and then dying) mother, Agnes, another older friend, Yolanda, and her sister, Mary. In 1978 she began a series called "Silver Lining," portraying older married couples, often in surprising and ambiguous ways. Subsequent projects include "Seattle Faces" (1982) and a series of portraits of her former WASP sisters, published in 1990 as *For God, Country and the Thrill of It: Women Airforce Service Pilots in WWII*. An earlier retrospective volume, *Silver Lining*, was published in 1983. Stylistically Noggle's work has been straightforward, usually black-and-white, usually made with a 35-mm. camera; and occasionally she has given her pictures a slightly aggressive edge with a wide-angle lens and electronic flash.

Widely exhibited, Noggle's work is in numerous public collections, the three largest concentrations being the San Francisco Museum of Modern Art, California; the Museum of Contemporary Photography, Columbia College, Chicago, Illinois; and Northlight Gallery at Arizona State University, Tempe. Noggle has been honored with three fellowships from the National Endowment for the Arts (NEA) (1975, 1978, 1988), and she was a recipient of a Guggenheim fellowship (1982).

Gretchen Garner

Bibliography

Artner, Alan. "Anne Noggle Exhibition Paints Portrait of Age-Ravaged Youth." *Chicago Tribune* (February 10, 1984).

Bright, Deborah. "Anne Noggle: A Retrospective Exhibit." *New Art Examiner* (March 1984).

Butler, Susan. "So How Do I Look? Women Before the Camera." *Photo Communique* (Fall 1987): 24–35.

Coke, Van Deren. *History of Photography in New Mexico*. Albuquerque: University of New Mexico Press, 1979.

Dorfman, Elsa. "New Wrinkles." *Women's Review of Books* 2:6 (March 1985).

Grover, Jan Zita. "Anne Noggle's Problematic Portraits." *Afterimage* 8:4 (November 1980): 1, 5–7.

Jussim, Estelle. "Touched by Life." *Boston Review* 11:1 (February 1986): 22–23.

Newhall, Beaumont. "Southwest Bookshelf [Review of Silver Lining]." *New Mexico Magazine* (July 1984): 33.

Noggle, Anne. "The Long, Short, Fat, Skinny Photographs of Capt. Anne Noggle." *Camera* 35 (January–February 1973): 60–67, 72, 78.

———, and Margery Mann. *Women of Photography: An Historical Survey*. San Francisco Museum of Modern Art, 1975.

———. *Silver Lining*. Essay by Jan Zita Grover. Albuquerque: University of New Mexico Press, 1983.

———. *For God, Country and the Thrill of It: Women Airforce Service Pilots in WWII*. Texas A&M University Press, 1990.

Nordman, Maria (1943–)

Known for her controlled, deconstructible sculptures and the play and interplay of light, space, and sound upon these temporal works, the artist Maria Nordman was born in Gorlitz, Silesia, Germany. She studied at the Max Planck Institute in Stuttgart, Germany; and went to the University of California at Los Angeles (UCLA) where, by 1967, she was awarded her Bachelor of Fine Arts and Master of Arts degrees. The following year Nordman combined research and travel in Europe and, on her return to California, accepted a position as editorial assistant to the architect Richard Neutra (1969–1970).

Nordman has held almost a dozen solo exhibitions of her work between 1967 and 1985 in Europe and the United States, including the Pasadena Museum of Modern Art, California (1972); Galleria Franco Toselli, Milan, Italy (1974); Museo d'Artista, Florence, Italy (1976); "5 Public Proposals for an Open Place," Rosamund Felsen Upstairs Gallery, Los Angeles, California (1978), which travelled to Galerie Saman, Geneva, Switzerland (1979); Westfalischer Kunstverein, Westfalischer Landesmuseum, Munster, Germany (1983); and others. Her work has been selected for many group exhibitions in the United States and Europe, such as the "Biennale," Venice, Italy (1976); "Documenta 6," Kassel, Germany (1977); "André/Buren/Nordman: Space as Support," University of California at Berkeley (1979); "Pier and Ocean: Construction in the Art of the 70s," Hayward Gallery, London, England (1980), which travelled to the Rijksmuseum Kroller-Müller, Otterlo, the Netherlands; "The First Show," Museum of Contemporary Art, Los Angeles, California (1983); "Nel mezzo della primavera," Galleria Pieroni, Rome, Italy (1984); "Promenades," Parc Lullin, Geneva, Switzerland (1985); and others.

There are those who assert that Nordman's work is related to that created by her peers: Michael Asher, Eric Orr, Barbara Munger, or Jim Turrell. Her work, however, would seem to suggest a style all its own.

Bibliography
Marks, Claude. *World Artists: 1950–1980*. H.W. Wilson, Publishers, 1984.
Plagens, Peter. "Maria Nordman." *Artforum* 12:6 (February 1974): 40–44.
Pohlen, Annelie. "Munster. Maria Nordman, Westfalischer Kunstverein." *Artforum* 22:7 (March 1984): 101.
Wortz, Melinda. "Los Angeles, Maria Nordman, 315 No. Alameda/166 N. Central." *Artforum* 22:2 (October 1983): 82.

Norfleet, Barbara (1926–)

Born in Lakewood, New Jersey, the photographer/curator/educator Barbara Norfleet earned a Bachelor's degree at Swarthmore College, Pennsylvania (1947); received a Master of Arts degree in social relations from Radcliffe College, Harvard University, Cambridge, Massachusetts (1950); and a Doctorate degree in social relations psychology from the same institution the following year.

Norfleet has held solo exhibitions of her photographs in museums and galleries in the United States, including Light Impressions Gallery, Rochester, New York, and the John Michael Kohler Arts Center, Sheboygan, Wisconsin (1992); Brent Sikkema Fine Art, New York City and Howard Yezersky Gallery, Boston, Massachusetts (1990); International Center of Photography, New York City, (1987); George Eastman House, Rochester, New York and the Museum of Art, Oregon State University, Corvallis (1986); Friends of Photography, Carmel, California (1984); Washington Women's Art Center, Washington, D.C. (1982); Harvard University, Cambridge, Massachusetts (1979); and others. Her work has been invited to many distinguished group exhibitions and travelling shows in the United States and abroad: from Houston, Texas, to Paris, France; Boston, Massachusetts; Turin, Italy; New York City; Barcelona, Spain; Washington, D.C.; Anvers, Belgium; Québec, Canada; and Rumelange, Luxembourg.

Norfleet has received many honors and awards, including the Aaron Siskind award (1991); National Endowment for the Arts (NEA) fellowships in photography (1982, 1984–1985); a Guggenheim Foundation fellowship (1984); two Massachusetts artist's fellowships in photography (1982, 1987); a Printing Industries of America graphic arts award (1987); and a National Endowment for the Humanities research grant to collect and organize the photography archive at Harvard University with respect to the social history of America (1975, 1977). Her work is represented in private, public, and corporate permanent collections, including the Museum of Modern Art (MoMA), New York City; Boston Museum of Fine Arts; Harvard University, and Massachusetts Institute of Technology (MIT)—both in Cambridge, Massachusetts; Corcoran Gallery of Art, Washington, D.C.; George Eastman House, Rochester, New York; the Polaroid Collection; the Coca Cola Collection; and others.

Bibliography
Norfleet, Barbara. *All the Right People*. New York Graphic Society, 1986.
———. "Studio Photographers and Two Generations of Baby Raising." *Photo Communique* (Spring 1988).
———. *Manscape with Beasts*. Harry N. Abrams, 1990.
Who's Who in American Art. 19th ed. R.R. Bowker Co., 1991–1992.

Noriega, Adelaida (1931–)

Born in Mexico, Adelaida Noriega studied watercolor, drawing, mixed media, and sculpture. She works in bronze, patinated plaster, and alabaster.

Noriega's first approach to sculpture was figurative; in her second phase, she searched for and found more synthetic forms. In 1978 Noriega won the silver rose prize for her works in the competition of the Feria de las Flores in San Ángel, Mexico.

Bibliography
Alvarez, José Rogelio, et al. *Enciclopedia de México*. Secretaría de Educación Pública, 1987.

Norton, Ann Weaver (c. 1910–1982)

Born in Selma, Alabama, the sculptor Ann Weaver Norton studied at the National Academy of Design, the Art Students League, and the Cooper Union—all in New York City. Norton then spent five years as an apprentice to Alexander Archipenko and John Hovannes, among others; in the 1940s she taught at the Norton Gallery School of Art, West Palm Beach, Florida.

Norton's "megalith" sculptures—vertical towers of handmade bricks or wood—were exhibited at the Clocktower, Institute of Art and Urban Resources (1978), and the Max Hutchinson Gallery (1981)—both in New York City; and other venues, including the permanent exhibit on the grounds of her home in West Palm Beach, Florida.

Norton was awarded a fellowship from the National Endowment for the Arts (NEA) (1981); her work is represented in permanent collections in the United States and abroad, such as the Detroit Institute of Art, Michigan; High Museum of Art, Atlanta, Georgia; Los Angeles County Museum of Art, California; Norton Gallery, West Palm Beach, Florida; the Musée Rodin, Paris, France; and others.

Bibliography
Ann Norton: Gateways. New York: Max Hutchinson Gallery, 1980.
Glueck, Grace. "Ann Norton, Sculptor, Says She's Like Tip of an Iceberg." *The New York Times* (March 26, 1978).
Morris, Diana. "Women's Art: Miles Apart (Aaron Berman Gallery, New York City)." *Women Artists News* 7:5 (March–April 1982): 15–16.
Obituary. *The New York Times* (February 4, 1982).

Norton, Elizabeth (1887–)

Born in Chicago, Illinois, the sculptor/printmaker Elizabeth Norton learned her craft at the School of the Art Institute of Chicago, Illinois; the Art Students League, and the National Academy of Design—both in New York City.

In addition to a solo exhibition at the California State Library, Sacramento (1942) and others, Norton's work was included in many group shows, such as the Golden Gate Exhibition, San Francisco (1939), California Miniature Print Society (1941), and California Society of Etchers (1942)—all in California; National Academy of Design (1942), and the American Color Print Society (1944)—both in New York City; the Wichita Art Association, Kansas (1946); and others.

Norton is a member of the American Federation of Arts, the California Printmakers and the California Society of Etchers. Her work is represented in many private and public permanent collections, including the Art Institute of Chicago, Illinois; California State Library, Sacramento, and Stanford University, Palo Alto—both in California; Library of Congress, Washington, D.C.; New York Public Library, New York City; Yale University, New Haven, Connecticut; and others.

Bibliography
American Art Annual. Vol. 28. American Federation of Arts, 1932.
Flint, Jane Altic. *Provincetown Printers: A Woodcut Tradition.* National
Museum of American Art, Smithsonian Institution, 1983.
Library of Congress. *American Prints in the Library of Congress: A Cata-
log of the Collection.* Johns Hopkins Press, 1970.

Norvell, Patsy (1942–)

Mathematics, feminism, and nature entered Patsy Norvell's artistic practice successively, each enriching what had come before. In college she
followed dual majors in mathematics and sculpture. The feminist movement of the early 1970s set her to thinking about what is permissible
in art. When her art subsequently moved outdoors she was prompted
to consider how she might recapture nature for interior spaces.

Born in Greenville, South Carolina, Norvell grew up in
Poughkeepsie, New York. In 1964 she earned her Bachelor of Arts de-
gree at Bennington College, Vermont, where she had studied with Tony
Smith, David Smith, and Anthony Caro. After a year in San Francisco,
California, she moved to New York City, where she has lived since.
During the next several years she taught mathematics and edited textbooks in that subject for a living; earned a Master of Arts degree in
fine arts from Hunter College, New York City (1970), and continued a
series of "space frames," which she had initiated as an undergraduate.
These were conceptual works—first in painted steel, later in wood—
which explored issues of volume, limits, surface, and transparency.

Around 1970 Norvell turned her attention to process as an ingre-
dient of her work, which she now constructed from commonplace materials with ordering and stacking techniques. Soon, rethinking the
nature and purpose of her art from a feminist perspective, she began to
admit autobiographical references into her work and to expand its limits with nontraditional techniques, such as sewing and pleating, and
novel materials. "Hair Quilt" (1972–1973) was a five-by-eight-foot wall
piece made from cuttings of her friends' hair and Scotch "Magic" tape.

Since the mid-1970s Norvell has conceived her work in terms of
environmental space. Attracted to fences for their symbolic as well as
formal characteristics, she investigated their possibilities in such works
as "Inside Out" (1976), a monumental parabola, which initiated a series of large outdoor pieces. The most ambitious of these, "Lifeline"
(1976) brought time and movement into the aesthetic experience: the
viewer walked through a sequence of spaces bearing reference to
Norvell's own life history.

In 1979, prompted by the desire to work also for indoor spaces
and by a long-standing preoccupation with transparency, Norvell began to use glass as an abstract structure. "Glass Garden" (1979–1980)
can be installed either indoors or outdoors as a functional greenhouse
or as pure space. In subsequent glass works Norvell frequently has
incorporated botanical motifs in the imagery she etches (by "sandblast-
ing") on it. This technique has seen fruition in various formats, among
them a major collaborative installation commissioned by the Norton
Gallery of Art in Palm Beach, California (1982) from Norvell and her
husband, the painter Robert Zakanitch; a number of multi-panel, move-
able screens, including "Traveler" (1982) and "Climber" (1982); and
installations in several public interiors, including the lobby of the new
Home Savings of America Tower in Los Angeles, California (1988).

In recent years Norvell has also worked on a variety of outdoor

projects for public urban spaces. "Copperheads" (1983–1985), a se-
ries of faux-marble columns with copper tops, articulates the Federal
Court House plaza in Bridgeport, Connecticut. Six perforated steel
newsstands, realized in collaboration with the architect Frances
Halsband, were scheduled for installation along the Avenue of the
Americas in New York City during 1993.

Ann Lee Morgan

Bibliography
Feinberg, Jean E. *Patsy Norvell: Ten Years 1969–1979.* Exhibition Catalog.
Poughkeepsie, New York: Barrett House and Vassar College Art Gallery, 1979.
Norvell, Patsy. "Patsy Norvell." *Glass Art Society Journal.* 1984–1985.
Perreault, John. "The Greenhouse Effect." *SoHo News* (April 9, 1980): 23.

Nourse, Elizabeth (1859–1938)

Born in Cincinnati, Ohio, Elizabeth Nourse was a well-known expatriate painter of European peasants. Nourse studied from 1874 to 1881
at the McMicken School of Design in her native city, and, upon graduation, declined a teaching post there in order to remain a painter. In
1882 she studied at the Art Students League, New York City, attending a life class taught by William Sartain, and the next year she was
back in Cincinnati, supporting herself through her painting. In 1887
she moved to Paris, France, where she enrolled at the Académie Julian
and worked closely with Jules Lefèbvre. Beginning in 1889 she began
a series of extended trips—with her paintbrushes and pigments—to
Russia and the Ukraine, Italy, Holland, and North Africa.

Nourse's genre paintings are in general closer to the French and
American nineteenth-century realists than to the impressionists, although
occasional experiments with impressionism occurred in such sunlit landscapes as "Summer Hours" (1895, Newark Museum) and "La Reverie"
(c. 1910, College-Conservatory of Music, University of Cincinnati).

Nourse's first acceptance into the Paris Salon Exhibition, France
was in 1888 with a painting entitled "La Mère." She continued to exhibit regularly in the Paris Salons until 1920 and was elected to the
prestigious Société Nationale des Beaux-Arts in 1901. Nourse returned
to America only once: in 1893, when she had three paintings selected
for the World's Columbian Exposition in Chicago and for an exhibition
of 100 of her works at the Cincinnati Art Museum, which was followed
by an exhibition of 61 paintings at the V.G. Fischer Art Gallery in Washington, D.C. She continued to exhibit internationally every year until
1924.

Eleanor Tufts

Bibliography
Burke, Mary Alice Heekin. *Elizabeth Nourse, 1859–1938, A Salon Career.*
National Museum of American Art, 1983.
Tufts, Eleanor. *American Women Artists, 1830–1930.* National Museum
of Women in the Arts, 1987.

Noyes, Bertha (1876–1966)

Born in Washington, D.C., the painter Bertha Noyes studied at the
Corcoran School of Art in her native city and took further work with
Charles Hawthorne.

Noyes exhibited work in many exhibitions and was a member of
arts organizations, including the American Federation of Arts, the Arts

Group of Washington, the Washington Society of Artists, and Washington Watercolor Club—all in Washington, D.C.; the Boston Art Club and Provincetown Art Association—both in Massachusetts; National Association of Women Painters and Sculptors, New York City; Newport Art Association; and others. Her work is represented in private and public permanent collections.

Bibliography
American Art Annual. Vol. 28. American Federation of Arts, 1932.
Catalogue of Paintings, Drawings . . . Christie, Manson & Woods, July 2, 1968.
Fielding, Mantle. *Dictionary of American Painters, Sculptors, and Engravers.* Modern Books and Crafts, 1974.

Núñez, Dulce Maria (1950–)

Born in Mexico City, Mexico, the painter Dulce Maria Núñez had her first one-person exhibition there at the Sala Wagner in 1975. She studied at the National School of Painting and Sculpture in her native city (1975–1978) and at the Centro de Investigación y Experimentación Plástica (1978–1980). In 1981 Núñez studied silk-screen technique with Jan Hendrix in Mexico City. She also held solo shows at the Galería José Clemente Oroszco (1982) and at the Galería OMR (1989)—both in Mexico City.

Núñez collages together traditional Mexican imagery, juxtaposing in an often ironical way representations ranging from Pre-Columbian deities to popular wrestlers, in order to confront and question what she considers the fabrication of a nationalistic mythic identity. Her work also deals with the position of women in Mexican society, and, in a work such as "Tonantzin-Guadalupe" (1988), she blends and merges representations of women icons in Mexico from different traditions and times to suggest their interchangeability.

In 1981 Núñez was included in the exhibition "Women Artists of Mexico," which opened in Berlin, Germany, and then travelled to other museums. She participated in the "First Latin American Biennial of Fine Arts" held in 1984 in Havana, Cuba. In 1988 she exhibited in "Rooted Visions" at the Museum of Contemporary Hispanic Art and in 1990 in "Aspects of Contemporary Mexican Painting" at the Americas Society—both in New York City.

Susan Aberth

Bibliography
Pontiatowska, Elena. "Dulce Maria Núñez, una nueva pintora." *La Jornada* (September 1989).
———. *Mitos y realidades de Dulce Maria Núñez.* Mexico City: Galería OMR, 1989.
———. "Dulce Maria Núñez." *Nuevos Momentos del Arte Mexicano (New Moments in Mexican Art).* Exhibition Catalog. New York: Parallel Project, 1990, pp. 116–21.
Sullivan, Edward. *Aspects of Contemporary Mexican Painting.* New York: Americas Society Art Gallery, 1990, pp. 74–79.

Nutaraluk Aulatjut, Elizabeth (1914–)

Elizabeth Nutaraluk Aulatjut, a Canadian Inuit sculptor, was born near Ennadai Lake, 200 miles inland from the community of Arviat (Eskimo Point), Northwest Territories. She and the surviving members of her own large family were airlifted to Arviat in 1957 after enduring a decade of famine. Her first carvings were bartered for food while she was still living on the land. She still supports much of her family with her art income.

Nutaraluk Aulatjut carves depictions of mothers and children almost exclusively, using only small hand tools, such as axes and files. Dominating her roughly-hewn sculptures are the large heads of the mothers, their facial features crudely gouged, their braided hair represented by cross-hatched lines.

Nutaraluk Aulatjut's work has been exhibited in about thirty group shows across Canada, and in the United States and Europe, and is represented in the collections of the Art Gallery of Ontario, Toronto, and the Winnipeg Art Gallery, Manitoba—both in Canada. She was invited by the Canadian government to attend the opening of a touring sculpture/Inuit exhibition in Philadelphia, Pennsylvania, in 1973.

Ingo Hessel

Bibliography
Blodgett, Jean. *Grasp Tight the Old Ways: Selections from the Klamer Family Collection of Inuit Art.* Toronto: Art Gallery of Ontario, 1983.
Hessel, Ingo. "Artists from Ennadai Lake." *Inuktitut* 62 (Winter 1985): 25–30.
———. "Arviat Stone Sculpture." *Inuit Art Quarterly* 5:4 (Winter 1990): 4–15.
Winnipeg Art Gallery. *Eskimo Point/Arviat.* Winnipeg Art Gallery, 1982.

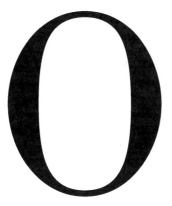

Oakley, Violet (1874–1961)

A native New Yorker, the muralist and stained-glass designer Violet Oakley studied at the Art Students League, New York City; the Pennsylvania Academy of Fine Arts, Philadelphia, under the aegis of Cecilia Beaux and Joseph De Camp; the Académie Montparnasse, Paris, France; and with Howard Pyle at the Drexel Institute, Philadelphia, Pennsylvania—where she met and soon came to live with Elizabeth Shippen Green and Jessie Wilcox Smith—both illustrators in the Howard Pyle tradition.

At Pyle's suggestion, Oakley turned to and conquered stained-glass design and later received a commission for eighteen murals for the new state capitol at Harrisburg, Pennsylvania, one of which was "The Opening of the Book of Law" in the Supreme Court room. Another depicted "The Spirit of the World Today as Prophesized by William Penn." Commissions for further work rolled in. Oakley also was responsible for the decoration of the alumnae house at Vassar College, Poughkeepsie, New York; All Angels Church, New York; and others. She taught mural painting at the Pennsylvania Academy of Fine Arts, Philadelphia (1913–1917), and, ten years later in Switzerland, sketched the League of Nations, New York City, in session. On behalf of world peace Oakley exhibited these works widely.

Oakley won myriad honors and medals for work in the United States and abroad, and was an associate of the National Academy of Design, New York City; and a member of the Philadelphia Watercolor Club, Pennsylvania; the New York Watercolor Club, the American Federation of Arts, and American Institute of Architects (AIA) (honorary)—all in New York City; Circulo de Bellas Artes, Madrid, Spain; and others.

Bibliography

Dunford, Penny. *Biographical Dictionary of Women Artists in Europe and America since 1850.* University of Pennsylvania Press, 1989.

Goodman, Helen. "Women Illustrators of the Golden Age of American Illustration." *Woman's Art Journal* 8:1 (Spring–Summer 1987): 13–22.

"Honored at the Pennsylvania Academy." *Art Digest* 14:10 (February 15, 1940): 13.

Likos, Patricia. "Violet Oakley (1874–1961)." *Philadelphia Museum of Art Bulletin* 75:325.

O'Banion, Nance (1949–)

A mixed-media artist, best known for her constructions of painted bamboo, hand-made paper, and electrical wire, Nance O'Banion was born on June 7, 1949, in Oakland, California, and raised in San Leandro, California. She received both Bachelor of Arts (1971) and Master of Arts (1973) degrees from the University of California, Berkeley. During this extended study at Berkeley she was influenced by Ed Rossbach's love of history and creative problem-solving, Sam Francis's non-objective painting, and Mary Dumas's creative approach to printed textiles. O'Banion's work has a strong awareness of context that is partially a result of a broad design curriculum that included classes in primitive art, philosophy, and architectural design.

O'Banion's first solo exhibition was at Casa Peralta in San Leandro, California, in 1973. With a background in textiles her earliest work was on the loom. However, she pioneered creative explorations of hand-made paper and produced a series of works shown in the group exhibition, "Fiberworks '76," at the TransAmerica Gallery in San Francisco,

California. This was an exhibition of the faculty of Fiberworks Center for the Textile Arts. O'Banion was a founder of the Fiberworks Center for the Textile Arts and played an active role as instructor and administrator there until 1984.

It was during this time also that O'Banion developed her unique constructions of painted bamboo slats, electrical wire, hand-made painted paper and linen thread—emotionally charged work with only occasional references to recognizable forms. In 1979 she had her first of many solo exhibits at the Allrich Gallery in San Francisco, titled "Disappearance/Appearance." In 1982 she completed a large-scale public project, "Billboard Series" (twelve-by-fifteen-by-ten-feet) for the San Francisco International Airport, California, which led to many large public commissions, including one for the Sheraton Hotel in Tokyo, Japan. Also in 1982 she had her second solo exhibit at the Allrich Gallery, which marked the beginning of her free-standing work. She continues to explore constructions both on and off the wall in exhibitions, such as "Windows, Curtains, Maps and Rocks," at the Kaufman Gallery, Houston, Texas (1985), and "Science in Action: At Home" at the Allrich Gallery, San Francisco (1987).

O'Banion has also had solo exhibits at Hestkobgard, Birkerod, Denmark, where she was artist-in-residence, and at Gallery CoCo in Kyoto, Japan. Her work was included in "Craft Today USA," which opened at the Musée des Art Décoratifs, Paris, France, and travelled throughout Europe (1989–1991), and "Craft Today: Poetry of the Physical," which opened at the American Craft Museum, New York City, and travelled throughout the United States (1986–1988), as well as "Architextures '85," Musée des Arts Décoratifs, Paris, France. She received National Endowment for the Arts (NEA) fellowships (1982, 1988), and has been an associate professor in the printmaking and textile departments of the California College of Arts and Crafts, Oakland, California, from 1974 to the present.

Claire Campbell Park

Bibliography
Craft Today: Poetry of the Physical. New York: American Craft Museum, 1986.
Frechette, Marie. "Nance O'Banion." *Textile/Art* (Autumn 1983).
Levin, Melinda. "Nance O'Banion: Defying Categorization." *Oakland Museum Association Magazine* (September–October 1983).
Making Paper. New York: American Craft Museum, 1982.
Rowley, Kathleen. "Nance O'Banion: A Willful Balance." *Fiberworks Newsletter* (Summer 1981).

Ocharán, Leticia (1942–)

Born in Villahermosa, Tabasco, Mexico, Leticia Ocharán studied painting with maestro Salvador Bribiesca (1965–1967) and was tutored by José Marin Bosqued and Jesús Alvarez Amaya in the Escuela de Iniciación Artistica of the National Institute of Fine Arts (1967–1969). Ocharán learned printmaking under Mariano Paredes, Sara Jiménez, and Alejandro Alvarado in Mexico City. She also studied printmaking in the Taller de Gráfica Popular, Mexico City (1968–1972) and took a special course in intaglio with maestro Mario Reyes in his workshop.

Ocharán is currently a professor of art at the Cárcel Preventiva of the Federal District (1967 to the present); and in the Taller Infantil del INBA (1975 to the present). She taught art at the la Casa del Lago (1973–1976); in the Escuela de Iniciación Artistica, Número 4 (1976–

1977), in the Manuel Bartolomé Casió School (1974–1976); and in the faculty of architecture of the University of Mexico (1977–1978).

Ocharán is cofounder and printmaking maestra of the Taller de Expresión Artistica (1979). Up to the first quarter of 1988 she participated in twenty-six solo and forty-six group exhibitions in Mexico and abroad, most recently in the "VI Biennial of Engraving," San Juan, Puerto Rico (1983); and in exhibitions at the Museum of the Constituyentes; the Museum of Fine Arts, Toluca; the Unidad Cultural Zacatenco of the National Polytechnical Institute (1984); and the El Rélox Cultural Center (1987, 1988).

Ocharán was cofounder of the Museum of Modern Art of Morelia (1972) and the Museum of Modern Art of Patzcuaro (1973); of Solaridad in Santiago, Chile (1972); of Contemporary Art in Acambaro (1976); of Latin American Printmaking in San Juan, Puerto Rico (1979); and of the Sala Mexicana of Contemporary Painting in the Franklin Rawson Museum, San Juan, Argentina (1980). Her work has been exhibited in the great capitols such as Moscow, Russia; Montevideo, Uruguay; Buenos Aires, Argentina; and San Juan, Puerto Rico; it has also been judged equally important in the major cities of Poland, Peru, Argentina, Bulgaria, Turkey, the former East Germany, and the United States.

Ocharán has generated illustrations for the reviews *Fem*, *Nueva Vida*, *Manaté*, and *Sin Embargo*; for the newspaper, *El Dia*, and for many books, among which are *Variaciones de invierno* by Juan Bautista Villaseca (1976) and *Aquí con mis hermanos* by Enrique Gonzáles Rojo, Margarita Paz Paredes, and Roberto Lopez Moreno (1979).

Ocharán has been awarded prizes in the Salón de la Plástica Mexicana (1976) and the INBA (1978)—both in Mexico City, Mexico. All of her work turns on the theme of woman and sexual relationships.

Bibliography
Alvarez, José Rogelio, et al. *Enciclopedia de México*. Secretaría de Educación Pública, 1987.
SAHAGUN: Segundo Concurso Nacional de Pintura. Galería de Auditorio Nacional/INBA. Mexico, 1981.

Odjig, Daphne (1919–)

Born on the Wikwemikong Indian reservation, Manitoulin Island, Ontario, Canada, Daphne Odjig, a member of the Odawa tribe, learned the craft of painting by assimilating, through careful observation, the techniques of her father and grandfather. However, she noted, "I don't want to be a painter of the Indian past, I'm beyond depicting legends . . . I like to paint what I feel."

Between 1967 and 1989 Odjig held thirty solo exhibitions of her works in galleries throughout Canada, including the Lakehead Art Centre, Port Arthur, Ontario (1967); Warehouse Gallery of Native Art, Winnipeg, Manitoba (1974); Lefebre Gallery, Edmonton, Alberta (1977); Pollock Gallery, Toronto, Ontario (1979); Children of the Raven Gallery, Vancouver, British Columbia (1980); Robertson Gallery, Ottawa, Ontario (1980, 1982, 1985, 1989); Gallery Phillip, Toronto, Ontario (1984, 1986, 1987, 1989); and others. Her work has been invited to many group shows throughout the world, such as the Indians of Canada Pavilion, Expo '70, Osaka, Japan (1970); Gallery Anthropos, London, England (1973); Laurentian University, Sudbury, Ontario (1976); the Oklahoma Museum of Art, Oklahoma City (1978); "Kinder des Nanabush," Interversa, Hamburg, Germany (1979); "Contemporary

Indian and Inuit Art of Canada," United Nations, New York City (1983); "Challenges," Meervaart Cultural Centre, Amsterdam, Holland (1985); "Woodlands: Contemporary Art of the Anishnabe," Thunder Bay Art Gallery, Ontario (1989); and many others.

Odjig has received many honors for her works in painting and printmaking, including an arts grant for a tour and exhibition of her paintings at the Smotra Folklore Festival in Yugoslavia (1971); a scholarship and appointment as resident artist at the Foundation Studio, Visby, Island of Gotland, Sweden, from the Swedish Brucebo Foundation (1973), and a bursary from the Manitoba Arts Council the same year; the Canada Silver Jubilee Medal (1977); honorary Doctorate degrees from Laurentian University (1982), and the University of Toronto (1985); an appointment to the Order of Canada, C.M. (1987); election to the Royal Canadian Academy of Art, R.C.A. (1989); and others.

Odjig's work is represented in numerous private, public, and corporate permanent collections in Canada and elsewhere, including the Canadian Museum of Civilization, Ottawa; the government of Israel, Jerusalem; McMichael Canadian Art Collection, Kleinburg, Ontario; Montréal Museum of Fine Art, Québec; Sir Wilfred Laurier University, Waterloo, Ontario; the Canada Council Art Bank, Ottawa; the Winnipeg Art Gallery, Manitoba; and a host of others.

Bibliography
Heard Museum Archives. Phoenix, Arizona.
Houle, Robert, "Odjig: An Artist's Transition." *Native Perspective* 3:2 (1978): 42–43.

O'Hara, Sheila (1953)

Born in Kobe, Japan, the fiber artist Sheila O'Hara earned a Bachelor of Fine Arts degree in textiles *with distinction* at the California College of Arts and Crafts, Oakland (1976), under the aegis of Trudi Germonprez and Kay Sekimachi. Earlier (1974) she spent a semester at the Philadelphia College of Art (now the University of the Arts), Pennsylvania.

O'Hara has held solo exhibitions of her woven structures in galleries, including "Architexture: Recent Tapestries," Center for Tapestry Arts, New York City (1990); Elaine Potter, San Francisco, California (1988); Modern Master Tapestries, New York City (1982, 1985); and the Western Women's Bank, San Francisco, California (1980). Her work has been invited to myriad group exhibitions throughout the United States and abroad, such as "Fiber Arts/New Directions for the Nineties," Manchester Institute of Arts and Sciences, New Hampshire (1992); "Art & Industry: The Jacquard Project," a travelling show, Museum for Industrial Culture, Nurnberg, Germany and the United States (1991); "The Fifth Annual International Textile Design Contest," The Space, Tokyo, Japan (1990); "Frontiers in Fiber: The Americans," a travelling show, North Dakota Museum of Art, Grand Forks, and a two-year Asian tour (1988–1990); "13th International Biennial of Tapestry," Musée Cantonal des Beaux-Arts, Lausanne, Switzerland (1987); "Charlottenborg Invitational," Copenhagen, Denmark (1986); "Weavings, Glass, and Wood," Following Sea, Honolulu, Hawaii (1981); and many others.

O'Hara's work is represented in private, corporate and museum permanent collections, including the American Craft Museum, New York City; Cooper-Hewitt Museum, New York City; San Francisco Museum of Fine Arts, California; Minneapolis Institute of Art, Minnesota; Oakland Museum, California; Arthur Andersen & Co., Denver, Colorado; Standard Oil of Ohio, San Francisco, California; Lloyds Bank International Ltd., New York City; Komatsu Store Co., Ltd., Tokyo, Japan; and others. A computer-assisted loom coupled with O'Hara's sense of humor and virtuoso skills enables her to create unique tapestries, such as "Mount Olympics" (1985), which portrays three life-sized contemporary skiers slaloming through Doric woven columns.

Bibliography
Lalena, Constance. "Professional Pursuits: Sheila O'Hara." *Handwoven* (September–October 1989): 88–91.
Mattera, Joanne. "Tapestries of Our Time." *Metropolis* (January–February 1985): 37–43.
O'Hara, Sheila. "Back to the Future." *Weaver's Magazine* (Fourth Quarter 1990): 30–35.
Pearson, Katherine. *American Crafts: A Source Book for the Home.* Stewart, Tabori & Chang, 1983.
Schira, Cynthia. "The Jacquard Project." *American Craft* (February–March 1992): 38–41.

Ohe, Katie (1937–)

Born on a secluded farm near Peers, Alberta, Canada, Katie Ohe became one of the province's most celebrated multimedia sculptors. Born Katherine Minna von der Ohe, she created three-dimensional objects early on. From the age of ten she has worked to support herself and her obsession with sculpture. She studied art at P.I.T.A. (now the Alberta College of Art); worked under the tutelage of Luke Lindoe, Marion Nicoll, and others; and received her four year diploma in fine arts in 1960. The previous year was spent on a National Gallery of Canada study award grant, at the Montréal School of Art and Design, investigating child art education with Arthur Lismer. On a Reeves scholarship, Canada Council grant, and tuition scholarship, Ohe took graduate work at the Clay Club (now the Sculpture Center), New York City (1961–1963), where she worked with Dorothy Denslow and Sahl Swarz.

Ohe has held solo exhibitions of her work in galleries and universities, including the University of Saskatoon, Saskatchewan (1962); 1640 Gallery, Montréal, Québec (1966); Illingworth Kerr Gallery, Alberta College of Art (1976, 1991); and the Glenbow Museum (1989)— all in Calgary, Alberta, Canada; and others. Her work has been selected for group museum exhibitions in Europe, Japan, Canada, and the United States, such as the Sculpture Center, New York City (1960–1970); National Gallery, Ottawa, Canada (1964); "Bradford Print Biennial," England (1974); "Venice Biennale," Italy (1975); "International Print Exhibition," Ljubljana, Yugoslavia (1975); "Kunstverein Zu Frechen," International Print Show, Germany (1975); "Alberta Art Foundation," Canada House Gallery, travelled to London, Brussels, Paris, and New York City (1975–1976); "Royal Canadian Academy," Nickle Arts Museum, Calgary (1982); and many others.

Married to the artist Harry Kiyooka (her strongest supporter), Ohe has taught sculpture for more than thirty years (1959–1991) in various institutions in Calgary, giving back to others part of that which she received; in the same vein, she has executed innumerable public sculpture commissions between 1962 and 1989. Ohe has received awards and honors for her work, including Canada Council grants (1962, 1968,

1973); a sculpture award in a Winnipeg exhibition (1964); the Allied Arts medal from the Royal Architectural Institute of Canada (1984); the Young Women's Christian Association (YWCA) arts and culture award (1989); the prestigious Alberta College of Art, Governor General's medal of excellence (1991); and others.

Ohe's sculpture has gone through several metamorphoses from the 1960s to the present, even as the sculptor herself has changed, grown, learned myriad industrial techniques and processes, allowed and encouraged the public to interact with her work, and maintained her commitment to her work. She wrote, "I believe a work of Art is only complete when the initial perceptual conception is spiritually satisfied." Ohe added, "Participation is an important element of my sculpture; movement alters the work perceptively, and changes the perceptual mode of each element . . . transmuting its spatial tensions."

Ohe's work is housed in the permanent collections of Alberta House, England; Sculpture Center, New York City; University of Calgary, Alberta; the Canada Council Art Bank, Ottawa; Edmonton Centre, Alberta; Alberta Art Foundation, Edmonton; and other institutions.

Bibliography

Katie Ohe. A Catalog. The Illingworth Kerr Gallery, Alberta College of Art, 1991.

Roukes, Nicholas. *Alberta Sculpture Survey '89*. The Triangle Gallery of Visual Arts, 1989.

Tousley, Nancy. "Movable Sculptures Evoke Sci-Fi Imagery." *Calgary Herald* (July 19, 1989).

Who's Who in American Art. 19th ed. R.R. Bowker Co., 1991–1992.

O'Keeffe, Georgia (1887–1986)

An American painter, most closely identified with certain subjects—notably gigantic flowers and sun-bleached animal bones, Georgia O'Keeffe was also an important pioneer in the field of total abstraction.

Born near Sun Prairie, Wisconsin, O'Keeffe wanted to be an artist from the age of ten. She studied one year at the Art Institute of Chicago, Illinois, and then in New York City at the Art Students League, where her teachers included William Merritt Chase and Kenyon Cox. Despite considerable success—she won the prize for still-life painting and was a popular student and model—O'Keeffe became frustrated with working in what she saw as a derivative, essentially conservative style. She left the Art Students League in 1908 and returned to Chicago, where she supported herself for nearly five years as a commercial artist.

While recuperating from a severe illness during the summer of 1912 O'Keeffe attended a class at the University of Virginia, where she was exposed to the ideas of Arthur Wesley Dow, whose interest in Oriental art and simplified shapes had a decisive influence on her own work. While teaching art in the Texas public schools O'Keeffe made a trip back to New York to study with Dow himself at Columbia University's Teacher's College. The next year marked O'Keeffe's artistic breakthrough. After critically surveying the work she had produced up to that point and determining that all of it had been influenced by other artists, O'Keeffe destroyed virtually everything she had made before 1915 and embarked on an intense exploration of abstract form in an attempt to forge her own, personal style. She did so, first in a series of remarkably spare charcoal drawings which she sent to Anita Pollitzer, a painter friend in New York. Pollitzer was so impressed by

the power of these pictures that she took them to Alfred Stieglitz, the avant-garde photographer, editor, and gallery owner whose establishment, known as "291" (for its address on Fifth Avenue), had discovered, presented, and supported an impressive roster of innovative European and American artists. Stieglitz, in turn, liked the drawings so much that he included them in a group exhibition—without O'Keeffe's knowledge. When she found out O'Keeffe travelled to New York to complain; Stieglitz convinced her to let him keep the works on view, and so began the legendary relationship between the twenty-nine-year-old painter and the fifty-two-year-old art dealer. O'Keeffe joined Stieglitz's stable of first-generation modernists which included Max Weber, Marsden Hartley, and John Marin; he mounted her first solo show in 1917. They began living together and, in 1924, were married.

The couple resided in New York City and vacationed in the Lake George, New York, area, and both the newly-built Manhattan skyscrapers and the lush, green woods around the lake found their way onto O'Keeffe's canvases—but transformed, and highly stylized. O'Keeffe's paintings, which had attracted considerable attention from the start, continued to generate excitement and controversy—and in 1928 an anonymous Frenchman purchased six small canvases for twenty-five thousand dollars, a record price for so few pieces by a living American. O'Keeffe first visited New Mexico in 1929, and immediately fell in love with the desert landscape. While Stieglitz was alive she remained in New York, but spent every summer in the Southwest. In 1949, after Steiglitz had died and his estate been settled, O'Keeffe moved to the isolated town of Abiquiu, New Mexico, where she stayed the rest of her life. Retrospective exhibitions of O'Keeffe's work were held at the Brooklyn Museum (1927), the Museum of Modern Art (MoMA) (1945), and the Whitney Museum of American Art (1970)—all in New York City; the Art Institute of Chicago, Illinois (1943); the Worcester Art Museum, Massachusetts (1960); the Amon Carter Museum of American Art, Fort Worth, Texas (1966); and the National Gallery of Art in Washington, D.C. (1987). Long before O'Keeffe's death she had become recognized as a major figure in twentieth-century American art; her stature is reflected by the fact that her obituary appeared on the front page of the first (news) section of *The New York Times*, rather than being relegated to "Arts & Leisure."

The most remarkable thing about O'Keeffe was the audacity and uniqueness of her early work. In 1916 even the most avant-garde European painters were just beginning to experiment with pure abstraction; three years after the Armory Show, the American tradition of artistic realism remained strong, and the other members of Stieglitz's stable showed clear ties to various European modernist movements. In contrast O'Keeffe's art—while it contains elements of surrealism (for example, in the irrational juxtaposition of a pink rose and a cow's skull), and precisionism (as observed in her tightly-controlled brushwork and clear-cut edges)—cannot be labeled: it is simply O'Keeffe.

Although her principal art-historical contributions were made with the charcoal and watercolor abstractions made between 1915 and 1920, O'Keeffe continued to produce challenging, though largely representational, images for another seventy years. And it was through these paintings—of flowers, buildings, and bones—that she became known to subsequent generations. O'Keeffe worked on all sorts of scales—from seven-by-nine-inch still lifes to the monumental "Sky Above Clouds IV" (1965), which measures eight-by-twenty-four feet. And, while she chose not to depict the people or pets that were closest to her, clearly the inanimate subjects she did paint—whether seashells, barns, or rocky hills—held great personal significance. All of O'Keeffe's *oeuvre*—youthful and mature, representational and abstract, large-scale and small—demonstrates the same aesthetic concerns, most notably with the simplification of form. Throughout her life, O'Keeffe was fascinated—almost obsessed—with particular shapes, such as the door opening onto the patio of her desert house, which she would paint innumerable times. Viewers have searched for—and often found—symbolic meanings in O'Keeffe's repeated forms, but the artist consistently denied that there was symbolism in her work. For example, critics tended to take O'Keeffe's many pictures of animal bones as evidence of her interest in the theme of death (and, clearly, she was a sophisticated painter well acquainted with the *vanitas* theme popular in seventeenth-century Dutch still-life paintings, where a human or animal skull was often included as a reminder of mortality); however, she always said she painted cow-skulls, and other bones because they were part of the landscape around her, and because of her interest in their physical forms. Indeed, in her series of "Pelvis" paintings (1943–1945), O'Keeffe comes progressively closer to her subject, making pictures of the sky as seen through one hole in the bone, and of the hole itself. The later paintings in this series are so abstract, in terms of both form and color, that they no longer read as "bones" at all. Similarly, in her celebrated flower paintings, such as the six-part "Jack in the Pulpit" series (1930), O'Keeffe moves from an iconic image of a single flower, surrounded by a mass of curving foliage, to a design study of green, brown, and purple elements, which have lost their identity as either blossoms or leaves. O'Keeffe's flowers—which she began producing in 1924—scandalized many viewers, who commented on the erotic content of these enormous, close-up images, reflecting the popularity of Freudian theory at the time. As usual, the artist maintained that there were no sexual aspects or other hidden agendas in her pictures; she also disagreed with writers who suggested that the inspiration for their size had anything to do with the photographic enlargements made by Stieglitz and his colleagues—O'Keeffe simply explained that she had painted her flowers big in order to attract people's attention.

Bibliography
Cowart, Jack, and Juan Hamilton. *Georgia O'Keeffe: Art and Letters.* New York Graphic Society, 1987.
Lisle, Laurie. *Portrait of an Artist: A Biography of Georgia O'Keeffe.* Rev. ed. University of New Mexico Press, 1986.
O'Keeffe, Georgia. *Georgia O'Keeffe.* Viking, 1977.
Pollitzer, Anita. *A Woman on Paper: Georgia O'Keeffe.* Simon and Schuster, 1988.
Stieglitz, Alfred. *Georgia O'Keeffe: A Portrait by Alfred Stieglitz.* Viking, 1979.

Okheena, Mary (1955–)

In recent years Mary Okheena has become a forceful presence in the annual print collections from Holman, Northwest Territories, Canada. This young Inuit artist started drawing and printmaking at the Holman Eskimo Co-operative as a teenager. The daughter of printmaker and sculptor Jimmy Memorana, Okheena is part of the third generation of organized graphic artists in the Canadian Arctic. As such her art combines a uniquely Inuit aesthetic and cultural tradition with Southern cultural influences and Western artistic devices.

Okheena began her professional artistic career by translating other artists' images into prints, which appear in the 1979 and 1980–1981 annual Holman print collections. Okheena excels at the stencil technique, achieving subtle and luminous gradations of color. It was in 1986 when Okheena began to apply the print medium to her own images. In this and in subsequent years (1986–1991) Okheena's images have constituted an integral and dynamic component of Holman's graphic collections. Okheena has consistently explored the aesthetic possibilities of animal and human forms, abstracting and exploiting their formal qualities in works such as "Musk-ox Waiting for the Tide to Cross Water" (1986) and "Cold and Hungry" (1986). She ingeniously creates visual metaphors as in "Mouth of the River" (1987) and "Songs of Animals" (1986), and frequently injects her work with a sense of fun and exuberance for life.

Okheena was commissioned in 1988 to create a print for Northwest Territories (NWT) Telephones which was reproduced on the cover of the NWT telephone directory. She has had two solo shows at Arctic Arts Gallery in Yellowknife, Northwest Territories (1989, 1990). The Canadian Museum of Civilization in Ottawa and the Prince of Wales Museum in Yellowknife have Okheena's prints in their permanent collections.

Annalisa R. Staples

Bibliography
Graburn, Nelson H.H. "Some Problems in the Understanding of Contemporary Inuit Art." Ottawa: Paper from a Conference on *Fine Arts of the Arctic*, 1988.
Holman Annual Prints. Catalogs: 1979, 1980–1981, 1986–1991. Holman Eskimo Co-operative Ltd.
Inuit Art Enthusiasts' Newsletter. 31 (April 1986).
Jackson, Marion E. "Influences of Acculturation on Contemporary Canadian Inuit Graphic Art." Ann Arbor: Paper from *Acculturation and Amerindian Art*, 1988.
Kalvak/Emerak Memorial Portfolio. Catalog. Holman Eskimo Co-operative Ltd., 1987.
Magrath, Robin. "The Influence of Comics on Inuit Art and Literature." *Inuit Art Quarterly* 4:1 (1987).
Souchotte, Sandra. "Women to Watch in the Yukon and N.W.T." *Chatelaine* (May 1987): 84–86.
Watt, Virginia J. "Holman Island Graphics 1986." A review. *Inuit Art Quarterly* 1:1 (1986): 11.

Okittuq, Maudie Rachel (1944–)

A sculptor, working both in whalebone and soapstone, Maudie Rachel Okittuq is one of the few women carvers from Spence Bay in the Central Canadian Arctic. She was born in 1944 in a hunting camp at Thom Bay in the eastern part of the Boothia Peninsula. At the age of twenty-one, she moved into the settlement of Spence Bay, where she has been carving since 1968.

The Netsilik Eskimo in the Central Arctic seem to have retained a strong connection to their ancient spiritual beliefs, even though most people have converted to Christianity. This is evident in the work of Okittuq, who comes from a shamanic family. Shamans were believed to have animal helpers or "familiars" which assisted them in the exercise of their shamanic powers. Shamans could also change into the shape of these helping spirits. Many of Okittuq's sculptures can be interpreted as depictions of shamans who are in various stages of transformation or accompanied by spirit helpers or familiars who can be seen on the figure's head, shoulder, or escaping the mouth.

Okittuq's other favorite theme is "Sedna," the sea goddess, who is a central figure in ancient Inuit mythology. She was believed to have power over all sea animals. According to traditional beliefs, Sedna would withhold the sea animals out of anger after taboos had been broken. The shaman then would have to go and visit and placate her. Okittuq shows both aspects of Sedna—the angry and the serene—in many of her sculptures.

The artist claims that the nature and shape of the stone tend to inspire her. Rather than force her will upon the material, she tends to be guided by its inherent form. This impression is reinforced by the fact that many of her pieces are modelled in the round with little concern for a frontal view. In the case of whalebone she uses the organic shapes of the material to full advantage.

Among the various exhibits which have featured Okittuq's work the most notable are "Inuit Art in the 1970s," which toured Canada in 1979–1980 and "In the Shadow of the Sun," which travelled in Canada and Europe in 1988–1989.

Maria Muehlen

Bibliography
Hoffman, Gerhard, ed. *Im Schatten der Sonne: Zeitgenoessische Kunst der Indianer und Eskimos in Kanada.* (In the Shadow of the Sun: Contemporary Art of the Canadian Indians and Eskimos). Stuttgart: Edition Cantz. Ottawa: Canadian Museum of Civilization, 1988, pp. 509–11.
Wight, Darlene. "Focus on Artists: The Central Arctic." *Inuit Arts and Crafts* 2 (December 1984): 22–33.

Okubo, Mine (1912–)

Born in Riverside, California, the painter Mine Okubo attended Riverside Junior College (1933–1934) and then went on to earn both Bachelor's and Master's degrees from the University of California at Berkeley (1935–1936). Winning a Bertha Henicke Taussig travelling fellowship from her alma mater, Okubo toured Europe for a year and a half.

After two solo exhibitions at the San Francisco Museum of Modern Art, California (1940–1941), Okubo was interned, along with many other *nisei*, at Tanforan Relocation Camp, San Bruno, California, and Central Utah Relocation Camp, Topaz, Utah (1942–1944), where, at the latter camp, she served as art editor and illustrator of *Trek.* Other solo shows included the Mortimer Levitt Gallery, New York City (1951); Image Gallery, Stockbridge, Massachusetts (1968); "Mine Okubo: An American Experience," Oakland Art Museum, California (1972); Riverside City College Gallery, California (1974); Western Association of Art Museums, a travelling show (1974–1975); "Citizen 13660: Evacuation Art," Seibu Corporation of America, a travelling exhibition shown throughout Japan (1976); Thousand Branches Gallery, San Francisco, California (1980); "Mine Okubo: A Retrospective 1942–1985," Catherine Gallery, New York City (1985); and others. She has exhibited work in myriad group shows throughout the United States and abroad.

Between 1944 and 1952 Okubo worked as an illustrator for magazines and periodicals, including *Fortune, Time, The New York Times, San Francisco Chronicle,* and others. Her visual account of the relocation camp ordeal was published in 1946 by the Columbia University Press,

titled *Citizen 13660.* Earlier, Okubo created murals for the Federal Arts Programs; she continued to draw and paint no matter the conditions.

Okubo has won many awards and honors. She is a teacher and lecturer, as well as a many-talented artist. Her work is in private and public permanent collections and in venues including Fort Ord, Government Island, Oakland Hospitality House, and Treasure Island, California.

Bibliography
Okubo, Mine. *Citizen 13660.* Columbia University Press, 1946.
Welchman, John C. "Turning Japanese." *Artforum* Vol. 27 (April 1989): 152–56.

Olazábul, Eugenia Rendon de

Founder of the Foto 18-A studio, Eugenia Rendon de Olazábul honed her photographic skills between 1960 and 1967. Her first solo exhibition was held at the International Center of Photography, New York City (1965). Since then Olazábul has had many solo shows, including the Galería OMR, Mexico City (1989, 1990), and has participated in numerous group exhibitions, such as the Centro Cultural/Arte Contemporaneo, Mexico City (1986); and others.

Olazábul's photographs have been published in *Foto Zoom, Artes de México, Vogue,* the Spanish edition of *Harper's Bazaar,* and in many other North American magazines. Her film, *Palenque,* won the Ariel prize in 1975; ten years later, she published a bilingual (Spanish/English) edition of her book, *Espinas—Thorns.* Her cacti series of color photographs utilizes and plays with light in a manner not unlike the French impressionists. Examples of her work are represented in private and public permanent collections.

Bibliography
La Mujer en México. Text by Linda Nochlin. Centro Cultural/Arte Contemporaneo. Mexico City. 1990.

Olds, Elizabeth (1896–1990)

The first female Guggenheim Foundation fellow in art, Elizabeth Olds was born in Minneapolis, Minnesota. Writer of children's books, painter, and printmaker—she studied at a number of institutions, including the University of Minnesota, and the Minneapolis School of Art—both in her native city, and the Art Students League, New York City, where she settled in 1921. During her Guggenheim period in France (1926–1927), Olds studied with the American painter George Luks; trained as a bareback horse rider; and performed with the Cirque d'Hiver in Paris.

For more than five decades Olds's works were exhibited in solo and group shows in major museums throughout the United States, including the Metropolitan Museum of Art (1942), the Museum of Modern Art (MoMA), the Whitney Museum of American Art (1945–1947, 1956); and the Brooklyn Museum International Watercolor Exhibitions (1949, 1953, 1955, 1957)—all in New York City. Her works honed in on the joys and sorrows of the "little people" during the Great Depression of the 1930s, in the social realistic style of the times. Olds won prizes for her lithographs and watercolors in shows at the Philadelphia Print Club, Pennsylvania (1937); the Art Alliance, Philadelphia (1938); the Baltimore Museum of Art, Maryland (1944); and others.

Examples of Olds's works are in the permanent collections of the Metropolitan Museum of Art and the Brooklyn Museum—both in New

York City; the Baltimore Museum of Art, Maryland; the Philadelphia Museum, Pennsylvania; the San Francisco Museum of Art, California; and many others.

Bibliography
Prescott, Kenneth W., and Susan E. Arthur. *Elizabeth Olds: A Retrospective Exhibition.* The R.G.K. Foundation, 1986.
Rubenstein, Charlotte S. *American Women Artists.* G.K. Hall, 1983.
Who's Who in American Art. Vol. 1. American Federation of Arts, 1935.

O'Leary, Diane (1935–)

The Comanche painter Diane O'Leary (Opeche-Nah-Se) was born in Waco, Texas, and spent her first seven years on the Seneca Indian reservation. She attended Bacone College, Muskogee, Oklahoma and Texas Christian University, Fort Worth, where she received Bachelor of Arts and Bachelor of Fine Arts degrees; Harvard University, Cambridge, Massachusetts, where she earned a Master of Arts degree in physics; and Stanford University, California, where she received a Master's degree in music. O'Leary never enrolled in a single art course. Her graduate specializations were in Southwestern archeology, Baroque literature and music.

Not until she was thirty-three years of age did O'Leary embark upon a career as a visual artist. She studied painting with Emil Bisttram and Eric Gibbard, lithography with Linton Kistler, and received occasional critiques from Georgia O'Keeffe, who became the greatest influence in her life. Earlier on, she worked as a registered nurse, was active on the Comanche Tribal Council, and worked in nuclear physics for the Atomic Energy Commission.

O'Leary has exhibited her work widely, including group shows at the Signature Gallery, Scottsdale (1977, 1978, 1981, 1984); Rosequist Gallery, Tucson (1986); a two-person show at the Heard Museum, Phoenix (1972); a solo exhibition at the Elaine Horwitch Gallery, Scottsdale (1973)—all in Arizona; and many others. In her brilliant-colored, hard-edged paintings, O'Leary often employs symbols: "Circles represent a number of different things in Indian symbolism. I use them primarily to denote the passage of time or to refer to either the sun or moon . . . ."

O'Leary's works are in public and private permanent collections, including the Denver Art Museum, Colorado; Harvard University, Cambridge, Massachusetts; the Guggenheim Museum, the Brooklyn Museum, and New York University—all in New York City; the University of Texas, Austin; Stanford University, California; and many others.

Bibliography
Broder, P.J. *American Indian Painting and Sculpture.* Abbeville Press, 1981, pp. 108–09.
Heard Museum Archives. Phoenix, Arizona.
"Joan Cawley Gallery." *Scottsdale Magazine* (Autumn 1987): 158.
Profile 1987: An Artist's Directory of Native American Art. Southwest Art, 1987, p. 14.

Oleszko, Patricia (1947–)

Born in Michigan, the performance artist Patricia Oleszko earned a Bachelor of Fine Arts degree from the University of Michigan, Ann Arbor (1970). She has held solo and group exhibitions, events, and performances throughout the United States and abroad, including "Holidaze," Central Park, and Macy's Thanksgiving Parade (1972), and "Sewn, Stitched, and Stuffed," Museum of Contemporary Craft (1973)—both in New York City; "Pat Oleszko: Body Sculpture," Patterson State College, New Jersey, and "Pat Oleszko: Soft Sculpture," Tyler School of Art, Temple University, Philadelphia (1974); "Rehearse—All Inter-Erupted and Ball-Arena Hi Jinx," Royal Academy of Art, Copenhagen, Denmark; and "Pat Superstar," a documentary on German television (1975); "Peepholeszko," Gallery 38, Copenhagen, and Artpark, Lewiston, New York (1976); "Hand/Some/Show," P.S.1, Long Island, New York (1978); "Taxi Show and Lineup" (1976) and "The Stage Show," Museum of Modern Art (MoMA), New York City (1979); "The Pats Reviewed," Modern Art Galleries, Vienna, Austria (1979); "Oleszko Under Glass," P.S.122, New York City (1988); "Nora's Art," Maryland Art Place, Baltimore, and The Kitchen, New York City (1990, 1993); and others.

Winner of awards and honors, Oleszko has taught at Flint Junior Community College, Michigan (1969); was artist-in-residence at Artpark, Lewiston, New York (1976); received grants from the New York State Council on the Arts (1973, 1980, 1987); fellowships from the National Endowment for the Arts (NEA) (1978, 1985, 1987); a grant from the Massachusetts Council on the Arts (1988); and a Guggenheim Foundation fellowship (1990).

Bibliography
Banes, Sally. "Under Cover and Covering Up." *Village Voice* (March 8, 1984): 79.
Gussow, Mel. "A Vaudeville Landscape Full of Amazon Balloons." *The New York Times* (February 24, 1993): B3.
Lonier, Terri. "Altered Ego: An Interview with Pat Oleszko." *Fiberarts* 10:1 (January–February 1983): 26–29.
Oleszko, Pat. "Sorcerers and Apprentices." *Artforum* 25:3 (December 1986): 117–21.
Weisburg, Ruth. "Personifications of Myth." *Artweek* 15:20 (May 19, 1984): 6.

Ondaatje, Kim (1928–)

Born in Toronto, Ontario, Canada, the writer/printmaker/painter Kim Ondaatje studied briefly at the Ontario College of Art, Toronto; earned a Bachelor's degree in English and psychology from McGill University, Montréal, Québec (1952); and a Master's degree in English from Queen's University, Kingston, Ontario, while on scholarship there. She returned to the visual arts after having taught English for five years.

Ondaatje has held solo exhibitions in museums and galleries in Canada, including the Jerold Morris Gallery, Toronto (1969); "Kim Ondaatje: A Retrospective," Merton Gallery, Toronto (1971); McLaughlin Gallery, Oshawa (1972)—all in Ontario; and many others. Her work has been included in group shows, such as the "97th Annual Exhibition, Ontario Society of Artists, Toronto (1969); Montréal Museum of Fine Arts, Québec (1970); "Graphics '72," Art Gallery of Brant, Brantford, Ontario (1972); London Public Library and Art Museum, Ontario, a travelling show (1972); and others.

Ondaatje has won many honors and purchase awards for serigraphy and other media. Her work is represented in private, corporate, and public permanent collections in Canada and the United States, including the London Public Library and Art Museum, Ontario; Montréal Museum of Fine Arts; Owens Art Gallery, Sackville, New Brunswick; Seattle Art Museum, Washington; University of Western Ontario, London; Windsor Public Art Gallery, Ontario; and many others.

Bibliography
Fleisher, Pat. "Profile: Kim Ondaatje." *Artmagazine* 2:7 (Spring 1971): 6–7.
Lord, Barry. "Mass Prints." *Artmagazine* 8:31–32 (March–April 1977): 14–17.
Ondaatje, Kim. "The Quilt in the Jet Age." *Canadian Antiques Collector* 10:4 (July–August 1975): 48–50.

Ono, Yoko (1933–)

A pioneer in the field of performance art, Yoko Ono developed a style that encompassed several media, including poetry, music, conceptual object sculpture, and filmmaking. Known primarily to the public as the wife of the late John Lennon, she made substantial contributions of her own to avant-garde film and conceptual art that were largely ignored until after Lennon's death.

Born in Tokyo, Japan, Ono attended Gakushin University there before transferring to Sarah Lawrence College, Bronxville, New York, to study poetry and music. At the end of the 1950s she was part of a circle of artists that included John Cage, Merce Cunningham, and Yvonne Rainer. One of her first public performances, *A Piece for Strawberries and Violins*, had Rainer standing up and sitting down before a table stacked with dishes for ten minutes before smashing the dishes in accompaniment to rhythmic background of repeated syllables, a tape of moans and words spoken backwards, and an aria of the high-pitched wails that later became Ono's trademark.

In the early 1960s Ono was part of a Dada-influenced art movement that became known as Fluxus. Her works in this period are characterized by a minimalistic simplicity, the use of everyday objects, and an inextricable link between the viewer's actions or experiences and the ideas being portrayed. Her "Painting to Hammer a Nail" (1961) provided a hammer, nails, a wood panel, and instructions to use them. Often her works directed "viewers" to participate in some way—"Painting to See the Room Through" (1961) placed a peep-hole in a canvas; "Painting to Shake Hands" (1962) offered her hand to shake through a hole in the canvas—and the instructions that accompanied many of her works are included in her book, *Grapefruit* (1964). Notable public showings of her works include "Alchemical Wedding," Albert Hall, London (1967); "Evening with Yoko Ono," Birmingham, Alabama (1968), and "Yoko Ono," Whitney Museum of American Art, New York City (1989).

In 1966 Ono began making films, contributing substantially to the field of avant-garde cinema but receiving little recognition until the Whitney Museum of American Art, New York City, mounted a showing of her works in 1989 and the American Federation of Arts, Washington, D.C., released a collection of her films in 1990. She contributed three films to the Fluxfilm Program in 1966: two one-shot films shot at 2000 frames per second, *Eyeblink* and *Match*, and *No. 4 (Bottoms)*—an eighty-minute sequence of buttocks of walking males and females.

Ono worked with John Lennon on several film projects, beginning with *Film No. 5 (Smile)* (1968, 51 minutes). This film records Lennon's face at 333 frames per second in various phases of smiling. They collaborated on a series of films between 1968 and 1971, including *Two Virgins* (1968), *Bed-In* (1969), *Rape* (1969), and *Imagine* (1971). In the 1980s she made several music videos documenting her recovery from Lennon's death.

Helen Hayes

Bibliography
Macdonald, Scott. "Yoko Ono: Ideas on Film." *Film Quarterly* 43 (Fall 1989): 2–23.
McCormick, Carlo. "Yoko Ono Solo." *Artforum* 27 (February 1989): 116–21.
Golson, G. Barry. *The Playboy Interviews with John Lennon and Yoko Ono.* Playboy Press, 1981.
Who's Who of American Women, 1992. Marquis Who's Who, Inc., 1992.

Oonark, Jessie (1906–1985)

Jessie Oonark was born in the area of northern Canada known as the Barren Lands, north and west of the present-day village of Baker Lake, Northwest Territories, where she settled in the late 1950s. Her childhood and young adulthood were spent in the traditional pursuits of an Inuit woman: dressing caribou and sealskins, and making parkas and other items of traditional clothing. Oonark began her career as a graphic artist in 1959, when a Canadian biologist working in Baker Lake gave her art supplies. Her talent was immediately recognized, and she was soon making drawings for sale. A selection of Oonark's drawings were sent from Baker Lake to Cape Dorset, the only Inuit settlement issuing prints at the time. Works by Oonark were included in the first Cape Dorset print editions ("Tattooed Faces," "Inland Eskimo Woman," 1960; "Peoples of the Inland" (1961)—all signed "Una." She was the only outsider ever included in the Cape Dorset print program.

Oonark was a major force in the development of the graphic arts program at Baker Lake in the 1960s and 1970s. Her singular talent was rewarded by an art advisor at Baker Lake who gave Oonark her own studio and a small salary to allow her the freedom of full-time artistic creativity. (She had previously been working as a janitor at the local church.) Between 1970 and 1985 more than 100 of Oonark's drawings were translated into prints and issued in the annual Baker Lake print editions.

A strong, bold graphic sense informs all of Oonark's work. Traditional dress, women's facial tattoos, and shamanistic themes are common in her art, yet they usually appear as isolated, fragmentary forms, shaped into a graphically bold image rather than a comprehensible narrative. Oonark is also well known as a textile artist, whose wool and felt wall-hangings reveal her as a master of color and form. Her best-known and most ambitious textile commission is a large wool and felt wall-hanging (Untitled, 1973), four-by-six-meters in size, which hangs in the foyer of the National Arts Center in Ottawa, Ontario, Canada.

Oonark was elected to membership in the Royal Canadian Academy of Arts in 1975; she was awarded the Order of Canada in 1984. Her work has been included in almost every major exhibit of Inuit art ever organized.

Janet Catherine Berlo

Bibliography
Berlo, Janet C. "The Power of the Pencil: Inuit Women in the Graphic Arts." *Inuit Art Quarterly* 5:1 (1990): 16–26.
Blodgett, Jean. *Grasp Tight the Old Ways.* Toronto: Art Gallery of Ontario, 1983.
Blodgett, Jean, and Marie Bouchard. *Jessie Oonark: A Retrospective.* Winnipeg Art Gallery, 1986.
Driscoll, Bernadette. "Tattoos, Hairsticks, and Ulus: The Graphic Art of Jessie Oonark." *Arts Manitoba* 3:4: 12–19.

Ordóñez, Sylvia (1956–)

The painter Sylvia Ordóñez, known for her introspective self-portraits, richly colored still lifes, and haunting landscapes, has exhibited widely throughout Mexico since the 1970s. She studied abroad for a number of years in Paris, France, and at the Slade School in London, England, but her first exhibition was in her native city of Monterrey, Nuevo León, Mexico, in 1977. In 1978 she won fifth prize in the Bienal de Pintores Jóvenes organized by the Instituto Nacional de Bellas Artes, and first prize in the Fifth Congreso de Arte Pittorico de Fomento Industrial y Comercio de Monterrey—both in Mexico. Ordóñez travelled to Barcelona, Spain, in 1979 to study printmaking at the Escuela de Artes y Oficios.

In 1990 Ordóñez's work was included in the important exhibition, "Women in Mexico," organized by Edward Sullivan for the National Academy of Design in New York City, which travelled to various art institutions in the United States and Mexico throughout 1991. Also in 1990 Ordóñez was shown in New York's SoHo under the auspices of the Parallel Project's "New Moments in Mexican Art" exhibition series which showcased works by leading contemporary Mexican painters. The artist continues to live and work in the small village of Villa de Garcia, Nuevo León, Mexico.

Susan Aberth

Bibliography

Cavazos, Patricia Garcia. "Sylvia Ordóñez." *Nuevos Momentos del Arte Mexicano (New Moments in Mexican Art).* Exhibition Catalog. New York: Parallel Projects, 1990, pp. 122–25.

Mexico. The New Generations. San Antonio Museum of Art, 1985.

Pintura Mexicana de hoy. Tradición e innovación. Monterrey: Centro Cultural Alfa, 1989.

Sullivan, Edward. *Women in Mexico.* Mexico City: Centro Cultural, Arte Contemporaneo, 1990, pp. 80–83.

Orkin, Ruth (1921–1985)

Born in Boston, Massachusetts, Ruth Orkin was a self-taught photographer—her husband was a photographer and her mother was the silent film actress Mary Ruby.

Orkin worked as a messenger for MGM in 1943; soaked up the background; became intrigued with the persons in front of and behind the camera; and used her own camera to take candid shots of people on and off the sets. The following year she moved to New York City and began her career as a free-lance photographer working for many of the popular magazines of the time.

Orkin won awards and honors for her black-and-white prints; in 1959 she was named one of the "Top Ten Women Photographers in the U.S." as a result of a poll taken by the Professional Photographers of America. Earlier on (1953), a film she codirected, *Little Fugitive*, won the coveted Silver Lion of San Marco award at the Venice Film Festival.

Orkin's photographs are in private and public permanent collections including, among others, the Metropolitan Museum of Art, and the Museum of Modern Art (MoMA)—both in New York City.

Bibliography

Auer, Michele, and Michel Auer. *Encyclopedie Internationale des Photographes de 1839 a nos jours.* Editions Camera Obscura, 1985.

A Photo Journal: Ruth Orkin. Viking Studio Books, 1981.

Walsh, George, Colin Naylor, and Michael Held. *Contemporary Photographers.* Saint Martin's Press, 1982.

Witkin, Lee D., and Barbara London. *The Photograph Collector's Guide.* New York Graphic Society, 1979.

Ortiz Pérez, Emilia (1917–)

Born in Tepic, Nayarit, in Mexico, Emilia Ortiz Pérez studied painting with Vizcarra in Guadalajara and in the Academy of San Carlos in Mexico City. In 1940 Ortiz held an exhibition of her drawings and paintings, which were based upon her observations of the indigenous world. She is best known for her watercolors.

Since 1940 Ortiz has had some fifteen solo exhibitions in Mexico and abroad. She is also a cartoonist, a caricaturist, and a poet. Her book, *De mis soledades vengo,* a prizewinner, was published in 1986 by the Fundación Dr. Julian Gascon Mercado.

Bibliography

Alvarez, José Rogelio, et al. *Enciclopedia de México.* Secretaría de Educación Pública, 1987.

Osborne, Lyndal (1940–)

Lyndal Osborne was born in Australia and received her first art education at the National Art School in Sydney in 1961. She completed graduate studies at the University of Wisconsin in Madison, receiving a Master of Fine Arts degree in printmaking in 1971. Her first teaching assignment was at the University of Houston, Texas, for one year, and, since then, she has been a member of the faculty of the University of Alberta, Canada, primarily engaged in printmaking instruction.

Osborne's art is strongly tied to her Australian background. From early childhood she has learned to appreciate beauty in the forms of the natural world. Over the years these forms have become internalized and have become a major source of inspiration. On one level the images attract by their visual appearance and concreteness as defined by the artist. They represent purely visual reality and provoke optical sensations. On another level the artist creates ambiguity by the use of forms which have associations with objects belonging to a different reality. Taken out of their context and put in a new one they lose their primary meaning. In this way the artist creates a mood of mystery and evokes associations with non-specific rituals in which simple objects are involved.

For several years Osborne has been working mostly in lithography. She uses photographs of found objects and makes sculptural forms constructed of organic material to help work out ideas. She now employs drawing very extensively in her prints and builds up the image by overlaying many colored drawings to achieve the final result. In her latest work color plays a leading role: hot reds, poisonous violets, strange greens and yellows create an unusual world, which in turn becomes an expression of eroticism.

Osborne's work has been accepted into many national and international print exhibitions over the past twenty years. Some of these include biennales and triennales in such cities as Wakayana and Tokyo, Japan; Seoul, Korea; Ibiza, Spain; Bradford, England; Miami, Florida; and San Francisco, California; Fredrikstad, Norway; Cracow, Poland; Ljubljana, Yugoslavia; Reykjavik, Iceland; Fremantle, Australia; Frechen, Germany; Varna, Bulgaria; and Taiwan, China.

Several solo exhibitions have been shown in Canadian cities, the most recent a retrospective called "Songs of the Stone" in the Edmonton Art Gallery in 1990. A smaller version of this show toured four cities in Argentina in 1990–1991. Her works are owned by numerous collectors and in important institutional collections such as the National Gallery of Canada, Ottawa, and the Canada Art Bank.

Marytka Kosinski

Bibliography

Lyndal Osborne: Songs of the Stone. Exhibition Catalog by Roger Boulet, Director. Alberta: Edmonton Art Gallery, 1990, p. 28.
Contemporary Art Print of the World. 2 vols. Misool Congron Sa, Seoul, Korea, in cooperation with Intern Art Center, Kyoto, Japan, 1989.
Printmaking in Alberta 1945–1985 by Bente R. Cochran. University of Alberta, 1989, pp. 116–18.
Contemporary Edmonton Prints. Exhibition Catalog by Bente R. Cochrane. Alberta: Edmonton Art Gallery, 1988, pp. 15, 17.
Edmonton Prints: Brazil. Catalog to accompany a Brazilian tour, 1984. Organized by the Society of Northern Alberta Print Artists.

Oshuitoq, Ningeeuga (1918–1980)

Born in a camp along the southern shore of Baffin Island in the early decades of the twentieth century, and raised by her grandparents, Ningeeuga Oshuitoq lived much of her life in the traditions of her Inuit heritage. It was not until 1960 when she was in her forties that she and her family moved to Cape Dorset, then a rapidly-growing Arctic settlement of more than 200 people. Before relocating to Cape Dorset, she and others from her camp had visited the community sporadically for trade and celebration. Less than a year after moving to Cape Dorset, Ningeeuga was diagnosed with tuberculosis and was subsequently hospitalized in southern Canada for four years. Shortly after her return to Cape Dorset in 1965 she became interested in the fledgling arts and crafts program in the community and began to experiment with drawing. One of her images was selected for the 1966 Cape Dorset annual print collection. Between 1966 and the time of her death in 1980, twenty-six of Ningeeuga's drawings were used as print images in nine Cape Dorset annual print collections from 1966–1968, 1973–1974, and 1977–1980.

Ningeeuga draws inspiration for the subject matter of her images from her imagination and from her experience living on the land in the traditional Inuit culture. She developed a distinctive personal style with strong curvilinear forms in her representations of Inuit women, children, birds, and imaginary creatures, and the design elements often take priority over representational accuracy. Rubber-legged children and dogs romp happily across her pages, and she often embellishes her simple line drawings with lines, balls, and circles enhancing their interest and design qualities.

Ningeeuga's engaging artwork has been included in several internationally touring exhibitions of Inuit art and is included in significant permanent collections, including the Art Gallery of Ontario, Toronto; Canadian Museum of Civilization, Ottawa; Prince of Wales Northern Heritage Centre, Yellowknife; Amon Carter Museum of American Art, Fort Worth, Texas; Canadian Guild of Crafts, Montréal; Simon Fraser Gallery, Burnaby, British Columbia; and the Art Gallery of York University, Downsview, Ontario.

Marion E. Jackson

Bibliography

Cape Dorset Annual Print Collection Catalogs: 1966–1968, 1973–1974, 1977–1980.
Department of External Affairs Canada. *Graphic Art by Eskimos of Canada: Second Collection.* Ottawa: Department of External Affairs, 1970.
Furneaux, Patrick, and Leo Rosshandler. *Arts of the Eskimo: Prints.* Montréal: Signum Press in association with Oxford University Press, 1974.
Goetz, Helga. *The Inuit Print/L'estampe Inuit.* Ottawa: National Museums of Canada, 1977.
Jackson, Marion, and Judith Nasby. *Contemporary Inuit Drawings.* Guelph, Ontario: Macdonald Stewart Art Centre, 1987.
Simon Fraser Gallery. *The Art of the Eskimo.* Burnaby, British Columbia: Simon Fraser University, 1971.
York University Art Gallery. *Eskimo Carvings and Prints from the Collection of York University.* Downsview, Ontario: York University, 1971.

Osorio, Luz (1860–1935)

Luz Osorio was born in Paplanta, Vera Cruz, Mexico. It is assumed, by most authorities, that she studied in the Academy of Fine Arts in Puebla under the aegis of Francisco Morales. Her painting, "Una Virgen Cristiana," won first prize in the 2nd exhibition of the Sociedad Poblana de Artisanos; she also painted "La Papenteca," a portrait of an indigenous youth seated on a boulder, with a pitcher at his side, and a small calabash cup in his hands.

Osorio married the politician and impresario Carlos B. Zetina, gave birth to ten children, and then abandoned art.

Bibliography

Alvarez, José Rogelio, et al. *Enciclopedia de México.* Secretaría de Educación Pública, 1987.

Otis, Jeanne (Edmonds) (1940–)

Born in Hackensack, New Jersey, ceramic artist Jeanne (Edmonds) Otis is known for her colorful hand-built and salt-glazed porcelain wall constructions. As a young child she moved with her family to the Midwest, where she was raised on the north side of Chicago, Illinois. From an early age Otis knew she wanted to be an artist and was encouraged in her artistic pursuits by both of her parents. In 1957, following graduation from high school, she entered DePauw University in Greencastle, Indiana, where she received her Bachelor of Arts degree in art in 1961.

Throughout the 1960s Otis taught art classes at the elementary and high school levels in Indiana, Missouri, and Ohio, where she also exhibited her work in local and regional exhibitions. During the time she spent in Ohio, she took additional art classes at Denison University, Granville. She had been introduced to ceramics during her years at DePauw University by Richard Peeler, but it was not until 1971, when Ralph Komives was hired as the new ceramics instructor at Denison, that she was inspired to turn from painting to clay as her primary medium.

From 1971 to 1972 Otis underwent significant changes in her life. She was divorced from her husband, Tim Otis, whom she had married during her sophomore year at DePauw University, and, as a single parent with two daughters, made the decision to enter graduate school at Ohio State University in Columbus with an emphasis in clay. She completed her Bachelor of Fine Arts degree at Denison University in 1973 and that same year studied ceramics on a scholarship with Cynthia Bringle at the Penland

School of Crafts in North Carolina. She received her Master of Fine Arts degree in ceramics from Ohio State University in 1974.

Otis's early work in clay combines the use of the vessel form with a sense of humor and a love for fiber and surface design, which she had retained since learning how to sew as a child. Known as her "Dude Pots," each "Dude" was "dressed" in a ceramic costume, such as the baggy blue jeans and red suspenders of her "Lost Dutchman Prospector Coffeepot" (1975), to reflect the character's vocation and personality.

For another major series, which was influenced by her interest in antique quilts, Otis created actual quilt patterns in clay that were meant to either hang on the wall or function as dinner plates. This body of work, which integrated her background in painting and her sense of color and surface design, became the transition to her larger-scale abstract wall constructions.

In the summer of 1975, following a semester of teaching a general crafts course at San Diego State University in California, Otis moved to Arizona to accept a position in ceramics at Arizona State University, Tempe. As happens to many artists who move to the Southwest, Otis's palette began to change and reflect the softer, more light reflective colors of her new desert surroundings. She also began to break the square patterns she had developed with her "ceramic quilts" and work with broken circles and free-form shapes that have an affinity to art deco. In 1982 Otis created her first piece, "Fool's Puzzle," which incorporated overlapping elements.

Otis has never been concerned with a technology for its own sake, rather her masterful command of glaze techniques developed from her problem-solving efforts to create a wide variety of colors to enrich her palette. Similarly her search for the right clay body led her to experiment with porcelain for her wall pieces.

As a painter Otis has worked in a style reminiscent of the figurative paintings of California Bay area artist Richard Diebenkorn and was influenced by the color harmonies of Milton Avery. Similar sensibilities of color and formal relationships are visible in her contemporary work in clay. Referred to as "color dialogues," Otis's wall constructions also have an architectonic quality in their balanced interconnection of parts. Otis acknowledges the sophisticated detail in the work of her architect husband, Robert Fronske, whom she married in 1976, as an additional source of inspiration.

Since the early 1970s Otis has exhibited nationally and internationally in more than seventy solo and group exhibitions. Her work is in the collections of Hughes Aircraft Corporation, Los Angeles, California; Arizona State University Art Museum, Tempe, Barrows Neurological Institute, Phoenix, and Valley National Bank, Payson—all in Arizona; and the Hyatt Regency Hotel, San Antonio, Texas.

Lucinda H. Gedeon

Bibliography

Herman, Lloyd E. *American Porcelain: New Expressions in an Ancient Art.* Timber Press, 1980.

Toth, Beth. "Jeanne Otis: A Color Dialogue." *Ceramics Monthly* (January 1988): 40–42.

Ott, Sabina (1955–)

A native New Yorker, the painter/printmaker Sabina Ott earned a Bachelor of Fine Arts degree at the San Francisco Art Institute, California (1979), and, two years later, a Master of Fine Arts degree from the same school.

Ott's large oil and encaustic paintings on wooden panels have been seen in solo exhibitions in galleries and museums, including the Marsha Mateyka Gallery, Washington, D.C. (1993); Los Angeles County Museum of Art, California (1992); Charles Cowles Gallery, New York City (1985, 1987, 1989, 1992); Pence Gallery, Santa Monica (1987, 1988, 1990, 1991), Rena Bransten Gallery, San Francisco (1989), and San Francisco Museum of Modern Art (1989)—all in California; Galerie am Moritzplatz, Berlin, Germany (1987); Davies/Long Gallery (1985, 1986), and Los Angeles Institute of Contemporary Art (1983)—both in Los Angeles, California; and others. Her work has been invited to group exhibitions, such as "Breakdown," Rose Art Museum, Brandeis University, Waltham, Massachusetts (1992); "42nd Biennial Exhibition of Contemporary American Painting," Corcoran Gallery of Art, Washington, D.C. (1991); "Images Transformed," Oakland Museum (1992), and "La Brazil Projects," Municipal Art Gallery, Barnsdall Park, Los Angeles (1990)—both in California; "Words and Images: Seven Corporate Commissions," Cleveland Center for Contemporary Art, Ohio (1989); "Contemporary Diptychs: Divided Visions," Whitney Museum of American Art at Equitable Center (1987), and Piezo Electric Gallery (1985)—both in New York City; and others.

Ott was the recipient of a new talent award, Los Angeles County Museum of Art, California (1986); she received an artist-in-residence grant, Djerassi Foundation, Woodside, California (1989); and a National Endowment for the Arts (NEA) grant (1990). She has taught on the graduate faculty of the Art Center of Design, Pasadena, California, since 1986, and has been on the faculty at California State University, Los Angeles, since 1990. Panelist and art juror, Ott is active in professional arts and political organizations, including the Women's Action Coalition, Los Angeles, California (1992 to the present); Foundation for Art Resources (1991 to present); and others. Her work is represented in private, public, and corporate permanent collections, including the Metropolitan Museum of Art and Chase Manhattan Bank—both in New York City; Los Angeles County Museum of Art and Oakland Museum of Art—both in California; Contemporary Art Museum, Honolulu, Hawaii; Corcoran Gallery of Art, Washington, D.C.; Dayton-Hudson Foundation, Minneapolis, Minnesota; Brandeis University, Waltham, Massachusetts; and many others.

Bibliography

Anderson, Michael. "Sabina Ott at Pence Gallery." *Artissues* 21 (January–February 1992): 39.

Fazzolari, Bruno. "Down to Basics: Images Transformed at the Oakland Museum." *Artweek* (April 28, 1992): 23.

Westfall, Stephen. "Sabina Ott at Charles Cowles." *Art in America* (March 1990): 199.

Owens-Hart, Winnie (1949–)

Born in Washington, D.C., the ceramist/sculptor/educator Winnie Owens-Hart earned a Bachelor of Fine Arts degree from the Philadelphia College of Art, Pennsylvania (now the University of the Arts); and a Master of Fine Arts degree from Howard University, Washington, D.C.

Owens-Hart has held solo exhibitions, including "Dreams, Visions, Nightmares and the Real World," Bloomsburg, Pennsylvania (1988); and "Winnie Owens-Hart: An Exhibition of African American Contemporary/Traditional Ceramics," CRT's Craftery Gallery, Hartford, Connecticut (1983); among others. Her work has been invited to or included in many group shows in the United States and abroad, such as "Influences: Contemporary African and African-American Art" (she was both curator and exhibiting artist), Hood College, Frederick, Maryland (1989); "VOICES: An Exhibition of Works by 14 Afro-American Artists," Community Folk Art Gallery, Syracuse, New York (1987); "Black Women Visual Artists in Washington, D.C.," Bethune Museum-Archives, Inc., Washington, D.C. (1986); "Biennale Internationale de Ceramique d'Art, Vallauris, France (1984); "Forever Free: Art by African-American Women 1862–1980," a travelling exhibition, Illinois State University, Normal (1981); and others.

Owens-Hart's work is represented in private and public permanent collections, including Howard University, Washington, D.C.; Syracuse University, New York; and many others. "Trimesters" (1990), offers many statements about Owens-Hart: first, it is a narrative piece composed of three female torsos, hands throwing a pot, and a symbol for swimming; second, she uses clay freely to express her innermost feelings (in this instance, her daughter's birth); third, she carries on the African tradition in clay, yet imbues that tradition with her singular approach.

Bibliography

Atungaye, Monifa. "Winnie Owens-Hart." *Ceramics Monthly* (September 1988).
Hall, Robert L. *Gathered Visions: Selected Works by African American Women Artists*. Anacostia Museum. Smithsonian Institution Press, 1992.
Scarupa, Harriet Jackson. "Winnie Owens: Messenger in Clay." *New Directions* (October 1979).

Ox, Jack (1948–)

Born in Denver, Colorado, the painter/conceptual artist Jack Ox earned a Bachelor of Fine Arts degree from the San Francisco Art Institute, California (1969); and received a Master of Fine Arts degree from the University of California at San Diego (1977).

Ox has held solo exhibitions of work in the United States and abroad, including the Brooklyn Academy of Music, New York (1982); Contemporary Arts Center, New Orleans, Louisiana (1983); "Music to My Eyes," Pyramid Gallery, Rochester, New York (1984); "On the Wall, On the Air," Haydn Gallery, Massachusetts Institute of Technology (MIT) (1984); "Vom Klang Der Bilder," Staatgalerie Stuttgart, Germany (1985); "Capriccio," Palais des Beaux Arts, Brussels, Belgium (1986); and others.

Her work has been invited to group exhibitions in many venues in the United States and Europe; it is represented in private, public, and corporate permanent collections, including Atlantic Richfield Corporation, Dallas, Texas; Dartmouth College, Hanover, New Hampshire; General Electric Corporation, Ridgefield, Connecticut; the University of Iowa, Iowa City; and others.

Bibliography

Ox, Jack, with Peter Frank. "The Systematic Translation of Musical Composition into Paintings." *Leonardo* 17:3 (1984).
Ratcliff, Carter. "Looking at Sound." *Art in America* 68:3 (March 198): 87–95.
Who's Who in American Art. 17th ed. R.R. Bowker Co., 1986.

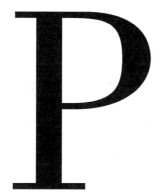

Pacheco, Maria Luisa (1919–1982)

Born in La Paz, Bolivia, the painter/illustrator/designer Maria Luisa Pacheco studied at the Academia de Bellas Artes in her native city with Cecilio Guzman Derojas and Jorge de la Reza (1934); and at the Academia de San Fernando, Madrid, Spain (1951–1952). She also studied with Daniel Vasquez Díaz while in Madrid (1952). From 1956 until her death she lived in New York City.

Pacheco held solo exhibitions in museums and galleries, including the Galería Sudamericana, New York City (1956, 1958); the Pan American Union, Washington, D.C. (1957); Rose Fried Gallery (1962), Bertha Schaefer Gallery (1965, 1967), and Zegri Gallery (1968)—all in New York City; and others. Her work was included in many prestigious group shows throughout the United States: from New York City to Los Angeles, California; Washington, D.C.; Dallas, Texas; Omaha, Nebraska; Tulsa, Oklahoma; and Newport, Rhode Island.

Winner of honors and awards, Pacheco received Guggenheim Foundation fellowships (1957, 1959, 1960). She was an illustrator for *Life* magazine in the mid-1950s and taught at her alma mater in La Paz, Bolivia (1950–1951). Examples of her work are in private, public, and corporate permanent collections, including the Dallas Museum of Fine Arts, Texas; IBM Corporation, Washington, D.C.; the Guggenheim Museum, New York City; Museum of Modern Art of Latin America, Washington, D.C.; the University of Texas at Austin; and others.

Bibliography

Claure, Rigobeto Villarroel. *Art in Latin America Today: Bolivia*. Pan American Union, 1963.

The Latin American Spirit: Art and Artists in the United States, 1920–1970. Harry N. Abrams, 1988.

Pacheco, Martha (1957–)

Born in Guadalajara, Jalisco, Mexico, Martha Pacheco studied at the School of Fine Arts of the University of Guadalajara from 1976 to 1981. Her drawings and paintings reveal the influence of Javier Campos Cabello, with whom she worked at the Institute of Visual Research, Jaliscience, Mexico.

The subject matter of Pacheco's work, insofar as it can be described up to 1987, consists of disemboweled animals and nude or half-clothed personages in urban settings of the 1940s and 1950s; there is a certain fearfulness, an ambiguity, a disconcerting air about her compositions which say much about today's society.

Pacheco's style emerged full-blown in 1983; she has had solo shows at the Casa de la Cultura Jaliscience (1982) and at the Galería Magritte (1984 and 1986)—both in Guadalajara, Jalisco. Some of her group exhibitions in Mexico include "Pintores Escultores y una Bicicleta Descompuesta," Institute of Visual Research, Casa de la Cultura, Jaliscience (1982); "V Salón del Retrato," IVR, Galería Municipal Jaime Torres Bodet, Guadalajara (1983); "35 en el 85," Forum of Art and Culture, Guadalajara (1985); "13 de Occidente" (1986) and "Imágenes traspuestas" (1987)—both in the Museum of Modern Art, Mexico City; and the VII Encuentro Nacional de Arte Joven in Aguascalientes (1987), in which she won the prize for drawing.

Bibliography
Algunos de Guadalajara: Pintura y Gráfica. INBA, 1987.
Imágenes Traspuestas. Museo de Arte Moderno. Bosque de Chapultepec, 1987.

Paeff, Bashka (1893–1979)

Born in Minsk, Russia, the sculptor Bashka Paeff (Mrs. Samuel Waxman) studied with Bela Pratt at the Massachusetts Normal School and the School of the Boston Museum of Fine Arts—both in Massachusetts.

A member of several professional arts organizations, she exhibited work for many years with the National Academy of Design and the National Sculpture Society—both in New York City; and others.

Paeff's sculpture is represented in private and public permanent collections. She was commissioned to create fountains (her *Boy and Bird* fountain in the Boston Public Garden is the best known); war memorials; bronze reliefs and bas-reliefs of many outstanding individuals, including Martin Luther King, Jr.; Oliver Wendell Holmes; and others. Her work is sited in venues in Massachusetts such as the State House and Boston University—both in Boston; Harvard University Medical Library and Law Library; and Massachusetts Institute of Technology (MIT)—all in Cambridge.

Bibliography
"Bashka Paeff, Sculptor of 'Boy and Bird,' '85'" Obituary. *The New York Times* (January 26, 1979): A23.
Dodd, Loring Holmes. *Golden Moments in American Sculpture*. Dresser, Chapman, and Grimes, 1967.
Fielding, Mantle. *Dictionary of American Painters, Sculptors, and Engravers*. Modern Books and Crafts, 1974.

Page, Marie Danforth (1869–1940)

A painter of portraits (and occasionally of landscapes), the native Bostonian Marie Danforth Page began her art instruction at seventeen with the painter Helen Knowlton, and continued until 1889. From 1890 to 1895 she studied with Frank W. Benson and Edmund C. Tarbell at the Boston Museum School, Massachusetts.

Page exhibited her work for the first time at the Boston Art Club in 1894. Upon her marriage to Calvin G. Page in 1896 the couple settled on Marlborough Street in Boston, where the artist had a studio on the top floor. After a trip to Europe in 1903, when she copied Velázquez's paintings in Spain, she took a summer course at Harvard University, Cambridge, Massachusetts, with Denman Ross in color theory and tonal relationships. Her first solo exhibition of fifteen portraits was held in 1902. When three of her paintings were accepted for the Panama-Pacific International Exposition in 1915, she travelled through the Panama Canal to attend the exhibition in San Francisco, California, and receive a bronze medal. The National Academy of Design, New York City, awarded her the Shaw prize the following year and elected her an associate in 1927. Her portraits were very popular and commanded handsome fees. In Boston she exhibited at the Walter Kimball and Vose galleries and at the Guild of Boston Artists, and she always sustained a lively record of participation in national exhibitions. Today many of her paintings are in private collections, and six portraits of professors (painted between 1928 and 1931) are at Harvard University, Cambridge, Massachusetts.

Eleanor Tufts

Bibliography
Fairbrother, Trevor J. *The Bostonians: Painters of an Elegant Age, 1870–1930*. Boston: Museum of Fine Arts, 1986.
Hoppin, Martha J. *Marie Danforth Page, Back Bay Portraitist*. Springfield, Massachusetts: George Walter Vincent Smith Art Museum, 1979.
Tufts, Eleanor. *American Women Artists, 1830–1930*. National Museum of Women in the Arts, 1987.

Page, P.K. (1916–)

Born in Swanage, Dorset, England, the poet/painter/printmaker P.K. (Patricia Kathleen) Page emigrated to Canada in 1919. The wife of a Canadian High Commissioner, Page has lived and worked in many countries throughout the world.

Winner of honors and awards for her poetry, Page has held solo exhibitions in museums and galleries in Canada and abroad, including the Picture Loan Society, Toronto (1960); Art Gallery of Greater Victoria, British Columbia (1965); and others. Her work has been included in many group shows, including those sponsored by the National Gallery of Canada, Ottawa, and "Three Poet Artists," Burnaby Art Gallery, British Columbia (1978). Examples of her work are represented in private and public permanent collections.

Bibliography
Frances, Anne. "P.K." *Canadian Art* 20:1 (January–February 1963): 42–45.
Three Poet Artists: Eldon Grier, P.K. Page, Joe Rosenblatt. A Catalog. Burnaby Art Gallery, 1978.

Palau, Marta (1934–)

Born in Albesa, Lérida, Spain, Marta Palau emigrated to Mexico when she was six years old. She studied at la Escuela de Pintura y Escultura (La Esmeralda), Mexico City (1955–1965), and took classes in printmaking with Guillermo Silva Santamaria. Palau went to San Diego State University, California, to take advanced printmaking techniques with Paul Lingren; she also learned to make tapestries in Barcelona, Spain.

Palau affirms that her compositions are the products of caprice—of accident—serendipity; with respect to her collage, "Sellos de la España Sellada," however, the critic Rita Eder sees the combination of her brushstrokes and collaged work in a darker vein.

At the end of the 1950s Palau did a suite of prints based upon the legends of the Minotaur, playing on humor and eroticism. At that time she used the arts of the palmists and the zodiac as a pretext to investigate the limits of color. At the Third Salon of Independents (1979), she exhibited "Ambientación alquímica," a work scribbled over with formulae and cabalistic numbers. Palau showed thirteen serigraphs in 1981, the central theme of which was the figure of Lázaro Cárdenas. In sculpture she has constructed three-dimensional, tubular labyrinths which she terms "doors of time"; and in tapestries she wove such works as "La Cascada," "La Guerra Florida," "El Hombre de los Hongos," and "Mis Caminos son Terrestres," solely with natural Mexican fibers.

Palau has participated in more than forty exhibitions throughout the Americas, including the Jewish Community Center in San Diego and the La Jolla Museum of Art—both in California; the Galería Juan Martín and the Galería Pecanin—both in Mexico City, Mexico. In 1963 Palau's work was exhibited in Tokyo, Japan, and the Far East. Her most recent show took place in the National Salon of the Palace of Fine Arts,

Mexico (1985). The government of the state of Michoacan, Mexico, sponsored the publication of her book titled *Marta Palau* (1985).

Bibliography
Alvarez, José Rogelio, et al. *Enciclopedia de Mexico.* Secretaría de Educación Pública, 1987.
The Texas Quarterly: Image of Mexico II. The University of Texas, Autumn 1969.

Palfi, Marion (1907–1978)

Born in Berlin, Germany, the photographer Marion Palfi studied her craft and received a general education in Europe before emigrating to the United States.

Palfi taught photography at several institutions in the Los Angeles area between the mid-1960s and the mid-1970s, including the University of California at Los Angeles (UCLA) Extension and Chouinard–California Institute of the Arts, Valencia; Inner City Cultural Center; and the Woman's Building. Earlier on, she taught at the New School for Social Research, New York City.

Winner of awards and honors, Palfi received a Rosenwald fellowship (1946); a Guggenheim Foundation fellowship (1967); and a National Endowment for the Arts (NEA) fellowship (1974). Her compassionate black-and-white photographs of senior citizens, children, minorities and the disadvantaged illustrated and illuminated problems that were difficult to comprehend. Representative examples of her work are in private and public permanent collections, including the Museum of Modern Art (MoMA) and the New York Public Library—both in New York City; San Francisco Museum of Modern Art, California; University of Kansas, Lawrence; the Museum of Port-au-Prince, Haiti; and others.

Bibliography
Browne, Turner, and Elaine Partnow. *Macmillan Biographical Encyclopedia of Photographic Artists and Innovators.* Macmillan, 1983.
Witkin, Lee, and Barbara London. *The Photograph Collector's Guide.* London, 1979.

Palliser, Minnie (1928–)

Canadian Inuit artist Minnie Palliser was born in 1928 in a camp south of Inukjuaq (Port Harrison) in Arctic Québec. In 1947 she married George Palliser and moved into that community, where they continue to live with their children and grandchildren.

Originally encouraged by James Houston, Palliser has been carving since the late 1940s. Her pieces are usually small, compact, and comfortably rounded. Palliser's concern for the preservation of her culture is apparent in the traditional subject matter of her carvings. Her focus has been almost exclusively on mothers, fathers, and children. Her cachet is a textured effect, achieved with tiny nail pricks that represent fur trim and accent the contrasting materials.

After some experimenting with basketry and doll-making, Palliser finds that carving in stone brings her the most pleasure. Her work has been shown in galleries across Canada and the United States, including six exhibitions in the 1980s alone. She is also a traditional throat singer—an accomplishment that has taken her to many performances, including two European tours.

    Mary Craig

Bibliography
Inuit Artist Index Arranged by Last Name. Indian and Northern Affairs Canada, 1990.

Palmer, Adelaide C. (c. 1851–1928)

Born in Oxford, New Hampshire, the painter Adelaide C. Palmer was a student of John J. Enneking. Palmer was a member of the Copley Society, Boston, Massachusetts (1893).

Bibliography
American Art Annual. Vol. 28. American Federation of Arts, 1932.
Fielding, Mantle. *Dictionary of American Painters, Sculptors, and Engravers.* Modern Books and Crafts, 1974.
Woman's Who's Who of America. American Commonwealth Co., 1914.

Palmer, Jessie A. (1882–1956)

Born in Lawrence, Texas, the painter Jessie A. Palmer studied with John Carlson, Frank Reaugh, and Martha Simkins. Winner of prizes and awards, Palmer received the Evert's medal at the Dallas Woman's Forum, Texas (1924); first prizes at the Texas-Oklahoma fairs (1926, 1927); honorable mentions at the Texas Fine Arts Association and an exhibition in Nashville, Tennessee (1929).

Palmer was a member of the Amarillo Arts Association, Texas; the Reaugh Art Club; the Southern States Art League; and the Texas Fine Arts Association. Examples of her work are in private and public permanent collections, including the Travis School and the Dallas Woman's Forum—both in Dallas, Texas; and others.

Bibliography
American Art Annual. Vol. 28. American Federation of Arts, 1932.
Fielding, Mantle. *Dictionary of American Painters, Sculptors, and Engravers.* Modern Books and Crafts, 1974.
O'Brien, Esse Forrester. *Art and Artists of Texas.* Tardy Publishing Co., 1935.

Palmer, Pauline (1867–1938)

Born in McHenry, Illinois, the painter Pauline Palmer studied with William Merritt Chase, Kenneth Hayes Miller, and Charles Hawthorne. She took further work in Paris, France, with Collin, Courtois, Prinet, and Simon.

Winner of awards and honors, Palmer won a bronze medal at the St. Louis Exposition, Missouri (1904); the Young Fortnightly prize (1907); the Marshall field prize (1907); the Thompson portraiture prize (1914); the Cahn honorable mention (1916); the Rosenwald purchase prize (1916); the Carr prize (1917); the Butler purchase prize (1920); the fine arts building prize (1924); Rosenwald prize (1926)—all at the Art Institute of Chicago, Illinois; she also won prizes or honorable mentions at the Society of Women Artists Exhibition (1915); the Chicago Art Guild (1915); Chicago Society of Artists (1920); National Association of Women Painters and Sculptors (1924); Chicago Galleries Association (1928, 1929, 1931); and others.

Member and president of the Chicago Painters and Sculptors, Palmer also belonged to the Chicago Arts Club; the Chicago Galleries Association; Grand Central Galleries, New York City; and others. Representative examples of her work can be found in private and public permanent collections, including the Academy of Fine Arts, Elgin, Illinois; the Art Institute of Chicago, the Arche Club, the Klio Association, and the Nike Club—all in Chicago, Illinois; Aurora Art Association, Illinois; Delgado Museum of Art, New Orleans, Louisiana; Muncie Art Association, Indiana; Rockford Art Association, Illinois; San Diego Museum of Art, California; and many others.

Bibliography
American Art Annual. Vol. 28. American Federation of Arts, 1932.
Obituary. *Who's Who in American Art.* Vol. 3. American Federation of Arts, 1940.
Pattison, James W. "Water-color Exhibition at the Art Institute." *Brush and Pencil* 4:3 (1899): 149–58.

Panneton, Louise (1926–)

Born in Trois Rivieres, Québec, Canada, the painter/fiber artist Louise Panneton studied individually with several artists, including Leon Bellefleur, Jordi Bonet, and Geraldine Bourbeau. She took further work at the Académie Julian, Paris, France; studied with Pauline Labrèque and Pierre Daquin; and studied tapestry at the University of Québec with further tapestry research in Spain and North Africa.

Panneton has held many solo exhibitions in museums and galleries in Québec, including Grenier des Artistes, Grand Piles (1967); Galerie Jacques Lacroix, Chicoutimi (1968); Galerie du Vieux, Trois Rivières (1970); Galerie l'Apogée, Saint-Sauveur-des-Monts (1971, 1973); and others. Her paintings were exhibited in group shows, such as the Galerie Zanettin, Québec City (1962), and others until 1967. She showed tapestries at many venues from 1967 on, including "La Nouvelle Tapisserie Québecoise," Musée d'Art Contemporain, Montréal (1978); and others. Examples of Panneton's work are in private and public permanent collections, including the Ministry of Intergovernmental Affairs, Québec City; the Town Hall, Trois Rivières; Musée du Québec; and others.

Bibliography
Benoit, Luc. "Trois Rivières: Lousie Panneton; l'écheveau et la tapisserie." *Vie des arts* (Autumn 1974): 73–74.
Cloutier-Cournoyer, Francoise. *La Nouvelle Tapisserie Québecoise.* A Catalog. Montréal, Québec: Musée d'Art Contemporain, 1978.

Pardo, Silvia (1941–)

Born in Mexico, Silvia Pardo studied art at the Ibero-American University in her native city. She did illustration for the reviews *El Rehilete* and *Zarza,* and, in 1953, took third place in a drawing exhibition sponsored by the United Nations. She is an excellent portraitist whose work in pencil or wash, in the late 1960s, elicited praise from the critics for its old-master-like draftsmanship.

Pardo enjoyed two solo shows before 1969; she participated in many group shows, including the Galería Kusak, the Galería Misrachi, the Salón de las Plástica Mexicana, the Museum of Modern Art, the National Institute of Fine Arts, and the Galería Pardo (where she exhibited oils and ink drawings in 1985 and 1987)—all in Mexico City, Mexico.

Bibliography
Alvarez, José Rogelio, et al. *Enciclopedia de Mexico.* Secretaría de Educación Pública, 1987.

The Texas Quarterly: Image of Mexico II. The University of Texas, Autumn 1969.

Park, Madeleine Fish (1891–1960)

Born in Mount Kisco, New York, the sculptor Madeleine Fish Park studied at the Art Students League, New York City.

Winner of honors and awards, she exhibited work in many galleries and museums in the United States and abroad, including the American Women's Association (1933, 1940); the Architectural League, New York City; Art Institute of Chicago, Illinois; Hudson Valley Art Association, New York (1944); Museum of Modern Art (MoMA), New York City; Salon des Beaux-Arts, Paris, France; San Francisco Museum of Art, California; Whitney Museum of American Art, New York City; and myriad others.

Park was a member of the Allied Artists of America; American Federation of Arts; Art Workers' Club for Women; the Chappaqua Art Guild; National Sculpture Society; National Association of Women Artists; the Society of Medallists; and others. Her work is represented in many private and public permanent collections.

Bibliography
American Art Annual. Vol. 30. American Federation of Arts, 1934.
Obituary. *Who's Who in American Art.* Vol. 8. American Federation of Arts, 1962.

Parker, Olivia (1941–)

Leading the revival of interest in still-life photography in the 1970s, Olivia Parker's work has been compared both to that of Chardin and to that of Joseph Cornell. Like Chardin, Parker described lovingly each ordinary object in her pictures, and, like Cornell, her often fanciful and dreamlike effects are achieved through the juxtaposition of improbable objects. Parker's earlier arrangements tended to be within boxes or compartmented structures, similar to Cornell's. Unlike Cornell's, however, her constructions are always ephemeral. Neither the delicate fruit and flowers nor her extraordinary lighting effects (mixed daylight and filtered tungsten light) last more than a moment, and as Parker states, "Although my work may move close to the other visual arts in that I make what I photograph, it remains purely photographic in its final form." Photographic composition—that is, one perfect point of view—is important in her work as well: "I like the implications of visual edges: the swollen limits of a ripe pear touching a hard line of light, downy feathers confined by a metal grid, a mirror scattering its surfaces into nothing, or the thin shell of a bright face, its edges already deteriorating into darkness."

Parker was trained in painting and art history; she earned her Bachelor of Arts degree at Wellesley College, Massachusetts, in 1963. Parker began working in photography in 1970 and, by 1975, had abandoned painting altogether. As the mother of two young children she found still-life photography a convenient and accessible genre, and it has remained central to her work, even though her most recent series, "The Possession of Animals," incorporates photographs of live animals, and the occasional portrait makes an appearance in her work. The objects that frequent her still lifes—old pictures, voluptuous flowers, mica, shells, ancient scientific diagrams and maps, old messages, game parts, and weathered instruments—suggest the range of her intellectual interests, and her strong attraction to the concepts that explained and animated the past. Also, "Games, those dependent on both chance and thought, creep into my pictures," and her playful titles often suggest a story: "The Devil's Tea Party," "Isabella's Bit of the Florida Coast," "Starlight Games," "The Quarrellers."

Made with a large view-camera, Parker's first still lifes were contact-printed on black-and-white silver chloride paper, and then partially toned in selenium. The resulting "split-toned" images combined areas of silvery grey with warm deep brown. This early work was collected in the monograph, "Signs of Life" (1978). In the same year she began working in color with Polaroid materials of all formats, from four-by-five to the large twenty-by-twenty-four Polaroid studio camera. Easily making a transition to color, Parker is a brilliant colorist, exploiting particularly the rich intensities of the Polaroid material. Her second monograph, "Under the Looking Glass" (1983), a collection of color pictures, was a production of the publications department of the Polaroid Corporation. Parker returned to monochrome in her third published collection, "Weighing the Planets" (1987), although she continues her color work as well. Since 1987 she has also worked with positive Cibachrome material, both directly in-camera and as an enlarging material.

Parker's work has been critically acclaimed from its first appearance, and it is widely exhibited and published internationally. Although she has no regular academic connection, Parker has been active as a lecturer and workshop leader. Her work can be found in many public collections, among them the Polaroid Collection, the Art Institute of Chicago, Illinois; the International Museum of Photography at George Eastman House (Rochester); the Museum of Modern Art (MoMA), New York City; the Fogg Museum, Harvard University, Cambridge, Massachusetts; the Victoria & Albert Museum, London, England; the High Museum, Atlanta, Georgia; the California Museum of Photography, Riverside; and the Tokyo Fuji Art Museum, Japan.

Gretchen Garner

Bibliography

Hoy, Anne. *Fabrications*. Abbeville Press, 1987.

Parker, Olivia. *Under the Looking Glass*. New York Graphic Society, Little Brown, 1983.

———. [Portfolio with essay by Henry Horenstein], *Popular Photography* (December 1986): 60–67.

———. [Portfolio with essay by Evelyn Roth], *American Photographer* (January 1987): 46–47.

———. *Weighing the Planets*. Boston: New York Graphic Society, Little Brown, 1987.

Rathbone, Belinda, ed. *One of a Kind*. David R. Godine, 1979, pp. 66–67.

Rosenblum, Naomi. *World History of Photography*. Abbeville Press, 1984, pp. 591, 593.

Stone, Jim, ed. *Darkroom Dynamics*. Curtin and Van Nostrand Reinhold, 1979.

Sullivan, Constance, ed. *Legacy of Light*. Alfred A. Knopf, 1987.

Tucker, Jean S. *The Modernist Still Life Photographed*. The University of Missouri Press, 1989, 42, 44.

Walsh, Naylor, and Held Walsh, eds. *Contemporary Photographers*. St. Martin's Press, 1982, pp. 588–89.

Weiley, Susan. "New Light on Color." *ARTnews* (October 1985): 82–89.

Parks, Louise (1945–)

The African-American painter Louise Parks earned a Bachelor of Fine Arts degree from Pratt Institute, Brooklyn, New York, and a Master of Fine Arts degree from Hunter College, New York City.

Parks held a solo exhibition at the Cinque Gallery, New York City, and has exhibited her work in many group shows. "Tapestry #4" (1970), an almost four-by-nine-foot, mixed-media work, is laden with expressive energy and dynamic color, and is typical of Parks's efforts of this period.

Bibliography

Afro-American Artists: New York and Boston. A Catalog. The Museum of the National Center of Afro-American Artists, and the Museum of Fine Arts, Boston, 1970.

Parra, Carmen (1944–)

Born in Mexico City, Mexico, Carmen Parra pursued her early interest in anthropology by attending the National School of Anthropology and History, Mexico, from 1961 to 1964. The visual arts, at that juncture in her life, became her sole concern: she studied at the Accademia delle Belle Arti, Rome, Italy (1964–1965); la Escuela de Pintura y Escultura (La Esmeralda), Mexico City (1967); and the Royal College of Arts, London, England, where she studied "Graphics in Cinema" (1970).

Between 1966 and 1990 Parra held more than thirty solo exhibitions of her work in Mexico, South America, and France, including "Retratos de Bertold Brecht," Edvard Munch Gallery, Mexico City (1968); "Morte do bicicleta," Oca Gallery, Rio de Janeiro, Brazil (1969); "Tour Eiffel, Norriture Principal pour des Poissons d'Ornement," Forum Sarcelles, Paris, France (1976); "Papalotl, grafito de Dios," Casa de la Cultura de Morelia, Michoacan, Mexico (1982); "Querétaro: ciudad barroca," Exconvento del Desierto de Los Leones, Estado de Mexico (1990); and many others. Her work has been invited to myriad group exhibitions in France, Germany, and Mexico, such as "La Nouvelle Peinture Mexicaine," Casa de Mexico, Paris, France, and the Galerie Verriere, Lyon, France (1975); "La Creación Feminina," Goethe Institute, Mexico City, and Kunstler Haus Bethanier, Berlin, Germany (1980); "De Santos y Santitos," Pecanins Gallery, Mexico City (1983); and many more prestigious shows throughout her country, to the present.

Painter, printmaker, stage and costume designer, book illustrator, muralist, and filmmaker—Parra moves easily from one medium of expression to another. She has won awards for her work, including a first prize at the Primavera Otono, Fiesta Primavera Otono, Mexico City (1981), and has executed several large murals during her prestigious career.

Parra works in series: she transmutes through visual metaphor the essence of William Blake, Jorge Luis Borges, and Rainer Maria Rilke; she re-creates angels, butterflies, bull fights, and golden rain in a personal, evocative manner. Her work is housed in many permanent public and private collections throughout the world, including the Museo de Arte Moderno, Mexico City, and the Universidad Nacional Autónoma de Mexico.

Bibliography

Alvarez, José Rogelio, et al. *Enciclopedia de Mexico*. Special Edition, 1987.

Parra, Carmen. *Retratos. Homage to Sergio Fernandez*. Mexico: Metropolitan Autonomous University, 1984.

Who's Who in American Art. 19th ed. R.R. Bowker Co., 1991–1992.

Parraguirre, Maria Luisa

Maria Luisa Parraguirre studied at la Escuela de Pintura y Escultura (La Esmeralda), Mexico City, Mexico, from 1965 to 1972. A printmaker, she worked in the Taller del Molina de Santo Domingo and, in 1976, was given a grant to continue her art studies in Paris, France.

Parraguirre returned to Mexico the following year and, since then, has offered printmaking classes in the educational establishment from which she graduated; she has exhibited her work in Mexico since 1971 and has shown in Czechoslovakia and Poland (1975); Switzerland (1976); and Venezuela (1977).

Parraguirre makes woodcuts, intaglios, and mixed-media prints; her renderings of vegetables are painstakingly done, while her representations of the figure have become increasingly abstract.

Bibliography

Alvarez, José Rogelio, et al. *Enciclopedia de Mexico.* Secretaría de Educación Pública, 1987.

Parrish, Clara Weaver (1861–1925)

A landscape and figure painter, etcher, and stained glass designer, Clara Weaver was born on the family plantation outside Selma, Alabama. Her parents, William and Lucia Weaver, brought her up in Selma after the Civil War. In the early 1880s her parents sent her to New York City to study at the Art Students League with William Merritt Chase, W. Siddons Mowbray, Kenyon Cox, and J. Alden Weir.

In the twentieth century Parrish maintained a studio in Paris, France, as well as in New York City. During periods in Paris she studied with Alphonse Mucha, with Gustav Courtois at the Academy Colarossi, and with Raphael Collin at Fonteney aux Roses, near Paris.

In 1887 she married William Peck Parrish, a stock broker. After living in Birmingham, Alabama for two years, they moved to New York City. A daughter, born in 1889, lived only sixteen months, and her husband died in 1901.

Louis Comfort Tiffany employed Parrish as a designer in the 1890s. She participated in the design of windows for St. Michael's Episcopal Church in New York City and designed many windows and at least one mosaic mural for Alabama churches.

Parrish exhibited in the 1893 World's Columbian Exposition, the 1897 Centennial and International Exposition, Nashville, Tennessee; the 1899 Greater America Exposition, Omaha, Nebraska; the 1900 Exposition Universelle, Paris, France; and the 1910 Appalachian Exposition, Knoxville, Kentucky. She also held exhibits at the Royal Academy, London, England; the Paris Salon, France; the Pennsylvania Academy of Fine Arts, Philadelphia; the Newark Free Public Library, New Jersey; the Albright-Knox Art Gallery, Buffalo, New York; the MacDowell Club; the Gibbes Art Gallery, Charleston, South Carolina; the Books Memorial Art Gallery, Memphis, Tennessee; the Pen & Brush Club, New York City; and the Little Art Gallery, Birmingham, Alabama. She participated in group shows with the Woman's Art Club; the American Watercolor Society; the New York Watercolor Club; and the National Arts Club—all in New York City; the Boston Art Club, Massachusetts; the Art Club of Philadelphia, Pennsylvania; and the Nebraska Art Association. E. Bonneau & Fils, Paris, France, held a solo exhibition of her paintings in 1910.

Parrish won many awards, including the Watrous prize at the Woman's Art Club, New York City (1901, 1913), and silver medals at the Appalachian Exposition in Knoxville, Tennessee (1910) and the Panama Pacific Exposition in San Francisco, California (1915) and the award for best painting at the National Arts Club, New York City (1924). She was a member of the New York Watercolor Club, the National Association of Women Painters and Sculptors, the Women's Art Club and the National Arts Club—all in New York City. The Sturdivant Museum Association and the Siegel Gallery—both in Selma, Alabama—own collections of her work.

Phyllis Peet

Bibliography

Brown, C. Reynolds. *Clara Weaver Parrish.* Alabama: Montgomery Museum of Fine Arts, 1980.

Parsons, Betty (1900–1982)

A native New Yorker, the affluent painter, sculptor, collector, and noted art dealer Betty Parsons, after a brief marriage, a Paris divorce, and a ten-year stay in France, studied sculpture with Renée Praha and, later, with Antoine Bourdelle and Ossip Zadkine.

Parsons exhibited widely in museums and galleries in the United States and abroad, including Bennington College, Vermont (1968); "Betty Parsons: Paintings, Gouaches, and Sculpture 1955–68," Whitechapel Gallery, London, England (1968); "Women Choose Women," New York Cultural Center (1973); "Betty Parsons Retrospective: An Exhibition of Paintings and Sculpture," Montclair Art Museum, New Jersey (1974); "American Art in the Newark Museum," the Newark Museum, New Jersey (1981); and others.

As a New York City dealer, Parsons was best known for launching the careers of many abstract expressionists and helping women artists—among them Barbara Chase-Riboud, Agnes Martin, and Anne Ryan. Examples of her work are in private and public permanent collections, including the National Collection of Fine Arts, Smithsonian Institution, Washington, D.C.

Bibliography

Brenson, Michael. "Betty Parsons, Art Dealer, 82: Pioneer in New York School." *The New York Times* (July 24, 1982).

Lichtenstein, Grace. "Betty Parsons: Still Trying to Find the Creative World in Everything." *Art News* 78:3 (March 1979): 52–56 and cover.

Withers, Josephine. "Betty Parsons." *Women Artists in Washington Collections.* University of Maryland and Women's Caucus for Art, 1979.

Patten, Christine Taylor (1940–)

Christine Taylor Patten lives and works in New Mexico; she came first to Santa Fe and then to Taos. She was born in Los Angeles, California, where she earned a Bachelor of Fine Arts degree at the Otis Art Institute. She studied with R. Buckminster Fuller, among others. The impact of Fuller's ideas regarding the search for harmonic relationships between man and the environment is evident in Patten's work.

Patten's work is concerned with deepening the experience of seeing through the process of making art. This depth of seeing experience, she feels, gives her clues to seeing life. As one aspect of her abiding interest in light, above all in laser beams, she constructs holograms. But most often she draws, "to extract the contents," as she quotes the Webster definition in explanation of her chosen medium.

In Patten's drawings line is generated out of line, in the way that crystals form, or cells divide. She uses a crow quill pen and ink on handmade paper to create her abstract imagery. First she establishes a parent line, which she observes, and then responds to with another. She then proceeds with the next line and the next, each growing out of the previous one. Ultimately her drawings—frequencies of sound or heartbeats recorded as pulsations on a screen—as, literally, in life, seem attuned to forces in nature—like the patterns of waves, whether of water, gravity, or sound.

A consideration of the intricate makeup of the universe and its cycles—simple to complex—always returning, infinitely small or grand, micro, that is, or macro, is Patten's fundamental theme. The work itself is cyclical. Large drawings—some of them ranging to many feet—which appear simple at a distance but are actually complex, alternate with smaller, simpler drawings.

Patten's holograms, which by their nature show no impression of the artist's hand, are based totally on thought disclosed by means of light. The observer stands in a certain position before a seemingly empty, transparent block, and then, as his position changes, the image, a shell, say, or some other natural object, appears suspended, reconstructed in the air as colored light.

"Seeing more than we normally see," the mysterious act of seeing, which, though we perform it we do not understand, becomes still more mysterious; the sense of wonder is increased, Patten believes. Both in the holograms and the drawings her goal is to bring the unseen to visibility.

Many of her exhibitions have been in colleges, universities, and museums in California and New Mexico, including Seaver College Art Department of Pepperdine University, Malibu, California (1989); the Jonson Gallery of the University of New Mexico, Albuquerque (1989, 1990); the Museum of Fine Arts of the Museum of New Mexico, Albuquerque, where her work is part of the permanent collection; and Pasadena City College, California (1991). She also exhibits in galleries in both states.

Barbara Cortright

Bibliography
The Spirit that Wants Me: A New Mexico Anthology. Sandia Publishing, 1991.
Expressive Drawing. Joseph Mugnaini, Davis, 1988.

Patterson, Margaret Jordan (1867–1950)

Born on shipboard off the coast of Surabaja, Indonesia, Margaret Jordan Patterson was the daughter and granddaughter of sea captains. Patterson studied at Pratt Institute, Brooklyn, New York, under the aegis of Arthur Wesley Dow in 1895; she was a teacher of art in the public schools of Portsmouth, New Hampshire, and then in Boston, Massachusetts.

Patterson made the grand tour of Europe when she was thirty-two years old and spent many summers taking further trips in France, Italy, and elsewhere. She did additional study with Claudio Castellucho in Italy and with Ermenagildo Anglada-Camarasa in Paris, France, where, about 1910, she learned to make color woodcuts in sessions with the American artist, Ethel Mars.

Patterson's first solo exhibition of prints occurred at the Galerie Levesque, Paris, France (1913); this was followed by another show at the Galerie Barbazanges. The following year Patterson exhibited a clutch of prints at Herman Dudley Murphy's studio in Boston, Massachusetts, and, soon afterward, mounted a full-scale solo show at the Louis Katz Gallery in New York City.

Patterson won a number of honors and awards for her work, including an honorable mention at the Panama-Pacific International Exposition in San Francisco, California (1915); and a medal from the Philadelphia Watercolor Club, Pennsylvania (1939); among others. She exhibited her prints and paintings in many shows throughout the country.

Bibliography
American Art Annual. Vol. 28. American Federation of Arts, 1932.
Who's Who in American Art. Vol. 3. American Federation of Arts, 1940.

Peabody, Amelia (1890–)

Born in Marblehead Neck, Massachusetts, the sculptor Amelia Peabody studied at the Boston Museum School of Fine Arts, Massachusetts, and also with Charles Grafly. She was a member of several arts organizations, including the American Artists Professional League; American Federation of Arts; the Boston Art Guild; the Boston Sculptors Society; the Copley Society of Boston; North Shore Art Association; and others.

Peabody exhibited her sculpture in galleries and museums, including the "Exhibition of American Sculpture," sponsored by the National Sculpture Society, held at the California Palace of the Legion of Honor, San Francisco, California (1929); the "Fiftieth Annual Exhibition," National Association of Women Painters and Sculptors, New York City (1942); and others. Representative examples of her work are housed in private and public permanent collections, including the Boston Museum of Fine Arts, Massachusetts, and others.

Bibliography
American Art Annual. Vol. 28. American Federation of Arts, 1932.
Archives of American Art. *Collection of Exhibition Catalogs.* G.K. Hall, 1979.
Who's Who in American Art. Vol. 10. American Federation of Arts, 1970.

Peacock, Jan (1955–)

Jan Peacock was born in Barrie, Ontario, Canada, but she spent the better part of her early years in a small town northwest of metropolitan Toronto. Peacock showed no particular early inclinations toward a career in art, but she was inspired in the middle-1970s by a very unorthodox professor, Robert McKaskell, in the department of visual arts at the University of Western Ontario in London, Canada. McKaskell, one of those inventive free-thinkers who continually turned the academic environment on its head, was preoccupied with performance art and had considerable impact on those students who drifted away from the still-dominant formal investigations toward issues of content.

Like those of a slightly later student of McKaskell, Joyann Saunders, Peacock's works began with a prolonged self-examination, but were always tempered with a linguistic play directly inspired by Marcel Duchamp. One example, made before she received her Bachelor of Fine Arts degree in 1978, was the grotesque phallic pun, "A Pole in the Air, Enamoured" (private collection, Winnipeg). With this heady mixture of play and conceptual provocation under her arm, as it were, she made her way to the University of California at San Diego, where she studied with the conceptual artist Newton Harrison, among others. Although she had started making videos with linguistic preoccupations earlier, there she clearly made that electronic medium her own. She earned a Master of Fine Arts degree in 1981.

Peacock began exhibiting internationally before graduation, first in the Biennale Internationale de Paris, France (1980), and since then at shows across the United States, including New York City and Washington, D.C. Most recently she has come to public attention in the prestigious "Canadian Biennial of Contemporary Art" at the new National Gallery of Canada in Ottawa (1989). There she displayed "The Road Rises to Meet You" (1986), a major installation with two videotapes, a variety of sculptural props and slide projections, and accompanying texts. The various sources of information—visions of a tumbling couple, landscapes, news reports, and domestic chats—seem to suggest that a coherent picture will emerge, but it does not, indicating that just below the surface of our expectations lies a zone of profound unfamiliarity with the "real" world around us.

Peacock teaches at the Nova Scotia College of Art and Design in Halifax, Canada, which has had a certain reputation for advanced critical and intellectual art.

Robert J. Belton

Bibliography

Nemiroff, Diana. *Canadian Biennial of Contemporary Art/Biennale Canadienne d'Art Contemporain.* Exhibition Catalog. Ottawa: National Gallery of Canada (October 6–December 3, 1989).

Peak, Elizabeth J. (1952–)

Born in Fort Belvoir, Virginia, the painter/printmaker Elizabeth J. Peak attended the University of Nebraska, Lincoln (1970–1972); earned a Bachelor's degree in sculpture at the University of California at Santa Barbara (1974); studied printmaking with Michael Mazur at Brandeis University, Waltham, Massachusetts (Fall 1974); and worked with Gabor Peterdi at Yale University, New Haven, Connecticut, where she received a Master of Fine Arts degree in printmaking (1977).

Peak has held solo exhibitions in galleries and universities, including the Franz Bader Gallery, Washington, D.C. (1988, 1990); American University, Washington, D.C. (1987); Morehead State University, Kentucky (1986); Clark University, Worcester, Massachusetts (1985); Hobart-William Smith Colleges, Geneva, New York (1983); Bowdoin College, Brunswick, Maine (1982); and others. Her work has been invited to many group exhibitions, such as "Trees," Bowdoin College, Brunswick, Maine (1991); Corcoran Gallery of Art, Washington, D.C. (1992); various North American "Annuals" of the Boston Printmakers (1981, 1987, 1989–1991); "Prints: Washington," the Phillips Collection, Washington, D.C. (1988); "Gallery Artists," Jane Haslem Gallery, Washington, D.C. (1984, 1985, 1986); "Contemporary American Monotypes," Chrysler Museum, Norfolk, Virginia (1985); "Urban Landscapes," Wilhelm Gallery, Houston, Texas (1984); "Prints International: 1990," Silvermine Guild, New Canaan, Connecticut (1990); and many others.

Visiting artist, artist-in-residence, and guest curator at galleries, colleges, and universities throughout the United States—Peak has taught at American University, Washington, D.C. (1986–1987); College of the Holy Cross, Worcester, Massachusetts (1983–1986); Bowdoin College, Brunswick, Maine (1980–1982); and Connecticut College, New London

(1978–1979). Winner of many honors and awards for her work, Peak garnered the juror's cash award for etching at the 43rd North American Print Exhibition of the Boston Printmakers, Massachusetts (1991); the Berthe von Moschzisker prize at the Print Club's 62nd Annual International Competition, Philadelphia, Pennsylvania (1986); and many others. Her work is represented in private, public, and corporate permanent collections, including Yale University, New Haven, Connecticut; Smithsonian Institution, Washington, D.C.; Bowdoin College, Brunswick, Maine; American University, Washington, D.C.; Santa Cruz Museum, California; Honolulu Academy of Art, Hawaii; Otis Elevator, Boston, Massachusetts; National Institute of Health, Washington, D.C.; and many others.

Bibliography

Tucker, Patricia. "Medium as Message." *Museum and Arts* (July–August 1991).
Hollen, Sharron. "Virginia Artist Captures Landscapes in Nebraska." *Lincoln Journal* (1989).
Who's Who in American Art. 19th ed. R.R. Bowker Co., 1991–1992.

Peale, Mary Jane (1827–1902)

Mary Jane Peale of the famous Philadelphia, Pennsylvania, family of artists had role models in the cousins of her father: Sarah Peale, Anna Claypoole Peale, and Margaretta Angelica Peale—all successful painters. A granddaughter of James Willson Peale, she was born in New York City but spent most of her professional life in Philadelphia, Pennsylvania. She had the distinction of knowing that she wanted to be a painter before her father, Rubens Peale, a museum director, decided to turn to painting. Thus, she became her father's teacher during the last decade of his life.

Peale studied painting with her uncle, Rembrandt Peale, and with Thomas Sully. Her work consisted of still lifes and portraits. Her "Still Life" in the Mead Art Museum, Amherst College, Massachusetts, and "Still Life Bowl of Fruit" at William Doyle Galleries, New York City, are typical of her depictions of various realistic, succulent fruits knit together in a complex design and displayed on a wooden table top. Her "Small Bouquet of Flowers," Coe Kerr Gallery, New York City, has a wispy look comparable to the delicate paintings of her contemporary, Odilon Redon. An example of her portraiture is "Rubens Peale" (1860, Southern Alleghenies Museum of Art) in which her father is palpably portrayed, with white hair and wearing hexagonal steel-rimmed glasses.

Eleanor Tufts

Bibliography

Gerdts, William H., and William Burke. *American Still-Life Painting.* Praeger, 1971.
Tufts, Eleanor. *American Women Artists, 1830–1930.* National Museum of Women in the Arts, 1987.

Pearce, Helen Spang (1895–)

Helen Spang Pearce's early experience of Pennsylvania Dutch folk art in her birthplace, Reading, Pennsylvania, stimulated her feeling for design. As a young girl she began to draw and create designs. She then went on to attend the Philadelphia School of Design for Women, Pennsylvania.

Despite these eastern roots, however, Pearce is known for her paintings of New Mexico. In 1941 she moved to Albuquerque, New Mexico, where she became a student at the University of New Mexico, studying with Raymond Jonson, Kenneth Adams, and Randall Davey. Jonson was a founding member of the New Mexico Transcendentalists, along with Emil Bisttram. Their focus on the spiritual aspects of the New Mexico landscape through abstract art was important in Pearce's development. She and other women artists in New Mexico organized Las Artistas, a group whose work was shown in several exhibitions at the Museum of Fine Arts in Santa Fe, New Mexico, and other exhibition spaces throughout the state.

Pearce's paintings are based on the real landscape but are abstract rather than realistic in their simplification of natural forms and their emphasis on strong curves and broad color planes.

Barbara Cortright

Bibliography
Eldredge, Charles C., Julie Schimmel, and William H. Truetner. *Art in New Mexico, 1900–1945: Paths to Taos and Santa Fe.* Abbeville Press, 1986.
Fisher, Reginald Gilbert. "Pearce, Helen." *An Art Directory of New Mexico.* Santa Fe Museum of New Mexico, 1947.
Who's Who in American Art. Vol 9. American Federation of Arts, 1965, p. 362.
Who's Who of American Women. A.N. Marquis Company, 1958, p. 99.

Pecanins, Ana Maria

Born in Barcelona, Spain, Ana Maria Pecanins emigrated to Mexico in 1951. Between 1951 and 1963 Pecanins made many trips to the United States, where she travelled in the West and also painted.

Pecanins has had many solo exhibitions in cities throughout North America, including Mexico City, Mexico; San Francisco, California; Phoenix and Scottsdale, Arizona; and Santa Fe, New Mexico.

Bibliography
The Texas Quarterly: Image of Mexico II. The University of Texas, Winter 1969.

Pelaez, Amelia (1897–1968)

Born in Santa Clara, Cuba, the painter Amelia Pelaez studied in many institutions, including the Academia de San Alejandro, Havana, Cuba, with Leopold Romanach (1915–1924); the Art Students League, New York City (1924); Académie de la Grande Chaumière, l'École des Beaux-Arts, L'École de Louvre, and with Alexandra Exter, in Paris, France (1927–1934).

Pelaez held but one solo exhibition in New York—at the Galería Norte (1941); however, her work appeared in many group shows, such as the "Latin American Exhibition of Fine and Applied Arts," Riverside Museum, New York City (1939–1940); San Francisco Museum of Art, California (1942, 1945); Brooklyn Museum, New York (1943, 1949); Museum of Modern Art (MoMA), New York City (1943, 1944, 1967); Pan American Union, Washington, D.C. (1946, 1947, 1952, 1959); "The United States Collects Latin American Art," Art Institute of Chicago, Illinois (1959); and others. Examples of her work are in private and public permanent collections, including the Museum of Modern Art of Latin America, Washington, D.C.

Bibliography
Portner, Leslie Judd. "Cuban Modern Paintings." *Pan American Union* (1950): 67–69.
The Latin American Spirit: Art and Artists in the United States, 1920–1979. Harry N. Abrams, 1988.

Pell, Ella Ferris (1846–1922)

Born in St. Louis, Missouri, the painter, sculptor, and illustrator Ella Ferris Pell studied with William Rimmer at the Design School for Women at Cooper Union in New York City, graduating in 1870. A review in the New York *Evening Post* of 1868 praised her sculpture of "Puck." In 1872 she embarked on a five-and-a-half-year trip to Europe, North Africa, and the Near East. When she returned to the United States and began exhibiting at the National Academy of Design, New York City, in the early 1880s, her entries consisted of paintings done during her travels, such as "La Annunziata" and "Water Vendor, Cairo, Egypt."

In the 1880s Pell studied in Paris, France, at the Académie des Beaux-Arts des Champs-Élysées with Jean-Paul Laurens, Jacques-Fernand Humbert, and Gaston Casimir Saint-Pierre—teachers respectively of history painting, religious painting, and portraiture and genre. The Paris Salon of 1889, France, accepted her painting entitled "The Angel Making Adam See the Consequences of His Sin," and the Paris Salon of 1890 accepted her "Portrait of Mme T." and "Salomé" (a subject painted by her teacher, Humbert, in 1880). Pell returned to New York City in the 1890s. She illustrated Paul Tyner's love story, *Through the Invisible,* which was published in 1897, and had work accepted for reproduction by the chromolithographer Louis Prang (e.g., Christmas cards, Easter designs, and figures). Her large painting, "Agnus Dei" (1899, Columbus Museum of Art), and two mystical paintings date from this period: "The Evolution of Soul" and "Storm Gods of Riz-Veda." Although her work stems from the academic tradition, Pell showed a streak of independence in her interpretations. She is buried in a pauper's grave in Fishkill Rural Cemetery in New York, and fifty-eight oil paintings have been deposited with the Pell Family Collection at Fort Ticonderoga Museum.

Eleanor Tufts

Bibliography
Eldredge, Charles C. *American Imagination and Symbolist Painting.* New York: Grey Art Gallery, New York University, 1979.
Tufts, Eleanor. *American Women Artists, 1830–1930.* National Museum of Women in the Arts, 1987.

Pelletier, Helene (1954–)

Helene Pelletier was born in Grand Falls, New Brunswick, Canada—a province that is part of the original Acadian homeland. Her identity as an Acadian is central to her art-making. After completion of her Bachelor of Fine Arts degree at the Université de Moncton, New Brunswick, in 1978, Pelletier moved to Winnipeg, Manitoba, becoming part of the Acadian diaspora that has spread throughout North America. She now lives in St. Boniface, across the river from Winnipeg and, historically, the most significant French-speaking community in the west of Canada.

For a number of years Pelletier was involved in the Centre Culturel Franco-Manitobain; she continues to be a cultural community activist. Her own work acknowledges, in a poignant blend of affection, wistfulness, and desperation, the solidarity and anxiety that comes from being part of a marginalized, though vigorous, community whose advocates must vigilantly lay claim to its defining characteristics. Pelletier is one of a small number of artists in Canada whose first aim is to represent a community to itself.

Pelletier's largest works take the form of *tableaux vivants* which address issues of poverty, child rearing, women's gossip networks, and the fragility of human vanity. The expressive heads and articulate hands of the life-size figures, meticulously dressed in period clothes, often the 1950s, are modelled in clay—her favorite medium. Along with smaller pieces and portrait heads in clay the *tableaux vivants,* including "Helene Kurtis–Salon de Beauté" and "J'ai un Extrème Regret de Vous Avoir Rencontrer," reveal a skillful assimilation of the gauche humor of folk art (a strong presence in the prairie provinces and New Brunswick) and funk ceramics (a West Coast import now well established through the work of Joe Fafard and Victor Cicansky). Her work is characterised by the satirical treatment—sometimes gentle, sometimes biting—of the francophone culture, including the contortions that French Canadian women must go through to conform and not to conform to the dominant culture.

Pelletier has participated in numerous group exhibitions and has had solo exhibitions at the Centre Culturel Franco-Manitobain and the Galerie d'art at the Université de Moncton, where she maintains close ties with the Acadian community.

Charlotte Townsend-Gault

Bibliography
McElroy, Randal. "Exhibits Explore Female Fantasies." *Winnipeg Free Press* (November 12, 1988).
"Nobody's Fool." Winnipeg: *The Daily Graphic* (March 10, 1986).
"Se faire belle à tout Prix: Helene Pelletier au Centre Culturel Franco-Manitobain." St. Boniface: *Le Culturel* (November 1988).
Whiteway, Doug. "Madam Trop." *Winnipeg Free Press* (December 4, 1984.)

Pelton, Agnes (1881–1961)

Born of American parents in Stuttgart, Germany, Agnes Pelton spent her early childhood in Europe. When her father died in 1890, Pelton and her mother returned to Brooklyn, New York, where her mother opened the Pacific School of Music. At fourteen Pelton attended Pratt Institute in Brooklyn, receiving a certificate in 1900. She studied landscape with Arthur Wesley Dow that summer in Ipswich, Massachusetts. She spent the next year in Italy, and, on her return to America, studied for four summers with Hamilton Easter Field in Ogunquit, Maine, where she had her first solo exhibition in 1911.

Pelton was invited to exhibit in the New York Armory Show of 1913, New York City, and submitted two paintings, "The Vine Wood" and "Stone Age." Her activities in New York City accelerated in 1915 when she participated in a Women's Suffrage Exhibition at Macbeth Galleries and had a solo exhibition at the Dora Brophy Gallery. In 1917 she was included in an "Imaginative Paintings" exhibition at the Knoedler Galleries, New York City, and two years later had a solo exhibition of "Pastels of Taos Landscape and Indian Portraits" at the Museum of New Mexico in Santa Fe.

A versatile painter, Pelton chose her subjects from a wide range of landscapes, portraits, and flowers. Her subsequent travels included Hawaii and the Near East, and always she exhibited her latest work upon return. In addition to her studio in New York City she maintained a studio in a windmill on Long Island in the 1920s. Her turning away from figurative art can be marked by her 1929 exhibitions of "Abstractions" in Pasadena, Los Angeles, California, and New York City. California became her adopted state in 1931 when she settled in Cathedral City.

In 1938 Raymond Jonson invited Pelton to become one of the founding members of the Transcendental Painting Group. One-woman exhibitions of her abstractions continued to be held through the 1940s and 1950s in the leading museums of California. She often wrote poetry to accompany her works. "Orbits" (1934, Oakland Museum), a twilight painting, came to her "in the midst of smoke tree studies." She called "The Fountains" (1926, private collection) "a symbolic vision."

Eleanor Tufts

Bibliography
Stainer, Margaret. *Agnes Pelton.* Fremont, California: Ohlone College Art Gallery, 1989.
Tufts, Eleanor. *American Women Artists, 1830–1930.* National Museum of Women in the Arts, 1987.

Peña, Tonita (Quah Ah) (1895–1949)

A pioneer in her artistic activities, Tonita Peña helped lead the way for many Native American artists through her dual roles as one of the first Native Americans of either sex to master the tools of easel painting and as the first Native American woman to make a career of easel painting.

Born in San Ildefonso Pueblo, New Mexico, on June 13, 1895, Peña was raised in a Tewa-speaking community whose strong artistic heritage included expression in the form of song, ceremonial dance, woven and embroidered textiles, decorated pottery, and ceremonial objects. Art was not identified as something separate but rather was part of everyday life. Men were the weavers and makers of ceremonial items to be worn or carried. Women made and painted the pottery. Easel painting and other forms of Western art were completely foreign to these and other native peoples of the Southwest.

At the end of the nineteenth century and turn of the twentieth century, paper, colored pencils, and watercolor paints were introduced to a few Native American individuals as part of the growing interaction between Anglo-Americans and Southwest Native Americans. Some of the first Native Americans to produce watercolor paintings as artwork for sale to outsiders (largely as the result of encouragement from outsiders) were from San Ildefonso Pueblo, particularly a man named Crescencio Martinez (d. 1918). Growing up in San Ildefonso, Peña became aware of this activity, and she joined the ranks of the early experimenters with this art form.

Peña actually began painting as a young child at San Ildefonso Pueblo day school when her teacher, Esther B. Hoyt, encouraged her and a few others to paint with watercolors, drawing upon the Pueblo ceremonies for inspiration. This was a significant source of encouragement for Peña and also was her only formal training.

After her mother died Peña was raised in Cochiti Pueblo by her aunt, Martina Vigil, a potter. Although thoroughly exposed to the art and craft of the Pueblo woman's traditional medium of artistic expression in clay, Peña chose to reject the confines that came with the manufacture of pottery, including its inherent stylistic and social regimentation, and to pursue a medium that allowed for individual expression—not a traditional concept in the Pueblo world, and particularly not for a woman.

Other Pueblo people were doing some painting with watercolors during the early years of the twentieth century, but they were all men. By the late teens and early 1920s there were several acknowledged artists in this "new" art form, among them Peña's half-brother, Romando Vigil (1902–1978). Vigil's wife was the sister of Martinez's wife. Martinez's nephew, Alfonso Roybal (Awa Tsireh) (1898–1955), occasionally painted along with his uncle and was soon acclaimed for his skill. These San Ildefonso painters, along with Fred Kabotie (Hopi) and Velino Shije Herrera (Zia Pueblo) and a few others, were known as the first generation of Native American easel painters, all of them earning regular income from their artwork. Together, but working individually, they created a style now known as "traditional," consisting mostly of representational figures in activities of everyday (including ceremonial) life, with little, if any, foreground or background setting. Peña was a member of this group of artists and was the only woman painter of her generation.

Peña's paintings are known for their sense of movement and meticulous detail. She often portrayed women in her paintings, and sometimes did images of pottery on which appropriate designs were painted with exact precision. Her preferred medium was transparent watercolor.

Early encouragement for Peña's efforts came from Edgar Lee Hewett of the Museum of New Mexico and School of American Research and from Kenneth Chapman of the Laboratory of Anthropology—all in Santa Fe, New Mexico. Peña was commissioned to paint murals for the Society of Independent Artists (1933); Chicago World's Fair, Illinois; Santa Fe Indian School, New Mexico; and James W. Young's Rancho La Canada (c. 1933). Her work was exhibited regularly at a number of museums and galleries, including the Heard Museum, Phoenix, Arizona; the Museum of New Mexico, Albuquerque; the National Gallery of Art, Washington, D.C.; and the Philbrook Art Center, Tulsa, Oklahoma; and was included in two major travelling exhibits, the "Exposition of Indian Tribal Arts" (1931–1933), and the United States Information Agency's (USIA) European tour of "Contemporary American Indian Painting" (1955–1956). She is well-represented in museum and private collections, among them the Cincinnati Art Museum, Ohio; the City Art Museum of St. Louis, Missouri; the Corcoran Gallery of Art, Washington, D.C.; the Denver Art Museum, Colorado; the Gilcrease Institute of American History and Art, Tulsa, Oklahoma; the Museum of the American Indian, Heye Foundation, New York City; the Museum of Northern Arizona, Flagstaff; and the Southwest Museum, Los Angeles, California. La Fonda Hotel in Santa Fe, New Mexico, has acquired many of her paintings.

An established artist, Peña served on occasion as an art instructor at Santa Fe Indian School and Albuquerque Indian School—both in New Mexico—where she inspired others to follow her example. Pablita Velarde, of Santa Clara Pueblo, New Mexico, credits her meeting with Peña, during a visit of Peña's to Santa Fe Indian School when Velarde was a student, as a major influence on her own decision to paint.

While Peña was pursuing her career as an artist she was also busy carrying out the responsibilities of wife and mother at Cochiti Pueblo, where she continued to live after marrying. At one point her husband was governor of the pueblo. Of her six children, one, Joe Hilario Herrera (1923–) went on to become a renowned artist himself, originally inspired, he said, by watching his mother paint when he was a boy.

Tryntje Van Ness Seymour

Bibliography
Dunn, Dorothy. *American Indian Painting of the Southwest and Plains Areas*. University of New Mexico Press, 1968.

Seymour, Tryntje Van Ness. *When the Rainbow Touches Down*. Phoenix, Arizona: The Heard Museum, 1989.
Snodgrass, Jeanne O. *American Indian Painters: A Biographical Directory*. Vol. XXI, part 1. Contributions from the Museum of the American Indian, Heye Foundation. New York: Museum of the American Indian, Heye Foundation, 1968.
Tanner, Clara Lee. *Southwest Indian Painting: A Changing Art*. University of Arizona Press, 1973.

Penalba, Alicia (1918–)

Born in Buenos Aires, Argentina, the sculptor Alicia Penalba studied at the Escuela Superior de Bellas Artes in her native city; studied sculpture with Ossip Zadkine in Paris, France; and attended the Académie de la Grande Chaumière, also in Paris, France.

Penalba has held solo exhibitions in museums and galleries in the United States and elsewhere, including the Otto Gerson Gallery, and the Fine Arts Associates Gallery, New York City (1960); Devorah Sherman Gallery, Chicago, Illinois (1962); Bonino Gallery, New York, and the Phillips Collection, Washington, D.C. (1966); and others. Her work has been shown in group exhibitions, including the Guggenheim Museum, New York City (1958, 1962); Cleveland Museum of Art, Ohio (1960); Carnegie Institute's "Internationals," Pittsburgh, Pennsylvania (1964, 1967, 1970); Aldrich Museum of Contemporary Art, Ridgefield, Connecticut (1964); and many others.

Penalba has won a French embassy scholarship and other honors and awards; her sculpture graces many private and public permanent collections, including the Albright-Knox Art Gallery, Buffalo, New York; Carnegie Institute, Pittsburgh, Pennsylvania; Isaac Delgado Museum, New Orleans, Louisiana; Hirshhorn Museum and Sculpture Garden, Washington, D.C.; and others.

Bibliography
Penalba, Alicia. *Alicia Penalba*. Lausanne: Alice Paoli Gallery, 1967.
"Show by Artists of Seven Nations." *The New York Times* (February 16, 1958).
The Latin American Spirit: Art and Artists in the United States, 1920–1970. Harry N. Abrams, 1988.

Penman, Edith (1860–1929)

An oil and watercolor painter, etcher, and potter, Edith Penman was born in England but grew up in the United States. She attended Cooper Union School of Design for Women in New York City. A versatile artist in the mode of the arts and crafts movement, Penman became known for her landscape and floral paintings, landscape etchings, and for her development of new ceramic glazes.

In Penman's etchings, fifty of which were published by Christian Klackner, she preferred to portray the effects of light on water, depicting landscapes of river and coastal views or of atmospheric winter scenes. She exhibited with the New York Etching Club, New York City, which also published one of her etchings in its catalog. Penman also showed work in the woman's building at the 1893 World's Columbian Exposition in Chicago, Illinois; at the National Academy of Design, New York City; the Museum of Fine Arts, Boston, Massachusetts; the Union League Club, New York City; the Boston Art Club, and the Boston Society of Artists—both in Massachusetts; the Fort Worth Museum of Art, Texas; and the Nebraska

Art Association. She participated in group shows with the Boston Society of Arts and Crafts, Massachusetts; the Woman's Art Club of New York, New York City, and the National Association of Women Painters and Sculptors, New York City, for which she served as treasurer for years. In the 1920s she maintained studios in New York City in the Van Dyck Studio Building and at Briarcliff, where she exhibited her pottery.

Phyllis Peet

Bibliography
C. Klackner Gallery. *Klackner's American Etchings*. New York: C. Klackner, 1988.
"Exhibition of 12 Painters, Women, at the MacDowell Club." *The New York Times* (March 8, 1914): 18.
"Edith Penman." [Obituary] *Art Digest* 3 (Mid-January 1929): 12.
Peet, Phyllis. *American Women of the Etching Revival*. Atlanta: High Museum of Art, 1988, p. 63.

Penn, Barbara (1952–)

Born in Pittsburgh, Pennsylvania, Barbara Penn is known for her constructions and installations. She earned a Bachelor's degree from the State University of New York (SUNY) at New Paltz (1973); received a Bachelor of Fine Arts degree from the San Francisco Art Institute, California (1983); attended the Skowhegan School of Painting and Sculpture, Maine (1985); and was awarded a Master of Fine Arts degree from the University of California at Berkeley (1986).

Penn's work has been exhibited throughout the United States since the early 1980s. Her solo exhibitions include the Gallery Paule Anglim, San Francisco, California (1990, 1991); and the Galerie Nalepa, Berlin, Germany (1991). Her work has been included in group shows, such as the Obere Galerie in Haus am Lutzowplatz, Berlin, Germany (1992); "Choice," A.I.R. Gallery, New York City (1991); and "Order of Intuition: Aspects of Bay Area Abstract Painting," Palo Alto Cultural Center, California (1989).

In 1990 Penn was the recipient of artist's residency grants from the Millay Colony for the Arts, Austerlitz, New York, and Yaddo, Saratoga Springs, New York. Her combined media works provide visual references to symbols of wholeness, fragility, separation, pain, chance, choice, risk, and transformation. The installations appear to begin from a game-like place and evolve into a profound and poetic visual voyage that becomes spiritually and psychologically provocative.

Moira Geoffrion

Bibliography
Cebulski, Frank. "Barbara Penn." *Artweek* (January 10, 1991).
Schipp, Renée. "Der Turmbau zu Babel im Spiegel Zeitgenossischen Kunstschaffens." *Berliner Morgenpost* (March 12, 1991).
Sternborg, Auke. "Sprachverwirrung in Der Tagesspiegel." *Feuilleton* (March 27, 1991).

Pepper, Beverly (1924–)

New York-born sculptor and painter Beverly Pepper now lives and works in an ancient castle in Perugia, Italy. Her formal education includes a Bachelor of Fine Arts degree from Pratt Institute and studies at the Art Students League—both in New York City. She also studied with Ferdinand Léger and André L'Hôte in Paris, France, after her move to Europe in 1948.

In a varied and eclectic career Pepper has created no typical style, but continues to explore a wide range of problems. In the 1940s she worked as an art director for New York advertising firms and then moved into expressionistic paintings on social themes. She began to work in sculpture in 1960 with a series of wood and bronze works.

In 1962 Pepper was invited to show sculpture in Spoleto, Italy, along with David Smith and Alexander Calder. The geometric, welded sculptures she created for this exhibition were her first metal works. Throughout the remainder of the 1960s Pepper made a series of stainless-steel boxes—some painted, some mirrored, and some with gashes in them as if ripped by teeth.

Pepper began to work with environmental pieces in 1971 when she created "Land Canal Hillside" in Dallas, Texas. This was followed by "Amphisculpture" in 1974 on the grounds of the AT&T facility in Bedminster, New Jersey, and works in Dartmouth, New Hampshire (1977) and Sol y Ombra Park, Barcelona, Spain (1986). During this period Pepper also made site-specific monumental sculptures including steel columns for the Piazza di Todi in Todi, Italy (1974).

Pepper sculpted several series of works, including a series with a ladder-like appearance from 1977 which examines welded sculpture from the inside out. She also created a series of "tents or pyramids" such as "Excalibur" (1976) at the San Diego Federal Courthouse, which is a grouping of bright red, planted stainless steel-triangular forms. In 1983 Pepper exhibited a group of imaginary steel tools in Central Park, New York.

As insurance against the difficulties involved with working with large metal sculpture over the years, Pepper returned to painting with an exhibition of abstract paintings at the Charles Cowles Gallery, New York City, in 1987.

Pepper was awarded National Endowment for the Arts (NEA) grants in 1975 and 1979 and received the award for best art in steel from the Iron and Steel Institute in 1970. She took part in the Venice Biennale in 1972 and was included in "Monumental Sculpture of the Seventies" at the Houston Fine Arts Museum, Texas, 1975. Her works have been exhibited throughout the world, and are included in many permanent collections including Albright-Knox Art Gallery, Buffalo, New York; Massachusetts Institute of Technology (MIT) and Fogg Art Museum, Harvard University—both in Cambridge, Massachusetts; and Metropolitan Museum of Art, New York City.

Judith Sealy

Bibliography
Fry, Edward. *Beverly Pepper, Sculpture*. San Francisco Museum of Art, 1975.
Munro, Eleanor. *Originals: American Women Artists*. Simon and Schuster, 1979, pp. 345–54.
Rubenstein, Charlotte Streifer. *American Women Artists*. G.K. Hall, 1982, pp. 361–65.
Solomon, Deborah. "Woman of Steel." *Art News* 86 (December 1987): 112–17.
Thompson, Walter. "Beverly Pepper: Dramas in Space." *Arts Magazine* 62 (Summer 1988): 52–55.

Peralta, Irma (1936–)

Born in Mexico, Irma Peralta studied ceramics at Mexico City College with Frank González (1954); sculpture with Geles Cabrera (1955); and design and artisanry at the National Institute of Fine Arts—all in Mexico City, Mexico.

Peralta earned her teacher's certificate in 1966; the previous year she inaugurated the First Salon of Modern Ceramics under the patronage of the then Department of Tourism, and, in 1970, she formed the Cone 10 Ceramists, to popularize the technique of stoneware.

Peralta exhibited her work at the Palace of Fine Arts, Mexico City (1971), and at the annual art fair held at the residence of the U.S. ambassador. From 1971 to 1976 she taught at the Talleres Sabatinos in the Museum of Cultures. Subsequently, she exhibited her ware in the House of Matsumoto, and in the gallery of the Hebrew Sports Center.

Bibliography

Alvarez, José Rogelio, et al. *Enciclopedia de Mexico*. Secretaría de
  Educación Pública, 1987.

Pereira, Irene Rice (1902–1971)

Highly regarded during the 1940s for her innovative paintings on glass, Irene Rice Pereira spent most of her adult life in New York City. Her birth certificate indicates that she was born Irene M. Rice on August 5, 1902, although most biographies give her year of birth as 1907—a result of her fibbing about her age.

Enrolling in the Art Students League, New York City, in 1927, she studied with Richard F. Lahey, William von Schlegell, and, more significantly, Jan Matulka, whose class she attended from 1929 until 1931. Her classmates included David Smith, Dorothy Dehner, Lucille Corcos, Edgar Levy, and Burgoyne Diller. Through these associations, she met Stuart Davis, Arshile Gorky, Frederick Kiesler, and John Graham. While at the Art Students League she also met Humberto Pereira, whom she married in 1929. Although they divorced in 1938, she continued to use the name "I. Rice Pereira" professionally, despite subsequent marriages to George Wellington Brown in 1942 and George Reavey in 1950—both marriages ending in divorce. She used her first initial only to offset any discrimination that otherwise might be attached to the work of a woman artist.

In 1931 she travelled to Europe, studied for one month at the Académie Moderne in Paris, France, and then spent the month of December in Algeria, where she encountered the Sahara, significant to her for its sense of infinite space and pervasive light.

Returning home in 1932, Pereira began to make large paintings of ship anchors and machinery, several of which were exhibited in her first one-artist show at the ACA Gallery in New York City in 1933. She experimented briefly with social realism during the mid-1930s when she was a member of the American Artists Congress and the United American Artists. She was on the original faculty of the Works Progress Administration Federal Art Project (WPA/FAP) Bauhaus-inspired Design Laboratory in 1936 and remained with the school through its change of sponsorship in 1939. She began to experiment with total abstraction late in 1938, and she made her first glass painting the next winter.

After working and exhibiting at Hilla Rebay's Museum of Non-Objective Painting from 1940 until 1942, Pereira began a two-year association with Peggy Guggenheim's Art of This Century Gallery, where she was given a one-artist show in January, 1944. About 1945 she began to construct multi-planar glass paintings, with two panes of corrugated glass, reverse-painted with geometric figures, held in a shadow-box frame over a painted panel. The forms within these paintings appear to ripple with the viewer's change in position. By this time, she had immersed herself in a study of Carl Jung's psychoanalytic theories, scientific theories of the space-time continuum, and alchemy, and these multiplanar glass paintings may be interpreted on three metaphorical levels: as the stratiform levels of the psyche, the fluid structure of space-time, and the alchemical vessel containing the watery *prima materia*. Pereira abandoned painting on glass in 1953, the year she was given a retrospective exhibition at the Whitney Museum of American Art, New York City.

George Reavey, a writer with a long association with European surrealists, reinforced Pereira's interest in alchemy and introduced her to neo-Platonic mysticism, upon which her own light metaphysics was based. She began to write philosophical essays and books based upon an eclectic synthesis of Bauhaus utopianism, Jungianism, alchemy, quantum theory, and neo-Platonism in 1951 with "Light and the New Reality." This essay was her first attempt to express her belief that space and time are bound together by light into a whole that transcends physical reality. Her most readable book, *The Nature of Space*, self-published in 1956 and later republished by the Corcoran Gallery of Art, Washington, D.C., reflects her interest in the works of neo-Kantian philosopher Ernst Cassirer. The most sumptuously illustrated of her books was *The Lapis*, published in 1957. Difficult to read and understand, her more than twenty published and unpublished manuscripts nevertheless provide clues to understanding her abstract paintings of the late 1950s and 1960s. The angular "U" and "Z" motifs characteristic of these works were, for her, archetypal symbols of unity that become markers or signposts in what may most easily be understood as mental landscapes.

Pereira died on January 11, 1971, in Marbella, Spain, a month after moving from New York.

Karen A. Bearor

Bibliography

Bearor, Karen A. "Irene Rice Pereira: An Examination of Her Paintings and
  Philosophy." Ph.D. dissertation, University of Texas at Austin, 1988.
Baur, John I.H. *Loren MacIver; I. Rice Pereira*. Macmillan Company, 1953.
Pereira, Irene Rice. "Light and the New Reality." *The Palette* (Spring
  1952): 2–11.
———. *The Nature of Space, A Metaphysical and Aesthetic Inquiry*.
  Corcoran Gallery of Art, 1968.
Washington, D.C., Smithsonian Institution, Archives of American Art. I.
  Rice Pereira Papers.

Perlin, Rae (1910–)

Newfoundland is a large, rocky island that is sparsely populated and in which one is in constant contact with nature. This is as true today as it was when Rae Perlin was a young woman. Even the city of St. John's ranges itself around a large natural harbor that insists upon making the presence of a wild and unpredictable sea an unremitting factor in the lives of the people who have chosen to settle in this inhospitable environment. It is this environment that has influenced Perlin as much as her passion for art.

Before she turned twenty Perlin had made her way from her birthplace in St. John's, Newfoundland, to New York City, where she discovered her love of art. Having trained as a nurse she was able to supplement her studies, and she spent the 1940s studying with Samuel Brecher and Hans Hofmann. Early in the 1950s she moved to Europe where she studied for five years, first at la Académie de la Grande Chaumière and then at Académie Ranson—both in Paris, France. In 1959 she returned to Newfoundland to pursue her career as an artist. She works in watercolor, pastel, and oil, producing representational landscapes, portraits, and figures in which she tries to incorporate her own spiritual searches. She is committed to the Baha'i faith and considers this commitment an important part of her art-making.

In addition to her work as an artist, Perlin plays an active role in the community life of St. John's. In 1982 she had her first solo exhibition at Memorial University Art Gallery and in 1985 at the Pollyanna Gallery, St. John's. In addition to this she has written art criticism and in 1986 began a book of commentaries that will include her drawings and sketches.

Janice Helland

Bibliography
Rae Perlin, Sketches and Studies. St. Johns Memorial University Art Gallery, c. 1982.

Perry, Clara Greenleaf (1871–1960)

Born in Long Branch, New Jersey, the painter/sculptor Clara Greenleaf Perry was a pupil of Robert Henri—the artist associated with the "Ashcan School." She was a member of the Copley Society of Boston; the National Association of Women Painters and Sculptors, New York City; and the Washington Art Club. Her work is represented in private and public permanent collections.

Bibliography
American Art Annual. Vol. 30. American Federation of Arts, 1934.
Clement, Clara Erskine. *Women in the Fine Arts.* Houghton Mifflin, 1904.
Fielding, Mantle. *Dictionary of American Painters, Sculptors, and Engravers.* Modern Books and Crafts, 1974.

Perry, Lilla Cabot (1848–1933)

A painter of portraits and of landscapes, Lilla Cabot Perry was born into the Boston-Brahmin Cabot family. In 1874 she married Thomas S. Perry and gave birth to three daughters, who often served as subjects of her paintings. In January 1886 she began private lessons with the painter Robert Vonnoh, and, in November 1886, she enrolled at the Cowles School of Art to study with Dennis Bunker.

Perry took her family to France in 1887 for a stay of over two years, so that she could study at the Académie Colarossi and the Académie Julian, and during the summer of 1889, she met Claude Monet at Giverny. For the next two decades the Perrys spent as many summers as possible next door to Monet. Her painting, "Alice on the Path" (1891), hangs in Monet's house today, and among the eight pictures she exhibited at the World's Columbian Exposition in 1893 were several painted at Giverny. Her landscapes ("Giverny Landscape, in Monet's Garden," c. 1897, and "Haystacks," c. 1896, both

Richard H. Love Gallery), as well as scenes of figures by open windows ("La Petite Angèle," 1889, Hirschl and Adler Galleries and "Marie at the Window," Autumn 1921, Vose Galleries), are impressionistically painted.

On the family's third trip to Europe (1894–1897), they went to Spain so that Perry could copy paintings by Velázquez and Jusepe de Ribera. In 1896 she had paintings accepted for shows in Paris, France, and Berlin, Germany, and the next year in Florence, Italy, Dresden, Germany, and Munich, Germany. Because of a teaching position offered to her husband, she travelled in 1898 to Tokyo, Japan, where she remained for three years absorbing at first-hand *Japanisme* and continuing with her painting of both landscape and portraiture.

In 1903 Perry bought a farm in Hancock, New Hampshire, that reminded her of Normandy. After her death a memorial exhibition was held at the Boston Art Club, Massachusetts, to show her latest paintings, including a winter landscape in Hancock painted the day before she died.

Among her awards were bronze medals at the St. Louis Exposition, Missouri (1904), and the Panama-Pacific International Exposition, San Francisco, California (1915). She was a founder of the Guild of Boston Artists (1914) and its first secretary. She had a number of solo exhibitions there, and her paintings were also included in annual exhibitions at the Pennsylvania Academy of Fine Arts, Philadelphia, and the Corcoran Gallery of Art, Washington, D.C.

Eleanor Tufts

Bibliography
Birmingham, Dors. "'The Black Hat' by Lilla Cabot Perry." *Currier Gallery of Art Bulletin* (Fall 1986): 2–23.
Lilla Cabot Perry: A Retrospective Exhibition. New York: Hirschl & Adler Galleries, 1969.
Tufts, Eleanor. *American Women Artists, 1830–1930.* National Museum of Women in the Arts, 1987.
Ward, Lisa. "Lilla Cabot Perry." M.A. thesis, University of Texas, 1985.

Perry, Mary Chase (1867–1961)

Born in Hancock, Michigan, the ceramist Mary Chase Perry studied painting with Frans Bischoff in Detroit, Michigan. She studied china painting, among other courses, at the Cincinnati School of Design, Ohio (1887–1889) and also took work at the Detroit Art Museum School, Michigan.

One of Perry's neighbors in Detroit, Horace J. Caulkins, invented a portable, kerosene-fueled kiln for the firing of dental porcelains which, at Perry's insistence, he converted for china painting. The new device was named the "Revelation" kiln, and Perry travelled throughout the United States demonstrating its usefulness. The kiln soon was adopted as the standard kiln for American ceramists. In 1903, with Caulkins as partner, Perry opened the Pewabic Pottery and, a year later, exhibited work at the Louisiana Purchase International Exposition, St. Louis, Missouri. She prospered as a result of sales and of commissions in sites such as St. Paul's Cathedral, Detroit, Michigan (1908); Rice Institute, Houston, Texas (1913); the National Shrine of the Immaculate Conception, Washington, D.C. (1923–1931); Detroit Institute of Arts; and others. After her death the pottery was donated to Michigan State University, East Lansing.

Bibliography
Bleicher, Fred, et al. "Pewabic Pottery: An Official History." *Arts Ceramica.* 1977.
Clark, Garth. *American Ceramics: 1896 to the Present.* Abbeville Press, 1987.
Robinson, Adelaide A. "Mary Chase Perry: The Potter." *Keramik Studio* 6:10 (1905).

Peterson, Jennie Christine (Jane) (1876–1965)

Considered by her contemporaneous critics to be one of America's most prolific and brilliant painters, landscape, floral, and portrait painter Jane Peterson was born in Elgin, Illinois, to Julius and Kate Peterson. She was married twice, each time briefly. When she was fifty she married corporate lawyer M. Bernard Philipp, who died four years later. In 1939, she was married for less than a year to New Haven physician James S. McCarty.

Peterson's mother lent her $300 in 1895 to study at the Pratt Institute, Brooklyn, New York. She entered Arthur Wesley Dow's class the next year when he began to teach there. After graduating in 1901 Peterson studied at the Art Students League, New York City, while working as drawing supervisor of public schools in Brooklyn. She taught in Elmira, New York; served as drawing supervisor of public school teachers in Boston, Massachusetts; then taught at the Maryland Institute in Baltimore for three years before she went to Europe in 1907.

In London, England, Peterson studied with Frank Brangwyn, then went to Paris, France, and studied with Jacques-Emile Blanche, Charles Cottet, and Claudio Castelucho. She made her first of many visits to Venice, Italy, to paint before she returned to the United States. In 1909 she went to Madrid, Spain, to study with Joaquín Sorolla y Bastida and travelled in Egypt and Algeria. Thirty years later she studied with modernist André L'Hôte in Paris.

In 1913 Peterson began to teach at the Art Students League, New York City. She joined Louis Comfort Tiffany in 1916 for his transcontinental painting exhibition in his private railway car. Peterson travelled frequently, painting in the United States from Maine to Florida, in the West, and as far north as British Columbia. She painted almost annually in Europe and spent six months in Turkey in 1924.

Peterson began to exhibit with solo shows in 1908 at the Société des Artistes Français, Paris, France; then at the St. Botolph Club, Boston, Massachusetts; the Knoedler Gallery, New York City; and at Bandann's Art Gallery, Baltimore, Maryland. In 1910 and 1914 she had solo exhibitions at the Art Institute of Chicago, Illinois. She also participated in group shows with the American Watercolor Society and the New York Society of Painters—both in New York City; the Baltimore Watercolor Club, Maryland; the North Shore Arts Association, Gloucester, Massachusetts. Other shows include the Buffalo Fine Arts Academy, New York; the Corcoran Gallery of Art, Washington, D.C., the National Academy of Design, and the National Arts Club—both in New York City; the Palm Beach Art League, Florida; the Pennsylvania Academy of Fine Arts, Philadelphia; the Toledo Museum of Art, Ohio; the J.B. Speed Memorial Art Museum, Louisville, Kentucky; the Syracuse Museum of Fine Arts and the Vassar College Art Gallery, Poughkeepsie—both in New York; and the Wichita Art Museum, Kansas. She also showed her work at the 1915 Panama-Pacific International Exposition in San Francisco, California, and at many galleries, including the Grand Central Galleries, Anderson Galleries, Milch Galleries, and Ehrich Gallery—all in New York City, and the Copley Gallery and Robert C. Vose Galleries, Boston, Massachusetts. Her work has been collected by many museums, including the Baltimore Museum of Art, Maryland; the Brooklyn Museum, New York; the Delaware Art Museum, Baltimore; the High Museum of Art, Atlanta, Georgia; the Metropolitan Museum of Art, New York City; and the Pennsylvania Academy and the Philadelphia Museum of Art—both in Philadelphia.

Peterson was selected the "most outstanding individual of the year" for artistic achievement by the American Historical Society in 1938. During World War II she produced four portraits representing women in each branch of the military which were auctioned for $211,000 to build a war memorial. Peterson was a member of the American Watercolor Society, the National Association of Women Painters and Sculptors, the New York Watercolor Club—all in New York City—and the Allied Artists of America and served on the board of trustees of the Metropolitan Museum of Art, New York City.

Phyllis Peet

Bibliography
Hirschl & Adler Galleries, Inc. *Jane Peterson: A Retrospective Exhibition.* Hirschl & Adler Galleries, Inc., 1970.
Jonathan, Joseph J. *Jane Peterson: An American Artist.* Boston, Massachusetts: Privately printed, 1981.
Peterson, Jane. "Why I Paint Flowers." *Garden Magazine* 36 (September 1922): 31.
———. *Flower Painting.* New York: Art Books for All, 1946.

Peterson, Margaret (1902–)

Born in Seattle, Washington, the painter Margaret Peterson earned a Bachelor's degree from the University of California at Berkeley, where she studied with Hans Hofmann and Worth Ryder. She received a Master's degree from the same institution, then went to Paris, France, where she studied with Vaclav Vytlacil and André L'Hôte (1931–1932).

Widely travelled in North and Central America, especially concerned with Native American myth and symbol in Canada, Mexico, and the United States, Peterson has held solo exhibitions of her work in many venues, including the Palace of the Legion of Honor, San Francisco, California (1933, 1960); Biblioteca Nacional, Mexico (1934); San Francisco Art Museum, California (1950, 1958, 1973); Art Gallery of Greater Victoria, British Columbia (1953, 1959, 1962, 1978); and many others. Her work has been included in prestigious group shows, such as the Biennial Exhibitions of Canadian Art, National Gallery, Ottawa (1961, 1963); the São Paulo Biennale, Brazil (1963); and others.

Peterson has earned many awards and honors, and her work is represented in private and public permanent collections, including the Confederation Memorial Building, Charlottetown, Prince Edward Island, Canada; National Gallery of Canada, Ottawa; Oakland Art Museum, California; Palace of the Legion of Honor, San Francisco, California; University of Victoria, British Columbia; and others.

Bibliography
Creative Canada. Vol. 2. University of Toronto Press, 1972.
Margaret Peterson: A Retrospective. A Catalog. Art Gallery of Greater Victoria, 1978.

Pfaff, Judy (1946–)

Born in London, England, Judy Pfaff has lived and worked in the United States since she was thirteen years old. She earned her Bachelor's degree in 1971 from Washington University, St. Louis, Missouri. Two years later, she received her Master of Fine Arts degree from Yale University, New Haven, Connecticut, where she studied painting with Al Held.

Pfaff held her first solo exhibition in 1974 and has had her work shown in many prestigious solo and group shows, including the Albright-Knox Art Gallery, Buffalo, New York (1982); Holly Solomon Gallery, New York (1983, 1985), and Whitney Biennial, Whitney Museum of American Art (1981)—both in New York City; Hirshhorn Museum and Sculpture Garden, Washington, D.C. (1981); Wacoal Art Center, Tokyo, Japan (1985); the John Weber Gallery, New York City (1986); and many others. "Superette" (1986), a typical recent work of "visual music," is a huge thirty-three-foot mixed-media installation, which was designed particularly for its venue in the John Weber Gallery. (It can be reassembled.) Pfaff uses ordinary "garden variety" materials in an uncommon way, on the specific site, to create her installations.

Honored for her works, the widely-travelled Pfaff received a Creative Artists Public Service (CAPS) grant from the State of New York (1976); two fellowships from the National Endowment for the Arts (NEA) (1979, 1986); a Guggenheim Foundation fellowship (1983); and a Bessie award (1984). Her works are in the permanent collections of prestigious museums, including the Albright-Knox Art Gallery, Buffalo, New York; the Whitney Museum of American Art, New York City; and many others.

Bibliography

Collings, Betty. "Judy Pfaff." *Arts Magazine* 55:3 (November 1980): 4.
Gill, Susan. "Beyond the Perimeters. The Eccentric Humanism of Judy Pfaff." *Arts Magazine* 61:2 (October 1986): 77–79.
Heller, Nancy. *Women Artists*. Abbeville Press, 1987.
Nadelman, Cynthia. "Judy Pfaff." *Art News* 82:4 (April 1983): 151.

Pflug, Christiane (Schütte) (1936–1972)

Born in Berlin, Germany, Christiane (Schütte) Pflug was a highly impressionable four-year-old when her father died of tuberculosis. In the years following his death, Pflug's mother—who was not legally married to her father—attempted to distract her with a vacation to Bavaria. During the visit the child was startled by a roomful of dolls seen in flashes of lightning. It seems possible that she was traumatized by such experiences, given the nature of her artistic development. From 1943 on, her mother seems to have moved her about in Austria and Germany, originally to avoid the war. By 1951 the fifteen-year-old had already left school and moved in with her grandparents in Berlin.

Pflug soon expressed an interest in fashion design, no doubt inspired by her mother, who did such work until the war years disrupted things. She was sent to Paris, France, to study *haute couture* in 1953, but her fate was drastically changed on New Year's Eve, when she met Michael Pflug, a medical student with a strong interest in modern art. He encouraged her to take up landscape painting, in spite of her complete lack of formal training. Works such as "Palais de justice, Paris" (1954) are a bit naive in handling, but they are all the more forceful for it. She married Pflug in the summer of 1956, followed by a two-year period in Tunisia, where her husband did his internship. Her works of the period are mostly modest still lifes in gloomy colors, though some-

how reminiscent of Henri Matisse. She had two daughters, Esther (1957) and Ursula (1958).

Pflug came to Canada to join her mother in 1959. She did not paint again until 1960, when her husband joined her there. Prominent Toronto art dealer Avrom Isaacs happened to see some of the landscapes Pflug had painted from an apartment window on a busy Yonge Street. He invited her to show at his gallery in 1962. (Isaacs later showed works by Pflug's two daughters, then aged seven and eight.) Gloom was still the operative word in some of these works. "Dead Pigeon" (1961) is a notable example. It was only after her first show that she began the series of large doll-paintings for which she is most generally recognized, largely due to the full-fledged retrospective at the Winnipeg Art Gallery, Canada, in 1966. (This gallery was the first and the most consistent in its support, mounting two other shows, in 1974 and 1979.) In most of her doll paintings, a simple domestic interior—often a kitchen—is given a strange, almost surrealist twist, by removing virtually every trace of human irregularity and replacing human forms with blank, staring dolls. An oft-cited source for these images is the magic realism of the Dutch School.

The Pflugs bought a house on Birch Avenue in Toronto, Ontario, Canada, in 1967, and Pflug's paintings were for a time rather pleasantly preoccupied with activities around the neighborhood school and the life of the street in general. Her colors were brighter and her compositions a little more expansive, but the views were still claustrophobic, as it were—the world always seen from an upstairs window. The last of the series, "Cottingham School with Black Flag" (1971–1972), is psychologically loaded to the point of oppressiveness: at first glance a colorful vision of green trees against a backdrop of hydro lines and apartment buildings, it soon revolves into a compressed space in the foreground, devoid of figures but for one, almost unnoticed, peering from an upstairs window. The foliage of the trees starts to resemble birds in flight—echoed by a tiny bird-like aircraft in the distance. The image resonates with a desire for escape, but from what? Some uncharitable voices have suggested that her husband was overbearing, but the painting itself offers no evidence to this effect. Instead, the image shows a Canadian flag on its pole just left of center: its normally brilliant red has become dead black.

It was to be Pflug's last work. On April 4, 1972, she took her own life with a drug overdose. She was on the Toronto islands—a weekend escape of sorts for Torontonians in the downtown area.

Robert J. Belton

Bibliography

Davis, Ann. *The Drawings of Christiane Pflug*. Winnipeg Art Gallery, 1979.

Phillips, Helen (1913–1995)

Born in Fresno, California, the sculptor Helen Phillips studied at the California Institute of the Arts (1931–1935), and won a travelling scholarship to Paris, France (1936). She also studied for a short time at Atelier 17, New York City, later marrying its founder, Stanley William Hayter. Except for some years before and after World War II—when she was in the United States as an exhibiting artist—Phillips lived and worked in Paris.

Phillips's first solo exhibition occurred in 1954 and her work was invited to group exhibitions, including the American Cultural Centre,

Paris, France (1958). Earlier on, Phillips entered the competition for the "Monument to the Unknown Political Prisoner" winning in the French section along with seven others. Her work is represented in private and public permanent collections in France and the United States.

Bibliography
Dunford, Penny. *Biographical Dictionary of Women Artists in Europe and America since 1850.* University of Pennsylvania Press, 1989.
Mackay, J. *Dictionary of Western Sculptors in Bronze.* 1978.

Phillips, Marjorie Acker (1895–1985)

Born in Bourbon, Indiana, the painter Marjorie Acker Phillips studied with Gifford Beal, Kenneth Hayes Miller, and Boardman Robinson. Married to the Washington collector Duncan Phillips, she was a member of the Society of Washington Artists, Washington, D.C.

Phillips's work was shown in many solo and group exhibitions, including the Kraushaar Art Galleries (1924); the "Second Biennial Exhibition of Contemporary American Painting," Whitney Museum of American Art (1934); the Marlborough Gallery (1973)—all in New York City; and many others. Her work is represented in private and public permanent collections, including the Phillips Memorial Gallery, Washington, D.C.; the Whitney Museum of American Art, New York City; Yale University, New Haven, Connecticut; and others.

Bibliography
American Art Annual. Vol. 28. American Federation of Arts, 1932.
Goodrich, Lloyd, and John I.H. Baur. *American Art of Our Century.* Praeger, 1961.
Willand, Susan. "Marjorie Phillips." *Women Artists in Washington Collections.* Ed. Josephine Withers. University of Maryland, College Park, and Women's Caucus for Art, 1979.

Pierce, Florence (1918–)

The sculptor Florence Pierce was born in Washington, D.C., and began her education as an artist at the Duncan Phillips Collection Studio School in her native city in 1935. She moved to New Mexico in 1936, and completed her education in Taos at Emil Bisttram's School of Art. This experience, coupled with an exposure to the New Mexican atmosphere became the deciding influence in her life as an artist. She was the youngest member of the group known as the New Mexico Transcendentalists. These artists maintained a commitment to abstract art in the West somewhat similar to that consistently supported by the American Abstract Artists in the eastern part of the country at a time when the social realists were dominant.

It is difficult to imagine Pierce's art divorced from the light and space of New Mexico, though her aim is to achieve a timeless and indeed placeless expression. She sees it as the distillation of contemplation and the mysterious and ineffable which transcends immediate sense experience. These ideas she carries out in large—in fact, to human scale—abstract forms which have remained constant from archaic times to the present: triangles, squares, and circles. To express luminosity she makes use of translucent media: resin, fiberglass, epoxy, which both retain and allow light to pass through. Colors are pale, subtle, and elegant. The quality of light is emphasized through gradations which range from the nearly opaque to the nearly transparent. Textural distinctions, though

very delicate, play a significant part in her sculpture, as does a finely drawn balance between symmetry and asymmetry. Her term for her sculptures is "lucamorphs," a word coined by the artist.

Like Piet Mondrian, Pierce has consistently concerned herself with universal forms, but though the basic geometry has come down from pre-history, her dynamic spatial division and use of contemporary materials mark Pierce's art as uncompromisingly modern.

Recognition outside New Mexico has developed slowly—she was included in an exhibition at the Worcester Museum, "American Abstract art of the '30s and '40s, the Second Wave," in September, 1991. In New Mexico her work has been regularly exhibited in museums and galleries from the 1940s. Invitation to an alcove show for 1991 at the Museum of Fine Arts in Santa Fe, 1990–1991, is an indication of the continued regard in which she has been held in her home state.

Barbara Cortright

Bibliography
"Art Throb." *Lear's Magazine* (November 1989).
Brown, Love, and Raven. "Exposures, Women and Their Art." 1989.
Quantam, University of New Mexico, 1987.

Pierce, Leona (1922–)

Born in Santa Barbara, California, the daughter of schoolteachers, Leona Pierce attended Scripps College, Claremont, California (1940–1942), where she studied with Millard Sheets, before going on to Chouinard Art Institute, Los Angeles, California. With the encouragement of Donald and Esther Bear in 1945, Pierce took further study at the Art Students League in New York City where, that summer, she worked with Yasuo Kuniyoshi and Cameron Booth. She took evening classes with Stuart Davis at the New School for Social Research, New York City.

Winner of a Philip Rosenthal scholarship for painting (1948) and a Tiffany fellowship in graphic arts (1951–1952), Pierce is also the recipient of purchase prizes and awards for her woodcuts from the Brooklyn Museum, New York City (1949), the Philadelphia Print Club, Pennsylvania (1950); the Library of Congress Print Annual, Washington, D.C. (1950); the New Britain Print Annual, Connecticut (1951); the Bradley University Print Annual, Peoria, Illinois (1952); the University of Southern California Print Annual, Los Angeles (1952); and the Society for American Graphic Artists Print Exhibition, New York City (1953). She also received commissions for woodcuts from the Museum of Modern Art (MoMA) (1957), the International Graphic Arts Society (1953), and the Seven Arts Society (1955)—all in New York City.

Pierce first exhibited her woodcuts in a solo show in 1947 and again in 1949 and 1951 at the Santa Barbara Museum of Art, California. She has had more than thirty solo shows of her work in the United States and abroad. These include the Weyhe Gallery, New York City (1951, 1954, 1959, 1962); Mills College, Oakland, California (1951); the Philadelphia Art Alliance, Pennsylvania (1952); the University of Maine, Orono (1956); and the Rye Public Library, New York (1959). With her printmaker-husband, Antonio Frasconi, Pierce participated in two-person shows of woodcuts from 1950 to 1990 at the Berkeley Store Gallery, California (1991).

Pierce's work has been in many group exhibitions throughout the world, including MoMA (1953, 1955–1956); and the Society of

American Graphic Artists (1954)—both in New York City; the International Exposition of Graphic Art, Yugoslavia (1955); the United States Information Agency (USIA) travelling show in the Far East (1962); "American Prints 'Round the World," sponsored by the Society of American Graphic Artists and the USIA (1962); "Women Printmakers Past and Present: 1400 to 1973," the New York Public Library exhibition of part of its permanent collection, in a show curated by Elizabeth Ross (1973); and others. Her work is in the permanent collection of the MoMA, Brooklyn Museum, and New York Public Library—all in New York City; Library of Congress, Washington, D.C.; Philadelphia Museum of Art, Pennsylvania; and the Institute of Contemporary Art, Boston, Massachusetts. It may also be seen at Cornell University, Ithaca, New York; the Santa Barbara Museum of Art, California; Bradley University, Peoria, Illinois; and others. "Slides" (1957), is a typical color woodcut of joyous children in an urban playground; in a sense, it sings of the promise of a better world.

Bibliography
Adlow, Dorothy. "Slides." *Christian Science Monitor* (July 1957).
"Fifteen American Printmakers." A Catalog. Muncie, Indiana: Ball State Art Gallery, 1964.
Heller, Jules. *Printmaking Today*. 2nd edition. Holt, Rinehart & Winston, 1972.
"Leona Pierce Shares Life's Work." *Darien News* (March 1981).

Pincus, Laurie (1951–)

A native New Yorker, the painter/installationist Laurie Pincus grew up in Los Angeles, California. She attended Bard College, Annandale-on-Hudson, New York (1970–1971) and earned a Bachelor's degree from Sarah Lawrence College, Bronxville, New York (1975).

Pincus has held solo exhibitions in museums and galleries in the United States and abroad, including the Valerie Miller Gallery, Palm Desert, California (1991); "Special Project," Fuji Television, Tokyo, Japan (1990); "10-Year Survey Show," Loyola Marymount University, Los Angeles, California (1989); Judy Youens Gallery, Houston, Texas (1988); "Sleepwalkers and Art," Allrich Gallery, San Francisco, California (1987); Galería Gráfica Tokio, Tokyo, Japan (1986); "Sleepwalkers, Gangsters and the Junior League," Jan Baum Gallery, Los Angeles, California (1986); and others. Her work has been invited to many group exhibitions, such as "Hats and Headgear," San Francisco International Airport (1992); and "External Fantasies, Internal Realities," Security Pacific Gallery, the Plaza, Los Angeles (1991)—both in California; "America Pop Culture Today 3," La Foret Museum, Tokyo, Japan (1989); Helander Gallery, Palm Beach, Florida (1988); "Southern California Artists," Lancaster Arts Festival, Ohio (1987); "Los Angeles Painters on the Edge," Quay Gallery, San Francisco (1985); and "Humor in Art," Los Angeles Institute of Contemporary Art (1981)—both in California; "Invitational: New in New York," Monique Knowlton Gallery, New York City (1981); and many others.

Pincus's painted wood figures, tableaus, and paintings—based upon childhood dreams and adult perspicacity—are represented in many private and public permanent collections.

Bibliography
America Pop Culture Today. Vol. 3. Seibundo Shinkosha Publishing, 1990.
Brown, Betty. *Exposures: Women and Their Art*. New Sage Press, 1989.
Caine, Barry. "Artist Brings Her 'Inside People' to Life." *San Francisco Herald* (July 1987).
Hyndman, Robert. "The Make-Believe World of Laurie Pincus." *Daily Pilot Notebook* 3:6 (February 6, 1987).
Marrow, Maeva. *Inside the L.A. Artist*. Peregrine Smith, 1988.
Smith, Mark Chalen. "Pincus Puts TV's Fantasy into Her Art." *Los Angeles Times* (October 1987).

Pindell, Howardena (1943–)

Howardena Pindell's multi-faceted art records an individual's spiritual journey, but it also engages issues of racial and social justice. As an African-American woman Pindell is particularly well-situated to observe inequity and oppression, but she transcends simplistic responses to inhumanity. Her art tolerates ambiguity and human frailty. Its aesthetic appeal reflects Pindell's observation that a "unifying factor" among spiritual traditions is "a concern for the visual expression of the 'divine' through beauty."

Pindell grew up in Philadelphia, Pennsylvania, where she was born. After earning a Bachelor of Fine Arts degree at Boston University, Massachusetts, and a Master of Fine Arts degree at Yale University, New Haven, Connecticut, she accepted a curatorial position at the Museum of Modern Art (MoMA), New York City. Her earlier work had been figurative, but in New York City, Pindell began to paint sensuous, large-scale abstractions, although more overt content continued in her smaller, mixed-media assemblages.

In 1979 Pindell left the museum to join the faculty at the State University of New York (SUNY) at Stony Brook. In the same year she suffered severe physical injuries and temporary loss of memory in an automobile crash, and the following year she travelled to Japan to spend seven months absorbing a culture that deeply affected her thinking. In the aftermath of these events Pindell's art intensified both personally and politically. Her controversial 1980 video, *Free, White and 21*, set the pace. In this performance Pindell played both her Black self and a White alter ego who raise unsettling racist issues as they hurl accusations at each other. Until that time most of Pindell's art had not been issue-oriented, but in the 1980s she confronted the political dimension of her private concerns.

Most notably in a series of major mixed-media paintings grouped under the rubric of "Autobiography," she explored the intersection of her own experience with history and world events. "Autobiography: Water/Ancestors/Middle Passage/Family Ghosts" (1988) centers on the outline of her own body. Her somber visage, partially covered with white make-up, draws us to the middle of a surrealistic field upon which float additional faces, eyes, the outline of a slave ship, and other symbolic elements. Whereas Pindell's personal odyssey predominates in this work, another example from the series, "Autobiography: Air/CS560," deals directly with difficult political issues. Here, four life-sized bodies representing major racial skin colors—black, brown, yellow, and white—drift like corpses on a sea of cut-out words and phrases, along with a news photograph of a wounded Palestinian. "Beaten" recurs numerous times, along with "assassination," "shot," "censorship," "broken," "how dare you question," and other journalistic allusions to violent suppression of individual rights. Ominously, the title refers to a nerve gas of American manufacture.

Ann Lee Morgan

Bibliography
Feinberg, Mark. "Painter Pindell Discovers that More than the Gallery Walls Are All-White." *In These Times* 20:26 (September 1989): 21.
Sheffield, Margaret. "The New Work." Introduction to *Howardena Pindell: Autobiography*. Exhibition Catalog. New York: Cyrus Gallery, 1989.
Verdino-Sullwold, Carla Maria. "Howardena Pindell: Volcanic View of the Self." *Crisis* 97 (January 1990): 13, 38.
Wilson, Judith. "Howardena Pindell." *Ms.* 8 (May 1980): 66–70.

Pineda, Marianna (1925–)

Born in Evanston, Illinois, Marianna Pineda studied sculpture with various masters at several institutions, including Carl Milles at Cranbrook Academy of Art, Bloomfield Hills, Michigan (Summer 1942); Simon Moselsio at Bennington College, Vermont (1942–1943); Raymond Puccinelli at the University of California, Berkeley (1943–1945); Oronzio Maldarelli at Columbia University, New York City (1945–1946); and with Ossip Zadkine in Paris, France (1949–1950).

Pineda has held many solo exhibitions of her sculpture and drawings in galleries, museums, and colleges, including "Four Decades of Drawings," the College of William and Mary, Williamsburg, Virginia (1992); "The EVE CELEBRANT Series," Judi Rotenberg Gallery, Boston, Massachusetts (1990); "Search for the Queen," Contemporary Arts Center, Honolulu, Hawaii (1982); "Twenty Years of Sculpture," Newton College, Massachusetts (1972); Swetzoff Gallery, Boston, Massachusetts (1956, 1963, 1964); and others. Her work has been invited to numerous group exhibitions between 1944 and 1992, such as "Crossection," World Financial Center (1992); and "167th Juried Exhibition," National Academy of Design (1992); American Academy and Institute of Arts and Letters (1961); "Recent Sculpture," a travelling show, Museum of Modern Art (MoMA) (1959); Whitney Museum of American Art (1953, 1954, 1955, 1957, 1959); "American Sculpture," and Metropolitan Museum of Art (1951)—all in New York City; "American Painters and Sculptors," Galerie 8, Paris, France (1950); and many others.

Winner of honors and awards for her work, Pineda was the recipient of gold medals and prizes from the National Sculpture Society, New York City (1986, 1988, 1991); an artists award and a gold medal from the National Academy of Design (1987, 1988)—all in New York City. Among other honors she was elected an associate fellow (1983) and academician (1986) of the National Academy of Design. Her public sculptures include an eight-foot bronze of the last Queen of Hawaii, "The Spirit of Lill'uokalani"; "Twirling," a two-figure group for East Boston Housing for the Elderly, Massachusetts; a monumental "Oracle," for Radcliffe College, Cambridge, Massachusetts; and many more.

Pineda's work is represented in private and public permanent collections, including the Addison Gallery of American Art, Phillipps Academy, Andover; Boston Museum of Fine Arts; Fogg Art Museum, Harvard University, Cambridge; and Radcliffe College, Harvard University, Cambridge—all in Massachusetts; Dartmouth College, Hanover, New Hampshire; Collection of the state of Hawaii; Walker Art Center, Minneapolis, Minnesota; Muscarelle Museum of Art, Williamsburg, Virginia; and others.

Bibliography
Pilgrims and Pioneers: New England Women in the Arts. Midmarch Arts, 1987.
Rubenstein, Charlotte S. *American Women Sculptors*. G.K. Hall, 1990.
Watson-Jones, Virginia. *Contemporary American Women Sculptors*. Oryx Press, 1986.

Pingwartok, Ulayu (1904–1978)

Ulayu Pingwartok, a Canadian Inuit graphic artist, was born near Lake Harbour on southwestern Baffin Island on April 7, 1904. She lived a traditional lifestyle on the land until her move into the settlement of Cape Dorset in 1959. Like many Cape Dorset Inuit, Ulayu was encouraged in the early 1960s to produce drawings for the annual print collections. She created drawings in various media until a year before her death in February 1978.

Charming in their straightforward simplicity and descriptiveness, Ulayu's images are a testament to the artist's keen observation of nature and domestic life. Many early prints are portraits of birds, with an emphasis on delineation of plumage. Her later prints generally depict traditional camp life, concentrating on the activities of women. An accomplished seamstress herself, Ulayu carefully rendered clothing patterns and styles. Shelter, in the form of summer tents and winter igloos, is another recurring theme.

Thirty of Ulayu's seven hundred drawings were translated into prints for ten annual Cape Dorset collections between 1965 and 1979. Her work was included in fifteen group exhibitions in Canada and the United States, including the landmark touring show, "The Inuit Print." A solo exhibition of her prints and drawings, "Ulayu," toured in 1982–1984. Her work is represented in the collections of the National Gallery of Canada, the Canadian Museum of Civilization, the McMichael Canadian Art Collection, and the Winnipeg Art Gallery.

Ingo Hessel

Bibliography
Indian and Northern Affairs Canada. *Ulayu*. Exhibition Catalog. Indian and Northern Affairs Canada, 1981.

Pinto, Jody (1942–)

A native New Yorker, the environmental sculptor Jody Pinto studied at the Pennsylvania Academy of Fine Arts, Philadelphia, where she won a Cresson European fellowship (1967), and then went on to earn a Bachelor of Fine Arts degree from the Philadelphia College of Art (now the University of the Arts) in 1973.

Pinto has held many solo exhibitions of her work at galleries and museums in the United States and abroad, including "Approach to a Bridge," an installation, Real Art Ways, Hartford, Connecticut (1988); Hal Bromm Gallery, New York City (1978, 1979, 1980, 1981, 1983, 1985, 1987); Marian Locks Gallery, Philadelphia (1980, 1987); Richard Demarco Gallery, Edinburgh, Scotland (1979); and others. Her work has been invited to myriad group shows around the world, such as "Public Art Proposals," International Public Art Fair, Yokohama, Japan (1992); "New York Now—Works on Paper," Nordyllands Kunstmuseum, Aalborg, and Randers Kunstmuseum—both in Denmark (1984); Venice Biennale, Italy; "New York 1980," Banco Gallery, Brescia, Italy; and Tel-Hai 80 Conference, Upper Galilee, Israel—all in 1980; "Sounding the Depths: 150 Years of American Watercolors," a travelling show, Milwaukee Art Museum, Wisconsin (1990); "Outside In: Socrates Sculpture Park," City Gallery (1987); and "Drawing Acquisitions 1978–1981," Whitney Museum of American Art (1981)—both in New York City; "Dwelling," Institute of Contemporary Art, Philadelphia (1978); and others.

Pinto is best known, however, for her environmental sculpture—with its dry-stacked fieldstone terraces and native flora works on two-acre sites, or on master plan extensions, one-mile long, including landscaping, footpaths, pedestrian bridges, and outdoor theaters, or in designing structures for children's play and exploration. In these works her sensitivity and creativity emerge, as may be seen in "Papago Park/City Boundary," Phoenix, Arizona (1990–1992); and many other projects. She has received awards and honors for her work, including grants or fellowships from the National Endowment for the Arts (NEA) (1979); the Pennsylvania Council on the Arts (1981); and the New Jersey Council on the Arts (1982) and design honors awards from the American Institute of Architects (AIA) (1988); the American Society of Landscape Architects (1992); and others.

Pinto's work may be viewed at various sites across the United States and is represented in museum and corporate permanent collections, including the Guggenheim Museum, the Whitney Museum of American Art, and Chemical Bank—all in New York City; Philadelphia Museum of Fine Art and Hunt Manufacturing Co.—both in Pennsylvania; the State University of New York (SUNY) at Purchase; and others.

Bibliography

Cummings, Paul. "Jody Pinto Talks with Paul Cummings." *Drawing* 9:1 (1987): 10–14.

Raven, Arlene. "Classical Myth and Imagery in Contemporary Art." *The Village Voice* (May 10, 1988): 100.

Schwendenwein, Jude. "Breaking Ground: Art in the Environment." *Sculpture* (September–October 1991): 40.

Smith, Shaw. "Documenting FINGERSPAN." *New Art Examiner* (April 1989): 53.

Piper, Adrian (1948–)

Despite working consistently in the art world since 1970, multi-media artist Adrian Piper has just begun to receive her due recognition. Recent attention given to multi-culturalism coincides with her longtime concern as an African-American with issues of racism.

Born in New York City, Piper relates most of her work to her experience growing up in Harlem as a light-skinned black woman, and attending on scholarship a wealthy, mostly white, school. The ambivalence and difficulties of her position are reflected in a work of text and image, "Political Self-Portrait #2 (Race)" (1978), in which she describes her experience as "gray" rather than "black" and comments on the "white racist ideology" that victimizes both blacks and whites.

Piper developed her career as an artist while simultaneously teaching philosophy. She received her Doctorate degree in philosophy from and has taught that subject at the University of Michigan, Ann Arbor; the University of California at San Diego, and currently at Wellesley College, Massachusetts. She attended the School of Visual Arts in New York City from 1966 to 1969. Influenced by the conceptual art of Sol Lewitt, for whom she worked as an assistant in 1969, her first works were conceptually based. She focused on text and seriality, for example.

Although a strong conceptual bias continues to underlie much of Piper's work, in 1970 she began to investigate her own experience in a series of performances entitled *Catalysis*, in which she went out in public looking or acting offensively. For example, she soaked her clothes in foul-smelling substances and then rode the subway; she filled her bag with ketchup and then, while riding the bus, foraged in it for keys; she played a tape recording of belches in a library. These acts not only tested the limits of her own ego boundaries, but also aimed to catalyze viewers' reactions and reflection toward "otherness."

Over the past decade, Piper's often confrontational video installations and performances elucidate the triggering mechanisms of racism, and its effect on African-American people. In the walk-in installation, *Four Intruders Plus Alarm Systems* (1980), four menacing black male faces confront the viewer, and earphones narrate possible reactions ranging from subtle to overt racism. Other pieces, such as *Vanilla Nightmares* (1986), consider gender and class exploitation as well as racism. This photo-text series is based on advertising images in *The New York Times* to which Piper overlaid her own charcoal drawings of stereotypic images of black sexuality. Her critical writings, as sophisticated as one would expect from her background as a professor of philosophy, also attempt to uproot even the more subtle forms of racism.

Piper has received two National Endowment for the Arts (NEA) visual artists fellowships, and her work has been shown in galleries since the late 1960s. In 1987 the Alternative Museum in New York City organized a travelling retrospective entitled "Adrian Piper: Reflections 1967–87." She is represented in New York City by the John Weber Gallery.

Patricia Mathews

Bibliography

Als, Hilton. "Darling." *Artforum* 29 (March 1991): 100–04.

Johnson, Ken. "Being and Politics." *Art in America* 78 (September 1990): 154–61.

Lippard, Lucy. *From the Center: Feminist Essays on Women's Art.* Dutton, 1976, pp. 107–08, 167–71.

Piper, Adrian. "Two Conceptions of the Self." *Philosophical Studies* 48 (September 1985).

———. "Ideology, Confrontation, and Political Self-Awareness: An Essay, 1982." *Blasted Allegories: An Anthology of Writings by Contemporary Artists.* Ed. B. Wallis. New Museum of Contemporary Art, 1987, pp. 129–33.

———. "A Paradox of Conscience." *New Art Examiner* 16 (April 1989): 27–31.

Sims, Lowery Stokes. "The Mirror, the Other." *Artforum* 28 (March 1990): 111–15.

Welish, M., E. Hayt-Atkins. "In This Corner: Adrian Piper's Agitprop." *Arts Magazine* 65 (March 1991): 43–51.

Wilson, Judith. "In Memory of the News and of Ourselves: The Art of Adrian Piper." 16/17 (Autumn–Winter 1991): 39–64.

Piper, Jane (1916–1991)

Jane Piper was a distinguished painter and teacher, known for her colorful, spatially-oriented paintings, meditations on still lifes, and landscapes. Piper studied with Arthur B. Carles and with Hans Hofmann, as well as with Earl Horter, and at the Pennsylvania Academy of Fine Arts and the Barnes Foundation—both in Philadelphia, Pennsylvania.

Long known as one of Philadelphia's leading painters, Piper spent her summers in Wellfleet, Massachusetts, painting and participating in exhibitions in the Provincetown area. Piper was also well known as an influential teacher, and many of her former students continued to seek her advice and support over the years. Piper taught at the Philadelphia College of Art, Pennsylvania, from 1956 until her retirement in 1985. She also taught at the Philadelphia Museum of Art, Pennsylvania, from 1954 to 1956 and at the New York Studio School, New York City, and the Pennsylvania Academy of Fine Arts, Philadelphia, in 1986.

Piper had one-person exhibitions throughout the country. Her work is represented in many public and private collections, including the Philadelphia Museum of Art and the Carnegie Institute Museum of Art, Pittsburgh—both in Pennsylvania; the Brooklyn Museum and National Academy of Design—both in New York City; and the Corcoran Gallery of Art and the Phillips Collection—both in Washington, D.C. Her work is represented by the Mangel Gallery in Philadelphia.

In 1986–1987 Piper had a travelling retrospective of paintings from 1940 to 1985. The show went to James Madison University in Harrisonburg, Virginia; the Pennsylvania Academy of Fine Arts in Philadelphia; and the State University of New York (SUNY) in Oswego. In January 1991 she had another retrospective at the New York Studio School, New York City. A memorial service was held for her at the Philadelphia Museum of Art, Pennsylvania, in September 1991; and an exhibition of her work and the work of her former students was held at the Mangel Gallery for the month of November 1991.

Piper was the wife of the noted sociologist E. Digby Baltzell, and the mother of painter Jan Baltzell, and architect Eve Baltzell.

Larry Day

Bibliography
Florescu, Michael. "Jane Piper." *Arts* (May 1981): 18.
Piper, Jane. "Remembering Arthur B. Carles." *Arts* (March 1988): 73–75.
Scott, William P. "Continuity and Change: Conversations with Jane Piper." *American Artist* (November 1978): 76–81, 122–24.
———. "Jane Piper." *Art in America* (December 1986): 142–43.
Wolanin, Barbara A. "Interview with Jane Piper." New York: Archives of American Art, 1986. Unpublished.
———. "Jane Piper: Retrospective 1940–1985." Catalog of travelling exhibition organized for James Madison University, Harrisonburg, Virginia, 1986–1987, n.p.

Pitseolak, Ashoona (1904–1983)

One of Canada's best known artists, the Inuit graphic artist known simply as Pitseolak was born on Nottingham Island in Hudson's Bay. She lived the last twenty-five years of her life in the settlement of Cape Dorset, where she became one of the most famous, and certainly the most prolific Inuit graphic artist. Pitseolak produced more than 7,000 original drawings in her twenty-four-year artistic career. Over 200 of her drawings were translated into prints and issued in the Cape Dorset annual collections from 1960 to 1983. Pitseolak's oral autobiography, illustrated with her own drawings, was published in 1971.

The subject matter of Pitseolak's prints and drawings is generally the traditional way of life of the Inuit before the coming of the Whites. Scenes of camp life, fording a river with dogs, or sewing a skin tent remind both artist and viewer of what life was like for previous generations, before the appearance of airplanes, snowmobiles, and satellite dishes. Pitseolak's narrative drawings serve as a means of recapturing these old ways and making them vivid for younger generations of Inuit.

Pitseolak's work has been included in scores of Inuit art shows, including "The Family of Pitseolak," Robertson Galleries (1967), and "The Inuit Print," National Museum of Man (1977)—both in Ottawa; "The Coming and Going of the Shaman," Winnipeg Art Gallery (1978); and "Arctic Mirror," Canadian Museum of Civilization, Ottawa (1990). A solo print retrospective (1962–1970) was held at the Canadian Guild of Crafts, Montréal, in 1971. Pitseolak was made a member of the Royal Canadian Academy of Art in 1974, and the Order of Canada was conferred upon her in 1977.

Janet Catherine Berlo

Bibliography
Annual Cape Dorset Print Catalogs 1960–1983. West Baffin Eskimo Co-operative Ltd., Cape Dorset, Northwest Territories, Canada.
Berlo, Janet C. "The Power of the Pencil: Inuit Women in the Graphic Arts." *Inuit Art Quarterly* 5:1 (1990): 16–26.
Eber, Dorothy, ed. *Pitseolak: Pictures out of My Life*. University of Washington Press, 1971.
Humez, Jean. "Pictures in the Life of Eskimo Artist Pitseolak." *Woman's Art Journal* 2:2 (1982): 30–36.

Pitt, Sheila (1940–)

Born in Philadelphia, Pennsylvania, Sheila Pitt is known for her innovative large-scale prints, which combine monotype and woodcut techniques. Her educational background includes studies at Temple University, Philadelphia, where she received a Bachelor's degree in biology and mathematics education (1961); studies in scientific illustration at the University of Arizona, Tucson (1977–1979); and further study with Lynn Schroeder and Andrew Polk, which led to her Master of Fine Arts degree from the University of Arizona (1987).

A faculty member at the University of Arizona, Pitt has exhibited her prints throughout the United States, including solo shows at Gallery Route One, Point Reyes, California (1991, 1993); Matrix Gallery, Sacramento, California (1991); Oregon State University, Corvallis (1989); and the Schloss Wolfsburg, Wolfsburg, Germany (1987). Her numerous group exhibitions include the Hunterdon National Print Exhibit, Clinton, New Jersey (1992); ARC Gallery, Chicago, Illinois (1992); "Scratching the Surface," a national print invitational exhibition at the Visual Arts Center of Alaska (1989), which included Jim Dine, Mauricio Lasansky, Jasper Johns, and David Salle, among others.

Pitt has earned awards and honors, including a University of Arizona faculty incentive grant (1991) to develop a series of prints titled, "Coming Up for Air: Woman Submerged and Surfacing." Her current work addresses the issue of women living, working, and almost drowning in an unhealthy environment. She employs the metaphor of women in water and their struggle to surface from the liquid depths of that environment to confront powerful and serious contemporary concerns of women in our society. She shows the relationship between societal controls upon women's role today and the breeding of animals. Her concern for women's freedom for self-control and equality has been a constant theme throughout her printmaking career.

Moira Geoffrion

Bibliography
Perkins, Ann, and Rita, Townsend. *Bitter Fruit*. Hunter House Publishers, 1991.

Pixley, Anne Flaten (1932–)

Anne Flaten Pixley was born in Paris, France; her parents were Americans of Norwegian descent. Presently she divides her time between Venice, California, and Bellegarde, France—a village between Nîmes and Arles. She grew up and was educated in Minnesota, taking her Bachelor of Arts degree there from St. Olaf College in Northfield. Though she studied for a time at the Art Students League in New York City, she earned her Master of Fine Arts degree at Claremont Graduate School in California.

Pixley was trained as a painter, but her first exhibited works, the "Post and Paper" series, were constructed of paper—large rectangles made from a frame of wooden posts on the wall with slits in which many small squares of the artist's hand-made paper are inserted in a grid pattern. The effect is suggestive of growing leaves reordered by geometry.

While the initial aspect of Pixley's work is one of great simplicity in keeping with her aim of expressing the large idea through an economy of means, there is an interior complexity in the color and texture of the squares. Edge and surface are important components of the work. The color itself is an intrinsic part of the paper, itself a tissue of fibers dyed in several colors optically mixed.

The work is diagonally organized, top to bottom, left to right, because Pixley sees light as a diagonal shape. Edges and density give notice of its presence; that presence is expressed through the diagonal form. As in nature, which has always been an important source for Pixley, from the snows of Minnesota to the green vistas of rural France, the view changes with the changing light, with changing points of observation, even with successive viewing.

Because there is always process in sense perception—and it is the process of the perception of light, not an object in nature, which Pixley is concerned to represent—her works evolve decision by decision and are never preconceived. To inspire the act of seeing as opposed to simply looking—an act occasioned by intense looking at the work, but not ending with the work—is her goal.

The phenomenology of Merleau-Ponty, which focused on sense perception through the embodied mind, was important to her in arriving at this goal. Thus, as Pixley attempts to picture process, so is the viewing a process, never static, always in flux.

Pixley followed the post and paper works, for example, with a reexamination of the drawing studies she had made to determine the color for the papers and arrived at large drawings made by the same creative process: one colored mark determining the next. These became fields of colored lines, some seemingly at random, widely spaced yet diagonally directed, some interwoven like a mesh, some clustered rhythmically in bursts against a grid. Always the border, which is formed from within the work by the cessation of line, the clearing of the space, is important. Density and edges, in the drawings as in the constructions, are significant.

Later watercolors consist of simple basic shapes in one color, varied by differences in the opaqueness or transparency of the wash in accord with the same principle.

As John Cage has used random sound to intensify hearing, so Pixley has made use of chance in constructing her works, so that viewing is not passive but rather a coming to see. As Cage has expressed it in a 1964 catalog essay for an exhibition of works by Jasper Johns, "the endlessly changing ancient task: the imitation of nature is her manner of operation." In a related sense, a Zen garden is not intended to be the object that one sees but rather represents an impulse to seeing. Pixley has gained much of her perception from the East.

Pixley has exhibited widely in the United States, Europe, and Japan in galleries, museums, colleges, and universities. Exhibitions include those of the Biennale Internationale in Lausanne, Switzerland; the Los Angeles Institute of Contemporary Art, California; Galerie Maronie Kyoto, Japan; American Cultural Center, Tel Aviv, Israel; and Musée Ziem, Martigues, France. Her work is included in the public collections of Security Pacific Bank; Musée Ziem, Martigues, and Musée Reattu, Arles—both in France.

Barbara Cortright

Bibliography
Anne Flaten Pixley. Exhibition Catalog. Villeneuve d'Ascq: Musée d'Art Modern, 1986.
Anne Flaten Pixley/Drawings 1983–1987. Exhibition Catalog. Rancho Cucamonga, California: Rex W. Wignall Museum/Gallery, Chaffey College, 1987.

Platt, Eleanor (1910–1974)

Born in Woodbridge, New Jersey, the sculptor Eleanor Platt studied at the Art Students League, New York City (1929–1933). Winner of honors and awards, Platt won the Chaloner prize (a three-year scholarship) in 1940; four years later, she was the recipient of a $1,000 grant from the American Academy and Institute of Arts and Letters, New York City; and in 1945 she received a Guggenheim Foundation fellowship.

Platt executed many commissions of famous persons, including busts of "Associate Justice Louis D. Brandeis" for the U.S. Supreme Court; "Judge Learned Hand" for the Harvard University Law School, Cambridge, Massachusetts; "Albert Einstein" for the Metropolitan Museum of Art, New York City; and "Chief Justice Earl Warren" for the National Lawyers Club, Washington, D.C. Her works are represented in private and public permanent collections.

Bibliography
"Eleanor Platt Dies; Sculptor Was 64." Obituary. *The New York Times* (September 7, 1974).
Gardner, Albert TenEyck. *American Sculpture: A Catalogue of the Collection of the Metropolitan Museum of Art*. New York Graphic Society, 1965.
Who's Who in American Art. Vol. 4. American Federation of Arts, 1947.

Plochmann, Carolyn Gassan (1926–)

Born in Toledo, Ohio, the painter Carolyn Gassan Plochmann studied at the School of Design, Toledo Museum of Art, Ohio (1943–1947); earned a Bachelor's degree from the University of Toledo (1947), and, two years later, received a Master of Fine Arts degree from the University of Iowa, Iowa City, as George W. Stevens fellow from the Toledo Museum of Art. Plochmann also studied with Alfeo Faggi in Woodstock, New York (1950), and enrolled in a postgraduate dissection anatomy course at Southern Illinois University, Carbondale.

Plochmann has been given more than thirty-five solo exhibitions between 1952 and 1992, including the Toledo Museum of Art, Ohio (1955, 1965); a retrospective show and others at the Evansville Museum of Arts and Science, Indiana (1962, 1973, 1979, 1990–1991); Bresler Galleries, Milwaukee, Wisconsin (1958, 1967); Kennedy Galleries, New York City (1973, 1981, 1983, 1987, 1989); and the Knoxville Museum of Art, Tennessee (1990). From 1942 to 1989 her work has been invited to myriad group exhibitions throughout the United States and Mexico, such as the Carnegie Institute, Pittsburgh, Pennsylvania (1943); Butler Institute of American Art, Youngstown, Ohio (1951, 1953–1955, 1957, 1959, 1961, 1964); Ohio University, Athens (1951–1952, 1954–1955, 1957, 1965); University of Iowa, Iowa City (1957, 1983); la Escuela Nacional de Artes Plásticas, Mexico City (1963); Weyhe Gallery, New York City (1968); "West '80, '85, and '86: Art and the Law," travelling shows to State Bar Associations and museums throughout the United States; and many others.

Plochmann has garnered numerous awards and honors for almost five decades, such as eight first prizes at Toledo Federation of Art societies between 1942 and 1968; purchase awards at the Butler Institute of American Art (1951); seven Evansville Museum of Arts and Science purchase awards between 1955 and 1967; the West Collection (1985); and others. Plochmann taught at the School of Design, Toledo Museum of Art (1946–1947) and at Southern Illinois University, Carbondale (1949–1950). Her work is represented in private and public permanent collections in the United States, including the University of Iowa, Iowa City; University of Toledo, Ohio; Southern Illinois University Libraries, Carbondale; the collection of Mr. and Mrs. Arthur Magill, Greenville, South Carolina; University of Chicago Libraries Collection, Illinois; and others.

Bibliography

Carolyn Plochmann: A Charmed Vision. Essay by Matthew Daub. Foreword by Otto Wittman. Evansville Museum of Arts and Science, 1990.
Hoving, Thomas. *Connoisseur* (March 1983).
University Portrait: Nine Paintings by Carolyn Plochmann. Foreword by R. Buckminster Fuller. Southern Illinois University Press, 1959.

Pogue, Stephanie Elaine (1944–)

Born in Shelby, North Carolina, the African-American printmaker/educator Stephanie E. Pogue earned a Bachelor of Fine Arts degree from Howard University, Washington, D.C.; received a Master of Fine Arts degree from Cranbrook Academy of Art, Bloomfield Hills, Michigan; and also studied with George Baer, James Porter, and Mavis Pusey.

Pogue has held solo exhibitions of her etchings, monotypes, and other prints in museums and galleries in the United States and abroad, including the Castle Gallery, Hyattsville, Maryland (1989); the City Museum, Arondelovac, previously in Yugoslavia (1985); and others. Her semi-abstract landscapes and figure works have been invited to or included in many major print exhibitions throughout the world, such as "Black Women Artists: North Carolina Connections," North Carolina Central University, Durham (1990); "Black Arts Festival Exhibition," Spelman College, Atlanta, Georgia (1988); "The Art of Black America in Japan: Afro-American Modernism," Tokyo and Chiba—both in Japan (1987); "International Print Exhibit," Taipei City Museum of Fine Arts, Taiwan (1983); "Migraciones: Una Exhibición de Artistas Gráficos Afro-Americanos," El Museo de Arte Moderna la Tertulia, Cali, Colombia (1976); and others.

An award winner and printmaking teacher who is widely-travelled, Pogue recently drew upon both her personal experience and individual essence to create a series of "Self Portraits" (1989) subtitled, "Anxiety," "Discovery," and "Cinnamon Toast"—titles that speak eloquently to all of us. Examples of her work are in private and public permanent collections, including the Arkansas Art Center, Little Rock; Fisk University, Nashville, Tennessee; the Studio Museum in Harlem, New York City; University of North Dakota, Grand Forks; the Whitney Museum of American Art, New York City; and others.

Bibliography

Driskell, David C. "New Works by Stephanie Pogue." *American Literature Forum* 19:1 (Spring 1985).
Hall, Robert L. *Gathered Visions: Selected Works by African American Women Artists.* Anacostia Museum, Smithsonian Institution Press, 1992.
Lewis, Samella, and Bob Biddle. *International Review of African-American Art* 6:4 (1986).

Poitras, Jane Ash (1951–)

Born in Fort Chipewayan, Alberta, Canada, the painter/printmaker Jane Ash Poitras earned a Bachelor of Science degree in microbiology from the University of Alberta, Edmonton (1977). Five years later, after having switched her interests to the arts in the same university, she received a Bachelor of Fine Arts degree in printing; and, in 1985, Poitras obtained her Master of Arts degree in printmaking from Columbia University, New York City.

Poitras has had examples of her work shown in solo and group exhibitions in Canada, the United States, Europe, and Asia, including the Canadiana Galleries, Edmonton, Alberta (1981); "International Independent Exhibition of Prints," Prefectual Gallery, Kanagawa, Japan (1984); "Contemporary American Prints," Brooklyn Museum, New York (1986); Los Angeles Celebration of Canadian Contemporary Native Art," Southwest Museum, Los Angeles, California (1987); "Zeitgenossische Kunst der Indianer und Eskimos in Kanada," Dortmund, Germany, then travelling throughout Canada (1988); Musée des Beaux-Arts, Paris, France (1989); and many others. Her solo shows include the Robert Vanderleelie Gallery (1984, 1985), and the Vik Gallery—both in Edmonton, Alberta (1985, 1987); University of British Columbia, Vancouver (1987); and others.

Winner of many awards for her work, Poitras received the Lady Rodney scholarship (1972); a Graphex purchase award (1978); bursaries from Indian and Northern Affairs, Ottawa, Ontario, Canada (1981–1985); a Syncrude Canada scholarship (1983–1985); the Helen R. Elser scholarship, Columbia University, New York City (1984–1985); and many others. Her work is in the permanent collections of museums and other prestigious institutions in Canada and the United States, including the Alberta Art Foundation, Edmonton; the Brooklyn Museum and Columbia University—both in New York City; the Canada Council Art Bank, Ottawa; the House of Commons, Ottawa, Ontario, Canada; McMichael Art Gallery, Kleinburg, Ontario, Canada; and others.

Bibliography

Buehler, Clint. "The Travels of Jane Ash Poitras." *Visual Arts Newsletter—Alberta Culture* 6:4 (August 1984).
Hanna, Deirdre. "Jane Ash Poitras." *Now Magazine* 8:47 (August 1989).
Matousek, Phylis. "Printmaker Finds Year a Series of High Points." *Edmonton Journal* (August 17, 1985).

Pondick, Rona (1952–)

Born in Brooklyn, New York, the sculptor Rona Pondick earned a Bachelor's degree from Queens College, New York City (1974), and, three years later, received a Master of Fine Arts degree from Yale University, New Haven, Connecticut.

Pondick held a solo exhibition at the Madeleine Carter Gallery, Boston, Massachusetts (1984), and has had her work invited to many group exhibitions, including the Zabriskie Gallery and fiction/nonfiction—both in New York City (1987), among many others.

Winner of honors and awards, Pondick was the recipient of the Fannie B. Pardee prize in sculpture (1987), and a grant from the Ludwig Vogelstein Foundation. Her works are represented in private and public permanent collections. "GTRPSB01386" (1986), a typical monotype of the period, roils across the picture plane in curvilinear energy-laden forms that suggest sexuality.

Bibliography

Brenson, Michael. "Peter Flaccus, Helen Miranda Wilson, and Rona Pondick." *The New York Times* (July 3, 1987): C23.

Cohen, Ronny. "New Abstraction V." *Print Collectors Quarterly* (March–April 1987): 12–14.

Kingsley, April. *Emerging Sculptors 1986*. A Catalog. Sculpture Center, 1986.

Poor, Anne (1918–)

Perhaps the most singular achievement of Anne Poor, primarily known as a landscape painter and muralist, was her assignment as the only woman artist/correspondent in the U.S. armed forces during World War II.

When Poor was seven, her mother, writer Bessie Breuer, married the artist, Henry Varnum Poor, who encouraged Anne's desire to be an artist. Poor studied at the Art Students League, New York City, with Alexander Brook, William Zorach, and Yasuo Kuniyoshi. She spent 1937 in Paris, France, under auspices of Vermont's Bennington College, attending the Académie Julian and the École Fernand Léger and studying painting with Jean Lurçat and Abraham Rattner.

In 1938 Poor began to assist her stepfather with fresco murals. By the early 1940s she had won her own Works Progress Administration (WPA) mural commissions. Poor has since done several other murals and in 1948 won the Edwin Austen Abbey memorial fellowship for mural painting, enabling her to study in Italy and Greece.

Poor enlisted in the Women's Army Corps (WAC) in 1943, becoming a photo-technician, then an official artist/correspondent for the War Artists Unit. She spent a year in the Pacific recording in fluid sketches evacuations of the wounded for the Air Transport Command.

Poor first exhibited in the 1942 "Artists for Victory" show at the New York City's Metropolitan Museum of Art. She had her first solo show in 1943 at the American-British Art Center, New York City. Poor has since had numerous solo and group exhibitions.

Following the war Poor lectured at the Skowhegan School in Maine, staying on to become a faculty member, director, board member, and trustee. Whenever possible she travelled with her sketchbook. A trip to Greece resulted in a charming collaborative book with author Henry Miller.

Poor won first prize in the National Academy Arts Contest in 1944. She has twice won the Benjamin Altman landscape prize from the National Academy of Design in New York City (1971, 1981) and the Academy's Henry War Ranger purchase fund prize in 1972. The National Academy of Arts and Letters awarded Poor their Hassam award in 1972 and 1977. Poor's work is in several U.S. museums and in many public and private collections.

Sylvia Moore

Bibliography

Bearor, Karen A. "Anne Poor." *American Women Artists: The Twentieth Century*. Exhibition Catalog. Tennessee: Knoxville Museum of Art, 1989.

Burchfield, Charles. Exhibition Catalog Essay. American/British Art Center, 1944.

Gussow, Allan. *A Sense of Place: The Artist and the American Land*. Friends of the Earth, 1979.

Moore, Sylvia. "Anne Poor." *Women's Art Journal* (Fall–Winter 1982).

Pootoogook, Napatchie (1938–)

Born at Sako, a traditional Inuit camp on the southwest coast of Baffin Island, Northwest Territories, Canada, Napatchie Pootoogook is the only surviving daughter of one of Inuit art's most important figures, Pitseolak Ashoona. Along with her sculptor brothers, Kiawak and Kaka Ashoona, and her graphic artist sisters-in-law, Mayureak and Sorosiluto Ashoona, Napatchie belongs to a family with a strong artistic identity that has contributed significantly to the reputation of Cape Dorset art and the printmaking studio of the West Baffin Eskimo Co-operative. In the mid-1950s, while living at Kiaktuuq, she married Eegyvudluk Pootoogook (b. 1931), son of the important camp leader, Pootoogook, who has since become one of the main printers in the Cape Dorset studio. Like her mother, Napatchie began drawing in the late 1950s. Since 1960 her work has been included in almost every annual collection of Cape Dorset prints. Napatchie and her husband moved into Cape Dorset in 1965, where they have continued to live, except for a two-year stay in Iqaluit in the early 1970s.

Although much of her early work, such as the print "Eskimo Sea Dreams" (1960), presents a lyrical, dream-like reflection of Inuit beliefs in the spirit world, the main thrust of her prints and drawings since the mid-1970s has been more concerned with recording traditional life, clothing, and local Inuit history. In prints such as "Atchealka's Battle" (1978), "The First Policeman I Saw" (1978), "Nascopie Reef" (1989), and "Whaler's Exchange" (1989), Napatchie uses a vigorous, energetic figurative style to bring to life significant events of the past. Like her sister-in-law, Sorosiluto, Napatchie participated in the acrylic painting/drawing workshops established by the West Baffin Co-operative in 1976. Her interest in landscape and Western notions of spatial composition would seem to grow out of this experience. Most recently Napatchie has been working directly in the lithographic medium and experimenting with life drawing as a preparatory stage toward the print image. For Inuit art, works such as her large (112-by-80-cm.) color lithograph, "My New Accordion" (1989), are a part of a new direction in figurative drawing and scale.

Napatchie is represented in the collections of the National Gallery of Canada, Ottawa; the Canadian Museum of Civilization, Hull/Ottawa; and the Art Gallery of Ontario, Toronto.

Marie Routledge

Bibliography

Barz, Sandra. *Inuit Artists Print Workbook.* New York: Arts and Culture of the North, 1981.

———. *Canadian Inuit Print Artist/Printer Biographies.* New York: Arts and Culture of the North, 1990.

———. *Inuit Artists Print Workbook. Vol. II.* New York: Arts and Culture of the North, 1990.

Cape Dorset, West Baffin Eskimo Co-operative. Catalogs of the Cape Dorset Annual Graphics Collections: 1960–1967, 1970, 1977–1983, 1985, 1989–1991.

Jackson, Marion E. "The Ashoonas of Cape Dorset: In Touch with Tradition." *North/Nord* 29:3 (Fall 1982): 14–18.

Pop Chalee (1906–)

Pop Chalee (Blue Flower), also known as Merina Lujan, is a Native American from the Taos Pueblo in New Mexico. Throughout her career she devoted herself to the flat, two-dimensional, "traditional" style of Indian painting.

In the 1930s Pop Chalee attended The Studio art classes taught by Dorothy Dunn at the Santa Fe Indian School, New Mexico. Under the jurisdiction of the U.S. government's Bureau of Indian Affairs, The Studio was the first school of its kind to encourage Native American artists. It was during this period, Pop Chalee explained, that the school was visited by Walt Disney, who offered jobs in his California studio to some of the art students. It was also during this visit that he was inspired to create his well-known Bambi character for the motion pictures.

From the start of her attendance in Dunn's classes, Pop Chalee shone in the forefront. With a market ready for her paintings in Santa Fe, she established her own studio there, following graduation in 1937. Two years later she was commissioned—along with the now-legendary Native American artists Awa Tsireh, Joe H. Herrera, Pablita Velarde, Harrison Begay, and Popovi Da—to do murals at Maisel's Trading Post in Albuquerque, New Mexico. The idea to use Native American artists had been suggested to the building's architect by Santa Fe muralist Olive Rush. Each artist—except Pop Chalee—chose to depict traditional tribal subjects. She chose, instead, to paint an imaginary forest scene. Later she developed variations of this scene in smaller, easel-size paintings.

Pop Chalee's smaller paintings were often done on black French paper, with opaque watercolor (only occasionally with casein paints), in a full range of colors which have become her own unique color combinations. Without exception her forest scenes contain trees, each totally inventive species and colors. With deer as the central figures, the remainder of the scene contains pairs—or families—of birds, rabbits, squirrels, skunks, and bears. Tiny flowers—also in pairs—in a wide range of colors are sprinkled throughout. Though all design elements of the forests are carefully placed to suggest foregrounds and backgrounds, there are no true ground lines.

Pop Chalee's forest scenes are reminiscent of the painting techniques used in East India—the native home of her mother. While reflecting on the source of her inspiration for these particular scenes, the artist maintained that it was the Taos mountains and animals—the same ones that play a major role in her native Pueblo religion. One of her atypical easel-sized paintings of a forest scene, "The Enchanted Forest," was included (in color) in the catalog for "Night of the First Americans" exhibition, held in 1982 at the John F. Kennedy Center for the Performing Arts, Washington, D.C.

Pop Chalee did two murals for Hinkel's Santa Fe department store in 1943. Later, before the building was destroyed, the seven-by-ten-foot forest scene was removed for installation at the Santa Fe Indian School. The five-by-five-foot buffalo hunt scene was taken to the University of New Mexico, Albuquerque. Another large mural was commissioned by the Santa Fe Railroad depicting Zuni Pueblo ceremonial figures called *Shalakos.* It has now been installed at the Millicent Rogers Museum in Taos, New Mexico.

In the 1940s Pop Chalee was commissioned to paint twelve murals for the Albuquerque Airport Terminal building. The murals remained there until major construction was begun on expansion of the airport's facilities. They then were removed and placed in storage for the next two decades. In 1989–1990 they were taken from storage to undergo extensive conservation, under the artist's supervision. In 1990 the murals were hung in specially constructed, individually lighted areas, of the new Albuquerque International Airport's second-level Great Hall.

Pop Chalee is known, too, for her paintings of a mythological horse. Based on a Taos Pueblo myth, each high-stepping animal is magnificently Arabian-like. With head and neck held proudly erect, it appears even more theatrical through the effect of non-traditional colors applied to tinted paper. Without exception the exaggerated mane and tail are dramatically presented by flowing white hair which begins in a mass on the body and ends in finite strands that encompass a large area of the overall design. Two other well-known Indian painters, Woody Crumbo and Percy Sandy, also painted the same myth, with a central horse not dissimilar to Pop Chalee's design.

Pop Chalee was born in Utah and spent most of her life away from her father's pueblo of Taos. During the 1940s, she told Indian legends and talked about Indian art on a radio program aired from Phoenix, Arizona.

In 1960 one of Pop Chalee's paintings was selected by Oscar B. Jacobson, art professor at the University of Oklahoma and known for his work with Kiowa Indian painters, to be included in *American Indian Painters,* a portfolio that is eagerly sought by collectors of Native American art.

In the 1950s Pop Chalee and her Navajo husband, Edward Lee (Ntay), operated an art and ornamental iron works business in Scottsdale, Arizona. During this period she and her husband also toured twenty-one cities in the United States to promote the motion picture, *Annie Get Your Gun.* The barely five-foot-tall painter was a colorful promoter, dressed in a white, Pueblo-style dress which was complemented with elaborate silver and turquoise jewelry. Her dark hair, dramatically parted in the middle, was worn in braids which fell almost to her waist.

With a long and distinguished career of exhibiting her paintings, Pop Chalee's work was shown at the First Annual Indian Exposition and Congress (1937), and at the Annual American Indian Week (1938) in Tulsa, Oklahoma. Other showings include the Contemporary American Indian Painting Exhibition at the National Gallery of Art (1953), and at the 2nd Annual Invitational Exhibition of American Indian Paintings at the U.S. Department of the Interior (1965)—both in Washington, D.C.; Southwest Museum, Los Angeles, California; Elliott O'Hara School, Biddeford, Maine; Russell Sage Foundation, Gallery of Living

Artists, New York City; Heard Museum, and Fred Wilson Gallery, Phoenix, Arizona; Buck Saunders Gallery, Scottsdale, Arizona; and numerous showings at the Annual Inter-Tribal Indian Ceremonials, Gallup, New Mexico. She rarely entered competitions, but she did receive the Grand award at Gallup in 1938. In 1970 Pop Chalee shared the spotlight with Patrick Swazo Hinds, a progressive painter from Tesuque Pueblo, at the Heard Museum in Phoenix, Arizona.

Pop Chalee is represented in many public collections, including the Thomas Gilcrease Institute of American History and Art, Tulsa, Oklahoma; Heard Museum, Phoenix, Arizona; Museum of Northern Arizona's Katherine Harvey Collection, Flagstaff; Museum of New Mexico, Santa Fe; Stanford University, California; and others.

Jeanne O. Snodgrass King

Bibliography
Dunn, Dorothy. *American Indian Painting of the Southwest and Plains Areas.* University of Mexico Press, 1968, pp. 319–20.
Silbermann, Arthur. *100 Years of Native American Painting.* Oklahoma Museum of Art, 1978, p. 48.
Snodgrass, Jeanne O. *American Indian Painters. A Biographical Directory.* Museum of the American Indian, Heye Foundation, 1968, pp. 148–49.
Tanner, Clara Lee. "Contemporary Indian Art." *Arizona Highways* 26 (February 1950): 22–29.
———. "Southwest Indian Painting." *University of Arizona Press & Arizona Silhouettes* (1957): 80–81.
Wilson, Maggie. "Darling of the Resort Owners, Pet of the Art Collectors Back in Town." *The Arizona Republic* (February 22, 1970): 2M.

Popescu, Beaty (1954–)

Beaty Popescu was born in Montréal, Québec, Canada, but because her parents moved to Germany when she was in her teens, she completed her high school education in West Germany, then studied biology for one year at Heidelberg University before entering the National Academy of Fine Arts in Stuttgart. After two years at the National Academy of Fine Arts (1975–1977), Popescu returned to Canada and completed her Bachelor of Fine Arts degree at York University, Toronto, in 1981. A fine arts scholarship enabled her to work in an independent program at the Banff School of Fine Arts, Alberta (1981–1982), and she also began showing in group exhibitions: Chroma Zone Gallery, Toronto, and Open Space Gallery, Victoria—both in 1982. By the time Popescu registered in the Master of Fine Arts program at the Nova Scotia College of Art and Design (1983), she had begun her career as an artist. She graduated from the Nova Scotia College of Art and Design in 1985 and currently teaches in the department of visual arts at Memorial University, Newfoundland.

Popescu has an impressive list of exhibitions, but her most interesting contribution to date was for "The Embodied Viewer" (Glenbow Art Museum, Calgary, 1991). Her installation of objects and drawings, "Emergence-Drawings" and "Emergence-Objects" clearly shows her Jungian interest in a holistic relationship between mind and body. In an exhibition that itself focused on the exchange and interaction between viewer and artwork, Popescu emphasized art as a reminder of our "bodiness" in a technologically-oriented world that tends to make our minds "top-heavy." Her concern is for a centeredness that might emerge from an aware unification of the material and the spiritual. Her

work "emerges" as organic gouache drawings from black grounds or as natural objects (feathers, bones, etc.) peeking out from inside sculpted shapes made from layered paper (often pages torn from atlases). Her representations are often informed by her dreams and her sensations—particularly those obtained in nature, for example, walking on a beach, listening to the waves and the birds—and they interact with a viewer at that level as well: at a level that goes beyond the rational conscious mind and suggests to us that we communicate with our own deeper selves.

Janice Helland

Bibliography
The Embodied Viewer. Calgary: Glenbow Art Gallery, 1991.
O'Neill, Colleen. *Emergence.* Memorial University of Newfoundland, 1991.

Porter, Katherine (1941–)

The Iowa-born expressionist painter of abstract political and moral landscapes, Katherine Porter studied at Colorado College, Colorado Springs (1959–1961), and earned a Bachelor's degree from Boston University, Massachusetts (1963).

Porter has held many solo exhibitions in museums and galleries across the United States, including "Katherine Porter: Works on Paper 1969–1979," Museum of Fine Arts, San Francisco, California (1980); "Drawings," Dartmouth College, Hanover, New Hampshire (1981); Arts Club of Chicago, Illinois (1983); "Retrospective," Brandeis University, Waltham, Massachusetts (1985); "Katherine Porter," David McKee (1985); "Katherine Porter," Sidney Janis Gallery, New York City (1987); and others. Her work has been invited to many prestigious group exhibitions, such as the "Biennials" of the Whitney Museum of American Art, New York City (1976, 1981); and others.

Winner of honors and awards, Porter received a fellowship from the National Endowment for the Arts (NEA) (1972); an honorary Doctorate from Colby College, Waterville, Maine (1984); and others. Examples of her paintings are in private and public permanent collections, including the Fogg Art Museum., Harvard University, Cambridge, Massachusetts; High Museum, Atlanta, Georgia; the Guggenheim Museum, the Whitney Museum of American Art, and the Museum of Modern Art (MoMA)—all in New York City; and others.

Bibliography
Edelman, Robert G. "Katherine Porter at Sidney Janis." *Art in America* 75:3 (March 1987): 135.
Krantz, Les, ed. *The New York Art Review.* Macmillan, 1982.
Russell, John. "Juicy Abstractions by Katherine Porter." *The New York Times* (February 27, 1981).
Wadsworth, Susan M. "Political and Moral Landscapes: The Paintings of Katherine Porter." *Arts Magazine* 62:1 (September 1987): 84–87.

Porter, Liliana (1941–)

Born in Buenos Aires, Argentina, Liliana Porter studied printmaking at the Ibero-American University and at the Institute of Applied Arts—both in Mexico City, Mexico. Her first solo exhibition occurred in 1959 at the now-defunct Galería Proteo in Mexico City. In these intervening years Porter has had many solo exhibitions in Mexico, Argentina, Canada, the United States, and Uruguay.

Porter has had her work accepted in group exhibitions in Tokyo,

Japan; Mexico City, Mexico; New York City; Buenos Aires, Argentina; and Switzerland, to name but a clutch of shows. She has been associated with the Pratt Graphic Art Center in New York City as an advanced student and as cofounder and director of the New York Graphic Workshop.

Porter's work is in many major collections in Mexico and abroad, including the Museum of Modern Art (MoMA) in New York City; the University of Texas at Austin; the Museum of Modern Art in Caracas, Venezuela; and the Stedelijk Museum in Amsterdam, the Netherlands. She has had many shows at the Galería Pecanins in Mexico City, Mexico.

A pictorial illusionist, Porter creates collage drawings, screen prints, and intaglios that provide a wry combination of visual delights; real and painted shadows, real and printed three-dimensional objects, fragments of photos and picture postcards, pencil and crayon lines drawn on gallery walls leading the viewer into her exhibitions, images of apples, toy figurines, open books—all are unified, magically, to provide a fresh look at some very old ideas.

Bibliography

Collins, James. "Liliana Porter, Hundred Acres Gallery." *Artforum* 12:6 (February 1974): 74–75.
Frank, Peter. "Reviews." *Art News* 72:4 (April 1973): 73.
Heartney, Eleanor. "Liliana Porter." *Arts Magazine* 59:3 (November 1984): 36.
The Texas Quarterly: Image of Mexico II. The University of Texas, Winter 1969.

Pratt, Elspeth (1953–)

Elspeth Pratt became known in the mid-1980s as a Canadian sculptor in the bricolage mode (found materials assemblage) favored by other Vancouver-area artists such as Mowry Baden, Roland Brener, and Lynda Gammon.

Pratt studied political science and painting at several Canadian universities before obtaining a Master of Fine Arts degree from the University of British Columbia (1984). The following year she had a solo exhibition at the Contemporary Art Gallery in Vancouver. In 1986 her sculpture was included in "Broken Muse," a major group exhibition organized by the Vancouver Art Gallery to acknowledge local postmodernist artmaking. The latter exhibition established the critical context for her work, which tends to deconstruct the modernist values embodied in concepts of technological progress, standardization, and transcendence.

Pratt builds her work from commonly-used materials such as doorskin, cardboard, standard cuts of lumber, and wire mesh. The work is paradoxically fragile in structure. "That Was Then This Is Now" (1986) typically compounds the formal indeterminacy of her practice by depending equally on wall and floor for support. The sculpture's abstractness and casually dispersed assembly are reminiscent of American post-minimalist practice. Later works depart from this precedent, using appropriated titled and photographic components to bind the reductive modernist vocabulary to sophisticated notions of intertextuality.

Exhibited with the work of Bernie Miller and Robert McNealy in 1990, Pratt's "From Here to Eternity" (1990) proposed a feminist rereading of two familiar narratives; the mass-cultural myth concerning "how the West was won," and Clement Greenberg's prophesy that "it is for a self-sufficiency like sculpture's, and sculpture's alone, that both painting and architecture now strive" (1958). "From Here to Eternity" achieves these effects by opposing fully exposed, makeshift construc-

tion to a subject matter suggesting nineteenth-century railway technology. It mimics constructivist sculpture but incorporates representational elements. In this way the sculpture subverts its presumed (because abstract) autonomy as an art object while implying the decay of modernist culture.

Ingrid Jenkner

Bibliography

Jenkner, Ingrid, and Greg Bellerby. *Material Remains*. Exhibition Catalog. Vancouver: Charles H. Scott Gallery, 1991.
Linsley, Robert. *Architettura: Astrazione*. Exhibition Catalog. Rome: Sala 1, 1989.
Pakasaar, Helga, and Keith Wallace. *Broken Muse*. Exhibition Catalog. Vancouver: Vancouver Art Gallery, 1986.

Pratt, Mary (West) (1935–)

Born in Fredericton, New Brunswick, Canada, and educated in art from the age of six, Mary (West) Pratt was only eleven when she first exhibited in an international show of children's art in the Luxembourg in Paris, France. Between 1950 and 1953 she was studying on an occasional basis with Canadian luminaries as varied as Fritz Brandtner and Lawren Harris, both of whom advocated abstraction. But it was the regional interests of the Maritime provinces and Alex Colville's cool realism that would have the decisive influence on both Pratt and her husband, painter Christopher Pratt, with whom she worked on set decorations in 1955, and married two years later. Immediately after their marriage, the Pratts left for Glasgow, Scotland, where Christopher entered the School of Fine Arts. After a brief itinerant period the couple settled in Sackville, New Brunswick, where both registered at the Mount Allison School of Fine Arts in the Bachelor of Fine Arts program. They both graduated in 1961, teaching on an occasional basis.

In 1962 Pratt began to "paint in a corner of the dining-room," as she would put it (in characteristically self-effacing terms). Around 1964 she read Betty Friedan's *The Feminine Mystique*, but she opted for the time being to let her husband's needs determine the course of events. Washing the floor in the bedroom one day in 1968, however, she found herself fascinated by evanescent effects of light on the transient facets of rumpled bedsheets. About a year later, Pratt's husband noted that photographs would help her fix such passing moments, so she could paint them later at leisure. With this, the future course of her work was secured, for it would consist largely of brilliantly photographic transcriptions of humble, everyday scenes of domestic life. Most of these are oil on canvas, but the results vary from the limpidity of watercolor to a nearly hallucinatory translucency that rivals Jan Vermeer.

Pratt's subjects are often oriented toward traditionally female domestic tasks, such as food preparation, and frequently include everyday items such as eggs in a basket, preserves on a shelf, split cod fillets, or turkey wrapped in astonishingly convincing tin foil. The statements that accompany the paintings are equally unpretentious: "These preserves were a gift from a friend," or "This speaks about the pleasures of a young woman's involvement with cosmetics." On occasion, however, Pratt has entered into unfamiliar territory, more realistic than Colville's but similarly disquieting in its strange serenity. An example is her "Service Station" (1978), which shows in brutal detail a portion of a slaughtered moose carcass hanging from the back of a tow-truck, almost in a parody of Rembrandt's famous slaughtered ox. But her intentions were regional: "Images like this are fairly common in rural Canada . . . . [The man who killed it] had no idea that I would be upset by this moose. But it screamed 'murder, rape, clinical dissection, torture,' all the terrible nightmares hanging right in front of me. I couldn't understand why he hadn't thought of all that."

Pratt's first solo show was mounted at the Memorial University Art Gallery, St. John's, Newfoundland, and it was followed by such a string of virtuoso performances that a partial retrospective was mounted and circulated in the Maritimes in 1973, while a more thorough survey was organized in 1981 by the London Regional Art Gallery in Ontario. Her fame has grown since then in leaps and bounds, helped by a renewed interest in photo-realist painting in general and by her inclusion in an exhibition of 1975 called "Some Canadian Women Artists," assembled by the National Gallery of Canada, Ottawa. Among the manifestations of her fame are a documentary produced by the Canadian Broadcasting Corporation and requests for book illustrations. She shows principally in Toronto, Calgary, and Vancouver, but she continues to live and work in the Maritimes, part of the year in a converted cottage-studio in Salmonier, in rural Newfoundland.

Robert J. Belton

Bibliography
Gwyn, Sandra, and Gerta Moray. *Mary Pratt*. Toronto: McGraw-Hill Ryerson, 1989.

Prellwitz, Edith Mitchell (1865–1944)

Born in South Orange, New Jersey, the painter Edith Mitchell Prellwitz learned her craft at the Art Students League, New York City, and took further work at the Académie Julian, Paris, France, with William Adolphe Bouguereau, Gustave Courtois, and Tony Robert-Fleury.

Winner of honors and awards, Prellwitz exhibited work in museums and galleries in the United States and abroad, including the Salon des Beaux-Arts, Paris, France; National Academy of Design, New York City (1894, 1929); the Atlanta Exposition, Georgia (1895); Pratt Institute, Brooklyn, New York (1899); Pan-American Exposition, Buffalo, New York (1901); and others. Her work is represented in private and public permanent collections, including a mural she painted for the Universalist Church in Southold, New York.

Bibliography
American Art Annual. Vol. 1. Macmillan, 1899.
A Circle of Friends: Art Colonies of Cornish and Dublin. University of New Hampshire, 1985.
Obituary. *Who's Who in American Art.* Vol. 4. American Federation of Arts, 1947.

Premio Real, Alexandrine de (1920–)

Born in Paris, France, Alexandrine de Premio Real has lived in Mexico since 1951. She studied at la Escuela de Pintura y Escultura (La Esmeralda), Mexico City, Mexico, and at the Académie Julien in Paris, France, where she had her first solo show in 1948.

Premio's work, "Mercado Mexicano," is in the permanent collection of the Museum of Tel Aviv, Israel, and "Espacio de Golondrinas" may be seen in the Club de Industriales of Mexico City. She works in enamels, monotypes, oils, and watercolor.

Bibliography
Alvarez, José Rogelio, et al. *Enciclopedia de Mexico.* Secretaría de Educación Pública, 1987.

Price, M. Elizabeth (1875–1960)

Born in Martinsburg, West Virginia, the painter M. Elizabeth Price studied at the Pennsylvania Museum and School of Industrial Art and the Pennsylvania Academy of Fine Arts, Philadelphia.

Price was a member of many art associations, including the Allied Artists of America, the Art Alliance of Philadelphia, American Artists Professional League, American Woman's Association, the Fine Arts Society of Arkansas, the Pennsylvania Academy of Fine Arts fellowship, and the National Association of Women Painters and Sculptors. Her work was exhibited in many venues, including the "Fiftieth Anniversary Exhibition 1889–1939: National Association of Women Painters and Sculptors," American Fine Arts Building, New York City (1939), and is represented in private and public permanent collections.

Bibliography
American Art Annual. Vol. 28. American Federation of Arts, 1932.
American Watercolors and Drawings, Philadelphia Collection XI. Frank S. Schwarz and Son, 1981.
Who's Who in American Art. Vol. 8. American Federation of Arts, 1962.

Prophet, Nancy Elizabeth (1890–1960)

Born in Warwick, Rhode Island, the African-American sculptor Nancy Elizabeth Prophet studied at l'École des Beaux-Arts, Paris, France; the Rhode Island School of Design, Providence; and taught at Spelman College and Atlanta University—both in Atlanta, Georgia.

Prophet held exhibitions of her figurative, expressive, three-dimensional sculpture in wood at the Harmon Foundation (1930); and the Whitney Museum of American Art (1935, 1937)—both in New York City; and elsewhere. She is the winner of the Otto H. Kahn prize (1929) and the Greenough prize at the Newport Art Association (1932). Representative examples of her work are in private and public permanent collections, including the Rhode Island School of Design, Providence, and the Whitney Museum of American Art, New York City.

Bibliography
Cederholm, Theresa. *Afro-American Artists: A Bio-Bibliographical Directory.* Boston Public Library, 1973.
Hedgepeth, Chester M. *Twentieth Century African-American Writers and Artists.* American Library Association, 1991.
Locke, Alain. "The American Negro as Artist." *American Magazine of Art* 23:3 (September 1931): 211–20.
Spradling, Mary. *In Black and White.* Vol. 1. Gale, 1980.

Pudlat, Mary (1923–)

A prolific Canadian Inuit artist, Mary Pudlat retains clear memories of her early years living in the traditional Inuit hunting lifestyle in the area near Povungnituk in Arctic Québec. Orphaned as a teenager, she lived for a while with her brother in Ivujivik before moving to Baffin Island in the early-1940s. There she married Samuelie Pudlat in 1943 and continued to live in the traditional semi-nomadic camps along the south shore of Baffin Island until she and her husband and children moved permanently to Cape Dorset in 1963.

At the time of Pudlat's arrival in Cape Dorset the new West Baffin Eskimo Co-operative fine arts program was gaining momentum, and she began to explore her own talent for sculpting in soapstone and for drawing. Pudlat's artwork, tentative at first, became increasingly confident. Like many other Inuit artists she turned to her experience on the land for inspiration, carving and drawing birds, fish, human figures, and activities from the traditional culture. The selection of one of Pudlat's images of a bear for inclusion in the 1964–1965 Cape Dorset print collection gave her initial encouragement, but the demands of her young family and custodial work that she occasionally performed for the Co-operative left her limited time for her art in the years that followed. After her husband's death in 1979, however, and with her children becoming more independent, Pudlat returned to drawing during the 1980s. Pudlat's images have served as the basis for thirty-four Cape Dorset prints; her work is included in the annual collections for 1964–1966, 1979–1980, and 1984–1990. In addition Pudlat's work has been included in a number of museum exhibitions, including "Inoonoot Eskima: Grafick och Skulptur fran Cape Dorset och Povungnituk," shown at Stockholm, Sweden, in 1967, and "The Last and First Eskimos" in Fort Worth, Texas, in 1984. Examples of Pudlat's art are also included in significant public art collections, including the Metropolitan Museum of Art, New York City; Canadian Museum of Civilization, Ottawa; Royal Ontario Museum, Toronto; Macdonald Stewart Art Centre, Guelph, Ontario; Simon Fraser University Gallery, Burnaby, British Columbia; and the London Regional Art Gallery, London, Ontario.

Marion E. Jackson

Bibliography

Cape Dorset Annual Print Collection Catalogs: 1964–1966, 1979–1980, 1984–1990.

Queens Museum. *Eskimo Art.* New York: Queens Museum, 1974.

Pugh, Sarah Mabel (1891–1986)

Born in Morrisville, North Carolina, the painter/printmaker Sarah Mabel Pugh graduated from the Peace Institute (1913), where she studied under Ruth Huntington Moore. She attended classes in life drawing and illustration at the Art Students League, New York City; won a four-year scholarship to the Pennsylvania Academy of Fine Arts, Philadelphia; and was a recipient of the Cresson traveling scholarship, which allowed her to tour and study in Europe.

Pugh worked as an illustrator for several book publishers and magazines in New York City (1926–1936), then returned to a full-time job as a teacher and head of the art department at Peace Institute until 1960. She was author and illustrator of a children's book, *Little Carolina Bluebonnet* (1933).

Pugh exhibited work locally, regionally, and nationally, including venues as disparate as the Brooklyn Museum, the National Academy of Design, National Association of Women Artists and the New York World's Fair (1939)—all in New York City; and the Southern States Art League. Her most successful mediums in printmaking were relief prints and lithographs, though she also pulled monotypes and painted portraits. "Sarah's Piano" (c. 1925), a technically-proficient and convincing woodcut, won a prize at the 10th Exhibition of the Southern States Art League. Many of her works are represented in the North Carolina Museum of Art at Raleigh and elsewhere.

Bibliography

Archives of American Art. *A Checklist of the Collection.* Smithsonian Institution, 1975.

Mahony, Bertha E., and Elinor Whitney. *Contemporary Illustrators of Children's Books.* Women's Educational and Industrial Union, 1930.

Nine From North Carolina. A Catalog. Essay by Caroline Hickman. North Carolina State Committee and the National Museum of Women in the Arts, 1989.

Pukingrnak, Nancy (1940–)

Nancy Pukingrnak was born in the Chantrey Inlet area of the Keewatin region of the Northwest Territories. As a young child she led a traditional nomadic existence at the inlet and along the banks of the Back River, living in igloos in the winter and tents in the summer and subsisting on a diet of caribou and fish. She was brought to the nearby settlement of Baker Lake in the spring of 1958 following a difficult winter marked by a severe shortage of land foods in the Back River area. In a dramatic rescue by the Canadian armed forces, a starving Pukingrnak and her mother, Jessie Oonark, were airlifted to safety. Pukingrnak settled permanently in Baker Lake and married shortly thereafter. She has given birth to eleven children, seven of whom are still living.

With encouragement from her mother, who went on to become one of Canada's most successful artists, and her sister, Victoria Mamnguqsualuk—both enthusiastically involved in the arts and crafts program initiated at Baker Lake by the Federal government in the early 1960s—Pukingrnak started carving in 1962 and did her first drawings in 1969. Pukingrnak's other siblings, Josiah Nuilaalik, Janet Kigusiuq, Mary Yuusipik, Miriam Nanurluk, and William Noah, also became established, successful artists in their own right.

Pukingrnak has forged an equally successful name for herself in the field of Inuit art. She is best known for her drawings and sculpture but also works in fabric. Her grandmother's stories of bygone days and Inuit mythology as well as her own childhood memories serve as an endless source of inspiration. Three recurrent themes dominate Pukingrnak's work—intimate domestic scenes of life on the land, lively depictions of "Qiviuq," the legendary Inuit hero, and graphic portrayals of "Qavaq," the mythological multi-headed creature with clawed hands and feet and a tail who preys on human beings.

In her art making, Pukingrnak combines old skills with new ones. She is intimately familiar with the traditional life of the Inuit and is herself a meticulous sewer of caribou skin clothing. Yet exposure to books, magazines, and television over the past thirty years has had a profound influence on her view of the world. Pukingrnak's incorporation of Western conventions of spatial perspective distinguishes her art from that of older Inuit artists who draw without reference to space.

Pukingrnak's work was first exhibited in 1974 at a showing of Baker Lake sculpture mounted by the Canadian Guild of Crafts in Montréal. Her artistic talent surfaced at a time when Inuit art was receiving widespread recognition as a new and exciting art form. Pukingrnak quickly earned recognition for her unique artistic ability. In 1976 the Upstairs Gallery, Winnipeg, mounted a solo exhibition of her drawings and sculpture. In 1978 her drawings were featured in a two-person show shared with Baker Lake artist Simon Tookoome. That same year her works appeared in three group exhibitions held throughout Canada.

Pukingrnak's drawings and sculpture have since appeared in thirteen additional group exhibitions, two of which toured internationally to Chicago, Illinois, and Denmark in 1983 and 1984, respectively. Pukingrnak first contributed a drawing to the Baker Lake Annual Print Collection in 1982; her drawings were again selected for the 1983–1984, 1986, and 1987 collections. Her print, "Rescued from Two-Faced Monsters" (1986–23), was reproduced on the cover of the 1986 Baker Lake Print Collection catalog. In January 1989 Pukingrnak and her sister, Janet Kigusiuq, were guests of honor when the exhibition, "Contemporary Inuit Drawings," mounted in 1987 by the Macdonald Stewart Art Centre, opened at the National Gallery of Canada.

Pukingrnak's work can be found in the permanent collections of the Canadian Museum of Civilization and the Department of Indian Affairs and Northern Development—both in Ottawa; the Winnipeg Art Gallery; the Macdonald Stewart Art Centre, Guelph and the Art Gallery of Ontario, Toronto—both in Ontario.

Marie Bouchard

Bibliography
Blodgett, Jean. *The Coming and Going of the Shaman: Eskimo Shamanism and Art.* Winnipeg Art Gallery, 1979.
———. *Grasp Tight the Old Ways: Selections from the Klamer Family Collection of Inuit Art.* Toronto: Art Gallery of Ontario, 1983.
Bouchard, Marie. "Making Art in Baker Lake." *Inuit Art Quarterly* 4:3 (Summer 1989): 6–9.
Driscoll, Bernadette. *Inuit Myths, Legends and Songs.* Winnipeg Art Gallery, 1982.
Jackson, Marion E. *Contemporary Inuit Drawings.* Guelph: Macdonald Stewart Art Centre, 1987.
Macduff, Alistair, and George M. Galpin. *Lords of the Stone.* Vancouver: Whitecap Books, 1982.

Purcell, Ann (1941–)

Born in Arlington, Virginia, Ann Purcell earned a Bachelor's degree in painting from the Corcoran School of Art and George Washington University—both in Washington, D.C. (1973), after independent study in Mexico (1969–1971). She also did graduate work at New York University, , where she received a Master of Arts degree in liberal studies (1989).

Purcell has held solo exhibitions in galleries, including the Villa Roma Gallery, San Miguel de Allende, Mexico (1971); Pyramid Galleries, Washington, D.C. (1978); Tibor de Nagy Gallery, New York City (1978, 1980); Osuna Gallery, Washington, D.C. (1981, 1983, 1987); Philip Dash Gallery, New York City (1986, 1987); and others. Her work has been invited to many group exhibitions in the United States and abroad, such as the Misrachi Gallery, Mexico City, Mexico (1971); "Five Washington Artists," Corcoran Gallery of Art, Washington, D.C. (1976); United States Information Agency (USIA), a travelling exhibit to American embassies in the Middle East (1974–1976); "Washington Painters," Rutgers University, New Brunswick, New Jersey (1976); "New York Collection: '78–'79," Albright-Knox Art Gallery, Buffalo, New York (1978–1979); James Madison University, Harrisonburg, Virginia (1982); Hokin/ Kaufman Gallery, Chicago, Illinois (1983); "Center for the Book Arts Exhibit" and "Primal Forces," the Cooper Union, New York City (1989, 1990); Franz Bader Gallery, Washington, D.C. (1990); "Collage," Osuna Gallery (1990); "Beauty and Eloquence," Art in Embassies Program, Kathmandu, Nepal (1992); "Spare Parts," Organization of Independent Artists, Marine Midland Bank, New York City (1992–1993); and others.

Winner of awards and honors for her abstract expressionist paint-

ings, Purcell was the recipient of a Pollack-Krasner Foundation grant (1989); a Lester Hereward Cooke foundation grant for mid-career achievement in painting (1988); and a fellowship at the MacDowell Art Colony, Peterborough, New Hampshire (1975). She has been a guest lecturer at Indiana State University, Terre Haute (1983); the National Museum of American Art, Washington, D.C. (1988), and Long Island University, New York (1989); and has taught at the Corcoran School of Art, and the Smithsonian Institution (1974–1979)—both in Washington, D.C.; and at Parsons School of Design, New York City (1983–1985).

Purcell's work is represented in private, public, and corporate permanent collections, including the Phillips Collection, the Corcoran Gallery of Art, and Embassy of Italy, Washington, D.C.—all in Washington, D.C.; Santa Barbara Museum, California; New Orleans Museum of Art, Louisiana; Virginia Museum of Fine Arts, Richmond; Salt Lake City Museum, Utah; Pepsico Collection, New York; AT&T; Embassy of Sweden, Stockholm; and others.

Bibliography
Cameron, Dan. "Ann Purcell." *Arts Magazine* (November 1983).
Forgey, Benjamin. "A Virtuoso Talent Finds a Firm Footing." *The Washington Star* (January 18, 1981).
Livingston, Jane. *Five Washington Artists.* Garamond Press, 1976.
Who's Who in American Art. 19th ed. R.R. Bowker Co., 1991–1992.

Putnam, Brenda (1890–1975)

Born in Minnesota, the sculptor Brenda Putnam as a teenager studied at the Boston Museum School of Art, Massachusetts (1905–1907); the Art Students League, New York City; and the Corcoran School of Art, Washington, D.C. She also studied with J.E. Fraser, Charles Grafly, and Bela Pratt.

Winner of many awards and honors, Putnam was a member of several arts organizations, including the National Sculpture Society, the National Arts Club of New York, National Association of Women Painters and Sculptors, and the Grand Central Art Galleries—all in New York City. Her first stylistic prize-winning phase (1910–c. 1925), consisted of representational portraits, cherubs, and animals for garden fountains and sundials. Displeased with her work, Putnam travelled to Florence, Italy, and, in time, found a new approach in the work and ideas of Alexander Archipenko.

Putnam exhibited work in galleries and museums, including in New York City "Small Bronzes by Great Sculptors as Prizes," Grand Central Galleries (1926); "Contemporary American Sculpture," National Sculpture Society, and the California Palace of the Legion of Honor (1929); the 40th, 45th, and 46th Annual Exhibitions of the National Association of Women Painters and Sculptors (1931, 1936, 1937); and many others. Examples of her work are in private and public permanent collections, including the Corcoran Gallery of Art, the Folger Shakespeare Memorial Library, and the U.S. Capitol building—all in Washington, D.C.; Brookgreen Gardens, South Carolina; Dallas Museum of Art, Texas; and others.

Bibliography
Art in the United States Capitol. U.S. Government Printing Office, 1976.
Dunford, Penny. *Biographical Dictionary of Women Artists in Europe and America since 1850.* University of Pennsylvania Press, 1989.
Obituary. *The New York Times* (November 2, 1975): 67.
Putnam, Brenda. *The Sculptor's Way.* Farrar and Rinehart, 1939.

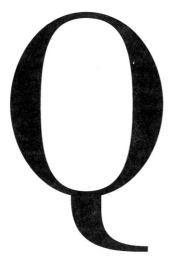

Qaulluaryuk, Ruth (1932–)

Both a draftsperson and a textile artist, Ruth Qaulluaryuk is best known for her lyrical depictions of the Arctic, particularly its abundant wildlife, dense, colorful vegetation, and virgin spaces. Qaulluaryuk has no formal training as an artist, but, like many Inuit women of her generation, she had adapted her traditional sewing skills and aesthetic sensibilities to the making of wall-hangings and drawings.

Born and raised in the remote Back River area of the Keewatin region of the Northwest Territories, Canada, Qaulluaryuk lived a traditional nomadic existence until the late 1950s, when a severe shortage of land foods led to starvation among the Inuit in the Central Arctic. Qaulluaryuk and her family reluctantly moved to the nearby settlement of Baker Lake in the early 1970s to find relief from the hardships of camp life and to enable the children to go to school. Hers was one of the last families to do so.

In order to contribute to the family income Qaulluaryuk turned her hand to sewing clothing and craft items for sale to the newly established Arts and Crafts program operated by the federal government. Her artistic career was launched in 1974 when two of her wall-hangings appeared in the "Crafts from Arctic Canada" exhibition sponsored by the Canadian Eskimo Arts Council. That same year Qaulluaryuk's drawing "Tundra with River" (1974) was selected for the 4th edition of the Baker Lake Annual Print Collection. "Hundreds and Hundreds, Herds of Caribou" (1975), printed in the following year's collection, firmly established Qaulluaryuk's reputation as an artist.

She has since contributed three additional drawings to the annual print collections, and her drawings, prints, and wall-hangings have been featured in twenty group exhibitions held in Canada and the United States. Her works are in the permanent collections of the National Gallery of Canada, Ottawa; the Canadian Museum of Civilization, Ottawa; the Macdonald Stewart Art Centre, Guelph, Ontario; the Winnipeg Art Gallery; the Prince of Wales Northern Heritage Centre, Yellowknife; and the Simon Fraser Gallery, Simon Fraser University, Burnaby.

Qaulluaryuk is the daughter of Baker Lake artist Luke Anguhadluq. Her husband, Josiah Nuilaalik, is also an artist in Baker Lake. They have seven children and numerous grandchildren.

Marie Bouchard

Bibliography

Canadian Eskimo Arts Council. *Crafts From Arctic Canada*. Toronto: Herzig-Somerville Ltd., 1974.

Department of Indian and Northern Affairs. *Chisel and Brush/Le Ciseau et la Brosse*. Ottawa: Department of Indian Affairs and Northern Development, 1984.

Gillmor, Alison. "Uumajut: Animal Imagery in Inuit Art." *Arts Manitoba* 4:3 (Summer 1985): 20–23.

Jackson, Marion E. *Contemporary Inuit Drawings*. Guelph: Macdonald Stewart Art Centre, 1987. [A drawing by Qaulluaryuk was incorrectly attributed to Francis Kaluraq in this exhibition. See p. 60.]

National Museum of Man. *The Inuit Print/L'Estampe Inuit*. Ottawa: National Museums of Canada, 1977.

Schrager, Reissa. "Chisel and Brush." *Inuit Art Quarterly* 1:3 (1986): 12–13.

Qinnuayuak, Lucy (1915–1982)

Lucy Qinnuayuak is a prolific graphic artist, well known for illustrations of her favorite theme—the bird image, either singularly or in groups, and in all sorts of situations or relationships. She also depicts other themes which spring from her personal interpretation of the

Canadian Inuit traditional way of life. She was born in Salluit, in northern Québec. At a very young age Qinnuayuak, along with her mother and sister, moved to Baffin Island, Northwest Territories, where they lived in Cape Dorset and in several outpost camps. She met her husband, Tikituk, a sculptor and graphic artist, at Supujuak camp where they enjoyed a traditional way of life. In the early 1960s they moved to Cape Dorset.

Qinnuayuak started to draw in the 1950s while living in Supujuak camp. Her drawings were turned into graphics from 1961 until 1983, excluding 1973. She also created her own plastic repertoire of forms that clearly defines the aesthetic values in her works. Over the years she has drawn all kinds of birds in various poses—the features of their eyes and feathers connecting them to each other. In her compositions movement and stability are often ambiguously juxtaposed.

At the end of the 1970s Qinnuayuak began working with acrylic paint in conjunction with other mixed media. Her compositions from that period are colorful, extremely vibrant, and powerful. They are also much more elaborate and complex with a broader story line. Qinnuayuak's art is realistic and humorous, and it reflects the traditional Inuit way of life.

As part of the first generation of Inuit graphic artists, Qinnuayuak made an important contribution to the Cape Dorset graphic art movement. Her works are represented in Canadian and international galleries. All of her graphics and some drawings are in the National Inuit Art Collection at the Canadian Museum of Civilization in Hull, and a selection of nine prints and two drawings are in the National Gallery of Canada in Ottawa. Her works have been featured in several minor and major exhibitions.

Qinnuayuak was honored when one of her designs was chosen for an Olympic banner and displayed at the Art Gallery of Ontario, Toronto, in 1976. It was one of ten drawings selected from 400 submitted. In 1984, the stone block of her stonecut print, "Large Bear" (1961), was donated to the Tate Gallery in London, England, by Sir Charles Gimpel. Today it is on extended loan to the Scott Polar Research Institute in Cambridge, England.

Odette Leroux

Bibliography
Blodgett, Jean. *Grasp Tight the Old Ways: Selections from the Klamer Family Collection of Inuit Art*. Toronto: Art Gallery of Ontario, 1983.
Eber, Dorothy Harley. "Visits with Pia." *The Beaver* (Winter 1983): 20–27.
———. "Lucy Qinnuayuak." *The Canadian Encyclopedia*. Ed. James H. Marsh. Hurtig Publishers (1985): 1042.
Jackson, Marion E. *Contemporary Inuit Drawings*. Guelph, Ontario: Macdonald Stewart Art Centre, 1987.
Van Raalte, Sharon. "Inuit Women and Their Art." *Communiqué* (May 1975): 21–23.

Qiyuk, Miriam Marealik (1933–)
Miriam Marealik Qiyuk is one of the eight surviving children of the Inuit artist Jessie Oonark, from Baker Lake in Canada's Northwest Territories. Qiyuk grew up in the traditional camp lifestyle and moved to Baker Lake while in her twenties. She is married to the artist Silas Qiyuk.

In the early 1960s Qiyuk began to do wall-hangings and carvings. Due to an unfortunate allergic reaction to wool, she had to dis-

continue producing textile works around 1980. Her carvings often deal with the episode of an Inuit legend in which the adventurous hero Kiviuq eventually marries a bird-woman. In these carvings, birds and human figures, delicately rendered, are entwined in a timeless sleep and appear to grow out of what is often an irregularly shaped flat piece of stone.

The artist's work has been featured in countless exhibitions in Canada and the United States, including "Crafts from the Arctic Canada," which travelled Canada in 1974; "Inuit Art in the 1970s," which toured Canada in 1978 and 1980; and "Arctic Vision," which toured the United States between 1984 and 1986.

Maria Muehlen

Bibliography
Blodgett, Jean. "Christianity and Inuit Art." *The Beaver* (Autumn 1984): 16–25.
Macduff, Alistair, and George M. Caplin. *Lords of the Stone*. White Cap Books, 1982.
Swinton, George. "Eskimo Art Reconsidered." *Artscanada* (December 1971–January 1972): 85–94.

Quijano, Yolanda (1933–)
Born in Mérida, Yucatan, Mexico, Yolanda Quijano abandoned a career in medicine to enter and study at Escuela de Pintura y Escultura (La Esmeralda) in Mexico City (1969–1961). Her first solo show in painting occurred in 1965. The following year she won first prize in an "Homage to Posada" exhibition organized by the Instituto Nacional de la Juventud Mexicana.

Since 1971 Quijano has also worked in sculpture. Through June 1988, she exhibited her work in fifty shows, twenty of which were solo affairs: "Complicidad para Subsistir" was shown in the Salón de la Plástica Mexicana (1980); "Frutos Vespertinas" in Cuernavaca (1984); and "Teorema Onírico" in the Perisur of the City of Mexico (1986) and in Monterrey (1987).

Quijano has received many prizes, among which are the Nuevos Valores award of the Salón de la Plástica Mexicana (1963), a gold medal in Mérida (1973) and another of silver granted by the National Institute of Fine Arts (1976).

Bibliography
Alvarez, José Rogelio, et al. *Enciclopedia de Mexico*. Secretaría de Educación Pública, 1987.

Quintana, Georgina (1956–)
Born in Mexico, Georgina Quintana studied Spanish literature at the University of Mexico (1974–1976); printmaking in the workshop of maestro Mario Reyes (1974); and drawing with professor Héctor Xavier R. She also studied in la Escuela de Pintura y Escultura (La Esmeralda), Mexico City (1977–1980) and took advanced work abroad.

A painter, Quintana exhibited her work in various cultural institutions in Mexico, including those in Campeche (1979), Morelia (1980), and in Aguascalientes (1982, 1983, 1984); in the galleries of Arte Contemporáneo (1984, 1987), OMR (1987), and Tata Vasco de Querétaro (1980, 1987); and in the First Diego Rivera Biennial, at which she won honorable mention (1984).

In 1985 Quintana was awarded the Antonio Robles prize. Among her most representative and, perhaps, better-known exhibitions are

"Espacio Violente" and "La Piñata" at the Academy of San Carlos, Mexico City. Quintana has mastered a great many media and techniques; in Barcelona, Spain, she took courses in the fabrication of handmade paper.

Bibliography
Alvarez, José Rogelio, et al. *Enciclopedia de Mexico.* Secretaría de Educación Pública, 1987.

Qumaluk, Leah Nuvalinga (Sala) (1934–)

Leah Nuvalinga (Sala) Qumaluk was born April 17, 1934, in Inukjuaik (Port Harrison) Arctic Québec and moved to Povungnituk with her husband, Josie Qumaluk, in 1954. A carver at first, Qumaluk began to draw and experiment with stoneblock printing in 1960.

During her professional career Qumaluk authored, and in most cases printed, at least ninety-five prints, of which the overwhelming majority were stonecuts. In addition she printed hundreds of additional editions for other artists. This prodigious output was accomplished by designing and cutting blocks at home, and then putting in a nine-to-five job in the print shop. Qumaluk often ignored the typical Povungnituk device of framing the image with the rough border of the uncut block. In the 1960s her imagery was dominated by mythological themes or demons conjured from her own imagination. At the insistence of the cooper she switched to tamer depictions of animals and traditional life. Her output slowed by the later 1970s, and in 1985 she retired completely.

Qumaluk was represented in sixteen annual Povungnituk print collections of the Canadian Museum of Civilization, the Winnipeg Art Gallery, the McMichael Canadian Art collection, and the Musée du Québec.

Mary Craig

Bibliography
Barz, Sandra. *Canadian Inuit Print Artist/Printer Biographies.* Art & Culture of the North, 1990.

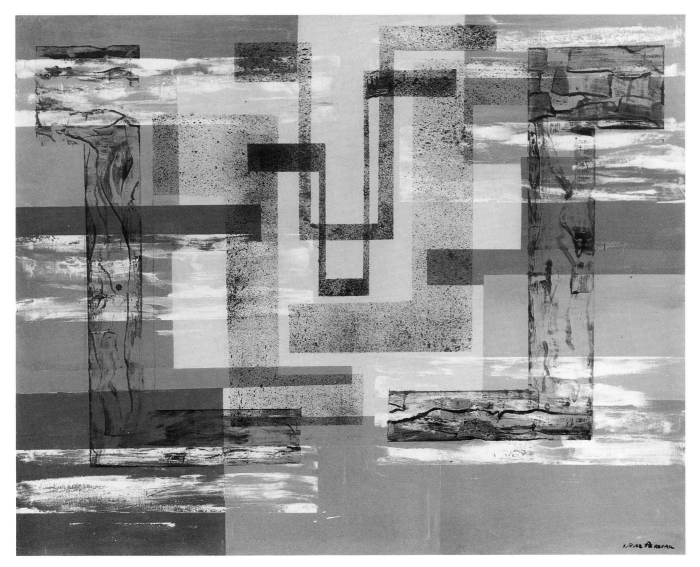

Irene Rice Pereira. Landscape of the Absolute. *1955. Oil on canvas. 40 × 50 inches.*
Collection of Whitney Museum of American Art. Gift of Richard Adler.

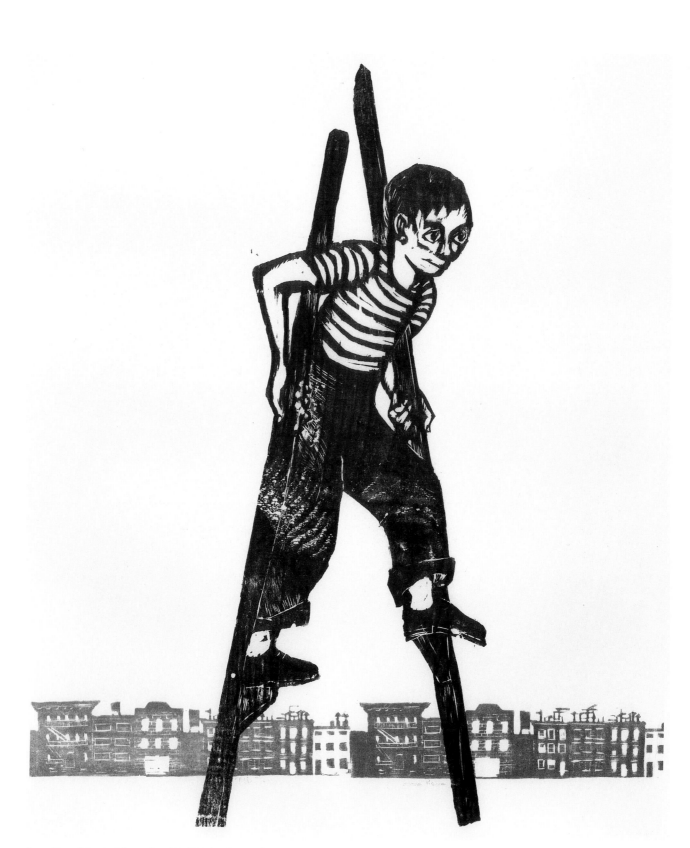

Leona Pierce. Stilts #1. *Color woodcut. 26 × 20 inches. Courtesy the artist.*

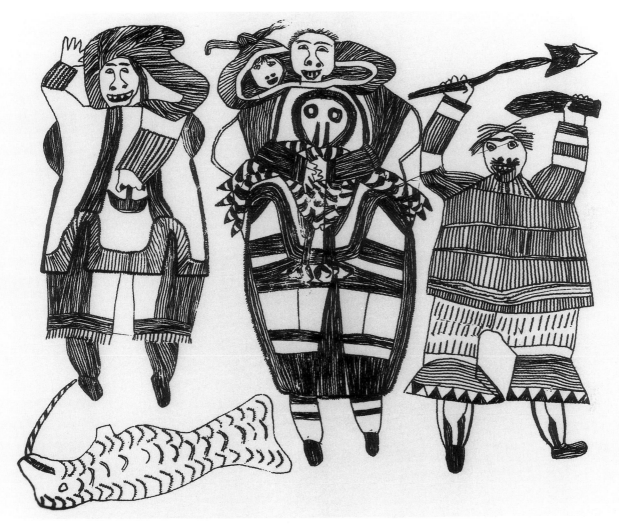

Ashoona Pitseolak. Happy Family. *1963. Engraving. 24.50 × 29.75 cm. Courtesy West Baffin Eskimo Cooperative, Cape Dorset, NWT, Canada.*

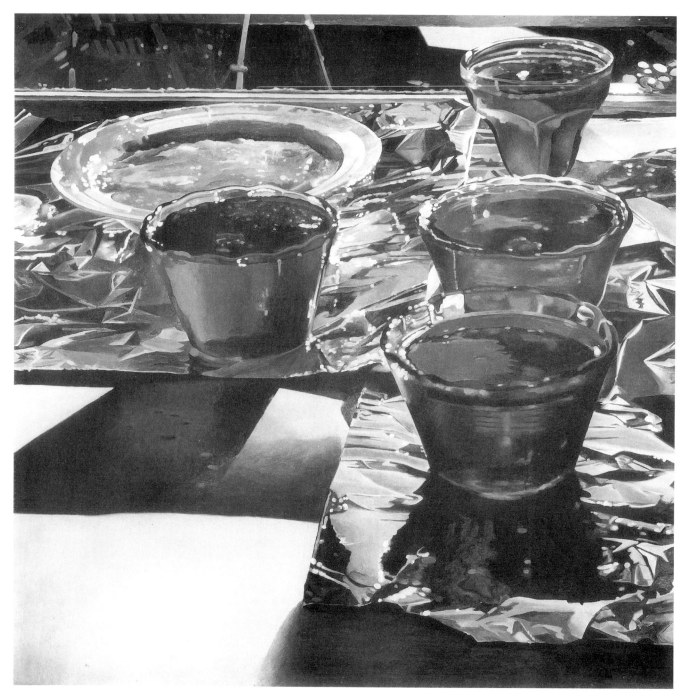

Mary Pratt. Red Currant Jelly. *1972. Oil on masonite. 45.9 × 45.6 cm.*
National Gallery of Canada.

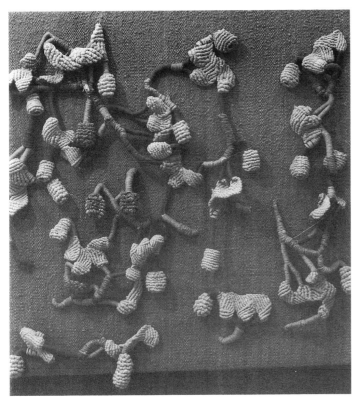

Marta Palau. La bufadora. *1978. Mural tapestry. 187 × 182 × 28 cm.*
Collection Museo de Arte Moderno, INBA.

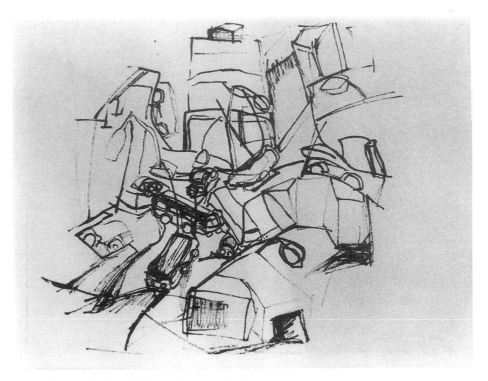

Georgina Quintana. Untitled. *1956. India ink on paper. 46 × 33 cm.*
Archivo CENIDIAP-INBA.

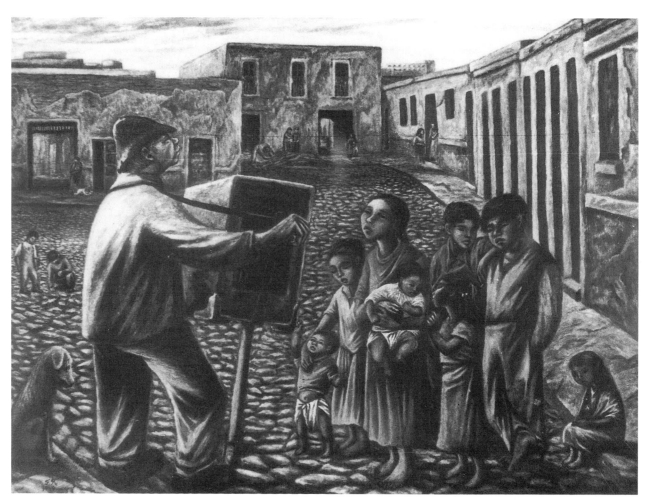

Fanny Rabel. Callejon de la amagura. *1949. Tempera and oil on masonite.*
95 × 122 cm. Archivo CENIDIAP-INBA. Private collection.

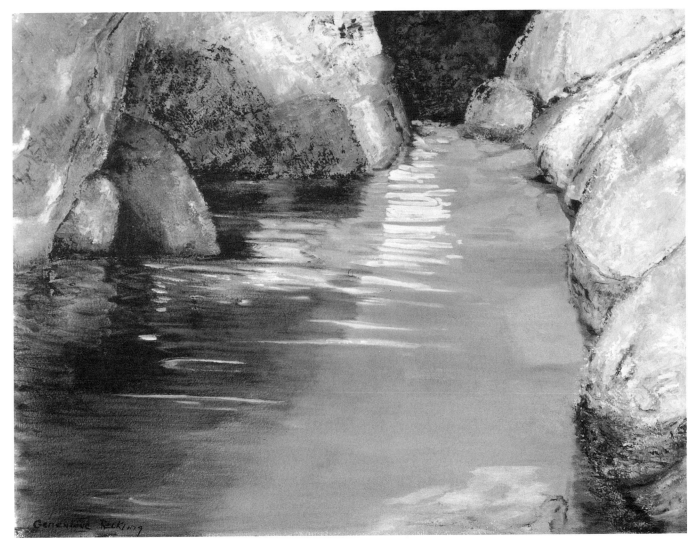

Genevieve Reckling. Cave of the Poet. *1988. Oil on paper. 23 × 30 inches.*
Courtesy the artist.

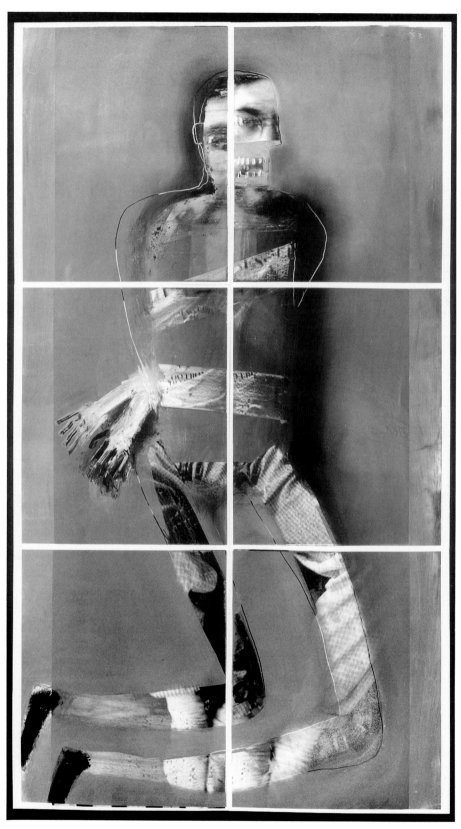

Holly Roberts. Bound Man Kneeling *(6 panels). 1992.*
Oil on gelatin silver print. Courtesy the artist.

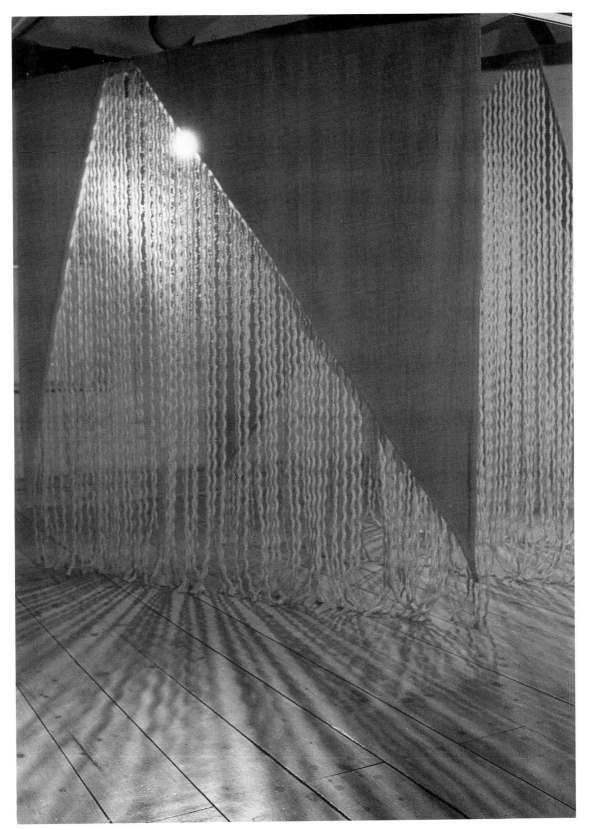

Mariette Rousseau-Vermette. Portes Secretes (Secret Doors). *1983-1984.*
Wool and twine. 4 units, each 250 × 250 cm. Courtesy the artist.

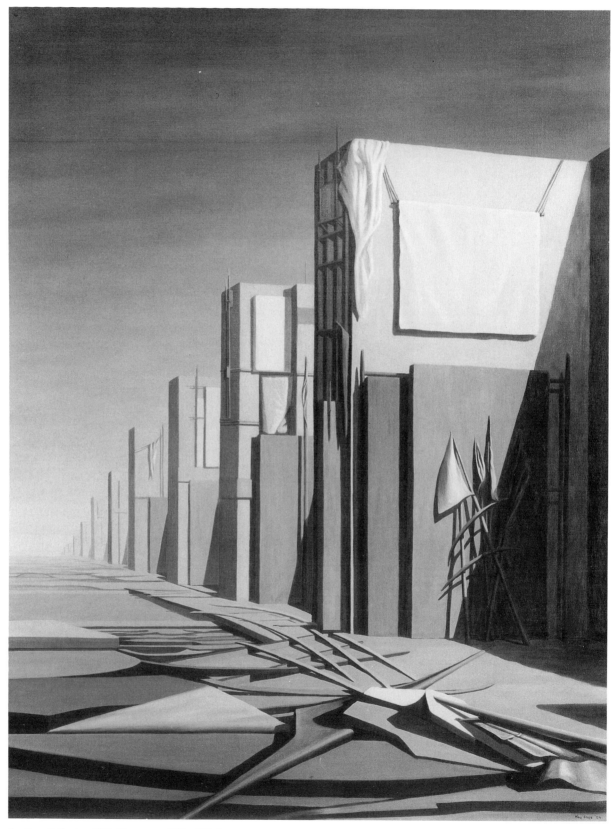

Kay Sage. No Passing. *1954. Oil on canvas. 51¹/₄ × 38 inches.*
Collection of Whitney Museum of American Art.

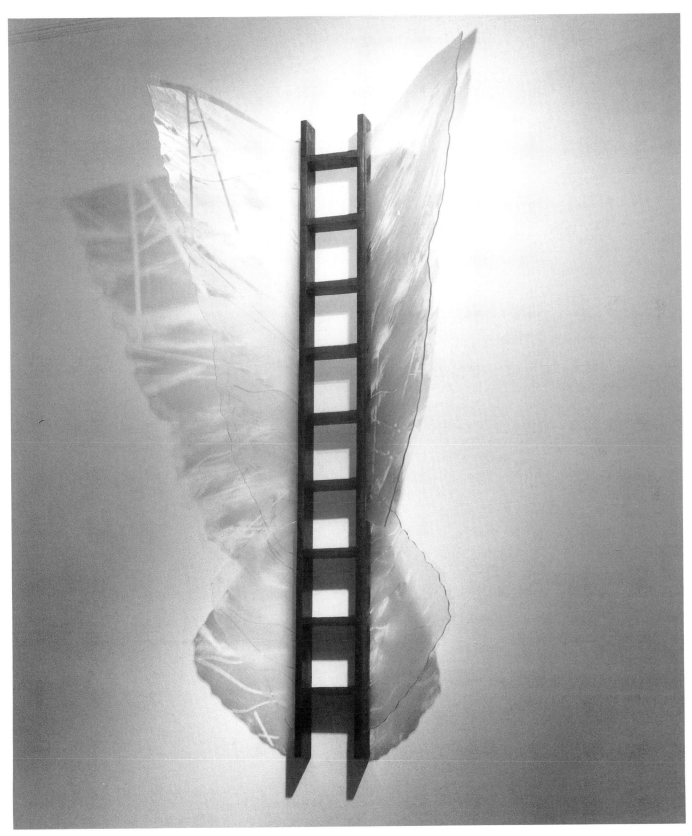

Norie Sato. Wings of Transmission: Vertical Sync. *1990.*
Wood, wax, pigment, etched glass. 76 × 37 × 15 inches. Courtesy the artist.

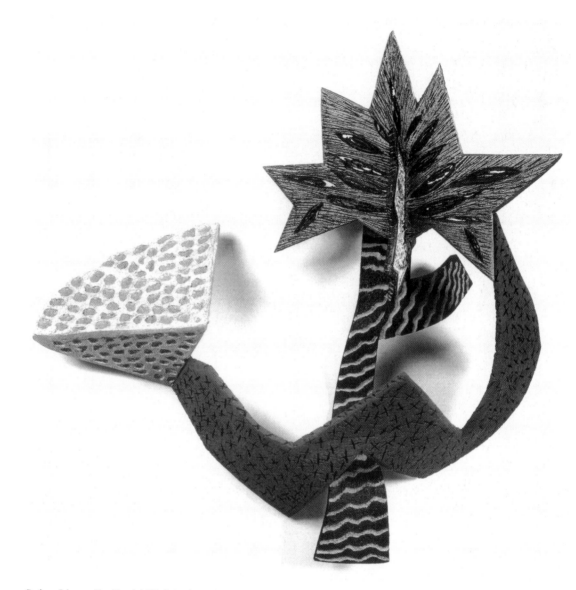

Barbara Schwartz. Head Land. *1992. Painted cast aluminum.*
35 × 34 × 13 inches. Courtesy the artist.

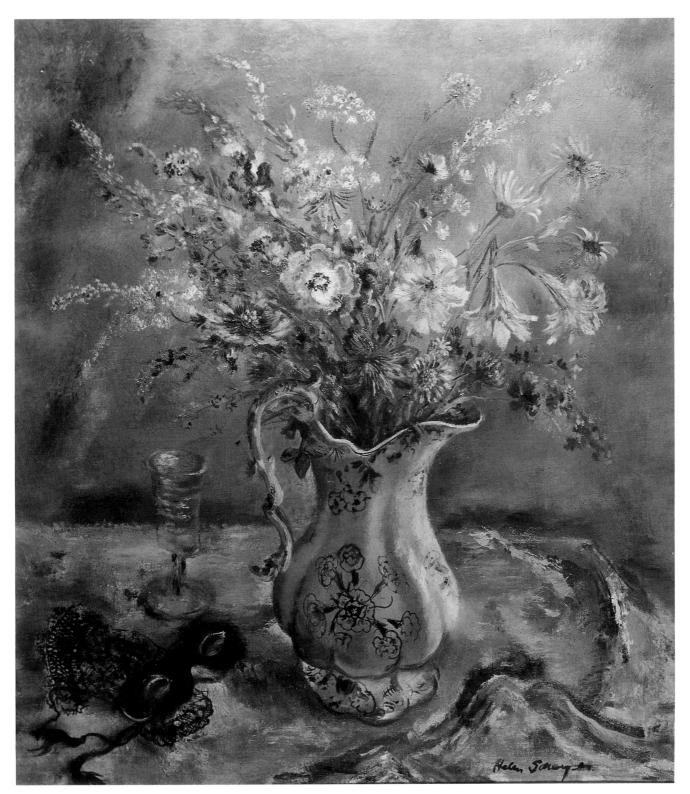

Helen Sawyer. Arrangement with Pitcher and Green Glass, *n.d. Oil on canvas. 30 × 25
inches. Copyright ©1994 by the Indianapolis Museum of Art. Gift of Mrs. and Mrs. Wendell
F. Coler in memory of their daughter Jean Coler.*

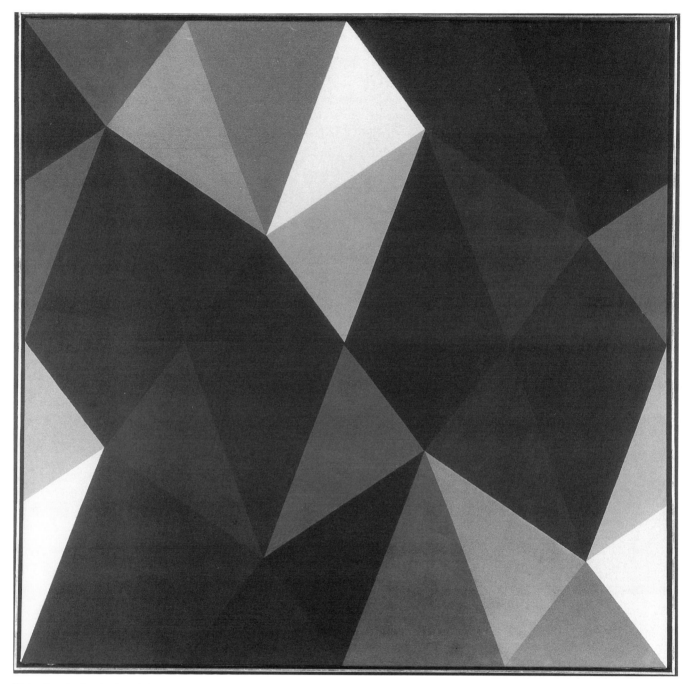

Marian Scott. Artifact. Acrylic on duck canvas. 152.4 × 152.4 cm.
National Gallery of Canada. Royal Canadian Academy of Arts diploma work,
deposited by the artist, Montréal, 1976.

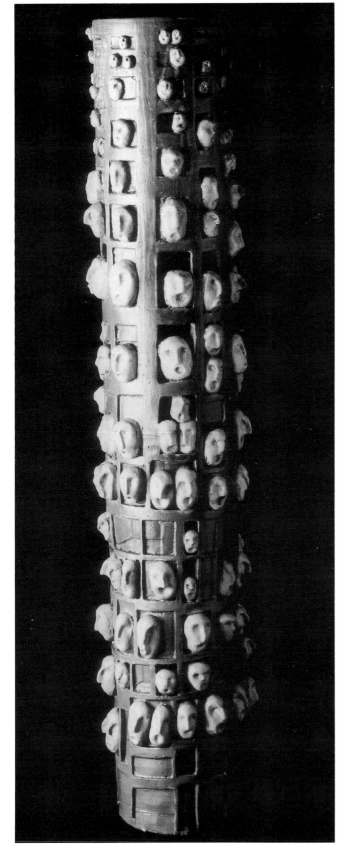

Sarai Sherman. Tower of Babel. *1983. Majolica porcelain.*
36 × 6 inches. Courtesy the artist.

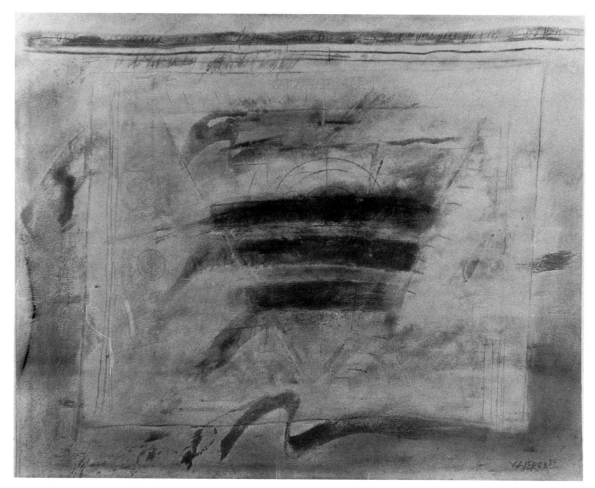

Susana Sierra. Forma silente. *1983. Oil on canvas.*
130 × 160 cm. Archivo CENIDIAP-INBA.

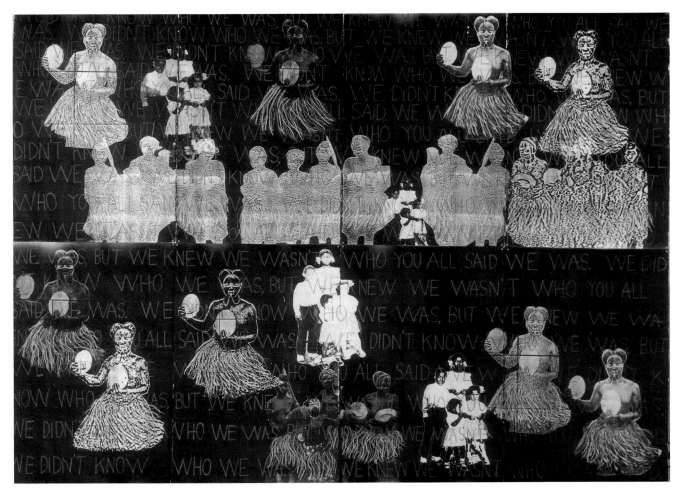

*Clarissa T. Sligh. Who We Was. 1993. Installation: Caran d'Ache crayon on
Cyanotype and engraved plastic. 90 × 240 inches. Courtesy the artist.*

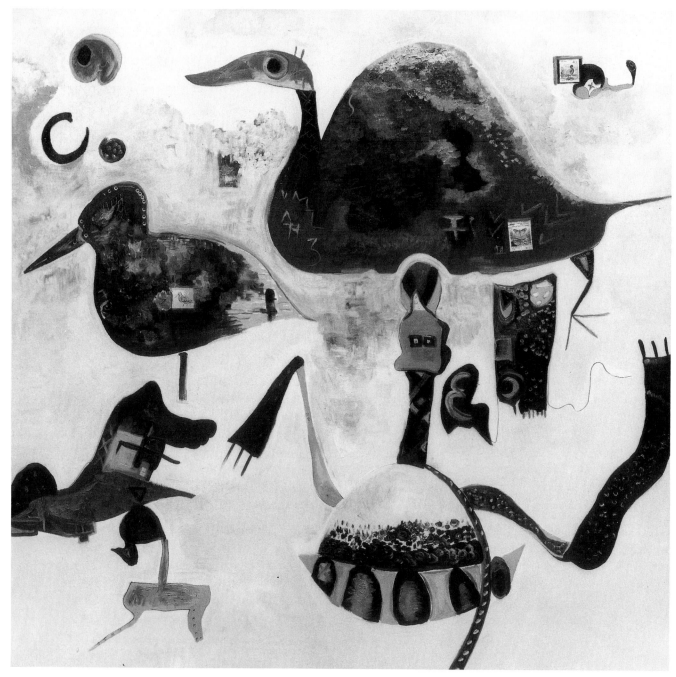

Lila Snow. DNA Birds. *1992. Oil on canvas. 40 × 40 inches. Courtesy the artist.*

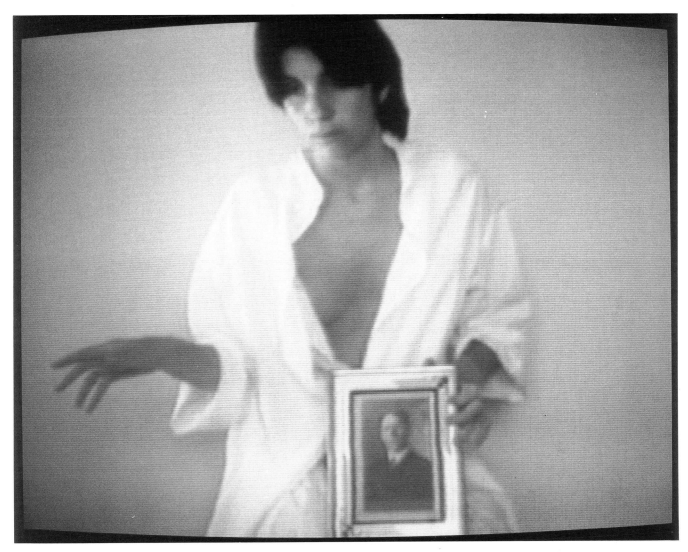

Lisa Steele. The Ballad of Dan Peoples. *1976. B/w videotape, 8:00 minutes on ³/₄" cassette.*
National Gallery of Canada.

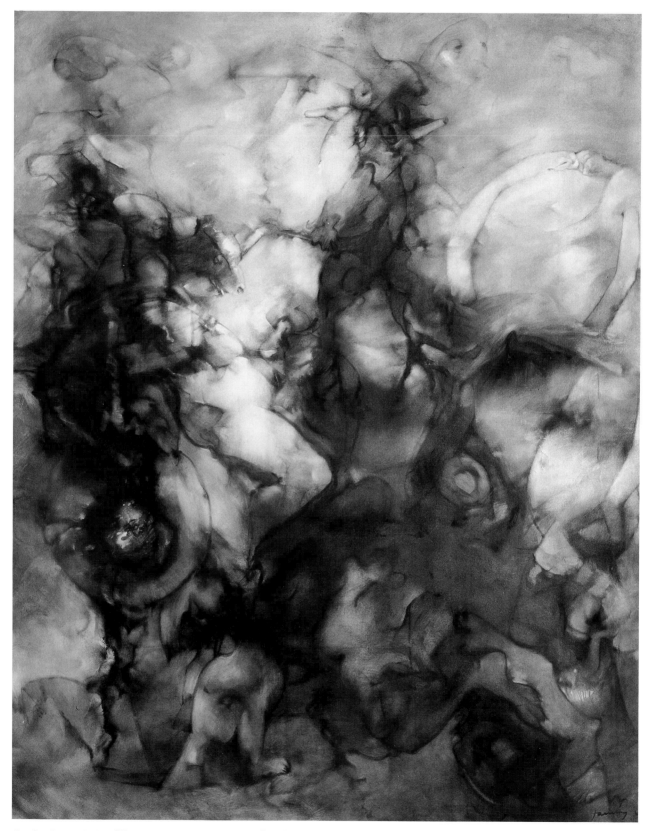

Dorothea Tanning. Paris and Vicinity. 1962. Oil on canvas. 100 × 78¾ inches.
Collection of Whitney Museum of American Art. Gift of Alexander Iolas Gallery.

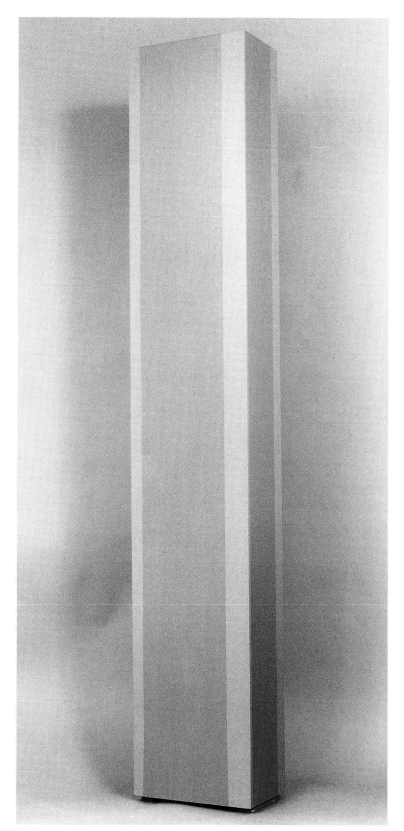

Anne Truitt. Summer Dryad. *1971. Acrylic on wood. 76 × 13 × 8 inches.*
Courtesy The National Museum of Women in the Arts. Gift of the Holladay Foundation.

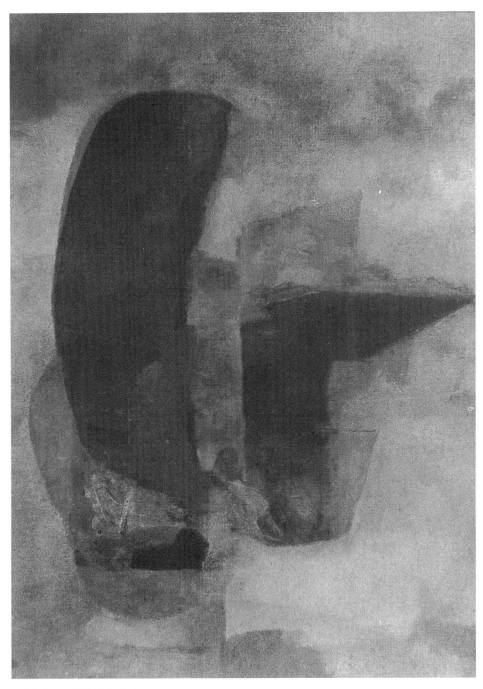

Cordelia Urueta. Al filo de la obsidiana. *1964. Oil on canvas. 109 × 150 cm.*
Archivo CENIDIAP-INBA. Private collection.

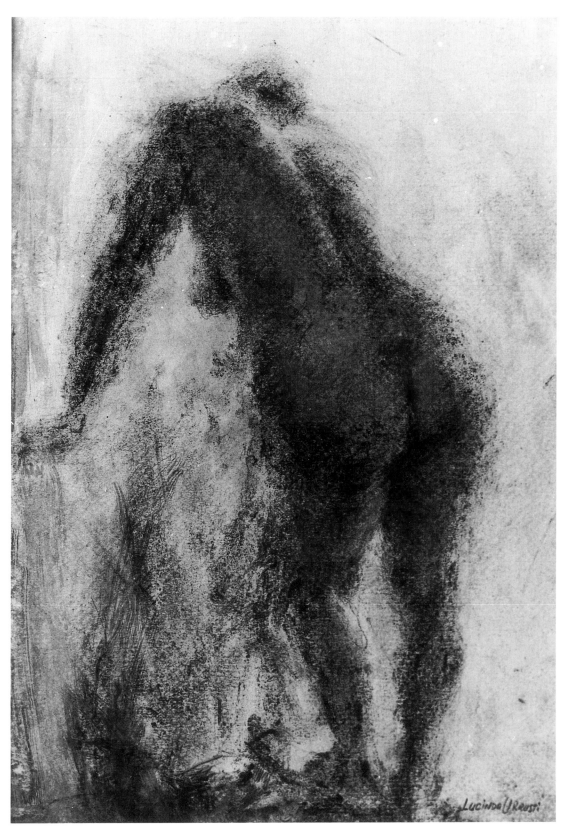

Lucinda Urrusti. Desnudo gris., *n.d. Pigment. 33 ×25 cm. Archivo CENIDIAP-INBA.*
Collection of the artist.

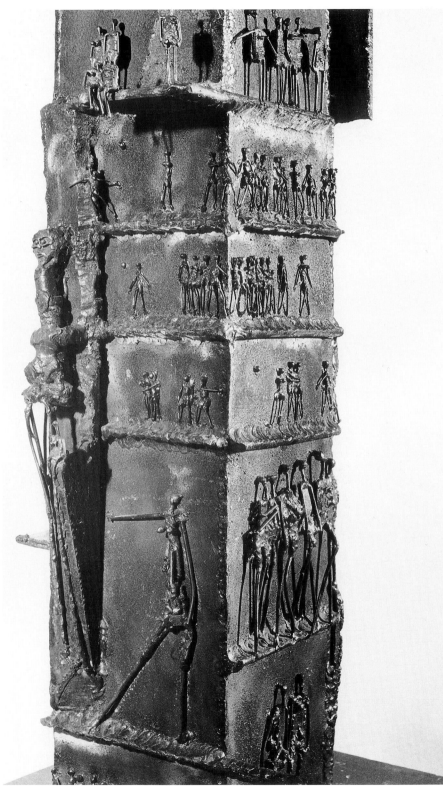

Agnese Udinotti. Stele #2 (detail). Welded steel. 42 × 12 × 10 inches.
Private collection, Paris, France.

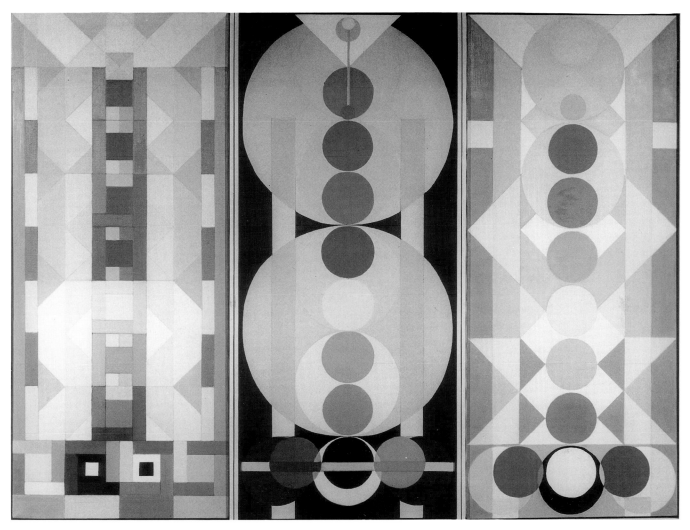

Charmion von Wiegand. Triptych, Number 700. *1961. Oil on canvas. 3 panels, overall:*
42¹/₄ × 54 inches. Collection of Whitney Museum of American Art. Gift of Alvin M. Greenstein.

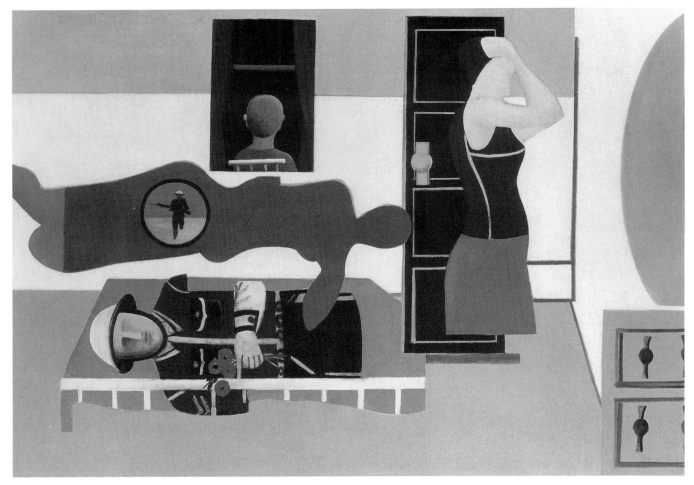

Esther Warkov. Memorial to a Dead Lover. *1966. Oil on canvas. 113.8 × 162.3 cm.*
National Gallery of Canada.

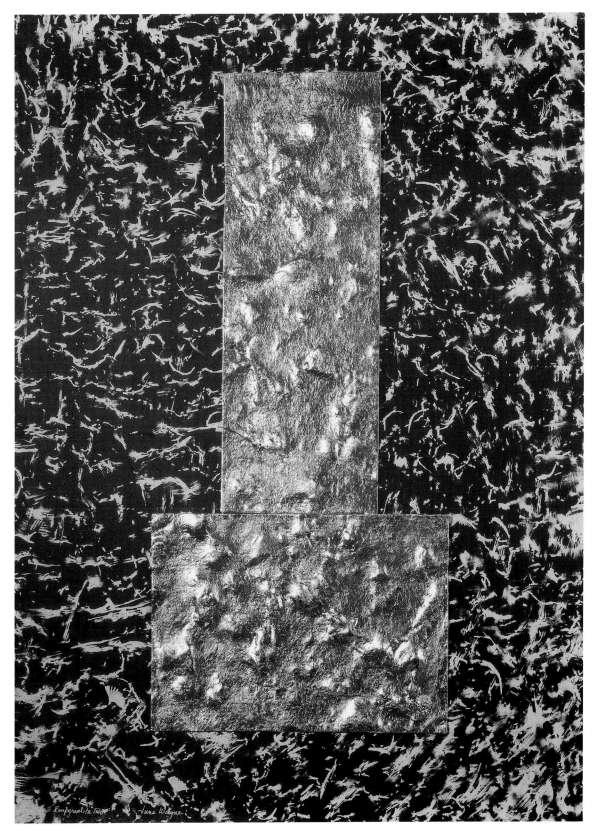

June Claire Wayne. Empyrealite Two. *1988. Lithograph, molded paper, silver leaf.*
31 × 22 inches. Courtesy the artist.

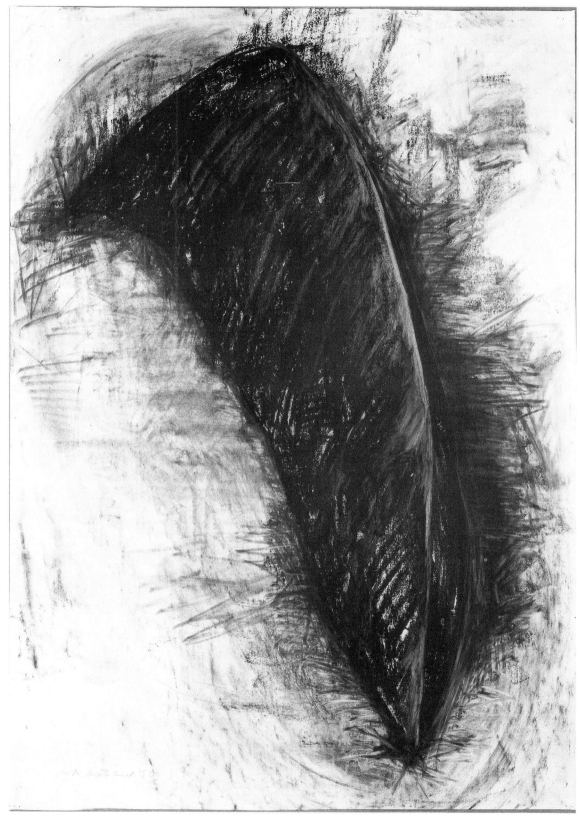

Mia Westerlund. Untitled No. 2. *1980. Charcoal on wove paper.*
151.5 × 107.5 cm. National Gallery of Canada, Ottawa.

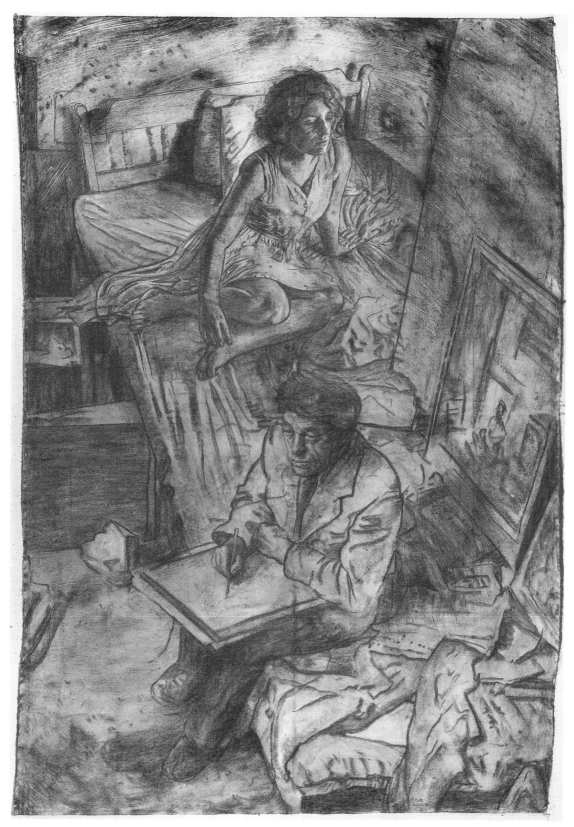

Ruth Weisberg. Alone, Together. *1989. Charcoal, graphite, oil, and wax on unstretched canvas. 46½ × 63¾ inches. Courtesy the artist.*

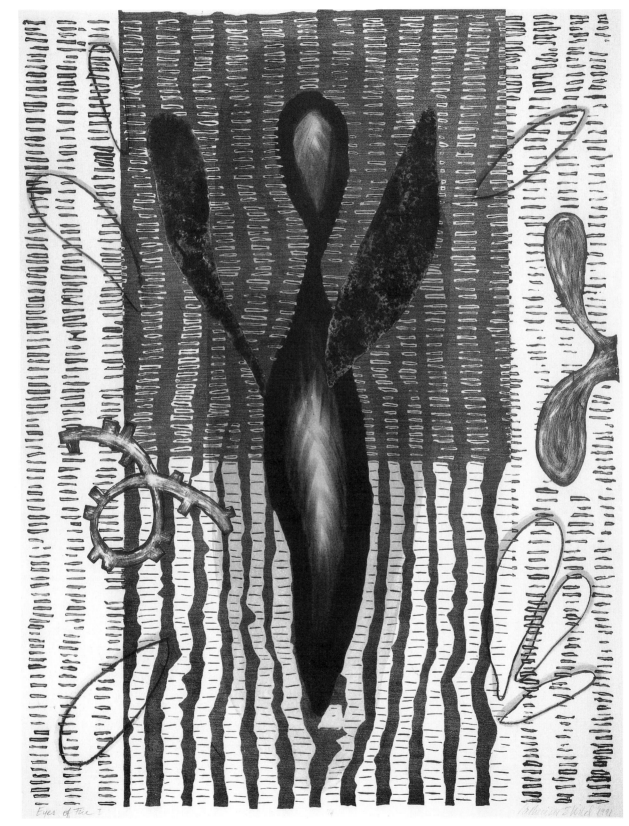

Catherine E. Wild. Eyes of Fire I. 1991. Lithograph. 41 × 29 inches. Courtesy the artist.

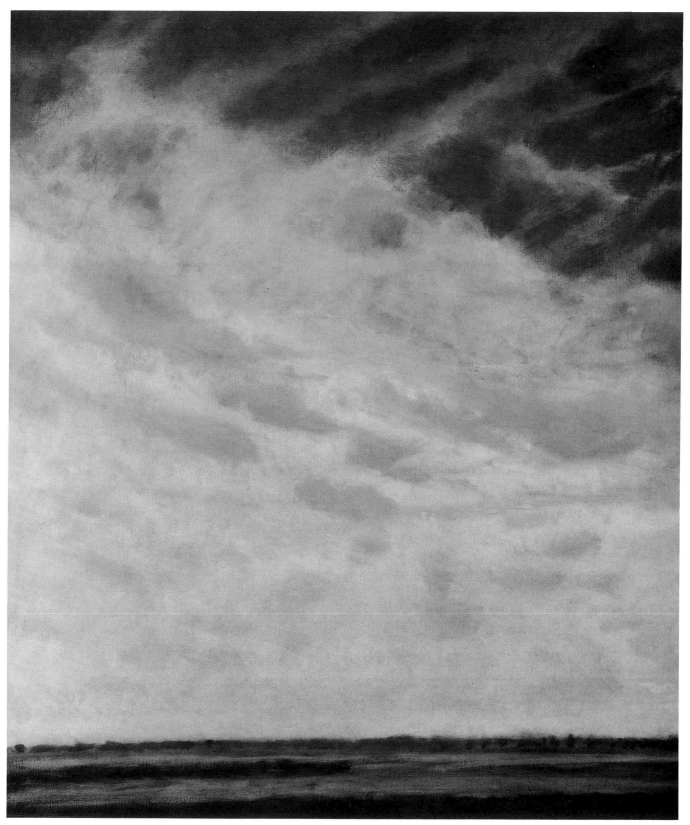

Jane Wilson. Salt Marsh. 1993. Oil on linen. 70 × 60 inches.
Courtesy Fischbach Gallery, New York.

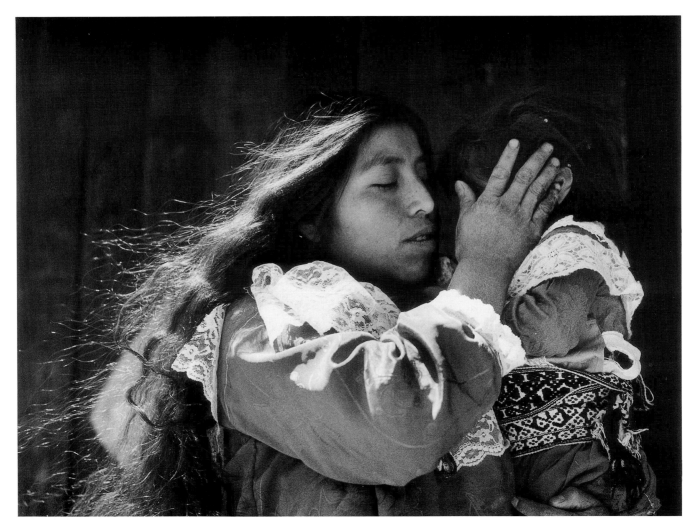

Mariana Yampolsky. Carisia-Caress. 1992. Silver gelatin print.
6¹/₄ × 8¹/₄ inches. Courtesy the artist.

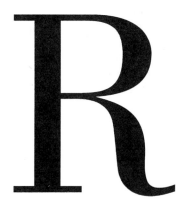

Rabel, Fanny (1924–)

Born in Poland, Fanny Rabel has lived in Mexico since 1938. She studied art in night school (1939); at la Escuela de Pintura y Escultura (La Esmeralda) (1940–1945); and at the School of the Book Arts (1945–1948)—all in Mexico City. While at La Esmeralda she had the good fortune to work under Frida Kahlo, Diego Rivera, Carlos Orozco Romero, and Francisco Zúñiga.

Rabel was an assistant to Diego Rivera in 1948, when he painted murals in the National Palace. In 1950 she became a member of the Taller de Gráfica Popular and of the Salón de la Plástica Mexicana. She painted a 125-square-meter mural in the Hebrew Sports Center (1957), another in the Pavilion of the Mexican Revolution at the VI Book Fair (1960), and a fifty-square-meter mural titled "Ronda del Tiempo," in the scholar's section of the National Museum of Anthropology (1964).

Rabel's first exhibition in Mexico occurred in 1951 and, from then on, she has shown in Tel Aviv, Israel; Montréal, Canada; Santiago, Chile; São Paulo, Brazil; Paris, France; Warsaw, Poland; Peking, China; Lima, Peru; Cordoba, Argentina; New York City; Los Angeles, California; and Tokyo, Japan. Her works are in the permanent collections of the Museum of Modern Art (MoMA), New York City; the Bibliothèque Nationale de Paris, France; the Royal Academy of Denmark; the Library of Congress, Washington, D.C.; the Franklin Rawson Museum in San Juan, Argentina; and in many distinguished private collections.

In 1959 the Taller de Gráfica Popular published Rabel's monograph, *Niños de Mexico*, which contains twenty-seven original prints; up to 1987 she had shown her work in eighty solo exhibitions and participated in sixty-four group shows, including "La Gente y la Ciudad Desquiciada" in the galleries Guadalupe Posada and at the Secretary of the Treasury building (1981); "Opera Prima" in the Salón de la Plástica Mexicana (1984); and "Mujeres en la Plastica" (1986).

Rabel is especially noted as a portraitist. She donated her mural, "Hacia la Salud," to the Children's Hospital in 1982; in 1984 she began an eighty-six-square-meter mural, "La Familia Mexicana," for the Register of Deeds. Alaíde Foppa writes, "Formed within Mexican realism and tied to the Taller de Gráfica Popular, [Rabel] has almost always managed to escape overly dogmatic expression through the lyric vein that nourishes her painting."

Bibliography
Alvarez, José Rogelio, et al. *Enciclopedia de Mexico*. Secretaría de
    Educación Pública, 1987.
Gual, Enrique F. *La Pintura de Fanny Rabel*. 1968.
Rabel, Fanny. *Requiem por una Ciudad: 40 Obras de Fanny Rabel*.
    La Universidad Nacional Autónoma de Mexico, 1984.
The Texas Quarterly: Image of Mexico II. The University of Texas. Autumn 1969.

Rady, Elsa (1943–)

A ceramist, known for her highly refined wheel-thrown porcelain vessels, Elsa Rady was born in New York City and currently maintains her studio in Venice, California. An important influence on Rady's work has been her mother, Lily Mehlamn, who was a dancer with the Martha Graham Dance Company in the 1930s. The flowing yet severely pure forms that Rady is known for find their antecedents in the sinuous elements of early modern dance.

In 1966, after graduating from Chouinard Art School in Los Angeles, California, Rady became successful making Chinese-influenced pots for the crafts fair circuit. From 1966 to 1968 she also worked as a contract designer to Interpace, Franciscan China Corporation in Glendale, California, and completed a ceramic mural for the Jules Stein Eye Institute at the University of California at Los Angeles (UCLA), and three murals for Disneyland in Anaheim, California. Rady had her first solo show at The American Hand gallery in Washington, D.C., in 1979 and since then had had more than fifteen gallery exhibitions throughout the United States. Her most recent exhibitions have been at the Holly Solomon Gallery in New York City (1990) and at the Isetan Art Museum in Tokyo, Japan (1991).

Rady received a National Endowment for the Arts (NEA) fellowship grant (1981) and a California Arts Council grant (1983). Her porcelains are in the collections of the Smithsonian Institution's Renwick Gallery in Washington, D.C.; Boston's Museum of Fine Arts, Massachusetts; the Los Angeles County Museum of Art, California; and the Victoria & Albert Museum of Art in London, England.

Elena Karina Canavier

Bibliography
Axel, Jan, and Karen McReady. *Porcelain: Traditions and New Visions.* Watson-Guptill, 1981, p. 40–41, 74, 75, 118–19, 130, 133.
Clark, Garth. *American Ceramics, 1987 to the Present.* Abbeville Press, 1987, pp. 126, 292.
Levine, Elaine. *The History of American Ceramics, 1607 to the Present.* Harry N. Abrams, 1988, pp. 261, 263.

Rainer, Yvonne (1934–)

During the 1960s Yvonne Rainer declared, "No!" to the spectacle, virtuosity, and make-believe of classical and modern dance. In place of technique and expression she investigated ordinary movement executed by trained and untrained dancers. By the 1970s her choreography returned to a narrative form. She showed an interest in directing and, eventually, abandoned dance for film.

The penultimate post-modern choreographer and performance artist, Rainer founded the Judson Dance Theater in New York City with Steve Paxton and Ruth Emerson. Their crowning achievement was *The Mind is a Muscle* (1966). This three-part performance piece included work by Paxton and David Gordon. Rainer contributed *Trio A*, a piece reworked until 1974, which became her signature work.

Born in San Francisco, California, Rainer moved to New York City in 1956. She abandoned her acting aspirations to study ballet and also study at the Martha Graham Studio. In 1960 she summered in San Francisco, California, working with Trisha Brown and Ann Halprin. The latter exposed Rainer to the use of hand-held props in dance. Returning to New York City, she studied at the Merce Cunningham Studio, repeatedly participating in Robert Dunn's compositional workshop. From 1961 to 1965 she danced with James Waring.

Rainer's movement style was eclectic, repetitious, and surreal, arbitrarily intertwining sounds—including squawks and squeals—with everyday gestures. In *The Bells* (1961), she fiddled with her fingers; *Three Seascapes* (1962) included a conflict with a coat. By 1964 task-oriented movement had developed into *Room Service*, with minimalist action determined by the manipulation of functional objects, such as furniture and mattresses.

This activity-generated, gamelike choreography exploded the illusionary myths of ballet and modern dance. Familiar movement—little leaps, walking, and low steps with relaxed feet—in place of concern for body shape and design, reduced dance to a workmanlike pursuit. The traditional concept of a dance vocabulary evaporated and was replaced with the language of mundane movement.

Stripping dance to pure and austere action burst the bubble of the dancer as superhuman. Effort was neither hidden nor emphasized. In 1965 Rainer's manifesto, *A Quasi-Survey of Some Minimalist Tendencies*, was an analysis of *Trio A* in relation to minimalism as practiced by sculptors. She said, ". . . no to spectacle. No to virtuosity, no to transformations, magic and make-believe . . . ." Free of embellishments, Rainer liberated dancers from the pressure of performing, allowing them to explore raw movement. She changed the way dance is looked at and critically analyzed. She sought to restore a fundamental integrity to the basic elements of movement.

By 1974, Rainer's choreography showed a renewed interest in narrative. *This is the Story of a Woman Who* (1974), is performed with words projected on a backdrop. This fragmented personal history, in the language of pulp fiction, was read by an actress onstage and seen as gigantic typed memoranda.

Kiana Dicker

Bibliography
Banes, Sally. *Terpsichore in Sneakers.* Houghton Mifflin, 1980.
Cohen, Selma Jeanne. *Next Week, Swan Lake.* Wesleyan University Press, 1986.
Croce, Arlene. *Going to the Dance.* Alfred A. Knopf, 1982.
Siegel, Marcia B. *The Shapes of Change.* Houghton Mifflin, 1979.

Rakine, Marthe (c. 1906–)

Born in Moscow, Russia, the painter Marthe Rakine began her formal art education at L'École d'Art Décoratifs, Paris, France (1926). She took various classes at the Sorbonne, and held her first exhibition (1932); studied at the Académie de la Grande Chaumière under the aegis of Othon Friesz in the mid-1930s; and also at the Ontario College of Art, Toronto, Canada (1949–1950).

Rakine has held solo exhibitions in museums and galleries in Canada, including Hart House, University of Toronto (1951); Picture Loan Society, Toronto (1952); Laing Galleries, Toronto (1953); Montréal Museum of Fine Arts (1954); Waddington Galleries, Montréal (1957); and others. Her work has been invited to many prestigious group shows, such as the Carnegie International Exhibition, Pittsburgh, Pennsylvania (1952); and others.

Examples of Rakine's paintings can be found in private and public permanent collections in Canada, including the Agnes Etherington Art Centre, Kingston, Ontario; Art Gallery of Ontario, Toronto; Hart House, University of Toronto; National Gallery of Canada, Ottawa; and many others.

Bibliography
Baird, Joseph. "The Art of Marthe Rakine." *Canadian Art* 11:1 (Autumn 1953): 19–22.
Weelen, Guy. *Marthe Rakine.* Presses Litteraires de France, 1949.

Rand, Ellen Emmet (1876–1941)

At the turn of the century the Emmet family in New York boasted several popular painters: the three sisters Rosina, Lydia, and Jane, and their younger cousin, Ellen Emmet, who was born in San Francisco to parents who had travelled there during the gold rush. Rand's family moved back to New York after her father's death in 1884. Her art instruction consisted of drawing lessons at a very early age with Dennis Bunker in Boston, Massachusetts; classes at the Art Students League, New York City, from 1889 to 1893, then study one summer with William Merritt Chase at Shinnecock on Long Island; and three years in Paris, France, in the studio of Frederick MacMonnies, who had just switched from sculpting to painting.

On her return to New York City in 1900 Rand took a studio in Washington Square and became so busy with portrait commissions that Durand-Ruel Galleries, New York City, gave her a one-woman exhibition as early as 1902, and ninety of her paintings were shown at Boston's Copley Hall, Massachusetts, in 1906. Her marriage to William B. Rand in 1911 and the birth of three sons in the next three years did not prevent her from resuming her career. In fact her income supported the family. During the school year the children stayed with her at East 57th Street, New York City, where she maintained a bustling new studio, and they spent the summers in Salisbury, Connecticut, on a farm which her husband ran and where she kept a second studio.

Rand exhibited extensively, garnering many medals. The National Academy of Design, New York City, elected her an associate in 1926 and an academician in 1934. Among her 800 portraits are "Henry James" (1900, collection of Leon Edel), "Pablo Casals" (c. 1905, collection of John A. Rand), and "President Franklin D. Roosevelt" (1934, FDR Library, Hyde Park, New York).

Eleanor Tufts

Bibliography

Cummings, Hildegard. *Good Company: Portraits by Ellen Emmet Rand.* William Benton Museum of Art, University of Connecticut, 1984.

Hoppin, Martha J. *The Emmets: A Family of Women Painters.* Pittsfield, Massachusetts: Berkshire Museum, 1982.

Tufts, Eleanor. *American Women Artists, 1830–1930.* National Museum of American Art, 1987.

Randolph, Lynn (1938–)

Born in New York City, the painter Lynn Randolph earned a Bachelor of Fine Arts degree at the University of Texas, Austin (1961).

Randolph has held a number of solo exhibitions of her work in the United States. Her most recent one-person shows include "Lynn Randolph," the Graham Gallery, Houston, Texas (1984, 1986, 1991); and "Lynn Randolph," the Mary Ingraham Bunting Institute, Radcliffe College, Harvard University, Cambridge, Massachusetts (1990). Her paintings have been invited to many group exhibitions, such as "Iconoclasm in Contemporary Texas Art," Museum of Fine Arts, Houston (1992), "A Sense of Place: Recent Acquisitions in Contemporary Texas Art," San Antonio Museum of Art (1991), and "Everyday Miracles: Retablos, Ex-votos, and Contemporary Texas Artists," Contemporary Art Museum, Houston (1990)—all in Texas; "Acts of Faith: Politics and the Spirit," Cleveland State University, Ohio (1988); "Life within Life," Collins Gallery, San Francisco, California (1986); "Texas Artists," Contemporary Arts Center, New Orleans, Louisiana (1980); and others.

Winner of awards and honors for her work, Randolph was the recipient of a fellowship at Radcliffe College, Harvard University, Cambridge, Massachusetts (1989–1990); a residency at Yaddo, Saratoga Springs, New York (1987); and was named by the Mayor of the city of Houston, Texas, as one of sixteen artists "who have contributed greatly to the development of our growing and vibrant art community."

Randolph is a writer, set designer, and an active lecturer at meetings of professional art organizations and universities. Her paintings are represented in private, public, and corporate permanent collections, including the San Antonio Museum of Art and Museum of Fine Arts, Houston—both in Texas; Prudential Insurance Co.; the Mary Ingraham Bunting Institute of Radcliffe College, Harvard University, Cambridge, Massachusetts; and others. "The Shepherdess" (1989), a typical Randolph oil, is composed of a young woman in an eerie Southwestern landscape conjuring up four bloody-mouthed hyena heads wearing four-in-hand ties; there are two sheep at her side among the cacti, and lightning bolts from her hands draw fire from the monsoon sky.

Bibliography

Connelly, David. *Art Papers* (January–February 1992): 66.

Frick, Thomas. "Lynn Randolph at the Bunting Institute." *Art in America* (December 1990): 176.

Lauter, Estella. *Quadrant* XXIII:7 (Spring 1991): 40.

Moore, Sylvia, ed. *No Bluebonnets, No Yellow Roses: Essays on Texas Women in the Arts.* Midmarch Arts Press, 1988.

Rankin, Joan (1927–)

Born in Calgary, Alberta, Canada, the multitalented artist Joan Rankin creates abstract works in virtually all of the visual arts mediums—painting, sculpture, stained glass, photography, painting, wall hangings, clay, wood, and textiles.

Rankin earned a Bachelor's degree in fine arts from the University of Saskatchewan, Canada, after study with Nicola Bjelajac, Augustus Kenderdine, and Kenneth Lochhead. In summers during the early to mid-1960s she attended the well-known Emma Lake Workshops, Saskatchewan, where she studied with such notables as Clement Greenberg, Jules Olitski, Lawrence Alloway, and Frank Stella. In 1969 she received a Master's degree in art education from Concordia University, Montréal, where she worked under the aegis of Yves Gaucher and Alfred Pinsky.

Painting instructor, art director, art supervisor, and scriptwriter—Rankin has held solo exhibitions in museums and galleries from Moose Jaw, Saskatchewan, to Toronto and Montréal. Her work has been included in many group shows throughout Canada. Examples of her award-winning output are in private and public permanent collections, including Concordia University, Montréal; Moose Jaw Art Museum and Regina Public Library—both in Saskatchewan; and many others.

Bibliography

Greenberg, Clement. "Clement Greenberg's View of Art on the Prairies: Painting and Sculpture in Prairie Canada Today." *Canadian Art* 20:2 (March–April 1963).

Saskatchewan: Art and Artists. Regina: Norman Mackenzie Art Gallery, 1978.

Stevens, Pat, and Barry Stevens. "Joan Rankin." *Arts West* 3:2 (March–April 1978): 18–22.

Raphael, Shirley (1937–)

Born in Montréal, Québec, Canada, Shirley Raphael is a painter, printmaker, and maker of colorful banners. Raphael learned her craft at many institutions, including the School of the Montréal Museum of Fine Arts; and Sir George Williams University (now Concordia University)—both in Montréal, Canada; Boston University, Massachusetts; l'École des Beaux-Arts, Montréal, where she studied printmaking with Janine Leroux-Guillaume and Robert Savoie; Instituto Allende, San Miguel de Allende, Mexico; Atelier Libre, Sadye Bronfman Cultural Centre, Montréal; Atelier Libre of Pierre Ayot, Montréal; and workshops with artists, including Larry Rivers, Andrew Stasik, and others.

Raphael has held solo exhibitions in museums and galleries throughout Canada and abroad: from Sudbury, Ontario to London, England; from Burnaby, British Columbia, to Montréal, Québec.

She has won honors and awards, has travelled widely, and has had her work included in many prestigious group shows, such as the "Canadian Printmakers Showcase," Ottawa (1973); the International Art Fair, Basel, Switzerland (1974); "Banners," the British Commonwealth Institute, London, England (1975); and others. Examples of her work are in private, public, and corporate permanent collections, including the Art Gallery of Toronto, and National Library, Ottawa—both in Ontario, Canada; Dartmouth College, Hanover, New Hampshire; Montréal Museum of Fine Arts, Québec, Canada; Pepsi Cola Company, New York City; and many others.

Bibliography

McMann, Evelyn de R. *Royal Canadian Academy of Arts, Exhibitions and Members, 1880–1979.* University of Toronto Press, 1981.

Tomlin, Fergus. "Unlimited Media—Unlimited Concepts." *Artmagazine* 6:21 (1975).

Raull, Regina (1933–)

Born in Bilbao, Spain, Regina Raull came to Mexico early in her childhood. She studied at the Academy of San Carlos in Mexico City. A painter, her principal solo exhibitions took place in the Galería Misrachi, Mexico City (1963); the Ateneo Veracruzano (1969); a show organized on the occasion of the visit of Spain's King Juan Carlos I to Mexico (1978); the Palacio de Cristal, Madrid, Spain (1979); and the Saddleback Galleries, Los Angeles, California (1973, 1977).

Raull has participated in many group shows in Mexico and in Europe. Among her murals, the best-known are: "La Educación en la Época Mexica," in the National Museum of Anthropology, Mexico City; "Atención y Rehabilitación," in a children's hospital; and "El Origin de la Vida," in an institution that is part of the office of the secretary of health. In 1971, during the Christmas holidays, Raull executed several "luminous" murals in the center of Mexico City.

Bibliography

Alvarez, José Rogelio, et al. *Enciclopedia de Mexico.* Secretaría de Educación Pública, 1987.

Ravenscroft, Ellen (1876–1949)

Born in Jackson, Mississippi, the painter/printmaker Ellen Ravenscroft studied with William Merritt Chase and Robert Henri. She did further study with Castellucho in Paris, France.

Winner of awards and honors, Ravenscroft won the portrait prize at the Catherine Lorillard Wolfe Club, New York City (1908); the prize for landscape painting at the same institution (1915); a special prize and honorable mention at the Kansas City Art Institute (1923); and others. Her work is represented in private and public permanent collections.

Bibliography

American Art Annual. Vol. 28. American Federation of Arts, 1932.

Fielding, Mantle. *Dictionary of American Painters, Sculptors, and Engravers.* Modern Books and Crafts, 1974.

Obituary. *Who's Who in American Art.* Vol. 5. American Federation of Arts, 1953.

Ravlin, Grace (1873–1956)

Born in Kaneville, Illinois, the painter Grace Ravlin studied at the Art Institute of Chicago, Illinois; the Pennsylvania Academy of Fine Arts, Philadelphia, under William Merritt Chase; and with Menard and Simon in Paris, France.

Ravlin was a member of several arts organizations, including the Société Nationale des Beaux-Arts, and the Peintres Orientalistes Français, Paris, France (1912); and the Salon d'Automne. She has received many awards and honors, including the third medal at the Amis des Arts, Toulon, France (1911); the silver medal at the Panama-Pacific International Exposition, San Francisco, California (1915); the Field and Butler prizes at the Art Institute of Chicago, Illinois (1922); and others. Her work is represented in private and public permanent collections, including the Arche Club, Chicago, Art Institute of Chicago, Vanderpool Art Association, and city of Chicago Collection—all in Illinois; the government of France; Musée de Luxembourg, France; Los Angeles County Museum of Art, California; Newark Museum, New Jersey; and others.

Bibliography

American Art Annual. Vol. 28. American Federation of Arts, 1932.

Dawdy, Doris Ostrander. *Artists of the American West: A Biographical Dictionary.* Vol. 2. Sage Books, 1980.

Robertson, Edna, and Sarah Nestor. *Artists of the Canyons and Caminos, Santa Fe: The Early Years.* Peregrine Smith, 1976.

Raymond, Evelyn (1908–)

Born in Duluth, Minnesota, the artist Evelyn Raymond was honored by the Minnesota Statehood Centennial Commission (1958) as the first woman sculptor to place a statue of a woman in the U.S. Capitol, Washington, D.C. Raymond studied sculpture with Charles S. Wells at the Minneapolis School of Art, Minnesota (1928–1930); spent the next two years studying painting with Cameron Booth; and in 1932 went to the Art Students League, New York City, where she studied sculpture with William Zorach.

Raymond held solo exhibitions in Minnesota at the Walker Art Center, Minneapolis (1948); Hennepin Avenue Methodist Church, Minneapolis (1968); College of St. Thomas, St. Paul (1983); and others. Her award-winning work has been included in group shows in her native state and commissioned examples are sited at many venues, including the College of St. Thomas, St. Paul; Minnesota Museum of Art, St. Paul; St. Olaf College, Northfield; the University of Minnesota; U.S. Capitol; Walker Art Center; and others.

Bibliography
Annual Regional Sculpture Exhibition. Walker Art Center, 1944–1947.
Art in the United States Capitol. U.S. Government Printing Office, 1976.
Paine, Sylvia. "Evelyn Raymond." *WARM Journal* (Autumn 1982): 4–7.
Watson-Jones, Virginia. *Contemporary American Women Sculptors*. Oryx Press, 1986.

Raymond, Lilo (1922–)

Born in Frankfurt, Germany, the photographer Lilo Raymond learned her craft through seminars with David Vestal (1961–1963). Raymond has held many solo exhibitions and has participated in group exhibitions throughout the United States and abroad, including "Still Life in Photography," Helios Gallery, New York City (1976); Contrasts Gallery, London, England (1980); Photo West, Carmel, California (1982); and others.

Recipient of a Creative Artists Public Service (CAPS) grant from the New York State Council on the Arts (1978), Raymond has offered photographic seminars at prestigious venues, including the Maine Photographic Workshop, Rockport; the International Center for Photography and the New School for Social Research—both in New York City, where she has contributed her wisdom to seminars in photography since 1978. Examples of her work are in private and public permanent collections, such as the High Museum, Atlanta, Georgia; Isaac Delgado Museum, New Orleans, Louisiana; Metropolitan Museum of Art and the Museum of Modern Art (MoMA)—both in New York City; and others.

Bibliography
Beaton, Sir Cecil. *The Magic Image*. Little Brown & Co., 1975.
Blodgett, Richard. *A Collector's Guide*. Ballantine Books, 1979.

Ream, Vinnie (1847–1914)

The sculptor Vinnie Ream, born in Madison, Wisconsin, is best known for her marble statue of Abraham Lincoln in the Rotunda of the U.S. Capitol. In her teens, while working in the post office, she studied with the sculptor Clark Mills. She asked President Lincoln to sit for her, and although he was too busy for formal sittings, he permitted her to model him in his office as he worked. Thus she was very familiar with his features when a competition was announced for a statue after his assassination. The model that she submitted was selected, making her the first female artist to receive a government commission ($10,000). Once her over-life-size plaster cast was ready for transference to marble in 1869 she travelled to Italy to select the Carrara marble and supervise the stone cutters.

Ream studied in Paris, France, with Léon J.F. Bonnat, and in Rome, Italy, with Luigi Majoli, and for six months she maintained a studio in Rome, Italy. She also modeled from life the composer Franz Liszt and Cardinal Antonelli, the papal secretary of state, and created at least two ideal marble works of semi-nude females, "Passion Flower" and "Spirit of Carnival" (both in the State Historical Society of Wisconsin, Madison).

After her return to Washington Ream received her second government commission: a statue of Admiral Farragut. This ten-foot statue, standing today in Farragut Square, is composed of bronze melted down from the propellers of the admiral's flagship. While working on this memorial, Ream married a lieutenant, Richard L. Hoxie in 1878, and for a few years devoted herself to her husband and a son. Two of her neoclassical sculptures, "The West" (1866–1868, Wisconsin State Capitol) and "Miriam's Song of Triumph," were exhibited at the World's Columbian Exposition of 1893.

Before her marriage Ream had done bust portraits of General Custer, Horace Greeley, Senator John Sherman, and two congressmen. When she returned to sculpting, she accepted commissions for two bronze statues to be placed in the U.S. Capitol: "Sequoya" (1912) and "Governor Samuel Kirkwood" (1913). On the tomb of Ream and her husband, General Hoxie, in Arlington National Cemetery, Virginia, stands a bronze replica of her serene marble statue, "Sappho" (the original of which is in the National Museum of American Art, Smithsonian Institution, Washington, D.C.).

Eleanor Tufts

Bibliography
Tufts, Eleanor. *American Women Artists, 1830–1930*. National Museum of Women in the Arts, 1987.
Wilkins, Thurman. "Ream, Vinnie." *Notable American Women*, vol. 3. Belknap Press, Harvard University Press, 1971.

Rebay, Hilla von (1890–1967)

Born into opulence in Germany, the non-objective painter Hilla von Rebay studied at the Académie Julian, Paris, France, beginning in 1909. A theosophist, she exhibited widely in group shows in France and Germany prior to World War I and, owing to the influence of Jean Arp, held two solo exhibitions at Der Sturm Gallery, Berlin, Germany. She settled in the United States in 1927; championed the cause of abstract art; persuaded Irene and Solomon R. Guggenheim to buy non-objective works; and became the Guggenheim Foundation's first curator and the first director of the Guggenheim Museum, New York City. Von Rebay also showed her own paintings and collages in galleries in the United States (1927–1962), among them French and Co., New York City (1962).

Bibliography
Archives of American Art. *Collection of Exhibition Catalogs*. G.K. Hall, 1979.
Dunford, Penny. *Biographical Dictionary of Women Artists in Europe and America since 1850*. University of Pennsylvania Press, 1989.
Lukach, Joan M. "Rebay, Hilla." *Notable American Women: The Modern Period*. Harvard University Press, 1980.
Who's Who in American Art. Vol. 3. American Federation of Arts, 1940.

Reckling, Genevieve (1930–)

Born in St. Louis, Missouri, Genevieve Reckling's family moved to Houston, Texas, when she was five years old. For a time she lived in the shadow of the Houston Museum of Fine Arts and as a teenager attended classes at the Houston Museum of Fine Arts School, where her precocious talent was awarded various exhibition prizes. By her mid-teens Reckling had been regularly exposed to the stimulation of an art-filled environment with all its discussions, polemics, and stimulating ambience. She then attended the University of Texas at Austin for a year. She married at nineteen, had children early, and continued her studies at Arizona State University, Tempe, after moving to Phoenix, Arizona, from Los Angeles, California.

Reckling's first solo exhibition was at the Meredeth Long Gallery in Houston, Texas, in 1971, and she began showing regularly with the Suzanne Brown Gallery in 1975 and in 1984 joined the Marilyn Butler Gallery—both in Scottsdale, Arizona.

Throughout her life Reckling has travelled extensively throughout the United States, Mexico, Europe, Hawaii, and Tahiti. Her romantic paintings often depict the images seen in these travels. She has also produced various editions of lithographs in workshops in San Francisco, California; Santa Fe, New Mexico; and Scottsdale, Arizona. For the past decade Reckling's work has evoked the richness of the Western landscape, the poetic and soft colors of the desert, of canyon streams, and secret private corners of majestic rock formations and quiet pools. Her contemporary approach to landscape painting invokes both realism and abstraction in a balance that provides the viewer with a very personal vision.

Reckling's exhibitions include solo shows at the Dublin Gallery, Los Angeles, California; Marilyn Butler Fine Arts, Scottsdale, Arizona; C.G. Rein galleries, Houston, Texas, and Scottsdale, Arizona. Her extensive record in group exhibitions include "The Best of the West" invitational, Colorado Springs Art Center, 1986; Albright-Knox Art Gallery, Buffalo, New York, 1985; "In Celebration of Excellence," Elaine Starkman Gallery, New York City; "American Art Now, Paintings in the 1980s," Museum of Arts and Science, Columbus, Georgia, 1984; and others. Her works can be found in the collections of the Scottsdale Center for the Arts; Arizona State University Art Museum; Hughes Aircraft Company; Dunn and Bradstreet Corp.; Phoenix Art Museum; Tucson Museum of Art; Aetna Life and Casualty—all in Arizona; Colorado Springs Center for the Arts; and elsewhere.

In 1983, with over thirty other artists, Reckling went on a river raft trip through the Grand Canyon. The experience was of particular importance in the evolution of her work. Since that time images of water have become an increasingly prevalent component of her landscape paintings. She continues her vital explorations into many aspects of the mystery of water, its reflections, movement, transparency, sparkling qualities, and other features—all of which have become themes in her romantic paintings.

Leonard Lehrer

Bibliography
Kotrozo, Carol. "Four Arizona Women." *Artspace* (Fall 1982): 36–39.
Locke, Donald. "A Sidelong Look at Cowboy Art." *Artspace* (April 1981): 24.
Nordling, Karl. "Moods of Water." *Scottsdale Magazine* (March–April 1986): 25–27.
Perlman, Barbara. "Flowers Are Not the Point." *Arizona Arts and Lifestyle* (Fall 1980): 34–41.

Redgrave, Helen Felicity (1920–)

English-born Helen Felicity Redgrave emigrated to Canada in 1942 and initiated her art career by studying at Sheridan College, Oakville, Ontario (1968–1970); the University of Guelph, Ontario, where she earned a Bachelor of Fine Arts degree after study with Gene Chu, John Fillion, and Walter Palchinski (1970–1973); and the University of Toronto, where she received a Bachelor's degree in art education under John Elderfield and Roald Nasgaard (1974–1975).

A teacher for many years, Redgrave has held solo exhibitions in museums and galleries, including Tartu College, University of Toronto,

(1974), and Damkjar Galleries, Burlington (1975)—both in Ontario; Mount St. Vincent University, Halifax, Nova Scotia (1976); Harbourfront Community Gallery, Toronto (1978); "Felicity Redgrave," Art Gallery of Nova Scotia, a travelling show (1978), and Dresden Gallery (1982)—both in Halifax; and others. Her work has been included in many group shows, such as the "Black Exposition," Memorial University, Newfoundland (1975); "Atlantic Graphics," Mount St. Vincent University, Halifax (1976); "Forum '76," Montréal Museum of Fine Arts, Québec (1976); and others. Examples of her meticulous work are in private and public permanent collections, including Mount St. Vincent University, Halifax, Novia Scotia; Sheridan College, Oakville, Ontario; the University of Ontario, Toronto; and others.

Bibliography
Laurette, Patrick C. *Felicity Redgrave.* A Catalog. Art Gallery of Nova Scotia, 1978.

Reese, Claudia

Born in Des Moines, Iowa, the ceramist/sculptor Claudia Reese studied at the School for American Craftsmen, Rochester Institute of Technology, New York, in the summer of 1969. Previously she attended the State University of New York (SUNY) at Albany. Reese earned a Bachelor's degree from Connecticut College, New London (1971), and, three years later, received a Master of Fine Arts degree from Indiana University, Bloomington.

Reese has held solo exhibitions in the United States and abroad, including Takashimaya, Tokyo (1991); Daimaru Department Store, Kobe (1990)—both in Japan; Savoir Faire Gallery and the Seiba Department Store—both in Tokyo, Japan in 1989; "Claudia Reese: Recent Sculpture," Southwest Craft Center, San Antonio (1988); and "Claudia Reese: Recent Sculpture," R.S. Levy Gallery, Austin (1987)—both in Texas. She also had solo exhibitions at "Recent Sculpture," Willingheart Gallery, Austin, Texas (1984); and "Work in Clay," Purdue University, West Lafayette, Indiana (1981). Her work reflects a certain wit and fantasy and has been invited to more than sixty group exhibitions: from Corpus Christi, Texas, to La Jolla, California; from Las Cruces, New Mexico, to Paris, France; from Scarsdale, New York, to Sheboygan, Wisconsin—and it is represented in private and public permanent collections.

Bibliography
Carlozzi, Annette. *Fifty Texas Artists.* Chronicle Books, 1986.
Lavatelli, Mark. "New Talent in Texas." *Artspace* (Summer 1984).
McCombie, Mel. "Claudia Reese." *Art News* (November 1987).
Watson-Jones, Virginia. *Contemporary American Women Sculptors.* Oryx Press, 1986.

Reichek, Elaine (1943–)

Born in New York City, Elaine Reichek earned a Bachelor's degree at Brooklyn College, New York (1963), and then attended Yale University, New Haven, Connecticut, where she received a Bachelor of Fine Arts degree the following year.

A conceptual artist, Reichek has held many solo exhibitions of her work in galleries and universities, including the Parsons Dreyfus Gallery, New York City (1978, 1979); "Special Projects: Artist's Bedrooms," Institute for Art and Urban Resources, P.S.1, Long Island City,

New York (1979); Rutgers University, New Brunswick, New Jersey (1980); A.I.R. Gallery, New York City (1981, 1985, 1987); "Houses," with Vito Acconci and Ira Joel Haber, Snug Harbor Museum, Staten Island, New York (1985); "Revenge of the Coconuts: A Curiosity Room," 56 Bleeker Street Gallery, New York City (1988); "Native Intelligence," a travelling show from New York University, New York City, to South Carolina, Ohio, and Washington (1992); and others. Her work has been invited to numerous group exhibitions in the United States and abroad, such as "Out of the House," Whitney Museum Downtown, New York City (1978); "USA: Women Artists," Museo de Arte Contemporanea, São Paulo, Brazil (1980); Lunds Kunsthalle, Lund, Sweden (1981); "Women Sculptor's Drawings," Max Hutchinson Gallery, New York City (1982); "Neue Stofflichkeit," Frauen Museum, Bonn, Germany (1984); "New York Art Now: Correspondences," a travelling show, La Forêt Museum, Tokyo, Japan (1985); "Words and Images with a Message," Women's Studio Workshop, Rosendale, New York (1990); "Burning in Hell," Franklin Furnace, New York City (1991); "PHOTOWORKS," Michael Klein, Inc., New York City (1992); and many others.

Reichek has been a guest lecturer at diverse institutions on equally diverse topics throughout the United States. Her work is represented in private and public permanent collections, including the Portland Art Museum, Oregon; Norton Gallery of Art, West Palm Beach, Florida; Best Products, Inc., Ashland, Virginia; and others.

Bibliography
Adams, Brooks. An Interview. *Art in America* (July 1989).
Goldberg, Vicki. "Context is All—Or Nothing." *The New York Times* (July 7, 1991): 25–26.
Miller, Charles V. "Domestic Science." *Artforum* (March 1989).
Princenthal, Nancy. "Elaine Reichek's Native Intelligence." *The Print Collector's Newsletter* (July–August 1992): 94–95.

Reid, Leslie Mary Margaret (1947–)

Born in Ottawa, Ontario, Canada, the painter/printmaker Leslie Mary Margaret Reid studied at Queen's University, Kingston, Ontario, under the aegis of Ralph Allen and Stanley Swain, where she received a Bachelor's degree in art history (1964–1967). Reid then took studio work at the Byam Shaw School of Art, London, England (1968–1970); and printmaking at the Chelsea School of Art (1970–1971); about five years later, she took a course in photolithography at the Slade School of Fine Art, London, England, from Stanley Jones.

Reid has held solo exhibitions in museums and galleries in Canada and abroad, including Gallery Zella 9, London, England (1973); Algonquin College, Ottawa (1975), Gallery Graphics, Ottawa (1976, 1978), and Mira Godard Gallery, Toronto (1978, 1981)—all in Ontario; Canadian Cultural Center, Paris, France (1980); Galerie Jolliet, Montréal, Québec (1982); and others. An inspirational teacher, her large-scale paintings and prints have been included in many prestigious group shows, such as Marlborough Graphics, New York City (1974); "12th International Biennial of Graphic Art, Ljubljana, Yugoslavia (1977); 7th International Print Biennial, Cracow, Poland (1978); "Canadian Contemporary Prints," National Gallery of Canada, Ottawa (1978); Festival Internationale de la Peinture, Cages sur Mer, France (1979); and others. Examples of her work are in private and public permanent collections throughout Canada.

Bibliography
Babinska, Anna. "Leslie Reid: Light Distilled." *Artmagazine* 11:45 (September–October 1979): 47–49.
Graham, Mayo. *Some Canadian Women Artists*. A Catalog. National Gallery of Canada, 1975–1976.
Leslie Reid. A Catalog. Paris, France: Canadian Cultural Center, 1980.

Reid, Mary Hiester (1854–1921)

Born in Reading, Pennsylvania the painter Mary Hiester Reid studied at the School of Design, Philadelphia, Pennsylvania (1872), and with Thomas Eakins; she took further study at the Académie Colorossi, Paris, France, under the aegis of Dagnan-Bouveret and others.

Widely travelled in Europe, Reid was a resident of Toronto, well-known for her still-life paintings, and an elected associate member of the Royal Canadian Academy and the Ontario Society of Artists. She held joint exhibitions with her husband, George Reid, and others, including Oliver, Coate and Company, Toronto (1888); Art Metropole, Toronto (1912); Royal Ontario Museum, Toronto (1915); and others. In 1922 a memorial exhibition of Reid's work—more than 300 paintings—was held at the Art Gallery of Ontario, Toronto.

Examples of 's her paintings are in private and public permanent collections, including the Art Gallery of Ontario, Laurentian University, Sudbury, National Gallery of Canada, Ottawa—all in Ontario; and many others.

Bibliography
MacBeth, Madge. "Canadian Women in the Arts." *Maclean's* 27:12 (October 1914): 23–25, 105–08.
Memorial Exhibition of Paintings by Mary Hiester Reid, ARCA, OSA. A Catalog. Toronto, Ontario: Art Gallery of Ontario, 1922.

Reindel, Edna (1900–)

Born in Detroit, Michigan, the painter and muralist Edna Reindel learned her craft at Pratt Institute, Brooklyn, New York. Reindel was one of several artists called upon to paint murals for the Works Progress Administration (WPA).

Reindel exhibited work in museums and galleries, including the Whitney Museum of American Art, New York City (1934, 1937, 1938, 1940); Carnegie Institute, Pittsburgh, Pennsylvania (1937, 1938, 1944–1946); the Art Institute of Chicago, Illinois (1934, 1945); and others.

Examples of Reindel's work are in private and public permanent collections, including Ball State Teachers College (now Ball State University), Muncie, Indiana; the Metropolitan Museum of Art and the Whitney Museum of American Art—both in New York City; a U.S. post office mural, Swainsboro, Georgia; and others.

Bibliography
American Art Annual. Vol. 28. American Federation of Arts, 1932.
Paintings and Mural Sketches. New York: MacBeth Gallery, 1937.
Second Biennial Exhibition of Contemporary American Painting. Whitney Museum of American Art, 1934.

Reinertson, Lisa (1955–)

Born in Washington, D.C., Lisa Reinertson earned a Bachelor's degree from the University of California at Davis with highest honors in 1982. She studied at the Skowhegan School of Painting and Sculpture, Maine (1983), and, the following year, received a Master of Fine Arts degree from the University of California at Davis.

Reinertson has held a number of solo exhibitions of her work throughout California, including the James Snidle Gallery, Chico (1992); Natsoulas/Noveloso Gallery, Davis (1991); University of the Pacific, Stockton (1990); "Introductions," Dorothy Weiss Gallery, San Francisco (1987); Southern Exposure Gallery, San Francisco (1986); Shackleford and Sears Gallery, Davis (1985); the Art Works Gallery, Sacramento (1985); and others. Her work has been invited to thirty-five group exhibitions between 1981 and 1991, such as "Sculptural Perspectives for the Nineties," Muckenthaler Cultural Center, Fullerton, California (1991); "California Ceramic Sculptors/IV Concorso Della Ceramica D'Arte," Savona, Italy (1990); "Contemporary Ceramics: The Artists of TB9," California State University, Fullerton (1989); "Dr. Martin Luther King Sculpture Proposal," Kalamazoo Institute for the Arts, Michigan (1988); "Twelfth International Sculpture Conference," Gallery Space, San Francisco, California (1982); and others.

Winner of six awards and honors for her sculpture, Reinertson was commissioned to create two seven-foot bronze figures for Arco Stadium and a bronze for the University of California Medical Center, Sacramento (1991); a bronze portrait of Martin Luther King Jr. for the City of Kalamazoo, Michigan (1989), and a clay portrait of King for the King Hall Law School at University of California at Davis (1987). She has been an assistant professor of ceramics at California State University, Chico, since 1987, and has lectured widely. Her work is represented in private and public permanent collections from New York to California.

Bibliography

Crane, Carolyn. "Up Front, 2nd Annual California Conference." *Ceramics Monthly* (September 1991).

Klein, Elaine. "Proposed King Park Centerpiece on Display." *Kalamazoo Gazette* (July 15, 1988).

Simon, Richard. "A Fair of the Art." *Sacramento Union* (August 17, 1985).

Remington, Deborah (1935–)

Over a period of thirty years Deborah Remington's work has developed with remarkable consistency from its beginnings within the abstract expressionist traditions of the San Francisco Bay Area. By 1965, when she painted "Haddonfield" (Whitney Museum of American Art), the iconic majesty of her work had firmly established her position among the front ranks of American abstract painters. The distinctive, polished surfaces of the paintings of the 1960s and 1970s gave way in the 1980s to a re-emergence of the brushstroke; simultaneously, her work became less rigid in its structure, while retaining an intensely personal palette of fiery reds, steel-cold greys, strangely hot blues, and vivid contrasts of dark and light.

Born in Haddonfield, New Jersey, Remington attended high school in Pasadena, California, then went to San Francisco, California, for study at the San Francisco Art Institute—the school that, under the direction of Douglas MacAgy, had become the central force for advanced painting on the West Coast. There, in the 1950s, she studied with Clyfford Still, who "made you question all your assumptions," as well as with Elmer Bischoff, Ed Corbett, David Park, and Hassell Smith. After leaving the school she spent three years in the Far East; in Japan she studied classical and contemporary calligraphy—study that provided important discipline for her later work—and engaged in a brief career as an actress. Returning to San Francisco she concentrated on drawing during the early 1960s—work that culminated in her "breakthrough" painting, "Statement" (1963, San Francisco Museum of Modern Art).

In 1965 Remington established a studio in New York City, where she continues to work. Although primarily a painter she has also created several series of extraordinary color lithographs, principally at Tamarind Institute in Albuquerque, New Mexico (1973–1980). Her work, which is represented in numerous public and private collections in the United States and Europe, was the subject of a major retrospective exhibition organized in 1984 by the Newport Harbor Art Museum, California.

Clinton Adams

Bibliography

Ashton, Dore. *American Art Since 1945.* Oxford University Press, 1982.

Deborah Remington: A 20-Year Survey. Exhibition Catalog. Essay by Dore Ashton. Biography and bibliography. California: Newport Harbor Art Museum, 1984.

Kuspit, Donald B. "Deborah Remington: Autonomy and Absence in the Visual Koan." *Art International* 23:3/4 (Summer 1979): 17–23.

Robins, Corinne. "Deborah Remington: Paintings without Answers." *Arts Magazine* 51 (April 1977): 140–41.

Replinger, Dot (1924–)

Born in Chicago, Illinois, the fiber artist Dot Replinger earned a Bachelor's degree in art education at the Art Institute of Chicago, where she studied with Carolyn Howlett and Else Regensteiner.

Replinger has held many solo exhibitions in galleries and museums in the Midwest, including the Edward Sherbeyn Gallery, Chicago, Illinois (1970); Knoll International, St. Louis, Missouri (1971); Octagon Art Center Gallery, Evanston (1980), Kankakee Historical Museum (1983), Paris Centennial Museum (1985), and Parkland College Art Gallery, Champaign (1987)—all in Illinois; and others. Her work has been invited to many national group exhibitions, such as "Southern Tier," Corning, New York, where she won a jury award (1969); "Craft Multiples," a travelling show, Renwick Gallery, Washington, D.C. (1975–1980); Marietta Crafts National, Ohio (1975, 1977); "Clay and Fiber: 15 Viewpoints," Wustum Museum, Racine, Wisconsin (1978); "Fiber Forms '78," Cincinnati Art Museum, Ohio (1978); "Artists Invitational," Museum of Arts, Evansville, Indiana (1978); and others.

Winner of awards and honors for her fiber works, Replinger was the recipient of a National Endowment for the Arts (NEA) craftsman fellowship (1976); the Buckman textile award (1969); the A.A.U.W. interest group award at the Mississippi River Crafts Show, Memphis, Tennessee; and purchase prizes at the Mid-States Craft Exhibition, Evansville, Indiana (1968, 1975). She won first place awards (1971, 1974, 1991) at the Oakbrook Center Invitational, Illinois; and honorable mention prizes (1973, 1975, 1980, 1983); and received awards at the North Shore Art League Craft Show, Northbrook, Illinois (1974, 1979, 1980). Her commissioned work hangs in private and public permanent collections, including Amerinvesco; Caterpillar International; Sinai Temple; Champaign Public Library; and State of Illinois Building, Chicago—all in Illinois; Waterfront Place, Seattle, Washington; and many others.

Bibliography
The Fiberarts Design Book I. Hastings House, Publishers, 1980.
Who's Who in American Art. 19th ed. R.R. Bowker Co., 1991–1992.

Reynal, Jeanne (1903–)

Born in White Plains, New York, the mosaicist Jeanne Reynal studied in Paris, France, and apprenticed to Boris Anrep (1930–1938).

Reynal's work has been seen in many solo and group exhibitions in the United States and abroad, including the "1954 Annual Exhibition of Contemporary American Sculpture, Watercolors, and Drawings," Whitney Museum of American Art, New York City (1954); San Francisco Museum of Art, California, a travelling exhibition to Amarillo, Texas; Boston, Massachusetts; Lincoln, Nebraska; and Montréal, Québec, Canada (1964); "Women Artists of America 1707–1964," the Newark Museum, New Jersey (1965); Betty Parsons Gallery, New York City (1971); "Women Choose Women," New York Cultural Center (1973); Bodley Gallery, New York City (1976); and many others.

Reynal's mosaics run the gamut of approaches: from large non-objective panels as in "Reincarnation Lullabies" (1961), and "Nanyuki" (1970), a three-dimensional standing sculpture, to wry and delightful portraits of noted personages, such as Buckminster Fuller, Marcel Duchamp, King Faisal, Martha Graham, and Mrs. Onassis.

She executed many mosaic commissions, including the Nebraska State Capitol building; the Ford Foundation, White Plains, New York; and her work is represented in private and public permanent collections such as the Museum of Modern Art (MoMA), and the Whitney Museum of American Art—both in New York City; Walker Art Center, Minneapolis, Minnesota; and others.

Bibliography
Ashton, Dore, Lawrence Campbell, et al. *The Mosaics of Jeanne Reynal.* October House, 1969.
DeKooning, Elaine. "Jeanne Reynal, Mosiac Portraits." *Craft Horizons* 36:4 (August 1976): 32–35.
Gerdts, William H. "Reynal Makes a Mosaic." *Art News* 52 (December 1953): 34–36, 51–53.
Wooster, Ann-Sargent. "Jeanne Reynal and Ethel Schwabacher (Bodley). *Art News* 75:3 (March 1976): 142.

Rheaume, Jeanne Leblanc (1915–)

Born in Montréal, Québec, Canada, the painter Jeanne Leblanc Rheaume was a student at l'École des Beaux-Arts in her native city (1934–1936); she also studied under the aegis of Harold Beament, Lilias Torrance Newton, and Goodridge Roberts at the Art Association of Montréal.

Rheaume has held solo exhibitions in museums and galleries in Canada and abroad, including the Galerie de l'Atelier, Québec (1949, 1955); Dominion Gallery, Montréal (1951, 1953); Galleria Il Camino, Rome, Italy (1955); Pavillon Hélène de Champlain, Montréal (1958); Institut Français, Florence, Italy (1959); Galerie l'Art Français, Montréal (1972, 1975, 1981); Wallack Galleries, Ottawa (1979, 1982); and many others. Her paintings have been included in many prestigious group shows since the 1940s.

A longtime resident of Florence, Italy, Rheaume has won prizes and honors for her work. Examples of her paintings are in private and public permanent collections, including the Art Gallery of Hamilton, Ontario; Art Gallery of Vancouver, British Columbia; Canada Council Art Bank, Ottawa; and Montréal Museum of Fine Arts—all in Canada; Maison du Québec, Paris, France; and many others.

Bibliography
Chevalier, Willie. "Jeanne Rheaume et la rigueur." *Vie des arts* 20:78 (Spring 1975): 26–27.
MacDonald, Colin S. *A Dictionary of Canadian Artists.* Canadian Paperbacks, 1984.
Westbridge, Anthony, ed. *Canadian Art Sales Index.* Vancouver, 1985.

Rhoades, Katharine Nash (1885–1965)

Late in the first decade of the twentieth century, the avant-garde painter and poet Katharine Nash Rhoades, accompanied by Malvina Hoffman and Marion Beckett, went to Paris, France. A rich rebel, she was drawn to the visual excitement found at Alfred Stieglitz's Gallery 291, New York City, and held her first solo exhibition of paintings there in 1915.

Rhoades's works during that period were not unlike those shown by the pre-World War I paintings of Matisse and his friends. Unfortunately, Rhoades burned most of her early work in the 1920s; some paintings survive that show an awareness of Cubism.

Rhoades also contributed poems and illustrations to the journals *291* and *Camera Work,* which proclaimed, in visual and written terms, her strong feminist views; further, she was a prime mover in the establishment and administration of the New York City Dada group and equally active in the establishment of the Freer Gallery, Washington, D.C.

Bibliography
"Art Notes." *The New York Times* (January 30, 1915): 8.
Dunford, Penny. *Biographical Dictionary of Women Artists in Europe and America since 1850.* University of Pennsylvania Press, 1989.
Devree, Howard. "A Reviewer's Notebook." *The New York Times* (March 17, 1935): 7.
Homer, William Innes, et al. *Avant-Garde Painting and Sculpture in America 1910–1925.* Delaware Art Museum, 1975.

Rice, Jacqueline Ione (1941–)

Born in Orange, California, the ceramist Jacqueline Ione Rice earned a Bachelor's degree from the University of Washington, Seattle (1968), where she studied with Fred Bauer, Howard Kottler, and Robert Sperry. Two years later she received a Master of Fine Arts degree from the same institution.

An educator as well as an artist, Rice has taught at the Kansas City Art Institute (1971–1973); the University of Michigan, Ann Arbor (1973–1977); and since 1977 has been head of the ceramics department at the Rhode Island School of Design, Providence.

Rice received a Mellon grant in 1984, which she used to research indigenous pottery. This study, in turn, led to her designing tableware for Grazia—a majolica factory in Deruta, Italy. She works in wood and handmade paper in addition to the complex, sculptural clay forms and innovative tableware for which she is known.

Bibliography
Clark, Garth. *American Ceramics: 1896 to the Present.* Abbeville Press, 1987.

Richards, Lucy C. (early twentieth century)

Born in Lawrence, Massachusetts, the sculptor Lucy C. Richards studied at the Boston Museum School of Fine Arts, Massachusetts; with Kops in Dresden and Eustritz in Berlin, Germany; and at the Académie Julian, Paris, France.

Richards was a member of several arts organizations, including the Guild of Boston Artists, and the Copley Society of Boston—both in Massachusetts; the National Association of Women Painters and Sculptors, New York City; and others. She exhibited work at the "Annual Exhibition of Painting and Sculpture," Art Institute of Chicago, Illinois (1912), among other venues. Her work is represented in private and public permanent collections.

Bibliography

American Art Annual. Vol. 28. American Federation of Arts, 1932.

Fielding, Mantle. *Dictionary of American Painters, Sculptors, and Engravers.* Modern Books and Crafts, 1974.

Pattison, James W. "Annual Exhibition of Painting and Sculpture, Art Institute of Chicago." *Fine Arts Journal* 27:6 (December 1912): 791–99.

Richardson, Constance Coleman (1905–)

The landscape painter Constance Coleman Richardson grew up in Indianapolis, Indiana, where her father was a professor. After attending Vassar College, Poughkeepsie, New York, she studied from 1925 to 1928 at the Pennsylvania Academy of Fine Arts, Pennsylvania, where she met Edgar P. Richardson, a fellow painting student, who became an art historian and her husband. She worked in Indianapolis from 1928 to 1930. Upon their marriage in 1931, the Richardsons moved to Detroit, Michigan, and lived there for more than thirty years while Edgar served as editor of *The Art Quarterly* and director of the Detroit Institute of Arts.

During the summers that Richardson and her husband spent in the hills of Vermont and New York state she painted rural landscapes. When they were based in the Midwest she painted along the Great Lakes. Then she discovered the West, and many subsequent vacations were spent in Wyoming, where she worked outdoors making oil sketches that she later converted to finished oil paintings on gesso-grounded masonite. Often her husband served as the model for the sole figure inhabiting her paintings of the Western expanse.

Richardson's realistic landscape paintings were included in exhibitions on both coasts and in the Midwest in the 1930s, receiving numerous prizes. In addition to her exhibitions at the Macbeth Gallery in New York City in the 1940s and 1950s, she was given an exhibition at the M.H. De Young Memorial Museum, San Francisco, California, in 1947. Her work was included in the Pennsylvania Academy of Fine Arts, Philadelphia, and the Detroit Institute of Art, Michigan, biennial exhibitions of 1957 and 1959; the Kennedy Galleries in New York City in the 1960s and in 1970. She lives in Philadelphia, Pennsylvania.

Eleanor Tufts

Bibliography

Bruner, Louise. "The Paintings of Constance Richardson." *American Artist* 25:1 (January 1961): 21–25, 64–66.

Rubinstein, Charlotte Streifer. *American Women Artists.* G.K. Hall, 1982.

Tufts, Eleanor. *American Women Artists, 1830–1930.* National Museum of Women in the Arts, 1987.

Richardson, Margaret Foster (1881–c. 1945)

The Boston portrait painter Margaret Foster Richardson was born in Winnetka, Illinois, and arrived in Boston, Massachusetts, in 1900 to study painting at the Massachusetts State Normal Art School. After studying there for five years with Joseph DeCamp and Ernest L. Major, she entered Edmund C. Tarbell's portrait class at the Boston Museum School in 1905, and from 1906 to 1908 was a special student acting as Anson Cross's assistant.

Richardson had a solo exhibition in 1910 at the Copley Gallery in Boston. Her first award came in 1911 when she won the Harris bronze medal (and $300 prize) at the Art Institute of Chicago, Illinois. This was followed by the Maynard portrait prize at the National Academy of Design, New York City, in 1913. Her remarkably original and vital "Self-Portrait, A Motion Picture" (1912, Pennsylvania Academy of Fine Arts) was exhibited at the Pennsylvania Academy in 1913 before she departed on her own study tour of the art galleries of Europe—starting in Spain, and continuing to Italy, Austria, Germany, Holland, Belgium, France, and England.

Among Richardson's early works are paintings in the Tarbell/DeCamp style (inspired by the painter Jan Vermeer), such as the "Seated Woman" (1909, Sotheby's New York), a single figure in a domestic interior replete with still-life objects; the realistic scene is rendered in a soft, poetic tonality. Her greatest body of work lies in portraiture; among her subjects were "Mary Baker Eddy," founder of the Christian Science Church; "Professor Robert H. Richards" of the Massachusetts Institute of Technology (MIT), Cambridge, Massachusetts; "Dr. William E. Huntington," former president of Boston University, Massachusetts; "Admiral Phelps" for the *U.S.S. Phelps*; portraits of headmasters of the Boston, Massachusetts, public schools; and portraits for the American Legion Post in Lynn, Massachusetts, and for the public library in Lawrence, Massachusetts.

Eleanor Tufts

Bibliography

Tufts, Eleanor. *American Women Artists, 1830–1930.* National Museum of Women in the Arts, 1987.

Rideout, Alice (c. 1872–)

Born in Marysville, California, the figurative sculptor Alice Rideout, even as a child, knew she would one day be a sculptor. Rideout studied privately with Rupert Schmidt; attended the San Francisco School of Design, California; and won her first commission before her twentieth birthday.

Rideout's drawings and maquette for the sculptural commission at the Woman's Building of the World's Columbian Exposition, Chicago, Illinois (1893), prevailed against all others; she employed workmen to do the rough, preliminary work on the stone figures for the pediment leaving the final stages for her own hands. Nothing but speculation abounds as to the remainder of Rideout's career.

Bibliography

Banks, Charles Eugene. *The Artistic Guide to Chicago and the World's Columbian Exposition.* R.S. Pearle Co., 1893.

Elliott, Maude Howe, ed. *Art and Handicraft in the Woman's Building of the World's Columbian Exposition, Chicago, 1893.* Rand, McNally and Co., 1894.

Weimann, Jeanne Madeline. *The Fair Women.* Academy Chicago, 1981.

Rieger, Patricia (1952–)

Born in Portland, Maine, the ceramic sculptor Patricia Rieger studied at several institutions of higher learning, including Goddard College, Plainfield, Vermont, where she earned a Bachelor's degree (1976); the New York State College of Ceramics, Alfred University, New York, where she received a Bachelor of Fine Arts degree (1983); and the University of North Carolina at Chapel Hill, where, three years later, she was awarded a Master of Fine Arts degree.

Rieger has had her work invited to, or included in many group exhibitions in the United States and abroad, such as "Northern Telecom's Annual Exhibition of North Carolina Sculpture," Research Triangle Park (1985–1988), at which she won a purchase award; "Patricia Rieger and Xavier Toubes," Ceramicas de Sargadelos, Lugo, Spain (1986); Butler Institute of Art, Youngstown, Ohio (1987); "Wittes Ende Show," the Signature Shop and Gallery, Atlanta, Georgia (1988); "Recent Ceramic Work by Three Alfred Graduates," Martha Scheider Gallery, Inc., Chicago, Illinois (1989); and others.

Winner of a visual arts fellowship from the Southern Arts Federation (1987), Rieger creates highly personal, occasionally whimsical, sometimes absurd human and animal ceramic sculptures. "Two Views, One Window" (1986), a glazed earthenware piece, is typical of her work of this period.

Bibliography

Nine from North Carolina: An Exhibition of Women Artists. North Carolina State Committee and the National Museum of Women in the Arts, 1989.

Rifka, Judy (1945–)

A native New Yorker, the multi-talented Judy Rifka attended Hunter College, New York City (1963–1966), and the New York Studio School, also in New York City, where she studied with Philip Guston (1966); she also studied at the Skowhegan School of Painting and Sculpture, Maine.

Painter, video artist, and book artist—Rifka is an artist who takes risks and woos chance not unlike a jazz musician. She has held solo exhibitions and installations in museums and galleries in the United States and abroad, including Franklin Furnace (1977), and Printed Matter (1980)—both in New York City; Museum für (sub) Kultur, Berlin, and Hamburg—both in Germany (1981); "Judy Rifka: Major Works 1981–1984," Knight Gallery, Charlotte, North Carolina (1984); "Judy Rifka: Installation," Gracie Mansion, New York City (1985); and others. Her work is represented in private and public permanent collections, including the Boston Museum of Fine Arts, Massachusetts; New York Public Library and Whitney Museum of American Art—both in New York City; Toledo Museum of Art, Ohio; University of North Carolina, Greensboro; and others.

Bibliography

Brenson, Michael. "Judy Rifka." *The New York Times* (January 25, 1985).
Howe, Katherine. "Judy Rifka at Brooke Alexander." *Image and Issues* (July–August 1983).
Smith, Roberta. "Intermural Painting." *Village Voice* (February 23, 1982).

Ringgold, Faith (1930–)

The paintings, soft sculpture, installations, performance art, and quilts of Faith Ringgold narrate African-American history and racial politics from a highly personal, feminist perspective.

Born in New York City, Ringgold was raised in Harlem during the Depression in the wake of the African-American literary and visual arts movement known as the Harlem Renaissance. Frequently sick with asthma as a small child, Ringgold began drawing and painting to pass the time. She attended the City College of New York, where she received a Bachelor of Science degree in fine art in 1955 and a Master of Arts degree in art in 1959. During the 1950s she married classical and jazz pianist Robert Earl Wallace (1950), and had two children: Michael Faith Wallace and Barbara Faith Wallace. This marriage ended in divorce in 1956. She subsequently married Burdette Ringgold in 1962.

Motivated by the civil rights and black power movements in the 1960s, Ringgold's work began to address issues of American racism and the ironies of American democratic ideals. Many of her first political paintings were inspired by the writings of James Baldwin and Amiri Baraka. Her "American People" series (1963–1967) included powerful images utilizing the American flag and iconic figures. Works such as "The American Dream" (1964), "God Bless America" (1962), "The Flag is Bleeding" (1967), and "Die" (1967) challenged the American establishment. In 1968 she actively participated in the protests against the Whitney Museum of American Art and the Museum of Modern Art (MoMA)—both in New York City, for not being more inclusive of artists of color.

As an African-American feminist in the 1970s, Ringgold turned from painted images on canvas, which were associated with Western European-American traditions, to fabric pieces, cloth paintings, and soft sculpture, which combined African and feminine craft sensibilities. Many of her early fabric works were made in collaboration with her mother, fashion designer and dressmaker Wili Posey. By the end of the decade she had expanded into the realm of multi-media installation and performance art to make her social and political statements. During this period Ringgold also made her first story quilt.

Quilt-making, which to Ringgold was so closely tied to her early family memories, as well as being so connected with women's lives, became an effective medium for the artist to express her ideas. Combining pictures, symbols, and a written narrative, Ringgold's social content found a feminist context.

In her painted story quilts (1980–1988) Ringgold's narrations varied from her own telling of Alice Walker's novel, *The Color Purple* ("The Purple Quilt," 1986), to her enchanting "Tar Beach" (1988), a work that depicts a family on the rooftop of a Harlem brownstone on a hot summer night, to her documenting of her own successful attempts at dramatic weight loss, in "Change: Faith Ringgold's . . . Weight Loss" (1986).

While Ringgold's work became less politically obvious in the late 1980s, at its base are still her strong convictions as an African-American feminist artist. As the decade changed Ringgold began another avenue of expression. In 1990 she published her first children's book, *Tar Beach*. Since her graduation from City College, New York City, in 1955, Ringgold has also had a career as a teacher. She taught in the New York City public schools between 1955 and 1973; she has lectured widely; and, in 1984, she joined the faculty of the University of California, San Diego. A twenty-year retrospective of her work was mounted at the Studio Museum in Harlem in New York in 1984.

Ringgold has received a number of awards, including a National Endowment for the Arts (NEA) award in sculpture in (1978); an honorary Doctorate degree from the Moore College of Art, Philadelphia, Pennsylvania (1986); and a Guggenheim Foundation fellowship (1987). She was also awarded an honorary Doctorate degree at the College of Wooster, Ohio, that same year. She received a New York Foundation for the Arts award for painting; and, in 1990, a major exhibition of her work, "Faith Ringgold: A 25-Year Survey," began a national tour to twelve venues. Her work is included in the collections of the Guggenheim Museum, the Metropolitan Museum of Art, the Museum of Modern Art (MoMA), and the Studio Museum of Harlem—all in New York City; the Newark Museum, New Jersey; and the High Museum, Atlanta, Georgia; among others.

Lucinda H. Gedeon

Bibliography

Flomenhaft, Eleanor, et al. *Faith Ringgold: A 25-Year Survey*. Hempstead, New York: Fine Arts Museum of Long Island, 1990.

Gouma-Peterson, Thalia. "Faith Ringgold's Narrative Quilts." *Arts Magazine* (January 1987): 66–68.

———, and Kathleen McMannus Zurko, eds. *Faith Ringgold: Painting, Sculpture and Performance*. Ohio: The College of Wooster Art Museum, 1985.

Ringgold, Faith. "Being My Own Woman." *Confirmation: An Anthology of African American Women*. Ed. Amiri Baraka and Amina Baraka. William Morrow, 1983.

Roth, Moira. "The Field and the Drawing Room." *Faith Ringgold Change: Painted Story Quilts*. New York: Bernice Steinbaum Gallery, 1987.

Wallace, Michele, ed. *Faith Ringgold: Twenty Years of Painting, Sculpture and Performance (1963–1983)*. New York: Studio Museum in Harlem, 1984.

Rippon, Ruth (1927–)

Born in Sacramento, California, the ceramist/sculptor Ruth Rippon earned a Bachelor's degree at the California College of Arts and Crafts, Oakland (1947). Two years later, after study with Antonio Prieto, she received a Master of Fine Arts degree from the same institution. She also studied with Joan Jockwig Pearson while on a scholarship at the San Francisco School of Fine Arts, California.

Rippon has held many solo exhibitions between 1948 and 1987, including Gumps, San Francisco (1953), Artists Contemporary Gallery, Sacramento (1960, 1965, 1967, 1969, 1972, 1974, 1977, 1979, 1981, 1987), Barrios Art Gallery, Sacramento (1961–1964), Humboldt State College, Arcata (1961), Chico State College (1965)—all in California; "Ruth Rippon Retrospectives," Crocker Art Gallery, Sacramento, California (1971, 1983); and the University of Rochester, New York (1976); Sacramento City College (1978), and College of Holy Names, Oakland (1982)—both in California; and many others throughout the United States. Her work has been invited to many group exhibitions, such as the California State Fair (1948–1956, 1958–1961, 1964–1966, 1972, 1980); Syracuse National Ceramic Exhibition, New York (1949, 1958); Pacific Coast Ceramic Exhibition, San Francisco, California (1951–1954); Wichita Decorative Arts and Ceramics Show, Kansas (1949, 1954, 1959–1962); Museum of Contemporary Craft, New York City (1956); "World Tour: Ceramics and Textiles," United States Information Agency (USIA) (1957); Mills College Invitational, Oakland (1962), San Francisco Potters Annual, M.H. De Young Memorial Museum, San Francisco (1965–1966, 1968); Artists Contemporary Gallery, Sacramento (1979, 1981); Michael Himovitz Gallery, Sacramento

(1982)—all in California; and others.

A professor of art at California State University at Sacramento, Rippon has been the recipient of twenty-four awards between 1948 and 1985 for her ceramic work, in addition to such commissions as a casserole dish for the home of the vice-president of the United States; a life-sized clay sculpture, "The Lollies" (1984), installed at the Pavilions Shopping Center, Sacramento; "Woman with Shells," sited at Freeport Square, Sacramento; "Mother with Children," also at the Pavilions Shopping Center—all in California; and many private commissions of large-scale sculptural work. Examples of her work are located in private, public, and corporate permanent collections, including the Crocker Art Gallery, Sacramento; Chico State College; San Francisco Art Commission; Antonio Prieto Memorial Collection, Mills College, Oakland—all in California; Memorial Museum, Rochester, New York; and many others.

Bibliography

"Stunning Exhibit of Rippon's Art." *Sacramento Bee* (November 1979).

"Ceramist for the Moment." *Pioneer Magazine* (January 1980).

"Rippon's Art is Reassuring." *Sacramento Union* (November 1980).

Ristvedt-Henderek, Milly (1942–)

Born in Kimberley, British Columbia, the painter Milly Ristvedt-Henderek studied at the Vancouver School of Art, British Columbia, under the aegis of Roy Kiyooka (1960–1964).

Ristvedt-Henderek has held solo exhibitions in galleries and museums in Canada, including the Carmen Lamanna Gallery, Toronto (1968, 1969 1970); Galerie Joliet, Québec (1974, 1975, 1978, 1979); Algonquin College, Ottawa (1977); Klonaridis, Inc., Toronto (1979, 1981, 1984); Martin Gerard Gallery, Edmonton, Alberta (1980, 1982); Galerie Don Stewart, Montréal (1980, 1982, 1983); Moore Gallery Ltd., Hamilton, Ontario (1985); and more. Her paintings have been included in many prestigious group shows, since the "Centennial Awards Exhibition," Art Gallery of Ontario, Toronto (1967).

Ristvedt-Henderek has been an inspiring teacher for many years and a winner of prizes and honors; her work is represented in private, public, and corporate permanent collections in Canada and elsewhere, including the Art Gallery of Hamilton, Ontario; the Art Gallery of Ontario, Toronto; Boston Museum of Fine Arts, Massachusetts; Canada Council Art Bank, Ottawa; Montréal Museum of Fine Arts; Musée d'Art Contemporain, Montréal; Shell Oil, Canada Ltd.; and many others.

Bibliography

Burnett, David, and Marilyn Schiff. *Contemporary Canadian Art*. Mel Hurtig, 1983.

Wilkin, Karen. *Milly Ristvedt-Henderek: Paintings of a Decade*. A Catalog. Queen's University, 1979–1980.

———. *Canada x Ten*. A Catalog. Edmonton Art Gallery, 1974.

Robbins, Ellen (1828–1905)

Born in Watertown, Massachusetts, Ellen Robbins was a self-taught watercolorist, specializing in flowers and autumn leaves. She had one year of study at the School of Design in Boston, Massachusetts. When she could find no one in Boston offering instruction in watercolor she took the initiative herself and painted her first watercolor of violets at the Forest Hills Cemetery. She conceived the idea of painting in albums and began by selling a volume of twenty watercolors for $25. Before long she had created a vogue for her albums of autumn leaves. She also realized that she could fill a vacuum in Boston, and she offered classes in "Flower and Autumn Leaf Painting." At the outset she travelled by trolley car from Watertown, but in later years she moved into Boston.

As early as 1850 Robbins began spending summers on the Isles of Shoals off the New Hampshire coast. The poet Celia Thaxter maintained both a literary salon and a special garden which provided endless subject matter for visiting artists. Robbins, handicapped by a lame leg since birth, was not prevented from travelling, and in 1873 she sailed for Europe with her sister, Martha, to see both art and flowers.

Robbins's paintings of flowers are awesome for their beauty and for their size. "Peonies" (1887, Watertown Free Public Library), for example, is especially large for a watercolor, measuring twenty-four inches by thirty-six and one quarter inches. In addition to the profusion of blossoms in these works there is a variety of bowls, such as the blue-and-white design of houses and foliage in "Peonies" and a translucent spherical green vase in "Carnations and Poppies" (1888, Worcester Art Museum). Her paintings, reproduced in chromolithographs by Louis Prang, were very popular in England. She also painted a long frieze of flowers for the Browning Room at Wellesley College, Massachusetts, but it was destroyed in a fire and is known today only in photographs.

Eleanor Tufts

Bibliography
Gerdts, William H. *Down Garden Paths: The Floral Environment in American Art.* Associated University Presses, 1983.
Robbins, Ellen. "Reminiscences of a Flower Paints." *New England Magazine* 14:4 (June 1896): 440–51, and 5 (July 1986): 532–45.
Tufts, Eleanor. *American Women Artists, 1830–1930.* National Museum of Women in the Arts, 1987.

Robert, Louise (1941–)

Born in Montréal, Québec, Canada, Louise Robert grew up in a cosmopolitan cultural atmosphere of anti-authoritarian *automatisme* inspired by Paul-Émile Borduas. However, unlike the *automatistes* (or their near relatives, the abstract expressionists), Robert is a thoroughgoing post-modernist who questions the assumptions of free abstraction and the notion of self-expression. Her work thus bears some resemblances to action painting, but it also includes ironic phrases—for example, "À ne pas lire" (Not to Be Read)—which draw the viewer's attention to the linguistic variability of visual signs. Other works include an illegible calligraphy reminiscent of Cy Twombly's. Most recently her images evoke colorful landscapes not unlike the works of Jack Bush, but she usually includes some linguistically disorienting element.

Robert J. Belton

Bibliography
Burnett, David. *Cineplex Odeon: The First Ten Years*, 1989.

Roberts, Holly (1951–)

The eerie and compelling images of Holly Roberts's paintings derive much of their emotive content from the uncommon tension that exists between her painterly technique and the neutral, photographic surface upon which she works. The photographs that serve her as jumping-off points become "palimpsests," ultimately to be buried or erased by the forms that cover them. The strange animals that are her frequent subjects emerge from a nighttime world in which the spirits walk and anything is possible.

Born in Boulder, Colorado, Roberts came to her unique combination of photography and painting after study in Mexico and Ecuador, and at the University of New Mexico, Albuquerque, where she earned a Bachelor of Arts degree with special distinction (1973); and Arizona State University, where she earned a Master of Fine Arts degree (1981).

First active as a printmaker, Roberts served as curator at Tamarind Institute, Albuquerque, New Mexico, from 1973 to 1978. Her painted photographs have been seen in frequent exhibitions during the 1980s, including solo shows at the Linda Durham Gallery, Santa Fe, New Mexico (1987, 1989); Jayne H. Baum Gallery, New York City (1989); Ehlers/Caudill Gallery, Chicago, Illinois (1989); and Friends of Photography, San Francisco, California (1990). She lives and works in Zuni, New Mexico.

Clinton Adams

Bibliography
Grundberg, Andy, and Kathleen McCarthy Gauss. *Photography and Art: Interactions since 1946.* Abbeville Press, 1987, pp. 183, 202, 255.
Hirsch, Robert. *Exploring Color Photography.* William C. Brown, 1989.
Holly Roberts. Friends of Photography (1990).

Roberts, Malkia

Born in Washington, D.C., the African-American painter/educator Malkia Roberts earned a Bachelor's degree from Howard University in her native city, and received a Master of Fine Arts degree from the University of Michigan, Ann Arbor.

Roberts has held solo exhibitions in galleries in the United States, including "Awake the Echoes," Gallery Antigua, Miami, Florida (1988); "Odyssey: Paintings by Malkia Roberts," King-Tisdell Cottage, Savannah, Georgia (1987); and others. Her work has been included in many group shows, such as "Influences: Contemporary African and African-American Art," Hood College, Frederick, Maryland (1989); "Afro-American Abstract Artists," Evans-Tibbs Collection, Washington, D.C. (1986); "Through Women's Hands," Volta Place Gallery, Washington, D.C. (1983); "The Second Atlanta Life African-American National Art Competition and Exhibition," Atlanta Life Insurance Company, Georgia (1982); and others.

Roberts's work is represented in private and public permanent collections, including Atlanta University, Georgia; Evans-Tibbs Collection, Washington, D.C.; and others. Behind layered veils of color, the strongly-sensed female figure in the painting "Guardian" (1986) provides a fleeting glimpse of Roberts's approach: "women of color" are the caretakers of culture and the family—the custodians of tradition. The multi-layered oil and acrylic is filled with mystery in a non-traditional vision.

Bibliography
Atkinson, Edward J. *Black Dimensions in Contemporary American Art.* 1971.
Hall, Robert L. *Gathered Visions: Selected Works by African American Women Artists.* Anacostia Museum, Smithsonian Institution Press, 1992.
Lewis, Samella. *Art: African American.* 1978.

Robertson, Sarah (1891–1948)

Born in Montréal, Québec, Canada, the painter Sarah Robertson was a student of William Brymner and Maurice Cullen at the Art Association of Montréal (1910–1920), where she held a junior scholarship (1912).

Prone to sickness, yet dedicated to landscape painting, Robertson exhibited regularly at the Royal Canadian Academy; the Art Association of Montréal; the Art Gallery of Ontario, Toronto; with the Beaver Hall Group; and with the infamous Group of Seven—all in Canada. Her work was also invited to many exhibitions outside of Canada, including the British Empire Exposition, Wembley, England (1924–1925); "Contemporary Canadian Artists," Corcoran Gallery of Art, Washington, D.C. (1930); "A Century of Canadian Art," Tate Gallery, London, England (1938); the New York World's Fair (1939), and the Riverside Museum (1947)—both in New York City; and others. Three years after her death the National Gallery of Canada, Ottawa, organized a memorial travelling retrospective exhibition.

Robertson's work is represented in private and public permanent collections, including the Art Gallery of Hamilton, Ontario, Canada; the National Gallery of Canada, Ottawa; the Courtauld Institute of Art, London, England; and many others. "Coronation" (1937), a visual reference to the previous year's coronation of King George VI, suggests exuberant crowds of people through the depiction of fluttering flags, trees, and marks of red-orange—in a rhythmic unity.

Bibliography

Meadowcroft, Barbara. *Sarah Robertson: Retrospective Exhibition*. A Catalog. Walter Klinkhoff Gallery, Montréal, 1991.

McCullough, Nora. *The Beaver Hall Group*. National Gallery of Canada, 1966.

Robinson, Charlotte (1924–)

The painter/printmaker Charlotte Robinson was born in San Antonio, Texas, and studied at New York University (1947–1948), New York City, then spent the next three years in Germany, studying with Gisbert Palmie in Garmisch. Returning to the United States Robinson attended the Corcoran School of Art, Washington, D.C., where she worked with Eugene Weiss.

Robinson has held numerous solo exhibitions of her work in the United States and abroad, including Casino Estoril, Lisbon, Portugal (1962); the Art Gallery, Chapel Hill, North Carolina (1967, 1968, 1970); Fendrick Gallery, Washington, D.C. (1979); Sol del Rio, San Antonio, Texas (1978); Arlington Art Center, Virginia (1981); Fordham University, New York City (1990); Iowa State University, Ames (1991); de Andino Fine Arts, Washington, D.C. (1990, 1992); and others. Her work has been invited to myriad group exhibitions in the United States, Europe, Asia, and Africa, such as the Amadis Gallery, Madrid, Spain (1962); Galerie Saint-Placide, Paris, France (1963); Carus Gallery, New York City (1964, 1965); "4 American Artists," United States Information Agency (USIA) Cultural Center, Nairobi, Kenya (1975); "60th Annual International Competition: The Print Club," Philadelphia, Pennsylvania (1984); "American Herstory: Women and the U.S. Constitution," Atlanta College of Art, Georgia (1988); "Beauty and Eloquence, American Women Artists," Art in Embassies Program, Kathmandu, Nepal (1991); "The Twentieth Year Invitational Show," Rutgers University, New Brunswick, New Jersey (1992); and many others.

A popular lecturer, Robinson has won awards and honors for her work, including the Concourse award, Corcoran School of Art, Washington, D.C. (1952); a scholarship award from the Telfair Academy of Art, Savannah, Georgia (1959); two National Endowment for the Arts (NEA) grants (1977, 1978–1981); and a fellowship at the Virginia Center for the Creative Arts, Sweet Briar (1985). Her work is represented in private, public, and corporate permanent collections, including the Imperial Calcasieu Museum, Lake Charles, Louisiana; Museo Reina Sofía, Madrid, Spain; Museo Nacional de Arte Contemporanea, Lisbon, Portugal; McNay Art Museum, San Antonio, Texas; Caldwell College, New Jersey; National Museum of Women in the Arts and the White House—both in Washington, D.C.; AT&T; and many others. "A Black Place" (1990), an oil on canvas, presents a visual metaphor for an ordered, serene, abstract landscape/seascape seen from the artist's window/soul; it runs the gamut of a cool palette with occasional hot accents.

Bibliography

Braddy, Jason. "Painter Charlotte Robinson Raises Water Quality Issues." *Ames Daily Tribune* (September 7, 1991): 2.

Lippard, Lucy. "Up, Down and Across: A New Frame for New Quilts." Essay in *The Artist and the Quilt*. Alfred A. Knopf, 1983.

McKoy, Mary. "Charlotte Robinson at de Andino." *The Washington Post* (December 22, 1990): D1.

Richard, Paul. "Robinson's Reflections." *The Washington Post* (November 19, 1988): C2.

Robson, Frances (1959–)

The photographer Frances Robson was born in Meadow Lake, Saskatchewan, Canada. Since the mid-1980s she has been concerned with documenting the activities of various women's groups in Saskatchewan, which meet regularly for social, career, cultural, recreational, or personal reasons. Robson describes her interest in this "women and community" project as stemming from the desire to portray individuals as part of a larger supportive group; to explore women's relationships with other women; and to document the social history of women's groups. Robson's most recent work is concerned with the representation of the role of women belly dancers in Western and Middle Eastern cultures. Over the past two years she has travelled extensively in Turkey, Egypt, Morocco, Spain, and Greece to complete this project.

Robson received a Bachelor of Arts degree in English from the University of Saskatchewan (1981) and a Master of Fine Arts degree from the School of the Art Institute of Chicago, Illinois (1985). She also studied photography at the University of Ottawa, Ontario (1981–1983). Since 1980 solo exhibitions of her work have been held in Saskatchewan, Alberta, and Ontario, and her photographs have been included in group shows across Canada and the United States. Robson's work is represented in the collections of the Canadian Museum of Contemporary Photography in Ottawa and the Art Institute of Chicago, Illinois, among others. She presently lives in Saskatoon where she teaches photography at the University of Saskatchewan.

Lynne S. Bell

Bibliography

Borsa, Joan. "Another Prairies." The Art Gallery at Harbourfront, 1986.

———. *Making Space*. Presentation House Gallery, 1988.

McLellan. "Frances Robson: Women and Community." Norman Mackenzie Art Gallery, 1987.

Rockburne, Dorothea (1934–)

Born in Montréal, Québec, Canada, Dorothea Rockburne is known for her "structures" that derive in part from the Golden Section and a dancer's concern for breaking through the grid. To overcome an infirm childhood she swam her way to health and self-reliance, read widely, and revealed a passion for drawing and painting. Between 1947 and 1950 Rockburne studied at l'École des Beaux-Arts, Montréal, Québec. She took further work at Black Mountain College, North Carolina, graduating in 1956, after study with Philip Guston, Esteban Vicente, Jack Tworkov, and what she describes as "wonderful" dance classes with Merce Cunningham.

Rockburne's work has been seen in more than three dozen solo exhibitions in galleries and museums in the United States and abroad, including the Bykert Gallery, New York City (1970, 1972, 1973); Galerie Ileana Sonnabend, Paris, France (1971); Galleria Toselli, Milan, Italy (1972, 1973, 1974); John Weber Gallery (1976, 1978), the Museum of Modern Art (MoMA) (1981), and Xavier Fourcade (1981, 1982, 1985, 1986)—all in New York City; "A Painting Retrospective," Rose Art Museum, Brandeis University, Waltham, Massachusetts (1989); André Emmerich Gallery, New York City (1988, 1989, 1990, 1991, 1992); D.P Fong and Spratt Galleries, San José, California (1992); and others. Her work has been selected for showing in more than 250 group and travelling exhibitions in Europe and the United States, such as "Paperworks," MoMA, New York City (1970); "Rockburne, Fisher, Ryman," the New Gallery, Cleveland, Ohio (1971); Spoleto Festival, Italy (1972); "Modern Painting: 1900 to the Present," Museum of Fine Arts, Houston, Texas (1975); "Zeichnung Heute—Drawing Now," MoMA, New York City, a travelling show to Kunsthaus, Zurich, Switzerland; Staatliche Kunsthalle, Baden-Baden, Germany; Graphische Sammlung Albertina, Vienna, Austria; and the Tel Aviv Museum, Israel (1976); Whitney Biennial, Whitney Museum of American Art, New York City (1977, 1979); "Documenta 6," Kassel, Germany (1977); "The 1970s: New American Painting," a travelling show through Europe, New Museum, New York City (1980); "The Americans: The Collage," Contemporary Arts Museum, Houston, Texas (1983); Nuova Citta, Brescia, Italy (1987); "Recent Acquisitions," Guggenheim Museum, New York City (1989); "El Sueño de Egipto: La Influencia del Arte Egipto en el Arte Contemporaneo," El Centro Cultural/Arte Contemporaneo, A.C., Mexico City, Mexico (1991); and others.

A resident in New York City since the mid-1950s, Rockburne has garnered honors and awards for her work, including a Guggenheim Memorial Foundation fellowship (1972–1973); a painting award from the Art Institute of Chicago, Illinois (1972); a fellowship from the National Endowment for the Arts (NEA), Washington, D.C. (1974); and the creative arts award from Brandeis University, Waltham, Massachusetts (1985). She was a visiting artist at the Skowhegan School of Painting and Sculpture, Maine (1984); was appointed Milton and Sally Avery distinguished professor at Bard College, Annandale-on-Hudson, New York (1985); and was awarded Grossman artist-in-residence at Lafayette College, Easton, Pennsylvania (1992).

Layered, one unit superimposed upon another, a kind of quiescent visual philosophy (as in "Narcissus," 1984), Rockburne's work is not "easy" for the viewer. She notes, "I've never wanted to understand my work in a so-called logical way. Like love, it should remain undefined . . ."

Rockburne's work is in a host of permanent public and private collections, including the Corcoran Gallery of Art, Washington, D.C.; Fogg Art Museum, Harvard University, Cambridge, Massachusetts; High Museum of Art, Atlanta, Georgia; Minneapolis Art Institute, Minnesota; Museum of Fine Arts, Houston, Texas; Museum of Modern Art (MoMA), the Whitney Museum of American Art, and Guggenheim Museum—all in New York City; Ludwig Museum, Aachen, Germany; Auckland City Art Museum, New Zealand; Art Gallery of Toronto, Ontario, Canada; and others.

Bibliography

Belz, Carl, and Susan L. Stoops. *Dorothea Rockburne*. A Catalog. The Rose Art Museum, Brandeis University, 1989.

Brenson, Michael. "Concentrated Passion of the Circle and the Square." *The New York Times* (February 15, 1991): C18.

Licht, J. "Work and Method." An Interview. *Art & Artists* (March 1972): 32.

Storr, Robert. "Rockburne's Wager." Intro. to Catalog. *Dorothea Rockburne: Pascal and Other Concerns*. André Emmerich Gallery, 1988.

Yau, John. "Light and Dark." Intro. to Catalog. *New Works: Cut-Ins*. André Emmerich Gallery, 1988–1989.

Rodríguez, Otilia (1876–1959)

Born in Zacatecas, Mexico, Otilia Rodríguez studied at the Academy of San Carlos, Mexico City, under the aegis of Felix Parra, José Maria Velasco, and Joaquín Ramírez, and showed her student drawings in the 1898 exposition of the INBA.

President Porfirio Díaz rewarded her, in 1905, with an annuity of twenty pesos a month and a grant with which to take advanced studies in Europe. However, Rodríguez passed up this opportunity in order to marry Sóstenes Ortega, another of her teachers.

Before her marriage Rodríguez worked as an illustrator for the newspaper *El Imparcial*, and then taught drawing and painting in the schools and offered private lessons. Her landscape paintings reflect the style of her teacher, Velasco. Since she never sold any of her work, almost all of her paintings remained in the hands of her friends and family.

Rodríguez's most important works include: "Niños Jugendo en Chapultepec," "Rocas de Chapultepec," "La Vecinda," "La Hacienda de los Morales," "Vista desde el Castillo de Chapultepec," "La Villa de Guadalupe," and "Fuente del Bosque de Chapultepec." In his book, *Velasco y sus Discípulos*, Javier Perez de Salazar reproduced two copies of Landesio executed by Otilia Rodríguez: "Paisaje de un Valle" and "Convento Franciscano."

Bibliography

Alvarez, José Rogelio, et al. *Enciclopedia de Mexico*. Secretaría de Educación Pública, 1987.

Rogers, Barbara (1937–)

Both a painter and an educator, Barbara Rogers was born in Newcomerstown, Ohio, and received her Bachelor of Science degree from Ohio State University, Columbus, and a Master of Arts degree from the University of California at Berkeley.

Rogers has exhibited widely from the 1970s to today. Her work has been shown in numerous group shows throughout the United States, and she has had several solo shows, for instance at the San Francisco Museum of Modern Art and the University of the Pacific Gallery, Stockton—both in California; the Marianne Deson Gallery in Chicago, Illinois; the Linda Farris Gallery, Washington, D.C.; and the Michael Berger Gallery, Pittsburgh, Pennsylvania. Her most recent two-person show was a travelling show in Germany in 1991. Her works have been collected by museums, including the San Francisco Museum of Modern Art, the Oakland Art Museum, and the University of California Art Museum, Berkeley—all in California; she is represented in several corporate collections.

Rogers has been a visiting instructor at several schools, including the University of California at Berkeley, the University of Washington in Seattle, and the San Francisco Art Institute, California. She was on the faculty at San José State University and then joined the painting department at San Francisco Art Institute—both in California. She is now on the faculty at the University of Arizona, Tucson, and has received two grants from the university to support her research.

Rogers's work has been characterized by its super-realistic depictions of tropical gardens, erotic subjects, and architectural fragments. Her paintings have been about imaginative, dreamy, and exotic romance. In the early 1990s, however, her style changed dramatically, as Rogers began to investigate abstraction as a new way to articulate her ideas about nature. Her works contain abstract biomorphic forms, photographs, and even organic debris. Her work has moved from romance to a new Romantic sensibility in which nature is the fragile frame for human life, not the stage set.

Paul Ivey

Bibliography
Albright, Thomas. *Art in the San Francisco Bay Area 1945–1980.* University of California Press, 1985.
Ivey, Paul. *Barbara Rogers. Catalog Essay for Exhibition "Bilder Über Dem Wasser."* Bonn: USIS, 1991.
Posey, Ernest. "The Artist and the Airbrush." *Airbrush World* (September 1982).

Rogers, Gretchen (1881–1967)

The American impressionist painter Gretchen Rogers was a member of the Guild of Boston Artists and the winner of a silver medal at the Panama-Pacific International Exposition, San Francisco, California (1915).

Bibliography
American Art Annual. Vol. 28. American Federation of Arts, 1932.
Fairbrother, Trevor J. *The Bostonians: Painters of an Elegant Age, 1870–1930.* Boston: Museum of Fine Arts, 1985.
Weber, Nicholas Fox. "Rediscovered American Impressionists." *American Art Review* 3:1 (1976): 109.

Romano, Clare (1922–)

Born in Palisade, New Jersey, the printmaker/painter Clare Romano earned a Bachelor of Fine Arts degree from the Cooper Union School of Art, New York City; studied at l'École des Beaux-Arts, Fontainebleau, France (1949); and, on a Fulbright grant, studied at the Instituto Statale d'Arte, Florence, Italy (1958–1959). She also attended the New School for Social Research, New York City.

Romano has held more than seventy solo exhibitions in museums and galleries throughout the world, including the Galleria Segno Grafico, Venice, Italy (1992); Benton Gallery, Southampton, New York (1986, 1987, 1991); Jane Haslem Gallery, Washington, D.C. (1981, 1988); New Jersey State Museum, Trenton (1984); "Three Decades of Prints," a travelling show, Australian Arts Council (1983); Galerie Lometsch, Kassel, Germany (1979); Galerie Daberkow, Frankfurt, Germany (1977); the Print Club, Philadelphia, Pennsylvania (1967); and many others. Her paintings and prints have been invited to myriad national and international group exhibitions—from the Museum of Modern Art (MoMA), the Metropolitan Museum of Art, and the Whitney Museum of American Art—all in New York City—to United States Information Agency (USIA) travelling shows in Poland, Romania, Yugoslavia, South America, Africa, and the Far East. She received many other invitations from Stockholm, Sweden, to Carrara, Italy; from Grenchen, Switzerland, to San Juan, Puerto Rico; from London, England, to the Netherland Antilles; from Ugo da Carpi, Italy, to Lima, Peru, and the United States.

Winner of more than forty awards and honors between 1951 and 1991, Romano was a recipient of the Benjamin West Clinedinst memorial medal for artistic merit, artists' fellowship, New York City (1991); the rank of national academician, National Academy of Art, New York City (1979); a Fulbright grant to Florence, Italy (1958–1959); MacDowell Colony fellowships, Peterborough, New Hampshire (1974, 1976, 1978, 1982, 1987); a Tiffany Foundation grant (1952); and prizes, medals, and purchase awards at major national exhibitions throughout the United States.

Professor of printmaking at Pratt Institute, Brooklyn, New York, since 1964, Romano is a prolific writer, and has been a visiting artist at the Pennsylvania Academy of Fine Arts, Philadelphia; Vermont Studio School, Johnson; Queensland College of Art, Brisbane, Australia; United States Information Agency artist-in-residence, Yugoslavia, with Graphic Arts USA (1965–1966); University of Washington, Seattle; and many others. She has executed, on commission, murals, woodcuts and other printmaking media, especially collagraphs—the printmaking process long associated with her name. Her works are represented in distinguished private, public, and corporate permanent collections around the world.

Bibliography
Delatiner, Barbara. "Review." *The New York Times* (June 10, 1990).
Raynor, Vivien. "Review." *The New York Times* (May 5, 1985).
Romano, Clare, with John Ross and Tim Ross. *The Complete Collagraph.* Free Press, Macmillan, 1980.
———. *The Complete Printmaker.* Free Press, Macmillan, 1989.

Roosevelt, Adelheid Lange (1878–1962)

Born in St. Louis, Missouri, the cubist sculptor Adelheid (Heidi) Lange Roosevelt, of German descent, was brought to Germany by her mother after the death of her father. Roosevelt studied architecture for some years at the Polytechnique, Zurich, Switzerland, and returned to the United States to work for one of the architects of the St. Louis World's Fair (1903–1906).

A member of the St. Louis Artist's Guild, Roosevelt and her husband went to Paris, France (1912–1913), where she met many of the avant-garde Cubists, especially Raymond Duchamp-Villon, in whose studio she worked. She exhibited two works in the Salon d'Automne, Paris, France (1913); returned to the United States just prior to the start of World War I (as did so many American artists abroad); held a solo show of abstract work at the de Zayas Modern Gallery, New York City (1916); showed at the inaugural exhibition of the Society of Independent Artists, New York City (1917); and others. Her work is represented in private and public permanent collections, including the Helen Foresman Spencer Museum of Art, University of Kansas, Lawrence.

Bibliography
Hyland, Douglas, and Marilyn Stokstad. *Catalogue of the Sculpture Collection.* Helen Foresman Spencer Museum of Art, the University of Kansas, Lawrence, 1981.
Vanguard American Sculpture, 1913–39. Rutgers University Press, 1975.

Rose, Leatrice

A native New Yorker, the painter Leatrice Rose graduated from the Cooper Union School of Art (1945); attended the Art Students League (1946); and did further work at the Hans Hofmann School (1946)—all in New York City.

Rose has held solo exhibitions in galleries in New York City, including the Hansa Gallery (1954), Zabriskie Gallery (1965), Tibor de Nagy Gallery (1975, 1978, 1981, 1982), Armstrong Gallery (1985), and Cyrus Gallery (1989). She also held a solo exhibit at the Benton Gallery, Southampton (1987); and other locations. Her work has been invited to group exhibitions, such as the "Annual," Whitney Museum of American Art (1950); "Nine Painters," Tibor de Nagy Gallery (1951); "Annuals," Stable Gallery (1955, 1957); "Portrait Show," Zabriskie Gallery (1960); "American Flowers" (1966); and "Women Choose Women," New York Cultural Center (1973)—all in New York City; also in New York state venues, including the "New York Collection '78–'79," Albright-Knox Art Gallery, Buffalo (1979); "A Painter's Appreciation of Realism," Munson-Williams-Proctor Institute, Utica (1982); "1+1=2," a travelling show, Bernice Steinbaum Gallery, New York City (1984); Benton Gallery, Southampton (1987); "In Memory of John Meyers," Kouros Gallery, New York City (1988); "Invitational," American Academy and Institute of Arts and Letters, New York City (1992); and many others.

Rose has received awards and honors for her work, including grants from Yaddo, Saratoga Springs, New York (1972); New York State Council for the Arts (1974); Ingram Merrill Foundation and the American Association of University Women (1974, 1975); the National Endowment for the Arts (NEA) (1977); Esther and Adolph Gottlieb Foundation (1980, 1988); and painting awards from the National Academy of Design (1974, 1992), and the American Academy and Institute of Arts and Letters (1992)—both in New York City. Rose has been teaching painting at the Art Students League, New York City, since 1987, and has been a guest lecturer at many colleges and universities. Her work is represented in private, public, and corporate permanent collections, including Syracuse University, New York; Metropolitan Museum of Art, New York City; Guild Hall Museum, East Hampton, New York; Amerada Hess Corporation; Ciba-Geigy; and others.

Bibliography
Bass, Ruth. "Review." *Art News* (May 1981).
Campbell, Lawrence. "Leatrice Rose at Armstrong." *Art in America* 73:10 (October 1985): 154–55.
Guest, Barbara. "Leatrice Rose." *Arts Magazine* 59:10 (Summer 1985): 13.
Who's Who in American Art. 19th ed. R.R. Bowker Co., 1991–1992.

Rosenberg, Rosa (1921–1981)

Born in Lenberg, Poland, Rosa Rosenberg arrived in Mexico at the age of two. She studied painting privately and, in 1966, won first place in the competition, Nuevos Valores, held under the auspices of the Hebrew Sports Center. Rosenberg exhibited her work from 1968 through 1975; her last exhibition occurred at the latter date in the Palace of Fine Arts.

In the judgment of Ignacio Flores-Antuñez, Rosenberg's paintings are "manifestations of emotive states where anguish slips in like an accusatory presence."

Bibliography
Alvarez, José Rogelio, et al. *Enciclopedia de Mexico.* Secretaría de Educación Pública, 1987.

Rosenfield, Ethel (1910–)

Born in Poland, the sculptor Ethel Rosenfield studied part-time at l'École des Beaux-Arts, Montréal, Québec, Canada, under the aegis of Louis Archambault, Sylvia Daoust, and Armand Filion (1957–1960), before becoming a full-time student (1960–1962).

Rosenfield has held solo exhibitions in museums and galleries in Canada, including the Mansfield Book Mart (1964); and Galerie Martin (1966)—both in Montréal; and others. Her work has been included in two-person and group shows in Canada, such as the St. Laurent Art Society (1962); "Ethel Rosenfield, Sculptor," Association des Sculpteurs de Québec (1972); and Au Lutin Qui Bouffe (1953)—all in Montréal; Loranger Gallery, Toronto, Ontario (1978); and others.

Examples of Rosenfield's sensuous sculpture are in private and public permanent collections, including Concordia University, Montréal (formerly Sir George Williams University); the Musée Contemporain d'Art Moderne, Montréal; Storm-King Art Center, Ellenville, New York; and others.

Bibliography
Ayre, Robert. *Ethel Rosenfield, Sculpteur.* A Catalog. Montréal, Québec: Association des Sculpteurs de Québec, 1972.
Naiman, Sandra. "All Women in this Group of Seven." *Toronto Sun* (September 25, 1978).

Rosenthal, Doris (1895–1971)

Born in Riverside, California, the painter/printmaker Doris Rosenthal studied with George Bellows and John Sloan at the Art Students League, New York City; she also studied at Columbia University, in the same city.

Rosenthal exhibited widely in solo and group shows, including the "Second Biennial of American Painting," Whitney Museum of American Art (1934); "American Painting Today 1950, A National Competitive Exhibition," Metropolitan Museum of Art (1950); and the Midtown Galleries (1941, 1952, 1955, 1957)—all in New York City; and myriad others.

Recipient of a Guggenheim Foundation fellowship to Mexico (1931–1932), Rosenthal kept mining themes from this research and from other travels—inwardly, as well. She was a teacher of painting and drawing at summer schools offered by Columbia University, and a member of arts organizations, including the National Association of Women Painters and Sculptors, New York City. Her work is represented in private and public permanent collections.

Bibliography
American Art Annual. Vol. 28. American Federation of Arts, 1932.
Reese, Albert. *American Prize Prints of the 20th Century*. American Artists Group, Inc., 1949.
Samuels, Peggy, and Harold Samuels. *The Illustrated Biographical Encyclopedia of Artists of the American West*. Doubleday, 1976.
"Shows Fruits of a Scholarship in Mexico." *Art Digest* 8:10 (February 15, 1934): 29.

Rosenthal, Rachel (1926–)

". . . [T]o me, the propagation of ideas, beliefs, and world views is the most important and significant thing I can do with the time allotted . . . . I believe in expressing things with vigor and passion. I want to perform in a way that will make people uneasy with the easy way out. We can't afford to go easy on ourselves in these times." Thus wrote Rachel Rosenthal in 1988.

A native of France, whose family fled Paris before the Nazi occupation during World War II, Rosenthal was reared in New York City. Although she studied with the painter Hans Hofmann and with Meyer Schapiro, Columbia University's well-known art historian and critic, Rosenthal maintained her interest in the theater. In the decade after the war's end she travelled back and forth between the absurdist theater of Paris and Merce Cunningham's New York City-based performing arts company, which included such luminaries as John Cage and the budding notables Jasper Johns and Robert Rauschenberg.

In 1956 Rosenthal founded the Instant Theater in Los Angeles, California, a workshop dedicated to improvisational performance—which had a ten-year existence. Not until the early 1970s did Rosenthal, through Miriam Schapiro, become part of the Woman's Art Movement—a relationship that, in some way, fostered Rosenthal's interest in performance art.

Rosenthal's first performance, "Replays," based upon her mother's death, was produced in 1975. This was followed by works that became less and less autobiographical as Rosenthal explored themes of ecological destruction, nuclear power, feminism, aging, animal rights, and others. Her works have been performed in Europe and the United States, including *Soldier of Fortune* (1981), *L.O.W. in Gaia* (1986), and *Pangaean Dreams* (1991), to name but a clutch of titles in which she roars, screams, laments, and rages in the voices of various personae. Rosenthal dominates the stage with her powerful presence and shaved head, accompanied by slides of paintings and texts or video, and an integrated musical score.

Bibliography
Durland, Steven. "Rachel Rosenthal." *High Performance* 10: 3 (1987) 36–37.
Exposures, Women and Then Art. NewSage Press, 1989.
Holden, Stephen. "Holding Hu-person-ity Up to Ridicule." *The New York Times* July 25, 1991.
Raven, Arlene. "Rachel Rosenthal." *High Performance* 10:4 (1987): 71–72.
Rosenthal, Rachel. "Rachel Rosenthal." *High Performance* 11 (Spring–Summer 1988): 65–66.

Roser, Ce

Born in Philadelphia, Pennsylvania, the painter/video artist Ce (Cecilia) Roser studied at the Berlin Fine Arts Academy, Germany (1952–1953).

Roser's work has been seen in myriad solo and group exhibitions in the United States and abroad, including the "International Watercolor Biennial," Brooklyn Museum (1963); and "Women Choose Women," New York Cultural Center (1973)—both in New York City; "Art and Poetry," Tweed Museum of Art, Duluth, Minnesota (1977); "New Acquisitions," Guggenheim Museum, New York City (1982); "New Spaces/New Faces," East Hampton Guild Hall Museum, New York (1987); "International Travelling Show," Tikanoja, Rovaniemi, and Josensuu Art Museums—all in Finland (1988); and others.

Roser is a member of the American Abstract Artists; founder of Women in the Arts, and its initial executive coordinator (1974–1976); and a member of Women's Caucus for Art. Her work is represented in private and public permanent collections, including the Bibliothèque Nationale, Paris, France; Brooklyn Museum, Guggenheim Museum, and the Museum of Modern Art (MoMA)—all in New York City; National Museum of Art, Washington, D.C.; Newark Museum of Art, New Jersey; and others.

Bibliography
Daniell, Rosemary. "Elegant Explosions East and West Mingle in Roser Act." *Atlanta Constitution* (July 5, 1967).
Dunlop, Lane. "Review." *Arts Magazine* (September 1977).
Marter, Joan. "Review." *Arts Magazine* (February 1980).

Rosler, Martha (1943–)

A native of Brooklyn, New York, the video/performance artist Martha Rosler first studied at the Art School of the Brooklyn Museum, New York; earned a Bachelor's degree at Brooklyn College, New York (1965); and received a Master of Fine Arts degree from the University of California at San Diego (1974).

Rosler has taught film, photography, and media in universities in the United States and Canada, and has held solo performances, solo and group exhibitions in museums and galleries in the United States and abroad since the early 1970s, including the Long Beach Museum of Art, California (1977); the Whitney Museum of American Art, New York City (1977, 1979, 1983, 1987); A-Space, Toronto, Canada (1979); Institute of Contemporary Arts, London, England (1980); and many others.

Rosler has received fellowships from the National Endowment for the Arts (NEA) (1975–1977, 1980); examples of her work are held in private and public permanent collections, including the Museum of Modern Art (MoMA), New York City; Centro de Arte y Comunicación,

Buenos Aires, Argentina; Long Beach Museum of Art, California; Contemporary Arts Museum, Houston, Texas; and other venues. Rosler's work ranges across political and social themes, from Vietnam and Chile to the role of woman as producer/consumer of food, and other recent concerns—using wry humor insinuated into narrative.

Bibliography
Buchloh, Benjamin H.D. "From Gadget Video to Agit Video: Some Notes of Four Recent Video Works." *Art Journal* 45:3 (Fall 1985): 217–27.
Gever, Martha. "An Interview with Martha Rosler." *Afterimage* 9:3 (October 1981): 10–17.
Kuspit, Donald. "The Art of Memory/The Loss of History." *Artforum* 24:7 (March 1986): 120–21.
Lippard, Lucy. "Caring: Five Political Artists." *Studio International* 193:987 (March 1977): 197–207.

Rossman, Ruth Scharff (1914–)

Born in Brooklyn, New York, the figurative painter Ruth Scharff Rossman studied at several institutions, including the Cleveland Institute of Art, and Case Western Reserve University, Cleveland—both in Ohio, where she earned a Bachelor's degree; the Kahn Institute of Art, and the University of California at Los Angeles (UCLA); and with Rico Lebrun and Sueo Serisawa in Los Angeles, California.

Rossman has exhibited work in museum and gallery group and solo shows, including "Recent Painting USA: The Figure," a travelling show, Museum of Modern Art (MoMA), New York City (1962–1963); Heritage Gallery, Los Angeles, California (1963, 1966); Crescent Gallery, New Orleans, Louisiana (1977, 1978); the Rocky Mountain National, Colorado (1977, 1981); Los Angeles Museum of Science, Industry, and Art (now the Los Angeles County Museum of Art) (1978); and the University of Judaism, Los Angeles (1979)—both in California; and many others.

A teacher of art early on, Rossman has won prizes and honors, including purchase awards at the Pennsylvania Academy of Fine Arts, Philadelphia (1965); the Los Angeles Annual All-City Exhibition, California (1965, 1969); the Rocky Mountain National, Colorado (1977); and others.

Examples of Rossman's work are in private and public permanent collections, including Brandeis University, Waltham, Massachusetts; National Watercolor Society, New York City; the Pennsylvania Academy of Fine Arts, Pennsylvania; Redlands University, California; and many others. "Women on Park Bench" (1961), an expressionistic oil on masonite, is typical of her paintings of this period. Rossman's observations of life in an urban environment are transmuted magically into a vigorous work of visual art.

Bibliography
Recent Painting USA: The Figure. A Catalog. Museum of Modern Art, 1962.
Who's Who in American Art. 15th ed. R.R. Bowker Co., 1982.

Roth, Evelyn Margaret (1936–)

Born on a farm in Mundare, Alberta, Canada, the wry-humored fabric artist/sculptor/performing artist Evelyn Margaret Roth worked as a librarian at the University of British Columbia when she joined Intermedia Vancouver and stretched her many talents with the group

(1965–1969): earlier on, she studied dance, fencing, and the design of clothing.

Roth creates events to elicit audience participation, such as her fifty-foot inflatable salmon prop which she designed for a performance at the Salmon Festival, Queen Charlotte Islands, British Columbia (the performance has been repeated at the Edinburgh Festival, Scotland, and in many venues in Australia and the South Pacific). She has also created sculptured "wearables" from discarded clothing and has had them worn in dance-theater events. Rarely does she make "objects" for sale.

Lecturer at universities in Canada and the United States, Roth has given many workshops and has had her work recorded and shown on national and international television.

Bibliography
Crawford, Lee. "Keeping Them in Stitches, Fabric Art is More Than Quilting." *Western Living* 11:10 (October 1981): 92–94, 99.
Godfrey, Stephen. "The Shape of Roth." Toronto: *Globe and Mail* (December 6, 1986).
Murray, Joan. "Some Contemporary Women Artists in Canada: An Introduction." *Fireweed: A Women's Literary amd Cultural Journal* 3:4 (Summer 1979): 86–101.

Rothenberg, Susan (1945–)

Born in Buffalo, New York, Susan Rothenberg is a Guggenheim fellow in painting (1980) and a Creative Artists Public Service (CAPS) grantee from the State of New York (1976–1977). She earned her Bachelor of Fine Arts degree at Cornell University, Ithaca, New York (1966), and took further work at George Washington University and the Corcoran School of Art—both in Washington, D.C.

Rothenberg has held many solo and group exhibitions in prestigious venues throughout the United States and Europe, including the Willard Gallery, New York City (1976, 1977, 1979, 1983); the Mayor Gallery, London, England (1979); the Stedelijk Museum, Amsterdam, the Netherlands (1982); Whitney Museum of American Art, New York City (1979); the Biennale, Venice, Italy (1980); Nicola Jacobs Gallery, London, England (1985); the Los Angeles County Museum of Art, California (1987); and many others.

Rothenberg worked as Nancy Graves's assistant (1970) and found her own metaphor in the horse paintings that emerged in 1973. These mostly monochromatic horse paintings continued, with variations in treatment of surface, color, space, and figure-ground relationships, gradually moving toward the human figure in the 1980s. Her work can be found in the permanent collections of the Akron Art Museum, Ohio; Albright-Knox Art Gallery, Buffalo, New York; Art Museum of South Texas, Corpus Christi and Museum of Fine Arts, Houston—both in Texas; Museum of Modern Art (MoMA) and the Whitney Museum of American Art—both in New York City; Walker Art Center, Minneapolis, Minnesota; and many others.

Bibliography
Bell, Jane. "Susan Rothenberg." *Art News* 86:5 (May 1987): 147.
Heller, Nancy G. *Women Artists*. Abbeville Press, 1987.
Malen, Lenore. "Susan Rothenberg." *Art in America* 87:1 (January 1988): 129.
Who's Who in American Art. 19th ed. R.R. Bowker Co., 1991–1992.

Rothschild, Judith (1921–1993)

A native New Yorker, the artist Judith Rothschild earned a Bachelor's degree from Wellesley College, Massachusetts; studied with Reginald Marsh at the Art Students League, New York City; attended the Cranbrook Academy of Art, Bloomfield Hills, Michigan; studied with Hans Hofmann and Karl Knaths; and with Stanley William Hayter at Atelier 17, New York City.

Rothschild's work was exhibited in solo and group exhibitions in the United States and abroad, including the Annely Juda Gallery, London, England; Galleria Milan, Italy, and Liatowich Gallery, Basle, Switzerland (1973–1974); Gallery Gmurzynska, Cologne, Germany (1979–1981); Thorne Art Gallery, New Hampshire (1982); and many others. Founder and president of the American Abstract Artists Association and one of the founders of the Long Point Gallery, a cooperative, in Provincetown, Massachusetts, she was a board member of the American Federation of Arts, Washington, D.C.; the MacDowell Colony, Peterborough, New Hampshire; the New York Studio School, New York City; and the Provincetown Fine Arts Work Center, Massachusetts.

Rothschild was artist-in-residence at Syracuse University, New York (1970–1971); guest artist at Pratt Institute (summer 1974); and guest artist, Rhode Island School of Design, Providence (summers 1975, 1976, 1977). Her abstract oils and collages are represented in private, public, and corporate permanent collections in the United States and abroad, including the Metropolitan Museum of Art and the Whitney Museum of American Art—both in New York City; City Art Gallery, Auckland, New Zealand; First National Bank of Chicago, Illinois; Fogg Art Museum, Harvard University, Cambridge, Massachusetts; and others.

Bibliography
Lambert, Bruce. "Judith Rothschild, 71, a Painter; Began Foundation to Help Artists." *The New York Times* (March 10, 1993): B9.
Who's Who in American Art. 19th ed. R.R. Bowker Co., 1991–1992.

Rotraut (Uecker) (1938–)

Born in Rerik, East Germany, the painter Rotraut (Uecker) moved to a farm in the Mecklenburg area at the age of nine. Rotraut followed her artist-brother Gunther Uecker—the leading member of the ZERO group—to Düsseldorf, Germany, where she enrolled in evening art classes. Rotraut became an assistant to Yves Klein in the late 1950s and, in turn, sat for him, married him, and gave birth to his only son three months after Klein's death in 1962. Difficult though it was, being the wife of a well-known artist, Rotraut pursued her own work and her own destiny as a painter.

At the age of twenty-one Rotraut held her first solo exhibition at the New Vision Gallery, London, England. From 1959 to 1989 she held many solo shows at galleries, including the Galerie Amstel 47, Amsterdam, the Netherlands (1964); Antwerp Gallery, Belgium (1976); Riva Yares Gallery, Scottsdale, Arizona (1987, 1990); Pascal de Sarthe Gallery, San Francisco, California (1987–1988); Galerie Gilbert Brownstone, Paris, France (1988); "Thirty Years of Painting," a retrospective exhibition at Gallery 44, Kaarst, BRD (1989); Keeser Bohbot, Hamburg, Germany (1990); Arizona State University, Tempe (1992); and others.

Rotraut's work has been selected for exhibition in group shows throughout the world, such as the Laboratoire 32, Nice, France (1958); Carl Van Der Voort, Ibiza, Spain (1973); Schwartz Bild, Munich, Germany (1975); UNESCO, Paris, France (1976); Centre Georges Pompidou, Paris, France (1977); Galerie 44, Kaarst, BRD (1987); Kaibundo Gallery, Kobe, Japan (1989); Arizona State University, Tempe (1991–1992); and many others. "Galaxy" (1987), is not atypical of one of her series of paintings: a large work (six-by-thirteen-feet), it is a skyscape of cosmic reveries—the evening sky seen in childhood, remembered and re-created in her Arizona desert studio. Examples of her work can be found in many private and public collections throughout the world. She has lived in Arizona since 1982.

Bibliography
Giraudy, Daniele. "Rotraut: Indigo Mood." *Cimaise* (January–February 1989).
Pincus-Witten, Robert. "Entries: Nice Again." *Arts Magazine* (December 1988).
Restany, Pierre. "Rotraut: Lumiere-Mouvement-Espace." *Galeries Magazine* (December 1987).
Tullmann, Greta. "Interview mit Rotraut." *AB 40* (February 1990).

Rousseau-Vermette, Mariette (1926–)

Born at Trois-Pistoles, Québec, Canada, the noted tapestry artist Mariette Rousseau-Vermette studied art at l'École des Beaux-Arts, Québec (1944–1948); with Dorothy Liebes in San Francisco, and at the Oakland College of Arts and Crafts (1948–1949)—both in California; and during 1952, 1964, 1972–1973, she researched different tapestry techniques in Europe and Asia.

Rousseau-Vermette has held solo exhibitions of her work throughout Canada, the United States, and Europe, including the Musée des Beaux-Arts, Montréal (1961); Galerie Camille Hebert, Montréal (1964); New-Design Gallery, Vancouver (1964); Musée du Québec, a retrospective (1972); Centre Culturel Canadien, Paris, France (1974); Grace Borgenicht Gallery, New York City (1977); Galerie Alice Pauli, Lausanne, Switzerland (1978); Mira Godard Gallery, Montréal, Toronto, and Calgary; and many others. She has had her work invited to distinguished group exhibitions throughout the world, such as the Biennale Internationale de la Tapisserie, Lausanne, Switzerland (1962, 1965, 1967, 1971, 1977); "Art et Architecture," Triennale de Milan, Italy (1968); "Contemporary Tapestries," a travelling exhibition, the Museum of Modern Art (MoMA), New York City (1968–1969); "International Exhibition," Québec and Canada Pavillions, Osaka, Japan (1970); "Fibre Works: The Americans and Japan," Museum of Modern Art, Kyoto, Japan (1977); and myriad other two and three-person shows.

Designer of sets and costumes for the theater, Rousseau-Vermette was head of fiber-visual arts at the Banff School of Fine Arts, Alberta, Canada (1979–1985), she has won many honors and awards, including a Canada Council grant (1968), a certificate of honor granted by la Conférence Canadienne des Arts (1974), membership in the Royal Canadian Academy of Arts and election to same (1971, 1973 to the present); officer of the Order of Canada (1976); and many others. Her brilliant tapestries are in major private, public, and corporate permanent collections throughout the world, including theater curtains for the Kennedy Center, and the Canadian Embassy Theatre—both in Washington, D.C.; the Canadian Art Centre, Ottawa; and Place des Arts, Montréal. One of her tapestries graces the ceiling of the Roy Thomson Hall, Toronto; and others are to be found in the National Gallery of

Canada, Ottawa; Museum of Modern Art, Kyoto, Japan; Metropolitan Museum of Art and Rockefeller Center—both in New York City; Alcoa, Pittsburgh, Pennsylvania; Exxon, and myriad others.

Bibliography
Constantine, Mildred, and Jack Lenor Larsen. *Beyond Craft: The Art Fabric.* Van Nostrand Reinhold, 1973.
———. "The New Art Expression." *American Fashions and Fabrics.* An Interview. No. 118. (Winter 1979).
Jarry, Madeleine. *L'art de la tapisserie du XXieme siecle.* Office du Livre, Fribourg, 1973.
Ouvrard, Helene. *La Tapisserie Murale: Mariette Rousseau-Vermette.* Les Editions Formart, Inc., 1972.

Rubalcava, Cristina (1940–)

Born in San Ángel, Mexico, Cristina Rubalcava studied painting in Mexico, Eastbourne, England, and in Paris, France. In 1972 she published a book of her drawings made when she was between two and four years of age. Shortly thereafter Rubalcava began to participate in the Salons de la Jeune Peinture and won the Cannes international prize, France (1974).

One of Rubalcava's paintings, titled "Les Avatars de Miss Liberty," was shown in the Centre Georges Pompidou, Paris, France (1977), and, soon after, thirty works with the umbrella theme, "La Vie Conjugale," were exhibited in the Wally Findlay Galleries in New York City. Rubalcava also exhibited the series, "The Business Men," in the same city.

Despite the fact that she lives in Europe, Rubalcava frequently exhibits her work in Mexico. She illustrated a book on Augustín Lara in the recent past. Rubalcava has a daring sense of humor: she executed a work depicting English policemen in the nude which, it appeared, stirred up a minor scandal.

Bibliography
Alvarez, José Rogelio, et al. *Enciclopedia de Mexico.* Secretaría de Educación Pública, 1987.

Rubenstein, Meridel (1948–)

New Mexico is the home of Meridel Rubenstein's complex narrative photographs, and the land and its people have provided her themes. After her first encounter with serious photography at Massachusetts Institute of Technology (MIT), Cambridge, studying under Minor White, Rubenstein went west in 1973 to New Mexico, where she enrolled in the graduate photography program at the University of New Mexico, Albuquerque, and received her Master of Fine Arts degree in 1977. She remained in that state and, since 1985, has divided her year between her Santa Fe, New Mexico, home and San Francisco, California, where she is on the faculty of San Francisco State University.

Rubenstein's point of departure has been the portrait, and in connection with that, the landscape—"I want to understand how we are connected to this place we call home." In her first project in New Mexico, "La Gente de la Luz" (1977), Rubenstein blended landscapes into her portrait images to suggest a seamless connection between them; frequently the images involved a handwritten text as well, adding a third level of information. These works defined Rubenstein's style of pictures as well as goals: "I've tried to increase, in an additive sense, the levels of information one can absorb visually from an image." In "The Lowriders" (1980), a fairly straightforward color documentary series, Rubenstein photographed the culture of the Hispanic "low-rider" customized automobiles.

For a survey sponsored by the New Mexico Museum of Fine Arts, Rubenstein again worked in color on "Habitats" (1983–1985), image-sequences of three traditional dwelling sites in New Mexico. In 1981 she began exploring less documentary themes in "Lifelines" (1981–1984), assemblages of objects, landscapes, and existing portraits. These large palladium prints are generalized images about relationships and life-marking ritual moments, compared to her earlier portraits. In 1985 she began a series called "Labyrinths and Constellations," centered loosely on the myth of the Minotaur. In combinations of stage tableaus of nude figures and ritual objects in a dark abandoned site, Rubenstein has attempted "images that would recreate the experience of trying to become whole. The Labyrinth seemed a good model for the complexity of this process." Departing from her seamless blends or rephotographed collages, these palladium prints were mounted on several levels in low-relief, framed with burnished steel frames, giving the large works a new physicality and presence.

Continuing the large, steel-framed pieces, Rubinstein's current subject is Los Alamos, New Mexico—the site of the development of the atomic bomb. Part of a collaborative project with Steina and Woody Vasulka and Ellen Zqeig called "The Meeting," Rubenstein contributed wide-ranging and intuitive combinations of the specifics of individual life with photographs suggesting powerful and ominous forces. "Home" (1987), for example, is a vertical series of four images beginning with a man crouching naked at the mouth of a cave at the bottom and an eerie satellite dish facing the heavens at the top; in between is a swallows' nest and a bleak landscape, forcing the viewer to see these disparate elements in connection.

Honored with two National Endowment for the Arts (NEA) survey grants (1978, 1982), an NEA inter-arts grant (1988–1989), and an NEA photographer's fellowship (1983), Rubenstein has also received a Guggenheim Foundation fellowship (1981) and a Ferguson grant from the Friends of Photography (1977). Her work is widely exhibited and is in several public collections, including the Center for Creative Photography, Tucson, Arizona; the Denver Museum of Art, Colorado; the Museum of Fine Arts, Houston, Texas; the San Francisco Museum of Modern Art, California; the Minneapolis Institute of Arts, Minnesota; the Fine Arts Museum, University of New Mexico, Albuquerque, and the New Mexico Museum of Fine Arts, Santa Fe—both in New Mexico; and the California Museum of Photography, University of California, Riverside.

Gretchen Garner

Bibliography
Blake, Robert. "Mythical Circuits." *San Francisco Camerawork Quarterly* 14:3 (Fall 1987): 13, 20, 89.
Bloom, John. "Interview with Meridel Rubenstein." *Photo Metro* (September 1988): 4–11.
Coke, Van Deren. *Photography in New Mexico.* Albuquerque: University of New Mexico Press, 1979.
Garner, Gretchen. *Reclaiming Paradise: American Women Photograph the Land.* Duluth: Tweed Museum of Art, University of Minnesota, 1987, pp. 38–89.

Jussim, Estelle, and Elizabeth Lindquist-Cock. *Landscape as Photograph.* Yale University Press, 1985, pp. 17, 18, 128, 130.

Rubenstein, Meridel. *La Gente de la Luz.* Santa Fe: New Mexico Museum of Fine Arts, 1977.

Smith, Joshua P., and Merry A. Foresta. *The Photography of Invention: American Pictures of the 1980s.* Washington: The National Museum of American Art, and Massachusetts: The MIT Press, 1989, pp. 166–67.

Solnit, Rebecca. "Uncommon Perceptions." *Sierra* (July–August 1989): 42–49.

Tamblyn, Christine. "Meridel Rubenstein, Gregory Mahoney." *ARTnews* 89:10 (December 1988): 170–71.

Yates, Steve. *The Essential Landscape.* University of New Mexico Press, 1985, pp. 23, 24, 132–35.

———. "The Feminine Portrait: Photographs by Gilpin, Noggle, and Rubenstein." *El Palaccio* (Santa Fe): 92:1 (Summer–Fall 1986): 26–33.

Rubin, Eleanor (1940–)

Born in Hollywood, California, the printmaker Eleanor Rubin earned a Bachelor's degree from Brandeis University, Waltham, Massachusetts (1962), and received a Master's degree in education from Harvard University, Cambridge, Massachusetts, the following year.

Rubin has held solo and two-person exhibitions in museums and galleries in the United States, and has had her work invited to group exhibitions, including "Imprint of the Imagination," Newton Art Center, Massachusetts (1984); "Museum without Walls," Summer's World Center for the Arts, Worcester, Massachusetts (1986); "Twin Sisters: A Visual Connection," Brown University, Providence, Rhode Island (1987); "Eleanor Rubin: Bear Rising and Other Images," Plum Gallery, Kensington, Maryland (1987, 1990); Blue Mountain Gallery, New York City (1992); "The Transferred Image," Starr Gallery, Newton (1992), and "Her Heart Could Not Contain," Erik H. and Joan M. Erikson Center, Cambridge (1991)—both in Massachusetts ; and others.

Rubin has been the recipient of grants from Massachusetts councils and foundations for the arts (1984, 1986, 1987); and has been artist-in-residence at the Centrum Frans Masereel, Kasterlee, Belgium (1988). Panelist and lecturer at professional arts organizations, Rubin holds active memberships in the Boston Visual Arts Union, American Association of Museums, Boston Printmakers, Women's Caucus for Art, and others. Her work is represented in private and public permanent collections, including the Museum of Fine Arts and Boston Public Library—both in Boston, Massachusetts; California College of Arts and Crafts, Oakland; the Photo/Graphics Gallery, New Canaan, Connecticut; and others.

Bibliography
Sisters: A Complex Destiny. A Catalog. Women's Caucus for the Arts, 1987.

Standish, Dana. "All That's Fit to Print." *Newton Tab* (November 16, 1983).

Temin, Christine. "Studio Open House: New Look." *Boston Globe* (December 7, 1992): Cal. Mag. 36.

Van Siclen, Bill. "Hera Gallery Faces Grief Head On." *Providence Journal-Bulletin* (November 22, 1991).

Rubin, Sandra Mendelsohn (1947–)

Born in Santa Monica, California, the painter Sandra Mendelsohn Rubin studied at the University of California at Los Angeles (UCLA), where she earned a Bachelor of Fine Arts degree (1976) and a Master of Fine Arts degree three years later.

Rubin has shown her art in solo exhibitions at the Los Angeles County Museum of Art, California (1985); the Claude Bernard Gallery, New York City (1987); and others. Her work has been included in group exhibitions in the United States and abroad, such as the "Exhibition of Contemporary Los Angeles Artists," Nagoya City Museum, Japan (1982); "A Heritage Renewed," University of California at Santa Barbara (1983); "American Realism: Twentieth Century Drawings and Watercolors," San Francisco Art Museum, California (1986); "California Cityscapes," San Diego Museum of Art, California (1991); and others.

Winner of awards and honors, Rubin received a young talent purchase award from the Los Angeles County Museum of Art, California (1980); and fellowship grants from the National Endowment for the Arts (NEA) (1981, 1991); plus others. Examples of her work are in private and public permanent collections, including the Boise Art Museum, Idaho; Los Angeles County Art Museum, Santa Barbara Museum of Art, UCLA—all in California; and others.

Bibliography
Beckett, Wendy. *Contemporary Women Artists.* Phaidon Press Ltd., 1988.

Edgerton, Anne C., and Maurice Tuchman. "Young Talent Awards: 1963–1983." *Bulletin, Los Angeles County Museum of Art* 27 (1983): 54.

Sandra Mendelsohn Rubin: Paintings and Drawings. A Catalog. New York: Claude Bernard Gallery, 1987.

Ruellan, Andrée (1905–)

The painter Andrée Ruellan is known for her urban genre scenes of New York and the American South. Born in New York City on April 6, 1905, Ruellan was a prodigy who first exhibited her work at the age of eight, assisted by her childhood mentor, Robert Henri. She entered the Art Students League, New York City, on a scholarship and studied with Maurice Sterne and Leo Lentelli; in 1922 she won the opportunity to study with Sterne in Rome, Italy. The following year Ruellan moved to Paris, France, where she worked with Charles Dufresne and Per Krogh at the Académie Suedoise, and first attempted lithography with Desjobert. She held her first one-woman exhibit at the Sacre du Printemps Gallery, Paris, France, in 1925.

After marrying the artist John Taylor in 1929, Ruellan settled in Woodstock, New York. She exhibited her paintings, drawings, and prints in national and one-woman shows from the 1930s through the 1970s. Ruellan also painted murals for post offices in Emporia, Virginia (1940), and Lawrenceville, Georgia (1941).

Ruellan won a third prize for her painting "Charleston" at the Worcester Museum's 1938 Biennial in Massachusetts. In 1945 she received the Pennell Memorial medal at the Pennsylvania Academy of Fine Arts, Philadelphia, as well as a grant from the American Academy and National Institute of Arts and Letters, New York City. She was a Guggenheim Foundation fellow in France from 1950–1951. Ruellan's work can be found in the collections of the Whitney Museum of American Art and the Metropolitan Museum of Art—both in New York City; and other major museums.

Peggy J. Hazard

Bibliography
Adams, Clinton. *American Lithographers 1900–1960*. University of New
    Mexico Press, 1983.
Marling, Karal Ann. *Woodstock, An American Art Colony, 1902–1977*.
    Vassar College Art Gallery, 1977.
Reese, Albert. *American Prize Prints of the 20th Century*. American Artists
    Group, 1949.
Salpeter, Harry. "About Andrée Ruellan." *Coronet* 5 (December 1938): 90–98.
Watson, Ernest W. "An Interview with Andrée Ruellan." *American Artist*
    7 (October 1943): 8–13.

Rush, Olive (1873–1966)

Born in Fairmount, Indiana, the painter Olive Rush studied her craft
in the United States and abroad; she was a member of several arts organizations, including the New York Watercolor Club, New York City;
the Wilmington Society of Fine Arts, Delaware; and others.

Winner of prizes and awards, Rush received an honorable mention
at the Richmond Art Association, Virginia (1919); first prize at the John
Herron Art Institute, Indianapolis, Indiana (1919); Tri Kappa prize, Hoo-
sier Salon (1931); honorable mention at the "Annual Exhibition," Denver Museum of Art, Colorado (1931); and others. Representative examples
of her work are in private and public permanent collections, including
the Art Museum, Worcester, Massachusetts; Brooklyn Museum, New York
City; John Herron Art Institute, Indianapolis, Indiana; La Fonda Hotel,
Santa Fe, New Mexico; Nathaniel Hawthorne School, Indianapolis, Indiana; Phillips Memorial Gallery, Washington, D.C.; St. Andrews Church,
Wilmington, Delaware; and others.

Bibliography
Burnet, Mary Q. *Art and Artists of Indiana*. Century Co., 1921.
Who's Who in American Art. Vol. 1. American Federation of Art, 1935.
Women Artists in the Howard Pyle Tradition. Chadds Ford, Pennsylvania:
    Brandywine River Museum, 1975.

Rutherford, Erica (1923–)

The film and theater designer Erica Rutherford was born in Edinburgh,
Scotland, and studied at the Royal Academy for Dramatic Art, London,
England; the Slade School of Fine Arts in the same city; and the Accademia
Florence, Italy. She had a successful career in theater design, which was
carried out in England, South Africa, Spain, and the United States.

Upon retirement Rutherford settled in Canada and became a prolific painter and printmaker. She has held solo exhibitions in museums
and galleries in Canada and abroad, including the Leicester Galleries,
London (1961–1964); Galería Ivan Spence, Ibiza, Spain (1961–1966);
Galerie San Jorge, Madrid, Spain (1962); Ashgate Gallery, Farnham,
England (1966, 1970, 1974); Pollock Gallery (1975, 1981) and the Pascal Gallery, Toronto, Canada (1981, 1983); Gallery 1667, Halifax, Nova
Scotia (1986); and many others. She has won many awards and honors,
and her work has been included in group exhibitions in many countries.

Rutherford was also an illustrator of children's books. Examples
of her work are in private, public, and corporate permanent collections, including the Arts Council of Great Britain; Burnaby Art Gallery, British Columbia; Canada Council Art Bank, Ottawa; Corcoran
Gallery of Art, Washington, D.C.; the government of Prince Edward
Island Art Collection; Stephens College, Columbia, Missouri; University of Wales, Cardiff; and many others.

Bibliography
Atlantic Print Exhibition. A regional travelling exhibition. Halifax: Art
    Gallery of Nova Scotia.
Huser, Glen. "Cats are Stars in Children's Books." *Edmonton Journal*
    (November 2, 1986).
Kritzwiser, Kay. "Patients Turn Art Critics for Hospital Collection." *Globe
    and Mail* (March 3, 1982).

Ryan, Anne (1889–1954)

Born in Hoboken, New Jersey, Ann Ryan was a mother, painter,
printmaker, writer, set and costume designer—but, in particular, she
was a collagist of extraordinary sensitivity. Ryan attended St. Elizabeth's
College near Morristown, New Jersey, majored in literature, and published a book of poetry, *Lost Hills*, in 1925. Six years later she free-
lanced as a writer, lived in Majorca, and travelled through Europe, not
unaware of modern European art.

Supported by Hans Hofmann and Anthony Smith in her desire to
paint, Ryan embarked on a career as a plastic artist five years after
she had returned to the United States. She learned and mastered engraving techniques at Atelier 17, New York City, with Stanley William
Hayter in 1941, and held her inaugural solo exhibition of paintings
and intaglio prints at the Marquis Gallery, New York City, in 1943.

Ryan took further study with Louis Schanker (1945), acquiring the
technical knowledge needed for creating color woodcuts; she exhibited
her prints with the *Vanguard*—a group of experimental printmakers—at
the Brooklyn Museum, New York (1946). That same year Ryan held a solo
show of twenty-two color woodcuts at the Marquis Gallery, New York City.
She also was given solo shows at the Betty Parsons Gallery (1954), and
the Metropolitan Museum of Art (1989)—both in New York City; and others. Posthumous exhibitions were held at the Stable Gallery (1963),
Fischbach Gallery (1968), Kraushaar Galleries (1957), Marlborough Galleries (1974), and the Brooklyn Museum (1974)—all in New York City.

Winner of honors and awards for her work, Ryan received a purchase prize at the 2nd Annual National Print Exhibition at the Brooklyn Museum, New York (1948), among others, and, in the next six years,
began to make the first of more than 400 small collages and 100 color
woodcuts. Her work graces many permanent public and private collections in the United States.

Bibliography
Anne Ryan: Collages 1948–1954. A Catalog. New York: André Emmerich
    Gallery, 1979.
Ashbery, John. "A Place for Everything." *Art News* 69:1 (March 1970):
    32–33, 73–75.
Baro, Gene. *Thirty Years of American Printmaking Including the 20th
    National Print Exhibition*. Brooklyn Museum, 1976.
Faunce, Sarah C. *Anne Ryan Collages*. Brooklyn Museum, 1974.
Frank, Peter. "Anne Ryan at the National Collection of Fine Arts." *Art in
    America* 62:5 (September–October 1974): 117–18.
Kramer, Hilton. "Anne Ryan: Bigness on a Small Scale." *The New York
    Times* (February 3, 1968).
Windham, Donald. "A Note on Anne Ryan." *Botteghe Oscura* 22 (1958):
    267–71.

Ryerson, Margery Austen (1886–1989)

Born in Morristown, New Jersey, the painter/printmaker Margery Austen Ryerson studied with Charles W. Hawthorne and Robert Henri. She was a member of the Allied Artists of America, New York City; the California Printmakers; Grand Central Art Galleries, New York City; Provincetown Art Association, Massachusetts; Society of American Etchers; and the Washington Watercolor Club, Washington, D.C.

Ryerson exhibited her paintings and etchings widely in the United States and abroad, including portraits at the Grand Central Art Galleries, New York City (1942); Mount Holyoke College, South Hadley, Massachusetts, and the Weyhe Gallery, New York City (1973). Ryerson won many awards and honors, including the Emil Fuchs prize, Brooklyn Society of Etchers, New York (1924); and others. Her work is represented in private and public permanent collections, including the Bibliothèque Nationale, Paris, France; Brooklyn Museum and New York Public Library—both in New York City; Cleveland Museum of Art, Ohio; Smithsonian Institution, Washington, D.C.; the Uffizi Gallery, Florence, Italy; and others.

Bibliography

Ely, Catherine Beach. "Margery Austen Ryerson." *Art in America* 13:15 (August 1925): 283–88.

Movalli, Charles. "A Conversation with Margery Ryerson." *American Artist* 40 (November 1976): 58–63, 95–99.

Rubenstein, Charlotte Streifer. *American Women Artists*. G.K. Hall, 1982.

Ryerson, Margery. "Sketching Faces from the TV Screen." *American Artist* 33:6 (Summer 1969): 68–70.

S

Saar, Alison (1956–)

Sculptor/assemblage artist Alison Saar had the advantage of growing up with one of the great collage/assemblage artists of the modern period—her mother, Betye Saar. Born in Los Angeles, California, Saar was the second of three daughters. She would often accompany her mother when she was making prints; while her mother worked she would give her daughter clay to play with to keep her out of danger. Saar's father, an artist/conservator, was influential as well. He gave Saar drawing lessons and took her, along with her sisters, to museums. Saar later worked with her father for eight years as an art conservator, learning to carve in the process. During this period she was exposed to art from a wide range of cultures. Her multi-racial heritage—she is white on her father's side and African, Native American, and Irish on her mother's—also broadened her perspectives.

Saar studied studio art and art history at Scripps College, Claremont, California, receiving a Bachelor of Arts degree in 1978. She was able to study there with one of the leading African-American art historians, Dr. Samella Lewis, and wrote a thesis on African-American folk art. She received a Master of Fine Arts degree from Otis Art Institute, Los Angeles, California, in 1981.

Although Saar's work differs in many ways from that of her mother—such as in its use of larger, single figures—both artists became attracted to the mystical and spiritual, especially as it exists in found materials. Both are rooted in an aesthetic defined through African-American and American cultures, and both artists' works have appealing, animated surfaces. Saar's work is more spunky and overtly dynamic than the more mystical and lyrical, shimmering presence of her mother's works.

Saar's first body of work after graduate school, in the early to mid-1980s, was a series of mostly life-size collaged figural sculptures which emphasized spiritual qualities or ambivalent moral qualities of often consciously clichéd figures from street hustlers to athletes, Joe Louis, and Afro-Caribbean deities. The first example of this genre is the black seated male figure, "Si j'étais blanc" of 1981. Often crudely carved of wood, with ceramic or glass shards or nails embedded in their body cavities, or covered in tin or other discarded materials, or painted in bright blue or red, these figures engage cultural stereotypes with an enlivening combination of irony, wit, and empathy. Judith Wilson has suggested that these works exemplify the new African-American aesthetic called "neohoodooism," in which the Western tradition is decentered in favor of modes from other cultures. Saar particularly draws from images and processes used in Africa and Mexico. Her figures tend to come from black cultures, but some are of American Indians or Chicanos. Her next group of works included a series of life-sized black-and-white drawings of similar characters, "Shamans, Saints and Sinners," which she describes as "modern fetishes of the magic and mystery of the urban underground." Saar has also done a number of installation works ("Love Potion #9," 1988; "Crossroads," 1989) in which single figures are united with other elements to represent larger ideas with a wide range of interpretive sources from Christian to African. Her most recent works often reveal some secret desire, power, or spiritual wound contained within the boundaries of the body. They have a strong sense of tangible presence in their funky, chunky forms, their glittering surfaces, and their bright colors.

Saar moved to New York in 1983 as artist-in-residence at the Studio Museum in Harlem. In 1985 she held another residency at the Roswell Museum of Art, Albuquerque, New Mexico, and again at the Washington Project for the Arts in Washington, D.C., in 1986. She now lives in New York City.

Patricia Mathews

Bibliography

Shepherd, Elizabeth, ed. *The Art of Betye and Alison Saar: Secrets, Dialogues, Revelations.* Exhibition Catalog. Essays by Lucy Lippard, Ishmael Reed, and Judith Wilson. Wight Art Gallery, UCLA, 1990.

Wilson, Judith. "Hexes, Totems and Necessary Saints: A Conversation with Alison Saar." *Real Life Magazine* 29 (Winter 1988–89).

———. "Down to the Crossroad. The Art of Alison Saar." *Third Text* 10 (Spring 1990): 25–44.

Saar, Betye (1926–)

The sculptor and installation artist Betye Saar is best known for her assemblage and collage boxes that incorporate references to the occult as well as political commentary on the African-American experience.

Born in Los Angeles, California, as a child Saar watched the visionary Simon Rodia construct his Watts Tower out of fragments of glass, ceramic shards, bottle tops, mirrors, and other refuse. Both the collage technique and the visionary aspect of this work influenced her own aesthetic development. Her interest in mysticism and the occult was also stimulated at an early age. She was clairvoyant and psychic until the age of six, when her father died.

Saar received a Bachelor of Arts degree from the University of California at Los Angeles (UCLA) in 1949, married an artist, and had three daughters, one of whom, Alison, went on to become an artist herself. Saar then returned to school, receiving a Master's degree in graphic design at California State University at Long Beach. Only then, at the age of thirty-four, did she decide to become an artist.

Saar became acquainted in the late 1960s with the boxes of Joseph Cornell and began to assemble her own small boxes from objects. She had already evinced a penchant for collecting small objects, a compulsion she would later refer to as "power-gathering" because of her belief that found, used objects contained natural forces. Early on in her career she developed her own personal symbology that continues to inhabit her works.

Saar's assemblages from the late 1960s and early 1970s ranged from mystical evocations that sometimes incorporated African motifs, such as "House of Tarot" (1966) and "Black Girl's Window" (1969), to revolutionary statements that rupture stereotypes about blacks such as "The Liberation of Aunt Jemima" (1972), in which Aunt Jemima carries a gun and wears a Black Power fist as a skirt. These boxes have a magical, poignant, jewel-like quality to them, and often reflect nostalgic memory fragments of her childhood.

Saar's work continues to be cross-cultural, in part because of her own mixed blood—African, Irish, and Native American—in part because of her travels, and in part because of her intense empathy for others. More recently she has produced installations as well as assemblages, such as "Mojotech" (1988), a mixed-media installation created during a residency at Massachusetts Institute of Technology (MIT), Cambridge, which refers to the relationship between mysticism and science. She has also done some collaborations with her daughter, Alison Saar.

Saar has had a number of solo exhibitions and now teaches art at Otis-Parsons Institute in Los Angeles, California.

Patricia Mathews

Bibliography

Clothier, Peter. *Betye Saar.* Exhibition Catalog. Los Angeles: The Museum of Contemporary Art, 1984.

Rituals: The Art of Betye Saar. Exhibition Catalog. New York: The Studio Museum in Harlem, 1980.

Shepherd, Elizabeth, ed. *The Art of Betye and Alison Saar: Secrets, Dialogues, Revelations.* Exhibition Catalog. Essays by Lucy Lippard, Ishmael Reed, and Judith Wilson. Wight Art Gallery, UCLA, 1990.

Tucker, Marcia. *Betye Saar.* Whitney Museum of American Art, 1975.

Sadowska, Krystyna (1912–)

Born in Lublin, Poland, the many-talented, prize-winning artist Krystyna Sadowska earned a degree from the Warsaw Academy of Fine Arts, Poland (1930–1934); studied painting at the Académie de la Grande Chaumière, Paris, France (1940); and learned ceramics at the Central School of Arts and Crafts, London, England (1945–1946). Earlier, she taught weaving in Parana, Brazil, on behalf of the Polish government.

Sadowska has held many solo exhibitions in museums and galleries, including St. George's Gallery, London, England (1946); Rio de Janeiro, Brazil (1947); Henry Morgan Gallery, Montréal, Québec (1950), Memorial Library, Halifax, Nova Scotia (1953), the Dorothy Cameron Gallery, Toronto, Ontario (1964), and Art Gallery of Windsor, Ontario (1977)—all in Canada; and others. Her work has been included in prestigious national and international group shows and her commissioned works—sculpture, batiks, tapestries—are in venues across Canada.

Sadowska has earned international honors and awards from the governments of France and Brazil for tapestries; she has been equally honored for her ceramics, batiks, and other media. Examples of her sculptural works are in private, corporate, and public permanent collections in Canada, including Calgary House, Alberta; Ontario Government Project, Queen's Park, Toronto; Royal Bank Plaza, Toronto; University of Waterloo; and many others.

Bibliography

Ayre, Robert. "Ceramics in Canada." *Studio* 154:777 (December 1957): 168–75.

Fraser, Ted. *Krystyna Sadowska: Sculptures, Drawings, Collages, Batiks, Paintings.* A Catalog. Art Gallery of Windsor, 1977.

Sage, Kay (1898–1963)

Kay (Katherine Linn) Sage was born in Albany, New York, to a wealthy, conservative senator, Henry Manning Sage, and his wife. As a child Sage frequently travelled to Europe with her mother, returning to Italy and France every year. After her parents divorced she lived with her mother in San Francisco, California, for two years and then in New York City. By the time she finished school at age fifteen she had attended seven different schools. During World War I Sage worked as a translator for the Censorship Bureau from 1917 to 1918. When the war ended she returned to Europe to study art in Italy, spending time with a group in Rome sketching landscapes. She took classes for a few months in 1924 at the Scuola Liberale delle Belle Arti in Milan, Italy.

In 1927 she married Prince Ranieri de San Faustino and for almost ten years lived life as a princess in Rome and Rapallo—both in Italy. She eventually grew tired of the lifestyle of the idle rich, divorced her husband, and turned back to her painting. She had her first solo exhibition in 1936 at the Galleria del Milione in Milan. Her paintings at that time were abstract expressions that loosely dealt with perspective and the idea of infinite distance, which held her interest for many years. Her first volume of poetry, written under her married name of Kay di San Faustino, was published the next year. *Piove in Giardino* was a book of children's verse illustrated by Sage with watercolors of animals, circus performers, and musicians. By 1937 Sage sold her jewelry, resumed her maiden name, and moved to Paris, France.

In Paris she became active in the surrealist movement in the arts. She had a single painting in the 1938 Salon des Surindépendants show which attracted the attention of artists André Breton and Yves Tanguy. They felt that a man must have painted this mechanical painting and sought to meet the artist. Two years later Sage and Tanguy were married.

With the outbreak of World War II Sage had to return to the United States and went back to New York City. She had her first show in the United States at the Pierre Matisse Gallery in New York City and, with the help of Yvon Deblos—the French minister of education—planned a series of solo shows in New York for artists working in Paris. The first artist who exhibited was Tanguy. Sage gave financial support to many of the artists who came to the United States, notably Breton. She also bought many works of art by her friends and amassed a superior collection of surrealist and twentieth-century art.

Sage and Tanguy moved to a nineteenth-century farmhouse in Woodbury, Connecticut, in 1941. They had separate studios in a divided barn on the property and both painted surrealistic works but with different results. Tanguy's canvases dealt with organic, sculptural objects painted against a stark, dream-like background. Sage consciously avoided his influence and stuck with a rigid architectural draftsmanship in her works, but pitted structures against the desolate hallucinatory plains popular in the surrealist movement ("The Torment of the Poet" [1941]).

In her painting "In the Third Sleep" (1944), Sage used the gameboard motif, often seen in Giorgio de Chirico's work, bringing in strong light sources against a parched landscape. The painting won the Watson F. Blair purchase prize, and it was exhibited at the Art Institute of Chicago, Illinois.

Tanguy and Sage usually exhibited their work separately but were convinced in 1954 to have an exhibit together at the Wadsworth Athenaeum in Hartford, Connecticut. Critics commented on the similarities and differences in their paintings, saying that Tanguy was more concerned with animistic forms while Sage used complex architectural angles in her works.

Tanguy died the following year, and Sage became more and more reclusive. She continued to write poetry and by the late 1950s had four volumes published, the best known being *The More I Wonder,* in 1957. She continued to paint until 1958 when her eyesight began to fail. In 1959 she attempted suicide with a drug overdose. Catherine Viviano, hoping to lift her spirits, organized a retrospective showing of Sage's works in her New York gallery in 1960. Sage was encouraged and began doing collages which were exhibited the following year, and also began cataloging Tanguy's paintings.

Despite encouragement from friends and the public, Sage shot herself in the heart in January 1963. She bequeathed 100 works of art to the Museum of Modern Art (MoMA) in New York City and left the largest legacy of unrestricted purchase funds for the museum. The Herbert F. Johnson Museum at Cornell University in Ithaca, New York, had a retrospective exhibition of her work in 1977. Her paintings are in the permanent collections of many museums, including the Philadelphia Museum of Art, Pennsylvania; the San Francisco Museum of Art, California; the Whitney Museum of American Art, New York City; and others.

Nancy Knechtel

Bibliography
Chadwick, Whitney. *Women Artists and the Surrealist Movement.* Little Brown and Co., 1985.
Contemporary Artists. 2nd ed. 1983, p. 809.
Kay Sage 1898–1963. Herbert F. Johnson Museum, Cornell University, 1977.

Sahler, Helen Gertrude (1877–1950)

Born in Carmel, New York, the sculptor Helen Gertrude Sahler studied at the Art Students League, New York City, and took further study with H.A. MacNeill and Enid Yandell.

Sahler exhibited work in many shows, such as the National Sculpture Society's "Contemporary American Sculpture," California Palace of the Legion of Honor, San Francisco, California (1929). She was a member of many art organizations, including the Art Alliance of Philadelphia, Pennsylvania; Allied Artists of America, National Association of Women Painters and Sculptors, and New York Municipal Art Society—all in New York City; American Federation of Arts, Washington, D.C.; Connecticut Academy of Fine Arts, Westport; the MacDowell Colony, Peterborough, New Hampshire; North Shore Art Association, Long Island, New York; and the Numismatic Society.

Examples of Sahler's sculpture and numismatic commissions are in private and public permanent collections, including the Brush Memorial, Hackley Chapel, Tarrytown, New York; the Numismatic Museum, New York; St. Marks Church, Fall River, Massachusetts; and others.

Bibliography
American Art Annual. Vol. 28. American Federation of Arts, 1932.
Obituary. *The New York Times* (December 4, 1950): 29.
Who's Who in American Art. Vol. 4. American Federation of Arts, 1947.

Saila, Pitaloosie (1942–)

The graphic artist Pitaloosie Saila chooses people, compositions of people, and animals, birds, Canadian Inuit traditional events, and Inuit mythical figures and spirits as her subjects. Born in Cape Dorset, Northwest Territories, Pitaloosie experienced camp life and, because of severe illness, was exposed to southern lifestyles and cultures. She lived in Halifax, Montréal, and Hamilton, Ontario, between 1950 and 1957 where she learned to speak English and some French. In 1960 she married sculptor Pauta Saila. They live in Cape Dorset where they have an active and committed life with their children and grandchildren.

Pitaloosie started to draw in the early to mid-1960s. In 1968 some of her drawings were turned into graphics, and they have regularly been part of the Cape Dorset annual graphics collections. Throughout her artistic career, Pitaloosie has treated a wide range of themes and has developed personal styles that range from pure realism to formal/abstract, and that include compositions blending both styles. She tends to stylize and to reduce to the essential, the shape of a single subject. Powerful compositions are the result. Some of Pitaloosie's works are uniquely striking for their unconventional style, their modernist approach, and their intelligent use of color and texture. Like other Cape

Dorset artists, Pitaloosie uses her art to express her concerns and to be in her own way a chronicler of the traditional Inuit way of life.

Pitaloosie belongs to the second generation of Inuit graphic artists. Her well-defined style has been enriched and broadened and yet still reflects the aesthetic of the graphic art movement from the Cape Dorset school. Since 1968 several museums and galleries across Canada, the United States and abroad, have acquired her works. All her graphics are in the National Inuit Art Collection at the Canadian Museum of Civilization in Hull, and a selection of eleven graphics and two drawings are in the National Gallery of Canada in Ottawa. Her two-dimensional works are shown on a regular basis in all types of exhibitions. Over the years Pitaloosie has been honored several times. The reproduction of her stonecut print, "Fisherman's Dream" (1971) on a twelve-cent stamp on November 18, 1977, is particularly notable.

Odette Leroux

Bibliography

Blodgett, Jean. *Grasp Tight the Old Ways: Selections from the Klamer Family Collection of Inuit Art.* Toronto: Art Gallery of Ontario, 1983.

Canadian Eskimo Arts Council. *Transcript of the Interview with Pitaloosie Saila.* Ottawa: Department of Indian and Northern Affairs, 1985.

Saila, Pitaloosie. "Pitaloosie Saila Talks About Old Age, Her First Drawing, White People and Other Things." *Inuit Art Quarterly* 2:3 (Summer 1987): 10–12.

Van Raalte, Sharon. "Inuit Women and Their Art." *Communique* (May 1975): 21–23.

St. Croix, Mother (1854–1940)

Born in Clermont-Ferand, France, the photographer Mother St. Croix (Marie Sourant) entered a convent when she was in her late teens and left France for the Ursuline convent in New Orleans, Louisiana, in 1873. It was not until her mid-forties that she began to practice photography—a result of receiving her first camera from the Zion Company, Paris, France.

Taking large format photographs (up to sixteen-by-twenty-inch plates) of students and life in the cloistered Ursuline orders, St. Croix expressed her beliefs and ideas through her work. Representative examples of that work are in private and public permanent collections, including the New Orleans Museum of Art and the Ursuline Convent of New Orleans—both in Louisiana; and others.

Bibliography

Freeman, Tina. *The Photographs of Mother St. Croix.* New Orleans Museum of Art, 1982.

Salinger, Joan A. (1951–)

Born in Detroit, Michigan, Joan A. Salinger is known for her unique, experimental, color photographs. Salinger earned a Bachelor of Fine Arts degree *magna cum laude* from the University of Michigan, Ann Arbor (1973), and, three years later, received a Master of Fine Arts degree from the Cranbrook Academy of Art, Bloomfield Hills, Michigan, where she studied photography with Carl Toth.

An instructor in photography in several Los Angeles, California area art schools and colleges, Salinger has won awards and honors, including grants from the Michigan Council for the Arts, and the National Endowment for the Arts (NEA); she also participated in the artist-in-schools program in Flint, Michigan (1976–1977), as the result of a grant from the Charles Stewart Mott Foundation.

Salinger's work is represented in private, public, and corporate permanent collections, including the Flint Community Schools; K-Mart Corporation, Troy; and the Michigan Art Education Association, Lansing—all in Michigan; New Orleans Museum of Art, Louisiana; Northern Virginia College, Alexandria; and others.

Bibliography

Browne, Turner, and Elaine Partnow. *Macmillan Biographical Encyclopedia of Photographic Artists and Innovators.* Macmillan, 1983.

Catalogue 1. A Catalog. Washington, D.C.: Sander Gallery, 1979.

Saloma, Alicia (1924–)

Alicia Saloma was born in Moroleón, Guanajuato, Mexico. A grant awarded her by Ernesto García Cabral allowed her to study in the Academy of San Carlos (1938–1940) and in Escuela de Pintura y Escultura (La Esmeralda) (1960–1966)—both in Mexico City. Her art teachers were Fernando Castro Pacheco and Nicolás Moreno.

In 1967 Saloma was given a solo exhibition in the Galería Chapultepec of the Instituto Nacional de Bellas Artes, Mexico City. She won first prize in the 7th Annual Art Exhibition of the Foreign Friends of Acapulco and also showed her work in the Instituto Francés de América Latina (1960, 1963), the Galería de Arte Caribe de Nueva York (1967, 1970), in Nice, France (1969), and in Kansas and Pittsburgh, Pennsylvania (1972). Her work is represented in the collections of the Pacific National Bank, Los Angeles, California; the Museum of Modern Art, Santiago, Chile; and the Museum of Modern Art, Morelia, Mexico. Saloma has painted in oil, with acrylics, and in encaustic; she has made wood engravings and linoleum cuts; she has also produced sculpture, under the direction of Rosa Castello; and painted murals, guided by the painter Armando López Carmona. Her work may be described as belonging to the neo-realist, constructivist style.

Bibliography

Alvarez, José Rogelio, et al. *Enciclopedia de Mexico.* Secretaría de Educación Pública, 1987.

Sampson, Atlanta Constance (1897–)

Born on a Midwestern farm, the painter Atlanta Constance Sampson left Detroit, Michigan, where she was teaching art, and moved to New York City in the 1940s. She studied with Hans Hofmann, worked at various part-time jobs, lived in a one-room apartment, created a prodigious amount of charcoal drawings, oils, and watercolors over the next half century—ever seeking a solo exhibition.

Sampson held her first solo exhibition at the National Arts Club, New York City (1988). She was then ninety-one years old. Her work has also been exhibited in the Rotunda of the U.S. Capitol building, Washington, D.C., and privately. She now lives in Iowa.

Bibliography

Adam, John. "Discovered at 91." *Art News* 92 (January 1993): 22.

Campbell, Lawrence. "National Arts Club, New York: Exhibit." *Art in America* 77 (January 1989): 148–49.

Samualie, Eliyakota (1939–1987)

A Canadian Inuit graphic artist and sculptor, Eliyakota Samualie was born in a coastal camp near Cape Dorset, Northwest Territories. Since her father died when she was very young, Eliyakota was raised for many years by her maternal grandparents. She moved into Cape Dorset in the early 1960s to live with her mother. Though Eliyakota never married, she raised one adopted child until her death in 1987.

Eliyakota began drawing in the early 1960s while still living on the land. Her drawings were first translated into prints for the 1970 annual Cape Dorset collection. Eliyakota's imagery consisted mainly of bird forms, occasionally combined with human, spirit, or flesh elements. Her drawings and the resulting print images are notable for their precision, stylization, and symmetry. Line and composition are tightly controlled; Eliyakota's birds are not merely depicted, they are displayed. This rather decorative style occasionally resembles that of the renowned Cape Dorset artist, Kenojuak Ashevak.

Eliyakota was represented in twelve Cape Dorset print collections. Her drawings, prints, and occasional sculptures have been featured in about fifteen group and two solo exhibitions. Works by Eliyakota can be found in the collections of the National Gallery of Canada, and the Canadian Museum of Civilization—both in Ottawa, the Art Gallery of Ontario, Toronto; and the Winnipeg Art Gallery, Manitoba.

Ingo Hessel

Bibliography
Hobbs, Anna. "From Cape Dorset: The Vivid Imagery of Our Inuit Artists." *Canadian Living* (November 1982): 41–47.

Sands, Ethel (1873–1962)

Born in Newport, Rhode Island, the painter Ethel Sands divided her time between her residences in England and France. Sands studied with Eugène Carrière in Paris, France; she became a British citizen in 1900; and shared her life with Nan Hudson, whom she met in Paris.

Sands showed her still-life and figure paintings in many solo exhibitions and had her work accepted at the Salon d'Automne, Paris, France (1904); five years later, she was accepted as a member. Sands and Hudson held a two-person show in London, England, among others, and became founding members of the London Group (1913). During World War I and World War II Sands was a nurse; afterwards she engaged in sustained travel until her life-long partner Hudson's deteriorating physical condition required her presence. Hudson died in 1957.

Much of Sands's output was destroyed in the bombing of London or stolen from her home in France, yet a fine example of her work may be seen in the Tate Gallery, London.

Bibliography
Cooper, E. *The Sexual Perspective: Homosexuality and Art in the Last 100 Years.* 1986.
Waters, G. *Dictionary of British Artists Working 1900–1940.* 1975.

Sanford, Marion (1904–c. 1986)

Born in the Province of Ontario, Canada, the sculptor Marion Sanford was raised in Warren, Pennsylvania. She studied painting at the Pratt Institute, Brooklyn, New York, and worked as a stage and costume designer, but was truly interested in sculpture. She studied direct carving for a brief period at the Art Students League, New York City, but essentially taught herself.

Sanford's first exhibitions of women farm workers (her forte) date from 1937, though there were sales of portrait busts earlier on. She was elected an associate member of the National Academy of Design and was also elected to membership in the National Sculpture Association—both in New York City. Examples of her work are represented in private and public permanent collections, including Brookgreen Gardens, South Carolina; the Corcoran Gallery of Art, Washington, D.C.; and others.

Bibliography
Dunford, Penny. *Biographical Dictionary of Women Artists in Europe and America since 1850.* University of Pennsylvania Press, 1989.
Proske, Beatrice. *Brookgreen Gardens Sculpture.* South Carolina, 1968.

Sanin, Fanny

Born in Bogotá, Colombia, the non-figurative painter Fanny Sanin earned a degree in Fine Arts from the University of the Andes, Bogotá (1960); she did graduate work in printmaking at the University of Illinois, Urbana, and took further study at the Chelsea School of Art and the Central School of Art, London, England. She has lived in Bogotá, Colombia; London, England; Mexico City, Mexico; and, since 1971, in New York City.

Sanin has held many solo exhibitions in prestigious museums and galleries since 1961, including the Modern Art Gallery, Monterrey (1964), and the National University, Mexico City (1965)—both in Mexico; Colseguros Gallery, Bogotá, Colombia (1966); Museum of Fine Arts, Caracas, Venezuela (1967); AIA Gallery, London, England (1968); and Pan American Union Gallery, Washington, D.C. (1969). Between 1969 and 1991 Sanin offered solo shows almost every year: from Monterrey, Mexico, to Caracas, Venezuela; from New York City to Medellín and other cities in Colombia; from Lafayette, Indiana, to the Inter-American Art Gallery, Miami-Dade Community College, Florida (1991). Her paintings have been invited to more than sixty group exhibitions in the United States, South and North America, and Europe. Winner of awards and honors, Sanin won a prize at the VIII November Salon, Monterrey, Mexico (1963); the First Edinburgh Open 100, Scotland (1967); the Medellín Award, Il Coltejer Art Biennial, Bogotá, Colombia (1970); the Canadian Club Award, U.S. Art Tour, New York City (1985); and others.

"Acrylic No. 3" (1981), a typical work of the period—abstract in nature, enriched by a personal approach to color that makes other "geometric" works pale by comparison—offers a sense of serenity, calm, peace—despite its creation in the maelstrom of an urban environment.

Sanin's work is represented in private, public, and corporate permanent collections, including the Museum of Modern Art (MoMA), and Chemical Bank—both in New York City; Museum of Modern Art, Mexico City, Mexico; Museum of Modern Art, and University of the Andes—both in Bogotá, Colombia; Museum of Art, Warsaw, Poland; Puerto Rico Institute of Culture, San Juan; UNICEF Collection; Valencia Ateneum, Venezuela; National Museum of Women in the Arts, Washington, D.C.; and others in Colombia, Venezuela, Mexico, England, Canada, France, Puerto Rico, Germany, Australia, Spain, and the United States.

Bibliography

Fanny Sanin: At the Edge. A Catalog. Essay by Dr. Donald B. Goodall. Miami-Dade Community College, 1981.

Fanny Sanin. A Catalog. Essay by Peter Frank. New York: Phoenix Gallery, 1982.

Fanny Sanin. A Catalog. Essay by John Stringer. Bogotá: Museum of Modern Art, 1986.

Fanny Sanin. A Catalog. Essay by Mario Amaya. New York: Schiller-Wapner Gallery, 1986.

Russell, John. "Fanny Sanin." *The New York Times* (19 February 1982): C26.

Sargent, Jean McNeil (Braley) (1925–)

Born in Wilkesboro, North Carolina, Jean McNeil (Braley) Sargent won a scholarship to the School of Professional Art, New York City (1944–1947) and began her professional art career as a textile designer and commercial artist. She studied painting at the Art Students League, New York City (1957); and printmaking at La Reparata Graphic Center, Florence, Italy (1975), and Pratt Graphic Center, New York City (1976). She earned a Bachelor's degree at the University of California at San Diego (1977); studied advanced printmaking at New York University, New York City, with Krishna Reddy (1982), and also with the master printmaker Stanley William Hayter at Atelier 17, Paris, France (1980, 1981, 1983).

A painter and printmaker, Sargent has had her work shown in myriad solo and group exhibitions in the United States and abroad—from Los Angeles, California, to Yokohama, Japan; from Boston, Massachusetts, to Bombay, India; from New York City to Guadalajara, Mexico.

Sargent has won a number of awards and honors for her work; she is an arts activist in the San Diego, California, community, and was cofounder of the Printmakers Atelier, La Jolla, California, with Françoise Gilot. Sargent taught at a number of institutions, including a community college in San Diego, and Mira Costa College, Oceanside—both in California; and the Corcoran School of Art, Washington, D.C. Her work is in many private and public permanent collections, such as the National Archives, Washington, D.C.; Pratt Graphics Center, New York City; Bibliothèque Nationale, Paris, France; the Embassy of New Zealand, Washington, D.C.; and others.

Bibliography

La Brecque, Eric. "On Channel 37 . . ." *Del Mar Surfcomber* (August 21, 1985): 7.

Petersen, Martin. "On View." *Applause* (November 1980): 22.

Who's Who in American Art. 19th ed. R.R. Bowker Co., 1991–1992.

Sargent, Margaret (1892–1978)

Born in Wellesley, Massachusetts, the painter/sculptor Margaret Sargent studied with Gutzon Borglum and Woodbury; she was a member of the National Society of Women Painters and Sculptors, New York City.

Bibliography

American Art Annual. Vol. 28. American Federation of Arts, 1932.

The Feminine Gaze: Women Depicted by Women 1900–1930. Whitney Museum of Art, 1984.

Moore, Honor. "My Grandmother Who Painted." *The Writer on Her Work*. W.W. Norton, 1980.

Sartain, Emily (1841–1927)

A native of Philadelphia, Pennsylvania, Emily Sartain was born into a family of printmakers and painters, and was encouraged and taught, early on, by her father. Sartain studied at the Pennsylvania Academy of Fine Arts in her native city (1864–1870). She travelled throughout Europe over the next four years, and won a medal at the Centennial Exposition in 1876 for a work shown the preceding year at the Paris Salon, France.

Known primarily as an art educator, Sartain was principal of the Philadelphia School of Design for Women, Pennsylvania (1886–1920)—the first industrial design school for women in the United States. Founder and president of the Plastic Club, Philadelphia, Sartain won two medals at exhibitions held at the Pennsylvania Academy of Fine Arts, Philadelphia; showed at the National Academy of Design, New York City; and in other venues until she was in her late forties. Sartain's printmaking specialty was mezzotint engraving, an example of which is in the collection of the Print Room of the New York Public Library, New York City.

Bibliography

Gilchrist, Agnes A. "Sartain, Emily." *Notable American Women 1607–1950*. Vol. 3. Harvard University Press, 1971.

Goodman, Helen. "Emily Sartain: Her Career." *Arts Magazine* 61:9 (May 1987): 61–65.

Hanaford, Phebe A. *Daughters of America*. True & Co., 1882.

Sasaki, Tomiyo (1943–)

Born in Vernon, British Columbia, Canada, the video artist and installationist Tomiyo Sasaki initially studied at the Alberta College of Art, Calgary, Alberta, Canada (1962–1965); did further study in painting and sculpture at the San Francisco Art Institute, California, where she earned a Bachelor of Fine Arts degree (1967); and received a Master of Arts degree from the California College of Arts and Crafts, Oakland (1969).

Sasaki has held many solo exhibitions and installations in museums and galleries in the United States and abroad, including the Media Studies Center, Buffalo, New York (1976); the Museum of Modern Art (MoMA) (1977), and the Anthology, Film and Video Archives (1980)—both in New York City; "Spawning Sockeyes," an installation at P.S.1, Institute for Art and Urban Resources, Long Island City, New York (1985); and others. Her videos explore and transmute the fauna of exotic locales.

Winner of awards and honors, Sasaki received Creative Artists Public Service (CAPS) grants (1872, 1976); grants from the Canada Council (1969–1974, 1976, 1981–1982); and fellowships from the National Endowment for the Arts (NEA) (1982), the Guggenheim Memorial Foundation (1983), the New York Foundation for the Arts (1985); and others. Examples of her work are in private and public permanent collections, including the National Gallery of Canada, Ottawa; the New York Public Library, New York City; and others.

Bibliography

Art Video Retrospectives and Perspectives. Charleroi, Belgium: Palais des Beaux-Arts, 1983.

Lord, Barry. "The Eleven O'Clock News in Colour." *Artscanada* 27 (June 1970): 4–20.

Making Their Mark: Women Artists Move into the Mainstream 1970–1985. Abbeville Press, 1989.

Sato, Norie (1949–)

Born in Sendai, Japan, the printmaker/video artist/mixed media installationist Norie Sato earned a Bachelor of Fine Arts degree at the University of Michigan, Ann Arbor (1971), and, three years later, received a Master of Fine Arts degree from the University of Washington, Seattle. Sato has held numerous solo exhibitions of her work in galleries and museums in the United States, including "Norie Sato," Index Gallery, Clark College, Vancouver, Washington (1991); "New Work," Elizabeth Leach Gallery, Portland, Oregon (1991); "Wings of Transmission," Linda Farris Gallery (1990), and "In Public: Seattle 1991," Seattle Arts Commission—both in Seattle, Washington. At the Linda Farris Gallery, Sato has also exhibited solo shows of prints (1989); works on paper and glass (1986, 1987); and on paper and video (1981, 1983). Her "Video Viewpoints" exhibition was offered at the Museum of Modern Art (MoMA), New York City (1980).

From 1976 to 1991 Sato has had her work invited to many group exhibitions in the United States and abroad, such as "Vanishing Boundaries," Intermedia Arts Gallery, St. Paul, Minnesota (1991); "Computers and the Creative Process," a travelling show, University of Oregon, Eugene (1989); "Glass: Material in the Service of Meaning," Tacoma Art Museum, Washington (1991); "Young America—Not in New York," Dolan/Maxwell Gallery, Philadelphia, Pennsylvania (1987); "Documents Northwest: The PONCHO series," Seattle Art Museum, Washington (1984); "Impressions I: Experimental Prints," Institute of Contemporary Art of the Virginia Museum, Richmond (1983); "19 Artists—Emergent Americans," Guggenheim Museum, New York City (1981); "New York, Seattle, Los Angeles," travelling to Europe, Japan, and throughout the United States, organized by MoMA (1980), and "8 West Coast Printmakers," Brooklyn Museum (1978)—both in New York City; and many others.

Sato's video "trees" and large-scale works on paper require the viewer to rethink old clichés of broadcast images and to ponder the visual beauty of her ever-changing two-dimensional surfaces. She has won a number of commissions, honors, and awards for her work, including an artists fellowship from the Washington State Arts Commission (1989–1990); the Betty Bowen memorial art award from the Seattle Art Museum, Washington (1983); artists fellowships and a planning grant from the National Endowment for the Arts (NEA) (1979, 1980, 1982); and others. Her work is represented in private and public permanent collections, including the Brooklyn Museum and the Guggenheim Museum—both in New York City; city of Seattle Public Art Collection and Seattle Art Museum—both in Washington; Hawaii State Cultural Foundation, Honolulu; Philadelphia Museum of Art, Pennsylvania; Purdue University, West Lafayette, Indiana; and many others.

Bibliography

Baro, Gene. "19 Artists: Emergent Americans." *Art International* (March–April 1981).

Carlsson, Jae. "Norie Sato." *Artforum* (October 1989): 182.

"Norie Sato." *Northwest Originals: Washington Women and Their Art.* MatriMedia, Inc., 1990.

Wooster, Ann Sargent. "Centerfold: Video." *The Village Voice* (April 1–7, 1981).

Sauer, Jane (1937–)

Born in St. Louis, Missouri, the fiber artist/sculptor Jane Sauer earned a Bachelor of Fine Arts degree from Washington University in her native city (1959). She has won honors and awards for her waxed linen "baskets" and other objects, including a National Endowment for the Arts (NEA) fellowship (1984); a biennial visual artists grant from the Missouri Arts Council (1986); and others.

Sauer's work has been exhibited in solo and group shows in the United States and abroad, including "American Baskets: The Eighties," the Chicago Public Library Cultural Center, Illinois; and Grand Rapids and Jackson, Michigan (1988); "Current Exhibition: Jane Sauer," St. Louis Art Museum, Missouri (1988); "The Tactile Vessel: New Basket Forms," a travelling show through 1991, Erie Art Museum, Pennsylvania (1989); "Crafts Today USA," a travelling show touring Europe and Russia, American Craft Museum, New York City, through 1991; and others.

Sauer's work is represented in many private and public permanent collections, including the Bellas Artes Gallery, Santa Fe, New Mexico, and others. "Rationality" (1989), an interlaced, waxed linen, basket-like object, was slowly built up by Sauer in this archaic technique: creating both surface and structure sans tools. She also creates knotted sculptures.

Bibliography

Degener, Patricia. "Emotive Basketry." *American Crafts Magazine* (August–September 1986): 42–45.

Pulleyn, Rob, ed. *The Basketmaker's Art.* Lark Books, 1986.

Van Deventer, M.J. "Jane Sauer." *Art Gallery International* (May–June 1989): 42–45.

Saunders, Joyan (1954–)

Photographer Joyan Saunders was born in Newfoundland, Canada, but she did not study art until she went to Cambrian College in Sudbury, Ontario, in 1972. She subsequently took a Bachelor of Fine Arts degree at the University of Western Ontario, which encouraged sharply critical practices and art forms then still unusual in academic circles. This was further strengthened by Master of Fine Arts studies at Montréal's Concordia University and—like Jan Peacock before her—at the University of California at San Diego. There she continued to develop her interest in photo-documentation of performance-like incidents presented with a cinematic sensibility.

Saunders's first solo show was at the Forest City Gallery in London, Ontario—an artist-run alternative gallery for experimental work. Since then she has shown in a variety of locales, including an important show of feminist art at the Montréal Museum of Contemporary Art, Québec, in 1982. Her work is not unlike that of Cindy Sherman's, but it was developed well before Sherman was the star she is today, and it is both more narrative and less commercially polished in appearance.

Robert J. Belton

Bibliography

Art et féminisme. Montréal: Musée d'art contemporain (March 11–May 2, 1982).

Joyan Saunders: Prescriptions. Buffalo: CEPA Gallery and Montréal: Artexte, 1984.

Perspektief 31:2 (April 1988): 57–66.

Sauret, Nunik (1951–)

Born in Mexico, Nunik Sauret studied at la Escuela de Pintura y Escultura (La Esmeralda), Mexico City, and, in 1976, joined the Taller de Grabado del Molino of Santo Domingo. She has exhibited her work in some twenty solo shows and participated in many group shows, including the Biennials of Printmaking in Yugoslavia (1979); Norway (1980); and Colombia and Puerto Rico (1981).

Sauret makes prints in various techniques including etching, drypoint, aquatint, mezzotint, and engraving. Although she also makes drawings and paintings, her greatest accomplishments have been attained as a printmaker. A constant theme in her work is the depiction of fruits and vegetables with erotic overtones.

Bibliography

Alvarez, José Rogelio, et al. *Enciclopedia de Mexico*. Secretaría de Educación Pública, 1987.

Savage, Anne (1896–1971)

Born in Montréal, Québec, Canada, the landscape painter Anne Savage was a member of the Beaver Hall Group. Savage studied at the Art Association of Montréal with William Brymner and Maurice Cullen (1914–1918) and also at the Minneapolis School of Art, Minnesota (1920–1921).

Savage often exhibited with the Group of Seven, which included her friend, A.Y. Jackson, and her work was shown in many group exhibitions, such as the British Empire Exposition, Wembley, England (1924–1925); with other Canadian painters in Paris, France (1927); the Corcoran Gallery, Washington, D.C.; the New York World's Fair (1939); a travelling retrospective organized by the National Gallery of Canada, Ottawa (late 1960s); and others. President of the Canadian Group of Painters (1949, 1960), Savage taught art for twenty-five years at Baron Byng High School, Montréal, and, from 1947 to 1952, was supervisor of the Protestant School Board of Greater Montréal.

Savage's work is represented in many private and public permanent collections. "The Plough" (c. 1931), an oil on canvas in the collection of the Montréal Museum of Fine Arts, Québec, depicts a plough which dominates a landscape of rhythmic, rolling hills; painted so convincingly, it strongly suggests the presence of the farm worker.

Bibliography

Braide, Janet. *Anne Savage—Her Expression of Beauty*. Montréal Museum of Fine Arts, 1979.

McCullough, Nora. *The Beaver Hall Group*. National Gallery of Canada, 1966.

Samuels, Peggy, and Harold Samuels. *The Illustrated Biographical Encyclopedia of Artists of the American West*. Doubleday, 1976.

Savage, Augusta Christine (Fells) (1892–1962)

A sculptor and influential teacher in New York City's Harlem, Augusta Christine (Fells) Savage broke racial barriers during her career and aided many young African-American artists. She was born on February 29, 1892, in Green Cove Springs, Florida—one of fourteen children of a Methodist minister. She said she made her earliest sculptures out of the local red clay as a child, displeasing her father who opposed the making of "graven images." But she persisted and was talented enough to teach a clay modeling class at her high school in West Palm Beach, Florida.

She attended Tallahassee State Normal School, Florida, for a year, and in 1919 she won a $25 dollar prize at the Palm Beach county fair. Encouraged, she sought commissions unsuccessfully in Jackson, Florida, and then headed to New York City, arriving with $4.60 and a letter of introduction from a county fair official to sculptor Solon Borglum. With Borglum's aid, she enrolled at the Cooper Union, New York City, where she studied with George Brewster from 1921 to 1923.

In 1923 her application for a scholarship to attend a summer art school at the Palace of Fontainebleau in France was returned after the American screening committee learned she was African-American. Savage responded publicly in letters and newspaper interviews, with support from advocates such as African-American educator and author W.E.B. Du Bois, and Alfred Martin of the Ethical Culture Society. In the lean years ahead Savage studied with Herman A. MacNeil and Onorio Ruotuolo while laboring in factories and laundries. She had to turn down a scholarship to study in Rome, Italy, in 1926 because of lack of money, but she kept working, completing busts of Du Bois and African-American leader Marcus Garvey. She most often portrayed African-Americans and African-American figurative themes. Her breakthrough came with "Gamin," a head of a jaunty African-American street youth, that won her a Julius Rosenwald Foundation fellowship in 1929, finally enabling her to study in Europe for two and a half years. She worked in Paris, France, with Felix Beuneteaux at the Académie de la Grande Chaumière and portrait sculptor Charles Despiau. She exhibited at Grand Palais salons.

Returning to New York City during the Depression era, Savage started a Harlem art school with a grant from the Carnegie Foundation, Pittsburgh, Pennsylvania. Her school, initially located in a one-room apartment, had varying names over the years: the Savage School of Arts and Crafts, Savage Studios, and Uptown Art Laboratory. When an exhibition of her students' work was held at the 138th Street YWCA (Young Women's Christian Association) in 1935, featuring many Harlem scenes, Savage told an interviewer she wanted to teach them "the essentials without making them bound down with academic tradition, which will spoil the freshness of their work." By 1936 she had founded the Harlem Art Center, an African-American showcase school for the Federal Art Project of the Works Progress Administration (WPA/FAP). She also organized a club—the Vanguard—and was active in the Harlem Artists' Guild. She aided many African-American artists, including William E. Artis, Norman Lewis, Ernest Crichlow, Elton C. Fax, Robert Savon Pious, and Jacob Lawrence.

Savage's own work took a back seat to her role as educator and promoter. "It was always in me how much I'd been kept down," she once said. "If I can inspire one of these youngsters . . . my monument will be in their work." However, she exhibited in the 1920s and 1930s at the 135th Street branch of the New York Public Library, Anderson Galleries, the Architectural League, and the Argent Galleries, appearing in the first shows of the Harmon Foundation, organized to boost African-American art. Many of her works were made only in plaster because of cost considerations, and have not been preserved. In the 1930s she exhibited a wood carving entitled "Envy" and "Martiniquaise," a woman's head in black Belgian marble, as well as "After the Glory," a condemnation of war in plaster, and "Realization." Her "Gamin" and "La Citadelle—Freedom" in bronze are in the Howard University Gallery of Art, Washington, D.C. The plaster of the

"Gamin" is in the National Museum of American Art, Washington, D.C. Her small bronze, waist-length "Pugilist" is in the New York Public Library's Schomburg collection, New York City. "Faun," in cast cement, is in the Du Sable Museum of African-American History, Chicago, Illinois, while her 1928 bronze, "Green Apples," is in the Beinecke Rare Book and Manuscript Library, Yale University, New Haven, Connecticut.

Savage's last major commission was "Lift Every Voice," which stood outside the Contemporary Art Building at the 1939 New York World's Fair. Savage said it was inspired by a song of the same name by James Weldon Johnson, which she called "the national Negro anthem." Her sculpture was in the shape of a harp, with a choir of African-American singers forming the strings and "the arm and hand of the creator" forming the soundboard. A youth kneels in front holding a bar of notes. The whole was made of plaster, finished to resemble black basalt. It was destroyed after the fair.

Savage failed in her attempt to open a Salon of Contemporary Negro Art in Harlem after the WPA art project ended. In 1945 she "retired" to Saugerties, New York, where she worked for a mushroom grower and largely abandoned her art. Savage had married three times and had one daughter, Irene.

Cynthia Mills

Bibliography
Bearden, Romare, and Harry Henderson. *Six Black Masters of American Art*. Zenith Books, 1972, pp. 76–98, 104, 106–07.
Donaldson, Jeff R. *Generation "306"—Harlem, New York*. Ph.D. dissertation. Northwestern University, 1974, pp. 53–56, 105–08, 161–62.
Igoe, Lynn Moody. *250 Years of Afro-American Art: An Annotated Bibliography*. R.R. Bowker Co., 1981, pp. 1080–83.
Logan, Rayford W., and Michael R. Winston, eds. *Dictionary of American Negro Biography*. (Entry by Elton C. Fax). W.W. Norton & Co., 1982, pp. 542–43.
New York Public Library artist's files.
Reynolds, Gary, and Beryl J. Wright. *Against the Odds: African-American Artists and the Harmon Foundation*. Newark, New Jersey: The Newark Museum, 1989, pp. 18, 23, 104, 139, 242, 248, 251–53.
Rubenstein, Charlotte Streifer. *American Women Artists*. Hall & Co., 1982, pp. 115, 158–260, 265.
Schomburg Center for Research in Black Culture. *Augusta Savage and the Art Schools of Harlem*. New York, 1988.

Savage, Naomi (1927–)

By exploring and creating new art forms, Naomi Savage expanded the medium of photography. Born on June 25, 1927, in Princeton, New Jersey, Savage began her photographic studies in 1943, with Berenice Abbott at the New School for Social Research in New York City. She continued her education at Bennington College in Vermont, where she studied art, photography, and music from 1944 to 1947. The next year was spent with her uncle, Man Ray, in California, where she was exposed to his innovative techniques and attitudes about art. In 1950 she married David Savage—an architect/sculptor—and they moved with him to Paris, France, where they remained for several years.

Over the past thirty years Savage has participated in a number of individual and group exhibitions, including one in Trenton, New Jersey, entitled "Two Generations of Photography; Man Ray and Naomi Savage," in 1969. Her work can be found in the permanent collections of the Museum of Modern Art (MoMA) in New York City; Fogg Art Museum at Harvard University, Cambridge, Massachusetts; Museum of Fine Art in Houston, Texas; and the Madison Art Center in Wisconsin.

Savage has been the recipient of the Cassandra Foundation award in 1970, followed by the National Endowment for the Arts (NEA) photography fellowship in 1971. In the same year she was commissioned by the Lyndon Baines Johnson Library at Austin, Texas, to make a mural of president's portraits, which she did on five eight-by-ten-foot photo-engraved plates. Savage also received the silver award, Art Directors Club in 1976.

Combining past and present techniques with traditional black-and-white still photography, Savage creates images that range from portraits and landscapes to abstract designs. Her techniques include solarization, silk-screen, high-contrast toning, gum-bichromate prints, images on porcelain, and many techniques of her own design.

Melissa J. Guenther

Bibliography
Browne, Turner, and Elaine Partnow. *Macmillan Biographical Encyclopedia of Photographic Artists and Innovators*. Macmillan and Collier Macmillan, 1983.
Lewis, Peggy. *Two Generations of Photography: Man Ray and Naomi Savage*. Exhibition Catalog. Trenton, New Jersey, 1969.
Walsh, George, Coline Naylor, and Michael Held, eds. *Contemporary Photographers*. St. Martin's Press, 1982.
Witkin, Lee D., and Barbara London. *The Photographer Collector's Guide*. New York Graphic Society, 1979.

Sawyer, Helen Alton (1900–)

Born in Washington, D.C., the painter Helen Alton Sawyer studied at the National Academy of Design, New York City; and with Charles Hawthorne, the painter, Johansen, and Wells M. Sawyer, her father. She married Jerry Farnsworth, whom she first met on Cape Cod, Massachusetts, when they both studied with Hawthorne.

Sawyer and Wells M. Sawyer held a two-person exhibition at the Babcock Galleries, New York City (1921). She also showed in solo and group exhibitions and was a member of several arts organizations, including the Provincetown Art Association, Massachusetts; Washington Art Club and the Washington Society of Artists—both in Washington, D.C.; and the Yonkers Art Association, New York.

Bibliography
American Art Annual. Vol. 28. American Federation of Arts, 1932.
Watson, Ernest W. *Twenty Painters*. Watson-Guptill, 1950.

Scaravaglione, Concetta (1900–1975)

A sculptor known for her monumental stone and metal figures, Concetta Scaravaglione was born and raised on New York City's Lower East Side. As a teenager Scaravaglione won silver and bronze medals in New York City's National Academy of Design free sculpture class for female students; beginning in 1920 she spent three years at the Art Students League, also in New York City, where her teachers included Boardman Robinson, Forbes Watson, and John Sloan. In 1924 Scaravaglione won a scholarship to work with Robert Laurent;

later she studied under Theodore Roszak.

Scaravaglione began exhibiting her work in 1925; she had her first one-woman show in 1941 at the Virginia Museum of Fine Arts, Richmond, and her first solo show in New York, thirty-three years later, at the Kraushaar Gallery. Her sculptures are in the permanent collections of the Whitney Museum of American Art and Museum of Modern Art (MoMA)—both in New York City; and the National Museum of American Art—Washington, D.C. A gifted instructor, she taught at New York University, New York City; Black Mountain College, North Carolina; Sarah Lawrence College, Bronxville, and Vassar College, Poughkeepsie—both in New York.

Scaravaglione received several important government commissions, including "Railway Mail Carrier, 1862" (1935), a cast aluminum figure for the federal post office building; and "Agriculture" (1937), a limestone relief at the Federal Trade Commission building—both in Washington, D.C. Her fourteen-foot-tall "Woman with Mountain Sheep" of 1939 was unveiled at that year's New York World's Fair; and "Girl with Gazelle" (1936) was reproduced on the covers of both *Art Digest* and *Newsweek*. Scaravaglione was awarded the Widener gold medal at the Pennsylvania Academy of Fine Arts, Philadelphia, in 1934; in 1947 she became the first woman to win the Prix de Rome.

Bibliography

Rubinstein, Charlotte Streifer. *American Women Artists: From Early Indian Times to the Present.* Avon, 1982, pp. 255–57.
Scaravaglione, Concetta. "My Enjoyment in Sculpture." *Magazine of Art* 32 (August 1939): pp. 450–55.
Washington, D.C., Smithsonian Institution, Archives of American Art. Concetta Scaravaglione Papers (microfilm roll 1622).

Schapiro, Miriam (1923–)

A leading force in the feminist art movement that emerged in the early 1970s, Miriam Schapiro was born in Toronto, Canada, but spent most of her childhood in New York City, where her father, Theodore Schapiro, earned his living as an industrial designer and director of the Rand School of Social Science. Her mother, Fannie (Cohen) Schapiro was extremely supportive of her daughter's early aspirations to become an artist. It was therefore with warm parental encouragement that Schapiro enrolled as a teenager in Victor D'Amico's Saturday classes at the Museum of Modern Art (MoMA) and in evening drawing classes sponsored by the Works Progress Administration's Federal Art Project (WPA/FAP)—both in New York City. In 1943 she entered Hunter College, New York City, but soon transferred to the University of Iowa, Iowa City, from which she received her Bachelor of Arts degree in 1945, a Master of Arts degree in 1946, and a Master of Fine Arts degree in 1949.

In 1946 Schapiro met and married fellow student Paul Brach, and four years later the couple moved to Columbia, Missouri, where Brach taught at the University of Missouri and Schapiro taught children's art. In 1952 they settled in New York City. There Schapiro worked at a variety of jobs, including teaching children's art and working for a real estate firm. Meanwhile she was also pursuing her career as a studio artist and was soon showing her work at a number of galleries. In 1958 she opened her first solo exhibition at the André Emmerich Gallery, New York City.

During her first years back in New York City, Schapiro's paint-

ings belonged to the abstract expressionist school. By the early 1960s, however, her work, though continuing to be abstract, became considerably more structured and geometric in character. In either case, Schapiro had already begun to express feminist themes in her art. Thus, a number of paintings dating from the 1950s, such as "Interview" and "Bouquet," embodied covert statements regarding female identity in a man's world. In the decade following, feminist concerns became more apparent in her works, and many of them, including her "Shrine" series, were expressions of the artist's struggle to come to terms with her aspiration as a creative being and the tensions they spawned in the face of the traditional view of womanhood. Her hard-edged, geometric composition of 1968, titled "Big Ox," represented the end of that struggle. Schapiro regarded this piece, as she later put it herself, as a visual declaration that "male-assertive, logical, measured and reasonable thoughts" could reside "in a female body."

After moving with her husband to La Jolla, California, in 1967, Schapiro continued to work as a studio artist but also became a lecturer in art at the University of California, San Diego. In 1970 she joined the faculty of the California Institute of the Arts, Valencia, and shortly thereafter allied herself with Judy Chicago to found and codirect the California Institute of the Arts feminist art program.

The collaboration with Chicago marked a watershed in Schapiro's career. For among its most tangible fruits was Womanhouse—an enterprise that opened in 1972 where women artists were invited to share in transforming an old Hollywood mansion into a totally female environment. As her contribution to this project Schapiro worked in tandem with Sherry Brody to create "The Dollhouse"—a structure divided into six compartments and decorated with bits of fabric, mementos, and miniature household objects that were meant to evoke female life and fantasy. In the course of working on this piece and directing the Womanhouse project in general, Schapiro's professional perspective underwent radical change. Instead of attempting to express herself in idioms largely defined by a masculine art world, she would henceforth seek the inspiration for her work in the traditional feminine experience.

In short the domestic decorative arts that were generally associated with women and that she had once dismissed as beneath her concerns as a serious artist became primary sources for her self-expression. One of the pieces most emblematic of this shift is the artist's "Again Sixteen Windows" (1973), which echoed a grid composition she had done eight years previously. Whereas the earlier picture, titled simply "Sixteen Windows," had been void of decorative embellishment, the grid and the spaces that it framed in this later work were defined by an array of flowered and checked patterns unmistakably evocative of home and hearth. Composing this and other works from scraps of cloth, embroidery, buttons, and rickrack, Schapiro gave birth to a new subcategory of collage which she terms "femmage" and through which she sought, as one critic put it, to "create a valid imagery of women's consciousness."

As she began taking new approaches to her own work in the early 1970s, Schapiro was also rapidly becoming a leading presence in the campaign to help other women artists establish a strong identity within the art world. In 1974 the Feminist Art Program produced under her guidance "Anonymous Was A Woman," which, among other things, featured seventy-one letters from professional women artists to the young members of their sex who aspired to joining their profession. In the year following she collaborated with her students in the Feminist Program in publishing *Art: A Woman's Sensibility*—a volume devoted to the writings and works of seventy-six American women artists.

In 1975, following a retrospective exhibition of her work at the University of California, San Diego, Schapiro moved back to New York. Shortly thereafter, a book on Japanese kimonos, which Sherry Brody had given her, inspired the idea for one of her most ambitious pieces. The result was "The Anatomy of a Kimono," a grouping of painted and fabric panels collectively measuring more than six-and-a-half-by-fifty feet, that went on view at the André Emmerich Gallery, New York City, in 1976. Four years later another retrospective exhibition of Schapiro's work was organized which eventually travelled to nine sites throughout the country.

The recipient of a number of honors, including an honorary Doctorate degree from the College of Wooster, Ohio, Schapiro is represented today in many private and public collections. Among the museums that own her work are the Museum of Modern Art (MoMA), and the Whitney Museum of American Art—both in New York City; and the National Gallery of Art, and Hirshhorn Museum and Sculpture Garden—both in Washington, D.C.

Frederick S. Voss

Bibliography
Bradley, Paula W. "Miriam Schapiro: The Feminist Transformation of an Avant-Garde Artist." Unpublished Ph.D. dissertation, University of North Carolina, Chapel Hill, 1982.
Frank, Elizabeth. "Miriam Schapiro: Formal Sentiments." *Art in America* 70 (May 1982): 106–10.
Kuspit, Donald. Interview with Miriam Schapiro. *Art in America* 65 (September 1977): 83.
Miriam Schapiro, A Retrospective: 1953–1980. Ohio: The College of Wooster, 1980.
New Paintings by Miriam Schapiro. Bernice Steinbaum Gallery, 1986.
Nochlin, Linda. "Recent Work of Miriam Schapiro." *Arts Magazine* 48 (November 1973): 38–41.
Schapiro, Miriam. "The Education of Women as Artists: Project Womanhouse." *Art Journal* 31 (Spring 1972): 268–70.
Stofflet, Mary. "Miriam Schapiro." *Arts Magazine* 51 (May 1977): 12.

Scheer, Elaine (1958–)

As a graduate student at the San Francisco Art Institute, California, Elaine Scheer received the Isaac Walters sculpture award in 1980 and a merit scholarship in 1981, graduating with a Master of Fine Arts degree the following year.

A native of Los Angeles, California, Scheer began exhibiting ceramic sculpture and drawings in 1978 as an undergraduate student at Sonoma State University in Rohnert Park, California, where she had her first solo show. After graduating with honors and distinction in 1979, she was invited in 1981 to exhibit in a two-person show at the Diego Rivera Gallery in San Francisco, California, and the John Bolles Gallery in Santa Rosa, California. Visiting artist assignments between 1983 and 1990 included the San Francisco Art Institute, California; Brigham Young University, Provo, Utah; the Art Institute of Chicago, Illinois; and Memphis State University, Tennessee.

Scheer's sculptures have been included in a number of competitive exhibits, among them the Westwood Clay National (1981), the 3rd Annual Monarch Tile National Ceramic Competition (1988), and the 22nd Annual Ceramics Invitational, University of Wisconsin, Whitewater (1991). In 1986 she was invited to develop a mixed-media outdoor installation at Muir Beach, California. "Peace Theater" juxtaposed classroom chairs with a grave and a six-foot-high globe-like ball of earth, clay, and straw. Scheer was interviewed on KRON, San Francisco, California, to discuss the work's interaction with peace and environmental groups. That same year Scheer spent three months as an arts/industry resident at the Kohler Company, sponsored by the John Michael Kohler Art Center, Sheboygan, Wisconsin. Using this opportunity to expand the scale and style of her work, she developed a series of ceramic sculptures for outdoor environments.

Since 1988 Scheer has been teaching at the University of Wisconsin at Madison and is now an associate professor of ceramics and mixed media. "Storytelling Tree" (1990) was in the faculty show of 1990–1991 and continues her exploration of creating spaces that interact with the viewer. In 1991 Scheer had a one-person show—a ceramics and mixed-media installation at Artemisia Gallery in Chicago, Illinois.

Elaine Levin

Bibliography
Dragat, T. "A Cue From Nature." *Metier* (Fall 1986): 6.
Levin, Elaine. *The History of American Ceramics.* Harry N. Abrams, 1988.
Moore, Sylvia, ed. *Yesterday and Tomorrow: California Women Artists.* Midmarch Arts, 1989.
"Peace Theater." *Women of Power* 6 (Spring 1987): 82.
Scheer, Elaine. "Thoughts on the Panel Discussion: The Map Is Not the Territory." *NCECA Journal* 11 (1990–1991).

Scheer, Sherie (1940–)

Born in Estherville, Iowa, the free-lance photographer Sherie Scheer earned Bachelor's and Master's degrees from the University of California at Los Angeles (UCLA) (1969, 1971).

Known for her panoramic photographs Scheer, in a sense, takes photographs of photographs and then works on the finished product with oils. That is, she takes individual shots, butts them together, re-shoots and then paints the resultant print.

Representative examples of her work are in private, public, and corporate permanent collections in the United States and abroad, including the National Gallery of Australia, Canberra; Gallery Van Haarlem, the Netherlands; Center for Creative Photography, Tucson, Arizona; Harvard University, Cambridge, Massachusetts; Security Pacific National Bank, Los Angeles, California; University of Oklahoma, Norman; and many others.

Bibliography
Art in America (March–April 1978).
Photographic Directions, Los Angeles, 1979. A Catalog. Los Angeles: Security Pacific National Bank, 1979.
Popular Photography (December 1977).

Schille, Alice (1869–1955)

Upon graduation from high school in her native city of Columbus, Ohio, Alice Schille enrolled at the Columbus Art School in 1887. After two years there she went to New York City to study painting at the Art Students League with H. Siddons Mowbray, Kenyon Cox, and William Merritt Chase, who called her his best student at the time. Chase invited her to his new summer school at Shinnecock and later purchased two of her paintings. During 1893–1894, while she attended classes at the Pennsylvania Academy of Fine Arts, Philadelphia, she had work accepted for the academy's annual exhibition. She then spent six years in Europe, where she studied briefly at Académie Colarossi in Paris, France; copied Velázquez at the Prado; painted the seashore in Holland and Belgium; and exhibited two paintings in a special show at the Louvre, Paris, France, in 1900.

From 1902 to 1942 Schille taught at the Columbus Art School, Ohio, spending her summers in travel and regularly submitting paintings to annual national exhibitions. She garnered many awards, among them the Corcoran prize from the Washington Watercolor Club (1908); a gold medal at the Panama-Pacific International Exposition, San Francisco (1915), and first prize at the Philadelphia Watercolor Club, Pennsylvania (1932). Her first solo exhibition was at the Cincinnati Art Museum, Ohio, in 1911, which included watercolors of the Dalmatian coast.

Schille generally painted landscapes, often including people, in watercolor as she went on her extensive travels to Europe, North Africa, and Central America. She frequently created a mosaic-like effect in her paintings, leaving the white of the paper showing between little squares of color. For her portraits she reserved the use of oil.

Eleanor Tufts

Bibliography

Alice Schille, A.W.S. Boston: Vose Galleries, 1982.
Owings, Edna. "The Art of Alice Schille." *International Studio* 50 (August 1913): 31–33.
Tufts, Eleanor. *American Women Artists, 1830–1930*. National Museum of Women in the Arts, 1987.
Wells, Gary. "Alice Schille: Painter from the Midwest." *Art and Antiques* 6 (September–October 1983): 64–71.

Schira, Cynthia (1934–)

Born in Pittsfield, Massachusetts, the contemporary weaver and fiber artist Cynthia Schira earned a Bachelor's degree from the Rhode Island School of Design, Providence (1956); studied the art of tapestry at L'École d'Art Décoratif, Aubusson, France (1956–1957), and received a Master of Fine Arts degree from the University of Kansas, Lawrence (1967).

Schira has held a number of solo exhibitions of her work in museums and galleries, including the Franklin Parrasch Gallery, New York City (1991); Miller/Brown Gallery, San Francisco, California (1985, 1988); Renwick Gallery, National Museum of American Art, Smithsonian Institution, Washington, D.C. (1987); Hadler/Rodriguez Galleries, New York City (1978, 1982, 1985); Museum Bellerive, Zurich, Switzerland (1979); and others. Her weavings have been invited to group exhibitions throughout the world—from Tulsa, Oklahoma to Kyoto, Japan; from Sheboygan, Wisconsin to Nürnberg, Germany; from New York City to Lodz, Poland. Schira has carried out commissions both large and small—from a four-by-thirty-two-foot tapestry for the Galleria Bank, Houston, Texas (1977) to a five-by-seven-foot weaving for the Prince Kuhio Hotel in Hawaii (1979)—and many others.

Professor of design at the University of Kansas, Lawrence, Schira has lectured widely, given many workshops, shared her expertise, and served as juror for major competitions. She has won many awards and honors for her work, embracing fellowships from Textron (1956); the National Endowment for the Arts (NEA) (1974, 1983); Kansas Arts Commission (1990); an honorary Doctorate degree from the Rhode Island School of Design, Providence (1989); and others. Her work is represented in private and public permanent collections in the United States and abroad, including the Metropolitan Museum of Art, American Craft Museum, and Cooper-Hewitt Museum—all in New York City; Philadelphia Museum of Art, Pennsylvania; Museum Bellerive, Zurich, Switzerland; the Art Institute of Chicago, Illinois; the Spencer Museum of Art, University of Kansas, Lawrence; and many others.

Bibliography

American Craftspeople Project: The Reminiscences of Cynthia Schira. Special Collections, University Library, Columbia University, 1988.
Corwin, Nancy. "Image into Structure." *Surface Design Journal* 14:1 (Fall 1989).
Duesenbury, Mary. "Cynthia Schira." *New Art Examiner* 15:1 (September 1987).
Talley, Charles. "Evocative Landscape Weaving." *Artweek* 19:15 (April 16, 1988).

Schmid Esler, Annemarie (1937–)

Annemarie Schmid Esler's innovative work in clay employs cast forms in sculpture, assemblage, and installation, and combines the sensibility of California pop and surrealist elements. Paintings and large graphic drawings complement the ceramics.

Born in Winnipeg, Manitoba, Canada, Schmid Esler obtained a Bachelor of Arts degree at the University of Manitoba, and did postgraduate work at the University of Munich and the Alberta College of Art. She has exhibited extensively in Canada, the United States, Europe, and Japan, including "Ceramics International," London, England (1972); "Ceramics in Contemporary Art," Sopolt, Poland (1979); and "International Ceramics," Seattle, Washington (1984). She lives in Calgary.

Early work influenced by California pop features miniature ceramic beds in lavishly embellished porcelain, often based on fairy-tales. Subsequent delicate porcelain cups are nostalgic. Robust clay plates inspired by the prairie landscape have elements added, surfaces modified, and textures impressed into the wet clay.

Around 1980 Schmid Esler began to use a cast crow in mysterious, sometimes surrealistic assemblages incorporating cupboards or box-like structures in clay, and miscellaneous materials. They evoke the ambience of rural homesteads while the silent, watchful crows convey the feeling of psychic or physical isolation of the prairies.

Schmid Esler explores the metaphoric and meditative potential of sculpture and pushes beyond the vessel-making tradition of clay. In the "Temple" series (1983), architectural enclosures are structured from clay tubes and sticks on raised platforms. Some have a strong formal presence while in others fallen and leaning forms suggest chaotic disarray. The "Cityscape" series of 1986–1987, with its contorted ruins, deals with issues of cultural and personal destruction and desolation. Recent work in the "Odyssey" series concentrates on individual geometric shapes placed on steel shelves.

Patricia Ainslie

Bibliography

Doyon, Carola, Lorne Falk, and Jean Weir. *Restless Legacies: Contemporary Craft Practice in Canada*. Calgary: Olympic Arts Festival, 1988.

Greenfield, Valerie. *Annemarie Schmid Esler: Fourteen Years*. Calgary: Alberta College of Art, 1987.

Storr-Britz, Hildegarde. *Contemporary International Ceramics*. Cologne: Dumont Verlag, 1980.

Schmidt, Katherine (1898–1978)

Born in Xenia, Ohio, the American realist painter Katherine Schmidt studied at the Art Students League, New York City, with George Bridgman, Kenneth Hayes Miller, and John Sloan.

A member of the American Society of Painters, Sculptors, and Gravers, New York City, Schmidt held solo exhibitions in many museums and galleries, including the Carnegie Institute, Pittsburgh, Pennsylvania (1940); Metropolitan Museum of Art, and the Whitney Museum of American Art—both in New York City; the Newark Museum, New Jersey; the University of Nebraska, Omaha; and others. Examples of her work are in private and public permanent collections, including the Metropolitan Museum of Art and the Whitney Museum of American Art—both in New York City; the National Museum of American Art and the Smithsonian Institution, Washington, D.C.; and others.

Bibliography

Baigell, Matthew, and Julia Williams, eds. *Artists against War and Fascism, Papers of the First American Artists' Congress*. Rutgers University Press, 1986.

Shanks, John Arthur. "Katherine Schmidt Shubert 1898–1978, A Selective View of Her Art (Whitney Museum of American Art)." *Women Artists News* 7:6 (Summer 1982): 30.

The Neglected Generation of American Realist Painters: 1930–1948. Kansas: Wichita Art Museum, 1981.

Schneemann, Carolee (1939–)

An American painter, filmmaker, and performance artist—Carolee Schneemann is best known for having used her own body as an art object within her works. She explored the notion of "flesh as material," using dreams and sexuality as the sources of her imagery. Her extensive study of the history of women and female imagery in art yielded a focus on "vulvic space," of which snakes and umbrellas (her central metaphor for sex) were an outward model.

Schneemann was the first artist to work with dancers in a medium that combined 1960s happenings, improvisation, and group dance works with artistic media and concepts. In the early 1960s her performance work began with the Judson Dance Theater—a seminal New York group that included Trisha Brown, Yvonne Rainer, and Steve Paxton. Her first major work in this period—*Eye Body* (1963)—was a solo work that explored "the image values of flesh as material." *More Than Meat Joy* (1964)—her most influential work—was a loosely scripted group piece in which the performers improvised with sausages, chickens, and raw fish. It was well-received in London, England; Paris, France; and New York City; with London being the only place in which it was performed as designed—in the nude.

Schneemann's paintings have been exhibited extensively in New York and Europe. Her works are characterized by their use of found objects and collage/assemblage techniques. Her work also includes a number of films, the most famous of which, *Fuses* (1965–1968), depicts her in sexual interactions with her former husband, James Tenney. Like much of her work, it is considered by some to be pornographic and sexually exploitive and by others to be an intellectually challenging demythification of beauty and the body—a work in which the body is one of many materials through which Schneemann explores sensuality and human experience.

After 1973 Schneemann stopped doing large performance works, concentrating instead on painting, filmmaking, and solo performance work. Key works in this period include *Kitch's Last Meal* (1973–1978), a film juxtaposing images of life in the country with the final days in the life of her cat; *Interior Scroll* (1975), a solo performance work in which Schneemann pulls a ten-foot scroll from her vagina and reads from it; and a series of paintings focusing on Lebanon and Palestine.

Schneemann has taught courses on women artists and the representation of women at the Art Institute of Chicago, Illinois; Rutgers University, New Brunswick, New Jersey; and the universities of Ohio, Colorado, and California. She has published four books, including a catalog of her work called *More Than Meat Joy* (1979).

Helen Hayes

Bibliography

Castle, Ted. "Carolee Schneemann: The Woman Who Uses Her Body as Her Art." *Artforum* 19 (November 1980): 64–70.

Dunford, Penny. *A Biographical Dictionary of Women Artists in Europe and America since 1850*. Harvester Wheatsheaf, 1990, p. 267.

Kuspit, Donald. "Carolee Schneemann." *Artforum* 23 (April 1985): 92.

Schneemann, Carolee. *More Than Meat Joy*. Documentext, 1979.

———. *Carolee Schneemann: Early and Recent Work*. Documentext, 1983.

Schneider, Rosalind (1932–)

A native New Yorker, Rosalind Schneider earned a Bachelor's degree from Empire State College, State University of New York (SUNY) (1984), after previous study at the School of Fine Arts, Syracuse University, New York (1950–1951) and the Art Students League, New York City (1956–1960), where she studied under Morris Kantor and held the Bernard Klonis merit scholarship (1957–1958).

Schneider's career, like ancient Gaul, can be divided into three parts: painting, sculpture, and filmmaking. During the 1960s she explored painting and showed "Abstract Paintings," at the Amel Gallery, New York City; Butler Institute of American Art, Youngstown, Ohio; and the Corcoran Gallery of Art, Washington, D.C.—all in 1963. By 1964–1965 she was showing "Illuminated Sculpture" at Amel Gallery in New York City; and in 1974 she was the first film artist to show "Experimental Film," at the Hirshhorn Museum and Sculpture Garden, Washington, D.C. She also exhibited with the "New American Filmmakers" at the Whitney Museum of American Art, New York City (1973); and "Expanded Cinema" at the Institute of Contemporary Art, London, England (1976). "Film as Art" and variations thereof were screened at the University of Virginia, Charlottesville; Mount Holyoke College, South Hadley, Massachusetts (1973); Virginia Commonwealth University, Richmond, and Lafayette College, Easton, Pennsylvania (1974).

In succeeding years Schneider screened a group of her films in Reykjavik, Iceland, which in time became the foundation for her dimensional pieces and media installations, such as *Earth Saga*—a film multi-projection piece, including sculpture—shown at the Thorpe Intermedia Gallery, New York City (1981); and *Egyptian Dialogue*—a work that utilized video projections on a sculpture-based installation, within a painted environment, advancing Schneider's concepts and perceptual vision—which was built for the Bronx Museum, New York (1988).

Eleven recent installations (1981 to 1990) are site-oriented projects: including *Yosemite Loop*, which projects moving film on the sculptured surface and was shown at A.I.R. Gallery, New York City (1983); and the video projected piece, *The Horse as Landscape*, built for the Hudson River Museum's show, *The Nature of the Beast* (1989), and subsequently shown at the Islip Museum, New York (1990), and at the Foster Goldstrom Gallery, New York (1990). Schneider showed "Earth Passageways," a group of paintings incorporating altered photographs as a structured base at SoHo 20 Gallery, New York City (1992).

Schneider's work is represented in private and public permanent collections, including the Donnell Film Library, New York; the United States Information Agency (USIA) Film Collection, Washington, D.C.; Nynex, New York; and others.

Bibliography

Groce, George. *The Artist as Filmmaker.* An Interview. CBS, St. Louis, Missouri (November 1974).

Gross, Arlene. "A Woman and Her Films." *The Feminist Bulletin* (May 1975): 10.

Nold, Fred. *Installation: Video and Sculpture.* State of the Arts. Channel 19, New York (1989).

Sturken, Marita. "Rosalind Schneider: Artist Filmmaker." *Art and Cinema Journal* (June 1980).

Schoenfeld, Flora (1873–1960)

The painter/printmaker Flora Schoenfeld was born in Lanark, Illinois; studied at the School of the Art Institute of Chicago, Illinois; and taught Saturday classes there until 1904. Schoenfeld also studied with Charles Hawthorn, B.J.O. Nordfeldt, and William Zorach in Provincetown, Massachusetts; and with Albert Gleizes, Fernand Léger, and Natalia Goncharova in Paris, France. Schoenfeld exhibited widely in Paris, Chicago, and Provincetown, travelling frequently between the United States and Europe. She lived in Chicago and was a non-resident member of the New York Society of Women Artists, and other professional art organizations.

Bibliography

Flint, Janet Altic. *Provincetown Printers: A Woodcut Tradition.* National Museum of American Art, 1983.

Who's Who in American Art. Vol. 1. American Federation of Arts, 1935.

Wolf, Amy J. *New York Society of Women Artists 1925.* New York, ACA Galleries, 1987.

Schreiber, Charlotte Mount (1834–1922)

Born in England, the painter Charlotte Mount Schreiber emigrated to Canada as an adult of forty-one years. She lived on the property now utilized by Erindale College, Ontario.

Schreiber's paintings were exhibited with the Royal Academy when she lived and worked in England. A true activist in Toronto's art community, Schreiber was a member of the Ontario Society of Artists; the first female member of the Royal Canadian Academy of Arts; and a board member of the Ontario School of Art and Design. Examples of her work are in private and public permanent collections.

Bibliography

Fleisher, Pat. "Love or Art." *Art Magazine* 5:15 (Fall 1973): 19.

Weaver, Emily P. "Pioneer Canadian Women: Mrs. Charlotte M. Schreiber, Painter." *Canadian Magazine* 49 (May 1917): 32–36.

Schuller, Grete (Margaret) (c. 1900–1984)

Born in Vienna, Austria, the sculptor Grete (Margaret) Schuller studied at the Vienna Lyzeum; the Vienna Kunstakademie; and the Art Students League, New York City, where she worked under William Zorach. Schuller took further work at the Sculpture Center, New York City.

Winner of many prizes and honors, Schuller was particularly known for her sculptures of animals. She exhibited widely, including the National Academy of Arts and Letters (1955), and the Sculpture Center (1958)—both in New York City; University of Notre Dame, Indiana (1959); Detroit Institute of Arts, Michigan (1959–1960); Pennsylvania Academy of Fine Arts, Philadelphia (1959–1960); "150 Years of American Art," Westbury Garden, New York (1960); and many others. Schuller was a member of major professional associations, such as the National Sculpture Society, Allied Artists of America, the Audubon Artists Society, the Sculptors League, and the National Association of Women Artists—all in New York City. Her works are represented in private and public permanent collections, including the American Museum of Natural History, New York City; the Boston Museum of Science, Massachusetts; the Norfolk Museum of Art, Virginia; and the collection of the late Thomas J. Watson, chairman of IBM.

Bibliography

Grete Schuller. A Catalog. New York. Sculpture Center, 1958.

Obituary. *The New York Times* (June 18, 1984).

Who's Who in American Art. Vol. 14. American Federation of Arts, 1980.

Schuster, Donna Norine (1883–1953)

The California painter Donna Norine Schuster studied at the School of the Art Institute of Chicago, Illinois, and with Edmund C. Tarbell and William Merritt Chase.

A plein air painter, Schuster won many honors and awards, including a gold medal and painting prize at the Minnesota State Art Exposition (1913, 1914); a silver medal at the Northwestern Exhibition, St. Paul Institute for the Arts, Minnesota (1915); a silver medal for watercolors at the Panama-Pacific International Exposition, San Francisco, California (1915); a silver medal at the Panama-California Exposition, San Diego, California (1915); first prize in watercolors and oils, Phoenix, Arizona (1918, 1919, 1920); first prize, California Watercolor Society (1926); first honorable mention, Statewide Exhibition, Santa Cruz, California (1931); and others.

Schuster was president of the California Watercolor Society; and a member of the California Art Club, the Society of Independent Artists, and West Coast Arts; and others.

Bibliography
American Art Annual. Vol. 28. American Federation of Arts, 1932.
Donna Norine Schuster (1883–1953). California: Downey Museum of Art, 1977.
Impressionism, The California View, Painting 1890–1930. The Oakland Museum, 1981.

Schwalb, Susan (1944–)

Susan Schwalb's specialty is the exacting drawing technique—silverpoint. Since 1975 she has focused on this Renaissance medium, evolving innovative methods that have transformed the instrument into a vehicle for expressive abstractions.

A graduate of the High School of Music and Art, New York City, Schwalb earned a Bachelor of Fine Arts degree from Carnegie-Mellon University, Pittsburgh, Pennsylvania (1965). She has held fellowships at the MacDowell Colony, Peterborough, New Hampshire (1974, 1975, 1989), Yaddo, Saratoga Springs, New York (1981), and the Virginia Center for the Creative Arts, Richmond (1973).

Schwalb's earliest series of silverpoint drawings was based on the orchid and limited to black and white. The drawings were given solo exhibitions at Rutgers University, New Brunswick, New Jersey (1977); and Loyola University, Chicago, Illinois (1978), and were shown in numerous group exhibitions. Schwalb then turned to abstraction. For a time she burned and tore paper, juxtaposing precise silverpoint lines upon a dramatic ground. Schwalb next worked on a series of triptychs that were granted a solo exhibition at the American Center in Belgrade and elsewhere in Yugoslavia in 1983, sponsored by the United States Information Agency (USIA).

In 1984 Schwalb began to do large-scale works incorporating color, using line to build up a vibrating, luminous surface. She continues to explore the contrast between colored and metallic paint, subtle toning, precise linear effects, and abstract forms.

Schwalb's work is represented in many public collections, including the Arkansas Arts Center Foundation in Little Rock; Boston Public Library; and Fogg Art Museum, Harvard University, Cambridge—both in Massachusetts; Chase Manhattan Bank, New York City; and the Norton Gallery of Art, West Palm Beach, Florida. In 1985 Schwalb's drawings were in the first historical survey of American silverpoint, "The Fine Line: Drawing with Silver in America," originating at the Norton Gallery of Art.

Sylvia Moore

Bibliography
Breslow, Stephen. "Four Women Artists: Thompson/Schwalb/Pachner/Hirt." *Atlanta Art Papers* (March–April 1988).
Dreishpoon, Douglas. "The Fine Line: Drawing with Silver." *Arts* (September 1985).
Earley, Sandra. "Art: The Siren Song of Silverpoint." *The Wall Street Journal* (September 11, 1985).
Faxon, Alicia, and Sylvia Moore. *Pilgrims and Pioneers: New England Women in the Arts.* Midmarch Arts, 1987.
Glueck, Grace. "Imagery From the Jewish Consciousness." *The New York Times* (June 6, 1982).
Miller, Lynn, and Sally Swenson. *Lives and Works: Talks with Women Artists.* Scarecrow Press, 1981.

Schwarcz, June (1918–)

Born in Denver, Colorado, enamelist June Schwarcz received her education at several institutions, including the University of Colorado, Boulder (1936–1938); the University of Chicago, Illinois (1938–1939); and Pratt Institute, Brooklyn, New York (1939–1941). She also studied intermittently at the La Jolla Art Center, California, and the Institute of Design, Chicago, Illinois, where she worked under the aegis of Laszlo Moholy-Nagy.

Schwarcz has held thirteen solo exhibitions of her work in the United States, Germany, and Switzerland between 1957 and 1990, including the La Jolla Art Center, California (1957); Museum of Contemporary Craft, New York City (1966); Arizona State University, Tempe (1970); Museum Bellerive, Zurich, Switzerland (1971); Schmeckmuseum Pforzheim, Germany (1972); San Francisco Folk Crafts and Folk Art Museum, California (1983); Franklin Parrasch Gallery, New York City (1990); and others.

In addition to two- and three-person exhibitions, Schwarcz's work has been invited to group exhibitions throughout the world, such as the "20th Ceramic International Exhibition," Syracuse Museum, New York (1958); "American Craftsmen Invitational, University of Washington, Seattle (1966); "Third, Fourth, Sixth, and Tenth International Biennials: Art of Enamel," Limoges, France (1975, 1978, 1982, 1990); "Craft, Art and Religion," Vatican Museum, Rome, Italy (1978); "Enamel Today," Goldsmiths Hall, London, England (1981); "International Enamel Exhibition," Coburg Fine Arts Society, Germany (1981); "Silver, New Forms and Expression," Fortunoff, New York City (1990); and many others.

Schwarcz's work is represented in private, public, and corporate permanent collections in the United States and abroad, including the American Craft Museum, New York City; Oakland Art Museum, California; Denver Art Museum, Colorado; Renwick Gallery, National Collection of Fine Arts, Smithsonian Institution, Washington, D.C.; Minneapolis Museum of Art, Minnesota; Arizona State University, Tempe; Kunstgewerbemuseums, Zurich, Switzerland; Neutrogena Corp.; and others.

Bibliography
Bennett, Jamie. "June Schwarcz: A Conversation with Jamie Bennett." *Metalsmith* (Summer 1983).
Lynn, Vanessa. "Focus: June Schwarcz—The Malleable Vessel." *Metalsmith* 10:3 (Summer 1990).
Ventura, Anita. "June Schwarcz: Electroforming with Enamel." *Crafts Horizons* (November 1965).
Who's Who in American Art. 19th ed. R.R. Bowker Co., 1991–1992.

Schwartz, Barbara (1948–)

Originally from Philadelphia, Pennsylvania, the daughter of a sculptor, Barbara Schwartz received her Bachelor of Fine Arts degree in 1970 from the Carnegie-Mellon University in Pittsburgh, Pennsylvania. After college she lived in Paris, France, and has subsequently travelled through Mexico and the Far East. Since 1970 she has lived in New York City and has shown successfully at the Willard Gallery (1976, 1978, 1979, 1981) and at Hirschl and Adler Modern Gallery (1983, 1987, 1990)—both in that city. She has participated in many museum exhibitions and has had solo shows in Chicago, Illinois; Miami, Florida; Los Angeles,

California; Seattle, Washington; and Pittsburgh, Pennsylvania.

Schwartz is best known for her jubilant and idiosyncratic fusion of painting and sculpture into polychrome reliefs—initially in plaster, then subsequently in hand-made paper, patinated bronze, and, most recently, in cast and painted aluminum. In their wit, chroma, and formal invention, these works recall Alexander Archipenko's and Pablo Picasso's early twentieth-century reliefs.

The artist considers herself as much a painter as a sculptor. At the moment her work falls into three modes: polychrome wall reliefs, monotypes, and architectural commissions, which employ many elements. Her art reveals a profound affinity with primitive art; Jeanne Siegel in 1976 noted the similarity of the "Affinbandi" series to African sculpture, and in 1983 David Schapiro wrote of the relation of the cast bronzes to Sepik river sculpture. The most recent works—both sculpture and monotypes—have a kinetic urgency inspired by Western and Eastern dance, a choreography which the artist codes into compelling abstract rhythms. In imagery the monotypes relate to the present sculpture, and in mood they recall the fragile spontaneity of the plaster and paper works. Schwartz's eccentric vocabulary of forms comes from a diversity of sources: art historical memory—Cubism, futurism, African art. Her subtle use of curvilinear motifs derives from abstract patterns in nature.

Schwartz is represented in many private collections and in such public collections as the Albright-Knox Art Gallery, Buffalo, New York; the Cincinnati Art Museum, Ohio; the Neuburger Museum, State University of New York (SUNY), Purchase; the Guggenheim Museum, New York City; the Museum of Contemporary Art, Chicago, Illinois; and the Utah Museum of Fine Arts in Salt Lake City. The artist has taught sculpture for thirteen years at the School of Visual Arts, New York City; she also taught at the Brooklyn Museum School, Parsons School of Design, Hunter College, and the Cooper Union—all in New York City; and the Rhode Island School of Design, Providence. Among her commissioned architectural sculptures is "Marina Square Dispersions" (1986), in Singapore, and "Fidelity Dispersions" (1990) in Dallas, Texas. She is married to the sculptor Art Schade and lives in Manhattan and Clermont, New York.

Margaret Sheffield

Bibliography
Gerrit, Henry. "Barbara Schwartz at Hirschl and Adler Modern." Review. *Art in America* (July 1987): 122, 123 (photograph).
Robins, Corrine. *The Pluralist Era: American Art 1968–1981.* New York: Harper & Row, 1984.
Russel, John. *The New York Times* (October 18, 1976).
Shapiro, David. *Barbara Schwartz 1983 at Hirschl and Adler Modern 1983.* A Catalog.
Siegel, Jeanne. Review. *Art in America* (May–June 1975).
———. "Barbara Schwartz' Affinbandi II." *Arts Magazine* (January 1977).
Stein, Harvey. *Artists Observed.* Harry N. Abrams, 1986.

Schwartz, Therese (1928–)

A native New Yorker, the painter/writer Therese Schwartz studied at several institutions, including the Corcoran School of Art and American University—both in Washington, D.C., and the Brooklyn Museum Art School, New York.

Schwartz has held solo exhibitions in museums and galleries in the United States and abroad, including the Andrea Ross Gallery, Santa Monica, California (1990); Humphrey Fine Art, New York City (1987, 1989, 1992); ARCO International Art Fairs, Madrid, Spain, and Galería Casa Negret, Bogotá, Colombia (1988); Galerie Fabian Walter, Basel, Switzerland (1986); Tallgrass Fine Arts, Kansas City, Missouri (1981); Landmark Gallery, New York City (1976, 1978); Rutgers University, New Brunswick, New Jersey (1973); East Hampton Gallery, New York (1964, 1966); Parma Gallery, New York City (1959–1961); Howard University, Washington, D.C. (1952); and others.

Schwartz's paintings have been invited to many group exhibitions and are represented in private, public, and corporate permanent collections, such as the Brooklyn Museum and New School for Social Research—both in New York City; William Rockhill Nelson Gallery of Art, Kansas City, Missouri; Smithsonian Institution, Washington, D.C.; Syracuse University, New York; Lehigh University, Bethlehem, Pennsylvania; Ciba-Geigy Corporation, Ardsley, New York; Kunstmuseum, Basel, and Kunsthaus, Zurich, Switzerland; and others. "Collaged Painting" (1988), a large, gridded abstract work, is rich in color, texture, and visual metaphor.

Bibliography
Heartney, Eleanor. "Therese Schwartz at Humphrey Fine Art." *Art in America* 75:10 (October 1987): 182–83.
Henry, Gerrit. "Therese Schwartz at Humphrey Fine Art." *Art in America* (July 1992).
Knaus, David. "Therese Schwartz: Taking the Square." *Helicon Nine:* 8 (1983).
Who's Who in American Art. 19th ed. R.R. Bowker Co., 1991–1992.

Schwarz, Judith (1944–)

Born in British Columbia, Canada, the sculptor Judith Schwarz earned a Bachelor's degree from the University of British Columbia (1966); studied at the Vancouver Art School, British Columbia (1973–1976); and received a Master of Fine Arts degree from York University, Toronto (1978).

Schwarz has held many solo exhibitions in galleries and museums throughout Canada and abroad, including "Installation on Site," Mercer Union (1979), and S.L. Simpson Gallery (1981, 1984, 1986, 1988)—both in Toronto; "Cella: An Installation," P.S.1, Long Island City, New York (1982); "Judith Schwarz," Art Gallery of Windsor, Ontario (1989); and others. Her work has been included in or invited to numerous group exhibitions in North America and Europe, such as "Ambiance/Stimuli," Alternative Museum, New York City (1982); "Exposition Canadiense," Instituto de Cultura de Yucatan, Mexico (1985); "York Faculty Show," Zhejiang Academy of Fine Arts, Hangzhou, China (1986); "Waterworks," London Regional Art Gallery, Ontario (1987); "A Meeting: An Exhibition by Canadian and Dutch Artists," Stichting Artichoc, Oss, the Netherlands (1989); and many others.

Winner of awards and honors, Schwarz received various grants from the Canada Council (1979, 1980, 1984, 1985, 1986, 1987); Ontario Arts Council (1979, 1986, 1987, 1988); York University (1987, 1989); and others. Using natural and industrial materials, such as oak and steel, Schwarz creates outdoor abstract sculptures that fit the Canadian environment. She also creates works for the interior. A recent commission (1990) involved a bronze sculpture fountain for Hotel Deck, Skydome, Toronto, titled "Spiral Fountain."

Representative examples of Shwartz's work can be found in private, corporate, and public permanent collections, including the Canada Council Art Bank, Ottawa, National Gallery of Canada, Ottawa, and York University, Toronto—all in Ontario; the City of Vancouver, British Columbia; University of Oregon, Eugene; and others.

Bibliography
Dault, Gary Michael. *A Meeting/Een moeting.* Exhibition Catalog. Jan Cunen Museum, Oss, Netherlands, 1989.
Dewdney, Christopher. "Enigmatic Emblematic." *Canadian Art* (Winter 1989).
Hassan, Jamelie. "Judith Schwarz at Forest City Gallery." *C Magazine* (Sprint 1985).
20x20, Italia/Canada. Exhibition Catalog. Galeria Blue and Galeria Dove Le Tigre, Milan, Italy, 1979.

Scott, Marian Mildred Dale (c. 1906–1994)

Marian Mildred Dale Scott was born in Montréal, Québec, Canada, on June 26, 1906. The dates are not certain, but it is known that she studied at l'École des Beaux-Arts in Montréal and later at the Slade School in London, England, where she painted in a manner reminiscent of Amedeo Modigliani. She had returned to Montréal by the time of the Depression, when art was considered an irrelevant commodity in some circles; she did produce a few social realist scenes of local people enduring deprivation.

Between 1935 and 1938 Scott taught at a Children's Art Center, believed to have been founded by the socialist Norman Bethune, along with fellow teacher and experimental painter Fritz Brandtner. This experience influenced her later development; inspired by Brandtner's aggressive assimilation of new stylistic tendencies, particularly in recent French painting, Scott too began to look at models ranging from late Matisse to current surrealism. Her immediate circle helped in this, for in 1939 she joined John Lyman's Contemporary Art Society, much preoccupied with relative modernist autonomy. Her first solo exhibition took place at the Grace Horne Gallery in Boston, Massachusetts (1944). Her first Canadian solo show would wait over thirty years until 1977.

Scott has only recently come back into focus as an interesting contributor to the history of Canadian art. This may have been due in part to the fact that she was a woman in a patriarchal system, of course, and in part to Canada's nationalistic preoccupations, which the Contemporary Art Society generally tried to play down. It may also have been because her work varied in style rather precipitously. Early paintings such as "People in a Park" (1935) are composed in fluid and organic colored lines, rather like a Raoul Dufy but more solid in approach. In the mid-1940s a series of "cell" paintings ("Cell and Crystal" [1945], "Cell and Fossil" [1946], and others) returned to the unusual fusion of quasi-architectural forms and automatist linear components seen in the early paintings of surrealist André Masson. Yet again, and quite abruptly, she turned to a sharply simplified realism rather like Charles Sheeler's precisionism, as in "Fire Escape" (1947). In the 1960s she was painting colored abstractions, some in triangular fan formations.

Robert J. Belton

Bibliography
Visions and Visionaires: Ten Canadian Women Artists 1914–1945. Ontario: London Regional Art Gallery, 1983.

Scott, Mary (1948–)

A Canadian painter, Mary Scott is known for her critical paintings which examine the nature and history of painting and representation. Her early works explore the medium and conceptual framework of painting through the use of non-traditional tools and supports, as, for example, the works in which she applied the paint with a syringe, the ridges of thread-like paint build upon themselves and become the support as well as the ground. Incorporated in some of these works were appropriated texts which retained a central position in her later works. Since 1982 Scott's work has been initiated by her readings: French Feminism, psychoanalytic theory and criticism, social/cultural feminist criticism, literary criticism, and literature by women. Her image sources include Leonardo da Vinci, soft-porn magazines and Robert Mapplethorpe photographs.

Scott attended the University of Calgary, earning her Bachelor of Fine Arts degree with distinction in 1978; and the Nova Scotia College of Art and Design, where she was awarded a Master of Fine Arts degree in 1980. She has taught at the Banff Centre, the Nova Scotia College of Art and Design, and the Alberta College of Art.

Scott has had solo exhibitions at Gallery 111 in Winnipeg, Manitoba (1987); and the Southern Alberta Art Gallery in Lethbridge, Alberta (1989); as well as others. She has been in numerous group exhibitions including the Canadian Biennial of Contemporary Art at the National Gallery of Canada, Ottawa (1989). Her work is included in the collections of the Glenbow Museum, the National Gallery of Canada, the University of Lethbridge Art Gallery, the Canada Council Art Bank, and the Nickle Arts Museum. The Canada Council has awarded her several "B" grants.

Scott has shown a strong commitment to the art community through her involvement not only as a teacher but also as an art administrator who cofounded and codirected art galleries, including Stride Gallery (1985–1986).

Vera Lemecha

Bibliography
Conley, Christine. *Politically Speaking.* Women in Focus, 1988.
Dahle, Sigrid. *Textu(r)al Strategies.* Gallery 111, University of Manitoba, 1987.
Fischer, Barbara. *She Writes in White Ink.* Walter Phillips Gallery, Banff Centre, 1985.
Grenville, Bruce. *Active Surplus.* Power Plant, 1987.
———. *Mary Scott.* Lethbridge, Alberta: Southern Alberta Art Gallery, 1989.
McAlear, Donna. *Striving for Ideal Resolution.* Nickle Arts Museum, 1988.
Nemiroff, Diana, and Jessica Bradley. *Songs of Experience.* National Gallery of Canada, 1986.
———. *Canadian Biennial of Contemporary Art.* National Gallery of Canada, 1989.

Scott (Palchinski), Sylvia (1946–)

Born in Regina, Saskatchewan, Canada, the multimedia, multi-talented artist Sylvia Scott (Palchinski) studied at the Instituto de Allende, San Miguel, Mexico (1967); earned a diploma from the Alberta College of Art, Calgary (1968); and won a fellowship to the Gloucestershire School of Art and Design, Gloucester, England (1973).

Scott has held many solo exhibitions in museums and galleries in Canada and abroad: from the Vestvagoy Kommune, Norway, to the rooftops in New York City; from Vancouver, British Columbia, to the Venice Biennal, Italy, and Documenta, Kassel, Germany; from La Push, Washington, to Alpach, Austria.

Scott has won awards and honors, and has taught art for more than two decades. Her work has been included in prestigious group shows in Canada, England, and the United States. Examples of her output can be found in private and public permanent collections, such as the Agnes Etherington Art Centre, Kingston, Ontario; Canada Council Art Bank, Ottawa; Ontario Institute for Studies in Art Education, Toronto; Vancouver Art Gallery, British Columbia; and others.

Bibliography
Lippard, Lucy. *Overlay.* Pantheon, 1983.
MacDonald, Colin S. *A Dictionary of Canadian Artists.* Vol. 5. Canadian Paperbacks, 1988.
Palchinski, Sylvia. "Sylvia Palchinski: A Letter." *Artscanada* 30:1 (February–March 1973): 34–38.

Scudder, Janet (1869–1940)

Janet Scudder, who became famous for her garden sculptures, was among the wave of American artists who went to Paris, France, at the turn of the century. Although her residence in Paris lasted for forty-five years, her fountain sculptures were as popular with American clients as those made by her contemporaries who remained in America and were members of the National Sculptors' Society.

Born in Terre Haute, Indiana, Scudder, at the age of eighteen, entered the Cincinnati Academy of Art, Ohio, for its three-year program and studied sculpture with Louis Rebisso. Upon graduation in 1891 she moved to Chicago, Illinois, where she was hired as one of the female assistants, known as "White Rabbits," in Lorado Taft's studio, working with Taft on his sculptural projects for the World's Columbian Exposition. With the money she earned Scudder departed for Paris in 1893, accompanied by Zulime Taft (Lorado's sister). Because Scudder had admired Frederick MacMonnies's sculpture at the Columbian Exposition she insisted upon studying with him in Paris, and within a year she became one of his assistants. When her money ran out she returned to New York City and secured enough commissions for portrait medallions to move back to Paris in 1896. She was the first American woman to have her portrait medallions accepted by the Musée du Luxembourg, Paris, France.

A trip to Italy introduced Scudder to the youthful nude figures of Roman and Renaissance art, and back in Paris she modeled "Frog Fountain," which resulted in new commissions from American art patrons for garden sculpture. She bought a villa on the edge of Paris at St. Cloud and was able to experiment in her own garden with new sculptural ideas.

At the time of World War I Scudder helped to organize the Lafayette Fund for war relief; and upon America's entry into the war she served overseas with the YMCA and the Red Cross. She even turned her house over to the YMCA (Young Men's Christian Association). In 1925 the French government recognized her humanitarian aid by making her a chevalier of the Legion of Honor.

Success came to her early in the twentieth century when the architect Stanford White bought the "Frog Fountain" and recommended that she make four more. In this popular bronze sculpture, typical of her realistic nude statues of children, an animated little boy, balancing himself on one foot by stretching out his arms, peers down at three frogs through whose open mouths open spray is emitted. The Art Institute of Chicago, Illinois, acquired "Fighting Boys Fountain," and "Young Diana" received honorable mention at the Paris Salon of 1911, France. She won a silver medal at the Panama-Pacific International Exposition, San Francisco, California, in 1915, and was named an associate member of the National Academy of Design, New York City, in 1920. She received the Olympiad medal at Amsterdam, the Netherlands (1928), and a silver medal at the Paris Exposition, France (1937). In the fall of 1939 she returned to New York City and the next summer rented a cottage in Rockport, Massachusetts, where she died.

Eleanor Tufts

Bibliography
Lewis, W. Williams, II. "Scudder, Janet." *Notable American Women.* Vol. 3. Belknap Press of Harvard University Press, 1971.
Scudder, Janet. *Modeling My Life.* Harcourt, Brace and Co., 1925.
Tufts, Eleanor. *American Women Artists, 1830–1930.* National Museum of Women in the Arts, 1987.

Seabrook, Georgette (1916–)

Born in Charleston, South Carolina, the African-American painter Georgette Seabrook, after study with Gwendolyn Bennett at the Harlem Art Center in New York City (early 1930s), took further work in the city at Cooper Union Art School. She specialized in portraiture and mural painting.

Seabrook's work has been exhibited in galleries and museums, including Atlanta University, Georgia, and the Harlem Art Workshop Exhibition, New York City (1933); the Baltimore Museum of Art, Maryland (1939); the American Negro Exposition, Chicago, Illinois (1940); the Library of Congress, Washington, D.C. (1940); and others. Her work is represented in private and public permanent collections, including the New York Public Library, New York City; and others.

Bibliography
Cederholm, Theresa. *Afro-American Artists: A Bio-Bibliographical Directory.* Boston Public Library, 1973.
Hedgepeth, Chester M., Jr. *Twentieth-Century African-American Writers and Artists.* American Library Association, 1991.
Porter, James A. *Modern Negro Art.* Arno Press, 1969.

Seaman, Laurie (1952–)

Laurie Seaman was born in Montréal, Québec, Canada, and moved in 1968 to London, Ontario, which was then enjoying the height of its reputation as a major regional center of serious art. She received no technical training until she enrolled in the Bachelor of Fine Arts program at the University of Western Ontario from 1981 to 1985, although she recalled that she drew a great deal as a child and frequently read historical novels and biographies about artists. Her work is an *alla prima* realism—often involving figures in apparently casual situations, but hinting at deeper levels of content regarding communication and the lack thereof. Her most well-known work is "She Now Owns the Bar" (1989), a feminist portrait of a local entrepreneur fashioned after Edouard Manet's "Bar at the Folies-Bergère" (1881–1882). It won first prize at a juried Western Ontario show at the London Regional Art Gallery in 1989.

Robert J. Belton

Bibliography
Lawson, Shelly. "Struggle of Growing up Revealed in Young Artist's Work." *London Free Press* (May 21, 1988): E6.

Sears, Sarah Choate (1858–1935)

Born in Cambridge, Massachusetts, the painter Sarah Choate Sears studied with several painters, including Dennis M. Bunker, Joseph De Camp, Edmund C. Tarbell, and Ross Turner. She has won many awards in the United States and abroad, including the Evans prize at the American Watercolor Society, New York City (1893); a medal at the World's Columbian Exposition, Chicago, Illinois (1893); honorable mention at the Paris Exposition, France (1900); a bronze medal at the Pan-American Exposition, Buffalo, New York (1901); a silver medal at the Charleston Exposition, South Carolina (1902); a silver medal at the St. Louis Exposition, Missouri (1904); and others.

Sears was a member of the New York Watercolor Club and the National Art Club—both in New York City; the Philadelphia Watercolor Club, Pennsylvania; the Copley Society of Boston, the Boston Watercolor Club, and is a life member of the Boston Society of Arts and Crafts—all in Massachusetts. Her work is represented in private and public permanent collections.

Bibliography
American Art Annual. Vol. 28. American Federation of Arts, 1932.
Clement, Clara Erskine. *Women in the Fine Arts.* Houghton Mifflin, 1904.
Pierce, Patricia Jobe. *Edmund C. Tarbell and the Boston School of Painting, 1889–1980.* Hingham, Massachusetts: Pierce Galleries, 1980.

Seath, Ethel (1879–1963)

Born in Montréal, Québec, Canada, the painter Ethel Seath studied with William Brymner, Maurice Cullen, and Edmond Dyonnet at the Art Association of Montréal. She did further study in Provincetown, Massachusetts with Charles Hawthorne. Earlier, to help support her family, Seath was an illustrator at *The Montréal Witness*. Her work soon earned her a post at *The Montréal Star* (1901), where it became a distinctive feature in the *Weekly Star.* Giving up her career as an illustrator, Seath taught art at a private girl's school, The Study, Montréal, from 1917 to 1962. She also taught at the Montréal Museum of Fine Arts.

Seath's paintings were invited to many group exhibitions in Canada and abroad, including the British Empire Exposition, Wembley, England (1924–1925); "Contemporary Canadian Artists," Corcoran Gallery of Art, Washington, D.C. (1930); "A Century of Canadian Art," Tate Gallery, London, England (1938); the New York World's Fair (1939), and the Riverside Museum—both in New York City (1947); and others. Her work was also included in a travelling retrospective exhibition of the Beaver Hall Group, which was organized by the National Gallery of Canada, Ottawa, in 1966.

Seath's work is represented in many private and public permanent collections, including the Art Gallery of Ontario, Toronto, Canada. "Cactus," (1938), a still-life of pears and a potted cactus on a windowsill, presents the solidity of a Cézanne.

Bibliography
Hicks, Laureen. "Ethel Seath Retires after 45 Years." *The Montréal Star* (October 26, 1962).
Little, Roger. "Ethel Seath: A Retrospective Exhibition." Montréal: Walter Klinkhoff Gallery, 1987.
Who's Who in American Art. Vols. 4–5. American Federation of Arts, 1947, 1953.

Seidler, Doris (1912–)

Born in London, England, the painter/printmaker Doris Seidler studied with Stanley William Hayter at Atelier 17, New York City.

Seidler has exhibited her prints in major exhibitions throughout the United States and abroad, including Atelier 17, the Brooklyn Museum, the Jewish Museum, and the Whitney Museum of American Art—all in New York City; the 1st and 2nd Hawaii National Print Exhibitions, Honolulu; the Vancouver Art Gallery, British Columbia; Pennsylvania Academy of Fine Arts, Philadelphia; Society of American Graphic Artists; and others.

Winner of many awards and honors, author of many articles, including one on Douglass Howell for *Impression 4* (Fall 1958), her work is represented in private and public permanent collections, such as the Brooklyn Museum, New York City; Library of Congress and Smithsonian Institution—both in Washington, D.C.; Philadelphia Museum of Art, Pennsylvania; and many others.

Bibliography
Seidler, Doris. "Douglass Howell—Papermaker." *Impression 4: A Magazine of the Graphic Arts.* Los Angeles (Fall 1958): 6–9.
Who's Who in American Art. 15th ed. R.R. Bowker Co., 1982.

Seigel, Judy (1930–)

Although she never imagined being anything other than an artist, Judy Seigel never dreamed she would be a photographer. Now she calls herself "artist-photographer," to suggest the many processes—including paint—she uses. When invited to speak to students at her alma mater—Cooper Union in New York City—she tells us about her photography class there in the 1950s: "We spent the entire semester lighting one wine bottle and one drape. Then the teacher came around with an old wooden studio camera and took one shot of each set-up. He said his assistant developed them but nothing was good enough to print."

In her last year at art school Seigel had to decide whether to be a "fine" art or graphics major. That was the heyday of abstract expressionism, and its spirit of messianism hung thickly in the classroom. "I knew I didn't have a mission to save the world through brushstrokes," she recalls, so she decided she must be a graphic artist. After graduation (with highest honors), she entered the world of New York advertising art. Always a "good drawer," she was soon staff illustrator at an agency and then a free-lancer, doing children's books and general illustration in a wide range of "artistic" styles. Within a few years she'd been in all the field's annuals: the Graphis Annual, the Society of Illustrators Annual, the Art Directors Annual.

But once the novelty of seeing her work in a newspaper going to a million people wore off, Seigel found carrying out other people's ideas, as well as the loss of quality in reproduction (especially with the printing techniques of the day) demoralizing. She realized she did, after all, have to be a "fine artist" and make art she cared deeply about. As soon as finances permitted, she quit commercial work to paint—and to raise a family.

Even as a commercial artist Seigel had been known for experimental techniques. Now, after a period of painting "fauvish" cityscapes, she turned to acrylics, inventing a variety of processes which moved in and out of abstraction. Prophetically these works looked photographic, and were sometimes mistaken for large abstract photographs. Imagery she found in the Museum of Modern Art (MoMA) exhibit, "Photography into Printmaking," New York City (1968), like solarizing and infrared, had an uncanny resemblance to paint techniques she'd been developing and she began to think of the paintings as "analogs" to such photographic effects. Computer and video graphics were other inspirations: Her "Channel Six" series, for instance, was inspired by the vertical roll of an out-of-kilter TV monitor.

Although drawn to such experimental effects, Seigel had no interest in actually doing photography until an unrelated project led her into the darkroom. Photographing the "T-shirts of 1978" as a document of street literature, finding herself with negatives of 1,600 people in "statemental" T-shirts, she learned to print them in a darkroom inherited from her son. This sub-cellar, deep below the New York City streets, evolved into an alchemist's laboratory, full of equipment Seigel devised for her own style of working. (When *Modern Photography* did a feature on it, they called it a "dungeon," but she sees it more as "grotto.")

In any event, having discovered the miracles of photography, Seigel plunged into study, beginning graduate work at Pratt Institute, Brooklyn, New York, in 1980 and experimenting with chemical processes as she had with paint. Her discoveries included unprecedented iridescent effects achieved by toning black-and-white photographs with as many as fifteen different chemical baths. She printed by "solarizing" for the "Mackie line" edge effect that had fascinated her since painting days, making one-of-a-kind toned and solarized photographs. On some she added paint in the style of Persian miniatures, seeing the Mackie line as the photographic equivalent of the exquisite outlines of those works. Her toned and/or painted works were exhibited at the Bronx Museum "Photo Start" show; Seigel's "Sa'di Photographer, F-64 Observer," the announcement image, was purchased by MoMA, New York City, among other collections, and featured in almost every photography magazine.

Seigel began to suspect that through studying photo chemistry and old photography manuals (which she collected), she had learned more about these processes than anyone else still living—or more than anyone she could find. The photo industry had lost interest in old processes as it moved into color and the amateur market—a fact that reinforced Seigel's interest in some even older processes—the hand-applied emulsions of nineteenth-century photography. Mixed on the spot and applied to artists' paper, they freed one from the vagaries of mass manufacturers. More important, they created a luscious velvety effect and tactile surface that to an artist and "drawer" felt like home. One process—gum bichromate—she describes as a "perfect hybrid" between photography and paint. Having adapted these techniques to modern requirements, Seigel plans a book based on her research. Meanwhile, she teaches the processes at Pratt Institute and the International Center for Photography—both in New York City. When she entered photography the field was still dominated by the pure, "straight" philosophy of Ansel Adams and his F-64 group. Seigel became an advocate of what she called "crooked photography," an ironic and *imperfect*

style. Speaking on "Synthetic Color in Photography" at the Pratt Institute Color Conference, she claimed photography as a "mark-making tool" with the same privileges to "fold, spindle and mutilate" as any other modern art medium. Her paper was featured in *exposure*, the journal of the Society for Photographic Education, the following year, but even as late as 1989, when she was guest speaker at a photography conference at Bryn Mawr, Pennsylvania, she found such ideas a revelation to historians and academics.

While evolving these processes, Seigel was finding her subject in New York City—which she had once painted in watercolors and oils. Now she transformed subways, streets, denizens, and landmarks, with and without added paint. The Empire State Building, New York City, became "The Single Best Building in the World." The Statue of Liberty, New York City, appeared in "Eating Man Arrives Liberty Island." Other titles such as "Why the Staten Island Ferry is Better than the Verrazzano Bridge" and "The Sun Takes Bite Out of the World Trade Center," defined their New York City subjects while extending them.

In 1985 Seigel began photographing Times Square, New York City, then being torn down for redevelopment. Her scenes ranged from drug sales and porn shops to theater-goers and kids out for a good time. Street signs and marquees often became self-captions: "Gone with the Wind," "Nerds in Paradise," "God Save New York City." Seeking a balance between process and document, she found printing the more than 500 rolls of film from the project turning into the labor of a lifetime, but began lecturing about the work and exhibiting images so far. She also started to write her Times Square experience—reflections on the phantasmagoria of the metropolis, race relations, human archetypes, street photography, tensions between "art" photography and documentary photography and between "art" and "photography." In this project her subject has fully emerged—the combination of reality and process.

Cynthia Navaretta

Bibliography

Calhoun, Catherine. "Rediscover 'Solarized' Printing." *Modern Photography* (June 1986).

Grundberg, Andy. "Photography View." *The New York Times* (October 31, 1982).

Preston, Malcolm. "The Process is the Message." *Newsday* (June 22, 1985).

Ruth, Sura. "Judy Seigel." *Professional Women Photographers Newsletter* (March–April–May 1986).

Schwarty, Therese. "Painting and Photography: A Painter's View." *Annual Journal of the Society for Contemporary Photography* (1984).

Van Camp, Louis. "Gallery Shows as Marketing Tools." *Studio Photography* (May 1986).

Sekimachi, Kay (1926–)

Although Kay Sekimachi has been a lifelong resident of the San Francisco Bay area, California, she is an internationally recognized textile artist and teacher. For nearly forty years she has been a pioneer in creating unique sculptural forms using a wide variety of textile and basketry techniques.

Sekimachi began weaving in 1949 after studying drawing and design at the California College of Arts and Crafts in Oakland from 1946 to 1949. She feels that she mastered the loom and developed personal aesthetic expression only after two summer classes with Trude Guermonprez—one of the great modern textile artists.

During the early 1960s Sekimachi invented the basic textile sculpture forms which won world acclaim and the accolade of "classics." Limiting herself to the use of a single nylon monofilament in either black or transparent white and the single technique of a loom-controlled, multi-harness weaving, she produced an impressive series of vertical diaphanous hangings. These three-dimensional weavings probably are the most delicate-appearing sculptures ever made. There were no precedents for these textile creations; there have been no significant continuations. In the mid-1970s Sekimachi completed the last of these complex and time-consuming works which defined her personal aesthetic.

In the early 1970s Sekimachi began investigating card-weaving, split-ply twining, and the creation of box forms using a multi-harness loom. Sekimachi explored every technique and every material as a possibility for new projects. Her card-weaving developed into long and narrow *kawas* as "rivers" and, later, *marugawas* or "round rivers"; her split-ply twining developed into a superb series of flat hangings, and her woven pieces were delicate linen constructions—often nesting boxes.

Three-dimensional forms—primarily in paper—became the leading focus of her creative activity in the 1980s. She created countless baskets, boxes, nests, columns, and shrines—often using Stocksdale bowls for shaping, layers of paper or linen for texture, hand and machine stitching for contrasts and simple decoration or in place of lamination. Some works were dyed, some of natural colors; all were simple and elegant objects to hold gently with hands or eyes.

In 1985 Sekimachi was honored for her distinctive and life-long achievements in the crafts by being elected a fellow of the American Craft Council. This is the highest honor awarded to craftsmen in America.

In addition to many solo shows Sekimachi has participated in several exhibitions with Bob Stocksdale and innumerable group exhibitions throughout the United States, Europe, and Japan. Her work was featured in the two most important crafts shows of the 1980s: "The Eloquent Object" organized by the Philbrook Museum of Art, Tulsa, Oklahoma (1987); and the much-acclaimed "Poetry of the Physical" at the American Craft Museum, New York City (1986). In the fall of 1993 a Stocksdale and Sekimachi retrospective opened at the Palo Alto Cultural Center in California.

Sekimachi has taught or conducted special workshops at most major educational centers for the crafts in the United States, including the Arrowmont School of Arts and Crafts in Gatlinburg, Tennessee; Mendocino Art Center in California; Haystack Mountain School of Crafts in Deer Isle, Maine; Anderson Valley Ranch in Snowmass, Colorado; California College of Arts and Crafts in Oakland; the University of Washington in Seattle; and the Rhode Island School of Design in Providence.

Among the many public collections in which Sekimachi's work is represented are the American Craft Museum in New York City; Renwick Gallery of the Smithsonian Institution, Washington, D.C.; Musée des Arts Décoratif in Paris, France; the National Museum of Modern Art in Kyoto, Japan; Royal Scottish Museum, Edinburgh; the Minneapolis Institute of Arts in Minnesota; and the Arizona State University Art Museum in Tempe.

Rudy H. Turk

Bibliography

Constantine, Mildred, and Jack Lenor Larsen. *Beyond Craft: The Art Fabric.* Van Nostrand Reinhold Co., 1973.

Gedeon, Lucinda H. *Fiber Concepts.* Arizona State University Art Museum, 1989.

Sekimachi, Kay. *Trude Remembered, The Tapestries of Trude Guermonprez.* California: Oakland Museum, 1982.

Shermeta, Margo. *Meeting Ground: Basketry Traditions and Sculptural Forms.* Arizona State University Art Museum, 1990.

Talley, Charles. "Kay Sekimachi: Successful on Her Own Terms." *Fiberarts* (September–October 1982): 72–74.

Selvin, Nancy (1943–)

Born in Los Angeles, California, the ceramist Nancy Selvin earned a Bachelor's degree from the University of California at Berkeley (1969) and, the following year, received a Master of Arts degree after study with Peter Voulkos and Ron Nagle.

Selvin has held solo exhibitions of her work in the United States, including "Nancy Selvin," Sybaris Gallery, Royal Oak, Michigan (1992); Grossmont College, El Cajon, California (1990); "New Directions," Leverett Center, Massachusetts (1988); Elements, New York City (1984); "New Work," Anhalt Gallery, Los Angeles (1981), and Quay Gallery, San Francisco (1976, 1979)—both in California; and others. Her work has been invited to group exhibitions in the United States and abroad, such as the "Cup as Metaphor," Sybaris Gallery, Detroit, Michigan (1991); "Aha Hana Lima," Academy of Art, Honolulu, Hawaii (1989); "Monumental Women," SOMAR Gallery, San Francisco, California (1987); Oxford Gallery, England (1983); "Kanazawa Invitational," Japan (1982); Earthenware USA," Hand and Spirit Gallery, Scottsdale, Arizona (1981); "5th Annual Ceramic Invitational," University Art Gallery, Ogden, Utah (1978); "Images of Cups," Anderson Gallery, Palo Alto, California (1976); "Objects," Lee Nordness Gallery, New York City (1971); and many others.

Selvin has taught and has given workshops and lectures in the United States and abroad. A director of university and college ceramic programs since 1970, she is presently on the staff of the San Francisco State University as lecturer in ceramics. Selvin's bold yet sensitive "Looking Through Glass" (1991), is a typical example of her large-scale work: a ten-by-sixty-foot mixed-media installation, occupying eight adjoining store-front windows of a Berkeley, California, downtown parking garage, it presented her work to a peripatetic and, perhaps, new public.

Selvin's work is represented in private, public, and corporate permanent collections, including the Los Angeles County Museum of Art, and Oakland Museum—both in California; Hokkoku Shimbun, Tokyo, Japan; Arizona State University, Tempe; the collection of Joan Mondale, Washington, D.C.; Kaiser Permanente Collection, Boulder, Colorado; Nora Eccles Museum, Logan, Utah; and others.

Bibliography

Attie, Shimon. "Nancy Selvin." *Artweek* (March 21, 1991): 15.

Clowes, Jody. "Nancy Selvin." *American Craft* (August–September 1992).

Levin, Elaine. *The History of American Ceramics.* Harry N. Abrams, 1988.

Moore, Sylvia, ed. *Yesterday and Tomorrow: California Women Artists.* Midmarch Press, 1989.

Speight, Charlotte. "Choices: An Interview." *Studio Potter* (December 1991).

Semmel, Joan (1932–)

A native New Yorker, Joan Semmel attended the High School of Music and Art, graduated from the Cooper Union (1952), married, had a child, and studied art with Morris Kantor at the Art Students League (1958–1959)—all in New York City. She was awarded a Bachelor of Fine Arts degree from Pratt Institute, Brooklyn, New York, in 1963, and a Master of Fine Arts degree from the same institution nine years later.

Upon the completion of her undergraduate degree, Semmel left for a seven-year stay in Spain with her family and created the time to paint bold, vivid abstract expressionist works. Once she was separated from her husband, Semmel returned to the United States with her two children and encountered the feminist movement. Her works became figurative and erotic and they centered on the female nude from a woman's point of view—all headless self images.

Semmel has had a number of solo exhibitions of her work throughout the years in galleries and institutions such as the Lerner-Heller Gallery (1975, 1977, 1978, 1979, 1981), and 112 Greene Street, curated by Lowery S. Sims (1984)—both in New York City; Manhattanville College, Purchase, New York (1985); University of Missouri at St. Louis (1986); Benton Gallery, Southhampton, New York (1987); Gruenebaum Gallery, New York City (1987); "Joan Semmel: Recent Work," East Hampton Center for Contemporary Art, New York (1989); "Through the Looking Glass," Bernice Steinbaum Gallery, New York City (1989); "At the Water's Edge," Tampa Museum of Art, Florida (1990); Nathan Contemporaries, and "Sex and Subtext," at the Ceres Gallery—both in New York City (1990). Her paintings have been invited to group exhibitions in national and international shows, including the Salon de Mayo, Barcelona (1965), and the Concurso Nacional, Madrid (1967–1969)—both in Spain; "Contemporary Nudes," One Penn Plaza (1988), and "Guerrilla Girls Exhibition," the Palladium (1986)—both in New York City; "Feministiche Kunst International," Haags Gemeentemuseum, the Hague, the Netherlands (1979); Newport Beach Museum, California (1979); "Contemporary Women: Consciousness and Content," Brooklyn Museum (1977), the Whitney Downtown Museum (1977), and the Queens Museum (1975)—all in New York City; to name but a few.

Semmel teaches painting at the Mason Gross School of Art, Rutgers University, New Brunswick, New Jersey, and was a member of Women in the Arts and the Women's Ad Hoc Committee. In "Locker Line" (1989), a not atypical oil from a recent series, Semmel explores, in a sensuous and painterly manner, isolation and narcissism in a woman's locker room.

Semmel's honors include an Office of Education EPDA fellowship (1970–1972); a Creative Artists Public Service (CAPS) program award from the New York State Council on the Arts (1975–1976); and two grants from the National Endowment for the Arts (NEA) (1980, 1985). Her work is represented in major permanent collections in the United States and abroad, including the Museum of Modern Art, Barcelona, Spain; the James A. Michener Collection at the University of Texas at Austin; the Museum of Plastic Arts, Montevideo, Uruguay; the Chrysler Museum, Norfolk, Virginia; the New Jersey State Museum of Art, Trenton; the National Museum of Women in the Arts, Washington, D.C.; and many others.

Bibliography

Alberts, Calvin. *Figure Drawing Comes to Life.* 2nd ed. Prentice-Hall, 1987.

Alloway, Lawrence. *Joan Semmel.* Sharadin Gallery, Kutztown State College, 1980.

Brown, Betty Ann, and Arlene Raven. *Exposures: Women and Their Art.* NewSage Press, 1989.

Marter, Joan. "Joan Semmel's Portrait: Personal Confrontations." *Arts Magazine* 58:9 (May 1984): 104–06.

Westfall, Stephen. "Joan Semmel at Gruenebaum." *Art in America* 76:1 (January 1988): 137–38.

Sewell, Lydia Amanda Brewster (1859–1926)

Born in North Elba, Essex County, New York, the painter Lydia Amanda Brewster Sewell studied at the Art Students League, New York City, with William Merritt Chase; she took further work at the Académie Julian, Paris, France, with Charles Émile Carolus-Duran and Tony Robert-Fleury.

Winner of honors and awards, Sewell exhibited work in museums and galleries, including the National Academy of Design, New York City (1888, 1903); the Columbian Exposition, Chicago, Illinois (1893); the Pan-American Exposition, Buffalo, New York (1901); Charleston Exposition, South Carolina (1902); St. Louis Exposition, Missouri (1904); and others. Examples of her work are in private and public permanent collections.

Bibliography

Elliott, Maud Howe, ed. *Art and Handicraft in the Women's Building of the World's Columbian Exposition, Chicago, 1893.* Rand McNally and Co., 1894.

Naylor, Maria, ed. *The National Academy of Design Exhibition Record 1861–1900.* New York: Kennedy Galleries, 1973.

Obituary. *American Art Annual.* Vol. 26. American Federation of Arts, 1929.

Shaffer, Mary (1943–)

Born in Waterboro, South Carolina, the sculptor/glass artist Mary Shaffer earned a Bachelor of Fine Arts degree from the Rhode Island School of Design, Providence (1965).

Since the mid-1970s Shaffer has held solo exhibitions of her sculptural glass in museums and galleries in the United States and abroad: from O.K. Harris in New York City (1975, 1977, 1979, 1982, 1985) to Gallery SM, Frankfurt, and Galerie von Finkelstein, Hannover—both in Germany; Museum Bellerive, Zurich, Switzerland—all in 1981; and many others. Her work has been included in many group shows throughout the world, some of them travelling widely, such as "New Glass: A Worldwide Survey," which toured the United States, Great Britain, France, and Japan (1979–1984); "Americans in Glass 1984," which toured museums and galleries in the United States, Germany, Denmark, Great Britain, the Netherlands, Switzerland, and Sweden; and others.

Shaffer's sculptures are composed of transparent and opaque materials, such as glass, metal, and tile, and are represented in private, public, and corporate permanent collections, including the Corning Museum of Glass, New York; the Lannon Foundation, West Palm Beach, Florida; Museum Bellerive, Zurich, Switzerland; Musée de Verre et Atelier du Verre de Sars Poteries, France; the National Museum of Modern Art, Tokyo, Japan; and others.

Bibliography

Ballerini, Julia. "Mary Shaffer's Glass." *Craft Horizons* 34:1 (February 1979): 24–27.

Glass in the Modern World. Kyoto, Japan: National Museum of Modern Art, 1981.

Sculptural Glass. Tucson Museum of Art, 1983.

Watson-Jones, Virginia. *Contemporary American Women Sculptors.* Oryx Press, 1986.

Sharpe, Geraldine (1929–1968)

An artist whose untimely death ended her career when she had only just begun to achieve renown, Geraldine Sharpe may be recognized as a superb photographer of her time when her work is better known. Sharpe left behind two bodies of work: the landscapes made in the late 1950s up to 1962, and the work she did in 1962 in Ghana.

Most of Sharpe's landscapes were made between 1957 and 1962 when she was an assistant to Ansel Adams after graduating from the San Francisco Art Institute, California. Often Sharpe's pictures were made in the same locations as some of Adams's classic images, and there was doubtless a mutual sharing and influence between the two, yet we see in Sharpe's landscapes a vision more tragic than in Adams. Their forms— bare trees, moving water, an abandoned house, an upturned tree whose roots become a haunting female form—are the raw material of melancholy. Her dark tonalities enforce her dark vision. Adams recognized Sharpe's talent but also found her temperament difficult. The feeling was probably mutual, and they parted on the occasion of her Guggenheim Foundaton fellowship that enabled her to travel to Ghana in 1962.

Sharpe made no landscapes in Ghana. The African pictures are of people, seen intimately and empathetically. After only a few months in Ghana, Sharpe was badly injured in an automobile accident. A leg that would not mend demanded her return to the United States. Adams had another assistant by then, but with his help she was offered a job as chief photographer at Winterthur Museum in Delaware, far from her California home. She took the job but eventually lost it, and a few months later she was dead.

Geraldine Sharpe's photographs are in the possession of friends and family in northern California. Although several were published as Polaroid advertisements in *Aperture* in the early 1960s, and one portfolio was published by that journal in 1960, few have entered public collections.

Gretchen Garner

Bibliography

Adams, Ansel. "Gerry Sharpe." Exhibition Catalog. Carmel, California: Friends of Photography (May–June 1969).

Garner, Gretchen. *Reclaiming Paradise: American Women Photograph the Land.* Duluth: Tweed Museum of Art, University of Minnesota, 1987, pp. 26–27.

Invitational Exhibition 10/American Photographers 10. Milwaukee: School of Fine Arts, University of Wisconsin (March 1965).

Sharpe, Geraldine. "Ten Photographs: Portfolio." *Aperture* 8:4 (1960): 174–84.

Shatter, Susan (1943–)

Acclaimed for her large-scale watercolors and oils of unpeopled landscapes, Susan Shatter was born in New York and was educated at various institutions, including the University of Wisconsin, Madison (1961); the Skowhegan School of Painting and Sculpture, Maine (1964); Pratt Institute, Brooklyn, New York, where she worked under the aegis of Alex Katz and received her Bachelor of Fine Arts degree in 1965; and Boston University, Massachusetts, where she was a student of the figurative painter James Weeks, and earned her Master of Fine Arts degree in 1972.

Painter, exhibiting artist, university and art school teacher, wife, and mother—Shatter appears to have realized her goals. She had her first solo exhibition at the Fischbach Gallery, New York City, at the age of twenty-nine, and has had sixteen others up to 1991 in distinguished galleries from New York City to San Francisco, California. Her work has been invited to no less than 100 group exhibitions such as "Painterly Realism," Smith College, Northampton, Massachusetts (1970); Knoedler Gallery (1971), and Fischbach Gallery (1972)—both in New York City; "Boston Watercolor Today," Museum of Fine Arts, Massachusetts (1976); "American Painterly Realism," Heath Gallery, Atlanta, Georgia (1978); "Grand Canyon Perspectives," Denver Museum of Natural History, Colorado (1985); "Realist Watercolors," the Pennsylvania State University, University Park (1990); and hosts of others.

Widely travelled (to research, photograph, and make on-site watercolor sketches all over the world—some for studio translation and permutation), Shatter appears to be in love with raw canyons, bleak coastlines, and young mountainous terrain seen from high vantage points. "Zabriskie Point" (1990), a large Death Valley, California, watercolor, reflects Shatter's recent approach to color and two-dimensionality.

Shatter enjoys an academic career as well, having taught, among other institutions, at the University of Pennsylvania, Philadelphia (1974–1975, 1979, 1982–1984); Bennington College, Vermont (1979); and the Skowhegan School of Painting and Sculpture, Maine (1977, 1979, 1988–1991), where she has been a board member (1979 to the present) and chair of the board (1988–1991). She has won grants from the Massachusetts Creative Artists Humanities (1975); the Radcliffe Institute fellowship (1975–1976); Ingram-Merrill Foundation (1976–1977); the National Endowment for the Arts (NEA) (1980, 1987); and the New York State Foundation for the Arts (1985). Her work is included in major public, private, and corporate permanent collections, including the Philadelphia Museum of Art, Pennsylvania; the Boston Museum of Fine Arts, Massachusetts; the Art Institute of Chicago, Illinois; the Utah Museum of Fine Art, Salt Lake City; and many others.

Bibliography

Gerrit, Henry. "Susan Shatter at Fischbach." *Art in America* 75:6 (June 1987): 156–57.

Hurwitz, Lori. "Susan Shatter." *American Artist* (December 1990): 28–32.

Kuspit, Donald B. "Susan Shatter at Fischbach." *Art in America* 70:9 (October 1982): 135.

Shaw-Clemons, Gail (1953–)

Born in Washington, D.C., the African-American mixed-media artist and printmaker Gail Shaw-Clemons earned both her Bachelor's and Master of Fine Arts degrees from the University of Maryland, College Park.

Shaw-Clemons has held solo exhibitions in galleries, including "Art Reach Milwaukee," a travelling show, and Terra Rouge Gallery—

Shaw-Clemons, Gail **505**

both in Milwaukee, Wisconsin (1988); and others. Her work has been included in many group shows in the United States, such as Diverse Works Gallery, Houston, Texas (1988); Museum of Science and Industry, Chicago, Illinois (1987); Fonda del Sol Visual Art and Media Center, Washington, D.C. (1985); the Tanner Gallery, Los Angeles, California (1984); Evans-Tibbs Collection, Washington, D.C. (1983); and others.

Shaw-Clemons's work is represented in private and public permanent collections, including Atlanta Life Insurance, Georgia; Maret School, Washington, D.C.; Milwaukee Arts Commission, Wisconsin; and others. Her mixed-media fantasies are environmentalist-oriented warnings of things-to-come expressed in non-threatening form and content, as in "Never Take for Granted the Air You Breathe" (1990), wherein an other-wordly female figure is posed in front of a window through which one can solely view fish and underwater plant life.

Bibliography

Hall, Robert L. *Gathered Visions: Selected Works by African American Women Artists.* Anacostia Museum. Smithsonian Institution Press, 1992.

Krantz, Les. "Gail Shaw-Clemons." *Chicago Art Review* (1989).

Thorson, Alice. "Trauma of Love, Fragility of Psyche." *Washington Times* (November 24, 1988).

Shea, Judith (1948–)

Born in Philadelphia, Pennsylvania, the sculptor Judith Shea earned an Associate in Arts degree (1969) and, six years later, received a Bachelor of Fine Arts degree—both from Parsons School of Design, New York City.

Between 1976 and 1993 Shea held more than twenty-four solo exhibitions in the United States, including "Judith Shea," Max Protetch Gallery, New York City (1991, 1993); "Judith Shea," Laumeier Sculpture Park, St. Louis, Missouri, and "Judith Shea/Monuments and Statues," Whitney Museum of American Art, New York City (1992); "Forefront: Judith Shea," National Museum of Women in the Arts," Washington, D.C. (1990); Willard Gallery, New York City (1980, 1981, 1983, 1984, 1986); the Women's Center Gallery, Yale University, New Haven, Connecticut (1978); and others. Her work has been invited to myriad group exhibitions throughout the United States and abroad, such as "Figurative Contemporary Sculpture," Albuquerque Museum, New Mexico (1993); "Encontros: Luso Americanos de Arte Contemporanea," Gulbenkian Foundation, Lisbon, Portugal (1989); "Figurative Impulses," Santa Barbara Museum of Art, California (1988); "Drawings," Barbara Krakow Gallery, Boston, Massachusetts (1986); "Stockholm International Art Exposition," Willard Gallery, New York City, a travelling exhibition to Sweden (1982); "The Soft Land/II Soffice Paese," Palazzo Farnese, Cortona, Italy (1981); "The Handwrought Object, 1776–1976," Cornell University, Ithaca, New York (1976); and many others.

Shea was awarded two National Endowment for the Arts (NEA) fellowships for her work (1984, 1986); she was commissioned by dance and theater companies to create clothing designs (she is a former fashion student), and was also the recipient of a Guggenheim Foundation sculptor-in-residence fellowship at Chesterwood, Massachusetts (1989). Her figurative sculptures are, presently, haunting metaphors of statuary and fabric.

Shea's work is represented in private and public permanent collections in the United States, including the Neuberger Museum, State University of New York (SUNY) at Purchase; Chase Manhattan Bank, and Brooklyn Museum—both in New York City; Dallas Museum of Fine Arts, Texas; Walker Art Center, Minneapolis, Minnesota; Hirshhorn Museum and Sculpture Garden, Washington, D.C.; and many others.

Bibliography

Marincola, Paula. "Judith Shea's Contemporary Kore." *Artforum* (Summer 1990): 134–39.

Schjeldahl, Peter. "Metaphysics of Skin." *The Village Voice* (April 16, 1991): 99.

Taplin, Robert. "Judith Shea at Max Protetch Gallery." *Art in America* (October 1991): 151–52.

Who's Who in American Art. 19th ed. R.R. Bowker Co., 1991–1992.

Shechter, Laura (1944–)

Born in Brooklyn, New York, the virtuoso realist painter Laura Shechter earned a Bachelor's degree in fine arts, with honors, from Brooklyn College, New York (1965), and was the recipient of a Kratter scholarship that year. Her work was further honored by a Creative Artists Public Service (CAPS) grant from the New York State Council on the Arts (1981–1982).

Shechter has held twenty-two solo exhibitions of her work in galleries and museums in the United States, including the Forum Gallery, New York City (1976, 1980, 1983); Capricorn Gallery, Bethesda, Maryland (1977, 1990); Pucker/Safrai Gallery, Boston, Massachusetts (1981); Van Straaten Gallery, Chicago, Illinois (1983); University of Richmond, Virginia (1991); Katharina Rich Perlow Gallery, New York City (1992); and others. Her drawings, paintings, and prints have been invited to group exhibitions in the United States and abroad, such as "Selections in Contemporary Realism," Akron Art Institute, Ohio (1974); "16 Realistas," Centro Colombo Americano, Bogotá, Colombia (1979); "American Drawing in Black and White," Brooklyn Museum, New York (1980–1981); "The Fine Line: Drawing with Silver in America," a travelling show, Norton Gallery, West Palm Beach, Florida (1985–1986); "Echo Press: A Decade of Printmaking," Indiana University, Bloomington (1990); "New Viewpoints: Contemporary Women Realists," Seville World Exposition, Spain (1992); and others.

Curator, panelist, artist-in-residence, and lecturer at colleges and universities—Shechter has been a faculty member at Parsons School of Design (1984) and at the National Academy of Design (1985–1988)—both in New York City. Her work is represented in private, public, and corporate permanent collections, including the Albright-Knox Art Gallery, Buffalo, New York; Brooklyn Museum, New York Public Library, and Chemical Bank—all in New York City; Arizona State University, Tempe; Art Institute of Chicago, Illinois; Israel Museum, Jerusalem, and Tel Aviv Museum—both in Israel; 3M Corporation; and many others.

Bibliography

Merritt, Robert. "Painter's Progress Easily Seen in Exhibit." *Richmond Times-Dispatch* (September 12, 1991): A–10.

Raynor, Vivian. "Precision for Precision's Sake." *The New York Times* (May 21, 1989).

Widing, Eric. "Laura Shecter." *American Artist* (April 1987): 36–41.

Who's Who in American Art. 19th ed. R.R. Bowker Co., 1991–1992.

Sheerer, Mary Gwen (1865–1954)

Born in Covington, Kentucky, the ceramist Mary Gwen Sheerer was raised in New Orleans, Louisiana. A scholarship to the Cincinnati School of Design, Ohio, allowed her to study with Frank Duveneck, among others.

Sheerer was employed by Sophie Newcomb Memorial College, New Orleans, Louisiana, to teach ceramics and drawing (1894), eventually becoming a professor of ceramics and drawing—a post she held until her retirement in 1931. Sheerer was given the responsibility for selecting qualitative student ceramic work for sale to the public. The ceramic objects produced in Newcomb's pottery were not unlike those produced in professional studios at that time; for example, the Newcomb pottery won the grand prize at the Panama-Pacific International Exposition, San Francisco, in 1915.

Sheerer won many awards and honors during her lifetime. In 1925 she was a delegate on the Hoover Commission to the Exposition Internationale des Arts Décoratifs et Industriels Modernes, Paris, France; and from 1924 to 1927 she was chair of the art division of the American Ceramic Society, which elected her a fellow in 1931.

Bibliography
Poesch, Jessie. *Newcomb Pottery: An Enterprise for Southern Women.* Schiffer Publishing, 1984.
Sheerer, Mary G., and Paul E. Cox. "Newcomb Pottery." *American Ceramic Society Journal* 1 (August 1918).
Smith, Kenneth E. "Ceramics at Newcomb College." *Design* 46 (December 1944).

Sheets, Nan Jane (1885–)

Born in Albany, Illinois, the painter/printmaker Nan Jane Sheets studied with many teachers, including Hugh Breckenridge, Kathryn E. Cherry, John Carlson, Nellie Knopf, Robert Reid, Birger Sandzen, A. Thayer, and E.L. Warner.

Sheets received honors and awards, including the Birger Sandzen prize at an exhibition of the Broadmoore Art Academy (1924); a purchase prize at the Kansas City Art Institute, Missouri (1924); a prize in landscape at the Southern States Art League (1929); and others. She was a member of the Oklahoma Art Association, Tulsa; the Art League of Oklahoma City; the MacDowell Colony, Peterborough, New Hampshire; the North Shore Art Association; National Association of Women Painters and Sculptors, New York City; the Southern States Art League; and the American Federation of Arts, Washington, D.C. Her work is represented in private and public permanent collections, including the Kansas City Art Institute, Missouri.

Bibliography
American Art Annual. Vol. 28. American Federation of Arts, 1932.
Dawdy, Doris Ostrander. *Artists of the American West.* Vol. 1. Swallow Press, 1974.
Who's Who in American Art. Vol. 10. American Federation of Arts, 1970.

Shelton, Margaret (1915–1984)

Margaret Shelton worked in pencil, watercolor, and oil, but she is particularly notable for her block prints, producing 174 between 1936 and 1984. Her art celebrates the diversity and beauty of the Alberta landscape, the endless prairie, and the majestic Rocky Mountains.

Shelton was born in Bruce near Edmonton, Alberta, Canada, and was raised in Rosedale in southeastern Alberta. She studied at the Provincial Institute of Technology and Art in Calgary from 1933 and at the Banff School of Fine Arts, where she was awarded a fine art diploma in 1938. Her two most influential teachers—Alfred Leighton and Henry Glyde—had studied in London, England, at the Royal College of Art, and introduced their students to the formal principles of English art.

Early drawings showed Shelton's fine draftsmanship and precise, realistic rendering. She worked extensively out of doors, producing a large body of sensitive drawings and watercolors of the landscape and the industrial area near Rosedale.

In 1936, under Glyde's influence, Shelton began to make linocuts, initially printed only in black. As her work matured she developed a lively interaction of forms and a great variety of detailed surface patterning. After instruction with the newly arrived Walter Phillips—internationally recognized for his color woodcuts in the Japanese manner—Shelton began to make color linocuts.

Shelton exhibited locally with the Alberta Society of Artists and the Calgary Sketch Club. In the 1940s she exhibited with the national print societies in Toronto, the Canadian Society of Graphic Art, and the Society of Canadian Painter-Etchers and Engravers.

Shelton made an important contribution to the revival of the block print in Canada due to the veracity and consistent quality of her work. An exhibition of her prints was held at the Burnaby Art Gallery, British Columbia, in 1981, and at the Glenbow Museum, Calgary, in 1985. She died in Calgary.

Patricia Ainslie

Bibliography
Ainslie, Patricia. *Images of the Land: Canadian Block Prints 1919–1945.* Calgary: Glenbow Museum, 1984.
———. *Margaret Shelton: Block Prints 1936–1984.* Calgary: Glenbow Museum, 1985.
Tousley, Nancy. "Isolation Plagued Prolific Alberta Artist." *Calgary Herald* (February 19, 1986).

Shepherd, Kara (1911–)

Born on her parent's farm in Culpepper, Virginia, the surrealist painter Kara Shepherd expressed an interest in art early on and received encouragement from her father and mother. Shepherd studied at the Philadelphia School of Art, Pennsylvania (1926); the Art Students League (1950), and Fordham University (1960)—both in New York City; l'École des Beaux-Arts, Fontainebleu, France (1962–1964); and Arizona State University, Tempe (1979–1980). Her mystical landscapes are represented in private and public permanent collections.

Bibliography
Artists of the Black Community/USA. A Catalog. Phoenix: The Arizona Bank Galleria, 1988.

Sherman, Cindy (1954–)

Born in Glen Ridge, New York, the photographer Cindy Sherman received her Bachelor of Arts degree from the State University of New York (SUNY) at Buffalo in 1976. Although she began her academic training in painting she transferred into photography during her junior year of college. Sherman's earliest images include a series of black-and-white self-portraits documenting a progression from wearing no makeup to a final image of total transformation via makeup. In 1975 her series "Cutouts" was composed of storyboard-like collaged self-portraits. Between 1977 and 1980 Sherman produced "Untitled Film Stills," a series of very grainy, eight-by-ten-inch black-and-white photographs, which have the appearance of "film noir" movie stills. Sherman—artist, model, actress, and director—then turned to color photography. While her photographs retain their self-portraiture format, they are never autobiographical; instead, they cull our vast mass-media memory banks of cultural clichés from sources such as fashion advertising, women's magazines, television soap operas and B movies. The objectified women she personifies are victims, icons of modern isolation which address issues of female identity and oppression, and negate the individuality of personality.

The scale of her photographs have grown to the larger-than-life size, over four-by-eight-feet. They remain untitled; Sherman says she leaves them untitled to maintain ambiguity so that no single reading is forced on them.

Sherman received a Guggenheim Foundation fellowship at age twenty-nine—one of the youngest to receive the fellowship. Her photographs are in major collections worldwide and have been widely exhibited nationally and internationally.

Laine Sutherland

Bibliography

Ball, Edward. "The Beautiful Language of My Century: From the Situationists to the Simulationists." *Arts Magazine* 63 (January 1989): 65–72.

Gambrell, Jamey. "Cindy Sherman, Metro Pictures." *Art Forum* 20 (January 1982): 85–86.

———. "Marginal Acts." *Art in America* 71 (March 1984): 115–18.

Johnson, Ken. "Cindy Sherman and the Anti-Self: An Interpretation of Her Imagery." *Arts Magazine* 62 (November 1987): 47–53.

Marzorati, Gerald. "Imitation of Life." *Artnews* 82 (September 1983): 79–87.

Sherman, Cindy. *Cindy Sherman.* Pantheon Books, 1984.

Sherman, Sarai (1922–)

Born in Philadelphia, Pennsylvania, the painter/sculptor/printmaker Sarai Sherman earned Bachelor of Fine Arts and Bachelor of Science degrees in education from the Tyler School of Fine Arts, Temple University, in her native city; she received a Master of Arts degree in art history and painting from the University of Iowa, Iowa City.

Sherman has held solo exhibitions in galleries in the United States and abroad, including ACA Gallery, New York City (1951, 1955, 1958, 1960); Galleria La Nuova Pesa, Rome (1961), and Galleria Viotti, Turin (1963)—both in Italy; Forum Gallery, New York City (1963, 1967, 1970, 1974, 1986); Fairweather-Hardin Gallery, Chicago, Illinois (1964); Museum of Contemporary Art, Skopje, Yugoslavia (1965); Galerie Weltz, Salzburg, Austria, and Salon Tribune-Mladih, Novi Sad, Yugoslavia (1966); Galleria dell'Orso, Milan, (1973), and Studio 5, Bologna (1976)—both in Italy; Madison Gallery, Toronto, Canada (1979); Galleria Giulia, Rome, Italy (1982); and many others. Her work has been invited to myriad group exhibitions throughout the world—from Iowa City, Iowa, to Palermo, Sicily; New York City; Sucasne-Umenie,

Bratislava, Czechoslovakia; Urbana, Illinois; Haifa, Israel; Youngstown, Ohio; Acireale, Italy; and many others.

Sherman has won awards and honors for her work in various media, including a Pepsi Cola award (1945); a Fulbright Foundation fellowship to Italy (1952–1954); a painting award from the American Academy and Institute of Arts and Letters, New York City (1964) and their Childe Hassam Prize (1970); many medals, citations, and prizes in exhibitions throughout Italy; the Proctor prize, National Academy of Design, New York City (1976); and others. Her drawings, prints, paintings, and ceramic sculpture show Sherman's past and present concern with humankind's inhumanity to one another, where form and content are one. Her sculptural work of the 1980s, in porcelain, presents serene animal and human forms for one to contemplate, metaphors for peace and war, life and death. Between 1987 and 1992 Sherman has been at work on a private commission in Cortona, Italy, creating paintings, sculpture and architectural trompe l'oeil for a centuries-old family chapel.

Sherman's work is represented in private and public permanent collections, including the Museum of Modern Art (MoMA) and the Whitney Museum of American Art—both in New York City; Syracuse University, New York; Hirshhorn Museum and Sculpture Garden, Washington, D.C.; National Gallery of Modern Art, Rome, and the Uffizi Gallery, Florence—both in Italy; Jerusalem Museum, Israel; National Gallery of Modern Art, Bratislava, Czechoslovakia; International Museum of Modern Art, Skopje, Yugoslavia; Gramsci Museum, Ghilarza, Sardinia; and many others.

Bibliography

Goodrich, Lloyd, and Edward Bryant. *Forty Artists under Forty from the Collections of the Whitney Museum of American Art.* Praeger, 1962.

Sarai Sherman, A Retrospective: 1945–1982. Essays by Carlo Ludovico Ragghianti and Mario Penelope. Nuovedizioni Enrico Vallechi, 1983.

Sarai Sherman. A Catalog. New York City: Forum Gallery, 1986.

Sarai Sherman: Ceramic Sculpture. Toronto: Madison Gallery, 1986.

Sherwood, Rosina Emmet (1854–1948)

A painter in oil, watercolor, and pastel, Rosina Emmet Sherwood was a member of the Emmet family of artists. Her earliest instruction in art probably came from her mother, Julia Pierson Emmet, who had studied with the New York painter Daniel Huntington. After a trip to Europe in 1876–1877, Sherwood became one of William Merritt Chase's first pupils at his Tenth Street Studio in New York City, and by 1881 she was ready for her own studio in this building. In 1884, accompanied by her younger sister Lydia, she travelled to Paris, France, and studied with Tony Robert-Fleury at the Académie Julian. After her return to New York City she married Arthur Sherwood in 1887 and had five children. Despite her busy schedule as wife and mother, Sherwood continued working, often using her family as subjects. For instance, in "Family at Christmas" (c. 1902, Collection of Rosamond Sherwood), all the children are depicted, including Robert Emmet Sherwood who grew up to be the famous Pulitzer-prize-winning playwright.

Some of Rosina Sherwood's earliest works were illustrations—for *Harper's Magazine*, among other publications. Another early success occurred in 1880 when, out of 600 designs submitted for Louis Prang & Company's open competition for Christmas cards for the American Art-Gallery, New York, she won the first prize of $1,000. She was commissioned to paint a mural for the Woman's Building at the World's Columbian Exposition in 1893; the six-figure allegorical composition was entitled "The Republic's Welcome to Her Daughters." Landscapes in watercolor survive from the around-the-world trip she took in 1922. Although much of her work today remains in family hands, her portrait of "Archer Huntington" (1892) hangs at the Hispanic Society of America in New York.

Eleanor Tufts

Bibliography
Hoppin, Martha J. *The Emmets: A Family of Women Painters*. Pittsfield, Massachusetts: Berkshire Museum, 1982.
Tufts, Eleanor. *American Women Artists, 1830–1930*. National Museum of Women in the Arts, 1987.

Shonnard, Eugenie Frederica (1886–1978)

Born in Yonkers, New York, the painter/sculptor Eugenie Frederica Shonnard studied sculpture in Paris, France, with Antoine Bourdelle and Auguste Rodin.

Shonnard exhibited in many solo exhibitions, including "Eugenie Shonnard," the Governor's Gallery (1976), and "An Exhibition of the Sculpture of Eugenie Shonnard," Museum of New Mexico Art Gallery, Santa Fe (1954)—both in Santa Fe, New Mexico; and group shows, such as "Exhibition of American Sculpture," the National Sculpture Society, New York City (1923); and others. She was a member of the Art Alliance; the National Association of Women Painters and Sculptors and an associate member of the National Sculpture Society—both in New York City. Representative examples of her work are in private and public permanent collections, including the Metropolitan Museum of Art, New York City; Brookgreen Gardens, South Carolina; and others.

Bibliography
American Art Annual. Vol. 28. American Federation of Arts, 1932.
Bell, Enid. "The Sculpture of Eugenie Shonnard." *American Artist* 30 (June 1966): 62–67, 87–89.
Rubenstein, Charlotte Streifer. *American Women Artists*. G.K. Hall, 1982.

Shore, Henrietta Mary (1880–1963)

Born in Toronto, Ontario, Canada, the landscape and still-life painter/printmaker Henrietta Mary Shore studied with Laura Muntz in her native city. Shore also studied at the Art Students League, New York City, with William Merritt Chase and, later, with Robert Henri; she took further work at Heatherly's Art School, London, England; and in Holland.

Shore emigrated to California (1913) and, two years later, won a medal at the Pan-Pacific International Exposition, San Francisco, California. In 1920 she began a three-year stay in New York City, turning out semi-abstract paintings, perceived by the local critics as works having the symbolism and rare quality of those painted by Georgia O'Keeffe during the same period. Returning to California, she became a friend of Edward Weston; she painted and taught painting, lived in Carmel, painted six murals in Monterey, California, during the mid-1930s—as did so many other professional artists—and had a difficult time in her later years. Shore exhibited widely in the United States, Canada, and Europe and her works are in private and public permanent collections.

Bibliography
A Woman's Vision: California Painting into the 20th Century. San Francisco: Maxwell Galleries, 1983.
Armitage, Merle. *Henrietta Shore*. E. Weyhe, 1933.
Henrietta Shore, A Retrospective Exhibition: 1900–1963. Intro. by Jo Farb Hernandez. Monterey Peninsula Museum of Art, 1986.
Maddows, Ben. *Edward Weston: 50 Years*. Aperture, 1973.

Shuttleworth, Claire (1868–1930)

Born in Buffalo, New York, the painter Claire Shuttleworth became a resident of Chippewa, Ontario, Canada. She studied in Buffalo, New York; at the Art Students League, New York City, with George Bridgman and others; and took further study in Paris, France, with Raphael Collin and Luc Olivier Merson.

Winner of honors and awards, Shuttleworth exhibited in museums and galleries in the United States and abroad, including the Buffalo Society of Arts, New York (1910, 1929); many of the Salons des Beaux-Arts, Paris, France; and others. She was particularly intrigued with the study of moving water and, specifically, with the Niagara river.

Shuttleworth was a member of the American Federation of Arts and National Association of Women Painters and Sculptors—both in New York City; the Buffalo Society of Arts, New York; the Rockport Art Association; and others. Her work is represented in private and public permanent collections, such as the Amot Art Galleries, Elmira, and the Buffalo Historical Society—both in New York; and others.

Bibliography
Catalogue of a Collection of Paintings, Sketchings, and Studies of the Niagara River by Claire Shuttleworth. Buffalo, New York: Albright Art Gallery, 1920.
Green, Laura Moss. "Minglestreams." *Saturday Night* 43:2 (November 26, 1927): 51.
Obituary. *American Art Annual*. Vol. 28. American Federation of Arts, 1932.
Shuttleworth, Claire. "Sketching along the Niagara." *Buffalo Arts Journal* (May 1925): 15–17.

Sidauy, Mily (1943–)

An expressionist Mexican sculptor, Mily Sidauy studied her craft at the Taller de Matusha Corkidi and has been exhibiting work since 1977 in many group and solo shows. Winner of awards and honors, Sidauy's work is represented in private and public permanent collections.

Bibliography
Mujeres Mexicanas: Quien es Quien. Mexico, D.F.: Editorial Antena, S.A., 1980–1981.

Siegel, Irene (1932–)

A painter and printmaker, Irene Siegel has made her career in the Chicago, Illinois, area where she was born and raised. She attended Northwestern University, Evanston, Illinois, where she studied painting with George Cohen, and graduated with honors in 1953. After a year of graduate work at the University of Chicago, she attended the Illinois Institute of Technology (IIT)—both in Chicago, Illinois, as the recipient of a Moholy-Nagy scholarship. She received a Master of Science degree from IIT in 1955.

Siegel's detailed, surreal images led her to be grouped with the Chicago imagists in the 1960s. Her work was regularly included in the "Chicago Artists and Vicinity" exhibitions at the Art Institute of Chicago, Illinois. In 1967 she produced twenty-one meticulously drawn, brightly-colored lithographs during a fellowship at the Tamarind.

Siegel taught at the University of Illinois at Chicago from 1971 until 1982. Her output in the 1970s varied considerably in approach, combining realism, surrealism, and abstraction. A 1978 solo exhibition of conceptual pieces at the Young Hoffman Gallery in Chicago combined written remarks with pastel drawings of simple motifs. She enjoyed the pluralism in the art world of the period, stating: "Nonalignment is freedom."

In 1985 a local controversy developed over a mural Siegel was commissioned to paint for the meeting room of the New Sulzer Regional Library in Chicago as part of a "percent for art" program. Interpreting her neo-expressionist treatment of Virgil's "Aenid" as condoning graffiti and violence, the community called for its destruction. After several months of public debate the library was dedicated with the mural in place.

Paula Wisotzki

Bibliography
Schulze, Franz. "Right Thing, Right Place, Right Time." *Art News* 77 (November 1978): 151.

Sierra, Susana (1942–)

Born in Mexico, the painter Susana Sierra initially studied the history of art in France and Italy before returning to Mexico to pursue studies in philosophy, pre-Columbian art, and the visual arts at the Escuela Nacional de Artes Plásticas.

Sierra has held solo exhibitions in museums and galleries in Mexico and abroad, and her work has been included in many group shows, such as the "X Bienal de Jovenes," Paris, France; the Smithsonian Institution, Washington, D.C.; and others. One of her solo exhibitions took place at the Museum of Modern Art in her native city. She has earned honors and awards, including a purchase prize in the Salon de Pintura at the Palacio de Bellas Artes, Mexico City. Her work is represented in private and public permanent collections.

Bibliography
Mujeres Mexicanas: Quien es Quien. Mexico, D.F.: Editorial Antena, 1980–1981.

Sigler, Hollis (1948–)

Born in Gary, Indiana, the painter Hollis Sigler earned a Bachelor of Fine Arts degree at the Moore College of Art, Philadelphia, Pennsylvania (1970) and, three years later, received a Master of Fine Arts degree from the School of the Art Institute of Chicago, Illinois.

Sigler has held many solo exhibitions in museums and galleries and has had her work included in prestigious group shows, including the "1981 Biennial Exhibition," Whitney Museum of American Art, New York City (1981); "The Anxious Edge," Walker Art Museum, Minneapolis, Minnesota (1982); "Back to the USA," a travelling show, Bonn and Stuttgart—both in Germany (1983); "Selections–Art since 1945," Museum of Modern Art (MoMA), New York City (1985); "Thirty-Ninth Corcoran Biennial of Contemporary American Painting," Washington, D.C. (1985); Akron Art Museum, Ohio (1986); National Museum of Women in the Arts, Washington, D.C., and Printworks Gallery, Chi-

cago, Illinois (1991); "Interiors," Steven Scott Gallery, Baltimore, Maryland (1992); "Face to Face: Self Portraits by Chicago Artists," David Adler Cultural Center, Libertyville, Illinois (1992); and others.

Sigler has taught drawing and painting at Columbia College, Chicago, Illinois, since 1978; she has earned many honors and awards, such as the Emilie L. Wild prize for painting from the Art Institute of Chicago, Illinois (1980); the chairman's grant and the individual artist grant from the Illinois Council on the Arts (1986); a fellowship from the National Endowment for the Arts (NEA) (1987); and many others.

Examples of her paintings are in private and public permanent collections, including the Indianapolis Museum of Art, Indiana; Madison Art Center, Wisconsin; Museum of Contemporary Art, Chicago; the Seattle Art Museum, Washington; and others.

Bibliography
Brown, Raven. *Women and Their Art*. NewSage Press, 1989.
Intimate/INTIMATE. Curated by Charles S. Mayer and Bert Brouwer. Terre Haute: Indiana State University, 1986.
Moser, Charlotte. "Hollis Sigler." *Art News* 85:4 (April 1986): 143.

Simmons, Laurie (1949–)

A photographer, well known for her tableaux which include small human-like figures which are often playful and ironic, Laurie Simmons was born in New York City. She was educated at Tyler School of Fine Arts at Temple University in Philadelphia, Pennsylvania, and graduated with a Bachelor of Fine Arts degree in 1971.

Simmons began to gain attention with the Marlborough Gallery, New York City, exhibit "Color Photography: Five New Views," in 1981. In the early 1980s she showed in several important American and European venues, including the important "Image Scavengers Show" at the Institute of Contemporary Art in Philadelphia, Pennsylvania, in 1982. Her work was included in the 1985 Whitney Museum of American Art Biennial, New York City, and the Sydney Biennale, Australia, in 1986. She is represented by Metro Pictures in New York City.

Generally, Simmons works with gender stereotypes found in unusual places: from human bodies in swimming pools, to ventriloquist's dummies and children's dolls. The works are also about narrative and the human process of giving inanimate objects both feelings and meanings. Her work also points to the illusionary quality of the photograph in capturing this narrative in a two-dimensional medium. Simmons's recent work is exemplified in her black-and-white photograph "Walking House" (1989), which is comparable to earlier surrealist objects. A model suburban house sits atop a "great pair of legs." Through combining these two images, an irony about the suburban housewife and the idealized media image of the model female is critically engaged and is both a humorous parody and beguiling metaphor about the construction of gender in our society.

Paul Ivey

Bibliography
Kalina, Richard. "Review of Laurie Simmons at Metro Pictures." *Art in America* 78:2 (February 1990): 174.
Klein, Michael R. "Laurie Simmons." *Arts* 55:9 (May 1981): 4.
Simmons, Laurie. "Ventriloquism." *ArtForum* 26, 4 (December 1987): 93–99.
Woodward, Richard. "Review of Laurie Simmons at Metro Pictures." *ArtNews* 87:5 (May 1988): 161.

Simon, Jewel Woodard (1911–)

Born in Houston, Texas, the multi-talented African-American painter, poet, sculptor, printmaker, and composer Jewel Woodard Simon earned a Bachelor of Arts degree with highest honors from Atlanta University, Georgia (1931). She taught and was department head of mathematics at Jack Yates High School, Houston, Texas (1931–1939). In 1934 Simon began private art instruction on Saturday mornings with Bertha L. Hellman. She married Edward Lloyd Simon (1939) and, after two years of travel, they moved to Atlanta, Georgia. She also studied painting with Hale Woodruff (1946) and sculpture with Alice Dunbar (1947) and, despite existing racism, was the first African-American to enter and graduate from the Atlanta College of Art, Georgia (1962–1967). Further, Simon was invited to create lithographs at Tamarind Institute, University of New Mexico, Albuquerque (1981).

Simon has held many solo exhibitions throughout the United States and abroad, and has had her work invited to group exhibitions, including the New York World's Fair (1939), Art USA (1958), and the International Society of Artists—all in New York City; the High Museum of Art, Atlanta, and Macon Museum—both in Georgia; Ringling Museum, Sarasota, Florida; Alpha Kappa Alpha Sorority, Atlanta, Georgia; Oakland Museum, California; University of Connecticut, Storrs (1970); Clark College, Atlanta, Georgia (1973); Carver Museum, Tuskegee, Alabama (1974); "Experiment in Friendship," a travelling show, New Zealand, Russia, Germany, Denmark, and Sweden (1966–1967); and Japan (1978); Ariel Gallery, SoHo, New York City (1991). She shows annually at the Atlanta Museum of Art, Georgia, and other institutions.

Simon has received many awards and honors, including six purchase prizes at exhibits of the Atlanta Historical Society, Georgia; the James Weldon Johnson art award of the NAACP; the Leading Lady award from the American Association of University Women; the Golden Dove Heritage award from Alpha Kappa Alpha, Kappa Omega chapter (1979) and the Bronze Jubilee award (1981). She is active in many social, religious, and civic organizations, and her work is represented in private and public permanent collections, including Atlanta University, Georgia; Carver Museum, Tuskegee, Alabama; Du Sable Museum of African-American History, Chicago, Illinois; Kiah Museum, Savannah, Georgia; Ringling Museum, Sarasota, Florida; and others.

Bibliography
Brown, Marion. *The Negro in the Fine Arts*. Vol. 2. Negro Heritage Library, 1970.
Lewis, Samella S., and Ruth C. Waddy. *Black Artists on Art*. 1969.
Who's Who in American Art. 19th ed. R.R. Bowker Co., 1991–1992.

Singer, Susi (1895–1955)

Susi Singer was born in Austria and lived in Vienna, where she earned a reputation in the field of ceramic sculpture. She was a scholarship student at the Kunstgewerbeschule, studying briefly with Michael Powolny. In 1992 she joined the Wiener Werkstatte (Vienna Workshop) and taught herself to handle clay. Her talent with the material was acknowledged in the 1925 Paris Exposition, France, with a prize for her sculpture. That same year she established her own studio at Grunbach am Schneeberg, continuing to sell some of her sculptures through the Wiener Werkstatte.

Singer's ceramics were first exhibited in America in the International Exhibition of Ceramics at the Metropolitan Museum of Art, New York City, in 1928. Her figurative sculptures, influenced by the rural community around her, connect her to the themes and style of eighteenth-century tabletop figurines. Her work continued to win prizes at international exhibitions, in London, England, in 1934 and in Brussels, Belgium, in 1935. But the financial chaos engulfing Austria, the death of her husband in a tragic accident in 1938, and the signs of an approaching war convinced Singer, who was Jewish, that she must emigrate to America, where previously she had found a market for her whimsical sculptures.

Crippled by a bone disease caused by the malnutrition prevalent in Austria after World War I Singer, hobbling on two canes, and accompanied by her two-year-old son, arrived in Pasadena, California, in 1939. Moving to Hollywood in 1941, Singer set up a studio in her small apartment where she produced her hand-built figurines influenced by Oriental ceramics and her observations of people in the local community.

In 1946 Singer received a fellowship to work at Scripps College in Claremont, California, for a year. There she produced a large group of sculptures which were exhibited by the college in 1974, and also by a local gallery and at the Pasadena Art Institute, California. Other Los Angeles, California, galleries showcased her work in succeeding years. Her work during these years began to incorporate more realistic details and to artfully combine glazed with unglazed areas.

Singer was a major link between the figurative ceramic movement that began in Europe in the 1920s which subsequently inspired American ceramists.

Elaine Levin

Bibliography
Bielheimer, Ruth. "Prominent Viennese Ceramic Artist Becomes Pasadenan." *Star News* 22 (December 1939): 22.
Levin, Elaine. "Vally Weiselthier/Susi Singer." *American Craft* 46:6 (December 1986–January 1987): 46–51.
Rochowanski, I.W. "Die Plasikerin Susi Singer." *Deutsche Kunst und Dekoration* 64 (September 1929): 402.

Singleton, Becky (1952–)

The photographer Becky Singleton was born and raised in Toronto, Canada, and attended the Ontario College of Art from 1970 to 1973. In 1974 she moved to London, Ontario, where a strong regional school had already developed. She immediately began showing smaller works in group shows, frequently winning small Ontario Arts Council project costs grants and rather larger Canada Council grants. Apart from those Singleton has been remarkably successful in avoiding the market-based recuperation and commodification of many other contemporary artists. Her most well-known work is the so-called "How to . . ." series (1981), which includes a large photograph of a robust woman standing expressionlessly in front of the camera, wearing only a pair of panties and some accessories identified by a caption: "How to wear galoshes while wearing a party hat." The result draws attention to and pokes fun at the way advertising operates only in the grammatical realm called the imperative, thus revealing itself as authoritarian at the root. Singleton now lives and works in Toronto.

Robert J. Belton (with Lana Pitkin)

Bibliography
Burnett, David, and Marilyn Schiff. *Contemporary Canadian Art*. Hurtig, 1983.

Sinton, Nell (1910–)

Born in San Francisco, California, the painter Nell Sinton attended Saturday morning classes at the California School of Fine Arts (1922–1923) and, three years later, began formal study there with Lucien Labaudt and Maurice Sterne (1926–1928, 1937–1938). She apprenticed to Sterne and assisted with his Federal Art Project (FAP) murals in the bay area (1938–1940).

Sinton's first solo exhibition was held at the Raymond & Raymond Gallery, San Francisco, California (1947). Further solo shows followed at the California Palace of the Legion of Honor, San Francisco (1949), and Santa Barbara Museum of Art (1950)—both in California; Bolles Gallery, New York City and San Francisco, California (1962); Quay Gallery (now Braunstein/Quay), New York City and San Francisco, California (1966, 1969, 1971, 1974, 1977–1980, 1983, 1986–1987, 1989); San Francisco Museum of Art (1970), Jacqueline Anhalt Gallery, Los Angeles (1972), and "30-Year Retrospective," Mills College, Oakland (1981)—all in California; and others. Her work has been invited to myriad group exhibitions throughout the United States, between 1940 and 1992.

Sinton has been a lecturer, art juror, and teacher at various institutions. Examples of her paintings, scrolls, and constructions are in many private, public, and corporate permanent collections, including AT&T, New Jersey; Chase Manhattan Bank, New York City; Oakland Museum of Art, San Francisco Museum of Art, and the University of California at Berkeley—all in California; and others.

Bibliography
Baker, Kenneth. "Review." *San Francisco Chronicle* (November 1990).
Berkson, Bill. "Review." *Artforum* (March 1987).
Shere, Charles. "Thirty Year Retrospective." *Oakland Tribune*. 1981.
Who's Who in American Art. 19th ed. R.R. Bowker Co., 1991–1992.

Sisto, Elena (1952–)

Born in Boston, Massachusetts, the painter Elena Sisto earned a Bachelor's degree in art and art history from Brown University, Rhode Island School of Design, Providence, and took graduate work at the New York Studio School of Drawing, Painting, and Sculpture, New York City.

Sisto has held solo exhibitions at the Stephen Wirtz Gallery, San Francisco, California (1993); Germans Van Eck Gallery, New York City (1992); University of Missouri at St. Louis (1991); Damon Brandt Gallery (1990), and Vanderwoude Tannenbaum Gallery (1984, 1986)—both in New York City; and others. She has held two-person exhibitions at Germans Van Eck Gallery, New York City (1991); and Winston Gallery, Washington, D.C. (1987). Her work has been invited to group shows throughout the United States: from Los Angeles, California, to Ithaca, New York; Waterville, Maine; San Francisco, California; Chicago, Illinois; New York City; Greensboro, North Carolina; and Norfolk, Connecticut; and others.

Sisto has earned honors and awards, including National Endowment for the Arts (NEA) fellowships (1989–1990, 1983–1984), and a residency at the Millay Colony (1987) among others. She has been an active guest lecturer at colleges and art schools since 1986 and has taught painting and drawing at several institutions, including Columbia University, New York City (1990–1992); the New York Studio School, New York City (1987–1992); Rhode Island School of Design, Providence (1987–1991); and the State University of New York (SUNY) at Purchase (1988). Her work is represented in private and public permanent collections.

Bibliography
Hagen, Charles. "Elena Sisto." *Artforum* (Summer 1990).
———. "Elena Sisto." *The New York Times* (December 4, 1992).
Pardee, Hearne. "Elena Sisto." *Art News* (September 1990).
Smith, Roberta. "Elena Sisto." *The New York Times* (June 28, 1991).
Westfall, Stephen. "Elena Sisto." *Art in America* (February 1987).

Skoff, Gail (1949–)

Born in Los Angeles, California, the photographer Gail Skoff received her Bachelor of Fine Arts (1972) and Master of Fine Arts (1979) degrees from the San Francisco Art Institute, California. Between 1976 and 1985 she taught photography at the University of California Extension, Berkeley, and at the Associated Students of the University of California Studio, where she also worked as darkroom supervisor and photo curator. She was the recipient of a National Endowment for the Arts (NEA) fellowship in 1976. Her photographs have been widely exhibited and are in major collections nationally and internationally.

Skoff states that her interest is in the "magical transformation of reality through hand coloring . . . [creating] photographs where time and space are suspended, and a new world emerges separate from my everyday life." She explores the world for environments where contemporary life as she knows it does not exist. In early work Skoff photographed costumed models then hand-colored the prints to produce romantic and mysterious images. She has also photographed exotic people and foreign lands. Skoff has broken boundaries that very few women have crossed by journeying into the landscape to photograph. She photographed uninhabited lands: deserts, prairies, and unusual land formations. Through the dramatic manipulations of hand-coloring, masking, drawing, painting, and toning, these prints are transformed into extraordinarily surreal panoramic landscapes. Skoff removed every clue as to date to further push her illusion of timelessness. The most recent photographs are of large organic, abstracted forms. Skoff says she has been influenced by photographer Julia Margaret Cameron and painter Georgia O'Keeffe.

Laine Sutherland

Bibliography
Auer, Michel. *Photographers Encyclopaedia International: 1839 to the Present*. Editions Camera Obscura, 1985.
David, Douglas, and Maggie Malone. "The Young Romantics." *Newsweek* (March 19, 1979).
Fischer, Hal. "San Francisco [review]." *Artforum* 18 (May 1980): 87.
Garner, Gretchen. *Reclaiming Paradise: American Women Photograph the Land*. Duluth, Minnesota: Tweed Museum of Art, 1987.

Skoglund, Sandra (1946–)

Both a sculptor and photographer, Sandy Skoglund was born in Boston, Massachusetts, received her Bachelor of Arts degree from Smith College, Northampton, Massachusetts, in 1968 and went on to the University of Iowa, Iowa City, to finish a Master of Fine Arts degree in 1972.

Skoglund has exhibited widely in the 1980s. Her installations or her photographs of these installations have appeared in exhibitions at the Fogg Art Museum at Harvard University, Cambridge, Massachusetts; the Fort Worth Art Museum, Texas; Leo Castelli Gallery and the International Center of Photography—both in New York City; the Institute of Contemporary Art, London, England; and the Museum of Contemporary Art in Chicago, Illinois. Her work was also featured in the 1981 Whitney Museum of American Art Biennial, New York City.

Skoglund received the emerging artist award from the National Endowment for the Arts (NEA) (1980) and won an award from the New York Foundation for the Arts (1988). She has taught at Hartford Art School, Connecticut, and is now associate professor of art at Rutgers University, New Brunswick, New Jersey. She is represented by Castelli Graphics in New York City. Her work has been collected by a number of museums, including the Metropolitan Museum of Art, New York City; the St. Louis Museum of Art, Missouri; the Dallas Museum of Art, Texas; the Wadsworth Athenaeum, Hartford, Connecticut; the Baltimore Museum of Art, Maryland; and the Denver Museum of Art, Colorado. Her work is also represented in several corporate collections.

Skoglund's sculptural tableaux are meticulously created. They are muted environments frequently overrun with small animals—often painted in day-glow colors. Her photographs of the life-size installations preserve what writer Ingrid Sischy calls a "frozen slice of unchecked imagination." Her subject is often the unconscious dread of a suburban America—how human beings relate, and often fear, the social and especially the natural world. Her installations—made up of everyday objects and multiple sculpted animal forms—are all unified in her photographic practice which creates the illusion of domestic apocalypse.

One of Skoglund's most well-known works, "Revenge of the Goldfish" (1981), represents a twilight bedroom where a young man has awakened to a fantasy of large goldfish swimming about the room. Skoglund's works are visually arresting and invite many interpretations—psycho-sexual ones and broader, socially engendered ones.

Paul Ivey

Bibliography

Heartney, Eleanor. "Review of Sandy Skoglund at P.P.O.W." *Art in America* 79:11 (November 1991): 153.

Richardson, Nan. "Sandy Skoglund, Wild at Heart." *ArtNews* 90:4 (April 1991): 115–19.

Skoglund, Sandy. "Spirituality in the Flesh: A Project for ArtForum." *ArtForum* 30 (February 1991): 76–77.

Slavin, Arlene (1942–)

A native New Yorker, the painter/printmaker/muralist Arlene Slavin earned a Bachelor of Fine Arts degree at the Cooper Union, New York City (1964), and, three years later, received a Master of Fine Arts degree from Pratt Institute, Brooklyn, New York.

Slavin has held solo exhibitions in galleries throughout the United States and abroad, including "Screen Retrospective," Centre College, Danville, Kentucky (1992); Yeshiva University, New York City (1991); Educational Testing Service, Princeton, New Jersey (1990); "Simultaneous Landscapes," Katharina Rich Perlow Gallery, New York City (1988); "Print Retrospective," American Embassy, Belgrade, Yugoslavia (1984); "Sea World," a 214-foot mural installation, University of Colorado, Colorado Springs (1981); "Aquarium," a 115-foot mural installation, Pratt Institute (1981), Alexander F. Milliken Gallery (1979, 1980, 1981), Brooke Alexander (1976); Fischbach Gallery (1973, 1974)—all in New York City; and others. Her work has been invited to myriad group exhibitions, such as "Screens, Fans, Gates, Doors," Benton Gallery, Southampton (1991), and "Creatures Large and Small," Elaine Benson Gallery, Bridgehampton (1984–1985, 1987, 1989, 1991)—both in New York; "Screening," Cadme Gallery, Philadelphia, Pennsylvania (1987); "Large Drawings," Winnipeg Art Gallery, Canada, a travelling show (1985–1986); "Collector's Choice," Virginia Art Museum, Richmond (1981); "Painting and Sculpture Today," the Contemporary Arts Center, Cincinnati, Ohio (1974); and many others.

Slavin has recently been awarded a number of public commissions in New York City, including the metal work for the main stairway of the De Soto School (1992); a fifty-five-foot steel fence for the sculpture garden of the Henry Street Settlement (1992); a cut steel sculpture/bench for Central Park (1989); three acrylic on wood folding screens (each eight-by-ten-feet) for the Hudson River Museum, Yonkers (1983); and others. Her multipanelled screens encompass acrylic-painted and cut-out flora and fauna and they exist as free-standing forms in space.

Between 1967 and 1979 Slavin taught briefly at various universities as a visiting artist or critic; has lectured widely from coast to coast; and was the recipient of a grant in printmaking from the National Endowment for the Arts (NEA) (1977–1978). Her work is represented in private, public, and corporate permanent collections, including the Metropolitan Museum of Art, Brooklyn Museum, and Albert Einstein College of Medicine—all in New York City; Fogg Art Museum, Harvard University, Cambridge, Massachusetts; University of California at Berkeley; Smithsonian Institution, Washington, D.C.; Heckscher Museum, Huntington, New York; Prudential Life Insurance Co., New Jersey; and many others.

Bibliography

"Birds." Talk of the Town. *The New Yorker* (March 19, 1979): 32–33.

Crossman, Christopher B. *Painterly Panels*. Heckscher Museum, 1987.

Levin, Gail. "Arlene Slavin at Yeshiva University Critique." *Art Times* (October 1991): 5.

Van Gelder, Pat. "Animals as Subjects in Contemporary Art." *American Artist* (May 1989): 44–50, 96–100.

Sleigh, Sylvia

Realist painter Sylvia Sleigh was born in Landudno, Wales, and studied at the Brighton School of Art, England. She emigrated to the United States in 1961 and, two years later, held her first American solo exhibition at Bennington College, Vermont.

Sleigh has also held solo shows at universities and galleries in New York City, including SoHo 20, A.I.R. Gallery, the New School for Social Research, Fordham University, and G.W. Einstein Co., Inc. Further exhibitions were held at the University of Rhode Island, Kingston; Douglass College, Rutgers University, New Brunswick, New Jersey; Ohio State University, Columbus; Northwestern University, Evanston, Illinois; and others. Her most recent exhibitions include the Steibel Modern Gallery, New York City (1992), and "Invitation to a Voyage and Other Works," which was shown at the Milwaukee Art Museum, Wisconsin; Butler Institute of Art, Youngstown, Ohio; and Ball State University, Muncie, Indiana (1990).

Sleigh's work has been invited to myriad group exhibitions in such venues as Tokyo, Japan; New York City; Denver, Colorado; Stamford, Connecticut; Philadelphia, Pennsylvania; and Chicago, Illinois. She has received honors and awards, including the Edith Kreeger Wolf distinguished professorship at Northwestern University, Evanston, Illinois (1977); a National Endowment for the Arts (NEA) fellowship (1982); and a grant from the Pollack-Krasner Foundation (1985). In addition to Northwestern University, Sleigh has taught at the State University of New York (SUNY) at Stony Brook, and at the New School for Social Research, New York City. Her oils are represented in many private and public permanent collections.

Bibliography

Frueh, Joanna. "Chicago: Sylvia Sleigh at Zaks." *Art in America* 74:1 (January 1986): 143, 145.

Henry, Gerrit. "Sylvia Sleigh at G.W. Einstein." *Art in America* 71:6 (Summer 1983): 158.

Rubinstein, Charlotte S. *American Women Artists.* G.K. Hall, 1982.

Sylvia Sleigh: Recent Paintings. A Catalog. Essay by Donald B. Kuspit. G.W. Einstein Co., Inc., 1980.

Sligh, Clarissa T. (1939–)

Born in Washington, D.C., Clarissa T. Sligh earned a Bachelor's degree from Hampton Institute, Virginia (1961), on a four-year scholarship. She received a Bachelor of Fine Arts degree from Howard University, Washington, D.C. (1972); attended the Skowhegan School of Art, Maine, on scholarship (1972); was awarded a Master of Business Administration degree at the University of Pennsylvania, Philadelphia (1973); and studied photography at the International Center of Photography, New York City (1979, 1980). Sligh has worked on NASA's Manned Space Flight Program; was an analyst on Wall Street, New York City; a school desegregation plaintiff in the 1950s; and is an artist/photographer and filmmaker. Widely travelled, she is a noted lecturer, panelist, art juror, workshop leader, visiting artist and, most recently, distinguished visiting artist/teacher at Carleton College, Northfield, Minnesota.

Sligh has held solo exhibitions in galleries throughout the United States, including the Center for Photography, Woodstock, New York, and Carleton College, Northfield, Minnesota (1992); Syracuse University, New York, and the Rhode Island School of Design, Providence (1991); White Columns, New York City, and Moore College of Art, Philadelphia, Pennsylvania (1990); C.E.P.A. Satellite Space, Buffalo, New York (1987); Modernage Discovery Gallery, New York City (1982); and others. Her photographs and other visual works have been invited to eighty-eight group exhibitions in the United States and abroad between 1981 and 1992, such as "Bridges and Boundaries: African-Americans and American Jews," a travelling show, coast-to-coast, the Jewish Mu-

seum (1992), "Recent Acquisitions," Museum of Modern Art (MoMA) (1991), and "Profiles: Four African-American Women Artists," the French Embassy (1991)—all in New York City; "Learn to Read Art: Artists' Books," Art Gallery of Hamilton, Ontario, Canada (1990); "Cheney Goodman and Schwerner, The Mississippi Three, The Struggle Continues," SoHo 20 Gallery, New York City (1990); "Le Mois de la Photo," Montréal, Québec, Canada (1989); "Autobiography: Herstory," Castelli Gallery (1987), "Artists as Filmmakers," A.I.R. Gallery, New York City (1983, 1985), and "Art against Intervention in Central America," Westbeth Gallery (1984)—all in New York City; and many others.

Winner of awards and honors, Sligh was the recipient of an "Artiste en France" residency from the government of France (1992); a grant from the New York State Council on the Arts (1990); an Art Matters grant (1989); grants from the National Endowment for the Arts (NEA) and the New York Foundation for the Arts (1988); an Amelia Earhart fellowship, Zonta International (1962); and others. Her work is represented in private and public permanent collections, including the Museum of Modern Art (MoMA), and the Schomberg Center for Research in Black Culture, New York Public Library—both in New York City; Australian National Gallery, Canberra; National Museum of Women in the Arts, Washington, D.C.; University of Arizona, Tucson; Dartmouth College, Hanover, New Hampshire; and others.

Bibliography

Hagen, Charles. "How Racial and Cultural Differences Affect Art." *The New York Times* (August 23, 1991).

Marks, Laura U. "Healing the Cultural Body: Clarissa Sligh's Unfinished Business." *Center Quarterly* 50 (1992): 18–22.

Raven, Arlene. "Not a Pretty Picture: Can Violent Art Heal?" *Village Voice* (June 17, 1986).

Van Proyen, Mark. "Clarissa Sligh." *Artweek* 21:36 (November 1, 1990): 17.

Sloan, Jeanette Pasin (1946–)

Born in Chicago, Illinois, the painter/printmaker Jeanette Pasin Sloan earned a Bachelor of Fine Arts degree at Marymount College, Tarrytown, New York (1967), and, two years later, received a Master of Fine Arts degree from the University of Chicago, Illinois.

Sloan has held many solo exhibitions in galleries throughout the United States, including the Peltz Gallery, Milwaukee, Wisconsin (1989, 1990); Butters Gallery, Portland, Oregon (1989, 1991); Camino Real Gallery, Boca Raton, Florida (1990); G.W. Einstein Co., Inc., New York City (1977, 1979, 1980, 1983, 1985); Landfall Press Gallery, Chicago, Illinois (1978); Tatischeff Gallery, Santa Monica, California (1989); Roger-Ramsay Gallery, Chicago, Illinois (1989, 1992); and others. Her works have been invited to myriad group exhibitions, such as "Interiors," Steven Scott Gallery, Baltimore, Maryland (1992); "Face to Face: Self-Portraits by Chicago Artists," Chicago Cultural Center (1992), and "Realism Re-Examined," Landfall Press Exhibit, Federal Reserve Bank of Chicago (1991)—both in Illinois; "Presswork: The Art of Women Printmakers," a travelling show, National Museum of Women in the Arts, Washington, D.C. (1991); "Water-Color: Contemporary Currents," Riverside Art Museum, California (1989); "National Drawing Invitational," Arkansas Art Center, Little Rock (1987); "59th Annual International Competition," the Print Club, Philadelphia, Pennsylvania (1983); National Academy of Design, New York City (1980); "Recent

Acquisitions," National Collection of Fine Arts, Smithsonian Institution, Washington, D.C. (1978); and many others.

Sloan received the Watson F. Blair prize at the "79th Exhibition by Artists of Chicago and Vicinity," Art Institute of Chicago, Illinois (1981); and the Benton Spruance prize for her lithograph, "Silver Bowls," at the Philadelphia Print Club, Pennsylvania (1983). She has been a lecturer and artist-in-residence at leading art institutes and universities in the United States and Canada, including the University of Texas at Austin (1989); the University of Notre Dame, Indiana (1986); and the University of Regina, Canada (1986). Sloan also received a fellowship from the Illinois Arts Council (1986). Her work is in many private, public, and corporate permanent collections, such as the Nippon Lever Corporation, Tokyo, Japan; Art Institute of Chicago, Illinois; Chase Manhattan Bank, the Metropolitan Museum of Art, and the New York Public Library—all in New York City; Fogg Art Museum, Harvard University, Cambridge, Massachusetts; Yale University Art Gallery, New Haven, Connecticut; and others.

Bibliography

"Jeanette P. Sloan." *Print Collectors Newsletter* 17:4 (September–October 1986).

Gerritt, Henry. "Jeanette P. Sloan." *Art in America* (June 1985).

Holg, Garrett. "Review of Exhibition at Roger Ramsay Gallery, Chicago." *New Art Examiner.* Vol. 14 (March 1987): 14.

Meticulous Realist Drawing. A Catalog. Essay by Ronny Cohen. Squibb Gallery, 1989.

Raynor, Vivien. "Precision for Precision's Sake in a Show by Virtuoso Realists." *The New York Times* (May 21, 1989).

Smith, Alexis (1949–)

Born in Los Angeles, California, the conceptual artist Alexis Smith earned a Bachelor's degree at the University of California at Irvine.

Smith has presented more than thirty-five solo exhibitions, performances, and installations in museums and galleries in the United States and abroad, including the Riko Mizuno Gallery, Los Angeles (1974); Whitney Museum of American Art, New York City (1975); University of California at San Diego (1976, 1991); Holly Solomon Gallery, New York City (1977, 1978, 1979, 1981); De Appel, an installation, Amsterdam, the Netherlands (1979); Margo Leavin Gallery (1982, 1988, 1990), and Rosamund Felsen Gallery (1978, 1980, 1982)—both in Los Angeles, California; "Alexis Smith," a major retrospective, Whitney Museum of American Art, New York City, and the Museum of Contemporary Art, Los Angeles, California (1992); and others. Her work has been invited to myriad group exhibitions throughout the world in such venues as Walnut, California; Paris, France; Boston, Massachusetts; Miami, Florida; Nagoya, Japan; Dublin, Ireland; Helsinki, Finland; and Mexico City, Mexico.

On commission Smith has created collage works in permanent painted installations, stone monuments, outdoor tiled walkways, and other public and private projects; she has published "artist's books," posters, billboards, editions of prints, and *ex libris* designs for museums, universities, and other institutions. In addition to lecturing widely and participating in art school programs throughout the United States, Smith has taught at private and public universities, including the Universities of California at Irvine, San Diego, and Los Angeles (UCLA),

between 1985 and 1990.

Winner of many honors, Smith won a new talent award from the Los Angeles County Museum of Art, California (1974); fellowship grants from the National Endowment for the Arts (NEA) (1976, 1987); and others. In addition to her site installations and other public art, Smith's work is represented in many private, public, and corporate permanent collections.

Bibliography

Hopkins, Henry. *California Painters: New Work.* Chronicle Books, 1989.

Kimmelman, Michael. "Flotsam, Jetsam and Quotes in Collages by Alexis Smith." *The New York Times* (November 29, 1991): B1, B4.

Knight, Christopher. "Alexis Smith Plays the Name Game." *Elle Magazine* (December 1991): 128–30.

Who's Who in American Art. 19th ed. R.R. Bowker Co., 1991–1992.

Smith, Barbara T. (1931–)

Born in Pasadena, California, the performance artist (a deficient term in this case), Barbara T. Smith earned a Bachelor's degree *cum laude* from Pomona College, Claremont (1953); attended Chouinard Art Institute, Los Angeles (1965); participated in workshops with Alex Hay in Los Angeles (1968), and Steve Paxton, Santa Monica (1969); and received a Master of Fine Arts degree from the University of California at Irvine (1971)—all in her native state.

Smith has created solo performances in venues from Sydney, Australia, to New York City; Los Angeles, California; Bangkok, Thailand; Victoria, British Columbia; and Berlin, Germany. She has collaborated with Judy Chicago, Suzanne Lacy, Coco Gordon, and others in performances ranging in sites from Kathmandu, Nepal to San Francisco, and New York. Her recent solo exhibitions include "This Is It," Glenmore Guest House, Dharamsala, India (1992); "Bottom Line," Highways, Santa Monica (1990), and "Ground Zero," Social and Public Art Resource Center, Venice (1989)—both in California. Her shows include photographs, drawings, sculpture, lithography, documentation, books, installations, and other diverse media.

Between 1965 and 1990 Smith's work has been invited to group exhibitions in galleries and museums in the United States and abroad, such as "Modern Buddhist Art II," Hofheim, Germany (1990); "Making Their Mark: Women Artists Move into the Mainstream, 1970–1985," a travelling show, Cincinnati Art Museum, Ohio (1989); "A Southern California Collection," Cirrus Gallery, Los Angeles (1987); Cornell University, Ithaca, New York (1981); "100+: Current Directions in Contemporary Art," Los Angeles Institute of Contemporary Art, California (1978); "Museum of Drawers," Berne, Switzerland (1973); and many others.

Initiated by Smith, her "21st Century Odyssey" redefined and transmuted the ancient Greek tale of Odysseus and Penelope, except that Smith (Odysseus) circumnavigated the real world in her quest and her collaborator scientist, Dr. Ron L. Walford (Penelope), was sealed in the well-publicized Biosphere 2 in Oracle, Arizona, for two years. Their media-linked conversations and communications (from special sites on Smith's odyssey) were the bases of art works, meditations, prayer cycles, technology and community survival.

Smith has been a visiting artist, guest artist, and lecturer at universities and colleges throughout the United States and abroad; she has received many honors and awards, including National Endowment for the Arts (NEA) grants (1974, 1979, 1985); residencies at Dorland Mountain

Colony (1982); Capp Street Project, San Francisco (1984); Djerassi Foundation, Woodside, California (1987); Social and Public Art Resource Center, Venice, California (1989); and others. Her work is represented in private and public permanent collections, including the Archives of the Venice Biennale, Italy; Brooke Alexander, New York City; Cornell University, Ithaca, New York; Museum of Modern Art (MoMA), New York City; Museum of Conceptual Art, San Francisco, California; and others.

Bibliography

Brown, Betty Ann. *Yesterday and Tomorrow: California Women Artists.* Midmarch Arts, 1989.

Festa, Angelika. "Pageant of the Holy Squash." *High Performance* 47:12:3. (1989).

Goode, Starr. "An Interview with Barbara T. Smith." *The Goddess in Art.* Group W, Cable Television, 1986.

Heiman, Andrea. "Odyssey: A Dialogue between Two Worlds." *The Los Angeles Times* (July 7, 1992).

Smith, Jaune Quick-to-See (1940–)

Born on the Flathead Reservation in Montana, Native American artist Jaune Quick-to-See Smith is of Flathead, French-Cree, and Shoshone parentage. Her early years were itinerant ones, as she traveled with her father who was a horse trader. The saddles, ropes, and the colors of worn leather in her father's bunk house all affected her sense of color and texture. After her training in art education at Framingham State College, Massachusetts (where she earned a Bachelor of Arts degree in 1976), and painting at the University of New Mexico (where she earned a Master of Arts degree in 1980), Smith achieved international recognition within the worlds of Native American art and mainstream modern art.

Smith's work merges Native American pictographic imagery with modernist color and sign theory. The signs and symbols of Native American art history have a particular resonance for her. Of the Indian influences in her work, Smith mentions pictographs, skin robes, ledger book art, and muslin paintings. Contemporary feminist aesthetics and traditional Indian women's arts of skin sewing, beadwork and cloth patterning are joined in her work. Smith uses paint on canvas, pastel, printmaking, as well as multimedia collage images that combine calico, wallpaper, and paint. The calico squares recall the calico dresses worn for ceremonies since the mid-19th century by women of her tribes. Muslin fragments evoke the feedsacks she fashioned into shirts as a child.

In addition to exhibiting her work internationally, Smith has served as a spokesperson for Native American activism and Native American artists, both traditional and modernist. She has curated or juried numerous shows of Native arts, including *Women of Sweetgrass, Cedar, and Sage* (American Indian Community House Gallery, New York, 1985). She has been a visiting professor or critic in art departments throughout North America, including the Institute of American Indian Arts (Santa Fe, New Mexico) and Washington University (St. Louis, Missouri). Smith's work is represented in numerous museum collections, including the Minneapolis Institute of Art, Minnesota; the Newark Art Museum, New Jersey; the University of Oklahoma Museum of Art; the Heard Museum, Phoenix, Arizona; the St. Louis Art Museum, Missouri; the Denver Art Museum, Colorado; the National Museum of American Art, Washington, D.C.; and the Museum of Mankind, in Vienna, Austria.

Janet C. Berlo

Bibliography

Archuleta, Margaret, and Rennard Strickland. *Shared Visions: Native American Painters and Sculptors in the Twentieth Century.* Phoenix: The Heard Museum, 1991, p. 57.

Brown, Betty Ann, and Arlene Raven. *Exposures: Women and Their Art.* New Sage Press, 1989, pp. 54–55.

Hammond, Harmony, and Jaune Quick-to-See Smith. *Women of Sweetgrass, Cedar, and Sage: Contemporary Art by Native American Women.* New York: American Indian Community House, 1985.

Highwater, Jamake. *The Sweet Grass Lives On.* Lippincott, 1980, pp. 179–80.

Wade, Edwin, and Rennard Strickland. *Magic Images: Contemporary Native American Art.* Tulsa: Philbrook Art Center, 1981, pp. 80–81.

Smith, Jo-An (1933–)

Born in Eugene, Oregon, the designer/goldsmith Jo-An Smith studied at the University of Washington, Seattle (1950–1952); Indiana University, Bloomington (1965); privately in Buenos Aires, Argentina (1966); in San Salvador, El Salvador (1967); and Panama, before earning a Bachelor's degree at the University of Texas, El Paso (1971) and a Master of Arts degree from New Mexico State University, Las Cruces, four years later.

In the 1970s Smith's work appeared in national and international shows. Most recently it has been invited to group exhibitions, including "Wearable Art," State University of New York (SUNY) at Potsdam (1989); "Treasure Trio," Las Cruces Renaissance Craft Fair, New Mexico (1986–1989); "Art and Apparel Exhibition," Georjess (1986), and "Art's a Poppin," Dona Ana Arts Council (1985–1988)—all in Las Cruces, New Mexico; "The Metalsmith," Phoenix, Arizona, and Seattle, Washington (1976–1977); and others.

A distinguished member of the Society of North American Goldsmiths and the Dona Ana Arts Council, Smith has won many awards and honors for her finely-crafted jewelry. She created a commemorative piece for the Bicentennial, Smithsonian Institution, Washington, D.C., and, since 1985, has fashioned the awards for teaching excellence conferred by New Mexico State College, Las Cruces. Her work is represented in private and public permanent collections, including New Mexico State University, Las Cruces; the Smithsonian Institution, Washington, D.C.; Texas A&M University, El Paso; and many others.

Bibliography

Who's Who in American Art. 19th ed. R.R. Bowker Co., 1991–1992.

Smith, Jori (1907–)

After a general education, the painter Jori Smith studied at l'École des Beaux-Arts, Montréal, Québec, Canada, until 1929, when she left to study with Edwin Holgate. She has held many solo exhibitions in museums and galleries in Canada, including the Galerie Dominion, Montréal (1955); Galerie Katel, Montréal (1976); and others.

Smith's work has been included in group shows in Canada and abroad, such as the Art Gallery of Ontario, Toronto (1945); "Artes Gráficas do Canada," National Museum of Fine Arts, Rio de Janeiro, Brazil (1946); "The Development of Painting in Canada, 1665–1945," Musée des Beaux-Arts, Montréal (1955); Waddington Gallery, Montréal (1955–1957); "Peinture Canadienne des années 30," a travelling show, National Gallery of Canada, Ottawa (1975); and others. Her paintings are metaphors of the social and political conditions of her time; examples of her work are represented in private and public permanent collections in Canada.

Bibliography
Gautier, Ninon. "Rencontre avec Jori Smith," *Le Collectionneur* 3:11 (1981): 11–14.
Trois Generations d'Art Québecois, 1940, 1950, 1960. Montréal: Musée d'Art Contemporain, 1976.

Smith, Sherri (1943–)

Born in Chicago, Illinois, the fiber artist/sculptor Sherri Smith earned a Bachelor's degree, Phi Beta Kappa, from Stanford University, California (1965); and a Master of Fine Arts degree in weaving and textile design from Cranbrook Academy of Art, Bloomfield Hills, Michigan, two years later.

Smith worked for Dorothy Liebes, Inc. (1968) and Boris Kroll Fabrics, New York City (1969) before the start of her academic career. She has since taught at Colorado State University, Fort Collins (1971–1974), and at the University of Michigan, Ann Arbor, since 1974.

Smith has held many solo exhibitions, including the Museum of the Southwest, Midland, Texas (1973); Craftsmen's Gallery, Scarsdale, New York, and Joseph Magnin Gallery, Denver, Colorado (1974); Hackley Art Museum, Muskegon, Michigan (1975); Colorado Springs Fine Arts Center (1976); Hadley Gallery, New York City (1978); and others. Her work has been invited to group exhibitions in the United States and abroad, including "Wall Hangings," Museum of Modern Art (MoMA) (1969), and the Museum of Contemporary Craft (1969)—both in New York City; Biennale of Tapestry, Lausanne, Switzerland (1971–1977); "Fiber Structures," Denver Art Museum, Colorado (1972); University of Iowa, Iowa City (1973); "Three-Dimensional Fibers," Govett-Brewster Art Gallery, New Plymouth, New Zealand (1974); Museum of Contemporary Art, Chicago, Illinois, and Kansas City Art Institute, Missouri (1976); "Fiber Works," Cleveland Museum of Art (1977), and Cincinnati Art Museum (1978)—both in Ohio; and others.

Smith received a Young American fellowship grant from the American Craft Council, and a silver medal at the "3rd Tapestry Triennale," Lodz, Poland (1978). Her work is represented in private, public, and corporate permanent collections, including the Art Institute of Chicago, Illinois; AT&T, New York City; Borg-Warner Corporation; Colorado Springs Fine Arts Center; Dubai Airport Hotel, Saudi Arabia; Hackley Art Museum; Hyatt Regency Hotel, Québec, Canada; IBM, Atlanta, Georgia; and others.

Bibliography
Constantine, Mildred, and Jack Lenor Larsen. *The Art Fabric: Mainstream.* Van Nostrand Reinhold, 1981.
"Sherri Smith Tapestries." *Handweaver and Craftsman* 26:6 (November–December 1974): 46–47.
Who's Who in American Art. 19th ed. R.R. Bowker Co., 1991–1992.

Smith, Shirley

Born in Wichita, Kansas, the painter Shirley Smith earned a Bachelor of Fine Arts degree at Kansas State University, Manhattan, and also studied at the Art Students League, New York City, and the Provincetown Workshop Art School, Massachusetts.

Smith's most recent solo exhibitions were held in galleries such as Art/EX Gallery, Stamford Museum and Nature Center, Connecticut (1987), and the American Academy and Institute of Arts and Letters Invitational, New York City (1990). Her work has been invited to many group shows, including "American Painting 1970," Virginia Museum of Art, Richmond (1970); "Recent Acquisitions & Lyrical Abstraction," Whitney Museum of American Art, New York City (1971); "From the Museum Collection: Art by Women," University of California at Berkeley (1973); "Auditorium Installation Exhibition," Everson Museum, Syracuse, New York (1976–1979); and New York City venues, including "Views by Women Artists," Women's Caucus for Art (1982); "161st Annual Exhibition," National Academy of Design (1986); "Animal Life" (1987), and "Nature in Art" (1988)—both at One Penn Plaza. Smith's award-winning work is represented in private, public, and corporate permanent collections, including the Aldrich Museum of Contemporary Art, Ridgefield, Connecticut; Phoenix Art Museum, Arizona; Prudential Insurance Company of America, Newark, New Jersey; University of California at Berkeley; Whitney Museum of American Art, New York City; and others.

Bibliography
Campbell, Lawrence. "Review." *Art News* (February 1973).
Kingsley, April. "Review." *Art International* (March 1973).
Mayer, Rosemary. "Review." *Arts* (February 1973).

Snow, Lila (1927–)

A prize-winning sculptor, painter, and assemblage artist, Lila Snow has a remarkably diverse background, and equally varied interests. The Brooklyn, New York, native earned a Bachelor of Science degree in chemistry and worked for some years in that field; not surprisingly, she often incorporates references to scientific phenomena in her art. She married the physicist George Snow, and raised three children, while continuing to be active in many other arenas. She has published art criticism; done graphic design; performed in a modern-dance company; taught the first women's studies course offered at the University of Maryland (1972); served as associate director of the Washington Women's Art Center, Washington, D.C. (1977–1979); and, most recently, has been a successful, politically-oriented performance artist.

Snow received her art training at the Corcoran School of Art and the American University—both in Washington, D.C., and cites instructors Ed McGowin and Tom Green as two of her most important influences. Since 1972 she has exhibited her work regularly in both solo and group shows in half a dozen states, plus Italy, France, and Japan. The bulk of Snow's work consists of assembled wall-sculptures, made largely from found objects. She takes elements as disparate as the cardboard cores from bolts of cloth, Styrofoam packing boxes for delicate scientific instruments, and cigar boxes, and transforms them—using bits of colored paper, postage stamps, miniature plastic toys, and innumerable other items gathered during her residencies in Europe and Japan.

While her works are essentially abstract—demonstrating a highly sophisticated sense of texture and design—Snow's pieces also refer to aspects of her own life, and to current events. During the 1970s, for example, she made art strongly critical of Watergate, and of U.S. involvement in the Vietnam War. More recently she has dealt with such subjects as George Orwell's *1984*, nuclear proliferation, and the Clarence Thomas/Anita Hill Supreme Court hearings.

Throughout her career Snow has used collage to express her ideas on a variety of cultural themes. In the past several years, however, the artist has also been working on a striking series of oil paintings exploring motifs encountered during recent trips to Africa; these canvases integrate Snow's strong coloristic sense with collage and calligraphy, in a highly innovative way.

Bibliography

Heller, Nancy G. "Lila Snow's Paper Politics." *The Washington Post* (June 18, 1985): D–7.

Shenker, Israel. "The Physicist as a Soft-Shoe Man." *The New York Times* (February 4, 1976): B–4.

Thern-Smith, Linda. "Lila Snow: Collages and Paintings." *Washington Review* (February–March 1992): 25.

Welzenbach, Michael. "Artist as Unarmed Disarmer." *The Washington Post* (January 20, 1990): C–2.

Snowden, Sylvia (1942–)

Born in Raleigh, North Carolina, the African-American painter Sylvia Snowden earned both her Bachelor of Fine Arts and Master of Fine Arts degrees from Howard University, Washington, D.C.

Snowden has held solo exhibitions in galleries and museums, including "Paintings by Sylvia Snowden," M. Hanks Gallery, Santa Monica, California (1989); "Large Works on Paper," Brody's Gallery, Washington, D.C. (1987); and others. Her work has been included in many prestigious group shows in the United States and abroad, such as "African-American Contemporary Art," Museo Civico d'Arte di Gibellina, Sicily, Italy (1990); "Introspectives: Contemporary Art by Americans and Brazilians of African Descent," California Afro-American Museum, Los Angeles, California (1989); "Secrets," Gallery 10 Ltd., Washington, D.C. (1988); "The Art of Black America in Japan," International Cultural Exchange Association, Tokyo, Japan (1987); "Myth and Ritual," Touchstone Gallery, Washington, D.C. (1986); and others.

Snowden's work is represented in private and public permanent collections, including Hampton University, Virginia; Howard University, Washington, D.C.; and others. "Miss Phoebe's Quilt" (1990), a not atypical recent painting, reveals a heavily-impastoed, expressionistic work based upon the riot of color and texture used in quiltmaking by the artist's grandmother.

Bibliography

Lazarus, Elizabeth. "The Experience Exhibited." *The Washington Post* (August 24, 1986).

McElroy, Guy C., Richard J. Powell, and Sharon F. Patton. *African-American Artists, 1880–1987: Selections from the Evans-Tibbs Collection.* Washington, D.C., 1989.

Thorson, Alice. "Sylvia Snowden Engaging Expressionism." *New Art Examiner* (October 1988).

Snyder, Joan (1940–)

Joan Snyder is best known for her expressionistic, mixed-media paintings. Snyder received her Bachelor of Arts degree from Douglass College, Rutgers University, New Brunswick, New Jersey, in 1962 and her Master of Fine Arts degree from Rutgers University in 1966.

Snyder has had approximately thirty solo exhibitions in galleries and museums throughout the United States since she began exhibiting her work in 1970. She has had solo exhibitions at Los Angeles Institute of Contemporary Art, Century City, California (1976); Neuberger Museum, State University of New York (SUNY) at Purchase (1978); Wadsworth Athenaeum, Hartford, Connecticut (1981); and Hirschl and Adler Modern Gallery, New York City (1985, 1988, 1990). Snyder has also participated in more than eighty group exhibitions throughout the United States, Europe, and China. Her paintings are in the permanent collections of museums throughout the United States, including Boston Museum of Fine Arts, Massachusetts; Metropolitan Museum of Art, Museum of Modern Art (MoMA), Whitney Museum of American Art, and Jewish Museum—all in New York City; the Fogg Art Museum, Harvard University, Cambridge, Massachusetts; and the High Museum of Art, Atlanta, Georgia.

Snyder began painting expressionist portraits and landscapes in the 1960s. In the early 1970s she began to focus on "stroke paintings," in which the paint strokes became her subject matter. In 1974 she began addressing the issues raised by the feminist movement in her "flock/membrane paintings." Certain images, such as trees, fields, crosses, fishbones, and abstract totems recur in her work to reflect the themes of transcendence and redemption. Snyder's work is deeply personal and autobiographical: her life experiences—the joy of her daughter Molly's birth in 1979, an earlier miscarriage, a divorce, her relationships with friends and lovers—are all reflected in her painting. "Beanfield with Music for Molly" (1984) was a celebration of fertility, both that of nature and that of the artist herself. "Moonfield" (1986) evokes a poetic and spiritual landscape—a personal view of the universal preoccupation with moon-viewing. Her "Landscape of the Spirit" (1990) depicts draped white forms in an ambiguous, expressionistic landscape fashioned of silk, velvet, straw, and paint on linen. The use of three-dimensional additive materials and found objects has been a recurrent theme in Snyder's work for many years.

Inspired by several articles in the *Christian Science Monitor* on the exploitation of children, Snyder next embarked on a series of paintings, including "Boy in Afghanistan" (1988), "Small Brothers from Nicaragua" (1988), and "Morning Requiem (For the Children)" (1987–1988), that focused on the suffering of children around the world. With paintings such as "Weedfield with Music" (1990), Snyder returned to nature as a primary thematic source. Although her palette remained primarily dark, subsequent paintings tended once again to be more personal than political.

Rhonda Cooper

Bibliography

Alloway, Lawrence. "Art; Joan Snyder's New Paintings . . . ." *The Nation* (June 4, 1973): 733.

Dore, Ashton. *Joan Snyder.* Catalog Essay. Boston, Massachusetts: Nielsen Gallery, 1991.

Gill, Susan. "Painting from the Heart." *Art News* (April 1987).

Henry, Gerrit. "Joan Snyder: True Grit." *Art in America* (February 1986).

Herrera, Hayden. *Joan Snyder.* Catalog Essay. Neuberger Museum, State University of New York, College of Purchase, 1978, pp. 2–38.

———. *Joan Snyder Collects Joan Snyder.* Catalog Essay. California: Santa Barbara Contemporary Arts Forum, 1988, pp. 11–33.

Perl, Jed. "Houses, Fields, Gardens, Hills." *New Criterion* (February 1986).

Smith, Roberta. "Artwork that Strikes up Conversations with Viewers." *The New York Times* (April 1, 1988).

Snyder, Joan. "An untitled statement." *Studio International Journal of Modern Art* (July–August 1974).

Tucker, Marcia. "The Anatomy of a Stroke: Recent Paintings by Joan Snyder." *Artforum* (May 1971): 42–45.

Snyder, Kit-Yin

Born in China and raised in New York City, Kit-Yin Snyder is best known for her site-specific experimental sculpture. Snyder originally intended to pursue a career in architecture. She earned a Bachelor of Science degree in electrical engineering and a Master's degree in mathematics, before receiving her Master of Fine Arts degree in sculpture from Claremont College, California, in 1979. She taught ceramics at Swarthmore College, Pennsylvania, for many years before leaving the teaching field to devote herself to the creation of large-scale works for alternative and public spaces.

In 1979 Snyder originated her standard module of hand-made, transparent wire-mesh bricks. Interested in Greek and Roman classical ruins as sculpture, she began incorporating elements of architecture into her installations. Since 1979 Snyder has presented over twenty installations throughout the United States and Europe.

Funded by a National Endowment for the Arts (NEA) grant, Snyder produced her first outdoor installation, "Two Part Invention," in Bryant Park in 1981 during an artist-in-residency for the Public Art Fund in New York City. She created her largest work, "Córdoba," in 1983 at the City University of New York (CUNY) Graduate Center. The effect of direct light on the open-mesh structures lent an illusion of solidity to the airy work, challenging the viewer's perception of reality. By manipulating various light sources into her work Snyder suggests that our experience of the world is an illusion that can be easily manipulated. Snyder's "Hadrian's Retreat" at the Sculpture Center in New York City and "Hadrian's Improvisation," an outdoor installation at the Hudson River Museum in Yonkers, New York (both of 1984), incorporated reflecting pools that refer to the Roman emperor Hadrian's villa near Tivoli, Italy. Like the play of light on her wire-mesh structures, the ever-changing images in the reflecting pools remind the viewer of the elusive nature of reality.

In 1986 Snyder designed "Throne Room" as one of the sets for a production of "The Memory Theatre of Julio Camillo," produced by the Creation Company (through the auspices of Creative Time, Inc.) inside the anchorage of the Brooklyn Bridge. Snyder created her own production in a set/installation of Luigi Pirandello's *Cost è (Si Vi Pare) (Right You Are if You Think You Are)* with theatrical lighting and a voice-over: a theater setting without actors. Subsequent set/installations include "Enrico IV (Henry IV)" at the University Art Gallery at the State University of New York (SUNY), Stony Brook (1990), in which Snyder combined a theatrical stage setting with reflecting pools and a voice-over narration of Pirandello's play.

Snyder has received numerous awards, including a studio residency at P.S.1, Long Island City, New York (1980); National Endowment for the Arts (NEA) fellowships (1980, 1982, 1986); a Creative Artists Public Service (CAPS) fellowship for sculpture (1981); and a fellowship in sculpture from the New York Foundation for the Arts (1986, 1991). She has received awards for excellence in design for her installation in Margaret Mitchell Square, commissioned by the city of Atlanta, Georgia (1986); and an excellence in design award from the Art Commission of New York City for an installation in collaboration with Richard Haas for the White Street Detention Center (1989–1990).

Rhonda Cooper

Bibliography

Braff, Phyllis. "Links to Ecological Themes." *New York Times*, Long Island section (September 2, 1990).

Busch, Akiko. "Artists Who Make Architecture." *Metropolis* (August–September 1981).

Cooper, Rhonda. *Kit-Yin Snyder: Enrico IV*. Exhibition Catalog. University Art Gallery, State University of New York at Stony Brook, 1990.

Gordon, Alastair. "11 Artists 'Emerge' at Gallery in East Hampton: Collector's Choice of Emerging Artists—1990 and *Enrico IV* by Kit-Yin Snyder." *Newsday* (August 31, 1990).

Verre, Philip. *Shared Space*. Exhibition Catalog. The Bronx Museum of the Arts, 1983.

Sokolowski, Linda (1943–)

Born in Utica, New York, Linda Sokolowski studied at the Rhode Island School of Design, Providence, where she received her Bachelor of Fine Arts degree in 1965. Six years later she earned a Master of Fine Arts degree at the University of Iowa, Iowa City, where she studied with James Lechay and Mauricio Lasansky.

Sokolowski has held nine solo exhibitions between 1974 and 1991, six of which were at the Kraushaar Galleries, New York City. She also held solo shows at the State University of New York (SUNY) at Binghamton (1978); and Thayer Academy, Braintree, Massachusetts (1975). Her work has been invited to a host of group exhibitions throughout the United States, including the "30th Annual Hassam Fund Exhibition," American Academy and Institute of Arts and Letters, New York City (1978); "Annual Drawing and Small Sculpture Show," Ball State University, Muncie, Indiana (1977, 1978); Drake University, Des Moines, Iowa (1986); Hamilton College, Clinton, New York (1981); Randolph-Macon Woman's College, Lynchburg, Virginia (1984, 1990); "More Than Land or Sky . . . ," National Museum of American Art, Smithsonian Institution, Washington, D.C. (1981); "The 165th Annual Exhibition," National Academy of Design, New York City (1990); and others.

Sokolowski teaches at Harpur College, SUNY at Binghamton. She has received honors and awards for her work, including a Childe Hassam purchase award from the American Academy and Institute of Arts and Letters, New York City (1978); a purchase award from the Library of Congress, Washington, D.C. (1984); and research grants from SUNY, Binghamton (1979, 1990).

Sokolowski's works are in public, private, and corporate permanent collections, including Ball State University, Muncie, Indiana; SUNY at Potsdam; Portland Museum of Art, Maine; IBM, New York City; the University of Iowa, Iowa City; Oak Ridge Art Center, Tennessee; Portland Museum, Maine; and many others. "Sea Wall" (1991), is typical of Sokolowski's work: this collage evokes a sense of great magical space in a small format. She writes, ". . . the paper works rely more on independent cut-out shapes. These solo (or act), often as three-dimensional objects against washed grounds or as interactive characters on a stage."

Bibliography
Beckett, Wendy. *Contemporary Women Artists*. Universe Books, 1988.
Raynor, Vivien. "A Show Meant to Give Pleasure." *The New York Times* (July 16, 1989).
Who's Who in American Art. 19th edition. R.R. Bowker Co., 1991–1992.

Solomon, Rosalind (1930–)

Born in Highland Park, Illinois, the photographer Rosalind Solomon earned a Bachelor's degree in political science from Goucher College, Baltimore, Maryland (1951), and worked for the Experiment in International Living as director of the southern region (1965–1968). She began the study of photography independently in 1968, then studied privately with Lisette Model in New York City (1974–1976).

Recent solo exhibitions of Solomon's work were held in the United States and abroad, including "Rosalind Solomon: Disconnections," Instituto de Estudios Norteamericas, Barcelona, Spain (1992); "Rosalind Solomon," Photo Gallery International, Tokyo, Japan (1991); "Rosalind Solomon: Photos 1976–1987," a travelling show, Etherton Gallery, Tucson, Arizona. Other important exhibitions were held at the Museum of Modern Art (MoMA), New York City (1986); Museum Voor Volkenkunde, Rotterdam, the Netherlands (1988); "Rosalind Solomon: Earthrites," a travelling show, Musée de Photographie, Antwerp, Belgium (1988); "Portraits in the Time of AIDS," a travelling show, New York University, New York City (1988); and two travelling shows sponsored by the International Museum of Photography, George Eastman House, Rochester, New York: "Rosalind Solomon: Ritual Photographs 1975–1985," and "Rosalind Solomon: India"—both in 1982; and many others.

Solomon's photographs were invited to myriad group exhibitions in galleries and museums in such venues as Basel, Switzerland, to La Jolla, California; Oslo, Norway; Woodstock, New York; Kansas City, Kansas; Madrid, Spain; Paris, France; Houston, Texas; Tokyo, Japan, and Chatanooga, Tennessee. She has won honors and awards, including a Guggenheim Foundation fellowship (1979–1980); fellowships from the American Institute of Indian Studies (1981–1984) and the National Endowment for the Arts (NEA); and awards from Art Matters, Inc. (1988).

Visiting artist at universities and colleges throughout the United States, Solomon has executed many limited edition projects between 1973 and 1990, including books, photographs, memorabilia, installations, and found objects. Her work is represented in private, public, and corporate permanent collections, including the Museum of Modern Art (MoMA), and the Metropolitan Museum of Art—both in New York City; Bibliothèque Nationale, Paris, France; National Museum of American Art, and the Library of Congress—both in Washington, D.C.; Canadian Centre for Architecture, Montréal, Canada; Museo de Fotografía, Mexico City, Mexico; Israel Museum, Tel Aviv; Museum Voor Volkenkunde, Rotterdam, the Netherlands; Victoria & Albert Museum, London, England; and many others.

Bibliography
Grundberg, Andy. "Portraits Return in a New Perspective." *The New York Times* (June 26, 1988).
Novak, Ralph. "The Indomitable Spirit by Photographers + Friends United Against AIDS." *People Magazine* (April 1990).
"Portraits from the Planet." *Images Ink* (April 1990).
Sullivan, Connie. *Women Photographers*. Harry N. Abrams, 1990.

Sonneman, Eve (1946–)

Born in Chicago, Illinois, the photographer Eve Sonneman earned a Bachelor of Fine Arts degree from the University of Illinois, Champaign (1967), and, two years later, received a Master of Fine Arts degree from the University of New Mexico, Albuquerque. She has earned awards and honors, including a Boskop Foundation grant in the arts (1969); a grant from the Institute of Art and Urban Resources of New York (1977); a grant from the Polaroid Corporation for research in Polavision (1978); National Endowment for the Arts (NEA) fellowships (1971, 1978); and others.

Sonneman has been on the art faculty of a number of institutions, including her present post at the School of Visual Arts, Cooper Union College of Art and Architecture, and City University of New York (CUNY)—all in New York City; and Rice University, Houston, Texas. Representative examples of her work are in private and public permanent collections in the United States and abroad, such as the Bibliothéque Nationale, Paris, France; the Metropolitan Museum of Art, and the Museum of Modern Art (MoMA)—both in New York City; the National Gallery of Australia, Canberra; Art Institute of Chicago, Illinois; Center for Creative Photography, Tucson, Arizona; International Museum of Photography, George Eastman House, Rochester, New York; Menil Foundation, Houston, Texas; and many others.

Bibliography
Nuridsany, Michel. "Eve Sonneman: l'instant et le moment." *Le Figaro* (November 21, 1977).
Photographers in New York. Japan: Seibundo Shindosha, 1973.
Szarkowski, John. *Mirrors and Windows*. 1978.

Soreff, Helen

A native New Yorker, the painter Helen Soreff earned a Bachelor of Fine Arts degree at the Atlanta Art Institute, Georgia, where she was both a High Museum of Art scholar and a Beaux-Arts scholar (1952); the following year, Soreff took further work at the Art Students League, New York City. Still later, she studied at New York University, New York City, and at C.W. Post College, Long Island University, where she received a Master's degree (1976).

Soreff's work has been exhibited in solo and group exhibitions, including the Mercer Gallery (1977), Bertha Urdang Gallery (1977, 1978), Condeso-Lawler Gallery (1983), Clocktower and Graham Modern Gallery (1986), and "Lines of Vision," Blum Helman Gallery (1989)—all in New York City; Guild Hall Museum, East Hampton, New York (1987–1989); and many others. She has received awards and honors, including an Adolph Gottlieb Foundation grant (1986), and a fellowship from the New York Foundation for the Arts (1987). Her work is represented in private and public permanent collections.

Bibliography
Cyphers, Peggy. "Review." *Arts Magazine* (October 1989).
Frank, Peter. "Review." *Kunstforum* (January–February 1990).
Thompson, Walter. "Review." *Art in America* (November 1989).

Soto, Dolores (1869–c. 1964)

Born in Tulancingo, Hidalgo, Mexico, Dolores Soto was the favorite of José Maria Velasco in the Académia de Bellas Artes. In the 1891 exposition, Soto showed thirty-one paintings.

There is an extensive article written about her in *El Album de la Mujer* (June 17, 1888). She participated in the Columbian Exposition in Chicago, Illinois, and painted many large works. Soto worked primarily for herself, her friends, and her acquaintances.

Bibliography

Alvarez, José Rogelio, et al. *Enciclopedia de Mexico*. Secretaría de Educación Pública, 1987.

Spencer, Lilly Martin (1822–1902)

Born in Exeter, England, to a family who moved in 1830 to New York and then settled in Marietta, Ohio, the painter Lilly Martin Spencer spent her youth and had her first exhibition in Ohio in 1841. That autumn she carried her paintings to an exhibition in Cincinnati, Ohio, where she stayed for the next eight years.

Spencer took art lessons from John Insco Williams, and in 1844 she married Benjamin Rush Spencer, an English tailor, who lost his job the next year and fell ill. Once he recuperated he turned to preparing the canvases and frames for his wife's paintings and helped with domestic duties. Meanwhile, she maintained a studio in downtown Cincinnati. Although she exhibited and sold her paintings in Cincinnati, the lure of great patronage attracted her to New York City, just as it appealed to other artists at this time for the same reason. The Spencers moved to New York City in 1848, and, within two years, she was exhibiting at the National Academy of Design, New York City, where she took evening drawing classes and of which she was elected an honorary member. She continued to exhibit almost annually at the academy. *Sartain's Magazine* of 1849 took note of Spencer's arrival in New York City and wrote that the Art-Union had already purchased two of her paintings.

To cope with the expenses of a growing family the Spencers moved in 1858 to Newark, New Jersey, where Spencer painted, among other works, a life-size portrait of the landlord's children, "Children of Marcus L. Ward," Newark Museum. They moved again in 1879 to Highland, New York, overlooking the Hudson River. In 1900, ten years after her husband's death, Spencer returned to New York City.

Spencer's high-spirited genre paintings are quite anecdotal and frequently need their titles for the viewer to understand their full import: such as "Peeling Onions" (c. 1852, Memorial Art Gallery, University of Rochester) and "Kiss Me and You'll Kiss the 'Lasses" (1856, Brooklyn Museum). The figures are very realistically painted in bright, crisp colors. In addition to her sprightly genre scenes and portraits Spencer painted still lifes of fruits, luxuriantly displayed at the corner of a table.

Eleanor Tufts

Bibliography

Bolton-Smith, Robin, and William H. Truettner. *Lilly Martin Spencer: The Joys of Sentiment*. National Collection of Fine Arts, Smithsonian Institution Press, 1973.

Tufts, Eleanor. *American Women Artists, 1830–1930*. National Museum of Women in the Arts, 1987.

Spero, Nancy (1926–)

Nancy Spero's recent paintings show powerful, yet delicately-rendered, collaged figures of women that float freely in unconfined space. They are hand-printed on long paper scrolls that wrap around gallery walls. Her scrolls have a biting political edge, yet they simultaneously evoke an enigmatic inner resonance which establishes their kinship with ancient hieroglyphs that assume the mythological function of art. Like Egyptian tomb paintings, from which, in part, they are derived, they engage the viewer in a transformative process.

Born in Cleveland, Ohio, Spero studied at the School of the Art Institute of Chicago, Illinois, from 1945 to 1949 under the German Fauvist-expressionist painter Paul Wieghardt. Her early work was influenced by Oskar Kokoschka, Jean Dubuffet, and primitive artifacts in Chicago's Field Museum of Natural History. In 1951 she married Leon Golub, another Art Institute graduate who would become a well-known existentialist painter. By 1960 they had three sons. Alienated from the formalist tendencies of abstract expressionism which dominated the American art world during the 1950s and early 1960s, they lived largely in Italy and France. There, Spero began her "Black Paris Paintings" (1958–1966)—introspective, archetypal pictures of lovers, mothers, monsters, and prostitutes, executed in oil on canvas. They are murky, indistinct apparitions that emerge out of the unconscious night.

Spero and Golub returned to New York City in 1964, where they still share a studio divided down the middle. Although her work had been enthusiastically received in Paris, minimalism and pop art were being promoted in New York City, and her unfashionable pictures were ignored. In rebellion against the art world establishment, she rejected the traditional high-art medium of oil on canvas for the more fragile materials of gouache and ink on paper. Provoked by the irrational violence of the Vietnam War and frustrated by her artistic isolation, she began to paint raw, explosive, surrealistic visions of metamorphosing sexual, insectile, bombs, planes, and helicopters.

Spero's characteristic scrolling format evolved while she worked on the "Codex Artaud" series (1971–1972), which combines her own pictographic notations with fragments of tortured mystical poetry by Antonin Artaud—a French surrealist who advocated the use of nonrational ritual to alter the viewer's consciousness and disrupt conventional assumptions about reality. Spero identified with Artaud's determination to cross forbidden boundaries and with his perception of himself as a pariah. Because she felt that her woman's voice would not be heard, she adopted his anguished words as her own. But she became uncomfortable speaking through a male persona. By the mid-1970s she had read the theories of French feminists, such as Helene Cixous, who propose a feminine form of expression based upon the decentered rhythms of the female body. Spero's subsequent work concentrates exclusively on women as subject in a quest to discover a visual language that is an appropriate metaphor for female experience.

Spero has been involved in a number of feminist and anti-imperialist art groups over the past three decades, and her art reflects her political commitment. "Torture in Chile" (1974) was her first explicitly feminist work. It is based on graphic written accounts of women as political victims from Amnesty International files, presented in the context of a Mesopotamian myth about the torture and dismemberment of the goddess Tiamat. One of her most ambitious scrolls, "Notes on Women in Time" (1976–1979; twenty inches by 215 feet), analyzes patriarchal constructions of femininity by juxtaposing ninety-six quotations about women, taken primarily from the works of noted male intellectuals, with images of self-confident, vigorous women who exalt in their freedom from male-defined feminine roles.

Spero's work in the 1980s rarely includes writing, and much of it is colorful and celebratory. "Hera Totem" (1985), a tall and narrow vertical scroll, cites goddess imagery from diverse historical discourses to create a non-verbal icon that provides the contemporary feminist drive for the social empowerment of women with a mythological foundation. But the euphoria of these utopian visions of feminine transcendence is periodically qualified by apocalyptic images. "Mourning Woman/Irradiated" (1985), a somber, horizontal scroll, depicts women appropriated from both Western and non-Western contexts in weary and defeated poses. They are rendered in a smeared and broken style that suggests the painful disintegration of flesh. Spero's recent work is an optimistic embodiment of exhilarating possibilities that is haunted by a wary recognition of the fragility of dreams. Her art has been applauded in avant-garde circles, but it is not yet represented in the collection of any major American institution.

Marilyn Lincoln Board

Bibliography

"Dialogue: An Exchange of Ideas between Dena Shottenkirk and Nancy Spero." *Arts Magazine* (May 1987): 34–35.

King, Elaine. *Nancy Spero: The Black Paris Paintings*. Exhibition Catalog. Hewlett Gallery, Carnegie-Mellon University, 1985.

Kuspit, Donald. "From Existence to Essence." *Art in America* (January 1984): 86–94.

Miller, Lynn, and Sally Swenson. *Lives and Works: Talks with Women Artists*. Scarecrow Press, 1981.

Nancy Spero. Exhibition Catalog. Essays by Lisa Tickner and Jon Bird. London: Institute of Contemporary Arts, 1987.

Nancy Spero: Works since 1950. Exhibition Catalog. Essays by Dominique Nahas, Jo-Anna Isaak, Robert Storr, and Leon Golub. Syracuse, New York: Everson Museum of Art, 1987.

Robbins, Corinne. "Nancy Spero: 'Political' Artist of Poetry and the Nightmare." *The Feminist Art Journal* (Spring 1975): 19–22, 48.

Sperry, Ann

Born in the Bronx, New York, the sculptor Ann Sperry earned a Bachelor's degree at Sarah Lawrence College, Bronxville, New York, where she studied with Theodore Roszak and William Rubin. In addition to the polychromed, welded steel sculpture which secured her reputation, Sperry designed a 334-foot long fence and gate commissioned by the Seattle Arts Commission, Washington (1988) and provided a functional uplift to the headquarters of the New England Telephone Company, Boston, Massachusetts (1990–1992). During the past decade, she also designed artist's books, furniture, and sets and costumes for contemporary ballet and opera.

Sperry has held simultaneous solo exhibitions in museums and galleries in 1992, including Timothy Brown Fine Arts, Aspen, Colorado; Sapporo International Exchange Plaza Gallery, Sapporo, Japan; and A.I.R. Gallery, New York City. She has offered indoor and outdoor installations on sites and in galleries, such as Aspen Art Park, Colorado (1991); Jayne Baum Gallery, New York City (1988); American Federation of Architects, Washington, D.C. (1985); and the College Art Association meeting in New Orleans, Louisiana (1980); among others. Sperry has also held one-person shows at the Lerner-Heller Gallery, New York City (1980, 1982); Benson Gallery, Bridgehampton, New York (1970, 1972, 1975); Jacqueline Anhalt Gallery, Los Angeles, California (1970, 1972); and many others. Her work has been invited to myriad group shows from New York City to Berlin, Germany; Palo Alto, California; Verona, Italy; Tesuke, New Mexico; and Westport, Connecticut.

In local, regional, national and international venues and institutions, Sperry has been a panelist, teacher, guest artist, lecturer, and writer; she edited *Helicon Nine* magazine; and is also a member of the Public Art Commission, Riverside South, and board member of Volunteer Lawyers for the Arts—all in New York City. Her work is represented in private, public, and corporate permanent collections in the United States and abroad, including Fondation Deutsch, Lausanne, Switzerland; Everson Museum of Art, Syracuse, New York; Brandeis University, Waltham, Massachusetts; Tel Aviv Museum, Israel; Library of Congress, Washington, D.C.; Bibliothèque Nationale, Paris, France; New York Public Library, New York City; Atlantic Richfield, Los Angeles, California; and more.

Bibliography

Floria, David, and Annette Carlozzi. *Sculpture/Aspen '88*. A Catalog. Aspen Art Museum, 1988.

Glower, Ron. "Seeking Allusions to Otherness." *Artweek* (March 29, 1988).

Kingsley, April, and John Perreault. *Ann Sperry: New Work/A Twelve-Year Survey*. A Catalog. New York: Newhouse Gallery, 1987.

"Review." *Hokkai Times*. Sapporo, Japan (July 15, 1992).

Squire, Maud Hunt (1873–c. 1955)

Born in Cincinnati, Ohio, the painter/printmaker Maud Hunt Squire studied at the art academy in her native city (1894–1898). She developed a friendship with Ethel Mars, a fellow student, that lasted throughout their lives.

Squire and Mars lived in Paris, France, from 1903 until 1915, when the start of World War I forced them to return to the United States. They moved to Provincetown, Massachusetts, and both were active printmakers in the burgeoning art scene. Some years later they retraced their steps to France and spent the rest of their days in Vence and in European travel.

A member of the Société des Dessinateurs et des Humoristes in Paris, France, Squire illustrated children's books, and exhibited work in the Pan-Pacific International Exposition, San Francisco, California (1915), as well as Provincetown, Massachusetts, Paris, France, and other venues. Her work is represented in private and public permanent collections.

Bibliography

Dunford, Penny. *Biographical Dictionary of Women Artists in Europe and America since 1850*. University of Pennsylvania Press, 1989.

Flint, Janet. *Provincetown Printers*. National Museum of American Art, 1983.

Stack, Gael (1941–)

Born in Chicago, Illinois, the painter Gael Stack earned a Bachelor of Fine Arts degree at the University of Illinois, Champaign (1970), and, two years later, received a Master of Fine Arts degree from Southern Illinois University, Carbondale.

Stack has held solo exhibitions in galleries and art centers throughout the United States, including the Mitchell Gallery, Carbondale (1972); Graphics Gallery, San Francisco, California (1974); Beitzel Fine Arts, New York City (1988); Meredith Long Gallery, Houston (1975–1981), Janie C. Lee Gallery, Houston (1983, 1985, 1987, 1989), "Gael Stack: A Survey 1974–1989," University of Houston and Dallas Museum of Art (1989), "Recent Paintings," Moody Gallery, Houston (1990–1992), and "Gael Stack: Revealing Clues," Amarillo Art Center (1992)—all in Texas; and others. Her work has been invited to myriad group exhibitions in the United States and abroad—from Zurich, Switzerland, to Aspen, Colorado; Paris, France; Texas City, Texas; Frankfurt, Germany; Muncie, Indiana; San Miguel de Allende, Mexico; Oslo, Norway; and New York City.

Stack's work is represented in distinguished private and public permanent collections, including the Guggenheim Museum, New York City; Yale University, New Haven, Connecticut; Museum of Fine Arts, Houston; the Menil Collection, Houston; Dallas Museum of Fine Art; and San Antonio Museum of Art—all in Texas; and others.

Bibliography
Chadwick, Susan. "Solo Exhibition at Moody Gallery." *The Houston Post* (April 2, 1990): 3–13.
Gambrell, Jamey. "Art Capital of the Third Coast." *Art in America* (April 1987): 186–202.
Hill, Ed, and Suzanne Bloom. "Gael Stack." *Artforum* (March 1986).
Johnson, Patricia C. "Flashes of Insight." *Houston Chronicle* (February 22, 1992): D1, 5.

Staffel, Doris (1921–)

A painter and teacher who has had a wide influence on a large number of young artists and students, Doris Staffel has created a strong place for herself in the cultural world of Philadelphia, Pennsylvania. In her work and in her questioning and persuasive teaching she has explored many of the tenets of modernism, and she has continuously striven for those forms that most clearly and forcefully expressed her knowledge and her beliefs. Staffel's work has recently shifted from a dominantly symbolic format to a powerful figurative one. Long known for both her drawing and her painting, she has concentrated on drawing since the late 1980s.

Staffel was educated at Tyler School of Art, Temple University, Philadelphia, Pennsylvania, where she received a Bachelor of Science degree and a Bachelor of Fine Arts degree in 1944; Iowa University, Iowa City, where she received a Master of Arts degree in 1946; and at the Naropa Institute in Boulder, Colorado, where she studied Buddhist iconography in 1975. She has taught in Pennsylvania at the Philadelphia Museum of Art, where she was a staff lecturer from 1954 to 1958 and at the University of the Arts (formerly the Philadelphia College of Art) from 1958 to 1991.

Staffel has had numerous one-person shows in the United States and abroad and has participated in many group shows, the two most recent being a four-person exhibition at the Moore College of Art, Philadelphia, Pennsylvania, in 1990 and a drawing show at the University of Indiana, Bloomington, in 1988. Her work is in many collections—public and private.

Larry Day

Bibliography
Scott, William P. "Doris Staffel at Jessica Berwind Gallery." *Art in America* Vol. 81 (November 1993): 134–35.
Staffel, D. "Untitled." *Art in America*. Vol. 73 (April 1985): 78.
Who's Who in American Art. 20th ed. R.R. Bowker Co., 1993–1994.

Stanton, Elizabeth Cady (1894–)

A native New Yorker, the painter Elizabeth Cady Stanton studied with several well-known teachers and painters, including Cecilia Beaux, George Bridgman, F. Luis Mora, and Albert Sterner. She is a member of the American Federation of Arts, the Barnard Club, the National Association of Women Painters and Sculptors, and the Tiffany Foundation—all in New York City. Her work is represented in private and public permanent collections.

Bibliography
American Art Annual. Vol. 28. American Federation of Arts, 1932.
Fielding, Mantle. *Dictionary of American Painters, Sculptors, and Engravers*. Modern Books and Crafts, 1974.
Who's Who in American Art. Vol. 8. American Federation of Arts, 1962.

Stanton, Lucy May (1875–1931)

Born in Atlanta, Georgia, Lucy May Stanton painted small watercolor portraits on ivory. She was introduced to painting at the age of seven, when oil paints were given to her and she studied with a French artist, Madame Seato, in New Orleans, Louisiana, where her father's business took the family in the winter. She also studied painting at Southern Female Seminary in La Grange, Georgia, and painted watercolors in Venice, Italy, while touring Europe with her father in 1889–1890. After graduation from Southern Baptist College for Women, Walnut Ridge, Arkansas, in 1895, she stayed for another year assisting her painting teacher, and she also began her professional career by painting three miniature portraits of the soprano, Adelina Patti. In 1896 she left for three years of study in Paris, France: first privately with Augustus Koopman, then at the Académie de la Grande Chaumière, plus miniature painting with Virginia Reynolds and anatomy at the Sorbonne.

During the first decade of the twentieth century she opened studios in several different cities, including Atlanta, Georgia; New York City; Los Angeles, California; and Paris, France. In the next decade her studios were in Athens, Georgia; North Carolina; New York City; and Boston, Massachusetts.

From 1899 to 1931 she exhibited more than 100 miniatures at the Pennsylvania Society of Miniature Painters as well as a total of ninety-three works (mostly miniatures) at the Pennsylvania Academy of Fine Arts—both in Philadelphia. She also exhibited at the Royal Society of Miniaturists in London, England, in 1914 and at the Panama-Pacific International Exposition in San Francisco, California, in 1915. Among her awards were a blue ribbon at the Paris Salon, France, of 1906 and a medal of honor at the Concord Art Association, Massachusetts, in 1923. She had solo exhibitions at galleries in New York City; Boston, Massachusetts; Baltimore, Maryland; and New Orleans, Louisiana.

Among her works—primarily Southern subjects—are "Joel Chandler Harris" (1912, National Portrait Gallery), "Congressman Howell Cobb" (1912, U.S. Capitol), and "North Carolina Mountain Woman" (c. 1913–1915, Metropolitan Museum of Art).

Eleanor Tufts

Bibliography
Forbes, W. Stanton. *Lucy M. Stanton, Artist.* Emory University, 1975.
Tufts, Eleanor. *American Women Artists, 1830–1930.* National Museum of Women in the Arts, 1987.

Stathacos, Chrysanne (1951–)

Born in Buffalo, New York, Chrysanne Stathacos spent twelve years in Canada and is an American/Canadian citizen. She received her Bachelor of Fine Arts degree at York University, Toronto, Canada, after studies at the Cleveland Institute of Arts, Ohio. Stathacos's work has been included in numerous solo and group exhibitions, including "Monumenta" at YYZ, Toronto; "O Kromazone" at the Institute Unzeit in West Berlin, Germany; solo exhibitions at Mercer Union, Toronto; the Burchfield Art Center, Buffalo, New York; as well as group exhibitions at the White Columns ("Lyric") and Amy Lipton Gallery ("The New Metaphysics") in New York City.

Early work by Stathacos consisted of large drawings and mixed-media figurative work on canvas constructed with fluorescent oil sticks, paints, bits of metal, and plaster scraps. Metaphysical and cosmological interests continue from these early works into later pieces by Stathacos in which she uses innovative printmaking methods. She prints objects found in nature—such as leaves, flowers, and hair—directly onto the etching press allowing the objects to "trace their own impressions," without the interference of the observations of the artist. In this way Stathacos feels that she directly participates in nature's process in the hopes of finding a unifying pattern that is the basis of reality.

Stathacos has curated various exhibitions, including "Sex and Language" for Garnet Press Gallery, Toronto, and "The Abortion Project" for Artists' Space and Simon Watson Gallery in New York City. Her work is in the collections of the Albright-Knox Art Gallery, Buffalo, and Rochester Memorial Art Gallery—both in New York; the Art Gallery of Hamilton, Ontario; among others.

Linda Jansma

Bibliography
Holubizky, Ihor. "Chrysanne Stathacos." *Arts Magazine* (November 1991).
Ouroborours. Buffalo, New York: Burchfield Arts Center, n.d.

Steele, Lisa (1947–)

Born in Kansas City, Missouri, Lisa Steele came to Canada in 1968 with no formal art education—though she did attend the University of Missouri, Columbia—making her first videotape production in 1972. Since then she has shown across Canada, the United States, South America, and Europe. In 1980 she represented Canada at the Venice Video Biennale, Italy, and in 1989 she was given a joint retrospective at the Art Gallery of Ontario, Toronto.

Steele's works, such as *The Gloria Tapes* (1979–1980), explore the representation of social and autobiographical issues as experienced by women, yet her technique of direct storytelling, in which the artist often plays the protagonist, draws the viewer into the narrative in more or less the same manner as conventional film. The result draws attention to the media complacency of the beholder and complicity in the subjugation that such media imply. In keeping with these meditations on what it is to be a woman—the object of another's gaze—Steele is an active member of two outspoken groups called Film and Video Against Censorship and Feminists Against Censorship, which made something of a stir in the middle-1980s. Her basic argument is that the objectivization of women in advertising is every bit as dangerous as that in pornography, and that eliminating only the latter effectively destroys only a symptom of a social problem that remains untouched.

Steele is an active social commentator, a teacher at the Ontario College of Art, Toronto, and a prime mover in the development of a healthy artists' video community in Canada through such centers as V/Tape. In 1985 she was honored with the first prize at the Vienna Video Biennal, Italy, for a collaboration with Kim Tomczak.

Robert J. Belton (with Lana Pitkin)

Bibliography
Bailey, Cameron. "Lisa Steele and Kim Tomczak." *Now* 9:10 (November 9–15, 1989): 20.
Robertson, Clive. "Lisa Steele: The Recent Tapes." *Centerfold* (June–July 1979): 248–54.
Steele, Lisa. "Gendering in the Mass Media." *Women against Censorship.* Ed. V. Burstyn. Douglas and McIntyre, 1985.

Stein, Sandy (1946–)

Born in Dallas, Texas, the sculptor Sandy Stein, after two years of premedical training in the mid-1960s, earned a Bachelor of Fine Arts degree in sculpture from the University of Texas at Dallas (1979); did further study in sculpture at Bethany College, Lindborg, Kansas (1981), and at the American Academy of Paros, Greece (1982). Two years later she travelled to France and Spain to engage in independent study.

Stein has held solo exhibitions in museums and galleries from Dallas, Texas, to Athens, Greece, and has had her work included in group shows throughout the Southwest, but particularly in her native state since the late 1970s. Examples of her rugged stone sculptures and work in other materials are represented in private, public, and corporate permanent collections, including the Dallas Museum of Art, the collection of the city of Dallas, and San Antonio Art Institute—all in Texas; and many others.

Bibliography
Annual Delta Art Exhibition. Little Rock: Arkansas Art Center, 1979.
Ennis, Michael. "Public Gestures." *Texas Monthly* (May 1985): 172, 174–75.
Fifth Texas Sculpture Symposium. Dallas: Connemara Conservancy, 1985.
Watson-Jones, Virginia. *Contemporary American Women Sculptors.* Oryx Press, 1986.

Steinhouse, Tobie (1925–)

Born in Montréal, Québec, Canada, the painter/printmaker Tobie Steinhouse studied at Sir George Williams University (now Concordia University) in her native city; won a scholarship to the Art Students League, New York City, where she studied with Morris Kantor and Harry Sternberg (1946–1947); l'École des Beaux-Arts, Paris, France, and continued further study and painting with Arpad Szenes (1948–1957). She also created intaglio prints under the aegis of Stanley William Hayter at Atelier 17, Paris, France (1961–1962). Earlier, during World War II, Steinhouse did engineering drafting and illustrated a manual for the Royal Canadian Air Force.

Winner of awards and honors, Steinhouse has held solo exhibitions in museums and galleries in Canada and abroad. She has had her work included in prestigious group exhibitions, such as the international printmaking biennials in Santiago, Chile; Bradford, England; Menton, France; and many others. She has published numerous portfolios of color etchings and other intaglio works, and is represented in private and public permanent collections, including Confederation Art Gallery, Charlottetown, Prince Edward Island; the External Affairs Ministry of Canada, Moscow Embassy, Russia; McMichael Conservancy Collection, Kleinburg, Ontario; Montréal Museum of Fine Arts, Québec; National Gallery of Canada, Ottawa; and others.

Bibliography
Nixon, Virginia. "Tobie Steinhouse: Songes et lumiere." *Vie des arts* 67 (Summer 1972): 29–31, 86–87.
Who's Who in American Art. 15th ed. R.R. Bowker Co., 1982.

Steinke, Bettina (1913–)

Portrait painter Bettina Steinke, daughter of "Jolly Bill" Steinke of national radio fame, was born in Biddeford, Maine, and enrolled in the Fawcett Art School, Newark, New Jersey, after graduation from high school. She then attended Cooper Union and the Phoenix Art School—both in New York City—where she decided to devote herself to portraiture.

Steinke's first commission in 1937—painting murals in the Children's Studio of the National Broadcasting Company—included a portrait of "Dr. Walter Damrosch" at the piano. NBC hired her as resident artist to make sketches of its celebrities, such as "Fred Allen," "Kate Smith," "Rudy Vallee," and others, and the broadcasting company published a souvenir book of the NBC Symphony Orchestra that included 100 of her charcoal portraits of Arturo Toscanini and the individual players.

Steinke left NBC in 1939 to set up her own studio. In 1940, the American Association of Composers, Authors and Publishers (ASCAP) commissioned her to make portraits of some of its member musicians and composers, including "Jerome Kern." Other commercial commissions followed and, during World War II years, she painted portraits not only of "President Franklin D. Roosevelt," "General Douglas MacArthur," and "General Dwight D. Eisenhower," but sketched enlisted men and the wounded in hospitals.

In 1946 Steinke married photo-journalist Don Blair and for ten years they travelled South and Central America and the Arctic photographing and sketching for such clients as Standard Oil of New Jersey and Hudson's Bay Company. In 1956 they settled in Taos, New Mexico, where Steinke began genre painting in addition to commissioned portraits. They moved to Santa Fe, New Mexico, in 1970. Steinke divides her time between commissioned portraits of chief executive officers, bankers, and the renowned, and genre painting that has won numerous awards. Her oil painting entitled "Father and Daughter at the Crow Fair" was awarded the Prix de West in 1978 by the National Cowboy Hall of Fame and Western Heritage Center, Oklahoma City, Oklahoma, at the annual exhibition of the National Academy of Western Art.

Steinke works in oil, pastel, and charcoal. Her paintings are included in the permanent collections of the Gilcrease Museum, Tulsa, and National Cowboy Hall of Fame and Western Heritage Center, Oklahoma City—both in Oklahoma; Frye Museum, Seattle, Washington; Indianapolis Museum of Art, Indiana; Albuquerque Museum, New Mexico; and hundreds of other public and private collections. Her latest retrospective was held at the Gilcrease Museum, Tulsa, Oklahoma, in May 1987. She is a founding member of the National Academy of Western Art.

Barbara Kramer

Bibliography
Hedgpeth, Don. *Bettina: Portraying Life in Art.* Northland Press, 1978.
Who's Who in American Art. 15th ed. R.R. Bowker Co., 1982.

Steir, Pat (1940–)

A native of Newark, New Jersey, Pat Steir (born Iris Patricia Sukoneck) grew up in a New Jersey suburb of Philadelphia. As a youth she studied music, poetry, art, and philosophy. From 1956 until 1962 she attended Boston University, Massachusetts, and the Pratt Institute, Brooklyn, New York, where she studied etching and lithography and earned a Bachelor of Fine Arts degree in 1961. While at Pratt Institute, Steir also worked with Philip Guston and Richard Lindner. Her paintings of the 1960s show Lindner's influence. Most of these early paintings were destroyed by the end of that decade. After completing her formal education she continued painting but supported herself by working as a book designer and art director for Harper & Row Publishers in New York City.

In 1970 Steir began to exhibit what she considers her first mature work. The paintings and drawings she produced between 1970 and 1975 express both her literary and aesthetic aspirations. In this body of work words and images come together on otherwise blank canvases. Utilizing a linear approach these works reflect Steir's reassessment of her personal imagery. She simply marked out with a large "X" anything she wished to change. Composed of verbal and visual images, these works are autobiographical, consisting of poetic fragments of her personal history and ideas. For one entire year she produced only drawings. In 1975 and 1976 Steir abandoned earlier ambitious projects and focused on the study of details in language in her work. She examined the differences between words and images—their graphic fundamentals—and presented isolated words and images as "icons." In 1973 she produced her first color lithographs for Landfall Press in Chicago, Illinois.

Since 1977, with few exceptions, Steir has limited her work to paintings and prints, often one based upon the other. For example, the oil and canvas work, "Form, Illusion, Myth: Abstraction, Belief, Desire" (1981), was preceded by the etching of the same year, "Abstraction, Belief, Desire" (eleven plates grouped as a triptych). The latter was made at Crown Point Press, Oakland, California, where she started working in 1976. Prints—especially monotypes—became her outlet for drawing. In her 1985 series "After Turner I" and "After Turner II," she combines etching with monotype to achieve her final product. That same year, at the Museum of Modern Art (MoMA) in New York City, "New Work on Paper III" introduced some of these works. In 1982 Steir went to Japan twice with Crown Point Press to produce woodcuts.

Despite their random appearance Steir's gestural marks and images are arranged logically—often placed within a grid pattern or structured by a central square or rectangular form—intensifying the dichotomy of order and disorder. "The Breughel Series (A Vanitas of Styles)" of 1982–1984, a sixty-four-panel work, points out a series of art historical vignettes through which is illustrated the "tension" of visual stimulation throughout (art) historical periods. Her iconography, steeped in the symbolism associated with the theories of Carl Jung in addition to her own art historical studies, is portrayed through elements such as animals, body parts, flowers, and landscape. Words and various scribbles, diagrams, and symbolic marks correspond to the personalized pictorial images or comment on communication itself (as in her seven print series "The Burial Mound Series," 1976).

While the framework of Steir's art is the autobiographical visualization of images, she consciously encompasses them within the larger history of which art history is a part. With her latest paintings ("Waterfall of the Fundiments," 1990), Steir returns again to nature. The layering techniques continue, this time with a black-and-white palette. Instead of written and pictorial images, here the use of paint drips allude more to her abstract expressionist roots.

Steir has had many individual exhibitions in the United States and in Europe: her first solo show was at the Terry Dintenfass Gallery in New York City in 1964 and in 1971 she began annual one-woman exhibitions in that city. She has received grants from the National Endowment for the Arts (NEA) and in 1982 was awarded a Guggenheim Foundation fellowship.

Adeline Lee Karpiscak

Bibliography

Broun, Elizabeth. *Form Illusion Myth, Prints and Drawings of Pat Steir.* Helen Foresman Spencer Museum of Art, University of Kansas, 1983.

Castle, Ted. "Pat Steir and the Science of the Admirable." *Artforum* 20 (May 1982): 47–55.

Gardner, Paul. "Pat Steir: Seeing through the Eyes of Others." *ArtNews* 84 (November 1985): 80–88.

New Work on Paper III. Essay by Bernice Rose. New York: Museum of Modern Art, 1985.

Pat Steir, Etchings and Paintings. Crown Point Gallery, 1981.

Plous, Phyllis. *Contemporary Drawing/New York.* Santa Barbara: University of California Art Museum, 1978.

Ratcliff, Carter. *Pat Steir Paintings.* Harry N. Abrams, 1986.

Solomon, Elke M. *Recent Drawings: William Allan, James Bishop, Vija Celmins, Brice Marden, Jim Nutt, Alan Saret, Pat Steir, Richard Tuttle.* American Federation of the Arts, 1975.

Willi, Juliane, et al. *Pat Steir: Prints 1976–1988.* Geneva: Cabinet des Estampes, Musée d'Art et d'Histoire; London: Tate Gallery, 1988.

Stephens, Alice Barber (1858–1932)

One of the most successful illustrators of the late nineteenth century, Alice Barber Stephens was also a painter, teacher, wood-engraver, photographer, wife, and mother. She was born on a farm near Salem, New Jersey, and, when the family moved to Philadelphia, Pennsylvania, she completed her public school education there. By 1873 she was enrolled as a full-time student at the Philadelphia School of Design for Women, Pennsylvania, where she learned wood-engraving. Also at that time her illustrations began to appear in *Scribner's Monthly*. In the fall of 1876 she entered the Pennsylvania Academy of Fine Arts, Philadelphia, and studied with Thomas Eakins. Upon graduation in 1880 she became a professional illustrator; her works appeared in *Harper's*, *Century*, *Cosmopolitan*, *Collier's*, *McClure's*, and *Frank Leslie's Weekly*. She also offered classes in her Philadelphia studio. In 1886–1887 she was in Paris, France, studying at the Académie Julian and Académie Colarossi. She exhibited a pastel and an engraving at the Paris Salon of 1887, France, and she also sketched in

Italy. On her return to the United States she became a leading illustrator, contributing regularly to the *Ladies Home Journal*.

From 1883 to 1893 Stehpens taught life classes at the Philadelphia School of Design and exhibited oil paintings at the Pennsylvania Academy of Fine Arts annually from 1884 through 1890, winning the prize of best painting by a resident woman artist for her "Portrait of a Little Boy" (1890). In June 1890 she married Charles Hallowell Stephens, a former classmate in the Pennsylvania Academy of Fine Arts who was then teaching there. She continued to paint, signing her illustrations with her married name. A change occurred in her work in the 1890s when half-tone reproduction processes enabled her to add color to her illustrations. Her six illustrations depicting women in contemporary settings (including "The Woman in Business," "The Dinner Party," and others) in the *Ladies Home Journal* of 1897 exemplify her particularly painterly, stylist compositions. In 1897 she cofounded with Emily Sartain the Plastic Club, in Philadelphia, Pennsylvania—the oldest art club for women in continuous existence in the United States; the next year she had an exhibition of eighty of her works there. Among the many books she illustrated are Nathaniel Hawthorne's *The Marble Faun* (1900), Louisa May Alcott's *Little Women* (1902), and Kate Douglas Wiggin's *Mother Carey's Chickens* (1911).

Eleanor Tufts

Bibliography

Brown, Ann Barton. *Alice Barber Stephens, A Pioneer Woman Illustrator.* Brandywine River Museum, 1984.

Tufts, Eleanor. *American Women Artists, 1830–1930.* National Museum of Women in the Arts, 1987.

Stephenson, Susanne G. (1935–)

Born in Canton, Ohio, the ceramist Susanne G. Stephenson earned a Bachelor of Fine Arts degree at Carnegie-Mellon University, Pittsburgh, Pennsylvania (1957), and, three years later, received a Master of Fine Arts degree from the Cranbrook Academy of Art, Bloomfield Hills, Michigan.

Stephenson has held many solo exhibitions in galleries and museums, including Collectors Gallery, Kalamazoo, Michigan (1967); Canton Art Institute, Ohio (1972); Habitat Gallery, Dearborn (1973), Hackley Art Museum, Muskegon (1975), Midland Center for the Arts (1977), Kidd Gallery, Birmingham (1981)—all in Michigan; Garth Clark Gallery, Los Angeles, California (1984, 1987, 1990); Carnegie Institute, Pittsburgh, Pennsylvania (1985); Martha Schneider Gallery, Highland Park, Illinois (1986, 1988); Eastern Michigan University, Ypsilanti (1989); Schneider-Bluhm-Loeb Gallery, Chicago, Illinois (1991); and others. Her work has been invited to many group exhibitions in the United States and abroad—from Fukuoka, Japan, to Camden, New Jersey; the Bronx, New York; Faenza, Italy; London, England; Los Angeles, California; Brussels, Belgium; Tempe, Arizona; and Auckland, New Zealand; among others.

Professor of art at Eastern Michigan University, Ypsilanti, since 1963, Stephenson has also taught at the University of Michigan, Ann Arbor (1960). Her work has garnered more than fifteen ceramic and designer-craftsmen awards, including a Michigan Foundation for the Arts award (1985), an Arts-Midwest regional visual arts fellowship and a Michigan Council for the Arts Creative Artists Public Service (CAPS) grant (1987–1988). Her work is represented in private, public, and corporate permanent collections, including the Butler Art Institute, Youngstown, Ohio; Museum of Contemporary Craft, New York City; State

University of New York (SUNY) at Fredonia; Arizona State University, Tempe; El Paso Museum of Art, Texas; Victoria & Albert Museum, London, England; Plains Museum of Art, Morehead, Minnesota; Burroughs Corporation, Detroit, Michigan; and many others.

Bibliography

Clark, Garth. *American Potters: The Work of Twenty Modern Masters.* Watson-Guptill, 1981.

Finkel, Marilyn. "Susanne Stephenson." *Craft Horizons* 37:6 (December 1977): 69–70.

Koplos, Janet. "Alterations—The Ceramics of Susanne Stephenson." *American Crafts* 1: (1983).

Who's Who in American Art. 19th ed. R.R. Bowker Co., 1991–1992.

Sterbak, Jana (1955–)

A Czech-born Canadian sculptor and installation artist based in Montréal, Québec, Canada, Jana Sterbak is internationally recognized for her works centering on the female body as the site of certain social and cultural manifestations. Sterbak finds the label "feminist" too confining a description of her practice. Her ironic, often humorous outlook is informed as much by her witnessing the aftermath of the "Prague Spring," as by feminist cultural theory and studies in the history of art. Works such as "Seduction Couch" (1986), a Récamier-style, audibly electrostatically charged steel chaise, and "Bed Room" (1987), a series of beds with pillowcases embroidered with slogans connoting the psycho-pathology of "normal" sexual relations, metaphorically equate personal repression with social oppression.

Other frequently exhibited works of Sterbak's have been described as "Clothes for an Alienated Subject." These include "I Want You To Feel the Way I Do . . ." (1984–1985), a free-standing dress of live, uninsulated wire with wall-projected text, and "Vanitas—Flesh Dress for Albino Anorexic" (1988), a chemise sewn together from flank steak which is either worn by a model (performed) or suspended on a dressmaker's dummy. Such requiems for romance, in which the body is excruciatingly present only in absentia, appeal through the senses to a constellation of social and intellectual issues surrounding women's oppression. Sterbak's art poses questions about the boundary between the inert and the living, about social persuasion and individual identity, and ultimately about freedom and control.

Sterbak has participated in several group exhibitions that explore the social construction of the self and the power relations embedded in representation. Among them are "The Impossible Self," Winnipeg Art Gallery (1988), and "Group Material," Dia Foundation, New York City (1988). The National Gallery of Canada, Ottawa, mounted a ten-year survey of her work in 1991.

Ingrid Jenkner

Bibliography

Andreae, Janice. "Jana Sterbak." *Parachute* 49 (December 1987–February 1988): 29.

Greenberg, Reesa. "Jana Sterbak." *C Magazine* 16 (December 1987): 50–53.

Nemiroff, Diana. *Canadian Biennial of Contemporary Art.* Exhibition Catalog. Ottawa: National Gallery of Canada, 1989.

———, and Milena Kalinsokova. *Jana Sterbak: States of Being.* Exhibition Catalog. Ottawa: National Gallery of Canada, 1991.

Sterbak, Jana. "Malevolent Heart (Gift)." *Parachute* (September–November 1982): 29.

Sterne, Hedda (Lindenberg) (1916–)

Best known for being the only woman among the New York School artists photographed as "The Irascibles" in 1950, Hedda (Lindenberg) Sterne has painted in a variety of styles during her long career.

Born in Bucharest, Rumania, by the age of eleven Sterne was fluent in English, French, and German, as well as her native Rumanian. From 1932 to 1934 she studied art history and philosophy at Bucharest University. Leaving the university before receiving a degree, she travelled to Vienna, Austria, and Paris, France, to study art. She was introduced to the surrealist circle by Victor Brauner, a family friend, and in 1938 she exhibited in the Paris Salon des Surindépendants, France. That same year, she married Ben Sterne.

Sterne arrived in the United States in 1941—one of the artist-refugees fleeing the war in Europe. Because of her familiarity with the surrealist artists she gravitated to Peggy Guggenheim's Art of This Century Gallery in New York City. There her work came to the attention of Betty Parsons, who, in the fall of 1943, presented Sterne's first solo exhibition in the United States, beginning an association between dealer and artist that continued for almost four decades.

Unlike many artist-refugees of the World War II era, whose stays in the United States were temporary, Sterne chose to remain, becoming a citizen in 1944. In that same year she divorced Sterne and subsequently married artist and cartoonist Saul Steinberg, a fellow Rumanian whom she had met in New York City.

In the late 1940s and 1950s Sterne's work was dominated by machine imagery. In these paintings surrealist-inspired anthropomorphized machines were gradually replaced by more abstract forms which evoked a machine-powered, man-made environment through the curves of a freeway overpass or the patterns formed by the girders of a skyscraper.

Nina Lean's famous photograph of "The Irascibles" documents Sterne's link to the New York School; however, as with the other women associated with abstract expressionists, Sterne never enjoyed the fame achieved by her male colleagues. While she shared those artists' belief in the importance of the process of painting, she never settled into the personalized mark-making typical of abstract expressionism.

It has been noted that there is little distinction between drawing and painting for Sterne—a characteristic especially evident in the portraits she has produced throughout her career. The late 1960s and 1970s represented a period of experimentation for Sterne. Intense, surrealistic studies of lettuce (1967) gave way to a series of generic faces called "Everyone" (1970). "Diary, June–October 1976" captured the rhythms of the artist's life through the pattern of text written in small squares with the line running horizontally one day and vertically the next. In the early 1980s a series of paintings of geometric forms have allowed Sterne to explore structure and space.

Paula Wisotzki

Bibliography

Hedda Sterne: Forty Years. New York: Queens Museum, 1985.

Hedda Sterne Retrospective. New Jersey: Montclair Art Museum, 1977.

Rubinstein, Charlotte Streifer. *American Women Artists: From Early Indian Times to the Present.* Avon, 1982, pp. 275–76.

Sterne, Hedda. "From Studio to Gallery." *Arts Digest* 29 (October 15, 1954): 4.

Sterrenburg, Joan (1941–)

A professor of fine arts at Indiana University, Bloomington, Joan Sterrenburg began as a textile artist and began papermaking in the mid-1970s. Her childhood experiences watching quiltmaking and rugmaking were formative. She was educated at the University of Wisconsin, Madison, where she received a Bachelor of Arts degree (1963); Stanford University, California, where she worked towards a Master of Arts degree (1964); and the University of California at Berkeley, where she was awarded a Master of Arts degree (1970). Sterrenburg studied with Ed Rossbach at the University of California at Berkeley and with Lillian Elliott. She has taught at several prominent crafts schools, including Haystack Mountain School of Crafts, Maine; Penland School of Crafts, North Carolina; and Arrowmont School of Crafts, Gatlinburg, Tennessee. She received a National Endowment for the Arts (NEA) crafts fellowship (1979), and numerous crafts awards; her work is in many corporate and museum collections, including AT&T in Atlanta, Georgia; Washington State Arts Commission; IBM; Illinois State University, Normal; and the St. Louis Museum of Art, Missouri. Sterrenburg's work has been published in *Craft Today*, *USA*, *American Craft*, *Fiberarts*, *Interior Design*, and *Crafts Horizons*, and in several books on basketry and soft sculpture. Her work in papermaking has been supported by research grants from Indiana University, Bloomington.

In her work Sterrenburg particularly enjoys establishing systems that generate illusionistic ambiguity, usually as a result of the interaction of colors. In her early fiber work, such as her series of "Plaited Ikats," the vertical modular units and diagonal grid pattern were animated by variations of resist-dyed color modulations, creating a play of constants against variables. In the 1980s she realized she was not tied to materials, but was creating modular systems of established structures with random elements. Her later work focused on modularity and its changing configurations of color and structural layering which are components of her work. Color in her paper works results from mixing pigments into the pulp, creating a subtly varied color pattern along with her layering of units. Her current work in paper and mixed-media focuses on personal shrines and draws on Plato's allegory of the cave and on Indonesian puppet theater. Her travel and research in Japan, Thailand, and Indonesia has inspired an interest in the rites of passage. She recently was awarded a grant to co-teach an honors course on the cycles of nature and of life with a colleague in anthropology.

Julie F. Codell

Bibliography

Craft Today: USA. New York: American Craft Council, 1989.

Held, Shirley E. *Weaving: A Handbook of the Fiber Arts*. Holt, Rinehart & Winston, 1978, pp. 189, 238, 288, 296.

Meilach, Dona. *Soft Sculpture and Other Soft Art Forms*. Crown Publishers, 1974, pp. 100–01.

Van Gelder, Lydia. *Ikat*. Watson-Guptill, 1980, pp. 20–21.

Stettheimer, Florine (1871–1944)

Born in Rochester, New York, the painter Florine Stettheimer studied at the Art Students League, New York City, from 1892 to 1895, principally with H. Siddon Mowbray and Kenyon Cox; she then had a private studio in New York City until 1906 when she went to Europe with her mother and two of her sisters, Carrie and Ettie. She took painting lessons in Munich, Stuttgart, and Berlin—all in Germany—and visited the major art museums in Italy, Switzerland, and France. The outbreak of World War I in 1914 forced her return to New York City, where the Knoedler Galleries gave her a solo exhibition in 1916. The next year she joined the Independent Society of Artists and participated in its annual exhibitions until 1926, when she resigned. In 1924 she was invited to show with the Carnegie International Exhibition in Pittsburgh, Pennsylvania, and in 1931 she began to exhibit with the American Society of Painters, Printers, and Gravers, New York City. She was included in the First Biennial Exhibition of Contemporary American Painting at the Whitney Museum of American Art, New York City (1932).

With her mother and sisters Stettheimer created a famous salon at Alwyn Court—a château-like building on West 58th Street, New York City—and her circle of friends included avant-garde artists, musicians, dancers, and writers, such as Marcel Duchamp, Elie Nadelman, Gaston Lachaise, Virgil Thomson, Cecil Beaton, Carl Van Vechten, and Henry McBride. Meanwhile Stettheimer maintained a studio in the Beaux-Arts building in which she painted portraits of her family and friends. In 1929 an especially important collaboration occurred when Virgil Thomson asked her to do the sets and costumes of Gertrude Stein's *Four Saints in Three Acts*, for which he had just written the music. The opera opened at the Wadsworth Athenaeum theater in Hartford, Connecticut, in 1934, before going to New York City.

Stettheimer's last series of paintings consisted of large-scale canvas tributes to Manhattan called "Cathedrals of New York." She was still working on "Cathedrals of Art" (Metropolitan Museum of Art) when illness necessitated two operations in 1942; two years later she died in the New York Hospital.

Stettheimer's style of painting was uniquely her own creation with no obvious concessions to new modernist modes except for amusing liberties with perspective. Her figures were often rendered in wispy, calligraphic sketches, culminating in pointed, dainty toes, and her palette was festively bright. Her paintings are in the leading American art museums.

Eleanor Tufts

Bibliography

Heins, Barbara. "Florine Stettheimer and the Avant-garde American Portrait." Doctoral Dissertation. Yale University, 1986.

McBride, Henry. *Florine Stettheimer*. New York: Museum of Modern Art, 1946.

Sussman, Elisabeth. *Florine Stettheimer: Still Lifes, Portraits and Pageants, 1910–1942*. Boston: Institute of Contemporary Art, 1980.

Tufts, Eleanor. *American Women Artists, 1830–1930*. National Museum of Women in the Arts, 1987.

Tyler, Parker. *Florine Stettheimer: A Life in Art*. Farrar, Straus & Co., 1963.

Stevens, May (1924–)

May Stevens was born in Boston, Massachusetts, and studied at the Massachusetts College of Art, in her native city, the Art Students League in New York City, and the Académie Julian in Paris, France. Her first solo exhibition was in Paris in 1951, and her first New York City show was at the Galeries Moderne in 1955. Known for her large oil and acrylic paintings she also incorporates collages of media articles—words play an important role in the meaning and impact of Stevens's works. Her works in the 1950s show an active political participation in the civil rights movement dealing with racial strife and patriarchal power. In the early 1960s she did a series titled "Freedom Riders," which dealt with publicized bus burnings in Alabama, and then did prints of the dead "Malcolm X," taken from drawings she had done after she saw him laid out in his casket in Harlem, New York. Aware of her own working-class background and some of its prejudices, she did a series entitled "Big Daddy," showing her father in front of a television, wearing an undershirt, ready for the attack with various army symbols around him. Predominantly using red, white, and blue as her palette, she includes a Ku Klux Klan hood with his regalia. Whitney Chadwick states Stevens "first gave visual form to the growing gulf between the White American dream and Black American reality."

Into the 1970s Stevens's works concentrated on feminist issues. Also a poet and writer, she founded *Heresies*, a progressive feminist journal and continually showed an interest in the historical role of women. Stevens began exploring the situation of women in male society in photomontages, paintings, and murals. In "Mysteries and Politics" (1978) she painted an assembly of women from history—famous and unknown people all celebrated on canvas, herself among them. Her best-known series deals with the situation of women where in a poignant series called "Ordinary/Extraordinary" she juxtaposes images of her mother—Alice Stevens—with the socialist leader Rosa Luxemburg. These works show the contrasts of the lives of a housewife with limitations in her world, and an active political activist. She relies heavily on photographic images drawn from her family collections as well as public archives. In 1989 Stevens' "One Plus or Minus One" was installed at the New Museum of Contemporary Art in New York City and later at a gallery in Northern Ireland. The work included two photomurals, each eleven-by-seventeen-feet, with texts that grouped multiple images of men broken by a focal point—a solitary female image: Rosa Luxemburg. The murals were attached to the walls like billboards and were torn down at the end of each installation.

Stevens has received numerous awards including the New York State Council on the Arts Creative Artists Public Service (CAPS) award in graphics (1974), a National Endowment for the Arts (NEA) grant in painting in 1983, and a Guggenheim Foundation fellowship in painting (1986). She has works in the collections of the Whitney Museum of American Art and the Brooklyn Museum—both in New York City; and the San Francisco Museum of Modern Art, California; among others. In 1989 she exhibited at the Kunsthalle, Düsseldorf, West Germany; the Museum of Contemporary Art, São Paulo, Brazil; and in the Indochina Arts Project. In 1990 she had work in the Kremlin show, Moscow, Russia. She currently teaches at the School of Visual Arts in New York City.

Nancy Knechtel

Bibliography

Chadwick, Whitney. *Women, Art and Society*. Thames and Hudson, 1990.

Jacobsen, Carol. "Two Lives: Ordinary/Extraordinary." *Art in America* (February 1989): 153–57 ff.

Rosa/Alice. Universe Books, 1988.

Who's Who in American Art. 18th ed. R.R. Bowker Co., 1989–1990.

Stewart, Hilda (Pocock) (1892–1978)

A painter known for her portrait miniatures in watercolor on ivory, Hilda (Pocock) Stewart was born in London, England. As a child she received art instruction from both her parents, who were accomplished artists and exhibitors at the Royal Academy in London. Her mother, Alicia Shellshear, taught her how to paint portrait miniatures on ivory. In 1908 she attended anatomy lectures at the Royal Academy and enrolled in the Regent Street Polytechnic School of Art, where she specialized in arts and crafts stained wood design under Harry Theaker and Winifred Stamp.

Stewart exhibited her first miniature with the Royal Academy in 1910 and was elected a full member of the Royal Society of Miniature Painters in 1916. During the war years of 1914 to 1918, she taught part time at the Regent Street Polytechnic, while executing commissions for portrait miniatures. During these years her arts and crafts design work won an award in the National School of Art Competitions and was featured in *The Studio* magazine.

After her marriage Stewart moved in 1921 to the small prairie community of Luseland in Saskatchewan, Canada. There she continued to paint portrait miniatures and landscapes in watercolor. She taught as an art instructor at Regina College (1935–1936), and in Saskatoon at the University of Saskatchewan (1936–1948). She was an active member of the Saskatoon art community during this period, exhibiting regularly with the Saskatoon Art Association. Retiring to Vancouver in 1948 she continued to be active as an artist for many years.

Lynne S. Bell

Bibliography

Anon. "Decorative Woodwork by Students of the Polytechnic Institute." *The Studio* 68 (1916): 192–201.

Bell, Lynne S. *Hilda Stewart R.M.S.: An Essay in Retrieving History*. Mendel Art Gallery, 1990.

Holme, Charles, ed. "Arts and Crafts: A Review of the Work Executed by Students in the Leading Art Schools of Great Britain and Ireland." *The Studio*, special 16–18 (Autumn 1916).

Stiebel, Hanna (1923–)

Born in Tel Aviv, Israel, the sculptor Hanna Stiebel studied with Manolo Pasqual at the New School for Social Research, New York City (1955–1956); earned a Bachelor of Fine Arts degree in sculpture from the Cranbrook Academy of Art, Bloomfield Hills, Michigan (1962); and received a Master of Fine Arts degree in sculpture, the following year, after graduate study with Julius Schmidt. She also did research in bronze casting with Bruno Bearzi at the Università degli Studi di Firenze, Italy (1963–1964); and took advanced work in museology at Wayne State University, Detroit, Michigan (1975–1976).

Stiebel has held solo exhibitions in museums and galleries in the United States and abroad and has had her work included in myriad group shows. She has won honors and awards in several sculpture competitions, and examples of her work are represented in private, public, and corporate permanent collections, including such venues as the Meadowbrook Art Gallery Sculpture Park, Rochester; City of Pontiac Phoenix Center Pedestrian Plaza; and Interlochen Music Academy—all in Michigan; Lake Fairlee Art Camp, Vermont; and many others.

Bibliography
Michigan Collects Michigan Art. Pontiac Art Center, 1976.
Redstone, Louis G., and Ruth R. Redstone. *Public Art: New Directions.* McGraw-Hill, 1981.
Watson-Jones, Virginia. *Contemporary American Women Sculptors.* Oryx Press, 1986.

Stone, Sylvia (1928–)

The sculptor Sylvia Stone was born in Toronto, Canada; studied privately in her native city; took further work at the Art Students League, New York City; married, had children, divorced, and married the painter Al Held.

Stone has held many solo exhibitions in museums and galleries, including the André Emmerich Gallery, New York City (1972, 1975, 1977, 1979, 1980); Bennington College, Vermont (1977); and others. Her work has been included or invited to many group exhibitions in the United States and abroad, such as "14 Sculptors—Industrial Edge," Walker Art Center, Minneapolis, Minnesota (1969); the "Sculpture Annuals," Whitney Museum of American Art, New York City (1969, 1971, 1973); "200 Years of American Sculpture," Hayward Gallery, London, England (1975); the "3rd Biennale of Small Sculpture," Budapest, Hungary (1975); and many others.

Winner of awards and honors, Stone received a Creative Artists Public Service (CAPS) award from the New York State Council on the Arts (1971); a grant from the National Endowment for the Arts (NEA) (1976); and others. Her abstract work is represented in private, public, and corporate permanent collections, including the Aldrich Museum of Contemporary Art, Ridgefield, Connecticut; the Wadsworth Athenaeum, Hartford, Connecticut; Walker Art Center, Minneapolis, Minnesota; Whitney Museum of American Art, New York City; Xerox Corporation; and others.

Bibliography
Kramer, Hilton. "Sylvia Stone (Emmerich)." *The New York Times* (November 7, 1980).
Munro, Eleanor. *Originals: American Women Artists.* Simon and Schuster, 1979.
Rubinstein, Charlotte S. *American Women Artists.* G.K. Hall, 1982.

Stoppert, Mary (1941–)

Born in Flint, Michigan, the sculptor Mary Stoppert earned a Bachelor's degreee at Western Michigan University, Kalamazoo (1964); attended Wayne State University, Detroit, Michigan (1964–1965); and, three years later, received a Master of Fine Arts degree from the School of the Art Institute of Chicago, Illinois.

Stoppert has held solo exhibitions in galleries and museums in the United States and has shown in many group exhibitions: from "Six Contemporary Sculptors," Northern Illinois University, De Kalb, Illinois (1975) to "American Women Artists," São Paulo, Brazil (1980), among others. A professor of art at Northeastern Illinois University, Chicago, Stoppert has won honors and awards, including the Logan prize (1974); the Curtis prize (1977) at the Art Institute of Chicago; and the presidential merit award from Northeastern Illinois University, Chicago (1979).

Stoppert's work is represented in private and public permanent collections, including the Michael C. Rockefeller Arts Center Gallery, Fredonia, New York; Museum of Contemporary Art, Chicago, Illinois; Northern Illinois University, De Kalb; and others. Her "Queen's Ring" series of mixed-media installations evokes a strange and wondrous mythic culture.

Bibliography
American Women Artists 1980. Museu de Arte Contemporanea da Universidad de São Paulo, 1980.
Chicago: The City and Its Artists 1945–1978. University of Michigan, 1978.
Watson-Jones, Virginia. *Contemporary American Women Sculptors.* Oryx Press, 1986.

Stout, Renee (1958–)

Born in Junction City, Kansas, the African-American sculptor Renee Stout earned a Bachelor of Fine Arts degree at Carnegie-Mellon University, Pittsburgh, Pennsylvania.

Stout has held solo exhibitions in universities and galleries, including "Recent Sculpture," B.R. Kornblatt Gallery (1991) and Chapel Gallery, Mount Vernon College (1987)—both in Washington, D.C.; and others. Her work has been included in many group shows in the United States, such as "Black Art—Ancestral Legacy: The African Impulse in African-American Art," Dallas Museum of Art, Texas (1989); Marie Martin Gallery, Washington, D.C. (1988); Carlow College, Pittsburgh, Pennsylvania (1987); Wayland House Gallery, Washington, D.C. (1986); the Museum of Science and Industry, Chicago, Illinois (1985); and others.

Stout seeks inspiration for her mixed-media sculptures in the spiritual "magic" to be found in many cultures, but especially African, Native American, and Hispanic. Her work seems that of a gifted sorceress, employing fetishes and other spell-struck objects in an aesthetic unity. Representative examples of her work are in private and public permanent collections, including Allegheny Community College, Pittsburgh, Pennsylvania; Dallas Museum of Art, Texas; and others.

Bibliography
Fleming, Lee. "Casting Spells." *Museum & Arts Washington* (March–April 1990).
Hall, Robert L. *Gathered Visions: Selected Works by African American Women Artists.* Anacostia Museum, Smithsonian Institution Press, 1992.
McKenna, Maureen A. *Black Art—Ancestral Legacy: The African Impulse in African-American Art.* A Catalog. 1989.

Strider, Marjorie (1939–)

Born in Guthrie, Oklahoma, the painter/sculptor Marjorie Strider earned a Bachelor's degree at the Kansas City Art Institute, Missouri, and a Bachelor of Fine Arts degree at the University of Oklahoma, Norman, whereupon she left the Midwest for New York City.

Strider has held many solo exhibitions throughout the United States, including Pace Gallery (1965, 1966), and Nancy Hoffman Gallery (1973, 1974)—both in New York City; Colby-Sawyer College, New London, New Hampshire (1978); Bernice Steinbaum Gallery, New York City (1983, 1984); Alexandria Museum, Louisiana (1983); University of Arizona, Tucson (1984); Dickinson College, Carlisle, Pennsylvania (1985); "Broadway Windows," an outdoor installation, New York University (1988–1990), Belleview Park, an outdoor installation (1991), and André Zarre Gallery (1993)—all in New York City; and others.

Between 1963 and 1993 her work has been invited to more than ninety-five group exhibitions in the United States and abroad, such as the "First International Girlie Exhibition," Pace Gallery, New York City (1964); Felix Handschin Gallery, Basel, Switzerland (1970); "Whitney Annual," Whitney Museum of American Art, New York City (1970); "Outdoor Sculpture," Kunsthalle Museum, Hamburg, Germany (1972); "The Male Nude," School of Visual Arts (1973), and Museum of Modern Art (MoMA) penthouse (1975)—both in New York City; "The Drawing Biennale," Lisbon, Portugal (1981); "Let's Play House," Bernice Steinbaum Gallery, New York City (1986); "Contemporary Sculpture," an outdoor installation, Chesterwood, Massachusetts (1991); André Zarre Gallery, New York City (1992); and many others.

Filmmaker, visiting lecturer, performance artist, and panelist in museums, art schools, and universities in Europe and the United States—Strider has been teaching at the School of Visual Arts, New York City, since 1969. She has won many honors and awards for her work, including grants from the Richard Florsheim Foundation (1992); the Pollack-Krasner Foundation (1991); Massachusetts Council on the Arts (1986); and the National Endowment for the Arts (NEA) (1974, 1980). She was artist-in-residence and a fellow at various institutions (1973–1978), including the MacDowell Colony, Peterborough, New Hampshire.

Strider's work is represented in private, public, and corporate permanent collections, including the Guggenheim Museum, New York City; Albright-Knox Art Gallery, Buffalo, New York; New York University, New York City; Hirshhorn Museum and Sculpture Garden, Washington, D.C.; Wadsworth Atheneum, Hartford, Connecticut; First National Bank, Seattle, Washington; Newark Museum, New Jersey; and many others.

Bibliography
An Industrious Art. The Fabric Workshop. Norton, 1992.
Rubinstein, Charlotte S. *American Women Sculptors*. G.K. Hall, 1991.
Van Wagner, Judith K. *Marjorie Strider: 10 Years 1970–1980*. Greenvale, New York: Long Island University, 1982.
Watson-Jones, Virginia. *Contemporary American Women Sculptors*. Oryx Press, 1986.

Strunck, Gisela-Heidi (1945–)

Born in Deggendorf, Germany, the artist Gisela-Heidi Strunck studied literature and philosophy in universities in Madrid, Spain; Florence, Italy; Athens, Greece; and Oslo, Norway (1962–1966), before enrolling in the University of Dallas, Irving, Texas (1970–1974) to study ceramics and sculpture.

Strunck has held solo exhibitions in museums and galleries in the United States since 1976, and has had her work appear in two-person and group shows throughout her adopted state and in Gallery Aquinas, South Bend, Indiana (1980); Wichita Art Museum, Kansas (1981); Arkansas Art Center, Little Rock (1984); and Ana's Kitchen Art Services, Hot Springs, Arkansas (1984); among others.

Strunck has earned honors and awards for her mixed-media sculptures. Her work is represented in private, public, and corporate permanent collections, including the First National Bank of Chicago, Dallas, Texas; IS, Incorporated, Mill Valley, California; University of Dallas, Irving, Texas; and others.

Bibliography
Fifth Texas Sculpture Symposium. Dallas: Connemara Conservancy, 1985.
Kutner, Janet. "Dallas: Five Artists, Four Shows, Three Dimensions." *Art News* 76:3 (March 1977): 95–98.
Twenty-Seventh Annual Delta Art Exhibition. Little Rock: Arkansas Art Center, 1984.
Watson-Jones, Virginia. *Contemporary American Women Sculptors*. Oryx Press, 1986.

Stuart, Michelle

The archaic, reciprocal bond between humankind and the earth is for Michelle Stuart both physical and spiritual, extending through the immemorial ages. She uses varied strategies and artistic media to investigate this relationship and draw attention to the passage of time, which inexorably unites all.

Born in Los Angeles, California, Stuart grew up there and studied for a year at the Chinouard Art Institute. Dissatisfied, she left to spend a year in Mexico, where she worked as an assistant to Diego Rivera, followed by another three years in Europe. After moving to New York City in 1958, she took courses in the humanities at the New School for Social Research, in that same city.

In the experimental 1960s and the early 1970s Stuart contributed to and drew from significant new interests in conceptualism, minimalism, process, and earthworks. In 1973 she began to make earth scrolls: large-scale, muslin-backed paper hangings produced by rubbing varied colors of earth into their surfaces. Simple but monumental, these works of great aesthetic presence evoke the majesty of nature as well as the passing of geological time. Soon she began to make her own paper, which she colored and tied together into what she called rock books. Inscrutable, they testify to the human desire—and perhaps inability—to know the world.

Stuart also worked directly on the land during the 1970s. "Niagara Gorge Path Relocated" (1975), at Artpark in Lewiston, New York, consisted of a 460-foot scroll unfurled down a rocky, overgrown hillside where the Niagara River once ran. On a plateau overlooking the Columbia River in Oregon, Stuart arranged 3,400 rocks in the wheel-like configuration. "Stone Alignments/Solstice Cairns" (1979) oriented to the summer solstice and recalling prehistoric ritual structures.

During the 1980s Stuart produced indoor installations, usually incorporating sound, as in "Correspondences" (1981) and "Ashes in Arcadia" (1988), but she also returned to her origins in more traditional painterly and sculptural concerns. These newly conceived works often incorporate insights stimulated by travel in Asia, especially Japan and the Himalayas. She addresses the cross-cultural meaning of gardens as physical and metaphorical places of tranquility in "Silent Gardens" (1984–1987), eight panels nearly eight-by-twelve-feet each, and "Paradisi," which measures sixteen-and-one-half-by-thirty-three feet. Both of these works comprise modular encaustic units inlaid with bits of the natural world, such as rocks and plants. "The Four Seasons" (1987), installed at the College of Wooster in Ohio, consists of four bronze panels based on vegetation, some of which were cast from actual flowers, leaves, and branches. For a recent commission, "Tabula" (1989–1992), in the lobby of a new Manhattan high school, Stuart created more than thirty marble panels etched with images relating to discovery, knowledge, and the cosmos.

Ann Lee Morgan

Bibliography

Duvert, Elizabeth. "With Stone, Star, and Earth: The Presence of the Archaic in the Landscape Visions of Georgia O'Keeffe, Nancy Holt, and Michelle Stuart." In *The Desert Is No Lady: Southwestern Land-scapes in Women's Writing and Art.* Ed. Vera Norwood and Janice Monk. Yale University Press, 1987.

Lovelace, Cary. "Michelle Stuart's Silent Gardens." *Arts Magazine* 63 (September 1988): 76–79.

Munro, Eleanor. *Originals: American Women Artists.* Simon and Schuster, 1979.

Van Wagner, Judy Collischan. *Michelle Stuart: Voyages.* Exhibition Catalog. New York: Hillwood Art Gallery, Long Island University, 1985.

Stussy, Maxine Kim (1923–)

A native of Los Angeles, California, the sculptor Maxine Kim Stussy attended the University of Southern California, University Park (1943), and earned a Bachelor's degree from the University of California at Los Angeles (UCLA) (1947). She also did research and further study in England, France, Germany, and Italy (1959, 1963).

Stussy has exhibited work in museums and galleries in the United States and abroad, including the Los Angeles County Museum of Art (1954, 1958, 1959, 1961), Zara Gallery, San Francisco (1977), and Coslow Gallery, Los Angeles (1989)—all in California; Galleria Schneider, Rome, Italy (1959); Denver Art Museum, Colorado (1960); and others. Examples of her commissioned works are in private and public collections and are located in many California venues. Most recently, Stussy completed a commission of a bronze horse in Westport, Connecticut (1992).

Bibliography

Reinoehl, Kathleen. "The Many Faces of Maxine Kim Stussy." *American Artist Magazine* (July 1875).

Who's Who in American Art. 20th ed. R.R. Bowker Co., 1993–1994.

Sullivan, Françoise (1925–)

Born in Montréal, Québec, Canada, the painter/sculptor/choreographer Françoise Sullivan studied at l'École des Beaux-Arts, Montréal (1941–1945) before going on to New York City to study modern dance (1946–1947). She was part of the "Automatiste Group" and signed the manifesto, "Le Refus Global," in 1948.

Sullivan has held solo exhibitions in museums and galleries in Canada and abroad, including "Retrospective: 12 Years of Painting," Musée du Québec (1993); the Galerie Dominion and Galerie Circa, Montréal (1990); "Actions Documentées," Place des Arts (1987); Galerie Montcalm, Hull (1985, 1987); "Peintures Récentes," Galerie Joliet, Montréal (1983); "Peintures Récentes, Actions Documentées," Video, Galerie Sans Nom, Moncton, New Brunswick (1982); "Chi e Pandora?" Installation, Galeria Unimedia, Genoa, Italy (1981); "Retrospective," Musée d'Art Contemporain, Montréal (1981); Galeria Dove Le Tigre, Milan, Italy (1979); Forest City Gallery, London, Ontario (1978); and others. Her work has been invited to many group exhibitions throughout Canada and Europe, such as "Kunst aus Canada," Galerie Clara Maria Sels, Dusseldorf, Germany (1992); "Présence Québecoise," Ferme du Buisson, Marne La Vallée, France (1992); "Présence Québecoise," Chateau de Biron, Dordogne, France (1992); "Naissance et Persistance de la Sculpture," Musée du Québec, Canada (1992); "Gilles Daigneault Propose . . . ," Galerie Palardy, Montréal (1989); "La Peinture a Montréal, Un Second Regard," a travelling show through Nova Scotia and the Maritimes (1985); "International Festival of Women Artists," Carlsberg Glyptothek Museum, Copenhagen, Denmark (1980); and many others.

Among her many awards and honors Sullivan received le Prix Borduas from the province of Québec (1987); the Martin Lynch Staunton award, Canada Council (1984); "Biennial," second prize, Sadye Bronfman Centre, Montréal (1982); Québec province sculpture prize, Ministry of Cultural Affairs (1963); and Le Prix Maurice-Cullen (for painting), l'École des Beaux-Arts, Montréal (1943). She was named to the Royal Canadian Academy of Arts (1992).

Sullivan's career as a choreographer has paralleled her notable approach to the visual arts. She participated in the "Festival International de Nouvelle Danse" and her most recent works were performed at L'Agora de la Danse, Montréal (1992). Her visual works are represented in private, public, and corporate permanent collections, including Air Canada, Montréal; the Art Bank, Canada Council, Ottawa; National Gallery of Canada, Ottawa; National Bank of Canada, Montréal; Art Gallery of Ontario; and many others.

Bibliography

Daigneault, Gilles. *L'Art au Québec depuis Pellan. Une Histoire des prix Borduas.* Musée du Québec, 1988.

Gravel, Claire. "Françoise Sullivan: La Parole Retrouvée." *Vie des Arts* (March 1988).

Lapointe, Manon. "Françoise Sullivan: Renouer avec la Presence du Passe." *ETC* (Spring 1988).

Saint-Pierre, Marcel. "The Rhetoric of Dreams." *Vanguard* (Summer 1986).

Sutton, Carol (1945–)

Carol Sutton was born in Norfolk, Virginia, and took a Bachelor of Fine Arts degree at the Richmond Professional Institute. She later received a Master of Fine Arts degree from the University of North Carolina at Chapel Hill. In 1970 she moved to Toronto, where she eventually met some representatives of the school of post-painterly abstraction that flourished under the guidance of critic Clement Greenberg. Unlike the flat lyrical abstractions of Jack Bush—one of the artists who influenced her most directly—Sutton's paintings are more expressively personal, with sometimes strident color effects established by sprays, spatters, and gestural sweeps that emerge from and mix with one another in an indeterminate, vaporous space. The results are not unlike a cross between the more sober color fields of Jules Olitski and the late textured paintings of Larry Poons. A characteristic example is "Eye of the Oval," commissioned by the Cinéplex Odéon Corporation for a theater in Orlando, Florida, in 1987.

Robert J. Belton

Bibliography

Burnett, David. *Cineplex Odeon: The First Ten Years.* 1989.

Swann, Valetta (d. 1973)

Valetta Swann was an English painter who studied at the Central School of Art in London, England. Not atypically, she made many study trips to the major museums of Europe. Swann exhibited her work at the Zak

Gallery during her fifteen-month residence in Paris, France.

Married to the noted anthropologist Bronislaw Malinowski, Swann accompanied her husband to the United States when he was appointed to teach anthropology at Yale University, New Haven, Connecticut, in 1939. Swann often went with her husband on his many anthropological field trips to Oaxaca, Mexico. After the death of her husband Swann took up residence in New York City (1942–1945) and, during that period, exhibited her paintings at the Palace of Fine Arts in Mexico City, Mexico. Swann settled in Mexico in 1946 and lived there until her death in 1973.

Her works reveal the cultural influences of her adopted country and of its pre-Columbian art and artifacts. Swann had nineteen solo exhibitions in various institutions and galleries, seven of which were in the Palace of Fine Arts, Mexico City, Mexico.

Bibliography

Alvarez, José Rogelio, et al. *Enciclopedia de Mexico*. Secretaría de Educación Pública, 1987.

Fernández, Justino. *Arte moderno y contemporáneo de Mexico*. 1952.

The Texas Quarterly: Image of Mexico II. The University of Texas, Autumn 1969.

Swartz, Beth Ames (1936–)

A predominantly abstract painter, known for the identification of her art with spiritual and environmental themes, Beth Ames Swartz was born in New York City, where she grew up. The family spent summers in the Adirondacks. Though her grandparents on both sides were Jewish immigrants, her parents were not actively religious. As a girl Swartz's creative tendencies were encouraged at home through lessons in drawing, painting, and dancing, and she began weekly lessons at the Art Students League, New York City, in 1948. She graduated from the High School of Music and Art, New York City, in 1953 and Cornell University, Ithaca, New York, in 1956. In 1959 she received a Master of Arts degree in art education; married Melvin Swartz, a law student; moved to Arizona, where she combined public school teaching in order to devote herself full time to painting; and had her first solo show in a local gallery in 1967. She then began to expand her exhibition outside the local area.

The Arizona landscape became a source of inspiration for her painting, though it had at first seemed strange and forbidding. The theme of the inherent conflicts in nature, cycles of destruction and renewal, conflict, and destruction involved in settlement by man underlay her series on the elements and the eventual fire painting series, for which she received recognition beyond her immediate environs in the "Ten Take Ten" exhibition at the Colorado Springs Fine Arts Center, Colorado (1977), and the First Western States Biennial (1978). To make the fire paintings she exploited the effects of burning and mutilating paper, and added paint and ornamental collage to create heavily-textured abstractions. Each was begun with her own fire ritual.

A growing interest in spiritual sources led Swartz to investigate Jewish history and thought, including the Kaballa, and subsequently to visit Israel and the sites associated with Jewish heroines. This investigation resulted in the series, "Israel Revisited." Its major theme is the feminine aspect of the divine principle, the Sheckinah, in Judaism. The works were constructed in layers which incorporated earth from the sites in Israel and were crumpled and ornamented with metallic elements to achieve a three-dimensional, light-refracting surface.

Swartz's continuing preoccupation with spiritual modes of thought as manifested throughout the world in Native American and Eastern religions led her to further reading and inquiry and to an expansion of concept which included shamanic healing of body and mind and healing of the earth through concern for the environment. Her work is in the collections of the Phoenix Art Museum, Arizona; the Brooklyn Art Museum and the Jewish Museum—both in New York City; and the Smithsonian Institution, Washington, D.C.

Barbara Cortright

Bibliography

Nelson, Mary Carroll. *Connecting: The Art of Beth Ames Swartz*. Northland Press, 1984.

Rand, Harry. "Some Notes on the Recent Art of Beth Ames Swartz." *Arts Magazine* (September 1981): 92–96.

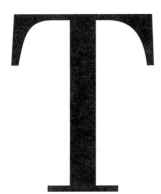

Tacha, Athena (1936–)

Professor of sculpture at Oberlin College, Ohio, since 1973, Athena Tacha was born in Larissa, Greece. Tacha received a Master of Arts degree in sculpture from the National Academy of Fine Arts, Athens, Greece (1959); a Master of Arts degree in art history from Oberlin College, Ohio, two years later; and a Doctorate degree in aesthetics from the Sorbonne, University of Paris, France (1963). She was awarded an honorary Doctor of Fine Arts degree from the College of Wooster, Ohio, in 1990.

Tacha's work has been seen in more than a dozen solo exhibitions in galleries and museums in the United States, including the Zabriskie Gallery (1979, 1981), and the Max Hutchinson Gallery (1984)—both in New York City; and the High Museum of Art, Atlanta, Georgia, a retrospective show which included more than 100 works of sculpture, drawing, "conceptual" photography plus large color photographs of her public commissions (1989). During the same year Tacha held another solo show at the Cleveland Center for Contemporary Art, Ohio, of installations, sculpture, and drawing. Her work has also been selected for numerous group exhibitions throughout the world, including the Venice Biennale, Italy (1980). Between 1975 and 1990 more than a score of Tacha's public commissions have been executed in various parts of the United States—from "Connections," a city-block park with terraced gardens in Franklin Town, Philadelphia, Pennsylvania, to "Ice Walls," a twenty-five-foot-long glass block work at the Museum of History and Art in Anchorage, Alaska.

Tacha won first prize in sculpture at the "May Show," Cleveland Museum of Art, Ohio (1968, 1971, 1979); a grant from the National Endowment for the Arts (NEA) (1975); and a fellowship at the Center for Advanced Visual Studies, Massachusetts Institute of Technology (MIT), Cambridge (1974). Her work is in the permanent collection of the Allen Art Museum, Oberlin College, Ohio; the Cleveland Museum of Art, Ohio; the Museum of Fine Arts, Houston, Texas; the National Collection of Fine Arts, Washington, D.C.; and the Hirshhorn Museum and Sculpture Garden in Washington, D.C.

Bibliography

Johnson, Ellen H. "Nature as Source of Athena Tacha's Art." *Artforum* (January 1981): 58–62.

Lippard, Lucy. "Athena Tacha's Public Sculpture." *Arts Magazine* (October 1988): 68–71.

Marter, Joan. "Athena Tacha's Sculpture: Outdoor Sites Transformed." *Sculpture* (July–August 1987): 12–15.

Tacha, Athena. "Rhythm as Form." *Landscape Architecture* (May 1978): 196–205.

Who's Who in American Art. 19th ed. R.R. Bowker Co., 1991–1992.

Tahedl, Ernestine (1940–)

Known for her abstract landscapes that honor the Canadian reverence for nature, Ernestine Tahedl was elected to the Royal Canadian Academy of Arts and the Ontario Society of Artists. Tahedl was born and educated in Vienna, Austria. She attended the Vienna Academy of Applied Arts where she received a Master of Arts degree in graphic arts (1961). For the next two years, before she emigrated to Canada, Tahedl collaborated with her father, Professor Heinrich Tahedl, in designing and executing stained-glass commissions.

Between 1971 and 1991 Tahedl held thirty-eight solo exhibitions of her work throughout Canada, Europe, and the United States, including the Canadian Guild of Crafts, Montréal (1968); the Wiener Secession, Vienna, Austria (1971); l'École des Beaux-Arts, Montpelier, France (1974); Goethe-Institut, Montréal (1977); Vered International Art Gallery, East Hampton, New York (1979); Lefèbvre Galleries, Edmonton, Canada (1980); Gallery Quan (1984, 1986) and Gallery Quan-Schieder (1987, 1988, 1990)—both in Toronto, Canada; and others. She has executed many commissions in Canadian churches, universities, libraries, and other private and public venues. She also did restoration work in the Christkoenigs Church in Klagenfurt, Austria (1989), and published *Circle of Energy (1981)*, a portfolio of etchings in an edition of forty-eight.

Tahedl's work has been invited to many group exhibitions throughout the world, including the Pleiades Gallery, New York (1978); Les Métiers de l'art, Musée des Arts Décoratifs, Paris, France (1980); the Wesleyan International Exhibition of Prints and Drawings, Macon, Georgia, which travelled throughout the United States (1980–1981); the 15th International Biennial of Graphic Art, Ljubljana, Yugoslavia (1983); the Art Gallery at Harbourfront, Toronto, Canada (1985); Hanga Annual Print Exhibition, Metropolitan Museum of Fine Art, Tokyo, Japan (1985, 1986, 1987); International Biennial Print Exhibition, Taipei, Taiwan (1985, 1987); and many others.

Tahedl's work is housed in permanent public, corporate, and private collections throughout Canada, the United States, France, Austria, El Salvador, and Switzerland. She has won prizes and honors for her work, including a Canada Council arts award (1967); a purchase award at the Concours Artistiques du Québec and the allied arts medal of the Royal Architectural Institute of Canada (1966); the bronze medal of the Vienna International Exhibition of Paintings (1963); and others.

Bibliography

Gagnon, Claude-Lyse. "Les Vitraux d'Ernestine Tahedl." *Vie des Arts* (Hiver 1967–1968): 63–64.

Robert, Guy. *Art Actuel au Québec*. Iconia, 1983.

Russ, Joel, and Lou Lynn. *Contemporary Stained Glass*. Doubleday, 1985.

Simard, Guy. *Verriers du Québec*. Marcel Broquet, Inc., 1989.

Who's Who in American Art. 19th ed. R.R. Bowker Co., 1991–1992.

Tait, Agnes (1894–1981)

Agnes Tait was born in New York City and studied there at the National Academy of Design (1908–1918). Her paintings and, especially, her prints were exhibited widely throughout the United States, reflecting her long and fruitful career, including the "Forty-Fifth Annual Exhibition," National Association of Women Painters and Sculptors (1936); the New York World's Fair (1939); "Fourteen American Women Printmakers of the '30s and '40s," Weyhe Gallery (1973)—all in New York City; and "Women Artists: 1550–1950," Los Angeles County Museum, California (1976). She also painted decorative panels, portraits, and landscapes.

In 1941 Tait moved to Santa Fe, New Mexico, where she saturated herself in the culture of the Southwest, illustrated children's books, and focussed her energies on pulling prints.

Bibliography

"Agnes Tait in Santa Fe." *Art Digest* 19 (March 15, 1945): 18.

Harris, Ann Sutherland, and Linda Nochlin. *Women Artists: 1550–1950*. Alfred A. Knopf, 1976.

Pena, Lydia M. "In the American Scene: The Life and Times of Agnes Tait." *Woman's Art Journal* 5:1 (Spring–Summer 1984): 35–39.

———. *The Life and Times of Agnes Tait*. New Mexico: Roswell Museum and Art Center, 1984.

Takaezu, Toshiko (1929–)

Born in Papeekeo, Hawaii, the ceramist, sculptor, weaver, and painter Toshiko Takaezu enrolled in Saturday classes at the Honolulu Art School (1947–1949); attended the University of Hawaii (1948, 1951)—both in Hawaii; and Cranbrook Academy of Art, Bloomfield Hills, Michigan, where she studied clay with Maija Grotell.

Takaezu has held many solo exhibitions throughout the United States, including the University of Wisconsin, Madison (1955); Cleveland Institute of Art, Ohio (1959, 1961); Peabody College for Teachers, Nashville, Tennessee (1961); Gallery 100, Princeton, New Jersey (1965); Lewis and Clark College, Portland, Oregon (1971); Florida Junior College, Jacksonville (1975, 1985); Hau-Pulamamau, Kuakini Hospital, Honolulu, Hawaii (1987); Montclair Art Museum, New Jersey (1988); University of Bridgeport, Connecticut (1989); and others. Her work has been invited to group exhibitions in the United States and throughout the world—from Brussels, Belgium, to Tulsa, Oklahoma; Prague, Czechoslovakia; Princeton, New Jersey; Kyoto, Japan; Geneva, Switzerland; New York City; and many others.

Takaezu has won many honors and awards for her work, including a McInerny Foundation grant (1952); a Tiffany Foundation grant (1964); a National Endowment for the Arts fellowship (1980); and a Living Treasure award, Honolulu, Hawaii (1987). She has taught at universities and art schools in the United States, including Cranbrook Academy of Art, Bloomfield Hills, Michigan; University of Wisconsin, Madison; Cleveland Institute of Art, Ohio; Honolulu Academy of Art, Hawaii; and Princeton University, New Jersey. Recently, Takaezu wrote, "In my life I see no difference between making pots, cooking and growing vegetables . . . there is a need for me to work in clay . . . it gives me many answers for my life."

Takaezu's work is represented in private, public, and corporate permanent collections, such as the Smithsonian Institution, Washington, D.C.; Museum of Contemporary Craft and Metropolitan Museum of Art—both in New York City; Honolulu Academy of Art, Hawaii; New Jersey State Museum, Trenton, and Newark Museum—both in New Jersey; Philadelphia Museum of Art, Pennsylvania; University of New Hampshire, Durham; Baltimore Museum, Maryland; Johnson Wax Collection, Racine, Wisconsin; Arizona State University, Tempe; National Museum, Bangkok, Thailand; Toledo Museum, Ohio; and many more.

Bibliography

Levin, Elaine. *The History of American Ceramics*. Harry N. Abrams, 1987.

Manhart, Tom, and Marcia Manhart. *The Elegant Object*. Philbrook Museum of Art, 1987.

Schmidt, James. "Toshiko Takaezu." *Ceramics Monthly* (January 1990): 36–37.

Toshiko Takaezu: Four Decades. A Catalog. Essays by Paul J. Smith and Sherman E. Lee. Montclair Art Museum, 1990.

Takashima, Shizuye (1928–)

Born in Vancouver, British Columbia, Canada, the painter/printmaker/illustrator Shizuye Takashima earned a Bachelor's degree from the Ontario College of Art, Toronto, Canada (1953); studied weaving at the Fine Arts Institute, San Miguel de Allende, Mexico (1965); and printmaking at the Pratt Graphic Art Center, New York City (1966).

Widely-travelled throughout the United States, Canada, Europe, and the Far East as a result of grants from the Canada Council, Takashima has held many solo exhibitions in galleries, such as the Upstairs Gallery, Toronto (1959, 1960, 1961); Waddington Galleries, Ltd., Montréal (1963, 1967); Jerrold Morris International Gallery, Toronto (1963, 1964); Burnaby Art Gallery, British Columbia (1965, 1978); Gallery House Sol, Georgetown, Ontario (1984); and others. Her work has been invited to group exhibitions, including the Art Gallery of Ontario (1959, 1960); Hamilton Art Gallery, Ontario (1961); Hart House, University of Toronto (1961); Montréal Museum of Fine Arts and the "VI Biennial Exhibition," National Gallery, Ottawa (1965)—all in Canada; Gallery Potpourri, Long Island, New York (1971); "Mystic Circle," a travelling show across Canada, Burnaby Art Gallery, British Columbia (1974); "Japanese-Canadian Artists," a travelling show through Ontario, National Gallery, Ottawa (1977); Gallery House Sol (1982); "Canada at Bologna," a travelling show through Amsterdam, the Netherlands, Paris, France, and Toronto, Canada, of children's book illustrations (1990–1991); and others.

Takashima's work is represented in private, public, and corporate permanent collections, including the National Gallery, Ottawa; Burnaby Art Gallery, British Columbia; Robert McLaughlin Gallery, Oshawa, Ontario; Imperial Oil, Ltd., Calgary, Alberta; McGill University, Montréal; University of Sherbrooke, Québec; and many others. Her autobiographical novel, *A Child in Prison Camp*, one of five required readings in Canadian senior schools, has been cited for its literary and artistic merit, and won awards and diplomas in Canada, the United States, Japan, and Italy. It was transformed into a musical by the Fuji Drama Company of Tokyo, Japan, in 1975.

Bibliography
Mathews, Robin. "Review." *The Canadian Forum* (August 1961).
Silcox, David P. "Review." *Canadian Art Magazine* 78 (1962).
Takashima, Shizuye. *A Child in Prison Camp*. Tundra Books of Montréal, 1971–1989.
Who's Who in American Art. 19th ed. R.R. Bowker Co., 1991–1992.

Tanguma, Marta (1938–)

Born in Mexico, painter/sculptor Marta Tanguma exhibited her first works (nineteen oils) in the Casa de la Paz of the Organismo de Promoción Internacional de Cultura, Mexico City (1968). Two years later she painted a mural, "Vibración Lumínica," for the Instituto de Hipnosis Médica, Mexico City.

Tanguma's chief sculptures include "Combinatorio" (five modular pieces, 1971); "Formas Tridemensionales" (wood faced with aluminum, 1972); "Obelisco Circulante, Andrómeda" (five wooden forms) and "Cosmos," for the Museo Tecnológico de la Comisión Federal de Electricidad, Mexico City (1974, 1975); "La Fuente," for the Canoas Park in Monterrey (1975); "Conviviencia Infantil," for the Instituto Mexicano de Seguro Social, Mexico City (1975); "Agua" (five triangles in polyester resin, 1976) for Acapulco; "Polimerografias" (1977); various murals for the Metro Station at Coyoacan (1981–1982); "Familia Cosmica" (polyester resin, 1986) and "Robots y Cosmos" (1986–1987) exhibited in the Metro stations. Tanguma primarily employs petroleum-derived plastics for her sculptures.

Bibliography
Alvarez, José Rogelio, et al. *Enciclopedia de Mexico*. Secretaría de Educación Pública, 1987.

Tannahill, Mary Harvey (1863–1951)

A painter, printmaker, embroiderer, and creator of batiks, Mary Harvey Tannahill was born on the family plantation in Warren County, North Carolina, and from 1865 was raised in New York City, where she studied with Kenyon Cox and Arthur Wesley Dow. Owing to her parents' support and financial security, she knew from early childhood that she would be an artist.

Tannahill's first public essays were in miniature paintings (watercolors on ivory), which she exhibited with the Philadelphia Society of Miniature Painters, Pennsylvania. She worked in other media as well.

A denizen of Provincetown, Massachusetts, having spent more than thirty summers there, Tannahill learned the art of relief printing from Blanche Lazzell. She soon turned out the white-line color woodcuts associated with the Provincetown, Massachusetts, area and exhibited with the Provincetown group. For forty years Tannahill showed her—at first glance—seemingly naive work with many professional art organizations, including the Panama-Pacific International Exposition, San Francisco, California (1915); the Society of Independent Artists (1917, 1922, 1925), and the National Association of Women Painters and Sculptors (1939)—both in New York City; and others. Examples of her work are in private and public permanent collections in the United States and abroad, such as the Newark Public Library, New Jersey; the Bibliothèque Nationale, Paris, France; and many others.

Bibliography
Eight Southern Women. South Carolina: Greenville County Museum of Art, 1986.
"Painters of Miniatures." *The New York Times* (February 2, 1902): 10.
Wolf, Amy. *New York Society of Women Artists: 1925*. New York: ACA Galleries, 1987.

Tanning, Dorothea (1913–)

Born and raised in Galesburg, Illinois, Dorothea Tanning led what she describes in her autobiography as an uneventful life, except for her experience as a teenager working for the public library, which instilled a yearning for new experiences and exotic locales.

Tanning's first real encounter of the outer world took place in 1932, when she very briefly studied at the Art Institute of Chicago, Illinois, but that was soon to be overshadowed by a whirlwind of international activity. In 1936 she saw the epoch-making exhibition, "Fantastic Art, Dada, Surrealism," at the Museum of Modern Art (MoMA), New York City, whereupon she resolved to visit Paris, France, and to immerse herself into the artistic and intellectual community. She did not arrive there until 1939, however, and to her disappointment, discovered that the approach of World War II had stifled creativity and sent artists into exile. Frustrated, she visited an uncle in Stockholm, Sweden, and painted a few portraits.

Tanning's misfortune began to be redressed in the 1940s, when she left conventional portraiture behind in favor of disturbing paintings with enigmatic themes clearly inspired by surrealism. "Children's Games" (c. 1942), for example, shows wild-haired children tearing strips of wallpaper to reveal a female torso painted in the manner of René Magritte. Some of these works were shown at the Julian Levy Gallery in New York City, a well-known center of surrealist activity in the war years. There they came to the attention of the famous and redoubtable surrealist Max Ernst, who later appeared at Tanning's door to judge her painting for an exhibition of women painters. He was immediately taken by Tanning's self-portrait, showing her bare-breasted, in a skirt of thorns, standing in an endless corridor of doorways next to a creature like a winged lemur. Ernst named the work "Birthday" (1942), and he proceeded to introduce Tanning to the members of his circle. Her first solo exhibition, also at the Julian Levy Gallery, soon followed in 1944, but with little financial success. Tanning and Ernst married in 1946, and they lived in Sedona, Arizona; Provence, and Paris—both in France; at various times until 1976, when Ernst died.

Tanning continued to paint and to make theater decor throughout her maturity, but her endeavors were largely overshadowed by Ernst's. This was particularly unfortunate, for she had already distinguished herself as a painter of noteworthy individuality, allowing the representation of specific figures—such as nude adolescents and her dog, Katchina—to coalesce gradually with an increasingly painterly manipulation of form and color. By 1966, when the first full-length book on her work was published, her atmospheric fields of suggestive shapes were generally recognized as veiled erotic metamorphoses inspired by surrealist automatic procedures. In this, her mature work is quite unlike that of other women loosely affiliated with surrealism, such as Leonora Carrington and Kay Sage.

Although she has continued to paint since the 1960s, Tanning has begun to turn to other media. For example her "Chambre 202, Hôtel du Pavot" (1970) in the Centre Pompidou, Paris, France, features three-dimensional versions of her more anthropomorphic forms clad in various textiles. More recently she has revealed herself to be a writer of considerable breadth and imagination. Her autobiography, entitled "Birthday" in memory of Ernst, is deeply poetic in both imagery and structure.

Although Tanning had retrospective shows in the Casino Communale, Knokke-Le-Zoute (1967), and in the Centre National d'Art Contemporain, Paris (1974), her artistic stature is only now being fully recognized. She continues to live and work in New York City.

Robert J. Belton

Bibliography
Bosquet, Alain. *La peinture de Dorothea Tanning*. Jean-Jacques Pauvert, 1966.
Chadwick, Whitney. *Women Artists and the Surrealist Movement*. Thames and Hudson, 1985.
Tanning, Dorothea. *Birthday*. Lapis Press, 1986.

Tarragó, Leticia (1940–)

Born in Orizaba, Veracruz, Mexico, Leticia Tarragó studied at la Escuela de Pintura y Escultura (La Esmeralda) in Mexico City and in the Taller Libre de Grabado, both in the National Institute of Fine Arts, where at the age of fourteen she won first prize in the annual student competition. Tarragó also studied drawing with Dr. Atl (Gerardo Murillo) and printmaking with Guillermo Silva Santamaría in Mexico; she took advanced work in the graphic arts in Warsaw, Poland, and has been exhibiting her work since 1959.

In 1958 Tarragó won first prize (a trip to Europe) in the KLM Airlines international poster competition. She won the honors in engraving from the Salón de la Plástica Mexicana in 1962, and, five years later, she won the highly-esteemed 30,000-peso award, the national prize in printmaking, from the National Institute of Fine Arts, which was presented to her by Augustín Yañez, the secretary of education.

From 1968 to 1970 Tarragó worked in Switzerland and Holland with a group of printmakers. She has offered classes in the University of Veracruz and in the Instituto Allende de San Miguel de Allende, Guanajuato. Together with Fernando Vilchis she founded the printmaking workshop in the Benito Juarez University in Oaxaca.

Tarragó works in etching and aquatint. Her works offer a surprising lyricism often based on child-like reminiscences; she re-creates the universe of the child with a peculiar innocence—a universe inhabited by animals, balloons, and circus scenes. She likes to describe unusual visual happenings. Her work resides in many major public and private collections.

Bibliography
Alvarez, José Rogelio, et al. *Enciclopedia de Mexico*. Secretaría de Educación Pública, 1987.
The Texas Quarterly: Image of Mexico II. The University of Texas, Autumn 1969.

Tasseor Tutsweetok, Lucy (1934–)

Lucy Tasseor Tutsweetok, an Inuit sculptor, was born in Nunalla, Manitoba, Canada. After her father's death she lived with her grandparents in and around Nunalla and Churchill. She married Richard Tutsweetok in Rankin Inlet in 1960 and moved to Arviat (Eskimo Point), Northwest Territories, soon after. She began carving in the early 1960s.

After several false starts, Tasseor Tutsweetok became inspired by the memory of sand drawings that she and her grandfather (whom she considers to be the greatest influence on her life) had made when she was a child. Tasseor Tutsweetok's sculptures, representing mothers and children or family groups, are carved in a semi-abstract style in which the human figure is rarely fully defined. Human subjects are suggested by heads, arms, and legs which emerge from the stone. Subtle variations in the positioning or expression of heads and faces are clues to understanding the meaning of specific sculptures.

Tasseor Tutsweetok's work has been exhibited since 1970 in about forty group shows in Canada, the United States, and Europe, including the landmark Sculpture/Inuit world tour of 1971–1973. Her sculptures are in the permanent collections of the National Gallery of Canada, Ottawa; the Canadian Museum of Civilization, Ottawa; the Art Gallery of Ontario; and the Winnipeg Art Gallery, Manitoba. Tasseor Tutsweetok attended the opening of Sculpture/Inuit in Philadelphia, Pennsylvania, in 1973 and was invited to attend the opening of the new National Gallery in Ottawa in 1988.

Ingo Hessel

Bibliography
Canadian Eskimo Arts Council. *Sculpture/Inuit: Masterworks of the Canadian Arctic*. University of Toronto Press, 1971.
Hessel, Ingo. "Arviat Stone Sculptures." *Inuit Art Quarterly* 5:4 (Winter 1990): 4–15.
Winnipeg Art Gallery. *Eskimo Point/Arviat*. Winnipeg Art Gallery, 1982.
Zepp, Norman. *Pure Vision: The Keewatin Spirit*. Regina: Norman Mackenzie Art Gallery, 1986.

Tatya, Winnie (1931–)

Winnie Tatya lives in Baker Lake—a small settlement in Canada's Northwest Territories. She belongs to a group of women who have been producing appliqué wall-hangings since the 1960s.

Tatya was born in a family camp in the Garry Lake area and moved to Baker Lake at the age of thirty-seven so that her children could attend school there. Soon after she moved to Baker Lake she learned to apply her traditional sewing skills to a new medium: the sewing of cut-out felt images onto a surface of duffel by means of embroidery floss. Like the other wall-hanging artists in Baker Lake, Tatya has developed her individual stitching to suit her needs for expression. Her images consist of static, carefully arranged compositions which often show a central image surrounded by smaller ones in symmetrical fashion. She also uses the multiple image in which one motif is repeated all over the picture plane, with slight variations introducing variety and rhythmical tension. Her work has been shown in numerous sales and cultural exhibitions in Canada and the United States, particularly in the early 1980s.

Maria Muehlen

Bibliography

Butler, Sheila. "Wallhangings from Baker Lake." *The Beaver* (Autumn 1972): 26–31.

Muehlen, Maria. "Baker Lake Wallhangings: Starting from Scraps." *Inuit Art Quarterly* (Spring 1989): 6–11.

Whitton, Elizabeth. "The Baker Lake Eskimo and Their Needlecraft." (Inuit Art Section, unpublished manuscript.)

Tauch, Waldine Amanda (1892–1986)

Born in Schulenburg, Texas, the sculptor Waldine Amanda Tauch studied with Pompeo Cappini. Tauch received many commissions for fountains, memorials, and liturgical pieces. She exhibited widely in galleries and museums, including "Contemporary American Sculpture," National Sculpture Society, and the California Palace of the Legion of Honor (1929); the "Forty-Fifth Annual Exhibition," National Association of Women Painters and Sculptors (1936)—all in New York City; and others.

Tauch was a member of the American Artist's Professional League, National Association of Women Painters and Sculptors, Society of Western Sculptors, and the Southern States Art League. Her work is represented in private and public permanent collections, including the Grace Lutheran Church and Witte Memorial Museum—both in San Antonio, Texas; Henderson Memorial, Winchester, Kentucky; Monument to Civil and World War Heroes and Pioneers, Bedford, Indiana; and others.

Bibliography

American Art Annual. Vol. 28. American Federation of Arts, 1932.

Hutson, Alice. *From Chalk to Bronze, A Biography of Waldine Tauch.* Shoal Creek Publishers, 1978.

O'Brien, Esse Forrester. *Art and Artists of Texas.* Tardy Publishing Co., 1935.

Tawney, Lenore (1907–)

A seminal figure in the development of fiber arts in post-World War II America, Lenore Tawney was a pioneer in the medium of woven sculpture. She was born in Lorain, Ohio, where her early years were spent in a Catholic convent school. Oppressed by the school's strict demands for conformity, Tawney left home as soon as she was able. Following two years of study at the University of Illinois in Champaign/Urbana, in 1946 she began her artistic training at the Chicago Institute of Design, Illinois. Among Tawney's early teachers were Bauhaus emigré Laszlo Moholy-Nagy, abstract expressionist painter Emerson Woelffer, and avant-garde sculptor Alexander Archipenko.

Trained originally as a sculptor, Tawney also studied the rudiments of studio weaving with Marli Ehrmann in 1949. Fiber did not become her principal medium until 1954, however, when she learned tapestry weaving from Finnish weaver Martta Taipale at the Penland School of Crafts, North Carolina. After six weeks of intensive study at Penland, Tawney returned to Chicago and began to make her mark in the field of fiber art.

In 1957 Tawney left Chicago and moved to Coenties Slip in New York City, where she maintained a studio in the same building as avant-garde artists Jack Youngerman, Robert Indiana, Ellsworth Kelly, and Agnes Martin. As these painters and others of their generation were attempting to resolve problems of form by replacing the sensuousness of color with black and white, so Tawney began to limit her palette to the color of natural linen and black to investigate woven form and structure.

An early one-person exhibit of Tawney's work in November 1961 at the Staten Island Museum displayed her innovative use of Peruvian gauze techniques and loosely woven or exposed warp, for which she had to invent a special reed. This exhibition marked the beginning of a revolution in the field of contemporary fiber arts that took a traditional and functional medium into the realm of the non-utilitarian. Tawney was one of the first artists to take fiber off the wall and design woven forms that were to be hung in space and appreciated as three-dimensional sculpture. Her "Cloud" series, begun in 1978 with a work that incorporated 2,000 white linen threads which fell in varying lengths from a blue horizontally hung canvas "sky," became her trademark. Incorporating transparency as a design element and hanging panels of fiber one in front of the other to create perceptual illusions are among her innovative approaches to the medium.

Tawney is also acclaimed for her small and intimate collages and assemblages in which sticks, feathers, bones, and eggs are combined into mystical and devotional statements informed by poetic writing, Zen, Siddha meditation, and Jungian philosophy. Often placed in boxes reminiscent of those of Joseph Cornell, her materials and images reflect the oneness of the profoundly spiritual and natural worlds Tawney inhabits.

Lucinda H. Gedeon

Bibliography

Anonymous. "Lenore Tawney: Her Designs Show Imaginative Departure from Traditional Tapestry Techniques." *Handweaver and Craftsman* 13:2 (Spring 1962): 6–9.

Henry, Gerrit. "Cloudworks and Collage." *Art in America* (June 1986): 116–21.

Hoff, Margo. "Lenore Tawney: The Warp is Her Canvas." *Craft Horizons* (November–December 1957): 14–19.

Howard, Richard. "Tawney." *Craft Horizons* (February 1975): 46–47.

Magnan, Kathleen Nugent, ed. *Lenore Tawney: A Retrospective.* Exhibition Catalog. Rizzoli, 1990.

Taylor, Ann (1941–)

Born in Rochester, New York, Ann Taylor is known for her paintings, mainly of landscapes, whose scenes are so stripped of detail they seem abstractions of the landscape rather than responses to a particular place. Taylor's later work has developed as increasingly abstract, replacing views of the landscape as a whole with geometric segments of it, as if seen through windows. These segments then become elements of form played off against large areas of atmospheric space.

Taylor was interested in nature and the natural scene from early childhood, especially because her parents were devoted to bird watching and sometimes allowed her to accompany them. Until she went away to school she lived in rural surroundings and was able to spend time alone absorbing the beautiful countryside of upstate New York and the shores of Lake Ontario and the Finger Lakes. There were also long summers with the family at Higgins Lake in Michigan. These experiences with shores, water, and sky culminated in paintings of landscape in which clouds and shorelines were her first concerns.

Although Taylor began with the study of music and literature when she attended Vassar College, Poughkeepsie, New York, she discovered her bent toward painting was stronger than these interests and eventually left Vassar to live in New York City. In 1962 she received a Bachelor's degree in American literature from the New School for Social Research, New York City. This choice was dictated by her strong feeling of empathy with Ralph Waldo Emerson and the New England transcendentalists, whose sense of nature she considered basic to her paintings. She studied painting briefly, on an individual basis, with Julian Levi, and began exhibiting in 1964. Interspersed with studio painting, she made a number of extensive trips to Alaska, across the United States, Yucatan, the Bahamas, North Africa, England, and the continent. These varied landscapes, as well as a wish to express the sensation of movement through them in her "Acceleration" series, extended the range of her subject matter, particularly in portraying mountain peaks. In 1984 a retrospective exhibition of her work opened at the Rochester Museum and Science Center and travelled to other museums and art centers in the United States.

Barbara Cortright

Bibliography
Cortright, Barbara. *The Reach of Solitude: The Paintings of Ann Taylor.* Middlebury, Vermont: Paul S. Eriksson, 1983.
Women Artists in America II. University of Tennessee Press, 1975.

Taylor, Anna Heyward (1879–1956)

Born in Columbia, South Carolina, the painter/printmaker Anna Heyward Taylor studied with William Merritt Chase, Charles Hawthorne, Lathrop, Meijer, and B.J.O. Nordfeldt.

Taylor's paintings and woodcuts were shown in many galleries and museums, including "Contemporary Art of the United States," New York World's Fair, IBM building, New York City (1940); "Women Printmakers," Philadelphia Museum of Art, Pennsylvania (1956); and others. She was a member of several arts organizations, including the Charleston Art Association, Columbia Art Association, and Columbia Sketch Club—all in South Carolina; National Arts Club, National Association of Women Painters and Sculptors, and Society of Independent Artists—all in New York City; Southern States Art League; and the Washington Art Club, Washington, D.C. Her work is represented in private and public permanent collections.

Bibliography
American Art Annual. Vol. 28. American Federation of Arts, 1932.
Flint, Janet Altic. *Provincetown Printers: A Woodcut Tradition.* National Museum of American Art, 1983.
Obituary. *Who's Who in American Art.* Vol. 7. American Federation of Arts, 1959.

Taylor, Grace Martin (1903–)

Painter, printmaker, teacher, and arts administrator, Grace Martin Taylor was born in Morgantown, West Virginia. She received both her Bachelor's and Master's degrees from West Virginia University in her native city.

Taylor was a student of Hugh Henry Breckenridge, Arthur B. Carles, and Henry McCarter at the Pennsylvania Academy of Fine Arts, Philadelphia, in 1922; three years later, on a visit to Provincetown, Massachusetts, she learned the technique of the white-line color woodcut from Blanche Lazzell. In various summers spent in Provincetown, Taylor took further study with Fritz Pfeiffer and Hans Hofmann. She also studied at Ohio University, Athens; the Art Institute of Chicago, Illinois; and the Art Students League, New York City, as well as with Emil Bisttram in Taos, New Mexico.

Taylor's first solo exhibition of prints occurred in 1938 at the College of William and Mary, Williamsburg, Virginia. Other solo shows of paintings and prints were held at Ohio University (1945); "Artist of the Year," West Virginia University (1958, 1967); and the West Virginia University Creative Arts Center (1974). Her work was invited to many group exhibitions throughout the United States, including "Fifty Color Prints of the Year," California Printmaker's Society (1933); the Metropolitan Museum of Art (1943), National Academy of Design (1944, 1948), and American Watercolor Society (1958, 1959)—all in New York City; American Drawing Biennial, Norfolk Museum, Virginia (1965); Contemporary Gallery, Palm Beach, Florida (1967); Smithsonian Institution, Washington, D.C. (1985); and others.

One of the founding members of the American Color Print Society in Philadelphia, Pennsylvania, Taylor has garnered a number of honors and awards for her work, such as first prize at the Seven State Exhibition, Intermont College, Virginia (1948); first prize and juror's award, Three State Annual Exhibition, Huntington Galleries (1954, 1964); and others. Her work is in the permanent collection of the American Color Print Society, Philadelphia, Pennsylvania; the Charleston Art Gallery, West Virginia; and the Hallmark Company. Between 1934 and 1956 Taylor was associated with Mason College of Music and Fine Arts as associate professor, department head, president, and dean when she retired to take up teaching once more at Morris Harvey College, and lecturing for West Virginia University's extension program.

Taylor has worked in many media as painter and printmaker: oils, casein, acrylics, watercolor, drawing, and relief printing. Her works are composed of free, yet structured abstractions, which pose profound, enigmatic questions of aesthetic value.

Bibliography
Acton, David. *A Spectrum of Innovation: Color in American Printmaking 1890–1960.* Norton, 1990.
Who's Who in American Art. 19th ed. R.R. Bowker, 1991–1992.

Taylor, Janet (Roush) (1941–)

Fiber artist and tapestry weaver Janet (Roush) Taylor was born and raised in Lima, Ohio. From early childhood Taylor escaped into a world of drawn line and color, and, by the time she was thirteen years old, her goal was to attend art school. She took as many art classes as possible in high school and, with scholarship monies, parental loans, and wages earned from a number of part-time jobs, she entered the Cleveland Institute of Art, Ohio, in 1959. Her initial interests were in graphic and interior design, but, in her junior year, upon the advice of Joseph McCullough, the director of the art institute, Taylor changed the focus of her major to weaving and textile design.

In June 1963 Taylor received her Bachelor of Fine Arts degree from the Cleveland Institute of Art and that September entered graduate school at Syracuse University, New York . At Syracuse University her mentor was textile designer Donald Waterson, from whom Taylor received highly valued encouragement and support. Upon receipt of her Master of Fine Arts degree in textile design and weaving in 1965, Taylor moved to New York City where she soon secured a coveted position as a designer/colorist for the Jack Lenor Larsen Design Studio. While working for Larsen, Taylor executed a major commission of thirty-two tapestries after designs by Larsen and architect Louis Kahn for the Unitarian Church in Rochester, New York. Living in New York exposed Taylor to a wealth of stimuli and the work of fiber artist Lenore Tawney—a pioneer in woven sculptural forms—made a particularly strong impression on her. In 1966 she married architect Hugh Taylor and the following year relocated to Philadelphia, Pennsylvania. For the next year Taylor continued to work for Larsen, who sent designs and materials for her to weave. In 1968 she assumed her first teaching post at Moore College of Art in Philadelphia, Pennsylvania. When Taylor's husband accepted a teaching position at Kent State University in 1969, the couple moved to Ohio.

During Taylor's first year in Kent her tapestries took a new direction. She began to weave simple geometries, which evolved into major architectural statements, undoubtedly influenced by the field trips and endless hours of photographing architectural edifices with her husband. An additional profound and lasting impact on Taylor's work came from the two trips made in 1969 and 1973 to the Southwest, where she was immediately drawn to the geometric elements, stark simplicity, and directness of Navajo weaving.

In 1975 Taylor's son Christopher was born, and, the following year, she moved to Arizona to accept a teaching position and coordinate the fiber arts program at Arizona State University, Tempe. Although her professional career was well-grounded, her marriage unfortunately was not, and Taylor was divorced in 1981.

Having previously encompassed geometric-optical illusions using high-intensity color of almost equal value, Taylor's palette in the Southwest became much softer, and landscape elements became the most dominant motif. Boulders and rock forms inspired carefully-painted studies, which were translated into large-scale tapestries. Since her move to Arizona Taylor continues to work in tapestry, and the landscape of the Southwest is the dominant inspiration for her imagery.

In addition to her university positions Taylor has taught as a guest artist at Arrowmont School of Arts and Crafts in Gatlinburg, Tennessee; the Penland School of Crafts in North Carolina; and Haystack Mountain School of Crafts in Deer Isle, Maine. She has executed commissions for the Corpus Christi National Bank, Texas; the Valley National Bank in Phoenix, the Boulder's Resort, Carefree, Westcourt in the Buttes Resort, Tempe, and the Scottsdale Cultural Council—all in Arizona; and the Neshaminy Interplex Business Center in Trevose, Pennsylvania. Since the late 1960s Taylor has exhibited nationally and internationally in more than sixty solo and group exhibitions. In addition her works are in the permanent collections of the Cleveland Institute of Art, Ohio; Syracuse University, Ithaca, New York; the Pauli collection, Zurich, Switzerland; the IBM Corporation, Tucson, and Arizona State University Art Museum, Tempe—both in Arizona.

Lucinda H. Gedeon

Bibliography

Arizona Art Forms. Five-minute videotape. Tempe, Arizona: KAET Television.

Bevlin, Marjorie E. *Design through Discovery*. Holt, Rinehart & Winston, 1977.

Fisher, Jan. "Color Conversations." *Woman Image Now* 4 (1989–1990): 37–39.

Larsen, Jack Lenor, and Mildred Constantine. *Beyond Craft: The Art of Fabric*. Van Nostrand, 1973.

Taylor, Janet, and Star M. Sacks. "The Artist as Teacher." *Continuum*. Tempe: Arizona State University College of Fine Arts, 1981, pp. 22–23.

Teller, Jane Simon (1911–)

Born in Rochester, New York, the artist Jane Simon Teller attended the Rochester Institute of Technology, New York (1920–1922); Skidmore College, Saratoga Springs, New York (1929–1930); and earned a Bachelor's degree from Barnard College, New York City (1933). She learned sculpture and woodcarving while working for the Works Progress Administration (WPA), New York City, and through study with Aaron J. Goodelman and Karl Nielson (1935); and studied welding with Ibram Lassaw (1951).

Teller has held many solo exhibitions in the United States, including a retrospective show at the Montclair Art Museum, New Jersey (1985). She has had her work invited to myriad group exhibitions, including the Whitney Museum of American Art (1962), and Museum of Modern Art (MoMA)—both in New York City; the American Embassy, Tokyo, Japan (1975); Squibb Gallery, Princeton (1982), and Montclair Art Museum (1984)—both in New Jersey; and others.

Teller has won honors and awards, including a sculpture prize at the "Fiftieth Anniversary Exhibition," Philadelphia Art Alliance, Pennsylvania (1960); a purchase award at the New Jersey State Museum (1971), and purchase prizes at Trenton State College (1972–1979)—both in Trenton, New Jersey. In addition to her commissioned work in venues throughout the United States, Teller's work is represented in private and public permanent collections, including the Dresden Museum, Germany; Newark Museum and Princeton University—both in New Jersey; Rockefeller University and Skidmore College, Saratoga Springs—both in New York; and many others.

Bibliography

De Paoli, Geri. "Jane Teller's Sculptures and Drawings: Powerful Presence in the 'Big Rhythm.'" *Woman's Art Journal* 8:1 (Spring–Summer 1987): 28–32.

Miller, David. *Jane Teller Retrospective*. Skidmore College, 1986.

Women's Caucus for Art Honor Awards. Houston: National Women's Caucus for Art, 1988.

Watson-Jones, Virginia. *Contemporary American Women Sculptors*. Oryx Press, 1986.

Tennent, Madge (1889–1972)

The painter Madge Tennent (Madeleine Grace Cook Tennent) was born in Dulwich, England—a suburb of London. She drew images from the age of four and travelled widely: when she was five, her family left for Capetown, South Africa; five years later they moved to a farm in Kent, England. She studied briefly at the Capetown School of Art when she was twelve; the following year, she attended the Académie Julian in Paris, France, where she worked under the aegis of William Bouguereau and Marcel Baschet; and, at sixteen, she was back in South Africa. She also lived in New Zealand, British Samoa, and, with her husband and two sons, settled in Hawaii (1923).

Tennent's first solo exhibition was at the Crossroads Studio, Honolulu, Hawaii. From 1930 to 1944 her rich and vibrant paintings of the Hawaiian people were seen in many museums and galleries, including the Ferargil Gallery, New York City; Wertheim Gallery, London, England; Bernheim-Jeune Galleries, Paris, France; Grossman and Moody Gallery, Honolulu, Hawaii; and others. Her work was invited to or seen in juried group exhibitions, such as the "First National Exhibition of American Art," New York City (1936, 1937); the "Independent" show of the Association of Honolulu Artists, Hawaii (1939); and others. Examples of her work are in private, public, and corporate permanent collections, including the Pietermaritzburg Municipal Art Gallery, South Africa; IBM, New York; the Honolulu Academy of Arts, Hawaii; and others.

Bibliography

Prithwish, Neogy. *Artists of Hawaii: 19 Painters and Sculptors.* Vol. 1. University Press of Hawaii, 1974.

Tennent, Arthur. *The Art and Writing of Madge Tennent.* Island Heritage, 1977.

Tennent, Madge. *Autobiography of an Unarrived Artist.* Brentano's for Columbia University Press, 1949.

Tewi, Thea (1915–)

Born in Berlin, Germany, the sculptor Thea Tewi graduated from the Staatliche Kunstakademie in her native city, having studied with Bruno Paul (1935). After becoming an American citizen, she also studied in New York City at the Sculpture Center (1953–1956); the Art Students League (1954–1955); and at the New School for Social Research with Seymour Lipton and Manolo Pascual (1955). She later studied at the Fonderia Tomasi, Pietrasanta, Italy, where she researched the lost wax process and bronze casting (1970–1972).

Tewi has held solo exhibitions in galleries and art centers, including the Village Art Center, New York City (1961); Maurice Villency Gallery, Roslyn Heights, New York (1968); Sala Michelangelo, Carrara, Italy (1969); University of Notre Dame, Indiana (1970); Main Place Gallery, Dallas, Texas (1971); Hallway Galleries, Washington, D.C. (1976, 1980); Randall Galleries (1977, 1979, 1981, 1983), Vorpal Gallery (1987, 1988), Brooklyn Botanic Garden (1988) and the New York Academy of Sciences (1992)—all in New York City; and many others. Her work has been invited to group shows throughout the United States and abroad: from New York City to Paris, France; from Norwalk, Connecticut, to Seravezza, Italy; from Springfield, Massachusetts, to Carrara, Italy, and University Park, Pennsylvania.

"Sea Snail," "Spindle Shell," and "On a Breaking Wave" are examples of stone sculpture (her favorite choice of material) in which she carved marble and onyx to explore new ideas and experiences.

Tewi's work is represented in private, public, and corporate permanent collections, including the National Collection of Fine Arts, Smithsonian Institution, Washington, D.C.; Cincinnati Art Museum, Ohio; Chrysler Art Museum, Norfolk, Virginia; University of Notre Dame, Indiana; Bank of Tokyo, Japan; Citicorp, New York City; Parks Department, New York City; Pfizer Corporation; and many others.

Bibliography

Alexis, Karin. "Profiles: Thea Tewi." *Art Voices/South* 3:6 (November–December 1980): 51.

Meilach, Donna Z. *Contemporary Stone Sculpture.* Crown, 1970.

Watson-Jones, Virginia. *Contemporary American Women Sculptors.* Oryx Press, 1986.

Who's Who in American Art. 19th ed. R.R. Bowker Co., 1991–1992.

Thecla (Connell), Julia (1896–1973)

Desire, loneliness, and a droll scrutiny of life provisioned Julia Thecla (Connell)'s wistful surrealism. With her remarkably accomplished and flexible technique, she illustrated the power of beauty and the utility of fantasy.

Thecla grew up in rural Illinois and studied briefly at what is now Illinois State University in Normal. She taught for several years before moving to Chicago, Illinois, probably in 1920. There she took classes at the School of the Art Institute of Chicago and discarded her last name, along with much of her past. Despite her introverted personality, by around 1930 she had become actively engaged in the exhibitions, organizations, and social activities that constituted Chicago's art life. At the same time her paintings overcame the delicate innocence of her earlier efforts. Stronger, more complex imagery now suggested familiarity with the work of Odilon Redon and the European surrealists, as well as Chicago artists such as Ivan LeLorraine Albright and Gertrude Abercrombie. Later in life she withdrew, lost her studio, and eventually died in obscure poverty in a Catholic home.

Idealized self-portraits in many works suggest the autobiographical impulse for Thecla's creativity. In the mysterious "Last Lover" (1936), the disembodied hand of death offers the Thecla-persona a final bouquet. Representing the artist at the height of her powers, the imaginary landscape, "Undiscovered Place" (1951), represents a safe haven for the psyche. In later works from the 1950s, such as "Guarded Ones" (1955), Thecla's increasingly fluid technique conjures an insubstantial world where reality and fantasy effortlessly intermingle.

Ann Lee Morgan

Bibliography

McKenna, Maureen A. *Julia Thecla, 1896–1973.* Springfield: Illinois State Museum, 1984.

Thiewes, Rachelle (1952–)

Born in Owatonna, Minnesota, the goldsmith and jeweler Rachelle Thiewes attended Western Illinois University, Macomb (1970–1972); earned a Bachelor's degree at Southern Illinois University, Carbondale (1974); and attended Kent State University, Ohio, where she received a Master of Fine Arts degree (1976).

Thiewes has held solo exhibitions in universities and galleries in the United States, including "Rachelle Thiewes," Dartmouth College,

Hanover, New Hampshire (1991); "Rachelle Thiewes: New Work," Jewelers'werk Galerie, Washington, D.C. (1989); "Rachelle Thiewes," CDK Gallery, New York City (1989); "Rachelle Thiewes," Elaine Potter Gallery, San Francisco, California (1986); and others. Between 1972 and 1992 her work has been invited to more than 135 two-person and group exhibitions in the United States and abroad—from Perth, Western Australia, to Edinboro, Pennsylvania; Ankara, Turkey; Scottsdale, Arizona; Moscow, Russia; Little Rock, Arkansas; Helsinki, Finland; New York City; Ketchum, Idaho; Honolulu, Hawaii; and Woodstock, Vermont.

A professor of art at the University of Texas, El Paso, since 1976, Thiewes has won many awards and honors for her work, including a National Endowment for the Arts (NEA) fellowship (1988); two merit awards at "Gold '82," an international gold competition, International Gold Corporation, New York City (1982); and other awards in exhibitions at the Phoenix Art Museum, Arizona (1977); Southern Illinois University, Carbondale (1974); and Geneva Arts Festival, Illinois (1972, 1973). Her work is represented in private and public permanent collections, including the Arkansas Art Center, Little Rock; Art Institute of Chicago, Illinois; Evansville Art Museum, Indiana; the University of Texas, El Paso; and others.

Bibliography
Amendolara, Sue. "Rachelle Thiewes." *Metalsmith* (Fall 1989).
Dinoto, Andrea. "Intersecting Visions." *American Craft* (August–September 1992).
Lynn, Vanessa S. "Provocative Performers: The Intimate Abstractions of Rachelle Thiewes." *Metalsmith* (Summer 1987).
Seymour, Liz. "New Drama in Silver." *Southern Accents* (March 1991).

Thomas, Alma (1892–1978)

Born in Columbus, Georgia, the African-American painter Alma Thomas earned a Bachelor's degree from Howard University, Washington, D.C., and did graduate work at Columbia University, New York City, where she received a Master's degree in art education. Howard University honored Thomas with a retrospective exhibition (1966)—one of many solo and group exhibitions that showed her work. The Corcoran Gallery of Art, Washington, D.C., also gave her a retrospective show (1972).

Thomas held solo shows in galleries and museums, including "Alma Thomas," Fisk University, Nashville, Tennessee (1971); "Alma Thomas," the Whitney Museum of American Art (1972), and "Alma W. Thomas: Recent Paintings 1975–1976," Martha Jackson West (1976)—both in New York City; and many others after her death, such as "Alma Thomas," National Museum of American Art, Washington, D.C. (1982). Thomas's work is represented in private and public permanent collections, including the Corcoran Gallery of Art, George Washington University, the National Museum of Women in the Arts, the Phillips Collection, and Howard University—all in Washington, D.C.; and others. "Wind Dances with Flower Beds" (1968), an acrylic on canvas, is not atypical of the expert abstractions she painted during this period.

Bibliography
Atkinson, J. Edward, ed. *Black Dimensions in Contemporary American Art.* New American Library, 1971.
Fine, Elsa Honig. *The Afro-American Artist.* Holt, Rinehart & Winston, 1973.
Foresta, Merry A. *A Life in Art: Alma Thomas, 1891–1978.* National Museum of American Art, 1981.

National Museum of Women in the Arts. Harry N. Abrams, 1987: 84–85, 235.

Thorne-Thompsen, Ruth (1943–)

A photographer known for her innovative and exclusive use of a pinhole camera, Ruth Thorne-Thompsen was born in New York City. She attended Southern Illinois University in Carbondale and received her Bachelor of Fine Arts degree in painting in 1970. Three years later, Thorne-Thompsen completed her Bachelor of Arts degree in photography at Columbia College, Chicago, and went on to the School of the Art Institute of Chicago—both in Illinois, where she earned her Master of Fine Arts degree in photography in 1976. Currently, Thorne-Thompsen is an adjunct professor at Columbia College and has been there since 1974.

Thorne-Thompsen has received the National Endowment for the Humanities summer fellowship, which took her to Paris, France, in 1979, and the John Quincy Adams fellowship in 1976. Her work can be found in the permanent collections of the Art Institute of Chicago and the Museum of Contemporary Art—both in Chicago, Illinois; the Graham Nash Collection in Los Angeles, and the San Francisco Museum of Modern Art—both in California; as well as the Bibliothèque Nationale in Paris, France.

Thorne-Thompsen works well with a small, homemade camera, which has a removable back, a pinhole aperture, and no lens. This camera produces grainy, black-and-white images with blurred boundaries and distorted perspective. They resemble the nineteenth-century exploration photographs of Maxime DuChamp in the Near East and of Francis Frith in the Middle East. Thorne-Thompsen is not interested in fooling the viewer with her unrealistic images of the world, but with renewing the mystery of old photographic procedures and strengthening the history of photography. Her ongoing work is entitled "Expedition Series."

Melissa J. Guenther

Bibliography
Browne, Turner, and Elaine Partnow. *Macmillan Biographical Encyclopedia of Photographic Artists and Innovators.* Macmillan and Collier Macmillan, 1983.
Edwards, Owen. "Tripping the Light Fantastic." *Photographer* XII:3 (March 1984).
Stand, Marc. "Lost in Space." *Vogue* (June 1984).

Titcomb, Mary Bradish (1856–1927)

The painter Mary Bradish Titcomb, born in Windham, New Hampshire, studied at the Female Academy in nearby Derry before attending the Massachusetts Normal Art School in Boston. Upon receiving her diploma in June 1887 she accepted a position teaching drawing in the public schools of Brockton, Massachusetts. On a leave of absence in 1895 she went to Paris, France, to study at the Académie Julian with Jules Lefèbvre. She resumed her teaching in Brockton until 1901 when she resigned to devote herself full-time to her own painting. From 1901 to 1909 she studied at the Boston Museum School, Massachusetts, with Edmund C. Tarbell, Frank W. Benson, and Philip L. Hale. Her sketchbooks of 1892 to 1909 give evidence of travel to lakes and mountains in Maine and New Hampshire (1892, 1897); Nogales, Arizona (1898, 1902) to visit her brother and his family; Canada (1899, 1901); Spain

(1906); and Brittany (1909).

Starting in 1895, when Titcomb joined the Copley Society, Boston, Massachusetts, she began exhibiting regularly in Boston and won the watercolor prize at the C.E. Cobb Gallery. From 1904 through 1927 she participated in twenty-nine exhibitions at the Pennsylvania Academy of Fine Arts, Philadelphia. To avoid any possible prejudice in juried shows, she began signing her name "M. Bradish Titcomb" in 1905.

A celebrated sale occurred in 1915 when President Woodrow Wilson bought her "Portrait of Geraldine J" at the Corcoran Gallery of Art's 5th Exhibition of Oil Paintings by Contemporary American Artists, Washington, D.C. Later the actress Jane Russell identified the sitter as her mother, and, when she could not buy the portrait from the Woodrow Wilson House in Washington, D.C., she had a copy made.

The major body of Titcomb's work consists of impressionistic landscapes, oftentimes including human figures. She was a member of "The Group" which showed at the Worcester Art Museum, Massachusetts (1917, 1919), and at the Detroit Institute of Art, Michigan (1918). She also participated in many national exhibitions, such as the annual exhibitions at the Art Institute of Chicago, Illinois; the "First Annual Exhibition of Selected Paintings by American Artists" at the Detroit Institute of Art, Michigan (1915); and three paintings in the Panama-Pacific International Exposition, San Francisco, California (1915). In 1920 she moved to Marblehead, Massachusetts, and exhibited at the North Shore Art Association of Gloucester the summer before her death in October 1927.

Eleanor Tufts

Bibliography
Tufts, Eleanor. *American Women Artists, 1830–1930.* National Museum of Women in the Arts, 1987.

Tod, JoAnne (1953–)

JoAnne Tod was born and raised in Montréal, Québec, Canada, and educated at the Ontario College of Art in Toronto, Canada (1970–1974). Her first group exhibition took place at the little-known Gallery 76 in Toronto in 1973. Since then she has had solo shows in some of the more prestigious Canadian galleries. The first of these was held in 1979 in the alternative artist-run space called YYZ (after the Toronto Airport code), and, since 1984, she has been represented by the private and very influential Carmen Lamanna Gallery, Toronto. Tod's exhibition themes are usually politically charged—the first one was called "Mao: Six Uncommissioned Portraits." In Canada she is considered one of the more important feminist painters participating in the current critique of representation. Her style is a brand of flat, unexpressive realism, but her content is unmistakable. It usually features images of women drawn from popular culture, but they are reworked or combined with other elements in such a way as to undermine the expectations that determined the content of the image in its original context. A well-known example is her "Self-Portrait" (1982), which is less a true self-portrait than a symbolic image of the plight of woman in consumer society. It shows a young beauty in an evening gown and fur stole of the sort found in fashion magazines of the 1950s and early 1960s. She stands on the steps of the Lincoln Memorial in Washington, D.C., opening her arms in a gesture of acceptance or greeting which is all the more ambiguous in that her pose is aligned with the conspicuously

phallic Washington Monument in the distance. Most unnerving of all is a text simply printed across the hem of her garment: "'Neath my arm is the colour of Russell's Subaru." Tod thus calls into question several layers of female roles and expectations: clothing, glamor, nostalgia, political endeavor, and consumerism. Her greatest international exposure in any single show was at the "Songs of Experience" assembled at the National Gallery of Canada, Ottawa, in 1986.

Robert J. Belton

Bibliography
Bradley, Jessica, and Diana Nemiroff. *Songs of Experience.* Ottawa: National Gallery of Canada, 1986.
Monk, Philip. *Struggles with the Image.* Toronto: Gallery YYZ, 1988.
Moorhouse, Ashleigh. *Art, Sight, and Language.* Kapuskasing: Penumbra, 1989.

Tolmács, Helena

Born in Monterrey, Nuevo León, Mexico, Helena Tolmács studied the plastic arts in the University of Nuevo León (1949–1952), and the history of art in the Technological Institute of Monterrey (1951). She was a professor of art in both institutions (1952–1955) and then she moved to Mexico City.

From 1949 to 1955 Tolmács exhibited her work in her native city; since 1956 she has shown every year in the Salón de la Plástica Mexicana, Mexico City, and, since 1969, in the collection of the gallery, the Molino de Santo Domingo. Her work is in many museums in Mexico and abroad, and is also in distinguished private collections in Jaffa, Israel; Santiago, Chile; Oradea, Rumania; Sacramento, California; and San Juan, Puerto Rico.

Bibliography
Alvarez, José Rogelio, et al. *Enciclopedia de Mexico.* Secretaría de Educación Pública, 1987.

Toogood, Wendy (1947–)

Wendy Toogood makes impeccably crafted fiber constructions. Utilizing a wide variety of textures and colors, she produces vibrant images strongly influenced by folk art and kitsch. Born in Bristol, she settled in Calgary, Alberta, Canada, in 1952. She graduated from the Alberta College of Art, Calgary, in 1969, and studied at the Instituto Allende, Mexico. She teaches at the Alberta College of Art.

Toogood's extensive exhibitions include "Four Hangings," National Gallery of Canada, Ottawa (1970); "Mikrokosma," Canada, United States, and Europe (1983–1985); and "Frontiers," Japan and Australia (1984). Her early work featuring the human head evolved about 1972 into flying humanoid forms. These witty, darting, appliquéd figures became a consistent motif. "Cloth Construction" (1979), a mural commission in three large panels, is a collage of brightly colored fabrics and patterns handsewn onto a cotton backing and quilted for structural strength. Bias tape "drawing" carries a flowing rhythm across the panels.

Around 1982 Toogood developed a purely abstract formal vocabulary of line, color, and texture. New glitzy materials were added to her existing "palette" of herringbone tweeds, silks, printed cottons, taffetas, sequined fabrics, synthetic metallic fabrics, Spandex, photographic animal-skin prints, and vinyls. In "Strong Winds" (1985), a four-panel construction commissioned for Expo '86 in Vancouver, the landscape theme dictated a horizontal composition. Large, simple, vertical forms suggest mountains and teepees. Areas of solid color are offset with concentrations of linear "drawn" marks.

Recently Toogood has broken away from the restrictions of a rectangular format. Working directly on the wall rather than flat on the floor has changed the way the pieces are made. Some fabrics are draped, hung, or furled, creating more tactile and three-dimensional compositions.

Patricia Ainslie

Bibliography
Laviolette, Mary-Beth. *Wendy Toogood.* Lethbridge: Southern Alberta Art Gallery, 1988.
Tousely, Nancy. "Toogood's Strong Winds to Blow over Expo." *Calgary Herald* (December 22, 1985).
Townsend-Gault, Charlotte. "New Image Alberta." *Vanguard* 12:2 (1983): 20–21.

Toral, Maria Teresa (1912–)

Born in Madrid, Spain, Maria Teresa Toral studied drawing and chemistry in the School of Arts and Crafts in her native city (1930–1936) and took further study in printmaking at the National Institute of Fine Arts, Mexico City, Mexico, with Guillermo Silva Santamaría (1959–1963). A naturalized citizen of Mexico, she exhibited in her new country for the first time in 1963; this was followed by shows in Spain and in Israel.

A teacher of physics and chemistry at the Polytechnic Institute and at the University of Mexico, Toral participated in the International Exhibition of Miniature Prints at the Pratt Center for Contemporary Printmaking in New York City (1968–1969). In 1972 she received an honorable mention in the Salón de la Plástica Mexicana, Mexico City. Toral's work is in the permanent collections of museums in Chile, Canada, Mexico, the United States, Holland, Israel, and Czechoslovakia. As a printmaker Toral makes etchings, serigraphs, and mixed-media works. Her thematic material is many-sided and often concerned with the world of the child.

Bibliography
Alvarez, José Rogelio, et al. *Enciclopedia de Mexico.* Secretaría de Educación Pública, 1987.
Nelken, Margarita. *Siete Años de Grabado de Maria Teresa Toral.* n.d.
The Texas Quarterly: Image of Mexico II. The University of Texas, Autumn 1969.

Torr, Helen (1886–1967)

A romantic who transformed objects into symbols of her feelings, Helen Torr was a talented painter among the first generation of American modernists. However, her output was small, and she lived in the shadow of her more celebrated husband, Arthur Dove.

Torr grew up in Philadelphia, Pennsylvania, and studied at the Drexel Institute and the Pennsylvania Academy of Fine Arts—both in Philadelphia. Her first marriage ended in 1921 when she and Dove fell in love in Westport, Connecticut. Aboard the sailboat that soon provided their home on Long Island Sound, the art of both partners flourished in an atmosphere of mutual encouragement. In the late 1920s they resided on shore at Halesite, Long Island, New York, and in 1933 they moved to Dove's hometown of Geneva, New York, where they remained for five years. Returning to Long Island, they lived in Centerport, New York, where Torr stayed on but did not paint after Dove's death in 1946.

Most of Torr's work dates to the 1920s and early 1930s. It ranged from the bold abstraction of the undated 1920s charcoal, "On Board Ship," to an incisive realism, exemplified by her self-portrait, "I" (1933). In most of her paintings, natural objects provide the basis for stylized interpretation, as in "Sea Shell" (1928) and "Along the Shore" (1932). Although much of her work superficially resembles Dove's, her vision was characteristically more specific than his, and her compositions are more tightly conceived and executed. Torr's dominant tone is meditative, often verging on melancholy, and her deft sense of the decorative rarely fails.

Ann Lee Morgan

Bibliography
DePietro, Anne Cohen. *Arthur Dove and Helen Torr: The Huntington Years.* Huntington, New York: Heckscher Museum, 1989.
Gatling, Eva Ingersoll. Introduction to *Helen Torr 1886–1967.* Huntington, New York: Heckscher Museum, and New York: Graham Gallery, 1972.
Leff, Sandra. Introduction in *Helen Torr 1886–1967.* New York: Graham Gallery, 1980.
Roos, Jane Mayo. "Helen Torr." *Arts* 54:9 (May 1980).

Touchette, Charleen (1954–)

Born in the textile-mill town of Woonsocket, Rhode Island, Charleen Touchette is a member of the Pied Noir (Blackfeet) tribe. Touchette attended Bard College, Annandale-on-Hudson, New York, where she received her Bachelor of Arts degree in 1975.

Lecturer on women's art and contemporary Native American art, Touchette has curated exhibitions at Willamette University, Salem, Oregon, and the Six Directions Gallery, in the same city. She received a grant from the Metropolitan Arts Commission, Portland, Oregon, in the recent past.

Touchette paints themes in series, based upon her French-Canadian/Native American upbringing. Works such as "Tes Filles: Memories, Dreams, and Reflections of a Canuck/Pied Noir Girlhood," "Grandmother Telling Stories," "Shadow Mama with Babes," and "Reindeer Woman Vision" are typical of this period.

"Deer Woman Vision" (1983), an acrylic painting on linen of a snake, a horned and nude woman, and four profiled horses in the sky, is described by the artist as "a woman of peace who brings vision and power. The jade green serpent spiraling into the electric blue twilight sky is a good spirit helper who brings a message from the center of the Earth to protect the Earth Mother." She also writes, "My art expresses what it feels like to be a woman, daughter, granddaughter, and sister. It is simultaneously mythological, autobiographical, and spiritual. My imagery is inspired by my dreams, memories, and visions."

Touchette's works have been invited to many exhibitions, including "Women of Sweetgrass, Cedar, and Sage," American Indian Community House Gallery, New York City (1985); "Visage Transcended: Contemporary Native American Masks, American Indian Contemporary Arts, San Francisco, California (1985); and others.

Bibliography
Heard Museum Archives. Phoenix, Arizona.

Townsend, Martha (1956–)

Martha Townsend was born in Ottawa, Ontario, Canada. She received a Bachelor of Fine Arts degree from the Nova Scotia College of Art and Design, Halifax, in 1978. She eventually moved to Montréal, Québec, Canada, where she taught at Concordia University and worked at Yajima Gallery, Artexte, and for the Steinberg collection. She moved to Brooklyn, New York, in 1991.

Townsend's earlier work invested the tradition of the found object with the conceptual play of language. Works such as "Burying Eve" (1985), an inverted garden spade with a wedding band embedded in the center, were shown at her first important solo show at Powerhouse—a women's gallery in Montréal. The "Bull" (1987)—an iron bowl and coil of a bull tether—and "Link" (1987)—an iron bale hook and chain links—were exhibited at Art 45 in 1987 and in the 1988 exhibition, "Enchantment/Disturbance," curated by Renée Baert for Toronto's Power Plant Gallery.

In 1988 and 1989 Townsend worked at Strokestown House, County Roscommon, Ireland, in part to explore her ancestors' roots. Her installation, "La Chasse-Galerie," explored the connections between the histories of Ireland and Québec. The centerpiece of the work, a canoe, figures prominently in the Québecois legend of La Chasse-Galerie.

Townsend's work shifted in 1988, borrowing the elemental forms of minimalism, particularly the sphere and the wedge, but executed in sensual and evocative materials. This work was shown at Mercer Union in Toronto and Art 45 in Montréal in 1988 and 1990, respectively. The work included "Morning Sphere" (1988), a stained cedar sphere around which a suede band had been fitted.

Townsend's blackened wooden sphere, "Orb" (1992), five feet in diameter, was shown at "Diagonales," an exhibition curated for the Centre Internationale d'Art Contemporain, and again in a solo show at Lethbridge's Southern Alberta Art Gallery. She has exhibited throughout Canada and has participated in group shows in New York, Berlin, and France. She has given numerous public lectures and has been the recipient of many senior grants from Québec's Ministry of Cultural Affairs and the Canada Council. Her work is included in both public and private collections.

Cyril Reade

Bibliography

Baert, Renée. *Enchantment/Disturbance*. Toronto: The Power Plant, 1988.

Fraser, Ted. *Artifact: Memory and Desire*. Stratford Gallery, 1989.

Laing, Carol. *Interview with Martha Townsend*. Mercer Union, 1989.

Randolph, Jeanne. "The Predicament of Meaning." *Martha Townsend*. The Southern Alberta Art Gallery, 1992.

St.-Gelais, Thérèse. *Diagonales Montréal: Martha Townsend*. Editions Parachute, 1992.

Treiman, Joyce (Wahl) (1922–)

Joyce (Wahl) Treiman's figurative painting examines the human condition, sometimes through images inspired by her personal experiences, and other times through mythic themes. Born in Evanston, Illinois, Treiman began taking drawing lessons at the age of eight. While in high school she attended life-drawing classes at the School of the Art Institute of Chicago, Illinois, and spent time sketching in the galleries of the museum. These early experiences were the foundation of a lifelong commitment to drawing. In 1943 she earned a Bachelor of Fine Arts degree at the University of Iowa, Iowa City, having studied paint-

ing with Philip Guston. Her early work was strongly influenced by his version of social realism. She also found Guston's approach to teaching inspiring, using it as a model for her own work in the classroom when she held positions as visiting artist later in her career.

After college Treiman returned to the Chicago area. She married Kenneth Treiman in 1945, and, in the late 1940s, exhibited regularly, showing images of isolated, troubled individuals still related to Guston's figures. Around 1950 she came under the influence of Willem de Kooning's work, and sought subjects from mythology and the Old Testament, which she expressed through abstracted forms, eventually experimenting with a series of abstract expressionist-inspired, non-representational works in the late 1950s.

Treiman and her family moved to Los Angeles, California, in 1960, where she started painting figural compositions again. For a time the images seemed to materialize out of abstract forms worked on the canvas, but, in the mid-1960s, she returned to more conventional figures which were planned in advance. Among her best-known works the paintings of the late 1960s and early 1970s depicted enigmatic relationships among disparate figures, each demanding the individual attention of the viewer. Laden with symbolism these works—for example, "The Birthday Party" (1966–1967)—were not anecdotal, but based on images from the inner world of the artist.

Concern with her relationship to artists from the past—stimulated by several trips to Europe in the 1960s—led Treiman to paint a series of works in homage to the painters she admired most, including Bonnard, Eakins, Monet, Sargent, and Toulouse-Lautrec. Another group of works reflect life in the Western United States through the depiction of its landscape and legendary inhabitants: Native Americans and cowboys. The many social types to be found in her paintings also populate her drawings, prints, and sculptures.

Like many artists who painted figurative works in the 1960s and 1970s, Treiman has received little widespread recognition. However, she has steadily built an impressive record, participating in numerous solo and group exhibitions. She has won many prizes and has been the recipient of several important fellowships, including those of Tiffany Foundation (1947), Tupperware Art Fund (1955), and Ford Foundation (1963).

Paula Wisotzki

Bibliography

Joyce Treiman: A Retrospective. Essays by Lester D. Longman and Maurice Bloch. Los Angeles Municipal Art Gallery, 1978.

Joyce Treiman: Paintings, 1961–1972. Intro. by William Wilson. La Jolla Museum of Contemporary Art, 1972.

Rubinstein, Charlotte Streifer. *American Women Artists: From Early Indian Times to the Present*. Avon, 1982, pp. 338–41.

Trejo, Paulina (1925–)

Born in Quatrociénegas, Coahuila, Mexico, Paulina Trejo studied at the Academy of San Carlos, Mexico City (1943–1947). A painter and printmaker, Trejo has exhibited her work in Mexico and abroad since 1944; the most recent exhibitions were on the occasions of the 150th anniversary of the founding of the city of Ocampo, Coahuila (1978); the 50th birthday of the National School of Graphic Arts, Mexico City; and the competition, "Vamos a Retratar a Diego," convened by the Salón de la Plástica Mexicana, Mexico City.

Bibliography
Alvarez, José Rogelio, et al. *Enciclopedia de Mexico.* Secretaría de
    Educación Pública, 1987.

Trieff, Selina (1934–)

Born in Brooklyn, New York, the painter Selina Trieff attended the Art
Students League, New York City, where she studied with Morris Kantor.
She also worked under the aegis of Hans Hofmann at his school in the
same city. Trieff earned a Bachelor's degree from Brooklyn College, where
she studied with Mark Rothko and Ad Reinhardt (1955).

Trieff has had solo and group exhibitions of her work in many
galleries and museums in the United States and abroad, including
"Work on Paper," Brooklyn Museum, New York (1975); Galleri Anna,
Göteborg, Sweden (1979); "Contemporary Figure Painting," Hewra
Gallery, Wakefield, Rhode Island (1979); Artes Gallery, Oslo, Norway
(1984); Graham Modern Gallery, New York City (1986, 1987, 1988);
Ruth Bachofner Gallery, Santa Monica, California (1987); and others.

Winner of honors and awards, Trieff has been instructor of drawing
at the New York Institute of Technology since 1975. She is a member of
the College Art Association, Women's Caucus for Art, and Women in the
Arts. She was a visiting artist at the University of Notre Dame, Indiana
(1976) and also taught at the New York Studio School, Pratt Institute,
and the National Academy of Design—all in New York City. Examples
of her work are in private, public, and corporate permanent collections,
including the Brooklyn Museum and the New York Public Library;
Bayonne Jewish Center, New Jersey; Notre Dame University, Indiana;
Prudential Life Insurance Company; and others.

Bibliography
Campbell, Lawrence. "Selina Trieff at Graham Modern." *Art in America* 74:12
    (December 1986): 138–140.
Marter, Joan. "Confrontations: The Paintings of Selina Trieff." *Arts Magazine*
    60:10 (Summer 1986): 51–53.
Russell, John. "Selina Trieff, Graham Gallery." *The New York Times* (June 12,
    1987): Y18.

Truitt, Anne (1921–)

Lauded for the writing of her memoirs, Ann Truit is a reader of the
classics. She holds honorary Doctorate degrees for her sculpture from
the Corcoran School of Art, Washington, D.C., the Kansas City Art
Institute, Missouri; St. Mary's College of Maryland, Maryland City, and
the Maryland Institute College of Art, Baltimore—both in Maryland.
Truitt was born in Baltimore, Maryland, and received her Bachelor's
degree in psychology from Bryn Mawr College, Pennsylvania (1943).
She also studied art at the Institute of Contemporary Art, Washington, D.C. (1948–1949), and the Dallas Museum of Fine Arts (1950),
Texas. Earlier she was a psychologist at Massachusetts General Hospital in Boston.

Truitt has held many solo exhibitions of her sculpture in galleries and museums in the United States and Japan, including the André
Emmerich Gallery, New York City (1963, 1965, 1969, 1975, 1980,
1986, 1991); Minami Gallery, Tokyo, Japan (1964, 1967); Baltimore
Museum of Fine Arts, Maryland (1969, 1974, 1992); the Whitney Museum of American Art, New York City (1973); Osuna Gallery, Washington, D.C. (1979, 1981, 1986, 1989, 1992); the Neuberger Museum,
State University of New York (SUNY) at Purchase (1986); and others. Her richly-painted, color-banded, wood structures and her drawings were invited to group exhibitions in the United States, Japan,
and Germany, including "Black, White, and Grey," Wadsworth Athenaeum, Hartford, Connecticut (1964); "Color and Space," Minami
Gallery, Tokyo, Japan (1966); "Amerikanische Zeichnungen 1930–
1980," Stadtische Galerie, Frankfurt, Germany (1985); and others.

Truitt earned the title professor emerita and teaches at the University of Maryland. She was awarded a Guggenheim Foundation fellowship (1971); two National Endowment for the Arts (NEA) fellowships
(1972, 1977); and an Arts Council grant from the government of Australia (1981). Her work is housed in the permanent collections of prestigious museums and galleries, such as the National Gallery of Art,
Hirshhorn Museum and Sculpture Garden, and National Museum of
American Art—all in Washington, D.C.; the Albright-Knox Art Gallery, Buffalo, New York; Metropolitan Museum of Art, Museum of Modern Art (MoMA), and Whitney Museum of American Art—all in New
York City; Museum of Fine Arts, Houston, Texas; St. Louis Museum of
Art, Missouri; Walker Art Center, Minneapolis, Minnesota; and others.

Bibliography
Baro, Gene. "Anne Truitt at the Corcoran." *Art in America* (July–August 1974).
Greenberg, Clement. "Changer: Anne Truitt, American Artist Whose Painted
    Structures Helped to Change the Course of American Sculpture." *Vogue*
    (May 1968).
Heller, Nancy G. *Women Artists.* Abbeville Press, 1987.
Plagens, Peter. "The Heart of the Matter." *Newsweek* (March 30, 1992): 66.
Truitt, Anne. *DAYBOOK: The Journal of an Artist.* Pantheon Books, 1982.
———. *Turn: The Journal of an Artist.* Viking Penguin Press, 1986.

Tulurialik, Ruth Annaqtuusi (1934–)

A Canadian Inuit artist best known for her exuberant drawings, bright-
colored wool duffel wall-hangings, and energetic stoneblock prints produced through the Sanavik Co-operative at Baker Lake, Northwest Territories, Ruth Annaqtuusi Tulurialik did not turn to art until she was
in her mid-thirties. Tulurialik was born in a traditional Inuit camp along
the Kazan River in the Keewatin district of Arctic Canada before the
establishment of permanent communities in the Canadian North. As
an infant she was adopted by her aunt and uncle, Elisapee Unuqnuq
and Thomas Tapatai, and was raised in the area that was to become the
community of Baker Lake during the 1950s.

Having worked a number of years as an interpreter for the nursing station, child care worker, and cook, Tulurialik became very interested in the arts and crafts projects that were introduced in her community during the 1960s under the auspices of the Canadian federal
government. She first tried her hand at wool duffel wall-hangings but
has become better known for her strongly gestural drawings and for
the stonecut and stencil prints based on her drawings.

Tulurialik draws inspiration for her art from the traditional ways
of her Inuit culture, filling her compositions with extremely imaginative depictions of Arctic animals, Inuit in traditional dress, women with
facial tatoos, shamans and spirits, fantastic birds and fish, and transformational images. Her drawings—usually in colored pencil—are
highly-complex in organization and frequently fill the entire page with
color. She characteristically overlays one hue over another to create

complex and textured skeins of color and often extends the background nearly to the edge of the page, creating a narrow border which she leaves blank to frame her drawings. The figures in Tulurialik's drawings are firmly outlined and filled with color, and she makes occasional use of "voice balloons" to indicate sounds or words expressed by the highly active humans, animals, and spirits that occupy the vibrant world she creates.

Tulurialik has been drawing regularly since 1970. Sixteen of her drawings have been used as the basis for prints produced through the annual Baker Lake print collections. Tulurialik's work is represented in the Baker Lake print collections for the years 1971–1973, 1975, 1977, 1980, and 1983–1987. With the assistance of a Canada Council Explorations grant in 1984 Tulurialik and David Pelly collaborated to produce a collection of stories to accompany a selection of her original drawings; this collection was published under the title *Qikaaluktut—Images of Inuit Life* by Oxford University Press in 1986. That same year a major solo exhibition of forty-two of Tulurialik's drawings, "The Vital Vision: Drawing by Ruth Annaqtuusi Tulurialik," was organized and circulated by the Windsor Gallery of Art, Ontario.

Tulurialik's highly-esteemed drawings, prints, and wall-hangings have been widely exhibited in group exhibitions and are held in such important public collections as the Art Gallery of Ontario, Toronto; government of the Northwest Territories; Macdonald Stewart Art Centre, Guelph; McMichael Collection, Kleinburg, Ontario; National Museum of Civilization, Ottawa; Prince of Wales Northern Heritage Centre, Yellowknife; Sanavik Co-operative, Baker Lake; and the Winnipeg Art Gallery, Manitoba.

Marion E. Jackson

Bibliography

Art Gallery of Ontario. *The People Within.* Toronto: Art Gallery of Ontario, 1976.

Baker Lake annual print collection catalogs: 1971–1973, 1975, 1977, 1980, 1983–1987.

Blodgett, Jean. *The Coming and Going of the Shaman.* Winnipeg Art Gallery, 1978.

Department of Indian and Northern Affairs. *A Face Like the Sun.* Ottawa: Department of Indian and Northern Affairs, 1973.

———. *We Lived by Animals.* Ottawa: Department of Indian and Northern Affairs, 1975.

Driscoll, Bernadette. *Inuit Myths, Legends and Songs.* Winnipeg Art Gallery, 1982.

———, and Sheila Butler. *Baker Lake Prints & Print Drawings 1970–76.* Winnipeg Art Gallery, 1983.

Goetz, Helga. *The Inuit Print/L'estampe Inuit.* Ottawa: National Museums of Canada, 1977.

Fry, Jacqueline, and Sheila Butler. *Baker Lake Drawings.* Winnipeg Art Gallery, 1972.

Jackson, Marion, and Judith Nasby. *Contemporary Inuit Drawings.* Guelph, Ontario: Macdonald Stewart Art Centre, 1987.

Jackson, Marion E., and David F. Pelly. *The Vital Vision: Drawings by Ruth Annaqtuusi Tulurialik.* Ontario: Windsor Gallery of Art, 1986.

Tulurialik, Ruth Annaqtuusi, and David F. Pelly. *Qikaaluktut—Images of Inuit Life.* Oxford University Press, 1986.

Turnbull, Grace H. (1880–1976)

Born in Baltimore, Maryland, the sculptor Grace H. Turnbull exhibited work in group shows, including the 45th and 50th "Annual Exhibitions," National Association of Women Painters and Sculptors, New York City (1936, 1942); and others. Winner of honors and awards, Turnbull was a recipient of the Whitelaw Reid first prize, Paris, France (1914). Representative examples of her work are in private and public permanent collections, including the Metropolitan Museum of Art, New York City.

Bibliography

American Art Annual. Vol. 28. American Federation of Arts, 1932.

Schnier, Jacques. *Sculpture in Modern America.* University of California Press, 1948.

Turnbull, Grace H. *Chips from My Chisel: An Autobiography.* Richard R. Smith, 1953.

Turner, Helen Maria (1858–1958)

Born in Louisville, Kentucky, the painter/pastellist Helen Maria Turner studied at the Artist's Association of New Orleans, Louisiana; the Art Students League, Cooper Union, and Teachers College, Columbia University—all in New York City, with William Merritt Chase, Kenyon Cox, and Douglas Volk.

Between 1897 and 1933 Turner showed regularly in juried exhibitions at the American Association of Miniature Painters, New York City, and many others in the United States and abroad, including the School of the Art Institute of Chicago, Illinois; Luxembourg Museum, Paris, France (1919); Corcoran Gallery of Art, Washington, D.C.; 14th International, Venice, and the 2nd International, Rome—both in Italy (1924); National Academy of Design, New York City; Pennsylvania Academy of Fine Arts, Philadelphia; the Watercolor Club and the Women's Art Club—both in New York City; and others.

Turner participated in a two-person show with sculptor Harriet Whitney Frishmuth, which toured the United States; she held a joint exhibition with Walter Griffin at the Memorial Art Gallery, Rochester, New York (1917), and, that same year, held a solo show at the Milch Gallery, New York City. Her work was honored in a travelling retrospective exhibition (1983–1984).

Winner of many awards, Turner was the recipient of the Elling prize for landscapes, New York Women's Club (1912); the Agar prize, National Association of Women Painters and Sculptors; the Shaw memorial prize, National Academy of Design (1913), second prize at the National Arts Club (1922); a gold medal from the National Arts Club (1927)—all in New York City; the Altman prize (1921) and the Maynard prize (1927); and others. She was elected an associate of the National Academy of Design, New York City (1913), and a national academician.

Turner taught art at St. Mary's Academy, Dallas, Texas (1893–1894) and at the YWCA (Young Women's Christian Association) in New York City (1902–1919). She was a member of many prestigious art associations, including the New York Watercolor Club, National Association of Portrait Painters, National Arts Club, American Federation of Arts, American Artists Professional League, and the Southern States Art League. Her work is represented in private and public permanent collections, such as the Corcoran Gallery of Art and Phillips Memorial Gallery—both in Washington, D.C.; Detroit Institute of Arts, Michigan; Delgado Museum, New Orleans, Louisiana; Houston Art Museum,

Texas; Metropolitan Museum of Art and the National Arts Club—both in New York City; Newark Art Museum, New Jersey; Norfolk Museum, Virginia; and others.

Bibliography

An Exhibition of Paintings by Six American Women. St. Louis City Art Museum, 1918.

Buff, Barbara. "Cragsmoor, An Early American Art Colony." *Antiques* 114 (November 1978): 1056–67.

Helen M. Turner: A Retrospective Exhibition. Cragsmoor Free Library, New York, 1983.

The New York Times [New Jersey edition] (January 15, 1984): 24.

Tuu'luq, Marion (c. 1910–)

Working in isolation in the small arctic community of Baker Lake, Northwest Territories, Marion Tuu'luq is far removed from the acclaim her art has received. For more than twenty years she produced wall-hangings and drawings, laboriously and lovingly portraying a world that is sometimes real, sometimes imaginary but always brimming with life, joy, and the bright colors, rich textures, and elegant forms that have become her trademark.

Tuu'luq was born around 1910 at Back River, northwest of Baker Lake, where she led a traditional, humble existence. She married twice and gave birth to sixteen children, only four of whom are alive.

Tuu'luq's artistic career began shortly after she and her family, escaping the disease and famine ravaging the barren lands at that time, resettled in Baker Lake in 1961. She emerged from these difficult times tough in mind and body, generous in spirit and with her sense of humor surprisingly intact. Like many other Inuit women, Tuu'luq quickly adapted her sewing skills to the local arts and crafts project established by the federal government as a source of income for the displaced Inuit. She did her first drawings in the mid-1960s and sewed clothing items and small cloth "pictures"—small scenes sewn onto a fabric background—for a sewing project managed by the wife of the local Anglican minister.

After the death of her mother, Tuu'luq, still only a child, taught herself the difficult task of cutting and sewing the bulky caribou skin clothing essential for survival—a skill traditionally passed on from mother to daughter. She developed a tiny, regular, precise stitch so important in the sewing of skins. To her growing technical ability she added an intimate knowledge of her medium, of pattern and design and painstakingly crafted clothing which not only fit properly but which were also distinctively decorated with inlaid designs in contrasting colors of fur.

Tuu'luq's artistic ability flowed naturally from her traditional skills and rich experiences on the land—the visual organization and manual dexterity developed in her past guiding her eyes and hands. Her talent flourished under the nurturing guidance of artists Jack and Sheila Butler, who arrived in Baker Lake in 1969 to serve as craft officers for the community. The Butlers introduced her to beadwork and encouraged the making of drawings and large-scale wall-hangings. Tuu'luq favored the fabric medium and developed a fascination for heavily embroidered surface patterns rendered in bright colors. At times her visual interpretations were preconceived but most often she just picked up her scissors and started cutting images, developing her theme as she went along.

Anthropomorphic figures, abstract stylized designs, and the single image of a woman's face are common motifs in Tuu'luq's work. She exploits these images repeatedly to portray old and new beliefs and the easy existence man had with animals. According to Tuu'luq the image of the female face has existed in her mind since before she started producing art. It appears in her visual vocabulary perhaps as a means of self-contemplation and an acknowledgment of the respect paid to human existence in Inuit culture.

The prestigious exhibition "Crafts from Arctic Canada," mounted by the Canadian Eskimo Arts Council in Ottawa in 1974, launched Tuu'luq's artistic career. Since then her wall-hangings and drawings have been exhibited regularly in national and international group exhibitions. In 1976 her work appeared in a two-person exhibition shared with her artist husband, Luke Anguhadluq. That same year Public Works Canada commissioned Tuu'luq to create a wall-hanging for the Penetanguishene Post Office in Ontario. In 1978 she was elected a member of the Royal Canadian Academy of Arts. In 1980 her wall-hangings were featured in a solo exhibition at the Upstairs Gallery in Winnipeg. She was also one of the women chosen to produce a wall-hanging for the Northwest Territories Pavilion at Expo '86 in Vancouver. Most recently Tuu'luq's wall-hangings were featured in the 1989 Canadian Museum of Civilization's touring exhibition, "In the Shadow of the Sun": *Zeitgenossische Kunst der Indianer und Eskimos in Kanada.*

While known particularly for her fabric art, Tuu'luq has also contributed drawings to thirteen of the Baker Lake Annual Print Collections. "Creatures of the World" (1987), based on Tuu'luq's drawing, was chosen for the cover of the 1987 print collection catalog. In recognition of her artistic accomplishments and her contribution to Inuit Art, Tuu'luq received an Honorary Doctor of Laws degree from the University of Alberta in June 1990. She is the first Inuk to be so recognized by the university and only the second Inuit artist in Canada to receive an honorary degree.

Tuu'luq's work can be found in the permanent collections of the Winnipeg Art Gallery; the Department of Indian Affairs and Northern Development, Ottawa; the Canadian Museum of Civilization, Hull; the Prince of Wales Northern Heritage Centre, Yellowknife; the Macdonald Stewart Art Centre, Guelph; the Simon Fraser Gallery, Burnaby; the Canada Council Art Bank, Ottawa; and in the Klamer Family Collection, Art Gallery of Ontario, Toronto.

Marie Bouchard

Bibliography

Baker, Marilyn. "The Tapestries of Marion Tuu'luq." *Branching Out* 7:2 (1980).

Blodgett, Jean. *Grasp Tight the Old Ways: Selections from the Klamer Family Collection of Inuit Art.* Toronto: Art Gallery of Ontario, 1983.

Tuu'luq/Anguhadluq. The Winnipeg Art Gallery, 1976.

Butler, Sheila. "Wall Hangings from Baker Lake." *The Beaver* (Autumn 1972).

Department of Information, Government of the Northwest Territories. "Stories by Marion Anguhadluq." *Northern People* (1976).

Ingram, Mathew. "From Igloo to Art Gallery." *Alberta Report* (June 1990).

Jackson, Marion, and Judith Nasby. *Contemporary Inuit Drawings.* Guelph: Macdonald Stewart Art Centre, 1987.

"Marion Tuu'luq Receives Honorary Degree." *Inuit Art Quarterly* 5:3 (Summer 1990).

Muehlen, Marial. "Baker Lake Wall-Hangings: Starting From Scraps." *Inuit Art Quarterly* 4:2 (Spring 1989).

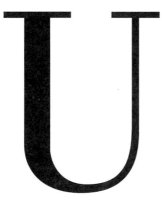

U

Udinotti, Agnese (1940–)

Born in Athens, Greece, the poet/sculptor/painter Agnese Udinotti earned a Bachelor's degree (1962) and a Master's degree (1963) from Arizona State University, Tempe.

Udinotti has held many solo and two-person exhibitions in museums and galleries in the United States and abroad, including Arizona State University, Tempe (1962, 1975); Tucson Art Center (1965)—both in Arizona; Hellenic-American Union (1968) and New Forms Gallery (1969, 1973–1974, 1977, 1992)—both in Athens, Greece; Albert White Gallery, Toronto, Canada (1969, 1971); Vorpal Gallery, San Francisco, California (1969, 1971, 1973); Galerie Balans, Amsterdam, the Netherlands (1973–1975, 1978); Elaine Horwitch Gallery, Scottsdale, Arizona (1973, 1974); French Institute, Salonica, Greece (1977); Museo Nacional de Oaxaca, Mexico (1978); Galerie 1–2–3, San Salvador, El Salvador (1978); "9th Panhellenic Exhibitions," a travelling show to Paris and London, UNESCO (1979); Udinotti Gallery, Scottsdale, Arizona (annually 1981–1988, 1992); "25-Year Retrospective," Greek Sculptors Guild, Athens, Greece (1989); and many others. Her work has been invited to myriad group exhibitions in the United States and Europe: from Yuma, Arizona, to Edinburgh, Scotland; from San Francisco, California, to Stuttgart, Germany; from Marietta, Ohio, to Volos, Greece; from Moorhead, Minnesota, to Paris, France.

Winner of honors and awards for her painting and sculpture, Udinotti was poetry editor of the magazine *Chimera*, and honorary advisor to the American Biographical Institute. Her work is represented in private, public, and corporate permanent collections, including the Phoenix Art Museum; Valley National Bank, Phoenix; Arizona State University, Tempe—all in Arizona; the Ministry of Education of Greece; National Gallery of Athens; and Vorres Museum of Art, Paiania—all in Greece; Stanford University, Palo Alto, California; National Museum of Women in the Arts, and the General Services Administration, Washington, D.C.; and many others. "Relief" (1987), a welded steel sculpture not atypical of her work of this period, seems to synthesize Udinotti's concerns and anxieties: man's inhumanity to man; man vs. man-made structures; what is beautiful, what is ugly; and others.

Bibliography

Three Generations of Greek Women Artists. A Catalog. National Museum of Women in the Arts, 1989.

Udinotti. Foreword by Rudy Turk. Northland Press, 1973.

Udinotti, Agnese. *Udinotti: A Biography*. Paradise House, Inc., 1989.

Watson-Jones, Virginia. *Contemporary American Women Sculptors*. Oryx Press, 1986.

Who's Who in American Art. 19th ed. R.R. Bowker Co., 1991–1992.

Ugalde, Ana (1925–)

Born in San Juan del Río, Querétaro, Mexico, Ana Ugalde studied painting with Prometeo Barragán and José Ramos Castillo. She exhibited for the first time in the Galería del Grupo Preparatoriano 20–24 (1958); she painted the murals in the Museo Regional de San Diego in Acapulco (1951); and participated with Antonio López Sáenz, Martha Rojas, and Enrique Carreón in producing works for the temple museum annex of the Castillo de Chapultepec (1959). Along with Héctor Trillo, Martha Rojas, and Prometeo Barragán, she participated in creating decorative works for the pre-Hispanic rooms of the Museo de la Ciudad de Mexico

(1963); and participated in assembling and decorating the Oaxaca Room of the Museo Nacional de Antropología, Mexico City (1964). Ugalde offers classes in painting and restoration; her most recent projects were undertaken in the Sagrario Metropolitano and in the Temple of the Profera in Mexico City. In addition to her many mural and restoration projects, Ugalde continues to work at easel painting.

Bibliography

Alvarez, José Rogelio, et al. *Enciclopedia de Mexico*. Secretaría de Educación Pública, 1987.

Ukeles, Mierle Laderman (1939–)

Sculptor, performance and environmental artist, Mierle Laderman Ukeles was born in Denver, Colorado. She attended the University of Colorado, Boulder (summers 1958–1963); earned a Bachelor's degree from Barnard College, New York City (1961); took studio classes at Pratt Institute, Brooklyn, New York (1962–1964); received a 5th-year certificate for teaching art in the university from the University of Denver, Colorado (1966); and obtained a Master of Arts degree from New York University, New York City, in inter-related arts (1974).

Ukeles has received more than fifty grants, artist's fellowships, commissioned projects, and awards for art in public places, inter-arts projects, and for curating and designing, including nine fellowships from the National Endowment for the Arts (NEA) (1977–1991); seven commissions and other awards from the New York State Council on the Arts and the New York Foundation on the Arts (1979–1991); a Guggenheim Foundation fellowship (1985–1986); a Creative Artists Public Service (CAPS) fellowship (1983–1984); and others dating back to 1976. She was artist member of a design team for a twelve-mile extension of an Oregon rail system (1992); created sculptural work and bridge lighting for the Strawberry Mansion Bridge, Philadelphia, Pennsylvania (1992); engaged in many landfill and sanitation projects, including "Flow City" (1983–1992), a chain of interactive environments for the public to bear witness to the processes of maintenance, sanitation, and waste disposal in New York City's Marine Transfer Facility; designed "The Social Mirror," a twenty-cubic-yard garbage collection truck sheathed in tempered glass mirrors, completed in 1983; created "Vulniswagendans," a futurist ballet for ten garbage vehicles in a public square with sound accompaniment, at the International Art Festival, Rotterdam, Holland (1985); and others.

Ukeles's performances and other works have been invited to myriad group exhibitions in galleries and museums in the United States and abroad. Videos, television, audio, and radio programs have documented and/or presented her public art to new audiences. She lectures widely on a broad range of public art topics from Seattle, Washington, to Washington, D.C.; from New York City, to Jerusalem, Israel; from Los Angeles, California, to Philadelphia, Pennsylvania.

Bibliography

Cembalest, Robin. "The Ecological Art Explosion." *Art News* 90:6. 96–105.
Gablik, Suzy. "Socially Conscious Creativity Helps Heal Society's Ills." *The Utne Reader* 50 (March–April 1992): 63–64.
Heartney, Eleanor. "Skeptics in Utopia." *Art in America* 80:7 (July 1992): 76–81.
Lippard, Lucy R. "Sniper's Nest—The Garbage Girls." *Z Magazine* 4:12 (December 1991): 80–83.

Phillips, Patricia C. "Public Art: Waste Not." *Art in America* 77:2 (February 1989): 47, 49, 51.

Ulmann, Doris (1884–1934)

The photographer Doris Ullman, best known for her pictorialist portraits of the people of remote Appalachia and the deep south of the United States, was born in New York City into a very wealthy family. In 1900 she enrolled in teacher training at the Ethical Culture Society School in her native city, where Lewis Hine taught. After graduation Ulmann enrolled at Teacher's College, Columbia University, New York City, where she studied psychology and law before registering for a photography class taught by Clarence H. White. White had a great influence on the development of her career in photography. He and Ullman were also active members of the Pictorial Photographers of America.

Between 1918 and 1925 Ullman produced three large groups of portraits which were published as bound, limited edition portfolios of photogravures: *Twenty-Four Portraits of the Faculty of Physicians and Surgeons of Columbia University*, *A Book of Portraits of the Medical Department of the Johns Hopkins University*, and *A Portrait Gallery of American Editors*.

After 1918 Ullman also made portraits of celebrities of the art world and society. Among her subjects were "Sinclair Lewis," "Waldo Frank," "Thomas Wolfe," "Robert Frost," "William Butler Yeats," "Lillian Gish," "Paul Robeson," "Martha Graham," "Anna Pavlova," "Max Weber," "Ansel Adams," "Albert Einstein," "Helen Keller," "John Dewey," "Sherwood Anderson," and "President Calvin Coolidge." In 1927 she was introduced to folk music documentarian John Jacob Niles. For six to eight months a year, until her death in 1934, they travelled the back roads of the rural south, Niles serving as assistant, guide, and companion. Niles collected folk ballads, and Ulmann made portraits.

While Ullman could have chosen to use modern photography equipment, she chose instead to use a glass-plate view camera and tripod without the benefit of shutter or light meter. Ulmann used the platinum process for most of her work; however, she also made oil and gum-bichromate and bromoil prints.

Laine Sutherland

Bibliography

Featherstone, David. *Doris Ulmann, American Portraits*. University of New Mexico Press, 1985.
Nikles, John Jacob, and Jonathan Williams. *The Appalachian Photographs of Doris Ulmann*. The Jargon Society, 1971.

Urban, Reva (1925–)

Born in Coney Island, Brooklyn, New York, the painter/sculptor Reva Urban studied at the Art Students League, New York City, on a Carnegie scholarship (1943–1945). Her first series of explosive solo painting exhibitions took place at the Peridot Gallery, New York City (1958, 1960); she also showed a large triptych at the "International," Carnegie Institute, Pittsburgh, Pennsylvania (1958); and exhibited pastels at the "International Exhibition," Salzburg, Austria (1959). She introduced "shaped canvas" paintings at the University of Colorado at Boulder (1958, 1960); held solo shows of paintings and pastels at Gres Gallery, Washington, D.C., and Chicago, Illinois (1961, 1962); showed large paintings at "Documenta III," Kassel, Germany (1964); and held many other exhibitions, solo and group, in major cities in the United States and Germany.

"Hugo's Cabinet" (1965), a sculpted canvas and cabinet painting, fuses painting and sculpture—the abstract and the figural—in a commanding strategy of intense color and organic form. Winner of honors and awards, Urban held a Yaddo fellowship, Saratoga Springs, New York (1960) and also received a Tamarind fellowship, Albuquerque, New Mexico (1962) to create a suite of lithographs. Her work is represented in private and public permanent collections, including the Alverthorp Gallery, Jenkintown, Pennsylvania; the Art Institute of Chicago, Illinois; Finch College and the Museum of Modern Art (MoMA)—both in New York City; University of California at Berkeley; and many others.

Bibliography
Selz, Peter. *Reva Urban. A Catalog.* University Art Collection, University of California at Berkeley, 1966.
Wagstaff, Sam Jr. "Reva." American Abstract Painters and Sculptors, 1962.
Who's Who in American Art. 19th ed. R.R. Bowker Co., 1991–1992.

Urrusti, Lucinda (1930–)

Born in Melilla, Spanish Morocco, Lucinda Urrusti has lived in Mexico since 1939. After an academic education, Urrusti gave some thought to architecture as a profession, but turned instead to art, and studied at la Escuela de Pintura y Escultura (La Esmeralda) (1950–1953). Some of the teachers with whom she studied art include Federico Cantú, Jesús Guerrero Galván, and Agustín Lazo. Urrusti also had a brief assistantship with Ricardo Martínez de Hoyas. A painter, Urrusti won first prize in the Salón de Otoño of the National Institute of Fine Arts, Mexico City (1953); she won another first prize in the Jovenes Valores exhibit at the Salón de la Plástica Mexicana, Mexico City (1957), and had this honor repeated in the Second Salón de la Plástica Feminina, Mexico City. She has also worked in the field of museography.

Urrusti had her first solo exhibition in 1958, and her work was seen in group exhibitions starting in 1953. Solo shows of her output have been mounted in the Palace of Fine Arts, Mexico City, and in galleries such as Diana, Lourdes Chumacero, and Summa Artis—all in Mexico City. As of 1979 she showed primarily in the United States. She lives alternately between New York City and Mexico City, painting flora and fauna, portraits, nudes, and landscapes.

Bibliography
Alvarez, José Rogelio, et al. *Enciclopedia de Mexico.* Secretaría de Educación Pública, 1987.
The Texas Quarterly: Image of Mexico II. The University of Texas, Autumn 1969.

Urueta, Cordelia (1908–)

Born in Coyoacán, a suburb of Mexico City, Cordelia Urueta was reared in a family of intellectuals and early on displayed a great interest in art. Urueta studied painting with Alfred Ramos Martinez in the Coyoacán Open-Air School of Painting. In 1929 she visited New York City where her uncle, the poet José Juan Tablada, showed her sketches to Alma Reed, winning their inclusion in a group show of Mexican painters presented at the Delphic Studios. This put her in contact with the great Mexican artists: José Clemente Orozco and Rufino Tamayo.

In 1932 Urueta began to teach drawing at the primary school at the Secretaria de Educación Pública, Mexico City. She married the painter Gustavo Montoya in 1938 and they travelled to Europe, both obtaining diplomatic positions in Paris, France. There Urueta met many well-known contemporary artists and, accompanied by David Alfaro Siqueiros, visited Georges Braque. When World War II broke out, Urueta was transferred to New York, where she lived for three years, and again familiarized herself with the art scene. In 1943 she returned to Mexico and resumed teaching. Also at this time she sought out the legendary painter Dr. Atl to discuss the vocation of painting.

In 1950 Urueta was one of the founding members of the Salón de la Plástica Mexicana, Mexico City, and in 1955 she was included in the first Bienal Interamericana held in Mexico City and received an honorable mention when it was held next in 1960. Participating in the VI Bienal Internacional in São Paulo, Brazil, Urueta received another honorable mention. In 1964 her work was included in the inaugural exhibition at the Museo de Arte Moderno in Mexico City. Urueta obtained first prize in painting at the Salón de Invierno del Salón de la Plástica Mexicana. In 1967 she participated in the Museo de Arte Moderno's "Tribute to Frida Kahlo" exhibition and also had a one-person show at the prestigious Galería de Arte Mexicano, Mexico City, which would now represent her. She has had numerous solo and group shows both in Mexico and abroad, where her abstract style and different modes of expression make her work intriguing, yet difficult to classify.

Susan Aberth

Bibliography
Espejo, Beatriz. *Historia de la Pintura Mexicana.* Mexico City, 1989, pp. 241–45.
Keith, Delmari R. *Galería de Arte Mexicano. Historia y Testimonios.* Mexico City, 1985.
Pintura Mexicana (Mexican Painting) 1950–1980. New York: IBM Gallery, 1990.

Uyauperq Aniksak, Margaret (1905–)

A Canadian Inuit sculptor, Margaret Uyauperq Aniksak was born just inland from the community of Arviat (Eskimo Point), Northwest Territories, on the west coast of Hudson Bay. Uyauperq Aniksak's family moved to Churchill, Manitoba, for several years, then back to Arviat. She married Paul Aniksak there in 1938, and began stone carving in the mid-1960s.

In a community whose stone sculpture is notable for its roughness, lack of detail and compactness, Uyauperq Aniksak's work could be considered fairly naturalistic. Facial features, hair braids, and clothing details are carefully rendered, making her depictions of the mother-and-child theme especially sensitive and poignant. Uyauperq Aniksak also produces fabric collage wall-hangings, which illustrate traditional camp life. These incorporate bleached caribou skin, sealskin, felt, and beadwork. She is considered to be Arviat's leading producer of the soft white caribou suede used in fine clothing and crafts.

Uyauperq Aniksak's work has been exhibited in Canada, the United States, and Europe, including the international Sculpture/Inuit show of 1971–1973. Her works are in the collections of the National Gallery of Canada, the Canadian Museum of Civilization, the Art Gallery of Ontario; and the Winnipeg Art Gallery.

Ingo Hessel

Bibliography
Hessel, Ingo. "Arviat Stone Sculpture." *Inuit Art Quarterly* 5:4 (Winter 1990): 4–15.
Winnipeg Art Gallery. *Eskimo Point/Arviat.* Winnipeg Art Gallery, 1982.

V

Valentien, Anna Marie (1862–1947)

Born in Cincinnati, Ohio, the ceramist/sculptor Anna Marie Valentien was also a printer of books. Valentien studied at the Art Academy in her native city and worked at the noted Rookwood Pottery (1884–1905). Three years after she joined Rookwood Pottery and married its chief decorator, Albert R. Valentien, they went to Paris, France, where she studied with Auguste Rodin, Antoine Bourdelle, and others.

Winner of many awards and honors, Valentien received a gold medal at the Atlanta Exposition, Georgia (1895); a collaborative gold medal at the Pan-California Exposition, San Diego, California (1915); two further gold medals at the same exposition the following year; the highest award and cash prize at the Sacramento State Fair, California (1919); and others.

Returning home, Valentien tried to persuade the Rookwood Pottery to adopt a "sculptural" style; however, few pieces were manufactured in that style, and, in 1907, the Valentiens moved to San Diego, California, where they set up the Valentien Pottery. She was a member of the La Jolla Art Association; San Diego Art Guild; and the San Diego Fine Arts Society—all in California. Her works are represented in private and public permanent collections.

Bibliography
American Art Annual. Vol. 28. American Federation of Arts, 1932.
Garth, Clark. *American Ceramics 1896 to the Present*. Abbeville Press, 1987.
Kamerling, Bruce. "Anna & Albert Valentien: The Arts and Crafts Movement in San Diego." *Arts and Crafts Quarterly* 1:4 (July 1987): 1, 12–20.
Ode to Nature: Flowers and Landscapes of the Rookwood Pottery, 1880–1940. A Catalog. New York: Jordan-Volpe Gallery, 1980.
Peck, Herbert. *The Book of Rookwood Pottery*. Crown, 1968.
Valentine, John. "Rookwood Pottery." *House Beautiful* (September 4, 1898).

Van Derpool, Karen (1946–)

Born in Troy, New York, the fiber artist Karen Van Derpool earned a Bachelor's degree at State University of New York (SUNY) (1968) and, two years later, received a Master of Fine Arts degree from the Tyler School of Art, Temple University, Philadelphia, Pennsylvania. She took further work at the Haystack Mountain School of Crafts, Deer Isle, Maine, and the School for American Craftsmen, Rochester, New York.

Van Derpool's work in fibers has been seen in solo and group exhibitions in the United States and abroad, including "Weaving Unlimited," Portland Art Museum, Oregon (1973); the "3rd International Exhibition of Miniature Textiles," British Craft Centre, London, England (1978); "Art in Crafts," Bronx Museum (1978), and Museum of American Craft (1980)—both in New York City; "Art Fabric: Mainstream," San Francisco Museum of Modern Art, California (1981); "Fiber National '85," Adams Memorial Gallery, Dunkirk, New York (1985); and others.

Van Derpool is a professor at California State University, Chico, and a winner of honors and awards. Her work is represented in private and public permanent collections, such as Ball State University, Muncie, Indiana; the First National Bank of Boston, Massachusetts; and others.

Bibliography
Park, Betty. "Felting." *Fiberarts* (November–December 1980).
Schlossman, Betty. "Reviews: Clay, Fiber, Metal by Women Artists." *Art Journal* 37:4 (Summer 1978).

Van Halm, Renée (1949–)

Renée van Halm was born in Amsterdam, Holland, and came to Canada as a young girl. She studied at the Vancouver School of Art until 1975, when she entered the Master of Fine Arts program at Concordia University in Montréal, Québec. She began exhibiting in group shows immediately upon graduation, and she has had solo shows since 1908 in every year but 1987.

Van Halm's work loosely bridges the post-modernist categories of neoexpressionism, installation art, appropriated imagery, and autobiography. Her works are typically large, free-standing "paintings" which allude very obliquely to such things as Italian Quattrocento architecture and Gothic iconography. A well-known example would be "In Pausing, She is Implicated in a Well-Structured Relationship" (1982), which was inspired by an anonymous Gothic drawing. The work consists of a simplified and brightly painted portico through which one sees disembodied feet. To the right a tiny free-standing figure advances toward a small doorway in a wall painted gesturally in blue and violet. The vision of the Virgin Mary and Elizabeth is thus not represented *per se*, but is the foundation of a metaphor which the artist has described as "the process of rebirth which occurs each time we move from the security of a known situation to one in which we feel vulnerable."

Van Halm's work is of the intellectual sort that used to be disparaged as literary. In Toronto, where she now lives and works, this allusive approach is part and parcel of the so-called critique of representation.

Robert J. Belton

Bibliography
Grenville, Bruce. *The Allegorical Image in Recent Canadian Painting.* Kingston: Agnes Etherington Art Centre, 1985.
———. "Renée van Halm: S.L. Simpson Gallery." *Parachute* 52 (September–November 1988).
Murray, Joan. *The Best of Contemporary Canadian Art.* Hurtig, 1987.
Nemiroff, Diana, and Jessica Bradley. *Songs of Experience.* Ottawa: National Gallery of Canada, 1986.

Van Hoesen, Beth (1926–)

Born in Boise, Idaho, the printmaker Beth Van Hoesen learned her craft through study in several institutions, including la Escuela de Pintura y Escultura (La Esmeralda), Mexico City, Mexico (1945); San Francisco Art Institute, California (1946–1947, 1951–1952); Stanford University, California, where she earned a Bachelor's degree (1948); and l'École des Beaux-Arts, Fontainebleu, France (1948–1951). During the same years she took additional work at the Académie Julian and the Académie de la Grande Chaumière, Paris, France.

Van Hoesen's prints have been exhibited in many solo and group shows throughout the United States and abroad, in galleries and museums, such as the M. H. De Young Memorial Museum, San Francisco (1959), Achenbach Foundation, Palace of the Legion of Honor, San Francisco (1961, 1974), Santa Barbara Museum (1963, 1974, 1976), Crocker Art Gallery, Sacramento (1966), and Oakland Museum (1975, 1980)—all in California; Brooklyn Museum, New York (1962, 1966, 1968, 1977); "Continuing American Graphics," Osaka, Japan (1970); Hawaii National Print Exhibition, Honolulu (1971, 1980); John Berggruen Gallery, San Francisco, California (1982, 1985, 1987); Art Museums Association of America, a travelling exhibition (1983–1985); and many others.

Van Hoesen is an author and winner of awards and honors; her work is represented in private, public, and corporate permanent collections, including the San Francisco Museum of Modern Art, Achenbach Foundation, and Palace of the Legion of Honor—all in San Francisco, California; Stanford University, California; Arizona State University, Tempe; Museum of Modern Art (MoMA) and Brooklyn Museum—both in New York City; Art Institute of Chicago, Illinois; Victoria & Albert Museum, London, England; and many others. Van Hoesen's prints—especially her intaglios—are unique and precise weddings of form, content, and technique—to which are added a delightful imagination.

Bibliography
Van Hoesen, Beth. *A Collection of Wonderful Things.* Scrimshaw, 1972.
———. *Creatures.* Chronicle Books, 1987.
———. "Prints and Photographs Published." *Print Collectors Newsletter* Vol. 14 (January–February 1984): 215.
———. "Wild Things: Animals in Contemporary West Coast Art." *Artweek* Vol. 24 (June 3, 1993): 4.

Van Ness, Beatrice Whitney (1888–1981)

Born in Chelsea, Massachusetts, the painter Beatrice Whitney Van Ness studied with several artists, including Benson, Hale, Pratt, and Tarbell. Winner of awards and honors, Van Ness received the Julian A. Shaw prize at the National Academy of Design, New York City (1914); a silver medal at the Panama-Pacific International Exposition, San Francisco, California (1915); and others. Representative examples of her work are in private and public permanent collections, including the National Museum of Women in the Arts, Washington, D.C.

Bibliography
American Art Annual. Vol. 28. American Federation of Arts, 1932.
Fielding, Mantle. *Dictionary of American Painters, Sculptors, and Engravers.* Modern Books and Crafts, 1974.
National Museum of Women in the Arts. Harry N. Abrams, 1987.

Van Vliet, Claire (1933–)

Claire Van Vliet is the proprietor of the Janus Press, founded in 1955 and located in Newark, Vermont, since 1966. Janus' publications—books, pamphlets, and broadsides—number approximately 100. Many have been designed, illustrated, type-set, printed (sometimes on paper made by the artist), and bound by Van Vliet in a well-equipped studio, print shop, and bindery of her own design. Born in Ottawa, Canada, the artist has lived in the United States since 1947. She received her Bachelor of Arts degree from San Diego State University in 1952, and her Master of Fine Arts degree from Claremont Graduate School in 1954—both in California; then served printing apprenticeships at a newspaper in Oberursel, Táunus, Germany (1955–1957) and with the Pickering Press in Maple Shade, New Jersey (1958–1959), before launching a teaching career at the Philadelphia College of Art (now the University of the Arts), Pennsylvania, the University of Wisconsin, Madison, and privately with many Janus Press apprentices.

Since settling in Vermont, Van Vliet has been concerned mainly with Janus Press, but she also has been an artist-in-residence and lecturer throughout the United States, Canada, Great Britain, and New Zealand. Primarily a publisher of first-edition poetry, Van Vliet illustrated several Franz Kafka texts in the 1960s. In the 1970s she was a pioneer in the use of colored paper pulps for book illustration, and more recently she has developed a variety of distinctive non-adhesive book structures.

Van Vliet also has created a significant body of watercolors, drawings, etchings, lithographs, woodcuts, and paperworks in her own studio and at printmaking and papermaking workshops in the United States, Canada, and abroad, including UM Grafik, Copenhagen, Denmark; Tandem Press, Madison, Wisconsin; Magnolia Editions, Oakland, California; Twinrocker Handmade Paper Mill, Brookston, Indiana; and MacGregor-Vinzani paper studio, Whiting, Maine. Her primary subject in paperworks has been Vermont landscapes. However, Van Vliet's landscape interest recently expanded to include the American Southwest, thanks to her receipt, in 1990, of the John D. and Catherine T. MacArthur Foundation award, which allowed her the time and funds to travel. Van Vliet's works have been the subject of about forty solo exhibitions in the United States, Canada, and Scandinavia.

Ruth E. Fine

Bibliography
Cate, P. Dennis. *Claire Van Vliet Printmaker and Printer*. New Brunswick, 1975.
Fine, Ruth E. *The Janus Press, 1976–1980*. Burlington, 1982.
———. *The Janus Press, 1981–1990*. Burlington, 1992.
Lehrer, Ruth Fine. *The Janus Press, 1955–1975*. Burlington, 1976.
Rothe, Wolfgang. *Kunst Zu Kafka*. Stuttgart, 1979.
Scott, David. *Claire Van Vliet—Prints*. Burlington, 1971.
Taylor, W. Thomas. "Claire Van Vliet's Janus Press." *American Craft* (February–March 1987): 52–59, 66.

Varian, Dorothy (1895–1985)

A native New Yorker, the painter Dorothy Varian was a member of the National Association of Women Painters and Sculptors, New York City, and exhibited her work at other galleries and museums, including the "Second Biennial Exhibition of Contemporary American Painting," at the Whitney Museum of American Art, New York City (1934), among others.

Varian's work is represented in private and public permanent collections, including the Whitney Museum of American Art, New York City; the Phillips Memorial Gallery, Washington, D.C.; and others.

Bibliography
American Art Annual. Vol. 28. American Federation of Arts, 1932.
American Art at the Newark Museum. A Catalog. The Newark Museum, 1981.
Goodrich, Lloyd, and John I.H. Baur. *American Art of Our Century*. Praeger, 1961.

Varo, Remedios (1908–1963)

Born in Angles, Spain, the surrealist painter Remedios Varo early on exhibited a talent for art—which was encouraged by her family. She made many drawings throughout her childhood and painted her first work at the age of twelve. After attending a convent school she was sent to the Escuela de Artes y Oficios; took further study at the Escuela de Bellas Artes; and became a full-time student at the Academia de San Fernando (1924)—all in Madrid, Spain—where she studied painting under the aegis of Manuel Bendito-Vives.

After a first marriage to a friend and fellow student at the Academia de San Fernando (1930), Varo was introduced to the inner circles of the surrealist movement in Paris, France. She returned to Barcelona, Spain, married a revolutionary French poet, and left for Paris (1937). She was arrested and interned by the Germans (1940) and went to live in Mexico (1941). Varo had to do commercial artwork to survive, yet continually expressed her innermost feelings in precision-like paintings and drawings of her childhood, her dreams and fantasies, to wed science, art, and a rich imagination in personal terms from 1923 to her death forty years later.

Varo's paintings were invited to many group exhibitions, including the Academía de San Fernando, Madrid (1934); and "Logicophobists," Glorieta Catalonia-Librería, Barcelona (1936)—both in Spain; "Surrealist Objects and Poems," London Gallery, England (1937); "Exposition Internationale du Surréalisme Organisée par la Revue Mizue," Nippon Salon, Tokyo, Japan (1937); "Exposition Internacionale del Surrealismo," Galería de Arte Mexicano, Mexico City, and touring to California, New York, and Peru (1940); "La Surréalisme en 1947: Exposition Internationale du Surréalisme," Galerie Maeght, Paris, France (1947); Galería Diana, Mexico City (1955); "Salon Frida Kahlo," Galería de Arte Contemporaneo, Mexico City (1956); and "Group Exhibition to Aid Spanish Political Prisoners," El Ateneo Español de Mexico, Mexico City (1961).

Varo was given solo shows at the Galería Diana, Mexico City (1956); Galería Juan Martin, Mexico City (1962); and a major retrospective of 124 of her works at the Palacio de Bellas Artes, Mexico City, subsequent to her death (1964); and others at the Museo de Arte Moderno, Mexico City (1971–1983). Three years later her work appeared in solo exhibitions at the New York Academy of Sciences and the National Academy of Science, Washington, D.C. Examples of her work have been shown in group exhibitions in the United States and Europe, including the cities of Barcelona and Madrid, Spain; Lausanne, Switzerland; Lyon and Paris, France; Milan, Italy; Munich, Germany—and are housed in many permanent collections.

Bibliography
Chadwick, Whitney. *Women Artists and the Surrealist Movement*. Thames and Hudson, 1985.
Kaplan, Janet A. *Unexpected Journeys: The Art and Life of Remedios Varo*. Abbeville Press, 1988.
Orenstein, Gloria F. "Art History and the Case for the Women of Surrealism." *JGE: The Journal of General Education* 27 (Spring 1975): 31–54.

Vasulka, Steina (1940–)

Born in Reykjavik, Iceland, the video artist Steina Vasulka studied at the State Conservatory of Music, Prague, Czechoslovakia (1959–1963) and played in the Iceland Symphony Orchestra.

Vasulka and her husband, Woody, created videos separately and together, and made a significant contribution to the art of video by founding The Kitchen—an electronic arts gallery in New York City (1971). The Vasulkas also brought about the creation of new electronic hardware to produce their works.

Throughout the 1970s Vasulka exhibited solo and collaborative videos (with her husband) in many venues in the United States and abroad, including the Global Village, New York City (1971); the State University of New York (SUNY) at Buffalo (1974), and the Experimental Television Center, Binghamton (1978)—both in New York; Carnegie Institute, Pittsburgh, Pennsylvania (1982); The Kitchen, New York City, and the Centre Georges Pompidou, Paris, France (1983–1984); and "Steina et Woody Vasulka," a retrospective, MBXA/Cinédoc (1984)—both in Paris, France; and many others.

Winner of honors and awards, Vasulka garnered a Guggenheim Foundation fellowship (1976); a National Endowment for the Arts (NEA) grant; a grant from the New York State Council on the Arts; a production grant from the Southwest Independent Production Fund, Houston, Texas (1982); and others. Examples of her work are in private and public permanent collections, including the Aarhus Kunstmuseum, Denmark; Akron Art Institute, Ohio; Museum of Modern Art (MoMA), New York City; Virginia Museum of Fine Arts, Richmond; and others.

Bibliography
Haller, Robert. "Interview with Steina." *Video Texts: 1983.*
Lalanne, Dorothée. "Promenade Electronique." *Vogue,* Paris ed. (June–July 1984): 178–83.
Making Their Mark: Women Artists Move into the Mainstream, 1970–85. Abbeville Press, 1989.

Velarde, Pablita (Tse Tsan) (1918–)

One of the best known of her generation of easel painters of Native American heritage, Pablita Velarde was born in Santa Clara Pueblo, New Mexico, on September 19, 1918. Named Tse Tsan (Golden Dawn) in her native Tewa language, Velarde left the Tewa world of Santa Clara at the age of six, when she and her sisters were sent to Saint Catherine's Indian School in Santa Fe, New Mexico. There they spent their girlhood years except for summers when they returned home. In 1932 Velarde transferred to Santa Fe Indian School where she entered the eighth grade and became one of only two female students (her sister Rosita was the other) in Dorothy Dunn's first class of the newly-created, and later to become famous, Santa Fe Indian School art program (the Studio).

Attendance at Dunn's classes was the only formal art training Velarde received. While a student at the Studio Velarde had the opportunity to meet Tonita Peña, who was staying at the school while working on a mural project there. The meeting had a major influence on Velarde's life, for Peña was herself a Tewa woman, and in her confidence and success as a fine artist she served as a role model for Velarde (whose own mother had died when Velarde was three). Velarde credits Peña for giving her "the strength to dare," since easel painting, along with the concept of signed individual artwork, was still a relatively new art form to Native Americans, and it was particularly venturesome for a woman.

Shortly after Velarde's first year at the Studio—when she was in her young teens—one of her paintings was displayed at Chicago's Century of Progress exhibit, Illinois. With this first recognition Velarde's enthusiasm for painting increased. After graduating from the Studio in 1936 Velarde got a job as an assistant art teacher at the Santa Clara Day School. In 1939, as a result of urging by artist Olive Rush, Velarde was commissioned to do a mural on the facade of Maisel Trading Post

in downtown Albuquerque, New Mexico. Shortly afterward Velarde, just twenty years old, was hired to work as artist-in-residence at Bandelier National Monument in northern New Mexico, where she painted a series of paintings portraying traditional Pueblo Indian life. During two different periods of tenure between 1939 and 1948, Velarde painted numerous detailed paintings for Bandelier National Monument.

In 1940 Velarde built a studio at Santa Clara. She later moved to Albuquerque where she met and married Herbert Hardin. The couple had two children, Helen (1943–1984), who had a notable career as a painter exploring modern techniques and creating her own style, and Herbert (1944–), who became a sculptor. Velarde made Albuquerque her home for most of the rest of her life, returning occasionally to nearby Santa Clara.

Velarde exhibited her work regularly and won a number of top prizes, including the grand award (1953) and trophy award (1968), Philbrook Art Center, Tulsa, Oklahoma; the Scottsdale grand award, Arizona (1965); and first prizes at the Inter-Tribal Indian Ceremonial, Gallup, New Mexico (1969, 1971). In 1954 the French government honored her with the *Palmes d'Academiques.* She has had solo shows at the Museum of New Mexico, Santa Fe; the Philbrook Art Center, Tulsa, Oklahoma; and Enchanted Mesa gallery, Albuquerque, New Mexico; and her work is included in the collections of a wide selection of museums. The Museum of New Mexico commissioned her to paint large panels for a travelling exhibit. She also painted a mural for the Indian Pueblo Cultural Center in Albuquerque, New Mexico.

In 1960 Velarde published a number of traditional Santa Clara stories in a book form, illustrated with a group of her paintings. The book, *Old Father, the Storyteller,* received notice as one of the Best Western Books of 1961 and won further renown for its author/artist.

Throughout her career Velarde, like many of her Native American contemporaries, chose to portray scenes from Pueblo life or symbols and images of importance to Pueblo people. She has worked in casein and tempera, and occasionally in oils, but Velarde is particularly known for her mastery and regular use, as a mature artist, of *fresco secco*—a technique she learned while a student of Dorothy Dunn's and which she was inspired to use because of her familiarity with the sand-painting, kiva-mural, and rock-art legacy (including ancient pictographs and petroglyphs) of her ancestors. Velarde's painstaking procedure relies on the use of natural earth colors which she collects in the form of rock and sand and then hand-grinds on a *metate* (grinding stone) until she has pulverized them to a fine powder. Keeping her colors separate, she mixes the powder with a binder (glue) and water, then applies them to her painting surface, usually masonite, sometimes applying as many as seven layers.

Velarde has followed her interest in the traditions of her people through her depictions of them in paintings and, in later years, through lectures and storytelling. In 1977 Velarde was singled out to receive the New Mexico governor's award for outstanding achievement in the arts. In 1984 the National Park Service, through the Harper's Ferry Historical Association, released a videotape about her career, *Pablita Velarde: An Artist and Her People.*

Tryntje Van Ness Seymour

Bibliography
Dunn, Dorothy. *American Indian Painting of the Southwest and Plains Areas.* University of New Mexico Press, 1968.

Nelson, Mary Carroll. *Pablita Velarde: The Story of An American Indian.* Dillon Press, 1971.

Scott, Jay. *Changing Woman: The Life and Art of Helen Hardin.* Northland Press, 1989.

Seymour, Tryntje Van Ness. *When the Rainbow Touches Down.* Phoenix: The Heard Museum, 1989.

Silberman, Arthur. *100 Years of Native American Painting.* Oklahoma City: The Oklahoma Museum of Art, 1978.

Snodgrass, Jeanne O. *American Indian Painters: A Biographical Directory.* Contributions from the Museum of the American Indian, Heye Foundation. Vol. XXI, part 1. New York: Museum of the American Indian, Heye Foundation, 1968.

Tanner, Clara Lee. *Southwest Indian Painting: A Changing Art.* University of Arizona Press, 1973.

Velarde, Pablita. *Old Father, the Storyteller.* Globe, Arizona: Dale Stuart King, 1960.

Vidotto, Elena Bonafonte (1934–)

With her diminutive, exquisitely-detailed still lifes, Elena Bonafonte Vidotto carries on a painting tradition long popular in both her native Italy and her adopted country—the United States. Born in Milan, Vidotto trained under Augusto Colombo at that city's Art Academy; won a scholarship for further study in Austria; and, beginning in the early 1960s, lived on and off in New York City, where she was a pupil at the Art Students League and the School of Visual Arts.

Both skillful and prolific, Vidotto quickly established herself as a successful portrait and still-life painter. She exhibited regularly at galleries in Italy and New York City, and hit upon the unusual practice of holding annual shows of her new work on board the Italian ocean liners she took to visit her relatives each summer. These shipboard displays attracted considerable attention, including the interest of a prominent Kenyan couple who, in 1969, invited Vidotto to visit their Nairobi home. She did so, and spent two years in East Africa, painting a series on the Masai and other indigenous peoples. Vidotto has also worked in South Africa, Mexico, and Jamaica; she has participated in group exhibitions in Italy, Switzerland, and in several cities of the United States. In 1975 Vidotto acquired U.S. citizenship (via a marriage, which was later dissolved) and moved to Washington, D.C., where she continues to reside today, supporting herself with portrait commissions. But her real artistic love is still lifes—a couple of cracked eggs, a basket of mushrooms, or a bunch of keys suspended from a nail driven into a wooden door—all painstakingly rendered with oils on wooden panels or carefully gessoed boards, and all remarkably real-looking. Although she has work in the permanent collections of several institutions (notably the National Museum of Women in the Arts, Washington, D.C.), the bulk of Vidotto's paintings are in private hands.

Bibliography

Hemsing, Jan. "The Lonely Lemons." *Kenya Weekly News* (May 12, 1969): 18–19.

Unsigned. "Elena Bonafonte Vidotto." *American Artist* (June 1987): 35.

Villaseñor Zepeda, Elena (1944–)

Born in Sahuayo, Michoacan, Mexico, Elena Villaseñor Zepeda first studied with maestro Luis Sahagún (1967–1968), then at the School of Watercolor (1969–1971), before attending la Escuela de Pintura y Escultura (La Esmeralda) (1972–1975)—all in Mexico City. She also studied printmaking at the Art Students League in New York City.

A partial listing of Villaseñor's solo shows in Mexico City include: The Iron and Steel Institute (1975); Molino de Santo Domingo (1977); Galería Chapultepec, INBA (1978); Galería San Angel (1980); and the Galería Etceterum (1986).

In addition to the twenty-one group shows to which Villaseñor contributed work from 1973 to 1980, a sampling of newer shows include: Contemporary Printmaking in Mexico: 1972–1982, BANAMEX, and the Annual Painting Exhibition in the Palace of Fine Arts (1982); "Mujeres Artistas—Artistas Mujeres" at the Museum of Fine Arts, Toluca, Mexico, the IV Exhibition of Latin American Printmaking, Fundación Cultural de Curitiba, Brazil, and "La Noche de las Escrituras" at the Convent at Tepoztlán, Morelia (1982); "Pintura Erótica Mexicana" at Factory Place, Los Angeles, California (1985); "Cinco Artistas" at the Galería Artforum, Mexico City (1986) and, in the same year, a travelling show sponsored by INBA, which opened at the Galería Crowne Plaza.

Villaseñor won first place in printmaking at INBA during the Concurso Día del Arbol y Fiesta del Bosque, Mexico City (1979, 1980); she was awarded second place in the Concurso Sor Juana Inés de la Cruz (1980); another second place in the Concurso de Pintura la Ciudad, INBA (1981); and she won a prize in the Fourth Exhibition of Latin American Printmaking in Curitiba, Brazil (1984).

Villaseñor's painting, "El Estanque" (1987), is typical of her figurative, decorative, myth-like style, which emerged about 1980; the work depicts three women who seem to be cavorting in a flower-decorated pond. Her color and form appear to derive from the fairs and fiestas, the legends and rites, the very soul and heart of Mexico.

Bibliography

Imágenes Traspuestas. Museo de Arte Moderno. Bosque de Chapultepec, 1987.

Segundo Concurso Nacional de Pintura. Galería del Auditorio Nacional/ INBA, 1981.

von Rydingsvard, Ursula (1942–)

Professor of sculpture in the graduate division at the School of Visual Arts in New York City since 1986, Ursula von Rydingsvard was born in Deensen, a village in north central Germany. One of seven children of Polish origin, she spent her childhood on a collective farm and, at the end of World War II, in a wooden barracks in a refugee camp until 1952, when her family emigrated to the United States.

After two years of study at the University of New Hampshire, Durham, von Rydingsvard transferred to the University of Miami, Coral Gables, Florida, where she received her Bachelor's degree in 1964 and a Master of Arts degree the following year. She did further graduate work at the University of California at Berkeley (1969–1970) and obtained a Master of Fine Arts degree from Columbia University, New York City, in 1975.

Between 1977 and 1993 von Rydingsvard has had nearly twenty solo exhibitions of her work in the United States and abroad, including the National Museum of Women in the Arts, Washington, D.C. (1993); Lorence-Monk Gallery, New York City (1991); Cranbrook Art Museum, Bloomfield Hills, Michigan (1989); Studio Bassanese, Trieste, Italy (1985); 55 Mercer Street, New York City (1977, 1979, 1980); and a 10-year retrospective at the Storm King Art Center, Mountainville, New York (1992).

Von Rydingsvard's work has been invited to many group exhibitions in universities, museums, and galleries across the United States and Europe, such as "Jestesmy," at the Central Bureau for Art Exhibitions, Warsaw, Poland (1991); the Philip Morris branch of the Whitney Museum of Contemporary Art, New York City (1990); Walker Art Center, Minneapolis, Minnesota (1990); Addison Gallery, Phillips Academy, Andover, Massachusetts (1989); the Metropolitan Museum of Art, New York City (1989); the Brooklyn Museum, New York (1989); P.S.1, Long Island City, New York (1978); the Corcoran Gallery of Art, Washington, D.C. (1975); and many others.

Von Rydingsvard has been the recipient of a number of grants and awards, including a National Endowment for the Arts (NEA) grant (1986–1987, 1979); a Griswald travelling grant from Yale University, New Haven, Connecticut (1985); a Guggenheim Foundation fellowship (1983); a Creative Artists Public Service (CAPS) grant (1980); grants from the America the Beautiful Fund and the New York State Council on the Arts (1978); and a Fulbright-Hays travel grant (1975).

Prior to her current professorial appointment at the School for Visual Arts, von Rydingsvard taught at various institutions between 1978 and 1986, including Pratt Institute, Brooklyn, and Fordham University, Bronx—both in New York City; and Yale University, New Haven, Connecticut. Von Rydingsvard is a transformed post-minimalist whose cut, sawn, chipped, chewed, and glued cedar works are rife with haunting memories of her childhood. Her work is in the permanent public collections of the Brooklyn Museum and the Metropolitan Museum of Art—both in New York City; the Detroit Art Institute, Michigan; the Walker Art Center, Minneapolis, Minnesota; and other well-known institutions.

Bibliography
Berman, Avis. "Ursula von Rydingsvard: Life under Siege." *Art News* (December 1988).
Brenson, Michael. "Setting Free the Images in Big Beams of Wood." *The New York Times* (April 1, 1988): C32.
Tully, Judd. "Ursula von Rydingsvard." *Arts Magazine* (May 1980): 22.
Who's Who in American Art. 19th edition. R.R. Bowker Co., 1991–1992.

von Wiegand, Charmion (c. 1896–1985)

An abstract painter, Charmion von Wiegand was born in Chicago, Illinois, grew up in San Francisco, California, and attended high school in Berlin, Germany, where her journalist father was a foreign correspondent. She studied at Barnard College, New York City, and started out at the school of journalism at Columbia University, New York City, later transferring to the department of art and archaeology. She then studied at New York University, New York City, with Richard Offner.

Von Wiegand started painting in 1926, receiving encouragement from her friend, painter Joseph Stella. She spent some time as a journalist in Moscow and returned in the 1930s to wed Joseph Freeman, a founder of the *New Masses* magazine and later of the *Partisan Review.* Von Wiegand became an editor for *Art Front*—the magazine of the Artist's Union—and also wrote for the Federal Art Project (FAP). Her painting at this time was influenced by friend and mentor Piet Mondrian, whom she had interviewed in 1941. He suggested she join the American Abstract Artists group in 1942, and she eventually was

its president from 1951 to 1953.

Von Wiegand had her first solo exhibition at the Rose Fried Gallery, New York City, in 1942, and, in 1945, she was in Peggy Guggenheim's 1945 Women's Show at the Art of This Century. By the later 1940s she had found her expertise in collages, putting together bright combinations of lace, cards, and hand-printed materials. In 1948 she organized an important show of Kurt Schwitter's collages with Naum Gabo and Katherine Dreiser and continued to exhibit her own collages throughout the 1950s.

As von Wiegand grew more interested in Tibetan Buddhist art, her collages and paintings drew more from Eastern religious symbolism ("Dark Journey: Collage #207," 1958). She received first prize at the Cranbrook Academy of Art Religious Art Exhibition, Bloomfield Hills, Michigan (1969), and had a retrospective showing of her work at the Noah Goldowsky Gallery, New York City (1974). She also has had exhibitions at the Beaubourg in Paris, France; Yale University, New Haven, Connecticut; and the Albright-Knox Art Gallery in Buffalo, New York. Her works are in the permanent collections of the Cleveland Museum of Art, Ohio; the Hirshhorn Museum and Sculpture Garden, Washington, D.C.; the Newark Museum, New Jersey; and the Museum of Modern Art (MoMA), New York City.

Nancy Knechtel

Bibliography
Collins, Jim. *Women Artists in America: 18th Century to the Present 1790–1980.* Apollo, 1980.
Cummings, Paul. *Dictionary of Contemporary American Artists.* St. Martin's Press, 1988, p. 646.
Rubenstein, Charlotte Streifer. *American Woman Artists: From Early Indian Times to the Present.* Avon, 1982, pp. 296–98.

Vonnoh, Bessie Potter (1872–1955)

Success came early to St. Louis-born Bessie Potter Vonnoh, who at age twenty-two already had her own studio in Chicago, Illinois. Her family had moved to Chicago in 1874, and, at age eighteen, she enrolled at the Art Institute of Chicago for sculpture classes with Lorado Taft. She became one of the female assistants called the "White Rabbits" in Taft's studio, working on the sculpture for the World's Columbian Exposition of 1893. She modeled the figure "Art" for the Illinois State building. Taft related that it was at this exposition that Vonnoh saw the small bronzes of Paul Troubetskoy, which influenced her to experiment with bronze figurines. Today most of the museums in the United States have at least one of her small bronzes: "The Young Woman" (1896), "Girl Dancing" (1897), "Daydreams" (1903), the group entitled "Motherhood" (1903), or "The Fan" (c. 1910). Her fame soon spread beyond Chicago, and she exhibited several pieces at the Tennessee Centennial of 1897. More remarkably she was commissioned by the Fairmount Park Art Association, Philadelphia, Pennsylvania, to model a colossal portrait bust of "Major-General S.W. Crawford" as part of a Civil War memorial. This was followed by a similar commission to sculpt a marble bust of "Vice President James S. Sherman" in 1911 for the U.S. Senate building, Washington, D.C.

In 1895 Vonnoh travelled to Paris, France, where she met Auguste Rodin, and she also made a trip to Florence, Italy, to see Renaissance sculpture before marrying in 1899 Robert Vonnoh, a painter whom she had met in Taft's studio. They made their home in New York and later in the artists' colony in Lyme, Connecticut. Meanwhile she began to receive prizes: a bronze medal for "The Young Mother" at the Paris Exposition of 1900, France; an honorable mention at the Pan-American Exposition, Buffalo, New York (1901); a gold medal at the St. Louis Exposition, Missouri (1904); the Shaw prize at the National Academy of Design, New York City, for "Enthroned" (1904); and a silver medal at the Panama-Pacific International Exposition in San Francisco, California (1915). In 1913 the Brooklyn Museum, New York, gave her an exhibition, and she had work accepted into the Armory Show, also in New York City. During the 1920s and 1930s Vonnoh turned to life-sized statues: a bird fountain for Ormand Beach Park, Florida; a bird bath of two children for the Audubon Society's bird sanctuary near Theodore Roosevelt's grave at Oyster Bay, Long Island (1925); and a group of children for the fountain memorializing Frances Hodgson Burnett (author of Little Lord Fauntleroy) in the Children's Garden, Central Park (1937). In 1906 she became an associate member of the National Academy of Design, New York City, and in 1921 she received its gold medal and was made an academician. She was elected to the National Institute of Arts and Letters, New York City, in 1931. She

was adept at modeling both the nude and the clothed figure, in the latter case favoring Grecian drapery. Although Vonnoh's bronze figurines were usually static, her sculpted dance pieces were quite naturally lively, graceful works (such as "Allegresse," 1921).

Vonnoh and her husband had several two-person exhibitions in New York galleries in the second and third decades of the twentieth century. They were living on the French Riviera at Nice when he died in 1933. She returned to New York but tapered off in her work. In 1948 she married Edward Keyes, who passed away nine months later. She died in New York City five months before her eighty-third birthday.

Eleanor Tufts

Bibliography

Rubinstein, Charlotte Streifer. *American Women Artists*. G.K. Hall, 1982.

Tufts, Eleanor. *American Women Artists, 1830–1930*. National Museum of Women in the Arts, 1987.

Ultan, Roslye B. "Bessie Potter Vonnoh: American Sculptor." M.A. thesis, American University, 1973.

W

Wachtel, Marion Kavanaugh (1875–1954)

Born in Milwaukee, Wisconsin, the painter Marion Kavanaugh Wachtel studied at the Art Institute of Chicago, Illinois, and with William Merritt Chase.

Wachtel was a plein air painter identified with the California school of painting and a member of several arts organizations, including the California Watercolor Society, the Pasadena Painters, and Ten Painters of Los Angeles—all in California; and the New York Watercolor Club, New York City. Her work is represented in private and public permanent collections, such as the California State Building, Sacramento, the Friday Morning Club, Los Angeles, and the Woman's Club, Hollywood—all in California; the Cedar Rapids Museum, Iowa; and others.

Bibliography

A Woman's Vision: California Painting into the 20th Century. A Catalog. San Francisco: Maxwell Galleries, 1983.

American Art Annual. Vol. 28. American Federation of Arts, 1932.

Kovinick, Phil. *The Woman Artist in the American West 1860–1960.* Fullerton, California: Muckenthaler Cultural Center, 1976.

Wald, Sylvia (1915–)

Born in Philadelphia, Pennsylvania, Sylvia Wald studied at the Moore Institute of Art in her native city. She hitchhiked to New York City before graduation and settled there at the end of the 1930s.

At the age of twenty-three Wald won a national competition in painting and in sculpture sponsored by the ACA Gallery, New York City (1939), which led to a successful solo exhibition in that gallery in both media. More painting and sculpture invitations to exhibit followed in the 1940s, including the Philadelphia Museum of Art, and Carnegie Institute, Pittsburgh—both in Pennsylvania; Whitney Museum of American Art and Metropolitan Museum of Art (MoMA)—both in New York City; and the Phillips Memorial Gallery, Washington, D.C.; among others.

Married to a medical practitioner, Wald accompanied him on his World War II assignment to an army hospital in Louisville, Kentucky. After watching Harry Gottlieb make a screen print one afternoon, Wald, a quick study, made screen prints throughout her four-year stay and was also fortunate to make friends with the art critic and historian Justus Bier, who played no small part in her aesthetic outlook. The Library of Congress, Washington, D.C., acquired one of her prints from this period during the show, "100 Fine Prints of the Year" (1944).

Wald returned to New York at the end of the war, secured a small country place, discovered gardening and painting out-of-doors, and experimented and found a more spontaneous, creative way to make screen prints during this period of transition.

In the 1950s Wald produced a large body of work, had many exhibitions, and won awards in painting and printmaking. Her work became more abstract as she searched and researched her private thoughts and feelings. In 1955 the Museum of Modern Art (MoMA), New York City, in its major international exhibition, "Fifty Years of American Art: Salute of France," included Wald's work.

A solo exhibition of Wald's paintings and prints at the Deborah Sherman Gallery in Chicago, Illinois (1960), marked a significant moment in her career: she divided her time between urban and country living and focused on painting. The death of her husband in 1963 brought trauma. In the company of friends, she went abroad for the first time, and was indelibly impressed by what she saw in the Musée de l'Homme, Paris, France.

Returning home, in solitude and despair, Wald spent more time in her country studio; she gave up painting and began to work in three-dimensions using wire, string, and plaster to create white sculptures—a glimpse of future work. Another severe personal loss occurred: Wald's mother died.

In 1967 Wald returned to Europe and visited Greece, Spain, and France. Two years later, with her new artist-husband, Wald began a new and different life involving much travel, including Canada, Central America, South America, India, France, Korea, Japan, Hong Kong, Thailand, and China. These enriching experiences found expression in larger and free-standing paper and canvas collage constructions, some with wire, string, bamboo, bird images, or feathers.

Wald has had more than fifty group exhibitions in major museums throughout the United States and abroad since 1939, including, among others: the Amon Carter Museum, Fort Worth, Texas (1991); the Museum of Fine Arts, Boston, Massachusetts (1991); the Brooklyn Museum, New York (1975); the American Art Gallery, Copenhagen, Denmark (1965–1966); the Palace of Fine Arts, Mexico City, Mexico (1959); and the National Gallery of Modern Art, Rome, Italy (1957). She has been honored with more than a dozen solo exhibitions, including the Fullhouse Gallery, Princeton, New Jersey (1984) and Amerika Haus, Munich, Germany (1979).

A cross-section of important public institutions that house her work in their permanent collections include: the Metropolitan Museum of Art, Museum of Modern Art (MoMA), Brooklyn Museum, Whitney Museum of American Art, and the Guggenheim Museum—all in New York City; the National Gallery, Washington, D.C.; the National Gallery of Canada, Ottawa; Bibliothèque Nationale, Paris, France; Victoria & Albert Museum, London, England; and others.

Bibliography

Acton, David. *A Spectrum of Innovation: Color in American Printmaking 1890–1960.* Norton, 1990.

Peterdi, Gabor. *Printmaking: Methods Old and New.* Macmillan, 1959.

The Brooklyn Museum Bulletin. Vol. XIV, 1952.

WalkingStick, Kay (1935–)

Kay WalkingStick is best known for her paintings, which combine geometric abstraction with abstracted landscapes. Her multi-layered paintings reflect an interest in the mysteries of life. WalkingStick often paints in diptych form, each half depicting a different view of the same landscape. The reverberations between the two juxtaposed views—one naturalistic and the other an abstraction—reflect WalkingStick's intuitive unification of momentary perception and permanent memory.

WalkingStick, a member of the Cherokee Nation of Oklahoma received her Bachelor of Fine Arts degree from Beaver College, Glenside, Pennsylvania (1959) and her Master of Fine Arts degree from Pratt Institute, Brooklyn, New York (1975). She began exhibiting her paintings in 1969. Since her solo exhibition at the SoHo Center for the Visual Arts in New York City in 1976, she has had more than twenty solo shows in galleries and museums throughout the United States. A solo exhibition focusing on her work from 1974 through 1990 was organized in 1991 by the Hillwood Art Museum of Long Island University, C.W. Post campus in Brookville, New York, and subsequently travelled to the Heard Mu-

seum in Phoenix, Arizona. Other solo exhibitions have been presented at Morris Museum, Morristown, New Jersey (1992) and at M-13 Gallery in New York City (1987, 1990). WalkingStick has participated in more than fifty-five group exhibitions throughout the United States, Canada, Europe, and Israel. They include "Autobiography, In Her Own Image," curated by Howardena Pindell at Intar Gallery (1988), and "The Decade Show, Framework of Identity in the 1980s" at the New Museum of Contemporary Art (1990)—both in New York City; and "Shared Visions, Native American Painters and Sculptors of the 20th Century" at the Heard Museum in Phoenix, Arizona (1991). Her paintings are in public and private collections throughout the United States and Israel, including the San Diego Museum of Fine Arts, California; Albright-Knox Art Gallery, Buffalo, and the Johnson Museum at Cornell University in Ithaca—both in New York; the Israel Museum in Jerusalem; and the Heard Museum in Phoenix, Arizona.

WalkingStick has taught painting and drawing at Fairleigh Dickinson University, Rutherford (1970–1973); Upsala College, East Orange (1975–1979); Art Center of North New Jersey (1978–1985); and Montclair Art Museum (1986–1988)—all in New Jersey; Cornell University, Ithaca (1988–1990); and the State University of New York (SUNY) at Stony Brook (1990 to the present)—both in New York. Her 1989 interview with artist George Longfish, "Like a Longfish Out of Water," appeared in the *Northeast Indian Quarterly*, American Indian Program of Cornell University, vol. VI, no. 3, Fall 1919. Her article "Democracy, Inc.: Kay WalkingStick on Indian Law," appeared in the November 1991 edition of *Artforum*.

WalkingStick has received many awards and honors, including a Danforth Foundation graduate fellowship for women (1973–1975); New Jersey State Council on the Arts fellowship awards (1981, 1985–1986); a National Endowment for the Arts (NEA) visual artist fellowship in painting (1983–1984); and a Richard A. Florsheim art fund award (1991). She has served as a panelist for the New York State Council on the Arts (1986–1987); the New Jersey State Council on the Arts (1987); the New York Foundation for the Arts (1989), and Arts Midwest in Minneapolis, Minnesota (1990).

Rhonda Cooper

Bibliography

Archuleta, Margaret, and Rennard Strickland. *Shared Visions, Native American Painters and Sculptors of the 20th Century.* Phoenix, Arizona: Heard Museum, 1991.

Braff, Phyllis. "A Special Regard for Nature's Forces." *The New York Times* (April 14, 1990).

Cotter, Holland. *Kay WalkingStick, Paintings 1974–1990.* Brookville, New York: Hillwood Art Museum, 1991.

Jones, Kellie. "Kay WalkingStick." *The Village Voice*, New York (May 16, 1989).

Krane, Susan, with Robert Evan and Helen Raye. *The Painting and Sculpture Collection: Acquisitions since 1972.* Albright-Knox Art Gallery, Hudson Hills Press, 1987.

Lippard, Lucy R. *Mixed Blessings.* Pantheon Books, 1991, pp. 109, 185, 186.

Raynor, Vivien. "The Male Figure, Dual Images, and Landscapes." *The New York Times* (March 26, 1989).

van Wagner, Judith Collishan. *Lines of Vision, Drawings by Contemporary Women.* Hudson Hills Press, 1989, p. 145.

Walter, Martha (1875–1976)

A plein-air painter of landscapes and a portraitist, Martha Walter was born in Philadelphia, Pennsylvania. She studied at the Pennsylvania Academy of Fine Arts, Philadelphia, with William Merritt Chase, and won the Toppan prize in 1902 and a two-year Cresson travelling scholarship in 1903, which enabled her to study in Paris, France, as well as to visit Italy, Holland, and Spain. She enrolled at the Académie de la Grande Chaumière in Paris but, finding its approach too classical, she transferred to the Académie Julian, also in Paris. The academic tradition was not to her liking, so she established her own studio on the Rue de Bagneaux with several other young American women artists. In 1909 she won the Pennsylvania Academy's Mary Smith prize for the best work by a woman, and exhibited in its annuals for over fifty years, winning a gold medal in 1923.

World War I caused Walter to return to the United States. She set up studios in New York City and Boston, Massachusetts, painting the beaches of Atlantic City, New Jersey, and Gloucester, Massachusetts. In the next decades she pursued an international career, teaching at the New York School of Art and in Brittany. In 1922 the Galerie Georges Petit gave her an exhibition from which the French government purchased her painting, "The Plaid Cape," for the Musée du Luxembourg—both in Paris. In the 1930s she exhibited at the Milch Galleries in New York City and began her travels in North Africa. Among the thirty-nine works listed in her 1931 exhibition are "Portrait of Her Majesty, the Queen of Spain," "Spanish Gypsies," and "Goat Market, North Africa." In 1941 the Art Club of Chicago, Illinois, exhibited seventy-eight of her oil paintings and watercolors, and, in 1955, the Woodmere Museum in Philadelphia, Pennsylvania, exhibited 135 of her paintings, including her "Ellis Island" series. Her paintings, characterized by bright, vivid colors and a white pigment saturated with light, are in the Toledo Museum, Ohio; the Terra Museum of American Art and the Art Institute of Chicago—both in Chicago, Illinois; Detroit Institute of Art, Michigan; and Milwaukee Art Center, Wisconsin.

Eleanor Tufts

Bibliography

David, Carl E. "Martha Walter." *American Art Review* 4:5 (May 1978): 84–90.

Tufts, Eleanor. *American Women Artists, 1830–1930*. National Museum of Women in the Arts, 1987.

Wapner, Grace Bakst

A native New Yorker, the ceramist/sculptor Grace Bakst Wapner earned a Bachelor's degree at Bennington College, Vermont. Before completing her degree she spent a year in New York City attending the Sculpture Center and the New School for Social Research, where she studied with Paul Feeley.

Wapner has held solo exhibitions in galleries and universities, including the 55 Mercer Gallery (1973–1975, 1977–1978, 1982, 1984), and Bernice Steinbaum Gallery (1987, 1989, 1992)—both in New York City; the Gallery of July and August, Woodstock, New York (1975, 1977); Drew University, Madison, New Jersey (1984); Washington Square, Washington, D.C. (1992); and others. Her work has been invited to many group exhibitions between 1964 and 1992 in museums and galleries, such as "Totems," Elana Zaney Gallery, Shady, New York

(1992); "Artists of the Mohawk Region, Hudson Region," State University of New York (SUNY) at Albany (1991); "Invitational Group Show," Woodstock Artists Association, Woodstock, New York (1966–1967, 1973, 1981, 1983, 1991); "Group Show," Bernice Steinbaum Gallery (1987–1990), the Hess Trust (1982, 1983), and "Women in American Architecture: A Historic and Contemporary Perspective," Brooklyn Museum (1977)—all in New York City; and others.

In "Nomads, Lovers, Artists and Thieves" (1991), a recent work of bronze and porcelain, Wapner fuses and transmutes these disparate materials to create a spidery metaphor for human and biological growth and development. Her work is represented in private and public permanent collections.

Bibliography

Art Now. Gallery Guide: Downtown, New York. (May 1992).

Galligan, Gregory. "Grace Bakst Wapner." *Ceramics Monthly* (Summer 1987).

Henry, Sara. "Grace Wapner." *Ceramics Monthly* (September 1987).

Warashina, Patti (1940–)

Born in Spokane, Washington, the ceramist/sculptor Patti Warashina earned a Bachelor of Fine Arts degree at the University of Washington, Seattle (1962), and, two years later, was awarded a Master of Fine Arts degree from the same institution.

Between 1962 and 1992 Warashina has held thirty-two solo exhibitions in galleries throughout the United States, including the Phoenix Art Gallery, New York City (1962); Left Bank Gallery, Flint, Michigan (1968); Contemporary Crafts Museum, Portland, Oregon (1969); Grossmont College, San Diego, California (1976); University of Nevada, Las Vegas (1978); Tucson Art Museum, Arizona (1982); University of New Mexico, Albuquerque (1983); Jane Hartsook Gallery (1989), and Helen Druitt Gallery (1991)—both in New York City; Bellevue Art Museum, Washington (1991); University of Montana, Missoula (1992); and others. Warashina's work has been invited to more than 325 group exhibitions in the United States and abroad, such as "24th Ceramic National Exhibition," Syracuse, New York (1962, 1964, 1966); "Contemporary Ceramic Art: USA, Canada, Mexico, Japan," National Museum of Modern Art, Tokyo, Japan (1971); "International Exhibition of Ceramics," Victoria & Albert Museum, London, England (1972); "Poetry of the Physical," a travelling exhibition, American Craft Museum, New York City (1986); "Shattered Self," a travelling show to Colorado, California, and Europe, the Society for Art in Crafts, Pittsburgh, Pennsylvania (1988); "1st Perth International Crafts Triennial," Art Gallery of Western Australia (1989); and myriad others.

A professor of art at the University of Washington, Seattle, and a widely-known lecturer, Warashina has won awards and honors for her work, including two National Endowment for the Arts (NEA) awards (1975–1976, 1986–1987); the governor's special commendation award in the arts, Olympia (1980), a commissioned sculpture from the Seattle Arts Commission, honoring northwest artists of significant accomplishment and sited at the Seattle Opera House (1986), and the 1992 honors program award from the King County Arts Commission, Seattle (1992)—all in Washington; and others. Her work is represented in private, public, and corporate permanent collections, including the Henry Art Gallery, Seattle, Washington; Sea of Japan Exposition, Kanazawashi, and National Museum of Modern Art, Tokyo—both in Japan;

Wustum Museum of Fine Arts and Johnson Wax Collection—both in Racine, Wisconsin; Brooks Memorial Art Museum, Memphis, Tennessee; Palomar College, San Marcos, California; Detroit Art Institute, Michigan; University of Colorado, Boulder; Everson Museum, Syracuse, New York; Art Gallery of Western Australia, Perth; Palm Beach Community College, Florida; and others.

Bibliography
Grieve Watkinson, Patricia. "Patti Warashina." *American Ceramics* 10:1 (Spring 1992): 18–25.
Harrington, LaMar. *Ceramics in the Pacific Northwest: A History*. University of Washington Press, 1979.
Kangas, Matthew. *American Craft* 40:2 (April–May 1980): 2–8.
Klemperer, Louise. "Surreal or So Real? The Little World of Patti Warashina." *American Ceramics* 4:2, pp. 38–47.
Who's Who in American Art. 19th ed. R.R. Bowker Co., 1991–1992.

Ward, Catharine Weed Barnes (1851–1913)

Born January 10, 1851, in Albany, New York, Catharine Weed Barnes Ward was internationally known during her lifetime as a photographer, lecturer, and editor. Educated at the Albany Female Academy, New York, and the Friends' School of Providence, Rhode Island, Ward enrolled in 1869 at Vassar College, Poughkeepsie, New York. Poor health, however, prevented her from completing her studies there. Interested in music and painting, Ward began photography studies in 1886 at the instigation of her mother. Skill came quickly, and, on October 2, 1887, an item in *The Argus*, Albany, New York, mentioned her as a successful amateur photographer.

In a portrait studio built in her home in Albany, Ward made photographs and lantern slides which won competitions in New York City and Buffalo, New York; Boston, Massachusetts; and Washington, D.C. (1888–1891). At the same time she contributed numerous articles to *Outing* and *Frank Leslie's Weekly*. In May 1890 Barnes was made editor of a column entitled "Woman's Work" for the *American Amateur Photographer*, and, in February 1892, she became coeditor of that magazine with F.C. Beach. During a trip to England and Scotland in July 1892 she was invited to address the Photographic Convention of the United Kingdom at Edinburgh, Scotland.

A member of the Society of Amateur Photographers of New York and the New York Camera Club—both in New York City; the Postal Photographic Club; and an honorary member of the Chicago Camera Club, Illinois, Ward was the only woman on a committee of six to act as judge of the photographic exhibit at the Columbian World's Exposition, Chicago, Illinois, in 1893. On July 15, 1893, she married H. Snowden Ward, a well-known photographer, lecturer, and author of London, England.

While living in London, England, Ward continued as editor of *American Amateur Photographer* until 1895, when she resigned to work with her husband as a coeditor of the *Photogram*. Ward provided photographs for several of her husband's books, including *Shakespeare's Town and Times* (1896); *The Real Dicken's Land* (1903); *The Canterbury Pilgrimages* (1904); and *The Land of Lorna Doone* (1908). She also provided lantern slides as illustrations for a series of lectures in England and the United States given by her husband.

After her husband's death in 1911, Ward continued to make her home in Hadlow, England, where she was an active member of the Tunbridge Wells Photographic Society. She died in 1913 and is buried in the family plot in Albany, New York.

Elizabeth Poulson

Bibliography
American Amateur Photographer. Brunswick, Maine: 1889–1895.
Hines, Richard, Jr. "Women in Photography." *The Photographic Times* 242 (May 1899).
National Cyclopaedia of American Biography. James T. White and Company, 1898.
Who Was Who in America (1892–1942). Vol. I. A.N. Marquis Company, 1943.

Ward-Brown, Denise (1953–)

Born in Philadelphia, Pennsylvania, the African-American sculptor/printmaker/educator Denise Ward-Brown earned a Bachelor of Fine Arts degree at the Tyler School of Art, Temple University, Philadelphia; and received a Master of Fine Arts degree from Howard University, Washington, D.C.

Ward-Brown has held solo exhibitions in galleries, including "New Work," Jones Troyer Fitzpatrick, and "Assemblage," The "O" Street Studio (1989)—both in Washington, D.C., among others. Her work has been invited to or included in many group shows, such as "Next Generation: Southern Black Aesthetic," Southeastern Center for Contemporary Arts, Winston-Salem, North Carolina (1990); "People Who Make Prints," Northern Virginia Community College, Annandale (1989); "Four Artists," Notre Dame College, Baltimore, Maryland (1989), and "Bridges to the African-American Aesthetic," Strathmore Hall Arts Center, Rockville (1988)—both in Maryland; "Afro-American Art, Now," George Washington University, Washington, D.C. (1987); and others.

Ward-Brown's recent sculpture is composed mainly of cast-off objects and materials (usually of wood) that are transmuted into layered abstract compositions based upon the life experience of the artist. Her work is represented in private and public permanent collections, including the Office of the Mayor, Washington, D.C.

Bibliography
Hall, Robert L. *Gathered Visions: Selected Works by African American Women Artists*. Anacostia Museum, Smithsonian Institution Press, 1992.
James, Curtia. "Denise Ward-Brown." *New Art Examiner* (December 1989).
Lewis, Jo Ann. "The Myth Masters." *The Washington Post* (March 1, 1986).

Waring, Laura Wheeler (1887–1948)

Laura Wheeler Waring was born in Hartford, Connecticut, where her father was a Congregational minister and her mother a musician. Upon graduation from Oberlin College, Ohio, she attended the Pennsylvania Academy of Fine Arts, Philadelphia (1918–1924). On a Cresson travelling scholarship she enrolled for further study at the Académie de la Grande Chaumière in Paris, France (1924–1925). She returned to America and, in 1927, received the Harmon Foundation's gold award in fine arts. Her work then began to be included in major exhibitions at such museums as the Art Institute of Chicago, Illinois (1933); the Pennsylvania Academy of Fine Arts, Philadelphia (1935, 1938); the Dallas Museum of Fine Arts, Texas (1936); and Howard University, Washington, D.C. (1937, 1939, 1949), a retrospective exhibition of forty paintings.

Primarily a portraitist, Waring is best known for the commission she shared with Betsy Graves Reyneau of "Outstanding Americans of Negro Origin" for the Harmon Foundation. She painted portraits of "Marian Anderson" (1944, full-length standing, looking majestic in a long evening dress), "W.E.B. DuBois" (c. 1945, seated at a table with a serious expression on his face), "Harry Thacker Burleigh" (his arms folded across his chest), and "James Weldon Johnson" (1943, seated against an evocative poetic background)—all in the National Portrait Gallery, Washington, D.C. She also did the portrait of "Alma Thomas" in the reds and greens favored by Thomas (1947, Howard University). In her portrait of "Anna Washington Derry" (1927, National Museum of American Art) she shows her ability to convey a sensitive, poignant face in a probing manner. In addition she painted many still lifes, landscapes, and genre scenes (such as "Jazz Dancer I" c. 1939).

Waring was an instructor of art at Cheyney State Teachers College (now Cheyney State College) in Pennsylvania, for many years before becoming head of the department, while her husband served as a professor in the romance language department at Lincoln University, Pennsylvania. Two of her portraits can be seen at Cheyney State College, Pennsylvania—one in Carnegie Library and the other in Burleigh Hall.

Eleanor Tufts

Bibliography
Bontemps, Arna Alexander. *Forever Free: Art by African-American Women 1862–1980.* Alexandria, Virginia. 1980.
Igoe, Lynn Moore, with Janes Igoe. *250 Years of Afro-American Art: An Annotated Bibliography.* R.R. Bowker Co., 1981.
Tufts, Eleanor. *American Women Artists, 1830–1930.* National Museum of Women in the Arts, 1987.

Warkov, Esther (1941–)

Born in Winnipeg, Manitoba, the artist Esther Warkov studied at the Winnipeg School of Art (1958–1961). She is a Canadian figurative painter whose works carry on the classical ascetic spirit associated with a northern country—but, with a difference. Warkov's singular social commentary is based, in part, on a life that asks questions. Her paintings may be analyzed for their form, color, or satiric bite—to no avail. Form and content are one.

Warkov has exhibited in many solo and group shows in Canada and abroad, including "Expo '67," Montréal, Québec, Canada; Museum of Modern Art, Paris, France (1973); Albright-Knox Art Gallery, Buffalo, New York (1974); and many others. She has received honors and awards for her work, including Canada Council bursaries (1967–1972) and grants (1973–1974). Representative examples of Warkov's work may be found in private and public permanent collections in Canada, including the Beaverbrook Art Gallery, Fredricton, New Brunswick; Museum of Fine Arts, Montréal; the National Gallery, Ottawa; Vancouver Art Gallery, British Columbia; Winnipeg Art Gallery, Manitoba; and others.

Bibliography
Lumsden, Ian G. "Warkov." *Vie des arts* 66 (Spring 1972): 58–61, 90–91.
Milne, Marlene. "Esther Warkov: Mixing Memory and Desire." *Arts Manitoba* 1:3–4 (Winter 1978): 79–81.
Tamplin, Illi-Maria, Curator. *Manitoba Flashback.* A Catalog. Ontario: Art Gallery of Peterborough, 1981.

Wasey, Jane (1912–)

A resident of Maine, born in Chicago, Illinois, the sculptor Jane Wasey studied with Paul Landowski in Paris, France; with Simon Moselsio in New York City; and with John Flanagan and Heinz Warneke.

Wasey has held solo exhibitions in museums and galleries in the United States, including the Montross Gallery (1934), and the Delphic Studio (1935)—both in New York City; Philbrook Art Museum, Tulsa, Oklahoma (1945); Weathervanes Contemporaries (1954), and Kraushaar Galleries (1955, 1971, 1986)—both in New York City; and others. Her work has been invited to many distinguished group exhibitions in the United States and abroad, such as the Albright-Knox Art Gallery, Buffalo, New York; Audubon Artists, Brooklyn Museum, the Sculptors Guild, Metropolitan Museum of Art, and Whitney Museum of American Art—all in New York City; Burlington Galleries, London, England; Art Institute of Chicago, Illinois; Colby College, Waterville, Maine; Pennsylvania Academy of Fine Arts and Philadelphia Museum of Art—both in Philadelphia, Pennsylvania; and others.

Winner of honors and awards, Wasey was the recipient of the Phillips memorial prize, Architectural League (1955); the Mrs. John Henry Hammond award, National Association of Women Artists (1951); the Lighthouse prize (1951); Avery memorial prize (1951); first prize for sculpture, Parrish Art Museum (1951); the Guild Hall prize (1951–1956); and others.

Wasey's work is represented in private and public permanent collections, including Arizona State University, Tempe; University of Colorado, Boulder; Dartmouth College, Hanover, New Hampshire; University of Maine, Orono; Pennsylvania Academy of Fine Arts, Philadelphia; Whitney Museum of American Art, New York City; and many others. Her three-dimensional portrait of André, a harbor seal beloved by the residents of Rockport, Maine, is on permanent display in that city's Marine Park.

Bibliography
Brumme, C. Ludwig. *Contemporary American Sculpture.* Crown, 1948.
Hill, M. Brawley. *Women: A Historical Survey of Works by Women Artists.* North Carolina Museum of Art, 1972.
Meilach, Dona Z. *Contemporary Stone Sculpture.* 1970.
The Arizona State College Collection of American Art. A Catalog. Text by Paula R. Kloster. Arizona State College, 1954.
Who's Who in American Art. 19th ed. R.R. Bowker Co., 1991–1992.

Wasserman, Barbara (1934–)

Born in New York City, Barbara Wasserman received her formal education at New York University, New York City, and Hofstra College, Hempstead, New York. She had her work accepted in a group exhibition at the New York City Center in 1958 and, the following year, at the Village Arts Center in New York City.

In 1959 Wasserman settled in Mexico City, Mexico, and had her first solo exhibition at the Galería Diana there in 1960. She has enjoyed many more solo shows at galleries and institutes, including the Mexican-North American Institute of Cultural Relations, the Galería Pecanins in Mexico City, and the Smolin Gallery in New York City. Wasserman won a prize for watercolor at the National Academy of Design, New York City, in 1958.

Bibliography
The Texas Quarterly: Image of Mexico II. The University of Texas, Winter 1969.

Watson, Genna (1948–)

Born in Baltimore, Maryland, the artist Genna Watson earned a Bachelor of Fine Arts degree from the Maryland Institute College of Art, Baltimore, where she studied with Roger Majorowicz (1970). She studied sculpture at Washington University, St. Louis, Missouri (1971–1973); and received a Master of Fine Arts degree in sculpture from the University of Wisconsin at Madison, where she studied with Art Schade.

An award-winning sculptor, Watson has held solo exhibitions and has had her work invited to group exhibitions throughout the United States, including the "Twenty-First Area Exhibition: Sculpture," Corcoran Gallery of Art, Washington, D.C. (1978); "Uncommon Visions," University of Rochester, New York (1979); "Body and Soul: Recent Figurative Sculpture," a travelling show, Contemporary Arts Center, Cincinnati, Ohio (1985); and others. Her mixed-media installations, as seen in her solo show at Fendrick Gallery, Washington, D.C. (1982), challenge the viewer. Her work is represented in private and public permanent collections.

Bibliography

Richard, Paul. "Galleries: Women in Shadow, At Tartt, Watson's Haunting Sculptures." *The Washington Post* (March 21, 1987): B2.

Rubenfeld, Florence. "Reviews East Coast: Genna Watson, The Athenaeum." *New Art Examiner* 11:8 (May 1984): II 4.

Watson-Jones, Virginia. *Contemporary American Women Sculptors.* Oryx Press, 1986.

Watson, Helen Richter (1926–)

Born in Laredo, Texas, the artist Helen Richter Watson earned a Bachelor's degree in functional ceramics from Scripps College, Claremont, California (1947), and a Master of Fine Arts degree in the same specialty from Claremont Graduate School and University Center, California (1949). She did further work in functional ceramics at the Wichita Art Association, Kansas (1950); studied with Bernard Leach (1950) and Margaret Wildenhain (1960); and carried her specialty even further at Alfred University, New York (1966). Winner of awards and honors, Watson received a Swedish government grant for the study of arts and crafts, Stockholm (1952–1953); a twenty-four-foot sculpture commission for the Nueces County Courthouse, awarded by the Bicentennial Committee of Corpus Christi, Texas (1976); a distinguished alumna award from Scripps College (1978); and others. She has held solo exhibitions in galleries and museums in California, Texas, and Oklahoma and has shown her work in many group exhibitions throughout the United States.

A professor of ceramics at Otis Art Institute, Los Angeles, California, Watson has completed many commissions which grace public venues in the West. Her love for clay originated in childhood and grew from simple pot-making to symbolic, abstract, monumental, architectural stoneware forms. Her work is represented in private, public, and corporate permanent collections, including Christ Church, Laredo, and Tyler Bank and Trust Company—both in Texas; and San Antonio Community Hospital, Ontario; Scottish Rite Masonic Temple, Los Angeles; and Scripps College, Claremont—all in California; and many others.

Bibliography

First Annual Distinguished Alumna Exhibition. Scripps College, 1978.

"Helen Richter Watson: Monumental Sculpture." *Ceramics Monthly* 28:4 (April 1980): 56–57.

Watson-Jones, Virginia. *Contemporary American Women Sculptors.* Oryx Press, 1986.

Who's Who in American Art. 19th ed. R.R. Bowker Co., 1991–1992.

Wayne, June Claire (1918–)

Born in Chicago, Illinois, June Claire Wayne is a painter, printmaker, writer, industrial designer, designer of tapestries, and founding director of the world-renowned Tamarind Lithography Workshop, to name but a clutch of her talents and proclivities.

A bookish, only child of a divorced couple (her grandmother raised her, while her mother worked to support them), she drew incessantly. Wayne became bored with high school and dropped out in her third year, even though she passed the entrance examinations to the University of Chicago, Illinois. She left home at the age of sixteen, found employment, and coped with life.

Wayne's first solo exhibition of small watercolors and drawings occurred in 1935 at the Diana Court Bookshop Gallery in Chicago, Illinois. The following year, as a guest of Mexico's Department of Public Education, she travelled to Mexico City to paint, and there she had a solo exhibition at the Palacio de Bellas Artes. Over the next ten years, during which time she continued to paint, Wayne worked in the art galleries of Marshall Field and Company, Chicago, Illinois (1937), participated in the easel painting project of the Illinois Works Progress Administration Federal Art Project (WPA/FAP) (1938); and moved to New York City in 1939 to work as an industrial designer. When Pearl Harbor erupted in 1941, Wayne moved to California where she was certified as a production illustrator. Meanwhile she taught herself to write radio scripts (1942), and returned to Chicago in 1943 as a staff writer for WGN Radio. At the war's end she returned to California.

In 1947 Wayne discovered the magic of creating a lithograph on stone in the Los Angeles, California, print shop of Lynton Kistler. Her prodigious output in this medium continues to the present. Between 1947 and 1956 she became interested in aspects of optics in visual narrative; became intrigued with "eyepaths" in two- and three-dimensional space; and pursued investigations of symbol systems—all of which were realized in her paintings and prints. This analytical activity led to the "Kafka Series," the "Optics Series," the "Fable Series," the "Justice Series," and culminated in solo exhibitions at the Santa Barbara Museum (1950, 1953), the San Francisco Museum of Art (1950)—both in California; the Art Institute of Chicago, Illinois (1952); the Contemporaries Gallery, New York City (1953), and the Art Museum of La Jolla (1954), and the M.H. de Young Memorial Museum, San Francisco (1956)—both in California.

Early in her career Wayne's work manifested an interest in the problem of movement, in relationships between focal and peripheral vision, in allegory and in symbolized ambiguity, and in the play of polar opposites—all in metaphor. Her techniques and methods, her images and symbols present an organic totality.

In the mid 1950s Wayne's wide-ranging interest in all things related to the visual arts, music, science, and literature became clear. She became a consultant to a Ford Foundation discussion series for adults titled, "You and Modern Art." She went to France to create lithographs on stone with the printer Marcel Durassier, which culminated in her "Livre d'Artiste, Songs and Sonnets of John Donne" (1958).

Wayne's Tamarind Avenue studio in Los Angeles, California, as a result of her proposal to the Ford Foundation, became the world-famous Tamarind Lithography Workshop which she founded and directed during its inaugural decade (1960–1970). In addition, she produced the "Lemming Series" and many other unique lithographs (1960–1970). By 1971 she was making tapestry cartoons and was collaborating with three French tapestry weaveries. She wrote an eight-part public television series on the artist and the art world which included segments filmed with Louise Nevelson, Françoise Gilot, Grace Glueck, and many other art world personalities. Her post-Tamarind work opened at the Municipal Art Gallery of Los Angeles, California (1973), in the same year that she produced the film, *Four Stones For Kanemitsu*, which took an Oscar nomination. Two years later she began "The Dorothy Series," a biography of her mother in lithographs, a project that spanned four years.

In the 1980s Wayne created nine suites of lithographs, and an audio-visual slide show that became a program on PBS. In 1988 she did a unique collaboration with Otto Piene and the Massachusetts Institute of Technology (MIT) Institute for Advanced Visual Studies in which her galactic images were projected onto a twenty-foot balloon sphere as she, herself, in a parachute harness, flew from twelve Piene balloons during the WESTWEEK celebration at the Pacific Design Center, West Hollywood, California (1988). In this period she also created paintings, collages, and many lithographs.

Wayne has been awarded four honorary Doctorate degrees from distinguished art colleges and has won scores of awards and purchase prizes for her works in many media. Her art may be found in dozens of public and private collections in the United States, Europe, and Australia. Among the museums are the Museum of Modern Art (MoMA), New York City; the National Gallery of Art and the Library of Congress, Washington, D.C.; the Bibliothèque Nationale, Paris, France; the Bibliothèque Royale de Belgique, Bruxelles, Belgium; the Australian National Gallery in Canberra, and the Queensland Art Gallery in Brisbane, Australia.

Bibliography

Adams, Clinton. *American Lithographers: 1900–1960*. University of New Mexico Press, 1984.

Baskett, Mary W. *The Art of June Wayne*. Harry N. Abrams, 1969.

Kester, Bernard. *June Wayne: The Djuna Set*. Exhibition Catalog. The Fresno Art Museum, 1988. (Paintings.)

Gilmour, Pat. *June Wayne: The Djuna Set*. Exhibition Catalog. The Fresno Art Museum, 1988. (Prints.)

Munro, Eleanor. *Originals: American Women Artists*. Simon and Schuster, 1979.

Raven, Arlene. *June Wayne: The Djuna Set*. Exhibition Catalog. The Fresno Art Museum, 1984.

Weber, Idelle (1932–)

Born in Chicago, Illinois, the photo-realist painter and printmaker Idelle Weber studied at Scripps College, Claremont, California, and at the University of California at Los Angeles (UCLA), where she obtained Bachelor's and Master's degrees.

Weber has held solo exhibitions in museums and galleries in the United States and abroad, and has had her work included in many prestigious group shows, including the Guggenheim Museum, New York City (1964); Wadsworth Athenaeum, Hartford, Connecticut (1966, 1974); the Whitney Downtown, New York City (1975); "Realismus und Realitat," Darmstadt, Germany (1975); Smithsonian Institution, National Collection of Fine Arts, Washington, D.C. (1976); "American Artists '76: A Celebration," McNay Art Institute, San Antonio, Texas (1976); O.K. Harris Gallery (1977, 1979, 1983), and New York Graphic Society—both in New York City: and the Pennsylvania Academy of Fine Arts, Philadelphia (1981); Ruth Siegel Contemporary Gallery, New York City (1984, 1986); and many others.

Winner of awards and honors, Weber is a university teacher at the graduate level. Examples of her work are in private and public permanent collections, including the Albright-Knox Art Gallery, Buffalo, New York; San Francisco Museum of Modern Art, California; Smithsonian Institution, National Collection of Fine Arts, Washington, D.C.; Worcester Art Museum, Massachusetts; Yale University, New Haven, Connecticut; and many others.

Bibliography

Goodyear, Frank, Jr. *Contemporary American Realism since 1960*. Boston: New York Graphic Society and Pennsylvania Academy of Fine Arts, 1981.

Henry, Gerrit. "Idelle Weber at Ruth Siegel." *Art in America* 74:3 (March 1986): 151–52.

Real, Really Real, SUPER REAL. Essays by Sally Booth-Meredith, Alvin Martin, Linda Nochlin, and Philip Pearlstein. Texas: San Antonio Museum of Art, 1981.

Weber, Trudi (1945–)

Born in Zurich, Switzerland, Trudi Weber has lived in Mexico from infancy. A self-taught painter, she developed child-like themes and painted in a naive style. Weber has exhibited her work since 1965. Fritz Laufer, in writing about her work, noted that, "Her paintings are full of the joy of life, of simple and pleasant thoughts that touch the heart of mankind."

Bibliography

Alvarez, José Rogelio, et al. *Enciclopedia de Mexico*. Secretaría de Educación Pública, 1987.

Weems, Katherine Lane (1899–1990)

Born in Boston, Massachusetts, the animal sculptor Katherine Lane Weems studied at the School of the Museum of Fine Arts, Boston. She also studied with Charles Grafly, Anna Hyatt Huntington, and Brenda Putnam.

A national and international prize winner for many years, Weems made a film for the Museum of Fine Arts titled, *From Clay to Bronze* (1930), which included a technical lecture-demonstration on the subject of sculpture. Three years later she executed several large directly-carved, animal relief panels on a brick wall for a biological laboratory at Harvard University, Cambridge, Massachusetts—and her career burgeoned. Among many other exhibitions, Weems showed in the "Fortieth Annual Exhibition," National Association of Women Painters and Sculptors, New York City (1931); and the "122nd Annual Exhibition," the Pennsylvania Academy of Fine Arts, Pennsylvania (1927).

Weems was a member of the National Academy of Design and the

National Sculpture Society—both in New York City; and other professional art organizations. Her work is represented in private and public permanent collections, including the Pennsylvania Academy of Fine Arts, Philadelphia; Brookgreen Gardens, South Carolina; and others.

Bibliography

Ambler, Louise Todd. *Katherine Lane Weems, Sculpture and Drawings.* Boston Athenaeum, 1987.

Greenthal, Kathryn, Paula M. Kozol, and Jan Seidler Ramirez. *American Figurative Sculpture in the Museum of Fine Arts.* Boston: Museum of Fine Arts, 1986.

Weems, Katherine Lane, as told to Edward Weeks. *Odds Were Against Me: A Memoir.* Vantage Press, 1985.

Weinrich, Agnes (1873–1946)

Agnes Weinrich, a printmaker and painter, was born on an opulent farm near Burlington, Iowa. She attended Burlington Institute College and did further study at Iowa Wesleyan College in Mount Pleasant.

After their father died in 1899, Weinrich and her sister Helen travelled to Paris, France, and Berlin, Germany, to study art and music respectively, and to avail themselves of the Grand Tour.

Weinrich attended the School of the Art Institute of Chicago, Illinois (1905), and the following year, when she and her sister moved to Provincetown, Massachusetts, she studied briefly with Charles Webster Hawthorne and Blanche Lazzell. She also attended the Art Students League, New York City, to work with anatomy teacher George Bridgman, and William de Leftwich Dodge.

Weinrich was in the forefront of the "modernist" movement in the Provincetown Art Association, where she exhibited her paintings and color woodcuts (1917–1920). The infamous Armory Show in New York City (1913) made a deep and lasting impression upon her and, perhaps, explains the origin of her strong abstract paintings and prints.

Weinrich's brother-in-law Karl Knaths owed much to her sensibilities and visual ideas; the two worked in separate studios in the house Knaths built for himself, Weinrich and her sister (his wife). In 1927 the Provincetown Art Association, finally persuaded by Weinrich and others, sponsored a separate "modern" exhibition along with the regular "conservative" show. Weinrich, Knaths, and Blanche Lazzell were among the jurors for the "modern" show. Ten years passed before the Association sponsored a "combined" exhibition.

Weinrich had solo exhibitions in Boston, Chicago, and Washington, D.C., and produced work until her death in Provincetown in 1946. Her oils, "Plants and Fruit" and "Still Life with Leaves," both in the Phillips Collection, Washington, D.C., are worthy examples of her abstract, vigorous style.

Bibliography

Acton, David. *A Spectrum of Innovation: Color in American Printmaking 1890–1960.* Worcester Art Museum, 1990.

Flint, Janet. *Provincetown Printers: A Woodcut Tradition.* Exhibition Catalog. National Museum of American Art, Smithsonian Institution, 1983.

Seckler, Dorothy Gees. *Provincetown Painters 1890s–1970s.* Everson Museum of Art, 1977.

The Phillips Collection, A Summary Catalog. The Phillips Collection, 1985.

Weintraub, Annette (1946–)

A native New Yorker, the multi-faceted artist Annette Weintraub earned a Bachelor of Fine Arts degree at Cooper Union, New York City (1967), and a Master of Fine Arts degree three years later from the University of Pennsylvania, Philadelphia.

Weintraub has shown paintings, prints, drawings, electronic art, and artist's books in more than thirty exhibitions in the United States and abroad, including "Concrete Erections," Michael Ingbar Gallery of Architectural Art, New York City (1993); "Third International Symposium on Electronic Art," Gallery Ars Multiplicata, Sydney, Australia (1992); "ACM SIGGRAPH Travelling Art Show," Boston Computer Museum, Massachusetts (1991–1992); "Fifth Annual Juried Show of Computer Art and Video," Fine Arts Museum of Long Island, New York (1987–1988); "CADE '86," Association for Computer Art and Design Education, Sheridan College, Toronto, Canada (1986); "Woman, Inside and Out," Gallery Yves Arman, New York City (1983); and many others.

A professor of art at the City College, City University of New York (CUNY), Weintraub has been associated with that university since 1981. She has won honors and awards, including an artist's fellowship from the New York Foundation for the Arts (1991); resident grants from Yaddo, Saratoga Springs, New York (1979, 1989); and others. Weintraub has lectured and presented workshops in many institutions. Examples of her work are in private, corporate, and public permanent collections, including the Aldrich Museum of Contemporary Art, Ridgefield, Connecticut; Fine Arts Museum of Long Island, New York; Lehigh University, Bethlehem, Pennsylvania; Wichita Art Museum, Kansas; Best Products Company, Ashland, Virginia; AT&T; and others.

Bibliography

Gosden, Margaret. "Art & Soul." *Women Artists News* (Spring 1985).

Preston, Malcolm. "An Interest in Surface Design." *Newsday* (November 17, 1982).

"Screen Test." *MacWeek* (August 21, 1990): 31.

Weir, Irene (1862–1944)

Though she has been hidden from history by the fame of her artist-uncles—Julian Alden Weir and John Ferguson Weir—and her artist-grandfather—Robert Walter Weir—influential teachers as well as painters, Irene Weir had a long and significant career as a painter, etcher, poster designer, muralist, teacher, lecturer, and writer. Weir was born in St. Louis, Missouri, to Walter Weir, a teacher, and Annie Field Andrews Weir, a homemaker. She attended the Yale School of Fine Arts, New Haven, Connecticut, where her uncle John taught for years, in 1881–1882 and completed a Bachelor of Fine Arts degree in 1906. She also studied with her uncle Julian, John H. Twachtman, and Joseph Pennell. She took classes at the Art Students League, New York City, and the Académie des Beaux-Arts, Paris, France, and received a diploma from l'École des Beaux-Arts Américaine in Fontainbleau, France (1923).

After teaching drawing in the New Haven, Connecticut, public school system from 1887 to 1890, Weir served as director of the Slater Museum School of Art in Norwich, Connecticut, until early 1893, when she began to teach art in the Brookline, Massachusetts public schools. Moving to New York City in 1910, she became director of the fine arts department at the Ethical Culture School and then founded the School of Design and Liberal Arts in 1917, serving as its director until 1929. Murals she painted include those for the Washington Cathedral and New York City's Westside Prison.

Weir wrote articles for *Art News, Parnassus, Art Digest, Touchstone,* and *Art World* magazines, as well as two books on art, *The Greek Painter's Art* (1905) and *Outlines of Courses in Design, Representation and Color for High School Classes,* with Elizabeth Stone (1910). Her biography of her grandfather, *Robert W. Weir, Artist,* was published in 1947, three years after her death. Weir was a member of the New York Watercolor Society, the National Association of Women Painters and Sculptors, Art Alliance of America, the National Society of Etchers, and the New York Society of Craftsmen—all in New York City; the London Lyceum Club, England; the 20th Century Club, and the Society of Independent Artists.

Weir exhibited at the Pratt Institute, the Brooklyn Museum, the National Arts Club, the Art Alliance of America, the Art Students League, the Brooklyn Society of Etchers, the National Association of Women Painters and Sculptors, the New York Society of Watercolor Painters, the Architectural League, and the New York Society of Arts and Crafts—all in New York City; the Corcoran Gallery of Art, Washington, D.C., Vassar College Art Gallery, Poughkeepsie, and the Syracuse Museum of Fine Arts—both in New York; Princeton University Gallery, New Jersey; and Yale University School of Fine Art, New Haven, Connecticut. Galleries that exhibited her work include the Anderson Galleries, the Montross Galleries, and the Macbeth Galleries—all in New York City; and the Grafton Galleries, London, England.

Phyllis Peet

Bibliography

"Irene Weir." Artists Files, Art Department, The New York Public Library.
"Irene Weir." *Notable American Women.* Vol. 3. 1971, pp. 557–58.
"Irene Weir." [Obituary.] *The New York Times* (March 23, 1944).

Weisberg, Ruth (1942–)

Ruth Weisberg is an artist who works primarily in painting, lithography, and drawing. She is professor of fine arts at the University of Southern California (USC), Los Angeles, and she previously served as chair, studio art department (1986–1987), as well as acting associate dean for the school of architecture and fine arts for two years. She received her Bachelor's and Master's degrees from the University of Michigan, Ann Arbor, in 1963 and 1965, respectively, as well as a special citation in painting and printmaking from the Accademia di Belle Arti, Perugia, Italy. After a year at Stanley William Hayter's Atelier 17 in Paris, France, she taught for several years at Eastern Michigan University, Ypsilanti.

Weisberg's recent honors include the distinguished artist award, Fresno Art Museum, California (1990); the National Women's Caucus for Art mid-career achievement award (1988); and the University of Michigan's outstanding achievement award for alumni, Ann Arbor (1987); Phi Kappa Phi faculty recognition award for creative work, University of Southern California, Fresno (1986); and the third annual Vesta award in the visual arts given by the Women's Building, Los Angeles, California (October 1984). In 1979 Weisberg was commissioned to create a lithograph for the Graphic Arts Council, Los Angeles County Museum, California; and, in January 1979, a Weisberg lithograph was presented to Georgia O'Keeffe as part of a ceremony honoring her at the White House. For the academic year 1969–1970 Weisberg was awarded a Ford Foundation grant, which was administered by the Near Eastern Center of the University of California at Los Angeles (UCLA).

Weisberg has had more than sixty solo and two-person exhibitions since 1967, including "A Print Retrospective," Fresno Art Museum, California; "The Scroll," Hebrew Union College, New York City; and the Skirball Museum, Hebrew Union College, Los Angeles, California (1988–1989); Associated American Artists, New York City (1987, 1990); Jack Rutberg Fine Arts, Los Angeles, California (1983, 1985, 1988); the Alice Simsar Gallery, Ann Arbor, Michigan (1968, 1969, 1972, 1974, 1977, 1988); "A Circle of Life," Fisher Gallery, University of Southern California; Carnegie-Mellon University, Pittsburgh (1986), Philadelphia Print Club, and the University of Pittsburgh—all in Pennsylvania; University of Richmond, Virginia (1985); and others.

Weisberg has shown in more than 150 group exhibitions, including "American Women Artists: The 20th Century," Knoxville Museum of Art, Tennessee; "Recent Figurative Prints," Associated American Artists, New York City (1987); "The Years of Passage 1969–1975," Fresno Arts Center and Museum, California (1987); "Movie Tone Muse," One Penn Plaza, New York City; "Modern American Printmaking," a travelling exhibition opening in Hannover, Germany, and travelling to seven locations in West Germany and Madrid, Spain (1985–1986); "American Women in Art," United Nations Conference on Women, Nairobi, Kenya (1985); "Spectrum Los Angeles," Hartje Gallery, Berlin and Frankfurt—both in West Germany (1985); "Self-Portraits," Gallery in the Plaza, Security Pacific Bank, Los Angeles, California (1985); "Olympiad: Summer '84 Exhibition," Koplin Gallery, Los Angeles, California (1984); "National Women's Art Exhibition," Louisiana World Exposition, New Orleans, Louisiana (1984); "Atelier Nord International Exhibition," Gallery F15, Jeloya, Oslo, and Tromso Art Association—all in Norway (1982); "Twentieth Century Masters of Lithography," Art Institute of Chicago, Illinois (1978).

Weisberg's work can be found in the following collections: the Achenbach Foundation for Graphic Arts, Fine Arts Museum, San Francisco, and the Oakland Museum—both in California; Grunwald Foundation for the Graphic Arts, University of California at Los Angeles (UCLA), Los Angeles County Museum of Art; and the Skirball Museum at Hebrew Union College—all in Los Angeles, California; Arizona State University Art Museum, Tempe; the Art Institute of Chicago and the Spertus Museum of Chicago—both in Illinois; the Dance Collection at Lincoln Center and the New York Public Library—both in New York City; Detroit Institute of Arts, Michigan; the Bibliothèque Nationale, Paris, France; the National Gallery of Art and the National Museum of Women in the Arts—both in Washington, D.C.; the Norwegian National Museum, Oslo, the Oslo Municipal Museum, and the Trondheim Municipal Museum—all in Norway; Portland Art Museum, Oregon; Indianapolis Museum of Art, Indiana; University of Michigan Museum of Art, Ann Arbor; Joslyn Art Museum, Omaha, Nebraska; University of Texas, Austin; and others.

Weisberg served as the 1990–1992 president of the College Art Association (CAA) and was cochair of studio sessions for the San Francisco, California, meetings (1989). She founded the Southern California chapter of the WCA in 1976. She serves on the national advisory board of the Tamarind Institute, and the advisory boards of the Los Angeles Artists Equity and the Woman's Building—both in Los Angeles, California. Weisberg formerly was vice-president of the Graphic Arts Council, Los Angeles County Museum of Art. She is a past president of the Los Angeles Printmaking Society. As director of the Kelyn Press, Weisberg has published two limited-edition books, *Tom O'Bedlam's Song* and *The Shtetl, A Journey and a Memorial*—both of which include her original prints. Weisberg has been a contributing editor of *Artweek*, and has written numerous articles for other publications, including *Women's Studies Quarterly, New York,* and *The Tamarind Papers,* Albuquerque, New Mexico. She has lectured, demonstrated, juried, and curated exhibitions at the invitation of more than fifty institutions.

Leonard Lehrer

Bibliography
Brown, Betty Ann, and Arlene Raven. *Exposures: Women and Their Art.* New Sage Press, 1989.
Clothier, Peter. "Ruth Weisberg at U.S.C." *Art in America* (April 1986).
Gouma-Peterson, Thalia. "Passage in Cyclical Time: Ruth Weisberg's Scroll. *Art Magazine* (February 1988).
Lerman, Ora. "Autobiographical Journey." *Arts Magazine* (May 1985).
Wortz, Melinda. "Ruth Weisberg." *Art News* (January 1984).

Weiss, Lee (1928–)

Born in Inglewood, California, the watercolorist Lee Weiss studied briefly at the California College of Arts and Crafts, Oakland (1946–1947), then with Eric Oback at San José State College (1957) and with Alexander Nepote (1958).

Weiss has held more than ninety-five solo exhibitions in galleries and museums, including the Walker Art Center, Minneapolis, Minnesota (1960); California Palace of the Legion of Honor, San Francisco, California (1962); Neville-Sargent Gallery, Chicago, Illinois (1990, 1992); Franz Bader Gallery, Washington, D.C. (biannually 1966–1972, and biannually 1973–1987); Gallery Madison 90, New York City (1974 and biannually 1977–1991); Garver Gallery, Madison, Wisconsin (1973, 1975, and biannually 1976–1992); "25-Year Retrospective," Wustum Museum of Fine Arts, Racine, Wisconsin (1987); and myriad others. Her work has been invited to more than seventy group exhibitions throughout the United States and abroad—from Tokyo, Japan, to Beloit, Wisconsin; Tours, France; Las Vegas, Nevada; Taipei, Taiwan; Toronto, Canada; Los Angeles, California; Youngstown, Ohio; and New York City.

Recipient of more than eighty honors, awards, certificates of merit, commissions, and purchase prizes, Weiss is a member and fellow of the American Watercolor Society, New York City, and the National Watercolor Society, California; she is a lifetime member of the Wisconsin Painters and Sculptors. She was one of four Americans invited to show at the Rosoh-kai Watercolor Exhibition, Setagawa Museum (1988–1990), and in the Meguro Museum, Tokyo, Japan (1991–1992); and others.

Weiss recently was quoted as saying, "I like the unexpected and grabbing it by the tail. . . All these years of work with watercolor have been constant discovery. . . A good painting should have some mystery, some magic." Her watercolors are represented in private, public, and corporate permanent collections, including the University of Wisconsin, Madison, Milwaukee Art Center, Wustum Museum of Fine Arts, Racine, and Dean Witter Co., Milwaukee—all in Wisconsin; Loyola University, Chicago, Illinois; National Academy of Design and the Hearst Corporation—both in New York City; National Museum of American Art, Smithsonian Institution, and the Phillips Collection—all in Washington, D.C.; and many others.

Bibliography
Davis, Tom. "Lee Weiss." *Wisconsin Trails* (July–August 1991).
Doherty, Stephen. "Lee Weiss." *Watercolor '91* (Fall 1991).
Raupe, Bebe. "The Regional Showcase." *The Artist's Magazine* (September 1991).
Weiss, Lee, and Bruce Pepich. *Lee Weiss Watercolors III.* Winchell Art Publications, 1990.

Welch, Mabel R. (d. 1959)

Born in New Haven, Connecticut, the painter Mabel R. Welch studied at the Art Students League, New York City, under the aegis of Cox and Robert Reid; she took further study in Paris, France, with Garrido, Lazar, Scott, and Van der Weyden.

Winner of awards and honors, Welch received a silver medal at the Panama-Pacific International Exposition, San Francisco, California (1915); a medal of honor at the Pennsylvania Academy of Fine Arts, Pennsylvania (1920); and others. She was a member of several arts organizations, including the American Society of Miniature Painters, MacDowell Club, and National Association of Women Painters and Sculptors—all in New York City; and the Pennsylvania Society of Miniature Painters.

Among the many group exhibitions in which Welch's work was displayed are the "Fiftieth Anniversary Exhibition 1889–1939," National Association of Women Painters and Sculptors (1939), and "Portraits by Distinguished American Artists," Grand Central Art Galleries (1942)—both in New York City. Further examples are to be found in private and public permanent collections.

Bibliography
American Art Annual. Vol. 28. American Federation of Arts, 1932.
Lounsbery, Elizabeth. "American Miniature Painters." *Mentor* 4:23 (January 5, 1917): 11.
Rucker, Kathryn. "Some Miniatures by Mabel Welch." *Art and Decoration* 3:9 (July 1913): 305.

Wellman, Joyce E. (1949–)

A native New Yorker, the African-American painter/printmaker Joyce E. Wellman studied at the Maryland Institute College of Art, Baltimore; and earned a Master of Arts degree from the University of Massachusetts, Amherst.

Wellman has held a number of solo exhibitions, including "Art in Public Places," Court House Square, Arlington, Virginia (1989); "Metro Art Program," First American Bank, Washington, D.C. (1989); and others. Her work has been included in many group shows, such as "Saluting Ellington: Selected Works of Five Washington Artists," Washington D.C. Commission on the Arts and Humanities (1990); "Introductions," June Kelly Gallery, New York City (1988); "Made by Hand: Works on Paper," Minneapolis College of Art and Design, Minnesota (1988); "Black Women Visual Artists in Washington, D.C.," Bethune Museum Archives, Washington, D.C. (1986); "1270 Women Art Exhibition," Metropolitan Museum of Art Community Programs, New York City (1974); and others.

Signs, symbols, energy-laden marks, wry ideas and a spiritual presence are presented in Wellman's mixed-media abstractions, such as "Egg on a Leg" (1989). Her work is represented in private and public permanent collections, including the Evans-Tibbs Collection, Washington, D.C.; the National Urban League, New York City; and others.

Bibliography
Hall, Robert L. *Gathered Visions: Selected Works by African American Women Artists*. Anacostia Museum, Smithsonian Institution Press, 1992.
Powell, Rick. *From the Potomac to the Anacostia: Art and Ideology in the Washington Area*. 1989.
Thorson, Alice. "Common Bonds." *City Paper* (February 8, 1991).

Welsh, Ruth (1949–)

Born in Prince Albert, Saskatchewan, Canada, the ceramic sculptor/painter Ruth Welsh earned a Bachelor's degree from the University of Saskatchewan, Saskatoon (1970). She studied ceramic sculpture, painting, and printmaking intermittently with many noted artists at different venues (1970–1984); and earned a Bachelor of Fine Arts degree from her alma mater (1985).

Welsh has held solo exhibitions of paintings and ceramic sculpture between 1975 and 1990 throughout the province of Saskatchewan, and has had her work invited to or included in juried group shows at the Shoestring Gallery, Saskatoon (1973, 1974, 1976); Mendel Art Gallery, Saskatoon (1975, 1977, 1986, 1988, 1989); the Ontario Crafts Council, Toronto, Ontario (1979); and many others.

Winner of many awards and honors, Welsh is also an inspiring art educator. Examples of her work are in private, corporate, and public permanent collections, including the cities of Regina and Weyburn, Saskatchewan; Indusmin Ltd., Toronto, Ontario; Mendel Art Gallery, Saskatoon; and others.

Bibliography
Canadian Artists in Exhibition. Roundstone Press, 1974.
Newman, Marketa, ed. *Biographical Dictionary of Saskatchewan Artists: Women Artists*. Fifth House Publishers, 1990.

Wendt, Julia Bracken (1871–1942)

Born in Apple River, Illinois, the sculptor Julia Bracken Wendt learned her craft at the Art Institute of Chicago, Illinois, under the aegis of Lorado Taft (1887–1892).

Wendt's work was exhibited in museums, galleries, and expositions, including the Chicago Municipal Art League, Illinois (1905); the Panama-Pacific International Exposition, San Francisco, California (1915), and California Art Club (1918)—both in California; "Contemporary American Sculpture," National Sculpture Society and the California Palace of the Legion of Honor (1929)—both in New York City; and many others.

Winner of awards and honors, Wendt was a member of art associations in Chicago, Illinois; Los Angeles, and Laguna Beach—both in California; she was also a teacher at Otis Art Institute, Los Angeles, California. Examples of her work are in private and public permanent collections, including the Los Angeles County Museum of Art, California; and others.

Bibliography
Maxwell, Everett C. "The Art of Julia Bracken Wendt, Noted Sculptress." *Fine Arts Journal* 23 (November 1910): 271–78.
Moure, Nancy, et al. *Southern California Artists 1890–1940*. Laguna Beach Museum of Art, 1979.
100 Years of California Sculpture. California: The Oakland Museum, 1982.
Nineteenth Century American Women Artists. Whitney Museum of American Art, Downtown Branch, 1976.

Wenzel, Carmen (1931–)

Born in Puebla, Mexico, Carmen Wenzel studied the plastic arts with Martín Serrano in the University of the Americas, Cholula, Mexico, and with Robert Horne in Sunset Center, Carmel, California.

A sculptor, Wenzel exhibited for the first time in 1972 in the Auditorio of the Reforma de Puebla. She executed a religious sculpture that was seven meters high for the church in Huejotzingo. This was followed by exhibits of her work in Centro de Arte Moderno in Guadalajara; Galería Arvil; Casa de la Cultura in Aguascalientes; Universidad Autónoma of Zacatecas; and the Instituto Panameño de Arte.

In 1977 Wenzel completed "Encuentro Cósmico" for the University of the Americas in Cholula. Through the end of 1988 she had exhibited her bronze and aluminum sculptures in twenty-five shows.

Bibliography
Alvarez, José Rogelio, et al. *Enciclopedia de Mexico*. Secretaría de Educación Pública, 1987.

Westbrook, Adell (1935–)

Born in Little Rock, Arkansas, the African-American painter Adell Westbrook earned a Bachelor's degree from the University of Maryland, College Park, and received a Master of Fine Arts degree from the Catholic University of America, Washington, D.C.

Westbrook has exhibited her work in solo and group shows, including the Henri Gallery, Washington, D.C. (1985); Montgomery College, Rockville, Maryland (1981); "Emerging Artists," The Art Barn Association Gallery, National Park Service, Washington, D.C. (1981); the Catholic University of America, Washington, D.C. (1980); and others.

Westbrook's work is represented in private and public permanent collections. "Solar, No. 4" (1985) presents a vibrant view of the artist's universe employing scores of circular forms—some textured—on a floating ground.

Bibliography
Hall, Robert L. *Gathered Visions: Selected Works by African American Women Artists*. Anacostia Museum, Smithsonian Institution Press, 1992.

Westerlund, Mia (1942–)

Mia Westerlund was born in New York City and educated at the National Academy of Fine Arts. After her education she married, had two children, and moved to Toronto, Canada. There she attended artists' workshops in the early 1970s, where she began to explore fiberglass and polyester resin. The forms she developed were of the simple, visually monolithic sort common to most minimalist public sculptures of the period. In her later works, such as "Muro Series IX" (1976), she stopped using fiberglass and turned to cast concrete. Apart from the resultant changes from flexibility and volume to opaque mass and more textured, "pictorial" surface, the types of forms she preferred—especially tall, thin wedges—remained more or less the same.

Robert J. Belton (with Lana Pitkin)

Bibliography
White, Peter. "Mia Westerlund's Pictorial Sculpture." *Parachute* 13 (Winter 1978): 36–38.

Westfall, Carol D. (1938–)

Born in Everett, Pennsylvania, the fiber artist/printmaker/sculptor Carol D. Westfall earned a Bachelor of Fine Arts degree at the Rhode Island School of Design, Providence (1960); received a Master of Fine Arts degree from the Maryland Institute College of Art, Baltimore (1972); and took post-graduate work at a number of institutions, including the University of Maryland, College Park; Instituto Allende, San Miguel de Allende, Mexico; Haystack Mountain School of Crafts, Deer Isle, Maine; Peters Valley School of Crafts, New Jersey; Weavers' Service Center, Bharat Nagar, Delhi, India; School of the Visual Arts, New York City; and Penland School of Crafts, North Carolina.

Westfall has held many solo exhibitions in the United States and abroad and has had her work invited to myriad group exhibitions in museums throughout the world, including the Galería Kin, Mexico City, Mexico, and the Florence Dahl Gallery, New York City (1976); the "7th Biennial of Tapestry," Lausanne, Switzerland, and the Galerie Jardin des Arts, Paris, France (1975); "The Dyer's Art," Tucson Museum of Art, Arizona (1977); "Fiber as Art," Manila, the Philippines (1980); "The Web of India," American Center, New Delhi, and Ruth Kaufman Gallery, New York City (1981); "The New Basket: Vessel for the Future," Brainard Art Gallery, Potsdam, New York, which toured the United States and Africa (1984); "In Recognition of Excellence," Montclair Museum, New Jersey (1986); "Interlacing," American Craft Museum, New York City (1987); "International Textile Competition," Kyoto Municipal Museum, Japan (1989); "8th International Biennial of Miniature Textiles," Savaria Museum, Szombathelyi, Hungary (1990); "Innovative Quilts," Gallery Elena, Taos, New Mexico; and "The Fan," Galerie Philharmonie, Liege, Belgium (1991); and many others.

Westfall has been a professor of fiber arts at Montclair State College, New Jersey, since 1972; she is a world-traveler, teacher, art juror, lecturer, workshop leader, and artist-in-residence in centers and universities around the globe. She has received many honors and awards for her work, such as the merit award, American Crafts Awards; master print award, Rutgers University Center for Innovative Printmaking, Mason Gross School of the Arts, New Brunswick, New Jersey (1988); two fellowship grants from the New Jersey State Council on the Arts (1976, 1987); and an Indo-American fellowship (1980–1981). Her work is represented in private, public, and corporate permanent collections, including the Delaware Museum of Art, Wilmington; New Jersey State Museum, Trenton, Montclair State College, Newark Public Library, and Rutgers University, New Brunswick—all in New Jersey; Rhode Island School of Design, Providence; Goucher College, Baltimore, Maryland; and many others.

Bibliography
Schlossman, Betty L. "Review: Clay, Fiber, Metal by Women Artists." *Art Journal* 37:4 (Summer 1978): 330–32.
7th International Biennial of Tapestry, Lausanne, Switzerland. Musée Cantonal des Beaux-Arts, 1975.
Westfall, Carol, and Suellen Glashausser. *Plaiting, Step by Step.* Watson-Guptill, 1976.
Znamierowski, Nell. *Fiber: The Artist's View.* Long Island University, 1983.

Wharton, Margaret (1943–)

Born in Portsmouth, Virginia, Margaret Wharton received her Bachelor's degree from the University of Maryland, College Park, in 1965. During the next ten years she discovered the chair and the book as a metaphor for art-making, and earned a Master of Fine Arts degree from the Art Institute of Chicago, Illinois (1975).

Wharton's first solo exhibition took place at the Phyllis Kind Gallery, Chicago, Illinois, in 1976; she had eleven more solo shows at the Kind galleries in Chicago, Illinois, and New York City between 1977 and 1991. In 1981–1982 another solo exhibition by Wharton, sponsored by the Museum of Contemporary Art, Chicago, travelled to Texas, Florida, and South Carolina. Her work has been invited to many group exhibitions throughout the United States and the United Kingdom, including "Making Their Mark: Women Artists Today, A Documentary Survey 1970–1985," a travelling exhibition seen at the Cincinnati Art Museum, Ohio; the New Orleans Museum of Art, Louisiana; the Denver Art Museum, Colorado; and the Pennsylvania Academy of Fine Arts, Philadelphia (1988–1990); "Chair as Object as Statement," at the University of Wisconsin, Eau Claire (1988); "Fetish Art: Obsessive Expression," Rockford Art Museum, Illinois (1986); "Drawing in Air," Ceolfrith Gallery, Sunderland Arts Centre, England, which also travelled to Wales and Leeds (1983–1984); "Sculpture Then and Now," James Mayor Gallery, London, England (1983); "Dead or Alive," Lerner-Heller Gallery, New York City, a travelling show (1982); and many others.

Wharton won the Anna Louise Raymond award in the "Fellowship Show" at the Art Institute of Chicago, Illinois (1975), and the Logan prize (1974) in the "Chicago and Vicinity Show" at the same institution. She completed commissions for the Museum of Contemporary Art (1985) and the Chicago Public Library, West Lawn branch (1986)—both in Chicago, Illinois. Wharton has also been awarded grants from the National Endowment for the Arts (1980, 1988).

Her work is in major public and private permanent collections, including the Art Institute of Chicago and Museum of Contemporary Art—both in Chicago, Illinois; the Corcoran Gallery of Art, Washington, D.C.; the Dallas Museum, Texas; the Madison Art Center, Wisconsin; Seattle Art Museum, Washington; and the Whitney Museum of American Art, New York City.

Sawing chairs and books, reworking the parts in myriad and wondrous metaphorical ways, and rearranging them in two and three-dimensional space provides a gourmet's fare for the intellect and imagination of the viewer; Wharton never fails to entice the spectator to mull over her work.

Bibliography

Artner, Alan G. "Margaret Wharton's High Standards." *Chicago Tribune* (March 10, 1988): 9.

Brown, Betty Ann, and Arlene Raven. *Exposures: Women and Their Art.* NewSage Press, 1989.

Glauber, Robin. "Chairs as Metaphor: The Sculpture of Margaret Wharton." *Arts Magazine* 56:1 (September 1981): 84.

Jacob, Mary Jane. *Margaret Wharton.* A Catalog. Chicago, Illinois: Museum of Contemporary Art, 1981.

Wheeler (Keith), Dora (1857–1940)

Born in Jamaica, New York, the painter Dora Wheeler (Keith) studied at the Art Students League, New York City; was a pupil of William Merritt Chase; and also studied in Paris, France.

An associate member of the National Academy of Design, New York City (1906), and other arts organizations, Wheeler won the Louis Prang prizes in 1885 and 1886 and an honorable mention at the Pan-American Exposition, Buffalo, New York (1901). Earlier, she exhibited at the World's Columbian Exposition, Chicago, Illinois (1893), and Albany, New York (1894). Her work is in private and public permanent collections, including the New York Historical Society.

Bibliography

American Art Annual. Vol. 28. American Federation of Arts, 1932.

Elliott, Maude Howe, ed. *Art and Handicraft in the Women's Building of the World's Columbian Exposition, Chicago, 1893.* Rand, McNally and Co., 1894.

Weimann, Jeanne Madeline. *The Fair Women.* Academy Chicago, 1981.

White, Elizabeth (1892–)

Born at Old Oraibi on the Third Mesa of the Hopi Reservation in Arizona, Elizabeth White, whose family name was Qoyawayma, was given the first name of Polinsaysi, which means Butterfly Sitting among the Flowers in the Breeze. White was one of the first Oraibi children to obtain an education and become a teacher; Mennonite missionaries on the reservation introduced her to the Christian religion. They educated her in their school in the hopes that she would champion their beliefs in the field. When she tried, however, she met with vindictiveness from her people.

White taught at the Tuba City Boarding School and the Hotevilla Government Day School. She attended Northern Arizona University, Flagstaff, and the University of California at Los Angeles (UCLA) to qualify formally as an Indian Service teacher. At a later period she taught on the Navajo Reservation in Chinle, Arizona, and in Toadlena, New Mexico, before returning full circle through Polacca to home base in Oraibi. She met Lloyd White in the Toadlena and was married in 1931 for some years until they divorced.

White is a multi-talented individual whose expression, after retirement, found its outlet in writing and music; her book, *The Sun Girl,* published in 1945, was one of the fifty best books of the year. Still searching for a better medium through which to convey her ideas, she rediscovered ceramics and, on her own, found and developed a pearly clay that, as much as the form of her work, denotes it as hers. Her ware is in many public and private collections in the United States.

Bibliography

Monthan, Guy, and Doris Monthan. *Art and Indian Individualists, The Art of Seventeen Contemporary Southwestern Artists and Craftsmen.* Northland Press, 1975.

Whitehead, Frances Yeatts (1953–)

Born in Berea, Kentucky, the sculptor Frances Yeatts Whitehead earned a Bachelor of Fine Arts degree from East Carolina University, Greenville, North Carolina (1975), and, three years later, received a Master of Fine Arts degree from Northern Illinois University, De Kalb.

Whitehead exhibited work in solo and group shows, including "Meeting Ground: Basketry Traditions and Sculptural Forms," the Forum, St. Louis, Missouri, and Arizona State University, Tempe (1990); "Standing Ground: Sculpture by American Women," the Contemporary Arts Center, Cincinnati, Ohio (1987); "Recent Acquisitions," Museum of Contemporary Art, Chicago, Illinois (1987); Sculpture Chicago Program, commissioned construction and exhibition of large-scale works, Chicago, Illinois (1986); and others.

Winner of artist's grants from the National Endowment for the Arts (NEA) (1986) and the Illinois Arts Council (1985), Whitehead uses metals (zinc and copper) and other outmoded materials such as gutta percha, shellac, and celluloid in her sculpture, unrelated to the nature of the specific works. "Cigale" (1989), an elegant, small, square "funnel" of wire screen and shellac is, basically, a circle in a square—a cool form to pique and challenge the viewer. Whitehead's work is represented in private and public permanent collections.

Bibliography

Bonesteel, Michael. "Medium Cool." *Art in America* (December 1987): 139–47.

Leucking, Steve. "Review." *Sculpture Magazine* (January 1990).

Meeting Ground: Basketry Traditions and Sculptural Forms. A Catalog. St. Louis, Missouri: The Forum, and Tempe: Arizona State University, 1990.

Whitehorse, Emmi (1956–)

Born in Crownpoint, New Mexico, Emmi Whitehorse earned a Bachelor of Arts degree in painting at the University of New Mexico, Albuquerque (1980), and, two years later, received a Master of Fine Arts degree in printmaking.

Whitehorse has held solo exhibitions of her work in many galleries in the United States and Europe, including the Hartje Gallery, Frankfurt, Germany (1986); the Marilyn Butler Gallery, Scottsdale, Arizona (1985); Akmak Gallery, West Berlin, Germany (1984); the Galleria del Cavallino, Venice, Italy (1984); and others. She has had her work invited to many group exhibitions, such as the Stremmel Galleries, Reno, Nevada (1986); "Woman of Sweet Grass, Sage and Cedar," a travelling show, the A.I.C.H. Gallery, New York City (1985); "Artists under Thirty," the Silvermine Guild, New Canaan, Connecticut (1985); "Modern Native American Abstraction," a travelling show, the Philadelphia Art Alliance, Pennsylvania (1983); the Heard Museum, Phoenix, Arizona (1981); the University of North Dakota, Grand Forks (1980); the Pueblo Culture Center, Albuquerque, New Mexico (1978); and others.

Whitehorse's work is in a number of permanent public, corporate, and private collections, including the Heard Museum, Phoenix, Arizona; the Wheelwright Museum, Santa Fe, New Mexico; Ivan

Chermayoff Associates, New York City; IBM, Tarrytown, New York; Prudential Insurance Corporation, Newark, New Jersey; and others.

Bibliography

Highwater, Jamake. "Noble Savages and Wild Indians." *New York Arts Journal* (1980): 24.

The Grey Canyon Artists. Video interview. The University of North Dakota, 1980.

Traugot, Joseph. "Emmi Whitehorse, Kin'nah'zin." *Artspace* (Summer 1982): 40–41.

Whiten, Colette (1945–)

Colette Whiten was born in Birmingham, England, and became a Canadian citizen in 1975, after she graduated from the Ontario College of Art in Toronto. She came to public attention almost immediately upon graduation, especially for her plaster casts from living figures. Unlike sculptor George Segal, who popularized the technique and who used the resultant figures very much as anonymous entities, Whiten was very concerned with the individuality of her figures. After a time she became increasingly preoccupied with the strange contraptions used to help support her model's limbs, and she began to explore their residual associations with instruments of torture.

By the late 1970s Whiten had returned from the objects themselves to the curious perceptual phenomena they created. She exhibited the concave casts themselves, not the positives made from them, and she lit them in such a way that the viewer was unable to decide whether the figures were hollow or sculpture in the round. This smacked a little of novelty art, and she returned for a time to casting. After a small hiatus in her activity she turned to a kind of art-embroidery which differentiated itself from "craft" in the plain (*i.e.*, nondecorative and anti-traditional) nature of the subjects involved, like businessmen proudly standing beside their latest automotive acquisition.

Whiten is very well-respected in Canada. She has received a number of important public commissions, the most notorious of which is a series of cut-out figures on the grounds of the Queen Street Mental Health Centre in Toronto. She has shown in solo exhibitions almost annually for over a decade with the influential Carmen Lamanna Gallery. In 1990 she received a prestigious arts award from the city of Toronto.

Robert J. Belton

Bibliography

Shaw, Catherine Elliott. *The Canadian Contemporary Figure.* London: McIntosh Gallery, University of Western Ontario (October–November 1988).

Whitlock, An (1944–)

Born in Guelph, Ontario, Canada, the sculptor, multi-media and installation artist An Whitlock received her education in industrial design at the Ontario College of Art, Toronto. Whitlock uses pins, rubber, graphite, plaster, waxed paper, barbed wire, and other unorthodox materials to create enigmatic, beautifully crafted, highly personal works.

Whitlock has held more than twenty solo exhibitions in galleries and museums throughout Canada since 1973, including the Art Gallery of Ontario, Toronto (1974); the Alberta College of Art, Calgary (1976); the Grunwald Gallery, Toronto (1981, 1988); Powerhouse, Montréal (1984); the Toronto Sculpture Garden (1989); Art Gallery of Hamilton (1991); and others. Her work has been invited to many group exhibitions, such as "Hangings," Art Gallery of Ontario, Toronto (1972); "Inaugural Exhibition," Espace, Montréal (1974); "Some Canadian Artists," National Gallery of Canada, Ottawa (1975); "Four Places," Vancouver Art Gallery, British Columbia (1977); "50th Anniversary: Contemporary Outdoor Sculpture," Guild Inn, Toronto (1982); "Reflections: Contemporary Art Since 1964," National Gallery of Canada, Ottawa (1983); "Flight Pattern Uninterrupted," Definitely Superior, Thunder Bay (1989); and others.

Lecturer, visiting artist, and artist-in-residence at a number of Canadian universities from the mid-1970s through the mid-1980s— Whitlock has won awards and honors, including seven grants each from the Canada Council and the Ontario Arts Council (1972–1988). Examples of her work can be found in private, public, and corporate permanent collections, including the National Gallery of Canada, Ottawa; Art Gallery of Ontario, Toronto; the Canada Council Art Bank, Ottawa; Alberta College of Art, Calgary; Kitchener-Waterloo Regional Art Gallery; McCarthy & McCarthy; and many others.

Bibliography

Burnett, David, and Marilyn Schiff. *Contemporary Canadian Art.* Hurtig Publishers, 1983.

"Hangings." A review. *Artscanada* (April–May 1971): 74.

Mays, John Bentley. "Calm Amid the Waxed Paper, Barbed Wire." *The Globe and Mail* (June 20, 1981): 11.

———. "The House Whitlock Built Definitely Not a Home." *The Globe and Mail* (December 22, 1989): 67.

Whitney, Anne (1821–1915)

Born in Watertown, Massachusetts, Anne Whitney was tutored at home and given one year of study at a girls' school in Bucksport, Maine. Whitney taught school in Salem, Massachusetts, from 1847 to 1849, and, from December 1850 to May 1851, travelled by boat to New Orleans via Cuba. During these years she wrote poetry, and, in 1859, a book of her collected poems was published. Her interests then shifted to sculpture, and she spent 1859–1860 studying anatomy at a hospital in Brooklyn, New York; in Philadelphia, Pennsylvania she attended lectures by William Trost Richards and studied drawing at the Pennsylvania Academy of Fine Arts. Her earliest known extant sculpture is "Bust of Laura Brown" (1859, National Museum of American Art) and her earliest full-length life-size work is a marble statue of "Lady Godiva" (1860–1861, private collection).

Whitney began her sculpting in a shed on the family property in Belmont, Massachusetts. In 1861 she took a studio on Tremont Street in Boston, Massachusetts, next to William Rimmer's studio, where she received private instruction. Her abolitionist concerns kept her in Boston until the Civil War ended. Her colossal sculpture of "Africa" was created during this time, and her "Godiva" was exhibited in Boston, Massachusetts, and New York City to high acclaim.

In 1867 Whitney travelled to Rome, Italy, and remained for four years. Two neoclassical works from this period are "Lotus Eater" (Newark Museum) and "Chaldean Shepherd" (Smith College Museum of Art).

In a more polemic and realistic vein was her sculpture of the Haitian liberator, "Toussaint L'Ouverture" (now lost). The summer of 1868 she visited Munich's famous foundry to learn about casting in bronze—the medium she chose for her sculpture "Roma."

On her return to Boston, Whitney received a commission in 1873 from the state of Massachusetts for a marble statue of "Governor Samuel Adams" for the U.S. Capitol building. Whitney went to Italy in 1875 to select the Carrara marble and to supervise the transference of her plaster cast to stone. She spent that summer in Ecouen, France; a turn to realism is marked in her bronze sculpture "Le Modèle" (Museum of Fine Arts, Boston) from this period as well as in her "Roma." Five years later the city of Boston requested that her "Governor Samuel Adams" be cast in bronze for placement near Faneuil Hall.

In 1875, Whitney won an anonymous competition for a statue of "Senator Charles Sumner" to be erected in the Boston Public Garden. She was given the prize money but denied the commission because she was a woman. In 1900 the life-size bronze sculpture of "Sumner" was commissioned for Harvard Square, Cambridge, where it is today. Whitney did many portrait busts, including "William Lloyd Garrison," "President James Walker" of Harvard University, "President Alice Freeman Palmer" of Wellesley College, Massachusetts, "Harriet Beecher Stowe," "Frances E. Willard," "Lucy Stone," and others. She has also created several public monuments, including the colossal bronze statue of "Leif Ericsson" (1885), which still stands in front of the Commonwealth Avenue mall in Boston.

Eleanor Tufts

Bibliography
Gerdts, William H. *The White, Marmorean Flock.* Vassar College Art Gallery, 1972.
Payne, Elizabeth Rogers. "Anne Whitney, Sculptor." *Art Quarterly* 24:3 (1962): 244–61.
———. "Anne Whitney, Art and Social Justice." *Massachusetts Quarterly* 12:2 (1971): 245–60.
Tufts, Eleanor. *American Women Artists, 1830–1930.* National Museum of Women in the Arts, 1987.

Whitney, Gertrude Vanderbilt (1878–1942)

Born in New York City, the sculptor Gertrude Vanderbilt Whitney astonished socialite friends when she began to study sculpture seriously. She studied with Hendrik Christian Andersen, with James Earle Fraser at the Art Students League in New York City, and, finally, with Andrew O'Connor in Paris, France.

In 1901 Whitney received her first major commission from the Buffalo Exposition, New York, where she created the life-sized figure "Aspiration." She showed work successfully in several important venues including the St. Louis World's Fair, Missouri (1904); the National Academy, New York City, where she won a prize (1910); Paris Salon, France, for which she won a prize (1913); American Art Dealers Association, for which she won a medal (1932); Chicago World's Fair, Illinois (1933); and the New York World's Fair, New York City (1939).

Specializing in public art projects, Whitney has created several monuments including "Aztec Fountain," Washington, D.C. (1912); "Fountain of El Dorado," Lima, Peru (originally shown at the Panama-Pacific International Exposition in San Francisco, California (1915);

"The Washington Heights War Memorial," New York City (1922); "Buffalo Bill Cody," Wyoming (1924); and Columbia Memorial, Palos, Spain (1929). Her most famous work is the "Titanic Memorial," Washington, D.C. (1931). This eighteen-foot-high figure in granite takes the shape of a cross to symbolize resurrection.

Whitney was important in her support of other artists and for American art generally. In 1915 she founded the Friends of Young Artists, and later organized the Whitney Studio Club and the Whitney Studio Galleries as a place for young artists to work and to show their work—all in New York City. In 1931, her collection of American art having been refused by the Metropolitan Museum of Art, New York City, Whitney opened her own museum—the Whitney Museum of American Art. Originally showing Whitney's personal and eclectic collection of art, today the Whitney Museum is probably the most important museum of modern American art in the country.

Judith Sealy

Bibliography
Friedman, B.H. *Gertrude Vanderbilt Whitney: A Biography.* Doubleday, 1978.
Nickerson, Ruth. "A Vanguard of American Women Sculptors." *Sculpture Review* 35 (Winter 86–87): 16–24.
Rubinstein, Charlotte Streifer. *American Women Artists.* Avon, 1982, pp. 186–88.

Whitney, Isabel Lydia (1884–1962)

Born in Brooklyn, New York, the muralist Isabel Lydia Whitney studied with Arthur Wesley Dow, Hayley Lever, and Howard Pyle. A memorial exhibition of her drawings and watercolors was held in her honor at the gallery of the Pen & Brush Club, New York City (1962).

Whitney was a member of several arts organizations, including the Brooklyn Society of Modern Art, the Brooklyn Watercolor Club, National Arts Club, Salons of America, and the Society of Independent Artists—all in New York City. Her work is represented in private and public permanent collections.

Bibliography
American Art Annual. Vol. 28. American Federation of Arts, 1932.
Gerdts, William H. *Women Artists of America 1707–1964.* The Newark Museum, 1965.
Who's Who in American Art. Vol. 3. American Federation of Arts, 1940.

Whittome, Irene (1942–)

Born in Vancouver, Canada, Irene Whittome studied painting and drawing at the Vancouver School of Art from 1959 to 1963, where she worked with painter Jack Shadbolt. She moved to Paris, France, in 1963 and studied engraving at Atelier 17, run by Stanley William Hayter, between 1965 and 1968. When she returned to Montréal, Québec, Canada, she began teaching undergraduate courses and, in 1974, taught in the Master's program at Concordia University.

From 1963 until 1976 Whittome entered her prints and drawings in exhibitions in Japan, Great Britain, Belgium, France, Yugoslavia, Argentina, Poland, Austria, Canada, Germany, Italy, Switzerland, and Spain. Her work was acquired by numerous public collections including the Bibliothèque Nationale de Paris, France; the Municipal Museum, Birmingham, England; and the Museum of Modern Art in Buenos Aires, Argentina; as well as collections across Canada.

In 1969 Whittome began to accumulate materials and objects, retaining the idea of repetition from her experience as a printmaker. "White Museum I" and "White Museum II" (both 1975) are collections of diverse materials, standardized cases, and repeated gestures of wrapping. In 1979 Whittome developed the classroom theme in a work entitled "Model One—Work at School/Classroom 208" at P.S.1 in New York City. In choosing to work with references to the museum and the school Whittome examined the relationship between individual imagination and social institutions. The Montréal Museum of Fine Arts organized a major travelling exhibition of her work from 1975 to 1980, including "White Museum I," "White Museum II," "Paperwork," "Vancouver," and "The Classroom."

From 1980 to 1982 Whittome worked on "Installation Room 901," in which a large black cross was painted on the wall and white pigment spread on canvas on the floor. She presented this studio work to the public for the Musée d'Art Contemporain's "Repères" exhibition, simultaneously exhibiting at the Yajima gallery and museum. She presented drawings and a maquette for "Incunabula for a Bridge" at Cornell University's Herbert F. Johnson Museum of Art, Ithaca, New York, in 1984 and, later that year, at the Utsukushi-ga-hara Open-Air Museum in Hakone, Japan, where it won third prize. The twenty-foot-high wooden structure is permanently installed at this site.

Whittome prepared "Individuelle Mythologien, Kassel 1972—Montréal 1985" for Centre International d'Art Contemporain de Montréal's 1985 "Aurora Borealis" exhibition, painting the walls, floor, and ceiling red and, in characteristic repetitive insistence, hung the walls with drawings and photographs referencing Kassel's 1972 "Documenta V."

Whittome worked on "Musée des Traces" between 1985 and 1989 in an unused Montréal garage—its first exhibition site. A fiberglass replica of a giant leatherback turtle found on the banks of the St. Lawrence River occupied the center of the room. Objects displayed on stands and shelves and in glass cases as well as framed photographs completed this personal museum. Toronto's Art Gallery in Ontario reconstructed the museum in 1990. A replica of a turtle was also the focus of related work. In "Illuminati" (1987), prepared for Montréal's Musée d'Art Contemporain's exhibition, "Elementa naturae," the giant tortoise was housed in an outdoor construction which included large stones rescued from a demolished building; "Shamash" (1988) was shown in Toronto's Power Plant exhibit, "The Historical Ruse: Art in Montréal"; and "Ho T'u" (1988) was shown first at the Musée d'Histoire Naturelle in La Rochelle and then acquired by the Musée des Beaux-Arts et d'Histoire Naturelle in Valence, France. Whittome was commissioned to cast a bronze turtle for Bankers' Hall in Calgary, Alberta.

Whittome began to work again with the idea of a museum with "Musée Noir" for the inaugural exhibition, "Pour la Suite du Monde," of the new Musée d'Art Contemporain and a simultaneous exhibition at the Samuel Lallouz Gallery, Montréal, in 1992. She has received many awards, including the Gershon Iskowitz prize in 1992—a prize awarded to a Canadian artist for outstanding achievement.

Cyril Reade

Bibliography

Falk, Lorne. "Irene F. Whittome: Interviewed by Lorne Falk." *C Magazine* 13 (Spring 1987): 44–49.

Fry, Jacqueline. *Irene Whittome 1975–1980*. The Montréal Museum of Fine Arts, 1980.

———. *Le Musée des Traces d'Irene Whittome*. Editions Parachute, 1989.

Gale, Peggy. "At the Silent Centre: Tracing Personal and Cultural History with Irene Whittome." *Canadian Art* 6:3 (September 1989): 88–93.

Godmer, Gilles, and Réal Lussier. *Pour la Suite du Monde*. Musée d'Art Contemporain, 1992.

Gosselin, Claude, Norman Thériault, and René Blouin. *Aurora Borealis*. Centre International d'Art Contemporain de Montréal, 1985.

Nemiroff, Diana. "Accumulating Intuition: Irene Whittome." *Vanguard* 10:1 (February 1981): 8–15.

Pontbriand, Chantal. *The Historical Ruse: Art in Montréal*. The Power Plant, 1988.

Thériault, Norman. *Québec 75*. Institut d'Art Contemporain, 1975.

Trudel, Jean. "L'Imaginaire Comme Objet de Curiosité." *Parachute* 57 (January–February–March 1990): 4–9.

Widmer, Gwen (1945–)

Born in Chicago, Illinois, the photographer Gwen Widmer earned a Bachelor's degree from Goshen College, Indiana (1967), and received a Master of Fine Arts degree from the School of the Art Institute of Chicago, Illinois (1973).

The wife of a photographer, Widmer is on the art faculty at the University of Northern Iowa, Cedar Falls; earlier she taught at the University of Illinois, Champaign/Urbana (1972–1974). She has won awards and honors, including a grant from the Iowa Arts Council (1978); fellowships in photography from the National Endowment for the Arts (NEA) (1975, 1980); and others.

Many of Widmer's large-format photographs are "altered" with mixed-media and some bear the mark-making of drawing and/or writing. Representative examples of Widmer's work are in private and public permanent collections, including Humboldt State University, Arcata, California; J.B. Speed Museum, Louisville, Kentucky; Kalamazoo Institute of the Arts, Michigan; Madison Art Center, Wisconsin; and others.

Bibliography

Color. Time-Life Series, 1980.

Photographers Midwest Invitational. A Catalog. Minneapolis, Minnesota: Walker Art Center, 1973.

Popular Photography 75:2 (1974).

Wieland, Joyce (1931–)

Sometimes considered one of the more important Canadian artists of the second half of the twentieth century, Joyce Wieland has distinguished herself as a painter, designer, and filmmaker in both the commercial and avant-garde senses. Born in Toronto, Ontario, Canada, Wieland studied commercial art at the Central Technical School under the landscape painter Carl Schaeffer, and others. A visit to Europe in the early 1950s strengthened her desire to become a fine artist, but when she returned to Canada, she could find only commercial employment as a film animator for a small firm called Graphics Associates. There she met her husband to be, painter, filmmaker, and musician Michael Snow, in 1954.

From that point forward their artistic careers were intertwined.

After some unremarkable initial exhibitions in Hamilton and Toronto, Wieland joined the Isaacs Gallery in Toronto—a major center of cultural ferment. In 1962 she first showed the large, brightly colored stain paintings that earned her recognition. Filled with organic forms and lyrically translucent atmospheres, these works have something in common with American color-field painting, but they also display an interest in the figure and a personal sensibility that is usually described as a sort of feminist modernism.

Anxious to make a name in an international context, Snow insisted that the couple move to New York City in 1963. Initially reluctant, Wieland soon appreciated the move for the way it raised her consciousness about her home country. This, fused with an interest in collaborative quiltmaking she had been developing since 1961, eventually led to the creation of a number of striking inventions which are at one and the same time reclamations of traditional female handicraft as art and assertions of a characteristically Canadian nationalism. (The latter component is no doubt why these works have typically been overlooked as predecessors of Judy Chicago's similar craft collectivism.) Things came to a head in 1971, when the National Gallery in Ottawa mounted an exhibition entitled "True Patriot Love," in which stuffed quilts and wall-hangings were emblazoned with slogans such as "J'aime le Canada" and "Down with U.S. Imperialism."

Back in Canada in the early 1970s, Wieland gradually turned from quilting activities to a greater interest in film. Her paintings of the middle 1960s—such as "Nature Mixes" (1963) and "Boat Tragedy" (1964)—foreshadow this development, for they are divided into panels with sequentially developing images. In addition the impact of Snow's substantial achievements in this arena must have been considerable. The most famous of Wieland's avant-garde films was *Reason over Passion* (1969), which was part travelogue, part political satire, and part modernist experiment. The title is a tongue-in-cheek paraphrase from a speech by then prime minister of Canada and media celebrity Pierre Trudeau. That alone earned her the title of pop artist.

Although Wieland continued to paint and make quilts in the middle-1970s, much of her energy was directed at *The Far Shore*—a standard narrative film of 1976 that dealt in veiled terms with a near-legendary predecessor of the Group of Seven, landscape painter Tom Thomson. Given that Thomson represented an earlier nationalistic love of the homeland, and since he drowned under moderately mysterious circumstances, it is perhaps not surprising that she should want to treat him in unabashedly Romantic terms. What is not so clear, however, is why the film was a critical and commercial failure.

Perhaps because she was discouraged, or perhaps because her public was discouraged, Wieland stayed out of the limelight until 1987, when the Art Gallery of Ontario staged a major retrospective exhibition. It included some exceptionally delicate circular paintings with evocative sprites cavorting in Dionysian abandon, as if underwater (e.g., "What They Do at Sunrise," 1982). Her most striking recent work is "Artist on Fire" (1983), a neo-expressionist vision of Wieland, now separated from Snow, as a cloven-hooved painter in flames, working at an easel in front of something like the Petit Trianon at Versailles. The canvas bears an image of a priapic god kissing a bird. She is now as celebrated as before, but this time passion is more clearly in the ascendant.

Robert J. Belton

Bibliography
True Patriot Love. Ottawa: National Gallery of Canada, 1971.
Joyce Wieland. Toronto: Art Gallery of Ontario, 1987.

Wieselthier, Vally (1895–1945)

The Paris Exposition of 1925, which identified the art deco movement, awarded silver and gold medals for whimsical, figurative ceramic sculpture to Austrian artist Vally Wieselthier. A 1920 graduate of Vienna's Kunstgewerbeschule, Wieselthier began selling her work through the Wiener Werkstatte, Austria, where she became head of the ceramics department. After her figurines were acclaimed at the international Exhibition of Ceramic Art held at the Metropolitan Museum of Art, New York City, in 1928, she made her first visit to America. A one-person show and several commissions followed.

In 1929 Wieselthier joined Rockwell Kent, Paul Poiret, and others to form Contempora, an artists' collective for which she designed women's accessories and produced life-size figurative sculptures. Her stylized portrait heads of women epitomized the "flapper" look of the 1920s. Her fresh, more expressive use of clay influenced the work of Viktor Schreckengost, Russell Aitken, and R. Guy Cowan. The American contacts she made encouraged her to move to New York City in 1932.

During the Depression Wieselthier designed ware for Sebring Pottery of Ohio. Her large figures of women as nature goddesses found a market as garden sculpture and department store mannequins. Between 1929 and 1945 she had five one-person shows at galleries in Detroit, Michigan; Chicago, Illinois; and New York City. Her work was accepted for a sculpture show at the Whitney Museum of American Art, New York City, in 1940. In 1938, 1939, and 1940, the National Ceramic Exhibitions at the Syracuse Museum, New York (now the Everson Museum of Art) included her sculptures, and, in 1946, a few months after her death, "Taming the Unicorn" (1945), won first prize.

Elaine Levin

Bibliography
Canfield, Ruth. "The Pottery of Vally Wieselthier." *Design* 31:6 (November 1929): 103–05.
Siple, Ella S. "The International Exhibition of Ceramic Art." *The American Magazine of Art* 19:11 (November 1928): 602–19.
Wieselthier, Vally. "Ceramics." *Design* 31:6 (November 1929): 101–02.
———. "Studying Art in Vienna: A Brief Autobiography." *Arts and Decoration* 44 (February 1936): 28–29+.

Wiitasalo, Shirley (1949–)

Born in Toronto, Ontario, Canada, Shirley Wiitasalo studied at the Ontario College of Art in that city from 1967 to 1968 under François Thépot. Since 1969 she has shown her work across Canada and abroad, exhibiting regularly at the Carmen Lamanna Gallery, Toronto, since 1973. Due to the innovative nature of her painting, Wiitasalo was featured in a number of thematic shows investigating new trends in figurative art in the early 1980s, including "Fiction," Art Gallery of Ontario, Toronto (1982); "Subjects in Pictures," YYZ Artists Outlet, Toronto (1984; and "Late Capitalism," Art Gallery at Harbourfront, Toronto (1985). A solo touring exhibition of her work was organized by the Art

Gallery of Ontario in 1987.

Wiitasalo has developed a personal visual language in her paintings, which, as reviewer Gary Michael Dault points out, have been variously interpreted as "dream imagery, psychological allegories, emblems of late capitalism, subversive fiction." In fact the work resists interpretation and the wealth of responses to it attests to its resonance. In evoking the culture of suburban middle-class consumerism (with which her personal relationship is as ambiguous as her rendering of it on canvas), Wiitasalo communicates a sense of desire or of desiring—a recurring theme in her painting. Desire here—or its frustration—is an unbridgeable gap between the self and the objective world, heightened and sanctioned by advertising and related media. In an untitled painting from 1982, for example, Wiitasalo takes a picture of an ordinary suburban house, probably appropriated from an illustrated advertisement for real estate, and couples it with an oily blackish reflection that shows not the house, but a schematic "dream" castle and a ripple-deformed number that could be an asking price. The picture is divided by a horizon line with the house/reflection image sitting on it like a setting sun—a further symbol of the unattainable. Wiitasalo frequently uses images made up of reflections or shadows, such as the layering of images in consciousness, and, although her images may seem ambiguous, interpretation often brings flashes of understanding and even provocation.

For Wiitasalo the viewer's relationship to the painting is a meaningful part of the work, and much of her recent work questions what the viewer brings to a picture. Viewers can read, for example, "Black & White" (1987) in various ways, depending on the point of view. The black border delineates a cave-like opening, which could be interpreted as an eye-hole in a mask or skull. The white central area, like lighted space, encloses human figures with two dark, again cave-like openings beyond them, representing alternatively, again, a mask or skull, or the mushroom cloud of a nuclear explosion. In deciding what the image is, the viewer must determine where the artist places onlookers in relation to the objects or spaces depicted. In the particular case of "Black & White," onlookers can be considered dead, or near-death, or looking back at life itself at the moment of annihilation. Alternatively, the viewer might posit a kind of symbolic passage—coming out of darkness into light? The questions raised by Wiitasalo's sparely rendered, loosely brushed images are always engaging, as much an inquiring into the psychological, communicative nature of painting as a social commentary.

Janice Seline

Bibliography
Monk, Philip. *Shirley Wiitasalo*. Toronto: Art Gallery of Ontario, 1987.
Dault, Gary Michael. "Subversive Action." *Canadian Art* (Spring 1988): 62–67.

Wild, Catherine E. (1954–)

A printmaker, mixed-media artist, and teacher, Catherine E. Wild was born and raised in Montréal, Canada. She attended the Nova Scotia College of Art and Design, Halifax, in 1973; however, her art education began in earnest in 1974 at Concordia University, Montréal, studying under Jennifer Dickson and Jack Damer. Brief interests in painting, drawing, and sculpture yielded to lithography and abstrac-tion, which Wild found intriguing and difficult. She moved to Vancouver in 1977 for further study with Bob Evermon at the Emily Carr College of Art.

In 1979 Wild began Master of Fine Arts studies at the University of Wisconsin at Madison, working in printmaking and low relief paper constructions with Jack Damer, Warrington Colescott, and Victor Kord. Graduate school was intensely competitive and intellectually galvanizing, particularly as few students shared Wild's commitment to abstraction. The experience reinforced her own artistic self-reliance, supplying insights and critical tools that she transferred to her work and later to teaching.

Returning to British Columbia in 1982, Wild received a Canada Council grant to prepare an exhibition at the Richmond Arts Center. She also taught in 1983–1984 at the University of Alberta, a seminal experience in a highly professional department. In 1984 Wild's creative activities ground to a halt for nearly a year with the death of her mother—the second death in her immediate family in five years.

Wild returned to Concordia University as a teacher in 1984 for two years, and headed the lithography area at Arizona State University, Tempe, in 1986–1988. She now teaches at Montréal's John Abbott College and lectures throughout North America.

Wild's earliest works in all-over pattern, rhythm, and repetition are as much a personal meditation on perception as a dialogue with her media. With works such as "Allure for Love" (1982), "Tango" (1984), and "Spectrum" (1982), intense color and organic shapes begin intruding on hitherto austere, monochromatic backgrounds. She has since shown a bolder, more intuitive use of color and form.

Works accepted into major juried exhibitions include "It Was Your Time" (1985), shown at the 17th International Biennial of Graphic Arts in Ljubljana, and at the 1986 Burnaby Print Biennial, where it received the purchase award, and "Black Desire" (1987), which was selected for International Prints II by the Silvermine Guild Gallery. Wild's work has been selected twice by Philadelphia's Print Club, Pennsylvania, winning the board of governors prize in printmaking in 1986 for "Shadow Dancing" (1986); "Curl" was shown in 1988. "Spectrum" (1982) was shown at the Graphex 9 at the Art Gallery of Brant; and "Deep Freeze" (1985) was shown at the 21st Bradley National Print and Drawing Exhibition (1987), where Wild received the juror's merit award.

Wild has had solo exhibitions at Galerie Don Stewart, Montréal (1985), the Tyler School of Art, Temple University, Philadelphia, Pennsylvania (1987); and Montréal's Canal Complex (1991). Her works are owned by the state of Illinois, the Contemporary Print Collection of Burnaby Art Gallery, and the Kelly Lavoie and Steinberg Collections in Montréal.

Spyro Rondos

Bibliography
Graphex 9. Exhibition Catalog. Brantford, Ontario. The Art Gallery of Brant, 1984, p. 65.
Newsprints 2:6–7 (1986): 43.
1987 International Biennial of Graphic Art. Exhibition Catalog. Ljubljana, Yugoslavia, p. 351.
The Print Club. Exhibition Catalog. Philadelphia, Pennsylvania: 62nd Annual International Competition, 1986, p. 16.

Wildenhain, Marguerite (1896–1985)

Born in Lyon, France, Marguerite Wildenhain moved to Germany with her family, beginning her formal art training in sculpture at the Berlin School of Fine and Applied Arts. When the Bauhaus opened in 1919 she left her job as a designer of porcelain for a factory in Thuringia and apprenticed as the first potter at the workshop in Dornburg under master potter Max Krehan, and sculptor Gerhard Marcks.

In 1926, as a certified pottery master, Wildenhain became chairman of the ceramics department at the Municipal School for Arts and Crafts in Halle Saale. At the same time she designed production models for Royal Berlin Porcelain. When the Nazis came to power in Germany she was forced to leave. She fled to Putten, Holland, where she established a pottery workshop and continued as a designer for Regout Porcelain in Maastricht. In 1940, when the Nazis invaded Holland, Wildenhain left for America on the last ship braving the mine-filled harbor.

A teaching position at the California College of Arts and Crafts kept Wildenhain in Oakland, California, until 1942, when she founded Pond Farm Pottery located north of San Francisco, California, in Guerneville. Here in a rural area she established a workshop and opened a summer school. In a short time the school's reputation drew students from around the world. Her philosophy about making pottery the center of one's life along with the Bauhaus dictum that ceramics was an art form on the same level as painting and sculpture, inspired several generations of students.

Wildenhain responded to Pond Farm's rural location by adapting textures from nature as surface embellishment for her pottery. Her expertly thrown ware was exhibited and sold first in stores and galleries in San Francisco. Beginning in 1952 she accepted invitations to travel to colleges around the country conducting workshops that included the Bauhaus message and her commitment to a life in clay. Also around this time she began incorporating figures as part of the vessel's surface. Narrative themes illustrating current events, mythology, Bible stories and life at Pond Farm decorated her expertly thrown ware.

In the 1960s, after a trip to Peru, where she attended the World Crafts Council meeting, Wildenhain added images characteristic of that country. On bowls, vases, tiles, sculptures, and wall plaques Wildenhain portrayed village life, the Aymara and Quechua Indians, the sheepherders and the animals of the Andes. Inevitably the two-dimensional figures moved into three dimensions in a primitive style that contrasts with the perfect form of her thrown ware. More interested in form than color, her ware never emphasized the glaze, and her small figurative sculpture followed Native American and Peruvian pottery in their disregard for glazes.

In the early years Wildenhain's pottery sold at Gump's in San Francisco and later in stores in Chicago, Illinois, and Dallas, Texas. Once Wildenhain's reputation was established, customers would come directly to Pond Farm for their purchases. An active member of the American Craft Council, she was elected their Western representative, and exhibited regularly in group shows. Between 1942 and 1976 she had seven solo shows. Her two books, *Pottery: Form and Expression* (1962) and *The Invisible Core* (1973), along with numerous articles, her summer school, and the workshops she held at colleges around the country established Wildenhain as a major influence on the development of studio pottery in America.

Elaine Levin

Bibliography

Petterson, Richard B. "Marguerite Wildenhain." *Ceramics Monthly* 25:3 (March 1977): 21–28.

Prothro, Hunt. "Marguerite Wildenhain: Sustained Presence." *American Craft* 40:4 (August–September 1980): 28–31.

Wildenhain, Marguerite. *Development of the Pond Farm Pottery and School.* Wildenhain Papers, Archives of American Art, Smithsonian Institution, Washington, D.C.

———. *The Invisible Core: A Potter's Life and Thoughts.* Pacific Books, 1973.

———. *Pottery: Form and Expression.* New York: American Craftsmen's Council, 1962.

Wilke, Hannah (1940–1993)

Performance art and sculpture that make erotic and feminist statements, often simultaneously, are hallmarks of Hannah Wilke's work. Beginning in the 1960s Wilke's art, much of which is autobiographical, could be identified as an example of how the women's movement was affecting the art world.

In works such as Wilke's "Starification Object Series (S.O.S.)" (1975), she and other women artists worked to reverse the male tradition of using women's bodies as anonymous objects in art. In the performance piece "S.O.S.," Wilke decorated her semi-nude body with pieces of chewed gum she had sculpted into the vaginal images that became one of her trademarks. The resulting poses, which are documented in photographs, examine and parody the roles Wilke and other women play in society.

The majority of Wilke's art emerged from New York City's Ronald Feldman Gallery after her graduation from Temple University's Tyler School of Fine Arts, Philadelphia, Pennsylvania, with a Bachelor's degree in 1961. The vaginal designs she used in "S.O.S." evolved from her art school work. Wilke, who was born Arlene Hannah Butter in New York City on March 7, 1940, also received a Bachelor of Science degree from Temple University in 1962.

Again, vaginal images, representing "176 Single-Fold Gestural Sculptures" (1973–1974), were the centerpiece of her second one-woman New York City exhibition, "Floor Show, 1974" at Feldman Gallery. In addition to the terra cotta images themselves, the way the sculptures were sold carried a message. Each piece was sold separately. The sculptures were interpreted as representing both the individuality of women as well as the unity of womanhood.

In her art Wilke not only worked with visual images, but also played with words and language. When titling her works and series she used puns and gave new meaning to words and cliches. "Needed Eraser-Her" (1973–1977) expressed her perspective of anti-feminist sentiments.

A retrospective of Wilke's work was presented by the University of Missouri, St. Louis, in 1989. The exhibition featured her sculptures, drawings, watercolors, photographs/conceptual art, mixed media, and videos. Among the works included in the retrospective were pieces from the "So Help Me Hannah" series (1978–1984), nude black-and-white photographs of Wilke taken in seedy settings combined with text from prominent male thinkers, such as James Joyce and Karl Marx, to examine gender issues; "I Object: Memoirs of a Sugargiver" (1977–1978), Cibachrome diptych self-portraits, critiquing Marcel Duchamp's portrayal of the female figure in "Étant donnés;" "In Memorium: Selma Butter (Mommy)" (1979–1983), a mixed-media series that focused on

Wilke's mother, who was dying from cancer, and issues associated with women and aging; and "Venus Pareve" (1982–1984), ten-inch cast plaster self-portraits, each painted a different color, that probe the image of the ideal woman.

Among the works in Wilke's recent shows have been abstract watercolor self-portraits from the "B.C." series (1986–1988). In June 1987, during work on the series, Wilke was diagnosed with cancer. The watercolors, which form a visual diary, were exhibited at Feldman Gallery with pieces Wilke had done earlier about her mother's bout with cancer.

Melissa D. Olson

Bibliography
Berman, Avis. "A Decade of Progress, But Could a Female Chardin Make a Living?" *Art News* 79:8 (October 1980): 73–78.
Frueh, Joanna. *Hannah Wilke: A Retrospective.* University of Missouri Press, 1989.
Kimmelman, Michael. "Hannah Wilke." *The New York Times* (September 29, 1989). sect. III, p. 30, col. 5.
Lippard, Lucy R. "The Pains and Pleasures of Rebirth: Women's Body Art." *Art in America* 64:3 (May–June 1976): 73–81.
Nemser, Cindy. "Four Artists of Sensuality." *Arts Magazine* 49:7 (March 1975): 73–75.
Rother, Moira. *The Amazing Decade: Women and Performance Art in America 1970–1980.* Astro Artz, 1983.
Savitt, Mark. "Hannah Wilke: The Pleasure Principle." *Arts Magazine* 50:1 (September 1975): 56–57.
Siegel, Judy. "Between the Censor and the Muse?" *Women Artists News* 11:5 (Winter 1986–1987): 4, 47–48.
Tannenbaum, Judith. "Hannah Wilke." *Art Magazine* 48:8 (May 1974): 62.

Wilson, Anne (1949–)

A mixed-media artist, best known for her constructions referring to animal hides, Anne Wilson was born on April 16, 1949, in Detroit, Michigan. Raised in Michigan, she attended Cranbrook Academy of Art, Bloomfield Hills, where she studied with Gerhardt Knodel, and received a Bachelor of Fine Arts degree in 1972. Wilson continued her studies at the California College of Arts and Crafts, Oakland. Sculptor Bella Feldman, and textile artist Lillian Elliott, were strong influences and she graduated with a Master of Fine Arts degree in 1976.

Wilson began exhibiting professionally in 1972 in "Objects and Images," Parrish Art Museum, Southampton, New York. Her early work was based on clothing forms. In 1983 she began to make "urban furs," exhibited at the Miller/Brown Gallery, San Francisco, California. She continued her exploration of the tensions and contradictions of the organic and synthetic in the modern world through related woven and painted series exhibited in "Fiber R/Evolution," University of Wisconsin, Milwaukee (1986), and "Craft Today: Poetry of the Physical," the American Craft Museum (1987), among others. In the exhibit "Tangents," Maryland Institute, Baltimore (1987–1988), Wilson first exhibited work that was constructed of synthetic felt stitched with linen fur and painted to more convincingly allude to actual hide. This series of work has also been included in the "6th International Triennale of Tapestry," Central Museum of Textiles, Lodz, Poland, and the "14th International Biennial of Tapestry," Musée Cantonal des Beaux-Arts,

Lausanne, Switzerland.

Wilson is the recipient of a National Endowment for the Arts (NEA) fellowship in both 1982 and 1988, and the Tiffany Foundation award in 1989. Her work is included in the collections of the Art Institute of Chicago, Illinois, and the M.H. de Young Memorial Museum, San Francisco. Wilson has been an associate professor at the School of the Art Institute of Chicago, Illinois, since 1979.

Claire Campbell Park

Bibliography
Maryland Institute. *Tangents: Art in Fiber.* Baltimore: College of Art, 1987.
Spector, Buzz. "Anne Wilson: Urban Furs." *American Craft* (February–March 1988).
University Art Museum, University of Wisconsin, Milwaukee. *Fiber R/Evolution,* 1986.

Wilson, Jane (1924–)

Born in the southern Iowa town of Seymour, Jane Wilson grew up knowing landscapes that seemingly went on forever, sensing the textures of tilled earth, drinking in the dynamic skies over rolling expanses—memories that would find their way, metamorphosed, into her future paintings.

Wilson received her Bachelor's degree from the University of Iowa, Iowa City, in 1945; she earned a Master of Arts degree in art history at the same institution two years later. After teaching for two years at her alma mater, Wilson and her writer-critic husband, John Gruen, moved to New York City. She has been an adjunct faculty member at many colleges and universities such as Pratt Institute (1967–1970), the Cooper Union (1976), Parsons School of Design (1973–1983, 1989–1990), and Columbia University, School of the Arts, as associate professor (1975–1988) and professor and acting chair (1986–1988)—all in New York City. She was visiting artist at the University of Wisconsin, Madison; Kansas City Art Institute, Missouri; University of Iowa, Iowa City; the American University, Washington, D.C.; Dartmouth College, Hanover, New Hampshire; and others.

Wilson has won prizes and grants from the Ingram Merrill Foundation (1963); Tiffany Foundation (1967); the American Academy and Institute of Arts and Letters, New York City, Childe Hassam purchase fund (1972–1973, 1981), and the award in art (1985); the National Academy of Design, New York City, Ranger purchase prize (1977), Adolph and Clara Obrig prize (1985, 1987), and the Benjamin Altman prize (1990); and the Eloise Spaeth award for distinguished achievement in painting from the Guild Hall Museum, East Hampton, New York (1988). Her still lifes, landscapes, and shorescapes are multilayered works that haunt the viewer long after seeing them; they evoke myriad responses as paintings even as they prod and provoke one's memory banks. "City on a Plain" (1990) elicits wonderment and nodding of the head at the painterly magic of light, space, and atmosphere.

Wilson had her forty-third solo exhibition in the United States, most recently at Fischbach Gallery, New York City (1991). Her paintings have been invited to major group exhibitions throughout her career and are in the permanent public collections of the Whitney Museum of American Art, Museum of Modern Art (MoMA), Metropolitan Museum of Art, and New York University—all in New York City; the Smithsonian Institution and the Hirshhorn Museum and Sculpture Garden—both in Washington, D.C.; and the Museum of Foreign Art, Sophia, Bulgaria—

to name a small selection. She has been a member of the National Academy of Design, New York City, since 1979 and has served on its council (1980–1986, 1989–1992). She has served on the board of governors of the Skowhegan School of Painting and Sculpture, Maine (1981–1990) and was chair (1984–1986). Wilson has been a member of the American Academy and Institute of Arts and Letters, New York City, since 1991.

Bibliography
Gardner, Paul. "Jane Wilson's Weather Eye." *Art News* 84:10 (December 1985): 56–60.
Gruen, John. *The Party's Over Now: Reminiscences of the Fifties.* Viking Press, 1972.
Jane Wilson: Landscapes and Still Life: 1960–1990. A Catalog. Modlin Fine Arts Center, University of Richmond, 1990.
Rubinstein, Charlotte Streifer. *American Women Artists.* G.K. Hall, 1982.

Wilson, Martha (1947–)

Founder and director of the Franklin Furnace Archive, New York City (1976), the performance artist Martha Wilson earned a Bachelor's degree from Wilmington College, Ohio (1969), and, two years later, received a Master of Arts degree from Dalhousie University, Nova Scotia, Canada.

Wilson has performed as a soloist and has also followed the collaborative path for many years, performing with Jacki Apple (1972) and, since 1978, with Disband, a group of five artists who collaborate on various projects in addition to their private work.

Wilson's work has ranged from concern with individual identity to broader themes; she has taught at the School of Visual Arts, New York City, and at Dalhousie University, Novia Scotia, Canada.

Bibliography
Burnham, L. "Per/for/mance: American Performance Artists in Italy." *High Performance* (Summer 1980).
Lippard, Lucy. *Get the Message.* 1984.
Roth, M. *The Amazing Decade: Women and Performance Art, 1970–1980.* 1983.

Wilson, May (1905–1986)

Born in Baltimore, Maryland, the assemblage sculptor May Wilson produced a great quantity of work, little of which was seen by the general public. She took correspondence school courses in art; separated from her husband; and, by 1966, was creating whimsical, three-dimensional, spray-painted, mono-colored fantasies from the detritus of daily life.

Wilson's work was exhibited in solo and group shows, some of which travelled widely, including "New Idea, New Media Show," Martha Jackson Gallery (1960), "Assemblage," a travelling show, Museum of Modern Art (MoMA) (1962), and "1970 Sculpture Annual," Whitney Museum of American Art (1970)—all in New York City; and others in Washington, D.C., and Detroit, Michigan. However, from 1970 through the time of her death, Wilson had little or nothing to do with dealers, and so informed them.

Wilson won awards at the Baltimore Museum of Art exhibitions, Maryland (1952, 1959). Her work graces the permanent collections of the Baltimore Museum of Art, Maryland; Corcoran Gallery of Art, Washington, D.C.; Dela Banque de Pariset, Brussels, Belgium; Goucher College, Baltimore, Maryland; the Whitney Museum of American Art, New York City; and others.

Bibliography
1970 Sculpture Annual. New York: Whitney Museum of American Art, 1970.
Obituary. *Art in America* 75:1 (January 1987): 160.
Wilson, Bill. "Grandma Moses of the Underground." *Art & Artists* (May 1968).
Who's Who in American Art. 15th ed. R.R. Bowker Co., 1982.

Wingate, Arline (1906–)

A native New Yorker, the sculptor Arline Wingate studied and worked in New York City; Paris, France; Madrid, Spain; Stockholm, Sweden; and Rome, Italy.

A member of the Sculptors Guild, New York City, Wingate has exhibited her work in museums and galleries throughout the United States and abroad, including the Metropolitan Museum of Art, Whitney Museum of American Art, and Brooklyn Museum—all in New York City; the Wadsworth Atheneum, Hartford, Connecticut; Pennsylvania Academy of Fine Arts, Philadelphia, Pennsylvania; Petit Palais, Paris, France; Ghent Museum, Belgium; Museo de Bellas Artes, Buenos Aires, Argentina; Burlington Galleries, London, England; and others.

Wingate's sculptures are represented in private, public, and corporate permanent collections, such as Syracuse University, Parrish Museum, Southampton, and Guild Hall Museum, East Hampton—all in New York; National Museum of Stockholm, Sweden; Ghent Museum, Belgium; Newark Museum, New Jersey; Norfolk Museum, Virginia; Birmingham Museum, Alabama; Farnsworth Museum, Rockland, Maine; Wichita University, Kansas; Hirshhorn Museum and Sculpture Garden, Washington, D.C.; and many others.

Bibliography
Russo, Alexander. *Profiles on Women Artists.* University Publications of America, 1985.
Who's Who in American Art. 19th ed. R.R. Bowker Co., 1991–1992.

Winkel, Nina (1905–)

Born in Borken-Westfalen, Germany, the sculptor Nina Winkel studied at the Kunstgewerbe Schule (School for Arts and Crafts) Essen (1921); the Staatliche Kunstakademie, Düsseldorf (1922–1923); and the Kunstgewerbe Schule Abteilung Staedel-Museum, Frankfurt-am-Main (1929–1931)—all in Germany—where she studied under the aegis of Joseph Hartwig and Richard Scheibe.

Winkel has held many solo exhibitions in museums and galleries in the United States and abroad since 1944 and has had her work invited to group shows throughout the United States in sites such as the Whitney Museum of American Art (1950, 1954), the Metropolitan Museum of Art (1951–1952), the American Academy and Institute of Arts and Letters (1951)—all in New York City—and the University of Nebraska, Lincoln (1949).

Winkel has received many awards, honors, and commissions, including an honorary Doctorate degree from the State University of New York (SUNY) at Plattsburgh (1985); Elizabeth Watrous gold medals (1945, 1978), Samuel F.B. Morse gold medal (1964), and the artists fund prize for best sculpture (1979)—all from the National Academy of Design, New York City; a purchase prize, National Sculpture Society, New York City (1981); and others. Her work is represented in private and public permanent collections in the United States and abroad, including "Justice Protectress" at the Supreme Court of New York; Albert Schweitzer School, Wiesbaden, Germany; the University of Notre Dame, Indiana; City of Borken-Westfalen, Germany; Nabu Manufacturing Corporation, Ottawa, Canada; and many others.

Bibliography

Dryfoos, Nancy. "Nina Winkel . . . Her Copper Sculpture." *National Sculpture Review* 20:4 (Winter 1971–1972): 18–19.

Hale, Nathan Cabot. *Welded Sculpture*. Watson-Guptill, 1968.

National Sculpture Society Annual Exhibition. New York: National Sculpture Society, 1946–1983.

Watson-Jones, Virginia. *Contemporary American Women Sculptors*. Oryx Press, 1986.

Winokur, Paula (1935–)

Born in Philadelphia, Pennsylvania, the ceramist Paula Winokur earned a Bachelor of Fine Arts degree and a Bachelor of Science in education degree from the Tyler School of Art, Temple University, Philadelphia, Pennsylvania (1958), and studied ceramics at Alfred University, New York, during the summer of that year.

Between 1962 and 1991 Winokur has held more than twenty solo exhibitions throughout the United States, including Napa Valley College, California (1991); Helen Druitt Gallery, New York City (1978, 1982, 1988, 1990); Chatham College, Pittsburgh, Pennsylvania (1981); College of William and Mary, Williamsburg, Virginia (1980); Contemporary Crafts, Portland, Oregon (1976); the American Hand Gallery, Washington, D.C. (1971); and others. Her ceramic works have been invited to many group exhibitions in the United States and abroad: from Jenkintown, Pennsylvania to Sheboygan, Wisconsin; San José, California; New York City; Chicago, Illinois; Calgary, Canada; Gent, Belgium; and others.

Art juror, workshop leader and widely-known lecturer/demonstrator of ceramic techniques and processes—Winokur has been an assistant professor of ceramics at Beaver College, Glenside, Pennsylvania since 1973. She has received and executed a number of commissions to create a variety of works, such as fireplace installations, entries and conference rooms, large planters, and limited edition plates. She has earned honors and awards, including National Endowment for the Arts (NEA) fellowships (1976, 1988); a craftsman's fellowship from the Pennsylvania Council on the Arts (1986); an honorary fellowship from the National Council on Education in the Ceramic Arts (1983); and others. Her work is represented in private, public, and corporate permanent collections, including the American Craft Museum and Peat/Marwick Associates—both in New York City; Arizona State University, Tempe; Alberta Potters Association, Calgary, Canada; Philadelphia Museum of Fine Arts, Pennsylvania; Witte Museum of Art, San Antonio, Texas; and many others.

Bibliography

Dormer, Peter. *The New Ceramics: Trends and Traditions*. Thames & Hudson, 1986.

Levin, Elaine. *The History of American Ceramics*. Harry N. Abrams, 1988.

Peterson, Susan. *The Craft and Art of Clay*. Prentice-Hall, 1991.

Sozanski, Edward J. "Paula Winokur: A Review." *Philadelphia Inquirer* (December 24, 1987).

Winsor, Jackie V. (Jacqueline) (1941–)

A Canadian-born American sculptor, Jackie Winsor had her work featured in a mid-career retrospective exhibit at the Museum of Modern Art (MoMA), New York City, in 1979. She became well known for the forty tightly bound wood and fiber constructions she had completed. Although still remembered for her remarkably sensitive use of earthbound materials within the minimalist aesthetic, Winsor has moved away from these materials in the past decade to work with metal and painted plaster, although she continues to employ simple cubes and rectangular forms.

In the 1970s Winsor made highly tactile structures with materials such as saplings, brick, ropes, and planks of wood. Although she utilized the primary structures of minimalism her work evoked the romantic worlds of the pastoral even when she incorporated metal mesh and wire, rather than the machine aesthetic implied by much contemporary metal sculpture. Winsor's early work even included a sensuous performance piece, "Up and/or Down" (1971), in which one-quarter-ton thick rope was passed between a man and a woman positioned above and below a hole in the floor of a building. Rope figured prominently in her work of this decade—for all its natural allusions, she became interested in incorporating it in her work because it was one of the industrial materials manufactured in the neighborhood in which she lived in the Lower East Side of New York.

"Bound Grid" (1971–1972), made of saplings wrapped tightly with hemp in a grid structure, is typical of Winsor's sculpture in its powerful evocation of primitive ritual. The obviously handcrafted bundles reinforce a sense of process and give emphasis to handcraft. Although her use of raw organic materials is most striking within the sterile atmosphere of museums and galleries, Winsor has made site-specific works as well, which connote human presence in otherwise uninhabited places. Her "30 to 1 Bound Trees" (1971), made of thirty white birch saplings bound together with a live tree at its core, evokes the windswept empty landscape of its site in Halifax, Nova Scotia.

Born in Newfoundland, Winsor moved with her family to Boston, Massachusetts, in 1951. She took her Bachelor of Fine Arts degree at Massachusetts College of Art, Boston, in 1965 and her Master of Fine Arts degree at Douglass College, Rutgers University, New Brunswick, New Jersey, in 1967. In 1968 her first solo exhibit was held at the Douglass College Gallery, Rutgers University. She was awarded a Guggenheim Foundation fellowship in 1978.

Much of Winsor's work in the past decade has been shown at the Paula Cooper Gallery in New York City. In 1986 she exhibited a group of three-foot-high cubes of plaster and wood, some with mirrored surfaces, which recalled cubes of the previous decade such as "Sheet Rock Piece" (1976). Like her earlier structures, small openings in the center of each face allowed viewers to peer inside the cubes. Instead of reinforcing the raw materials of the exterior, the interiors of the new work consisted of surprising, intensely-colored surfaces. In 1990 Winsor moved her sculpture off the floor onto the wall. In these simple rectangular structures, plain wooden framing surrounds sunken, painted recessions. In a further remove from the honest materialism of minimalist sculpture, Winsor appears to be gravitating toward the illusionistic sphere of painting. Recalling Josef Albers' "Homage to the Square" series, the sunken areas are sometimes painted so that they appear to advance instead of recede.

Debora A. Rindge

Bibliography
Lippard, Lucy. "Jackie Winsor." *Artforum* 12 (February 1974): 56–58; reprinted in Lucy Lippard, *From the Center: Feminist Essays on Women's Art.* E.P. Dutton, 1976, pp. 202–09.
Jackie Winsor. New York: Museum of Modern Art, 1979.
Pincus-Witten, Robert. "Winsor Knots: The Sculpture of Jackie Winsor." *Arts Magazine* 51 (June 1977): 127–33.
Smagula, Howard. *Currents: Contemporary Directions in the Visual Arts.* 2nd ed. Prentice-Hall, 1989, pp. 150–60.

Wolcott, Marion Post (1910–1990)

Daughter of a family physician, born in Bloomfield, New Jersey, the photographer Marion Post Wolcott studied modern dance with Ruth St. Denis at the New School for Social Research, New York City, and with Doris Humphrey at New York University in the same city.

Wolcott interned in elementary education one summer at Vassar College, Poughkeepsie, New York; taught in a New England mill town and at a private boarding school in Cambridge, Massachusetts; posed for life drawing classes; studied and travelled in Europe for two years; saw and heard Hitler at a Nazi rally, which reinforced her antifascist leanings; borrowed a professional camera from the photographer Trude Fleischmann, in Austria, and used it well. Returning to the United States, she taught at a progressive institution, Hessian Hills School, Croton-on-Hudson, New York. She became a free-lance photographer and associated with actors and directors of the Group Theatre in New York City, and was the only female photographer employed (in a group of ten) by the *Evening Bulletin* in Philadelphia, Pennsylvania. In July 1938, during the Great Depression, Wolcott began her professional photographic career for the celebrated Farm Security Administration, which included Dorothea Lange, Ben Shahn, and Walker Evans, to create, for three short years, some of the most memorable photographs of rural America.

Wolcott married in 1941 and devoted the remainder of her life to her family. Her work is represented in many permanent collections, including the Metropolitan Museum of Art and International Center of Photography—both in New York City; the Art Institute of Chicago, Illinois; Houston Museum of Fine Arts, Texas; National Gallery of Canada, Ottawa; the George Eastman House, Rochester, New York; and others.

Bibliography
Hendricks, Paul. *Looking for the Light: The Hidden Life of Marion Post Wolcott.* Alfred A. Knopf, 1992.
Stein, Sally. *Marion Post Wolcott.* A Monograph. Carmel, California: Friends of Photography, 1983.

Wolfe, Ann (1905–)

Born in Mlawa, Poland, the sculptor Ann Wolfe earned a Bachelor's degree from Hunter College, New York City; studied sculpture in Manchester, England, and Paris, France; and worked under Charles Despiau at the Académie de la Grande Chaumière, Paris, France.

Wolfe has held many solo exhibitions in galleries and museums, including the Worcester Art Museum (1939) and the Grace Horne Gallery, Boston (1941)—both in Massachusetts; Whyte Gallery, Washington, D.C. (1946); Hamline University, St. Paul (1951), Walker Art Center, Minneapolis (1955), Minneapolis Institute of Arts (1964), and Westlake Gallery, Minneapolis (1970)—all in Minnesota; and many others.

Winner of honors and awards, Wolfe has shown her work in myriad regional and national group shows throughout the United States. Her sculpture is represented in public and private permanent collections, such as Children's Hospital and Hamline University—both in St. Paul, Minnesota; City University of New York (CUNY), and Colgate University, Hamilton—both in New York; Jerusalem Museum, Israel; National Museum of Korea, Seoul; Museum of Western Art, Moscow, Russia; University of California at Berkeley; and others.

Bibliography
Watson-Jones, Virginia. *Contemporary American Women Sculptors.* Oryx Press, 1986.
Who's Who in American Art. 19th ed. R.R. Bowker Co., 1991–1992.

Wood, Beatrice (1893–)

Acting and painting vied for Beatrice Wood's attention as a young student. Born in San Francisco, California, Wood studied art and acting in New York City and Paris, France. When World War I began in 1914, Wood returned to New York City to concentrate on an acting career. In 1916 she began a close friendship with Marcel Duchamp and other members of the New York City Dada group taking refuge from the war in Europe. She participated in the group's varied activities, producing drawings for avant-garde magazines and designing posters. Duchamp became her mentor, influencing her thinking about art and introducing her to other emigré artists and to art collectors Walter and Louise Arensberg, whose aesthetic judgments and modern art sensibility impressed the young artist.

When the Dadaists returned to Europe after the war and the Arensbergs moved to California, Wood became involved in Eastern religions, following Indian philosopher Krishnamurti to Europe. Trips to Los Angeles, California, beginning in 1923, resulted in a permanent move there five years later. Wood had purchased a set of luster glazed ware during a previous trip to Europe and decided in 1933, at age forty, that she would make a teapot to match. She innocently enrolled in an adult education ceramics class at Hollywood High School, California, a move that propelled her into a lifetime career in clay.

Wood's teapot never materialized, but her imagination was fired when she made some small figurines that promptly sold, inflating her confidence about becoming a ceramist. She studied briefly with Glen Lukens at the University of Southern California, Los Angeles, and with Gertrud and Otto Natzler, established her own studio in Hollywood in 1941. Department stores ordered her functional ware, and, in 1944, she had a solo exhibit at America House in New York City.

In 1946 Krishnamurti settled in Ojai, California—a small community northwest of Los Angeles—establishing a private school for young children. Wood followed in 1948, relocating her studio and teaching part-time at the school. The luster glaze she had originally sought was elusive but, with some further instruction from Vivika and Otto Heino, she persevered, finally developing a palette of luster glaze colors unique for the ceramics of the period. Her lusterwares were exhibited in Hawaii and at several Los Angeles galleries.

In 1961 Wood was sent to India by the U.S. State Department at the request of the Indian government. Travelling to fourteen cities, she lectured on American potters and exhibited her work. She in turn was enthralled by the naive and direct expression of feelings in the folk art she saw and by the national dress for women—the sari. The loose-fitting and glamorous sari worn with bangles and beads became her regular apparel. She returned to India in 1965 and 1972, visiting also in Israel, Nepal, and Afghanistan.

Figurative sculpture, tiles, and plaques of figures in bas relief remained a somewhat hidden part of Wood's ceramics. During the 1960s and 1970s a few figures accompanied shows of her exotic lusterware. Mostly she made them for her own amusement. Perhaps because the subject matter concerned the relationship between men and women, hints of liaisons and disappointments in love that reflected her own experiences, she did not readily display her sculptures. Then, too, the exotic beauty of her luster glazes on bowls, chalices, vases, and plates were in demand. Yet the whimsical expressive use of clay apparent in her handling of figures began to creep into her functional ware as bas relief figures on bowls and chalices. The figures were displayed in the gallery area of her Ojai home. A 1973 retrospective of her work included her sculptures and lusterware and travelled from the Phoenix Art Museum, Arizona, to venues around the country.

Between 1970 and 1980 her work was exhibited almost yearly at the Zachary Waller Gallery in Los Angeles, California. In 1978 Wood's ceramics, drawings, and her earlier work with the Dadaists were part of a series of exhibits in Syracuse, New York; Philadelphia, Pennsylvania; and New York City. Her work in "A Century of Ceramics in the United States," at the Everson Museum of Art in Syracuse, New York, in 1979, curated by Garth Clark, subsequently brought her a one-person exhibition at Clark's newly opened gallery in Los Angeles, California, in 1981. Wood took inspiration from this new representation and, at age eighty-eight, began a large body of new works. A video documentary of her life was produced in 1982, and a Dada Ball in honor of her ninetieth birthday was held in Los Angeles the following year.

The 1980s also became the decade in which Wood's figurative sculpture was exhibited for its own sake, in a gallery in Santa Fe, New Mexico, and in an exhibit that travelled from the Oakland Museum (1989) to the Craft and Folk Art Museum of Los Angeles (1990)—both in California. Sexual games, variations on the theme of prostitution, and a pessimistic attitude toward marriage are themes Wood returns to frequently, poking fun at traditional attitudes. Wood considers herself an artist rather than a serious sculptor, working in a consciously naive fashion to comment on the human comedy.

Elaine Levin

Bibliography

Clark, Garth. "Beatrice Wood." *American Craft* 43:4 (August–September 1983): 25–26.

Hare, Denise. "The Lustrous Life of Beatrice Wood." *Craft Horizons* 38:3 (June 1978): 26–31.

Naumann, Francis M. "Beatrice Wood." *American Craft* 43, 4 (August–September 1983): 24.

———. *Intimate Appeal: The Figurative Art of Beatrice Wood.* California: Oakland Museum, 1989.

Wood, Beatrice. *The Angel Who Wore Black Tights.* Rogue Press, 1982.

Wood, Elizabeth Wyn (1903–1966)

A founding member of the Sculptors' Society of Canada, Elizabeth Wyn Wood was one of the earliest proponents of modernism in Canadian sculpture. Her contribution was unique in that she turned to the Canadian landscape as a vehicle for artistic expression around the time that Canada's national school of landscape painters—the Group of Seven—was doing the same in paint. Wood also contributed to the arts in Canada through her involvement in the Canadian Arts Council, acting as its organizing secretary from 1944–1945, chair of the international relations committee from 1944–1948, and vice-president from 1948–1949.

Born in Orillia, Ontario, Canada, Wood studied at the Ontario College of Art, Toronto, from 1921–1926, specializing in sculpture in her postgraduate year. She subsequently married her sculptor instructor, Emanuel Hahn (1881–1957), then spent one year at the Art Students League, New York City, studying with Robert Laurent and Edward McCarten.

In 1927 Wood began exploring spatial relationships between elements found in nature—first in drawings made with a lithographic pencil of subjects observed at the Hahn cottage on the Pickerel River in northern Ontario. The different elements would be treated as planes in relief, and the sculpture would employ such new and unconventional materials as aluminum, tin, and glass. For an early example of these works, "Passing Rain" (1928), Wood won the Willingdon arts award for sculpture in 1930. The marble version was purchased by the National Gallery of Canada, Ottawa, that same year.

Architectural sculpture and monuments also occupied Wood throughout her career. Her major works in this field were the "Welland-Crowland War Memorial" (1939); four carvings for the approach plaza to Rainbow Bridge, Niagara Falls, Ontario (1940–1942); two relief carvings for the Bank of Montréal building in Toronto (1947–1948); the Leacock Memorial in Orillia Public Library (1949); and the monument to King George VI at Niagara Falls, Ontario, in 1963. As well as being involved in the Canadian Arts Council, Wood was one of the founding members of the Sculptors' Society of Canada (SSC) in 1928, and its president from 1933–1935. She was the author of the Brief of the SSC to the Royal Commissions on National Development in the Arts, Letters and Sciences submitted to the Massey Commission in 1949. Wood was also active as a teacher at Central Technical School, Toronto, from 1929 to 1958.

Christine Boyanoski

Bibliography

Luckyj, Natalie. *Visions and Victories: Ten Canadian Women Artists 1914–45.* London Regional Art Gallery, 1983.

Voaden, Herman. "Elizabeth Wyn Wood." *Maritime Art* II:5 (June–July 1942): 145–49.

Who's Who in Ontario Art. Reprint from the Ontario Library Review (February 1949).

Wood, Elizabeth Wyn. "A National Program for the Arts in Canada." *Canadian Art* I:3 (February–March 1944): 93–95, 127–28.

Woodham, Jean (1925–)

Born in Midland City, Alabama, the sculptor Jean Woodham earned a Bachelor's degree from Auburn University, Alabama; took three years of postgraduate work at the Sculpture Center, New York City; and, as a result of a national competition sponsored by the University of Illinois, Urbana, was awarded a fourth year of independent study in New York City.

Woodham has held eighteen solo exhibitions in museums and galleries throughout the United States and abroad, and has had her work invited to many group exhibitions, including "The Coming of Age of American Sculpture: The First Decades of the Sculpture Guild, 1930s–1950s," a travelling show, Hofstra University, Hempstead, New York (1992); "14th International Sculpture Conference, Sculptors Guild, Philadelphia, Pennsylvania (1992); and "Seven Sculptors: Inaugural Art Exhibition, Norwalk Community College, Connecticut (1992). She has also shown her work at the Whitney Museum of American Art, New York City; Boston Museum of Fine Arts, Massachusetts; Pennsylvania Academy of Fine Arts, Philadelphia; New Burlington Galleries, London, England; Museo de Arte Moderno, Mexico City; Museo Nacional de Bellas Artes, Buenos Aires, Argentina; Albright-Knox Art Gallery, Buffalo, New York; Heller Gallery and Sculpture Center—both in New York City; and others.

Winner of awards and honors, Woodham received the Finch award, "Art of the Northeast U.S.A.," Museum of Modern Art (MoMA), New York City (1985); the Djerassi Foundation grant for creative sculpture (1983); a medal of honor, National Association of Women Artists (1974); a Carlson Foundation grant for a retrospective exhibition (1970); and others. Currently president of the Sculptors Guild, Inc., New York City (her third term), Woodham also received citations for contributions to the arts from the governor of Alabama (1989); United Nations (1988); the governor of Connecticut (1987); and the Connecticut General Assembly (1986). Her large-scale work and other sculptures are represented in 150 private, public, and corporate permanent collections, including a twenty-eight-foot sculpture at the Harry S. Truman High School, New York City; and others at Auburn University, Alabama; Central Connecticut State University, New Britain; Foreign Art Museum, Sofia, Bulgaria; Norfolk Museum of Arts and Sciences, Virginia; Nynex Corporate Headquarters; General Electric Credit Corporation; and many others.

Bibliography

Padovano, Anthony. *The Process of Sculpture.* Doubleday, 1981.
Watson-Jones, Virginia. *Contemporary American Women Sculptors.* Oryx Press, 1986.
Who's Who in American Art. 19th ed. R.R. Bowker Co., 1991–1992.
Williams, Arthur. *Sculpture Technique: Form and Content.* Davis Publications, 1989.

Woodlock, Ethelyn Hurd (1907–)

From the age of six, when she drew a trolley car, Ethelyn Hurd Woodlock knew she was going to be an artist. Born in Hallowell, Maine, the surrealist and magic realist painter received her basic art education at the Copley School of Commercial Art in Boston, Massachusetts, and spent many years studying still life and perspective.

An indefatigable worker (her self-portrait series, started in 1943, numbers 116 paintings), Woodlock exhibited her paintings at thirty-five of the "Annuals" held at the National Academy of Fine Arts; showed innumerable times at the National Arts Club; and was one of the first New Jersey women asked to join the Salmagundi Club (1974)—all in New York City. "Please Forward," a typical Woodlock painting from the permanent collection of the National Museum of Women in the Arts, Washington, D.C., is one of four works included in "New Viewpoints: Contemporary American Realists," in the Seville Expo '92, Spain. The painting, a *trompe l'oeil* representation of cancelled Civil War letters,

a feather, pince-nez spectacles, and a key has been likened, by many, to Harnett; Woodlock sees the work as an example of magic realism.

Woodlock has received many awards and honors for her paintings, including the "Best Traditional Oil" from the National Association of Women Artists (1973); "Best Still Life" (1971) and a gold medal (1973) from the Catherine Lorillard Wolfe Art Club (1971); two "Best in Show" awards from the American Artists Professional League of New Jersey; the "Award of Highest Merit" from the Bergen County Artists Guild (1975); an Allied Artists award (1977); "Best in Show" award at the Ringwood Manor State Annual (1978); four national awards for her miniature paintings; and many others in New Jersey and Florida.

Art juror, teacher, lecturer on art, shells, and ghosts (she wrote that her eighteen-room Victorian mansion had five good but sad ghosts)—Woodlock is the author of an illustrated autobiography titled *Dreams Have Wings.*

Bibliography

Who's Who in American Art. 19th ed. R.R. Bowker Co., 1991–1992.
Woodlock, Ethelyn Hurd. *Dreams Have Wings.* Privately printed. 1985.

Woodman, Betty (1930–)

Born in Norwalk, Connecticut, the prize-winning ceramist Betty Woodman attended the School for American Craftsmen, Alfred University, Alfred, New York (1948–1950).

In addition to a commission executed for the Denver Municipal Airport, Colorado (1991)—a solo work—Woodman has held solo exhibitions in galleries and museums in the United States and abroad, including "Betty Woodman," Wadsworth Athenaeum, Hartford, Connecticut (1992); "Lobby Project: Betty Woodman," Museum of Modern Art (MoMA), New York City (1988, 1989, 1991); "Opera Selecta: The Work of Betty Woodman, 1975–1990," Het Kruithuis Den Bosch, the Netherlands (1990); Greenberg Gallery, St. Louis, Missouri (1987); Max Protetch Gallery, New York City (1983, 1984, 1986, 1980, 1990, 1991); "The Ceramics of Betty Woodman," Albright College, Reading, Pennsylvania (1985); Douglas Drake Gallery, Kansas City, Missouri (1984); Galleria Pirra, Torino, Italy (1980); and many others. Her work has been invited to myriad group exhibitions throughout the world: from New York City to Shigaraki-yaki, Japan; Seattle, Washington; Paris, France; Amersfoort, Holland; Arvada, Colorado; Syracuse, New York; Cardiff, Wales; London, England; and Tokyo, Japan—and others.

Woodman has won many honors and awards, including a Fulbright-Hays scholarship to Florence, Italy (1966); National Endowment for the Arts (NEA) fellowships (1980, 1986); the governor's award in the arts, Colorado (1987); awards from the Atelier Experimental de Recherche et de Création, Manufacture National de Sèvres, France (1985, 1986, 1988); and others.

A professor in the department of fine arts at the University of Colorado at Boulder since 1979, Woodman has taught ceramics at other institutions and has served as panelist, workshop and seminar leader, art juror, guest printmaker, and lecturer in the United States and abroad. Her works are represented in private and public permanent collections in the United States, Canada, England, Italy, and the Netherlands, including the Boston Museum of Fine Arts, Massachusetts; Brooklyn Museum, Metropolitan Museum of Art, and the Whitney Museum of American Art—all in New York City; Carnegie-

Mellon University, Pittsburgh, Pennsylvania; Denver Art Museum, Colorado; Het Kruithuis, Den Bosch, the Netherlands; International Ceramic Museum, Faenza, Italy; Los Angeles County Museum of Art, California; Museum of Decorative Arts of Montréal, Canada; Arizona State University, Tempe; the Victoria & Albert Museum, London, England; and many others.

Bibliography
Brenson, Michael. "Betty Woodman." *The New York Times* (April 22, 1988).
Clark, Garth. *American Potters: The Work of Twenty Modern Masters.* Watson-Guptill, 1981.
Koplos, Janet. "From Function to Form." *Art in America* (November 1990): 166–71.
Miro, Marsha. "History Inspires Superb Potter." *Detroit Free Press* (July 22, 1986): 3F.

Woodward, Mabel May (1877–1945)

Born in Providence, Rhode Island, the painter Mabel May Woodward studied in New York City with several artist/teachers, including William Merritt Chase, Cox, and Du Mond. This "rediscovered" American Impressionist painter belonged to several arts organizations, such as the Providence Art Club, Providence Watercolor Club—both in Rhode Island; and the Provincetown Art Association, Massachusetts. Representative examples of her work are in private and public permanent collections.

Bibliography
American Art Annual. Vol. 28. American Federation of Arts, 1932.
A Century of American Painting, 1850–1950. Columbus, Ohio: Keny and Johnson Gallery, 1981.
Important American Paintings, Drawings and Sculpture. Sotheby's, New York (May 31, 1984): Lot 187 and 201.

Wooten, Mary Bayard Morgan (1876–1959)

Born in New Bern, North Carolina, the photographer Mary Bayard Morgan Wooten studied at the State Normal and Industrial College (now the University of North Carolina at Greensboro) from 1892 to 1894.

Wooten worked as an art instructor at the Arkansas School for the Deaf, and established an art program at the Georgia School for the Deaf. She returned to New Bern, Arkansas, from a broken marriage with two young sons and the problems of earning a living. With the help of friends she sold hand-painted calendars and other merchandise and soon pasted photographs on the calendars. Then she read everything she could find on the subject, studied with the photographer Nace Brock (1908), received commissions for portraits and other subjects—all of which led to her becoming a first-rate photographer.

In time Wooten became the official photographer at Fort Bragg, North Carolina; she held the same post for the Carolina Playmakers; and was the yearbook photographer for the University of North Carolina, Chapel Hill (1920–1940).

Wooten's work is represented in private and public permanent collections, including the University of North Carolina at Chapel Hill, and others. "Mrs. Holyfield" (c. 1930–1934) shows Wooten at her best: revealing the inner dignity as well as the outer reality of a mountain woman of the Blue Ridge country, seated in a chair, hands folded on her lap, an enigmatic smile on her wrinkled face.

Bibliography
Nine from North Carolina: An Exhibition of Women Artists. Essay by Caroline Mesrobian Hickman. The North Carolina State Committee and The National Museum of Women in the Arts, Washington, D.C., 1989.

Wörner Baz, Marysole (1936–)

Born in Mexico, Marysole Wörner Baz exhibited her paintings for the first time in 1955. She honed her approach to painting by working in Paris, France (1957). Examples of her work are in the Museo de Bellas Artes, Mexico City, Mexico; the Museum of Modern Art, Tel Aviv, Israel; and in Birmingham, Alabama, and the Art Center in Texas.

Wörner Baz has also executed stone sculptures and has had solo shows in the Galerías Proteo, Mexico; and New York City; Galería Merkup, Mexico City (annually, since 1961); the Palacio de Bellas Artes, Mexico City, los Museos de Arte y Historia, Ciudades Juárez and Monterrey—all in Mexico; and in group exhibitions in the United States, France, Canada, and Venezuela.

Bibliography
Alvarez, José Rogelio, et al. *Enciclopedia de Mexico.* Secretaría de Educación Pública, 1987.

Wright, Alice Morgan (1881–1975)

One of the earliest American modernist sculptors, Alice Morgan Wright was a native of Albany, New York. After graduation from Smith College, Northampton, Massachusetts, in 1904, she pursued art study in New York City at the Art Students League under Hermon Atkins MacNeil and James Earle Fraser. In 1909, the year her work was first exhibited at the National Academy of Design, New York City, she sailed for Paris, France, where she enrolled in classes at the Académie Colarossi. While abroad she exhibited at the Paris Girls Club (1910); at the Royal Academy in London, England (1911), at the Paris Salon (1912), and at the Salon d'Automne, also in Paris (1913). Also during this period Wright became actively involved in the women's suffrage movement, and, in 1912, travelled to London to participate in a public demonstration. She was arrested and jailed in Holloway Prison with Emmeline Pankhurst. Wright continued to campaign for votes for women in America.

Returning to the United States in 1914, Wright established a studio in Macdougal Alley in New York, and soon became involved with the avant-garde. Marius de Zayas presented her work at his Modern Gallery in 1916, and, in 1917, she participated at the first exhibition mounted by the Society of Independent Artists. Wright was fascinated by modern dance, and several of her sculptures were inspired by Isadora Duncan, Ruth St. Denis, and Waslaw Nijinsky. She maintained her New York City studio until about 1920, when she returned to Albany, New York. By 1930 Wright had ceased to sculpt and exhibit her work. She was increasingly absorbed by animal welfare and became internationally famous for her activist work for the humane treatment of animals. Her sculpture is in the permanent collection of the Hirshhorn Museum and Sculpture Garden and the Folger Shakespeare Library—both in Washington, D.C.; the Albany Institute of History and Art, New York; and Brookgreen Gardens, South Carolina.

Betsy Fahlman

Bibliography
Alice Morgan Wright Papers. Northampton, Massachusetts, Smith College, Sophia Smith Collection.
Fahlman, Betsy. *Sculpture and Suffrage: The Art and Life of Alice Morgan Wright (1881–1975)*. New York: Albany Institute of History and Art, 1978.
Marter, Joan, Roberta K. Tarbell, and Jeffrey Wechsler. *Vanguard American Sculpture 1913–1939*. Rutgers University Art Gallery, 1979.
Rubinstein, Charles Streifer. *American Women Artists*. G.K. Hall, 1982.
———. *American Women Sculptors: A History of Women Working in Three Dimensions*. G.K. Hall, 1990.

Wright, Catherine Morris (1899–)

Born in Philadelphia, Pennsylvania, the painter Catherine Morris Wright studied at the Pennsylvania Academy of Fine Arts, Philadelphia, and with Leopold Seyffert and Henry B. Snell.

Winner of honors and awards, Wright received an honorable mention at an exhibition of the Philadelphia Art Club (1924), among others. She exhibited in many galleries and associations, including "C.M. Wright, A.N.A.: Retrospective Exhibition 1915–1951," Newport Art Association, Rhode Island (1952); "Catherine Morris Wright Retrospective Exhibition," Woodmere Art Gallery, Philadelphia, Pennsylvania (1954); and others.

An associate of the National Academy of Design, New York City, Wright was also a member of several arts organizations, including the American Federation of Arts, Washington, D.C.; American Watercolor Society and the New York Watercolor Club—both in New York City; Baltimore Watercolor Club, Maryland; and Newport Art Association, Rhode Island. Her work is represented in private and public permanent collections.

Bibliography
American Art Annual. Vol. 28. American Federation of Arts, 1932.
Huber, Christine Jones. *The Pennsylvania Academy and Its Women*. Pennsylvania Academy of Fine Arts, 1973.
Watts, Harvey M. "The Art of Catherine Morris Wright." *Art and Archeology* 32 (July–August 1931): 17–27.
Wright, Catherine Morris. *The Color of Life*. Houghton Mifflin, 1957.

Wrinch, Mary Evelyn (1877–1969)

Painter and printmaker Mary Evelyn Wrinch was born in Kirby-le-Soken, Essex, England. She emmigrated to Canada in 1885, settling in Bronte, Ontario. Wrinch first studied art while enrolled at Bishop Strachan School in Toronto where she attended a china painting class. At the age of sixteen she entered the Central School of Art (now the Ontario College of Art), studying under Robert Holmes, G.A. Reid, and Laura Muntz. Intrigued at an early age by the art of painting miniatures, Wrinch studied under miniature painter Alyn Williams, at the Grosvenor Life School in London, England, in 1897; she also took courses in life drawing under Walter Donne. In 1899 she continued her study of miniature painting under Alice Beckington at the Art League (later the Art Students League) in New York City.

Wrinch first exhibited her work at the age of seventeen at the annual Ontario Society of Artists Exhibition in 1894. She was elected a member of the Ontario Society of Artists in 1901 and was the first woman to become an officer in a major Canadian arts orga-nization when she was elected vice-president and treasurer from 1924 to 1925. Elected an associate of the Royal Canadian Academy in 1918, Wrinch was also a member of the Society of Canadian Painter-Etchers and Engravers and the Canadian Handicraft Association. Wrinch became the second wife to her former instructor, G.A. Reid, in 1922.

While her early miniature paintings met with critical approval, Wrinch decided to turn her attention to painting the Canadian landscape. She was one of the first Canadian artists to visit Northern Ontario, having stayed in a cottage on Lake Muskoka as early as 1906. Her work is characterized by its rich colors and flat patterning which was influenced by Gauguin and is shown in such works as "After a Snowfall" (1920). Around 1928 Wrinch began the final phase of her career by making linoleum block prints. In these works Wrinch continued to use bold colors and a decorative approach. She used as many as nine different blocks for her prints, which depicted themes of the Canadian north as well as flowers from her garden in Wychwood Park, Toronto.

Linda Jansma

Bibliography
Dickman, Chris. *The Prints of Mary Wrinch*. Durham Art Gallery, 1980.
Murray, Joan. "Mary Wrinch: Canadian Artist." *Canadian Collector* (September 1969): 16–19.

Wyle, Florence (1881–1968)

Born in Trenton, Illinois, Florence Wyle seemed an unlikely candidate to become a well-known sculptor in Canada, which fostered very little sculpture beyond commemorative monuments in the early part of the century. She took pre-medical studies at the University of Illinois, Urbana, from 1900, but in 1903 she abruptly transferred to the school of the Art Institute of Chicago, Illinois. There, in 1905, she met Frances Loring, with whom she was to spend her entire life after 1909.

Wyle taught modelling at the Art Institute of Chicago between 1906 and 1909, and she received her first major commission from that institute in 1907. After a stay in New York City she moved to Toronto in 1913 to join Loring, who had gone there the year before. The two artists were personally and professionally inseparable from that point on. Both were members of many artists' organizations, and both tirelessly promoted the cause of sculpture in Canada, as hostesses—they were known as "the Girls"—artists, and jurists. They particularly encouraged younger women sculptors, including Frances Gage and Elizabeth Wyn Wood. In 1920 both joined the Ontario Society of Artists, but withdrew in 1933, when all the sculptor members formed a new Sculptor's Society of Canada. They were reinstated in 1948. The Royal Canadian Academy welcomed Wyle as an associate from 1920, but she was not a full member until 1938, when she became the first female sculptor so recognized. In 1953 she won a Coronation medal for her endeavors.

Wyle received a number of commissions for memorials in her lifetime, but her most endearing works are smaller, more intimate figures. In them one can find traces of the work of sculptors as varied as F.W. MacMonnies, Augustus Saint-Gaudens, Aristide Maillol, and even Constantin Brancusi. Her work, however, never became abstract. Wyle had a great feeling for natural materials and polished, idealized surfaces. Her "Draped Torso" (1939) and "Sea and Shore" (c. 1950) are reminiscent of the handling of the figure in Hiram Power's famous "Greek Slave" of 1843. Wyle's works, however, are thoroughly modern in the truncation of the limbs and stylization of certain surface features.

Little scholarly attention was paid to her work until 1983, when her estate made a substantial donation of works to the Art Gallery of Ontario, Toronto, which mounted an excellent, comprehensive critical exhibition in 1987.

Robert J. Belton

Bibliography
Boyanoski, Christine. *Loring and Wyle: Sculptors' Legacy*, 1987.
Sisler, Rebecca. *The Girls: A Biography of Frances Loring and Florence Wyle*, 1972.

Y

Yamaguchi, Yuriko (1948–)

A native of Osaka, Japan, Yuriko Yamaguchi was already twenty-three years old when she emigrated to the United States with her family. She has now spent another twenty-four years in her adopted country, where she has made both her career and her home.

In 1974 Yamaguchi earned a Bachelor of Arts degree at the University of California, Berkeley, and, in the same year, had her first one-person show at the Japanese Cultural Center, San Francisco, California. By that time she had already participated in four juried group exhibitions, and decided that she wanted to continue her formal education. After a year of directed studies at Princeton University, New Jersey, Yamaguchi moved to the Washington, D.C., area, where she has lived ever since. As a graduate student (in the painting department) at the University of Maryland, College Park, Yamaguchi worked with Richard Klank and Anne Truitt, and eventually determined that her principal interest lay in three-dimensional art. She received her Master of Fine Arts degree in sculpture from the University of Maryland in 1979.

From the beginning her sculptural work—small, carved, and painted wooden shapes, typically attached to the wall to form intriguing patterns—was recognized by teachers and critics for its originality and strength. After a period working as a commercial designer (while her husband pursued his own postgraduate education) Yamaguchi decided to devote herself to making art full time. Since 1980 her work has appeared in numerous group exhibitions on both the east and west coasts of the United States, in Germany, and Japan.

Yamaguchi has had one-person exhibitions at the Foundry Gallery (1981), Gallery 10 (1982), Gallery K (1984), the Washington Project for the Arts (1984), and the Middendorf Gallery (1987, 1989)—all in Washington, D.C. She is currently represented in that city by the Baumgartner Gallery, where she had a solo show in the spring of 1993, and by the Penine Hart Gallery in New York City. In recent years Yamaguchi has begun to work on a larger scale and to receive public commissions.

Yamaguchi has work in numerous private and public collections, including the Paper Museum, Tokyo, Japan; the Hyatt Regency Hotel, Washington, D.C.; and the Artery Organization, Bethesda, Maryland. In 1985 she won first place in "Artquest," sponsored by the University Museum of California State University; she has also received Virginia Museum fellowships (1985–1986, 1988–1989), a Mid-Atlantic States visual arts residency grant (1986–1987), and many other awards. The artist has also taught—at the Art League School, Alexandria, Virginia (1980–1983) and the University of Maryland, College Park (1982–1984, 1986); since 1988 she has been on the faculty of the Corcoran School of Art, Washington, D.C.

Bibliography

Lewis, Jo Ann. "Finding Her Form, Locally." *The Washington Post* (October 27, 1984): C2.

Smith, Linda Thern. "An Interview with Washington Sculptor Yuriko Yamaguchi." *Washington Review* (April–May 1985): 24–25.

Yampolsky, Mariana (1925–)

Mariana Yampolsky, a versatile Mexican artist best known for her photography, was born in Chicago, Illinois, on September 6, 1925. She moved to Mexico and became a citizen of that country after completing her Bachelor of Arts degree in the humanities at the University of Chicago, Illinois (1945). She enrolled in laEscuela de Pintura y Escultura (La Esmeralda) in Mexico City in 1945 and joined the Taller de Gráfica Popular, Mexico's outstanding graphic arts center, where she worked as a printmaker until 1958. She also studied photography with Lola Alvarez Bravo at the prestigious Academia de San Carlos—both in Mexico City. Her projects during that period included illustrations for several publications under the direction of the Bauhaus architect, Hannes Meyer.

Yampolsky was a founding member of the Salón de la Plástica Mexicana (1951) and worked as an illustrator for several major newspapers, including *El Nacional, Excelsior,* and *El Día,* from 1956 to 1962. During the latter part of that period (1960–1962) she also travelled extensively in Europe and the Near East.

In 1963 Yampolsky collaborated in the making of Carmen Toscano's documentary film about the Mexican Revolution, *Memorias de un Mexicano,* and served as an advisor to the Fondo Editorial de la Plástica Mexicana for a book on a great printmaker, José Guadalupe Posada. During the next few years (1964–1967) she co-edited, with artist Leopoldo Méndez, the book *Lo Efímero y Eterno del Arte Popular Mexicano,* published by the Fondo Editorial de la Plástica Mexicana in 1970; her responsibilities included intensive research and photography of popular art throughout the country. Following that project she served as photographer for the Olympic Committee at the 1968 Summer Olympics in Mexico City.

In the early 1970s Yampolsky worked as a planner and graphic coordinator of a series of government-produced free textbooks for school children. Later (1978–1981) she edited illustrated children's books (*Enciclopedia Infantil Colibri*) as well as a series of art books for the Secretaría de Educación Pública and Editorial Salvat.

The first book of Yampolsky's own photographs, *La Casa en la Tierra,* was published in 1981, with an introductory text by Elena Poniatowska. Other books followed: *El Casa que Canta, El Raíz y el Camino,* and *Estancias del Olvido,* also with introductions by Elena Poniatowska. Much of her photography (she works exclusively in black and white) concerns the daily life of ordinary people and the popular architecture of rural Mexico.

Yampolsky's graphic art and photography have been exhibited in Japan at "Arte Mexicano" (1955); the United States at a solo exhibition at the Center for Creative Photography, Tucson, Arizona (1980); Switzerland at "Fotografie Latinamerika," Kunsthaus, Zurich (1981); Norway at "Mexikansk Fotografi," a solo exhibition at Gallery Cannon, Milan, Italy; England, a solo exhibition at Photographers' Gallery, London (1985); Cuba, Australia, and Mexico at "Exposición Internacional de Mujeres Fotógrafas," a travelling show (1975); "Mexico-Berlin, la Creación Feminina," Goethe Institut (1980); 1st and 2nd "Muestra de Fotografía Latinoamericana Contemporánea" (1978, 1981); and numerous others. Her photographs are in collections in Mexico and abroad, including the Museo de Arte Moderno, Mexico City; California Museum of Photography; University of Chicago, Illinois; and others.

Martha Davidson

Bibliography
Yampolsky, Mariana. *La Casa en la Tierra.* Intro. by Elena Poniatowksa. Mexico City: Instituto Nacional Indigenista, 1981.
———. *El Raíz y el Camino.* Intro. by Elena Poniatowska. Mexico City: Secretaría de Educación Pública, 1985.
———. *La Casa que Canta.* Mexico City: Secretaría de Educación Pública, 1985.
———. *Estancias del Olvido.* Intro. by Elena Poniatowska. Mexico City: Educación Gráfica, 1987.

Yandell, Enid (1870–1934)

Born in Louisville, Kentucky, the figurative sculptor Enid Yandell studied at the Cincinnati Art Academy, Ohio; worked as an assistant to Karl Bittner in New York City; and studied in Paris, France, with Frederick MacMonnies.

Yandell produced the caryatids that supported the roof garden of the Women's Building at the Chicago Exposition, Illinois (1893); "Pallas Athene," a monumental work for the Nashville Exposition, Tennessee (1897); the Carrie Brown Memorial Fountain, Providence, Rhode Island (1901); and others. She exhibited a work in the infamous Armory Show, New York City (1913); executed many portrait busts and other small-scale works; designed a tankard for Tiffany's; was a member of the National Sculpture Society, New York City; and taught on Martha's Vineyard, Massachusetts. Examples of her work are in private and public permanent collections.

Bibliography
Clement, Clara Erskine. *Women in the Fine Arts.* Houghton Mifflin, 1904.
Rubinstein, Charlotte Streifer. *American Women Artists.* G.K. Hall, 1982.
Taft, Lorado. *The History of American Sculpture.* Macmillan, 1924.

Yáñez, Puri (1936–)

Born in Murcia, Spain, Puri Yáñez arrived in Mexico with her parents, who were political refugees, when she was three years old. She studied interior decoration at the University of Women, Mexico City (1952–1955) after an academic education and, knowing that she wanted to be an artist, went to the Ibero-American University, Mexico City, to study under the aegis of Jorge González Camarena (1956–1958).

A painter affiliated with the "school" of surrealism, Yáñez has participated in thirty-one exhibitions, thirteen of which were solo shows. Her first solo show occurred in 1965 at the Galería Excelsior, under the auspices of the National Institute of Fine Arts, Mexico City. Yáñez also had solo exhibitions at the Galería José Maria Velasco and the Galería Chapultepec. Coincident with the 1968 Cultural Olympics, her work was included in several group shows. Her outstanding exhibitions include "Arte y Libros," Monterrey (1976); "Homenaje a Federico García Lorca," Galería Pro Arte (1977); "Las Leyendas de las Calles de Mexico," Museo de la Ciudad de Mexico (1978); "Surrealismo de Puri Yáñez," the Italian embassy in Mexico (1981); "Magia y Fantasia," Instituto Mexicano-Norteamericano de Relaciones Culturales (1983); and "25 Oleos," Galería El Agora (1984)—all in Mexico. Yáñez has also exhibited her work abroad.

Bibliography
Alvarez, José Rogelio, et al. *Enciclopedia de Mexico.* Secretaría de Educación Pública, 1987.
The Texas Quarterly: Image of Mexico II. The University of Texas, Autumn 1969.

Yang, Yan-Ping (1934–)

Born in Beijing, China, Yan-Ping Yang is best known for her large-scale paintings of lotus flowers, rocky landscapes, and abstracted paintings of calligraphy. She received a degree in architecture from Qinghua University in 1958 and worked as an architect for eight years before being granted a transfer to the art designing section at Beijing Art Company. Within two years Yang was allowed to enter the oil painting section at Beijing Art Company and continued her independent study of traditional Chinese painting. In 1980 she became an artist of the Beijing Art Academy. In 1986 Yang and her husband, the artist Shan-qing Zeng, received fellowships from the Committee on Education Exchange with China at the State University of New York (SUNY) at Stony Brook, where Yang and Zeng were given visiting artist status from the University's department of art.

Yang began exhibiting her work in 1974 when she participated in a group exhibition at the Chinese National History Museum in Beijing. She subsequently participated in many group exhibitions at the Chinese National Fine Art Museum in Beijing and the Beijing Artists Association. Her paintings were included in a number of group exhibitions sent from China to Japan, France, and America. These included a travelling exhibition entitled "Contemporary Chinese Painting: An Exhibition from the People's Republic of China" that was shown in San Francisco, California; New York City; Ithaca, New York; Denver, Colorado; Indianapolis, Indiana; Kansas City, Missouri; Minneapolis, Minnesota; and Birmingham, Alabama. In 1985 Yang's work appeared in a two-person exhibition at BAWAG Art Gallery in Vienna, Austria. Yang's first one-person exhibition was held in the Chinese Artists' Gallery at the Chinese National Fine Arts Museum in Beijing in 1985. Since her arrival in the United States she has had nearly twenty one- and two-person shows in the United States, Europe, Japan, and Taiwan. Her solo exhibitions have been presented by the Johnson Gallery at Middlebury College, Vermont (1987); the United Nations in Vienna, Austria (1987); Gallery Beer-Sheeba in Tokyo, Japan (1987); Gallery Vindobona in Bad Kissingen, Germany (1988); Takashimaya Art Gallery in Tokyo, Japan (1989, 1990); the World Bank Art Society, Washington, D.C. (1990); Hsiung Shih Art Gallery, Taipei, Taiwan (1990); Davidson Gallery, Seattle, Washington (1991); and Alisan Fine Arts Gallery in Hong Kong (1991). Her group shows have included "Contemporary Chinese Painting" at the Krannert Art Museum, University of Illinois, Champaign, Illinois (1988); "The Faculty Show '91" at the University Art Gallery at SUNY, Stony Brook (1991); "Chinese Women Artists Show" at the Chinese Culture Foundation of San Francisco, California (1991); and "Collecting the 20th Century" at the British Museum, London, England (1991), which included her painting "Lotus" (1985).

Yang's paintings are in numerous private and public collections throughout the world, including the British Museum, London, England; the Beijing Artists' Association, the National Historical Museum in Beijing—both in China; Hobart and William Smith College, Geneva, New York; Miami University, Oxford, Ohio; and the Krannert Art Museum in Champaign, Illinois. She has served as an artist-in-residence at SUNY at Stony Brook since her arrival in 1986. She has also served as an artist-in-residence at the Austrian Summer Institute in Vienna during the summers of 1985, 1986, and 1987 and at Miami University in Oxford, Ohio, in the fall in 1986.

Yang's paintings include elements of both traditional Chinese painting and the Western art she learned as a student in China. Her lifelong interests in Chinese poetry, literature, and Taoism have strongly influenced her work. Like the scholar-painters of eleventh-century China, Yang maintains that the purpose of painting is to express the mind of the artist and not to formally represent the natural world. When laboring in the Chinese countryside during the Cultural Revolution, Yang used her rest periods to sketch from life. Her direct observations of the changes in color and light during various times and seasons greatly influenced her later work.

With the end of the Cultural Revolution, Yang was able to begin the perfection of her own innovative style. The paintings she made between 1978 and 1981, such as "Mountain Spirit" and "Towering Mountain," were done in a very fine line against subdued mottled backgrounds and were often thematically grounded in Chinese literature. During the 1980s Yang focused on landscapes and on paintings of calligraphy that are expressionistic renditions of poems and thoughts of the artist. In "Cai nu de gao" (literally, "Talent woman virtue high") Yang abstracted archaic Chinese characters to produce a painting that uses both picture and text to reveal the mind of the artist.

Yang began painting lotus flowers in 1981. Admired in China for its beauty and purity, the lotus was a traditional Buddhist symbol. Yang's memories of a lotus pond near her home in Beijing, where she first became interested in how the lotus plant changed with the seasons, served as the inspiration for her paintings. Between 1981 and 1989 Yang painted many images of the lotus pond, especially in the late autumn and early winter when the plants begin to bend with adversity. In "Deep Autumn" (1985), the intertwining pink and gray lotus stalks are depicted amid the bold red, purple, orange, and black lotus leaves. In "Winter Lotus Pond" (1991), Yang uses wetter inktones and overlapping forms to capture the stillness and beauty of the pond. Recent landscape paintings, such as "Morning with Mist" (1990) and "Snow Peak of a Rocky Mountain" (1991) continue to focus on texture and color. They depict mountains and snow very differently from the way in which they are depicted in traditional Chinese landscape painting, although Yang retains the convention of a high horizon line. Yang has said that she was influenced by the sight of the Rocky Mountains in the western United States. The colors, shapes, and surface patterns she uses derive neither from traditional Chinese forms nor from Western art; rather, they reflect her own unique style while retaining the strength and capturing the essence of her subject as did the best work of China's scholar-painters. Her evocative and powerful style continues to evolve as she searches within herself for something that is neither Chinese nor Western but uniquely her own.

Rhonda Cooper

Bibliography

Cahill, James. "Painting of Yang Yan-Ping." *Hsiung Shih Art Monthly* (December 1990): 146–53.

———. "The Paintings of Yang Yan-Ping." *Lotus/Landscape/Yang Yan-Ping*. Taiwan: Hsiung Shih Art Books Company, 1990.

Cohen, Joan Lebold. *The New Chinese Painting 1949–1986*. Harry N. Abrams, 1987, pp. 55, 128–30.

Kiyohi Ko Munakata. "Bright Starts in a New Era." *Contemporary Chinese Painting*. Exhibition Catalog. Krannert Art Museum, 1983.

Sullivan, Michael. "The Calligraphic Works of Yang Yan-Ping." *Apollo* 291 (May 1986): 346–49.

Yaegashi, Haruki. *Yang Yan-Ping Exhibition*. Exhibition Catalog. Tokyo: Gallery Beer-Sheeba, 1987.

Yanik, Dorothy Cavalier

Painter, printmaker, teacher, and designer—Dorothy Cavalier Yanik in recent years has devoted most of her time to extremely subtle and articulately modulated prints and drawing as well as teaching at the Carnegie-Mellon University in Pittsburgh, Pennsylvania, and, most recently, at the Maryland Institute College of Art in Baltimore.

Yanik studied at Yale University, New Haven, Connecticut, under Josef Albers, earning a Bachelor of Fine Arts degree in 1963, and at the Maryland Institute College of Art where she received a Master of Fine Arts degree in 1975. Prior to her work at Carnegie-Mellon University, Yanik taught at the Philadelphia College of Art, Pennsylvania (1965–1967); Catholic University (1977–1978), Trinity College (1973–1979), and American University (1975–1982)—all in Washington, D.C.; and Arizona State University, Tempe, Arizona (1982–1984).

Yanik has participated in numerous solo and group exhibitions, the most recent being a selection of her work at the Franz Bader Gallery in Washington, D.C., in 1989. Yanik is a slow, meticulous worker, and her brilliantly crafted realism is in many public and private collections, including the U.S. State Department Art Bank; Millbank, Tweed, Hadley & McCloy of New York and Los Angeles; University Museum Art Collections, Arizona State University, Tempe; and EMI Records, New York City. Her prints are currently represented by Orion Editions and Gallery in New York City and the Jane Haslem Gallery in Washington, D.C. Yanik has also collaborated with a master photographer creating two editions at the Photography Collaborative Facility and with a master printer on a collograph edition at the Print Research Facility—both at Arizona State University, Tempe, in 1983–1984. She has also lectured at various colleges throughout the country and served as a juror for numerous exhibitions.

Larry Day

Bibliography
American Drawings: Realism/Idealism. Boca Raton Museum, Florida, 1987.
Arizona Highways (October 1985).
Recent Work and Catalogue Raisonné. Tempe, Arizona: Visual Arts Research Institute, Arizona State University, 1986.
"The Nation." *Art News* (December 1980).
22nd Area Exhibition: Works on Paper. Exhibition Catalog. Washington, D.C.: Corcoran Gallery of Art, 1980.
U.S. Department of State—Art Bank. Exhibition Catalog, 1988.

Yanish, Elizabeth (1922–)

Born in St. Louis, Missouri, Elizabeth Yanish is known for her abstract bronze, steel, or wood sculptures. Yanish studied at Washington University in her native city, and also at Denver University, Colorado; and with Edgar Britton, Angelo Di Benedetto, Frank Vavra, and Wilbur Verhelst.

Yanish has held many solo exhibitions in the United States and abroad, including the Beaux-Arts Gallery (1962), and International House (1963)—both in Denver, Colorado; Contemporaries Gallery, Santa Fe, New Mexico (1963); 7th Red Door (1964), Southern Colorado State College (1966)—both in Pueblo, Colorado; Woodstock Gallery, London, England (1973); a retrospective show at L.B. Baumerder Gallery, Denver, Colorado (1982); and others. Her work has been invited to group exhibitions in the United States and abroad: from Newport, Rhode Island, to Salt Lake City, Utah; Oklahoma City, Oklahoma; Lucca, Italy; Greeley, Colorado; Muncie, Indiana; and others.

Yanish has served as an art juror, member, and past-president of several professional art organizations; has given lecture/demonstrations before art club audiences, public schools, and colleges; and has completed interior sculptures for churches and public buildings, such as the Beth Israel Hospital, BMH Synagogue, Colorado State Bank, Colorado Women's College, and Denver General Hospital—all in Denver, Colorado; Congregation Har Ha-Sham, Boulder, and the Faith Bible Chapel, Arvada—both in Colorado.

Yanish has received awards and honors, including first place in the First Annual National Space Art Exhibition, U.S. Air Force Academy, Colorado Springs, Colorado (1962); the McCormick Award, Ball State Teachers College, Muncie, Indiana (1964); and a first prize at the American Association of University Women's annual exhibition, Southern Colorado State College, Pueblo (1968). Her work is represented in private and public permanent collections.

Bibliography
Manson, John. "Elizabeth Yanish: Sculptor." *Artists of the Rockies* 1:1 (Winter 1974): 10–11.
Who's Who in American Art. 19th ed. R.R. Bowker Co., 1991–1992.

Yazbek, Charlotte

Born in Puebla, Mexico, the sculptor Charlotte Yazbek studied clay modelling, direct carving, drawing, and painting with Uxio Souto, Hermilo Casteñeda, Pedro Medina Guzmán, and Mathias Goeritz (1952–1962). From 1970 to 1976 she was consultant in artisanry for the government of Mexico.

From 1960 to 1987 Yazbek participated in thirty-four group exhibitions, one of which was outside of Mexico, at Universal Studios, Beverly Hills, California. Her solo shows include the Galerías Fulton (1963, 1964); Art Collector, New York City (1967); Weintraub, Beverly Hills, California (1965); Du Bose (1968) of Texas; and the Mexican Pavilion of the World's Fair in New York City (1964).

Yazbek's sculpture is in many permanent collections including eighteen monumental works in the Parque Cuautitlán Izcalli in the state of Mexico; the group, "La Familia," in the Unidad Adolfo López Mateos; twelve works in the gardens of La Escondida, in Avándaro; a portrait of Carlos "Hank" González in Santiago Tianguistengo; and seven bronzes and many others in the Centro de Servicios Administrativos of the Nation, including "Adagio II" (Ciudad Nezahualcóyotl), "Los Novios" (Ecatepec), "Vendedor de Esperanzas" (Tlalnepantla), "Cazador de Estrellas" (Atlacomulco), "El último Unicornio" (Valle de bravo), and "Buscador de Pájaros" and "Muchacha de la Luna" (Toluca). Other works include "Los Novios," in the Paseo de los Niños Héroes, in Chapultepec; "Adagio," in the rotunda of the Paseo de los Niños Héroes; "El Hombre Roto," in the Museo de Arte Moderno; and the busts of Habib Estéfano and Antonio Fajer in the Galería de Hombres Ilustres del Centro Libanés—all in Mexico City.

Salvador Elizando, in the book, *Charlotte Yazbek*, wrote, "I feel that this artist has managed to arrive at the ideal point at which she realizes her internal harmony and the harmonious relationship that obtains between her sculpture and the space in which it dwells. That is to say, the harmony between nature and art." Among her little-known pictorial work is a notable self-portrait (1981).

Bibliography

Alvarez, José Rogelio, et al. *Enciclopedia de Mexico*. Secretaría de
    Educación Pública, 1987.
Elizondo, Salvador. *Charlotte Yazbek*.

Youngblood, Daisy (1945–)

Born in Ashville, North Carolina, the ceramist Daisy Youngblood studied at Virginia Commonwealth University, Richmond (1963–1967).
Youngblood is a figurative ceramist who does not deal in metaphor;
her work deals with the harsh realities of today.

Bibliography

Henry, Gerrit. "Daisy Youngblood at Barbara Gladstone." *Art in America*
    72 (April 1984).
McTwigan, Michael. *In the Eye of the Beholder: A Portrait of Our Time*. State
    University of New York at New Palz, 1985.
Silverthorne, Jeanne. "Daisy Youngblood." *Artforum* (April 1984).

Z

Zeitlin, Harriet (1929–)

Born in Philadelphia, Pennsylvania, the painter/printmaker Harriet Zeitlin earned a Bachelor of Fine Arts degree at the University of Pennsylvania and the Pennsylvania Academy of Fine Arts—both in Philadelphia—on a four-year scholarship (1946–1950). She did additional study at the Barnes Foundation, Merion, Pennsylvania (1948–1950); enrolled in printmaking classes at the University of California at Los Angeles (UCLA) (1963–1969); and studied photography at Santa Monica City College, California (1980–1981).

Zeitlin has held solo exhibitions in galleries and museums, including Art Harris Gallery (1970), and Jacqueline Anhalt Gallery (1972, 1975)—both in Los Angeles, California; Weyhe Gallery, New York City (1976); United States Information Agency (USIA) Bicentennial Exhibition, a travelling show throughout India (1976); San Antonio Library, Texas (1983); Whittier College (1984), Santa Monica Library (1989), the Santa Barbara Museum of Art, and the Monterey Peninsula Museum of Art—all in California; and others. Her work has been invited to many group exhibitions throughout the United States, such as the "160th Annual," Pennsylvania Academy of Fine Arts, Philadelphia (1965); Pratt Institute, New York City (1968); "Collage and Assemblage," Los Angeles Institute of Contemporary Art, California (1975); Suzanne Gross Gallery, Philadelphia, Pennsylvania (1979); "Three from Los Angeles," Riverside Museum, California (1984); "Wall Works," L.A. Art Core, California (1986); "Women and the U.S. Constitution," Atlanta College of Art, Georgia (1988); Bernice Steinbaum Gallery, New York City (1990); and others.

Zeitlin has taught printmaking, mask making, quiltmaking, and painting in public and private university extension classes, and in her own studio—to children and adults throughout the Santa Monica and Los Angeles, California, area. She has won prizes and awards for her work, including second prize, Atlanta College of Art, Georgia (1988), and grants from the California Arts Council (1977–1978), and the City of Los Angeles (1990–1991)—both in California. Her work is represented in private, public, and corporate permanent collections, including the Los Angeles County Museum of Art, University of California at Los Angeles (UCLA), and Fluor Corporation, Irvine—all in California; Library of Congress, Washington, D.C.; the U.S. Embassy, New Delhi, India; and others.

Bibliography

Women and the Constitution. A Catalog. Georgia: Atlanta College of Art, 1988.
The Definitive Contemporary American Quilt. A Catalog. New York City: Bernice Steinbaum Gallery, 1990.
Who's Who in American Art. 19th ed. R.R. Bowker Co., 1991–1992.

Zelt, Martha (1930–)

Born in Washington, Pennsylvania, the printmaker Martha Zelt earned a Bachelor's degree from Temple University, Philadelphia, Pennsylvania. She also studied at Connecticut College, New London; the Pennsylvania Academy of Fine Arts, Philadelphia; the New School for Social Research, New York City, with Antonio Frasconi; Museo Arte Moderno, São Paulo, Brazil, with Johnny Friedlaender; and the University of New Mexico, Albuquerque, with Garo Antreasian.

Lithographs and other works by Zelt have appeared in many group exhibitions in the United States and abroad, including the International Biennale, São Paulo, Brazil (1961); the Annual National Exhibitions at the Pennsylvania Academy of Fine Arts, Philadelphia (1961–1970); "30 Years of American Printmaking," Brooklyn Museum, New York (1976); and "New Ways with Paper," National Collection of Fine Arts, Washington, D.C. Her solo exhibitions include the Peale Galleries, Pennsylvania Academy of Fine Arts (1972), and the Print Club, Philadelphia (1975)—both in Pennsylvania; Brooklyn Museum, New York (1980); Carnegie Institute, Pittsburgh, Pennsylvania (1981); Tamarind Institute, Albuquerque, New Mexico (1983, 1986); and many others.

Zelt's academic career has encompassed the teaching of printmaking at the Pennsylvania Academy (1968–1982); the Philadelphia College of Art (now the University of the Arts) (1969–1982)—both in Pennsylvania; and the University of North Carolina at Chapel Hill (1981). She was chair of the department of art, Virginia Intermont College, Bristol (1985–1989); and distinguished visiting professor, University of Delaware, Newark (1988–1989).

Zelt has received many honors and awards, including the Cresson travelling award (1954) and the Scheidt memorial travelling award from the Pennsylvania Academy of Fine Arts and a fellowship from the Print Club (1965)—both in Philadelphia, Pennsylvania; and a grant from the Roswell Museum, New Mexico (1982). Her work is represented in private and public permanent collections, including the Brooklyn Museum, New York; Carnegie Institute, Pittsburgh, Pennsylvania Academy of Fine Arts, Philadelphia, and Philadelphia Museum of Art—all in Pennsylvania; Princeton University, New Jersey; and others.

Bibliography
Romano, Clare, and John Ross. *The Complete Printmaker*. Macmillan, 1990.

Zimmerman, Elyn (1945–)

Born in Philadelphia, Pennsylvania, the sculptor/environmental artist Elyn Zimmerman earned a Bachelor's degree from the University of California at Los Angeles (UCLA) (1968), and, four years later, was awarded a Master of Fine Arts degree from the same institution, having worked with Robert Irwin and Richard Diebenkorn.

Zimmerman has held solo exhibitions in museums and galleries in the United States and abroad, including the University Art Museum, Berkeley (1974), California Institute of Technology, Pasadena (1975)—both in California; Institute for Art and Urban Resources, P.S.1, New York City (1977); Museum of Contemporary Art, Chicago, Illinois (1979); Galleria del Cavallino, Venice, Italy (1981); Hudson River Museum, Yonkers, New York (1982); University of South Florida, Tampa (1991); 65 Thompson Street, New York City (1992); and others. Her work has been invited to many group exhibitions, such as the "Whitney Biennial," Whitney Museum of American Art, New York City (1974); Biennale of Sydney, Australia (1976); "Eight Artists: The Elusive Image," Walker Art Center, Minneapolis, Minnesota (1979); "Drawings: The Pluralist Decade," Venice Biennale, Italy, and Institute for Contemporary Art, Philadelphia, Pennsylvania (1980); "Artist as Social Designer," Los Angeles County Museum of Art, California (1985); "Sculpture for Public Spaces," Marisa Del Re Gallery, New York City (1986); "Green," Max Protetch Gallery, New York City (1991); and others.

For more than a decade Zimmerman has completed large-scale, outdoor projects comprised of gardens, multiple water features, including waterfalls and pools, granite boulders, seating areas, and so forth, for private and public institutions, such as the National Geographic So-

ciety, Washington, D.C. (1984); O'Hare International Center, Chicago, Illinois (1987); Dade County Justice Center, North Miami, Florida (1989); First Market Tower Plaza, San Francisco, California (1991); and others.

Winner of awards and honors for her work, Zimmerman received a Japan-U.S. creative exchange fellowship (1981); a Bessie award for the set design of "Memory Theater of Giulio Camillo," New York City (1986); National Endowment for the Arts (NEA) fellowships (1976, 1980); and others. Her work is represented in private, public, and corporate permanent collections, such as the Los Angeles County Museum of Art, California; Whitney Museum of American Art, New York City; Neuberger Museum, SUNY at Purchase; Chase Manhattan Bank; General Mills Corporation; and many more.

Bibliography
Berman, Avis. "Public Sculpture's New Look." *Art News* 90:7 (September 1991).
Castagliola, M.E. "Elyn Zimmerman: Sanctuary." *Art Papers* (September–October 1991).
Rubenstein, Charlotte. *American Women Sculptors*. G.K. Hall, 1990.
Treib, Marc. *Elyn Zimmerman: A Decade of Projects*. A Catalog. 1988.

Zorach, Marguerite Thompson (1887–1968)

The painter Marguerite Thompson Zorach was an early exponent of Fauvism and Cubism in America. Born in Santa Rosa, California, and raised in Fresno, California, Zorach was taken to Paris, France, in 1908 by her aunt, Harriet Adelaide Harris, a teacher and amateur painter, and on the day of arrival she attended the Salon d'Automne, thus getting her first exposure to Fauvism. She remained for four years, meeting Gertrude Stein and Pablo Picasso, becoming a friend of Ossip Zadkine, and studying at La Palette, an art school run by John Duncan Fergusson, a "Post-Impressionist." This is the term Zorach would later use to describe herself, believing that it described all modern movements after impressionism, including Fauvism.

In 1911 Zorach exhibited at the Salon of the Société des Artistes Indépendents and at the Salon d'Automne—both in Paris, France—before she departed with her aunt on a trip around the world. While studying at La Palette she met William Zorach, another American artist, whom she married after her return to America in December 1912. Zorach and her husband lived in New York after their marriage and often spent their summers in New England. In 1923 they bought a farm in Maine, where the colder climate in the summers was conducive to their art and good for their two children. In her later work Zorach continued to apply her paint in brilliant, unmixed colors but combined with a more Cubistic style of sharp, wedge-shaped forms. She painted the human figure as well as landscapes.

Zorach exhibited California landscapes at the Royal Galleries in Los Angeles, California, in 1912 and had one of her works in the New York Armory Show of 1913. Both Zorach and her husband were in the Forum show at the Anderson Galleries, New York City, in 1916. She received a silver medal at the California Place of the Legion of Honor in 1919. Thereafter she had periodic solo exhibitions in New York City at such venues as the Montross Gallery (1923); several at the Downtown Gallery; Knoedler Galleries (1944); and Kraushaar Galleries (1953, 1957, 1962, 1968). She also did embroidered tapestries between 1918 and 1924. She became the founder and first president of the New York Society of Women Artists in 1925. Her work is in the permanent collections of the National Museum of American Art, the Whitney Museum of American Art, the Museum of Modern Art (MoMA), the Metropolitan Museum of Art—all in New York City; and the Newark Museum, New Jersey.

Eleanor Tufts

Bibliography

Rubenstein, Charlotte Streifer. *American Women Artists: From Early Indian Times to the Present.* G.K. Hall, 1982.

Tarbell, Robert K. *Marguerite Zorach: The Early Years, 1908–1920.* Smithsonian Institution, 1973.

Tufts, Eleanor. *American Women Artists, 1830–1930.* National Museum of Women in the Arts, 1987.

Zucker, Barbara M. (1940–)

Philadelphia, Pennsylvania-born sculptor Barbara M. Zucker took her Bachelor of Science degree from the University of Michigan, Ann Arbor, and then studied at the Cranbrook Academy of Design, Bloomfield Hills, Michigan, and the Kokoschka School of Vision, Austria, before finalizing her formal education with a Master of Arts degree at Hunter College, New York City. Zucker has taught at La Guardia Community College, Long Island, New York; Fordham University, New York City; Philadelphia College of Art, Pennsylvania; University of Vermont, Burlington; and Yale University, New Haven, Connecticut. She has been artist-in-residence at Florida State University, Tallahassee; and Princeton University, New Jersey.

While working at a New York City gallery in the 1960s, Zucker created sculptures in a figurative style in a series of works based on the common chair. In sculptures such as "Giraffe Chair" (1965), and "Alice-in-Land" (1967) she explored the known attributes of a chair while giving the form a more iconic presence. In the 1970s Zucker moved into installation pieces with work such as "Dragon Pearls" (1972). She also began to use a flocking material sprayed on metal as an intricate part of her sculptures. Two forms—fans and niches or arches—figure strongly in works of the late 1970s such as "Meeting Curves" (1979). In "Plume II" and "Cadillac Coral" (both 1980), Zucker continues to explore the fan shape, but creates a more totemic, monumental and formal form which appears also in "Three–Two" (1982). "Two Triangles" (1983), for the Old Greenwich public library, Connecticut, shows the continuance of this bolder, abstracted movement in her work. "Olive Oil" (1984) is an abstracted figurative form which Zucker hopes is the first of a series that will be motor-driven to interact with the viewer.

Zucker received a National Endowment for the Arts (NEA) fellowship grant in 1975 and a Reader's Digest fellowship award to work at Giverny in 1990. She has had solo shows at the A.I.R. Gallery, 112 Green Street Gallery, Robert Miller Gallery, Pam Adler Gallery, and the Sculpture Center—all in New York City. She was a co-founder of the A.I.R. Gallery in New York City in 1972 and an editorial assistant on *Art News* from 1974 to 1981. She is still an active contributor to varied journals including *Art News*, *Village Voice*, *Art Journal*, and *Women's Studies*.

Zucker's works appear in the permanent collections of the Whitney Museum of American Art and Chase Manhattan Bank—both in New York City, and the American Can Company.

Judith Sealy

Bibliography

Donadio, Emmie. "Coming Alive at a Certain Time." *Arts Magazine* 59 (June 1985): 78–81.

Faust, Gretchen. *Arts Magazine* 64 (September 1989): 93.

Stavitsky, Gail. *Arts Magazine* 60 (December 1985): 120.

Van Wagner, Judith Collischan. "Barbara Zucker's Activated Objects." *Arts Magazine* 59: (June 1985): 82–84.

Zwick, Rosemary (1925–)

Born in Chicago, Illinois, the printmaker/sculptor Rosemary Zwick earned a Bachelor of Fine Arts degree at the University of Iowa, Iowa City (1945), where she studied with Phillip Guston and Humberto Albrizio. She studied printmaking with Max Kahn in evening classes at the School of the Art Institute of Chicago, Illinois (1946–1947); took education courses at De Paul University (1947–1948); and studied aesthetics at the University of Illinois at Chicago Circle (1979)—all in Chicago, Illinois.

Zwick has held many solo exhibitions in galleries throughout the midwestern United States, including the Contemporary Arts Gallery (1950); Chicago Public Library (1953, 1963); Newman Brown Gallery (1953); Findlay Galleries (1956); Frank Ryan Gallery (1958); University of Chicago Center for Continuing Education (1965); Mundelein College (1968); Northeastern Illinois University (1969); and Old Town Art Center (1990)—all in Chicago, Illinois. She has also shown at the Alley Theater, Houston, Texas (1959); Indiana University, Bloomington (1964); Evanston Public Library, Illinois; and others. Her work has been invited to many group exhibitions throughout the United States, such as "Chicago Artists and Vicinity," Art Institute of Chicago, Illinois (1947–1952, 1954, 1956); Boston Society of Independent Artists, Massachusetts (1951, 1961); the Print Club, Philadelphia, Pennsylvania (1950, 1951); Library of Congress Print Annual, Washington, D.C. (1952); Union League of Chicago, Illinois (1955, 1974); Houston Museum of Modern Art, Texas (1956); Museum of Contemporary Craft, New York City (1957); Isaac Delgado Museum of Art, New Orleans, Louisiana (1958); Wichita Ceramic National Exhibitions, Kansas (1963, 1966, 1968); Chicago Historical Society, Illinois (1979); Indiana Museum of Art, South Bend (1992); and others.

Zwick has completed a number of ceramic relief and sculpture commissions at the Wonderland Shopping Center, Livonia, Michigan (1959); Motorola Company, Chicago (1960), Public Library, Bedford Park (1981), and the Unitarian Church, Evanston (1991)—all in Illinois, where she created a large ceramic relief and a seven-by-eighteen-foot acrylic mural. Her work is represented in private, public, and corporate permanent collections, including the Standard Oil Company of Indiana; U.S. Post Office, San Francisco, California; Antioch College, Yellow Springs, Ohio; various public schools in Phoenix, Arizona, Evanston, Illinois, and Reaves, Illinois; Motorola Company, Chicago, Illinois; and others.

Bibliography

Buchwald, Wesley. *Craftsmen in Illinois.* Illinois Art Education Association, 1965.

Kenny, John B. *Ceramic Design.* Chilton, 1963.

Redstone, Louis. "Art in Architecture." *Art Voices* (January–February 1981).

Who's Who in American Art. 19th ed. R.R. Bowker Co., 1991–1992.

Index

The country or countries in which the artist lived and worked appears in brackets.

Photographic Sources